CASES AND MATERIALS ON CONSTITUTIONAL LAW

FIFTH EDITION

David Crump
John B. Neibel Professor of Law
University of Houston

Eugene Gressman
Professor Emeritus of Law
University of North Carolina

David S. Day
Professor of Law
University of South Dakota

Charles W. "Rocky" Rhodes
Godwin Ronquillo PC Research Professor of Law
South Texas College of Law

Library of Congress Cataloging-in-Publication Data

Crump, David.
Cases and materials on constitutional law / David Crump, Eugene Gressman, David S. Day — 5th ed.
p. cm.
Includes index.
ISBN 978-1-4224-7015-2 (hardbound)
1. Constitutional law—United States—Cases. I. Gressman, Eugene, 1917- II. Day, David S. III. Title.
KF4550.C78 2009
342.73—dc22

2008053509

NOTE TO USERS

To ensure that you are using the latest materials available in this area, please be sure to periodically check the LexisNexis Law School web site for downloadable updates and supplements at www.lexisnexis.com/lawschool.

Editorial Offices
744 Broad Street, Newark, NJ 07102 (973) 820-2000
201 Mission St., San Francisco, CA 94105-1831 (415) 908-3200
www.lexisnexis.com

MATTHEW◆BENDER

(2009–Pub.479)

PREFACE

Organization and Methodology. This book is mostly traditional in approach. It begins with judicial review, deals next with legislative and executive powers, and contains coverage of individual rights in the latter half. The landmark cases, from *Marbury v. Madison* to *Brown v. Board of Education* to *Bush v. Gore* and beyond, are present, and coverage in this volume extends through the Court's term ending in July, 2008. Our goal is to provide a comprehensive, traditionally organized set of materials that is presented in a concise and manageable format.

Special Features. However, there is more to the book than traditional organization and approach. The following is a description of some of the special features that we have included.

SPECIAL FEATURES

"Applied" Constitutional Law: Study of Actual Litigation Documents. In addition to traditional case materials, the book includes documents from actual litigation. Complaints and answers, motions, briefs, orders, and record excerpts, all are reproduced for the student to see and study. In Chapter 1, testimony of Professors Tribe and Wright in a legislative hearing concerning the Pennzoil-Texaco dispute is reproduced to show the legislative function in enforcing the Constitution. An Appendix to Chapter 3 contains litigation documents from an actual preemption case; and Chapter 11 is followed by an appendix entitled, "The Story of a First Amendment Case," Finally, Chapter 7, which is entitled "The Anatomy of a Constitutional Case," is unique among constitutional law casebooks: it reproduces major documents from start to finish in a single constitutional case, so that students may see how such a case is developed in the real world. We believe that these materials will give the student a feel for the skills required to litigate constitutional issues. In addition, they show that constitutional law is not made only by the Supreme Court, but also in legislatures, state and federal trial courts, and intermediate appellate courts. And these "real world" materials will help the student to understand the theory of constitutional law better, because each example contains a knotty constitutional question — in its procedural context.

Encouraging Reading of the Constitution: Constitutional Theory and History. We have placed the Constitution at the beginning of the book, not at the end. We want to encourage the student to read the Constitution. Toward that end, we also have inserted reading assignments, with specific references to constitutional text, throughout the book. And in the preface that contains the Constitution, we have included source documents and commentary that will introduce the student to constitutional history. Finally, in Chapters 1 and 9, we have inserted appendices that emphasize constitutional theory.

A "User Friendly" Book. Above all, we have tried to produce a book that makes the fundamentals easy for the student to grasp. Complex chapters (such as those on federalism, equal protection, and the first amendment) are introduced by text that gives the student a "road map" of the issues. The cases are edited with student comprehension in mind, and explanations of difficult principles are inserted in brackets. Our notes and questions are self-contained; they do not require the student to consult outside sources. We know that constitutional law requires intense work in class, and it generates questions than can be appreciated only through Socratic dialogue — but one philosophy is that it is best for the student to come to class having actually understood the material in the book. The class then does not need to consist solely of helping to get across the basics, and the professor can raise more interesting issues.

Problems Taken From Actual Litigation Situations. Most of the Chapters contain from one to a dozen problems. In almost every instance, the problems are taken from actual litigation situations, such as controversies decided by lower courts. The problems are real. For example, the abortion cases are followed by a problem on forced cesarean sections, which have generated court decisions in more than a dozen states. In the speech chapter, a problem about rap music that allegedly encourages violence, based upon pending litigation, is included. Also included is a problem about the notorious "Hit Man" case, in which a hired assassin followed a manual called "Hit Man," written so as to give directions to killers. There are also problems about the *Hopwood* case and about Proposition 209, and many, many others.

State Constitutional Law. One chapter contains another coverage of state constitutional law. As the chapter indicates Supreme Court Justice William J. Brennan Jr. has called state constitutionalism the "most important" development in constitutional law of recent years. Our coverage is very brief, because few professors will have time for more. But it should serve at least to introduce the student to the length and breadth of state constitutional law.

The "Embarrassing" (or Frightening?) Second Amendment. Our book is unique in covering the militia clauses and second amendment right to bear arms. The Chapter contains *District of Columbia v. Heller.* The second amendment hasn't been addressed in many other Supreme Court opinions, and it makes an excellent exercise in interpretation. Guns and violence are, moreover, an important societal issue. This coverage will help future attorneys to sort out the conflicting views of the National Rifle Association and gun control forces.

Careful Case Selection and Editing to Produce a Comprehensive, but Compact Book. We have included "major" cases in more complete text, "squib" cases (or paragraph cases) that are more heavily edited, and note cases. Our objective is to produce a book in which major cases can be read and discussed in depth, squib cases provide additional points — and notes provide detail in compact form. We have attempted to provide a "comprehensive" set of materials.

For this Fifth Edition, several Chapters have been partially modified and streamlined. The materials in Chapter 1 on Conditions of Constitutional Adjudication have been reorganized and supplemented. Similarly, part of Chapter 11 (Free Speech) has been changed to reflect current doctrinal developments. Other Chapters have received minor modifications and consolidations. Many Notes have been added. The new reference Notes enhance the opportunities for students to pursue topics further.

It remains our hope that we have produced a book that will be particularly useful to counteract the constitutional law professor's occupational frustration in not having sufficient time to develop this complex area of law.

We hope that you will enjoy the book as much as we and our students have.

David Crump
University of Houston

Eugene M. Gressman
University of North
Carolina (Emeritus)

David S. Day
University of South Dakota
School of Law

Charles W. "Rocky" Rhodes
South Texas
College of Law

TABLE OF CONTENTS

TABLE OF CONTENTS

TABLE OF CONTENTS

TABLE OF CONTENTS

TABLE OF CONTENTS

TABLE OF CONTENTS

TABLE OF CONTENTS

TABLE OF CONTENTS

TABLE OF CONTENTS

TABLE OF CONTENTS

TABLE OF CONTENTS

TABLE OF CONTENTS

TABLE OF CONTENTS

Chapter 7   THE ANATOMY OF A CONSTITUTIONAL CASE: *REDI-MART, INC. v. LONDON RETAIL MERCHANTS ASSOCIATION* ... **399**

TABLE OF CONTENTS

TABLE OF CONTENTS

TABLE OF CONTENTS

TABLE OF CONTENTS

TABLE OF CONTENTS

TABLE OF CONTENTS

TABLE OF CONTENTS

TABLE OF CONTENTS

TABLE OF CONTENTS

TABLE OF CONTENTS

TABLE OF CONTENTS

TABLE OF CONTENTS

TABLE OF CONTENTS

TABLE OF CONTENTS

TABLE OF CONTENTS

TABLE OF CONTENTS

TABLE OF CONTENTS

Chapter 0
PREFATORY CHAPTER
THE CONSTITUTION AND ITS ADOPTION

§ 0.01 TEXT OF THE CONSTITUTION

[Preamble]

We the people of the United States, in Order to form a more perfect Union, establish Justice, insure domestic Tranquility, provide for the common defence, promote the general Welfare, and secure the Blessings of Liberty to ourselves and our Posterity, do ordain and establish this Constitution for the United States of America.

Article I.

Section 1. All legislative Powers herein granted shall be vested in a Congress of the United States, which shall consist of a Senate and House of Representatives.

Section 2. The House of Representatives shall be composed of Members chosen every second Year by the People of the several States, and the Electors in each State shall have the Qualifications requisite for Electors of the most numerous Branch of the State Legislature.

No Person shall be a Representative who shall not have attained to the Age of twenty five Years, and been seven Years a Citizen of the United States, and who shall not, when elected, be an Inhabitant of that State in which he shall be chosen.

Representatives and direct Taxes shall be apportioned among the several States which may be included within this Union, according to their respective Numbers, which shall be determined by adding to the whole Number of free Persons, including those bound to Service for a Term of Years, and excluding Indians not taxed, three fifths of all other Persons.[1] The actual Enumeration shall be made within three Years after the first Meeting of the Congress of the United States, and within every subsequent Term of ten Years, in such Manner as they shall by Law direct. The number of Representatives shall not exceed one for every thirty Thousand, but each State shall have at Least one Representative; and until such enumeration shall be made, the State of New Hampshire shall be entitled to chuse three, Massachusetts eight, Rhode-Island and Providence Plantations one, Connecticut five, New York six, New Jersey four, Pennsylvania eight, Delaware one, Maryland six, Virginia ten, North Carolina five, South Carolina five, and Georgia three.

When vacancies happen in the Representation from any State, the Executive Authority thereof shall issue Writs of Election to fill such Vacancies.

The House of Representatives shall chuse their Speaker and other Officers; and shall have the sole Power of Impeachment.

Section 3. The Senate of the United States shall be composed of two Senators from each State, [chosen by the Legislature thereof,][2] for six Years; and each Senator shall have one Vote.

Immediately after they shall be assembled in Consequence of the first Election, they shall be divided as equally as may be into three Classes. The Seats of the Senators of the first Class shall be vacated at the Expiration of the second Year, of the second Class at the Expiration of the fourth Year, and of the third Class at the Expiration of the sixth Year, so that one third may be chosen every second Year; [and if Vacancies happen by Resignation, or otherwise, during the Recess of the Legislature of any State, the

---

[1] Changed by section 2 of the Fourteenth Amendment.

[2] Changed by the Seventeenth Amendment.

Executive thereof may make temporary Appointments until the next Meeting of the Legislature, which shall then fill such Vacancies.][3]

No Person shall be a Senator who shall not have attained to the Age of thirty Years, and been nine Years a Citizen of the United States, and who shall not, when elected, be an Inhabitant of that State for which he shall be chosen.

The Vice President of the United States shall be President of the Senate, but shall have no Vote, unless they be equally divided.

The Senate shall chuse their other Officers, and also a President pro tempore, in the Absence of the Vice President, or when he shall exercise the Office of President of the United States.

The Senate shall have the sole Power to try all Impeachments. When sitting for that Purpose, they shall be on Oath or Affirmation. When the President of the United States is tried, the Chief Justice shall preside: And no Person shall be convicted without the Concurrence of two thirds of the Members present.

Judgment in Cases of Impeachment shall not extend further than to removal from Office, and disqualification to hold and enjoy any Office of honor, Trust or Profit under the United States: but the Party convicted shall nevertheless be liable and subject to Indictment, Trial, Judgment and Punishment, according to Law.

Section 4. The Times, Places and Manner of holding Elections for Senators and Representatives, shall be prescribed in each State by the Legislature thereof; but the Congress may at any time by Law make or alter such Regulations, except as to the Places of chusing Senators.

The Congress shall assemble at least once in every Year, and such Meeting shall be [on the first Monday in December,][4] unless they shall by Law appoint a different Day.

Section 5. Each House shall be the Judge of the Elections, Returns and Qualifications of its own Members, and a Majority of each shall constitute a Quorum to do Business; but a smaller Number may adjourn from day to day, and may be authorized to compel the Attendance of absent Members, in such Manner, and under such Penalties as each House may provide.

Each House may de its Members for disorderly Behaviour, and, with the Concurrence of two thirds, expel a Member.

Each House shall keep a Journal of its Proceedings, and from time to time publish the same, excepting such Parts as may in their Judgment require Secrecy; and the Yeas and Nays of the Members of either House on any question shall, at the Desire of one fifth of those Present, be entered on the Journal.

Neither House, during the Session of Congress, shall, without the Consent of the other, adjourn for more than three days, nor to any other Place than that in which the two Houses shall be sitting.

Section 6. The Senators and Representatives shall receive a Compensation for their Services, to be ascertained by Law, and paid out of the Treasury of the United States. They shall in all Cases, except Treason, Felony and Breach of the Peace, be privileged from Arrest during their Attendance at the Session of their respective Houses, and in going to and returning from the same; and for any Speech or Debate in either House, they shall not be questioned in any other Place.

No Senator or Representative shall, during the Time for which he was elected, be appointed to any civil Office under the Authority of the United States, which shall have

---

[3] Changed by the Seventeenth Amendment.

[4] Changed by section 2 of the Twentieth Amendment.

been created, or the Emoluments whereof shall have been encreased during such time; and no Person holding any Office under the United States, shall be a Member of either House during his Continuance in Office.

Section 7. All Bills for raising Revenue shall originate in the House of Representatives; but the Senate may propose or concur with Amendments as on other Bills.

Every bill which shall have passed the House of Representatives and the Senate, shall, before it becomes a Law, be presented to the President of the United States; If he approves he shall sign it, but if not he shall return it, with his Objections to that House in which it shall have originated, who shall enter the Objections at large on their Journal, and proceed to reconsider it. If after such Reconsideration two thirds of that House shall agree to pass the Bill, it shall be sent, together with the Objections, to the other House, by which it shall likewise be reconsidered, and if approved by two thirds of that House, it shall become a Law. But in all such Cases the Votes of both Houses shall be determined by yeas and Nays, and the Names of the Persons voting for and against the Bill shall be entered on the journal of each House respectively. If any Bill shall not be returned by the President within ten Days (Sundays excepted) after it shall have been presented to him, the Same shall be a Law, in like Manner as if he had signed it, unless the Congress by their Adjournment prevent its Return, in which Case it shall not be a Law.

Every Order, Resolution, or Vote to which the Concurrence of the Senate and House of Representatives may be necessary (except on a question of Adjournment) shall be presented to the President of the United States; and before the Same shall take Effect, shall be approved by him, or being disapproved by him, shall be repassed by two thirds of the Senate and House of Representatives, according to the Rules and Limitations prescribed in the Case of a Bill.

Section 8. The Congress shall have Power To lay and collect Taxes, Duties, Imposts and Excises, to pay the Debts and provide for the common Defence and general Welfare of the United States; but all Duties, Imposts and Excises shall be uniform throughout the United States;

To borrow Money on the credit of the United States;

To regulate Commerce with foreign Nations, and among the several States, and with the Indian Tribes;

To establish an uniform Rule of Naturalization, and uniform Laws on the subject of Bankruptcies throughout the United States;

To coin Money, regulate the Value thereof, and of foreign Coin, and fix the Standard of Weights and Measures;

To provide for the Punishment of counterfeiting the Securities and current Coin of the United States;

To establish Post Offices and post Roads;

To promote the Progress of Science and useful Arts, by securing for limited Times to Authors and Inventors the exclusive Right to their respective Writings and Discoveries;

To constitute Tribunals inferior to the supreme Court;

To define and punish Piracies and Felonies committed on the high Seas, and Offenses against the Law of Nations;

To declare War, grant Letters of Marque and Reprisal, and make Rules concerning Captures on Land and Water;

To raise and support Armies, but no Appropriation of Money to that Use shall be for a longer Term than two Years;

To provide and maintain a Navy;

To make Rules for the Government and Regulation of the land and naval Forces;

To provide for calling forth the Militia to execute the Laws of the Union, suppress Insurrections and repel Invasions;

To provide for organizing, arming, and disciplining the Militia, and for governing such Part of them as may be employed in the Service of the United States, reserving to the States respectively, the Appointment of the Officers, and the Authority of training the Militia according to the discipline prescribed by Congress;

To exercise exclusive Legislation in all Cases whatsoever, over such District (not exceeding ten Miles square) as may, by Cession of particular States, and the Acceptance of Congress, become the Seat of the Government of the United States, and to exercise like Authority over all Places purchased by the Consent of the Legislature of the State in which the Same shall be, for the Erection of Forts, Magazines, Arsenals, dock-Yards, and other needful Buildings;—And

To make all Laws which shall be necessary and proper for carrying into Execution the foregoing Powers, and all other Powers vested by this Constitution in the Government of the United States, or in any Department or Officer thereof.

Section 9. The Migration or Importation of such Persons as any of the States now existing shall think proper to admit, shall not be prohibited by the Congress prior to the Year one thousand eight hundred and eight, but a Tax or duty may be imposed on such Importation, not exceeding ten dollars for each Person.

The Privilege of the Writ of Habeas Corpus shall not be suspended, unless when in Cases of Rebellion or Invasion the public Safety may require it.

No Bill of Attainder or ex post facto Law shall be passed.

No Capitation, or other direct, Tax shall be laid, unless in Proportion to the Census or Enumeration herein before directed to be taken.

No Tax or Duty shall be laid on Articles exported from any State.

No Preference shall be given by any Regulation of Commerce or Revenue to the Ports of one State over those of another: nor shall Vessels bound to, or from, one State, be obliged to enter, clear, or pay Duties in another.

No Money shall be drawn from the Treasury, but in Consequence of Appropriations made by Law; and a regular Statement and Account of the Receipts and Expenditures of all public Money shall be published from time to time.

No Title of Nobility shall be granted by the United States: And no Person holding any Office of Profit or Trust under them, shall, without the Consent of the Congress, accept of any present, Emolument, Office, or Title, of any kind whatever, from any King, Prince, or foreign State.

Section 10. No State shall enter into any Treaty, Alliance, or Confederation; grant Letters of Marque and Reprisal; coin Money; emit Bills of Credit; make any Thing but gold and silver Coin a Tender in Payment of Debts; pass any Bill of Attainder, ex post facto Law, or Law impairing the Obligation of Contracts, or grant any Title of Nobility.

No State shall, without the Consent of the Congress, lay any Imposts or Duties on Imports or Exports, except what may be absolutely necessary for executing its inspection Laws: and the net Produce of all Duties and Imposts, laid by any State on Imports or Exports, shall be for the Use of the Treasury of the United States; and all such Laws shall be subject to the Revision and Control of the Congress.

No State shall, without the Consent of Congress, lay any Duty of Tonnage, keep Troops, or Ships of War in time of Peace, enter into any Agreement or Compact with another State, or with a foreign Power, or engage in War, unless actually invaded, or in such imminent Danger as will not admit of delay.

Article II.

Section 1. The executive Power shall be vested in a President of the United States of America. He shall hold his Office during the Term of four Years, and, together with the Vice President, chosen for the same Term, be elected, as follows:

Each State shall appoint, in such Manner as the Legislature thereof may direct, a Number of Electors, equal to the whole Number of Senators and Representatives to which the State may be entitled in the Congress: but no Senator or Representative, or Person holding an Office of Trust or Profit under the United States, shall be appointed an Elector.

[The Electors shall meet in their respective States, and vote by Ballot for two Persons, of whom one at least shall not be an Inhabitant of the same State with themselves. And they shall make a List of all the Persons voted for, and of the Number of Votes for each; which List they shall sign and certify, and transmit sealed to the Seat of the Government of the United States, directed to the President of the Senate. The President of the Senate shall, in the Presence of the Senate and House of Representatives, open all the Certificates, and the Votes shall then be counted. The Person having the greatest Number of Votes shall be the President, if such Number be a Majority of the whole Number of Electors appointed; and if there be more than one who have such Majority, and have an equal Number of Votes, then the House of Representatives shall immediately chuse by Ballot one of them for President; and if no Person have a Majority, then from the five highest on the List the said House shall in like Manner chuse the President. Butin chusing the President, the Votes shall be taken by States, the Representation from each State having one Vote; A quorum for this Purpose shall consist of a Member or Members from two thirds of the States, and a Majority of all the States shall be necessary to a Choice. In every Case, after the Choice of the President, the Person having the greatest Number of Votes of the Electors shall be the Vice President. But if there should remain two or more who have equal Votes, the Senate shall chuse from them by Ballot the Vice President.][5]

The Congress may determine the Time of chusing the Electors, and the Day on which they shall give their Votes; which Day shall be the same throughout the United States.

No Person except a natural born Citizen, or a Citizen of the United States, at the time of the Adoption of this Constitution, shall be eligible to the Office of the President; neither shall any person be eligible to that Office who shall not have attained to the Age of thirty five Years, and been fourteen Years a Resident within the United States.

[In Case of the Removal of the President from Office, or of his Death, Resignation, or Inability to discharge the Powers and Duties of the said Office, the Same shall devolve on the Vice President, and the Congress may by Law provide for the Case of Removal, Death, Resignation or Inability, both of the President and Vice President, declaring what Officer shall then act as President, and such Officer shall act accordingly, until the Disability be removed, or a President shall be elected.][6]

The President shall, at stated Times, receive for his Services, a Compensation, which shall neither be encreased nor diminished during the Period for which he shall have been elected, and he shall not receive within that Period any other Emolument from the United States, or any of them.

Before he enter on the Execution of his Office, he shall take the following Oath or Affirmation:—"I do solemnly swear (or affirm) that I will faithfully execute the Office of President of the United States, and will to the best of my Ability, preserve, protect and defend the Constitution of the United States."

---

[5] Superseded by the Twelfth Amendment.

[6] Modified by the Twenty-Fifth Amendment.

Section 2. The President shall be Commander in Chief of the Army and Navy of the United States, and of the Militia of the several States, when called into the actual Service of the United States; he may require the Opinion, in writing, of the principal Officer in each of the executive Departments, upon any Subject relating to the Duties of their respective Offices, and he shall have Power to grant Reprieves and Pardons for Offenses against the United States, except in Cases of Impeachment.

He shall have Power, by and with the Advice and Consent of the Senate, to make Treaties, provided two thirds of the Senators present concur; and he shall nominate, and by and with the Advice and Consent of the Senate, shall appoint Ambassadors, other public Ministers and Consuls, Judges of the supreme Court, and all other Officers of the United States, whose Appointments are not herein otherwise provided for, and which shall be established by Law: but the Congress may by Law vest the Appointment of such inferior Officers, as they think proper, in the President alone, in the Courts of Law, or in the Heads of Departments.

The President shall have Power to fill up all Vacancies that may happen during the Recess of the Senate, by granting Commissions which shall expire at the End of their next Session.

Section 3. He shall from time to time give to the Congress information of the State of the Union, and recommend to their Consideration such Measures as he shall judge necessary and expedient; he may, on extraordinary Occasions, convene both Houses, or either of them, and in Case of Disagreement between them, with Respect to the Time of Adjournment, he may adjourn them to such Time as he shall think proper; he shall receive Ambassadors and other public Ministers; he shall take Care that the Laws be faithfully executed, and shall Commission all the Officers of the United States.

Section 4. The President, Vice President and all civil Officers of the United States, shall be removed from Office on Impeachment for, and Conviction of, Treason, Bribery, or other high Crimes and Misdemeanors.

Article III.

Section 1. The judicial Power of the United States, shall be vested in one supreme Court, and in such inferior Courts as the Congress may from time to time ordain and establish. The Judges, both of the supreme and inferior Courts, shall hold their Offices during good Behaviour, and shall, at stated Times, receive for their Services, a Compensation, which shall not be diminished during their Continuance in Office.

Section 2. The judicial Power shall extend to all Cases, in Law and Equity, arising under this Constitution, the Laws of the United States, and Treaties made, or which shall be made, under their Authority;—to all Cases affecting Ambassadors, other public Ministers and Consuls;—to all Cases of admiralty and maritime Jurisdiction;—to Controversies to which the United States shall be a Party;—to Controversies between two or more States;—between a State and Citizens of another State;—between Citizens of different States—between Citizens of the same State claiming Lands under Grants of different States, and between a State, or the Citizens thereof, and foreign States, Citizens or Subjects.

In all Cases affecting Ambassadors, other public Ministers and Consuls, and those in which a State shall be Party, the supreme Court shall have original Jurisdiction. In all the other Cases before mentioned, the supreme Court shall have appellate Jurisdiction, both as to Law and Fact, with such Exceptions, and under such Regulations as the Congress shall make.

The Trial of all Crimes, except in Cases of Impeachment; shall be by Jury; and such Trial shall be held in the State where the said Crimes shall have been committed; but when not committed within any State, the Trial shall be at such Place or Places as the Congress may by Law have directed.

Section 3. Treason against the United States, shall consist only in levying War against them, or in adhering to their Enemies, giving them Aid and Comfort. No Person shall be convicted of Treason unless on the Testimony of two Witnesses to the same overt Act, or on Confession in open Court.

The Congress shall have Power to declare the Punishment of Treason, but no Attainder of Treason shall work Corruption of Blood, or Forfeiture except during the Life of the Person attained.

Article IV.

Section 1. Full Faith and Credit shall be given in each State to the public Acts, Records, and judicial Proceedings of every other State; And the Congress may by general Laws prescribe the Manner in which such Acts, Records and Proceedings shall be proved, and the Effect thereof.

Section 2. The Citizens of each State shall be entitled to all Privileges and Immunities of Citizens in the several States.

A Person charged in any State with Treason, Felony, or other Crime, who shall flee from Justice, and be found in another State, shall on Demand of the executive Authority of the State from which he fled, be delivered up, to be removed to the State having Jurisdiction of the Crime.

[No Person held to Service or Labour in one State, under the Laws thereof, escaping into another, shall, in Consequence of any Law or Regulation therein, be discharged from such Service or Labour, but shall be delivered upon Claim of the Party to whom such Service or Labour may be due.][7]

Section 3. New States may be admitted by the Congress into this Union; but no new State shall be formed or erected within the Jurisdiction of any other State; nor any State be formed by the Junction of two or more States, or Parts of States, without the Consent of the Legislatures of the States concerned as well as of the Congress.

The Congress shall have Power to dispose of and make all needful Rules and Regulations respecting the Territory or other Property belonging to the United States; and nothing in this Constitution shall be so construed as to Prejudice any Claims of the United States, or of any particular State.

Section 4. The United States shall guarantee to every State in this Union a Republican Form of Government, and shall protect each of them against Invasion; and on Application of the Legislature, or of the Executive (when the Legislature cannot be convened) against domestic Violence.

Article V.

The Congress, whenever two thirds of both Houses shall deem it necessary, shall propose Amendments to this Constitution, or, on the Application of the Legislatures of two thirds of the several States, shall call a Convention for proposing Amendments, which, in either Case, shall be valid to all Intents and Purposes, as Part of this Constitution, when ratified by the Legislatures of three fourths of the several States, or by Conventions in three fourths thereof, as the one or the other Mode of Ratification may be proposed by the Congress; Provided that no Amendment which may be made prior to the Year One thousand eight hundred and eight shall in any Manner affect the first and fourth Clauses in the Ninth Section of the first Article; and that no State, without its Consent, shall be deprived of it's equal Suffrage in the Senate.

Article VI.

All Debts contracted and Engagements entered into, before the Adoption of this Constitution, shall be as valid against the United States under this Constitution, as under the Confederation.

---

[7] Superseded by the Thirteenth Amendment.

This Constitution, and the Laws of the United States which shall be made in Pursuance thereof; and all Treaties made, or which shall be made, under the Authority of the United States, shall be the supreme Law of the Land; and the Judges in every State shall be bound thereby, any Thing in the Constitution or Laws of any State to the Contrary notwithstanding.

The Senators and Representatives before mentioned, and the Members of the several State Legislatures, and all executive and judicial Officers, both of the United States and of the several States, shall be bound by Oath or Affirmation, to support this Constitution; but no religious Test shall ever be required as a Qualification to any Office or public Trust under the United States.

Article VII.

The Ratification of the Conventions of nine States, shall be sufficient for the Establishment of this Constitution between the States so ratifying the Same.

Done in Convention by the Unanimous Consent of the States present the Seventeenth Day of September in the Year of our Lord one thousand seven hundred and Eighty seven and of the Independence of the United States of America the Twelfth. . . .

Amendment I. [1791]

Congress shall make no law respecting an establishment of religion, or prohibiting the free exercise thereof; or abridging the freedom of speech, or of the press; or the right of the people peaceably to assemble, and to petition the Government for a redress of grievances.

Amendment II. [1791]

A well regulated Militia, being necessary to the security of a free State, the right of the people to keep and bear Arms, shall not be infringed.

Amendment III. [1791]

No Soldier shall, in time of peace be quartered in any house, without the consent of the Owner, nor in time of war, but in a manner to be prescribed by law.

Amendment IV. [1791]

The right of the people to be secure in their persons, houses, papers, and effects, against unreasonable searches and seizures, shall not be violated, and no Warrants shall issue, but upon probable cause, supported by Oath or affirmation, and particularly describing the place to be searched, and the persons or things to be seized.

Amendment V. [1791]

No person shall be held to answer for a capital, or otherwise infamous crime, unless on a presentment or indictment of a Grand Jury, except in cases arising in the land or naval forces, or in the Militia, when in actual service in time of War or public danger; nor shall any person be subject for the same offence to be twice put in jeopardy of life or limb; nor shall be compelled in any criminal case to be a witness against himself, nor be deprived of life, liberty, or property, without due process of law; nor shall private property be taken for public use without just compensation.

In all criminal prosecutions, the accused shall enjoy the right to a speedy and public trial, by an impartial jury of the State and district wherein the crime shall have been committed; which district shall have been previously ascertained by law, and to be informed of the nature and cause of the accusation; to be confronted with the witnesses against him; to have compulsory process for obtaining witnesses in his favor, and to have the Assistance of Counsel for his defence.

Amendment VII. [1791]

In Suits at common law, where the value in controversy shall exceed twenty dollars, the right of trial by jury shall be preserved, and no fact tried by a jury shall be otherwise re-examined in any Court of the United States, than according to the rules of the common law.

Amendment VIII. [1791]

Excessive bail shall not be required, nor excessive fines imposed, nor cruel and unusual punishments inflicted.

Amendment IX. [1791]

The enumeration in the Constitution, of certain rights, shall not be construed to deny or disparage others retained by the people.

Amendment X. [1791]

The powers not delegated to the United States by the Constitution, nor prohibited by it to the States, are reserved to the States respectively, or to the people.

Amendment XI. [1795]

The Judicial power of the United States shall not be construed to extend to any suit in law or equity, commenced or prosecuted against one of the United States by Citizens of another State, or by Citizens or Subjects of any Foreign State.

Amendment XII. [1804]

The Electors shall meet in their respective states and vote by ballot for President and Vice-President, one of whom, at least, shall not be an inhabitant of the same state with themselves; they shall name in their ballots the person voted for as President, and in distinct ballots the person voted for as Vice-President, and they shall make distinct lists of all persons voted for as President, and of all persons voted for as Vice-President, and of the number of votes for each, which lists they shall sign and certify, and transmit sealed to the seat of the government of the United States, directed to the President of the Senate;—The President of the Senate shall, in the presence of the Senate and House of Representatives, open all the certificates and the votes shall then be counted;—The person having the greatest number of votes for President, shall be the President, if such number be a majority of the whole number of Electors appointed; and if no person have such majority, then from the persons having the highest numbers not exceeding three on the list of those voted for as President, the House of Representatives shall choose immediately, by ballot, the President. But in choosing the President, the votes shall be taken by states, the representation from each state having one vote; a quorum for this purpose shall consist of a member or members from two-thirds of the states, and a majority of all the states shall be necessary to a choice. [And if the House of Representatives shall not choose a President whenever the right of choice shall devolve upon them, before the fourth day of March next following, then the Vice-President shall act as President, as in the case of the death or other constitutional disability of the President.—][8] The person having the greatest number of votes as Vice-President, shall be the Vice-President, if such number be a majority of the whole number of Electors appointed, and if no person have a majority, then from the two highest numbers on the list, the Senate shall choose the Vice-President; a quorum for the purpose shall consist of two-thirds of the whole number of Senators, and a majority

---

[8] Superseded by section 3 of the Twentieth Amendment.

of the whole number shall be necessary to a choice. But no person constitutionally ineligible to the office of President shall be eligible to that of Vice-President of the United States.

Amendment XIII. [1865]

Section 1. Neither slavery nor involuntary servitude, except as a punishment for crime whereof the party shall have been duly convicted, shall exist within the United States, or any place subject to their jurisdiction.

Section 2. Congress shall have power to enforce this article by appropriate legislation.

Amendment XIV. [1868]

Section 1. All persons born or naturalized in the United States and subject to the jurisdiction thereof, are citizens of the United States and of the State wherein they reside. No State shall make or enforce any law which shall abridge the privileges or immunities of citizens of the United States; nor shall any State deprive any person of life, liberty, or property, without due process of law; nor deny to any person within its jurisdiction the equal protection of the laws.

Section 2. Representatives shall be apportioned among the several States according to their respective numbers, counting the whole number of persons in each State, excluding Indians not taxed. But when the right to vote at any election for the choice of electors for President and Vice President of the United States, Representatives in Congress, the Executive and Judicial officers of a State, or the members of the Legislature thereof, is denied to any of the male inhabitants of such State, being twenty-one years of age, and citizens of the United States, or in any way abridged, except for participation in rebellion, or other crime, the basis of representation therein shall be reduced in the proportion which the number of such male citizens shall bear to the whole number of male citizens twenty-one years of age in such State.

Section 3. No person shall be a Senator or Representative in Congress, or elector of President and Vice President, or hold any office, civil or military, under the United States, or under any State, who, having previously taken an oath, as a member of Congress, or as an officer of the United States, or as a member of any State legislature, or as an executive or judicial officer of any State, to support the Constitution of the United States, shall have engaged in insurrection or rebellion against the same, or given aid or comfort to the enemies thereof. But Congress may by a vote of two-thirds of each House, remove such disability.

Section 4. The validity of the public debt of the United States, authorized by law, including debts incurred for payment of pensions and bounties for services in suppressing insurrection or rebellion, shall not be questioned. But neither the United States nor any State shall assume or pay any debt or obligation incurred in aid of insurrection or rebellion against the United States, or any claim for the loss or emancipation of any slave; but all such debts, obligations and claims shall be held illegal and void.

Section 5. The Congress shall have power to enforce, by appropriate legislation, the provisions of this article.

Amendment XV. [1870]

Section 1. The right of citizens of the United States to vote shall not be denied or abridged by the United States or by any State on account of race, color, or previous condition of servitude.

Section 2. The Congress shall have power to enforce this article by appropriate legislation.

Amendment XVI. [1913]

The Congress shall have power to lay and collect taxes on incomes, from whatever source derived, without apportionment among the several States, and without regard to any census or enumeration.

Amendment XVII. [1913]

The Senate of the United States shall be composed of two Senators from each State, elected by the people thereof, for six years; and each Senator shall have one vote. The electors in each State shall have the qualifications requisite for electors of the most numerous branch of the State legislatures.

When vacancies happen in the representation of any State in the Senate, the executive authority of such State shall issue writs of election to fill such vacancies: *Provided*, That the legislature of any State may empower the executive thereof to make temporary appointments until the people fill the vacancies by election as the legislature may direct.

This amendment shall not be so construed as to affect the election or term of any Senator chosen before it becomes valid as part of the Constitution.

Amendment XVIII. [1919; repealed, 1933]

[**Section 1.** After one year from the ratification of this article the manufacture, sale, or transportation of intoxicating liquors within, the importation thereof into, or the exportation thereof from the United States and all territory subject to the jurisdiction thereof for beverage purposes is hereby prohibited.

Section 2. The Congress and the several States shall have concurrent power to enforce this article by appropriate legislation.

Section 3. This article shall be inoperative unless it shall have been ratified as an amendment to the Constitution by the legislatures of the several States, as provided in the Constitution, within seven years from the date of the submission hereof to the States by the Congress.]

Amendment XIX. [1920]

The right of citizens of the United States to vote shall not be denied or abridged by the United States or by any State on account of sex.

Congress shall have power to enforce this article by appropriate legislation.

Amendment XX. [1933]

Section 1. The terms of the President and Vice President shall end at noon on the 20th day of January, and the terms of Senators and Representatives at noon on the 3d day of January, of the years in which such terms would have ended if this article had not been ratified; and the terms of their successors shall then begin.

Section 2. The Congress shall assemble at least once in every year, and such meeting shall begin at noon on the 3d day of January, unless they shall by law appoint a different day.

Section 3. If, at the time fixed for the beginning of the term of the President, the President elect shall have died, the Vice President elect shall become President. If a President shall not have been chosen before the time fixed for the beginning of his term, or if the President elect shall have failed to qualify, then the Vice President elect shall act as President until a President shall have qualified; and the Congress may by law provide for the case wherein neither a President elect nor a Vice President elect shall have qualified, declaring who shall then act as President, or the manner in which one who is to act shall be selected, and such person shall act accordingly until a President or Vice President shall have qualified.

Section 4. The Congress may by law provide for the case of the death of any of the persons from whom the House of Representatives may choose a President whenever the right of choice shall have devolved upon them, and for the case of the death of any of the persons from whom the Senate may choose a Vice President whenever the right of choice shall have devolved upon them.

Section 5. Sections 1 and 2 shall take effect on the 15th day of October following the ratification of this article.

Section 6. This article shall be inoperative unless it shall have been ratified as an amendment to the Constitution by the legislatures of three-fourths of the several States within seven years from the date of its submission.

Amendment XXI. [1933]

Section 1. The eighteenth article of amendment to the Constitution of the United States is hereby repealed.

Section 2. The transportation or importation into any State, Territory, or possession of the United States for delivery or use therein of intoxicating liquors, in violation of the laws thereof, is hereby prohibited.

Section 3. This article shall be inoperative unless it shall have been ratified as an amendment to the Constitution by conventions in the several States, as provided in the Constitution, within seven years from the date of the submission hereof to the States by the Congress.

Amendment XXII. [1951]

Section 1. No person shall be elected to the office of the President more than twice, and no person who has held the office of President, or acted as President, for more than two years of a term to which some other person was elected President shall be elected to the office of the President more than once. But this Article shall not apply to any person holding the office of President when this Article was proposed by the Congress, and shall not prevent any person who may be holding the office of President, or acting as President, during the term within which this Article becomes operative from holding the office of President or acting as President during the remainder of such term.

Section 2. This article shall be inoperative unless it shall have been ratified as an amendment to the Constitution by the legislatures of three-fourths of the several States within seven years from the date of its submission to the States by the Congress.

Amendment XXIII. [1961]

Section 1. The District constituting the seat of Government of the United States shall appoint in such manner as the Congress may direct:

A number of electors of President and Vice President equal to the whole number of Senators and Representatives in Congress to which the District would be entitled if it were a State, but in no event more than the least populous State; they shall be in addition to those appointed by the States, but they shall be considered, for the purposes of the election of President and Vice President, to be electors appointed by a State; and they shall meet in the District and perform such duties as provided by the twelfth article of amendment.

Section 2. The Congress shall have power to enforce this article by appropriate legislation.

Amendment XXIV. [1964]

Section 1. The right of citizens of the United States to vote in any primary or other election for President or Vice President, for electors for President or Vice President, or for Senator or Representative in Congress, shall not be denied or abridged by the United States or any State by reason of failure to pay any poll tax or other tax.

Section 2. The Congress shall have power to enforce this article by appropriate legislation.

Amendment XXV. [1967]

Section 1. In case of the removal of the President from office or of his death or resignation, the Vice President shall become President.

Section 2. Whenever there is a vacancy in the office of the Vice President, the President shall nominate a Vice President who shall take office upon confirmation by a majority vote of both Houses of Congress.

Section 3. Whenever the President transmits to the President pro tempore of the Senate and the Speaker of the House of Representatives his written declaration that he is unable to discharge the powers and duties of his office, and until he transmits to them a written declaration to the contrary, such powers and duties shall be discharged by the Vice President as Acting President.

Section 4. Whenever the Vice President and a majority of either the principal officers of the executive departments or of such other body as Congress may by law provide, transmit to the President pro tempore of the Senate and the Speaker of the House of Representatives their written declaration that the President is unable to discharge the powers and duties of his office, the Vice President shall immediately assume the powers and duties of the office as Acting President.

Thereafter, when the President transmits to the President pro tempore of the Senate and the Speaker of the House of Representatives his written declaration that no inability exists, he shall resume the powers and duties of his office unless the Vice President and a majority of either the principal officers of the executive department or of such other body as Congress may by law provide, transmit within four days to the President pro tempore of the Senate and the Speaker of the House of Representatives their written declaration that the President is unable to discharge the powers and duties of his office. Thereupon Congress shall decide the issue, assembling within forty-eight hours for that purpose if not in session. If the Congress, within twenty-one days after receipt of the latter written declaration, or, if Congress is not in session, within twenty-one days after Congress is required to assemble, determines by two-thirds vote of both Houses that the President is unable to discharge the powers and duties of his office, the Vice President shall continue to discharge the same as Acting President; otherwise, the President shall resume the powers and duties of his office.

Amendment XXVI. [1971]

Section 1. The right of citizens of the United States, who are eighteen years of age or older, to vote shall not be denied or abridged by the United States or by any State on account of age.

Section 2. The Congress shall have power to enforce this article by appropriate legislation.

Amendment XXVII. [1992]

No law, varying the compensation for the services of the Senators and Representatives, shall take effect until an election of Representatives shall have intervened.

§ 0.02 SOURCE DOCUMENTS FROM WHICH CONSTITUTIONAL PRINCIPLES WERE DRAWN

INTRODUCTORY NOTE: SEPARATION OF POWERS, FROM THE GREEK PHILOSOPHERS TO MAGNA CARTA TO MONTESQUIEU TO MADISON

A Written Constitution with Delegated Powers. Written constitutions in which power is delegated by the people are a comparatively recent invention. The United States Constitution was one of the first. A more common source of governing authority, at the time, was God. The ruler tended to claim power by divine right. Nevertheless, most of the ideas that shaped the Constitution of the United States were not new.

The Influences on the Framers. The delegates to the Constitutional Convention were elite and well-educated. Many had read the great philosophers in the original Latin or Greek. Therefore,we start this section with an excerpt from Plato's Dialogues on the separation of powers (a subject on which Aristotle and other Greek philosophers also wrote). Ideas came, also, from such sources as Magna Carta, the English Bill of Rights, and pre-constitutional colonial documents. The Founders particularly were influenced by such political philosophers as Locke, Hobbes, Hume, and Montesquieu, as well as the economics of Adam Smith. In some instances, the antecedents are the clear sources even of the precise words used. For example, the eighth amendment contains language virtually identical to that in the English Bill of Rights, and the due process clause traces to the concept of the "law of the land" in Magna Carta.

Tracing the Separation-of-Powers Concept. In these excerpts, we emphasize the constitutional concept of separation of powers as it was influenced by source documents. As the above examples indicate, this is not the only concept in the Constitution that was shaped by historical forces, but it happens to be one that is readily traceable.

PLATO, DIALOGUES (LAWS XI), 875–76. [The Athenian Stranger:] [N]o man's nature is able to know what is best for human society; or knowing, always able and willing to do what is best. [If] [a person] be possessed of absolute and irresponsible power, he will never remain firm in his principles or persist in regarding the public good as primary in the state, and the private good as secondary. . . .

[Cleinias:] Then what is to be the inference?

Ath. The inference is, that some things should be left to courts of law; others the legislator must decide for himself . . .

MAGNA CARTA Ch. 12, 14, 17–18 (1215). [The great barons met John, King of England, at Runnymede, where they made demands based upon grievances of their time. The resulting Great Charter contains sixty-three chapters, written in the form of promises by King John. Chapters 12 and 14 provide for meetings of the "common counsel" to consent to the imposition of "scutage" or "aid"—a crude analog of the modern notion that there should be no taxation without representation in some kind of legislative branch. As for the judicial branch, Chapter 17 freed suitors from the King's custom of having his Court travel about the countryside and abroad with him, and Chapter 18 similarly provided a small measure of independence for courts and preservation of basic kinds of claims. Chapters 39 and 40, respectively, contain the famous requirement that the processes of justice conform to the "law of the land," as well as the "open courts" provision (which, curiously, has made its way into the majority of state constitutions, but not into the federal Constitution). Thus, the separation of powers in Magna Carta is rudimentary, but significant. As one commentator says, "These Chapters [on courts and administration of justice], above all others, have made Magna Carta a symbol to later ages and have contributed most significantly to Anglo-American concepts of justice." A.E.D. Howard, *Magna Carta: Text and Commentary* 12 (1964). The text follows:]

12. No scutage or aid shall be imposed in Our Kingdom unless by common counsel thereof, except to ransom Our person, make Our eldest son a Knight, and once to marry Our eldest daughter. . . .

14. For obtaining the common counsel of the Kingdom concerning the assessment of aids . . . or of scutage, We will cause to be summoned . . . the archbishops, bishops, abbots, earls, and great barons; We will also cause to be summoned, generally . . . all those who hold lands directly of Us, to meet on a fixed day, but with at least forty days notice, and at a fixed place. . . .

17. Common Pleas shall not follow Our Court, but shall be held in some certain place.

18. Recognizances of novel disseisin, mort d'ancestor, and darrein presentment shall be taken only in their proper counties, and in this manner: We or, if We be absent from the realm, Our Chief Justiciary, shall send two justiciaries through each county four times a year, and they, together with four knights elected out of each county by the people thereof, shall hold the said assizes in the county court, on the day and in the place where that court meets. . . .

39. No free man shall be taken, imprisoned, disseised, outlawed, banished, or in any way destroyed, nor will We proceed against or prosecute him, except by the lawful judgment of his peers and by the law of the land.

40. To no one will We sell, to none will We deny or delay, right or justice. . . .

C. WALKER, RELATIONS AND OBSERVATIONS, HISTORICAL AND POLITICK, UPON THE PARLIAMENT BEGUN ANNO DOM. 1640 (1648). [T]he King by Himselfe can neither make, repeal, or alter any one law.

[N]or can the King by Himselfe, or joyntly with the Lords and Commons judge what the Law is; this is the office of the sworn Judges. . . . Now for any one man, or any Assembly, Court, or Corporation of men . . . to usurpe these three powers: 1. The Governing Power. 2. The Legislative Power. 3. And the Judicative Power, unto themselves, is to make themselves the highest Tyrants, and the people the basest slaves in the world; for to govern supremely by a Law made, and interpreted by themselves according to their own pleasure, what can be more boundlesse and arbitrary?

J. LOCKE, SECOND TREATISE §§ 143, 144, 159 (1689).

143. *The Legislative* Power is that which has a right to *direct* how *the Force of the Commonwealth* shall be imploy'd for preserving the Community and the Members of it. . . .

144. But because the Laws that are at once, and in a short time made, have a constant and lasting force, and need a *perpetual Execution*, or an attendance thereunto: Therefore'tis necessary that there should be a *Power always in being* which should see to the *Execution* of the Laws . . . and thus the *Legislative* and *Executive Power* come often to be separated. . . .

159. [T]he Legislative and Executive Power are in distinct hands . . . in all moderated Monarchies and well-framed Governments. . . .

11 MONTESQUIEU, SPIRIT OF THE LAWS Ch. 6 (1748). In every government there are three sorts of power: [1] the legislative; [2] the executive in respect of things dependent on the law of nations; and [3] the executive in regard to matters that depend on the civil law.

By virtue of the first, the prince or magistrate enacts [laws]. By the second, he makes peace or war, sends or receives embassies, establishes the public security, and provides against invasions. By the third, he punishes criminals, or determines the disputes that arise between individuals. The latter we shall call the judiciary power, and the other simply the executive power of the state. . . .

When the legislative and executive powers are united in the same person, or in the same body of magistrates, there can be no liberty; because apprehensions may arise, less the same monarch or senate should enact tyrannical laws, [and] execute them in a tyrannical manner. . . .

[T]he legislative body being composed of two parts, they check one another by the mutual privilege of rejecting. They are both restrained by the executive power, as the executive is by the legislative.

These three powers should naturally form a state of repose or inaction. But as there is a necessity for movement in the course of human affairs, they are forced to move, but still in concert. . . .

CONSTITUTION OF THE [PRE-CONSTITUTIONAL] STATE OF VIRGINIA (1776). The legislative, executive, and judiciary departments, shall be separate and distinct, so that neither exercise the Powers properly belonging to the other; nor shall any person exercise the powers of more than one of them at the same time, except that the Justices of the County Courts shall be eligible to either House of Assembly. . . .

MADISON, THE FEDERALIST NO. 47: SEPARATION OF POWERS WITHIN THE FEDERAL GOVERNMENT. [This work, which relies heavily upon an explication of Montesquieu's *Spirit of the Laws*, is excerpted in § 0.05 of this Chapter.]

NOTES AND QUESTIONS

(1) *"Separation of Powers" as Versus "Checks and Balances."* Although the doctrine of separation of powers and the concepts of checks and balances often are thought of together, they are (at least superficially) contradictory. In fact, opponents of the Constitution charged that it "distributed and blended" government power among the three branches "in such a manner as to destroy all symmetry . . . and to expose some of the essential parts . . . to the danger of being crushed by the disproportionate weight of other parts." Madison, *The Federalist* No. 47. The opponents quoted Montesquieu in their efforts to defeat ratification on this ground. Consider whether Montesquieu's theory, as expressed in *Spirit of the Laws*, justifies the opponent's charges. For Madison's response, see below.

(2) *What Significance Should be Given to the Fact that the Federal Constitution, Unlike the Virginia Constitution, Does Not Expressly Provide for Separation of Powers?: The Example of the "Legislative Veto" Case— INS v. Chadha, 462 U.S. 919 (1983).* In a number of enactments, Congress provided that a single house could disapprove, and thereby "veto," administrative actions of certain kinds. In *Chadha*, a litigant challenged one of these provisions on the ground that it violated the separation of powers. The argument was that this "legislative veto" effectively bypassed the requirement of legislation enacted by both houses, which was supposed to be subject to the veto power of the executive and interpreted by the courts. Consider whether the text and history of the Constitution support or oppose this argument. Notice that the federal Constitution, unlike the Virginia Constitution of 1776 and many current state constitutions, does not provide expressly for separation of powers; the argument for the separation of powers doctrine in the federal Constitution is a structural one, based upon the parallel formats of the first three articles. Does the absence of express text connote more flexibility? Consider, also, whether Montesquieu's theory, which heavily influenced Madison (the "Father of the Constitution") and other Framers, contemplates a flexible, rather than watertight, separation. *See The Federalist* No. 47, § 0.05 below. [Note: In *Chadha*, which is reproduced in Chapter 5, below, the Supreme Court struck down a legislative veto provision on separation of powers grounds.]

§ 0.03   EVENTS THAT LED TO THE CONSTITUTIONAL CONVENTION

ARTICLES OF CONFEDERATION (1781)

Article I. The Stile of this Confederacy shall be "The United States of America."

Article II. Each state retains its sovereignty, freedom, and independence, and every Power, Jurisdiction and Right, which is not by this Confederation expressly delegated to the United States, in Congress assembled. . . .

Article IX. The United States in Congress assembled, shall have the sole and exclusive right and power of determining on peace and war, except in cases mentioned in the sixth article—of sending and receiving ambassadors—entering into treaties and alliances [and other listed foreign policy powers].

The United States in Congress assembled shall also be the last resort on appeal in all disputes . . . between two or more states. . . .

The United States in Congress assembled shall also have the sole and exclusive right and power of regulating the alloy and value of coins struck by their own authority, or by that of the respective states—fixing the standard of weights and measures throughout the United States—regulating the trade and managing all affairs with the Indians . . .—establishing or regulating post offices from one state to another . . . and exacting such postage on the papers passing thro' the same as may be requisite to defray the expenses of the said office—appointing all officers of the land forces, in the service of the United States, excepting regimental officers. . . .

NOTES AND QUESTIONS

(1) *The "Nationalist" Franklin-Dickinson Draft of the Articles; the "States Rights" Position that Prevailed.* During the Revolutionary War, Benjamin Franklin proposed what he called the "Articles of Confederation and perpetual Union." Later, when the Continental Congress appointed a committee to draft a Declaration of Independence and Articles of Confederation, the committee delegated John Dickinson of Pennsylvania to begin the task. Dickinson was an advocate of strong central government and borrowed heavily from Franklin's plan, although omitting Franklin's proposal for a power over "general commerce." (Interestingly, neither Franklin nor Dickinson proposed that the national government have a general power to tax.) Dickinson's Article III provided that "each colony [which was what Dickinson called them, rather than "states"] shall retain and enjoy as much of its present Laws, Rights and Customs, as it may think fit . . . in all matters that shall not interfere with the Articles of Confederation." States rights advocates, however, prevailed in Congress, and Article III instead was written narrowly to confine the Confederation to "expressly delegated" powers. Consider how sharply this provision differs from the comparable provisions in the current Constitution—particularly the "necessary and proper" clause, the commerce clause, and the taxing power.

(2) *Superpowers and Economic Problems.* Despite advocates of state sovereignty, pressures toward union persisted for economic reasons and because of the military threat from superpowers of the day, particularly England, Spain, and France. No state could resist, but a "more perfect union" providing for the "common defense" might. *See* C. Bowen, Miracle at Philadelphia, 25–26 (1986). (The authors appreciate Professor Myron Moskovitz's formulation of this issue.)

(3) *Failure of the Articles of Confederation: From Shay's Rebellion to States' Aggravations of General Economic Collapse; Madison's Explanation.* Western lands were an early source of difficulty under the Articles of Confederation. Virginia claimed the Pacific Ocean as its western border, and Maryland, exploiting the requirement of

unanimity under the Articles, held out for nationalization of western lands. Britain's maintenance of garrisons in the Great Lakes area, in violation of the Treaty of Paris, slowed the opening of the Northwest Territory. Depredations by Indian tribes and by the Spanish on the south and west were major concerns, for which the Confederation provided inadequate response. Post-war depression had left small farmers in debt throughout the Confederation, and in Massachusetts, they sought the enactment of laws that would have enabled them to pay less value to their creditors in paper money. The Massachusetts legislature refused, and the result was Shay's Rebellion—a serious attempt to take over the state government, prevented only by the militia. (The modern analog would be a well-organized effort by the Ku Klux Klan to take over New York.) Shay's Rebellion profoundly shook what John Jay called "the better kind of people." In economic matters, the absence of a general taxing power was particularly difficult: "Requisitions" from states were paid as a matter of grace, war debt accumulated, and the phrase "not worth a Continental" originated. The absence of general commerce powers also prevented the Confederation government from dealing with economic problems—and these economic causes, as Madison explained, were among the major motivations for the Constitutional Convention. Consider the following.

MADISON, STATEMENT OF THE CAUSES OF THE CONSTITUTIONAL CONVENTION, 5 ELLIOT'S DEBATES ON THE FEDERAL CONVENTION OF 1787, 109–122. The principal difficulties which embarrassed the progress, and retarded the completion, of the plan of confederation, may be traced to—first the natural repugnance of the parties to a relinquishment of power; secondly, a natural jealously of its abuse in other hands than their own; thirdly, the rule of suffrage among parties [*i.e.*, the states] whose inequality and size did not correspond with that of their wealth, or of their military or free populations; fourthly, the selection and definition of the powers, at once necessary to the federal head, and safe to the several members.

To these sources of difficulty, incident to the formation of all such confederacies, were added two others. . . . [The first was the case of Crown Lands and Western Lands.]

The other source of dissatisfaction was the peculiar situation of some of the states, which, having no convenient ports for foreign commerce, were subject to be taxed by their neighbors, through whose ports their commerce was carried on. New Jersey, placed between Philadelphia and New York, was likened to a cask tapped at both ends; and North Carolina, between Virginia and South Carolina, to a patient bleeding at both arms. The Articles of Confederation provided no remedy for the complaint. . . .

But the radical infirmity of the "Articles of Confederation" was the dependence of Congress on the voluntary and simultaneous compliance with its requisitions by so many independent communities, each consulting more or less its particular interest and convenience, and distrusting the compliance of the other. . . .

At the date of the Convention, the aspect and retrospect of the political condition of the United States could not but fill the public mind with a gloom which was relieved only by a hope that so select a body would devise an adequate remedy for the existing prospective evils so impressively demanding it.

It was seen that the public debt, rendered so sacred by the cause in which it had been incurred, remained without any provision for its payment. [T]he want of authority in Congress to regulate commerce had produced in foreign nations, particularly Great Britain, a monopolizing policy. . . . The same want of a general power over commerce led to an exercise of the power, separately, by the states, which not only proved abortive, but engendered rival, conflicting, and angry regulations. . . .

[I]n the internal administration of the states, a violation of contracts had become familiar, in the form of depreciated paper made a legal tender, of property substituted for money, of instalment laws, and of the occlusions of the courts of justice, although evident that all such interferences effect the rights of other states, relatively creditors, as well as citizens creditors within the state. . . .

As a natural consequence of this distracted and disheartening condition of the Union, the federal authority had ceased to be respected abroad. [A]t home, it had lost all confidence and credit; the unstable and unjust career of the states had also forfeited the respect and confidence essential to order and good government, involving a general decay of confidence and credit between man and man. . . .

Such were the defects . . . for which the Convention were to provide a remedy. . . .

§ 0.04 THE CONSTITUTIONAL CONVENTION

JAMES KIRBY MARTIN, IN THE COURSE OF HUMAN EVENTS: AN INTERPRETIVE EXPLORATION OF THE AMERICAN REVOLUTION
Ch IX (1979)*

[*I. Who Were the Founders?: A Convention of Nationalist Aristocrats.*]

[The vast majority of the leaders who assembled in Philadelphia] looked back over recent events [besetting Confederation America] with horror; they wanted to look forward with hope. On the surface these national constitution makers were a diverse lot. A few were quite young, such as James Madison and Alexander Hamilton, both in their thirties; some were aged, such as the octogenarian Benjamin Franklin; most were passing beyond their middle years, such as George Washington, Robert Morris, and John Dickinson. They were not sent from heaven, as some commentators have implied; rather, they ostensibly came as representatives from the states. Only a handful of them were localists. Of the fifty-five men who attended the convention during its three and a half months of deliberations, thirty-nine had at one time or another served in Congress; twenty-one were former Continental army officers. Their focus on problems no doubt reflected the national orientation of their previous office-holding experiences. . . .

[T]he nationalists were clearly dominant. Among those in attendance were Washington, Franklin, Madison, Hamilton, Robert Morris, Gouverneur Morris, John Dickinson, Charles Pinckney, and James Wilson. . . .

Of those who attended, there were a few dissidents, clearly out of step with the dominating nationalists. Typical was Luther Martin of Maryland, a schoolteacher turned lawyer who had developed a reputation for his large drinking capacity. Martin spoke rarely, but when he did his words came out as huge gusts of wind. Few objected when Martin gave up and left the convention in complete disgust over the proceedings.

Generally, the delegates, whether nationalists or antinationalists, were not representative of the people, socially or economically. There were no freehold farmers, artisans, or day laborers among their numbers. On the contrary, the delegates were by and large men of wealth, high social standing, and extensive formal education. [M]any were public creditors. Of the fifty-five delegates, some thirty held significant amounts of federal public securities. Thus, the creation of a fiscally solvent national government capable of paying off the national debt could potentially reward these men with handsome monetary profits.

Personal economic gain, however, represents far too narrow a basis to explain why these delegates gathered in Philadelphia. That factor may have lurked in the background, as did the question of protecting property against paper money, legal tender, and debt stay laws, comprehended by the nationalists in images of anarchy associated with convulsive incidents like Shay's Rebellion. [C]onstitution making gave them an opportunity to release pent-up frustrations because they now had the opportunity to redistribute power and authority. . . .

Recent events, threatening on so many fronts, epitomized what was wrong. But events alone do not fully explain why the nationalists often thought that

---

Confederation . . . [America] was on the brink of ruin. Elbridge Gerry captured the essence of the answer when he exclaimed about an "excess of democracy" and the people as "dupes of pretended patriots." An essential tenet of the political theory of the time was that liberty could be destroyed from below as well as from above, by self-serving commoners as well as by willful monarchs. "[W]e have been guarding against an evil that old States are most liable to, excess of power in the rulers," Benjamin Franklin pointed out after the convention, "but our present danger seems to be defect of obedience in the subjects. . . ."

[A]lthough men of exalted socioeconomic standing, they lacked comparable political power, which they assumed was their natural heritage as established socioeconomic stewards. They continued presuming that social stability depended upon an indivisible relationship between the leaders and the led in state and society, whether in monarchical or republican systems. The problem, they believed, was that the decentralized authority in the states had weakened that relationship, leaving confusion and a harvest of anarchy in its wake. The wrong men had got into power, and the republican order was suffering its death throes because of democratic and demagogic excesses.

[II. The Convention Begins.]

The convention was supposed to open on May 14, 1787, yet not enough delegates had appeared by the appointed date. The convention finally got started on May 25, and George Washington modestly accepted a unanimous invitation to take the president's chair. Next, a committee mapped out rules of procedure, including a decision to keep all deliberations secret. The delegates did not want to confuse the public with contradictory daily reports, especially if they altered early decisions later on in their proceedings. Moreover, they wanted complete frankness in debates. Some nationalist delegates preferred the veil of secrecy to prevent public pressure against their plan to go far beyond their instructions and to create a new government.

[III. Randolph Submits the Virginia Plan.]

The crucial moment arrived once procedural questions were disposed of and it was agreed that each state delegation should have one vote. [O]n Tuesday, May 29, energetic Edmund Randolph rose from his chair and explained the outline of a new plan of government. . . .

The debate over the Virginia Plan went on for the next two weeks, and it helped to precipitate one of three major crises that the convention would experience. In presenting the plan, Randolph urged boldness upon the delegates. The Virginians recommended a three-tiered structure of government, including a bicameral legislature and a national executive. The lower house was "to be elected by the people of the several states," while the upper house was "to be elected by those of the first, out of a proper number of persons nominated by the individual [state] Legislatures." In turn, the national executive was to be selected by a full session of the new national legislature. The plan also called for a national judiciary, which, besides regular judicial assignments, would have the power, in conjunction with the executive, to veto legislation. Not only would the national legislature "enjoy the . . . Rights vested in Congress by the Confederation"; it could also "legislate in all cases to which the separate States are incompetent, or in which the harmony of the United States may be interrupted by the exercise of individual Legislation." The Virginia Plan did not enumerate specific powers, but the national legislature was to have the authority "to negative all laws passed by the several States, contravening in the opinion of the National Legislature the articles of Union. . . ."

By and large, the convention reacted favorably. . . .

In the formulation of the Articles of Confederation, one of the hottest debates had centered on the question of whether each state would enjoy equal voting power in Congress, as opposed to the notion of representation according to population. Equality for the states had been the clear choice in 1777. Now, 10 years later, the Virginia Plan called for proportional representation for the lower house. The fear among delegates from the "small" states (Connecticut, New Jersey, and Delaware for example) was that the "large" states (such as Massachusetts, Pennsylvania, and Virginia) would use superior voting strength to undermine and destroy the interests of the small states. . . .

[IV. Paterson Puts Forward the "Small States' Plan."]

On June 15, William Paterson of New Jersey rallied the delegates from the less populous states. He laid before the convention what has since been called the "New Jersey Plan." [T]he New Jersey Plan countered the Virginia Plan on several fronts. It called for a unicameral national legislature in which each state enjoyed equal voting strength. . . .

Paterson's presentation unleashed a wicked round of debate, not over the distribution of powers between state and nation, but over the question of representation. He thought that the convention was erring in pushing the assumptions of the Virginia Plan so boldly. His proposal was more in the spirit of the original convention charge. More important, it did not sacrifice the small states. "Destroy this balance of equality," exhorted Paterson, "and you endanger the rights of lesser societies by the danger of usurpation in the greater. . . ."

[D]ebating quickly gave way to day-by-day picking and haggling. A few members made vague noises about leaving. To make matters worse, Luther Martin gained the floor and harangued the assemblage for two days running. . . .

[V. The Great Compromise: Different Representation in House and Senate.]

The delegates, tired and worn down by the extremely humid weather, finally sorted out the issues and labored toward what is known as the "Great Compromise." They at last focused on complementary points in the Virginia and New Jersey Plans and fused them together. First, they settled on a three-tiered structure of government, harking back to Britain's balanced model as essential for the protection of the liberties of all groups. Second, they agreed that the central government was to be supreme over the states. Now the new national government could serve as the ultimate check upon democratic licentiousness when the state governments could no longer contain popular pressures from below. Third, the new national government was to have a vast increase in specified powers. Fourth, representation in the lower house was to be proportional to population, while the states would retain equal voting strength in the upper house, called the Senate. The less populous states thus could protect their interests at the senatorial level. Indeed, what the Great Compromise did was to fuse the competing plans into a coherent whole. The convention had cleared one of its highest hurdles by the middle of July.

[VI. The North-South Split and Compromise: Slave Trade and Property Issues.]

Differences over the mode of representation set off the second major controversy. Questions about representation provoked questions about how the expanded powers of the national government were to affect particular interests. The debates did not follow the localist-nationalist split; rather, they proceeded along North-South lines.

The South was particularly sensitive about the subject of slavery. [T]he reality . . . was that a frontal assault on slavery would have driven the southern delegates from the convention and probably from the union. This would have destroyed all prospects for achieving social and political stability and national longevity through constitutional change. Clearly, the latter had the highest priority on the nationalist agenda.

Similar attitudes did not prevail about the slave trade. It was a touchy and rancorous issue, but it could be discussed. The Lower South took a rigid position. "If the Convention thinks that North Carolina, South Carolina, and Georgia will ever agree to the plan, unless their right to import slaves be untouched," threatened John Rutledge, "the expectation is vain." The Upper South was more flexible. Slave labor had become an economic burden in some areas there, particularly in the face of the long-term decline in the productivity of tobacco plantations. Upper South delegates thus were susceptible to compromise because of the economic woes of debt-ridden planters.

All told, southern delegates were intensely aware of their minority status in the union. They wanted special protection through explicit constitutional provisions, but without emasculating the thrust toward the centralization of authority. Furthermore, they demanded a decennial census. In the 1780s everyone assumed, because of the undeveloped state of the territory north of the Ohio River and the southwestern course of population movement into Kentucky and Tennessee, that the southern frontier would be the most likely spawning ground of new states—states accepting the institution of slavery and thereby identifying with southern interests. . . .

What it boiled down to was that northern and southern interests, as one slaveholding South Carolinian blurted out, were "different as the interests of Russia and Turkey. . . ."

In the end, both sides conceded points in a series of piecemeal agreements. The North won on import duties, the adoption of which would require only majority votes in Congress. That effectively appeased the middle states' commercial leaders who had persistently advocated permanent revenue sources from tariffs for the national government. The South carried the day on commercial treaties; the Senate was to have exclusive jurisdiction over treaties of all kinds, with a two-thirds' vote necessary for ratification. In effect, the South had gained de facto veto control over formal commercial arrangements with other nations. The real losers were the states, not the sectional interests involved.

The South also gained the decennial census and the counting of a slave as three-fifths of a . . . person—this was originally a part of the Great Compromise—for purposes of calculating representation in the lower house. . . .

At the same time, the South conceded that slaves would not only count for representation but also for purposes of direct taxation. It perhaps is not ironic that southern delegates, insisting that slaves were inviolate property, should have been so willing to award them three-fifths' human status. [T]he South never achieved expected majority status, and some Northerners became more resistant to the continuing spread of slavery westward as the nineteenth century unfolded, all of which ultimately shattered the carefully drawn compromise of the Constitutional Convention.

[C]ooperation and consensus in the face of recent crises represented the spirit of the moment, even to the point that the Deep South delegates reluctantly conceded to Congress the right to prohibit the importation of slaves after twenty years. Moreover, their delegates accepted the point that newly imported slaves could be taxed at a modest rate. [A]t the same time, the concession on the slave trade was a prime factor in getting a fugitive clause into the final document as a *quid pro quo*. The "supreme law of the land" thus mandated the return of all runaway slaves to their plantation owners. . . .

[T]he compromise, in temporarily muting sectional ill will, helped to solidify that alliance [of citizens of propertied wealth] in the short run, just as the whole new edifice further secured property by providing additional checks against the popular fury associated with so-called democratic licentiousness.

[*VIII. The Problems of the Presidency.*]

Having come this far, the delegates were not about to run aground on the third area of disagreement—the national presidency. In post-convention commentary, Madison confided to Jefferson that questions surrounding the executive were "peculiarly embarrassing." He elaborated: "On the question whether it should consist of a single person, or a plurality of co-ordinate members, on the mode of appointment, on the duration of office, on the degree of power, on the re-eligibility, tedious and reiterated discussions took place. . . ."

Even more vexing than defining the powers of the President was the problem of procedures for electing the chief executive. The nationalists were not advocates of direct popular elections. Too much electioneering could lead the President to bow to public opinion and favor unwise legislation or, perhaps worse yet, to manipulate public opinion and the public will for demagogic purposes. Likewise, direct popular election would always favor candidates from the more populous states. The awkward scheme of an electoral college thus seemed the best solution to both problems. . . . None of the delegates imagined how differently the process would actually work, largely because they did not think in terms of the formation of national political parties.

[*VIII. The Judiciary: Postponing the Issue.*]

It was early September before these issues had been settled. The delegates were tired and worn down by their own interminable nitpicking. Eager to go home, they gave up on the matter of designing a full-blown national judiciary. They simply provided for a Supreme Court and left to the first Congress the task of creating a network of inferior federal courts. . . .

[*XI. A Second Beginning.*]

Thirty-nine delegates (actually a colleague from Delaware affixed John Dickinson's signature) signed the completed document on Monday, September 17. A few still in attendance begged off. Edmund Randolph was one, indicating that he wanted to keep his options open—a polite way of saying that he did not want formal association with the Constitution if it failed of ratification. The implication was that it might hurt his burgeoning political career back home.

One key to a less anxious future, the delegates reasoned, was the proposed concentration of decision-making authority in the central government. Powers that had been in the jurisdiction of the states under the Articles now were to be exercised in the common interest on the national level, including those of taxation, the regulation of interstate and foreign commerce, the making of foreign treaties, the coining of money and the regulation of its value, the funding of a public debt, and the raising and maintenance of armies and navies. Moreover, Congress could legislate whatever was "necessary and proper" to assure the creation of a strong new nation. From this perspective, the Constitution resolved nationalist frustrations over the diffuseness and even utter absence of decision making in the Confederation era. . . .

MADISON, RECORDS OF THE FEDERAL CONVENTION (1787)

[Here, we continue using the separation-of-powers doctrine as an illustration of the historical development of the Constitution, as we did in a preceding section on source documents. Our focus is on the debates in the Constitutional Convention, as the Framers grappled with the relationship among the executive, legislative and judicial branches.]

[June 2, 1787] [Mr. Dickinson] went into a discourse of some length, the sum of which was, that Legislative, Executive, & Judiciary departments ought to be made as independent. as possible; but that such an Executive as some seem to have in contemplation was not consistent with a republic; that a firm Executive could only exist in a limited monarchy. [I]n place of these attachments we must look out for something else. One source of stability is the double branch of the Legislature. The division of the Country into distinct States formed the other principal source of stability. . . .

[June 4, 1787] [M]r. Gerry doubts whether the Judiciary ought to form a part of [the legislative process], as they will have a sufficient check agst. encroachments on their own department by their exposition of the laws, which involved a power of deciding on the constitutionality. In some States, the Judges had actually set aside laws as being agst. the Constitution. This was done too with general approbation. It was quite foreign from the nature of Ye office to make them judges of the policy of public measures. He moves to postpone the clause in order to propose "that the National Executive shall have a right to negative any Legislative Act which shall not be afterwards passed by _____ parts [left blank in original] of each branch of the National Legislature. . . ."

Mr. Wilson thinks neither the original proposition nor the amendment go far enough. If the Legislative, Executive & Judiciary ought to be distinct & independent, The Executive ought to have an absolute negative. Without such a Self-defence the Legislature can at any moment sink it into non-existence. . . .

The question to postpone in order to take Mr. Gerry's proposition into consideration was agreed to. . . . [Here, an amendment was proposed by Wilson and Hamilton to remove the words "unless by __ parts of each branch of the national legislature", thereby giving the executive an absolute veto.]

Mr. Gerry sees no necessity for so great a control over the legislature as the best men in the Community would be comprised in the two branches of it.

Docr. Franklin, said he was sorry to differ from his colleague from whom he had a very great respect, on any occasion, but he could not help it on this. He had had some experience of this check in the Executive on the Legislature, under the proprietary Government of Pena. The negative of the Governor was constantly made use of to extort money. No good law whatever could be passed without a private bargain with him. [Franklin] was afraid, if a negative [*i.e.,* an absolute veto] should be given as proposed, that more power and money would be demanded, till at last eno' would be gotten to influence & bribe the legislature into a complete subjection to the will of the Executive.

Mr. Sherman was agst. enabling any one man to stop the will of whole. [Wilson and Hamilton's amendment ultimately was defeated.]

[June 6, 1787] Mr. Wilson moved to reconsider the vote excluding the judiciary from a share in the revision of the laws, and to add after "National Executive" the words "with a convenient number of the national judiciary"; remarking the expediency of reinforcing the Executive with the influence of that Department. . . .

Mr. Gerry felt the Executive, while standing alone wd. be more impartial than when he cd. be covered by the sanction & seduced by the sofestry of the Judges. . . .

[August 15, 1787] Mr. Govr. Morris, suggested the expedient of an absolute negative in the Executive. He could not agree that the Judiciary which was part of the Executive, should be bound to say that a direct violation of the Constitution was law. [H]e enlarged on the tendency of the Legislative Authority to usurpe on the Executive and wished the section to be postponed, in order to consider of some more effectual check than requiring two-thirds only to overrule the negative of the Executive.

Mr. Sherman. Can one man be trusted better than all the others if they all agree? This was neither wise or safe. He disapproved of Judges meddling in politics and parties. We have gone far enough in forming the negative as it now stands.

[Having thus settled upon a veto power in the executive, excluded the judiciary from the legislative or veto process, and allowed the legislature to override a veto by a two-thirds vote in each house, the Convention rejected further efforts to amend these provisions.]

§ 0.05   RATIFICATION OF THE CONSTITUTION AND ADOPTION OF THE BILL OF RIGHTS

[A]   The Federalists, The Opponents, and The Debates on Ratification

Here, as in the preceding sections on source documents and on convention debates, we use the separation-of-powers doctrine as an illustration of the historical development of the Constitution.

MADISON, THE FEDERALIST NO. 47: SEPARATION OF POWERS WITHIN THE FEDERAL GOVERNMENT AND CHARGES OF OPPONENTS. One of the principal objections inculcated by the more respectable adversaries to the Constitution, is its supposed violation of the political maxim, that the legislative, executive, and judiciary departments ought to be separate and distinct. [Critics charge that in the Constitution] [t]he several departments of power are distributed and blended in such a manner as at once to destroy all symmetry and beauty of form, and to expose some of the essential parts of the edifice to the danger of being crushed by the disproportionate weight of other parts.

Unification of Power As a Definition of Tyranny. [T]he accumulation of all powers, legislative, executive, and judiciary, in the same hands . . . may justly be pronounced the very definition of tyranny. Were the federal Constitution, therefore, really chargeable with the accumulation of power, or with a mixture of powers having a dangerous tendency to such an accumulation, no further arguments would be necessary to inspire a universal reprobation. . . . [B]ut the charge cannot be supported, and . . . the maxim on which it relies has been totally misconceived and misapplied. . . .

[Montesquieu and] the British Constitution. The oracle who is always consulted and cited on this subject is the celebrated Montesquieu. The British Constitution was to Montesquieu what Homer has been to the didactic writers on epic poetry. . . .

On the slightest view of the British Constitution, we must perceive that the legislative, executive, and judiciary departments are by no means totally separate and distinct from each other. The executive magistrate forms an integral part of the legislative authority. [A]ll the members of the judiciary department are appointed by him, can be removed by him on the address of the two Houses of Parliament. [O]ne branch of the legislative department forms also a great constitutional counsel to the Executive Chief [and] is the sole depository of judicial power in cases of impeachment, .and is invested with the supreme appellate jurisdiction in all other cases. The judges, again, are so far connected with the legislative department as often to attend and participate in its deliberations. . . .

Montesquieu's Theory Examined. From these facts, by which Montesquieu was guided, it may clearly be inferred that, in saying "there can be no liberty where the legislative and executive powers are united in the same person. . . ." . . ., he did not mean that these departments ought to have no *partial agency* in, or no *control* over, the acts of each other. His meaning, as his own words import, and still more conclusively as illustrated by the example . . ., can amount to no more than this, that where the *whole* power of one department is exercised by the same hands which possessed the *whole* power of another department, the fundamental principles of a free constitution are subverted. . . .

States Mix Departments. [Madison here gives examples of checks and balances in the governments of the respective states.]

All [State] Provisions Open to Criticism. [I] wish not to be regarded as an advocate for the particular organizations of the several state governments. [I]n some instances the fundamental principle under consideration has been violated by too great a mixture. . . . What I have wished to evince is, that the charge brought against the proposed Constitution, of violating the sacred maxim of free government, is warranted neither by the real meaning annexed to that maxim by its author [Montesquieu], nor by the sense in which it has hitherto been understood in America [in the states].

NOTES AND QUESTIONS

(1) *The Publication of the Federalist and Its Influence.* The authors of the Federalist were Alexander Hamilton and John Jay, in addition to Madison. All were Federalists and advocates of strong national government. The Federalist was published widely in newspapers, and these articles were a major influence on the ratification process. Of course, they view the Constitution through Federalist eyes; it has aptly been said there are two Constitutions, the draft produced in Philadelphia and the "Federalist Constitution." Consider the following question: To what extent should the views expressed in the Federalist be considered in interpreting the Constitution, given the nature of their influence on the interpretations that led to ratification?

(2) *The Opposition: Luther Martin's Example.* As the following section shows, there was significant opposition to the Constitution. State's rights advocates, particularly those from Maryland, and among those, particularly Luther Martin, were vociferous in their arguments. They raised everything from federalism concerns to the absence of a Bill of Rights (*see* below).

(3) *The Debates in the State Conventions; Ratification; the Bill of Rights.* Ratification depended upon affirmative votes in at least nine states in conventions set up for the purpose. Delaware, the first state to ratify, did so unanimously; the others were fragmented. Debate often was heated, as it was in the Constitutional Convention. Consider the following materials, which describe the political "deal" that was struck to secure ratification, at last, in Virginia and New York: The price was Madison's commitment to the adoption, by amendment, of a Bill of Rights.

[B]   The Bill of Rights and The Fourteenth Amendment

HITTNER, THE BILL OF RIGHTS AND THE RATIFICATION
OF THE CONSTITUTION
95 New Age 53, 54–58 (1987)[*]

[M]ost of us equate our Constitution with the precious freedoms it grants us—the freedom to practice the religion of our choice without government interference; the right to express freely our political and social views; the right to read the views of others in an open and free press; and the sanctity of our homes against unreasonable government intrusion. Yet, these freedoms, which we now view as synonymous with the United States Constitution, were not a part of the original document. . . .

[M]any of the framers regarded any Bill of Rights as superfluous. They simply saw no necessity to extend prohibitions into areas to which they believed the Federal Power did not extend in the first instance. Furthermore, many of the framers of the Constitution saw a danger in any attempt to list a Bill of Rights. Alexander Hamilton, in Federalist No. 84, warned against the inclusion of "various exceptions to powers which are not granted; and on this very account, would afford a colorable pretext to claim more than was granted. For why declare that things shall not be done which there is no power to do?" Moreover, James Wilson argued that in an attempt to set forth important rights, some inevitably would be overlooked and possibly be viewed as waived.

[E]ven before the document was presented to the state conventions for ratification, the campaign against the Constitution began. The loudest voices of objection came from

---

[*] Copyright © 1987 by *The New Age*. Reprinted with permission.

states' rights politicians, known as the Anti-Federalists. Many were not motivated entirely by a sincere fear that the Constitution without a Bill of Rights was inadequate to protect individual rights, but, by exploiting this issue, they hoped to defeat the Constitution altogether or force a second constitutional convention which would deny Congress the power to regulate commerce and to tax. Their objections to the omission of a Bill of Rights, however, struck a responsive chord in the mass of the people. . . .

By June 21, 1788, the Constitution had been ratified by nine states, the requisite number for its adoption. However, Virginia and New York had yet to approve the document, and it was inconceivable that the new union could survive without the inclusion of these two states. The apprehensions of the people by now had been considerably fanned, and the issue of the Bill of Rights produced vigorous political battles in the conventions of those two states.

In the New York convention, efforts to defeat the Constitution were led by Governor George Clinton, while ratification of the document was championed by Alexander Hamilton. The Virginia debate pitted James Madison against Patrick Henry, who demanded that a Bill of Rights be included.

In Virginia, it appeared that Madison and his supporters would be unable to muster sufficient votes to secure ratification. Hamilton wrote to Madison, expressing the belief that Virginia's action would determine the outcome in New York. The prospect of losing Virginia and, subsequently, New York—the proposed union's commercial center—made compromise inevitable.

Madison and George Nicholas worked out a strategy which was adopted by the advocates of ratification: the Virginia convention would ratify the Constitution and ask for subsequent amendments. Madison would pledge himself to help secure the amendments. [N]ews of Virginia's ratification reached the New York Convention and shortly thereafter New York became the 11th state to ratify, by a vote of 30 to 27.[9]

Considering himself "bound in honor and in duty" to follow through on the commitment made in Virginia, James Madison, the Federalist, became the champion of the Bill of Rights in the First Congress, refuting arguments against the amendments which had earlier been advanced by members of his own party. To those who believed that there was no need for a Bill of Rights because the powers of the Federal Government were limited and enumerated in the Constitution, Madison pointed out the fact that Congress was authorized to make all laws "necessary and proper" to implement the enumerated powers. . . .

Similarly, Madison refuted the contention that the declaration of rights established by the individual states constituted an adequate protection of personal liberties: "[S]ome States have no bills of rights, [and] there are others provided with very defective ones. . . ."

[T]he Bill of Rights formally became part of the Constitution in December, 1791.

The Bill of Rights was born out of fear of . . . an unrestrained strong central government. Madison, however, would have extended the Bill of Rights to ensure protection of the people from abuses by the State Government as well. He set forth this proposal before the first Congress in 1789:

> I should, therefore, wish to extend this interdiction, and add that no states shall violate the equal rights of conscience, freedom of the press, or trial by jury in criminal cases. . . . [I]t must be admitted on all hands that the State Governments are as liable to attack these invaluable privileges as the General Government is, and therefore ought to be as cautiously guarded against.

Madison's proposal, although approved by the House, could not muster the required

---

[9] It is interesting to note that North Carolina ratified the Constitution in 1789 only after Congress formally proposed the Bill of Rights; in 1790 Rhode Island became the 13th and final state to ratify.

two-thirds vote in the state-minded Senate. It was not until the post-Civil War period, with the ratification of the 14th amendment, that the United States Constitution provided citizens with a shield against the potentially abusive wielding of power by the states.

[In modern times, by construction of the 14th amendment,] the Court began to hold that certain provisions of the Bill of Rights . . . must be assumed to apply to the states as well as to the Federal Government. Rights guaranteed by the fourth, fifth, and sixth amendments were "selectively incorporated"; by the end of the 1960's, the Supreme Court had adopted all but a few of the Bill of Rights guarantees as protections against abuses by the state governments.

[Truly] the institution of the Bill of Rights has proved to be a "monumental afterthought. . . ."

CONSTITUTIONAL HISTORY: SUGGESTIONS FOR FURTHER READING

The most important primary sources of information about the founding are James Madison's Notes of Debates in the Federal Convention of 1787 (W.W. Norton 1987) and The Federalist Papers (pseudonymously co-authored by Madison, Alexander Hamilton, and John Jay to advocate ratification of the Constitution). For a collection of primary sources, see M. Farrand, Records of the Federal Convention of 1787 (Yale Univ. Press 1911).

For scholarly analysis, see, e.g., C. Van Doren, The Great Rehearsal (The Viking Press, 1948, reprinted 1987); C. Rossiter, 1787: The Grand Convention (McMillan & Co. 1966, reprinted 1987); R. Bernstein, Are We to Be a Nation?: The Making of the Constitution (Harvard Univ. Press 1987). See generally Steiner & Van Beck, *A More (or Less) Perfect List of Bicentennial Books*, 25 Hous. Lawyer 24 (1987) (describing Bernstein's work as "[t]he best Bicentennial book to appear thus far"). See also L. Levy, Encyclopedia of the American Constitution (1987) (four-volume work).

For lighter reading, see C. Bowen, Miracle at Philadelphia (Little, Brown & Co. 1966, reprinted 1986); see also C. Mee, The Genius of the People (Harper & Row, Publishers 1987). A popular history can be found in F. Barbash, The Founding: A Dramatic Account of the Writing of the Constitution (Simon & Schuster 1987).

Chapter 1

JUDICIAL POWER AND ITS LIMITS

§ 1.01 JUDICIAL REVIEW: ITS NATURE AND ITS APPROPRIATENESS

A. HAMILTON, THE FEDERALIST NO. 78, at 490 (B. Wright ed. 1961). Whoever attentively considers the different departments of power must perceive that, in a government in which they are separated from each other, the judiciary . . . will always be the least dangerous to the political rights of the Constitution; because it will be least in a capacity to annoy or injure them. . . . The judiciary . . . has no influence over either the sword or the purse; no direction either of the strength or of the wealth of the society; and can take no active resolution whatever. It may be said to have neither force nor will, but merely judgment; and must depend upon the aid of the executive arm even for the efficacy of its judgments.

[A] Can the Courts Overrule Congress?

Can the Courts Overrule Congress? In the United States, it often is taken for granted that the answer is yes. But that answer should not be accepted uncritically. The Constitution does not expressly address the issue.

Is Our History of Judicial Review an American Anomaly? In fact, some Western democracies deny the judiciary any power to countermand decisions of the legislative branch (or they restrict that power). That state of affairs provides workable government, including protection of individual rights, in such sophisticated democracies as England. Furthermore, in the United States, the judiciary has no monopoly on the enforcement of the Constitution, and indeed the members of the legislative and executive branches have duties to protect it—and they take an oath to do so.

The Pre-Marbury History. Since the text of the Constitution does not explicitly provide for judicial authority to overrule Congress (or the Executive Branch), the decision in *Marbury v. Madison* (below) may seem to constitute unjustified overreaching by the Court. Certainly, both original critics (such as Jefferson) and more modern critics (such as former Attorney General Meese) consider the *Marbury* decision questionable.

What if the Constitution's history suggested that the Framers intended for judicial review even though the concept was not textually expressed? In this regard, consider Alexander Hamilton in FEDERALIST NO. 78:

> The interpretation of the laws is the proper and peculiar province of the courts. A constitution is, . . . and must be regarded by the judges as, a fundamental law. It therefore belongs to them to ascertain its meaning as well as the meaning of any particular act proceeding from the legislative body.

THE FEDERALIST NO. 78 at 492 (Hamilton) (B. Wright ed. 1961).

The Pre-Marbury Precedent. Also, consider the precedent in the states and the lower federal courts. While the conventional wisdom on this question was that, before *Marbury*, judicial review was rarely exercised, a recent comprehensive study concludes that there was a more substantial body of case law supporting the doctrine. Dean William Michael Treanor has identified thirty-one cases where a statute was invalidated. Dean Treanor also found seven decisions where, although the statute was upheld, at least one judge asserted that the statute was unconstitutional. *See* William Michael Treanor, *Judicial Review Before Marbury*, 58 STAN. L. REV. 455 (2005). While this historical information does not necessarily *justify* judicial review, it would suggest that Chief Justice Marshall's analysis might not be as unique or radical as some critics have charged. Dean Treanor's research indicates that *Marbury* may instead have been a synthesis of an existing body of precedent.

[1]   Inferring Judicial Review from the American Written Constitution: *Marbury v. Madison*

NOTE ON THE HISTORICAL BACKGROUND OF *MARBURY v. MADISON*

The Federalists Lose the Presidential Election of 1800. During the administration of President George Washington, two political parties fought for dominance: the Federalists and the Anti-Federalists (also known as the Democratic-Republicans). John Adams, a leading Federalist, defeated Thomas Jefferson in the presidential election of 1796. Adams turned out to be an unpopular president, and his administration lost support. In the 1800 presidential election, Jefferson, a leading Anti-Federalist, defeated Adams.

The Federalists' Efforts to Retain Control of the Judicial Branch: The Appointment of Chief Justice John Marshall. After Jefferson's election in 1800, Adams remained president until the end of his term of office on March 4, 1801. The final months of the Adams administration were a busy period for the Federalists as they sought to retain control of the federal government through the judicial branch. Keeping control of the Supreme Court was particularly important to Adams and the Federalists, and when Oliver Ellsworth resigned as Chief Justice of the United States in December 1800, Adams attempted to reappoint John Jay, who had served as the nation's first Chief Justice. But Jay refused reappointment (he had resigned to become Governor of New York, expressing the opinion that the United States Supreme Court would never amount to much!). Adams then turned to his very capable Secretary of State, John Marshall. The Senate confirmed Marshall's nomination as Chief Justice on January 27, 1801, and he took office eight days later, on February 4, 1801. In addition to his new post as Chief Justice, Marshall remained Secretary of State until the end of President Adams' administration on March 4, 1801. Thus, for a crucial one-month period, Marshall served as both Secretary of State and Chief Justice of the United States.

The Federalist Court-Packing Plan. During February, while Marshall held both posts, Congress passed two important pieces of legislation designed to entrench a Federalist judiciary. The Circuit Court Act doubled the number of federal judges and permitted Adams to appoint sixteen judges to the newly created Federal Circuit Court. A later enactment permitted Adams to appoint 42 justices of the peace for the District of Columbia and Alexandria, Virginia.

The "Midnight" Judges. These "midnight" appointments went almost exclusively to good Federalists. In the case of the District of Columbia and Alexandria judges, Senate confirmation was completed only one day before Jefferson was to become president. Adams signed all the commissions, and Secretary of State John Marshall—with help from his younger brother—attempted to sign, seal, and have delivered all of the commissions during the last hours of President Adams' administration.

Non-Delivery of Marbury's Commission. Jefferson became president, however, before all the commissions were delivered, and he and his Secretary of State, James Madison, refused to deliver the commissions Adams and Marshall had left behind. This action was not surprising, since Jefferson and his party had opposed Adams' midnight appointments. One of the judges who did not get his commission was William Marbury—who later became the protagonist in *Marbury v. Madison.*

Marbury's Original Mandamus Action in the Supreme Court Under the Judiciary Act. Section 13 of the Judiciary Act of 1789 contained a provision for mandamus jurisdiction in the Supreme Court. Under the purported authority of this provision, Marbury brought an original action for mandamus in the Supreme Court late in 1801. The Court set the case for argument in 1802 and ordered Madison to "show cause why mandamus should not issue." Madison refused even to appear. However, Congress abolished part of the Court's 1802 term at the same time as it repealed the Circuit Court Act, and the case was not heard until February 1803.

Marshall's Political Dilemma—Solved by Judicial Review. The case presented Marshall with a considerable political dilemma. No doubt he was personally inclined to rule in favor of the Federalist claims and order President Jefferson to deliver the commissions. However, if the Court did that, there were two probable consequences: (1) President Jefferson would ignore the order, and (2) Chief Justice Marshall and the other Federalist judges on the Court would have to be impeached. Marshall solved the dilemma by holding that the Supreme Court could not be given the original mandamus jurisdiction that Congress allegedly had conferred by Section 13 of the Judiciary Act. The reason: Section 13, wrote Marshall, was repugnant to the Constitution. The Court's power of judicial review was a logical necessity to this conclusion.

The Context and Consequence of Marshall's Solution. Marshall's solution has been called brilliant. Jefferson and the Anti-Federalists won a small battle: Marbury did not get his commission. But the judiciary won the war: the Court claimed the power of judicial review and the authority to declare unconstitutional acts of the legislative or executive branches.

TEXT OF THE CONSTITUTION

Art. I, § 1: All legislative Powers herein granted shall be vested in a Congress of the United States. . . .

Art. II, § 1: The executive Power shall be vested in a President of the United States. . . .

Art. III, § 1: The judicial Power shall be vested in one supreme Court, and in such inferior Courts as Congress shall from time to time ordain and establish . . . .

§ 2: The judicial Power shall extend to all Cases, in Law and Equity, arising under this Constitution, the Laws of the United States, and Treaties made . . . under their Authority;. . . .

In all Cases affecting Ambassadors, other public Ministers and Consuls, and those in which a State shall be a Party, the supreme Court shall have original Jurisdiction. In all the other Cases before mentioned, the supreme Court shall have appellate Jurisdiction, . . . with such Exceptions, and under such Regulations as the Congress shall make. . . .

ALSO READ: Art. VI, cl. 2–3 (the supremacy and oath-of-office clauses).

MARBURY v. MADISON
5 U.S. (1 Cranch) 137 (1803)

[T]he following opinion of the Court was delivered by the CHIEF JUSTICE [JOHN MARSHALL]. . . .

At the last term . . . a rule was granted in this case, requiring the secretary of state to show cause why a mandamus should not issue, directing him to deliver to William Marbury his commission. . . .

In the order in which the court has viewed this subject, the following questions have been considered and decided.

1st. Has the applicant a right to the commission he demands?

2d. If he has a right, and that right has been violated, do the laws of his country afford him a remedy?

3d. If they do afford a remedy, is it a mandamus issuing from this court?

The first object of inquiry is,

1st. Has the applicant a right to the commission he demands?

His right originates in an act of congress passed in February, 1801, concerning the District of Columbia. . . .

It appears, from the affidavits, that in compliance with this law, a commission for William Marbury, as a justice of the peace for the county of Washington, was signed by John Adams, then President of the United States; after which the seal of the United States was affixed to it; but the commission has never reached the person for whom it was made out. . . .

To withhold his commission, therefore, is an act deemed by the court not warranted by law, but violative of a vested legal right.

This brings us to the second inquiry; which is,

2d. If he has a right, and that right has been violated, do the laws of this country afford him a remedy? . . .

The government of the United States has been emphatically termed a government of laws, and not of men. It will certainly cease to deserve this high appellation, if the laws furnish no remedy for the violation of a vested legal right. . . .

The conclusion from this reasoning is, that where the heads of departments are the political or confidential agent of the executive, merely to execute the will of the President, or rather to act in cases in which the executive possesses a constitutional or legal discretion, nothing can be more perfectly clear than that their acts are only politically examinable. But where a specific duty is assigned by law, and individual rights depend upon the performance of that duty, it seems equally clear that the individual who considers himself injured, has a right to resort to the laws of this country for a remedy. . . .

It remains to be inquired whether,

3d. He is entitled to the remedy for which he applies. This depends on,

1st. The nature of the writ applied for; and,

2d. The power of this court.

1st. The nature of the writ.

Blackstone, in the 3d volume of his Commentaries, page 110, defines a mandamus to be "a command issuing in the king's name from the court of king's bench, and directed to any person, corporation, or inferior court of judicature within the king's dominions, requiring them to do some particular thing therein specified, which appertains to their office and duty, and which the court of king's bench has previously determined, or at least supposes, to be consonant to right and justice. . . ."

. . . Or, in the words of Lord Mansfield, the applicant, in this case, has a right to execute an office of public concern, and is kept out of possession of that right.

These circumstances certainly concur in this case. . . .

This, then, is a plain case for a mandamus, either to deliver the commission, or a copy of it from the record; and it only remains to be inquired,

[2d] Whether it can issue from this court.

The act to establish the judicial courts of the United States authorizes the Supreme Court "to issue writs of mandamus in cases warranted by the principles and usages of law, to any courts appointed, or persons holding office, under the authority of the United States."

The Secretary of State, being a person holding an office under the authority of the

United States, is precisely within the letter of the description, and if this court is not authorized to issue a writ of mandamus to such an officer, it must be because the law is unconstitutional, and therefore absolutely incapable of conferring the authority, and assigning the duties which its words purport to confer and assign.

The constitution vests the whole judicial power of the United States in one Supreme Court, and such inferior courts as congress shall, from time to time, ordain and establish. This power is expressly extended to all cases arising under the laws of the United States; and, consequently, in some form, may be exercised over the present case; because the right claimed is given by a law of the United States.

In the distribution of this power it is declared that "the Supreme Court shall have original jurisdiction in all cases affecting ambassadors, other public ministers and consuls, and those in which a state shall be a party. In all other cases, the Supreme Court shall have appellate jurisdiction. . . ."   *orig. juris.*

It cannot be presumed that any clause in the constitution is intended to be without effect; and, therefore, such a construction is inadmissible, unless the words require it. . . .

To enable this court, then, to issue a mandamus, it must be shown to be an exercise of appellate jurisdiction, or to be necessary to enable them to exercise appellate jurisdiction. . . .   *hold*

The authority, therefore, given to the Supreme Court, by the act establishing the judicial courts of the United States, to issue writs of mandamus to public officers, appears not to be warranted by the constitution; and it becomes necessary to inquire whether a jurisdiction so conferred can be exercised.

The question, whether an act, repugnant to the constitution, can become the law of the land, is a question deeply interesting to the United States; but, happily, not of an intricacy proportioned to its interest. It seems only necessary to recognize certain principles, supposed to have been long and well established, to decide it. . . .

. . . The powers of the legislature are defined and limited; and that those limits may not be mistaken, or forgotten, the constitution is written. To what purpose are powers limited, and to what purpose is that limitation committed to writing, if these limits may, at any time, be passed by those intended to be restrained? The distinction between a government with limited and unlimited powers is abolished, if those limits do not confine the persons on whom they are imposed, and if acts prohibited and acts allowed, are of equal obligation. It is a proposition too plain to be contested, that the constitution controls any legislative act repugnant to it; or, that the legislature may alter the constitution by an ordinary act.

Between these alternatives there is no middle ground. The constitution is either a superior paramount law, unchangeable by ordinary means, or it is on a level with ordinary legislative acts, and, like other acts, is alterable when the legislature shall please to alter it.

If the former part of the alternative be true, then a legislative act contrary to the constitution is not law: if the latter part be true, then written constitutions are absurd attempts, on the part of the people, to limit a power in its own nature illimitable. . . .

This theory is essentially attached to a written constitution, and, is consequently, to be considered, by this court, as one of the fundamental principles of our society. . . .

It is emphatically the province and duty of the judicial department to say what the law is. Those who apply the rule to particular cases, must of necessity expound and interpret that rule. If two laws conflict with each other, the courts must decide on the operation of each.

So if a law be in opposition to the constitution; if both the law and the constitution apply to a particular case, so that the court must either decide that case conformably to the law, disregarding the constitution; or conformably to the constitution, disregarding the law; the court must determine which of these conflicting rules governs the case. This is of the very essence of judicial duty. . . .

Those, then, who controvert the principle that the constitution is to be considered, in court, as a paramount law, are reduced to the necessity of maintaining that courts must close their eyes on the constitution, and see only the law.

This doctrine would subvert the very foundation of all written constitutions. . . .

That it thus reduces to nothing what we have deemed the greatest improvement on political institutions, a written constitution, would of itself be sufficient, in America, where written constitutions have been viewed with so much reverence, for rejecting the construction. But the peculiar expressions of the constitution of the United States furnish additional arguments in favour of its rejection.

The judicial power of the United States is extended to all cases arising under the constitution.

Could it be the intention of those who gave this power, to say that in using it the constitution should not be looked into? That a case arising under the constitution should be decided without examining the instrument under which it arises? . . .

There are many other parts of the constitution which serve to illustrate this subject.

It is declared that "no tax or duty shall be laid on articles exported from any state." Suppose a duty on the export of cotton, of tobacco, or of flour; and a suit instituted to recover it. Ought judgment to be rendered in such a case? Ought the judges to close their eyes on the constitution, and only see the law?

The constitution declares "that no bill of attainder or ex post facto law shall be passed."

If, however, such a bill should be passed, and a person should be prosecuted under it; must the court condemn to death those victims whom the constitution endeavors to preserve?

"No person," says the constitution, "shall be convicted of treason unless on the testimony of two witnesses to the same overt act, or on confession in open court."

Here the language of the constitution is addressed especially to the courts. It prescribes, directly for them, a rule of evidence not to be departed from. If the legislature should change that rule, and declare one witness, or a confession out of court, sufficient for conviction, must the constitutional principle yield to the legislative act?

From these, and many other selections which might be made, it is apparent, that the framers of the constitution contemplated that instrument as a rule for the government of courts, as well as of the legislature.

Why otherwise does it direct the judges to take an oath to support it? This oath certainly applies in an especial manner, to their conduct in their official character. How immoral to impose it on them, if they were to be used as the instruments, and the knowing instruments, for violating what they swear to support! . . .

Why does a judge swear to discharge his duties agreeably to the constitution of the United States, if that constitution forms no rule for his government? If it is closed upon him, and cannot be inspected by him?

If such be the real state of things, this is worse than solemn mockery. To prescribe, or to take this oath, becomes equally a crime.

It is also not entirely unworthy of observation, that in declaring what shall be the supreme law of the land, the constitution itself is first mentioned; and not the laws of the United States generally, but those only which shall be made in pursuance of the constitution, have that rank.

Thus, the particular phraseology of the constitution of the United States confirms and strengthens the principle, supposed to be essential to all written constitutions, that a law repugnant to the constitution is void; and that courts, as well as other departments, are bound by that instrument.

The rule must be discharged. _C O._

NOTES AND QUESTIONS ON THE *MARBURY* OPINION

(1) *The Existence of Judicial Review Under the American Constitution: Marbury v. Madison, 5 U.S. (1 Cranch) 137 (1803).* Marbury sued the Jefferson Administration after Madison refused to deliver his judicial commission. Marbury brought his claim directly in the Supreme Court under Section 13 of the Judiciary Act of 1789, passed by the first Congress. But, even though the term *judicial review* does not appear in the text of the Constitution, the Court, per Chief Justice Marshall, held that it had authority to engage in judicial review of the actions of Congress and then invalidated Section 13.

The rest of American constitutional law derives from the Court's conclusion that judicial review exists. The following Notes develop aspects of the *Marbury* decision and its fundamental holding recognizing judicial review. Recent scholarship (in conjunction with the 200th anniversary of *Marbury*) includes the Symposium Issue, 38 Wake Forest Law Review 313 (2003). Students may find the articles by Professors Suzanna Sherry and Robert F. Nagel particularly helpful. *See also* Sanford Levinson and Jack M. Balkin, *What Are the Facts of Marbury v. Madison,* 20 Const. Comment. 255 (2003).

(2) *Does Marshall's Supremacy Clause Reasoning "Beg a Critical Question?": Van Alstyne, A Critical Guide to Marbury v. Madison, 1969 Duke L.J. 1, 22–23 (1969).* Professor Van Alstyne's work, which is among the most influential commentaries on the case, suggests that in his analysis of the supremacy clause, Marshall missed the point:

> The point is that Marshall arguably may have begged a critical question, *i.e.,* he failed to acknowledge and thus to answer a question critical to the position he takes. *Assuming that an act repugnant to the Constitution is not a law "in pursuance thereof" and thus must not be given effect as the supreme law of the land, who, according to the Constitution, is to make the determination as to whether any given law is in fact repugnant to the Constitution itself?* Such alleged repugnance is ordinarily not self-demonstrating . . . Marshall never confronts this question. His substitute question, whether a law repugnant to the Constitution still binds the courts, *assumes* that such "repugnance" has appropriately been determined by those granted such power under the Constitution. It is clear, however, that the supremacy clause itself cannot be the clear textual basis for a claim by the judiciary that this prerogative to determine repugnancy belongs to it.

Congress has the duty to construe and follow the Constitution, and the Supremacy Clause could as plausibly—indeed, perhaps more plausibly—have been read as devolving this ultimate power upon Congress, rather than the Court. Is this criticism persuasive?

(3) *Deriving Judicial Review from the Judicial Power Granted by Article III: Graglia, Judicial Review on the Basis of "Regime Principles:" A Prescription for Government by Judges, 26 S. Tex. L.J. 435, 436 (1985).* Marshall reasons that, "it is emphatically the province and duty of the judicial department to say what the law is," and uses this famous dictum as the basis for a conclusion that the judicial duty includes resolving constitutional conflicts. Perhaps this reasoning is open to criticism, however, on the ground that there was only doubtful precedent for regarding the judicial power as including the setting aside of parliamentary acts. The English position at the time was typified by the statement of Lord Chief Justice Holt in *City of London v. Wood,* 12 Mod. 669 (1700): "An act of parliament can do no wrong, though it may do several things that

---

look pretty odd." Therefore, perhaps the unusual nature of judicial review indicates that, if a part of the Constitution, it would be expressed. Consider the following analysis by Professor Graglia:

> Even as so limited [by Hamilton and Marshall]—to disallowing statutes in irreconcilable variance with the Constitution—the power is an extraordinary one, without precedent in either English or civil law—so extraordinary, indeed, that the absence of explicit provision for it in the Constitution might well be taken as establishing that no such power was granted by those who ratified the Constitution. If enforcing the Constitution is what judicial review meant in fact, however, it would be of no great importance, hardly meriting discussion. Very few occasions for its exercise would arise, because the Constitution contains few limitations on self-government, and those limitations are almost never violated.

> One unfamiliar with the Constitution could easily get the impression from . . . defenses of judicial review, that the Constitution is an esoteric and lengthy document, like, say, the Bible or the Talmud, or at least the Tax Code, in which one might by sufficient study find all manner of interesting things. It is therefore important to emphasize at the outset of a discussion of judicial review that the Constitution is very short and straightforward, easily printed with all amendments on fewer than twenty pages and apparently quite easy to understand. . . .*

Is Graglia's view persuasive? On the other hand, could Marshall's statement have derived from the FEDERALIST No. 78, at 521 (P. Ford Ed. 1898)? Alexander Hamilton said:

> The interpretation of the laws is the proper and peculiar province of the courts. A constitution is, in fact, and must be regarded by the judges as, a fundamental law. It therefore belongs to them to ascertain its meaning as well as the meaning of any particular act proceeding from the legislative body.

Can judicial review be justified by the extension, in Article III, of the judicial power to "all cases arising under the Constitution?" Note that a case easily can arise under the Constitution and not involve invalidation of an act of Congress (*e.g.*, a damages suit against a state officer for violating the plaintiff's rights under the Constitution).

(4) *Marshall's Reliance on the Judicial Oath: Eakin v. Raub, 12 S. & R. 330 (Pa. 1825).* Does the "judicial oath" provision of Article VI, cl. 3, add anything to Marshall's argument? Officers of the other branches are required to take a similar oath. Consider *Eakin v. Raub*, 12 S. & R. 330 (Pa. 1825) (Gibson, J., dissenting):

> The oath to support the Constitution is not peculiar to the judges, but is taken indiscriminately by every officer of the government. . . .

> [The judges do not do a positive act in violation of the Constitution] if the law has been passed according to the forms established in the Constitution. The fallacy of the question is, in supposing that the judiciary adopts the acts of the legislature as its own. . . . [T]he fault is imputable to the legislature, and on it the responsibility exclusively rests. . . .

(5) *Is the Whole of the Argument Better than the Sum of its Parts?* Van Alstyne, *supra*, at 29, suggests that item-by-item criticism of Marshall's opinion may do it an "unfairness." As Van Alstyne sees the opinion, "each argument, and each textual fragment on which the argument rested, may not seem especially compelling by itself. However, perhaps the separate pieces support each other, the fragments draw together, and the 'whole' of Marshall's argument is much better than each part separately considered." Is this conclusion persuasive (or should we expect constitutional opinions to be logical in a syllogistic way)?

---

* Copyright © 1985 by Lino A. Graglia and the *South Texas Law Journal*. Reprinted by permission.

(6) *Other Criticisms of Marshall's Opinion.* Judicial review is not the only controversial aspect of Marshall's opinion. Among the arguable flaws that have been exposed by Van Alstyne and others are the following:

(a) *Should Marshall have considered jurisdiction only?* It generally is considered improper for a court that concludes that it lacks jurisdiction then to proceed to render an opinion on the merits. Why, then, did Marshall consider Marbury's entitlement to the commission as the "first" issue? The answer may lie in Marshall's political motives. His opinion enabled Marshall to give Jefferson and the antifederalists a stern lecture (ostensibly above politics) on the impropriety of their conduct.

(b) *Did the existence of a "right" to Marbury's commission imply the existence of a remedy?* Marshall's dictum that right implies remedy has been challenged frequently. "In the few cases where the executive's removal power has been successfully challenged, moreover, the only *remedy* ever granted was a judgment for salary. Restoration to the office itself apparently has never been granted to an official removed by the President." Van Alstyne, *supra* at 10. In *Myers v. United States*, 272 U.S. 52 (1926), Chief Justice Taft expressly disapproved this holding of *Marbury*.

(c) *Should the constitutional issue have been avoided by construction of the act of Congress in question?* When a statute is ambiguous, a court generally should prefer a construction that will avoid the constitutional question. *See, e.g., United States v. Security Industrial Bank*, 459 U.S. 70 (1982). In construing Section 13 of the Judiciary Act, however, Marshall's opinion never seriously considers this approach; indeed, it can be argued that he went out of his way to find the provision unconstitutional. The nub of the question was whether Section 13 required the Supreme Court to entertain a mandamus proceeding that originated in that Court, as opposed to one involving review of a lower court proceeding. The relevant text of Section 13 is as follows:

[T]he Supreme Court shall have exclusive jurisdiction of all controversies of a civil nature [for which the Constitution provides original jurisdiction in the Supreme Court]. . . . The Supreme Court shall also have appellate jurisdiction from the circuit courts and courts of the several states, . . . and shall have power to issue . . . writs of mandamus, in cases warranted by the principles and usages of law, to any courts appointed, or persons holding office, under the authority of the United States.

Couldn't this provision have been subjected to a narrowing construction that would have avoided confronting its unconstitutionality?

(d) *Should Marshall have recused himself?: Aetna Life Ins. Co. v. Lavoie, 475 U.S. 813 (1986).* In *Aetna* the Supreme Court held that a judge should recuse himself whenever the circumstances "would offer a possible temptation to the average . . . judge to . . . lead him not to hold the balance nice, clear and true" between the parties. This standard is a requirement of due process. In *Martin v. Hunter's Lessee*, reproduced in a later section of this chapter, Marshall did not sit because, as an owner of some of the property involved, he had a financial interest in the outcome of the case. Didn't Marshall's involvement in the events leading to Marbury's suit require his recusal?

(7) *Some of the Historical Background of Marbury.* In assessing the constitutionality of the Judiciary Act of 1789, consider the following facts: The legislation in question, § 13 of the Judiciary Act of 1789, had been enacted by the first Congress. The first Congress, of course, included James Madison, the "Father of the Constitution," and 18 others who had been members of the Constitutional Convention. Section 13 of the Judiciary Act had been sponsored by a special Senate Judiciary Committee of leading lawyers, five of whose eight members had been members of the Constitutional Convention. The Judiciary Act had been drafted by the head of the committee, Oliver

Ellsworth, who was the leading lawyer of the day, and the leading member of the Convention's five-man Committee of Detail. Oliver Ellsworth would soon become Chief Justice of the United States Supreme Court. Ellsworth and his Committee of Detail had drafted Article III of the Constitution. Section 13 had been approved by President Washington, who had been President of the Constitutional Convention.

The Judiciary Act of 1789 was in large measure the product of the Framers themselves. The same people who drafted Article III drafted the Judiciary Act of 1789. There is no evidence that any of these members of the Constitutional Convention as members of Congress questioned the provision which the *Marbury* Court later found unconstitutional.

These facts pose the issue: Since essentially the same people wrote Article III of the Constitution and wrote the Judiciary Act of 1789, what is the likelihood that, a few months after writing the Constitution, they would write a statute which was inconsistent with (and thereby unconstitutional under) the Constitution? *See generally* JAMES BRADLEY THAYER, JOHN MARSHALL (Da Capo Press ed. 1974).

[2] Judicial Review and the Madisonian Dilemma: Reconciling Democratic Governance with Minority Protection

BICKEL, THE LEAST DANGEROUS BRANCH 19, 27 (1962).* Nothing can finally depreciate the central function that is assigned in democratic theory and practice to the electoral process; nor can it be denied that the policy-making power of representative institutions, born of the electoral process, is the distinguishing characteristic of this system. Judicial review works counter to this characteristic. . . .

[D]emocracies do live by the idea, central to the process of gaining the consent of the governed, that the majority has the ultimate power to displace the decision-makers and to reject any part of their policy. With that idea, judicial review must achieve some measure of consonance.

UNITED STATES v. CAROLENE PRODUCTS, CO. 304 U.S. 144 (1938). This opinion hinted, in dictum, at a means by which judicial review might generally honor majority rule but emphasize protection of minority rights in those cases in which such protection was most needed. Justice Stone's opinion for the Court upheld a statute regulating commerce in milk. The Court determined that the statute had a "rational basis." In a famous footnote, however, *id.* at 152–53 n.4, Justice Stone distinguished certain kinds of cases for which a rational basis might be insufficient, and stricter scrutiny might be warranted. In so doing, he arguably provided the basis for two different levels of judicial review—that applicable to cases generally, and a stricter kind applicable to three special cases, defined as follows:

> There may be narrower scope for operation of the presumption of constitutionality when legislation appears on its face to be within a specific prohibition of the Constitution, such as those of the first ten amendments. . . .
>
> It is unnecessary to consider now whether legislation which restricts those political processes which can ordinarily be expected to bring about repeal of undesirable legislation, is to be subjected to more exacting judicial scrutiny . . . than are most other types of legislation. . . .
>
> Nor need we inquire whether similar considerations enter into the review of statutes, directed at particular religious, or national, or racial minorities . . .; whether prejudice against discrete and insular minorities may be a special condition, . . . which may call for a correspondingly more searching judicial inquiry.

NOTES AND QUESTIONS ON THE RELATIONSHIP OF
JUDICIAL REVIEW TO DEMOCRACY

(1) *Is Judicial Review "Anti-Democratic?"* Supreme Court Justice Robert H. Jackson called the Court "anti-democratic," and Justice Felix Frankfurter wrote of the Court's "stupendous powers" of judicial review that were a "limitation on popular government." Justices (and all federal judges) have life tenure (Art. III, § 1), subject to removal only by impeachment (Art. II, § 4). Thus, when the Court strikes down an act of Congress, "we are confronted by the fact that the one non-elective and non-removable element in the government rejects the conclusion of the two elective and removable branches." LEVY, JUDICIAL REVIEW 13–15 (1967).

(2) *The Constitutional Provisions Insulating Article III Judges from the Majoritarian Political Processes.* The materials above and the previous Note have highlighted a central difference between judicial decision-making (i.e., judicial review) and decision-making by other governmental entities (*i.e.*, Congress; state legislators, etc.): the Framers gave Article III judicial decision-makers lifetime tenure and thereby gave these judges a great deal of "insulation" (*i.e.*, freedom) from the political accountability faced by other decision-makers (*e.g.*, the Executive). *See* Art. III, § 1. The Framers, who were experienced participants in the colonial political processes, also provided that Article III judges should "receive for their Services, a Compensation, which shall not be diminished during their Continuance in Office." *Id.* The Framers understood that the independence created by lifetime tenure could be undercut if the Congress could simply lower judicial compensation in response to counter-majoritarian decisions; the Framers sought to avoid the situation where Judges performing their Article III duties were driven from the position by financial reasons. Thus, the Compensation Clause was intended to complement the lifetime tenure provision of Article III.

In *United States v. Hatter*, 532 U.S. 557 (2001), some federal judges claimed that the imposition of certain Medicare taxes violated the Compensation Clause. The Court, per Justice Breyer, held that, while Article III Judges could be subjected to general, non-discriminatory taxes, the Compensation Clause prohibited a tax which "singles out judges for specially unfavorable treatment." Justices Scalia and Thomas dissented in part. The *Hatter* decision contains an extensive discussion of the history and policies underlying the Compensation Clause, and you should consider the role of the Framers' intent to create "judicial independence" as you review the materials in this casebook.

(3) *Ely's Thesis that Judicial Review Can Counteract Failures of Democracy: J. Ely, Democracy and Distrust (1980).* In this enormously influential book, Dean Ely argues that judicial review actually can be representation-reinforcing—that is, it can enhance, rather than frustrate, democracy. It can do so, Ely argues, if it defers to the political branches when they would naturally be expected to further the democratic process, but provides for a stricter standard to check what might be called failures of democracy. As Ely puts it,

> [T]he representation-reinforcing orientation whose contours I have sketched . . . is not inconsistent with, but on the contrary is entirely supportive of, the American system of representative democracy. It recognizes the unacceptability of the claim that appointed and life-tenured judges are better reflectors of conventional values that elected representatives, devoting itself instead to policing the mechanisms by which the system seems to insure that our elected representatives will actually represent. . . .

> The approach to constitutional adjudication recommended here . . . intervenes only when the "market," in our case the political market, is systematically malfunctioning. (A referee analogy is also not far off: the referee is to intervene only when one team is gaining unfair advantage, not because the "wrong" team has scored.). . . In a representative democracy value determinations are to be made by our elected representatives, and if in fact most of us disapprove we can vote them out of office. Malfunction occurs when the *process* is undeserving of

trust, when (1) the ins are choking off the channels of political change to ensure that they will stay in and the outs will stay out, or (2) though no one is actually denied a voice or a vote, representatives beholden to an effective majority are systematically disadvantaging some minority out of simple hostility or a prejudiced refusal to recognize commonalities of interest, and thereby denying that minority the protection afforded other groups by a representative system.*

Is this thesis persuasive, or does it break down in the face of criticism? First, consider who is to determine when "representation-reinforcing" intervention is needed, and what form it should take. Ely says that only judges are "in a position objectively to assess claims—though no one could suppose the evaluation won't be full of judgment calls. . . ." *Id.* 101–03. Secondly, by invoking principles outside the Constitution to interpret it, how can Ely insure that judges will stop there rather than reading in other extra-constitutional principles that reflect their personal preferences? *Cf.* Bork, *Styles in Constitutional Theory*, 26 S. Tex. L. Rev. 383, 390 (1985), who argues: "Some theorists . . . would have courts make democracy more democratic. [Dean Ely], who is a non-interpretivist whether he knows it or not, takes this tack. The difficulty is that there is neither a constitutional nor an extra-constitutional basis for making the Constitution more democratic than the Constitution is." Does this argument lead to a rejection of Ely's thesis?

(4) *The Madisonian Dilemma: Reconciling Minority Rights with Majority Rule.* The central problem of judicial review concerns the resolution of what has been called the Madisonian dilemma: a Madisonian democracy, such as the United States, holds that majorities generally are entitled to rule simply because they are majorities but that individuals, even when in the minority, must have some protection from majority control. But neither majority nor minority can be trusted to draw the dividing line, because tyranny either by one or by the other inevitably would follow. Bork, *supra*, at 383.

(5) *"Discrete and Insular Minorities:" The Carolene Products Formula for Resolving the Madisonian Dilemma.* The *Carolene Products* formula would protect, first, minority rights contained in a "specific prohibition of the Constitution. . . ." Thus the right of citizens in tiny Rhode Island to two senators should prompt closer scrutiny on judicial review if larger states formed a majority sufficient to remove Rhode Island's senators by act of Congress. Further, *Carolene Products* would scrutinize "legislation which restricts [the] political processes;" Judge Ely's thesis is influenced by this prong of the formula. Finally, *Carolene Products* would protect "discrete and insular minorities," such as religious, or national, or racial groups. This prong, however, is subject to varying analyses. For example, in the abortion context, which group is the appropriate discrete and insular minority for protection, if any: women? pregnant women? fetuses/unborn children? persons who care deeply about the right to life? In other contexts, could it happen that white males might be considered a discrete and insular minority? Consider how this definitional framework can be given meaning—and how it can be limited so that every case does not involve competing claims of discrete and insular minorities.

[3] The Court's Political Environment: Separation of Powers, Independent Duties of Co-ordinate Branches, and the Problem of Defiance

COOPER v. AARON, 358 U.S. 1 (1958). Following the Court's decision in *Brown v. Board of Education*, 349 U.S. 294 (1955), the people of Arkansas amended their Constitution to direct the Arkansas legislature to oppose "in every constitutional manner the un-constitutional desegregation decisions . . . of the United States

Supreme Court." The day before the opening of Central High School in Little Rock, the governor of Arkansas dispatched units of the Arkansas National Guard to place the school "off limits" to black students. Thereafter, at the request of the Little Rock school board, the district court granted a two-and-one-half-year suspension of the school board's court-approved desegregation program. In response to this attempt at interposition and nullification, the Supreme Court issued a judgment four days after argument, only later issuing its opinion:

> Opinion of the Court by the CHIEF JUSTICE, MR. JUSTICE BLACK, MR. JUSTICE FRANKFURTER, MR. JUSTICE DOUGLAS, MR. JUSTICE BURTON, MR. JUSTICE CLARK, MR. JUSTICE HARLAN, MR. JUSTICE BRENNAN, and MR. JUSTICE WHITTAKER. . . .

> The constitutional rights of respondents are not to be sacrificed or yielded to the violence and disorder which have followed upon the actions of the Governor and Legislature. . . .

> What has been said, in the light of the facts developed, is enough to dispose of the case. However, we should answer the premise of the actions that the Governor and Legislature that they are not bound by our holding in the *Brown* case. . . .

> Article VI of the Constitution makes the Constitution the law of the land. . . . It follows that the interpretation of the Fourteenth Amendment enunciated by this Court in the *Brown* case is the supreme law of the land. . . .

NOTES AND QUESTIONS ON THE POLITICAL POSITION OF THE SUPREME COURT

(1) *Interposition and Nullification.* The theory that a state may "interpose" its sovereignty to insulate it from, and thereby "nullify," an order of the federal courts, has occasionally surfaced and is illustrated in *Cooper v. Aaron. See* Note, *Interposition v. Judicial Power— A Study of Ultimate Authority in Constitutional Questions,* 1 RACE REL. L. REP. 465 (1956). Although thoroughly discredited by (and before) *Cooper v. Aaron,* such incidents threaten the legitimacy of the Court at least temporarily. Note the highly unusual designation of the opinion as by each individual justice, rather than as a per curiam opinion or as an opinion of the Court delivered by one justice. Is it likely that the Court had concerns that its order might otherwise be neither obeyed nor enforced given the political considerations?

(2) *Enforcement by the President.* Ultimately, President Eisenhower ordered troops under the authority of the United States to carry out the enforcement of desegregation orders in Arkansas. Could the President, acting within his authority as commander-in-chief and exercising his proper constitutional authority, have declined to do so on the ground that the commitment of troops would be militarily unsound, or that it would likely result in a high number of civilian casualties, or that the resulting deprivation of political freedom to the Arkansas voting majority would be counterproductive?

(3) *Presidential Interpretations of Judicial Review: Do Presidents have Authority Akin to Interposition and Nullification?* Over the years, Presidents frequently have articulated doctrines that avoid ultimate Supreme Court authority over Presidential functions. For example,

(a) *Thomas Jefferson, Letter to Mrs. John Adams, September 11, 1804, in 8 Works of Thomas Jefferson 310–31 (1897):* "You seem to think it devolved on the judges to decide on the validity of the sedition law. But nothing in the Constitution has given them a right to decide for the executive, more than to the executive to decide for them. Both . . . are equally independent in the sphere of action assigned to them. The judges, believing the law constitutional, had a right to pass a sentence of fine and imprisonment. . . . But the executive, believing the law to be unconstitutional, was bound to remit the execution of it;

because that power has been confided to him by the Constitution."

(b) *James Madison, in 4 Elliott, Debates on the Federal Constitution 550 (1836):* "However true, therefore, it may be that the judicial department is, in all questions submitted to it by the forms of the Constitution, to decide in the last resort, this resort must necessarily be deemed the last in relation to the authorities of the other departments of the government; not in relation to the rights of the parties to the constitutional compact, from which the judicial, as well as the other departments, hold their delegated trust."

(c) *Abraham Lincoln, in 6 Richardson, Messages and Papers of the Presidents 5, 9–10 (1897):* "I do not forget the position assumed by some that constitutional questions are to be decided by the Supreme Court, nor do I deny that such decisions must be binding in any case upon the parties to a suit as to the object of that suit, while they are also entitled to very high respect and consideration in all parallel cases by all other departments of the government. . . . At the same time, the candid citizen must confess that if the policy of the government upon vital questions affecting the whole people is to be irrevocably fixed by decisions of the Supreme Court, . . . the people will have ceased to be their own rulers. . . ."

(4) *The Avoidance of Constitutional Questions: United States v. Security Industrial Bank, 459 U.S. 70 (1982).* In *Security Industrial Bank,* the government contended that bankruptcy legislation was properly construed to void a lien held by the bank. The court of appeals struck the statute down as a violation of the "taking of property" clause of the fifth amendment. The Supreme Court expressly held that it was required to "address" the constitutional issue, but would not "decide" it, because of "the cardinal principle that this Court will first ascertain whether a construction of the statute is fairly possible by which the constitutional question may be avoided." The Court therefore carefully reviewed the facts in light of previous taking clause cases, found a "substantial" constitutional question—and then avoided the question by adopting a construction of the statute making it prospective only so that it did not destroy the bank's lien. Is this reasoning wasteful (or even disingenuous)?

PROBLEM A

CONSTITUTIONAL CRISIS NO. 1. Congress passes an Act. The President seeks to enforce it. But opponents set up a test case, and the Supreme Court ultimately declares the Act unconstitutional. An overwhelming majority in both houses of Congress conclude that the Supreme Court is wrong, and Congress passes the Act verbatim, a second time. Question 1: Should the President sign the bill? Question 2: How does (or should) our constitutional system resolve which opinion, legislative or judicial, the President should honor—or whether he should decide independently? Question 3: If the Congress has passed the Act by a margin large enough to override a veto, can the President justify enforcement by the possibility that the Court may change its mind?

PROBLEM B

CONSTITUTIONAL CRISIS NO. 2. The Supreme Court renders a decision in a particular case that arguably protects interests related to the freedom of speech. But the members of Congress strongly conclude that the "freedom of speech" at issue is illusory, and that the decision in fact violates real constitutional rights of other persons—rights related to privacy or enjoyment of property. Question 1: Does Congress have power to pass an Act countermanding the Supreme Court's constitutional decision? Question 2: Does Congress have an affirmative constitutional duty to do so?

NOTE ON OTHER NATIONS' APPROACHES TO JUDICIAL REVIEW

England. In England, "a sovereign Parliament can lay down what the limits of judicial control shall be. . . . Judicial review is thus effectively excluded." R. DAVID & J. BRIERLEY, MAJOR LEGAL SYSTEMS IN THE WORLD TODAY 381–82 (1985). Furthermore, England lacks a written constitution. Nevertheless, England has a compelling doctrine of constitutionalism, because "[i]n England tradition and democratic attitudes constitute a powerful political reality." Thus, the unwritten "constitution" in England "is composed of a series of rules, sometimes in the form of legislative provisions but most often judicial in origin, which guarantee fundamental rights and freedoms and limit the arbitrary exercise of power by established authorities"—but it is Parliament that ultimately interprets this unwritten Constitution, subject only to "the force of public opinion." *Id.* 383.

Australia. The Australian constitution provides for a parliamentary system. Australia differs from England, however, and more closely resembles the United States, in that it is a union of states. The states have important protections against the federal government, and it is perhaps for that reason that Australia recognizes the power of judicial review. The High Court of Australia is predominantly a non-constitutional court, since the absence of a bill of rights reduces its role in constitutional litigation; but "[t]he High Court . . . plays a much more significant role in restraining federal power to regulate [with respect to the states] than does the Supreme Court of the United States." Barrett, *A Parliamentary System of Government in a Federal State—The Australian Experience*, 19 U.C. DAVIS L. REV. 153, 186–93 (1985).

The Former Soviet Union. "The supreme organ of state power of the USSR is the Supreme Soviet of the USSR." It "is empowered to decide all questions assigned to the jurisdiction of the USSR by the present constitution." Sov. Const. art. 108. The Supreme Court of the USSR "is elected by the Supreme Soviet." Art. 153. Although judges are declared to be "independent," Art. 155, this structure precludes judicial review; the "independence of judges has nothing whatever to do with an attempt to strike a balance between the judicial and the legislative powers. Judges, while applying the law, must be sensitive to the directives given by the Communist Party and the government." R. DAVID & J. BRIERLEY, *supra*, at 261–62; *see generally* W. SIMONS, THE CONSTITUTIONS OF THE COMMUNIST WORLD 386–90 (1980). In Russia today, the constitutional court has greater power than under the old USSR.

Germany. The traditional German conception of the separation of powers held that statutes were the sole source of law and that there was no role for the courts other than the enforcement of the law created by a sovereign parliament. In 1951, however, partly in response to the atrocities of the National Socialist regime, West Germany created a Federal Constitutional Court. [There also is a constitutional court in each of the "Lander" (states).] The Federal Constitutional Court has broad powers of judicial review, comparable to those of the United States Supreme Court. Within a remarkably short period of time, the role of this court had become firmly established. "Indeed, the German experience seems to show that judicial review, once regarded as a unique feature of American constitutionalism, can flourish in constitutional traditions substantially different from the American." A. KATZ, LEGAL TRADITIONS AND SYSTEMS: AN INTERNATIONAL HANDBOOK 90, 97–99 (1986).

[B]   Review of State Court Decisions

INTRODUCTORY NOTE

State Court Judgments after Marbury v. Madison. Marbury established the power of the Court to subject federal statutes to judicial review. By implication, the Court's reasoning might seem to include the states. But the states then were accustomed to greater sovereign independence than we would conceive them to have today, and judicial review of state judgments remained in doubt.

The Separate Importance of Judicial Review of State Judgments. Some have suggested that the Supreme Court's power to review state judgments is even more important than its power over federal judgments. For example, Justice Oliver Wendell Holmes wrote that he did not think the United States would come to an end if the Court lost its power to invalidate an act of Congress, but "I do think the Union would be imperiled if we could not make the declaration as to the laws of the several states." O. HOLMES, COLLECTED LEGAL PAPERS 295–96 (1920). It can be argued that a strong national government would be impossible without this power. The issue of jurisdiction over state judgments received definitive treatment in 1816, when the Court decided *Martin v. Hunter's Lessee.*

MARTIN v. HUNTER'S LESSEE
14 U.S. (1 Wheat.) 304 (1816)

[Following the Revolutionary War, Virginia confiscated lands owned by British subjects, including Martin. It granted a portion of Martin's land to Hunter. Hunter then sued Martin in ejectment in a Virginia state court. The Virginia Court of Appeals held for Hunter. The United States Supreme Court then reversed the Virginia Court of Appeals and issued a mandate directing the Virginia court to enter judgment for Martin.

[The Virginia court refused to obey the Supreme Court's mandate for the following reasons:

> The [Virginia] court is unanimously of the opinion that the appellate power of the Supreme Court of the United States does not extend to this court under a sound construction of the Constitution of the United States . . . and that obedience to [the Supreme Court's] mandate [should] be declined by the court. The United States Supreme Court then reviewed the case a second time, to determine whether its decision was binding on the Virginia court.]

MR. JUSTICE STORY delivered the opinion of the Court. . . .

The Constitution of the United States was ordained and established, not by the states in their sovereign capacities, but emphatically, as the Preamble of the Constitution declares, by "the people of the United States." [T]he people had a right . . . to make the powers of the state governments, in given cases, subordinate to those of the nation. . . .

The third article of the Constitution is that which must principally attract our attention. The 1st section declares, "The judicial Power of the United States shall be vested in one supreme Court, and in such other inferior Courts as the Congress may, from time to time ordain and establish. . . ."

. . . The language of the article throughout is manifestly designed to be mandatory upon the legislature. . . . The judicial power of the United States *shall be vested* (not may be vested) in one supreme Court, and in such inferior courts as Congress may, from time to time ordain and establish. . . . The judicial power must, therefore, be vested in some court, by Congress. . . .

If, then, it is a duty of Congress to vest the judicial power of the United States, it is a duty to invest the *whole judicial power.* . . .

It being, then, established that the language of this clause is imperative, the next question is as to the cases to which it shall apply. The answer is found in the Constitution itself. The judicial power shall extend to all the cases enumerated in the Constitution. . . .

If the Constitution meant to limit the appellate jurisdiction to cases pending in the courts of the United States, it would necessarily follow that the jurisdiction of these courts would, in all the cases enumerated in the Constitution, be exclusive of state tribunals. How otherwise could the jurisdiction extend to *all* cases arising under the Constitution, laws, and treaties of the United States. . . ? If some of these cases might be entertained by state tribunals, and no appellate jurisdiction as to them should exist, then the appellate power would not extend to *all*, but to some, cases. . . .

[I]t is plain that the framers of the Constitution did contemplate that cases within the judicial cognizance of the United States not only might but would arise in the state courts, in the exercise of their ordinary jurisdiction. With this view, the sixth article declares, that "This Constitution, and the laws of the United States which shall be made in pursuance thereof, and all treaties made, or which shall be made, under the authority of the United States, shall be the supreme law of the land, and the judges in every state shall be bound thereby, anything in the Constitution or laws of any state to the contrary notwithstanding. . . ."

It is a mistake that the Constitution was not designed to operate upon the states, in their corporate capacities. It is crowded with provisions which restrain or annul the sovereignty of the states in some of their highest branches of their prerogative. . . .

It is further argued, that no great public mischief can result from a construction which will limit the appellate power of the United States to cases in their own courts: first, because state judges are bound by an oath to support the Constitution of the United States, and must be presumed to be men of learning and integrity; and secondly, because Congress must have an unquestionable right to remove all cases within the scope of the judicial power from the state courts to the courts of the United States. . . . As to the first reason—admitting that the judges of the state courts are, and always will be, of as much learning, integrity, and wisdom, as those of the courts of the United States, (which we very cheerfully admit), it does not aid the argument. . . . The Constitution has presumed (whether rightly or wrongly, we do not inquire) that state attachments, state prejudices, state jealousies, and state interests, might sometimes obstruct, or control, or be supposed to obstruct or control, the regular administration of justice. . . .

This is not all. A motive of another kind, perfectly compatible with the most sincere respect for state tribunals, might induce the grant of appellate power over their decisions. That motive is the importance, and even necessity of *uniformity* of decision throughout the whole United States, upon all subjects within the purview of the Constitution. Judges of equal learning and integrity, in different states, might differently interpret a statute, or a treaty of the United States, or even the Constitution itself.

We have not thought it incumbent on us to give any opinion upon the question, whether this Court have authority to issue a writ of mandamus to the [Virginia] court of appeals to enforce the former judgments, as we do not think it necessarily involved in the decision of this cause.

It is the opinion of the whole Court, that the judgment of the court of appeals of Virginia, rendered on the mandate in this cause, be reversed, and the judgment of the district court, held at Winchester, be, and the same is hereby affirmed.

[JOHNSON, J., Concurring:]

It will be observed in this case, that the court disavows all intention to decide on the right to issue compulsory process to the state courts; thus leaving us, in my opinion, where the Constitution and laws place us—supreme over persons and cases as far as our judicial powers extend, but not asserting any compulsory control over the state tribunals.

NOTES AND QUESTIONS

(1) *Non-Enforcement of the Judgment.* Note the Supreme Court's avoidance of a potential constitutional crisis by its withholding of a second mandate, and its direct affirmance of the trial court. The political difficulties of enforcement against defiant state authorities are illustrated by *Cooper v. Aaron*, in the preceding section, above.

(2) *The Refusal to Review Judgments Resting upon "Independent and Adequate" State Grounds.* The Constitution does not expressly define the extent of jurisdiction over state judgments. The Court has declined to review state judgments that rest upon "independent and adequate" state law grounds. The difficulty is that many state supreme court opinions intermix state and federal law. In *Michigan v. Long*, 463 U.S. 1032 (1983), Justice O'Connor, writing for the majority, concluded that if the four corners of the state court opinion did not reflect a plain statement of an independent and adequate state ground for the holding, the Court would presume that there were no such grounds and that it had jurisdiction. Justice O'Connor pointed out that state courts easily could avoid this result by including the requisite plain statement. Justice O'Connor further noted that this treatment of the jurisdictional issue achieved "the consistency that is necessary," in that there is an "important need for uniformity in federal law" that goes unsatisfied "when we fail to review an opinion that rests primarily upon federal grounds. . . ."

APPENDIX TO § 1.01: CONSTITUTIONAL LAW IN PRACTICE—THE USE OF CONSTITUTIONAL ARGUMENTS TO SUPPORT AND OPPOSE PROPOSED LEGISLATION RELATING TO THE PENNZOIL-TEXACO DISPUTE

NOTE ON THE USE OF CONSTITUTIONAL ARGUMENTS TO OPPOSE LEGISLATION OR ITS ENFORCEMENT

Constitutional Arguments in the Legislative Process. It should be remembered that every member of Congress and the President each takes an oath to defend the Constitution. Thus, opponents of a proposed enactment sometimes argue to legislators (or to the executive, as leader of the party or in support of exercise of the veto power) that the legislation would be unconstitutional. These kinds of arguments may be expressed in documents that look very much like briefs that would be filed in a court, or they may be set out in informal letters, by word of mouth, or in lobbying campaigns.

The Pennzoil-Texaco Legislative Dispute as an Example. The famous Pennzoil-Texaco dispute provides a dramatic illustration of the use of constitutional arguments against the enactment of legislation. Consider the following materials.

NOTE ON THE BACKGROUND TO THE *PENNZOIL-TEXACO* LEGISLATIVE DISPUTE

Pennzoil's Judgment and Texaco's Dilemma. Pennzoil Company obtained a trial-court judgment of more than $10 billion against Texaco Inc., based upon the largest jury verdict in history. Texaco appealed, alleging numerous errors. However, the governing procedural law of Texas provided that Pennzoil could execute on the judgment regardless of the appeal unless Texaco posted a bond in the full amount of the judgment, plus interest and costs. It also could impose liens upon Texaco's real property. Although it had net worth exceeding the amount of the judgment, Texaco would have been unable to avoid bankruptcy if required to post such a bond, or if its realty were subjected to liens.

The Proposed Legislation Providing for Judicial Discretion. Reacting to this situation, and recognizing that the laws of 39 states plus the federal government provided for greater judicial flexibility in the treatment of liens and bonds, state legislators filed bills to change the Texas law. The principal bills, which were supported by Texaco but opposed by Pennzoil, would have allowed a judgment debtor to avoid liens or execution by posting a bond in an amount to be set by the trial court. *See generally Texaco Resumes Appeal of $11 Billion Damages*, HOUSTON CHRONICLE, May 14, 1987, § 2, at 1, col. 2.

The Constitutional Arguments For and Against the "Texaco Bills." In addition to other lobbying efforts, Pennzoil presented the testimony of Professor Laurence Tribe of Harvard, who gave his opinion that the Texaco bills were unconstitutional. Texaco countered with the opinion of Professor Charles Alan Wright of the University of Texas, who just as firmly maintained that they were constitutional.

OPINION OF PROFESSOR LAURENCE TRIBE ON THE UNCONSTITUTIONALITY OF S.B. 1414

(Unpublished document presented in connection with Professor Tribe's testimony before the Texas Senate Judiciary Committee, April 25, 1987.)

Mr. Chairman and Members of the Judiciary Committee:

I am honored to appear before this Committee today to testify on [S.B. 1414]. . . . To introduce myself, I should inform the Committee that I am here as a representative of the Pennzoil Company but I am expressing as well my own constitutional views. I hold a chair as the Tyler Professor of Constitutional Law, Harvard Law School. . . .

The accompanying memorandum explains my conclusion that the proposed statute would accomplish nothing but constitutional mischief. It would distort the law of Texas to enact a special rule for Texaco, violating the Fourteenth Amendment of the United States Constitution. . . .

The new rules that Texaco seeks as a special favor are in many respects profoundly unwise. But, even if those rules embodied sound policy, retroactive application of such rules to *trial judgments rendered before the new rules took effect* . . . would unconstitutionally take property without just compensation. . . .

I. The [Proposed Act] Works a Taking Without Just Compensation in Violation of the Fifth and Fourteenth Amendments

Section 11 of the Act, on its face, would apply the proposed legislation to resolve the security questions arising in *Pennzoil v. Texaco*, currently on appeal in the Texas courts. Under Texas law extant when the Pennzoil judgment was entered, that judgment is final pending appeal. . . .

A. The State May Not Retroactively Destroy the Property Rights Already Created by Texas Law As Incidents of Pennzoil's Judgment. . . .

When judgment was entered in Pennzoil's favor in December 1985, and *affirmed* by the Court of Appeals in February 1987, existing Texas law gave Pennzoil important rights by virtue of that judgment: a right to judgment liens against Texaco's property, a right to a bond or other security in the full amount of that judgment pending appeal, and a right to enforce that judgment forthwith if full security were not provided by Texaco. . . .

The Supreme Court has long held that a creditor's security interests are a form of property. *See, e.g., United States v. Security Industrial Bank*, 459 U.S. 70, 76 (1982); *Armstrong v. United States*, 364 U.S. 40, 44 (1960); *Louisville Bank v. Radford*, 295 U.S. 555, 590 (1935). Although the "'bundle of rights' which accrues to a secured party is obviously smaller than that which accrues to an owner in fee simple," the Court has rejected "the proposition that differences such as these relegate the secured party's interest to something less than property. . . ."

In *Security Industrial Bank*, the Supreme Court reviewed a change in federal bankruptcy law that, retroactively applied, would have enabled debtors to avoid liens that had been perfected by creditors prior to the enactment of the law. The Court held that allowing debtors to avoid these liens "would result in a complete destruction of the property right of the secured party. . . ." . . . And it is settled that one has a property right in pursing whatever claims or causes of action are created by state law. *See Logan v. Zimmerman Brush Co.*, 455 U.S. 422, 428–30 (1982). . . .

[Later sections of the memorandum, incorporated into Professor Tribe's testimony, further developed the taking argument and also concluded that S.B. 1414 violated the Equal Protection and Supremacy Clauses. Those parts are omitted here.]

OPINION OF PROFESSOR CHARLES ALAN WRIGHT ON THE CONSTITUTIONALITY OF S.B. 1414

(Unpublished document presented through the testimony of David Boies and Professor David Crump before the Texas Senate Judiciary Committee, April 25, 1987.)

My name is Charles Alan Wright. I hold the William B. Bates Chair for the Administration of Justice at The University of Texas Law School, where since 1955 I have taught Constitutional Law. I have represented Texaco in its litigation with Pennzoil both in federal and state courts, . . . but my rule for myself . . . is that I will not take a position on behalf of a client unless it represents what I would be willing to teach to my students as the law. . . .

I respect greatly the scholarly work done in the area of constitutional law by my friend Larry Tribe. Much as I admire his work, however, on occasion I find that I disagree with him. That is the case here. . . . In my judgment, the constitutionality of Senate Bill 1414 is clear beyond question.

Professor Tribe's principal argument is that Pennzoil had property rights by virtue of its judgment against Texaco, specifically "a right to judgment liens against Texaco's property, a right to a bond or other security in the full amount of that judgment pending appeal, and a right to enforce that judgment forthwith if full security were not provided by Texas." The retroactive application of S.B. 1414, he contends, would be unconstitutional. He is wrong on both counts.

Senate Bill 1414 studiously avoids any interference with vested property rights that might be subject to constitutional challenge. Section 11 of the bill provides that

> this Act shall not apply nor be applicable (1) to existing judgment liens filed on the effective date of this Act or (2) to those pending cases where on the effective date of this Act a good and sufficient bond has been filed and approved, or deposits have been made in accordance with Tex. Rev. [sic] Civ. P. 47.

Pennzoil had no judgment liens, it had no bond in the full amount of the judgment, and it is wholly uncertain whether it ever had any claim to either as a condition to appeal. Professor Tribe confuses the trial, judgment, and appeal on the one hand, with the security provisions of Texas law on the other. . . .

It is quite apparent that the proposed legislation does not present a retroactivity problem. It has no effect on any security interest Pennzoil has in the judgment because Pennzoil has no security interest at all. As it is well aware, now that Texaco has been forced into bankruptcy, Pennzoil is at most merely one of Texaco's unsecured creditors.

Even if we suppose that this legislation raises problems of retroactivity, which it clearly does not, and that Pennzoil had the rights it now claims, this Legislature has full power to adopt different rules that would not provide for those rights. No one knows better than Professor Tribe that complaints about the retroactivity of legislation are, for the most part, a meaningless shibboleth [citing L. Tribe, *American Constitutional Law* 48 (1979 Supp.)]. . . .

Pennzoil has no [v]ested property right. [Even if retroactive], [l]egislation affecting it must meet only the undemanding rules applied generally to retroactive economic and social legislation. A unanimous Court, in *Pension Benefit Guaranty Corp. v. R.A. Gray & Co.*, 467 U.S. 717 (1984), [said:]

> We further explained that the strong deference accorded legislation in the field of national economic policy is no less applicable when that legislation is applied retroactively. Provided that the retroactive application of a statute is supported by a legitimate legislative purpose furthered by rational means, judgments about the wisdom of such legislation remain within the exclusive province of the legislative and executive branches. 467 U.S. at 729.

It is difficult to think of a more rational, indeed compelling, legislative purpose than the one that animates S.B. 1414. As recited in Section 2(8) of the bill, it is "to protect the rights of access by judgment debtors to the appellate courts of the State of Texas and the United States Supreme Court to present a meaningful appeal by due course of law. . . ."

[Professor Wright's statement further developed his response to the taking argument. It also disposed of Professor Tribe's equal protection argument by a single citation to *New Orleans v. Dukes*, 427 U.S. 297, 303–04 (1976). Those portions of the statement are omitted here. Professor Wright's conclusion:]

For the foregoing reasons, I think that Senate Bill 1414 would easily survive any constitutional test.

NOTES AND QUESTIONS

(1) *The Aftermath.* Some members of the Senate committee expressed opposition to the "retroactivity" feature of the bill, as they characterized it. Because the majority disagreed, the bill was favorably reported out of committee—but only by a four-to-three vote. Weeks later, the parallel House committee reported favorably by a five-to-three vote. Houston Chronicle, Tuesday, May 12, 1987, § 2, at 1, col. 2. However, the bill failed to clear the full legislature.

(2) *Constitutional and Nonconstitutional Arguments: A "Red Herring?"* The influence of the constitutional arguments in the Pennzoil-Texaco legislative dispute should not be exaggerated, because both sides lobbied hard in other ways. Texaco stressed the unfairness of the lien and bond provisions, not only to it, but to other litigants. Concerned for their jobs, Texaco employees filled the Senate gallery. Pennzoil argued that S.B. 1414 would make it harder for victorious plaintiffs to collect, that the bill was "special interest" legislation, and that Texaco had no prospect of emerging from Chapter 11 protection anyway. The question arises, then, what use was made of the constitutional arguments? Do you suppose that a constitutional scholar's opinion could be used simply as a red herring? Is that what Pennzoil (or Texaco) was doing?

(3) *How Should the Legislature Judge the Constitutionality of Legislation?* Perhaps the legislature's function should be to impose a higher (or at least separate) constitutional standard than the decisions of courts would imply, because of the legislature's independent duty to preserve the Constitution. But perhaps this approach would mean an unduly restrictive "super-Constitution," which would prevent needed legislation by the cumulation of prohibitions that would not be imposed by any branch alone. Perhaps, then, the conscientious legislator would simply read and follow the court decisions. But wouldn't that approach avoid the legislature's independent duty?

(4) *"Risk" of Unconstitutionality Due to the "Generality" and "Uncertainty" of Constitutional Law: Should the Legislature Simply "Let it Rip?"* Imagine that a legislator refuses to vote for any legislation posing a substantial "risk" of unconstitutionality. That approach would frustrate a great deal of needed legislation. The "mushy" nature of constitutional decisions means that constitutionality often is subject to some doubt. Are there times when a legislator should "let it rip" and vote for legislation that seems wise, even if there is substantial risk of its later invalidation?

§ 1.02   LIMITING JUDICIAL POWER

[A]   The "Case or Controversy" Requirement

[1]   Advisory Opinions and Nonadversary Procedures

Read U.S. Const. Art. III, § 2, cl. 1 (the case or controversy requirement).

INTRODUCTORY NOTE: ADVISORY OPINIONS

What Is an Advisory Opinion? Imagine that your Constitutional Law class decides that it wants to find out the answer to an interesting, but unresolved, constitutional question. Therefore, you and your fellow students nominate one member of the class to sue another in an action for a declaratory judgment, which you plan to bring in the federal district court nearest you. The loser won't be hurt, because the sole objective is to get the court to render a judgment answering your interesting question. What you are seeking is known as an "advisory opinion."

Pragmatic Reasons for Avoiding Advisory Opinions. Since no one really cares who wins, neither side is likely to develop the facts or brief the case vigorously. And, of course, limited judicial resources are consumed in deciding a question that may never need to be decided.

Origins of the Prohibition on Advisory Opinions. Your Constitutional Law class would not succeed because the federal courts will not render advisory opinions. This doctrine surfaced as early as 1793 when Thomas Jefferson, as Secretary of State, submitted twenty-nine questions to the Court, dealing with various issues of international law. In his reply to President Washington on behalf of the Court, Chief Justice Jay concluded that advisory opinions were prohibited because of " . . . the lines of separation drawn by the Constitution between the three departments of the government. These being in certain respects checks upon each other, . . . are considerations which afford strong arguments against the propriety of our extra-judicially [issuing advisory opinions], especially as the power given by the Constitution to the President, of calling on the heads of the departments for opinions, seems to have been purposely as well as expressly united to the executive department." 3 H. JOHNSTON, CORRESPONDENCE AND PUBLIC PAPERS OF JOHN JAY 486–89 (1911).

MUSKRAT v. UNITED STATES
219 U.S. 346 (1911)

[In 1902, Congress distributed to certain individual Cherokee Indians lands owned by the Cherokee tribe. In 1906, however, it passed an Act to change the distribution. Since it was concerned that the change might be unconstitutional, Congress provided in the 1906 Act that four named individuals could file suit against the United States in the Court of Claims on behalf of all claimants under the 1902 Act, with a right of appeal to the Supreme Court. The Court of Claims upheld the constitutionality of the changed distribution. Muskrat and other named claimants then appealed to the Supreme Court in accordance with the 1906 Act.]

The first question in these cases, as in others, involves the jurisdiction of this court to entertain the proceeding, and that depends upon whether the jurisdiction conferred is within the power of Congress, having in view the limitations of the judicial power, as established by the Constitution of the United States.

[Here, the Court quoted sections 1 and 2 of Article III of the Constitution.

[It then discussed *Hayburn's Case*, 1 L. Ed. 436, 2 Dall. 409, which concerned an Act of Congress that assigned the circuit courts the task of determining the amount of veterans' disability pay, subject to revision by the Secretary of War and Congress. The Act was struck down as unconstitutional on the basis of the following propositions:]

> "That by the Constitution of the United States, the government thereof is divided into three distinct and independent branches, and that it is the duty of each to abstain from, and to oppose, encroachments on either.

> "That neither the legislative nor the executive branches can constitutionally assign to the judicial any duties but such as are properly judicial, and to be performed in a judicial manner.

> "That the duties assigned to the circuit courts by this act are not of that description, and that the act itself does not appear to contemplate them as such; inasmuch as it subjects the decisions of these courts, made pursuant to those duties, first to the consideration and suspension of the Secretary at War, and then to the revision of the legislature; whereas by the Constitution, neither the Secretary at War, nor any other executive officer, nor even the legislature, are authorized to sit as a court of errors on the opinions of this court. . . ."

As we have already seen, by the express terms of the Constitution, the exercise of the judicial power is limited to "cases" and "controversies." Beyond this it does not extend, and unless it is asserted in a case or controversy within the meaning of the Constitution, the power to exercise it is nowhere conferred.

. . . A "case" was defined by Mr. Chief Justice Marshall as early as the leading case of *Marbury v. Madison*, 2 L. ed. 60, 1 Cranch, 137, to be a suit instituted according to the regular course of judicial procedure. . . .

It is therefore evident that there is neither more nor less in this procedure than an attempt to provide for a judicial determination, final in this court, of the constitutional validity of an act of Congress. Is such a determination within the judicial power conferred by the Constitution, as the same has been interpreted and defined in the authoritative decisions to which we have referred? We think it is not. That judicial power, as we have seen, is the right to determine actual controversies arising between adverse litigants, duly instituted in courts in proper jurisdiction.

. . . [I]t is true the United States is made a defendant to this action, but it has no interest adverse to the claimants. The object is not to assert a property right as against the government, or to demand compensation for alleged wrongs because of action upon its part. The whole purpose of the law is to determine the constitutional validity of this class of legislation, in a suit not arising between parties concerning a property right necessarily involved in the decision in question, but in a proceeding against the government in its sovereign capacity, and concerning which the only judgment required is to settle the doubtful character of the legislation in question. Such judgment will not conclude private parties, when actual litigation brings to the court the question of the constitutionality of such legislation. In a legal sense the judgment could not be executed, and amounts in fact to no more than an expression of opinion upon the validity of the acts in question. . . .

[Reversed and dismissal ordered.]

NOTES AND QUESTIONS

(1) *The Case in Favor of Advisory Opinions.* There might be compelling reasons for a legislature to obtain a clear declaration of constitutionality before, not after, passing a particular law. Consider a proposed tax, which Congress concludes is wise policy and probably is constitutional, but it fears crippling losses of collected revenues if refund

suits invalidate the tax five to ten years later. Congress faces a classic "Catch-22": It cannot pass the law without a declaration of constitutionality, but it cannot obtain that declaration unless it first passes the law.

(2) *State Provisions for Advisory Opinions.* For these reasons, some states (*e.g.,* Massachusetts) empower the judicial branch to render advisory opinions on proposed legislation. The problem is one of limiting the demands upon the judiciary and avoiding the disadvantages associated with advisory opinions (*see* the next note).

(3) *The Case Against Advisory Opinions.* Since advisory opinions are not binding on any parties, they might subtly denigrate the power and respect of the courts. The lack of incentive to develop the case is a concern, and indeed there is the possibility that collusive suits might result in decisions based on deliberately skewed facts and briefing. The courts may be over-burdened. Perhaps more importantly from a systemic perspective, advisory opinions may infringe the separation of powers. *See generally* Brilmayer, *The Jurisprudence of Article III: Perspectives on the "Case or Controversy" Requirement,* 93 HARV. L. REV. 297 (1979); Tushnet, *The Sociology of Article III: A Reply to Professor Brilmayer,* 93 HARV. L. REV. 1698 (1980); Brilmayer, *A Reply,* 93 HARV. L. REV. 1727 (1980).

PROBLEM C

A CONSTITUTIONAL AMENDMENT AUTHORIZING ADVISORY OPINIONS ON PENDING LEGISLATION, BASED UPON THE MASSACHUSETTS STATE CONSTITUTION. In Massachusetts, "Each branch of the legislature, as well as the governor or the council, shall have authority to require the opinions of the justices of the supreme judicial court, upon important questions of law, and upon solemn occasions." *See* Mass. Const. Pt. 2, Ch. 3, Art. II. Imagine that a similarly worded provision has been proposed as an amendment to the United States Constitution. Would you favor the amendment?

(1) *Arguments For and Against.* What are the arguments in favor of such a provision? The arguments against?

(2) *Judicial Power to Avoid the Question?* Perhaps it would be wiser to grant the judicial branch the power to decline to issue a particular advisory opinion. Should the Massachusetts provision be redrafted or interpreted to give the high court discretion? In fact, the Supreme Judicial Court of Massachusetts has found some "wiggle room" in it—by finding violations of the separation of powers doctrine, or by failing to find an "important question of law" or a "solemn occasion"! *See, e.g., Opinion of the Justices to Senate,* 386 Mass. 1201, 436 N.E.2d 935 (Mass. 1982) (refusing to answer question regarding vagueness of proposed measure on grounds of absence of important question and need to preserve separation of powers).

WEBSTER v. REPRODUCTIVE HEALTH SERVICES, 492 U.S. 490 (1989). Plaintiffs filed suit attacking a 1986 Missouri statute restricting abortions. [Longer excerpts from the Court's treatment of the substantive issues appear in Chapter 9, below.] The preamble to the statute contained "findings" that "[t]he life of each human being begins at conception" and that "unborn children have protectible interests in life, health, and well-being." The statute also required that all state laws be interpreted to provide to unborn children the same rights enjoyed by other persons under the federal Constitution. Plaintiffs included in their prayer a request for an injunction against enforcement of these provisions and a declaration of unconstitutionality. The Court, per Chief Justice Rehnquist, decided several other challenges presented by plaintiffs but refused to decide whether this preamble language was constitutional:

> The State contends that the preamble itself is precatory and imposes no substantive restrictions on abortions. . . . Appellees, on the other hand, insist that the preamble is an operative part of the Act intended to guide the interpretation of other provisions of the Act. They maintain, for example, that

the preamble's definition of life may prevent physicians in public hospitals from dispensing certain forms of contraceptives, such as the intrauterine device. . . .

It will be time enough for federal courts to address the meaning of the preamble should it be applied to restrict the activities of appellees in some concrete way. Until then, this Court "is not empowered to decide . . . abstract propositions, or to declare . . . principles or rules of law which cannot affect the result as to the thing in issue in the case before it."

Justice Blackmun, joined by Justices Brennan and Marshall, and Justice Stevens dissented.

[2]   Other Conditions of Adjudication: Standing

NOTE ON STANDING AND RELATED DOCTRINES

The case or controversy requirement of Article III sometimes surfaces in other forms, such as standing, ripeness, or mootness. *See generally* Monaghan, *Constitutional Adjudication: The Who and When,* 82 YALE L.J. 1363 (1973). Standing, the most litigious of these concepts, asks the question whether a particular plaintiff is in a proper position to challenge some form of governmental action. Has the plaintiff acted solely to promote principles of good government? Or has the plaintiff truly been adversely affected or injured by the governmental action? The plaintiff may also be confronted with ripeness and mootness problems. The plaintiff cannot institute suit before some kind of adverse impact or injury has occurred; such premature action would render the suit unripe for purposes of federal jurisdiction under Article III. At the other end of the spectrum, once a concrete controversy has been properly put in litigation, the lawsuit may become moot by the occurrence of some event outside the record.

MASSACHUSETTS v. MELLON and **FROTHINGHAM v. MELLON**, 262 U.S. 447 (1923). These were the leading cases on constitutional standing before 1968. Frothingham challenged the constitutionality of the federal Maternity Act of 1921, an Act that provided for payments to the states for programs designed to reduce maternal and infant mortality, on the ground that its enactment exceeded the constitutional powers of Congress. She alleged that she was injured as a taxpayer, in that the Act would increase the taxes she would pay to the federal government. The State of Massachusetts, both as an entity and as a representative of its citizens, asserted a parallel claim. The Supreme Court held that neither claim was justiciable. The state had presented only "abstract questions of political power, of sovereignty, of government," and Frothingham as a federal taxpayer could not show the requisite kind of injury:

> [A taxpayer's] interest in the moneys of the treasury . . . is shared with millions of others; is comparatively minute and indeterminable; and the effect upon future taxation . . . [is] so remote, fluctuating, and uncertain that no basis is afforded [for judicial decision].
>
> . . . We have no power per se to review and annul acts of Congress on the ground they are unconstitutional. That question may be considered only when the justification for some direct injury suffered or threatened, presenting a justiciable issue, is made to rest upon such an act. . . .

NOTE ON THE LIBERALIZATION OF CONSTITUTIONAL STANDING: FROM *FROTHINGHAM* TO THE PRESENT DAY

The *Frothingham* case emphasized the requirement that the plaintiff show a "direct" injury, and it implied that standing would not exist if the injury was shared with other citizens generally. More recent cases have avoided overruling this test but have liberalized it.

"Personal Stake" and "Concrete Adverseness which Sharpens the Presentation of Issues:" Baker v. Carr, 369 U.S. 186 (1962). The plaintiffs in *Baker v. Carr* complained that the legislature had apportioned voting districts so as to dilute their votes. Thus, the claimed injury was suffered, if at all, together with many other citizens, and it was subject to fluid shifts as populations changed. Nonetheless, the Court held that standing existed. Justice Brennan's statement of the test has become famous:

> Have the appellants alleged such a personal stake in the outcome of the controversy as to assure that concrete adverseness which sharpens the presentation of issues upon which the court so largely depends for illumination of difficult constitutional questions? This is the gist of the question of standing. . . .

369 U.S. at 204. This test may have some utility, but it is subject to criticism, since it does not indicate what kind or degree of personal stake or adverseness is required, except by referring to the sharpening of the dispute. However, *Baker v. Carr* clearly had the result of liberalizing standing. [*Baker* is reproduced below in the section on political questions.]

A More Liberal Approach to Taxpayer Standing: Flast v. Cohen, 392 U.S. 83 (1968). In this case, taxpayers sued to prevent expenditure of federal funds in religious schools for instruction and textbooks in mathematics, reading, etc. Despite the similarity of the case to *Frothingham*, the Supreme Court held the plaintiffs had standing under the following two-part test:

> First, the taxpayer must establish a logical link between that status and the type of legislative enactment attacked. Thus, a taxpayer will be a proper party to allege the unconstitutionality only of exercises of . . . the taxing and spending [powers]. . . . Secondly, the taxpayer must establish a nexus between that status and the precise nature of the constitutional infringement alleged. Under this requirement, the taxpayer must show that the challenged enactment exceeds specific constitutional limitations imposed on the congressional taxing and spending power and not simply that the enactment is generally beyond the powers delegated to Congress by Art. I, § 8. . . .

392 U.S. at 102. Ms. Frothingham would have met the first prong of the test, but not the second; the plaintiffs in *Flast* met that prong as well, since they argued a violation of the first amendment prohibition upon establishment of religion (and not merely the nonexistence of underlying power). But the *Flast* test was strictly construed in some of the later decisions. *See* Note (3) after *Bender v. Williamsport* below.

The Current Tests for Standing: Article III and Prudential Requirements. In recent years, the Supreme Court has tried to clarify standing requirements for those who seek to challenge the constitutionality of governmental action. Two basic categories of tests have been established—the Article III requirements and the prudential or discretionary requirements.

The Article III requirements, which cannot be waived or altered by statute, are threefold: (1) the plaintiff must show some actual or threatened injury, economic or otherwise; (2) the injury must be fairly traceable to the actions of the governmental defendant; and (3) the injury must be redressable by a decision favorable to the plaintiff. *Valley Forge Christian College v. Americans United for Separation of Church and State,* 454 U.S. 464 (1982).

Supplementing these Article III minima are various prudential or discretionary requirements. Each factor comes armed with exceptions, the invocation of which often depends upon the Court's desire to engage in constitutional lawmaking in a particular case. These discretionary factors include the following: (1) the plaintiff must normally assert personal legal rights, not those of third parties; (2) the Court usually refrains from adjudicating questions of wide public importance that amount to "generalized grievances" common to all citizens; (3) a plaintiff claiming economic injury, due to governmental action favoring the plaintiff's competitors, must normally fall within "the

zone of interests" protected or regulated by the statutory provision in question. *E.g.,*
Association of Data Processing Organizations v. Camp, 397 U.S. 150 (1970).

BENDER v. WILLIAMSPORT AREA SCHOOL DISTRICT, 475 U.S. 534 (1986).
A group of high school students in Williamsport, Pennsylvania formed a prayer club
called "Petros" and sought to meet during regular student activity periods. Upon denial
of permission by school officials, the students successfully sued for the right in a federal
district court. The School Board complied with the decision rather than appeal, but one
member of the Board, John C. Youngman, sought to appeal the judgment. Although the
court of appeals held that he had standing and decided in his favor, the Supreme Court
ultimately held that he lacked standing to do so:

> [The] obligation to notice defects in a court of appeals' subject-matter
> jurisdiction assumes a special importance when a constitutional question is
> presented. In such cases we have strictly adhered to the standing requirements
> to ensure that our deliberations will have the benefit of adversary presentation
> and a full development of the relevant facts. . . .

> The first paragraph of the complaint alleged that the action was brought
> against the defendants "in their individual and official capacities." App. 13.
> There is, however, nothing else in the complaint, or in the record on which the
> District Court's judgment was based, to support the suggestion that relief was
> sought against any School Board member in his or her *individual* capacity.
> Certainly the District Court's judgment granted no such relief. . . . Since the
> judgment against Mr. Youngman was not in his individual capacity, he had no
> standing to appeal in that capacity. . . .

> As a member of the School Board sued in his official capacity Mr. Youngman
> has no personal stake in the outcome of the litigation and therefore did not have
> standing to file the notice of appeal. . . .

Justices Burger, White, Rehnquist, and Powell dissented.

NOTES AND QUESTIONS

(1) *Standing under the Baker v. Carr Standard: Personal Stake, Concrete Adver-*
sity, and Sharpening. Remember the *Baker* approach: to have standing, a litigant must
show that his "personal stake" creates a "concrete" adversity that "sharpens" the
dispute. Board Member Youngman obviously felt strongly, had a sharply defined dispute
with other Board Members, and obviously briefed the issues well, because the court of
appeals held in his favor and against Petros! Doesn't *Baker v. Carr* support Youngman's
claim of standing in *Williamsport? Perhaps Williamsport* demonstrates the ineffectiveness of the broad *Baker v. Carr* test. For another perspective, indicating that the *Baker*
approach may not sufficiently limit the judicial roles, *see* Scalia, *The Doctrine of*
Standing as an Essential Element of the Separation of Powers, 17 SUFFOLK U. L. REV.
881 (1983). *See generally* Nichol, *Rethinking Standing,* 72 CAL. L. REV. 68 (1984); Spann,
Expository Justice, 131 U. PA. L. REV. 585 (1983).

(2) *"Jus Tertii" or Standing to Present Rights of Third Persons: Singleton v. Wulff,*
428 U.S. 106 (1976). In some instances, a litigant asserts rights that belong more
immediately to other persons, and yet is himself the more appropriate person to bring
the challenge. In *Singleton,* for example, physicians were allowed to assert rights of
their patients in attacking a statute regulating abortions. The physicians could show a
direct economic injury, and they "arguably" were within the "zone of interests"
protected by the constitutional rules at issue. "Jus tertii" means "rights of third
persons." Indeed, it might be said that this principle is involved in school cases such as
Bender v. Williamsport, whenever a parent seeks to challenge conditions under which
a child goes to school. The person most immediately affected is the child, but the parent
is an appropriate person to sue.

Another, quite different example is provided by *Edmonson v. Leesville Concrete Co.*, 500 U.S. 614 (1991), in which the Court held that a potential juror, excluded by a peremptory challenge exercised on the basis of race, suffered a violation of equal protection—which, in turn, could be asserted by a litigant in the trial. Edmonson, a black, claimed that Leesville had exercised peremptory challenges with the motivation of excluding blacks from jury service. The Supreme Court focussed upon the allegedly violated rights of the excluded jurors, rather than upon Edmonson's—but held that Edmonson had standing to assert the rights of the excluded jurors.

(3) *A Narrowing of the Flast Exception: Hein v. Freedom From Religion Foundation, Inc., 127 S. Ct. 2553 (2007).* President Bush, by Executive Orders, created a White House Office to ensure that "faith-based community groups" would be eligible to compete for federal agency financial support. No Congressional legislation authorized this office, nor did Congress specifically appropriate money for the Office's activities; the Office was funded only through general Executive Branch appropriations. Freedom From Religion Foundation, Inc. (FFRF), an organization opposed to Government endorsement of religion, sued the Office and its directors, claiming that the promotion of the faith-based community groups violated the Establishment Clause. (*See* Chapter 12, below.) Although the court of appeals ruled that FFRF had standing under the *Flast* exception, the Supreme Court, per Justice Alito (5-4), reversed and denied standing.

Justice Alito's plurality opinion rejected the challengers' claim for at least two reasons: (1) the challenge was brought against the Executive Branch, not Congressional action under Art. I, § 8; and (2) the challenge was brought against purely Executive Branch expenditures and not Congressional appropriations under the Taxing and Spending powers. Justice Alito also reasoned that, if "abuses" were to develop, the challenger's recourse was to seek Congressional action rather than seek Article III judicial relief. The plurality thus read *Flast* narrowly.

Justice Scalia (for Justice Thomas) concurred only in the judgment. Justice Scalia would simply overrule *Flast.* Four Justices, in an opinion by Justice Souter, dissented.

(4) *A Return to the Historical Roots of Article III Standing: DaimlerChrysler Corp. v. Cuno, 547 U.S. 332 (2006).* The State of Ohio and the city of Toledo sought to encourage DaimlerChrysler Corporation to expand its Toledo operations by offering a state franchise tax credit and a local property tax exemption. Plaintiffs, a group of state and local taxpayers, challenged these economic development "subsidies" on dormant Commerce Clause grounds. [*See* § 3.02 below.] The Court, per Chief Justice Roberts, held that the taxpayers did not have standing to challenge either the state franchise tax credit or the local property tax exemption. The Court relied on the venerable pre-*Lujan* decisions of *Frothingham* and *Doremus.* The Court also rejected the plaintiffs' argument that the Court should create a *Flast*-type exception for dormant Commerce Clause claims.

Justice Ginsburg concurred. For an analysis of the issues in *Cuno, see* Bradford C. Monk, *Prudential Standing and the Dormant Commerce Clause: Why the "Zone of Interests" Test Should not Apply to Constitutional Cases,* 48 ARIZ. L. REV. 23 (2006).

LUJAN v. DEFENDERS OF WILDLIFE, 504 U.S. 555 (1992). Section 7(a)(2) of the Endangered Species Act requires each federal agency to consult with the Secretaries of the Interior and of Commerce to insure that actions funded by it are not likely to jeopardize endangered or threatened species. At first, both Secretaries promulgated a joint regulation extending this requirement to actions taken in foreign nations, but a subsequent joint rule limited its coverage to the United States and to the high seas. Defenders of Wildlife and other environmental organizations filed suit for declaratory and injunctive relief, on the theory that the new regulation, omitting coverage of species in foreign territory, was inconsistent with the governing statutes.

The Court, per Justice Scalia, held that the plaintiffs lacked standing. The Court's holding was based upon the "injury in fact" test and focussed upon the affidavits of two Defenders members, Joyce Kelly and Amy Skilbred. Kelly's affidavit claimed that she would "suffer harm in fact" because of the American role in overseeing the rehabilitation of the Aswan High Dam on the Nile and in developing Egypt's master water plan, which she alleged would threaten the endangered Nile crocodile, whose habitat she had observed "and intend[s] to do so again, and hope[s] to observe the crocodile directly." Skilbred's affidavit alleged that she had observed habitats of endangered species in Sri Lanka whose habitat would be reduced by agency-funded projects, injuring her because she intended to go back to Sri Lanka but had no current plans: "I don't know [when]. . . ." The Court rejected these theories, as well as other theories advanced by plaintiffs:

> Over the years, our cases have established that the irreducible constitutional minimum of standing contains three elements: First, the plaintiff must have suffered an "injury in fact"—an invasion of a legally-protected interest which is (a) concrete and particularized, and (b) "actual or imminent, not 'conjectural' or 'hypothetical.' " Second, there must be a causal connection between the injury and the conduct complained of—the injury has to be "fairly . . . trace[able] to the challenged action of the defendant, and not . . . th[e] result [of] the independent action of some third party not before the court." Third, it must be "likely," as opposed to merely "speculative," that the injury will be "redressed by a favorable decision. . . ."

> [The affidavits in this case] contain no facts, however, showing how damage to the species will produce "imminent" injury to Mss. Kelly and Skilbred. [A]nd the affiants' profession of an "inten[t]" to return to the places they had visited before—where they will presumably, this time, be deprived of the opportunity to observe animals of the endangered species—is simply not enough. Such "some day" intentions—without any description of concrete plans, or indeed even any specification of when the some day will be—do not support a finding of the "actual or imminent" injury that our cases require.

Justice Blackmun, joined by Justice O'Connor, dissented and observed, "[A] reasonable finder of fact could conclude, based not only upon their statements of intent to return, but upon their past visits to the project sites, as well as their professional backgrounds, that it was likely that Kelly and Skilbred would [soon] make a return trip to the project areas." He went on to say:

> I fear the Court's demand for detailed descriptions of future conduct will do little to weed out those who are genuinely harmed from those who are not. More likely, it will resurrect a code-pleading formalism in federal court summary judgment practice, as federal courts, newly doubting their jurisdiction, will demand more and more particularized showings of future harm. [Just to survive summary judgment, for example,] a Federal Torts Claims Act plaintiff alleging loss of consortium should make sure to furnish this Court with a "description of concrete plans" for her nightly schedule of attempted activities.

NOTES AND QUESTIONS

(1) *The Core of the Modern Standing Doctrine after Lujan.* As the *Lujan* decision indicates, the Court considers three elements to be the "irreducible constitutional minimum" for standing: (1) injury-in-fact; (2) causation; and (3) redressability by the relief requested. *Lujan,* 504 U.S. at 560. This "injury-in-fact" standard is sometimes described as injury that is "concrete and particularized" and "actual or imminent." The dissenters consider *Lujan* as concentrating too narrowly on the particularity of the allegations or evidence of immediacy of harm. You should consider the extent to which the majority's insistence on better evidence of immediacy serves the goal of satisfying the "Case or Controversy" requirement of Article III.

(2) *The Spectrum of "Harms" Within the Standing Doctrine.* While the Court in *Lujan* has confirmed that injury-in-fact will satisfy standing, the Court has repeatedly indicated that, at the other end of the spectrum, certain kinds of "injuries" are not

constitutionally sufficient to satisfy the standing doctrine. In particular, the Court has determined that "ideological injuries" and purely "subjective injuries" do not satisfy the standing requirement. *See Sierra Club v. Morton*, 405 U.S. 727 (1972). The Court considers allegations of ideological injuries and purely subjective injuries to be, in essence, the type of "generalized grievance" that the standing doctrine seeks to exclude. For such ideological (often political) disputes, the Court would have the allegedly injured parties take their grievance to the political process. Falling between the prohibited ideological and purely subjective injuries and the injury-in-fact situation are the types of injuries which are characterized as "expressive harms." The expressive harms are found in several contexts, particularly in the case of the Establishment Clause and the Equal Protection Clause. *See generally* Note, *Expressive Harms and Standing*, 112 HARV. L. REV. 1313 (1999).

(3) *The Constitutional Standing Requirement of "Judicial Redressability": Steel Co. v. Citizens for a Better Environment, 523 U.S. 83 (1998).* An environmental group sued a steel manufacturer under the Emergency Planning and Community Right-to-Know Act (EPCRA) for an alleged failure to perform required reporting. The manufacturer, when notified of the plaintiff's intent to sue, filed the overdue forms and sought to dismiss the action. The Supreme Court, per Justice Scalia, applied the *Lujan* analysis, and held that the plaintiff lacked standing. The Court held that the plaintiff's claim did not satisfy the judicial redressability element of standing because none of the relief sought would reimburse the plaintiff for any loss allegedly caused by the manufacturer's late reporting. There were four concurring opinions. *See F.E.C. v. Akins*, 523 U.S. 420 (1998). *See also Adarand Constructors, Inc. v. Mineta*, 534 U.S. 103 (2001).

(4) *The Lujan Standard Applied to States Acting in their Sovereign Capacity: Massachusetts v. Environmental Protection Agency, 549 U.S. 497 (2007).* Lead by Massachusetts, several states, local governments and environmental organizations petitioned for a review of an order of the Environmental Protection Agency (EPA). The EPA Order had denied a petition for rule-making which sought to regulate "greenhouse gas emissions" from motor vehicles under the Clean Air Act. Although the substance of this case involved the Court's interpretation of provisions of the Clean Air Act, the initial issue was whether the states and other organizations had standing. The EPA (Bush Administration) argued that, because the greenhouse gas emissions inflict widespread harm, the doctrine of standing presents an insuperable jurisdictional obstacle. The Court, per Justice Stevens, disagreed and ruled that Massachusetts did have standing and that the lawsuit could go forward.

Although the Court relied upon the *Lujan* factors, and particularly on Justice Kennedy's *Lujan* concurrence, the Court concluded that an important distinction was that Massachusetts was not a "private individual" but a "sovereign entity." The Court found precedential support for this distinction in the 1907 decision of *Georgia v. Tennessee Copper Co.*, where Justice Holmes, writing for the Court, recognized "that states are not normal litigants for purposes of invoking federal jurisdiction." Because Massachusetts had its own state lands affected by the greenhouse gas emissions, the state's sovereignty interest, according to the Court, had to receive deference. The Court also recognized that the Clean Air Act created a procedural right to challenge the rejection of rule-making authority. The Court then held that "given that procedural right and Massachusetts' stake protecting its quasi sovereign interests, the commonwealth is entitled to special solicitude in our standing analysis." The Massachusetts decision might be read as a case where the state satisfies the *Lujan* criteria, or alternatively, as a case where state sovereignty creates an exception to the *Lujan* criteria.

Chief Justice Roberts dissented on the standing issue (joined by Justices Scalia, Thomas and Alito.) Basically the Chief Justice's dissent asserted that the Court was improperly relaxing Article III standing requirements. Justice Scalia dissented on the merits of the Court's interpretation of the Clean Air Act.

(5) *What about Present, but Indirect, Harm when Persons More Directly Harmed have not Sued?: United States v. Hays, 515 U.S. 737 (1995).* In *Hays*, the plaintiffs claimed that Louisiana's congressional redistricting plan was a "racial gerrymander" violative of the Equal Protection Clause. The focus of the claim was a newly-created district with a majority of minority voters, Louisiana's District 4. District 4 also had an odd geographic shape, but none of the plaintiffs resided in District 4. The Supreme Court, per Justice O'Connor, applied the three criteria from *Lujan*, and held that since these plaintiffs were not residents of the allegedly gerrymandered district, they did not have standing. The Court concluded that mere allegations of race consciousness on the part the Legislature which created District 4 were not sufficient to satisfy *Lujan's* injury-in-fact requirement. While the *Hays* decision would seem to establish a clear standing requirement for racial gerrymander cases (*i.e.,* the challenger should be a resident of the allegedly gerrymandered district), isn't *Hays* distinguishable from *Lujan* because the injury to the plaintiffs in *Hays* is far less speculative (and more direct) than in *Lujan*? Hence, should the *Lujan* criteria have been used? The Court has applied its *Hays* standard to subsequent redistricting cases. *See, e.g., Bush v. Vera,* 517 U.S. 952 (1996).

(6) *Do Members of Congress Who "Lose" A Floor Vote have Standing to Challenge the Act?: The First Line-Item Veto Case, Brought before the Veto Was Used— Raines v. Byrd, 521 U.S. 811 (1997).* Senator Robert Byrd and other members of Congress, who had voted against the Line Item Veto Act ("the Act"), challenged the constitutionality of the Act. Although the District Court had found that the Act diluted the legislators' Article I voting power and that this was a sufficient "institutional injury" to give them Article III standing, the Supreme Court, per Chief Justice Rehnquist, applied the standing criteria from *Lujan* and held that the members of Congress lacked standing to bring this claim. The Court distinguished the leading "legislative standing" case, *Coleman v. Miller,* because the votes of the legislators here "were given full effect. They simply lost that vote." The Court noted that Congress had a remedy available—repealing the Act—and that other, proper plaintiffs could (and undoubtedly would) challenge the Act once it went into effect.

Justices Stevens and Breyer dissented separately. Justice Breyer argued that the standing issue should be considered in light of "the systematic nature, seriousness, and immediacy of the harm." How would Justice Breyer's three factors differ from the criteria in *Lujan*?

(7) *The Actual Injury Element of Standing: Adarand Constructors, Inc. v. Mineta, 534 U.S. 103 (2002) (Adarand II).* In *Adarand Constructors, Inc. v. Peña,* 515 U.S. 200 (1995), the Court handed down a landmark affirmative action decision that the strict scrutiny standard governs affirmative action programs of the federal government as well as of the states. [The *Adarand I* decision is covered in § 10.03 below.] After a complicated procedural history on remand, the Supreme Court granted certiorari a second time to review whether the Department of Transportation (DOT) disadvantaged business enterprise (DBE) program survived strict scrutiny. But during the briefing schedule, Adarand shifted its argument to focus on a different DBE program. The Supreme Court, in a *per curiam* opinion, dismissed the writ of certiorari as improvidently granted in part because Adarand lacked standing to challenge this other program. The Court recognized the national importance of the affirmative action issues, but it insisted that satisfaction of conditions of justiciability (including standing) were constitutional "thresholds."

[3] Other Conditions of Adjudication Requirements: Ripeness

(1) *"Ripeness" and Prematurity.* The ripeness requirement is closely related to the advisory opinion, standing, and mootness doctrines (indeed all may be viewed as different special cases of the same basic idea), but refers to the notion that the claim has not matured because all conditions or events that must concur to create the

required injury have not yet come into existence. *See, e.g., Anderson v. Green*, 513 U.S. 557 (1995). In *Anderson*, the challengers claimed that California's durational residency requirement law providing *differential payment* of welfare benefits, for the first year of California residency, violated their equal protection rights. Although the challengers prevailed in the lower courts, the Court, in a *per curiam* decision, held that the case was not ripe because, subsequent to the initiation of the action, the federal government had removed the necessary permission for California to use its differential payment program. Without this permission, California could not operate the program. The Court refused to address the equal protection claim (under *Sosna v. Iowa*, below in § 10.04).

(2) *The Factors in the Ripeness Analysis: Ohio Forestry Association, Inc. v. Sierra Club, 523 U.S. 726 (1998).* After exhausting administrative remedies, the Sierra Club challenged the lawfulness of the National Forest Service's land and resource management plan for a National Forest in Ohio, contending that the plan permitted excessive logging and "clearcutting." The Court of Appeals found that, although no site specific logging had taken place, the action was ripe and that the government's plan violated the applicable federal statute. On the ripeness issue, the Supreme Court, per Justice Breyer, unanimously reversed. In deciding the ripeness issue, at least in the context of judicial review of an agency's decision, the Court identified several factors:

> (1) whether delayed review would cause hardship to the plaintiffs; (2) whether judicial intervention would inappropriately interfere with further administrative action; and (3) whether the court's would benefit from further factual development [by the agency] of the issues presented.

> Since the Court concluded that all three factors favored judicial non-intervention, the Court held that the case was not ripe and remanded it to the lower courts and agency.

(3) *Competing Formulations of the Standard for Determining Ripeness: National Park Hospitality Ass'n v. Department of the Interior, 538 U.S. 803 (2003).* The National Park Service (NPS) implemented regulations that purported to exempt concession contracts from the Contract Dispute Act of 1978 (CDA). Concessioners brought a facial challenge to these regulations on the basis that the CDA did apply to concession contracts, but the lower courts upheld the regulations. The Supreme Court, per Justice Thomas, held that the concessioners' action was not ripe and, therefore, vacated the judgments.

The doctrinal significance of this decision is the Court's statement of the standard: "Determining whether administrative action is ripe for judicial review requires us to evaluate (1) the fitness of the issues for judicial review and (2) the hardship to the parties of withholding court consideration." The Court held that the concessioners' claim did not satisfy either prong of this standard because the NPS was not empowered to administer the CDA, and the regulations did not interfere with the concessioners' business. Compare this two-prong standard to the *Ohio Forestry* three-prong standard (above). Justice Breyer, author of *Ohio Forestry*, dissented.

[4] Other Conditions of Adjudication Requirements: Mootness

(1) *Mootness: The Case or Controversy Requirement That A Case Must Be "Alive" At All Stages of Judicial Review-Arizonans For Official English v. Arizona, 520 U.S. 43 (1997).* This decision is typical of a case in which the federal courts would find that a controversy—although once alive—had become moot. The State of Arizona, by a ballot initiative, passed a state constitutional provision establishing, *inter alia*, that the state's official "language" would be only English. A state employee challenged the English-Only provision, and the federal District Court held that the provision was, on overbreadth grounds, unconstitutional. While the case was on appeal, the employee voluntarily left government employment. Although the matter had been ruled upon by

the Court of Appeals, the unanimous Supreme Court, per Justice Ginsburg, vacated the lower courts' judgments and remanded. The Court held that, when the employee-challenger left state employment, her claims became moot since her concerns about facing job-related discipline had been removed. With her voluntary departure from her job, the employee's potential injuries (and, hence, her claim) was no longer "alive."

(2) *Mootness: The Exception for Cases "Capable of Repetition, Yet Evading Review": Roe v. Wade, 410 U.S. 113 (1973).* What happens if a claimant's status changes during appeals, so that the relief sought is no longer needed? Imagine, for example, that the plaintiff in a prison reform case is paroled shortly after trial, but before judgment. The case arguably is moot, because the plaintiff no longer claims any injury. In *Roe v. Wade*, plaintiffs challenged abortion laws; Supreme Court review would have been beyond the reach of any case if standing were strictly construed, because it always takes more than nine months to reach that forum! The Court labelled the issue "capable of repetition, yet evading review"-and found standing for that reason. *See also Davis v. Federal Election Commission*, 128 S. Ct. 2759 (2008). One mechanism that has been used to address this problem is for the plaintiffs to file their suit as a class action, with a fluid group always having rights at issue, and representative parties changing if necessary. In *Bender v. Williamsport*, the same problem arose, because students who were members of Petros when suit was brought had graduated by the time the case reached the Supreme Court. The court of appeals solved this problem by granting a motion to add new plaintiffs who were currently enrolled as students, 741 F.2d 538, 542 n.4 (3d Cir. 1984), but it could not overcome the lack of an appellant with standing.

(3) *An Example of Non-Mootness even after Repeal of a Challenged Law: Northeastern Florida Chapter of the Associated General Contractors v. City of Jacksonville, 508 U.S. 656 (1993).* A Jacksonville ordinance set aside 10% of the City's contracts for minority business enterprises. The Associated General Contractors challenged this racial and gender preference on equal protection grounds. After the Supreme Court granted certiorari, Jacksonville repealed its ordinance and argued that the case was moot. But the city had substituted another ordinance which, although different, still contained racial and gender preferences. The Court, per Justice Thomas, rejected the City's mootness argument on the ground that "a defendant's voluntary cessation of a challenged practice does not deprive a federal court of its power to determine the legality of the practice." The new ordinance might disadvantage the Contractors "to a lesser degree than the old one, but . . . it still disadvantages them in the same fundamental way." The City's argument would enable the City to "moot a case by . . . replacing [an offending ordinance] with one that differs only in some insignificant respect."

Justice O'Connor, joined by Justice Blackmun, dissented. "When a challenged statute expires or is repealed or is significantly amended pending review, and the only relief sought is prospective, the Court's practice has been to dismiss the case as moot." Here, the ordinance was not closely similar, according to the dissenters; it "clearly was written to remedy the constitutional defects that petitioner alleged." Is this reasoning correct? Should there be a new challenge, if the plaintiffs want to bring one, with new evidence and new issues—or is the majority more persuasive in arguing that such an approach would enable the City to frustrate review by subterfuge?

(4) *Non-Mootness Even Though The Defendant Has Complied With Federal Permit Requirements: Friends of the Earth v. Laidlaw Environmental Services, 528 U.S. 167 (2000).* Environmental groups brought an action against the holder of pollution discharge permit pursuant to the citizen suit provision of the Clean Water Act (CWA). The District Court found that there had been numerous violations of the permit's mercury discharge limits and imposed a penalty of $405,000.00, but the court denied injunctive relief. The environmental groups appealed, and the defendant came into full compliance with the permit's requirements. The Court of Appeals vacated and

remanded on the grounds that the defendant's compliance rendered any claim for injunctive relief moot.

The Supreme Court, per Justice Ginsburg, reversed because the court of appeals had misapplied the "law on post-commencement mootness." The Court decided that a "defendant's voluntary cessation of allegedly unlawful conduct ordinarily does not suffice to moot a case." The Court also held that the plaintiffs had standing under the *Lujan* standards [below], and this holding drew a vigorous dissent from Justice Scalia. *See also, City of Erie v. Pap's A.M.*, 529 U.S. 277 (2000), below in § 11.06.

(5) *Mootness And The Voluntary Cessation By The Challenger: City News and Novelty, Inc. v. City of Waukesha, 531 U.S. 278 (2001).* While numerous decisions, such as *Northeastern Florida Chapter*, above, hold that the voluntary cessation of the challenged practice by the government defendant will not ordinarily moot a case, the Court has often observed, as in *City News*, that voluntary cessation of action by a challenger will suffice to moot a case. When the City News enterprise voluntarily withdrew its application for license renewal (and closed its business), the Court, per Justice Ginsburg, held that the controversy with the city was moot. As a practice tip, you should remember that adding a claim for monetary damages (to claims for prospective relief) will be a means to avoid mootness even if the challenger's circumstances would change during the course of the litigation.

PROBLEM D

A "CASE OR CONTROVERSY?": HILL v. PRINTING INDUSTRIES OF THE GULF COAST, 422 U.S. 937 (1975). A section of the Election Code of the (imaginary) State of West York provides that all election campaign literature must contain the name and address of the printer. The statute is based upon legislative findings that it is important to be able to identify the printer in order to prevent "dirty tricks," such as falsely attributed smears, during election campaigns. A printing industry trade organization challenges the statute as violative of the first amendment guaranty of freedom of speech and association, arguing that candidates will have greater difficulty obtaining printers willing to print their literature because of the statute. A lower federal court agrees with this argument and declares the statute unconstitutional. The state appeals to the Supreme Court—but during the appeal, mindful of the absence of enforceable regulatory provisions, the state legislature repeals the statute and replaces it with another set of laws that does not require identification of the printer.

(1) *Mootness.* Does the repeal of the statute render the case moot? [In *Printing Industries*, above, the Supreme Court entered a one-paragraph order remanding the case for a determination whether it was moot. The trial court dismissed. Was the dismissal correct?]

(2) *Ripeness; Advisory Opinions.* But assume that the state's position is that it wishes to know whether the repeal was necessary; it would like to "repeal the repeal," so that the printer-identification provision is still in effect. Does this claimed interest or injury affect the outcome of the case? Alternatively, imagine that there are some printers who fear prosecution because they refused to comply with the statute before the time it was repealed. Does this claimed interest or injury affect the result?

(3) *Standing.* Does Printing Industries of the Gulf Coast, as a trade association, have standing to sue? If so, can it base its claim on the first amendment rights of candidates for election, whom it claims will be hindered in their ability to contract for printing? [In *Printing Industries*, above, the lower court answered yes to both questions; was this conclusion correct?]

[B] The Political Question Doctrine: An Exception to Judicial Review

NOTE ON THE HISTORY AND MEANING OF THE POLITICAL QUESTION DOCTRINE: HOW TO READ THE CASE OF *BAKER v. CARR*

Political Questions as Reflecting Separation of Powers, Judicial Function, and Prudential Limits. The "political" question doctrine really reflects a complex of at least three underlying concerns. First, it reflects respect for the separation of powers, in avoiding decisions expressly given by the Constitution to the executive or legislative branches. Secondly, some decisions are inappropriate for the judicial function, because they involve non-judicial discretion or lack of judicially determinable standards. Finally, it encompasses what might be called "prudential" concerns, or judicial deference as a matter of policy, such as the avoidance of embarrassment to other branches or of interference with pronouncements where consistency especially is important. These concerns are summarized in somewhat different form in *Baker v. Carr*, below.

Luther v. Borden: Development of the Political Question Doctrine. Historically, the leading case following the doctrine was *Luther v. Borden*, 48 U.S. (7 How.) 1 (1849). Plaintiff alleged a trespass by the defendants, who, in turn, claimed that they were acting for the legitimate government of Rhode Island pursuant to military orders to arrest the plaintiff for insurrection. The plaintiff countered by claiming that the government of Rhode Island had been altered by the people of that State in what since has become known as Dorr's Rebellion, and the defendants therefore did not legitimately represent the state. Thus, what appeared to be a trespass case depended upon a court's determining which of two competing groups in an insurrection should be recognized as the government of Rhode Island. The Supreme Court, in an opinion by Chief Justice Roger Taney, refused to decide the issue, labelling it a political question. Justice Taney cited the "Guaranty" Clause of the Constitution, which provides: "The United States shall guarantee to every State in this union a Republican Form of Government. . . ." To Taney, the general reference to the United States meant that "it rests with Congress to decide what government is the established one in a State." That legislative decision "is binding on every other department of the government, and could not be questioned in a judicial tribunal." If the judiciary intervened, Taney feared such consequences as court interference with the President's orders to "troops in the service of the United States" when they sought to maintain the guaranty.

The Apportionment Cases: Background to Baker v. Carr. In a later series of cases, citizens in various states sought to challenge dilution of their votes because of malapportionment. State legislatures tended not only to gerrymander districts, but to make them of unequal size, so that geographical areas in which the majority opposed the majority party had more voters and fewer representatives per voter. In *Colegrove v. Green*, 328 U.S. 549 (1946), plaintiffs claimed that population shifts, together with legislative inaction, had produced malapportionment that denied them equivalent votes; the Supreme Court denied relief, leaving the justiciability of the question ambiguous. It remained for *Baker v. Carr* to consider the question more generally.

The Modern Disarray (or Disappearance?) of the Political Question Doctrine. Since *Luther v. Borden*, the political question doctrine has shrunk dramatically, and many issues that it would seem at first blush to insulate from review have been decided by courts. Professor Wright says, "No branch of the law of justiciability is in such disarray as the doctrine of the 'political question.'" C. WRIGHT, THE LAW OF FEDERAL COURTS 74 (4th ed. 1983). At least one commentator argues that the doctrine has disappeared and that only isolated categories of nonjusticiable matters remain. Henkin, *Is There a "Political Question Doctrine?"*, 85 YALE L.J. 597 (1976).

BAKER v. CARR
369 U.S. 186 (1962)

claim

[Plaintiffs complained that they were "denied the equal protection of the laws . . . by virtue of the debasement of their votes" under the Tennessee apportionment statute of 1901. During the sixty intervening years, population changes made the 1901 statute "unconstitutional and obsolete," and no reapportionment had since passed the Tennessee legislature. Plaintiffs asked for a declaration of unconstitutionality, an injunction against further elections under the statute, and, until the Tennessee legislature passed a proper law, a decree imposing "a reapportionment by mathematical application" of federal census figures (or a decree requiring completely statewide

PH

elections for all offices). The district court dismissed on jurisdictional grounds and for want of a justiciable question, without distinguishing these two grounds.]

hold

In light of the District Court's treatment of the case, we hold today only (a) that the court possessed jurisdiction of the subject matter; (b) that a justiciable cause of action is stated upon which appellants would be entitled to appropriate relief; and (c) because appellees raise the issue before this Court, that the appellants have standing to challenge the Tennessee apportionment statutes. . . .

Jurisdiction of the Subject Matter.

[The Court first held that since the controversy fell within a properly applicable jurisdictional statute, it had jurisdiction. But justiciability, it concluded, was a separate issue.]

Justiciability.

In holding that the subject matter of this suit was not justiciable, the District Court relied on *Colegrove v. Green, supra,* and subsequent *per curiam* cases. The court stated: "From a review of these decisions there can be no doubt that the federal rule . . . is that the federal courts . . . will not intervene in cases of this type to compel legislative reapportionment." We understand the District Court to have read the cited cases as compelling the conclusion that since the appellants sought to have a legislative apportionment held unconstitutional, their suit presented a "political question" and was therefore nonjusticiable. We hold that this challenge to an apportionment presents no nonjusticiable "political question." The cited cases do not hold the contrary.

Of course the mere fact that the suit seeks protection of a political right does not mean it presents a political question. Such an objection "is little more than a play upon words." *Nixon v. Herndon,* 273 U.S. 536. . . . Rather, it is argued that apportionment cases, whatever the actual wording of the complaint, can involve no federal constitutional right except one resting on the guaranty of a republican form of government, and that complaints based on that clause have been held to present political questions which are nonjusticiable.

. . . The nonjusticiability of a political question is primarily a function of the separation of powers. Much confusion results from the capacity of the "political question" label to obscure the need for case-by-case inquiry. . . . [We must] analyze representative cases and [i]nfer from them the analytical threads that make up the political question doctrine. We shall then show that none of those threads catches this case.

Validity of enactments: In *Coleman v. Miller, 307 U.S. 433,* this Court held that the questions of how long a proposed amendment to the Federal Constitution remained open to ratification, and what effect a prior rejection had on a subsequent ratification, were committed to congressional resolution and involved criteria of decision that necessarily escaped the judicial grasp. Similar considerations apply to the enacting process. . . .

Prominent on the surface of any case held to involve a political question is found a textually demonstrable constitutional commitment of the issue to a coordinate political department; or a lack of judicially discoverable and manageable standards for resolving it; or the impossibility of deciding without an initial policy determination of a kind clearly for nonjudicial discretion; or the impossibility of a court's undertaking independent resolution without expressing lack of the respect due coordinate branches of government; or an unusual need for unquestioning adherence to a political decision already made; or the potentiality of embarrassment from multifarious pronouncements by various departments of one question.

Unless one of these formulations is inextricable from the case at bar, there should be no dismissal for non-justiciability on the ground of a political question's presence. . . .

Republican form of government: Luther v. Borden, 12 L.Ed. 581, 7 How. 1, though in form simply an action for damages for trespass was, as Daniel Webster said in opening the argument for the defense, "an unusual case." The defendants, admitting an otherwise tortious breaking and entering, sought to justify their action on the ground that they were agents of the established lawful government of Rhode Island, which State was then under martial law to defend itself from active insurrection; that the plaintiff was engaged in that insurrection; and that they entered under orders to arrest the plaintiff. . . . The plaintiff's right to recover depended upon which of the two groups was entitled to such recognition; but the lower court's refusal to receive evidence or hear argument on that issue, its charge to the jury that the earlier established or "charter" government was lawful, and the verdict for the defendants, were affirmed upon appeal to this Court. . . .

Clearly, several factors were thought by the Court in *Luther* to make the question there "political"; the commitment to the other branches of the decision as to which is the lawful state government; the unambiguous action by the President, in recognizing the charter government as the lawful authority; the need for finality in the executive's decision; and the lack of criteria for which a court could determine which form of government was republican. . . .

We come, finally, to the ultimate inquiry whether our precedents as to what constitutes a nonjusticiable "political question" bring the case before us under the umbrella of that doctrine. A natural beginning is to note whether any of the common characteristics which we have been able to identify and label descriptively are present. We find none: The question here is the consistency of state action with the Federal Constitution. We have no question decided, or to be decided, by a political branch of government coequal with this Court. Nor do we risk embarrassment of our government abroad, or grave disturbance at home if we take issue with Tennessee as to the constitutionality of her action here challenged. Nor need the appellants, in order to succeed in this action, ask the Court to enter upon policy determinations for which judicially manageable standards are lacking. Judicial standards under the Equal Protection Clause are well developed and familiar, and it has been open to courts since the enactment of the Fourteenth Amendment to determine, if on the particular facts they must, that discrimination reflects *no* policy, but simply arbitrary and capricious action. . . .

Reversed and remanded.

Mr. Justice Whittaker did not participate in the decision of this case.

[The concurring opinions of Justices Douglas and Stewart are omitted.]

Mr. Justice Clark, concurring. . . .

The controlling facts cannot be disputed. It appears from the record that 37% of the voters of Tennessee elect 20 of the 33 Senators while 40% of the voters elect 63 of the

99 members of the House. . . .

[T]ennessee's apportionment is a crazy-quilt without rational basis. . . .

Although I find the Tennessee apportionment statute offends the Equal Protection Clause, I would not consider intervention by this Court into so delicate a field if there were any other relief available to the people of Tennessee. But the majority of the people of Tennessee have no "practical opportunities for exerting their political weight at the polls" to correct the existing "invidious discrimination." Tennessee has no initiative and referendum. I have searched diligently for other "practical opportunities" present under the law. I find none other than through the federal courts. . . . It is said that there is recourse in Congress and perhaps that may be, but from a practical standpoint this is without substance. To date Congress has never undertaken such a task in any State. . . .

MR. JUSTICE FRANKFURTER, whom MR. JUSTICE HARLAN joins, dissenting.

. . . [T]he Court does not vouchsafe the lower courts—state and federal—guidelines for formulating specific, definite, wholly unprecedented remedies for the inevitable litigations that today's umbrageous disposition is bound to stimulate in connection with politically motivated reapportionments in so many States. . . . To charge courts with the task of accommodating the incommensurable factors of policy that underlie these mathematical puzzles is to attribute, however flatteringly, omnicompetence to judges. The Framers of the Constitution persistently rejected a proposal that embodied this assumption. . . .

The *Colegrove* doctrine, in the form in which repeated decisions have settled it, was not an innovation. It represents long judicial thought and experience. From its earliest opinions this Court has consistently recognized a class of controversies which do not lend themselves to judicial standards and judicial remedies. To classify the various instances as "political questions" is rather a form of stating this conclusion than revealing of analysis. . . .

The influence of these converging considerations—the caution not to undertake decision where standards meet for judicial judgment are lacking, the reluctance to interfere with matters of state government in the absence of an unquestionable and effectively enforceable mandate, the unwillingness to make courts arbiters of the broad issues of political organization historically committed to other institutions and for whose adjustment the judicial process is ill-adapted—has been decisive of the settled line of cases, reaching back more than a century, which holds that Art. IV, § 4, of the Constitution, guaranteeing to the States "a Republican Form of Government," is not enforceable through the courts. . . .

What, then, is this question of legislative apportionment? Appellants invoke the right to vote and to have their votes counted. But they are permitted to vote and their votes are counted. They go to the polls, they cast their ballots, they send their representatives to the state councils. Their complaint is simply that the representatives are not sufficiently numerous or powerful—in short, that Tennessee has adopted a basis of representation with which they are dissatisfied. Talk of "debasement" or "dilution" is circular talk. One cannot speak of "debasement" or "dilution" of the value of a vote until there is first defined a standard of reference as to what a vote should be worth. What is actually asked of the Court in this case is to choose among competing bases of representation—ultimately, really, among competing theories of political philosophy—in order to establish an appropriate frame of government for the State of Tennessee and thereby for all the States of the Union. . . .

To find such a political conception legally enforceable in the broad and unspecific guarantee of equal protection is to rewrite the Constitution. *See Luther v. Borden, supra.* Certainly, "equal protection" is no more secure a foundation for judicial judgment of the permissibility of varying forms of representative government than is

"Republican Form. . . ." For a court could not determine the equal-protection issue without in fact first determining the Republican-Form issue, simply because what is reasonable for equal-protection purposes will depend upon what frame of government, basically, is allowed. To divorce "equal protection" from "Republican Form" is to talk about half a question.

The notion that representation proportioned to the geographic spread of population is so universally accepted as a necessary element of equality . . . that it must be taken to be the standard of a political equality preserved by the Fourteenth Amendment—that it is, in appellants' words "the basic principle of representative government"—is, to put it bluntly, not true. However desirable and however desired by some among the great political thinkers and framers of our government, it has never been generally practiced, today or in the past. . . .

[At this point, Justice Frankfurter reviews apportionment practices of (1) Great Britain; (2) the Colonies and the Union; (3) the states at the time of ratification of the Fourteenth Amendment, and those later admitted; and (4) contemporary states. His detailed review convinces him that the historical understanding does not justify the majority's conclusions. It shows "that there is not—as there has never been—a standard by which the place of equality as a factor in apportionment can be measured."]

Dissenting opinion of Mr. Justice Harlan, whom Mr. Justice Frankfurter joins. . . .

In short, there is nothing in the Federal Constitution to prevent a State, acting not irrationally, from choosing any electoral legislative structure it thinks best suited to the interests, temper, and customs of its people. . . . A State's choice to distribute electoral strength among geographical units, rather than according to a census of population, is certainly no less a rational decision of policy than would be its choice to levy a tax on property rather than a tax on income. Both are legislative judgments entitled to equal respect from this Court. . . .

NOTES AND QUESTIONS

(1) *The Aftermath of Baker v. Carr—"One Person, One Vote:" Reynolds v. Sims, 377 U.S. 533 (1964).* In *Baker,* the Court avoided foreshadowing an intention to impose strict mathematical formulas upon state reapportionment. But in a line of cases that began with *Reynolds v. Sims, supra,* the Court interpreted the equal protection clause as requiring apportionment according to population—a principle that since has become known as "one person, one vote." [The cases are discussed, below, in the chapter of this book on Equal Protection.] Was the Court inexorably pushed to the one person one vote principle by the lack of any other suitable judicial standard after *Baker v. Carr*? And if so, don't Justices Harlan and Frankfurter have a point in saying that representation by population, or representation by geographic areas, are two different methods that simply pose differences of political philosophy?

(2) *Following the Point of Justices Frankfurter and Harlan: A Case that Shows the Political Nature of the "Equality" Issue.* Imagine the (hypothetical) state of Winnemac, which has one major urban area, the City of Zenith, but whose population is 90% rural. If the state is apportioned according to population, urban residents fear that their votes will be "diluted" in the sense that voters with rural values and political agendas will always outvote them. Therefore, the state, at its constitutional convention, devises an apportionment scheme that weights the votes of urban residents more heavily than they otherwise would be weighted, to compensate for the greater mass of rural voters. But the principle of one person, one vote seems to indicate that such a plan is unconstitutional. In such a situation, the point of Justices Frankfurter and Harlan is that it is a "political" judgment, not susceptible of judicial standards, to require apportionment by population in the one person, one vote mold. For another example, consider the United

States Senate, which contains two Senators per state, not apportioned by population. Do these Justices have a point? If so, is it about justiciability—or about the merits?

(3) *Gerrymandering; Redistricting by Incumbents to Protect their Safe Seats; Etc.* Is there an equal protection violation if the dominant political party, while observing the principle of "one person, one vote," draws district lines so as to concentrate the maximum number of opposition party voters in the fewest possible districts (thereby reducing the number of their representatives)? More to the point, is this question justiciable? Consider the following case.

DAVIS v. BANDEMER, 478 U.S. 109 (1986). Indiana Democrats alleged that a previous Republican majority in the state legislature had reapportioned by a political gerrymander that violated their right to equal protection of the laws. In fact, Democratic candidates for the Indiana House received 51.9% of statewide votes but won only 43 of 100 seats. In Marion and Allen Counties, Democrats drew 46.6% of the vote, but only three of 21 Democrat candidates were elected. Relying upon these and similar statistics, the district court held that the reapportionment was unconstitutional and ordered the legislature to prepare a new plan. A majority of the Supreme Court reversed on the merits but held that equal protection claims for political gerrymandering could be justiciable. The majority noted that the Court repeatedly had said that if districting "would operate to minimize or cancel the voting strength of racial *or political* elements in the population," it would "raise a constitutional question." The majority then relied directly on the analysis of *Baker v. Carr* to hold that the gerrymandering issue was not a political question:

Six Justices concurred in this holding. Justices Powell and Stevens would have gone farther and affirmed the district court; accordingly, they dissented on the merits. Justice Powell's opinion found "a paradigm example of unconstitutional discrimination against the members of a political party that happened to be out of power."

Justice O'Connor, joined by Chief Justice Burger and Justice Rehnquist, concurred separately. These three justices would have reversed on the ground that the issue was a nonjusticiable political question:

> I would hold that the partisan gerrymandering claims of major political parties raise a nonjusticiable political question that the judiciary should leave to the legislative branch as the Framers of the Constitution unquestionably intended. . . .
>
> To turn these matters over to the federal judiciary is to inject the courts into the most heated partisan issues. . . .
>
> . . . If members of the major political parties are protected by the Equal Protection Clause from dilution of their voting strength, then members of every identifiable group . . . should be able to bring similar claims. Federal courts will have no alternative but to attempt to recreate the complex process of legislative apportionment in the context of adversary litigation in order to reconcile the competing claims of political, religious, ethnic, racial, occupational, and socioeconomic groups. . . .
>
> In my view, where a racial minority group is characterized by the "traditional indicia of suspectness" and is vulnerable to the political process, . . . individual voters who belong to that group enjoy some measure of protection . . . [from] political gerrymandering. . . .
>
> Clearly, members of the Democratic and Republican parties cannot claim that they are a discrete and insular group vulnerable to exclusion from the political process by some dominant group: these political parties *are* the dominant groups, and the Court has offered no reason to believe that they are incapable of fending for themselves through the political process. Indeed, there is good reason to think that political gerrymandering is a self-limiting enterprise. In order to gerrymander, the majority must weaken some of its safe

seats. . . . Similarly, an overambitious gerrymander can lead to disaster for the legislative majority. . . . There is no proof before us that political gerrymandering is an evil that cannot be checked or cured by the people or by the parties themselves. Absent such proof, I see no basis for concluding that there is a need, let alone a constitutional basis, for judicial intervention.

NOTES AND QUESTIONS

(1) *The "Failures-of-Democracy" Theory: Does it Support Justice O'Connor's View? Does it Support Baker v. Carr in the First Place?* Justice O'Connor apparently would limit judicial intervention to those cases in which the evil "cannot be checked or cured by the people or the parties themselves," such as when a majority oppresses a "discrete and insular" minority. A racial gerrymander, in which a legislature minimizes the affects of black voters, is an example. The majority responded to this argument by saying, "Justice O'Connor's factual assumptions are by no means obviously correct: It is not clear that political gerrymandering *is* a self-limiting enterprise or that other groups will have any great incentive to bring gerrymandering claims, given the requirement of a showing of discriminatory intent." Is this analysis correct?

A related question concerns the failures-of-democracy theory in *Baker v. Carr.* Is intervention justified in *Baker v. Carr* because arguably the "evil cannot be checked or cured by" the political process?

(2) *The Original Intention: Lack of Support for Judicial Review in Vote Dilution Cases?* In *Baker*, Justice Frankfurter painstakingly documented the practices in Great Britain, Colonial America, and States before and after ratification of the Fourteenth Amendment, to show that the drafters of the basic Constitution and of the Fourteenth Amendment did not contemplate the justiciability of equal protection claims for vote dilution. Justice O'Connor maintains that the Founders "unquestionably" intended to leave the matter to the legislative branch. If Frankfurter and O'Connor are right, does that mean that *Baker* and *Davis* are incorrectly decided?

(3) *"Judicially Manageable Standards."* Is Justice O'Connor correct in asserting that there are no judicially manageable standards for political gerrymandering, given that the Court will be driven to consider "rough proportionality" among diverse groups for whom proportionality will require conflicting divisions of the pie? In other words, consider whether proportional representation by political parties may require one reapportionment plan, while proportional representation by racial, religious, or socio-economic groups might each require different plans.

(4) *Revisiting Davis and Political Gerrymandering: Vieth v. Jubelirer, 541 U.S. 267 (2004).* As a result of the 2000 census, Pennsylvania lost two congressional districts. Both Houses of the Pennsylvania Legislature and the Governor were controlled by the Republicans. The Republican majority passed a redistricting scheme that favored Republicans. Challengers Vieth and Furey were Democrats who sued claiming, *inter alia*, that the Republican scheme was, under Davis, an impermissible political gerrymander.

The *Vieth* Court, per Justice Scalia's plurality opinion, concluded that the Pennsylvania political gerrymandering controversy was "nonjusticiable." Relying on much of the reasoning from Justice O'Connor's opinion in *Davis*, the Scalia opinion found that the judiciary lacked discoverable and meaningful standards to review, under Art. I, § 2, a purely "political" gerrymander. Justice Kennedy's concurrence provided the fifth vote to dismiss, but he refused to foreclose all possibility of judicial relief if some limited and precise rationale could be found to review certain redistricting cases. Justices Stevens, Souter, Ginsburg, and Breyer dissented.

Read U.S. Const. Art. I, § 3, cl. 6 (the Impeachment Clause).

NIXON v. UNITED STATES
506 U.S. 224 (1993)

CHIEF JUSTICE REHNQUIST delivered the opinion of the Court.

[Judge Walter L. Nixon (no relation to President Nixon) was convicted before a jury upon two counts of making false statements to a grand jury. He refused to resign his federal judgeship and continued to draw his salary while in prison. The House of Representatives adopted and presented articles of impeachment against him. The Senate then invoked Senate Impeachment Rule XI, which allows the appointment of a committee to "receive evidence and take testimony," after which the full Senate ultimately voted to convict and remove Nixon. He then filed suit for a declaratory judgment that the conviction was void, arguing that the constitutional power to "try" all impeachments required the full Senate to take part in evidentiary hearings.

[The District Court dismissed on the ground that this claim was a nonjusticiable political question, and the Court of Appeals affirmed. Here, the Supreme Court also affirms the dismissal.]

A controversy is nonjusticiable—i.e., involves a political question—where there is "a textually demonstrable constitutional commitment of the issue to a coordinate political department; or a lack of judicially discoverable and manageable standards for resolving it. . . ." *Baker v. Carr*, 369 U.S. 186, 217 (1962). [A]s the discussion that follows makes clear, the concept of a textual commitment to a coordinate political department is not completely separate from the concept of a lack of judicially discoverable and manageable standards for resolving it; the lack of judicially manageable standards may strengthen the conclusion that there is a textually demonstrable commitment to a coordinate branch.

In this case, we must examine Art. I, § 3, cl. 6, to determine the scope of authority conferred upon the Senate by the Framers regarding impeachment. It provides:

> The Senate shall have the sole Power to try all Impeachments. When sitting for that Purpose, they shall be on Oath or Affirmation. When the President of the United States is tried, the Chief Justice shall preside: And no Person shall be convicted without the Concurrence of two thirds of the Members present.

The language and structure of this Clause are revealing. The first sentence is a grant of authority to the Senate, and the word "sole" indicates that this authority is reposed in the Senate and nowhere else. The next two sentences specify requirements to which the Senate proceedings shall conform: the Senate shall be on oath or affirmation, a two-thirds vote is required to convict, and when the President is tried the Chief Justice shall preside.

Petitioner argues that the word "try" in the first sentence imposes by implication an additional requirement on the Senate in that the proceedings must be in the nature of a judicial trial. [P]etitioner concludes from this that courts may review whether or not the Senate "tried" him before convicting him. [Note that the Chief Justice now engages in a textual and historical analysis.]

There are several difficulties with this position which lead us ultimately to reject it. The word "try," both in 1787 and later, has considerably broader meanings than those to which petitioner would limit it. Older dictionaries define try as "[t]o examine" or "[t]o examine as a judge." See 2 S. Johnson, A Dictionary of the English Language (1785). In more modern usage the term has various meanings. For example, try can mean "to examine or investigate judicially," "to conduct the trial of," or "to put to the test by experiment, investigation, or trial." Webster's Third New International Dictionary 2457 (1971). [B]ased on the variety of definitions, we cannot say that the Framers used the word "try" as an implied limitation on the method by which the Senate might proceed in trying impeachments. . . .

The conclusion that the use of the word "try" in the first sentence of the Impeachment Trial Clause lacks sufficient precision to afford any judicially manageable standard of review of the Senate's actions is fortified by the existence of the three very specific requirements that the Constitution does impose on the Senate when trying impeachments: the members must be underoath, a two-thirds vote is required to convict, and the Chief Justice presides when the President is tried. These limitations are quite precise, and their nature suggests that the Framers did not intend to impose additional limitations on the form of the Senate proceedings by the use of the word "try" in the first sentence.

Petitioner devotes only two pages in his brief to negating the significance of the word "sole" in the first sentence of Clause 6. [W]e think that the word "sole" is of considerable significance. [T]he common sense meaning of the word "sole" is that the Senate alone shall have authority to determine whether an individual should be acquitted or convicted. The dictionary definition bears this out. "Sole" is defined as "having no companion," "solitary," "being the only one," and "functioning . . . independently and without assistance or interference." Webster's Third New International Dictionary 2168 (1971). If the courts may review the actions of the Senate in order to determine whether that body "tried" an impeached official, it is difficult to see how the Senate would be "functioning . . . independently and without assistance or interference. . . ."

[The Chief Justice then provided analysis based on the "legislative history" of the Senate trial provision.] The Framers labored over the question of where the impeachment power should lie. Significantly, in at least two considered scenarios the power was placed with the Federal Judiciary. [D]espite these proposals, the Convention ultimately decided that the Senate would have "the sole Power to Try all Impeachments." According to Alexander Hamilton, the Senate was the "most fit depositary of this important trust" because its members are representatives of the people. . . .

There are two additional reasons why the Judiciary, and the Supreme Court in particular, were not chosen to have any role in impeachments. First, the Framers recognized that most likely there would be two sets of proceedings for individuals who commit impeachable offenses—the impeachment trial and a separate criminal trial. In fact, the Constitution explicitly provides for two separate proceedings. The Framers deliberately separated the two forums to avoid raising the specter of bias and to ensure independent judgments. . . . [C]ertainly judicial review of the Senate's "trial" would introduce the same risk of bias as would participation in the trial itself.

Second, judicial review would be inconsistent with the Framers' insistence that our system be one of checks and balances. In our constitutional system, impeachment was designed to be the *only* check on the Judicial Branch by the Legislature. [N]ixon's argument would place final reviewing authority with respect to impeachments in the hands of the same body that the impeachment process is meant to regulate.

Nevertheless, Nixon argues that judicial review is necessary in order to place a check on the Legislature. Nixon fears that if the Senate is given unreviewable authority to interpret the Impeachment Trial Clause, there is a grave risk that the Senate will usurp judicial power. The Framers anticipated this objection and created two constitutional safeguards to keep the Senate in check. The first safeguard is that the whole of the impeachment power is divided between the two legislative bodies, with the House given the right to accuse and the Senate given the right to judge. This split of authority "avoids the inconvenience of making the same persons both accusers and judges; and guards against the danger of persecution from the prevalency of a factious spirit in either of those branches." The second safeguard is the two-thirds supermajority vote requirement. . . .

In addition to the textual commitment argument, we are persuaded that the lack of finality and the difficulty of fashioning relief counsel against justiciability. *See Baker v. Carr.* We agree with the Court of Appeals that opening the door of judicial review to the procedures used by the Senate in trying impeachments would "expose the political life of the country to months, or perhaps years, of chaos." This lack of finality would manifest itself most dramatically if the President were impeached. The legitimacy of any successor, and hence his effectiveness, would be impaired severely, not merely while the judicial process was running its course, but during any retrial that a differently constituted Senate might conduct if its first judgment of conviction were invalidated. Equally uncertain is the question of what relief a court may give other than simply setting aside the judgment of conviction. Could it order the reinstatement of a convicted federal judge, or order Congress to create an additional judgeship if the seat had been filled in the interim?

Petitioner finally contends that a holding of nonjusticiability cannot be reconciled with our opinion in *Powell v. McCormack*, 395 U.S. 486 (1969). The relevant issue in *Powell* was whether courts could review the House of Representatives' conclusion that Powell was "unqualified" to sit as a Member because he had been accused of misappropriating public funds and abusing the process of the New York courts. We stated that the question of justiciability turned on whether the Constitution committed authority to the House to judge its members' qualifications, and if so, the extent of that commitment. . . .

[T]he claim by the House that its power to "be the Judge of the Elections, Returns and Qualifications of its own Members" was a textual commitment of unreviewable authority was defeated by the existence of this separate provision specifying the only qualifications which might be imposed for House membership. The decision as to whether a member satisfied these qualifications *was* placed with the House, but the decision as to what these qualifications consisted of was not. [The Court there concluded that the case was justiciable and held that Representative Powell's exclusion was unconstitutional.]

In the case before us, there is no separate provision of the Constitution which could be defeated by allowing the Senate final authority to determine the meaning of the word "try" in the Impeachment Trial Clause. We agree with Nixon that courts possess power to review either legislative or executive action that transgresses identifiable textual limits. [B]ut we conclude, after exercising that delicate responsibility, that the word "try" in the Impeachment Clause does not provide an identifiable textual limit on the authority which is committed to the Senate.

For the foregoing reasons, the judgment of the Court of Appeals is

Affirmed.

[The concurring opinion of JUSTICE STEVENS is omitted.]

JUSTICE WHITE, with whom JUSTICE BLACKMUN joins, concurring in the judgment.

[I] find no [prohibition of the Court's jurisdiction] and would therefore reach the merits of the claim. I concur in the judgment because the Senate fulfilled its constitutional obligation to "try" petitioner. . . .

[E]ven taking a wholly practical approach, I would prefer not to announce an unreviewable discretion in the Senate to ignore completely the constitutional direction to "try" impeachment cases. When asked at oral argument whether that direction would be satisfied if [t]he Senate, without any procedure whatsoever, unanimously found the accused guilty of being "a bad guy," counsel for the United States answered that the

Government's theory "leads me to answer that question yes. . . ."

Of course the issue in the political question doctrine is *not* whether the Constitutional text commits exclusive responsibility for a particular governmental function to one of the political branches. There are numerous instances of this sort of textual commitment, *e.g.*, Art. I, § 8, and it is not thought that disputes implicating these provisions are nonjusticiable. Rather, the issue is whether the Constitution has given one of the political branches final responsibility for interpreting the scope and nature of such a power. . . .

[Having thus disagreed with the Court's opinion on justiciability, these Justices next proceed to concur in the result by rejecting Petitioner Nixon's argument on the merits.] In short, textual and historical evidence reveals that the Impeachment Trial Clause was not meant to bind the hands of the Senate beyond establishing a set of minimal procedures. Without identifying the exact contours of these procedures, it is sufficient to say that the Senate's use of a factfinding committee under Rule XI is entirely compatible with the Constitution's command that the Senate "try all impeachments." Petitioner's challenge to his conviction must therefore fail. . . .

JUSTICE SOUTER, concurring in the judgment.

I agree with the Court that this case presents a nonjusticiable political question. Because my analysis differs somewhat from the Court's, however, I concur in its judgment by this separate opinion.

As we cautioned in *Baker v. Carr*, "the "political question' label" tends "to obscure the need for case-by-case inquiry. . . ."

One can, nevertheless, envision different and unusual circumstances that might justify a more searching review of impeachment proceedings. If the Senate were to act in a manner seriously threatening the integrity of its results, convicting, say, upon a coin-toss, or upon a summary determination that an officer of the United States was simply " 'a bad guy,' " judicial interference might well be appropriate. . . .

NOTES AND QUESTIONS

(1) *Distinguishing Powell v. McCormack from Nixon: Is the Distinction Persuasive?* In *Powell*, the Court struck down the exclusion of Representative Powell by the House of Representatives. The question, said the Court, was not a political question and was justiciable. Chief Justice Warren reasoned that the "textually demonstrable commitment" to the House of the power to "be the Judge of the Elections, Returns and Qualifications of its Members" extended "only to the qualifications set forth in the Constitution." The express qualifications consisted of specific age, citizenship, and residence requirements, and the Court concluded that the textual commitment to Congress did not embrace Powell's exclusion for "misconduct" such as improper use of public funds.

In *Nixon*, note that the Court relies on the Senate's "sole power to try" impeachments, and on the oath, the two-thirds vote and the provision for the Chief Justice to preside, and distinguishes *Powell* on these grounds. Is the distinction persuasive? Or is the congressional power to "be the Judge," with its three specific qualifications, parallel to the Senate's "sole power to try" impeachments, and its three specific procedural requirements?

(2) *State-Imposed Term Limitations on Congressional Service: Do They Present a Political Question or Are They Justiciable?* In *U.S. Term Limits, Inc. v. Thornton*, 514 U.S. 779 (1995), the Court, per Justice Stevens, held that term limits imposed by state constitutional law on members of Congress were unconstitutional. The grounds for the decision, the original intent of the Congressional "Qualifications Clauses," is considered in § 3.06 below. The Court revisited *Powell v. McCormack*, above, but the *Thornton* decision did not focus on the political question doctrine issue. The Court determined, at

least implicitly, that the term limitations issue did not satisfy the criteria for a political question, as set forth above in *Nixon*. For further analysis of *Powell*, see § 3.06 below.

(3) *Effectiveness of Enactments, Especially Constitutional Amendments: Coleman v. Miller, 307 U.S. 433 (1939)*. Plaintiffs in *Coleman* were Kansas state legislators who had lost the legislative vote on ratification of an amendment to the United States Constitution. They alleged that the amendment had failed to obtain the requisite ratifications by three-fourths of the states within a reasonably contemporaneous time period as the Constitution allegedly contemplated for amendments. The Constitution provides for adoption of amendments "as the . . . Mode of Ratification may be proposed by the Congress," Art. V, and custom provided for the Congressional "promulgation of the adoption of the amendment." The Supreme Court held that the validity of the enactment presented a political question, to be determined by Congress.

(4) *The President Unilaterally Abrogates a Treaty and Avoids Adjudication: Goldwater v. Carter, 444 U.S. 997 (1979)*. President Carter announced recognition of the People's Republic of China as the sole government of China. In a related action, he unilaterally announced the termination of the Mutual Defense Treaty between the United States and Taiwan, which the People's Republic regarded as a rival government of a part of China. A group of Senators sought injunctive or declaratory relief to prevent termination of the Taiwan Treaty, to which the Senate had consented in accordance with the Constitution. The Supreme Court, without further explanation, entered a one-sentence order remanding the case with directions to dismiss. Apparently, the Court concluded that the case was nonjusticiable.

Justice Powell concurred on the ground that "a dispute between Congress and the President is not ready for judicial review unless and until each branch has taken action asserting its constitutional authority." Here, "a few Members of Congress" had sued, but "Congress has taken no official action." The case therefore was "not ripe for judicial review."

Four members of the Court concurred, in an opinion by Justice Rehnquist, on the ground that "the basic question presented by this case is 'political' and therefore nonjusticiable because it involves the authority of the President in the conduct of our country's foreign relations and the extent to which the Senate or the Congress is authorized to negate the action of the President." Three Justices dissented.

(5) *What if There is Actual Conflict between the President and Congress?: Japan Whaling Ass'n v. American Cetacean Society, 478 U.S. 221 (1986)*. Would the result in *Goldwater v. Carter* be different, as Justice Powell's opinion seems to suggest, if there had been actual conflict between the President and Congress? In *Japan Whaling, supra*, it appeared that such a conflict existed, in that the President arguably had failed to enforce whaling quota treaties by sanctions against other nations, particularly Japan, when they were required by statute. All of the justices regarded the question as justiciable (although the majority held for the President's authority on the merits). The majority opinion, by Justice White, reasoned that "the courts have authority to construe treaties and executive agreements, and it goes without saying that interpreting congressional legislation is a recurring and accepted task for the federal courts." Is this decision consistent with *Goldwater v. Carter*, and does it suggest that actual conflict would have changed the result in that case?

(6) *Mandatory Ballot Recounts and the Presidential Election: Do they Present a Political Question?* In *Bush v. Gore*, 531 U.S. 98 (2000), the Supreme Court said no. The Court, in a *per curiam* opinion, held that the state court order requiring manual recounts of Presidential ballots only in selected counties and without uniform standards for ascertaining the "voter's intent" violated the equal protection rights of candidate Bush (and his supporters). Although the text of Article II and of the Twelfth Amendment set forth procedures for a Congressional resolution of disputes about Presidential elections, the Court declined to apply the political question doctrine as some of the dissenters (*e.g.*, Justice Breyer) urged. The decision is set forth in § 5.08 below.

(7) *Further Research on the Political Question Doctrine.* For further examination, you might consider the following articles: Arthur Bonfield, *The Guarantee Clause of Article IV, Section 4: A Study in Constitutional Desuetude*, 46 MINN. L. REV. 513 (1962); Mark A. Graber, *Resolving Political Questions Into Judicial Questions: Tocqueville's Thesis Revisited*, 21 CONST. COMMENT. 485 (2004); Louis Michael Seidman, *The Secret Life of the Political Question Doctrine*, 37 J. MARSHALL L. REV. 441 (2004).

PROBLEM E

THE TWENTY-SEVENTH AMENDMENT: CONGRESS EXERCISES ITS POWER TO DETERMINE THE VALIDITY OF AN ENACTMENT DRAFTED BY JAMES MADISON AND RATIFIED 203 YEARS LATER. The Twenty-Seventh Amendment prohibits Congress from voting itself a pay increase until an election has intervened. The language was drafted by James Madison and won its first state ratification in 1789. But it took more than 200 years until, in 1992, Michigan became the thirty-eighth state to ratify it, making out the requisite three-quarters of the states. Modern amendments usually have been accompanied by time limits for ratification (typically, seven years), but the 1789 Congress placed no such limit on ratification of the Twenty-Seventh Amendment. The substantive question is, was the Amendment ratified within a "reasonable" time? But the more interesting question is, who decides the validity of the enactment, Congress or the Court? *See 1789 Amendment Is Ratified but Now the Debate Begins*, N.Y. TIMES, May 8, 1992, § A, at 1, col. 3.

House Speaker Thomas Foley promptly called for hearings to "confirm" the amendment—both because of doubts about its validity and because of a desire to maintain Congress' assertedly "exclusive" authority to determine validity of such an enactment. The Amendment was politically popular, and it was confirmed by overwhelming votes in both Houses. A remaining question, however: Is it possible for a challenge to the "reasonableness" of the two-centuries' ratification time to reach the Supreme Court, and for it to be considered justiciable? (Such a challenge seems unlikely as a practical matter, for structural and political reasons.)

PROBLEM F

THE "VIETNAM CASE." During the pendency of the Vietnam War, there were repeated efforts to obtain adjudications of the illegality of that war. The prototype case was that of a draftee refusing induction or a serviceman directed to Vietnam who sued to prevent that result or was prosecuted for refusing. The arguments were diverse; they ranged from assertions that the failure of Congress to exercise its exclusive authority to declare war under Art. I, § 8 of the Constitution made the President's conduct of war unconstitutional, to arguments based upon international law and international agreements, including the United Nations Charter, that allegedly made the war illegal. The courts considered dozens of these "Vietnam cases," but none resulted in a decision on the merits.

(1) *Standing, Ripeness, Mootness, Etc.* It should be apparent that some plaintiffs in Vietnam Cases would have difficulties in overcoming barriers of standing, ripeness, mootness, etc. For example, a recent draftee probably could not show actual injury, or a claim that was ripe for adjudication, when he had not been and might never be sent to Vietnam.

(2) *Textual Commitment.* Does the "textual commitment" prong of the *Baker* analysis support a conclusion that the Vietnam Case is a political question? Is this argument supported by Justice Powell's related ripeness reasoning in *Goldwater v. Carter*, in that Congress, to which the power to declare war was textually committed, had not taken action to curb President's authority to conduct the war?

(3) *Judicially Manageable Standards.* Does this prong of the *Baker v. Carr* political question analysis allow the judiciary to avoid the Vietnam Case? Note that although Congress has authority to declare war, the President is Commander-in-Chief of the

military forces and has arguable authority to undertake uses of force short of war; is there a lack of judicially manageable standards for determining when this authority ends and Congress' authority becomes exclusive? *See Dalton v. Spector*, 511 U.S. 462 (1994).

(4) *Risk of Foreign or Domestic Disturbance.* Does the Vietnam Case involve an area in which the nation particularly needs to "speak with one voice?" A decision adverse to the President might leave military commanders uncertain whom to obey. But if the question is a pure question of law, under *Powell v. McCormack* and *Japan Whaling*, does the judicial responsibility to declare the law prevail even in the face of "embarrassment from multifarious pronouncements"? Or are some conflicts of this kind too serious to tolerate?

[C]   Congressional Power to Limit Jurisdiction

> Read Art. III, § 2, cl. 2 (Congress' power over Supreme Court jurisdiction); Art. III, § 1 (Congress' power over inferior courts).

EX PARTE McCARDLE
74 U.S. (7 Wall.) 506 (1869)

[McCardle was held in custody by military authorities, although he was not in the military service, on the charge that he had published "articles alleged to be incendiary and libelous, in a newspaper of which he was editor" in violation of the post-Civil War Reconstruction Acts. He filed a petition for a writ of habeas corpus, which the lower courts denied, holding that the Reconstruction laws in question were constitutional. McCardle then appealed to the Supreme Court under the authority of then-existing jurisdictional statutes. After the Supreme Court had acknowledged its jurisdiction, received briefs, and heard oral argument, but before it could decide the case, Congress passed an act providing that the jurisdictional statute under which McCardle had appealed, "for the exercise of any such jurisdiction by the Supreme Court on any appeals which have been or may hereafter be taken, be, and the same is hereby repealed." The Supreme Court's opinion, upholding this exercise of Congressional authority, left standing the decisions of the lower courts refusing habeas corpus to McCardle.]

Mr. Chief Justice Chase delivered the opinion of the Court. . . .

It is quite true, as was argued by the counsel for the petitioner, that the appellate jurisdiction of this court is not derived from Acts of Congress. It is, strictly speaking, conferred by the Constitution. But it is conferred "with such exceptions and under such regulations as Congress shall make. . . ."

The source of that jurisdiction, and the limitations of it by the Constitution and by statute, have been on several occasions subjects of consideration here. In the case of *Durousseau v. U. S.*, 6 Cranch, 312; *Wiscart v. Dauchy*, 3 Dall. 321, particularly, the whole matter was carefully examined, and the court held, that while "the appellate powers of this court are not given by the Judicial Act, but are given by the Constitution:" they are, nevertheless, "limited and regulated by that Act, and by such other Acts as have been passed on the subject." The court said, further, that the Judicial Act was an exercise of the power given by the Constitution to Congress "of making exceptions to the appellate jurisdiction of the Supreme Court."

"They have described affirmatively," said the court, "its jurisdiction, and this affirmative description has been understood to imply a negation of the exercise of such appellate power as is not comprehended within it."

The principle that the affirmation of appellate jurisdiction implies the negation of all such jurisdiction not affirmed having been thus established, it was an almost necessary consequence that Acts of Congress, providing for the exercise of jurisdiction, should come to be spoken of as Acts granting jurisdiction, and not as Acts making exceptions to the constitutional grant of it.

The exception to appellate jurisdiction in the case before us, however, is not an inference from the affirmation of other appellate jurisdiction. . . . It is hardly possible to imagine a plainer instance of positive exception.

We are not at liberty to inquire into the motives of the Legislature. We can only examine into its power under the Constitution; and the power to make exceptions to the appellate jurisdiction of this court is given by express words.

What, then, is the effect of the repealing Act upon the case before us? We cannot doubt as to this. Without jurisdiction the court cannot proceed at all in any cause. Jurisdiction is power to declare the law, and when it ceases to exist, the only function remaining to the court is that of announcing the fact and dismissing the cause. . . .

Counsel seem to have supposed, if effect be given to the repealing Act in question, that the whole appellate power of the court, in cases of habeas corpus, is denied. But this is in error. The Act of 1868 does not except from that jurisdiction any cases but appeals from circuit courts under the Act of 1867. It does not affect the jurisdiction which was previously exercised. . . .

The appeal of the petitioner in this case must be dismissed for want of jurisdiction.

NOTES AND QUESTIONS

(1) *How Broad is Congress' Power to Create Exceptions to the Supreme Court's Jurisdiction?* The *McCardle* case appears, at first blush, to sanction extensive congressional authority to curtail the Court's appellate jurisdiction. *See also* Casto, *The First Congress' Understanding of Its Authority over the Federal Courts' Jurisdiction*, 26 B.C. L. REV. 1101, 1102 (1985) (concluding that early interpretations "demonstrate a general acceptance of extensive congressional control over federal court jurisdiction"). But *McCardle* should not be read too expansively. It did no more than sustain the repeal of an 1867 habeas corpus statute that authorized appeals to the Supreme Court from certain habeas corpus rulings of the federal circuit courts. As the last sentence of the *McCardle* opinion indicates, the repealer statute "does not affect the [habeas corpus] jurisdiction which was previously exercised" under other jurisdictional statutes. Indeed, shortly after the *McCardle* decision, the Court reaffirmed its power to review habeas corpus rulings under these other statutes, and expressly limited the *McCardle* decision to its peculiar circumstances. *Ex parte Yerger*, 75 U.S. (8 Wall.) 85 (1869). *Yerger* also labeled the *McCardle*-type exception to the Court's appellate jurisdiction as "unusual and hardly to be justified except upon some imperious public exigency."

(2) *Constitutional Limitations on the Power to Create Exceptions: United States v. Klein, 80 U.S. (13 Wall.) 128 (1872).* The *Klein* decision is an important counterpoint to *McCardle*. It indicates that there are constitutional limits to the congressional power to create exceptions to the Court's appellate jurisdiction over lower federal court decisions. *Klein* invalidated a congressional "exception" to appellate jurisdiction over a class of cases arising in the then-new federal Court of Claims. The exception clearly reflected congressional dissatisfaction with an earlier Supreme Court decision (*United States v. Padelford*, 76 U.S. (9 Wall.) 531 (1870)) that established, as a rule of decision in this class of cases, that presidential pardons of southerners constituted proof of loyalty to the Union for purposes of a statute authorizing suits in the Court of Claims to secure the return of property seized in the southern states during the Civil War. The Court held the statutory "exception" unconstitutional as being directed at two impermissible ends: (a)

the "exception" was deemed to impair the effect of a presidential pardon and thus infringed on the Executive's pardoning power; (b) the "exception" was designed to force the judiciary to abandon the rule of evidence established in *Padelford* and therefore interfered with the exercise of judicial power. *See also* Gressman and Gressman, *Necessary and Proper Roots of Exceptions to Federal Jurisdiction*, 51 Geo. Wash. L. Rev. 495 (1983).

(3) *Other Possible Constitutional Limits on Creating Exceptions Respecting Review of Lower Federal Court Decisions.* Both *McCardle* and *Klein* deal only with "exceptions" to the Court's appellate jurisdiction over lower federal courts, and only *Klein* speaks to limitations on the congressional "exceptions" power. But the Court did note in *United States v. Bitty*, 208 U.S. 393, 399–400 (1908), that in establishing "exceptions" Congress must have "of course due regard to all the provisions of the Constitution." And so, in addition to the limits mentioned in *Klein*, it has been suggested that the Due Process Clause of the Fifth Amendment, including its equal protection stand, might impose constitutional hazards for "exceptions" legislation that is invidiously discriminatory or without rational basis. *See* Sager, *The Supreme Court, 1980 Term—Foreword: Constitutional Limitations on Congress' Authority to Regulate the Jurisdiction of the Federal Courts*, 95 Harv. L. Rev. 17, 78–80 (1981). If Congress were to except from the Court's appellate jurisdiction all free speech cases arising in the lower federal courts, would that not violate the First Amendment?

[D] The Supreme Court's Jurisdiction under Current Statutes

NOTE ON SUPREME COURT JURISDICTIONAL STATUTES

Jurisdiction to Review Federal Court Judgments. The Supreme Court's power to review the judgments and opinions of lower federal courts is, for the most part, confined to cases in the 13 federal courts of appeals. In 28 U.S.C. § 1254(1), the Court is empowered to review cases "in the courts of appeals . . . [b]y writ of certiorari granted upon the petition of any party to any civil or criminal case, before or after rendition of judgment or decree." It does not matter whether that judgment is final or interlocutory or whether any written opinion has been rendered by the court of appeals.

Any party, aggrieved or not by a judgment of a federal district court, can seek certiorari under § 1254(1) "before . . . rendition of judgment or decree" by a court of appeals. Such review is reserved, however, for extremely important cases, such as a district court judgment invalidating an important federal statute, where the public interest demands quick resolution of the case by the Supreme Court.

In addition, § 1254(2) provides that the Supreme Court can review, by way of "certification" by a court appeals, any difficult question of law encountered by that court in any civil or criminal case pending before it. This procedure is rarely invoked. The Supreme Court discourages courts of appeals from certifying such matters and prefers that they use their *en banc* procedures (whereby all the active circuit judges hear the case) rather then bothering the Supreme Court at this juncture.

In 1988, Congress abolished the Supreme Court's jurisdiction to review, by way of a mandatory appeal, decisions of courts of appeals holding state statutes or city ordinances unconstitutional. Such holdings remain reviewable by way of certiorari. The Court's jurisdiction to review federal court decisions by direct appeal, rather than certiorari, is now severely limited to a handful of cases that Congress has specified be heard by special three-judge federal district courts. Appeals may be taken from such courts directly to the Supreme Court in reapportionment cases and in cases arising under the Civil Rights Act of 1964, the Voting Rights Act of 1965 and the Presidential Election Campaign Fund Act, as well as certain kinds of antitrust cases.

Jurisdiction to Review State Court Judgments. Congress has provided, in 28 U.S.C. § 1257(a), that the Supreme Court may review by writ of certiorari "final judgments or decrees rendered by the highest court of a State in which a decision could be had," where (1) the validity of a federal treaty or statute has been drawn in question, (2) the validity of a state statute has been drawn in question as being repugnant to the Constitution or laws of the United States, or (3) any title, right, privilege, or immunity is set up or claimed under the Constitution, treaties or laws of the United States.

Congress in 1988 eliminated all kinds of mandatory appeals from state court decisions. The Supreme Court's jurisdiction to review state court judgments is now exclusively by writ of certiorari. That means that the Court has total discretion either to grant or deny a petition for a writ of certiorari seeking review of a state court judgment.

Note that § 1257(a) confines the Supreme Court's certiorari jurisdiction to those state court judgments that are "final" rather than "interlocutory" in nature. And the judgment must be that of the highest court of a state in which a decision could be had. Finally, note that to be reviewable by the Supreme Court a state court judgment must address or at least involve a properly raised question arising under the federal Constitution, treaties or statutes. The Court has no jurisdiction whatsoever to review matters of state law.

The Outmoded Distinctions Between the Certiorari and the Appeal Jurisdictions. As indicated above, in 1988 Congress eliminated virtually all of the Supreme Court's jurisdiction to review federal or state court judgments by way of appeal. The Supreme Court, with but a few minor federal statutory exceptions, is now truly an "all-certiorari" tribunal.

Thus we no longer need be concerned with the distinctions between appeals and certiorari cases. Nor need we seek to understand the subterfuges used by the Court itself to avoid giving full and meaningful review to all appeals as of right. The Court can now utilize its certiorari jurisdiction to maximize control of its docket.

The litigant who petitions the Court for a writ of certiorari has no "right" to have the petition granted or the case reviewed. The petition is little more than a plea that the Court exercise its discretion—which is the essence of certiorari—to grant review. Most petitions are denied, without explanation and without constituting any kind of precedent. In recent years, when more than 4000 petitions have been filed each term, more than 95 percent have been denied.

For a complete and authoritative guide to the Supreme Court's jurisdiction and procedures, see R. Stern, E. Gressman & S. Shapiro, Supreme Court Practice (6th ed. 1986). For a discussion of the curtailment of mandatory appeals in favor of certiorari, *see* Boskey and Gressman, *The Supreme Court Bids Farewell to Mandatory Appeals*, 121 F.R.D. 81 (1988).

Original Jurisdiction: The Supreme Court as the "Trial" Court. The Supreme Court has original jurisdiction in a narrow class of cases defined by the Constitution, particularly those "in which a State shall be a Party." U.S. Const. art. III, § 2. Typical examples would include suits by one state against another concerning boundaries, water rights, or the right to tax. *Cf. Ohio v. Wyandotte Chemicals Corp.*, 401 U.S. 493 (1971) (Court had, but declined to exercise, original jurisdiction of suit by state against alleged polluters of Lake Erie).

NOTE ON PROCEDURE FOR REVIEW BY CERTIORARI OR APPEAL

The Petition for Certiorari. Invocation of the Supreme Court's discretionary jurisdiction is an esoteric art. The petitioner or applicant takes the first step by filing a timely petition for writ of certiorari; a petition is timely if filed within 90 days of the judgment below in a civil case, or within 60 days in a criminal case. The purpose of this document is not to argue the merits of the case or the error of the court below. Instead, the purpose is to persuade and convince the Court that there are "special and important reasons" (in the language of the Court's rule 17.1) why the Court should take time to hear and decide the case on its merits, which includes the filing of briefs on the merits and oral argument before the Court. The most persuasive consideration appears to be a demonstration that the issue involved is one of truly national importance, a consideration that often controls even where the lower courts are in conflict on an issue. Paradoxically, a demonstration that the case or the issue is unique, or is an aberration, may be counterproductive. Nor is the error involved in the decision below any guarantee that certiorari will be granted. The Supreme Court simply does not engage in error-correction, absent some issue of national significance. *See* R. STERN, E. GRESSMAN & S. SHAPIRO, SUPREME COURT PRACTICE, ch. 6 (6th ed. 1986).

Grant or Denial of Certiorari; The "Rule of Four." Affirmative votes by four members of the Court suffice to grant certiorari. This convention is known as the "Rule of Four." Denial of certiorari is of no precedential value, and the principle is well established that it means only that there were not four members of the Court who chose to hear this particular case at this time. *See Hughes Tool Co. v. Trans World Airlines*, 409 U.S. 363 (1973); Linzer, *The Meaning of Certiorari Denials*, 79 COLUM. L. REV. 1227 (1979).

Principles Guiding the Certiorari Decision. Justice to the individual parties is the concern underlying the provision for intermediate appellate review; contrary to popular conceptions, however, it is not the purpose of certiorari. Supreme Court rule 17.1 sets out certain circumstances in which certiorari is indicated. Among the most important are those in which there are intolerable conflicts on nationally important issues between courts of appeals, or between a court of appeals and a state court of last resort, or those in which substantial issues of federal law have not been, but should be, decided by the Supreme Court. Thus review by certiorari addresses systemic problems, rather than problems of individual justice.

[E]   Stare Decisis

PAYNE v. TENNESSEE, 501 U.S. 808 (1991). To what extent is the Supreme Court bound by its own prior decisions, through the principle of *stare decisis*? Should it be bound never to change them, or should it decide each case by re-examining every relevant decided case, or should its approach be somewhere in between? In *Payne*, a capital case, the Court held that evidence of impact of the crime on victims' survivors was not barred by the Eighth Amendment. To do so, the Court had to overrule two recent decisions—and, in the process, per Chief Justice Rehnquist, it had to consider the effect of *stare decisis*:

> [The Supreme Court of Tennessee] rejected Payne's contention that the admission of [victim impact evidence] constituted prejudicial violations of his rights under the Eighth Amendment as applied in *Booth v. Maryland*, 482 U.S. 496 (1987) and *South Carolina v. Gathers*, 490 U.S. 805 (1989). . . .

> The *Booth* Court began its analysis with the observation that the capital defendant must be treated as a " 'uniquely individual human bein[g],' " and therefore the Constitution requires the jury to make an individualized determination as to whether the defendant should be executed based on the " 'character of the individual and the circumstances of the crime.' " [T]o the extent that victim impact evidence presents "factors about which the defendant was unaware, and that were irrelevant to the decision to kill," the Court concluded, it has nothing to do with the "blameworthiness of a particular defendant. . . ."

> *Booth* and *Gathers* were based on two premises: that evidence relating to a particular victim or to the harm that a capital defendant causes a victim's family do not in general reflect on the defendant's "blameworthiness," and that only evidence relating to "blameworthiness" is relevant to the capital sentencing decision. However, the assessment of harm caused by the defendant as a result of the crime charged has understandably been an important concern of the

criminal law, both in determining the elements of the offense and in determining the appropriate punishment. Thus, two equally blameworthy criminal defendants may be guilty of different offenses solely because their acts cause differing amounts of harm. "If a bank robber aims his gun at a guard, pulls the trigger, and kills his target, he may be put to death. If the gun unexpectedly misfires, he may not. His moral guilt in both cases is identical, but his responsibility in the former is greater." *Booth*, 482 U.S. at 519 (Scalia, J., dissenting). . . .

We thus hold that if the State chooses to permit the admission of victim impact evidence and prosecutorial argument on that subject, the Eighth Amendment erects no *per se* bar. [T]here is no reason to treat such evidence differently than other relevant evidence is treated.

Payne and his *amicus* argue that despite these numerous infirmities in the rule created by *Booth* and *Gathers*, we should adhere to the doctrine of *stare decisis* and stop short of overruling those cases. *Stare decisis* is the preferred course because it promotes the evenhanded, predictable, and consistent development of legal principles, fosters reliance on judicial decisions, and contributes to the actual and perceived integrity of the judicial process. [N]evertheless, when governing decisions are unworkable or are badly reasoned, "this Court has never felt constrained to follow precedent." *Stare decisis* is not an inexorable command; rather, it "is a principle of policy and not a mechanical formula of adherence to the latest decision." This is particularly true in constitutional cases, because in such cases "correction through legislative action is practically impossible." Considerations in favor of *stare decisis* are at their acme in cases involving property and contract rights, where reliance interests are involved; the opposite is true in cases such as the present one involving procedural and evidentiary rules.

Applying these general principles, the Court has during the past 20 Terms overruled in whole or in part 83 of its previous constitutional decisions. *Booth* and *Gathers* were decided by the narrowest of margins, over spirited dissents challenging the basic underpinnings of those decisions. They have been questioned by members of the Court in later decisions, and have defied consistent application by the lower courts. [R]econsidering these decisions now, we conclude for the reasons heretofore stated, that they were wrongly decided and should be, and now are, overruled. We accordingly affirm the judgment of the Supreme Court of Tennessee.

JUSTICES O'CONNOR, SCALIA, and SOUTER each wrote concurring opinions.

JUSTICES MARSHALL, BLACKMUN, and STEVENS dissented. JUSTICE MARSHALL wrote the following:

> Power, not reason, is the new currency of this Court's decision-making. [N]either the law nor the facts supporting *Booth* and *Gathers* underwent any change in the last four years. Only the personnel of this Court did. [T]he majority declares itself free to discard any principle of constitutional liberty which was recognized or reaffirmed over the dissenting votes of four Justices and with which five or more Justices *now* disagree.

> [T]he majority today sends a clear signal that scores of established constitutional liberties are now ripe for reconsideration, thereby inviting the very type of open defiance of our precedents that the majority rewards in this case. . . .

PLANNED PARENTHOOD v. CASEY, 508 U.S. 833 (1992). This case is excerpted more extensively in Chapter 9, *below*. The Court, per Justice O'Connor, applied the doctrine of *stare decisis* in refusing to overrule the "essential holding" of *Roe v. Wade*, 410 U.S. 113 (1973), which protected a woman's "fundamental" right to terminate her pregnancy by abortion. The Court based this holding on "a series of prudential and pragmatic considerations," including (1) that *Roe* had not "proven unworkable," (2) that many people had "organized intimate relationships" in "reliance" upon availability of abortion if contraception failed, (3) that no "evolution of legal principle" had left *Roe's* central rule an "anachronism," (4) that no change in *Roe's* "factual underpinning" had left it obsolete, (5) that a comparison with decisions that had overruled previous lines of decisions (*e.g., Brown v. Board of Education*) "confirmed" the argument for upholding *Roe*, and (6) that overruling *Roe* would appear to be the result of political considerations, undermine public confidence, and weaken the Article III Judicial Power.

Four Justices dissented in an opinion by Chief Justice Rehnquist that criticized the Court's "newly minted" theory of *stare decisis*.

[F] "Amending the Constitution": Through Article V and Otherwise

NOTE ON CONSTITUTIONAL AMENDMENTS

One limit on the Court's exercise of judicial review would be the amendment process under Article V. [You should review Article V in the Prefatory Chapter.] The Article V procedures have been implemented on certain occasions to overrule Supreme Court decision. For example, the Eleventh Amendment (limiting federal court jurisdiction over suits involving the State as a defendant) was adopted to overrule *Chisholm v. Georgia*, 2 U.S. 419 (1793). [*See* § 3.05 below.] Some 170 years later, the Twenty-Sixth Amendment (eighteen-year-old voting in state elections) was adopted to overrule *Oregon v. Mitchell*, 400 U.S. 112 (1970). [*See* § 14.02 below.] Despite these examples, however, most observers suggest that the Article V procedures are only part of the process of constitutional change.

At this point, you should consider two ideas as "working hypotheses." First, even though the Framers may have contemplated the frequent use of the Article V procedures to change the federal constitution (including "correcting" Supreme Court decisions), the Article V procedures have not really been used that frequently. We have, after all, only twenty-seven amendments in 220 years.

A second hypothesis, for your consideration, is that a great deal of constitutional change has happened outside of the Article V procedures. Indeed, the judicial review process you are currently studying has been, in many instances, a functional substitute for Article V. For further reading, *see* David A. Strauss, *The Irrelevance of Constitutional Amendments*, 114 HARV. L. REV. 1457 (2001) (outlining various modalities of "constitutional change" beyond the Article V procedures).

Appendix 1

THEORIES OF JUDICIAL REVIEW: HOW SHOULD THE JUDGES READ THE CONSTITUTION?

[A] ORIGINALISM, NON-ORIGINALISM, AND TEXTUALISM

INTRODUCTORY NOTE

Originalism and Textualism. "Originalism" refers to a jurisprudence of original intentions, or the belief that "the Supreme Court must, or at least should, refer to the meaning that constitutional provisions had in the 'original understanding.'" Simon, *The Authority of the Framers of the Constitution: Can Originalist Interpretation Be Justified?*, 73 CAL. L. REV. 1482 (1985). *See also* Maltz, *Some New Thoughts on an Old Problem: The Role of the Intent of the Framers in Constitutional Theory*, 63 B.U. L. REV. 811 (1983). "Textualism" allows the judge to focus upon the words of the text and to arrive at an interpretation based on principles derived from the document itself. *See* Laycock, *Taking Constitutions Seriously: A Theory of Judicial Review*, 59 TEX. L. REV. 343 (1981).

The Brennan-Meese Debate. In 1985, two styles of constitutional interpretation were illustrated in a debate between Attorney General Edwin Meese (an originalist) and Supreme Court Justice William Brennan (who clearly is a non-originalist, but whose views the reader must consider to determine whether he is a "non-interpretivist"). The participants to the debate "presented two starkly contrasting views of the essence of the Constitution. Simplified, Meese and his fellow conservatives see the Constitution as a compact. . . . Hence, powers not enumerated in the Constitution to the federal government cannot be assumed by the federal government. Justice Brennan, by contrast, sees the Constitution as more than a contract, as a declaration that the values of individual liberty transcend the scope of government restriction, whether that government be local, state, or national." Marcotte, *Federalism and the Rise of State Courts*, 73 A.B.A. J. 60 (1987).

MEESE, THE SUPREME COURT OF THE UNITED STATES: BULWARK OF A LIMITED CONSTITUTION
27 S. TEX. L. REV. 455 (1986)[*]

By fulfilling its proper function, the Supreme Court contributes not only to institutional checks and balances, but also to the moral undergirding of the entire constitutional edifice. . . .

But that is not to suggest that the Justices are a body of platonic guardians. Far from it. . . .

In considering [recent] areas of adjudication—Federalism, criminal law, and religion—one may conclude that far too many of the Court's opinions were, on the whole, mere policy choices rather than articulations of constitutional principle. The voting blocs and the arguments all reveal a greater allegiance to what the Court thinks constitutes sound public policy rather than a deference to what the Constitution, its text and intention, may demand. . . .

What, then, should a constitutional jurisprudence actually be? It should be a *jurisprudence of original intention.* By seeking to judge policies in light of principles, rather than remold principles in light of policies, the Court could avoid both the charge of incoherence *and* the charge of being either too conservative or too liberal.

A jurisprudence seriously aimed at the explication of original intention would produce defensible principles of government that would not be tainted by ideological predilection.

This belief in a *jurisprudence of original intention* also reflects a deeply rooted commitment to the idea of democracy. The Constitution represents the consent of the governed to the structures and powers of the government. The Constitution is the fundamental will of the people; that is the reason the Constitution is the fundamental law. To allow the Court to govern simply by what it views at the time as fair and decent, is a scheme of government no longer popular; the idea of democracy has suffered. The permanence of the Constitution has been weakened. A constitution that is viewed as only what the judges say it is, is no longer a constitution in the true sense of the term. . . .

BRENNAN, THE CONSTITUTION OF THE UNITED STATES: CONTEMPORARY RATIFICATION
27 S. Tex. L. Rev. 433 (1986)[*]

The amended Constitution of the United States entrenches the Bill of Rights and the Civil War amendments and draws sustenance from the bedrock principles of another great text, the Magna Carta. So fashioned, the Constitution embodies the aspiration to social justice, brotherhood, and human dignity that brought this nation into being. . . . Like every text worth reading, it is not crystalline. . . . Its majestic generalities and ennobling pronouncements are both luminous and obscure. This ambiguity, of course, calls forth interpretation, the interaction of reader and text. . . .

. . . Precisely because coercive force must attend any judicial decision to countermand the will of a contemporary majority, the Justices must render constitutional interpretations that are received as legitimate. . . . [T]he debate is really a debate about how to read the text, about constraints on what is legitimate interpretation.

There are those who find legitimacy in fidelity to what they call "the intentions of the Framers." In its most doctrinaire incarnation, this view demands that Justices discern exactly what the Framers thought about the question under consideration and simply follow that intention in resolving the case before them. It is a view that feigns self-effacing deference to the specific judgments of those who forged our original social compact. But in truth it is little more than arrogance cloaked as humility. It is arrogant to pretend that from our vantage we can gauge accurately the intent of the Framers on application of principle to specific, contemporary questions. . . . Typically, all that can be gleaned is that the Framers themselves did not agree about the application or meaning of particular constitutional provisions and hid their differences in cloaks of generality. . . .

Perhaps most importantly, while proponents of this facile historicism justify it as a depoliticization of the judiciary, the political underpinnings of such a choice should not escape notice. A position that upholds constitutional claims only if they were within the specific contemplation of the Framers in effect establishes a presumption of resolving textual ambiguities against the claim of constitutional right. . . . This is a choice no less political than any other; it expresses antipathy to claims of the minority to rights against the majority. Those who would restrict claims of right to the values of 1789 specifically articulated in the Constitution turn a blind eye to social progress and eschew adaption of overarching principles to changes of social circumstance.

. . . One cannot read the text without admitting that it embodies substantive value choices; it places certain values beyond the power of any legislature. . . .

To remain faithful to the context of the Constitution, therefore, an approach to

---

interpreting the text must account for the existence of these substantive value choices and must accept the ambiguity inherent in the effort to apply them to modern circumstances. The Framers discerned fundamental principles through struggles against particular malefactions of the Crown; the struggle shapes the particular contours of the articulated principles. But our acceptance of the fundamental principles has not and should not bind us to those precise, at times anachronistic, contours. Successive generations of Americans have continued to respect these fundamental choices and adopt them as their own guide to evaluating quite different historical practices. . . .

Current Justices read the Constitution in the only way that we can: as twentieth-century Americans. We look to the history of the time of framing and to the intervening history of interpretation. But the ultimate question must be: What do the words of the text mean in our time? For the genius of the Constitution rests not in any static meaning it might have had in a world that is dead and gone, but in the adaptability of its great principles to cope with current problems and current needs. . . .

NOTES AND QUESTIONS

(1) *The "Adaptability" of Originalism to the Conditions of "Twentieth Century Americans."* Attorney General Meese later answered Justice Brennan's "current problems" argument as follows:

> At the deepest level, a jurisprudence of original intention does two things. First, it seeks to discern the meaning of the text of the Constitution by understanding the intentions of those who framed, proposed, and ratified it. The intentions of the Framers supply us with our original principles. Second, a jurisprudence of original intention is not confined to the circumstances from which those original principles sprang. Rather, those principles can be applied to new circumstances, circumstances often unforeseen by the Founders themselves. . . .

Lecture by Attorney General of the United States Edwin Meese, III, at the University of Dallas (February 27, 1986) (reprinted with permission of Mr. Meese). Reconsider Justice Brennan's criticisms in light of these subsequent remarks by Attorney General Meese.

(2) *"Selective" Originalism?* If (as Justice Brennan argues) all original intentions cannot be discerned and applied, is there room for a jurisprudence of selective original intention, *i.e.*, application of those principles that *can* be discerned and applied?

(3) *Does Originalism Really Embody a "Political" Judgment Against Individual Rights?* Reconsider Justice Brennan's argument that originalism "establishes a presumption of resolving textual ambiguities against the claim of constitutional right." Might there be instances in which the original understanding would support the claim of constitutional right when contemporary textual interpretation would not? Thus "opponents of the [Vietnam] war eager to return to the original understanding of the War Power are not likely to be eager to return to what was probably the rather conservative initial understanding of freedom of speech." Levinson, *Fidelity to Law and the Assessment of Political Activity*, 27 STAN. L. REV. 1185, 1200 n.68 (1975). And consider *Park Lane Hosiery Co. v. Shore*, 439 U.S. 322 (1979), in which the majority, including Justice Brennan, decided against the right to jury trial. In a solitary dissent based upon the original understanding, Justice Rehnquist would have held in favor of the constitutional right: "If a jury would have been impaneled in a particular kind of case in 1791, then the seventh amendment requires a jury trial today. . . ."

(4) *An Outspoken Defense of Originalism—R. Berger, Government by Judiciary: The Transformation of the Fourteenth Amendment, 363–64, 407–08, 417–18 (1977).* Professor Raoul Berger's is perhaps the most outspoken defense of originalism:

> Current indifference to the "original intention"—shorthand for the meaning attached by the framers to the words they employed in the Constitution and its Amendments is a relatively recent phenomenon. . . . We are told that the Framers intended to leave it "to succeeding generations [meaning judges] . . . to rewrite the 'living' constitution anew," an argument opposed to historical fact. The sole and exclusive vehicle of change the Framers provided was the amendment process; judicial discretion and policymaking were in high disfavor; all "agents and servants of the people" were to be "bound by the chains" of a "fixed Constitution. . . ."
>
> Why is the "original intention" so important? The answer was long since given by Madison: if "the sense in which the Constitution was accepted and ratified by the Nation . . . be not the guide in expounding it, there can be no security for consistent and stable government, more than for a faithful exercise of its powers. . . ." This it was that caused Jefferson to say, "Our peculiar security is in the possession of a written constitution. Let us not make it a blank paper by construction. . . ."
>
> The historical records all but incontrovertibly establish that the framers of the Fourteenth Amendment excluded both suffrage and segregation from its reach; they confined it to protection of carefully enumerated rights against State discrimination, deliberately withholding federal power to supply those rights where they were not granted by the State to anybody, white or black. This was a limited—tragically limited—response to the needs of blacks newly released from slavery; . . . nonetheless, it was all the sovereign people were prepared to do in 1868.
>
> Given the clarity of the framers' intention, it is on settled principles as good as written into the text. To "interpret" the Amendment in diametrical opposition to that intention is to rewrite the Constitution. . . . The Court, it is safe to say, has flouted the will of the framers and substituted an interpretation in flat contradiction of the original design: to leave suffrage, segregation, and other matters to State governance. It has done this under cover of the so-called "majestic generalities" of the Amendment—"due process" and "equal protection"—which it found "conveniently vague," without taking into account the limited aims those terms were meant to express. When Chief Justice Warren asserted that "we cannot turn back the clock to 1868," he in fact rejected the framers' intention as irrelevant. Such conduct impels one to conclude that the Justices are becoming a law unto themselves. . . .

Berger would not, he says, repudiate all non-original decisions: "It would . . . be utterly unrealistic and probably impossible to undo the past in the face of the expectations that the segregation decisions, for example, have aroused in our black citizenry—expectations confirmed by every decent instinct." But "the difficulty of the rollback cannot excuse the *continuation* of such unconstitutional practices." *Id.* 412–13. Without respect for the limits on power provided by originalism, says Berger, "the entire democratic structure is undermined and the way is paved from Weimar to Hitler." *Id.* 410. Is this reasoning persuasive?

(5) *Theoretical Justifications of Originalism.* For a short but lucid description of theoretical justifications for originalism, *see* Simon, *The Authority of the Framers of the Constitution: Can Originalist Interpretation Be Justified?*, 73 CAL. L. REV. 1482,

---

1484–85 (1985).* First, it can be claimed that originalism is implicit in the concept of a written constitution. This claim receives justification from the setting out of procedures for amendment in the document itself, but it ultimately rests on the principle that originalism is inherent in such a document.

A "Contract" Basis for Originalism. The Constitution was adopted by signatures in a convention, and ratified by states as separate parties, in a manner analogous to a contract. As an alternative to a view of the document as a literal contract, it may be claimed that social contract reasoning supports originalism.

Theories of Democracy as Support for Originalism. Originalism checks the power of the Supreme Court and avoids the frustration of democracy. To the extent that it rests upon expressions of consent by the people in ratification, enforcement of constitutional requirements against democratic results remains democratic.

Justification of Originalism by Reference to Extrinsic Values. Finally, it can be argued that originalism is justified by values of certainty, predictability, and efficiency and that it therefore produces good and just results. [Simon generally rejects these arguments.]

(6)   *Rejection of Originalism as Controlled by the Dead Hand From the Grave.* Consider whether the following reasoning, taken from J. ELY, DEMOCRACY AND DISTRUST 11 (1980),** is persuasive:

> The [constitutional] amendments most frequently in issue in court . . .—to the extent that they ever represented the "voice of the people"—represent the voice of people who have been dead for a century or two. There were those who worried about this even at the beginning. Noah Webster opined that "the very attempt to make perpetual constitutions, is the assumption of a right to control the opinions of future generations; and to legislate for those over whom we have as little authority as we have over a nation in Asia." And Jefferson wrote to Madison " 'that the earth belongs in usufruct to the living;' that the dead have neither powers nor rights over it." His suggestion was that the Constitution expire naturally every 19 years. . . .

(7)   *Arguments Against Originalism Based Upon the Exclusion of the Majority of the Population from the Electorate.* One difficulty with originalism, at least to the extent it is based upon contract theories, is that most of the population of voting age at the time of adoption of the Constitution was denied the right to vote. By some estimates, roughly 80% of the potential electorate was excluded. *See* Simon, *supra*, at 1498 n.44 and authorities therein cited. Does this consideration destroy originalism? (If so, doesn't it also destroy the Constitution?)

(8)   *What if the Original Intention was that the Original Intention Would Not be Authoritative?: Powell, The Original Understanding of Original Intent,* 98 HARV. L. REV. 885, 948 (1985).*** Based upon a historical analysis, Professor Powell concludes that originalism cannot be based upon the understanding of the framers, because that understanding did not include a recognition that their intent was authoritative:

> It is commonly assumed that the "interpretive intention" of the Constitution's framers was that the Constitution would be construed in accordance with what future interpreters could gather of the framers' own purposes, expectation, and intentions. Inquiry shows that assumption to be incorrect. . . . Early interpreters usually applied standard techniques of statutory construction to

---

the Constitution. When a consensus eventually emerged on a proper theory of constitutional interpretation, it indeed centered on "original intent." But at the time, that term referred to the "intentions" of the sovereign parties to the constitutional compact, as evidenced in the Constitution's language and discerned through structural methods of interpretation; it did not refer to the personal intentions of the framers or of anyone else. . . . [The] debate [concerning interpretation] cannot be resolved, . . . and should not be affected, by the claim or assumption that modern intentionalism was the original presupposition of American constitutional discourse. Such a claim is historically mistaken.

Reconsider the argument of R. Berger, above, who argued that the concept of a "living" constitution was "an argument opposed to historical fact" and quoted Madison and Jefferson in support of originalism. Is this position reconcilable with Powell's conclusions?

(9) *Is a Synthesis of Originalism and Textualism Appropriate (Or Possible)?* Perhaps it is possible to use originalism for the purpose of construing ambiguous language when the intention is relatively clear and when it can accurately be applied to present-day conditions. Such would be the approach of R. Berger, *supra*, to the due process and equal protection clauses. Other interpretative methods then could be used for "unambiguous" provisions or for those for which there is no clear evidence of original intent. But this theory supplies no criteria by which to determine that a provision is unambiguous— *cf.* Tushnet, *A Note on the Revival of Textualism in Constitutional Theory*, 58 S. Cal. L. Rev. 683, 686–88 (1985) (purporting to show that even a provision such as the thirty-five year age minimum for the President is "obviously vulnerable" to conflicting interpretations).

(10) *"Open Textured" Provisions: Should Interpretation Honor the Generality of the Constitutional Text?: J. Ely, Democracy and Distrust.* Furthermore, the "synthesis" approach may reflect a lack of respect for the actual language of the Constitution, in its generality. For example, "We know from its history that [the equal protection clause] was meant particularly to combat inequality toward blacks. We also know, however—and would likely presume it even if we didn't—that the decision to use general language, not tied to race, was a conscious one." If we interpret such "open textured" provisions restrictively to honor the intent of the drafters, do we hereby violate the intent expressed by their choice of general, inclusive language?

[B] INTERPRETIVISM AND SUPPLEMENTATION (OR NON-INTERPRETIVISM?)

INTRODUCTORY NOTE

Interpretivism and Supplementation (or Non-Interpretivism). The interpretivist position is that every constitutional decision should reflect an interpretation of the Constitution. A particular decision may reflect original intent or it may derive from other textual interpretation, but it should be composed of values derived from the Constitution. The non-interpretivist position, on the other hand, is that judges can (indeed must) use values derived from external sources. One cannot adequately give meaning to the Constitution, the supplementers or non-interpretivists would say, merely by reading its language and history. (It should be added that some modern theorists reject the distinction and maintain that both approaches amount to "interpreting" the Constitution. In effect, these theorists would say that we are "all" interpretivists, and the real debate is about whether and how much to supplement.)

Justifications for Supplementation: Open-Textured Guarantees, Non-Textual Decisions, and the Evolutionary Nature of a Constitution. Supplementers can point to such open phrases as "freedom of speech," "due process," and "equal protection," which are more evocative of a broad philosophy than they are descriptive, and which are far more general in phrasing than the historical concerns that produced them. Further, they can point to a wide variety of existing decisions that do not seem justifiable by interpretation alone, and yet are embedded in our constitutional law; *Roe v. Wade*, 410 U.S. 113 (1973), the abortion decision, is a prime example. Further, the nature of a constitution as a fundamental document arguably supports a flexible and evolutionary reading.

Supplementation (or Non-Interpretivism) and Democratic Theory: A. Bickel, The Least Dangerous Branch, 24–26 (1962). Some supplementation theories are based upon the conception that judges are more appropriate guardians of fundamental liberties or "enduring general values" than are legislators or executives. Bickel's work is among the most influential statements of this position. Bickel argued that "courts have certain capacities for dealing with matters of principle that legislators and executives do not possess." He recognized the fundamental conflict of Madisonian democracy produced by this theory of judicial review, and he sought to rationalize judicial review so that, if not fully consistent with democratic theory, it at least would not be anti-democratic. This result would be achieved by scholarship that sorted "enduring" from nonenduring values:

> [When] the pressure for immediate results is strong enough and emotions ride high enough, [legislators] will ordinarily prefer to act on expediency rather than take the long view. . . . Not merely respect for the rule of established principles but the creative establishment and renewal of a coherent body of principled rules—that is what our legislators have proven themselves ill-equipped to give us. Judges have, or should have, the leisure, the training, and the insulation to follow the ways of the scholar in pursuing the ends of government. This is crucial in sorting out the enduring values of a society. . . . [Judges can] appeal to men's better natures, to call forth their aspirations, which may have been forgotten in the moment's hue and cry. . . .*

The Problems of Neutrality and Consistency: Wechsler, Toward Neutral Principles of Constitutional Law, 73 HARV. L. REV. 1, 15 (1959). One of the persistent difficulties with supplementation is the appearance that it is result-oriented: rather than neutral principles, the judge may impose his idiosyncratic preferences. Wechsler's construction emphasized the "words of the constitutional provisions" and posited that "history has weight in elucidation of the text," in order to ensure these neutral principles:

> I put it to you that the main constituent of the judicial process is precisely that it must be genuinely principled . . . on analysis and reasons quite transcending the immediate result that is achieved. To be sure, the courts decide . . . only the case they have before them. But must they not decide on grounds of adequate neutrality and generality, tested not only by the instant application but by others that the principles imply?**

PROBLEM G

JUSTICE BRENNAN ON THE DEATH PENALTY ORIGINALISM, TEXTUALISM, SUPPLEMENTATION, AND NON-INTERPRETIVISM. "As I interpret the Constitution," says Justice Brennan, "capital punishment is under all circumstances cruel and unusual punishment prohibited by the Eighth and Fourteenth Amendments. This is a position of which I imagine you are not unaware." Brennan, *The Constitution of the United States: Contemporary Ratification*, 27 S. TEX. L. REV. 433, 443–44 (1986). He justifies this conclusion as follows:

> . . . I view the Eighth Amendment's prohibition of cruel and unusual punishments as embodying to a unique degree the moral principles that

---

substantively restrain the punishments our civilized society may impose. . . . Foremost among the moral principles recognized in our cases and inherent in the prohibition is the primary principle that the state . . . must treat its citizens in a manner consistent with their intrinsic worth as human beings. . . . [A]n executed person has lost the very right to have rights, now or ever. For me, then, the fatal constitutional infirmity of capital punishment is that it treats members of the human race as non-humans, as objects to be toyed with and discarded. Capital punishment is, indeed, "cruel and unusual." It is thus inconsistent with the fundamental premise of the Constitution that even the most base criminal remains a human being possessed of some potential, at least, for common human dignity.[*]

(1) *Comparing Originalism.* How would this position compare with a jurisprudence of original intention?

(2) *Textualist Interpretivism?* To what extent does Justice Brennan's justification reflect interpretation based upon principles derived from the text of the Constitution? If you are skeptical, note that Justice Brennan quotes the language and finds in the Constitution the principle that "even the most based criminal is 'human' and 'possessed' of some potential . . . for common human dignity." Is this textualism, or is it non-interpretivism?

(3) *Supplementation (or Non-Interpretivism)?* Justice Brennan also refers to the "moral principles recognized in our cases." Are the moral principles to which Justice Brennan refers derived from the Constitution? If not, can their use in decisionmaking be justified?

(4) *Consistency; Neutral Principles.* Will the moral principles expounded by Justice Brennan support consistent results, reached without application of the personal values of the individual judge? Consider the following: Is life imprisonment without possibility of pardon or parole just as unconstitutional as capital punishment under Brennan's analysis, if it can be read as denying a "base criminal's" dignity or "intrinsic worth"? Conversely, might some judges in some cases calculate that the "intrinsic worth" of an individual murderer in a heinous case is such as to support capital punishment? Are these "neutral" principles?

(5) *Can One Justify Supplementation (or Non-Interpretivism) by Interpreting "Cruel and Unusual Punishment" as Evolutionary and Open-Textured?* Perhaps the very language, "cruel and unusual," admits of a textual interpretation of evolving standards— *i.e.*, perhaps it refers to contemporaneous (or even progressive) notions of cruelty and unusualness. If so, does this interpretation justify non-interpretivism in the form of importation of contemporary moral philosophy? If so, from where can Justice Brennan draw these principles? [Note that he cannot draw them from current popular consensus.]

BREST, THE FUNDAMENTAL RIGHTS CONTROVERSY: THE ESSENTIAL CONTRADICTIONS OF NORMATIVE CONSTITUTIONAL SCHOLARSHIP, 90 YALE L.J. 1063, 1064 (1981).[**] The controversy [over the legitimacy of judicial review in a democratic polity] is currently manifested in the body of scholarship that centers on substantive due process decision such as *Griswold v. Connecticut* [which struck down a Connecticut statute prohibiting use of contraceptives as applied to married couples], *Eisenstadt v. Baird* [which extended *Griswold* to unmarried persons], *Roe v. Wade* [the abortion decision], and *Doe v. Commonwealth's Attorney* [which upheld a prohibition upon private consensual homosexual conduct]. The judges and scholars who support judicial intervention usually acknowledge that the rights at stake—variously described in terms of privacy, procreational choice, sexual autonomy, lifestyle choices, and intimate association, are not satisfied by the text or original history of the Constitution. They argue that the judiciary is nonetheless authorized, if not duty-bound, to protect individuals against government interference with these rights, which can be discovered in conventional morality or derived through the methods of philosophy and adjudication. . . .

BREST, THE MISCONCEIVED QUEST FOR
THE ORIGINAL UNDERSTANDING
60 B.U. L. Rev. 204, 228–29, 238 (1980)*

Several features of adjudication commend it as a plausible method for deriving and applying Bickel's "fundamental" values or Ely's "representation-reinforcing" values. Judges—especially federal judges—are relatively independent officials. Cases are presented through arguments based on precedent, policy, and principle, by parties who stand equally before the court. The court must justify its decisions by articulating reasons for them. The concreteness of the dispute, and the method of "testing" a result by articulating a governing principle and applying it to this and similar cases—real or hypothetical—induce the court to take responsibility for its decisions and to look beyond the circumstances of the particular dispute. And although the court gives strong presumptive weight to its precedents, the presumption is defeasible: Precedents are modified and even overruled to reflect perceived changes in social needs and values. Therefore, a doctrine that survives over a period of time has the approval of court composed, in effect, of all the judges who have ever had occasion to consider and apply it.

This is, of course, an idealized description of the Anglo-American "case" or "common law" method, which derives legal principles from custom, social practices, conventional morality, and precedent. Most American constitutional doctrines have evolved through adjudication, for it is the method of moderate originalism in the many cases where original sources alone cannot resolve the controversy before the court.

The only difference between moderate originalism and nonoriginalist adjudication is one of attitude toward the text and original understanding. For the moderate originalist, these sources are conclusive when they speak clearly. For the nonoriginalist, they are important but not determinative. Like an established line of precedent at common law, they create a strong presumption, but one which is defeasible in the light of changing public values. . . . The presumption is most likely to be overcome in adjudication under broad clauses involving issues of equality and liberty, where legal and moral principles are closely intertwined. . . .

[This] argument . . . is addressed chiefly to those who would have the judiciary serve the ends of constitutional government by enforcing "fundamental values" or by playing a "representation-reinforcing" role. . . . The burden of my argument is that nonoriginalist adjudication serves these ends better than either strict or moderate originalism. To put it bluntly, one can better protect fundamental values and the integrity of democratic processes by protecting them than by guessing how other people meant to govern a different society a hundred or more years ago.

BORK, STYLES IN CONSTITUTIONAL THEORY
26 S. Tex. L.J. 383 (1985)**

The problem in this area of constitutional theory always has been, and always will be, the resolution of what has been called the Madisonian dilemma. The United States was founded on what we now call a Madisonian system, one which allows majorities to rule in wide areas of life simply because they are majorities, but which also holds that

---

individuals have some freedoms that must be exempt from majority control. The dilemma is that neither the majority nor the minority can be trusted to define the proper spheres of democratic authority and individual liberty. The first would court tyranny by the majority; the second, tyranny by the minority.

It is not at all clear that the framers assigned the federal judiciary a major role in the resolution of this dilemma. . . . But over time it came to be thought that the resolution of the Madisonian problem—the definition of majority power and minority freedom was primarily the function of the judiciary and, especially, the function of the Supreme Court. . . .

Today, the reigning theory is that interpretation may be impossible, and is certainly inadequate. The majority of theorists would assign to judges not the task of defining values found in the Constitution but the task of creating new values and hence new rights for individuals against the majority. These value-creating theories are sometimes referred to as non-interpretivism. . . .

It is little short of astounding to reread today the wide-ranging, free-handed task Bickel would then—he had second thoughts in later years—have assigned to the Supreme Court:

> The function of the Justices . . . is to immerse themselves in the tradition of our society and of kindred societies that have gone before, in history and in the sediment of history which is law, and . . . in the thought and the vision of the philosophers and the poets. The Justices will then be fit to extract "fundamental presuppositions" from their deepest selves, but in fact from the evolving morality of our tradition.

It is tempting to say at this point that nothing could be further from the theories of Story, Cooley, and Thayer than constitutional law, if it can be called that, drawn from prolonged immersion in the visions of poets. It is tempting to say that, but, as you will see, it is possible to get still further away from the old tradition.

One is doubtless familiar with the next stage of theory. Dean Harry Wellington would create new constitutional rights by employing "the *method of philosophy*" to determine the "conventional morality" of our society. Professor Ronald Dworkin seeks a "fusion of constitutional law and moral theory." . . . Professor Thomas Grey suggests that there is a "higher law" of unwritten "natural rights" which courts are to enforce.

Professor Richard Parker promises a new constitutional theory which will "take seriously and work from (while, no doubt, revising) the classical conception of a republic, including its elements of relative equality, mobilization of the citizenry, and civic virtue." This, it seems, is to be constitutional theory as written by the Committee on Public Safety. . . .

The progression by no means stops there. It could not stop there. The nature of the non-interpretive enterprise is such that its theories must end in constitutional nihilism and the imposition of the judge's merely personal values on the rest of us. The reason is that none of these theorists has been able—and I venture to suggest none ever will be able—to build a philosophical structure that starts from accepted premises and logically demonstrates the answers, or the range of allowable answers, to questions not answered by the written Constitution. . . .

This failure will become apparent—indeed, it is already apparent as each of the non-interpretive theorists convincingly destroys all the others' systems—and that is why the inevitable end to non-interpretivist, value-choosing theory is constitutional nihilism. Professor Paul Brest, a non-interpretivist, bravely acknowledges this: "the controversy over the legitimacy of judicial review in a democratic polity . . . is essentially incoherent and unresolvable" since "no defensible criteria exist" "to assess theories of judicial review," and, therefore, "the Madisonian dilemma is in fact unresolvable. . . ."

A second reason that non-interpretivism ends in nihilism is that it has proved wholly unable to meet a condition most theorists have accepted as indispensable—consistency with democratic control of government. Alexander Bickel explained why that is essential. . . .

Bickel not only posed the problem, he essayed an answer which in my opinion no one writing afterward has improved upon. That answer came in two parts. The first was one of relative institutional capacities; courts are simply better than legislatures in dealing with principles of long-run importance as opposed to immediate problems. . . .

The second step in Bickel's argument is that the courts' commands are not really final. Speaking of the resistance to the decision in *Brown v. Board of Education*, Bickel wrote:

> The Supreme Court's law . . . could not in our system prevail—not merely in the very long run, but within the decade—if it ran counter to deeply felt popular needs or convictions, or even if it was opposed by a determined and substantial minority and received with indifference by the rest of the country. This, in the end, is how and why judicial review is consistent with the theory and practice of political democracy. This is why the Supreme Court is a court of last resort presumptively only. . . .

Both steps in the argument—superior institutional capacity and lack of finality—are essential, but, unfortunately, neither can survive examination.

Even if we assume that courts have superior capacities for dealing with matters of principle, it does not follow that courts have the right to impose more principle upon us than our elected representatives give us. . . .

The non-interpretivist's contention that the Court is not final and hence is not undemocratic, or at least not unacceptably so, must also be rejected. It is true that an outraged people can, if it persists, overturn a Supreme Court decision. That necessarily means that there would be little democratic control over a non-interpretivist court. . . . The theory assumes, as one of my clerks put it, that in the long run none of us will be dead. . . .

Many non-interpretive theorists have responded to this anti-democratic difficulty by simply dropping Bickel's condition from the discussion. Perry . . . [concludes] as follows:

> If I were unable to defend constitutional policymaking by the judiciary as consistent with the principle of electorally accountable policymaking, then, given my commitment to constitutional policymaking by the judiciary, I would have to question the axiomatic character of the principle of electorally accountable policymaking. In a word, if judicial rule and democracy come into conflict, Perry will have to question the desirability of democracy. . . .

The institutions and traditions of the American republic, including the historic Constitution, are our best chance for happiness and safety. . . .

It is at least worth considering that Justice Story may have had hold of a profound truth when he said that "[u]pon subjects of government . . . metaphysical refinements are out of place. A constitution . . . is addressed to the common sense of the people; and never was designed for trials of logical skill, or visionary speculation."

NOTES AND QUESTIONS

(1) *"Open-Textured" Constitutional Provisions: How Would an Originalist Like Judge Bork Construe Them?* Reconsider such constitutional phrases as due process, equal protection, freedom of speech, or cruel and unusual punishment, and consider how an interpretivist would decide upon their meanings. In particular, consider the possibility that an interpretivist might give weight to the drafters' deliberate choice of general language as embodying an evolutionary standard. If so, paradoxically perhaps

both originalist and textualist theories of interpretivism call for supplementation (non-interpretivism?) to supply contemporary values!

As a concrete example, consider whether the Constitution, through the due process, equal protection, right to counsel, or cruel and unusual punishment clauses, requires the appointment of an attorney at state expense for an indigent defendant accused of a capital crime. Assume that the original understanding would justify his trial (and execution, upon conviction) without counsel. Can the constitutional guarantees in question be construed appropriately without reference to supplementary principles? If not, is Judge Bork wrong—or does the example simply reinforce the thread of Judge Bork's argument that the Constitution must be the starting point for constitutional reasoning?

(2) *Is Judge Bork's Reference to American "Institutions and Traditions" and to a "Constitution . . . Addressed to the Common Sense of the People" a Call for Supplementation (or Non-Interpretivism)?* Note that the "institutions and traditions of the American republic," which Bork says are to be considered as well as the "historic Constitution," might imply support for what he calls non-interpretivist principles. A Constitution "addressed to the common sense of the people" might be read as incorporating a sense of public morality through which extra-constitutional non-interpretivist notions could be imported. Do these considerations weaken Judge Bork's argument?

(3) *What Would an Interpretivist Do About Existing Non-Interpretivist Decisions That Have Acquired Legitimacy?* Brest points out that a non-suplementary interpretivism cannot justify certain existing decisions that are embedded in our constitutional law. What would Bork do with these decisions, which arguably include the school desegregation cases from *Brown v. Board of Education* on? However, when a holding is extra-constitutional, and we decide to keep it because of extra-constitutional reasons found in popular acceptance or settled expectations, isn't this reasoning ipso facto non-interpretivist?

(4) *Supplemental (or Non-Interpretivist) Theories Deriving Adjudicatory Principles: Natural Law, Conventional Morality, Contemporary Moral Philosophy, and Enhancement of Democracy.* For examples of efforts to derive coherent supplemental theories, *see* R. DWORKIN, TAKING RIGHTS SERIOUSLY (1977) (contemporary moral philosophy); J. ELY, DEMOCRACY AND DISTRUST (1980) (compensation for failures of political processes to achieve open democracy); Grey, *Do We Have an Unwritten Constitution?*, 27 STAN. L. REV. 703 (1975) (referring to natural law or "higher law principles" as "deeply embedded in our constitutional traditions"); Wellington, *Common Law Rules and Constitutional Double Standards: Some Notes on Adjudication*, 83 YALE L.J. 221 (1973) (use of reason and conventional morality).

(5) *Support for Brest's Theory of Adjudication From the Founders.* In support of Brest's theory that the process of adjudication itself helps to identify constitutional values, consider the experience of James Madison. As a Congressman, he concluded that Congress lacked power to create the first national bank, and he therefore opposed it. Twenty years later, he accepted the Supreme Court's contrary conclusion—and, as President, signed the bill authorizing the second bank. As he explained,

> It could not but happen, and was foreseen at the birth of the Constitution, that difficulties and differences of opinion might occasionally arise in expounding terms and phrases necessarily used in such a charter . . . and that it might require a regular course of practice to liquidate and settle the meaning of some of them.

Letter from James Madison to Judge Spencer Roane, in 3 LETTERS AND OTHER WRITINGS OF JAMES MADISON 143, 145 (1865), quoted in Powell, *The Original Understanding of Original Intent*, 98 HARV. L. REV. 885, 941 (1985).

(6) *The Bork Supreme Court Nomination and the Senate's Refusal to confirm.* President Reagan nominated Judge Bork to the Supreme Court. The resulting Senate hearings generated intense debate about the proper role of the Senate in "advising and consenting" to such nominations—particularly with respect to the question whether (and to what extent) the Senate should consider Judge Bork's constitutional views. *See* Symposium, *The Bork Nomination*, 9 CARDOZO L. REV. 1 (1987).

NOTE ON PROFESSOR BOBBIT'S "SIX MODALITIES" OF CONSTITUTIONAL ARGUMENT

Professor Philip Bobbit has described six methods, or six "modalities," of constitutional argument. PHILIP BOBBIT, CONSTITUTIONAL FATE (1982). Professor Bobbit's methods are adaptable to virtually any constitutional question (and in fact they may be adaptable to questions of statutory construction or to the interpretation of other kinds of legal instruments). *See, e.g.,* Sanford Levinson, *The Embarrassing Second Amendment*, 99 YALE L.J. 637 (1989) (applying Professor Bobbit's six modalities to the interpretation of the Second Amendment militia clause and right to keep and bear arms). Professor Bobbit's six modalities are:

(1) *Textual*: argument that considers the words and language of the text. For example, an interpretation of the First Amendment as absolute (or as establishing "preferred" rights), because it provides that "Congress shall make *no* law" abridging the freedom of speech, is based upon a textual argument.

(2) *Historical*: argument that relies upon the intention of the drafters, the events that produced the provision, or similar kinds of appeals to history. For example, an interpretation of the First Amendment as limited rather than absolute, because the Founders arguably saw it as more restricted in scope than modern readers might, or because their public interpretation arguably did not protect certain kinds of utterances (*e.g.,* defamation or sedition), would be based upon historical arguments. (Originalism, therefore, is identified with this modality.)

(3) *Structural*: argument that infers relationships among the entities set up or recognized by the Constitution and interprets its provisions accordingly. Thus, the Constitution assigns roles to different branches of government, to the States, to the people, etc. An interpretation of the First Amendment that gives political speech a preferred position because it enables the people better to perform their function in electing, guiding and checking the government, for example, uses a structural argument.

(4) *Doctrinal*: argument that refers to the tradition of received wisdom, usually to the precedential implications of the Supreme Court's decisions. For example, an argument that First Amendment freedoms are preferred rights because the Supreme Court said so in a given case is a doctrinal argument.

(5) *Prudential*: argument that depends upon the practical consequences of differing interpretations, or in other words, "policy" argument. An interpretation of the First Amendment that excludes child pornography, on the ground that its protection is not necessary to robust public debate, can be called a prudential argument.

(6) *Ethical*: argument that relies on moral or ethical grounds. This modality sometimes may seem indistinguishable from the fifth modality, that of prudential argument; there is, however, a difference. Whereas prudential argument emphasizes the consequences of an interpretation in the practical sense, ethical argument emphasizes the rightness-or-wrongness of moral content of the interpretation. For example, a reading of the First Amendment that excludes child pornography on the ground that its protection by the government would be immoral, either because the material damages children or because viewing it is wrong, is an ethical argument.

NOTES AND QUESTIONS

(1) *Different Modes of Argument as Applied to the Constitutionality of the Death Penalty.* Recall Justice Brennan's absolutist position on the unconstitutionality of the Death Penalty. Consider ways in which each of the suggested modes of argument—textual, historical, structural, doctrinal, prudential, and ethical—could be used (or are used) to support Justice Brennan's view, or, for that matter, the opposing view.

(2) *Different Modes of Argument as Applied to the Justiciability of Impeachment.* Recall the various opinions of the Justices in *United States v. Nixon*, in which the majority held that an attack upon the Senate's use of a committee to "try" impeachments was nonjusticiable. Consider ways in which each of the suggested modes of argument—textual, historical, structural, doctrinal, prudential, and ethical—could be used (or are used) to support the majority's view or the opposing view.

(3) *Are Some Modes of Interpretation Generally Superior to Others? The Originalist's View as an Example.* Originalism appear to have broad appeal among scholars, although its acceptance is not universal and the extent of its persuasiveness differs widely among them. A reader who insists on relatively strict originalism probably will regard the historical approach as controlling and consider textual, structural or doctrinal approaches as authorized when history permits them (or in the case of the text, as a historical source). Such a view might see prudential considerations as often disfavored and ethical arguments as almost always disfavored (since ethical arguments, especially when contrary to original intent, arguably seek to promote propositions preferred by the reader even though more definite interpretations oppose them). Can you explain the apparent paradox that many people, even though they might consider the Constitution with a degree of reverence reserved for an important ethical statement, nevertheless might regard ethical arguments about its interpretation as suspect?

PROBLEM H

THE SECOND AMENDMENT AS INTERPRETED BY THE NATIONAL RIFLE ASSOCIATION—OR BY ADVOCATES OF GUN CONTROL. Read the Second Amendment. Notice that it contains both a militia clause and a right to keep and bear arms, and it does not make the relationship between the two completely clear. Some gun lobbyists might argue that the Amendment provides a personal, individual right to possess arms of indefinite number and description. Some gun control advocates might argue, however, that the right is qualified by the militia clause and thus is to be exercised by the people collectively, in connection with a well-regulated militia. There are surprisingly few Supreme Court decisions on point. Describe how the various modes of argument—textual, historical, structural, doctrinal, prudential and ethical—could be used to support either interpretation. (If you want guidance, you might consult Chapter 15 of this book, which considers the Second Amendment, as well as Professor Levinson's article, *The Embarrassing Second Amendment*, cited above.)

Chapter 2
CONGRESSIONAL POWER

§ 2.01 NATIONAL LEGISLATIVE POWER: ITS NATURE AND LIMITS

[A] The Federalist Vision of Strong Central Government

MADISON, THE FEDERALIST NO. 10: VIOLENCE OF PARTIES RESTRAINED BY A STRONGER FEDERAL UNION

Among the numerous advantages promised by a well-constructed Union, none deserves to be more accurately developed than its tendency to break and control the violence of faction. . . .

Party Conflicts Make for Disorder. . . . By a faction, I understand a number of citizens, whether amounting to a majority or minority of the whole, who are united and actuated by some common impulse of passion, or of interest, adverse to the rights of other citizens, or to the permanent and aggregate interests of the community. . . .

Pure Democracy No Cure for Factionalism. [A] pure democracy, by which I mean a society consisting of a small number of citizens, who assemble and administer the government in person, can admit of no cure for the mischiefs of faction. There is nothing to check the inducements to sacrifice the weaker party or an obnoxious individual. . . .

Republican Government Refines Popular Passions. A republic, by which I mean a government in which the scheme of representation takes place, opens a different prospect, and promises the cure for which we are seeking. . . .

The two great points of difference between a democracy and a republic are: first, the delegation of the government, in the latter, to a small number of citizens elected by the rest; secondly, the greater number of citizens, and greater sphere of country, over which the latter may be extended. . . .

Larger Republic Better than Small. [I]f the proportion of fit characters be not less in the large than in the small republic, the former will present a greater option, and consequently a greater probability of a fit choice. . . .

Large Unions Include a Greater Diversity of Interests. Hence, it clearly appears, that the same advantage which a republic has over a democracy, in controlling the effects of faction, is enjoyed by a large over a small republic,—is enjoyed by the Union over the States composing it. Does the advantage consist in the substitution of representatives whose enlightened views and virtuous sentiments render them superior to local prejudices and to schemes of injustice? It will not be denied that the representation of the Union will be most likely to possess these requisite endowments. . . .

[B] Enumerated, Implied, and Inherent Powers

NOTE: CONGRESS' POWERS IN A FEDERAL SYSTEM

A Federal System. The United States is a federal system of government. It is a union in which a central or overall government has acknowledged powers, but in which individual state governments have separate existences and authority. (Switzerland, Canada, and Australia similarly are federations, with quite different characteristics.) The Constitution originated in dissatisfaction with the relative efficacies of state and national governments under the Articles of Confederation that preceded it.

The Articles of Confederation, Article II. This localism was deliberately featured in the Articles of Confederation. Article II provided, "Each state retains its sovereignty, freedom, and independence, and every power, jurisdiction and right, which is not by this confederation expressly delegated to the United States in Congress assembled." The Constitution was intended to form, as its preamble says, "a more perfect Union" than the Articles of Confederation.

The Constitution's Approach to the Powers of Congress. The Virginia delegation to the Constitutional Convention, through Edmund Randolph, submitted proposed language that would have authorized Congress "to legislate in all cases to which the separate States are incompetent, or in which the harmony of the United States may be interrupted by the exercise of individual legislation." I F. FARRAND, RECORDS OF THE FEDERAL CONVENTION OF 1787, at 47, 53 (1911); II *Id.* at 25–27, 181–82. The Convention rejected proposals that would have confined Congress' power narrowly; it also rejected a broad proposal by Hamilton, which would have allowed Congress to "pass all laws which they shall judge necessary to the common defense and general welfare of the Union." The delegates instead endorsed Randolph's approach, in a rewritten resolution, as follows:

"Resolved, that the national legislature ought

"1. to possess the legislative rights vested in Congress by the confederation; and

"2. moreover, to legislate in all cases for the general interests of the Union; and

"3. also in those to which the states are separately incompetent; or

"4. in which the harmony of the United States may be interrupted by the exercise of individual legislation."

The Convention voted to send this resolution to the Committee of Detail, which was the drafting committee. That group then generated language closely similar to the words adopted as Article I, § 8 of the Constitution, setting forth the principal powers of Congress. *Id.*

Enumerated Powers. One way in which to set up a legislature is to empower it to legislate only in permitted areas or in permitted ways. The Articles of Confederation, which restricted the national government to "expressly delegated" powers, was a strict embodiment of the enumerated powers concept. The United States Constitution also contains enumerated powers—but with a difference.

Implied and Inherent Powers. Although the Constitution creates a government of enumerated powers, it has been interpreted as providing for implied powers related to those that are enumerated and thus it frees Congress from the restrictions of the "expressly delegated" language of the Articles of Confederation. Note that implied powers, strictly speaking, must be related to enumerated ones. Congress may exercise authority to condemn property to build a post office—not because condemnation is a kind of authority Congress "ought" to have, but because it is implied from Congress' postal power enumerated in Art. I, § 8. A separate doctrine of "inherent" power would attribute to Congress those kinds of power that are inherent in the legislature of a general government. This theory, however, has seldom been advanced by courts as justification for acts of Congress (its principal valid use might be said to be in connection with the management of foreign affairs, which is not a power enumerated in the Constitution).

The Necessary and Proper Clause. The Constitution provides that Congress also has power to pass laws "necessary and proper" to the carrying out of its enumerated powers. Understandably, this provision was the focal point of attack by those who preferred stronger states and a weaker union. Its precise interpretation was a matter of conjecture. Did it provide Congress with a broad field of action, in which anything related to an enumerated power was "necessary" and hence authorized, or did it place a stricter requirement of necessity on implied powers? Consider the following explanation by James Madison.

MADISON, THE FEDERALIST NO. 44: LIMITATIONS ON STATE POWERS AND A BROAD INTERPRETATION OF FEDERAL POWERS DEFENDED

. . . [Among the powers of Congress are included] the several powers and provisions by which efficacy is given to all rest.

1. Of these and first is, the "power to make all laws which shall be necessary and proper for carrying into execution the foregoing powers. . . ."

Few parts of the Constitution have been assailed with more intemperance than this; yet on a fair investigation of it, no part can appear more completely invulnerable. . . .

Limitation to Express Powers Not Desirable. Had the convention taken the . . . method of adopting the second article of Confederation, it is evident that the new Congress would be continually exposed, as their predecessors have been, to the alternative of construing the term *"expressly"* with so much rigor, as to disarm the government of all real authority whatever, or with so much latitude as to destroy altogether the force of the restriction. . . .

Complete Enumeration of Powers Not Possible. Had the convention attempted a positive enumeration of the powers necessary and proper for carrying their other powers into effect, the attempt would have involved a complete digest of laws on every subject to which the Constitution relates; accommodated too, not only to the existing state of things, but to all the possible changes which futurity may produce. . . .

Implied Powers Unavoidable. Had the Constitution been silent on this head, there can be no doubt that all the particular powers requisite as means of executing the general powers would have resulted to the government, by unavoidable implication. [W]herever a general power to do a thing is given, every particular power necessary for doing it is included. . . .

State Protection against Abuses. If it be asked what is to be the consequence, in case the Congress shall misconstrue this part of the Constitution, and exercise powers not warranted by its true meaning, I answer, the same as if they should misconstrue or enlarge any other power vested in them. . . . In the first instance, the success of the usurpation will depend on the executive and judiciary departments, which are to expound and give effect to the legislative acts; and in the last resort a remedy must be obtained from the people, who can, by the election of more faithful representatives, annul the acts of the usurpers. . . .

Read U.S. Const. Art. I, § 8 (powers of Congress); also, consider Art. III, § 1 (court jurisdiction power); Art. III, § 2 (admiralty clause); Art. IV, § 3 (national property clause); Art. IV, § 4 (guaranty clause); Art. IV, § 1 (full faith and credit clause); and Amend. XIV, § 5 (power to enforce civil rights amendments).

PROBLEM A

WHAT CONSTITUTIONAL GRANT OF POWER TO CONGRESS, IF ANY, SUPPORTS THE FEDERAL FLAG DESECRATION STATUTE? The Federal Flag Protection Act of 1989 provides that whoever "knowingly mutilates, defaces, physically defiles, burns, maintains on the floor or ground or tramples upon any flag of the United States" can be fined or imprisoned. The Act has been held inapplicable to certain cases, but the Supreme Court has not struck it down on its face or in its entirety. Consider the constitutionality of this law under each of the following theories:

(a) *Does the Flag Desecration Statute Violate a Constitutional Prohibition?* *Cf. Texas v. Johnson*, 491 U.S. 397 (1989) (holding that a conviction under a related state law, as applied to defendant's act of burning the flag, violated the first amendment, but refusing to strike down the law on its face); *see also United States v. Eichman*, 496 U.S. 310 (1990) (striking down conviction under 1989 Flag Protection Act). We shall consider this issue in greater depth in the chapter on freedom of speech, below.

(b) *Can the Statute Be Justified by Reference to Any of the Enumerated Powers of Congress?* In *Spence, supra*, neither the majority nor the dissenters had an easy time identifying the interest(s) advanced by such a law, but all perceived at least some arguable claims of legitimacy. The majority cited the "interest in preserving the national flag as an unalloyed symbol of our country," as well as the need "to prevent the appropriation of a revered national symbol." Justice Rehnquist, in dissent, emphasized "preserving the flag as 'an important symbol of nationhood and unity,'" observing that "the flag is a national property, and the Nation may regulate those who would make, imitate, sell, possess or use it." Can these interests be related to *enumerated* powers of Congress in Art. I, § 8 (such as the war, military, militia, preservation-of-union, or patent and copyright powers)? In the alternative, do they fall under powers elsewhere enumerated (such as the national property clause of Art. IV, § 3)? If not within the enumerated powers, is a flag desecration statute within the *implied* powers of Congress (does the necessary and proper clause help here)? Finally, if such a law is not within the enumerated or implied powers, is there an *"inherent"* power of a confederated government to designate and protect a revered symbol of national unity?

NOTE ON THE BACKGROUND TO THE NATIONAL BANK CASE

The Federalists, the Anti-Federalists, and the First National Bank. Soon after the adoption of the Constitution, Treasury Secretary Alexander Hamilton, a prominent Federalist, recommended that Congress charter a government bank. Over vigorous opposition from anti-Federalists, Congress passed an act creating the first Bank of the United States. President Washington, who then was uncommitted on the issue, requested the advice of Secretary of State Thomas Jefferson and of Attorney General Edmund Randolph, concerning whether he should sign or veto the measure. Both vigorously expressed the opinion that the bank charter was outside the power of Congress and unconstitutional. Jefferson had criticized Federalist efforts to charter a national mining business:

I do not know whether it is understood that [state legislatures are] incompetent [to charter a business corporation], or merely that we have concurrent [power] under the sweeping clause [*i.e.*, the necessary and proper clause]. Congress are authorized to defend the nation. Ships are necessary for defense; copper is necessary for ships; mines, necessary for copper; a company necessary to work the mines; and who can doubt this reasoning who has ever played at "This is the House that Jack Built?" Under such a process of filiation of the necessities the sweeping clause makes clean work.

1 C. WARREN, THE SUPREME COURT IN UNITED STATES HISTORY 501 (1926). But President Washington also requested (and ultimately followed) Hamilton's opinion, which fore-shadowed the reasoning of the Supreme Court when it considered the question years later. According to Hamilton, every enumerated power of Congress "includes, by force of the term, a right to employ all the means requisite" to make the power effective, unless the means were somehow inconsistent with provisions of the Constitution. *See* HAMMOND, *The Bank Cases, in* QUARRELS THAT HAVE SHAPED THE CONSTITUTION 37–38 (J.

Garraty ed. 1966). The bank was unpopular, and it became more so. By the time its charter expired in 1811, the Anti-Federalists were in office and allowed it to pass into oblivion.

The Second National Bank. But five years later, the Republicans were a different party; in the process of achieving dominance, they had acquired the allegiance of entrepreneurs and businesspeople. The national treasury, as it happened, was in desperate straits. The Republicans decided that a government bank was necessary after all. Unfortunately, the second national bank was unpopular too. The causes included poor lending practices (which ended unavoidably in foreclosures) as well as actual corruption and self-dealing. And, of course, there remained the principled opposition of those who regarded the federal government as strictly limited to enumerated powers and who saw the bank, with its eighteen branches from Portsmouth to Savannah, and from New Orleans to Cincinnati, as infringing the sovereignty of the states.

The States Fight the Bank; Maryland's Test Case. Georgia, Kentucky, Maryland, North Carolina, Ohio, and Tennessee enacted taxes upon the bank or its notes. The taxes were not revenue-motivated: they were intended to destroy the bank's branches within those states. In May, 1818, a man named John James, acting to obtain evidence for the State of Maryland, demanded of James W. McCulloch, the bank's cashier in Baltimore, the statutory penalty of $100 per unstamped note. McCulloch refused, Maryland sued, and the result was the Supreme Court's decision in an opinion by Chief Justice Marshall that consolidated the expansion of federal power.

McCulloch v. Maryland: The Opinion. Chief Justice Marshall's opinion contains at least four major themes. *First*, it concludes that the source of the power granted in the Constitution was not the states, but rather the people directly. The Constitution therefore is not a mere compact among the states but a more fundamental document. *Second*, the opinion emphasizes the flexibility of this fundamental document. This part of the opinion contains the famous dictum, "[W]e must never forget that it is a *constitution* we are expounding." *Third*, Marshall interprets the necessary and proper clause to authorize Congressional action of broad scope—not tied merely to that which is strictly "necessary" for carrying out enumerated powers. He follows the view expressed by Hamilton in support of the first National Bank. *Fourth*, Marshall holds that state efforts to frustrate federal exercises of power are invalid, with the famous statement that the power to tax is "the power to destroy."

McCulloch's Reliance on the Necessary and Proper Clause. The Court could find no specific congressional power to establish a national bank; but Congress could rationally conclude that the establishment of a bank was "necessary and proper" to the execution of at least five of its vested powers: to lay and collect taxes, to borrow money, to regulate commerce, to conduct a war, and to raise and support an army and navy.

McCULLOCH v. MARYLAND
17 U.S. (4 Wheat.) 316 (1819)

The following opinion was delivered by the CHIEF JUSTICE [JOHN MARSHALL]. . . .

[Against the factual background detailed above, the Court here upholds Congress' *Hold.* exercise of power to charter the Second National Bank.]

In discussing this question, the counsel for the state of Maryland have deemed it of some importance, in the construction of the constitution, to consider that instrument not as emanating from the people, but as the act of sovereign and independent states. The powers of the general government, it has been said, are delegated by the states, who alone are truly sovereign; and must be exercised in subordination to the states, who alone possess supreme dominion.

It would be difficult to sustain this proposition. The convention which framed the constitution was indeed elected by the state legislatures. But the instrument, when it came from their hands, was a mere proposal, without obligation, or pretensions to it. It was reported to the then existing Congress of the United States, with a request that it might "be submitted to a convention of delegates, chosen in each state by the people thereof, under the recommendation of its legislature, for their assent and ratification." . . . It is true, they assembled in their several states and where else should they have assembled? The government proceeds directly from the people; is "ordained and established" in the name of the people. . . .

The government of the Union, then (whatever may be the influence of this fact on the case), is, emphatically, and truly, a government of the people. [I]ts powers are granted by them, and are to be exercised directly on them, and for their benefit.

This government is acknowledged by all to be one of enumerated powers. . . . But the question respecting the extent of the powers actually granted, is perpetually arising. . . .

Among the enumerated powers, we do not find that of establishing a bank or creating a corporation. But there is no phrase in the instrument which, like the articles of confederation, excludes incidental or implied powers; and which requires that everything granted shall be expressly and minutely described. Even the 10th amendment, which was framed for the purpose of quieting the excessive jealousies which had been excited, omits the word "expressly," and declares only that the powers "not delegated to the United States, nor prohibited to the states, are reserved to the states or to the people" . . . A constitution, to contain an accurate detail of all the subdivisions of which its great powers will admit, and of all the means by which they may be carried into execution, would partake of a prolixity of a legal code, and could scarcely be embraced by the human mind. It would probably never be understood by the public. Its nature, therefore, requires, that only its great outlines should be marked, its important objects designated, and the minor ingredients which compose those objects be deduced from the nature of the objects themselves.

In considering this question, then, we must never forget that it is a *constitution* we are expounding.

Although, among the enumerated powers of government, we do not find the word "bank" or "incorporation," we find the great powers to lay and collect taxes; to borrow money; to regulate commerce; to declare and conduct a war; and to raise and support armies and navies. The sword and the purse, all the external relations, and no inconsiderable portion of the industry of the nation, are entrusted to [it]. . . . [I]t may with great reason be contended, that a government, entrusted with such ample powers, on the due execution of which the happiness and prosperity of the nation so vitally depends, must also be entrusted with ample means for their execution. [T]hroughout this vast republic, from the St. Croix to the Gulf of Mexico, from the Atlantic to the Pacific, revenue is to be collected and expended, armies are to be marched and supported. The exigencies of the nation may require that the treasure raised in the north should be transported to the south, that raised in the east conveyed to the west, or that this order should be reversed. . . . [B]ut it is denied that the government has its choice of means; or, that it may employ the most convenient means, if, to employ them, it be necessary to erect a corporation.

The creation of a corporation, it is said, appertains to sovereignty. This is admitted. But to what portion of sovereignty does it appertain? . . . In America, the powers of sovereignty are divided between the government of the Union, and those of the States. They are each sovereign, with respect to the objects committed to it, and neither sovereign with respect to the objects committed to the other. . . . The power of creating a corporation, though appertaining to sovereignty, is not, like the power of making war, or levying taxes, or of regulating commerce, a great substantive and independent power, which cannot be implied as incidental to other powers, or used as a means of executing them. . . . No sufficient reason is, therefore, perceived, why it may not pass as incidental to those powers which are expressly given, if it be a direct mode of executing them.

But the consideration of the United States has not left the right of Congress to employ the necessary means for the execution of the powers conferred on the government to general reasoning. To its enumeration of powers is added that of making "all laws which shall be necessary and proper, for carrying into execution the foregoing powers, and all other powers vested by this constitution, in the government of the United States, or in any department thereof."

The counsel for the State of Maryland have urged various arguments, to prove that this clause, though in terms a grant of power, is not so in effect; but is really restrictive of the general right, which might otherwise be implied, of selecting means for executing the enumerated powers. . . .

[T]he argument on which most reliance is placed, is drawn from the peculiar language of this clause. . . . The word "necessary" is considered as controlling the whole sentence, and as limiting the right to pass laws for the execution of the granted powers, to such as are indispensable, and without which the power would be nugatory. That it excludes the choice of means, and leaves to Congress, in each case, that only which is most direct and simple.

Is it true that this is the sense in which the word "necessary" is always used? Does it always import an absolute physical necessity, so strong that one thing, to which another may be termed necessary, cannot exist without that other? We think it does not. If reference be had to its use, in the common affairs of the world, or in approved authors, we find that it frequently imports no more than that one thing is convenient, or useful, or essential to another. . . .

A thing may be necessary, very necessary, absolutely or indispensably necessary. . . . This word, then, like others, is used in various senses; and, in its construction, the subject, the context, the intention of the person using them, are all to be taken into view. . . . It must have been the intention of those who gave these powers to insure, as far as human prudence could insure their beneficial execution. . . . To have prescribed the means by which government should, in all future time, execute its powers, would have been to change, entirely, the character of the instrument, and gave it the properties of a legal code. It would have been an unwise attempt to provide, by immutable rules, for exigencies which, if foreseen at all, must have been seen dimly, and which can be best provided for as they occur. . . . If we apply this principle of construction to any of the powers of the government, we shall find it so pernicious in its operation that we shall be compelled to discard it. . . .

Take, for example, the power "to establish post-offices and post-roads." This power is executed by the single act of making the establishment. But, from this has been inferred the power and duty of carrying the mail along the post-road, from one post office to another. And, from this implied power, has again been inferred the right to punish those who steal letters from the post-office, or rob the mail. It may be said, with some plausibility, that the right to carry the mail, and to punish those who rob it, is not indispensably necessary to the establishment of a post-office and post-road. . . .

But the argument which most conclusively demonstrates that error of the construction contended for by the counsel for the state of Maryland, is founded on the intention of the convention, as manifested in the whole clause. . . . We think so for the following reasons:

1st. The clause is placed among the powers of Congress, not among the limitations on those powers.

2nd. Its terms purport to enlarge, not to diminish the powers vested in the government. It purports to be an additional power, not a restriction on those already granted. . . . If no other motive for its insertion can be suggested, a sufficient one is found in the desire to remove all doubts respecting the right to legislate on that vast mass of incidental powers which must be involved in the constitution, if that instrument be not a splendid bauble.

We admit, as all must admit, that the powers of the government are limited, and that its limits are not to be transcended. But we think the sound construction of the constitution must allow to the national legislature that discretion, with the respect to the means by which the powers it confers are to be carried into execution, which will enable that body to perform the high duties assigned to it, in the manner most beneficial to the people. Let the end be legitimate, let it be within the scope of the constitution, and all means which are appropriate, which are plainly adapted to that end, which are not prohibited, but consist with the letter and spirit of the constitution, are constitutional. . . .

It being the opinion of the court that the act incorporating the bank is constitutional, and that the power of establishing a branch in the state of Maryland might be properly exercised by the bank itself, we proceed to inquire:

2. Whether the state of Maryland may, without violating the constitution, tax that branch?

[The Court went on to hold, in this portion of the opinion, that the Maryland tax was unconstitutional. It reasoned: "The great principle is, that the constitution and the laws made in pursuance thereof are supreme. . . . From this, other propositions are deduced as corollaries. . . . These are, 1st, that a power to create implies a power to preserve. 2d. That a power to destroy, if wielded by a different hand [*i.e.*, by a state government], is hostile to . . . these powers to create and preserve. 3d. That where this repugnancy exists, that authority which is supreme must control, not yield to that over which it is supreme."]

NOTES AND QUESTIONS

(1) *The Aftermath of McCulloch: Continued Corruption, Continued Opposition—Osborn v. Bank of the United States, 22 U.S. (9 Wheat.) 738 (1824).* The popular reaction to *McCulloch* was one of shock and outrage. "The masses could understand the Tenth Amendment [reserving powers to the states and people] but not the subtleties of Hamilton and Marshall, according to whom the Constitution meant yes when it said no." HAMMOND, *supra*, at 39. It did not help that McCulloch, together with other officers of the bank, later was formally accused of embezzling from it. But the resistance to the bank was nowhere so vigorous as in Ohio, where a legislative committee criticized the Supreme Court's decision as the result not only of a misreading of the Constitution, but as reflecting "inadvertence or connivance" on the part of Maryland in presenting its claims as "throughout an agreed case," since the facts were stipulated. Ohio treasurer Ralph Osborn defied a federal injunction, sent agents who entered the Chillicothe, Ohio office of the bank, and took specie and banknotes sufficient to pay the state tax by force. The bank ultimately obtained a federal court order for return of the money, which Osborn's successor defied; he was arrested by federal officers, who took possession of his keys and physically retrieved the bank's funds. Perhaps fortunately, there was considerable delay before the Ohio bank litigation reached the Supreme Court, where, in *Osborn v. Bank of the United States*, *supra*, it reaffirmed the reaffirmation of the holding that Congress had authority to charter the bank. *See generally* HAMMOND, *supra*, at 39–46.

(2) *President Jackson's Veto of the Bank Charter Renewal; An Era of Strictly Limited Federal Power.* In 1832, Congress passed an act renewing the bank's charter. President Andrew Jackson vetoed this enactment, on the ground, among others, that it was unconstitutional, and that the executive had an independent obligation to defend the Constitution. HAMMOND, *supra*, at 46–47.

(3) *Did the People Really Delegate Congressional Power Directly—Or Did They Do So Through the States?: Hodel v. Virginia Surface Mining & Reclamation Ass'n, 452*

U.S. 264 (1981). Marshall's holding that the people acted directly to delegate powers in the Constitution is important to his reasoning, because it supports a strong national government that is not beholden to the states. But in *Virginia Surface Mining, supra,* Justice Rehnquist, concurring, asserts instead that the people acted through the mechanism of their state governments in making the delegation. As Marshall acknowledges, they acted in conventions set up by state legislatures, and had acted through state delegations to the Constitutional Convention. Is Justice Rehnquist's theory viable, and what, if any, difference would it make?

(4) *Rejection of "Inherent" Power and Limitation of Enumerated Powers: Kansas v. Colorado, 206 U.S. 46 (1907).* In this case, Kansas complained that Colorado had improperly diverted and deprived Kansas of waters of the Arkansas River. Colorado relied in part upon federal statutes providing for the reclamation of arid lands. The Court held that the powers of Congress did not include the reclamation at issue. If Congress had concerned itself with the navigability of the River, it would have been justified by the commerce clause, and if it had reclaimed land within a federal territory as opposed to a state it would have been justified by the national property clause; as it acted, however, it was justified by neither. "[N]o one of [Congress' powers], by any implication, refers to the reclamation of arid lands." The Court then turned to an argument based upon the theory of inherent power:

> [The] argument runs substantially along this line: All legislative power must be vested in either the state or the national government; no legislative powers belong to a state other than those which affect solely the internal affairs of that state; consequently all powers which are national in their scope must be found vested in the Congress of the United States. But the proposition [i]s in direct conflict with the doctrine that this is a government of enumerated powers. . . . This natural construction of the original body of the Constitution is made absolutely certain by the 10th Amendment.

Is the Court convincing in arguing that the commerce power does not support arid land reclamation? Is the rejection of inherent power convincing?

(5) *The Tenth Amendment.* As *Kansas v. Colorado* demonstrates, the Tenth Amendment was a tool used by limited-power advocates, as the necessary and proper clause was used by central government advocates. We shall consider the Tenth Amendment in Chapter 3, *below.*

(6) *Foreign Affairs: A Legitimate Use of Inherent Power? Fong Yue Ting v. United States, 149 U.S. 698 (1893).* The Constitution nowhere delegates a general power over foreign affairs. Does Congress therefore lack this power, or is it to be justified as inherent in national sovereignty? The restrictive approach of *Kansas v. Colorado, supra,* contrasts sharply with the language of the Court in *Fong Yue Ting:* "The United States are a sovereign and independent nation and are vested with the entire control of international relations and with all the powers of government necessary to maintain that control. . . . The power [over foreign affairs] is to be regulated by treaty or act of Congress."

CITY OF BOERNE v. FLORES, 521 U.S. 507 (1997). The Religious Freedom Restoration Act (RFRA) was prompted by a decision of the Supreme Court upholding state laws of general application that incidentally burdened some individuals' free exercise of religion. Specifically, in *Employment Div. v. Smith,* 494 U.S. 872 (1990), Smith had been fired from his job as a drug rehabilitation counselor because he ingested peyote in a ceremony of the Native American Church. The Court there read the Free Exercise Clause as applicable only to laws that target religious exercises. The Court thus held that neutral or generally applicable laws, like Oregon's general drug laws, are not covered by that Clause even though they may incidentally have substantial impact on some individuals' religious exercises. RFRA was designed to change that result. Henceforth, said RFRA, all generally applicable laws that had this substantial impact could not be enforced unless they survive strict scrutiny, *i.e.*, they are found to serve some "compelling" government interest.

The power of Congress upon which RFRA was based was the power to enforce the Fourteenth Amendment. But the sweep of the Act was enormous; it affected zoning, environmental, penal, welfare, health, and prison regulations, as well as laws of every other possible description. This case, for example, arose because a church administered by Bishop Flores sought to avoid complying with the City of Boerne's historic preservation ordinance so that it could construct an addition to its building. The Supreme Court, per Justice Kennedy, struck down RFRA as unconstitutional on the ground, among others, that it exceeded Congress's power to enforce the Fourteenth Amendment.

For an insightful commentary, *see* Eugene Gressman, *Some Thoughts on the Necessary and Proper Clause*, 31 SETON HALL L. REV. 37 (2000). *See generally* JOSEPH M. LYNCH, NEGOTIATING THE CONSTITUTION: THE EARLIEST DEBATES OVER ORIGINAL INTENT (1999).

§ 2.02 THE COMMERCE POWER AND ITS DEVELOPMENT

[A] The Early Commerce Clause: From the Founding to the 1930s

NOTE ON THE ORIGINS OF THE COMMERCE POWER

The Economic Motivations for the Constitutional Conventions. Contrary to popular impressions, the protection of individual liberties was not the motive for the Constitutional Convention. The Bill of Rights, notwithstanding its importance, was added by amendments. Instead, economic conditions in the post-Revolutionary War era, under the Articles of Confederation, were the primary motivation. A postwar depression produced severe friction between classes of people who considered themselves creditors and those who sympathized with debtors, producing state legislation and monetary policies aimed at out-of-state creditors. Trade wars were common; so were efforts to tax goods intended for shipment to other states. New Jersey, for example, lacked a major port of its own, but was situated between New York and Philadelphia, and so taxes by its bordering states led it to be compared to a "keg tapped at both ends."

The Commerce Power. The earlier Articles of Confederation denied Congress any power to regulate interstate commerce. They likewise contained no limitation upon the power of the states to regulate, or to tax, interstate commerce. The resulting abuses led the Framers to draft the Constitution differently.

[1] What is "Commerce among the Several States?": Early Development

Read U.S. Const. Art. I, § 8, cl. 3 (the commerce power). Also, consider Art. I, § 10 (restrictions on state power).

GIBBONS v. OGDEN
22 U.S. (9 Wheat.) 1 (1824)

[The New York legislature granted Livingston and Fulton the exclusive right to navigate waters of the state by steam vessel. Ogden acquired this exclusive right by assignment from Livingston and Fulton. He sought an injunction to prevent Gibbons from operating a competing steamship service between New York City and Elizabethtown, New Jersey, under a federal license allowing his boats to be used "in the coasting trade." This license was issued pursuant to the Federal Licensing Act, and Gibbons claimed that it protected his right to engage in the trade. The New York courts upheld the state law creating Ogden's monopoly as constitutional and granted the injunction. Gibbons appealed. In this opinion, the Supreme Court reverses on the basis of the commerce clause.]

MR. CHIEF JUSTICE MARSHALL delivered the opinion of the Court. . . .

The subject to be regulated is commerce; and our constitution being, as was aptly said at the bar, one of enumeration, and not of definition, to ascertain the extent of the power it becomes necessary to settle the meaning of the word. The counsel for the appellee would limit it to traffic, to buying and selling, or the interchange of commodities, and do not admit that it comprehends navigation. This would restrict a general term, applicable to many objects, to one of its significations. Commerce, undoubtedly, is traffic, but it is something more; it is intercourse. It describes the commercial intercourse between nations, and parts of nations, in all its branches, and is regulated by prescribing rules for carrying on that intercourse. . . .

. . . All America understands, and has uniformly understood, the word "commerce" to comprehend navigation. It was so understood, and must have been so understood, when the constitution was framed. The power over commerce, including navigation, was one of the primary objects for which the people of America adopted their government, and must have been contemplated in forming it. . . .

To what commerce does this power extend? The constitution informs us, to commerce "with foreign nations, and among the several states, and with the Indian tribes."

It has, we believe, been universally admitted that these words comprehend every species of commercial intercourse between the United States and foreign nations. No sort of trade can be carried on between this country and any other, to which this power does not extend. . . .

The subject to which the power is next applied, is to commerce "among the several states." The word "among" means intermingled with. A thing which is among others, is intermingled with them. Commerce among the states cannot stop at the external boundary line of each state, but may be introduced into the interior.

It is not intended to say that these words comprehend that commerce which is completely internal, which is carried on between man and man in a state, or between different parts of the same state, and which does not extend to or affect other states. Such a power would be inconvenient, and is certainly unnecessary.

Comprehensive as the word "among" is, it may very properly be restricted to that commerce which concerns more states than one. The phrase is not one which would probably have been selected to indicate the completely interior traffic of a state, because it is not an apt phrase for that purpose; and the enumeration of the particular classes of commerce to which the power was to be extended, would not have been made had the intention been to extend the power to every description. . . . The completely internal commerce of a state, then may be considered as reserved for the state itself.

But, in regulating commerce with foreign nations, the power of Congress does not stop at the jurisdictional lines of the several states. It would be a very useless power if it could not pass those lines. The commerce of the United States with foreign nations, is that of the whole United States. Every district has a right to participate in it. The deep streams which penetrate our country in every direction, pass through the interior of almost every state in the Union, and furnish the means of exercising this right. . . . If it exists within the states, if a foreign voyage may commence or terminate at a port within a state, then the power of Congress may be exercised within a state. . . .

We are now arrived at the inquiry, What is this power?

It is the power to regulate; that is, to prescribe the rule by which commerce is to be governed. This power, like all others vested in Congress, is complete in itself, may be exercised to its utmost extent, and acknowledges no limitations, other than are prescribed in the constitution. . . . The wisdom and the discretion of Congress, their identity with the people, and the influence which their constituents possess at elections, are, in this, as in many other instances, as that, for example, of declaring war, the sole restraints on which they have relied, to secure them from its abuse. They are the restraints on which the people must often rely solely, in all representative governments. . . .

[The Court went on to examine the act of Congress by which Gibbons was licensed to ply the "coasting trade." It concluded that the act and license authorized him to conduct the steamship operations he was conducting, in spite of New York's prohibition. "[T]he act of a state inhibiting the use of [navigable waters or ports] to any vessel having a license under the act of Congress comes, we think, in direct collision with that act," and hence the New York monopoly was invalid.

[The Court's extensive consideration of the commerce clause as a restriction on the powers of the states is omitted here and is considered separately in Chapter 3, below. The concurring opinion of Justice Johnson is also omitted.]

[*Reversed.*]

NOTES AND QUESTIONS

(1) *Popular Reaction. Gibbons v. Ogden* has been described as "the only popular [decision] which Marshall ever rendered." Dangerfield, *The Steamboat Case, in* QUARRELS THAT HAVE SHAPED THE CONSTITUTION 49, 60–61 (J. Garraty ed. 1966). It resulted in an explosion in numbers of interstate steamships, particularly traveling about New York, where few before had existed, and in reductions of fares. Perhaps more importantly, "the railroad, the telegraph, the telephone, the oil and the gas pipelines, the airplane, as they moved across state borders, all came under the protection of *Gibbons v. Ogden.*" *Id.* Even so, critics of the decision ranged from those who profited from the slave trade and foresaw federal intervention to statesmen such as Thomas Jefferson, who saw it as validating excessive federal power.

(2) *"Commerce" as "Intercourse"—Are Intangibles, such as Insurance Contracts, Included?: Paul v. Virginia, 75 U.S. (8 Wall.) 168 (1869).* Marshall's definition of commerce as "intercourse" would seem to reach virtually any contract or transaction, whether it concerned tangibles or intangibles, business or pleasure. However, a Court more disposed to the limiting of Congressional power emerged under the leadership of Chief Justice Chase in the latter half of the nineteenth century; and in *Paul,* the Court held that insurance contracts, even if interstate, did not involve "articles of commerce" and hence were subject to state but (by implication) not federal regulation. This odd decision was overruled in modern times by *United States v. South Eastern Underwriters Ass'n,* 322 U.S. 533 (1944).

(3) *Commerce "Among" the Several States as "That Commerce that Concerns More States than One:" Hanley v. Kansas City Southern Ry Co., 187 U.S. 617 (1903).* Imagine transportation between two points within the same state in which part of the route is a loop outside the state; is the trip "commerce among the several states"? Yes, the Court held, in *Hanley, supra.* What about a telegraphic message sent from one point in North

Carolina to another over wires that cross a point in Virginia? *See Western Union Tel. Co. v. Speight*, 254 U.S. 17 (1920) (held, yes; following *Hanley*). What about baggage porter services performed entirely within a state at the point of departure on an interstate trip? *See New York, N.H. & H. R. Co. v. Nothnagle*, 346 U.S. 128 (1953) (held, yes). Note that Marshall interprets "among the several states" as applying to "that commerce which concerns more states than one."

(4) *The Concept of "Plenary" Powers.* The *Gibbons* decision developed the interpretation of the interstate commerce power. It also contained a famous (and often-cited) general description of all the "plenary" powers of Congress. The Court described Congressional power as "plenary" because "it is complete in itself, may be exercised to its utmost extent, and acknowledges no limitations, other than are prescribed in the constitution." It is important to understand that plenary powers analysis has traditionally assumed that a Congressional power is "complete in itself."

Even so, there still remains a question whether all powers of Congress are "plenary." Under *Gibbons*, it would seem that all Article I, Section 8 powers (like the interstate commerce power) are plenary. But, what about powers granted elsewhere in the basic constitutional text? Also, what about powers granted to Congress by various Amendments? Further discussion can be deferred until you study the *Flores* decision in Chapter 14.02.

THE DANIEL BALL, 77 U.S. (10 Wall.) 557 (1871). The Daniel Ball was a small vessel operating entirely within the State of Michigan. She shuttled on the Grand River between the cities of Grand Rapids and Grand Haven, was constructed so as to draw only two feet of water, and was incapable of navigating the waters of Lake Michigan. However, it was admitted that some items that she carried were destined ultimately for places outside Michigan, or originated outside. The Court held that the Daniel Ball was required to be inspected and licensed under applicable federal laws and that the extension of federal authority over it did not exceed the commerce power:

> There is, undoubtedly, an internal commerce which is subject to the control of the States. . . . [I]nasmuch as [the Daniel Ball's] agency in the transportation was entirely within the limits of the State, and she did not run in connection with, or in continuation of, any line of vessels or railway leading to other States, it is contended that she was engaged entirely in domestic commerce. But this conclusion does not follow. So far as she was employed in transporting goods destined for other States, or goods brought from without the limits of Michigan and destined to places within that State, she was engaged in commerce between the States, and however limited that commerce may have been, she was, so far as it went, subject to the legislation of Congress. She was employed as an instrument of that commerce. . . . The fact that several different and independent agencies are employed in transporting the commodity, some acting entirely in one State, and some acting through two or more States, does in no respect alter the character of the transaction. To the extent in which each agency acts in that transportation, it is subject to the regulation of Congress.

NOTES AND QUESTIONS

(1) *"Between" the States: Must the Activity Cross a State Line?* The *Daniel Ball* refers to commerce "between" states, which sounds more restrictive than commerce "among" the several states. The word implies, perhaps, that the crossing of a state line might be necessary in the activity regulated, although the holding contradicts this inference. But it prompts the question: Would the Daniel Ball have been subject to Congress' power if it never carried goods that were shipped interstate, but if it competed with or otherwise affected interstate shipping by others? The modern answer, as we shall see from cases that follow, is yes.

(2) *Is there any Non-Interstate Commerce Left?* A vessel like the Daniel Ball probably could never escape being in interstate commerce, if it carries even some

articles that somebody else ultimately carries in interstate commerce. Thus, the petitioners in *The Daniel Ball* argued that "if the position here asserted be sustained, [C]ongress may take the entire control of the commerce of the country." Is this contention correct?

[2] The Commerce Power during the "Dual Federalism" Era: From the Late 1800s to the 1930s

INTRODUCTORY NOTE: THE DUAL FEDERALISM ERA

The Interstate Commerce Act, the Sherman Act, and Dual Federalism: A Stricter View of the Commerce Power. In the late 1800s, Congress vastly increased the potential reach of federal law by enacting the Interstate Commerce Act, which created an important independent regulatory commission, and by the Sherman Antitrust Act. It also attempted to exert authority over certain kinds of harmful or morally objectionable products. These actions prompted closer judicial scrutiny. In fact, the Court tended to regard regulatory power as split into two distinct parts: Congress' power and state power. In some cases, the Court's analysis tended to view these different arenas as non-overlapping. If state regulatory power existed, federal power, according to this theory, did not. Hence the name, dual federalism. The difficulty was that the real world rarely categorizes itself so neatly.

"Manufacturing" as Distinguished from Commerce. One cornerstone of the dual federalism approach was to treat manufacturing as excluded from the commerce power. The states, under this theory, could regulate manufacturing, but Congress could not. Again, the world rarely is so neatly divided.

UNITED STATES v. E.C. KNIGHT CO., 156 U.S. 1 (1895). The Government alleged that the defendants had conspired to monopolize the manufacture of refined sugar in violation of the Sherman Antitrust Act. The Court upheld a dismissal of the complaint because "it does not follow that an attempt to monopolize [t]he manufacture was an attempt . . . to monopolize commerce." The effect was not sufficiently "direct" upon interstate commerce—and "manufacturing" was not "commerce":

> The regulation of commerce applies to the subjects of commerce and not to matters of internal police. Contracts to buy, sell, or exchange goods to be transported among the several states, the transportation and its instrumentalities . . . may be regulated, but this is because they form part of interstate trade or commerce. The fact that an article is manufactured for export to another state does not itself make it an article of interstate commerce. . . .

> In *Gibbons v. Ogden,* . . . and other cases often cited, the state laws, which were held inoperative, were instances of direct interference with . . . interstate or international commerce; yet in [other cases], state legislation which . . . affected interstate commerce and persons engaged in it, has been frequently sustained because the interference was not direct. . . .

THE SHREVEPORT RATE CASE (HOUSTON, EAST & WEST TEXAS RY. v. UNITED STATES)
234 U.S. 342 (1914)

[The Texas Railroad Commission prescribed commodity rates for intrastate railroad carriage between Houston or Dallas and points in east Texas. These rates were much lower than rates between Shreveport, Louisiana, and points in Texas of comparable distance. Shreveport competed with Dallas and Houston for the trade of the intervening territory, and the Interstate Commerce Commission found that the lower intrastate rates "unjustly discriminated in favor of traffic within the state of Texas." For example, "a rate of 60 cents carried first-class traffic a distance of 160 miles to the eastward from Dallas, while the same rate would carry the same class of traffic only 55 miles into Texas from Shreveport. The first-class rate from Houston to Lufkin, Texas, 118.2 miles, was 50 cents per 100 pounds, while the rate from Shreveport to the same point, 112.5 miles, was 69 cents."

[An Act of Congress gives the Interstate Commerce Commission broad authority to set aside any "unreasonable preference" or discrimination by a railroad. Therefore, at the same time that it set interstate rates from Shreveport to Texas points, the Commission invalidated the intrastate Texas rates. In this opinion, the Supreme Court upholds this action under the commerce power.]

Mr. Justice Hughes delivered the opinion of the Court:. . . .

The point of the objection to the order is that, as the discrimination found by the Commission to be unjust arises out of the relation of intrastate rates, maintained under state authority, to interstate rates that have been upheld as reasonable, its correction was beyond the Commission's power. Manifestly the order might be complied with, and the discrimination avoided, either by reducing the interstate rates from Shreveport to the level of the competing intrastate rates, or by raising these intrastate rates to the level of the interstate rates, or by such reduction in the one case and increase in the other as would result in equality. The holding [below] was that the order relieved the appellants from further obligation to observe the intrastate rates, and that they were at liberty to comply with the Commission's requirements by increasing these rates sufficiently to remove the forbidden discrimination. The invalidity of the order in this aspect is challenged upon [the ground] [t]hat Congress is impotent to control the intrastate charges of an interstate carrier even to the extent necessary to prevent injurious discrimination against interstate traffic. . . .

. . . It is of the essence of [Congress' commerce] power that, where it exists, it dominates. Interstate trade was not left to be destroyed or impeded by the rivalries of local government. The purpose was to make impossible the recurrence of the evils which had overwhelmed the Confederation, and to provide the necessary basis of national unity by insuring "uniformity of regulation against conflicting and discriminating state legislation." By virtue of the comprehensive terms of the grant, the authority of Congress is at all times adequate to meet the varying exigencies that arise, and to protect the national interest by securing the freedom of interstate commercial intercourse from local control. *Gibbons v. Ogden*. . . .

. . . Its authority, extending to these interstate carriers as instruments of interstate commerce, necessarily embraces the right to control their operations in all matters having such a close and substantial relation to interstate traffic that the control is essential or appropriate to the security of that traffic, to the efficiency of the interstate service, and to the maintenance of conditions under which interstate commerce may be conducted upon fair terms and without molestation or hindrance.

. . . Wherever the interstate and intrastate transactions of carriers are so related that the government of the one involves the control of the other, it is Congress, and not the state, that is entitled to prescribe the final and dominant rule, for otherwise Congress would be denied the exercise of its constitutional authority, and the state, and not the nation, would be supreme within the national field. . . .

[Here, the Court discusses two previous decisions: *Baltimore & O. Ry. Co. v. ICC*, 221 U.S. 612 (1911), in which regulation of the hours of labor of interstate workers was extended also to intrastate ones because it was impractical to separate them, and *Southern Ry. Co. v. United States*, 222 U.S. 20 (1911), upholding extension of the Safety Appliance Act to intrastate rail operations to enhance the safety of interstate traffic.]

While these decisions sustaining the Federal power relate to measures adopted in the interest of the safety of persons and property, they illustrate the principle that Congress in the exercise of its paramount power, may prevent the common instrumentalities of interstate and intrastate commercial intercourse from being used in their intrastate operations to the injury of interstate commerce. This is not to say that Congress possesses the authority to regulate the internal commerce of a state, as such, but that it does possess the power to foster and protect interstate commerce, and to take all measures necessary or appropriate to that end, although intrastate transactions of interstate carriers may thereby be controlled.

This principle is applicable here. We find no reason to doubt that Congress is entitled to keep the highways of interstate communication open to interstate traffic upon fair and equal terms. . . . It is immaterial, so far as the protecting power of Congress is concerned, that the discrimination arises from intrastate rates as compared with interstate rates. . . .

It is to be noted [t]hat the power to deal with the relation between the two kinds of rates, as a relation, lies exclusively with Congress. . . . It is for Congress to supply the needed correction where the relation between intrastate and interstate rates presents the evil to be corrected, and this it may do completely, by reason of its control over the interstate carrier in all matters having such a close and substantial relation to interstate commerce that it is necessary or appropriate to exercise the control for the effective government of that commerce. . . .

[W]e conclude that the order of the Commission now in question cannot be held invalid upon the ground that it exceeded the authority which Congress could lawfully confer.

NOTES AND QUESTIONS

(1) *The "Direct Effect" Test of E.C. Knight versus the "Close and Substantial Relationship" Test of Shreveport.* Notice that in *E.C. Knight* (the manufacturing case), the Court distinguished between state and federal power by whether the effect on interstate commerce was "direct." Is the Court's later decision in *Shreveport* consistent with this "direct effect" test? Notice that the regulated railroad rates at issue were entirely intrastate, and it is only by virtue of their effect on interstate rates that the ICC can regulate them—but is this effect "direct"? The *Shreveport* Court does not overrule *E.C. Knight*, but it uses a different approach: it asks whether the regulation has a "close and substantial relation" to interstate commerce. This test appears to allow a wider scope of power over commerce for Congress. Which approach is the more accurate interpretation of the Constitution?

(2) *The "Current of Commerce" Theory: Swift & Co. v. United States, 196 U.S. 375 (1905).* The Government alleged that Swift and others conspired not to bid against each other in order to fix prices in stockyards in which they purchased cattle. The activity in question took place entirely within a single state. Justice Holmes, for the Court, upheld the application of the Sherman Act: "[C]ommerce among the States is not just a technical legal concept, but a practical one, drawn from the course of business. When cattle are sent for sale from a place in one State, with the expectation that they will end their transit, after purchase, in another, and when in effect they do so, with only the interruption necessary to find a purchaser . . ., the current thus existing is a current of commerce among the States. . . ." Is this test helpful? [Wouldn't it apply to manufacturing, if manufacturing is part of the "current of commerce?" Does the test furnish any practical limits upon the commerce power?]

(3) *When is an Interstate Journey Not Interstate Commerce?— During the Cab Ride to the Railroad Station: United States v. Yellow Cab Co., 332 U.S. 218, 230–32 (1947).* In this case, the Court held that a taxicab ride to the railroad station, to start an interstate journey, was not interstate commerce; and therefore, monopolization of local cab service could not be prohibited by the Federal antitrust laws:

In a sense, of course, a traveler starts an interstate journey when he boards a conveyance near his home. . . . Indeed, the terminal points of an interstate journey may be traced even further to the moment when the traveler leaves

[h]is room or office and descends [t]he building by elevator.

But interstate commerce is an intensely practical concept drawn from the normal and accepted course of business. . . .

Here we believe that the common understanding is that a traveler [b]egins his interstate movement when he boards the train at the station and that his journey ends when he disembarks at the station in the city of destination. What happens prior or subsequent to that rail journey [i]s not a constituent part of the interstate movement. The traveler has complete freedom to arrive at or leave the station by taxicab, trolley, bus, subway, elevated train, private automobile, his own two legs, or various other means of conveyance. [Taxicab service] is contracted for independently of the railroad journey and may be utilized whenever the traveler so desires. [T]o the taxicab driver, it is just another local fare.

Note the contrast between this holding and *The Daniel Ball*, above. Also, consider whether this holding is consistent with the current of commerce theory set out in the preceding note.

(4) *Commerce as Including Professional Football Leagues—but Not Professional Baseball(!?)* In *Federal Baseball Club v. National League*, 259 U.S. 200 (1922), the Court held that professional baseball involved "personal activity" by players rather than commerce, and the fact that they travelled interstate in order to accomplish the object did not make it subject to Congress' power. Professional baseball thus was exempt from the antitrust laws. Later, in *Toolson v. New York Yankees*, 346 U.S. 356 (1953), the Court noted that Congress had considered the question and had not itself, since *Federal Baseball Club*, acted to cover baseball by the antitrust laws—and so, "[w]ithout re-examination of the underlying issues," the Court affirmed "on the authority of *Federal Baseball Club* . . . so far as that decision determines that Congress had no intention of including the business of baseball within the scope of the federal antitrust laws." Then, in *Radovich v. National Football League*, 352 U.S. 445 (1957), the Court held that professional football was commerce and was subject to the antitrust laws. What part of this reasoning is correct? *Cf. Flood v. Kuhn*, 407 U.S. 258 (1972) (upholding baseball's antitrust exemption because of Congressional inaction, although the Chief Justice expressed "grave reservations" and three Justices argued that the Court should "admit the error" of *Federal Baseball Club*).

NOTE ON THE POLICE POWER

States' Control over "Matters of Internal Police." As the *E.C. Knight* case indicates, the Court conceived of states as having power over "matters of internal police," which was different, in its view at that time, from the commerce power of Congress. The police power is difficult to define. In some usages it refers to the states' authority to protect the health, welfare or morals of the people; it also connotes the regulation of particularly local matters.

Police Power versus Economic Regulation: Congressional Bans on Interstate Trade of a Harmful or Objectionable Nature. Constitutional issues arose, however, when Congress sought to prohibit trade in articles that were viewed as harmful or morally objectionable. When Congress invoked a flat prohibition upon a given activity, there was the question whether Congress was "regulating"—or whether it was doing something else. Could Congress destroy a given kind of trade as an adjunct of its power to regulate it? And there was the related question whether Congress could use the commerce power to address moral evils.

Police Power and the Negative Commerce Clause. It should not be forgotten that the police power defines the scope of state power in many cases. We shall return to the question of state power, and consider the validity of state regulation affecting interstate commerce, in the next chapter.

CHAMPION v. AMES (THE LOTTERY CASE)
188 U.S. 321 (1903)

[Appellant Champion was convicted of violating the Federal Lottery Act of 1895, which made it a crime to cause lottery tickets to be "carried from one state to another." By habeas corpus, he challenged the constitutionality of the Act on the theory that it exceeded the powers of Congress. The Supreme Court first heard argument in 1901. Apparently, the case produced significant controversy within the Court, which ordered reargument that year, then ordered a second reargument in 1902, and did not decide the case until 1903—and then by a five-to-four margin.]

Mr. Justice Harlan delivered the opinion of the Court: . . .

We have said that the carrying from state to state of lottery tickets constitutes interstate commerce, and that the regulation of such commerce is within the power of Congress under the Constitution. Are we prepared to say that a provision which is, in effect, a *prohibition* of the carriage of such articles from state to state is not a fit or appropriate mode for the *regulation* of that particular kind of commerce? . . .

In determining whether regulation may not under some circumstances properly take the form or have the effect of prohibition, the nature of the interstate traffic which it was sought by the act of May 2d, 1895, to suppress cannot be overlooked. When enacting that statute Congress no doubt shared the views upon the subject of lotteries heretofore expressed by this court. In *Phalen v. Virginia*, 8 How. 163, 168, after observing that the suppression of nuisances injurious to public health or morality is among the most important duties of government, this court said: "Experience has shown that the common forms of gambling are comparatively innocuous when placed in contrast with the widespread pestilence of lotteries. The former are confined to a few persons and places, but the latter infests the whole community; it enters every dwelling; it reaches every class; it preys upon the hard earnings of the poor; it plunders the ignorant and simple. . . ."

If it be said that the [lottery act] of 1895 is inconsistent with the 10th Amendment, . . . the answer is that the power to regulate commerce among the states has been expressly delegated to Congress.

Besides, Congress, by that act, does not assume to interfere with traffic or commerce in lottery tickets carried on exclusively within the limits of any state, but has in view only commerce of that kind among the several states. . . . [C]ongress only supplemented the action of those states perhaps all of them which, for the protection of the public morals, prohibit the drawing of lotteries, as well as the sale or circulation of lottery tickets, within their respective limits. It said, in effect, that it would not permit the declared policy of the states, which sought to protect their people against the mischiefs of the lottery business, to be overthrown or disregarded by the agency of interstate commerce. . . .

Mr. Chief Justice Fuller, with whom concur Mr. Justice Brewer, Mr. Justice Shiras, and Mr. Justice Peckham, dissenting: . . .

An invitation to dine, or to take a drive, or a note of introduction, all become articles of commerce under the ruling in this case, by being deposited with an express company for transportation. This in effect breaks down all the differences between that which is, and that which is not, an article of commerce, and the necessary consequence is to take from the states all jurisdiction over the subject so far as interstate communication is concerned. It is a long step in the direction of wiping out all traces of state lines, and the creation of a centralized government. . . .

NOTES AND QUESTIONS

(1) *Importance of the Lottery Case.* This case confirmed the authority of Congress, over the objection that it was exercising a kind of "national police power," to prohibit articles of commerce from interstate trade—and perhaps more importantly, to define which articles were harmful or objectionable, within limits. This power could be claimed as the basis for a wide variety of different kinds of regulation that might otherwise be seen as prohibited; and it was so claimed, with mixed results.

(2) *Reliance on the Lottery Case to Prohibit Objectionable Articles or Activities: Hoke v. United States, 227 U.S. 308 (1913).* In *Hoke*, the Court upheld the Mann Act, which prohibits transportation of women across state lines for prostitution or other immoral purposes, and it relied on the *Lottery Case* in doing so. In *Caminetti v. United States*, 242 U.S. 470 (1917), it extended this result to noncommercial applications of the Mann Act. In *Hipolite Egg Co. v. United States*, 220 U.S. 45 (1911), the Court upheld the Pure Food and Drug Act, which prohibited not only interstate transportation of adulterated food and drugs, but also their intrastate sale and use in some circumstances.

(3) *The Child Labor Case.* In the decision that follows, the Court sharply limited this expansion of the commerce power, using the Tenth Amendment to do so.

Read U.S. Const. Amend. X (reservation of powers to states and people).

HAMMER v. DAGENHART (THE CHILD LABOR CASE), 247 U.S. 251 (1918). A federal statute prohibited interstate shipment of any article from a firm that within the preceding thirty days had employed children under fourteen (or had employed children fourteen to sixteen except under specified hours and conditions). Plaintiff Dagenhart, as next friend of his children, sued to enjoin enforcement of this statute on the ground that it exceeded the commerce power and, also, violated the tenth amendment. The district court held the statute unconstitutional. In this opinion, on appeal, the Supreme Court affirms the holding of unconstitutionality.

In *Gibbons v. Ogden*, Chief Justice Marshall [s]aid:

It is the power to regulate, that is, to prescribe the rule by which commerce is to be governed." In other words, the power is one to control the means by which commerce is carried on, which is directly the contrary of the assumed right to forbid commerce from moving and thus destroy it as to particular commodities. . . .

In [the Lottery Case], the use of interstate transportation was necessary to the accomplishment of harmful results. In other words, although the power over interstate transportation was to regulate, that could only be accomplished by prohibiting the use of the facilities of interstate commerce to effect the evil intended.

This element is wanting in the present case. . . . The act in its effect does not regulate transportation among the states, but aims to standardize the ages at which children may be employed in mining and manufacturing within the states. The goods shipped are of themselves harmless. . . .

It is further contended that the authority of Congress may be exerted to control interstate commerce in the shipment of child-made goods because of the effect of the circulation of such goods in other states where the evil of this class of labor has been recognized by local legislation. . . . In other words, that the unfair competition thus engendered may be controlled by closing the channels of interstate commerce to manufacturers in those states where the local laws do not meet what Congress deems to be the more just standard of other states.

There is no power vested in Congress to require the states to exercise their police power so as to prevent possible unfair competition. . . .

In our view the necessary effect of this act is [t]o regulate the hours of labor of children in factories and mines within the states, a purely state authority. . . .

Mr. Justice Holmes dissented:

[I] had thought that the propriety of the exercise of a power admitted to exist in some cases was for the consideration of Congress alone, and that this court always had disavowed the right to intrude its judgment upon questions of policy or morals. . . .

The act does not meddle with anything belonging to the states. . . . But when they seek to send their products across the state line they are no longer within their rights. [U]nder the Constitution such commerce belongs not to the states, but to Congress to regulate. It may carry out its views of public policy whatever indirect effect they may have upon the activities of the states. . . .

NOTES AND QUESTIONS

(1) *Distinguishing the Child Labor Case from the Lottery Case and the Mann Act Case, etc.* In what ways is the Child Labor Case distinguishable from *Champion v. Ames* (the Lottery Case), *Hoke v. United States* (the Mann Act Case), or *Hipolite Egg Co. v. United States* (the Pure Food and Drug Act Case)? Undoubtedly you have noted that in each of those cases, the arguable harm occurred in the state where the product was used or activity undertaken, whereas in the Child Labor Case the harm was at the site of production or manufacture. Should that distinction make a difference? But notice that, in the Child Labor Case, proponents of the law can make a much stronger argument that states with protective regulation are at a competitive disadvantage. The Court rejected that reasoning; should it have?

(2) *The Child Labor Tax Case— The Court Again Frustrates Congress' Effort to Reduce Child Labor: Bailey v. Drexel Furniture Co., 259 U.S. 126 (1922).* Congress promptly responded to the Child Labor decision by enacting a tax upon employers who used child labor. This enactment, of course, was based upon the taxing power, which is not linked to commerce or to interstate activity. The Court held that the enactment involved a "penalty" rather than a "tax" and invalidated it. We shall reconsider this decision in the section on the taxing power, below.

[B]   The Great Depression, the New Deal, and the Direct-Indirect Effects Doctrine: A Case Study in the Need to Limit Constitutional Law

NOTE ON THE BACKGROUND TO THE *SCHECHTER POULTRY* CASE

The National Recovery Act as a Response to the Great Depression. When the early 1930s saw the national economy slide into deep depression, it was perhaps natural that many looked to the national government to solve the problem, whether or not it fit within the notions of "commerce" found in the more restrictive decisions of the Supreme Court. President Franklin D. Roosevelt promised a "New Deal," and as a key ingredient of that policy, Congress enacted the National Industrial Recovery Act of 1933. The Act contained provisions for minimum wages, maximum hours, collective bargaining, consumer protection, and industrial codes prohibiting unfair competition. The New Dealers hoped to break the disastrous spiral of deflation by raising wages, and in addition they "primed the pump" by large public works expenditures. The National Recovery Administration, which had responsibility for implementation of the

Act, authorized employers to display the sign of the Blue Eagle, and the slogan, "We Do Our Part," which signified compliance with the applicable industrial code.

The Industrial Codes. The NRA sought to negotiate codes of fair competition within each industry together with representatives of business, labor, and consumer interests (although it often was charged that the views of the former generally prevailed). When approved by the President, these codes had the force of law and carried criminal penalties for their violation. Eventually, the codes covered not only concentrated heavy industries such as steel and automobiles but also such lesser ones as the burlesque theatre, corncob pipe, and animal soft-hair industries (the last employed only forty-five persons, but had its own detailed set of regulations). Many of the codes set minimum prices, prohibited rebates, or even limited production quotas; consumer protection regulations in the macaroni industry prohibited noodles of less than 5.5 percent egg, artificially colored, or wrapped in yellow paper.

The Poultry Industry and the Schechter Case. The Code of Fair Competition for the Live Poultry Industry of the Metropolitan Area in and about the City of New York was an example of the proliferation of the codes. It prohibited the selling of uninspected or unfit birds, set minimum wages of fifty cents an hour, set maximum hours of forty-eight per week, and regulated such odd practices as "straight killing" (the customer had to accept "run of the coop," or birds selected by chance, rather than choose the best). The four Schechter brothers, some of whom had survived testifying as witnesses at early federal racketeering trials and had maintained a living in the gangster-ridden, cutthroat competition of the New York poultry industry of the 1930s, were convicted before a jury of violating provisions of the Metropolitan Area code dealing with straight killing, wages and hours, and diseased chickens, of which witnesses testified that they had sold thousands of pounds at four to eight cents below market prices. The conviction was upheld by the Court of Appeals, and it became the test case for the NRA when it reached the Supreme Court. The Schechters' lawyer, during argument, explained straight killing: " . . . you have got to put your hand in the coop and take out whichever chicken comes to you. . . ." Justice McReynolds ominously inquired, "And it was for that your client was convicted?" "Yes," was the response, "and fined $5, 000 and given three months in jail." *See generally* Friedel, *The Sick Chicken Case, in* QUARRELS THAT HAVE SHAPED THE CONSTITUTION 191 (J. Garraty ed. 1966). The result was the following opinion.

A.L.A. SCHECHTER POULTRY CORP. v. UNITED STATES, 295 U.S. 495 (1935). A unanimous Court reversed the eighteen-count convictions of the corporation and its principals for various violations of the Metropolitan Area Code. Chief Justice Hughes' opinion held that enforcement of the Code in these circumstances exceeded the commerce power:

> . . . Extraordinary conditions may call for extraordinary remedies. But . . . [e]xtraordinary conditions do not create or enlarge constitutional power. . . . Such assertions of extra-constitutional authority were anticipated and precluded by the explicit terms of the Tenth Amendment. . . .

> Were these transactions *"in"* interstate commerce? [A]lmost all the poultry coming to New York is sent there from other states. But the code provisions, as here applied, do not concern the transportation of the poultry. . . . [It] was trucked to [defendants'] slaughterhouses in Brooklyn for local disposition. The interstate transaction in relation to that poultry then ended. . . .

> The undisputed facts thus afford no warrant for the argument that the poultry handled by defendants at their slaughterhouse markets was in a "current" or "flow" of interstate commerce. . . . *See Swift & Co. v. United States.* . . .

> Did the defendants' transactions directly "affect" interstate commerce. . . ? The power of Congress extends not only to the regulation of transactions which are part of interstate commerce, but to the protection of the commerce from

injury. . . . We have held that, in dealing with common carriers, the dominant authority of Congress necessarily embraces the right to control their intrastate operations in all matters having a close and substantial relationship to interstate commerce. . . . *The Shreveport Case.* . . .

[T]here is a necessary and well-established distinction between direct and indirect effects. . . . [W]here the effect of intrastate transactions is merely indirect, such transactions remain within the domain of state power. . . .

The Government also makes the point that efforts to enact state legislation establishing high labor standards have been impeded by the belief that unless similar action is taken generally, commerce will be diverted from the states adopting such standards. . . .

It is not the province of the Court to consider the economic advantages of such a centralized system. It is sufficient to say that the Federal Constitution does not provide for it. . . .

NOTES AND QUESTIONS

(1) *Extending the Schechter Holding and the Direct-Indirect Effects Doctrine: Carter v. Carter Coal Co., 298 U.S. 238 (1936).* Shortly after *Schechter*, the Court used similar direct-indirect reasoning to strike down wage and hour regulations promulgated pursuant to the Bituminous Coal Conservation Act of 1935, which was a response to the depressed condition of the coal industry. Justice Sutherland, for the Court, reasoned, "The word 'direct' implies that the activity or condition invoked or blamed shall operate proximately—not mediately, remotely, or collaterally—to produce the effect." Coal mining was "production" and was not itself commerce.

(2) *Invalidating the Agricultural Adjustment Act: United States v. Butler, 297 U.S. 1 (1936).* In the same time period, the Court struck down the Agricultural Adjustment Act. The *Butler* case, in which this result was reached, is considered below in connection with the spending power.

(3) *President Roosevelt's Response to the Schechter Decision: National Economic Problems versus a "Horse-and-Buggy" Court.* The immediate holding of *Schechter* was not a serious problem for the administration; actually the NRA had become an administrative nightmare. The Act was about to expire without administration efforts at renewal. But the *Schechter* reasoning was a disaster for the New Deal. President Roosevelt said that its implications were "more important than any decision probably since the *Dred Scott* case." "The big issue," he added, "is this: Does this decision mean that the United States has no control over any national economic problem?" The United States was the only country in the world that had not determined how it was to proceed in addressing national economic problems, "and we have been relegated to the horse-and-buggy definition of interstate commerce." The phrase "horse and buggy" found its way "into newspaper headlines throughout the country." Friedel, *The Sick Chicken Case, supra,* at 207–208.

(4) *The Court Packing Plan.* The President also proposed a forceful solution to the problem. After his landslide re-election in 1936, he proposed legislation that would have allowed appointment of an additional Supreme Court Justice for each sitting justice over seventy years of age who had served for ten years, until there were fifteen justices, or six more than before. Not coincidentally, there were six sitting justices over seventy years old who had more than ten years' service, so that President Roosevelt would instantly have six appointments to make and, with existing justices who were thought favorable to most New Deal legislation, a clear majority on the Court. The Constitution does not specify the number of justices but, as might be expected, this transparent effort to change the existing number to change the majority elicited strong opposition. The plan ultimately was defeated in Congress, but the defeat was due partly to the changes

of position of some justices, who shifted the majority of the Court. Chief Justice Hughes and Justice Roberts are generally credited with changing their views. See below.

[C] Expansion and Breakthrough: National Economic Problems as Objects of the Commerce Power

NLRB v. JONES & LAUGHLIN STEEL CORP., 301 U.S. 1 (1936). The National Labor Relations Act protected union organizing activities as well as collective bargaining. It was a response to breakdowns in the national economy due to violent labor disputes, which Congress sought to channel instead into the mechanisms set up by the Act. Chief Justice Hughes' opinion for the Court upheld the Act as a valid exercise of the commerce power. Jones and Laughlin's business involved coal from one state or from another, and steel production in yet another. Although recognizing that the stream-of-commerce rationale might apply to Jones & Laughlin's sprawling, nationwide business, the Chief Justice "[did] not find it necessary" to address that issue, resting decision instead on a broader view of the commerce power:

> The congressional authority to protect interstate commerce from burdens and obstructions is not limited to transactions which can be deemed to be a part of a "flow" of interstate or foreign commerce. Burdens and obstructions may be due to injurious action springing from other sources. The fundamental principle is that the power to regulate commerce is the power to enact "all appropriate legislation" for its protection and advancement [citing *The Daniel Ball*]. [T]hat power is plenary and may be exerted to protect interstate commerce "no matter what the source of the dangers which threaten it. . . ."

> That intrastate activities, by reason of close and intimate relation to interstate commerce, may fall within federal control is demonstrated in the case of carriers who are engaged in both interstate and intrastate transportation [citing *The Shreveport Case*]. . . .

> [T]he fact that the employees here concerned were engaged in production is not determinative. The question remains as to the effect upon interstate commerce of the labor practice involved. . . .

> Experience has abundantly demonstrated that the recognition of the right of employees to self-organization and to have representatives of their own choosing for collective bargaining is often an essential condition of industrial peace. . . . [T]he question is not essentially different in the case of employees in industries of such a character that interstate commerce is put in jeopardy from the case of transportation companies.

NOTES AND QUESTIONS

(1) *Comparing Chief Justice Hughes' Opinion in Jones & Laughlin with His Earlier Opinion in Schechter.* Is *Jones & Laughlin* consistent with *Schechter*? Earlier, Chief Justice Hughes insisted upon the direct-indirect distinction and concluded that a centralized system for stimulating commercial activity was unconstitutional. If the Chief Justice did change his views, it may be difficult to say why. Whether the court packing plan (which he vigorously opposed), or increasing disruptions of the economy by labor unrest of national impact, or new perceptions owing to reconsideration of the argument, may have been the cause is unknown. He was joined by Justices Brandeis, Stone, Cardozo, and Roberts.

(2) *Jones & Laughlin and Marshall's View in McCulloch and Gibbons.* It might be suggested that the opinion in *Jones & Laughlin* is more reminiscent of Marshall's view in such cases as *McCulloch* and *Gibbons v. Odgen* than of some precedent since Marshall. How do the two views compare?

(3) *The Dissent of the "Four Horsemen" in Jones & Laughlin.* Justices McReynolds, Van Devanter, Sutherland, and Butler (known as the "Four Horsemen" for their

persistent votes against New Deal legislation and related laws) dissented in *Jones & Laughlin*. Justice McReynolds said, "Every consideration brought forward to uphold the Act before us was applicable to support the Acts held unconstitutional in [*Schechter* and other cases]. . . . The Act puts into the hands of a Board power of control over purely local industry beyond anything heretofore deemed permissible." But soon none of the Four Horsemen remained on the Court, and thus *United States v. Darby* resulted in a unanimous Court.

UNITED STATES v. DARBY
312 U.S. 100 (1941)

Mr. Justice Stone delivered the opinion of the Court:

The two principal questions raised by the record in this case are, *first*, whether Congress has constitutional power to prohibit the shipment in interstate commerce of lumber manufactured by employees whose wages are less than a prescribed minimum or whose weekly hours of labor at that wage are greater than a prescribed maximum, and, *second*, whether it has power to prohibit the employment of workmen in the production of goods "for interstate commerce" at other than prescribed wages and hours. . . .

Appellee demurred to an indictment found in the district court for southern Georgia charging him with violation of § 15(a) (1) (2) and (5) of the Fair Labor Standards Act. . . . The district court sustained the demurrer and quashed the indictment and the case comes here on direct appeal. . . .

The Fair Labor Standards Act set up a comprehensive legislative scheme for preventing the shipment in interstate commerce of certain products and commodities produced in the United States under labor conditions as respects wages and hours which fail to conform to standards set up by the Act. Its purpose [i]s to exclude from interstate commerce goods produced for the commerce and to prevent their production for interstate commerce, under conditions detrimental to the maintenance of the minimum standards of living necessary for health and general well-being; and to prevent the use of interstate commerce as the means of competition in the distribution of goods so produced, and as the means of spreading and perpetuating such substandard labor conditions among the workers of the several states. . . .

The demurrer [c]hallenged the validity of the Fair Labor Standards Act under the Commerce Clause and the Fifth and Tenth Amendments. The district court quashed the indictment in its entirety upon the broad grounds that the Act, which it interpreted as a regulation of manufacture within the states, is unconstitutional. It declared that manufacture is not interstate commerce. . . .

The prohibition of shipment of the proscribed goods in interstate commerce. Section 15(a)(1) prohibits, and the indictment charges, the shipment in interstate commerce, of goods produced for interstate commerce by employees whose wages and hours of employment do not conform to the requirements of the Act. [T]he only question arising under the commerce clause with respect to such shipments is whether Congress has the constitutional power to prohibit them.

While manufacture is not of itself interstate commerce the shipment of manufactured goods interstate is such commerce and the prohibition of such shipment by Congress is indubitably [within its power]. . . .

[The] power to regulate commerce is the power "to prescribe the rule by which commerce is governed." *Gibbons v. Ogden*. . . . It extends not only to those regulations which aid, foster and protect the commerce, but embraces those which prohibit it. . . . It is conceded that the power of Congress to prohibit transportation in interstate commerce includes noxious articles, *Lottery Case (Champion v. Ames)*, *Hipolite Egg Co. v. United States, cf. Hoke v. United States,* . . . stolen articles, . . . kidnapped persons, . . . and articles such as intoxicating liquor or convict-made goods, traffic in which is restricted by the laws of the state of destination. . . .

But it is said that the present prohibition falls within the scope of none of these categories; that while the prohibition is nominally a regulation of the commerce, its motive or purpose is regulation of wages and hours of persons engaged in manufacture, the control of which has been reserved to the states and upon which Georgia and some of the states of destination have placed no restriction; that the effect of the present statute is not to exclude the prescribed articles from interstate commerce in aid of state regulation . . . but instead, under the guise of a regulation of interstate commerce, it undertakes to regulate wages and hours within the state contrary to the policy of the state which has elected to leave them unregulated.

The power of Congress over interstate commerce "is complete in itself, may be exercised to its utmost extent, and acknowledges no limitations other than are prescribed in the Constitution." *Gibbons v. Ogden.* . . . Congress, following its own conception of public policy concerning the restrictions which may appropriately be imposed on interstate commerce, is free to exclude from the commerce articles whose use in the states for which they are destined it may conceive to be injurious to the public health, morals or welfare, even though the state has not sought to regulate their use. . . .

Such regulation is not a forbidden invasion of state power merely because either its motive or its consequence is to restrict the use of articles of commerce within the states of destination and is not prohibited unless by other constitutional provisions. It is no objection to the assertion of the power to regulate interstate commerce that its exercise is attended by the same incidents which attend the exercise of the police power of the states. . . . The motive and purpose of a regulation of interstate commerce are matters for the legislative judgment upon the exercise of which the Constitution places no restriction and over which the courts are given no control. . . .

Whatever their motive and purpose, regulations of commerce which do not infringe some constitutional prohibition are within the plenary power conferred on Congress by the Commerce Clause. Subject only to that limitation, presently to be considered, we conclude that the prohibition of the shipment interstate of goods produced under the forbidden substandard labor conditions is within the constitutional authority of Congress.

holding

In the more than a century which has elapsed since the decision of *Gibbons v. Ogden,* these principles of constitutional interpretation have been so long and repeatedly recognized by this Court as applicable to the Commerce Clause, that there would be little occasion for repeating them now were it not for the decision of this Court twenty-two years ago in *Hammer v. Dagenhart* . . . . In that case it was held by a bare majority of the Court over the powerful and now classic dissent of Mr. Justice Holmes setting forth the fundamental issues involved, that Congress was without power to exclude the products of child labor from interstate commerce. . . .

Hammer v. Dagenhart has not been followed. The distinction on which the decision rested was that Congressional power to prohibit interstate commerce is limited to articles which in themselves have some harmful or deleterious property—a distinction which was novel when made and unsupported by any provision of the Constitution—has long since been abandoned. . . .

The conclusion is inescapable that *Hammer v. Dagenhart* was a departure from the principles which have prevailed in the interpretation of the Commerce Clause both before and since the decision and that such vitality, as a precedent, as it then had has long since been exhausted. It should be and now is overruled.

Validity of the wage and hour requirements. Section 15(a)(2), and §§ 6 and 7, require employers to conform to the wage and hour provisions with respect to all employees engaged in the production of goods for interstate commerce. As appellee's employees are not alleged to be "engaged in interstate commerce" the validity of the prohibition turns on the question whether the employment [o]f employees engaged in the production of goods for interstate commerce is so related to the commerce and so affects it as to be within the reach of the power of Congress to regulate it.

Congress may . . . by appropriate legislation regulate intrastate activities where they have a substantial effect on interstate commerce.

. . . A recent example is the National Labor Relations Act for the regulation of employer and employee relations in industries in which strikes, induced by unfair labor practices named in the Act, tend to disturb or obstruct interstate commerce. *See National Labor Relations Bd. v. Jones & Laughlin Steel Corp.* . . .

Congress, having by the present Act adopted the policy of excluding from interstate commerce all goods produced for the commerce which do not conform to the specified labor standards, it may choose the means reasonably adapted to the attainment of the permitted end, even though they involve control of intrastate activities. Such legislation has often been sustained with respect to powers, other than the commerce power granted to the national government, when the means chosen, although not themselves within the granted power, were nevertheless deemed appropriate aids to the accomplishment of some purpose within an admitted power of the national government.

. . . A familiar like exercise of power is the regulation of intrastate transactions which are so commingled with or related to interstate commerce that all must be regulated if the interstate commerce is to be effectively controlled. *Shreveport Case.* . . .

We think also that § 15(a)(2) now under consideration, is sustainable independently of § 15(a)(1), which prohibits shipment or transportation of the proscribed goods. As we have said the evils aimed at by the Act are the spread of substandard labor conditions through the use of the facilities of interstate commerce for competition by the goods so produced with those produced under the prescribed or better labor conditions; and the consequent dislocation of the commerce itself caused by the impairment or destruction of local businesses by competition made effective through interstate commerce. The Act is thus directed at the suppression of a method or kind of competition in interstate commerce which it has in effect condemned as "unfair," as the Clayton Act has condemned other "unfair methods of competition" made effective through interstate commerce. . . .

The means adopted by § 15(a)(2) for the protection of interstate commerce by the suppression of the production of the condemned goods for interstate commerce is so related to the commerce and so affects it as to be within the reach of the commerce power. . . .

So far as *Carter v. Carter Coal Co.* . . . is inconsistent with this conclusion, its doctrine is limited in principle by the decisions under the Sherman Act and the National Labor Relations Act, which we have cited and which we follow.

Our conclusion is unaffected by the Tenth Amendment. . . . The amendment states but a truism that all is retained which has not been surrendered. There is nothing in the history of its adoption to suggest that it was more than declaratory of the relationship between the national and state governments as it had been established by the Constitution before the amendment or that its purpose was other than to allay fears that the new national government might seek to exercise powers not granted, and that the states might not be able to exercise fully their reserved powers. . . .

NOTES AND QUESTIONS

(1) *The "Substantial Effect" Doctrine in Darby: How Does It Differ from Previous Approaches? Darby says that Congress may regulate intrastate activities having a "substantial effect on interstate commerce."* This formulation should be contrasted with

the direct-indirect approach of *Schechter* and the "close and substantial relation" approach of *Shreveport*.

(2) *The Commerce-Prohibiting Technique as a Means of Exercising a National Police Power: The Overruling of the Child Labor Case.* Note that the overruling of the Child Labor Case enables Congress to use its power to prohibit commerce as a means of exercising a national police power over "local" activities. The "motive" is irrelevant when Congress does so. After *Darby*, is there *any* activity that is not within the scope of this Congressional power?

(3) *Competition among States Causing Them to "Race to the Bottom" as a Proper Concern of the Commerce Power.* *Darby* accepts the so-called "race to the bottom" reasoning, or in other words the agreement that the commerce power is a necessary corrective to the tendency of the states to avoid consumer, health and safety regulations because other states that compete for the same commerce do not have similar regulations. Note that the Court expressly overrules the Child Labor decisions and limits the New Deal decisions that reject this rationale.

(4) *The Tenth Amendment as an Ineffective "Truism"* Note the Court's treatment of the Tenth Amendment as a truism. Will it, in practice, be irrelevant as a limit upon Congressional power as a result of this reasoning? *See* the cases in Chapter 3, below, limiting certain incursions upon state power.

PROBLEM B

FEDERAL REGULATION OF MARRIAGE, AS HYPOTHESIZED IN JONES & LAUGHLIN. The Court of Appeals, in *Jones & Laughlin*, rejected the Government's arguments by the observation that "almost anything—marriage, birth, and death—may in some fashion affect commerce." Justice McReynolds appended this opinion to his dissent, in support of his arguments for a direct-indirect test; he evidently viewed federal regulation of marriage as an outlandish hypothesis. But after *Darby*, perhaps it is less outlandish. Could Congress validly enact a comprehensive act regulating marriages in all fifty states, by setting minimum ages, testing and license requirements, etc., on the theory that marriage and divorce "substantially affect" commerce? If not, could it accomplish the same result by prohibiting persons whose marriages failed to conform to national regulations from travelling in interstate commerce? And, finally, are there reasons to believe that Congress would have motives not to to enact this hypothetical legislation, even if it has that power?

[D]   The Modern Commerce Power

[1]   Large Accumulations of Small Effects

 WICKARD v. FILBURN
317 U.S. 111 (1942)

M<small>R</small>. J<small>USTICE</small> J<small>ACKSON</small> delivered the opinion of the Court:

[The Agricultural Adjustment Act of 1938 was designed to prevent wheat surpluses in order to avoid "abnormally low or high wheat prices." It directed the Secretary of Agriculture to determine a national acreage allotment for the annual wheat crop, and this allotment was to be apportioned to states, counties, and individual farms. Under certain circumstances, these allotments could be replaced by mandatory quotas. Roscoe C. Filburn, the appellee, was subject to a quota of 11.1 acres at a normal yield of 20.1 bushels per acre; however, he sowed 23 acres, harvested 239 bushels from the excess acreage, and was subjected to a penalty of 49 cents a bushel, or $117.11 in all. Customarily, Filburn sold a portion of his crop, used some for home consumption, and used some to feed poultry and livestock within his farm acreage. The lower court enjoined collection of the penalty, citing the "equities of the case," among other reasons. The Supreme Court reversed, holding that the penalty was a valid exercise of the commerce power.]

[T]he question would merit little consideration since our decision in *United States v. Darby* [e]xcept for the fact that this Act extends federal regulation to production not intended in any part for commerce but wholly for consumption on the farm. The Act includes a definition of "market" and its derivatives so that as related to wheat in addition to its conventional meaning it also means to dispose of "by feeding (in any form) to poultry or livestock which, or the products of which, are sold, bartered, or exchanged, or to be so disposed of." Hence, marketing quotas not only embrace all that may be sold without penalty but also what may be consumed on the premises. . . .

Appellee says that this is a regulation of production and consumption of wheat. Such activities are, he urges, beyond the reach of congressional power under the Commerce Clause, since they are local in character, and their effects upon interstate commerce are at most "indirect." In answer the Government argues that the statute regulates neither production nor consumption, but only marketing; and, in the alternative, that if the Act does go beyond the regulation of marketing it is sustainable as a "necessary and proper" implementation of the power of Congress over interstate commerce. . . .

At the beginning Chief Justice Marshall described the federal commerce power with a breadth never yet exceeded. *Gibbons v. Ogden.* He made emphatic the embracing and penetrating nature of this power by warning that effective restraints on its exercise must proceed from political rather than from judicial processes. . . . [Here, the Court discussed such cases as *United States v. E.C. Knight Co.* (holding that manufacturing was not commerce) and other decisions, which it labelled "restrictive," that used the direct-indirect distinction. It concluded:] In some cases sustaining the exercise of federal power over intrastate matters the term "direct" was used for the purpose of stating, rather than of reaching, a result; in others it was treated as synonymous with "substantial" or "material;" and in others it was not used at all. Of late its use has been abandoned in cases dealing with questions of federal power under the Commerce Clause.

In the *Shreveport Rate Cases*, the Court held that railroad rates of an admittedly intrastate character and fixed by authority of the state might, nevertheless, be revised by the Federal Government because of the economic effects which they had upon interstate commerce. The opinion of Mr. Justice Hughes found federal intervention constitutionally authorized because of "matters having . . . a close and substantial relation to interstate traffic. . . ."

The Court's recognition of the relevance of the economic effects in the application of the Commerce Clause exemplified by this statement has made the mechanical application of legal formulas no longer feasible. Once an economic measure of the reach of the power granted to Congress in the Commerce Clause is accepted, questions of federal power cannot be decided simply by finding the activity in question to be "production" nor can consideration of its economic effects be foreclosed by calling them "indirect. . . ."

[E]ven if appellee's activity be local and though it may not be regarded as commerce, it may still, whatever its nature, be reached by Congress if it exerts a substantial economic effect on interstate commerce, and this irrespective of whether such effect is what might at some earlier time have been defined as "direct" or "indirect. . . ."

The wheat industry has been a problem industry for some years. Largely as a result of increased foreign production and import restrictions, annual exports of wheat and flour from the United States during the ten-year period ending in 1940 averaged less than 10 per cent of total production, while during the 1920s they averaged more than 25 per cent. The decline in the export trade has left a large surplus in production which in connection with an abnormally large supply of wheat and other grains in recent years caused congestion in a number of markets; tied up railroad cars; and caused elevators in some instances to turn away grains, and railroads to institute embargoes to prevent further congestion. . . .

During 1941 producers who co-operated with the Agricultural Adjustment program received an average price on the farm of about $1.16 a bushel as compared with the world market price of 40 cents a bushel.

Differences in farming conditions, however, make these benefits mean different things to different wheat growers. . . .

Except in regions of large-scale production, wheat is usually grown in rotation with other crops; for a nurse crop for grass seeding; and as a cover crop to prevent soil erosion and leaching. Some is sold, some kept for seed, and a percentage of the total production much larger than in areas of specialization is consumed on the farm and grown for such purpose. . . .

The effect of consumption of home-grown wheat on interstate commerce is due to the fact that it constitutes the most variable factor in the disappearance of the wheat crop. Consumption on the farm where grown appears to vary in an amount greater than 20 per cent of average production. . . .

[T]hat appellee's own contribution to the demand for wheat may be trivial by itself is not enough to remove him from the scope of federal regulation where, as here, his contribution, taken together with that of many others similarly situated, is far from trivial. . . . [citing *Darby*].

. . . One of the primary purposes of the Act in question was to increase the market price of wheat and to that end to limit the volume thereof that could affect the market. It can hardly be denied that a factor of such volume and variability as home-consumed wheat would have a substantial influence on price and market conditions. This may arise because being in marketable condition such wheat overhangs the market and if induced by rising prices tends to flow into the market and check price increases. But if we assume that it is never marketed, it supplies a need of the man who grew it which would otherwise be reflected by purchases in the open market. Home-grown wheat in this sense competes with wheat in commerce. The stimulation of commerce is a use of the regulatory function quite as definitely as prohibitions or restrictions thereon. This record leaves us in no doubt that Congress may properly have considered that wheat consumed on the farm where grown if wholly outside the scheme of regulation would have a substantial effect in defeating and obstructing its purpose to stimulate trade therein at increased prices. . . .

Reversed.

NOTES AND QUESTIONS

(1) *Judicial Adoption of the New Deal's Most Expansive Theory of Interstateness:
Wickard v. Filburn, 317 U.S. 111 (1942).* Filburn challenged the constitutionality of the New Deal's Agricultural Adjustment Act, arguing that, with respect to his home-grown wheat, Congressional regulation exceeded the scope of the interstate commerce power. The Court, per Justice Jackson, disagreed. Although Filburn argued that growing his wheat was "local" in nature, the Court found sufficient "interstateness" to justify Congressional regulation. As such, *Wickard* is more expansive than the earlier theories of interstateness. *Wickard* came to represent the theory that Congress may find interstateness in the cumulative effect of intrastate activities on interstate commerce. Watch for the limiting of the *Wickard* rationale in later decisions, especially *United States v. Lopez* below.

(2) *Is a "Drop in the Bucket" Enough to Affect Commerce? Wickard v. Filburn* has sometimes been said to embody the "drop in the bucket" doctrine, in that Filburn's own production and consumption was the proverbial drop in the bucket. Notice, however, that the Court's reasoning emphasizes the accumulation of many "drops"; this accumu-

lation is what produces the "substantial effect" that the Court finds upon interstate commerce. The question remains: Just what are the limits of the federal commerce power after *Wickard v. Filburn*? It is clear, for example, that it is no longer limited by the "local activity" or "production-is-not-commerce" doctrines of earlier cases, and it may be appropriate to speculate whether there are *any* limits whatsoever. *Cf. Maryland v. Wirtz*, 392 U.S. 183 (1968) (Harlan, J.) ("Congress may [not] use a relatively trivial impact on commerce as an excuse for broad general regulation of state or private activities"). Is this "trivial effects" dictum a meaningful, or useful, test?

(3) *Congressional (i.e., Self-Imposed) Limits on the Commerce Power.* The *Wickard* opinion cites *Gibbons v. Ogden* as "warning that effective restraints on [the commerce power] must proceed from political rather than judicial processes." Will political processes (together with Congress' own enforcement of the Constitution) restrain the exercise of the commerce power to its proper sphere?

[2] Civil Rights Protection and the Commerce Power

 HEART OF ATLANTA MOTEL, INC. v. UNITED STATES
379 U.S. 241 (1964)

Mr. Justice Clark delivered the opinion of the Court.

[A corporate motel operator sued for an injunction against enforcement of the public accommodations sections of the Civil Rights Act of 1964, which provided: "All persons shall be entitled to the full and equal enjoyment of the goods, services, facilities, privileges, advantages, and accommodations of any place of public accommodation, as defined in this section, without discrimination or segregation on the ground of race, color, religion, or national origin." Section 201 further defined covered accommodations as including "any inn, hotel, motel, or other establishment which provides lodging to transient guests," if its operations "affect commerce or if discrimination or segregation by it is supported by state action," with certain inapplicable exceptions. The district court upheld the statute as constitutional. On direct appeal to the Supreme Court, Heart of Atlanta asserted among other arguments that the statute exceeded the commerce power, which Congress had cited as a basis for the Act.]

1. *The Factual Background and Contentions of the Parties.*

[A]ppellant owns and operates the Heart of Atlanta Motel which has 216 rooms available to transient guests. [I]t is readily accessible to interstate highways 75 and 85 and state highways 23 and 41. Appellant solicits patronage from outside the State of Georgia through various national advertising media, including magazines of national circulation; it maintains over 50 billboards and highway signs within the State, soliciting patronage for the motel; it accepts convention trade from outside Georgia and approximately 75% of its registered guests are from out of State. . . .

4. *Application of Title II to Heart of Atlanta Motel.*

It is admitted that the operation of the motel brings it within the provisions of § 201(a) of the Act and that appellant refused to provide lodging for transient Negroes because of their race or color and that it intends to continue that policy unless restrained.

[T]he legislative history of the Act indicates that Congress based the Act on § 5 and the Equal Protection Clause of the Fourteenth Amendment as well as its power to regulate interstate commerce under Art I, § 8, cl. 3, of the Constitution.

The Senate Commerce Committee made it quite clear that the fundamental object of Title II was to vindicate "the deprivation of personal dignity that surely accompanies denials of equal access to public establishments." At the same time, however, it noted that such an objective has been and could be readily achieved "by congressional action based on the commerce power of the Constitution." S. Rep. No. 872 at 16–17. . . . [S]ince the commerce power is sufficient for our decision here we have considered it alone. . . .

6. *The Basis of Congressional Action.*

While the Act as adopted carried no congressional findings the record of its passage through each house is replete with evidence of the burdens that discrimination by race or color places upon interstate commerce. This testimony included the fact . . . that Negroes in particular have been the subject of discrimination in transient accommodations, having to travel great distances to secure the same; that often they have been unable to obtain accommodations and have had to call upon friends to put them up overnight; and that these conditions have become so acute as to require the listing of available lodging for Negroes in a special guidebook which was itself "dramatic testimony to the difficulties" Negroes encounter in travel. These exclusionary practices were found to be nationwide, the Under Secretary of Commerce testifying that there is "no question that this discrimination in the North still exists to a large degree" and in the West and Midwest as well. This testimony indicated a qualitative as well as quantitative effect on interstate travel by Negroes. The former was the obvious impairment of the Negro traveler's pleasure and convenience that resulted when he continually was uncertain of finding lodging. As for the latter, there was evidence that this uncertainty stemming from racial discrimination had the effect of discouraging travel on the part of a substantial portion of the Negro community. We shall not burden this opinion with further details since the voluminous testimony presents overwhelming evidence that discrimination by hotels and motels impedes interstate travel.

7. *The Power of Congress Over Interstate Travel.*

[Here, the Court discussed the breadth of the commerce power recognized in *Gibbons v. Ogden* and its progeny, including *Wickard v. Filburn* (the "cumulative effects" case). It also discussed the *Lottery Case* and similar extensions of the power, covering allegedly harmful articles or activities.]

That Congress was legislating against moral wrongs in many of these areas rendered its enactments no less valid. In framing Title II of this Act Congress was also dealing with what it considered a moral problem. But that fact does not detract from the overwhelming evidence of the disruptive effect that racial discrimination has had on commercial intercourse. It was this burden which empowered Congress to enact appropriate legislation, and, given this basis for the exercise of its power, Congress was not restricted by the fact that the particular obstruction to interstate commerce with which it was dealing was also deemed a moral and social wrong.

It is said that the operation of the motel here is of a purely local character. But, assuming this to be true, "[i]f it is interstate commerce that feels the pinch, it does not matter how local the operation which applies the squeeze. . . ."

We, therefore, concluded that the action of the Congress in the adoption of the Act as applied here to a motel which concededly serves interstate travelers is within the power granted it by the Commerce Clause of the Constitution, as interpreted by this Court for 140 years. It may be argued that Congress could have pursued other methods to eliminate the obstructions it found in interstate commerce caused by racial discrimination. But this is a matter of policy that rests entirely with the Congress not with the courts. How obstructions in commerce may be removed—what means are to be employed—is within the sound and exclusive discretion of the Congress. It is subject only to one caveat—that the means chosen by it must be reasonably adapted to the end permitted by the Constitution. We cannot say that its choice here was not so adapted. The Constitution requires no more.

Affirmed.

[JUSTICES BLACK, DOUGLAS and GOLDBERG each wrote concurring opinions, which, since they also were applicable to *Katzenbach v. McClung*, below, are appended to that decision.]

 KATZENBACH v. McCLUNG
379 U.S. 294 (1964)

MR. JUSTICE CLARK delivered the opinion of the Court.

[Section 201 of the Civil Rights Act of 1964 also covers any "restaurant principally engaged in selling food for consumption on the premises," if "it serves or offers to serve interstate travelers or a substantial portion of the food which it serves . . . has moved in interstate commerce." The district court enjoined enforcement of this provision against Ollie's Barbecue, a small restaurant owned by Ollie McClung, which had no substantial interstate patronage. The case was consolidated for argument in the Supreme Court with *Heart of Atlanta, supra.*]

. . . There is no claim that interstate travelers frequented the restaurant. The sole question, therefore, narrows down to whether Title II, as applied to a restaurant annually receiving about $70,000 worth of food which has moved in commerce, is a valid exercise of the power of Congress.

As we noted in *Heart of Atlanta Motel* both Houses of Congress conducted prolonged hearings on the Act. . . . The record is replete with testimony of the burdens placed on interstate commerce by racial discrimination in restaurants. A comparison of per capita spending by Negroes in restaurants, theaters, and like establishments indicated less spending, after discounting income differences, in areas where discrimination is widely practiced. . . .

It goes without saying that, viewed in isolation, the volume of food purchased by Ollie's Barbecue from sources supplied from out of state was insignificant when compared with the total foodstuffs moving in commerce. But, as our late Brother Jackson said for the Court in *Wickard v. Filburn*:

> That appellee's own contribution to the demand for wheat may be trivial by itself is not enough to remove him from the scope of federal regulation where, as here, his contribution, taken together with that of many others similarly situated, is far from trivial. . . .

Here . . . Congress has determined for itself that refusals of service to Negroes have imposed burdens both upon the interstate flow of food and upon the movement of products generally. Of course, the mere fact that Congress has said when particular activity shall be deemed to affect commerce does not preclude further examination by this Court. But where we find that the legislators, in light of the facts and testimony before them, have a rational basis for finding a chosen regulatory scheme necessary to the protection of commerce, our investigation is at an end. The only remaining question—one answered in the affirmative by the court below—is whether the particular restaurant either serves or offers to serve interstate travelers or serves food a substantial portion of which has moved in interstate commerce.

The appellees urge that Congress, in passing the Fair Labor Standards Act and the National Labor Relations Act, made specific findings which were embodied in those statutes. Here, of course, Congress has included no formal findings. But their absence is not fatal to the validity of the statute, see *United States v. Carolene Products Co.*, 304 U.S. 144, 152 (1938), for the evidence presented at the hearings fully indicated the nature and effect of the burdens on commerce which Congress meant to alleviate.

Confronted as we are with the facts laid before Congress, we must conclude that it had a rational basis for finding that racial discrimination in restaurants had a direct and adverse effect on the free flow of interstate commerce.

MR. JUSTICE BLACK, concurring:

I recognize [t]hat some isolated and remote lunchroom which sells only to local people and buys almost all its supplies in the locality may possibly be beyond the reach of the power of Congress to regulate commerce, just as such an establishment is not covered by the present Act. But we do not consider the effect on interstate commerce of only one isolated, individual, local event, without regard to the fact that this single local event when added to many others of a similar nature may impose a burden on interstate commerce by reducing its volume or distorting its flow [citing *Wickard v. Filburn*]. . . .

MR. JUSTICE DOUGLAS, concurring.

[I] would prefer to rest on the assertion of legislative power contained in § 5 of the Fourteenth Amendment which states: "The Congress shall have power to enforce, by appropriate legislation, the provisions of this article"—a power which the Court concedes was exercised at least in part in this Act.

A decision based on the Fourteenth Amendment would have a more settling effect, making unnecessary litigation over whether a particular restaurant or inn is within the commerce definitions of the Act or whether a particular customer is an interstate traveler. . . . And that construction would put an end to all obstructionist strategies and finally close one door on a bitter chapter in American history.

JUSTICE GOLDBERG, concurring:

[The Senate Commerce Committee made clear its conclusion that the 1964 Act was not merely a matter of economics when it said:] " . . . Discrimination is not simply dollars and cents, hamburgers and movies; it is the humiliation, frustration, and embarrassment that a person must surely feel when he is told that he is unacceptable as a member of the public because of his race or color. . . ."

[Eliminating this effect of discrimination] is the primary purpose of the Act. . . . The cases cited in the Court's opinions are conclusive that Congress could exercise its powers under [either] the commerce clause [or the fourteenth amendment] to accomplish this purpose.

NOTES AND QUESTIONS

(1) *Why Did Congress Rely upon the Commerce Power (as Opposed to Relying solely upon the Civil Rights Amendments)?* The Fourteenth Amendment empowers Congress to "enforce" its provisions, and it might seem that this source of power would be more appropriate as a basis for Civil Rights Acts. But the provisions of the Fourteenth Amendment assert that "no state" may deny due process or equal protection of the laws to any person. But there was substantial doubt whether Heart of Atlanta Motel, Ollie's Barbecue, and similar firms were really sufficiently related to state action. Notice Justice Douglas' disquiet with this reasoning; is Justice Douglas' argument persuasive?

(2) *A National Police Power?* These civil rights cases seem to establish a national police power that extends to "drops in the bucket" under the same reasoning as that in *Wickard v. Filburn.* Notwithstanding the value of upholding the Civil Rights Act, does this national police power hold any adverse implications for individual liberties?

(3) *Congressional Self-Limitation in Both Title IV (Public Accommodations) and Title VII (Employment Discrimination) of the Civil Rights Act.* Congress remains obligated to enforce the Constitution itself. In addition, Congress is composed of elected

representatives who respond to values of their constituents, including the value of refraining from maximum exercise of the commerce power. Thus, Title VII, which prohibits discrimination in employment, applies only to an employer "engaged in an industry affecting commerce who has fifteen or more employees." 42 U.S.C. § 2000e (1978). Although *Wickard v. Filburn* might support a prohibition of discrimination even by sporadic, part-time, single-employee firms, might it be that Congress concluded that this fifteen-employee threshold was an appropriate means of ensuring its own conformity to the limits of the commerce power?

PROBLEM C

THE CIVIL RIGHTS ACT AND SMALL PRIVATE BOARDING HOUSES. The public accommodations section of the Civil Rights Act of 1964, in its coverage of inns and places of lodging, contains an exception for "an establishment located within a building which contains not more than five rooms for rent or hire and which is actually occupied by the proprietor of such establishment as his residence." This exemption reflected the concerns of legislators who objected to the encroachment of federal regulation upon private homeowners who took in one or two boarders. Consider, first, the question of the commerce power. If Congress had extended the Act to cover small private boarding houses, would it have violated the Constitution as construed in *Wickard v. Filburn* and *Katzenbach v. McClung*? Second, is it likely that the legislators would have considered the efficiency of enforcement, the homeowner's lesser ability to keep statistics showing compliance, or even the individual's interest in personal autonomy to discriminate on silly grounds within the intimate surroundings of the home?

[3]　Criminalizing Local Activities under the Commerce Power

PEREZ v. UNITED STATES, 402 U.S. 146 (1971). Perez was convicted of making an "extortionate extension of credit" in violation of the federal Consumer Credit Protection Act. He argued that this criminal statute exceeded the commerce power. The Court, through Mr. Justice Douglas, observed that Perez was "one of the species known as 'loan sharks' which Congress found are in large part under the control of 'organized crime.'" Congress, in its reports, had found that "[e]ven where extortionate credit transactions are purely intrastate in character, they nevertheless directly affect interstate and foreign commerce." The reports "supplied Congress with the knowledge that the loan shark racket provides organized crime with its second most lucrative source of revenue, extracts millions from the pockets of people, coerces its victims into the commission of crimes against property, and causes the takeover by racketeers of legitimate businesses." Rejecting the "impassioned plea of petitioner that all that is involved in loan sharking is a traditionally local activity," the Court concluded: "It appears, instead, that loan sharking in its national setting is one way organized interstate crime holds its guns to the heads of the poor and rich alike and syphons funds from numerous localities to finance its national operations."

Justice Stewart dissented: "In order to sustain this law we would, in my view, have to be able at the least to say that Congress could rationally have concluded that loan sharking is an activity with interstate attributes that distinguish it in some substantial respect from other local crime. But it is not enough to say that loan sharking is a national problem, for all crime is a national problem. It is not enough to say that some loan sharking has interstate characteristics, for any crime may have an interstate setting. . . . The definition and prosecution of local crime are reserved to the States under the Ninth and Tenth Amendments."

PROBLEM D

THE "H. RAP BROWN LAW." The Civil Rights Act of 1968 was not limited to prohibitions of racial discrimination. It also contained the "H. Rap Brown law," which was a response to the activities of black activist H. Rap Brown, who achieved national visibility in the mid-1960s and precipitated racial riots in various locations during his interstate travels. Specifically, the Act made it a crime to "travel in interstate or foreign commerce or use any facility of interstate commerce" such as the mails, telephone, or television, "with intent—(A) to incite a riot; (B) to organize, promote, encourage, participate in, or carry on a riot; (C) to commit any act of violence in furtherance of any riot; or (D) to aid or abet any person in inciting or participating in or carrying on a riot [under certain circumstances]. . . ." 18 U.S.C. § 2101. Note that the states have laws criminalizing incitement of riots, and these laws arguably could more efficiently be prosecuted, in that they can and do dispense with the cumbersome requirement of proving that the criminal intent coincided with the crossing of a state line. Is the federal statute constitutional under the majority view in *Perez?* Would Mr. Justice Stewart regard it as constitutional?

[4] The Commerce Power Today: What are the Limits?

HODEL v. VIRGINIA SURFACE MINING AND RECLAMATION ASS'N, 452 U.S. 264 (1981). The federal Surface Mining Control and Reclamation Act of 1977 contained restrictions on private surface mining and requirements for environmental restoration. The Mining Association alleged that the Act exceeded the commerce power because its "principal goal is regulating the use of private lands within the borders of the states. . . . Consequently, appellees contend that the ultimate issue presented is " 'whether land *as such* is subject to regulation under the Commerce Clause, *i.e.*, whether land can be regarded as being 'in commerce.' " Justice Marshall, for the Court, refused to "accept either appellee's framing of the question or the answer they would have us supply:"

> The task of a court that is asked to determine whether a particular enactment is valid under the commerce clause is relatively narrow. The court must defer to a congressional finding that a regulated activity affects interstate commerce, if there is any rational basis for the finding [citing *Heart of Atlanta* and *Katzenbach v. McClung*]. . . .

> Thus, when Congress has determined that an activity affects interstate commerce, the courts need inquire only whether the finding is rational. [The Surface Mining Act] recites the congressional finding that "many surface mining operations result in disturbances of surface areas that burden and adversely affect commerce and the public welfare by destroying or diminishing the utility of land for commercial, industrial, residential, recreational, agricultural, and forestry purposes, by causing erosion and landslides, by contributing to floods, by polluting the water, by destroying fish and wildlife habitats, by impairing natural beauty, by damaging the property of citizens, by creating hazards dangerous to life and property, by degrading the quality of life in local communities, and by counteracting governmental programs and efforts to conserve soil, water, and other natural resources."

> The legislative records provides ample support for these statutory findings. The Surface Mining Act became law only after six years of the most thorough legislative consideration. Committees of both Houses of Congress held extensive hearings. . . .

> The denomination of an activity as a "local" or "intrastate" activity does not resolve the question whether Congress may regulate it under the Commerce Clause. . . . [citing *Jones & Laughlin, United States v. Darby, Wickard v. Filburn*, and *Katzenbach v. McClung*.] Here, Congress rationally determined

that regulation of surface coal mining is necessary to protect interstate commerce from adverse effects that may result from that activity. . . .

Moreover, the Act responds to a congressional finding that nationwide "surface mining and reclamation standards are essential in order to ensure that competition among interstate sellers of coal produced in different states will not be used to undermine the ability of the several states to improve and maintain adequate standards on coal mining operations. . . ." The prevention of this sort of destructive interstate competition is a traditional role for congressional regulation under the commerce clause [citing *Darby*]. . . .

Chief Justice Burger, concurring, was concerned "that we often seem to forget the doctrine that laws enacted by Congress under the Commerce Clause must be based on a *substantial* effect on interstate commerce. However, I join in the Court's opinion in [this case and in *Hodel v. Indiana*, below] because in them the Court acknowledges and reaffirms that doctrine."

HODEL v. INDIANA, 452 U.S. 2376 (1981). The Court, per Mr. Justice Marshall, applied its holding in *Hodel v. Virginia Surface Mining*, above, to uphold the "prime farmland" protections of the Surface Mining Act, even though a federal interagency report had concluded that these protections applied only to 21, 800 acres annually, or "0.006% of the total prime farmland acreage in the Nation." The Court pointed out that this 0.006% of acreage produced 0.04% of the national corn production, accounting for a value of $5.16 million, "which surely is not an insignificant amount of commerce." "A Court may invalidate legislation enacted under the Commerce Clause only if it is clear that there is no rational basis for a congressional finding that the regulated activity affects interstate commerce, or that there is no reasonable connection between the regulatory means selected and the asserted ends. . . . We are not convinced that the District Court had reliable grounds to reach either conclusion in this case." In the first place, said the Court, the interagency report did not examine the full impact of surface mining on agriculture, nor did it conclude that the impact was too negligible for federal regulation. "[More important] the pertinent inquiry . . . is not how much commerce is involved but whether Congress could rationally conclude that the regulated activity affects interstate commerce."

Justice Rehnquist concurred specially, observing that "one of the greatest 'fictions' of our federal system is that the Congress exercises only those powers delegated to it, while the remainder are reserved to the States or to the people." He added:

Though there can be no doubt that Congress in regulating surface mining has stretched its authority to the "nth degree," our prior precedents compel me to agree with the Court's conclusion. I therefore concur in the judgments of the Court.

There is, however, a troublesome difference between what the Court does and what it says. In both cases, the Court asserts that regulation will be upheld if Congress had a rational basis for finding that the regulated activity affects interstate commerce. . . . In my view, the Court misstates the test. [I]t has long been established that the commerce power does not reach activity which merely "affects" interstate commerce. There must be a showing that the regulated activity has a *substantial effect* on interstate commerce [citing *Jones & Laughlin, Shreveport, Wickard v. Filburn,* and *Heart of Atlanta,* among other cases]. [But] it may be that I read too much into the Court's choice of language. In the *Virginia* case, for example, it does mention at one point that Congress did have a "rational basis for concluding that surface coal mining has substantial effects on interstate commerce."

NOTES AND QUESTIONS

(1) *The "Effect" Test Versus the "Substantial Effect" Test: NLRB v. Fainblatt, 306 U.S. 601 (1939).* Is Justice Rehnquist right in distinguishing a test depending upon "substantial" effect from one depending only upon "effect" on interstate commerce? Given that small "effects" on interstate commerce are the inevitable result of any human activity, doesn't the size (or substantiality) of the effect logically have to be considered if the effects test is to escape meaninglessness? And if so, are Justices Rehnquist and Burger correct when they infer that that really may be what the Court means?

(2) *The "Rational Basis" Test.* But note that the test, in any event, is not whether the Court finds a substantial effect; it is whether Congress could have had any "rational basis" for concluding that there was such an effect. Thus the Court will not invalidate a statute even when it finds no substantial effect, if Congress found such an effect and was not irrational in doing so. What does this principle do to the commerce power as a practical matter? Are you left to conclude that there are no meaningful limits on the commerce power? *Cf.* Epstein, *The Proper Scope of the Commerce Powers*, 73 Va. L. Rev. 1387 (1987); Cirillo & Eisenhofer, *Reflection on the Constitutional Commerce Power*, 60 Temp. L.Q. 901 (1987).

⚖ UNITED STATES v. LOPEZ
514 U.S. 549 (1995)

Chief Justice Rehnquist delivered the opinion of the Court.

[The respondent, Alfonso Lopez, Jr. ("Lopez"), was a 12th grade student at a San Antonio, Texas, high school. He carried a concealed .38 caliber handgun and five bullets to school. The school officials discovered the gun and initiated Lopez's prosecution. Lopez was initially charged under Texas state law, but these charges were dismissed after federal prosecutors charged Lopez with violating the Gun-Free School Zones Act of 1990 ("the Act").

[In the Act, Congress made it a crime for any person "knowingly to possess a firearm" within 1, 000 feet of any public, parochial or private school. Lopez moved to dismiss, claiming that Congress did not have authority under the commerce power to pass the Act. The District Court denied Lopez's motion to dismiss, convicted him and sentenced him to six months' imprisonment. The court of appeals applied the "substantial effect" standard and reversed. Here, the Supreme Court agreed with the use of the substantial effect standard for the commerce clause and affirmed, holding the Act unconstitutional.]

[T]he Act neither regulates a commercial activity nor contains a requirement that the possession be connected in any way to interstate commerce. We hold that the Act exceeds the authority of Congress "[t]o regulate Commerce . . . among the several States . . . " U.S. Const., Art. I, § 8, cl. 3 . . .

We start with first principles. The Constitution creates a Federal Government of enumerated powers. See U.S. Const., Art. I, § 8. . . .

[T]he Court, through Chief Justice Marshall, first defined the nature of Congress' commerce power in *Gibbons v. Ogden,* . . . The commerce power "is the power to regulate; that is, to prescribe the rule by which commerce is to be governed. This power, like all others vested in Congress, is complete in itself, may be exercised to its utmost extent, and acknowledges no limitations, other than are prescribed in the constitution." The *Gibbons* Court, however, acknowledged that limitations on the commerce power are inherent in the very language of the Commerce Clause.

In *A.L.A. Schecter Poultry Corp. v. United States,* 295 U.S. 495, 550 (1935), the Court struck down regulations that fixed the hours and wages of individuals employed by an intrastate business because the activity being regulated related to interstate commerce only indirectly. In doing so, the Court characterized the distinction between direct and indirect effects of intrastate transactions upon interstate commerce as "a fundamental one, essential to the maintenance of our constitutional system."

[I]n the watershed case of *NLRB v. Jones & Laughlin Steel Corp.*, 301 U.S. 1, (1937), the Court upheld the National Labor Relations Act against a Commerce Clause challenge, and in the process, departed from the distinction between "direct" and "indirect" effects on interstate commerce. ("The question [of the scope of Congress' power] is necessarily one of degree"). The Court held that intrastate activities that "have such a close and substantial relation to interstate commerce that their control is essential or appropriate to protect that commerce from burdens and obstructions" are within Congress' power to regulate. . . .

In *Wickard v. Filburn*, [moreover] the Court upheld the application of amendments to the Agricultural Adjustment Act of 1938 to the production and consumption of homegrown wheat. [T]he *Wickard* Court emphasized that although Filburn's own contribution to the demand for wheat may have been trivial by itself, that was not "enough to remove him from the scope of federal regulation where, as here, his contribution, taken together with that of many others similarly situated, is far from trivial."

[These "New Deal" decisions] ushered in an era of Commerce Clause jurisprudence that greatly expanded the previously defined authority of Congress under that clause. . . .

But even these modern-era precedents which have expanded congressional power under the Commerce Clause confirm that this power is subject to outer limits. . . . [T]he Court has . . . undertaken to decide whether a rational basis existed for concluding that a regulated activity sufficiently affected interstate commerce. *See e.g.*, *Hodel v. Virginia Surface Mining & Reclamation Assn., Inc.*, 452 U.S. 264 (1981). . . .

Consistent with this structure, we have identified three broad categories of activity that Congress may regulate under its commerce power. First, Congress may regulate the use of the channels of interstate commerce. Second, Congress is empowered to regulate and protect the instrumentalities of interstate commerce, or persons or things in interstate commerce, even though the threat may come only from intrastate activities. Finally, Congress' commerce authority includes the power to regulate those activities having a substantial relation to interstate commerce, *i.e.*, those activities that substantially affect interstate commerce.

Within this final category, admittedly, our case law has not been clear whether an activity must "affect" or "substantially affect" interstate commerce in order to be within Congress' power to regulate it under the Commerce Clause. . . . We conclude, consistent with the great weight of our case law, that the proper test requires an analysis of whether the regulated activity "substantially affects" interstate commerce.

We now turn to consider the power of Congress, in the light of this framework, to enact [the Act]. The first two categories of authority may be quickly disposed of: The Act is not a regulation of the use of the channels of interstate commerce, nor is it an attempt to prohibit the interstate transportation of a commodity through the channels of commerce; nor can the Act be justified as a regulation by which Congress has sought to protect an instrumentality of interstate commerce or a thing in interstate commerce. Thus, if the Act is to be sustained, it must be under the third category as a regulation of an activity that substantially affects interstate commerce.

First, we have upheld a wide variety of congressional Acts regulating intrastate economic activity where we have concluded that the activity substantially affected interstate commerce. . . . Where economic activity substantially affects interstate commerce, legislation regulating that activity will be sustained.

Even *Wickard*, which is perhaps the most far reaching example of Commerce Clause authority over intrastate activity, involved economic activity in a way that the possession of a gun in a school zone does not. . . .

[The Act] is a criminal statute that by its terms has nothing to do with "commerce" or any sort of economic enterprise, however broadly one might define those terms.[1]

[I]t cannot, therefore, be sustained under our cases upholding regulations of activities that arise out of or are connected with a commercial transaction, which viewed in the aggregate, substantially affects interstate commerce. Second, [the Act] contains no jurisdiction element which would ensure, through case-by-case inquiry, that the firearm possession in question affects interstate commerce. . . .

Although as part of our independent evaluation of constitutionality under the Commerce Clause we of course consider legislative findings, and indeed even congressional committee findings, regarding effect on interstate commerce, . . . The Government concedes that "[n]either the statute nor its legislative history contain[s] express congressional findings regarding the effects upon interstate commerce of gun possession in a school zone." [The Court noted that a subsequent Congress made findings, in another statute, about the effect of school firearms on interstate commerce, but that the Government here did not rely on those later findings.] We agree with the Government that Congress normally is not required to make formal findings as to the substantial burdens that an activity has on interstate commerce. But to the extent that congressional findings would enable us to evaluate the legislative judgment that the activity in question substantially affected interstate commerce, even though no such substantial effect was visible to the naked eye, they are lacking here. . . .

The Government's essential contention [i]s that we may determine here that [the Act] is valid because possession of a firearm in a local school zone does indeed substantially affect interstate commerce. The Government argues that possession of a firearm in a school zone may result in violent crime and that violent crime can be expected to affect the functioning of the national economy in two ways. First, the costs of violent crime are substantial, and, through the mechanism of insurance, those costs are spread throughout the population. Second, violent crime reduces the willingness of individuals to travel to areas within the country that are perceived to be unsafe. *Cf. Heart of Atlanta Motel.* The Government also argues that the presence of guns in schools poses a substantial threat to the educational process by threatening the learning environment. A handicapped educational process, in turn, will result in a less productive citizenry. That, in turn, would have an adverse effect on the nation's economic well-being. As a result, the Government argues that Congress could rationally have concluded that the Act substantially affects interstate commerce.

We pause to consider the implications of the Government's arguments. The Government admits, under its "costs of crime" reasoning, that Congress could regulate not only all violent crime, but all activities that might lead to violent crime, regardless of how tenuously they relate to interstate commerce. Similarly, under the Government's "national productivity" reasoning, Congress could regulate any activity that it found was related to the economic productivity of individual citizens: family law (including marriage, divorce, and child custody), for example. . . . Thus, if we were to accept the Government's arguments, we are hard-pressed to posit any activity by an individual that Congress is without power to regulate.

Justice Breyer [in dissent] focuses, for the most part, on the threat that firearm possession in and near schools poses to the educational process and the potential economic consequences flowing from that threat. [T]his analysis would be equally

---

[1] Under our federal system, the " 'States possess primary authority for defining and enforcing the criminal law.' " [W]hen Congress criminalizes conduct already denounced as criminal by the States, it effects a " 'change in the sensitive relation between federal and state criminal jurisdiction.' " United States v. Enmons, 410 U.S. 396, 411–412 (1973) (quoting United States v. Bass, 404 U.S. 336, 349 (1971)). The Government acknowledges that [the Act] "displace[s] state policy choices in . . . that its prohibitions apply even in States that have chosen not to outlaw the conduct in question." . . .

applicable, if not more so, to subjects such as family law and direct regulation of education.

[J]ustice Breyer rejects our reading of precedent and argues that "Congress . . . could rationally conclude that schools fall on the commercial side of the line." Again, Justice Breyer's rationale lacks any real limits because, depending on the level of generality, any activity can be looked upon as commercial. Under the dissent's rationale, Congress could just as easily look at child rearing as "fall[ing] on the commercial side of the line" because it provides a "valuable service—namely, to equip [children] with the skills they need to survive in life and, more specifically, in the workplace." . . .

. . . The possession of a gun in a local school zone is in no sense an economic activity that might, through repetition elsewhere, substantially affect any sort of interstate commerce. Respondent was a local student at a local school; there is no indication that he had recently moved in interstate commerce, and there is no requirement that his possession of the firearm have any concrete tie to interstate commerce.

To uphold the Government's contentions here, we would have to pile inference upon inference in a manner that would bid fair to convert congressional authority under the Commerce Clause to a general police power of the sort retained by the States. [T]o do so would require us to conclude that the Constitution's enumeration of powers does not presuppose something not enumerated, cf. *Gibbons v. Ogden*, and that there never will be a distinction between what is truly national and what is truly local, cf. *Jones & Laughlin Steel*. This we are unwilling to do.

Affirmed.

JUSTICE KENNEDY, with whom JUSTICE O'CONNOR joins, concurring.

The history of the judicial struggle to interpret the Commerce Clause during the transition from the economic system the Founders knew to the single, national market still emergent in our own era counsels great restraint before the Court determines that the Clause is insufficient to support an exercise of the national power. That history gives me some pause about today's decision, but I join the Court's opinion with these observations on what I conceive to be its necessary though limited holding. . . .

Of the various structural elements in the Constitution, separation of powers, checks and balances, judicial review, and federalism, only concerning the last does there seem to be much uncertainty respecting the existence, and the content, of standards that allow the judiciary to play a significant role in maintaining the design contemplated by the Framers.

[T]here is irony in this, because of the four structural elements in the Constitution just mentioned, federalism was the unique contribution of the Framers to political science and political theory. . . . Though on the surface the idea may seem counterintuitive, it was the insight of the Framers that freedom was enhanced by the creation of two governments, not one. . . .

The theory that two governments accord more liberty than one requires for its realization two distinct and discernable lines of political accountability: one between the citizens and the Federal Government; the second between the citizens and the States. . . . Were the Federal Government to take over the regulation of entire areas of traditional state concern, areas having nothing to do with the regulation of commercial activities, the boundaries between the spheres of federal and state authority would blur and political responsibility would become illusory. *See New York v. United States* [ch. 3, below]. The resultant inability to hold either branch of the government answerable to the citizens is more dangerous even than developing too much authority to the remote central power. . . .

If a State or municipality determines that harsh criminal sanctions are necessary and wise to deter students from carrying guns on school premises, the reserved powers of the States are sufficient to enact those measures. Indeed, over 40 States already have criminal laws outlawing the possession of Firearms on or near school grounds. . . .

The statute now before us forecloses the States from experimenting and exercising their own judgment in an area to which States lay claim by right of history and expertise, and it does so by regulating an activity beyond the realm of commerce in the ordinary and usual sense of that term. . . .

JUSTICE THOMAS, concurring.

[A]lthough I join the majority, I write separately to observe that our case law has drifted far from the original understanding of the Commerce Clause. In a future case, we ought to temper our Commerce Clause jurisprudence in a manner that both makes sense of our more recent case law and is more faithful to the original understanding of that Clause.

We have said that Congress may regulate not only "Commerce . . . among the several states," but also anything that has a "substantial effect" on such commerce. This test, if taken to its logical extreme, would give Congress a "police power" over all aspects of American life. Unfortunately, we have never come to grips with this implication of our substantial effects formula. [I]ndeed, on this crucial point, the majority and Justice Breyer agree in principle: the Federal Government has nothing approaching a police power. . . .

[I]t seems to me that the power to regulate "commerce" can by no means encompass authority over mere gun possession, any more than it empowers the Federal Government to regulate marriage, littering, or cruelty to animals, throughout the 50 States. Our Constitution quite properly leaves such matters to the individual States, notwithstanding these activities' effects on interstate commerce. Any interpretation of the Commerce Clause that even suggests that Congress could regulate such matters is in need of reexamination.

JUSTICE STEVENS, dissenting. . . .

Guns are both articles of commerce and articles that can be used to restrain commerce. Their possession is the consequence, either directly or indirectly, of commercial activity. In my judgment, Congress' power to regulate commerce in firearms includes the power to prohibit possession of guns at any location because of their potentially harmful use; it necessarily follows that Congress may also prohibit their possession in particular markets. The market for the possession of handguns by school-age children is, distressingly, substantial. Whether or not the national interest in eliminating that market would have justified federal legislation in 1789, it surely does today.

JUSTICE SOUTER, dissenting.

In reviewing congressional legislation under the Commerce Clause, we defer to what is often a merely implicit congressional judgment that its regulation addresses a subject substantially affecting interstate commerce "if there is any rational basis for such a finding." . . . If that congressional determination is within the realm of reason, "the only remaining question for judicial inquiry is whether 'the means chosen by Congress [are] reasonably adapted to the end permitted by the Constitution.' " . . .

There is today, however, a backward glance at both the old pitfalls, as the Court treats deference under the rationality rule as subject to gradation according to the commercial or noncommercial nature of the immediate subject of the challenged regulation. The distinction between what is patently commercial and what is not looks much like the old distinction between what directly affects commerce and what touches it only indirectly. . . . Thus, it seems fair to ask whether the step taken by the Court today does anything but portend a return to the untenable jurisprudence from which the Court extricated itself almost 60 years ago. . . .

JUSTICE BREYER, with whom JUSTICE STEVENS, JUSTICE SOUTER, and JUSTICE GINSBURG join, dissenting.

The issue in this case is whether the Commerce Clause authorizes Congress to enact a statute that makes it a crime to possess a gun in, or near, a school. In my view, the statute falls well within the scope of the commerce power as this Court has understood that power over the last half-century.

I

In reaching this conclusion, I apply three basic principles of Commerce Clause interpretation. First, the power to "regulate Commerce . . . among the several States," U.S. Const., Art. I, § 8, cl. 3, encompasses the power to regulate local activities insofar as they significantly affect interstate commerce. . . . I use the word "significant" because the word "substantial" implies a somewhat narrower power than recent precedent suggests. . . .

Second, in determining whether a local activity will likely have a significant effect upon interstate commerce, a court must consider, not the effect of an individual act (a single instance of gun possession), but rather the cumulative effect of all similar instances (*i.e.*, the effect of all guns possessed in or near schools). *See, e.g., Wickard, supra.* . . .

Third, the Constitution requires us to judge the connection between a regulated activity and interstate commerce, not directly, but at one remove. Courts must give Congress a degree of leeway in determining the existence of a significant factual connection between the regulated activity and interstate commerce—both because the Constitution delegates the commerce power directly to Congress and because the determination requires an empirical judgment of a kind that a legislature is more likely than a court to make with accuracy. The traditional words "rational basis" capture this leeway. Thus, the specific question before us [is] not whether the "regulated activity sufficiently affected interstate commerce," but, rather, whether Congress could have had "a *rational basis*" for so concluding. . . .

II

Applying these principles to the case at hand, we must ask whether Congress could have had a *rational basis* for finding a significant (or substantial) connection between gun-related school violence and interstate commerce. Or, to put the question in the language of the *explicit* finding that Congress made when it amended this law in 1994: Could Congress rationally have found that "violent crime in school zones," through its effect on the "quality of education," significantly (or substantially) affects "interstate" or "foreign commerce"?

Having found that guns in schools significantly undermine the quality of education in our Nation's classrooms, Congress could also have found, given the effect of education upon interstate and foreign commerce, that gun-related violence in and around schools is a commercial, as well as a human, problem. Education, although far more than a matter of economics, has long been inextricably intertwined with the nation's economy. . . .

The economic links [between guns and education] seem fairly obvious. Why then is it not equally obvious, in light of those links, that a widespread, serious, and substantial physical threat to teaching and learning *also* substantially threatens the commerce to which that teaching and learning is inextricably tied? That is to say, guns in the hands of six percent of inner-city high school students and gun-related violence throughout a city's schools must threaten the trade and commerce that those schools support. The only question, then, is whether the latter threat is (to use the majority's terminology) "substantial." And, the evidence of (1) the *extent* of the gun-related violence problem, (2) the *extent* of the resulting negative effect on classroom learning, and (3) the *extent* of the consequent negative commercial effects, when taken together, indicate a threat to trade and commerce that is "substantial." At the very least, Congress could rationally have concluded that the links are "substantial." . . .

NOTES AND QUESTIONS

(1) *The Court Strikes Down a Congressional Action Based on the Interstate Commerce Power: United States v. Lopez, 514 U.S. 549 (1999).* For the first time in nearly 60 years, the Supreme Court struck down a congressional program adopted under the interstate commerce power. In *Lopez*, the Court, per Chief Justice Rehnquist, held that the Gun-Free School Zone Act exceeded the scope of congressional power under the interstate commerce clause. The Chief Justices's plurality opinion relied upon the reasoning that school violence was not "commerce." The plurality opinion, joined by the concurrence of Justice Kennedy (and Justice O'Connor), also addressed the issue regarding the proper standard for judicial review of congressional action when Congress relied upon the commerce power to regulate what is essentially intrastate activities. [This issue was flagged for you in the Notes following *Hodel* above.] The *Lopez* Court held that the proper standard was the "substantially affects" interstate commerce rather than merely "affects" interstate commerce.

The reasoning of the Kennedy concurrence differed in a number of respects from Chief Justice Rehnquist's plurality opinion. The four dissenting Justices, in opinions by Justices Souter and Breyer, disagreed with the suggestion that Congress's commerce power was limited to the regulation of "commercial" activities. The dissents also disagreed with the use of the "substantially affects" standard. There was also a concurrence by Justice Thomas arguing for an "originalist" approach to the commerce clause issues. These various issues and arguments are explored further in the Notes below.

(2) *The Cumulative Effects Doctrine of Wickard v. Filburn: Is the Majority Faithful to It?* It may be correct that one gun-toting student, such as Lopez, cannot alone have a substantial effect on commerce. But the Court has recognized a cumulative effects doctrine: it isn't Lopez alone, but all the potential gun-toting students taken together that count. The majority distinguishes *Wickard* on the ground that it involved economic activity (on-premises consumption of home-grown wheat) in a way that schools do not. Is this reasoning persuasive?

(3) *The "Rational Basis" Test for Reviewing Congress's Conclusions about Substantial Effects: How Does the Court Treat It?* The Court acknowledges the rule that Congress is to be upheld if there is a "rational basis" for finding a substantial effect. Implicitly, the Court finds no such rational basis, emphasizing the lack of Congressional findings, the difference between the school setting and prior cases in which Congress may have gained expertise, and the Court's independent judicial duty. Is this reasoning persuasive—or has the Court deviated from a true rational basis approach?

(4) *The Lopez Recasting of the Commerce Clause Precedents.* The *Lopez* plurality opinion characterized the commerce clause precedents as falling into three categories: (1) Congressional attempts to regulate the "channels of interstate commerce;" (2) Congressional efforts to regulate the "instrumentalities" (*e.g.*, aircraft) that are involved in interstate commerce; (3) Congress may regulate where intrastate activities have a "substantial effect" on interstate commerce. The *Lopez* Court treated firearms and school violence as falling only into the substantial effects on interstate commerce category. The categorization of the precedents into this three part analysis is one of the remarkable features of the *Lopez* plurality opinion. Critics have not often focused on this restructuring. Even supporters of the results in *Lopez* have acknowledged that the

plurality opinion "reconfigured the precedents." LAURENCE TRIBE, AMERICAN CONSTITU-
TIONAL LAW 819 (3d ed. 2000).

(5) *"Channels" of Interstate Commerce, "Instrumentalities," and "Substantial
Effects."* The Court acknowledges that, in addition to regulating substantial effects on
interstate commerce, Congress may regulate the "channels" of interstate commerce
(*e.g.,* interstate travel) and its "instrumentalities" (*e.g.,* aircraft). Most firearms are
shipped interstate, and it is therefore likely that the usual person in Lopez's position is
carrying a gun that has travelled in interstate commerce. Could this reasoning sustain
the statute at issue, on a regulation-of-channels-for-interstate-firearms rationale?

(6) *Original Intent and Lopez: When "the States are Separately Incompetent."*
Consider whether the majority's approach can be justified from original intent. *See*
Justice Thomas' concurrence, above. As we saw earlier in this chapter, the Founders
rejected a broad grant of power to Congress advocated by Hamilton and instead they
adopted Randolph's proposal allowing legislation "for the general interests of the
Union" and when "the states are separately incompetent." From this, the Committee on
Detail drafted the Commerce Clause. The Founders thought they were creating a union
with limited powers. Does original intent support the result in *Lopez?* Is this original
intent approach more easily defended than the majority's approach? *See generally*
Deborah Jones Merritt, *Commerce!,* 94 MICH. L. REV. 674 (1995).

(7) *Original Intent and Justice Thomas.* Justice Thomas's concurrence in *Lopez*
calls for a return to a narrower perspective on the scope of Congressional power under
the commerce clause. Justice Thomas argued that even the "substantial effects"
standard is broader than the Framers' intent with respect to the clause. In particular,
Justice Thomas argued that the Framers understanding of the term "commerce" was
much narrower than the Court had given to that term. Justice Thomas argued that the
term "commerce" should be limited to certain "transactions" and "transportation"
pursuant to those types of economic transactions. The other four Justices in the *Lopez*
majority declined to join Justice Thomas's approach.

Many in academia have been critical of Justice Thomas's approach. One of the leading
constitutional scholars has reviewed both Justice Thomas's opinion and his critics'.
Randy E. Barnett, *The Original Meaning of the Commerce Clause,* 68 U. CHI. L. REV.
101 (2001). Professor Barnett concludes that Justice Thomas was correct that the
Framers considered the term commerce to mean the "trade or exchange of goods"
(including the means of transporting them) and not the broader notion of any "gainful
activity." Of course, just because the Framers used the term commerce in a narrower
scope than it might be used today does not necessarily limit Congress's powers. Should
it?

(8) *Congressional Regulation of "Social" Issues as Compared to "Economic"
Issues.* A number of scholars have suggested that the real issue here is not necessarily
a broader or narrower scope of the term "commerce," or even how the two hundred
years of commerce clause precedents should be read, but that the real issue is just at
what point is there any limit on Congressional ability to regulate with respect to certain
"social" issues (here loosely defined as "non-commercial" matters). Such social issues
had traditionally been the provence of state regulation under state police powers. The
facts of *Lopez* demonstrate that the state of Texas had taken steps to address school
area violence. In fact, Lopez was initially charged under state law. As the plurality
opinion in *Lopez* indicated, when the states appear to be competent to address a
problem, and where the problem is essentially of a "social" nature, what is the rationale
for allowing Congress to regulate these matters especially in the name of a power that
is texturally connected to "commerce"? For a thoughtful analysis, *see* Debra Jones
Merritt, *The Third Translation of The Commerce Clause: Congressional Power to
Regulate Social Problems,* 66 GEO. WASH. L. REV. 1206 (1998).

PROBLEM E

FALLOUT FROM LOPEZ IN OTHER CONTEXTS: DOES LOPEZ THREATEN FEDERAL LAWS ADVANCING INTERESTS AS DIVERSE AS ARBITRATION AGREEMENTS AND ABORTION CLINIC ACCESS? The Federal Freedom of Access to Clinic Entrances Act ("FACE") is a federal law that, among other subjects, makes it a crime to intimidate a woman entering an abortion clinic. This FACE Act has been challenged on the ground that access to local abortion clinics, even if inhibited, does not substantially affect interstate commerce. Is the FACE Act made unconstitutional by the *Lopez* reasoning? (A majority of courts considering the question have upheld the Act.) Also, consider the decision of the Court, in the same term as *Lopez*, in *Allied-Bruce Terminix, Inc. v. Dobston*, 513 U.S. 265 (1995). There, the Court upheld an application of the Federal Arbitration Act to a local termite inspection and eradication contract by observing:

> The parties do not contest that the transaction in this case, in fact, involved interstate commerce. In addition to the multistate nature of Terminix and Allied-Bruce, the termite-treating and house-repairing material used by Allied-Bruce in its (allegedly inadequate) efforts to carry out the terms of the Plan, came from outside Alabama.

But isn't this reasoning inconsistent with *Lopez*? If *Allied-Terminix* is correct, and if it is enough that supplies moved in interstate commerce or that one party is a multistate entity, perhaps the result would change in *Lopez* if the gun had come from another state—or if the defendant was an employee of a Fortune 500 company! Does this outcome make sense—or is application of the Federal Arbitration Act unconstitutional under *Lopez*? There also have been similar constitutional attacks on the Child Support Recovery Act (upheld in some courts, invalidated in at least one), the prohibition on possession of firearms by felons, the federal Carjacking Act (generally upheld), and other enactments. *See* Eric Grossman, *Where Do We Go From Here? The Aftermath and Application of United States v. Lopez*, 33 Hous. L. Rev. 795 (1996).

UNITED STATES v. MORRISON
529 U.S. 598 (2000)

Chief Justice Rehnquist delivered the opinion of the Court.

In these cases we consider the constitutionality of 42 U.S.C. § 13981, which provides a federal civil remedy for the victims of gender- motivated violence. . . .

I

Petitioner Christy Brzonkala enrolled at Virginia Polytechnic Institute (Virginia Tech) in the fall of 1994. In September of that year, Brzonkala met respondents Antonio Morrison and James Crawford, who were both students at Virginia Tech and members of its varsity football team. Brzonkala alleges that, within 30 minutes of meeting Morrison and Crawford, they assaulted and repeatedly raped her. After the attack, Morrison allegedly told Brzonkala, "You better not have any . . . diseases." Complaint § 22. In the months following the rape, Morrison also allegedly announced in the dormitory's dining room that he "like[d] to get girls drunk and. . . . " *Id.*, § 31. The omitted portions, quoted verbatim in the briefs on file with this Court, consist of boasting, debased remarks about what Morrison would do to women, vulgar remarks that cannot fail to shock and offend.

Brzonkala alleges that this attack caused her to become severely emotionally disturbed and depressed. She sought assistance from a university psychiatrist, who prescribed antidepressant medication. Shortly after the rape Brzonkala stopped attending classes and withdrew from the university. . . .

In December 1995, Brzonkala sued Morrison, Crawford, and Virginia Tech in the

United States District Court for the Western District of Virginia. Her complaint alleged that Morrison's and Crawford's attack violated § 13981. . . . Morrison and Crawford moved to dismiss this complaint on the grounds that it failed to state a claim and that § 13981's civil remedy is unconstitutional. The United States, petitioner in No. 99-5, intervened to defend § 13981's constitutionality.

The District Court . . . held that Brzonkala's complaint stated a claim against Morrison and Crawford under § 13981, but dismissed the complaint because it concluded that Congress lacked authority to enact the section under either the Commerce Clause or § 5 of the Fourteenth Amendment. [The Court of Appeals affirmed.]

Section 13981 was part of the Violence Against Women Act of 1994. It states that "[a]ll persons within the United States shall have the right to be free from crimes of violence motivated by gender." 42 U.S.C. § 13981(b). To enforce that right, subsection (c) declares:

> "A person (including a person who acts under color of any statute, ordinance, regulation, custom, or usage of any State) who commits a crime of violence motivated by gender and thus deprives another of the right declared in subsection (b) of this section shall be liable to the party injured, in an action for the recovery of compensatory and punitive damages, injunctive and declaratory relief, and such other relief as a court may deem appropriate. . . . "

Although the foregoing language of § 13981 covers a wide swath of criminal conduct, Congress placed some limitations on the section's federal civil remedy. Subsection (e)(1) states that "[n]othing in this section entitles a person to a cause of action under subsection (c) of this section for random acts of violence unrelated to gender or for acts that cannot be demonstrated, by a preponderance of the evidence, to be motivated by gender." Subsection (e)(4) further states that § 13981 shall not be construed "to confer on the courts of the United States jurisdiction over any State law claim seeking the establishment of a divorce, alimony, equitable distribution of marital property, or child custody decree."

Every law enacted by Congress must be based on one or more of its powers enumerated in the Constitution. . . . Congress explicitly identified the sources of federal authority on which it relied in enacting 13981. It said that a "federal civil rights cause of action" is established "[p]ursuant to the affirmative power of Congress . . . under section 5 of the Fourteenth Amendment to the Constitution, as well as under section 8 of Article I of the Constitution." We address Congress' authority to enact this remedy under each of these constitutional provisions in turn.

II

Due respect for the decisions of a coordinate branch of Government demands that we invalidate a congressional enactment only upon a plain showing that Congress has exceeded its constitutional bounds. See United States v. Lopez, 514 U.S., at 568 (Kennedy, J., concurring); United States v. Harris, 106 U.S., at 635. With this presumption of constitutionality in mind, we turn to the question whether § 13981 falls within Congress' power under Article I, § 8, of the Constitution. Brzonkala and the United States rely upon the third clause of the Article, which gives Congress power "[t]o regulate Commerce with foreign Nations, and among the several States, and with the Indian Tribes."

As we discussed at length in Lopez, our interpretation of the Commerce Clause has changed as our Nation has developed. See Lopez, 514 U.S., at 552–557 (Kennedy, J., concurring); id., at 584, 593–599 (Thomas, J., concurring). We need not repeat that detailed review of the Commerce Clause's history here; it suffices to say that, in the years since NLRB v. Jones & Laughlin Steel Corp., 301 U.S. 1 (1937), Congress has had considerably greater latitude in regulating conduct and transactions under the Commerce Clause than our previous case law permitted. See Lopez, 514 U.S., at 555–556; id., at 573–574 (Kennedy, J., concurring).

Lopez emphasized, however, that even under our modern, expansive interpretation of the Commerce Clause, Congress' regulatory authority is not without effective bounds. . . .

As we observed in Lopez, modern Commerce Clause jurisprudence has "identified three broad categories of activity that Congress may regulate under its commerce power." 514 U.S., at 558. "First, Congress may regulate the use of the channels of interstate commerce." 514 U.S., at 558, (citing Heart of Atlanta Motel, Inc. v. United States, 379 U.S. 241 (1964); United States v. Darby, 312 U.S. 100 (1941)). "Second, Congress is empowered to regulate and protect the instrumentalities of interstate commerce, or persons or things in interstate commerce, even though the threat may come only from intrastate activities." 514 U.S., at 558 (citing Shreveport Rate Cases, 234 U.S. 342 (1914). "Finally, Congress' commerce authority includes the power to regulate those activities having a substantial relation to interstate commerce, . . . i.e., those activities that substantially affect interstate commerce." 514 U.S., at 558–559 (citing Jones & Laughlin Steel, *supra*.)

Petitioners do not contend that these cases fall within either of the first two of these categories of Commerce Clause regulation. They seek to sustain § 13981 as a regulation of activity that substantially affects interstate commerce. Given § 13981's focus on gender-motivated violence wherever it occurs (rather than violence directed at the instrumentalities of interstate commerce, interstate markets, or things or persons in interstate commerce), we agree that this is the proper inquiry.

Since Lopez most recently canvassed and clarified our case law governing this third category of Commerce Clause regulation, it provides the proper framework for conducting the required analysis of § 13981. In Lopez, we held that the Gun-Free School Zones Act of 1990, 18 U.S.C. § 922(q)(1)(A), which made it a federal crime to knowingly possess a firearm in a school zone, exceeded Congress' authority under the Commerce Clause. Several significant considerations contributed to our decision.

First, we observed [in *Lopez*] that § 922(q) was "a criminal statute that by its terms has nothing to do with 'commerce' or any sort of economic enterprise, however broadly one might define those terms." Id., at 561. . . .

Both petitioners and Justice Souter's dissent downplay the role that the economic nature of the regulated activity plays in our Commerce Clause analysis. But a fair reading of *Lopez* shows that the noneconomic, criminal nature of the conduct at issue was central to our decision in that case. . . . *Lopez's* review of Commerce Clause case law demonstrates that in those cases where we have sustained federal regulation of intrastate activity based upon the activity's substantial effects on interstate commerce, the activity in question has been some sort of economic endeavor.

The second consideration that we found important in *Lopez* was that the statute contained "no express jurisdictional element which might limit its reach to a discrete set of firearm possessions that additionally have an explicit connection with or effect on interstate commerce." Id., at 562. Such a jurisdictional element may establish that the enactment is in pursuance of Congress' regulation of interstate commerce.

Third, we noted that neither § 922(q) " 'nor its legislative history contain[s] express congressional findings regarding the effects upon interstate commerce of gun possession in a school zone.' " Ibid. While "Congress normally is not required to make formal findings as to the substantial burdens that an activity has on interstate commerce," 514 U.S., at 562, the existence of such findings may "enable us to evaluate the legislative judgment that the activity in question substantially affect[s] interstate commerce, even though no such substantial effect [is] visible to the naked eye." 514 U.S., at 563.

Finally, our decision in *Lopez* rested in part on the fact that the link between gun possession and a substantial effect on interstate commerce was attenuated. . . .

We rejected in Lopez these "costs of crime" and "national productivity" arguments because they would permit Congress to "regulate not only all violent crime, but all activities that might lead to violent crime, regardless of how tenuously they relate to interstate commerce." . . .

With these principles underlying our Commerce Clause jurisprudence as reference points, the proper resolution of the present cases is clear. Gender-motivated crimes of violence are not, in any sense of the phrase, economic activity. While we need not adopt a categorical rule against aggregating the effects of any noneconomic activity in order to decide these cases, thus far in our Nation's history our cases have upheld Commerce Clause regulation of intrastate activity only where that activity is economic in nature.

Like the Gun-Free School Zones Act at issue in Lopez, § 13981 contains no jurisdictional element establishing that the federal cause of action is in pursuance of Congress' power to regulate interstate commerce. . . .

In contrast with the lack of congressional findings that we faced in *Lopez*, § 13981 is supported by numerous findings regarding the serious impact that gender-motivated violence has on victims and their families. But the existence of congressional findings is not sufficient, by itself, to sustain the constitutionality of Commerce Clause legislation. As we stated in *Lopez*, " '[S]imply because Congress may conclude that a particular activity substantially affects interstate commerce does not necessarily make it so.' " 514 U.S., at 557, n. 2. Rather, " '[w]hether particular operations affect interstate commerce sufficiently to come under the constitutional power of Congress to regulate them is ultimately a judicial rather than a legislative question, and can be settled finally only by this Court.' " 514 U.S., at 557, n. 2.

In these cases, Congress' findings are substantially weakened by the fact that they rely so heavily on a method of reasoning that we have already rejected as unworkable if we are to maintain the Constitution's enumeration of powers. Congress found that gender-motivated violence affects interstate commerce:

> "by deterring potential victims from traveling interstate, from engaging in employment in interstate business, and from transacting with business, and in places involved in interstate commerce; . . . by diminishing national productivity, increasing medical and other costs, and decreasing the supply of and the demand for interstate products." H.R. Conf. Rep. No. 103-711, at 385, U.S. Code Cong. & Admin.News 1994, pp. 1803, 1853.

Accord, S.Rep. No. 103-138, at 54. Given these findings and petitioners' arguments, the concern that we expressed in *Lopez* that Congress might use the Commerce Clause to completely obliterate the Constitution's distinction between national and local authority seems well founded. See *Lopez, supra*, at 564. The reasoning that petitioners advance seeks to follow the but-for causal chain from the initial occurrence of violent crime (the suppression of which has always been the prime object of the States' police power) to every attenuated effect upon interstate commerce. If accepted, petitioners' reasoning would allow Congress to regulate any crime as long as the nationwide, aggregated impact of that crime has substantial effects on employment, production, transit, or consumption. Indeed, if Congress may regulate gender-motivated violence, it would be able to regulate murder or any other type of violence since gender-motivated violence, as a subset of all violent crime, is certain to have lesser economic impacts than the larger class of which it is a part.

[W]e accordingly reject the argument that Congress may regulate noneconomic, violent criminal conduct based solely on that conduct's aggregate effect on interstate commerce. The Constitution requires a distinction between what is truly national and what is truly local. *Lopez*, 514 U.S., at 568. . . .

III

Because we conclude that the Commerce Clause does not provide Congress with authority to enact § 13981, we address petitioners' alternative argument that the section's civil remedy should be upheld as an exercise of Congress' remedial power under § 5 of the Fourteenth Amendment. [See § 14.02 below.] . . .

The principles governing an analysis of congressional legislation under § 5 are well settled. Section 5 states that Congress may " 'enforce,' by 'appropriate legislation' the constitutional guarantee that no State shall deprive any person of 'life, liberty or property, without due process of law,' nor deny any person 'equal protection of the laws.' " However, "[a]s broad as the congressional enforcement power is, it is not unlimited." Oregon v. Mitchell, 400 U.S. 112, 128 (1970). In fact, as we discuss in detail below, several limitations inherent in § 5's text and constitutional context have been recognized since the Fourteenth Amendment was adopted.

Petitioners' § 5 argument is founded on an assertion that there is pervasive bias in various state justice systems against victims of gender- motivated violence. This assertion is supported by a voluminous congressional record. [P]etitioners contend that this bias denies victims of gender-motivated violence the equal protection of the laws and that Congress therefore acted appropriately in enacting a private civil remedy against the perpetrators of gender-motivated violence to both remedy the States' bias and deter future instances of discrimination in the state courts.

As our cases have established, state-sponsored gender discrimination violates equal protection unless it " 'serves "important governmental objectives and . . . the discriminatory means employed" are "substantially related to the achievement of those objectives." ' " United States v. Virginia, 518 U.S. 515 (1996). However, the language and purpose of the Fourteenth Amendment place certain limitations on the manner in which Congress may attack discriminatory conduct. These limitations are necessary to prevent the Fourteenth Amendment from obliterating the Framers' carefully crafted balance of power between the States and the National Government. Foremost among these limitations is the time-honored principle that the Fourteenth Amendment, by its very terms, prohibits only state action. . . .

The force of the doctrine of *stare decisis* behind these decisions stems not only from the length of time they have been on the books, but also from the insight attributable to the Members of the Court at that time. Every Member had been appointed by President Lincoln, Grant, Hayes, Garfield, or Arthur—and each of their judicial appointees obviously had intimate knowledge and familiarity with the events surrounding the adoption of the Fourteenth Amendment.

Petitioners contend that two more recent decisions have in effect overruled this longstanding limitation on Congress' § 5 authority. [The Court distinguished these decisions.] . . .

Petitioners alternatively argue that, unlike the situation in the Civil Rights Cases, here there has been gender-based disparate treatment by state authorities, whereas in those cases there was no indication of such state action. . . .

But even if that distinction were valid, we do not believe it would save § 13981's civil remedy. For the remedy is simply not "corrective in its character, adapted to counteract and redress the operation of such prohibited [s]tate laws or proceedings of [s]tate officers." Civil Rights Cases, 109 U.S., at 18. Or, as we have phrased it in more recent cases, prophylactic legislation under § 5 must have a "congruence and proportionality between the injury to be prevented or remedied and the means adopted to that end." Florida Prepaid Postsecondary Ed. Expense Bd. v. College Savings Bank, 527 U.S. 627 (1999); Flores, 521 U.S., at 526. [See § 14.02 below.] Section 13981 is not aimed at proscribing discrimination by officials which the Fourteenth Amendment might not itself proscribe; it is directed not at any State or state actor, but at individuals who have committed criminal acts motivated by gender bias.

In the present cases, for example, § 13981 visits no consequence whatever on any Virginia public official involved in investigating or prosecuting Brzonkala's assault. The section is, therefore, unlike any of the § 5 remedies that we have previously upheld. For example, in Katzenbach v. Morgan, 384 U.S. 641 (1966), Congress prohibited New York from imposing literacy tests as a prerequisite for voting because it found that such a requirement disenfranchised thousands of Puerto Rican immigrants who had been educated in the Spanish language of their home territory. That law, which we upheld, was directed at New York officials who administered the State's election law and prohibited them from using a provision of that law. In South Carolina v. Katzenbach, 383 U.S. 301 (1966), Congress imposed voting rights requirements on States that, Congress found, had a history of discriminating against blacks in voting. The remedy was also directed at state officials in those States. . . .

Section 13981 is also different from these previously upheld remedies in that it applies uniformly throughout the Nation. Congress' findings indicate that the problem of discrimination against the victims of gender-motivated crimes does not exist in all States, or even most States. By contrast, the § 5 remedy upheld in Katzenbach v. Morgan, *supra*, was directed only to the State where the evil found by Congress existed, and in South Carolina v. Katzenbach, *supra*, the remedy was directed only to those States in which Congress found that there had been discrimination.

For these reasons, we conclude that Congress' power under § 5 does not extend to the enactment of § 13981.

IV

Petitioner Brzonkala's complaint alleges that she was the victim of a brutal assault. But Congress' effort in § 13981 to provide a federal civil remedy can be sustained neither under the Commerce Clause nor under § 5 of the Fourteenth Amendment. If the allegations here are true, no civilized system of justice could fail to provide her a remedy for the conduct of respondent Morrison. But under our federal system that remedy must be provided by the Commonwealth of Virginia, and not by the United States. The judgment of the Court of Appeals is

Affirmed.

JUSTICE THOMAS, concurring.

The majority opinion correctly applies our decision in *United States v. Lopez*, and I join it in full. I write separately only to express my view that the very notion of a "substantial effects" test under the Commerce Clause is inconsistent with the original understanding of Congress' powers and with this Court's early Commerce Clause cases. By continuing to apply this rootless and malleable standard, however circumscribed, the Court has encouraged the Federal Government to persist in its view that the Commerce Clause has virtually no limits. Until this Court replaces its existing Commerce Clause jurisprudence with a standard more consistent with the original understanding, we will continue to see Congress appropriating state police powers under the guise of regulating commerce.

JUSTICE SOUTER, with whom JUSTICE STEVENS, JUSTICE GINSBURG, and JUSTICE BREYER join, dissenting.

The Court says both that it leaves Commerce Clause precedent undisturbed and that the Civil Rights Remedy of the Violence Against Women Act of 1994, 42 U.S.C. § 13981, exceeds Congress's power under that Clause. I find the claims irreconcilable and respectfully dissent.

I

Our cases, which remain at least nominally undisturbed, stand for the following propositions. Congress has the power to legislate with regard to activity that, in the aggregate, has a substantial effect on interstate commerce. See Wickard v. Filburn, 317 U.S. 111. The fact of such a substantial effect is not an issue for the courts in the first instance, ibid., but for the Congress, whose institutional capacity for gathering evidence and taking testimony far exceeds ours. By passing legislation, Congress indicates its conclusion, whether explicitly or not, that facts support its exercise of the commerce power. The business of the courts is to review the congressional assessment, not for soundness but simply for the rationality of concluding that a jurisdictional basis exists in fact. . . .

One obvious difference from United States v. Lopez is the mountain of data assembled by Congress, here showing the effects of violence against women on interstate commerce. Passage of the Act in 1994 was preceded by four years of hearings, which included testimony from physicians and law professors; from survivors of rape and domestic violence; and from representatives of state law enforcement and private business. . . .

Congress thereby explicitly stated the predicate for the exercise of its Commerce Clause power. Is its conclusion irrational in view of the data amassed? True, the methodology of particular studies may be challenged, and some of the figures arrived at may be disputed. But the sufficiency of the evidence before Congress to provide a rational basis for the finding cannot seriously be questioned.

Indeed, the legislative record here is far more voluminous than the record compiled by Congress and found sufficient in two prior cases upholding Title II of the Civil Rights Act of 1964 against Commerce Clause challenges. . . .

II

The Act would have passed muster at any time between *Wickard* in 1942 and *Lopez* in 1995, a period in which the law enjoyed a stable understanding that congressional power under the Commerce Clause, complemented by the authority of the Necessary and Proper Clause, Art. I. § 8 cl. 18, extended to all activity that, when aggregated, has a substantial effect on interstate commerce. . . .

Thus the elusive heart of the majority's analysis in these cases is its statement that Congress's findings of fact are "weakened" by the presence of a disfavored "method of reasoning." This seems to suggest that the "substantial effects" analysis is not a factual enquiry, for Congress in the first instance with subsequent judicial review looking only to the rationality of the congressional conclusion, but one of a rather different sort, dependent upon a uniquely judicial competence.

This new characterization of substantial effects has no support in our cases (the self-fulfilling prophecies of *Lopez* aside), least of all those the majority cites.

Since adherence to these formalistically contrived confines of commerce power in large measure provoked the judicial crisis of 1937, one might reasonably have doubted that Members of this Court would ever again toy with a return to the days before NLRB v. Jones & Laughlin Steel Corp., which brought the earlier and nearly disastrous experiment to an end. And yet today's decision can only be seen as a step toward recapturing the prior mistakes. Its revival of a distinction between commercial and noncommercial conduct is at odds with *Wickard*, which repudiated that analysis, and the enquiry into commercial purpose, first intimated by the *Lopez* concurrence, see *Lopez*, *supra*, (opinion of Kennedy, J.), is cousin to the intent-based analysis employed in *Hammer*, *supra*, but rejected for Commerce Clause purposes in *Heart of Atlanta*, *supra* and *Darby*, *supra*. . . .

If we now ask why the formalistic economic/noneconomic distinction might matter today, after its rejection in *Wickard*, the answer is not that the majority fails to see causal connections in an integrated economic world. The answer is that in the minds of the majority there is a new animating theory that makes categorical formalism seem useful again. Just as the old formalism had value in the service of an economic conception, the new one is useful in serving a conception of federalism. . . .

The objection to reviving traditional state spheres of action as a consideration in commerce analysis, however, not only rests on the portent of incoherence, but is compounded by a further defect just as fundamental. The defect, in essence, is the majority's rejection of the Founders' considered judgment that politics, not judicial review, should mediate between state and national interests as the strength and legislative jurisdiction of the National Government inevitably increased through the expected growth of the national economy. . . .

JUSTICE BREYER, with whom JUSTICE STEVENS joins, and with whom JUSTICE SOUTER and JUSTICE GINSBURG join as to Part I-A, dissenting.

No one denies the importance of the Constitution's federalist principles. Its state/federal division of authority protects liberty—both by restricting the burdens that government can impose from a distance and by facilitating citizen participation in government that is closer to home. The question is how the judiciary can best implement that original federalist understanding where the Commerce Clause is at issue.

I

The majority holds that the federal commerce power does not extend to such "noneconomic" activities as "noneconomic, violent criminal conduct" that significantly affects interstate commerce only if we "aggregate" the interstate "effect[s]" of individual instances. Justice Souter explains why history, precedent, and legal logic militate against the majority's approach. I agree and join his opinion. I add that the majority's holding illustrates the difficulty of finding a workable judicial Commerce Clause touchstone—a set of comprehensible interpretive rules that courts might use to impose some meaningful limit, but not too great a limit, upon the scope of the legislative authority that the Commerce Clause delegates to Congress. . . .

A

Consider the problems. The "economic/noneconomic" distinction is not easy to apply. Does the local street corner mugger engage in "economic" activity or "noneconomic" activity when he mugs for money? See Perez v. United States, 402 U.S. 146 (1971) (aggregating local "loan sharking" instances); United States v. Lopez, 514 U.S. 549, 559 (1995) (loan sharking is economic because it consists of "intrastate extortionate credit transactions"). . . .

Given my conclusion on the Commerce Clause question, I need not consider Congress' authority under 5 of the Fourteenth Amendment. Nonetheless, I doubt the Court's reasoning rejecting that source of authority. . . .

The majority adds that Congress found that the problem of inadequacy of state remedies "does not exist in all States, or even most States." But Congress had before it the task force reports of at least 21 States documenting constitutional violations. And it made its own findings about pervasive gender-based stereotypes hampering many state legal systems, sometimes unconstitutionally so. The record nowhere reveals a congressional finding that the problem "does not exist" elsewhere. Why can Congress not take the evidence before it as evidence of a national problem? This Court has not previously held that Congress must document the existence of a problem in every State prior to proposing a national solution. And the deference this Court gives to Congress' chosen remedy under § 5, *Flores*, suggests that any such requirement would be inappropriate. . . .

NOTES AND QUESTIONS

(1) *The Federal Violence Against Women Act Held Unconstitutional: United States v. Morrison, 529 U.S. 598 (2000).* Congress passed the Violence Against Women Act (VAWA). Its provisions included the creation of a victim's federal civil action against the private individuals causing the harm. In this case, a female college student sued, *inter alia,* two college football players for allegedly raping her. The football players defended, *inter alia,* on the grounds that the VAWA was beyond Congressional powers. The Supreme Court, per Chief Justice Rehnquist, agreed with the football players. The Court (5 - 4) held that the civil cause of action provision of VAWA was unconstitutional. The Court held that Congress exceeded its authority under the interstate commerce power [relying on the *Lopez* decision, *supra*] and under § 5 of the Fourteenth Amendment [relying on the *Flores* decision, *infra* Chapter 14]. The same four Justices dissenting in *Lopez* dissented here.

(2) *The Relationship of Lopez and Morrison.* The *Morrison* majority acknowledged that the record assembled by Congress to support the VAWA was much greater than the record regarding school zone violence in *Lopez.* But, a better showing of effects on interstate commerce did not save the VAWA. In addition to the Court's statements, consider the following suggestion.

As you noted above, the reasoning of the Chief Justice in *Lopez* was quite different than the *Lopez* concurrence (by Justice Kennedy). There had been much academic and other speculation as to which of the competing approaches would control future interstate commerce clause cases. The *Morrison* decision suggests that Chief Justice Rehnquist's approach now commands a majority. Under the *Lopez/Morrison* approach, the Court apparently first asks whether the subject matter of the Congressional action at issue is "economic" or "noneconomic." When the activity is considered (by the Judiciary) as noneconomic (as in "education" or "gender-based violence"), the Court will not permit Congress to aggregate the effects of the noneconomic activity to establish the requisite "substantial effects" on interstate commerce. Under the *Lopez/Morrison* approach, there is a judicially enforceable limit—in addition to the political process—on Congressional power to regulate the conduct of the States.

(3) *Justice Thomas and Original Intent.* In his concurring opinion, Justice Thomas again called for a full repudiation of the "substantial effects" standard. Justice Thomas argued that: "Until this Court replaces its existing Commerce Clause jurisprudence with a standard more consistent with the original understanding, we will continue to see Congress appropriating state police powers under the guise of regulating commerce." Justice Thomas apparently considered Congress as untrustworthy to exercise power to protect persons against gender-based violence. Consider again the Court's trust in (or deference to) Congress in *Heart of Atlanta* and other pre-*Lopez* decisions. Should the Court afford more deference to Congress (as a democratically-accountable entity) or would you agree with Justice Thomas? *See also Jones v. United States,* 529 U.S. 848 (2000) (narrow construction of a federal statute, per Justice Ginsburg, to avoid the constitutional issue). [*See generally* § 3.03 below and *Reno v. Condon,* 528 U.S. 141 (2000).]

(4) *Congressional Commerce Clause Power to Regulate "Channels of Interstate Commerce" and "Instrumentalities of Interstate Commerce": Pierce County, Wash. v. Guillen, 537 U.S. 129 (2003).* Both *Lopez* and *Morrison* involved the "substantial effects" theory of interstate commerce, but the Court repeatedly indicated that Congress' commerce power also covered two other categories of action: regulation of the "channels of interstate commerce" and regulation of the "instrumentalities of interstate commerce." *Pierce County* addressed an exercise of the commerce power where Congress based its action on the "channels" and "instrumentalities" theories.

Congress passed the Hazard Elimination Program (Program) to improve highway safety. The Program provides money to state and local governments to improve the most hazardous sections of their roads. Eligibility for Program funding requires state governments to evaluate the roads by compiling data on accidents. [For the personal injury lawyer, this was a "dream come true"—a centralized data base for future cases.] When local governments were reluctant to compile the accident data, Congress sought to encourage them to comply by passing § 409 of the Program which declared that accident data compiled for the Program "shall not be admitted into evidence in Federal or State court." Thus, Congress dictated part of the evidence law for state court actions. The Washington Supreme Court held that § 409 exceeded Congressional power (under the Commerce or Spending Clauses). The Supreme Court, per Justice Thomas, unanimously reversed, holding that § 409 was within Congress' commerce power.

While the Court was not as explicit as in other decisions, *see Eldred v. Ashcroft* below, the Court held that "Congress could reasonably believe that adopting [§ 409] . . . would result in . . . greater safety on our Nation's roads." The Court stated that § 409 could be viewed "as legislation aimed at improving safety in the channels of commerce and increasing protection for the instrumentalities of interstate commerce." This reasoning and language comports with the rational basis standard.

Remember that Justice Thomas has taken the narrowest view (of any Justice) regarding the scope of the commerce power. In *Pierce County*, however, he writes for the Court upholding the power of Congress to control the admissibility of evidence in State courts in state law tort actions. Would the Framers have intended that the commerce power gave Congress control over the admissibility of evidence for tort law claims in state court? *See generally*, Mark R. Killenbeck, *The Physics of Federalism*, 51 KAN. L. REV. 1 (2002).

(5) *Some Limits of the Lopez/Morrison Interpretation of the Commerce Clause: Citizens Bank v. Alafabco, Inc., 539 U.S. 52 (2003).* The Citizens Bank, a lender, sought to compel Alafabco, the borrower, to arbitrate a financial dispute under the Federal Arbitration Act (FAA). The dispute arose from a series of commercial loan transactions and debt-restructuring agreements all occurring in Alabama. The Alabama Supreme Court decided that the FAA's arbitration provision was outside the scope of Congressional power because the set of transactions between the parties had not had a "substantial effect on interstate commerce." The Supreme Court, in a *per curiam* opinion, reversed on the Commerce Clause issue.

The Court held that

> Congress' Commerce Clause power may be exercised in individual cases without showing any specific effect upon interstate commerce if in the aggregate the economic activity in question would represent a general practice . . . subject to federal control. . . . Only the general practice need bear on interstate commerce in a substantial way.

See Note (8) after *Lopez*, above. *See generally* J. Randy Beck, *The Heart of Federalism: Pretext Review of Means-End Relationships*, 36 U.C. DAVIS L. REV. 407 (2003).

GONZALES v. RAICH
545 U.S. 1 (2005)

JUSTICE STEVENS delivered the opinion of the Court.

California is one of at least nine States that authorize the use of marijuana for medicinal purposes. The question presented in this case is whether the power vested in Congress by Article I, § 8, of the Constitution "[t]o make all Laws which shall be necessary and proper for carrying into Execution" its authority to "regulate Commerce with foreign Nations, and among the several States" includes the power to prohibit the local cultivation and use of marijuana in compliance with California law.

I

California has been a pioneer in the regulation of marijuana. In 1913, California was one of the first States to prohibit the sale and possession of marijuana, and at the end of the century, California became the first State to authorize limited use of the drug for medicinal purposes. In 1996, California voters passed Proposition 215, now codified as the Compassionate Use Act of 1996. The proposition was designed to ensure that "seriously ill" residents of the State have access to marijuana for medical purposes, and to encourage Federal and State Governments to take steps towards ensuring the safe and affordable distribution of the drug to patients in need. . . .

Respondents Angel Raich and Diane Monson are California residents who suffer from a variety of serious medical conditions and have sought to avail themselves of medical marijuana pursuant to the terms of the Compassionate Use Act. They are being treated by licensed, board-certified family practitioners, who have concluded, after prescribing a host of conventional medicines to treat respondents' conditions and to alleviate their associated symptoms, that marijuana is the only drug available that provides effective treatment. . . .

Respondents . . . brought this action against the Attorney General of the United States and the head of the DEA seeking injunctive and declaratory relief prohibiting the enforcement of the federal Controlled Substances Act (CSA), 84 Stat. 1242, 21 U.S.C. § 801 et seq., to the extent it prevents them from possessing, obtaining, or manufacturing cannabis for their personal medical use. . . .

The District Court denied respondents' motion for a preliminary injunction. *Raich v. Ashcroft*, 248 F.Supp.2d 918 (N.D.Cal.2003). . . .

A divided panel of the Court of Appeals for the Ninth Circuit reversed and ordered the District Court to enter a preliminary injunction. . . . The Court of Appeals distinguished prior Circuit cases upholding the CSA in the face of Commerce Clause challenges by focusing on what it deemed to be the "separate and distinct class of activities" at issue in this case: "the intrastate, noncommercial cultivation and possession of cannabis for personal medical purposes as recommended by a patient's physician pursuant to valid California state law." The court found the latter class of activities "different in kind from drug trafficking" because interposing a physician's recommendation raises different health and safety concerns, and because "this limited use is clearly distinct from the broader illicit drug market—as well as any broader commercial market for medicinal marijuana—insofar as the medicinal marijuana at issue in this case is not intended for, nor does it enter, the stream of commerce." . . .

The obvious importance of the case prompted our grant of certiorari. The case is made difficult by respondents' strong arguments that they will suffer irreparable harm because, despite a congressional finding to the contrary, marijuana does have valid therapeutic purposes. The question before us, however, is not whether it is wise to enforce the statute in these circumstances; rather, it is whether Congress' power to regulate interstate markets for medicinal substances encompasses the portions of those markets that are supplied with drugs produced and consumed locally. Well-settled law controls our answer. The CSA is a valid exercise of federal power, even as applied to the troubling facts of this case. We accordingly vacate the judgment of the Court of Appeals.

II

[T]he main objectives of the CSA were to conquer drug abuse and to control the legitimate and illegitimate traffic in controlled substances. Congress was particularly concerned with the need to prevent the diversion of drugs from legitimate to illicit channels.

To effectuate these goals, Congress devised a closed regulatory system making it unlawful to manufacture, distribute, dispense, or possess any controlled substance except in a manner authorized by the CSA. 21 U.S.C. §§ 841(a)(1), 844(a). The CSA categorizes all controlled substances into five schedules. § 812. . . .

In enacting the CSA, Congress classified marijuana as a Schedule I drug. 21 U.S.C. § 812(c). . . . By classifying marijuana as a Schedule I drug, as opposed to listing it on a lesser schedule, the manufacture, distribution, or possession of marijuana became a criminal offense, with the sole exception being use of the drug as part of a Food and Drug Administration pre-approved research study.

The CSA provides for the periodic updating of schedules and delegates authority to the Attorney General, after consultation with the Secretary of Health and Human Services, to add, remove, or transfer substances to, from, or between schedules. § 811. Despite considerable efforts to reschedule marijuana, it remains a Schedule I drug.

III

Respondents in this case do not dispute that passage of the CSA, as part of the Comprehensive Drug Abuse Prevention and Control Act, was well within Congress' commerce power. Brief for Respondents 22, 38. Nor do they contend that any provision or section of the CSA amounts to an unconstitutional exercise of congressional authority. Rather, respondents' challenge is actually quite limited; they argue that the CSA's categorical prohibition of the manufacture and possession of marijuana as applied to the intrastate manufacture and possession of marijuana for medical purposes pursuant to California law exceeds Congress' authority under the Commerce Clause.

In assessing the validity of congressional regulation, none of our Commerce Clause cases can be viewed in isolation. As charted in considerable detail in *United States v. Lopez*, our understanding of the reach of the Commerce Clause, as well as Congress' assertion of authority thereunder, has evolved over time. The Commerce Clause emerged as the Framers' response to the central problem giving rise to the Constitution itself: the absence of any federal commerce power under the Articles of Confederation. . . .

[Our c]ases have identified three general categories of regulation in which Congress is authorized to engage under its commerce power. First, Congress can regulate the channels of interstate commerce. *Perez v. United States*, 402 U.S. 146 (1971). Second, Congress has authority to regulate and protect the instrumentalities of interstate commerce, and persons or things in interstate commerce. *Ibid.* Third, Congress has the power to regulate activities that substantially affect interstate commerce. *Ibid. NLRB v. Jones & Laughlin Steel Corp.*, 301 U.S. 1, 37 (1937). Only the third category is implicated in the case at hand.

Our case law firmly establishes Congress' power to regulate purely local activities that are part of an economic "class of activities" that have a substantial effect on interstate commerce. *See, e.g., Wickard v. Filburn*, 317 U.S. 111, 128–129 (1942). . . .

Wickard thus establishes that Congress can regulate purely intrastate activity that is not itself "commercial," in that it is not produced for sale, if it concludes that failure to regulate that class of activity would undercut the regulation of the interstate market in that commodity.

The similarities between this case and *Wickard* are striking. Like the farmer in *Wickard*, respondents are cultivating, for home consumption, a fungible commodity for which there is an established, albeit illegal, interstate market. . . . Here too, Congress had a rational basis for concluding that leaving home-consumed marijuana outside federal control would similarly affect price and market conditions.

More concretely, one concern prompting inclusion of wheat grown for home consumption in the 1938 Act was that rising market prices could draw such wheat into the interstate market, resulting in lower market prices. *Wickard*, 317 U.S., at 128. The parallel concern making it appropriate to include marijuana grown for home consumption in the CSA is the likelihood that the high demand in the interstate market will draw such marijuana into that market. . . .

Nonetheless, respondents suggest that *Wickard* differs from this case in three respects: (1) the Agricultural Adjustment Act, unlike the CSA, exempted small farming operations; (2) *Wickard* involved a "quintessential economic activity"—a commercial farm—whereas respondents do not sell marijuana; and (3) the *Wickard* record made it clear that the aggregate production of wheat for use on farms had a significant impact on market prices. Those differences, though factually accurate, do not diminish the precedential force of this Court's reasoning.

The fact that Wickard's own impact on the market was "trivial by itself" was not a sufficient reason for removing him from the scope of federal regulation. . . . And while it is true that the record in the *Wickard* case itself established the causal connection between the production for local use and the national market, we have before us findings by Congress to the same effect.

[I]n assessing the scope of Congress' authority under the Commerce Clause, we stress that the task before us is a modest one. We need not determine whether respondents' activities, taken in the aggregate, substantially affect interstate commerce in fact, but only whether a "rational basis" exists for so concluding. *Lopez*, 514 U.S., at 557; *Katzenbach v. McClung*, 379 U.S. 294, 299–301 (1964); *Heart of Atlanta Motel, Inc. v. United States*, 379 U.S. 241, 252–253 (1964). Given the enforcement difficulties that attend distinguishing between marijuana cultivated locally and marijuana grown elsewhere, and concerns about diversion into illicit channels, we have no difficulty concluding that Congress had a rational basis for believing that failure to regulate the intrastate manufacture and possession of marijuana would leave a gaping hole in the CSA. Thus, as in *Wickard*, when it enacted comprehensive legislation to regulate the interstate market in a fungible commodity, Congress was acting well within its authority to "make all Laws which shall be necessary and proper" to "regulate Commerce . . . among the several States." U.S. Const., Art. I, § 8. That the regulation ensnares some purely intrastate activity is of no moment. As we have done many times before, we refuse to excise individual components of that larger scheme.

IV

To support their contrary submission, respondents rely heavily on two of our more recent Commerce Clause cases. In their myopic focus, they overlook the larger context of modern-era Commerce Clause jurisprudence preserved by those cases. Moreover, even in the narrow prism of respondents' creation, they read those cases far too broadly. Those two cases, of course, are *Lopez* and *Morrison*. . . .

The Court of Appeals . . . isolat[ed] a "separate and distinct" class of activities that it held to be beyond the reach of federal power, defined as "the intrastate, noncommercial cultivation, possession and use of marijuana for personal medical purposes on the advice of a physician and in accordance with state law." 352 F.3d, at 1229. . . . The question, however, is whether Congress' contrary policy judgment, *i.e.*, its decision to include this narrower "class of activities" within the larger regulatory scheme, was constitutionally deficient. We have no difficulty concluding that Congress acted rationally in determining that none of the characteristics making up the purported class, whether viewed individually or in the aggregate, compelled an exemption from the CSA; rather, the subdivided class of activities defined by the Court of Appeals was an essential part of the larger regulatory scheme. . . .

The congressional judgment that an exemption for such a significant segment of the total market would undermine the orderly enforcement of the entire regulatory scheme is entitled to a strong presumption of validity. Indeed, that judgment is not only rational, but "visible to the naked eye," *Lopez*, 514 U.S., at 563, under any commonsense appraisal of the probable consequences of such an open-ended exemption.

Second, limiting the activity to marijuana possession and cultivation "in accordance with state law" cannot serve to place respondents' activities beyond congressional reach. The Supremacy Clause unambiguously provides that if there is any conflict between federal and state law, federal law shall prevail. . . .

V

Respondents also raise a substantive due process claim and seek to avail themselves of the medical necessity defense. These theories of relief were set forth in their complaint but were not reached by the Court of Appeals. We therefore do not address the question whether judicial relief is available to respondents on these alternative bases. We do note, however, the presence of another avenue of relief. As the Solicitor General confirmed during oral argument, the statute authorizes procedures for the reclassification of Schedule I drugs. But perhaps even more important than these legal avenues is the democratic process, in which the voices of voters allied with these respondents may one day be heard in the halls of Congress. Under the present state of the law, however, the judgment of the Court of Appeals must be vacated. The case is remanded for further proceedings consistent with this opinion.

It is so ordered.

JUSTICE SCALIA, concurring in the judgment.

I agree with the Court's holding that the Controlled Substances Act (CSA) may validly be applied to respondents' cultivation, distribution, and possession of marijuana for personal, medicinal use. I write separately because my understanding of the doctrinal foundation on which that holding rests is, if not inconsistent with that of the Court, at least more nuanced. . . .

I

Our cases show that the regulation of intrastate activities may be necessary to and proper for the regulation of interstate commerce in two general circumstances. Most directly, the commerce power permits Congress not only to devise rules for the governance of commerce between States but also to facilitate interstate commerce by eliminating potential obstructions, and to restrict it by eliminating potential stimulants. See *NLRB v. Jones & Laughlin Steel Corp.*, 301 U.S. 1, 36–37 (1937). That is why the Court has repeatedly sustained congressional legislation on the ground that the regulated activities had a substantial effect on interstate commerce. . . .

JUSTICE O'CONNOR, with whom THE CHIEF JUSTICE and JUSTICE THOMAS join as to all but Part III, dissenting.

We enforce the "outer limits" of Congress' Commerce Clause authority not for their own sake, but to protect historic spheres of state sovereignty from excessive federal encroachment and thereby to maintain the distribution of power fundamental to our federalist system of government. *United States v. Lopez; NLRB v. Jones & Laughlin Steel Corp.* One of federalism's chief virtues, of course, is that it promotes innovation by allowing for the possibility that "a single courageous State may, if its citizens choose, serve as a laboratory; and try novel social and economic experiments without risk to the rest of the country." *New State Ice Co. v. Liebmann*, 285 U.S. 262, 311 (1932) (Brandeis, J., dissenting).

This case exemplifies the role of States as laboratories. The States' core police powers have always included authority to define criminal law and to protect the health, safety, and welfare of their citizens. Exercising those powers, California (by ballot initiative and then by legislative codification) has come to its own conclusion about the difficult and sensitive question of whether marijuana should be available to relieve severe pain and suffering. Today the Court sanctions an application of the federal Controlled Substances Act that extinguishes that experiment, without any proof that the personal cultivation, possession, and use of marijuana for medicinal purposes, if economic activity in the first place, has a substantial effect on interstate commerce and is therefore an appropriate subject of federal regulation. In so doing, the Court announces a rule that gives Congress a perverse incentive to legislate broadly pursuant to the Commerce Clause—nestling questionable assertions of its authority into comprehensive regulatory schemes—rather than with precision. That rule and the result it produces in this case are irreconcilable with our decisions in *Lopez, supra,* and *United States v. Morrison.* Accordingly I dissent. . . .

II

Even assuming that economic activity is at issue in this case, the Government has made no showing in fact that the possession and use of homegrown marijuana for medical purposes, in California or elsewhere, has a substantial effect on interstate commerce. . . .

There is simply no evidence that homegrown medicinal marijuana users constitute, in the aggregate, a sizable enough class to have a discernable, let alone substantial, impact on the national illicit drug market—or otherwise to threaten the CSA regime. . . .

In this regard, again, this case is readily distinguishable from *Wickard.* . . .

Relying on Congress' abstract assertions, the Court has endorsed making it a federal crime to grow small amounts of marijuana in one's own home for one's own medicinal use. This overreaching stifles an express choice by some States, concerned for the lives and liberties of their people, to regulate medical marijuana differently. If I were a California citizen, I would not have voted for the medical marijuana ballot initiative; if I were a California legislator I would not have supported the Compassionate Use Act. But whatever the wisdom of California's experiment with medical marijuana, the federalism principles that have driven our Commerce Clause cases require that room for experiment be protected in this case. For these reasons I dissent.

JUSTICE THOMAS, dissenting.

Respondents Diane Monson and Angel Raich use marijuana that has never been bought or sold, that has never crossed state lines, and that has had no demonstrable effect on the national market for marijuana. If Congress can regulate this under the Commerce Clause, then it can regulate virtually anything—and the Federal Government is no longer one of limited and enumerated powers. . . .

NOTES AND QUESTIONS

(1) *The Interstate Commerce Power and "Medical Marijuana": Gonzales v. Raich, 545 U.S. 1 (2005).* In 1970, Congress adopted a comprehensive regulatory scheme (the CSA) for various drugs, including marijuana, which made possession or use of such drugs illegal under federal law. Nevertheless, in recent years, nine states have passed laws authorizing the "medicinal use" of marijuana. California's "Compassionate Use Act" allowed "seriously ill" state residents to have access to marijuana under a doctor's prescription. The challengers, Raich and Monson, sought to use medical marijuana that was "home-grown." When federal authorities threatened criminal prosecutions, the challengers, and their physicians, argued that Congress did not have the power, under the interstate commerce power, to regulate "medical marijuana." The Supreme Court, per Justice Stevens, disagreed with the challengers (and California). The Court held that Congress could constitutionally exercise its interstate commerce power over the

intrastate, noncommercial cultivation and possession of cannabis for personal medical purposes as recommended by a patient's physician pursuant to California law.

The Court distinguished (and limited) the *Lopez* and *Morrison* decisions (above). Justice Scalia concurred only in the judgment; he offered a more "nuanced" analysis relying on the Necessary and Proper Clause. Justice O'Connor, Chief Justice Rehnquist, and Justice Thomas dissented. Compared to *Lopez* and *Morrison*, the main change in voting alignment was Justice Kennedy.

(2) *The Sky Is Not Falling: Rational Basis Remains, Even After the Lopez Decision, The Governing Standard For the Congressional Exercise of a Plenary Power.* The common understanding, since the New Deal era, was that judicial review of the exercise of one of Congress' "plenary powers" would be conducted under the deferential "rational basis" standard. [This is reviewed extensively in Ch. 3, below, in the *Garcia* decision.] The *Lopez* and *Morrison* decisions created uncertainty whether the Court was continuing to use the rational basis standard. [Similarly, the Court's decisions regarding the Section 5 power of Congress suggested that the Court was not using rational basis for review of that power.] The use of rational basis means that Congress (the democratically accountable branch of government) will make the final decision on important issues. Any other (*i.e.*, "higher") judicial review standard may take decision-making authority away from Congress—and, perhaps, give the authority to the federal courts.

To the extent that *Lopez* and *Morrison* suggested the use of a standard higher than rational basis, they envisioned a more active judicial role. The *Raich* decision, by confirming that the governing standard is rational basis, upholds the broad scope of the plenary power of Congress under the interstate commerce power. The *Raich* Court's use of legislative purpose is examined in David L. *Franklin, Facial Challenges, Legislative Purpose, and the Commerce Clause*, 92 IOWA LAW REVIEW 41 (2006).

(3) *The Medical Marijuana Movement and Justice Stevens' Reliance on the "Political Process."* The majority's opinion in *Raich*, while confirming the applicability of the rational basis standard, primarily focused on a discussion of precedent—distinguishing (and limiting) *Lopez* and *Morrison*. At the very end of Justice Stevens' majority opinion, the Court discussed two alternative "avenues of relief" available to California and, more generally, the proponents of the medical marijuana movement. According to the Court, one alternative is a renewed effort to reclassify marijuana under the CSA. (Of course, as the majority opinion recognized, this reclassification effort has repeatedly failed.) The Court, however, also pointed to another alternative: "perhaps even more important than these legal avenues is the democratic process,. . . ." It is somewhat curious that Justice Stevens would refer to the "political process" as just another "avenue of relief." The "political process," after all, is the underlying rationale for the Court's use of the deferential rational basis standard of judicial review and not just an "avenue of relief." Is the majority changing the terminology of the "federalism" debate? Is this why Justice Scalia presented his "nuanced" concurrence? Is reliance on the political process to resolve social controversies "overreaching," as Justice O'Connor argued in her dissent? *See generally* Kurt T. Lash, *James Madison's Celebrated Report of 1800: The Transformation of the Tenth Amendment*, 74 GEO. WASH. L. REV. 165 (2006).

(4) *A Supreme Court Justice and Former State Legislator: Justice O'Connor's Dissent.* Justice O'Connor submitted the lead dissent. Her dissent emphasized the Brandeisian theme of American "federalism": the States may serve as social "laboratories" to test new ideas and that the federal government should not thwart such valuable "experimentation," especially where no "fundamental rights" are implicated. Justice O'Connor was the only member of the Court who had ever served as an elected state legislator (and, more doctrinally, as a "democratically accountable" official). Would her experience (including being majority leader of the Arizona Senate) favorably dispose her

to trust state legislators—and their good faith experiments? In *Raich*, the majority's adoption of the rational basis standard essentially cuts off this argument, but you should watch for this theme.

There is a remarkable passage in Justice O'Connor's opinion where she indicates that she voted in the case in a fashion inconsistent with her own, personal views on medical marijuana. This opinion should be compared to Justice Kennedy's concurrence in *Texas v. Johnson*, the first flag-burning decision (below in Chapter 11).

§ 2.03   THE TAXING, SPENDING, AND OTHER POWERS

[A]   The Taxing Power as an Instrument of Regulation

THE CHILD LABOR TAX CASE (BAILEY v. DREXEL FURNITURE CO.), 259 U.S. 34 (1922). After the Court had overturned the Congressional prohibition upon interstate shipment of products of child labor in the *Child Labor Case (Hammer v. Dagenhart*, above), Congress imposed a tax upon the net profit of any firm that knowingly employed child labor. In an opinion by Chief Justice Taft, the Court then proceeded to strike down the tax as well. "It is defended upon the ground that it is a mere excise tax, levied by the Congress of the United States under its broad power of taxation conferred by article I, § 8 of the Federal Constitution. . . . ," said the court. "But this Act is more. . . . [A] court must be blind to see that the so-called tax is imposed to stop the employment of children within the age limits prescribed. Its prohibitory and regulatory effects are palpable." The Court then applied the reasoning of *Hammer v. Dagenhart* to hold this penalty unconstitutional.

[handwritten margin notes: "Facts" and "hold."]

Read U.S. Const. Art. I, § 8, cl. 1 (the taxing power).

NOTES AND QUESTIONS

(1) *Advantages of Taxation as a Means of Regulation; Inevitable Regulatory Effects of Taxes; Anomalous Nature of Child Labor Tax Holding.* Every tax has the effect, to a greater or lesser degree, of discouraging consumption of the taxed item. Thus a tax upon gasoline (or crude oil) decreases gasoline consumption. This effect provides an argument in favor of permitting Congress to consider regulatory results when it exercises the taxing power, if only for the purpose of avoiding the undue suppression of desirable conduct. Indeed, might it be more sound, from the point of view of an economist, to regulate by taxation rather than prohibition in some cases? Once these principles are recognized, drawing lines about taxes as "penalties" or as unduly "oppressive" becomes difficult, and it is perhaps for that reason that the holding of the *Child Labor Tax Case* is anomalous. As with the interstate commerce decisions relying on the Court's ascertainment of a "bad" Congressional motive, the tax "motive" decisions were subsequently overruled.

(2) *No Interstate Effect Requirement for the Taxing Power; Greater Potential Breadth than the Commerce Power.* On the other hand, note that the taxing power is not limited, as is the commerce power, by interstate considerations. If the taxing power can be used for regulatory purposes even in the absence of any revenue motivation, won't it overwhelm whatever limitations still remain on the commerce power, slight though they may be? Cf. *United States v. Constantine*, 296 U.S. 287 (1935) (striking down as penalty a federal tax on liquor dealers operating in states where selling liquor was illegal; tax would "usurp" powers of the states). Note, however, that *Constantine* was decided in the same year as the *Schechter Poultry* case and has similarly been repudiated.

UNITED STATES v. KAHRIGER
345 U.S. 22 (1953)

Mr. Justice Reed delivered the opinion of the Court.

[The Court in this case upheld the occupational tax provisions of the federal Revenue Act of 1951, including a provision that required persons in the business of accepting wagers to register and pay ten percent of all wager receipts as a tax. Persons licensed under state law were exempted. Kahriger attacked the law as an attempt to "penalize illegal intrastate gambling through the regulatory features of the Act and [to infringe] the police power which is reserved to the states." The legislative history included statements by members of Congress disclosing a desire to penalize or eliminate illegal gamblers or "put [them] out of business." The district court struck down the tax on the authority of *United States v. Constantine, supra.* The Supreme Court here reverses, pointing out that *Sonzinsky v. United States, 300 U.S. 506 (1937),* had sustained a tax on transfers of illegal firearms shortly after *Constantine.*]

Appellee would have us say that because there is legislative history indicating a congressional motive to suppress wagering, this tax is not a proper exercise of such taxing power. . . .

It is conceded that a federal excise tax does not cease to be valid merely because it discourages or deters the activities taxed. Nor is the tax invalid because the revenue obtained is negligible. Appellee, however, argues that the sole purpose of the statute is to penalize only illegal gambling in the states through the guise of a tax measure. . . . But regardless of its regulatory effect, the wagering tax produces revenue. . . .

It is axiomatic that the power of Congress to tax is extensive and sometimes falls with crushing effect on businesses deemed unessential or inimical to the public welfare, or where, as in dealings with narcotics, the collection of the tax also is difficult. As is well known, the constitutional restraints on taxing are few. "Congress cannot tax exports, and it must impose direct taxes by the rule of apportionment, and indirect taxes by the rule of uniformity. . . ." The remedy for excessive taxation is in the hands of Congress, not the courts. . . .

The difficulty of saying when the power to lay uniform taxes is curtailed, because its use brings a result beyond the direct legislative power of Congress, has given rise to diverse decisions. In that area of abstract ideas, a final definition of the line between state and federal power has baffled judges and legislators.

. . . Where federal legislation has rested on other congressional powers, such as the Necessary and Proper Clause or the Commerce Clause, this Court has generally sustained the statutes, despite their effect on matters ordinarily considered state concern. When federal power to regulate is found, its exercise is a matter for Congress. Where Congress has employed the taxing clause a greater variation in the decisions has resulted. . . .

. . . It is hard to understand why the power to tax should raise more doubts because of indirect effects than other federal powers.

Reversed [i.e., tax upheld].

Mr. Justice Jackson, concurring.

I concur in the judgment and opinion of the Court, but with such doubt that if the minority agreed upon an opinion which did not impair legitimate use of the taxing power I probably would join it. . . .

[H]ere is a purported tax law which requires no reports and lays no tax except on specified gamblers whose calling in most states is illegal. . . . This is difficult to regard as a good-faith revenue measure, despite the deference that is due Congress. On the contrary, it seems to be a plan to tax out of existence the professional gambler whom it has been found impossible to prosecute out of business. . . .

[But] the evil that will come from this statute will probably soon make itself manifest to Congress. The evil of a judicial decision impairing the legitimate taxing power by extreme constitutional interpretations might not be transient. . . .

[The dissenting opinion of MR. JUSTICE BLACK, joined by MR. JUSTICE DOUGLAS, concluding that the registration feature violated the prohibition upon self-incrimination, is omitted.]

MR. JUSTICE FRANKFURTER, dissenting.

Two generalizations may . . . safely be drawn from [the] series of cases [dealing with taxing as regulation]. Congress may make an oblique use of the taxing power in relation to activities with which Congress may deal directly, as for instance, commerce between the States. Thus, if the dissenting views of Mr. Justice Holmes in *Hammer v. Dagenhart* . . . had been the decision of the Court, as they became in *United States v. Darby*, the effort to deal with the problem of child labor through an assertion of the taxing power in the statute considered in the *Child Labor Tax Case* would by the latter case have been sustained. However, when oblique use is made of the taxing power as to matters which substantively are not within the powers delegated to Congress, the Court cannot shut its eyes to what is obviously, because designedly, an attempt to control conduct which the Constitution left to the responsibility of the States, merely because Congress wrapped the legislation in the verbal cellophane of a revenue measure.

NOTES AND QUESTIONS

(1) *Other Constitutional Provisions Restraining the Taxing Power.* What if Congress were to impose an excise tax upon persons living in New York and California but nowhere else? What if it taxed at a 100% rate? There are other provisions of the Constitution (specifically the uniformity requirement of art. I, § 8, cl. 1 and the taking clause of the Fifth Amendment) that address these issues.

(2) *When, If Ever, Is a "Regulatory" Tax Unconstitutional Today?* Justice Frankfurter's opinion would test the limits of the regulatory taxing power by making it coterminous with all other powers of Congress; *i.e.,* if it is within the scope of the commerce power, or the copyright power, or the post office power, it can be reached and regulated through the mechanism of a tax. Is this reasoning persuasive? Notice that, today, it would mean few restrictions on the taxing power because of the long reach of the commerce power (which may be a reason why there are few modern cases raising the issue).

(3) *The Court Overrules Kahriger's Specific Holding without Disturbing its Reasoning: Marchetti v. United States, 390 U.S. 39 (1968).* The type of tax at issue in *Kahriger* later was held unconstitutional in *Marchetti* on self-incrimination grounds under the Fifth Amendment. That decision did not affect the reasoning about the taxing power.

[B]   The Spending Power: "Insurance" Plans, Transfer Payments, and Inducements for State Regulation

> Read U.S. Const. Art. I, § 8, cl. 1 (taxing and spending powers)

UNITED STATES v. BUTLER, 297 U.S. 1 (1935), through Justice Roberts, struck down the Agricultural Adjustment Act of 1933. The Act attempted to balance production and consumption of agricultural commodities by empowering the Secretary of Agriculture to enter into contracts with farmers for reduction of acreage planted, in exchange for "rental or benefit payments." The program was to be funded with a tax upon the processing of the agricultural commodities at issue. Those challenging the Act could do so because they were subject to the tax and hence had standing to challenge it, although the thrust of the attack was upon the regulatory aspects of federal spending for benefit payments. In an opinion rendered in the same year as the *Schechter Poultry* case and reflecting similar philosophy, the Court concluded that the Act invaded the reserved powers of the states:

> The clause thought to authorize the legislation . . . confers upon the Congress power "to lay and collect Taxes, Duties, Imposts and Excises, to pay the debts and provide for the common Defence and general Welfare of the United States." It is not contended that this provision grants power to regulate agricultural production on the theory that such legislation would promote the general welfare. The Government concedes that the phrase "to provide for the general welfare" qualifies the power to "lay and collect taxes. . . ."

> Since the foundation of the nation sharp differences of opinion have persisted as to the true interpretation of the [general Welfare] phrase. Madison asserted it amounted to no more than a reference to the other powers enumerated in the subsequent clauses of the same section. . . . Hamilton, on the other hand, maintained the clause confers a power separate and distinct from those later enumerated, is not restricted in meaning by the grant of them, and Congress consequently has a substantive power to tax and to appropriate, limited only by the requirement that it shall be exercised to provide for the general welfare of the United States. . . . Mr. Justice Story, in his commentaries, espouses the Hamiltonian position. . . . Study of all of these leads us to conclude that the reading advocated by Mr. Justice Story is the correct one. While, therefore, the power to tax is not unlimited, its confines are set in the clause which confers it, and not in those of § 8 which bestow and define the legislative powers of the Congress. It results that the power of Congress to authorize expenditure of public moneys for public purposes is not limited by the direct grants of legislative power found in the Constitution. . . .

> . . . Wholly apart from that question, another principle embedded in our Constitution prohibits the enforcement of the Agricultural Adjustment Act. The Act invades the reserved powers of the states. It is a statutory plan to regulate and control agricultural production, a matter beyond the powers delegated to the federal government. The tax, the appropriation of the funds raised, and the direction for their disbursement, are but parts of the plan. They are but a means to an unconstitutional end.

> . . . To forestall [enactments of this kind], the Tenth Amendment was adopted. . . .

> . . . The power to confer or withhold unlimited benefits is the power to coerce or destroy. If the cotton grower elects not to accept the benefits, he will

receive less for his crops; those who receive payments will be able to undersell him. . . . The coercive purpose and intent of the statute is not obscured by the fact that it has not been perfectly successful. . . .

But if the plan were one for purely voluntary cooperation it would stand no better. . . . At best it is a scheme for purchasing with federal funds submission to federal regulation of a subject reserved to the states.

Justice Stone, joined by Justices Brandeis and Cardozo, dissented, believing that the spending power is "in addition to the legislative power and not subordinate to it. This independent grant of the power of the purse, and its very nature, involving in its exercise the duty to insure expenditure within the granted power, presuppose the capacity to impose such conditions as will render the choice effective." The majority's reasoning would lead to absurd results, said the dissenters: "The government may give seeds to farmers, but may not condition the gift upon their being planted in places where they are most needed or even planted at all. The government may give money to the unemployed, but may not ask that those who get it shall give labor in return, or even use it to support their families. . . . All that, because it is purchased regulation infringing state powers, must be left for the states, who are unable or unwilling to supply the necessary relief."

NOTES AND QUESTIONS

(1) *"Conditional" Grants.* The majority as well as the dissent assumed that Congress could attach "conditions" to the benefits it dispensed pursuant to the spending power. Furthermore, it concluded that the spending power was independent of the other powers. However, it determined that the enactment at issue was not a mere "conditioned" grant, but instead was a detailed regulatory plan that violated the Tenth Amendment because it "invaded" the regulatory powers reserved to the states. What is likely to happen to the scope of the spending power when as in the commerce power cases considered above, the tenth amendment later is viewed more restrictively (or even as an ineffective "truism")? Consider *Steward Machine Co. v. Davis* and *South Dakota v. Dole*, below.

(2) *"Coercion:" Is it Relevant?* The dissenters denied that the Act in question was "coercive," reasoning that it did not threaten loss to those who refused cooperation, but only provided a benefit to those who did. Is this reasoning persuasive? Should the "coercion" factor make any difference in this context?

(3) *The Limits of the Spending Power: Are There Any?* The dissent also stated, "The Constitution requires that public funds shall be spent for a defined purpose, the promotion of the general welfare." Does this "defined" purpose serve to limit the spending power, or is it limited only by the specific prohibitions of the Constitution? Consider the following cases. In examining what, if any, limits exist for the exercise of the Spending Power; consider also *New York v. United States*, 505 U.S. 144 (1992), below in § 3.03. Although primarily a Commerce Clause decision, the Congressional legislation at issue there also involved the Spending Power, and the Court held that certain "take title" provisions of the Low-Level Radioactive Waste Policy Amendments Act were unconstitutional. For commentary on the Spending Power, *see* David E. Engdahl, *The Spending Power*, 44 Duke L.J. 1 (1994); Lynn A. Baker, *Conditional Federal Spending After Lopez*, 95 Colum. L. Rev. 1911 (1995).

STEWARD MACHINE CO. v. DAVIS, 301 U.S. 548 (1937). The Court here upheld sections III and IX of the Social Security Act, which imposed an excise tax upon employers of eight or more, the proceeds of which were commingled with other federal revenue and "not earmarked in any way." However, the employer was entitled to a 90 percent credit against the tax for all state unemployment taxes paid to a state plan that qualified with the requirements of the federal Act. The clear effect of the enactment was to induce states to set up unemployment compensation programs conforming to federal policy. The Act required qualifying state payments to be paid immediately into the federal Unemployment Trust Fund and to be disbursed by the Secretary of the Treasury when "duly requisitioned" by a state "from the amounts standing to its credit." The Act also authorized federal appropriations in the form of grants to states for unemployment compensation administration, although no money had yet been appropriated.

The excise is not void as involving the coercion of the States in contravention of the Tenth Amendment or of restrictions implicit in our federal form of government. . . .

To draw the line intelligently between duress and inducement there is need to remind ourselves of facts as to the problem of unemployment that are now matters of common knowledge. . . .

The difficulty with the petitioner's contention is that it confuses motive with coercion. "Every tax is in some measure regulatory. To some extent it interposes an economic impediment to the activity taxed as compared with others not taxed." In like manner every rebate from a tax when conditioned upon conduct is in some measure a temptation. But to hold that motive or temptation is equivalent to coercion is to plunge the law in endless difficulties. Even on that assumption the location of the point at which pressure turns into compulsion, and ceases to be inducement, would be a question of degree,—at times, perhaps, of fact. The point had not been reached when [the states at issue in this case] made their choice. . . .

In ruling as we do, we leave many questions open. We do not say that a tax is valid, when imposed by act of Congress, if it is laid upon the condition that a state may escape its operation through the adoption of a statute unrelated in subject matter to activities fairly within the scope of national policy and power. No such question is before us. . . .

[Affirmed.]

Justice McReynolds dissented: "That portion of the Social Security legislation here under consideration, I think, exceeds the power granted to Congress. It unduly interferes with the orderly government of the State by her own people and otherwise offends the Federal Constitution. . . ." Justices Van Devanter, Butler, and Sutherland also dissented.

> Read U.S. Const. Amend. XXI (repeal of prohibition; validation of state laws governing intoxicating liquor).

 SOUTH DAKOTA v. DOLE
483 U.S. 203 (1987)

CHIEF JUSTICE REHNQUIST delivered the opinion of the Court.

[South Dakota permitted 19-year-olds to purchase beer containing up to 3.2% alcohol. A federal statute required the Secretary of Transportation to withhold a percentage of the federal highway funds that otherwise would be payable to any state "in which the purchase or public possession of any alcoholic beverage by a person who is less than twenty-one years of age is lawful." South Dakota sought a declaration that the statute was an unconstitutional violation of (1) the limits of the spending power and (2) the Twenty-First amendment.

[The Court began by recognizing that the Twenty-First amendment "grants the States virtually complete control over whether to permit importation or sale of liquor and how to structure the liquor distribution system," citing *California Retail Liquor Dealers Ass'n v. Midcal Aluminum, Inc.*, 445 U.S. 97, 110 (1980). The twenty-first amendment, "the bounds of which have escaped precise definition," thus raised a difficult question concerning whether Congress could legislate a national drinking age—if it had sought to "legislate directly." However, in this particular statute, "Congress has acted indirectly under its spending power to promote uniformity in the States' drinking ages," said the Court. Consequently, "[a]s we explain below, we find this legislative effort within constitutional bounds even if Congress may not regulate drinking ages directly."]

[I]ncident to [the spending] power, Congress may attach conditions on the receipt of federal funds, and has repeatedly employed the power "to further broad policy objectives by conditioning receipt of federal moneys upon compliance by the recipient with federal statutory and administrative directives" [citing *Fullilove v. Klutznick*, 448 U.S. 448 (1980) (upholding grants conditioned upon recipients' setting aside ten percent for minority business enterprises); *Steward Machine Co. v. Davis*; and other cases]. [O]bjectives not thought to be within Article I's "enumerated legislative fields" [citing *United States v. Butler*] may nevertheless be attained through the use of the spending power and the conditional grant of federal funds.

The spending power is of course not unlimited . . ., but it instead is subject to several general restrictions articulated in our cases. The first of these limitations is derived from the language of the Constitution itself: the exercise of the spending power must be in pursuit of "the general welfare," [C]ourts should defer substantially to the judgment of Congress [in this determination]. Second, we have required that if Congress desires to condition the States' receipt of federal funds, "it must do so unambiguously . . . enabl[ing] the States to exercise their choice knowingly, cognizant of the consequences of their participation" [citing *Pennhurst State School & Hosp. v. Halderman*, 451 U.S. 1 (1981) (provision in mental health grants encouraging "least restrictive" settings for treatment did not entitle mentally retarded persons to enforce rights thereto by private suit)]. . . . Third, our cases have suggested (without specific elaboration) that conditions on federal grants might be illegitimate if they are unrelated "to the federal interest in particular national projects or programs." Finally, we have noted that other constitutional provisions might provide an independent bar to the conditional grant of federal funds. . . .

South Dakota does not seriously claim that [the statute] is inconsistent with any of the first three restrictions mentioned above. . . . Congress found that the differing drinking ages in the states created particular incentives for young persons to combine their desire to drink with their ability to drive, and that this interstate problem required a national solution. . . . A presidential commission concluded that the lack of uniformity in the states' drinking ages created "an incentive to drink and drive" because "young persons commut[e] to border states where the drinking age is lower." [Hence, the Court concluded, the statute served the general welfare, was "directly related to one of the main purposes for which highway funds are expended safe interstate travel," and imposed conditions that "could not be more clearly stated by Congress."]

The remaining question about the validity of [the statute]—and the basic point of disagreement between the parties—is whether the Twenty-First Amendment constitutes an "independent constitutional bar" to the conditional grant of federal funds. Petitioner . . . asserts that "Congress may not use the spending power to regulate that which it is prohibited from regulating directly under the Twenty-First Amendment. . . ." But our cases show that this "independent constitutional bar" limitation on the spending power is not of the kind petitioner suggests. *United States v. Butler*, for example, established that the constitutional limitations on Congress when exercising the spending power are less exacting than those on its authority to regulate directly. . . .

[The "independent constitutional bar" concept] stands for the unexceptionable proposition that the power may not be used to induce the states to engage in activities that would themselves be unconstitutional. Thus, for example, a grant of federal funds conditioned on invidiously discriminatory state action or the infliction of cruel and unusual punishment would be an illegitimate exercise of the Congress' broad spending power. . . .

[The Court further held that "a perceived Tenth Amendment limitation on congressional regulation of state affairs [does] not concomitantly limit the range of conditions placed on federal grants."]

Our decisions have recognized that in some circumstances the financial inducement offered by Congress might be so coercive as to pass the point at which "pressure turns into compulsion." *Steward Marchine Co. v. Davis.* . . .

. . . [A]ll South Dakota would lose if she adheres to her chosen course as to a suitable minimum drinking age is 5% of the funds obtainable under specified highway grant programs. . . . Here Congress has offered relatively mild encouragement. . . . But the enactment of [drinking age] laws remains the prerogative of the states not merely in theory but in fact.

JUSTICE O'CONNOR dissented, saying: "[T]he Court's application of the requirement that the condition imposed be reasonably related to the purpose for which the funds are expended, is cursory and unconvincing." Congress could insist on safe highway construction, "[b]ut it is not entitled to insist as a condition of the use of highway funds that the state impose or change regulations in other areas of the state's social and economic life because of an attenuated or tangential relationship to highway use or safety. . . ." Furthermore, the regulation of drinking ages "falls squarely within the scope of those powers reserved to the States by the Twenty-first Amendment. . . . Congress simply lacks power under the Commerce Clause to displace state regulation of this kind." Justice Brennan dissented separately.

NOTES AND QUESTIONS

(1) *The Constitutional Standard for "Conditions" Under the Spending Power: South Dakota v. Dole, 483 U.S. 203 (1987).* Congress sought to "encourage" a national 21 year-old minimum drinking age by conditioning 5% of a state's federal highway funding on compliance, which States like South Dakota (with its 19 year-old drinking age for 3.2 beer) would lose unless they changed their laws. (Congress has also employed the same approach for highway speed limits and safety belt requirements.) South Dakota argued that this type of program exceeded Congressional power and that the program was unconstitutional as "coercive." The Court rejected the coercion argument because the program was a "relatively mild encouragement" and the State could, after all, simply forgo the money (like its neighbor, Wyoming). As to the scope of the Spending Clause powers, the Court identified a four-part test. You should compare the *Dole* standard to the rational basis standard used for other plenary powers (*i.e.*, the two-part test: whether Congress had a legitimate interest and whether the means selected were rationally related to the achievement of that interest).

When South Dakota initiated the case, no other state would join them. Why not? Also, when South Dakota initiated the case, the *National League of Cities* decision [§ 3.03] had not yet been overruled by the 1995 *Garcia* decision. Given that *National League of Cities* was still "good law" (for the commerce power) in 1995, how would you structure your argument regarding the scope of the spending power? Perhaps the leading article on the *Dole* doctrine is Professor David E. Engdahl, *The Contract Thesis of the Federal Spending Power*, 52 S.D. L. REV. 496 (2007).

(2) *Spending Conditions as Analogous to "A Contract:" Pennhurst State School & Hosp. v. Halderman, supra.* In *Pennhurst*, the Court, through Justice Rehnquist, observed that "legislation enacted pursuant to the spending power is much in the nature of a contract: in return for federal funds, the States agree to comply with federally imposed conditions. The legitimacy of Congress' power to legislate under the spending power thus rests on whether the state voluntarily and knowingly accepts the terms of the 'contract.' " Thus a Congressional preference for treatment in the "least restrictive" setting pursuant to the use of federal mental health funds is not a binding condition if its language and legislative history shows it to be merely encouragement rather than a condition. Justices White, Brennan, and Marshall dissented because they thought the language clear.

(3) *Limits on the Spending Power as Analogous to "A Contract:" Barnes v. Gorman, 536 U.S. 181 (2002), and Gonzaga University v. Doe, 536 U.S. 273 (2002).* In *Barnes*, a unanimous Supreme Court, per Justice Scalia, vacated a jury's punitive damages award in a suit brought by a paraplegic seeking damages under the Americans with Disabilities Act and the Rehabilitation Act for mistreatment while in police custody. The Court held that state recipients of federal funds do not implicitly consent to the potential for "liability for punitive damages."

In *Gonzaga University v. Doe*, 536 U.S. 273 (2002), the Court vacated damage claims awarded under the Family Educational Rights and Privacy Act of 1974. Per Chief Justice Rehnquist, the Court relied upon the *Pennhurst* holding that Congress must unambiguously intend to establish an individual right and held that the spending legislation at issue provided no basis for private remedies through 42 U.S.C. § 1983, even in cases brought by a beneficiary of the Act. *See* Annie M. Horner, Gonzaga v. Doe*: The Need for Clarity in the Clear Statement Test*, 52 S.D. L. Rev. 537 (2007).

(4) *The "Independent Bar" Element of the Dole Four-Part Standard: United States v. American Library Ass'n, 539 U.S. 194 (2003).* In *Dole*, the Twenty-First Amendment did not constitute an "independent bar" to the Congressional exercise of the spending power. In *American Library Ass'n*, the Court, per Chief Justice Rehnquist (the author of *Dole*), rejected the library challengers' argument that conditioning federal funds on installing anti-pornography software on library computers was outside the spending power. The Court reasoned that public libraries remained free to simply decline the federal funds. Given the high cost of the computer technology, how many municipal libraries can afford to decline federal funds? Or, like South Dakota and highway funding in *Dole*, are the public entities actually now "hostages" to the federal hand-outs? *See* Tonnis H. Venhuizen, *United States v. American Library Association: The Supreme Court Fails to Make the South Dakota v. Dole Standard a Meaningful Limitation on the Congressional Spending Power*, 52 S.D. L. Rev. 565 (2007).

(5) *The "Independent Bar" Prong of the Dole Standard: Rumsfeld v. Forum For Academic And Institutional Rights, Inc., 547 U.S. 47 (2006).* Congress passed, pursuant to the spending power, the Solomon Amendment which required the Department of Defense to deny funding to any higher education institution that refused to give military recruiters the same access as other campus recruiters. An association of law schools (FAIR) challenged the Solomon Amendment on freedom of speech and freedom of association grounds (arguing that these were "independent constitutional bars"). The Court, per Chief Justice Roberts, concluded that the Solomon Amendment did not compel any speech or otherwise violate FAIR's freedoms of speech or expressive association. The unanimous Court then held that the Solomon Amendment did not transgress any independent constitutional bar under *Dole*, and thereby upheld the exercise of the spending power. *See* Note (4) above. The Court emphasized that "FAIR has attempted to stretch a number of First Amendment doctrines well beyond the sorts of activities these doctrines protect." *See* Chapter 11.09 below.

hold.

(6) *The Court Rejects a Lopez-Style Attack on the Congressional Spending Power: Sabri v. United States, 541 U.S. 600 (2004).* Under its spending power, Congress passed

18 U.S.C. § 666(a)(2), which makes it a federal felony to bribe any state or local official of an entity that receives at least $10,000 in federal funds. Sabri offered three separate bribes to a Minneapolis councilman to facilitate his construction business. Sabri was indicted for violating § 666(a)(2). Sabri made a motion to dismiss the indictment on two grounds: (1) the indictment required proof of a "nexus" to the federal funds; and (2) Congress lacked the authority to pass § 666(a)(2). Although the trial court had agreed with Sabri, the Supreme Court ruled for the government and upheld the constitutionality of § 666(a)(2).

The Court, per Justice Souter, rejected Sabri's *Lopez*-style challenge. Relying on the spending power as bolstered by the authority under the Necessary and Proper Clause, the Court held that § 666(a)(2) was constitutional because it "addressed the problem at the sources of bribes, by rational means, to safeguard the integrity of the state, local and tribal recipients of federal dollars." The Court also rejected Sabri's argument based on the *Lopez* and *Morrison* decisions; these were distinguishable because it was not necessary to pile "inference upon inference" to understand that § 666(a)(2) was designed "to protect spending objects from the menace of local administrators on the take."

(7) *Further Research on the Spending Power.* In the post-*Lopez* world, there is revived interest in the scope of Congressional power under the Spending Clause. For further research, consider the following articles: Lynn A. Baker, *Lochner's Legacy for Modern Federalism: Pierce County v. Guillen As a Case Study*, 85 B.U. L. Rev. 727 (2005); Mitchell N. Berman, *Coercion Without Baselines: Unconstitutional Conditions in Three Dimensions*, 90 Geo. L.J. 1 (2001); Richard W. Garnett, *The New Federalism, The Spending Power and Federal Criminal Law*, 89 Cornell L. Rev. 1 (2003). *See generally*, *Symposium on South Dakota v. Dole*, 52 S.D. L. Rev. 454 (2007).

[C]   Other Congressional Powers

NOTES AND QUESTIONS

(1) *The Borrowing Power of Art. I, § 8, cl. 2.* This power is one of the foundations of the national banking system and of the Federal Reserve System. *Cf. McCulloch v. Maryland, supra.* But it has been interpreted, as have other powers, to increase the authority of Congress in non-obvious ways. For example, it has been used to support devaluation of the currency, *Norman v. Baltimore & O. R.R. Co.*, 294 U.S. 240 (1935), taxes upon state bank notes designed to drive them out of circulation, *Veazie Bank v. Fenno*, 75 U.S. (8 Wall.) 533 (1869), and overriding of state property laws that otherwise would govern the rights to proceeds of federal bonds, *Free v. Bland*, 369 U.S. 663 (1962) (bond ownership not governed by Texas community property law, but by federal law).

(2) *Abolition or Curtailment of the Borrowing Power? The Federal Deficit.* The growth of federal deficits has given rise to suggestions for an amendment to the Constitution to require a balanced budget, or to authorize a "line-item" veto (by which the president could eliminate single expenditures from a spending bill without vetoing the entire bill), as well as deficit reduction legislation in Congress (some of which we consider below, in the chapter on Presidential power). There also have been suggestions for the outright elimination of the borrowing power.

When viewed aside from partisan rhetoric, are any of these ideas worth considering? If a balanced budget amendment were adopted, how would it allow for extraordinary years, such as those of a Great Depression or World War (perhaps by super-majorities or by explicit exceptions)? Would it be enforceable (could the Supreme Court, for example, determine that it had been violated and, through the power of judicial review, order compliance? Would that sort of enforcement be essential)? With respect to the line-item veto, most states provide comparable authority to their governors; should the federal government do so also?

(3) *The Copyright and Patent Powers.* Consider the copyright and patent powers of Art. I, § 8, cl. 8. Imagine that Congress takes action having the effect of awarding patents to an "inventor" of a perpetual motion machine and to Albert Einstein for recognition of the relationship, "E = mc2." Would these actions be constitutional? [Do the terms "Science and useful Arts," "Authors and Inventors," and "Writings and Discoveries" embrace these situations? Is Congress due deference for so determining?] *See generally* M. Nimmer, Nimmer on Copyright (1976). Might the copyright and patent powers be used in a regulatory fashion, to allow reach of federal law to regulate conduct that could not be reached by other powers?

(4) *The Copyright Power as a Plenary Power: Eldred v. Ashcroft, 537 U.S. 186 (2003).* The power to grant copyrights is one of the powers of Congress found in Art. I, § 8. In the 1998 Copyright Term Extension Act (CETA), Congress enlarged the duration of copyrights by 20 years. Congress provided that this enlarged term would apply to both future and existing copyrights. The plaintiffs were businesses and individuals suffering harm from the enlargement of copyright terms because their products or services built on copyrighted works that have gone into the public domain. The plaintiffs advanced various constitutional theories, including a First Amendment free speech claim. For present purposes, the plaintiffs argued that CETA exceeded the scope of Congressional power. The lower courts ruled for the federal government.

The Supreme Court, per Justice Ginsburg, affirmed. The Court first held that CETA did not violate the Copyright Clause's "limited Times" requirement. The Court then asked "whether [CETA] is a rational exercise of the legislative authority conferred by the Copyright Clause." The Court held that Congress had at least three legitimate reasons for CETA: (1) an intent to conform American copyright law with the law of the European Union; (2) an intent to respond to "increases in human longevity"; and (3) an intent to respond to an increased "parents age when their children are born." The Court concluded that "we find that CETA is a rational enactment; we are not at liberty to second-guess congressional determinations and policy judgments of this order, however debatable or arguably unwise they may be."

(5) *The Indian Commerce Clause and The Treaty Clause as Plenary Powers: United States v. Lara, 541 U.S. 193 (2004).* In this criminal prosecution, the Court was required to examine the scope of Congressional power under the Indian Commerce Clause (and, on these facts, the Treaty Clause). Mr. Billy Jo Lara was an enrolled member of the Turtle Mountain Band of Chippewa Indians in North Dakota. He was married to a member of another tribe in North Dakota, the Spirit Lake Tribe, and lived there with his family. The Spirit Lake Tribe banned him from the reservation, but he ignored the order. Federal officers stopped him for questioning, and he struck one of the officers. Lara was prosecuted by the Spirit Lake Tribe in tribal court and, following his conviction, he served a jail sentence. Subsequently, the Federal Government charged Lara in Federal District Court with assaulting a federal officer. Lara defended on the grounds of double jeopardy. The Government contended that there was no double jeopardy problem because the tribal court was exercising its "inherent sovereignty" rather than any "delegated authority" from Congress.

In a highly fragmented decision, the Court, per Justice Breyer's plurality opinion, reaffirmed that the Indian commerce power was a "plenary" power. The plurality concluded that Congress had the power to relax previously established restrictions on tribal sovereign authority. The plurality also determined that Congress had relaxed its restrictions on tribal authority over nonmember Indians. Thus, because the Spirit Lake tribe was exercising its "inherent tribal authority" against Lara, a nonmember Indian, there was no double jeopardy problem. [Students will remember, from their criminal law course, that one of the exceptions to double jeopardy is the "dual sovereign" doctrine.]

The *Lara* Court was highly splintered in terms of rationale. Justice Stevens concurred. Justices Kennedy and Thomas concurred in the judgment only. Justices Souter and Scalia dissented. [For further discussion of the Treaty Power, *see* § 5.03

below.] *See* Judith Resnik, *Tribes, Wars, and the Federal Courts: Applying the Myths and the Methods of Marbury v. Madison to Tribal Courts' Criminal Jurisdiction*, 36 ARIZ. ST. L.J. 77 (2004). *See generally* Robert G. Natelson, *The Original Understanding of the Indian Commerce Clause*, 85 DEN. U. L. REV. 201 (2007).

(6) *The Foreign Affairs Power; the War and Military Powers; the Treaty Power.* Congress has a recognized power in foreign affairs, although the contours of that power are not clearly marked. The power is not tied to particular clauses, except that it is related to some (such as the foreign commerce power). The war and military powers are expressly provided for in Art. 1, § 8. The Senate's role in ratifying treaties is the source of another "power" of Congress. Because each of these powers war, foreign affairs and treaties also involves presidential power, our consideration of these areas is postponed until the chapter on presidential power.

(7) *Power to Enforce the Fourteenth Amendment (and Other Amendments).* Several of the amendments to the Constitution explicitly provide that Congress has power to enforce them. These provisions arguably vest Congress with latitude to expand upon the self-enforcing meaning of the relevant amendments. Enforcement of the Fourteenth Amendment is particularly important; in addition, legislation of considerable impact has been based upon the Thirteenth and Fifteenth Amendments. Consideration of these issues is postponed to Chapter 14 on congressional enforcement of civil rights.

Chapter 3

FEDERALISM: NATIONAL POWER AS AFFECTING THE POWERS OF THE STATES

NOTE: WHAT THIS CHAPTER IS ABOUT

In this chapter, we take up questions dealing with the distribution of power between the federal and state governments. Collectively, these issues are sometimes referred to as problems of "federalism."

Preemption of State Power by Congress. One aspect of federalism is the Supremacy Clause, which means that national power overcomes inconsistent exercises of state power. The concept is fairly simple: if Congress passes an act, the states cannot countermand it. Nevertheless, the concept of preemption often is more difficult than this simple statement would imply.

Preemption by Negative Implication: The Commerce Clause as a Restraint on State Power. In fact, there are instances in which Congressional *in* action may displace state power. This concept is referred to as the "negative" or "dormant" commerce clause. If a legislative matter peculiarly affects interstate commerce and Congress has not acted, there may be a negative implication that Congress intended the matter to remain unregulated.

Privileges and Immunities. The Constitution requires the states evenhandedly to afford privileges and immunities to citizens and noncitizens alike.

State Sovereignty. Is there a core area of state sovereignty that cannot be preempted? Occasionally, Congress has attempted to regulate the manner in which state lawmaking is done, for example. This is currently the most controversial issue considered in this chapter.

§ 3.01 PREEMPTION OF STATE POWER BY CONGRESSIONAL ACTION: THE SUPREMACY CLAUSE

Read U.S. Const. Art. VI, cl. 2 (the Supremacy Clause). Consider, also, *id.* cl. 3 (state officers' oath to support Constitution).

THE CONCEPT OF PREEMPTION

The Effect of the Supremacy Clause. Imagine that a state legislature passes an act providing, "newspapers shall no longer be permitted in this state." Since the Constitution provides for the freedom of speech and of the press, and since the Constitution and federal laws are the "supreme Law of the Land," the state law in question therefore is of no effect.

Express Preemption by Congress. Congress sometimes includes express statements in its enactments, to the effect that particular categories of state statutes or decisional law are preempted.

Implied Preemption. Often, however, a preemption problem is not controlled by any clear statement of Congress. Thus, preemption often is inferred as a matter of Congressional intent to displace possibly inconsistent state regulation.

[A] Implied Preemption

PENNSYLVANIA v. NELSON, 351 U.S. 934 (1956). Nelson, an acknowledged Communist Party member, was convicted in the state courts of a violation of the Pennsylvania Sedition Act, which included a prohibition against bringing the federal government into "contempt or disrepute" or "excit[ing] against them the hatred of the good people of the United States." The Pennsylvania Supreme Court held that sedition acts respecting the federal government were preempted by the federal Smith Act, "which prohibits the knowing advocacy of the overthrow of the government of the United States by force and violence." The United States Supreme Court, per Warren, Ch. J., upheld this reversal of Nelson's conviction:

> *First*, "[t]he scheme of federal regulation [is] so pervasive as to make reasonable the inference that Congress left no room for the states to supplement it." [The Court described the provisions of the Smith Act, Internal Security Act, and other acts, which included various prohibitions, regulation of organizations, registration requirements, and other sanctions, and concluded: "Taken as a whole, they evince a Congressional plan which makes it reasonable to determine that no room has been left for the states to supplement it."]

> *Second*, the federal statutes "touch a field in which the federal interest is so dominant that the federal system [must] be assumed to preclude enforcement of state laws on the same subject." [The Court described systems of national defense, Congress' "all-embracing program for resistance to the various forms of totalitarian aggression," and the role of the FBI in responding to sedition.]

> *Third*, enforcement of state sedition acts presents a serious danger of conflict with the administration of the federal program. Since 1939, in order to avoid a hampering of uniform enforcement of its program by sporadic local prosecutions, the federal government has urged local authorities not to intervene in such matters, but to turn over to the federal authorities immediately and unevaluated all information concerning subversive activities. . . .

PACIFIC GAS & ELECTRIC CO. v. STATE ENERGY RESOURCES CONSERVATION AND DEVELOPMENT COMMISSION
461 U.S. 190 (1983)

MR. JUSTICE WHITE delivered the opinion of the Court:

[Section 25524.1(b) of the California Public Resources Code conditioned the building of any nuclear power plant upon the state energy commission's finding that there would be "adequate capacity" for temporary storage of the plant's spent fuel. Section 25524.2 imposed a moratorium on new nuclear plants until the United States approved a means for permanent disposal of high level nuclear wastes. The district court held that these California laws were preempted by the federal Atomic Energy Act. The court of appeals reversed. Here, the Supreme Court upholds the court of appeals, concluding that section 25524.2 is not preempted and that the challenge to section 25524.1(b) is not ripe for review.]

[A]bsent explicit preemptive language, Congress' intent to supersede state law altogether may be found from a " 'scheme of federal regulation . . . so pervasive as to make reasonable the inference that Congress left no room for the States to supplement it,' because the 'Act of Congress may touch a field in which the federal interest is so dominant that the federal system will be assumed to preclude enforcement of state laws on the same subject,' or because 'the object sought to be obtained by the federal law and the character of obligations imposed by it may reveal the same purpose. . . .' " Even where Congress has not entirely displaced state regulation in a specific area, state law is preempted to the extent that it actually conflicts with federal law. Such a conflict arises when "compliance with both federal and state regulations is a physical impossibility," *Florida Lime & Avocado Growers, Inc. v. Paul*, 373 U.S. 132, 142–43 (1963), or where state law "stands as an obstacle to the accomplishment and execution of the full purposes and objectives of Congress." *Hines v. Davidowitz*, 312 U.S. 52, 67 (1941).

Petitioners, the United States, and supporting *amici*, present three major lines of argument as to why § 25524.2 is pre-empted. First, they submit that the statute—because it regulates construction of nuclear plants and because it is allegedly predicated on safety concerns—ignores the division between federal and state authority created by the Atomic Energy Act, and falls within the field that the Federal Government has preserved for its own exclusive control. Second, the statute, and the judgments that underlie it, conflict with decisions concerning the nuclear waste disposal issue made by Congress and the Nuclear Regulatory Commission. Third, the California statute frustrates the federal goal of developing nuclear technology as a source of energy. We consider each of these contentions in turn.

Even a brief perusal of the Atomic Energy Act reveals that, despite its comprehensiveness, it does not at any point expressly require the States to construct or authorize nuclear powerplants or prohibit the States from deciding, as an absolute or conditional matter, not to permit the construction of any further reactors. Instead, petitioners argue that the Act is intended to preserve the Federal Government as the sole regulator of all matters nuclear, and that § 25524.2 falls within the scope of this impliedly pre-empted field. But as we view the issue, Congress, in passing the 1954 Act and in subsequently amending it, intended that the federal government should regulate the radiological safety aspects involved in the construction and operation of a nuclear plant, but that the States retain their traditional responsibility in the field of regulating electrical utilities for determining questions of need, reliability, cost, and other related state concerns. . . .

[Here, the Court considered in detail the legislative history of the Atomic Energy Act and concluded as follows:] This account indicates that from the passage of the Atomic Energy Act in 1954, through several revisions, and to the present day, Congress has preserved the dual regulation of nuclear-powered electricity generation: the Federal Government maintains complete control of the safety and "nuclear" aspects of energy generation; the States exercise their traditional authority over the need for additional generating capacity, the type of generating facilities to be licensed, land use, ratemaking, and the like.

. . . State safety regulation is not pre-empted only when it conflicts with federal law. Rather, the Federal Government has occupied the entire field of nuclear safety concerns, except the limited powers expressly ceded to the States. When the Federal Government completely occupies a given field or an identifiable portion of it, as it has done here, the test of pre-emption is whether "the matter on which the State asserts the right to act is in any way regulated by the Federal Act. . . ." A state moratorium on nuclear construction grounded in safety concerns falls squarely within the prohibited field. . . .

That being the case, it is necessary to determine whether there is a nonsafety rationale for § 25524.2. California has maintained . . . that § 25524.2 was aimed at economic problems, . . . not radiation hazards. The California Assembly Committee on Resources, Land Use, and Energy, . . . reported that the waste disposal problem was "largely economic or the result of poor planning, *not* safety related. . . ."

[W]e accept California's avowed economic purpose as the rationale for enacting § 25524.2. Accordingly, the statute lies outside the occupied field of nuclear safety regulation.

Petitioners' second major argument concerns federal regulation aimed at the nuclear waste disposal problem itself. It is contended that § 25524.2 conflicts with federal regulation of nuclear waste disposal, with the NRC's decision that it is permissible to continue to license reactors, notwithstanding uncertainty surrounding the waste disposal problem, and with Congress' recent passage of legislation directed at that problem. . . .

The NRC's imprimatur, however, indicates only that it is safe to proceed with such plants, not that it is economically wise to do so. Because the NRC order does not and could not compel a utility to develop a nuclear plant, compliance with both it and § 25524.2 is possible. Moreover, because the NRC's regulations are aimed at insuring that plants are safe, not necessarily that they are economical, § 25524.2 does not interfere with the objective of the federal regulation. . . .

Finally, it is strongly contended that § 25524.2 frustrates the Atomic Energy Act's purpose to develop the commercial use of nuclear power. It is well established that state law is pre-empted if it "stands as an obstacle to the accomplishment and execution of the full purposes and objectives of Congress. . . ."

There is little doubt that a primary purpose of the Atomic Energy Act was, and continues to be, the promotion of nuclear power. The Act itself states that it is a program "to encourage widespread participation in the development and utilization of atomic energy for peaceful purposes to the maximum extent consistent with the common defense and security and with the health and safety of the public." 42 U.S.C. § 2013(d). . . .

The Court of Appeals is right, however, that the promotion of nuclear power is not to be accomplished "at all costs." . . . Congress has allowed the States to determine—as a matter of economics—whether a nuclear plant vis-à-vis a fossil fuel plant should be built. . . . Given this statutory scheme, it is for Congress to rethink the division of regulatory authority in light of its possible exercise by the States to undercut a federal objective. . . .

Affirmed.

Justice Blackmun, with whom Justice Stevens joins, concurring in part and concurring in the judgment.

I join the Court's opinion, except to the extent it suggests that a State may not prohibit the construction of nuclear power plants if the State is motivated by concerns about the safety of such plants. . . .

[C]ongress has occupied not the broad field of "nuclear safety concerns," but only the narrower area of how a nuclear plant should be constructed and operated to protect against radiation hazards. States traditionally have possessed the authority to choose which technologies to rely on in meeting their energy needs. Nothing in the Atomic Energy Act limits this authority, or intimates that a State [m]ay not consider the features that distinguish nuclear plants from other power sources. . . .

NOTES AND QUESTIONS

(1) *The Issue, in Preemption Cases, is Congressional Intent: Expressions of Intent Not to Preempt, as Well as Expressions of Intent to Preempt, Will be Honored.* Very little constitutional law is involved in preemption cases. There rarely is any question that Congress has the raw power to preempt, and therefore the sophisticated issue in most preemption cases is the intent of Congress. As was stated in *Swift & Co. v. Wickham,* 382 U.S. 111, 120 (1965), the question "is never one of interpretation of the Federal Constitution but inevitably one of comparing two statutes." Thus, if Congress expressly states that it does *not* intend to preempt state regulation, or if the legislative history contains controlling statements to that effect, the courts should honor state laws. *E.g., Askew v. American Waterways Operators, Inc.,* 411 U.S. 325 (1973) (since legislative history together with text of federal water pollution legislation indicated Congressional intent to leave states free to legislate regarding pollution liability to state, state pollution liability laws were not preempted). Similarly, the courts should honor controlling

expressions of intent to preempt. *E.g.*, Fidelity Federal Savings & Loan Ass'n v. De La Cuesta, 458 U.S. 141 (1982) *(honoring express preemption of state regulation of lending agreement clauses provided for by federal law).*

(2) *Should the Court Indulge a Presumption in Favor of Preemption—or Against It?: The Effects of Pervasive Regulatory Systems, Strong National Interests, and State Interests.* But often, the issue simply is unclear, and the Court must infer Congressional intent from conflicting or ambiguous indications. In such a situation, should the Court be inclined toward a finding of preemption, so as to uphold the federal policy? Or should it indulge a presumption against preemption, and strain to harmonize state and federal regulations, so that the state law can be upheld? When intent is to be inferred from diffuse indications, such as the inference of an attempt to occupy the field by a less than comprehensive regulatory scheme, the Court often has preferred not to find preemption. *E.g., Florida Lime & Avocado Growers Ass'n v. Paul*, 373 U.S. 132 (1963) (intent to occupy the field is inferable only when "unmistakable," *i.e.*, when "the nature of the regulated subject matter permits no other conclusion"). *But cf. Burbank v. Lockheed Air Terminal*, 411 U.S. 624 (1973) (majority concluded that "pervasive control" over airport noise and safety indicated Congressional intent to occupy the field). Another factor, implied by the *Burbank* case, is whether the issue traditionally is of national concern, or of state concern. *E.g., Maurer v. Hamilton*, 309 U.S. 598 (1940) (Pennsylvania prohibition of automobile transport trucks carrying cars over their cabs was not preempted, despite express determination by the Interstate Commerce Commission that cars over cabs were safe, because of traditional strong state interest in highway safety).

(3) *Federal Railroad Safety Act Preempts State Tort Law Regarding Certain Railroad Crossing Accidents: Norfolk Southern Railway Co. v. Shanklin, 529 U.S. 344 (2000).* In *Shanklin*, the plaintiff's theory was that the defendant railroad had negligently failed to maintain adequate warning devices at grade crossing. The railroad defended, *inter alia*, on the grounds that it had met the Federal Railroad Safety Act (FRSA) standards and that the FRSA preempted state tort law. [Please note, as a matter of practice, that *Shanklin* demonstrates how constitutional issues frequently arise even in garden-variety tort cases.] The Supreme Court, per Justice O'Connor, agreed with the railroad. The Court held that, as to warning devices installed with federal funds, the FRSA preempted the subject matter of the adequacy of railroad crossing warning devices. Under this decision, the states will not be able to set higher (*i.e.*, more strict) standards for railroad crossing warning devices than those established by FRSA.

(4) *Federal Statute Preempts State Tort Law Claim Based on Defective Design Because of an Actual Conflict: Geier v. American Honda Motor Co., Inc., 529 U.S. 861 (2000).* In *Geier*, the plaintiff's tort law claim was based on the theory that the manufacture was negligent in failing to equip the automobile with a driver's side airbag. The manufacturer defended on the grounds that the National Traffic and Motor Vehicle Safety Act both expressly and impliedly preempted the negligence claim. The Supreme Court, per Justice Breyer, held that the claim was not preempted by the express preemption provision but that the claim was preempted because it actually conflicted with a Federal Department of Transportation regulation. As such, the *Geier* decision illustrates both types of preemption.

(5) *State Legislation Restricting State Agencies Ability to Purchase Goods or Services from Companies Doing Business with a Disfavored Foreign Country was Preempted: Crosby v. National Trade Council, 530 U.S. 363 (2000).* Massachusetts passed a law barring state entities from purchasing goods or services from any company doing business with the foreign nation of Myanmar (Burma). After the state law was enacted, Congress passed, pursuant to its Foreign Commerce power, an act imposing a set of mandatory and conditional sanctions on Burma. The federal statute delegated power to the Executive branch to implement the sanctions and monitor Burma's

"progress to democratization." The Massachusetts statute was challenged by a national trade association, as being inconsistent with the provisions of the federal act.

The Supreme Court, per Justice Souter, agreed with the challengers. Referring to the principles set forth in this section, the Court held that the Massachusetts statute was impliedly preempted. The Court determined that implied preemption existed for three reasons: (1) the state statute was an obstacle to Congressional intent to delegate discretion to the President regarding policies toward Burma; (2) the state statute exceeded and interfered with Congressional intent to limit economic pressure to a selected range; and (3) the state statute conflicted with the Executive's authority to speak for the country regarding democratization and other reform in Burma. Justices Scalia and Thomas concurred in the judgment. Wasn't this an "easy" case? Compare the federal interest in this case (uniformity in foreign relations) with those in Notes (3) and (4) above. Or, as critics such as Professor Sanford Levinson have suggested, was the decision "complacent displacement of state authority in the name of non-existent one-voice nationalism"? Sanford Levinson, *Compelling Collaboration With Evil? A Comment On Crosby v. National Foreign Trade Council*, 69 FORDHAM L. REV. 2189 (2001).

(6) *Implied Preemption Arising from the "Inherently Federal Character" of the Regulatory Scheme: Buckman Co. v. Plaintiffs' Legal Committee, 531 U.S. 341 (2001).* Patients alleging injuries from orthopedic bone screws placed in their spines brought an action against a "consultant" based on a Pennsylvania state law authorizing claims for "fraud" on the Food and Drug Administration (FDA); they argued that the consultant helped the manufacturer secure FDA approval through fraudulent misrepresentations. Although the court of appeals had permitted the state law "fraud on the FDA" claim, the Supreme Court, per Chief Justice Rehnquist, disagreed. The Court held that relationship between the FDA and the manufacture was "inherently federal in character" and that, under conflict analysis, the state law was impliedly preempted. [There was some discussion of "presumptions" which might be compared to Note (2) above.] Justice Stevens (joined by Justice Thomas) concurred only in the judgment.

(7) *Avoidance of Preemption Issues Through Narrow Construction of Federal Law: United States v. Oakland Cannabis Buyers' Cooperative, 532 U.S. 483 (2001).* This was the "Medical Marijuana" case that seemed to raise a preemption issue because distribution of marijuana is prohibited by the federal Controlled Substances Act ("CSA") while possession of marijuana for medical purposes was permitted by California state law (passed as a result of a state initiative). This "conflict" was caused by the federal government suing the Oakland Cannabis Buyers' Cooperative ("Cooperative") which distributed marijuana to persons qualified under state law. The Cooperative sought to assert a "medical necessity" defense. Although the court of appeals had recognized the necessity defense (and set up the preemption issue), the Supreme Court, per Justice Thomas, avoided the constitutional issue by narrowly construing the CSA to prohibit the necessity defense. Three Justices, per Justice Stevens, concurred only in the judgment, criticized the "overbroad language" of the majority and emphasized that the case only involved *distribution*—and not possession. Would the assertion of the necessity defense by a medically qualified patient—rather than a distributor—present a more compelling case for the Court to address the preemption issues?

PROBLEM A

IS MURDER IN THE WORKPLACE PREEMPTED BY OSHA? ILLINOIS v. CHICAGO MAGNET WIRE CORP., 56 U.S.L.W. 2022 (Ill. App. 1st Dist. June 29, 1987). A Cook County, Illinois, grand jury voted indictments against a manufacturing firm and five of its officers, charging each with various offenses under Illinois criminal statutes for workers' injuries owing to allegedly unsafe workplace conditions maintained by the defendants. The trial court dismissed the indictment, holding that the federal Occupational Safety and Health Act preempted the state from application of its criminal law to conditions regulated as to occupational safety and health issues by the federal government. The court of appeals agreed, emphasizing the "comprehensiveness" of the federal act, in addition to "the fact that the states have been afforded the opportunity to develop their own regulatory schemes" in conformity with OSHA. What importance should be attached to the traditionally strong interest of the state in criminal laws against murder and assault? To the fact that the state was attempting to apply laws of general application? To the comprehensiveness of the federal regulatory scheme, or possibilities of inconsistency? The Illinois Supreme Court ultimately reversed and held that the state murder statute was not preempted. 534 N.E.2d 962 (Ill. 1989). In addition, in *English v. General Electric Co.*, 496 U.S. 72 (1990), the Supreme Court suggested that criminal laws would not be preempted by nuclear safety legislation.

[B] Express Preemption

INGERSOLL-RAND CO. v. McCLENDON
498 U.S. 133 (1991)

JUSTICE O'CONNOR delivered the opinion of the Court.

[The Employee Retirement Income Security Act ("ERISA") enacted a uniform regulatory scheme for private employee benefit plans. The Act contains a civil enforcement system as well as a prohibition on interference with rights protected under the Act. ERISA also contains a broad express preemption of "any and all State laws insofar as they may now or hereafter relate to any [covered] employee benefit plan."]

[Respondent McClendon was fired by Ingersoll-Rand, purportedly as part of a company-wide reduction in force. He claimed that Ingersoll-Rand's principal reason was to avoid making contributions to his pension fund. He did not, however, assert any claim under ERISA or its anti-interference provisions; instead, he alleged various tort and contract theories under Texas state law. The Texas Supreme Court, although recognizing that McClendon could be terminated at will under applicable Texas law, created a "public policy" exception allowing suit by a person whose termination was motivated principally by an employer's desire to avoid pension contribution. The Texas court distinguished ERISA's preemption language by the observation that McClendon was "*not* seeking lost *pension benefits* but [was] instead seeking future lost wages, mental anguish and punitive damages as a result of a wrongful discharge."

[The Supreme Court, per JUSTICE O'CONNOR, here unanimously reversed.]

"The [ERISA] pre-emption clause is conspicuous for its breadth." Its "deliberately expansive" language was "designed to 'establish pension plan regulation as exclusively a federal concern.'" The key to § 514(a) is found in the words "relate to." Congress used those words in their broad sense, rejecting more limited pre-emption language that would have made the clause "applicable only to state laws relating to the specific subjects covered by ERISA." Moreover, to underscore its intent that [the preemption] be expansively applied, Congress used equally broad language in defining the "state laws" that would be pre-empted. Such laws include "all laws, decisions, rules, regulations, or other State action having the effect of law. . . ."

"A law 'relates to' an employee benefit plan, in the normal sense of the phrase, if it has a connection with or reference to such a plan." Under this "broad common-sense meaning," a state law may "relate to" a benefit plan, and thereby be pre-empted, even if the law is not specifically designed to affect such plans, or the effect is only indirect. Pre-emption is also not precluded simply because a state law is consistent with ERISA's substantive requirements.

Notwithstanding its breadth, we have recognized limits to ERISA's pre-emption clause. In *Mackey v. Lanier Collection Agency & Service, Inc.*, 486 U.S. 825 (1988), the Court held that ERISA did not pre-empt a State's general garnishment statute, even though it was applied to collect judgments against plan participants. . . . Moreover, under the plain language of § 514(a) the Court has held that only state laws that relate to benefit *plans* are pre-empted. *Fort Halifax Packing Co. v. Coyne*, 482 U.S. 1, 23 (1987). Thus, even though a state law required payment of severance benefits, which would normally fall within the purview of ERISA, it was not pre-empted because the statute did not require the establishment or maintenance of an ongoing plan.

Neither of these limitations is applicable to this case. We are not dealing here with a generally applicable statute that makes no reference to, or indeed functions irrespective of, the existence of an ERISA plan. Nor is the cost of defending this lawsuit a mere administrative burden. Here, the existence of a pension plan is a critical factor in establishing liability under the State's wrongful discharge law. As a result, this cause of action relates not merely to pension benefits, but to the essence of the pension *plan* itself. . . .

[T]he Texas cause of action makes specific reference to, and indeed is premised on, the existence of a pension plan. In the words of the Texas court, the cause of action "allows recovery when the plaintiff proves that the principal reason for his termination was the employer's desire to avoid contributing to or paying benefits under the employee's pension fund." Thus, in order to prevail, a plaintiff must plead, and the court must find, that an ERISA plan exists and the employer had a pension-defeating motive in terminating the employment. Because the court's inquiry must be directed to the plan, this judicially created cause of action "relate[s] to" an ERISA plan. . . .

The conclusion that the cause of action in this case is pre-empted [i]s supported by our understanding of the purposes of that provision. Section 514(a) was intended to ensure that plans and plan sponsors would be subject to a uniform body of benefit law; the goal was to minimize the administrative and financial burden of complying with conflicting directives among States or between States and the Federal Government. . . . Allowing state based actions like the one at issue here would subject plans and plan sponsors to burdens not unlike those that Congress sought to foreclose through [the preemption]. . . . It is foreseeable that state courts . . . might develop different substantive standards applicable to the same employer conduct, requiring the tailoring of plans and employer conduct to the peculiarities of the law of each jurisdiction. Such an outcome is fundamentally at odds with the goal of uniformity that Congress sought to implement. . . .

[The Court here goes on to hold that even if there were no express preemption, the Texas cause of action would still be struck down under the implied preemption doctrine, because it "conflicts directly" with ERISA's creation of an exclusive remedy for interference with protected pension rights.]

The judgment of the Texas Supreme Court is reversed.

CIPOLLONE v. LIGGETT GROUP, INC., 505 U.S. 504 (1992). The Federal Cigarette Labeling and Advertising Act ("1965 Act") required a warning label on every package of cigarettes. Section 5 of the Act was captioned "Preemption" and provided: "(a) No statement relating to smoking and health, other than the [prescribed] statement . . ., shall be required on any cigarette package," and "(b) No [such] statement [s]hall be required in the advertising of any cigarettes [which] are labelled in conformity with" the requirement. In 1969, Section 5(b) was amended (by the "1969 Act") to provide: "No requirement or prohibition based on smoking and health shall be imposed under state law with respect to the advertising or promotion of any cigarettes [lawfully] labelled."

The complaint in this case alleged that Rose Cipollone had contracted lung cancer and died as a result of smoking defendants' cigarettes. The jury found Rose Cipollone 80% responsible so that her estate recovered no damages, but it awarded $400,000 to her husband for loss of consortium. The defendants contended that federal preemption protected them from any liability based on their conduct after 1965.

The Supreme Court, per Justice Stevens, held that certain of the plaintiffs' common-law claims were preempted. It began by holding that "the pre-emptive scope [i]s governed entirely by the express language in § 5," and that implied preemption was excluded. "Such reasoning is a variant of the familiar principle of *expressio unius est exclusio alterius:* Congress' enactment of a provision defining the pre-emptive reach of a statute implies that matters beyond that reach are not preemptive." The Court proceeded to hold that the 1965 Act did not provide any defense against common law actions.

With respect to the 1969 Act (the Amendments), however, the Court found that "the plain language of the preemption provision [i]s much broader." First, the later Act bars not simply "statements" but rather "requirement[s] or prohibition[s] [i]mposed under state law." Second, the later act reaches beyond statements "in the advertising" to obligations "with respect to the advertising or promotion" of cigarettes. But this broader scope "does not mean that [the 1969 Act] preempts all common law claims." Instead, "we must fairly—but in light of the strong presumption against preemption—narrowly construe the precise language of § 5(b) [in the 1969 Act] and we must look to each of petitioner's common law claims to determine whether it is in fact preempted." The Court considered each category of damage actions to determine whether the state-law duty that was the predicate constituted a "requirement or prohibition based on smoking and health [i]mposed under state law with respect to [a]dvertising or promotion":

Failure to Warn: . . . [I]nsofar as claims under [Petitioner's] failure to warn theory require a showing that respondents' post-1969 advertising or promotions should have included additional, or more clearly stated, warnings, those claims are preempted. The Act does not, however, preempt petitioner's claims that rely solely on respondents' testing or research practices or other actions unrelated to advertising or promotion.

Breach of Express Warranty: . . . A manufacturer's liability for breach of an express warranty derives from, and is measured by, the terms of that warranty. Accordingly, the "requirements" imposed by an express warranty claim are not "imposed under state law," but rather imposed by the warrantor. . . .

[A]ccordingly, to the extent that petitioner has a viable claim for breach of express warranties made by respondents, that claim is not preempted by the 1969 Act.

Fraudulent Misrepresentation: . . . [S]uch claims are not predicated on a duty "based on smoking and health" but rather on a more general obligation—the duty not to deceive. [B]oth the 1965 and the 1969 Acts explicitly reserve the FTC's authority to identify and punish deceptive advertising practices—an authority that the FTC had long exercised and continues to exercise. This indicates that Congress intended the phrase "relating to smoking and health" [t]o be construed narrowly, so as not to prescribe the regulation of deceptive advertising. . . .

Conspiracy to Misrepresent or Conceal Material Facts:[T]he predicate duty [under state law] underlying this claim is a duty not to conspire to commit fraud. [T]his duty is not preempted by § 5(b) [because] it is not a preemption "based on smoking and health" as that phrase is properly construed. . . .

Justice Blackmun, joined by Justices Kennedy and Souter, dissented in part. These Justices would have found no preemption of common-law claims, based upon "the states' traditional ability to protect the heath and safety of their citizens" and a principle against preemption "in the absence of clear and unambiguous evidence that Congress intended that result." Thus, "[o]ur precedents do not allow us to infer a scope of preemption beyond that which is clearly mandated by Congress' language. In my view, neither version of the federal legislation at issue here provides the kind of unambiguous evidence of congressional intent necessary to displace state common-law damages claims."

Finally, Justice Scalia, joined by Justice Thomas, dissented in part. These Justices would have found "complete" preemption of the common-law claims under the 1969 Act:

> Today's decision announces what, on its face, is an extraordinary and unprecedented principle of federal statutory construction: that express preemption provisions must be construed narrowly, "in light of the presumption against the preemption of state police power regulations." . . . Under the supremacy clause, our job is to interpret Congress' decrees of preemption neither narrowly nor broadly, but in accordance with their apparent meaning. If we did that job in the present case, we would find, under the 1965 Act, preemption of the petitioner's failure-to-warn claims; and under the 1969 Act, we would find preemption of the petitioner's claims complete. . . .

> The results seem odder still when one takes into account the second new rule that the Court announces. . . . Once there is an express preemption provision, [the Court would hold that] all doctrines of implied preemption are eliminated. . . . [W]ith regard to implied "conflict" preemption— *i.e.*, where state regulation actually conflicts with federal law, or where state regulation "stands as an obstacle to the accomplishment and execution" of Congress' purposes—the Court's second new rule works mischief. . . .

NOTES AND QUESTIONS

(1) *Express Preemption: Determining Congressional Intent.* When Congress has included an explicit preemption provision in a statute (such as ERISA), there is really no issue that Congress intended to assert the supremacy of federal law. There is, however, an issue as to the intended *scope* of Congressional action. In express preemption, the choice of language by Congress determines the scope of preemptive effect. For example, as in *McClendon*, 498 U.S. 133, *supra*, the use of the broad term "relate to" indicates an intent to make the subject matter "exclusively a federal concern." The *Cipollone* decision, however, demonstrates that the preemption provision "relating to smoking and health" will not be construed to cover certain common law tort claims which arguably rest on different common law duties. These cases demonstrate that, even in express preemption cases, the Congressional choice of terms must be interpreted (by the Article III courts) in a manner consistent with the applicable constitutional history, structure and values.

(2) *A Presumption against Preemption Generally—or Only against Preemption of Traditional State Areas of Regulation?* Justice Scalia criticizes the majority for its "extraordinary and unprecedented" presumption against preemption. Perhaps the majority's statement would be more persuasive if it were written in terms of upholding "historic" or "traditional" state regulations, since Congress would know about such regulations and ordinarily would respect them. Many past decisions defer to traditional state power, at least in the implied pre-emption area; *see Pacific Gas & Electric.*

(3) *The Elimination of Implied Preemption by an Express Preemption.* Justice Scalia also criticizes the majority for ruling out implied preemption whenever there is express preemption. This principle could have the ironic result of narrowing the field of federal supremacy merely because Congress has expressed its intention to provide for federal supremacy! Justice Scalia apparently would presume against "field" preemption in such a case, but not against "conflict" preemption. The Court, however, argues that express language means that Congress has considered the alternatives and eliminated them; is this reasoning (the "expressio unius" principle) persuasive?

(4) *Should Preemption be Construed Broadly, or Narrowly—or Neither? Comparing McClendon and Cipollone.* The Court's decisions contain statements justifying both

broad construction of preemption—and narrow. Justice Scalia's choice is neither; his approach is, "it depends." He apparently would use all available rules of statutory construction to decide what is, after all, a question of statutory intent. Is this view persuasive? Or would it be better, in this area, for Congress to have a few clear principles so that it can know how its language will be read?

(5) *Congress Can Influence Whether Preemption is Broad or Narrow, by Switching its Language from "Relating To" to "Determining."* In *Morales v. Trans World Airlines*, 504 U.S. 374 (1992), the majority pointed out that an earlier (rejected) draft of the Act in question had not contained the broad "relating to" language, but instead was limited to state laws "*determining*" airline fares. "[R]elating to" is broader than "determining," said the majority. Presumably, therefore, if Congress wishes to confine its preemption, it can use the "determining" language, but if it wants to preempt more broadly, it can negate all state laws that "relate to" the subject of its legislation. But as *Cipollone* demonstrates, preemption cases still are highly fact-specific.

(6) *Express Preemption, ERISA and the Court's Use of Presumption: Egelhoff v. Egelhoff Ex. Rel. Breiner, 532 U.S. 141 (2001).* The children of intestate's first marriage sued intestate's second wife, seeking life insurance proceeds and pension benefits (from an ERISA-covered plan). Intestate and the second wife had divorced shortly before his death. The second wife was designated as the beneficiary of his ERISA-covered pension plan. Under Washington law, the designation of a spouse as the beneficiary of a nonprobate asset was revoked automatically upon divorce. The second wife argued, however, that ERISA preempted the Washington statute and left her as the beneficiary. The Supreme Court, per Justice Thomas, agreed that the State law was preempted. The Court's interpretation was based not only on a textual and precedential analysis, but also on a policy concern that the Washington statute "interferes with nationally uniform plan administration."

The Court, in dictum, discussed the existence of "preemption presumptions," stating that: "There is indeed a presumption against preemption in areas of traditional state regulation such as family law." The Court said this presumption was "overcome" on the facts of the case. Justice Scalia, for Justice Ginsburg, concurred. Justice Breyer, joined by Justice Stevens, dissented, rejecting a "literal" interpretation of ERISA. The dissenters would have applied a presumption against preemption because this was an area traditionally governed by state law. The use of a presumption whenever Congress would regulate in an area "traditionally" regulated by the state may be a pro-Federalism technique similar to some of the interpretative methodologies you reviewed in Chapter 2. Consider here, again, the *Lopez* and *Morrison* decisions above.

(7) *Interpreting the Preemption Clause of the Medical Device Amendments Through Competing Lenses: Riegel v. Medtronic, Inc., 128 S. Ct. 999 (2008).* The Medical Device Amendments of 1976 (MDA) established a rigorous pre-market review process for new medical devices designed for sustaining human life. The MDA contains an express preemption provision, which provides, in pertinent part, that the states are prohibited from applying any requirement "(1) which is different from, or in addition to, any requirement applicable under this chapter to the device, and (2) which relates to the safety or effectiveness of the device . . . ." Relying on this provision, the lower courts dismissed a lawsuit brought by the Riegels against Medtronic for damages arising from the rupture of one of Medtronic's balloon catheters after it was over-inflated.

The Supreme Court, in an opinion by Justice Scalia, affirmed. While cautioning that not every device regulation was a "requirement" concerning safety or effectiveness that could have preemptive force under the MDA, the Court held that the pre-market approval process for the catheter, which involved an individualized safety review, was such a "requirement" that preempted any common-law claims, such as the Riegels, that were "different from, or in addition to" the requirements imposed by federal law. Justice Ginsburg dissented, arguing that there was no indication that Congress, in enacting the MDA, intended to preempt state common-law suits at all. Instead, she maintained that the preemption clause was designed to establish a uniform administrative regulatory scheme, without impacting tort law claims for damages. Justice Stevens, in a concurring opinion, agreed with Justice Ginsburg that the purpose of the preemption provision was uniformity, but he concluded that the Court was bound by the MDA's text, which established a broader preemptive effect.

Assuming that Justices Stevens and Ginsburg correctly identified the purpose of the MDA, which should control for preemption analysis—the text or the legislative intent? On one hand, the Court has frequently indicated that the "purpose of Congress is the ultimate touchstone of preemption analysis." *See Cipollone v. Liggett Group, Inc.*, 505 U.S. 504, above. On the other hand, one might argue that the text is the best indication of purpose. How should this issue be resolved?

(8) *Expressing Congressional Purpose Through Previously Interpreted Language: Rowe v. New Hampshire Motor Transport Ass'n, 128 S. Ct. 989 (2008).* One method for Congress to ensure that the scope of an express preemption provision matches its intent is to borrow preemption language previously interpreted by the Supreme Court. In 1994, Congress borrowed the preemption language from the Airline Deregulation Act, which had been interpreted by the Supreme Court in *Morales v. Trans World Airlines, Inc.*, 504 U.S. 374 (1992), discussed above in Note (5), in enacting a federal statute preempting state trucking regulation. The *Rowe* Court, relying on its prior interpretation of the same language in *Morales*, had little difficulty in holding that a Maine tobacco law regulating the delivery of tobacco to customers within the state was preempted because it "related to a price, route, or service of any motor carrier."

§ 3.02 THE NEGATIVE COMMERCE CLAUSE: RESTRICTIONS ON STATE POWER TO AFFECT INTERSTATE COMMERCE

INTRODUCTORY NOTE: THE TWO FACES OF THE COMMERCE CLAUSE

The Commerce Clause as Analogous to Two Clauses: An "Affirmative" Grant to Congress and a "Negative" Restriction on the States. To understand the material that follows, it is necessary to perceive that the commerce clause really is two clauses contained in the same language. On the one hand, it is an affirmative grant to Congress of power to regulate commerce. On the other hand, it has the effect of restraining state power to regulate interstate commerce. This latter conception is called the "negative" or "dormant" commerce clause.

The "Negative" or "Dormant" Commerce Clause. The negative effect of restriction on the states flows from the affirmative grant of power to Congress. One explanation runs as follows: Congress has the power to regulate interstate commerce, but if it declines to regulate a particular aspect of that commerce, the Congressional silence is tantamount to a Congressional expression of intent to leave the area unregulated, and hence to protect it from state regulation. *See* Sholley, *The Negative Implications of the Commerce Clause*, 3 U. CHI. L. REV. 556 (1936).

The Vagueness of this Negative Implication Theory. Reasoning by negative implication is tricky business, and the "Congressional silence" theory easily can be lampooned. Consider the following: "Now Congress has a wonderful power that only judges and lawyers know about. Congress has a power to keep silent. Congress can regulate interstate commerce just by not doing anything about it. Of course, when Congress keeps silent, it takes an expert to know what it means. But the judges are experts." POWELL, THE STILL SMALL VOICE OF THE COMMERCE CLAUSE, PROCEEDINGS, NATIONAL TAX ASSOCIATION 337, 338–39 (1937), cited in J. NOWAK, R. ROTUNDA & J. YOUNG, CONSTITUTIONAL LAW 267 n.4 (3d ed. 1986). Today, the rationales for the doctrine focus on protecting national economic unity, protecting outsiders to the political process, and supporting individual economic liberty.

The Original Intent and the Negative Commerce Power. The negative commerce power has definite roots in the concerns of the drafters of the Constitution. Under the Articles of Confederation, states had strong motivations to favor local interests. Discriminatory regulations and duties, abrogations of contracts in favor of residents, reliance on unstable paper money, and taxes on interstate commerce were particular problems. Consider the following excerpt from *The Federalist.*

MADISON, THE FEDERALIST NO. 42: POWERS OVER FOREIGN AND INTERSTATE AFFAIRS. . . . The defect of power in the existing confederacy to regulate the commerce between its several members . . . [has] been clearly pointed out by experience. . . . A very material object of [the commerce] power was the relief of the states which import and export through other states. . . . Were these at liberty to regulate the trade between state and state, it must be foreseen that ways would be found out to load the articles of import and export, during the passage through their jurisdiction, with duties which would fall on the makers of the latter and the consumers of the former. . . .

The necessity of a superintending authority over the reciprocal trade of confederated states, has been illustrated by other examples as well as our own. In Switzerland where the Union is so very slight, each canton is obliged to allow merchandises a passage through its jurisdiction into other cantons, without an augmentation of the tolls. . . . Among the restraints imposed by the Union of the Netherlands on its members, one is, that they shall not establish imposts disadvantageous to their neighbors, without the general permission. . . .

[A] The Early Development of the Negative Commerce Clause

NOTE ON THE POLICE POWER IN THE ERA OF "SELECTIVE EXCLUSIVITY"

The Early Dual Federalism Approach to the Commerce Power: Mutual (or "Selective") Exclusivity. As we have seen in the preceding chapter, some of the Supreme Court's early decisions were based on the assumption that the existence of federal power meant the absence of state power, and vice versa. Of course, the world is rarely so neat, and insistence upon such unattainable precision created an unpredictable jurisprudence. Furthermore, as the federal power expanded, this mutual exclusivity (or, as it sometimes has been called, "selective exclusivity") approach would have wiped out state power.

The Police Power. The early decisions were premised on the notion that the power to provide for the local health, welfare, and morals was the essential province of the states. As we have seen in the preceding chapter, this concept is known as the "police power." This power historically was used to justify the kind of state regulation that seemed necessary but that arguably affected interstate commerce.

Modern Approaches: Overlapping Power and "Cooperative Federalism" in a Framework of National Supremacy. As we shall see later in this Chapter, the original mutual-exclusivity-coupled-with-police-power concept of state and federal power has given way to recognition that there must as a practical matter be an area of overlap, in which either the state or the federal authority may regulate. But for now, we turn to the Supreme Court's early conceptions of the negative commerce clause.

Read U.S. Const. Art. I, § 8, cl. 3 (the commerce power). Also, consider Art. I, § 10 (restrictions on state power) and U.S. Const. Amend. X (powers reserved to states and people).

GIBBONS v. OGDEN, 22 U.S. (9 Wheat.) 1 (1924). [Ogden sought an injunction to prevent Gibbons from operating a steamship service in violation of the monopoly granted by New York state, which Ogden had acquired. Gibbons held a federal license allowing his boats to be used "in the coasting trade." The New York courts upheld the state law creating Ogden's monopoly and granted the injunction. In this opinion by Chief Justice Marshall, the Supreme Court reversed on the basis of the commerce clause.

[Portions of the Court's opinion dealing with the commerce clause as an affirmative grant of power to Congress are reproduced in § 2.02, *supra*. The Court, of course, held that Congress had the necessary regulatory power. Here, we reproduce the Court's treatment of the commerce clause as a restriction on the powers of the states:]

But it has been urged with great earnestness, that although the power of Congress to regulate commerce with foreign nations, and among the several states, be co-extensive with the subject itself, and have no other limits than are prescribed in the constitution, yet the states may severally exercise the same power within their respective jurisdictions. In support of this argument, it is said that they possessed it as an inseparable attribute of sovereignty, before the formation of the constitution, and still retain it, except so far as they have surrendered it by that instrument; that this principle results from the nature of the government, and is secured by the tenth amendment; that an affirmative grant of power is not exclusive, unless in its own nature it be such that the continued exercise of it by the former possessor is inconsistent with the grant, and that this is not of that description. . . .

The grant of the power to lay and collect taxes is, like the power to regulate commerce, made in general terms, and has never been understood to interfere with the exercise of the same power by the states; and hence has been drawn an argument which has been applied to the question under consideration. But the two grants are not, it is conceived, similar in their terms or their nature. Although many of the powers formerly exercised by the states, are transferred to the government of the Union, yet the state governments remain, and constitute a most important part of our system. The power of taxation is indispensable to their existence, and is a power which, in its own nature, is capable of residing in, and being exercised by, different authorities at the same time.

. . . When, then, each government exercises the power of taxation, neither is exercising the power of the other. But, when a state proceeds to regulate commerce with foreign nations, or among the several states, it is exercising the very power that is granted to Congress, and is doing the very thing which Congress is authorized to do. There is no analogy, then, between the power of taxation and the power of regulating commerce.

But the inspection laws are said to be regulations of commerce, and are certainly recognized in the constitution, as being passed in the exercise of a power remaining with the states.

That inspection laws may have a remote and considerable influence on commerce, will not be denied; but that a power to regulate commerce is the source from which the right to pass them is derived, cannot be admitted. The objects of inspection laws is to improve the quality of articles produced by the labor of the country; to fit them for exportation; or, it may be, for domestic use. They act upon the subject before it becomes an article of foreign commerce, or of commerce among the states, and prepare it for that purpose. . . .

The acts of Congress, passed in 1796 and 1799, empowering and directing the officers of the general government to conform to, and assist in the execution of the quarantine and health laws of a state, proceed, it is said, upon the idea that these laws are constitutional. . . . But they do not imply an acknowledgment that a state may rightfully regulate commerce with foreign nations, or among the states; for they do not imply that such laws are an exercise of that power, or enacted with a view to it. On the contrary, they are treated as quarantine and health laws, are so denominated in the acts of Congress, and are considered as flowing from the acknowledged power of a state, to provide for the health of its citizens. . . .

It has been contended by the counsel for the appellant, that, as the word "to regulate" implies in its nature, full power over the thing to be regulated, it excludes, necessarily, the action of all others that would perform the same operation on the same thing. That regulation is designed for the entire result, applying to those parts which remain as they were, as well as to those which are altered. It produces a uniform whole, which is as much disturbed and deranged by changing what the regulating power designs to leave untouched, as that on which it has operated.

There is great force in this argument, and the court is not satisfied that it has been refuted.

[Having thus sketched the argument in favor of the dormant or negative commerce clause, and stated that the court was "not satisfied" that it had been refuted, Chief Justice Marshall did not further analyze the issue. He went on to conclude that Gibbons' license for "the coasting trade" constituted a license to ply the steamboat trade along the route that New York had prohibited "and the act of a state inhibiting the use of [a steamboat] having a license under the Act of Congress, comes, we think, in direct collision with that Act."]

[Reversed.]

NOTES AND QUESTIONS

(1) *Gibbons v. Ogden as Introducing, but Not Definitively Establishing, the Negative Commerce Clause.* Because the New York monopoly conflicted with actual Congressional regulation, Marshall did not definitively address the negative commerce clause argument. The argument, of course, was that since Congress' power to regulate commerce was exclusive, even Congressional silence constituted a prohibition of state regulation. This was, as a historical matter, the gist of the negative or dormant commerce clause.

(2) *A Case to Compare With Gibbons: Willson v. Black Bird Creek Marsh Co., 27 U.S. (2 Pet.) 245 (1829).* The Delaware legislature authorized construction of a dam that blocked navigable waters. The owners of the sloop *Sally,* a federally licensed vessel, broke down the dam; they later were held liable for damages. The question: Could Delaware lawfully legislate in a manner that not only affected interstate commerce, but actually obstructed it? In a terse opinion, which provides a sharp stylistic contrast to his elaborate opinion in *Gibbons,* Chief Justice Marshall upheld the Delaware law:

> . . . The value of the property on [the] banks must be enhanced by excluding the water from the marsh, and the health of the inhabitants probably improved. Measures calculated to produce these objects [a]re undoubtedly within those which are reserved to the states. . . .
>
> If Congress had passed any Act which bore upon the case. . . , we should feel not much difficulty in saying that a state law coming in conflict with such Act

would be void. But Congress has passed no such Act. . . .

    We do not think that the [state] Act empowering the Black Bird Creek Marsh Co. to place a dam across the creek can [b]e considered as repugnant to the power to regulate commerce in its dormant state. . . .

Is this reasoning consistent with the language, in *Gibbons*, finding "great force" in the argument that Congress' power over interstate commerce is "exclusive?"

    (3) *Distinguishing Black Bird Creek from Gibbons: Nondiscriminatory Legislation, Important Local Purposes, and Seriousness of the Interstate Effect.* Perhaps the obstruction in *Black Bird Creek* still can be reconciled with *Gibbons*, despite *Gibbons'* implication that Congress' power is exclusive. First, the dam legislation in *Black Bird Creek* arguably was nondiscriminatory, while the monopoly in *Gibbons* deliberately favored local interests. Second, the dam could be justified by undeniable local interests in health and welfare in a way unrelated to interstate commerce, but this could not be done in *Gibbons*. As we shall see, these factors have become important determinants of the modern negative commerce clause.

COOLEY v. BOARD OF WARDENS OF THE PORT OF PHILADELPHIA
53 U.S. (12 How.) 299 (1851)

MR. JUSTICE CURTIS delivered the opinion of the Court:

[An Act of the Pennsylvania legislature required vessels arriving at or departing the port of Philadelphia to "receive a pilot," or, if it should "refuse or neglect to take a pilot," to pay half the required pilotage fee to the "Society for the Relief" of pilots. Cooley was adjudged liable by a state court for the half-pilotage penalty. He appealed to the Supreme Court, claiming that the Pennsylvania Act violated the negative commerce clause, as well as the port preference clause and the constitutional prohibition upon duties on imports, exports, or tonnage. After holding that the Act was not an unconstitutional duty and did not violate the port preference clause, the Court addressed and rejected Cooley's negative commerce clause argument.]

The Act of Congress of the 7th of August, 1789, sec. 4, is as follows: "That all pilots in the bays, inlets, rivers, harbors, and ports of the United States, shall continue to be regulated in conformity with the existing laws of the States, respectively, wherein such pilots may be, or with such laws as the States may respectively hereafter enact for the purpose, until further legislative provision shall be made by Congress."

If the law of Pennsylvania, now in question, had been in existence at the date of this Act of Congress, we might hold it to have been adopted by Congress, and thus made a law of the United States, and so valid. . . .

But the law on which these actions are founded was not enacted till 1803. What effect, then, can be attributed to so much of the Act of 1789 as declares that pilots shall continue to be regulated in conformity "with such laws as the States may respectively hereafter enact for the purpose, until further legislative provision shall be made by Congress"?

    . . . The grant of commercial power to Congress does not contain any terms which expressly exclude the States from exercising an authority over its subject matter. If they are excluded it must be because the nature of the power, thus granted to Congress, requires that a similar authority should not exist in the States. . . .

    . . . Now, the power to regulate commerce embraces a vast field, containing not only many, but exceedingly various subjects, quite unlike in their nature; some imperatively demanding a single uniform rule, operating equally on the commerce of the United States in every port; and some, like the subject now in question, as imperatively demanding that diversity, which alone can meet the local necessities of navigation. . . .

[W]hatever subjects of this power are in their nature national, or admit only of one uniform system, or plan of regulation, may justly be said to be of such a nature as to require exclusive legislation by Congress. That this cannot be affirmed of laws for the regulation of pilots and pilotage is plain. The Act of 1789 contains a clear and authoritative declaration by the first Congress, that the nature of this subject is such, that until Congress should find it necessary to exert its power, it should be left to the legislation of the States; that it is local and not national; that it is likely to be the best provided for, not by one system, or plan of regulations, but by as many as the legislative discretion of the several States should deem applicable to the local peculiarities of the ports within their limits. . . .

We have not adverted to the practical consequences of holding that the States possess no power to legislate for the regulation of pilots, though in our apprehension these would be of the most serious importance. For more than sixty years this subject has been acted on by the States, and the systems of some of them created and of others essentially modified during that period. . . .

We are of opinion that this state law was enacted by virtue of a power, residing in the State to legislate; that it is not in conflict with any law of Congress; [and] that this law is therefore valid, and the judgment of the Supreme Court of Pennsylvania in each case must be affirmed.

NOTES AND QUESTIONS

(1) *The Local-Versus-National-Regulation Distinction in Cooley: Is it Viable?* *Cooley* reasons that states may regulate local matters, for which different treatment from state to state is appropriate, whereas Congress may regulate matters of national concern, which require uniform national treatment. Is this test viable? [The problem is that the Court is not particularly well-suited for determining whether a given problem "requires" a national solution as opposed to treatment tailored to local conditions. Couldn't one claim, for example, that uniform national regulation of pilotage is desirable, so that vessels plying interstate waters need not deal with unfamiliar (and possibly subtly discriminatory) regulations in each port?]

(2) *Congressional Authorization of State Regulation in the Aftermath of Court Prohibition: From Leisy v. Hardin, 135 U.S. 100 (1890), to Wilkerson v. Rahrer, 140 U.S. 545 (1891).* What should happen if Congress expressly authorizes a given kind of state regulation, thus removing the negative implication of the commerce clause? The clearest example is to be found in a pair of late-nineteenth century decisions concerning liquor regulation. In *Leisy v. Hardin*, the Court held that a state could not prohibit the sale of liquor imported into the state, if it was sold in the "original packages." This "original package doctrine" viewed the commodity as part of a continuous stream of commerce, and, in turn, it furthered the mutual exclusivity view of Congressional and state power. The *Leisy* decision, however, was unpopular, and Congress promptly passed the Wilson Act, which subjected intoxicating liquors to the state police power "to the same extent and in the same manner as those such liquors had been produced in such state." In the *Rahrer* case, the Court upheld the Wilson Act by convoluted reasoning. The Congress, it said, could not "transfer legislative power to a state, nor sanction a state law in violation of the Constitution." But in *Leisy v. Hardin*, the Court had not held that the state lacked power; state law simply had collided with the prohibition of the negative commerce clause. Thus, in the Wilson Act, "Congress did not use terms of permission to the state to act, but simply removed an impediment to the enforcement of the state laws [c]reated by the absence of a specific utterance on its part. . . ."

(3) *Confusion and Inconsistency in the Negative Commerce Clause: Insurance Regulation, from Paul v. Virginia, 75 U.S. (8 Wall.) 168 (1869) to Prudential Ins. Co. v. Benjamin, 328 U.S. 408 (1946).* The Court originally held in *Paul v. Virginia* that insurance was not "commerce" and therefore was not subject to Congressional regulation. This holding, anomalous though it was, ushered in pervasive state regulation of the insurance business, which continues to this day. The decision ultimately was

overruled in *United States v. South Eastern Underwriters Ass'n*, 322 U.S. 533 (1944). Ironically this latter decision threatened to undermine state authority over the insurance business—and because of *Paul v. Virginia*, state regulation was all there was. Congress therefore passed the McCarran Act, which provided that "the business of insurance . . . shall be subject to the laws of the several states which relate to the regulation or taxation of such business." The series of decisions came full circle[1] in *Prudential, supra*, in which the Court upheld the McCarran Act, while acknowledging the confusion and inconsistency in prior negative commerce clause decisions:

> The continuing adjustment has filled many of the great constitutional gaps of Marshall's time and later. But not all of the filling has been lasting. Great emphases of national policy swinging between nation and states in historic conflicts have been reflected, variously and from time to time, in premise and therefore in conclusion of particular dispositions. In turn, their sum has shifted and reshifted the general balance of authority, inevitably producing some anomaly of logic and of result in the decisions.

This statement probably could equally describe the modern decisions under the negative commerce clause. Negative inferences remain a tricky business!

PROBLEM B

PENNSYLVANIA v. WHEELING & BELMONT BRIDGE CO., 54 U.S. (13 How.) 518, 14 L. Ed. 249 (1852). A year after *Cooley v. Board of Wardens*, the Court faced a difficult situation of interstate rivalry in the *Wheeling & Belmont Bridge* case. The State of Pennsylvania sued to remove defendant's bridge, pointing out that it obstructed a navigable river, directed trade away from Pennsylvania, and reduced tolls and revenues of the state. The Virginia legislature had passed an act authorizing defendant to construct the bridge, and after the suit was filed, it passed a supplementary act affirming that it was "of lawful height." In an original proceeding brought by Pennsylvania before the Supreme Court, the Court found that the bridge did, in fact, seriously obstruct navigation. How should the Court, then, decide the case?

(1) *Applying Gibbons, Black Bird Creek, and Cooley: Is the State Police Power Predominant in Wheeling & Belmont Bridge, or Is there a Need for National Regulation?* Notice the superficial similarity of the *Wheeling & Belmont Bridge* case to *Black Bird Creek*, in which the state police power was upheld. But consider, also, the later local-versus-national-regulation approach of *Cooley*. Under these authorities, should Pennsylvania's view, or Virginia's statutes, prevail?

(2) *The Court's Actual Holding in Wheeling & Belmont Bridge.* The Court, per Justice McLean, concluded that the Virginia laws authorizing the bridge were unconstitutional: "No state law can hinder or obstruct the free use of a [shipping] license granted under an act of Congress." The Court's order required the bridge to be raised higher. Chief Justice Taney dissented, relying on *Black Bird Creek* and saying: "The United States and Virginia are the only sovereignties which can exercise any power over the river where the bridge is erected. Virginia has authorized it. . . . Congress has made no regulation declaring such a structure unlawful. . . ." Which of these views do you think is correct? When a state law provides important local benefits, but also imposes a serious burden on commerce, who should decide its appropriateness, and how?

(3) *Congress Reverses the Court's Decision: Pennsylvania v. Wheeling & Belmont Bridge Co., 59 U.S. (18 How.) 421, 15 L. Ed. 435 (1856) ("Wheeling & Belmont II").*

---

[1] Perhaps it did not come "full" circle. In a modern decision, *Metropolitan Life Ins. Co. v. Ward*, 470 U.S. 869 (1985) (Powell, J.), the Court held that state taxation that applied a higher rate to out-of-state insurers than to domestic ones was unconstitutional even if authorized by the McCarran Act. The mechanism for the decision, however, was not the negative commerce clause, but the equal protection clause of the fourteenth amendment. Justice O'Connor dissented, joined by Justices Brennan, Marshall, and Rehnquist.

Congress passed an act the next year, legislatively reversing the Court and declaring that the bridge was a lawful structure (and, with a dash of overkill, also declaring it to be a post road)! Pennsylvania's second proceeding in the Court resulted in an opinion upholding the constitutionality of this act of Congress. Does this outcome indicate that Virginia's law was a proper exercise of the police power? If so, was Pennsylvania simply bound to suffer the consequences of Virginia's decision? What does the decision indicate about the role of Congress in negative commerce clause cases?

[B]   The Modern Standard under the Negative Commerce Clause

NOTE ON (1) DISCRIMINATION AND (2) THE *PIKE* FORMULATION

(1)   *Discrimination Against Interstate Commerce.* The modern approach asks, first, whether state regulation is evenhanded. This issue is sometimes put in terms of discrimination against interstate commerce. Discriminatory regulation is upheld only if it passes a least-onerous-alternative test (*i.e.*, it must protect an important and legitimate state interest that cannot be advanced by any reasonable alternative means).

(2)   *Undue Burdens on Interstate Commerce created by Ostensibly Evenhanded State Regulation: Pike v. Bruce Church, Inc., 397 U.S. 137 (1970).* The *Pike* case often is said to embody the modern negative commerce clause test in the event of nondiscrimination:

> Where the statute regulates evenhandedly to effectuate a legitimate local public interest, and its effects on interstate commerce are only incidental, it will be upheld unless the burden imposed on such commerce is clearly excessive in relation to the putative local benefits. If a legitimate local purpose is found, then the question becomes one of degree. And the extent of the burden that will be tolerated will of course depend on the nature of the local interest involved, and on whether it could be promoted as well with a lesser impact on interstate activities. . . .

397 U.S. at 142 (citations omitted). The student should be aware that this brief sketch of the modern approach is necessarily simplistic. In any event, we start with the first of these two situations: discrimination.

[1]   Discrimination Against Interstate Commerce: The "Strictest Scrutiny" Standards

INTRODUCTORY NOTE

There are several analytical concepts that are commonly used, by the courts and the commentators, when discussing the discrimination tier of the dormant Commerce Clause. Watch for these in the cases below. The cases describe three *types* of discrimination: facial discrimination; discriminatory purpose; and discriminatory effect. These are the three theories used by challengers to demonstrate state discrimination against interstate commerce *and* to secure the high level of scrutiny associated with the discrimination tier.

The second set of concepts are commonly called the *modes* of discrimination. There are four modes: tariff-type discrimination; exclusionary discrimination; economic protectionism discrimination; and isolationism discrimination.

The third set of concepts are the three *rationales* commonly offered for heightened scrutiny. There are three rationales, from narrowest to broadest: National Political Unity rationale (similar to the Privileges and Immunities Doctrine of Article IV, Section 2); the Political Process rationale (similar to the rationale in equal protection);

and Individual Economic Liberty (similar to the rationales in the Privileges and Immunities and Substantive Due Process doctrine).

These analytical tools are used by the courts and by the lawyers in dormant Commerce Clause cases. You should watch for reference to them.

DEAN MILK CO. v. CITY OF MADISON, 340 U.S. 349 (1951). This case exemplifies the modern approach to an overtly discriminatory regulation. An ordinance of the City of Madison, Wisconsin prohibited importation and sale of pasteurized milk unless processed within a five-mile radius of the city's center. The ordinance also limited the city's responsibility for inspection, which was a condition to importation and sale, to a twenty-five mile radius. In an opinion by Justice Clark, over the dissent of Justices Black, Douglas, and Minton, the Court held the ordinance unconstitutional because it discriminated against interstate commerce and could not be justified by the absence of any less onerous alternative:

> In thus erecting an economic barrier protecting a major local industry against competition from without the state, Madison plainly discriminates against interstate commerce. This it cannot do, even in the exercise of its unquestioned power to protect the health and safety of its people, if reasonable nondiscriminatory alternatives, adequate to conserve legitimate local interests, are available. . . . A different view, that the ordinance is valid simply because it professes to be a heath measure, would mean that the commerce clause of itself imposes no limitations on state action. . . , save for the rare instance where a state artlessly discloses an avowed purpose to discriminate against interstate goods. . . .

> It appears that reasonable and adequate alternatives are available. If the City of Madison prefers to rely upon its own officials for inspection of distant milk sources, such inspection is readily open to it without hardship for it could charge the actual and reasonable cost of such inspection to the importing producers and processors. . . . The [Model Milk Ordinance recommended by the United States Public Health Service] imposes no geographical limitation on location of milk sources and processing plants but excludes from a municipality milk not produced and pasteurized in conformity to standards as high as those enforced by the receiving city. . . .

NOTES AND QUESTIONS

(1) *The Elusiveness of "Discrimination" as a Determinative Factor. Dean Milk* reflects a strong skepticism about determining discrimination from the face of the statute. It has been suggested that the "single justification" for judicial invalidation of state legislation under the negative commerce clause lies in "the process-oriented protection of representational government." Eule, below at §§ [8]. If so, the degree to which in-staters have transferred the burden to out-of-staters, rather than the face of the statute, should be determinative. Does this reasoning lead to the conclusion that deference to state legislative findings is inappropriate even for laws that seem nondiscriminatory? *See West Lynn Creamery, Inc. v. Healy*, 512 U.S. 188 (1994) (the Court relied, in part, on the absence of a "political check" (*i.e.*, participation in the state's political process by nonresident milk producers) to decide that a Massachusetts assessment-and-subsidy tax scheme was "discrimination").

(2) *The Difficulty with Evaluation of Less Burdensome Alternatives: Criticizing Dean Milk.* But assuming that a particular state law does favor local interest at the expense of out-of-staters, and thus appears to be "discriminatory," the evaluation of "less burdensome" alternatives, as in *Dean Milk*, also contains hidden difficulties. Might a national authority undervalue local interests? Perhaps it will evaluate as "less burdensome" those alternatives which are more burdensome for the locality, or which

achieve the local purpose less effectively. Do these considerations weigh in favor of at least some deference even to facially discriminatory regulation based upon state legislative findings?

CITY OF PHILADELPHIA v. NEW JERSEY, 437 U.S. 617 (1978). A New Jersey statute prohibited importation of most solid or liquid waste from outside the state. In-state waste, however, could still be disposed of in New Jersey landfills. Out-of-state cities, together with New Jersey landfill operators, attacked the statute under the negative commerce clause. The New Jersey Supreme Court held that the "slight" burden on interstate commerce was outweighed by valid local health and environmental concerns and that the statute did not discriminate economically. The Supreme Court, per Justice Stewart, here reverses and invalidates the statute:

> The opinions of the Court through the years have reflected an alertness to the evils of "economic isolation" and protectionism, while at the same time recognizing that incidental burdens on interstate commerce may be unavoidable when a State legislates to safeguard the health and safety of its people. Thus, where simple economic protectionism is effected by state legislation, a virtually per se rule of invalidity has been erected. . . . The clearest example of such legislation is a law that overtly blocks the flow of interstate commerce at a State's borders. . . .

> [The Court rejects the argument that the prohibition is aimed at environmental protection rather than economic protection, because it is implemented by discrimination against out-of-staters.] Contrary to the evident assumption of the state court and the parties, the evil of protectionism can reside in legislative means as well as legislative ends. Thus, it does not matter whether the ultimate aim of [this law] is to reduce the waste disposal costs of New Jersey residents or to save remaining open lands from pollution, for we assume New Jersey has every right to protect its residents' pocketbooks as well as their environment. And it may be assumed as well that New Jersey may pursue those ends by slowing the flow of *all* waste into the State's remaining landfills, even though interstate commerce may incidentally be affected. But whatever New Jersey's ultimate purpose, it may not be accomplished by discriminating against articles of commerce coming from outside the State unless there is some reason, apart from their origin, to treat them differently. . . .

Justice Rehnquist dissented, viewing the prohibition as similar to a quarantine against disease and as a permissible regulation to protect health and safety of the State's residents. Justice Rehnquist also argued that "garbage" was not "commerce" and, therefore, the dormant Commerce Clause doctrine did not apply.

NOTES AND QUESTIONS

(1) *Philadelphia v. New Jersey as "Round One" in the Interstate Garbage Battles.* New Jersey's outright prohibition of imported waste was less sophisticated than later generations of garbage restrictions. Rounds two and three involved local plans, taxes, and fees. See below.

(2) *"Round Two": Fort Gratiot Sanitary Landfill, Inc. v. Michigan Department of Natural Resources, 504 U.S. 353 (1992).* In "Round Two," the *Fort Gratiot* case involved a Michigan law that prohibited waste from being imported into a given county unless it was done pursuant to a comprehensive waste management plan adopted by the county. Defenders of the law argued that it more clearly was a health and safety regulation than New Jersey's prohibition had been, and that it applied even to waste transfers within the State as long as they went from one county to another. The Court relied on *Philadelphia v. New Jersey* in striking down the Michigan law. The companion case, *Chemical Waste*, concerned an Alabama law imposing a fee of $25.60 per ton on all hazardous wastes, but imposing an additional $ 72.00 for each ton "generated outside of Alabama." Among other arguments, Alabama claimed that the extra fee compensated for environmental

risks created by transportation on Alabama's highways over the longer distances necessary on average to import waste. Again, the Court relied on *Philadelphia v. New Jersey* in reversing, although it suggested that an across-the-board per-ton fee, a per-mile tax on waste transportation, or an evenhanded cap on total waste tonnage would all be acceptable. Again, Chief Justice Rehnquist dissented: "[T]he Court gets it exactly backward. . . . [I]t is the 34 States that have no hazardous waste facility whatsoever, not to mention the remaining States with facilities all smaller than [Alabama's], that have isolated themselves."

(3) *Quarantine as an Analogy.* Justice Rehnquist's dissents also invoked cases upholding quarantines, *i.e.*, border blockages designed to contain diseases. Is this analogy persuasive, or is it perhaps too facile, since the waste regulations all allowed in-staters to traffic in the "quarantined" material?

(4) *"Round Three": The Oregon Waste Case.* "Round Three" in the garbage wars, involving a still more sophisticated kind of differential treatment of in- and out-of-staters, was resolved in the following case.

OREGON WASTE SYSTEMS v. DEPARTMENT OF ENVIRONMENTAL QUALITY OF THE STATE OF OREGON
511 U.S. 93 (1994)

JUSTICE THOMAS delivered the opinion of the Court.

Two Terms ago, in *Chemical Waste Management, Inc. v. Hunt*, 504 U.S. 334 (1992), we held that the negative Commerce Clause prohibited Alabama from imposing a higher fee on the disposal in Alabama landfills of hazardous waste from other States than on the disposal of identical waste from Alabama. In reaching that conclusion, however, we left open the possibility that such a differential surcharge might be valid if based on the costs of disposing of waste from other States . . . Today, we must decide whether Oregon's purportedly cost-based surcharge on the instate disposal of solid waste generated in other States violates the Commerce Clause.

I

[Oregon levied a wide range of fees on solid waste landfill operations as part of the state's comprehensive solid waste disposal plan. The state legislature imposed a fee of 85 cents per ton on waste generated in-state and a "surcharge" (of $2.25 per ton) for disposal of "waste generated out-of-state." Although the legislature required that the surcharge be based on "cost to the State of Oregon," petitioners challenged the allegedly cost-based fee under the dormant Commerce Clause. The state courts upheld the fee system.]

II

The Commerce Clause provides that "[t]he Congress shall have Power . . . [t]o regulate Commerce . . . among the several States." Art. I, § 8, cl. 3. Though phrased as a grant of regulatory power to Congress, the Clause has long been understood to have a "negative" aspect that denies the States the power unjustifiably to discriminate against or burden the interstate flow of articles of commerce. . . . The Framers granted Congress plenary authority over interstate commerce in "the conviction that in order to succeed, the new Union would have to avoid the tendencies toward economic Balkanization that had plagued relations among the Colonies and later among the States under the Articles of Confederation." *Hughes v. Oklahoma*, 441 U.S. 322 (1979).

[C]onsistent with these principles, we have held that the first step in analyzing any law subject to judicial scrutiny under the negative Commerce Clause is to determine whether it "regulates evenhandedly with only 'incidental' effects on interstate commerce, or discriminates against interstate commerce". . . . As we use the term here, "discrimination" simply means differential treatment of in-state and out-of-state economic interests that benefits the former and burdens the latter. If a restriction on commerce is discriminatory, it is virtually *per se* invalid. [B]y contrast, nondiscriminatory regulations that have only incidental effects on interstate commerce are valid unless "the burden imposed on such commerce is clearly excessive in relation to the putative local benefits." *Pike v. Bruce Church, Inc.*, 397 U.S. 137 (1970).

In *Chemical Waste*, we easily found Alabama's surcharge on hazardous waste from other States to be facially discriminatory because it imposed a higher fee on the disposal of out-of-state waste than on the disposal of identical in-state waste. We deem it equally obvious here that Oregon's $2.25 per ton surcharge is discriminatory on its face. The surcharge subjects waste from other States to a fee almost three times greater than the $0.85 per ton charge imposed on solid in-state waste. The statutory determinant for which fee applies to any particular shipment of solid waste to an Oregon landfill is whether or not the waste was "generated out-of-state." Ore. Rev. Stat. § 459.297(1) (1991). It is well-established, however, that a law is discriminatory if it "tax[es] a transaction or incident more heavily when it crosses state lines than when it occurs entirely within the State." *Chemical Waste, supra.*[2]

Respondents argue, and the Oregon Supreme Court held, that the statutory nexus between the surcharge and "the [otherwise uncompensated] costs to the State of Oregon and its political subdivision of disposing of solid waste generated out-of-state," necessarily precludes a finding that the surcharge is discriminatory. We find respondents' narrow focus on Oregon's compensatory aim to be foreclosed by our precedents. As we reiterated in *Chemical Waste*, the purpose of, or justification for, a law has no bearing on whether it is facially discriminatory. . . . Consequently, even if the surcharge merely recoups the costs of disposing of out-of-state waste in Oregon, the fact remains that the differential charge favors shippers of Oregon waste over their counterparts handling waste generated in other States. In making that geographic distinction, the surcharge patently discriminates against interstate commerce.

III

Because the Oregon surcharge is discriminatory, the virtually per se rule of invalidity provides the proper legal standard here, not the *Pike* balancing test. As a result, the surcharge must be invalidated unless respondents can "sho[w] that it advances a legitimate local purpose that cannot be adequately served by reasonable nondiscriminatory alternatives" [citing *New Energy Co. of Indiana v. Limbach*, 486 U.S. 269 (1988) and *Chemical Waste*.] Our cases require that justifications for discriminatory restrictions on commerce pass the "strictest scrutiny." *Hughes, supra.* The State's burden of justification is so heavy that "facial discrimination by itself may be a fatal defect." *Id.*

At the outset, we note two justifications that respondents have *not* presented. No claim has been made that the disposal of waste from other States imposes higher costs on Oregon and its political subdivisions than the disposal of in-state waste. Also, respondents have not offered any safety or health reason unique to nonhazardous waste from other States for discouraging the flow of such waste into Oregon. *Cf. Maine v. Taylor*, 477 U.S. 131 (1986) (upholding ban on importation of out-of-state baitfish into Maine because such baitfish were subject to parasites completely foreign to Maine baitfish). [That case was one of the rare instances in which a discriminatory state

---

[2] The dissent argues that the $2.25 per ton surcharge is so minimal in amount that it cannot be considered discriminatory, even though the surcharge expressly applies only to waste generated in other States. The dissent does not attempt to reconcile that novel understanding of discrimination with our precedents, which clearly establish that the degree of a differential burden or charge on interstate commerce "measures only the *extent* of the discrimination" and "is of no relevance to the determination whether a State has discriminated against interstate commerce." *Wyoming v. Oklahoma*, 502 U.S. 487 (1992). . . .

statute survived strict scrutiny. Inspection for parasites was technologically unworkable, and Maine, there, was able to demonstrate that there was no alternative that protected its interests without discriminating against interstate commerce. Importation of baitfish would have threatened Maine's environment in a way that could not be prevented absent a ban. But those conditions are not present in the case at bar.] Consequently, respondents must come forward with other legitimate reasons to subject waste from other States to a higher charge than is levied against waste from Oregon.

[R]espondents' principal defense of the higher surcharge on out-of-state waste is that it is a "compensatory tax" necessary to make shippers of such waste pay their "fair share" of the costs imposed on Oregon by the disposal of their waste in the State. [T]hough our cases sometimes discuss the concept of the compensatory tax as if it were a doctrine unto itself, it is merely a specific way of justifying a facially discriminatory tax as achieving a legitimate local purpose that cannot be achieved through nondiscriminatory means. *See Chemical Waste, supra.* [U]nder that doctrine, a facially discriminatory tax that imposes on interstate commerce the rough equivalent of an identifiable and "substantially similar" tax on intrastate commerce does not offend the negative Commerce Clause.

[A]lthough it is often no mean feat to determine whether a challenged tax is a compensatory tax, we have little difficulty concluding that the Oregon surcharge is not such a tax. Oregon does not impose a specific charge of at least $2.25 per ton on shippers of waste generated in Oregon, for which the out-of-state surcharge might be considered compensatory. In fact, the only analogous charge on the disposal of Oregon waste is $0.85 per ton, approximately one-third of the amount imposed on waste from other States. Respondents' failure to identify a specific charge on intrastate commerce equal to or exceeding the surcharge is fatal to their claim.

[R]espondents' final argument is that Oregon has an interest in spreading the costs of the in-state disposal of Oregon waste to all Oregonians. That is, because all citizens of Oregon benefit from the proper in-state disposal of waste from Oregon, respondents claim it is only proper for Oregon to require them to bear more of the costs of disposing of such waste in the State through a higher general tax burden. At the same time, however, Oregon citizens should not be required to bear the costs of disposing of out-of-state waste, respondents claim. The necessary result of that limited cost-shifting is to require shippers of out-of-state waste to bear the full costs of in-state disposal, but to permit shippers of Oregon waste to bear less than the full cost.

We fail to perceive any distinction between respondents' contention and a claim that the State has an interest in reducing the cost of handling in-state waste. . . . To give controlling effect to respondents' characterization of Oregon's tax scheme as seemingly benign cost-spreading would require us to overlook the fact that the scheme necessarily incorporates a protectionist objective as well.

[R]espondents counter that if Oregon is engaged in any form of protectionism, it is "resource protectionism," not economic protectionism. It is true that by discouraging the flow of out-of-state waste into Oregon landfills, the higher surcharge on waste from other States conserves more space in those landfills for waste generated in Oregon. Recharacterizing the surcharge as resource protectionism hardly advances respondents' cause, however. Even assuming that landfill space is a "natural resource," "a State may not accord its own inhabitants a preferred right of access over consumers in other States to natural resources located within its borders." *Philadelphia, supra.*

[W]e recognize that the States have broad discretion to configure their systems of taxation as they deem appropriate. [A]ll we intimate here is that their discretion in this regard, as in all others, is bounded by any relevant limitations of the Federal Constitution, in this case the negative Commerce Clause. Because respondents have offered no legitimate reason to subject waste generated in other States to a discriminatory surcharge approximately three times as high as that imposed on waste generated in Oregon, the surcharge is facially invalid under the negative Commerce Clause.

hold.

[*The Court reversed.*] *C·O'*

CHIEF JUSTICE REHNQUIST, with whom JUSTICE BLACKMUN joins, dissenting.

[N]otwithstanding the identified shortage of landfill space in the Nation, the Court notes that it has "little difficulty" concluding that the Oregon surcharge does not operate as a compensatory tax, designed to offset that loss of available landfill space in the State caused by the influx of out-of-state waste. The Court reached this nonchalant conclusion because the State has failed "to identify a specific charge on *intrastate* commerce equal to or exceeding the surcharge." (emphasis added). The Court's myopic focus on "differential fees" ignores the fact that in-state producers of solid waste support the Oregon regulatory program through state income taxes and by paying, indirectly, the numerous fees imposed on landfill operators and the dumping fee on in-state waste. . . .

Far from neutralizing the economic situation for Oregon producers and out-of-state producers, the Court's analysis turns the Commerce Clause on its head. Oregon's neighbors will operate under a competitive advantage against their Oregon counterparts as they can now produce solid waste with reckless abandon and avoid paying concomitant state taxes to develop new landfills and clean up retired landfill sites. . . . If anything, striking down the fees works to the disadvantage of Oregon businesses. They alone will have to pay the "nondisposal" fees associated with solid waste: landfill siting, landfill clean-up, insurance to cover environmental accidents, and transportation improvement costs associated with out-of-state waste being shipped into the State. [T]he Court today leaves States with only two options: become a dumper and ship as much waste as possible to a less populated State, or become a dumpee, and stoically accept waste from more densely populated States.

[I] think that the $2.25 per ton fee that Oregon imposed on out-of-state waste works out to similar "fair approximation" of the privilege to use its landfills. Even the Court concedes that our precedents do not demand anything beyond "substantia[l] equivalen[cy]" between the fees charged on in-state and out-of-state waste. [The Chief Justice had earlier calculated that, for the typical nonresident waste producer, Oregon's surcharge worked out to be a cost increase of $0.14 per week.] The $0.14 per week fee imposed on out-of-state waste producers qualifies as "substantially equivalent" under the reasonableness standard of [the Court's precedents].

[I]t escapes me how an additional $0.14 per week cost for the average solid waste producer constitutes anything but the type of "incidental effects on interstate commerce" endorsed by the majority. Even-handed regulations imposing such incidental effects on interstate commerce must be upheld unless "the burden imposed on such commerce is clearly excessive in relation to the putative local benefits." *Pike, supra* . . . .

NOTES AND QUESTIONS

(1) *The Dormant Commerce Clause: A Two-Tiered Model.* As indicated in the Introductory Notes, the modern Dormant Commerce Clause Doctrine appears to have two "tiers" or standards. As demonstrated by the majority opinion in *Oregon Waste Systems* above, the upper tier (the more stringent tier) is employed when the court determines that a state regulation is "discriminatory" against interstate commerce. The regulation in *Oregon Waste* is "facially discriminatory." On the discrimination tier, a state regulation can be "discriminatory" even if it is facially neutral. On the discrimination tier, the Court uses what it calls the "strictest scrutiny" standard (in *Oregon Waste*). Note that the state has won only one case on the discrimination tier. *See Maine*

v. Taylor, 477 U.S. 131 (1986). The second, or lower, tier of the modern Dormant Commerce Clause Doctrine is illustrated mainly by the undue burden standard. This standard applies to non-discriminatory regulations that have only incidental effects on interstate commerce, but even these regulations are unconstitutional if the burden imposed on interstate commerce is considered an "undue burden." Watch for the use of these two tiers below. Note that, in certain cases, the Court is not completely clear as to which tier is being employed. The key issue of "discrimination" sometimes is difficult to determine. *See* David S. Day, *The "Mature" Rehnquist Court and the Dormant Commerce Clause Doctrine: The Expanded Discrimination Tier*, 52 S.D. L. REV. 1 (2007).

(2) *The Threshold Issue of "Discrimination" For Purposes of the Dormant Commerce Clause Doctrine?: General Motors Corp. v. Tracy, 519 U.S. 278 (1997).* The state of Ohio imposed sales and use taxes on sellers of natural gas, but Ohio exempted local distribution companies (LDC). LDC entities served small and residential buyers and were highly regulated by Ohio. General Motors purchased its natural gas for Ohio facilities from an out-of-state, non-LDC seller and, accordingly, had to pay the use taxes. Arguing that Ohio's tax exemption for LDC's was "discriminatory" against interstate commerce, General Motors sued for a refund of the use taxes.

The Supreme Court, per Justice Souter, upheld Ohio's tax scheme. The Court determined that the distinction in tax treatment between highly regulated sellers (the LDC's) and other sellers was not "discriminatory." The Court found no impermissible burden on interstate commerce largely because it determined, as a "threshold," that highly regulated LDC's and other sellers were not similarly situated. The Court concluded, borrowing from its antitrust doctrines, that LDC's served different "markets" than other sellers. Hence, the Court applied only a form of the rational basis test. Justice Stevens was the only dissenter.

(3) *A Facially Discriminatory Real Estate Tax Violates the Dormant Commerce Clause Doctrine: Camps Newfound/Owatonna, Inc. v. The Town of Harrison, Maine, 520 U.S. 564 (1997).* The state of Maine had a statute which provided charitable and philanthropic organizations with an exemption from local property taxes. The state tax exemption, however, did not apply to those charitable organizations whose property served mainly the interests of out-of-state (non-Maine) persons. The church-owned campground in *Camps* operated a summer camp in the Maine wilderness whose clientele was 95% non-Maine residents. Under the circumstances, the town denied the church's application for exemption from real estate property taxes. Although the Supreme Court of Maine had upheld the Maine taxing scheme against a Dormant Commerce Clause challenge, the Supreme Court, per Justice Stevens, reversed. The Court held that the Maine tax scheme was facially discriminatory with respect to interstate commerce and that Maine could not satisfy the virtual *per se* standard of the doctrine's upper tier.

Justice Scalia dissented. Justice Thomas also dissented arguing, more broadly, that the Court should abandon its Dormant Commerce Clause Doctrine since the doctrine had no textual basis or, according to Justice Thomas, any historical basis.

(4) *Discrimination in Interstate Commerce Regarding "Direct Shipment" Wine Sales: Granholm v. Heald, 544 U.S. 460 (2005).* Many states regulate the sale and importation of wine through a three-tier system requiring separate licenses for producers, wholesalers, and retailers. Michigan and New York were states with such systems. In recent years, the wine industry had undergone two significant changes. First, there were now over 3,000 wineries in the country. Second, the wholesale market for wine had consolidated; the number of licensed wholesalers had dropped from 1600 to 600. Increasing the winery-to-wholesaler ratio means that many small wineries do not produce enough wine or have sufficient consumer demand for their wine to make it economical for wholesalers to carry their products. These economic circumstances caused many small wineries to rely on "direct shipping" to reach new markets. Twenty-six states allowed direct shipping of wine with various restrictions; thirteen of

those states had "reciprocity laws" which allowed direct shipment from wineries outside the state provided the state of origin afforded similar nondiscriminatory treatment to the reciprocal state.

The Michigan and New York schemes allowed in-state, but not out-of-state, wineries to make direct sales to consumers. There were a number of differences between Michigan and New York. The Michigan statute provided an "exception" for the forty (40) in-state wineries. Because of the exception, in-state wineries were able to make direct shipments to Michigan consumers whereas out-of-state wineries could not. New York's system also had exceptions, primarily an exception for an out-of-state winery that was willing and able to establish a "branch factory office or store room within New York." The cost of establishing a "physical presence" (*i.e.*, an in-state facility), however, was prohibitive for most small wineries.

The Michigan and New York regulatory systems were challenged on dormant Commerce Clause grounds. The lower courts had split on the dormant Commerce Clause issues, but the Supreme Court, per Justice Kennedy, struck down both of the state regulatory schemes. The Court indicated that "the current patchwork of laws . . . is essentially the product of an ongoing low-level trade war." The Court concluded that allowing these states to discriminate against out-of-state wine invites the type of "balkanization" and multiplication of preferential trade areas destructive of the very purpose of the Commerce Clause.

The Court concluded that both direct shipping laws "discriminated" against interstate commerce. The existence of the exceptions in both states was a basis for finding "facial discrimination." The Court also found that there was "discrimination in effect." In the case of Michigan, the Court reasoned that the "two extra layers of overhead increased the cost of out-of-state wines to Michigan consumers." In the case of the New York, the Court held that its "physical presence" requirement was "just an indirect way of subjecting all out-of-state wineries, but not local ones to the three-tier system." The physical presence requirement ran up the cost of doing business for out-of-staters and also increased the costs to consumers in New York, thereby encouraging consumers to buy in-state produced wine. *See* David S. Day, *The Expanded Concept of Facial Discrimination in the Dormant Commerce Clause Doctrine*, 40 CREIGHTON L. REV. 497 (2007).

After concluding that the state regulatory schemes were "discriminatory," the majority applied the *per se* standard. The majority also decided that the Twenty-First Amendment did not include the authority to "discriminate against interstate commerce."

There were two dissents. Justice Stevens, for Justice O'Connor, dissented on "original intention" grounds. The longer dissent, by Justice Thomas (joined by Chief Justice Rehnquist, Justice Stevens, and Justice O'Connor), disagreed with the historical analysis of the majority opinion. Justice Thomas basically concluded that the Twenty-First Amendment allows the states to discriminate against interstate commerce. Justice Thomas characterized the majority opinion as "this confused mishmash of elite opinion."

[2]   Embargoes

PROBLEM C

WHAT IF A STATE REQUIRES GARBAGE TO BE DUMPED LOCALLY? THE "REVERSE OREGON WASTE" CASE: WASTE SYSTEMS CORP. v. MARTIN COUNTY, MINN., 784 F. Supp. 641 (D. Minn. 1992). In a "reverse twist" on the garbage cases that banned imports, two Minnesota counties enacted ordinances that were embargoes or prohibitions on the export of garbage. In other words they actually *required*(!) all waste generated in the counties to be disposed at a new facility built by the two counties. An Iowa corporation that operated a landfill in Iowa challenged the constitutionality of these ordinances, because before their enactment, two-thirds of the waste generated in the counties had been disposed of at the Iowa landfill. The disposal cost at the new Minnesota facility was $70 per ton, while the Iowa charges were $30 per ton. Are the Minnesota laws discriminatory, and are they unconstitutional? [The facility director admitted that the purpose was "for us to get all of the garbage" and "to assure the financial success of the (Minnesota) facility." The district court reasoned that the Minnesota ordinances were economic protectionism that could not survive strict scrutiny.]

A More Interesting Question: Does this case, by its illustration of a clearer kind of economic protectionism, make it easier to argue that the Oregon, Michigan and Alabama laws at issue in *Oregon Wastes, Fort Gratiot* and *Chemical Waste* are *not* "economic protectionism," but rather "*environmental* protectionism"? (Or are both kinds of cases equally examples of discrimination against commerce, and therefore equally unconstitutional?)

C & A CARBONE, INC. v. TOWN OF CLARKSTOWN, 511 U.S. 383 (1994). This case presented a system similar to the "reverse twist" referenced in Problem C above. Seeking to comply with various governmental regulations concerning bulk solid waste, Clarkstown closed its old landfill and built a new "solid waste transfer station." In order to finance this transfer station, Clarkstown passed an ordinance requiring all solid waste haulers, including Carbone, to deposit solid waste at the transfer station. The city also established a higher-than-market fee for use of the transfer station. The Court, per Justice Kennedy, held that the flow control ordinance violated the "well-settled principles of our Commerce Clause jurisprudence."

Justice O'Connor concurred in the judgment, but she would have applied the "undue burden" standard from *Pike*, 397 U.S. 137, *supra*. Justice Souter, joined by Chief Justice Rehnquist and Justice Blackmun, dissented. Justice Souter argued that the ordinance's "[p]rotection of the public fisc is a legitimate local benefit directly advanced by the ordinance. . . ." The dissent concluded that "[t]he Commerce Clause was not passed to save the citizens of Clarkstown from themselves." *See United Haulers Association, Inc.* below.

[3] The Prohibition upon "Projecting Legislation into other States"

BROWN-FORMAN DISTILLERS CORP. v. NEW YORK LIQUOR AUTHORITY, 476 U.S. 573 (1986). New York State required every liquor distiller or producer to sell at a price no higher than the lowest price that the distiller charged anywhere else in the United States. The Supreme Court, per Marshall, J., held that this statute violated the negative commerce clause. The Court did not rely upon a discrimination rationale, because the appellant conceded that the statute was "even-handed." Instead, the Court emphasized the fact that the statute enabled New York to "project its legislation into" other states:

> Appellant does not dispute that New York's . . . law regulates all distillers of intoxicating liquors evenhandedly, or that the state's asserted interest—to assure the lowest possible prices for its residents—is legitimate. Appellant contends that these factors are irrelevant, however, because the lowest-price [law] falls within that category of direct regulations of interstate commerce that the commerce clause wholly forbids. This is so, appellant contends, because the [law] effectively regulates the price at which liquor is sold in other states. . . .

> We agree with appellants . . . that . . . New York's [law] regulates out-of-state transactions in violation of the commerce clause. Once a distiller has posted prices in New York, it is not free to change its prices elsewhere in the United States during the relevant month. Forcing a merchant to seek regulatory approval in one state before undertaking a transaction in another directly regulates interstate commerce. *Edgar v. MITE Corp.*, [discussed below]; *see*

also Baldwin v. G.A.F. Seelig, Inc., 294 U.S. at 522 (regulation tending to "mitigate the consequences of competition between the states" constitutes direct regulation). While New York may regulate the sale of liquor within its borders, and may seek low prices for its residents, it may not "project its legislation into [other states] by regulating the price to be paid" for liquor in those states.

That the [law] is addressed only to sales of liquor in New York is irrelevant if the "practical effect" of the law is to control liquor prices in other states. . . .

NOTES AND QUESTIONS

(1) *State Efforts to Regulate the High-Stakes Game of National Corporate Take-overs: Edgar v. MITE Corp., 457 U.S. 624 (1982), as Compared to CTS Corp. v. Dynamics Corp. of America, 481 U.S. 69 (1987).* What happens when a major investor from one state makes a hostile tender offer to take over a corporation that is another state's largest private employer? The answer: The second state's legislature gets into the act, of course. These two complex decisions deal with that problem; the first struck down the state regulation and the second upheld it.

(2) *The Projection-of-Regulation and Multi-State Interference Rationales: Are They Simply Different Ways to Express the Discrimination Concern, or are They a Different Concern?* The *Brown-Forman, MITE,* and *CTS* cases deal with the issue of one state "projecting its regulation" into other states, and with the possible problem of interference with interstate commerce that can result from many states enacting inconsistent regulations. Are these concerns really just a complicated form of the discrimination problem? *See generally* Regan, *Siamese Essays: (I) CTS Corp. v. Dynamics Corp. of America and Dormant Commerce Clause Doctrine; (II) Extraterritorial State Legislation,* 85 MICH. L. REV. 1865 (1987). For an interesting analysis of a different but related issue, *see* Note, *The Commerce Clause Limitation on the Power to Condemn a Relocating Business,* 96 YALE 1343 (1987).

[4] "Nondiscriminatory" Regulation: The Balancing Test

BIBB v. NAVAJO FREIGHT LINES, INC., 359 U.S. 520 (1959). An Illinois regulation required contour mudflaps for trucks. The result was that truckers could not use in Illinois a mudflap design that was legal in forty-five other states; furthermore, Illinois-approved mudflaps could not be used in Arkansas, which allowed only straight mudflaps. There was some evidence that the Illinois design reduced safety by causing heat buildup in brake drums, and the trial court found that it created no safety advantages. The Court invalidated the Illinois requirement under the negative commerce clause, with the following observations:

> This is one of those cases—few in number—where local safety measures that are nondiscriminatory place an unconstitutional burden on interstate commerce. This conclusion is especially underlined by the deleterious effect which the Illinois law will have on the "interline" operation of interstate motor carriers [*i.e.*, those in which long-haul truckers exchange loads]. The conflict between the Arkansas regulation and Illinois regulation also suggests that this regulation of mudguards is not one of those matters "admitting of diversity of treatment, according to the special requirements of local conditions. . . ."

SOUTHERN PACIFIC CO. v. ARIZONA
325 U.S. 761 (1945)

MR. CHIEF JUSTICE STONE delivered the opinion of the Court.

The Arizona train limit law . . . makes it unlawful for any person or corporation to operate within the state a railroad train of more than fourteen passenger or seventy freight cars. . . . [The Arizona trial court, after making extensive findings, held the law unconstitutional, but the Arizona Supreme Court reversed and upheld the statute. Here, the United States Supreme Court holds the Arizona law unconstitutional under the negative commerce clause.] . . .

[T]he matters for ultimate determination here are the nature and extent of the burden which the state regulation of interstate trains, adopted as a safety measure, imposes on interstate commerce, and whether the relative weights of the state and national interest involved are such as to make inapplicable the rule, generally observed, that the free flow of interstate commerce and its freedom from local restraints in matters requiring uniformity of regulation are interests safeguarded by the commerce clause from state interference.

[T]he facts found by the state trial court showing the nature of the interstate commerce involved, and the effect upon it of the train limit law, are not seriously questioned. . . .

The findings show that the operation of long trains, that is trains of more than fourteen passenger cars and more than seventy freight cars, is standard practice over the main lines of the railroads of the United States, and that, if the length of trains is to be regulated at all, national uniformity in the regulation adopted, such as only Congress can prescribe, is practically indispensable to the operation of an efficient and economical national railway system. . . . Outside of Arizona, where the length of trains is not restricted, appellant runs a substantial proportion of long trains. In 1939 on its comparable route for through traffic through Utah and Nevada from 66 to 85% of its freight trains were over 70 cars in length and over 43% of its passenger trains included more than fourteen passenger cars.

In Arizona, approximately 93% of the freight traffic and 95% of the passenger traffic is interstate. Because of the Train Limit Law appellant is required to haul over 30% more trains in Arizona than would otherwise have been necessary. [T]he additional cost of operation of trains complying with the Train Limit Law in Arizona amounts for the two railroads traversing that state to about $1,000,000 a year. [M]ore locomotives and more manpower are required; the necessary conversion and reconversion of train lengths at terminals and the delay caused by breaking up and remaking long trains upon entering and leaving the state in order to comply with the law, delays the traffic and diminishes its volume moved in a given time, especially when traffic is heavy. . . .

[F]requently it is not feasible to operate a newly assembled train from the New Mexico yard nearest to Arizona, with the result that the Arizona limitation governs the flow of traffic as far east as El Paso, Texas. For similar reasons the Arizona law often controls the length of passenger trains all the way from Los Angeles to El Paso.

If one state may regulate train lengths, so may all the others, and they need not prescribe the same maximum limitation. . . . The serious impediment to the free flow of commerce by the local regulation of train lengths and the practical necessity that such regulation, if any, must be prescribed by a single body having a nation-wide authority are apparent.

The trial court found that the Arizona law had no reasonable relation to safety, and made train operation more dangerous. . . . [T]he decisive question is whether in the circumstances the total effect of the law as a safety measure in reducing accidents and casualties is so slight or problematical as not to outweigh the national interest in keeping interstate commerce free from interferences which seriously impede it and subject it to local regulation which does not have a uniform effect on the interstate train journey which it interrupts.

[H]ere examination of all the relevant factors makes it plain that the state interest is outweighed by the interest of the nation in an adequate, economical railway transportation service, which must prevail. *Reversed.*

MR. JUSTICE BLACK, dissenting.

[W]hat the Court decides today is that it is unwise governmental policy to regulate the length of trains. I am therefore constrained to note my dissent.

For more than a quarter of a century, railroads and their employees have engaged in controversies over the relative virtues and dangers of long trains. Railroads have argued that they could carry goods and passengers cheaper in long trains than in short trains. They have also argued that while the danger of personal injury to their employees might in some respects be greater on account of the operation of long trains, this danger was more than offset by an increased number of accidents from other causes brought about by the operation of a much larger number of short trains. These arguments have been, and are now, vigorously denied. . . .

[I]t is significant, however, that American railroads never once asked Congress to exercise its unquestioned power to enact uniform legislation on that subject, and thereby invalidate the Arizona law. That which for some unexplained reason they did not ask Congress to do when it had the very subject of train length limitations under consideration, they shortly thereafter asked an Arizona state court to do. . . ..

[A] century and a half of constitutional history and government admonishes this Court to leave that choice to the elected legislative representatives of the people themselves, where it properly belongs both on democratic principles and the requirements of efficient government. . . .

MR. JUSTICE DOUGLAS, dissenting.

. . . My view has been that the courts should intervene only where the state legislation discriminated against interstate commerce or was out of harmony with laws which Congress had enacted. . . . It seems to me particularly appropriate that that course be followed here. For Congress has given the Interstate Commerce Commission broad powers of regulation over interstate carriers. . . . It is in a position to police the field. And if its powers prove inadequate for the task, Congress, which has paramount authority in this field, can implement them. . . .

NOTES AND QUESTIONS

(1) *Who Should Find the Facts that Determine Constitutional Issues—The Courts or the Legislatures?* Notice Justice Black's criticism of the Court for acting as a "super-legislature" in making its own determination of the facts, and of the proper balance of safety considerations. Doesn't he have a point? But notice, also, that Chief Justice Stone and a majority may have a point in saying that the consequences of allowing a state legislature to make findings governing impact upon interstate commerce may have "destructive consequences to the commerce of the nation." What is the proper balance between these two positions?

(2) *Uneven Weighting in the Southern Pacific Balancing Test: "Slight or Problematical" Local Benefits Do Not Justify "Interferences Which Seriously Impede" Interstate Commerce.* At one point in the opinion, Chief Justice Stone says that the "decisive question" is whether the advancement of the state interest is "so slight or problematical as not to outweigh the national interest in keeping interstate commerce free from interferences which seriously impede it. . . ." Notice that this statement of the balancing test is skewed in favor of upholding the state law, because it would result in a determination of unconstitutionality only when national harm heavily outweighed local gain. Does the uneven weighting of interests take some of the sting out of the Court's sitting as a super-legislature, if that is what it has done?

NOTE ON HOW TO READ THE *PIKE* CASE

A Widely Quoted Statement of the Modern Test. The case that follows contains perhaps the most widely quoted test of the modern negative commerce clause. The test has been excerpted earlier in this chapter, at the beginning of these negative commerce clause materials, and it is contained in the first full quoted paragraph of the Court's opinion that follows.

The Facts of Pike v. Bruce Church. The statute in question in this case is facially evenhanded. The facts are convoluted. It may be helpful to focus upon the parties' ultimate motives: Arizona wants Bruce Church's high-quality cantaloupes labeled as packed in Arizona, but Bruce Church wants to pack them, more cheaply, just across the border in California.

PIKE v. BRUCE CHURCH, INC.
397 U.S. 137 (1970)

MR. JUSTICE STEWART delivered the opinion of the Court.

[Bruce Church produced cantaloupes of unusually high quality near Parker, Arizona at a farm Bruce Church had developed out of the desert. Since it would have cost $200,000 to build packing facilities there, it shipped the cantaloupe harvest in bulk just across the border to Blythe, California, where it operated "centralized and efficient packing shed facilities." It sorted, inspected, packed, and shipped from Blythe. The Arizona Fruit and Vegetable Standardization Act, however, provided that all cantaloupes grown in Arizona and offered for sale must be "packed in regular compact arrangement in closed standard containers approved by the supervisor. . . ." Supervisor Pike, acting under the authority of the statute, entered an order preventing Bruce Church from shipping to Blythe because the bulk cantaloupes were not packed in Arizona, and because they consequently failed to identify these high-quality, Arizona-grown cantaloupes as having been packed in Arizona. The packaging in California would have complied otherwise with all the regulations of the Arizona statute. The district court granted a preliminary injunction against the enforcement of this order to prevent eminent loss of a year's crop, which would have cost Bruce Church approximately $700,000; it later made the injunction permanent. In this opinion, a unanimous Supreme Court rules against the state of Arizona.]

Although the criteria for determining the validity of state statutes affecting interstate commerce have been variously stated, the general rule that emerges can be phrased as follows: Where the statute regulates evenhandedly to effectuate a legitimate local public interest, and its effects on interstate commerce are only incidental, it will be upheld unless the burden imposed on such commerce is clearly excessive in relation to the putative local benefits. . . . If a legitimate local purpose is found, then the question becomes one of degree. And the extent of the burden that will be tolerated will of course depend on the nature of the local interest involved, and on whether it could be promoted as well with a lesser impact on interstate activities. . . . At the core of the Arizona Fruit and Vegetable Standardization Act are the requirements that fruits and vegetables shipped from Arizona meet certain standards of wholesomeness and quality, and that they be packed in standard containers in such a way that the outer layer or exposed portion of the pack does not "materially misrepresent" the quality of the lot as a whole. The impetus for the Act was the fear that some growers were shipping inferior or deceptively packaged produce, with the result that the reputation of Arizona growers generally was being tarnished and their financial return concomitantly reduced. It was to prevent this that the Act was passed in 1929. The State has stipulated that its primary purpose is to promote and preserve the reputation of Arizona growers by prohibiting deceptive packaging. . . .

But application of the Act through the appellant's order to the appellee company has a far different impact, and quite a different purpose. . . . The appellant's order would forbid the company to pack its cantaloupes outside Arizona, not for the purpose of keeping the reputation of its growers unsullied, but to enhance their reputation through the reflected good will of the company's superior produce. The appellant, in other words, is not complaining because the company is putting the good name of Arizona on an inferior or deceptively packaged product, but because it is not putting that name on a product that is superior and well packaged. As the appellant's brief puts the matter, "It is within Arizona's legitimate interest to require that interstate cantaloupe purchasers be informed that this high quality Parker fruit was grown in Arizona."

Although it is not easy to see why the other growers of Arizona are entitled to benefit at the company's expense from the fact that it produces superior crops, we may assume that the asserted state interest is a legitimate one. But the State's tenuous interest in having the company's cantaloupes identified as originating in Arizona cannot constitutionally justify the requirement that the company build and operate an unneeded $200,000 packing plant in the State. The nature of that burden is, constitutionally, more significant than its extent. For the Court has viewed with particular suspicion state statutes requiring business operations to be performed in the home State that could more efficiently be performed elsewhere. Even where the State is pursuing a clearly legitimate local interest, this particular burden on commerce has been declared to be virtually per se illegal. . . . *Toomer v. Witsell*, 334 U.S. 385.

The appellant argues that the above cases are different because they involved statutes whose express or concealed purpose was to preserve or secure employment for the home State, while here the statute is a regulatory one and there is no hint of such a purpose. But in *Toomer v. Witsell, supra*, the Court indicated that such a burden upon interstate commerce is unconstitutional even in the absence of such a purpose. In *Toomer* the Court held invalid a South Carolina statute requiring that owners of shrimp boats licensed by the State to fish in the maritime belt off South Carolina must unload and pack their catch in that State before "shipping or transporting it to another State." What we said there applies to this case as well:

> There was also uncontradicted evidence that appellants' costs would be materially increased by the necessity of having their shrimp unloaded and packed in South Carolina ports rather than at their home bases in Georgia where they maintain their own docking, warehousing, refrigeration and packing facilities. In addition, an inevitable concomitant of a statute requiring that work be done in South Carolina, even though that will be economically disadvantageous to the fishermen, is to divert to South Carolina employment and business which might otherwise go to Georgia; the necessary tendency of the statute is to impose an artificial rigidity on the economic pattern of the industry. . . .

While the order issued under the Arizona statute does not impose such rigidity on an entire industry, it does impose just such a strait-jacket on the appellee company with respect to the allocation of its interstate resources. Such an incidental consequence of a regulatory scheme could perhaps be tolerated if a more compelling state interest were involved. But here the State's interest is minimal at best—certainly less substantial than a State's interest in securing employment for its people. If the Commerce Clause forbids a State to require work to be done within its jurisdiction to promote local employment, then surely it cannot permit a State to require a person to go into a local packing business solely for the sake of enhancing the reputation of other producers within its borders.

The judgment is *Affirmed.*

NOTES AND QUESTIONS

(1) *The Nondiscrimination Tier of the Dormant Commerce Clause Doctrine: Pike v. Bruce Church, Inc., 397 U.S. 137 (1970).* When the state regulatory scheme is "nondiscriminatory," the applicable dormant Commerce Clause standard derives from the *Pike* decision. In *Pike*, Arizona regulated the processing and packaging of

cantaloupes. In order to enhance the state's reputation for high-quality produce, Arizona regulators insisted that Bruce Church, Inc. (and other growers) process and package the cantaloupes in Arizona rather than at Bruce Church's existing California facility. In effect, the nondiscriminatory Arizona regulation would require Bruce Church to spend over $200,000 (in 1960s dollars) to build an Arizona packaging facility. Bruce Church sued under the dormant Commerce Clause.

The Supreme Court, per Justice Stewart, unanimously ruled in favor of Bruce Church even though the Court found the Arizona regulation to be nondiscriminatory. The *Pike* Court articulated the standard (Note (2) below) that later came to be known as the "undue burden" test.

(2) *A Widely Quoted, But Not Self-Executing Test.* You should identify and absorb the *Bruce Church* test, contained in the first quoted paragraph of the opinion. Additionally, it may be worthwhile to compare it with the following statements from other cases:

> Under that general rule [of *Bruce Church*] we must inquire (1) whether the challenged statute regulates evenhandedly with only "incidental" effects on interstate commerce, or discriminates against interstate commerce either on its face or in practical effect; (2) whether the statute serves a legitimate local purpose; and, if so (3) whether alternative means could promote this local purpose as well without discriminating against interstate commerce. *Hughes v. Oklahoma, supra,* 441 U.S. at 336.

> This Court has adopted what amounts to a two-tiered approach to analyzing state economic regulation under the commerce clause. When a state statute directly regulates or discriminates against interstate commerce, or when its effect is to favor in-state economic interests over out-of-state interests, we have generally struck down the statute without further inquiry. . . . When, however, a statute has only indirect effects on interstate commerce and regulates evenhandedly, we have examined whether the state's interest is legitimate and whether the burden on interstate commerce clearly exceeds the local benefits [citing *Bruce Church*]. We have also recognized that there is no clear line separating the category of state regulation that is virtually *per se* invalid under the commerce clause, and the category subject to the *Pike v. Bruce Church* balancing approach. In either situation, the critical consideration is the overall effect of the statute on both local and interstate activity. *Brown-Forman Distillers Corp. v. New York State Liquor Authority, supra,* 106 S. Ct. at 2084.

Arguably, every restatement of the test in different words has the effect of subtly altering its meaning. Note, also, the *Brown-Forman* admission that there is "no clear line separating. . . ." the various tests and the "overall effect of the statute on both local and interstate activity" is the ultimate consideration.

PROBLEM D

RECONSIDERING PENNSYLVANIA v. WHEELING & BELMONT BRIDGE CO. [IN PROBLEM B ABOVE]: WOULD VIRGINIA'S OBSTRUCTION OF NAVIGATION PASS THE BRUCE CHURCH BALANCING TEST? In the *Wheeling & Belmont Bridge* case, Virginia authorized the construction of a bridge that obstructed navigation, diverted traffic, and caused Pennsylvania to complain that its tolls and revenues were reduced. But the bridge provided local benefits to Virginians, which presumably constituted the motivation for their building of the bridge.

(1) *Would the Bridge Be Discriminatory; and if Not, Would It Pass the Bruce Church Test?* The first question is, does the Virginia law authorizing the bridge discriminate against interstate commerce? (Perhaps it does not do so on its face, but consider whether it should be treated as discriminatory under, for example, the political check theory.) Second, assuming the bridge authorization is considered "evenhanded"

rather than "discriminatory," what should be the result of applying the *Bruce Church* test to this obstruction of commerce? Consider whether the "incidental" burden on interstate commerce is "clearly excessive" in relation to the "putative local benefits," as well as whether the benefits can be obtained by means having a "lesser impact" on commerce. Should there be deference to the Virginia legislature?

(2) *Congress' Role in Ensuring Navigation.* If obstructions to navigation become sufficiently serious, Congress presumably will act to provide a nationwide plan for allowable river obstructions. Does the presence of this Congressional alternative provide a political check that compensates for the arguable absence of a political check within Virginia?

NOTES AND QUESTIONS

(1) *The Commerce Clause as a Protection of "Individual" Rights: Dennis v. Higgins, 498 U.S. 439 (1991).* In this case, the Supreme Court expressly held, per Justice White, that the Commerce Clause confers "rights, privileges, or immunities" within the meaning of 42 U.S.C. § 1983 (the Civil Rights Remedies Statute), rather than merely allocating power between federal and state governments. Dennis ran a motor carrier business and claimed that the state of Nebraska had imposed discriminatory and retaliatory taxes and fees upon him, in violation of the Commerce Clause. You might also reconsider the Commerce Clause decisions upholding civil rights legislation, such as *Heart of Atlanta* and *Katzenbach v. McClung* in Chapter 2 above. Are these examples relevant to deciding whether the rationale for the dormant Commerce Clause doctrine should include protection of individual rights as well as protection of national economic unity and protection of political outsiders (*i.e.*, nonresidents)?

(2) *The Third Generation of Flow-Control Ordinances: United Haulers Ass'n Inc. v. Oneida-Herkimer Solid Waste Management Authority, 550 U.S. 330 (2007).* The Oneida-Herkimer Solid Waste Management Authority (WMA) operated a waste sorting facility under a flow-control ordinance that was nearly identical to the flow-control ordinance in *Carbone*, above. The only difference, for dormant Commerce Clause purposes, was that the WMA waste sorting facility was *owned* by the public entities. Nonetheless, for the Court's plurality, per Chief Justice Roberts, this was enough to distinguish *Carbone* and uphold this ordinance. [*ordinance upheld*]

Beyond deciding that the ordinance was not discriminatory, the plurality opinion also applied a version of the "undue burden" standard and upheld the ordinance. Since Justice Scalia and Thomas reject any reliance on the undue burden (*Pike*) standard [*see* § 3.02[B][8] below], they did not join that part of Roberts' opinion. Justice Scalia concurred in part. In a much longer opinion, Justice Thomas concurred only in the judgment; he called for the rejection of the entire dormant Commerce Clause doctrine because it is "untethered from the written constitution." [*wow, Thomas*]

Justice Alito wrote a dissenting opinion, concluding that the Oneida-Herkimer ordinance was discriminatory and that the reasoning of *Carbone* controlled. The Alito dissent did not address the Court's undue burden analysis.

The Court's reliance on "public ownership" to determine that the ordinance was not discrimination against interstate commerce may make a doctrinally significant statement. This analysis appeared to rely on the reasoning of the "market participant" sub-doctrine. [§ 3.02[B][8] below]. *See* Kenneth L. Karst, *From Carbone to United Haulers: The Advocates' Tales*, 2007 Sup. Ct. Rev. 237; *see also American Trucking Association Inc. v. Michigan Public Service Commission*, 545 U.S. 429 (2005).

(3) *The Nondiscrimination Tier: The Reliance on Judicial Assessment of the Effects of Nonpurposeful State Regulation.* Cases on the nondiscrimination tier are cases where the state regulation is not facially or purposefully discriminatory. In other words, they are "effects" cases. The critics (Justices Scalia and Thomas) of the nondiscrimination tier are concerned that a state regulatory scheme would be struck

down only because of its effects on interstate commerce. The effects may be the result of mere state negligence. Compare this doctrine to equal protection or free speech.

(4) *Further Research on the "Undue Burden" Test of the Dormant Commerce Clause Doctrine: Academic Commentary.* The undue burden test from *Pike* is the most controversial aspect of the dormant Commerce Clause doctrine. On the Court, the *Pike* test has been rejected by Justices Scalia and Thomas. For further information, *see* § 3.02[B][8] below. For academic commentary on the *Pike* decision, *see* David S. Day, *Revisiting Pike: The Origins of the Nondiscrimination Tier of the Dormant Commerce Clause Doctrine,* 27 HAMLINE L. REV. 45 (2003); Donald Regan, *The Supreme Court and State Protectionism: Making Sense of the Dormant Commerce Clause,* 84 MICH. L. REV. 1091 (1986); Mark Tushnet, *Rethinking the Dormant Commerce Clause,* 1979 WIS. L. REV. 125.

[5] Subsidies to In-State Residents

WEST LYNN CREAMERY, INC. v. HEALY, 512 U.S. 186 (1994). Faced with a declining in-state dairy industry, Massachusetts developed a two-part "pricing order." First, Massachusetts imposed an "assessment" on all fluid milk sold by dealers to Massachusetts retailers. The assessment applied evenhandedly to milk produced in-state and out-of-state and was, therefore, non-discriminatory. Second, the proceeds of the assessment were distributed to Massachusetts dairy farmers as a "local subsidy." Analogizing the Massachusetts pricing order to a "protective tariff or customs duty," the Court, per Justice Stevens, held the program unconstitutional under the negative Commerce Clause. . . .

> Because of their distorting effects on the geography of production, tariffs have long been recognized as violative of the Commerce Clause. In fact, tariffs against the products of other States are so patently unconstitutional that our cases reveal not a single attempt by any State to enact one. Instead, the cases are filled with state laws that aspire to reap some of the benefits of tariffs by other means. . . .

> Under these cases, Massachusetts' pricing order is clearly unconstitutional. Its avowed purpose and its undisputed effect are to enable higher cost Massachusetts dairy farmers to compete with lower cost dairy farmers in other States.

> [E]ven granting respondent's assertion that both components of the pricing order would be constitutional standing alone,[3] the pricing order nevertheless must fall. A pure subsidy funded out of general revenue ordinarily imposes no burden on interstate commerce, but merely assists local business.

> [B]y conjoining a tax and a subsidy, Massachusetts has created a program more dangerous to interstate commerce than either part alone. Nondiscriminatory measures, like the evenhanded tax at issue here, are generally upheld, in spite of any adverse effects on interstate commerce, in part because "[t]he existence of major in-state interests adversely affected . . . is a powerful safeguard against legislative abuse." [H]owever, when a nondiscriminatory tax is coupled with a subsidy to one of the groups hurt by the tax, a state's political processes can no longer be relied upon to prevent legislative abuse, because one of the in-state interests which would otherwise lobby against the tax has been mollified by the subsidy. . . .

Justice Scalia, joined by Justice Thomas, concurred in the judgment. Chief Justice Rehnquist, with Justice Blackmun, dissented mainly on the ground that the negative

---

[3] We have never squarely confronted the constitutionality of subsidies, and we need not do so now. We have, however, noted that "[d]irect subsidization of domestic industry does not ordinarily run afoul" of the negative Commerce Clause. New Energy Co. of Indiana v. Limbach, 486 U.S., at 278. . . .

Commerce Clause doctrine should not apply to a "subsidy" such as the Massachusetts distribution. Regarding the majority's concern for the exclusion of the out-of-state producers from the state's normal political processes, the Chief Justice concluded that "[a]nalysis of interest group participation in the political process may serve many useful purposes, but serving as a basis for interpreting the dormant Commerce Clause is not one of them." Should judicial review under the negative Commerce Clause doctrine attempt to protect interstate commerce because such commerce is "powerless" in the state political process or is proper consideration limited to the impact of state regulation on the national economy? Who is right on the "political check" issue: the majority or the Chief Justice's dissent?

PROBLEM E

A SUBSIDY ADMINISTERED INDEPENDENTLY FROM ANY PARTICULAR TAX AND PAID FROM GENERAL REVENUES, BUT LIMITED TO RESIDENTS: CONSTITUTIONAL? In the case above, the problem with the subsidy appears to center on its linkage with the tax. There is generally no prohibition on subsidies to in-staters funded from general tax revenues, and Justice Stevens's opinion appears to preserve this principle. Therefore, what if Massachusetts (1) imposed a milk tax that was payable into general revenues and collected by the State Treasurer and (2) simultaneously adopted a subsidy program, independently administered by the Department of Agriculture, payable from general revenues to dairy farmers who are financially distressed as determined by individual application of defined criteria of need? Analyze whether this plan would produce a different result than the case above.

[6]   The Importance of Fact Litigation as to Burdens

RAYMOND MOTOR TRANSPORTATION, INC. v. RICE, 434 U.S. 429 (1978). Wisconsin's statutes generally prohibited trucks longer than fifty-five feet or pulling more than one other vehicle to be operated on state highways without permits. Appellants were truckers who were denied permits to operate 65-foot double-trailer units. At trial, they presented extensive, uncontradicted evidence that the 65-foot doubles were as safe as, if not safer than, 55-foot singles when operated on limited-access four-lane divided highways. They also showed without contradiction that since they were prevented from using interline transfers of doubles unless they circumvented the state or hauled them through separately, the Wisconsin statutes caused disruption, delay, and increased costs. Finally, the truckers' evidence showed that Wisconsin routinely made exceptions for various vehicles over fifty-five feet in length. The Supreme Court, per Powell, J., struck down the regulations under the negative commerce clause.

Justice Blackmun, joined by three other justices, concurred but wrote separately to "emphasize the narrow scope of today's decision." The concurring justices pointed out that the Court was not engaging in balancing in derogation of the legislature. "[I]f safety justifications are not illusory, the Court will not second-guess legislative judgment about their importance in comparison with the related burdens on interstate commerce. . . . Here, the Court does not engage in a balance of policy; it does not make a legislative choice. Instead, after searching the factual records developed by the parties, it concluded that the safety interests have not been shown to exist as a matter of law."

KASSEL v. CONSOLIDATED FREIGHTWAYS CORP., 450 U.S. 662 (1981). Iowa, unlike other nearby states, prohibited the use of 65-foot double-trailer trucks even on divided highways. The appellant trucking company produced evidence, similar to that in *Raymond Motor Transportation, Inc. v. Rice*, showing that the Iowa law caused it disruption, delay, and increased costs. Iowa defended the law as a reasonable safety measure (and also showed that it reduced Iowa road wear by diverting traffic to other states). The district court, after receiving conflicting evidence, made fact findings to the effect that the 65-foot doubles were as safe as shorter trucks, and it held that the state law impermissibly burdened interstate commerce. Justice Powell's opinion for the plurality affirmed and thus struck down the Iowa law:

> But the incantation of a purpose to promote the public health or safety does not insulate a state law from commerce clause attack. Regulations designed for that salutary purpose nevertheless may further the purpose so marginally, and interfere with commerce so substantially, as to be invalid under the commerce clause. . . . This "weighing" by a court requires—and indeed the constitutionality of the state regulation depends on—"a sensitive consideration of the weight and nature of the state regulatory concern in light of the extent of the burden imposed on the course of interstate commerce. . . ."

> Statistical studies supported the view that 65-foot doubles are at least as safe overall as 55-foot singles and 60-foot doubles. . . .

> [The Iowa law was subject to exemptions for livestock or farm vehicles and for cities abutting other states. This " 'border cities exemption' also suggests that Iowa's statute may not have been designed to ban dangerous trucks, but rather to discourage interstate truck traffic."] . . . Iowa seems to have hoped to limit the use of its highways by deflecting some through traffic. . . .

> In sum, the statutory exemptions, their history, and the arguments Iowa has advanced in support of its law in this litigation, all suggest that the deference traditionally accorded a state's safety judgment is not warranted. . . . The controlling factors are thus the findings of the district court, accepted by the court of appeals, with respect to the relative safety of the types of trucks at issue, and the substantiality of the burden on interstate commerce.

Justice Brennan, joined by Justice Marshall, concurred. Lastly, Justice Rehnquist, joined by the Chief Justice and Justice Stewart, dissented: "Iowa introduced evidence supporting the relation between vehicle length and highway safety." The district court was wrong in approaching the case as though the question were the relative safety of different truck lengths: "The question . . . is whether the Iowa legislature has acted rationally in regulating vehicle lengths and whether the safety benefits from this regulation are more than slight or problematical." Note that Justice Rehnquist argued for the use of a rational basis standard. This scrutiny is lower than either tier of the doctrine. Moreover, under rational basis, the state would always prevail.

NOTES AND QUESTIONS

(1) *Congress Legislates National Standards, Mooting Rice and Kassel: Surface Transportation Assistance Act of 1982, Pub. L. 97-424, 96 Stat. 2097, and Department of Transportation Appropriations Act of 1983, Pub. L. 97-369, 96 Stat. 1765.* In these two enactments, Congress provided nationwide standards for truck lengths and related issues, so that the narrow holdings of *Rice* and *Kassel* no longer control. Does this legislation say anything about these decisions as constitutional law?

(2) *The Effect of Kassel on Criticism of the Court as a "Super-Legislature" and upon the Unevenly-Weighted Balance Issue.* Other cases demonstrate the dilemma of undue deference to state protectionism versus the Court's acting as a "super-legislature."

PROBLEM F

THE DELAWARE "SUPERCOLLIER" CASE: NORFOLK SOUTHERN CORP. v. OBERLY, 822 F.2d 388 (3d Cir. 1987). The only east coast anchorage between Maine and Mexico that can accommodate very large coal vessels, known as "supercolliers," when they are fully loaded, is Big Stone Anchorage in Delaware Bay. Plaintiff, a coal shipper, wishes to establish a major coal transshipment station at that point. The Delaware Coastal Zone Act, however, provides that "offshore gas, liquid, or solid bulk product transfer facilities which are not in operation on June 28, 1971, are prohibited in the coastal zone [which includes the area in question] and no permit may be issued therefor." Plaintiff alleges that this law, as applied to it, violates the negative commerce clause. *Norfolk Southern Corp. v. Oberly, supra.*

(1) *Should There Be Heightened Scrutiny or a Presumption of Unconstitutionality?* The plaintiff claims that the Delaware law "overtly blocks the flow of interstate commerce at a State's borders" and hence is subject to a presumption of unconstitutionality, citing *Philadelphia v. New Jersey.* Is the contention correct?

(2) *How Should the Balancing Test Be Applied?* Plaintiff argues, in the alternative, that the burden upon interstate commerce is "clearly excessive" in comparison to putative local benefits, when considered in light of alternatives with lesser impact (*e.g.*, selective permitting, environmental standards, etc.). Is this contention correct? [Note: the Third Circuit, in *Norfolk Southern*, 822 F.2d 388, *supra*, rejected both of plaintiff's contentions, holding the Delaware law nondiscriminatory and also holding that, in the words of the *Bruce Church* test, the burden was not "clearly excessive" in light of putative local benefits which included protection of the coastal zone from pollution and blight. Do you think the Supreme Court would have agreed?]

[7] The States' Own Purchases, Sales, and Resources in the Marketplace

The State is Permitted Some Room to "Discriminate" by Managing Its Own Resources to Favor Its Citizens. Imagine that the state of New York holds a ceremonial state dinner at which it serves wine purchased at public expense. Naturally, it serves New York, rather than California, wine (and California may do the opposite). Question: Is this overt state "discrimination" a violation of the negative commerce clause? Answer: It has been held not to be, on the theory that the state, in its management of its own resources, is entitled to prefer its own citizens. Its market choices are like public welfare payments.

An Example: White v. Massachusetts Council of Construction Employers, Inc., 460 U.S. 204 (1983). In the *White* case, the City of Boston required city-funded construction projects to be performed by a work force that consisted at least half of Boston residents. The Court upheld this requirement against a negative commerce clause challenge. It covered "a discrete, identifiable class of economic activity in which the city is a major participant. Everyone affected by the order is, in a substantial if informal sense, 'working for the city.' "

State Efforts to Stretch this Principle. Sometimes, states have attempted to justify measures that were essentially protectionist by overbroad characterizations of their own roles in the marketplace. In *Hughes v. Oklahoma* (the seined minnows case), for example, the state unsuccessfully attempted to sustain its regulation on the theory that its wildlife was a state resource. *See also Hicklin v. Orbeck*, 437 U.S. 518, 533 (1978) (invalidating Alaskan hiring preferences related to oil and gas resources). Consider, also, the following case.

REEVES, INC. v. STAKE
447 U.S. 429 (1980)

MR. JUSTICE BLACKMUN delivered the opinion of the Court:

[In 1919, South Dakota's then-prevailing Progressive Political Movement concluded that regional cement shortages had "interfered with and delayed both public and private enterprises," and that they were "threatening the people of this state." South Dakota's unique solution was to build, at state expense, a state-owned cement plant, operated by the State Cement Commission. For more than fifty years, this state project supplied both state residents and out-of-state buyers. In 1978, however, a cement shortage caused the State Cement Commission to announce that it was confining its sales of cement to residents of the state. This decision forced the petitioner, an out-of-state buyer, to cut its business severely. It sued, and the district court granted an injunction preventing South Dakota from confining its sales to residents. The court of appeals reversed, concluding that the state had "simply acted in a proprietary capacity" to favor its residents, as permitted by *Hughes v. Alexandria Scrap Corp.*, 426 U.S. 794 (1976). Here, the Supreme Court affirms (by 5-4 vote) the court of appeals and holds that South Dakota's restrictive sales policy is not invalidated by the negative commerce clause.]

Alexandria Scrap concerned a Maryland program designed to remove abandoned automobiles from the State's roadways and junkyards. To encourage recycling, a "bounty" was offered for every Maryland-titled junk car converted into scrap. [A] new law imposed more exacting documentation requirements on out-of-state than in-state processors. By making it less remunerative for suppliers to transfer vehicles outside Maryland, the reform triggered a "precipitate decline in the number of bounty-eligible hulks supplied to appellee's [Virginia] plant from Maryland sources." Indeed, "[t]he practical effect was substantially the same as if Maryland had withdrawn altogether the availability of bounties on hulks delivered by unlicensed suppliers to licensed non-Maryland processors. . . ."

. . . In the Court's view, however, *Alexandria Scrap* did not involve "the kind of action with which the Commerce Clause is concerned." Unlike prior cases voiding state laws inhibiting interstate trade, "Maryland has not sought to prohibit the flow of hulks, or to regulate the conditions under which it may occur. Instead, it has entered into the market itself to bid up their price, . . . as a purchaser, in effect, of a potential article of interstate commerce," and has restricted "its trade to its own citizens or businesses within the State."

Having characterized Maryland as a market participant, rather than as a market regulator, the Court found no reason to "believe the Commerce Clause was intended to require independent justification for [the State's] action." The Court couched its holding in unmistakably broad terms. "Nothing in the purposes animating the Commerce Clause prohibits a State, in the absence of congressional action, from participating in the market and exercising the right to favor its own citizens over others."

The basic distinction drawn in *Alexandria Scrap* between States as market participants and States as market regulators makes good sense and sound law. As that case explains, the Commerce Clause responds principally to state taxes and regulatory measures impeding free private trade in the national marketplace. . . . There is no indication of a constitutional plan to limit the ability of the States themselves to operate freely in the free market. . . .

Restraint in this area is also counseled by considerations of state sovereignty, the role of each State " 'as guardian and trustee for its people,' " and "the long recognized right of trader or manufacturer, engaged in an entirely private business, freely to exercise his own independent discretion as to parties with whom he will deal." [G]iven these factors, *Alexandria Scrap* wisely recognizes that, as a rule, the adjustment of interests in this context is a task better suited for Congress than this Court.

South Dakota, as a seller of cement, unquestionably fits the "market participant" label more comfortably than a State acting to subsidize local scrap processors. Thus, the general rule of *Alexandria Scrap* plainly applies here. Petitioner argues, however, that the exemption for marketplace participation necessarily admits of exceptions. While conceding that possibility, we perceive in this case no sufficient reason to depart from the general rule.

In finding a Commerce Clause violation, the District Court emphasized "that the Commission . . . made an election to become part of the interstate commerce system." [T]his argument is not persuasive. It is somewhat self-serving to say that South Dakota has "exploited" the interstate market. An equally fair characterization is that neighboring States long have benefited from South Dakota's foresight and industry. . . .

Undaunted by these considerations, petitioner advances four more arguments for reversal:

First, petitioner protests that South Dakota's preference for its residents responds solely to the "non-governmental objectiv[e]" of protectionism. . . .

We find the label "protectionism" of little help in this context. The State's refusal to sell to buyers other than South Dakotans is "protectionist" only in the sense that it limits benefits generated by a state program to those who fund the state treasury and whom the State was created to serve. . . .

Second, petitioner echoes the District Court's warning:

If a state in this union, were allowed to hoard its commodities or resources for the use of their own residents only, a drastic situation might evolve. For example, Pennsylvania or Wyoming might keep their coal, the northwest its timber, and the mining states their minerals. The result being that embargo may be retaliated by embargo and commerce would be halted at state lines. . . . This argument, although rooted in the core purpose of the Commerce Clause, does not fit the present facts. Cement is not a natural resource, like coal, timber, wild game, or minerals. [W]hatever limits might exist on a State's ability to invoke the *Alexandria Scrap* exemption to hoard resources which by happenstance are found there, those limits do not apply here. . . .

[Here, the court rejects petitioner's third and fourth arguments, which were based on the alleged competitive advantage given to South Dakota businesses and the claim that South Dakota should be required to replicate a free market. "The very reason South Dakota built its plant was because the free market had failed adequately to supply the region with cement"]

The judgment of the United States Court of Appeals is affirmed.

MR. JUSTICE POWELL, with whom MR. JUSTICE BRENNAN, MR. JUSTICE WHITE, and MR. JUSTICE STEVENS join, dissenting.

[South Dakota's] policy represents precisely the kind of economic protectionism that the Commerce Clause was intended to prevent. . . .

Unlike the market subsidies at issue in *Alexandria Scrap*, the marketing policy of the South Dakota Cement Commission has cut off interstate trade. The State can raise such a bar when it enters the market to supply its own needs. In order to ensure an adequate supply of cement for public uses, the State can withhold from interstate commerce the cement needed for public projects.

The State, however, has no parallel justification for favoring private, in-state customers over out-of-state customers. In response to political concerns that likely would be inconsequential to a private cement producer, South Dakota has shut off its cement sales to customers beyond its borders. That discrimination constitutes a direct barrier to trade "of the type forbidden by the Commerce Clause, and involved in previous cases. . . ." *Alexandria Scrap*. The effect on interstate trade is the same as if the state legislature had imposed the policy on private cement producers. The Commerce Clause prohibits this severe restraint on commerce. . . .

SOUTH-CENTRAL TIMBER DEVELOPMENT, INC. v. WUNNICKE, 467 U.S. 82 (1984). Alaska announced that it would sell a quantity of timber from state-owned lands, but that, pursuant to a requirement imposed by state statute, "primary manufacture within the state of Alaska" would be required as a special provision in all contracts. Thus, a purchaser would be required to process the timber in Alaska before exporting it. South-Central, an Alaskan timber logging company, operated no processing facilities in the state, although it exported Alaskan logs, typically to Japan.

It claimed that the Alaskan sales policy violated the commerce clause. In the Supreme Court, the plurality opinion by Justice White, struck down the Alaska sales policy:

> There are sound reasons for distinguishing between a state's preferring its own residents in the initial disposition of goods when it is a market participant and a state's attachment of restrictions on dispositions subsequent to the goods coming to rest in private hands. First, simply as a matter of intuition a state market participant has a greater interest as a "private trader" in the immediate transaction than it has in what its purchaser does with the goods after the state no longer has an interest in them. Second, downstream restrictions have a greater regulatory effect than do limitations on the immediate transaction. Instead of merely choosing its own trading partners, the state is attempting to govern the private, separate economic relationships of its trading partners. . . .

> [The Alaskan processing contract policy exhibits a] protectionist nature [that subjects it to] the rule of virtual *per se* invalidity [citing *Bruce Church* and *Philadelphia v. New Jersey*.]

Justice Rehnquist, joined by Justice O'Connor, dissented: "In my view, the line of distinction drawn in the plurality opinion between the State as market participant and the State as market regulator is both artificial and unconvincing."

NOTES AND QUESTIONS

(1) *The State as Market Participant Distinguished from the State as Regulator: Is South-Central Timber Consistent with Alexandria Scrap and White?* In each of these cases, the state's effort is to channel its benefits and bounty to its citizens. Some cases involve attempts to do so directly, as in *Reeves, Inc. v. Stake;* in other cases, it has attempted to do so through middlemen—as in *White, South-Central Timber*, and (less obviously) *Alexandria Scrap*. Justice Rehnquist's dissent in *South-Central* is based on the premise that the economic effect is the same. Is he correct?

(2) *The Distinction Between the State as Government and the State as Entrepreneur: Are the Dissenters in Reeves Correct?* The dissenters in *Reeves* see a difference between the state when it acts in a public, governmental capacity, and when it acts to run a business that any private entrepreneur could conduct. If this distinction were viable, the state could reserve its cement for necessary public works, such as the construction of courthouses or highways—but it could not discriminate against interstate commerce for sales for commercial purposes, such as building private homes. Is this argument persuasive, in the sense that it better reflects the true meaning of the commerce clause? In the alternative, does it better reflect the sovereignty of the states, as protected by the tenth amendment?

(3) *The Sovereignty Issue: The State as a State.* Does it make a difference whether *Reeves, Inc. v. Stake* is decided on the basis that the commerce clause simply does not reach the state's conduct, or on the basis that the state has sovereign power to function as a market participant under the tenth amendment or other constitutional protections? This issue of state sovereignty— *i.e.*, the extent to which the states are immune from Congressional regulation—is a complex subject, which we take up in the next section.

(4) *Upholding State Tax Exemptions for a State's Own Municipal Bonds: Department of Revenue of Kentucky v. Davis, 128 S. Ct. 1801 (2008).* Kentucky, like almost all States, exempts from its state income tax the interest earned on municipal bonds issued by it (or its political subdivisions), but it does tax the interest on bonds issued by other States. The Davises, Kentucky taxpayers, paid taxes on their out-of-state bonds and then challenged the Kentucky tax scheme as a violation of the dormant Commerce Clause. Although the Kentucky courts agreed with the challengers, the Supreme Court ruled in favor of the State.

Justice Souter's majority opinion relied on *United Haulers*, above, to conclude that the tax scheme was non-discriminatory because the state was merely favoring the traditional governmental function of issuing bonds to pay for public projects rather than favoring local entities over substantially similar out-of-state interests. In a section of the opinion for only a plurality, Justice Souter also defended the result under the market participant exception. He contended that Kentucky was participating in the interstate and intrastate bond markets, and the fact that it was also acting as a regulator by establishing the differential taxing scheme did not prevent the application of the market participant exception. The final section of the opinion for the Court rejected the application of the undue burden/*Pike* standard.

There were four concurrences. Justice Stevens concurred on the grounds that Kentucky was merely engaged in a borrowing scheme for financing public projects. Chief Justice Roberts concurred only on the basis of his reasoning in *United Haulers*. Justices Scalia and Thomas concurred on their theories calling for the abandonment of the *Pike* standard or the entire doctrine. The dissents, by Justices Kennedy and Alito, disagreed with any expansion of the market participant exception or of the traditional government function analysis of *United Haulers*.

[8] Should the Dormant Commerce Clause Jurisprudence Be Abandoned?

AMERICAN TRUCKING ASSOCIATIONS, INC. v. SMITH, 496 U.S. 167 (1990). This decision is noteworthy primarily because of the concurring opinion of Justice Scalia repudiating all of the "so-called 'negative' Commerce Clause jurisprudence." The issue before the Court was whether the invalidation of a flat tax on highway use in *American Trucking Co. v. Scheiner*, 483 U.S. 266 (1987), on the ground that it violated the negative commerce clause, should be applied retroactively—a result that would impose high refund obligations on many states. The plurality, together with Justice Scalia, held that the *Scheiner* holding should be applied prospectively only, thus sparing the states an unexpected disaster. Justice Scalia believed that invalidation of the tax in *Scheiner* was wrong in the first place:

> I dissented in *Scheiner*, and in that case and elsewhere have registered my disagreement with the so-called "negative" Commerce Clause jurisprudence. . . . This disagreement rests on more than my view (by no means mine alone) that the jurisprudence is a "quagmire," that it has been "arbitrary, conclusory, and irreconcilable with the constitutional text," since its inception in the last century, and that it has only worsened with age. I believe that this jurisprudence takes us, self-consciously and avowedly, beyond the judicial role itself. . . .
>
> Presuming law from congressional silence is quite different from the normal judicial task of interpreting and applying text, or determining and applying common-law tradition. The principal question to be asked, of course, is what would a reasonable federal regulator of commerce intend—which is no different from the question a legislator himself must ask. That explains, I think, why no body of our decisional law has changed as regularly as our "negative" Commerce Clause jurisprudence. [T]hat also explains why our exercise of the "negative" Commerce Clause function has ultimately cast us in the essentially legislative role of weighing the imponderable—balancing the importance of the State's interest in this or that (an importance that different citizens would assess differently) against the degree of impairment of commerce. [W]hatever it is that we are expounding in this area, it is not a Constitution. . . .

NOTES AND QUESTIONS

(1) *Reliance Interests after Reversal of the Dormant Commerce Clause Jurisprudence: Quill Corp. v. North Dakota, 508 U.S. 808 (1991).* In this case, Justice Scalia cited his *American Trucking* decision as a basis for rejecting an earlier decision that

prohibited state taxation of interstate mail-order purchases. He would have safeguarded reliance interests by following the earlier decision purely as a matter of *stare decisis*, leaving ultimate resolution of the issue to Congress.

(2) *Democracy and Protectionism: The Negative Commerce Clause as Depending Upon the Absence of a "Political Check." Julian N. Eule, Laying the Dormant Commerce Clause to Rest*, 91 Yale 425, 443–45 (1982). If regulation is nondiscriminatory—that is, if it falls evenhandedly on those whose votes impose it and those upon whom it is imposed—there arguably is a political check upon the magnitude of the burden. But if in-staters can find a way to "export" the costs of regulation to out-of-staters, democratic checks will be absent. Thus Eule, *supra*, concludes: "When regulations promulgated by a legislative body fall solely or predominantly on a group represented in the legislature, there is cause to believe that the enactment will be rationally based, efficacious, and no more burdensome than is necessary to achieve the proffered purpose." Is this reasoning useful in determining whether "discrimination" is present? *See also* Maltz, *How Much Regulation is Too Much?—An Examination of Commerce Clause Jurisprudence*, 50 Geo. Wash. L. Rev. 47 (1981); Tushnet, *Rethinking the Dormant Commerce Clause*, 1979 Wis. L. Rev. 125.

(3) *Evaluating Alternate Approaches that Justice Scalia Might Use to Achieve His "Stated Goal" of Retrenchment in the Negative Commerce Jurisprudence—Day, The Rehnquist Court and the Dormant Commerce Clause Doctrine: The Potential Unsettling of the "Well-Settled Principles,"* 22 U. Tol. L. Rev. 675 (1991). Justice Scalia testified at his Senate confirmation hearings: "I assure you, I have no agenda." In this provocative article, Professor Day argues that the Justice has developed at least a "stated goal" of retrenchment in the negative commerce clause area. The article considers how and whether that goal could be achieved. One method, based upon his past opinions, would be for Justice Scalia to persuade the Court to require "explicit" or "facial" discrimination, thereby removing the Court from any case of nonexplicit protectionism (and perhaps permitting States to accomplish the result by artifice). A second method would be to require "invidious" or "purposeful" discrimination, thereby permitting protectionism when the state's invidious motivation is not provable. Professor Day concludes that "[a]doption of Justice Scalia's 'explicitness' standard would be, to borrow his own phraseology, 'just terrible,'" but the article then proceeds to handicap the chances for success.

(4) *Would Abolition of the Negative Commerce Clause Be "Terrible" in Light of Congress's Authority to Legislate the Same Results Under the Positive Commerce Clause?* Even if an explicitness standard that allowed discrimination to be done by artifice would be "just terrible," perhaps a total abolition of the negative commerce clause would be acceptable, since Congress can countermand protectionism that becomes too terrible. See the notes following the *Kassel* case, above. In fact, Congress could simply excerpt the language of *Pike v. Bruce Church*, above, and pass it as a statute, couldn't it? The result: greater fidelity to the constitutional text, an end to the jumbled legislative-like decisions of the Justices, and an ability to adjust the system (e.g., to allow environmental protection). Would this be better?

(5) *The Court's Further Experience With The Idea of Abandoning the Negative Commerce Clause Jurisprudence: South Central Bell Telephone v. Alabama, 526 U.S. 160 (1999).* In *South Central Bell*, the State explicitly argued, much along the lines outlined in this subsection and by Justice Scalia's opinions, that the Court should abandon its rigorous scrutiny under the dormant commerce clause. The Court unanimously refused, in an opinion by Justice Breyer, to jettison its venerable doctrine. Justice Scalia joined the majority. Justice Thomas joined Justice Scalia in advocating the abandonment of the dormant Commerce Clause doctrine. Only Justice Thomas, in a concurrence, signaled a willingness to reconsider the 170 year-old doctrine.

As to its substantive merits, the *South Central Bell* decision involved Alabama's corporate "franchise" tax. Although the franchise tax applied to both domestic and non-Alabama corporations, the standards for calculating the amount of the tax were significantly more burdensome on non-Alabama corporations such as South Central Bell. The Court determined, under its *Oregon Waste* analysis [above], that the Alabama franchise tax fell into the "discrimination tier" (because it "favored" Alabama corporations over nonresident corporations) and that Alabama could not justify this differential burden. Would the abandonment urged by Alabama serve the goals of the dormant commerce clause doctrine or of federalism? Or, was Alabama's argument more likely the product of a losing position (*i.e.*, a facially "discriminatory" state regulation)? *See also United Haulers*, 127 S. Ct. 1786, above at §§ 3.02[B][4], Note (4).

§ 3.03 THE SOVEREIGNTY ISSUE AND THE TENTH AMENDMENT: STATES "AS STATES"

[A] Just What is the Place of a State in the Constitutional Hierarchy?: The Original Understanding

BARBASH, THE FOUNDING
65–68 (1987)[*]

[The Virginia Plan, for which Madison was the principal architect and Randolph the primary spokesperson, called for a legislature with proportional representation. The lower house would be elected directly by the people, in proportion to population; it, in turn, would select the members of a smaller, upper house from candidates submitted by state legislatures (and for that matter, the national legislature also would select the executive and judicial officers).

[Early in the convention, the Virginia Plan encountered little opposition. Delegates from smaller states had not realized how many more legislators Virginia and other populous states would have than they. When the light finally dawned, the schism between the big and little states threatened to break up the convention. Barbash describes what happened:]

And even as they spoke, a sheet of paper was circulating among the delegates from the small states with the numbers on it, and though it only confirmed the obvious, the tabulation made the obvious more vivid. At the top of the paper were the names of ten states. Beside each name was a number-a projection of the number of representatives each would have in a new Congress based on proportional representation.

Georgia-1.

Delaware-1.

Rhode Island-2.

[Here the other states were listed beside numbers that ranged from 3 for New Hampshire to 8 each for New York and Connecticut.]

At the bottom were the names of the other three states Massachusetts, Pennsylvania and Virginia. Beside each of those, as well, was a number, also representing the state's potential strength in the new government.

Massachusetts-14.

Pennsylvania-12.

Virginia-16.

The implication was clear to everyone. Under the Virginia Plan, Massachusetts, Pennsylvania and, of course, Virginia would have the controlling interest in the new Congress. [T]hey could also control the choice of the President and of the judges. . . .

The small states had always said they would be "swallowed up" if they lost their equality. The phrase evoked much more than a loss of power in the union: it reflected a deep concern for their sovereignty and their identities and their rights and liberties.

Equality of the states was the heart of federalism.

Madison was equally intense on the subject. Of all the characteristics of the old order, none so interfered with his vision of nationhood as the principle of one state, one vote.

It was impure: As he saw it, this was to be a government constituted by the people, not by states, and the people rather than states should be represented.

It was unjust: Why should the power of 700,000, the population of Virginia, equal the strength of 59,000, the population of Delaware . . . ?

In truth, the delegates knew they were in for a long and bitter confrontation. On June 6, Edmund Randolph wrote: ". . . the prospect of a very long sojournment here has determined me to bring up my family."

[The little states' plan, of which William Paterson of New Jersey was a principal proponent, called (of course) for equalization of states' votes in the Congress, as the Articles of Confederation provided for. Ultimately, Roger Sherman presented the Connecticut plan, which called for a lower house with representation according to population, and an upper house with representation by states. Upon this plan was based perhaps the greatest single compromise of the Convention: our bicameral Congress, with a House of Representatives elected according to population and a Senate with two senators per state.]

NOTES AND QUESTIONS

(1) *Original Understanding No. 1: State Sovereignty is Inviolable.* From this Constitutional history, one might conclude that the states are endowed with inviolable sovereignty. Certainly that was the preference of many delegates from the smaller states. Some, when they spoke of "my country," did not mean the United States; they meant the states of which they were citizens. [There are other evidences of this version of the original understanding; the Tenth Amendment is an example.]

(2) *Original Understanding No. 2: State Sovereignty was Granted a Measure of Political Protection by the House-Senate Compromise, but Beyond that, States are Subject to Congressional Regulation.* An opposing view of the original understanding, however, might take the very compromise as evidence of less protection for state sovereignty. The small states got equal representation in the Senate. In that body, they could block House initiatives by the large states that might threaten their sovereignty. They agreed upon a political check-and thus the deal was struck.

[B] The Extent of State Immunity from National Regulation

Read U.S. Const. Amend. X (powers reserved to people and states); also, consider *id.* Art. I §§ 2–4 (Senate and House of Representatives).

STATE SOVEREIGNTY PRIOR TO THE *NATIONAL LEAGUE OF CITIES* CASE

The Problem of State Sovereignty. Imagine that Congress passes a law precisely determining the manner of supervision of state employees, such as police officers and firefighters. Or imagine that Congress imposes a tax upon state courthouses, prescribes procedures for state legislatures, or countermands a state's designation of its state bird. Finally, imagine that Congress abolishes a state and merges it with another, or abolishes all of the states. Would any of these actions be unconstitutional?

Early Decisions: New York's Bottled Waters and California's Railroad. When New York operated a state-owned mineral water bottling business, the Court held that it was not immune from federal taxation-but it pointedly observed that the same ruling might not apply to the state's governmental activities. "Only a state can own a state house. . . . These could not be included for purposes of federal taxation [w]ithout taxing the state as a state." Even so, Justices Black and Douglas dissented on the ground that the tax infringed the state's power of sovereignty. *New York v. United States*, 326 U.S. 572 (1946).

Regulation of State Employees and the Wirtz and Fry Cases: Maryland v. Wirtz, 392 U.S. 183 (1968); Fry v. United States, 421 U.S. 542 (1975). What about federal regulation of state employees engaged in purely governmental activities? In *Wirtz*, the Court considered Congress' extension of federal minimum wage requirements to certain employees of state and local institutions. The Court held that state governments had no immunity from such regulation, although it made the general statement that "the utter destruction of the state as a sovereign political entity" was not within the power of Congress. In *Fry* the Court upheld the application to state government employees of wage and price controls designed to suppress inflation. But the Court took the opportunity to observe that the tenth amendment was "not without significance." Congress, it said, "may not exercise power in a fashion that impairs the states' integrity or their ability to function effectively in a federal system."

NATIONAL LEAGUE OF CITIES v. USERY, 426 U.S. 833 (1976). We include only brief excerpts from this decision, because it was reversed in the *Garcia* case, which you will encounter in a few pages, and which contains the same arguments.

The Fair Labor Standards Act sets minimum wages and maximum hours for most kinds of employment. In 1974, Congress extended these provisions to state employees generally, exempting only narrow categories such as executive, administrative or professional employees. The lower federal courts relied upon *Wirtz*, above, to uphold the Act against a constitutional challenge. The Supreme Court, per Justice Rehnquist, reversed by a five-to-four majority, overruled *Wirtz*, and concluded that the Act infringed states' sovereignty:

> This Court has never doubted that there are limits upon the power of Congress to override state sovereignty, even when exercising its otherwise plenary powers to tax or to regulate commerce. . . . In *Fry, supra,* the Court recognized that an express declaration of this limitation is found in the Tenth Amendment:

> > While the Tenth Amendment has been characterized as a "truism," stating merely that "all is retained which has not be surrendered," . . . it is not without significance. The Amendment expressly declares the constitutional policy that Congress may not exercise power in a fashion that impairs the States' integrity or their ability to function effectively in a federal system.

> Judged solely in terms of increased costs in dollars, [the states'] allegations show a significant impact on the functioning of the governmental bodies involved. The metropolitan government of Nashville and Davidson County, Tenn., for example, asserted that the Act will increase its costs of providing

essential police and fire protection, without any increase in service or in current salary levels, by $938,000 per year. . . .

Increased costs are not, of course, the only adverse effects. . . . [C]alifornia asserted that it could not comply with the overtime costs (approximately $750,000 per year) which the Act required to be paid to California highway patrol cadets during their academy training program. California reported that it had thus been forced to reduce its academy training program from 2,080 hours to only 960 hours. . . .

Justice Blackmun concurred, stating that although he was not "untroubled" by certain possible implications of the Court's opinion, he regarded the result as "necessarily correct." Justice Stevens dissented. Justice Brennan, joined by Justices White and Marshall, also dissented:

The reliance of my Brethren upon the Tenth Amendment as an "express declaration of [a state sovereignty] limitation," . . . must astound scholars of the Constitution. . . .

Judicial restraint in this area merely recognizes that the political branches of our government are structured to protect the interests of the States, as well as the Nation as a whole, and that the States are fully able to protect their own interests. . . .

NOTES AND QUESTIONS

(1) *Dean Choper's "Federalism Proposal" in Contradistinction to Usery:* Choper, *The Scope of National Power Vis-á-Vis the States: The Dispensability of Judicial Review, 86 Yale 1552 (1977).* In contradistinction to *National League of Cities,* Dean Choper advanced what he called his "Federalism Proposal": "[T]he federal judiciary should not decide constitutional questions respecting the ultimate power of the national government vis-á-vis the states. . . . [This issue] should be treated as nonjusticiable with final resolution left to the political branches." The crux of Dean Choper's argument is "that state representation in the national executive and legislature places the President and Congress in a trustworthy position to view the issues involved in federalism disputes." Is this view persuasive? Part of Dean Choper's concern was that federalism cases may "sap" the Court's energy so that it cannot adequately consider cases involving individual rights—but don't important rights of individuals sometimes depend upon issues of federalism?

(2) *The Difficulty of Containing and Justifying the National League of Cities Immunity; Its Coordination with Necessary or Desirable Federal Regulation.* The scope of the immunity established by *National League of Cities* for traditional governmental functions that were necessary for the integrity of the State was not clear immediately after the decision. The series of decisions that followed reflected efforts to rationalize *National League of Cities* with appropriate federal intrusions into state sovereignty.

(3) *Defining the Scope of Immunity: Hodel v. Virginia Surface Mining & Reclamation Ass'n, 452 U.S. 264 (1981).* This case dealt with Congressionally authorized regulation of surface mining. The regulation displaced state power over the mining lands at issue; states were allowed to perform certain regulatory functions, but only if they adopted federal standards in doing so. The surface mining association alleged that the federal act infringed state sovereignty principles. The Court limited *National League of Cities* by a three-part test. First, the states' sovereignty immunized them only from federal actions that regulated the states "as states," rather than regulating commercial activities or private persons. Second, the state functions at issue must be "indisputably attributes of state sovereignty. Finally, the regulation must directly impair the states' ability "to structure integral operations in areas of traditional [state] functions." Since

federal regulation of surface mining did not infringe these tests, it was not unconstitutional.

(4)   *Regulation of Quasi-Commercial Activities, Employment Discrimination, and Public Utilities Commissions: United Transportation Union v. Long Island RR. Co., 455 U.S. 678 (1982), EEOC v. Wyoming, 460 U.S. 226 (1983), and FERC v. Mississippi, 456 U.S. 742 (1982).* A year later, the Court faced the question whether a state-owned railroad was immune from federal regulation. New York argued that transportation was a traditional government function, but the Court viewed operation of inter-city railroads as outside the function of states "as states." Then, by a five-to-four majority, the Court held that Wyoming constitutionally could be prohibited from discharging park and game wardens at age 55. The Court had difficulty in determining whether the federal law regulated an "indisputable attribute of state sovereignty," labeling this phrase from *National League of Cities* "somewhat unclear."

Then, the Public Utility Regulatory Policies Act of 1978 ("PURPA") required the states to "consider" specific federally proposed utility rate standards for public utility operations, with the "consideration" to be done in accordance with detailed procedural rules. If a state's public utility commission did not do so, its utility regulation would be taken over by the federal government. By a six-to-three majority, the Court upheld the Act. Since the Congress could have preempted the field of public utility regulation, it had not violated the Constitution by its "cooperative federalism." In a sharply worded dissent, however, Justice O'Connor disagreed, joined by Chief Justice Burger and Justice Rehnquist. PURPA had "directly impaired" the states' traditional functions. Justice O'Connor actually saw the Act as an attempt to "kidnap"(!) state commissions by the use of federal power.

(5)   *The Overruling of National League of Cities-and the Possibility of Its Resurrection. National League of Cities* had a short life. Nine years later, Justice Blackmun switched his vote, made the dissenters a majority, and joined in overruling it.

GARCIA v. SAN ANTONIO METROPOLITAN TRANSIT AUTHORITY
469 U.S. 528 (1985)

MR. JUSTICE BLACKMUN delivered the opinion of the Court.

[Employees of the San Antonio Metropolitan Transit Authority (SAMTA), a state-created entity operating an urban mass transit system, sued to enforce wage and hour provisions of the Fair Labor Standards Act. The FLSA is described in *United States v. Darby*, Ch. 2, above. When Congress extended it to state employees, its effect was to confine narrowly the patterns of hourly work and wages for which the states could employ most kinds of workers. On the strength of *National League of Cities*, the trial court held for the transit authority. It concluded that metropolitan mass transit, unlike the city railroad at issue in *United Transportation Union v. Long Island RR. Co.*, *supra*, was a traditional function of the state "as a state" and that it met the other prongs of the *Virginia Surface Mining* test. After receiving briefs on this issue, however, the Supreme Court ordered new briefs, focusing on the issue whether *National League of Cities* should be overruled. Here, with the four *National League of Cities* dissenters joining Justice Blackmun, the Court overrules that decision.]

Our examination of this "function" standard applied in these and other cases over the last eight years now persuades us that the attempt to draw the boundaries of state regulatory immunity in terms of "traditional governmental function" is not only unworkable but is inconsistent with established principles of federalism and, indeed, with those very federalism principles on which *National League of Cities* purported to rest. That case, accordingly, is overruled.

The prerequisites for governmental immunity under *National League of Cities* were summarized by this Court in *Hodel*, *supra*. Under that summary, four conditions must be satisfied before a state activity may be deemed immune from a particular federal regulation under the Commerce Clause. First, it is said that the federal statute at issue must regulate "the 'States as States.' " Second, the statute must "address matters that are indisputably 'attribute[s] of state sovereignty.' " Third, state compliance with the federal obligation must "directly impair [the States'] ability 'to structure integral operations in areas of traditional governmental functions.' " Finally, the relation of state and federal interests must not be such that "the nature of the federal interest . . . justifies state submission."

The controversy in the present cases has focused on the third *Hodel* requirement—that the challenged federal statute encroach on "traditional governmental functions." The District Court voiced a common concern: "Despite the abundance of adjectives, identifying which particular state functions are immune remains difficult." Thus, courts have held that regulating ambulance services, . . . licensing automobile drivers, . . . operating a municipal airport, . . . performing solid waste disposal, . . . and operating a highway authority, . . . are functions *protected* under *National League of Cities*. At the same time, courts have held that issuance of industrial development bonds, . . . regulation of intrastate natural gas sales, . . . regulation of traffic on public roads, . . . regulation of air transportation, . . . operation of a telephone system, . . . leasing and sale of natural gas, . . . operation of a mental health facility, . . . and provision of in-house domestic services for the aged and handicapped, . . . are *not* entitled to immunity. We find it difficult, if not impossible, to identify an organizing principle that places each of the cases in the first group on one side of a line and each of the cases in the second group on the other side. . . .

We believe, however, that there is a more fundamental problem at work here, a problem that explains why *[N]ational League of Cities* is unlikely to succeed regardless of how the distinctions are phrased. . . . The essence of our federal system is that within the realm of authority left open to them under the Constitution, the States must be equally free to engage in any activity that their citizens choose for the common weal, no matter how unorthodox or unnecessary anyone else—including the judiciary—deems state involvement to be. Any rule of state immunity that looks to the "traditional," "integral," or "necessary" nature of governmental functions inevitably invites an unelected federal judiciary to make decisions about which state policies it favors and which ones it dislikes. "The science of government . . . is the science of experiment," and the States cannot serve as laboratories for social and economic experiment, if they must pay an added price when they meet the changing needs of their citizenry by taking up functions that an earlier day and a different society left in private hands. . . .

We therefore now reject, as unsound in principle and unworkable in practice, a rule of state immunity from federal regulation that turns on a judicial appraisal of whether a particular governmental function is "integral" or "traditional. . . ."

[A]part from the limitation on federal authority inherent in the delegated nature of Congress' Article I powers, the principal means chosen by the Framers to ensure the role of the States in the federal system lies in the structure of the Federal Government itself. It is no novelty to observe that the composition of the Federal Government was designed in large part to protect the States from overreaching by Congress. . . . The significance attached to the States' equal representation in the Senate is underscored by the prohibition of any constitutional amendment divesting a State of equal representation without the State's consent.

The effectiveness of the federal political process in preserving the States' interests is apparent even today in the course of federal legislation. On the one hand, the States have been able to direct a substantial proportion of federal revenues into their own treasuries in the form of general and program-specific grants in aid. [M]oreover, at the same time that the States have exercised their influence to obtain federal support, they have been able to exempt themselves from a wide variety of obligations imposed by Congress under the Commerce Clause. . . .

These cases do not require us to identify or define what affirmative limits the constitutional structure might impose on federal action affecting the States under the Commerce Clause. *See Coyle v. Oklahoma*, 221 U.S. 559 (1911). . . .

National League of Cities v. Usery is overruled. . . .

[handwritten: doesn't infringe state's sovereignty]

JUSTICE POWELL, with whom The Chief Justice, JUSTICE REHNQUIST, and JUSTICE O'CONNOR join, dissenting. . . .

Whatever effect the Court's decision may have in weakening the application of *stare decisis*, it is likely to be less important than what the Court has done to the Constitution itself. [D]espite some genuflecting in Court's opinion to the concept of federalism, today's decision effectively reduces the Tenth Amendment to meaningless rhetoric when Congress acts pursuant to the Commerce Clause. . . .

The Framers believed that the separate sphere of sovereignty reserved to the States would ensure that the States would serve as an effective "counterpoise" to the power of the federal government.

As I view the Court's decision today as rejecting the basic precepts of our federal system and limiting the constitutional role of judicial review, I dissent.

JUSTICE REHNQUIST, dissenting.

. . . [The] judgment in this case should be affirmed, and I do not think it incumbent on those of us in dissent to spell out further the fine points of a principle that will, I am confident, in time again command the support of a majority of this Court. . . .

JUSTICE O'CONNOR, with whom JUSTICE POWELL and JUSTICE REHNQUIST join, dissenting.

. . . Just as surely as the Framers envisioned a National Government capable of solving national problems, they also envisioned a republic whose vitality was assured by the diffusion of power not only among the branches of the Federal Government, but also between the Federal Government and the States. . . .

. . . Because virtually every *state* activity, like virtually every activity of a private individual, arguably "affects" interstate commerce, Congress can now supplant the States from the significant sphere of activities envisioned for them by the Framers. . . . As a result, there is now a real risk that Congress will gradually erase the diffusion of power between state and nation on which the Framers based their faith in the efficiency and vitality of our Republic. . . .

[The Federal] [G]overnment has, with this Court's blessing, undertaken to tell the States the age at which they can retire their law enforcement officers, and the regulatory standards, procedures, and even the agenda which their utilities commissions must consider and follow. *See EEOC v. Wyoming; FERC v. Mississippi*, 456 U.S. 742 (1982). The political process has not protected against these encroachments on state activities, even though they directly impinge on a State's ability to make and enforce its laws. With the abandonment of *National League of Cities*, all that stands between the remaining essentials of state sovereignty and Congress is the latter's underdeveloped capacity for self-restraint. . . .

NOTES AND QUESTIONS

(1) *Just How Far Does Garcia Go? Can the Federal Government Legislate About Where the State Capital Shall Be? Coyle v. Smith, 221 U.S. 559 (1911).* Garcia concerned a federal statute based upon a generally accepted federal interest, which, although it intruded into state sovereignty, did not reach the deepest core of that concept. One arguably open question is whether Congress will be upheld if it legislates

to promote minimal federal interest, in a core state sovereignty area. For example, what if Congress attempted to dictate to a state where its capital should be? It might seem that Congress would not undertake such silly action. However, it has, in *Coyle, supra*. The location of the capital was "essentially and peculiarly" within the state's power, said the Court, and it held Congress' action unconstitutional. Would the same result obtain today, after *Garcia*?

(2) *The Political Check of a Popularly Elected President and Bicameral Congress.* Recall Dean Choper's thesis, expressed after *National League of Cities*, that federal intrusions into state power should constitute nonjusticiable questions, because the structure of Congress and the Presidency provided adequate protection. After *Garcia*, does it seem that the thesis still is correct? Does the *Coyle* case cast light upon it? *See also* Note, *The Tenth Amendment after Garcia: Process-Based Procedural Protections*, 135 U. Pa. L. Rev. 1657 (1987); *Cf.* Lopez, *The Constitutional Doctrines of State Immunity from Federal Regulation and Taxation after Garcia*, 4 J.L. & Pol. 89 (1987); Redish & Drizin, *Constitutional Federalism and Judicial Review: The Role of Textual Analysis*, 62 N.Y.U. L. Rev. 1 (1987).

Read U.S. Const. Art. 1, § 10, cl. 3 (the compact clause).

NEW YORK v. UNITED STATES
505 U.S. 144 (1992)

JUSTICE O'CONNOR delivered the opinion of the Court.

[Congress enacted the Low-Level Radioactive Waste Policy Amendments Act of 1985 against a background of looming and serious shortages of disposal sites for low-level radioactive waste in the obligation to provide for the disposal of waste generated within their borders. It contains three provisions setting forth "incentives." First, the "monetary incentives" provide that states with disposal sites may impose a surcharge on waste from other states, the Secretary of Energy collects and escrows a portion of this surcharge, and states achieving a series of "milestones" in developing disposal sites receive portions of this fund. Second, the "access" incentives authorize sited states gradually to increase the cost of access for waste generated in states that do not meet federal guidelines, and then to deny access altogether. Finally, the "take title" incentive provides that a state that fails to provide for the disposal of all internally generated waste by a particular date must take title to and possession of the waste upon request, and it becomes liable for all damages suffered by the generator or owner as a result of its failure promptly to take possession.

[New York State and two of its counties filed this suit to declare the three incentives provisions unconstitutional under the Tenth Amendment and under the Guarantee Clause of Article IV, § 4 (which directs the United States to "guarantee to every State [a] Republican Form of Government"). The District Court dismissed the complaint, and the Court of Appeals affirmed. Here, the Court upholds the monetary and access incentives, but it reverses as to the third ("take title") incentive and holds it unconstitutional.]

II

A

[The federal-state allocation of power] can be viewed in either of two ways. In some cases the Court has inquired whether an Act of Congress is authorized by one of the powers delegated to Congress in Article I of the Constitution. *See, e.g., [M]cCulloch v. Maryland.* In other cases the Court has sought to determine whether an Act of Congress invades the province of state sovereignty reserved by the Tenth Amendment. *See, e.g., Garcia v. San Antonio Metropolitan Transit Authority.* In a case like this one, [t]he two inquiries are mirror images of each other. . . .

It is in this sense that the Tenth Amendment "states but a truism that all is retained which has not been surrendered." *United States v. Darby.* [C]ongress exercises its conferred powers subject to the limitations contained in the Constitution. [T]he Tenth Amendment [r]estrains the power of Congress, but this limit is not derived from the text of the Tenth Amendment itself, which, as we have discussed, is essentially a tautology. Instead, the Tenth Amendment confirms that the power of the Federal Government is subject to limits that may, in a given instance, reserve power to the States. . . .

B . . .

This case . . . concerns the circumstances under which Congress may use the States as implements of regulation; that is, whether Congress may direct or otherwise motivate the States to regulate in a particular field or a particular way. . . .

1

As an initial matter, Congress may not simply "commandee[r] the legislative processes of the States by directly compelling them to enact and enforce a federal regulatory program." *Hodel v. Virginia Surface Mining & Reclamation Assn., Inc.* In *Hodel*, the Court upheld the Surface Mining Control and Reclamation Act of 1977 precisely because it did not "commandeer" the States into regulating mining. [T]he Constitution has never been understood to confer upon Congress the ability to require the States to govern according to Congress' instructions. *See Coyle v. Oklahoma* [the state-capital location case].

Indeed, the question whether the Constitution should permit Congress to employ state governments as regulatory agencies was a topic of lively debate among the Framers. . . .

2

This is not to say that Congress lacks the ability to encourage a State to regulate in a particular way, or that Congress may not hold out incentives to the States as a method of influencing a State's policy choices. Our cases have identified a variety of methods, short of outright coercion, by which Congress may urge a State to adopt a legislative program consistent with federal interests. Two of these methods are of particular relevance here. First, under Congress' spending power, "Congress may attach conditions on the receipt of federal funds." [*South Dakota v. Dole*] [S]econd, where Congress has the authority to regulate private activity under the Commerce Clause, we have recognized Congress' power to offer States the choice of regulating that activity according to federal standards or having state law pre-empted by federal regulation. . . .

[B]y either of these two methods, as by any other permissible method of encouraging a State to conform to federal policy choices, the residents of the State retain the ultimate decision as to whether or not the State will comply. [S]tate governments remain responsive to the local electorate's preferences; state officials remain accountable to the people. [I]f the citizens of New York, for example, do not consider that making provision for the disposal of radioactive waste is in their best interest, they may elect state officials who share their view. That view can always be preempted under the Supremacy Clause if is contrary to the national view, but in such a case it is the Federal Government that makes the decision in full view of the public, and it will be federal officials that suffer the consequences if the decision turns out to be detrimental or unpopular. But where the Federal Government directs the States to regulate, it may be state officials who will bear the brunt of public disapproval, while the federal officials who devised the regulatory program may remain insulated from the electoral ramifications of their decision. Accountability is thus diminished when, due to federal coercion, elected state officials cannot regulate in accordance with the views of the local electorate in matters not pre-empted by federal regulation. . . .

III

[C]onstrued as a whole, the Act comprises three sets of "incentives" for the States to provide for the disposal of low level radioactive waste generated within their borders. We consider each in turn.

A

The first set of incentives works in three steps. First, Congress has authorized States with disposal sites to impose a surcharge on radioactive waste received from other States. Second, the Secretary of Energy collects a portion of this surcharge and places the money in an escrow account. Third, States achieving a series of milestones receive portions of this fund. . . .

The Act's first set of incentives [i]s thus well within the authority of Congress under the Commerce and Spending Clauses. [I]t is not inconsistent with the Tenth Amendment.

B

In the second set of incentives, Congress has authorized States and regional compacts with disposal sites gradually to increase the cost of access to the sites, and then to deny access altogether, to radioactive waste generated in States that do not meet federal deadlines. As a simple regulation, this provision would be within the power of Congress to authorize the States to discriminate against interstate commerce. . . .

C

The take title provision is of a different character. [I]n this provision, Congress has crossed the line distinguishing encouragement from coercion. . . .

The take title provision offers state governments a "choice" of either accepting ownership of waste or regulating according to the instructions of Congress. Respondents do not claim that the Constitution would authorize Congress to impose either option as a freestanding requirement. On one hand, the Constitution would not permit Congress simply to transfer radioactive waste from generators to state governments. [T]he same is true of the provision requiring the States to become liable for the generators' damages. [O]n the other hand, the second alternative held out to state governments—regulating pursuant to Congress' direction—would, standing alone, present a simple command to state governments to implement legislation enacted by Congress. As we have seen, the Constitution does not empower Congress to subject state governments to this type of instruction. . . .

[T]he take title provision appears to be unique. No other federal statute has been cited which offers a state government no option other than that of implementing legislation enacted by Congress. Whether one views the take title provision as lying outside Congress' enumerated powers, or as infringing upon the core of state sovereignty reserved by the Tenth Amendment, the provision is inconsistent with the federal structure of our Government established by the Constitution.

IV

A

[T]he United States [a]rgues that the Constitution envisions a role for Congress as an arbiter of interstate disputes. The United States observes that federal courts, and this Court in particular, have frequently resolved conflicts among States. . . . The United States suggests that if the Court may resolve such interstate disputes, Congress can surely do the same under the Commerce Clause. . . .

[W]hile the Framers no doubt endowed Congress with the power to regulate interstate commerce in order to avoid further instances of the interstate trade disputes that were common under the Articles of Confederation, the Framers did not intend that Congress should exercise that power through the mechanism of mandating state regulation. . . .

B

The sited State respondents focus their attention on the process by which the Act was formulated. [R]espondents note that the Act embodies a bargain among the sited and unsited States, a compromise to which New York was a willing participant and from which New York has reaped much benefit. Respondents then pose what appears at first to be a troubling question: How can a federal statute be found an unconstitutional infringement of State sovereignty when state officials consented to the statute's enactment?

The answer follows from an understanding of the fundamental purpose served by our Government's federal structure. The Constitution does not protect the sovereignty of States for the benefit of the States or state governments as abstract political entities, or even for the benefit of the public officials governing the States. To the contrary, the Constitution divides authority between federal and state governments for the protection of individuals. . . .

Where Congress exceeds its authority relative to the States, therefore, the departure from the constitutional plan cannot be ratified by the "consent" of state officials. . . .

[T]he facts of this case raise the possibility that powerful incentives might lead both federal and state officials to view departures from the federal structure to be in their personal interests. Most citizens recognize the need for radioactive waste disposal sites, but few want sites near their homes. As a result, [i]t is likely to be in the political interest of each individual official to avoid being held accountable to the voters for the choice of location. If a federal official is faced with the alternatives of choosing a location or directing the States to do it, the official may well prefer the latter, as a means of shifting responsibility for the eventual decision. If a state official is faced with the same set of alternatives—choosing a location or having Congress direct the choice of a location—the state official may also prefer the latter, as it may permit the avoidance of personal responsibility. The interests of public officials thus may not coincide with the Constitution's intergovernmental allocation of authority.

[N]or does the State's prior support for the Act estop it. . . . New York has never joined a regional radioactive waste compact. [T]hat a party collaborated with others in seeking legislation has never been understood to estop the party from challenging that legislation in subsequent litigation. . . .

VII

[Much] of the Constitution is concerned with setting forth the form of our government. . . . The result may appear "formalistic" in a given case to partisans of the measure at issue, because such measures are typically the product of the era's perceived necessity. But the Constitution protects us from our own best intentions. . . .

States are not mere political subdivisions of the United States. . . . [T]he Constitution instead "leaves to the several States a residuary and inviolable sovereignty," The Federalist No. 39, reserved explicitly to the States by the Tenth Amendment.

Whatever the outer limits of that sovereignty may be, one thing is clear: The Federal Government may not compel the States to enact or administer a federal regulatory program. [T]he judgment of the Court of Appeals is accordingly affirmed in part [as to the mandatory and access incentives] and reversed in part [as to the "take title" provision].

JUSTICE WHITE, with whom JUSTICE BLACKMUN and JUSTICE STEVENS join, concurring in part and dissenting in part.

[These Justices would have upheld all of the challenged incentives, including the "take title" provisions.]

I

My disagreement with the Court's analysis begins at the basic descriptive level of how the legislation at issue in this case came to be enacted. The [Act] resulted from the efforts of state leaders to achieve a state-based set of remedies to the waste problem. . . .

II

Even were New York not to be estopped from challenging the take title provision's constitutionality, I am convinced that, seen as a term of an agreement entered into between the several States, this measure proves to be less constitutionally odious than the Court opines. First, the practical effect of New York's position is that because it is unwilling to honor its obligations to provide in-state storage facilities for its low-level radioactive waste, other States with such plants must accept New York's waste, whether they wish to or not. [I] do not understand the principle of federalism to impede the National Government from acting as referee among the States to prohibit one from bullying another.

[T]he Court's holding [here] [e]ssentially misunderstands that the 1985 take title provision was part of a complex interstate agreement about which New York should not now be permitted to complain. . . .

[The opinion of JUSTICE STEVENS, concurring in part and dissenting in part, is omitted.]

NOTES AND QUESTIONS

(1) *What, Now, Is the Status of the Debate over National League of Cities v. Garcia?* The Court ostensibly avoids overruling *Garcia* (and, indeed, ostensibly cites it with approval). But the dissenters are unpersuaded by the majority's distinction of *Garcia* (which is made on the ground that *Garcia* concerned a generally applicable law, governing both States and individuals, whereas this Low-Level Waste Act can be applied *only* to States in their sovereign capacities). Furthermore, a majority rationale for *Garcia* was that "process" (*i.e.*, the bicameral Congress) protects states—but the

majority here rejects that rationale. And perhaps most significantly, the Rehnquist-O'Connor viewpoint now has mustered a majority. Regarding *New York v. United States, see* H. Jefferson Powell, *The Oldest Question of Constitutional Law*, 79 Va. L. Rev. 633 (1993). Does *New York v. United States* undermine *Garcia*?

(2) *Conditional Pre-Emption.* What result, if Congress merely tacked on a (highly coercive) provision that if any State failed to comply with the Act, the Federal Secretary of Energy would designate disposal sites in that State? [Answer: That simple addition would appear to solve the problem, even under Justice O'Connor's reasoning. See whether you can explain why, in terms of Congress' power to pre-empt "conditionally"—and also, see whether you can articulate why members of Congress (as Justice O'Connor demonstrates) might have selfish political motives to avoid this solution.]

(3) *Compacts, Agreements to Compacts, Congressional Conditions Attached to Compacts, and Estoppel.* Notice how the majority differs from the dissent, which would accept far more informal manifestations of "agreement" to a compact by a State. The dissent apparently reasons that the Act became a "compact" that was agreed to by New York, that Congress consented, that Congress added the take title provision as a condition, and (by implication) that New York agreed to this provision as well—or, in the alternative, that New York is estopped to avoid the effect of the Act. In fact, New York (or at least, its responsible officials) engaged in an extensive pattern of conduct that indicated acceptance, to its advantage and arguably to other States' detriment; the dissent paints a dismal picture of New York as having successfully "suckered" the other States.

(4) *The Constitution as "Protecting Us from Our Best Intentions."* The majority's response to this argument of the dissent is that the Constitution is concerned with the "form" in which an action is undertaken, and that the prescribed formalism should not yield to current exigencies. Is this reasoning a protection of individual liberty to hold officials accountable, as the majority would have it—or is the dissent correct in calling it a "civics lecture" that rings "hollow"? *See* Justice Kennedy's concurring opinion in the *Lopez* case in Chapter 2.

(5) *An Anticommandeering Principle as a Limit on Congressional Power: Printz v. United States, 521 U.S. 898 (1997).* In *Printz*, the Court held that the Brady Hand Gun Violence Prevention Act's provisions requiring state and local enforcement officers to conduct background checks on prospective hand gun purchasers and to perform related tasks was unconstitutional because it improperly commandeered state executive branch resources to implement the program. The state executive resources were protected by principles of state sovereignty. The *Printz* decision, as well as the earlier *New York* decision, have come to stand for an *anticommandeering principle*: while Congress may preempt state law and may enact incentives for states to adopt federally approved standards (through the spending power), Congress may not force the states to enact federal regulations directly nor may it direct state officials to carry out a federal regulatory program. The anticommandering principle is a narrower scope of protection for States than that afforded by the *National League of Cities*, but you should examine the parallels in results and in reasoning.

(6) *State Sovereignty as a Limit on Congressional Power.* The *Printz* Court relied on "three sources": historical understanding and practice, the Constitution's structure, and precedent. Justice Scalia emphasized that these sources must be considered "in that order." Which of three, if any, did you find determinative? What role, if any, should policy considerations play in the analysis (such as the dissenters urge)?

(7) *The Role of Congressional Intent.* The Court's holding appears to rest on historical, structural and precedential reasoning. Yet, the Court concludes that "the whole object of the [Brady Act is] to direct the functioning of the state executive. . . ." If Congress had had some other purpose, and direction to the state official was merely

"incidental," would the Court still strike down the congressional action? Wouldn't Congress, or its lawyers, always be able to identify some permissible objective, if that were the test?

(8) *New York and Lopez: What are the Connections to the Court's Reasoning in Printz?* The Court might have approached the Brady Act issue as did the *Lopez* majority [Ch. 2 above], asking whether Congress had the prerequisites for exercising a plenary power. Instead, the Court relied more on its "state sovereignty" approach from, *e.g., New York v. United States* above. Thus, the constitutional flaw is that the Congressional effort invaded the authority left to the states. Note the Court's reliance on the "dual sovereignty" concept that formed, in *Lopez*, the basis for Justice Kennedy's "swing" vote. Would the Court have done better to emphasize the intrastate character of the object of regulation, as in *Lopez?*

(9) *Further Applications of Lopez and Printz: Reno v. Condon, 528 U.S. 141 (2000).* Congress passed the Driver's Privacy Protection Act (DPPA) which restricted a state's ability to disclose a driver's personal information without consent. The State of South Carolina sued to enjoin enforcement. Although the lower courts agreed with South Carolina, the Supreme Court, per Chief Justice Rehnquist, reversed. The Court held that the DPPA was constitutionally proper under the interstate commerce power. [*See* § 2.02 above.] The Court also held that the DPPA did not violate the principles of federalism under *Printz* and other decisions in this section. You should recognize the interaction and overlap of the Court's analysis in these "federalism" decisions—whether the decision appears here or in Chapter 2.

ALDEN v. MAINE, 527 U.S. 706 (1999). Earlier in this subchapter, you examined the *National League of Cities* decision and the decision which explicitly overruled it, the *Garcia* decision. Both of those decisions had arisen from the Congressional attempt to apply the Fair Labor Standards Act ("FSLA") to the States (in the States' roles as employers of workers). The *Alden* decision arose from the "private enforcement" provisions of the FSLA. The *Alden* plaintiffs, state probation officers and juvenile caseworkers, first sued Maine in federal court to enforce the FSLA standards; this action was dismissed because Maine asserted an Eleventh Amendment defense. [*See* § 3.05 below.]

The *Alden* plaintiffs then refiled their claims in state court, relying on the conventional understanding that the Eleventh Amendment did not affect actions brought in state court to enforce congressionally-adopted, federal standards. [*See* § 3.05, Note (7).] In *Alden*, the Supreme Court, per Justice Kennedy, held that Congress did not have the authority to override a pre-constitutional concept of state sovereign immunity and, therefore, individuals like the *Alden* plaintiffs could not sue the State, even in state court. Justice Kennedy explained the 5-4 majority's reasoning in terms similar to the *Printz* rationale [above]:

> A power to press a state's own courts into Federal service is the power first to turn the state against itself and ultimately to commandeer the entire political machinery of state against its will and at the behest of individuals.

The four Justices dissenting in *Alden*, per Justice Souter, disagreed with the Court's history: "There is almost no evidence that the generation of the Framers thought sovereign immunity was fundamental. . . ." The dissent also questioned the majority's reliance on an original intentionist approach:

> The framers intentions and expectations count so far as they point to the meaning of the Constitution's text or the fair implications of its structure, but they do not hover over the instrument to veto any application of its principles to a world the framers could not have anticipated.

The *Alden* decision seems to demonstrate the overlap between the "state sovereignty" concepts [§ 3.03] and the Eleventh Amendment [§ 3.05]. The *Alden* decision means that Congress cannot create a private cause of action against a State under the

FSLA enforceable either in federal court or in state court. Apparently, the only constitutionally permissible means of FSLA enforcement against a state is an action brought by the federal government agency. What are the chances that the Labor Department will have sufficient resources to bring all the actions on behalf of the 4.7 million state employees whose federal rights are violated by the State employers? Do you agree with a leading commentator: "While the Supreme Court did not overrule the *Garcia* decision, which upheld the extension of Federal Labor law to the states, that was likely to be [*Alden's*] practical effect?" Linda Greenhouse, *States Are Given New Legal Shield By Supreme Court*, N.Y. TIMES, June 24, 1999, at 1.

FEDERAL MARITIME COMMISSION v. SOUTH CAROLINA PORTS AU-THORITY, 535 U.S. 743 (2002). In *Alden v. Maine*, above, the Court appeared to determine that, in addition to Eleventh Amendment immunity, the States had a separate, pre-constitutional immunity from suit. This concept of state sovereign immunity was confirmed and expanded in *Federal Maritime*.

A cruiseline company, South Carolina Maritime Services, Inc. (Maritime Services), wanted permission to berth a cruise ship at port facilities owned by South Carolina. The State Ports Authority (SCSPA) denied berthing permission because the cruise ships offered "gambling activities." Maritime Services filed a complaint with the Federal Maritime Commission (FMC), a Congressionally-created agency with jurisdiction over maritime commerce. Maritime Services wanted injunctive relief and a form of monetary damages from the State. The State defended this Article II administrative agency action on the grounds of state sovereign immunity under *Alden*. Although the FMC ruled that the *Alden*-type immunity applied only before judicial tribunals and not Executive Branch agencies, the court of appeals reversed. Here, the Supreme Court, per Justice Thomas, affirmed, holding that state sovereign immunity barred the FMC from adjudicating a private party's complaint against a non-consenting State. Justices Stevens, Souter, Ginsburg and Breyer dissented.

At one level, the Court performed a comparison between judicial adjudication (as in *Alden*) and the FMC agency adjudication. The Court concluded that the "formalized administrative adjudications" before the FMC were sufficiently similar to judicial adjudication to implicate state sovereign immunity. At this comparative level, the decision is not particularly remarkable.

Other aspects of the Court's opinion, however, are quite expansive. First, the Court stated that the Eleventh Amendment immunity was "only one particular exemplification of [state sovereign immunity]." Clarifying a point left unresolved in *Alden*, the Court concluded that the state sovereign immunity concept is broader than the States' Eleventh Amendment protection.

The Court repeatedly asserted that the "pre-eminent purpose of state sovereign immunity is to accord States the dignity that is consistent with their status as sovereign entities." This, of course, is a broader rationale than the concept of protecting the state treasury.

After *Federal Maritime*, Congressional power to authorize suit against a non-consenting State is faced with three constraints. Absent a valid abrogation by Congress, the Eleventh Amendment bars Congress from creating federal judicial remedies against the states. The *Alden* decision bars Congress from creating state judicial remedies against the states. The *Federal Maritime* decision then bars Congress from creating judicial-type administrative remedies against the states. And *Federal Maritime's* language suggests that the Court's concept of state sovereign immunity may contain further constraints on Congressional power.

Justice Stevens dissented, on historical grounds. He disagreed with the majority's expanded "dignity" preservation rationale. Justice Breyer also dissented, much as he had in the Court's recent abrogation and plenary powers decisions. He issued a lengthy critique of the *Alden* decision. He argued that the so-called alternative remedies left to Congress were inadequate to achieve legitimate Congressional goals.

The *Federal Maritime* decision may have, as the Court concluded, little "practical" significance. The language of the decision, however, promises further reliance by the States in any dispute with the federal government. *See generally* Joanne C. Brant, *The Ascent of Sovereign Immunity*, 83 Iᴀ. L. Rᴇᴠ. 767 (1998).

§ 3.04 THE INTERSTATE PRIVILEGES AND IMMUNITIES CLAUSE

Read U.S. Const. Art. IV, § 2, cl. 1 (interstate privileges and immunities).

INTRODUCTION TO ARTICLE IV: THE PRIVILEGES AND IMMUNITIES CLAUSE

Article IV, Section 2's Privileges and Immunities Clause is one of the major components of American federalism. Along with the plenary powers of Article I, Section 8 (Chapter 2 above), the Privileges and Immunities Clause expresses the Framer's intent to forge a national economic and political unit. One of the early judicial interpretations of the Clause was the Supreme Court's decision in *Paul v. Virginia*, 75 U.S. (8 Wall) 168 (1868). The *Paul* Court described the Framer's goal for the Clause:

> It was undoubtedly the object of the clause in question to place the citizens of each State upon the same footing with citizens of other States, so far as the advantages resulting from citizenship in those States are concerned. It relieves them from the disabilities of alienage in other States; it inhibits discriminating legislation against them by other States; it gives them the right of free ingress into other States, and egress from them; it insures them in other States the same freedom possessed by the citizens of those States in the acquisition and enjoyment of property and in the pursuit of happiness; and it secures to them in other States the equal protection of their laws. It has been justly said that no provision of the Constitution has tended so strongly to constitute the citizens of the United States one people as this.

> Indeed, without some provision of the kind removing from the citizens of each States the disabilities of alienage in other States, and giving them equality of privilege with citizens of those States, the Republic would have constituted little more than a league of States; it would not have constituted the Union which now exists.

In *Piper* and the other decisions below, watch for the modern Court's reliance on these goals or constitutional policies.

SUPREME COURT OF NEW HAMPSHIRE v. PIPER
470 U.S. 274 (1985)

Jᴜsᴛɪᴄᴇ Pᴏᴡᴇʟʟ delivered the opinion of the Court:

[Kathryn Piper lived in Vermont, 400 yards from the New Hampshire border. She passed the New Hampshire bar examination but was denied admission to the bar because a New Hampshire Supreme Court rule limited admission to residents of the state. A federal district court held that the New Hampshire rule violated the interstate privileges and immunities clause, and an equally divided court of appeals affirmed. Here, the Supreme Court affirms the invalidation of the New Hampshire bar residency rule.]

[The interstate Privileges and Immunities Clause] was intended to "fuse into one

Nation a collection of independent, sovereign States." *Toomer v. Witsell*, 334 U.S. 385, 395 (1948). Recognizing this purpose, we have held that it is "[o]nly with respect to those 'privileges' and 'immunities' bearing on the vitality of the Nation as a single entity" that a State must accord residents and nonresidents equal treatment. *Baldwin v. Montana Fish & Game Comm'n*, [436 U.S. 371, 383 (1978)]. In *Baldwin*, for example, we concluded that a State may charge a nonresident more than it charges a resident for the same elk-hunting license. Because elk-hunting is "recreation" rather than "a means of livelihood," we found that the right to a hunting license was not "fundamental" to the promotion of interstate harmony.

Derived, like the Commerce Clause, from the fourth of the Articles of Confederation [which provided that free inhabitants of States "shall be entitled to all privileges and immunities of free citizens in the several States . . . and shall enjoy therein all the privileges of trade and commerce. . . ."], the Privileges and Immunities Clause was intended to create a national economic union. It is therefore not surprising that this Court repeatedly has found that "one of the privileges which the Clause guarantees to citizens of State A is that of doing business in State B on terms of substantial equality with the citizens of that State." *Toomer v. Witsell*. . . . [I]n *Toomer*, the Court held that nonresident fishermen could not be required to pay a license fee of $2,500 for each shrimp boat owned when residents were charged only $25 per boat. [I]n *Hicklin v. Orbeck*, 437 U.S. 518 (1978), we found violative of the Privileges and Immunities Clause a statute containing a resident hiring preference for all employment related to the development of the State's oil and gas resources. . . .

[The Court rejected the State's argument that lawyers "are bound up with the exercise of judicial power and the administration of justice" and that, since they "exercise" state power on a daily basis, they should be outside the protection of the Privileges and Immunities Clause. Although recognizing that the State might have legitimate reasons for limiting the right to vote or to hold elective office to its own citizens, the Court reasoned that "a lawyer is not [a 'political'] officer of the State in any political sense." Membership in the bar instead is a privilege or immunity protected by the clause.]

The conclusion that [the New Hampshire rule] deprives residents of a protected privilege does not end our inquiry. "[L]ike many other constitutional provisions, the Privileges and Immunities Clause is not an absolute. . . ." The clause does not preclude discrimination against nonresidents where: (i) there is a substantial reason for the difference in treatment; and (ii) the discrimination practiced against nonresidents bears a substantial relationship to the State's objective [citing *United Building & Construction Trades Union v. Mayor & Council of Camden*, 465 U.S. 208 (1984)]. In deciding whether the discrimination bears a close or substantial relationship to the State's objective, the Court has considered the availability of less restrictive means.

The Supreme Court of New Hampshire offers several justifications for its refusal to admit nonresidents to the bar. It asserts that nonresident members would be less likely: (i) to become, and remain, familiar with local rules and procedures; (ii) to behave ethically; (iii) to be available for court proceedings; and (iv) to do *pro bono* and other volunteer work in the State. . . .

[The Court summarily rejected the first two justifications, finding "no evidence" that nonresident lawyers will be less informed and "no reason" to believe that they will be less ethical.]

There is more merit to [the State's] assertion that a nonresident member of the bar at times would be unavailable for court proceedings. [N]evertheless, we do not believe that this type of problem justifies the exclusion of nonresidents from the state bar. . . . The trial court . . . may require any lawyer who resides at a great distance to retain a local attorney who will be available for unscheduled meetings and hearings.

[The Court rejected the final justification, finding it "reasonable to believe" that nonresident lawyers will perform their share of *pro bono* services. Furthermore, they "could be required to represent indigents and perhaps to participate in formal legal aid work."]

In summary, [the State] neither advances a "substantial reason" for its discrimination against nonresident applicants to the bar, nor demonstrates that the discrimination practiced bears a close relationship to its proffered objectives. . . .

JUSTICE REHNQUIST, dissenting.

This [decision] may not be surprising to those who view law as just another form of business frequently practiced across state lines by interchangeable actors. . . . The decision will be surprising to many, however, because it so clearly disregards the fact that the practice of law is—almost by definition—fundamentally different from those other occupations that are practiced across state lines without significant deviation from State to State. . . .

The Framers of our Constitution undoubtedly wished to ensure that the newly created Union did not revert back to its component parts because of interstate jealousies and insular tendencies, and it seems clear that the Art. IV Privileges and Immunities Clause was one result of these concerns. But the Framers also created a system of federalism that deliberately allowed for the independent operation of many sovereign States, each with [its] own laws created by [its] own legislators and judges. . . .

It is but a small step from these facts to the recognition that a state has a very strong interest in seeing that its legislators and judges come from among the constituency of state residents, so that they will better understand the local interests to which they will have to respond. . . .

Unlike the Court, I would take the next step, and recognize that the State also has a very "substantial" interest in seeing that its lawyers are members of that constituency. . . .

In addition, I find the Court's "less restrictive means" analysis both ill-advised and potentially unmanageable. [S]uch an analysis, when carried too far, will ultimately lead to striking down almost any statute on the ground that the Court could think of another "less restrictive" way to write it. This approach to judicial review . . . tends to place courts in the position of second-guessing legislators on legislative matters. . . .

NOTES AND QUESTIONS

(1) *Reconsidering Local-Hire Provisions in Public Works Contracts: White v. Massachusetts Council of Construction Employers, supra.* In the *White* case, which is considered in a previous section, the Court upheld a Boston city ordinance requiring public works contractors to fill at least 50% of all construction jobs with city residents. The Court concluded that since the city's funds were at issue, the city was a participant in the marketplace, and the ordinance therefore was not a violation of the negative commerce clause. The Court did not decide whether the ordinance violated the privileges and immunities clause, because "[w]e did not grant certiorari on the issue and remand without passing on its merits." What result, if the Court had passed upon it? *See also* Laycock, *Equality and the Citizens of Sister States*, 15 FLA. ST. U. L. REV. 431 (1987). *See generally* Bogen, *The Privileges and Immunities Clause of Article IV*, 37 CASE W. L. REV. 794 (1987). Consider the following case.

(2) *United Building and Construction Trades Council v. City of Camden, 465 U.S. 208 (1984).* In this case, the Supreme Court subjected an ordinance similar to that in *White* to privileges-and-immunities-clause examination. The city argued that it was not denying privileges of "state" citizenship; residency in the city was the issue, and many residents of the state were denied the same privileges. The Court, per Justice Rehnquist, rejected this reasoning, holding that the city was a political subdivision of the

state. However, the Court remanded for a determination whether the ordinance burdened protected privileges and immunities and, if so, whether it could be justified by Camden's arguments:

> The resident hiring preference is designed, the city contends, to increase the number of employed persons living in Camden and to arrest the "middle class flight" currently plaguing the city. The city also argues that all non-Camden residents employed on public work projects, whether they reside in New Jersey or Pennsylvania, constitute a "source of the evil at which the statute is aimed." That is, they "live off" Camden without "living in" Camden.

Is this proffered justification valid? Justice Blackmun dissented, saying: "I do not find 'beggar thy neighbor' economic policies any more attractive when practiced by municipalities than when practiced by states or nations."

(3) *An Expansive Interpretation of the Privileges and Immunities Clause: Lunding v. New York Tax Appeals Tribunal, 522 U.S. 287 (1998).* Nonresident taxpayers challenged, under *inter alia* the Privileges and Immunities clause, a provision of the New York state income tax law that effectively denied a state income tax deduction for alimony paid only to nonresident taxpayers while granting the deduction to New York residents. This provision cost the challenger, a lawyer practicing in New York, an additional $3,724 in New York taxes. As suggested below, in Note (4), Lunding challenged the disparity under equal protection, negative Commerce Clause, and Privileges and Immunities claims. Relying on the *Piper* standard for the Privileges and Immunities claim, the Supreme Court, per Justice O'Connor, struck down New York's alimony deduction scheme because New York had not provided a "substantial reason" for the differential treatment of nonresidents. *See Piper supra.* Justice Ginsburg, for the Chief Justice and Justice Kennedy, dissented because Lunding's former spouse also was a nonresident and, hence, her "alimony" income escaped from New York taxation. The dissenters urged that the standard for state tax laws be lower than the *Piper* standard; the dissenters would uphold the state tax law as long as it resulted in a "reasonably fair distribution of burdens" between residents and nonresidents. Is the *Piper* standard too high or should states be afforded more regulatory latitude?

Another "expansive" decision regarding Article IV Privileges and Immunities was *Doe v. Bolton,* 410 U.S. 179 (1973). [*Doe* is the companion case to *Roe v. Wade. See* Chapter 9 below.] In *Doe,* the Court, per Justice Blackmun, held that access to health care (for abortion services) was a fundamental right under Article IV and that the state's residency requirement did not satisfy the substantial reason standard.

(4) *Further Commentary on Article IV, § 2's Privileges and Immunities Doctrine: Saenz v. Roe, 526 U.S. 489 (1999).* In *Saenz,* the Supreme Court, per Justice Stevens, held that a California statute limiting the welfare benefits paid to residents of less than one year's duration to the level of the person's prior state residence violated the right to travel under the Equal Protection doctrine. [*See* § 10.03[B][3] below.] As part of the majority's discussion of the sources of the right to travel jurisprudence, the Court relied on its Article IV, § 2 caselaw. For further research on this topic, you should review the *Saenz* decision. For further research, *see generally* George F. Carpinello, *State Protective Legislation and Nonresident Corporations: The Privileges and Immunities Clause as a Treaty of Nondiscrimination,* 73 Iₐ. L. Rᴇᴠ. 351 (1988); Jonathan D. Varat, *State Citizenship and Interstate Equality,* 48 U. Cʜɪ. L. Rᴇᴠ. 487 (1981).

(5) *The "Mutually Reinforcing Relationship" Between the Privileges and Immunities Clause and the Negative Commerce Clause.* More than once the Supreme Court has noted the "mutually reinforcing relationship" between the Privileges and Immunities Clause of Article IV and the negative side of the Commerce Clause, "a relationship that stems from their common origin in the Fourth Article of the Articles of Confederation and their shared vision of federalism." *Hicklin v. Orbeck,* 437 U.S. 518, 531–532 (1978). The Court itself uses commerce clause precedents to "reinforce" its privileges and immunities analyses, and vice versa.

However, there are certain distinctions between the Art. IV Privileges and Immunities doctrine and the dormant Commerce Clause doctrine. One of the chief differences is that the Court has held that a corporation does not have standing under Article IV because, at the time of the framing of Article IV, a corporation was not considered a "citizen." *See Paul v. Virginia*, 75 U.S. (8 Wall.) 168 (1868). Many academics have called for the overruling of *Paul*. *See* Carpinello, *supra* Note (5). Another doctrinal difference is that a dormant Commerce Clause challenger does not have to be an out-of-stater, while Article IV only protects out-of-state residents. Finally, Article IV doctrine protects only those interests considered "fundamental rights." *See Piper* above. There is no "fundamental right" threshold in dormant Commerce Clause doctrine. Should there be one? *See generally* Brannon P. Denning, *Why the Privileges and Immunities Clause of Article IV Cannot Replace the Dormant Commerce Clause Doctrine*, 88 MINN. L. REV. 384 (2003).

(6)   *A Violation of Article IV Privileges and Immunities Clause May Be Proven "In Effect": Hillside Dairy v. Lyons, 539 U.S. 59 (2003).* Out-of-state dairies that sold raw milk to processors in California brought an action challenging part of California's milk pricing and pooling regulations. The processors of fluid milk were required to pay a "premium price" for raw milk, and part of this premium was placed in a pool and rebated to California producers. Certain processors (who were buying raw milk more cheaply out-of-state) did not have to pay into the pool. When California amended its regulations to require pool contributions for some out-of-state purchases, out-of-state producers (who lost business) brought this action under various theories, including Article IV's Privileges and Immunities Clause.

The lower court had dismissed the Article IV claim because the regulations did not discriminate *on their face* based on citizenship or residence. The Supreme Court, per Justice Stevens, reversed. In this regard, the Court held, unanimously, that an Article IV claim could be maintained even in the absence of an express statement in the statute identifying out-of-state citizenship as a basis for different treatment. The Court reserved the issue whether a differential effect alone sufficed under Article IV, reasoning that the statutory class was a proxy for out-of-state citizenship. The Court's decision also involved a dormant Commerce Clause analysis.

§ 3.05   THE ELEVENTH AMENDMENT

Read U.S. Const. Amend. XI (states' immunity from federal suits).

INTRODUCTORY NOTES

(1)   *The Textual and Historical Context of the Eleventh Amendment.* The Eleventh Amendment was adopted to overturn the Supreme Court decision in *Chisholm v. Georgia*, 2 U.S. 419 (1793). *Chisholm* involved a diversity action by non-citizens of Georgia against the State of Georgia. Georgia had claimed "sovereign immunity" as its defense, but the Supreme Court upheld the money damage award against Georgia. The popular and political reaction was intense, and Congress quickly passed the Eleventh Amendment. The amendment, by the terms of the text, seemed to prohibit the federal courts from hearing damage cases where a state was a defendant when the basis for Federal Jurisdiction was diversity of citizenship.

(2)   *The Expansion of the Scope of the Eleventh Amendment's Immunity.* In *Hans v. Louisiana*, 134 U.S. 1 (1890), the Supreme Court held that the Eleventh Amendment, despite its apparent textual limitation to diversity actions, also prohibited a citizen of a state from suing her own State under federal question jurisdiction. *Hans* seemed to

expand the scope of the Eleventh amendment's damage immunity for States. In fact, today, there are competing theories of the Eleventh Amendment: the "Diversity" theory and the "Immunity" theory. Under the "Diversity" theory, the Amendment is considered to ban only those damage actions against a State which are brought by non-citizens of the State. This narrow interpretation of the Eleventh Amendment still has advocates today. *See* Justice Souter's dissent in *Seminole Tribe* below. Under the "Immunity" theory, the scope of the Eleventh Amendment is broader: even citizens of a state cannot sue their own state for damages in federal court.

In any Eleventh Amendment problem, the first issue is which theory of the scope of the Eleventh Amendment Immunity will the Court use. When the Court uses a broad immunity (the Immunity theory), the states are immune under almost all circumstances from any damage liability.

(3) *The Eleventh Amendment as Protecting "Arms of the State," such as State Agencies, but Not Distinct Entities, such as Cities or Counties.* Another "threshold" issue in most Eleventh Amendment cases is whether a particular agency or entity is part of the "State" (or part of some other governmental entity—federal or local); this is sometimes called the "arm of the State" issue. In *Regents of the University of California v. Doe*, 519 U.S. 425 (1997), the Court, per Justice Stevens, held that a state-operated scientific laboratory sued for breach of contract would be considered part of the State (and, hence, immune under the Eleventh Amendment) even though the laboratory was indemnified by the federal government. The Court focused on the *legal* consequences, rather than the *financial* consequences, of the suit against the laboratory. But other decisions hold that cities (municipal corporations), counties and other distinct entities are not "arms of the State" even though they are created by it, and the Eleventh Amendment does not generally protect cities or other entities that are separate from the State.

(4) *The "Consent" and "Abrogation" Issues in Eleventh Amendment Doctrine.* In addition to the issue regarding the scope of the Eleventh Amendment's immunity, there are two other issues in the doctrine. First, a state may "consent" to a waiver of its Eleventh Amendment immunity. Second, even if a state does not waive its immunity, the Court has recognized that, under some circumstances, Congress may "abrogate" the Eleventh Amendment immunity. For example, in *Fitzpatrick v. Bitzer*, 427 U.S. 445 (1976), the Court held that, pursuant to Section 5 of the 14th Amendment, Congress had abrogated the Eleventh Amendment immunity for purposes of attorneys' fees awards against the State. *See* 42 U.S.C. § 1988. The principle case in this section, *Seminole Tribe of Florida v. Florida*, below, addresses the abrogation issue.

(5) *Suits against Individual Officials, either for Prospective Injunctive Relief or for Damages in Their Individual (but Not Representative) Capacities, are Outside the Eleventh Amendment.* The easiest and most common way of avoiding the Eleventh Amendment is to name the pertinent state official as a party defendant. This brings into play the doctrine established in *Ex parte Young*, 209 U.S. 123 (1908). Under that doctrine, the state official acts *ultra vires* and commits an illegal act when the official attempts to enforce an allegedly unconstitutional statute. The official "is stripped of his official or representative character and is subject in his person to the consequences of his individual conduct." *Ex Parte Young*, 209 U.S. at 160.

But the Court has subsequently limited the *Ex parte Young* doctrine to suits that seek only prospective injunctive relief or personal damages against the state official. If the suit seeks retrospective relief from the state treasury, such as past damages, the *Ex parte Young* "fiction" dictates that the state official resumes "his official or representative character" and that the state is the real party in interest.

(6) *The Apparent Expansion of the Eleventh Amendment in Seminole Tribe, below.* The *Seminole Tribe* decision, however, has injected a new limitation into the *Ex parte Young* doctrine. It appears to hold that, "where Congress has prescribed a detailed remedial scheme for the enforcement against a State of a statutorily created right" and

where the federal statute does not explicitly or implicitly involve state officers in that enforcement scheme, then a court should "hesitate" before "permitting an action against a state officer based upon *Ex parte Young*." Look for this issue below.

(7) *The Scope of the Ex parte Young Exception to Eleventh Amendment Immunity: Verizon Md., Inc. v. Public Service Comm'n of Maryland, 535 U.S. 635 (2002).* Following the *Seminole Tribe* decision, there were a number of issues regarding the scope of the *Ex parte Young* exception, as suggested by the prior notes. Besides the "detailed remedial scheme" issue, the Court's plurality opinion in *Idaho v. Coeur d' Alene Tribe of Idaho*, 521 U.S. 261 (1997) appeared to suggest a further narrowing of the *Ex parte Young* doctrine. But in the *Verizon Maryland* decision, the Court, per Justice Scalia, resisted the State's argument to narrow *Ex parte Young*. The Court, with no dissents, held that, as long as the claim sought only prospective injunctive or declaratory relief, the *Ex parte Young* exception would apply. The Court also determined that the federal statutory provisions at issue would not constitute a "detailed and exclusive remedial scheme" which might qualify for an exclusion from *Ex parte Young*. Justice Kennedy concurred; Justice Souter also submitted a concurring opinion.

(8) *The Eleventh Amendment, Pre-Constitutional State Sovereign Immunity and Suits in State Courts Based on Federal Rights: Alden v. Maine, 527 U.S. 706 (1999).* The conventional wisdom, for many generations of constitutional law students, was that, whatever the scope of the Eleventh Amendment regarding suits in federal courts, the Eleventh Amendment did not restrict suits *in state courts* which sought to enforce federal law.

In *Alden v. Maine*, the Supreme Court may have overturned this conventional wisdom. *Alden* was an action, brought in state court pursuant to the Fair Labor Standards Act ("FSLA") against the State employer for violations of the FSLA. The Court, in a 5-4 opinion by Justice Kennedy, relied on a pre-Eleventh Amendment, pre-constitutional concept of state sovereign immunity which, according to the majority, was broader than the Eleventh Amendment's immunity. The Court held that, as to nonconsenting States (such as Maine), neither the Constitution's adoption nor congressional action in passing the FSLA abrogated the State's sovereign immunity and that Congress could not abrogate a State's immunity in its own courts. Justice Souter, for Justices Stevens, Ginsburg and Breyer, dissented in a lengthy opinion decrying the majority's "absolutism."

Thus, as to any private rights under the FSLA, an unconsenting State could not be sued in federal court because of the Eleventh Amendment and could not be sued, after *Alden*, in its own state courts. After *Alden*, is any enforcement mechanism left or is an action by the federal government agency against the state the only remedy? [The Eleventh Amendment topic must necessarily receive brief treatment here, but you should consider this case along with the *College Savings Bank* decision below in this section and the materials in §§ 3.03, 3.06, and 14.02.]

SEMINOLE TRIBE OF FLORIDA v. FLORIDA, 517 U.S. 44 (1996). In the Indian Gaming Regulatory Act (IGRA), Congress allowed an Indian tribe to conduct gaming activities only after entering into a valid compact between the tribe and the State in which the gaming activities were located. Under the IGRA, States were required to "negotiate in good faith" with a tribe towards the formation of a compact. The IGRA provided that a tribe may sue a State in federal court in order to compel performance of the duty of good faith negotiations. In the Act, Congress also provided a remedial scheme assertable by a tribe that claims its rights were violated; this scheme was complex, but limited.

When negotiations between Florida and the Seminole Tribe of Florida broke down, the Seminole Tribe sued Florida and its Governor in federal district court. The defendants moved to dismiss the complaint on the grounds that the suit violated Florida's Eleventh Amendment immunity. The district court denied the motion to dismiss, but the court of appeals reversed, holding that the Indian Commerce Clause of

Article I, § 8 did not grant Congress the power to abrogate the Eleventh Amendment. In this decision, the Supreme Court, per Chief Justice Rehnquist, affirmed the court of appeals, holding that Congress did not have power to abrogate under the Indian Commerce Clause. The Court, in so holding, overruled *Pennsylvania v. Union Gas Company*, 491 U.S. 1 (1990).

Congress' intent to abrogate the States' immunity from suit must be obvious from "a clear legislative statement." This rule arises from a recognition of the important role played by the Eleventh Amendment and the broader principles that it reflects. . . .

[H]ere, we agree with the parties, with the Eleventh Circuit in the decision below, and with virtually every other court that has confronted the question that Congress has provided an "unmistakably clear" statement of its intent to abrogate.

[Therefore,] our inquiry into whether Congress has the power to abrogate unilaterally the States' immunity from suit is narrowly focused on one question: Was the Act in question passed pursuant to a constitutional provision granting Congress the power to abrogate? Previously, in conducting that inquiry, we have found authority to abrogate under only two provisions of the Constitution. [First], we recognized that the Fourteenth Amendment, by expanding federal power at the expense of state autonomy, had fundamentally altered the balance of state and federal power struck by the Constitution. [The Fourteenth Amendment, unlike the Commerce Clause, was passed *after* the Eleventh Amendment and thus altered the power balance.—Eds.]

[I]n only one other case has congressional abrogation of the States' Eleventh Amendment immunity been upheld. In *Pennsylvania v. Union Gas Co.*, 491 U.S. 1 (1989), a plurality of the Court found that the Interstate Commerce Clause, Art. I, § 8, cl. 3, granted Congress the power to abrogate state sovereign immunity, stating that the power to regulate interstate commerce would be "incomplete without the authority to render States liable in damages.". . .

[I]n five years since it was decided, *Union Gas* has proven to be a solitary departure from established law. Reconsidering the decision in *Union Gas*, we conclude that none of the policies underlying *stare decisis* require our continuing adherence to its holding. The decision has, since its issuance, been of questionable precedential value, largely because a majority of the Court expressly disagreed with the rationale of the plurality. . . . We feel bound to conclude that *Union Gas* was wrongly decided and that it should be, and now is, overruled. . . .

In overruling *Union Gas* today, we reconfirm that the background principle of state sovereign immunity embodied in the Eleventh Amendment is not so ephemeral as to dissipate when the subject of the suit is an area, like the regulation of Indian commerce, that is under the exclusive control of the Federal Government. . . . The Eleventh Amendment restricts the judicial power under Article III, and Article I cannot be used to circumvent the constitutional limitations placed upon federal jurisdiction.

The majority also ruled against the Seminole Tribe on its *Ex parte Young* theory. The Court held that the *Ex parte Young* exception to Eleventh Amendment immunity would not apply when Congress had a "carefully crafted and intricate remedial scheme" in the statute.

Where Congress has created a remedial scheme for the enforcement of a particular federal right, we have, in suits against federal officers, refused to supplement that scheme with one created by the judiciary. Here, of course, the question is not whether a remedy should be created, but instead is whether the Eleventh Amendment bar should be lifted, as it was in *Ex parte Young*, in order to allow a suit against a state officer. Nevertheless, we think that the same general principle applies: therefore, where Congress has prescribed a detailed remedial scheme for the enforcement against a State of a statutorily created right, a court should hesitate before casting aside those limitations and permitting an action against a state officer based upon *Ex parte Young*.

[Here], the fact that Congress chose to impose upon the State a liability which is significantly more limited than would be the liability imposed upon the state office under *Ex parte Young* strongly indicates that Congress had no wish to create the latter. . . . We hold that *Ex parte Young* is inapplicable to petitioner's suit against the Governor of Florida, and therefore that suit is barred by the Eleventh Amendment and must be dismissed for a lack of jurisdiction.

Justice Stevens dissented. Justice Souter, for Justices Ginsburg and Breyer, also dissented. The Souter dissent included an extensive historical analysis and a critique of the *Hans* decision.

NOTES AND QUESTIONS

(1) *Congressional Power Under Article I, § 8 and Abrogation of the State's Eleventh Amendment Immunities: Seminole Tribe of Florida v. Florida, 517 U.S. 44 (1996).* In the principal case above the Supreme Court, per Chief Justice Rehnquist, held that the Indian Commerce Clause power of Art.I, § 8 did not provide Congress with authority to abrogate the States' immunities under the Eleventh Amendment. The *Seminole Tribe* decision, in conjunction with other abrogation decisions in Note (4) above, suggested that only those Congressional powers conferred after the Eleventh Amendment was adopted could be the source of authority to abrogate. Thus, *Seminole Tribe* was widely recognized, in the context of federalism, as a decision favoring the States.

The Court later rejected, or at least stepped back from, this broad reading of *Seminole Tribe*. In *Central Virginia Community College v. Katz*, 546 U.S. 356 (2006), the Court, per Justice Stevens, held that the Bankruptcy Clause, Art. I, § 8, cl. 4, gave Congress power to abrogate state sovereign immunity (including the version found in the Eleventh Amendment) even though the Bankruptcy Clause pre-dated the Eleventh Amendment. The majority was composed of the *Seminole Tribe* dissenters *plus* Justice O'Connor. Justice Thomas dissented (for Chief Justice Roberts and Justices Scalia and Kennedy).

(2) *Expanding Abrogation Doctrine to the Due Process Clause of the Fourteenth Amendment: College Savings Bank v. Florida Prepaid Postsecondary Education Expense Board, 527 U.S. 666 (1999).* In *College Savings Bank*, a private entity sued a Florida State agency for "false and misleading advertising" under the Lanham Act and the Trademark Remedy Clarification Act ("TRCA"). The plaintiff responded to Florida's Eleventh Amendment defense by arguing that Congress had abrogated the immunity by passing TRCA, pursuant to § 5 of the Fourteenth Amendment, to protect "property rights" secured by the Due Process Clause. By asserting abrogation under § 5, the plaintiff sought to avoid the implications of *Seminole Tribe*.

The Supreme Court, per Justice Scalia, held that, even if TRCA had been passed pursuant to § 5, the authority under the Due Process Clause did not include the authority to abrogate. The Court also held that there had not been any waiver by Florida of its Eleventh Amendment immunities. Justices Breyer, Stevens, Souter, and Ginsburg dissented. [This decision should be considered together with the *Alden v. Maine* decision in Note (8) above and with a companion case from Florida set forth in § 14.02 below.]

§ 3.06   ATTEMPTS BY THE STATE TO CONTROL THE FEDERAL GOVERNMENT

NOTE ON THE FEDERAL GOVERNMENT'S IMMUNITY FROM EFFORTS BY THE STATES TO DISADVANTAGE IT

McCulloch v. Maryland and Intergovernmental Tax Immunity in the Modern Cases: "The Power to Destroy." You should recall *McCulloch v. Maryland* from Chapter 2. There, several states had imposed onerous taxes on the National Bank or its notes in an effort to prevent the bank from operating. Chief Justice Marshall invalidated these taxes, citing the Supremacy Clause and observing that state power to tax the federal government was the "power to destroy" it. Today, more than 150 years later, cases still arise that reflect efforts of the states to impose taxes that discriminate against the federal government. *See, e.g., Davis v. Michigan Dep't of Treasury,* 489 U.S. 803 (1989) (holding that it is unconstitutional for a state to grant income tax exemptions to state employees while taxing federal employees and denying them the exemption); *Reich v. Collins,* 513 U.S. 106 (1995) (holding that it was unconstitutional for a state to abolish its refund remedy after collecting discriminatory taxes from federal employees).

More Subtle Questions of State Power to Influence the Federal Government: U.S. Term Limits, Inc. v. Thornton. On the other hand, it is arguable that the founders intended the states to be a countervailing force that would help limit the power of the national government. *See, e.g., United States v. Lopez,* in § 2.02 above (Kennedy, J., concurring). The Constitution grants or reserves certain powers to the states; for example, the states are authorized to prescribe the "Times, Places and Manner of Holding Elections for Senators and Representatives," subject to Congressional alteration. What does this power include? May a state add to the three required qualifications of age, citizenship and residence, stated in the Constitution for Congress? Specifically, may it impose term limits? Consider the following, and note the focus on originalism, textualism and historical analysis.

U.S. TERM LIMITS, INC. v. THORNTON
514 U.S. 211 (1995)

Justice Stevens delivered the opinion of the Court.

[Arkansas, one of the petitioners, was one of over twenty-five states that passed state laws directed at limiting the terms of members of the federal Congress. Generally, these efforts were designed to remove so-called "career" politicians. States that passed such laws relied, in part, on the Elections Clause, which gives the States power to regulate the "Times, Places and Manner" of holding elections, including federal elections. In the instant Arkansas case, the voters passed (by 60% vote) an amendment to the Arkansas constitution ("Amendment 73") prohibiting the name of an otherwise eligible candidate for Congress from appearing on the general election ballot if the candidate already had served three terms in the House or two terms in the Senate. The candidate might still be elected by write-in balloting.

[The respondents challenged Amendment 73 on the ground that the states assertedly had no authority to add to the three requirements (age, citizenship and residency) for congressional service established by the Qualifications Clauses of Art. I, § 2, cl. 2 and Art. I, § 3, cl. 3. The Arkansas state courts agreed with the respondents that the constitutional qualifications are "fixed." Here the Supreme Court affirms.]

II

Twenty-six years ago, in *Powell v. McCormack*, 395 U.S. 486 (1969), we reviewed the history and text of the Qualifications Clauses in a case involving an attempted exclusion of a duly elected Member of Congress. The principal issue was whether the power granted to each House in Art. I, § 5, to judge the "Qualifications of its own Members" includes the power to impose qualifications other than those set forth in the text of the Constitution. In an opinion by Chief Justice Warren for eight Members of the Court, we held that it does not. . . .

Powell [in sum] establishes two important propositions: first, that the "relevant historical materials" compel the conclusion that, at least with respect to qualifications imposed by Congress, the Framers intended the qualifications listed in the Constitution to be exclusive; and second, that that conclusion is equally compelled by an understanding of the "fundamental principle of our representative democracy . . . 'that the people should choose whom they please to govern them.'" . . .

III

Petitioners argue that the Constitution contains no express prohibition against state-added qualifications, and that Amendment 73 is therefore an appropriate exercise of a State's reserved power to place additional restrictions on the choices that its own voters may make. We disagree for two independent reasons. First, we conclude that the power to add qualifications is not within the "original powers" of the States, and thus is not reserved to the States by the Tenth Amendment. Second, even if States possessed some original power in this area, we conclude that the Framers intended the Constitution to be the exclusive source of qualifications for members of Congress, and that the Framers thereby "divested" States of any power to add qualifications. . . .

In short, as the Framers recognized, electing representatives to the National Legislature was a new right, arising from the Constitution itself. The Tenth Amendment thus provides no basis for concluding that the States possess reserved power to add qualifications to those that are fixed in the Constitution. . . . In the absence of any constitutional delegation to the States of power to add qualifications to those enumerated in the Constitution, such a power does not exist.

Even if we believed that States possessed as part of their original powers some control over congressional qualifications, the text and structure of the Constitution, the relevant historical materials, and, most importantly, the "basic principles of our democratic system" all demonstrate that the Qualifications clauses were intended to preclude the States from exercising any such power and to fix as exclusive the qualifications in the Constitution. . . .

The available affirmative evidence indicates the Framers' intent that States have no role in the setting of [Congressional] qualifications. . . .

[At this point, the majority discussed textual, structural and historical evidence regarding the Framers' intent]. . . . The Framers feared that the diverse interests of the States would undermine the national Legislature, and thus they adopted provisions intended to minimize the possibility of state interference with federal elections. . . .

Similarly, we believe that state-imposed qualifications, as much as congressionally imposed qualifications, would undermine the second critical idea recognized in *Powell*: that an aspect of sovereignty is the right of the people to vote for whom they wish. Again, the source of the qualification is of little moment in assessing the qualification's restrictive impact.

Finally, state-imposed restrictions, unlike the congressionally imposed restrictions at issue in *Powell*, violate a third idea central to this basic principle: that the right to choose representatives belongs not to the States, but to the people. . . . The Congress of the United States, therefore, is not a confederation of nations in which separate sovereigns are represented by appointed delegates, but is instead a body composed of representatives of the people. . . .

Permitting individual States to formulate diverse qualifications for their representatives would result in a patchwork of state qualifications, undermining the uniformity and the national character that the Framers envisioned and sought to ensure. . . .

IV

Petitioners argue that, even if States may not add qualifications, Amendment 73 is constitutional because it is not such a qualification, and because Amendment 73 is a permissible exercise of state power to regulate the "Times, Places and manner of Holding Elections." We reject these contentions. . . .

V

The merits of term limits, or "rotation," have been the subject of debate since the formation of our Constitution, when the Framers unanimously rejected a proposal to add such limits to the Constitution. The cogent arguments on both sides of the question that were articulated during the process of ratification largely retain their force today. . . .

. . . [any such change must come] through the Amendment procedures set forth in Article V. . . .

[*Affirmed.*]

JUSTICE KENNEDY, concurring.

[T]he majority and dissenting opinions demonstrate the intricacy of the question whether or not the Qualifications Clauses are exclusive. In my view, however, it is well settled that the whole people of the United States asserted their political identity and unity of purpose when they created the federal system. The dissent's course of reasoning suggesting otherwise might be construed to disparage the republican character of the National Government, and it seems appropriate to add these few remarks to explain why [the dissent's] course of argumentation runs counter to fundamental principles of federalism.

Federalism was our Nation's own discovery. The Framers split the atom of sovereignty. It was the genius of their idea that our citizens would have two political capacities, one state and one federal, each protected from incursion by the other. . . .

The political identity of the entire people of the Union is reinforced by the proposition, which I take to be beyond dispute, that, though limited as to its objects, the National Government is and must be controlled by the people without collateral interference by the States. . . . The States have no power, reserved or otherwise, over the exercise of federal authority within its proper sphere. . . . That the States may not invade the sphere of federal sovereignty is as incontestable, in my view, as the corollary proposition that the Federal Government must be held within the boundaries of its own power when it intrudes upon matters reserved to the States. *See United States v. Lopez, supra.* . . .

JUSTICE THOMAS, with whom the CHIEF JUSTICE, JUSTICE O'CONNOR, and JUSTICE SCALIA join, dissenting.

I dissent. Nothing in the Constitution deprives the people of each State of the power to prescribe eligibility requirements for the candidates who seek to represent them in Congress. The Constitution is simply silent on this question. And where the Constitution is silent, it raises no bar to action by the States or the people.

I

Because the majority fundamentally misunderstands the notion of "reserved" powers, I start with some first principles. Contrary to the majority's suggestion, the people of the States need not point to any affirmative grant of power in the Constitution in order to prescribe qualifications for their representatives in Congress, or to authorize their elected stated legislators to do so. . . .

These basic principles are enshrined in the Tenth Amendment, which declares that all powers neither delegated to the Federal Government nor prohibited to the States "are reserved to the States respectively, or to the people." . . .

In short, the notion of popular sovereignty that undergirds the Constitution does not erase state boundaries, but rather tracks them. . . .

[T]he majority's essential logic is that the state governments could not "reserve" any powers that they did not control at the time the Constitution was drafted. . . .

The majority is [however] quite wrong to conclude that the people of the States cannot authorize their state governments to exercise any powers that were unknown to the States when the Federal Constitution was drafted. Indeed, the majority's position frustrates the apparent purpose of the Tenth Amendment's final phrase. . . .

II . . .

. . . Because the text of the Qualifications Clauses does not support its position, the majority turns instead to its vision of the democratic principles that animated the Framers. But the majority's analysis goes to a question that is not before us: whether Congress has the power to prescribe qualifications for its own members. [But] the democratic principles that contributed to the Framers' decision to withhold this power from Congress do not prove that the Framers also deprived the people of the States of their reserved authority to set eligibility requirements for their own representatives. [Justice Thomas provided here an extensive textual and historical analysis of the various clauses referenced by the majority.]. . .

The Qualifications Clauses do prevent the individual States from abolishing all eligibility requirements for Congress. This restriction on state power reflects the fact that when the people of one State send immature, disloyal, or unknowledgeable representatives to Congress, they jeopardize not only their own interests but also the interests of the people of other States. Because Congress wields power over all the States, the people of each State need some guarantee that the legislators elected by the people of other States will meet minimum standards of competence. The Qualifications Clauses provide that guarantee: they list the requirements that the Framers considered essential to protect the competence of the National Legislature.

If the people of a State decide that they would like their representatives to possess additional qualifications, however, they have done nothing to frustrate the policy behind the Qualifications Clauses. . . .

[In this part of his dissent, Justice Thomas provided an extensive review of what he called the "historical evidence." This history is presented in five parts: (1) the history of the Qualifications Clauses at the 1787 Constitutional Convention; (2) the history of four other provisions referenced by the majority; (3) the history of the Qualifications Clauses during the ratification process; (4) the history of state election qualification laws in the post-ratification era; and (5) the history of certain Congressional controversies regarding qualifications for Congressional office. Justice Thomas argued that the historical evidence does not support and, in most cases, repudiates the majority's position. He concluded:]

The prohibition that today's majority enforces is found nowhere in the text of the Qualifications Clauses. In the absence of evidence that the Clauses nonetheless were generally understood at the time of the framing to imply such a prohibition, we may not use the Clauses to invalidate the decisions of a State or its people. . . .

NOTES AND QUESTIONS

(1) *State-Imposed Term Limitations on Congressional Service: U.S. Term Limits v. Thornton, 514 U.S. 211 (1995).* The Court holds, by a 5-4 majority, that state efforts to impose term limits on members of Congress violate the Qualifications Clauses because the Constitution's three explicitly-stated criteria (age, citizenship, and residence) are fixed and exclusive. Although the majority concedes that the term limits movement may serve salutary reform goals (such as freeing Congress from entrenched incumbents), the majority concludes that the use of term limits would require a Constitutional amendment under Article V. But perhaps the majority puts too little emphasis on the Elections Clauses by which the states are given power to fix the "manner" of holding elections for federal offices. When "the people" of a state decide to design their elections to decrease chances of incumbents, whether in an attempt to level the playing field or for some other reason, aren't "the people" of that state doing exactly what the majority emphasizes—electing whom they please—even if they do happen to use term limits as part of the "manner" of doing so?

(2) *Theories of Judicial Review and Thornton: What Role Should Historical Analysis Play?* In the majority, concurring and dissenting opinions, at least four theories of judicial interpretation are extensively displayed: textualism, historical analysis, precedential reasoning and policy-based analysis. Both the majority and dissent purport to be directed at ascertaining the Framers' Intent (*i.e.*, "original intent") regarding the Qualification Clauses. You will want to review the Appendix to Chapter 1 regarding Originalism and Interpretivism. Which of the *Thornton* opinions, if any, employs an Originalist approach?

(3) *Is the Real Issue in Thornton a Concern for Federalism, or "Individual Liberty"?* In Justice Kennedy's short concurring opinion, he concluded that the term limits amendment violated "fundamental principles of federalism." He argued, by citation to the *Lopez* decision, that "the States may not invade the sphere of federal sovereignty. . . ." Justice Kennedy argued that, to protect individual liberty, the "Framers split the atom of sovereignty." By having strong state governments, the Federalism system protects individual liberty against coercion by the Federal government and vice versa. *See generally* Kathleen M. Sullivan, *Dueling Sovereignties: U. S. Term Limits v. Thornton*, 109 Harv. L. Rev. 78 (1995).

(4) *State Primary Election Systems and Federal Control Under the "Elections Clause:" Foster v. Love, 522 U.S. 67 (1998).* Under the Elections Clause, Art I, § 4, cl. 1, Congress had established a national November date for the biennial elections to Congress. Since 1978, Louisiana had adopted a statutory scheme for conducting Congressional elections known as an "open primary" in which all candidates, regardless of party, appear on the ballot and all voters, regardless of party, are entitled to vote. If one candidate receives a majority of the "open primary" vote, that candidate is considered as "elected" under Louisiana law and no further vote is taken in November. Although a November vote may be taken if no candidate secured a majority, over 80% of Louisiana's Congressional elections had been ended with the open primary. The respondents were Louisiana voters who challenged the constitutionality of the open primary scheme under the Elections Clause. Relying heavily on *Thornton, supra*, the Supreme Court unanimously held, per Justice Souter, that if a State would hold an election, for congressional offices, the Elections Clause requires that the election may not be consummated prior to the federal election day. Doesn't this decision, when read together with *Thornton*, significantly restrict the State's flexibility in structuring its election system to accommodate local needs or preferences or should we understand that such "restrictions" were intended by the Framers?

Appendix 3

CONSTITUTIONAL LAW IN PRACTICE—NEGATIVE COMMERCE CLAUSE AND PREEMPTION ARGUMENTS IN *PENNZOIL CO. v. TEXACO, INC.*

BACKGROUND TO THE PENNZOIL-TEXACO DISPUTE

Pennzoil's State-Court Judgment Against Texaco. Pennzoil Co. obtained a judgment for more than $11 billion against Texaco Inc. on the ground that Texaco had interfered with Pennzoil's alleged contract to purchase an interest in Getty Oil Co. The purchase agreement was expressly made subject to the completion of a "definitive merger agreement," which never was completed. The parties described it in their press releases as merely an "agreement in principle" which would not be binding. Nevertheless, Pennzoil's theory was that the agreement in principle ripened into a binding contract when Pennzoil's basic offer was approved by Getty's board of directors and when expressions of assent such as handshakes and champagne toasts were exchanged between the negotiators for the parties. Texaco claimed to have relied upon the documents, assurances from Getty that there was no binding contract, and similar indications that it was not acting unlawfully. Nevertheless, the jury in a Texas state court found that Pennzoil did have a binding contract and that Texaco knew of the contract and knowingly interfered with it.

Texaco's Federal Litigation to Stay the Judgment Pending Appeal. Texas law did not provide Texaco with an effective means for staying enforcement of the judgment pending appeal. Therefore, Texaco commenced an action in New York federal court under 42 U.S.C. § 1983 (the civil rights remedies law) and other statutes to enjoin enforcement of the Texas judgment pending appeal. [It also lobbied the Texas legislature in an effort to obtain a change in Texas law governing enforcement pending appeal. That action involved a clash of constitutional issues that is set forth in Chapter 1, above.]

Texaco's Negative Commerce Clause Argument. Among other arguments, Texaco claimed that the judgment together with the Texas appeals laws violated the negative commerce clause. Stated simply, the argument presupposed that the national market in securities purchases, and particularly the market in control shares of purchased corporations, would be harmed by the Texas interference-with-contract principles. The resulting uncertainty on the part of any major purchaser, as to whether it might be subjected to very large damages because a jury later might find that a non-definitive agreement was binding, would substantially deter such purchases in interstate commerce.

Texaco's Supremacy Clause (or Preemption) Arguments. Texaco also argued that these Texas laws were preempted by various federal laws, including a federal securities statute called the Williams Act.

Texaco's Other Arguments. These negative commerce clause and preemption arguments were not Texaco's only arguments. It had several others, including due process, equal protection, and full faith and credit clause arguments. However, we have focused here upon the negative commerce clause and preemption arguments because they are capable of being isolated and studied separately.

Pleadings, Fact Gathering, Evidence, and Briefing. In practice, constitutional law does not consist merely of the rarified task of generating abstract arguments. It also requires the use of procedures to frame the dispute, prove the facts, and advocate outcomes. We here reproduce excerpts from Texaco's federal complaint for injunction and from evidence, which was in affidavit form.

TEXACO'S COMPLAINT

UNITED STATES DISTRICT COURT
SOUTHERN DISTRICT OF NEW YORK

TEXACO, INC., **Plaintiff,** –against– **PENNZOIL COMPANY,** **Defendant.**	**85 Civ. 9640 (CLB)** *AMENDED COMPLAINT*

Plaintiff Texaco Inc. ("Texaco") . . . avers:

NATURE OF THE ACTION

1. On November 19, 1985, in an action entitled *Pennzoil Company v. Texaco, Inc.* ("*Pennzoil v. Texaco*" or the "*Pennzoil* action"), a jury in the District Court for the 151st Judicial District of Texas (the "Texas Court") rendered a verdict against Texaco and in favor of defendant Pennzoil Company ("Pennzoil") . . ., on Pennzoil's claim that Texaco tortiously interfered with an alleged contract between Pennzoil and Getty Oil Company ("Getty Oil") and related entities for the purchase of 3/7ths of Getty Oil's common stock. . . . According to Pennzoil's theory, Texaco committed this tort by making a tender offer, at Getty Oil's invitation, for all of Getty Oil's shares . . ., which offer was higher than a competing offer by Pennzoil and was accepted by Getty Oil's directors and by the overwhelming majority of its shareholders.

2. On December 10, 1985, the Texas Court entered judgment on that verdict in the amount of $11,120,976,110.83 (the "Judgment"). . . . A copy of the Judgment is annexed hereto as Exhibit A.

3. As set forth below, the Judgment rests upon the purported legal principle (hereinafter the "*Pennzoil* rule") that damages for tortious inducement of breach of contract may be imposed when (among other things) (a) the parties to the purported contract have expressly agreed not to be bound thereby pending drafting and execution of a definitive written instrument and have failed to reach agreement on crucial terms; (b) the defendant did not have actual knowledge of the existence of the purported contract; and (c) the defendant acted only after being solicited to make a competitive bid by one of the parties to the alleged contract, who represented that the defendant was free to bid.

4. As set forth below, the *Pennzoil* rule (a) impermissibly burdens interstate commerce by deterring competitive tender offers and therefore violates the Commerce Clause; [and] (b) conflicts with, and is therefore preempted by, the Securities Exchange Act of 1934, 15 U.S.C. §§ 78n(d), 78n(e) and 78bb (the "Williams Act"), which promotes and provides a framework for competing tender offers. . . .

5. As set forth below, although the Constitution and laws of Texas entitle Texaco to appeal as of right from the Judgment, the Texas Rules of Civil Procedure . . . require Texaco to post a supersedeas bond in the amount of the entire Judgment, plus interest and costs, in order to secure a stay of execution of the Judgment pending appeal. . . .

6. As set forth below, application of these provisions of Texas procedural law (hereinafter the "supersedeas and lien provisions") will destroy Texaco as a going concern, thus insulating the Judgment and the *Pennzoil* rule from review in the Texas appellate courts or, if necessary, in the Supreme Court of the United States. . . .

[Paragraphs 7 through 63 of the complaint, dealing with Parties, Jurisdiction, venue, common fact allegations, and various other subjects are omitted here.]

FIRST CAUSE OF ACTION
(Commerce Clause)

64. Texaco realleges the averments of Paragraphs 1 through 63 above as if fully set forth herein.

65. In *Edgar v. MITE Corp.*, 457 U.S. 624 (1982), the United States Supreme Court held that state action inhibiting initiation of interstate tender offers impermissibly burdened interstate commerce and thereby violated the Commerce Clause.

66. By deterring the making of a competing tender offer where the target and a given bidder have conducted any substantial negotiations, the Judgment and the *Pennzoil* rule place substantial, direct, adverse and undue burden upon interstate commerce.

67. Application of the [Texas judgment enforcement] provisions to prevent appellate review of the Judgment and the *Pennzoil* rule will render this impermissible burden upon interstate commerce permanent and irremediable, in violation of the Commerce Clause.

SECOND CAUSE OF ACTION
(Supremacy Clause—Williams Act)

68. Plaintiff realleges the averments of Paragraphs 1 through 67 above as if fully set forth herein.

69. By deterring the making of competing tender offers in the manner permitted and encouraged by the Williams Act [a federal statute regulating tender offers], the Judgment and the *Pennzoil* rule contravene paramount federal laws and impair and frustrate paramount federal interests in preserving competition and maximizing investment values. In addition, by deterring competing bids, the Judgment and the *Pennzoil* rule confer a substantial tactical advantage upon initial offerors over targets, in contravention of Williams Act policies favoring a "neutral" balance between target and offeror.

70. By virtue of their direct conflict with the Williams Act and its policies, the Judgment and the *Pennzoil* rule are rendered void and of no legal effect under the Supremacy Clause.

71. Application of the [Texas judgment enforcement] provisions to bar appellate review of the Judgment and the *Pennzoil* rule will render permanent and irremediable their conflict with and disruption of the federal regulatory scheme established by the Williams Act.

72. Application of the [Texas judgment enforcement] provisions to bar appellate review of the Judgment and the *Pennzoil* rule is therefore void and of no legal effect under the Williams Act and the Supremacy Clause.

[Other Claims, which include due process, equal protection, and other theories, are here omitted.]

[The Complaint prays for a temporary restraining order, preliminary and permanent injunctions, and other relief.]

[The Complaint is supported by various affidavits and other attachments demonstrating the facts upon which the TRO is requested. One affidavit, that of Economist Lester Thurow, is excerpted here.]

AFFIDAVIT SUPPORTING PRAYER FOR TRO

UNITED STATES DISTRICT COURT
SOUTHERN DISTRICT OF NEW YORK

TEXACO, INC.,		
	Plaintiff,	**85 Civ. 9640 (CLB)**
–against–		*AMENDED COMPLAINT*
PENNZOIL COMPANY,		**AFFIDAVIT OF LESTER C. THUROW**
	Defendant.	

STATE OF NEW YORK,

COUNTY OF NEW YORK, ss.:

LESTER C. THUROW, being duly sworn deposes and says:

1. I am Gordon Y. Billiard Professor of Management and Economics at the Sloan School of Management of the Massachusetts Institute of Technology. I earned a doctorate in Economics at Harvard University in 1964. I have been a member of the M.I.T. faculty since 1968.

2. I am aware of the $11.1 billion judgment entered by a Texas trial court against Texaco in an action commenced by Pennzoil, which I refer to herein as "the *Pennzoil* action." I understand that there are provisions of Texas law that permit Pennzoil to enforce its $11.1 billion judgment, even before Texaco's appeal can be heard and decided.

3. For purposes of this affidavit, I assume the following facts [which are set forth in other witnesses' factual affidavits, also attached to the Complaint]:

(a) Pennzoil claims that Texaco induced the breach of a contract under which Pennzoil was to acquire from the Getty Oil Company and other Getty entities 3/7ths of Getty Oil Company's outstanding common stock for a price of $112.50 per share ($2.6 billion);

(b) Getty Oil Company and Pennzoil, a day after they allegedly reached this agreement, issued press releases stating that they had "an agreement in principle" which was "subject to the execution of a definitive agreement";

(c) Getty Oil Company and Pennzoil thereafter continued to negotiate unsuccessfully on various terms and never reached agreement on those terms;

(d) the Getty entities and Pennzoil never agreed on and never signed a "definitive agreement";

(e) while Pennzoil and the Getty entities were attempting to negotiate a more definitive agreement, representatives of the Getty entities approached Texaco and invited Texaco to make a higher bid for Getty Oil Company;

(f) representatives of the Getty entities told Texaco that they had no prior contract with Pennzoil and were free to deal with Texaco;

(g) Texaco responded with an offer to purchase 100% of Getty Oil Company's stock for $125 per share and later raised its offer to $128 per share;

(h) the directors and shareholders of Getty Oil Company approved the Texaco proposal;

(i) Pennzoil claims that it is entitled to recover $7.53 billion in damages as a result of Texaco's alleged interference, and the jury awarded that amount; and

(j) the jury awarded Pennzoil punitive damages in the amount of $3 billion.

4. If, as I have assumed to be the case, the Texas trial court entered the $11.1 billion judgment against Texaco on a record that reflected these facts, then the Pennzoil judgment announces a new and dangerous rule, which I refer to herein as "the *Pennzoil* rule." The *Pennzoil* rule would provide that:

(a) parties who have an "agreement in principle" which is explicitly subject to the negotiation and signing of a definitive agreement can nonetheless be bound to multi-billion dollar obligations even when the definitive agreement has never come into existence and has never been signed;

(b) a jury can find that parties have agreed to a complex, multi-billion dollar, multi-party transaction, even where, after the "agreement in principle", the parties continued to negotiate actively and unsuccessfully on various terms that were important to them;

(c) a purchaser can be found liable for inducing a breach of contract even though, against the background facts described in (a) and (b) above, the seller informed the purchaser that there was no prior contract, and explicitly asked the purchaser to make a higher bid; and

(d) the purchaser can thereby expose itself to liability in an amount that is far greater than the value of the contract with which it allegedly has interfered.

5. It is my opinion that the *Pennzoil* rule may have serious negative effects on the functioning of the national economy. Our national economy is based upon a system of competitive capitalism in which the person who is willing to pay the highest price receives the benefit of any investment opportunity. In the context of the sale of companies, this system should encourage a public auction in which the highest bidder wins. This system furthers two primary goals:

(a) it allocates the nation's resources to their highest values uses; and

(b) it maximizes the value of shareholders' investment in publicly held companies.

6. To be sure, the free and open competition for investment opportunities is constrained by the law of contracts. Once two parties have entered into binding contract, the competition is over. Bidders who arrive after that point have arrived too late. The timeliness of the bid is an important part of the competition. Parties to a contract must be able to rely on their contract once they have it.

7. Thus, competitive capitalism is based on two fundamental propositions:

First, there should be free and open competition among parties seeking investment opportunities.

Second, when the competition is over, the parties must be able to rely on their contracts.

8. For competitive capitalism to work, there must be rules concerning when the auction is still open and when the auction is over. These rules must be clearly articulated and must be applied in an objective, consistent and predictable manner. Otherwise, those participating in the competition cannot discern the rules and guide their conduct in accordance with them:

(a) The rules concerning contract formation must define a reasonably clear line indicating when a contract has been achieved. Parties involved in negotiations must be able to determine, in advance, *which* actions will have the effect of binding them.

(b) The rules concerning when a party may be held liable for interfering with contract must also be clear. Investors competing hard for investment opportunities must be able to determine in advance when the auction is over, and should be held liable only when they induce a breach of contract after they *know* the competition is over. . . .

10. The result in the *Pennzoil* action represents a significant threat to the national economy for two reasons:

First, it has established the *Pennzoil* rule, which is at variance with the rules of competitive capitalism as generally understood.

Second, and even more importantly, it suggests that there may be no reliable rules—the rules may be whatever a local jury decides they are, and an investor who competes is at risk that some jury somewhere may decide that it broke the rules. . . .

12. If potential competitive bidders believe that they are at risk that a local jury somewhere may (a) determine that their conduct was somehow unethical, and (b) award money damages many times the size of any conceivable harm done to the first bidder as a result of losing its proposed transaction, they will be deterred from making a competitive bid. The risk that the first bidder will sue, and will win the kind of judgment that Pennzoil has won, may be too great to bear.

13. The uncertainty created by the *Pennzoil* rule and the *Pennzoil* action will inevitably chill the competitive capitalism that is a necessary and desirable part of our national economy. If, as I assume to be the case, Texaco may not be able to secure meaningful appellate review of the judgment without being crippled financially, the *in terrorem* effect on the national economy will be exacerbated.

[signed:] Lester C. Thurow

Sworn to before me this
29th day of December, 1985.
[signed by Notary Public]

NOTES AND QUESTIONS

(1) *Fact Development in Constitutional Litigation.* Sometimes constitutional issues can be presented without development of adjudicative facts, and often the "lawmaking" facts are sufficiently clear so that they do not require development either. But there are some cases in which fact development is crucial. Recall the contrast between the *Rice* and *Kassel* cases, excerpted earlier in this chapter, in which the votes of several justices were influenced by the development of facts supporting constitutional justifications in *Kassel* but not in *Rice*. Is Texaco's negative commerce argument benefited by the fact development illustrated in Professor Thurow's affidavit? On the other hand, might there be reasons for *not* developing facts of this kind?

(2) *Analyzing the Preemption and Negative Commerce Clause Arguments Submitted by Texaco.* What should be the outcome of the preemption arguments presented by Texaco? Consider whether there are strong national interests, whether securities regulation is pervasive, and the nature and strength of the state's interests in applying its law. Also, how should the negative commerce clause argument be evaluated? Consider the tests that the cases in this chapter have set forth: whether the state law principles are discriminatory; whether they otherwise fit in the "virtually per se unconstitutional" category; and, finally, whether the burden on interstate commerce outweighs the legitimate state benefits achieved by the state law principles in question.

(3) *The Outcome: Pennzoil Co. v. Texaco Inc., 481 U.S. 1 (1987)* . The district court granted the requested relief, holding that the preemption and negative commerce clause arguments were valid. The court of appeals affirmed on other grounds. The Supreme Court reversed without reaching the merits. It held that the federal courts had no jurisdiction to consider these issues and that they should have been presented instead to the Texas courts, which had jurisdiction over the judgment. The judgment on the merits was affirmed by the Texas Court of Appeals. The Texas Supreme Court declined

to review the case; Texaco petitioned a bankruptcy court for relief; and, finally, the case was settled while Texaco's petition for certiorari was pending.

Chapter 4
STATE TAXATION OF INTERSTATE COMMERCE

§ 4.01 THE HISTORICAL CONCERNS: DISCRIMINATION, MULTIPLE BURDENS (APPORTIONMENT), JURISDICTION, AND FAIR RELATIONSHIP

INTRODUCTORY NOTE

State Taxation and the Negative Commerce Clause. The issue of state taxation of interstate commerce bears some resemblance to that of state regulation, although there are some different and special concerns. The problem can be brought sharply into focus by imagining that the state taxes only products that are exported from the state, so as to export the burden of supporting its government. But there also are more subtle problems.

The Concerns: Discrimination, Multiple Burdens, Jurisdiction to Tax, and Fair Relationship. The prohibition of discrimination against interstate commerce is one firmly entrenched principle. As this principle relates to state taxes, however, there are several problems. First, as in the case of regulation, discrimination in taxation often can be artfully concealed. A second problem is that of different states imposing the same tax on the same object, so that interstate commerce is subjected to cumulative burdens not imposed on commerce within a single state. Apportionment of the tax, so that each state taxes only that share fairly attributable to it, is generally the solution to this multiple burdens problem. Third, the state must have jurisdiction to tax, supported by a nexus between the taxed activity and the state. Finally, the cases express a requirement of a fair relationship between the taxed activity and some state benefits, although the relationship need not be tailored to the cost to the state of the taxed activity.

WESTERN LIVE STOCK v. BUREAU OF REVENUE
303 U.S. 250 (1938)

Mr. Justice Stone delivered the opinion of the Court.

[New Mexico imposed a tax upon the gross receipts of certain kinds of businesses, including publication of newspapers and magazines. The statute provided: "But the gross receipts of the business of publishing newspapers or magazines shall include only the amounts received for the sale of advertising space." Western Live Stock was a monthly trade magazine that was wholly prepared, edited, and published within the state, although it was distributed nationally and gained revenue from many states. Its publishers argued that the tax infringed the commerce clause "because it is measured by gross receipts which are to some extent augmented by appellants' maintenance of an interstate circulation of their magazine." The state courts upheld the tax. The Supreme Court, per Justice Stone, here affirms.]

It was not the purpose of the commerce clause to relieve those engaged in interstate commerce from their just share of state tax burden even though it increases the cost of doing the business. "Even interstate business must pay its way," and the bare fact that one is carrying on interstate commerce does not relieve him from many forms of state taxation which add to the cost of his business. . . .

. . . On the other hand, local taxes, measured by gross receipts from interstate commerce, have often been pronounced unconstitutional. The vice characteristic of those which have been held invalid is that they have placed on the commerce burdens of such a nature as to be capable in point of substance of being imposed, . . . or added to, . . . with equal right by every state which the commerce touches, merely because interstate commerce is being done, so that without the protection of the commerce clause it would bear cumulative burdens not imposed on local commerce. . . . The multiplication of state taxes measured by the gross receipts from interstate transactions would spell the destruction of interstate commerce and renew the barriers to interstate trade which it was the object of the commerce clause to remove.

It is for these reasons that a state may not lay a tax measured by the amount of merchandise carried in interstate commerce, . . . or upon the freight earned by its carriage. . . . Taxation measured by gross receipts from interstate commerce has been sustained when fairly apportioned to the commerce carried on within the taxing state . . . and in other cases has been rejected only because the apportionment was found to be inadequate or unfair. . . .

In the present case the tax is, in form and substance, an excise conditioned on the carrying on of a local business, that of providing and selling advertising space in a published journal, which is sold to and paid for by subscribers, some of whom receive it in interstate commerce. The price at which the advertising is sold is made the measure of the tax. . . .

. . . The tax is not one which in form or substance can be repeated by other states in such manner as to lay an added burden on the interstate distribution of the magazine. [R]eceipts from subscriptions are not included in the measure of the tax. It is not measured by the extent of the circulation of the magazine interstate. All the events upon which the tax is conditioned—the preparation, printing and publication of the advertising matter, and the receipt of the sums paid for—it occur in New Mexico and not elsewhere. . . . The dangers which ensure from the imposition of a tax measured by gross receipts derived directly from interstate commerce are absent. . . .

Affirmed [and tax upheld].

NOTES AND QUESTIONS

(1) *Discrimination.* Justice Stone points out that a tax would be unconstitutional, if, for example, it was "measured by the amount of merchandise carried in interstate commerce" or by "the freight earned by its carriage." These discrimination concerns, in the state tax area, are analogous to those concerning regulation of commerce generally. Notice that the Court could not workably prohibit taxes upon property merely because it has traveled in interstate commerce. That approach would create a kind of "reverse discrimination," because the out-of-state company would obtain an arbitrary advantage over in-state businesses which would be subject to the tax.

(2) *Multiple Burdens and Fair Apportionment: Western Live Stock.* Notice Justice Stone's implication that a gross receipts tax measured by the circulation of Western Live Stock magazine would be unconstitutional. The reason: If New Mexico could impose a gross receipts tax based upon circulation sold elsewhere, every other state in which the publisher did business could impose a similar gross receipts tax, taxing transactions in every other state. These multiple burdens would place interstate commerce at a competitive disadvantage with intrastate commerce, exemplified by a hypothetical magazine that is published and has all its circulation in a single state. But notice that Justice Stone upholds a tax upon all advertising receipts, on the theory that the publication of the advertising matter occurs only in New Mexico, and hence the tax cannot "be repeated by other states" so as to create multiple burdens. But is this analysis accurate? Couldn't another state, at least in theory, impose a tax on part of the same advertising revenue, if it were apportioned so that it fell only upon the part of the advertising revenue derived from circulation in the taxing state? After all, even a tax upon circulation receipts would not be unconstitutional; it would be unconstitutional only if unapportioned.

BRANIFF AIRWAYS, INC. v. NEBRASKA STATE BOARD OF EQUALIZATION AND ASSESSMENT, 347 U.S. 590 (1954). Nebraska imposed an apportioned ad valorem tax on Braniff's flight equipment. In other words, it imposed a tax measured by the value of Braniff's airplanes that landed in the state, subject to an apportionment formula that took into account the fact that the airplanes were elsewhere part of the time. The apportionment formula was complex. It depended upon the arithmetical average of three ratios: (1) Braniff's ratio of Nebraska landings to its total landings nationwide; (2) its ratio of revenue tons in Nebraska to revenue tons nationwide; and (3) its ratio of Nebraska originating revenues to nationwide originating revenues. Braniff objected to the tax, pointing out that it had an average of only eighteen landings in Nebraska per day, and that the same airplanes were not regularly involved. It argued that Nebraska lacked jurisdiction to impose the tax and also that it could not show a fair relationship between the imposition of tax burdens and benefit derived from it by the State. The Supreme Court, per Justice Reed, upheld the tax:

> The argument upon which appellant depends ultimately . . . is that its aircraft never "attained a taxable situs within Nebraska. . . ."

> . . . So far as due process is concerned the only question is whether the tax in practical operation has relation to opportunities, benefits, or protection conferred or afforded by the taxing state. . . .

> Thus the situs issue devolves into the question of whether eighteen stops per day by appellant's aircraft is sufficient contact with Nebraska to sustain that state power to levy an apportioned ad valorem tax on such aircraft. We think such regular contact is sufficient to establish Nebraska's power to tax even though the same aircraft do not land every day and even though none of the aircraft is continuously within the state. The basis of the jurisdiction is the habitual employment of the property within the state. [Braniff] rents its ground facilities and pays for fuel it purchases in Nebraska. [It has] the opportunity to exploit the commerce, traffic, and trade that originates in or reaches Nebraska. Approximately one-tenth of [Braniff's] revenue is produced by the pick-up and discharge of Nebraska freight and passengers. Nebraska certainly affords protection during such stops and these regular landings are clearly a benefit to appellant.

Justice Frankfurter dissented. He pointed out that the states could, as a practical matter, use different apportionment formulas to impose multiple burdens on interstate commerce. "It is one thing . . . for the individual states to determine what factors should be taken into account and how they should be weighted. It is quite another for Congress to devise, as the Civil Aeronautics Board recommended it should, a scheme of apportionment binding on all of the states. . . . It is the diverse and fluctuating exercise of power by the various states, even where based on concededly relevant factors, which imposes an undue burden on interstate commerce." Justice Frankfurter also was concerned that a tax upon "planes which pause for a few moments" provided a way to cumulate taxes unfairly against Braniff, which already paid taxes for the services it enjoyed in Nebraska. "In fact it pays approximately $22,000 a year for the use of the airport, $14,000 a year in gasoline taxes, and appropriate property taxes on office equipment, trucks and other items permanently in Nebraska."

NOTES AND QUESTIONS

(1) *Jurisdiction and Fair Relationship.* Jurisdiction to tax is not precisely the same as, but is closely analogous to, the familiar kind of jurisdiction to adjudicate controlled by the *International Shoe* line of cases, which you studied in your Civil Procedure course. It also is closely related to the notion of a "fair relationship" between the burdens imposed by the state and benefits to the taxpayer. Since the benefits may be highly intangible (as Justice Reed's reasoning demonstrated), the relationship may be very

rough. *Cf.* McHugh & Reed, *The Due Process Clause and the Commerce Clause: Two New and Easy Tests for Nexus in Tax Cases,* 90 W. VA. L. REV. 31 (1987).

(2) *Apportionment Formulas and Justice Frankfurter's Concern.* Doesn't Justice Frankfurter have a point? Imagine that state X is the site of Braniff's busiest ticket office, although its airports do not handle much traffic; state X decides to maximize its revenue by apportioning according to ticketing revenues. State Y, on the other hand, maximizes its tax revenue by apportioning according to the number of in-state landings, because its airport is a regional transfer point. Couldn't cumulative burdens be imposed in this manner? [On the other hand, isn't this an inherent and unavoidable concern, at least theoretically, as to every state revenue measure that affects interstate businesses?]

§ 4.02   THE MODERN CASES AND THE FOUR-PART TEST

NOTE ON THE DEMISE OF THE "PRIVILEGE TAX" DOCTRINE

In *Spector Motor Service v. O'Connor,* 340 U.S. 602 (1951), the Court struck down an apportioned net income tax imposed on a corporation "for the privilege of carrying on or doing business within the state." The Court reasoned that the state could tax intrastate business of an interstate firm, but it could not do so by a "direct" tax on the "privilege" of doing business within the state, because that amounted to a direct tax upon interstate commerce. The dissenters pointed out that the tax was fairly apportioned and nondiscriminatory. In fact, it appeared that a tax with the same practical effect could have been constructed, and it would have had a far better chance of being sustained, if only it had not been worded in terms of taxing the "privilege" of doing business in the state. This "privilege tax" doctrine was applied in several cases to strike down taxes based upon adequate jurisdiction, which were fairly apportioned, which were nondiscriminatory, and which bore a fair relationship to state services. The results were not consistent, and the reasoning seemed artificial and arbitrary. In the following case, the Court abandoned the privilege tax doctrine, and it adopted, instead, a four-part test based upon practical factors.

COMPLETE AUTO TRANSIT, INC. v. BRADY
430 U.S. 274 (1977)

MR. JUSTICE BLACKMUN delivered the opinion of the Court:

[Mississippi imposed what it called "privilege taxes" for the "privilege of engaging or continuing in business or doing business within this state," measured by gross proceeds, apportioned to sales or income from transactions within the state. Complete Auto provided a contract service that picked up rail-delivered new cars at Jackson, Mississippi, and delivered them to Mississippi dealers. The Mississippi Tax Commission assessed taxes against Complete Auto for its sales of transportation services within Mississippi. Complete Auto objected on the grounds that it provided but one part of an interstate movement, and that the tax, assessed as a "privilege" tax, was unconstitutional. The Mississippi Supreme Court upheld the tax, stating: "It will be noted that the taxpayer has a large operation in this state. It is dependent upon the State for police protection and other state services the same as other citizens. It should pay its fair share of taxes so long, but only so long, as the tax does not discriminate against interstate commerce, and there is no danger of interstate commerce being smothered by cumulative taxes of several states." The United States Supreme Court, in a unanimous opinion, here affirms.]

Appellant, in its complaint . . ., did *not* allege that its activity which Mississippi taxes does not have a sufficient nexus with the state; or that the tax discriminates against interstate commerce; or that the tax is unfairly apportioned; or that it is unrelated to services provided by the state. . . .

Appellant's attack is based solely on decisions of this Court holding that a tax on the "privilege" of engaging in an activity in the state may not be applied to an activity that is part of interstate commerce. *See, e.g., Spector Motor Service v. O'Connor.* . . . This rule looks only to the fact that the incidence of the tax is "privilege of doing business;" it deems irrelevant any consideration of the practical effect of the tax. The rule reflects an underlying philosophy that interstate commerce should enjoy a sort of "free trade" immunity from state taxation.

Appellee [the Mississippi Tax Commission], in its turn, relies on decisions of this Court stating that "[I]t was not the purpose of the commerce clause to relieve those engaged in interstate commerce from their just share of state tax burden even though it increases the cost of doing the business." *Western Live Stock v. Bureau of Revenue* . . . . These decisions have considered not the formal language of the tax statute but rather its practical effect, and have sustained a tax against commerce clause challenge when the tax is applied to an activity with a substantial nexus with the taxing state, is fairly apportioned, does not discriminate against interstate commerce, and is fairly related to the services provided by the state.

. . . Under the present state of the law, the *Spector* rule, as it has come to be known, has no relationship to economic realities. Rather it stands as a trap for the unwary draftsman. . . .

Not only has the philosophy underlying the rule been rejected, but the rule itself has been stripped of any practical significance. If Mississippi had called its tax one on "net income" or on the "going concern value" of appellant's business, the *Spector* rule could not invalidate it. . . . Simply put, the *Spector* rule does not address the problems with which the commerce clause is concerned. Accordingly, we now reject the rule of *Spector Motor Service, Inc. v. O'Connor*, . . . and that case is overruled.

[T]he judgment of the Supreme Court of Mississippi [upholding the tax] is affirmed.

NOTES AND QUESTIONS

(1) *A Tax Struck Down on Grounds of Discrimination: Maryland v. Louisiana, 451 U.S. 725 (1981).* Louisiana placed a "first-use tax" upon any natural gas brought into Louisiana which had not previously been subject to taxation by another state or the United States. The primary incidence of the tax was on gas produced in the federal Outer Continental Shelf (OCS), processed in Louisiana, shipped through pipelines, and sold for the most part to out-of-state customers. Furthermore, the tax was subject to a number of exemptions and credits, which had the effect of removing the tax in most instances in which gas was sold for Louisiana consumption to Louisiana taxpayers. The Supreme Court, per Justice White, struck down the tax:

> . . . In this case, the Louisiana First-Use Tax unquestionably discriminates against interstate commerce in favor of local interests as the necessary result of various tax credits and exclusions. . . . OCS gas consumed in Louisiana . . . is exempt from the First-Use Tax. . . . Finally, [because of the credits available to utilities,] Louisiana consumers of OCS gas are thus substantially protected against the impact of the First-Use Tax. . . . OCS gas moving out of the state, however, is burdened with the First-Use Tax. . . .

(2) *A Tax that Successfully Exported Burdens of the State: Commonwealth Edison Co. v. Montana, 453 U.S. 609 (1981).* Montana's severance tax on each ton of coal mined in the state was levied at rates that depended upon the value, energy content, and method of extraction, but it could equal at maximum thirty percent of the contract sales price. The Supreme Court, per Justice Marshall, upheld the tax:

> Appellants do not dispute that the Montana tax satisfied the first two prongs of the *Complete Auto Transit* test. [Jurisdiction to tax is present because "a substantial [n]exus of the severance of coal is established in Montana," and

there is no requirement of apportionment because "the severance can occur in no other state."]

Appellants assert that the Montana tax "discriminate[s] against interstate commerce" because ninety percent of Montana coal is shipped to other states under contracts that shift the tax burden primarily to non-Montana utility companies and thus to citizens of other states. But the Montana tax is computed at the same rate regardless of the final destination of the coal, and there is no suggestion here that the tax is administered in a manner that departs from this even-handed formula. We are not, therefore, confronted here with the type of differential tax treatment of interstate and intrastate commerce that the Court has found in other "discrimination" cases. *See, e.g., Maryland v. Louisiana.* . . .

Appellants argue that they are entitled to an opportunity to prove that the amount collected under the Montana tax is not fairly related to the additional costs the state incurs because of coal mining. Thus, appellant's objection is to the *rate* of the Montana tax, and even then, their only complaint is that the *amount* the state receives in taxes far exceeds the *value* of the services provided to the coal mining industry. . . . [A]ppellants have completely misunderstood the nature of the inquiry under the fourth prong of the *Complete Auto Transit* test. . . .

[T]here is no requirement under the due process clause that the amount of general revenue taxes collected from a particular activity must be reasonably related to the value of services provided to the activity. . . .

(3) *The "Fair Relationship" Prong as Illustrated in Consolidated Edison Co. v. Montana.* The fourth prong of the *Complete Auto* test is that the taxed activities must have a "fair relationship" to state services or benefits. But the Montana tax case makes it clear that the "relationship" need not have anything to do with the amount of tax. Once it is determined that a particular kind of tax can be imposed, the tax may be imposed in any rate or amount. Notice that Montana citizens thus are able to export to other states much of the cost of their government. Theoretically, Montana could impose a tax such that ninety-nine percent or more of the out-of-state purchaser's payment went to pay the Montana exaction. Is there any limit on this taxation? (Note that competitive market imposes some limits, and the incidence of the tax on non-exempt Montanans also is a consideration; but won't a rational state legislature nevertheless maximize revenues from a tax that exports burdens as clearly as the coal tax does? Note, also, that other states reciprocally may export burdens to Montana.)

(4) *Mail-Order Purchases from Out of State The Court Continues to Grapple with the Complete Auto Test: Quill Corp. v. North Dakota, 504 U.S. 298 (1992).* North Dakota attempted to impose its state use tax on out-of-state mail-order houses that sold to North Dakotans. Although a previous decision, *National Bellas Hess, Inc. v. Department of Revenue of Illinois,* 386 U.S. 753 (1967), had held that mail-order houses lacked sufficient connection with the state, the Supreme Court of North Dakota declined to follow *Bellas Hess* because "the tremendous social, economic, commercial, and legal innovations" of the past quarter-century allegedly had rendered its holding "obsole[te]." North Dakota concluded that the *Complete Auto* case had inaugurated a different test that focussed on the practical effect of the challenged tax. The Court, per Justice Stevens, rejected this argument on *stare decisis* grounds, although it held that Congress could change the rule and allow state taxation of mail-order sales if it chose to:

In sum, although in our cases subsequent to *Bellas Hess* [w]e have not adopted a similar bright-line, physical-presence requirement, our reasoning in those cases does not compel that we now reject the rule that *Bellas Hess* established in the area of sales and use taxes. To the contrary, the continuing value of a bright-line rule in this area and the doctrine and principles of *stare decisis* indicate that the *Bellas Hess* rule remains good law. . . .

This aspect of our decision is made easier by the fact that the underlying issue is not only one that Congress may be better qualified to resolve, but also one that Congress has the ultimate power to resolve. . . . Indeed, in recent years Congress has considered legislation that would "overrule" the *Bellas Hess* rule. . . . Accordingly, Congress is now free to decide whether, when, and to what extent the states may burden interstate mail-order concerns with a duty to collect use taxes.

Justice White dissented in part because he favored "giving *Bellas Hess* the complete burial it justly deserve[d]." Justice Scalia, joined by Justices Kennedy and Thomas, concurred separately because he adhered to his reasoning in the *American Trucking* case that the negative commerce clause jurisprudence was erroneous (Ch. 3, above). He would have adhered to *Bellas Hess* solely as a matter of *stare decisis:* "[T]he *Bellas Hess* rule has engendered substantial reliance and has become part of the basic framework of a sizeable industry," and "I do not share Justice White's view that we may disregard these reliance interests because it has become unreasonable to rely upon *Bellas Hess.*"

Chapter 5

PRESIDENTIAL POWER AND RELATED POWERS OF CONGRESS; SEPARATION OF POWERS

§ 5.01 EXECUTIVE VERSUS LEGISLATIVE POWER

[A] Chapter Introduction: Imperial Presidency or Imperial Congress?

NOTES AND QUESTIONS

(1) *The Realpolitik of the Presidency: Difficulty in Defining the Lawful Limits of Presidential Power.* Consider the following excerpt from L. Tribe, American Constitutional Law 209 (2d ed. 1988)[*]:

> Whether imperial or simply magisterial—or as "close to the people" as ambition and the media can make it—the American Presidency will never be easy to locate within our constitutional framework. [F]or [t]he President is a person as well as an institution; and, unlike other institutions, the Presidency is led by an individual elected by the entire Nation to secure its survival, to represent it to the world, and to voice its aspirations to all the people. Thus it is only by an extraordinary triumph of constitutional imagination that the Commander in Chief is conceived as commanded by law.

Perhaps in no other area of constitutional law is the impact of real politics on court decisions more apparent than in those examining the balance of power between executive and Congress. Although the Constitution, writings of the Framers, and decisional history provide a sketch of the way the distribution of national powers was meant to function, in practice the resolution of separation of powers issues has more often been the product of intense political struggle and uneasy compromise.

(2) *The Framers and the "Imperial" Presidency.* The Framers in 1787 created the Article II Executive. One of the recurring questions in this area of Constitutional law is whether the Framers intended for a "strong" or "weak" Presidential figure.

Some historical information may be helpful. As of 1776, there was widespread concern about a "strong executive"; after all, that model was the King. Most states, with the exception of New York, initially established weak executives (although some states subsequently strengthened gubernatorial powers before the Constitutional Convention). The Articles of Confederation, moreover, had a weak executive.

Against this historical preference for weak executives, consider the actions of the Framers. While most state executives had no veto, the Framers gave the President the veto power (even though a two-thirds vote of Congress can override a veto). Many state executives did not possess an appointment or nomination power; the Framers, in contrast, gave the President the power to nominate all Officers and to make recess appointments. The Framers gave the President the power to pardon (below § 5.07). Similarly, the Framers gave the President power to make treaties (below § 5.03), subject to the approval of two-thirds of the Senate. The Framers also gave the President the power as Commander in Chief of the military and the power to execute federal law. Considered cumulatively, the Framers' actions suggest that they rejected the weak executive approach in favor of a stronger executive model.

(3) *Why Have a Separation of Powers Doctrine?* The impression that an "imperial" President or Congress is dangerous assumes that the concept of separation of powers is

---

[*] Copyright © 1988 by Foundation Press, Inc. Reprinted by permission.

an essential prerequisite to democratic government. *Cf.* Wright, *The Modern Separation of Powers: Would James Madison Have Untied Ulysses?* 18 COLUM. L. REV. 69 (1987). This argument is periodically raised by constitutional reformers who argue that in the 21st century the United States cannot afford the separation of powers and its dispersal of control and subsequent loss of efficiency and the ability for a quick action. Consider the following, from Schlesinger, *Shielded from an Imperial President*, OUTLOOK, May 20, 1986, at 1:*

> [H]igh-minded and capable Americans argue today for reforming the Constitution. [T]he most basic challenge [c]omes from those reformers who challenge [t]he separation of powers. . . .

> The Committee on the Constitutional System, co-chaired by three distinguished Americans, Sen. Nancy Landon Kassebaum, R-Kan., Douglas Dillon, the former secretary of the Treasury, and Lloyd Cutler, a former counsel to President Jimmy Carter, mounted a thoughtful re-examination of the whole question. "The checks and balances inspired by the experience of the 18th century," the Committee declares, "have led repeatedly, in the 20th century, to governmental stalemate and deadlock, to an incapacity to make quick and sharp decisions in the face of urgent problems."

In domestic policy, the separation of powers, it is argued, inhibits concerted action by the executive and Congress to deal with the budget deficit, the trade deficit and other agonizing questions. In foreign policy, some add, the consequences may be even more disastrous. Consider the justifications for the separation of powers posited by the Framers. Can these reasons answer the charge that the technological realities of the 21st century require an executive to act quickly?

> *The Federalist No. 47 (1787) (Madison).* "The accumulation of all powers, legislative, executive, and judiciary in the same hands, whether of one, a few, of many and whether hereditary self-appointed, or elective, may justly be pronounced the very definition of tyranny. [But this does] not mean that these departments ought to have no *partial agency* in, or no *control* over, the acts of each other. . . . [It only means] that where the *whole* power of one department is exercised by the same hands which possess the *whole* power of another department, the fundamental principles of a free constitution are subverted."

> *The Federalist No. 48 (1787) (Madison).* "It is agreed on all sides that the powers properly belonging to one of the departments ought not to be directly and completely administered by either of the other departments. It is equally evident that none of them ought to possess, directly or indirectly, an overruling influence over the others in the administration of their respective powers. [The] most difficult task is to provide some practical security for each, against the invasion of the others. . . ."

(4) *Should the Court Try to Resolve Separation of Powers Issues?* Many commentators believe a judicial resolution of such conflicts is inadvisable. Professor Choper has argued:

> The federal judiciary should not decide constitutional questions concerning the respective powers of Congress and the President vis-a-vis another; rather, the ultimate constitutional issues of whether executive action (or inaction) violates the prerogatives of Congress or whether legislative action (or inaction) transgresses the realm of the President should be held to be nonjusticiable, their final resolution to be remitted to the interplay of the national political process.

---

* Reprinted by consent of author. Professor Schlesinger cautions that he here is stating the views of others.

J. CHOPER, JUDICIAL REVIEW AND THE NATIONAL POLITICAL PROCESS 263 (1980).* Is judicial review of separation of powers issues unconstitutional for this reason?

[B] Sources of Executive Power

Read U.S. Const. Art. II (the Executive).

NOTES AND QUESTIONS

(1) *What is the Source and Scope of the Executive's Power?* Article II of the Constitution sets out the powers and duties of the President. Section 1 vests the "executive Power" in the President and describes the length of the term of office, the election process, qualifications, succession, compensation, and oath of office. Section 2 describes the President's role as "Commander-in-chief" and the powers to grant pardons, make treaties, appoint officials, and fill vacancies. Section 3 mandates that the Executive present to Congress information about the State of the Union, recommend legislation deemed "necessary and expedient," "take Care that the Laws be faithfully executed," and commission officers. Section 4 describes the conduct for which the President, Vice President and federal officials may be removed by impeachment.

(2) *Are There Any Inherent Presidential Powers Not Explicitly Stated in the Constitution?* The ambiguous language used in the Constitution to describe the President's powers suggests that the Framers did not intend exclusively to define the scope or means of Executive authority. Presidents have argued, and the Court has occasionally agreed, that implicit powers of the Executive can be inferred from the Commander in Chief power, the "take Care" clause, and the vesting of executive power in the President. When you read *Youngstown Sheet & Tube Co. v. Sawyer*, below (The Steel Seizure Case), notice how the various Justices interpret Article II's description of the Executive's powers.

(3) *Who Defines the Scope of the Executive's Inherent Powers?* Unless the power exercised is constitutionally questionable enough to cause the intervention of the legislature or bring the matter before the judiciary, the President is generally free to define the scope of his own authority. The exercise of this discretion depends greatly on the personal philosophy of the individual in office. Consider the contrasting views of Presidents Theodore Roosevelt and William H. Taft:

> "[The President is] a steward of the people bound actively and affirmatively to do all he could for the people. [It is] not only his right but his duty to do anything that the needs of the Nation demand, unless such action [is] forbidden by the Constitution or by the law."

T. ROOSEVELT, AUTOBIOGRAPHY 372 (1914).

> "The true view of the Executive function is . . . that the President can exercise no power which cannot be fairly and reasonably traced to some specific grant of power or justly implied and included within such express grant as proper and necessary to its exercise."

W. H. TAFT, OUR CHIEF MAGISTRATE AND HIS POWERS 139–40 (1925).

(4) *Are There Any Limits on the Executive's Inherent Powers?* The forces of political accommodation and the reluctance of the Court to entertain separation of powers disputes has produced a sparsity of judicial decisions interpreting the range of the

Executive's power. These decisions do, however, indicate the Court's belief that it has the constitutional authority to define and establish the limits of Executive power. If the Executive and Legislative branch are constitutionally established as equals to the Judiciary, are they obliged to follow the Court's ruling on a separation of powers issue?

YOUNGSTOWN SHEET & TUBE CO. v. SAWYER
[THE STEEL SEIZURE CASE]
343 U.S. 579 (1952)

Mr. Justice Black delivered the opinion of the Court.

We are asked to decide whether the President was acting within his constitutional power when he issued an order directing the Secretary of Commerce to take possession of and operate most of the Nation's steel mills. The mill owners argue that the President's order amounts to law-making, a legislative function which the Constitution has expressly confided to the Congress and not to the President. The Government's position is that the order was made on findings of the President that his action was necessary to avert a national catastrophe which would inevitably result from a stoppage of steel production, and that in meeting this grave emergency the President was acting within the aggregate of his constitutional powers as the Nation's Chief Executive and the Commander in Chief of the Armed Forces of the United States. The issue emerges here from the following series of events:

In the latter part of 1951, a dispute arose between the steel companies and their employees over terms and conditions that should be included in new collective bargaining agreements. Long-continued conferences failed to resolve the dispute. [The President invoked legislatively created procedures involving the Federal Mediation and Conciliation and the Federal Wage Stabilization Boards to no avail.] [O]n April 4, 1952, the [Steelworkers] Union gave notice of a nation-wide strike called to begin at 12:01 a.m. April 9. The indispensability of steel as a component of substantially all weapons and other war materials led the President to believe that the proposed work stoppage would immediately jeopardize our national defense and that governmental seizure of the steel mills was necessary in order to assure the continued availability of steel. Reciting these considerations for his action, the President, a few hours before the strike was to begin, issued Executive Order 10340. . . .

. . . [T]he next morning the President sent a message to Congress reporting his action. Twelve days later he sent a second message. Congress has taken no action.

Obeying the Secretary's orders under protest, the companies brought proceedings against him in the District Court. Their complaints charged that the seizure was not authorized by an act of Congress or by any constitutional provisions. [T]he United States asserted that a strike disrupting steel production for even a brief period would so endanger the well-being and safety of the Nation that the President had "inherent power" to do what he had done power "supported by the Constitution, by historical precedent, and by court decisions." [H]olding against the Government on all points, the District Court on April 30 issued a preliminary injunction restraining the Secretary from "continuing the seizure and possession of the plant . . . and from acting under the purported authority of Executive Order No. 10340." On the same day the Court of Appeals stayed the District Court's injunction. . . .

The President's power, if any, to issue the order must stem either from an act of Congress or from the Constitution itself. There is no statute that expressly authorizes the President to take possession of property as he did here. . . . There are two statutes which do authorize the President to take both personal and real property under certain conditions. However, the Government admits that these conditions were not met. . . .

Moreover, the use of the seizure technique to solve labor disputes in order to prevent work stoppages was not only unauthorized by any congressional enactment; prior to this controversy, Congress had refused to adopt that method of settling labor disputes. When the Taft-Hartley Act was under consideration in 1947, Congress rejected an amendment which would have authorized such governmental seizures in cases of emergency.

. . . The contention is that presidential power should be implied from the aggregate of his powers under the Constitution. Particular reliance is placed on provisions in Article II which say that "the executive Power shall be vested in a President . . .;" that "he shall take Care that the Laws be faithfully executed;" and that he "shall be Commander in Chief of the Army and Navy of the United States."

The order cannot properly be sustained as an exercise of the President's military power as Commander in Chief of the Armed Forces. The Government attempts to do so by citing a number of cases upholding broad powers in military commanders engaged in day-to-day fighting in a theater of war. Such cases need not concern us here. Even though "theater of war" [may] be an expanding concept, we cannot with faithfulness to our constitutional system hold that the Commander in Chief of the Armed Forces has the ultimate power as such to take possession of private property in order to keep labor disputes from stopping production. This is a job for the Nation's lawmakers, not for its military authorities.

Nor can the seizure order be sustained because of the several constitutional provisions that grant executive power to the President. In the framework of our Constitution, the President's power to see that the laws are faithfully executed refutes the idea that he is to be a lawmaker . . . The first section of the first article says that "All legislative Powers herein granted shall be vested in a Congress of the United States. . . ."

The power of Congress to adopt such public policies as those proclaimed by the order is beyond question. [But the] Constitution did not subject this law-making power of Congress to presidential or military supervision or control.

It is said that other Presidents without congressional authority have taken possession of private business enterprises in order to settle labor disputes. But even if this be true, Congress has not thereby lost its exclusive constitutional authority to make laws necessary and proper to carry out the powers vested by the Constitution. . . .

The Founders of this Nation entrusted the law-making power to the Congress alone in both good and bad times. . . .

The judgment of the District Court is affirmed.

MR. JUSTICE JACKSON, concurring in the judgment and opinion of the Court. . . .

Presidential powers are not fixed but fluctuate, depending upon their disjunction or conjunction with those of Congress. . . .

1. When the President acts pursuant to an express or implied authorization of Congress, his authority is at its maximum, for it includes all that he possesses in his own right plus all that Congress can delegate. In these circumstances, and in these only, may he be said (for what it may be worth) to personify the federal sovereignty. If his act is held unconstitutional under these circumstances, it usually means that the Federal Government as an undivided whole lacks power. A seizure executed by the President pursuant to an Act of Congress would be supported by the strongest of presumptions and the widest latitude of judicial interpretation, and the burden of persuasion would rest heavily upon any who might attack it.

2. When the President acts in absence of either a congressional grant or denial of authority, he can only rely upon his own independent powers, but there is a zone of twilight in which he and Congress may have concurrent authority, or in which its distribution is uncertain. Therefore, congressional inertia, indifference or quiescence

may sometimes [e]nable, if not invite, measures on independent presidential responsibility. In this area, any actual test of power is likely to depend on the imperatives of events and contemporary imponderables rather than on abstract theories of law.

3. When the President takes measures incompatible with the expressed or implied will of Congress, his power is at its lowest ebb, for then he can rely only upon his own constitutional powers minus any constitutional powers of Congress over the matter. Courts can sustain exclusive Presidential control in such a case only by disabling the Congress from acting upon the subject. Presidential claim to a power at once so conclusive and preclusive must be scrutinized with caution, for what is at stake is the equilibrium established by our constitutional system.

Into which of these classifications does this executive seizure of the steel industry fit? It is eliminated from the first by admission, for it is conceded that no congressional authorization exists for this seizure. . . .

Can it then be defended under flexible tests available to the second category? It seems clearly eliminated from that class because Congress has not left seizure of private property an open field but has covered it by three statutory policies inconsistent with this seizure. . . . None of these were invoked. In choosing a different and inconsistent way of his own, the President cannot claim that it is necessitated or invited by failure of Congress to legislate upon the occasions, grounds and methods for seizure of industrial properties.

This leaves the current seizure to be justified only by the severe tests under the third grouping, where it can be supported only by any remainder of executive power after substraction of such powers as Congress may have over the subject. In short, we can sustain the President only by holding the seizure of such strike-bound industries is within his domain and beyond control by Congress. . . .

The Solicitor General seeks the power of seizure in three clauses of the Executive Article, the first reading, "The executive Power shall be vested in a President of the United States of America."

I cannot accept the view that this clause is a grant in bulk of all conceivable executive power but regard it as an allocation to the presidential office of the generic powers thereafter stated.

The clause on which the Government next relies is that "The President shall be Commander in Chief of the Army and Navy of the United States. . . ."

[T]he Constitution expressly places in Congress, power "to raise and *support* Armies" and "to *provide* and *maintain* a Navy. . . ."

We should not use this occasion to circumscribe, much less to contract, the lawful role of the President as Commander-in-Chief. I should indulge the widest latitude of interpretation to sustain his exclusive function to command the instruments of national force, at least when turned against the outside world for the security of our society. [W]hat the power of command may include I do not try to envision, but I think it is not a military prerogative, without support of law, to seize persons or property because they are important or even essential for the military and naval establishment.

The third clause in which the Solicitor General finds seizure powers is that "he shall take Care that the Laws be faithfully executed. . . ." That authority must be matched against words of the Fifth Amendment that "No person shall be [d]eprived of life, liberty, or property, without due process of law. . . ." One gives a governmental authority that reaches so far as there is law, the other gives a private right that authority shall go no farther. These signify about all there is of the principle that ours is a government of laws, not of men, and that we submit ourselves to rulers only if under rules.

MR. JUSTICE BURTON, concurring in both the opinion and judgment of the Court. . . .

The present situation is not comparable to that of an imminent invasion or threatened attack. . . . Nor is it claimed that the current seizure is in the nature of a military command addressed by the President, as Commander-in-Chief, to a mobilized nation waging, or imminently threatened with, total war.

MR. JUSTICE CLARK, concurring in the judgment of the Court. . . .

I conclude that where Congress has laid down specific procedures to deal with the type of crisis confronting the President, he must follow those procedures in meeting the crisis; but that in the absence of such action by Congress, the President's independent power to act depends upon the gravity of the situation confronting the nation. I cannot sustain the seizure in question because here, [C]ongress had prescribed methods to be followed by the President in meeting the emergency at hand.

MR. JUSTICE DOUGLAS, concurring. . . .

[T]he seizure of the plant is a taking in the constitutional sense. [T]hough the seizure is only for a week or a month, the condemnation is complete and the United States must pay compensation for the temporary possession. . . .

The President has no power to raise revenues. That power is in the Congress by Article I, Section 8 of the Constitution. . . . The branch of government that has the power to pay compensation for a seizure is the only one able to authorize a seizure or make lawful one that the President had effected. . . .

MR. JUSTICE FRANKFURTER, concurring.

[I]n formulating legislation for dealing with industrial conflicts, Congress could not more clearly and emphatically have withheld authority than it did in 1947. [P]revious seizure legislation had subjected the powers granted to the President to restrictions of varying degrees of stringency. . . . The President could not ignore the specific limitations of prior seizure statutes. No more could he act in disregard of the limitation put upon seizure by the 1947 act. . . .

To be sure, the content of the three authorities of government is not to be derived from an abstract analysis. The areas are partly interacting, not wholly disjoint. The Constitution is a framework for government. Therefore the way the framework has consistently operated fairly establishes that it has operated according to its true nature. Deeply embedded traditional ways of conducting government cannot supplant the Constitution or legislation, but they give meaning to the words of a text or supply them. It is an inadmissibly narrow conception of American constitutional law to confine it to the words of the Constitution and to disregard the gloss which life has written upon them. In short, a systematic, unbroken, executive practice, long pursued to the knowledge of the Congress and never before questioned, engaged in by Presidents who have also sworn to uphold the Constitution, making as it were such exercise of power part of the structure of our government, may be treated as a gloss on "executive Power" vested in the President by § 1 of Art. II. . . .

The only other instances of seizures are those during the periods of the first and second World Wars. In his eleven seizures of industrial facilities, President Wilson acted, or at least purported to act, under authority granted by Congress. Thus his seizures cannot be adduced as interpretations by a President of his own powers in the absence of statute.

Down to the World War II period, then, the record is barren of instances comparable to the one before us. Of twelve seizures by President Roosevelt prior to the enactment of the War Labor Disputes Act in June, 1943, three were sanctioned by existing law, and six others were effected after Congress, on December 8, 1941, had declared the existence of a state of war. In this case, reliance on the powers that flow from declared war has been commendably disclaimed by the Solicitor General. . . . Nor do [this President's actions here] come to us sanctioned by long-continued acquiescence of Congress giving decisive weight to a construction by the Executive of its powers. . . .

MR. CHIEF JUSTICE VINSON, with whom MR. JUSTICE REED and MR. JUSTICE MINTON, join, dissenting. . . .

Those who suggest that this is a case involving extraordinary powers should be mindful that these are extraordinary times. A world not yet recovered from the devastation of World War II has been forced to face the threat of another and more terrifying global conflict. [W]e . . . assume without deciding that the courts may go behind a President's finding of fact that an emergency exists. But there is not the slightest basis for suggesting that the President's finding in this case can be undermined. . . .

Secretary of Defense Lovett swore that "a work stoppage in the steel industry will result immediately in serious curtailment of production of essential weapons and munitions of all kinds." He illustrated by showing that 84% of the national production of certain alloy steel is currently used for production of military-end items and that 35% of total production of another form of steel goes into ammunition, 80% of such ammunition now going to Korea. The Secretary of Defense stated that: "We are holding the line [in Korea] with ammunition and not with the lives of our troops. . . ."

The broad power granted by Article II to an officer on duty 365 days a year cannot, it is said, be invoked to avert disaster. Instead, the President must confine himself to sending a message to Congress recommending action. Under this messenger-boy concept of the Office, the President cannot even act to preserve legislative programs from destruction so that Congress will have something left to act upon. [U]nder this view, the gravity of the emergency and the immediacy of the threatened disaster are considered irrelevant as a matter of law.

NOTES AND QUESTIONS

(1) *Aftermath: The Court Handed Down its Decision Only Two Months after President Truman had Seized the Steel Industry.* The district court entered its injunction on April 30, 1952. Bypassing the court of appeals, the Supreme Court granted certiorari four days later and heard oral argument on May 12 and 13. The Court issued its 130-page opinion on June 2. Was the Court justified in acting on such an expedited timetable? Alternatively, why did the Court act so hastily on such an important issue?

In retrospect, the constitutional and political consequences of Truman's actions appear far more significant than the economic and military fears that had motivated the seizure. After the Court's decision, the union struck for fifty-three days. No steel shortage materialized, and the industry owners finally negotiated an agreement similar to the Wage Stabilization Board's recommendations.

(2) *Justice Jackson's Tripartite Approach: Widely Followed Opinion in the Steel Seizure Case.* Justice Jackson's opinion has proved the most influential of all those in the *Steel Seizure Case.* Consider whether Justice Jackson's three-part approach offers a more functional alternative to Justice Black's formulation. Justice Jackson's *functional* approach is generally contrasted to Justice Black's *formalistic* approach (indeed, his original intentionist analysis). Watch for the continuing competition between these approaches in subsequent decisions. Perhaps Justice Jackson's approach is less helpful given the ambiguity of Congressional intent and the vagueness of Article II's grant of Executive authority.

(3) *"It is an Inadmissibly Narrow Conception of American Constitutional Law to Confine it to the Words of the Constitution and to Disregard the Gloss Which Life has Written upon Them."* Justice Frankfurter's willingness to recognize powers which have

accrued to the presidency through time, custom, and perhaps indifference seems antithetical to Justice Black's conception that Executive power "must stem either from an act of Congress or from the Constitution itself." Is Justice Frankfurter's position more persuasive because it implicitly acknowledges the subtle shifts a system of government makes to accommodate the changing demands and concerns required by contemporary society?

(4) *Evaluating the Steel Seizure Case in Terms of the Policies Underlying the Separation of Powers Doctrine.* Was either efficiency served or tyranny averted by the *Steel Seizure Case* decision? Is this an example of a decision that should have been left to the political process rather than the Judiciary? Consider the fact that 1952 was a pivotal election year since Truman's announcement that he would not seek reelection left the Presidency wide open. Although many in the Republican-controlled Congress actually supported President Truman's action, they may have purposefully refused to take the initiative in order to further damage the image of a Democratic President. Does this stalemate further justify the involvement of the Court, or does it provide greater support for the argument that the matter should have been left alone?

(5) *Revisiting the Steel Seizure Decision.* The *Steel Seizure* decision was, on the occasion of its fiftieth anniversary, the object of renewed scholarly examination. The current wars against terrorism and in Iraq also create renewed interest in the scope of Executive power. Students can review the Symposium Issue of *Constitutional Commentary: Youngstown at Fifty*, 19 Const. Comment. 1 (2002). While all the articles are thoughtful, students will particularly benefit from Michael Stokes Paulsen, *Youngstown Goes to War*, 19 Const. Comment. 215 (2002).

[C] The President's Exercise of Quasi-Legislative Powers

INTRODUCTORY NOTE

Although the principle of separation of powers is a central element of the governmental structure envisioned by the Framers, it is modified in significant ways by the equally important concept of "checks and balances." In a system where the doctrine of separation of powers was strictly applied, the three governmental branches would be virtually autonomous, exclusively pursuing their respective legislative, executive, and judicial functions. "Checks and balances," however, suggests that the branches of government must be held accountable to each other by structural mechanisms which can permit them to restrain each other. This section will examine four of the primary ways the President can exert legislative power through the veto, pocket veto, impoundment, and line-item veto.

[1] The Presidential Veto

The Veto as an Instance of Legislative Power in the President. The most significant and direct constitutional acknowledgment of the Executive's legislative function is the President's veto power. Justice White observed that it was "obviously not considered an . . . *executive* function" by the Framers because it gives the President "an important role" in the legislative process. *Buckley v. Valeo*, 424 U.S. 1, 285 (1976) (White, J., concurring). Woodrow Wilson similarly commented that "[I]n the exercise of his power of veto, which is [h]is most formidable prerogative, the President acts not as the executive but as the third branch of the legislature." Wilson, Congressional Government 54 (1884).

The Limits of the Presidential Veto: No "Line-Item Veto." The Constitution does not allow a President selectively to exercise the veto power over particular portions of a bill. [Why not? Most governors of the states *do* have such a "line-item veto."] The presidential power to approve or veto extends to "Every Bill which shall have passed the House of Representatives and the Senate." That indicates that the approval or veto must relate to the precise form and content of the bill that passed the two Houses. Otherwise, if the President could pick and choose those portions of a bill to be either approved or vetoed, the resulting law would be fragmented; it would not represent the true form or content of the bill considered and passed by the two Houses. *See* Gressman, *Is the Item Veto Constitutional?*, 64 N.C. L. Rev. 819 (1986).

Is There any Limit on the Reasons for a Veto? Nor does the Constitution state the reasons for which a President may invoke the veto power. Is it possible to argue that the President should only be permitted to veto legislation on the grounds that it is unconstitutional? This question became a very controversial topic during the early 19th Century. President Jackson "resolved" the issue by aggressively vetoing bills that he did not like on the merits. The practice has been perpetuated by all subsequent Presidents. Is this an example of a "gloss which life has written" on the Constitution, of the kind that Justice Frankfurter described in the *Steel Seizure Case?*

[2] The (Statutory) Line-Item Veto

Congress Passes a Statute Setting Up a Line-Item Veto. Although Congress was unable to muster the necessary two-thirds votes to promulgate a constitutional amendment providing for a line-item veto, it did enact a statute that, through complex mechanisms, combines Congressional procedures and Presidential signature requirements to create the same effect as a limited line-item veto.

Is the Statutory Line-Item Veto Constitutional? If one focuses on the constitutional text alone, one can construct an argument that the statutory line-item veto did not offend its provisions. Opponents, however, see the text differently, and they emphasize functional arguments about the structure of the Constitution, such as the transfer of power from the Congress to the President that the new veto brings about. The first challenge to the line-item statute was dismissed on standing grounds. *See* Chapter 1. *See* also the separations of powers materials below.

CLINTON v. CITY OF NEW YORK
529 U.S. 417 (1998)

JUSTICE STEVENS delivered the opinion of the Court.

[As an effort to control federal spending, Congress passed the Line Item Veto Act (the Act). The Act provided that, in addition to the Presidential veto power found in the Presentment Clause of Art. I, § 7, cl. 2, the President would have the authority, *inter alia*, to "cancel" items of "new direct spending" and "any limited tax benefit." The President had to follow certain procedures, and a simple majority vote of both Houses of Congress could override any cancellation. After the Supreme Court rejected the initial challenge brought by members of Congress, *see* Chapter 1.02 above, President Clinton exercised his authority, canceling both spending and taxation provisions. One appellee, the City of New York, challenged the spending cancellation; the other appellee, the Snake River farmers cooperative, challenged the cancellation of a "tax break" provision. The District Court determined that the appellees had standing and, on the merits, that the Act violated the Presentment Clause and the Separation of Powers doctrine. The federal government sought an expedited review directly with the Supreme Court. Here, the Court affirms on the standing and Presentment Clause issues.]

IV

The Line Item Veto Act gives the President the power to "cancel in whole" three types of provisions that have been signed into law: "(1) any dollar amount of discretionary budget authority; (2) any item of new direct spending; or (3) any limited tax benefit." It is undisputed that the New York case involves an "item of new direct spending" and that the Snake River case involves a "limited tax benefit" as those terms are defined in the Act. It is also undisputed that each of those provisions had been signed into law pursuant to Article I, § 7, of the Constitution before it was canceled.

The Act requires the President to adhere to precise procedures whenever he exercises his cancellation authority. In identifying items for cancellation he must consider the legislative history, the purposes, and other relevant information about the items. He must determine, with respect to each cancellation, that it will "(i) reduce the Federal budget deficit; (ii) not impair any essential Government functions; and (iii) not harm the national interest." Moreover, he must transmit a special message to Congress notifying it of each cancellation within five calendar days (excluding Sundays) after the enactment of the canceled provision. It is undisputed that the President meticulously followed these procedures in these cases.

A cancellation takes effect upon receipt by Congress of the special message from the President. If, however, a "disapproval bill" pertaining to a special message is enacted into law, the cancellations set forth in that message become "null and void." The Act sets forth a detailed expedited procedure for the consideration of a "disapproval bill," but no such bill was passed for either of the cancellations involved in these cases. A majority vote of both Houses is sufficient to enact a disapproval bill. The Act does not grant the President the authority to cancel a disapproval bill, but he does, of course, retain his constitutional authority to veto such a bill.

[I]n both legal and practical effect, the President has amended two Acts of Congress by repealing a portion of each. "[R]epeal of statutes, no less than enactment, must conform with Art. I." *INS v. Chadha*, 462 U.S. 919, 954 (1983). There is no provision in the Constitution that authorizes the President to enact, to amend, or to repeal statutes. . . .

There are important differences between the President's "return" of a bill pursuant to Article I, § 7, and the exercise of the President's cancellation authority pursuant to the Line Item Veto Act. The constitutional return takes place before the bill becomes law; the statutory cancellation occurs after the bill becomes law. The constitutional return is of the entire bill; the statutory cancellation is of only a part. Although the Constitution expressly authorizes the President to play a role in the process of enacting statutes, it is silent on the subject of unilateral Presidential action that either repeals or amends parts of duly enacted statutes.

There are powerful reasons for construing constitutional silence on this profoundly important issue as equivalent to an express prohibition. The procedures governing the enactment of statutes set forth in the text of Article I were the product of the great debates and compromises that produced the Constitution itself. Familiar historical materials provide abundant support for the conclusion that the power to enact statutes may only "be exercised in accord with a single, finely wrought and exhaustively considered, procedure." *Chadha*, 462 U.S., at 951. Our first President understood the text of the Presentment Clause as requiring that he either "approve all the parts of a Bill, or reject it in toto." What has emerged in these cases from the President's exercise of his statutory cancellation powers, however, are truncated versions of two bills that passed both Houses of Congress. They are not the product of the "finely wrought" procedure that the Framers designed.

V

The Government advances two related arguments to support its position that despite the unambiguous provisions of the Act, cancellations do not amend or repeal properly enacted statutes in violation of the Presentment Clause. First, relying primarily on *Field v. Clark*, 143 U.S. 649 (1892), the Government contends that the cancellations were merely exercises of discretionary authority granted to the President by the Balanced Budget Act and the Taxpayer Relief Act read in light of the previously enacted Line Item Veto Act. Second, the Government submits that the substance of the authority to cancel tax and spending items "is, in practical effect, no more and no less than the power to 'decline to spend' specified sums of money, or to 'decline to implement' specified tax measures." Neither argument is persuasive. . . .

Thus, the conclusion in *Field v. Clark* that the suspensions mandated by the Tariff Act were not exercises of legislative power does not undermine our opinion that cancellations pursuant to the Line Item Veto Act are the functional equivalent of partial repeals of Acts of Congress that fail to satisfy Article I, § 7.

The Government's reliance upon other tariff and import statutes, discussed in *Field*, that contain provisions similar to the one challenged in *Field* is unavailing for the same reasons. . . .

. . . More important, when enacting the statutes discussed in *Field*, Congress itself made the decision to suspend or repeal the particular provisions at issue upon the occurrence of particular events subsequent to enactment, and it left only the determination of whether such events occurred up to the President. The Line Item Veto Act authorizes the President himself to effect the repeal of laws, for his own policy reasons, without observing the procedures set out in Article I, § 7. The fact that Congress intended such a result is of no moment. Although Congress presumably anticipated that the President might cancel some of the items in the Balanced Budget Act and in the Taxpayer Relief Act, Congress cannot alter the procedures set out in Article I, § 7, without amending the Constitution.

Neither are we persuaded by the Government's contention that the President's authority to cancel new direct spending and tax benefit items is no greater than his traditional authority to decline to spend appropriated funds. The Government has reviewed in some detail the series of statutes in which Congress has given the Executive broad discretion over the expenditure of appropriated funds. . . . In those statues, as in later years, the President was given wide discretion with respect to both the amounts to be spent and how the money would be allocated among different functions. It is argued that the Line Item Veto Act merely confers comparable discretionary authority over the expenditure of appropriated funds. The critical difference between this statute and all of its predecessors, however, is that unlike any of them, this Act gives the President the unilateral power to change the text of duly enacted statutes. Note of the Act's predecessors could even arguably have been construed to authorize such a change.

If there is to be a new procedure in which the President will play a different role in determining the final text of what may "become a law," such change must come not by legislation but through the amendment procedures set forth in Article V of the Constitution. *Cf. U.S. Term Limits, Inc. v. Thornton*, 514 U.S. 779, 837 (1995).

The judgment of the District Court is affirmed.

JUSTICE KENNEDY, concurring.

A nation cannot plunder its own treasury without putting its Constitution and its survival in peril. The statute before us, then, is of first importance, for it seems undeniable the Act will tend to restrain persistent excessive spending. Nevertheless, for the reasons given by Justice Stevens in the opinion for the Court, the statute must be found invalid. Failure of political will does not justify unconstitutional remedies.

I write to respond to my colleague Justice Breyer, who observes that the statute does not threaten the liberties of individual citizens, a point on which I disagree. The argument is related to his earlier suggestion that our role is lessened here because the two political branches are adjusting their own powers between themselves. To say the political branches have a somewhat free hand to reallocate their own authority would seem to require acceptance of two premises: first, that the public good demands it, and second, that liberty is not at risk. The former premise is inadmissible. The Constitution's structure requires a stability which transcends the convenience of the moment. The latter premise, too, is flawed. Liberty is always at stake when one or more of the branches seek to transgress the separation of powers.

Separation of powers was designed to implement a fundamental insight: concentration of power in the hands of a single branch is a threat to liberty. The Federalist states the axiom in these explicit terms: "The accumulation of all powers, legislative, executive, and judiciary, in the same hands . . . may justly be pronounced the very definition of tyranny." The Federalist No. 47, p. 301 (C. Rossiter ed., 1961). So convinced were the Framers that liberty of the person inheres in structure that at first they did not consider a Bill of Rights necessary. It was at Madison's insistence that the First Congress enacted the Bill of Rights. It would be a grave mistake, however, to think a Bill of Rights in Madison's scheme then or in sound constitutional theory now renders separation of powers of lesser importance.

In recent years, perhaps, we have come to think of liberty as defined by that word in the Fifth and Fourteenth Amendments and as illuminated by the other provisions of the Bill of Rights. The conception of liberty embraced by the Framers was not so confined. They used the principles of separation of powers and federalism to secure liberty in the fundamental political sense of the term, quite in addition to the idea of freedom from intrusive governmental acts. The idea and the promise were that when the people delegate some degree of control to a remote central authority, one branch of government ought not possess the power to shape their destiny without a sufficient check from the other two. In this vision, liberty demands limits on the ability of any one branch to influence basic political decisions. . . .

The principal object of the statute, it is true, was not to enhance the President's power to reward one group and punish another, to help one set of taxpayers and hurt another, to favor one State and ignore another. Yet these are its undeniable effects. The law establishes a new mechanism which gives the President the sole ability to hurt a group that is a visible target, in order to disfavor the group or to extract further concessions from Congress. The law is the functional equivalent of a line item veto and enhances the President's powers beyond what the Framers would have endorsed.

It is no answer, of course, to say that Congress surrendered its authority by its own hand; nor does it suffice to point out that a new statute, signed by the President or enacted over his veto, could restore to Congress the power it now seeks to relinquish. That a congressional cession of power is voluntary does not make it innocuous. The Constitution is a compact enduring for more than our time, and one Congress cannot yield up its own powers, much less those of other Congresses to follow. Abdication of responsibility is not part of the constitutional design. . . .

JUSTICE SCALIA, with whom JUSTICE O'CONNOR joins, and with whom JUSTICE BREYER joins as to Part III, concurring in part and dissenting in part.

[I]n my view, the Snake River appellees lack standing to challenge the President's cancellation of the "limited tax benefit," and the con-stitutionality of that action should not be addressed. I think the New York appellees have standing to challenge the President's cancellation of an "item of new direct spending"; I believe we have statutory authority (other than the expedited-review provision) to address that challenge; but unlike the Court I find the President's cancellation of spending items to be entirely in accord with the Constitution. . . .

[I] turn, then, to the crux of the matter: whether Congress's authorizing the President to cancel an item of spending gives him a power that our history and traditions show must reside exclusively in the Legislative Branch.

Certain Presidents have claimed Executive authority to withhold appropriated funds [to impound the funds] even absent an express conferral of discretion to do so. . . . President Nixon, the Mahatma Ghandi of all impounders, asserted at a press conference in 1973 that his "constitutional right" to impound appropriated funds was "absolutely clear." Our decision two years later in *Train v. City of New York*, 420 U.S. 35 (1975), proved him wrong, but it implicitly confirmed that Congress may confer discretion upon the executive to withhold appropriated funds, even funds appropriated for a specific purpose. . . .

JUSTICE BREYER, with whom JUSTICE O'CONNOR and JUSTICE SCALIA join as to Part III, dissenting.

II

I approach the constitutional question before us with three general considerations in mind. First, the Act represents a legislative effort to provide the President with the power to give effect to some, but not to all, of the expenditure and revenue-diminishing provisions contained in a single massive appropriations bill. And this objective is constitutionally proper. . . .

Second, the case in part requires us to focus upon the Constitution's generally phrased structural provisions, provisions that delegate all "legislative" power to Congress and vest all "executive" power in the President. *See* Part IV, *infra*. The Court, when applying these provisions, has interpreted them generously in terms of the institutional arrangements that they permit. *See, e.g., Mistretta v. United States*, 488 U.S. 361, 412 (1989) (upholding delegation of authority to Sentencing Commission to promulgate Sentencing Guidelines); . . .

Third, we need not here referee a dispute among the other two branches. . . .

These three background circumstances mean that, when one measures the literal words of the Act against the Constitution's literal commands, the fact that the Act may closely resemble a different, literally unconstitutional, arrangement is beside the point. To drive exactly 65 miles per hour on an interstate highway closely resembles an act that violates the speed limit. But it does not violate that limit, for small differences matter when the question is one of literal violation of law. No more does this Act literally violate the Constitution's words. *See* Part III, *infra*. . . .

V

In sum, I recognize that the Act before us is novel. In a sense, it skirts a constitutional edge. But that edge has to do with means, not ends. The means chosen do not amount literally to the enactment, repeal, or amendment of a law. Nor, for that matter, do they amount literally to the "line item veto" that the Act's title announces. . . . The Constitution, in my view, authorizes Congress and the President to try novel methods in this way. Consequently, with respect, I dissent.

NOTES AND QUESTIONS

(1) *The Federal Spending Crisis and the Constitutionality of the Line Item Veto Approach.* The *Clinton* Court held that the congressional effort to restrain congressional spending embodied in the Line Item Veto Act violated the Presentment Clause because it added to the Executive's role without amending the Constitution. The three "dissenting" Justices would have afforded more deference to the congressional reform effort.

(2) *The Role of the Framers' Intent.* The *Clinton* decision, like the *Thornton* decision above, appears to embody judicial review based on an assessment of the Framer's Intent. The *Clinton* majority concluded that the Framers had established a "checks and balances" mechanism where the Executive's role was confined to an all-or-nothing "veto." The dissenters either disagreed regarding the Framers Intent or would afford Congress more latitude to solve national "problems" with creative measures.

(3) *Another Concurrence by Justice Kennedy.* Justice Kennedy concurred, reasoning much as he had in his concurrences in the *Lopez* decision (plenary powers), § 2.02 above, and *Thornton* (term limits), § 3.06 above. Justice Kennedy again argued that the "structural" provisions of the Constitution serve the goal of individual liberty as much as the textually explicit provisions such as the Bill of Rights or the Fourteenth Amendment. Why would a concern for "individual liberty" be a preferrable mode of interpretation than the majority's focus, through text and history, on the Framer's Intent?

[3]   The Pocket Veto

An Absolute Veto? The Constitutional Convention explicitly refused to allow the President an absolute veto over legislation and provided that any veto could be overturned by a two-thirds vote from both Houses. Similarly, the Framers were careful to state that a Bill left unsigned by the President for ten days would automatically become law "unless the Congress by their Adjournment prevent its Return, in which Case it shall not be a Law." Art I, § 7, cl. 2. Ironically, this provision has been invoked by Presidents to permit an absolute veto under certain circumstances.

How the Pocket Veto Works. The possibility of pocket veto arises when the Executive is presented with a bill within ten days of a Congressional adjournment. If the President does not act on the bill until Congress adjourns he is thereby prevented from "return[ing]" it to Congress. As a result, the bill is effectively killed, without the possibility of a Congressional override, and must again be passed by both Houses and delivered to the President for approval.

The Limits of the Pocket Veto. The scope of this power has been explored in the few cases which interpret what type of congressional recess constitutes an adjournment. The pocket veto can unquestionably be invoked at the conclusion of each two-year Congressional session. In *The Pocket Veto Case*, 279 U.S. 655 (1929), the Supreme Court extended the reach of the veto to include the interim break between annual sessions. However, in *Wright v. United States*, 302 U.S. 583 (1938), the Court held that a three-day Senate adjournment, where an officer of the Congress had been designated to receive the bill, did not "prevent its Return" as required by the Constitution for exercising a pocket veto. (The Court suggested that a ten-day adjournment of both houses would be sufficient to give rise to a pocket-veto opportunity.)

Why Do We Need the Pocket Veto? Consider whether the pocket veto serves a constitutional purpose. In *Wright*, the Court suggested that Art I, § 7, cl. 2 served two "fundamental" purposes by ensuring that the President have a "suitable opportunity" to consider bills presented to him and that Congress likewise have sufficient time to consider Executive objections in determining whether to override a veto.

[4]   Impoundment

How Impoundment Works. In addition to the veto and pocket-veto powers, the President can also directly affect legislation through the impoundment of appropriated funds. This highly controversial power is exercised when the President delays or refuses to spend Congressionally authorized funding. Unlike the veto and pocket-veto powers, which require that an objectionable Bill be rejected in its entirety, impoundment enables the President selectively to spend and withhold funds on different provisions of a bill.

The Executive Position Supporting Impoundment. Presidents have justified impoundment as an inherent power vested in the Executive to "maintain fiscal control and to coordinate fiscal policy." *Joint Hearings on S. 373 Before an Ad Hoc Subcomm. on Impoundment of Funds of the Sen. Comm. on Government Operations and the Subcomm. on Separation of Powers of the Sen. Judiciary Comm.*, 93d Cong., 1st Sess. 839 (1973). From the Jefferson administration through the early 1960s, impoundment was used without challenge in controlling defense appropriations. Furthermore, Congress explicitly sanctioned the power of impoundment by delegating it to the President in legislation like the 1964 Civil Rights Act, whose title VI authorized the withholding of funds in an effort to fight segregation. Former Deputy Attorney General Sneed argued that impoundment was necessary to effectuate the Executive's economic policies because "The harsh reality is that time and time again Congress has passed swollen appropriation acts and failed to levy the taxes necessary to avoid inflation. [Presidents] have been forced to resort to their veto power and, ultimately, to impounding of appropriations." *Id.* at 268. Can impoundment also be justified as a "gloss" on the Constitution?

The Separation-of-Powers Problem Posed by Impoundment. During the Johnson and Nixon administrations, however, debate over the constitutionality of the power grew as the use of impoundment began to spread to social welfare programs. Rather than merely controlling spending and avoiding program deficits, impoundment was used to effectuate Executive policy priorities. Furthermore, Congress is traditionally regarded as having the "power of the purse" and the mandate to enact legislation. *See* Levison & Mills, *Impoundment: A Search for Legal Principles*, 26 U. FLA. L. REV. 191, 195 (1974). It is argued that the "power to repeal or nullify a law is a legislative power. Since impoundment in effect repeals a law, the President violates this provision when he withholds funds. . . . An appropriations act constitutes a law which the President must faithfully execute." Mikva & Hertz, *Impoundment of Funds—the Courts, the Congress and the President: A Constitutional Triangle*, 69 NW. L. REV. 335, 376–380 (1974). Constitutional support for that argument is found in the Court's statement in *Kendall v. United States*, 37 U.S. (12 Pet.) 524, 613 (1838), that "To contend that the obligation imposed on the President to see the laws faithfully executed, implies a power to forbid their execution [for whatever reason], is a novel construction of the Constitution, and entirely inadmissible." *See also* Gressman, *Take Care, Mr. President*, 64 N.C. L. REV. 381 (1986) ("the Executive's power of execution does not include a power to ignore or disobey what Congress has provided"). But could it be argued that impoundment is in fact necessary to effectuate a Congressional purpose, such as combating inflation or balancing the budget? In the 1973 Joint Hearings on impoundment, it was argued that President Nixon

> . . . was confronted in the 1973 budget with laws consisting of appropriation acts, . . . the 1946 Full Employment Act, . . . debt ceilings, [and] the Economic Stabilization Act. [H]e was looked to by Congress and certainly by the public as one having a very profound responsibility for price stability. Now when we put all that together, the problem is how best to faithfully execute the laws.

Is Impoundment Permitted Under a Steel Seizure Case Analysis? Previous exercises of the impoundment power had avoided controversy because they had either been explicitly authorized by Congress or implicitly permitted by an express constitutional grant of Executive power. Impounding defense appropriations, for example, can be justified under the President's powers as Commander-in-Chief. Under Justice Black's analysis in the *Steel Seizure Case*, this distinction is significant because it brings the Executive action within an express constitutionally delegated power. But impoundment conflicts with a congressional directive to spend the appropriated funds, bringing the exercise of the power within Justice Jackson's third category. Can a *Steel Seizure Case* argument be made in favor of impoundment?

Court Rulings. The Supreme Court has never ruled on the constitutionality of impoundment. However, in *Train v. City of New York*, 420 U.S. 35 (1975), the Court rejected President Nixon's claim that the Federal Water Pollution Control Act permitted the executive to withhold funds, as a matter of statutory construction. Similarly, the vast majority of lower court decisions have refused to allow the impoundment of funds, holding that the congressional appropriations were mandatory rather than discretionary.

The Impounding Control Act of 1974. The increasing controversy over President Nixon's broad assertion of the impoundment power culminated in the passage (over a Presidential veto) of the Congressional Budget and Impounding Control Act, 31 U.S.C. § 1301. The Act recognizes two forms of impoundment: deferral of budget authority and rescission of budgetary authority, and it prescribes separate procedures for resolving each confrontation.

Practical Effect of the Act. In practical terms, the Act has been very successful in defusing a complicated separation of powers conflict. Subsequent Presidents have uniformly adhered to the provisions of the statute. Should this "tradition" make a difference in an analysis of the statute's constitutionality?

Constitutionality of the Impoundment Act as "Structural" Legislation. Professor Tribe has described this statute, along with the 1973 War Powers Resolution [also in this Chapter, below], as "structural legislation—legislation altering processes and patterns of government decision-making—of great significance in the constitutional evolution of legislative-executive relations." L. TRIBE, AMERICAN CONSTITUTIONAL LAW 157 (1978); *see also* Dam, *The American Fiscal Constitution*, 44 U. CHI. L. REV. 271 (1977). Rather than enunciating specific policies, it attempts to regulate basic governmental processes and structures. Note that while the Act is perceived as an example of executive and legislative compromise and accommodation, it was passed over an executive veto. Is the Impoundment Act constitutional?

[D]   The Legislature's Exercise of Quasi-Executive Powers: Bicameralism and Presentment

INTRODUCTORY NOTE

The Proliferation of Administrative Agencies Decreases Congressional Control. The increasing involvement of the government in American society has required the creation of agencies to devise specific policies for carrying out broad Congressional mandates. However, once Congress delegated to the Executive the necessary authority to establish an agency, it lost primary control over the way the particular agency decided to effectuate the congressional policies.

Congress Looks to the One-House (or Two-House) "Legislative Veto" as a Solution. In order to retain some control, Congress began to insert "legislative veto" provisions in its statutes. This mechanism took a variety of forms. Depending on the particular provision, a one- or two-House resolution by the legislature enabled it to disapprove, or "veto," the proposed administrative action. This legislative veto was constitutionally vulnerable, however, because it omitted steps generally required for enactment of bills into law.

Actual Use of the Legislative Veto. By the early 1980s, about 200 Acts contained legislative veto provisions. However, from 1930 to 1982 Congress had only exercised a total of 230 vetoes. Of these, nearly half involved the deportation of aliens under the immigration and naturalization laws; roughly a quarter were exercised under the Impoundment Act; an eighth rejected some of the many internal reorganization efforts of the federal government by the President. Of the remaining thirty vetoes only some involved significant political issues like foreign relations, defense, and international commerce. The rest dealt with regulatory matters. Strauss, *Was There a Baby in the Bathwater? A Comment on the Supreme Court's Legislative Veto Decision*, 1983 DUKE L.J. 789, 790–91 (1983).

Reread U.S. Const. Art. I, § 1 (vesting all legislative power in Congress); Art. I, § 7, cl. 2 (requiring every bill to be presented to the Executive); Art. I, § 7, cl. 3 (every order, resolution or vote requiring the concurrence of both the House and Senate must be presented to Executive).

I.N.S. v. CHADHA
462 U.S. 919 (1983)

CHIEF JUSTICE BURGER delivered the opinion of the Court.

[These cases present] a challenge to the constitutionality of the provision in § 244(c)(2) of the Immigration and Nationality Act, 66 Stat. 216, as amended, 8 U.S.C. § 1254(c)(2), authorizing one House of Congress, by resolution, to invalidate the decision of the Executive Branch, pursuant to authority delegated by Congress to the Attorney General of the United States, to allow a particular deportable alien to remain in the United States.

I

Chadha is an East Indian who was born in Kenya and holds a British passport. He was lawfully admitted to the United States in 1966 on a nonimmigrant student visa. His visa expired on June 30, 1972. [A] deportation hearing was held before an Immigration Judge on January 11, 1974. Chadha conceded that he was deportable for over-staying his visa and the hearing was adjourned to enable him to file an application for suspension of deportation under § 244(a)(1) of the Act. . . .

[T]he Immigration Judge found that Chadha met the requirements of § 244(a)(1): he had resided continuously in the United States for over seven years, was of good moral character, and would suffer "extreme hardship" if deported.

Pursuant to § 244(c)(1) of the Act, the Immigration Judge suspended Chadha's deportation and a report of the suspension was transmitted to Congress. . . .

Once the Attorney General's recommendation for suspension of Chadha's deportation was conveyed to Congress, [either House of] Congress had the power under § 244(c)(2) of the Act, 8 U.S.C. § 1254(c)(2), to veto the Attorney General's determination that Chadha should not be deported [by adopting a resolution stating that it "does not favor the suspension of such deportation."]

. . . Representative Eilberg . . . introduced a resolution opposing "the granting of permanent residence in the United States to [six] aliens," including Chadha. [S]o far as the record before us shows, the House consideration of the resolution was based on Representative Eilberg's statement from the floor that

> [i]t was the feeling of the committee, after reviewing 340 cases, that the aliens contained in the resolution [Chadha and five others] did not meet these statutory requirements, particularly as it relates to hardship; and it is the opinion of the committee that their deportation should not be suspended.

The resolution was passed without debate or recorded vote. [T]he resolution was not treated as an Art. I legislative act; it was not submitted to the Senate or presented to the President for his action.

[T]he Immigration Judge reopened the deportation proceedings to implement the

House order deporting Chadha. [O]n November 8, 1976, Chadha was ordered deported pursuant to the House action. . . .

[The court of appeals struck down § 244(c)(2) as an unconstitutional infringement of the separation of powers.] [W]e now affirm. . . .

III [A]

[J]ustice White undertakes to make a case for the proposition that the one-House veto is a useful "political invention," and we need not challenge that assertion. [B]ut policy arguments supporting even useful "political inventions" are subject to the demands of the Constitution which defines powers and, with respect to this subject, sets out just how those powers are to be exercised. . . .

B

The Presentment Clauses

The records of the Constitutional Convention reveal that the requirement that all legislation be presented to the President before becoming law was uniformly accepted by the Framers. Presentment to the President and the Presidential veto were considered so imperative that the draftsmen took special pains to assure that these requirements could not be circumvented. During the final debate on Art. I, § 7, cl. 2, James Madison expressed concern that it might easily be evaded by the simple expedient of calling a proposed law a "resolution" or "vote" rather than a "bill." As a consequence, Art. I, § 7, cl. 3 was added.

The decision to provide the President with a limited and qualified power to nullify proposed legislation by veto was based on the profound conviction of the Framers that the powers conferred on Congress were the powers to be most carefully circumscribed. It is beyond doubt that lawmaking was a power to be shared by both Houses and the President. . . .

The President's role in the lawmaking process also reflects the Framers' careful efforts to check whatever propensity a particular Congress might have to enact oppressive, improvident, or ill-considered measures. The President's veto role in the legislative process was described later during public debate on ratification: . . .

". . . The primary inducement to conferring the power in question upon the Executive is, to enable him to defend himself; the secondary one is to increase the chances in favor of the community against the passing of bad laws, through haste, inadvertence, or design." The Federalist No. 73, at 458 (A. Hamilton). [T]he Presentment Clauses [also] serve the important purpose of assuring that a "national" perspective is grafted on the legislative process. . . .

C

Bicameralism

The bicameral requirement of Art. I, §§ 1, 7, was of scarcely less concern to the Framers than was the Presidential veto and indeed the two concepts are interdependent. . . .

Hamilton argued that a Congress comprised of a single House was antithetical to the very purposes of the Constitution. Were the Nation to adopt a Constitution providing for only one legislative organ, he warned:

"[W]e shall finally accumulate, in a single body, all the most important prerogatives of sovereignty, and thus entail upon our posterity one of the most execrable forms of government that human infatuation ever contrived. Thus we should create in reality that very tyranny which the adversaries of the new Constitution either are, or affect to be, solicitous to avert." The Federalist No. 22, p. 135 (H. Lodge ed. 1888). . . .

However familiar, it is useful to recall that apart from their fear that special interests could be favored at the expense of public needs, the Framers were also concerned, although not of one mind, over the apprehensions of the smaller states. . . . It need hardly be repeated here that the Great Compromise, under which one House was viewed as representing the people and the other the states, allayed the fears of both the large and small states.

We see therefore that the Framers were acutely conscious that the bicameral requirement and the Presentment Clauses would serve essential constitutional functions. The President's participation in the legislative process was to protect the Executive Branch from Congress and to protect the whole people from improvident laws. The division of the Congress into two distinctive bodies assures that the legislative power would be exercised only after opportunity for full study and debate in separate settings. . . . It emerges clearly that the prescription for legislative action in Art. I, §§ 1, 7, represents the Framers' decision that the legislative power of the Federal Government be exercised in accord with a single, finely wrought and exhaustively considered, procedure.

IV

[B]eginning with this presumption, we must nevertheless establish that the challenged action under § 244(c)(2) is of the kind to which the procedural requirements of Art. I, § 7, apply. Not every action taken by either House is subject to the bicameralism and presentment requirements of Art. I. [W]hether actions taken by either House are, in law and fact, an exercise of legislative power depends not on their form but upon "whether they contain matter which is properly to be regarded as legislative in its character and effect."

Examination of the action taken here by one House pursuant to § 244(c)(2) reveals that it was essentially legislative in purpose and effect. . . . [C]ongress has *acted* and its action has altered Chadha's status. . . .

The legislative character of the one-House veto in these cases is confirmed by the character of the congressional action it supplants. Neither the House of Representatives nor the Senate contends that, absent the veto provision in § 244(c)(2), either of them, or both of them acting together, could effectively require the Attorney General to deport an alien once the Attorney General, in the exercise of legislatively delegated authority[16] had determined the alien should remain in the United States. Without the challenged provision in § 244(c)(2), this could have been achieved, if at all, only by legislation requiring deportation.

Finally, we see that when the Framers intended to authorize either House of Congress to act alone and outside of its prescribed bicameral legislative role, they narrowly and precisely defined the procedure for such action. There are four provisions in the Constitution, explicit and unambiguous, by which one House may act alone with the unreviewable force of law, not subject to the President's veto:

(a) The House of Representatives alone was given the power to initiate impeachments. Art. I, § 2, cl. 5;

(b) The Senate alone was given the power to conduct trials following impeachment on

---

[16] Congress protests that affirming the Court of Appeals in these cases will sanction "lawmaking by the Attorney General. . . . Why is the Attorney General exempt from submitting his proposed changes in the law to the full bicameral process?". . . When the Attorney General performs his duties pursuant to § 244, he does not exercise "legislative" power. The bicameral process is not necessary as a check on the Executive's administration of the laws because his administrative activity cannot reach beyond the limits of the statute that created it—a statute duly enacted pursuant to Art. I, §§ 1, 7.

charges initiated by the House and to convict following trial. Art. I, § 3, cl. 6;

(c) The Senate alone was given final unreviewable power to approve or to disapprove Presidential appointments. Art. II, § 2, cl. 2;

(d) The Senate alone was given unreviewable power to ratify treaties negotiated by the President. Art. II, § 2, cl. 2. . . .

The veto authorized by § 244(c)(2) doubtless has been in many respects a convenient shortcut; the "sharing" with the Executive by Congress of its authority over aliens in this manner is, on its face, an appealing compromise. [B]ut it is crystal clear from the records of the Convention, contemporaneous writings and debates, that the Framers ranked other values higher than efficiency. . . .

V

We hold that the congressional veto provision in § 244(c)(2) is severable from the Act and that it is unconstitutional. Accordingly, the judgment of the Court of Appeals is

Affirmed.

JUSTICE POWELL, concurring in the judgment. . . .

[I]n my view, the case may be decided on a narrower ground. When Congress finds that a particular person does not satisfy the statutory criteria for permanent residence in this country it has assumed a judicial function in violation of the principle of separation of powers. Accordingly, I concur only in the judgment. . . .

JUSTICE WHITE, dissenting.

Today, the Court not only invalidates § 244(c)(2) of the Immigration and Nationality Act, but also sounds the death knell for nearly 200 other statutory provisions in which Congress has reserved a veto.

The prominence of the legislative veto mechanism in our contemporary political system and its importance to Congress can hardly be overstated. It has become a central means by which Congress secures the accountability of executive and independent agencies. Without the legislative veto, Congress is faced with a Hobson's choice: either to refrain from delegating the necessary authority, leaving itself with a hopeless task of writing laws with the requisite specificity to cover endless special circumstances across the entire policy landscape, or in the alternative, to abdicate its law-making function to the Executive Branch and independent agencies. [T]he device is known in every field of governmental concern: reorganization, budgets, foreign affairs, war powers, and regulation of trade, safety, energy, the environment, and the economy.

I

[D]uring the 1970s the legislative veto was important in resolving a series of major constitutional disputes between the President and Congress over claims of the President to broad impoundment, war, and national emergency powers. The key provision of the War Powers Resolution, 50 U.S.C. § 1544(c), authorizes the termination by concurrent resolution of the use of armed forces in hostilities. A similar measure resolved the problem posed by presidential claims of inherent power to impound appropriations. Congressional Budget and Impoundment Control Act of 1974, 31 U.S.C. § 1403. . . .

This history of the legislative veto also makes clear that it has not been a sword with which Congress has struck out to aggrandize itself at the expense of the other branches—the concerns of Madison and Hamilton. Rather, the veto has been a means of defense, a reservation of ultimate authority necessary if Congress is to fulfill its designated role under Art. I as the Nation's lawmaker. [T]o be sure, the President may have preferred unrestricted power, but that could be precisely why Congress thought it essential to retain a check on the exercise of delegated authority. . . .

II

[T]he Constitution does not directly authorize or prohibit the legislative veto. Thus, our task should be to determine whether the legislative veto is consistent with the purposes of Art. I and the principle of separation of powers which are reflected in the Article and throughout the Constitution. We should not find the lack of a specific constitutional authorization for the legislative veto surprising, and I would not infer disapproval of the mechanism from its absence. From the summer of 1787 to the present, the Government of the United States has become an endeavor far beyond the contemplation of the Framers. . . .

III

[T]he power to exercise a legislative veto is not the power to write new law without bicameral approval or Presidential consideration. The veto must be authorized by statute and may only negative what an Executive department or independent agency has proposed. On its face, the legislative veto no more allows one House of Congress to make law than does the Presidential veto confer such power upon the President. . . .

The rise of administrative bodies probably has been the most significant legal trend of the last century. . . . They have become a veritable fourth branch of the government, which has deranged our three-branch legal theories. . . .

NOTES AND QUESTIONS

(1) *Is There Anything Left of the Legislative Veto After Chadha?: Process Gas Consumers Group v. Consumers Energy Council, 463 U.S. 1216 (1983).* Consider whether a two-house legislative veto, or a veto over a truly independent regulatory agency, should survive after *Chadha.* In *Process Gas*, two weeks after the decision in *Chadha*, the Court summarily affirmed, per curiam, two lower court decisions invalidating legislative vetoes. Both cases involved independent regulatory agencies (the Federal Energy Regulatory Commission and the FTC) and the latter involved a two-house veto. Justice White dissented:

> I cannot agree that the legislative vetoes in these cases violate the requirements of Article I of the Constitution. Where the veto is placed as a check upon the actions of the independent regulatory agencies, the Article I analysis relied upon in *Chadha* has a particularly hollow ring. [T]hese regulations have the force of law without the President's concurrence; nor can he veto them if he disagrees with the law that they make. The President's authority to control independent agency law-making, which on a day-to-day basis is non-existent, could not be affected by the existence or exercise of the legislative veto.

(2) *Should the Court Have Ruled so Broadly in Chadha?* Justice Powell concurred narrowly on the grounds that the particular veto used in *Chadha* was adjudicatory and therefore impermissible. Is it meaningful to distinguish legislative vetoes where Congress acts in a quasi-judicial capacity? Are some types of legislative vetoes more justifiable than others? For an analysis of a related problem, *see* G. C. Smith, *From Unnecessary Surgery to Plastic Surgery: A New Approach to the Legislative Veto Severability Cases,* 24 HARV. J. ON LEGIS. 397 (1987).

(3) *How Do the Various Opinions Reflect the Justices' Views on Separation of Powers?* Justice White seems to perceive the separation of powers issue in a much more flexible manner than the majority. Since Congress and the President approved both the initial act and the denial of suspension of deportation, no separation of powers issues are implicated. Is this analysis persuasive?

In contrast, Chief Justice Burger's analysis is based on strict textual grounds. Since the decision to reverse the suspension of Chadha's deportation was "law-making," it required the consent of the Senate and the approval of the President. Is this approach convincing? Consider whether there is a persuasive argument that the veto is not "law-making" (as Justice White argues).

(4) *Are the Separation of Powers Principles Furthered or Hindered by the Court's Decision?* It is unlikely that the Framers could have envisioned the massive growth of the administrative state, and thereby executive power, in the 21st century. Can the argument be made that the legislative veto is therefore essential to maintaining the separation of powers balance created by the Framers? Perhaps the legislative veto can be justified as a necessary means to "check and balance" the "fourth branch" of government.

Furthermore, Congress possesses other means of controlling the use of its delegated authority: (a) "Sunset" legislation establishes a fixed date at which the delegated authority will expire. This enables Congress to consider how its delegated power has been used before delegating further authority; (b) "Report and wait" provisions can provide that before rules promulgated by the agency become effective Congress must have the opportunity to legislate on the subject. The Federal Rules of Civil Procedure are currently subject to such a provision; (c) Alternatively, an agency's authority can be limited to an advisory capacity, requiring a joint resolution of Congress before its actions are approved; (d) Oversight hearings also provide a means to monitor or supervise agency action; (e) Congressional control over the budget of an agency provides another means of accountability; (f) Finally, Congress can always revoke part or all of the agency's authority if it is approved by both Houses and the President. What is the relative effectiveness of these "solutions," and would any of them be unconstitutional after *Chadha*?

[E]   Congressional Delegation of Quasi-Legislative Power to "Independent Regulatory Agencies" or Officers

INTRODUCTORY NOTE

The Nondelegation Doctrine. Although the Constitution is silent on the issue of Congressional delegation of authority to the Executive, Article I, sec. 1 requires that "All legislative Powers herein granted shall be vested in a Congress." In the late 1920s, on the eve of the making of the contemporary administrative state, the Supreme Court held that a valid delegation must establish "an intelligent principle to which the person or body authorized to take action is directed to conform." Otherwise, Congress would not be retaining "all" its legislative authority. *J. W. Hampton, Jr. & Co. v. United States*, 276 U.S. 394, 409, Treas. Dec. 42706 (1928). This doctrine has also been justified on policy grounds as a means of promoting Congressional accountability, increasing predictability, and preventing the political insulation which can foster an improper or unfair exercise of power.

The Restrictive View: The Panama Refining and Schechter Cases. Aggressive delegation of authority to the Executive in the 1930s through the New Deal legislation brought on the first, and only, major assertions of the nondelegation doctrine by the Supreme Court. In *Panama Refining Co. v. Ryan*, 293 U.S. 388 (1935), the Court invalidated a provision of the National Industrial Recovery Act of 1933 (NIRA) which delegated to the Executive the authority to prohibit the interstate transportation of oil violating state mandated production quotas. The Court held that the statute did not sufficiently direct the Executive's actions and therefore impermissibly delegated legislative discretion to the President. Similarly, in *Schechter Poultry Corp. v. United States*, 295 U.S. 495 (1935), the Supreme Court rejected a statute authorizing the

Executive to promulgate a "live poultry code" which established regulations governing the sale and quality of chickens, unfair competition, and employee wage and hour limits. The Court stated:

> The Congress is not permitted to abdicate or to transfer to others the essential legislative function with which it is thus vested. . . .
>
> What is meant by "fair competition" as the term is used in the Act? Does it refer to a category established in the law, and is the authority to make codes limited accordingly? Or is it used as a convenient designation for whatever set of laws the formulators of a code for a particular trade or industry may propose and the President may approve [as] being wise and beneficent provisions for the government of the trade and industry . . . ?

The Death of the Nondelegation Doctrine. Panama Refining and *Schechter* are the only two cases in which federal statutes ever have been invalidated on nondelegation grounds. Subsequent decisions have repeatedly distinguished *Schechter* and approved a broad variety of generalized delegations. The Court has upheld statutes authorizing the Executive to promulgate regulations on vague "fair," "reasonable," and "public interest" standards.

YAKUS v. UNITED STATES, 321 U.S. 414 (1944), is typical of this modern approach towards the delegation of authority to individuals and agencies in the Executive branch. *Yakus* involved a challenge to the Emergency Price Control Act, which allowed the Office of Price Administration to fix maximum prices of commodities and rents. The Act declared the policy of preventing wartime inflation, directed the Administrator to give consideration to prevailing prices, and mandated that the prices set be "fair and equitable." The Court upheld the statute:

> The Act is unlike the National Industrial Recovery Act . . . considered in *Schechter* . . . which proclaimed in the broadest terms its purpose "to rehabilitate industry and to conserve natural resources." It prescribed no method of attaining that end save by the establishment of codes of fair competition, the nature of whose permissible provisions was left undefined. . . .
>
> The essentials of the legislative function are the determination of the legislative policy and its formulation and promulgation as a defined and binding rule of conduct—here the rule, with penal sanctions, that prices shall not be greater than those fixed by maximum price regulations which conform to standards and will tend to further the policy which Congress has established. [I]t is no objection that the determination of facts and the inferences to be drawn from them in the light of the statutory standards and declaration of policy call for the exercise of judgment, and for the formulation of subsidiary administrative policy within the prescribed statutory framework. . . . [O]nly if we could say that there is an absence of standards for the guidance of the Administrator's action, so that it would be impossible in a proper proceeding to ascertain whether the will of Congress has been obeyed, would we be justified in overriding its choice of means for effecting its declared purpose of preventing inflation.

NOTES AND QUESTIONS

(1) *Should the Nondelegation Doctrine be Revived?* Although *Schechter* has never been followed, it also has never been explicitly overruled. Consider the argument for the nondelegation doctrine by Justice Rehnquist in *Industrial Union Department v. American Petroleum Institute*, 448 U.S. 607 (1980) (Rehnquist, J., concurring):

> We ought not to shy away from our judicial duty to invalidate unconstitutional delegations of legislative authority solely out of concern that we should thereby reinvigorate discredited constitutional doctrines of the pre-New Deal era. [If] we are ever to reshoulder the burden of ensuring that Congress itself

makes the critical policy decisions, these are surely the cases in which to do it. . . .

See also American Textile Manufacturers Institute v. Donovan, 452 U.S. 490, 543–48 (1981) (Rehnquist, J., joined by Burger, C.J., dissenting on nondelegation grounds). Is Justice Rehnquist's justification for the nondelegation doctrine persuasive? *Compare* Chief Justice Rehnquist's reasoning in *Lopez* and *Morrison*, above in Chapter 2.

(2) *Introduction to Bowsher v. Synar (The "Gramm-Rudman-Hollings Case"), below.* Although the nondelegation doctrine largely has been ignored by the Court for over fifty years, the separation of powers issues underlying the legislative delegation of power remain significant. Their form, however, has changed. The *Gramm-Rudman-Hollings* case, which follows, examines the constitutionality of a statute which delegates significant responsibility to an "independent" government officer: the Comptroller General. Although the officer is nominated by the President from a list prepared by Congress, he is removable only by Congress. As in *Chadha* the issue is, once again, whether the congressional action unconstitutionally violates separation of powers principles by permitting the legislative branch to intrude too far into the Executive branch.

Read U.S. Const. Art. II, § 2 (giving executive authority to appoint "officers" with advice and consent of Senate); Art. II, § 4 (providing for removal of "officers").

BOWSHER v. SYNAR
478 U.S. 714 (1986)

CHIEF JUSTICE BURGER delivered the opinion of the Court.

The question presented by these appeals is whether the assignment by Congress to the Comptroller General of the United States of certain functions under the Balanced Budget and Emergency Deficit Control Act of 1985 violates the doctrine of separation of powers. *[handwritten:] issue*

I

On December 12, 1985, the President signed into law the Balanced Budget and Emergency Deficit Control Act of 1985, 2 U.S.C.A. § 901 *et. seq.* (Supp.1986), popularly known as the "Gramm-Rudman-Hollings Act." The purpose of the Act is to eliminate the federal budget deficit. To that end, the Act sets a "maximum deficit amount" for federal spending for each of fiscal years 1986 through 1991. The size of that maximum deficit amount progressively reduces to zero in fiscal year 1991. If in any fiscal year the federal budget deficit exceeds the maximum deficit amount by more than a specified sum, the Act requires across-the-board cuts in federal spending to reach the targeted deficit level, with half of the cuts made to defense programs and the other half made to non-defense programs. The Act exempts certain priority programs from these cuts. § 255.

These "automatic" reductions are accomplished through a rather complicated procedure, spelled out in § 251, the so-called "reporting provisions" of the Act. Each year, the Directors of the Office of Management and Budget (OMB) and the Congressional Budget Office (CBO) independently estimate the amount of the federal budget deficit for the upcoming fiscal year. . . .

The Comptroller General, after reviewing the Directors' reports, then reports his conclusions to the President. § 251(b). The President in turn must issue a "sequestration" mandating the spending reductions specified by the Comptroller General. § 252. There follows a period during which Congress may by legislation reduce spending to obviate, in whole or in part, the need for the sequestration order. If such reductions are not enacted, the sequestration order becomes effective and the spending reductions included in that order are made.

Anticipating constitutional challenge to these procedures, the Act also contains a "fallback" deficit reduction process to take effect "[i]n the event that any of the reporting procedures described in section 251 are invalidated." § 274(f). Under these provisions, the report prepared by the Directors of OMB and the CBO is submitted directly to a specially-created Temporary Joint Committee on Deficit Reduction, which must report in five days to both Houses a joint resolution setting forth the content of the Directors' report. Congress then must vote on the resolution under special rules, which render amendments out of order. If the resolution is passed and signed by the President, it then serves as the basis for a Presidential sequestration order. . . .

III

We noted recently that "[t]he Constitution sought to divide the delegated powers of the new Federal Government into three defined categories, Legislative, Executive, and Judicial." *INS v. Chadha.* The declared purpose of separating and dividing the powers of government, or course, was to "diffus[e] power the better to secure liberty." *Youngstown Sheet & Tube Co. v. Sawyer*, (Jackson, J., concurring). Justice Jackson's words echo the famous warning of Montesquieu, quoted by James Madison in The Federalist No. 47, that " 'there can be no liberty where the legislative and executive powers are united in the same person, or body of magistrates'. . . ."

The Constitution does not contemplate an active role for Congress in the supervision of officers charged with the execution of the laws it enacts. The President appoints "Officers of the United States" with the "Advice and Consent of the Senate . . ." Article II, § 2. Once the appointment has been made and confirmed, however, the Constitution explicitly provides for removal of Officers of the United States by Congress only upon impeachment by the House of Representatives and conviction by the Senate. . . .

. . . To permit the execution of the laws to be vested in an officer answerable only to Congress would, in practical terms, reserve in Congress control over the execution of the laws. . . . The structure of the Constitution does not permit Congress to execute the laws; it follows that Congress cannot grant to an officer under its control what it does not possess.

Our decision in *INS v. Chadha*, 462 U.S. 919 (1983), supports this conclusion. In *Chadha*, we struck down a one house "legislative veto" provision by which each House of Congress retained the power to reverse a decision Congress had expressly authorized the Attorney General to make. . . . To permit an officer controlled by Congress to execute the laws would be in essence, to permit a congressional veto. Congress could simply remove, or threaten to remove, an officer for executing the laws in any fashion found to be unsatisfactory to Congress. This kind of congressional control over the execution of the laws, *Chadha* makes clear, is constitutionally impermissible. . . .

[W]ith these principles in mind, we turn to consideration of whether the Comptroller General is controlled by Congress.

IV

Appellants urge that the Comptroller General performs his duties independently and is not subservient to Congress. We agree with the District Court that this contention does not bear close scrutiny. The critical factor lies in the provisions of the statute defining the Comptroller General's office relating to removability. Although the

Comptroller General is nominated by the President from a list of three individuals recommended by the Speaker of the House of Representatives and the President pro tempore of the Senate, *see* 31 U.S.C. § 703(a)(2), and confirmed by the Senate, he is removable only at the initiative of Congress. He may be removed not only by impeachment but also by Joint Resolution of Congress "at any time" resting on any one of the following bases: "(i) permanent disability; (ii) inefficiency; (iii) neglect of duty; (iv) malfeasance; or (v) a felony or conduct involving moral turpitude." 31 U.S.C. § 703(e)(1). . . .

Against this background, we see no escape from the conclusion that, because Congress [retained] removal authority over the Comptroller General, he may not be entrusted with executive powers. The remaining question is whether the Comptroller General has been assigned such powers in the Balanced Budget and Emergency Deficit Control Act of 1985.

V

The primary responsibility of the Comptroller General under the instant Act is the preparation of a "report." This report must contain detailed estimates of projected federal revenues and expenditures. The report must also specify the reductions, if any, necessary to reduce the deficit to the target for the appropriate fiscal year. The reductions must be set forth on a program-by-program basis. . . .

Appellants suggest that the duties assigned to the Comptroller General in the Act are essentially ministerial and mechanical so that their performance does not constitute "execution of the law" in a meaningful sense. On the contrary, we view these functions as plainly entailing execution of the law in constitutional terms. Interpreting a law enacted by Congress to implement the legislative mandate is the very essence of "execution" of the law. Under § 251, the Comptroller General must exercise judgment concerning facts that affect the application of the Act. He must also interpret the provisions of the Act to determine precisely what budgetary calculations are required. Decisions of that kind are typically made by officers charged with executing a statute.

The executive nature of the Comptroller General's functions under the Act is revealed in § 252(a)(3) which gives the Comptroller General the ultimate authority to determine the budget cuts to be made. Indeed, the Comptroller General commands the President himself to carry out, without the slightest variation (with exceptions not presented), the directive of the Comptroller General as to the budget reductions. . . .

. . . The judgment and order of the District Court are affirmed.

JUSTICE STEVENS, with whom JUSTICE MARSHALL joins, concurring in the judgment.

[I] agree with the Court that the "Gramm-Rudman-Hollings" Act contains a constitutional infirmity so severe that the flawed provision may not stand. I disagree with the Court, however, on the reasons why the Constitution prohibits the Comptroller General from exercising the powers assigned to him by § 251(b) and § 251(c)(2) of the Act. It is not the dormant, carefully circumscribed congressional removal power that represents the primary constitutional evil. Nor do I agree with the conclusion of both the majority and the dissent that the analysis depends on a labeling of the functions assigned to the Comptroller General as "executive powers." Rather, I am convinced that the Comptroller General must be characterized as an agent of Congress because of his longstanding statutory responsibilities; that the powers assigned to him under the Gramm-Rudman-Hollings Act require him to make policy that will bind the Nation; and that, when Congress, or a component or an agent of Congress, seeks to make policy that will bind the Nation, it must follow the procedures mandated by Article I of the Constitution—through passage by both Houses and presentment to the President.

In short, even though it is well settled that Congress may delegate legislative power to independent agencies or to the Executive, and thereby divest itself of a portion of its lawmaking power, when it elects to exercise such power itself, it may not authorize a lesser representative of the Legislative Branch to act on its behalf. It is for this reason that I believe § 251(b) and § 251(c)(2) of the Act are unconstitutional. . . .

JUSTICE WHITE, dissenting.

The Court, acting in the name of separation of powers, takes upon itself to strike down the Gramm-Rudman-Hollings Act, one of the most novel and far-reaching legislative responses to a national crisis since the New Deal. . . . I will . . . address the wisdom of the Court's willingness to interpose its distressingly formalistic view of separation of powers as a bar to the attainment of governmental objectives through the means chosen by the Congress and the President in the legislative process established by the Constitution.

I

[A]ppropriating funds is a peculiarly legislative function, and one expressly committed to Congress by Art. I, § 9, which provides that "[n]o Money shall be drawn from the Treasury, but in Consequence of Appropriations made by Law." . . . Delegating the execution of this legislation that is, the power to apply the Act's criteria and make the required calculations to an officer independent of the President's will does not deprive the President of any power that he would otherwise have or that is essential to the performance of the duties of his office. . . .

[T]he Act vesting budget-cutting authority in the Comptroller General represents Congress' judgment that the delegation of such authority to counteract ever-mounting deficits is "necessary and proper" to the exercise of the powers granted the Federal Government by the Constitution; and the President's approval of the statute signifies his unwillingness to reject the choice made by Congress. *Cf. Nixon v. Administrator of General Services* [in this Chapter, below]. Under such circumstances, the role of this Court should be limited to determining whether the Act so alters the balance of authority among the branches of government as to pose a genuine threat to the basic division between the lawmaking power and the power to execute the law. Because I see no such threat, I cannot join the Court in striking down the Act.

JUSTICE BLACKMUN, dissenting.

[I]n my view [t]he plaintiffs, now appellees, are not entitled to the relief they have requested. Appellees have not sought invalidation of the 1921 provision that authorizes Congress to remove the Comptroller General by joint resolution; indeed, it is far from clear they would have standing to request such a judgment. The only relief sought in this case is nullification of the automatic budget-reduction provisions of the Deficit Control Act. . . . Any incompatibility, I feel, should be cured by refusing to allow congressional removal—if it ever is attempted—and not by striking down the central provisions of the Deficit Control Act. . . . I cannot see the sense of invalidating legislation of this magnitude in order to preserve a cumbersome, 65-year-old removal power that has never been exercised and appears to have been all but forgotten until this litigation.

NOTES AND QUESTIONS

(1) *Commentary. Bowsher* has generated considerable commentary. *See, e.g.,* Banks & Strauss, *Bowsher v. Synar: The Emerging Judicialization of the Fisc,* 28 B.C. L. REV. 659 (1987); Gifford, *The Separation of Powers Doctrine and the Regulatory Agencies after Bowsher v. Synar,* 55 GEO. WASH. L. REV. 441 (1987); Swan, *The Political Economy of the Separation of Powers: Bowsher v. Synar,* 17 CUM. L. REV. 795 (1987).

(2) *The Cumulative Effect of Chadha and Bowsher.* Professor Elliott writes, "What is haunting about *Chadha* is the revelation that the Supreme Court has not yet

developed a theory to harmonize administrative lawmaking and the Constitution." If necessary, he adds, the law will survive the demise of the legislative veto, but "[t]here will be real trouble" if the Court "has forgotten that there is more to the Constitution than just words." Elliott, *INS v. Chadha: The Administrative Constitution, the Constitution, and the Legislative Veto*, 1983 SUP. CT. REV. 125, 176.

EUGENE GRESSMAN, SEPARATION OF POWERS: THE THIRD CIRCUIT DIMENSION
19 SETON HALL L. REV. 491, 493–94, 498, 501 (1989).*

Striking vacillations in the Court's approach to the separation doctrine occurred during the reign of Chief Justice Burger. The Court alternately swung between a literalist or simplistic approach and a functional or pragmatic approach that balances the conflicting interests of the competing branches. The literalist approach, hewing closely to the constitutional text, is an unruly child of modern theories of interpretivism. It is grounded in the belief that the three great branches of government "should be kept separate in all cases in which they were not expressly blended." On the other hand, the functional version contemplates that Congress "will integrate the dispersed powers into a workable government [and] enjoins upon [the] branches separateness but interdependence, autonomy but reciprocity."

As illustrated by its decisions in *Immigration & Naturalization Service v. Chadha* and *Bowsher v. Synar*, the Burger Court was capable of applying the separation doctrine in its most literal and formal sense. . . .

Somewhat surprisingly, the Rehnquist Court made its choice rather quickly but quite decisively. In 1988, the Court ruled in *Morrison v. Olson* [below] that [C]ongress can vest in the judicial branch the appointment of a special prosecutor to investigate and prosecute ethical indiscretions by high executive branch officials. In 1989, the Court ruled in *Mistretta v. United States* [also below] that [C]ongress can establish a Sentencing Commission, place it within the judicial branch, authorize it to establish nationwide sentencing guidelines, require designated federal judges to serve on the Commission and to share authority with non-judicial members, and empower the President to appoint the members and remove them for cause only.

What is significant about the *Morrison* and *Mistretta* rulings, apart from their near-unanimity, is their studied refusal to embrace the literalist version of the separation doctrine, so warmly endorsed earlier by the Burger Court in *Chadha* and *Bowsher*. Indeed, both *Morrison* and *Mistretta* consciously reiterate, endorse and apply the functional approach. . . .

 ## MORRISON v. OLSON
487 U.S. 654 (1988)

CHIEF JUSTICE REHNQUIST delivered the opinion of the Court.

[The 1978 Ethics in Government Act 28 U.S.C. §§ 49 and 591 granted authority to a Special Division of the United States Court of Appeals for the District of Columbia Circuit to appoint "independent counsel" to investigate and prosecute possible criminal wrongdoing by certain high executive branch officials. Section 592 of the Act provided that the Attorney General must apply to this division of the Court for appointment of an independent counsel whenever an initial investigation disclosed "reasonable grounds to believe that further investigation [was] warranted." The purpose of the enactment was to ensure that conflicts of interest within the executive branch would not compromise investigations or prosecutions of executive officers. An independent counsel could be removed only "by the personal action of the Attorney General and only for good cause,

---

physical disability, mental incapacity, or other condition that substantially impairs the performance of the independent counsel's duties."

[*Morrison v. Olson* involved a constitutional challenge, by recipients of grand jury subpoenas, to the appointment under § 592 of independent counsel Alexia Morrison, a lawyer in a private firm in Washington, D.C. The Court of Appeals, by a two-to-one vote, struck down the statute as a violation of the separation of powers principle, of the appointments clause of Article II, and of the provisions of Article III governing the authority and independence of the judiciary.

[The Supreme Court reversed and upheld the statute. First, the Court rejected the argument that the statute violated the appointments clause of Article II, § 2, cl. 2. The appointments clause provides that the President shall appoint "Officers of the United States," but that Congress may vest the appointment of "inferior Officers" in "the Courts of Law, or in the Heads of Departments." The independent counsel, according to the Court, was an "inferior" officer, because such an officer was subject to removal by a higher executive branch official (the Attorney General), had a restricted role limited to investigation and prosecution of certain crimes, had limited jurisdiction, and held office only temporarily. As an "inferior" officer, an independent counsel lawfully could be appointed by the judicial branch.

[Second, the appointment did not violate the limits on judicial power imposed by Article III, because the "inferior officers" provision in the appointments clause was a separate source of judicial power. Furthermore, the D.C. Circuit special division's exercise of the powers granted to it did not pose any threat to the impartial and independent adjudication of claims, because the members of the division, as well as the division itself, were prevented from adjudicating the exercise of an independent counsel's official duties. Finally, the Court turned to the argument that the statute violated separation of powers principles by impermissibly interfering with the functions of the executive branch.]

A

Two Terms ago we had occasion to consider whether it was consistent with the separation of powers for Congress to pass a statute that authorized a government official who is removable only by Congress to participate in what we found to be "executive powers." *Bowsher v. Synar*, 478 U.S. 714, 730 (1986). We held in *Bowsher* that "Congress cannot reserve for itself the power of removal of an officer charged with the execution of the laws except by impeachment." . . .

Unlike [*Bowsher*,] this case does not involve an attempt by Congress itself to gain a role in the removal of executive officials other than its established powers of impeachment and conviction. The Act instead puts the removal power squarely in the hands of the Executive Branch; an independent counsel may be removed from office, "only by the personal action of the Attorney General, and only for good cause." . . .

[O]ur present considered view is that the determination of whether the Constitution allows Congress to impose a "good cause"-type restriction on the President's power to remove an official cannot be made to turn on whether or not that official is classified as "purely executive." The analysis contained in our removal cases is designed not to define rigid categories of those officials who may or may not be removed at will by the President, but to ensure that Congress does not interfere with the President's exercise of the "executive power" and his constitutionally appointed duty to "take care that the laws be faithfully executed" under Article II. [T]he characterization of the agencies in [such cases as] *Humphrey's Executor* [a]s "quasi-legislative" or "quasi-judicial" in large part reflected our judgment that it was not essential to the President's proper execution of his Article II powers that these agencies be headed up by individuals who were removable at will. . . .

Considering for the moment the "good cause" removal provision in isolation from the other parts of the Act at issue in this case, we cannot say that the imposition of a "good cause" standard for removal by itself unduly trammels on executive authority. [A]s we noted above, [t]he independent counsel is an inferior officer under the Appointments Clause, with limited jurisdiction and tenure and lacking policymaking or significant administrative authority. Although the counsel exercises no small amount of discretion and judgment in deciding how to carry out her duties under the Act, we simply do not see how the President's need to control the exercise of that discretion is so central to the functioning of the Executive Branch as to require as a matter of constitutional law that the counsel be terminable at will by the President. . . .

B

The final question to be addressed is whether the Act, taken as a whole, violates the principle of separation of powers by unduly interfering with the role of the Executive Branch. . . .

We observe first that this case does not involve an attempt by Congress to increase its own powers at the expense of the Executive Branch. Unlike some of our previous cases, most recently *Bowsher v. Synar*, this case simply does not pose a "dange[r] of congressional usurpation of Executive Branch functions." [S] *ee also INS v. Chadha.* Indeed, with the exception of the power of impeachment[,] Congress retained for itself no powers of control or supervision over an independent counsel.

Similarly, we do not think that the Act works any *judicial* usurpation of properly executive functions. As should be apparent from our discussion of the Appointments Clause above, the power to appoint inferior officers such as independent counsels is not in itself an "executive" function in the constitutional sense, at least when Congress has exercised its power to vest the appointment of an inferior office in the "courts of Law." . . .

Finally, we do not think that the Act "impermissibly undermine[s]" the powers of the Executive Branch, or "disrupts the proper balance between the coordinate branches [by] prevent[ing] the Executive Branch from accomplishing its constitutionally assigned functions." It is undeniable that the Act reduces the amount of control or supervision that the Attorney General and, through him, the President exercises over the investigation and prosecution of a certain class of alleged criminal activity. . . . Nonetheless, the Act does give the Attorney General several means of supervising or controlling the prosecutorial powers that may be wielded by an independent counsel. Most importantly, the Attorney General retains the power to remove the counsel for "good cause." . . . [I]n addition, [t]he Act requires that the counsel abide by Justice Department policy unless it is not "possible" to do so. Notwithstanding the fact that the counsel is to some degree "independent" and free from Executive supervision to a greater extent than other federal prosecutors, in our view these features of the Act give the executive Branch sufficient control over the independent counsel to ensure that the President is able to perform his constitutionally assigned duties. . . .

JUSTICE SCALIA, dissenting.

The present case began when the Legislative and Executive Branches became "embroiled in a dispute concerning the scope of the congressional investigatory power," which—as is often the case with such interbranch conflicts—became quite acrimonious. In the course of oversight hearings into the administration of the Superfund by the Environmental Protection Agency (EPA), two subcommittees of the House of Representatives requested and then subpoenaed numerous internal EPA documents. The President responded by personally directing the EPA Administrator not to turn over certain of the documents, and by having the Attorney General notify the congressional subcommittees of this assertion of executive privilege. In his decision to assert executive privilege, the President was counseled by appellee Olson. . . . [T]he House's response was to pass a resolution citing the EPA Administrator, who had possession of the documents, for contempt. [T]he United States Attorney, however, a member of the Executive Branch, initially took no steps to prosecute the contempt citation. . . . After further haggling, the two Branches eventually reached an agreement giving the House subcommittees limited access to the contested documents.

Congress did not, however, leave things there. Certain Members of the House remained angered by the confrontation, particularly by the role played by the Department of Justice. Accordingly, staff counsel of the House Judiciary Committee were commissioned [t]o investigate the Justice Department's role in the controversy. That investigation lasted 2 1/2 years, and produced a 3,000-page report issued by the Committee over the vigorous dissent of all but one of its minority-party members. That report [w]as sent to the Attorney General along with a formal request that he appoint an independent counsel to investigate Mr. Olson and others.

[M]erely the political consequences (to him and the President) of seeming to break the law by refusing to do so would have been substantial. How could it not be, the public would ask, that a 3,000-page indictment drawn by our representatives over 2 1/2 years does not even establish "reasonable grounds to believe" that further investigation or prosecution is warranted with respect to at least the principal alleged culprit? But the Act establishes more than just practical compulsion. [The Attorney General] *had* a duty to comply unless he could conclude that there were "*no reasonable grounds to believe*," not that prosecution was warranted, but merely that "*further investigation*" was warranted.

Thus, by the application of this statute in the present case, Congress has effectively compelled a criminal investigation of a high-level appointee of the President in connection with his actions arising out of a bitter power dispute between the President and the Legislative Branch. . . .

The Court concedes that "[t]here is no real dispute that the functions performed by the independent counsel are 'executive' ". . . . [G]overnmental investigation and prosecution of crimes is a quintessentially executive function.

As for the [further] question, whether the statute before us deprives the President of exclusive control over that quintessentially executive activity: The Court does not, and could not possibly, assert that it does not. That is indeed the whole object of the statute. . . .

[I]t is ultimately irrelevant *how much* the statute reduces presidential control. The case is over when the Court acknowledges, as it must, that "[i]t is undeniable that the Act reduces the amount of control or supervision that the Attorney General and, through him, the President exercises over the investigation and prosecution of a certain class of alleged criminal activity. . . ."

Under our system of government, the primary check against prosecutorial abuse is a political one. The prosecutors who exercise this awesome discretion are selected and can be removed by a President, whom the people have trusted enough to elect. Moreover, when crimes are not investigated and prosecuted fairly, nonselectively, with a reasonable sense of proportion, the President pays the cost in political damage to his administration. . . . That result, of course, was precisely what the founders had in mind when they provided that all executive powers would be exercised by a *single* Chief Executive. . . .

That is the system of justice the rest of us are entitled to, but what of that select class consisting of present or former high-level executive-branch officials? [A]n independent counsel is selected, and the scope of her authority prescribed, by a panel of judges. What if they are politically partisan, as judges have been know to be, and select a prosecutor antagonistic to the administration, or even to the particular individual who has been selected for this special treatment? There is no remedy for that, not even a political one. . . . Can one image a less equitable manner of fulfilling the Executive responsibility to investigate and prosecute? . . .

[Justice Scalia also concluded that the Act violated other constitutional provisions—including the appointments clause, because he believed an independent counsel was not an "inferior" officer. Those portions of the dissent are omitted here. Note that Congress did not renew the Independent Counsel Act after the Impeachment of President Clinton.]

MISTRETTA v. UNITED STATES
488 U.S. 361 (1989)

JUSTICE BLACKMUN delivered the opinion of the Court.

[The Sentencing Reform Act of 1984 created the United States Sentencing Commission, designated it as an "independent commission in the judicial branch," and gave it authority to set binding guidelines and determinate sentences for federal criminal cases. The resulting standards consisted of ranges of sentences and guidelines for the exercise of discretion, depending on detailed factors pertaining to the defendant and the crime. The purpose of the Act was to redress a perception of serious disparity in sentencing and to remove the disadvantages of discretionary parole.

[The Act provides for the Commission to have seven voting members, who are appointed by the President with the advice and consent of the Senate and who serve six-year terms. "At least three of the members shall be Federal judges selected after considering a list of six judges recommended to the President by the Judicial Conference of the United States." The President can remove a member only for "neglect of duty or malfeasance in office."

[Petitioner Mistretta, both before and after his conviction by guilty plea for conspiracy to distribute cocaine, attacked the guidelines on the grounds (1) that Congress had delegated excessive lawmaking authority to the Commission and (2) that the Act violated the doctrine of separation of powers. In developing these arguments, he contended that the Act transgressed the grant of judicial power in Article III (a) by placing a policymaking body in the judicial branch, (b) by requiring Article III judges to serve on it and to share power with nonjudges, and (c) by subjecting them to Presidential removal for cause.

[The district court rejected these arguments. There was no court of appeals decision because the Supreme Court granted certiorari before judgment owing to the public importance of the controversy, which affected the legality of virtually every federal sentence. Here, the Court upholds the Act.]

III

Delegation of Power

Petitioner argues that in delegating the power to promulgate sentencing guidelines for every federal criminal offense to an independent Sentencing Commission, Congress has granted the Commission excessive legislative discretion in violation of the constitutionally based nondelegation doctrine. We do not agree.

The nondelegation doctrine is rooted in the principle of separation of powers that underlies our tripartite system of government. The Constitution provides that "[a]ll legislative Powers herein granted shall be vested in a Congress of the United States," U.S. Const., Art. I § 1, and we long have insisted that "the integrity and maintenance of the system of government ordained by the Constitution," mandate that Congress generally cannot delegate its legislative power to another Branch. . . . [S]o long as Congress "shall lay down by legislative act an intelligible principle to which the person or body authorized to [exercise the delegated authority] is directed to conform, such legislative action is not a forbidden delegation of legislative power."

Applying the "intelligible principle" test to congressional delegations, our jurisprudence has been driven by a practical understanding that in our increasingly complex society, replete with ever changing and more technical problems, Congress simply cannot do its job absent an ability to delegate power under broad general directives. [A]ccordingly, this Court has deemed it "constitutionally sufficient if Congress clearly delineates the general policy, the public agency which is to apply it, and the boundaries of this delegated authority. . . ."

[Here, the Court detailed the seven offense characteristics and eleven offender characteristics that Congress had required the Commission to consider, as well as specifications as to life imprisonment, repeat offenders, probation, and other aspects of sentencing. It concluded:] In other words, although Congress granted the Commission substantial discretion in formulating guidelines, in actuality it legislated a full hierarchy of punishment—from near maximum imprisonment, to substantial imprisonment, to some imprisonment, to alternatives—and stipulated the most important offense and offender characteristics to place defendants within these categories. . . .

Congress has met [the] standard here. The Act sets forth more than merely an "intelligible principle" or minimal standards. . . .

IV

Separation of Powers

[I]n applying the principle of separated powers in our jurisprudence, we have sought to give life to Madison's view of the appropriate relationship among the three coequal Branches. [S]eparation of powers, he wrote, "d[oes] not mean that these [three] departments ought to have no *partial agency* in, or no *control* over the acts of each other," but rather "that where the *whole* power of one department is exercised by the same hands which possess the whole power of another department, the fundamental principles of a free constitution, are subverted." The Federalist No. 47. . . .

In adopting this flexible understanding of separation of powers, we simply have recognized Madison's teaching that the greatest security against tyranny [l]ies not in a hermetic division between the Branches, but in a carefully crafted system of checked and balanced power within each Branch. "[T]he greatest security," wrote Madison, "against a gradual concentration of the several powers in the same department, consists in giving to those who administer each department, the necessary constitutional means, and personal motives, to resist encroachments of the others." The Federalist No. 51. . . .

It is this concern of encroachment and aggrandizement that has animated our separation-of-powers jurisprudence and aroused our vigilance against the "hydraulic pressure inherent within each of the separate Branches to exceed the outer limits of its power." . . . For example, [we have] invalidated attempts by Congress to exercise the responsibilities of other Branches or to reassign powers vested by the Constitution in either the Judicial Branch or the Executive Branch. *Bowsher v. Synar.* . . . By the same token, we have upheld statutory provisions that to some degree commingle the functions of the Branches, but that pose no danger of either aggrandizement or encroachment. *Morrison v. Olson.* . . .

[Mistretta] argues that Congress, in constituting the Commission as it did, effected an unconstitutional accumulation of power within the Judicial Branch while at the same time undermining the Judiciary's independence and integrity. Specifically, petitioner claims that in delegating to an independent agency within the Judicial Branch the power to promulgate sentencing guidelines, Congress unconstitutionally has required the Branch, and individual Article III judges, to exercise not only their judicial authority, but legislative authority—the making of sentencing policy—as well. Such rulemaking authority, petitioner contends, may be exercised by Congress, or delegated by Congress to the Executive, but may not be delegated to or exercised by the Judiciary.

At the same time, petitioner asserts, Congress unconstitutionally eroded the integrity and independence of the Judiciary by requiring Article III judges to sit on the Commission, by requiring that those judges share their rulemaking authority with non-judges, and by subjecting the Commission's members to appointment and removal by the President. . . .

A

Location of the Commission

The Sentencing Commission unquestionably is a peculiar institution within the framework of our Government. Although placed by the Act in the Judicial Branch, it is not a court and does not exercise judicial power. [O]ur constitutional principles of separated powers are not violated, however, by mere anomaly or innovation. [C]ongress' decision to create an independent rulemaking body to promulgate sentencing guidelines and to locate that body within the Judicial Branch is not unconstitutional unless Congress has vested in the Commission powers that are more appropriately performed by the other Branches or that undermine the integrity of the Judiciary.

According to express provision of Article III, the judicial power of the United States is limited to "Cases" and "Controversies." *See Muskrat v. United States.* In implementing this limited grant of power, we have refused to issue advisory opinions or to resolve disputes that are not justiciable. . . .

Nonetheless, we have recognized significant exceptions to this general rule and have approved the assumption of some nonadjudicatory activities by the Judicial Branch. [W]e have recognized the constitutionality of a "twilight area" in which the activities of the separate Branches merge. . . .

That judicial rulemaking, at least with respect to some subjects, falls within this twilight area is no longer an issue for dispute. [W]e specifically have held that Congress, in some circumstances, may confer rulemaking authority on the Judicial Branch. In *Sibbach v. Wilson & Co.*, 312 U.S. 1 (1941), we upheld a challenge to certain rules promulgated under the Rules Enabling Act of 1934 which conferred upon the Judiciary the power to promulgate Federal Rules of Civil Procedure. . . .

In light of this precedent and practice, we can discern no separation-of-powers impediment to the placement of the Sentencing Commission within the Judicial Branch. [T]he sentencing function long has been a peculiarly shared responsibility among the Branches of government. . . . Indeed, the legislative history of the Act makes clear that Congress' decision to place the Commission within the Judicial Branch reflected Congress' "strong feeling" that sentencing has been and should remain "primarily a judicial function. . . ." . . .

We agree with petitioner that the nature of the Commission's rulemaking power is not strictly analogous to this Court's rulemaking power under the enabling acts. [T]he degree of political judgment about crime and criminality exercised by the Commission and the scope of the substantive effects of its work does to some extent set its rulemaking powers apart from prior judicial rulemaking.

We do not believe, however, that the significantly political nature of the Commission's work renders unconstitutional its placement within the Judicial Branch. . . .

B

Composition of the Commission

We now turn to petitioner's claim that Congress' decision to require at least three federal judges to serve on the Commission and to require those judges to share their authority with non-judges undermines the integrity of the Judicial Branch.

[W]e find Congress' requirement of judicial service somewhat troublesome, but we do not believe that the Act impermissibly interferes with the functioning of the Judiciary.

The text of the Constitution contains no prohibition against the service of active federal judges on independent commissions such as that established by the Act. The Constitution does include an Incompatibility Clause applicable to national legislators:

> No Senator or Representative shall, during the Time for which he was elected, be appointed to any civil Office under the Authority of the United States, which shall have been created, or the Emoluments whereof shall have been increased during such time; and no Person holding any Office under the United States, shall be a Member of either House during his Continuance in Office.

U.S. Const., Art. I, § 6, cl. 2. No comparable restriction applies to judges, and we find it at least inferentially meaningful that at the Constitutional Convention two prohibitions against plural office-holding by members of the judiciary were proposed, but did not reach the floor of the Convention for a vote.

Our inferential reading that the Constitution does not prohibit Article III judges from undertaking extrajudicial duties finds support in the historical practice of the Founders after ratification. [Here, the Court gave many examples, ranging from John Marshall's simultaneous service as Secretary of State and Chief Justice to Earl Warren's simultaneous service as head of the Commission to Investigate the Assassination of President Kennedy and Chief Justice.]

This is not to suggest, of course that every kind of extrajudicial service under every circumstance necessarily accords with the Constitution. [T]he ultimate inquiry remains whether a particular extrajudicial assignment undermines the integrity of the Judicial Branch. . . .

In our view, petitioner significantly overstates the mandatory nature of Congress' directive that at least three members of the Commission shall be federal judges, as well as the effect of this service on the practical operation of the Judicial Branch. Service on the Commission by any particular judge is voluntary. The Act does not conscript judges for the Commission. No Commission member to date has been appointed without his consent. . . .

Moreover, we cannot see how the service of federal judges on the Commission will have a constitutionally significant practical effect on the operation of the Judicial Branch. We see no reason why service on the Commission should result in widespread judicial recusals. That federal judges participate in the promulgation of guidelines does not affect their or other judges' ability impartially to adjudicate sentencing issues. . . .

We are somewhat more troubled by petitioner's argument that the Judiciary's entanglement in the political work of the Commission undermines public confidence in the disinterestedness of the Judicial Branch. . . . The legitimacy of the Judicial Branch ultimately depends on its reputation for impartiality and nonpartisanship. That reputation may not be borrowed by the political Branches to cloak their work in the neutral colors of judicial action.

Although it is a judgment that is not without difficulty, we conclude that the participation of federal judges on the Sentencing Commission does not threaten, either in fact or in appearance, the impartiality of the Judicial Branch. We are drawn to this conclusion by one paramount consideration: that the Sentencing Commission is devoted exclusively to the development of rules to rationalize a process that has been and will continue to be performed exclusively by the Judicial Branch. . . .

C

Presidential Control

[T]he notion that the President's power to appoint federal judges to the Commission somehow gives him influence over the Judicial Branch or prevents, even potentially, the Judicial Branch from performing its constitutionally assigned functions is fanciful. [W]e simply cannot imagine that federal judges will comport their actions to the wishes of the President for the purpose of receiving an appointment to the Sentencing Commission.

The President's removal power over Commission members poses a similarly negligible threat to judicial independence. The Act does not, and could not under the Constitution, authorize the President to remove, or in any way diminish the status of Article III judges, as judges. . . . [C]ongress specified in the Act that the President may remove the Commission members only for good cause. [*See*] *Morrison*. . . .

V

We conclude that in creating the Sentencing Commission—an unusual hybrid in structure and authority—Congress neither delegated excessive legislative power nor upset the constitutionally mandated balance of powers among the coordinate Branches. [A]ccordingly, we hold that the Act is constitutional. . . .

JUSTICE SCALIA, dissenting.

While the products of the Sentencing Commission's labors have been given the modest name "Guidelines," they have the force and effect of laws, prescribing the sentences criminal defendants are to receive. A judge who disregards them will be reversed. I dissent from today's decision because I can find no place within our constitutional system for an agency created by Congress to exercise no governmental power other than the making of laws.

I . . .

Petitioner's most fundamental and far-reaching challenge to the Commission is that Congress' commitment of such broad policy responsibility to any institution is an unconstitutional delegation of legislative power. [E]xcept in a few areas constitutionally committed to the Executive Branch, the basic policy decisions governing society are to be made by the Legislature. Our Members of Congress could not, even if they wished, vote all power to the President and adjourn *sine die*. . . .

In short, I fully agree with the Court's rejection of petitioner's contention that the doctrine of unconstitutional delegation of legislative authority has been violated because of the lack of intelligible, congressionally prescribed standards to guide the Commission.

II

Precisely because the scope of delegation is largely uncontrollable by the courts, we must be particularly rigorous in preserving the Constitution's structural restrictions that deter excessive delegation. The major one, it seems to me, is that the power to make law cannot be exercised by anyone other than Congress, except in conjunction with the lawful exercise of executive or judicial power. . . .

[S]trictly speaking, there is *no* acceptable delegation of legislative power. As John Locke put it almost three hundred years ago, "[t]he power of the *legislative* being derived from the people by a positive voluntary grant and institution, can be no other, than what the positive grant conveyed, which being only to make laws, and not to make *legislators*, the *legislative* can have no power to transfer their authority of making laws, and place it in other hands." J. Locke, *Second Treatise of Government* 87 (R. Cox ed. 1982). [I]n the present case, however, a pure delegation of legislative power is precisely what we have before us. It is irrelevant whether the standards are adequate, because they are not standards related to the exercise of executive or judicial powers; they are, plainly and simply, standards for further legislation.

The lawmaking function of the Sentencing Commission is completely divorced from any responsibility for execution of the law or adjudication of private rights under the law. It is divorced from responsibility for execution of the law not only because the Commission is not said to be "located in the Executive Branch" ([I] doubt whether Congress can "locate" an entity within one Branch or another for constitutional purposes by merely saying so); but, more importantly, because the Commission neither exercises any executive power on its own, nor is subject to the control of the President who does. . . .

III

Today's decision follows the regrettable tendency of our recent separation-of-powers jurisprudence, *see Morrison*, to treat the Constitution as though it were no more than a generalized prescription that the functions of the Branches should not be commingled too much—how much is too much to be determined, case-by-case, by this Court. The Constitution is not that. Rather, as its name suggests, it is a prescribed structure, a framework, for the conduct of government. In designing that structure, the framers *themselves* considered how much commingling was, in the generality of things, acceptable, and set forth their conclusions in the document. . . .

NOTES AND QUESTIONS

(1) *Contrasting the Court's "Functional" Approach in Mistretta to its "Formalism" in Chadha.* In *Mistretta*, the majority looks to the actual effect of the enactment, determining that it will not in fact undermine the independence of branches that is the object of separation of powers—but Justice Scalia prefers to rely on the formal structure set up by the Constitution as he sees it. (The Independent Counsel case, *Morrison v. Olson*, presented a similar division of the Court.) But in *Chadha*, the majority relied upon a formal approach to the structure set up by the constitutional text—over the dissent of Justice White, who would have taken a functional approach emphasizing the values underlying the separation of powers. Has the Court shifted its approach from one of formalism to one of functionalism? *See generally* Gressman, *Separation of Powers: The Third Circuit Dimension*, 19 SETON HALL L. REV. 901 (1989).

(2) *The Dangers of Concentrating Power in the Judiciary: Gressman, Inherent Judicial Power and Disciplinary Due Process, 18 Seton Hall L. Rev. 541 (1989).* There is no political check, as such, to prevent an independent counsel responsible to the judiciary from accumulating a staff of ten persons, or 100, or 1,000—or from spending $100,000, or $1 million, or $10 million, in the prosecution of a single individual. In another context, Gressman notes that the courts traditionally have disciplined attorneys without the intervention of other branches—and thus they act in a legislative capacity when they promulgate codes of conduct, in an executive capacity when they initiate prosecutions, and in a judicial capacity when they adjudicate disciplinary cases:

> In political theory, the accumulation of all such governmental powers [over attorney discipline] in the hands of any group of judges is a classic violation of the separation of powers concept. . . .
>
> We need not and do not here charge that the courts' exercise of inherent power to control and regulate lawyers is an exercise in tyranny, in violation of

the separation of powers doctrine. It is enough to note that this inherent power is indeed composed of all governmental powers respecting the practice of law. In this context, courts legislate. They execute. They adjudicate. We can only trust that the courts use all these powers in a responsible fashion, eschewing the excesses that such concentration of power makes possible. The pressure toward (and difficulty of) improving attorneys' professionalism is such that there are genuine questions, according to Gressman, concerning whether the level of due process should be lowered with respect to attorney discipline. When should the potential for the excesses that Gressman identifies become a constitutional bar to the accumulation of power in the judiciary?

(3) *Separation of Powers Between Congress and the Judiciary: Miller v. French, 530 U.S. 327 (2000).* Congress passed the Prison Litigation Reform Act (PLRA). The PLRA contained a provision that created, upon application by a state, an automatic stay of certain judicial decrees concerning unconstitutional conditions in state prisons. Certain prisoners, beneficiaries of a judicial decrees, sought to enjoin the PLRA's automatic stay provision as a violation of separation of powers. The Supreme Court, per Justice O'Connor, disagreed with the prisoners. The Court held that the automatic stay provision did not encroach on Article III powers and, rather, was merely part of certain new standards established by Congress for prospective relief. Four Justices dissented, fully or in part.

§ 5.02 JUDICIAL EXERCISE OF QUASI-LEGISLATIVE POWERS

NOTES AND QUESTIONS

(1) *"Judicial Power to Tax?": Missouri v. Jenkins, 495 U.S. 33 (1990).* A federal court enters a school desegregation decree. However, tax revenues raised pursuant to state law by the local school district are inadequate to fund the remedial order. May the court order or authorize taxation inconsistent with state law? In *Jenkins*, the Court held that Fourteenth Amendment desegregation principles permit a federal court to authorize local school districts to levy increased property taxes to fund a remedial order, and that the Tenth Amendment was not thereby violated. However, said the Court, the district court should not impose the tax increase itself when the local jurisdiction is willing to do so, and when enjoining implementation of state law to the contrary would be sufficient to obtain compliance.

(2) *Judicial Power to Order the Adoption of Legislation?: Spallone v. United States, 493 U.S. 265 (1990).* May a federal district court order members of a legislative body to enact legislation, and then hold in contempt those members who refuse? In *Spallone*, the Court determined that the City of Yonkers, New York, had engaged in racial discrimination by deliberately concentrating its public and subsidized housing in one predominantly non-white quadrant. Ultimately, the city entered into a consent decree, committing the city to adopt legislation conditioning future construction of multi-family housing on the inclusion of a certain percentage of assisted units. But members of the city council, who had not been parties to the agreement, refused to vote for the legislation in question and instead, the council declared a moratorium on all public housing construction, in defiance of the district court's order. The court held the city in contempt and, in an unusual action, also adjudicated the recalcitrant council members in contempt, subjecting them to fines of $500 per day. Later, two council members switched their votes, allowing the city to comply with the court's decrees, but four council members were subjected to fines.

The Supreme Court, without defining the ultimate power of federal judges to hold legislators in contempt, reversed. It held that the district court had abused its discretion under traditional equitable principles, since it had acted without first imposing fines against the city alone and allowing a reasonable time for these fines to elicit the city's compliance.

(3) *Relationship of These Issues to Issues Raised in Chapter 1 (Judicial Power).* You should recognize the relationship between these issues and those raised in Chapter 1, concerning judicial power. These separation-of-powers cases may be distinguished on the ground that they involve affirmative acts of "quasi-legislation," as opposed to judicial review, but both problems are fundamentally related to the Madisonian dilemma of protecting minority rights while reconciling that protection with the principles of democratic governance.

§ 5.03 FOREIGN OR EXTERNAL AFFAIRS

[A] The Treaty Power

Read U.S. Const. Art. II, § 2 (the treaty power of the President, with Senate's advice and consent), Art. VI (treaties as part of the "supreme Law of the Land").

INTRODUCTORY NOTE

Federalism and the Treaty Power. Article VI of the Constitution declares that treaties are the supreme law of the land, and Article II, section 2 gives the President and Congress the right to make treaties. Treaties would therefore seem to override state or local laws.

Are There Any Constraints on the Treaty Power? In *DeGeofroy v. Riggs*, 133 U.S. 258 (1890), Justice Field stated that the treaty power does not extend "so far as to authorize what the Constitution forbids," but that the power does extend to "any matter which is properly the subject of negotiation with a foreign country." What are proper subjects for negotiation? Are there subjects which must not be regulated by treaties and are, instead, properly the subjects of state regulations?

MISSOURI v. HOLLAND
252 U.S. 416 (1920)

Mr. Justice Holmes delivered the opinion of the Court.

This is a bill in equity brought by the State of Missouri to prevent a game warden of the United States from attempting to enforce the Migratory Bird Treaty Act. . . . The ground of the bill is that the statute is an unconstitutional interference with the rights reserved to the States by the Tenth Amendment. . . .

On December 8, 1916, a treaty between the United States and Great Britain was proclaimed by the President. It recited that many species of birds in their annual migrations traversed many parts of the United States and of Canada, that they were of great value as a source of food and in destroying insects injurious to vegetation, but were in danger of extermination through lack of adequate protection. It therefore provided for specified closed seasons and protection in other forms, and agreed that the two powers would take or propose to their lawmaking bodies the necessary measures for carrying the treaty out. The above mentioned act of July 3, 1918 entitled an act to give effect to the convention, prohibited the killing, capturing or selling any of the migratory birds included in the terms of the treaty except as permitted by regulations compatible with those terms to be made by the Secretary of Agriculture. . . . It is said that a treaty cannot be valid if it infringes the Constitution, that there are limits, therefore, to the treaty-making power, and that one such limit is that what an act of Congress could not do unaided, in derogation of the powers reserved to the States, a treaty cannot do. . . .

. . . We do not mean to imply that there are no qualifications to the treaty-making power; but they must be ascertained in a different way. It is obvious that there may be matters of the sharpest exigency for the national well being that an act of Congress could not deal with but that a treaty followed by such an act could, and it is not lightly to be assumed that, in matters requiring national action, "a power which must belong to and somewhere reside in every civilized government" is not to be found. . . .

The treaty in question does not contravene any prohibitory words to be found in the Constitution. The only question is whether it is forbidden by some invisible radiation from the general terms of the Tenth Amendment. We must consider what this country has become in deciding what that amendment has reserved.

[T]he whole foundation of the State's rights is the presence within their jurisdiction of birds that yesterday had not arrived, tomorrow may be in another State and in a week a thousand miles away. If we are to be accurate we cannot put the case of the State upon higher ground than that the treaty deals with creatures that for the moment are within the state borders, that it must be carried out by officers of the United States within the same territory, and that but for the treaty the State would be free to regulate this subject itself.

As most of the laws of the United States are carried out within the States and as many of them deal with matters which in the silence of such laws the State might regulate, such general grounds are not enough to support Missouri's claim. Valid treaties of course "are as binding within the territorial limits of the States as they are elsewhere throughout the dominion of the United States. . . ."

Here a national interest of very nearly the first magnitude is involved. It can be protected only by national action in concert with that of another power. . . . We see nothing in the Constitution that compels the Government to sit by while a food supply is cut off and the protectors of our forests and our crops are destroyed. It is not sufficient to rely upon the States. . . . We are of the opinion that the treaty and statute must be upheld. . . .

NOTES AND QUESTIONS

(1) *Are there any State Laws Which Would Override a Treaty?* Consider ALI, RESTATEMENT (SECOND) FOREIGN RELATIONS LAW OF THE UNITED STATES, § 40 (1965): "An international agreement of the United States must relate to the external concerns of the nation as distinguished from matters of purely internal nature." Can a clear distinction really be made between "internal" and "external" considerations? Doesn't the treaty in *Missouri v. Holland* affect both internal affairs and our relationship with Great Britain?

(2) *Are There Other Sources of Foreign Affairs Power Besides the Treaty Power?* In *Perez v. Brownell*, 356 U.S. 44 (1958), the Court decided that Congress had the right to take away the citizenship of a native-born American because he had voted in a foreign election. The court stated that, "Although there is in the Constitution no specific grant to Congress of power to enact legislation for the effective regulation of foreign affairs, there can be no doubt of the existence of this power in the law-making organ of the Nation. [T]he States that joined together to form a single nation and to create, through the Constitution, a Federal Government to conduct the affairs of that nation must be held to have granted that Government the powers indispensable to its functioning effectively in the company of sovereign nations."

(3) *Revisiting the Treaty Power.* For further research, readers should consult Michael P. Van Alstine, *Federal Common Law In An Age of Treaties*, 89 CORNELL L.

REV. 892 (2004); Curtis A. Bradley, *The Treaty Power and American Federalism*, 97 MICH. L. REV. 390 (1998); Edward T. Swaine, *Does Federalism Constrain the Treaty Power?*, 103 COLUM. L. REV. 403 (2003).

[B]   Executive Proclamations and Agreements

INTRODUCTORY NOTE

As was seen in *Missouri v. Holland*, certain foreign affairs powers which are not specifically mentioned in the Constitution nonetheless vest in the federal government. The issue in *United States v. Curtiss-Wright*, below, is how much authority the legislature may delegate to the executive in the area of foreign affairs. The issue raises several questions. How much power does the legislature have in the area of foreign affairs? Where does this power come from? How much of the power can be constitutionally delegated to the President? Does the President's authority in foreign affairs come from Congress, the Constitution, or both?

UNITED STATES v. CURTISS-WRIGHT EXPORT CORP.
299 U.S. 304 (1936)

MR. JUSTICE SUTHERLAND delivered the opinion of the Court.

On January 27, 1936, an indictment was returned in the court below, the first count of which charges that appellees . . . conspired to sell in the United States certain arms of war, namely, fifteen machine guns, to Bolivia . . . in violation of the Joint Resolution of Congress approved May 28, 1934, and the provisions of a proclamation issued on the same day by the President of the United States pursuant to authority conferred by section 1 of the resolution. . . .

[T]he Joint Resolution follows: *"Resolved by the Senate and House of Representatives of the United States of America in Congress assembled*, That if the President finds that the prohibition of the sale of arms and munitions of war in the United States to those countries now engaged in armed conflict in the Chaco may contribute to the reestablishment of peace between those countries, and if . . . he makes proclamation to that effect, it shall be unlawful to sell, except under such limitations and exceptions as the President prescribes, any arms or munitions of war in any place in the United States to the countries now engaged in that armed conflict. . . .

"Sec. 2. Whoever sells any arms or munitions of war in violation of section 1 shall, on conviction, be punished by a fine not exceeding $10,000 or by imprisonment not exceeding two years, or both."

[The defendant, Curtiss-Wright, argues] that the Joint Resolution effects an invalid delegation of legislative power to the executive. . . .

Whether, if the Joint Resolution had related solely to internal affairs, it would be open to the challenge that it constituted an unlawful delegation of legislative power to the Executive, we find it unnecessary to determine. The whole aim of the resolution is to affect a situation entirely external to the United States, and falling within the category of foreign affairs. . . .

The two classes of powers are different, both in respect of their origin and their nature. The broad statement that the federal government can exercise no powers except those specifically enumerated in the Constitution, and such implied powers as are necessary and proper to carry into effect the enumerated powers, is categorically true only in respect of our internal affairs. . . . [S]ince the states severally never possessed international powers, such powers could not have been carved from the mass of state powers but obviously were transmitted to the United States from some other source.

The Union existed before the Constitution, which was ordained and established among other things to form "a more perfect Union." [T]he Framers' Convention was called and exerted its powers upon the irrefutable postulate that though the states were several their people in respect of foreign affairs were one.

It results that the investment of the federal government with the powers of external sovereignty did not depend upon the affirmative grants of the Constitution. The powers to declare and wage war, to conclude peace, to make treaties, to maintain diplomatic relations with other sovereignties, if they had never been mentioned in the Constitution, would have vested in the federal government as necessary concomitants of nationality.

[I]n this vast external realm, with its important, complicated, delicate and manifold problems, the President alone has the power to speak or listen as a representative of the nation. He *makes* treaties with the advice and consent of the Senate; but he alone negotiates. Into the field of negotiation the Senate cannot intrude; and Congress itself is powerless to invade it. As Marshall said in his great argument of March 7, 1800, in the House of Representatives, "The President is the sole organ of the nation in its external relations, and its sole representative with foreign nations."

[I]t is quite apparent that if, in the maintenance of our international relations, embarrassment—perhaps serious embarrassment—is to be avoided and success for our aims achieved, congressional legislation which is to be made effective through negotiation and inquiry within the international field must often accord to the President a degree of discretion and freedom from statutory restriction which would not be admissible were domestic affairs alone involved. Moreover, he, not Congress, has the better opportunity of knowing the conditions which prevail in foreign countries, and especially is this true in time of war. . . .

reas.

NOTES AND QUESTIONS

(1) *Justice Sutherland's Statement that the President's Authority to Issue the Proclamation in Question Stems from Both the Congressional Resolution and the Constitution.* If the power comes from the Constitution, wouldn't the President be able to exercise it even if Congress were silent? What if Congress had disapproved the President's Proclamation in *Curtiss-Wright?*

(2) *The Court's View of the Executive Power in Foreign Affairs as Particularly Large.* Consider the Court's statement that the President is "the sole organ of the federal government" in the foreign affairs field. What are the constitutional limits on the President's power to act in foreign affairs? Are there any congressional limits on the President's power? Reconsider *Youngstown,* above. This question will be considered further in the context of the War Powers Resolution, below. For an excellent analysis of related issues, *see* Paust, *Is the President Bound by the Supreme Law of the Land?—Foreign Affairs and National Security Reexamined,* 9 HASTINGS CONST. L.Q. 719 (1982).

[C] Executive Agreements Based on Unclear Congressional Authority

INTRODUCTORY NOTE

Curtiss-Wright dealt with a case of specific congressional authorization of a President's actions. When congressional authorization is not as clear, what powers does the President have? *Dames & Moore v. Regan* deals with President Carter's settlement agreement with Iran for the release of U.S. hostages. Does the power to make such agreements lie within the Executive, or must Congress approve?

DAMES & MOORE v. REGAN

453 U.S. 654 (1981)

JUSTICE REHNQUIST delivered the opinion of the court.

I

On November 4, 1979, the American Embassy in Tehran was seized and our diplomatic personnel were captured and held hostage. In response to that crisis, President Carter, acting pursuant to the International Emergency Economic Powers Act, 50 U.S.C. §§ 1701–1706 (1976 ed., Supp. III) (hereinafter IEEPA), declared a national emergency on November 14, 1979, and blocked the removal or transfer of "all property and interests in property of the Government of Iran, its instrumentalities and controlled entities and the Central Bank of Iran which are or become subject to the jurisdiction of the United States. . . ."

On December 19, 1979, petitioner Dames & Moore filed suit in the United States . . . against the Government of Iran, the Atomic Energy Organization of Iran, and a number of Iranian banks. In its complaint, petitioner alleged that its wholly owned subsidiary, Dames & Moore International, S. R. L., was a party to a written contract with the Atomic Energy Organization, and that the subsidiary's entire interest in the contract had been assigned to petitioner. [P]etitioner contended [that] it was owed $3,436,694.30 plus interest for services performed under the contract prior to the date of termination. The District Court issued orders of attachment directed against property of the defendants. . . .

On January 20, 1981, the Americans held hostage were released by Iran pursuant to an Agreement entered into the day before. . . . The Agreement stated that "[i]t is the purpose of [the United States and Iran] . . . to terminate all litigation as between the Government of each party and the nationals of the other, and to bring about the settlement and termination of all such claims through binding arbitration." In furtherance of this goal, the Agreement called for the establishment of an Iran-United States Claims Tribunal which would arbitrate any claims not settled within six months. [U]nder the Agreement, the United States is obligated "to terminate all legal proceedings in United States courts involving claims of United States persons and institutions against Iran and its state enterprises, to nullify all attachments and judgments obtained therein, to prohibit all further litigation based on such claims, and to bring about the termination of such claims through binding arbitration. . . ."

On January 19, 1981, President Carter issued a series of Executive Orders implementing the terms of the agreement. . . .

Meanwhile, [p]etitioner moved for summary judgment in the District Court against the Government of Iran and the Atomic Energy Organization, but not against the Iranian banks. The District Court granted petitioner's motion and awarded petitioner the amount claimed under the contract plus interest. Thereafter, petitioner attempted to execute the judgment by obtaining writs of garnishment and execution in state court in the State of Washington, and a sheriff's sale of Iranian property in Washington was noticed to satisfy the judgment. However, . . . the District Court stayed execution of its judgment pending appeal by the Government of Iran and the Atomic Energy Organization. The District Court also ordered that all prejudgment attachments obtained against the Iranian defendants be vacated and that further proceedings against the bank defendants be stayed in light of the Executive Orders discussed above.

On April 28, 1981, petitioner filed this action in the District Court for declaratory and injunctive relief against the United States and the Secretary of the Treasury, seeking to prevent enforcement of the Executive Orders and Treasury Department regulations implementing the Agreement with Iran. In its complaint, petitioner alleged that the actions of the President and the Secretary of the Treasury [w]ere unconstitutional. . . .

II

The parties and the lower courts have all agreed that much relevant analysis is contained in *Youngstown Sheet & Tube Co. v. Sawyer*.

[W]e have in the past found and do today find Justice Jackson's classification of executive actions into three general categories analytically useful. . . . [However,] Justice Jackson himself recognized that his three categories represented "a somewhat over-simplified grouping," and it is doubtless the case that executive action in any particular instance falls, not neatly in one of three pigeonholes, but rather at some point along a spectrum running from explicit congressional authorization to explicit congressional prohibition. . . .

IV

Although we have concluded that the IEEPA constitutes specific congressional authorization to the President to nullify the attachments and order the transfer of Iranian assets, there remains the question of the President's authority to suspend claims pending in American courts. [I]n terminating these claims through Executive Order No. 12294 the President purported to act under authority of both the IEEPA and 22 U.S.C. § 1732, the so-called "Hostage Act". . . .

Concluding that neither the IEEPA nor the Hostage Act constitutes specific authorization of the President's action suspending claims, however, is not to say that these statutory provisions are entirely irrelevant to the question of the validity of the President's action. We think both statutes highly relevant in the looser sense of indicating congressional acceptance of a broad scope for executive action in circumstances such as those presented in this case. [T]he IEEPA delegates broad authority to the President to act in times of national emergency with respect to property of a foreign country. The Hostage Act similarly indicates congressional willingness that the President have broad discretion when responding to the hostile acts of foreign sovereigns. . . .

[C]ongress cannot anticipate and legislate with regard to every possible action the President may find it necessary to take or every possible situation in which he might act. [T]he enactment of legislation closely related to the question of the President's authority in a particular case which evinces legislative intent to accord the President broad discretion may be considered to "invite" "measures on independent presidential responsibility," *Youngstown* (Jackson, J., concurring). At least this is so where there is no contrary indication of legislative intent and when, as here, there is a history of congressional acquiescence in conduct of the sort engaged in by the President. It is to that history which we now turn.

Not infrequently in affairs between nations, outstanding claims by nationals of one country against the government of another country are "sources of friction" between the two sovereigns. *United States v. Pink*, 315 U.S. 203, 225 (1942). To resolve these difficulties, nations have often entered into agreements settling the claims of their respective nationals. As one treatise writer puts it, international agreements settling claims by nationals of one state against the government of another "are established international practice reflecting traditional international theory." L. Henkin, *Foreign Affairs and the Constitution* 262 (1972). [T]here has also been a longstanding practice of settling such claims by executive agreement without the advice and consent of the Senate. . . .

Crucial to our decision today is the conclusion that Congress has implicitly approved the practice of claim settlement by executive agreement. This is best demonstrated by Congress' enactment of the International Claims Settlement Act of 1949 [which provided] a procedure whereby funds resulting from future settlements could be distributed. To achieve these ends Congress created the [F]oreign Claims Settlement Commission, and gave it jurisdiction to make final and binding decisions with respect to claims by United States nationals against settlement funds. . . .

In addition to congressional acquiescence in the President's power to settle claims, prior cases of this Court have also recognized that the President does have some measure of power to enter into executive agreements without obtaining the advice and consent of the Senate. In *United States v. Pink*, 315 U.S. 203 (1942), for example, the Court upheld the validity of the Litvinov Assignment, which was part of an Executive Agreement whereby the Soviet Union assigned to the United States amounts owed to it by American nationals so that outstanding claims of other American nationals could be paid. . . .

In light of all the foregoing—the inferences to be drawn from the character of the legislation Congress has enacted in the area, such as the IEEPA and the Hostage Act, and from the history of acquiescence in executive claims settlement—we conclude that the President was authorized to suspend pending claims pursuant to Executive Order No. 12294. As Justice Frankfurter pointed out in *Youngstown*, "a systematic, unbroken, executive practice, long pursued to the knowledge of the Congress and never before questioned . . . may be treated as a gloss on "Executive Power' vested in the President by § 1 of Art. II. . . ."

The judgment of the District Court is accordingly affirmed. . . .

NOTES AND QUESTIONS

(1) *Did the Court Evade the Separation of Powers Doctrine in Dames & Moore?* Consider the following: "Under a conventional separation-of-powers analysis, the President would have to justify his actions either by an express delegation from Congress or by his own independent, plenary powers. The Court, however, failed to find either an express delegation or a plenary power to settle or suspend claims. In order to justify the claims suspension, the Court put forth a novel doctrine of implied congressional consent." *The Supreme Court, 1980 Term*, 95 HARV. L. REV. 93, 194 (1981). Did the Court indeed apply a faulty analysis? Note that Justice Rehnquist, once a clerk to Justice Jackson, declined to apply the Jackson three-part test and used, instead, Justice Frankfurter's "historical gloss" theory of separation of powers.

(2) *The Realpolitik of the Decision.* Professor Arthur S. Miller has suggested that the Court's decision in *Dames & Moore* was baldly political, forced on the Court by the popularity of President Carter's settlement:

> To understand the Supreme Court's decision in *Dames & Moore v. Regan*, one should perceive at the outset that it is basically a compromise between harsh international reality and abstract constitutional norms. Although crafted in familiar lawyers' language, Justice William H. Rehnquist's opinion for the Court reeks with the odor of compromise forced by necessity. Principle, as usual, gave way to realpolitik.

Miller, *Dames & Moore v. Regan: A Political Decision by a Political Court*, 29 UCLA L. REV. 1104, 1127 (1982). Is the *Dames & Moore* decision "political?" If so, consider what it is that is wrong with using politics to decide cases. Was the Court so concerned with public opinion that it did not reach a reasoned decision?

[D] The Limits of Executive Power

MEDELLÍN v. TEXAS, 128 S. Ct. 1346 (2008). The International Court of Justice, which resolves disputes between members of the United Nations, ruled, in a dispute brought by Mexico against the United States, that 51 Mexican nationals were entitled to reconsideration of their state court convictions due to the states' failure to inform them of their consular rights. This reconsideration, according to the ICJ, was required irrespective of procedural rules requiring timely preservation of complaints. After the ICJ's ruling, President George W. Bush issued a Memorandum that the United States would comply by "having State courts give effect to the decision." Despite the ICJ decision and the Presidential Memorandum, the Texas Court of Criminal Appeals dismissed the application for writ of habeas corpus filed by one of these Mexican nationals, Medellín, because he did not timely raise his complaint. The Supreme Court granted certiorari to address whether Texas had to reconsider Medellín's claim.

The Court, per Chief Justice Roberts, held that neither the ICJ ruling nor the Presidential Memorandum was directly enforceable federal law. First, despite the fact that the ICJ ruling was an international law obligation of the United States, nothing in the relevant treaties, according to the Court, suggested that the decision was automatically binding in state courts. Because the treaties thus were not self-executing and Congress had not enacted an implementation statute, Texas was not bound by the ICJ's judgment.

The Court next considered whether the Presidential Memorandum was enforceable federal law. While recognizing the compelling international concerns supporting the President's action, the Court reasoned that such concerns did not allow the disregard of "first principles" requiring all executive actions to "'stem either from an act of Congress or from the Constitution itself.'" Employing Justice Jackson's tripartite scheme from the *Steel Seizure Cases*, above, the Court held that the President was within the third zone in attempting to implement a non-self-executing treaty:

> [T]he Constitution . . . divides the treaty-making power between the President and the Senate. . . . If the Executive determines that a treaty should have domestic effect of its own force, that determination may be implemented "in mak[ing]" the treaty, by ensuring that it contains language providing for domestic enforceability [and by obtaining] the Senate['s] requisite two-thirds vote. . . . [However,] the terms of a non-self-executing treaty can become domestic law only in the same way as any other law—through passage of legislation . . . . When the President asserts the power to "enforce" a non-self-executing treaty by unilaterally creating domestic law, he acts in conflict with the implicit understanding of the ratifying Senate. His assertion of authority . . . is therefore within Justice Jackson's third category, . . .

Because his authority fell within the third zone, the Court concluded that any claimed Congressional "acquiescence" was irrelevant (although the Court did not believe that Congress had acquiesced in any event).

The Court also rejected the President's claim that his authority to settle foreign claims under executive agreements, as discussed in *Dames & Moore*, above, authorized the Presidential Memorandum:

> The claims-settlement cases involve a narrow set of circumstances: the making of executive agreements to settle civil claims between American citizens and foreign governments or foreign nationals. They are based on the view that "a systematic, unbroken, executive practice, long pursued to the knowledge of the Congress and never before questioned," can "raise a presumption that the [action] had been [taken] in pursuance of its consent." . . .
>
> The President's Memorandum is not supported by a "particularly longstanding practice" of congressional acquiescence, . . . Indeed the Government has not identified a single instance in which the President has attempted (or Congress has acquiesced in) a Presidential directive issued to state courts,. . . The Executive's narrow and strictly limited authority to settle international claims disputes pursuant to an executive agreement cannot stretch so far as to support the current Presidential Memorandum.

Justice Stevens concurred, urging that, although the Court reached the right conclusion on a difficult issue, Texas should protect "the honor and integrity of the Nation" by voluntarily complying with the ICJ ruling. Justice Breyer, joined by Justices Souter and Ginsburg, dissented, arguing that the ICJ judgment was enforceable in state courts under the relevant treaties.

What should the President have done to ensure compliance with the ICJ ruling and keep the United States from breaching its international law obligations? Should he have requested Congress to enact implementing legislation? Were there ways he could have "encouraged" Texas to comply without attempting to mandate compliance? Should the Executive be "the sole organ of the federal government" in matters of foreign affairs, or is it appropriate to divide authority between the Executive and Congress, and sometimes between the federal government and the states, as indicated in *Medellín*?

§ 5.04   THE WAR AND MILITARY POWERS AND THE COMMANDER-IN-CHIEF

[A]   The Extent of the War Power

Reread U.S. Const. Art. I, § 8, cls. 11–16; Art. II, § 1, cl. 1; Art. II, § 2, cl. 1 (war and military powers; executive power; commander-in-chief clause).

WOODS v. CLOYD W. MILLER CO., 333 U.S. 138 (1948). After the end of World War II, Congress passed the Housing and Rent Act of 1947, which continued rent controls initially imposed during World War II. A landlord who increased his rents beyond those allowed challenged the law on the ground that, because the war had ended, Congress did not have power under the War Power to pass the statute. Justice Douglas, writing for the Court, disagreed:

> [T]he war power includes the power "to remedy the evils which have arisen from its rise and progress" and continues for the duration of that emergency. Whatever may be the consequences when war is officially terminated, the war power does not necessarily end with the cessation of hostilities. . . .
>
> The legislative history of the present Act makes abundantly clear that there has not yet been eliminated the deficit in housing which in considerable measure was caused by the heavy demobilization of veterans and by the cessation or reduction in residential construction during the period of hostilities due to the allocation of building materials to military projects. Since the war effort contributed heavily to that deficit, Congress has the power even after the cessation of hostilities to act to control the forces that a short supply of the needed article created. If that were not true, the Necessary and Proper Clause, Art. I, § 8, cl. 18, would be drastically limited in its application to the several war powers.

Woods shows that domestic regulations are permitted under Congress' war power and that the regulations need not end when hostilities are terminated. The *Woods* court also conceded that these wide-ranging powers could lead to a usurpation of states' rights under the Ninth and Tenth Amendments. What are the limits on Congress' use of the war powers to regulate the domestic economy during wartime? In peacetime? The *Woods* court suggests that there are limits on the use of war powers once hostilities have ceased—based upon the length of time since fighting ended and the relationship between the war and the regulation.

[B]   Separation of Powers and the War Power

INTRODUCTION TO THE WAR POWERS RESOLUTION

Expanded Executive Power in the War and Military Areas. Article I of the Constitution gives the legislative branch the power to declare war. Article II names the

President Commander-in-Chief of the armed forces. How should the power to engage in armed conflict be divided between the two branches? In the twentieth century, the Executive became the dominant force in waging war. The Executive committed American troops to the Vietnam War for over a decade in the 1960s and 1970s without Congress ever declaring war.

The War Powers Resolution. Congress feared that the President was usurping legislative war powers, and in 1973 it passed the War Powers Resolution over President Nixon's veto. Proponents hailed the Resolution as a return to the Constitutional notion of checks and balances in the area of war powers. Critics called the Resolution an unconstitutional encroachment on the Executive's legitimate powers which would weaken American foreign policy.

THE WAR POWERS RESOLUTION

§ 2. Purpose and Policy

(a) Congressional declaration

It is the purpose of this chapter to fulfill the intent of the framers of the Constitution of the United States and insure that the collective judgment of both the Congress and the President will apply to the introduction of United States Armed Forces into hostilities, or into situations where imminent involvement in hostilities is clearly indicated by the circumstances, and to the continued use of such forces in hostilities or in such situations. . . .

(c) Presidential executive power as Commander-in-Chief; limitation

The constitutional powers of the President as Commander-in-Chief to introduce United States Armed Forces into hostilities, or into situations where imminent involvement in hostilities is clearly indicated by the circumstances, are exercised only pursuant to (1) a declaration of war, (2) specific statutory authorization, or (3) a national emergency created by attack upon the United States, its territories or possessions, or its armed forces.

§ 3. Consultation; initial and regular consultations

The President in every possible instance shall consult with Congress before introducing United States Armed Forces into hostilities or into situations where imminent involvement in hostilities is clearly indicated by the circumstances, and after every such introduction shall consult regularly with the Congress until United States Armed Forces are no longer engaged in hostilities or have been removed from such situations.

§ 4. Reporting requirement

(a) Written report; time of submission; circumstances necessitating submission; information reported

In the absence of a declaration of war, in any case in which United States Armed Forces are introduced to [into imminent hostilities], the President shall submit within 48 hours to the Speaker of the House of Representatives and to the President pro tempore of the Senate a report, in writing, setting forth to [information required by this section]. . . .

[Section (c) of this provision requires periodic reports to Congress, no less often than once every six months]

§ 5. Congressional action . . .

(b) Termination of use of United States Armed Forces; exceptions; extension period

Within sixty calendar days after a report is submitted or is required to be submitted pursuant to section 1543(a)(1) of this title, whichever is earlier, the President shall terminate any use of United States Armed Forces with respect to which such report was submitted (or required to be submitted), unless the Congress (1) has declared war or has enacted a specific authorization for such use of United States Armed Forces, (2) has extended by law such sixty-day period, or (3) is physically unable to meet as a result of an armed attack upon the United States. Such sixty-day period shall be extended for not more than an additional thirty days if the President determines and certifies to the Congress in writing that unavoidable military necessity respecting the safety of United States Armed Forces requires the continued use of such armed forces in the course of bringing about a prompt removal of such forces.

(c) Concurrent resolution for removal by President of United States Armed Forces

Notwithstanding subsection (b) of this section, at any time that United States Armed Forces are engaged in hostilities outside the territory of the United States, its possessions and territories without a declaration of war or specific statutory authorization, such forces shall be removed by the President if the Congress so directs by concurrent resolution. . . .

§ 8. Interpretation of joint resolution

(a) Inferences from any law or treaty

Authority to introduce United States Armed Forces into hostilities or into situations wherein involvement in hostilities is clearly indicated by the circumstances shall not be inferred—

> (1) from any provision of law (whether or not in effect before November 7, 1973), including any provision contained in any appropriation Act, unless such provision specifically authorizes the introduction of United States Armed Forces into hostilities or into such situations and states that it is intended to constitute specific statutory authorization within the meaning of this chapter; or

> (2) from any treaty heretofore or hereafter ratified unless such treaty is implemented by legislation specifically authorizing the introduction of United States Armed Forces into hostilities or into such situations and stating that it is intended to constitute specific statutory authorization within the meaning of this chapter. . . .

(d) Constitutional authorities or existing treaties unaffected; construction against grant of Presidential authority respecting use of United States Armed Forces

Nothing in this chapter—

> (1) is intended to alter the constitutional authority of the Congress or of the President, or the provisions of existing treaties; or

> (2) shall be construed as granting any authority to the President with respect to the introduction of United States Armed Forces into hostilities or into situations wherein involvement in hostilities is clearly indicated by the circum-stances which authority he would not have had in the absence of this chapter. . . .

NOTES AND QUESTIONS

(1) *Professor Carter's View: The War Powers Resolution is Constitutional Because it "Defines" the War Power.* Professor Stephen L. Carter concludes that the Resolution is constitutional, in essence because it "defines" the key term. The War Powers Resolution is nothing more or less than a "Congressional definition of the word 'war' in Article I. . . ." Carter, *The Constitutionality of the War Powers Resolution*, 70 VA. L. REV. 101, 117 (1984). But should the legislature define the meaning of "war" or should the judiciary? Does the "necessary and proper" clause give Congress the right to pass the resolution, on the grounds that for Congress to declare war it must first define the term? (If Congress may define "war," isn't it acting as a judge in its own case for separation of powers purposes?)

(2) *The Constitution Arguably Gives the President the Power to "Repel Sudden Attack," But Not to Declare War.* Opponents of the War Powers Resolution argue that

in temporary, defensive situations the President should be able to act unilaterally for the nation. Authority to do so comes from power as Commander-in-Chief and general executive power, it is argued. In the large gray area between repulsion of sudden attack and a full-scale war, does the Executive or the Legislature have the power to send troops? Do the two branches share the power?

In the mission to rescue the American hostages in Iran in 1980, President Carter did not consult Congress prior to the rescue attempt. Could it be argued that he was merely executing a policy Congress would surely have approved? Or should Congress be involved in such strategic decisions as when to attempt a rescue?

(3) *Former Secretary of State Cyrus Vance Argues that Because Military Powers are Split Between the Executive and the Legislature, a Coordination of the Efforts of the Two Branches Will Produce the Best Results.* Vance stresses the importance of consultation between the President and Congress before the President takes military action:

> I believe that the "consultation" required by the War Powers Resolution means, first, that the congressional leadership should be given all information about a planned action that is material to a judgment about its advisability; second, that the congressional leadership should receive that information sufficiently in advance of the planned action to permit a reasonable opportunity to absorb the information, consider its implications, and form a judgment before irrevocable decisions are made by the President; and third, that the congressional leadership should have a real opportunity to communicate its views to the President or at least to his closest advisors.

Vance, *Striking the Balance: Congress and the President Under the War Powers Resolution*, 133 U. PA. L. REV. 79, 90–91 (1984).*"Consultation," then, as used in the War Powers Resolution, would still leave the final decision to commit troops to the Executive. Should this satisfy the Constitutional concerns of opponents of the War Powers Resolution? Where does Congress get the authority to force the President to "consult"?

(4) *The President as Wielding "All" War Powers in Practice.* Newell L. Highsmith asserts that: "The dispute between the President and Congress over which branch of the United States government has the power to commit American forces to war is based on a conflict between two weighty authorities: the Constitution and two hundred years of history and tradition. [Constitutional] provisions seem relatively unambiguous: the President is to direct the armed forces that Congress chooses to establish and maintain in such endeavors as Congress chooses to pursue. [I]n practice, however, all war powers usually have been wielded by the President." Highsmith, *Policing Executive Adventurism: Congressional Oversight of Military and Paramilitary Operations*, 19 HARV. J. ON LEGIS. 327, 328 (1982).

(5) *Presidents, Since 1973, Have Criticized and Often Ignored the War Powers Resolution.* Michael Glennon suggests that "Presidents . . . cannot reasonably be expected to cede to the Congress any greater role in the decision-making process than the Congress *legitimately* and *clearly* demands." Glennon, *The War Powers Resolution: Sad Record, Dismal Promise*, 17 LOY. L.A. L. REV. 657, 660 (1984). Glennon states that "what is needed from the Resolution's authors is a clear and succinct and convincing statement as to precisely *why* it is constitutional," and argues that the War Powers Resolution is justified by the "fluctuating" powers approach used in *Dames & Moore v. Regan.* Under this approach, "the scope of the President's power is a function of the concurrence or non-concurrence of the Congress; once Congress acts, its negative provides 'the rule of the case.' " Glennon believes this analysis explains why the President is empowered to act in emergencies, but why the power lasts only so long as Congress concurs with the President's actions.

---

(6) *The Mayaguez Incident as an Example of a President's Sidestepping the Resolution.* In May, 1975, Cambodian forces seized an American merchant vessel, the S.S. Mayaguez, and took it to Koh Tang Island. President Ford ordered U.S. military forces to recapture the Mayaguez and rescue its crew members. Forty American marines were killed. President Ford did not consult with Congress before beginning the rescue efforts. While the hostilities were occurring, a White House official phoned several Senators and Congressmen to inform them of what was taking place. They were not asked for their opinions, and it is doubtful that they were "consulted" as the War Powers Resolution requires. Subsequently, the President issued a report to Congress about the incident. He "took note" of the War Powers Resolution, but he cited his authority as Chief Executive and Commander-in-Chief of the armed forces as having given him authority to take action. President Ford argued that the President always retains power to protect American lives and property. Aside from the constitutional question, his Mayaguez action was immensely popular with the electorate.

Was President Ford correct in his analysis of presidential power? If it requires the President to do more than President Ford did, is the War Powers Resolution constitutional? For an analysis of related issues, *see* Paust, *The Seizure and Recovery of the Mayaguez*, 85 YALE L.J. 774 (1976).

(7) *The Executive War Powers and Access to the Federal Courts: The "Enemy Combatant Detainees" Decisions.* In a trilogy of decisions, the Supreme Court considered, *inter alia*, the constitutional separation of powers issues arising out of the war in Afghanistan following the September 11 attack on New York City and the Pentagon. All three cases involve claims by persons who had been "indefinitely detained" by the Defense Department in U.S. military prisons, either in the U.S. or at Guantanamo Bay, Cuba. In all three cases, the Executive branch argued, in the alternative, that its detention actions had been authorized by Congress in the Authorization for Use of Military Force Act ("AUMF") passed to authorize action against al Qaeda and the Taliban. As such, these cases do not present any separation of powers issue under the War Powers Act (above). Rather, the issue here is a separation of powers conflict between the Article III Judiciary and the Executive (arguably authorized by Congress).

The differences between the cases largely relate to the status of the detainee. In *Rasul v. Bush*, 542 U.S. 466 (2004), the detainees were aliens (2 Australian and 12 Kuwait citizens) held at Guantanamo Bay. In *Hamdi v. Rumsfeld*, 542 U.S. 507 (2004), the detainee was a U.S. citizen held incommunicado in a military brig in South Carolina. Finally, in *Rumsfeld v. Padilla*, 542 U.S. 426 (2004), Padilla was a U.S. citizen brought to New York as a witness in the investigation of the September 11 terrorist attacks; he was also held in a military brig in South Carolina.

The *Hamdi* decision turned on procedural due process considerations, and it is reviewed in § 8.03 below. In *Padilla*, the Court, per Chief Justice Rehnquist, held that the District Court did not have habeas jurisdiction because Padilla did not sue the commander of the brig; this conclusion drew four dissenters—Stevens, Souter, Ginsburg, and Breyer. (This 5-4 lineup was, of course, common in the Rehnquist Court.)

In *Rasul*, the Court, per Justice Stevens, held that federal habeas statute conferred jurisdiction on the District Courts to hear the claims of non-citizen detainees; the *Rasul* majority did not spell out any details, indicating a cases by case approach. Justice Kennedy concurred; Justice Scalia (for the Chief Justice and Justice Thomas) dissented.

These three consolidated decisions involve multiple statutory and constitutional issues. As a matter of separation of powers doctrine, it appears that eight Justices have rejected the Executive's argument that it had the power to indefinitely detain persons it had determined to be "enemy combatants." While some of the eight Justices would give the Executive somewhat more latitude, only Justice Thomas would agree to defer completely. The Courts will apparently serve as a "check and balance" on the Executive and Congressional war powers. *See generally* Jide Nzelibe, *A Positive Theory of the War-Powers Constitution*, 91 Ia. L. Rev. 993 (2006).

In response to the 2004 trilogy, the Bush Administration sought to "try" certain "detainees" in military commission tribunals—instead of in the federal court system or military court-martials. The rights of the defendants in the proposed military commission trials would be much narrower than these other alternatives. In *Hamdan v. Rumsfeld*, 548 U.S. 557 (2006), the Court decided that the President lacked authority to impose the military commission tribunal in Hamdan's case. Hamdan, a detainee from Afghanistan, had not been determined to be a prisoner of war.

More generally, the Court repudiated the Bush Administration's plan to use the commission tribunals. The Court, per Justice Stevens (who was awarded a Bronze Star as a WWII navy officer), held that the commission tribunals were not authorized by Congress and violated a provision of the Geneva Conventions, which the United States had signed. Justice Kennedy concurred, relying on the *Steel Seizure* decisions [§ 5.01 above]. Justice Breyer concurred, emphasizing that Congress had never authorized the tribunals. Justices Scalia, Thomas and Alito dissented. The reliance on the Geneva Conventions is, in some circles, controversial as reliance on "international law." There are a range of other alternatives that, with Congressional authorization, may be employed in the further stages of the conflict regarding the detainees.

(8)   *Constitutional Habeas Protections for Detainees at Guantanamo Bay: Boumediene v. Bush, 128 S. Ct. 2229 (2008).* After the *Hamdan* decision, Congress enacted the Military Commissions Act of 2006 (MCA), which provided statutory authorization for military commissions and stripped the federal courts of jurisdiction to address habeas corpus petitions filed by detainees designated as enemy combatants. Detainees held at Guantanamo Bay, Cuba challenged the constitutionality of the habeas ban. The Supreme Court, in a 5-4 decision, held that the Constitution protected the detainees' habeas corpus rights.

Justice Kennedy's opinion for the Court rejected the Government's position that the detainees were barred from the writ because they were designated as enemy combatants and were held outside the sovereign territory of the United States. Instead of adopting such a formalistic approach, the Court employed a functional analysis derived from its prior precedents examining several factors, including the process that the detainees had received, the nature of the locales where they were apprehended and detained, and the practical obstacles to judicial resolution. These factors led the Court to conclude that the detainees had habeas corpus rights, and that the procedures established by the MCA and the Detainee Treatment Act were not an adequate substitute for these constitutionally protected rights.

Chief Justice Roberts, joined by Justices Scalia, Thomas, and Alito, dissented, claiming the Court invalidated "the most generous set of procedural protections ever afforded aliens detained by this country as enemy combatants." Justice Scalia, in a separate dissent for the same Justices, maintained that neither the common-law history of the writ nor the Court's precedents authorized habeas protection for these alien enemies detained during an ongoing war outside the United States.

As Chief Justice Roberts pointed out, the majority's decision overrode the clear determination of both political branches regarding the appropriate procedural protections for those held as enemy combatants in a military conflict. Was this decision, as the Chief Justice charged, merely an "unelected, politically unaccountable" judiciary seeking "control of federal policy regarding enemy combatants"? Or was ascertaining the constitutionally required procedures in these cases—some involving individuals held for over six years without any hearing, and others involving individuals apprehended thousands of miles from any active battlefield—particularly the province of the judiciary?

§ 5.05 EXECUTIVE AND LEGISLATIVE PRIVILEGE; IMMUNITIES

[A] Legislative Immunity

Read U.S. Const. Art. I, § 6, cl. 1 (privilege from arrest, speech or debate clause).

NOTE ON THE SPEECH OR DEBATE CLAUSE

Art. I, § 6, cl. 1 of the Constitution is known as the Speech or Debate Clause. Its rationale is that legislators will be more candid in their debates if they know they cannot be called into court for what they say.

In *United States v. Brewster*, 408 U.S. 501 (1972), the Supreme Court held, 6-3, that the Speech or Debate Clause did not preclude prosecution of a former Senator for accepting a bribe. The majority held that the clause does not protect "all conduct relating to the legislative process." Instead, it protects only "against inquiry into acts which occur in the regular course of the legislative process." In *Doe v. McMillan*, 412 U.S. 306 (1973), a subcommittee report on the District of Columbia school system mentioned certain students by name as having committed crimes or been involved in other disciplinary problems. Parents of the students mentioned in the report sued for invasion of privacy. The Court held that the suit was partially blocked by the Speech or Debate Clause. Immunity attached to the introduction of the report at Committee hearings and to vote for publication of the report. However, immunity did not extend to those who distributed the report to the public, even though they were authorized by Congress to do so. The reason is that the dissemination was beyond the realm of the "legislative function."

In *Hutchinson v. Proxmire*, 443 U.S. 111 (1979), the Court held that press releases and newsletters are not subject to legislative immunity. The Court therefore allowed a defamation suit based on statements Senator Proxmire made in a press release and newsletters to go forward.

[B] Executive Privilege for Confidential Information

INTRODUCTORY NOTE

The Watergate controversy increased debate about the scope of executive privilege. President Nixon had tape recorded conversations which might have been useful to the Congressional and Special Prosecutor's investigation of the Watergate break-in and cover up. President Nixon claimed executive privilege and argued that he did not have to obey a court order to turn over the tapes. In *United States v. Nixon*, the Supreme Court attempted to determine the scope of executive power to deny information requested by the other branches of government. The purpose of executive privilege and its separation of powers analysis are keys to the decision.

UNITED STATES v. NIXON

418 U.S. 683 (1974)

MR. CHIEF JUSTICE BURGER delivered the opinion of the Court. . . .

On March 1, 1974, a grand jury of the United States District Court for the District of Columbia returned an indictment charging seven named individuals with various offenses, including conspiracy to defraud the United States and to obstruct justice. Although he was not designated as such in the indictment, the grand jury named the President, among others, as an unindicted coconspirator. On April 18, 1974, upon motion of the Special Prosecutor, . . . a subpoena *duces tecum* was issued [t]o the President. . . . This subpoena required the production, in advance of the September 9 trial date, of certain tapes, memoranda, papers, transcripts or other writings relating to certain precisely identified meetings between the President and others. . . . On May 1, 1974, the President's counsel filed a "special appearance" and a motion of quash the subpoena under Rule 17(c). This motion was accompanied by a formal claim of privilege. . . .

On May 20, 1974, the District Court denied the motion to quash and the motions to expunge and for protective orders. . . .

[The President sought review in the Court of Appeals on May 24. Later the same day, the Special Prosecutor petitioned the Supreme Court for a writ of certiorari before judgment, which the Court granted a week later.]

The Claim of Privilege

A . . .

In the performance of assigned constitutional duties each branch of the Government must initially interpret the Constitution, and the interpretation of its powers by any branch is due great respect from the others. [M]any decisions of this Court, however, have unequivocally reaffirmed the holding of *Marbury v. Madison*, 1 Cranch; 137, 2 L.Ed. 60 (1803), that "[i]t is emphatically the province and duty of the judicial department to say what the law is. . . ."

B

In support of his claim of absolute privilege, the President's counsel urges two grounds, one of which is common to all governments and one of which is peculiar to our system of separation of powers. The first ground is the valid need for protection of communications between high Government officials and those who advise and assist them in the performance of their manifold duties; the importance of this confidentiality is too plain to require further discussion. Human experience teaches that those who expect public dissemination of their remarks may well temper candor with a concern for appearances and for their own interests to the detriment of the decision making process. Whatever the nature of the privilege of confidentiality of Presidential communications in the exercise of Art. II powers, the privilege can be said to derive from the supremacy of each branch within its own assigned area of constitutional duties. Certain powers and privileges flow from the nature of enumerated powers; the protection of the confidentiality of Presidential communications has similar constitutional underpinnings.

The second ground asserted by the President's counsel in support of the claim of absolute privilege rests on the doctrine of separation of powers. Here it is argued that the independence of the Executive Branch within its own sphere insulates a President from a judicial subpoena in an ongoing criminal prosecution, and thereby protects confidential Presidential communications.

hold.

need more rec[d]

would upset the constr. balance

However, neither the doctrine of separation of powers, nor the need for confidentiality of high-level communications, without more, can sustain an absolute, unqualified Presidential privilege of immunity from judicial process under all circumstances. [A]bsent a claim of need to protect military, diplomatic, or sensitive national security secrets, we find it difficult to accept the argument that even the very important interest in confidentiality of Presidential communications is significantly diminished by production of such material for *in camera* inspection with all the protection that a district court will be obliged to provide. [T]o read the Art. II powers of the President as providing an absolute privilege as against a subpoena essential to enforcement of criminal statutes on no more than a generalized claim of the public interest in confidentiality of nonmilitary and nondiplomatic discussions would upset the constitutional balance of "a workable government" and gravely impair the role of the courts under Art. III.

C

Since we conclude that the legitimate needs of the judicial process may outweigh Presidential privilege, it is necessary to resolve those competing interests in a manner that preserves the essential functions of each branch. The right and indeed the duty to resolve that question does not free the Judiciary from according high respect to the representations made on behalf of the President. . . .

But this presumptive privilege must be considered in light of our historic commitment to the rule of law. This is nowhere more profoundly manifest than in our view that "the twofold aim [of criminal justice] is that guilt shall not escape or innocence suffer." [T]he need to develop all relevant facts in the adversary system is both fundamental and comprehensive. The ends of criminal justice would be defeated if judgments were to be founded on a partial or speculative presentation of the facts. [T]o ensure that justice is done, it is imperative to the function of courts that compulsory process be available for the production of evidence needed either by the prosecution or by the defense. . . .

[T]he interest in preserving confidentiality is weighty indeed and entitled to great respect. However, we cannot conclude that advisers will be moved to temper the candor of their remarks by the infrequent occasions of disclosure because of the possibility that such conversations will be called for in the context of a criminal prosecution. . . .

hold.

We conclude that when the ground for asserting privilege as to subpoenaed materials sought for use in a criminal trial is based only on the generalized interest in confidentiality, it cannot prevail over the fundamental demands of due process of law in the fair administration of criminal justice. The generalized assertion of privilege must yield to the demonstrated, specific need for evidence in a pending criminal trial. . . .

E

[A]t this stage the District Court is not limited to representations of the Special Prosecutor as to the evidence sought by the subpoena; the material will be available to the District Court. It is elementary that *in camera* inspection of evidence is always a procedure calling for scrupulous protection against any release or publication of material not found by the court, at that stage, probably admissible in evidence and relevant to the issues of the trial for which it is sought. That being true of an ordinary situation, it is obvious that the District Court has a very heavy responsibility to see to it that Presidential conversations, which are either not relevant or not admissible, are accorded that high degree of respect due the President of the United States. . . .

Affirmed.

NOTES AND QUESTIONS

(1) *Did the Supreme Court Have Power to Review President Nixon's Decision Not to Turn Over the Tapes?* Nixon argued, first, that since he was still in office, he was immune to judicial process. Therefore, he would have to be impeached and removed from office before he could be amenable to judicial proceedings. This position had some historical backing. In *Mississippi v. Johnson*, 71 U.S. (4 Wall.) 475 (1867), the Court refused to hear a suit to enjoin President Johnson from enforcing the Reconstruction Acts. The Court stated that courts did not possess the power to issue injunctions against sitting presidents. Nixon's counsel relied on this case in his arguments. The Court did not give the argument much weight; in fact, the point was not separately discussed. Should impeachment be the only remedy available against a sitting President? Should the Court get involved in a dispute between Congress and the President, or is that a political question?

(2) *The Scope of Judicial Review of Presidential Assertions of Privilege.* President Nixon's second argument related to the scope of executive privilege. He asserted that the absolute power to determine the scope of executive privilege lies with the Executive branch. While the Court held that one branch's interpretation of its powers is due great respect from the other branches, it maintained that, as Marshall stated in *Marbury*, "it is emphatically the province and duty of the judicial department to say what the law is." Did the Court go too far in this assertion of judicial supremacy? As Professor Gerald Gunther has pointed out, "there is nothing in *Marbury v. Madison* that precludes a constitutional interpretation which gives final authority to another branch." Gunther, *Judicial Hegemony and Legislative Autonomy: The Nixon Case and the Impeachment Process*, 22 UCLA L. Rev. 30, 34 (1974). There are some political questions the Court refuses to decide. Why shouldn't this be one of them? (Did the fact that the nation was looking to the Court to end the standoff between Nixon and the Special Prosecutor play a role?)

(3) *The Court's Balancing Approach.* Once the Court decided that the scope of executive privilege was a justiciable question, it proceeded to weigh the Executive's need for confidentiality against the prosecutor's and the judiciary's need for the tapes. Did the Court act properly in using a balancing test, which is far more uncertain protection for advisers depending on confidentiality than a more specific categorical test?

(4) *The Privilege and Congressional Demands for Information.* The *Nixon* case did not address the question of when executive privilege withstands Congressional demands for information (sometimes pursuant to impeachment investigations). Is this a question the Judiciary should decide, or is it a political question to be settled by Congress and the Executive? In *Senate Select Committee on Presidential Campaign Activities v. Nixon*, 498 F.2d 725 (D.C. Cir. 1974), a Senate committee had requested Nixon's tapes pursuant to its investigation. The D.C. Circuit held that the Committee's need for the information was outweighed by Nixon's executive privilege. The court stated that a claim of executive privilege is presumptively valid and can be overcome only when there is an important countervailing need for the information. The court thus used a balancing test similar to that in *Nixon*.

(5) *Continued Assertion of Executive Privilege by Article II Officials: Cheney v. United States District Court, 542 U.S. 367 (2004).* President Bush formed the National Energy Policy Development Group (NEPDG), and he made Vice President Cheney a member. A public interest group and an environmental group brought a civil action against the NEPDG and Cheney for alleged violation of certain procedural and disclosure requirements of the Federal Advisory Committee Act (FACA). The plaintiffs propounded some broad discovery requests. Cheney and the defendants objected to the breadth and relevancy of the requests. Subsequently, the trial court entered certain discovery orders. Cheney and the defendants then sought a writ of mandamus vacating the orders. Although the court of appeals declined to issue mandamus, the Supreme

Court, per Justice Kennedy, ordered the appellate court to reconsider Cheney's entitlement to the writ.

The Supreme Court's opinion addressed a number of issues related to the procedural posture of the case. The court of appeals had concluded that the *Nixon* decision put the burden on the defendants to assert and to substantiate an executive privilege claim before seeking mandamus. But the *Cheney* Court distinguished *Nixon* on several grounds: (1) *Nixon* involved a criminal action and *Cheney* was a civil action; (2) the discovery in *Cheney* had the potential to be disruptive of certain Executive functions; and (3) unlike the "precisely identified" subpoenaes in *Nixon*, the discovery requests were "overly broad" (*i.e.*, asked "for everything under the sky"). The *Cheney* Court concluded that the lower courts should reconsider the breadth of and the basis for the discovery against the Vice President, especially in light of separation of powers concerns. Two Justices (Ginsburg and Souter) dissented.

[C] Executive Immunity against Liability for Damages

NIXON v. FITZGERALD, 457 U.S. 731 (1982). Ernest Fitzgerald, a management analyst with the Air Force, lost his job after revealing to Congress that cost-overruns on the C-5A transport plane could approximate $2 billion dollars. He brought a civil suit against President Nixon seeking damages on the grounds that Nixon was responsible for his wrongful discharge. In a 5-4 decision, the Court held that the President possessed absolute immunity from liability for damages in a civil action. Justice Powell, writing for the Court, stated that Nixon, as a former President, "is entitled to absolute immunity from damages liability predicated on his official acts. We consider this immunity a functionally mandated incident of the President's unique office, rooted in the constitutional tradition of the separation of powers and supported by our history." Justice Powell reasoned that the President would be too preoccupied to perform his Constitutional duties if his every action were subject to civil suits. Hence, "we think it appropriate to recognize absolute Presidential immunity from damages liability for acts within the 'outer perimeter' of his official responsibility." Justice Powell argued that this rule would still leave "sufficient protection against misconduct on the part of the Chief Executive. There remains the constitutional remedy of impeachment. . . . The President is subjected to constant scrutiny by the press." He also cited "vigilant oversight by Congress" and a desire to be reelected as checks on the President's actions.

Justice White, in dissent, argued that "the President should have the same remedial obligations toward those whom he injures as any other federal officer." [In *Harlow v. Fitzgerald*, 457 U.S. 800 (1982), the Court decided that presidential aides are not absolutely immune from civil suits, although they have the same qualified "good faith" immunity as other executive officers. Should the President be singled out as not having to be concerned with civil liability for his official actions, when other executive officials may be liable?]

Although the "Watergate era" has largely passed, issues regarding "executive privilege" and "Presidential immunities" remain part of the constitutional landscape. For example, although *Nixon v. Fitzgerald*, *supra*, held that the President was immune from damage liability "for acts within the 'outer perimeter' of his official responsibility," should Presidential immunity extend to acts *before* a President assumed the office (or was even nominated by a party)? Or, alternatively, should the federal courts defer any civil litigation concerning a sitting President until the President leaves office? Which approach, if any, is supported by the decisions in this Section?

CLINTON v. JONES, 520 U.S. 681 (1997). In this highly publicized case, the plaintiff (Jones) brought a civil action against President Clinton for acts (allegedly constituting sexual harassment) which occurred *before* Clinton took office as President. Based largely on *Nixon v. Fitzgerald*, President Clinton sought to dismiss the suit on the grounds of executive immunity or, alternatively, to stay all proceedings until he left office. The federal district court upheld Clinton's request for staying the proceedings, but the Court of Appeals reversed. In *Clinton*, the Supreme Court, per Justice Stevens, affirmed the court of appeals determining that, under the circumstances, the separation of powers doctrine did not require any broad stay of the litigation or any "temporary immunity" until the President left office.

The Court accepted, from *Nixon v. Fitzgerald*, the theory that the President had absolute immunity for damage liability, but the Court differentiated President Clinton's alleged acts from the conduct in *Fitzgerald* because they occurred before Clinton became President. The majority reasoned that: "The principal rationale for affording certain public servants immunity from suits for money damages arising out of their official acts is inapplicable to unofficial conduct."

The Court rejected Clinton's separation of powers argument by holding that, in deciding whether the sexual harassment claim would go forward subject to the generally applicable Rules of Civil Procedure, the Court was not encroaching on any "Executive" function. The Court also rejected Clinton's policy argument that predicted a "flood" of lawsuits against future Presidents, expressing "confidence" in the ability of the lower courts to avoid frivolous or abusive lawsuits. The Court also noted that, if warranted, Congress might enact legislation giving the President more immunity than other litigants.

§ 5.06   THE APPOINTMENTS POWER, POWER OVER PERSONNEL, AND NATIONAL PROPERTY POWER

[A]   The Appointments Power

Read U.S. Const. Art. 2, § 2, Cl. 2 (the Appointments Clause).

INTRODUCTORY NOTE

The Appointments Clause, Art. II, § 2, cl. 2, was designed to assure separation of powers by giving the Executive the sole authority to appoint officials to enforce the law. The legislature thereby avoids entanglement with the Executive. Though Congress may create agencies to administer laws, it may not appoint the members of the agencies. The Court [in *Buckley v. Valeo*, below] has defined "Officer of the United States" as "any appointee exercising significant authority pursuant to the laws of the United States."

BUCKLEY v. VALEO, 424 U.S. 1 (1976). The 1974 amendments to the Federal Election Campaign Act created an eight-member Federal Election Commission which has broad responsibility for administering the Act. Among its duties, the Commission had record keeping, disclosure and investigative functions, as well as extensive rulemaking and adjudicative and enforcement powers. The Commission was composed of the Secretary of the Senate and the Clerk of the House of Representatives (as non-voting, *ex officio* members), two members appointed by the President *pro tempore* of the Senate, two members appointed by the Speaker of the House of Representatives, and two members appointed by the President. Each of the six voting members had to be confirmed by the majority of both houses of Congress.

The Supreme Court held that, given the powers exercised by the Commission, the method of appointing its members both ran afoul of the separation of powers and violated Art. II, § 2, cl. 2. It violated the separation of powers because, anticipating *Bowsher*, "the Legislative Branch may not exercise executive authority by retaining the power to appoint those who will execute its laws." It violated the "Appointments Clause" because the Commissioners were not appointed in any of the ways set forth in Art. II, § 2, cl. 2. Even if the Commissioners were not "Officers of the United States" who had to be appointed by the President and confirmed by the Senate under the first part of the clause, the Act did not vest their appointment "in the Courts of Law, or in the Heads of Departments" the alternatives provided in the second part of the clause. Moreover, given the scope of the powers the Commission possessed, the Commissioners were clearly "Officers of the United States" within the meaning of the Appointments Clause. The Commission's powers were not limited to aiding Congress to legislate and went well beyond "those powers which Congress might delegate to one of its own committees. . . ." Instead, the Commissioners exercised broad administrative powers, including the authority to promulgate rules to implement the Act and to conduct civil litigation to enforce it, which made them "Officers of the United States."

[B]   Presidential Power Over Personnel and Property

NOTES AND QUESTIONS

(1) *The Removal of Executive Officers from Office.* How may Executive officers be removed from office? The Constitution is silent on the issue, but it has been addressed by the Supreme Court. In *Myers v. United States*, 272 U.S. 52 (1926), the Court held unconstitutional a Congressional provision that certain types of postmasters, appointed by the President, could not be removed by the President without the consent of the Senate. Chief Justice Taft reasoned that since the President was empowered to enforce the laws, he should have the responsibility for deciding who to appoint as officers and which officers should be removed. Therefore, congressional limitations on the President's right to remove officers were held unconstitutional.

However, in *Humphrey's Executor v. United States*, 295 U.S. 602 (1935), the Court held that Congress may restrict the President's right to remove a federal official who holds a quasi-legislative or quasi-judicial role. The case involved Congressional restrictions on the removal of Federal Trade Commissioners, and the Court held that *Myers* applied only to "purely executive officers."

(2) *Control Over Presidential Property.* In *Nixon v. Administrator of General Services*, 433 U.S. 425 (1977), the Court upheld the Constitutionality of the Presidential Recordings and Materials Preservation Act of 1974. The Act directed the General Services Administration (GSA) to take custody of Richard Nixon's papers and tape recordings, screen them, and return to him those that were personal and private. The rest would be kept in the GSA's possession for determination of their historical value. President Nixon had alleged that the Act violated separation of powers principles. The Court rejected this view as requiring too much separateness between the three branches of government. The Court stressed that a "flexible approach" to separation of powers analysis was necessary. Proper inquiry, the Court reasoned, "focuses on the extent to which [the Act] prevents the Executive Branch from accomplishing its constitutionally assigned functions." The Court concluded that the Act would not be "unduly disruptive of the Executive Branch."

§ 5.07 THE PARDON POWER

Read U.S. Const. Art. II, § 2 (the pardon power).

NOTE ON THE PARDON POWER

The Pardon Power was used by President Ford on September 8, 1974, in his controversial decision to pardon Richard Nixon of "all offenses" he committed "or may have committed" while President. President Ford was acting according to Art. II, § 2 of the Constitution. This power has been interpreted in a very broad fashion. In *Ex parte Garland*, 71 U.S. (4 Wall.) 333 (1866), the Court held that the legislature may not control the President's exercise of the pardon power. *Cf.* Buchanan, *The Nature of a Pardon Under the United States Constitution*, 39 Ohio St. L.J. 36 (1978).

More recently, in *Schick v. Reed*, 419 U.S. 256 (1974), the breadth of the President's power once again was affirmed. The Court held that the President had the power, in commuting a death sentence to life imprisonment, to require that there be no possibility of parole. The Court stated that, since the pardon power derives directly from the Constitution, it cannot be limited by Congress and the President may impose any condition "which does not otherwise offend the Constitution." In 2001, the country's attention was again directed to the pardon power when questions arose in Congress and the media regarding certain "last minute" pardons granted by President Clinton. One pardon involved political supporters of President Clinton's spouse in her campaign for a New York Senate seat. Should Congress investigate, or legislate, the scope of the pardon power?

The recent uses of the pardon power, although a "plenary" power, have been controversial. President George H.W. Bush, while a lame-duck President, pardoned witnesses in the ongoing Iran-Contra scandal; in particular, the pardons impeded any possible investigation into whether he, as Vice President, may have misled the Independent Counsel.

President Clinton granted 140 pardon hours before leaving office, including pardons to his brother Roger Clinton, Whitewater figure Susan McDougal, former cabinet member Henry Cisneros, former CIA Director John Deutch, and fugitive financier Marc Rich, whose ex-wife donated more than $1 million to Democratic causes, including donations to the Clintons.

The second President Bush commuted the criminal sentence of Lewis "Scooter" Libby, who was convicted for perjury and obstruction of justice in the investigation of the outing of Valerie Plame as a CIA operative. Do these examples indicate that Congress should investigate, or legislate, the scope of the pardon power? Could the President's use of the pardon power serve as the grounds for impeachment? *See generally* Sanford Levinson, Our Undemocratic Constitution, 112–113 (2006).

§ 5.08 THE ELECTORAL COLLEGE AND PRESIDENTIAL ELECTIONS

Read U.S. Const. Art. II, § 1 and the Twelfth Amendment

NOTES ON THE ELECTORAL COLLEGE

(1) *The Framers' Invention: The Electoral College.* (You undoubtedly "studied" it as a high school student, but it probably seemed like just another arcane topic. Well, now you can read *Bush v. Gore* below—nothing arcane there!)

(2) *The 2000 Presidential Election Trilogy.* During a few weeks following the 2000 Presidential election, the Supreme Court exercised the judicial review authority and announced three decisions regarding the role of manual recounting in the state of Florida's tabulation of votes in the Presidential election between Governor George Bush and Vice President Al Gore. The *Bush* trilogy raises various issues concerning equal protection, Article II powers, federalism and the political question doctrine. Watch for these as you read below.

(3) *The Background for Bush II: Judicial Resolution of an Electoral College Dispute.* The Presidential election of 2000 in the State of Florida was excruciatingly close: Governor George Bush (the Republican) had only a 1,784 vote margin over Vice President Al Gore (the Democrat) and this margin shrank to only a few hundred votes during the various recounts. At stake were Florida's 25 electoral college votes. Moreover, because of the nation-wide closeness of the electoral college vote, whoever won Florida would win the Presidency.

Pursuant to state law, Gore sought manual recounts in only four counties. Bush resisted these recounts, arguing: (1) that, as conducted, the manual recounts violated his equal protection rights and (2) that the procedures ordered by the Florida Supreme Court violated Article II standards (including transgressing the "safe harbor" decision by the Florida Legislature). The Florida Supreme Court essentially agreed with the Gore request and ordered the manual recounting to continue.

In the first decision, *Bush v. Palm Beach County Canvassing Bd.*, 531 U.S. 70 (2000), the Supreme Court, in an unanimous *per curiam* opinion, reversed the Florida Supreme Court and signaled that Bush's Article II argument was considered colorable. On remand, the Florida Supreme Court essentially agreed again with the Gore position. This lead to another expedited "appeal" by Bush.

In the second opinion, *Bush v. Gore*, 531 U.S. 1046 (2000) (*Bush I*), the Supreme Court stayed the manual recounts and accepted certiorari on the merits of Bush's petition for certiorari. *Bush I* was a 5-4 decision, with Justices Stevens, Souter, Ginsburg, and Breyer dissenting. Justice Scalia filed a concurring opinion. [You may study Justices Stevens and Scalia's opinions regarding "irreparable harm" in your Remedies courses.] The Court heard oral argument on an expedited schedule and issued the *Bush II*, 531 U.S. 98 (2000), opinion.

The *Bush II* opinion involves three basic opinions, and you should keep the differences in mind as you read it. First, there is the *per curiam* opinion (by Justices O'Connor and Kennedy); it pursues an equal protection analysis. Second, there is a concurring opinion by Chief Justice Rehnquist; it focuses on the Article II considerations. Third, there are opinions by the four dissenting Justices. Consider these below.

BUSH v. GORE
531 U.S. 98 (2000)

PER CURIAM.

On December 8, 2000, the Supreme Court of Florida ordered that the Circuit Court of Leon County tabulate by hand 9,000 ballots in Miami-Dade County. It also ordered the inclusion in the certified vote totals of 215 votes identified in Palm Beach County and 168 votes identified in Miami-Dade County for Vice President Albert Gore, Jr., and Senator Joseph Lieberman, Democratic Candidates for President and Vice President. The Supreme Court noted that petitioner, Governor George W. Bush asserted that the net gain for Vice President Gore in Palm Beach County was 176 votes, and directed the Circuit Court to resolve that dispute on remand. The court further held that relief would require manual recounts in all Florida counties where so-called "undervotes" had not been subject to manual tabulation. The court ordered all manual recounts to begin at once. Governor Bush and Richard Cheney, Republican Candidates for the Presidency and Vice Presidency, filed an emergency application for a stay of this mandate. On December 9, we granted the application, treated the application as a petition for a writ of certiorari, and granted certiorari.

The proceedings leading to the present controversy are discussed in some detail in our opinion in *Bush v. Palm Beach County Canvassing Bd.*, 531 U.S. 70 (2000) *(per curiam) (Bush I)*. On November 8, 2000, the day following the Presidential election, the Florida Division of Elections reported that petitioner, Governor Bush, had received 2,909,135 votes, and respondent, Vice President Gore, had received 2,907,351 votes, a margin of 1,784 for Governor Bush. Because Governor Bush's margin of victory was less than "one-half of a percent . . . of the votes cast," an automatic machine recount was conducted under § 102.141(4) of the election code, the results of which showed Governor Bush still winning the race but by a diminished margin. Vice President Gore then sought manual recounts in Volusia, Palm Beach, Broward, and Miami-Dade Counties, pursuant to Florida's election protest provisions. A dispute arose concerning the deadline for local county canvassing boards to submit their returns to the Secretary of State (Secretary). The Secretary declined to waive the November 14 deadline imposed by statute. The Florida Supreme Court, however, set the deadline at November 26. We granted certiorari and vacated the Florida Supreme Court's decision, finding considerable uncertainty as to the grounds on which it was based. Bush I. On December 11, the Florida Supreme Court issued a decision on remand reinstating that date.

On November 26, the Florida Elections Canvassing Commission certified the results of the election and declared Governor Bush the winner of Florida's 25 electoral votes. On November 27, Vice President Gore, pursuant to Florida's contest provisions, filed a complaint in Leon County Circuit Court contesting the certification. He sought relief pursuant to § 102.168(3)(c), which provides that "[r]eceipt of a number of illegal votes or rejection of a number of legal votes sufficient to change or place in doubt the result of the election" shall be grounds for a contest. The Circuit Court denied relief, stating that Vice President Gore failed to meet his burden of proof. He appealed to the First District Court of Appeal, which certified the matter to the Florida Supreme Court.

Accepting jurisdiction, the Florida Supreme Court affirmed in part and reversed in part. *Gore v. Harris*, 772 So.2d. 1243 (2000). The court held that the Circuit Court had been correct to reject Vice President Gore's challenge to the results certified in Nassau County and his challenge to the Palm Beach County Canvassing Board's determination that 3,300 ballots cast in that county were not, in the statutory phrase, "legal votes."

The Supreme Court held that Vice President Gore had satisfied his burden of proof under § 102.168(3)(c) with respect to his challenge to Miami-Dade County's failure to tabulate, by manual count, 9,000 ballots on which the machines had failed to detect a vote for President ("undervotes"). Noting the closeness of the election, the Court explained that "[o]n this record, there can be no question that there are legal votes within the 9,000 uncounted votes sufficient to place the results of this election in doubt." A "legal vote," as determined by the Supreme Court, is "one in which there is a 'clear indication of the intent of the voter.'" The court therefore ordered a hand recount of the 9,000 ballots in Miami-Dade County. . . . [T]he Supreme Court further held that the Circuit Court could order "the Supervisor of Elections and the Canvassing Boards, as well as the necessary public officials, in all counties that have not conducted a manual recount or tabulation of the undervotes . . . to do so forthwith, said tabulation to take place in the individual counties where the ballots are located."

The Supreme Court also determined that both Palm Beach County and Miami-Dade County, in their earlier manual recounts, had identified a net gain of 215 and 168 legal votes for Vice President Gore. Rejecting the Circuit Court's conclusion that Palm Beach County lacked the authority to include the 215 net votes submitted past the November 26 deadline, the Supreme Court explained that the deadline was not intended to exclude votes identified after that date through ongoing manual recounts. As to Miami-Dade County, the Court concluded that although the 168 votes identified were the result of a partial recount, they were "legal votes [that] could change the outcome of the election." The Supreme Court therefore directed the Circuit Court to include those totals in the certified results, subject to resolution of the actual vote total from the Miami-Dade partial recount.

The petition presents the following questions: whether the Florida Supreme Court established new standards for resolving Presidential election contests, thereby violating Art. II, § 1, cl. 2, of the United States Constitution and failing to comply with 3 U.S.C. § 5, and whether the use of standardless manual recounts violates the Equal Protection and Due Process Clauses. With respect to the equal protection question, we find a violation of the Equal Protection Clause.

II

A

The closeness of this election, and the multitude of legal challenges which have followed in its wake, have brought into sharp focus a common, if heretofore unnoticed, phenomenon. Nationwide statistics reveal that an estimated 2% of ballots cast do not register a vote for President for whatever reason, including deliberately choosing no candidate at all or some voter error, such as voting for two candidates or insufficiently marking a ballot. See Ho, More Than 2M Ballots Uncounted, AP Online (Nov. 28, 2000); Kelley, Balloting Problems Not Rare But Only In A Very Close Election Do Mistakes And Mismarking Make A Difference, Omaha World-Herald (Nov. 15, 2000). . . .

B

The individual citizen has no federal constitutional right to vote for electors for the President of the United States unless and until the state legislature chooses a statewide election as the means to implement its power to appoint members of the Electoral College. U.S. Const., Art. II, § 1. This is the source for the statement in *McPherson v. Blacker*, 146 U.S. 1 (1892), that the State legislature's power to select the manner for appointing electors is plenary; it may, if it so chooses, select the electors itself, which indeed was the manner used by State legislatures in several States for many years after the Framing of our Constitution. History has now favored the voter, and in each of the several States the citizens themselves vote for Presidential electors. When the state legislature vests the right to vote for President in its people, the right to vote as the legislature has prescribed is fundamental; and one source of its fundamental nature lies in the equal weight accorded to each vote and the equal dignity owed to each voter. The State, of course, after granting the franchise in the special context of Article II, can take back the power to appoint electors.

The right to vote is protected in more than the initial allocation of the franchise. Equal protection applies as well to the manner of its exercise. Having once granted the right to vote on equal terms, the State may not, by later arbitrary and disparate treatment, value one person's vote over that of another. See, *e.g.*, *Harper v. Virginia Bd. of Elections*, 383 U.S. 663, 665 (1966).

There is no difference between the two sides of the present controversy on these basic propositions. Respondents say that the very purpose of vindicating the right to vote justifies the recount procedures now at issue. The question before us, however, is whether the recount procedures the Florida Supreme Court has adopted are consistent with its obligation to avoid arbitrary and disparate treatment of the members of its electorate.

Much of the controversy seems to revolve around ballot cards designed to be perforated by a stylus but which, either through error or deliberate omission, have not been perforated with sufficient precision for a machine to count them. In some cases a piece of the card—a chad—is hanging, say by two corners. In other cases there is no separation at all, just an indentation.

The Florida Supreme Court has ordered that the intent of the voter be discerned from such ballots. For purposes of resolving the equal protection challenge, it is not necessary to decide whether the Florida Supreme Court had the authority under the legislative scheme for resolving election disputes to define what a legal vote is and to mandate a manual recount implementing that definition. The recount mechanisms implemented in response to the decisions of the Florida Supreme Court do not satisfy the minimum requirement for non- arbitrary treatment of voters necessary to secure the fundamental right. Florida's basic command for the count of legally cast votes is to consider the "intent of the voter." This is unobjectionable as an abstract proposition and a starting principle. The problem inheres in the absence of specific standards to ensure its equal application. The formulation of uniform rules to determine intent based on these recurring circumstances is practicable and, we conclude, necessary.

The law does not refrain from searching for the intent of the actor in a multitude of circumstances; and in some cases the general command to ascertain intent is not susceptible to much further refinement. In this instance, however, the question is not whether to believe a witness but how to interpret the marks or holes or scratches on an inanimate object, a piece of cardboard or paper which, it is said, might not have registered as a vote during the machine count. The factfinder confronts a thing, not a person. The search for intent can be confined by specific rules designed to ensure uniform treatment.

The want of those rules here has led to unequal evaluation of ballots in various respects. As seems to have been acknowledged at oral argument, the standards for accepting or rejecting contested ballots might vary not only from county to county but indeed within a single county from one recount team to another. . . .

In addition, the recounts in these three counties were not limited to so- called undervotes but extended to all of the ballots. The distinction has real consequences. A manual recount of all ballots identifies not only those ballots which show no vote but also those which contain more than one, the so- called overvotes. Neither category will be counted by the machine. This is not a trivial concern. At oral argument, respondents estimated there are as many as 110,000 overvotes statewide. As a result, the citizen whose ballot was not read by a machine because he failed to vote for a candidate in a way readable by a machine may still have his vote counted in a manual recount; on the other hand, the citizen who marks two candidates in a way discernable by the machine will not have the same opportunity to have his vote count, even if a manual examination of the ballot would reveal the requisite indicia of intent. Furthermore, the citizen who marks two candidates, only one of which is discernable by the machine, will have his vote counted even though it should have been read as an invalid ballot. The State Supreme Court's inclusion of vote counts based on these variant standards exemplifies concerns with the remedial processes that were under way.

That brings the analysis to yet a further equal protection problem. The votes certified by the court included a partial total from one county, Miami- Dade. The Florida Supreme Court's decision thus gives no assurance that the recounts included in a final certification must be complete. . . . This accommodation no doubt results from the truncated contest period established by the Florida Supreme Court in *Bush I*, at respondents' own urging. The press of time does not diminish the constitutional concern. A desire for speed is not a general excuse for ignoring equal protection guarantees.

In addition to these difficulties the actual process by which the votes were to be counted under the Florida Supreme Court's decision raises further concerns. That order did not specify who would recount the ballots. The county canvassing boards were forced to pull together ad hoc teams comprised of judges from various Circuits who had no previous training in handling and interpreting ballots. Furthermore, while others were permitted to observe, they were prohibited from objecting during the recount.

The recount process, in its features here described, is inconsistent with the minimum procedures necessary to protect the fundamental right of each voter in the special instance of a statewide recount under the authority of a single state judicial officer. Our consideration is limited to the present circumstances, for the problem of equal protection in election processes generally presents many complexities. . .

Upon due consideration of the difficulties identified to this point, it is obvious that the recount cannot be conducted in compliance with the requirements of equal protection and due process without substantial additional work. It would require not only the adoption (after opportunity for argument) of adequate statewide standards for determining what is a legal vote, and practicable procedures to implement them, but also orderly judicial review of any disputed matters that might arise. In addition, the Secretary of State has advised that the recount of only a portion of the ballots requires that the vote tabulation equipment be used to screen out undervotes, a function for which the machines were not designed. If a recount of overvotes were also required, perhaps even a second screening would be necessary. Use of the equipment for this purpose, and any new software developed for it, would have to be evaluated for accuracy by the Secretary of State, as required by Fla. Stat. § 101.015 (2000). . . .

Because it is evident that any recount seeking to meet the December 12 date will be unconstitutional for the reasons we have discussed, we reverse the judgment of the Supreme Court of Florida ordering a recount to proceed. . . . [Reversed and remanded.]

CHIEF JUSTICE REHNQUIST, with whom JUSTICE SCALIA and JUSTICE THOMAS join, concurring.

We join the *per curiam* opinion. We write separately because we believe there are additional grounds that require us to reverse the Florida Supreme Court's decision.

I

We deal here not with an ordinary election, but with an election for the President of the United States. . . .

In most cases, comity and respect for federalism compel us to defer to the decisions of state courts on issues of state law. That practice reflects our understanding that the decisions of state courts are definitive pronouncements of the will of the States as sovereigns. Cf. *Erie R. Co. v. Tompkins*, 304 U.S. 64 (1938). Of course, in ordinary cases, the distribution of powers among the branches of a State's government raises no questions of federal constitutional law, subject to the requirement that the government be republican in character. See U.S. Const., Art. IV, § 4. But there are a few exceptional cases in which the Constitution imposes a duty or confers a power on a particular branch of a State's government. This is one of them. Article II, § 1, cl. 2, provides that "[e]ach State shall appoint, in such Manner as the *Legislature* thereof may direct," electors for President and Vice President. (Emphasis added.) Thus, the text of the election law itself, and not just its interpretation by the courts of the States, takes on independent significance.

In *McPherson v. Blacker*, 146 U.S. 1 (1892), we explained that Art. II, § 1, cl. 2, "convey[s] the broadest power of determination" and "leaves it to the legislature exclusively to define the method" of appointment. A significant departure from the legislative scheme for appointing Presidential electors presents a federal constitutional question.

3 U.S.C. § 5 informs our application of Art. II, § 1, cl. 2, to the Florida statutory scheme, which, as the Florida Supreme Court acknowledged, took that statute into account. Section 5 provides that the State's selection of electors "shall be conclusive, and shall govern in the counting of the electoral votes" if the electors are chosen under laws enacted prior to election day, and if the selection process is completed six days prior to the meeting of the electoral college. As we noted in *Bush v. Palm Beach County Canvassing Bd.*,

> "Since § 5 contains a principle of federal law that would assure finality of the State's determination if made pursuant to a state law in effect before the election, a legislative wish to take advantage of the 'safe harbor' would counsel against any construction of the Election Code that Congress might deem to be a change in the law."

If we are to respect the legislature's Article II powers, therefore, we must ensure that postelection state-court actions do not frustrate the legislative desire to attain the "safe harbor" provided by § 5.

In Florida, the legislature has chosen to hold statewide elections to appoint the State's 25 electors. Importantly, the legislature has delegated the authority to run the elections and to oversee election disputes to the Secretary of State (Secretary), and to state circuit courts. Isolated sections of the code may well admit of more than one interpretation, but the general coherence of the legislative scheme may not be altered by judicial interpretation so as to wholly change the statutorily provided apportionment of responsibility among these various bodies. In any election but a Presidential election, the Florida Supreme Court can give as little or as much deference to Florida's executives as it chooses, so far as Article II is concerned, and this Court will have no cause to question the court's actions. But, with respect to a Presidential election, the court must be both mindful of the legislature's role under Article II in choosing the manner of appointing electors and deferential to those bodies expressly empowered by the legislature to carry out its constitutional mandate.

In order to determine whether a state court has infringed upon the legislature's authority, we necessarily must examine the law of the State as it existed prior to the action of the court. Though we generally defer to state courts on the interpretation of state law, there are of course areas in which the Constitution requires this Court to undertake an independent, if still deferential, analysis of state law. . . .

This inquiry does not imply a disrespect for state *courts* but rather a respect for the constitutionally prescribed role of state *legislatures*. To attach definitive weight to the pronouncement of a state court, when the very question at issue is whether the court has actually departed from the statutory meaning, would be to abdicate our responsibility to enforce the explicit requirements of Article II.

II

Acting pursuant to its constitutional grant of authority, the Florida Legislature has created a detailed, if not perfectly crafted, statutory scheme that provides for appointment of Presidential electors by direct election. Fla. Stat. § 103.011 (2000) . . . .

The state legislature has also provided mechanisms both for protesting election returns and for contesting certified election results. Section 102.166 governs protests. Any protest must be filed prior to the certification of election results by the county canvassing board. . . .

Contests to the certification of an election, on the other hand, are controlled by § 102.168. The grounds for contesting an election include "[r]eceipt of a number of illegal votes or rejection of a number of legal votes sufficient to change or place in doubt the result of the election." § 102.168(3)(c). . . .

But as we indicated in our remand of the earlier case, in a Presidential election the clearly expressed intent of the legislature must prevail. And there is no basis for reading the Florida statutes as requiring the counting of improperly marked ballots, as an examination of the Florida Supreme Court's textual analysis shows. . . . For the court to step away from this established practice, prescribed by the Secretary of State, the state official charged by the legislature with "responsibility to . . . [o]btain and maintain uniformity in the application, operation, and interpretation of the election laws," § 97.012(1), was to depart from the legislative scheme.

III

The scope and nature of the remedy ordered by the Florida Supreme Court jeopardizes the "legislative wish" to take advantage of the safe harbor provided by 3 U.S.C. § 5. December 12, 2000, is the last date for a final determination of the Florida electors that will satisfy § 5. Yet in the late afternoon of December 8th—four days before this deadline—the Supreme Court of Florida ordered recounts of tens of thousands of so-called "undervotes" spread through 64 of the State's 67 counties. This was done in a search for elusive—perhaps delusive—certainty as to the exact count of 6 million votes. But no one claims that these ballots have not previously been tabulated; they were initially read by voting machines at the time of the election, and thereafter reread by virtue of Florida's automatic recount provision. No one claims there was any fraud in the election. The Supreme Court of Florida ordered this additional recount under the provision of the election code giving the circuit judge the authority to provide relief that is "appropriate under such circumstances." Fla. Stat. § 102.168(8) (2000).

Surely when the Florida Legislature empowered the courts of the State to grant "appropriate" relief, it must have meant relief that would have become final by the cut-off date of 3 U.S.C. § 5. In light of the inevitable legal challenges and ensuing appeals to the Supreme Court of Florida and petitions for certiorari to this Court, the entire recounting process could not possibly be completed by that date . . . . But the federal deadlines for the Presidential election simply do not permit even such a shortened process. . . .

Given all these factors, and in light of the legislative intent identified by the Florida Supreme Court to bring Florida within the "safe harbor" provision of 3 U.S.C. § 5, the remedy prescribed by the Supreme Court of Florida cannot be deemed an "appropriate" one as of December 8. It significantly departed from the statutory framework in place on November 7, and authorized open-ended further proceedings which could not be completed by December 12, thereby preventing a final determination by that date.

For these reasons, in addition to those given in the *per curiam*, we would reverse.

JUSTICE STEVENS, with whom JUSTICE GINSBURG and JUSTICE BREYER join, dissenting.

The Constitution assigns to the States the primary responsibility for determining the manner of selecting the Presidential electors. See Art. II, § 1, cl. 2. When questions arise about the meaning of state laws, including election laws, it is our settled practice to accept the opinions of the highest courts of the States as providing the final answers. On rare occasions, however, either federal statutes or the Federal Constitution may require federal judicial intervention in state elections. This is not such an occasion.

The federal questions that ultimately emerged in this case are not substantial. . . .

Even assuming that aspects of the remedial scheme might ultimately be found to violate the Equal Protection Clause, I could not subscribe to the majority's disposition of the case. As the majority explicitly holds, once a state legislature determines to select electors through a popular vote, the right to have one's vote counted is of constitutional stature. As the majority further acknowledges, Florida law holds that all ballots that reveal the intent of the voter constitute valid votes. . . .

In the interest of finality, however, the majority effectively orders the disenfranchisement of an unknown number of voters whose ballots reveal their intent—and are therefore legal votes under state law—but were for some reason rejected by ballot-counting machines. It does so on the basis of the deadlines set forth in Title 3 of the United States Code. But, as I have already noted, those provisions merely provide rules of decision for Congress to follow when selecting among conflicting slates of electors. They do not prohibit a State from counting what the majority concedes to be legal votes until a bona fide winner is determined. . . .

What must underlie petitioners' entire federal assault on the Florida election procedures is an unstated lack of confidence in the impartiality and capacity of the state judges who would make the critical decisions if the vote count were to proceed. Otherwise, their position is wholly without merit. The endorsement of that position by the majority of this Court can only lend credence to the most cynical appraisal of the work of judges throughout the land. It is confidence in the men and women who administer the judicial system that is the true backbone of the rule of law. Time will one day heal the wound to that confidence that will be inflicted by today's decision. One thing, however, is certain. Although we may never know with complete certainty the identity of the winner of this year's Presidential election, the identity of the loser is perfectly clear. It is the Nation's confidence in the judge as an impartial guardian of the rule of law.

I respectfully dissent.

JUSTICE SOUTER, with whom JUSTICE BREYER joins and with whom JUSTICE STEVENS and JUSTICE GINSBURG join with regard to all but Part C, dissenting.

The Court should not have reviewed either Bush v. Palm Beach County Canvassing Bd., or this case, and should not have stopped Florida's attempt to recount all undervote ballots, by issuing a stay of the Florida Supreme Court's orders during the period of this review. If this Court had allowed the State to follow the course indicated by the opinions of its own Supreme Court, it is entirely possible that there would ultimately have been no issue requiring our review, and political tension could have worked itself out in the Congress following the procedure provided in 3 U.S.C. § 15. The case being before us, however, its resolution by the majority is another erroneous decision. . . .

A

The 3 U.S.C. § 5 issue is not serious. That provision sets certain conditions for treating a State's certification of Presidential electors as conclusive in the event that a dispute over recognizing those electors must be resolved in the Congress under 3 U.S.C. § 15. . . . And even that determination is to be made, if made anywhere, in the Congress.

B

The second matter here goes to the State Supreme Court's interpretation of certain terms in the state statute governing election "contests," Fla. Stat. § 102.168 (2000); there is no question here about the state court's interpretation of the related provisions dealing with the antecedent process of "protesting" particular vote counts, § 102.166, which was involved in the previous case, *Bush v. Palm Beach County Canvassing Board.* . . .

The starting point for evaluating the claim that the Florida Supreme Court's interpretation effectively re-wrote § 102.168 must be the language of the provision on which Gore relies to show his right to raise this contest: that the previously certified result in Bush's favor was produced by "rejection of a number of legal votes sufficient to change or place in doubt the result of the election." None of the state court's interpretations is unreasonable to the point of displacing the legislative enactment quoted.

In sum, the interpretations by the Florida court raise no substantial question under Article II. . . .

C

It is only on the third issue before us that there is a meritorious argument for relief, as this Court's *Per Curiam* opinion recognizes. It is an issue that might well have been dealt with adequately by the Florida courts if the state proceedings had not been interrupted, and if not disposed of at the state level it could have been considered by the Congress in any electoral vote dispute. But because the course of state proceedings has been interrupted, time is short, and the issue is before us, I think it sensible for the Court to address it.

Petitioners have raised an equal protection claim (or, alternatively, a due process claim, see generally *Logan v. Zimmerman Brush Co.*, 455 U.S. 422 (1982)), in the charge that unjustifiably disparate standards are applied in different electoral jurisdictions to otherwise identical facts. . . . . I can conceive of no legitimate state interest served by these differing treatments of the expressions of voters' fundamental rights. The differences appear wholly arbitrary.

In deciding what to do about this, we should take account of the fact that electoral votes are due to be cast in six days. I would therefore remand the case to the courts of Florida with instructions to establish uniform standards for evaluating the several types of ballots that have prompted differing treatments, to be applied within and among counties when passing on such identical ballots in any further recounting (or successive recounting) that the courts might order. . . .

JUSTICE GINSBURG, with whom JUSTICE STEVENS joins, and with whom JUSTICE SOUTER and JUSTICE BREYER join as to Part I, dissenting.

I

The Chief Justice acknowledges that provisions of Florida's Election Code "may well admit of more than one interpretation." But instead of respecting the state high court's province to say what the State's Election Code means, The Chief Justice maintains that Florida's Supreme Court has veered so far from the ordinary practice of judicial review that what it did cannot properly be called judging. . . . There is no cause here to believe that the members of Florida's high court have done less than "their mortal best to discharge their oath of office," and no cause to upset their reasoned interpretation of Florida law. . . .

By holding that Article II requires our revision of a state court's construction of state laws in order to protect one organ of the State from another, The Chief Justice contradicts the basic principle that a State may organize itself as it sees fit. Article II does not call for the scrutiny undertaken by this Court. . . .

JUSTICE BREYER, with whom JUSTICE STEVENS and JUSTICE GINSBURG join except as to Part I-A-1, and with whom JUSTICE SOUTER joins as to Part I, dissenting.

I

The political implications of this case for the country are momentous. But the federal legal questions presented, with one exception, are insubstantial.

A

1

The majority raises three Equal Protection problems with the Florida Supreme Court's recount order: first, the failure to include overvotes in the manual recount; second, the fact that *all* ballots, rather than simply the undervotes, were recounted in some, but not all, counties; and third, the absence of a uniform, specific standard to guide the recounts. As far as the first issue is concerned, petitioners presented no evidence, to this Court or to any Florida court, that a manual recount of overvotes would identify additional legal votes. The same is true of the second, and, in addition, the majority's reasoning would seem to invalidate any state provision for a manual recount of individual counties in a statewide election. The majority's third concern does implicate principles of fundamental fairness. The majority concludes that the Equal Protection Clause requires that a manual recount be governed not only by the uniform general standard of the "clear intent of the voter," but also by uniform subsidiary standards (for example, a uniform determination whether indented, but not perforated, "undervotes" should count). . . . I agree that, in these very special circumstances, basic principles of fairness may well have counseled the adoption of a uniform standard to address the problem. In light of the majority's disposition, I need not decide whether, or the extent to which, as a remedial matter, the Constitution would place limits upon the content of the uniform standard.

2

Nonetheless, there is no justification for the majority's remedy, which is simply to reverse the lower court and halt the recount entirely. . . .

By halting the manual recount, and thus ensuring that the uncounted legal votes will not be counted under any standard, this Court crafts a remedy out of proportion to the asserted harm. And that remedy harms the very fairness interests the Court is attempting to protect. The manual recount would itself redress a problem of unequal treatment of ballots. . . .

B

The remainder of petitioners' claims, which are the focus of The Chief Justice's concurrence, raise no significant federal questions. . . .

II

Despite the reminder that this case involves "an election for the President of the United States," no preeminent legal concern, or practical concern related to legal questions, required this Court to hear this case, let alone to issue a stay that stopped Florida's recount process in its tracks. . . .

Of course, the selection of the President is of fundamental national importance. But that importance is political, not legal. And this Court should resist the temptation unnecessarily to resolve tangential legal disputes, where doing so threatens to determine the outcome of the election.

The Constitution and federal statutes themselves make clear that restraint is appropriate. They set forth a road map of how to resolve disputes about electors, even after an election as close as this one. That road map foresees resolution of electoral disputes by *state* courts.

To the contrary, the Twelfth Amendment commits to Congress the authority and responsibility to count electoral votes. A federal statute, the Electoral Count Act, enacted after the close 1876 Hayes-Tilden Presidential election, specifies that, after States have tried to resolve disputes (through "judicial" or other means), Congress is the body primarily authorized to resolve remaining disputes.

The legislative history of the Act makes clear its intent to commit the power to resolve such disputes to Congress, rather than the courts . . .

The decision by both the Constitution's Framers and the 1886 Congress to minimize this Court's role in resolving close federal presidential elections is as wise as it is clear. However awkward or difficult it may be for Congress to resolve difficult electoral disputes, Congress, being a political body, expresses the people's will far more accurately than does an unelected Court. And the people's will is what elections are about. . . .

NOTES AND QUESTIONS

(1) *Manual Recount Procedures, the Electoral College and Equal Protection: Bush v. Gore, 531 U.S. 98 (2000).* In *Bush II*, the Supreme Court, in the *per curiam* opinion, held that the manual recount of the Presidential election ordered by the Florida Supreme Court (to discern the "intent of the voter") violated Governor Bush's rights under the equal protection doctrine because the state court had not provided specific, state-wide standards to avoid arbitrary treatment of voters. The concurrence, by Chief Justice Rehnquist, would have also held that the state court's procedures would have violated the principles of Article II. The dissenters—Justices Stevens, Souter, Ginsburg, and Breyer—disagreed with the Article II analysis and, to a lesser extent, the *per curiam* opinion's equal protection analysis. Some of the issues raised by this controversy are examined below.

(2) *State Manual Recount Procedures and Equal Protection.* As you will examine in Chapter 11, the right to vote in state elections is considered as a "fundamental right" for purposes of equal protection doctrine. The Court suggests that, when the state court ordered manual recounting on a less than state-wide basis and without standard recount procedures, this interpretation violated the fundamental rights of certain Florida voters. The majority suggested that, unless some specific standards were identified in advance, a manual recount to determine the "intent of the voter" would be so arbitrary as to violate the equal protection guarantee. The dissenters response here would emphasize the values of federalism, generally arguing that the Court should show some deference to the state courts even though this state election was for Presidential electors.

(3) *Presidential Elections and the Political Question Doctrine.* The Electoral College is a particular invention of the Framers, and they set forth the basic procedures in Article II. When historical experience (*i.e.*, the election of President Jefferson in 1800) demonstrated some problems, the Twelfth Amendment was passed to rectify them. The dissenters in *Bush II*, particularly Justice Breyer, argued that the provisions of Article II and the Twelfth Amendment demonstrate that there is a "textual commitment" of Electoral College disputes to Congress and, therefore, the federal courts should avoid deciding the "political question." *See* § 1.02 above. Reconsider Chief Justice Rehnquist's concurrence as arguing that the text of the Constitution must be "supplemented" by reference to 3 U.S.C. § 5 (the "safe harbor" statute) which is a Congressional decision about the role of the states in Electoral College disputes. Notice that the *per curiam* opinion avoids reliance on any Article II analysis. *See generally* Jack M. Balkin & Sanford Levinson, *Understanding the Constitutional Revolution*, 87 Va. L. Rev. 1045 (2001).

Given the importance of the 2000 Presidential election and the decisive role of the Supreme Court, there has been a large volume of academic (and popular) commentary. For further information, students can read the exchange of views between Professors Nelson Lund and Laurence H. Tribe in 19 CONST. COMMENT. 543–625 (2002). *See generally* Mark Tushnet, Essay, *Renormalizing Bush v. Gore: An Anticipatory Intellectual History*, 90 GEO. L.J. 113 (2001).

Chapter 6
CONSTITUTIONAL PROTECTION OF ECONOMIC RIGHTS

§ 6.01 CONSTITUTIONAL PROTECTION OF ECONOMIC, AS OPPOSED TO PERSONAL OR POLITICAL, RIGHTS

NOTE: DO ECONOMIC RIGHTS HAVE A STATUS SIMILAR TO THAT OF OTHER PERSONAL AND POLITICAL RIGHTS?

Lesser Protection for Economic Rights? The view often is expressed that such economic rights as the right to enforce contracts or to protect property are of lesser status than individual and political rights. In this view, the freedom from invasion of personal security, the right to vote, and the freedom of speech are more deserving of protection. [For arguments emphasizing the economic values of the Constitution, *see* Symposium, *The Constitution as an Economic Document*, 56 GEO. WASH. L. REV. 172 (1987); Powe, *Scholarship and Markets*, in *Id.*]

The Controversial Argument That Personal and Political Rights Depend Upon Economic Rights: Professor Friedman's View. The contrary view—and it is a controversial one—is that the ability to protect capital in private hands is necessary to other freedoms. According to this theory, if individuals can transform their accumulated wealth into printing presses, ink, and paper, they may be able to begin a newspaper; without the ability to protect wealth from government invasion, they may not be able to do so. One of the principal proponents of this view is Professor Milton Friedman. Consider the following:

> In a capitalist society, it is only necessary to convince a few wealthy people to get funds to launch any idea, however strange, and there are many such persons, many independent foci of support. . . . It is only necessary to persuade them that the propagation can be financially successful; that the newspaper or magazine or book or other venture will be profitable. The competitive publisher, for example, cannot afford to publish only writings with which he personally agrees; his touchstone must be the likelihood that the market will be large enough to yield a satisfactory return on his investment.

> [T]here are no such possibilities in the socialist society; there is only the all-powerful state.

> Let us stretch our imagination and suppose that a socialist government is aware of this problem and is composed of people anxious to preserve freedom. Could it provide the funds? . . . It could establish a bureau for subsidizing subversive propaganda. But how could it choose whom to support? If it gave to all who asked, it would shortly find itself out of funds.

> Moreover, freedom to advocate unpopular causes does not require that such advocacy be without cost. On the contrary, no society could be stable if advocacy of radical change were costless, much less subsidized.

> But we are not yet through. In a free market society, it is enough to have the funds. The suppliers of paper are as willing to sell it to the *Daily Worker* as to the *Wall Street Journal.* In a socialist society, it would not be enough to have the funds. The hypothetical supporter of capitalism would have to persuade a government factory making paper to sell to him, the government printing press to print his pamphlets, a government post office to distribute them among the people, a government agency to rent him a hall in which to talk, and so on.

> . . . So far as I know, none of the people who have been in favor of socialism and also in favor of freedom have really faced up to this issue, or made even a

respectable start at developing the institutional arrangements that would permit freedom under socialism. By contrast, it is clear how a free market capitalist society fosters freedom.

M. FRIEDMAN, CAPITALISM AND FREEDOM 17–19 (1962)*; *see also* M. & R. FRIEDMAN, FREE TO CHOOSE 65–69 (1980). Do these views have merit? To maintain other individual and political rights, will it be necessary for an independent judiciary to protect economic rights as zealously as, say, the freedom of speech?

The Argument Against Equivalent Protection of Economic Rights. There also are many commentators who would oppose or qualify Friedman's theory. In the first place, there is the argument that capitalism produces such serious harm to the common environment, because it does not motivate people to serve the common good, as to outweigh its putative advantages, at least in some instances. *Cf.* J. K. GALBRAITH, THE AFFLUENT SOCIETY (1958). Another view is that the capitalist claim of market superiority is exaggerated in that the market requires much more participation by government to produce regularity and predictability than market-supporting economists would admit. *Cf.* J. K. GALBRAITH, THE NEW INDUSTRIAL STATE (1967). Furthermore, a market economy by itself produces (and cannot redress) severe inequalities of income, including extremes of poverty. *See* R. DORFMAN, PRICES AND MARKETS Ch. 9 (3d ed. 1978); P. SAMUELSON & W. NORDHAUS, ECONOMICS ch. 34–35 (12th ed. 1983); *cf.* R. POSNER, ECONOMIC ANALYSIS OF LAW ch. 16 (3d ed. 1986). Finally, the agglomerations of wealth that Friedman sees as leading to political freedoms are seen by others as leading instead to the permanent oppression of a powerless underclass, with whom the wealthy have too little in common. Indeed, one of the most influential works of political economy in world history predicts an ultimate class struggle followed by a dictatorship of the proletariat for these reasons. K. MARX, DAS KAPITAL (1869).

Tushnet's View: Tushnet, A Note on the Revival of Textualism in Constitutional Theory, 58 S. CAL. L. REV. 683, 694 (1985). In critiquing Laycock's theory of liberal textualism, Tushnet points out that Laycock identifies objects which the Constitution positively values (such as national unity, individualism, personal autonomy, and private association) as well as "bad" values (such as state sovereignty). Tushnet says: "I would add private property and the social control thereof to the list" of values that the Constitution regards as "bad." Is Tushnet's proposal capable of justification, given that the Constitution expressly prohibits taking of property for public use without just compensation, makes property an object of the due process clause, and prohibits contract impairment by the states?

The View of the Current Supreme Court Majority: The Dolan Case Holds that Economic Protection is not a "Poor Relation." One of the Supreme Court's recent pronouncements regarding the constitutional status of "economic rights" is *Dolan v. City of Tigard*, 512 U.S. 374 (1994). In the *Dolan* decision, below § 6.03, the Court, per Chief Justice Rehnquist, stated that "[w]e see no reason why the [rights under the] Takings Clause of the Fifth Amendment, as much a part of the Bill of Rights as the First Amendment or Fourth Amendment, should be relegated to the status of a poor relation in these comparable circumstances." Are the Chief Justice's statements consistent with Friedman or one of Friedman's critics?

§ 6.02   SUBSTANTIVE DUE PROCESS AND BUSINESS REGULATION

[A]   Early Conceptions: Justice Chase's "Natural Rights" Theory

CALDER v. BULL, 3 U.S. (3 Dall.) 386 (1798) (Chase, J.). The Connecticut state legislature voided a probate decree and directed a rehearing according to new provisions of law. The Court, per Justice Chase, held that this Connecticut Act was not an invalid ex post facto law. This holding, however, is not as interesting as the following exchange between Justices Chase and Iredell, expressing sharply different views about constitutional limits on government power.

CHASE, JUSTICE. . . . The people of the United States erected their constitutions, or forms of government, to establish justice, to promote the general welfare, to secure the blessing of liberty, and to protect their persons and property from violence. The purposes for which men enter into society will determine the nature and terms of the social compact; and as they are the foundations of the legislative power, they will decide what are the proper objects of it: the nature, and ends of legislative power will limit the exercise of it. . . . An act of the legislature (for I cannot call it a law) contrary to the great first principles of the social compact, cannot be considered a rightful exercise of legislative authority. . . . A law that punished a citizen for an innocent action, or, in other words, for an act, which when done, was in violation of no existing law; a law that destroys, or impairs, the lawful private contracts of citizens; a law that makes a man a judge in his own cause; or a law that takes property from A and gives it to B. It is against all reason and justice for a people to entrust a legislature with such power; and therefore, it cannot be presumed that they have done it. . . .

IREDELL, JUSTICE. . . . If, then, a government, composed of legislative, executive and judicial departments, were established, by a Constitution, which imposed no limits on the legislative power, the consequence would inevitably be, that whatever the legislative power chose to enact, would be lawfully enacted, and the judicial power, could never interpose to pronounce it void. It is true, that some speculative jurists have held, that a legislative act against natural justice must, in itself, be void; but I cannot think that any court of justice would possess a power to declare it so. . . .

[T]herefore, . . . it has been the policy . . . of the people of the United States, when they framed the federal Constitution, to define with precision the objects of the legislative power, and to restrain its exercise within marked and settled boundaries. If any act of Congress, or of the legislature of a state, violates those constitutional provisions, it is unquestionably void. . . . If, on the other hand, the legislature of the Union, or the legislature of any member of the Union, shall pass a law, within the general scope of their constitutional power, the Court cannot pronounce it to be void, merely because it is, in their judgment, contrary to the principles of natural justice. The ideas of natural justice are regulated by no fixed standard; the ablest and the purest men have differed upon the subject. . . . There are then but two lights, in which the subject can be viewed. 1st. if the legislature pursue the authority delegated to them, their acts are valid. 2d. if they transgressed the boundaries of that authority, their acts are invalid. . . .

NOTES AND QUESTIONS

(1) *The Limited Influence of Chase's View: Comparing Fletcher v. Peck, 10 U.S. (6 Cranch) 87 (1810).* The Court generally has refrained from expressly embracing Justice Chase's rhetoric, at least in that it has not justified decisions by natural law alone. Often, however, the construction of constitutional restraints may be supplemented by natural law reasoning. Thus, in *Fletcher v. Peck, supra,* the Court suggested that a state might be "restrained by the general principles of our political institutions [or] by the words of the Constitution." But the Court's holding, that a legislature could not constitutionally set aside land titles rented to purchasers, was connected to the contract clause and other provisions of Art. I § 10.

(2) *Was Justice Chase Nevertheless a Good Prophet?* Consider the following: "In form, the Supreme Court has adopted the views of Justice Iredell and ruled that it only may invalidate acts of the legislative and executive branches on the basis of specific provisions of the Constitution. In substance, however, the beliefs of Justice Chase have prevailed as the Court continually has expanded its bases for reviewing the acts of other branches of government." J. NOWAK, R. ROTUNDA & J. YOUNG, CONSTITUTIONAL LAW 426 (3d ed. 1986).

(3) *The Early States as Unrestrained by Due Process, Taking of Property, or other Bill of Rights Constraints: Barron v. Mayor and City Council, 32 U.S. (7 Pet.) 243 (1833).* In *Barron,* the Court (per Chief Justice Marshall) squarely held that the Fifth Amendment prohibition on taking private property for public use without just compensation did not apply to the states. In fact, said the Court, the Bill of Rights restrained only the federal government: "The Constitution was ordained and established by the people of the United States for themselves, for their own government, and not for the government of the individual states." Since the enactment of the Fourteenth Amendment, the Due Process and Equal Protection Clauses of that provision, which do apply to the states, have provided the kind of protection that was lacking in *Barron;* but in the early days of the Republic, after the *Barron* decision, there were few federal constitutional restraints on states. The prohibitions of Article I § 10 were applicable to the states, and prevented such acts as imposts or duties on imports or exports, passage of paper money tender laws, or enactment of those attained. It also prohibits states from impairing the obligations of contracts. But *Barron* induced lawyers to look, generally unsuccessfully, for implied theories of natural law in the Constitution.

[B] The Fourteenth Amendment

Read U.S. Const. Amend. XIII (abolishing involuntary servitude) and Amend. XIV (the fourteenth amendment).

NOTE: SUBSTANTIVE DUE PROCESS AND THE HISTORICAL BASIS OF THE FOURTEENTH AMENDMENT

The Thirteenth Amendment and the Civil Rights Act of 1866. In 1865, near the end of the Civil War, the Thirteenth Amendment was ratified, prohibiting involuntary servitude. *See* Chapter 14, below. Desiring a broader protection for African Americans than merely freedom from slavery, Congress the next year passed the Civil Rights Act of 1866, which contained broad prohibitions against any states denying contract, property, or various other rights to any citizen on grounds of "race or color [or] previous condition" of servitude. The Thirteenth Amendment gave Congress the power to enforce its anti-slavery provisions, but there were doubts about the validity of basing broader legislative protections, such as those of the Civil Rights Act of 1866, upon the ostensibly narrow protections of the Thirteenth Amendment. *See generally* Buchanan, *The Quest for Freedom: A Legal History of the Thirteenth Amendment* (1976) [originally published in volumes 12 and 13 of the HOUSTON LAW REVIEW].

Adoption of the Fourteenth Amendment. Thus, a major impetus for promulgation of the Fourteenth Amendment was Congress' recognition of the possible need to provide a sound basis for the Civil Rights Act of 1866. The Fourteenth Amendment began as a congressional committee proposal for authorizing Congress to legislate on the subject. Later, Privileges or Immunities, Due Process, and Equal Protection Clauses were added, directly restraining the states. The amendment was ratified in 1868. *See* Maltz, *Reconstruction without Revolution: Republican Civil Rights Theory in the Era of the Fourteenth Amendment*, 24 HOUS. L. REV. 221 (1987).

"Procedural" Due Process and "Substantive" Due Process. On its face, the Due Process Clause seems to be concerned only with matters of procedure—with issues such as notice, a right to be heard, and the like. But the clause necessarily is broader, because it is bound up with the concept of "life, liberty or property" that the "process" is invoked to protect. Hence the concept of "substantive" due process: the clause may be used to protect against arbitrary state deprivations of life, liberty or property of various kinds, even if they do not pose issues that we normally would think of as procedural. According to this notion, a legislative enactment regulating the conduct of an individual or firm may be invalid if it impairs interests in life, liberty or property, even if the procedure by which it is enacted and enforced is, strictly speaking, not objectionable.

The Slaughter House Cases: Early Rejection of the Fourteenth Amendment as a Broad Charter of Economic Freedom. It was natural that this theory of substantive due process would be thrust into the void left by the absence of effective constitutional restraints on state impairment of economic interests. But there were several reasons for not accepting this theory. First, the history of the amendment suggested a primary purpose of protecting African American citizens. Second (and less obviously), substantive due process easily can be overasserted and then threatens to overwhelm desirable legislative prerogative. In any event, the Supreme Court's early analysis rejected the Privileges or Immunities, Due Process, and Equal Protection Clauses as general protections of economic rights, in the *Slaughter House Cases.*

THE SLAUGHTER HOUSE CASES, 83 U.S. (16 Wall.) 36 (1873). Independent butchers challenged Louisiana's grant of a monopoly to a particular firm to operate slaughterhouses in New Orleans. Their arguments were based upon the Privileges or Immunities, Due Process, and Equal Protection Clauses. The Court, per Justice Miller, emphasized the history of the Fourteenth Amendment in rejecting these challenges:

> The most cursory glance at these [civil rights amendments] discloses a unity of purpose, when taken in connection with the history of the times, which cannot fail to have an important bearing on any question of doubt concerning their true meaning. . . .

> The institution of African slavery, as it existed in about half the states of the Union . . . culminated in the effort, on the part of most of the states in which slavery existed, to separate from the federal government, and to resist its authority. This constituted the war of the rebellion. . . .

> In that struggle slavery, as a legalized social relation, perished. . . .

> . . . Among the first acts of the legislation adopted by several of the states in the legislative bodies . . . were laws which imposed upon the colored race onerous disabilities and burdens, and curtailed their rights in the pursuit of life, liberty and property. . . .

> [I]n the light of this recapitulation of events, . . . and on the most casual examination of the language of these amendments, no one can fail to be

impressed with the one pervading purpose found in them all, lying at the foundation of each, and without which none of them would have been even suggested; we mean the freedom of the slave race, the security and firm establishment of that freedom, and the protection of the newly made free men and citizens from the oppressions of those who had formerly exercised unlimited dominion over them.

We do not say that no one else but the negro can share in this protection. Both the language and spirit of these articles are to have their fair and just weight in any question of construction. Undoubtedly, while negro slavery alone was in the mind of the Congress which proposed the thirteenth [amendment] it forbids any other kind of slavery, now or hereafter. . . .

The 1st section of the fourteenth [amendment], to which our attention is more specially invited, opens with a definition of citizenship—not only citizenship of the United States, but citizenship of the states. It had been said by eminent judges that no man was a citizen of the United States except as he was a citizen of one of the states composing the Union. . . . [I]t had been held by this Court, in the celebrated *Dred Scott* case, only a few years before the outbreak of the civil war, that a man of African descent, whether a slave or not, was not and could not be a citizen of a state or of the United States. . . . To remove this difficulty primarily, and to establish a clear and comprehensive definition of citizenship which should declare what should constitute citizenship of the United States and also citizenship of a State, the [national citizenship] clause was framed. . . .

[I]t is only the [privileges and immunities of the citizens of the United States] which are placed by this clause under the protection of the federal Constitution, and . . . the [privileges and immunities of the citizen of the state], whatever they may be, are not intended to have any additional protection by this paragraph of the amendment. . . .

[The Court next distinguished the fourteenth amendment privileges and immunities clause from the interstate privileges and immunities clause of Art. IV § 2, which protects privileges and immunities of citizens of states. It inquired what rights were protected by that phrase.]. . .

. . . The first and the leading case on the subject is that of *Corfield v. Coryell,* 4 Wash. CC 371 (Pa. Cir. 1823): "The inquiry . . . is, what are the privileges and immunities of citizens of the several states? We feel no hesitation in confining these expressions to those privileges and immunities which are fundamental; which belong of right to the citizens of all free governments. . . . What these fundamental principles are, it would be more tedious than difficult to enumerate." "They may all, however, be comprehended under the following general heads: protection by the government, with a right to acquire and possess property of every kind, and to pursue and obtain happiness and safety, subject, nevertheless, to such restraints as the government may prescribe for the general good of the whole."

. . . Was it the purpose of the fourteenth amendment, by the simple declaration that no state should make or enforce any law which shall abridge the privileges and immunities of citizens of the United States, to transfer the security and protection of all the civil rights which we have mentioned, from the states to the federal government? . . .

We are convinced that no such results were intended by the Congress which proposed these amendments, nor by the legislatures of the states, which ratified them.

[W]e may hold ourselves excused from defining the privileges and immunities of citizens of the United States which no state can abridge, until some case involving those privileges may make it necessary to do so. [The Court went on to describe some such "United-States-protected" privileges and immunities, including the right to come to the seat of government "to assert any claim he may have upon" it, to have "free access to its seaports," and "to demand the care and protection of the federal government over his life, liberty, and property when on the high seas or within the jurisdiction of a foreign government."]

The argument has not been much pressed in these cases that the defendant's charter deprives the plaintiffs of their property without due process of law, or that it denies to them the equal protection of the law. . . . In the light of the history of these amendments, and the pervading purpose of them, which we have already discussed, it is not difficult to give a meaning to this [due process] clause. . . .

. . . We doubt very much whether any action of a state not directed by way of discrimination against the negroes as a class, or on account of their race, will ever be held to come within the purview of this provision. It is so clearly a provision for that race and that emergency, that a strong case would be necessary for its application to any other. . . .

Justice Field, joined by Justices Chase, Swayne, and Bradley, dissented. He agreed that the fourteenth amendment did not attempt to create new privileges or immunities, but concluded that the Civil Rights Act of 1866 "was supported upon the theory that citizens of the United States as such were entitled to the rights and privileges enumerated, and to deny any such citizen equality in these rights and privileges with others was, to the extent of the denial, subjecting him to an involuntary servitude." Therefore, the dissenters reasoned, the rights of "citizens of all free governments" must have been the objective of the fourteenth amendment privileges and immunities clause also. "This equality of right . . . in the lawful pursuits of life, . . . is the distinguishing privilege of citizens of the United States. . . . The fourteenth amendment, in my judgment, makes it essential to the viability of the legislation of every state that this equality of right should be respected."

NOTES AND QUESTIONS

(1) *The Slaughter House Cases and the Judicial Interpretation of the Fourteenth Amendment's Privileges or Immunities Clause.* The *Slaughter House Cases* rejected the independent butchers' challenge based on several Thirteenth and Fourteenth Amendment theories. The Court's interpretation of the Fourteenth Amendment's Privileges or Immunities Clause has been given great precedential weight since this was an early interpretation of the Clause by a Court that witnessed its ratification. The *Slaughter House* majority first distinguished between privileges or immunities granted by the States and *federal privileges or immunities* granted pursuant to national citizenship. The Court held that the Clause protected only federal privileges or immunities. As to all other privileges or immunities, the Court held that the States were free to define such rights and that judicial review would be deferential (*i.e.*, under rational basis review—to use the modern terminology). As suggested by the Introductory Notes, this interpretation had the effect of eviscerating the substantive content of the Privileges or Immunities Clause. The common understanding of the *Slaughter House* decision was that the Court's interpretation had nullified the Clause. *See Saenz v. Roe*, 526 U.S. 489, 521 (1999) (Thomas, J., dissenting); LAURENCE TRIBE, AMERICAN CONSTITUTIONAL LAW §§ 7-2; 7-3 (2d. ed 1988). For further research, review Richard L. Aynes, *The Continuing Importance of Congressman John A. Bingham and the Fourteenth Amendment*, 36 AKRON L. REV. 589 (2003); David S. Bogan, *Slaughter-House: Five Views of the Case*, 55 HASTINGS L.J. 333 (2003).

(2) *Possible Reinterpretation of the Privileges or Immunities Clause: Judicial and Academic Revisionism?* In § 10.03, you will read a right to interstate travel decision, *Saenz v. Roe*, 526 U.S. 489 (1999), where several of the Justices discuss the Privileges

or Immunities Clause and the *Slaughter House Cases*. This may suggest a willingness to revisit the narrow interpretation of the Clause imposed there. The academic commentaries have, for many years, called for revising—or overruling—the *Slaughter House* interpretation. The literature is extensive. For some of the "revisionism" debate, see James W. Fox, Jr., *Re-Readings and Misreadings: Slaughter-House, Privileges or Immunities and Section Five Enforcement Powers*, 91 Ky. L.J. 67 (2003); Kevin Christopher Newsom, *Setting Incorporationism Straight: A Reinterpretation of the Slaughter-House Cases*, 109 Yale L.J. 643, 649 (2000); William J. Rich, *Privileges or Immunities: The Missing Link in Establishing Congressional Power to Abrogate State Eleventh Amendment Immunity*, 28 Hastings Const. L.Q. 235 (2001); and Bryan H. Wildenthal, *The Lost Compromise: Reassessing the Early Understanding in Court and Congress on Incorporation of the Bill of Rights in the Fourteenth Amendment*, 61 Ohio St. L.J. 1051 (2001). Regarding the scope of the Section Five power, *see* Chapter 14.

MUNN v. ILLINOIS
94 U.S. 113 (1877)

Mr. Chief Justice Waite delivered the opinion of the Court:

[The Illinois assembly fixed by law the maximum price for grain storage in warehouses in Chicago and other cities. Plaintiffs attacked this regulation under the Negative Commerce Clause, Port Preference Clause, and Due Process and Equal Protection Clauses of the Fourteenth Amendment. The Court upheld the statute, dealing first with the fourteenth amendment.]

Every statute is presumed to be constitutional. The courts ought not to declare one to be unconstitutional, unless it is clearly so. . . .

When one becomes a member of society, he necessarily parts with some rights or privileges which, as an individual not affected by his relations to others, he might retain. . . . This does not confer power upon the whole people to control rights which are purely and exclusively private, . . . but it does authorize the establishment of laws requiring each citizen to so conduct himself, and so use his own property as not unnecessarily to injure another. . . . From this source came the police powers. . . . With the fifth amendment in force, Congress . . . conferred power upon the city of Washington "to regulate . . . the rates of wharfage at private wharfs, . . . the sweeping of chimneys, and to fix the rates of fees therefore . . . and the weight and quality of bread. . . ."

From this it is apparent that, down to the time of the adoption of the fourteenth amendment, it was not supposed that statutes regulating the use, or even the price of the use, of private property necessarily deprived an owner of his property without due process of law. . . .

This brings us to inquire as to the principles upon which this power of regulation rests, in order that we may determine what is within and what without its operative effect. Looking, then, to the common law, from whence came the right which the Constitution protects, we find that when private property is "affected with a public interest, it ceases to be *juris privati* only." Property does become clothed with a public interest when used in a manner to make it of public consequence, and affect the community at large. When, therefore, one devotes his property to a use in which the public has an interest, he, in effect, grants to the public an interest in that use, and must submit it to be controlled by the public for the common good, to the extent of the interest he thus has created. . . .

NOTES AND QUESTIONS

(1) *Property "Clothed with a Public Interest" as Versus Purely "Private" Property: Is there an Adequate Limiting Principle in the Munn Reasoning?* Perhaps Chief Justice Waite's distinction between objects of "public interest" and those of private interest has some degree of validity. Thus, for example, we would suppose that a law comprehensively regulating the conduct of a grain elevator might be more likely to be upheld than comprehensive regulation of one's pursuits in his own private home. But can't such very "private" property as the interiors of one's home become "clothed with a public interest" in some instances? *Compare Village of Belle Terre v. Boraas*, 416 U.S. 1 (1974) (upholding prohibition upon co-residence of persons not related by blood or marriage) with *Moore v. City of East Cleveland*, 431 U.S. 494 (1977) (striking down regulation that would require exclusion of blood relatives). Actually, doesn't a privately owned pocket comb become "clothed with a public interest" if it has sharp edges and is left in a place where it might injure someone? Is there a way that the reasoning of *Munn* can be used to fashion a test of what does, and does not, violate substantive due process? [Perhaps it can be done by inquiring whether the regulated *aspect* is one in which there is a legitimate public interest?]

(2) *The Nature and Extent of Regulation of Property "Clothed with a Public Interest."* If a business is "clothed with a public interest," *Munn* says it can be regulated, but it does not indicate whether there is any kind or extent of regulation that would be unacceptable. Would regulation be valid if it is arbitrary or nonsensical (*e.g.*, every grain elevator must have a skating rink attached)? Would it be valid if confiscatory (*e.g.*, if it regulated prices at such a low level that the most efficient managers could not run them except at a loss)?

(3) *Deference to the Legislature.* Chief Justice Waite announces a "presumption" of constitutionality that is to prevail unless there the contrary is clear. But notice that Chief Justice Waite does not state what kind of test is to be used to determine when the "presumption" of constitutionality is overcome. Is this aspect of the opinion a defect, and if so, why?

(4) *Trouble Arises after Munn as "Liberty of Contract" Begins to Convert the Court into a "Super-Legislature:" Mugler v. Kansas, 123 U.S. 623 (1887), and Allgeyer v. Louisiana, 165 U.S. 578 (1897).* In *Mugler*, the Court sustained prohibition of alcoholic beverages against a claim that it denied due process by putting liquor dealers out of business. *Mugler* appeared to approve deference to the legislature, but it sowed the seeds of a constitutional crisis, because it contained dictum requiring that the legislature's actions bear a "substantial relation" to protection of public health, morals or safety. Then, in *Allgeyer*, the Court used "liberty of contract" reasoning to strike down a Louisiana law requiring regulatory approval of out-of-state insurance contracts on in-state property. With *Allgeyer*, the substantive due process theory that the Court had rejected in the *Slaughter House Cases* became a basis for striking down any law that regulated the freedom to contract. The case that follows, *Lochner v. New York*, is the best known in this line of cases.

[C] "Liberty of Contract": A Case Study in the Need for Judicial Restraint

LOCHNER v. NEW YORK

198 U.S. 45 (1905)

Mr. Justice Peckham . . . delivered the opinion of the Court:

[A New York law limited the hours a bakery employee could work to ten per day and sixty per week. The New York Court of Appeals, by a four-to-three majority, upheld this statute as a health law. Here, the Supreme Court strikes it down as a violation of "liberty of contract."]

. . . The mandate of the statute, that "no employee shall be required or permitted to work," is the substantial equivalent of an enactment that "no employee shall contract or agree to work," more than ten hours per day; and, as there is no provision for special emergencies, the statute is mandatory in all cases. . . . The employee may desire to earn the extra money which would arise from his working more than the prescribed time, but this statute forbids the employer from permitting the employee to earn it.

The statute necessarily interferes with the right of contract between the employer and employees, concerning the number of hours in which the latter may labor in the bakery of the employer. The general right to make a contract in relation to his business is part of the liberty of the individual protected by the 14th Amendment of the Federal Constitution. *Allgeyer v. Louisiana*, 165 U.S. 578. . . . The right to purchase or to sell labor is part of the liberty protected by this amendment, unless there are circumstances which exclude the right. There are, however, certain powers, existing in the sovereignty of each state in the Union, somewhat vaguely termed police powers, the exact description and limitation of which have not been attempted by the courts. Those powers, broadly stated, and without, at present, any attempt at a more specific limitation, relate to the safety, health, morals, and general welfare of the public. Both property and liberty are held on such reasonable conditions as may be imposed by the governing power of the state in the exercise of those powers, and with such conditions the 14th Amendment was not designed to interfere. *Mugler v. Kansas*. . . .

It must, of course, be conceded that there is a limit to the valid exercise of the police power by the state. . . . Otherwise the 14th Amendment would have no efficacy. . . . In every case that comes before this court, therefore, where legislation of this character is concerned, and where the protection of the Federal Constitution is sought, the question necessarily arises: Is this a fair, reasonable, and appropriate exercise of the police power of the state, or is it an unreasonable, unnecessary, and arbitrary interference with the right of the individual to his personal liberty, or to enter into those contracts in relation to labor which may seem to him appropriate or necessary for the support of himself and his family? Of course the liberty of contract relating to labor includes both parties to it. The one has as much right to purchase as the other to sell labor.

This is not a question of substituting the judgment of the court for that of the legislature. If the act be within the power of the state it is valid, although the judgment of the court might be totally opposed to the enactment of such a law. But the question would still remain: Is it within the police power of the state? and that question must be answered by the court.

The question whether this act is valid as a labor law, pure and simple, may be dismissed in a few words. There is no reasonable ground for interfering with the liberty of person or the right of free contract, by determining the hours of labor, in the occupation of a baker. There is no contention that bakers as a class are not equal in intelligence and capacity to men in other trades or manual occupations, or that they are not able to assert their rights and care for themselves without the protecting arm of the state, interfering with their independence of judgment and of action. They are in no sense wards of the state. Viewed in the light of a purely labor law, with no reference whatsoever to the question of health, we think that a law like the one before us involves neither the safety, the morals, nor the welfare, of the public, and that the interest of the public is not in the slightest degree affected by such an act. The law must be upheld, if at all, as a law pertaining to the health of the individual engaged in the occupation of a baker. . . .

We think that there can be no fair doubt that the trade of a baker, in and of itself, is not an unhealthy one to that degree which would authorize the legislature to interfere with the right to labor, and with the right of free contract on the part of the individual, either as employer or employee. In looking through statistics regarding all trades and occupations, it may be true that the trade of a baker does not appear to be as healthy as some other trades, and is also vastly more healthy than still others.

. . . But are we all, on that account, at the mercy of legislative majorities? . . . In our large cities there are many buildings into which the sun penetrates for but a short time in each day, and these buildings are occupied by people carrying on the business of bankers, brokers, lawyers, real estate, and many other kinds of business, aided by many clerks, messengers, and other employees. Upon the assumption of the validity of this act under review, it is not possible to say that an act, prohibiting lawyers' or bank clerks, or others, from contracting to labor for their employers more than eight hours a day would be invalid. . . .

. . . We do not believe in the soundness of the views which uphold this law. On the contrary, we think that such a law as this, although passed in the assumed exercise of the police power, and as relating to the public health, or the health of the employees named, is not within that power, and is invalid. The net is not, within any fair meaning of the term, a health law, but is an illegal interference with the rights of individuals, both employers and employees, to make contracts regarding labor upon such terms as they may think best. . . .

It is manifest to us that the limitation of the hours of labor . . . has no such direct relation to, and no such substantial effect upon, the health of the employee, as to justify us in regarding the section as really a health law. It seems to us that the real object and purpose were simply to regulate the hours of labor between the master and his employees . . . in a private business, not dangerous in any degree to morals, or in any real and substantial degree to the health of the employees. Under such circumstances the freedom of master and employee to contract with each other in relation to their employment, and in defining the same, cannot be prohibited or interfered with, without violating the Federal Constitution. . . .

Mr. Justice Holmes dissenting: . . .

This case is decided upon an economic theory which a large part of the country does not entertain. If it were a question whether I agreed with that theory, I should desire to study it further and long before making up my mind. But I do not conceive that to be my duty, because I strongly believe that my agreement or disagreement has nothing to do with the right of a majority to embody their opinions in law. It is settled by various decisions of this court that state constitutions and state laws may regulate life in many ways which we as legislators might think as injudicious, or if you like as tyrannical, as this, and which, equally with this, interfere with the liberty to contract. Sunday laws and usury laws are ancient examples. A more modern one is the prohibition of lotteries. . . . The 14th Amendment does not enact Mr. Herbert Spencer's Social Statics. The other day we sustained the Massachusetts vaccination law. *Jacobson v. Massachusetts* . . . The decision sustaining an eight-hour law for miners is still recent. *Holden v. Hardy*, 100 U.S. 366. Some of these laws embody convictions or prejudices which judges are likely to share. Some may not. But a Constitution is not intended to embody a particular economic theory, whether of paternalism and the organic relation of the citizen to the state or of *laissez faire*. It is made for people of fundamentally differing views, and the accident of our finding certain opinions natural and familiar, or novel, and even shocking, ought not to conclude our judgment upon the question whether statutes embodying them conflict with the Constitution of the United States.

. . . I think that the word "liberty," in the 14th Amendment, is perverted when it is held to prevent the natural outcome of a dominant opinion, unless it can be said that a rational and fair man necessarily would admit that the statute proposed would infringe fundamental principles as they have been understood by the traditions of our people and our law. It does not need research to show that no such sweeping condemnation can be passed upon the statute before us. A reasonable man might think it a proper measure on the score of health. Men whom I certainly could not pronounce unreasonable would uphold it as a first installment of a general regulation of the hours of work. Whether in the latter aspect it would be open to the charge of inequality I think it unnecessary to discuss.

MR. JUSTICE HARLAN (with whom MR. JUSTICE WHITE and MR. JUSTICE DAY concurred) dissenting: . . .

It is plain that this statute was enacted in order to protect the physical well-being of those who work in bakery and confectionery establishments. It may be that the statute had its origin, in part, in the belief that employers and employees in such establishments were not upon an equal footing, and that the necessities of the latter often compelled them to submit to such exactions as unduly taxed their strength. Be this as it may, the statute must be taken as expressing the belief of the people of New York that, as a general rule, and in the case of the average man, labor in excess of sixty hours during a week in such establishments may endanger the health of those who thus labor. Whether or not this be wise legislation it is not the province of the court to inquire. . . . So that, in determining the question of power to interfere with liberty of contract, the court may inquire whether the means devised by the state are germane to an end which may be lawfully accomplished and have a real or substantial relation to the protection of health, as involved in the daily work of the persons, male and female, engaged in bakery and confectionery establishments. But when this inquiry is entered upon I find it impossible, in view of common experience, to say that there is here no real or substantial relation between the means employed by the state and the end sought to be accomplished by its legislation. *Mugler v. Kansas.* . . .

Professor Hirt in his treatise on the "Diseases of the Workers" has said: "The labor of the bakers is among the hardest and most laborious imaginable, because it has to be performed under conditions injurious to the health of those engaged in it. It is hard, very hard, work, not only because it requires a great deal of physical exertion in an overheated workshop and during unreasonably long hours, but more so because of the erratic demands of the public, compelling the baker to perform the greater part of his work at night, thus depriving him of an opportunity to enjoy the necessary rest and sleep,—a fact which is highly injurious to his health." Another writer says: "The constant inhaling of flour dust causes inflammation of the lungs and of the bronchial tubes. The eyes also suffer through this dust, which is responsible for the many cases of running eyes among the bakers. The long hours of toil to which all bakers are subjected produce rheumatism, cramps, and swollen legs.

" . . . The average age of a baker is below that of other workmen; they seldom live over their fiftieth year, most of them dying between the ages of forty and fifty. During periods of epidemic diseases the bakers are generally the first to succumb to the disease, and the number swept away during such periods far exceeds the number of other crafts in comparison to the men employed in the respective industries. When, in 1720, the plague visited the city of Marseilles, France, every baker in the city succumbed to the epidemic, which caused considerable excitement in the neighboring cities and resulted in measures for the sanitary protection of the bakers. . . ."

I do not stop to consider whether any particular view of this economic question presents the sounder theory. . . . It is enough for the determination of this case, and it is enough for this court to know, that the question is one about which there is room for debate and for an honest difference of opinion. . . .

NOTES AND QUESTIONS

(1) *The Lochner Era—Interventionist (or Activist) Judicial Review under Substantive Due Process: Lochner v. New York, 198 U.S. 45 (1905).* Today, in modern constitutional doctrine, the term "Lochnerizing" is an epithet that some Justices and lawyers use as an argument. In the *Lochner* decision, the Court (5-4) held that a New

York law regulating the work hours of bakers violated the substantive due process (*i.e.*, liberty of contract) rights of the bakery owner. This victory for economic rights was accomplished by the Court's use of a form of heightened scrutiny—here the "direct and substantial" relationship test. Note that both the majority and Justice Harlan's dissent used this heightened scrutiny. [Today, this level of scrutiny would be analogized to "intermediate scrutiny." *See* Ch. 10.]

(2) *The Modern "Rational Basis" Test: Justice Holmes' Dissent in Lochner.* Justice Holmes' objective approach, which inquires whether any "rational and fair" person might accept the basis for the law in question, is more closely akin to the type of scrutiny that would be applied today in a *Lochner*-type case. Justice Holmes' dissent is considered as one of the origins of the rational basis standard. *See* Ch. 2 (plenary powers) and Ch. 10 (equal protection). Notice that the majority's "direct and substantial" relationship approach entails a higher level of scrutiny. This test applies because the majority, perhaps mistakenly, has identified liberty of contract as a "fundamental" right. As we shall see in later chapters, the Court, even today, uses stricter scrutiny when fundamental rights are curtailed, requiring a "compelling" state interest or its equivalent. The key issue, perhaps, is that of determining which rights or interests are "fundamental."

(3) *Criticizing Lochner.* The *Lochner* decision is widely regarded as one of the least defensible in American constitutional history. Criticisms include the following:

a. *Heightened Scrutiny Where Rational Basis Should Suffice.* This criticism is partially developed in the preceding note.

b. *Judges' Idiosyncratic Preferences Prevail over Democratic Preferences Expressed in the Legislature.* The Court says, "this is not a question of substituting the judgment of the Court for that of the legislature," but the essence of its reasoning is the statement, "We do not believe in the soundness of the views which uphold this law."

c. *Unduly Narrow Concept of Legitimate Legislative Objectives.* Today, even if the New York statute were not viewed as a health law, it probably would be sustained simply as a regulation of the employment relationship. But the *Lochner* majority rejects this purpose, declaring that "the real object and purposes were simply to regulate the hours of labor," a purpose that the Court assumes is outside state legislative power.

d. *Undue Expansion of "Liberty" as Protected by the Fourteenth Amendment.* Perhaps one can criticize *Lochner* on the ground that the specially protected "liberty of contract" that the Court finds in the Fourteenth Amendment simply is not there to be found. The Civil Rights Act of 1866, which it was a major purpose of the Fourteenth Amendment to legitimize, was concerned with contract rights only as against discrimination on the basis of race, color, or previous servitude. By using the "liberty" concept of the Fourteenth Amendment to strike down a law that is nondiscriminatory and rationally based, the majority arguably has misconstrued that concept. [Notice that acceptance of this reasoning, however, would have other implications, such as leading to rejection of the allegedly fundamental right to abortion, *Roe v. Wade*, below, or birth control, *Griswold v. Connecticut*, below.]

e. *Unwarranted Assumption that "Liberty of Contract" in Fact Existed.* The majority assumed an arms-length labor market in which the employee could decide whether to work overtime. But many people, including many economists, would reject this hypothesis of equal bargaining power.

f. *Refusal to Consider Objectively the Evidence Related to Health.* Even if a court employs a general test that purports to defer to the legislature, it can sabotage democratic preferences by simply refusing to accept evidence demonstrating that particular legislation has a rational basis. Here, Justice Harlan quotes health evidence that arguably is quite compelling, but the majority concludes that there is no health issue—without dealing with the evidence.

g. *Assumption that the Legislative Appetite for Increasing Regulation is a One-Way Street, Which Only the Court Can Restrain.* The *Lochner* majority assumes that employers and employees would be at the mercy of increasingly regulation-minded legislatures without the Court's intervention. On the contrary, at some point the democratic imposition of regulation is self-limiting. In recent years, Congress has selectively decreased controls in such diverse industries as oil and gas production, trucking, airlines, and banking, and it has been motivated by nothing more than traditional democratic pressures in doing so.

(4) *Attempting to Defend Lochner: Natural Law, Traditional American Values, Originalism, and Textualism. Lochner* is such a convenient target that it is easy to regard the majority justices as raw, unprincipled usurpers. But the attempt to defend its (currently) unpopular views can, at the least, be an interesting exercise. Isn't it possible that, rather than imposing idiosyncratic preferences, the *Lochner* majority Justices thought they were applying objective principles derived from proper methods of constitutional construction? First, a natural law view of due process, valuing personal autonomy, presumably would value the freedom to contract and to choose employment. Second, laissez faire views, although not universally held, were firmly a part of the American political tradition. Third, perhaps the justices could justify treating the Constitution as an economic document. Justice Holmes' famous statement that "the Fourteenth Amendment does not enact Mr. Herbert Spencer's Social Statics" seems correct, and his conclusion that the "Constitution is not intended to embody a particular economic theory" is appealing. But textually, the Constitution includes protection of contracts against state abrogation, protection of property in both the Due Process and Taking Clauses, and numerous other economic provisions. Both mercantile interests in the north and agricultural interests in the south were interested in the formation of a union that would protect their economic interests, and the benefits of a competitive economy repeatedly were emphasized in the debates both in the convention and upon ratification. The Civil Rights Act of 1866 was heavily concerned with rights of contract and employment. In summary, the *Lochner* majority might have used natural law, traditional American political values, originalism, and textualism to support their reasoning, however strange their views might seem today. Are these arguments persuasive? If not, might the Justices have accepted them as objective justifications—and, if so, what does that acceptance say about the difficulty of judicial restraint?

(5) *Upholding Limits on Women's Hours: The "Brandeis Brief" and Muller v. Oregon, 208 U.S. 412 (1908).* Three years after *Lochner*, the Supreme Court considered whether a law limiting factory employment of *women* to ten hours was constitutional. Attorney (later Justice) Louis Brandeis persuaded the Court to uphold this law by approaching the Court as the super-legislature it had become. His brief demonstrated the link between the legislation and its purposes by arguing extensive factual evidence, of the kind that would be used to lobby a legislature. This technique, known as the "Brandeis Brief," still is useful today, but was particularly influential after *Lochner*, for obvious reasons. Brandeis succeeded in persuading the Court that women were at a "disadvantage" in the "struggle for subsistence" because they were members of the "weaker" gender—a notion to which, obviously, the Court no longer adheres.

NOTE: FROM *LOCHNER* TO *SCHECHTER POULTRY*: THE COURT USES THE COMMERCE CLAUSE AND SUBSTANTIVE DUE PROCESS TO CONTROL LEGISLATURES

The Relationship Between Lochner and Schechter Poultry. You should recall the New Deal constitutional crisis, which we dealt with in an earlier chapter in connection with the commerce power. From the late 1800s to the latter 1930s, the Court relied sometimes on limits it perceived in the Commerce Clause, and sometimes on substantive due process, to strike down business regulation that it thought interfered unduly with economic freedoms. Thus, the *Schechter Poultry* decision (which struck down codes promulgated under the National Industrial Recovery Act), *United States v. Butler* (which invalidated the Agricultural Adjustment Act), and *Carter v. Carter Coal Co.* (which struck down the Bituminous Coal Conservation Act), all bear a philosophical relationship to *Lochner*. Different constitutional provisions are involved, but both lines of decision involve relatively strict judicial scrutiny of rationales, coupled with refusal to defer to legislatures.

The Aftermath of Allgeyer and Lochner: Three and a Half Decades of Ascendancy of Economic Due Process. In *Coppage v. Kansas*, 236 U.S. 1 (1915), the Court invalidated a state law prohibiting "yellow dog" contracts, in which employees were required to promise not to join labor unions. The labor legislation objectives, which included redressing alleged inequalities in bargaining power, violated substantive due process. Justice Holmes dissented, echoing his views in *Lochner*. In *Adkins v. Children's Hospital*, 261 U.S. 525 (1923), the Court invalidated a minimum wage law for women, again on freedom of contract grounds.

Breakthrough: Nebbia v. New York, Below. Ultimately, the same factors that led to the New Deal breakthrough in the Commerce Clause cases also led to a revised view of substantive due process. National economic conditions, criticisms of the Court as a super-legislature, Congressional and popular acceptance of national labor legislation, tensions with the executive branch, and shifts in Court personnel, all contributed. Ironically, the specific holding of *Lochner* had long since been effectively overruled; *Bunting v. Oregon*, 243 U.S. 426 (1917), upheld a maximum hour law for factory workers—without mentioning *Lochner*. But the *Lochner* reasoning persisted until it was significantly curtailed in the following decision.

[D]   Substantive Due Process Recedes: The "Rational Basis" Test

NEBBIA v. NEW YORK
291 U.S. 502 (1934)

Mr. Justice Roberts delivered the opinion of the Court:

[The Court here sustains, as a legitimate exercise of the police power, New York's regulation of minimum prices for retail sales of milk. The underlying legislation was supported by extensive hearings and a lengthy report, which concluded that milk, although an essential item of diet, could not long be stored because of bacterial growth; that failure of producers to receive a reasonable return threatened "relaxation of vigilance against contamination;" that the state was heavily dependent upon the dairy industry and would suffer "serious economic loss" by its destruction, which was threatened by the "demoralization" of prices; and that this effect was caused by a complex surplus situation, which it was the purpose of the legislation to counteract.]

Under our form of government the use of property and the making of contracts are normally matters of private and not of public concern. The general rule is that both shall be free of governmental interference. But neither property rights nor contract rights are absolute. . . . Equally fundamental with the private right is that of the public to regulate it in the common interest. . . .

The Fifth Amendment, in the field of federal activity, and the Fourteenth, as respects state action, do not prohibit governmental regulation for the public welfare. They merely condition the exertion of the admitted power, by securing that the end shall be accomplished by methods consistent with due process. And the guaranty of due process, as has often been held, demands only that the law shall not be unreasonable, arbitrary, or capricious, and that the means selected shall have a real and substantial relation to the object sought to be attained. . . .

But we are told that because the law essays to control prices it denies due process. . . . [Nebbia's] position is that the Fourteenth Amendment requires us to hold the challenged statute void for this reason alone. The argument runs that the public control of rates or prices is per se unreasonable and unconstitutional, save as applied to businesses affected with a public interest; that a business so affected is one in which property is devoted to an enterprise of a sort which the public itself might appropriately undertake, or one whose owner relies on a public grant or franchise for the right to conduct the business, or in which he is bound to serve all who apply; in short, such as is commonly called a public utility; or a business in its nature a monopoly. The milk industry, it is said, possesses none of these characteristics, and, therefore, not being affected with a public interest, its charges may not be controlled by the state. . . .

. . . But if, as must be conceded, the industry is subject to regulation in the public interest, what constitutional principle bars the state from correcting existing maladjustments by legislation touching prices? We think there is no such principle. The due process clause makes no mention of sales or of prices any more than it speaks of business or contracts or buildings or other incidents of property. This view was negatived many years ago. *Munn v. Illinois*, 94 U.S. 113. The appellant's claim is, however, that this court . . . limited permissible legislation of that type to businesses affected with a public interest, and he says no business is so affected except it have one or more of the characteristics he enumerates. But this is a misconception. Munn and Scott held no franchise from the state. They owned the property upon which their elevator was situated and conducted their business as private citizens.

. . . Thus understood, "affected with a public interest" is the equivalent of "subject to the exercise of the police power"; and it is plain that nothing more was intended by the expression. . . .

It is clear that there is no closed class or category of businesses affected with a public interest, and the function of courts in the application of the Fifth and Fourteenth Amendments is to determine in each case whether circumstances vindicate the challenged regulation as a reasonable exertion of governmental authority or condemn it as arbitrary or discriminatory. . . .

So far as the requirement of due process is concerned, and in the absence of other constitutional restriction, a state is free to adopt whatever economic policy may reasonably be deemed to promote public welfare, and to enforce that policy by legislation adapted to its purpose. . . . If the laws passed are seen to have a reasonable relation to a proper legislative purpose, and are neither arbitrary nor discriminatory, the requirements of due process are satisfied. . . . And it is equally clear that if the legislative policy be to curb unrestrained and harmful competition by measures which are not arbitrary or discriminatory it does not lie with the courts to determine that the rule is unwise. . . . Times without number we have said that the Legislature is primarily the judge of the necessity of such an enactment, that every possible presumption is in favor of its validity, and that though the court may hold views inconsistent with the wisdom of the law, it may not be annulled unless palpably in excess of legislative power. . . .

. . . Price control, like any other form of regulation, is unconstitutional only if arbitrary, discriminatory, or demonstrably irrelevant to the policy the Legislature is free to adopt, and hence an unnecessary and unwarranted interference with individual liberty.

Tested by these considerations we find no basis in the due process clause of the Fourteenth Amendment for condemning the provisions of the Agriculture and Markets Law here drawn into question.

The judgment is affirmed.

Separate opinion of MR. JUSTICE MCREYNOLDS. . . .

Regulation to prevent recognized evils in business has long been upheld as permissible legislative action. But fixation of the price at which A, engaged in an ordinary business, may sell, in order to enable B, a producer, to improve his condition, has not been regarded as within legislative power. This is not regulation, but management, control, dictation—it amounts to the deprivation "of the fundamental right which one has to conduct his own affair honestly and along customary lines. . . ."

[P]lainly, I think, this Court must have regard to the wisdom of the enactment. At least, we must inquire concerning its purpose and decide whether the means proposed have reasonable relation to something within legislative power—whether the end is legitimate, and the means appropriate. If a statute to prevent conflagrations should require householders to pour oil on their roofs as a means of curbing the spread of fire when discovered in the neighborhood, we could hardly uphold it. Here, we find direct interference with guaranteed rights defended upon the ground that the purpose was to promote the public welfare by increasing milk prices at the farm. Unless we can affirm that the end proposed is proper and the means adopted have reasonable relation to it, this action is unjustifiable. . . .

. . . The ultimate welfare of the producer, like that of every other class, requires dominance of the Constitution. And zealously to uphold this in all its parts is the highest duty intrusted to the courts.

The judgment of the court below should be reversed.

MR. JUSTICE VAN DEVANTER, MR. JUSTICE SUTHERLAND, and MR. JUSTICE BUTLER authorize me to say that they concur in this opinion.

NOTES AND QUESTIONS

(1) *The Rational Basis Test.* The *Nebbia* Court uses some of the rhetoric of *Lochner*, in particular the requirement that "the means suggested shall have a real and substantial relation to the object sought to be obtained." But overall, the rhetoric closely resembles Justice Holmes' dissent in *Lochner*, embodying a "rational basis" test.

(2) *Demise of the "Affected with a Public Interest" Doctrine.* Note also the Court's treatment of the "affected with a public interest" doctrine of *Munn v. Illinois*. This phrase, says the Court, "is the equivalent of 'subject to the exercise of the police power'; and it is plain that nothing more was intended by the expression." Is anything left of *Munn v. Illinois*?

(3) *Burying "Freedom of Contract" and Resurrecting the Presumption of Constitutionality: West Coast Hotel Co. v. Parrish, 300 U.S. 379 (1937) and United States v. Carolene Products Co., 304 U.S. 144 (1938).* Three years after *Nebbia*, in *Parrish, supra,* the Court upheld a minimum wage for women, expressly holding that the state had legitimately considered and adjusted economic bargaining power. This decision confirmed the rejection of *Lochner*'s narrow concept of "legitimate legislative purpose." *Carolene Products* is notable for its firm statement of the presumption of constitutionality with respect to economic legislation, coupled with a clear statement of the rational basis test: "Regulatory legislation affecting ordinary commercial transactions is not to be pronounced unconstitutional unless . . . it is of such a character as to preclude the assumption that it rests upon some rational basis within the knowledge and experience of the legislators." In fact, we encountered *Carolene Products* in Chapter 1, while considering judicial review, because of its famous footnote 4—which suggests a narrower scope for the presumption of constitutionality when legislation (1) touches a specific prohibition of the Constitution, (2) restricts political processes, or (3) reflects "prejudice against discrete and insular minorities." Does this approach amount to an abdication of judicial responsibility in the economic arena?

(4) *Will the Courts Speculate about Hypothetical Legislative Purposes that the Legislature Did not Consider?* Thus far, we have been considering cases in which the legislative purpose was clear and the link to the means of achievement readily inferable. How should the Court treat legislation for which clear legislative purposes are lacking? Should the Court be willing to hypothesize legislative purposes and rationally related means? Consider the following.

WILLIAMSON v. LEE OPTICAL OF OKLAHOMA, INC., 348 U.S. 483 (1955). An Oklahoma statute made it unlawful for an optician to replace eyeglasses except with a written prescription from a licensed ophthalmologist or optometrist, who were health care professionals. The district court, although conceding that the police power of a state allowed regulation of the examination of eyes, found that through ordinary skills, the optician, as an artisan qualified to grind lenses, could duplicate or replace existing eyeglasses just as well as licensed health care professionals, and it therefore invalidated the Oklahoma law as an arbitrary interference with the opticians' right to do business. The Supreme Court, per Justice Douglas, reversed and upheld the law:

> The Oklahoma law may exact a needless, wasteful requirement in many cases. But it is for the legislature, not the courts, to balance the advantages and disadvantages of the new requirement. [T]he legislature might have concluded that the frequency of occasions when a prescription is necessary was sufficient to justify this regulation of the fitting of eyeglasses. [Or] the legislature may have concluded that eye examinations were so critical, not only for correction of vision but also for detection of latent ailments or diseases, that every change in frames and every duplication of a lens should be accompanied by a prescription from a medical expert. [I]t is enough that there is an evil at hand for correction, and that it might be thought that the particular legislative measure was a rational way to correct it.

DUKE POWER CO. v. CAROLINA ENVIRONMENTAL STUDY GROUP, INC., 438 U.S. 59 (1978). This Burger Court decision demonstrates the use of the rational basis test in the modern era. The Price-Anderson Act imposed a $560 million limitation on liability for nuclear accidents resulting from the operation of federally licensed nuclear power plants. It was based upon two Congressionally expressed purposes: protecting the public and encouraging the development of the nuclear energy industry. The district court held that the Act violated due process because "[t]he amount of recovery is not rationally related to the potential losses"; because "[t]he Act tends to encourage irresponsibility in matters of safety and environmental protection. . . ."; and, finally, because "[t]here is no quid pro quo" for the liability limitations, such as are found in a no-fault compensation system. The Supreme Court, per Chief Justice Burger, reversed and upheld the Act:

> [A]ppellees . . . urge a more elevated standard of review on the ground that the interests jeopardized by the Price-Anderson Act "are far more important than those in the economic due process and business-oriented cases where the traditional rationality standard has been invoked." . . . An intermediate standard . . . is thus recommended [by appellees] for our use here.
>
> [I]t is clear that Congress' purpose was to remove the economic impediments in order to stimulate the private development of electric energy by nuclear power while simultaneously providing the public compensation in the event of a catastrophic nuclear accident. . . . The liability-limitation provision thus emerges as a classic example of an economic regulation—a legislative effort to structure and accommodate "the burdens and benefits of economic life. . . ." That the accommodations struck may have profound and far-reaching consequences, contrary to appellees' suggestion, provides all the more reason for this Court to defer to the Congressional judgment unless it is demonstrably arbitrary or irrational. . . .

Assuming, arguendo, that the $560 million fund would not insure full recovery in all conceivable circumstances—and the hard truth is that no one can ever know—it does not by any means follow that the liability limitation is therefore irrational and violative of due process. . . . The reasonableness of the statute's assumed ceiling on liability was predicated on two corollary considerations—expert appraisals of the exceedingly small risk of a nuclear accident involving claims in excess of $560 million, and the recognition that, in the event of such an incident, Congress would likely enact extraordinary relief provisions to provide additional relief, in accord with prior practice. . . .

PROBLEM A

FLORIDA'S TORT REFORM AND INSURANCE ACT AND SUBSTANTIVE DUE PROCESS— SMITH v. DEPARTMENT OF INSURANCE, 507 So. 2d 1080 (Fla. 1987). As part of a comprehensive response to a perceived commercial insurance liability crisis, Florida's 1986 Tort Reform and Insurance Act placed a $450,000 limit (or "cap") on the recovery of non-economic damages (*i.e.*, on damages for pain and suffering). Plaintiffs attacked this provision on the ground, among others, that it demonstrably would under compensate the most seriously injured individuals and thus was distinguishable from the Price-Anderson Act at issue in *Duke Power*. Should the rational basis test be applied to legislation of this sort? If it is, should the legislation be sustained? [The Florida Supreme Court struck it down on the basis of the equal protection provisions of the federal Fourteenth Amendment and the Florida Constitution. It also held that the provision violated the Florida constitutional right of access to the courts.]

NOTES AND QUESTIONS

(1) *Hypothetical Purposes, Speculative Consequences, Complex Social Interactions, Unknown Future Events, and Legislative Flexibility to Fix Emerging Problems.* Notice the *Lee Optical* Court's willingness to hypothesize legitimate purposes to uphold legislation, even in the absence of any indication that the legislature considered them. Is this proper application of the rational basis test, or is it judicial abdication? Sometimes, the effects of regulatory legislation may be unknown; legislative history may reflect some strong doubts about its viability; and the majority may depend upon votes of legislators who candidly admit that complex social interactions may make the regulation unworkable. Should the Court sustain such legislation? *Cf. Permian Basin Area Rate Cases*, 390 U.S. 747 (1968)(granting deference to regulators to implement new theory on the ground that it embodied an "experiment"). What should be done if neither the Court nor the legislature can foresee the future of a given regulatory scheme? Notice the *Duke Power* Court's willingness to assume that, in the event of regulatory breakdown, Congress may step in to fix the problem. Is this reasoning simply the worst sort of judicial abdication? Or is it a proper application of the rational basis test, reflecting the conclusion that Congress has more flexibility than the Court does? For modern commentary on substantive due process, consider Hovenkamp, *The Political Economy of Substantive Due Process*, 40 STAN. L. REV. 379 (1988); Phillips, *Another Look at Economic Substantive Due Process*, 1987 WIS. L. REV. 265; Wright, *A Contractual Approach to Due Process*, 21 VAL. U.L. REV. 527 (1987); *see also FCC v. Beach Communications*, 508 U.S. 307 (1993) (any "conceivable" or "plausible" reason suffices under the Equal Protection clause, even if there is no indication that it ever was considered).

(2) *Can We Really Distinguish "Merely Economic" Regulation from Social Legislation that Impinges upon "Fundamental Rights"?* *Duke Power* demonstrates how treacherous distinctions between "mere economic" regulation and other legislation can be. Was the Court correct in regarding the Price-Anderson Act as an effort to

"structure and accommodate 'the burdens and benefit of economic life,' " or is the right of a person who suffers serious personal injury to recover an amount that reflects his damages a more "fundamental" right?

(3) *The Retroactive Application of Congressional Tax Legislation—The Court Confirms that "Rational Basis" is the Normal Standard for Reviewing Such Action: United States v. Carlton, 512 U.S. 26 (1994).* When Congress passes legislation with an intent to have it apply retroactively, the rational basis test is normally utilized. In *Carlton*, for example, Congress passed (in 1986) a tax provision which permitted an estate tax deduction for sales of certain stock. In late 1986, Carlton, as executor of an estate, purchased qualifying stock and sold it (at a loss of $631,000) two days later, generating a deduction of $5.3 million. Faced with an estimated loss to the Treasury of $7 billion, Congress passed (in December, 1987) an amendment to the provision which was intended to apply retroactively; this amendment nullified Carlton's strategy and denied the deduction to the estate.

Carlton claimed that the retroactive application of the 1987 amendment violated the Fifth Amendment's Due Process Clause, but applying rational basis scrutiny, the Court, per Justice Blackmun, rejected Carlton's claim. The Court held: (1) that the federal government had a "legitimate interest" in "curing" a mistake in the 1986 version of the tax code and (2) that the retroactive application was a means rationally related to the legitimate interest (*i.e.*, it saved the government $7 billion).

Many people would regard the destruction of reliance interests by retroactive legislation as "unfair" in the vernacular sense, but evidently it isn't unfair enough to be regarded as unconstitutional. (Should it be?)

The retroactive application of economic burdens has emerged as a factor in determining the constitutionality of congressional action under the Takings Clause. *See Eastern Enterprises v. Apfel*, 524 U.S. 498 (1998) and § 6.03[B] below.

PROBLEM B

DOES A SUNDAY CLOSING LAW WITH COMPREHENSIVE EXCEPTIONS REFLECT A (SECULAR) RATIONAL BASIS? READI-MART, INC. v. LONDON RETAIL MERCHANTS ASSOCIATION, Chapter 7, *infra*. A statute of the (hypothetical) state of West York provides a lengthy list of items that cannot be sold at retail on Sunday. The statute cannot be sustained merely as a pro-religion measure, because then it would violate the prohibition upon establishment of religion; to be upheld, it must reflect some *secular* rational basis. The state contends that this Sunday closing law insures that employees will have at least one day of rest per week.

Readi-Mart, Inc. wishes to merchandise all of its stock seven days per week, and it challenges the West York law on substantive due process grounds. Its expert testimony shows: (1) that the majority of people who work on Sunday are not employed in retail sales and hence are not affected by the day-of-rest rationale; (2) that the list of items whose sale is prohibited is not comprehensive, so that many if not most retail establishments stay open on Sunday, but simply decline to sell the prohibited items; (3) that competition among employers in the labor market, together with Federal labor legislation, are such that the West York Sunday Closing Law cannot possibly advance the purpose of providing employees a day of rest that they would not get without the law.

Given this evidence, should the law be struck down under the rational basis test if the day-of-rest rationale is the only proffered legislative purpose? Are there other legitimate purposes that can be hypothesized, to which the legislation is rationally related? And finally, if this legislation can be sustained on this evidence, can economic legislation *ever* be struck down on substantive due process grounds?

[E]   Equal Protection in the Economic Context

The current interpretation of the Equal Protection Clause is parallel to that of substantive due process in business regulation cases. The law will be upheld if it satisfies the deferential rational basis standard, just as a law satisfies due process if it reflects a rational basis. But the Equal Protection Clause was not always construed this way.

The Historical Invocation of Equal Protection to Restrict Business Regulation: Morey v. Doud, 354 U.S. 457 (1957). In *Morey*, an Illinois statute regulated currency exchange businesses but exempted American Express Company by name. The reason for the exemption was the legislature's determination, which was reasonably based, that American Express was so well established that its regulation was not necessary to protect the public. The Court struck down the statute on the ground that it created a "closed class" of favored businesses and thus was only "remotely" related to its purpose. *Morey* had significant impact for two reasons: first, it was decided after the substantive due process breakthrough of *Nebbia*, so that its equal protection reasoning was available for regulation-restricting arguments when due process was not, and second, its "closed class" reasoning was difficult to limit.

The Current "Reasonable Classification" Approach to Equal Protection in the Economic Context: New Orleans v. Dukes, 427 U.S. 297 (1976). Morey finally was *overruled*, in *Dukes*, which concerned a New Orleans city ordinance that prohibited pushcart vendors from plying their trade in that city's famous French Quarter. The ordinance "grandfathered" two longstanding vendors, and competitors claimed a denial of equal protection. The Court upheld the ordinance, including the "grandfather" clause, on the theory that preserving the positions of longstanding vendors reflected a "reasonable classification." *See also FCC v. Beach Communications, Inc.*, 508 U.S. 307 (1993) (any "conceivable" or "plausible" reason suffices, even if no evidence shows it was considered); but *see Allegheny Pittsburgh Coal Co. v. County Commission*, 488 U.S. 336 (1989) (unusual case of successful equal protection attack on tax system with dramatic inconsistencies).

Our Coverage of Due Process and Equal Protection in Future Chapters. We shall return to reconsider both due process and equal protection in other contexts in Chapters 7 through 10.

§ 6.03   TAKING OF PROPERTY WITHOUT JUST COMPENSATION

Read U.S. Const. Amend. V (the Taking Clause).

INTRODUCTORY NOTE ON THE TAKING CLAUSE DOCTRINE

The Supreme Court has developed, as in other areas, a doctrinal "model" for interpreting the Fifth Amendment's Taking Clause. Traditionally, the Court has used a two-tiered model. On the first tier, physical occupations or other possessory conduct was considered a *per se* taking. Other governmental regulations, which were not intentional takings, were considered as possible "regulatory" takings. *See* ERWIN CHEMERINSKY, CONSTITUTIONAL LAW 615–616 (2d ed. 2003); LAURENCE TRIBE, AMERICAN CONSTITUTIONAL LAW 587–602 (2d ed. 1988).

The Supreme Court, however, has recently suggested that it might switch to a four-tiered model. In *Lingle v. Chevron, U.S.A., Inc.*, 544 U.S. 2074 (2005), the Court rejected a Taking Clause challenge to a state scheme to cap rents paid by service station dealers to the oil company owners of the service stations. The Court stated:

> . . . We hold that the "substantially advances" formula is not a valid takings test, and indeed conclude that it has no proper place in our takings jurisprudence. In doing so, we reaffirm that a plaintiff seeking to challenge a government regulation as an uncompensated taking of private property may proceed under one of the other theories discussed above—by alleging a "physical" taking, a *Lucas*-type "total regulatory taking," a *Penn Central* taking, or a land-use exaction violating the standards set forth in *Nollan* and *Dolan*. Because Chevron argued only a "substantially advances" theory in support of its takings claim, it was not entitled to summary judgment on that claim. . . .

What are the advantages of the competing models? Which model best describes the cases considered below?

NOTE ON THE PURPOSES OF THE TAKING CLAUSE

The precise purposes of the Taking Clause in the original understanding are unclear. The following are among the policies, however, that it may be said to serve. For further commentary, *see* Professor Douglas W. Kmiec's article *The Original Understanding of the Taking Clause Is Neither Weak Nor Obtuse*, 88 COLUM. L. REV. 1630 (1988).

Preventing the Costs of Benefits to Society as a Whole From Being Shifted to a Small Part of Society. The clause is "a limit on government's power to isolate particular individuals for sacrifice to the general good," L. TRIBE, AMERICAN CONSTITUTIONAL LAW § 9-4 (2d ed. 1988). As the Supreme Court said in *Armstrong v. United States*, 364 U.S. 40 (1960): "The Fifth Amendment's guarantee that private property shall not be taken for a public use without just compensation was designed to bar government from forcing some people alone to bear public burdens which, in all fairness and justice, should be borne by the public as a whole." A change in the use of property may be desirable, but if so, the real question is not whether the benefit should be obtained but "upon whom the loss of the changes should fall." *Pennsylvania Coal Co. v. Mahon*, 260 U.S. 393 (1922).

Limiting Thoughtless and Excessive Government Intervention That Might Result From a Failure to Confront the Costs. If we focus upon the regulator, rather than upon the potentially small part of society "sacrificed" to the general good, we can perceive that the compensation requirement has a beneficial effect in that it requires the regulator to consider the costs of the regulation. This notion has been put in terms of restraining the "exuberance" of regulators. Hagman, Outline of Presentation, *The Compensation Issue: Theories of Liability for Damages From Planning and Land Use Controls*, ALI-ABA Program, Arlington, Virginia (March 26, 1980). If there is no need to pay for the property taken, the planner or regulator tends to focus on only the issues the regulator is interested in, without the restraint of weighing the real costs imposed upon other individuals, and, possibly, on the society as a whole.

Harmonizing Competing Social Needs. A regulatory taking may remove productive land from its best use, and jobs, commerce and products may be lost because firms as well as individuals will fear that their interests are unprotected. *See generally* Hagman, *supra*, at 2. This purpose really is a generalized version of the previous concern with restraining the exuberance of regulators; it emphasizes, however, that the costs imposed are borne not merely by targeted individuals, but by the larger society.

Inducing Investment Through Protecting Settled Expectations. The compensation requirement furthers the policy that "certain settled expectations of a focused and crystallized sort should be secure against government's disruption, at least without appropriate compensation." TRIBE, *supra*. Thus, the Supreme Court has emphasized the importance of just compensation when "investment-backed expectations" are invaded.

Penn Central Transportation Co. v. New York City, 438 U.S. 104, 124–25 (1978). There are "a number of expectancies embodied in the concept of 'property'—expectancies that, if sufficiently important, the government must condemn and pay for before it takes over the management of the landowner's property." *Kaiser Aetna v. United States*, 444 U.S. 164, 179 (1979).

In applying these policies to takings cases, the Court has developed a two-part doctrine. This doctrine is presented below.

[A]   Taking by Physical Invasion or by Destruction

LORETTO v. TELEPROMPTER MANHATTAN CATV CORP., 458 U.S. 419 (1982). A New York statute required a landlord to permit a cable television operator to install its equipment upon his property upon payment in an amount determined by a state commission. The state commission fixed this payment at a one-time $1 fee. After purchasing a building, Loretto discovered that both "crossover" and interior service cables had been placed on the roof pursuant to this statute. She sued, alleging that the statute effected a taking without just compensation. The Supreme Court, per Justice Marshall, agreed:

> When faced with a constitutional challenge to a permanent physical occupation of real property, this Court has invariably found a taking. As early as 1872, in *Pumpelly v. Green Bay Co.*, 80 U.S. (13 Wall.) 166, this Court held that the Defendant's construction, pursuant to state authority, of a dam which permanently flooded plaintiff's property constituted a taking. . . .
>
> . . . Such an appropriation is perhaps the most serious form of invasion of an owner's property interests. To borrow a metaphor . . . the government does not simply take a single "strand" from the "bundle" of property rights: it chops through the bundle, taking a slice of every strand.
>
> Our holding today is very narrow. . . . We do not . . . question the equally substantial authority upholding a state's broad power to impose appropriate restrictions upon an owner's *use* of his property. . . .

Justice Blackmun, joined by Justices Brennan and White, dissented. They objected to the use of a "rigid per se takings rule" in cases of permanent physical occupancy.

NOLLAN v. CALIFORNIA COASTAL COMMISSION
483 U.S. 825 (1987)

JUSTICE SCALIA delivered the opinion of the Court.

[To rebuild the residence on their beachfront lot, the Nollans were required to obtain a permit from the Coastal Commission. The Commission granted the permit, but as a condition, it required that the Nollans transfer to the state an easement allowing the public to walk along the beach across a strip of the Nollans' property just inland of the high tide line. The California Court of Appeal rejected the Nollans' argument that this condition constituted a taking. Here, the Supreme Court reverses.]

II

Had California simply required the Nollans to make an easement across their beachfront available to the public on a permanent basis in order to increase public access to the beach, rather than conditioning their permit to rebuild their house on their agreeing to do so, we have no doubt there would have been a taking. To say that the appropriation of a public easement across a landowner's premises does not constitute the taking of a property interest but rather, (as Justice Brennan contends) "a mere restriction on its use," is to use words in a manner that deprives them of all their ordinary meaning. [W]e have repeatedly held that, as to property reserved by its owner for private use, "the right to exclude [others is] 'one of the most essential sticks in the bundle of rights that are commonly characterized as property.'" *Loretto v. Teleprompter Manhattan CATV Corp.*, 458 U.S. 419, 433 (1982). In *Loretto* we observed that where governmental action results in "[a] permanent physical occupation" of the property, by the government itself or by others, "our cases uniformly have found a taking to the extent of the occupation, without regard to whether the action achieves an important public benefit or has only minimal economic impact on the owner." We think a "permanent physical occupation" has occurred, for purposes of that rule, where individuals are given a permanent and continuous right to pass to and fro, so that the real property may continuously be traversed, even though no particular individual is permitted to station himself permanently upon the premises. . . .

[G]iven, then, that requiring uncompensated conveyance of the easement outright would violate the Fourteenth Amendment, the question becomes whether requiring it to be conveyed as a condition for issuing a land use permit alters the outcome. We have long recognized that land use regulation does not effect a taking if it "substantially advance[s] legitimate state interests" and "does not den[y] an owner economically viable use of his land."

The Commission argues that a permit condition that serves the same legitimate police-power purpose as a refusal to issue the permit should not be found to be a taking if the refusal to issue the permit would not constitute a taking. We agree. Thus, if the Commission attached to the permit some condition that would have protected the public's ability to see the beach notwithstanding construction of the new house—for example, a height limitation, a width restriction, or a ban on fences—so long as the Commission could have exercised its police power (as we have assumed it could) to forbid construction of the house altogether, imposition of the condition would also be constitutional. Moreover (and here we come closer to the facts of the present case), the condition would be constitutional even if it consisted of the requirement that the Nollans provide a viewing spot on their property for passersby with whose sighting of the ocean their new house would interfere. . . .

The evident constitutional propriety disappears, however, if the condition substituted for the prohibition utterly fails to further the end advanced as the justification for the prohibition. . . . [H]ere, the lack of nexus between the condition and the original purpose of the building restriction converts that purpose to something other than what it was. The purpose then becomes, quite simply, the obtaining of an easement to serve some valid governmental purpose, but without payment of compensation. . . .

III

The Commission claims that it concedes as much, and that we may sustain the condition at issue here by finding that it is reasonably related to the public need or burden that the Nollans' new house creates or to which it contributes. We can accept, for purposes of discussion, the Commission's proposed test as to how close a "fit" between the condition and the burden is required, because we find that this case does not meet even the most untailored standards. The Commission's principal contention to the contrary essentially turns on a play on the word "access." The Nollans' new house, the Commission found, will interfere with "visual access" to the beach. That in turn (along with other shorefront development) will interfere with the desire of people who drive past the Nollans' house to use the beach, thus creating a "psychological barrier" to "access." The Nollans' new house will also, by a process not altogether clear from the Commission's opinion but presumably potent enough to more than offset the effects of the psychological barrier, increase the use of the public beaches, thus creating the need for more "access." These burdens on "access" would be alleviated by a requirement that the Nollans provide "lateral access" to the beach.

Rewriting the argument to eliminate the play on words makes clear that there is nothing to it. It is quite impossible to understand how a requirement that people already on the public beaches be able to walk across the Nollans' property reduces any obstacles to viewing the beach created by the new house. It is also impossible to understand how it lowers any "psychological barrier" to using the public beaches, or how it helps to remedy any additional congestion on them caused by construction of the Nollans' new house. We therefore find that the Commission's imposition of the permit condition cannot be treated as an exercise of its land use power for any of these purposes. . . .

We view the Fifth Amendment's property clause to be more than a pleading requirement, and compliance with it to be more than an exercise in cleverness and imagination. As indicated earlier, our cases describe the condition for abridgement of property rights through the police power as a "*substantial* advanc[ing]" of a legitimate State interest. We are inclined to be particularly careful about the adjective where the actual conveyance of property is made a condition to the lifting of a land use restriction, since in that context there is heightened risk that the purpose is avoidance of the compensation requirement, rather than the stated police power objective. . . .

Reversed.

JUSTICE BRENNAN, with whom JUSTICE MARSHALL joins, dissenting.

. . . The Coastal Commission, if it had so chosen, could have denied the Nollans' request for a development permit, since the property would have remained economically viable without the requested new development. Instead, the State sought to accommodate the Nollans' desire for new development, on the condition that the development not diminish the overall amount of public access to the coastline. . . .

The Court finds fault with this measure because it regards the condition as insufficiently tailored to address the precise type of reduction in access produced by the new development. The Nollans' development blocks visual access, the Court tells us, while the Commission seeks to preserve lateral access along the coastline. Thus, it concludes, the State acted irrationally. Such a narrow conception of rationality, however, has long since been discredited as a judicial arrogation of legislative authority. "To make scientific precision a criterion of constitutional power would be to subject the State to an intolerable supervision hostile to the basic principles of our Government. . . ."

Even if we accept the Court's unusual demand for a precise match between the condition imposed and the specific type of burden on access created by the appellants, the State's action easily satisfies this requirement. First, the lateral access condition serves to dissipate the impression that the beach that lies behind the wall of homes along the shore is for private use only. Furthermore, those persons who go down to the public beach a quarter-mile away will be able to look down the coastline and see that persons have continuous access to the tidelands, and will observe signs that proclaim the public's right of access over the dry sand.

The second flaw in the Court's analysis of the fit between burden and exaction is more fundamental. The Court assumes that the only burden with which the Coastal Commission was concerned was blockage of visual access to the beach. This is incorrect. The Commission specifically stated in its report in support of the permit condition that "[t]he Commission finds that the applicants' proposed development would present an increase in view blockage, *an increase in private use of the shorefront*, and that this impact would burden the public's ability to traverse to and along the shorefront. . . ."

The Court is therefore simply wrong that there is no reasonable relationship between the permit condition and the specific type of burden on public access created by the appellants' proposed development. Even were the Court desirous of assuming the added responsibility of closely monitoring the regulation of development along the California coast, this record reveals rational public action by any conceivable standard.

The fact that the Commission's action is a legitimate exercise of the police power does not, of course, insulate it from a takings challenge, for when "regulation goes too far it will be recognized as a taking." *Pennsylvania Coal Co. v. Mahon*, 260 U.S. 393, 415 (1922). Conventional takings analysis underscores the implausibility of the Court's holding, for it demonstrates that this exercise of California's police power implicates none of the concerns that underlie our takings jurisprudence. . . .

NOTES AND QUESTIONS

(1) *Loss of the Right to Exclude; Destruction of Value: Ruckelshaus v. Monsanto Co., 467 U.S. 986 (1984).* In *Monsanto*, plaintiff had submitted trade data to the Environmental Protection Agency (EPA) for the purpose of obtaining registration of certain pesticides. The agency disclosed some of the data publicly and used other data in evaluating the application of a subsequent applicant. The Court held that this confidential information was a kind of property that could be "taken" by either public disclosure or by appropriation for government use. During the period 1972 through 1978, the applicable statutes and regulations created a "reasonable, investment-backed expectation" that EPA would keep the data confidential upon its designation as such.

> The right to exclude others is generally "one of the most essential sticks in the bundle of rights that are commonly characterized as property. . . ." Once the data that constitute a trade secret are disclosed to others, or others are allowed to use those data, the holder of the trade secret has lost his property interest in the data. . . .

Is this analysis persuasive? If so, is it the loss of the right to exclude others, or the destruction of economic value in the property, that makes it so? Consider whether there is a parallel between the *Monsanto* "taking by disclosure" reasoning and the "permanent physical occupation" cases such as *Loretto* and *Nollan*.

(2) *Permanent, as Versus Temporary, Occupation: Block v. Hirsh, 256 U.S. 135 (1921).* The *Block* Court upheld a statute permitting tenants to remain in physical possession of their apartments for two years after the termination of their leases. Justice Blackmun, dissenting in *Loretto*, cited *Block* as establishing that "the Court's talismanic distinction between a continuous 'occupation' and a transient 'invasion' finds no basis in either economic logic or takings clause precedent." Isn't this reasoning correct, in that the holding in *Block* might have deprived the landowner forever of revenue that was perfectly real, even though it would have been earned during the temporary occupation? Does this reasoning undermine the *Loretto* Court's conclusion that there is something different about a permanent occupation?

(3) *The Type of "Invasion" or "Occupation" at Issue—Will Sound Waves Do? United States v. Causby, 328 U.S. 256 (1946).* The government builds an airport near existing residential land, and noise from takeoffs and landings makes them uninhabitable. A taking? Held, yes, in *Causby*. The airspace above real property is also "private property" for purposes of the Taking Clause. Consider the following case.

PHILLIPS v. WASH. LEGAL FOUNDATION, 524 U.S. 156 (1998). In this decision, the Court addressed a threshold issue in Takings Clause jurisprudence: What, for purposes of the Fifth Amendment's Takings Clause, constitutes "private property"? Texas had a program, the Texas' Interest on Lawyers Trust Account (IOLTA), where the interest earned on clients' "trust accounts" held by Texas lawyers in connection with the lawyer's legal practice (*e.g.*, retainers) was paid not to the client but to legal foundations which finance legal services for low-income persons. The IOLTA accounts were managed entirely by banks and private attorneys. Only one State (Indiana) did not have an IOLTA program. The rationale for these programs was based on the fact that the interest which might be earned on such trust accounts would not be sufficient to offset the accounting and other costs that would be incurred in attempting to obtain the interest for the client. In Texas, as elsewhere, the IOLTA programs were considered to have accomplished many positive results for the cause of delivering legal services to low-income people.

Notwithstanding the "social good" accomplished, the constitutionality of the Texas program was challenged by a legal foundation, a Texas attorney and a Texas business person whose funds were held in an IOLTA account. [Note the care taken by the challengers in establishing standing.] The plaintiffs claimed that the IOLTA program's channeling of the net interest income to the legal services foundations was a taking without just compensation violative of the Fifth Amendment. The Court, per Chief Justice Rehnquist, decided that the interest in the IOLTA account is the "private property" of the client. The Court did not address other issues, including whether a "taking" of private property had occurred and remanded for further consideration.

The Fifth Amendment, made applicable to the States through the Fourteenth Amendment, provides that "private property" shall not "be taken for public use, without just compensation," U.S. Const., Amdt. V. Because the Constitution protects rather than creates property interests, the existence of a property interest is determined by reference to "existing rules or understandings that stem from an independent source such as state law." *Board of Regents of State Colleges v. Roth*, 408 U.S. 564, 577 (1972). . . .

[W]e have never held that a physical item is not "property" simply because it lacks a positive economic or market value. . . . Our conclusion in this regard was premised on our longstanding recognition that property is more than economic value, it also consists of "the group of rights which the so-called owner exercises in his dominion of the physical thing," such "as the right to possess, use and dispose of it." While the interest income at issue here may have no economically realizable value to its owner, possession, control, and disposition are nonetheless valuable rights that inhere in the property. The government may not seize rents received by the owner of a building simply because it can prove that the costs incurred in collecting the rents exceed the amount collected.

The United States, as amicus curiae, additionally argues that "private property" is not implicated by the IOLTA program because the interest income generated by funds held in IOLTA accounts is "government-created value." We disagree. As an initial matter, this argument is factually erroneous. The interest income transferred to the TEAJA is not the product of increased efficiency, economies of scale, or pooling of funds by the government. . . . In other words, the State does nothing to create value; the value is created by respondents' funds. The Federal Government, through the structuring of its banking and taxation regulations, imposes costs on this value if private citizens attempt to exercise control over it. Waiver of these costs if the property is remitted to the State hardly constitutes "government-created value." . . .

This would be a different case if the interest income generated by IOLTA accounts was transferred to the State as payment "for services rendered" by the State. . . .

Four justices dissented. Justices Souter and Breyer wrote opinions arguing that the majority was improperly focusing only on the issue whether the IOLTA interest was "private property." Both dissenting opinions argued that this issue must be decided in the context of the other issues: whether a "taking" had occurred and whether the client had received "just compensation." Justice Breyer also concluded that, since no net interest at all would be earned on the IOLTA account without the pooling arrangement of the IOLTA programs, "I consequently believe that the interest earned is not the client's 'private property.' "

(4) *Revisiting Takings by State IOLTA Programs: Brown v. Legal Foundation of Washington, 538 U.S. 216 (2003).* The *Phillips* decision (above) held that interest earned on IOLTA accounts is the private property of the owner of the principal. Under the Washington IOLTA program, client funds are placed in IOLTA accounts when the funds

could not earn net interest for the client. The earnings from IOLTA accounts are used by the Legal Foundation to pay for legal services for the indigent and for certain educational activities. The challengers claimed that: (1) the placement of the funds in IOLTA accounts was a taking; and (2) the use of the interest from the IOLTA accounts was a taking that must be compensated under the Just Compensation Clause. While the lower courts ruled for the challengers, the Supreme Court, per Justice Stevens, upheld Washington's IOLTA program.

The Court held that the placement of the client funds in the IOLTA accounts was not a taking since the clients retained the beneficial interest in the funds. As to the transfer of the interest, the Court held that this was a *per se* taking under *Loretto*, above. The challengers, however, were denied any award under the Just Compensation Clause because the net interest would have been *zero*. The Court held that the amount of compensation was measured by the loss to the property owner and not by the gain to the government. Justice Scalia (for Rehnquist, Kennedy, and Thomas) dissented. In general, this decision cuts back on the significance of the *Phillips* decision.

(5) *"Proportionality": Must the Burden of the Inaction Bear Some Proportionality to the Benefit?: The Dolan Case.* What if the state, in order to protect values worth a few pennies, imposes costs in the millions of dollars on a land-owner? Consider the following case.

DOLAN v. CITY OF TIGARD, 512 U.S. 374 (1994). The city conditioned approval of Dolan's plans to expand her hardware store (and parking lot) upon her agreement to dedicate 10 percent of her property to (1) a public greenway adjacent to her property designed to minimize flooding and (2) a pedestrian and bicycle pathway designed to alleviate traffic congestion. She appealed, claiming that these land dedication exactments were not related to her proposed property development and were, therefore, an uncompensated taking. Although the city did not present evidence regarding her property's relationship to these exactments, the Oregon state courts upheld the city's position that it had, under *Nollan, supra*, presented sufficient evidence. The Supreme Court, per Chief Justice Rehnquist, reversed, holding that the city had failed its burden of proof to demonstrate a constitutionally sufficient justification for the two exactments. Following a review of the *Nollan* decision, the majority concluded:

> [I]n evaluating petitioner's claim, we must first determine whether the "essential nexus" exists between the "legitimate state interest" and the permit condition exacted by the city. *Nollan*. If we find that a nexus exists, we must then decide the required degree of connection between the exactions and the projected impact of the proposed development. We were not required to reach this question in *Nollan*, because we concluded that the connection did not meet even the loosest standard.

> [T]he second part of our analysis requires us to determine whether the degree of the exactions demanded by the city's permit conditions bear the required relationship to the projected impact of petitioner's proposed development.

> [W]e think the "reasonable relationship" test adopted by a majority of the state courts is closer to the federal constitutional norm than [other proposed standards]. But we do not adopt it as such, partly because the term "reasonable relationship" seems confusingly similar to the term "rational basis" which describes the minimal level of scrutiny under the Equal Protection Clause of the Fourteenth Amendment. We think a term such as "rough proportionality" best encapsulates what we hold to be the requirement of the Fifth Amendment.

> [B]ut simply denominating a governmental measure as a "business regulation" does not immunize it from constitutional challenge on the grounds that it violates a provision of the Bill of Rights. . . . We see no reason why the Takings Clause of the Fifth Amendment, as much a part of the Bill of Rights as the First Amendment or Fourth Amendment, should be relegated to the status of a poor

relation in these comparable circumstances.

[W]e conclude that the findings upon which the city relies do not show the required reasonable relationship between the floodplain easement and the petitioner's proposed new building.

[N]o precise mathematical calculation is required, but the city must make some effort to quantify its findings in support of the dedication for the pedestrian/bicycle pathway beyond the conclusory statement that it could offset some of the traffic demand generated.

Justice Stevens, for Justices Blackmun and Ginsburg, dissented from the Court's adoption of the "rough proportionality" standard because it placed the burden on the government rather than the challenger. Justice Souter also dissented.

NOTES AND QUESTIONS

The Limits of the Use of the Dolan "Rough-Proportionality" Standard for Taking Claims: City of Monterey v. Del Monte Dunes At Monterey Ltd, 526 U.S. 687 (1999). Although the main issue in the *Del Monte Dunes* decision was whether the challenger, in a takings case brought under 42 U.S.C. § 1983, had a Seventh Amendment right to a jury trial, the Supreme Court also addressed the proper scope of the *Dolan* "rough proportionality" standard. Plaintiff Del Monte Dunes ("the developer") sought to develop a 37.6 acre ocean-front parcel on the California coastline. For five years, the developer submitted development proposals to the City of Monterey; as each of the formal proposals was rejected by the City, the developer revised the next proposal to conform to the City's objections. The developer's proposals were eventually confined to the center or "bowl" of the property. Then, after five years, the City announced that, because the bowl area contained "sensitive buckwheat habitat," it would not allow development even in the bowl area.

The developer sued, claiming that "the shifting and sometimes inconsistent positions" asserted by the City had deprived the parcel of all value and constituted a "regulatory taking." The jury also heard evidence that, although always frustrating the developer, the City was planning to buy the parcel (at, of course, a low price), and the jury awarded the developer $1.45 million.

The Supreme Court, per Justice Kennedy, upheld the jury's verdict. For purposes of this subchapter, the Court's important observation (although dictum) was that . . . "we have not extended the rough-proportionality test of Dolan beyond the special context of exactions. . . ." Four Justices, in an opinion by Justice Souter, dissented from the Seventh Amendment holding, while agreeing with the Court's rejection of the rough-proportionality test for regulatory taking cases.

[B]   Taking by Regulation of Use

[1]   When Does "Regulation" Become "A Taking"?

PENN CENTRAL TRANSPORTATION CO. v. CITY OF NEW YORK
438 U.S. 104 (1978)

MR. JUSTICE BRENNAN delivered the opinion of the Court.

[The New York City Preservation Commission designated Grand Central Station, which Penn Central owned, as a "landmark." Pursuant to the City's Landmarks Preservation Law, this designation meant that Penn Central could not alter its exterior without Commission approval. It did have the right to transfer "development rights" from the landmark site to other, nearby lots, which arguably provided some economic benefit in exchange. Penn Central entered into a lease with UGP Properties, whereby

UGP was to construct a multi-story office building cantilevered over the station. The Commission rejected this development plan, and Penn Central filed suit, alleging that the Commission had thereby committed a taking of its property. Here, the Supreme Court holds that there was no taking and that compensation is not required.]

The question of what constitutes a "taking" for purposes of the Fifth Amendment has proved to be a problem of considerable difficulty. While this Court has recognized that the "Fifth Amendment's guarantee . . . [is] designed to bar Government from forcing some people alone to bear public burdens which, in all fairness and justice, should be borne by the public as a whole," *Armstrong v. United States*, 364 U.S. 140 (1960), this Court, quite simply, has been unable to develop any "set formula" for determining when "justice and fairness" require that economic injuries caused by public action be compensated by the government, rather than remain disproportionately concentrated on a few persons. . . .

In engaging in these essentially ad hoc, factual inquiries, the Court's decisions have identified several factors that have particular significance. The economic impact of the regulations on the claimant and, particularly, the extent to which the regulation has interfered with distinct investment-backed expectations are, of course, relevant considerations. So, too, is the character of the governmental action. A "taking" may more readily be found when the interference with property can be characterized as a physical invasion by government, *see, e.g., United States v. Causby*, 328 U.S. 256 (1946), than when interference arises from some public program adjusting the benefits and burdens of economic life to promote the common good. . . .

More importantly for the present case, in instances in which a state tribunal reasonably concluded that "the health, safety, morals, or general welfare" would be promoted by prohibiting particular contemplated use of land, this Court has upheld land-use regulations that destroyed or adversely affected recognized real property interests. Zoning laws are, of course, the classic example, *see Euclid v. Ambler Realty Co.*, 272 U.S. 365 (1926) (prohibition of industrial use), which have been viewed as permissible governmental action even when prohibiting the most beneficial use of the property. . . .

Zoning laws generally do not affect existing uses of real property, but "taking" challenges have also been held to be without merit in a wide variety of situations when the challenged governmental actions prohibited a beneficial use to which individual parcels had previously been devoted and thus caused substantial individualized harm. *Miller v. Schoene*, 276 U.S. 272 (1928), is illustrative. In that case, a state entomologist, acting pursuant to a state statute, ordered the claimants to cut down a large number of ornamental red cedar trees because they produced cedar rust fatal to apple trees cultivated nearby. [T]he statute [d]id not provide compensation for the value of the standing trees or for the resulting decrease in market value of the properties as a whole. A unanimous Court held that this latter omission did not render the statute invalid. The Court held that the State might properly make "a choice between the preservation of one class of property and that of the other". . . .

Goldblatt v. Hempstead,[369 U.S. 590 (1962),] is a recent example. There, a 1958 city safety ordinance banned any excavations below the water table and effectively prohibited the claimant from continuing a sand and gravel mining business that had been operated on the particular parcel since 1927. The Court upheld the ordinance against a "taking" challenge, although the ordinance prohibited the present and presumably most beneficial use of the property and had, like the regulations in *Miller* and *Hadacheck*, severely affected a particular owner. [B]ecause the restriction served a substantial public purpose, the Court thus held no taking had occurred. It is, of course, implicit in *Goldblatt* that a use restriction on real property may constitute a "taking" if not reasonably necessary to the effectuation of a substantial public purpose, . . . or perhaps if it has an unduly harsh impact upon the owner's use of the property.

Pennsylvania Coal Co. v. Mahon, 260 U.S. 393 (1922), is the leading case for the proposition that a state statute that substantially furthers important public policies may so frustrate distinct investment-backed expectations as to amount to a "taking." There the claimant had sold the surface rights to particular parcels of property, but expressly reserved the right to remove the coal thereunder. A Pennsylvania statute, enacted after the transactions, forbade any mining of coal that caused the subsidence of any house, unless the house was the property of the owner of the underlying coal and was more than 150 feet from the improved property of another. Because the statute made it commercially impracticable to mine the coal and thus had nearly the same effect as the complete destruction of rights claimant had reserved from the owners of the surface land, the Court held that the statute was invalid as effecting a "taking" without just compensation. . . .

Finally, government actions that may be characterized as acquisitions of resources to permit or facilitate uniquely public functions have often been held to constitute "takings." *United States v. Causby*, 328 U.S. 256 (1946), is illustrative. In holding that direct overflights above the claimant's land, that destroyed the present use of the land as a chicken farm, constituted a "taking," *Causby* emphasized that Government had not "merely destroyed property [but was] using a part of it for the flight of its planes. . . ."

B

[A]ppellants do not contest that New York City's objective of preserving structures and areas with special historic, architectural, or cultural significance is an entirely permissible governmental goal. They also do not dispute that the restrictions imposed on its parcel are appropriate means of securing the purposes of the New York City law. Finally, appellants do not challenge any of the specific factual premises of the decision below. They accept for present purposes both that the parcel of land occupied by Grand Central Terminal must, in its present state, be regarded as capable of earning a reasonable return, and that the transferable development rights afforded appellants by virtue of the Terminal's designation as a landmark are valuable, even if not as valuable as the rights to construct above the Terminal. In appellants' view none of these factors derogate from their claim that New York City's law has effected a "taking."

They first observe that the airspace above the Terminal is a valuable property interest, citing *United States v. Causby, supra*. They urge that the Landmarks Law has deprived them of any gainful use of their "air rights". . . .

[T]he submission that appellants may establish a "taking" simply by showing that they have been denied the ability to exploit a property interest that they heretofore had believed was available for development is quite simply untenable. . . . "Taking" jurisprudence does not divide a single parcel into discrete segments and attempt to determine whether rights in a particular segment have been entirely abrogated. In deciding whether a particular governmental action has effected a taking, this Court focuses rather both on the character of the action and on the nature and extent of the interference with rights in the parcel as a whole—here, the city tax block designated as the "landmark site."

Secondly, appellants, focusing on the character and impact of the New York City law, argue that it effects a "taking" because its operation has significantly diminished the value of the Terminal site. Appellants concede that the decisions sustaining other land-use regulations, which, like the New York City law, are reasonably related to the promotion of the general welfare, uniformly reject the proposition that diminution in property value, standing alone, can establish a "taking," see *Euclid v. Ambler Realty Co.*, 272 U.S. 365 (1926) (75% diminution in value caused by zoning law). . . .

Appellants, moreover, . . . argue that New York City's regulation of individual landmarks is fundamentally different from zoning or from historic-district legislation because the controls imposed by New York City's law apply only to individuals who own selected properties.

Stated baldly, appellants' position appears to be that the only means of ensuring that selected owners are not singled out to endure financial hardship for no reason is to hold that any restriction imposed on individual landmarks pursuant to the New York City scheme is a "taking" requiring the payment of "just compensation." Agreement with this argument would, of course, invalidate not just New York City's law, but all comparable landmark legislation in the Nation. We find no merit in it.

It is true, as appellants emphasize, that both historic-district legislation and zoning laws regulate all properties within given physical communities whereas landmark laws apply only to selected parcels. But, contrary to appellants' suggestions, landmark laws are not like discriminatory, or "reverse spot," zoning: that is, a land-use decision which arbitrarily singles out a particular parcel for different, less favorable treatment than the neighboring ones. In contrast to discriminatory zoning, which is the antithesis of land-use control as part of some comprehensive plan, the New York City law embodies a comprehensive plan to preserve structures of historic or aesthetic interest wherever they might be found in the city, and as noted, over 400 landmarks and 31 historic districts have been designated pursuant to this plan.

Equally without merit is the related argument that the decision to designate a structure as a landmark "is inevitably arbitrary or at least subjective, because it is basically a matter of taste," thus unavoidably singling out individual landowners for disparate and unfair treatment. [A] landmark owner has a right to judicial review of any Commission decision, and, quite simply, there is no basis whatsoever for a conclusion that courts will have any greater difficulty identifying arbitrary or discriminatory action in the context of landmark regulation than in the context of classic zoning or indeed in any other context.

Next, appellants observe that New York City's law differs from zoning laws and historic-district ordinances in that the Landmarks Law does not impose identical or similar restrictions on all structures located in particular physical communities.

. . . It is, of course, true that the Landmarks Law has a more severe impact on some landowners than on others, but that in itself does not mean that the law effects a "taking." Legislation designed to promote the general welfare commonly burdens some more than others. The owners of the brickyard in *Hadacheck*, of the cedar trees in *Miller v. Schoene*, and of the gravel and sand mine in *Goldblatt v. Hempstead*, were uniquely burdened by the legislation sustained in those cases.

In any event, appellants' repeated suggestions that they are solely burdened and unbenefited is factually inaccurate. This contention overlooks the fact that the New York City law applies to vast numbers of structures in the city in addition to the Terminal—all the structures contained in the 31 historic districts and over 400 individual landmarks, many of which are close to the Terminal. Unless we are to reject the judgment of the New York City Council that the preservation of landmarks benefits all New York citizens and all structures, both economically and by improving the quality of life in the city as a whole—which we are unwilling to do—we cannot conclude that the owners of the Terminal have in no sense been benefited by the Landmarks Law. . . .

Appellants' final broad-based attack would have us treat the law as an instance, like that in *United States v. Causby*, in which government, acting in an enterprise capacity, has appropriated part of their property for some strictly governmental purpose. Apart from the fact that *Causby* was a case of invasion of airspace that destroyed the use of the farm beneath and this New York City law has in nowise impaired the present use of the Terminal, the Landmarks Law neither exploits appellants' parcel for city purposes nor facilitates nor arises from any entrepreneurial operations of the city. The situation is not remotely like that in *Causby* where the airspace above the property was in the flight pattern for military aircraft.

C

Rejection of appellants' broad arguments is not, however, the end of our inquiry. . . . We now must consider whether the interference with appellants' property is of such a magnitude that "there must be an exercise of eminent domain and compensation to sustain [it]." *Pennsylvania Coal Co. v. Mahon.* That inquiry may be narrowed to the question of the severity of the impact of the law on appellants' parcel, and its resolution in turn requires a careful assessment of the impact of the regulation on the Terminal site.

Unlike the governmental acts in *Goldblatt, Miller, Causby, Griggs,* and *Hadacheck,* the New York City law does not interfere in any way with the present uses of the Terminal. . . . More importantly, on this record, we must regard the New York City law as permitting Penn Central not only to profit from the Terminal but also to obtain a "reasonable return" on its investment.

Appellants, moreover, exaggerate the effect of the law on their ability to make use of the air rights above the Terminal in two respects. First, it simply cannot be maintained, on this record, that appellants have been prohibited from occupying any portion of the airspace above the Terminal. While the Commission's actions in denying applications to construct an office building in excess of 50 stories above the Terminal may indicate that it will refuse to issue a certificate of appropriateness for any comparably sized structure, nothing the Commission has said or done suggests an intention to prohibit any construction above the Terminal. The Commission's report emphasized that whether any construction would be allowed depended upon whether the proposed addition "would harmonize in scale, material and character with [the Terminal]." Since appellants have not sought approval for the construction of a smaller structure, we do not know that appellants will be denied any use of any portion of the airspace above the Terminal.

Second, . . . it is not literally accurate to say that [appellants] have been denied *all* use of even those pre-existing air rights. [T]hey are made transferable to at least eight parcels in the vicinity of the Terminal, one or two of which have been found suitable for the construction of new office buildings. . . . While these rights may well not have constituted "just compensation" if a "taking" had occurred, the rights nevertheless undoubtedly mitigate whatever financial burdens the law has imposed on appellants and, for that reason, are to be taken into account in considering the impact of regulation.

On this record, we conclude that the application of New York City's Landmarks Law has not effected a "taking" of appellants' property. . . .

Affirmed.

MR. JUSTICE REHNQUIST, with whom the CHIEF JUSTICE and MR. JUSTICE STEVENS join, dissenting.

Of the over one million buildings and structures in the city of New York, appellees have singled out 400 for designation as official landmarks. . . . The question in this case is whether the cost associated with the city of New York's desire to preserve a limited number of "landmarks" within its borders must be borne by all of its taxpayers or whether it can instead be imposed entirely on the owners of the individual properties.

Only in the most superficial sense of the word can this case be said to involve "zoning." Typical zoning restrictions may, it is true, so limit the prospective uses of a piece of property as to diminish the value of that property in the abstract because it may not be used for the forbidden purposes. But any such abstract decrease in value will more than likely be at least partially offset by an increase in value which flows from similar restrictions as to use on neighboring properties. All property owners in a designated area are placed under the same restrictions, not only for the benefit of the municipality as a whole but also for the common benefit of one another. In the words of Mr. Justice Holmes, speaking for the Court in *Pennsylvania Coal Co. v. Mahon*, 260 U.S. 393, 415 (1922), there is "an average reciprocity of advantage."

[W]hile neighboring landowners are free to use their land and "air rights" in any way consistent with the broad boundaries of New York zoning, Penn Central, absent the permission of appellees, must forever maintain its property in its present state. The property has been thus subjected to a nonconsensual servitude not borne by any neighboring or similar properties.

Appellees have thus destroyed—in a literal sense, "taken"—substantial property rights of Penn Central. While the term "taken" might have been narrowly interpreted to include only physical seizures of property rights, "the construction of the phrase has not been so narrow. The courts have held that the deprivation of the former owner rather than the accretion of a right or interest to the sovereign constitutes the taking. . . ." Because "not every destruction or injury to property by governmental action has been held to be a taking in the constitutional sense," however, this does not end our inquiry. But an examination of the two exceptions where the destruction of property does *not* constitute a taking demonstrates that a compensable taking has occurred here.

As early as 1887, the Court recognized that the government can prevent a property owner from using his property to injure others without having to compensate the owner for the value of the forbidden use. . . . Nor is it relevant, where the government is merely prohibiting a noxious use of property, that the government would seem to be singling out a particular property owner. *Hadacheck, supra*, at 413. . . .

Appellees are not prohibiting a nuisance. . . . Instead, appellees are seeking to preserve what they believe to be an outstanding example of beaux-arts architecture. Penn Central is prevented from further developing its property basically because *too good* a job was done in designing and building it. . . .

Here, however, a multimillion dollar loss has been imposed on appellants. . . . Appellees have imposed a substantial cost on less than one one-tenth of one percent of the buildings in New York City for the general benefit of all its people. It is exactly this imposition of general costs on a few individuals at which the "taking" protection is directed.

NOTES AND QUESTIONS

(1) *Valid Public Purpose, Nature of Regulation, Investment-Backed Expectations, and Diminution in Value: Applying the Penn Central Factors to Pennsylvania Coal Co. v. Mahon, supra, and to Keystone Bituminous Coal Ass'n v. Debenedictis, 480 U.S. 470 (1987).* In *Pennsylvania Coal*, which is described in *Penn Central*, the mining company had obtained an express release of liability for surface damage. The surface owners obtained passage of a Pennsylvania law that prevented subsidence. The trial court found, as a fact, that the legislation was supported by nothing "except the private interests of the plaintiffs in the prevention of private injury." Justice Holmes' opinion for the Court emphasized (1) that a broad public interest was lacking and (2) that "the extent of the taking is great" because it abolished a valuable estate in land. Later, however, in *Keystone*, a five-to-four majority of the Court, per Justice Stevens, applied the *Penn Central* factors to what they saw as "a different set of 'particular facts.' " Pennsylvania's Bituminous Land Subsidence and Land Conservation Act prohibited coal mining causing subsidence to certain pre-existing structures, required fifty percent of the coal beneath certain structures to be kept in place, and authorized revocation of mining permits under certain circumstances. The Court upheld the Act:

[H]ere, . . . the Commonwealth is acting to protect the public interest in health, the environment, and the fiscal integrity of the area. That private individuals erred in taking a risk cannot estop the state from exercising its police power to abate activity akin to a public nuisance. The Subsidence Act is a prime example that "circumstances may so change in time . . . as to clothe with such a [public interest] what at other times . . . would be a matter of purely private concern. . . ."

[The Court held that the Subsidence Act was of general application and within the area of the state's protectible interests, unlike the enactment in *Pennsylvania Coal*, which protected relatively few landowners.]

[I]ndeed, petitioners have not even pointed to a single mine that can no longer be mined for a profit. . . .

Chief Justice Rehnquist, joined by Justices Powell, O'Connor, and Scalia, dissented: "[T]he Act works to extinguish Petitioners' interest in at least twenty-seven million tons of coal by requiring that coal be left in the ground and destroys their purchased support estates by returning to them financial liability for the subsidence." Is this analysis correct, or is the majority's analysis, including the distinction between *Keystone* and *Pennsylvania Coal*, more persuasive? *Cf.* Large, *The Supreme Court and the Takings Clause: The Search for a Better Rule*, 18 ENVTL. L.J. 3 (1987).

(2) *Investment-Backed Expectations and Diminution in Value as Opposed to "Adjustment of Rights for the Public Good": Andrus v. Allard, 444 U.S. 51 (1979).* The Eagle Protection Act and Migratory Bird Treaty Act prohibited commercial transactions in parts of birds legally killed before those birds came under the protection of the Acts. The Acts were aimed at preventing the killing of birds whose parts were indistinguishable from those killed earlier. A unanimous Court, in an opinion by Brennan, J., upheld the Acts:

The regulations challenged here do not compel the surrender of the artifacts, and there is no physical invasion or restraint upon them. . . . At least where an owner possesses a full "bundle" of property rights, the destruction of one "strand" of the bundle is not a taking, because the aggregate must be viewed in its entirety. . . .

It is, to be sure, undeniable that the regulations here prevent the most profitable use of appellees' property. Again, however, that is not dispositive. [A] reduction in the value of property is not necessarily equated with a taking. . . . In the instant case, it is not clear that appellees will be unable to derive economic benefit from the artifacts; for example, they might exhibit the artifacts for an admissions charge. [F]urther, perhaps because of its very uncertainty, the interest in anticipated gains has traditionally been viewed as less compelling than other property-related interests. . . .

Is this reasoning persuasive—or is it disingenuous? Interestingly, the Court never analyzed (or for that matter even mentioned) the element of "investment-backed expectations," which it emphasized heavily in such cases as *Penn Central* and *Keystone*, above. If you had purchased a stuffed bald eagle as an investment, with the quite reasonable expectation that its value would increase as eagles became increasingly rare, would you regard these Acts as having frustrated your expectations? On the other hand, perhaps the Court's decision (which was unanimous) can better be supported by focusing upon the nature of the regulation and the generality of the public purpose, which was not a deliberate effort to frustrate investment-backed expectations.

(3) *Complete Destruction of Value—How Does the Multi-Factor Test Work Then?: Hodel v. Irving, 481 U.S. 704 (1987) (O'Connor, J.).* The Indian Land Consolidation Act provided that an inherited interest in land would escheat to the tribe if it comprised less than 2 percent of the acreage and earned less than $100 in the preceding year. It was passed in response to a serious problem of fractionalization of Indian lands. No

compensation was provided. A unanimous Court held that this law violated the Takings Clause. Factors in favor of the statute included its broad public purpose, the lack of investment-backed expectations in the recipients (since they took by descent), and some degree of "reciprocity of advantage" since most heirs or devisees also were members of the tribe and would benefit from the land consolidation. However, the Court concluded:

> If we were to stop our analysis at this point, we might well find [the escheat provision] constitutional. But the character of the Government regulations here is extraordinary. [T]he regulation here amounts to virtually the abrogation of the right to pass on a certain type of property—the small undivided interest—to one's heirs. [E]ven the United States concedes that total abrogation of the right to pass property is unprecedented and likely to be unconstitutional.

The dimensions of the problem were illustrated by one parcel that earned $1,080 in annual rent and had 439 owners, one-third of whom received less than five cents a year. Given that testators could minimize and in fact avoid the escheat by traditional estate planning methods, is the Court's reasoning well taken?

LUCAS v. SOUTH CAROLINA COASTAL COUNCIL, 505 U.S. 1003 (1992). In 1986, petitioner Lucas paid $975,000 for two residential lots on a South Carolina barrier island. He intended to build single-family homes. In 1988, however, the state legislature enacted the Beachfront Management Act, which barred Lucas from erecting any permanent habitable structures on his land. Lucas filed suit, alleging that the Act effected a "taking" that required the payment of just compensation because it had deprived him of all "economically viable use" of the land. The state trial court agreed, finding that the Act rendered Lucas' parcels "valueless," and entered an award exceeding $1.2 million. The South Carolina Supreme Court reversed, holding that the legislature's uncontested findings that new construction in the coastal zone threatened a valuable public resource brought the case within that line of decisions allowing regulation without compensation to prevent "harmful or noxious uses" of property akin to public nuisances. The United States Supreme Court, per Justice Scalia, reversed and held that regulations denying a landowner all "economically viable use of his land" constitute one of the discrete categories of regulatory deprivations that require compensation "without the usual case-specific inquiry."

The Court suggested "that total deprivation of beneficial use is, from the landowner's point of view, the equivalent of a physical appropriation." Therefore, "in the extraordinary circumstance when no productive or economically beneficial use of land is permitted, it is less realistic to indulge our usual assumption that the legislature is simply 'adjusting the benefits and burdens of economic life,' *Penn Central Transportation Co.*, in a manner that secures an 'average reciprocity of advantage' to everyone concerned." Furthermore, such a regulation presents "a heightened risk that private property is being pressed into some form of public service under the guise of mitigating serious public harm."

As for the "harmful or noxious uses" principle, the South Carolina Court "was too quick to conclude that that principle decides the present case." A review of the relevant decisions demonstrated that the "harmful or noxious use" principle was merely the Court's early formulation of the police power justification necessary to sustain (without compensation) any regulatory diminution in value. Furthermore, the distinction between regulation that "prevents harmful use" and that which "confers benefits" is difficult, if not impossible, to discern on an objective, value-free basis. The difference "is often in the eye of the beholder." Here, for example, it was possible to describe in either fashion the concerns that inspired the South Carolina legislature: "One could say that imposing a servitude on Lucas' land is necessary in order to prevent his use of it from 'harming' South Carolina's ecological resources; or, instead, in order to achieve the 'benefits' of an ecological preserve." The Court then set out a "categorical" holding:

> Where the State seeks to sustain regulation that deprives land of all economically beneficial use, we think it may resist compensation only if the

logically antecedent inquiry into the nature of the owner's estate shows that the proscribed use interests were not part of his title to begin with. . . . [I]n the case of personal property, by reason of the State's traditionally high degree of control over commercial dealings, he ought to be aware of the possibility that new regulation might even render his property economically worthless. . . . In the case of land, however, we think the notion pressed by the Council that title is somehow held subject to the "implied limitation" that the State may subsequently eliminate all economically valuable use is inconsistent with the historical compact recorded in the Takings Clause that has become part of our constitutional culture.

Justice Kennedy concurred only in the judgment, emphasizing investment-backed expectations: The South Carolina Court had erred by relying on general legislative purposes "without a determination that they were in accord with the owner's reasonable expectations." Justice Blackmun dissented. He "question[ed] the Court's wisdom in issuing sweeping new rules to decide such a narrow case."

Justice Stevens dissented. "In my opinion," he wrote, "the Court is doubly in error. The categorical rule the Court establishes is an unsound and unwise addition to the law and the Court's formulation of the exception to that rule [*i.e.*, the restriction of nuisance principles to preexisting law] is too rigid and too narrow."

EASTERN ENTERPRISES v. APFEL, 524 U.S. 498 (1998). The petitioner, Eastern Enterprises (Eastern), had been a coal mine operator during the post-WWII years when historic agreements (*e.g.*, the 1950 agreement) were reached between the coal mine operators and the miners' union to provide benefit funds ("trusts")which covered the medical expenses of the miners and their dependents. Eastern was a signatory to the early trust agreements, but Eastern left the coal industry in 1965, ultimately selling off any interest in the coal industry. Eastern, thus, had left the coal industry before Congress passed ERISA in 1974 and the coal industry trusts were substantially restructured. For the coal industry trusts, the 1974 restructuring was not successful in dealing with the rapidly accelerating health care costs and the general decline of the coal industry. As more coal operators withdrew from the industry, the trusts were left without adequate funding. In 1992, Congress passed the Coal Industry Retiree Health Benefit Act (the Coal Act) and established a new fund (the Combined Fund) to provide lifetime health benefits to retirees. Congress mandated that the Combined Fund would be financed by premiums assessed coal operators who had signed the 1950 agreement (including Eastern), and the Social Security Administrator (Apfel) would assign retirees to coal operators according to an allocation formula designed to spread the costs of retiree medical benefits. Apfel eventually assigned Eastern over 1,000 retirees who, before 1964, had worked for Eastern; the cost to Eastern of these assigned lifetime benefits was estimated at $50 to $100 million.

Eastern sued Apfel for declaratory and injunctive relief. Eastern claimed that the retroactive nature of the Coal Act obligation and the substantial financial burden violated its substantive due process rights or, alternatively, constituted an impermissible taking. Although the lower courts ruled in favor of the federal government, the Supreme Court, per Justice O'Connor's plurality opinion, reversed and remanded. The plurality concluded that the Coal Act's allocation of retiree liability to Eastern may, in light of the adverse economic impact and the retroactive imposition of the liability, constitute a taking violative of the Fifth Amendment.

The plurality recognized that not every regulation creates a taking. The plurality announced that, for purposes of the Takings Clause, the constitutionality of a regulation is evaluated by examining the government's action under a standard of "fairness and justice." The plurality identified three factors for the Court's "regulatory takings analysis": (1) the adverse economic impact of the regulation; (2) the regulations' interference with reasonable investment backed expectations; and (3) "the character of the governmental action."

Applying these factors to Eastern's takings claim, the plurality determined that the Combined Fund assessment of $50 to $100 million to Eastern constituted a severe economic impact. The plurality found that the retroactive application (reaching back 30 to 50 years) of Combined Fund liability interfered with Eastern's reasonable investment expectations. The plurality found that Eastern had never had "notice" that, decades after leaving the industry, it might be liable for costly lifetime health benefits. Finally, the plurality found that the Coal Act was "quite unusual in character because it singled out certain employers, based on conduct far in the past and for conduct unrelated to any commitment made or injury caused."

Justice Kennedy concurred in the judgment (and dissented from the Takings Clause analysis). Justice Kennedy relied exclusively on a substantive due process analysis (and not the Takings Clause). His analysis turned on the retroactive nature and great severity of the burden, basically the same factors as Justice O'Connor's plurality opinion. Four Justices dissented.

NOTES AND QUESTIONS

(1) *Further (Post-Lucas) Dimensions of the "Regulatory Takings" Doctrine: Palazzolo v. Rhode Island, 533 U.S. 606 (2001).* Anthony Palozzolo was the owner of an ocean front parcel of land in Westerly on the Rhode Island coastline (in the "summer tourist" area). Palozzolo, who the Court emphasized was a "lifelong" Westerly resident, originally invested with others (in 1959). After his purchase of the property (which was mainly salt marsh land), Rhode Island established environmental legislation protecting "coastal wetlands." After Palozzolo gained sole ownership of the property, he sought to develop it.

The Rhode Island authorities essentially turned down his "commercial" development plans, although the state would permit him to build a residence on part of his land. Palozzolo eventually sued for inverse condemnation. Although the State courts ruled in favor of the State, the Supreme Court, per Justice Kennedy, agreed with Palozzolo, extended the protection against regulatory takings and remanded for further determination.

The Court first held that the claim was ripe. [*See* § 1.02(A)(2) above.] For purposes of this Chapter, the Court held that Palozzolo's acquisition of ownership after the effective date of the coastal wetlands regulation would not automatically bar his takings claim. The Court stated: "Future generations, too, have a right to challenge unreasonable limitations on the use and value of land." Finally, the Court remanded for consideration under the *Penn Central* decision, above. Justices O'Connor and Scalia filed concurring opinions (apparently aimed at each other). There were four dissenters—Justices Stevens, Souter, Ginsburg and Breyer.

(2) *Can a "Temporary" Moratorium on Construction Constitute a "Regulatory Taking": Tahoe-Sierra Preservation Council, Inc. v. Tahoe Regional Planning Agency, 535 U.S. 302 (2002).* The Tahoe Regional Planning Agency (TRPA) imposed two moratoria totaling 32 months on development in certain sensitive land areas in the Lake Tahoe Basin while it formulated a comprehensive land-use plan for the Basin. At the end of the 32 months, TRPA essentially banned all residential development. Real estate owners adversely affected by the moratoria sued claiming that TRPA's actions constituted, under the *Lucas* rule (above), a taking requiring compensation. The real estate owners did not pursue a theory based on *Penn Central*. The Supreme Court, per Justice Stevens, ruled for TRPA.

The Court held that the "temporary" nature of TRPA's moratoria precluded the application of the "categorical rule" from *Lucas*. The Court concluded that "in the regulatory taking context, we require a more fact specific inquiry." The Court further held that the proper analysis was based on the totality of the circumstances analysis from the *Penn Central* decision. The Court drew a sharp distinction between the "physical takings context [§ 6.03, above] and regulatory takings claims."

Chief Justice Rehnquist dissented because "a ban on all development lasting almost six years" should be considered a taking. Justice Thomas also dissented, citing the economist John Maynard Keynes and arguing that a "temporary taking" should be considered a compensable taking.

(3)   For further research on the Taking Clause jurisprudence, consider the following: Hanoch Dagan, *Takings and Distributive Justice*, 85 Va. L. Rev. 741 (1999); Jeb Rubenfeld, *Usings*, 102 Yale L.J. 1077 (1993); Herbert Hovenkamp, *The Takings Clause and Improvident Regulatory Bargains*, 108 Yale L.J. 801 (1999) (book review).

PROBLEM C

BALL DEVELOPMENT CO. v. CITY OF VIRGINIA CITY, APPENDIX, BELOW. The City of Virginia City requires that a new subdivision developer dedicate a certain percentage of its land to park space, in perpetuity. The Park Ordinance also allows the City, at its option, to demand cash payment of the market value of the specified portion of land, instead. The ordinance requires this dedication or payment no matter how much greenbelt and recreation space the subdivision plat includes; in fact, the needs created by the subdivision for park space or their fulfillment by the developer are irrelevant under the ordinance. Ball Development Company has proposed to build, on land that it owns, a subdivision with extensive private recreational facilities and greenbelt. As a condition of approving the plat, the City demands payment in cash for the market value of the percentage of land specified in its park ordinance. Is the City's action an unconstitutional taking? (The Appendix to this section, below, contains an expanded version of this problem, with litigation documents.)

[2]   Remedies for Takings: Inverse Condemnation

FIRST ENGLISH EVANGELICAL LUTHERAN CHURCH v. COUNTY OF LOS ANGELES, 482 U.S. 304 (1987). The County passed an ordinance providing that "[a] person shall not construct, reconstruct, place or enlarge any building or structure . . . within the outer boundary lines of the interim flood protection area located in Mill Creek Canyon . . .," which included property of the church. The church filed suit, alleging that the regulation amounted to a taking because it allegedly denied all use of the property. As a remedy, it sought damages on a theory of "inverse condemnation"; i.e., it sought to force the County to exercise the power of eminent domain and thereby purchase the land that it allegedly had taken by regulation. The California courts struck the damage allegations from the pleading, holding that no such remedy existed. The Supreme Court, per Justice Rehnquist, reversed and held that a remedy of damages by inverse condemnation for "temporary" regulatory takings was required by the Constitution:

Consideration of the compensation question must begin with direct reference to the language of the Fifth Amendment, which provides in relevant part that "private property [shall not] be taken for public use, without just compensation. . . ."

. . . Thus, government action that works a taking of property rights necessarily implicates the constitutional obligation to pay just compensation. *Armstrong v. United States*, 364 U.S. 40, 49 (1960).

We have recognized that a landowner is entitled to bring an action in inverse condemnation as a result of "the self-executing character of the constitutional provision with respect to compensation. . . ." [I]t has been established at least since *Jacobs v. United States*, 290 U.S. 13 (1933), that claims for just compensation are grounded in the Constitution itself:

The suits were based on the right to recover just compensation for property taken by the United States for public use in the exercise of its power of eminent domain. *That right was guaranteed by the Constitution. . . .* It rested upon the

Fifth Amendment. Statutory recognition was not necessary. A promise to pay was not necessary. . . .

While the Supreme Court of California may not have actually disavowed this general rule, we believe that it has truncated the rule by disallowing damages that occurred prior to the ultimate invalidation of the challenged regulation. The Supreme Court of California justified its conclusion at length, concluding that:

In combination, the need for preserving a degree of freedom in the land-use planning function, and the inhibiting financial force which inheres in the inverse condemnation remedy, persuade us that on balance mandamus or declaratory relief rather than inverse condemnation is the appropriate relief under the circumstances.

We, of course, are not unmindful of these considerations, but they must be evaluated in the light of the command of the Just Compensation Clause of the Fifth Amendment. The Court has recognized in more than one case that the government may elect to abandon its intrusion or discontinue regulations. . . . But we have not resolved whether abandonment by the government requires payment of compensation for the period of time during which regulations deny a landowner all use of his land.

In considering this question, we find substantial guidance in cases where the government has only temporarily exercised its right to use private property. [T]hough the takings were in fact "temporary," there was no question that compensation would be required for the Government's interference with the use of the property; the Court was concerned in each case with determining the proper measure of the monetary relief to which the property holders were entitled.

In the present case the interim ordinance was adopted by the county of Los Angeles in January 1979, and became effective immediately. Appellant filed suit within a month after the effective date of the ordinance and yet when the Supreme Court of California denied a hearing in the case on October 17, 1985, the merits of appellant's claim had yet to be determined. The United States has been required to pay compensation for leasehold interests of shorter duration than this. . . . [I]nvalidation of the ordinance or its successor ordinance after this period of time, though converting the taking into a "temporary" one, is not a sufficient remedy to meet the demands of the Just Compensation Clause.

Justice Stevens, joined in part by Justices Blackmun and O'Connor, dissented: "One thing is certain. The Court's decision today will generate a great deal of litigation. Most of it, I believe, will be unproductive. But the mere duty to defend the actions that today's decision will spawn will undoubtedly have a significant adverse impact on the land-use regulatory process." The dissenters concluded that the Due Process Clause, rather than the Takings Clause, should be the primary constraint on the use of unfair and dilatory procedures in the land-use area: "Cautious local officials and land use planners may avoid taking any action that might later be challenged and thus give rise to a damage action. Much important regulation will never be enacted, even perhaps in the health and safety area."

NOTES AND QUESTIONS

(1) *Deterrence of Useful Regulation Because of the Existence of the Inverse Condemnation Damage Remedy.* How persuasive is Justice Stevens' argument (the premise of which the majority accepts) that the inverse condemnation remedy will do harm in terms of deterrence of desirable regulation? Notice the type of ordinances most subject to deterrence: those in which (1) the validity of the ordinance is most doubtful and (2) the damages that it will impose are highest. Isn't this precisely the situation in which deterrence is most desirable? Or will the vagueness of the substantive law, as

exemplified in multi-factor decisions such as *Penn Central*, make the outcome so unpredictable that a rational calculus will be beyond the reach of public servants?

(2) *Will the Existence of the Inverse Condemnation Damage Remedy Make Courts Reluctant to Find Takings?* The inverse condemnation remedy may have an additional adverse effect: courts may be less willing to find the existence of takings, because of the fear of imposing astronomical liability on public servants or taxpayers. Is this result likely, and if so, what effect should it have upon the desirability of an inverse condemnation remedy?

[C] Problems Associated with Price Regulation

NOTE: PRICE REGULATION AND THE TAKINGS CLAUSE

The Propriety and Limits of Price Regulation: Munn v. Illinois, supra. Recall the Supreme Court's upholding of price regulation in industries "affected with a public interest." Actually, the modern constitutional view, after *Nebbia*, is that price regulation is permissible even in the absence of this showing.

When Price Regulation Becomes a Taking. But even if price regulation is constitutional as a general proposition, isn't it possible for it to *become* a taking? Imagine a public utility regulated by a city, which sets rates so low that no manager could make a profit. The investors' property is not usable in any other venture. By requiring them to submit their property to continued operation at a loss, has the city not taken it without just compensation?

The Hope Test: FPC v. Hope Natural Gas Co., 320 U.S. 591 (1943). In the *Hope* case, the Federal Power Commission acted pursuant to the Federal Natural Gas Act to determine "just and reasonable [maximum] rates" for Hope's sales of natural gas. The Commission used traditional utility regulation approaches, by determining the company's "original costs" and adding what it determined to be a "reasonable" return. The Supreme Court upheld the rate determination, reasoning as follows:

> From the investor or company point of view it is important that there be enough revenue not only for operating expenses but also for the capital costs of the business. These include service on the debt and dividends on the stock. . . . By that standard the return to the equity owner should be commensurate with returns on investments and other enterprises having corresponding risks. That return, moreover, should be sufficient to assure confidence in the financial integrity of the enterprise, so as to maintain its credit and to attract capital. . . .

> [B]y such a procedure the utility is made whole and the integrity of its investment maintained. No more is required. . . . Since there are no constitutional requirements more exacting than the standards of the [Natural Gas] Act, a rate order which conforms to the latter does not run afoul of the former.

Later, the Court said that "the just and reasonable standard of the Natural Gas Act 'coincides' with the applicable constitutional standards." *In re Permian Basin Area Rate Cases*, 390 U.S. 747, 770 (1968).

Modern Problems of Rate Regulation: Consumerism and Economic Efficiency. Classic utility regulation assumes a cost-plus-reasonable-return rate structure. If simplistically applied, however, this approach may impair efficiency, because the regulated utility recovers all costs, plus reasonable return, even if it is imprudent. Therefore, many regulatory bodies have adopted the approach of denying costs that were "imprudently" incurred. But this standard, too, introduces difficulties. Imagine a utility facing a crucial decision whether to build coal-fired or gas-fired boilers. Its prudence, and therefore its recovery of costs, will be judged by *hindsight*. This dilemma, in turn, may produce timid management, which opts for the course that best can be justified to regulators by hindsight rather than that which provides most effective consumer service. The regulatory response has been to consider prudence in terms of reasonable choice among a range of alternatives existing as of the time of the choice.

Efforts to Increase Efficiency—The Taking Issue: Duquesne Light Company v. Barasch, infra. What should happen if a utility, not acting imprudently, nevertheless creates excess capacity that is not usable? An unregulated private business would not be able to recover its costs for this capacity. As one utility colorfully put it in seeking Supreme Court review, "[Utility] investors do not have the opportunity to gain the profits Ford earned on the Mustang because they do not risk the losses Ford incurred on the Edsel." Yet regulators, quite understandably, have continued to search for ways in which to avoid the disincentive to efficiency created by cost-plus-return regulation, or by regulation based on historical costs. Instead, they have turned to other methodologies, such as requiring a plant to be actually "used and useful" before it may be included in the rate base. Might this approach result in denying utilities the "profits of the Mustang" while imposing upon them the "losses of the Edsel"—and thereby ultimately make them unable to obtain capital? Consider the *Duquesne* case that follows.

> [If a regulated public utility] were to charge a price . . . as a competitor does, [it] would be losing money. No matter how economists may extol the virtues of . . . charging for each unit of a product the addition to costs attributable to it . . ., the [regulated public utility] cannot afford to follow that policy.

R. DORFMAN, PRICES AND MARKETS 153 (3d ed. 1978). For an unregulated business, "in a particular year, errors in short-run planning or prediction may lead sellers to under- or over-estimate the demand for their products, and this in turn, may yield higher or lower prices or profits than expected. . . . But positive and negative windfalls should about cancel out over the long pull." R. Caves, *American Industry: Structure, Conduct, Performance* (5th ed. 1982). However, a regulated public utility cannot offset losses against "windfalls" occurring in "good" years, because its rate of return is regulated even in good years. Yet regulators, quite understandably, have continued to search for ways in which to avoid the disincentive to efficiency created by cost-plus-return regulation. Consider the case that follows.

DUQUESNE LIGHT CO. v. BARASCH, 488 U.S. 299 (1989). For many years, Pennsylvania had regulated utility rates on the basis of historical costs. Under that method, regulators considered the costs incurred by utilities (so long as they were incurred "prudently") and added a "reasonable" rate of return (theoretically, that for industries of comparable risk) and fixed prices at that level. During this regime of historical costs, the petitioners in Duquesne invested tens of millions of dollars in nuclear power plants because projections at that time indicated a growing demand for electricity and an enormous cost advantage to nuclear capacity. The Federal Department of Energy strongly encouraged petitioners and other utilities to invest in nuclear plants. But intervening events, including the a Middle-Eastern oil embargo and the accident at Three-Mile Island, radically changed the outlook both for the demand for electricity and for nuclear energy as a desirable way of meeting that demand. Ultimately, the petitioners canceled several plants. Nevertheless, in accordance with the historic costs doctrine, the petitioners sought to recoup their investment in these plants through regulated payments from ratepayers. The record before the Pennsylvania Public Utilities Commission included the finding of the administrative law judge that the utilities' expenditures "at every stage [prior to the nuclear plants' cancellation], were reasonable and prudent." The PUC, therefore, granted recovery of the costs in question.

The Pennsylvania Legislature, however, passed a statute that denied any recovery of capital investments that were not "used and useful in service to the public." The Pennsylvania Supreme Court concluded that this statute barred any recovery by petitioners of the costs of the cancelled nuclear plants. In response to petitioners' Taking Clause arguments, the state supreme court observed that the overall rates and returns allowed petitioners were adequate and concluded that "[T]he 'just compensation' safeguard[ed] to a utility by the [f]ederal Constitution is a reasonable return on the fair value of its property at the time it is being used for public service." The United States Supreme Court, per Chief Justice Rehnquist, affirmed:

> The guiding principle has been that the Constitution protects utilities from being limited to a charge for their property serving the public which is so "unjust" as to be confiscatory. . . . [I]f the rate does not afford sufficient compensation, the state has taken the use of utility property without paying just compensation and so violated the fifth and fourteenth amendments. *Smyth v. Ames*, 169 U.S. 466, 546 (1898). . . .

> At one time, it was thought that the Constitution required rates to be set according to the actual present value of the assets employed in the public service. This method, known as the "fair value" rule, is exemplified by the decision in *Smyth v. Ames, supra.* [I]n theory the *Smyth v. Ames* fair value standard mimics the operation of the competitive market. To the extent utilities' investments in plants are good ones (because their benefits exceed their costs) they are rewarded with an opportunity to earn an "above-cost" return, that is, a fair return on the current "market value" of the plant. To the extent utilities' investments turn out to be bad ones (such as plants that are canceled and so never used and useful to the public), the utilities suffer because the investments have no fair value and so justify no return.

> Although the fair value rule gives utilities strong incentive to manage their affairs well and to provide efficient service to the public, it suffered from practical difficulties which ultimately led to its abandonment as a constitutional requirement. . . . [In a footnote, Justice Rehnquist pointed out that the "most serious problem" perhaps was the "laborious and baffling task of finding the present value of the utility."]. . . .

> Forty-five years ago in the landmark case of *Federal Power Comm'n v. Hope Natural Gas Co.*, this Court abandoned the rule of *Smyth v. Ames*, and held that the "fair value" rule is not the only constitutionally acceptable method of fixing utility rates. In *Hope* we ruled that historical cost was a valid basis on which to calculate utility compensation. ("Rates which enable [a] company to operate successfully, to maintain its financial integrity, to attract capital, and to compensate its investors for the risks assumed certainly cannot be condemned as invalid, even though they might produce only a meager return on the so-called 'fair value' rate base.") [T]oday we reaffirm these teachings of *Hope Natural Gas:* "[I]t is not theory but the impact of the rate order which counts. If the total effect of the rate order cannot be said to be unreasonable, judicial inquiry . . . is at an end. . . ."

Justice Blackmun dissented on the ground that the Court lacked jurisdiction. Justice Scalia, joined by Justices White and O'Connor, concurred specially: "[I] think it important to observe, however, that while 'prudent investment' [n]eed not be taken into account as such in ratemaking formulas, it may need to be taken into account in assessing the constitutionality of the particular consequences produced by those formulas. We cannot determine whether [t]he government's action is confiscatory, unless we agree upon what the relevant 'investment' is. For that purpose, all prudently incurred investment may well have to be counted."

NOTES AND QUESTIONS

(1) *New Approaches to Efficiency Incentives in Rate Making: Kalt, Lee & Leonard, Reestablishing the Regulatory Bargain in the Electric Utility Industry, Discussion Paper No. E-87-02, Harvard Energy & Environmental Policy Center (1987).* Kalt, Lee, and Leonard describe various means by which regulators across the country have attempted to change the historic method of regulation. Massachusetts, for example, has attempted to measure the "value of the power" produced by a given facility and to use

this factor in determining what portion of costs to allow to be recovered. Other states, such as Connecticut, Pennsylvania, and New York, have begun "to selectively use preapproval cost recovery mechanisms, commonly referred to as 'cost caps,' to limit the consumer's exposure to future cost overruns and to provide rewards and penalties to the utility for good (or poor) management of the construction process." *Id.* at 34, 41. The latter approach involves the regulating body much more deeply in advance of construction; it allows high recovery for efficient construction and imposes losses on inefficient construction. But the consequences may be unattractive in some cases:

> If some projects come in with zero return, and others come in with allowed rates of return equal to the utility's cost of capital, the *expected return* of a firm as perceived by investors would be less than the cost of capital. . . . If the cost of capital is twelve percent, and the utility has a fifty percent chance of making no return, then it will have to be allowed a twenty-four percent return on its remaining investments. The consequence can be allowed rates of return that appear to provide exorbitant profits and concomitantly high electricity prices to projects that are approved for cost recovery. *Id.* 81–82.[*]

(2) *"Rent Control" for Gasoline Service Station Owners is Not a Taking: Lingle v. Chevron, U.S.A., Inc., 544 U.S. 528 (2005).* The Hawaii Legislature passed a law capping the rent that oil companies may charge dealers leasing company-owned service stations. The "rent cap" was the State's means to combat the perceived effect of market concentration on retail gasoline prices. Chevron, one of the largest oil companies in Hawaii, challenged the rent cap scheme as an unconstitutional taking. The case ultimately focused on what were the proper standards for determining whether a state regulatory scheme was a taking. The lower courts found that the rent cap scheme was a taking based on *Agins v. City of Tiburon*, 447 U.S. 255 (1980), and the purported "substantially advances" standard. The Supreme Court, per Justice O'Connor, reversed and ruled for the State. The Court unanimously held that the "substantially advances" standard was not the controlling test for the Taking Clause and remanded. The Court suggested that the Taking Clause doctrine may be governed by a four-part standard.

The rejection of the *Agins*-based test will not have broad consequences. But, the four-part doctrinal structure may suggest a rejection of the traditional two-tiered Taking Clause doctrine.

(3) *The New Regulation and the Taking Clause.* How does the Takings Clause impinge upon these new methods of regulation? Consider whether it may be more difficult for regulators to avoid takings as a consequence of pressure induced by the "new regulation."

[D]   The Public Purpose Requirement

HAWAII HOUSING AUTHORITY v. MIDKIFF, 467 U.S. 229 (1984). The Hawaii Land Reform Act of 1967 set up a land condemnation system whereby lessees of certain residential lots can request condemnation by the Hawaii Housing Authority (HHA) of the property on which they lived. The purpose of the Act is to reduce perceived evils of a land oligopoly traceable to the early high chiefs of the Hawaiian Islands. The HHA is required to hold a public hearing to determine whether the "public purposes" of the Act will be achieved by the grant of an application for condemnation, and the price to be paid by the government to the lessor then is set by a condemnation trial or by negotiation. Finally the HHA sells the land titles to the applicant lessees. The Court of Appeals reasoned that, since the Fifth Amendment requires that any taking be for a "public use," the Act was unconstitutional, because it was for a "private" purpose. A unanimous Supreme Court, per Justice O'Connor, reversed and upheld the Act.

---

[*] Copyright © 1987 by the Energy & Environmental Policy Center, John F. Kennedy School of Government, Harvard University. Reprinted with permission.

The starting point for our analysis of the Act's constitutionality is the Court's decision in *Berman v. Parker*, 348 U.S. 26, (1954). In *Berman*, the Court held constitutional the District of Columbia Redevelopment Act of 1945. That Act provided both for the comprehensive use of the eminent domain power to redevelop slum areas and for the possible sale or lease of the condemned lands to private interests. In discussing whether the takings authorized by that Act were for a "public use," the Court stated:

We deal . . . with what traditionally has been known as the police power. An attempt to define its reach or trace its outer limits is fruitless, for each case must turn on its own facts. The definition is essentially the product of legislative determinations addressed to the purposes of government, purposes neither abstractly nor historically capable of complete definition. . . . The "public use" requirement is thus coterminous with the scope of a sovereign's police powers. . . .

To be sure, the Court's cases have repeatedly stated that "one person's property may not be taken for the benefit of another private person without a justifying public purpose, even though compensation be paid."

. . . But where the exercise of the eminent domain power is rationally related to a conceivable public purpose, the Court has never held a compensated taking to be prescribed by the taking clause.

On this basis, we have no trouble concluding that the Hawaii Act is constitutional. The people of Hawaii have attempted, much as the settlers of the original 13 Colonies did, to reduce the perceived social and economic evils of a land oligopoly traceable to their monarchs. This oligopoly has, according to the Hawaii Legislature, created artificial deterrents to the normal functioning of the State's residential land market and forced thousands of individual homeowners to lease, rather than buy, the land underneath their homes. Regulating oligopoly and the evils associated with it is a classic exercise of a State's police powers. . . .

NOTES AND QUESTIONS

(1) *The Standard for Determining a "Public Use" Under the Takings Clause: Hawaii Housing Authority v. Midkiff, 467 U.S. 229 (1984).* The State of Hawaii passed the Hawaii Land Reform Act of 1967. It was designed to reduce the perceived social and economic evils of land oligopoly traceable to the pre-State monarchs. Under the Act, the State, at the request of a lessee, would condemn land and sell it to the lessee. The Act was challenged as an impermissible taking because there was no "public purpose." The Supreme Court, per Justice O'Connor (then, a new member of the Court), unanimously upheld the Act. The Court stated the standard of review: "where the exercise of eminent domain power is rationally related to a conceivable public purpose," it satisfies the public use requirement of the Fifth Amendment. The test, in other words, is the familiar rational basis standard. The deferential standard assumes that, if an error has occurred, the mistake will be corrected by the political process—not the courts.

(2) *A Challenge to the Rational Basis Standard for the Public Use Clause: Kelo v. City of New London, 545 U.S. 469 (2005).* Despite the unanimous *Midkiff* Court, the use of the rational basis standard was challenged by private homeowners in New London, Connecticut. The homeowners sued when the City sought to exercise its eminent domain power to complete an "economic development" plan where the property would be sold to private businesses; the plan was projected to create 1,000 jobs, to increase City tax revenues and to revitalize an economically distressed area. The sole issue was whether the taking from the private homeowners satisfied the "public use" requirement.

In a 5-4 decision, the Supreme Court, per Justice Stevens, held that the City's economic development plan satisfied the public use requirement. The key question was whether the Court would use the rational basis standard (from *Midkiff*) or some "heightened" scrutiny. Justice Stevens reasoned that the Court must afford a legislative body "broad latitude," but he did not address the rational basis standard directly.

Justice Kennedy concurred and quoted directly from *Midkiff*. Justice Kennedy, who taught constitutional law at the McGeorge Law School for many years, specifically referred to "a rational basis standard of review."

Justice O'Connor, the author of *Midkiff*, dissented, largely on the grounds that the rational basis standard was too low to protect the homeowners' private property rights. Justice Thomas also dissented, arguing that the Court had improperly converted the original textual meaning of "public use" into a "public purpose" inquiry. The dissenters apparently have doubts about the ability of the political process to correct the mistaken "taking." Twenty-one years after *Midkiff*, the well-settled doctrinal point is now a major conflict between the wings of the Court.

APPENDIX TO §§ 6.02–.03: CONSTITUTIONAL LAW IN PRACTICE—DUE PROCESS AND TAKING CLAUSE ISSUES IN *BALL DEVELOPMENT CO. v. CITY OF VIRGINIA CITY*

BACKGROUND TO THE DISPUTE: *BALL DEVELOPMENT CO. v. CITY OF VIRGINIA CITY*

The City's Park Dedication Ordinance. The City of Virginia City was a suburban community adjacent to a growing metropolitan area. It experienced phenomenal growth during the latter half of the 1970s and early 1980s, when projections showed that open space would be at a premium in a few years. Therefore, the city council enacted an ordinance requiring each developer to deed to the city a portion of the land upon which his project was to be located, to be used as a park. The amount of land was to be determined by the number of persons expected to reside in the development. The ordinance also provided that, if it chose to do so, the city could elect instead to exact from the developer a cash payment reflecting the market value of the requisite portion of the land. The payment would be used for park acquisition somewhere in the city, but it was to be paid to the general revenues. Compliance with the ordinance was made a condition for plat approval by the Virginia City Planning Commission, which was required for all land developments.

The Ball Development Case. Ball Development Company was the owner of several large tracts of land upon which the Meadowcreek Subdivision in Virginia City was partially completed. Meadowcreek contained extensive open space, together with very expensive recreational facilities. Having planned and installed these facilities, which were considerably in excess of the new park dedication requirements of the Virginia City ordinance, Ball development found itself facing demands for dedication or payment as a condition of plat approval for the uncompleted sections of Meadowcreek.

"Platmail"—Or Reasonable Regulation? Developers use a colorful name to describe ordinances like Virginia City's: They call it "platmail." But from the city's point of view, the requirement probably seemed natural, general, and attributable to the developer's own activities. After all, the city would not approve a subdivision with inadequate streets or sewers, each of which were required to be dedicated to the public. Why, then, should the city not be able to impose an across-the-board requirement designed to provide for open space?

These Materials Are Based Upon a Real Case: Berg Development Co. v. City of Missouri City, 603 S.W.2d 273 (Tex. Civ. App.—Houston [14th Dist.] 1980, writ ref'd n.r.e.). These materials are based upon a real case, with names, dates, and details changed. At the end, we note the actual holding of the real court. Does the ordinance give rise to an uncompensated taking? Does it deny Ball Development Company due process?

PLAINTIFF'S COMPLAINT ASSERTING TAKING, DUE PROCESS, AND OTHER CLAIMS

IN THE 240TH STATE DISTRICT COURT OF MANERO COUNTY, WEST YORK

BALL DEVELOPMENT CO. **vs.** **CITY OF VIRGINIA CITY**	**NO. CIV-88-1223**

PLAINTIFF BALL DEVELOPMENT COMPANY'S COMPLAINT

BALL DEVELOPMENT CO., Plaintiff, complains of CITY OF VIRGINIA CITY, Defendant, and would respectfully show as follows:

(1) Plaintiff is a corporation organized under the laws of the State of West York with its principal place of business in London, Manero County, West York. Defendant is a municipal corporation chartered under the laws of the State of West York and may be served by service upon its City Manager, John Stone.

(2) Plaintiff is the owner of real property within the boundaries of Virginia City, West York and Plaintiff desires to subdivide and develop a portion of such real property into and as a residential subdivision, known as Meadowcreek Section V.

(3) On December 19, 1987, the City of Virginia City, through its duly elected City Council, approved and enacted Ordinance No. 0-77-28, popularly known as the Park Dedication Ordinance, which Ordinance has been in effect at all material times mentioned herein and is now in effect, a true and correct copy of which is attached hereto as Exhibit "A" [Note: the Exhibit is omitted in this book] and incorporated herein by reference for all purposes.

(4) This Park Dedication Ordinance, in essence, requires any developer of a residential subdivision to dedicate a portion of its tract to be developed to the City of Virginia City for use as a public park, without any compensation to the developer. The Park Dedication Ordinance further provides that, at the option of Virginia City, the developer may be required to pay money to the City of Virginia City "for the purchase, improvement or maintenance of public parks within the City of Virginia City."

(5) Plaintiff is in the business of subdividing and developing real property for residential purposes. In this respect, Plaintiff is the owner of that tract of land located in Virginia City, Manero County, West York, known as Meadowcreek Section V. Pursuant to Art. 974a, Revised West York Civil Statutes, Plaintiff submitted a plat of Meadowcreek Section V, a residential subdivision, to the City Planning Commission and governing body of Virginia City for approval. The plat complied with all ordinances, regulations and requirements of the City of Virginia City and the provisions of § 4, Art. 974a with the exception of the Park Dedication Ordinance. Plaintiff was informed by officials of the City of Virginia City that the plat for Meadowcreek Section V was conditionally approved, subject to the submission by Plaintiff of a Deed of a portion of Meadowcreek Section V to the City of Virginia City as provided by the Park Dedication Ordinance.

(6) Subsequent to the conditional approval described herein, Defendant informed Plaintiff that it elected to receive a payment of money in lieu of a dedication of land, and that the amount of this payment would be $22,462.50. Thereafter, in order to mitigate damages which would result from the delay in approval of Plaintiff's plat, Plaintiff and Defendant entered into an Escrow Agreement with First National Bank of Virginia City as Escrow Agent, a true and correct copy of which is attached hereto to Exhibit "B" [Exhibit B also is omitted here]. By the terms of the Escrow Agreement, Plaintiff paid to the Escrow Agent the sum of $22,462.50, which is to be held by the Escrow

Agent pending the Court's determination of the validity of the Park Dedication Ordinance.

(7) The Park Dedication Ordinance is unconstitutional under Art. 1, § 17 of the Constitution of the State of West York and under the Fifth and Fourteenth Amendments of the Constitution of the United States, and therefore invalid, for the following reasons:

a. It is unreasonable, capricious and arbitrary.

b. It deprives Plaintiff of its property without due process of law.

c. It is discriminatory in nature.

d. It is not a proper or reasonable exercise of the police power of the Defendant City of Virginia City.

e. It amounts to a taking of Plaintiff's property for public use without adequate and fair compensation being made to Plaintiff, in that it unreasonably restrains Plaintiff's lawful use of its property for the purposes intended by Plaintiff.

f. It is unconscionably vague in numerous respects, such as vagueness in the methods to be utilized in determining the amount which must be paid to Virginia City should its City Council require payment of monies in lieu of dedication of land.

g. It fails to provide that should the City of Virginia City elect to receive money in lieu of land, that it will use such monies for the direct benefit of the residents or future residents of the subdivision in question, rather than for the public generally.

h. It does not require a showing of an increased need for park land which is specifically attributable to the particular subdivision being required to dedicate land or pay a fee in lieu thereof.

i. It is overly broad.

j. It fails to place time limitations on the City with respect to the use of any monies collected in lieu of land dedication.

(8) Plaintiff would further show that the Park Dedication Ordinance is beyond the scope of Defendant's power as a municipality. Art. 6081e of the West York Civil Statutes authorizes incorporated cities of the State of West York to acquire lands to be used for public parks "by gift, devise, or purchase, or by condemnation." The Park Dedication Ordinance represents an attempt by Defendant to circumvent Art. 6081e and accordingly is invalid because it is in direct contravention of the express methods set forth by the West York legislature, by which cities may acquire parks.

(9) Plaintiff would further show that it is the owner of undeveloped real property, other than Meadowcreek Section V, located within the boundaries of Defendant. Plaintiff's ownership of such other real property is also adversely affected by the Park Dedication Ordinance, which wrongfully limits Plaintiff's use of its land, which accordingly affects the market value of Plaintiff's land.

(10) Pursuant to the Uniform Declaratory Judgments Act, WEST YORK REV. CIV. STAT. ANN. Art. 2524-1, Plaintiff is entitled to a declaratory judgment that the Park Dedication Ordinance is unconstitutional and that it is invalid because it is beyond the scope of defendant's authority.

(11) Plaintiff would further show that, because Plaintiff's land is unique and because Plaintiff has no adequate remedy at law, Defendant and its officers and officials should be enjoined from enforcing or attempting to enforce the aforementioned Park Dedication Ordinance, either directly or indirectly.

WHEREFORE, PREMISES CONSIDERED, Plaintiff prays that Plaintiff have declaratory judgment against Defendant declaring the Park Dedication Ordinance to be unconstitutional and invalid, that a permanent injunction be entered enjoining Defendant, City of Virginia City, along with its officers and officials, from directly or indirectly enforcing or attempting to enforce the above-mentioned Park Dedication Ordinance, for costs of court in this behalf expended, and for such other and further relief as to which Plaintiff may be justly entitled.

Respectfully submitted,
PARKS & MAYER
By <u>**Thomas B. Engel**</u>

NOTE ON DEFENDANT'S ANSWER

The Defendant's answer consisted of a one-sentence general denial: "Defendant denies each and every allegation . . . of Plaintiff's complaint and demands strict proof thereof." This form of answer, which is permitted in West York, had the effect of simply placing in issue each required element of plaintiff's claim. If the suit had been filed in a federal court, Defendant would have been required to admit or deny each discrete allegation of the complaint, as follows: "Defendant admits the allegations of paragraph 1, 2, 3, 4, 5, and 6 of the Complaint. Defendant denies the allegations of paragraphs 7, 8, 9, 10, and 11, and of the prayer, of the Complaint."

PLAINTIFF'S MOTION FOR SUMMARY JUDGMENT
ON CONSTITUTIONAL AND OTHER CLAIMS

IN THE 240TH STATE DISTRICT COURT
ZERO COUNTY, WEST YORK

BALL DEVELOPMENT CO. **vs.** **CITY OF VIRGINIA CITY**	**NO. CIV-88-1223**

PLAINTIFF BALL DEVELOPMENT CO.'S MOTION
FOR SUMMARY JUDGMENT

Plaintiff BALL DEVELOPMENT CO. moves for summary judgment and would show the Court as follows:

(1) This motion is based upon the pleadings, the stipulations of facts entered into by the parties, and the affidavit of D. A. Ball, together with the exhibits thereto.

(2) These documents show that there is no genuine issue of material fact and that Plaintiff is entitled to judgment as a matter of law.

FOR THESE REASONS, Plaintiff prays that it be granted summary judgment for all relief prayed for in the complaint. . . .

STIPULATION OF FACTS (OFFERED IN SUPPORT OF MOTION FOR SUMMARY JUDGMENT)

IN THE 240TH STATE DISTRICT COURT OF MANERO COUNTY, WEST YORK

BALL DEVELOPMENT CO. vs. CITY OF VIRGINIA CITY	NO. CIV-88-1223

STIPULATION OF BOTH PARTIES AS TO FACTS

BALL DEVELOPMENT CO., Plaintiff and CITY OF VIRGINIA CITY, Defendant, by and through their respective attorneys of record, hereby stipulate to the following facts:

(1) Plaintiff is the owner of Meadowcreek Section V which is a proposed real estate development on a tract of land which is within the boundaries of the Defendant, City of Virginia City.

(2) On December 19, 1987 the city council of Virginia City enacted Ordinance No. 0-77-28.

(3) The attached Exhibit "A" [omitted] is a true and correct copy of such Ordinance No. 0-77-28.

(4) Since its enactment, the Ordinance has remained in effect, and is presently in effect.

(5) Prior to the filing of suit Plaintiff submitted a plat of Meadowcreek Section V, a residential subdivision, to the Planning Commission of Virginia City for approval.

(6) The plat complies with all requirements of Virginia City necessary for plat approval, except those requirements established by the Ordinance.

[The Stipulation also describes the City's initial refusal to approve the plat, the escrow agreement, the City's approval after that agreement, and various facts related to those facts. It is signed by the attorneys for both parties.]

AFFIDAVIT SHOWING FACTS SUPPORTING PLAINTIFF'S MOTION FOR SUMMARY JUDGMENT

IN THE 240TH STATE DISTRICT COURT OF MANERO COUNTY, WEST YORK

BALL DEVELOPMENT CO. vs. CITY OF VIRGINIA CITY	NO. CIV-88-1223

AFFIDAVIT IN SUPPORT OF PLAINTIFF BALL DEVELOPMENT CO.'S MOTION FOR SUMMARY JUDGMENT

STATE OF WEST YORK)

COUNTY OF MANERO)

Before the undersigned authority, on this day did personally appear D. A. Ball, the undersigned, who upon his oath did depose and state as follows:

My name is D. A. Ball, and I am a resident of Manero County, West York. I am employed as President of Ball Development Company, which is hereinafter sometimes referred to as the "Developer," and in that capacity am authorized to make this affidavit on its behalf. I was personally involved in the occurrences set forth in this affidavit and have personal knowledge of the facts stated herein.

Around December of 1982, the Developer's predecessor in interest initially acquired about 175 acres in Manero County, West York, within the boundaries of the City of Virginia City, which land was acquired for the purpose of developing into a residential subdivision to be known as Meadowcreek. Initially, Sections I and IV were platted for a residential subdivision, which Sections are approximately outlined in red on the attached Exhibit "A" [omitted].

After the utilities and streets had been established in Sections I and IV, and before any residents had moved into their homes in those Sections, the Developers deeded 4.059 acres of land in Meadowcreek to the Homeowners Association, Meadowcreek Association, Inc. This property was deeded to the Homeowners Association free and clear of any liens on December 26, 1974, and a true and correct copy of the Warranty Deed by which title was conveyed is attached hereto as Exhibit "B" [omitted].

The above-mentioned 4.059 acres constituted the site of the Meadowcreek Clubhouse, and the approximate boundaries of which are outlined in green on the attached Exhibit "C" [omitted]. The facilities and improvements thereon occupied a surface area of approximately 1 acres out of the 4.059 acres. The facilities included a clubhouse of approximately 5,500 square feet, the building of which cost the Developer approximately $100,000.00. The locker room in the clubhouse contained approximately 220 hand-built, wooden lockers. Also included in the clubhouse was a built-in ice maker, a bar, an indoor tennis pro shop, shower facilities, one large meeting room, two private offices for the Homeowners Association, and additional outdoor seating for the area where the bar overlooks the tennis courts. Included with the clubhouse were inside furnishings of an approximate value of $26,000.00, which included furniture of such brands as Henredon and Drexel.

[The affidavit describes, in detail, the tennis courts, large swimming pool, wading pool, landscaping, flower yards, etc., incorporated into the 4.059 acre common area.]

Section IV of Meadowcreek was developed into patio homes, and the approximate boundaries of Section IV are outlined in blue on the attached Exhibit "D" [omitted]. In December of 1974 the Developer deeded tract GG to the Meadowcreek Homeowners Association. Tract GG constitutes greenbelt areas for use by the residents of Section IV as park facilities and the approximate properties of Tract GG are outlined in green on the attached Exhibit "E" [omitted]. [The affidavit describes the greenbelt in detail. It goes on to describe the development of Sections II and III.]

The owners of patio homes in Section IV are, according to the bylaws of Meadowcreek Association, Inc., also permitted to fully utilize all of the facilities at the Meadowcreek Clubhouse referred to above. . . .

Because of the increase in the number of inhabitants of the subdivision resulting from Sections II and III, the Developer, at a cost of approximately $28,000.00, constructed two additional Laykold G-6 fully lighted tennis courts on the premises of the clubhouse site owned by the Homeowners Association. The Developer is presently under contract with Watts Pool Company to add another swimming pool at the Meadowcreek Clubhouse site. The contract provides for a 25-meter, Olympic racing pool. . . .

[The affidavit describes Section V, for which the city has attempted to exact the Park Ordinance payment, and its greenbelt and park entitlements. It concludes with the following:]

The Defendant City has failed and refused and does now fail and refuse, to consider whether these facilities, installed at great cost by the Developer, adequately address the need for park space, if any, created by the Meadowcreek Section at issue. Instead, the City has continued to insist upon the monetary exaction it claims by virtue of the Park Ordinance, which is to be paid to general revenues of the city. Based upon my experience and expertise in development, I believe this exaction is arbitrary and irrational and not reasonably based upon any need for park space attributable to the said Meadowcreek Section, to any other characteristic of that Section, or to any legitimate interest of the City. Likewise, I believe that it is a taking of the Developer's property for public use without just compensation and that it exhibits the other infirmities stated in Plaintiff's Complaint.

D. A. Ball

Signed and sworn to before me, the undersigned authority, on this the 2nd day of March, 1988.

Melba L. Gallott
Notary Public

NOTE ON THE DEFENDANT CITY'S CROSS-MOTION FOR SUMMARY JUDGMENT AND SUPPORTING FACTUAL MATERIAL

The City also filed a motion for summary judgment in its favor, which was similar in form to Plaintiff's motion. It was supported by the affidavit of the City Manager, which included the following:

> Due largely to the massive influx of people into the greater metropolitan area, the City of Virginia City has experienced a pronounced population growth during the past decade, and this growth is projected to continue in the future. [The affidavit details growth from a mere 604 persons in 1960 to a projected 60,000 in 1990.]

> The corporate limits of the City of Virginia City cover a superficial area of approximately 12,450 acres. . . . Immediately prior to the adoption of the ordinance in issue, Ordinance No. 0-77-28, the City of Virginia City had two (2) public parks consisting of a total of 0.88 acre.

> [T]he ordinance in issue, Ordinance No. 0-77-28, was an amendment to and is a part of a comprehensive subdivision ordinance.

> Under the provisions of said Ordinance No. 0-77-28, Ball Development Co. would be required to dedicate for public park purposes 1.797 acres of land within Meadowcreek Subdivision, Section V, or pay to the City the cash equivalent of the fair market value of such acreage. In the latter event, all money paid in lieu of the dedication of park land must be used exclusively for the purchase, improvement and maintenance of public parks within the City of Virginia City. The unimproved acreage in Meadowcreek Subdivision, Section V, had a fair market value of $12,500 per acre, was assessed for tax purposes on the basis of such value, and was assessed on the same basis for purposes of the Park Dedication Ordinance.

NOTES AND QUESTIONS

(1) *Applying the Due Process and Taking Clauses.* What should be the result? Should the court grant Ball Development's motion for summary judgment, or should it grant the City's cross motion? Consider the factors identified in the cases, including the following:

a. *Permanent Physical Occupation.* The ordinance obviously produces a permanent physical occupation of the real property exacted.

b. *Nature and Impact of the Regulation.* The ordinance is general and comprehensive, rather than narrowly targeted.

c. *Broad Public Purpose.* The legitimacy of efforts to create more park space is not subject to serious question, and it is designed to benefit the public generally.

d. *Sacrifice of the Few for the Benefit of the Many.* The present residents of Virginia City have acquired less than an acre of park space, but this ordinance shifts all of the cost of new park acquisition to those who will move to new subdivisions in the future—people who may be out-of-staters, speaking with different accents, with customs unfamiliar to local residents.

e. *Investment-Backed Expectations.* Ball Development and its predecessors acquired title and developed the land with the clearest kind of investment-backed expectations.

f. *Diminution in Value.* The parcel exacted by the ordinance is completely lost to the developer. On the other hand, the total property is not taken.

g. *Reciprocity of Advantage.* A comprehensive program to increase park space enhances the value of land throughout the city, providing some mutuality of benefit even to developers.

(2) *The Analogy to Taxation.* Could the City successfully have avoided all of the Taking Clause issues by simply imposing a tax on new real estate development, to be measured by the value of the land and the number of projected residents?

(3) *The Escrow Agreement and the Inverse Condemnation Remedy.* Notice that the City readily agreed to an escrow arrangement and approved the plat rather than allowing litigation delay to impose damages on the developer. The City probably could have faced the developer with a difficult dilemma by insisting on full compliance with the ordinance before plat approval, and it might well have been successful in forcing the developer to give up rather than face the massive losses that would result from years of delay. Would the City have agreed to the escrow arrangement if it had no fear of an inverse condemnation remedy?

(4) *The Result in the Real Case: Berg Development Co. v. City of Missouri City, supra.* In the real case, the trial judge decided in the city's favor and upheld the ordinance. The court of appeals, on the basis of the state (not federal) constitution, reversed and rendered judgment for the developer:

> It is beyond question that the ordinance before us involves a "taking, or . . . property loss to the owner not common to the general public" and, therefore, cannot be accomplished without compensation to the property owner. This is particularly evident when the provision of the ordinance which permits [the City] to receive funds in lieu of realty is considered. Clearly, with this provision, there is no room for the contention that appellee is merely regulating the use of appellant's realty. [W]e hold that the Parks dedication ordinance is void, being violative of [the developer's] constitutional rights under Tex. Const. art. 1, § 17 [which is parallel in wording to the federal taking clause, with slight differences].

> We do not hold that the ordinance would be constitutional if the "cash in lieu of realty" provision were deleted. It is our opinion that it would not. . . .

> While government can clearly require the dedication [by developers] of water mains and sewers as well as property for streets and alleys, we believe these to be distinguishable from the dedication of property for recreational purposes. The former bears a substantial relation to safety and health of the community while the latter does not. . . .

We are not unmindful of cases from other jurisdictions cited by [the City] which support its position. . . .

The state supreme court refused to review this decision, and since it was based on the state constitution, the City had no reasonable ground even to petition the United States Supreme Court for review. Is the court's distinction between parks and streets or sewers persuasive? What would have been the result under the federal Constitution? The court is quite correct in its recognition that other authority reaches the opposite result; *see, e.g., Associated Home Builders v. City of Walnut Creek*, 4 Cal. 3d 633 (1976). *Cf. City of College Station v. Turtle Rock Corp.*, 680 S.W.2d 802 (Tex. 1984) (state supreme court distinguished *Berg Development* in a case in which the ordinance required the city to use the exaction from the developer to provide neighborhood park space for the development within two years).

(5)   *The Impact of Dolan v. City of Tigard, 512 U.S. 374 (1994).* Following the Taking Clause doctrine from *Nollan, supra*, the *Dolan* case requires the government to bear the burden to prove a "rough proportionality" between the exactions demanded by the government's permit conditions and the projected impact of the property owner's proposed development. How would *Dolan's* allocation of the burden of persuasion on the Takings issue apply to the *Ball Development* case?

§ 6.04   THE CONTRACT CLAUSE

[A]   The Original Understanding

Read U.S. Const. Art. I § 10 (including the State Money, Bills of Credit, Tender, and Contracts Clauses).

NOTE ON THE HISTORICAL PURPOSE OF THE CONTRACT CLAUSE

The Historical Purpose of this Clause. The purposes of some constitutional provisions are ambiguous or unknown. Not so the Contract Clause. Its economic purpose, of safeguarding invested capital to assure credit at reasonable costs, is relatively clear.

Adam Smith's Wealth of Nations. Thirteen years before the adoption of the Constitution, Adam Smith published his famous work titled "An Inquiry into the Nature and Causes of the Wealth of Nations." Its description of the "invisible hand," by which the price system regulated production and consumption, spread rapidly. Within eight years, *Wealth of Nations* had been cited on the floor of Parliament. About the time of ratification of the Constitution, the Prime Minister of England stood when Adam Smith entered the room, saying, " . . . We are all your scholars." As one historian puts it, "[A]ll the western world became the world of Adam Smith." R. HEILBRONER, THE WORLDLY PHILOSOPHERS: THE LIVES, TIMES, AND IDEAS OF THE GREAT ECONOMIC THINKERS, 37, 46, 49, 50–52, 61–62 (1967). Adam Smith explained the need to enforce contracts:

> A defect in the law may sometimes raise the rate of interest considerably above what the condition of the country, as to wealth or poverty, would require. *When the law does not enforce the performance of contracts, it puts all borrowers nearly upon the same footing with bankrupts or people of doubtful credit in better regulated countries. The uncertainty of recovering his money makes the lender exact the same usurious interest which is usually required from bankrupts.*

SMITH, WEALTH OF NATIONS 112 (Oxford U. Press Ed. 1976) (emphasis added). Professors Tuttle and Perry state that acceptance of the ideas of Adam Smith was "well nigh universal" among the drafters of the Constitution. Economic historian Robert Heilbroner states that *Wealth of Nations* became an "economic blueprint" for the new American state. F. TUTTLE & J. PERRY, AN ECONOMIC HISTORY OF THE UNITED STATES 105 (1970); R. HEILBRONER, *supra*, at 37.

The Articles of Confederation: Impairment of the American Economy by Faithless Actions of the States. The American Revolution was followed by a severe postwar depression, which coincided with the Articles of Confederation. One principal motivation for the Constitutional Convention was the action of faithless states in trying to solve the problems of the post-war period by allowing paper securities to become worthless and by abrogating private contracts so as to benefit the state's own citizens at the expense of largely out-of-state creditors. Thus, James Madison explained the conditions that led to the Constitutional Convention as follows:

> In the internal administration of the states, a violation of contracts had become familiar, in the firm of depreciated paper made a legal tender, of property substituted for money, of installment laws, and of the occlusions of the courts of justice, although it was evident that all such interferences affected the rights of other states, relatively creditors, as well as citizens creditors within the state. . . .

> As a natural consequence of this disheartening condition of the Union, the federal authority had ceased to be respected abroad. . . . At home, it had lost all confidence and credit. . . .

V ELLIOTT'S DEBATES ON THE CONSTITUTION 120 (2d ed. 1901) (Madison). The authors of the FEDERALIST advanced similar causes: "The sober people of America are wary of the fluctuating policy which has directed the public councils," they wrote, "destroying" the economy by destroying "necessary confidence." They predicted that the Contract Clause would "give a regular course to the business of society." THE FEDERALIST No. 44.

The Economic Motivations for the Constitutional Convention. Historians repeatedly have observed that most of the concerns that led to the Constitutional Convention, as Madison explained, were economic. With reference to the Contract Clause, one commentator has written that "as long as a strong rationalization for capitalistic power existed in economic thought and opinion, the civil liberties and minorities rights argument was secondary." Lerner, *Minority Rule in the Constitutional Tradition, in* THE CONSTITUTION RECONSIDERED 195–97 (C. Reed ed. 1968). Another historian adds, "A principle of deep significance is written in [the paper money and contract clauses]. The economic history of the states between the revolution and the adoption of the Constitution is compressed in them." C. BEARD, AN ECONOMIC INTERPRETATION OF THE CONSTITUTION OF THE UNITED STATES 178–80 (1956).

The Debate in the Convention: The Economic Concerns. Debate on the Contract Clause in the Constitutional Convention was not extensive. However, such debate as there was supports the inference that the clause was motivated by the economic concerns mentioned by Madison. Records of the debate show the following entries for August 28:

> Article XII [predecessor to Section 10] being taken up:

> Wilson and Sherman: Moved to insert, after the words "coin money" the words "nor emit bills of credit, nor make anything but gold and silver a tender in payment of debts. . . ."

> Sherman: Thought this is a favorable crisis for crushing paper money. . . .

> [The state money clause passed overwhelmingly.]

> King: Moved to add . . . a prohibition on the states to interfere with private contracts.

G. Morris: This would be going too far. There are a thousand laws relating to bringing actions, limitations of actions, etc., which affect contracts. . . .

Sherman: Why then prohibit bills of credit?

Wilson: Was in favor of Mr. King's motion.

Madison: Admitted that inconveniences might arise from such a prohibition, but thought on the whole it would be overbalanced by the utility of it. . . .

The Contract Clause thus immediately followed the State Money Clause in the debate, and the delegates who had proposed that clause (Wilson and Sherman) immediately spoke for the Contract Clause, regarding it as similarly motivated to protect investment ("Why then prohibit bills of credit?"). The debate then turned to other economic issues, including embargoes, imposts, duties on imports, the taxing power, the general commerce power, and bankruptcy, and returned to the Contract Clause to refer it to the Committee on Style the following day. II F. FARRAND, RECORDS OF THE FEDERAL CONVENTION OF 1787, at 439–49, 596, 617–19 (Yale U. Press Ed. 1966). When Section 10 was adopted by the Convention a few days later, the only recorded comment was that of delegate Gerry of Massachusetts, who " . . . [E]ntered into observations inculcating the importance of public faith, and the propriety of the restraint put on the states from impairing the obligation of contracts. . . ." *Id.* 619.

Debates on Ratification: Concerns About Credit, Capital, Interest Rates and Foreign Debt. In those states in which the Contract Clause was actually debated during ratification, its purpose emerged as that of protecting the availability of capital in the economy at reasonable rates. For example, Charles Pinckney, one of the drafters of the Constitution and South Carolina's foremost spokesperson, began his remarks supporting ratification by decrying the "loss of credit" resulting from the "inefficacy of the Confederation." He attributed the calling of the Convention to the "destruction of commerce, of public credit, private confidence, and national character." Thereafter, he spoke directly in support of the Contract Clause as follows:

Henceforth, the citizens of the states may trade with each other without fear of tender-laws or laws impairing the nature of contracts. . . . Can this be done at present? It cannot. . . .

But above all, how much will this section tend to restore your credit with foreigners . . .! No more shall paper money, no more shall tender laws, drive their commerce from our shores and darken the American name in every country where it is known. . . .

IV ELLIOTT'S DEBATES, at 253–55, 333–34. In Pennsylvania, a legislator who had also been a convention delegate supported the Contract Clause by arguing that its absence had caused paper to pass at "twenty-five or thirty percent discount" in a neighboring state. II *id.* at 486. In states in which the Contract Clause was not directly mentioned, the need for protection of capital emerged as a foremost concern also. For example, in Massachusetts, one delegate supported limitation on the powers of the states by the following argument: "Our credit is reduced to so low an ebb, that American faith is a proverbial expression for perfidy, as punic faith was among the Romans." II *id.* at 143–44.

Early Case Authority Interpreting the Contract Clause: Emphasis of Its Economic Purposes. Chief Justice John Marshall was an author of several early Contract Clause cases. He had been one of the delegates to the Convention and was a strong believer in the economic function of the clause. In 1827, he gave the following statement of its purposes:

We cannot look back to the history of the . . . assemblage of the whole people by their representatives in the Convention . . . without being sensible of the great importance attached to the [Contract Clause]. The power of changing the relative situation of debtor and creditor, of interfering with contracts, a power which comes home to every man [and] touches the interests of all, . . .

had been used to such an excess by the state legislatures as to break in upon the ordinary intercourse of society and destroy all confidence between man and man. The mischief had become so great, so alarming as not only to impair commercial intercourse, and threaten the existence of credit, but to sap the morals of the people, and destroy the sanctity of private faith. To guard against the continuance of the evil . . . was one of the important benefits expected from a reform of the government.

Ogden v. Saunders, 25 U.S. [12 Wheat.] 237 (1827). Marshall "ought to have known what the framers of the Constitution intended [by the Contract Clause] better than any man on the Supreme bench." C. Beard, *supra.* Consider the following decision.

FLETCHER v. PECK, 10 U.S. [6 Cranch] 87 (1810). Peck purchased certain lands from the State of Georgia and sold them, in turn, to Fletcher. A later Georgia legislature concluded that the Act authorizing the sale to Peck had been tainted by corruption, in that members of the legislature had been promised shares in the land as a bribe, and this later legislature passed an Act rescinding the sale. Fletcher, who was an innocent third-party purchaser, then sued Peck, alleging a breach of title covenants in his deed. The Court, per Justice Marshall, held that there was no breach, because the rescinding Act was unconstitutional:

> Whatever respect might have been felt for the state sovereignties, it is not to be disguised that the framers of the Constitution viewed, with some apprehension, the violent acts which might grow out of the feelings of the moment; and that the people of the United States, in adopting that instrument, have manifested a determination to shield themselves and their property from the effects of those sudden and strong passions to which men are exposed. The restrictions on the legislative powers of the states are obviously founded in this sentiment. . . .

NOTES AND QUESTIONS

(1) *An Economic Purpose as Versus a Civil Liberties Approach: What is the Difference?* The Contract Clause could conceivably be viewed as a kind of protection of civil liberties—that is, as a protection against unfair treatment of a class of persons (those who rely upon contracts). But a historical analysis suggests that the original understanding was otherwise—that the purpose of the clause was to induce investors to put up capital at reasonable rates by enforcing their contracts and thus to benefit the economy as a whole. What difference in consequence flows from these two different purposes? [Suggestion: Is it possible that the investor would prefer the economic version of protection, in that it provides him with more protection than a "fairness" interpretation of the Contract Clause?]

(2) *Contrasting the Contract Clause and the Due Process Clause.* Many cases present both Due Process and Contract Clause issues. Sometimes, the courts have treated indiscriminately the cases decided under the two clauses. But in terms of both history and current doctrine, the two are different. The Due Process Clause protects against arbitrary or irrational treatment; its concern is fairness. An investor who has run the risk and succeeded is less interested in fairness than in strict enforcement of the bargain. Retroactive economic adjustment of the lot of debtor and creditor, to favor the former at the expense of the latter, may not appear irrational, arbitrary or unfair. The investor, interested in obtaining the full measure of reward from the risk he has run, would prefer a more specific protection and would wish the Contract Clause to be interpreted accordingly. Should it be?

(3) *To What Extent Should the Original Understanding Influence Us?: Simon, The Authority of the Framers of the Constitution: Can Originalist Interpretation Be Justified?, 73 Cal. L. Rev. 1482, 1496, 1501–02 (1985)*[*]:

> While the autonomy and welfare values that underlie consent theory cannot justify originalism as the exclusive method of constitutional interpretation, they might justify originalist interpretation of particular provisions. This will be true for any constitutional provisions that, because of reliance and expectation values, reasonably can be conceived to be like most ordinary contracts. . . . Constitutional provisions preventing . . . government from repudiating governmental contracts . . . fit this description to some extent. . . .
>
> In the interpretation of these types of provisions, the courts arguably ought to resolve ambiguity by reference to the plain meaning and/or original intent. . . .

Is this view persuasive?

(4) *The Contract Clause as a Guarantee of the Use of Personalty Free of Regulation: Dartmouth College v. Woodward, 17 U.S. [4 Wheat.] 518 (1819).* In the *Dartmouth College* case, the Court held that the Court could not make significant alterations to a charter granted to a private entity without violating the Contract Clause. But the holding was less significant than the reasoning. "The decision logically implied that all businesses or corporations chartered by the state had a right to use their property free of government regulation, because the limitation of the rights of the chartered businesses would violate the contract of the state." J. Nowak, R. Rotunda & J. Young, Constitutional Law Ch. 13, § I (3d ed. 1986). This interpretation, which seems far-reaching today because it amounted to a virtual guarantee of free enterprise exempt from most regulation, was particularly favored by Chief Justice Marshall. But later, in *Ogden v. Saunders, supra,* the Court rejected this anti-government-interference interpretation by holding that bankruptcy laws could be constitutional if prospectively applied.

[B] The Long Dark Age of the Contract Clause

CHARLES RIVER BRIDGE CO. v. WARREN BRIDGE CO., 36 U.S. [11 Pet.] 420 (1837). A state-chartered bridge company claimed that the contract created by its charter implied an agreement not to authorize competing bridges. It sued a bridge company that competed with its claimed monopoly. The Court reiterated its *Dartmouth College* holding that a charter or grant is a contract binding the state, but stated that it would construe such grants narrowly, to provide whenever possible for reasonable regulation under the police power.

STONE v. MISSISSIPPI

101 U.S. 814 (1880)

Mr. Chief Justice Waite delivered the opinion of the Court:

[The State of Mississippi chartered a private lottery company, which paid a sum of money to the state treasury and agreed to pay future sums in exchange for the right to conduct lotteries for twenty-five years. Four years later, Mississippi adopted a law making it illegal to conduct any lottery within the state. Here, the Supreme Court upholds the latter Mississippi law.]

All agree that the Legislature cannot bargain away the police power of a State. "Irrevocable grants of property and franchises may be made if they do not impair the supreme authority to make laws for the right government of the State: but no

---

Legislature can curtail the power of its successors to make such laws as they may deem proper to matters of police. . . ."

The question is, therefore, directly presented, whether, in view of these facts, the Legislature of a State can, by the charter of a lottery company, defeat the will of the People, authoritatively expressed, in relation to the further continuance of such business in their midst. We think it cannot. No Legislature can bargain away the public health or the public morals. . . .

In *Dart. Coll. v. Woodward* . . ., Chief Justice Marshall, when he announced the opinion of the court was careful to say, "That the framers of the Constitution did not intend to restrain States in the regulation of their civil institutions, adopted for internal government, and that the instrument they have given us is not to be so construed." The present case, we think, comes within this limitation. . . .

The contracts which the Constitution protects are those that relate to property rights, not governmental. It is not always easy to tell on which side of the line which separates governmental from property rights a particular case is to be put; but in respect to lotteries there can be no difficulty. They are not, in the legal acceptation of the term, *mala in se*, but as we have just seen, may properly be made *mala prohibita*. They are a species of gambling, and wrong in their influences. . . .

NOTES AND QUESTIONS

(1) *Impact of the Reasoning in Stone.* If the state cannot "bargain away" the right to alter regulations of public health, welfare, or morals, is anything left of the Contract Clause? Chief Justice Waite makes an effort to distinguish contracts that "relate to property rights" from those relating to such subjects as lotteries, on the ground that the latter, although not mala in se (evil in themselves), may be made mala prohibita (evil because prohibited). Consider whether, under the same reasoning, a legislature could retroactively make contracts providing for interest unlawful because it redefines usury laws to that effect, or could transform anticipated gains into mala prohibita by labeling them as windfall profit.

(2) *Economic Depression as Justifying Contract Abrogation for Debtors' Relief: Home Building & Loan Ass'n v. Blaisdell, 290 U.S. 398 (1934).* The *Blaisdell* decision is a landmark, in that it indicates that an "emergency" or other important public purpose can authorize contract impairment. The Minnesota Mortgage Moratorium Law, which was enacted during the Great Depression, allowed mortgage debtors to obtain emergency relief through authorized judicial proceedings that postponed sales and extended periods of redemption. Although conceding that the obligations of the mortgage contract were impaired, the Supreme Court upheld a state court holding that the statute was constitutional as an "emergency measure:"

> The statute does not impair the integrity of the mortgage indebtedness. The obligation for interest remains. . . . Aside from the extension of time, the other conditions of redemption are unaltered. . . .

> [T]he reasons which led to the adoption of [the contract] clause . . . are not left in doubt, and have frequently been described with eloquent emphasis. The widespread distress following the revolutionary period and the plight of debtors had called forth in the states an ignoble array of legislative schemes for the defeat of creditors and the invasion of contract obligations. [C]onfidence essential to prosperous trade had been undermined and the utter destruction of credit was threatened [citing the *Federalist* and Justice Marshall's statement in *Ogden v. Saunders*, above].

> But full recognition of the occasion and general purpose of the clause does not suffice to fix its precise scope. [T]he prohibition is not an absolute one and is not to be read with literal exactness like a mathematical formula. Justice Johnson, in *Ogden v. Saunders, supra*, . . . adverted to such a misdirected

effort in these words: "[B]ut to assign to contracts, universally, a literal purport, and to exact from them a rigid literal fulfillment, could not have been the intent of the Constitution. . . ."

Is this reasoning consistent with the original understanding, which the Court correctly sets forth? [Can an argument be made that, if an entire economic system is threatened with imminent collapse in which investors may not recover full value, the state acts consistently with the expectations of investors by enacting measures to prevent that collapse?]

[C]   The Renaissance of the Contract Clause

UNITED STATES TRUST CO. v. NEW JERSEY, 431 U.S. 1 (1977). Statutes concurrently passed by New York and New Jersey repealed a covenant made by the two states limiting the power of the New York Port Authority to subsidize rail passenger transportation from revenues and reserves pledged as security for bonds issued by the Port Authority. The trust company, as trustee for and holder of Port Authority bonds, sued for a declaration that this impairment of bond holders' security violated the Contract Clause. The Supreme Court, per Justice Blackmun, agreed and struck down the statutes. The Court began by citing *Home Building & Loan Ass'n v. Blaisdell, supra*:

> [*Blaisdell*] eschewed a rigid application of the contract clause to invalidate state legislation. Yet it did not indicate that the contract clause was without meaning in modern constitutional jurisprudence, or that its limitation on state power was illusory. . . .
>
> The states must possess broad power to adopt general regulatory measures without being concerned that private contracts will be impaired, or even destroyed, as a result. Otherwise, one would be able to obtain immunity from state regulation by making private contractual arrangements. This principle is summarized in Mr. Justice Holmes' well-known dictum: "One whose rights, such as they are, are subject to state restriction, cannot remove them from the power of the state by making a contract about them. . . ."
>
> When a state impairs the obligation of its own contract, the reserved-power doctrine has a different basis. [I]t is often stated that "the legislature cannot bargain away the police power of a state." *Stone v. Mississippi.* [I]n short, the contract clause does not require a state to adhere to a contract that surrenders an essential attribute of its sovereignty.
>
> In deciding whether a state's contract was invalid ab initio under the reserved-powers doctrine, earlier decisions relied upon distinctions among the various powers of the state. Thus the police power and the power of eminent domain were among those that could not be "contracted away," but the state could bind itself in the future exercise of the taxing and spending powers. [T]he power to enter into effective financial contracts cannot be questioned. Any financial obligation could be regarded in theory as a relinquishment of the state's spending power, since money spent to pay debts is not available for other purposes. [N]otwithstanding these effects, the Court has regularly held that the states are bound by their debt contracts.
>
> [Here,] [t]he states promised that revenues and reserves securing the bonds would not be depleted by the Port Authority's operation of deficit-producing passenger railroads. . . . Such a promise is purely financial and thus not necessarily a compromise of the state's reserved powers.
>
> Mass transportation, energy conservation, and environmental protection are goals that are important and of legitimate public concern. [The states] contend that these goals are so important that any harm to bond holders from repeal of the 1962 covenant is greatly outweighed by the public benefit. We do not accept

this invitation to engage in a utilitarian comparison of public benefit and private loss. [T]he Court has not "balanced away" the limitation on state action imposed by the contract clause. Thus a state cannot refuse to meet its legitimate financial obligations simply because it would prefer to spend the money to promote the public good rather than the private welfare of its creditors . . .

Justice Brennan, joined by Justice White and Marshall, dissented:

Decisions of this Court for at least a century have construed the contract clause largely to be powerless in binding a state to contracts limiting the authority of successor legislatures to enact laws in furtherance of the health, safety, and similar collective interests of the polity. [T]oday's decision . . . remolds the contract clause into a potent instrument for overseeing important policy determinations of the state legislature.

The dissenters also believed that the political process would protect bond holders:

[The states'] credibility in the credit market obviously is highly dependent upon exercising their vast lawmaking powers with self-restraint and discipline, and . . . few, if any, jurisdictions would choose to use their authority "so foolish[ly] as to kill a goose that lays golden eggs for them." [T]here is no reason to doubt that appellants' financial welfare is being adequately policed by the political processes and the bond marketplace itself.

ALLIED STRUCTURAL STEEL CO. v. SPANNAUS
438 U.S. 234 (1978)

Mr. Justice Stewart delivered the opinion of the Court.

[A Minnesota statute required employers who closed plants or terminated pension plans to provide benefits to any employees who had worked for more than ten years and to pay a "pension funding charge" if the fund was insufficient for that purpose. Allied's pension plan, adopted eleven years earlier, normally did not provide such rights until long after ten years' service. Allied had paid annual contributions to the fund based upon actuarial predictions. Since the new law increased its obligations, the fund was under endowed, and when Allied took steps to close its Minnesota operations, it was assessed a funding charge of $185,000. Here, the Supreme Court strikes down the Minnesota law as a violation of the Contract Clause.]

Although it was perhaps the strongest single constitutional check on state legislation during our early years as a Nation, the Contract Clause receded into comparative desuetude with the adoption of the Fourteenth Amendment, and particularly with the development of the large body of jurisprudence under the Due Process Clause of that Amendment in modern constitutional history. Nonetheless, the Contract Clause remains part of the Constitution. It is not a dead letter. And its basic contours are brought into focus by several of this Court's 20th-century decisions.

First of all, it is to be accepted as a commonplace that the Contract Clause does not operate to obliterate the police power of the States. "It is the settled law of this court that the interdiction of statutes impairing the obligation of contracts does not prevent the State from exercising such powers as are vested in it for the promotion of the common weal, or are necessary for the general good of the public, through contracts previously entered into between individuals may thereby be affected. This power, which, in its various ramifications, is known as the police power, . . . is paramount to any rights under contracts between individuals. . . ."

If the Contract Clause is to retain any meaning at all, however, it must be understood to impose *some* limits upon the power of a State to abridge existing contractual relationships, even in the exercise of its otherwise legitimate police power. The existence and nature of those limits were clearly indicated in a series of cases in this Court arising from the efforts of the States to deal with the unprecedented emergencies brought on by the severe economic depression of the early 1930s.

In *Home Building & Loan Ass'n v. Blaisdell*, 290 U.S. 398, the Court upheld against a Contract Clause attack a mortgage moratorium law that Minnesota had enacted to provide relief for homeowners threatened with foreclosure. . . . In upholding the state mortgage moratorium law, the Court found five factors significant. First, the state legislature had declared in the Act itself that an emergency need for the protection of homeowners existed. Second, the state law was enacted to protect a basic societal interest, not a favored group. Third, the relief was appropriately tailored to the emergency that it was designed to meet. Fourth, the imposed conditions were reasonable. And, finally, the legislation was limited to the duration of the emergency.

The *Blaisdell* opinion thus clearly implied that if the Minnesota moratorium legislation had not possessed the characteristics attributed to it by the Court, it would have been invalid under the Contract Clause of the Constitution. . . .

The most recent Contract Clause case in this Court was *United States Trust Co. v. New Jersey*, 431 U.S. 1. Evaluating with particular scrutiny a modification of a contract to which the State itself was a party, the Court in that case held that legislative alteration of the rights and remedies of Port Authority bondholders violated the Contract Clause because the legislation was neither necessary nor reasonable.

In applying these principles to the present case, the first inquiry must be whether the state law has, in fact, operated as a substantial impairment of a contractual relationship. The severity of the impairment measures the height of the hurdle the state legislation must clear. Minimal alteration of contractual obligations may end the inquiry at its first stage. Severe impairment on the other hand, will push the inquiry to a careful examination of the nature and purpose of the state legislation.

The severity of an impairment of contractual obligations can be measured by the factors that reflect the high value the Framers placed on the protection of private contracts. Contracts enable individuals to order their personal and business affairs according to their particular needs and interests. Once arranged, those rights and obligations are binding under the law, and the parties are entitled to rely on them.

Here, the company's contracts of employment with its employees include as a fringe benefit or additional form of compensation, the pension plan. The company's maximum obligation was to set aside each year an amount based on the plan's requirements for vesting. The plan satisfied the current federal income tax code and was subject to no other legislative requirements. And, of course, the company was free to amend or terminate the pension plan at any time. The company thus had no reason to anticipate that its employees' pension rights could become vested except in accordance with the terms of the plan. It relied heavily, and reasonably, on this legitimate contractual expectation in calculating its annual contributions to the pension fund.

The effect of Minnesota's Private Pension Benefits Protection Act on this contractual obligation was severe. The company was required in 1974 to have made its contributions throughout the pre-1974 life of its plan as if employees' pension rights had vested after 10 years, instead of vesting in accord with the terms of the plan. Thus a basic term of the pension contract—one on which the company had relied for 10 years—was substantially modified. . . .

Not only did the state law thus retroactively modify the compensation that the company had agreed to pay its employees from 1963 to 1974, but also it did so by changing the company's obligations in an area where the element of reliance was vital—the funding of a pension plan. . . .

[T]here is no showing in the record before us that this severe disruption of contractual expectations was necessary to meet an important general social problem. . . .

The only indication of legislative intent in the record before us is to be found in a statement in the District Court's opinion:

> It seems clear that the problem of plant closure and pension plan termination was brought to the attention of the Minnesota legislature when the Minneapolis-Moline Division of White Motor Corporation closed one of its Minnesota plants and attempted to terminate its pension plan.

But whether or not the legislation was aimed largely at a single employer, it clearly has an extremely narrow focus. It applies only to private employers who have at least 100 employees, at least one of whom works in Minnesota, and who have established voluntary private pension plans, qualified under § 401 of the Internal Revenue Code. And it applies only when such an employer closes his Minnesota office or terminates his pension plan. Thus, this law can hardly be characterized, like the law at issue in the *Blaisdell* case, as one enacted to protect a broad societal interest rather than a narrow class.

Moreover, in at least one other important respect the Act does not resemble the mortgage moratorium legislation whose constitutionality was upheld in the *Blaisdell* case. This legislation, imposing a sudden, totally unanticipated, and substantial retroactive obligation upon the company to its employees was not enacted to deal with a situation remotely approaching the broad and desperate emergency economic conditions of the early 1930s—conditions of which the Court in *Blaisdell* took judicial notice. . . .

This Minnesota law simply does not possess the attributes of those state laws that in the past have survived challenge under the Contract Clause of the Constitution. The law was not even purportedly enacted to deal with a broad, generalized economic or social problem. *Cf. Home Building & Loan Ass'n v. Blaisdell.* It did not operate in an area already subject to state regulation at the time the company's contractual obligations were originally undertaken, but invaded an area never before subject to regulation by the State. *Cf. Veix v. Sixth Ward Building & Loan Ass'n*, 310 U.S. 32, 38. It did not effect simply a temporary alteration of the contractual relationships of those within its coverage, but worked a severe, permanent, and immediate change in those relationships—irrevocably and retroactively. *Cf. United States Trust Co. v. New Jersey.* And its narrow aim was leveled, not at every Minnesota employer, not even at every Minnesota employer who left the State, but only at those who had in the past been sufficiently enlightened as voluntarily to agree to establish pension plans for their employees. . . .

[W]e . . . hold that if the Contract Clause means anything at all, it means that Minnesota could not constitutionally do what it tried to do to the company in this case.

MR. JUSTICE BRENNAN, with whom MR. JUSTICE WHITE and MR. JUSTICE MARSHALL join, dissenting.

In cases involving state legislation affecting private contracts, this Court's decisions over the past half century, consistently with both the constitutional text and its original understanding, have interpreted the Contract Clause as prohibiting state legislative Acts which, "[w]ith studied indifference to the interests of the [contracting party] or to his appropriate protection," effectively diminished or nullified the obligation due him under the terms of a contract. . . . But the Contract Clause has not, during this period, been applied to state legislation that, while creating new duties, in nowise diminished the efficacy of any contractual obligation owed the constitutional claimant. . . .

Today's decision greatly expands the reach of the Clause. The Minnesota Private Pension Benefits Protection Act (Act) does not abrogate or dilute any obligation due a party to a private contract; rather, like all positive social legislation, the Act imposes new, additional obligations on a particular class of persons. In my view, any constitutional infirmity in the law must therefore derive, not from the Contract Clause, but from the Due Process Clause of the Fourteenth Amendment. I perceive nothing in the Act that works a denial of due process and therefore I dissent. . . .

Historically, it is crystal clear that the Contract Clause was not intended to embody a broad constitutional policy of protecting all reliance interests grounded in private contracts. It was made part of the Constitution to remedy a particular social evil—the state legislative practice of enacting laws to relieve individuals of their obligations under certain contracts—and thus was intended to prohibit States from adopting "as [their] policy the repudiation of debts or the destruction of contracts or the denial of means to enforce them," *Home Building & Loan Ass'n v. Blaisdell*. But the Framers never contemplated that the Clause would limit the legislative powers of States to enact laws creating duties that might burden some individuals in order to benefit others. . . .

In sum, in my view, the Contract Clause has no applicability whatsoever to the Act, and because I conclude the Act is consistent with the only relevant constitutional restriction—the Due Process Clause—I would affirm the judgment of the District Court.

NOTES AND QUESTIONS

(1) *The Two-Stage Analysis, Heightened Scrutiny, and the Allied-Blaisdell Criteria.* Notice the method of analysis employed by Justice Stewart. First, the Court inquires whether there has been a "severe" impairment of a contract. In making this determination, it considers the "factors that reflect the high value the framers placed on the protection of private contracts," including the ability to "order personal and business affairs." If a "severe" impairment is found, the Court goes to the second stage—in which the legislation is subjected to heightened scrutiny, beyond that which would be implicated under the Due Process Clause. This second stage involves application of the *Allied-Blaisdell* criteria: whether the enactment is supported by strong needs, such as those in an emergency; whether it addresses a broad societal interest; whether the relief is appropriately tailored to the need; whether the conditions are reasonable; whether the legislation is limited to the duration of the need; and whether it operates in an area already subject to state regulation. Does this approach supply more than the Due Process Clause would require, or is it simply another form of balancing test, redundant of the Due Process Clause?

(2) *Originalism and Intentionalism: Is the Majority's Approach or That of Justice Brennan More Nearly Correct?* Notice that both the majority and dissent make appeals to the original intent of the Framers. The majority emphasizes the Framers' desire to protect private contracts so that individuals can order their affairs, creating binding obligations upon which the parties are "entitled to rely." Justice Brennan, on the other hand, emphasizes the post-revolutionary history as creating a concern for laws that relieved individuals of obligations, as distinguished from laws that created obligations. Which version of history is more nearly correct?

PROBLEM D

IS THE INDIANA MINERAL LAPSE ACT CONSTITUTIONAL?: TEXACO INC. v. SHORT, 454 U.S. 516 (1982). The Indiana Mineral Lapse Act provided that severed mineral estates (such as ownership of oil and gas in place, without surface ownership) would lapse after 20 years, or be merged with the surface estate, unless developed or preserved by certain document filings. The purpose of the Indiana Act was to reduce fragmentation of mineral interests, which can cause severe administrative problems and impediments to development when mineral owners proliferate by assignment, inheritance or other means. In *Texaco Inc. v. Short*, the owner of a lapsed mineral estate alleged that the Act violated both the Contract Clause and the Taking Clause. Consider the following questions.

(1) *Is There a Taking or Contract Clause Violation Under the Statute?* The Court found no violation of either clause.

(2) *Is the Result Consistent with the Original Understanding?* The Indiana Act results in the complete destruction of value of the estate, and it defeats interests created by private contracts. However, does the filing-or-development alternative make the enactment consistent with the intent of the framers? Would investors normally be deterred, or consider their expectations defeated, if required to file a document or develop the mineral estate within twenty years?

[D] Reburial of the Contract Clause?

ENERGY RESERVES GROUP v. KANSAS POWER & LIGHT CO.
459 U.S. 400 (1983)

Justice Blackmun delivered the opinion of the Court.

[Kansas Power & Light, a public utility, entered into long-term contracts to purchase gas from producers. Since the gas was produced and sold entirely within the State of Kansas, it then was not subject to any price regulation. As was customary in modern gas sales contracts, these contracts contained escalation clauses, which could cause prices to increase if other index prices, including governmentally regulated rates, increased. The Kansas legislature, however, subsequently enacted the Kansas Natural Gas Price Protection Act, which limited increases to lower rates than the contracts would have called for. The Kansas Act was a response to the Federal Natural Gas Policy Act, which ushered in a different method of national price regulation and was expected to result in higher rates. The court here upholds the Kansas Act, beginning by citing *Baisdell, United States Trust,* and *Allied.*]

The threshold inquiry is "whether the state law has, in fact, operated as a substantial impairment of a contractual relationship." *Allied Structural Steel Co.* . . .

[S]ignificant here is the fact that the parties are operating in a heavily regulated industry. . . . At the time of the execution of these contracts, Kansas did not regulate natural gas prices specifically, but its supervision of the industry was extensive and intrusive. Moreover, under the authority of § 5(a) of the 1938 Natural Gas Act, the Federal Power Commission (FPC) set "just and reasonable" rates for prices of gas both at the wellhead and in pipelines. Although prices in the intrastate market have diverged somewhat from those in the interstate market due to the recent shortage of natural gas, the regulation of interstate prices effectively limits intrastate price increases. [W]hile it is not entirely inconceivable that ERG in September 1975 anticipated the deregulation of gas prices introduced . . . in 1978, we think this is highly unlikely. . . . In exchange for these anticipated increases, KPL agreed to accept gas from the Spivey-Grabs field for the lifetime of that field. Thus, at the time of the execution of the contracts, ERG did not expect to receive deregulated prices.

. . . Price regulation existed and was foreseeable as the type of law that would alter contract obligations. . . .

To the extent, if any, the Kansas Act impairs ERG's contractual interests, the Kansas Act rests on, and is prompted by, significant and legitimate state interests. Kansas has exercised its police power to protect consumers from the escalation of natural gas prices caused by deregulation. The State reasonably could find that higher gas prices have caused and will cause hardship among those who use gas heat but must exist on limited fixed incomes.

Nor are the means chosen to implement these purposes deficient, particularly in light of the deference to which the Kansas Legislature's judgment is entitled. On the surface, the State's Act seems limited to altering indefinite price escalation clauses of intrastate contracts that affect less than 10% of the natural gas consumed in Kansas. To analyze properly the Kansas Act's effect, however, we must consider the entire state and federal gas price regulatory structure. Only natural gas subject to indefinite price escalator clauses poses the danger of rapidly increasing prices in Kansas.

[T]he Kansas Act simply brings the latter category into line with old interstate gas prices by limiting the operation of the indefinite price escalator clauses. [F]inally, the Act is a temporary measure that expires when federal price regulation of certain categories of gas terminates. The Kansas statute completes the regulation of the gas market by imposing gradual escalation mechanisms on the intrastate market, consistent with the new national policy toward gas regulation.

We thus resolve the constitutional issue against ERG.

NOTES AND QUESTIONS

(1) *Is Energy Reserves Group Consistent with Allied and with the Original Understanding?* Both parties in *Energy Reserves Group* anticipated increases in price. They could not know the amount of that increase, which depended upon various factors of limited predictability. The limited initial price, together with the escalation clauses, represented the consideration that the utility gave to induce ERG to commit its gas for the long term. Although various aspects of the oil and gas industry had been regulated in this market, price never had been. Finally, Kansas' law resulted in the payment of lower prices by in-state purchasers to a class of producers that included out-of-state investors. Is *Energy Reserves Group* consistent with the Court's prior decisions? Is it consistent with the original intention? *See* Powe, *Economic Make-Believe in the Supreme Court*, 4 Const. Comment. 385 (1986).

(2) *The Federal Government is Not Restrained by the Contract Clause, but May be Limited by Other Provisions: Connolly v. Pension Benefit Guaranty Corp., 475 U.S. 211 (1986).* The records of the Constitutional Convention reflect that when the Contract Clause was adopted as to the states, delegate Gerry of Massachusetts "alleged[ed] that Congress ought to be laid under the like prohibitions. [But] he was not 2ded." II F. Farrand, Records of the Federal Convention of 1787, at 619 (Yale U. Press. Ed. 1966). Notice the result: state governments are not allowed to abrogate contracts, but the federal government can do so. Of course, the federal government may in appropriate cases be restrained by other provisions, such as the Due Process or Takings Clauses. The *Connolly* case provides a typical example. The Multi-Employer Pension Plan Amendments Act of 1980 increased the obligations of an employer withdrawing from a plan. The Court held that a federal regulatory statute otherwise within the powers of Congress "may not be defeated by private contractual provisions."

Chapter 7

THE ANATOMY OF A CONSTITUTIONAL CASE: *REDI-MART, INC. v. LONDON RETAIL MERCHANTS ASSOCIATION*

§ 7.01 THE BACKGROUND TO THE "WEST YORK BLUE LAW" DISPUTE

INTRODUCTORY NOTE

What the Case in this Chapter is About. Several states have versions of what commonly are called "Blue Laws" or "Sunday Closing Laws." The case in this chapter concerns a dispute over the constitutionality of such a law. Redi-Mart, Inc. is a retail store selling hardware and other merchandise, and it wishes for economic reasons to remain open on consecutive Saturdays and Sundays to sell its merchandise. It contends that the state Blue Law is unconstitutional. The local Retail Merchants Association (whose members at least maintain a public posture of complying with the law) wish to see it enforced against Redi-Mart.

Where the Case Came From; Transformation to the (Hypothetical) "State of West York." These materials are based upon a real case called *Retail Merchants Association of Houston, Inc v. Handy Dan Hardware, Inc.*, 696 S.W.2d 44 (Tex. Ct. App.—Houston [1st Dist.] 1985, no writ). However, we have transformed the case to a hypothetical jurisdiction, the "State" of West York. It takes place in the "City" of London, which is in "Manero County," West York.

The Reconstruction of the Case Here. As in every case, some processes remained undocumented in the real case; in those instances, we have reconstructed or simulated typical processes. Details, times, places, events, and names have been changed (except the names of the lawyers, whom we wished to profile and who gave their consent). Nevertheless, the "core" of this altered case remains true to the original. The most important arguments, evidence, holdings, and legislative actions are true to the original.

What We Hope You Will Gain From This Case. The study of constitutional law tends to have an atmosphere of unreality about it. It involves neat, clear hypotheticals that do not depend upon the fearsomely difficult matter of fact development, and too often we tend to taste the heady wine of making policy choices without seeing the consequences. We hope to show that constitutional law applies not only in the Supreme Court, but also in other settings, such as legislatures, lower federal courts, state courts, and client counselling. We want to illustrate skills other than reading appellate opinions, such as writing briefs and memoranda, drafting pleadings, negotiating, marshaling and developing facts, and counselling clients, among others. We want to explore the difficulty of applying constitutional law because of its unpredictability—its "mushiness."

Why We Chose This Case. Although this dispute was a major event in the careers of both opposing lawyers, it is a humble case in constitutional terms. It never made it to the United States Supreme Court. We chose it, in fact, because it is more illustrative of typical constitutional practice, for that reason. It arose in a state court, and since the lawyers did not particularly care what tools they used to advance their clients' causes so long as those tools were legitimate, it intermixes state law issues with constitutional ones. The fact development is complex and interesting. Also, the case involves an astonishing array of constitutional issues—the first amendment religion and speech clauses, the commerce clause, equal protection, and several kinds of due process issues. The substantive due process question has overtones of the *Lochner* bogeyman—but it can be perceived as quite different from *Lochner.* Is this that rare case in which the legislation lacks a reasonable relationship to a legitimate state aim? Reproducing the events in the case show how different that question looks, when it is viewed in its factual context.

THE WEST YORK SUNDAY CLOSING LAW
W.Y. Civ. Stat. Ann. Art. 9001 (Vernon Supp. 1982–83)

[The West York Sunday Closing Law (or "Blue Law") prohibits a merchant from selling or offering for sale certain listed items on both consecutive days of Saturday and Sunday. Its legislative history demonstrates that, among other purposes, it is intended to insure that employees receive at least one day of rest each week. The Act contains various exceptions (including exemptions for "occasional" sales, sales for charitable purposes, and sales for "funeral or burial" purposes). The essence of the statute is the list of items whose sale is prohibited. It is enforceable by criminal penalties, although prosecutions have been few; it also is enforceable by injunction in an action brought either by the state or by an aggrieved private party, such as the Retail Merchants Association. The essence of the statute is its section 1, as follows:]

> Section 1. Any person, on both the two (2) consecutive days of Saturday and Sunday, who sells or offers for sale or shall compel, force or oblige his employees to sell any clothing; clothing accessories; wearing apparel; footwear; headwear; home, business, office or outdoor furniture; kitchenware; kitchen utensils; china; home appliances; stoves; refrigerators; air conditioners; electric fans; radios; television sets; washing machines; driers; cameras; metal hardware; tools, excluding non-power driven hand tools; jewelry; precious or semi-precious stones; silverware; watches; clocks; luggage; motor vehicles; musical instruments; recordings; toys, excluding items customarily sold as novelties and souvenirs; mattresses; bed coverings; household linens; floor coverings; lamps; draperies; blinds; curtains; mirrors; lawn mowers or cloth piece goods shall be guilty of a misdemeanor. Each separate sale shall constitute a separate offense.

NOTES AND QUESTIONS

(1) *Setting Up a Test Case.* Consider how you would wish to frame a challenge to the West York Blue Law if you represented Redi-Mart. You might advise your client to withhold sales during the pendency of an action for injunction and declaratory relief, in either state or federal court. Alternatively, you might advise your client that you think the statute is invalid and that it can make sales during the pendency of the declaratory-injunctive action. A wholly different route would be for the client to engage in violations of the statute, inviting prosecution or suit. This last course of action, obviously, is risky—will you be willing to advise your client on a course of conduct that may require a cash register operator to be arrested?—but it is possible that prosecution would frame the dispute in a way strategically advantageous to your client. [Lawyers in continuing education programs have been known to advise that if someone must go to jail, outside counsel should be sure that an attorney from the corporate legal department is the one who actually goes to jail, because the client will fight with primitive energy to get a loyal employee out of jail!] How would you advise your client?

(2) *Potential Liability: Civil, Criminal, and Contempt.* Consider the possibility that if it continues sales, the company may incur liability for very large damages, perhaps in suits brought by competitors for unfair competition, implied rights of action under the statute, or other theories. Consider, also, the liability of the client or its employees for criminal violations or for deliberate (or, inadvertent) violations once injunctive relief is granted. Since injunctive relief may be granted suddenly, the corporation probably ought to consider a contingency plan for insuring immediate compliance (a major undertaking). Finally, what liability will *you* have if the advice you give appears wrong by hindsight and causes large monetary liability?

(3) *"Client Centered" Counselling.* There naturally is likely to be great uncertainty about the answers to many of these questions, particularly that of the constitutionality of the statute under the various theories that can be asserted on Redi-Mart's behalf. Most codes governing lawyers' professional conduct require that a lawyer obtain the client's consent before undertaking a course of conduct that will cause a client to lose a substantial right or position. Given the mushiness of the questions at issue, how can you counsel your client so that the decisionmaking on these major issues is client-centered? How can you avoid making business decisions for the client, while giving the client the legal input that it needs to make those decisions?

(4) *Now That We Have Raised Questions 1 Through 3, It Should Be Added That You May Not Have The Luxury of Choosing!* A typical scenario for a dispute of this kind might well involve a client that simply violates an unpopular law whose enforcement has fallen into desuetude, which then suddenly is sued or suffers the arrest of its employees and needs immediate assistance.

DEFENDANT'S ATTORNEY'S MEMORANDUM TO THE FILE

November 20, 1983

MEMORANDUM TO: File

FROM: LINDA ADDISON

RE: *London Retail Merchants Ass'n v. Redi-Mart, Inc.:* **Service of Complaint, and My Initial Conferences with Client's Representatives**

Redi-Mart, Inc. has been sued by the local Retail Merchants Association, which seeks a preliminary injunction (fortunately, not a TRO) pursuant to W.Y. Rev. Civ. Stat. Ann. Art. 9001, the West York Blue Law. On behalf of the firm, I today entered into a fee engagement letter with Bruce L. McKisson, counsel to Redi-Mart. The hearing on the preliminary injunction is set for December 10, 1983, which is just fifteen days from now. [At this point, the memorandum contains a brief recitation of the underlying facts and discernible issues.]

I have advised Mr. McKisson that this preliminary injunction hearing may, as a practical matter, be the "whole ball game," because it will tend to establish the court's views for the issue of the permanent injunction. Before that time, it will be necessary to generate and produce detailed factual information to challenge the Blue Law. This information necessarily will include detailed statistical analyses, as well as presentation through expert witnesses. There is little time and the effort will require extensive cooperation from the client.

I advised Mr. McKisson that in my opinion, there was a chance, however remote, that Redi-Mart could incur liability for sales in nominal violation of the Blue Law. In addition, employees remain subject to a remote but appreciable threat of criminal prosecution. Because its legal department has considered these issues in the past, Mr. McKisson accepted the responsibility on its behalf to undertake to answer these questions.

In estimating attorneys fees for this proceeding, I indicated to Mr. McKisson that it easily could cost Redi-Mart on the order of $200,000 to $300,000 at the trial court level, depending on the complexity of the case, and that additional amounts would be required if the dispute is not resolved there and must go to the appellate courts.

NOTE ON THE LAWYERS IN THE "REAL" CASE

(1) *For the Plaintiff: Robert S. MacIntyre, Jr., of Houston's Baker, Brown, Sharman & Parker.* Bob MacIntyre (who represented the Retail Merchants Association) has a general civil litigation practice, which emphasizes business and

commercial matters but also includes real estate and insurance defense. He majored in biology at Kenyon College, graduating in 1969, and received his law degree from the University of Houston Law Center in 1973. In law school, he was president of the Student Bar Association, wrote for the Houston Law Review, and worked as a law clerk in several firms. Today, he is one of the senior litigators at Baker Brown, which numbers about 44 lawyers. Married to his wife, Kay, since 1975, he has two children, Robert Shaw III (10) and Shannon (6). For those who look for constitutional issues in every case, Bob MacIntyre's experience is an instructive indication to the contrary. As he puts it, the Blue Law dispute was "the only case that I've ever been involved in that depended on constitutional law."

(2) *For the Defense: Linda L. Addison of Houston's Fulbright & Jaworski.* Ms. Addison (who represented Redi-Mart) graduated from the University of Texas in 1973 and received her law degree there in 1976, serving as Managing Editor of the Texas Law Review. Today, she is a partner at Fulbright & Jaworski, which is one of the nation's largest firms, with more than 400 lawyers. She has climbed Mt. Kilimanjaro (in her junior year in college) and won a women's bench press competition. Her husband, Max, is a securities lawyer at Houston's Bracewell & Patterson. Ms. Addison writes a monthly column on the law of evidence in the Texas Bar Journal and likes to cook so much that she had her kitchen specially designed to hold her 190,000-BTU commercial stove. Her practice, like Mr. MacIntyre's, is made up of business, commercial, real estate, and personal injury litigation. Unlike Mr. MacIntyre, she has been lead counsel in one—but only one—other case that included substantial constitutional issues.

§ 7.02 THE PLEADINGS

COMPLAINT OF LONDON RETAIL MERCHANTS ASSOCIATION IN THE 280TH JUDICIAL DISTRICT COURT OF MANERO COUNTY, WEST YORK

LONDON RETAIL MERCHANTS ASSOCIATION, Plaintiff **v.** **REDI-MART, INC., Defendant**	**NO. 83-CIV-70032**

COMPLAINT FOR PRELIMINARY AND PERMANENT INJUNCTIONS

LONDON RETAIL MERCHANTS ASSOCIATION, Plaintiff, complains of REDI-MART, INC., Defendant, and would respectfully show the following:

1. Plaintiff is a West York corporation with its offices and principal place of business in London, Manero County, West York. Defendant is a West York corporation that operates eighteen (18) businesses in Manero County, West York, each known as REDI-MART or REDI-MART DO-IT-YOURSELF CENTER. Service of process can be had by serving Defendant's registered agent, Lawyer Service Corporation, Littlefield Building, Dublin, West York 78701.

2. Plaintiff is an association of local merchants operating as a nonprofit West York corporation. Its members have retail stores in approximately six hundred (600) locations and employ in excess of fifty thousand (50,000) persons throughout the London, Manero County area.

3. Plaintiff brings this action pursuant to W.Y. REV. CIV. STAT. ANN. Art. 9001 (Vernon Supp. 1982–83) (hereinafter Art. 9001), alleging that Defendant has violated the express terms of Section 1 of Art. 9001, by selling or offering for sale, and compelling, forcing or obliging its employees to sell, certain items listed therein on both consecutive days of Saturday and Sunday. Plaintiff has reason to believe that in the

past Defendant has repeatedly violated the spirit and language of Art. 9001, and has every intention of continuing its present unlawful course of conduct in the future. Specifically, Plaintiff will prove that on the two (2) consecutive days of Saturday, November 19, 1983, and Sunday, November 20, 1983, Defendant, acting through its officers, agents, servants and employees, at stores located at 11810 Bellaire Blvd. and 11210 North Freeway, London, West York, sold, offered for sale, compelled, forced or obliged its employees to sell certain proscribed items, namely one lamp, one electric drill, one light bulb, one fireplace set, one electric stapler, one electric "Weedeater," and one electric cord.

4. Defendant's sales and offers for sale of items listed in Section 1 of Art. 9001 were not exempted from the terms of that Section because they were not sales for charitable purposes, nor were they made for funeral or burial purposes. The items were not sold as part of the sale of real estate, nor in conjunction with the sale of real estate. Finally, the sales and offers for sale were not occasional sales by a person not engaged in the business of selling such items.

5. Defendant's conduct is in violation of Art. 9001, and as such, constitutes a public nuisance according to the terms of Section 4 of Art. 9001. Plaintiff has reason to believe that many other similar violations by Defendant have already occurred. Based upon Defendant's past conduct and Defendant's expressed intentions, Plaintiff represents that Defendant intends to continue this unlawful activity and continue to be a public nuisance. The threat of continuing harm is real and imminent. Unless the Defendant, its officers, agents, servants and employees, are restrained by injunction, as specifically authorized by Section 4 of Art. 9001, Plaintiff, as well as all the residents, citizens and taxpayers of London, West York, will suffer immediate and irreparable harm.

6. Plaintiff has no adequate remedy at law which would prevent the recurring violation of Art. 9001 by Defendant before a trial of this cause. Plaintiff would show that injunction is Plaintiff's sole source of immediate relief. Due to the nature of the injury complained of, Plaintiff contends that only a nominal bond should be required to secure Plaintiff's relief.

FOR THESE REASONS, Plaintiff prays that the Defendant be cited to appear and answer; that the Court set this application for preliminary injunction for hearing and order Defendant to show cause why a preliminary injunction should not be issued, commanding the Defendant, its officers, agents, servants, and employees to desist and refrain from directly or indirectly selling or offering for sale, or compelling, forcing or obliging Defendant's employees to sell, any item now or hereafter listed in W.Y. REV. CIV. STAT. ANN. Art. 9001, § 1 (Vernon Supp. 1982–1983) on the consecutive days of Saturday and Sunday. Plaintiff further prays that the temporary injunction be made permanent upon the final trial of this cause and that Plaintiff be awarded its costs and granted all such further relief, at law or in equity, to which Plaintiff may show itself justly entitled.

Respectfully submitted,
BAKER, BROWN, SHARMAN & PARKER
By <u>Robert S. MacIntyre, Jr</u>. . . .

THE STATE OF WEST YORK
COUNTY OF MANERO

BEFORE ME, the undersigned Notary Public, on this day personally appeared DANIELLE LYMAN, who being by me duly sworn, on her oath deposed and said that she is the duly authorized agent for the Plaintiff in the above-entitled and numbered cause; that she has read the above and foregoing Plaintiff's Original Petition and Application for Temporary and Permanent Injunction; and that all facts contained therein are within her personal knowledge and are true and correct.

DANIELLE LYMAN

SUBSCRIBED AND SWORN TO BEFORE ME on the 10th day of November, 1983, to certify which witness my hand and official seal.

Gloria P. Haverson
Notary Public in and for
Manero County, WEST YORK.

ANSWER OF REDI-MART RAISING CONSTITUTIONAL AND OTHER DEFENSES

IN THE 280TH JUDICIAL DISTRICT COURT OF MANERO COUNTY, WEST YORK

LONDON RETAIL MERCHANTS ASSOCIATION, Plaintiff v. **REDI-MART, INC., Defendant**	**NO. 83-CIV-70032**

ANSWER OF DEFENDANT REDI-MART, INC.

REDI-MART, INC., defendant, files this answer to the complaint of London Retail Merchants Association:

FIRST DEFENSE

1. *[NOTE: West York allows defendants to file a general denial. In the federal and many state courts, defendant would be required to answer each allegation, but here that process is shortened to a single sentence, as follows.]* Defendant asserts a general denial as is authorized by Rule 92 of the West York Rules of Civil Procedure, and defendant respectfully requests that the plaintiff be required to prove the charges and allegations against defendant by a preponderance of the evidence.

SECOND DEFENSE

2. For further answer herein, defendant would show that article 9001 is unconstitutional because it denies defendant due process and equal protection of law under both the state and federal constitutions.

THIRD DEFENSE

3. For further answer, defendant would show that the statute is unconstitutional because it violates defendant's rights under the Ninth Amendment to the Constitution of the United States of America.

FOURTH DEFENSE

4. For further answer, defendant would show that the statute is unconstitutional because it interferes with federal regulation of interstate commerce and violates the commerce clause of the United States Constitution.

FIFTH DEFENSE

5. For further answer, defendant would show that the statute is unconstitutional because it prohibits the sale of materials necessary to the freedoms of speech, press, and association and thereby violates the First Amendment to the United States Constitution.

SIXTH DEFENSE

6. For further answer, defendant would show that the statute is unconstitutional because it is a law respecting an establishment of religion and prohibiting the free exercise thereof, and it thereby violates both religion clauses of the First Amendment to the United States Constitution.

Defendant REDI-MART asks that the plaintiff take nothing; that defendant recover all costs; and that defendant have all other and further relief to which it is entitled.

FULBRIGHT & JAWORSKI
by Linda L. Addison

NOTES AND QUESTIONS

(1) *Generating Constitutional Theories In the Context of a Jumble of Facts.* Consider the following commentary: "It is easy for a law clerk to criticize attorneys who have presented a case when he drafts an opinion from their briefs. But it's harder to have clients come into your office and dump something on your desk and ask if there's something you can do, when you can't even tell if its a securities case, or a labor matter, or what." As a result, says [former federal district court law clerk Sal] Levatino, "If I went back now, thirteen years later, I'd have a whole lot more empathy for the attorneys." Crump, *How Judges Use Their Law Clerks*, 58 N.Y. St. B.J. 43, 45 (1986). This case did not appear on either lawyer's desk as a packaged dispute pitting the Blue Law against identified constitutional and state-law arguments; instead, it materialized gradually as a jumble of facts. Would you have recognized each of the constitutional arguments?

(2) *But Generating Arguments Isn't Enough: The Rule 11 "Reasonable Inquiry" Requirement.* From your Civil Procedure class, you should recall that Fed. R. Civ. P. 11 makes the attorney's signature a certification that, among other steps, he has undertaken a "reasonable inquiry," on the basis of which he has formed a belief that the pleading well grounded in both fact and law. If an attorney does not undertake such a reasonable inquiry, he or she is subject to sanctions. Therefore, if the attorney here simply asserts a commerce clause argument without first undertaking a reasonable inquiry, sanctions may be the result. Experienced attorneys document this inquiry carefully, and they base it upon repeatable steps, including documented client interviews, documentation of the existence or nonexistence of other witnesses, documented consultation of experts, demand letters or other communications with the adversary, documented legal research, and prompt discovery. Would you have asserted each of the theories stated in the defendant's answer, above, knowing that you could be subjected to sanctions? [In fact, in the real litigation, Linda Addison did not assert any of the first amendment arguments set out in this (edited) answer, although she evaluated each of them.] Consider the *McGowan* case, below.

(3) *Why the Suit Was Brought in State (Not Federal) Court: Louisville & Nashville R.R. v. Mottley, 211 U.S. 149 (1908).* Students sometimes ask why this case involving federal constitutional issues was filed in state court rather than federal court. Actually, state courts often decide federal constitutional questions. Here, in fact, a federal district court would not have had jurisdiction. The federal question statute confers jurisdiction on district courts only when the claim "arises under" federal law. 28 U.S.C. § 1331. Defenses based upon federal law, as in this case, do not confer jurisdiction. The *Mottley* case, which you may have read in your Civil Procedure course, is a leading decision on point.

McGOWAN v. MARYLAND, 366 U.S. 420 (1961). The Court, per Chief Justice Warren, held that Maryland's Sunday Closing Laws did not violate the establishment clause. The original Maryland enactment may have been "motivated by religious forces," but more recently, "secular justifications have been advanced for making Sunday a day of rest." Amended legislation had been supported by labor and trade organizations, and the law had been phrased and interpreted in accordance with a secular purpose:

> . . . The establishment clause does not ban federal or state regulation of conduct whose reason or effect merely happens to coincide or harmonize with the tenets of some or all religions. In many instances, the Congress or state legislatures conclude that the general welfare of society, wholly apart from religious considerations, demands such regulation. . . .

> [W]e . . . do not hold that Sunday legislation may not be a violation of the establishment clause if it can be demonstrated that its purpose—evidenced either on the face of the legislation, in conjunction with its legislative history, or in its operative effect—is to use the state's coercive power to aid religion.

Does this decision demonstrate that, ironically, the West York Sunday Closing Law is least vulnerable to the particular constitutional argument that, at first blush, might seem most obviously meritorious? Would it be more advisable for Redi-Mart's first amendment arguments (and for that matter, its commerce clause arguments) to be omitted from the Complaint?

§ 7.03 SIMULTANEOUS ACTIVITY IN THE LEGISLATIVE ARENA

NOTE ON LEGISLATIVE ACTIVITY

During and before this litigation—in fact, long before it—there was extensive activity in the West York legislature concerning the amendment or repeal of the Blue Law. A coalition called West York Citizens for Blue Law Repeal was particularly active in this endeavor, as were merchants associations, which were on the other side. We defer in-depth discussion of legislative activity to a later section of this chapter, but you should bear in mind that the legislative efforts—in which the attorneys for this plaintiff and this defendant participated—were of long duration.

§ 7.04 DISCOVERY, FACT-GATHERING, AND OTHER PRETRIAL ACTIVITY

REPORT OF DEFENDANT'S EXPERT DR. ARTHUR P. NELSON

[One of Defendant's expert witnesses was a business school professor who had extensive knowledge of labor markets. At Defendant's request, he produced the following report.]

Introduction

Article 9001 of the Civil Statutes of the State of West York—otherwise known as the West York Blue Law—attempts to guarantee West York retail workers a day of rest by restricting the sale of certain items on consecutive Saturdays and Sundays. In order to gauge the impact of these Blue Laws on the employment practices of West York retail firms, a statewide study was conducted under the direction of Dr. Arthur P. Nelson during the first two weeks of May, 1984. The following report on this study is divided into three parts.

PART I
EMPLOYMENT PATTERNS IN THE WEST YORK RETAIL SECTOR

. . . 1. The total number of people included in the definition of the West York work force stands at 7,821,000. This figure includes all types of work, agriculture and non-agriculture combined.

2. The total number of people included in the West York work force in non-agriculture occupations is 6,287,000.

3. More importantly for the concerns of this study are the figures on the total number of people employed in the West York work force in retail establishments. In 1984, this figure was 1,125,400.

4. Finally, what is the total number of people in the West York work force who are involved in firms which actually sell regulated merchandise as defined by the Blue Laws? This figure must be estimated for 1984 since it is no longer recorded by the Bureau of Census; however, if one relies on accurate historical trends—that is, the number of people historically employed in these firms in West York—one can estimate this figure to be about 281,350.

From these data, we can now derive a picture of the actual number of employees as a percentage of the work force who are covered or any way affected by the Blue Laws. The following results are instructive:

A. First of all, if one divides number "4" above by number "3," that is, the total work force involved in the selling of regulated merchandise by the total retail work force, one finds this figure to be 25.0%.

B. Furthermore, if one divides number "4" by number "2," that is, the regulated work force by the non-agriculture work force, one finds that the percentage of people involved in the regulated work force as it relates to the non-agriculture sector is 4.5%.

C. Finally, if one divides number "4" by number "1," that is, the regulated work force by the total work force, one finds that the total number of people in the regulated sector as it relates to the total work force is 3.6%.

This final figure derived under "C" above is perhaps the most significant for the purpose of this study. In essence, it demonstrates that only a very small percentage of the West York work force (3.6%) is subject to the constraints of the Blue Laws. Or, in other words, about 96.4% of the West York work force is unaffected and thus beyond the reach of the Blue Laws. . . .

PART II
SOCIAL CHANGE AND THE BLUE LAWS OF WEST YORK

The Blue Laws in West York . . . were written during a time that was vastly different from today. In the context of this earlier period, these statutes probably reflected both the values of the time and the nature of the retail business. . . .

The current generation of U.S. workers is perhaps the most work-oriented group in American history. The baby boom of the post-war era has gone to work in numbers that far exceeds anything we have ever seen. . . . [M]en and women share almost equally today in the activities of work outside the home. . . .

[W]ith the emergence of the multiple work force, we have also seen the rise of a significant number of people who wish to work on a part-time basis only. . . . As such, what was once considered a hardship—weekend work—now has become the preferred choice of a large number of workers in West York.

Changing Buying Habits

In the multi-worker family, weekends serve both their economic and recreational needs. . . . [T]he ability to shop at a convenient time actually enhances the economic welfare of the family because it allows them time to work. For this group, the "convenient time period" is from Friday night through Sunday. . . .

PART III

A STATEWIDE SURVEY OF EMPLOYMENT

PRACTICES IN THE RETAIL SECTOR
PERSONNEL PRACTICES IN WEST YORK RETAIL FIRMS
Objectives

A state-wide study of retailers in West York was conducted to determine whether retail establishments selling regulated merchandise as defined by Article 9001 of the Revised Civil Statutes of the State of West York differ from retail establishments selling unregulated merchandise in the extent to which they: 1. Keep their establishments open on consecutive Saturdays and Sundays; 2. Expect their retail sales employees to work more than six days per week; 3. Would not grant their employees a day of rest if there were no Blue Laws in effect in the State of West York.

[A discussion of the survey method is omitted here.]

[T]he results show that 92.7 percent of the retail establishments selling regulated merchandise and 91.0 percent of the retail establishments selling unregulated merchandise answered *no* to the question: "Would your firm require its full-time employees to work seven days a week if there were no Blue Laws in the State?" . . . [The study concludes that the West York Blue Law does not and cannot achieve or even enhance the purpose of providing a day of rest for West York workers.]

PLAINTIFF'S INTERROGATORIES
IN THE 280TH JUDICIAL DISTRICT COURT
OF MANERO COUNTY, WEST YORK

LONDON RETAIL MERCHANTS ASSOCIATION, Plaintiff **v.** **REDI-MART, INC., Defendant**	**NO. 83-CIV-70032**

PLAINTIFF'S INTERROGATORIES TO DEFENDANT

Plaintiff requests the defendant, by officers or agents, to answer under oath and accordance with Rule 33 of the West York Rules of Civil Procedure, the following interrogatories as they applied to the defendant. These interrogatories are to be deemed continuing interrogatories and the defendant shall promptly supply, by way of supplemental or amended answer, any additional responsive information that may become known to the defendant. . . .

1. Identify each person whom defendant expects to or may call as an expert witness at any hearing, specify the persons's office, occupation or title and his/her address, state the subject matter on which the expert is expected to testify, and state the substance of the facts and opinions to which the expert is expected to testify and a summary of the grounds for each opinion.

ANSWER: (1) Dr. Arthur P. Nelson, Associate Professor, Business School, West York Methodist University, Dublin, West York, who will testify concerning employment statistics in West York and concerning a survey of facts and attitudes regarding the Blue Law in West York, who will rely upon responses to that statewide study as factual information, as well as facts known to him through past study of the law in question, and who will testify, among other conclusions, that the law is not reasonably related to the purpose of providing a day of rest to persons employed in West York. (2) Dr. Harvey C. Bandemere, M.D., Ph.D., Associate Professor of Physiology, Harvard Medical School, Boston, Massachusetts 02139, who will consider facts and data reasonably available to an expert in public health, and who will testify that promotion of health, recreation, and welfare of the people of the state *is not reasonably related to the Blue Law. (3) Defendant does not know at this time what other experts it may present, although it may present others.*

[Plaintiff's other interrogatories and the answers thereto are omitted here. They could be expected to be extensive, dealing with such diverse subjects as other witnesses to be called by defendant, information on Redi-Mart's employees, policies regarding days and hours of work, items sold by Redi-Mart, and other subjects.]

NOTE ON PRODUCTION AND DEPOSITION DISCOVERY

It could be expected in a case of this kind that plaintiff would seek discovery of defendant's expert witnesses' reports as well as various other documents. These items would be obtained by request for production. In addition, it could be expected that plaintiff and defendant both would engage in extensive deposition discovery, both from experts and from other witnesses. Each party's interrogatories would attempt to obtain information concerning documents and witnesses that might be the subjects of further discovery. Each party might depose the other's employees and other witnesses. Depositions of experts, such as Dr. Nelson, could be expected to last several hours if not a day or more. For example, plaintiff would want to know Dr. Nelson's background (including his personal, employment, and educational history), his training or experience that qualifies him as an expert, the assignment that he was given (including any limitations on that assignment), all facts or data considered by him, all principles or knowledge that he considered in arriving at his conclusions, any particular kinds of information that he did not consider, any recognized deficiencies or methodological flaws in his research, any limitations on the validity of his conclusions, etc. Both sides could be expected to consult with their own experts in preparing to take depositions of opposition experts.

NOTE ON NEGOTIATION BETWEEN THE PARTIES

Settlement. A very high percentage of all litigation, probably well in excess of ninety percent, settles. In fact, a very high percentage of litigation involving constitutional issues also settles. Although this particular litigation over the West York Blue Law, given the kinds of issues of principle that are involved in it, seems unlikely to settle, it is surprising how often a case that the parties believe has no chance of settlement actually ends by being resolved that way. Should the parties, here, conduct negotiations toward settlement? It might be that an accommodation could be struck, by which the parties might agree to seek clarification from the court of the meaning of the statute and to have certain items that Redi-Mart sells declared to be non-prohibited, for example. That did not happen here, but settlement almost always is worth exploring.

Negotiation Over Matters Short of Settlement. Even if settlement is not a prospect, the attorneys negotiate extensively in every contested case. It often happens that many more matters are resolved by agreement than are contested. Here, for example, the parties negotiated concerning temporary relief, stipulations of evidence, timing, discovery, and many other matters.

Temporary Relief. Early in the case, the Retail Merchants Association proposed to Redi-Mart that it not sell prohibited items during the pendency of the litigation. After negotiations seeking an intermediate position, Redi-Mart agreed to this position, provided that it not be made part of the record.

Stipulation. The parties also entered into the following stipulation of fact.

STIPULATIONS OF EVIDENCE
IN THE 280TH JUDICIAL DISTRICT COURT
OF MANERO COUNTY, WEST YORK

LONDON RETAIL MERCHANTS ASSOCIATION, Plaintiff v. **REDI-MART, INC., Defendant**	**NO. 83-CIV-70032**

STIPULATION

LONDON RETAIL MERCHANTS ASSOCIATION, INC., Plaintiff, and REDI-MART, INC., Defendant, stipulate as follows:

1. THAT Defendant Redi-Mart, Inc. is engaged in the business of selling merchandise regulated by W.Y. REV. CIV. STAT. ANN. art. 9001 (Vernon Supp. 1982–1983).

2. THAT among the items sold by Redi-Mart, Inc. are lamps, hardware, power driven hand tools, home appliances and lawn mowers.

3. THAT Redi-Mart, Inc. and its employees sold these items on the two consecutive days of Saturday, November 19, 1983, and Sunday, November 20, 1983.

4. THAT Redi-Mart, Inc. has sold these items and others on consecutive Saturdays and Sundays since November 19th and 20th, 1983.

5. THAT the aforementioned sales were not occasional sales, were not for charitable purposes, were not for funeral or burial purposes, and were not done as a part of or in conjunction with the sale of real property.

Respectfully submitted

BAKER, BROWN, SHARMAN & PARKER

FULBRIGHT & JAWOR-SKI

By Linda L. Addison

By Robert S. MacIntyre, Jr.

NOTES AND QUESTIONS

(1) *The Skills of a Constitutional Lawyer.* Notice that Redi-Mart's constitutional defenses appear in a wholly different light when the facts are developed. An unpublished survey by the American Bar Foundation ranked "fact gathering" as the most important skill to practicing lawyers, above such skills as interpreting appellate opinions. As for negotiation, it is the "most highly developed skill in the practice of law." DeCotiis & Steele, *The Skills of the Lawyering Process,* 40 Tex. B.J. 483 (1977). This latter article, based on a study of skilled general practitioners, concluded that they spend large amounts of their time in "rapport building," advice and consultation, document preparation (although they did little expository writing), courthouse activities, and informal "continuing education," as well as negotiation. They also concluded that general practitioners do little reading "other than proofreading(!)" How would these conclusions differ for a lawyer involved in a case presenting constitutional issues? There can be little doubt that counselling, negotiating, and fact gathering remain essential to good practice in this context.

(2) *Experts.* Notice the effort that has been put by both sides into the employment, reporting, and discovery of experts. Why? Constitutional litigation usually involves not only adjudicative facts, but "quasi-legislative" facts as well. The latter category includes bodies of knowledge built up over broad ranges of experience. Consequently, experts are important to constitutional litigation.

(3) *The Effect of the Temporary Relief.* Plaintiff's attorney Robert S. MacIntyre, Jr. conveys his thoughts on the effect of the temporary relief as follows: "On walking through [Redi-Mart] on a Sunday, and seeing the aisles roped off, it occurred to me that I doubt I will ever see such a dramatic indication of the effect of what I do as a lawyer. It was a little bit frightening." Lawyers in other cases of great social impact report similar feelings.

§ 7.05   HEARING, "TRIAL," AND JUDGMENT

DEFENDANT'S TRIAL BRIEF

IN THE 280TH JUDICIAL DISTRICT COURT
OF MANERO COUNTY, WEST YORK

LONDON RETAIL MERCHANTS ASSOCIATION, Plaintiff **v.** **REDI-MART, INC., Defendant**	**NO. 83-CIV-70032**

DEFENDANT'S MEMORANDUM OF ARGUMENTS AND AUTHORITIES REGARDING THE UNCONSTITUTIONALITY OF ARTICLE 9001

[The brief begins with certain formal parts, such as a table of contents and index of authorities, which are omitted here. The argument portions of the brief began as follows:]

I. DEFENDANT'S CHALLENGE TO THE CONSTITUTIONALITY OF ARTICLE 9001 DIFFERS SIGNIFICANTLY FROM PREVIOUS CHALLENGES

[D]efendant will introduce into evidence the necessary factual and statistical background required for a proper review of the Blue Law. This evidence has been totally absent in any previous West York case.

Defendant's constitutional challenge here differs significantly from any previous challenge in several material respects: (1) previous West York and United States Supreme Court decisions were determined without a factual record demonstrating that the statute is not rationally related to its stated purpose; (2) defendant will demonstrate factually that substantial economic and social changes have occurred since the Blue Law was enacted, which render the statute unconstitutional today even if it was constitutional at the time of enactment; and (3) a trend has evolved among courts in other jurisdictions to strike down similar statutes. . . .

In summary, defendant will offer the testimony and statistical study of Dr. Arthur P. Nelson, Associate Professor of Organizational Behavior at the School of Business of West York Methodist University, to demonstrate that only 3.6 percent of the West York work force even is affected by the Blue Law. The Nelson testimony also establishes that there have been significant changes both within the retail sector itself and in general social and economic conditions. Dr. Harvey Bandemere, Associate Professor of Physiology at the Harvard Medical School, and the pre-eminent international expert in scheduling of people, will also testify as an expert. Dr. Bandemere will testify that the statute has no rational relationship to the health and recreation of the people of the State of West York, and in fact has a negative impact on their welfare. Additionally, defendant will offer the testimony of Martin Stein, Professor of Public Affairs at the School of Public Affairs at the University of West York at Dublin. Professor Stein, former Secretary of Health, Education and Welfare of the United States of America, will testify that there is no evidence that supports the proposition that selling or not selling a particular item on a particular day of the week has any impact on the welfare of those selling it or those purchasing it. . . .

II. SIGNIFICANT SOCIAL AND ECONOMIC CHANGES SINCE ARTICLE 9001 WAS ENACTED MAKE THE STATUTE CONSTITUTIONALLY INVALID

It is a well-settled principle of constitutional law that a statute valid when enacted may become invalid by a change in conditions to which it is applied. *Maine v. Taylor*, 106 S. Ct. 2440 (1986); *Nashville C & Stl. Ry. v. Walthers*, 294 U.S. 405 (1935); *Fort Worth and D.C. Ry. v. Welch*, 183 S.W.2d 730 (W.Y. App. 1944).

A. DRAMATIC CHANGES HAVE OCCURRED IN THE WORK FORCE SINCE ENACTMENT OF THE BLUE LAW

The testimony of Dr. Nelson will establish that the total work force in West York in 1984 consists of 7,821,000 persons, 1,125,400 of whom are employed by retail establishments. Of the retail work force, 281,350 are employed by businesses selling merchandise regulated under the Blue Law. Thus, . . . 96.4 percent of all employees in the State of West York are totally unaffected by the Blue Law. Today, there are three times as many employees working for retail establishments selling no merchandise regulated by the Blue Law as there are employed by retail business selling regulated business merchandise. Among the retail businesses selling no merchandise regulated by the Blue Law, 32.8 percent are open for business on consecutive Saturdays and Sundays. 19.8 percent of businesses selling regulated merchandise are open on consecutive Saturdays and Sundays. Almost all employers in West York, irrespective of whether they sell merchandise regulated under the Blue Law, provide their employees with a day of rest and would do so even if there were no Blue Law in this state. In fact, Dr. Nelson will testify, and his surveys demonstrate, that no statistically significant relationship exists between the type of merchandise a retailer sells and the retailer's decision to (1) be open on consecutive Saturdays and Sundays, (2) grant its employees a day of rest, and (3) grant its employees a day of rest if there were no Blue Law. . . . [This section of the brief continues with further examples of changes, including the effect of migration, working mothers, college students, the need for married couples to shop on Sunday when both work, and other similar factors.]

[The brief also contains other factual materials, as well as arguments of law. Those arguments are similar to arguments in the appellate briefs, which are excerpted below, and consequently they are omitted here. One section of the brief contains the following, which demonstrates an interesting manner of presenting facts to a court:] . . .

III. BECAUSE THE SELECTION OF MERCHANDISE REGULATED BY THE STATUTE IS ARBITRARY AND CAPRICIOUS, THE BLUE LAW VIOLATES DUE PROCESS

The Blue Law purports to promote a day of rest by prohibiting the sale of some 47 listed items. . . . However, even a cursory glance at the statute reveals the arbitrariness and capriciousness of the items regulated. The following items should be sufficient to demonstrate the statute's irrationality:

Can Be Sold	Cannot Be Sold
Hammer[*]	Nails[*]
Dictaphone	Television
Pillows	Mattresses
Cosmetics	Mirrors[*]
Food	Kitchen Utensils[*]
Screwdriver[*]	Screws[*]
Light bulbs	Lamps[*]
Film	Cameras

Lumber*	Electric Saw*
Wood Ladder*	Metal Ladder*

* Carried by Redi-Mart, Inc. . . .

NOTE ON PLAINTIFF'S TRIAL BRIEF

Plaintiff also filed a trial brief, summarizing what facts it expected to prove and arguing the law. That brief, which was similar in form to Defendant's trial brief although it argued for the opposite result, is omitted here.

NOTE ON, AND EXCERPTS FROM, PRELIMINARY INJUNCTION HEARING

[The hearing on the preliminary injunction actually was held in October, 1984, roughly ten months after it originally had been scheduled. This scheduling, which made it possible for both parties adequately to prepare, was a consequence of the parties' negotiations, including their agreement upon temporary relief.

[At the hearing, plaintiff proved a prima facie case, using stipulations and witnesses to show that Redi-Mart was violating, and intended to continue violating, the statute. Coverage of contested issues actually began with the defense. Ms. Addison presented Dr. Nelson, her other experts, and various witnesses, including several who testified to difficulties in understanding and applying the Blue Law. Mr. MacIntyre presented rebuttal evidence, which included experts who criticized flaws in defendant's experts methodology. The following are excerpts from some of the testimony. These excerpts are not intended to be comprehensive; instead, it is hoped that they will show the "flavor" of the hearing:]

THE COURT: Call your first witness.

MS. ADDISON: At this time, defendant would offer portions of the deposition of Arthur P. Nelson. [Ms. Addison then read the deposition excerpts, as follows:]

Q: Would you state your name and give your educational background and other qualifications, please?

A: Arthur P. Nelson. I am Associate Professor of Organizational Behavior at West York Methodist University. I have a Ph.D. from the University of Southern California in public affairs. At the business school, my primary interest is in the relationship to business of social changes in our society. I have had extensive experience with the preparation of reports and conduct of studies of that kind.

Q: In connection with the lawsuit of which this deposition is a part, have you been asked to make a study with respect to the so-called West York Blue Law?

A: Yes, I have. The study deals with the impact of the law on employment practices in the retail sector in the State of West York.

Q: Have you prepared the results of your study in written form?

A: Yes, I have.

Q: All right. We will mark this [the report] as Nelson Exhibit No. 1. [Whereupon the court reporter marked for identification Nelson Exhibit No. 1, entitled "The Blue Laws in West York: 1984."] Now, Mr. Nelson, . . . the first part of this study deals with employment patterns. Can you identify the sources of the numbers that were used in Part I of Nelson Exhibit No. 1?

A: The source of the employment pattern statistics was from the United States Bureau of Labor Statistics, 1984. [At this point, the deposition contains questions and answers exploring the statistics in Part I of the expert's report, which appears above.]

Q: Now, you have identified "retail workers," which is a fairly large figure, and "regulated" retail workers, a much smaller figure. Would you explain what those percentages are and what they mean?

A: The "retail workers" figure is the percentage of the West York labor pool that is employed in retail sales. By "regulated retail," I mean that percentage of retail sector employees who sell items covered by the West York Blue Law. That figure is very small: it is only 3.6 percent of the total work force in West York.

Q: Can you explain that figure in terms of the impact of the Blue Law?

A: It means that the Blue Law only potentially affects, at most, 3.6 percent of the total work force. In other words, more than 96 percent of the West York work force is completely unaffected, even potentially. Of course, on a professional note, I have to add that these statistics certainly don't support the notion that the Blue Law even so much as affects that 3.6 percent by aiding them in obtaining a "day of rest," but the point is that that 3.6 percent is the only segment of the work force that sells items regulated by the Blue Law.

[At this point, Ms. Addison continued with the reading of the deposition, which took the expert through each of the three parts of his report. Defense counsel then introduced portions of the deposition constituting cross-examination of Mr. Nelson. At the conclusion of the reading of the Nelson deposition, Ms. Addison called her first live witness, who was the president of her adversary, the Retail Merchants Association.]

MS. ADDISON: Your Honor, defendant would call Mr. David T. George as an adverse witness. . . .

Q: Would you state your full name for the record, please, sir; tell us how you are employed; and describe your employer?

A: David, middle initial T., George. I'm president of the London Retail Merchants Association. The LRMA is a full service trade association, including stores that occupy 600 locations in the City of London, doing three billion dollars worth of volume and employing 50,000 people. We have five service companies, a shipping corporation, a credit union, a consumer credit counselling service, and a security company. And then we have the main body of the Retail Merchants Association, which is a vast organization which organizes various groups in the retail sector as a forum for exchange of information in the City of London.

Q: Mr. George, let me hand you what has been marked as Defendant's Exhibit No. 7 and ask you if you can identify that, sir, as a copy of the membership list of the London Retail Merchants Association.

A: It is a list of our membership.

Q: Mr. George, it is true, is it not, and you have earlier testified that the Retail Merchants Association decided to take it upon itself to attempt to have the Blue Law enforced when both the City Attorney and the County Attorney told you that they would not enforce the statute?

MR. CONNOR [for the plaintiff]: Excuse me, Judge. I don't know what the relevance of this is. We have standing to bring this cause of action, and I object, because I don't think the question has any relevance.

MS. ADDISON: Your Honor, the LRMA does have standing, it's true. But one of our arguments is that it is unlawful for the state to delegate the enforcement of a penal statute to a private individual or entity. Second, because there will be an argument about selective enforcement, . . . defendant is taking the position that selective enforcement by a private entity is substantially more problematical from selective enforcement by a government body.

THE COURT: I will allow you to make a brief development of this issue. Maybe one question, or a few brief questions.

MS. ADDISON: Mr. George, it is true, is it not, that you have previously testified under oath that the LRMA decided to enforce the Blue Law when the City Attorney and County Attorney told you they would not enforce the statute?

A: Yes. . . . I have been on the job for six and a half years, and for the first four and a half years the City Attorney's office aided us in enforcement. I monitor and my staff monitors the Blue Law every week. . . . But the Deputy City Attorney and I had a meeting in which he told me that because of the case load it was becoming increasingly difficult for City Attorneys to undertake this job. . . . So I brought this to the attention of our Board of Directors who then directed me to employ counsel in the private sector in order to continue to pursue the monitoring of the Saturday-Sunday law.

Q: You do know, do you not, that Redi-Mart has direct competitors selling regulated merchandise in the London metropolitan area seven days a week in violation of the Blue Law?

A: Yes, I do.

Q: And you have not sued any of Redi-Mart's direct competitors, have you?

A: No.

Q: Do you also know, sir, that Redi-Mart has indirect competitors, by which I mean competitors who sell some regulated merchandise seven days a week in violation of the statute in the greater London metropolitan area?

A: Yes. That's true.

Q: Mr. George, let me hand you what has been introduced into evidence as Defendant's Exhibit No. 1, which includes a list of Redi-Mart's indirect competitors open seven days a week selling regulated merchandise. Some of those indirect competitors open seven days a week, competing with Redi-Mart, selling regulated merchandise, are members of the Retail Merchants Association, are they not?

A: Some of these establishments are members of the Retail Merchants Association, yes.

Q: Has the LRMA sued any of these competitors of Redi-Mart, who are members of the LRMA?

A: No.

Q: Mr. George, it is important to the Retail Merchants Association to make an example of Redi-Mart so that other competitors that are selling regulated merchandise seven days a week will fall into place, is that correct?

A: Well, I will say yes to that. . . .

[Ms. Addison elicited testimony that retailers open seven days a week in violation of the statute had "an unfair competitive advantage." The defense asked no questions of Mr. George at this time. Ms. Addison called her next witness, as follows:]

MS. ADDISON: We will now call Mr. Harold Ginszer.

Q: Would you please state your full name for the record, please, sir, and describe your employment?

A: Harold B. Ginszer. I'm with Ginszer's Food Fair, Inc., as executive vice president. . . . I'm also president of the Retail Grocers Association. . . .

Q: Will you tell the Court . . . whether to your knowledge there is any grocery store in town, anyone, that is complying with the West York Blue Law?

A: I know of no grocer that's in compliance with the Blue Law. This means Kroger's, Safeway, Eagle, Rice, Fiesta; and, of course, Ginszer's Food Fair. I know of no one that's in compliance with the Blue Law at this time. . . .

Q: Mr. Ginszer, are there certain products that you carry in your grocery store that you know for a fact are not governed by the Blue Law? Like grocery, for example?

A: Yes.

Q: Okay. And are there also certain other products, that you carry in your grocery stores, that you—well, that you're just not sure about whether they are governed by the Blue Law or not? If so, would you describe them?

A: There are items that are certainly in the gray area. I guess to start off with, there is in the Blue Law a section covering "toys," but it exempts novelty items, or things that are customarily sold as novelties. Could all of our toys be considered as "novelties" rather than "toys," and not be covered by the Blue Law? We also have things for babies like teething rings. Are teething rings considered a "toy" or are they considered something else? Some of the packages say "toy teething ring," but some just say "teething ring." Is it just the ones that say "toy" that you can't sell, or is it the ones that do not that you can sell?

Q: Do you know whether a teething ring is a "toy"?

A: I don't know. [The testimony also developed other examples of confusion as to covered items: Is a "bug zapper" covered as a "tool"? Is a Halloween mask covered as "wearing apparel"? or, alternatively, as "head wear"?, etc.]. . . .

[The hearing included the testimony of 16 witnesses, most of them either experts or retailers. It also included 60 exhibits. Typical examples of exhibits would include the lists referred to during Mr. George's testimony above. One of the exhibits consisted of Polaroid photographs, depicting men, women and children shopping, which were offered by Ms. Addison to show that "Sunday shopping was a " 'family' activity."]

NOTE ON STIPULATIONS, FINAL JUDGMENT, AND REQUEST FOR FINDINGS

Stipulations to Use of Preliminary Injunction Evidence as Evidence for Determination of Permanent Injunction. The parties stipulated that the evidence in the preliminary injunction hearing was to be considered as the evidence for the final injunction. This procedure avoided an additional hearing. The parties provided extensive additional briefs.

Trial Court's Initial Holding; Final Holding. The trial court granted a preliminary injunction. Ultimately, however, the trial judge entered a final judgment holding the statute unconstitutional, denying a permanent injunction, and dissolving the preliminary injunction. Excerpts from the judgment appear below.

Findings of Fact. The Retail Merchants Association made a written request for findings of fact and conclusions of law. Without findings of fact, the appellate court would not be able to review the question whether the facts as found by the trial judge supported the judgment. In addition, both parties filed proposed findings of fact. The general practice of trial judges is to rely heavily on these proposals.

JUDGMENT DECLARING STATUTE UNCONSTITUTIONAL

IN THE 280TH JUDICIAL DISTRICT COURT OF MANERO COUNTY, WEST YORK

LONDON RETAIL MERCHANTS ASSOCIATION, Plaintiff **v.** **REDI-MART, INC., Defendant**	**NO. 83-CIV-70032**

FINAL JUDGMENT

BE IT REMEMBERED that on the 8th day of October, 1984, came on for hearing the above entitled and numbered cause, wherein London Retail Merchants Association, Inc. is plaintiff and Redi-Mart, Inc. is defendant, and that both parties appeared by their respective attorneys of record and announced ready for trial and, no jury having been demanded, all matters of fact as well as of law were submitted to the Court for its hearing and determination. . . . [A]fter due deliberation, the Court announced its ruling in open court on October 9, 1984 that, because Article 9001, W.Y. Rev. Civ. Stat., violates the Constitution of the United States, the preliminary injunction previously granted herein should be dissolved, and that the permanent injunction should be denied.

Accordingly, it is ORDERED, ADJUDGED and DECREED that the preliminary injunction heretofore entered in this cause be dissolved, and the permanent injunction sought by plaintiff, London Retail Merchants Association, Inc., be in all things denied, and that all costs of court herein be taxed against the said plaintiff, for which costs the Clerk may have executive if they be not paid in due course.

SIGNED this 17th day of October, 1984.

Thomas R. Phillips[*]
Presiding Judge

APPROVED AS TO FORM ONLY:

APPROVED:
FULBRIGHT & JAWORSKI

BAKER, BROWN, SHARMAN & PARKER
By Robert S. MacIntyre, Jr.

By Linda L. Addison

. . . .

TRIAL COURT'S FINDINGS OF FACT AND CONCLUSIONS OF LAW

IN THE 280TH JUDICIAL DISTRICT COURT OF MANERO COUNTY, WEST YORK

LONDON RETAIL MERCHANTS ASSOCIATION, Plaintiff **v.** **REDI-MART, INC., Defendant**	**NO. 83-CIV-70032**

FINDINGS OF FACT AND CONCLUSIONS OF LAW

FINDINGS OF FACT

1. Of the total West York work force of 7,821,000 people, about 14% are employed by retail establishments.

2. Approximately 25% of those people employed by retail establishments are with firms which sell merchandise regulated by W.Y. Rev. Civ. Stat. Art 9001 ("Article 9001" or the "Blue Law").

3. In 1984, 281,350 people in West York were employed by businesses selling merchandise regulated under Article 9001.

4. The items regulated by Article 9001 are therefore sold by less than four percent of the West York work force. . . .

6. Many businesses which are regulated by the Blue Law are in fact open seven days a week.

---

[*] Judge Phillips later was appointed, and subsequently elected several times, as Chief Justice of the Texas Supreme Court.

7. Among the retail businesses selling no merchandise regulated by the Blue Law, almost one-third are open for business on consecutive Saturdays and Sundays.

[Findings 8 through 11 reflect the lack of achievement of a uniform day of rest and the lack of any effect of article 9001 in prompting employers to provide a day of rest.]

12. Merchandise classifications of Article 9001 bear no relationship to the achievement of a day of rest for workers each week in West York.

13. There is no relationship between Article 9001 and the health, recreation and welfare of the people of the State of West York.

14. The classifications of regulated items under Article 9001 are imprecise.

15. The imprecision of those classifications makes it impossible for many merchants to know whether their merchandising will comply with Article 9001. . . .

19. The increased divorce rate, the large number of women entering the work force, and the consequent growth in number of dual career families all have changed the fundamental practices of family structure that were uncontested assumptions when Article 9001 was enacted.

20. A larger percentage of families today have two or more wage earners than in 1961. . . .

24. The restriction of certain items for sale on successive Saturdays and Sundays causes an inconvenience to many prospective purchasers in West York.

25. Over fifty percent of those people employed in the retail sector work part-time. . . .

27. Weekend shopping is important to many retail businesses in avoiding the drop in productivity caused by idle capacity.

28. For many businesses, Sunday is in fact the most productive day of the week.

35. Several of the Association's own members are currently violating Article 9001.

36. The Association has not filed suit against any one of its members for violations of Article 9001.

37. The Association's purpose in bringing this suit is to prevent a competitive advantage by those selling merchandise seven days a week.

38. Sale of merchandise regulated by Article 9001 on consecutive Saturdays and Sundays does not have any discernible harmful effect upon the health, welfare or comfort of the people in a community in this State.

CONCLUSIONS OF LAW

1. This Court is not bound by earlier decisions . . . upholding the constitutionality of the Blue Law, since the record was not completely developed in any of the prior cases.

2. A statute that is constitutional when enacted may become unconstitutional by a change in the conditions to which it is applied.

3. Article 9001 violates the Fourteenth Amendment to the Constitution of the United States because the classifications it imposes do not bear any rational relationship to the legitimate state interest of achieving a common day of rest for the workers of West York under the actual facts to which it is applied. . . .

9. The operation of the Blue Law does not affect interstate commerce in any constitutionally objectionable manner.

SIGNED THIS <u>29th</u> day of November, 1984.

Thomas R. Phillips
Judge Presiding

§ 7.06 INTERMEDIATE APPEALS AND OTHER REVIEW

NOTE ON PERFECTION OF APPEAL

The Decision to Appeal. The London Retail Merchant's Association authorized Mr. MacIntyre to undertake an appeal of this adverse decision.

Mr. MacIntyre's File Memorandum. Perfection of an appeal is a far more complex matter than it appears at first blush. To take the case through intermediate review, the state supreme court, and petition for certiorari to the United States Supreme Court, Mr. MacIntyre likely would be required to comply with more than a dozen highly specific time deadlines, each of which needed to be computed from the rules and strictly complied with. This result must be accomplished in an atmosphere in which he had many other cases, each with its own shifting deadlines. Therefore, he would have begun the appeal by preparing a memorandum setting out the dates for the judgment, post-trial motions, notice of appeal, cost bond, and like matters.

Notice of Appeal and Cost Bond. The notice of appeal that Mr. MacIntyre filed, which was due thirty days after judgment or denial of post-trial motions, provided: "Notice is hereby given that London Retail Merchants Association, Plaintiff, hereby appeals to the West York Court of Appeals for the Fourteenth Circuit from the final judgment entered in this action on November 18, 1984." In addition, it was necessary for Mr. MacIntyre to file a cost bond, in the amount of $500, which was governed by the same deadline.

Preparation of the Record. Mr. MacIntyre was responsible, also, for securing preparation of the record from the court reporter, which included making satisfactory arrangements to pay the court reporter, and for preparing the transcript. Each of these documents was required to be filed within specific time deadlines. Other steps included payment for various fees, time limits for the state supreme court, and time limits for the United States Supreme Court.

Briefs. In most jurisdictions, briefs are governed by specific rules concerning content. The hypothetical West York rules reflected here are imitations of the Federal Rules of Appellate Procedure.

EXCERPTS FROM BRIEF OF APPELLANT IN COURT OF APPEALS

NO. 1-84-0798-CV
IN THE COURT OF APPEALS
FOR THE FOURTEENTH CIRCUIT OF WEST YORK

LONDON RETAIL MERCHANTS ASSOCIATION, INC.
v. REDI-MART, INC. . . .

BRIEF OF APPELLANT
ISSUES PRESENTED

1. Whether the district court erred in holding that the West York Sunday Closing Law violated the equal protection and due process clauses of the fourteenth amendment, when it repeatedly has been upheld by the United States Supreme Court and West York Supreme Court.

2. Whether the district court erred in holding that it was not bound by prior decisions because the record allegedly was not developed in any prior cases and because the statute, although not unconstitutional when enacted, became unconstitutional owing to changed conditions. . . .

[In a similar manner, defendant's brief set forth issues covering each of the major contested theories in the case.]

STATEMENT OF THE CASE

London Retail Merchants Association is an association of local merchants operating as a nonprofit West York corporation. Appellee Redi-Mart, Inc. operates eighteen retail outlets in Manero County, West York.

LRMA sued Redi-Mart seeking a preliminary and permanent injunction to prevent Redi-Mart from selling prohibited merchandise on successive Saturdays and Sundays pursuant to W.Y. Rev. Civ. Stat. Ann. Art. 9001 (Vernon Supp. 1984). (R.2.) . . . LRMA's application for preliminary injunction was granted; however, upon trial of the merits of LRMA's application for permanent injunction, the preliminary injunction was dissolved and the application for permanent injunction denied on the ground that Article 9001 violated the Constitution of the United States. R.18. LRMA then timely perfected this appeal.

The district court heard only testimony from interested witnesses complaining about the application of Article 9001 to them and college professors who were paid professional fees to testify. Following their testimony, the trial court made thirty-eight findings of fact, all of an evidentiary nature rather than ultimate issues, most of which have been rejected as of no probative value by prior appellate court decisions. . . .

[The statement of the case here summarized the evidence from appellant's point of view.]

SUMMARY OF ARGUMENT

1. Social and economic legislation is tested by the "rational basis" test, which provides that a statute will be struck down only if the state lacks a legitimate interest or if the statute bears no reasonable relation to it. The interest underlying Article 9001, which is to provide a day of rest to every West York employee, unquestionably is a legitimate state interest. Further, Article 9001 is reasonably related to this purpose, in that it increases the likelihood of such a day of rest for thousands of West York employees. Defendant has argued that the statute does not completely achieve this purpose or is not the best means of doing so, but this argument, even if correct, would not result in the invalidation of the statute.

2. . . . [Here, the appellant gave a brief statement of the arguments it intended to make on each issue set out at the beginning of the brief. The other arguments are omitted here.]

ARGUMENT

I. THE DISTRICT COURT ERRED IN HOLDING THAT THE WEST YORK SUNDAY CLOSING LAW LACKED ANY REASONABLE RELATIONSHIP TO A LEGITIMATE STATE INTEREST, PARTICULARLY WHEN THE UNITED STATES SUPREME COURT AND WEST YORK SUPREME COURT REPEATEDLY HAVE REJECTED THIS ARGUMENT.

In the last fifteen years, the issue of Article 9001's constitutionality has been before the appellate courts of West York on at least twelve different occasions. In three separate decisions, the West York Supreme Court has undertaken to write on the constitutionality of this statute. *Gibson Distributing Co. v. Downtown Development Ass'n of El Paso*, 572 S.W.2d 334 (W.Y. 1978); *Gibson Products Co. v. State*, 545 S.W.2d 128 (W.Y. 1976); *State v. Spartan's Industries*, 447 S.W.2d 407 (W.Y. 1969). On the last such occasion, *Gibson Distributing Co.*, West York Chief Justice Greenhill, writing for a unanimous Court, noted the Court's two previous decisions on the statute; held that the statute was a valid exercise of police power by the West York legislature; concluded that the statute was reasonably related to the public health and welfare; and held that this statute treated all merchants alike and therefore was not discriminatory or unconstitutional under the equal protection clause. The Chief Justice also noted that while there have been differences of opinion on the Court in the past, the Court "now regard [s] this matter as settled." 572 S.W.2d at 335. . . .

The LRMA concedes that there are some imperfections in Article 9001 and that it lacks mathematical precision and results in some inequality of impact on citizens. But these factors cannot result in the invalidation of the statute. "In the area of economic and social welfare, a state does not violate the equal protection clause merely because the classifications made by its law are imperfect." *United States Railroad Retirement Board v. Fritz*, 449 U.S. 166 (1980). Therefore, if the classification has some reasonable basis, "it does not offend the Constitution simply because the classification 'is not made with mathematical nicety or because in practice it results in some inequality.' " *Id.* In this regard, Redi-Mart's principal expert witnesses testified from the premise that the enactment of Article 9001 was meant to ensure or guarantee that *every* citizen of West York has Sunday off from work. (R.140, 141, 144, 169) Such a standard is not built into the law, nor is it required. The statute clearly states in Section 4 that it is meant "to promote" a day of rest. It becomes apparent after reviewing the testimony offered at trial, and upon consideration of the different levels of commercial activity in our community on weekends and weekdays, that Article 9001 does achieve its stated purpose. (CR. 267–70, 273–76, 294–95.) When one compares the commercial activity in our community on Saturdays and Sundays, this conclusion is even more obvious. Furthermore, the LRMA vigorously asserts that modest imperfections do not invalidate a statute or justify declaring it unconstitutional. *See Dandridge v. Williams, supra,* 397 U.S. at 485; *McGowan v. Maryland, supra.* . . .

A classic example of judicial intervention is found in *Lochner v. New York*, 198 U.S. 45 (1905). The *Lochner* court struck down a New York labor law which fixed the maximum number of working hours for bakery employees. . . . In a strong dissent, Justice Holmes stated: "This case is decided upon an economic theory which a large part of the country does not entertain. . . . [S]tate laws may regulate life in many ways which we as legislature might think as injudicious, or if you like as tyrannical. . . . Sunday laws . . . are ancient examples." The *Lochner* Court's unbridled intervention in economic regulation was curtailed by *Nebbia v. New York*, 291 U.S. 502 (1934). The Court declared that a state is free to adopt whatever economic policy may be deemed to promote the public welfare, and a law will be upheld if it has a reasonable relation to a proper legislative purpose and is neither arbitrary nor discriminatory.

In the decades following, the dissenting opinions of Justice Harlan and Holmes expressed in *Lochner* evolved into the Court's majority view, eventually culminating in the holding of *Williamson v. Lee Optical of Oklahoma*, 348 U.S. 483 (1955). In *Lee Optical*, the Court upheld protective legislation on the grounds that there *might* be a rational basis for the law. The Court stated: "[T]he law need not be in every respect logically consistent with its aims to be constitutional. It is enough that there is an evil at hand for correction, and that it might be though that the particular legislative measure was a rational way to correct it. . . . "

[Similar kinds of arguments developed each of the other issues framed by appellant. Those arguments are omitted here.]

CONCLUSION

. . . This Court should reverse the trial court's ruling and render judgment that Article 9001 is constitutional and directing the trial court to grant the permanent injunction for which the LRMA prayed.

Respectfully submitted,

BAKER, BROWN, SHARMAN & PARKER

By Robert S. MacIntyre, Jr.

EXCERPTS FROM BRIEF OF APPELLEE IN COURT OF APPEALS

NO. 1-84-0798-CV
IN THE COURT OF APPEALS
FOR THE FOURTEENTH CIRCUIT
OF WEST YORK

LONDON RETAIL MERCHANTS ASSOCIATION, INC.
v. REDI-MART, INC. . . .

BRIEF OF APPELLEE

ISSUES PRESENTED

[Again, formal parts of the brief, including the table of contents and table of authorities, are omitted here.]

ISSUES PRESENTED

1. Whether the trial judge's holding, that the West York Blue Law violates the due process and equal protection clauses, should be affirmed since it is supported by uncontested fact findings, which are based upon detailed expert and statistical evidence, to the effect that the enactment does not apply to more than ninety-six percent of West York employees and cannot advance its stated secular purpose of providing a day of rest to West York employees.

2. . . . [Appellant's brief contained other points, both responsive to and supplementary of issues framed by appellant, stated from appellee's point of view. Those issues are omitted here.]

STATEMENT OF THE CASE

Despite the requirements of W.Y. R. App. P. 414(e), the claimed factual recitations in LRMA's brief are seldom supported by *any* record references. Diffuse statements LRMA offers as facts are rife with error, improperly argumentative, and flawed by the omission of pertinent record references.

Redi-Mart is mystified by LRMA's false assertion that "the Court heard only testimony from interested witnesses" (LRMA's Brief at 2). Eight retailers, both direct and indirect competitors of Redi-Mart, testified regarding the hopeless confusion they face when attempting good-faith Blue Law compliance (R. 12–14, 26–29, 327–31 . . .). Redi-Mart also presented the testimony of three distinguished experts (R. 37–51, 52–108, 131–65), one of whom refused to accept compensation (R.50). LRMA itself presented the testimony of two retailers (R. 166–81, 262–96) and two experts (R. 182–254, 648–723), both of whom were "college professors who were paid a professional fee to testify," the very stone LRMA hurls from its glass house at Redi-Mart's experts. . . .

This is not just another Blue Law case. This is the first Blue Law case to present the appellate courts of West York with a fully developed fact record, a fact that LRMA has missed. Redi-Mart's evidence supports only one conclusion: the West York Blue Law is unconstitutional. . . .

Because LRMA has chosen not to challenge the sufficiency of the evidence supporting the district court's fact findings, they are binding on this court. . . . [At this point, appellant summarized the evidence and the fact findings. That summary is omitted here.]

SUMMARY OF ARGUMENT

[The summary of argument is omitted here.]

ARGUMENT

I. THE BLUE LAW VIOLATES THE EQUAL PROTECTION AND DUE PROCESS CLAUSES BECAUSE THERE IS NO RATIONAL RELATION-

SHIP BETWEEN THE STATUTE AND THE ACHIEVEMENT OF A DAY OF REST FOR WORKERS IN THE STATE OF WEST YORK.

Upon Redi-Mart's motion, Judge Phillips judicially noticed United States Bureau of Census and Department of Labor statistics showing that only fourteen percent of all workers in the State of West York are employed in the retail sector (FF1). Of these, no more than 281,350 (or twenty-five percent of the fourteen percent) are employed by retail establishments selling merchandise regulated under the Blue Law (FF3). . . . Therefore, the Blue Law affects at most only four percent of the total West York work force (FF4).

Judge Phillips' finding that the Blue Law does not achieve a uniform day of rest for the workers of West York (FF8–9) is further supported by Redi-Mart's evidence that there is no relationship between the Blue Law and an employer's policy of providing its employee with a day of rest(FF10–12). Merchandise classifications of Article 9001 bear no relationship to the achievement of a day of rest each week for West York workers. Merchandise classifications distinguish between items that are essentially identical, making the sale of some illegal without any rational relation to the actual or stated purposes of the Blue Law (FF16). Many businesses that are regulated by the Blue Law are in fact open seven days a week (FF6). Almost all employers, irrespective of whether they sell merchandise regulated by the Blue Law, provide their employees with a day of rest (FF10). . . .

[Appellee's Brief also contained extensive argument of the law, as well as argument of other issues. Those arguments are omitted here.]

CONCLUSION AND PRAYER

. . . Judge Phillips' unchallenged fact findings conclusively establish that the Blue Law is unconstitutional. Redi-Mart prays that Judge Phillips' judgment be affirmed. . . .

Respectfully submitted,

FULBRIGHT & JAWORSKI

by Linda L. Addison

NOTE ON FURTHER PROCEEDINGS, INCLUDING REPLY BRIEF AND ORAL ARGUMENT

Appellant's Reply Brief. Appellant was entitled to file a reply brief and did so. This brief was considerably shorter and answered only a few of the contentions raised by the appellee.

Oral Argument. Many courts consider oral argument less important than is popularly supposed, and many courts of appeals have local rules that allow them to dispense with it. Experienced appellate attorneys and judges generally agree that the briefs are far more important. Nevertheless, the Court heard oral argument in this case at the request of the parties. The following are excerpts from Linda Addison's notes for the oral argument:

1. KEEP IT SIMPLE—FOCUS ON WHAT I WANT

2. [Remember that the] case won't be won or lost on oral argument

Intro

not here today to talk about a day of rest for all West York workers

here to talk about a statute that exempts the employers of more than 96% of West Yorkers

here not because LRMA is interested in protecting a day of rest for the workers of West York here because LRMA enforces the Blue Law solely against its members' competitors to gain a competitive advantage, & does not enforce it against its own violating members . . .

if LRMA's view of constitution & precedent were right, we wouldn't have integrated schools in this country today

Overview

I. This ct. is not bound by prior Blue Law cases

II. [The district court's] finding of fact, [though, are binding on this court and all are supported by ample evidence and are unchallenged]

III. The 38 findings of fact establish unconst. [of statute] . . .

Body of Argument

I. This ct. [is] not bound by prior Blue Law Cases

A. Doctrine of stare decisis has ltd. applicability. Prior cases are not binding:

1. absent same facts, [or]

2. to issues not previously considered

B. LRMA [does] not dispute principles that limit application of doctrine of stare decisis (it only disputes whether records, issues were the same)

C. This case disting from all prior bec. of factual record

1. No prior case had fully developed record and this does

2. Significance of facts—judicial presumption of constitutionality in absence of evid to contrary—our [findings of fact] overcome [the presumption] for first time

D. This case disting because of issues not previously considered

1. Not rationally related to its purp under actual facts to which applied

2. Classifications not rationally related to its purp

3. [It does] not achieve a day of rest—findings of fact, emphasize

4. Underinclusive (less than 4%) . . .

II. Because LRMA not challenged suff of evid. supporting fundings of fact, they are binding on this court

A. They delib. chose not to challenge; 2 reasons

(1) futile—overwhelming evid (App. A)

(2) not want you to see how compelling it is—how only supports one conclusion

B. LRMA just IGNORES the findings of fact & implicitly asks you to ignore can't just ignore—38 findings supported by ample evidence . . .

III. [Findings of fact] estab unconst. [of art. 9001]

A. Why findings show unconst—no rational relationship—big picture:

purp of govt is to protect publ health & welfare; [does] it by promulgating legis. under police power; police power laws infringe on our liberty but OK if *RATIONALLY RELATED* to its purp & promotes publ health, safety & welfare eg [drunk driving laws]

if law not rationally related to achieve its purp—it's unconst. This is 1st case ever to show

[1] not protect pub health safety & welfare

[2] not rationally related to its purp

[3] not achieve day of rest; LRMA [does] not challenge these findings—& yet they say stat is const.

B. [In response to question from court, only] purp. is achieve a day of rest . . .

[Notes on various other issues appear in this document but are omitted here.]

CONCLUSION

A. Constitution protects us by requiring [that] laws be rationally related to their purposes & intelligible to people of common intelligence

B. We have before us a statute whose purp is to achieve a day of rest BUT

(1) that does not require any business to close on either Saturday or Sunday;

(2) that does not limit the # of days any man, woman or child can work;

(3) that allows a trade organization to use it to gain a compet adv & discriminate against non-members; and

(4) that allows the sale of hammers but not nails; screwdrivers but not screws; pillows but not mattresses; light bulbs but not lamps; [and] lumber but not saws.

We realize we are in the position of an underdog fighting 24 yrs of tradition & 15 yrs of case law; that's why we have the caliber record, brief we do & the record & [findings of fact] support only 1 conclusion. . . .

[Notes on various other issues appear in this document but are omitted here.]

CONCLUSION

Mr. MacIntyre's Argument for the Plaintiff. Mr. MacIntyre prepared an outline roughly similar to Ms. Addison's. Its principal thrust was that the Blue Law was the type of social and economic legislation in which the United States Supreme Court and state courts have said that the legislatures have wide latitude. He emphasized that the legislation did not affect any categories that would trigger heightened scrutiny, such as "suspect" classes or "fundamental" rights. He also made a major point of citing the prior decisions repeatedly upholding Sunday Closing Laws, including *McGowan v. Maryland*, above. As for Ms. Addison's argument concerning the fact findings, Mr. MacIntyre compliments its effectiveness: "From a procedural standpoint, I may have created difficulty for our case by not challenging the findings," he says. But that was a strategy choice, because "we probably would have stipulated to almost all of the fact findings, particularly those relating to changing buying habits, statistics, ability to make more money and the like." In the argument, however, he characterized these factors as "arguments of convenience, not of constitutionality." And he emphasized the principle that, in a constitutional case, the court is not nearly so rigidly bound by general findings as it is in other kinds of cases, but should review all of the evidence. Perhaps the most effective moment in Mr. MacIntyre's argument had little to do with the issues, and occurred during his rebuttal argument. Replying to Ms. Addison's repeated reference to her client as "the underdog" because it had the burden of proving lack of a rational basis, he told the Court: "That underdog sure can bite!"

Court of Appeals Opinion. The opinion of the court of appeals follows.

LONDON RETAIL MERCHANTS ASSOCIATION v. REDI-MART, INC.
—S.W.2d—(W.Y. App. 1985)

[Before WARREN, SMITH, and HOYT, JJ.]

WARREN, ASSOCIATE JUSTICE:

This case involves the constitutionality of article 9001 of the [West York] Revised Civil Statutes, commonly called the . . . "Blue Law." The [West York] Supreme Court has previously held the statute facially constitutional against contentions similar to those made by appellees in this case. The trial court, however, found that it was not bound by the previous decisions because the records before those courts were not fully developed. The court below held the statute unconstitutional and refused appellant's application to permanently enjoin appellees from violating the statute. Our main question on appeal is thus whether the evidence adduced at trial established that the statute is unconstitutional. We hold that the evidence failed to establish the statute's unconstitutionality and therefore reverse and remand the cause for entry of an order permanently enjoining appellee from violating article 9001.

[Here, the Court describes Redi-Mart, the statute, and the violations. This portion of the opinion is omitted.]

The first [state] Supreme Court . . . decision analyzing the constitutionality of the Blue Law is *State v. Spartan's Industries, Inc.*, 447 S.W.2d 407 ([W.Y.] 1969), *appeal dism'd*, 397 U.S. 590 (1970). [Here, the court discusses *Spartan's* as well as *Gibson Products* and *Gibson Distributing*, which were cited in the briefs, above.]

We agree, as a general proposition, that the amount of evidence presented in a prior case, or the extent of changes in society since a statute's enactment or the date of decision, may affect a decision's force as precedent and the validity of a statute previously upheld under constitutional attack. *See People v. Acme Markets, Inc.*, 37 N.Y.2d 326, 334 N.E.2d 555, 558 (1975) (fully developed record); *Nashville, C. & St. L.Ry. v. Walthers*, 294 U.S. 405, 415 (1935) (changed factual conditions). . . . Nevertheless, as a constitutional principle, appellee retains the burden of establishing that the statute is unconstitutional under the established standards of judicial review. We must therefore determine whether the evidence presented in the trial court shows that the statute violates the West York or United States Constitution.

At the hearing on the temporary injunction, the director of appellee's stores testified that his firm had difficulty complying with article 9001 because of his inability to determine what products fall within the statute's proscription, and that compliance with the Blue Law is costly in terms of lost business.

Appellee also provided the testimony of several expert witnesses. Professor [Martin Stein] of the University of West York, formerly Secretary of the United States Department of Health, Education, and Welfare, concluded that he could perceive no rational relationship between the statute's proscriptions and the health and welfare of the people of West York.

Dr. [Harvey C. Bandemere], professor at Harvard Medical School, testified that although the Blue Law was aimed at promoting desirable social goals, it is a "clumsy, inequitable, and archaic way of achieving those goals." Dr. [Bandemere], an authority of human adaptation to twenty-four hour day/night cycles, also testified that while he could find no "net positive effect" of the statute on health, welfare, and recreation, he did perceive a "net negative effect," including possible increases in pollution, possible increases in stress among family members, and inequities for two career/wage-earner households, students, and households headed by working mothers. . . .

Appellee also offered the deposition testimony of Dr. [Arthur Nelson], Associate Professor of Organizational Behavior at [West York] Methodist University Business School. Dr. [Nelson] concluded that only 3.6 percent of the total number of employees in West York are employed by businesses selling items regulated by the statute. . . .

Additionally, Dr. [Nelson] directed the preparation of a survey, which was admitted into evidence, regarding West York employment practices. From the survey, Dr. [Nelson] concluded that there was no statistically relevant relationship between a given firm's choice of whether to provide a day of rest to employees and whether it sold regulated or unregulated goods.

In rebuttal, appellant offered the testimony of [David Smith], assistant professor at West York A & M University in the Department of Marketing. Dr. [Smith] concluded that Dr. [Nelson's] survey had "serious methodological problems" and that it had little reliability as a scientific analysis of the effects of the West York Blue Law on the health and welfare of West Yorkers. Dr. [Smith] did not express an opinion as to the relationship between the statute and its goal of providing a day of rest for the citizens of the state. . . .

[A]ppellant [also] offered testimony of a retailer and of Dr. [Gregory George], an expert in demographic and market research. . . . Dr. [George] concluded for various reasons that the [Nelson] and [Bandemere] findings were wholly without scientific validity. . . .

After reviewing the evidence, the trial court made the following 38 findings of fact: [The appellate court here lists all of the trial court's findings of fact, followed by its conclusions of law].

Appellee contends that we are bound by the findings of fact made by the trial court because appellant has not specifically attacked the court's individual findings. As previously noted, however, our duty in reviewing the constitutionality of a provision is to determine whether the party challenging the enactment has carried its burden under the applicable standard of review. We thus turn to the various challenges asserted by appellee.

SUBSTANTIVE DUE PROCESS AND EQUAL PROTECTION

We regard the standard of review in causes such as this to be different from that applied in cases involving fundamental rights. Fundamental rights or interests are those guaranteed by the Bill of Rights of the United States Constitution or are in some manner traceable to the Constitution, or those that the court feels are preservative of other basic civil and political rights. See *Shapiro v. Thompson*, 394 U.S. 618 (1969); *Harper v. Virginia State Board of Elections*, 383 U.S. 663 (1966). Rights outside this ambit, such as those allegedly infringed upon by "Blue Laws" or "Sunday Closing Laws," are considered nonfundamental. [T]he reviewing court [in such a case] must review all of the evidence and determine whether it excludes the possibility that there is *any* rational relationship between the purpose of the statute and its effect, and whether the evidence excludes the possibility that the statute bears any rational relationship to an actual or articulated state interest. *McGowan v. Maryland*, 366 U.S. 420 (1961); *Williamson v. Lee Optical of Oklahoma*, 348 U.S. 483 (1955).

Review of the record demonstrates that Mr. [Stein's] testimony was not based on any substantive analysis of the statute. Dr. [Bandemere] merely concluded that the statute was not perfectly efficient in accomplishing a day of rest and that possible negative effects were observed. Finally, Dr. [Nelson's] study, though perhaps methodologically flawed, actually indicated some level of effectiveness of the statute in closing down retail businesses on weekends. . . .

Thus, while the means chosen by the legislature to secure commercial inactivity on the weekends may indeed operate "imperfectly or incompletely" since some merchants stay open all week regardless of the Blue Law, the imperfections do not rise to the level of an essentially arbitrary or discriminatory burden. . . .

We hold article 9001 not violative of the due process and equal protection clauses of the United States Constitution. We also hold that, under the tests applied, article 9001 does not violate the [State] Constitution. . . .

VAGUENESS

[Here, the Court holds that the statute is not unconstitutionally vague.]

DUE PROCESS AND THE PRIVATE ENFORCEMENT SCHEME

[Here, the court holds that the statute is not unconstitutional because of its provision for private suits for injunction, and it holds that the statute does not create an unconstitutional "irrebuttable presumption."]

EQUAL PROTECTION AND SELECTIVE ENFORCEMENT

[Here, the Court concludes that the statute does not violate the equal protection clause and is not unconstitutional because of selective enforcement.]

INTERSTATE COMMERCE

Finally, appellee argues . . . that enforcement of the . . . "Blue Law" imposes "an unconstitutional impairment of interstate commerce." Appellee contends that manufacturers outside the state cannot sell goods within the state on Sunday, and as a result, interstate commerce will be impaired.

Appellee cites no authority for the novel proposition that a statute of this nature, applying with equal force to West York and out-of-state producers selling goods in West York, violates the interstate commerce clause of the United States Constitution. *Cf. State v. Rockdale Assoc., Inc.,* 125 Vt. 495, 218 A.2d 718 (exemption for local producers allowing Sunday sales where out-of-state producers could not sell on Sunday held unconstitutional). Clearly, a state regulation affecting interstate commerce, assuming *arguendo* that ours is such a provision, will be upheld if the regulation is rationally related to a legitimate state end, and the regulatory burden is outweighed by the state interest. . . .

CONCLUSION

There is little doubt that the West York Blue Law is unpopular and archaic. As the . . . Court noted in *Spartan's Industries,* however, it is not our task to judge the wisdom or unpopularity of a legislative provision. . . .

The judgment is reversed and the cause is remanded for entry of an order permanently enjoining appellee from violating article 9001.

NOTE ON REHEARING AND ON STATE SUPREME COURT'S DENIAL OF DISCRETIONARY REVIEW

The Motion for Rehearing. Ms. Addison's motion for rehearing focused heavily upon the appellate court's failure to accept the trial judge's uncontested findings of fact and its substitution, instead, of its own review of the evidence. Her principal points were: "4. THE COURT OF APPEALS ERRED IN DISREGARDING THE TRIAL COURT'S FINDINGS OF FACT . . ." AND "5. THE COURT OF APPEALS ERRED IN USURPING THE FUNCTION OF THE TRIAL JUDGE BY SUBSTITUTING ITS JUDGMENT FOR HIS REGARDING THE UNCHALLENGED CREDIBILITY OF THE WITNESSES." The motion for rehearing, in fact, was successful to the extent that it promoted a further opinion from the Court of Appeals.

Court of Appeals' Opinion on Motion for Rehearing. The Court of Appeals opinion on rehearing included the following:

[A]ppellee contends that since the sufficiency of the evidence supporting the trial court's findings was not challenged, we are bound by those findings.

[S]everal of the lower court's "findings of fact" are in actuality "conclusions of law" [e.g., the finding of no reasonable relationship] and are thus reviewable under rules applicable to all cases. [I]n any event, where the constitutional issues involved are inextricably intertwined with the trial court's findings, proper consideration of those issues requires a review of the entire record. *Cf. Fiske v. Kansas*, 274 U.S. 380, 385–86 (1926). . . . Our review should not, however, include an evaluation of the credibility of witnesses since the trier of fact is the sole judge of credibility of witnesses [citing state authorities]. . . .

In sum, where a statute's constitutionality is challenged under the due process and equal protection clauses of the state and federal Constitutions, the reviewing court is required to examine all the evidence presented in an attempt to demonstrate the absence of any rational relationship between the statute's means and ends. On original submission, we reviewed all the evidence, . . . but absent an evaluation of witness credibility, in determining that appellee failed to meet its burden. . . . Appellee's motion for rehearing is overruled.

Denial of Review by the State Supreme Court. After the opinion on rehearing, within appropriate time deadlines, Redi-Mart filed an application for discretionary review by the state supreme court. That Court entered a one-sentence order: "The petition for discretionary review is denied." Similarly, it denied in one sentence Ms. Addison's motion for rehearing.

§ 7.07   PROCEEDINGS IN THE UNITED STATES SUPREME COURT

REDI-MART'S PETITION FOR
WRIT OF CERTIORARI

IN THE
SUPREME COURT OF THE UNITED STATES
OCTOBER TERM, 1986
REDI-MART, PETITIONER.

LONDON RETAIL MERCHANTS ASSOCIATION, RESPONDENT

On Appeal From the Supreme Court of the State of West York

PETITION FOR CERTIORARI TO THE SUPREME COURT
OF WEST YORK[*]

[The contents and form of the Petition are rigorously controlled by Supreme Court rules. Certain formal elements are omitted here, including the identification of parties, table of contents, table of authorities, statement of opinions and judgments below, statement of jurisdiction, and reproduction of the state statute involved.]

QUESTIONS PRESENTED

1. Does the West York Sunday Closing Law, W.Y. Rev. Civ. Stat. Ann. Art. 9001, violate the Due Process and Equal Protection clauses of the Fourteenth Amendment since more than ninety-six percent of employees are not in businesses even potentially affected by it, and since detailed statistical and other expert evidence demonstrates that it has no reasonable relationship to the legitimate state goal of providing employees with a day of rest?

2. . . . [The brief contains similar questions related to each of the other defensive theories or issues.] . . .

---

[*] In 1986, Redi-Mart could (and probably would) have used a different kind of request for review, namely an "appeal," rather than a petition for certiorari. But even then, certiorari was a permissible route. Today, certiorari would be Redi-Mart's only route, and hence we have used that format here.

STATEMENT OF THE CASE

[The statement of the case resembles the one set out in the LRMA brief in the court of appeals.]

REASONS FOR GRANTING THE WRIT

A. The Decision Below Conflicts with Other Decisions of Courts of Last Resort Concerning the Constitutionality of Closely Similar Statutes.

The opinions and judgment below conflict with recent decisions of other state supreme courts declaring similar Sunday Closing statutes unconstitutional. For example, in striking down Pennsylvania's Blue Law, the Pennsylvania Supreme Court explained:

> There is no fair and substantial relationship between the objective of providing a uniform day of rest and recreation and in permitting the sale of novelties but not Bibles and bathing suits; [or] in permitting the sale of fresh meat patties but not frozen meat patties; . . . . Likewise, we cannot find a fair and substantial relationship to the objective in permitting the sale of oriental rugs more than fifty years old while prohibiting the sale of the newer rugs, and permitting a table manufactured in 1877 to be sold but not one made in 1979; or in permitting the sale of newspapers but not magazines or books.

Kroger Co. v. O'Hara Township, 392 A.2d 266, 275 (Pa. 1978). Likewise, *People v. Abrahams*, 353 N.E.2d 574, 582–83 (N.Y. 1976), declared the New York Blue Law unconstitutional because it is possible, for instance:

> to buy beer but not cooked meals for home consumption; to eat meals in a restaurant but not drink therein; to purchase a thoroughbred horse at public auction but not to buy a less distinguished animal; . . . and, as in the case before us, to purchase drugs and medicine in a drug store but not to purchase most of the many other products sold in that same store, often on the very same counter. . . . It is apparent that [these categories are] a hodgepodge of unrelated exceptions legislated at the instances of whichever interest groups were best able to bring their views to the legislature's attention.

The West York statute, similarly, provides that hammers but not nails may be sold; pillows but not mattresses; cosmetics but not mirrors; food but not kitchen utensils; screwdrivers but not screws; light bulbs but not lamps; film but not cameras; lumber but not electric saws; and wood ladders but not metal ladders.

The Washington Supreme Court, in *County of Spokane v. Value-Mark, Inc.*, 419 P.2d 993, 997 (Wash. 1966), held that a municipal ordinance that prohibited Sunday sales of specifically enumerated goods could not be justified on the ground that it provided a day of rest:

> Nowhere does the ordinance imply that the police power is exerted for the health, welfare, morals and safety of the county by curtailing hours during which an employee . . . may be required by his employer to labor. So far as pertinent to Value-Mark . . . all of [its] departments may be maintained in full operation on Sunday as long as the clerks do not sell one of the prohibited items.

Like the Washington ordinance, the West York statute does not require businesses to close on either Saturday or Sunday, or require that the employees who work for those businesses refrain from work or limit their hours. The West York decision below squarely conflicts with these decisions in Pennsylvania, New York and Washington.

B. The Questions Presented Are Important.

Furthermore, the questions presented are important. This case will be first in which this Court has been presented with a fully developed factual record demonstrating the lack of reasonable relationship between the purpose of the statute, providing a day of rest to employees, and the means used, by restricting limited, but poorly defined, categories of goods dealt with by very few retail employees.

The evidence (as detailed in the statement of facts, above) shows that more than ninety-six percent of employees in West York work in businesses not even potentially affected by the statute. Further, the evidence demonstrates, with a high degree of statistical significance, and the trial court made an uncontested finding, that there was complete absence of correlation between regulation of items sold and the provision of a day of rest by employers in West York. Simply put, the statute does not and cannot enhance the provision of a day of rest to these employees.

The fact that this is the first Blue Law case in which this Court has been presented with a fully developed record makes a major difference in the substantiality of the questions involved. *Compare, e.g., Raymond Motor Transport, Inc. v. Rice*, 434 U.S. 429 (1978) (striking down truck-length regulation on ground that state had "failed to make even a colorable showing that its regulations contribute to highway safety") with *Cassell v. Consolidated Freightways Corp.*, 450 U.S. 662 (1981) (reconsidering, one year later, the issue raised in *Raymond* because the state had "made a more serious effort to support" the law in question).

Indeed, in *McGowan v. Maryland*, 366 U.S. 420 (1961), the Court issued an all-but-explicit invitation to the development of a record such as the one in this case. . . . This case raises the substantial question whether a case with a fully developed record, not present in *McGowan*, should produce a different result than that case. . . .

CONCLUSION

For these reasons, this Petition for Writ of certiorari should be granted.

Respectfully submitted,

FULBRIGHT & JAWORSKI

by Linda L. Addison. . . .

NOTES AND QUESTIONS

(1) *The Nature and Purpose of a Petition for Certiorari.* Notice that the Petition is not written, as are most briefs, to persuade the Court of the "rightness" of the Petitioner's position. Instead, it is written to demonstrate that the question is important. Therefore, the Petition highlights (1) conflicts among jurisdictions and (2) other indications that the questions presented are important. Note, also, that the Petition is very short and does not attempt to cover the issues exhaustively.

(2) *The Probability of Denial of Certiorari; Respondent's Opposition.* The respondent would file an Opposition to the Petition, which is similar in general appearance to the Petition and which would attempt to show that the questions are *not* important and that there is no real conflict. Here, it could be expected to emphasize the Supreme Court's prior decisions upholding Sunday Closing Laws. Only a tiny percentage of petitions filed by private parties are granted by the court.

§ 7.08   LEGISLATION MOOTS THE QUESTION

NOTE ON THE CAMPAIGN TO REPEAL THE WEST YORK
BLUE LAW

The Legislative Battle. The legislative campaign to repeal the West York Blue Law proceeded at the same time as the litigation outlined in this chapter. The battle was hard fought. Newspaper advertisements, with mail-in coupons, were headlined "Free the West York Shopper!" Twenty-seven retail stores announced a $300,000 advertising campaign to "drum up grass roots support." West York Citizens for Blue Law Repeal set up a toll-free telephone system. They generated letters to Representatives and Senators, as well as opinion-editorial page inserts for newspapers.

The Role of the Litigation Attorneys. Linda Addison was active in this legislative effort. As she wrote to her client, . . .

> It may . . . be of some consolation that, according to Senator Jones [the sponsor of the Blue Law repeal bill], the reversal of our judgment in the trial court in *London Retail Merchants Association v. Redi-Mart, Inc.* is exactly the shot in the arm the legislature needed to get the repeal bill through. While the argument we had been met with in the courts is that the Blue Law is a legislative matter, apparently a number of opponents to repeal were arguing that because the courts were apparently taking care of the problem, the legislature did not have to act. Apparently the reversal of our case disabused them of this notion. . . .

Redi-Mart stores began selling, "at nominal cost," T-shirts promoting the effort to "bust the Blue Law." Linda Addison, who is known for attention to detail, drafted a form letter for distribution to customers of Redi-Mart, addressed to their Senators or Representatives. She also participated in a campaign to insure that members of the press received letters and T-shirts, advising that "for the news media, the men should probably receive large t-shirts, and the women should receive medium."

The Repeal of the West York Blue Law by the Legislature During the Litigation. The legislative effort culminated in legislation described in Reyes, *Two Bills Filed to Cut Blue Law Repeal Opposition*, HOUSTON CHRONICLE, Mar. 1, 1985, § 2 at 1, col. 4:[*]

> It's round two in the legislative fight to repeal the state's Blue Law.

> Two bills filed Thursday are aimed at lessening opposition to repeal of the state's controversial Blue Law by exempting automobile dealers from the repeal proposal and guaranteeing that employees would receive at least a day off every seven days. . . .

> The proposed bills are mostly designed to soften opposition of the West York Automobile Dealers Association by effectively creating a Blue Law especially for the sale of motor vehicles.

> The repeal bills . . . would not allow the sale of motor vehicles on consecutive Saturdays and Sundays [but would repeal provisions applicable to all other retail merchandise] [Here, the article described lobbying efforts by automobile dealers that resulted in the retaining of the Blue Law for automobile sales.]

> Efforts to repeal the Blue Law are being led by several large retailers that include Sears Roebuck & Co., Target, Kroger, Joskes, Fiesta Mart, Southland Corp., K-Mart Corp., Eckerd Drugs and Zale Corp. . . .

A repeal provision similar to this proposal ultimately passed the West York legislature.

NOTES AND QUESTIONS

(1) *What Effect Does the Repeal Provision Have on the Constitutional Litigation?* Consider whether the repeal moots the case or controversy in the United States Supreme Court. What should the parties and the Court now do?

(2) *Is the New "Automobile Dealer Blue Law" Constitutional?* Notice that West York is left with a much narrower Blue Law, one that applies only to sales of motor vehicles, which apparently was obtained by effective lobbying by automobile dealers on their own behalf. Is this curtailment of the right to purchase automobiles reasonably related to a legitimate state purpose? Do you think it is a reasonable classification for purposes of equal protection?

---

[*] Copyright 1985 by the *Houston Chronicle*. Reprinted with permission.

Chapter 8

THE BASIC PROCEDURAL STRUCTURE OF DUE PROCESS AS A PROTECTION AGAINST STATE ACTION

§ 8.01 THE REQUIREMENT OF STATE ACTION (ALSO COVERED IN CHAPTER 13, BELOW)

INTRODUCTORY NOTE ON THE "STATE ACTION" REQUIREMENT

The Due Process Clause Applies Only to "State" Action, Not to "Private" Conduct: The Civil Rights Cases, 109 U.S. 3 (1883). By its terms, section 1 of the Fourteenth Amendment applies only to action by the state. It provides, ". . . nor shall any State" violate the due process or equal protection clauses. Ever since the *Civil Rights Cases, supra,* the Supreme Court consistently has held that these provisions do not apply to private actions that are not tied to the state or its agents. There are some clauses of the Constitution that apply directly to private individuals (*e.g.*, the Thirteenth Amendment, which abolishes slavery), but the Due Process and Equal Protection clauses do not. Thus, individuals and private businesses are usually free to discriminate even on invidious grounds without violating them.

Why Doesn't The Fourteenth Amendment Restrict Private Conduct Too? Although invidious discrimination by private individuals may be undesirable, the Constitution reflects the judgment that it would be worse to apply a blanket due process requirement to private conduct. In their private dealings, people need a degree of freedom to act in ways that would be illegal if done by the state—to prefer to associate with their friends rather than "afford due process" to strangers, to give just one crude example.

Distinguishing Truly Private Conduct from State Action. But sometimes, it can be difficult to distinguish between state action and private action. Much of our private activity is affected by state subsidies, incentives, or regulations. Also, some private actors perform functions that traditionally are governmental. When private conduct is intertwined with government action, the Court must decide whether the action is really attributable to the state.

Three Theories of State Action. There are at least three theories by which ostensibly private conduct can be treated as state action. First, (1) the private actor may be conducting a government function, or acting as a surrogate for the state. Second, (2) the state may be involved deeply enough in the private action so that it should be characterized as governmental action. Third, (3) the state may have encouraged the private action to such an extent that it becomes state action.

(1) *The Government Function Theory: From the Jaybird Primary Cases to the Company-Owned Town.* For the purpose of discriminating against African-Americans, political parties set up "private" primary elections for state offices (called Jaybird Primaries), and then limited them to white voters. In *Terry v. Adams,* 345 U.S. 461 (1953), the Supreme Court held that this so-called "private" activity was state action and was unconstitutional, since conducting an election is a governmental function. Earlier, in *Marsh v. Alabama,* 326 U.S. 501 (1946), the Court had held that a private company that owned an entire town was required to allow religious minorities to engage in speech-related activities on its property. Although the land was "private" in a sense, the company's actions became state action because its management of the entire town was a government function. But there are limits. In *Hudgens v. NLRB,* 424 U.S. 507 (1976), for example, the Court refused to hold that a shopping center owner was engaged in a governmental function when it excluded individuals who wanted to distribute handbills;

433

unlike the company town, the shopping center was engaged in private action, not state action. And finally, in *Jackson v. Consolidated Edison Co.*, 419 U.S. 345 (1974), the Court held that a private corporation did not perform a government function by conducting a utility business, and it was not bound by the due process clause when it cut off electrical service to a customer.

(2) *State Involvement or Symbiosis: From Lessees in State Buildings to Regulated Businesses.* In *Burton v. Wilmington Parking Authority*, 365 U.S. 715 (1961), a private business ran a coffee shop that discriminated against African-Americans. But the shop was located in space leased from the city, and the Court held that this discrimination was state action because of the "benefits mutually conferred" by the lease payments and the grant of the leasehold. But in *Moose Lodge No. 107 v. Irvis*, 407 U.S. 163 (1963), the Court held that a racially discriminatory private club located on private land did not become a state actor merely because it held a liquor license and was subject to extensive liquor regulations.

(3) *State Encouragement, Enforcement or Approbation.* In *Shelley v. Kraemer*, 334 U.S. 1 (1948), the Court held that racially discriminatory restrictive covenants for private housing were state action when they were enforced by the state. In *Reitman v. Mulkey*, 387 U.S. 369 (1967), upon a finding that a California state constitutional provision encouraged housing discrimination, the Court struck it down even though its express terms only removed prohibitions upon private activity. The limits of this theory, however, are illustrated by *Flagg Bros v. Brooks*, 426 U.S. 149 (1978), in which the Court upheld a state statute allowing a creditor to seize property without a due-process hearing. The state had not encouraged private seizures, but had merely refused to prohibit them. Consider the following illustrative case.

EDMONSON v. LEESVILLE CONCRETE CO., 500 U.S. 614 (1991). The issue in this case was whether it was unconstitutional for a private attorney, in litigation on behalf of a private client, to exercise peremptory challenges in a racially discriminatory manner (*e.g.*, by selectively removing African-Americans from the jury). The Court had already held that it was unconstitutional state action for a government prosecutor to do so in a criminal case; here, the Court extended that holding to private civil litigants.

The majority, in an opinion by Justice Kennedy, reasoned: (1) "A traditional function of government is evident here. The peremptory challenge is used in selecting an entity that is a quintessential government body [the jury], having no attributes of a private actor." The Court also applied both (2) state-involvement and (3) state-enforcement reasoning: "[W]ithout the direct and indispensable participation of the judge, who beyond all question is a state actor, the peremptory challenge system would serve no purpose." But Justice O'Connor, joined by the Chief Justice and Justice Scalia, dissented: "[T]he peremptory challenge is a mechanism for the exercise of *private* choice in the pursuit of fairness," and "the judge does not 'encourage' the use of a peremptory challenge at all." Which of these views is correct?

NOTES AND QUESTIONS

(1) *State Action and Private Action are Discussed Further in Chapter 13, Below.* Chapter 13 of this book is entitled "State Action vs. Private Action." It contains more extensive treatment of some of the cases cited above. You may or may not be assigned that chapter at this point, depending on your course outline.

(2) *Congressional Power to Protect Civil Rights against Private Action (Covered in Chapter 14).* Section 5 of the Fourteenth Amendment gives Congress power to "enforce" the Fourteenth Amendment "by appropriate legislation." This provision enables Congress to protect civil rights against private conduct that would not otherwise be reached by the Constitution. We already have seen the operation of the Civil Rights Act of 1964, for example, in Chapter 2, and we shall encounter other examples in Chapter 14.

§ 8.02   THE HISTORICAL DEVELOPMENT OF DUE PROCESS INTERPRETATION

[A]   The Search for Constitutional Protection of Personal Liberties Against State Governments

NOTE ON THE THEORIES THAT FAILED: PRIVILEGES AND IMMUNITIES, NATURAL LAW, ETC.

The Pre-Reconstruction History: No Bill-of-Rights Constraints Upon the States. As we saw in Chapter 6, the original Bill of Rights was inapplicable to the states. This omission induced lawyers to search for open-textured provisions that could be used as the basis of arguments for protection of natural or fundamental rights. The adoption of the Fourteenth Amendment gave new impetus to the search.

The Privileges and Immunities Clause of the Fourteenth Amendment. Reconsider the *Slaughter House Cases*, which are excerpted in Chapter 6, above. The plaintiffs in that case premised the thrust of their attack against defendants' monopoly upon the Privileges or Immunities clause of the Fourteenth Amendment. The much older decision in *Corfield v. Coryell* had given an expansive reading to the phrase "privileges and immunities." In the *Slaughter House Cases*, however, the Court consigned the Fourteenth Amendment Privileges or Immunities Clause to relative obscurity.

Natural Law. Reconsider *Calder v. Bull*, also in Chapter 6, above. Justice Chase's theory was that the social compact gave rise to rights protected by natural law, and that this principle was implicit in the Constitution. The theory had obvious deficiencies, however, and it rarely has been the explicit basis of constitutional decisionmaking.

Due Process, Judicial Restraint, and the Incorporation Debate. Of course, not every citizen would agree with the search for a broad constitutional protection of unenumerated personal liberties. Many might conclude that such a protection would produce the same mischief that the *Lochner* era witnessed. But the Due Process Clause remained as a viable part of the Constitution (or rather, it was resurrected after the *Slaughter House Cases*). At some point, it seemed that outrageous government action must violate the Due Process Clause if that clause was to avoid meaninglessness. How to imbue this little clause with meaning that was reasonably faithful to the need for restraint as well as to its text and purpose was a difficult problem then, as it still is today. One theory is that the Due Process Clause "incorporates" some or all of the specific guarantees of the Bill of Rights and applies them to the states. This theory has the advantages both of providing systematic protection and limiting judges to enumerated rights. But there is considerable disagreement concerning which protections of the Bill of Rights are incorporated and which are not, and there also is a fierce debate about the legitimacy of the incorporation process itself. It is to this incorporation debate, then, that we turn next.

[B]   The Incorporation Debate: The "Total Incorporation," "Selective Incorporation," "Ordered Liberty," "Fundamental Fairness," "American Scheme of Justice," and "Federalism" Theories

NOTES AND QUESTIONS ON THE INCORPORATION DEBATE

(1)   *Total Incorporation.* One theory that emerged after the adoption of the Fourteenth Amendment was that the Due Process Clause simply applied the entire Bill of Rights to the states. Although this "total incorporation" theory had the advantage of

simplicity and internal consistency, the Supreme Court consistently has declined to adopt it. The states have a considerable interest in the right to experiment with charging procedures that differ from the grand jury requirement of the Fifth Amendment, or with administrative procedures that they might prefer in civil cases to the precise kind of jury trial that is protected by the Seventh Amendment. Total incorporation would negate this interest.

(2) *Selective Incorporation.* The theory that the Court majority has followed is one of "selective incorporation." The Court has refused to apply certain Bill of Rights guarantees to the states—the Fifth Amendment grand jury provision and the Seventh Amendment right to jury trial in civil cases are among the few that it expressly has identified—while applying others. Thus the states are limited by the First Amendment's guaranty of freedom of speech and by the Taking Clause of the Fifth Amendment. Technically, it is inaccurate to say that these clauses themselves limit the states; the theory is that the Fourteenth Amendment Due Process Clause provides the limit, and its meaning is determined by incorporation of other clauses. But this theory, in turn, poses another problem: How are we to know precisely which clauses are incorporated, and which are not?

(3) *The "Fundamental Rights" and "Ordered Liberty" Approaches: From Palko v. Connecticut, 302 U.S. 319 (1937), to Adamson v. California, 332 U.S. 46 (1947).* As the Court asserted its authority in the economic arena, it searched for an incorporation principle in the personal liberties arena, and it ultimately articulated a standard by which "fundamental rights" were incorporated. Rights were fundamental, said the Court in *Palko*, if they were "implicit in the concept of ordered liberty." The freedom of speech thus was incorporated because it was essential to a free society; the requirement of a grand jury indictment, on the other hand, was not, because a society that valued both liberty and order could opt instead for examining trials or other screening mechanisms in criminal cases. After *Palko*, the selective incorporation issue arose again in *Adamson*, in which the court fragmented over the question whether the states must honor the federal privilege against self-incrimination. The following are excerpts from the opinions of three Justices:

REED, J., for the Court. . . . A right to a fair trial is a right admittedly protected by the due process clause of the fourteenth amendment. Therefore, appellant argues, the due process clause of the fourteenth amendment protects his privilege against self-incrimination. The due process clause of the fourteenth amendment, however, does not draw all the rights of the federal Bill of Rights under its protection. That contention was made and rejected in *Palko v. Connecticut.* . . . *Palko* held that such provisions of the Bill of Rights as were "implicit in the concept of ordered liberty" . . . became secure from state interference by the clause. But it held nothing more.

Specifically, the due process clause does not protect . . . the accused's freedom from giving testimony by compulsion in state trials that is secured to him against federal interference by the fifth amendment.[1] [F]or a state to require testimony from an accused is not necessarily a breach of the state's obligation to give a fair trial.

FRANKFURTER, J., concurring. . . . The [fourteenth] amendment neither comprehends the specific provisions by which the Founders deemed it appropriate to restrict the federal government nor is it confined to them. The due process clause of the fourteenth amendment has an independent potency, precisely as does the fifth amendment in relation to the federal. [T]he fifth amendment specifically . . . bars compelling a person to be a witness against himself in any criminal case, [and] it precludes deprivation of "life, liberty, or

---

[1] This specific holding has been overruled, as has the Court's general approach. *Cf. Duncan v. Louisiana,* below.

property, without due process of law." Are Madison and his contemporaries in the framing of the Bill of Rights charged with writing into it a meaningless clause? To consider "due process of law" as merely a shorthand statement of other specific clauses in the same amendment is to attribute to the authors and proponents of this amendment ignorance of, or indifference to, a historic conception which was one of the great instruments in the arsenal of constitutional freedom which the Bill of Rights was to protect and strengthen.

BLACK, J., dissenting. [M]y study of the historical events that culminated in the fourteenth amendment . . . persuades me that one of the chief objects . . . was to make the Bill of Rights applicable to the states. With full knowledge and import of the *Barron* decision [which held the Bill of Rights inapplicable to the states before the passage of the fourteenth amendment; *see* Chapter 6, above] the Framers and backers of the Fourteenth Amendment proclaimed its purpose to be to overturn the rule that case had announced. . . .

I would follow what I believe was the original purpose of the fourteenth amendment—to extend to all of the people of the nation the complete protection of the Bill of Rights.

(4)   *Rights "Fundamental to the American Scheme of Justice" as the Touchstone of Incorporation.* In *Duncan v. Louisiana,* below, the Court adopted what apparently is its current approach, incorporating those provisions of the Bill of Rights that it deems "fundamental to the American scheme of justice."

DUNCAN v. LOUISIANA, 391 U.S. 145 (1968). The Court, per Justice White, held in *Duncan* that the Fourteenth Amendment's Due Process Clause incorporated the right to jury trial as protected by the Sixth Amendment in criminal cases:

In resolving conflicting claims concerning the meaning of this spacious language [of the Due Process Clause], the Court has looked increasingly to the Bill of Rights for guidance; many of the rights guaranteed by the first eight amendments to the Constitution have been held to be protected against state action by the due process clause of the fourteenth amendment. That clause now protects the rights to compensation for property taken by the state; the rights of speech, press, and religion covered by the first amendment; the fourth amendment rights to be free from unreasonable search and seizure and to have excluded from criminal trials any evidence illegally seized; the right guaranteed by the fifth amendment to be free of compelled self-incrimination; and the sixth amendment rights to counsel, to a speedy and public trial, to confrontation of opposing witnesses, and to compulsory process for obtaining witnesses.

The test [for incorporation] has been phrased in a variety of ways in the opinions of this Court. The question has been asked whether a right is among those "fundamental principles of liberty and justice which lie at the base of all our civil and political institutions," . . . whether it is "basic to our system of jurisprudence," . . . and whether it is "a fundamental right, essential to a fair trial." [T]he position of Louisiana . . . is that the Constitution imposes on the states no duty to give a jury trial in any criminal case, regardless of the seriousness of the crime or the size of the punishment which may be imposed. Because we believe that trial by jury is fundamental to the American scheme of justice, we hold that the fourteenth amendment guarantees a right of jury trial in all cases which—were they to be tried in federal court—would come within the sixth amendment's guarantee.

Finally, Justice Harlan, joined by Justice Stewart, dissented: "The Court does not say that those who framed the fourteenth amendment intended to make the sixth amendment applicable to the states. And the Court . . . finds nothing unfair about the procedure by which the present appellant was tried. Nevertheless, . . . it holds, . . . that the due process clause incorporates the particular clause of the sixth amendment . . . including, as I read its opinion, the sometimes trivial accompanying baggage of judicial interpretation in federal contexts."

NOTES AND QUESTIONS ON THE LEGITIMACY OF INCORPORATION AND ON THE "JOT-FOR-JOT" THEORY OF INCORPORATION OF INTERPRETATIONS

(1) *Can Incorporation Be Justified by Originalism, Textualism, or Supplementation Reasoning (Non-Interpretivism)?* There is deep disagreement concerning whether the intent of the drafters of the Fourteenth Amendment involved incorporation of the Bill of Rights. As often happens, there is some evidence that they did so intend—and some evidence that they did not. *Compare, e.g.,* Justice Harlan's opinion in *Duncan,* above (finding no support for incorporation) with Justice Black's opinion in *Adamson* (which contains a lengthy appendix reflecting Fourteenth Amendment history purporting to show the drafters' desire to incorporate)."The preponderance of historical evidence . . . indicates that the drafters of the amendment did not specifically intend to apply all of [the Bill of Rights] to the states." J. NOWAK, R. ROTUNDA, & J. YOUNG, CONSTITUTIONAL LAW 364 (3d ed. 1986).

What about the text of the amendment? In *Adamson,* Justice Frankfurter makes interesting structural arguments against incorporation (he says that the federal Due Process Clause of the Fifth Amendment is identical but would be rendered meaningless if it merely restated rights that already are protected in the same Bill of Rights of which it is a part). But doesn't Justice Frankfurter's argument fail if we reason that state due process might, after all, be different from federal due process, or that the Fourteenth Amendment is not subject to his analysis since it is not part of the original Bill of Rights and therefore would not itself be rendered meaningless by incorporation? Finally, Justice Black supports his total incorporation theory by such values as preventing judicial activism. Is this a persuasive argument? For an evolutionary analysis, *see* Lewis & Trichter, *The Nationalization of the Bill of Rights: History, Development, and Current Status,* 20 WASHBURN L.J. 195 (1981).

(2) *Is All the "Accompanying Baggage" of Interpretation of Each Incorporated Amendment Also Incorporated?: Benton v. Maryland, 395 U.S. 784 (1969).* Notice the question raised by Justice Harlan in *Duncan:* If the due process clause does incorporate provisions of the Bill of Rights, does it also incorporate all of the interpretations of those provisions exactly as they have been applied to the federal government? Justice Harlan refers to the "sometimes trivial accompanying baggage" of interpretation that would thus be incorporated. Elsewhere, he criticizes the stifling of experimentation among the states with different approaches.

In *Benton v. Maryland, supra,* the Court (per Justice Brennan) said, "Once it is decided that a particular Bill of Rights guarantee is 'fundamental to the American scheme of justice,' the same constitutional standards apply against both the state and federal governments." And since the double jeopardy provision is part of the American scheme, he continued in *Benton,* it "must be judged, not by the watered-down standard enunciated in *Palko,* but under this Court's interpretation of the fifth amendment double jeopardy provision." Is this conclusion warranted? Consider the following.

JOHNSON v. LOUISIANA, 406 U.S. 365 (1972), and **APODACA v. OREGON,** 406 U.S. 404 (1972). In these companion cases, the Court, per Justice White, held that state criminal convictions by nonunanimous juries did not violate the due process clause, even as interpreted to incorporate the Sixth Amendment guarantee of jury trial. Justice White's opinions did not distinguish between standards applicable to the states and those applicable to the federal government. However, Justice Powell did so, criticizing the "jot-for-jot" theory of incorporation:

> POWELL, J., concurring: [I]n holding that the fourteenth amendment has incorporated "jot-for-jot" and "case for case" every element of the sixth amendment, the Court derogates principles of federalism that are basic to our system. In the name of uniform application of high standards of due process, the

Court has embarked upon a course of constitutional interpretation that deprives the states of freedom to experiment with adjudicatory processes different from the federal model. At the same time, the Court's understandable unwillingness to impose requirements that it finds unnecessarily rigid . . . has culminated in the dilution of federal rights that were, until these decisions, not seriously questioned. The doubly undesirable consequence of this reasoning process, labeled by Mr. Justice Harlan as "constitutional schizophrenia," . . . may well be detrimental to both the state and federal criminal justice systems.

§ 8.03 PROCEDURAL DUE PROCESS

INTRODUCTORY NOTE

By its literal terms, the Due Process Clause is a guarantee of state procedural regularity. Although that is not all it is, the procedural aspect of due process remains significant. The procedural due process guarantee is, compared to substantive due process, limited. Procedural due process does not prohibit a state from depriving a person of a protected interest. Instead, the procedural due process guarantee requires that any deprivation must not be arbitrary or capricious. Procedural due process, in other words, limits the state from *erroneously* depriving a person of a protected interest. *See Goldberg v. Kelly*, 397 U.S. 254 (1970).

In this section, we consider procedural due process. We shall encounter three basic issues: First, what "liberty" or "property" interests will be protected? Second, what kind of "deprivation" of "liberty or property" triggers due process protection? And third, what "process" is "due" in varying kinds of situations?

[A] What "liberty" or "property" Interests are Protected by Procedural Due Process?

NOTES AND QUESTIONS

(1) *Professor Reich and the New Property: Reich, The New Property, 73 Yale L.J. 733 (1964).* Professor Charles Reich anticipated *Goldberg v. Kelly* [below] by six years in this influential article. His insight was that government benefits in the form of statutory or administrative entitlements had created a new kind of "property." *See also* Terrell, *Liberty and Responsibility in the Land of "New Property": Exploring the Limits of Procedural Due Process*, 39 U. FLA. L. REV. 217 (1987). *Cf.* Eberle, *Procedural Due Process: The Original Understanding*, 4 CONST. COMMENT. 339 (1987).

(2) *The "High-Water Mark" of the Liberty-Or-Property Concept: Bell v. Burson, 402 U.S. 535 (1971).* In *Bell*, Mr. Justice Brennan extended his reasoning in *Goldberg v. Kelly* to strike down Georgia's Motor Vehicle Safety Responsibility Act. The Act, which was a substitute for mandatory liability insurance, provided that an uninsured automobile driver who was involved in an accident must satisfy all damage claims or post security to cover them, or his registration and driver's license would be suspended. The key factor in the Court's decision was that fault or innocence on the part of the driver was not an issue. In holding that this element was constitutionally required, the Court reasoned as follows:

> If the statute barred the issuance of licenses to all motorists who did not carry liability insurance . . ., the statute would not, under our cases, violate the fourteenth amendment. . . . [But] [once] licenses are issued, as in Petitioner's case, their continued possession may become essential to the pursuit of a livelihood. . . . In such cases, the licenses are not to be taken away without that procedural due process required by the fourteenth amendment. [T]his is but an application of the general proposition that relevant constitutional restraints limit state power to terminate an entitlement whether the entitlement is

denominated a "right" or a "privilege" [citing *Goldberg* and other cases].

Monaghan, *Of "Liberty" and "Property,"* 62 CORNELL L. REV. 401 (1977), concludes that *Bell* represents the "high-water mark" of the Court's then approach, which determined the existence of a liberty or property interest by measuring how "important" the right was to the individual. Notice the ironic result of *Bell v. Burson:* Georgia could prevent an indigent in Bell's position from driving, and indeed could have prevented him from driving in the first place, simply by imposing a requirement that he carry liability insurance. If it can do that, why can it not enact a Safety Responsibility Act, which actually provides him with greater freedom to drive and more flexible options after he has an accident?

(3) *The Pendulum Swings Back: Board of Regents v. Roth, 408 U.S. 564 (1972).* The holdings of *Goldberg, Bell,* and other cases involved liberal findings of liberty-or-property-deprivation, but the pendulum swung back in the *Roth* case. In *Roth,* an assistant professor at a state university, who had no contractual right to continued employment, alleged that the university's decision not to re-hire him was a violation of procedural due process since he had not had a pre-termination hearing. The Supreme Court upheld a summary judgment for the university, reasoning that in the absence of any statute, rule, or policy that created "a legitimate claim of entitlement" under state law, the claimant lacked the kind of "liberty or property" interest that could trigger due process.

The *Roth* decision established that, to determine whether a challenger had a protected property or liberty interest, the Court would look *outside* the Constitution to "an independent source such as state law." If a protected interest would exist, then the Court would look to the values *inside* the Constitution to determine what process was "due."

(4) *The Retreat from Roth: Arnett v. Kennedy, 416 U.S. 134 (1974) and Justice Rehnquist's "The Bitter With The Sweet."* Even the *Roth* reliance on state law to determine the existence of a protected interest was not enough of a change. Later, in *Kennedy,* a non-probationary employee protected by civil service was dismissed from his position in the federal Office of Economic Opportunity, allegedly for having made defamatory statements about other OEO employees. He was entitled, by statute, not to be discharged except for "cause," but in accordance with the same statute, he was denied a pre-termination hearing. The plurality opinion, by Justice Rehnquist, held that Kennedy was not denied any protected "liberty or property" interest:

> In *Board of Regents v. Roth*, we said: "Property interests, of course, are not created by the Constitution. Rather, they are created and their dimensions are defined by existing rules or understandings that stem from an independent source such as state law—rules or understandings that secure certain benefits and that support claims of entitlement to those benefits. . . ."

> Here, appellee did have a statutory expectancy that he not be removed other than for "such cause as will promote the efficiency of [the] service." But the very section of the statute which granted him that right [e]xpressly provided also for the procedure by which the cause was to be determined, and expressly omitted the procedural guarantees which appellee insists are mandated by the Constitution. . . .

> [W]here the grant of a substantive right is inextricably intertwined with the limitations on the procedures which are to be employed in determining that right, a litigant in the position of appellee must take the bitter with the sweet. . . .

Thus, the plurality held that sources outside the Constitution (such as state law) would control both the protected interest issue and the issue of what process was required.

Justice Powell concurred separately, rejecting the " 'wooden distinction' between 'rights' and 'privileges'," and instead balanced the government's "interest in being able to act expeditiously to remove an unsatisfactory employee" against appellee's "countervailing interests [in] the continuation of his public employment." [Note that the Court later made clear its rejection of the plurality reasoning in *Arnett. See Cleveland Board of Education v. Loudermill*, below.]

BISHOP v. WOOD
426 U.S. 341 (1976)

Mr. Justice Stevens delivered the opinion of the Court.

[A discharged city police officer alleged that his termination without a hearing denied him due process. The district court concluded that, under state law, a "permanent employee held his position at the will and pleasure of the city," and that removal was conditioned only on compliance with certain specified procedures which did not include a hearing. The court of appeals affirmed. Here, the Supreme Court holds that this state law foreclosed the finding of a liberty or property interest and that the discharged officer was entitled only to the procedures provided by state law, not to more extensive procedures that might be required by the due process clause.]

I

A city ordinance provides that a permanent employee may be discharged if he fails to perform work up to the standard of his classification, or if he is negligent, inefficient, or unfit to perform his duties. Petitioner first contends that even though the ordinance does not expressly so provide, it should be read to prohibit discharge for any other reason, and therefore to confer tenure on all permanent employees. In addition, he contends that his period of service, together with his "permanent" classification, gave him a sufficient expectancy of continued employment to constitute a protected property interest.

A property interest in employment can, of course, be created by ordinance, or by an implied contract. In either case, however, the sufficiency of the claim of entitlement must be decided by reference to state law. The North Carolina Supreme Court has held that an enforceable expectation of continued public employment in that State can exist only if the employer, by statute or contract, has actually granted some form of guarantee. *Still v. Lance*, 279 N.C. 254, 182 S.E.2d 403 (1971). . . .

In this case, as the District Court construed the ordinance, the City Manager's determination of the adequacy of the grounds for discharge is not subject to judicial review; the employee is merely given certain procedural rights which the District Court found not to have been violated in this case. The District Court's reading of the ordinance is tenable; it derives some support from a decision of the North Carolina Supreme Court, *Still v. Lance, supra;* and it was accepted by the Court of Appeals for the Fourth Circuit. These reasons are sufficient to foreclose our independent examination of the state-law issue.

Under that view of the law, petitioner's discharge did not deprive him of a property interest protected by the Fourteenth Amendment. . . .

II

Petitioner's claim that he has been deprived of liberty has two components. He contends that the reasons given for his discharge are so serious as to constitute a stigma that may severely damage his reputation in the community; in addition, he claims that those reasons were false. . . .

In *Board of Regents v. Roth*, we recognized that the nonretention of an untenured college teacher might make him somewhat less attractive to other employers, but nevertheless concluded that it would stretch the concept too far "to suggest that a person is deprived of 'liberty' when he simply is not rehired in one job but remains as free as before to seek another." This same conclusion applies to the discharge of a public employee whose position is terminable at the will of the employer when there is no public disclosure of the reasons for the discharge. . . .

Petitioner argues, however, that the reasons given for his discharge were false. . . . The truth or falsity of the City Manager's statement determines whether or not his decision to discharge the petitioner was correct or prudent, but neither enhances nor diminishes petitioner's claim that his constitutionally protected interest in liberty has been impaired. A contrary evaluation of his contention would enable every discharged employee to assert a constitutional claim merely by alleging that his former supervisor made a mistake.

The federal court is not the appropriate forum in which to review the multitude of personnel decisions that are made daily by public agencies. . . . We must accept the harsh fact that numerous individual mistakes are inevitable in the day-to-day administration of our affairs. . . . The Due Process Clause of the Fourteenth Amendment is not a guarantee against incorrect or ill-advised personnel decisions.

The judgment is *affirmed*.

MR. JUSTICE BRENNAN, with whom MR. JUSTICE MARSHALL concurs, dissenting.

[I] [f]ully concur in the dissenting opinions of Mr. Justice White and Mr. Justice Blackmun, which forcefully demonstrate the Court's error in holding that petitioner was not deprived of "property" without due process of law. I would only add that the strained reading of the local ordinance, which the Court deems to be "tenable," cannot be dispositive of the existence *vel non* of petitioner's "property" interest. There is certainly a federal dimension to the definition of "property" in the Federal Constitution; cases such as *Board of Regents v. Roth, supra,* held merely that "property" interests encompass those to which a person has "a legitimate claim of entitlement," and *can* arise from "existing rules or understandings" that derive from "an independent source *such as* state law." *Id.* (emphasis supplied). But certainly, at least before a state law is definitively construed as not securing a "property" interest, the relevant inquiry is whether it was objectively reasonable for the employee to believe he could rely on continued employment. . . . At a minimum, this would require in this case an analysis of the common practices utilized and the expectations generated by respondents, and the manner in which the local ordinance would reasonably be read by respondents' employees. . . .

These observations do not, of course, suggest that a "federal court is . . . the appropriate forum in which to review the multitude of personnel decisions that are made daily by public agencies." However, the federal courts are the appropriate forum for ensuring that the constitutional mandates of due process are followed by those agencies of government making personnel decisions that pervasively influence the lives of those affected thereby. . . .

MR. JUSTICE WHITE, with whom MR. JUSTICE BRENNAN, MR. JUSTICE MARSHALL, and MR. JUSTICE BLACKMUN join, dissenting.

I dissent because the decision of the majority rests upon a proposition which was squarely addressed and in my view correctly rejected by six Members of this Court in *Arnett v. Kennedy*.

The view was . . . rejected by Mr. Justice Marshall in an opinion joined by Mr. Justice Brennan and Mr. Justice Douglas in which it was correctly observed:

Accordingly, a majority of the Court rejects Mr. Justice Rehnquist's argument that because appellee's entitlement arose from statute, it could be conditioned on a statutory limitation of procedural due process protections, an approach which would render such protection inapplicable to the deprivation of any statutory benefit any "privilege" extended by Government—where a statute prescribed a termination procedure, no matter how arbitrary or unfair. It would amount to nothing less than a return, albeit in somewhat different verbal garb, to the thoroughly discredited distinction between rights and privileges which once seemed to govern the applicability of procedural due process. . . .

. . . The ordinance plainly grants petitioner a right to his job unless there is cause to fire him. Having granted him such a right it is the Federal Constitution, not state law, which determines the process to be applied in connection with any state decision to deprive him of it.

[The dissenting opinion of Mr. JUSTICE BLACKMUN, with whom MR. JUSTICE BRENNAN joined, is omitted.]

NOTES AND QUESTIONS

(1) *Is State Law Really the Determinant of Property Interests?* Justice Stevens' opinion simply defers to state law, holding that a determination of the non-existence of a state-law protected property interest forecloses consideration of the due process claim. First, is it correct to use state law in making this determination, which, after all, is ultimately the factor that decides a federal due process claim?

Second question: Is it correct, on the other hand, to regard state law as the *sole* determinant of the existence of a property interest, foreclosing further inquiry? One might imagine a case in which the state characterized employment contracts similarly to other contracts, but also enacted a statute providing: "No such contract may be construed to give rise to any liberty or property interest." Wouldn't federal law control over the conclusory state statute denying the existence of a liberty or property interest? *Cf.* Monaghan, *Of "Liberty" and "Property,"* supra (arguing that *Bishop* is wrongly reasoned, or at least wrongly phrased). *See also* Alexander, *The Relationship between Procedural Due Process and Substantive Constitutional Rights*, 39 U. FLA. L. REV. 217 (1987).

(2) *Short Deprivations: Goss v. Lopez, 419 U.S. 565 (1975). Goss* concerned an Ohio law that allowed public schools to suspend students for up to ten days without a hearing. The Court, per Justice White, struck down this statute, holding that " 'education is perhaps the most important function of state and local governments' . . . and the total exclusion from the educational process for more than a trivial period . . . is a serious event in the life of the suspended child. Neither the property interest in educational benefits temporarily denied nor the liberty interest in reputation, which is also implicated, is so insubstantial that suspensions may constitutionally be imposed by any procedure the school chooses, no matter how arbitrary."

Justice Powell, joined by the Chief Justice and Justices Blackmun and Rehnquist, dissented: "[H]owever one may define the entitlement to education provided by Ohio law, . . . a deprivation of not more than ten days' suspension from school, imposed as a routine disciplinary measure, does not assume constitutional dimensions."

(3) *The Court Rejects the "Bitter With the Sweet" Approach of Arnett v. Kennedy: Cleveland Board of Education v. Loudermill, 470 U.S. 532 (1985).* Loudermill stated on his employment application that he had never been convicted of a felony, but the Board of Education terminated him upon discovering that he had in fact been convicted of grand larceny. Under applicable state law, Loudermill was a "classified civil servant" and, by statute, could be terminated only for cause and through a process of administrative review. Loudermill sued, claiming that he was not afforded an opportu-

nity to respond to the dishonest-application charge or to challenge the dismissal. The Board argued that his due process claim was foreclosed by state law provisions defining both substantive and procedural rights, and that Loudermill must therefore take the "bitter with the sweet" according to *Arnett v. Kennedy*. The Supreme Court, per White, J. (and over the dissent of Rehnquist, J.), cited several intervening decisions undermining the bitter-with-the-sweet doctrine and then squarely rejected it, holding that Loudermill had been denied due process:

> In light of these holdings, it is settled that the "bitter-with-the-sweet" approach misconceives the constitutional guarantee. If a clearer holding is needed, we provide it today. The point is straightforward: the due process clause provides that certain substantive rights—life, liberty and property—cannot be deprived except pursuant to constitutionally adequate procedures. ". . . While the legislature may elect not to confer a property interest in [public] employment, it may not constitutionally authorize the deprivation of such an interest, once conferred, without appropriate procedural safeguards. . . ."

> In short, once it is determined that the due process clause applies, "the question remains what process is due. . . ." The answer to that question is not to be found in the [state] statute.

Is this reasoning persuasive? Can, or should, a state be able to influence the determination of "that process which is due" by coupling a grant of property right with procedures for its defeasance? Does the *Loudermill* Court's rejection of the bitter with the sweet theory cast doubt upon the validity of *Bishop v. Wood* (above)?

(4)   *Does Injury to Reputation Trigger the Due Process Clause? Paul v. Davis, 424 U.S. 693 (1976).* In *Paul*, the plaintiff sued a police chief who had publicized the allegation that he was an "active shoplifter" after criminal charges against him had been dismissed. (The case is dealt with in greater detail in Chapter 9, below.) The Court held that the plaintiff's reputation, standing alone, was not the kind liberty or property interests that would trigger procedrural due process. Read in the narrow fashion, *Paul* established that "reputation" is an exception to the *Roth* standard. Another exception is a claim of "false arrest." *See Albright v. Oliver*, 510 U.S. 266 (1994).

(5)   *Is a Mere "Claim" of a Property Right Itself a Property Right?* The answer is yes, as provided by *Logan v. Zimmerman Brush Co.*, 455 U.S. 422 (1982). Logan, whose employment with a private corporation was terminated allegedly because his disabled leg made it impossible for him to perform his duties, timely filed a charge of unlawful termination with the Illinois Fair Employment Practices Commission. Through inadvertence, the Commission scheduled its fact finding hearing five days after the expiration of a statutory 120-day deadline, and the Illinois courts held that this error committed by the Commission deprived it of jurisdiction and barred Logan's claim. The Supreme Court reversed:

> [A] cause of action is a species of property protected by the fourteenth amendment's due process clause. . . .

> [T]he view that Logan's . . . claim is a constitutionally protected one follows logically from the Court's . . . recent cases analyzing the nature of a property interest. The hallmark of property, the Court has emphasized, is an individual entitlement grounded in state law, which cannot be removed except "for cause. . . ." Once that characteristic is found, the types of interests protected as "property" are varied and, as often as not, intangible, relating "to the whole domain of social and economic fact."

Is this holding correct? Does it effectively overrule *Bishop v. Wood*? [Notice that the state supreme court had held that state law created no property interest, a holding analogous to the one that foreclosed further consideration in *Bishop*.]

(6) *Workers' Compensation Benefits as "Protected Property Interests" in Procedural Due Process: American Manufacturers Mutual Insurance Company v. Sullivan,
526 U.S. 66 (1999).* Like other states, Pennsylvania's Workers Compensation law
provided injured employees with medical benefit payments. Pennsylvania amended its
law to allow insurers to suspend payment of the benefits, without notice or an
opportunity to be heard, in any case where the insurer sought an administrative
"utilization review" of the "reasonableness" and "necessity" of the payment. The
challengers alleged that, assuming the actions of the insurers constituted "state action,"
the medical benefits were "property interests" protected by the Due Process Clause and
that these interests were being deprived without due process of law. Although the court
of appeals had agreed with the challengers, the Supreme Court, per Chief Justice
Rehnquist, disagreed and reversed.

The Court first held that the insurers' decisions were not "state action." [*See* Chapter
13 below.] Then, regarding the procedural due process issue, the Court held that the
challengers did not have a protected property interest in a payment prior to the
statutory authorized utilization review. The Court looked to the text of the Pennsylvania
law and concluded that the entitlement came into existence only after the review process
established the necessity and reasonableness of the charge. Although "the bitter-with-
the sweet" approach, discussed in Note (3) above was explicitly rejected in *Loudermill*,
the Chief Justice's reasoning here seems close to resurrecting that theory.

TOWN OF CASTLE ROCK (CO.) v. GONZALES, 545 U.S. 748 (2005). Fifteen
years after *DeShaney* (*see* Chapter 9), the Supreme Court revisited the issue of state
liability, for negligent or reckless conduct, under the Due Process Clause. While the
facts in *DeShaney* were described, by Chief Justice Rehnquist, as "undeniably tragic,"
Justice Scalia characterized the *Gonzales* case as involving "horrible facts." Jessica
Gonzales was estranged from her husband. She had secured a restraining order under
Colorado law preventing her husband from contact with her or their three daughters. In
violation of the restraining order, the husband abducted the three girls at approximately
5:00 p.m. Gonzales called the Castle Rock police and requested that they enforce the
restraining order. Under Colorado law (designed to reduce domestic violence and
abuse), the order said the police "shall use every reasonable means to enforce" the order.
Gonzales repeatedly (five times) contacted the police to request enforcement, but the
police made no efforts. At 3:20 a.m., the husband, in a suicidal rage, attacked the police
station with a semiautomatic handgun; the police returned fire and killed him. In the
husband's pickup, police found the bodies of all three daughters—murdered by the
husband.

Gonzales sued Castle Rock, under substantive due process (like *DeShaney*) and
procedural due process theories for the reckless or negligent enforcement of the
restraining order. The Tenth Circuit treated the case as a matter of procedural due
process and held that Gonzales had a protected "property" interest under Colorado law
in competent enforcement of the restraining order. The Supreme Court, per Justice
Scalia, disagreed and ruled for the City.

In a wide-ranging opinion, the Court held that any interest in enforcement of a
restraining order, even under the mandatory language of the Colorado scheme, was not
a sufficient entitlement to create a property interest. The Court noted that Gonzales was
only an *indirect* beneficiary of the statutory scheme, that her interest arose only
incidentally and that the police traditionally had *discretionary* authority, even under
the new Colorado statute. Justice Scalia's opinion did indicate that the people of
Colorado were "free to craft" a system of "better policing"—and that such a system
might create protectable property interests.

Justice Souter concurred, but rejected the majority's seeming adoption of a "direct-
indirect" model of analysis. Justice Souter said the flaw in Gonzales' case was her claim
of a "property interest in a state-mandated process in and of itself."

Justice Stevens (for Ginsburg) dissented. He concluded that Gonzales had a protected property interest because Colorado law gave her a "right to police assistance comparable to the right she would have possessed to any other service the government or a private firm might have undertaken to provide." According to Justice Stevens, she had a property interest in police security just as if a private security firm had contracted with her. You will note that the Court's conservative bloc frequently suggests that government is sometimes entitled to act like a "private business" (*e.g.*, public forum doctrine in Chapter 11; market-participant exception to the dormant Commerce Clause doctrine in Chapter 3); here, Justice Stevens argues that the government may face liability just like a private security firm would.

The *Castle Rock* Court concluded that the mother did not have a protected property interest in the restraining order procedure. Although reaching similar results, *City of Castle Rock* used a different analysis than *DeShaney*. *Castle Rock* focused on the existence (or nonexistence) of a "protected interest," while *DeShaney* conceded the existence of a protected interest and focused on whether the government conduct constituted a "deprivation."

PROBLEM A

THE TERMINATED "PROBATIONARY" TEACHER. This problem is not based upon any particular case, but it partakes of some characteristics of cases that arise daily throughout the United States. The West City Board of Education has terminated the employment of teacher Ralph Ripley on grounds of "conduct unbecoming the service." Three children have given written statements describing acts of sexual abuse allegedly practiced upon them by Ripley. Ripley has been employed for less than one year, and the West City Civil Service Code denominates him as a "probationary" employee. Although the Code details hearing procedures for termination of non-probationary employees, it contains no provisions for termination of probationary employees. The Principal at Ripley's school summoned him, presented him with the students' statements, demanded an explanation, and terminated him on the spot when Ripley refused to answer. Ripley points out that the employee handbook provides: "Ordinarily, probationary employees who satisfactorily complete their first year are granted protected permanent status unless their performance is unsatisfactory." Ripley vehemently denies the allegations of sexual abuse, and he alleges that his termination without a "hearing" violates due process.

(1) *A Liberty or Property Interest?* Does Ripley have a protected liberty or property interest that triggers the right to a hearing complying with due process?

(2) *Would You Take Ripley's Case on a Contingent Fee Basis?* Imagine that your estimate is that expenses of $6,000 aside from form fee, are the minimum necessary to present Ripley's claim in the courts, and since Ripley is an indigent you will have to advance that sum. Would you take his case on a contingent fee basis?

(3) *The School Board's Perspective.* If you represented the school board, would you recommend that it seek to redraft the Civil Service Code and employee handbook, and if so, how?

[B] What Kind of "Deprivation" of a Protected Interest Triggers Procedural Due Process?

What is required to have a deprivation under procedural due process? While it seems understandable that intentional conduct may trigger procedural due process, there are questions about whether negligent or reckless conduct can constitute a deprivation.

[1] Intentional Deprivations

GOLDBERG v. KELLY, 397 U.S. 254 (1970). The Court, per Justice Brennan, held that when public assistance is terminated, the welfare recipient must be afforded a hearing *before* the termination of welfare benefits. The decision widely is recognized as the beginning of a "revolution" in procedural due process, in which benefits earlier thought of as defeasible privileges became entitlements whose impairment was restricted. The statutes and regulations provided a full hearing only *after* discrimination. The Court began by acknowledging, "it is true, of course, that some governmental benefits may be administratively terminated without affording the recipient a pre-termination evidentiary hearing," but stated, "we agree with the district court that when welfare is discontinued only a pre-termination evidentiary hearing provides the recipient with procedural due process." It explained the conclusion thus:

> For qualified recipients, welfare provides the means to obtain essential food, clothing, housing, and medical care. . . . Thus the crucial factor in this context—a factor not present in the case of the blacklisted government contractor, the discharged government employee, [or] the taxpayer denied a tax exemption, [all of whom, under the case law, had no constitutional right to prior hearings]—is that termination of pending resolution of a controversy over eligibility may deprive an *eligible* recipient of the very means by which to live while he waits. . . .

> Moreover, important government interests are promoted by affording recipients a pre-termination evidentiary hearing. From its founding, the nation's basic commitment has been to foster the dignity and well-being of all persons within its borders. We have come to recognize that forces not within the control of the poor contribute to their poverty. [P]ublic assistance, then is not mere charity, but a means to "promote the general welfare, and secure the blessings of liberty to ourselves and our posterity. . . ."

> [The state] does not challenge the force of these considerations but argues that they are outweighed by countervailing government interests in conserving fiscal and administrative resources. [S]ummary adjudication protects the public fisc by stopping payments promptly upon discovery of reason to believe that a recipient is no longer eligible. [It] also conserves both the fisc and administrative time and energy by reducing the number of evidentiary hearings actually held.

> We agree with the district court, however, that these governmental interests are not overriding in the welfare context. The requirement of a prior hearing doubtless involves some greater expense, and the benefits paid to ineligible recipients pending decision at the hearing probably cannot be recouped, since these recipients are likely to be judgment-proof. But the state is not without weapons to minimize these increased costs. Much of the drain on fiscal and administrative resources can be reduced by developing procedures for prompt pre-termination facilities and by skillful use of personnel and facilities. . . .

> [The Court went on to describe the type of hearing required. This portion of the opinion is dealt with in the section on the "process that is due," below.]

Justice Black dissented:

> [I] do not think that the fourteenth amendment should be given such an unnecessarily broad construction. That amendment came into being primarily to protect Negroes from discrimination. [T]he Court, however, . . . in effect says the failure of the government to pay a promised charitable installment to an individual deprives that individual of *his own property*, in violation of the due process clause of the fourteenth amendment. It somewhat strains credulity to say that the government's promise of charity to an individual is properly belonging to that individual when the government denies that the individual is

honestly entitled to receive such a payment.

[2] Negligence By Government

PROBLEM B

NEGLIGENT (OR RECKLESS) FAILURE TO PREVENT CHILD ABUSE. The state placed two-year-old Tommy McDaniel in the foster care of Mr. and Mrs. Don Crozet. On April 2, Deborah Watkins, a caseworker with the Children's Protective Services Division of the State Department of Human Services, visited the foster home in response to reports by neighbors alleging abuse of Tommy. She found that Tommy had various burns, lacerations, contusions, and abrasions, and she heard Mr. Crozet's explanation that Tommy received these injuries by falling from his crib and playing near the stove. Ms. Watkins scheduled a follow-up visit the next month. However, five days later, on April 7, Tommy was dead, and Don Crozet was charged with his murder. The autopsy showed that Tommy died of massive subdural hemorrhage and internal injuries due to severe blows upon his face and abdomen and had numerous cigarette burns on his back, chest, face, penis, and scrotum. [This problem, too, is based upon no particular case but reflects circumstances that happen occasionally in many areas of the country. In fact, as the First Edition of this book was going to press, the Supreme Court granted certiorari in a remarkably similar case. *Deshaney v. Winnebago County Department of Social Services*, 489 U.S. 189 (1988). The decision in *DeShaney* is discussed in Chapter 9 because it was decided as a substantive due process analysis.] Do Tommy's natural parents have a claim against the state based upon its deprivation of his life without procedural due process by requiring his placement in the foster home and negligently (or recklessly) requiring his continued presence there? Consider the following decisions.

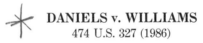

DANIELS v. WILLIAMS
474 U.S. 327 (1986)

Justice Rehnquist delivered the opinion of the Court.

[Daniels slipped on a pillow while he was an inmate at the Richmond, Virginia city jail. He sued Williams, a correctional deputy, on the allegation that Williams negligently left the pillow on the stairs. Daniels claimed that Williams' negligence "deprived" him of his "liberty" interest in freedom from bodily injury. Here, although accepting the existence of this liberty interest, the Supreme Court holds that its deprivation by a negligent act does not violate the Due Process Clause.]

[The Court begins its analysis by citing *Parratt v. Taylor*, 451 U.S. 527 (1981), in which Nebraska prison officials negligently lost an inmate's hobby kit. The *Parratt* Court held that this loss, "even though negligently caused, amounted to a deprivation" under the Due Process Clause. The *Parratt* Court also held, however, that since the inmate had available to him state procedures that could fully redress the deprivation by damages, there was no due process violation. In the present case, the Court's opinion points out that Williams had a potential sovereign immunity defense to Daniels' suit, and therefore it was not certain that the negligent deprivation would be redressed.]

[In *Parratt v. Taylor*], Justice Powell, concurring in the result, criticized the majority for "pass[ing] over" [the] important question of the state of mind required to constitute a "deprivation" of property. He argued that negligent acts by state officials, though causing loss of property, are not actionable under the Due Process Clause. To Justice Powell, mere negligence could not "wor[k] a deprivation in the *constitutional sense*." Not only does the word "deprive" in the Due Process Clause connote more than a negligent act, but we should not "open the federal courts to lawsuits where there has been no affirmative abuse of power. . . ." Upon reflection, we agree and overrule

Parratt to the extent that it states that mere lack of due care by a state official may "deprive" an individual of life, liberty or property under the Fourteenth Amendment.

The Due Process Clause of the Fourteenth Amendment provides: "[N]or shall any State deprive any person of life, liberty, or property, without due process of law." Historically, this guarantee of due process has been applied to *deliberate* decisions of government officials to deprive a person of life, liberty or property. . . . No decision of this Court before *Parratt* supported the view that negligent conduct by a state official, even though causing injury, constitutes a deprivation under the Due Process Clause. The history reflects the traditional and common-sense notion that the Due Process Clause, like its forebear in the Magna Carta, was " 'intended to secure the individual from the arbitrary exercise of the powers of government.' " . . . By requiring the government to follow appropriate procedures when its agents decide to "deprive any person of life, liberty, or property," the Due Process Clause promotes fairness in such decisions. And . . . it serves to prevent governmental power from being "used for purposes of oppression. . . ."

We think that the actions of prison custodians in leaving a pillow on the prison stairs, or mislaying an inmate's property, are quite remote from the concerns just discussed. Far from an abuse of power, lack of due care suggests no more than a failure to measure up to the conduct of a reasonable person. To hold that injury caused by such conduct is a deprivation within the meaning of the Fourteenth Amendment would trivialize the centuries-old principle of due process of law. . . .

NOTES AND QUESTIONS

(1) *More Serious Injury— Recklessness: Davidson v. Cannon, 474 U.S. 344 (1986).* Davidson sent a note reporting another inmate's threat. Prison officials took no action, and the other inmate seriously injured Davidson with a fork. The majority of the Supreme Court, per Justice Rehnquist, held that "the principles enunciated in *Daniels* [are] controlling here." The Court therefore denied Davidson's claim. Justice Brennan dissented, concluding that although merely negligent conduct could not work a constitutional deprivation, "I do believe . . . that official conduct which causes personal injury due to recklessness or deliberate indifference, does deprive a victim of liberty within the meaning of the fourteenth amendment." Justice Blackmun, joined by Justice Marshall, also dissented:

> When the State of New Jersey put Robert Davidson in its prison, it stripped him of all means of self protection. It forbade his access to a weapon . . . it forbade his fighting back. . . . It blocked all avenues of escape. . . .
>
> While I concur in the judgment in *Daniels*, I do not join the Court in extending that result to this case. It is one thing to hold that a commonplace slip and fall [d]oes not rise to the dignified level of a constitutional violation. [I]n these circumstances, I feel that Davidson was deprived of liberty by the negligence of the prison officials. Moreover, the acts of state officials in this case may well have risen to the level of recklessness.

Davidson was decided as the "companion" decision to *Daniels.* Taken together, they hold that neither negligence nor recklessness is sufficient to constitute a "deprivation" for purposes of the procedural due process doctrine.

(2) *Recklessness or "Deliberate Indifference to Serious . . . Need": Estelle v. Gamble, 429 U.S. 97 (1976).* In *Gamble,* a prison inmate claimed a due process violation owing to aggravation of his condition due to lack of medical care. The Court held that mere medical malpractice, although likely to state a claim under state law, could not rise to the level of a constitutional violation. However, "deliberate indifference" to a prisoner's "serious medical need" was sufficient to constitute cruel and unusual punishment under the prohibitions of the Eighth Amendment. Should this standard, which sometimes is regarded as indistinguishable from "recklessness," suffice to define

a due process deprivation? Is the holding consistent with the reasoning, in *Daniels*, that the due process clause is concerned with "abuse of power" by government? *See also City of Canton v. Harris*, 489 U.S. 378 (1989) (city's failure to offer adequate training to police officers may create liability under Due Process Clause, but is actionable only where the failure to train amounts to "deliberate indifference" to the constitutional rights of persons with whom the police may come into contact).

[C]   What Process Is "Due" (i.e., Constitutionally Required)?

INTRODUCTORY NOTE

Having examined the liberty or property interests whose deprivation will trigger due process, we turn now to the question: "What process is due" (*i.e.*, constitutionally required)? The answer always depends on the circumstances, because due process is a flexible concept. Here, although there are other possible components, we consider the following elements: (1) notice; (2) a "hearing"; (3) proof, evidence and discovery; (4) counsel; (5) an ostensibly "impartial" factfinder; (6) freedom from arbitrary application of law; (7) appeal; and (8) a timely remedy. As a general matter, the standard is set forth in the case below.

MATHEWS v. ELDRIDGE
424 U.S. 319 (1976)

MR. JUSTICE POWELL delivered the opinion of the Court.

[The Court here holds that termination of disability benefits under the Social Security Act, based upon a determination of recovery, does not require a pre-termination hearing. The Act required a recipient initially to demonstrate that he is eligible and to bear the continuing burden of showing impairment of such severity that he cannot perform any kind of gainful work. The Act and regulations provided recipients with pre-termination notice and an opportunity to present information, together with a right to a full post-termination hearing.]

In recent years this Court increasingly has had occasion to consider the extent to which due process requires an evidentiary hearing prior to the deprivation of some type of property interest even if such a hearing is provided thereafter. In only one case, *Goldberg v. Kelly*, has the Court held that a hearing closely approximating a judicial trial is necessary. In other cases requiring some type of pretermination hearing as a matter of constitutional right the Court has spoken sparingly about the requisite procedures. . . . More recently, in *Arnett v. Kennedy*, we sustained the validity of procedures by which a federal employee could be dismissed for cause. [F]ollowing dismissal, an evidentiary hearing was provided.

These decisions underscore the truism that "'[d]ue process,' unlike some legal rules, is not a technical conception with a fixed content unrelated to time, place and circumstances. . . ." "[D]ue process is flexible and calls for such procedural protections as the particular situation demands." . . .

[M]ore precisely, our prior decisions indicate that identification of the specific dictates of due process generally requires consideration of three distinct factors: First, the private interest that will be affected by the official action; second, the risk of an erroneous deprivation of such interest through the procedures used, and the probable value, if any, of additional or substitute procedural safeguards; and finally, the Government's interest, including the function involved and the fiscal and administrative burdens that the additional or substitute procedural requirement would entail. *See, e.g., Goldberg v. Kelly, supra.* . . .

Despite the elaborate character of the administrative procedures provided by the Secretary, the courts below held them to be constitutionally inadequate, concluding that due process requires an evidentiary hearing prior to termination. In light of the private and governmental interests at stake here and the nature of the existing procedures, we think this was error.

Since a recipient whose benefits are terminated is awarded full retroactive relief if he ultimately prevails, his sole interest is in the uninterrupted receipt of this source of income pending final administrative decision of his claim. His potential injury is thus similar in nature to that of the welfare recipient in *Goldberg*. . . .

Only in *Goldberg* has the Court held that due process requires an evidentiary hearing prior to a temporary deprivation. It was emphasized there that welfare assistance is given to persons on the very margin of subsistence. . . . Eligibility for disability benefits, in contrast, is not based upon financial need. Indeed, it is wholly unrelated to the worker's income or support from many other sources. . . .

As *Goldberg* illustrates, the degree of potential deprivation that may be created by a particular decision is a factor to be considered in assessing the validity of any administrative decisionmaking process. The potential deprivation here is generally likely to be less than in *Goldberg*, although the degree of difference can be overstated. . . .

An additional factor to be considered here is the fairness and reliability of the existing pretermination procedures, and the probable value, if any, of additional procedural safeguards. . . . In order to remain eligible for benefits the disabled worker must demonstrate by means of "medically acceptable clinical and laboratory diagnostic techniques," 42 U.S.C. § 423(d)(3), that he is unable "to engage in any substantial gainful activity by reason of any *medically determinable* physical or mental impairment . . ." § 423(d)(1)(A) (emphasis supplied). In short, a medical assessment of the worker's physical or mental condition is required. This is a more sharply focused and easily documented decision than the typical determination of welfare entitlement.

[T]o be sure, credibility and veracity may be a factor in the ultimate disability assessment in some cases. But procedural due process rules are shaped by the risk of error inherent in the truthfinding process as applied to the generality of cases, not the rare exceptions. The potential value of an evidentiary hearing, or even oral presentation to the decisionmaker, is substantially less in this context than in *Goldberg*. . . .

In striking the appropriate due process balance the final factor to be assessed is the public interest. This includes the administrative burden and other societal costs that would be associated with requiring, as a matter of constitutional right, an evidentiary hearing upon demand in all cases prior to the termination of disability benefits. . . .

Financial cost alone is not a controlling weight in determining whether due process requires a particular procedural safeguard prior to some administrative decision. But the Government's interest, and hence that of the public, in conserving scarce fiscal and administrative resources is a factor that must be weighed. At some point the benefit of an additional safeguard to the individual affected by the administrative action and to society in terms of increased assurance that the action is just, may be outweighed by the cost. Significantly, the cost of protecting those whom the preliminary administrative process has identified as likely to be found undeserving may in the end come out of the pockets of the deserving since resources available for any particular program of social welfare are not unlimited. . . .

But more is implicated in cases of this type than ad hoc weighing of fiscal and administrative burdens against the interests of a particular category of claimants. The ultimate balance involves a determination as to when, under our constitutional system, judicial-type procedures must be imposed upon administrative action to assure fairness. . . . In assessing what process is due in this case, substantial weight must be given to the good-faith judgments of the individuals charged by Congress with the administration of social welfare programs that the procedures they have provided assure fair consideration of the entitlement claims of individuals. This is especially so where, as here, the prescribed procedures not only provide the claimant with an effective process for asserting his claim prior to any administrative action, but also assure a right to an evidentiary hearing, as well as to subsequent judicial review, before the denial of his claim becomes final.

We conclude that an evidentiary hearing is not required prior to the termination of disability benefits and that the present administrative procedures fully comport with due process.

The judgment of the Court of Appeals is

Reversed.

MR. JUSTICE BRENNAN, with whom MR. JUSTICE MARSHALL concurs, dissenting.

[T]he Court's consideration that a discontinuance of disability benefits may cause the recipient to suffer only a limited deprivation is no argument. It is speculative. Moreover, the very legislative determination to provide disability benefits, without any prerequisite determination of need in fact, presumes a need by the recipient which is not this Court's function to denigrate. Indeed, in the present case, it is indicated that because disability benefits were terminated there was a foreclosure upon the Eldridge home and the family's furniture was repossessed, forcing Eldridge, his wife, and their children to sleep in one bed. Finally, it is also no argument that a worker, who has been placed in the untenable position of having been denied disability benefits, may still seek other forms of public assistance.

NOTES AND QUESTIONS

(1) *The Three-Part Standard for Determining What Procedures Are Constitutionally Required: Mathews v. Eldridge, 424 U.S. 319 (1976).* The Burger Court held that the determination of what process is due would be made by balancing three factors: (1) the private interest affected by state action; (2) the risk of erroneous deprivation from the existing procedures; and (3) the Government's interest, including fiscal and administrative burdens, that additional procedural protections (*e.g.*, providing an expert witness) would entail. This three-part balancing standard has been used, with some incidental modifications, since 1976. See the *Loudermill* decision below.

(2) *When Is a Pre-Termination Hearing Required, and of What Must It Consist?: Cleveland Board of Education v. Loudermill, 470 U.S. 532 (1985).* The Court held that Loudermill, who was fired for allegedly dishonestly answering that he was not an ex-felon when in fact he was, had a liberty or property interest in his employment as a security guard for the Board of Education. [That holding is set forth in the previous section.] The Court also applied the *Mathews v. Eldridge* criteria to determine that a pre-termination hearing was required and to describe its requirements:

> [The relevant factors] are the private interest in retaining employment, the governmental interest in the expeditious removal of unsatisfactory employees and the avoidance of administrative burdens, and the risk of an erroneous termination. *See Mathews v. Eldridge.* . . .
>
> First, the significance of the private interest in retaining employment cannot be gainsaid. . . .
>
> Second, some opportunity for the employee to present his side of the case is recurringly of obvious value in reaching an accurate decision.
>
> [Third], [t]he governmental interest in immediate termination does not outweigh these interests. [T]he employer shares the employee's interest in avoiding disruption and erroneous decisions; and until the matter is settled, the employee would continue to receive the benefit of the employee's labors. . . .

The foregoing considerations indicate that the pre-termination "hearing," though necessary, need not be elaborate. . . . *Mathews v. Eldridge.* . . .

[T]he tenured public employee is entitled to oral or written notice of the charges against him, an explanation of the employer's evidence, and an opportunity to present his side of the story. [T]o require more than this prior to termination would intrude to an unwarranted extent on the government's interest in quickly removing an unsatisfactory employee.

Justice Rehnquist dissented: "[The] customary 'balancing' inquiry conducted by the Court in this case reaches a result that is quite unobjectionable, but it seems to me that it is devoid of any principles which will either instruct or endure. [O]ne way to avoid this subjective and varying interpretation . . . is to hold that one who avails himself of government entitlements accepts the grant . . . along with its inherent limitations."

(3) *Due Process Without a Hearing?* Is it possible for due process to be satisfied with no hearing at all, even though impairment of a liberty or property interest is at stake? Consider the following cases.

INGRAHAM v. WRIGHT, 430 U.S. 651 (1977). The Court, per Justice Powell, held in Ingraham that the use of corporal punishment (*i.e.*, paddling) of students as a means of maintaining school discipline did not constitute cruel and unusual punishment and that the Due Process Clause did not require prior notice, an opportunity to be heard, or a hearing of any kind:

[T]eachers and school authorities are unlikely to inflict corporal punishment unnecessarily or excessively when a possible consequence of doing so is the institution of civil or criminal proceedings against them. . . .

But even if the need for advance procedural safeguards were clear, the question would remain whether the incremental benefit could justify the cost. . . .

[A] universal constitutional requirement would significantly burden the use of corporal punishment as a disciplinary measure. Hearings-even informal hearings-require time, personnel, and a diversion of attention from normal school pursuits. [T]eachers . . . may well prefer to rely on other disciplinary measures—which they may view as less effective—rather than confront the possible disruption that prior notice and a hearing may entail. . . .

[A]s noted in *Goss v. Lopez*, . . .: "Events calling for discipline are frequent occurrences and sometimes require immediate, effective action. . . ."

"At some point the benefit of an additional safeguard to the individual affected . . . and to society in terms of increased assurance that the action is just, may be outweighed by the cost." *Mathews v. Eldridge.* [W]e think that point has been reached in this case.

Justice White, joined by Justices Brennan, Marshall, and Stevens, dissented. As for the Due Process Clause, the dissenters concluded that it required a hearing: "not an 'elaborate hearing' before a neutral party, but simply 'an informal give-and-take between student and disciplinarian' " which gives the student "an opportunity to explain his version of the facts."

[1] Notice

NOTES AND QUESTIONS

(1) *Notice That is "Reasonably Calculated" to Apprise the Affected Person: The Progeny of Mullane v. Central Hanover Bank & Trust Co., 339 U.S. 306 (1950).* In *Mullane*, the Court held that New York could not cut off the rights of trust beneficiaries without "notice reasonably calculated, under all the circumstances, to apprise interested parties of the pendency of the action and afford them an opportunity to present their

objections." The Court interpreted this requirement in *Greene v. Lindsey*, 456 U.S. 444 (1982), to disallow service by posting on the tenant's door in eviction proceedings, since notices were "not infrequently" removed by children. Posting should be accompanied by mailed service, said the Court.

The Court followed the *Mullane* standard in *Jones v. Flowers*, 547 U.S. 220 (2006), holding that the notice sent by certified mail to an Arkansas taxpayer whose property was subject to a tax sale was insufficient when the certified mail was returned to the taxing authority as "unclaimed."

(2) *What Should Be Contained in the Notice?: Aguchak v. Montgomery Ward Co., 520 P.2d 1352 (Alaska 1974).* The Alaska Supreme Court, interpreting the Alaska constitutional due process clause, used *Mullane's* reasoning to require that the "form of summons . . . [adequately] inform . . . [the affected persons] of their rights and obligations in small claims proceedings. . . ." Although "[u]ndue expenses of collection will be passed on to the consumer through scarce and inexpensive credit," the Court nevertheless required that small claims defendants be apprised in terms understandable to a lay person of their rights after receipt of summons, including the right to request a change of venue. Is this decision correct? Must a defendant who may be a lay person be apprised of every important legal right that he might have, in terminology understandable to a lay person?

(3) *Prejudgment Seizure: When Can It Be Done Without Notice?— Connecticut v. Doehr, 501 U.S. 1 (1991).* Seizure by attachment, garnishment, sequestration or similar remedies obviously causes severe injury to some debtors, who might be able to avoid erroneous use of the remedy if they have notice. But creditors, in many instances, also have property interests at stake that may be lost if they are required to provide notice. How should this conflict be reconciled? The Supreme Court's decisions enable creditors to use *ex parte* seizure without notice in narrow instances, requiring sworn supporting testimony, neutral decisionmaking, and compelling circumstances. The *Doehr* case demonstrates that the absence of these factors may make seizure without notice unconstitutional.

(4) *An Unduly Expensive Notice Requirement May Comply With the Recipient's Due Process Rights But Violate Those of the Claimant: Boddie v. Connecticut, 401 U.S. 371 (1971).* The *Boddie* case brings home the point that due process must be governed by a balancing approach, at least in some applications. The Court held unconstitutional a system that required an average fee of $60, including service, to bring a divorce action, as applied to an indigent. What is the solution to this difficulty? Must the state and its taxpayers shoulder the burden by paying for service, or should it use less expensive service (which may be less likely to reach the defendant and less likely to provide notice)?

[2] A "Hearing"

GOLDBERG v. KELLY, 397 U.S. 254 (1970). The Court in *Goldberg* required a pre-termination hearing for welfare recipients. That portion of the opinion is contained in the preceding section. In these excerpts, the Court, per Justice Brennan, describes the kind of hearing that is required:

> We also agree with the district court, however, that the pre-termination hearing need not take the form of a judicial or a quasi-judicial trial. We bear in mind that the statutory [post-termination] "fair hearing" will provide the recipient with a full administrative review. Accordingly, the pretermination hearing has one function only: to produce an initial determination of the validity of the Welfare Department's grounds . . . in order to protect a recipient against an erroneous termination of his benefits. . . .

> [T]he hearing must be "at a meaningful time and in a meaningful manner." [I]n the present context, these principles require that a recipient have timely

and adequate notice detailing the reasons for a proposed termination, and an effective opportunity to defend by confronting any adverse witnesses and by presenting his own arguments and evidence orally. . . .

The City's procedures presently do not permit recipients to appear personally. . . . Thus a recipient is not permitted to present evidence to [the welfare] official orally, or to confront or cross-examine adverse witnesses. These omissions are fatal to the constitutional adequacy of the procedures.

The opportunity to be heard must be tailored to the capacities and circumstances of those who are to be heard. [W]ritten submissions are an unrealistic option for most recipients, who lack the educational attainment necessary to write effectively and who cannot obtain professional assistance. Moreover, written submissions do not afford the flexibility of oral presentations. . . .

[W]e do not say that counsel must be provided at the pre- termination hearing, but only that the recipient must be allowed to retain an attorney if he so desires. . . .

Finally, the decisionmaker's conclusion as to a recipient's eligibility must rest solely on the legal rules and evidence adduced at the hearing. [T]o demonstrate compliance with this elementary requirement, the decisionmaker should state the reasons for his determination and indicate the evidence he relied on, . . . though his statement need not amount to a full opinion or even formal findings of fact and conclusions of law. And, of course, an impartial decisionmaker is essential. [W]e agree with the district court that prior involvement in some aspects of a case will not necessarily bar a Welfare official from acting as a decisionmaker. He should not, however, have participated in making the determination under review. . . .

NOTES AND QUESTIONS

(1) *Decisions Unsuited to Resolution in a "Hearing": Board of Curators v. Horowitz, 435 U.S. 78 (1978).* In *Ingraham, supra,* the majority found no requirement for a hearing, essentially because the risk of erroneous deprivation was slight and the government's interest in avoiding a hearing was significant because of the need for prompt action. *Cf.* Note, *University Disciplinary Process: What's Fair, What's Due, and What You Don't Get,* 96 YALE L.J. 2132 (1987). What about a case in which the consequences of erroneous deprivation are severe and in which there is no need for prompt action, but the decision simply is one that is unsuited to resolution in a hearing? In *Horowitz, supra,* a medical student was dismissed during her final year of study for failure to meet academic standards. The Court detailed a lengthy history of inadequate clinical performance, punctuated by faculty reviews and warnings. The Court, per Justice Rehnquist, upheld the dismissal even though the student had not been given a "hearing" as such:

> Academic evaluations of a student, in contrast to disciplinary determinations, bear little resemblance to the judicial and administrative fact-finding proceedings to which we have traditionally attached a full-hearing requirement. [S]uch a judgment is by its nature more subjective and evaluative than the typical factual questions presented in the average disciplinary decision. Like the decision of an individual professor as to the proper grade for a student in his course, the determination whether to dismiss a student for academic reasons requires an expert evaluation of cumulative information and is not readily adapted to the procedural tools of judicial or administrative decisionmaking.

(2) *Updating Horowitz: Regents of the University of Michigan v. Ewing, 474 U.S. 214 (1985).* On a required national exam, Ewing received the lowest score ever recorded in the history of his program, and the school's Promotion and Review Board determined

not to allow him to re-take the examination even though its past practice had been to permit re-taking. A unanimous Court, per Stevens, J., upheld this action:

> [E]wing's failure of his medical boards, in the words of one of his professors, "merely culminate[d] a series of deficiencies. . . . In many ways, it's the straw that broke the camel's back." [H]is dismissal . . . rested on an academic judgment that is not beyond the pale of reasoned academic decisionmaking when viewed against the background of his entire career at the university. . . .

(3) *Is a "Hearing" Required Under Civil Forfeiture Provisions of Federal Anti-Drug Statutes?: United States v. James Daniel Good Real Property, 510 U.S. 43 (1993).* Good had pled guilty to a state drug charge and received a criminal sentence, including incarceration. Some four years after the drugs were found, the federal prosecutors instituted, pursuant to a federal statute, an *in rem* civil forfeiture action regarding Good's home—because of its role in the commission of a federal drug offense. After the federal authorities established, in an *ex parte* proceeding, probable cause to believe the real property was subject to the forfeiture provision, the federal authorities seized the rental proceeds of Good's home without prior notice to Good or without any adversarial hearing. Good contended that the forfeiture procedure violated his procedural due process rights since it denied him a hearing. The Court, per Justice Kennedy, agreed at least regarding real property, which is not moveable, noting that the Court's "precedents establish the general rule that individuals must receive notice and an opportunity to be heard before the Government deprives them of property," applying the *Mathews v. Eldridge* three-part standard. Four Justices dissented from, to use Chief Justice Rehnquist's terms, the "majority's expansive application of *Mathews.*"

(4) *Procedural Due Process Guarantee Does Not, By Itself, Protect a So-Called "Innocent" Spouse's Ownership Interest in an Automobile Against Civil Forfeiture: Bennis v. Michigan, 516 U.S. 442 (1996).* After the husband was convicted of "indecency" with a prostitute in an automobile jointly-owned by husband and wife, the prosecution sought a civil forfeiture of the car under Michigan's public nuisance "abatement" statute. Even though the wife had no knowledge of her husband's use of the car, the trial court did not allow her any offset for her ownership interest. The wife argued that, under procedural due process, she should be permitted to resist the abatement by showing she did not know about her husband's use of the car. The Supreme Court, per Chief Justice Rehnquist, rejected the wife's "innocent-owner" argument, reasoning that the forfeiture scheme, although harsh in some circumstances, served a legitimate governmental interest in deterring "illegal activity that contributes to neighborhood deterioration and unsafe streets." Four Justices dissented.

(5) *The Application of the Mathews Standard to Enemy Combatant Detainees: Hamdi v. Rumsfeld, 542 U.S. 507 (2004).* In one of the three "enemy combatant detainee" decisions, Hamdi, age 20, was a United States citizen captured in Afghanistan after the start of hostilities against the Taliban and al Qaeda. The federal government contended that he fought for the Taliban; his family contended that he was only in Afghanistan to do charitable relief work. The government had detained Hamdi at a series of locations; when his citizenship was discovered, he was held incommunicado in military brigs on U.S. territory. His family filed for a writ of habeas corpus. The President contended that the Congressional authorization of force, combined with the Executive commander-in-chief power, justified the detention. At the habeas hearing, the government had produced a declaration by a Defense Department official, the Mobbs Declaration, and the government contended that the Mobbs Declaration was all the "hearing" to which Hamdi was entitled. The court of appeals had agreed with the government. The Supreme Court, per Justice O'Connor's plurality opinion, disagreed with the Bush Administration and reversed.

In *Hamdi*, eight of the Justices rejected the Bush Administration's position that it could detain all enemy combatants indefinitely without permitting a hearing in a federal court. There were several competing rationales, however, among the eight Justices.

For present purposes, Justice O'Connor's plurality determined that Hamdi, as a U.S. citizen, was entitled to procedural due process. Applying the *Mathews* three-part balancing standard, the plurality held that Hamdi had to be given "notice of the factual basis for his classification," and a "fair opportunity to rebut the government's factual assertions before a neutral decisionmaker." The *Hamdi* Court referred to the *Mathews* standard as the "ordinary mechanism that we use for balancing such serious competing interests. . . ."

Justices Souter (and Ginsburg) concurred in the judgment but would have used broader grounds. Justice Scalia (for Justice Stevens) dissented from the O'Connor opinion but would also have reversed the lower court.

[3]　Proof by the Opponent, Evidence Development, and Discovery

SANTOSKY v. KRAMER, 455 U.S. 745 (1982). A New York court found that the Santoskys had permanently neglected their children, and it terminated their parental rights. The court applied the New York Family Court Act, which required only a "fair preponderance of the evidence," rather than a higher standard of proof sought by the Santoskys. The Supreme Court, per Justice Blackmun, reversed, requiring at least "clear and convincing evidence." The Court began by setting out the three factors specified by *Mathews v. Eldridge:* the private interests affected; the risk of error; and the countervailing government interests favoring the procedure. It concluded:

> [W]hen the state initiates a parental rights termination proceeding, it seeks not merely to infringe [a] fundamental liberty interest, but to end it. "[A] parent's interest in the accuracy and justice of a decision to terminate his or her parental status is, therefore, a commanding one."

> Thus, the first *Eldridge* factor—the private interest affected—weighs heavily against the use of the preponderance standard. . . .

> [W]e next must consider both the risk of erroneous deprivation of private interests resulting from use of a "fair preponderance" standard and the "likelihood that a higher evidentiary standard would reduce that risk. . . ."

> [A]n elevated standard of proof in a parental rights termination proceeding would alleviate "the possible risk that a factfinder might decide to [deprive] an individual based solely on a few isolated instances of unusual conduct [or] idiosyncratic behavior. . . ."

> Two state interests are at stake in parental rights termination proceedings—a *parens patriae* interest in preserving and promoting the welfare of the child and a fiscal and administrative interest in reducing the cost and burden of such proceedings. A standard of proof more strict than preponderance of the evidence is consistent with both interests. . . .

> The state's interests in finding the child an alternative permanent home arises only "when it is *clear* that the natural parent cannot or will not provide a normal family home for the child. . . ."

> [A] stricter standard of proof would reduce factual error without imposing substantial fiscal burdens upon the state. [T]hirty-five states already have adopted a higher standard by statute or court decision without apparent effect on the speed, form, or cost of their factfinding proceedings. . . .

> [T]he next question, then, is whether a "beyond a reasonable doubt" or a "clear and convincing" standard is constitutionally mandated. . . .

> [T]ermination proceedings often require the factfinder to evaluate medical and psychiatric testimony and to decide issues difficult to prove to a level of absolute certainty, such as lack of parental motive, absence of affection between parent and child, and failure of parental foresight and progress. [A] reasonable-

doubt standard would erect an unreasonable barrier to state efforts to free permanently neglected children for adoption.

Justice Rehnquist, joined by Chief Justice Burger and Justices White and O'Connor, dissented. "The state has an urgent interest in the welfare of the child." When the interests of the child and the state in a stable, nurturing home life are balanced against the interests of the parents, "it cannot be said that either set of interests is so clearly paramount as to require that the risk of error be allocated to one side or the other."

NOTES AND QUESTIONS

(1) *Did the Majority Miss the Point? Doesn't the Child Have an Interest That Also Is Commanding and of "Heavy" Weight, Namely the Interest in Not Being Abused, Beaten, or Neglected?* This is the point of the dissent. Perhaps one of the defects of the *Matthews v. Eldridge* approach is that it depends on correct evaluation of all the interests, including those of late children, who usually cannot hire lawyers.

(2) *Child Abuse Prevention: Can the State Remove the Child From the Environment on the Basis of Probabilities?* Often, a child may display injuries that create a probability of intentional abuse by a parent, but they do not furnish "clear" proof of abuse. In such circumstances, can the state remove the child temporarily as an emergency measure? If so, why can't it determine on the basis of the same evidence that return of the child to the same environment is excessively dangerous? Notice what Blackmun, J.'s, opinion means in such circumstances: The state must return the child to see whether she suffers further injuries, which will be detectable only by caseworker visits. Does the majority correctly analyze the "private" interest, or has it neglected to consider the private interests of the child? Is the dissent correct in its claim that there is no principled way to favor one interest over the other? *Cf.* Bell, *Decision Theory and Due Process: A Critique of the Supreme Court's Lawmaking for Burdens-of-Proof*, 78 J. CRIM. L. & CRIMINOLOGY 557 (1987); Note, *A Pre-Removal Hearing in Custody Decisions: Protecting the Foster Child*, 4 COOLEY L. REV. 375 (1987).

(3) *Cases In Which the State Has Opted for Burdening the Claimant with Clear and Convincing Evidence Requirements: Ohio v. Akron Center for Reproductive Health; Cruzan v. Director.* In the next chapter, we shall encounter other cases presenting a different, though related question: When may the state opt to burden a claimant with a clear and convincing proof requirement, as against the argument that it thus imposes an unconstitutional burden on a protected liberty interest? In *Akron*, the Court upheld a clear and convincing proof requirement for a minor seeking to avoid parental notification before obtaining an abortion; in *Cruzan*, it upheld the same standard for exercise of the right to withhold life support on behalf of an incompetent.

(4) *A Due Process Right to Discovery?: Brock v. Roadway Express, Inc., 481 U.S. 252 1740 (1987).* Pursuant to the Surface Transportation Assistance Act, the Secretary of Labor required Roadway Express to reinstate a discharged employee, upon a finding of reasonable cause to believe that the employee was discharged for refusing to violate safety standards or for whistle-blowing. The statute provided that, before such an order, the Secretary must give notice to the employer, and it must conduct an "expeditious" post-termination hearing. A plurality of the Court, per Justice Marshall, held that the statute reflected "a careful balance of the relative interests of the government, employee, and employer" and that the denial of a full pre-termination proceeding was not unconstitutional. Nevertheless, it concluded that the procedure was unconstitutional because it did not require the Secretary to inform the employer of the relevant evidence before the post-termination hearing:

> The district court correctly held that the Secretary's preliminary reinstatement order was unconstitutionally imposed in this case because Roadway was not informed of the relevant evidence supporting [the employee's] complaint and therefore was deprived of an opportunity to prepare a meaningful response. . . .

Is this decision, effectively holding that some amount of discovery is a requisite of due process, correct? Justice White, joined by Chief Justice Rehnquist and Justice Scalia, dissented. He concluded: "I would not ignore the strong interest the government may have in particular cases in not turning over the supporting information, including the names of the employees who spoke to the government and who corroborated [the employee's] claims."

[4] Counsel (And Funds For Expert Witnesses?)

LASSITER v. DEPARTMENT OF SOCIAL SERVICES, 452 U.S. 18 (1981). Lassiter, having been convicted of a brutal murder, had her parental rights terminated because she had "willfully left [her infant son] in foster care for more than two consecutive years" without attempting to correct the conditions that led to the foster care. Lassiter was indigent, and she claimed a due process denial in that the state was not required to provide counsel for her in the termination proceeding. The Supreme Court, per Justice Stewart, concluded that although counsel might well be required in some "complex" termination proceedings, the failure to appoint counsel here did not violate due process since there were no allegations upon which criminal charges could be based, no expert witnesses testified, there were no specially troublesome points of law, and counsel could not have made a "determinative" difference:

> The dispositive question . . . is whether the three *Eldridge* factors, when weighed against the presumption that there is no right to appointed counsel in the absence of at least a potential deprivation of physical liberty, suffice to rebut that presumption and thus to lead to the conclusion that the due process clause requires the appointment of counsel when a state seeks to terminate an indigent's parental status. [T]he parent's interest is an extremely important one (and may be supplemented by the dangers of criminal liability inherent in some termination proceedings); the state shares with the parent an interest in a correct decision, has a relatively weak pecuniary interest, and, in some but not all cases, has a possibly strong interest in informal procedures; and the complexity of the proceeding and the incapacity of the uncounselled parent could be, but would not always be, great enough to make the risk of an erroneous deprivation of the parent's rights insupportably high.

> If, in a given case, the parent's interests were at their strongest, the state's interests were at their weakest, and the risks of error were at their peak, it could not be said that the *Eldridge* factors did not overcome the presumption against the right to appointed counsel, and [due process might therefore require counsel]. But [n]either can we say that the Constitution requires the appointment of counsel in every parental termination proceeding. . . .

Justice Blackmun, joined by Justices Brennan and Marshall, dissented. They saw the parent's interest as "unique": "[T]he state's aim is not simply to influence the parent-child relationship but to *extinguish* it." In the view of the dissenters, the other two *Eldridge* factors also supported appointment of counsel, because the risk of erroneous deprivation without counsel was high and the state's interests "do not tip the scale against providing appointed counsel."

NOTES AND QUESTIONS

(1) *When Is Appointed Counsel Required?* Notice that the Court implies that appointment of counsel might be required in some, but not all, parental termination cases. Can you devise a general test to determine when due process requires appointment of counsel?

(2) *When Must the State Provide an Affected Person With An Expert Witness or Testing?: Little v. Streater, 452 U.S. 1 (1981).* The state law in the *Little* case made the mother's prima facie testimony on paternity virtually conclusive, and also made the

putative father's own testimony insufficient as a matter of law to overcome it. It did so in the face of inexpensive tests that could unambiguously negate paternity and for which the state could have recovered most of the relatively small cost from a federally funded program. The Court held that the state's refusal to pay the cost of these blood tests deprived a paternity suit defendant of a "meaningful opportunity to be heard" under these circumstances and therefore violated the due process clause. *See also Ake v. Oklahoma*, 470 U.S. 68 (1985) (state must provide criminal defendant with psychiatrist to serve as expert witness when insanity issue is raised).

[5] An Ostensibly "Impartial" Factfinder

WARD v. VILLAGE OF MONROEVILLE, 409 U.S. 57 (1972). Petitioner was convicted of a traffic offense in the Mayor's Court of Monroeville, Ohio. He claimed a violation of due process because the Mayor, who presided over the court, also was the chief executive of the village, a major part of whose income was derived from the fines imposed by him in his Mayor's Court. The Supreme Court of Ohio held that "such fact does not mean that a Mayor's impartiality is so diminished thereby that he cannot act in a disinterested fashion in a judicial capacity." The United States Supreme Court, per Brennan, J., stated, "We disagree with that conclusion":

> The issue turns . . . on whether the Mayor can be regarded as an impartial judge under the principles laid down by this Court in *Tumey v. Ohio*, 273 U.S. 510 (1927). There, contributions for prohibition law violations rendered by [a city Mayor] were reversed when it appeared that, in addition to his regular salary, the Mayor received $696.35 from the fees and costs levied by him against alleged violators. This Court held that "it certainly violates the fourteenth amendment and deprives a defendant in a criminal case of due process of law to subject his liberty or property to the judgment of a court, the judge of which has a direct, personal, substantial pecuniary interest in reaching a conclusion against him in his case. . . ."

> The fact that the Mayor there shared directly in the fees and costs did not define the limits of the principle. [T]he test is whether the Mayor's situation is one "which would offer a possible temptation to the average [person] as a judge to forget the burden of proof required to convict the defendant, or which might lead him not to hold the balance nice, clear and true between the state and the accused. . . ." Plainly that "possible temptation" may also exist when the Mayor's executive responsibilities for village finances may make him partisan to maintain the high level of contribution from the Mayor's Court.

Justice White, joined by Justice Rehnquist, dissented: "The Ohio Mayor who judged this case had no direct financial stake in its outcome. *Tumey v. Ohio* . . . is therefore not controlling, and I would not extend it."

NOTES AND QUESTIONS

(1) *Extending the Ward Reasoning to the Civil Context: Aetna Life Insurance Co. v. Lavoie, 475 U.S. 813 (1986).* In *Aetna*, one Justice of the Alabama Supreme Court cast the deciding vote in a case recognizing bad faith insurance claims for the first time, at a time when that Justice had pending at least one similar bad faith lawsuit against an insurer in a lower state court. The United States Supreme Court, per Burger, C.J., unanimously found a due process violation. It concluded that "a reasonable formulation of the issue is whether the situation is one 'which would offer a possible temptation to the average . . . judge to . . . lead him not to hold the balance nice, clear and true.' " *Ward v. Village of Monroeville.* . . ." Since this particular Justice's vote had the clear and immediate effect of enhancing both the legal status and the settlement value of his own case, the Court concluded that he had acted as "a judge in his own case."

(2) *Should the Ward and Aetna Courts Have Considered the Mathews v. Eldridge "Balancing" Factors?* Notice that the Court did not consider the three *Mathews v. Eldridge* balancing factors in either *Ward* or *Aetna*. Instead, it appears to have judged the violations by stricter standards. Perhaps this approach is justified, in that formal judicial proceedings are involved and the state's interest in not providing a different decisionmaker are not weighty. However, might there be instances in which the impartiality of the decisionmaker, just as other due process factors, should be subject to the *Mathews v. Eldridge* balancing test?

(3) *Extending the Ward and Aetna Reasoning to Private Adjudicators and to Alternate Dispute Resolution: Concrete Pipe and Products of California, Inc. v. Construction Laborers Pension Trust, 508 U.S. 602 (1993).* Federal pension legislation requires factual determinations to be made by the trustees when an employer withdraws from a pension trust. These determinations then fix the amount of money the employer owes as "withdrawal liability," unless an arbitration proceeding determines otherwise. The trustees, of course, have a fiduciary obligation to the trust beneficiaries, and thus they are biased; they have a motive to maximize the amount of money the employer owes. In this case, a withdrawing employer argued that adjudications by the trustees would deny it due process. The Supreme Court agreed; it extended *Ward* and *Aetna* to private adjudicators and to ADR situations, at least when they are mandated by government. "[D]ue process requires 'a neutral and detached judge in the first instance,' " said the Court, "and the command is no different when a legislature delegates adjudicative functions to a private party." The Court upheld the legislation, however, because it concluded that the real adjudication was the arbitration proceeding, which took place before disinterested arbiters who considered all the facts by a preponderance standard.

WASHINGTON v. HARPER, 494 U.S. 210 (1990). The Washington state penal system had a policy, denominated Policy 600.30, that allowed an inmate to be involuntarily medicated with antipsychotic drugs only if he (1) suffered from a "mental disorder" and (2) was "gravely disabled" or posed a "likelihood of serious harm to himself or others." Harper, an inmate who was involuntarily medicated, claimed a right to a more extensive hearing than he was provided. Under Policy 600.30, he was entitled only to a hearing before a special committee consisting of a psychiatrist, a psychologist, and a prison official, who could order involuntary medication if the psychiatrist was in the majority.

The Washington Supreme Court invalidated this procedure, holding that the due process clause required a judicial hearing with adversarial procedural protections in which the state had the burden of proof by "clear, cogent and convincing evidence," under a standard of "substituted judgment" for the inmate analogous to the medical treatment decision for an incompetent person. The United States Supreme Court, per Justice Kennedy, reversed, holding the state administrative procedures sufficient to comply with due process:

> The primary point of disagreement between the parties is whether due process requires a judicial decisionmaker. [N]one of the committee members may be involved, at the time of the hearing, in the inmate's treatment or diagnosis; members are not disqualified from sitting on the committee, however, if they have treated or diagnosed the inmate in the past. . . . [R]espondent contends that only a court should make the decision to medicate an inmate against his will. . . .

> The factors that guide us are well established. "Under *Mathews v. Eldridge*, we consider the private interests at stake in a governmental decision, the governmental interests involved, and the value of procedural requirements in determining what process is due under the Fourteenth Amendment."

> Respondent's interest in avoiding the unwarranted administration of antipsychotic drugs is not insubstantial. The forcible injection of medication into an

nonconsenting person's body represents a substantial interference with that person's liberty. [T]he drugs can have serious, even fatal, side effects. [T]ardive dyskinesia is a neurological disorder, irreversible in some cases, that is characterized by involuntary, uncontrollable movements of various muscles, especially around the face. [A] fair reading of the evidence [s]uggests that the proportion of patients treated with antipsychotic drugs who exhibit the symptoms of tardive dyskinesia ranges from 10% to 25%. . . .

Notwithstanding the risks that are involved, we conclude that an inmate's interests are adequately protected, and perhaps better served, by allowing the decision to medicate to be made by medical professionals rather than a judge. The Due Process Clause "has never been thought to require that the neutral and detached trier of fact be law trained or a judicial or administrative officer." . . . [I]ndependence of the decisionmaker is addressed to our satisfaction by these procedures. . . . [W]e reject also respondent's contention that the hearing must be conducted in accordance with the rules of evidence or that a "clear, cogent, and convincing" standard of proof is necessary. This standard is neither required nor helpful when medical personnel are making the judgment required by the regulations here.

Respondent contends that the Policy is nonetheless deficient because it does not allow him to be represented by counsel. We disagree. "[I]t is less than crystal clear why *lawyers* must be available to identify possible errors in *medical* judgment." Given the nature of the decision to be made, we conclude that the provision of an independent lay advisor who understands the psychiatric issues involved is sufficient protection. . . .

Justice Stevens, joined by Justices Brennan and Marshall, dissented:

[T]he critical defect in Policy 600.30 is the failure to have the treatment decision made or reviewed by an impartial person or tribunal. . . .

These decisionmakers have two disqualifying conflicts of interest. First, the panel members must review the work of treating physicians who are their colleagues and who, in turn, regularly review their decisions. . . . Second, the panel members, as regular staff of the Center, must be concerned not only with the inmate's best medical interests, but also with the most convenient means of controlling the mentally disturbed inmate. . . .

PROBLEM C

CHRYSLER CORPORATION v. TEXAS MOTOR VEHICLE COMMISSION, 755 F.2d 1192 (1985). Chrysler alleged that the Texas "Lemon Law" was unconstitutional as a violation of due process. The law provided a consumer remedy for defective new cars enforceable before the state Motor Vehicle Commission after simplified presentation of evidence. The majority of the members of the Motor Vehicle Commission, by statute, were required to be automobile dealers, with the rest being members or representatives of the public. Chrysler argued that the controlling influence of automobile dealers deprived it of an impartial decisionmaker since dealers would be motivated to find liability against manufacturers.

Is the Commission an Impartial Decisionmaker? Does the fact that a majority of the Commission consisted of automobile dealers deprive manufacturers, such as Chrysler, of due process? [The court held that it did not: "The predictors of bias here point in opposite directions. Perhaps the dealers on the Commission will be unsympathetic to manufacturers who contend that a claimed defect was only an inept repair effort by a dealer. Yet, we can equally speculate, if we are to speculate, that a dealer will be quick to find fault with his direct competitor—the dealer. Moreover, it is also possible that a dealer member of the Commission would tend to be biased in favor of manufacturers of his own make of car so that the brand he sells will not develop a reputation as a 'lemon.' [W]here the speculations tumble against each other . . . we cannot find that the decisionmaker is impermissibly biased in the constitutional sense." Is this reasoning persuasive?]

[6]   Freedom from Arbitrary Application of Law: Punitive Damages

NOTES AND QUESTIONS

(1) *Rational Choice of Applicable Law: Allstate Insurance Co. v. Hague, 449 U.S. 302 (1981).* In *Allstate,* the decedent had resided, obtained insurance, and been killed in Wisconsin, although he had worked in Minnesota and his widow had moved to Minnesota after his death for reasons unrelated to the litigation. The Minnesota courts had applied Minnesota law allowing plaintiffs to recover under multiple uninsured motorist policies, rather than Wisconsin law disallowing such "stacking." The Supreme Court held that the selection of applicable law must be based upon "a significant contact or significant aggregation of contacts, creating state interests, such that [the] choice . . . is neither arbitrary nor fundamentally unfair." Using this test, the Allstate plurality found Minnesota's contacts with the litigation sufficient to support that state's application of its own law. Is this holding correct? [A number of commentators have argued that the contacts in *Allstate* were insufficient to support choice of the forum's own law and that the Court should have found a due process violation. *See, e.g.,* Brilmayer, *Legitimate Interests in Multistate Problems: As Between State and Federal Law,* 79 Mɪᴄʜ. L. Rᴇᴠ. 1315, 1328–33 (1981); Silberman, *Can the State of Minnesota Bind the Nation?: Federal Choice-of-Law Constraints After Allstate Insurance Co. v. Hague,* 10 Hᴏғsᴛʀᴀ L. Rᴇᴠ. 103 (1981); Von Mehren & Trautman, *Constitutional Control of Choice of Law: Some Reflections on Hague,* 10 Hᴏғsᴛʀᴀ L. Rᴇᴠ. 35 (1981).]

(2) *Guidance and Control of the Jury: Pacific Mutual Life Ins. Co. v. Haslip, 499 U.S. 1 (1991).* Imagine that the jury is not told about any legal principles guiding its decision, or is not subject to control by judicial decision. Does the lack of jury guidance or control in the law violate due process? In the *Pacific Mutual* case, the Supreme Court held that due process was not violated by a large award of punitive damages against the insurer, for fraud perpetrated by its agent, because Alabama's procedures included jury instructions that explained that punitive damages are imposed for purposes of retribution and deterrence and that the jury must take into consideration the character and degree of wrong as shown by the evidence and the necessity of preventing similar wrongs. The state supreme court reviewed the award against a list of lawful standards, but Alabama had no procedure for conveying these controlling standards to the jury. Justice O'Connor dissented, emphasizing the lack of real control over the "powerful" and "devastating" nature of punitive damages: "States routinely authorize civil juries to impose punitive damages without providing them any meaningful instructions on how to do so. Rarely is a jury told anything more specific than 'do what you think best.' " *See also TXO Production Corp. v. Alliance Resources Corp.,* 509 U.S. 443 (1993) (upholding as not "grossly excessive" punitive damages of $10 million, which was more than 500 times the plaintiff's actual damages of $19,000, where jury instructions contained no specific criteria other than defendants' wealth, and state's appellate review was confined to general reasonableness).

For a contrast with *Haslip* (at least regarding the result), *compare Honda Motor Co. v. Oberg,* 512 U.S. 415 (1994), which held unconstitutional Oregon's appellate procedures that, although providing some protection against jury arbitrariness, did not provide any appellate review of the *size* of a punitive damage award, and consider the following.

BMW of NORTH AMERICA v. GORE, 517 U.S. 559 (1996). In *Gore,* the Court once again addressed a claim that a punitive damages award by a state court jury violated the procedural due process rights of a civil defendant. Respondent, Dr. Ira Gore, Jr., learned that his BMW sports sedan had actually been repainted by petitioner's (BMW) "vehicle preparation center" after the car had been exposed to acid rain in the shipping process from Germany. BMW had a policy of: (1) selling such repainted vehicles as "new" as long as the repair cost did not exceed three percent of the suggested retail price (approximately $41,000) and (2) *not* disclosing the repairs to the purchaser (or the dealer). Dr. Gore sued BMW in Alabama . . . .

To support his punitive damage claim, Gore showed that BMW had sold as new nearly 1,000 other cars, although only thirteen others were sold in Alabama. The jury awarded Gore $4,000 in actual damages. Then, the jury awarded Gore 4 million dollars in punitive damages. [Presumably, the calculation was 1000 repainted vehicles times $4000 diminished value.] Although the Alabama Supreme Court reduced the punitive damage award to $2 million (which was still 500 times the actual damages), the state Supreme Court ruled against BMW's defense that the punitive damage award violated procedural due process. . . . Here, applying the "grossly excessive" standard from *TXO*, the Court, per Justice Stevens, reversed and struck down the punitive damage award . . . .

> [E]lementary notions of fairness enshrined in our constitutional jurisprudence dictate that a person receive fair notice note only of the conduct that will subject him to punishment but also of the severity of the penalty that a State may impose. Three guideposts, each of which indicates that BMW did not receive adequate notice of the magnitude of the sanction that Alabama might impose for adhering to the nondisclosure policy adopted in 1983, lead us to the conclusion that the $2 million award against BMW is grossly excessive: the degree of reprehensibility of the nondisclosure; the disparity between the harm or potential harm suffered by Dr. Gore and his punitive damages award; and the difference between this remedy and the civil penalties authorized or imposed in comparable cases. . . .

> Perhaps the most important indicium of the reasonableness of a punitive damages award is the degree of reprehensibility of the defendant's conduct. . . .

> [I]n this case, none of the aggravating factors associated with particularly reprehensible conduct is present. The harm BMW inflicted on Dr. Gore was purely economic in nature. . . .

> [T]he second and perhaps most commonly cited indicium of an unreasonable or excessive punitive damages award is its ratio to the actual harm inflicted on the plaintiff. *See TXO*. . . .

> [T]he $2 million in punitive damages awarded to Dr. Gore by the Alabama Supreme Court is 500 times the amount of his actual harm as determined by the jury. Moreover, there is no suggestion that Dr. Gore or any other BMW purchaser was threatened with any additional potential harm by BMW's nondisclosure policy. . . .

> [C]omparing the punitive damages award and the civil or criminal penalties that could be imposed for comparable misconduct provides a third indicium of excessiveness. . . . In this case the $2 million economic sanction imposed on BMW is substantially greater than the statutory fines available in Alabama and elsewhere for similar malfeasance. . . .

> [T]he fact that BMW is a large corporation rather than an impecunious individual does not diminish its entitlement to fair notice of the demands that the several States impose on the conduct of its business. Indeed, its status as an active participant in the national economy implicates the federal interest in preventing individual States from imposing undue burdens on interstate commerce. While each State has ample power to protect its own consumers, none may use the punitive damages deterrent as a means of imposing its regulatory policies on the entire Nation. . . .

Justice Breyer, for Justices O'Connor and Souter, concurred, adding an appendix concerning historic rates of inflation. Justice Scalia, joined by Justice Thomas, dissented. . . .

> In earlier cases that were the prelude to this decision, I set forth my view that a state trial procedure that commits the decision whether to impose punitive damages, and the amount, to the discretion of the jury, subject to some judicial review for "reasonableness," furnishes a defendant with all the process that is "due." I do not regard the Fourteenth Amendment's Due Process Clause as a secret repository of substantive guarantees against "unfairness"—neither the unfairness of an excessive civil compensatory award, nor the unfairness of an "unreasonable" punitive award. What the Fourteenth Amendment's procedural guarantee assures is an opportunity to contest the reasonableness of a damages judgment in state court; but there is no federal guarantee a damages award actually *be* reasonable. . . .

Relying on concerns about federalism and possible interference with on-going "tort reform" efforts at the state level, Justice Ginsburg also dissented.

NOTES AND QUESTIONS

(1) *State Farm Mutual Auto Insurance Co. v. Campbell, 538 U.S. 408 (2003).* In *State Farm Mutual*, the Court, per Justice Kennedy, followed the principles of the *BMW* decision. The same majority as *BMW* held that a $145 million punitive damage award on a one million dollar compensatory judgment was excessive and violated procedural due process. The same Justices dissented. Justice Scalia again argued that the *BMW* approach created a substantive due process right which had no basis in the Due Process Clause. *See generally* Lindsay J. Efting, Note, *Punitive Damages: Will the Courts Still Punish the Wrongdoer After State Farm Mutual Automobile Insurance Co. v. Campbell?*, 49 S.D. L. Rev. 67 (2003).

(2) *Punitive Damage Award Based on a Jury's Desire to Punish Defendant for Harming Nonparties: Phillip Morris USA, v. Williams, 549 U.S. 346 (2007).* In the *Williams* decision, the Supreme Court continued to grapple with issues of procedural due process presented by large punitive damage awards. Like *Honda Motor Co.*, the *Williams* case arose in Oregon. Williams, the widow of a heavy smoker of Marlboro cigarettes, sued the manufacturer Phillip Morris USA, under theories of negligence and deceit. The trial court allowed the jury to consider "harm caused others" (*i.e.*, nonparties to the case). The jury found for Williams and awarded compensatory damages of $821,000 and punitive damages of $79.5 million. The manufacture appealed, arguing under *BMW of North America* that the nearly 100-to-1 ratio for punitive damages was "grossly excessive." On appeal, the manufacturer also argued that allowing the jury to consider harm caused to nonparties violated procedural due process.

Although the Oregon courts upheld the punitive damage award, the Supreme Court, per Justice Breyer, ruled that the award was unconstitutional and vacated the award. The Court did not reach the grossly excessive issue. Instead the Court held that "the Constitution's Due Process Clause forbids a state to use a punitive damages award to punish a defendant for injury that it inflicts upon nonparties who are, in the Court's terms, "strangers to the litigation." While the Court stated that consideration of harm to others might be constitutional as part of a determination of *reprehensibility*, the Court said that the procedural due process guarantee prohibited such consideration for purposes of *punishment*. The Court reasoned that, under these circumstances, the punitive damages "would amount to a taking of 'property' from the defendant without due process."

Four Justices dissented. Justices Stevens, Thomas and Ginsburg wrote opinions. Justice Ginsburg's dissent focused on one obvious problem created by the Court's analysis: when does permissible consideration for a *reprehensibility decision* end and impermissible consideration for *punishment* begin? Note that this decision suggests another defense to punitive damages apart from the "grossly excessiveness" defense.

[7] Appeal

NOTES AND QUESTIONS

(1) *Despite the Emphasis of Appellate Decisions in Law School Casebooks, Appeal Generally is Not a Due Process Requirement: Abney v. United States, 431 U.S. 651 (1977).* As the Court stated in *Abney,* "[I]t is well settled that there is no constitutional right to an appeal. [I]ndeed, for a century after this Court was established, no appeal as of right existed in criminal cases. . . ." If the state creates a right to appeal, numerous decisions hold that various due process rights (such as the right of an indigent to a state-provided transcript and to counsel) attach; the threshold right, however, is not a general due process creation.

(2) *Is There Ever a Due Process Right to an Appeal?: Gregg v. Georgia, 428 U.S. 153 (1976).* In *Gregg,* the Court upheld the Georgia procedure for imposing capital punishment. The process included an automatic appeal, which featured a sentence review. The Court regarded this process as "an important additional safeguard against arbitrariness and caprice" but did not expressly hold that appeal was required in capital cases as a condition of due process. In *Parker v. Dugger,* 498 U.S. 308 (1991), the Court went farther than it had in *Gregg,* and actually vacated a death sentence because of appellate review that it considered inadequate: "We have emphasized repeatedly the crucial role of meaningful appellate review in ensuring that the death penalty is not imposed arbitrarily or irrationally. We have held specifically that the Florida Supreme Court's system of independent review of death sentences minimizes the risk of constitutional error, and have noted the 'crucial protection' afforded by such review in jury override cases."

[8] A Timely and Effective Remedy

NOTES AND QUESTIONS

(1) *Can Systemic Civil Trial Delays Be Shown to Violate the Constitution?: Hittner & Osman, Federal Civil Trial Delays: A Constitutional Dilemma?, 31 S. Tex. L. Rev. 341 (1990).* Consider the following analysis:

> A young father is injured in a collision with a truck and is rendered a quadriplegic. He sues the defendant, a major moving van line, in state court. The defendant [r]emoves the suit to federal court where, because of clogged dockets, the plaintiff cannot expect to get to trial in less than three to four years.

> A businessman suing in state court for enforcement of payment pursuant to a contract that constitutes the major portion of his business finds his suit removed to federal court. A delay of several years in obtaining recovery would force him into bankruptcy. . . .

> [D]ebilitating docket congestion is occurring in the state courts as well as in the federal system. In Vermont, for example, the state Supreme Court recently issued a six month moratorium on civil jury trials because of what it termed the drastic reduction in availability of state judicial resources. . . .

[Hittner and Osman examine issues of justiciability, equal protection, access to the courts, due process, and right to jury trial, to conclude with litigation suggestions for such cases:]

> The foregoing discussion has depicted a constitutional challenge to court congestion as an uphill battle. [A] review of a few of the rare cases in which delays in reaching trial have been held unconstitutional provides some insight to the approach a successful constitutional challenger must take.

An adequate presentation of supporting statistics is essential. In *Mattos v. Thompson*, where the Supreme Court of Pennsylvania held that delays occasioned by the mandatory submission of medical malpractice claims to arbitration panels were oppressive and impermissibly infringed upon the constitutional right to a jury, the court reached that conclusion upon examination of an extensive statistical analysis presented by the plaintiff that revealed that 12.5% of the cases filed remained unresolved by the panels four years after filing, 38% remained unresolved after three years, 65% after two years, and 85% after one year. . . .

Decisions [also] shed some light on the extent of harm that will lead a court to reach such a conclusion. . . .

In *Waites v. Sondock*, the Texas Supreme Court examined the constitutionality of the Texas legislative continuance statute. . . . [F]inding that Mrs. Waites suffered irreparable injury by postponement of receipt of support payments critical to her ability to feed and support her children, the court concluded that under such circumstances the mandatory application of the legislative continuance statute violated the due process clause of both the state and federal constitutions and the access to the courts provision of the Texas Constitution.

[W] *aites* and [other] cases suggest that a court might find delays unconstitutional where they result in harm that cannot be remedied by the eventual right to trial. . . .

Are these cases appropriate for a holding that delay denies due process? What conditions should be required for such a holding?

(2) *A Meaningful Remedy: McKesson Corp. v. Florida Div. of Alcoholic Beverages and Tobacco, 496 U.S. 18 (1990).* The Florida Supreme Court concluded that McKesson Corporation had been required to pay unconstitutional liquor excise taxes because the Florida taxing scheme violated the commerce clause. Although the court enjoined the state from giving effect to discriminatory preferences for local distributors, it refused to provide McKesson a refund or any other form of relief for taxes it had already paid, claiming that "equitable considerations" opposed such relief. The United States Supreme Court, per Justice Brennan, held that if a state requires a taxpayer to pay first and only then to obtain review of the tax's validity, the due process clause requires the state to afford taxpayers "a meaningful opportunity to secure post-payment relief."

(3) *What State Law Alternatives will Satisfy the Hearing Requirement of Procedural Due Process?: Lujan v. G & G Fire Sprinklers, Inc., 121 U.S. 1446 (2001).* California statutes permitted the State—without notice or any hearing—to withhold money (and to impose penalties) from a public works subcontractor that failed to comply with the State's "prevailing wage" requirements. When payments were withheld to subcontractor G & G Fire Sprinklers, it sued, under 42 U.S.C. § 1983, and the district court and the Ninth Circuit held for the challenger because state law afforded no hearing at all. The Supreme Court, per Chief Justice Rehnquist, reversed.

While the Court confirmed the basic two-step doctrine from *Roth, supra,* the Court concluded that the lower courts had interpreted the hearing requirement too narrowly. Here, G & G Fire Sprinklers had a protected property interest that "can be fully protected by an ordinary breach-of-contract suit." Thus, since state law provided a meaningful remedy (albeit, a post-deprivation remedy), the hearing requirement of procedural due process was satisfied. The Chief Justice's reasoning here may be similar to the analysis offered twenty-five years earlier by then—Associate Justice Rehnquist in the alternative holding in *Paul v. Davis*, above. Should the availability of a federal remedy be precluded by the existence (in the Court's view) of an adequate state law remedy or should the plaintiff have a choice?

Appendix 8

SAMPLE PROCEDURES FOR STUDENT SUSPENSION OR EXPULSION

FRELS & COOPER, SCHOOL DISCIPLINE, POLICIES AND PROCEDURES: A PRACTICAL GUIDE 7–11, D6–D11*
(National School Boards Ass'n & Council of School Attys. ed. 1984)

There are many different ways for school districts to handle the hearing process. For example, many school districts provide that hearings concerning student discipline be held initially before the school board. Others provide that an upper level administrator hear the case. . . .

There are several benefits which may arise from having the building principal be responsible for the initial hearing. Having the principal hold the hearing helps assure that due process is afforded the student at the earliest time and at the lowest administrative level. Also, a relatively speedy appellate process is provided. Additionally, communication at this level is generally easier than if a hearing is held before the superintendent or at the board level. The chances of misunderstandings are reduced. . . .

Since the student is entitled to a fair hearing, the principal should avoid talking in great detail to those investigating the case. . . .

Some districts may choose, as an alternative, to have an administrative panel hear all long-term suspension cases in order to allow the principal to have a freer hand to investigate all discipline cases. When this option is chosen, the principal may present the evidence of the student's misconduct.

PROCEDURES FOR CONDUCTING A DUE PROCESS HEARING

[The procedures for investigation and notice are dealt with in a portion of this text that is omitted. *See* Specimen Letter # 3, which is included below.]

The first step in the hearing is for the principal to state the ground rules. He or she can read the outline (Specimen Outline # 4) with any appropriate additions to cover the specific case at hand. This outline should be handed out to all those in attendance so everyone will be apprised of the ground rules.

[T]he administration, usually the assistant principal, has the burden to go forward and present the administration's case that the student violated a rule and should be suspended. . . .

The principal should have the proceeding tape recorded. That tape recording can later be used for appeals to the superintendent and the board and eventually to prepare a transcript if the case should be [taken] to the courts. . . .

[T]he student, his or her parent, their representative, or their attorney, should certainly be allowed to cross-examine the witnesses put forth by the administration. The cross-examination should generally be allowed to go on for so long as the parent or their representative feels it is necessary. Time limits generally are not a good idea and simply raise the spectre of unfair treatment. The principal, however, may require that witnesses' testimony be relevant and that hearsay be avoided. In that regard, a principal should not rely solely on hearsay to make his or determination of whether the student committed the act(s) in question. . . .

---

* Copyright © 1984 by the National School Boards Association and Council of School Attorneys. Reprinted with permission.

After all the evidence has been presented, the principal should allow rebuttal evidence and then closing arguments. . . .

The notification letter informs the parent and student of the decision and of their right to appeal to the next administrative level (Specimen Letter # 5). The principal should make specific findings of fact about what he or she determined happened. . . . The principal should also delineate the appropriate punishment for any offense which the principal finds that the student committed.

Specimen Letter # 3
NOTICE OF HEARING AND
WITNESS LETTER (PRINCIPAL)
[For Suspension of More Than Ten Days]

(Parent or Guardian)	Hand Delivered or Certified Mail
(Address)	Return Receipt Requested
(Date)	

Dear (Parent or Guardian):

You have requested a hearing concerning the proposed suspension of (name) from school for misconduct and/or violation of District or school rules or regulations, specifically, (specific alleged misconduct) [*e.g.*, the possession of an item prohibited by Section 5 of the School Policy on Alcohol and Drugs, namely marijuana, on or about October 22, 1987, in and on school facilities].

Pursuant to your request, a hearing has been scheduled for (month) (day), (year) at (time) at (location of hearing). If this time for the hearing is not convenient, please do not hesitate to let me know so it can be rescheduled.

At the hearing, you will have the right to present any documentary or other evidence and any witnesses to refute the charges of misconduct. You may also present evidence and witnesses with respect to a proper punishment if the student is found to have committed the alleged offense(s). The Administration may present the following witnesses:

1. (Name of witness) , (nature of testimony) .
2. (Name of witness) , (nature of testimony) .

If additional witnesses are to be called by the administration, you will be notified as soon as possible. Rebuttal witnesses may also be presented by the Administration, but their identity and the nature of their testimony cannot be determined at this time. Documentary evidence may also be submitted. The documents which may be used (are attached) (will be presented to you prior to the hearing).

The hearing will be conducted as an informal hearing, and no strict rules of evidence will apply. However, the testimony or documents must be relevant and not hearsay. The Principal will rule on any objections to the presentation of witnesses or evidence that may be made by you or by the administration. The Administration's case in support of suspension will be presented by (name) , (title) unless you have an attorney. You and your child may be represented by another adult or an attorney. If you are to be represented by an attorney, the school district's attorney will present the Administration's case. If you will have another adult or an attorney represent your child, please let me know prior to the hearing so the school district's attorney can be present.

A COPY OF THE SCHOOL DISTRICT POLICIES REGARDING DISCIPLINE PROCEDURES IS ATTACHED TO THIS LETTER. PLEASE REVIEW THESE POLICIES. If you have any questions about the procedures to be followed at the hearing, the nature of the charges, or any other aspect of this matter, please do not hesitate to contact me.

Sincerely yours,

(Principal or Hearing Officer)

cc: The Student

Specimen Outline # 4
OUTLINE OF HEARING FOR STUDENT BEFORE
THE PRINCIPAL OR HEARING OFFICER

PRINCIPAL OR HEARING OFFICER: Today we are here for a hearing in the case of (name) . (Name) , a (classification) grade student at the (name) School, is charged with (describe) . It is proposed that he/she be expelled from school for the remainder of the term (or other time).

Both the Administration and the student will be given an opportunity to present testimony with respect to the incident involved in this case, any circumstances attendant to it, and any punishment that might be rendered if it is determined that (name) committed that act(s) in question. This procedure may be handled in one or two parts. In the first stage, only the issue of whether the student committed the acts of which he/she is charged will be considered. I will then make a decision as to whether the student committed those acts. If the student is found to have committed the acts, then punishment will be considered. The alternative is that I can consider whether the student committed the misconduct and the punishment at the same time. (Student's representative) which way do you want to do it? (Decide which procedure will be followed.)

(Name) is represented by an attorney (name) . The Administration will be represented by (name) . For the record, the following people are present: (list them) .

Each side will have a chance to present its witnesses and documentation in support of its position. This proceeding is being recorded to make a record of what transpires. The witnesses will be sworn in by (name) , a notary public. This will be conducted as an informal hearing, and no strict rules of evidence will apply; however, the testimony must not be hearsay, and it must be relevant. The attorneys may make such objections to testimony or documentation as they see fit and I, as Hearing Officer, will consider such objections.

As noted, the student is charged with (describe) . The student, through his parent, was notified of the charges and the time and date of this hearing. The Administration must show that the charges are supported by the evidence. The charges must be supported only by the evidence heard here today.

The Administration will present its case first, followed by the presentation of the student. Each of you may make a short opening statement if you wish.

(Opening statement by the Administration's representative.)

(Opening statement by the student's representative.)

PRINCIPAL OR HEARING OFFICER: (*Administration's representative*), *you may present your witnesses.* (The Administration's Representative presents witnesses.)

PRINCIPAL OR HEARING OFFICER: (*Student's representative*), *you may present your witnesses.* (The student's representative presents witnesses.)

PRINCIPAL OR HEARING OFFICER: (*Administration's representative*), *do you wish to present any rebuttal evidence?* (Presentation of rebuttal evidence by the administration's representative.)

PRINCIPAL OR HEARING OFFICER: *(Student's representative), do you wish to present anything further?*

PRINCIPAL OR HEARING OFFICER: *Do either of you wish to make closing statements?*

(Closing by Administration's representative.)

(Closing by Student's representative.)

PRINCIPAL OR HEARING OFFICER: I will now deliberate upon the evidence I have heard and will render a decision as quickly as possible. (The decision can be given verbally and followed up in writing, or the decision can be given in writing promptly after the hearing.)

NOTES AND QUESTIONS

(1) *Due Process.* Do the suggested procedures, in your view, provide "that process which is due" for a significant suspension or expulsion? Identify the components of due process and the ways in which they are met by the suggestions and forms that Frels and Cooper provide?

(2) *The Role of an Attorney for the Accused Student.* If you were the parent of a student whom the school district proposed to suspend for a lengthy time or expel, consider whether you would employ counsel to defend him or her. [Consider the amount that counsel might cost, which could be on the order of thousands of dollars.] At the hearing, what will be the role of the attorney for the accused student? Consider the relative importance of (1) objecting to procedures or persuading the person presiding to use enhanced procedures; (2) cross-examining the administration's witnesses concerning the infraction; (3) presenting defense testimony concerning the infraction; (4) presenting matters in mitigation of disposition or punishment; and (5) making persuasive arguments about the evidence. Which will likely be more important, the ability to argue about due process or the ability to present the case on the merits?

(3) *The Effects of Legally Circumscribed Procedures and of Defense Attorneys.* Before such cases as *Goldberg* and *Goss*, a school district might and often would provide a process analogous to that described by Frels and Cooper, but its obligation to do so was not judicially recognized. Might there be societal costs associated with the confining of student discipline by these judicial decisions? Consider whether this factor may transform educational decisions, such as whether the school's purposes require the removal of a disruptive student, into "legal" decisions that are controlled by the district's attorneys rather than by educators. Is that result desirable (or is the decision more than an "educational" one)? Consider, also, the role that this process creates for the principal, for fellow students who are called and cross-examined as witnesses, and for teachers who may be required to be witnesses against their students.

Chapter 9

DUE PROCESS: SUBSTANTIVE RIGHTS OF "PRIVACY" AND PERSONAL AUTONOMY

§ 9.01 THE FUNDAMENTAL RIGHTS CONTROVERSY

NOTES AND QUESTIONS

(1) *The Rational Basis Test for Most Legislation; "Strict Scrutiny" of Legislation That Impinges Upon "Fundamental Rights."* In the chapter on economic rights, we considered the rational basis test: most legislation will be upheld if it is supported by a rational basis. But if a particular right or interest protected by the Constitution is deemed "fundamental," it should have greater significance than mere protection from transparently arbitrary impairment. Therefore, courts have adopted a stricter scrutiny of statutes impinging upon fundamental rights. Typical formulations require the state to demonstrate a "compelling" state interest to support such a statute and also demonstrate that the government's means are necessary to the achievement of the compelling interest.

(2) *Non-Textual "Fundamental" Rights as Protected Even Though Not Enumerated.* Some fundamental rights—such as the "freedom of speech"—are textually explicit. Another aspect of the doctrine of fundamental rights is that there arguably are rights which, although not explicit in the text, are so fundamental that one or more open-textured provisions of the Constitution may be interpreted to protect them. Examples include the "right to vote in state elections" and the "right to marry." This concept of fundamental rights is controversial: it is arguably nondemocratic, and it is subject to the criticism that it enacts as positive constitutional law the preferences of individual judges.

(3) *Two Earlier Substantive Due Process Decisions Leading to the Modern View of Fundamental Rights: Pierce v. Society of Sisters, 268 U.S. 510 (1925), and Meyer v. Nebraska, 262 U.S. 390 (1923). Pierce* concerned a state law that required parents to place their children in public schools, thus prohibiting them from considering private or parochial education. The Court struck down the law, recognizing a basic, though non-textual, "liberty of parents . . . to direct the upbringing and education of [their] children. . . ." In *Meyer*, the Court invalidated a state law that prohibited the teaching of foreign languages to children. The Court held that the law had no "reasonable relation to any end within the competency of the state." These earlier substantive due process decisions have frequently been cited in modern cases recognizing fundamental rights.

(4) *Protection of Fundamental Rights By the Fourteenth Amendment and Other Sources.* By now, you may be regarding the Fourteenth Amendment as something of a chameleon. The majority in the *Slaughter House Cases* interpreted it in light of a primary thrust to provide equal rights to former slaves. In the chapter on procedural due process, we considered Justice Black's conclusion that the true intent of the Framers of the amendment was to incorporate totally the Bill of Rights, a theory that may be supported by some historical evidence but is opposed by other such evidence. Now, we look at the amendment as a protection of unenumerated, but "fundamental" human rights. Is it possible that the Framers had each of these widely different purposes in mind? Consider the following.

GRESSMAN, THE UNHAPPY HISTORY OF CIVIL RIGHTS LEGISLATION, 50 MICH. L. REV. 1323 (1952).* [The] concept of a paramount national citizenship to which fundamental rights adhered had been the basis of the 1866 Act and had been implicit in

---

* Copyright © 1952 by the University of Michigan Law Review Association. Reprinted by permission.

the whole movement to nationalize civil rights. [The National Citizenship Clause] was the necessary premise of all the remainder of the first section of the amendment, especially the privileges and immunities clause. The latter clause, forbidding the states from abridging the privileges or immunities of citizens of the United States, has real meaning only against a background of national citizenship accompanied by the basic rights of the individual. The promoters of the Fourteenth Amendment were not interested in prohibiting the states from interfering with the narrow, technical relationships of a citizen to the federal government. They were desirous of precluding the states from impinging upon the rights to life, liberty and the pursuit of happiness. And they thought of those rights as necessarily belonging to national citizenship, rights which they labeled privileges and immunities.

In light of subsequent developments, it is unfortunate that the framers of the amendment did not give a more definite indication as to the privileges and immunities which were intended to be placed under the protective umbrella of the federal government. The phrase "privileges or immunities" referred plainly enough, in the Framers' minds, to the fundamental rights of man, enumerated at least in part in the provisions of the 1866 Act. They felt that the Declaration of Independence and the Constitution itself had made self-evident the great rights which attached to those in allegiance to the federal government. And they knew that as long ago as 1823 the phrase "privileges and immunities of citizens," as used in article IV, section 2, of the Constitution had been judicially interpreted to include all fundamental rights [citing *Corfield v. Coryell*, which described privileges and immunities broadly and which the *Slaughter House* majority cited as showing that viewpoint]. Moreover, they may have feared that to enumerate the rights once again in the Fourteenth Amendment was not only redundant but might close the list and prevent subsequent recognition and protection of additional rights.

In any event, it was the privileges and immunities clause which the framers regarded as the core of section 1 of the amendment. The equal protection and due process clauses were treated by them as of secondary importance. . . .

Such was the intended nature of the Fourteenth Amendment upon its ratification on July 28, 1868. . . .

NOTES AND QUESTIONS

(1) *Given Professor Gressman's Views, Was the Slaughter House Majority Incorrect?* The history underlying the Fourteenth Amendment, including the dissatisfaction of many legislators with the Thirteenth Amendment as a sound basis for the more sweeping Civil Rights Act of 1866, is described in the chapter on economic rights. Was the *Slaughter House* majority correct in concluding that the amendment should be interpreted in accordance with this predominant purpose? Recall, also, Justice Black's theory, set forth in the procedural due process chapter, that the framers intended to incorporate the Bill of Rights, in part as a means of "limit[ing] the Supreme Court . . . to specific . . . protections only and keep[ing] judges from roaming at will in their own notions of what policies . . . are desirable and what are not." Is it likely that the framers of the Fourteenth Amendment intended to countermand this objective? On the other hand, history and text can be used as a basis for supporting Professor Gressman's theory. For example, if the Framers had only the narrow intention of enhancing the freedom of former slaves, why could they not have expressed that purpose (as they did in the Civil Rights Act of 1866) rather than using such broader terminology as "privileges or immunities" or "due process"?

(2) *Are Modern Fundamental Rights Such as Abortion or Birth Control Justifiable with Reference to the Intent of the Framers of the Amendment?* There is no evidence that the Framers considered abortion when adopting the Fourteenth Amendment. The Framers never considered the status of the birth control pill—since it was not invented until 1960. Can protection of these interests be justified as the application of a general

principle to a modern unanticipated problem? Are these rights, therefore, dependent upon non-interpretivist or supplementation justification—and, if so, is that justification persuasive?

(3)   *A Survey of the American People: A Firm (If Mistaken) Majority Belief That the Constitution Expressly Protects the Right to Privacy—Americans Certain of Right to Privacy, Houston Chronicle, Feb. 19, 1990, § A, at 2, col. 5.* The National Law Journal and Lexis surveyed 805 adults to mark the 200th anniversary of the Supreme Court. "The notion of a constitutional right to privacy is so firmly entrenched that a majority of those surveyed asserted—incorrectly—that the right is written into the Constitution." *Id.* The majority also believed that this right protected both homosexual conduct and a family's decision to end a relative's life support system. But the survey also showed that the people found this right as tricky as did the Supreme Court: a large majority said that it did not guarantee employees the right to refuse drug tests or the right of a minor to obtain an abortion without parental notification. Nearly six in ten Americans could not name a single Supreme Court Justice.

(4)   *A Complex Legal Concept, with at Least Five Separate, Shifting Meanings.* You may find the material in this chapter challenging. Professor Ken Gormley's article, *One Hundred Years of Privacy*, 1992 Wis. L. Rev. 1335, should provide valuable background and context. Professor Gormley concludes that privacy law actually consists of five subcategories: (1) Tort Privacy; (2) Fourth Amendment Privacy; (3) First Amendment Privacy; (4) Fundamental Decision Privacy; and (5) State Constitutional Privacy. His article traces each subcategory and demonstrates the interrelationships which have developed.

NOTE ON ROGER SHERMAN'S DRAFT OF A BILL OF RIGHTS

Discovery of the Sherman Draft. In 1985, James C. Hutson, the Chief of the manuscript division of the Library of Congress, found a handwritten document pasted in a volume of James Madison's papers. He did not examine it carefully until two years later—and in 1987, he discovered that it was a handwritten draft of a Bill of Rights by Roger Sherman of Connecticut. *See* N.Y. Times, July 29, 1987, at A1, col. 1. Sherman's draft contained many provisions similar to those of the current Bill of Rights—but it also provided a natural rights amendment.

Sherman's "Natural Rights" Amendment. Sherman's draft contained the following second amendment:

[2] The people have certain natural rights which are retained by them when they enter into Society. Such are the rights of Conscience in matters of religion; of acquiring property, and of pursuing happiness & Safety; of Speaking, writing, and publishing their Sentiments with decency and freedom; of peaceably assembling to consult their common good, and of applying to Government by petition or remonstrance for redress of grievances. Of these rights therefore they shall not be deprived by the Government of the United States.

Does the mention of "natural rights" in this draft imply broader protection than the current Bill of Rights (or does the apparently exclusive list that follows limit the grant)? As Hutson put it, the discovery of this piece of history "shows how little we know about" the writing of the Constitution. *Id.*

§ 9.02   REPRODUCTION, ABORTION, AND SEXUAL CONDUCT

SKINNER v. OKLAHOMA, 316 U.S. 535 (1942). Oklahoma's Habitual Criminal Sterilization Act authorized the sexual sterilization of a "habitual criminal," defined as a person three times convicted of a felony involving moral turpitude and sentenced to imprisonment. But the Act provided that certain offenses, such as embezzlement, would not be considered. Noting that a person convicted three times of larceny could be sterilized but a person similarly convicted of embezzling the same amounts could not be, the Court, per Justice Douglas, found a denial of equal protection. It premised this holding, however, on the "fundamental" nature of the right of marriage and procreation:

This case touches a sensitive and important area of human rights. Oklahoma deprives certain individuals of a right which is basic to the perpetuation of a race—the right to have offspring. . . .

[The Court here distinguishes *Buck v. Bell*, 274 U.S. 200 (1927), on the ground that although that case upheld sterilization of mentally deficient persons, the statute there required proof that the person would likely produce "socially undesirable offspring."]

[T]he instant legislation runs afoul of the equal protection clause, though we give Oklahoma that large deference which the rule of the foregoing cases requires. We are dealing here with legislation which involves one of the basic civil rights of man. Marriage and procreation are fundamental to the very existence and survival of the race. The power to sterilize, if exercised, may have subtle, far-reaching and devastating effects. In evil or reckless hands it can cause races or types which are inimical to the dominant group to witherand disappear. [S]terilization of those who have thrice committed grand larceny with immunity for those who are embezzlers is a clear, pointed, unmistakable discrimination. . . . We have not the slightest basis for inferring that that line has any significance in eugenics nor that the inheritability of criminal traits follows the neat legal distinctions which the law has marked between these two offenses.

Chief Justice Stone concurred separately, saying: "[W]hile the state may protect itself from the demonstrably inheritable tendencies of the individual which are injurious to society, the most elementary notions of due process would seem to require it to take appropriate steps to safeguard the liberty of the individual by affording him [s]ome opportunity to show that he is without such inheritable tendencies." Thus, the statute violated due process; the Chief Justice "seriously doubt[ed]" that the equal protection clause provided a basis for the decision.

Justice Jackson concurred separately for similar reasons, but added: "[T]here are limits to the extent to which a legislatively represented majority may conduct biological experiments at the expense of the dignity and personality and natural powers of a minority—even those who have been guilty of what the majority define as crimes."

NOTES AND QUESTIONS

(1) *The Narrow Basis, But Expansive Rhetoric, of the Skinner Majority.* Note that Justice Douglas' opinion for the majority would not strike down an involuntary sterilization program in the absence of discrimination that violated the equal protection clause. At the same time, Justice Douglas' majority reasoning concerning the fundamental nature of the individual interests in procreation is expansive, and it is tied to no identified constitutional doctrine. Why do you suppose Justice Douglas wrote the opinion in this manner?

(2) *Critiquing Buck v. Bell, supra.* Justice Holmes' opinion in *Buck v. Bell*, which upheld the involuntary sterilization of a third-generation mentally defective person, contains the notorious dictum that "three generations of imbeciles are enough." Is the decision defensible? If such a law were enacted today, would it be upheld?

[A]   Birth Control and the Basic Structure of Modern Substantive Due Process

Read U.S. Const. Amend. I, III, IV, V, and IX (Bill of Rights provisions cited in *Griswold*, below).

GRISWOLD v. CONNECTICUT
381 U.S. 479 (1965)

MR. JUSTICE DOUGLAS delivered the opinion of the Court.

[A Connecticut statute] provides: "Any person who uses any drug, medicinal article or instrument for the purpose of preventing conception shall be fined not less than $50 or imprisoned not less than sixty days nor more than one year or be both fined and imprisoned." [Griswold, executive director of the Planned Parenthood League of Connecticut, was convicted and fined $100 for abetting violations of this enactment because he] gave information, instruction, and medical advice to *married persons* as to the means of preventing conception. . . .

Coming to the merits, we are met with a wide range of questions that implicate the Due Process Clause of the Fourteenth Amendment. Overtones of some arguments suggest that *Lochner v. New York* should be our guide. But we decline that invitation. [W]e do not sit as a super-legislature to determine the wisdom, need, and propriety of laws that touch economic problems, business affairs, or social conditions. This law, however, operates directly on an intimate relation of husband and wife and their physician's role in one aspect of that relation.

The association of people is not mentioned in the Constitution nor in the Bill of Rights. The right to educate a child in a school of the parents' choice—whether public or private or parochial—is also not mentioned. Nor is the right to study any particular subject or any foreign language: Yet the First Amendment has been construed to include certain of those rights.

By *Pierce v. Society of Sisters*, the right to educate one's children as one chooses is made applicable to the States by the force of the First and Fourteenth Amendments. By *Meyer v. Nebraska*, the same dignity is given the right to study the German language in a private school. In other words, the State may not, consistently with the spirit of the First Amendment, contract the spectrum of available knowledge. . . .

The foregoing cases suggest that specific guarantees in the Bill of Rights have penumbras, formed by emanations from those guarantees that help give them life and substance. Various guarantees create zones of privacy. The right of association contained in the penumbra of the First Amendment is one, as we have seen. The Third Amendment in its prohibition against the quartering of soldiers "in any house" in time of peace without the consent of the owner is another facet of that privacy. The Fourth Amendment explicitly affirms the "right of the people to be secure in their persons, houses, papers, and effects, against unreasonable searches and seizures." The Fifth Amendment in its Self-Incrimination Clause enables the citizen to create a zone of privacy which government may not force him to surrender to his detriment. The Ninth Amendment provides: "The enumeration in the Constitution, of certain rights, shall not be construed to deny or disparage others retained by the people."

The Fourth and Fifth Amendments were described in *Boyd v. United States*, 116 U.S. 616, 630, as protection against all governmental invasions "of the sanctity of a man's home and the privacies of life." We recently referred in *Mapp v. Ohio*, 367 U.S. 643, 656, to the Fourth Amendment as creating a "right to privacy, no less important than any other right carefully and particularly reserved to the people."

We have had many controversies over these penumbral rights of "privacy and repose." *See, e.g.,. . . Skinner v. Oklahoma.* These cases bear witness that the right of privacy which presses for recognition here is a legitimate one.

The present case, then, concerns a relationship lying within the zone of privacy created by several fundamental constitutional guarantees. And it concerns a law which, in forbidding the *use* of contraceptives rather than regulating their manufacture or sale, seeks to achieve its goals by means having a maximum destructive impact upon that relationship. Such a law cannot standin light of the familiar principle, so often applied by this Court, that a "governmental purpose to control or prevent activities constitutionally subject to state regulation may not be achieved by means which sweep unnecessarily broadly and thereby invade the area of protected freedoms." *NAACP v. Alabama*, 377 U.S. 288, 307. Would we allow the police to search the sacred precincts of marital bedrooms for telltale signs of the use of contraceptives? The very idea is repulsive to the notions of privacy surrounding the marriage relationship.

We deal with a right of privacy older than the Bill of Rights—older than our political parties, older than our school system. Marriage is a coming together for better or for worse, hopefully enduring, and intimate to the degree of being sacred. It is an association that promotes a way of life, not causes; a harmony in living, not political faiths; a bilateral loyalty, not commercial or social projects. Yet it is an association for as noble a purpose as any involved in our prior decisions.

Reversed.

Mr. Justice Goldberg, whom The Chief Justice and Mr. Justice Brennan join, concurring.

I agree with the Court that Connecticut's birth-control law unconstitutionally intrudes upon the right of marital privacy, and I join in its opinions and judgment. Although I have not accepted the view that "due process" as used in the Fourteenth Amendment includes all of the first eight Amendments . . ., I do agree that the concept of liberty protects these personal rights that are fundamental, and is not confined to the specific terms of the Bill of Rights. My conclusion that the concept of liberty is not so restricted and that it embraces the right of marital privacy though that right is not mentioned explicitly in the Constitution is supported both by numerous decisions of this Court, referred to in the Court's opinion, and by the language and history of the Ninth Amendment. In reaching the conclusion that the right of marital privacy is protected, as being within the protected penumbra of specific guarantees of the Bill of Rights, the Court refers to the Ninth Amendment. I add these words to emphasize the relevance of that Amendment to the Court's holding. . . .

The Ninth Amendment . . . was proffered to quiet expressed fears that a bill of specifically enumerated rights could not be sufficiently broad to cover all essential rights and that the specific mention of certain rights would be interpreted as a denial that others were protected.

In presenting the proposed Amendment, Madison said:

> It has been objected also against a bill of rights, that, by enumerating particular exceptions to the grant of power, it would disparage those rights which were not placed in that enumeration. . . . This is one of the most plausible arguments I have ever heard urged against the admission of a bill of rights into this system; but, I conceive, that it may be guarded against. I have attempted it, as gentlemen may see by turning to the last clause of the fourth

resolution [the Ninth Amendment]. I Annals of Congress 439 (Gales and Seaton ed. 1834).

While this Court has had little occasion to interpret the Ninth Amendment, "[i]t cannot be presumed that any clause in the constitution is intended to be without effect." *Marbury v. Madison*. [T]o hold that a right so basic and fundamental and so deep-rooted in our society as the right of privacy in marriage may be infringed because that right is not guaranteed in so many words by the first eight amendments to the Constitution is to ignore the Ninth Amendment and to give it no effect whatsoever. . . .

A dissenting opinion suggests that my interpretation of the Ninth Amendment somehow "broaden [s] the powers of this Court." With all due respect, I believe that it misses the import of what I am saying. . . . Rather, the Ninth Amendment shows a belief of the Constitution's authors that fundamental rights exist that are not expressly enumerated in the first eight amendments and an intent that the list of rights included there not be deemed exhaustive. . . .

In determining which rights are fundamental, judges are not left at large to decide cases in light of their personal and private notions. . . . The Connecticut statutes here involved deal with a particularly important and sensitive area of privacy—that of the marital relation and the marital home.

Mr. Justice Harlan, concurring in the judgment.

I fully agree with the judgment of reversal, but find myself unable to join the Court's opinion. The reason is that it seems to me to evince an approach to this case very much like that taken by my Brothers Black and Stewart in dissent, namely: the Due Process Clause of the Fourteenth Amendment does not touch this Connecticut statute unless the enactment is found to violate some right assured by the letter or penumbra of the Bill of Rights.

In other words, what I find implicit in the Court's opinion is that the "incorporation" doctrine may be used to *restrict* the reach of Fourteenth Amendment Due Process. For me this is just as unacceptable constitutional doctrine as is the use of the "incorporation" approach to *impose* upon the States all the requirements of the Bill of Rights as found in the provisions of the first eight amendments and in the decisions of this Court interpreting them. . . .

In my view, the proper constitutional inquiry in this case is whether this Connecticut statute infringes the Due Process Clause of the Fourteenth Amendment because the enactment violates basic values "implicit in the concept of ordered liberty," *Palko v. Connecticut*, 302 U.S. 319, 325. . . . I believe that it does. While the relevant inquiry may be aided by resort to one or more of the provisions of the Bill of Rights, it is not dependent on them or any of their radiations. The Due Process Clause of the Fourteenth Amendment stands, in my opinion, on its own bottom.

Mr. Justice White, concurring in the judgment.

[S]tatutes regulating sensitive areas of liberty do, under the cases of this Court, require "strict scrutiny," *Skinner v. Oklahoma*. But such statutes, if reasonably necessary for the effectuation of a legitimate and substantial state interest, and not arbitrary or capricious in application, are not invalid under the Due Process Clause. . . .

In these circumstances one is rather hard pressed to explain how the ban on use by married persons in any way prevents use of such devices by persons engaging in illicit sexual relations and thereby contributes to the State's policy against such relationships. Neither the state courts nor the State before the bar of this Court has tendered such an explanation. . . . A statute limiting its prohibition on use to persons engaging in the prohibited relationship would serve the endposited by Connecticut in the same way, and with the same effectiveness, or ineffectiveness, as the broad anti-use statute under attack in this case. I find nothing in this record justifying the sweeping scope of this statute, with its telling effect on the freedoms of married persons, and therefore conclude that it deprives such persons of liberty without due process of law.

Mr. Justice Black, with whom Mr. Justice Stewart joins, dissenting.

[T]he Court talks about a constitutional "right of privacy" as though there is some constitutional provision or provisions forbidding any law ever to be passed which might abridge the "privacy" of individuals. But there is not. There are, of course, guarantees in certain specific constitutional provisions which are designed in part to protect privacy at certain times and places with respect to certain activities. Such, for example, is the Fourth Amendment's guarantee against "unreasonable searches and seizures." But I think it belittles that Amendment to talk about it as though it protects nothing but "privacy. . . ."

The due process argument which my Brothers Harlan and White adopt here is based, as their opinions indicate, on the premise that this Court is vested with power to invalidate all state laws that it considers to be arbitrary, capricious, unreasonable, or oppressive, or this Court's belief that a particular state law under scrutiny has no "rational or justifying" purpose, or is offensive to a "sense of fairness and justice." If these formulas based on "natural justice," or others which mean the same thing, are to prevail, they require judges to determine what is or is not constitutional on the basis of their own appraisal of what laws are unwise or unnecessary. The power to make such decisions is of course that of a legislative body. . . .

My Brother Goldberg has adopted the recent discovery that the Ninth Amendment as well as the Due Process Clause can be used by this Court as authority to strike down all state legislation which this Court thinks violates "fundamental principles of liberty and justice," or is contrary to the "traditions and [collective] conscience of our people." He also states, without proof satisfactory to me, that in making decisions on this basis judges will not consider "their personal and private notions." One may ask how they can avoid considering them. Our Court certainly has no machinery with which to take a Gallup Poll. [N]or does anything in the history of the Amendment offer any support for such a shocking doctrine. . . .

The Due Process Clause with an "arbitrary and capricious" or "shocking to the conscience" formula was liberally used by this Court to strike down economic legislation in the early decades of this century, threatening, many people thought, the tranquility and stability of the Nation. *See, e.g., Lochner v. New York.* That formula, based on subjective considerations of "natural justice," is no less dangerous when used to enforce this Court's views about personal rights than those about economic rights. . . .

Mr. Justice Stewart, whom Mr. Justice Black joins, dissenting.

Since 1879 Connecticut has had on its books a law which forbids the use of contraceptives by anyone. I think this is an uncommonly silly law. As a practical matter, the law is obviously unenforceable, except in the oblique context of the present case. . . . But we are not asked in this case to say whether we think this law is unwise, or even asinine. We are asked to hold that it violates the United States Constitution. And that I cannot do. . . .

The Court also quotes the Ninth Amendment, and my Brother Goldberg's concurring opinion relies heavily upon it. But to say that the Ninth Amendment has anything to do with this case is to turn somersaults with history. The Ninth Amendment, like its companion the Tenth,. . . "states but a truism that all is retained which has not been surrendered. . . ."

What provision of the Constitution, then, does make this state law invalid? The Court says it is the right of privacy "created by several fundamental constitutional guarantees." With all deference, I can find no such general right of privacy in the Bill of Rights, in any other part of the Constitution, or in any case ever before decided by this Court.

. . . If, as I should surely hope, the law before us does not reflect the standards of the people of Connecticut, the people of Connecticut can freely exercise their true Ninth and Tenth Amendment rights to persuade their elected representatives to repeal it. That is the constitutional way to take this law off the books.

NOTES AND QUESTIONS

(1)   *A "Fundamental Right" to Birth Control: Griswold v. Connecticut, 381 U.S. 479 (1965).* Although many states had historically banned access to contraceptives, only two states (Connecticut and Massachusetts) barred certain contraceptives by the 1960s. Connecticut's statute made it a criminal offense to use "any drug, medicinal article or instrument for the purpose of preventing conception. . . ." Under this statute, female contraceptives were prohibited, but condoms were allowed.

The statute was challenged by a married couple and doctors as a violation of the due process clause of the Fourteenth Amendment. (Notice that there was no equal protection claim because, on its face, the statute did not create any classifications). While the statute would satisfy the rational basis standard, the Court, per Justice Douglas, applied a heightened level of scrutiny and struck down the statute.

There were multiple opinions. Justice Douglas wrote the plurality. He relied on the "penumbras" of various Amendments to find that the constitution protected the "privacy right" of the married couple to decide whether to use birth control. Justice Goldberg concurred, based on the Ninth Amendment. Justice Harlan concurred, relying on the due process clause itself; he concluded that certain rights that were "implicit in the concept of ordered liberty" should receive heightened scrutiny. Justice White also concurred; he concluded that certain personal rights should receive "strict scrutiny."

There were two dissenters. The most famous dissent was Justice Stewart who, accepting the idea that the Connecticut statute was "unwise" and even "asinine," argued that there was no basis for judicial action. He would have left the issue to the political process.

The positions of the Justices are examined further in the Notes below. The *Griswold* decision and its reliance on the concept of "fundamental rights" is the pivotal decision in the modern substantive due process doctrine. The fundamental rights analysis of *Griswold* is, for example, the precedential model for the *Roe* decision, below. *See generally* Mary L. Dudziak, *Just Say No: Birth Control in the Connecticut Supreme Court Before Griswold v. Connecticut*, 75 Ia. L. Rev. 915 (1990).

(2)   *Expanding Griswold: Eisenstadt v. Baird, 405 U.S. 438 (1972), and Roe v. Wade, below. Griswold* was a watershed case. It is one of the most important bases of the abortion decision, *Roe v. Wade*, below; but in some ways, the most important expansion that followed *Griswold* was *Eisenstadt v. Baird*, in which the Court extended the right of contraception to the population generally. Having emphasized in *Griswold* that the distribution of contraceptives was to married persons, the Court shifted focus in *Eisenstadt* to hold that "the rights must be the same for the unmarried and the married alike." The Court reasoned, further, "if the right of privacy means anything, it is the right of the *individual*, married or single, to be free from unwarranted government intrusion into matters so fundamentally affecting a person as the decision whether to bear or beget a child" (emphasis in original). This interpretation—that individuals have a right to be free from "unwarranted government intrusion" and to "fundamental" rights, with the fundamental nature of the right being established by a comparison with the child bearing decision—implied the kind of broad protection of natural rights that had been sought by some since the *Slaughter House Cases*, and before.

(3)   *Criticizing Griswold and the Penumbra Theory. Griswold* is readily subject to criticism for its reasoning, even by those who find the result congenial. Consider the following:

a. *Result-Oriented Reasoning.* It may be difficult to escape the impression that Justice Douglas' opinion supports a result reached independently of its logic.

b. *Persuasiveness of the Penumbra Hypothesis.* Using intent to interpret a given constitutional provision has an appealing appearance of legitimacy. On the other hand, the use of "emanations" to discern a "penumbra" that does not partake of the expression of any provision is something else. One may argue that if the Framers intended to enact a broad protection of fundamental rights, it would seem that the expression of that meaning would be more conveniently discernible than by inference from numerous diffuse sources.

c. *Why Not Infer Other Penumbras? Isn't a "Free Enterprise Penumbra" Actually More Logical?* The same reasoning used by Justice Douglas could result in the discovery of numerous other penumbras, some of which might be equally legitimate yet absurd in consequences. For example, can one infer a penumbra for free enterprise, making businesses immune from regulation? A wide variety of provisions in the Constitution—ranging from the State Money Clause, Bills of Credit Clause, Contract Clause, and Takings Clause, to the Commerce Clause and like provisions, are designed to protect and foster economic activity. In fact, intentionalist support for this arguable penumbra is readily ascertainable. Consider Justice Marshall's opinion in *Ogden v. Saunders* [in the Contract Clause coverage, above], in which the argument was made that the Contract Clause, together with natural rights implied by the Constitution, was intended precisely to protect businesses against regulation. Is this penumbral argument persuasive?

d. *Lack of a Principled Basis for Distinguishing Economic Rights.* In order to avoid the *Lochner* catastrophe, Justice Douglas distinguishes substantive due process cases in the economic sphere. But is there a principled basis for the distinction? Might there be some people who would consider that the ability to carry on their life's work in a chosen profession (the liberty-of-contract-area) to be as fundamental as a right to purchase contraceptives?

e. *Lack of Principled Bases for Distinguishing Fundamental Rights.* The *Griswold* reasoning can be criticized for its dependence upon the idiosyncratic preferences of judges.

f. *Search-and-Seizure Reasoning Lacks Relevance or Persuasive Force.* One of the major underpinnings of Justice Douglas' approach is the concern that the marital bedroom will be subjected to unreasonable searches. But that concern could be enforced by prohibiting the searches, according to the terms of the Fourth Amendment. No search was involved in this case; in fact, Connecticut appears to have found means of enforcement that did not involve searches at all. (Could the same reasoning be used to strike down laws against heroin or machine guns, which normally are secreted?)

g. *Lack of Limits and Inconsistency in Implications.* The *Griswold* reasoning invites extension, without recognizing any principle that creates discernible limits. Contradictory implications seem likely. For example, the issue in *Eisenstadt v. Baird*—whether the *Griswold* principle protecting the marital relationship should be extended to unmarried couples—was certain to arise. Having extended the principle in *Eisenstadt*, the Court later,and just as inevitably, faced questions regarding whether adultery, incest, fornication, or homosexual activity implicated fundamental rights. Here, it drew the line. The result is that an unmarried individual has a fundamental right to access to contraceptives but can be prohibited from doing anything with them.

(4) *Defending the Griswold Reasoning.* But there also are ways to support the *Griswold* opinion:

a. *Defending the Penumbra Rationale.* One can criticize the penumbra recognized in *Griswold,* but it is much more difficult to criticize the basic concept of a penumbra. For example, isn't the doctrine of separation of powers a "penumbral" doctrine in the same sense as the rights at stake in *Griswold?* Some constitutions (*e.g.,* state constitutions) contain an explicit requirement of separation of powers; in the federal Constitution, the doctrine "emanates" from the structural parallelism of the first three articles establishing legislative, executive and judicial branches, and enumerating the powers of each. Similarly, the plenary powers of Congress have been interpreted, at least since *McCulloch,* to include "implied powers." *See* Chapter 2. The *Griswold* penumbra may be less readily discernible, but one might conclude that it is difficult to find the basic idea of a penumbra wholly lacking in legitimacy.

b. *The Argument That Fundamental Rights Were Within the Intent of the Framers of the Fourteenth Amendment: Reconsider Gressman, supra.* One readily can argue, as Gressman does, above, that the Privileges or Immunities Clause of the Fourteenth Amendment was intended to protect fundamental rights without specific enumeration. Although the vehicle for protection of the rights at issue in *Griswold* is due process rather than privileges and immunities, the transference of the purposes of the former clause to the latter thus arguably carries out the intent of the framers of the amendment.

c. *Reasoning From Natural Law: Reconsidering Calder v. Bull and Fletcher v. Peck.* Justice Chase's opinion in *Calder* and Justice Marshall's in *Fletcher* depend heavily upon natural law reasoning. In fact, Justice Chase would have relied directly upon the implication that the social compact underlying the Constitution created certain natural rights. For similar reasoning in the non-economic area, consider *Meyer v. Nebraska* and *Pierce v. Society of Sisters,* in a later section, below.

d. *The Difficulty of Avoiding Unacceptable Results If Some Protection of Fundamental Rights is Not Recognized.* It can be argued that, if we did not recognize *some* protection of unenumerated fundamental rights, the statute at issue in *Skinner,* authorizing sterilization of habitual criminals, would be constitutional. Even if that result were deemed acceptable, there would be no clear means of invalidating a hypothetical statute that authorized sterilization of persons in the general population, provided a rational basis (such as population control) could be shown.

e. *Importance of Marital and Sexual Privacy: G. Orwell, Nineteen Eighty-Four (1949).* Even those who criticize *Griswold* generally recognize the importance of marital privacy in a civilized society. George Orwell's famous work hypothesizes a totalitarian state that invades and controls marital and sexual privacy as a means of controlling its subjects.

f. *The Fourth Amendment Right to Be "Secure" in One's "Person."* The Fourth Amendment provides that the right of the people "to be secure in their persons, houses, papers and effects" against unreasonable searches and seizures "shall not be violated." Justice Douglas' opinion emphasizes the unreasonable search and seizure provision. But if instead one emphasizes the right of personal security protected by the amendment, the privacy rationale may be more strongly based than it otherwise appears.

g. *Avoiding State Imposition of Religious Values.* To what extent is the *Griswold* result based upon a unarticulated distaste for the imposition of religious values, in the form of a ban upon contraception, by the state—and can the decision be defended upon this ground?

h. *Equal Treatment of Men and Women or of Rich and Poor.* The *Skinner-Griswold-Eisenstadt* opinions have a strong undercurrent of equal protection in them; indeed, *Skinner* expressly is based upon the Equal

Protection Clause. Without birth control, the consequences of pregnancy fall far more heavily upon women than upon men (and they fall more heavily upon the poor than upon the wealthy). To what extent is *Griswold* arguably based upon these "quasi-equal protection" notions—and can it be defended on that basis?

(5) *The Third Amendment: Engblom v. Carey, 677 F.2d 957 (2d Cir. 1982).* This was the only case that "took the [third] amendment seriously." The Second Circuit held that New York Governor Carey acted unconstitutionally, when correctional officers went on strike, by quartering National Guard replacements in the state-owned, dormitory-style residences of the strikers at a prison. For the most part, it appears that most other citations to the Third Amendment fall into two categories: instances in which the courts have deemed the claims absurd or frivolous and rejected them summarily, or rare uses (as in *Griswold*) in which the Third Amendment is listed with or compared to other amendments. *See* Tom W. Bell, *The Third Amendment: Forgotten but Not Gone*, 2 Wm. & Mary Bill of Rts. J. 117, 118, 140–43 (1993). Do these two categories indicate that *Griswold's* use of the amendment is inappropriate?

(6) *Alternate Routes to the Result in Griswold: From Substantive Due Process to Privileges and Immunities to the Ninth Amendment.* Notice Justice Goldberg's view that the Ninth Amendment "shows a belief of the Constitution's authors that fundamental rights exist that are not expressly enumerated in the first eight amendments," and his conclusion that the rights at stake in *Griswold*, as fundamental rights, are among the unenumerated rights protected by that amendment. This approach may have the advantages of greater fidelity to the text, avoidance of diffuse inferences, and (at minimum) some deference to the intent of the founders, as expressed in their language. Is Justice Goldberg's reasoning appealing? (If so, how does one limit the fundamental rights that remain unenumerated and unrecognized in the Ninth Amendment?) *Cf.* Cooper, *Limited Government and Individual Liberty: The Ninth Amendment's Forgotten Lessons*, 4 J. L. & Pol. 63 (1987); Wells, *Means, Ends and Original Intent: A Response to Charles Coopers*, 4 J. L. & Pol. 81 (1987). Another pathway to the result in *Griswold* might be the Privileges and Immunities Clause, according to the logic of Professor Gressman's article set out above. Would this reasoning be preferable?

A third method of reaching the result might be that of Justice Chase in *Calder v. Bull*: to recognize that the Constitution is based upon a social compact, to infer that natural law is directly implicit in that compact, and to conclude that sexual and reproductive liberties are protected as fundamental. What advantages or disadvantages would follow from this approach? Still a fourth route to the result is shown by Justice Harlan's "ordered liberty" approach: the Fourteenth Amendment Due Process Clause does not merely incorporate the first ten amendments, but also "stands . . . on its own bottom," to protect rights fundamental to the concept of "ordered liberty." Is this approach better than Justice Douglas' penumbra? Justice Harlan argued that the standard for determining a fundamental right was whether the right was "implicit in the concept of ordered liberty." Justice Harlan found this standard in Justice Cardozo's opinion in *Palko v. Connecticut*, 302 U.S. 319 (1937). Does the Cardozo pedigree influence your assessment of the strength of this approach? *See Roe v. Wade*, below.

Another approach relying directly upon due process, but quite different from Justice Harlan's, is that of Justice White, who simply concluded that the Connecticut statute in *Griswold* lacked the requisite means-end relationship and might have validated a more narrowly drawn statute that was reasonably necessary to accomplish a substantial state interest. Yet another route would be to base the *Griswold* result on the Fourth Amendment protection of personal security and, of course, there may be other pathways to the result that we have not listed in this note. Are any of these routes legitimate, and if so, are they more so than Justice Douglas' reasoning in *Griswold? Cf.* Allen, *Taking Liberties: Privacy, Private Choice, and Social Contract Theory*, 56 U. Cin. L. Rev. 461 (1987).

(7) *The Modern Debate Over the Meaning of the Ninth Amendment.* In the 1980s, there was renewed interest in the proper interpretation of the Ninth Amendment which, rather simply, states: "The enumeration in the Constitution, of certain rights, shall not be construed to deny or disparage others retained by the people." In the post-New Deal era, the Ninth Amendment was interpreted as the equivalent of the Tenth Amendment. *See United Pub. Workers v. Mitchell,* 330 U.S. 75 (1947). The Tenth Amendment, you will remember, was "but a truism." *See Darby supra.* Thus, the Ninth Amendment lost any independent substantive content.

As you can see from the *Griswold* decision, Justice Goldberg's concurrence did not gather a majority. His Ninth Amendment analysis was largely relegated to "Notes" in Constitutional Law casebooks.

Probably as a result of the renewal of interest in the "original intentionism" school of interpretation during the Reagan Administration, scholars began to reexamine the history and function of the Ninth Amendment. At least five models have been advanced: (1) the state law rights model; (2) the residual rights model; (3) the individual natural rights model; (4) the collective rights model; and (5) the federalism model. These interpretative models, when applied, yield widely different results (much like the different models for separation of powers analysis). Further discussion is beyond the scope of this casebook, but a comprehensive overview may be found in: Randy Barnett, *The Ninth Amendment: It Means What It Says,* 85 Texas L. Rev. 1 (2006), and the authorities cited therein.

(8) *Striking Down Regulation of Contraceptive Sales: Carey v. Population Services International, 431 U.S. 678 (1977).* This case really involves an updating and extension of the result in *Griswold v. Connecticut,* above. A New York statute made it a crime (1) to distribute contraceptives to minors under sixteen, (2) for anyone other than a licensed pharmacist to distribute contraceptives to anyone, and (3) to advertise or display contraceptives. The plaintiff was a corporation engaged in the mail order retail sale of nonmedical contraceptives, and it regularly advertised in New York. The plurality, per Justice Brennan, struck down the statute on the authority of *Griswold.* "Read in light of its progeny," said the plurality, "the teaching of *Griswold* is that the Constitution protects individual decisions in matters of childbearing from unjustified intrusion by the state." Do the holdings of *Griswold, Eisenstadt v. Baird* and *Carey,* which apply to unmarried as well as married persons and (in the case of *Carey*) to persons under sixteen, imply a right of sexual autonomy?

[B]   Abortion and Substantive Due Process

ROE v. WADE
410 U.S. 113 (1973)

Mr. Justice Blackmun delivered the opinion of the Court.

This Texas federal appeal and its Georgia companion, *Doe v. Bolton,* present constitutional challenges to state criminal abortion legislation. The Texas statutes under attack here are typical of those that have been in effect in many States for approximately a century. The Georgia statutes, in contrast, have a modern cast and are a legislative product that, to an extent at least, obviously reflects the influences of recent attitudinal change, of advancing medical knowledge and techniques, and of new thinking about an old issue.

We forthwith acknowledge our awareness of the sensitive and emotional nature of the abortion controversy, of the vigorous opposing views, even among physicians, and of the deep and seemingly absolute convictions that the subject inspires. . . .

[W]e bear in mind, too, Mr. Justice Holmes' admonition in his now vindicated dissent in *Lochner v. New York.* . . .

I

The Texas statutes that concern us here are Arts. 1191–1194 and 1196 of the State's Penal Code. These make it a crime to "procure an abortion," as therein defined, or to attempt one, except with respect to "an abortion procured or attempted by medical advice for the purpose of saving the life of the mother." Similar statutes are in existence in a majority of the States.

II

Jane Roe, a single woman who was residing in Dallas County, Texas, instituted this federal action in March 1970 against the District Attorney of the county. . . .

Roe alleged that she was unmarried and pregnant; that she wished to terminate her pregnancy by an abortion "performed by a competent, licensed physician, under safe, clinical conditions"; that she was unable to get a "legal" abortion in Texas because her life did not appear to be threatened by the continuation of her pregnancy; and that she could not afford to travel to another jurisdiction in order to secure a legal abortion under safe conditions. She claimed that the Texas statutes were unconstitutionally vague and that they abridged her right of personal privacy, protected by the First, Fourth, Fifth, Ninth, and Fourteenth Amendments. By an amendment toher complaint Roe purported to sue "on behalf of herself and all other women" similarly situated. . . .

VI

It perhaps is not generally appreciated that the restrictive criminal abortion laws in effect in a majority of States today are of relatively recent vintage. [T]hey derive from statutory changes effected, for the most part, in the latter half of the 19th century. . . .

VII

Three reasons have been advanced to explain historically the enactment of criminal abortion laws in the 19th century and to justify their continued existence.

It has been argued occasionally that these laws were the product of a Victorian social concern to discourage illicit sexual conduct. Texas, however, does not advance this justification in the present case, and it appears that no court or commentator has taken the argument seriously.

A second reason is concerned with abortion as a medical procedure. When most criminal abortion laws were first enacted, the procedure was a hazardous one for the woman. . . .

Modern medical techniques have altered this situation. . . .

The third reason is the State's interest—some phrase it in terms of duty—in protecting prenatal life. Some of the argument for this justification rests on the theory that a new human life is present from the moment of conception. The State's interest and general obligation to protect life then extends, it is argued, to prenatal life. Only when the life of the pregnant mother herself is at stake, balanced against the life she carries within her, should the interest of the embryo or fetus not prevail. Logically, of course, a legitimate state interest in this area need not stand or fall on acceptance of the belief that life begins at conception or at some other point prior to live birth. In assessing the State's interest, recognition may be given to the less rigid claim that as long as at least *potential* life is involved, the State may assert interests beyond the protection of the pregnant woman alone. . . .

VIII

The Constitution does not explicitly mention any right of privacy. In a line of decisions, however, going back perhaps as far as *Union Pacific R. Co. v. Botsford*, 141

U.S. 250, 251 (1891), the Court has recognized that a right of personal privacy, or a guarantee of certain areas or zones of privacy, does exist under the Constitution. In varying contexts, the Court or individual Justices have, indeed, found at least the roots of that right in the First Amendment, *Stanley v. Georgia*, 394 U.S. 557, 564 (1969); in the Fourth and Fifth Amendments, *Terry v. Ohio*, 392 U.S. 1, 8–9 (1968); in the penumbras of the Bill of Rights, *Griswold v. Connecticut*; in the Ninth Amendment, *id.*, at 486 (Goldberg, J., concurring); or in the concept of liberty guaranteed by the first section of the Fourteenth Amendment, see *Meyer v. Nebraska*. These decisions make it clear that only personal rights that can be deemed "fundamental" or "implicit in the concept of ordered liberty," *Palko v. Connecticut*, 302 U.S. 319, 325 (1937), are included in this guarantee of personal privacy. They also make it clear that the right has some extension to activities relating to marriage, *Loving v. Virginia*, 388 U.S. 1, 12 (1967); procreation, *Skinner v. Oklahoma*, 316 U.S. 535, 541–542 (1942); contraception, *Eisenstadt v. Baird*; family relationships, *Prince v. Massachusetts*, 321 U.S. 158, 166 (1944); and child rearing and education, *Pierce v. Society of Sisters; Meyer v. Nebraska, supra.*

This right of privacy, whether it be founded in the Fourteenth Amendment's concept of personal liberty and restrictions upon state action, as we feel it is, or, as the District Court determined, in the Ninth Amendment's reservation of rights to the people, is broad enough to encompass a woman's decision whether or not to terminate her pregnancy. The detriment that the State would impose upon the pregnant woman by denying this choice altogether is apparent. Specific and direct harm medically diagnosable even in early pregnancy may be involved. Maternity, or additional offspring, may force upon the woman a distressful life and future. Psychological harm may be imminent. Mental and physical health may be taxed by child care. There is also the distress, for all concerned, associated with the unwanted child, and there is the problem of bringing a child into a family already unable, psychologically and otherwise, to care for it. In other cases, as in this one, the additional difficulties and continuing stigma of unwed motherhood may be involved. All these are factors the woman and her responsible physician necessarily will consider in consultation.

On the basis of elements such as these, appellant and some *amici* argue that the woman's right is absolute and that she is entitled to terminate her pregnancy at whatever time, in whatever way, and for whatever reason she alone chooses. With this we do not agree. . . . As noted above, a State may properly assert important interests in safeguarding health, in maintaining medical standards, and in protecting potential life. At some point in pregnancy, these respective interests become sufficiently compelling to sustain regulation of the factors that govern the abortion decision. . . .

We, therefore, conclude that the right of personal privacy includes the abortion decision, but that this right is not unqualified and must be considered against important state interests in regulation. . . .

Where certain "fundamental rights" are involved, the Court has held that regulation limiting these rights may be justified only by a "compelling state interest," and that legislative enactments must be narrowly drawn to express only the legitimate state interests at stake. *Griswold v. Connecticut.* . . .

IX

A. The appellee and certain *amici* argue that the fetus is a "person" within the language and meaning of the Fourteenth Amendment. In support of this, they outline at length and in detail the well-known facts of development. If this suggestion of personhood is established, the appellant's case, of course, collapses, for the fetus' right to life would then be guaranteed specifically by the Amendment. The appellant conceded as much on reargument. . . .

The Constitution does not define "person" in so many words. Section 1 of the Fourteenth Amendment contains three references to "person." The first, in defining "citizens," speaks of "persons born or naturalized in the United States." The word also appears both in the Due Process Clause and in the Equal Protection Clause. "Person" is used in other places in the Constitution. . . . But in nearly all these instances, the use of the word is such that it has application only postnatally. None indicates, with any assurance, that it has any possible prenatal application.

All this, together with our observation, *supra*, that throughout the major portion of the 19th century prevailing legal abortion practices were far freer than they are today, persuades us that the word "person," as used in the Fourteenth Amendment, does not include the unborn. . . .

This conclusion, however, does not of itself fully answer the contentions raised by Texas, and we pass on to other considerations.

B. The pregnant woman cannot be isolated in her privacy. She carries an embryo and, later, a fetus, if one accepts the medical definitions of the developing young in the human uterus. *See* Dorland's Illustrated Medical Dictionary, 478 479, 547 (24th ed. 1965). The situation therefore is inherently different from marital intimacy, or bedroom possession of obscene material, or marriage, or procreation, or education, with which *Eisenstadt* and *Griswold, Stanley, Loving, Skinner* and *Pierce* and *Meyer* were respectively concerned. As we have intimated above, it is reasonable and appropriate for a State to decide that at some point in time another interest, that of health of the mother or that of potential human life, becomes significantly involved. . . .

Texas urges that, apart from the Fourteenth Amendment, life begins at conception and is present throughout pregnancy, and that, therefore, the State has a compelling interest in protecting that life from and after conception. We need not resolve the difficult question of when life begins. When those trained in the respective disciplines of medicine, philosophy, and theology are unable to arrive at any consensus, the judiciary, at this point in the development of man's knowledge, is not in a position to speculate as to the answer. . . .

X

In view of all this, we do not agree that, by adopting one theory of life, Texas may override the rights of the pregnant woman that are at stake. We repeat, however, that the State does have an important and legitimate interest in preserving and protecting the health of the pregnant woman, whether she be a resident of the State or a non-resident who seeks medical consultation and treatment there, and that it has still *another* important and legitimate interest in protecting the potentiality of human life. These interests are separate and distinct. Each grows in substantiality as the woman approaches term and, at a point during pregnancy, each becomes "compelling."

With respect to the State's important and legitimate interest in the health of the mother, the "compelling" point, in the light of present medical knowledge, is at approximately the end of the first trimester. This is so because of the now-established medical fact, referred to above, that until the end of the first trimester mortality in abortion may be less than mortality in normal childbirth. It follows that, from and after this point, a State may regulate the abortion procedure to the extent that the regulation reasonably relates to the preservation and protection of maternal health. Examples of permissible state regulation in this area are requirements as to the qualifications of the person who is to perform the abortion; as to the licensure of that person; as to the facility in which the procedure is to be performed, that is, whether it must be a hospital or may be a clinic or some other place of less-than-hospital status; as to the licensing of the facility; and the like.

This means, on the other hand, that, for the period of pregnancy prior to this "compelling" point, the attending physician, in consultation with his patient, is free to determine, without regulation by the State, that, in his medical judgment, the patient's pregnancy should be terminated. If that decision is reached, the judgment may be effectuated by an abortion free of interference by the State.

With respect to the State's important and legitimate interest in potential life, the "compelling" point is at viability. This is so because the fetus then presumably has the capability of meaningful life outside the mother's womb. State regulation protective of fetal life after viability thus has both logical and biological justifications. If the State is interested in protecting fetal life after viability, it may go so far as to proscribe abortion during that period, except when it is necessary to preserve the life or health of the mother.

Measured against these standards, Art. 1196 of the Texas Penal Code, in restricting legal abortions to those "procured or attempted by medical advice for the purpose of saving the life of the mother," sweeps too broadly. . . . The statute, therefore, cannot survive the constitutional attack made upon it here.

[The concurring opinion of Justice Stewart is omitted.]

MR. JUSTICE DOUGLAS, concurring [in an opinion also applicable to *Doe v. Bolton*, below]. . . .

The Ninth Amendment obviously does not create federally enforceable rights. It merely says, "The enumeration in the Constitution, of certain rights, shall not be construed to deny or disparage others retained by the people." But a catalogue of these rights includes customary, traditional, and time-honored rights, amenities, privileges, and immunities that come within the sweep of "the Blessings of Liberty" mentioned in the preamble to the Constitution. Many of them, in my view, come within the meaning of the term "liberty" as used in the Fourteenth Amendment.

First is the autonomous control over the development and expression of one's intellect, interests, tastes, and personality.

These are rights protected by the First Amendment and, in my view, they are absolute, permitting of no exceptions.

Second is freedom of choice in the basic decisions of one's life respecting marriage, divorce, procreation, contraception, and the education and upbringing of children.

These rights, unlike those protected by the First Amendment, are subject to some control by the police power. Thus, the Fourth Amendment speaks only of "unreasonable searches and seizures" and of "probable cause." These rights are "fundamental," and we have held that in order to support legislative action the statute must be narrowly and precisely drawn and that a "compelling state interest" must be shown in support of the limitation. . . .

Third is the freedom to care for one's health and person, freedom from bodily restraint or compulsion, freedom to walk, stroll, or loaf.

These rights, though fundamental, are likewise subject to regulation on a showing of "compelling state interest. . . ."

MR. JUSTICE REHNQUIST, dissenting.

. . . I have difficulty in concluding, as the Court does, that the right of "privacy" is involved in this case. Texas, by the statute here challenged, bars the performance of a medical abortion by a licensed physician on a plaintiff such as Roe. A transaction resulting in an operation such as this is not "private" in the ordinary usage of that word. Nor is the "privacy" that the Court finds here even a distant relative of the freedom from searches and seizures protected by the Fourth Amendment to the Constitution, which the Court has referred to as embodying a right to privacy.

If the Court means by the term "privacy" no more than that the claim of a person to be free from unwanted state regulation of consensual transactions may be a form of "liberty" protected by the Fourteenth Amendment, there is no doubt that similar claims have been upheld in our earlier decisions on the basis of that liberty. . . . But that liberty is not guaranteed absolutely against deprivation, only against deprivation without due process of law. The test traditionally applied in the area of social and economic legislation is whether or not a law such as that challenged has a rational relation to a valid state objective. *Williamson v. Lee Optical Co.*, 348 U.S. 483, 491. The Due Process Clause of the Fourteenth Amendment undoubtedly does place a limit, albeit a broad one, on legislative power to enact laws such as this. If the Texas statute were to prohibit an abortion even where the mother's life is in jeopardy, I have little doubt that such a statute would lack a rational relation to a valid state objective under the test stated in *Williamson, supra*. But the Court's sweeping invalidation of any restrictions on abortion during the first trimester is impossible to justify under that standard, and the conscious weighing of competing factors that the Court's opinion apparently substitutes for the established test is far more appropriate to a legislative judgment than to a judicial one. . . .

While the Court's opinion quotes from the dissent of Mr. Justice Holmes in *Lochner v. New York*, 198 U.S. 45, 74, (1905), the result it reaches is more closely attuned to the majority opinion of Mr. Justice Peckham in that case. As in *Lochner* and similar cases applying substantive due process standards to economic and social welfare legislation, the adoption of the compelling state interest standard will inevitably require this Court to examine the legislative policies and pass on the wisdom of these policies in the very process of deciding whether a particular state interest put forward may or may not be "compelling." The decision here to break pregnancy into three distinct terms and to outline the permissible restrictions the State may impose in each one, for example, partakes more of judicial legislation than it does of a determination of the intent of the drafters of the Fourteenth Amendment.

To reach its result, the Court necessarily has had to find within the scope of the Fourteenth Amendment a right that was apparently completely unknown to the drafters of the Amendment. . . . By the time of the adoption of the Fourteenth Amendment in 1868, there were at least 36 laws enacted by state or territorial legislatures limiting abortion. . . .

There apparently was no question concerning the validity of this provision or of any of the other state statutes when the Fourteenth Amendment was adopted. The only conclusion possible from this history is that the drafters did not intend to have the Fourteenth Amendment withdraw from the States the power to legislate with respect to this matter. . . .

MR. JUSTICE WHITE, with whom MR. JUSTICE REHNQUIST joins, dissenting. . . .

[I] find nothing in the language or history of the Constitution to support the Court's judgments. The Court simply fashions and announces a new constitutional right for pregnant women and, with scarcely any reason or authority for its action, invests that right with sufficient substance to override most existing state abortion statutes. The upshot is that the people and the legislatures of the 50 States are constitutionally disentitled to weigh the relative importance of the continued existence and development of the fetus, on the one hand, against a spectrum of possible impactson the mother, on the other hand. As an exercise of raw judicial power, the Court perhaps has authority to do what it does today; but in my view its judgment is an improvident and extravagant exercise of the power of judicial review that the Constitution extends to this Court.

. . . In a sensitive area such as this, involving as it does issues over which reasonable men may easily and heatedly differ, I cannot accept the Court's exercise of its clear power of choice by interposing a constitutional barrier to state efforts to protect human life and by investing women and doctors with the constitutionally protected right to exterminate it. This issue, for the most part, should be left with the people and to the political processes the people have devised to govern their affairs. . . .

DOE v. BOLTON [COMPANION CASE TO ROE]
410 U.S. 179 (1973)

MR. JUSTICE BLACKMUN delivered the opinion of the Court.

In this appeal, the criminal abortion statutes recently enacted in Georgia are challenged on constitutional grounds.

[The Georgia law was more "modern" than the Texas statute in *Roe*. The Georgia law was based on three exceptions not contained in the Texas law: (1) serious and permanent injury to the woman's "health"; (2) fetal defect; and (3) pregnancy arising from rape. The Georgia law also had a "residency requirement for the woman; the residency requirement was attacked under substantive due process and the Article IV, § 2 Privileges and Immunities Clause, *See* Section 3.04 above.]

Section 26-1201 [which was based on the model Penal Code], with a referenced exception, makes abortion a crime, and § 26-1203 provides that a person convicted of that crime shall be punished by imprisonment for not less than one nor more than 10 years. Section 26-1202(a) states the exception and removes from § 1201's definition of criminal abortion, and thus makes noncriminal, an abortion "performed by a physician duly licensed" in Georgia when, "based upon his best clinical judgment" . . . an abortion is necessary because:

> (1) A continuation of the pregnancy would endanger the life of the pregnant woman or would seriously and permanently injure her health; or

> (2) The fetus would very likely be born with a grave, permanent, and irremediable mental or physical defect; or

> (3) The pregnancy resulted from forcible or statutory rape.

[The lower court struck the three numbered restrictive paragraphs from the statute. This holding, which the Supreme Court here sustains, meant that abortion was noncriminal if it merely was "necessary" in the physician's "best clinical judgment."]

A. *Roe v. Wade, supra*, sets forth our conclusion that a pregnant woman does not have an absolute constitutional right to an abortion on her demand. What is said there is applicable here and need not be repeated. . . .

C. Appellants argue that § 26-1202 (a) of the Georgia statutes, as it has been left by the District Court's decision, is unconstitutionally vague.

The vagueness argument is set at rest by the decision in *United States v. Vuitch*, 402 U.S. 62, 71–72 (1971), where the issue was raised with respect to a District of Columbia statute making abortions criminal "unless the same were done as necessary for the preservation of the mother's life or health and under the direction of a competent licensed practitioner of medicine." That statute has been construed to bear upon psychological as well as physical well-being.

We agree with the District Court that the medical judgment may be exercised in the light of all factors—physical, emotional, psychological, familial, and the woman's age—relevant to the well-being of the patient. All these factors may relate to health. This allows the attending physician the room he needs to make his best medical judgment. And it is room that operates for the benefit, not the disadvantage, of the pregnant woman.

D. The appellants next argue that the District Court should have declared unconstitutional three procedural demands of the Georgia statute: (1) that the abortion be performed in a hospital accredited by the Joint Commission on Accreditation of Hospitals; (2) that the procedure be approved by the hospital staff abortion committee; and (3) that the performing physician's judgment be confirmed by the independent examinations of the patient by two other licensed physicians. [Here, the Court strikes down each of these three requirements. As for the accredited hospital requirement, the State had failed to prove that "only the full resources of a licensed hospital" could satisfy relevant health concerns. The requirement of approval by a hospital committee was "unduly restrictive of the patient's rights and needs." The two-physician-concurrence provision was unnecessary since the statute required the woman's own physician to determine that "an abortion is necessary." "That should be sufficient," concluded the Court.]

E. The appellants attack the residency requirement of the Georgia law, as violative of the right to travel stressed in Shapiro v. Thompson, 394 U.S. 618 (1969), and other cases. A requirement of this kind, of course, could be deemed to have some relationship to the availability of post-procedure medical care for the aborted patient.

Nevertheless, we do not uphold the constitutionality of the residence requirement. It is not based on any policy of preserving state-supported facilities for Georgia residents, for the bar also applies to private hospitals and to privately retained physicians. There is no intimation, either, that Georgia facilities are utilized to capacity in caring for Georgia residents. Just as the Privileges and Immunities Clause, Const. Art. IV, § 2, protects persons who enter other States to ply their trade, so must it protect persons who enter Georgia seeking the medical services that are available there. *See* Toomer v. Witsell, 334 U.S. 385 (1948). A contrary holding would mean that a State could limit to its own residents the general medical care available within its borders. This we could not approve. . . .

MR. CHIEF JUSTICE BURGER, concurring [in an opinion also applicable to *Roe v. Wade*, above]. . . .

[F]or my part, I would be inclined to allow a State to require the certification of two physicians to support an abortion, but the Court holds otherwise. I do not believe that such a procedure is unduly burdensome, as are the complex steps of the Georgia statute, which require as many as six doctors and the use of a hospital certified by the JCAH.

I do not read the Court's holdings today as having the sweeping consequences attributed to them by the dissenting Justices; the dissenting views discount the reality that the vast majority of physicians observe the standards of their profession, and act only on the basis of carefully deliberated medical judgments relating to life and health. Plainly, the Court today rejects any claim that the Constitution requires abortions on demand.

MR. JUSTICE REHNQUIST, dissenting.

[S]ince, as indicated by my dissent in *Wade*, I view the compelling-state-interest standard as an inappropriate measure of the constitutionality of state abortion laws, I respectfully dissent from the majority's holding.

NOTES AND QUESTIONS

(1)   *The Legalization of Abortion as a Woman's Fundamental Right: Roe v. Wade, 410 U.S. 113 (1973).* In this post-*Griswold* substantive due process decision, the State of Texas had criminalized all abortions, with the exception of abortions necessary to save the life of the mother. Roe, a young single woman with an unwanted pregnancy, was the plaintiff. She alleged that her pregnancy was the result of a rape. (Although Roe recanted the rape story twenty years later, the case was adjudicated on the basis of a pregnancy created by a rape.) Even though as of 1973, several states (*e.g.*, New York and California) had liberalized their respective abortion laws, the Court analyzed Roe's claim against a historical background where most states had made access to abortion medical services largely illegal. The Texas law was one of the most restrictive laws on access to abortion.

The Court, per Justice Blackmun (a Nixon appointee), ruled (7-2) in favor of Roe's claim and struck down the Texas ban on abortion. The Court analyzed the case on textual, historical, precedential (*e.g.*, *Griswold*), and policy grounds; these are examined in the Notes below. For present purposes, you should recognize that *Roe* involved three basic holdings: (1) that, for federal constitutional purposes, a fetus is not a "person;" (2) that a woman has a "fundamental right" to have access to abortion-related medical services; and (3) that, applying the strict scrutiny standard to the asserted state interests in "maternal health" and "potential human life," the state: (a) could not prohibit abortions in the first trimester of pregnancy; (b) could require a woman to be "hospitalized" for second-trimester abortions, but could not ban pre-viability abortions; and (c) could ban all third trimester (post-viability) abortions.

The third holding, arising out of the application of strict scrutiny, was known as the "trimester system." Almost all states reformed their abortion regulations to conform to the trimester system of *Roe*. (Almost all states banned third-trimester abortions, but some, such as Colorado, continued to permit medically supervised third trimester abortions.) The trimester system was eventually overruled in the *Casey* decision below—when the Court changed the governing constitutional standard from strict scrutiny to "undue burden"—but it is discussed here because it was one of the basic holdings in *Roe*.

(2) *Did the Court in Roe v. Wade "Write a Statute"?* One aspect of *Roe v. Wade* that has been subjected to much criticism, and that is not present in *Skinner* or *Griswold*, is the detailed nature of the trimester holding, which actually depends upon express time deadlines. Justice Rehnquist criticizes the Court for judicial legislation; does the nature of the holding support the conclusion that the Court "wrote a statute"? Or is the holding simply one in which the Court was required by the nature of the conflicting interests to draw bright lines, as it has been on occasion in other areas? For more on the historical background of *Roe v. Wade, see* LINDA GREENHOUSE, BECOMING JUSTICE BLACKMUN (2005).

(3) *The Roe Standard for Determination of a Fundamental Right.* The determination that a woman has a "fundamental right" to terminate an unwanted pregnancy was one of the three basic holdings in *Roe*. The *Roe* Court stated that the standard it used to find a fundamental right is whether the "personal right" is "implicit in the concept of ordered liberty." The Court adopted this standard from Justice Harlan's concurrence in *Griswold*, above. As you may recall, Justice Harlan adopted this test from *Palko v. Connecticut*, 302 U.S. 319, 325 (1937). The *Palko* decision was authored by Justice Cardozo.

As mentioned above, the 1992 *Casey* decision overruled the trimester holding. But, as you will see, the *Casey* Court confirmed what it called the "central" holding of *Roe*. That central holding was the fundamental rights holding, based on the "implicit in the concept of ordered liberty" standard.

(4) *Discrete and Insular Minorities: Does Roe v. Wade Protect Them?—Recalling the Carolene Products Footnote.* In *United States v. Carolene Products*, in Chapter One *above*, the Court suggested that stricter standards of review might be applicable in three types of situations, including that in which rights of "discrete and insular minorities" were at stake. Assuming that this principle legitimately may be used to justify stricter scrutiny, is it properly invoked in *Roe v. Wade?*

Is it women who are the discrete and insular minority? If so, they are an unusual one, because they constitute a literal majority—but politically, they are not cohesive, and yet they are able to obtain majoritarian support for abortion rights because their number so inclined, coupled with men so inclined, constitute the majority. On the other hand, perhaps pregnant women are the discrete and insular minority at issue. But if it could be shown that the majority of such women do not desire abortions, is that definition of the class justifiable? Finally, one might regard the protected minority as pregnant women desiring but denied abortions, or as poor women who might seek abortions. But if we split the classes so finely, won't we find that a heavily impacted class that might be called a discrete and insular minority lurks within every statute?

One manner of criticizing the opinion might be to consider that fetuses/unborn children constitute the most discrete and insular of minorities, and that the Court has acted in a situation in which the majority has sought to protect precisely that class. This reasoning would picture the Court in the ironic position of countermanding majoritarian efforts to protect a discrete and insular minority.

Roe was decided, of course, as a substantive due process case. The issue, after *Griswold*, was whether the state regulation burdened a "fundamental right"—not whether it burdened a "suspect class." This note asks you to consider whether an equal protection—suspect class approach would be justifiable and whether it would reach different results. Perhaps the leading theorist who would have preferred that the abortion issue be approached under equal—protection—gender discrimination is Ruth Bader Ginsburg, *Some Thoughts on Autonomy and Equality in Relation to Roe v. Wade*, 63 N.C.L. REV. 375 (1985) (now, Justice Ginsburg).

(5) *The Dissents in Roe.* Justice White (a Kennedy appointment) dissented on what might be called "federalism" grounds. He argued that each state should be able to determine, through its political processes, what should be the appropriate posture on the abortion question. Justice Rehnquist (a Nixon appointment) dissented on somewhat different grounds. Justice Rehnquist rejected the Court's holding that the woman has a "fundamental right." Thus, absent a fundamental right, Justice Rehnquist would apply rational basis scrutiny (and would uphold the state regulation).

Notice Justice Rehnquist's approach: he would use a mere rationality test, not a strict scrutiny approach, and his conclusion is that much of the two statutes in question in *Roe* and *Doe* could be upheld on the basis of such a test. On the other hand, the majority invokes strict scrutiny. Only a statute that is (1) "narrowly drawn" to serve (2) a "compelling state interest" can survive such scrutiny. This test applies because of the conclusion that a "fundamental" right is at stake. Justice Blackmun's opinion finds a countervailing state interest in maternal health that is sufficiently compelling, but only during the second and third trimesters of a pregnancy, and the statute is not tailored sufficiently narrowly in the majority's view to this interest. The second compelling interest was the state's interest in the "potential life" of the fetus. This interest becomes compelling at the point of fetal viability (*i.e.*, when the lungs develop).

(6) *The "Person" Holding of Roe.* The *Roe* Court held that a fetus was not a "person" for purposes of the Fourteenth Amendment's Due Process Clause. As the Court explained, if a fetus were a person, then the State could satisfy strict scrutiny because it would have a compelling interest (in the life of the fetus), and it would have no less restrictive alternative than banning abortion services (as did the Texas law).

Many have recognized that this holding could be overturned by a constitutional amendment under Article V. This is the origin of the various proposed amendments that would define the term "person." Some of these would define a "person" as beginning at "conception."

(7) *Abortion and Privileges and Immunities: The Residency Requirement of Doe v. Bolton, 410 U.S. 179 (1973).* The *Doe* Court struck down the residency requirement. The Georgia challengers had relied primarily on a right of interstate travel. The Court, however, relied on Article IV, § 2. The *Doe* Court held that access to health care was a fundamental right for purposes of the Privileges and Immunities Clause and that the state could not satisfy the double substantiality standard. *See* § 3.04 and the *Piper* decision above.

PROBLEM A

DO COURT-ORDERED CESAREAN SECTIONS VIOLATE THE CONSTITUTIONAL RIGHT OF PRIVACY?: DEACONESS HOSPITAL v. McROBERTS, unreported trial court decision and unreported application for writ of prohibition, case number unavailable (Mo. Ct. App. May 1987), reported in INSIGHT MAGAZINE, June 22, 1987, at 58; accord, interview with Kent Karohl, judge presiding, by telephone from Houston, Texas (April 20, 1988).

On the eve of delivery, a pregnant woman countermands her physician's advice and chooses against cesarean section. She has three other children, all born via cesareans, and states that she does not want to undergo a fourth incision, fears the complications of surgery (including transfusion), and prefers a natural birth. Her physicians and hospital representatives, convinced that natural birth presents a significant risk of uterus rupture that would cause the death of her fetus/unborn child, go to court to force the woman to submit to cesarean section. [Note: This problem is not hypothetical; a nationwide survey found twenty-one cases in which court-ordered cesareans have been sought, with eighteen requests granted. *See Expert Says Court Use May* Deter Women Seeking Maternity Care, Houston Chronicle, May 13, 1987, at § 1, at 8, col. 2 (Associated Press).] Consider the following issues:

(1) *Can the State Prohibit Natural Birth and Require a Cesarean Section Against the Woman's Wishes?* Consider and apply the reasoning of *Roe v. Wade* to this situation. Can the cesarean section requirement be upheld under that reasoning? [Judge Karohl, in *McRoberts, supra,* states that he reviewed the trial judge's 6 p.m. decision at 7 p.m., on oral pleadings and on a partially oral report of the record, and, at the hospital, rendered an emergency oral decision that upheld the trial court's order requiring the cesarean.]

(2) *What If the Woman Finds Another Physician Who Concurs With Her Wishes?* The woman's right to follow the advice of her physician is a major concern in *Roe v. Wade.* What if the woman seeks another opinion and, after a search, finds a physician who supports her desire to give birth naturally, stating that he sees no significant risk and agrees that natural childbirth has advantages? Assume that the hospital and her former physicians remain strongly of the opinion that a cesarean is indicated. If the court concludes that there is "some" greater risk from natural rather than cesarean birth, as opposed to "significant" risk, would it act unconstitutionally in ordering a cesarean section?

(3) *Does the Unborn Child Have Rights Based Upon the Due Process Clause in These Circumstances?* Does the fetus/unborn child have relevant rights that are protected by the Due Process Clause in this circumstance? Is this fetus/unborn child a "person," and if so, when did he/she become one (or is it the fact that all concerned contemplate his/her becoming a "person" that makes the difference)? Is there is principled basis for weighing the fetus/unborn child's due process interests, if any, against those of the putative mother?

(4) *Negative Fallout From Forced Cesarean Sections: What is the Relevance of Discouraging Prenatal Care?* Some lawyers who have studied the problem of court-ordered cesarean sections argue that "this melange of the state and medicine is likely to harm more fetuses than it helps, since many women will quite reasonably avoid physicians altogether during pregnancy if failure to follow medical advice can result in forced treatment." Assuming it is true, what significance should this concern have?

[C]   Is Abortion a "Clash of Absolutes"—Or Is There Room for Persuasion?: "Serious, Respectful Debate" with "Greater Humility"

L. TRIBE, ABORTION: THE CLASH OF ABSOLUTES
238–41 (1990)*

It is an uncomfortable truth that the pro-choice movement draws its support disproportionately from various privileged elites. . . . Those who are pro-choice as a group tend to earn more that those who are pro-life; they have enjoyed more of modern society's ostensible benefits. . . . The pro-life movement, in turn, draws

---

disproportionately from the remaining groups, those "distanced from elite culture by their membership in relatively recent immigrant groups and in lower-status religious groups. . . ."

. . . [T]here is a pervasive sense of mutual distrust that arises from the conspicuously different social positioning and cultural orientation of the combatants in the abortion war.

Thus, pro-life adherents are quick to denounce those who favor choice as morally blind, deceived by their supposed sophistication into equating license with liberty and into rationalizing the murder of the helpless as a way to preserve the "quality of life. . . ."

Pro-choice advocates, for their part, tend to denounce the hypocrisy of pro-lifers and stress their supposed insensitivity to life in other settings (military adventurism, gun control, the death penalty) and their supposed lack of concern for babies and toddlers in such contexts as infant nutrition, day care, and aid to families with dependent children. At the same time . . . pro-choice advocates are quick to boast of their own broad-mindedness and respect for others, their devotion to democracy and to egalitarian values.

Where are those fine qualities, one might ask, when pro-choicers sometimes talk as though pro-life advocates are nasty and brutish types whose opinions don't deserve to be taken all that seriously? . . .

For both sides, therefore, a greater measure of humility seems in order. If we genuinely believe in the democratic principle of one person, one vote, then each of us will have to treat the votes, and hear the voices, of our "opponents" as being no less worthy or meaningful than our own.

On both sides of the abortion debate, this will require an unaccustomed and in some ways almost unnatural forbearance. Right to life advocates are inclined to respond to pleas for tolerance by insisting that the exclusion of the fetus from the processes of voting and debate distorts the discussion profoundly from the outset, for reasons that bear no proper relation to a moral or just outcome. . . .

And pro-choice advocates are inclined to react to pleas for mutual respect by insisting, no less vehemently, that it begs the question to attribute legitimacy to the views of those who would tell women how to lead their lives and what to do with their bodies. . . .

In the end, the answer to both sides is the same: *In a democracy, voting and persuasion are all we have.* Not even the Constitution is beyond amendment. And since we must therefore persuade one another even about which "rights" the Constitution ought to place beyond the reach of any temporary voting majority, *nothing*, neither life nor liberty, can be regarded as immune to politics writ large. . . .

. . . The lesson to be drawn from the arrogance of many pro-choice people who profess humility and mutuality is not that they should prove their democratic bona fides by sacrificing what they believe are fundamental rights, but that they should never take the rightness of their fundamental views as self-evident or think of their opponents as unworthy of engaging in serious, respectful debate. . . .

[D]　The Progeny of *Roe v. Wade*: Many Years of Grappling with Abortion-Related Issues

[1]　Abortion Consent, Notification, Etc.

NOTE ON THE *DANFORTH, BELLOTTI* AND *MATHESON* DECISIONS

After establishment of a fundamental right to terminate pregnancy, consent or notification of others became an early battleground. What if the woman's husband objected? What if a minorsought an abortion without her parents consent—and for that matter, what if she sought to avoid even notifying them? The Court struck down restrictive statutes in these areas.

Striking Down Requirements for Husbands' or Parents' Consent: Planned Parenthood v. Danforth, 428 U.S. 52 (1976). In this case, the Court, per Justice Blackmun, struck down a Missouri statute requiring a woman's husband to consent to her obtaining an abortion and also requiring consent of the parents of an unmarried teenager under age 18, unless a physician certified that the abortion was necessary to preserve her life.

Justice White, joined by Chief Justice Burger and Justice Rehnquist, dissented from the invalidation of the statute: "It is truly surprising that the majority finds in the United States Constitution . . . a rule that the state must assign a greater value to a mother's decision to cut off a potential human life by abortion than to a father's decision to let it mature into a live child. Such a rule cannot be found there, nor can it be found in *Roe v. Wade*. . . ." As for the parental consent requirement, "Missouri is entitled to protect the minor unmarried woman from making the decision in a way which is not in her own best interest, and it seeks to achieve this goal by requiring parental consultation and consent." Finally, Justice Stevens dissented from the parental-consent holding.

Adding a Judicial-Approval Escape Valve Does Not Salvage a Blanket Parental Consent Requirement: Bellotti v. Baird, 443 U.S. 622 (1979). This companion case to *Danforth* involved a Massachusetts statute that added an escape valve to the parental consent requirement, as follows: "If one or both of the mother's parents refuse . . . consent, consent may be obtained by order of a judge of the Superior Court for good cause shown, after such hearing as he deems necessary." The plurality concluded that, in order for parental consent requirements to stand, the state "must provide an alternative procedure" in which a minor can obtain the abortion by "show[ing] either: (1) that she is mature enough and well enough informed to make her abortion decision, in consultation with her physician, independently of her parent's wishes; or (2) that even if she is not able to make this decision independently, the desired abortion would be in her best interest." Therefore, the statute "[fell] short . . . in [both] respects."

NOTES AND QUESTIONS

(1) *An Unjustified Faith in Judicial or Administrative Abortion Decisionmaking?: Considering the "Alternative Procedure" Requirement of Baird.* Justice Stevens, joined by Justices Brennan, Marshall, and Blackmun, concurred in the judgment in *Baird*—but wrote separately to say, "the provision of an absolute veto to a judge—or, potentially, to an appointed administrator—is to me particularly troubling. [T]he only standard provided for the judge's decision is the best interest of the minor. That standard provides little real guidance to the judge, and his decision must necessarily reflect personal and societal values. . . ." Does the alternative procedure requirement in *Baird* repose unjustified faith in the judiciary?

(2) *Did the Court in Danforth and Baird Identify and Consider All of the Relevant Interests?* In *Danforth* and *Baird*, however, the Court considered only the husband's interest and the state's interest in the marriage relationship; it did not express any

concern for the interest in preserving potential life. What would have been the result if the Court had considered the *cumulative weight* of *all* interests restraining the abortion decision, thus combining the strength of the husband's interest, the state's interest in the marriage relationship, and the state's interest in potential life? *See* Regan, *Rewriting Roe v. Wade*, 77 MICH. L. REV. 1569 (1979).

(3) *Are There Other Interests At Stake?: Medical Malpractice or Safety Concerns; Avoidance of Undue Influence; "Fetal Pain."* In fact, does the preceding note really catalogue all of the relevant interests? Consider the following—

    a. *Undue Influence; Physician's Attitude Toward Abortion.* Might the state's relevant interests include protecting against the possibility that the ethical or philosophical opinions of the physician toward the pregnant woman's life choices might have undue influence upon the decision? In this regard, consider whether the parental or spousal consent requirements might serve to prevent this possibility from occurring.

    b. *Prevention of Malpractice; Safety Concern.* The Missouri statute also contained a ban on saline-method abortions, which was based ostensibly on safety concerns. Evidence showed the "danger of severe complications" after the first trimester; the Chief of Obstetrics at Yale University had testified that "physicians should be liable for malpractice if they chose saline over prostaglandin [methodology]." The latter method was shown by considerable evidence to have been safer, but the majority found that it was not readily available. Justice White criticized "[t]he majority's finding of fact" in this regard as "wholly unjustifiable."

    c. *Fetal Pain.* Does a fetus suffer pain from an abortion? Obviously, no living person has direct knowledge, although some have inferred that they do; this opinion is opposed by many others. The inference is based upon such evidence as the degree of development of the nervous system and photographic or motion picture recordations of fetuses by modern techniques within the womb during the actual event. Does this evidence, such as it is, create a cognizable state interest?

    d. *Other Interests.* Are there any additional interests that should be weighed in the balance?

PROBLEM B

NOONAN'S HYPOTHETICAL—THE FATHER WHO WISHES A CEREMONIAL BURIAL FOR THE FETUS. Professor Noonan points out that a husband, frustrated in his desire to prevent abortion by either persuasion or law, might so strongly believe that it represented the killing of his child that he might demand access to the remains of the fetus so as to provide it a ceremonial burial. But Professor Noonan concludes that the law's denial that the fetus is a person precludes its recognition of any legitimate interest in the husband to do so. Noonan, *The Root and Branch of Roe v. Wade*, 63 NEB. L. REV. 668, 678–79 (1984). Indeed, as Noonan points out, the Court struck down a requirement of "humane and sanitary" treatment of aborted fetuses in the *Akron* decision, below.

(1) *A Constitutionally Cognizable Interest in Burying the Fetus?* Does the father or husband have any right, or any interest short of a right that the Constitution does or should recognize, in this regard?

(2) *Is the Father's Interest Dependent Upon Personhood For the Fetus?* Is Noonan correct in concluding that the law cannot recognize the father's interest because it does not recognize that the fetus is a person?

(3) *The Woman's Interest In Avoiding Recognition of This Interest.* Does the woman, in turn, have a cognizable interest in avoiding implicit recognition of the

father/husband's beliefs, or even in preventing what she might regard as prurient preoccupation with the products of her bodily processes?

[2] Abortion Funding

Another battleground was abortion funding. Both the states and the federal government sought to restrict use of Medicaid money for this purpose. Some observers were surprised when a Court that had recognized a fundamental right, and protected it from consent and notice requirements, upheld the funding restrictions.

Upholding the Refusal to Fund Even Medically Necessary Abortions: Harris v. McRae, 448 U.S. 297 (1980). A series of provisions, collectively known as the Hyde Amendment, prohibited the use of federal Medicaid funds for abortions other than those necessary to save the life of the pregnant woman. A later version contained an exception for "instances where severe and long-lasting physical health damage to the mother would result if the pregnancy were carried to term when so determined by two physicians." The Court, per Justice Stewart, recognized that "the Hyde Amendment affects [t]he interest of a woman in protecting her health during pregnancy," but it nevertheless upheld the Hyde Amendment:

> [I]t simply does not follow that a woman's freedom of choice carries with it a constitutional entitlement to the financial resources to avail herself of the full range of protected choices. [A]lthough government may not place obstacles in the path of a woman's exercise of her freedom of choice, it need not remove those not of its own creation. Indigency falls in the latter category. . . .

> [T]o hold otherwise would mark a drastic change in our understanding of the Constitution. It cannot be that because government may not prohibit the use of contraceptives, [o]r prevent parents from sending their child to a private school, [g]overnment, therefore, has an affirmative constitutional obligation to insure that all persons have the financial resources to obtain contraceptives or send their children to private schools.

Justice Stevens, joined by Justices Brennan, Marshall, and Blackmun (each of whom wrote separately), dissented.

[3] The Third And Fourth Generations Of Abortion Statutes: Regulating The Circumstances Of Abortion

NOTE ON THE 1983 ABORTION DECISIONS: *AKRON* AND *ASHCROFT*

After *Danforth* and *Bellotti*, several cases arose involving statutes regulating the circumstances of abortion. Abortion advocates challenged various laws on the theory that they impermissibly burdened abortion or were unduly broad.

City of Akron v. Akron Center for Reproductive Health, Inc., 462 U.S. 416 (1983). The Court struck down five provisions in an Akron city ordinance, which (1) required that all abortions after the first trimester be performed in a hospital; (2) imposed a blanket parental notification requirement for unmarried minors; (3) required the physician to make certain specific disclosures, including a statement that the fetus was a "child" and was "human," as a condition of informed consent; (4) mandated a twenty-four hour waiting period; and (5) governed disposition of the remains of an aborted fetus, mandating "humane and sanitary" treatment. The Court concluded that these requirements imposed "significant" burdens upon the fundamental right to abortion.

Planned Parenthood Association v. Ashcroft, 462 U.S. 476 (1983), struck down a mandatory hospital requirement, but upheld statutory provisions requiring (1) a pathology report for each abortion, (2) a second physician during abortions after viability, and (3) parental consent for abortions involving minors, subject to an alternative procedure by which a juvenile court could authorize abortion if the minor was mature or if abortion was in her best interest.

The Court's Reaffirmation of Roe v. Wade; Justice O'Connor's Dissents. In the course of deciding these cases, particularly *Akron*, the Court majority reaffirmed its holding in *Roe v. Wade*. Justice O'Connor, joined by Justices White and Rehnquist, dissented. She concluded that the trimester framework, with its absolute deadlines, was fallacious: the fact that a state had a compelling interest after a certain point in time did not mean that it lacked legitimate interests before that point. Thus, in considering whether statutory requirements placed an "undue burden" on the right to abortion, the Court had failed adequately to consider the countervailing interests of the state. The "burden" inquiry raised "extremely sensitive issues," and "the appropriate forum for their resolution in a democracy is the legislature." Ultimately, Justice O'Connor's dissenting position prevailed in the *Casey* opinion below.

NOTE ON THE 1986 ABORTION DECISION
(*THORNBURGH v. AMERICAN COLLEGE OF OBSTETRICIANS AND GYNECOLOGISTS*)

The Issues in the Thornburgh Case: Thornburgh v. American College of Obstetricians and Gynecologists, 476 U.S. 747 (1986). The 1986 *Thornburgh* case concerned the constitutionality of six provisions in the Pennsylvania Abortion Control Act of 1982. These provisions did the following: (1) required "informed consent," as defined by the Act, for each abortion; (2) prescribed lengthy printed information to be given to the woman; (3) required reporting of detailed information about the abortion; (4) required a determination of viability; (5) required the physician in a postviability abortion to exercise the care that would be exercised if the child were intended to be born alive and to use the abortion technique most likely to cause the "unborn child" to be "aborted alive"; and (6) required a second physician to attend a postviability abortion.

"Undue Burdens" on the Abortion Decision. Justice Blackmun's opinion for the Court struck down all six questioned provisions. Most were struck down because they were "undue burdens" on the abortion decision, which was to be made by the pregnant woman with her physician's advice.

The Dissents. The most influential dissent was that of Justice O'Connor, joined by Justice Rehnquist; Chief Justice Burger and Justice White also dissented. Justice O'Connor restated the position set forth in her *Akron* dissents and added that the Court had gone "well beyond distortion of the 'unduly burdensome' standard."

NOTES AND QUESTIONS

(1) *Majority Sentiment Favoring the Right to Abortion.* A poll conducted in 1987 by the *National Law Journal* showed that a plurality of forty-four percent of judges concluded that *Roe v. Wade* was correctly decided. This percentage was more than double the seventeen percent who held the opinion that it should be overruled. NAT. L.J., Aug. 10, 1987, at S-12, col. 2. *Id.* In Texas, where *Roe v. Wade* arose, events show that majority sentiment has changed dramatically: forces seeking to limit abortion in 1987 were able to obtain passage of a law regulating third- trimester abortions only with great difficulty, and only because pro-abortion forces concluded that the law was acceptable. *See Pro-Lifers Hail Bill's Passage,* HOUSTON CHRONICLE, June 3, 1987, § 1, at 16, col. 5. Do these indications show that the *Roe v. Wade* holding is not necessary to protect the rights of minorities?

(2) *Updating the Politics of Abortion, 1990.* The politics of abortion in 1990 followed approximately the pattern that would be indicated by the polls described above. In Florida, a Bill restricting abortion favored by Florida's pro-life governor was soundly defeated, largely by the efforts of a pro-choice legislative committee. In Idaho, the legislature actually passed a restrictive abortion law, but Idaho's governor, although

himself pro life, stated: "I am concerned that this Bill may narrow it to a point where a woman who has suffered rape, who has suffered incest or the mother's life is in danger might not be able to receive an abortion," and added: "I am agonizing over it." Ultimately, he vetoed the Bill. *See* HOUSTON CHRONICLE, Mar. 23, 1990, § A, at 6, col. 1; HOUSTON CHRONICLE, Mar. 30, 1990, § A, at 3, col. 4.

(3) *Legislative Retrenchment of Roe v. Wade by Determination That Life Begins at Conception: The Human Life Bill.* The "Human Life Bill" repeatedly has been suggested or offered in Congress. This bill would have Congress find that the life of each human being "begins at conception" and declare that the term "person" as used in the Fourteenth Amendment includes all human beings, from the moment of conception. Congress has relatively broad authority, under section 5 of the Fourteenth Amendment, to "enforce, by appropriate legislation, the provisions of this [amendment]." Consider the following problem. For more on the scope of Congressional power, *see* Chapter 14.

PROBLEM C

THE MISSOURI HUMAN LIFE BILL AND THE CONSTITUTIONAL CHALLENGE AGAINST IT—REPRODUCTIVE HEALTH SERVICES v. WEBSTER, 662 F. Supp. 407 (W.D. Mo. 1987). The State of Missouri passed a statute similar to the proposed federal Human Life Bill. It promptly was challenged by abortion advocates under the *Roe v. Wade* line of cases. Consider the following questions:

(1) *Consequences of the Human Life Bill.* Would a state-enacted Human Life Bill disempower the state from permitting abortion even in the most acceptable circumstances (*e.g.*, in cases of rape, incest, or pregnancy endangering the life of the woman)? Presumably, the state could enact subsequent abortion-permitting legislation, but consider whether the Human Life Bill would require the state to protect the fetus/unborn child against deprivation of life.

(2) *Constitutionality.* Would a state Human Life Bill be constitutional? [In *Webster*, below, the Supreme Court held that this question was nonjusticiable since the declaration had not been used yet to decide any concrete questions]. Would the constitutional result be different if Congress acted under its constitutional authority to enforce the Fourteenth Amendment?

[4] The Webster Decision: An Assault Upon the Trimester Framework

The Issues at Stake in Webster v. Reproductive Health Services, 492 U.S. 490 (1989). This case concerned a Missouri statute restricting abortion. The Chief Justice's plurality opinion described the relevant provisions as follows:

> The first provision, or preamble, contains "findings" by the state legislature that "[t]he life of each human being begins at conception," and that "unborn children have protectable interests in life, health, and well-being." The Act further requires that all Missouri laws be interpreted to provide unborn children with the same rights enjoyed by other persons, subject to the Federal Constitution and this Court's precedents. Among its other provisions, the Act requires that, prior to performing an abortion on any woman whom a physician has reason to believe is 20 or more weeks pregnant, the physician ascertain whether the fetus is viable by performing "such medical examinations and tests as are necessary to make a finding of the gestational age, weight, and lung maturity of the unborn child." Section 188.029.

The Supreme Court held that the attacks on the preamble were nonjusticiable (*see* Chapter 1). However, the Court went on to uphold the viability-testing provisions by a fractured set of opinions.

Chief Justice Rehnquist's Opinion in Webster—Abandoning the Trimester System, but without Expressly Striking Down Roe. The Chief Justice and Justices White and Kennedy would have departed from the trimester framework, but they refrained from overruling *Roe v. Wade*:

We think that the doubt cast upon the Missouri statute by [prior] cases is not so much a flaw in the statute as it is a reflection of the fact that the rigid trimester analysis of the course of a pregnancy enunciated in *Roe* has resulted in subsequent cases like [*A*] *kron* making constitutional law in this area a virtual Procrustean bed. Statutes specifying elements of informed consent to be provided abortion patients, for example, were invalidated if they were thought to "structure . . . the dialogue between the woman and her physician." *Thornburgh v. American College of Obstetricians and Gynecologists*, 476 U.S. 747, 763 (1986). As the dissenters in *Thornburgh* pointed out, such a statute would have been sustained under any traditional standard of judicial review, or for any other surgical procedure except abortion. . . .

In the first place, the rigid *Roe* framework is hardly consistent with the notion of a Constitution cast in general terms, as ours is, and usually speaking in general principles, as ours does. The key elements of the *Roe* framework—trimesters and viability—are not found in the text of the Constitution or in any place else one would expect to find a constitutional principle. Since the bounds of the inquiry are essentially indeterminate, the result has been a web of legal rules that have become increasingly intricate, resembling a code of regulations rather than a body of constitutional doctrine. As Justice White has put it, the trimester framework has left the Court to serve as the country's "ex officio medical board with powers to approve or disapprove medical and operative practices and standards throughout the United States." *Planned Parenthood v. Danforth* (partial dissent).

In the second place, we do not see why the State's interest in protecting potential human life should come into existence only at the point of viability, and that there should therefore be a rigid line allowing state regulation after viability but prohibiting it before viability. The dissenters in *Thornburgh* would have recognized this fact by positing against the "fundamental right" recognized in *Roe* the State's "compelling interest" in protecting potential human life throughout pregnancy . . .

The tests that section 188.029 requires the physician to perform are designed to determine viability. [I]t is true that the tests in question increase the expense of abortion, and regulate the discretion of the physician in determining the viability of the fetus. [B]ut we are satisfied that the requirement of these tests permissibly furthers the State's interest in protecting potential human life, and we therefore believe section 188.029 to be constitutional. . . .

This case . . . affords us no occasion to revisit the holding of *Roe*, [a]nd we leave it undisturbed. To the extent indicated in our opinion, we would modify and narrow *Roe* and succeeding cases.

The Separate Opinions of Justices O'Connor, Stevens, and Scalia. Justice O'Connor agreed with the holding but refused to concur in the plurality's trimester reasoning. She concluded that it was "unnecessary" to reconsider the trimester framework "because these viability testing requirements [do not] conflict with any of the Court's past decisions." Separately, Justice Stevens reached a similar conclusion (although he dissented as to the preamble). On the other hand, Justice Scalia would have gone farther. He agreed with the dissenters that the plurality opinion "effectively would overrule *Roe v. Wade*," but added: "I think that should be done, but would do it more explicitly."

The Four Dissenters; Justice Blackmun's Opinion. Justice Blackmun, joined by Justices Brennan and Marshall, dissented from the upholding of the viability-testing provisions. In his opinion, Justice Blackmun criticized the plurality for "deceptive" reasoning, and added:

> [W]ith feigned restraint, the plurality announces that its analysis leaves *Roe* "undisturbed," albeit "modif(ied) and narrow(ed)." But this disclaimer is totally meaningless. [T]he simple truth is that *Roe* would not survive the plurality's analysis, and that the plurality provides no substitute for *Roe's* protective umbrella. I fear for the future. I fear for the liberty and equality of the millions of women who have lived and come of age in the 16 years since *Roe* was decided. I fear for the integrity of, and public esteem for, this Court. . . .

> [T]he plurality does not even mention, much less join, the true jurisprudential debate underlying this case: whether the Constitution includes an "unenumerated" general right to privacy as recognized in many of our decisions, most notably *Griswold v. Connecticut* and *Roe*, and, more specifically, whether and to what extent such a right to privacy extends to matters of childbearing and family life, including abortion. . . .

> For today, at least, the law of abortion stands undisturbed. For today, the women of this Nation still retain the liberty to control their destinies. But the signs are evident and very ominous, and a chill wind blows.

[E]   *Stare Decisis* or Failure of Duty?: The "Undue Burden" Standard of the *Casey* Decision

NOTE ON UNDERSTANDING *PLANNED PARENTHOOD v. CASEY*

In reading the following case, it may be helpful to preview the three groups into which the justices seem to be divided.

(1) *The "Undue Burden" Group: The Joint Opinion of Justices O'Connor, Kennedy, and Souter.* These justices' Joint Opinion is the Court's opinion, for the most part. It says that it reaffirms the "essential holding" of *Roe v. Wade* (but another group of justices disputes this assertion, and you will have to decide for yourself whether it is so). This group emphasizes a *stare decisis* rationale with multiple elements (this rationale too is a focal point of disagreement). But the Joint Opinion also rejects several aspects of *Roe* and its progeny, including the trimester framework and the strict scrutiny standard. In their place, it substitutes an "undue burden" standard: Before viability, a state may not impose an undue burden upon, meaning a "substantial obstacle" in the path of, a woman who seeks an abortion. This standard results in upholding certain requirements of the Pennsylvania statute at issue (including provisions for informed consent, a waiting period, parental consent, and reporting of information) while striking down others (particularly spousal notification).

(2) *The "Trimester" Group: The Separate Opinions of Justices Blackmun and Stevens.* Justice Blackmun joins in certain parts of the Joint Opinion, but he would preserve the trimester framework of *Roe v. Wade*, as well as the strict scrutiny requirement. His most strongly expressed concern, however, is that the five-to-four vote for reaffirming *Roe* may disappear with the change of one justice ("I am 83 years old. . . ."). Justice Stevens also writes a separate opinion.

(3) *The "Rational Basis" Group: The Opinions of Chief Justice Rehnquist and Justices White, Scalia, and Thomas.* This group would uphold the Pennsylvania statute in its entirety on the ground that it is rationally related to legitimate state interests. The group's opinions criticize the Joint Opinion's *stare decisis* methodology as well as the undue burden standard. These justices would overrule *Roe*. Of particular interest is the debate these justices hold with the majority concerning whether, and to what extent, the perceived legitimacy of the Court should bear upon the *stare decisis* analysis—including how to deal with the effects of public pressure and public expressions of opinion.

PLANNED PARENTHOOD v. CASEY
505 U.S. 833 (1992)

JUSTICE O'CONNOR, JUSTICE KENNEDY, and JUSTICE SOUTER announced the judgment of the Court and delivered the opinion of the Court with respect to Parts I, II, III, V-A, V-C, and VI, an opinion with respect to Part V-E, in which JUSTICE STEVENS joins, and an opinion with respect to Parts IV, V-B, and V-D.

I

Liberty finds no refuge in a jurisprudence of doubt. Yet 19 years after our holding that the Constitution protects a woman's right to terminate her pregnancy in its early stages, *Roe v. Wade*, 410 U.S. 113 (1973), that definition of liberty is still questioned. Joining the respondents as amicus curiae, the United States, as it has done in five other cases in the last decade, again asks us to overrule *Roe*.

At issue in these cases are five provisions of the Pennsylvania Abortion Control Act of 1982 as amended in 1988 and 1989. The Act [1] requires that a woman seeking an abortion give her informed consent prior to the abortion procedure, and [2] specifies that she be provided with certain information at least 24 hours before the abortion is performed. For a minor to obtain an abortion, the Act [3] requires the informed consent of one of her parents, but provides for a judicial bypass option if the minor does not wish to or cannot obtain a parent's consent. Another provision of the Act [4] requires that, unless certain exceptions apply, a married woman seeking an abortion must sign a statement indicating that she has notified her husband of her intended abortion. The Act [5] exempts compliance with these three requirements in the event of a "medical emergency," which is defined in [t]he Act. In addition to the above provisions regulating the performance of abortions, the Act [6] imposes certain reporting requirements on facilities that provide abortion services. . . .

After considering the fundamental constitutional questions resolved by *Roe*, principles of institutional integrity, and the rule of *stare decisis*, we are led to conclude this: the essential holding of *Roe v. Wade* should be retained and once again reaffirmed.

It must be stated at the outset and with clarity that *Roe*'s essential holding, the holding we reaffirm, has three parts. First is a recognition of the right of the woman to choose to have an abortion before viability and to obtain it without undue interference from the State. . . . Second is a confirmation of the State's power to restrict abortions after fetal viability, if the law contains exceptions for pregnancies which endanger a woman's life or health. And third is the principle that the State has legitimate interests from the outset of the pregnancy in protecting the health of the woman and the life of the fetus that may become a child. These principles do not contradict one another; and we adhere to each.

II

Constitutional protection of the woman's decision to terminate her pregnancy derives from the Due Process Clause of the Fourteenth Amendment. It declares that no State shall "deprive any person of life, liberty, or property, without due process of law." The controlling word in the case before us is "liberty." Although a literal reading of the Clause might suggest that it governs only the procedures by which a State may deprive persons of liberty, for at least 105 years, [s]ince *Mugler v. Kansas*, 123 U.S. 623, 660–661 (1887), the Clause has been understood to contain a substantive component as well, one "barring certain government actions regardless of the fairness of the procedures used to implement them. . . ."

[I]t is a promise of the Constitution that there is a realm of personal liberty which the government may not enter. We have vindicated this principle before. . . . The inescapable fact is that adjudication of substantive due process claims may call upon the

Court in interpreting the Constitution to exercise that same capacity which by tradition courts always have exercised: reasoned judgment. Its boundaries are not susceptible of expression as a simple rule. That does not mean we are free to invalidate state policy choices with which we disagree; yet neither does it permit us to shrink from the duties of our office. . . .

It is conventional constitutional doctrine that where reasonable people disagree the government can adopt one position or the other. *See, e.g., [W]illiamson v. Lee Optical of Oklahoma, Inc.*, 348 U.S. 483 (1955). That theorem, however, assumes a state of affairs in which the choice does not intrude upon a protected liberty. Thus, while some people might disagree about whether or not the flag should be saluted, or disagree about the proposition that it may not be defiled, we have ruled that a State may not compel or enforce one view or the other. *See West Virginia State Bd. of Education v. Barnette*, 319 U.S. 624 (1943); *Texas v. Johnson*, 491 U.S. 397 (1989).

Our law affords constitutional protection to personal decisions relating to marriage, procreation, contraception, family relationships, child rearing, and education. . . . [T]hese matters, involving the most intimate and personal choices a person may make in a lifetime, choices central to personal dignity and autonomy, are central to the liberty protected by the Fourteenth Amendment. At the heart of liberty is the right to define one's own concept of existence, of meaning, of the universe, and of the mystery of human life. Beliefs about these matters could not define the attributes of personhood were they formed under compulsion of the State.

These considerations begin our analysis of the woman's interest in terminating her pregnancy but cannot end it, for this reason: though the abortion decision may originate within the zone of conscience and belief, it is more than a philosophic exercise. Abortion is a unique act. It is an act fraught with consequences for others: for the woman who must live with the implications of her decision; for the persons who perform and assist in the procedure; for the spouse, family, and society which must confront the knowledge that these procedures exist, procedures some deem nothing short of an act of violence against innocent human life; and, depending on one's beliefs, for the life or potential life that is aborted.

Though abortion is conduct, it does not follow that the State is entitled to proscribe it in all instances. That is because the liberty of the woman is at stake in a sense unique to the human condition and so unique to the law. [H]er suffering is too intimate and personal for the State to insist, without more, upon its own vision of the woman's role, however dominant that vision has been in the course of our history and our culture. The destiny of the woman must be shaped to a large extent on her own conception of her spiritual imperatives and her place in society. . . .

[T]he reservations any of us may have in reaffirming the central holding of *Roe* are outweighed by the explication of individual liberty we have given combined with the force of *stare decisis*. We turn now to that doctrine.

III

A

The obligation to follow precedent begins with necessity, and a contrary necessity marks its outer limit. [N]o judicial system could do society's work if it eyed each issue afresh in every case that raised it. [A]t the other extreme, a different necessity would make itself felt if a prior judicial ruling should come to be seen so clearly as error that its enforcement was for that very reason doomed.

[I]t is common wisdom that the rule of *stare decisis* is not an "inexorable command," and certainly it is not such in every constitutional case. *See also Payne v. Tennessee* [Ch. 1, above]. Rather, when this Court reexamines a prior holding, its judgment is customarily informed by a series of prudential and pragmatic considerations designed to test the consistency of overruling a prior decision with the ideal of the rule of law, and to gauge the respective costs of reaffirming and overruling a prior case. Thus, for example, we may ask [1] whether the rule has proved to be intolerable simply in defying practical workability; [2] whether the rule is subject to a kind of reliance that would lend a special hardship to the consequences of overruling and add inequity to the cost of repudiation; [3] whether related principles of law have so far developed as to have left the old rule no more than a remnant of abandoned doctrine; or [4] whether facts have so changed or come to be seen so differently, as to have robbed the old rule of significant application or justification. . . .

1

Although *Roe* has engendered opposition, it has in no sense proven "unworkable," *see Garcia v. San Antonio Metropolitan Transit Authority*, 469 U.S. 528, 546 (1985), representing as it does a simple limitation beyond which a state law is unenforceable. While *Roe* has, of course, required judicial assessment of state laws affecting the exercise of the choice guaranteed against government infringement, and although the need for such review will remain as a consequence of today's decision, the required determinations fall within judicial competence.

2

The inquiry into reliance counts the cost of a rule's repudiation as it would fall on those who have relied reasonably on the rule's continued application. Since the classic case for weighing reliance heavily in favor of following the earlier rule occurs in the commercial context, where advance planning of great precision is most obviously a necessity, it is no cause for surprise that some would find no reliance worthy of consideration in support of *Roe*. . . .

To eliminate the issue of reliance that easily, however, one would need to limit cognizable reliance to specific instances of sexual activity. But to do this would be simply to refuse to face the fact that for two decades of economic and social developments, people have organized intimate relationships and made choices that define their views of themselves and their places in society, in reliance on the availability of abortion in the event that contraception should fail. The ability of women to participate equally in the economic and social life of the Nation has been facilitated by their ability to control their reproductive lives. The Constitution serves human values, and while the effect of reliance on *Roe* cannot be exactly measured, neither can the certain cost of overruling *Roe* for people who have ordered their thinking and living around that case be dismissed.

3

No evolution of legal principle has left *Roe*'s doctrinal footings weaker than they were in 1973. No development of constitutional law since the case was decided has implicitly or explicitly left *Roe* behind as a mere survivor of obsolete constitutional thinking. . . .

4

[W]e have seen how time has overtaken some of *Roe*'s factual assumptions: advances in maternal health care allow for abortions safe to the mother later in pregnancy than was true in 1973, *see Akron I*, and advances in neonatal care have advanced viability to a point somewhat earlier. But these facts go only to the scheme of time limits on the realization of competing interests, and [they] have no bearing on the validity of *Roe*'s central holding. . . . [W]henever it may occur, the attainment of viability may continue to serve as the critical fact, just as it has done since *Roe* was decided; which is to say that no change in *Roe*'s factual underpinning has left its central holding obsolete, and none supports an argument for overruling it.

5

[W]ithin the bounds of normal *stare decisis* analysis, then, and subject to the considerations on which it customarily turns, the stronger argument is for affirming *Roe's* central holding, with whatever degree of personal reluctance any of us may have, not for overruling it.

B

In a less significant case, *stare decisis* analysis could, and would, stop at the point we have reached. But the sustained and widespread debate *Roe* has provoked calls for some comparison between that case and others of comparable dimension. . . . Only two such decisional lines from the past century present themselves for examination, and in each instance the result reached by the Court accorded with the principles we apply today. [The plurality discussed the explicit overruling of *Adkins* and *Plessy*.] . . .

C

The examination of the conditions justifying the repudiation of *Adkins* by *West Coast Hotel* and *Plessy* by *Brown* is enough to suggest the terrible price that would have been paid if the Court had not *overruled*, as it did. In the present case, however, as our analysis to this point makes clear, the terrible price would be paid for overruling. . . .

The Court is not asked to [overrule such decision] very often, having thus addressed the Nation only twice in our lifetime, in the decisions of *Brown* and *Roe.* But when the Court does act in this way, its decision requires an equally rare precedential force to counter the inevitable efforts to overturn it and to thwart its implementation. [O]nly the most convincing justification under accepted standards of precedent could suffice to demonstrate that a later decision overruling the first was anything but a surrender to political pressure, and an unjustified repudiation of the principle on which the Court staked its authority in the first instance. So to overrule under fire in the absence of the most compelling reason to reexamine a watershed decision would subvert the Court's legitimacy beyond any serious question.

IV

From what we have said so far it follows that it is a constitutional liberty of the woman to have some freedom to terminate her pregnancy. [T]he woman's liberty is not so unlimited, however, that from the outset the State cannot show its concern for the life of the unborn, and at a later point in fetal development the State's interest in life has sufficient force so that the right of the woman to terminate the pregnancy can be restricted.

That brings us, of course, to the point where much criticism has been directed at *Roe*, a criticism that always inheres when the Court draws a specific rule from what in the Constitution is but a general standard. We conclude, however, that the urgent claims of the woman to retain the ultimate control over her destiny and her body [r]equire us to perform that function. Liberty must not be extinguished for want of a line that is clear. We conclude the line should be drawn at viability, so that before that time the woman has a right to choose to terminate her pregnancy. We adhere to this principle for two reasons. First, as we have said, is the doctrine of *stare decisis*. . . .

The second reason is that the concept of viability, as we noted in *Roe*, is the time at which there is a realistic possibility of maintaining and nourishing a life outside the womb, so that the independent existence of the second life can in reason and all fairness be the object of state protection that now overrides the rights of the woman. [W]e must justify the lines we draw. And there is no line other than viability which is more workable. . . .

The woman's right to terminate her pregnancy before viability is the most central principle of *Roe v. Wade*. It is a rule of law and a component of liberty we cannot renounce. . . .

Yet it must be remembered that *Roe v. Wade* speaks with clarity in establishing not only the woman's liberty but also the State's "important and legitimate interest in potential life.". . .

Roe established a trimester framework to govern abortion regulations. Under this elaborate but rigid construct, almost no regulation at all is permitted during the first trimester of pregnancy; regulations designed to protect the woman's health, but not to further the State's interest in potential life, are permitted during the second trimester; and during the third trimester, when the fetus is viable, prohibitions are permitted provided the life or health of the mother is not at stake. . . .

. . . [But a] framework of this rigidity was unnecessary and in its later interpretation sometimes contradicted the State's permissible exercise of its powers. . . .

We reject the trimester framework, which we do not consider to be part of the essential holding of *Roe. See Webster v. Reproductive Health Services.* [T]he trimester framework suffers from these basic flaws: in its formulation it misconceives the nature of the pregnant woman's interest; and in practice it undervalues the State's interest in potential life, as recognized in *Roe.* . . .

[T]he fact that a law which serves a valid purpose, one not designed to strike at the right itself, has the incidental effect of making it more difficult or more expensive to procure an abortion cannot be enough to invalidate it. Only where state regulation imposes an undue burden on a woman's ability to make this decision does the power of the State reach into the heart of the liberty protected by the Due Process Clause. . . .

The very notion that the State has a substantial interest in potential life leads to the conclusion that not all regulations must be deemed unwarranted. Not all burdens on the right to decide whether to terminate a pregnancy will be undue. In our view, the undue burden standard is the appropriate means of reconciling the State's interest with the woman's constitutionally protected liberty. . . .

A finding of an undue burden is a shorthand for the conclusion that a state regulation has the purpose or effect of placing a substantial obstacle in the path of a woman seeking an abortion of a nonviable fetus. A statute with this purpose is invalid because the means chosen by the State to further the interest in potential life must be calculated to inform the woman's free choice, not hinder it. . . .

[W]e give this summary [of the "undue burden" standard]:

(a) To protect the central right recognized by *Roe v. Wade* while at the same time accommodating the State's profound interest in potential life, we will employ the undue burden analysis as explained in this opinion. An undue burden exists, and therefore a provision of law is invalid, if its purpose or effect is to place a substantial obstacle in the path of a woman seeking an abortion before the fetus attains viability.

(b) We reject the rigid trimester framework of *Roe v. Wade.* To promote the State's profound interest in potential life, throughout pregnancy the State may take measures to ensure that the woman's choice is informed, and measures designed to advance this interest will not be invalidated as long as their purpose is to persuade the woman to choose childbirth over abortion. These measures must not be an undue burden on the right.

(c) As with any medical procedure, the State may enact regulations to further the health or safety of a woman seeking an abortion. Unnecessary health regulations that have the purpose or effect of presenting a substantial obstacle to a woman seeking an abortion impose an undue burden on the right.

(d) Our adoption of the undue burden analysis does not disturb the central holding of *Roe v. Wade*, and we reaffirm that holding. . . .

(e) We also reaffirm *Roe*'s holding that "subsequent to viability, the State in promoting its interest in the potentiality of human life may, if it chooses, regulate, and even proscribe, abortion except where it is necessary, in appropriate medical judgment, for the preservation of the life or health of the mother."

These principles control our assessment of the Pennsylvania statute, and we now turn to the issue of the validity of its challenged provisions.

V . . .

A

Because it is central to the operation of various other requirements, we begin with the statute's definition of medical emergency. . . . [W]e [c]onclude that, as construed by the Court of Appeals, the medical emergency definition imposes no undue burden on a woman's abortion right.

B

We next consider the informed consent requirement. Except in a medical emergency, the statute requires that at least 24 hours before performing an abortion a physician inform the woman of the nature of the procedure, the health risks of the abortion and of childbirth, and the "probable gestational age of the unborn child." . . .

[The Court here rejects arguments based upon physicians' First Amendment freedom of speech and the doctor-patient relationship, as well as the argument that the Pennsylvania statute is unconstitutional because it requires doctors personally to give the patient the required information rather than delegating this duty to their assistants.]

We are left with the argument that the various aspects of the informed consent requirement are unconstitutional because they place barriers in the way of abortion on demand. Even the broadest reading of *Roe*, however, has not suggested that there is a constitutional right to abortion on demand. *See, e.g., Doe v. Bolton.* Rather, the right protected by *Roe* is a right to decide to terminate a pregnancy free of undue interference by the State. [T]he informed consent requirement is not an undue burden on that right.

C

Section 3209 of Pennsylvania's abortion law provides, except in cases of medical emergency, that no physician shall perform an abortion on a married woman without receiving a signed statement from the woman that she has notified her spouse that she is about to undergo an abortion. The woman has the option of providing an alternative signed statement certifying that her husband is not the man who impregnated her; that her husband could not be located; that the pregnancy is the result of spousal sexual assault which she has reported; or that the woman believes that notifying her husband will cause him or someone else to inflict bodily injury upon her. . . .

The District Court heard the testimony of numerous expert witnesses, and made detailed findings of fact regarding the effect of this statute. . . .

[The scientific literature] and the District Court's findings reinforce what common sense would suggest. In well-functioning marriages, spouses discuss important intimate decisions such as whether to bear a child. But there are millions of women in this country who are the victims of regular physical and psychological abuse at the hands of their husbands. Should these women become pregnant, they may have very good reasons for not wishing to inform their husbands of their decision to obtain an abortion. Many may have justifiable fears of physical abuse, but may be no less fearful of the consequences of reporting prior abuse to the Commonwealth of Pennsylvania. . . . And many women who are pregnant as a result of sexual assaults by their husbands will be unable to avail themselves of the exception for spousal sexual assault, because the exception requires that the woman have notified law enforcement authorities within 90 days of the assault, and her husband will be notified of her report once an investigation begins. If anything in this field is certain, it is that victims of spousal sexual assault are extremely reluctant to report the abuse to the government; hence, a great many spousal rape victims will not be exempt from the notification requirement imposed by [Pennsylvania].

The spousal notification requirement is thus likely to prevent a significant number of women from obtaining an abortion. It does not merely make abortions a little more difficult or expensive to obtain; for many women, it will impose a substantial obstacle. . . .

This conclusion is in no way inconsistent with our decisions upholding parental notification or consent requirements. *See, e.g., Akron II.* Those enactments, and our judgment that they are constitutional, are based on the quite reasonable assumption that minors will benefit from consultation with their parents and that children will often not realize that their parents have their best interests at heart. We cannot adopt a parallel assumption about adult women. . . .

. . . These considerations confirm our conclusion that [the notification requirement] is invalid.

D

We next consider the parental consent provision. . . .

We have been over most of this ground before. Our cases establish, and we reaffirm today, that a State may require a minor seeking an abortion to obtain the consent of a parent or guardian, provided that there is an adequate judicial bypass procedure. Under these precedents, in our view, the one-parent consent requirement and judicial bypass procedure are constitutional. . . .

E

Under the recordkeeping and reporting requirements of the statute, every facility which performs abortions is required to file a report. . . . In the case of state-funded institutions, the information becomes public.

In *Danforth*, we held that recordkeeping and reporting provisions "that are reasonably directed to the preservation of maternal health and that properly respect a patient's confidentiality and privacy are permissible." We think that under this standard, all the provisions at issue here except that relating to spousal notice are constitutional. . . .

VI

Our Constitution is a covenant running from the first generation of Americans to us and then to future generations. [W]e accept our responsibility not to retreat from interpreting the full meaning of the covenant in light of all of our precedents. . . .

[The judgments are] affirmed in part and reversed in part, and the case is remanded for proceedings consistent with this opinion. . . .

JUSTICE BLACKMUN, concurring in part, concurring in the judgment in part, and dissenting in part.

I join parts I, II, III, V-A, V-C, and VI of the joint opinion of JUSTICES O'CONNOR, KENNEDY, and SOUTER.

Three years ago, in *Webster v. Reproductive Health Serv.*, four Members of this Court appeared poised to "cas[t] into darkness the hopes and visions of every woman in this country" who had come to believe that the Constitution guaranteed her the right to reproductive choice. (Blackmun, J., dissenting). All that remained between the promise of *Roe* and the darkness of the plurality was a single, flickering flame. Decisions since *Webster* gave little reason to hope that this flame would cast much light. But now, just when so many expected the darkness to fall, the flame has grown bright.

[I] fear for the darkness as four Justices anxiously await the single vote necessary to extinguish the light.

I

Make no mistake, the joint opinion of Justices O'Connor, Kennedy, and Souter is an act of personal courage and constitutional principle. . . .

[W]hile I believe that the joint opinion errs in failing to invalidate the [informed consent, waiting period, parental consent and reporting] regulations, I am pleased that the joint opinion has not ruled out the possibility that these regulations may be shown to impose an unconstitutional burden. The joint opinion makes clear that its specific holdings are based on the insufficiency of the record before it. [Justice Blackmun here cites the Court's reasoning concerning *stare decisis*, including the reference to *Roe*'s "premises of fact."] I am confident that in the future evidence will be produced to show that "in a large fraction of the cases in which [these regulations are] relevant, [they] will operate as a substantial obstacle to a woman's choice to undergo an abortion."

II . . .

C

Application of the strict scrutiny standard results in the invalidation of all the challenged provisions. Indeed, as this Court has invalidated virtually identical provisions in prior cases, *stare decisis* requires that we again strike them down.

III

At long last, the Chief Justice admits it. Gone are the contentions that the issue need not be (or has not been) considered. There, on the first page, for all to see, is what was expected: "We believe that *Roe* was wrongly decided, and that it can and should be *overruled*, consistently with our traditional approach to *stare decisis* in constitutional cases." If there is much reason to applaud the advances made by the joint opinion today, there is far more to fear from the Chief Justice's opinion.

The Chief Justice's criticism of *Roe* follows from his stunted conception of individual liberty. While recognizing that the Due Process Clause protects more than simple physical liberty, he then goes on to construe this Court's personal liberty cases as establishing only a laundry list of particular rights, rather than a principled account of how these particular rights are grounded in a more general right of privacy. This constricted view is reinforced by the Chief Justice's exclusive reliance on tradition as a source of fundamental rights. . . .

Even more shocking than the Chief Justice's cramped notion of individual liberty is his complete omission of any discussion of the effects that compelled childbirth and motherhood have on women's lives. [I]n short, the Chief Justice's view of the State's compelling interest in maternal health has less to do with health than it does with compelling women to be maternal.

Nor does the Chief Justice give any serious consideration to the doctrine of *stare decisis*. . . .

[The separate opinion of JUSTICE STEVENS, concurring in part and dissenting in part, is omitted. His opinion differs with the Court's rejection of the trimester framework, and although it uses the "undue burden" analysis, it would give stare decisis effect not only to *Roe* but to progeny of *Roe* such as *Akron I, Akron II* and *Thornburgh*.]

CHIEF JUSTICE REHNQUIST, with whom JUSTICE WHITE, JUSTICE SCALIA, and JUSTICE THOMAS join, concurring in the judgment in part and dissenting in part.

The joint opinion, following its newly-minted variation on stare decisis, retains the outer shell of *Roe v. Wade*, 410 U.S. 113 (1973), but beats a wholesale retreat from the substance of that case. We believe that *Roe* was wrongly decided, and that it can and should be *overruled*, consistently with our traditional approach to stare decisis in constitutional cases. We would adopt the approach of the plurality in *Webster* and uphold the challenged provisions of the Pennsylvania statute in their entirety.

I . . .

[P]etitioners insist that we reaffirm our decision in *Roe v. Wade*. . . .[1] [T]he state of our post-*Roe* decisional law dealing with the regulation of abortion is confusing and uncertain, indicating that a reexamination of that line of cases is in order. [T]he reexamination undertaken today leaves the Court no less divided than beforehand. [W]e conclude [that the "undue burden" standard] is an unjustified constitutional compromise, one which leaves the Court in a position to closely scrutinize all types of abortion regulations despite the fact that it lacks the power to do so under the Constitution.

[W]hile the language and holdings of [*Roe* and of *Doe v. Bolton*] appeared to leave States free to regulate abortion procedures in a variety of ways, later decisions based on them have found considerably less latitude for such regulations than might have been expected. . . .

[T]his state of confusion and disagreement warrants reexamination of the "fundamental right" accorded to a woman's decision to abort a fetus in *Roe*, with its concomitant requirement that any state regulation of abortion survive "strict scrutiny."

[W]e have held that a liberty interest protected under the Due Process Clause of the Fourteenth Amendment will be deemed fundamental if it is "implicit in the concept of ordered liberty." *Palko v. Connecticut*. Three years earlier, in *Snyder v. Massachusetts*, 291 U.S. 97 (1934), we referred to a "principle of justice so rooted in the traditions and conscience of our people as to be ranked as fundamental." These expressions are admittedly not precise, but our decisions implementing this notion of "fundamental" rights do not afford any more elaborate basis on which to base such a classification.

In construing the phrase "liberty" incorporated in the Due Process Clause of the Fourteenth Amendment, we have recognized that its meaning extends beyond freedom from physical restraint. [W]e have held that the term "liberty" includes a right to

---

[1] Two years after *Roe*, the West German constitutional court, by contrast, struck down a law liberalizing access to abortion on the grounds that life developing within the womb is constitutionally protected. Judgment of February 25, 1975, 39 BVerfGE 1 (translated in Jonas & Gorby, *West German Abortion Decision: A Contrast to Roe v. Wade*, 9 J. Marshall J. Prac. & Proc. 605 (1976)). In 1988, the Canadian Supreme Court followed reasoning similar to that of *Roe* in striking down a law which restricted abortion. *Morgentaler v. Queen*, 1 S.C.R. 30, 44 D.L.R. 4th 385 (1988).

marry, *Loving*; a right to procreate, *Skinner*; and a right to use contraceptives, *Griswold*; *Eisenstadt*. But a reading of these opinions makes clear that they do not endorse any all-encompassing "right of privacy."

In *Roe v. Wade*, the Court recognized a "guarantee of personal privacy" which "is broad enough to encompass a woman's decision whether or not to terminate her pregnancy." We are now of the view that, in terming this right fundamental, the Court in *Roe* read the earlier opinions upon which it based its decision much too broadly. Unlike marriage, procreation and contraception, abortion "involves the purposeful termination of potential life." The abortion decision must therefore "be recognized as *sui generis*, different in kind from the others that the Court has protected under the rubric of personal or family privacy and autonomy." *Thornburgh* (White, J., dissenting). . . . *See Michael H. v. Gerald D.* (To look "at the act which is assertedly the subject of a liberty interest in isolation from its effect upon other people [is] like inquiring whether there is a liberty interest in firing a gun where the case at hand happens to involve its discharge into another person's body"). . . .

II . . .

Stare decisis is defined in Black's Law Dictionary as meaning "to abide by, or adhere to, decided cases." [W]hile purporting to adhere to precedent, the joint opinion instead revises it. *Roe* continues to exist, but only in the way a storefront on a western movie set exists: a mere facade to give the illusion of reality. Decisions following *Roe*, such as *Akron I* and *Thornburgh*, are frankly *overruled*, in part under the "undue burden" standard expounded in the joint opinion.

In our view, authentic principles of *stare decisis* do not require that any portion of the reasoning in *Roe* be kept intact. "*Stare decisis* is not . . . a universal, inexorable command," especially in cases involving the interpretation of the Federal Constitution. Erroneous decisions in such constitutional cases are uniquely durable, because correction through legislative action, save for constitutional amendment, is impossible. . . .

The joint opinion also points to the reliance interests involved in this context in its effort to explain why precedent must be followed for precedent's sake. . . . But, as the joint opinion apparently agrees, any traditional notion of reliance is not applicable here. [R]eliance interests would not be diminished were the Court to go further and acknowledge the full error of *Roe*, as "reproductive planning could take virtually immediate account of" this action.

[S]urely it is dubious to suggest that women have reached their "places in society" in reliance upon *Roe*, rather than as a result of their determination to obtain higher education and compete with men in the job market, and of society's increasing recognition of their ability to fill positions that were previously thought to be reserved only for men. . . .

Apparently realizing that conventional *stare decisis* principles do not support its position, the joint opinion advances a belief that retaining a portion of *Roe* is necessary to protect the "legitimacy" of this Court. . . .

Taking the joint opinion on its own terms, we doubt that its distinction between *Roe*, on the one hand, and *Plessy* and *Lochner*, on the other, withstands analysis. . . .

[R]oe v. Wade adopted a "fundamental right" standard under which state regulations could survive only if they met the requirement of "strict scrutiny." While we disagree with that standard, it at least had a recognized basis in constitutional law at the time *Roe* was decided. The same cannot be said for the "undue burden" standard, which is created largely out of whole cloth by the authors of the joint opinion. It is a standard which even today does not command the support of a majority of this Court. And it will not, we believe, result in the sort of "simple limitation," easily applied, which the joint opinion anticipates. In sum, it is a standard which is not built to last.

In evaluating abortion regulations under that standard, judges will have to decide whether they place a "substantial obstacle" in the path of a woman seeking an abortion. In that this standard is based even more on a judge's subjective determinations than was the trimester framework, the standard will do nothing to prevent "judges from roaming at large in the constitutional field" guided only by their personal views. *Griswold v. Connecticut* (Harlan, J., concurring in judgment). . . .

[W]e think that the correct analysis is that set forth by the plurality opinion in *Webster*. A woman's interest in having an abortion is a form of liberty protected by the Due Process Clause, but States may regulate abortion procedures in ways rationally related to a legitimate state interest. *Williamson v. Lee Optical.* With this rule in mind, we examine each of the challenged provisions. . . .

IV

For the reasons stated, we therefore would hold that each of the challenged provisions of the Pennsylvania statute is consistent with the Constitution. It bears emphasis that our conclusion in this regard does not carry with it any necessary approval of these regulations. Our task is, as always, to decide only whether the challenged provisions of a law comport with the United States Constitution. If, as we believe, these do, their wisdom as a matter of public policy is for the people of Pennsylvania to decide.

JUSTICE SCALIA, with whom the CHIEF JUSTICE, JUSTICE WHITE, and JUSTICE THOMAS join, concurring in the judgment in part and dissenting in part.

My views on this matter are unchanged from those I set forth in my separate opinions in *Webster* and *Akron II*. The States may, if they wish, permit abortion-on-demand, but the Constitution does not require them to do so. The permissibility of abortion, and the limitations upon it, are to be resolved like most important questions in our democracy: by citizens trying to persuade one another and then voting. [A] State's choice between two positions on which reasonable people can disagree is constitutional even when (as is often the case) it intrudes upon a "liberty" in the absolute sense. Laws against bigamy, for example—which entire societies of reasonable people disagree with—intrude upon men and women's liberty to marry and live with one another. But bigamy happens not to be a liberty specially "protected" by the Constitution.

That is, quite simply, the issue in this case: not whether the power of a woman to abort her unborn child is a "liberty" in the absolute sense; or even whether it is a liberty of great importance to many women. Of course it is both. The issue is whether it is a liberty protected by the Constitution of the United States. I am sure it is not. I reach that conclusion not because of anything so exalted as my views concerning the "concept of existence, of meaning, of the universe, and of the mystery of human life." Rather, I reach it for the same reason I reach the conclusion that bigamy is not constitutionally protected—because of two simple facts: (1) the Constitution says absolutely nothing about it, and (2) the longstanding traditions of American society have permitted it to be legally proscribed. . . .[2]

[The Court's Opinion states:] "Liberty finds no refuge in a jurisprudence of doubt."

One might have feared to encounter this august and sonorous phrase in an opinion defending the real *Roe v. Wade*, rather than the revised version fabricated today by the authors of the joint opinion. The shortcomings of *Roe* did not include lack of clarity:

---

[2] The Court's suggestion that adherence to tradition would require us to uphold laws against interracial marriage is entirely wrong. Any tradition in that case was contradicted by a text an Equal Protection Clause that explicitly establishes racial equality as a constitutional value. *See Loving.* [T]he enterprise launched in *Roe*, by contrast, sought to establish—in the teeth of a clear, contrary tradition—a value found nowhere in the constitutional text.

Virtually all regulation of abortion before the third trimester was invalid. But to come across this phrase in the joint opinion—which calls upon federal district judges to apply an "undue burden" standard as doubtful in application as it is unprincipled in origin—is really more than one should have to bear. . . .

The Court's description of the place of *Roe* in the social history of the United States is unrecognizable. Not only did *Roe* not, as the Court suggests, resolve the deeply divisive issue of abortion; it did more than anything else to nourish it, by elevating it to the national level where it is infinitely more difficult to resolve. . . .

Roe's mandate for abortion-on-demand destroyed the compromises of the past, rendered compromise impossible for the future, and required the entire issue to be resolved uniformly, at the national level. At the same time, *Roe* created a vast new class of abortion consumers and abortion proponents by eliminating the moral opprobrium that had attached to the act. ("If the Constitution guarantees abortion, how can it be bad?"—not an accurate line of thought, but a natural one.) Many favor all of those developments, and it is not for me to say that they are wrong. But to portray *Roe* as the statesmanlike "settlement" of a divisive issue, a jurisprudential Peace of Westphalia that is worth preserving, is nothing less than Orwellian. [A]nd by keeping us in the abortion-umpiring business, it is the perpetuation of [d]isruption, rather than of any pax *Roe* ana, that the Court's new majority decrees. . . .

The Imperial Judiciary lives. It is instructive to compare this Nietzschean vision of us unelected, life-tenured judges—leading a Volk who will be "tested by following," and whose very "belief in themselves" is mystically bound up in their "understanding" of a Court that "speak [s] before all others for their constitutional ideals"—with the somewhat more modest role envisioned for these lawyers by the Founders. . . .

We should get out of this area, where we have no right to be, and where we do neither ourselves nor the country any good by remaining.

NOTES AND QUESTIONS

(1)　*The Emergence of the Undue Burden Standard for the Regulation of Abortion: Planned Parenthood v. Casey, 505 U.S. 833 (1992).* In the *Casey* decision, the Court, per a joint plurality of Justices O'Connor, Kennedy, and Souter, reviewed the various restrictions imposed by the Pennsylvania legislature. The Court (plurality plus two concurring Justices) first reaffirmed *Roe's* holding that a woman's decision to terminate an unwanted pregnancy was a fundamental right. The *Casey* plurality held, second, that the lesser standard of "undue burden" would be applied, rather than the strict scrutiny standard. The plurality also held, third, that all of Pennsylvania's restrictions—except the spousal notification requirement—did not impose an undue burden and, therefore, would be upheld.

It is generally understood that some of the restrictions upheld under the undue burden standard (*e.g.*, a required 24-hour waiting period) would not have survived strict scrutiny. Although the plurality acknowledged that a "spousal consent" requirement would have even been more restrictive, the plurality relied on extensive empirical data regarding spousal and domestic abuse of women to strike down the spousal notification requirement. Four Justices, as you can see from the opinions above, dissented. One of the dissenters, Justice White, left the Court the next year and was replaced by Justice Ginsburg.

(2)　*What Does the "Undue Burden" Standard Mean?* The plurality stated that an "undue burden exists if its purpose or effect is to place a substantial obstacle in the path of a woman seeking an abortion. . . ." This test indicated that a Court must consider the "effect" of a regulation when deciding whether the regulation was an "undue burden." In *Casey*, for example, consideration of the "effect" of the "spousal notification" provision was the basis for striking down the provision. The requirement of a woman who "seeks" an abortion evidently distinguishes regulations designed to persuade from those that impede; does this part of the test help make it objective?

(3) *The Stare Decisis Controversy.* The majority's analysis of *stare decisis* relies on certain factors from previous cases, such as (1) unworkability, (2) reliance interests, (3) undermining of legal reasoning by subsequent doctrine, and (4) undermining of factual assumptions. In some of these categories, the majority concedes that its reasoning is nontraditional (*e.g.*, reliance). The four opposing justices attack each prong of the analysis (*e.g.*, by pointing out that if protecting reliance interests meant protecting broad social customs, it would have resulted in reaffirmation of the "separate but equal" doctrine). Which side has the better argument concerning these four factors of stare decisis?

(4) *Beyond Traditional Stare Decisis: Cases of "Comparable Dimension" and Inquiries into "Legitimacy Under Fire."* The majority undertakes two lines of analysis that it suggests might not be necessary in a "less significant case": (1) it compares the grounds for overruling *Roe* to those in two cases of "comparable dimension" (*Plessy* and *Lochner*), and (2) it considers the cost to the Court's perceived legitimacy that would be paid by overruling rather than reaffirming *Roe.* The Court's reasoning apparently is that the "wrongness" of *Plessy* and *Lochner* was clearer at the time of overruling and that overruling a controversial decision under circumstances of perceived public pressure undermines legitimacy. The opposing justices appear to reason that a decision that the Court now considers erroneous should be *overruled*, and that the existence of public controversy should be excluded from consideration. Which view is correct?

(5) *Combining Stare Decisis and "Rightness-Wrongness" Considerations.* The stare decisis factors considered by the majority are not, however, the sole basis of decision; the Joint Opinion says that it also is based on "considering the fundamental constitutional questions resolved by *Roe.*" This consideration prompts the reader to ask what the Court should do if it evaluates a controversial prior decision as probably erroneous but it believes the error is debatable rather than clear. Perhaps the unclear probability of error then should combine with the judicial restraint embodied in the doctrine of stare decisis to result in reaffirmation of the prior decision. Does this line of thinking strengthen the majority's reasoning? This indicates that a Court will consider the effect of a regulation. In *Casey*, consideration of the effect of the spousal notice provision was determinative.

(6) *A Comparative Perspective: Poland's Post-Cold War Democracy Struggles With The Issues Involved in Abortion Rights*: Associated Press, *Poland Grapples with Abortion*, SIOUX CITY J., June 11, 1994, at B5. The political, ethical and moral issues which are intertwined with the constitutional questions investigated in this Chapter are not unique to the United States. For example, Poland's Parliament sought to address a widespread illegal abortion network in Poland and a large number of self-induced miscarriages. To this end, the Parliament has voted to ease its strict anti-abortion law by allowing a woman to have a legal abortion when she "is in difficult living conditions or a difficult personal situation." You might consider whether this Polish legal standard allows greater or lesser access to abortion than the American constitutional standard, which prohibits an "undue burden" on a woman seeking an abortion. For further comparative perspective, consider MARY ANN GLENDON, ABORTION AND DIVORCE IN WESTERN LAW (1987).

PROBLEM D

THE "UNDUE BURDEN" STANDARD OF PLANNED PARENTHOOD v. CASEY: WHAT ARE ITS MEANINGS AND RESULTS? Consider what outcome should be produced under the undue burden standard (*i.e.*, purpose or effect of creating a substantial obstacle) if a State regulates abortion in ways not contemplated by the Pennsylvania Act. (This analysis should help you to evaluate the utility of the undue burden standard as well as its meaning.) Specifically, what would be the result if a hypothetical jurisdiction were to enact (1) a statute that required women seeking abortions to attend four hours of classes taught by right-to-life organizations (is that a substantial obstacle, or merely persuasion)? (2) A statute that required spousal notification but included a broad, mandatory judicial bypass (*e.g.*, one that required state judges to dispense with the requirement for any woman who had substantial reason to fear any adverse reaction by her husband)? (3) A prohibition on use of an abortifacient pill (such as the drug known as RU486) on the grounds (a) that "it has not been proven safe and effective" or (b) that it would make abortion "too readily available" or (c) that it would "depreciate the state's interest in protecting potential human life?"

THE FIRST PARTIAL-BIRTH ABORTION DECISION: STENBERG v. CARHART, 530 U.S. 914 (2000). The *Carhart I* decision would be the Court's first pronouncement on the substance and scope of the "undue burden" standard established by the *Casey* decision. What would constitute a "substantial obstacle," in purpose or effect, to the exercise of a woman's fundamental right to abortion services?

For purposes of the *Carhart I* decision, you should understand that the most commonly used medical procedure for a late-term (post-viability) abortion is the dilation and evacuation (D&E) procedure. One variation of the D&E procedure is the dilation and extraction (D&X) procedure. [More detail is provided below in the second partial-birth abortion decision where the D&X procedure is called the "intact D&E" procedure.] Because the D&X procedure was considered close to infanticide, nearly 30 states criminalized the use of the D&X procedure, even when the woman's doctor considered it the most medically appropriate option for her. The Nebraska statute at issue here did not provide an exception of the woman's "health," although it did provide an exception for the woman's "life." The Nebraska statute was challenged on several grounds, including the theory that banning the D&X procedure created an undue burden, under *Casey*.

In the *Carhart I* decision, the Supreme Court, per Justice Breyer (who joined the Court after *Casey*), struck down the Nebraska statute. The Court first held that the Nebraska statute was unconstitutional because it lacked an exception for a woman's health. Second, the Court held that the criminalization of the D&X procedure created an undue burden on a woman's abortion rights, partially because the scope of the Nebraska law might inhibit doctors from using the D&E procedure and, in effect, ban all late-term abortions.

There were several concurring and dissenting opinions. Justice O'Connor concurred, emphasizing the "effect" aspect of the undue burden standard. Justices Stevens and Ginsburg also concurred; their opinions relied upon the undue burden standard, but emphasized the "purpose" aspect of the *Casey* standard.

Justice Scalia's dissent focused on his conclusion that the D&X procedure was "so horrible that the most clinical description of it evokes a shudder of revulsion." Justice Thomas dissented and repeated his view that *Roe* should be overruled. Justice Kennedy had a long dissent. On partial-birth abortion, he parted ways from his co-authors of the *Casey* plurality. Further discussion of Justice Kennedy's views can wait until the *Carhart II* decision, below, because there Justice Kennedy's dissent becomes the "new" Court's majority opinion.

NOTES AND QUESTIONS

(1) *The Post-Casey Application of the Undue Burden Standard to Partial Birth Abortion Regulations: Stenberg v. Carhart, 530 U.S. 914 (2000).* Although the political controversies regarding majoritarian regulation of abortion continued after the *Casey* decision, the *Carhart* decision in 2000 was the Court's first regarding abortion regulation since 1992. At issue in *Carhart* was a Nebraska statute (similar to laws in 30 other states) which criminalized the performance of certain abortion procedures after 12 weeks of gestation. The most common abortion procedure after 12 weeks was known as

"dilation and evacuation" (D & E). The Nebraska statute criminalized one of the D & E variations known as "dilation and extraction" (D & X). D & X was commonly referred to as "partial birth abortion." The trial court in *Carhart* had concluded, as a finding of fact, that the D & X procedure was superior to, and safer for the woman than, the other abortion procedures available after 12 weeks.

The Court, per Justice Breyer, held that the ban on the partial birth abortion procedure was unconstitutional. First, the Court held that Nebraska's law was unconstitutional because it lacked an exception for the preservation of the health of the woman. Second, the Court applied, in the alternative, the undue burden standard and struck down Nebraska's law. The Court found an undue burden on a woman's abortion rights in that the terms of the Nebraska restriction did not adequately distinguish between the D & E procedure and the D & X procedure.

(2) *The Doctrinal Controversy Regarding Abortion Regulation Continues.* Three Justices filed concurring opinions in *Carhart*. While the Court looked mainly at the "effect" of the restriction to determine the undue burden, Justice Ginsburg's concurring opinion also emphasized that, as she saw the facts, Nebraska's law had the impermissible "purpose" of restricting a woman's substantive due process rights.

Four Justices dissented. Switching sides from *Casey*, Justice Kennedy dissented in *Carhart* primarily on the grounds that the majority was misapplying the undue burden standard. Perhaps the most significant doctrinal development is that, in *Carhart*, the undue burden standard was accepted by a majority of the Court (including Justices Ginsburg and Breyer who joined the Court after *Casey*). Will this signal doctrinal stability? Or, as Justice Scalia's dissent suggested, is this just another "policy-judgment-couched-as-law"?

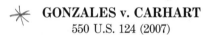

GONZALES v. CARHART
550 U.S. 124 (2007)

JUSTICE KENNEDY delivered the opinion of the Court.

[Following the *Stenberg v. Carhart* decision, above, Congress passed the Partial-Birth Abortion Ban Act of 2003 (the 2003 Act). The 2003 Act was somewhat more narrow than the Nebraska law struck down in *Carhart I*, and was based on Congressional "findings," many of which disagreed with the *Carhart I* Court's factual discussion. For example, Congress found as a fact that the intact D&E procedure was never medically necessary to the woman's health. The 2003 Act also did not include any "health exception," and therefore it directly challenged that holding of *Carhart I*.

The 2003 Act was challenged in three separate District Court actions. After a trial, each of the three District Courts found that the medical and scientific facts were contrary to the Congressionally-found facts, and enjoined the Attorney General of the United States from enforcing the 2003 Act. The Second, Eighth, and Ninth Circuits affirmed the grants of injunctive relief on appeal. The Supreme Court then granted certiorari to review the judgments of the Eighth and Ninth Circuits. Without overruling *Carhart I, Casey* or *Roe*, the Court, in a 5-4 decision by Justice Kennedy, upheld the 2003 Act.]

These cases require us to consider the validity of the Partial-Birth Abortion Ban Act of 2003 (Act), a federal statute regulating abortion procedures. In recitations preceding its operative provisions the Act refers to the Court's opinion in *Stenberg v. Carhart*, 530 U.S. 914 (2000), which also addressed the subject of abortion procedures used in the later stages of pregnancy. Compared to the state statute at issue in *Stenberg*, the Act is more specific concerning the instances to which it applies and in this respect more precise in its coverage. We conclude the Act should be sustained against the objections lodged by the broad, facial attack brought against it. . . .

I

A

The Act proscribes a particular manner of ending fetal life, so it is necessary here, as it was in *Stenberg*, to discuss abortion procedures in some detail. . . .

Abortion methods vary depending to some extent on the preferences of the physician and, of course, on the term of the pregnancy and the resulting stage of the unborn child's development. Between 85 and 90 percent of the approximately 1.3 million abortions performed each year in the United States take place in the first three months of pregnancy, which is to say in the first trimester. . . . The most common first-trimester abortion method is vacuum aspiration (otherwise known as suction curettage) in which the physician vacuums out the embryonic tissue. Early in this trimester an alternative is to use medication, such as mifepristone (commonly known as RU-486), to terminate the pregnancy. . . . The Act does not regulate these procedures.

Of the remaining abortions that take place each year, most occur in the second trimester. The surgical procedure referred to as "dilation and evacuation" or "D & E" is the usual abortion method in this trimester. . . . Although individual techniques for performing D & E differ, the general steps are the same. . . .

The abortion procedure that was the impetus for the numerous bans on "partial-birth abortion," including the Act, is a variation of this standard D & E. . . . For discussion purposes this D & E variation will be referred to as intact D & E. The main difference between the two procedures is that in intact D & E a doctor extracts the fetus intact or largely intact with only a few passes. There are no comprehensive statistics indicating what percentage of all D & Es are performed in this manner.

Intact D & E, like regular D & E, begins with dilation of the cervix. . . .

In an intact D & E procedure the doctor extracts the fetus in a way conducive to pulling out its entire body, instead of ripping it apart. . . .

Intact D & E gained public notoriety when, in 1992, Dr. Martin Haskell gave a presentation describing his method of performing the operation. In the usual intact D & E the fetus' head lodges in the cervix, and dilation is insufficient to allow it to pass. Haskell explained the next step as follows:

> " '. . . [T]he surgeon then forces the scissors into the base of the skull or into the foramen magnum. Having safely entered the skull, he spreads the scissors to enlarge the opening.
>
> " 'The surgeon removes the scissors and introduces a suction catheter into this hole and evacuates the skull contents. With the catheter still in place, he applies traction to the fetus, removing it completely from the patient.' "

H.R.Rep. No. 108-58, p. 3 (2003).

This is an abortion doctor's clinical description. . . .

D & E and intact D & E are not the only second-trimester abortion methods. Doctors also may abort a fetus through medical induction. . . . Doctors turn to two other methods of second-trimester abortion, hysterotomy and hysterectomy, only in emergency situations because they carry increased risk of complications. . . .

B

[T]he Act responded to *Stenberg* in two ways. First, Congress made factual findings. Congress determined that this Court in *Stenberg* "was required to accept the very questionable findings issued by the district court judge," § 2(7), 117 Stat. 1202, notes following 18 U.S.C. § 1531 (2000 ed., Supp. IV), p. 768, ¶ (7) (Congressional Findings), but that Congress was "not bound to accept the same factual findings," *ibid.*, ¶ (8).

Congress found, among other things, that "[a] moral, medical, and ethical consensus exists that the practice of performing a partial-birth abortion . . . is a gruesome and inhumane procedure that is never medically necessary and should be prohibited." *Id.*, at 767, ¶ (1).

Second, and more relevant here, the Act's language differs from that of the Nebraska statute struck down in *Stenberg*. . . .

II

The principles set forth in the joint opinion in *Planned Parenthood of Southeastern Pa. v. Casey*, 505 U.S. 833 (1992), did not find support from all those who join the instant opinion. See *id.*, at 979–1002 (SCALIA, J., joined by THOMAS, J., *inter alios*, concurring in judgment in part and dissenting in part). Whatever one's views concerning the *Casey* joint opinion, it is evident a premise central to its conclusion—that the government has a legitimate and substantial interest in preserving and promoting fetal life—would be repudiated were the Court now to affirm the judgments of the Courts of Appeals. . . .

We assume the following principles for the purposes of this opinion. Before viability, a State "may not prohibit any woman from making the ultimate decision to terminate her pregnancy." 505 U.S., at 879 (plurality opinion). It also may not impose upon this right an undue burden, which exists if a regulation's "purpose or effect is to place a substantial obstacle in the path of a woman seeking an abortion before the fetus attains viability.". . . On the other hand, "[r]egulations which do no more than create a structural mechanism by which the State, or the parent or guardian of a minor, may express profound respect for the life of the unborn are permitted, if they are not a substantial obstacle to the woman's exercise of the right to choose.". . . *Casey*, in short, struck a balance. The balance was central to its holding. We now apply its standard to the cases at bar. . . .

III. . .

C

A review of the statutory text discloses the limits of its reach. The Act prohibits intact D & E; and, notwithstanding respondents' arguments, it does not prohibit the D & E procedure in which the fetus is removed in parts.

The Act prohibits a doctor from intentionally performing an intact D & E. The dual prohibitions of the Act, both of which are necessary for criminal liability, correspond with the steps generally undertaken during this type of procedure. . . .

The identification of specific anatomical landmarks to which the fetus must be partially delivered also differentiates the Act from the statute at issue in *Stenberg*. . . .

By adding an overt-act requirement Congress sought further to meet the Court's objections to the state statute considered in *Stenberg*. . . .

Respondents have not shown that requiring doctors to intend dismemberment before delivery to an anatomical landmark will prohibit the vast majority of D & E abortions. The Act, then, cannot be held invalid on its face on these grounds.

IV

Under the principles accepted as controlling here, the Act, as we have interpreted it, would be unconstitutional "if its purpose or effect is to place a substantial obstacle in the path of a woman seeking an abortion before the fetus attains viability." *Casey*, 505 U.S., at 878, (plurality opinion). The abortions affected by the Act's regulations take place both previability and postviability; so the quoted language and the undue burden analysis it relies upon are applicable. The question is whether the Act, measured by its text in this facial attack, imposes a substantial obstacle to late-term, but previability, abortions. The Act does not on its face impose a substantial obstacle, and we reject this further facial challenge to its validity.

A

The Act's purposes are set forth in recitals preceding its operative provisions. A description of the prohibited abortion procedure demonstrates the rationale for the congressional enactment. The Act proscribes a method of abortion in which a fetus is killed just inches before completion of the birth process. . . . Under our precedents it is clear the State has a significant role to play in regulating the medical profession.

Casey reaffirmed these governmental objectives. The government may use its voice and its regulatory authority to show its profound respect for the life within the woman. . . .

The Act's ban on abortions that involve partial delivery of a living fetus furthers the Government's objectives. No one would dispute that, for many, D & E is a procedure itself laden with the power to devalue human life. Congress could nonetheless conclude that the type of abortion proscribed by the Act requires specific regulation because it implicates additional ethical and moral concerns that justify a special prohibition. . . .

Respect for human life finds an ultimate expression in the bond of love the mother has for her child. The Act recognizes this reality as well. Whether to have an abortion requires a difficult and painful moral decision. *Casey, supra,* at 852–853 (opinion of the Court). While we find no reliable data to measure the phenomenon, it seems unexceptionable to conclude some women come to regret their choice to abort the infant life they once created and sustained. . . . Severe depression and loss of esteem can follow. See *ibid.*

In a decision so fraught with emotional consequence some doctors may prefer not to disclose precise details of the means that will be used, confining themselves to the required statement of risks the procedure entails. From one standpoint this ought not to be surprising. Any number of patients facing imminent surgical procedures would prefer not to hear all details, lest the usual anxiety preceding invasive medical procedures become the more intense. This is likely the case with the abortion procedures here in issue. . . .

It is, however, precisely this lack of information concerning the way in which the fetus will be killed that is of legitimate concern to the State. *Casey, supra,* at 873 (plurality opinion). . . . The State has an interest in ensuring so grave a choice is well informed. It is self-evident that a mother who comes to regret her choice to abort must struggle with grief more anguished and sorrow more profound when she learns, only after the event, what she once did not know: that she allowed a doctor to pierce the skull and vacuum the fast-developing brain of her unborn child, a child assuming the human form.

It is a reasonable inference that a necessary effect of the regulation and the knowledge it conveys will be to encourage some women to carry the infant to full term, thus reducing the absolute number of late-term abortions. The medical profession, furthermore, may find different and less shocking methods to abort the fetus in the second trimester, thereby accommodating legislative demand. The State's interest in respect for life is advanced by the dialogue that better informs the political and legal systems, the medical profession, expectant mothers, and society as a whole of the consequences that follow from a decision to elect a late-term abortion.

It is objected that the standard D & E is in some respects as brutal, if not more, than the intact D & E, so that the legislation accomplishes little. What we have already said, however, shows ample justification for the regulation. Partial-birth abortion, as defined by the Act, differs from a standard D & E because the former occurs when the fetus is partially outside the mother to the point of one of the Act's anatomical landmarks. It was reasonable for Congress to think that partial-birth abortion, more than standard D & E, "undermines the public's perception of the appropriate role of a physician during the delivery process, and perverts a process during which life is brought into the world." Congressional Findings (14)(K), in notes following 18 U.S.C. § 1531 (2000 ed., Supp. IV), p. 769. There would be a flaw in this Court's logic, and an irony in its jurisprudence, were we first to conclude a ban on both D & E and intact D & E was overbroad and then to say it is irrational to ban only intact D & E because that does not proscribe both procedures. In sum, we reject the contention that the congressional purpose of the Act was "to place a substantial obstacle in the path of a woman seeking an abortion."

B

The Act's furtherance of legitimate government interests bears upon, but does not resolve, the next question: whether the Act has the effect of imposing an unconstitutional burden on the abortion right because it does not allow use of the barred procedure where " 'necessary, in appropriate medical judgment, for [the] preservation of the . . . health of the mother.' ". . . Here, by contrast, whether the Act creates significant health risks for women has been a contested factual question. The evidence presented in the trial courts and before Congress demonstrates both sides have medical support for their position. . . .

The question becomes whether the Act can stand when this medical uncertainty persists. The Court's precedents instruct that the Act can survive this facial attack. The Court has given state and federal legislatures wide discretion to pass legislation in areas where there is medical and scientific uncertainty. . . . See also *Stenberg, supra* (KENNEDY, J., dissenting). . . .

This traditional rule is consistent with *Casey*, which confirms the State's interest in promoting respect for human life at all stages in the pregnancy. Physicians are not entitled to ignore regulations that direct them to use reasonable alternative procedures. The law need not give abortion doctors unfettered choice in the course of their medical practice, nor should it elevate their status above other physicians in the medical community. . . .

Medical uncertainty does not foreclose the exercise of legislative power in the abortion context any more than it does in other contexts. The medical uncertainty over whether the Act's prohibition creates significant health risks provides a sufficient basis to conclude in this facial attack that the Act does not impose an undue burden.

The conclusion that the Act does not impose an undue burden is supported by other considerations. Alternatives are available to the prohibited procedure. . . .

Here the Act allows, among other means, a commonly used and generally accepted method [regular D&E], so it does not construct a substantial obstacle to the abortion right.

In reaching the conclusion the Act does not require a health exception we reject certain arguments made by the parties on both sides of these cases. On the one hand, the Attorney General urges us to uphold the Act on the basis of the congressional findings alone. Although we review congressional factfinding under a deferential standard, we do not in the circumstances here place dispositive weight on Congress' findings. The Court retains an independent constitutional duty to review factual findings where constitutional rights are at stake. . . .

As respondents have noted, and the District Courts recognized, some recitations in the Act are factually incorrect. . . . Whether or not accurate at the time, some of the important findings have been superseded. . . .

On the other hand, relying on the Court's opinion in *Stenberg*, respondents contend that an abortion regulation must contain a health exception "if 'substantial medical authority supports the proposition that banning a particular procedure could endanger women's health.' ". . . .

A zero tolerance policy would strike down legitimate abortion regulations, like the present one, if some part of the medical community were disinclined to follow the proscription. This is too exacting a standard to impose on the legislative power, exercised in this instance under the Commerce Clause, to regulate the medical profession. Considerations of marginal safety, including the balance of risks, are within the legislative competence when the regulation is rational and in pursuit of legitimate ends. When standard medical options are available, mere convenience does not suffice to displace them; and if some procedures have different risks than others, it does not follow that the State is altogether barred from imposing reasonable regulations. The Act is not invalid on its face where there is uncertainty over whether the barred procedure is ever necessary to preserve a woman's health, given the availability of other abortion procedures that are considered to be safe alternatives.

V

The considerations we have discussed support our further determination that these facial attacks should not have been entertained in the first instance. In these circumstances the proper means to consider exceptions is by as-applied challenge. . . .

JUSTICE THOMAS, with whom JUSTICE SCALIA joins, concurring.

I join the Court's opinion because it accurately applies current jurisprudence, including *Planned Parenthood of Southeastern Pa. v. Casey*. . . . I write separately to reiterate my view that the Court's abortion jurisprudence, including *Casey* and *Roe v. Wade*, has no basis in the Constitution. . . . I also note that whether the Act constitutes a permissible exercise of Congress' power under the Commerce Clause is not before the Court. The parties did not raise or brief that issue; it is outside the question presented; and the lower courts did not address it. . . .

JUSTICE GINSBURG, with whom JUSTICE STEVENS, JUSTICE SOUTER, and JUSTICE BREYER join, dissenting.

. . . Today's decision is alarming. It refuses to take *Casey* and *Stenberg* seriously. It tolerates, indeed applauds, federal intervention to ban nationwide a procedure found necessary and proper in certain cases by the American College of Obstetricians and Gynecologists (ACOG). It blurs the line, firmly drawn in *Casey*, between previability and postviability abortions. And, for the first time since *Roe*, the Court blesses a prohibition with no exception safeguarding a woman's health. . . .

I

A

As *Casey* comprehended, at stake in cases challenging abortion restrictions is a woman's "control over her [own] destiny." 505 U.S., at 869 (plurality opinion). . . . Thus, legal challenges to undue restrictions on abortion procedures do not seek to vindicate some generalized notion of privacy; rather, they center on a woman's autonomy to determine her life's course, and thus to enjoy equal citizenship stature.

In keeping with this comprehension of the right to reproductive choice, the Court has consistently required that laws regulating abortion, at any stage of pregnancy and in all cases, safeguard a woman's health. . . .

B

In 2003, a few years after our ruling in *Stenberg*, Congress passed the Partial-Birth Abortion Ban Act-without an exception for women's health. See 18 U.S.C. § 1531(a) (2000 ed., Supp. IV). The congressional findings on which the Partial-Birth Abortion Ban

Act rests do not withstand inspection, as the lower courts have determined and this Court is obliged to concede.

Many of the Act's recitations are incorrect. For example, Congress determined that no medical schools provide instruction on intact D & E. § 2(14)(B), 117 Stat. 1204, notes following 18 U.S.C. § 1531 (2000 ed., Supp. IV), p. 769, ¶ (14)(B) (Congressional Findings). But in fact, numerous leading medical schools teach the procedure. . . .

More important, Congress claimed there was a medical consensus that the banned procedure is never necessary. Congressional Findings (1), in notes following 18 U.S.C. § 1531 (2000 ed., Supp. IV), p. 767. But the evidence "very clearly demonstrate[d] the opposite.". . .

C

In contrast to Congress, the District Courts made findings after full trials at which all parties had the opportunity to present their best evidence. The courts had the benefit of "much more extensive medical and scientific evidence . . . concerning the safety and necessity of intact D & Es." *Planned Parenthood*, 320 F.Supp.2d, at 1014;. . .

According to the expert testimony plaintiffs introduced, the safety advantages of intact D & E are marked for women with certain medical conditions, for example, uterine scarring, bleeding disorders, heart disease, or compromised immune systems. See *Carhart*, 331 F.Supp.2d, at 924–929, 1026–1027;. . . Further, plaintiffs' experts testified that intact D & E is significantly safer for women with certain pregnancy-related conditions, such as placenta previa and accreta, and for women carrying fetuses with certain abnormalities, such as severe hydrocephalus. See *Carhart*, 331 F.Supp.2d, at 924, 1026–1027;. . .

Based on thoroughgoing review of the trial evidence and the congressional record, each of the District Courts to consider the issue rejected Congress' findings as unreasonable and not supported by the evidence. . . . The trial courts concluded, in contrast to Congress' findings, that "significant medical authority supports the proposition that in some circumstances, [intact D & E] is the safest procedure.". . .

Today's opinion supplies no reason to reject those findings. Nevertheless, despite the District Courts' appraisal of the weight of the evidence, and in undisguised conflict with *Stenberg*, the Court asserts that the Partial-Birth Abortion Ban Act can survive "when . . . medical uncertainty persists." This assertion is bewildering. Not only does it defy the Court's longstanding precedent affirming the necessity of a health exception, with no carve-out for circumstances of medical uncertainty, see *supra*, at 1641–1642; it gives short shrift to the records before us, carefully canvassed by the District Courts. . . .

II

A

The Court offers flimsy and transparent justifications for upholding a nationwide ban on intact D & E *sans* any exception to safeguard a women's health. Today's ruling, the Court declares, advances "a premise central to [*Casey's*] conclusion"— *i.e.*, the Government's "legitimate and substantial interest in preserving and promoting fetal life.". . . But the Act scarcely furthers that interest: The law saves not a single fetus from destruction, for it targets only a *method* of performing abortion. . . .

As another reason for upholding the ban, the Court emphasizes that the Act does not proscribe the nonintact D & E procedure. But why not, one might ask. Nonintact D & E could equally be characterized as "brutal," *ante*, at 1633, involving as it does "tear[ing] [a fetus] apart" and "ripp[ing] off" its limbs, *ante*, at 1620–1621, 1621–1622. "[T]he notion that either of these two equally gruesome procedures . . . is more akin to infanticide than the other, or that the State furthers any legitimate interest by banning one but not the other, is simply irrational." *Stenberg*, 530 U.S., at 946–947 (Stevens, J., concurring). . . .

Ultimately, the Court admits that "moral concerns" are at work, concerns that could yield prohibitions on any abortion. . . . Notably, the concerns expressed are untethered to any ground genuinely serving the Government's interest in preserving life. By allowing such concerns to carry the day and case, overriding fundamental rights, the Court dishonors our precedent. . . .

Revealing in this regard, the Court invokes an antiabortion shibboleth for which it concededly has no reliable evidence: Women who have abortions come to regret their choices, and consequently suffer from "[s]evere depression and loss of esteem." *Ante*, at 1634.[3] Because of women's fragile emotional state and because of the "bond of love the mother has for her child," the Court worries, doctors may withhold information about the nature of the intact D & E procedure.[4] The solution the Court approves, then, is *not* to require doctors to inform women, accurately and adequately, of the different procedures and their attendant risks. . . . Instead, the Court deprives women of the right to make an autonomous choice, even at the expense of their safety.[5]

This way of thinking reflects ancient notions about women's place in the family and under the Constitution-ideas that have long since been discredited. . . .

B

In cases on a "woman's liberty to determine whether to [continue] her pregnancy," this Court has identified viability as a critical consideration. See *Casey*, 505 U.S. 869–870 (plurality opinion). "[T]here is no line [more workable] than viability," the Court explained in *Casey*, for viability is "the time at which there is a realistic possibility of maintaining and nourishing a life outside the womb, so that the independent existence of the second life can in reason and all fairness be the object of state protection that now overrides the rights of the woman. . . .

Today, the Court blurs that line, maintaining that "[t]he Act [legitimately] appl[ies] both previability and postviability because . . . a fetus is a living organism while within the womb, whether or not it is viable outside the womb.". . .

One wonders how long a line that saves no fetus from destruction will hold in face of the Court's "moral concerns.". . . The Court's hostility to the right *Roe* and *Casey* secured is not concealed. Throughout, the opinion refers to obstetrician-gynecologists and surgeons who perform abortions not by the titles of their medical specialties, but by the pejorative label "abortion doctor.". . . A fetus is described as an "unborn child," and as a "baby," *ante*, at 1620, 1622–1623; second-trimester, previability abortions are referred to as "late-term," *ante*, at 1632; and the reasoned medical judgments of highly trained doctors are dismissed as "preferences" motivated by "mere convenience," *ante*, at 1620, 1638. . . .

---

[3] The Court is surely correct that, for most women, abortion is a painfully difficult decision. See *ante*, at 1633–1634. But "neither the weight of the scientific evidence to date nor the observable reality of 33 years of legal abortion in the United States comports with the idea that having an abortion is any more dangerous to a woman's long-term mental health than delivering and parenting a child that she did not intend to have . . . ." Cohen, Abortion and Mental Health: Myths and Realities, 9 GUTTMACHER POLICY REV. 8 (2006);

[4] Notwithstanding the "bond of love" women often have with their children, see *ante*, at 1633–1634, not all pregnancies, this Court has recognized, are wanted, or even the product of consensual activity. See *Casey*, 505 U.S., at 891 ("[O]n an average day in the United States, nearly 11,000 women are severely assaulted by their male partners. Many of these incidents involve sexual assault."). . . .

[5] Eliminating or reducing women's reproductive choices is manifestly *not* a means of protecting them. When safe abortion procedures cease to be an option, many women seek other means to end unwanted or coerced pregnancies. See, *e.g.*, World Health Organization, Unsafe Abortion: Global and Regional Estimates of the Incidence of Unsafe Abortion and Associated Mortality in 2000, pp. 3, 16 (4th ed. 2004).

III

A

The Court further confuses our jurisprudence when it declares that "facial attacks" are not permissible in "these circumstances," *i.e.*, where medical uncertainty exists. This holding is perplexing given that, in materially identical circumstances we held that a statute lacking a health exception was unconstitutional on its face. *Stenberg*, 530 U.S., at 930;. . .

Without attempting to distinguish *Stenberg* and earlier decisions, the majority asserts that the Act survives review because respondents have not shown that the ban on intact D & E would be unconstitutional "in a large fraction of relevant cases.". . . It makes no sense to conclude that this facial challenge fails because respondents have not shown that a health exception is necessary for a large fraction of second-trimester abortions, including those for which a health exception is unnecessary: The very purpose of a health *exception* is to protect women in *exceptional* cases.

B

If there is anything at all redemptive to be said of today's opinion, it is that the Court is not willing to foreclose entirely a constitutional challenge to the Act. . . .

The Court appears, then, to contemplate another lawsuit by the initiators of the instant actions. In such a second round, the Court suggests, the challengers could succeed upon demonstrating that "in discrete and well-defined instances a particular condition has or is likely to occur in which the procedure prohibited by the Act must be used." *Ante*, at 1638. One may anticipate that such a preenforcement challenge will be mounted swiftly, to ward off serious, sometimes irremediable harm, to women whose health would be endangered by the intact D & E prohibition. . . .

IV

Though today's opinion does not go so far as to discard *Roe* or *Casey*, the Court, differently composed than it was when we last considered a restrictive abortion regulation, is hardly faithful to our earlier invocations of "the rule of law" and the "principles of *stare decisis*.". . .

In sum, the notion that the Partial-Birth Abortion Ban Act furthers any legitimate governmental interest is, quite simply, irrational. The Court's defense of the statute provides no saving explanation. In candor, the Act, and the Court's defense of it, cannot be understood as anything other than an effort to chip away at a right declared again and again by this Court-and with increasing comprehension of its centrality to women's lives. When "a statute burdens constitutional rights and all that can be said on its behalf is that it is the vehicle that legislators have chosen for expressing their hostility to those rights, the burden is undue." *Stenberg*, 530 U.S., at 952 (Ginsburg, J., concurring) (quoting *Hope Clinic v. Ryan*, 195 F.3d 857, 881 (C.A.7 1999) (Posner, C. J., dissenting)). . . .

✳ NOTES AND QUESTIONS

(1) *The Second Partial-Birth Abortion Decision: Gonzales v. Carhart, 550 U.S. 124 (2007) (Carhart II)*. The Supreme Court struck down a Nebraska law prohibiting doctors from using an abortion procedure known as intact dilation and evacuation (intact D&E) in *Carhart I*, above. After President Bush took office, Congressional opponents of abortion succeeded in securing a federal law banning the intact D&E procedure (the Act) while allowing other abortion procedures, including the regular D&E. The lower courts struck down the Act, but the Supreme Court, per Justice Kennedy, upheld (5-4) the Act against the facial substantive due process claims of women and their doctors.

The Court held that the absence of a "health" exception did not mean the Act was unconstitutional (or constitute an undue burden). The Court also rejected a void-for-vagueness challenge. Finally, relying on the continued availability of other abortion procedures (including the regular D&E procedure), the Court held that the Act did not impose a substantial obstacle on a woman seeking a late-term, but previable, abortion. *See generally* Steven G. Calabresi, *Substantive Due Process After Gonzales v. Carhart*, 106 MICH. L. REV. 1517 (2008).

(2) *The Concurring and Dissenting Opinions.* Justice Thomas (for Justice Scalia) submitted a concurring opinion. Justice Thomas called, again, for overruling *Casey* and *Roe*.

The four dissenting Justices had been part of the majority in *Carhart I*, along with Justice O'Connor. But, Justice O'Connor had been replaced by Justice Alito (who voted with the Kennedy majority). [One Justice can, in some circumstances, make quite a difference.] Justice Ginsburg wrote for the dissenters. She argued that the Act imposed—in purpose *and* in effect—a substantial obstacle on a woman's decision. Consistent with her concurrence in *Carhart I*, Justice Ginsburg emphasized the purposeful nature of the Act, saying the Act "cannot be understood as anything other than an effort to chip away at a right declared again and again by the Court. . . ." Justice Ginsburg's opinion also spent time refuting various assertions made by the majority *in dicta*.

(3) *Whither Undue Burden?* The *Carhart II* Court "distinguished" *Carhart I* (rather than explicitly overruling it) on the ground that the federal Act was narrower than the Nebraska law. Otherwise, *Carhart II* suggests that the "effect" side of the undue burden standard depends on the availability of alternatives for the woman (and her physicians). The Court repeatedly emphasized that "[a]lternatives are available to the prohibited procedure." Since it is the woman's alternatives examined in the undue burden standard, this is contrary to strict scrutiny where only the state's alternatives are examined (as part of the narrow tailoring prong).

(4) *Abortion in the Political (Majoritarian) Process.* Not all action regarding abortion regulation has occurred in the judicial arena. For example, the South Dakota Legislature passed, and the Governor signed, a bill (HB 1215) that criminalized all abortions except for the life of the woman. (There were no other exceptions—for rape, incest, fetal defect or the health of the woman.) But, since South Dakota has "direct democracy," HB 1215 was referred to a popular vote. In the November 2006 election, the strict regulation was defeated by a 55% to 45% majority vote.

PROBLEM E

SENTENCING CHILD MURDERERS: REPRODUCTIVE RESTRICTIONS AS CONDITIONS OF PROBATION? Seventeen-year-old Tracy Wilder, in a Florida hospital, went into the bathroom to give birth to her baby. She then wrapped the infant in plastic, smothered her to death, and put her in a wastebasket. The Duvall County circuit court fashioned an unusual sentence when Wilder was convicted of this crime: She was to spend two years in prison followed by ten years of probation. But a key condition of the agreement under which Wilder could be released from confinement so early was that she remain on birth control (and receive psychological and birth control counseling) during the 10-year probationary period.

This sentence drew protests from both the Family Research Council and the American Civil Liberties Union, which usually were on opposite sides in cases involving reproduction, but which both argued that the sentence was unconstitutional. [Wilder's sentence was not unique, however. In an earlier Arizona case, a superior court judge had required use of contraception for a mother of two young children who nearly died when they were left unattended in an excessively hot apartment for two days, but then had abandoned the requirement as unenforceable after the woman became pregnant anyway. In an even more controversial Texas case, a convicted recidivist rapist offered to accept castration as a condition of probation but was refused by the trial judge when no physician could be found to perform such an operation.]

Is the birth control condition of probation for Wilder constitutional? What is the strength of her interest or right? What countervailing interests are there, and do they rise to a comparable level? What significance, if any, should be given to the fact that this probationary condition encourages the court to abbreviate Wilder's imprisonment, thereby increasing her freedom?

[F]　Sexual Conduct And Intimate Relationships

INTRODUCTORY NOTES AND QUESTIONS

(1) *Georgia Law Criminalizing Homosexual Sodomy Upheld Against Substantive Due Process Challenge: Bowers v. Hardwick, 478 U.S. 186 (1985).* Plaintiffs, a gay man and a heterosexual couple, challenged Georgia's law criminalizing certain intimate sexual conduct, including sodomy. The heterosexual couple's claim was dismissed for lack of standing. The court of appeals ruled that the gay man had a fundamental right to private and intimate association and that Georgia had to satisfy the strict scrutiny standard to justify its antisodomy law. The Supreme Court, per Justice White, disagreed and, in a 5 to 4 decision, reversed.

The Court first held that there was no substantive due process fundamental right to "engage in sodomy." Since there was no fundamental right, the Court applied only the rational basis standard. The Court then held that, for purposes of the rational basis test, the majoritarian notions of morality were a "legitimate governmental interest." Justice Powell concurred on "procedural" grounds.

There were four dissenters: Justices Blackmun, Brennan, Marshall, and Stevens. Justice Blackmun disagreed with the Court's formulation of the issue. Justice Stevens' dissent focused on the fact that the conduct occurred in the challenger's home and was, in his view, protected by the Fourth Amendment. Watch for the *Lawrence* decision below which revisited these issues.

(2) *Are Laws Against Private Acts of Adultery, Fornication, Incest, or Heterosexual Conduct Defined as Sodomy, Unconstitutional?* Justice White rejects the argument that consensual sexual behavior in private places such as the home is protected, expressing the concern that this reasoning would lead to the invalidation of laws against incest or like behavior performed in the home. Is this conclusion valid? Consider whether distinctions might be drawn on the ground of the state's possibly compelling interest in protecting the family or the marriage institution or preventing harm to minors or third persons. (Are some of the questioned practices, particularly fornication, protected by the implications of *Griswold*?) There has been substantial commentary on *Bowers*, much of it unfavorable. *E.g.*, Note, *Bowers v. Hardwick: The Invasion of Homosexuals' Right of Privacy*, 8 U. Bridgeport L. Rev. 229 (1987); Note, *Constitutional Law—An Imposition of the Justices' Own Moral Choices—Bowers v. Hardwick*, 9 Whittier L. Rev. 115 (1987); Note, *Bowers v. Hardwick: The Supreme Court Redefines Fundamental Rights Analysis*, 32 Vill. L. Rev. 221 (1987); *Cf.* Note, *Constitutional Law—The "Outer Limits" of the Right of Privacy: Bowers v. Hardwick*, 22 Wake Forest L. Rev. 629 (1987); *see also* Burnan, Morality, Sex and the Constitution: A Christian Perspective on the Power of Government to Regulate Private Sexual Conduct between Consenting Adults (1985); Buchanan, *Same-Sex Marriage: The Linchpin Issue*, 10 Dayton L. Rev. 541 (1985). Consider the Lawrence decision, below.

INTRODUCTORY NOTE

Before reading the *Lawrence* decision below, it may be helpful to read *Romer v. Evans*, 517 U.S. 620 (1996), an equal protection decision (authored by Justice Kennedy) below in Chapter 10. While the *Lawrence* decision overrules *Bowers*, the Court's reasoning is similar in many respects to *Romer*.

LAWRENCE v. TEXAS
539 U.S. 558 (2003)

Justice Kennedy delivered the opinion of the Court.

Liberty protects the person from unwarranted government intrusions into a dwelling or other private places. In our tradition the State is not omnipresent in the home. And there are other spheres of our lives and existence, outside the home, where the State should not be a dominant presence. Freedom extends beyond spatial bounds. Liberty presumes an autonomy of self that includes freedom of thought, belief, expression, and certain intimate conduct. The instant case involves liberty of the person both in its spatial and more transcendent dimensions.

I

The question before the Court is the validity of a Texas statute making it a crime for two persons of the same sex to engage in certain intimate sexual conduct.

In Houston, Texas, officers of the Harris County Police Department were dispatched to a private residence in response to a reported weapons disturbance. They entered an apartment where one of the petitioners, John Geddes Lawrence, resided. The right of the police to enter does not seem to have been questioned. The officers observed Lawrence and another man, Tyron Garner, engaging in a sexual act. The two petitioners were arrested, held in custody over night, and charged and convicted before a Justice of the Peace.

The complaints described their crime as "deviate sexual intercourse, namely anal sex, with a member of the same sex (man)." The applicable state law is Tex. Penal Code Ann. § 21.06(a) (2003). . . .

The petitioners . . . challenged the statute as a violation of the Equal Protection Clause of the Fourteenth Amendment and of a like provision of the Texas Constitution. Tex. Const., Art. 1, 3a. Those contentions were rejected. The petitioners, having entered a plea of *nolo contendere*, were each fined $200 and assessed court costs of $141.25.

The Court of Appeals for the Texas Fourteenth District considered the petitioners' federal constitutional arguments under both the Equal Protection and Due Process Clauses of the Fourteenth Amendment. After hearing the case en banc the court, in a divided opinion, rejected the constitutional arguments and affirmed the convictions. The majority opinion indicates that the Court of Appeals considered our decision in *Bowers v. Hardwick*, 478 U.S. 186 (1986), to be controlling on the federal due process aspect of the case. *Bowers* then being authoritative, this was proper.

We granted certiorari,. . .

II

We conclude the case should be resolved by determining whether the petitioners were free as adults to engage in the private conduct in the exercise of their liberty under the Due Process Clause of the Fourteenth Amendment to the Constitution. For this inquiry we deem it necessary to reconsider the Court's holding in Bowers. . . .

The facts in *Bowers* had some similarities to the instant case. . . . One difference between the two cases is that the Georgia statute prohibited the conduct whether or not the participants were of the same sex, while the Texas statute, as we have seen, applies only to participants of the same sex. . . . The Court, in an opinion by Justice White, sustained the Georgia law. Chief Justice Burger and Justice Powell joined the opinion of the Court and filed separate, concurring opinions. Four Justices dissented.

The Court began its substantive discussion in *Bowers* as follows: "The issue presented is whether the Federal Constitution confers a fundamental right upon homosexuals to engage in sodomy and hence invalidates the laws of the many States that still make such conduct illegal and have done so for a very long time." That statement, we now conclude, discloses the Court's own failure to appreciate the extent of the liberty at stake. To say that the issue in *Bowers* was simply the right to engage in certain sexual conduct demeans the claim the individual put forward, just as it would demean a married couple were it to be said marriage is simply about the right to have sexual intercourse. The laws involved in *Bowers* and here are, to be sure, statutes that purport to do no more than prohibit a particular sexual act. Their penalties and purposes, though, have more far-reaching consequences, touching upon the most private human conduct, sexual behavior, and in the most private of places, the home. The statutes do seek to control a personal relationship that, whether or not entitled to formal recognition in the law, is within the liberty of persons to choose without being punished as criminals.

This, as a general rule, should counsel against attempts by the State, or a court, to define the meaning of the relationship or to set its boundaries absent injury to a person or abuse of an institution the law protects. It suffices for us to acknowledge that adults may choose to enter upon this relationship in the confines of their homes and their own private lives and still retain their dignity as free persons. When sexuality finds overt expression in intimate conduct with another person, the conduct can be but one element in a personal bond that is more enduring. The liberty protected by the Constitution allows homosexual persons the right to make this choice.

Having misapprehended the claim of liberty there presented to it, and thus stating the claim to be whether there is a fundamental right to engage in consensual sodomy, the *Bowers* Court said: "Proscriptions against that conduct have ancient roots." In academic writings, and in many of the scholarly *amicus* briefs filed to assist the Court in this case, there are fundamental criticisms of the historical premises relied upon by the majority and concurring opinions in *Bowers*. . . .

At the outset it should be noted that there is no longstanding history in this country of laws directed at homosexual conduct as a distinct matter. . . . This does not suggest approval of homosexual conduct. It does tend to show that this particular form of conduct was not thought of as a separate category from like conduct between heterosexual persons.

Laws prohibiting sodomy do not seem to have been enforced against consenting adults acting in private. . . .

In *Bowers* the Court referred to the fact that before 1961 all 50 States had outlawed sodomy, and that at the time of the Court's decision 24 States and the District of Columbia had sodomy laws. 478 U.S., at 192–193. Justice Powell pointed out that these prohibitions often were being ignored, however. Georgia, for instance, had not sought to enforce its law for decades. *Id.*, at 197–198, n. 2 ("The history of nonenforcement suggests the moribund character today of laws criminalizing this type of private, consensual conduct"). . . .

In our own constitutional system the deficiencies in *Bowers* became even more apparent in the years following its announcement. The 25 States with laws prohibiting the relevant conduct referenced in the *Bowers* decision are reduced now to 13, of which 4 enforce their laws only against homosexual conduct. In those States where sodomy is still proscribed, whether for same-sex or heterosexual conduct, there is a pattern of nonenforcement with respect to consenting adults acting in private. The State of Texas admitted in 1994 that as of that date it had not prosecuted anyone under those circumstances. *State v. Morales*, 869 S.W.2d 941, 943.

Two principal cases decided after Bowers cast its holding into even more doubt. In *Planned Parenthood of Southeastern Pa. v. Casey*, 505 U.S. 833 (1992), the Court reaffirmed the substantive force of the liberty protected by the Due Process Clause. The *Casey* decision again confirmed that our laws and tradition afford constitutional protection to personal decisions relating to marriage, procreation, contraception, family relationships, child rearing, and education. . . .

Persons in a homosexual relationship may seek autonomy for these purposes, just as heterosexual persons do. The decision in *Bowers* would deny them this right.

The second post-*Bowers* case of principal relevance is *Romer v. Evans*, 517 U.S. 620 (1996). There the Court struck down class-based legislation directed at homosexuals as a violation of the Equal Protection Clause. *Romer* invalidated an amendment to Colorado's constitution which named as a solitary class persons who were homosexuals, lesbians, or bisexual either by "orientation, conduct, practices or relationships,"(internal quotation marks omitted), and deprived them of protection under state antidiscrimination laws. We concluded that the provision was "born of animosity toward the class of persons affected" and further that it had no rational relation to a legitimate governmental purpose. . . .

The central holding of *Bowers* has been brought in question by this case, and it should be addressed. Its continuance as precedent demeans the lives of homosexual persons. . . .

The foundations of *Bowers* have sustained serious erosion from our recent decisions in *Casey* and *Romer*. When our precedent has been thus weakened, criticism from other sources is of greater significance. In the United States criticism of *Bowers* has been substantial and continuing, disapproving of its reasoning in all respects, not just as to its historical assumptions. See, *e.g.*, C. Fried, Order and Law: Arguing the Reagan Revolution—A Firsthand Account 81–84 (1991); R. Posner, Sex and Reason 341–350 (1992). The courts of five different States have declined to follow it in interpreting provisions in their own state constitutions parallel to the Due Process Clause of the Fourteenth Amendment. . . .

To the extent *Bowers* relied on values we share with a wider civilization, it should be noted that the reasoning and holding in *Bowers* have been rejected elsewhere. The European Court of Human Rights has followed not *Bowers* . . . .

The doctrine of *stare decisis* is essential to the respect accorded to the judgments of the Court and to the stability of the law. It is not, however, an inexorable command. . . .

Bowers was not correct when it was decided, and it is not correct today. It ought not to remain binding precedent. *Bowers v. Hardwick* should be and now is overruled.

The present case does not involve minors. It does not involve persons who might be injured or coerced or who are situated in relationships where consent might not easily be refused. It does not involve public conduct or prostitution. It does not involve whether the government must give formal recognition to any relationship that homosexual persons seek to enter. The case does involve two adults who, with full and mutual consent from each other, engaged in sexual practices common to a homosexual lifestyle. The petitioners are entitled to respect for their private lives. The State cannot demean their existence or control their destiny by making their private sexual conduct a crime. . . . The Texas statute furthers no legitimate state interest which can justify its intrusion into the personal and private life of the individual.

Had those who drew and ratified the Due Process Clauses of the Fifth Amendment or the Fourteenth Amendment known the components of liberty in its manifold possibilities, they might have been more specific. They did not presume to have this insight. They knew times can blind us to certain truths and later generations can see that laws once thought necessary and proper in fact serve only to oppress. As the

Constitution endures, persons in every generation can invoke its principles in their own search for greater freedom. [Reversed].

JUSTICE O'CONNOR, concurring in the judgment.

The Court today overrules *Bowers v. Hardwick*. I joined *Bowers*, and do not join the Court in overruling it. Nevertheless, I agree with the Court that Texas' statute banning same-sex sodomy is unconstitutional. See Tex. Penal Code Ann. § 21.06 (2003). Rather than relying on the substantive component of the Fourteenth Amendment's Due Process Clause, as the Court does, I base my conclusion on the Fourteenth Amendment's Equal Protection Clause. . . .

This case raises a different issue than *Bowers*: whether, under the Equal Protection Clause, moral disapproval is a legitimate state interest to justify by itself a statute that bans homosexual sodomy, but not heterosexual sodomy. It is not. Moral disapproval of this group, like a bare desire to harm the group, is an interest that is insufficient to satisfy rational basis review under the Equal Protection Clause. Indeed, we have never held that moral disapproval, without any other asserted state interest, is a sufficient rationale under the Equal Protection Clause to justify a law that discriminates among groups of persons.

Moral disapproval of a group cannot be a legitimate governmental interest under the Equal Protection Clause because legal classifications must not be "drawn for the purpose of disadvantaging the group burdened by the law. . . ."

A State can of course assign certain consequences to a violation of its criminal law. But the State cannot single out one identifiable class of citizens for punishment that does not apply to everyone else, with moral disapproval as the only asserted state interest for the law. . . .

JUSTICE SCALIA, with whom THE CHIEF JUSTICE and JUSTICE THOMAS join, dissenting.

[M]ost of the rest of today's opinion has no relevance to its actual holding—that the Texas statute "furthers no legitimate state interest which can justify" its application to petitioners under rational-basis review (overruling *Bowers* to the extent it sustained Georgia's anti-sodomy statute under the rational-basis test). Though there is discussion of "fundamental proposition[s]," and "fundamental decisions," nowhere does the Court's opinion declare that homosexual sodomy is a "fundamental right" under the Due Process Clause; nor does it subject the Texas law to the standard of review that would be appropriate (strict scrutiny) if homosexual sodomy *were* a "fundamental right." Thus, while overruling the *outcome* of *Bowers*, the Court leaves strangely untouched its central legal conclusion: "[R]espondent would have us announce . . . a fundamental right to engage in homosexual sodomy. This we are quite unwilling to do." Instead the Court simply describes petitioners' conduct as "an exercise of their liberty"—which it undoubtedly is—and proceeds to apply an unheard-of form of rational-basis review that will have far-reaching implications beyond this case. . . .

II . . .

Texas Penal Code Ann. § 21.06(a) (2003) undoubtedly imposes constraints on liberty. So do laws prohibiting prostitution, recreational use of heroin, and, for that matter, working more than 60 hours per week in a bakery. But there is no right to "liberty" under the Due Process Clause, though today's opinion repeatedly makes that claim. The Fourteenth Amendment *expressly allows* States to deprive their citizens of "liberty," *so long as "due process of law" is provided*:. . .

IV

I turn now to the ground on which the Court squarely rests its holding: the contention that there is no rational basis for the law here under attack. This proposition is so out of accord with our jurisprudence--indeed, with the jurisprudence of *any* society we know—that it requires little discussion.

The Texas statute undeniably seeks to further the belief of its citizens that certain forms of sexual behavior are "immoral and unacceptable," *Bowers, supra*, at 196—the same interest furthered by criminal laws against fornication, bigamy, adultery, adult incest, bestiality, and obscenity. *Bowers* held that this *was* a legitimate state interest. The Court today reaches the opposite conclusion. . . . This effectively decrees the end of all morals legislation. If, as the Court asserts, the promotion of majoritarian sexual morality is not even a *legitimate* state interest, none of the above-mentioned laws can survive rational-basis review. . . .

One of the most revealing statements in today's opinion is the Court's grim warning that the criminalization of homosexual conduct is "an invitation to subject homosexual persons to discrimination both in the public and in the private spheres." It is clear from this that the Court has taken sides in the culture war, departing from its role of assuring, as neutral observer, that the democratic rules of engagement are observed. Many Americans do not want persons who openly engage in homosexual conduct as partners in their business, as scoutmasters for their children, as teachers in their children's schools, or as boarders in their home. They view this as protecting themselves and their families from a lifestyle that they believe to be immoral and destructive. The Court views it as "discrimination" which it is the function of our judgments to deter. So imbued is the Court with the law profession's anti-anti-homosexual culture, that it is seemingly unaware that the attitudes of that culture are not obviously "mainstream"; that in most States what the Court calls "discrimination" against those who engage in homosexual acts is perfectly legal; that proposals to ban such "discrimination" under Title VII have repeatedly been rejected by Congress, see Employment Non- Discrimination Act of 1994, S. 2238, 103d Cong., 2d Sess. (1994); Civil Rights Amendments, H.R. 5452, 94th Cong., 1st Sess. (1975); that in some cases such "discrimination" is *mandated* by federal statute, see 10 U.S.C. § 654(b)(1) (mandating discharge from the armed forces of any service member who engages in or intends to engage in homosexual acts); and that in some cases such "discrimination" is a constitutional right, see *Boy Scouts of America v. Dale*, 530 U.S. 640 (2000).

Let me be clear that I have nothing against homosexuals, or any other group, promoting their agenda through normal democratic means. Social perceptions of sexual and other morality change over time, and every group has the right to persuade its fellow citizens that its view of such matters is the best. That homosexuals have achieved some success in that enterprise is attested to by the fact that Texas is one of the few remaining States that criminalize private, consensual homosexual acts. But persuading one's fellow citizens is one thing, and imposing one's views in absence of democratic majority will is something else. I would no more *require* a State to criminalize homosexual acts—or, for that matter, display *any* moral disapprobation of them—than I would *forbid* it to do so. What Texas has chosen to do is well within the range of traditional democratic action, and its hand should not be stayed through the invention of a brand-new "constitutional right" by a Court that is impatient of democratic change. It is indeed true that "later generations can see that laws once thought necessary and proper in fact serve only to oppress," and when that happens, later generations can repeal those laws. But it is the premise of our system that those judgments are to be made by the people, and not imposed by a governing caste that knows best.

One of the benefits of leaving regulation of this matter to the people rather than to the courts is that the people, unlike judges, need not carry things to their logical conclusion. The people may feel that their disapprobation of homosexual conduct is strong enough to disallow homosexual marriage, but not strong enough to criminalize private homosexual acts—and may legislate accordingly. . . .

JUSTICE THOMAS, dissenting.

I join Justice Scalia's dissenting opinion. I write separately to note that the law before the Court today "is . . . uncommonly silly." *Griswold v. Connecticut*, 381 U.S. 479, 527 (1965) (Stewart, J., dissenting). If I were a member of the Texas Legislature, I would vote to repeal it. Punishing someone for expressing his sexual preference through noncommercial consensual conduct with another adult does not appear to be a worthy way to expend valuable law enforcement resources. . . .

NOTES AND QUESTIONS

(1) *Judicial Protection For Private Consensual Intimate Sexual Acts and Overruling Bowers: Lawrence v. Texas, 539 U.S. 558 (2003).* The *Bowers* decision, in 1985, had upheld, against a substantive due process challenge, Georgia's law criminalizing sodomy. In *Lawrence v. Texas*, the Court revisited the issue. This time, the case arose in Texas, and the Texas law criminalized certain intimate sexual conduct when the two persons were of the same sex. [Whereas the Georgia law had applied to both heterosexual and homosexual conduct, the Texas law applied only to homosexual conduct.]

In *Lawrence*, the Court, per Justice Kennedy, explicitly overruled *Bowers*. The Court, after a lengthy discussion of *stare decisis*, held that the "Texas statute furthers no legitimate state interest which can justify its intrusion into the personal and private life of the individual." Thus, because the Texas law lacked a "legitimate state interest," the law failed the rational basis test. The majority did not address the issue whether the prohibited conduct constituted a "fundamental right."

(2) *Justice O'Connor's Concurrence.* Justice O'Connor's concurring opinion is based on an equal protection analysis, but it is quite different than the majority's use of substantive due process analysis. But, since the rational basis standard for equal protection is the same as rational basis for substantive due process, she reached the same result as the majority.

(3) *Justice Scalia's Dissent.* Justice Scalia's dissent continued his criticism of the Court's analysis in *Roe, Casey, Romer* and the majority's (the "governing caste that knows best") judicial protection of "the so-called homosexual agenda." He also predicted that the state and federal laws prohibiting same-sex marriages would be the next target for judicial decisionmaking. Note that Justice O'Connor indicated that she would distinguish a same-sex marriage law from the anti-sodomy law in *Lawrence*.

(4) *The Relevance of the "Political Process."* Both the majority and the main dissent recognize that, since the *Bowers* decision, the number of States which have criminal prohibitions regarding sodomy have dropped-from 25 (in 1985) to 13 (in 2003). What did this mean for constitutional analysis? Justice Scalia argued that the Court was "impatient of democratic change." Did this indicate, as Justice Scalia asserts, that the majoritarian political process is working and, therefore, the judicial branch should defer on the issue? Or, as Justice Kennedy's majority opinion implied, did the continuing existence of such laws in 13 states demonstrate that judicial intervention was necessary—because the political process was *not* working?

(5) *Justice Thomas in Dissent.* Justice Thomas joined Justice Scalia, but he added a separate dissent relying on Justice Stewart's pithy dissent in *Griswold v. Connecticut*, above. Justice Thomas states—more broadly than any other dissenter—that he does not believe there is a "general right of privacy" even if the majority calls this right "liberty of the person both in its spatial and more transcendent dimensions." Remembering that Justice Stewart joined the *Roe v. Wade* majority, what weight would you give to Justice Stewart's *Griswold* dissent? More generally, should the *Lawrence* decision be read to have recognized a right of "sexual intimacy"? While the academic literature on *Lawrence*

is voluminous, students can find a thoughtful (and provocative) set of articles for further research in *Symposium: Gay Rights After Lawrence v. Texas*, 88 MINN. L. REV. 1017 (2004). *See generally* William D. Araiza, *Foreign and International Law in Constitutional Gay Rights Litigation: What Claims, What Use and Whose Law?*, 32 WILLIAM MITCHELL L. REV. 455 (2006); Charles W. "Rocky" Rhodes, *Liberty, Substantive Due Process, and Personal Jurisdiction*, 82 TUL. L. REV. 567 (2007). Regarding the continued controversy over Griswold, *see* Russell Shorto, *Contra-Contraception*, N.Y. TIMES (MAGAZINE), May 7, 2006, at 48.

APPENDIX TO § 9.02
READINGS ON THE CONSTITUTIONAL THEORY OF THE ABORTION CASES

[A]   The Interpretivism—Supplementation—Noninterpretivism Debate

ELY, THE WAGES OF CRYING WOLF: A COMMENT ON *ROE v. WADE*
82 YALE L.J. 920, 947–49 (1973)[*]

[I]t is difficult to see how [*Roe v. Wade*] will weaken the Court's position. [T]o the public the *Roe* decision must look very much like the New York legislature's recent liberalization of its abortion law. . . . *Roe v. Wade* seems like a durable decision.

It is, nevertheless, a very bad decision. Not because it will perceptibly weaken the Court—it won't; and not because it conflicts with either my idea of progress or what the evidence suggests is society's—it doesn't. It is bad because it is bad constitutional law, or rather because it is *not* constitutional law and gives almost no sense of an obligation to try to be. . . .

[T]he point that often gets lost in the commentary, and obviously got lost in *Roe*, is that . . . *before the Court* can get to the "balancing" stage, *before* it can worry about the next case and the case after that . . . it is under an obligation to trace its premises to the charter from which it derives its authority. A neutral and durable principle may be a thing of beauty and a joy forever. But if it lacks connection with any value the Constitution marks as special, it is not a constitutional principle and the Court has no business imposing it. I hope that will seem obvious to the point of banality. Yet those of us to whom it does seem obvious have seldom troubled to say so. And because we have not, we must share in the blame for this decision.

GREY, THE CONSTITUTION AS SCRIPTURE
37 STAN. L. REV. 1, 2 (1984)[**]

It is common to call the opposing schools of thought . . . "interpretivist" and "noninterpretivist," but this distorts the debate. If the current interest in interpretive theory . . . does nothing else, at least it shows that the concept of interpretation is broad enough to encompass any plausible mode of constitutional adjudication. We are all interpretivists; the real arguments are not over whether judges should stick to interpreting, but over what they should interpret and what interpretive attitudes they should adopt. Repenting past errors, I will therefore use the less misleading labels "textualists" and "supplementers" for, respectively, those who consider the text the sole legitimate source of operative norms in constitutional adjudication, and those who accept supplementary sources of constitutional law.

To these two schools, the last few years have added a third and fast-growing group

---

of constitutional theorists who reject the very question ("text alone, or text plus supplement?") to which textualists and supplementers propose different answers. According to these "rejectionists," judges are always interpreting the constitutional text, but this is not the kind of significant constraint on judicial activism that textualists think it is—the text, if read with an appropriately generous notion of context, provides as lively a Constitution as the most activist judge might need. . . .

[I]f, as rejectionists argue, the text when read in its appropriate context supplies norms that guide decisions like *Roe v. Wade* . . ., then the notion of what it means for a text to guide a decision has departed very far from the common understandings of both lawyers and ordinary people. To say that when judges decide cases like these they are getting all their law from the Constitution itself is bound to mislead. It is better for those of us who agree with these decisions to say that while the broad language of the Constitution delegates to judges the power to make them, their major premises come from such extra-textual sources as judicial precedent and the practices and ideals of social life. . . .

[B] What Kind Of "Supplementation" Or Noninterpretivism?

PERRY, ABORTION, THE PUBLIC MORALS, AND THE POLICE POWER: THE ETHICAL FUNCTION OF SUBSTANTIVE DUE PROCESS
23 U.C.L.A. L. Rev. 689, 690, 691–705 (1976)[*]

The basic and most cogent criticism of *Roe* . . . is not that the Court's opinion is inadequate, but rather that no conceivable rationale plausibly rooted in the Constitution can justify the Court's action in *Roe*.

[I] will attempt to show otherwise. Specifically, I will set forth a mode of inquiry for judicial review of statutes that, like the restrictive abortion legislation struck down in *Roe*, purport to serve the public morals, and I will demonstrate that this mode of inquiry has a constitutional basis, even though it requires the Court to apply values and norms not derived from the constitutional text. . . .

The founding fathers and, "perhaps by emulation," those who were responsible for the fourteenth amendment, intended that the specific content of the vague, ethical norms of the Constitution, including due process, remain to some extent an open question to be answered by each generation, for each generation. . . .

[T]he public morals are those commands proscribing nonobtrusive human behavior which, according to the conventions of the moral culture, merit the sanction of law behind them. Putting the matter in this fashion reveals an important distinction between the commands to which conventional moral culture subscribes and the commands to which it not only subscribes but believes should have the force of law and thus be legally binding on all, subscribers and nonsubscribers alike. [This distinction separates *"private"* from] *public* morals. There is a significant difference between doing something because one believes it to be morally right and wanting others compelled by the law to do that same thing whether or not *they* believe it as morally right. . . .

The conclusion seems reasonable that the Supreme Court and the judicial system over which it presides are quite competent to measure the metes and bounds of the public morals. This is not to say that the legislature is never competent, or that the Court owes the legislature no deference. The point is simply that the Court need not be paralyzed by self-doubt about its institutional ability to determine accurately the contours of the public morals. The Court, as it inquires whether a legislative act serves the public morals, need not assume the same highly deferential posture that it takes toward matters of social and economic policy. In the area of social and economic policy not only are social conventions by and large settled, but the legislature has a special expertise; neither of these observations holds true with respect to many issues in the public morals.

[U]ltimately, however, each individual Justice must map the relevant contours of conventional moral culture alone. Each Justice must ask whether particularized claims about that culture resonate with him or her. The Justices, after all, are not unfamiliar with conventional morals and attitudes; in truth it is unlikely that a very unconventional person would become a Justice of the Supreme Court. The collectivity which is the Supreme Court is, in this sense, a jury. . . .

GRANO, JUDICIAL REVIEW AND A WRITTEN CONSTITUTION IN A DEMOCRATIC SOCIETY
82 WAYNE L. REV. 1, 36 (1981)[*]

There are several problems with the approach that Professor Perry advocated. First, it is anomalous to give the Court power to go beyond the constitutional text only when majority sentiment supports the Court's thinking. . . . Second, Perry's thesis assumes that every piece of legislation should have majority backing—a thesis apparently shared by the single-issue groups that plague our politics. Moreover, Perry's thesis makes contemporary consensus the sole determinant of constitutionality. Indeed, essentially all Perry could find wrong with *Lochner* was that it "was predicated on an absurdly narrow 'reading' of the prevailing social attitudes (even of that pre-New Deal period)." Presumably, had public opinion been more strongly in the Court's favor, *Lochner* would have been correctly decided. Application of Perry's thesis also would necessarily demonstrate the constitutionality of many morals laws that other noninterpretivists, such as Professor Karst, would invalidate—laws forbidding incest, bigamy, and perhaps homosexuality. Conversely, had contemporary morality been in favor of strong prohibitions on abortion, and had a legislature nevertheless passed a permissive statute, Perry's thesis would have required the Court to invalidate such a statute and thereby give constitutional protection to the fetus.

Perry himself, however, could not rest with the ramifications of his thesis. Just one year after propounding it, he wrote:

> The specific position taken by a majoritarian society on a particular issue may be inconsistent with one or more basic moral principles to which society is committed. . . . In trying to ascertain conventional morality, a court should focus on the basic moral ideas to which society has long subscribed. Majoritarian views on specific issues of the day may be impulsive, irrational, or venal. *Basic moral ideas better indicate the true moral character of society* [citing Perry, *Constitutional "Fairness": Notes on Equal Protection and Due Process*, 63 VA. L. REV. 383, 388 n.26 (1977) (emphasis added)].

With this argument, Professor Perry assured complete subjectivity for his noninterpretivist approach. It could be argued, for example, that *Lochner* reflected the "basic moral principles" of America, at least up to the early twentieth century.

BENNETT, OBJECTIVITY IN CONSTITUTIONAL LAW
132 U. PA. L. REV. 445, 486 (1984)[**]

Roe v. Wade built on a series of prior decisions, some going back to much earlier courts, that protected the interests of adults with regard to procreation and those of parents with regard to children. It is plausible to see those prior decisions as opening a future that could accommodate *Roe v. Wade*. . . .

My point is not that *Roe v. Wade* was rightly decided, but that the debate about

---

whether the Supreme Court could legitimately invalidate laws prohibiting abortion is often misconceived. Viewed as a question of judicial objectivity, the legitimacy of *Roe v. Wade* turns not on whether there is some authoritative basis on which the Court can substitute its value judgment for that of the legislature but on whether the Court can successfully define its opinion as a natural outgrowth of what it had received. Perhaps my judgment that substantial continuity was demonstrated in *Roe v. Wade* is wrong. The continuity inquiry is not one to which authoritative answers are available. The legitimacy of *Roe v. Wade*, however, should be debated in terms of institutional continuity and of its substantive merits and not by reference to one or another dubious and inevitably incomplete standard of authoritativeness.

In contrast to *Roe v. Wade*, the state legislative apportionment cases, favorites of Ely, seem much less justifiable in terms of institutional continuity [citing *Baker v. Carr*]. . . .

Two years later, in *Reynolds v. Sims*, despite the embarrassing example of the constitutionally dictated basis for apportionment of the United States Senate, the Court held that *both* houses of the bicameral Alabama legislature were required under the equal protection clause to be apportioned on the basis of population. [T]o this day, legislative apportionment remains one of the few contexts in which the courts, in the name of the equal protection clause, mandate the values that legislatures must pursue rather than placing limited restrictions on the field of values that can legitimately be pursued. . . .

[C]   The Meaning of "Privacy": As Autonomy, As Freedom From Bodily Invasion, and As Other Concepts

HENKIN, PRIVACY AND AUTONOMY
74 COLUM. L. REV. 1410, 1411, 1424, 1430 (1974)*

In our day the Justices have newly recognized the "right to privacy." I think that denomination is misleading, if not mistaken. To date at least, the right has brought little new protection for what most of us think of as "privacy"—freedom from official intrusion. What the Supreme Court has given us, rather, is something essentially different and farther-reaching, an additional zone of autonomy, of presumptive immunity to governmental regulation. . . .

Jurisprudential uncertainties are aggravated, I think, because consideration has focused on defining the private right of Privacy, with little regard to our other balance, the competing "public good." There are, we have seen, intimations that the new zone of Privacy is characterized by activity done "in private," and sexual relations, to be sure, are usually conducted "in private," even today; but other activities are also generally secreted, done "in private," from burglary to espionage and conspiracies to overthrow governments. There are intimations that the right of privacy extends to activities that are intimate, and sexual relations, to be sure, are intimate, even today; but so are they in situations of statutory rape, prostitution, adultery, incest, homosexuality, and other forms of sodomy, which are still in almost every criminal code. . . . Control over one's body—made much of in the abortion debates—has not included the right to commit suicide,to reject medical treatment or vaccination, to refuse to make that body available to military service, or one's child's body and mind to compulsory elementary education. . . . Obviously, it is not from definitions of privacy or Privacy only, or even primarily, that we will learn why the state may forbid incest but not miscegenation, suicide but not abortion; may sterilize mental defectives but not forbid contraception. . . .

The answers, of course, must lie in the public goods that compete with "privacy" in these cases. The "goods" balance has never received refined scrutiny, for example, in applying the Bill or Rights; in the Privacy cases, it has hardly any scrutiny at all. The Court paid virtually no attention to the state's purpose or motive in outlawing contraception. The Court pronounced, without really telling us why, that before a fetus is quick the state has no proper interest to deny a woman's right to abortion, but that even then the mother's health is a sufficiently compelling interest justifying at least some interference with that Right of Privacy. It declared, but did not justify, that the life of the fetus thereafter is compelling enough, although less compelling, apparently, than the life or health of the mother. . . .

REGAN, REWRITING *ROE v. WADE*
77 Mich. L. Rev. 1569, 1570, 1589, 1596–97 (1979)*

Ultimately, my argument is an equal protection argument. I shall suggest that abortion should be viewed as presenting a problem in what we might call "the law of Samaritanism," that is, the law concerning obligations imposed on certain individuals to give aid to others. [I]f we require a pregnant woman to carry the fetus to term and deliver it—if we forbid abortion, in other words—we are compelling her to be a good Samaritan. [I]f we consider the special nature of the burdens imposed on pregnant women by laws forbidding abortion, we must eventually conclude that the equal protection clause forbids imposition of these burdens on pregnant women. . . .

My approach, however, is not a balancing approach at all. I do not argue that the sum of the woman's interest in having an abortion outweighs the sum of the state's interest in forbidding it. . . . The point of my argument is that the invasion of the woman's interest cannot be justified even on the ground that it is necessary to save the life of the fetus, so long as other potential [Good] Samaritans more eligible for compulsion are allowed to refuse much less burdensome and less invasive life-saving aid. . . .

Probably the most troublesome comparison, for my argument, is the comparison between the pregnant woman and the parent [because there are major areas in which parents can be forced to be Good Samaritans]. . . .

There are, however, significant differences between the parent and the pregnant woman who wants an abortion, differences which make parenthood look much more "voluntary" than unwanted pregnancy. . . .

CHEMERINSKY, RATIONALIZING THE ABORTION DEBATE:
LEGAL RHETORIC IN THE ABORTION CONTROVERSY
31 Buffalo L. Rev. 107, 142 (1982)**

[T]he best approach to the abortion issue would have been for the Court to declare that the decision whether to have an abortion is a private moral judgment which the state may not encourage, discourage, or prohibit. The Court could have held that a woman has the right at any point during her pregnancy to remove the fetus from her body. The state may set standards to insure that the fetus is removed in a manner most likely to guarantee its survival and it may require all steps necessary to keep the fetus alive once removed. . . . This approach overcomes the problems of *Roe v. Wade*, and while it is not without flaws, it could be defended as principled, non-arbitrary, and consistent with precedent.

First, the Court could articulate a legal principle to support its decision: it is the right of a person to decide what happens in and to his or her body. The state cannot compel a person to use her body to keep another person alive. . . .

Second, such a principle avoids arbitrary line-drawing by the Court. There is no need to decide whether or not the fetus is a person or at what point life begins. . . .

Furthermore, under this approach there is no need for an arbitrary balancing of the woman's rights versus those of the fetus. The fetus may have a right to life, but not a right to be kept in a woman's body against her will. . . .

[D] Personhood—And The Human Life Bill

EPSTEIN, SUBSTANTIVE DUE PROCESS BY ANY OTHER NAME: THE ABORTION CASES
1973 Sup. Ct. Rev. 159, 179–80*

What counts as a person under the Constitution? To this question, Mr. Justice Blackmun responds, as is his wont, by listing all the clauses of the Constitution which contain the word "person." Without discussion, he then concludes that it is not at all clear whether the term, as used in these clauses, was meant to include the unborn child. [But] Mr. Justice Blackmun is quite troubled because he thinks it possible that once an unborn child is treated as a person under the due process clause, then the Constitution forbids all abortions, even those performed to save the life of the mother.

There are several reasons why this position . . . must be rejected. In the first place, the due process clause still has its state action limitations [*i.e.*, it applies only to "the state" or those sufficiently closely connected to it]. There is no reason to suppose that the performance of an abortion by a private physician must constitute state action under the Constitution. . . .

Again, even if one adopts an expansive view of the state action requirement, it still does not follow that the unborn child has a right to life guaranteed to it under the Constitution. The Constitution does not prescribe a body of absolutes. "Balance of interests" tests are commonplace, given modern views on constitutional interpretation. [W]e could decide that the unborn child is a person under the Constitution and still leave it to state law to decide what complex of rights and duties attach to that status. . . .

NOONAN, THE ROOT AND BRANCH OF *ROE v. WADE*
63 Neb. L. Rev. 668, 673, 678–79 (1984)**

In one passage [in *Roe*] the Court spoke of the unborn before viability as "a theory of life," as though there were competing views as to whether life in fact existed before viability. [I]n another passage the Court spoke of life in the womb up to birth as "potential life." The Court's description was inaccurate if the Court meant to suggest that what was in the womb was pure potentiality, a zero that could not be protected by law. . . .

In [*Akron*] one can observe in the most concrete way the Court's discomfort before reality. The Court cannot uphold a requirement of humane burial without conceding that the being who is to be buried is human. A mask has been placed over this being. Even death cannot remove the mask. . . .

If the Court could . . . understand what humane and sanitary burial is, it might also perceive the reality of the extraordinary beauty of each human being put to death in the name of the abortion liberty and concealed from legal recognition by a jurisprudence that substitutes a judge's fiat for the truth.

ESTREICHER, CONGRESSIONAL POWER AND CONGRESSIONAL RIGHTS: REFLECTIONS ON PROPOSED "HUMAN LIFE" LEGISLATION
68 Va. L. Rev. 333, 338–40 (1982)*

Supporters of the "human life" bill present an argument consisting of two parts. The first treats the abortion ruling as essentially inconclusive because of the Court's institutional incapacity to resolve definitively the "factual" and moral issues of whether life begins at conception or some later point in the procreative process. As the argument runs, because the Court in *Roe* declined to define when life begins, it remains open to Congress, endowed with superior fact finding capability, to decide whether, prior to fetal viability, a governmental interest in protecting "life" is sufficient to overcome the woman's freedom of choice.

The second half of the argument addresses the fact that the Court in *Roe* rejected one state's effort to deny a woman's freedom of choice by declaring in a statute that life begins at conception. The argument asserts a superior competence in the national legislature to advance the protection of the fetus because of Congress' special responsibility and authority under section 5 of the fourteenth amendment, [which grants Congress power to "enforce" the amendment].

Although there is an outward plausibility to the "human life" position, the argument is fundamentally flawed. Congressional findings are entitled to great respect in any constitutional case, but there is no basis for claiming authority in Congress to displace the Court's definitive interpretations, whether that claim be founded on Congress' role as a national legislature or its enforcement authority under section 5. . . . In effect, the "human life" proposal attempts a legislative overruling of a Supreme Court interpretation of the Constitution, without traversing the thorny path of constitutional amendment. . . . *See City of Boerne, Texas v. Flores*, 521 U.S. 507 (1997).

§ 9.03   THE FAMILY

VILLAGE OF BELLE TERRE v. BORAAS, 416 U.S. 1 (1974). The village of Belle Terre adopted an ordinance restricting land use to one-family dwellings, defining the word "family" to mean one or more persons related by blood, adoption, or marriage, or not more than two unrelated persons, living and cooking together as a single house-keeping unit. The ordinance expressly excluded lodging, boarding, fraternity, or multi-dwelling houses. The Court, per Justice Douglas, upheld the ordinance, reasoning that it fell within the category of economic and sociallegislation not infringing fundamental rights and should be sustained since it bore a "rational relationship to a [permissible] state objective."

Justice Douglas emphasized environmental and family concerns: "A quiet place where yards are wide, people few, and motor vehicles restricted are legitimate guidelines in a land-use project addressed to family needs." Justices Brennan and Marshall dissented, with Justice Marshall concluding that the ordinance "unnecessarily burdens appellees' . . . freedom of association and their constitutionally guaranteed right to privacy" by negating the "selection of one's living companions" and the "right to 'establish a home.' "

MOORE v. EAST CLEVELAND
431 U.S. 494 (1977)

MR. JUSTICE POWELL announced the judgment of the Court, and delivered an opinion in which MR. JUSTICE BRENNAN, MR. JUSTICE MARSHALL, and MR. JUSTICE BLACKMUN joined.

East Cleveland's housing ordinance, like many throughout the country, limits occupancy of a dwelling unit to members of a single family. . . . But the ordinance contains an unusual and complicated definitional section that recognizes as a "family" only a few categories of related individuals. [The ordinance limited cohabitation to the spouse, unmarried children, parents, or parents-in-law of the "nominal head of the household," plus the spouse and dependent children of "not more than one dependent married or unmarried child of the nominal head of the household."] Because her family, living together in her home, fits none of these categories, appellant stands convicted of a criminal offense. [Ms. Moore violated the ordinance because two grandsons who were first cousins resided with her.] The question in this case is whether the ordinance violates the due process clause of the fourteenth amendment.

The city argues that our decision in *Village of Belle Terre v. Boraas* requires us to sustain the ordinance attacked here. Belle Terre, like East Cleveland, imposed limits on the types of groups that could occupy a single dwelling unit. Applying the constitutional standard announced in this Court's leading land-use case, *Euclid v. Ambler Realty Co.*, 272 U.S. 365 (1926), we sustained the Belle Terre ordinance on the ground that it bore a rational relationship to permissible state objectives.

But one overriding factor sets this case apart from *Belle Terre*. The ordinance there affected only *unrelated* individuals. [E]ast Cleveland, in contrast, has chosen to regulate the occupancy of its housing by slicing deeply into the family itself. . . .

When a city undertakes such intrusive regulation of the family, neither *Belle Terre* nor *Euclid* governs; the usual judicial deference to the legislature is inappropriate. "This court has long recognized that freedom of personal choice in matters of marriage and family life is one of the liberties protected by the Due Process Clause of the Fourteenth Amendment." A host of cases, tracing their lineage to *Meyer v. Nebraska* and *Pierce v. Society of Sisters*, have consistently acknowledged a "private realm of family life which the state cannot enter."

. . . [W]hen the government intrudes on choices concerning family living arrangements, this Court must examine carefully the importance of the governmental interests advanced and the extent to which they are served by the challenged regulation.

When thus examined, this ordinance cannot survive. The city seeks to justify it as a means of preventing overcrowding, minimizing traffic and parking congestion, and avoiding an undue financial burden on East Cleveland's school system. Although these are legitimate goals, the ordinance before us serves them marginally, at best. For example, the ordinance permits any family consisting only of husband, wife, and unmarried children to live together, even if the family contains a half dozen licensed drivers, each with his or her own car. At the same time it forbids an adult brother and sister to share a household, even if both faithfully use public transportation. The ordinance would permit a grandmother to live with a single dependent son and children, even if his school-age children number a dozen, yet it forces Mrs. Moore to find another dwelling for her grandson John, simply because of the presence of his uncle and cousin in the same household. . . .

The city would distinguish the cases based on *Meyer* and *Pierce*. It points out that none of them "gives grandmothers any fundamental rights with respect to grandsons" and suggests that any constitutional right to live together as a family extends only to the nuclear family—essentially a couple and their dependent children.

Ours is by no means a tradition limited to respect for the bonds uniting the members of the nuclear family. The tradition of uncles, aunts, cousins, and especially grandparents sharing a household along with parents and children has roots equally venerable and equally deserving of constitutional recognition. . . .

Whether or not such a household is established because of personal tragedy, the choice of relatives in this degree of kinship to live together may not lightly be denied by the State. *Pierce* struck down an Oregon law requiring all children to attend the State's public schools, holding that the Constitution "excludes any general power of the State to standardize its children by forcing them to accept instruction from public teachers only." By the same token the Constitution prevents East Cleveland from standardizing its children—and its adults—by forcing all to live in certain narrowly defined family patterns.

Reversed.

MR. JUSTICE BRENNAN, with whom MR. JUSTICE MARSHALL joins, concurring.

I join the plurality's opinion. I agree that the Constitution is not powerless to prevent East Cleveland from prosecuting as a criminal and jailing a 63-year-old grandmother for refusing to expel from her home her now 10-year-old grandson who has lived with her and been brought up by her since his mother's death when he was less than a year old. . . .

In today's America, the "nuclear family" is the pattern so often found in much of white suburbia. . . . The Constitution cannot be interpreted, however, to tolerate the imposition by government upon the rest of us of white suburbia's preference in patterns of family living. . . .

The "extended" form is especially familiar among black families. [E]ven in husband and wife households, 13% of black families compared with 3% of white families include relatives under 18 years old, in addition to the couple's own children. In black households whose head is an elderly woman, as in this case, the contrast is even more striking: 48% of such black households, compared with 10% of counterpart white households, include related minor children not offspring of the head of the household.

I do not wish to be understood as implying that East Cleveland's enforcement of its ordinance is motivated by a racially discriminatory purpose: The record of this case would not support that implication. But the prominence of other than nuclear families among ethnic and racial minority groups, including our black citizens, surely demonstrates that the "extended family" pattern remains a vital tenet of our society. [I]n prohibiting this pattern of family living as a means of achieving its objectives, appellee city has chosen a device that deeply intrudes into family associational rights that historically have been central, and today remain central, to a large proportion of our population.

MR. JUSTICE STEVENS, concurring in the judgment.

In my judgment the critical question presented by this case is whether East Cleveland's housing ordinance is a permissible restriction on appellant's right to use her own property as she sees fit. . . .

[S]ince this ordinance has not been shown to have any "substantial relation to the public health, safety, morals, or general welfare" of the city of East Cleveland, and since it cuts so deeply into a fundamental right normally associated with the ownership of residential property—that of an owner to decide who may reside on his or her property—it must fall under the limited standard of review of zoning decisions which this Court preserved in *Euclid*. . . . Under that standard, East Cleveland's unprecedented ordinance constitutes a taking of property without due process and without just compensation.

For these reasons, I concur in the Court's judgment.

MR. CHIEF JUSTICE BURGER, dissenting.

It is unnecessary for me to reach the difficult constitutional issue this case presents. Appellant's deliberate refusal to use a plainly adequate administrative remedy provided by the city should foreclose her from pressing in this Court any constitutional objections to the city's zoning ordinance. . . .

MR. JUSTICE STEWART, with whom MR. JUSTICE REHNQUIST joins, dissenting.

In *Village of Belle Terre v. Boraas*, the Court considered a New York village ordinance that restricted land use within the village to single-family dwellings. . . .

. . . The argument was made there that a municipality could not zone its land exclusively for single-family occupancy because to do so would interfere with protected rights of privacy or association. We rejected this contention, and held that the ordinance at issue "involve[d] no 'fundamental' right guaranteed by the Constitution, such as . . . the right of association, . . ." or any right of privacy, *cf. Griswold v. Connecticut; Eisenstadt v. Baird.*

The *Belle Terre* decision thus disposes of the appellant's contentions to the extent they focus not on her blood relationships with her sons and grandsons but on more general notions about the "privacy of the home." Her suggestion that every person has a constitutional right permanently to share his residence with whomever he pleases, and that such choices are "beyond the province of legitimate governmental intrusion," amounts to the same argument that was made and found unpersuasive in *Belle Terre*. . . .

[I] cannot agree. When the Court has found that the Fourteenth Amendment placed a substantive limitation on a State's power to regulate, it has been in those rare cases in which the personal interests at issue have been deemed " 'implicit in the concept of ordered liberty.' " *See Roe v. Wade, supra,* quoting *Palko v. Connecticut,* 302 U.S. 319, 325. The interest that the appellant may have in permanently sharing a single kitchen and a suite of contiguous rooms with some of her relatives simply does not rise to that level. To equate this interest with the fundamental decisions to marry and to bear and raise children is to extend the limited substantive contours of the Due Process Clause beyond recognition. . . .

[The dissenting opinion of JUSTICE WHITE is omitted.]

NOTES AND QUESTIONS

(1) *A Fundamental Right to Choose "Family" Composition: Moore v. East Cleveland, 431 U.S. 494 (1977).* The *Moore* decision is generally considered as establishing a fundamental right of family composition. Justice Powell's plurality opinion says that the Court must "examine carefully the governmental interests and the extent to which they are served when regulation intrudes upon family living arrangements." Thus, strict scrutiny would be the governing standard. [Note: as we shall see in the chapter on the Equal Protection Clause, below, that clause sometimes has been interpreted to require what is called "middle tier" review: review that is more exacting than a rational basis test, but not so exacting as strict scrutiny. Is Justice Powell's approach here analogous?]

(2) *The Fundamental Right to Marry: Zablocki v. Redhail, 434 U.S. 374 (1978).* In *Zablocki,* a Wisconsin statute provided that no resident of the state, having minor children not in his custodythat he was under a court order to support, could marry without court approval. The purpose was to ensure support and prevent the dependent children from becoming public charges. The Court, per Marshall, J., struck down the

statute, holding that "the right to marry is part of the fundamental 'right of privacy' implicit in the fourteenth amendment's due process clause," and that the statute was not sufficiently narrowly drawn to effectuate compelling state interests. Justice Rehnquist dissented, concluding that marriage was neither a fundamental right nor the proper subject of an intermediate standard of review; in his view, the statute should have been upheld because it satisfied the rational basis test. [For another decision recognizing the status of marriage as a fundamental right, *cf. Loving v. Virginia*, 388 U.S. 1 (1967) (state's prohibition of interracial marriage held an unconstitutional infringement of the fundamental right to marry). *See* Chapter 10.]

Consider the reasoning of the Court's marriage decision with the reasoning in Justice Scalia's plurality opinion in *Michael H* below.

MICHAEL H. v. GERALD D., 491 U.S. 110 (1989). Michael H. had an extramarital affair with Carole D. while she was married to Gerald D., as a result of which Victoria D. was born. At various times, Victoria was treated as the child of Gerald, and at various times that of Michael, while Carole lived with each of them and with another man at different times. Ultimately, reconciled with Gerald, Carole sought to deny Michael visitation of Victoria. She relied upon Cal. Evid. Code Ann. § 621, which provided that a child born to a married woman living with her husband is presumed to be a child of the marriage, a presumption that could be rebutted only by the husband or wife, and then only in limited circumstances.

Michael sued to establish paternity and the right of visitation; a guardian ad litem made a claim on the same basis for Victoria. The California courts applied the California statute and denied both paternity and visitation. Michael and Victoria then raised due process challenges in the Supreme Court. With a plurality opinion by Justice Scalia, the Court affirmed and rejected the due process challenge:

> Michael contends as a matter of substantive due process that because he has established a parental relationship with Victoria, protection of Gerald's and Carole's marital union is an insufficient state interest to support termination of that relationship. This argument is, of course, predicated on the assumption that Michael has a constitutionally protected liberty interest in his relationship with Victoria. . . .

> In an attempt to limit and guide interpretation of the [due process] clause, we have insisted not merely that the interests denominated as a "liberty" be "fundamental" (a concept that, in isolation, is hard to objectify), but also that it be an interest traditionally protected by our society. As we have put it, the due process clause affords only those protections "so rooted in the traditions and conscious of our people as to be ranked as fundamental. . . ."

> Thus, the legal issue in the present case reduces to whether the relationship between persons in the situation of Michael and Victoria has been treated as a protected family unit under the historic practices of our society, or whether on any other basis it has been accorded special protection. We think it impossible to find that it has. In fact, quite to the contrary, our traditions have protected the marital family (Gerald, Carole, and the child they acknowledge to be theirs) against the sort of claim Michael asserts. . . .

> We do not accept Justice Brennan's criticism that this result "squashes" the liberty that consists of "the freedom not to conform." It seems to us that reflects the erroneous view that there is only one side to this controversy—that one disposition can expand a "liberty" of sorts without contracting an equivalent "liberty" on the other side. Such a happy choice is rarely available. Here, to *provide* protection to an adulterous natural father is to *deny* protection to a marital father, and vice versa. If Michael has a "freedom not to conform" (whatever that means), Gerald must equivalently have a "freedom to conform." [O]ur disposition does not choose between these two "freedoms," but leaves that to the people of California. Justice Brennan's approach chooses one of them as

the constitutional imperative, on no apparent basis except that the unconventional is to be preferred.

[Justice Scalia rejected Victoria's claim as "if anything, weaker than Michael's," and supported by no history or tradition. Justice Scalia's opinion is commonly understood as arguing that the category of fundamental rights should be limited to those rights traditionally regarded by the majority as "fundamental."]

Justice O'Connor, joined by Justice Kennedy, concurred separately. Justice Stevens concurred in the judgment.

Justice Brennan, joined by Justices Marshall and Blackmun, dissented:

[B]y describing the decisive question as whether Michael and Victoria's interest is one that has been *"traditionally protected by* our society," (emphasis added), rather than one that society traditionally has thought important . . ., the plurality acts as if the only purpose of the due process clause is to confirm the importance of interests already protected by a majority of the states. . . .

In construing the fourteenth amendment to offer shelter only to those interests specifically protected by historical practice, moreover, the plurality ignores the kind of society in which our Constitution exists. We are not an assimilative, homogeneous society, but a facilitative, pluralistic one. . . . In a community such as ours, "liberty" must include the freedom not to conform. The plurality today squashes this freedom by requiring specific approval from history before protecting anything in the name of liberty. . . .

NOTES AND QUESTIONS

(1) *The Constitution and the Modern American Marriage: Michael H. v. Gerald D., 491 U.S. 110 (1989).* In a custody battle between the biological father of Victoria D. (Michael H.) and the biological mother (Carole D.) who was married to another man (Gerald D.), the substantive due process doctrine regarding the fundamental rights of marriage and childrearing came into conflict with facts that, for many Americans, seem to be a soap opera. In the plurality opinion, Justice Scalia rejected the biological father's claim of any "fundamental right." What was doctrinally significant was Justice Scalia's effort to narrow the standard for a fundamental right. Justice Scalia would add to the existing standard of "implicit in the concept of ordered liberty" (from *Griswold* and other decisions) the second requirement of "an interest traditionally protected by our society." While this was only a plurality decision, Justice Scalia's reasoning that *only traditionally recognized rights* could be "fundamental rights" has had continued vitality in subsequent cases. For further information about Justice Scalia's theory that *only traditionally recognized rights* might be considered fundamental, *see* Cass R. Sunstein, *Due Process Traditionalism*, 106 MICH. L. REV. 1543 (2008).

(2) *Parental Rights, Grandparent Visitation Rights and "The Best Interests of the Child" Standard: Troxel v. Granville, 530 U.S. 57 (2000).* In America's social climate where many children are born out-of-wedlock and over fifty percent of the marriages fail, issues of child custody and non-custodial visitation rights are common for many lawyers' practices. A particularly poignant issue is the question whether grandparents have some "right" to visitation with grandchildren. In the *Troxel* decision, the Supreme Court outlined, in a plurality opinion by Justice O'Connor, some of the constitutional dimensions. The *Troxel* case arose when paternal grandparents petitioned, under Washington's nonparent visitation statute, for visitation with the children of their deceased son. The children had been born out-of-wedlock [see the *Michael H* decision below], but they had had an on-going relationship with the paternal grandparents until the mother sought to limit their visitation to "one short visit per month." Over the mother's constitutional objection, the lower state court ordered two weekend visitations

per month and two weeks in the summer on the grounds that this was in the "best interest" of the children. The Washington Supreme Court reversed on federal constitutional grounds.

The Supreme Court, per Justice O'Connor, affirmed. The Court first held that the mother had, under substantive due process, a fundamental right to control the rearing of her children. Then, noting that Washington's statute was "breathtakingly broad" and did not require any deference [by the state court] to the parent's judgment, the Court held that the statute was not sufficiently tailored to achieve the state's purported interests. [The Court appeared to apply a version of strict scrutiny and concluded that the state failed the means prong.] The Court explicitly noted that the "narrower" statutory schemes of other states were not at issue. But, it is not hard to see a new generation of cases arising, especially in light of Justice Thomas' concurrence arguing that the states do not have a compelling interest in involuntary nonparent visitation. Justices Stevens, Scalia, and Kennedy all filed dissenting opinions.

§ 9.04 THE RIGHT TO INTERSTATE TRAVEL

EDWARDS v. CALIFORNIA
314 U.S. 160 (1941)

MR. JUSTICE BYRNES delivered the opinion of the Court.

[A California statute provided: "Every person . . . that brings or assists in bringing into the state any indigent person who is not a resident of the state, knowing him to be an indigent person, is guilty of a misdemeanor." Edwards, a California resident, used his automobile to transport his wife's brother, who arrived penniless, from Texas to California. For this act, Edwards was convicted under the statute. The Court here reverses on the basis of the Commerce Clause; the reader should consider alternative justifications for the holding.]

Article I, Section 8 of the Constitution delegates to the Congress the authority to regulate interstate commerce. And it is settled beyond question that the transportation of persons is "commerce," within the meaning of that provision. The issue presented in this case, therefore, is whether the prohibition . . . against the "bringing" or transportation of indigent persons into California is within the police power of that State. We think that it is not, and hold that it is an unconstitutional barrier to interstate commerce.

[T]he State asserts that the huge influx of migrants into California in recent years has resulted in problems of health, morals, and especially finance, the proportions of which are staggering. It is not for us to say that this is not true. We have repeatedly and recently affirmed, and we now reaffirm, that we do not conceive it our function to pass upon "the wisdom, need, or appropriateness" of the legislative efforts of the States to solve such difficulties.

But this does not mean that there are no boundaries to the permissible area of State legislative activity. There are. And none is more certain than the prohibition against attempts on the part of any single State to isolate itself from difficulties common to all of them by restraining the transportation of persons and property across its borders. . . .

It is difficult to conceive of a statute more squarely in conflict with this theory than the Section challenged here. [M]oreover, the indigent non-residents who are the real victims of the statute are deprived of the opportunity to exert political pressure upon the California legislature in order to obtain a change in policy. We think this statute must fail under any known test of the validity of State interference with interstate commerce. . . . *Reversed.*

MR. JUSTICE DOUGLAS, concurring.

I express no view on whether or not the statute here in question runs afoul of Art. I, Sec. 8 of the Constitution granting to Congress the power "to regulate Commerce with foreign Nations, and among the several States." But I am of the opinion that the right of persons to move freely from State to State occupies a more protected position in our constitutional system than does the movement of cattle, fruit, steel and coal across state lines. While the opinion of the Court expresses no view on that issue, the right involved is so fundamental that I deem it appropriate to indicate the reach of the constitutional question which is present.

The right to move freely from State to State is an incident of *national* citizenship protected by the privileges and immunities clause of the Fourteenth Amendment against state interference. Mr. Justice Moody in *Twining v. State of New Jersey*, 211 U.S. 78, 97, stated, "Privileges and immunities of citizens of the United States . . . are only such as arise out of the nature and essential character of the national government, or are specifically granted or secured to all citizens or persons by the Constitution of the United States." And he went on to state that one of those rights of *national* citizenship was "the right to pass freely from state to state." Now it is apparent that this right is not specifically granted by the Constitution. Yet before the Fourteenth Amendment it was recognized as a right fundamental to the national character of our Federal government. . . . That the right was implied did not make it any the less "guaranteed" by the Constitution. . . .

[S]ince the state statute here challenged involves such consequences, it runs afoul of the privileges and immunities clause of the Fourteenth Amendment.

MR. JUSTICE BLACK and MR. JUSTICE MURPHY join in this opinion.

MR. JUSTICE JACKSON, concurring.

While instances of valid "privileges or immunities" must be but few, I am convinced that this is one. I do not ignore or belittle the difficulties of what has been characterized by this Court as an "almost forgotten" clause. But the difficulty of the task does not excuse us from giving these general and abstract words whatever specific content and concreteness they will bear as we mark out their application, case by case. . . .

NOTES AND QUESTIONS

(1) *The (Implicit) Fundamental Right to Interstate Travel: Edwards v. California, 314 U.S. 160 (1941).* The *Edwards* majority relied on the plenary power of Congress to regulate interstate commerce. [*See* Chapter 2.] The concurring opinion by Justice Douglas relied on the Privileges or Immunities Clause of the Fourteenth Amendment to find that the Constitution recognized an implicit fundamental right to interstate travel. The Douglas opinion has become, over time, doctrinally controlling reading of the case, in much the same way the Justice Jackson's concurrence in the *Steel Seizure* case (*see* Chapter 5) has become the controlling opinion for separation of powers doctrine. Consider the following.

(2) *Foreign Travel: The Power of Congress and the President: Comparing Aptheker v. Secretary of State, 378 U.S. 500 (1964), with Haig v. Agee, 453 U.S. 280 (1981).* In *Aptheker*, the Court held that the right to travel abroad was an important aspect of the "liberty" guaranteed by the Due Process Clause of the fifth amendment. It therefore struck down a section of the Subversive Activities Control Act prohibiting members of Communist organizations from applying for passports. On the other hand, in *Agee*, the Court upheld the revocation of the passport of a citizen who announced his plans to travel abroad for the purpose of "expos[ing] CIA officers and agents . . . and tak[ing] the measures necessary to drive them out of the countries where they are operating," on the ground that his travel was likely to cause serious damage to national security or

foreign policy. It thus appears that the interest in traveling, including foreign travel, has a measure of substantive due process protection.

§ 9.05   OTHER ISSUES RELATED TO PRIVACY OR AUTONOMY: THE RIGHTS TO CONTROL ONE'S PERSONALITY, TO TREATMENT, TO DIE, OR TO BE LET ALONE

[A]   How Does the Court Really Discover Fundamental Rights: Is It a Two-Step Methodology?

DAVID CRUMP, HOW DO THE COURTS *REALLY* DISCOVER UNENUMERATED FUNDAMENTAL RIGHTS? CATALOGUING THE METHODS OF JUDICIAL ALCHEMY
19 Harv. J.L. & Pub. Pol'y 795 (1996)

This Article . . . concentrates upon the "hard question" that previous articles have treated less frequently: given that the courts seem to accept the charge of protecting unenumerated fundamental rights, precisely *how* have the courts in the real world gone about the business of recognizing them? . . .

The Court has used a strikingly large number of approaches, and these varying formulas lead to dramatically different results. Unfortunately, the Court has done little to indicate which of its inconsistent methodologies is to be preferred in a given case, beyond identifying the Justices who have written and joined each opinion. . . .

[The methods are] like the methods of a modern alchemy, conjuring up mystical formulae to conceal the sleight of hand by which a judge transforms the base metal of personal inclinations into the gold of fundamental rights. . . .

III. METHODOLOGIES FOR RECOGNIZING UNENUMERATED FUNDAMENTAL RIGHTS: WHAT ARE THE APPROACHES, AND WHEN ARE THEY JUSTIFIABLE? . . .

[The methods range] from the restrained approach of locating protected interests in the constitutional text to the generous test of evaluating interests by the importance they have for contemporary individuals. . . .

These methods lie along a continuum, all the way from hair-trigger formulas that can support a cornucopia of fundamental rights to stingy theories that protect virtually nothing that is not undeniably enumerated. . . .

[The Article here explores the origins and use by the Supreme Court of various "positive" methodologies for identifying fundamental rights: (A) confinement of fundamental rights to those explicitly protected in the text; (B) derivation from the text through the use of penumbral or structural arguments; (C) historical intentionalism or originalism; (D) evaluation of the private importance of the interest to the affected individual; (E) recognition of a history and tradition in which the interest is deeply rooted; (F) recognition of the interest as essential to ordered liberty; (G) recognition of the interest as fundamental to the American scheme of justice; (H) evaluation of the systemic importance of the interest; (I) natural law theories, ranging from the shock-the-conscience test to the Carolene Products formula; (J) categorization of the interest as economic or social on the one hand, or as a privacy or similarly favored interest on the other; and (K) identification in precedent of the Supreme Court or other Courts.

[The Article goes on to discuss advantages and disadvantages of each of these methods. For example, the importance-to-the-individual approach may be too broad, unprincipled, and unrestrained:]

For example, Professor Michelman challenged the [arguable] categorization of education as a fundamental rights by a famous question: "[W]hy education and not golf?" Professor Tribe responded,

> The time may come when constitutional law will answer the scholar's question . . . with a reply that is likely to make human sense—"because education is more important" [than golf]—and when this answer . . . will seem inescapable to those who take their lessons from life itself.

[But] one may conjure up the hypothetical case of an aspiring teenage golf professional who is denied access to a public course on [grounds that are rational but not compelling]. If that is not enough . . . we can hypothesize that the judge's brother is Arnold Palmer, and so this judge rightly can claim to know from "life itself" that golf is important—maybe even "fundamentally" important. . . . The intensity of this individual plaintiff's interest is aberrational and cannot be elevated above the interest in education without hamstringing proper state action and denigrating equal or greater interests of others. But—and this is the key point—judges who are fond of Arnold Palmer and are merely set free to "take their lessons from life itself" might hear the sympathetic case of the aspiring teenager and decide that golf is important enough.

It may seem silly, as Professor Tribe implies, to become overly analytical about this paper struggle between education and golf. But however silly it seems, the problem is not purely a "scholar's question." Real courts have used importance-to-the-individual reasoning to reach astonishingly silly (and astonishingly harmful) results in real cases. . . .

[But the Article concludes that, even with these defects, the importance-to-the-individual approach may be appropriate in some cases. It is the principal method used in the abortion cases, particularly *Roe v. Wade*. On the other hand, the deeply-rooted-in-history-and-tradition method arguably is more principled, restrained, and confined. But many would say that it is too restrictive:]

[C]ritics argue that there is a circularity to the history-and-tradition approach. It tests whether a given interest should be protected by asking whether it has been respected in the past. If the objective is to secure the interests of the minority, some would argue that such an approach is internally inconsistent, because if a right has been historically and traditionally respected, the majoritarian political process is likely to protect it independently of the courts. This method therefore can be criticized as extending protection only to those interests that need it least. In fact, it is arguable that this is precisely the point. . . .

[The Article concludes that a pluralistic system is better, and that it is appropriate for the Court to use different methods in different cases. However, the Court should use greater restraint with broad, mushy methods, such as importance-to-the-individual, than with more restrained approaches, such as history-and-tradition.]

[But the article argues that the Court's analysis cannot be limited to these "positive" methodologies. "Negative" methodologies also must be consulted.]

IV. "NEGATIVE" METHODOLOGIES: TESTING WHETHER AN INTEREST SHOULD BE FUNDAMENTAL BY INQUIRING INTO THE REASONS WHY IT SHOULD NOT BE

In addition to the positive methods described above for elevating an interest to fundamental status, the Supreme Court sometimes has used what might be called "negative" methodologies. It has asked about the reasons why the questioned interest should *not* be recognized as fundamental. This inquiry usually is not identified as separate from the positive tests, even though it arguably should be included in every opinion. . . .

In fact, this is the real defect in *Lochner*. The interest there in question was the liberty of contract, which anyone who enjoys working in a chosen profession would recognize as "important." But *Lochner* could not properly be decided on this basis alone.

In *Dandridge v. Williams*, the Supreme Court refused to recognize subsistence welfare, in the form of Aid to Families with Dependent Children, as a fundamental right. . . .

. . . Instead of emphasizing the reasons why it *should* categorize the questioned interest as fundamental, the *Dandridge* Court gave controlling weight to the reasons why it thought it *should not* do so. [It] could have been argued that the importance-to-the-individual approach would have supported an elevated status for the interest in subsistence. . . . Likewise, one can argue the systemic importance of the alleged right, in that, without the transfer payments represented by welfare, significant groups in the population cannot survive, much less participate in the political process. Furthermore, a society that values "ordered liberty" surely will furnish subsistence to its weakest members, and it even is arguable that the interest . . . is "deeply rooted in our Nation's history and tradition." But the Court was not persuaded by any of these "positive" arguments; instead, its emphasis was upon the *negative* consequences of judicial intervention in a quintessentially legislative problem.

This approach can be justified by the argument that it is self-defeating for the Court to intervene in a problem that . . . its intervention cannot help to solve. If there is anything that characterizes the problem of welfare assistance, it is its intractability. . . . Arguably there is an unusual need for government flexibility; the State needs breathing space, most of all, to experiment. . . .

In other words, *Lochner* is wrong because the Court considered only the positive arguments for recognizing an elevated liberty interest in the freedom to contract, and it did not evaluate the negative consequences of hamstringing legislatures by labeling this interest as a fundamental right. . . .

V. CONCLUSION . . .

As a concrete example, one might consider application of these methods to the complex of interests often lumped together as the putative "right to die." [At the time of this article, this issue had been considered by numerous courts, but the Supreme Court had not yet decided it. *See Washington v. Glucksberg*, below.]

The text of the Constitution contains no explicitly-elevated protection of these ["right-to-die"] interests, and penumbral or structural arguments are difficult to make in support of any of them. But the importance to the individual of each of these interests may be compelling, particularly if the individual is terminal, sentient, and severely affected by pain. On the other hand, the judicial restraint that should accompany the importance-to-the-individual methodology, coupled with contrary state interests such as protecting life, avoiding mistakes in choices, and considering rights of others, combine to counsel caution. And when we ask which of these interests is deeply rooted in our nation's history and tradition, it is probably that only the right to refuse treatment qualifies; a right to assisted suicide or euthanasia probably would not. None of the claimed interests, except arguably the right to refuse treatment, is likely to qualify under a minimalist ordered liberty approach, or under an approach emphasizing systemic importance. Thus, a judge who emphasized judicial restraint, and who considers ordered liberty or history and tradition to be appropriate tests, may decide that the right to refuse treatment deserves elevated status, but that other interests [such as assisted suicide] do not. This result is reinforced by consideration of the negative consequences, such as the effect on needed legislative flexibility, that would result from recognizing a comprehensive right to die as fundamental.

A judge who is more willing to read the Due Process Clause broadly might give weight to the importance-to-the-individual methodology and thereby decide in favor of assisted suicide. It is submitted, however, that the concern for judicial restraint in connection with this approach should be at its strongest. Furthermore, consideration of counterbalancing factors, such as the need for legislative flexibility, should countermand this result in any case short of the most compelling. . . .

[B] Personality, Reputation, and Related Issues

PAUL v. DAVIS
424 U.S. 693 (1976)

Mr. Justice Rehnquist delivered the opinion of the Court.

[Defendants distributed plaintiff's name and photograph on a flyer captioned, "active shoplifters." A shoplifting charge had been brought against plaintiff but had been dismissed. Plaintiff sued for damages under the civil rights remedies statute, 42 U.S.C. § 1983, for deprivation of his rights under both the procedural due process and the substantive due process doctrines. [For the procedural due process analysis in *Paul, see* Chapter 8.] Here, the Supreme Court upholds a dismissal of his claim under substantive due process.]

I

Respondent's due process claim is grounded upon his assertion that the flyer, and in particular the phrase "Active Shoplifters" appearing at the head of the page upon which his name and photograph appear, impermissibly deprived him of some "liberty" protected by the Fourteenth Amendment. His complaint asserted that the "active shoplifter" designation would inhibit him from entering business establishments for fear of being suspected of shoplifting and possibly apprehended, and would seriously impair his future employment opportunities. Accepting that such consequences may flow from the flyer in question, respondent's complaint would appear to state a classical claim for defamation actionable in the courts of virtually every State. . . .

If respondent's view is to prevail, a person arrested by law enforcement officers who announce that they believe such person to be responsible for a particular crime in order to calm the fears of an aroused populace, presumably obtains a claim against such officers under § 1983. And since it is surely far more clear from the language of the Fourteenth Amendment that "life" is protected against state deprivation than it is that reputation is protected against state injury, it would be difficult to see why the survivors of an innocent bystander mistakenly shot by a policeman or negligently killed by a sheriff driving a government vehicle, would not have claims equally cognizable under 1983.

It is hard to perceive any logical stopping place to such a line of reasoning. Respondent's construction would seem almost necessarily to result in every legally cognizable injury which may have been inflicted by a state official acting under "color of law" establishing a violation of the Fourteenth Amendment. We think it would come as a great surprise to those who drafted and shepherded the adoption of that Amendment to learn that it worked such a result, and a study of our decisions convinces us they do not support the construction urged by respondent. . . .

Respondent's complaint also alleged a violation of a "right to privacy guaranteed by the First, Fourth, Fifth, Ninth, and Fourteenth Amendments. . . ."

While there is no "right of privacy" found in any specific guarantee of the Constitution, the Court has recognized that "zones of privacy" may be created by more specific constitutionalguarantees and thereby impose limits upon government power. *See Roe v. Wade.* Respondent's case, however, comes within none of these areas. [I]n *Roe* the Court pointed out that the personal rights found in this guarantee of personal privacy must be limited to those which are "fundamental" or "implicit in the concept of ordered liberty" as described in *Palko v. Connecticut*, 302 U.S. 319, 325 (1937). The activities detailed as being within this definition were ones very different from that for which respondent claims constitutional protection—matters relating to marriage, procreation, contraception, family relationships, and child rearing and education. . . .

Respondent's claim is far afield from this line of decisions. He claims constitutional protection against the disclosure of the fact of his arrest on a shoplifting charge. His claim is based, not upon any challenge to the State's ability to restrict his freedom of action in a sphere contended to be "private," but instead on a claim that the State may not publicize a record of an official act such as an arrest. None of our substantive privacy decisions hold this or anything like this, and we decline to enlarge them in this manner.

[T]he judgment of the Court of Appeals holding otherwise is

Reversed.

MR. JUSTICE BRENNAN, with whom MR. JUSTICE MARSHALL concurs and MR. JUSTICE WHITE concurs in part, dissenting. . . .

[T]he Court by mere fiat and with no analysis wholly excludes personal interest in reputation from the ambit of "life, liberty, or property" under the Fifth and Fourteenth Amendments, thus rendering due process concerns never applicable to the official stigmatization, however arbitrary, of an individual. The logical and disturbing corollary of this holding is that no due process infirmities would inhere in a statute constituting a commission to conduct *ex parte* trials of individuals, so long as the only official judgment pronounced was limited to the public condemnation and branding of a person as a Communist, a traitor, an "active murderer," a homosexual, or any other mark that "merely" carries social opprobrium. The potential of today's decision is frightening for a free people. That decision surely finds no support in our relevant constitutional jurisprudence. . . .

NOTES AND QUESTIONS

(1) *The Two-Step Approach in Paul v. Davis: Does the Court Use Both Positive and Negative Methodologies?* Notice that the Court rejects "positive" arguments for reputation as a fundamental right. Thus, it holds that this interest is not "implicit in the concept of ordered liberty" and is not like other recognized privacy interests. Note also that the Court uses negative methodology: "There is no logical stopping point," and every injury traceable somehow to the state would be a Due Process violation implicating strict scrutiny. Which approach is a better way of answering the dissent?

(2) *Hair and Grooming as Aspects of Personality Protected By the Privacy Right: Kelley v. Johnson, 425 U.S. 238 (1976).* In *Kelley,* a policeman claimed that regulations limiting the length of his hair were unconstitutional. The Court, per Justice Rehnquist, held that the regulations did not violate any right guaranteed by the Fourteenth Amendment. Justice Rehnquist reasoned that the regulations had a rational basis in that they made police officers readily recognizable to the public and fostered esprit de corps. However, he emphasized that the plaintiff was an employee of the police department of the county, and not "a member of the citizenry at large." Justice Marshall, joined by Justice Brennan, dissented: "An individual's personal appearance may reflect, sustain, and nourish his personality and may well be used as a means of expressing his attitude and lifestyle. In taking control over a citizen's personal appearance, the government forces him to sacrifice substantial elements of his integrity and identity as well." The dissenters concluded that there was "no rational relationship between the challenged regulation and [the proffered] goals." Is the majority's reasoning correct, or that of the dissent? If the dissenters thought that the right of privacy was implicated, why did they invoke the rational basis test rather than strict scrutiny?

(3) *"Judicial Self-Restraint" Requires the "Utmost Care" When the Court Is Asked to "Break New Ground in this Field"— Due Process Does Not Guarantee Government Employees a Minimally Safe Work Place: Collins v. City of Harker Heights, 503 U.S. 115 (1992).* Plaintiff's husband died of asphyxia after entering a manhole to unstop a sewer line. Plaintiff alleged that he had a right to be "free from unreasonable risks of harm" and to be protected "from the [city's] custom and policy of deliberate indifference toward the safety of its employees." The Court, per Justice Stevens, unanimously rejected this "unprecedented" claim:

> [T]he Court has always been reluctant to expand the concept of substantive due process because guideposts for responsible decisionmaking in this uncharted area are scarce and open-ended. The doctrine of judicial self-restraint requires us to exercise the utmost care whenever we are asked to break new ground in this field. . . .

> [T]he due process clause of the Fourteenth Amendment was intended to prevent government "from abusing [its] power, or employing it as an instrument of oppression." *DeShaney.* . . .

> We also are not persuaded that the city's alleged failure to train its employees, or to warn them about known risks of harm, was an omission that can properly be characterized as arbitrary, or conscious-shocking, in a constitutional sense. . . . [W]e have previously rejected claims that the due process clause should be interpreted to impose federal duties that are analogous to those traditionally imposed by state tort law. . . .

 DESHANEY v. WINNEBAGO COUNTY DEPARTMENT OF SOCIAL SERVICES, 489 U.S. 189 (1989). The parents of infant Joshua DeShaney were divorced, and the court ordered that custody be placed with his father. The father moved to Winnebago County, Wisconsin, taking Joshua with him. Joshua then underwent a lengthy series of injuries, strongly indicating child abuse, but the Winnebago County Department of Social Services consistently failed to remove him from his environment after being notified or exposed to the injuries. Finally, the father beat four-year-old Joshua so severely that he fell into a life-threatening coma. Emergency brain surgery revealed a series of hemorrhages caused by traumatic injuries inflicted over a long period of time. Although Joshua did not die, he suffered brain damage so severe that he was expected to spend the rest of his life confined to an institution for the profoundly retarded. The father subsequently was tried and convicted of child abuse. Then, Joshua and his mother brought this action under the Civil Rights Statute, 42 U.S.C. § 1983, against the Department of Social Services and various individual employees alleging that they had deprived Joshua of his liberty without due process of law, by failing to intervene to protect him against a risk of violence at his father's hands of which they knew or should have known. Both the court of appeals and the Supreme Court, per Chief Justice Rehnquist, affirmed a summary judgment for the defendants, rejecting the claim:

> [N]othing in the language of the Due Process Clause itself requires the state to protect the life, liberty, and property of its citizens against invasion by private actors. The clause is phrased as a limitation on the state's power to act, not as a guarantee of certain minimal levels of safety and security. . . . [The Due Process Clause] was intended to prevent government "from abusing [its] power or employing it as an instrument of oppression" [citing *Davidson v. Cannon* and *Daniels v. Williams* from Ch. 8]. Its purpose was to protect the people from the state, not to ensure that the state protected them from each other. The Framers were content to leave the extent of governmental obligation in the latter area to the democratic political processes.

> [As] a general matter, then, we conclude that a state's failure to protect an individual against private violence simply does not constitute a violation of the Due Process Clause.

The majority rejected the argument, made by petitioners, that a constitutional duty had arisen out of a "special relationship" between the department and Joshua, created because the department knew that Joshua faced a special danger and had proclaimed its intention to protect him.

Justice Brennan, joined by Justices Marshall and Blackmun, dissented: "I would recognize, as the Court apparently cannot, that 'the State's knowledge of [an] individual's predicament' [and] its expressions of intent to help him can amount to a 'limitation of his freedom to act on his own behalf' or to obtain help from others. Thus, I would read [previous due process cases] to stand for the much more generous proposition that, if a state cuts off private sources of aid and then refuses aid itself, it cannot wash its hands of the harm that results from its inaction." Justice Brennan pointed out that the child welfare system in Wisconsin channeled all reports of suspected child abuse to local departments of social services, even if initially taken to sheriffs' offices or police departments or private citizens. Wisconsin law thus invited—indeed directed—citizens and governments to depend on local departments of social services to protect children from abuse. The state thus had guaranteed that "[I]f DSS ignores or dismisses these suspicions, no one will step in to fill the gap."

Justice Blackmun's dissent began in an unusual fashion: "Poor Joshua." He criticized the deductive reasoning of the majority.

NOTES AND QUESTIONS

(1) *The Fourteenth Amendment's Due Process Clause Does Not Impose Any "Affirmative Duties" on State Government: Revisiting DeShaney v. Winnebago County Department of Social Services, 489 U.S. 189 (1989).* Four-year-old Joshua DeShaney's father beat him so severely that the boy was confined to a state institution for the profoundly retarded. This pattern of physical abuse occurred largely during the time when the County's child protection services were supposedly overseeing the boy's situation. The Court, per Chief Justice Rehnquist, recognized that "[t]he facts of this case are undeniably tragic," but the majority rejected the substantive due process claim, reasoning, in part, that the Fourteenth Amendment did not impose any "affirmative duty" on the state to protect even children from private violence. What, if any, federal constitutional provisions impose "affirmative duties" on state government? *See generally* Barbara E. Armacost, *Affirmative Duties, Systematic Harms, and the Due Process Clause*, 94 MICH. L. REV. 982 (1996). While the conduct of the social worker was certainly "negligent" and could have been seen as "reckless," the Court held, in a footnote, that only purposeful (intentional) conduct violated substantive due process.

(2) *A Comparative Perspective: Should America Follow Columbia's Court And Recognize A Substantive Due Process Right To Possess Cocaine Or Marijuana?*—Mary Beth Sheridan, *Court throws Columbia into Turmoil by Decriminalizing Drugs*, HOUSTON CHRONICLE, May 10, 1994, § A at 8. Columbia's constitutional court recently ruled that laws criminalizing the possession and use of small amounts of marijuana, hashish, and cocaine violated the right "each person has to freely develop his personality." This decision triggered criticism by Columbia's President and by the United States.

Should there be a fundamental "liberty" (privacy) interest in developing one's personality under the Fourteenth Amendment? If such a right were found, how would its existence affect decisions like *Kelley v. Johnson* (the police officer's grooming case), *supra*? Note that the Colombian Court also has discovered a basic constitutional right to assisted suicide. *See* below.

PROBLEM F

IS THE PALM BEACH TOPLESS JOGGING ORDINANCE UNCONSTITUTIONAL?: DeWEESE v. TOWN OF PALM BEACH, 812 F.2d 1365 (1987). "Appellant Alan DeWeese is a male lawyer who lives in the town of Palm Beach,

Florida. He likes to run, and during the hot, humid Florida summers he runs without a shirt on. This activity offended the town fathers of Palm Beach so they passed a law against it, ordinance 21–48." The ordinance provides that it shall be unlawful for any person "to walk, run, jog, ride or otherwise be conveyed over or upon any street, alley, sidewalk, roadway, thoroughfare or other public place in the town of Palm Beach with the upper part of his or her body uncovered." It contained various exceptions for private residences, public beaches, and the like. DeWeese was stopped by a police officer and charged with violating the ordinance for jogging without a shirt. Is the ordinance unconstitutional?

[The Court of Appeals held that it was: "The town argues that the federal courts have no business meddling in the town's attempt to regulate the dress of its citizens. Translating this contention into legal language, the town's contention is that there is no liberty interest in matters of personal dress, protected by the Due Process Clause of the fourteenth amendment. It is true that the Supreme Court cases offer little guidance on this issue; *Kelley v. Johnson* assumes for purposes of that decision, but did not decide, that there was such a liberty interest. However, the issue is not an open question in this circuit; the law of this circuit plainly recognizes that the right of a citizen to choose his mode of personal hair grooming is 'within the great host of liberties protected by the fourteenth amendment from arbitrary state action. . . .' We think it is clear that the corresponding liberty interest in personal dress is similarly protected."]

[The Court went on to apply the rational basis test, finding that there was no legitimate interest of the municipality to which the Topless Jogging Ordinance was rationally related. Is this test the appropriate one, and is the conclusion correct? Does the application of the constitutional right of privacy to a topless jogging ordinance demean the Constitution, or does it stop an opening wedge toward state control of personality?]

[C]   Bodily Security and Freedom from Restraint

YOUNGBERG v. ROMEO
457 U.S. 307 (1982)

JUSTICE POWELL delivered the opinion of the Court.

[Although thirty-three years old, Nicholas Romeo was profoundly retarded, with the mental capacity of an eighteen-month-old child. While confined in the Pennsylvania state hospital system, he allegedly suffered injuries on at least sixty-three occasions during a period just over two years. Pursuant to the Fourteenth Amendment, he claimed (1) a right to safe conditions, (2) a right to freedom from bodily restraint, and (3) a right to training or "habilitation." The district court declined to submit the case to the jury on a due process basis, submitting it only on an eighth amendment cruel-and-unusual-punishment theory. Here, the Supreme Court reverses and remands, recognizing the first two claimed rights and requiring the lower courts to reconsider the third.]

II

A

[R]espondent's first two claims involve liberty interests recognized by prior decisions of this Court, interests that involuntary commitment proceedings do not extinguish. The first is a claim to safe conditions. In the past, this Court has noted that the right to personal security constitutes an "historic liberty interest" protected substantively by the Due Process Clause. . . .

Next, respondent claims a right to freedom from bodily restraint. In other contexts, the existence of such an interest is clear in the prior decisions of this Court. Indeed, "[l]iberty from bodily restraint always has been recognized as the core of the liberty protected by the Due Process Clause from arbitrary governmental action." This interest survives criminal conviction and incarceration. Similarly, it must also survive involuntary commitment.

B

Respondent's remaining claim is more troubling, In his words, he asserts a "constitutional right to minimally adequate habilitation." This is a substantive due process claim that is said to be grounded in the liberty component of the Due Process Clause of the Fourteenth Amendment. . . .

[O]n the basis of the record before us, it is quite uncertain whether respondent seeks any "habilitation" or training unrelated to safety and freedom from bodily restraints. In his brief to this Court, Romeo indicates that even the self-care programs he seeks are needed to reduce his aggressive behavior. And in his offer of proof to the trial court, respondent repeatedly indicated that, if allowed to testify, his experts would show that additional training programs, including self-care programs, were needed to reduce his aggressive behavior. If, as seems the case, respondent seeks only training related to safety and freedom from restraints, this case does not present the difficult question whether a mentally retarded person, involuntarily committed to a state institution, has some general constitutional right to training *per se*, even when no type or amount of training would lead to freedom.

In the circumstances presented by this case, and on the basis of the record developed to date, we . . . conclude that respondent's liberty interests require the State to provide minimally adequate or reasonable training to ensure safety and freedom from undue restraint. In view of the kinds of treatment sought by respondent and the evidence of record, we need go no further in this case.

III

A

We have established that Romeo retains liberty interests in safety and freedom from bodily restraint. Yet these interests are not absolute; indeed to some extent they are in conflict. In operating an institution such as Pennhurst, there are occasions in which it is necessary for the State to restrain the movement of residents—for example, to protect them as well as others from violence. Similar restraints may also be appropriate in a training program. And an institution cannot protect its residents from all danger of violence if it is to permit them to have any freedom of movement. The question then is not simply whether a liberty interest has been infringed but whether the extent or nature of the restraint or lack of absolute safety is such as to violate due process.

In determining whether a substantive right protected by the Due Process Clause has been violated, it is necessary to balance "the liberty of the individual" and "the demands of an organized society. . . ."

B

We think the standard articulated by Chief Judge Seitz affords the necessary guidance and reflects the proper balance between the legitimate interests of the State and the rights of the involuntarily committed to reasonable conditions of safety and freedom from unreasonable restraints. He would have held that "the Constitution only requires that the courts make certain that professional judgment in fact was exercised. It is not appropriate for the courts to specify which of several professionally acceptable choices should have been made. . . ."

[W]e vacate the decision of the Court of Appeals and remand for further proceedings consistent with this decision.

So ordered.

[The concurring opinion of JUSTICE BLACKMUN is omitted.]

CHIEF JUSTICE BURGER, concurring in the judgment.

I agree with much of the Court's opinion. However, I would hold flatly that respondent has no constitutional right to training, or "habilitation," *per se.* The parties, and the Court, acknowledge that respondent cannot function outside the state institution, even with the assistance of relatives. . . . The State did not seek custody of respondent; his family understandably sought the State's aid to meet a serious need.

I agree with the Court that some amount of self-care instruction may be necessary to avoid unreasonable infringement of a mentally retarded person's interests in safety and freedom from restraint; but it seems clear to me that the Constitution does not otherwise place an affirmative duty on the State to provide any particular kind of training or habilitation—even such as might be encompassed under the essentially standardless rubric "minimally adequate training," to which the Court refers.

NOTES AND QUESTIONS

(1) *The Liberty Interest in Avoiding Unwanted Drugs: Washington v. Harper, 494 U.S. 210 (1990).* The central question in this case was whether a judicial hearing was required before the state could treat a mentally ill prisoner with antipsychotic drugs against his will. In answering that question in the negative, per Justice Kennedy, the Court also considered the extent of substantive protection of the asserted liberty interests, using a rational basis standard:

> Respondent contends that the state, under the mandate of the Due Process Clause, may not override his choice to refuse antipsychotic drugs unless he has been found to be incompetent, and then only if the fact finder makes a substituted judgment that he, if competent, would consent to drug treatment. We disagree. . . .

> The legitimacy, and the necessity, of considering the state's interests in prison safety and security are well established by our cases. [T]he proper standard for determining the validity of a prison regulation claimed to infringe on an inmate's constitutional rights is to ask whether the regulation is "reasonably related to legitimate penological interests."

> [The state's policy] is a rational means of furthering the state's legitimate objectives. . . .

Justice Blackmun concurred separately. Justice Stevens, joined by Justices Brennan and Marshall, dissented in part.

(2) *Civil Commitment for "Sexually Violent Predators": Kansas v. Hendricks, 521 U.S. 346 (1997).* Hendricks, an inmate with a long history of pedophilia and criminal child molestation (who admitted that, if released, he could not "control the urge" to molest children and who refused other treatment), challenged Kansas' Sexual Violent Predator Act under a substantive due process theory. Hendricks had been civilly committed under the Act due to a finding that he was a pedophile and that pedophilia was either a "mental abnormality" or a "personality disorder." Although the Kansas Supreme Court had accepted Hendricks' substantive due process theory and invalidated the Act, the Supreme Court, per Justice Thomas, upheld the Act. The Court analogized the Act's civil commitment procedures to civil commitment of the mentally ill and emphasized that application of the Act did require a determination that the inmate was

"dangerous" to self or others. Justice Breyer, for Justices Stevens, Souter and, in part, Ginsburg, dissented on grounds other than substantive due process (*i.e.*, the dissent considered the Act an Ex Post Facto law).

(3) *Substantive Due Process Does Not Provide a "Liberty Interest" To Be Free From Criminal Prosecution Except Upon Probable Cause: Albright v. Oliver, 510 U.S. 1215 (1994).* Albright was charged with the sale of illegal substances. The charges against Albright, and numerous other defendants, were subsequently dismissed when it became clear that a confidential informant was fabricating information. Albright sued the city and Oliver, claiming that the police should have known the informant was fabricating and that he had a "liberty interest" to be free from prosecution except when the government would have probable cause. The Court, per Chief Justice Rehnquist's plurality opinion, rejected this substantive due process claim, relying on *Paul v. Davis* and *Collins v. City of Harker, supra.* Although the Court was highly divided (with six opinions), *Albright* confirms the Court's recent trend of rejecting "new" substantive due process claims.

[D]   Interests Regarding Death: Is There a "Right to Die"?

NOTES AND QUESTIONS

(1) *Distinguishing the Interest in Affirmatively Ending One's Life ("Assisted Suicide") from the Significant Interest in Refusing Treatment (Including an Interest in Dying by Removing Life Support): Cruzan v. Director, Missouri Department of Health, 497 U.S. 261 (1990).* Notice that the *Glucksberg* case does not deny that there is an important interest in refusing unwanted treatment, even in the event that the refusal may result in death. The interest in refusing unwanted treatment is deeply rooted in our nation's history and tradition, as tort cases based on the doctrine of informed consent demonstrate. For this reason, Chief Justice Rehnquist recognized in *Cruzan* that the interest in refusing treatment had become a "significant" interest. In summary, the claimed interest in assistance in affirmatively ending one's life is constitutionally weaker than the claimed interest in stopping treatment that would save one's life. Does the distinction make sense?

(2) *The Claimed Right in Cruzan Nevertheless Could Depend on Clear and Convincing Evidence.* Missouri, however, conditioned the right to refuse treatment on clear and convincing evidence of the person's choice. Since Mary Beth Cruzan was incompetent and vegetative, this standard was an obstacle to her asserted right to die, claimed by her parents and guardians. The Court upheld this difficult standard in *Cruzan.*

(3) *Popular Reaction to Cruzan: A "Living-Will Rush" and "Durable Powers."* After *Cruzan,* there was a public rush to execute living wills. A spokesperson for the Society for the Right to Die said, "We've had to get volunteers to help us man the phone line," and added: "That's the magic word right now—living wills." *See Right-to-Die Ruling Fuels Living Will Rush,* Houston Chronicle, July 2, 1990, § A, at 2, col. 5. A spokesperson for the American Bar Association's Commission on the Legal Problems of the Elderly, while recognizing the appropriateness of living wills, suggested consideration of a durable health care power of attorney, giving another individual authority to make health care decisions—because "medical technology changes by the year, if not by the minute," and a living will does not delegate flexible decisionmaking authority. *Id.*

WASHINGTON v. GLUCKSBERG
521 U.S. 702 (1997)

CHIEF JUSTICE REHNQUIST delivered the opinion of the Court.

[The state of Washington, although having a statutory basis for persons to decline medical treatment, had a long-standing criminal prohibition on any person assisting another person in a suicide. Respondents in the case were medical doctors who occasionally treated the terminally ill, three terminally ill patients who desired to have assistance (but who had died during the pendency of the case) and a nonprofit organization which assisted the dying. Petitioners were the State of Washington and its Attorney General. Advancing substantive due process and equal protection theories to challenge the Washington prohibition, the respondents brought this action in federal District Court. Although the District Court ruled for Washington, the en banc court of appeals held, on substantive due process grounds only, that the Washington prohibition was unconstitutional. Here, the Supreme Court reverses.]

I

We begin, as we do in all due-process cases, by examining our Nation's history, legal traditions, and practices. See, e.g., *Casey*, 505 U.S., at 849–850; *Cruzan*, 497 U.S., at 269–279. In almost every State—indeed, in almost every western democracy—it is a crime to assist a suicide. . . . Indeed, opposition to and condemnation of suicide—and, therefore, of assisting suicide—are consistent and enduring themes of our philosophical, legal, and cultural heritages.

More specifically, for over 700 years, the Anglo-American common-law tradition has punished or otherwise disapproved of both suicide and assisting suicide. . . .

That suicide remained a grievous, though nonfelonious, wrong is confirmed by the fact that colonial and early state legislatures and courts did not retreat from prohibiting assisting suicide. . . . And the prohibitions against assisting suicide never contained exceptions for those who were near death. . . . By the time the Fourteenth Amendment was ratified, it was a crime in most States to assist a suicide. *See Cruzan, supra*, at 294—295 (Scalia, J., concurring). . . .

Though deeply rooted, the States' assisted-suicide bans have in recent years been reexamined and, generally, reaffirmed. Because of advances in medicine and technology, Americans today are increasingly likely to die in institutions, from chronic illnesses. Public concern and democratic action are therefore sharply focused on how best to protect dignity and independence at the end of life, with the result that there have been many significant changes in state laws and in the attitudes these laws reflect. Many States, for example, now permit "living wills," surrogate health-care decisionmaking, and the withdrawal or refusal of life-sustaining medical treatment. At the same time, however, voters and legislators continue for the most part to reaffirm their States' prohibitions on assisting suicide. . . .

Thus, the States are currently engaged in serious, thoughtful examinations of physician-assisted suicide and other similar issues. [The Court here suggests that the "political processes" are functioning properly and that judicial intervention therefore is inappropriate.] . . .

Despite changes in medical technology and notwithstanding an increased emphasis on the importance of end-of-life decisionmaking, we have not retreated from [the traditional] prohibition. Against this backdrop of history, tradition, and practice, we now turn to respondents' constitutional claim.

[handwritten margin note: abandons the idea that the Due Process Clause is only about PDP and recognize SDP]

II

The Due Process Clause guarantees more than fair process, and the "liberty" it protects includes more than the absence of physical restraint. *Collins v. Harker Heights*, 503 U.S. 115 (1992). The Clause also provides heightened protection against government interference with certain fundamental rights and liberty interests. In a long line of cases, we have held that, in addition to the specific freedoms protected by the Bill of Rights, the "liberty" specially protected by the Due Process Clause includes the rights to marry, to have children, to direct the education and upbringing of one's children, to marital privacy, to use contraception, to bodily integrity, *Rochin v. California*, and to abortion. We have also assumed, and strongly suggested, that the Due Process Clause protects the traditional right to refuse unwanted lifesaving medical treatment. *Cruzan.*

But we "ha[ve] always been reluctant to expand the concept of substantive due process because guideposts for responsible decisionmaking in this unchartered area are scarce and open-ended." By extending constitutional protection to an asserted right or liberty interest, we, to a great extent, place the matter outside the arena of public debate and legislative action. We must therefore "exercise the utmost care whenever we are asked to break new ground in this field," lest the liberty protected by the Due Process Clause be subtly transformed into the policy preferences of the members of this Court.

Our established method of substantive-due-process analysis has two primary features: First, we have regularly observed that the Due Process Clause specially protects those fundamental rights and liberties which are, objectively, "deeply rooted in this Nation's history and tradition," and "implicit in the concept of ordered liberty," such that "neither liberty nor justice would exist if they were sacrificed," *Palko v. Connecticut*, 302 U.S. 319 (1937). Second, we have required in substantive-due-process cases a "careful description" of the asserted fundamental liberty interest. *Collins, supra*, at 125; *Cruzan, supra*, at 277–278.

Justice Souter, relying on Justice Harlan's dissenting opinion in *Poe v. Ullman*, would largely abandon this restrained methodology, and instead ask "whether [Washington's] statute sets up one of those 'arbitrary impositions' or 'purposeless restraints' at odds with the Due Process Clause of the Fourteenth Amendment." In our view, however, the development of this Court's substantive-due-process jurisprudence, described briefly above, has been a process whereby the outlines of the "liberty" specially protected by the Fourteenth Amendment . . . have at least been carefully refined by concrete examples involving fundamental rights found to be deeply rooted in our legal tradition. This approach tends to rein in the subjective elements that are necessarily present in due-process judicial review. In addition, by establishing a threshold requirement—that a challenged state action implicate a fundamental right—before requiring more than a reasonable relation to a legitimate state interest to justify the action, it avoids the need for complex balancing of competing interests in every case. . . .

As noted above, we have a tradition of carefully formulating the interest at stake in substantive-due-process cases. . . . The Washington statute at issue in this case prohibits "aid[ing] another person to attempt suicide," Wash. Rev. Code § 9A.36.060(1) (1994), and, thus, the question before us is whether the "liberty" specially protected by the Due Process Clause includes a right to commit suicide which itself includes a right to assistance in doing so.

We now inquire whether this asserted right has any place in our Nation's traditions. Here, as discussed above, we are confronted with a consistent and almost universal tradition that has long rejected the asserted right, and continues explicitly to reject it today, even for terminally ill, mentally competent adults. To hold for respondents, we would have to reverse centuries of legal doctrine and practice, and strike down the considered policy choice of almost every State. . . .

Respondents also rely on *Casey*. There, the Court's opinion concluded that "the essential holding of Roe v. Wade should be retained and once again reaffirmed.". . .

That many of the rights and liberties protected by the Due Process Clause sound in personal autonomy does not warrant the sweeping conclusion that any and all important, intimate, and personal decisions are so protected, and *Casey* did not suggest otherwise.

The history of the law's treatment of assisted suicide in this country has been and continues to be one of the rejection of nearly all efforts to permit it. That being the case, our decisions lead us to conclude that the asserted "right" to assistance in committing suicide is not a fundamental liberty interest protected by the Due Process Clause. The Constitution also requires, however, that Washington's assisted-suicide ban be rationally related to legitimate government interests. This requirement is unquestionably met here. As the court below recognized, Washington's assisted-suicide ban implicates a number of state interests. . . .

First, Washington has an "unqualified interest in the preservation of human life." The State's prohibition on assisted suicide, like all homicide laws, both reflects and advances its commitment to this interest. This interest is symbolic and aspirational as well as practical. . . .

Relatedly, all admit that suicide is a serious public-health problem, especially among persons in otherwise vulnerable groups. The State has an interest in preventing suicide, and in studying, identifying, and treating its causes. . . .

The State also has an interest in protecting the integrity and ethics of the medical profession. . . .

Next, the State has an interest in protecting vulnerable groups—including the poor, the elderly, and disabled persons—from abuse, neglect, and mistakes. . . . If physician-assisted suicide were permitted, many might resort to it to spare their families the substantial financial burden of end-of-life health-care costs.

The State's interest here goes beyond protecting the vulnerable from coercion; it extends to protecting disabled and terminally ill people from prejudice, negative and inaccurate stereotypes, and "societal indifference.". . .

Finally, the State may fear that permitting assisted suicide will start it down the path to voluntary and perhaps even involuntary euthanasia. . . .

We need not weigh exactingly the relative strengths of these various interests. They are unquestionably important and legitimate, and Washington's ban on assisted suicide is at least reasonably related to their promotion and protection. We therefore hold that Wash. Rev. Code § 9A.36.060(1) (1994) does not violate the Fourteenth Amendment, either on its face or "as applied to competent, terminally ill adults who wish to hasten their deaths by obtaining medication prescribed by their doctors."

Throughout the Nation, Americans are engaged in an earnest and profound debate about the morality, legality, and practicality of physician-assisted suicide. Our holding permits this debate to continue, as it should in a democratic society. The decision of the en banc Court of Appeals is reversed, and the case is remanded for further proceedings consistent with this opinion.

JUSTICE O'CONNOR, concurring.

The Court frames the issue in this case as whether the Due Process Clause of the Constitution protects a "right to commit suicide which itself includes a right to assistance in doing so," and concludes that our Nation's history, legal traditions, and practices do not support the existence of such a right. I join the Court's opinions because I agree that there is no generalized right to "commit suicide." But respondents urge us to address the narrower question whether a mentally competent person who is experiencing great suffering has a constitutionally cognizable interest in controlling the circumstances of his or her imminent death. I see no need to reach that question in the context of the facial challenges to the New York and Washington laws at issue here. . . .

JUSTICE STEVENS, concurring in the judgments.

The Court ends its opinion with the important observation that our holding today is fully consistent with a continuation of the vigorous debate about the "morality, legality, and practicality of physician-assisted suicide" in a democratic society. I write separately to make it clear that there is also room for further debate about the limits that the Constitution places on the power of the States to punish the practice. [Justice Stevens analogized the analysis of the assisted suicide issue to the Court's analysis of capital punishment:] . . .

JUSTICE SOUTER, concurring in the judgment.

The question is whether the statute sets up one of those "arbitrary impositions" or "purposeless restraints" at odds with the Due Process Clause of the Fourteenth Amendment. *Poe v. Ullman*, 367 U.S. 497 (1961) (Harlan, J., dissenting). I conclude that the statute's application to the doctors has not been shown to be unconstitutional, but I write separately to give my reasons for analyzing the substantive due process claims as I do, and for rejecting this one. . . . [Justice Souter presented an extensive discussion of Justice Harlan's dissenting opinion in *Poe* and substantive due process doctrine generally. He then applied his analysis to the assisted suicide issue concluding that:]

Legislatures, however, are not so constrained. The experimentation that should be out of the question in constitutional adjudication displacing legislative judgments is entirely proper, as well as highly desirable, when the legislative power addresses an emerging issue like assisted suicide. The Court should accordingly stay its hand to allow reasonable legislative consideration. While I do not decide for all time that respondents' claim should not be recognized, I acknowledge the legislative institutional competence as the better one to deal with that claim at this time.

JUSTICE GINSBURG, concurring in the judgments.

I concur in the Court's judgments in these cases substantially for the reasons stated by JUSTICE O'CONNOR in her concurring opinion.

JUSTICE BREYER, concurring in the judgments.

I do not agree with the Court's formulation of that claimed "liberty" interest. The Court describes it as a "right to commit suicide with another's assistance." But I would not reject the respondents' claim without considering a different formulation, for which our legal tradition may provide greater support. That formulation would use words roughly like a "right to die with dignity." But irrespective of the exact words used, at its core would lie personal control over the manner of death, professional medical assistance, and the avoidance of unnecessary and severe physical suffering—combined. . . .

I do not believe, however, that this Court need or now should decide whether or a not such a right is "fundamental." That is because, in my view, the avoidance of severe physical pain (connected with death) would have to comprise an essential part of any successful claim and because, as Justice O'Connor points out, the laws before us do not force a dying person to undergo that kind of pain. Rather, the laws of New York and of Washington do not prohibit doctors from providing patients with drugs sufficient to control pain despite the risk that those drugs themselves will kill. . . .

NOTES AND QUESTIONS

(1) *Is There A "Fundamental Right" To Assistance In Committing Suicide?* The *Glucksberg* Court held that, for purposes of a substantive due process claim, there was no "fundamental right"for an individual to have medical assistance in committing suicide. Absent a fundamental right, the challengers' claim received only rational basis scrutiny, and the *Glucksberg* Court upheld Washington's prohibition on assisting any suicide. [For the "equal protection" companion decision, *see Vacco v. Quill* below in § 10.03[B].] Note the importance to the Court's analysis of the conclusion that the "democratic processes" were historically and presently engaged with the various "right to die" issues. Note also that the Court suggested that fundamental rights must have been historically recognized. Remember Justice Scalia's plurality opinion in *Michael H.* (above).

(2) *Identifying Fundamental Rights After Glucksberg: A Two-Step Process?* What may be most significant in *Glucksberg* is the Court's methodology for determining whether an asserted interest is "fundamental." (Remember that identification as fundamental means that the interest normally is protected by "heightened scrutiny"; otherwise, it can be overcome by a mere "rational basis" asserted by the state.) The *Glucksberg* majority suggested that whether an asserted right is "fundamental" is determined by "two primary features," and it set forth a two-step analysis. The first step is "objective": whether the right is "implicit in the concept of ordered liberty" [from *Palko v. Connecticut*]. The second step is "a 'careful description' of the asserted fundamental liberty interest." Is this two step analysis consistent with the other substantive due process decisions you have reviewed in this Chapter, such as *Griswold, Roe v. Wade* or *Casey*? How does the "careful description" step in *Glucksberg* affect the range of interests that might be deemed "fundamental"? For another perspective on *Glucksberg* and *Quinn, see* Erwin Chemerinsky, *Washington v. Glucksberg Was Tragically Wrong*, 106 MICH. L. REV. 1543 (2008).

(3) *The Justification for a Two-Step Methodology in Identifying Fundamental Rights—Avoiding the "Lochner Monster": David Crump, How Do the Courts Really Discover Unenumerated Fundamental Rights?: Cataloguing the Methods of Judicial Alchemy, 19 Harv. J.L. & Pub. Pol'y 795 (1996).* This article anticipated the Court's two-step methodology in *Glucksberg*. Specifically, it proposes that the first step in identifying a fundamental right is to invoke one of the various formulas for marking it as warranting special protection, such as history and tradition, importance to the individual, textual identification in the Constitution, structural importance of the right, etc. But this analysis is not enough. This analysis, alone, would create numerous fundamental rights that the Court in fact has rejected, for good reason—they would prevent the democratic process from resolving conflicting claims closely related to the claimed right, conflicts that the Court cannot resolve within the judicial role. The right to work in one's chose profession, as in *Lochner*, is an example: A one-step analysis might recognize this right as fundamental. To avoid the *Lochner* monster, then, a second step is necessary. The Court must evaluate how much damage it would do by recognizing the right, or how much it would hamstring our democratic processes in protecting legitimate interests that conflict. The article calls this "the negative methodology." Is this what the Court's second step, requiring a "careful description," really means?

(4) *The Continuing Judicial and Political Controversy Regarding Assisted-Suicide: Gonzales v. Oregon, 546 U.S. 243 (2006).* Although *Glucksberg* had held that there was no "fundamental right" to physician-assisted suicide, the Right-To-Die-With-Dignity movement remained politically active. In *Gonzales v. Oregon*, the voters approved a ballot measure, the Oregon Death With Dignity Act (ODWDA). The drugs used by physicians under ODWDA are regulated by the federal Controlled Substances Act (CSA). In 2001, the Bush Administration issued an "Interpretive Rule" declaring that a physician's use of any CSA covered drug to assist suicide would not be a "legitimate medical practice" and, despite ODWDA, could be prosecuted criminally. The

challengers argued here that the Attorney General did not have the constitutional authority to override the State of Oregon's decision to permit certain assisted suicides. The Court, per Justice Kennedy, agreed with the challengers.

The Court addressed the case as if it were a matter of administrative law (and not a constitutional law issue). As a matter of federalism, however, the Court rejected the Bush administration's position because it would have constituted "a radical shift of authority from the States to the Federal Government to define general standards of medical practice in every locality." This reasoning seems parallel to the *Lopez* and *Morrison* decisions in Chapter 2 above. *See also* the *O Centro* decision in § 12.03.

Justice Scalia (who would normally join a *Lopez*-type analysis) dissented (for Chief Justice Roberts and Thomas). Justice Thomas dissented and criticized the majority for being inconsistent with *Gonzales v. Raich* above in Chapter 2. Should States be permitted to "experiment" with different approaches to the right to die? Would the same "political process" rationale from *Raich* apply to State experiments with "fundamental rights"—such as free speech or access to abortion?

NOTE ON OTHER NATIONS' CONSIDERATION OF THE "RIGHT TO DIE"

Serge F. Kovaleski, *Colombian High Court Legalizes Mercy Killing: Vatican Assails Assisted Suicide Decision*, HOUS. CHRONICLE, Aug. 24, 1997, at 28A, describes the decision of the Colombian Constitutional Court on this issue. Earlier, in 1994, Colombia's high court had held that use of marijuana and cocaine was protected as part of the constitutional right to develop one's personality (*see above*). In 1997, the Colombian court went on to hold that there was a constitutional protection against criminal responsibility for causing the death of a terminally ill person who had given clear authorization. In announcing the decision, the court's president explained, "The State has the duty to protect life, but this duty is not absolute—it has a limit. There is not just one morality. Every person can determine their own sense of life, whether it is sacred or not." (Compare the Joint Opinion in *Casey, supra*: "At the heart of liberty is the right to define one's own concept of existence, of meanings of the universe, and of the mystery of human life.")

This ruling made Colombia the only nation in the Western Hemisphere that recognized such a constitutional right. Relatively broad rights to die also are granted in the Netherlands, and Japan recognizes a more restricted right. Critics inside Colombia promptly denounced the Colombian decision on the ground, among others, that it was an invitation to manipulation of elderly persons by opportunistic relatives as well as likely to produce insurance fraud. The Vatican argued that the Colombian court had diminished the sanctity of life in a country that already had one of the world's highest violent death rates.

Chapter 10

EQUAL PROTECTION

§ 10.01   AN OVERVIEW OF EQUAL PROTECTION: THE THREE-TIERED APPROACH

> Read U.S. Const. Amend. XIV § 1 (the Equal Protection Clause).

NOTE ON THE OVERALL STRUCTURE OF THE EQUAL PROTECTION DECISIONS

Classifications as the Object of the Clause. The Equal Protection Clause addresses laws that classify persons. Of course, all laws must classify in some manner if they are to have any effect.

Identifying the Interests or Groups Affected by Classifications. Thus, a key question in equal protection analysis is: What interests, rights, or groups are affected by the classification at issue? In particular, this approach entails considering what persons are the objects of the alleged disadvantaged class (*e.g.*, whether they are African-Americans, women, or aliens) or what rights are burdened by the classification (*e.g.*, whether it affects the right to free speech or to travel interstate). If the classification would be a "suspect" one, or if the right would be "fundamental," the law is subject to a stricter kind of review.

The Three-Tiered System of Equal Protection Analysis. The Supreme Court has evolved what is sometimes called a three-tiered model of equal protection analysis, which depends upon what persons are classified and what rights or interests are burdened. The three tiers are: *first,* the *rational basis* (or reasonable classification) test, which is the lowest standard of review and which applies to the great mass of legislation; *second, "strict scrutiny,"* which is the most exacting kind of review and is triggered by laws impinging upon suspect classes or fundamental rights; and *third, "middle-tier review,"* which applies to rights or classes (*i.e.*, "quasi-suspect clauses") that the Court has deemed less sensitive than those triggering strict scrutiny, but more sensitive than those subject to the rational basis test.

The Imperfections of this Three-Tiered Model. Having set out this three-tiered model, we should immediately add that it does not perfectly describe or explain all of the Court's decisions. And as we shall see, certain Justices have expressly rejected it. *See, e.g.,* the dissents of Justice Marshall arguing for a "sliding scale," in *Dandridge v. Williams, San Antonio Independent School District v. Rodriguez,* and *Massachusetts Board of Retirement v. Murgia,* § 10.04, *below,* and the separate opinion of Justice Stevens, concurred in by Chief Justice Burger, in *Cleburne v. Cleburne Living Center,* also in this chapter *below.* The three-tiered model nevertheless is the doctrinally controlling standard, and you must understand it in order to understand most equal protection decisions. We will outline the tiers here, in the chronological order they developed within the equal protection doctrine.

The Lowest Level of Review: Rational Basis (or in some older cases, "Reasonable Classification"). The lowest level of review is closely analogous to the rational basis test for due process, which we have encountered in previous chapters. Most laws affecting economic rights, housing, education, living arrangements, taxes, employment, and a host of other issues, are governed by this standard. The question simply is whether the law is rationally related to a legitimate state interest.

The Highest Level of Review: Strict Scrutiny of Laws Affecting "Suspect Classes" or "Fundamental Rights"—The Requirement of a "Compelling State Interest" to Which the Law is "Narrowly" Tailored. What should be done if, for example, a state classifies people on the basis of race? That classification would bring it close to the historic core concerns of the Equal Protection Clause. These kinds of distinctions are described as *"suspect classifications"* and are subject to strict scrutiny, which requires a showing that they are "narrowly" tailored to advance a "compelling" (not merely a "legitimate") state interest. *See, e.g., Bakke v. Board of Regents,* 438 U.S. 265, 299 (1978) (reproduced *below*). Race, alienage, and nationality ("R-A-N") are the suspect classifications recognized by the Court (except that alienage classifications sometimes are subject only to the rational basis test, as we shall see). Additionally, a law is subject to strict scrutiny if it impinges upon a *"fundamental right."*

"Middle Tier" Equal Protection: A "Substantial" Relationship to an "Important" State Interest. The Court has found the world of legislation too complicated to be governed only by the strict scrutiny and rational basis approaches. Consequently, it has developed a "middle tier" of analysis for classifications that it considers sensitive but not so sensitive as to warrant the highest degree of scrutiny. Specifically, the Court has invoked this level of review for cases involving (1) gender, (2) illegitimacy, (3) children of illegal aliens ("G-I-C"), and (4) arguably, other classes. A statement of the middle tier standard might be that the state must show that the law is "substantially" (not merely rationally) related to the achievement of an "important" (not merely legitimate, but not so strong as to be compelling state interest. Consider the following problem, which is designed to introduce you to each of the three tiers of equal protection review.

PROBLEM A

WEST YORK'S FOURTH-OF-JULY PAGEANT. The hypothetical State of West York wishes to present a Fourth-of-July pageant portraying the tribulations of General George Washington and the revolutionary army at Valley Forge. The casting director, acting as the agent of the state, must choose among four actors who are competing to play the part of George Washington. The first actor is African-American; the second is white and bears a remarkable physical resemblance to the real George Washington; the third also is white but does not resemble George Washington at all; and the fourth is a woman. Assume that all four have equivalent acting ability. May the casting director consider the physical characteristics of the actors in choosing one of them?

[A suggested analysis: (1) The state, acting through its casting director, may not classify the black actor differently from the white ones on the basis of race unless it can show that its action is narrowly tailored to advance a compelling state interest. A pageant in which George Washington looks like the real George Washington may be a legitimate interest, and the desire to achieve it may be rational, but it hardly seems compelling. Conclusion: the state may not consider the black actor's race, even though it is not George Washington's race. (2)-(3) The state may, however, distinguish the white actor who resembles George Washington from the white actor who does not. This result may seem ironic, since an actor's resemblance to George Washington is as much an accident of birth as his race; the key point, however, is that distinctions on this basis do not impinge upon any suspect class, and therefore the rational basis test applies. The state has a legitimate interest in presenting a realistic pageant, and the selection of an actor who resembles George Washington is rationally related to that interest. (4) The casting director's consideration of the woman actor's gender apparently is governed by middle-tier scrutiny. The issue, therefore, is whether the state has an "important" interest that "substantially" is advanced by having a man play the part of George Washington (although recent decisional law suggests that the Court has increased this level of scrutiny). It may be that many casting directors in this situation would choose a man to play George Washington rather than a woman and would give little thought to the matter; as a matter of constitutional law, however, it is not a trivial matter to justify a state's decision to do so!]

Consider the following questions in connection with this problem and the suggested analysis.

(1) *The Viability of the Suggested Analysis.* Do you agree with the suggested analysis, and if not, why not?

(2) *Distinguishing Between the Black and White Actors.* If the above analysis is correct, and the state may not consider race at all, how is the casting director to choose between the black applicant and the white applicant who resembles George Washington, if they are indistinguishable in other respects?

(3) *Affirmative Action.* May the casting director select the black applicant on the basis of his race because of a policy in favor of increasing the number of black participants in the pageant? [Is that policy narrowly drawn to advance a compelling state interest? Should it have to be?]

§ 10.02 TRADITIONAL EQUAL PROTECTION: THE RATIONAL BASIS TEST

NOTES AND QUESTIONS

(1) *Traditional Equal Protection Analysis: An Introduction to the Rational Basis Standard.* At least since the New Deal era, the Court has addressed equal protection challenges (under the Fourteenth Amendment or the Fifth Amendment) with the rational basis standard—unless the regulating classification burdens a "suspect class" or a "fundamental right." The rational basis standard was discussed in Chapter 2, addressing the plenary powers of Congress, and in Chapter 3, concerning federalism issues. The following Notes (presented in chronological order) represent some of the historically prominent (*i.e.*, frequently cited) examples of rational basis review in the equal protection context.

(2) *Railway Express Agency, Inc. v. New York, 336 U.S. 106 (1949): Another Famous Jackson Concurrence.* A New York City ordinance forbid the placement of any advertising on motor vehicles; the City sought to prevent motorist distractions and, thereby, enhance public safety. The ordinance had an exception, however, for advertising about the business of the vehicle's owner. Thus, "owner-advertising" was permitted, but "for-hire" advertising was banned. Railway Express was a delivery company which sold "for-hire" advertising on the sides of its fleet of delivery trucks. Applying the rational basis standard, the Supreme Court, per Justice Douglas, upheld the ordinance and concluded: "It is no requirement of equal protection that all evils of the same genus be eradicated or none at all." The majority's rationale, therefore, relied on the idea that the legislative decisionmaker could act "one step at a time" without violating the equal protection doctrine (at least under rational basis scrutiny).

ordinance upheld

maj. rationale

Justice Robert Jackson provided a famous concurring opinion, discussing the rationale for equal protection review. He concluded that:

> I regard it as a salutary doctrine that cities, states and the Federal Government must exercise their power so as not to discriminate between their inhabitants except upon some reasonable differentiation fairly related to the object of regulation. This equality is not merely abstract justice. The framers of the Constitution knew, and we should not forget today, that there is no more effective practical guaranty against arbitrary and unreasonable government than to require that the principles of law which officials would impose upon a minority must be imposed generally. Conversely, nothing opens the door to arbitrary action so effectively as to allow those officials to pick and choose only a few to whom they will apply legislation and this to escape the political retribution that might be visited upon them of larger numbers were affected. Courts can take no better measure to assure that laws will be just than to require that laws be equal in operation.

(3) *"One Step At a Time": Williamson v. Lee Optical of Oklahoma, 348 U.S. 483 (1955).* Another famous equal protection opinion arose from an Oklahoma law authorizing only licensed opthalmologists or optometrists to make replacement lenses for glasses; an "optician" could make the lenses only if the consumer had a written prescription from an opthamologist or optometrist. The Court recognized that the effect of this "prescription requirement" was "to forbid the optician from fitting or duplicating lenses" even though the opticians were perfectly well qualified to do the job; for consumers, the Oklahoma law increased costs and created "a needless, wasteful requirement in many cases." The district court had struck down the prescription requirement, on equal protection and substantive due process grounds [*see* Chapter 6 above for the due process analysis].

The Supreme Court, per Justice Douglas, applied the rational basis standard; under this deferential review, the Court upheld the Oklahoma law. The Court's deference is apparent in its reasoning. Although the Oklahoma law was obviously "wasteful," the Court stated that "it is for the legislature, not the courts to balance the advantages and disadvantages of the [prescription] requirement."

In one of the classic formulations of rational basis scrutiny, the *Lee Optical* Court stated: "It is enough that there is an evil at hand for correction, and that *it might be thought* that the particular legislative measure was a rational way to correct it." (emphasis added).

Was the Court naíve about the political realities? The prescription requirement obviously favored the opthamologists and optometrists over the opticians in the competitive market for eyeglass lenses. The Court also certainly was aware that the opthamologists and optometrists were well-equipped to lobby for their economic interests. The Oklahoma scheme seemed grossly unfair to the politically weaker opticians (and to consumers). Yet, the *Lee Optical* Court was deferential. The rationale for rational basis scrutiny is succinctly summarized in *Vance v. Bradley*, 440 U.S. 93 (1979): "The Constitution presumes that, absent some reason to infer antipathy, even improvident decisions will eventually be rectified by the democratic process and that judicial intervention is generally unwarranted no matter how unwisely we may think a political branch has acted."

(4) *Underinclusion (and Overinclusion)—No Requirement of "Mathematical Nicety": United States Railroad Retirement Board v. Fritz, 449 U.S. 166 (1980).* Many problems of equal protection depend upon whether a given classification includes too many people or too few—whether it includes some whom the legislative purpose would not require impacting, or exempts some whose inclusion would further that purpose. The concept of overinclusion refers to the former; underinclusion refers to the latter. In the *Fritz* case, for example, Congress enacted a complex scheme to limit "windfalls" to individuals who qualified for both railroad retirement and social security; but the law allowed windfalls to some workers, and it was possible for workers with shorter employment histories to receive more than others with longer ones. The Court, per Justice Rehnquist, upheld the enactment: "If the classification has some 'reasonable basis,' it does not offend the Constitution simply because the classification 'is not made with mathematical nicety or because in practice it results in some inequality.' The problems of government are practical ones and may justify, if they do not require, rough accommodations—illogical, it may be, and unscientific." Justice Brennan, joined by Justice Marshall, dissented on the ground that the statute could only be upheld by reference to the "actual" purpose "identified by the state" in the enactment.

Perhaps the issue depends upon how large the underinclusion or overinclusion is. Should it have made a difference in *Fritz* whether the favored class was relatively small or relatively large, in relation to those not given windfalls? *Cf.* Farrell, *Equal Protection: Overinclusive Classifications and Individual Rights*, 41 ARK. L. REV. 1 (1988).

FITZGERALD v. RACING ASSOCIATION OF CENTRAL IOWA
539 U.S. 103 (2003)

JUSTICE BREYER delivered the opinion of the court.

[Iowa law permitted racetrack casinos and riverboat casinos to operate slot machines. As a source of state revenue, Iowa taxed the revenues generated by slot machines. The maximum tax rate for riverboat casinos was 20 percent. The maximum tax rate for racetrack casinos was 36 percent. The racetrack casino owners considered that this 20 percent/36 percent tax rate difference violated their federal equal protection rights. Here the Supreme Court, using the traditional standard, disagreed.]

Respondents, a group of racetracks and an association of dog owners, brought this lawsuit in state court challenging the 1994 legislation on the ground that the 20 percent/36 percent tax rate difference that it created violated the Federal Constitution's Equal Protection Clause, Amdt. 14, § 1. . . .

We here consider whether a difference in state tax rates violates the Fourteenth Amendment's mandate that "[n]o State shall . . . deny to any person . . . the equal protection of the laws," § 1. The law in question does not distinguish on the basis of, for example, race or gender. See, *e.g., Loving v. Virginia*, 388 U.S. 1 (1967); *United States v. Virginia*, 518 U.S. 515 (1996). It does not distinguish between in-state and out-of-state businesses. See, *e.g., Metropolitan Life Ins. Co. v. Ward*, 470 U.S. 869 (1985). Neither does it favor a State's long-time residents at the expense of residents who have more recently arrived from other States. Cf. *Hooper v. Bernalillo County Assessor*, 472 U.S. 612 (1985). Rather, the law distinguishes for tax purposes among revenues obtained within the State of Iowa by two enterprises, each of which does business in the State. Where that is so, the law is subject to rational-basis review:

> "[T]he Equal Protection Clause is satisfied so long as there is a plausible policy reason for the classification, the legislative facts on which the classification is apparently based rationally may have been considered to be true by the governmental decisionmaker, and the relationship of the classification to its goal is not so attenuated as to render the distinction arbitrary or irrational." *Nordlinger v. Hahn*, 505 U.S., 11–12 (1992) (citations omitted).

The Iowa Supreme Court found that the 20 percent/36 percent tax rate differential failed to meet this standard because, in its view, that difference "frustrated" what it saw as the law's basic objective, namely, rescuing the racetracks from economic distress. And no rational person, it believed, could claim the contrary.

The Iowa Supreme Court could not deny, however, that the Iowa law, like most laws, might predominately serve one general objective, say, helping the racetracks, while containing subsidiary provisions that seek to achieve other desirable (perhaps even contrary) ends as well, thereby producing a law that balances objectives but still serves the general objective when seen as a whole. See *Railroad Retirement Bd. v. Fritz*, 449 U.S. 166, 181 (1980) (STEVENS, J., concurring in judgment) (legislation is often the "product of multiple and somewhat inconsistent purposes that led to certain compromises"). After all, if every subsidiary provision in a law designed to help racetracks had to help those racetracks and nothing more, then (since any tax rate hurts the racetracks when compared with a lower rate) there could be no taxation of the racetracks at all.

Neither could the Iowa Supreme Court deny that the 1994 legislation, *seen as a whole*, can rationally be understood to do what that court says it seeks to do, namely, advance the racetracks' economic interests. Its grant to the racetracks of authority to operate slot machines should help the racetracks economically to some degree—even if its simultaneous imposition of a tax on slot machine adjusted revenue means that the law provides less help than respondents might like. At least a rational legislator might so believe. And the Constitution grants legislators, not courts, broad authority (within the bounds of rationality) to decide whom they wish to help with their tax laws and how much help those laws ought to provide. . . .

Once one realizes that not every provision in a law must share a single objective, one has no difficulty finding the necessary rational support for the 20 percent/36 percent differential here at issue. That difference, harmful to the racetracks, is helpful to the riverboats, which, as respondents concede, were also facing financial peril, Brief for Respondents 8. These two characterizations are but opposite sides of the same coin. Each reflects a rational way for a legislator to view the matter. And aside from simply aiding the financial position of the riverboats, the legislators may have wanted to encourage the economic development of river communities or to promote riverboat history, say, by providing incentives for riverboats to remain in the State, rather than relocate to other States. Alternatively, they may have wanted to protect the reliance interests of riverboat operators, whose adjusted slot machine revenue had previously been taxed at the 20 percent rate. All these objectives are rational ones, which lower riverboat tax rates could further and which suffice to uphold the different tax rates. . . .

IV

We conclude that there is "a plausible policy reason for the classification," that the legislature "rationally may have . . . considered . . . true" the related justifying "legislative facts," and that the "relationship of the classification to its goal is not so attenuated as to render the distinction arbitrary or irrational." Consequently the State's differential tax rate does not violate the Federal Equal Protection Clause. . . .

NOTES AND QUESTIONS

(1) *The Baseline of Equal Protection Analysis— The Rational Basis Standard: Fitzgerald v. Racing Association of Central Iowa, 539 U.S. 103 (2003).* The State of Iowa decided to tax slot machine revenue at riverboat casinos at a maximum of 20 percent while the revenues from the same slot machines located at racetrack casinos would be taxed at a maximum of 36 percent. For owners of racetrack casinos, this was considered "unfair."

In response to the equal protection claim brought by the "disadvantaged" racetrack casino owners, the Supreme Court, per Justice Breyer, applied the traditional rational basis test and rejected the claim. Iowa obviously had an interest in enhancing investment in the riverboat casino industry. Riverboat casinos were located on the Mississippi and Missouri rivers (which border Iowa), and they drew heavily from neighboring states (*e.g.*, Nebraska and Illinois). Thus, Iowa stood to profit from the taxes generated by non-Iowans gambling on the riverboat slot machines. By taxing racetrack casino revenues more heavily, Iowa in effect directed investment in gambling to its borders where the "customers" would more likely be non-Iowans.

(2) *The Rationale For the Rational Basis Standard.* As the main case and the Note cases repeatedly indicate, the traditional rational basis test is highly deferential. It is "a paradigm of judicial restraint." *Beach Communications.* The rationale for such judicial restraint is the Madisonian theory that, in a democracy, the federal courts should defer to the politically accountable officials. Thus, if Iowa's differential tax rate for slot machine revenue is "unfair" or otherwise some sort of "mistake," the victims of the mistake should take their grievance to the political process and win some appropriate relief. Note that, as Justice Breyer indicated in *Fitzgerald*, there are situations where the Court applies more rigorous levels of judicial scrutiny.

(3) *The Government Doesn't Always Win With the Rational Basis Test: Allegheny Pittsburgh Coal Co. v. County Commission, 488 U.S. 336 (1984).* Webster County valued land for tax purposes at the price at which it last sold. The Supreme Court, per Chief Justice Rehnquist, held this system unconstitutional under the rational basis test. It produced disparities in which some properties were values at eight to twenty times as

much as comparable properties, and although it did allow for some updating, the system would have taken at least 500 years to "equalize" Allegheny's properties. This case is an example of the relatively rare situation in which the state loses, even with the rational basis test.

(4) *Another Decision Where the Challengers Prevail, Allegedly Under the Rational Basis Standard: Was There Actually Heightened Scrutiny in Romer v. Evans, 517 U.S. 620 (1996)?* Although the likelihood of the government losing under the rational basis standard is very low, the Court recently ruled in favor of gay and lesbian challengers who contested a Colorado state constitutional amendment (Amendment 2) prohibiting any "special" treatment or preferred status based on sexual preference. [This *Romer* decision receives full treatment in Section 10.04[C] *below.*] Wouldn't Colorado have, to use the *Beach Communications* terminology, a *conceivable* legitimate interest in conserving scarce public resources (*e.g.*, funds to investigate discrimination claims) or in protecting religious liberty (*e.g.*, landlords whose religious beliefs are hostile to homosexual conduct), assuming the Court truly was using lowest-level scrutiny, as it said? Consider whether the Court really used heightened scrutiny, contrary to its opinion. *See also* the *Cleburne Living Center* decision at Section 10.04[G] *below.*

PROBLEM B

SPECIAL LIABILITY PROVISIONS FOR ASBESTOS PRODUCERS: IN RE ASBESTOS LITIGATION, 829 F.2d 1233 (3d Cir. 1987), *cert. denied, Owens-Illinois v. Danfield*, 485 U.S. 1029 (1988). In product liability cases, New Jersey allows manufacturers to avoid liability by showing that they did not and could not reasonably have known that their products were dangerous, based on available knowledge at the time of manufacture. But New Jersey apparently denies the use of this "state of the art" defense to manufacturers of one kind of products (and one kind only): asbestos products. Defendants, which were asbestos manufacturers, claimed that this New Jersey law denies them equal protection. Is this argument valid?

[The Third Circuit majority, in *In re Asbestos Litigation*, upheld the law. Two judges concurred in finding a rational basis for the classification, in that the New Jersey rule was based on a conclusion that the manufacturers in fact had available information that would have given them the requisite knowledge, and a firm rule denying the defense—even though not denied to other manufacturers about which an industry-wide conclusion could be reached—advanced the tort-system goals of risk-spreading, accident avoidance, and simplification of the fact-finding process. One judge dissented, pointing out that manufacturers of other products such as Agent Orange, the Dalkon Shield, and DES were not denied the defense despite similarly available information and similar effects in clogging the courts: "Only the asbestos industry is treated differently. This is just plain wrong." Which do you think is correct, the majority or the dissent?]

§ 10.03   THE "UPPER TIER": STRICT SCRUTINY AND "COMPELLING" GOVERNMENTAL INTERESTS

[A]   Race and Other "Suspect Classifications"

[1]   Before and After The Civil War Amendments

NOTE: BACKGROUND TO THE *DRED SCOTT* CASE

Congress' Early Efforts to Regulate Slavery. In this section, we consider suspect classifications, with special emphasis on race. We begin with the infamous *Dred Scott* case, which antedates the Civil War.

The power of Congress to regulate slavery in the territories was a lingering question before the Civil War. The Ordinance of 1787 outlawed slavery in the Northwest Territory, and the Missouri Compromise of 1820 forbade it in the Louisiana Territory north of thirty-six degrees, thirty minutes north latitude, except for the State of Missouri. Some Southerners (for whom a principal spokesman was John C. Calhoun) argued that these laws violated the rights of citizens to own property (*i.e.*, their slaves).

The Test Case: Dred Scott. Dred Scott was born a slave. He was the property of one Peter Blow, inherited by his daughter Elizabeth, sold to Dr. John Emerson, and ultimately left with Henry Blow, the son of his original owner. Catton, *The Dred Scott Case, in* QUARRELS THAT HAVE SHAPED THE CONSTITUTION 77, 78–79 (J. Garraty ed. 1966). Dr. Emerson had taken Scott to Wisconsin Territory, so that he lived on "free soil" for approximately five years, and the Missouri Compromise therefore arguably made him free. The contrary argument was that the Missouri Compromise was unconstitutional, and thus Dred Scott became the unlikely protagonist in one of the greatest constitutional battles in American history. Excerpts from this historic but unfortunate decision follow.

SCOTT v. SANDFORD [THE DRED SCOTT CASE], 60 U.S. (19 How.) 393 (1857). With seven different opinions, sprawling over more than 100 pages in the unofficial reporter, the Court held that Dred Scott was not free. Chief Justice Taney's majority opinion began by holding that slaves were not citizens: "The legislation of the states . . . shows, in a manner not to be mistaken, the inferior and subject condition of that [black] race at the time the Constitution was adopted." Therefore, the Interstate Privileges and Immunities Clause of Article IV, Section 2 did not protect Dred Scott. But the argument remained that the Missouri Compromise had freed him. "And the difficulty which meets us at the threshold of this part of the inquiry is, whether Congress is authorized to pass this law under any of the powers granted to it by the Constitution. . . .":

> The people of the United States have delegated to it certain enumerated powers, and forbidden it to exercise others. . . . And if the Constitution recognizes the right of property of the master in a slave, and makes no distinction between that description of property and other property owned by a citizen, no tribunal, acting under the authority of the United States, whether it be legislative, executive, or judicial, has a right to draw such a distinction, or deny to it the benefit of the provisions and guarantees which have been provided for the protection of private property against the encroachments of the government. . . .

> Upon these considerations, it is the opinion of the Court that the Act of Congress which prohibited citizens from holding and owning property of this kind in the territory of the United States north of the line therein mentioned, is not warranted by the Constitution, and is therefore void; and that neither Dred Scott himself, nor any of his family, were made free by being carried into this territory. . . .

NOTES AND QUESTIONS

(1) *The Reaction against the Court after the Dred Scott Decision.* "The tempest of malediction that burst over the judges [after the *Dred Scott* Case] seems to have stunned them; far from extinguishing the slavery controversy, they had fanned its flames and had, moreover, deeply endangered the security of the judicial arm of government. No such vilification as this had been heard even in the wrathful days following the Alien and Sedition Acts. . . ." R. MCCLOSKEY, THE AMERICAN SUPREME COURT 95–96 (1960). "This ruling was upset a few years later by marching armies, at the cost of much bloodshed, but the reversal came too late to be of any help to Dred Scott because he died before the Civil War began." Catton, *supra*, at 78.

(2) *The Thirteenth, Fourteenth, and Fifteenth Amendments.* The history of the Thirteenth and Fourteenth amendments was summarized earlier in this book, when those issues first were encountered in the chapter on substantive protection of economic rights. The Fifteenth Amendment, which protects the right to vote against denial on account of race, color, or previous condition of servitude, was the third in the series.

(3) *The Slaughter House Cases.* Recall the *Slaughter House* cases, in which the Court narrowly construed the Fourteenth Amendment Privileges and Immunities Clause and held that the Due Process and Equal Protection Clauses were a reaction to the issues of race and slavery. Does the *Dred Scott* holding, denying slaves citizenship or privileges and immunities, provide a background that supports the inference that the Fourteenth Amendment was targeted principally at these anti-slavery issues?

(4) *A Ringing Affirmation of the Fourteenth Amendment— And Some Lesser Precedents: Comparing Strauder v. West Virginia, 100 U.S. 303 (1879), with Pace v. State of Alabama, 106 U.S. 583 (1883).* In *Strauder*, which was one of the early post-Fourteenth-Amendment decisions, the Court struck down the defendant's murder conviction because the applicable state law excluded black citizens from serving on juries. The Court reasoned that the purpose of the Fourteenth Amendment, "in regard to the [African-American] race, for whose protection the amendment was primarily designed, [was] that no discrimination shall be made against them by law because of their color." But then, in *Pace*, the Court upheld an Alabama law which provided more severe penalties for interracial adultery and fornication that if the two participants were of the same race. The Justices reasoned that, although the law treated integrated activities more severely, it treated both races in precisely the same way.

Later, in school desegregation cases, *Strauder* would be used as precedent for the holding that the Fourteenth Amendment proscribed all state racial discrimination. But in the meantime, reasoning similar to that in *Pace* would be used to justify treatment that allegedly was "separate but equal."

[2] Express Racial Classifications

KOREMATSU v. UNITED STATES
323 U.S. 214 (1944)

Mr. Justice Black delivered the opinion of the Court.

[The petitioner, an American citizen of Japanese descent, was convicted in a federal district court for remaining in San Leandro, California, contrary to Civilian Exclusion Order No. 34 of the Commanding General of the Western Command, U.S. Army, which directed that after May 9, 1942, all persons of Japanese ancestry should be excluded from that "military area." No question was raised as to petitioner's loyalty to the United States.]

It should be noted, to begin with, that all legal restrictions which curtail the civil rights of a single racial group are immediately suspect. That is not to say that all such restrictions are unconstitutional. It is to say that courts must subject them to the most rigid scrutiny. Pressing public necessity may sometimes justify the existence of such restrictions; racial antagonism never can. . . .

Exclusion Order No. 34, which the petitioner knowingly and admittedly violated was one of a number of military orders and proclamations, all of which were substantially based upon Executive Order No. 9066, 7 Fed.Reg. 1407. That order, issued after we were at war with Japan, declared that "the successful prosecution of the war requires every possible protection against espionage and against sabotage to national-defense material, national-defense premises, and national-defense utilities. . . ."

One of the series of orders and proclamations, a curfew order, which like the exclusion order here was promulgated pursuant to Executive Order 9066, subjected all persons of Japanese ancestry in prescribed West Coast military areas to remain in their residences from 8 p.m. to 6 a.m. . . . . In *Kiyoshi Hirabayashi v. United States*, 320 U.S. 81, we sustained a conviction obtained for violation of the curfew order. The Hirabayashi conviction and this one thus rest on the same 1942 Congressional Act and the same basic executive and military orders, all of which orders were aimed at the twin dangers of espionage and sabotage. . . .

In the light of the principles we announced in the *Hirabayashi* case, we are unable to conclude that it was beyond the war power of Congress and the Executive to exclude those of Japanese ancestry from the West Coast war area at the time they did. True, exclusion from the area in which one's home is located is a far greater deprivation than constant confinement to the home from 8 p. m. to 6 a. m. Nothing short of apprehension by the proper military authorities of the gravest imminent danger to the public safety can constitutionally justify either. But exclusion from a threatened area, no less than curfew, has a definite and close relationship to the prevention of espionage and sabotage. The military authorities, charged with the primary responsibility of defending our shores, concluded that curfew provided inadequate protection and ordered exclusion. They did so, as pointed out in our *Hirabayashi* opinion, in accordance with Congressional authority to the military to say who should, and who should not, remain in the threatened areas.

Here, as in the *Hirabayashi* case, *supra*,". . . we cannot reject as unfounded the judgment of the military authorities and of Congress that there were disloyal members of that population, whose number and strength could not be precisely and quickly ascertained. We cannot say that the war-making branches of the Government did not have ground for believing that in a critical hour such persons could not readily be isolated and separately dealt with, and constituted a menace to the national defense and safety, which demanded that prompt and adequate measures be taken to guard against it."

Like curfew, exclusion of those of Japanese origin was deemed necessary because of the presence of an unascertained number of disloyal members of the group. [Because of] the finding of the military authorities that it was impossible to bring about an immediate segregation of the disloyal from the loyal, we sustained the validity of the curfew order as applying to the whole group. In the instant case, temporary exclusion of the entire group was rested by the military on the same ground. The judgment that exclusion of the whole group was for the same reason a military imperative answers the contention that the exclusion was in the nature of group punishment based on antagonism to those of Japanese origin. That there were members of the group who retained loyalties to Japan has been confirmed by investigations made subsequent to the exclusion. Approximately five thousand American citizens of Japanese ancestry refused to swear unqualified allegiance to the United States and to renounce allegiance to the Japanese Emperor, and several thousand evacuees requested repatriation to Japan. . . .

[W]e are not unmindful of the hardships imposed by it upon a large group of American citizens. But hardships are part of war, and war is an aggregation of hardships. All citizens alike, both in and out of uniform, feel the impact of war in greater or lesser measure. Citizenship has its responsibilities as well as its privileges, and in time of war the burden is always heavier.

[The Court refused to pass upon the validity of a portion of the order requiring Petitioner Korematsu to remain in an assembly or relocation center because he was not convicted of violating that portion of the order. It rejected the argument that it must consider that issue because curfew, exclusion and internment were all part of a single system in the order that Korematsu was required to comply with.]

It is said that we are dealing here with the case of imprisonment of a citizen in a concentration camp solely because of his ancestry, without evidence or inquiry concerning his loyalty and good disposition towards the United States. Our task would be simple, our duty clear, were this a case involving the imprisonment of a loyal citizen in a concentration camp because of racial prejudice. Regardless of the true nature of the assembly and relocation centers—and we deem it unjustifiable to call them concentration camps with all the ugly connotations that term implies—we are dealing specifically with nothing but an exclusion order. To cast this case into outlines of racial prejudice, without reference to the real military dangers which were presented, merely confuses the issue. Korematsu was not excluded from the Military Area because of hostility to him or his race. He was excluded because we are at war with the Japanese Empire, because the properly constituted military authorities feared an invasion of our West Coast and felt constrained to take proper security measures, because they decided that the military urgency of the situation demanded that all citizens of Japanese ancestry be segregated from the West Coast temporarily, and finally, because Congress, reposing its confidence in this time of war in our military leaders—as inevitably it must—determined that they should have the power to do just this. There was evidence of disloyalty on the part of some, the military authorities considered that the need for action was great, and time was short. We cannot—by availing ourselves of the calm perspective of hindsight—now say that at that time these actions were unjustified.

Affirmed.

MR. JUSTICE FRANKFURTER, concurring.

[T]he validity of action under the war power must be judged wholly in the context of war. That action is not to be stigmatized as lawless because like action in times of peace would be lawless. . . .

MR. JUSTICE ROBERTS.

I dissent, because I think the indisputable facts exhibit a clear violation of Constitutional rights.

This is not a case of keeping people off the streets at night as was *Kiyoshi Hirabayashi v. United States*, nor a case of temporary exclusion of a citizen from an area for his own safety or that of the community, nor a case of offering him an opportunity to go temporarily out of an area where his presence might cause danger to himself or to his fellows. On the contrary, it is the case of convicting a citizen as a punishment for not submitting to imprisonment in a concentration camp, based on his ancestry, and solely because of his ancestry, without evidence or inquiry concerning his loyalty and good disposition towards the United States. If this be a correct statement of the facts disclosed by this record, and facts of which we take judicial notice, I need hardly labor the conclusion that Constitutional rights have been violated.

MR. JUSTICE MURPHY, dissenting. . . .

Justification for the exclusion is sought . . . mainly upon questionable racial and sociological grounds not ordinarily within the realm of expert military judgment, supplemented by certain semi-military conclusions drawn from an unwarranted use of circumstantial evidence. Individuals of Japanese ancestry are condemned because they are said to be "a large, unassimilated, tightly knit racial group, bound to an enemy nation by strong ties of race, culture, custom and religion." . . .

The main reasons relied upon by those responsible for the forced evacuation, therefore, do not prove a reasonable relation between the group characteristics of Japanese Americans and the dangers of invasion, sabotage and espionage. The reasons appear, instead, to be largely an accumulation of much of the misinformation, half-truths and insinuations that for years have been directed against Japanese Americans by people with racial and economic prejudices—the same people who have been among the foremost advocates of the evacuation. . . . [Note that Professor Gressman served as Justice Murphy's law clerk.]

MR. JUSTICE JACKSON, dissenting.

Korematsu was born on our soil, of parents born in Japan. The Constitution makes him a citizen of the United States by nativity and a citizen of California by residence. No claim is made that he is not loyal to this country. . . .

[H]ad Korematsu been one of four—the others being, say, a German alien enemy, an Italian alien enemy, and a citizen of American-born ancestors, convicted of treason but out on parole—only Korematsu's presence would have violated the order. The difference between their innocence and his crime would result, not from anything he did, said, or thought, different than they, but only in that he was born of different racial stock.

Now, if any fundamental assumption underlies our system, it is that guilt is personal and not inheritable. . . .

It would be impracticable and dangerous idealism to expect or insist that each specific military command in an area of probable operations will conform to conventional tests of constitutionality. When an area is so beset that it must be put under military control at all, the paramount consideration is that its measures be successful, rather than legal. The armed services must protect a society, not merely its Constitution. . . .

[N]o court can require such a commander in such circumstances to act as a reasonable man; he may be unreasonably cautious and exacting. Perhaps he should be. . . .

The limitation under which courts always will labor in examining the necessity for a military order are illustrated by this case. How does the Court know that these orders have a reasonable basis in necessity? . . .

In the very nature of things military decisions are not susceptible of intelligent judicial appraisal. . . . Hence courts can never have any real alternative to accepting the mere declaration of the authority that issued the order that it was reasonably necessary from a military viewpoint. . . .

[B]ut if we review and approve, that passing incident becomes the doctrine of the Constitution. There it has a generative power of its own, and all that it creates will be in its own image. Nothing better illustrates this danger than does the Court's opinion in this case.

I should hold that a civil court cannot be made to enforce an order which violates constitutional limitations even if it is a reasonable exercise of military authority. The courts can exercise only the judicial power, can apply only law, and must abide by the Constitution, or they cease to be civil courts and become instruments of military policy.

. . . I do not suggest that the courts should have attempted to interfere with the Army in carrying out its task. But I do not think they may be asked to execute a military expedient that has no place in law under the Constitution. I would reverse the judgment and discharge the prisoner.

NOTES AND QUESTIONS

(1) *Applying Strict Scrutiny: A Narrowly Drawn Policy Serving a Compelling State Interest.* Justice Black's *Korematsu* opinion states the theory of strict scrutiny: Express racial classifications are "immediately suspect" and are subject to the "most rigid scrutiny;" they must be "justified" by "pressing public necessity." The language is similar to the modern test, which subjects suspect classifications to a strict-scrutiny requirement of a compelling governmental interest which they are narrowly drawn to serve. But notice that, while Justice Black's opinion requires a "pressing" necessity,

concludes that combating espionage and sabotage after Pearl Harbor qualifies, and reasons that the exclusion had a "definite and close" relationship to this goal, it nowhere expressly considers whether the military order was "narrowly" tailored to this purpose. Is this aspect of Justice Black's opinion a fatal flaw, in that it resulted in the inclusion of loyal individuals such as *Korematsu*? On the other hand, is Justice Jackson correct in holding that a court really cannot determine the propriety of a military order?

(2) *The United States Pays Compensation to Interned American Citizens of Japanese Ancestry.* Congress passed the Japanese-American Evacuation Claims Act of 1948, which paid $37 million for material losses suffered by internees in Korematsu's situation. But the actual losses were valued in the billions of dollars. During the 1970s, some of the Nisei (second-generation Japanese-Americans), who had been interned as young adults, began to take steps toward formal redress. In 1976, President Ford called the internment a "national mistake." Then, in 1981, Congress established a Commission, which denounced the internment as a "grave injustice" that resulted from "race prejudice, war hysteria, and a failure of political leadership."

The Nisei continued to press for reparations. Obstacles included the large costs of proposed legislation; apprehension that compensation would inspire large claims by other racial minorities (particularly blacks and American Indians); and the argument that the internment, however regrettable, was a necessary wartime precaution and might even have protected the Japanese Americans from hostile civilians. *Camps: A Dark Memory for Japanese-Americans; Former Internees Now Seek Redress*, HOUSTON CHRONICLE, July 19, 1987 § 1, at 2, col. 1. Ultimately, Congress passed and the President signed a $1.25 billion reparations Bill that would pay approximately $20,000 to each of thousands of Japanese-Americans who personally had been interned.

This event led members of the Congressional Black Caucus to seek remedies to compensate blacks for the legacy of slavery. Opponents argued that legal abolition of slavery had occurred more than a century before, whereas every compensated Japanese-American had personally been interned by force of law. The Bill "[did] not appear to have much support outside the Black Caucus." *Black Lawmakers Again Seek Slavery Reparations*, Houston Chronicle, May 30, 1990, § A, at 11, col. 1.

[a] Segregation, Including the Separate But Equal Doctrine

PLESSY v. FERGUSON, 163 U.S. 537 (1896). A Louisiana statute provided for separate railway carriages for whites and blacks. Plessy (who described himself as "seven-eighths Caucasian and one-eighth African blood" and stated that the "mixture of colored blood was not discernible in him") was ejected by a conductor for insisting upon sitting in a white-only coach and was imprisoned to answer a charge of violating the Louisiana statute. The Court, per Justice Brown, upheld the statute:

> We consider the underlying fallacy of the plaintiff's argument to consist in the assumption that the enforced separation of the two races stamps the colored race with a badge of inferiority. If this be so, it is not by reason of anything found in the act, but solely because the colored race choose to put that construction upon it. . . . The argument also assumes that social prejudices may be overcome by legislation, and that equal rights cannot be secured to the negro except by an enforced commingling of the two races. We cannot accept this proposition. . . .
>
> [The Court then noted that Plessy's rights might depend upon whether he was classified as black or white: "Under the allegations of his petition, it may undoubtedly become a question of importance whether, under the laws of Louisiana, the petitioner belongs to the white or colored race."]
>
> The judgment of the court below is therefore affirmed.

Justice Harlan dissented. First, he viewed Plessy's argument based on the Thirteenth

Amendment, which the majority summarily had rejected, as meritorious: "[The Thirteenth Amendment] not only struck down the institution of slavery as previously existing in the United States, but it prevents the imposition of any burdens or disability that constitute badges of slavery or servitude." Justice Harlan concluded that the Louisiana law violated this prohibition. Furthermore, it violated the Fourteenth Amendment:

> Everyone knows that the statute in question had its origin in the purpose, not so much to exclude white persons from railroad cars occupied by blacks, as to exclude colored people from coaches occupied by or assigned to white persons. . . .

> [B]ut in view of the Constitution, in the eye of the law, there is in this country no superior, dominant, ruling class of citizens. There is no caste here. Our Constitution is color-blind and neither knows nor tolerates classes among citizens. . . .

> In my opinion, the judgment this day rendered will, in time, prove to be quite as pernicious as the decision made by this tribunal in the *Dred Scott* Case.

NOTES AND QUESTIONS

(1) *The Separate But Equal Doctrine: Identifying the Flaw.* By now, the result in *Plessy* has been so firmly rejected that it is unusual to analyze why it is wrong; nevertheless, it may be useful to attempt to do so. Is it that separate accommodations for a minority race cannot be expected to be precisely equal, in the sense that the majority cannot be expected to care deeply about equality? Is it that separate but equal can *never* be equal even if the accommodations are precisely the same, because of the superior-inferior relationship between the two groups that the separation communicates? Or is it something else?

(2) *A Color-Blind Constitution: What Result for Affirmative Action or Race-Conscious Remedies?* Justice Harlan's famous dictum that the "Constitution is color-blind" is inspiring because it is a ringing rejection of the majority's reasoning. It may be a useful test in analyzing many constitutional problems. In some, however, it may be more controversial in its effects. Consider the result that such a principle might have in school desegregation cases. Would it mean that efforts to extirpate past practices could not succeed because they necessarily would take account of race? Would it mean that government could never undertake affirmative action?

(3) *Justice Harlan's Own Blindness to "Color Blindness": His Strange Treatment of Asian-Americans.* Justice Harlan's opinion contains an odd passage that singles out one group, the "Chinese race," and attempts to justify unequal treatment of individuals who belong to this group. Apparently, prejudice is an even stranger phenomenon than Justice Harlan might think. Justice Harlan explained that different treatment resulted because "the Chinese race" was "so different from our own." *Plessy*, 163 U.S. at 561. History seems to have given Justice Harlan's blind spot a quiet burial. *See also Cumming v. Board of Education*, 175 U.S. 528 (1899), below (opinion by Justice Harlan).

NOTE ON THE ROUTE FROM *PLESSY* TO *BROWN*: *McLAURIN, SWEATT*, ETC.

The Early Separate-But-Equal Decisions. From 1896 to 1954, the Supreme Court used the separate but equal doctrine. In early decisions, it often was casual about finding "equality." For example, in *Cumming v. Board of Education*, 175 U.S. 528 (1899), it upheld the closing of a black high school (male only) for "economic" reasons, even though the white high school (male only) was kept open and even though the white-only school board gave public money to a private school for white girls. The Cumming Court relied on the availability of other schools for the black males—in distant cities.

The Court Gradually Limits Separate but Equal. In 1938, the Court began a series of decisions that limited the separate but equal doctrine by making it difficult to comply with. In *State of Missouri ex. rel. Gaines v. Canada*, 305 U.S. 337 (1938), the State of Missouri offered to provide a black law school applicant an education outside the state but denied him entrance to the state's own law school because of his race. The Court reasoned that Missouri must provide the same opportunities to blacks that it did to whites, and that more intangible notions of similar quality would not suffice.

The Sweatt and McLaurin Cases: Narrow Construction of Separate-but-Equal Sets the Stage for Brown v. Board of Education. Then came the companion cases of *Sweatt v. Painter*, 339 U.S. 629 (1950), and *McLaurin v. Oklahoma State Regents*, 339 U.S. 637 (1950). The lawyer for the black students was Thurgood Marshall—later the first African-American Justice. In *Sweatt*, the trial court held that the University of Texas law school for Negroes was substantially equal to the University of Texas law school, but the Supreme Court reversed and held the two unequal because the latter school, which was reserved for whites, had broader course offerings, a more distinguished faculty, and other features that make for excellence in a law school. In *McLaurin*, a black graduate student was admitted to the state university, but was required to sit and perform other functions separately from white students; the Court held that his treatment was not equal because he was deprived of such aspects of education as meaningful exchange of views with other students. The decisions made clear the extraordinary difficulty of designing segregated educations that would not run afoul of the law. Furthermore, in *Sweatt*, the Court expressly reserved the question whether separate but equal remained constitutionally acceptable—a question it answered in the following case.

BROWN v. BOARD OF EDUCATION ("BROWN I")
347 U.S. 483 (1954)

Mr. Chief Justice Warren delivered the opinion of the Court.

These cases come to us from the States of Kansas, South Carolina, Virginia, and Delaware. . . .

In each of the cases, minors of the Negro race, through their legal representatives, seek the aid of the courts in obtaining admission to the public schools of their community on a nonsegregated basis. In each instance, they have been denied admission to schools attended by white children under laws requiring or permitting segregation according to race. This segregation was alleged to deprive the plaintiffs of the equal protection of the laws under the Fourteenth Amendment. In each of the cases other than the Delaware case, a three-judge federal district court denied relief to the plaintiffs on the so-called "separate but equal" doctrine announced by this Court in *Plessy v. Ferguson*. . . . In the Delaware case, the Supreme Court of Delaware adhered to that doctrine, but ordered that the plaintiffs be admitted to the white schools because of their superiority to the Negro schools.

The plaintiffs contend that segregated public schools are not "equal" and cannot be made "equal," and that hence they are deprived of the equal protection of the laws. . . .

[A]rgument was heard in the 1952 Term, and reargument was heard this Term on certain questions propounded by the Court.

Reargument was largely devoted to the circumstances surrounding the adoption of the Fourteenth Amendment in 1868. It covered exhaustively consideration of the Amendment in Congress, ratification by the states, then existing practices in racial segregation, and the views of proponents and opponents of the Amendment. This discussion and our own investigation convince us that, although these sources cast some light, it is not enough to resolve the problem with which we are faced. At best, they are inconclusive. The most avid proponents of the post-War Amendments undoubtedly intended them to remove all legal distinctions among "all persons born or naturalized in the United States." Their opponents, just as certainly, were antagonistic to both the letter and the spirit of the Amendments and wished them to have the most limited effect. What others in Congress and the state legislatures had in mind cannot be determined with any degree of certainty.

An additional reason for the inconclusive nature of the Amendment's history, with respect to segregated schools, is the status of public education at that time. In the South, the movement toward free common schools, supported by general taxation, had not yet taken hold. Education of white children was largely in the hands of private groups. Education of Negroes was almost nonexistent, and practically all of the race were illiterate. In fact, any education of Negroes was forbidden by law in some states. Today, in contrast, many Negroes have achieved outstanding success in the arts and sciences as well as in the business and professional world. It is true that public school education at the time of the Amendment had advanced further in the North, but the effect of the Amendment on Northern States was generally ignored in the congressional debates. Even in the North, the conditions of public education did not approximate those existing today. . . .

In the first cases in this Court construing the Fourteenth Amendment, decided shortly after its adoption, the Court interpreted it as proscribing all state-imposed discriminations against the Negro race. The doctrine of "separate but equal" did not make its appearance in this Court until 1896 in the case of *Plessy v. Ferguson, supra*, involving not education but transportation. American courts have since labored with the doctrine for over half a century. In *Cumming v. Board of Education of Richmond County*, 175 U.S. 528 (1899), the validity of the doctrine itself was not challenged. In more recent cases, all on the graduate school level, inequality was found in that specific benefits enjoyed by white students were denied to Negro students of the same educational qualifications. *State of Missouri ex rel. Gaines v. Canada*, 305 U.S. 337 (1938); *Sweatt v. Painter*, 339 U.S. 629 (1950); *McLaurin v. Oklahoma State Regents*, 339 U.S. 637 (1950). In none of these cases was it necessary to re-examine the doctrine to grant relief to the Negro plaintiff. And it *Sweatt v. Painter, supra*, the Court expressly reserved decision on the question whether *Plessy v. Ferguson* should be held inapplicable to public education.

In the instant cases, that question is directly presented. Here, unlike *Sweatt v. Painter*, there are findings below that the Negro and white schools involved have been equalized, or are being equalized, with respect to buildings, curricula, qualifications and salaries of teachers, and other "tangible" factors. Our decision, therefore, cannot turn on merely a comparison of these tangible factors in the Negro and white schools involved in each of the cases. We must look instead to the effect of segregation itself on public education.

In approaching this problem, we cannot turn the clock back to 1868 when the Amendment was adopted, or even to 1896 when *Plessy v. Ferguson* was written. We must consider public education in the light of its full development and its present place in American life throughout the Nation. . . .

Today, education is perhaps the most important function of state and local governments. Compulsory school attendance laws and the great expenditures for education both demonstrate our recognition of the importance of education to our democratic society. . . . In these days, it is doubtful that any child may reasonably be expected to succeed in life if he is denied the opportunity of an education. Such an opportunity, where the state has undertaken to provide it, is a right which must be made available to all on equal terms.

We come then to the question presented: Does segregation of children in public schools solely on the basis of race, even though the physical facilities and other "tangible" factors may be equal, deprive the children of the minority group of equal educational opportunities? We believe that it does.

In *Sweatt v. Painter*, in finding that a segregated law school for Negroes could not provide them equal educational opportunities, this Court relied in large part on "those qualities which are incapable of objective measurement but which make for greatness in a law school." In *McLaurin v. Oklahoma State Regents*, the Court, in requiring that a Negro admitted to a white graduate school be treated like all other students, again resorted to intangible considerations: ". . . his ability to study, to engage in discussions and exchange views with other students, and, in general, to learn his profession." Such considerations apply with added force to children in grade and high schools. To separate them from others of similar age and qualifications solely because of their race generates a feeling of inferiority as to their status in the community that may affect their hearts and minds in a way unlikely ever to be undone. The effect of this separation on their educational opportunities was well stated by a finding in the Kansas case by a court which nevertheless felt compelled to rule against the Negro plaintiffs:

> Segregation of white and colored children in public schools has a detrimental effect upon the colored children. The impact is greater when it has the sanction of the law; for the policy of separating the races is usually interpreted as denoting the inferiority of the negro group. A sense of inferiority affects the motivation of a child to learn. Segregation with the sanction of law, therefore, has a tendency to [retard] the educational and mental development of Negro children and to deprive them of some of the benefits they would receive in a racial[ly] integrated school system.

Whatever may have been the extent of psychological knowledge at the time of *Plessy v. Ferguson*, this finding is amply supported by modern authority.[1] Any language in *Plessy v. Ferguson* contrary to this finding is rejected.

We conclude that in the field of public education the doctrine of "separate but equal" has no place. Separate educational facilities are inherently unequal. Therefore, we hold that the plaintiffs [are] deprived of the equal protection of the laws guaranteed by the Fourteenth Amendment. This disposition makes unnecessary any discussion whether such segregation also violates the Due Process Clause of the Fourteenth Amendment. *[holding]*

Because these are class actions, because of the wide applicability of this decision, and because of the great variety of local conditions, the formulation of decrees in these cases presents problems of considerable complexity. . . . In order that we may have the full assistance of the parties in formulating decrees, the cases will be restored to the docket, and the parties are requested to present further argument on Questions 4 and 5 previously propounded by the Court for the reargument this Term.[2]

---

[1] K. B. Clark, *Effect of Prejudice and Discrimination on Personality Development* (Midcentury White House Conference on Children and Youth, 1950); Witmer and Kotinsky, *Personality in the Making* (1952), c. VI; Deutscher and Chein, *The Psychological Effects of Enforced Segregation: A Survey of Social Science Opinion*, 26 J. Psychol. 259 (1948); Chein, *What are the Psychological Effects of Segregation Under Conditions of Equal Facilities?* 3 Int. J. Opinion and Attitude Res. 229 (1949); Brumeld, *Educational Costs, in Discrimination and National Welfare* (MacIver, ed., 1949), 44–48; Frazier, *The Negro in the United States* (1949), 674–681. And *see generally* Myrdul, *An American Dilemma* (1944).

[2] 4. Assuming it is decided that segregation in public schools violates the Fourteenth Amendment

(*a*) would a decree necessarily follow providing that, within the limits set by normal geographic school districting, Negro children should forthwith be admitted to schools of their choice, or

(*b*) may this Court, in the exercise of its equity powers, permit an effective gradual adjustment to be brought about from existing segregated systems to a system not based on color distinctions?

5. On the assumption on which questions 4(*a*) and (*b*) are based, and assuming further that this Court will exercise its equity powers to the end described in question 4(*b*).

(*a*) should this Court formulate detailed decrees in these cases;

(*b*) if so, what specific issues should the decrees reach;

NOTES AND QUESTIONS

(1) *Overruling Separate But Equal: Brown v. Board of Education, 347 U.S. 483 (1954).* The *Brown* decision was a consolidation of four cases which challenged the *Plessy* Court's adoption of separate but equal as the controlling interpretation of the Equal Protection Clause. The challengers were represented by Thurgood Marshall (who later served as an Associate Justice on the Court). The *Brown* decision would generally be understood as the most important constitutional decision of the Twentieth Century. The *Brown* Court, per Justice Warren, unanimously overruled *Plessy* and held: "Separate educational facilities are inherently unequal."

Chief Justice Warren's opinion considers textual, historical, precedential, and policy grounds. The policy analysis was based on the Court's major premise: "Today education is perhaps the most important function of state and local governments." (Watch for reliance on this "premise" in many other equal protection decisions, including *Grutter* below.) Chief Justice Warren was in a unique position to make this claim, as he had served both as Governor and Attorney General of California before being appointed to the Court.

There are many academic works about the *Brown* decision. A recent Symposium Issue at 48 St. Louis U. L.J. 791 (2004) has numerous insightful articles. The following Notes examine some of the issues posed by the *Brown* decision and its progeny. *See* Ronald C. Griffin, *Jubilee*, 43 Washburn L.J. 353 (2004), for a compelling discussion of some of the post-*Brown* issues.

While almost all observers today recognize that the *Brown* decision, and the judicial review methodologies involved in it, were pivotal events in the history of American judicial review, there are some differing views. For example, Professor Robert Nagel questions the national significance of the *Brown* decision (and, therefore, any use of it as a "model" for judicial review) by arguing that the *Brown* decision (striking down statutory school segregation) was only correcting a "rogue" practice within a national culture of nondiscriminatory educational laws. *See* Robert Nagel, Constitutional Cultures 1–5 (1989).

(2) *Social Science as a Basis of the Court's Opinion.* The Court rejects the *Plessy* holding of non-stigmatization in part because "this [rejection] is amply supported by modern authority." Footnote eleven contains citations to works of social science that support the Court's conclusion. Is this reasoning (which has been subjected to much criticism) a sound basis for the Court's holding? The social sciences are not as accurate as other sciences, and their conclusions are more subject to reversal; does this consideration mean that a court should not rely upon social science because of a concern that constitutional holdings will be reversed by advances in the state of knowledge? [On the other hand, the *Plessy* court simply made an ex cathedra pronouncement that segregation did not connote inferiority. Is this sort of pronouncement any better than reliance on social science?]

(3) *The Historical Fourteenth Amendment as a Better Basis?* As previous materials in this book have shown, even if one concludes that racial equality before the law was not the only purpose of the Fourteenth Amendment, it certainly was a historical purpose. Might the Court have done better to emphasize this factor? The state of public education had changed, as the Court points out, from the time of adoption of the

---

(c) should this Court appoint a special matter to hear evidence with a view to recommending specific terms for such decrees;

(d) should this Court remand to the courts of first instance with directions to frame decrees in these cases, and if so what general directions should the decrees of this Court include and what procedures should the courts of first instance follow in arriving at the specific terms of more detailed decrees?

amendment to the date of decision of *Brown*. Consider whether the Court could have applied the historical purpose of the Fourteenth Amendment to education in its modern form. [Would reasoning of that kind perhaps have been disadvantageous in the view of some Justices, because it could have been construed to denigrate the use of the Fourteenth Amendment in other non-racial contexts, as the majority did in the *Slaughter-House Case*?] *See generally* William E. Nelson, *The Changing Meaning of Equality in Twentieth-Century Constitutional Law*, 52 WASH & LEE L. REV. 3 (1995). *See also Cooper v. Aaron, supra* in Chapter 1.

(4) *Justice Thomas's View; Rejection of Social Science Evidence and Stigma Theory in Missouri v. Jenkins, 515 U.S. 1139 (1995).* In *Jenkins*, the Court revisited the efforts of the federal district court to desegregate the Kansas City, Missouri public schools. The most interesting aspect of the decision, however, is the concurrence by Justice Thomas. Justice Thomas presented a wide-ranging critique of the school desegregation cases, including criticism of the view that the *Brown* decision, above, depended on the sociological and psychological data concerning the feelings of "inferiority" created by *de jure* segregation:

> Segregation was not unconstitutional [in *Brown*] because it might have caused psychological feelings of inferiority. Public school systems that separated blacks and provided them with superior educational resources—making blacks "feel" superior to whites sent to lesser schools—would violate the Fourteenth Amendment, whether or not the white students felt stigmatized, just as do school systems in which the positions of the races are reversed. Psychological injury or benefit is irrelevant to the question whether state actors have engaged in intentional discrimination—the critical inquiry for ascertaining violations of the Equal Protection Clause. The judiciary is fully competent to make independent determinations concerning the existence of state action without the unnecessary and misleading assistance of the social sciences.

(5) *Federal Equal Protection Under the Fifth Amendment Due Process Clause and School Desegregation: Bolling v. Sharpe,* 347 U.S. 497 (1954). The Equal Protection Clause, of course, applies only to the states; the federal government is subject to the Fifth Amendment Due Process Clause. However, that clause has been held to include an "equal protection component" that forbids invidious discrimination. In *Bolling*, which was a companion case to *Brown* and decided the same day, the Court held that the federal government could not operate racially segregated schools in the District of Columbia.

[b] Other Express Racial Classifications

LOVING v. VIRGINIA, 388 U.S. 1 (1967). A Virginia statute made interracial marriages involving white persons a crime. Loving, a white man, and his wife Mildred Jeter, a black woman, were convicted of cohabiting as husband and wife in Virginia. The Court (per Warren, C.J.) reversed the conviction:

> [T]he state argues that the meaning of the equal protection clause, as illuminated by the statements of the Framers, is only that state penal laws containing an interracial element as part of the definition of the offense must apply equally to whites and negroes in the sense that members of each race are punished to the same degree. . . .
>
> . . . In the case at bar, however, we deal with statutes containing racial classifications, and the fact of equal application does not immunize the state from the very heavy burden of justification which the fourteenth amendment has traditionally required of state statutes drawn according to race. . . .
>
> [A]t the very least, the equal protection clause demands that racial classifications, especially suspect in criminal statutes, be subjected to the "most rigid scrutiny," *Korematsu v. United States,* . . . and, if they are ever to be upheld,

they must be shown to be necessary to the accomplishment of some permissible state objective, independent of the racial discrimination which it was the object of the fourteenth amendment to eliminate. . . .

There is patently no legitimate overriding purpose independent of invidious racial discrimination which justifies this classification. The fact that Virginia prohibits only interracial marriages involving white persons demonstrates that the racial classifications must stand on their own justification, as measures designed to maintain white supremacy. . . .

Mr. Justice Stewart concurred, stating "I have previously expressed the belief that 'it is simply not possible for a state law to be valid under our Constitution which makes the criminality of an act depend upon the race of the actor.' . . . Because I adhere to that belief, I concur in the judgment of the Court."

NOTES AND QUESTIONS

(1) *Explicit Racial Classification and Marriage: Loving v. Virginia, 388 U.S. 1 (1967).* Richard Loving (a white man) and Mildred (a black woman) had been married for nine years, but their marriage was illegal in Virginia. They challenged Virginia's law. Virginia defended primarily on the theory that the antimiscenagation law burdened whites and blacks equally. The Court, per Chief Justice Warren, rejected this argument and ruled for the Lovings. The Court held that, even in a setting other than education, the state's use of racial classifications would be tested by the strict scrutiny standard. The Court further held that Virginia failed strict scrutiny because it did not have even a legitimate government interest (let alone a compelling interest).

Justice Potter Stewart's famous concurrence argued that state criminal laws where race was an essential element of the crime were *per se* invalid. Justice Stewart's approach was simpler than the majority's invocation of strict scrutiny, but it would be narrower because he would apply it only to criminal laws.

The *Loving* decision appeared the same year as a critically acclaimed movie, *Guess Who's Coming to Dinner*, which was a dramatic comedy examining attitudes toward interracial marriage. In 1967, the popular culture seemed to be far more accepting of interracial marriage than the laws of some states (especially in the South). Some have suggested that the *Loving* decision was an example of the Court "catching up" with the greater culture. With respect to interracial marriage, much has changed in America. While in 1970, only 0.7% of married couples were interracial, in 2005, 3.7% of married couples were interracial. *See* David Crary, Associated Press, *Interracial Marriage Flourishes 40 years after Landmark Ruling*, ARGUS LEADER, April 15, 2007, at 20.

(2) *What Test is Applied in Brown and Loving?* You should consider whether the test of strict scrutiny has varied from *Korematsu* to *Brown* to *Loving*. Is the Court still requiring that a suspect classification be supported by a compelling governmental interest to which the statute is narrowly drawn? Or are *Brown* and *Loving* such clearcut cases that the Court blurred the analysis? Consider, also, whether the simpler analysis favored by Justice Stewart—that a criminal conviction based upon racial classification is per se invalid—is better.

(3) *May a State Consider Race in Deciding Custody of Children? Palmore v. Sidoti, 466 U.S. 429 (1984).* In *Palmore*, a divorced white mother with custody of her white child married a blackman. The state courts transferred custody to the child's father, on the ground that the child should be spared "the social stigmatization that is sure to come." Applying strict scrutiny, the Court held that the concerns of the state court were probably real, but held that they could not supply the compelling interest that was required. Indeed, the Court held that the state could not give effect to private prejudices.

(4) *Adoption—May the State Consider Race? In re Gomez, 424 S.W.2d 656 (Tex. Civ. App. 1967).* In *Gomez*, a Texas state court considered a Texas law requiring that a

prospective adoptive parent be of the same race as the child intended to be adopted. It struck down this race-matching requirement as violative of equal protection. If the state were to consider race as merely one factor, and to base the decision upon the overall suitability of the adoptive parent, would that approach also violate equal protection? Does the state have a compelling interest in cultural compatibility, and if so, does consideration of race in these circumstances advance that interest sufficiently—or is this simply a case in which, irrespective of the importance of the private interest, race simply cannot be considered?

(5) *Unwritten State Policy of Racially Segregating Prisoners, Even If Only for Sixty Days, Violated Equal Protection Guarantee: Johnson v. California, 543 U.S. 499 (2005).* The California Department of Corrections (CDC) had an "unwritten policy" of racially segregating prisoners in prison "reception centers" for up to 60 days each time they entered a new correctional facility. The State initially relied on the unwritten and "temporary" nature of the policy to defend against the claim by Johnson, an African-American inmate, that the CDC policy violated his equal protection rights. After Johnson received appointed counsel (from a private Los Angeles law firm) and discovery was conducted, California justified the policy as necessary to avoid gang-related violence within the prisons. California also argued that the case was controlled by the deferential rational basis standard from *Turner v. Safley*, 482 U.S. 78 (1987).

The Supreme Court disagreed. The Court, per Justice O'Connor (5-3), held that the applicable standard, on remand, would be strict scrutiny. The Court suggested that California may have a compelling state interest in preventing gang-related violence, but that it would have to justify the 60-day segregation period as "narrowly tailored to serve a compelling state interest." *Johnson*, 543 U.S. at 509.

Justice Ginsburg (for Souter and Breyer) concurred. Justices Stevens, Thomas, and Scalia dissented. With a mere five-Justice majority, this issue may be revisited in other prison cases.

(6) *The Limits of "Racial" Discrimination—Can Ethnic, Religious, or Regional Groups Be "Suspect Classes?": The St. Francis College (Arabs) and Shaare Tefila (Jews) Cases, Below.* Thus far, we have been considering race as the term is narrowly understood today. But would official discrimination against (say) Roman Catholics or Jews, or against immigrants from the Middle East, be subject to strict scrutiny on the ground that it is tantamount to racial discrimination? The following decisions are not constitutionally based (they interpret civil rights legislation) but since the legislation derives from the Congressional power to enforce the Fourteenth Amendment, consider whether these decisions show the answer.

ST. FRANCIS COLLEGE v. AL-KHAZRAJI, 481 U.S. 604 (1987). The plaintiff, a United States citizen born in Iraq, alleged that the college was liable to him for denying him tenure on the basis of his "Arabian race." Because St. Francis was a private college, he sued under 42 U.S.C. § 1981, which prohibits certain racial discrimination even by private persons. The district court dismissed on the ground that § 1981 did not reach discrimination based on national origin and since the plaintiff was Caucasian, the alleged discrimination was not "racial." The Court of Appeals reversed this holding, as did the Supreme Court, per Justice White:

> The understanding of race in the 19th century . . . was different. . . .
>
> Encyclopedias of the 19th century . . . described race in terms of ethnic groups. [T]he 1863 version of the New American Encyclopedia divided the Arabs into a number of subsidiary races; represented the Hebrews as of the Semitic race; and identified numerous other groups as constituting races, including Swedes, Norwegians, Germans, Greeks, Finns, Italians, Spanish, Mongolians, Russians, and the like. . . .

SHAARE TEFILA CONGREGATION v. COBB, 481 U.S. 615 (1987). In this companion case, the Court (per Justice White) extended the holding of *St. Francis*

College to discrimination against Jews: "[T]he question before us is not whether Jews are considered to be a separate race by today's standards, but whether, at the time [the relevant civil rights legislation] was adopted, Jews constituted a group of people that Congress intended to protect. As is evident from . . . *St. Francis College*, . . . Jews and Arabs were among the peoples then considered to be distinct races and hence within the protection of the statute."

PROBLEM C

POLICY OF RACIAL MATCHING IN ADOPTIONS ATTACKED, HOUSTON CHRONICLE, Nov. 10, 1991, § C, at 1, col. 2. The Texas Department of Human Services had a written policy providing that the Department "prefers placement of children with adoptive parents whose race or ethnicity is the same as the child's." The Department "very, very seldom" crossed racial lines and did so only when placement has become extraordinarily difficult. Carol Eberhard, who had adopted a bi-racial baby girl six years earlier and would have liked to have adopted another mixed-race child, was disappointed when an African-American social worker told her that such a child should never be placed in an Anglo home. An organization called Our Adopted Friends opposed the state's policy, pointing out that it was discriminatory, resulted in keeping children in foster care too long, and prevented qualified couples from adopting.

Many states have similar, expressly racial policies. One state official explained: "Most people understand that children have a difficult enough time in the world without" the problems of a different-race family. Is such a state policy constitutional? [Is the state's interest in the child's welfare compelling, and is the policy narrowly targeted to serve it?]

[3] "De Facto" Discrimination or Discrimination In Effect: Discriminatory "Purpose" Is Required?

INTRODUCTORY NOTE ON INTENT AND IMPACT

In the preceding section, we dealt with racial classifications created by law, or what is called "de jure" discrimination. In this section, we deal with disparate racial impacts that are not expressly required by law. Of course, if administrators of a facially neutral law take it upon themselves to interpret and apply the law deliberately in a racially discriminatory manner, the outcome should not be different than if the written law required their interpretation. But on the other hand, the problem sometimes can be more subtle. What if the administrators have no racially discriminatory purpose, but the effect of their conduct is that the law impacts a somewhat larger percentage of black citizens than white ones because of social conditions? Admission to a law school on the basis of standardized test scores, for example, might present precisely this problem. In fact, it would be unrealistic to expect that any legislation would demonstrate precise statistical equality in its impact upon all ethnic groups, even if the legislation is facially neutral and evenhandedly administered.

A Requirement of Discriminatory "Purpose" Rather Than Discriminatory "Effect"; the Problem of Proof. The current position of the Court, after *Washington v. Davis*, below, is that disproportionate impact by itself is not sufficient to establish an equal protection violation; instead, discriminatory "purpose" is required. However, there also is the question of proof. Discriminatory purpose often is inferred from the effect of the law; for example, if administrators treated thousands of white persons uniformly in one way and thousands of blacks uniformly in another, an inference of discriminatory purpose might arise from these facts alone.

NOTE ON THE RELATIONSHIP BETWEEN INTENT AND EVIL: FROM THE STAR WARS LEGENDS TO THE SUPREME COURT OPINIONS

(1) *Is Evil Present Only Where There Is Intent?: The Philosophy of Boba Fett.* In the wonderful Star Wars legends (which occupy roughly the same place in today's popular culture as The Iliad did in Homer's time), Boba Fett is a bounty hunter. Exiled from his own planet, doing a job that may be needed but is not respected, Boba Fett accepts contracts to "collect" wanted people (excuse us; wanted *creatures*) in the name of an uncertain, shifting justice, depending on which society has contracted for his services. Boba Fett has a highly developed vocabulary, in which he expresses a precise (if cramped) philosophy of evil. It is a frontiersman's amalgamation of individual responsibility with fatalism:

> . . . Evil exists; it is intelligence in the service of entropy. When the side of a mountain slides down to kill a village, this is not evil, for evil requires intent. Should a sentient being cause that landslide, there is evil; and requires Justice as a consequence, so that civilization can exist. . . .

Daniel Keys Moran, *The Last One Standing: The Tale of Boba Fett, in* Star Wars: Tales of the Bounty Hunters 277–78 (Bantam Books, Kevin J. Anderson ed. 1996). (The authors acknowledge with appreciation that John David Crump, then age 11, called our attention to this passage.)

(2) *What Does "Intent" Mean (and for that Matter, What Does "Evil" Mean)?* Can't a natural disaster be considered "evil" at least in some senses? Maybe the notion that deliberate decisions must underlie a mountain slide before it can be called an evil thing is too narrow. Consider, also, whether intent truly is required for evil to exist. Suppose there is a person somewhere who could have prevented the mountain from sliding (or who could have warned the villagers), but this person didn't, and the reason was pure indifference. Isn't this omission "evil"? Are drunk drivers evil? Consider, also, whether people or institutions can produce evil results unintentionally, through negligence. Our law makes a major effort to address harm caused by negligence. We do not confine our deterrence mechanisms by a narrowly defined concept of intent.

(3) *What Does All This Have to Do With Constitutional Law?: The Supreme Court's Distinction between Discriminatory "Purpose" and Disparate "Impact."* The Supreme Court has something in common with Boba Fett. Its decisions require proof of "purposeful" discrimination to make out a case of racial inequity redressable under the Fourteenth Amendment. In other words, disparate "impact" is not enough under the Constitution. The similarity to Boba Fett isn't exact, of course, and you will need to evaluate the decisions for yourself. It is clear, however, that even if a government agency serves people of one race with different overall effects than people of another, the Court will not consider this circumstance alone as proof of illegality (at least, not if the disparate impact occurs "in spite of and not because of" race). In fact, even if the disparity arguably is preventable, and even if its eradication has been frustrated only by governmental inertia, one can interpret the decisions to deny redress under the Fourteenth Amendment in the absence of proof of intent. Boba Fett probably would approve.

(4) *Institutions and Racial Effects: How Can One Prove the "Intent" of an Institution, and Why Should It Be Required?—The Differing Views of People of Different Races.* Sometimes it will be hard to prove intent on the part of a large bureaucracy. In a major government agency, there are people of varying political philosophies and responsibilities, and a given instance of disparate racial impact may not be traceable to a particular policy, let alone to a person with racial animus. In fact, the decisions recognize these difficulties in various ways. For example, the Court has held that highly disparate impact, especially if it is unexplained by any legitimate cause, can suffice as proof of "intent" (is this really what it is?). Perhaps racial impact caused by bureaucratic indifference, then, ought to be as actionable as if it were caused by intent.

The answer to this question seems to depend on who is answering it. Polls show that Caucasian people tend to consider disparity to be racism only if it is linked to intent. *See below.* African-Americans, however, tend, in the polls, in greater proportion, to see racism in terms of disparate impact produced by the practices of an institution, whether it proceeds from intent or indifference. *Id.* Discussions of racial issues sometimes fail to bridge this gap.

(5) *In Defense of Intent: Does Boba Fett Have a Point?* But then again, it might be a mistake to rely purely on disparate impact. Here is an example. The Houston Rockets, twice World Champions in the National Basketball Association, have had relatively few Anglos or Hispanics as starting players. As of the date of this book, their three best known starters (Olajuwon, Drexler and Barkley) are African-Americans, as are most members of the team, past and present. Does this disparity mean that the composition of the Houston Rockets is illegal? Of course not. Many observers would conclude that the team is an excellent example of meritocracy. Notice, however, that a focus on disparate impact alone would convert the Rockets, quite unfairly, into outlaws. A requirement of intent avoids this result. You will have to decide for yourself, however, whether intent is really the best standard. Is there a better alternative?

YICK WO v. HOPKINS, 118 U.S. 356 (1886). San Francisco ordinances gave the Board of Supervisors discretion to refuse consent to operate laundries, except in buildings of brick or stone. This policy was ostensibly maintained for fire prevention and other purposes. Yick Wo, a native of China, had operated a laundry in the same wooden building for twenty-two years and had satisfactory inspections by fire wardens, but he was denied permission by the supervisors to continue operations. He was convicted and fined ten dollars for violation of the ordinance. The record established that "there were about 320 laundries in the City and County of San Francisco, of which about 240 were owned and conducted by subjects of China, and of the whole number, viz., 320, about 310 were constructed of wood, the same material that constitutes nine-tenths of the houses in the city of San Francisco." The Board had given permits to all non-Chinese applicants but one, but it had refused them to all Chinese applicants. The Court, per Justice Matthews, reversed the conviction:

> [T]he facts shown establish an administration directed so exclusively against a particular class of persons as to warrant and require the conclusion that, whatever may have been the intent of the ordinances as adopted, they are applied by the public authorities charged with their administration, and thus representing the state itself, with a mind so unequal and oppressive as to amount to a practical denial by the state of that equal protection of thelaws which is secured to the petitioners, as to all other persons, by the broad and benign provisions of the fourteenth amendment to the Constitution of the United States. Though the law itself be fair on its face, and impartial in appearance, yet, if it is applied and administered by public authority with an evil eye and an unequal hand, so as practically to make unjust and illegal discriminations between persons in similar circumstances, material to their rights, the denial of equal justice is still within the prohibition of the Constitution. . . .

> The present cases, as shown by the facts disclosed in the record, are within this class. It appears that both petitioners have complied with every requisite deemed by the law, or by the public officers charged with its administration, necessary for the protection of neighboring property from fire, or as a precaution against injury to the public health. No reason whatsoever, except the will of the supervisors, is assigned why they should not be permitted to carry on.

> [T]he fact of this discrimination is admitted. No reason for it is shown, and the conclusion cannot be resisted that no reason for it exists except hostility to the race and nationality to which the petitioners belong, and which, in the eye of the law, is not justified. [T]he imprisonment of the petitioners is therefore

illegal, and they must be discharged. . . .

WASHINGTON v. DAVIS
426 U.S. 229 (1976)

Mr. Justice White delivered the opinion of the Court.

[Two black applicants sued because their applications to become District of Columbia police officers were rejected on the basis of recruiting procedures which included a written personnel test. They contended that the test bore no relationship to job *arg.* performance and excluded a disproportionately high number of black applicants. The district court noted the absence of any claim of intentional discrimination, but it found that (a) the number of black police officers was not proportionate to the city's *district ct findings* population mix; (b) a higher percentage of blacks failed the test than whites; and (c) the test had not been validated to establish its reliability as a job performance predictor. Nevertheless, the district court held against the rejected applicants, because forty-four *district ct holding* percent of new police recruits were black, the department had affirmatively solicited blacks, the test was useful in predicting training performance, and it was not designed to discriminate against otherwise qualified blacks.

[The court of appeals, however, reversed; it applied a test established in *Griggs v. Duke Power Co.*, 401 U.S. 424 (1971), which held that in actions under Title VII of the Civil Rights Act of 1964, the employer had the burden of demonstrating that testing procedures were substantially related to job performance.

[Here, the Court reverses the court of appeals and reinstates the district court's *PH* judgment in favor of the government.]   *HOLDING*

Because the Court of Appeals erroneously applied the legal standards applicable to Title VII cases in resolving the constitutional issue before it, we reverse its judgment in respondents' favor. . . .

As the Court of Appeals understood Title VII, employees or applicants proceeding under it need not concern themselves with the employer's possibly discriminatory purpose but instead may focus solely on the racially differential impact of the challenged hiring or promotion practices. This is not the constitutional rule. We have never held that the constitutional standard for adjudicating claims of invidious racial discrimination is identical to the standards applicable under Title VII, and we decline to do so today.

The central purpose of the Equal Protection Clause of the Fourteenth Amendment is the prevention of official conduct discriminating on the basis of race. . . . But our cases have not embraced the proposition that a law or other official act, without regard to whether it reflects a racially discriminatory purpose, is unconstitutional *solely* because it has racially disproportionate impact.

Almost 100 years ago, *Strauder v. West Virginia*, 100 U.S. 303 (1880), established that the exclusion of Negroes from grand and petit juries in criminal proceedings violated the Equal Protection Clause, but the fact that a particular jury or a series of juries does not statistically reflect the racial composition of the community does not in itself make out an invidious discrimination forbidden by the Clause. "A purpose to discriminate must be present which may be proven by systematic exclusion of eligible jurymen of the proscribed race or by unequal application of the law to such an extent as to show intentional discrimination. . . ."

The school desegregation cases have also adhered to the basic equal protection principle that the invidious quality of a law claimed to be racially discriminatory must ultimately be traced to a racially discriminatory purpose. That there are both predominantly black and predominantly white schools in a community is not alone violative of the Equal Protection Clause. The essential element of *de jure* segregation is "a current condition of segregation resulting from intentional state action. *Keyes v.*

School Dist. No. 1, 413 U.S. 189, 205 (1973). The differentiating factor between *de jure* segregation and so-called *de facto* segregation . . . is *purpose* or *intent* to segregate."

This is not to say that the necessary discriminatory racial purpose must be express or appear on the face of the statute, or that a law's disproportionate impact is irrelevant in cases involving Constitution-based claims of racial discrimination. A statute, otherwise neutral on its face, must not be applied so as invidiously to discriminate on the basis of race. *Yick Wo v. Hopkins*, 118 U.S. 356 (1886). It is also clear from the cases dealing with racial discrimination in the selection of juries that the systematic exclusion of Negroes is itself such an "unequal application of the law . . . as to show intentional discrimination. . . ."

[N]ecessarily, an invidious discriminatory purpose may often be inferred from the totality of the relevant facts, including the fact, if it is true, that the law bears more heavily on one race than another. It is also not infrequently true that the discriminatory impact—in the jury cases for example, the total or seriously disproportionate exclusion of Negroes from jury venires—may for all practical purposes demonstrate unconstitutionality because in various circumstances the discrimination is very difficult to explain on nonracial grounds. Nevertheless, we have not held that a law, neutral on its face and serving ends otherwise within the power of government to pursue, is invalid under the Equal Protection Clause simply because it may affect a greater proportion of one race than of another. Disproportionate impact is not irrelevant, but it is not the sole touchstone of an invidious racial discrimination forbidden by the Constitution. Standing alone, it does not trigger the rule that racial classifications are to be subjected to the strictest scrutiny and are justifiable only by the weightiest of considerations. . . .

As an initial matter, we have difficulty understanding how a law establishing a racially neutral qualification for employment is nevertheless racially discriminatory and denies "any person . . . equal protection of the laws" simply because a greater proportion of Negroes fail to qualify than members of other racial or ethnic groups. Had respondents, along with all others who had failed [the test], whether white or black, brought an action claiming that the test denied each of them equal protection of the laws as compared with those who had passed with high enough scores to qualify them as police recruits, it is most unlikely that their challenge would have been sustained. [The test,] which is administered generally to prospective Government employees, concededly seeks to ascertain whether those who take is have acquired a particular level of verbal skill; and it is untenable that the Constitution prevents the Government from seeking modestly to upgrade the communicative abilities of its employees rather than to be satisfied with some lower level of competence, particularly where the job requires special ability to communicate orally and in writing. Respondents, as Negroes, could no more successfully claim that the test denied them equal protection than could white applicants who also failed. . . .

A rule that a statute designed to serve neutral ends is nevertheless invalid, absent compelling justification, if in practice it benefits or burdens one race more than another would be far-reaching and would raise serious questions about, and perhaps invalidate, a whole range of tax, welfare, public service, regulatory, and licensing statutes that may be more burdensome to the poor and to the average black than to the more affluent white.

[Reversed.]

MR. JUSTICE STEVENS, concurring. . . .

Frequently the most probative evidence of intent will be objective evidence of what actually happened rather than evidence describing the subjective state of mind of the actor. For normally the actor is presumed to have intended the natural consequences of his deeds. This is particularly true in the case of governmental action which is frequently the product of compromise, of collective decisionmaking, and of mixed motivation. It is unrealistic, on the one hand, to require the victim of alleged discrimination to uncover the actual subjective intent of the decisionmaker or, conversely, to invalidate otherwise legitimate action simply because an improper motive affected the deliberation of a participant in the decisional process. A law conscripting clerics should not be invalidated because an atheist voted for it.

My point in making this observation is to suggest that the line between discriminatory purpose and discriminatory impact is not nearly as bright, and perhaps not quite as critical, as the reader of the Court's opinion might assume. I agree, of course, that a constitutional issue does not arise every time some disproportionate impact is shown. On the other hand, when the disproportion is as dramatic as in . . . *Yick Wo v. Hopkins*, 118 U.S. 356 (1886), it really does not matter whether the standard is phrased in terms of purpose or effect. Therefore, although I accept the statement of the general rule in the Court's opinion, I am not yet prepared to indicate how that standard should be applied in the many cases which have formulated the governing standard in different language. . . .

NOTES AND QUESTIONS

(1) *The Role of "Discriminatory Impact" or "Disproportionate Effects" in Equal Protection Analysis: Washington v. Davis, 426 U.S. 229 (1976).* African-American applicants to the District of Columbia's police force were rejected because of inadequate scores on a written personnel test. They claimed that the use of the test violated the equal protection doctrine. The challengers relied on several facts: African-Americans failed the test at four times the rate as Caucasian applicants; the disproportionally low percentage of black police officers compared to the city's population; and the test had not been "validated" (for purposes of a Title VII employment discrimination claim). The trial court found that there had not been any intentional discrimination. The challengers, nonetheless, proceeded on a disparate impact theory under *Griggs v. Duke Power Co.*, 401 U.S. 424 (1971). The Supreme Court, per Justice White, declined to utilize the *Griggs* model. The Court held that the Equal Protection Clause is violated only by purposeful (or "invidious") discrimination. The Court concluded that "the invidious quality of a law claimed to be racially discriminatory must ultimately be traced to a racially discriminatory purpose." Put another way, when the government practice is facially-neutral and generally applicable, disproportionate impact alone is not enough to violate equal protection. Hence, effects alone are not enough, even when a suspect class is disproportionately burdened.

It is important to recognize that the requirement to demonstrate purposefulness is different from a theory of government "pretext." Subsequent decisions, below, examined various aspects of the purposefulness requirement.

(2) *Disproportionate Impact: What Significance Should It Have?* Consider whether the disproportionate impact of a law or government action should be ground for finding an equal protection violation, notwithstanding the Court's reasoning. Should, perhaps, a "substantial" disproportion suffice? A "substantial and unjustified" dispro-portion [perhaps this is sufficient under the Court's decision, because it supplies circumstantial proof]? Should a showing of disproportionate impact shift the burden to the government to justify the impact by neutral factors? *Cf.* Maltz, *Expansion of the Role of the Effects Test in Antidiscrimination Law: A Critical Analysis*, 59 NEB. L. REV. 345 (1980).

(3) *Opinion Polls Tend to Show That Whites Would Prefer an Intent Test, Blacks an Effects Test—"Blacks, Whites Differ on Definition of Racism,"* HOUSTON CHRONICLE, June 8, 1992, § A, at 1, col. 5. On some questions related to racism, blacks and whites seem to have similar opinions. But this report showed that blacks and whites tended to disagree on the central question of the definition of racism.

Blacks, the report showed, tended to see racism as an ongoing and pervasive condition of American life, while whites tended to think of it as individual actions or attitudes of bigotry that were the exception rather than the rule. Thus, whites tended to use the word "racism" to refer to explicit and conscious belief in racial superiority, whereas blacks meant something different by racism: a set of practices and institutions that resulted in the oppression of black people.

Is it possible that these two views would lead to two different perspectives on disproportionate impact? The first view, held by the majority of whites, tends to justify a requirement that constitutional violations must be predicated on discriminatory intent. The second view, held by the majority of blacks, obviously would afford more determinative significance to disproportionate impact even when proof of intent is lacking.

(4) *What if Government Acts With Knowledge Of, But in Spite of, Adverse Impact on a Minority—But Acts Without the Purpose of Causing It? Personnel Administrator of Massachusetts v. Feeney, 442 U.S. 256 (1979).* Massachusetts gave an "absolute" lifetime hiring preference to veterans for state positions if they merely obtained a passing score on an employment test. More than 98 percent of veterans were men, and thus the preference "operate[ed] overwhelmingly to the advantage of males." Nevertheless, the Court, per Justice Stewart, upheld the Massachusetts law, primarily because it was enacted "in spite of, and not because of," the disparate impact. The law was facially neutral, because "[v]eteran status is not uniquely male." As the majority saw it, "the dispositive question . . . is whether the appellee has shown that a gender-based discriminatory purpose has, at least in some measure, shaped" the Massachusetts law. But all evidence pointed to the conclusion, and the district court found, that the law was not motivated by a purpose of discriminating against women. Justice Marshall, joined by Justice Brennan, dissented. Although *Feeney* is a gender discrimination case, its reasoning has been extended to cases of disparate racial impact as well. *See McCleskey v. Kemp, below.* Is *Feeney* correctly reasoned?

(5) *"Selective Prosecution" Claims and "Purposeful" Discrimination: United States v. Armstrong, 517 U.S. 456 (1996).* In *Armstrong*, the Court revisited the "purposefulness" requirement in the context of a "selective prosecution" issue. In a prosecution for conspiracy to distribute crack cocaine, the defendants sought discovery to help establish their claim that the federal prosecutors had singled out African-Americans for prosecution. Although the district court ordered the government to provide the defendants with information, the Supreme Court, per Chief Justice Rehnquist, reversed, holding that the defendants had not met the "demanding" burden that is a predicate to obtaining discovery in a selective prosecution claim. The Court treated a selective prosection claim under "ordinary equal protection standards," stating that the challenger must demonstrate that the government policy "had a discriminatory effect and that it was motivated by a discriminatory purpose." The Court then determined that the defendants had not shown that non-black, similarly-situated defendants were not prosecuted for crack cocaine possession and, thus, had failed to establish even the "discriminatory effect" element of a selective prosecution claim. Justice Stevens dissented, arguing that the defendants had made the requisite evidentiary showing. Note that a high standard traditionally has been imposed upon claims of selective prosecution, to prevent criminal defendants from routinely seeking voluminous discovery. (But is this kind of case different? See the problems below.)

VILLAGE OF ARLINGTON HEIGHTS v. METROPOLITAN HOUSING DE-VELOPMENT CORP., 429 U.S. 252 (1977). In this case, the Court announced the various factors to be considered in determining discriminatory purpose. The Metropolitan Housing Development Corporation (MHDC) was a nonprofit developer that contracted to purchase a tract to build racially integrated low-and-moderate income housing. To do so, it needed to have the village planning committee grant it a zoning change from a single family to a multiple-family classification. At public hearings, both supporters and opponents mentioned that the project would be racially integrated. Opponents also argued that the area traditionally had been single-family and that rezoning would violate the village's policy of using multiple-family classifications primarily as a buffer between single-family and commercial or industrial zones (of which there were none in the area).

When the commission denied rezoning, MHDC sued, alleging a violation of equal protection. The district court found that there was no discriminatory purpose, but that the village had acted to maintain its zoning plan and protect property values. The court of appeals reversed, holding that the "ultimate effect" of the rezoning denial was racially discriminatory. The Supreme Court, per Justice Powell, reversed and upheld the village's action:

> Our decision last term in *Washington v. Davis* . . . made it clear that official action will not be held unconstitutional solely because it results in a racially disproportionate impact. . . .
>
> *Davis* does not require plaintiff to prove that the challenged action rested solely on racially discriminatory purposes. Rarely can it be said that a legislature or administrative body operating under a broad mandate made a decision motivated solely by a single concern, or even that a particular purpose was the "dominant" or "primary" one. In fact, it is because legislators and administrators are properly concerned with balancing numerous competing considerations that courts refrain from reviewing the merits of their decisions, absent a showing of arbitrariness or irrationality. But racial discrimination is not just another competing consideration. When there is proof that a discriminatory purpose has been a motivating factor in the decision, this judicial deference is no longer justified.
>
> Determining whether invidious discriminatory purpose was a motivating factor demands a sensitive inquiry into such circumstantial and direct evidence of intent as may be available. The impact of the official action—whether it "bears more heavily on one race than another," *Washington v. Davis,*—may provide an important starting point. Sometimes a clear pattern, unexplainable on grounds other than race, emerges from the effect of the state action even when the governing legislation appears neutral on its face. *Yick Wo v. Hopkins.* [B]ut such cases are rare. . . .
>
> The historical background of the decision is one evidentiary source, particularly if it reveals a series of official actions taken for invidious purposes. [T]he specific sequence of events leading up to the challenged decision also may shed some light on the decisionmaker's purposes. [F]or example, if the property involved here always had been zoned [multiple-family] but suddenly was changed to [single-family] when the town learned of MHDC's plans to erect integrated housing, we would have a far different case. Departures from the normal procedural sequence also might afford evidence that improper purposes are playing a role. Substantive departures too may be relevant, particularly if the factors usually considered important by the decisionmakers strongly favor a decision contrary to the one reached.
>
> The legislative or administrative history may be highly relevant, especially where there are contemporary statements by members of the decisionmaking body, minutes of its meetings, or reports. In some extraordinary instances, the members might be called to the stand at trial to testify concerning the purpose of the official action, although even then such testimony frequently will be barred by privilege. . . .
>
> We . . . have reviewed the evidence. The impact of the village's decision does arguably bear more heavily on racial minorities. [B]ut there is little about the sequence of events leading up to the decision that would spark suspicion. [T]he village is undeniably committed to single-family homes as its dominant residential land use. The rezoning request progressed according to the usual procedures.

The statements by the planning commission and village board members, as reflected in the official minutes, focused almost exclusively on the zoning aspects if the MHDC petition, and the zoning factors on which they relied are not novel criteria in the village's rezoning decisions. . . . The village originally adopted its buffer policy long before MHDC entered the picture and has applied the policy too consistently for us to infer discriminatory purpose from its application in this case. Finally, MHDC called one member of the village board to the stand at trial. Nothing in her testimony supports an inference of invidious purpose.

[R]espondents simply failed to carry their burden of proving the discriminatory purpose was a motivating factor in the village's decision. This conclusion ends the constitutional inquiry.

NOTES AND QUESTIONS

(1) *The "Motivating Factor" Test. Arlington Heights* makes clear the Court's holding that the racially discriminatory purpose need not be sole motivation of the action in order to trigger an equal protection violation, but it must be significant enough to be called a "motivating" factor. If there are two purposes, one invidious and one not, the second will not salvage the government's action unless the improper purpose is insubstantial. But note the interpretive difficulties that this standard may create. If one of five council members is motivated in part by a racially discriminatory purpose, is that purpose a "motivating factor" in the decision?

(2) *Legislative History Containing Racially Discriminatory Remarks May Invalidate a Statute That Otherwise Would Be Upheld: Hunter v. Underwood, 471 U.S. 222 (1985).* In *Hunter*, blacks and whites who were disenfranchised by an Alabama constitutional provision denying the vote to persons convicted of "any crime . . . involving moral turpitude" alleged that it denied them equal protection. The Court, per Justice Rehnquist, unanimously struck down the Alabama provision. It noted that the evidence of legislative intent in the record included the proceedings of the Constitutional Convention at which the Alabama provision was adopted, several historical studies, and the testimony of two expert historians. The evidence demonstrated "conclusively that [the provision] was enacted with the intent of disenfranchising blacks," so strongly, in fact, that counsel for Alabama conceded at oral argument that "I would be very blind and naive [to] try to come up and stand before this Court and say that race was not a factor in the enactment of [the provision]." The Court reasoned that other, legitimate purposes could not salvage this provision:

> At oral argument in this Court, the state suggested that, regardless of the original purpose of [the provision], events occurring in the succeeding eighty years had legitimated the provision. [W]ithout deciding whether [the Alabama provision] would be valid if enacted today without any impermissible motivation, we simply observe that its original enactment was motivated by desire to discriminate against blacks on account of race and the section continues to this day to have that effect. As such, it violates equal protection under *Arlington Heights*.

(3) *The Court Reaffirms the Arlington Heights Standard for Purposefulness: City of Cuyahoga Falls v. Buckeye Community Hope Foundation, 538 U.S. 188 (2003).* In the *Cuyahoga Falls* decision, the plaintiffs had applied for a permit to build low income housing in 1996. When some citizens filed a formal petition opposing the project, the city officials submitted the zoning issue to a voter referendum as required by the city charter. Soon thereafter, the city engineer denied plaintiffs' permits pending the outcome of the vote. The voters turned down the zoning reclassification, but the Ohio Supreme Court declared the referendum invalid in a 1998 decision and the city subsequently issued the permit. The plaintiffs sued in federal court, claiming that the city's *process* (specifically the use of the voter referendum procedure and the denial of the permits) had violated their equal protection rights.

The Court, per Justice O'Connor, decided that the plaintiffs had not satisfied the purposefulness standard of *Arlington Heights* and *Washington v. Davis*. The Court first held that the "proof of racially discriminatory intent or purpose is required" to demonstrate a violation of equal protection. The Court reasoned that, since here the attack was on the referendum petitioning process and not on the results of the referendum, the plaintiffs had not produced appropriate evidence that the *process* was racially motivated. This decision reaffirmed the purposefulness or invidiousness requirement for a successful equal protection claim.

The *Cuyahoga Falls* decision also confirmed the type of *evidence* that may be used to demonstrate discriminatory purpose. *See generally* IAN AYERS, PERVASIVE PREJUDICE (2000). To the extent that there may be a question about the admissibility of testimony by decision-makers, the Court stated that: "Again, statements made by decision makers or referendum sponsors during deliberation over a referendum may constitute relevant evidence of discriminatory intent in a challenge to an ultimately enacted initiative." Regarding the purposefulness requirement and its relation to "disparate impact" analysis, *see* Richard A. Primus, *Equal Protection and Disparate Impact: Round Three*, 117 HARV. L. REV. 494 (2003).

PROBLEM D

WEST YORK'S HYPOTHETICAL SICKLE-CELL ANEMIA PROGRAM. As a practical matter, the disease known as sickle-cell anemia affects only black persons. Its incidence among whites is negligible. Assume that the hypothetical state of West York undertakes a program to treat sickle-cell anemia. Its officials know that the program will result in the use of public funds collected from persons of all races to address a problem confined to a single race.

Is West York's sickle-cell anemia program constitutional? [You should consider, first, what test is applicable, and second, whether its requirements are met.] Would it make any difference if the funding of the sickle-cell program demonstrably resulted from curtailment of programs to combat other diseases shared by the population more generally, or diseases (*e.g.*, Tay-Sachs disease) disproportionately affecting non-black ethnic groups? Finally, what if the sponsor of the legislation announced an intent to "do something for African-American people?"

PROBLEM E

DO STIFFER PENALTIES FOR CRACK THAN FOR POWDERED COCAINE AMOUNT TO UNCONSTITUTIONAL RACIAL DISCRIMINATION? STATE v. RUSSELL, 477 N.W.2d 886 (Minn. 1991). Minnesota adopted sentencing laws whereby possession of three grams of crack cocaine could lead to a sentence of up to 20 years, while possession of an equal amount of powdered cocaine could lead to a maximum of only five years. The Minnesota Supreme Court accepted evidence tending to show that the use of crack was primarily by African-Americans (96.6 percent of those charged in the county with possession of crack in 1988 were black, while 79.6 percent charged with powder possession were white), and it concluded that little hard evidence supported a distinction between crack and powdered cocaine. (The evidence included police officers who testified from "street" experience that this quantity indicated drug dealing with crack but not with powder, and a chemist testified that there was evidence that crack, which is smoked rather than sniffed, is more associated with violence; but the court accepted contrary evidence on both points).

Question: On these facts, what should be the standard of review, strict scrutiny or rational basis? Should proof of intent to discriminate be required before strict scrutiny is invoked in this situation, and if so, is sufficient proof present here? [The Minnesota Court held that the crack law might trigger strict scrutiny, implying that the statistics showed that it was adopted because of rather than in spite of race; but it went on to hold that the law failed even the rational basis test under the state constitution. A dissenting opinion criticized what it called the "activist" majority for having "assumed" that the two forms of cocaine were identical when experts disagreed on that issue. Furthermore, the statistics were drawn from a sample of only 60 defendants in a single county, and the dissent concluded that the record was "barren" of evidence of discriminatory intent.]

Updating the Cocaine-and-Race Problem: The Federal Crack-Powder Differential. Federal law now provides a penalty differential such that it takes 100 times as much powder as crack cocaine for the same sentence to apply. The United States Sentencing Commission has proposed an amendment, for possible adoption by Congress, that would equalize the two. Attorney General Janet Reno, with backing of federal prosecutors, had vigorously opposed this change, on the ground that crack is more addictive, more associated with violence and more destructive for "the most vulnerable members of society." Question: Even if the impact of sentences is disparately harsh on African-Americans, does the inference of racism disappear when one considers the fact that victims of crack violence are also disproportionately African-American? ABA J., July, 1995, at 30. *See also United States v. Armstrong, above* (rejecting claim of selective prosecution).

(4) *Disproportionate Impact as Requiring an Immediate Neutral Explanation: Batson v. Kentucky, below.* Consider the following decision, which requires contemporaneous objection based upon statistical impact and allows contemporaneous explanation of nondiscriminatory purpose.

BATSON v. KENTUCKY
476 U.S. 79 (1986)

JUSTICE POWELL delivered the opinion of the Court.

[The prosecutor at Batson's trial used peremptory challenges to strike all four black persons on the venire. An all-white jury convicted Batson. Defense counsel moved to discharge the jury before it was sworn, alleging a denial of equal protection, but the trial judge observed that the parties were entitled to "strike anybody they want to." This conclusion, indeed, was supported by the Supreme Court's previous decision in *Swain v. Alabama*, 380 U.S. 202 (1965), which had held that disproportionate use of strikes in an individual case did not give rise to an equal protection violation; it was only if the prosecutor followed this pattern "in case after case, whatever the circumstances," that proof of discriminatory purpose could be adequate. Here, the Supreme Court modifies the rule of *Swain* and remands for further inquiry into the issue of discriminatory purpose.]

The standards for assessing a prima facie case in the context of discriminatory selection of the venire have been fully articulated since *Swain. See Washington v. Davis.* These principles support our conclusion that a defendant may establish a prima facie case of purposeful discrimination in selection of the petit jury solely on evidence concerning the prosecutor's exercise of peremptory challenges at the defendant's trial. To establish such a case, the defendant first must show that he is a member of a cognizable racial group, and that the prosecutor has exercised peremptory challenges to remove from the venire members of the defendant's race. Second, the defendant is entitled to rely on the fact, as to which there can be no dispute, that peremptory challenges constitute a jury selection practice that permits "those to discriminate who are of a mind to discriminate." Finally, the defendant must show that these facts and any other relevant circumstances raise an inference that the prosecutor used that practice to exclude the veniremen from the petit jury on account of their race. This combination of factors in the empanelling of the petit jury, as in the selection of the venire, raises the necessary inference of purposeful discrimination.

In deciding whether the defendant has made the requisite showing, the trial court should consider all relevant circumstances. For example, a "pattern" of strikes against black jurors included in the particular venire might give rise to an inference of discrimination. Similarly, the prosecutor's questions and statements during *voir dire* examination and in exercising his challenges may support or refute an inference of discriminatory purpose. These examples are merely illustrative. . . .

Once the defendant makes a prima facie showing, the burden shifts to the State to come forward with a neutral explanation for challenging black jurors. Though this requirement imposes a limitation in some cases on the full peremptory character of the historic challenge, we emphasize that the prosecutor's explanation need not rise to the level justifying exercise of a challenge for cause. But the prosecutor may not rebut the defendant's prima facie case of discrimination by stating merely that he challenged jurors of the defendant's race on the assumption—or his intuitive judgment—that they would be partial to the defendant because of their shared race. . . . Nor may the prosecutor rebut the defendant's case merely by denying that he had discriminatory motive or "affirming his good faith in individual selections." If these general assertions were accepted as rebutting a defendant's prima facie case, the Equal Protection Clause "would be but a vain and illusory requirement." The prosecutor therefore must articulate a neutral explanation related to the particular case to be tried. The trial court then will have the duty to determine if the defendant has established purposeful discrimination.

The State contends that our holding will eviscerate the fair trial values served by the peremptory challenge. . . .

While we recognize, of course, that the peremptory challenge occupies an important position in our trial procedures, we do not agree that our decision today will undermine the contribution the challenge generally makes to the administration of justice. The reality of practice, amply reflected in many state and federal court opinions, shows that the challenge may be, and unfortunately at times has been, used to discriminate against black jurors. [P]ublic respect for our criminal justice system and the rule of law will be strengthened if we ensure that no citizen is disqualified from jury service because of his race.

Nor are we persuaded by the State's suggestion that our holding will create serious administrative difficulties. In those states applying a version of the evidentiary standard we recognize today, courts have not experienced serious administrative burdens, and the peremptory challenge system has survived. . . .

In this case, petitioner made a timely objection to the prosecutor's removal of all black persons on the venire. Because the trial court flatly rejected the objection without requiring the prosecutor to give an explanation for his action, we remand this case for further proceedings. If the trial court decides that the facts establish, prima facie, purposeful discrimination and the prosecutor does not come forward with a neutral explanation for his action, our precedents require that the petitioner's conviction be reversed.

It is so ordered.

[The concurring opinions of Justices White, Marshall, Stevens, and O'Connor are omitted.]

Chief Justice Burger, joined by Justice Rehnquist, dissenting. . . .

[T]he peremptory challenge has been in use without scrutiny into its basis for nearly as long as juries have existed. It was in use among the Romans in criminal cases. . . .

[T]he Court's opinion, in addition to ignoring the teachings of history, also contrast with *Swain* in its failure to even discuss the rationale of the peremptory challenge. *Swain* observed:

The function of the challenge is not only to eliminate extremes of partiality on both sides, but to assure the parties that the jurors before whom they try the case will decide on the basis of the evidence placed for them and not otherwise. In this way the peremptory satisfies the rule that "to perform its high function in the best way, justice must satisfy the appearance of justice. . . ."

Permitting unexplained peremptories has long been regarded as a means to strengthen our jury system in other ways as well. One commentator has recognized:

The peremptory, made without giving any reason, avoids trafficking in the core of truth in most common stereotypes. [C]ommon human experience, common sense, psychological studies, and public opinion polls tell us that it is likely that certain classes of people statistically have predispositions that would make them inappropriate jurors for particular kinds of cases. But to allow this knowledge to be expressed in the evaluative terms necessary for challenges for cause would undercut our desire for a society in which all people are judged as individuals and in which each is held reasonable and open to compromise. [For example,] [a]lthough experience reveals that black males as a class can be biased against young alienated blacks who have not tried to join the middle class, to enunciate this in the concrete expression required of a challenge for cause is societally divisive. Instead, we have evolved in the peremptory challenge a system that allows the covert expression of what we dare not say but know is true more often than not. Babcock, *Voir Dire: Preserving "Its Wonderful Power,"* 27 Stan. L. Rev. 545, 553–554 (1975).

[That] the Court is not applying conventional equal protection analysis as shown by its limitation of its new rule to allegations of impermissible challenge *on the basis of race.* . . .

In short, it is quite probable that every peremptory challenge could be objected to on the basis that, because it excluded a venireman who had some characteristic not shared by the remaining members of the venire, it constituted a "classification" subject to equal protection scrutiny.

NOTES AND QUESTIONS

(1) *Unavoidable Racial Disparity in Criminal Justice Administration: McCleskey v. Kemp, 481 U.S. 279 (1987).* McCleskey was convicted of robbery-murder and sentenced to death. He presented a study sponsored by Iowa law professor David Baldus purporting to show that black defendants who killed white victims, as did McCleskey, have the greatest likelihood of receiving the death penalty. One of Baldus' models concluded that, even after taking account of thirty-nine nonracial variables, defendants charged with killing white victims were 4.3 times as likely to receive death sentences as defendants charged with killing blacks. The Court, per Justice Powell, refused to invalidate Georgia's death sentencing procedure on the basis of this study:

McCleskey . . . suggests that the Baldus study proves that the state as a whole has acted with a discriminatory purpose. He appears to argue that the state has violated the equal protection clause by adopting the capital punishment statute and allowing it to remain in force despite its allegedly discriminatory application. But " '[d]iscriminatory purpose'. . . implies more than intent as volition or intent as awareness of consequences. It implies that the decisionmaker, in this case a state legislature, selected or reaffirmed a particular course of action at least in part 'because of,' not merely 'in spite of,' its adverse effects upon an identifiable group." *Personnel Administrator of Massachusetts v. Feeney.*

[T]here [is] no evidence . . . that the Georgia legislature enacted the capital punishment statute to further a racially discriminatory purpose. . . .

Is this reasoning persuasive? Is it consistent with *Batson v. Kentucky*?

(2) *An Example of Peremptory Challenges with Explainable Differential Impact That Is Not Unconstitutional: Hernandez v. New York, 500 U.S. 352 (1991).* Defendant Hernandez raised a *Batson* challenge to the prosecutor's exclusion of two Latino venirepersons. The prosecutor explained first, that he was not certain even whether the two questioned jurors were Hispanics; second, he was "very uncertain that they would be able to listen and follow the interpreter," because they spoke Spanish. The prosecutor added that he had no reason to want to exclude Hispanics because "[e]ach of the complainants is a Hispanic." The plurality of the Supreme Court, per Justice Kennedy, affirmed the conviction. "[E]ven if we knew that a high percentage of bilingual jurors would hesitate in answering questions like these and, as a consequence, would be excluded under the prosecutor's criterion, that fact alone would not cause the criterion to fail the race neutrality test." This was so because "disparate impact should be given appropriate weight in determining whether the prosecutor acted with a forbidden intent, but it will not be conclusive in the preliminary race neutrality step of the *Batson* inquiry."

(3) *Extending Batson to Civil Litigants: Edmonson v. Leesville Concrete Co., 500 U.S. 614 (1991).* In this case, the Supreme Court, per Justice Kennedy, extended the *Batson* holding to all civil litigants. Although civil litigants normally are private, the Court attributed their action to the state, because "[t]he injury to excluded jurors would be the direct result of government delegation and participation [in the peremptory challenges]." (This state action issue is explored in depth in chapter 13, below, and was the more difficult issue in the case.)

(4) *Batson Also Applies to Criminal Defense Lawyers: Georgia v. McCollum, 505 U.S. 42 (1992).* In this case the Court, per Justice Blackmun, extended the *Batson* holding to criminal defendants. The Court reasoned: "Be it at the hands of the state or the defense, if a court allows jurors to be excluded because of group bias, it is a willing participant in a scheme that could undermine the very foundation of our system of justice—our citizens' confidence in it." [The case is further analyzed in ch. 13, below, concerning State Action vs. Private Action.]

(5) *Gender (J.E.B. v. Alabama, below) and Other Criteria Such as Religion, Social Class, Sexual Preference, Wealth, Education, etc.: How Far Will Batson be Extended?* As we shall see below, the Supreme Court has extended this principle to prohibit gender-based peremptories. But extending it to other criteria might destroy the viability of peremptory challenges. Some lower courts, for example, have refused to prohibit challenges based on religion, which arguably is defined by certain shared values and therefore may be more closely related to legitimate purposes of peremptory challenges.

[4] Equitable Remedies For Segregation in the Schools

BROWN v. BOARD OF EDUCATION ("BROWN II")
349 U.S. 294 (1955)

MR. CHIEF JUSTICE WARREN delivered the opinion of the Court.

[The Court's previous decision in this case, *Brown I*, appears earlier in this chapter. There, the Court overruled the separate but equal doctrine of *Plessy v. Ferguson.* Here, the Court considers what remedies should be ordered for unconstitutional school segregation.]

Full implementation of these constitutional principles may require a solution of varied local school problems. School authorities have the primary responsibility for elucidating, assessing, and solving these problems; courts will have to consider whether the action of school authorities constitutes good faith implementation of the governing constitutional principles. Because of their proximity to local conditions and the possible need for further hearings, the courts which originally heard these cases can best perform this judicial appraisal. Accordingly, we believe it appropriate to remand the cases to those courts.

In fashioning and effectuating the decrees, the court will be guided by equitable principles. Traditionally, equity has been characterized by a practical flexibility in shaping its remedies and by a facility for adjusting and reconciling public and private needs. [A]t stake is the personal interest of the plaintiffs in admissions to public schools as soon as practicable on a nondiscriminatory basis. To effectuate this interest may call for elimination of a variety of obstacles. [C]ourts of equity may properly take into account the public interest in the elimination of such obstacles in a systematic and effective manner. But is should go without saying that the vitality of these constitutional principles cannot be allowed to yield simply because of disagreement with them.

[T]he courts will require that the defendants make a prompt and reasonable start toward full compliance. [O]nce such a start has been made, the courts may find that additional time is necessary to carry out the ruling in an effective manner. The burden rests upon the defendants to establish that such time is necessary in the public interest and is consistent with good faith compliance at the earliest practicable date. To that end, the courts may consider problems related to administration, arising from the physical condition of the school plant, the school transportation system, personnel, revision of school districts and attendance areas into compact units to achieve a system of determining admission to the public schools on a nonracial basis, and revision of local laws and regulations which may be necessary in solving the foregoing problems. They will also consider the adequacy of any plans the defendants may propose to meet these problems and to effectuate a transition to a racially nondiscriminatory school system. During this period of transition, the courts will retain jurisdiction of these cases.

[The district courts shall] take such proceedings and enter such orders and decrees consistent with this opinion as are necessary and proper to admit to public schools on a racially nondiscriminatory basis with all deliberate speed the parties to these cases.

L. GRAGLIA, DISASTER BY DECREE: THE SUPREME COURT DECISIONS ON RACE AND THE SCHOOLS
33–45 (1976).*

The limited, almost tentative, approach of the Court to its decision invalidating school segregation is best illustrated by the fact that the Court failed to grant effective relief, even with regard to the nominal plaintiffs, individual black school children. If racial discrimination in the assignment of pupils to schools is unconstitutional, the remedy seems obvious and simple: assignment not based on race. . . . Although a year had already elapsed since *Brown I*, the Court required, not full compliance with that decision, but only "a prompt and reasonable start toward full compliance. . . ."

There was, however, little reason for this unprecedented allowance of delay except anticipated disagreement and resistance. . . . That the problems the district courts were authorized to consider did not usually require still more time was evident from the effective steps to end segregation quickly taken by the border states and the District of Columbia. "By the opening of the [1955] fall term in the following year only eight states remained completely segregated in their system of public schools; and more than a quarter of a million Negro children were attending desegregated schools in states which had the year before *required* segregation. . . ."

The assignment of children on a nonracial basis to their neighborhood schools is not usually an exceptionally difficult or time-consuming process. . . . The reasons for delay cited by the Court are not impressive. . . .

The Court's refusal to grant relief, even to the parties before it, was unfortunate for several reasons. First, it was likely to be interpreted—and it was—as vacillation, as uncertainty on the part of the Court that its new law would prevail. The refusal seemed to promise, despite the Court's disclaimer, that opposition would prove successful in achieving at least a more lengthy delay. . . . If a bitter pill is to be swallowed, it is probably better to require that it be swallowed at once. . . . The appearance of confidence and finality, even when the reality is lacking, can breed respect and acceptance.

Second, leaving the question of relief to the district courts with an explicit authorization of delay depending on "good faith" and "the public interest" put those courts in an untenable position. [T]he relevant local condition in this context was the intensity of the opposition to ending segregation. The only defense a local judge could have had for ending segregation was the clear and irresistible mandate of higher authority, and that mandate the Court did not provide.

[Third, the] Court's refusal to grant plaintiffs individual relief . . . in effect utilized the very classification by race it began by condemning. The most charitable interpretation is that the Court chose to ignore the interests of the individual blacks before it in favor of a supposed interest of racial groups—an approach that, as in *Plessy*, has been a major source of injustice to blacks throughout our history. . . .

By far the most unfortunate consequence of the Court's refusal to decree relief, however, was that it enormously complicated and confused the issues. Instead of a relatively simple requirement of "immediate" assignment to schools without regard to race, the Court introduced the ultimate complexities and uncertainties of an inquiry into "good faith" and "the public interest." In place of nonracial assignment, the requirement became the production of a "desegregation plan." . . . This issue—the acceptability of different desegregation plans was to be litigated for more than a decade. Under cover of the resulting confusion and delay, the original prohibition of segregation was metamorphosed into a requirement of integration. . . . That this drastic change had been made was never openly admitted and, therefore, did not have to be justified. . . .

For a decade after *Brown*, the most remarkable thing about the Supreme Court's action with respect to school segregation is that it acted so little. Having declared the war, it largely withdrew from the battle. . . .

[Here, Professor Graglia summarizes the early decisions after *Brown II*.]

The definitive answer to the question of delay came with the Court's pronouncement in 1969, in *Alexander v. Holmes County Board of Education*, that "every school district is to terminate dual school systems at once and to operate now and hereafter only unitary schools."

Thus the answer was finally given to what should have never been in question; present compliance with *Brown I* would be required. . . . But the question was answered too late for a return to the apparent simplicity of the *Brown I* requirement. By this time the federal courts at all levels had become long-accustomed to formulating and supervising methods of school assignment and to prodding school boards to ever more vigorous efforts. The courts' exertions had gained not only acceptance but endorsement and applause; the moral superiority of the judicial to the political process came to be widely recognized. . . . Moreover, the results of compliance with *Brown*, it soon became obvious, would be, for those who had endured the struggle, far from thoroughly satisfying: schools largely black and largely white would continue to exist in the South, as in the North. . . .

NOTES AND QUESTIONS

(1) *Should the Court Have Expressly Invoked the Aid of the Legislature to Remedy School Segregation? Should It Have Waited for Legislative Action?* The Civil Rights Act of 1964 resulted in desegregation of public accommodations, with a high level of

compliance, in a relatively short period of time. The moral authority, democratic force, investigative abilities, and flexibility of solutions that Congress could have brought to bear might have been superior to that of the Court. For example, Congress could use the spending power to encourage school desegregation. Would Congress have acted if the Court had not done so? (It did so during the Civil Rights Acts of the 1960s; those, however, came a decade after *Brown* and no doubt were encouraged by the moral force of that decision.) For a view that differs from Graglia's *see* Days, *School Desegregation Law in the 1980s: Why Isn't Anybody Laughing?*, 95 YALE L.J. 1737 (1986), *reviewing* P. DIMOND, BEYOND BUSING: INSIDE THE CHALLENGE TO URBAN SEGREGATION (1985) (discussing, among other issues, arguments that segregation in housing patterns would have resulted in segregation after assignment to neighborhood schools).

(2) *Should the Court Simply Have Ordered Desegregation, Now?* On the other hand, perhaps it persuasively can be argued that the Supreme Court, rather than calling for "all deliberate speed" and providing latitude for additional time, should simply have required the district courts to order local authorities to begin operating unitary (or at least neighborhood) schools during the very next term. *Cf.* L. Graglia, *Disaster by Decree: The Supreme Court's Decisions on Race and the Schools*, above. Would this solution have been preferable? [Notice that the Court ultimately came to the position, years later, of requiring prompt compliance. *See Green v. County School Board, below.*] *Cf.* Monaghan, *Law and the Negro Revolution: Ten Years After*, 44 B.U. L. REV. 467 (1964); Taylor, *Brown, Equal Protection and The Isolation of the Poor*, 95 YALE L.J. 1700 (1986).

(3) *"Freedom of Choice," Grade-by-Grade Plans, and Delays.* So-called freedom-of-choice plans allowed free transfers by students. In *Goss v. Board of Education*, 373 U.S. 683 (1963), the Court held that minority-to-majority transfers could not be permitted under such a plan because, obviously, they tended to perpetuate segregation. In *Rogers v. Paul*, 382 U.S. 198 (1965), the school district had adopted a grade-a-year plan, which meant that upper grades remained segregated by law; the Court reversed a lower court decision rejecting a challenge to this plan and indicated that delays no longer were tolerable. Perhaps the most dramatic single confrontation was in *Cooper v. Aaron*, 358 U.S. 1 (1958), which is reproduced in ch. 1 in the section on judicial review. The Court denied the City of Little Rock any additional time to comply with district court rulings and headed the opinion with all nine Justices' names to emphasize its unanimous judgment. Finally, in *Griffin v. County School Board*, 377 U.S. 218 (1964), the Court found itself required to hold that the closing of the public schools wholesale in a given county was a denial of equal protection to black students.

(4) *Requiring Compliance "Now."* Ultimately, the Court ordered denial of all motions for additional time and emphasized that the obligation of school districts was to terminate dual systems "now." Consider the following decision, which is indicative of the Court's frustration thirteen years after *Brown II*.

GREEN v. COUNTY SCHOOL BOARD, 391 U.S. 430 (1968). After remaining segregated until 1964, the New Kent County school board adopted a freedom-of-choice plan. The district court found that "the school board operates one white combined elementary and high school and one negro combined elementary and high school. There are no attendance zones. Each school serves the entire county." The Court, per Justice Brennan, required more immediate and drastic action:

> The pattern of separate "white" and "negro" schools in the New Kent County school system established under compulsion of state laws is precisely the pattern of segregation to which *Brown I* and *Brown II* were particularly addressed. . . .

> It is against this background that thirteen years after *Brown II* commanded the abolition of dual systems we must measure the effectiveness of respondent school board's "freedom-of-choice" plan to achieve that end. The school board contends that it has fully discharged its obligation by adopting a plan by which

every student, regardless of race, may "freely"choose the school he will attend. [B]ut that argument ignores the thrust of *Brown II*. [B] *rown II* was a call for the dismantling of well-entrenched dual systems. . . .

In determining whether respondent school board met that command by adopting its freedom-of-choice plan, it is relevant that this first step did not come until some eleven years after *Brown I* was decided and ten years after *Brown II* directed the making of a "prompt and reasonable start." [S]uch delays are no longer tolerable. [M]oreover, a plan that at this late date fails to provide meaningful assurance of prompt and effective disestablishment of a dual system is also intolerable. "The time for mere 'deliberate speed' has run out." [T]he burden on a school board today is to come forward with a plan that promises realistically to work, and promises realistically to work *now*. . . .

SWANN v. CHARLOTTE-MECKLENBURG BOARD OF EDUCATION
402 U.S. 1 (1971)

Mr. Chief Justice Burger delivered the opinion of the Court.

[In the late 1960s, the Charlotte-Mecklenburg school district remained heavily segregated. In response to court orders after numerous hearings, the school board submitted a plan calling for closing of some schools, pairing others (*i.e.*, combining pairs of schools into single units), and clustering still others (*i.e.*, combining multiple schools). The court rejected the plan and instead adopted a plan submitted by an appointed expert, John Finger (the Finger Plan), which called for "satellite" or non-contiguous zones and which required considerably more busing.

[The court of appeals reversed. On remand, the district court rejected a plan prepared by the Department of Health, Education and Welfare involving contiguous zoning and ordered the school district to accept the Finger Plan, or a plan earlier prepared by a minority of the board, or an earlier draft of the Finger Plan. The board chose the Finger Plan but appealed the district court's order. Here, a unanimous Court affirms the district court.]

The central issue in this case is that of student assignment, and there are essentially four problem areas:

> (1) to what extent racial balance or racial quotas may be used as an implement in a remedial order to correct a previously segregated system;

> (2) whether every all-Negro and all-white school must be eliminated as an indispensable part of a remedial process of desegregation;

> (3) what the limits are, if any, on the rearrangement of school districts and attendance zones, as a remedial measure; and

> (4) what the limits are, if any, on the use of transportation facilities to correct state-enforced racial school segregation.

(1) Racial Balances or Racial Quotas.

The constant theme and thrust of every holding from *Brown I* to date is that state-enforced separation of races in public schools is discrimination that violates the Equal Protection Clause. The remedy commanded was to dismantle dual school systems.

In this case it is urged that the District Court has imposed a racial balance requirement of 71%-29% on individual schools.

The District Judge went on to acknowledge that variation "from that norm may be unavoidable." This contains intimations that the "norm" is a fixed mathematical racial balance reflecting the pupil constituency of the system. If we were to read the holding of the District Court to require, as a matter of substantive constitutional right, any particular degree of racial balance or mixing, that approach would be disapproved and we would be obliged to reverse. The constitutional command to desegregate schools does not mean that every school in every community must always reflect the racial composition of the school system as a whole. . . .

We see therefore that the use made of mathematical ratios was no more than a starting point in the process of shaping a remedy, rather than an inflexible requirement. . . . In sum, the very limited use made of mathematical ratios was within the equitable remedial discretion of the District Court.

(2) *One-race Schools.*

The record in this case reveals the familiar phenomenon that in metropolitan areas minority groups are often found concentrated in one part of the city. . . .

[T]he existence of some small number of one-race, or virtually one-race, schools within a district is not in and of itself the mark of a system that still practices segregation by law. . . .

Where the school authority's proposed plan for conversion from a dual to a unitary system contemplates the continued existence of some schools that are all or predominately of one race, they have the burden of showing that such school assignments are genuinely nondiscriminatory. The court should scrutinize such schools, and the burden upon the school authorities will be to satisfy the court that their racial composition is not the result of present or past discriminatory action on their part.

An optional majority-to-minority transfer provision has long been recognized as a useful part of every desegregation plan. [T]he court orders in this and the companion *Davis* case now provide such an option.

(3) *Remedial Altering of Attendance Zones*

The maps submitted in these cases graphically demonstrate that one of the principal tools employed by school planners and by courts to break up the dual school system has been a frank and sometimes drastic gerrymandering of school districts and attendance zones. . . . More often than not, these zones are neither compact nor contiguous; indeed they may be on opposite ends of the city. As an interim corrective measure, this cannot be said to be beyond the broad remedial powers of a court.

Absent a constitutional violation there would be no basis for judicially ordering assignment of students on a racial basis. All things being equal, with no history of discrimination, it might well be desirable to assign pupils to schools nearest their homes. . . . The remedy for such segregation may be administratively awkward, inconvenient, and even bizarre in some situations and may impose burdens on some; but all awkwardness and inconvenience cannot be avoided in the interim period when remedial adjustments are being made to eliminate the dual school systems. . . .

(4) *Transportation of Students*

[B]us transportation has been an integral part of the public education system for years, and was perhaps the single most important factor in the transition from the one-room schoolhouse to the consolidated school. Eighteen million of the Nation's public school children, approximately 39%, were transported to their schools by bus in 1969–1970 in all parts of the country.

[T]he District Court's conclusion that assignment of children to the school nearest their home serving their grade would not produce an effective dismantling of the dual system is supported by the record.

Thus the remedial techniques used in the District Court's order were within that court's power to provide equitable relief; implementation of the decree is well within the capacity of the school authority.

[T]he trips for elementary school pupils average about seven miles and the District Court found that they would take "not over 35 minutes at the most." This system compares favorably with the transportation plan previously operated in Charlotte under which each day 23,600 students on all grade levels were transported an average of 15 miles one way for an average trip requiring over an hour. [D]esegregation plans cannot be limited to the walk-in school.

NOTES AND QUESTIONS

(1) *Equitable and Constitutional Limits to Non-Contiguous Zone and Busing.* The *Charlotte-Mecklenburg* decree obviously contemplated busing black children long distances to attend majority-white schools. If a black child is bused forty-five minutes per day each way to attend a school that white children attend in their neighborhood, has the black child been afforded equal protection of the laws? [Doctrinally, perhaps the result can be defended on the theory that it does not reflect purposeful discrimination against the black child but only the disparate impact of a systemwide plan, or, in other words, on the theory that the impact results "in spite of" and not "because of" the state's conduct, per *Feeney* and *McCleskey*, above. Is this argument persuasive?]

(2) *Individual Rights or Group ("Class") Rights?* The question posed in note (1) opens a deeper inquiry. Is the concern of the Equal Protection Clause that each *individual* shall be treated with equality before the law, or that major *classes* of people shall be treated without class discrimination? If the concern is with remedying discrimination against a group or class, adverse impacts upon individuals within the class may be the unavoidable result, as the question in note (1) indicates. Which model—that of individual or group—most accurately reflects the purpose of the equal protection clause? [Is it possible to make a synthesis? Perhaps elimination of group or class discrimination can be carried out so long as it does not have excessive effects on individuals. Perhaps it can be argued that desegregation is a value that is likely to enhance the interests of all individuals and, therefore, although equal treatment of individuals is a primary focus of the Equal Protection Clause, it cannot be achieved without recognition of group rights. Are these conceptions valid?]

(3) *Privately Created Segregation: White Flight, Resegregation, and Housing Patterns.* The Court in *Swann*, in a separate passage, also recognized that communities "will [not] remain demographically stable," and school authorities are not required to "make year-by-year adjustments." Further, the school board's duty is only to remedy purposeful segregation: "In the absence of a showing that either the school authorities or some other agency of the state has deliberately attempted to fix or alter demographic patterns to affect the racial compositions of the schools, further intervention by a district court should not be necessary." Consider, in this light, whether a school district has any obligation to (or indeed whether it even is constitutionally empowered to) remedy segregation which results from (1) private housing patterns not established by government, or (2) white flight resulting in resegregation after a desegregation order.

(4) *The Congressional Response: The Educational Amendments Act of 1974.* The Educational Amendments Act of 1974, passed after *Swann*, provided that no court or United States agency should take any action that would require a student to be transported other than to the school "closest or next closest to his place of residence" and prohibited transportation that would pose "a risk to the health of [any] student" or that would "impinge [] on the educational process" for any student. The Act also stated, however, that it was not intended to modify or diminish "the authority of the courts of the United States to enforce fully the fifth and fourteenth amendments." Consider whether restriction of available remedies would be constitutional in light of (1) the Equal Protection Clause, (2) Congress' authority to enforce the Fourteenth Amendment, and (3) separation of powers.

(5) *Desegregation Outside the South: Keyes v. School District (the Denver School Case), 413 U.S. 189 (1973).* One of the first cases outside the South, not involving express legal requirements of segregation, to reach the Court was *Keyes*, which involved the Denver school system. The record contained proof of purposeful administrative action creating segregation in a substantial portion of the school district. The Court reaffirmed that purposeful discrimination, and not merely impact, was required. However, it gave

great advantage to plaintiffs in proving discriminatory purpose, because it held that discriminatory purpose in a substantial part of the district shifted to the defendant the burden of disproving segregative intent in all other parts of the district. A major issue in the case concerned central city schools, which were heavily black, as to which little other evidence of segregative purpose existed. The Court also held that black and hispanic populations were to be aggregated to determine "one race" schools. The effect of *Keyes* was to retain the requirement of proof of discriminatory purpose, but to make it much easier to supply. Justice Rehnquist dissented.

COLUMBUS BOARD OF EDUCATION v. PENICK
443 U.S. 449 (1979)

MR. JUSTICE WHITE delivered the opinion of the Court.

The public schools of Columbus, Ohio, are highly segregated by race. In 1976, over 32% of the 96,000 students in the system were black. About 70% of all students attended schools that were at least 80% black or 80% white. Half of the 172 schools were 90% black or 90% white. . . .

The District Court's ultimate conclusion was that at the time of trial the racial segregation in the Columbus school system "directly resulted from [the Board's] intentional segregative acts and omissions," in violation of the Equal Protection Clause of the Fourteenth Amendment. Accordingly, judgment was entered against the local and state defendants enjoining them from continuing to discriminate on the basis of race in operating the Columbus public schools and ordering the submission of a systemwide desegregation plan. . . .

[First,] . . . [p]roof of purposeful and effective maintenance of a body of separate black schools in a substantial part of the system itself is prima facie proof of a dual school system and supports a finding to this effect absent sufficient contrary proof by the Board, which was not forthcoming in this case. *Keyes, supra.*

Second, both courts below declared that since the decision in *Brown II*, the Columbus Board has been under a continuous constitutional obligation to disestablish its dual school system and that it has failed to discharge this duty. . . .

Third, the District Court [f]ound that in the intervening years there had been a series of Board actions and practices [t]hat "intentionally aggravated, rather than alleviated," racial separation in the schools. These matters included the general practice of assigning black teachers only to those schools with substantial black student populations, a practice that was terminated only in 1974 as the result of a conciliation agreement with the Ohio Civil Rights Commission; the intentionally segregative use of optional attendance zones, discontiguous attendance areas, and boundary changes; and the selection of sites for new school construction that had the foreseeable and anticipated effect of maintaining the racial separation of the schools.

Against this background, we cannot fault the conclusion of the District Court and the Court of Appeals that at the time of trial there was systemwide segregation in the Columbus schools that was the result of recent and remote intentionally segregative actions of the Columbus Board.

Nor do we discern that the judgments entered below rested on any misapprehension of the controlling law. It is urged that the courts below failed to heed the requirements of *Keyes, Washington v. Davis*, and *Arlington Heights v. Metropolitan Housing Dev. Corp.*, that a plaintiff seeking to make out an equal protection violation on the basis of racial discrimination must show purpose. . . .

[T]he District Court correctly noted that actions having foreseeable and anticipated disparate impact are relevant evidence to prove the ultimate fact, forbidden purpose. Those cases do not forbid "the foreseeable effects standard from being utilized as one of the several kinds of proofs from which an inference of segregative intent may be properly drawn." Adherence to a particular policy or practice, "with full knowledge of the predictable effects of such adherence upon racial imbalance in a school system is one factor among many others which may be considered by a court in determining whether an inference of segregative intent should be drawn." The District Court thus stayed well within the requirements of *Washington v. Davis* and *Arlington Heights. See Personnel Administrator of Massachusetts v. Feeney*, 442 U.S. 256, 279 n.25, (1979). . . .

Because the District Court and the Court of Appeals committed no prejudicial errors of fact or law, the judgment appealed from must be affirmed.

[The concurring opinion of MR. CHIEF JUSTICE BURGER is omitted.]

MR. JUSTICE REHNQUIST, with whom MR. JUSTICE POWELL joins, dissenting.

The school desegregation remedy imposed on the Columbus school system by this Court's affirmance of the Court of Appeals is as complete and dramatic a displacement of local authority by the federal judiciary as is possible in our federal system. . . .

[T]he lower court's methodology would all but eliminate the distinction between *de facto* and *de jure* segregation and render all school systems captives of a remote and ambiguous past.

Today the Court affirms the Court of Appeals . . . in opinions so Delphic that lower courts will be hard pressed to fathom their implications for school desegregation litigation. . . .

"[D]iscriminatory purpose" and "systemwide violation" are to be treated as talismanic phrases which, once invoked, warrant only the most superficial scrutiny by appellate courts.

[C]oncepts such as "discriminatory purpose" and "systemwide violation" present highly mixed questions of law and fact. If district court discretion is not channelized by a clearly articulated methodology, the entire federal-court system will experience the disaffection which accompanies violation of Cicero's maxim not to "lay down one rule in Athens and another rule in Rome. . . ."

DAYTON BOARD OF EDUCATION v. BRINKMAN (DAYTON II)
443 U.S. 526 (1979)

MR. JUSTICE WHITE delivered the opinion of the Court.

The public schools of Dayton are highly segregated by race. In the year the complaint was filed, 43% of the students in the Dayton system were black, but 51 of the 69 schools in the system were virtually all white or all black. . . .

[The District Court held that] plaintiffs had failed to prove that acts of intentional segregation over 20 years old had any current incremental segregative effects. . . .

The Court of Appeals reversed. . . .

Given intentionally segregated schools in 1954, [t]he Court of Appeals was quite right in holding that the Board was thereafter under a continuing duty to eradicate the effects of that system, *Columbus*, and that the systemwide nature of the violation furnished prima facie proof that current segregation in the Dayton schools was caused at least in part by prior intentionally segregative official acts. Thus, judgment for the plaintiffs was authorized and required absent sufficient countervailing evidence by the defendant school officials. *Keyes*. . . .

. . . The Court of Appeals was also quite justified in utilizing the Board's total failure to fulfill its affirmative duty . . . to trace the current, systemwide segregation back to the purposefully dual system of the 1950s and to the subsequent acts of intentional discrimination *Columbus; Keyes; Swann.* [Affirmed.]

MR. JUSTICE REHNQUIST, with whom MR. JUSTICE POWELL joins, dissenting.

For the reasons set out in my dissent in *Columbus Board of Education v. Penick*, I cannot join the Court's opinion in this case. Both the Court of Appeals for the Sixth Circuit and this Court used their respective *Columbus* opinions as a roadmap, and for the reasons I could not subscribe to the affirmative duty, the foreseeability test, the cavalier treatment of causality, and the false hope of *Keyes* and *Swann* rebuttal in *Columbus*, I cannot subscribe to them here.

NOTES AND QUESTIONS

(1) *The Keyes Rule of Burden Shifting: As Applied in Columbus and Dayton II, Does It Obliterate the Purpose Requirement?* Does the application of the *Keyes* principles in *Columbus* and *Dayton II* have the effect of equating, as a practical matter, discriminatory purpose and discriminatory impact (or de jure and de facto segregation), despite the Court's theoretical retention of the purpose requirement?

(2) *The Doctrines of "Foreseeable and Anticipated Disparate Impact" and the "Presumptive Causal Link" to Pre-1954 Violations in Columbus and Dayton II.* In *Columbus*, the Court indicates that "actions having foreseeable and anticipated disparate impact" are relevant evidence of forbidden purpose. Does this formulation subtly change the rule of *Feeney* and *McCleskey*, to the effect that action taken in spite of, but not because of, disparate impact is not forbidden? In addition, in *Dayton*, a five-member majority recognizes a presumption that pre-1954 *de jure* segregation is causally connected to present segregated conditions. Notice the effect of this presumption: It supplies the proof of discriminatory purpose that plaintiffs need, shifting the burden of disproving purpose to the defendants. What effect will this approach have upon the requirement of proof of discriminatory purpose?

(3) *Taxes to Fund Remedial Decrees—Can a Federal Court Override State Law to Order Them?: Missouri v. Jenkins, 495 U.S. 33 (1990).* In this case, the district court overrode state law to authorize a local school district to levy increased property taxes to fund the court's remedial decree. The Supreme Court held that this order was within the district court's power to enforce the Fourteenth Amendment. Is the decision correct, and is it consistent with other decisions applying equitable principles to desegregation remedies?

(4) *The Interdistrict Remedies Issue: Milliken v. Bradley, below.* Some central metropolitan school districts are heavily populated by a single minority race. In such a situation, the elimination of past segregative practices may be impossible unless transportation across district lines is ordered. Furthermore, a desegregation decree in such a district may prompt white flight, such that resegregation will promptly result, unless interdistrict relief is available. In such a situation, may a district court ignore district lines, order interdistrict consolidation, or use other, similar remedies? Consider the following decision.

MILLIKEN v. BRADLEY, 418 U.S. 717 (1974). The district court found the Detroit public school system to be officially segregated. It concluded, however, that it could not accomplish desegregation within the confines of Detroit owing to the racial composition of the schools. It also concluded that the acts of the Detroit school board were attributable to the state as a whole. It therefore created a systemwide plan calling for transportation across a three-county metropolitan area, despite the fact that the eighty-five outlying school districts in these three counties were not parties to the action and there was no claim that they had committed any constitutional violation. The court of appeals affirmed. The Supreme Court, per Chief Justice Burger, reversed:

The [district] court's analytical starting point was its conclusion that school district lines are no more than arbitrary lines on a map drawn "for political convenience." [But] local autonomy has long been thought essential both to the maintenance of community concern and support for public schools and to quality of the educational process.

[E]ntirely apart from the logistical and other serious problems attending large-scale transportation of students, the consolidation would give rise to an array of other problems in financing and operating this new school system. Some of the more obvious questions would be: What would be the status and authority of the present popularly elected school boards? Would the children of Detroit be within the jurisdiction and operating control of a school board elected by the parents and residents of other districts? What board or boards would levy taxes for school boards in these . . . districts constituting the consolidated metropolitan area. . . ?

[I]t is obvious from the scope of the interdistrict remedy itself that absent a complete restructuring of the laws of Michigan relating to school districts the district court will become first, a de facto "legislative authority" to resolve these complex questions, and then the "school superintendent" for the entire area. . . .

[B]efore the boundaries of separate and autonomous school districts may be set aside by consolidating the separate units. . . , it must first be shown that there has been a constitutional violation within one district that produces a significant segregative effect in another district. [T]hus an inter-district remedy might be in order where the racially discriminatory acts of one or more school districts caused racial segregation in an adjacent district, or where district lines have been deliberately drawn on the basis of race. [C]onversely, without an interdistrict violation and interdistrict effect, there is no constitutional wrong calling for an interdistrict remedy.

Justice Douglas dissented, pointing out that the court of appeals had remanded to allow other affected school districts to be brought in as parties. Justice White also dissented, in an opinion joined by Justices Douglas, Brennan, and Marshall: "The core of my disagreement is that deliberate acts of segregation and their consequences will go unremedied, not because a remedy would be infeasible or unreasonable in terms of the usual criteria governing school desegregation cases, but because an effective remedy would cause what the Court considers to be undue administrative inconvenience to the state."

NOTES AND QUESTIONS

(1) *Creation of New School Districts: Wright v. City Council of Emporia, 407 U.S. 451 (1972), and United States v. Scotland Neck City Board of Education, 407 U.S. 484 (1972).* What should happen if authorities facing desegregation remedies decide to redesign school district lines? In *Emporia* and *Scotland Neck*, the Court held that creation of new school districts that would render an earlier desegregation order less effective was unconstitutional.

(2) *Resegregation by White Flight.* Does resegregation (or "white flight") constitute the sort of inter-district effect that can justify a remedy that transcends school district lines? Note the *Milliken* Court's reasoning, which does not appear to allow a remedy based on this factor.

FREEMAN v. PITTS
503 U.S. 467 (1992)

JUSTICE KENNEDY delivered the opinion of the Court.

[The district court in 1969 entered a consent decree approving a plan to dismantle *de jure* segregation in the DeKalb County School System (DCSS), which covers a major suburban area of Atlanta. The court retained jurisdiction. But in 1986, DCSS officials filed a motion for final dismissal of the litigation based upon the claim that DCSS had achieved unitary status.

[The district court found DCSS to be "an innovative school system that has traveled the often long road to unitary status almost to its end," noting that "the court has continually been impressed by the successes of the DCSS and its dedication to providing a quality education for all students within that system." It found that DCSS was a unitary system with regard to (1) student assignments, (2) transportation, (3) physical facilities, and (4) extracurricular activities, and ruled that it would order no further relief in those areas. However, the court said that vestiges of the dual system remained in the areas of (5) teacher and principal assignments, (6) resource allocation and (7) quality of education. It ordered DCSS to take measures to address the remaining problems.]

. . . [T]he Court of Appeals for the Eleventh Circuit reversed, holding that a district court should retain full remedial authority over a school system until it achieves unitary status in [all required] categories at the same time for several years. We now reverse the judgment of the Court of Appeals and remand, holding that a district court is permitted to withdraw judicial supervision with respect to discrete categories in which the school district has achieved compliance with a court ordered desegregation plan. A district court need not retain active control over every aspect of school administration until a school district has demonstrated unitary status in all facets of its system.

I

A. . . .

[T]he case before us requires an understanding and assessment of how DCSS responded to the directives set forth in *Green [v. New Kent County School Bd.*, 391 U.S. 430 (1968), which required school districts once segregated by law to promulgate plans that "promise[] realistically to work *now*" (emphasis in original)].

[A]fter [this] suit was filed, DCSS voluntarily began working with the Department of Health, Education and Welfare to devise a comprehensive and final plan of desegregation. The District Court in June 1969 entered a consent order approving the proposed plan, which was to be implemented in the 1969–1970 school year. [U]nder the plan all of the former *de jure* black schools were closed and their students were reassigned among the remaining neighborhood schools. . . .

Between 1969 and 1986 respondents sought only infrequent and limited judicial intervention into the affairs of DCSS. They did not request significant changes in student attendance zones or student assignment policies. In 1976 DCSS was ordered: to expand its Minority to Majority (M to M) student transfer program, allowing students in a school where they are in the majority race to transfer to a school where they are in the minority; to establish a bi racial committee to oversee the transfer program and future boundary line changes; and to reassign teachers so that the ratio of black to white teachers in each school would be, in substance, similar to the racial balance in the school population systemwide. From 1977 to 1979 the District Court approved a boundary line change for one elementary school attendance zone and rejected DCSSproposals to restrict the M to M transfer program. In 1983 DCSS was ordered to make further adjustments to the M to M transfer program. . . .

B

[A] critical beginning point is the degree of racial imbalance in the school district, that is to say a comparison of the proportion of majority to minority students in individual schools with the proportions of the races in the district as a whole. . . .

In the extensive record that comprises this case, one fact predominates: remarkable changes in the racial composition of the county presented DCSS and the District Court with a student population in 1986 far different from the one they set out to integrate in 1969. [T]he school system that the District Court ordered desegregated in 1969 had 5.6% black students; by 1986 the percentage of black students was 47%.

To compound the difficulty of working with these radical demographic changes, the northern and southern parts of the county experienced much different growth patterns. The District Court found that "[a]s the result of these demographic shifts, the population of the northern half of DeKalb County is now predominantly white and the southern half of DeKalb County is predominantly black." [B]etween 1975 and 1980 alone, approximately 64,000 black citizens moved into southern DeKalb County, most of them coming from Atlanta. During the same period, approximately 37,000 white citizens moved out of southern DeKalb County to the surrounding counties. . . .

Concerned with racial imbalance in the various schools of the district, respondents presented evidence that during the 1986–1987 school year DCSS had the following features: [50% of black students attended more-than-90%-black schools, and a large percentage of schools were disparate from the population as a whole]. . . .

Respondents argued in the District Court that this racial imbalance in student assignment was a vestige of the dual system, rather than a product of independent demographic forces. [R]espondents contended that DCSS had not used all available desegregative tools [including, *e.g.*, clustering and urban-to-suburban busing] in order to achieve racial balancing. . . .

[T]he District Court saw its task as one of deciding if petitioners "have accomplished maximum practical desegregation of the DCSS or if the DCSS must still do more to fulfill their affirmative constitutional duty." [T]he District Court made these findings:

[T]hese demographic shifts were inevitable as the result of suburbanization. . . ; blockbusting of formerly white neighborhoods leading to selling and buying of real estate in the DeKalb area on a highly dynamic basis; and the completion of Interstate 20, which made access from DeKalb County into the City of Atlanta much easier. . . .

The District Court added:

[A]bsent massive bussing, which is not considered as a viable option by either the parties or this court, the magnet school program and the M-to-M program, which the defendants voluntarily implemented and to which the defendants obviously are dedicated, are the most effective ways to deal with the effects on student attendance of the residential segregation existing in DeKalb County at this time.

In accordance with its factfinding, the District Court held that it would order no further relief in [certain areas emphasized by the *Green* case, specifically] the areas of student assignment, transportation, physical facilities and extracurricular activities. The District Court, however, did order DCSS to establish a system to balance teacher and principal assignments and to equalize per pupil expenditures throughout DCSS. . . .

[T]he Court of Appeals rejected the District Court's incremental approach [a]nd held that a school system achieves unitary status only after it has satisfied all six factors at the same time for several years. [T]he Court of Appeals held that petitioners bore the responsibility for the racial imbalance, and [w]ould have to take actions that "may be administratively awkward, inconvenient, and even bizarre in some situations," *Swann v. Charlotte Mecklenburg Bd. of Education*, 402 U.S. 1, 28 (1971), such as pairing and clustering of schools, drastic gerrymandering of school zones, grade reorganization, and busing. . . .

II

Two principal questions are presented. The first is whether a district court may relinquish its supervision and control over those aspects of a school system in which there has been compliance with a desegregation decree if other aspects of the system remain in noncompliance. As we answer this question in the affirmative, the second question is whether the Court of Appeals erred in reversing the District Court's order providing for incremental withdrawal of supervision in all the circumstances of this case.

A . . .

The objective of *Brown I* was made more specific by our holding in *Green* that the duty of a former *de jure* district is to "take whatever steps might be necessary to convert to a unitary system in which racial discrimination would be eliminated root and branch." We also identified various parts of the school system which, in addition to (1) student attendance patterns, must be free from racial discrimination before the mandate of *Brown* is met: (2) faculty, (3) staff, (4) transportation, (5) extracurricular activities and (6) facilities.

The concept of unitariness has been a helpful one in defining the scope of the district courts' authority. . . . But, as we explained last term in *Board of Education of Oklahoma City v. Dowell*, 111 S. Ct. 630, 636 (1991), the term "unitary" is not a precise concept. . . .

That the term "unitary" does not have fixed meaning or content is not inconsistent with the principles that control the exercise of equitable power. The essence of a court's equity power lies in its inherent capacity to adjust remedies in a feasible and practical way to eliminate the conditions or redress the injuries caused by unlawful action. Equitable remedies must be flexible if these underlying principles are to be enforced with fairness and precision. [T]he requirement of a unitary school system must be implemented according to this prescription.

Our application of these guiding principles in *Pasadena City Bd. of Education v. Spangler*, 427 U.S. 424 (1976), is instructive. There we held that a District Court exceeded its remedial authority in requiring annual readjustment of school attendance zones in the Pasadena school district when changes in the racial makeup of the schools were caused by demographic shifts "not attributed to any segregative acts on the part of the [school district]." . . .

Today, we make explicit the rationale that was central in *Spangler*. A federal court in a school desegregation case has the discretion to order an incremental or partial withdrawal of its supervision and control. [A] remedy is justifiable only insofar as it advances the ultimate objective of alleviating the initial constitutional violation. . . .

[R]eturning schools to the control of local authorities at the earliest practicable date is essential to restore their true accountability in our governmental system. When the school district and all state entities participating with it in operating the schools make decisions in the absence of judicial supervision, they can be held accountable to the citizenry, to the political process, and to the courts in the ordinary course. [Y]et it must be acknowledged that the potential for discrimination and racial hostility is still present in our country, and its manifestations may emerge in new and subtle forms after the effects of *de jure* desegregation have been eliminated. . . .

[A]mong the factors which must inform the sound discretion of the court in ordering partial withdrawal are the following: whether there has been full and satisfactory compliance with the decree in those aspects of the system where supervision is to be withdrawn; whether retention of judicial control is necessary or practicable to achieve compliance with the decree in other facets of the school system; and whether the school district has demonstrated, to the public and to the parents and students of the once disfavored race, its good faith commitment to the whole of the court's decree and to those provisions of the law and the constitution that were the predicate for judicial intervention in the first instance.

In considering these factors a court should give particular attention to the school system's record of compliance. . . .

B

We reach now the question whether [on the facts of this particular case] the Court of Appeals erred in prohibiting the District Court from returning to DCSS partial control over some of its affairs. . . .

The Court of Appeals was mistaken in ruling that our opinion in *Swann* requires "awkward," "inconvenient" and "even bizarre" measures to achieve racial balance in student assignments in the late phases of carrying out a decree, when the imbalance is attributable neither to the prior *de jure* system nor to a later violation by the school district but rather to independent demographic forces. [Here,] [t]he plan accomplished its objective in the first year of operation, before dramatic demographic changes altered residential patterns. . . .

[R]acial balance is not to be achieved for its own sake. [O]nce the racial imbalance due to the *de jure* violation has been remedied, the school district is under no duty to remedy imbalance that is caused by demographic factors. *Swann*. . . .

The effect of changing residential patterns on the racial composition of schools, though not always fortunate, is somewhat predictable. Studies show a high correlation between residential segregation and school segregation. [T]he District Court in this case heard evidence tending to show that racially stable neighborhoods are not likely to emerge because whites prefer a racial mix of 80% white and 20% black, while blacks prefer a 50%-50% mix.

Where resegregation is a product not of state action but of private choices, it does not have constitutional implications. It is beyond the authority and beyond the practical ability of the federal courts to try to counteract these kinds of continuous and massive demographic shifts. [R]esidential housing choices, and their attendant effects on the racial composition of schools, present an ever-changing pattern, one difficult to address through judicial remedies. . . .

As the *de jure* violation becomes more remote in time and these demographic changes intervene, it becomes less likely that a current racial imbalance in a school district is a vestige of the prior *de jure* system. The causal link between current conditions and the prior violation is even more attenuated if the school district has demonstrated its good faith. . . .

The requirement that the school district show its good faith commitment to the entirety of a desegregation plan so that parents, students and the public have assurance against further injuries or stigma also should be a subject for more specific findings. . . .

In contrast to the circumstances in *Penick*. . . , the District Court in this case stated that throughout the period of judicial supervision it has been impressed by the successes DCSS has achieved and its dedication to providing a quality education for all students, and that DCSS "has travelled the often long road to unitary status almost to its end." This, though, may not be the equivalent of a finding that the school district has an affirmative commitment to comply in good faith with the entirety of a desegregation plan, and further proceedings are appropriate for this purpose as well.

The judgment is reversed and the case is remanded to the Court of Appeals. [I]t should order further proceedings as necessary or order an appropriate remand to the District Court. . . .

JUSTICE THOMAS took no part in the consideration or decision of this case.

JUSTICE SCALIA, concurring. . . .

[O]ur post *Green* cases provide that, once state enforced school segregation is shown to have existed in a jurisdiction in 1954, there arises a presumption, effectively irrebuttable (because the school district cannot prove the negative), that any current racial imbalance is the product of that violation, at least if the imbalance has continuously existed, *see, e.g., Swann; Keyes.* . . .

But granting the merits of this approach at the time of *Green*, it is now 25 years later. [S]ince a multitude of private factors has shaped school systems in the years after abandonment of *de jure* segregation—normal migration, population growth (as in this case), "white flight" from the inner cities, increases in the costs of new facilities—the percentage of the current makeup of school systems attributable to the prior government enforced discrimination has diminished with each passing year, to the point where it cannot realistically be assumed to be a significant factor.

At some time, we must acknowledge that it has become absurd to assume, without any further proof, that violations of the Constitution dating from the days when Lyndon Johnson was President, or earlier, continue to have an appreciable effect upon current operation of schools. We are close to that time. . . .

[The concurring opinion of JUSTICE SOUTER is omitted.]

JUSTICE BLACKMUN, with whom JUSTICE STEVENS and JUSTICE O'CONNOR join, concurring in the judgment.

It is almost 38 years since this Court decided *Brown v. Board of Education*, 347 U.S. 483 (1954). In those 38 years the students in DeKalb County, Ga., never have attended a desegregated school system even for one day. . . .

I write separately for two purposes. First, I wish to be precise about my understanding of what it means for the District Court in this case to retain jurisdiction while relinquishing "supervision and control" over a subpart of a school system under a desegregation decree. Second, I write to elaborate on factors the District Court should consider in determining whether racial imbalance is traceable to board actions and to indicate where, in my view, it failed to apply these standards.

I

[T]hat the District Court's jurisdiction should continue until the school board demonstrates full compliance with the Constitution follows from the reasonable skepticism that underlies judicial supervision in the first instance. [I]t would seem especially misguided to place unqualified reliance on the school board's promises in this case, because the two areas of the school system the District Court found still in violation of the Constitution—expenditures and teacher assignments—are two of the *Green* factors over which DCSS exercises the greatest control. . . .

II

A

DCSS claims that it need not remedy the segregation in DeKalb County schools because it was caused by demographic changes for which DCSS has no responsibility. It is not enough, however, for DCSS to establish that demographics exacerbated the problem; it must prove that its own policies did not contribute. Such contribution can occur in at least two ways: DCSS may have contributed to the demographic changes themselves, or it may have contributed directly to the racial imbalance in the schools.

To determine DCSS' possible role in encouraging the residential segregation, the court must examine the situation with special care. . . .

> "People gravitate toward school facilities, just as schools are located in response to the needs of people. The location of schools may thus influence the patterns of residential development of a metropolitan area and have important impact on composition of inner-city neighborhoods." *Swann.*

[T]hus, schools that are demonstrably black or white provide a signal to these families, perpetuating and intensifying the residential movement.

School systems can identify a school as "black" or "white" in a variety of ways; choosing to enroll a racially identifiable student population is only the most obvious. The Court has noted: "[T]he use of mobile classrooms, the drafting of student transfer policies, the transportation of students, and the assignment of faculty and staff, on racially identifiable bases, have the clear effect of earmarking schools according to their racial composition. . . ."

In addition to exploring the school district's influence on residential segregation, the District Court here should examine whether school board actions might have contributed to school segregation. . . .

B

The District Court's opinion suggests that it did not examine DCSS' actions in light of the foregoing principles. The court did note that the migration farther into the suburbs was accelerated by "white flight" from black schools and the "blockbusting" of former white neighborhoods. [T]he court, in my view, failed to consider the many ways DCSS may have contributed to the demographic shifts. . . .

DCSS has undertaken only limited remedial actions since the 1976 court order. [D]CSS could have started and expanded its magnet and M-to-M programs more promptly; it could have built and closed schools with a view toward promoting integration of both schools and neighborhoods; redrawn attendance zones; integrated its faculty and administrators; and spent its funds equally. But it did not. DCSS must prove that the measures it actually implemented satisfy its obligation to eliminate the vestiges of *de jure* segregation originally discovered in 1969, and still found to exist in 1976.

III

[T]o be sure, changes in demographic patterns aggravated the vestiges of segregation and made it more difficult for DCSS to desegregate. But an integrated school system is no less desirable because it is difficult to achieve, and it is no less a constitutional imperative because that imperative has gone unmet for 38 years.

[A]ccordingly, in addition to the issues the Court suggests be considered in further proceedings, I would remand for the Court of Appeals to review [t]he District Court's finding that DCSS has met its burden of proving the racially identifiable schools are in no way the result of past segregative action.

NOTES AND QUESTIONS

(1) *Housing Patterns, "White Flight," and "Awkward . . ., Bizarre" Remedies: What Does the Court Hold?* The Court apparently holds that school segregation resulting from private choices in housing patterns is not remediable under the Constitution even if induced by white flight. Is this decision correct? Why, then, do you think that the court of appeals ordered remedies that it admitted might be "awkward" or "bizarre" (was it attempting merely to make a point or vindicate the court's authority)? *Cf.* David Crump, *From Freeman to Brown and Back Again: Principle, Pragmatism and Proximate Cause in the School Desegregation Decisions*, 68 WASH. L.

REV. 753 (1993) (observing that the courts ordering equitable remedies should consider both (1) whether it is principled and (2) whether it is pragmatically workable, and criticizing school desegregation decisions for failing to balance these criteria).

(2) *What about Housing Patterns That Result from De Jure Segregation?* But (as the concurring justices particularly point out), this principle does not apply if the housing patterns were "caused" by *de jure* segregation. That is, if certain schools officially are marked as "black" or "white,"and this designation causes racially distinguishable migration, the resulting housing choices cannot be considered purely private but instead are vestiges of *de jure* segregation. Notice that designations of black or white schools still may be official, *de jure* segregation even if they are informal. Indeed, they can result subtly from *de jure* actions affecting one of the many *Green* factors (*e.g.*, temporary buildings or faculty assignments). Thus, this issue is one of the main factors to be considered by the district court in its fact findings on remand.

(3) *Causation Issues: The Awkwardness of the Inquiry, and the Keyes and Columbus-Dayton Presumptions.* The awkward legal concept of causation underlies almost all of these issues. "Cause" is not a scientific or absolute concept; it instead is a legal conclusion, based upon multiple and conflicting factors, about fixing responsibility or blame. Recall the *Keyes* presumption (which infers *de jure* segregation in the entire school district upon proof that it exists in any part of the district) and the *Columbus-Dayton* presumption of causation (which means that if *de jure* segregation is proved ever to have existed in any part of a district, even before *Brown I*, it is presumed to be the cause of any racial imbalances in the present, even though it may be almost forty years later). These presumptions are difficult for school districts to overcome because they require the proving of a negative. Note that the DeKalb District succeeded in overcoming the presumption in this case by offering strong proof that private migration would have caused the result in any event. But the propriety of the presumptions remains a difficult issue. For example, because educators segregated schools in 1950 in a school district that today is administered by conscientious multiracial officials after a long history of desegregation efforts, should the school district today be "presumed" responsible for having "caused" every statistical difference in racial composition of each school? *See* David Crump, *supra*, 68 WASH. L. REV. 753 (1993).

(4) *Evaluating Equitable Remedies for School Desegregation: From Brown to Freeman and Back Again.* Perhaps *Brown II*, with its emphasis on "deliberate" speed and flexible remedies, encouraged intransigence—and perhaps it was inferior to more definite but less far-reaching remedies, such as immediate orders to assign pupils to neighborhood schools. Perhaps the do-it-now approach in *Green* should have been ordered much sooner. Perhaps *Swann*, with its approval of massive crosstown busing, engendered white flight that assured its own defeat (or perhaps *Swann* should have been decided earlier and even more forcefully). Perhaps *Milliken*, which effectively eliminated the consolidation of metropolitan districts as a remedy to white flight, was wrongly decided. Do you agree with any of these conclusions? *Freeman* provides a vantage point from which to reconsider the painful history of school desegregation remedies, all the way from *Brown II* to the present. [Why undertake such a study? Because there have been other occasions when the federal courts have been called upon to use unpopular remedies to alter unconstitutional conditions—crowded prisons are but one example—and these occasions will recur. *See* David Crump, *supra*, 68 WASH. L. REV. 753 (1993). Analyzing the history of school remedies may help us make better decisions in future cases.]

[5] Equitable Remedies Against Specific Employers for Past Discrimination

UNITED STATES v. PARADISE, 480 U.S. 149 (1987). In 1972, the Alabama Department of Public Safety was found to have systematically, and over a long time period, excluded blacks from employment. Eleven years later, the Department still had not adopted promotion procedures that did not disadvantage blacks, despite the order of the district court that it do so. The district court therefore ordered the Department to follow a "one-black-for-one-white promotion requirement," pursuant to which it would promote "one black trooper for each white trooper elevated in rank, as long as qualified black candidates were available, until the Department implemented an acceptable promotion procedure." The United States, through its Department of Justice, asserted that this order was unconstitutional. The Court upheld the order. The plurality opinion was by Justice Brennan, who was joined by Justices Marshall, Blackmun, and Powell:

> [T]he effects of [past discriminatory] policies [in the Department] remain pervasive and conspicuous at all ranks above the entry-level position. Of the 6 majors, *there is still not one black.* Of the 25 captains, *there is still not one black.* Of the 35 lieutenants, *there is still not one black.* Of the 65 sergeants, *there is still not one black.* Of the 66 corporals, *only four are black.* . . . Moreover, the department is *still* without acceptable procedures for advancement of black troopers into this structure, and it does not appear that any procedures will be in place within the near future. . . .

> It is now well established that government bodies, including courts, may constitutionally employ racial classifications essential to remedy unlawful treatment of racial or ethnic groups subject to discrimination. [B]ut although this Court has consistently held that some elevated level of scrutiny is required when a racial or ethnic distinction is made for remedial purposes, it has yet to reach consensus on the appropriate constitutional analysis. We need not do so in this case, however, because we conclude that the relief ordered survives even strict scrutiny analysis: it is "narrowly tailored" to serve a "compelling governmental purpose."

> The government unquestionably has a compelling interest in remedying past and present discrimination by a state actor. . . .

> While conceding that the District Court's order serves a compelling interest, the Government insists that it was not narrowly tailored to accomplish its purposes. . . . We cannot agree.

> In determining whether race-conscious remedies are appropriate, we look to several factors, including necessity for the relief and the efficacy of alternative remedies; the flexibility and duration of the relief, including the availability of waiver provisions; the relationship of the numerical goals to the relevant labor market; and the impact of the relief on the rights on third parties. . . .

> A. To evaluate the District Court's determination that it was *necessary* to order the promotion of eight whites and eight blacks to the rank of corporal at the time of the motion to enforce, we must examine the purposes the order was intended to serve. First, the court sought to eliminate the effects of the Department's "long term, open, and pervasive" discrimination, including the absolute exclusion of blacks from its upper ranks. Second, the judge sought to ensure expeditious compliance with the 1979 and 1981 Decrees by inducing the Department to implement a promotion procedure that would not have an adverse impact on blacks. . . .

> B. The features of the one-for-one requirement and its actual operation indicate that it is flexible in application at all ranks. The requirement may be waived if no qualified black candidates are available. [F]urther, it applies only when the Department needs to make promotions. Thus, if external forces, such as budget cuts, necessitate a promotion freeze, the Department will not be required to make gratuitous promotions to remain in compliance with the court's order.

Most significantly, the one-for-one requirement is ephemeral. . . . The requirement endures only until the Department comes up with a procedure that does not have a discriminatory impact on blacks—something the Department was enjoined to do in 1972 and expressly promised to do by 1980. . . .

C. We must also examine the relationship between the numerical relief ordered and the percentage of nonwhites in the relevant workforce. The original hiring order of the District Court required the Department to hire 50% black applicants until 25% of the state trooper force was composed of blacks; the latter figure reflects the percentage of blacks in the relevant labor market. [T]he enforcement order at issue here is less restrictive: it requires the Department to promote 50% black candidates until 25% of the rank in question is black, but *only* until a promotion procedure without an adverse impact on blacks is in place. . . .

D. The one-for-one requirement did not impose an unacceptable burden on innocent third parties. . . .

The one-for-one requirement does not require the layoff and discharge of white employees. . . . [B]ecause the one-for-one requirement is so limited in scope and duration, it only postpones the promotions of qualified whites. Consequently, like a hiring goal, it "impose[s] a diffuse burden, . . . foreclosing only one of several opportunities."

E. In determining whether this order was "narrowly tailored," we must acknowledge the respect owed a District Judge's judgment that specified relief is essential to cure a violation of the Fourteenth Amendment. . . .

[T]he judgment of the Court of Appeals, upholding the order of the District Court, is *Affirmed.*

Justice Powell concurred but wrote separately to emphasize his belief that the Court was required to apply strict scrutiny to any race-conscious remedy. Since "[t]he Court . . . has done this," he wrote, "I . . . join the opinion." On the other hand, Justice Stevens concurred only in the judgment, stating that a remedial decree against a party found guilty of past discrimination should be tested only by a standard of "reasonableness," *not* by strict scrutiny.

Justice White dissented in a separate opinion (omitted here). Finally, Justice O'Connor, joined by Chief Justice Rehnquist and Justice Scalia, also dissented:

[B]ecause the Court adopts a standardless view of "narrowly tailored" far less stringent than that required by strict scrutiny, I dissent. . . .

[T]he order at issue in this case clearly had one [legitimate] purpose, and [one] only—to compel the Department to develop a promotion procedure that would not have an adverse impact on blacks. . . .

[T]o survive strict scrutiny, the District Court order must fit with greater precision than any alternative remedy. The District Court had available several alternatives that would have achieved full compliance with the consent decrees without trammeling on the rights of nonminority troopers. The court, for example, could have appointed a trustee to develop a promotion procedure that would satisfy the terms of the consent decrees. . . . Alternatively, the District Court could have found the recalcitrant Department in contempt of court, and imposed stiff fines or other penalties for the contempt. . . .

[I]n its understandable frustration over the Department's conduct, however, the District Court imposed a racial quota without first considering the effectiveness of alternatives that would have a lesser effect on the rights of nonminority troopers. . . .

NOTES AND QUESTIONS

(1) *Strict Scrutiny, Intermediate Scrutiny, or Mere "Reasonableness:" Which of These Three Views Should Be the Standard for a Race-Conscious Remedy Against a Specific Actor Found to Have Discriminated?* In *Paradise*, Justice Powell's view ostensibly is emphasized: the plurality uses (1) strict scrutiny. It can be inferred, however, that Justice Brennan adheres to his preference for (2) intermediate review. And note that Justice Stevens advances a third approach: When there is a finding of past discrimination, the remedy should be evaluated by a standard of (3) mere "reasonableness." Which of these three views is most nearly correct? For an alternative analysis, *see* Note, *Affirmative Action and the Remedial Scope of Title VII: Procedural Answers to Substantive Questions*, 136 U. Pa. L. Rev. 625 (1987).

(2) *Remedying General Societal Discrimination Versus Remedying Actor-Specific Past Discrimination: The Constitutionality of "Quotas" Versus "Race (or Gender) as a Factor."* In *Paradise*, the Court upholds a one-for-one remedy that seems analogous to a quota, but it emphasizes the findings that the defendant is guilty of egregious past discrimination. In cases involving only general societal discrimination, however, the Court tends to approve rarely, and only when the "remedy" is not a quota. Do these considerations suggest that quotas should be used only for actor-specific past discrimination, whereas societal discrimination should be addressed only by using race (or gender) "as a factor"? *Cf.* Cox, *Some Thoughts on the Future of Remedial Race and Gender Preferences under Title VII*, 19 Val. U. L. Rev. 801 (1985); Rutherglen & Ortiz, *Affirmative Action under the Constitution and Title VII: From Confusion to Convergence*, 35 U.C.L.A. L. Rev. 298 (1988).

[6] Affirmative Action: Addressing General Societal Effects by "Benign" Consideration of Race—or "Reverse" Discrimination?

NOTE ON HOW TO READ THE *BAKKE* CASE

Justice Powell's Decision-Making Opinion. The *Bakke* case, which follows, is one of the Court's most significant affirmative action decisions. In an important sense, it is Justice Powell's decision. Four members of the Court (Justices Brennan, White, Marshall, and Blackmun) believed that the affirmative action plan adopted by the defendant, University of California, was constitutional. Four others (Justices Stevens, Burger, Stewart, and Rehnquist) concluded that the constitutional issue was not presented for decision and would have decided the case on narrower statutory grounds, holding the California plan illegal. Thus, in the end, it was Justice Powell's vote that determined the shape of the decision.

The Views of Justices Brennan et al. Justice Brennan and three other Justices would have upheld the California affirmative action program even though it featured the setting aside of a specific number of places for minority applicants. These Justices would not have used the highest level of scrutiny to examine an affirmative action plan; instead, they would have used an intermediate approach. The key to their reasoning is that the California affirmative action program was designed to assist discrete and insular minorities. It therefore necessarily used race-conscious remedies. Furthermore, it did not stigmatize the group that it disadvantaged (whites), according to these Justices, because whites were not a discrete and insular minority.

The Position of Justice Powell. Justice Powell, however, wrote that since the Fourteenth Amendment protects "persons" (*i.e.*, individual *persons*, as opposed to *classes* of people), a racial classification must be subjected to strict scrutiny and will be invalidated unless it is narrowly drawn to advance a compelling state interest. The California program, according to Justice Powell, failed this test because of the setting aside of specific numbers of places for minority applicants. But a different sort of program, exemplified by Harvard's affirmative action plan, in which race is a consideration but specific numbers of places are not set aside, would be constitutional, according to Justice Powell. His opinion found a compelling state interest served by such a program: the educational benefits that flow from a diverse student body. One major difference between Justice Powell and the Brennan group is Justice Powell's insistence that cases involving remedies for past discrimination are not analogous.

Richness and Complexity of the Opinions. Of course, this brief summary necessarily understates the richness of the issues in *Bakke.* It is a complex decision, and only a full reading can enable you to follow its twists and turns. *Cf.* Colker, *Anti-Subordination Above All: Sex, Race and Equal Protection,* 61 N.Y.U. L. REV. 1003 (1986); Kilgore, *Goals, Quotas, Preferences and Set-Asides: An Appropriate Affirmative Action Response to Discrimination?,* 19 VAL. U. L. REV. 829 (1985); Maltz, *Portrait of a Man in the Middle: Mr. Justice Powell, Equal Protection, and the Pure Classification Problem,* 40 OHIO ST. L.J. 941 (1979).

BOARD OF REGENTS v. BAKKE
438 U.S. 265 (1978)

MR. JUSTICE POWELL announced the judgment of the Court.

This case presents a challenge to the special admissions program of the petitioner, the Medical School of the University of California at Davis, which is designed to assure the admission of a specified number of students from certain minority groups.

For the reasons stated in the following opinion, I believe that so much of the judgment of the California court as holds petitioner's special admissions program unlawful and directs that respondent be admitted to the Medical School must be affirmed. For the reasons expressed in a separate opinion, my Brothers The Chief Justice, Mr. Justice Stewart, Mr. Justice Rehnquist and Mr. Justice Stevens concur in this judgment.

I also conclude for the reasons stated in the following opinion that the portion of the court's judgment enjoining petitioner from according any consideration to race in its admissions process must be reversed. For reasons expressed in separate opinions, my Brothers Mr. Justice Brennan, Mr. Justice White, Mr. Justice Marshall and Mr. Justice Blackmun concur in this judgment.

The Medical School of the University of California at Davis opened in 1968 with an entering class of 50 students. [O]ver the next two years, the faculty devised a special admissions program to increase the representation of "disadvantaged" students in each Medical School class. [The] program consisted of a separate admissions system operating in coordination with the regular admissions process. . . .

The special admissions program operated with a separate committee, a majority of whom were members of minority groups. On the 1973 application form, candidates were asked to indicate whether they wished to be considered as "economically and/or educationally disadvantaged" applicants; on the 1974 form the question was whether they wished to be considered as members of a "minority group," which the Medical School apparently viewed as "Blacks," "Chicanos," "Asians," and "American Indians. . . ."

[T]he applications then were rated by the special committee in a fashion similar to that used by the general admissions committee, except that special candidates did not have to meet the 2.5 grade point average cutoff applied to regular applicants. About one-fifth of the total number of special applicants were invited for interviews in 1973 and 1974. Following each interview, the special committee assigned each special applicant a benchmark score. The special committee then presented its top choices to the general admissions committee. The latter did not rate or compare the special candidates against the general applicants, but could reject recommended special candidates for failure to meet course requirements or other specific deficiencies. The special committee continued to recommend special applicants until a number prescribed by faculty vote were admitted. While the overall class size was still 50, the prescribed number was 8; in 1973 and 1974, when the class size had doubled to 100, the prescribed number of special admissions also doubled to 16. . . .

Allan Bakke is a white male who applied to the Davis Medical School in both 1973 and 1974. In both years Bakke's application was considered under the general admissions program, and he received an interview. His 1973 interview was with Dr. Theodore C. West, who considered Bakke "a very desirable applicant to [the] medical school." Despite a strong benchmark score of 468 out of 500, Bakke was rejected. . . .

[A]fter his 1973 rejection, Bakke wrote to Dr. George H. Lowrey, Associate Dean and Chairman of the Admissions Committee, protesting that the special admissions program operated as a racial and ethnic quota.

Bakke's 1974 application was completed early in the year. His student interviewer gave him an overall rating of 94, finding him "friendly, well tempered, conscientious and delightful to speak with." His faculty interviewer was, by coincidence, the same Dr. Lowrey to whom he had written in protest of the special admissions program. Dr. Lowrey found Bakke "rather limited in his approach" to the problems of the medical profession and found disturbing Bakke's "very definite opinions which were based more on his personal viewpoints than upon a study of the total problem." Dr. Lowrey gave Bakke the lowest of his six ratings, an 86; his total was 549 out of 600. Again, Bakke's application was rejected. . . . In both years, applicants were admitted under the special program with grade point averages, MCAT scores, and benchmark scores significantly lower than Bakke's. . . .

[T]he parties fight a sharp preliminary action over the proper characterization of the special admissions program. Petitioner prefers to view it as establishing a "goal" of minority representation in the Medical School. Respondent, echoing the courts below, labels it a racial quota.

This semantic distinction is beside the point: The special admissions program is undeniably a classification based on race and ethnic background. [Because of] the 16 special admissions seats, white applicants could compete only for 84 seats in the entering class, rather than the 100 open to minority applicants. Whether this limitation is described as a quota or a goal, it is a line drawn on the basis of race and ethnic status.

The guarantees of the Fourteenth Amendment extend to all persons. Its language is explicit: "No State shall . . . deny to any person within its jurisdiction the equal protection of the laws." It is settled beyond question that the "rights created by the first section of the Fourteenth Amendment are, by its terms, guaranteed to the individual. The rights established are personal rights. . . ."

[T]he guarantee of equal protection cannot mean one thing when applied to one individual and something else when applied to a person of another color. If both are not accorded the same protection, then it is not equal.

Nevertheless, petitioner argues that the court below erred in applying strict scrutiny to the special admissions program because white males, such as respondent, are not a "discrete and insular minority" requiring extraordinary protection from the majoritarian political process. [*United States v.*] *Carolene Products Co.* [ch. 1, *above*]. This rationale, however, has never been invoked in our decisions as a prerequisite to subjecting racial or ethnic distinctions to strict scrutiny. Nor has this Court held that discreetness and insularity constitute necessary preconditions to a holding that a particular classification is invidious. *See, e. g., Skinner v. Oklahoma ex rel. Williamson*, 316 U.S. 535, 541 (1942). [R]acial and ethnic classifications are subject to stringent examination without regard to these additional characteristics. . . .

Although many of the Framers of the Fourteenth Amendment conceived of its primary function as bridging the vast distance between members of the Negro race and the white "majority," *Slaughter-House Cases, supra,* the Amendment itself was framed in universal terms, without reference to color, ethnic origin, or condition of prior servitude. . . .

Petitioner urges us to adopt for the first time a more restrictive view of the Equal Protection Clause and hold that discrimination against members of the white "majority" cannot be suspect if its purpose can be characterized as "benign." The clock of our liberties, however, cannot be turned back to 1868. *Brown v. Board of Education.* It is far too late to argue that the guarantee of equal protection to *all* persons permits the recognition of special wards entitled to a degree of protection greater than that accorded others. "The Fourteenth Amendment is not directed solely against discrimination due to a 'two-class theory'—that is, based upon differences between 'white' and Negro."

Once the artificial line of a "two-class theory" of the Fourteenth Amendment is put aside, the difficulties entailed in varying the level of judicial review according to a perceived "preferred" status of a particular racial or ethnic minority are intractable. [A]s these preferences began to have their desired effect, and the consequences of past discrimination were undone, new judicial rankings would be necessary. The kind of variable sociological and political analysis necessary to produce such rankings simply does not lie within the judicial competence—even if they otherwise were politically feasible and socially desirable.

Moreover, there are serious problems of justice connected with the idea of preference itself. First, it may not always be clear that a so-called preference is in fact benign. Courts may be asked to validate burdens imposed upon individual members of a particular group in order to advance the group's general interest. . . . Nothing in the Constitution supports the notion that individuals may be asked to suffer otherwise impermissible burdens in order to enhance the societal standing of their ethnic groups. Second, preferential programs may only reinforce common stereotypes holding that certain groups are unable to achieve success without special protection based on a factor having no relationship to individual worth.

[T]hird, there is a measure of inequity in forcing innocent persons in respondent's position to bear the burdens of redressing grievances not of their making.

By hitching the meaning of the Equal Protection Clause to these transitory considerations, we would be holding, as a constitutional principle, that judicial scrutiny of classifications touching on racial and ethnic background may vary with the ebb and flow of political forces. . . .

Petitioner contends that on several occasions this Court has approved preferential classifications without applying the most exacting scrutiny. . . .

[The Court rejects the analogy to these lines of cases.]

[I]n this case, there has been no determination by the legislature or a responsible administrative agency that the University engaged in a discriminatory practice requiring remedial efforts. Moreover, the operation of petitioner's special admissions program is quite different from the remedial measures approved in those cases. It prefers the designated minority groups at the expense of other individuals who are totally foreclosed from competition for the 16 special admissions seats in every Medical School class. . . .

[T]he special admissions program purports to serve the purposes of: (i) "reducing the historic deficit of traditionally disfavored minorities in medical schools and in the medical profession;" (ii) countering the effects of societal discrimination; (iii) increasing the number of physicians who will practice in communities currently underserved; and (iv) obtaining the educational benefits that flow from an ethnically diverse student body. It is necessary to decide which, if any, of these purposes is substantial enough to support the use of a suspect classification.

[i] If petitioner's purpose is to assure within its student body some specified

racially invalid

percentage of a particular group merely because of its race or ethnic origin, such a preferential purpose must be rejected not as insubstantial but as facially invalid. Preferring members of any one group for no reason other than race or ethnic origin is discrimination for its own sake. This the Constitution forbids. *E.g., Loving v Virginia. . . .*

[ii] [T]he purpose of helping certain groups whom the faculty of the Davis Medical School perceived as victims of "societal discrimination" does not justify a classification that imposes disadvantages upon persons like respondent, who bear no responsibility for whatever harm the beneficiaries of the special admissions program are thought to have suffered. . . .

[iii] Petitioner identifies, as another purpose of its program, improving the delivery of health-care services to communities currently underserved. It may be assumed that in some situations a State's interest in facilitating the health care of its citizens is sufficiently compelling to support the use of a suspect classification. But there is virtually no evidence in the record indicating that petitioner's special admissions program is either needed or geared to promote that goal. . . .

[iv] The fourth goal asserted by petitioner is the attainment of a diverse student body. This clearly is a constitutionally permissible goal for an institution of higher education. Academic freedom, though not a specifically enumerated constitutional right, long has been viewed as a special concern of the First Amendment. The freedom of a university to make its own judgments as to education includes the selection of its student body. . . .

Thus, in arguing that its universities must be accorded the right to select those students who will contribute the most to the "robust exchange of ideas," petitioner invokes a countervailing constitutional interest, that of the First Amendment. In this light, petitioner must be viewed as seeking to achieve a goal that is of paramount importance in the fulfillment of its mission.

another issue

As the interest of diversity is compelling in the context of a university's admissions program, the question remains whether the program's racial classification is necessary to promote this interest. . . .

The experience of other university admissions programs, which take race into account in achieving the educational diversity valued by the First Amendment, demonstrates that the assignment of a fixed number of places to a minority group is not a necessary means toward that end. An illuminating example is found in the Harvard College program:

> In recent years Harvard College has expanded the concept of diversity to include students from disadvantaged economic racial and ethnic groups. Harvard College now recruits not only Californians or Louisianans but also blacks and Chicanos and other minority students.
>
> In Harvard College admissions the Committee has not set target-quotas for the number of blacks, or of musicians, football players, physicists or Californians to be admitted in a given year. . . .

In such an admissions program, race or ethnic background may be deemed a "plus" in a particular applicant's file, yet it does not insulate the individual from comparison with all other candidates for the available seats. . . .

This kind of program treats each applicant as an individual in the admissions process. The applicant who loses out on the last available seat to another candidate receiving a "plus" on the basis of ethnic background will not have been foreclosed from all consideration for that seat simply because he was not the right color or had the wrong surname. It would mean only that his combined qualifications, which may have included similar nonobjective factors, did not outweigh those of the other applicant. His qualifications would have been weighed fairly and competitively, and he would have no basis to complain of unequal treatment under the Fourteenth Amendment.

It has been suggested that an admissions program which considers race only as one factor is simply a subtle and more sophisticated—but no less effective—means of according racial preference than the Davis program. A facial intent to discriminate, however, is evident in petitioner's preference program and not denied in this case. No such facial infirmity exists in an admissions program where race or ethnic background is simply one element—to be weighed fairly against other elements—in the selection process. "A boundary line," as Mr. Justice Frankfurter remarked in another connection, "is none the worse for being narrow." *McLeod v Dilworth*, 322 U.S. 327, 329 (1944). . . .

[W]hen a State's distribution of benefits or imposition of burdens hinges on ancestry or the color of a person's skin, that individual is entitled to a demonstration that the challenged classification is necessary to promote a substantial state interest. Petitioner has failed to carry this burden. For this reason, that portion of the California court's judgment holding petitioner's special admissions program invalid under the Fourteenth Amendment must be affirmed.

In enjoining petitioner from ever considering the race of any applicant, however, the courts below failed to recognize that the State has a substantial interest that legitimately may be served by a properly devised admissions program involving the competitive consideration of race and ethnic origin. For this reason, so much of the California court's judgment as enjoins petitioner from any consideration of the race of any applicant must be reversed.

. . . [P]etitioner has conceded that it could not carry its burden of proving that, but for the existence of its unlawful special admissions program, respondent still would not have been admitted. Hence, respondent is entitled to the injunction, and that portion of the judgment must be affirmed. . . .

Opinion of MR. JUSTICE BRENNAN, MR. JUSTICE WHITE, MR. JUSTICE MARSHALL, and MR. JUSTICE BLACKMUN, concurring in the judgment in part and dissenting in part. . . .

[S]ince we conclude that the affirmative admissions program at the Davis Medical School is constitutional, we would reverse the judgment below in all respects. Mr. Justice Powell agrees that some uses of race in university admissions are permissible and, therefore, he joins with us to make five votes reversing the judgment below insofar as it prohibits the University from establishing race-conscious programs in the future.

Against this background, claims that law must be "color-blind" or that the datum of race is no longer relevant to public policy must be seen as aspiration rather than as description of reality. . . . Yet we cannot . . . let color blindness become myopia which masks the reality that many "created equal" have been treated within our lifetimes as inferior both by the law and by their fellow citizens.

Our cases have always implied that an "overriding statutory purpose" could be found that would justify racial classifications. *See, e. g., Loving v. Virginia; Korematsu v. United States.* . . .

We conclude, therefore, that racial classifications are not *per se* invalid under the Fourteenth Amendment. Accordingly, we turn to the problem of articulating what our role should be in reviewing state action that expressly classifies by race.

Unquestionably we have held that a government practice or statute which restricts "fundamental rights" or which contains "suspect classifications" is to be subjected to "strict scrutiny" and can be justified only if it furthers a compelling government purpose and, even then, only if no less restrictive alternative is available. But no fundamental right is involved here. Nor do whites as a class have any of the "traditional indicia of suspectness: the class is not saddled with such disabilities, or subjected to such a history of purposeful unequal treatment, or relegated to such a position of political powerlessness as to command extraordinary protection from the majoritarian political process." *United States v. Carolene Products Co.*, 304 U.S. 144, 152 n.4 (1938). . . .

On the other hand, the fact that this case does not fit neatly into our prior analytic framework for race cases does not mean that it should be analyzed by applying the very loose rational-basis standard of review that is the very least that is always applied in equal protection cases. . . .

Instead, a number of considerations—developed in gender-discrimination cases but which carry even more force when applied to racial classifications—lead us to conclude that racial classifications designed to further remedial purposes " 'must serve important and governmental objectives and must be substantially related to achievement of those objectives. . . .' "

In sum, because of the significant risk that racial classifications established for ostensibly benign purposes can be misused, . . . it is inappropriate to inquire only whether there is any conceivable basis that might sustain such a classification. Instead, to justify such a classification an important and articulated purpose for its use must be shown. In addition, any statute must be stricken that stigmatizes any group or that singles out those least well represented in the political process to bear the brunt of a benign program. . . .

Davis' articulated purpose of remedying the effects of past societal discrimination is, under our cases, sufficiently important to justify the use of race-conscious admissions programs where there is a sound basis for concluding that minority under representation is substantial and chronic, and that the handicap of past discrimination is impeding access of minorities to the Medical School. . . .

Finally, the conclusion that state education institutions may constitutionally adopt admissions programs designed to avoid exclusion of historically disadvantaged minorities, even when such programs explicitly take race into account, finds direct support in our cases construing congressional legislation designed to overcome the present effects of past discrimination.

These cases cannot be distinguished simply by the presence of judicial findings of discrimination, for race-conscious remedies have been approved where such findings have not been made. . . .

Properly construed, therefore, our prior cases unequivocally show that a state government may adopt race-conscious programs if the purpose of such programs is to remove the disparate racial impact its actions might otherwise have and if there is reason to believe that the disparate impact is itself the product of past discrimination, whether its own or that of society at large. There is no question that Davis' program is valid under this test. . . .

[The opinion here concluded that state action had "impair[ed] access to equal educational opportunity," citing cases decided under the separate but equal doctrine.]

[T]he second prong of our test—whether the Davis program stigmatizes any discrete group or individual and whether race is reasonably used in light of the program's objectives—is clearly satisfied by the Davis program.

It is not even claimed that Davis' program in any way operates to stigmatize or single out any discrete and insular, or even any identifiable, nonminority group. . . .

Accordingly, we would reverse the judgment of the Supreme Court of California holding the Medical School's special admissions program unconstitutional and directing respondent's admission, as well as that portion of the judgment enjoining the Medical School from according any consideration to race in the admissions process.

MR. JUSTICE MARSHALL. . . .

I agree with the judgment of the Court only insofar as it permits a university to consider the race of an applicant in making admissions decisions. I do not agree that petitioner's admissions program violates the Constitution. . . .

Since the Congress that considered and rejected the objections to the 1866 Freedmen's Bureau Act concerning special relief to Negroes also proposed the Fourteenth

Amendment, it is inconceivable that the Fourteenth Amendment was intended to prohibit all race-conscious relief measures.

While I applaud the judgment of the Court that a university may consider race in its admissions process, it is more than a little ironic that, after several hundred years of class-based discrimination against Negroes, the Court is unwilling to hold that a class-based remedy for that discrimination is permissible. In declining to so hold, today's judgment ignores the fact that for several hundred years Negroes have been discriminated against, not as individuals, but rather solely because of the color of their skins. It is unnecessary in 20th-century America to have individual Negroes demonstrate that they have been victims of racial discrimination; the racism of our society has been so pervasive that none, regardless of wealth or position, has managed to escape its impact. The experience of Negroes in America has been different in kind, not just in degree, from that of other ethnic groups. . . .

MR. JUSTICE BLACKMUN. . . .

I am not convinced, as Mr. Justice Powell seems to be, that the difference between the Davis program and the one employed by Harvard is very profound or constitutionally significant. The line between the two is a thin and indistinct one. In each, subjective application is at work. . . . The cynical, of course, may say that under a program such as Harvard's one may accomplish covertly what Davis concedes it does openly. I need not go that far, for despite its two-track aspect, the Davis program, for me, is within constitutional bounds, though perhaps barely so. It is surely free of stigma. . . .

[I]n order to get beyond racism, we must first take account of race. There is no other way. And in order to treat some persons equally, we must treat them differently. We cannot—we dare not—let the Equal Protection Clause perpetuate racial supremacy. . . .

MR. JUSTICE STEVENS, with whom the CHIEF JUSTICE, MR. JUSTICE STEWART, and MR. JUSTICE REHNQUIST join, concurring in the judgment in part and dissenting in part.

This is not a class action. The controversy is between two specific litigants. Allan Bakke challenged petitioner's special admissions program, claiming that it denied him a place in medical school because of his race in violation of the Federal and California Constitutions and of Title VI of the Civil Rights Act of 1964, 42 U.S.C. § 2000d *et seq.* . . .

The California Supreme Court, in a holding that is not challenged, ruled that the trial court incorrectly placed the burden on Bakke of showing that he would have been admitted in the absence of discrimination. The University then conceded "that it [could] not meet the burden of providing that the special admissions program did not result in Mr. Bakke's failure to be admitted." Accordingly, the California Supreme Court directed the trial court to enter judgment ordering Bakke's admission. Since that order superseded . . . the trial court's judgement, there is no outstanding injunction forbidding any consideration of racial criteria in processing applications.

It is therefore perfectly clear that the question whether race can ever be used as a factor in an admissions decision is not an issue in this case, and that discussion of that issue is inappropriate.

The University's special admissions program violated Title VI of the Civil Rights Act of 1964 by excluding Bakke from the Medical School because of his race. It is therefore our duty to affirm the judgment ordering Bakke admitted to the University.

Accordingly, I concur in the Court's judgment insofar as it affirms the judgment of the Supreme Court of California. To the extent that it purports to do anything else, I respectfully dissent.

NOTES AND QUESTIONS

(1) *The Famous Plurality (of One) Opinion By Justice Powell.* Justice Powell's opinion is considered the controlling opinion even though he wrote only for himself. Justice Powell's analysis has several parts. First, Justice Powell decided that equal protection protects "persons"—not "groups." Second, he decided that it was the "use of race in decisionmaking" that triggered strict scrutiny. Justice Powell rejected the argument that the "benign" use of race should be exempt from strict scrutiny. Justice Powell then concluded that three of the four interests advanced by UC-Davis *could* be compelling interests. This included "attainment of student body diversity." Finally, Justice Powell concluded that UC-Davis' set-aside a specific number of admissions and its separate committee did not satisfy the means prong because it was not sufficiently individualized. Watch for the subsequent interpretations of the Powell Plurality.

(2) *Criticizing the Bakke Reasoning.* Consider the following criticisms of the holding in *Bakke* and determine which, if any, you believe valid:

(a) *Irony of Requiring Past Discrimination for Specific Set-Asides.* A requirement of findings of past discrimination to support an affirmative action plan has the ironic result of investing a government entity with a "guilty" past with more flexibility than an "innocent" one. This reasoning, furthermore, means that the guilty agency has more room to disadvantage innocent individuals, such as Bakke. The reasoning would put a university in the awkward position of needing to admit past discrimination and seek to subject itself to judicial order so that it can accomplish the desired result. It thus discourages voluntary plans.

(b) *Condemnation of Visible Decisionmaking May Lead to "Fudged" Decisionmaking.* The preference for the Harvard plan, in which decisions are highly subjective but decisionmakers in fact may be likely to attempt to fill certain numbers of seats, arguably is simply a preference for less visible decisionmaking. The approach of the University of California arguably is more open and honest.

(c) *History of Class-Based Discrimination.* Although the Fourteenth Amendment protects persons, it protects them primarily with respect to classifications. Historically, minority group members have been disadvantaged—not as individuals, but as members of a class. Their repression has advantaged members of other classes. If this reasoning is accepted, perhaps Justice Powell's analysis fails at its beginning.

(d) *Lack of Analogy to Decisions Striking Down Disadvantages for Discrete and Insular Minorities.* An excluded white applicant from the University of California arguably has not been stigmatized in the same way as a black child who is required to attend a segregated school. Therefore, strict scrutiny arguably is inappropriate.

(e) *A Color-Blind Constitution; the Need for Avoiding Precise Racial Classifications, Interracial Squabbles About Entitlements, and Badges of Inferiority.* Perhaps the Powell decision also can be criticized by those supporting the conclusion that the Constitution is color-blind, as Justice Harlan said in his famous *Plessy* dissent. This doctrine is reinforced by practical considerations. Racial preferences may create the impression among the larger society that beneficiaries' accomplishments are devoid of achievement. The result may be a lowering of their own self-esteem. Furthermore, the process may involve government in close questions of racial classification: is a particular person a "Mexican-American" or not? The result of such inquiries may be destructive in the same way that the fascists' efforts to determine ethnic ancestry by percentage or by degree of relationship were harmful. Finally, official affirmative action may increase interracial tensions and actually exacerbate racial divisions.

Particularly if entitlements are important (as they are in education or employment), people may falsify their ethnic backgrounds, may band together in ethnic groups and seek political action on that basis, and may regard other ethnic groups as competitors.

(3) *Defending the Bakke Holding.* On the other hand, consider the following:

(a) *The Effect Upon Individuals in Bakke's Position.* Even if the concurring Justices are correct in pointing out that Bakke would not suffer the same stigma as a black child attending a segregated school, doesn't Bakke suffer very real psychological effects from what he understandably would perceive as racial discrimination against him?

(b) *The Relevance of Innocence.* While class-based remedies may be appropriate, particularly in remedying the effects of past individualized segregation, Justice Powell's approach has the effect of recognizing innocence—and minimizing disadvantage to innocent persons.

(c) *The Danger That "Benign" Quotas Will Become License for Disadvantaging Racial Minorities.* History is replete with instances in which apparently benign distinctions have been used to disadvantage minorities. For an example, consider *Goesart v. Cleary* and related decisions, below, in which the Court upheld a law "protecting" women by excluding them from certain professions. Justice Powell's opinion upholds affirmative action, but it draws an important symbolic line that may prevent benign distinctions from becoming invidious discriminations.

(d) *Reduction of the Need for Precise Categorization of Persons.* A quota system would exacerbate the disadvantages of classifying persons precisely as black, white, or otherwise. Justice Powell's approach, as he points out, decreases reliance on precise categorizations.

(e) *Less Visible Decisionmaking May Reduce the Harm.* Precisely because it is less visible, the decisionmaking involved in the Harvard plan, and Justice Powell's approach itself, may give less offense to competing members of different ethnic groups. Furthermore, because it recognizes broader criteria, those approaches may decrease somewhat the actuality of interracial competition.

PROBLEM F

FREE TUITION FOR BLACKS, Houston Chronicle, Mar. 7, 1990, § A, at 13, col. 1. Florida Atlantic University had 608 black students out of 11,310, and enrolled only 28 black freshmen in 1990. Facing increased targets for minority enrollment, the university implemented a novel idea—it publicly offered free tuition to every black freshman who met admission standards. The school was flooded with calls from across the nation, but an assistant to the state university's president also said, "We got a mass of calls from people who said they are angry." Is this state policy a denial of equal protection to white students, or is it valid affirmative action?

NOTE ON EMPLOYMENT-RELATED RACIAL PREFERENCES: THE *FULLILOVE, CROSON, METRO,* AND *ADARAND* CASES

The Court's Changing Battleground over Racial Preferences in Employment: The Fullilove, Croson, Metro Broadcasting, and Adarand Cases. A series of four cases tells the complicated story of the Supreme Court's views on affirmative action in employment. First, in the *Fullilove* case, the Court upheld certain preferences for minority contractors in federal projects, but it did not specify a level of scrutiny. Then, in *Croson,* the Court struck down a city's program for minority contractors, holding that States and cities must satisfy strict scrutiny. Next, in *Metro Broadcasting,* the Court revisited federal racial preferences and decided that they were different from similar actions by the States, because of Congress's power to enforce the Fourteenth Amendment. Finally, in *Adarand Constructors*, the Court overruled *Metro Broadcasting* and applied strict scrutiny to both State and federal affirmative action programs.

In this note, we shall try to help you to navigate the twists and turns of these four decisions. The vacillation results, in part, from shifting majorities on the Court, between Justices who prefer strict scrutiny and Justices who want lesser scrutiny of "benign" racial preferences or "remedial" programs.

(1) *The Fullilove Case: The Court Upholds a Federal Program without Specifying the Level of Scrutiny— Fullilove v. Klutznick, 448 U.S. 448 (1980).* The (Federal) Public Works Employment Act of 1977 required local public works projects to set aside ten percent of federal funds for contracts with minority business enterprises ("MBE"). These were defined as businesses owned by members of the following listed groups: African-Americans, Spanish-speaking persons, Asian-Americans, Indians, Eskimos, and Aleuts. The Act contained a flexible provision for waiver of the ten percent requirement if a contractor could show that the required level could not be achieved. By a 6-to-3 vote, with no majority opinion, the Court upheld this enactment. Chief Justice Burger delivered a plurality opinion for himself and Justices White and Powell, stating only that "careful" or "searching" evaluation was required:

> [C]ongress may employ racial or ethnic classifications in exercising its spending or other legislative powers only if those classifications do not violate the equal protection component of the due process clause of the Fifth Amendment. We recognize the need for careful judicial evaluation to assure that any Congressional program that employs racial or ethnic criteria to accomplish the objective of remedying the present effects of past discrimination is narrowly tailored to the achievement of that goal. . . .

> Here we deal with [t]he broad remedial powers of Congress [under § 5 of the Fourteenth Amendment, which authorizes Congress to enforce the Amendment]. It is fundamental that in no organ of government, state or federal, does there repose a more comprehensive remedial power than in the Congress, expressly charged by the Constitution with competence and authority to enforce equal protection guarantees. . . .

> Any preference based on racial or ethnic criteria must necessarily receive a most searching examination to make sure that it does not conflict with constitutional guarantees. [T]his opinion does not adopt, either expressly or implicitly, the formulas or analysis articulated in such cases as *University of California Regents v. Bakke*. [H]owever, our analysis demonstrates that the MBE provision would survive judicial review under either "test" articulated in the several *Bakke* opinions. . . .

Justice Powell concurred, applying "the analysis set forth in my opinion in . . . *Bakke*," or in other words, strict scrutiny. He found the requisite compelling interest in the need to redress continuing effects of past racial discrimination. On the other hand, Justice Marshall, joined by Justices Brennan and Blackmun, concurred separately to urge that strict scrutiny should not apply to "racial classifications that provide benefits to minorities for the purpose of remedying the present effects of past racial discrimination." These Justices advocated an intermediate level of scrutiny, requiring only that the racial classifications "serve[d] important government objectives and [were] substantially related to achievement of those objectives."

Justice Stewart, joined by Justice Rehnquist, dissented. He quoted Justice Harlan's dissent in *Plessy*: "Our Constitution is color-blind, and neither knows nor tolerates classes among citizens." The dissenters concluded that "[t]oday's decision is wrong for the same reason that *Plessy* was wrong. [U]nder our Constitution, the government may never act to the detriment of a person solely because of that person's race." As these dissenters saw it, "our statute books will once again have to contain laws that reflect the odious practice of delineating the qualities that make one person a negro and make another white." Justice Stevens also dissented.

(2) *The Croson Case: Strict Scrutiny Leads to the Invalidation of a City's MBE Program: City of Richmond v. J.A. Croson Co., 488 U.S. 469 (1989).* The City of Richmond adopted an MBE ordinance that was less flexible than the federal statute in *Fullilove* and required a greater set-aside (30%). The population of Richmond was approximately 50% black, and African-Americans actually held a majority on the City Council. The evidence relied upon by the City Council showed that there had been few minority contracts in recent years and few minority members in local contractors' associations; it also included testimony about general societal discrimination.

J.A. Croson Co. obtained a city contract by sealed bid. It had solicited bids from potential MBE subcontractors but received none, and it therefore sought a waiver. But after the contract was secured, an MBE belatedly offered a bid for certain fixtures—at a price that was 7% over market(!) Croson refused to accept this inflated bid. The City, however, refused the waiver. It also refused to increase the contract price, so that Croson lost its contract. Croson sued, claiming reverse discrimination.

A fragmented Supreme Court struck down the Richmond ordinance by distinguishing between federal remedial power (as in *Fullilove)* and the powers of the States. Justice O'Connor delivered what was partly a Court opinion, partly a plurality one:

> The principal opinion in *Fullilove*, written by Chief Justice Burger, did not employ "strict scrutiny" or any other traditional standard of equal protection review. . . .

> [H]is opinion stressed two factors in upholding the MBE set-aside. First was the unique remedial powers of Congress under § 5 of the Fourteenth Amendment. . . .

> The second factor emphasized by the principal opinion in Fullilove was the flexible nature of the 10% set-aside. [T]hus a waiver could be sought where minority businesses were not available to fill the 10% requirement or, more importantly, where an MBE attempted "to exploit the remedial aspects of the program by charging an unreasonable price, *i.e.*, a price not attributable to the present effects of prior discrimination." . . .

> That Congress may identify and redress the effects of society-wide discrimination does not mean that, *a fortiori*, the States and their political subdivisions are free to decide that such remedies are appropriate. . . .

> Absent searching judicial inquiry . . . , there is simply no way of determining what classifications are "benign" or "remedial" and what classifications are in fact motivated by illegitimate notions of racial inferiority or simple racial politics. Indeed, the purpose of strict scrutiny is to "smoke out" illegitimate uses of race by assuring that the legislative body is pursuing a goal important enough to warrant use of a highly suspect tool. . . .

> [A] generalized assertion that there has been past discrimination in an entire industry provides no guidance for a legislative body to determine the precise scope of the injury it seeks to remedy. It "has no logical stopping point." . . .

> It is sheer speculation how many minority firms there would be in Richmond absent past social discrimination. . . . Defining these sorts of injuries as "identified discrimination" would give local governments license to create a patchwork of racial preferences based on statistical generalizations about any particular field of endeavor. . . .

But Justices Marshall, Brennan and Blackmun dissented, arguing that strict scrutiny should not apply to racial preference laws denominated as "remedial:"

> In concluding that remedial classifications warrant no different standard of review under the Constitution than the most brute and repugnant forms of

state-sponsored racism, a majority of this Court signals that it regards racial discrimination as largely a phenomenon of the past, and that government bodies need no longer preoccupy themselves with rectifying racial injustice. I, however, do not believe this Nation is anywhere close to eradicating racial discrimination or its vestiges. . . .

Thus, the *Croson* case, like *Fullilove* before it, reflected a battle between Justices who sought strict scrutiny and those who wanted a lower level of scrutiny for "benign" or "remedial" laws. The strict scrutiny group thus prevailed in *Croson* as to State-ordered preferences, but the correct level for federally ordered ones, after *Fullilove*, remained unclear. In the next case, *Metro Broadcasting*, that issue arose again.

(3) *The Metro Broadcasting Case: Justices Brennan et al. Succeed in (Temporarily) Establishing an Intermediate Level of Review for Federal Racial Preferences— Metro Broadcasting, Inc. v. FCC, 497 U.S. 547 (1990)*. This case concerned two minority preference policies adopted by the FCC: First, in comparing applications for new broadcasting licenses, the FCC awarded an enhancement for minority ownership and management, and second, the FCC's distress sale policy allowed a broadcaster to transfer its license to a minority enterprise without the need of resolving the matter in a hearing. Although statistical evidence showed that only an insignificant fraction of licenses were held by minorities, the record did not show actual discrimination in the past, and therefore, the FCC did not base its policies on the purpose of remedying discrimination. Instead, it purported to act to satisfy its obligations under the Communications Act of 1934 to promote diversification of programming.

Metro Broadcasting attacked an order awarding a new television license to Rainbow Broadcasting in a comparative proceeding, in which the FCC had awarded a substantial enhancement to Rainbow because of its Hispanic ownership. A companion case attacked a distress sale to minority owners without a comparative hearing. The Supreme Court upheld both FCC policies. Justice Brennan, who had supported an intermediate kind of scrutiny in earlier decisions, forged a majority for his opinion in this case:

> It is of overriding significance in these cases that the FCC's minority ownership programs have been specifically approved—indeed, mandated—by Congress. In *Fullilove v. Klutznick*, Chief Justice Burger [o]bserved that [w]e are "bound to approach our task with appropriate deference to the Congress," a co-equal branch charged by the Constitution with the power " '[to] enforce, by appropriate legislation,' the equal protection guarantees of the fourteenth amendment". . . .
>
> A majority of the Court in *Fullilove* did not apply strict scrutiny to the race-based classification at issue. . . . [T]hree [m]embers would have upheld benign racial classifications that "serve important governmental objectives and are substantially related to achievement of those objectives." We apply that standard today. . . .
>
> Our decision last term in *Richmond v. J. A. Croson Co.*, concerning a minority set-aside program adopted by a municipality, does not prescribe the level of scrutiny to be applied to a benign racial classification employed by Congress. . . .
>
> [C]ongress and the FCC have selected the minority ownership policies primarily to promote programming diversity, and they urge that such diversity is an important governmental objective that can serve as a constitutional basis for the preference policies. We agree. . . .
>
> [J]ust as a "diverse student body" contributing to a "robust exchange of ideas" is a "constitutionally acceptable goal on which a race conscious university admissions program may be predicated," *University of California Regents v.*

Bakke, the diversity of view and information on the airwaves serves important first amendment values. . . .

We also find that the minority ownership policies are substantially related to the achievement of the government's interest. [W]ith respect to this "complex" empirical question, we are required to give "great weight to the decisions of Congress and the experience of the commission." . . .

Dissenting, Justice Kennedy, joined by Justice Scalia, cited *Plessy v. Ferguson* (the separate-but-equal case) and observed that its "standard of review and its explication have disturbing parallels to today's majority opinion that should warn us something is amiss here."

Justice O'Connor, joined by the Chief Justice, Justice Scalia, and Justice Kennedy, also dissented. She concluded that strict scrutiny was required, but she also argued that the FCC preference did not pass even the intermediate scrutiny suggested by the majority:

> The Constitution's guarantee of equal protection binds the federal government as it does the states, and no lower level of scrutiny applies to the federal government's use of race classifications. . . . [T]he Court has repeatedly indicated that "the reach of the equal protection guarantee of the fifth amendment is co-extensive with that of the fourteenth." *United States v. Paradise* (plurality opinion). . . .

> [E]ven if *Fullilove* applied outside a remedial exercise of Congress' § 5 power, it would not support today's adoption of the intermediate standard of review proffered by Justice Marshall but rejected in *Fullilove*. . . . [C]hief Justice Burger's opinion, joined by Justice White and Justice Powell, declined to adopt a particular standard of review but indicated that this Court must conduct "a most searching examination" and that courts must assure that any congressional program that employs racial or ethnic criteria to accomplish the objective of remedying the present effects of past discrimination is narrowly tailored to the achievement of that goal. . . .

> [T]he interest in increasing the diversity of broadcast viewpoints is clearly not a compelling interest. It is simply too amorphous, too insubstantial, and too unrelated to any legitimate basis for employing racial classifications.

> [T]he chosen means, resting as they do on stereotyping and so indirectly furthering the asserted end, could not plausibly be deemed narrowly tailored. . . .

> [T]he FCC's chosen means rests on the premise that differences in race, or in the color of a person's skin, reflect real differences that are relevant to a person's right to share in the blessings of a free society. [T]he policies impermissibly value individuals because they presume that persons think in a manner associated with their race. . . .

> Moreover, the FCC's programs cannot survive even intermediate scrutiny because race-neutral and untried means of directly accomplishing the governmental interests are readily available. The FCC could directly advance its interests by requiring licensees to provide programming that the FCC believes would add to diversity. . . .

(4) *The Adarand Constructors Case Overrules Metro Broadcasting (see below).* Justice Brennan's victory in *Metro Broadcasting* was temporary. Justice O'Connor's views later prevailed, and the Court applied strict scrutiny to both federal and state actions—as we shall see below in the *Adarand Constructors* case.

NOTES AND QUESTIONS ON *FULLILOVE, CROSON,* AND *METRO*

(1) *"Remedial" or "Benign" Racial Classifications: Can They Be Distinguished from Repressive Ones?* Notice Justice Kennedy's comparison of the majority's reasoning in *Metro Broadcasting* to that in *Plessy v. Ferguson.* Is the analogy persuasive? Or is there a difference? In *Metro*, the majority's reasoning upholds a preference for traditionally disadvantaged groups, whereas in *Plessy*, the regulation served further to stigmatize an already-disadvantaged group. Is this distinction persuasive—or is the "remedial" or "benign" nature of racial-preference legislation so elusive that strict scrutiny should apply even to these laws? [Might an Iranian-born applicant conclude that the classifications were not "benign" as to Iranian-Americans, for example, and endeavor to show that persons of Arab or Middle-Eastern extraction, though not favored by the FCC's preferences, were under-represented in station ownership statistics—and therefore were disadvantaged and denied equal protection by the preferences?]

(2) *Congress' Power to Enforce the Fourteenth Amendment, Compared to Federal Power Generally: The Breadth of the Court's Metro Broadcasting Holding.* In Chapter 14, we take up congressional enforcement of civil rights, and at that point we focus more closely upon Congress's power to enforce the Fourteenth Amendment under § 5. The majority's reasoning in *Metro*, however, does not appear to depend upon the scope of § 5. The holding validates racial classifications based upon the Communications Act, passed under the authority of the commerce power, insofar as they assertedly are "benign" and are substantially related to an important governmental objective. Under this approach, could "benign" racial classifications also be employed to protect the environment, to favor collective bargaining interests of labor unions, to assist in law enforcement, or for other purposes that might qualify as "important" but not "compelling"?

(3) *The Adarand Constructors Case (below): A Changed Majority of the Court Overrules Metro Broadcasting.* The *Croson* and *Metro* cases were hard-fought battles between those who favored strict scrutiny of racial preferences, such as Justices O'Connor, Scalia and Kennedy and Chief Justice Rehnquist, and those who favored intermediate-level review of "benign" or "remedial" legislation, such as Justices Brennan, Marshall and Blackmun. All three of these Justices left the Court, and with its changed composition, Justice O'Connor's view ultimately prevailed. In *Adarand Constructors, the Court overruled Metro.* Subsequent to *Adarand Constructors,* the Court denied certiorari in a much-watched case where the court of appeals had struck down an affirmative action plan at the University of Texas Law School. 64 U.S.L.W. 3765. Should there be a separate standard for affirmative action programs in educational settings or should the strict scrutiny test from *Adarand Constructors* govern?

ADARAND CONSTRUCTORS, INC. v. PEÑA
515 U.S. 200 (1995)

→overrules metro

JUSTICE O'CONNOR announced the opinion of the Court.

[Like most federal government agency contracts of the time, the Department of Transportation (DOT) contract at issue here contained a "subcontractor compensation clause" which gave a prime contractor a financial incentive (here, a 10% bonus) to hire subcontractors which qualified, under federal regulations, as "Disadvantaged Business Enterprises" ("DBE"). The DBE subcontractor clause was the affirmative action program at issue here when the DOT's prime contractor awarded the subcontract for highway guardrails to a DBE even though petitioner Adarand Constructors, Inc., which was not a DBE, had submitted the low bid. The DOT's subcontractor clause required the prime contractor to presume that a member of a racial minority or a woman was a "socially and economically disadvantaged individual" whose business could be certified as a DBE.

[Adarand sued, claiming that the DOT's affirmative action program violated the

Adarand (P's) claim

equal protection component of the Fifth Amendment. The lower federal courts applied the intermediate scrutiny standard of *Metro Broadcasting*, above, and ruled in favor of respondent DOT. The Supreme Court here vacates the court of appeals judgment, overrules *Metro*, and holds that, like state programs, federal affirmative action programs must satisfy the strict scrutiny standard established by *Croson*, above.]

The Government urges that "[t]he Subcontracting Compensation Clause program is . . . a program based on disadvantage, not on race," and thus that it is subject only to "the most relaxed judicial scrutiny." To the extent that the statutes and regulations involved in this case are race neutral, we agree. The Government concedes, however, that "the race-based rebuttable presumption used in some certification determinations under the Subcontracting Compensation Clause" is subject to some heightened level of scrutiny. The parties disagree as to what that level should be. . . .

A

In *Bolling v. Sharpe*, 347 U.S. 497 (1954), the Court for the first time explicitly questioned the existence of any difference between the obligations of the Federal Government and the States to avoid racial classifications. *Bolling* did note that "[t]he 'equal protection of the laws' is a more explicit safeguard of prohibited unfairness than 'due process of law.' " . . . But *Bolling* then concluded that, "[i]n view of [the] decision that the Constitution prohibits the states from maintaining racially segregated public schools, it would be unthinkable that the same Constitution would impose a lesser duty on the Federal Government." . . .

B

The Court's failure to produce a majority opinion in *Bakke, Fullilove*, and [other cases] left unresolved the proper analysis for remedial race-based governmental action. . . The Court resolved the issue, at least in part, in 1989. *Richmond v. J.A. Croson Co.* concerned a city's determination that 30% of its contracting work should go to minority-owned businesses. A majority of the Court in *Croson* held that "the standard of review under the Equal Protection Clause is not dependent on the race of those burdened or benefited by a particular classification," and that the single standard of review for racial classifications should be "strict scrutiny." . . .

[B]ut *Croson* of course had no occasion to declare what standard of review the Fifth Amendment requires for [a]ction taken by the Federal Government. . . .

Despite lingering uncertainty in the details, however, the Court's cases through *Croson* had established three general propositions with respect to governmental racial classifications. First, skepticism: " '[a]ny preference based on racial or ethnic criteria must necessarily receive a most searching examination,' " . . . Second, consistency: "the standard of review under the Equal Protection Clause is not dependent on the race of those burdened or benefited by a particular classification," . . . *i.e.*, all racial classifications reviewable under the Equal Protection Clause must be strictly scrutinized. And third, congruence: "[e]qual protection analysis in the Fifth Amendment area is the same as that under the Fourteenth Amendment." . . . Taken together, these three propositions lead to the conclusion that any person, of whatever race, has the right to demand that any governmental actor subject to the Constitution justify any racial classification subjecting that person to unequal treatment under the strictest judicial scrutiny. . . .

A year later, however, the Court took a surprising turn. *Metro Broadcasting, Inc. v. FCC* involved a Fifth Amendment challenge to two race-based policies of the Federal Communications Commission . . . [The *Metro Broadcasting* Court held] that "benign" federal racial classifications need only satisfy intermediate scrutiny, even though *Croson* had recently concluded that such classifications enacted by a State must satisfy strict scrutiny.

[B]y adopting intermediate scrutiny as the standard of review for congressionally mandated "benign" racial classifications, *Metro Broadcasting* departed from prior cases. . . .

The three propositions undermined by *Metro Broadcasting* all derive from the basic principle that the Fifth and Fourteenth Amendments to the Constitution protect persons, not groups. It follows from that principle that all governmental action based on race . . . should be subjected to detailed judicial inquiry to ensure that the personal right to equal protection of the laws has not been infringed. . . . Accordingly, we hold today that all racial classifications, imposed by whatever federal, state, or local governmental actor, must be analyzed by a reviewing court under strict scrutiny. [T]o the extent that *Metro Broadcasting* is inconsistent with that holding, it is overruled. . . .

[Regarding the argument—from *Metro Broadcasting*—that § 5 of the Fourteenth Amendment gives Congress power to establish race-based preferences and that the Court should defer in such matters to Congress, the Court noted that the DOT's subcontractor clause program was not based on § 5. Consequently, the Court concluded that "[w]e need not, and do not, address these differences today." The Court's avoidance of the § 5 issue was also noted by the dissenters, below.] . . .

Finally, we wish to dispel the notion that strict scrutiny is "strict in theory, but fatal in fact." *Fullilove, supra*, at 519 (Marshall, J., concurring in judgment). The unhappy persistence of both the practice and the lingering effects of racial discrimination against minority groups in this country is an unfortunate reality, and government is not disqualified from acting in response to it. . . . When race-based action is necessary to further a compelling interest, such action is within constitutional constraints if it satisfies the "narrow tailoring" test this Court has set out in previous cases. [Watch for this analysis later in the *Grutter* decision.

[Vacated and remanded.]

JUSTICE SCALIA, concurring in part and concurring in the judgment.

I join the opinion of the Court, except Part III-C, and except insofar as it may be inconsistent with the following: In my view, government can never have a "compelling interest" in discriminating on the basis of race in order to "make up" for past racial discrimination in the opposite direction. Individuals who have been wronged by unlawful racial discrimination should be made whole; but under our Constitution there can be no such thing as either a creditor or a debtor race. That concept is alien to the Constitution's focus upon the individual. . . . To pursue the concept of racial entitlement—even for the most admirable and benign of purposes—is to reinforce and preserve for future mischief the way of thinking that produced race slavery, race privilege and race hatred. In the eyes of government, we are just one race here. It is American. . . .

JUSTICE THOMAS, concurring in part and concurring in the judgment.

I agree with the majority's conclusion that strict scrutiny applies to all government classifications based on race. I write separately, however, to express my disagreement with the premise underlying Justice Stevens' and Justice Ginsburg's dissents: that there is a racial paternalism exception to the principle of equal protection.

That these programs may have been motivated, in part, by good intentions cannot provide refuge from the principle that under our Constitution, the government may not make distinctions on the basis of race. [T]here can be no doubt that the paternalism that appears to lie at the heart of this program is at war with the principle of inherent equality that underlies and infuses our Constitution. *See* Declaration of Independence ("We hold these truths to be self-evident, that all men are created equal, that they are endowed by their Creator with certain unalienable Rights, that among these are Life, Liberty, and the pursuit of Happiness").

These programs not only raise grave constitutional questions, they also undermine the moral basis of the equal protection principle . . . [T]here can be no doubt that racial paternalism and its unintended consequences can be as poisonous and pernicious as any other form of discrimination. So-called "benign" discrimination teaches many that because of chronic and apparently immutable handicaps, minorities cannot compete with them without their patronizing indulgence. Inevitably, such programs engender attitudes of superiority or, alternatively, provoke resentment among those who believe that they have been wronged by the government's use of race. These programs stamp minorities with a badge of inferiority and may cause them to develop dependencies or to adopt an attitude that they are "entitled" to preferences. . . .

JUSTICE STEVENS, with whom JUSTICE GINSBURG joins, dissenting.

Instead of deciding this case in accordance with controlling precedent, the Court today delivers a disconcerting lecture about the evils of governmental racial classifications. For its text the Court has selected three propositions, represented by the bywords "skepticism," "consistency," and "congruence." . . .

The Court's concept of skepticism is, at least in principle, a good statement of law and of common sense. Undoubtedly, a court should be wary of a governmental decision that relies upon a racial classification . . . But, as the opinions in *Fullilove* demonstrate, substantial agreement on the standard to be applied in deciding difficult cases does not necessarily lead to agreement on how those cases actually should or will be resolved . . .

The Court's concept of "consistency" assumes that there is no significant difference between a decision by the majority to impose a special burden on the members of a minority race and a decision by the majority to provide a benefit to certain members of that minority notwithstanding its incidental burden on some members of the majority. In my opinion that assumption is untenable. There is no moral or constitutional equivalence between a policy that is designed to perpetuate a caste system and one that seeks to eradicate racial subordination. Invidious discrimination is an engine of oppression, subjugating a disfavored group to enhance or maintain the power of the majority. Remedial race-based preferences [on the other hand] reflect the opposite impulse: a desire to foster equality in society. . . .

When a court becomes preoccupied with abstract standards, it risks sacrificing common sense at the altar of formal consistency. . . .

The Court's concept of "congruence" assumes that there is no significant difference between a decision by the Congress of the United States to adopt an affirmative-action program and such a decision by a State or a municipality. In my opinion that assumption is untenable. . . .

The Fourteenth Amendment [§ 5] directly empowers Congress at the same time it expressly limits the States. This is no accident. It represents our Nation's consensus, achieved after hard experience throughout our sorry history of race relations, that the Federal Government must be the primary defender of racial minorities against the States, some of which may be inclined to oppress such minorities. A rule of "congruence" that ignores a purposeful "incongruity" so fundamental to our system of government is unacceptable. . . .

JUSTICE SOUTER, with whom JUSTICE GINSBURG and JUSTICE BREYER join, dissenting.

[Justice Souter concluded that the strict scrutiny issue was not properly raised in the courts below; hence, the case must be decided on the basis of previously existing law. He added:]

In assessing the degree to which today's holding portends a departure from past practice, it is also worth noting that nothing in today's opinion implies any view of Congress's § 5 power and the deference due its exercise that differs from the views expressed by the *Fullilove* plurality. . . . Thus, today's decision should leave § 5 exactly where it is as the source of an interest of the national government sufficiently important to satisfy the corresponding requirement of the strict scrutiny test. . . . [*See* Chapter 14.]

JUSTICE GINSBURG, with whom JUSTICE BREYER joins, dissenting. . . .

The divisions in this difficult case should not obscure the Court's recognition of the persistence of racial inequality and a majority's acknowledgement of Congress' authority to act affirmatively, not only to end discrimination, but also to counteract discrimination's lingering effects. . . . Those effects, reflective of a system of racial caste only recently ended, are evident in our workplaces, markets, and neighborhoods. Job applicants with identical resumes, qualifications, and interview styles still experience different receptions, depending on their race. White and African-American consumers still encounter different deals. People of color looking for housing still face discriminatory treatment by landlords, real estate agents, and mortgage lenders. Minority entrepreneurs sometimes fail to gain contracts though they are the low bidders, and they are sometimes refused work even after winning contracts. Bias both conscious and unconscious, reflecting traditional and unexamined habits of thought, keeps up barriers that must come down if equal opportunity and nondiscrimination are ever genuinely to become this country's law and practice. . . .

NOTES AND QUESTIONS

(1) *"Benign" Racial Categories, "Gilded Cages," "Paternalism," or "False Equivalency?"* The *Adarand* Court overruled *Metro Broadcasting* and held that affirmative action programs of the federal government would be tested by the strict scrutiny standard. The majority rejects the concept that "benign" racial classifications can be distinguished, on the theory that they too easily can be misused once established (which might be called the golden cage argument—a "nice" cage is still a cage). Justice Thomas denies the existence of a "paternalism exception" to the Fourteenth Amendment. But the dissenters see these arguments as false equivalency. Comparing segregation to affirmative action is like equating a whites-only sign to "a welcome mat," according to the dissenters. Who has the better of this argument (are they both correct)?

(2) *Does the Majority's Argument Prove Too Much?: Recruitment and Scholarship as Distinguished from Preferences.* The use of racial preferences in recruiting for public employment, or in the distribution of public school scholarships, arguably remain as "open" issues. Imagine a state-agency employer that determines that a particular racial group is underrepresented among its personnel. The director therefore decides that he will visit several colleges this year where that underrepresented racial group is in the majority. Does the majority's reasoning make this "recruitment" decision unconstitutional? (What if the director decides that the expanded visits are necessary to avoid discrimination against the underrepresented group, but still the expansion is based on awareness of racial differences?)

(3) *Congress's Power to Enforce the Fourteenth Amendment.* The *Adarand* opinion holds that the same constraints apply to the Federal Government under the Fifth Amendment Due Process Clause as apply to the states under the Fourteenth Amendment Equal Protection and Due Process Clauses. But it does not fully explain why the differences in treatment of the Federal Government in those amendments do not make a difference in its powers. The Federal Government is not subject to any express equal protection constraint, although an "equal protection" component has been recognized based on the Fifth Amendment Due Process Clause. More importantly, the Fourteenth Amendment gives Congress power "to enforce . . . the provisions" of the Amendment.

The dissenters, quite understandably, emphasize this enforcement power. Is this issue indicative of a flaw in the majority's reasoning? Or, do the dissenters misunderstand the scope of Congressional power under Section 5? *See* Chapter 14.

PROBLEM G

THE HOPWOOD ISSUE: IS DIVERSITY A COMPELLING INTEREST? WHAT DOES IT MEAN? AND DOES A STATE VIOLATE THE EQUAL PROTECTION RIGHT OF SOME INDIVIDUALS IF IT USES RACE TO ACHIEVE IT? HOPWOOD v. TEXAS, *78 F.3d 932 (5th Cir. 1996).* Cheryl Hopwood was denied admission to the University of Texas Law School. She sued the State, alleging that the Law School's admission system afforded other applicants a preference on the basis of race in violation of the Fourteenth Amendment. There were disputes between the parties about the precise nature of the admission system and its proper characterization under *Bakke*, but this dispute proved not to be controlling because the Court held, contrary to Justice Powell's conclusion in *Bakke*, that a diverse student body was not a compelling interest:

. . . The law school maintains . . . that Justice Powell's formulation in *Bakke* is law and must be followed—at least in the context of higher education.

We agree with the plaintiffs that any consideration of race or ethnicity by the law school for the purpose of achieving a diverse student body is not a compelling interest under the Fourteenth Amendment. Justice Powell's argument in *Bakke* garnered only his own vote and has never represented the view of a majority of the Court in *Bakke* or any other case. Moreover, subsequent Supreme Court decisions regarding education state that non-remedial state interests will never justify racial classifications. Finally, the classification of persons on the basis of race for the purpose of diversity frustrates, rather than facilitates, the goals of equal protection. . . .

Thus, only one Justice concluded that race could be used solely for the reason of obtaining a heterogenous student body. As the *Adarand* Court states, the *Bakke* Court did not express a majority view and is questionable as binding precedent. 115 S. Ct. at 2109 ("The Court's failure in *Bakke* . . . left unresolved the proper analysis for remedial race-based government action.").

Since *Bakke*, the Court has accepted the diversity rationale only once in its cases dealing with race [in *Metro Broadcasting*]. In *Adarand*, the Court squarely rejected intermediate scrutiny as the standard of review for racial classifications, and *Metro Broadcasting* is now specifically overruled to the extent that it was in conflict with this holding. . . .

To believe that a person's race controls his point of view is to stereotype him. The Supreme Court, however, "has remarked a number of times, in slightly different contexts, that it is incorrect and legally inappropriate to impute to women and minorities 'a different attitude about such issues as the federal budget, school prayer, voting, and foreign relations.'" . . .

Instead, individuals, with their own conceptions of life, further diversity of viewpoint. Plaintiff Hopwood is a fair example of an applicant with a unique background. She is the now-thirty-two-year-old wife of a member of the Armed Forces stationed in San Antonio and, more significantly, is raising a severely handicapped child. Her circumstance would bring a different perspective to the law school. . . .

Questions: (1) *Stare Decisis.* Is the *Hopwood* court correct in concluding that it is not bound by Justice Powell's opinion in *Bakke*? (2) *The Effect of Adarand on Metro and Bakke.* After *Adarand*'s overruling of *Metro Broadcasting*, is diversity a permissible basis for the use of race as a discriminant in admissions? (3) *Recruitment, Matching, Scholarships, and the Borderland of Hopwood.* If the State cannot grant or deny admissions on the basis of any consideration of race, how far does the *Hopwood* principle go? Can the State use financial aid, with race as a plus factor, to achieve racial diversity? Can it "match" financial aid offered by another State outside the jurisdiction of this court (the Fifth Circuit)? And here is a more difficult question: Many people who agree with the *Hopwood* holding believe, nevertheless, that it is proper for the State to target its recruiting efforts to solicit applications from underrepresented ethnic or racial groups so long as the State does not consider race in granting or denying admission. If African-Americans are underrepresented at the State university, for example, the State might decide to send representatives to majority-black high schools to encourage applications. Does the *Hopwood* holding prohibit even this arguably "more benign" use of race? (4) *What Does "Diversity" Really Mean?* Consider whether the court is correct in its concept of diversity. It often is pointed out that law school discussions of the school desegregation cases would be cramped unless affirmative action ensured racial diversity. But perhaps it also could be argued that whatever their race, few law students endeavor to disagree with the holding in *Brown v. Board of Education*, and vigorous challenges to that decision might be enhanced by ensuring diversity of viewpoint, rather than race. Is it erroneous, or morally wrong, or simply futile, to use race as a proxy for diversity of viewpoint?

INTRODUCTORY NOTE TO *GRUTTER* AND *GRATZ*

After *Bakke*, there were several "open" issues regarding affirmative action in education. First, would the governing standard be "strict scrutiny" (as Justice Powell contended in *Bakke*)? Second, assuming strict scrutiny, would "intellectual diversity" or another type of "diversity" constitute a "compelling governmental interest"? Third, again assuming strict scrutiny, what type of "admissions process" would satisfy the means prong (least restrictive alternative)? Watch for the Court's resolution of these issues in the *Grutter* and *Gratz* decisions below. Then, note the often contrasting analysis in the *Seattle School District* decision from 2007.

GRUTTER v. BOLLINGER
539 U.S. 306 (2003)

JUSTICE O'CONNOR delivered the opinion of the Court.

This case requires us to decide whether the use of race as a factor in student admissions by the University of Michigan Law School (Law School) is unlawful.

I

A

The Law School ranks among the Nation's top law schools. It receives more than 3,500 applications each year for a class of around 350 students. Seeking to 'admit a group of students who individually and collectively are among the most capable,' the Law School looks for individuals with 'substantial promise for success in law school' and 'a strong likelihood of succeeding in the practice of law and contributing in diverse ways to the well-being of others.' More broadly, the Law School seeks 'a mix of students with varying backgrounds and experiences who will respect and learn from each other.' In 1992, the dean of the Law School charged a faculty committee with crafting a written admissions policy to implement these goals. In particular, the Law School sought to ensure that its efforts to achieve student body diversity complied with this Court's most recent ruling on the use of race in university admissions. See *Regents of Univ. of Cal. v. Bakke*, 438 U.S. 265 (1978). Upon the unanimous adoption of the committee's report by the Law School faculty, it became the Law School's official admissions policy.

The hallmark of that policy is its focus on academic ability coupled with a flexible assessment of applicants' talents, experiences, and potential 'to contribute to the learning of those around them.' The policy requires admissions officials to evaluate each applicant based on all the information available in the file, including a personal statement, letters of recommendation, and an essay describing the ways in which the applicant will contribute to the life and diversity of the Law School. In reviewing an applicant's file, admissions officials must consider the applicant's undergraduate grade point average (GPA) and Law School Admissions Test (LSAT) score because they are important (if imperfect) predictors of academic success in law school. The policy stresses that 'no applicant should be admitted unless we expect that applicant to do well enough to graduate with no serious academic problems.'

The policy makes clear, however, that even the highest possible score does not guarantee admission to the Law School. Nor does a low score automatically disqualify an applicant. Rather, the policy requires admissions officials to look beyond grades and test scores to other criteria that are important to the Law School's educational objectives. So-called 'soft variables' such as 'the enthusiasm of recommenders, the quality of the undergraduate institution, the quality of the applicant's essay, and the areas and difficulty of undergraduate course selection' are all brought to bear in assessing an 'applicant's likely contributions to the intellectual and social life of the institution.'

The policy aspires to 'achieve that diversity which has the potential to enrich everyone's education and thus make a law school class stronger than the sum of its parts.' The policy does not restrict the types of diversity contributions eligible for 'substantial weight' in the admissions process, but instead recognizes 'many possible bases for diversity admissions.' The policy does, however, reaffirm the Law School's longstanding commitment to 'one particular type of diversity,' that is, 'racial and ethnic diversity with special reference to the inclusion of students from groups which have been historically discriminated against, like African-Americans, Hispanics and Native Americans, who without this commitment might not be represented in our student body in meaningful numbers.' By enrolling a "critical mass' of [underrepresented] minority students,' the Law School seeks to 'ensur[e] their ability to make unique contributions to the character of the Law School.'

The policy does not define diversity 'solely in terms of racial and ethnic status.' Nor is the policy 'insensitive to the competition among all students for admission to the [L]aw [S]chool.' Rather, the policy seeks to guide admissions officers in 'producing classes both diverse and academically outstanding, classes made up of students who promise to continue the tradition of outstanding contribution by Michigan Graduates to the legal profession.'

B

Petitioner Barbara Grutter is a white Michigan resident who applied to the Law School in 1996 with a 3.8 grade point average and 161 LSAT score. The Law School initially placed petitioner on a waiting list, but subsequently rejected her application. In December 1997, petitioner filed suit in the United States District Court for the Eastern District of Michigan against the Law School, the Regents of the University of Michigan, Lee Bollinger (Dean of the Law School from 1987 to 1994, and President of the University of Michigan from 1996 to 2002), Jeffrey Lehman (Dean of the Law School), and Dennis Shields (Director of Admissions at the Law School from 1991 until 1998). Petitioner alleged that respondents discriminated against her on the basis of race in violation of the Fourteenth Amendment; Title VI of the Civil Rights Act of 1964, 78 Stat. 252, 42 U.S.C. § 2000d; and Rev. Stat. § 1977, as amended, 42 U.S.C. § 1981. . . .

During the 15-day bench trial, the parties introduced extensive evidence concerning the Law School's use of race in the admissions process. Dennis Shields, Director of Admissions when petitioner applied to the Law School, testified that he did not direct his staff to admit a particular percentage or number of minority students, but rather to consider an applicant's race along with all other factors. Shields testified that at the height of the admissions season, he would frequently consult the so-called 'daily reports' that kept track of the racial and ethnic composition of the class (along with other information such as residency status and gender). This was done, Shields testified, to ensure that a critical mass of underrepresented minority students would be reached so as to realize the educational benefits of a diverse student body. Shields stressed, however, that he did not seek to admit any particular number or percentage of underrepresented minority students.

Erica Munzel, who succeeded Shields as Director of Admissions, testified that 'critical mass' means 'meaningful numbers' or 'meaningful representation,' which she understood to mean a number that encourages underrepresented minority students to participate in the classroom and not feel isolated. Munzel stated there is no number, percentage, or range of numbers or percentages that constitute critical mass. Munzel also asserted that she must consider the race of applicants because a critical mass of underrepresented minority students could not be enrolled if admissions decisions were based primarily on undergraduate GPAs and LSAT scores. . . .

Kent Syverud was the final witness to testify about the Law School's use of race in admissions decisions. Syverud was a professor at the Law School when the 1992 admissions policy was adopted and is now Dean of Vanderbilt Law School. In addition to his testimony at trial, Syverud submitted several expert reports on the educational benefits of diversity. Syverud's testimony indicated that when a critical mass of underrepresented minority students is present, racial stereotypes lose their force because nonminority students learn there is no 'minority viewpoint' but rather a variety of viewpoints among minority students.

In an attempt to quantify the extent to which the Law School actually considers race in making admissions decisions, the parties introduced voluminous evidence at trial. . . .

In the end, the District Court concluded that the Law School's use of race as a factor in admissions decisions was unlawful. Applying strict scrutiny, the District Court determined that the Law School's asserted interest in assembling a diverse student body was not compelling because 'the attainment of a racially diverse class . . . was not recognized as such by *Bakke* and is not a remedy for past discrimination.' The District Court went on to hold that even if diversity were compelling, the Law School had not narrowly tailored its use of race to further that interest. . . .

Sitting en banc, the Court of Appeals reversed the District Court's judgment and vacated the injunction. . . .

We granted certiorari, 537 U.S. 1043 (2002), to resolve the disagreement among the Courts of Appeals on a question of national importance: Whether diversity is a compelling interest that can justify the narrowly tailored use of race in selecting applicants for admission to public universities.

II

A

We last addressed the use of race in public higher education over 25 years ago. In the landmark *Bakke* case, we reviewed a racial set-aside program that reserved 16 out of 100 seats in a medical school class for members of certain minority groups. The decision produced six separate opinions, none of which commanded a majority of the Court. . . .

Justice Powell provided a fifth vote not only for invalidating the set-aside program, but also for reversing the state court's injunction against any use of race whatsoever. The only holding for the Court in *Bakke* was that a 'State has a substantial interest that legitimately may be served by a properly devised admissions program involving the competitive consideration of race and ethnic origin.' Thus, we reversed that part of the lower court's judgment that enjoined the university 'from any consideration of the race of any applicant.'

Since this Court's splintered decision in *Bakke*, Justice Powell's opinion announcing the judgment of the Court has served as the touchstone for constitutional analysis of race-conscious admissions policies. Public and private universities across the Nation have modeled their own admissions programs on Justice Powell's views on permissible race-conscious policies. . . . We therefore discuss Justice Powell's opinion in some detail. [This discussion is omitted.] . . .

[W]e endorse Justice Powell's view that student body diversity is a compelling state interest that can justify the use of race in university admissions. . . .

III

A

Before this Court, as they have throughout this litigation, respondents assert only one justification for their use of race in the admissions process: obtaining 'the educational benefits that flow from a diverse student body.' Brief for Respondents Bollinger *et al.* i. In other words, the Law School asks us to recognize, in the context of higher education, a compelling state interest in student body diversity. . . .

Today, we hold that the Law School has a compelling interest in attaining a diverse student body.

The Law School's educational judgment that such diversity is essential to its educational mission is one to which we defer. . . .

As part of its goal of 'assembling a class that is both exceptionally academically qualified and broadly diverse,' the Law School seeks to 'enroll a 'critical mass' of minority students.' Brief for Respondents Bollinger *et al.* 13. The Law School's interest is not simply 'to assure within its student body some specified percentage of a particular group merely because of its race or ethnic origin.' *Bakke*, 438 U.S., at 307 (opinion of Powell, J.). That would amount to outright racial balancing, which is patently unconstitutional. Rather, the Law School's concept of critical mass is defined by reference to the educational benefits that diversity is designed to produce.

These benefits are substantial. As the District Court emphasized, the Law School's admissions policy promotes 'cross-racial understanding,' helps to break down racial stereotypes, and 'enables [students] to better understand persons of different races.' . . .

[In addition to "classroom" benefits,] in order to cultivate a set of leaders with legitimacy in the eyes of the citizenry, it is necessary that the path to leadership be visibly open to talented and qualified individuals of every race and ethnicity. Access to legal education (and thus the legal profession) must be inclusive of talented and qualified individuals of every race and ethnicity, so that all members of our heterogeneous society may participate in the educational institutions that provide the training and education necessary to succeed in America.

B

Even in the limited circumstance when drawing racial distinctions is permissible to further a compelling state interest, government is still 'constrained in how it may pursue that end: [T]he means chosen to accomplish the [government's] asserted purpose must be specifically and narrowly framed to accomplish that purpose.' *Shaw v. Hunt*, 517 U.S. 899, 908 (1996) (internal quotation marks and citation omitted). The purpose of the narrow tailoring requirement is to ensure that 'the means chosen 'fit' . . . th[e] compelling goal so closely that there is little or no possibility that the motive for the classification was illegitimate racial prejudice or stereotype.' *Richmond v. J. A. Croson Co.*, 488 *U.S.*, at 493 (plurality opinion).

Since *Bakke*, we have had no occasion to define the contours of the narrow-tailoring inquiry with respect to race-conscious university admissions programs. That inquiry must be calibrated to fit the distinct issues raised by the use of race to achieve student body diversity in public higher education. . . .

To be narrowly tailored, a race-conscious admissions program cannot use a quota system—it cannot 'insulat[e] each category of applicants with certain desired qualifications from competition with all other applicants.' *Bakke, supra*, at 315 (opinion of Powell, J.). Instead, a university may consider race or ethnicity only as a "plus' in a particular applicant's file,' without 'insulat[ing] the individual from comparison with all other candidates for the available seats.' *Id.*, at 317. In other words, an admissions program must be 'flexible enough to consider all pertinent elements of diversity in light of the particular qualifications of each applicant, and to place them on the same footing for consideration, although not necessarily according them the same weight.' *Ibid.*

We find that the Law School's admissions program bears the hallmarks of a narrowly tailored plan. As Justice Powell made clear in *Bakke*, truly individualized consideration demands that race be used in a flexible, nonmechanical way. . . .

That a race-conscious admissions program does not operate as a quota does not, by itself, satisfy the requirement of individualized consideration. When using race as a 'plus' factor in university admissions, a university's admissions program must remain flexible enough to ensure that each applicant is evaluated as an individual and not in a way that makes an applicant's race or ethnicity the defining feature of his or her application. The importance of this individualized consideration in the context of a race-conscious admissions program is paramount.

Here, the Law School engages in a highly individualized, holistic review of each applicant's file, giving serious consideration to all the ways an applicant might contribute to a diverse educational environment. The Law School affords this individualized consideration to applicants of all races. There is no policy, either *de jure or de facto*, of automatic acceptance or rejection based on any single 'soft' variable. Unlike the program at issue in *Gratz v. Bollinger, ante*, the Law School awards no mechanical, predetermined diversity 'bonuses' based on race or ethnicity. . . .

What is more, the Law School actually gives substantial weight to diversity factors besides race. . . .

Petitioner and the United States argue that the Law School's plan is not narrowly tailored because race-neutral means exist to obtain the educational benefits of student body diversity that the Law School seeks. We disagree. Narrow tailoring does not require exhaustion of every conceivable race-neutral alternative. Nor does it require a university to choose between maintaining a reputation for excellence or fulfilling a commitment to provide educational opportunities to members of all racial groups. Narrow tailoring does, however, require serious, good faith consideration of workable race-neutral alternatives that will achieve the diversity the university seeks. . . .

We are satisfied that the Law School adequately considered race-neutral alternatives currently capable of producing a critical mass without forcing the Law School to abandon the academic selectivity that is the cornerstone of its educational mission.

We acknowledge that 'there are serious problems of justice connected with the idea of preference itself.' *Bakke*, 438 *U.S.*, at 298 (opinion of Powell, J.). Narrow tailoring, therefore, requires that a race-conscious admissions program not unduly harm members of any racial group. . . .

We are satisfied with the Law School's admissions program does not. . . .

We are mindful, however, that '[a] core purpose of the Fourteenth Amendment was to do away with all governmentally imposed discrimination based on race.' *Palmore v. Sidoti*, 466 *U.S.* 429, 432 (1984). Accordingly, race-conscious admissions policies must be limited in time. This requirement reflects that racial classifications, however compelling their goals, are potentially so dangerous that they may be employed no more broadly than the interest demands. Enshrining a permanent justification for racial preferences would offend this fundamental equal protection principle. We see no reason to exempt race- conscious admissions programs from the requirement that all governmental use of race must have a logical end point. . . .

We take the Law School at its word that it would 'like nothing better than to find a race-neutral admissions formula' and will terminate its race-conscious admissions program as soon as practicable. See Brief for Respondents Bollinger *et al.* 34; *Bakke, supra,* at 317–318 (opinion of Powell, J.) (presuming good faith of university officials in the absence of a showing to the contrary). It has been 25 years since Justice Powell first approved the use of race to further an interest in student body diversity in the context of public higher education. Since that time, the number of minority applicants with high grades and test scores has indeed increased. We expect that 25 years from now, the use of racial preferences will no longer be necessary to further the interest approved today. . . .

JUSTICE GINSBURG, with whom JUSTICE BREYER joins, concurring. . . .

It is well documented that conscious and unconscious race bias, even rank discrimination based on race, remain alive in our land, impeding realization of our highest values and ideals. As to public education, data for the years 2000–2001 show that 71.6% of African-American children and 76.3% of Hispanic children attended a school in which minorities made up a majority of the student body. And schools in predominantly minority communities lag far behind others measured by the educational resources available to them. . . .

CHIEF JUSTICE REHNQUIST, with whom JUSTICE SCALIA, JUSTICE KENNEDY, and JUSTICE THOMAS join, dissenting.

I agree with the Court that, 'in the limited circumstance when drawing racial distinctions is permissible,' the government must ensure that its means are narrowly tailored to achieve a compelling state interest. I do not believe, however, that the University of Michigan Law School's (Law School) means are narrowly tailored to the interest it asserts. The Law School claims it must take the steps it does to achieve a 'critical mass' of underrepresented minority students. Brief for Respondents Bollinger *et al.* 13. But its actual program bears no relation to this asserted goal. Stripped of its 'critical mass' veil, the Law School's program is revealed as a naked effort to achieve racial balancing. . . .

Respondents explain that the Law School seeks to accumulate a 'critical mass' of *each* underrepresented minority group. But the record demonstrates that the Law School's admissions practices with respect to these groups differ dramatically and cannot be defended under any consistent use of the term 'critical mass.'

From 1995 through 2000, the Law School admitted between 1,130 and 1,310 students. Of those, between 13 and 19 were Native American, between 91 and 108 were African-Americans, and between 47 and 56 were Hispanic. If the Law School is admitting between 91 and 108 African-Americans in order to achieve 'critical mass,' thereby preventing African-American students from feeling 'isolated or like spokespersons for their race,' one would think that a number of the same order of magnitude would be necessary to accomplish the same purpose for Hispanics and Native Americans. Similarly, even if all of the Native American applicants admitted in a given year matriculate, which the record demonstrates is not at all the case, how can this possibly constitute a 'critical mass' of Native Americans in a class of over 350 students? In order for this pattern of admission to be consistent with the Law School's explanation of 'critical mass,' one would have to believe that the objectives of 'critical mass' offered by respondents are achieved with only half the number of Hispanics and one-sixth the number of Native Americans as compared to African- Americans. But respondents offer no race-specific reasons for such disparities. Instead, they simply emphasize the importance of achieving 'critical mass,' without any explanation of why that concept is applied differently among the three underrepresented minority groups. . . .

[T]he correlation between the percentage of the Law School's pool of applicants who are members of the three minority groups and the percentage of the admitted applicants who are members of these same groups is far too precise to be dismissed as merely the result of the school paying 'some attention to [the] numbers.' As the tables below show, from 1995 through 2000 the percentage of admitted applicants who were members of these minority groups closely tracked the percentage of individuals in the school's applicant pool who were from the same groups. . . .

The tight correlation between the percentage of applicants and admittees of a given race, therefore, must result from careful race based planning by the Law School. It suggests a formula for admission based on the aspirational assumption that all applicants are equally qualified academically, and therefore that the proportion of each group admitted should be the same as the proportion of that group in the applicant pool. . . .

The Court, in an unprecedented display of deference under our strict scrutiny analysis, upholds the Law School's program despite its obvious flaws. We have said that when it comes to the use of race, the connection between the ends and the means used to attain them must be precise. But here the flaw is deeper than that; it is not merely a question of 'fit' between ends and means. Here the means actually used are forbidden by the Equal Protection Clause of the Constitution.

JUSTICE KENNEDY, dissenting.

The separate opinion by Justice Powell in *Regents of Univ. of Cal. v. Bakke* is based on the principle that a university admissions program may take account of race as one, nonpredominant factor in a system designed to consider each applicant as an individual, provided the program can meet the test of strict scrutiny by the judiciary. 438 U.S. 265, 289–291, 315–318 (1978). This is a unitary formulation. If strict scrutiny is abandoned or manipulated to distort its real and accepted meaning, the Court lacks authority to approve the use of race even in this modest, limited way. The opinion by Justice Powell, in my view, states the correct rule for resolving this case. The Court, however, does not apply strict scrutiny. By trying to say otherwise, it undermines both the test and its own controlling precedents. . . .

The Court, in a review that is nothing short of perfunctory, accepts the University of Michigan Law School's assurances that its admissions process meets with constitutional requirements. The majority fails to confront the reality of how the Law School's admissions policy is implemented. The dissenting opinion by THE CHIEF JUSTICE, which I join in full, demonstrates beyond question why the concept of critical mass is a delusion used by the Law School to mask its attempt to make race an automatic factor in most instances and to achieve numerical goals indistinguishable from quotas. . . .

JUSTICE SCALIA, with whom JUSTICE THOMAS joins, concurring in part and dissenting in part.

I join the opinion of The Chief Justice. As he demonstrates, the University of Michigan Law School's mystical 'critical mass' justification for its discrimination by race challenges even the most gullible mind. The admissions statistics show it to be a sham to cover a scheme of racially proportionate admissions.

I also join Parts I through VII of Justice Thomas's opinion. I find particularly unanswerable his central point: that the allegedly 'compelling state interest' at issue here is not the incremental 'educational benefit' that emanates from the fabled 'critical mass' of minority students, but rather Michigan's interest in maintaining a 'prestige' law school whose normal admissions standards disproportionately exclude blacks and other minorities. If that is a compelling state interest, everything is. . . .

JUSTICE THOMAS, with whom JUSTICE SCALIA joins as to Parts I–VII, concurring in part and dissenting in part.

[I] believe blacks can achieve in every avenue of American life without the meddling of university administrators. Because I wish to see all students succeed whatever their color, I share, in some respect, the sympathies of those who sponsor the type of discrimination advanced by the University of Michigan Law School (Law School). The Constitution does not, however, tolerate institutional devotion to the status quo in admissions policies when such devotion ripens into racial discrimination. Nor does the Constitution countenance the unprecedented deference the Court gives to the Law School, an approach inconsistent with the very concept of 'strict scrutiny.'

No one would argue that a university could set up a lower general admission standard and then impose heightened requirements only on black applicants. Similarly, a university may not maintain a high admission standard and grant exemptions to favored races. The Law School, of its own choosing, and for its own purposes, maintains an exclusionary admissions system that it knows produces racially disproportionate results. Racial discrimination is not a permissible solution to the self-inflicted wounds of this elitist admissions policy. . . .

I

The majority agrees that the Law School's racial discrimination should be subjected to strict scrutiny. . . .

II

Unlike the majority, I seek to define with precision the interest being asserted by the Law School before determining whether that interest is so compelling as to justify racial discrimination. The Law School maintains that it wishes to obtain 'educational benefits that flow from student body diversity,' Brief for Respondents Bollinger *et al.* 14. This statement must be evaluated carefully, because it implies that both 'diversity' and 'educational benefits' are components of the Law School's compelling state interest. Additionally, the Law School's refusal to entertain certain changes in its admissions process and status indicates that the compelling state interest it seeks to validate is actually broader than might appear at first glance.

Undoubtedly there are other ways to 'better' the education of law students aside from ensuring that the student body contains a 'critical mass' of underrepresented minority students. Attaining 'diversity,' whatever it means, is the mechanism by which the Law School obtains educational benefits, not an end of itself. The Law School, however, apparently believes that only a racially mixed student body can lead to the educational benefits it seeks. How, then, is the Law School's interest in these allegedly unique educational 'benefits' not simply the forbidden interest in 'racial balancing,' that the majority expressly rejects?

A distinction between these two ideas (unique educational benefits based on racial aesthetics and race for its own sake) is purely sophistic—so much so that the majority uses them interchangeably.

The Law School's argument, as facile as it is, can only be understood in one way: Classroom aesthetics yields educational benefits, racially discriminatory admissions policies are required to achieve the right racial mix, and therefore the policies are required to achieve the educational benefits. It is the *educational benefits* that are the end, or allegedly compelling state interest, not 'diversity.' . . .

V

Putting aside the absence of any legal support for the majority's reflexive deference, there is much to be said for the view that the use of tests and other measures to 'predict' academic performance is a poor substitute for a system that gives every applicant a chance to prove he can succeed in the study of law. The rallying cry that in the absence of racial discrimination in admissions there would be a true meritocracy ignores the fact that the entire process is poisoned by numerous exceptions to 'merit.' . . .

VI

The absence of any articulated legal principle supporting the majority's principal holding suggests another rationale. I believe what lies beneath the Court's decision today are the benighted notions that one can tell when racial discrimination benefits (rather than hurts) minority groups, and that racial discrimination is necessary to remedy general societal ills. This Court's precedents supposedly settled both issues, but clearly the majority still cannot commit to the principle that racial classifications are *per se* harmful and that almost no amount of benefit in the eye of the beholder can justify such classifications. . . .

The silence in this case is deafening to those of us who view higher education's purpose as imparting knowledge and skills to students, rather than a communal, rubber-stamp, credentialing process. The Law School is not looking for those students who, despite a lower LSAT score or undergraduate grade point average, will succeed in the study of law. The Law School seeks only a facade—it is sufficient that the class looks right, even if it does not perform right.

The Law School tantalizes unprepared students with the promise of a University of Michigan degree and all of the opportunities that it offers. These overmatched students take the bait, only to find that they cannot succeed in the cauldron of competition. And this mismatch crisis is not restricted to elite institutions. . . .

NOTES AND QUESTIONS

(1) *Affirmative Action in Higher Education Admissions Processes: Grutter v. Bollinger, 539 U.S. 306 (2003) and Gratz v. Bollinger, 539 U.S. 244 (2003).* The *Grutter* (Law School admissions) and *Gratz* (undergraduate admissions) decisions are companion cases. In *Grutter*, a Caucasian female who was denied admission to Michigan Law School sued, claiming that the Law School's use of race as a "plus factor" was violative of the Equal Protection Clause. The Law School defended its practices on the grounds that it had a compelling state interest in the "intellectual diversity" of the student body and that its use of a "critical mass" approach in the context of individualized admissions screening process was narrowly tailored. Although the District Court, after a 15 day bench trial, had ruled against the Law School, the Supreme Court, per Justice O'Connor, held that the Law School's procedure satisfied the strict scrutiny standard. Four Justices (Rehnquist, Scalia, Kennedy, and Thomas) dissented.

(2) *The Status of "Intellectual Diversity" as a "Compelling State Interest": Do Grutter and Gratz Provide Clarification?* As you will recall from the *Bakke* decision (above), Justice Powell had discussed the four interests asserted by the University of California-Davis and had determined that three (*i.e.*, (1) remedying past discrimination; (2) serving historically underserved communities; and (3) obtaining an intellectually diverse student body) could be considered compelling state interests. Justice Powell's opinion also concluded that the asserted interest in assuring "some specified percentage of a particular group merely because of its race or ethnic origin" was not only not compelling but also not even legitimate.

The affirmative action decisions since *Bakke (Croson and Adarand)* had not addressed the "intellectually diverse student body" issue. These decisions focused on the governmental interests in remedying past discrimination or, arguably, in serving historically underserved communities. The Court had turned down the *Hopwood* case which did present the intellectual diversity issue. Note that in *Grutter* and *Gratz*, the Court declined to consider an interest in remedying past discrimination (which was not advanced by the University of Michigan even though the student-intervenors raised this argument).

Against this background, then, Justice O'Connor stated for the majority that "we hold that the Law School has a compelling interest in attaining a diverse student body." What had been the position of only Justice Powell in *Bakke*, now had the support of a majority of the Court. Thus, it might be expected that the *Grutter* opinion would provide needed clarification on this issue. But, did it?

The Powell opinion had stressed the importance of student body diversity as part of the University's academic freedom under the First Amendment. Student body diversity was important to the present-day educational function of the University. In contrast, the diversity interests accepted by Justice O'Connor's *Grutter* opinion seemed to focus beyond "learning outcomes" in the classroom; the majority included in the Law School's interest a concern for preparing "students for an increasingly diverse workforce and society." How the *Grutter* majority's conceptualization of an interest in "student body diversity" differs from Justice Powell's formulation of an intellectually diverse student body is not clear. At a minimum, however, it appears that the *Grutter* majority has allowed the University to project forward (*i.e.*, anticipate workforce and societal racial diversity) more than the Powell opinion did. Has the *Grutter* conception of "intellectual diversity" gotten too close to the concept of racial diversity "for its own sake" that Justice Powell rejected as "facially invalid"? This is just one of several issues which will undoubtedly be litigated in the post-*Grutter* era.

(3) *The Satisfaction of Strict Scrutiny.* The *Grutter* and *Gratz* decisions turn on the means prong of the strict scrutiny standard. The undergraduate admission system failed the means prong, but the Law School's "individualized" consideration and use of race as a "plus factor" to achieve a "critical mass" of selected minority students satisfied the narrow tailoring inquiry. Note that even the undergraduate program was far removed from the set-aside and two track admissions process of *Bakke* (and *Hopwood*). But the undergraduate program was not "tailored" enough. Apparently, if the weight given to race would be "determinative" (rather than just a "factor"), then a program will not satisfy the "narrow tailoring" prong. Again, given the great variety of admissions programs which developed after *Bakke*, one can anticipate that there will be much litigation about whether various "race-plus" programs are narrowly tailored. *See* David Crump, *The Narrow Tailoring Issue in the Affirmative Action Cases: Reconsidering the Supreme Court's Approval in Gratz and Grutter of Race-Based Decision-Making by Individualized Discretion*, 56 FLA. L. REV. 483 (2004). For a response to Professor Crump from one of the named defendants in *Grutter, see* Dennis J. Shields, *A Response to Profesor Crump's Narrow Tailoring Analysis of Grutter: Does It Matter How Many Angels Can Dance On the Head of A Pin?*, 56 FLA. L. REV. 761 (2004). *See also* Stephen B. Presser, *A Conservative Comment on Professor Crump*, 56 FLA. L. REV. 789 (2004).

(4) *The Political Response to the Supreme Court's Grutter Decision: A State Constitutional Provision Adopting the Dissenters' Colorblindness Position.* In 2006, in response to the *Grutter* decision, the voters of Michigan adopted a new provision to their state constitution. [*See* Chapter 16 for more on state constitutional law.] In pertinent part, Article 26, § 26 now reads:

§ 26 Affirmative Action Programs.

Sec. 26

(1) The University of Michigan . . . and any other public college or university, community college, or school district shall not discriminate against, or grant preferential treatment to, any individual or groups on the basis of race,

sex, color, ethnicity, or national origin in the operation of public employment, public education, or public contracting.

So, who won the University of Michigan cases? The public reaction ("backlash") was swift and actually much broader than just race. Is the Michigan majority's reaction similar to Arkansas in *Cooper v. Aaron*? Or, does the fact that *Grutter* held the affirmative action was permitted—but not required—distinguish the situation in *Cooper* (*see* Chapter 1 above)?

GRATZ v. BOLLINGER
539 U.S. 244 (2003)

CHIEF JUSTICE REHNQUIST delivered the opinion of the Court.

We granted certiorari in this case to decide whether 'the University of Michigan's use of racial preferences in undergraduate admissions violate[s] the Equal Protection Clause of the Fourteenth Amendment, Title VI of the Civil Rights Act of 1964 (42 U.S.C. § 2000d), or 42 U.S.C. § 1981.' Brief for Petitioners i. Because we find that the manner in which the University considers the race of applicants in its undergraduate admissions guidelines violates these constitutional and statutory provisions, we reverse that portion of the District Court's decision upholding the guidelines.

I

[The *Gratz* case involved the admissions of freshmen at the University of Michigan, a much larger program than the law school program addressed in *Grutter*. The undergraduate admissions program did not have the individualized screening of each file, instead awarding an automatic 20 points (of the 100 points required for admission) to a racial minority applicant.

The Court, per Chief Justice Rehnquist, applied strict scrutiny and held that the undergraduate admissions program did not satisfy the narrow tailoring prong. Note that the majority in *Gratz* is composed of the dissenters in *Grutter* plus Justice O'Connor.]

II

As they have throughout the course of this litigation, petitioners contend that the University's consideration of race in its undergraduate admissions decisions violates § 1 of the Equal Protection Clause of the Fourteenth Amendment, Title VI, and 42 U.S.C. § 1981. . . .

It is by now well established that 'all racial classifications reviewable under the Equal Protection Clause must be strictly scrutinized.' . . .

To withstand our strict scrutiny analysis, respondents must demonstrate that the University's use of race in its current admission program employs 'narrowly tailored measures that further compelling governmental interests.' . . . We find that the University's policy, which automatically distributes 20 points, or one-fifth of the points needed to guarantee admission, to every single 'underrepresented minority' applicant solely because of race, is not narrowly tailored to achieve the interest in educational diversity that respondents claim justifies their program. . . .

[Under this policy, race is] a decisive factor for virtually every minimally qualified underrepresented minority applicant. . . .

We conclude, therefore, that because the University's use of race in its current freshman admissions policy is not narrowly tailored to achieve respondents' asserted compelling interest in diversity, the admissions policy violates the Equal Protection Clause of the Fourteenth Amendment. We further find that the admissions policy also violates Title VI and 42 U.S.C. § 1981. Accordingly, we reverse that portion of the

District Court's decision granting respondents summary judgment with respect to liability and remand the case for proceedings consistent with this opinion.

JUSTICE O'CONNOR, concurring. . . .

Unlike the law school admissions policy the Court upholds today in *Grutter v. Bollinger* the procedures employed by the University of Michigan's (University) Office of Undergraduate Admissions do not provide for a meaningful individualized review of applicants. Cf. *Regents of Univ. of Cal. v. Bakke*, 438 U.S. 265 (1978) (principal opinion of Powell, J.). The law school considers the various diversity qualifications of each applicant, including race, on a case-by-case basis. See *Grutter v. Bollinger*, post. By contrast, the Office of Undergraduate Admissions relies on the selection index to assign every underrepresented minority applicant the same, *automatic* 20-point bonus without consideration of the particular background, experiences, or qualities of each individual applicant. And this mechanized selection index score, by and large, automatically determines the admissions decision for each applicant. The selection index thus precludes admissions counselors from conducting the type of individualized consideration the Court's opinion in *Grutter* requires. . . .

JUSTICE THOMAS, concurring.

I join the Court's opinion because I believe it correctly applies our precedents, including today's decision in *Grutter v. Bollinger*, post. For similar reasons to those given in my separate opinion in that case, see *post* (opinion concurring in part and dissenting in part), however, I would hold that a State's use of racial discrimination in higher education admissions is categorically prohibited by the Equal Protection Clause. . . .

JUSTICE BREYER, concurring in the judgment.

I concur in the judgment of the Court though I do not join its opinion. I join Justice O'Connor's opinion except insofar as it joins that of the Court. I join Part I of Justice Ginsburg's dissenting opinion, but I do not dissent from the Court's reversal of the District Court's decision. I agree with Justice Ginsburg that, in implementing the Constitution's equality instruction, government decisionmakers may properly distinguish between policies of inclusion and exclusion for the former are more likely to prove consistent with the basic constitutional obligation that the law respect each individual equally, see U.S. Const., Amdt. 14.

JUSTICE SOUTER, with whom JUSTICE GINSBURG joins as to Part II, dissenting.

. . . .

The cases now contain two pointers toward the line between the valid and the unconstitutional in race-conscious admissions schemes. *Grutter* reaffirms the permissibility of individualized consideration of race to achieve a diversity of students, at least where race is not assigned a preordained value in all cases. On the other hand, Justice Powell's opinion in *Regents of Univ. of Cal. v. Bakke*, 438 U.S. 265 (1978), rules out a racial quota or set-aside, in which race is the sole fact of eligibility for certain places in a class. Although the freshman admissions system here is subject to argument on the merits, I think it is closer to what *Grutter* approves than to what *Bakke* condemns, and should not be held unconstitutional on the current record. . . .

Without knowing more about how the Admissions Review Committee actually functions, it seems especially unfair to treat the candor of the admissions plan as an Achilles' heel. . . .

JUSTICE GINSBURG, with whom JUSTICE SOUTER joins, dissenting.

I

Educational institutions, the Court acknowledges, are not barred from any and all consideration of race when making admissions decisions. But the Court once again maintains that the same standard of review controls judicial inspection of all official race classifications. This insistence on 'consistency,' *Adarand*, 515 U.S., at 224, would be fitting were our Nation free of the vestiges of rank discrimination long reinforced by law, see *id.*, at 274–276, and n. 8 (Ginsburg, J., dissenting). But we are not far distant from an overtly discriminatory past, and the effects of centuries of law-sanctioned inequality remain painfully evident in our communities and schools. . . .

II

Examining in this light the admissions policy employed by the University of Michigan's College of Literature, Science, and the Arts (College), and for the reasons well stated by Justice Souter, I see no constitutional infirmity. . . .

The stain of generations of racial oppression is still visible in our society, see Krieger, 86 Calif. L. Rev., at 1253, and the determination to hasten its removal remains vital. One can reasonably anticipate, therefore, that colleges and universities will seek to maintain their minority enrollment—and the networks and opportunities thereby opened to minority graduates—whether or not they can do so in full candor through adoption of affirmative action plans of the kind here at issue. Without recourse to such plans, institutions of higher education may resort to camouflage. . . . If honesty is the best policy, surely Michigan's accurately described, fully disclosed College affirmative action program is preferable to achieving similar numbers through winks, nods, and disguises. . . .

[The dissenting opinion of Justice Stevens on standing grounds has been omitted.]

NOTES AND QUESTIONS

(1) *University Admissions Program, Operating Without "Individual" Application Review and With Reliance on a Point-System, Failed The Means Prong of Strict Scrutiny: Gratz v. Bollinger, 539 U.S. 244 (2003)*. While the Law School's admissions program survived strict scrutiny, the *Gratz* Court, per Chief Justice Rehnquist, held that the undergraduate admissions program failed the narrow tailoring prong of the strict scrutiny standard. The University of Michigan undergraduate admissions program was based on awarding "points" for various characteristics, and 100 points were required for admission. The program automatically awarded applicants from certain racial groups 20 points. The Court concluded that this point system did not provide the appropriate "individualized considerations" to meet the narrow tailoring requirement.

(2) *"Splitting the Baby": The Higher Education Admissions Cases of 2003.* As you can see, Justice O'Connor was the "swing vote." She voted, in *Grutter*, to uphold the Law School admissions program because it was sufficiently individualized and the use of race as a "plus factor" was not determinative; this, she concluded, was sufficient to satisfy narrow tailoring. In *Gratz*, Justice O'Connor concluded that the point system was a "mechanized selection" process which precluded "individualized consideration." Based on Justice O'Connor's opinions, it appears that a policy that focuses on "individualized consideration" and permits "nuanced judgments" will satisfy the narrow tailoring prong.

As a practical matter, will any large university undergraduate admissions program be able to provide individualized and nuanced judgments? What other approaches are available to such large public institutions?

(3)   *The Dissents in the Undergraduate Admission Case.* Justice Souter dissented because he concluded that the *Bakke* rule prohibited only quotas or set-asides. Is his reading of *Bakke* consistent with the Court's in these decisions?

Justice Ginsburg dissented regarding the application of strict scrutiny; she appears to favor a less rigorous standard. In that regard, she seems to parallel Justice Brennan in *Bakke*. Moreover, in one argument, Justice Ginsburg seems to assume that, even if the use of race were determined to be unconstitutional, "colleges and universities will seek to maintain their minority enrollment. . . ." Is she suggesting that the universities might engage in a form of "institutional civil disobedience"? For further examination of these decisions, *see* Evan Caminker, *A Glimpse Behind and Beyond Grutter*, 48 ST. LOUIS U. L.J. 889 (2004). *See also Symposium*, 21 CONST. COMM. 1 (2004).

PARENTS INVOLVED IN COMMUNITY SCHOOLS v. SEATTLE SCHOOL DISTRICT NO. 1
127 S. Ct. 2738 (2007)

CHIEF JUSTICE ROBERTS announced the judgment of the Court, and delivered the opinion of the Court with respect to Parts I, II, III-A, and III-C, and an opinion with respect to Parts III-B and IV, in which JUSTICES SCALIA, THOMAS, and ALITO join.

The school districts in these cases voluntarily adopted student assignment plans that rely upon race to determine which public schools certain children may attend. The Seattle school district classifies children as white or nonwhite; the Jefferson County school district as black or "other." In Seattle, this racial classification is used to allocate slots in oversubscribed high schools. In Jefferson County, it is used to make certain elementary school assignments and to rule on transfer requests. In each case, the school district relies upon an individual student's race in assigning that student to a particular school, so that the racial balance at the school falls within a predetermined range based on the racial composition of the school district as a whole. Parents of students denied assignment to particular schools under these plans solely because of their race brought suit, contending that allocating children to different public schools on the basis of race violated the Fourteenth Amendment guarantee of equal protection. The Courts of Appeals below upheld the plans. We granted certiorari, and now reverse.

I

Both cases present the same underlying legal question—whether a public school that had not operated legally segregated schools or has been found to be unitary may choose to classify students by race and rely upon that classification in making school assignments. Although we examine the plans under the same legal framework, the specifics of the two plans, and the circumstances surrounding their adoption, are in some respects quite different.

A

Seattle School District No. 1 operates 10 regular public high schools. In 1998, it adopted the plan at issue in this case for assigning students to these schools. The plan allows incoming ninth graders to choose from among any of the district's high schools, ranking however many schools they wish in order of preference.

Some schools are more popular than others. If too many students list the same school as their first choice, the district employs a series of "tiebreakers" to determine who will fill the open slots at the oversubscribed school. The first tiebreaker selects for admission students who have a sibling currently enrolled in the chosen school. The next tiebreaker depends upon the racial composition of the particular school and the race of the individual student. In the district's public schools approximately 41 percent of enrolled students are white; the remaining 59 percent, comprising all other racial groups, are classified by Seattle for assignment purposes as nonwhite. *Id.*, at 38a, 103a. If an oversubscribed school is not within 10 percentage points of the district's overall white/nonwhite racial balance, it is what the district calls "integration positive," and the district employs a tiebreaker that selects for assignment students whose race "will serve to bring the school into balance." *Id.*, at 38a. See *Parents Involved VII*, 426 F.3d 1162, 1169–1170 (C.A.9 2005) (en banc). . . .

Seattle has never operated segregated schools—legally separate schools for students of different races - nor has it ever been subject to court-ordered desegregation. It nonetheless employs the racial tiebreaker in an attempt to address the effects of racially identifiable housing patterns on school assignments. Most white students live in the northern part of Seattle, most students of other racial backgrounds in the southern part. . . .

Petitioner Parents Involved in Community Schools (Parents Involved) is a nonprofit corporation comprising the parents of children who have been or may be denied assignment to their chosen high school in the district because of their race. The concerns of Parents Involved are illustrated by Jill Kurfirst, who sought to enroll her ninth-grade son, Andy Meeks, in Ballard High School's special Biotechnology Career Academy. Andy suffered from attention deficit hyperactivity disorder and dyslexia, but had made good progress with hands-on instruction, and his mother and middle school teachers thought that the smaller biotechnology program held the most promise for his continued success. Andy was accepted into this selective program but, because of the racial tiebreaker, was denied assignment to Ballard High School. Parents Involved commenced this suit in the Western District of Washington, alleging that Seattle's use of race in assignments violated the Equal Protection Clause of the Fourteenth Amendment.

The District Court granted summary judgment to the school district, finding that state law did not bar the district's use of the racial tiebreaker and that the plan survived strict scrutiny on the federal constitutional claim because it was narrowly tailored to serve a compelling government interest. . . .

B

Jefferson County Public Schools operates the public school system in metropolitan Louisville, Kentucky. In 1973 a federal court found that Jefferson County had maintained a segregated school system and in 1975 the District Court entered a desegregation decree. Jefferson County operated under this decree until 2000, when the District Court dissolved the decree after finding that the district had achieved unitary status by eliminating "[t]o the greatest extent practicable" the vestiges of its prior policy of segregation.

In 2001, after the decree had been dissolved, Jefferson County adopted the voluntary student assignment plan at issue in this case. Approximately 34 percent of the district's 97,000 students are black; most of the remaining 66 percent are white. *McFarland v. Jefferson Cty. Public Schools*, 330 F.Supp.2d 834, 839–840, and n. 6 (W.D.Ky.2004) (McFarland I). The plan requires all nonmagnet schools to maintain a minimum black enrollment of 15 percent, and a maximum black enrollment of 50 percent. . . .

When petitioner Crystal Meredith moved into the school district in August 2002, she sought to enroll her son, Joshua McDonald, in kindergarten for the 2002–2003 school year. His resides school was only a mile from his new home, but it had no available space—assignments had been made in May, and the class was full. Jefferson County assigned Joshua to another elementary school in his cluster, Young Elementary. This school was 10 miles from home, and Meredith sought to transfer Joshua to a school in a different cluster, Bloom Elementary, which -like his resides school—was only a mile from home. See Tr. in *McFarland I*, pp. 1-49 through 1-54 (Dec. 8, 2003). Space was available at Bloom, and intercluster transfers are allowed, but Joshua's transfer was nonetheless denied because, in the words of Jefferson County, "[t]he transfer would have an adverse effect on desegregation compliance" of Young.

Meredith brought suit in the Western District of Kentucky, alleging violations of the Equal Protection Clause of the Fourteenth Amendment. . . .

III

A

It is well established that when the government distributes burdens or benefits on the basis of individual racial classifications, that action is reviewed under strict scrutiny. . . .

Without attempting in these cases to set forth all the interests a school district might assert, it suffices to note that our prior cases, in evaluating the use of racial classifications in the school context, have recognized two interests that qualify as compelling. The first is the compelling interest of remedying the effects of past intentional discrimination. See *Freeman v. Pitts*, 503 U.S. 467 (1992). Yet the Seattle public schools have not shown that they were ever segregated by law, and were not subject to court-ordered desegregation decrees. The Jefferson County public schools were previously segregated by law and were subject to a desegregation decree entered in 1975. In 2000, the District Court that entered that decree dissolved it, finding that Jefferson County had "eliminated the vestiges associated with the former policy of segregation and its pernicious effects," and thus had achieved "unitary" status. Jefferson County accordingly does not rely upon an interest in remedying the effects of past intentional discrimination in defending its present use of race in assigning students.

Nor could it. We have emphasized that the harm being remedied by mandatory desegregation plans is the harm that is traceable to segregation, and that "the Constitution is not violated by racial imbalance in the schools, without more." *Milliken v. Bradley*, 433 U.S. 267 (1977). Once Jefferson County achieved unitary status, it had remedied the constitutional wrong that allowed race-based assignments. Any continued use of race must be justified on some other basis.

The second government interest we have recognized as compelling for purposes of strict scrutiny is the interest in diversity in higher education upheld in *Grutter*. The specific interest found compelling in *Grutter* was student body diversity "in the context of higher education." *Ibid.* The diversity interest was not focused on race alone but encompassed "all factors that may contribute to student body diversity." . . .

The entire gist of the analysis in *Grutter* was that the admissions program at issue there focused on each applicant as an individual, and not simply as a member of a particular racial group. The classification of applicants by race upheld in *Grutter* was only as part of a "highly individualized, holistic review." As the Court explained, "[t]he importance of this individualized consideration in the context of a race-conscious admissions program is paramount." *Ibid.* The point of the narrow tailoring analysis in which the *Grutter* Court engaged was to ensure that the use of racial classifications was indeed part of a broader assessment of diversity, and not simply an effort to achieve racial balance, which the Court explained would be "patently unconstitutional."

In the present cases, by contrast, race is not considered as part of a broader effort to achieve "exposure to widely diverse people, cultures, ideas, and viewpoints," *ibid.*; race, for some students, is determinative standing alone. The districts argue that other factors, such as student preferences, affect assignment decisions under their plans, but under each plan when race comes into play, it is decisive by itself. It is not simply one factor weighed with others in reaching a decision, as in *Grutter*; it is the factor. Like the University of Michigan undergraduate plan struck down in *Gratz*, the plans here "do not provide for a meaningful individualized review of applicants" but instead rely on racial classifications in a "nonindividualized, mechanical" way. . . .

In upholding the admissions plan in *Grutter*, though, this Court relied upon considerations unique to institutions of higher education, noting that in light of "the expansive freedoms of speech and thought associated with the university environment, universities occupy a special niche in our constitutional tradition." The Court explained that "[c]ontext matters" in applying strict scrutiny, and repeatedly noted that it was addressing the use of race "in the context of higher education." The Court in *Grutter* expressly articulated key limitations on its holding—defining a specific type of broad-based diversity and noting the unique context of higher education—but these limitations were largely disregarded by the lower courts in extending *Grutter* to uphold race-based assignments in elementary and secondary schools. The present cases are not governed by *Grutter*.

B

Perhaps recognizing that reliance on *Grutter* cannot sustain their plans, both school districts assert additional interests, distinct from the interest upheld in *Grutter*, to justify their race-based assignments. In briefing and argument before this Court, Seattle contends that its use of race helps to reduce racial concentration in schools and to ensure that racially concentrated housing patterns do not prevent nonwhite students from having access to the most desirable schools. Brief for Respondents in No. 05-908, at 19. Jefferson County has articulated a similar goal, phrasing its interest in terms of educating its students "in a racially integrated environment." App. in No. 05-915, at 22. Each school district argues that educational and broader socialization benefits flow from a racially diverse learning environment, and each contends that because the diversity they seek is racial diversity—not the broader diversity at issue in *Grutter*—it makes sense to promote that interest directly by relying on race alone.

The parties and their *amici* dispute whether racial diversity in schools in fact has a marked impact on test scores and other objective yardsticks or achieves intangible socialization benefits. The debate is not one we need to resolve, however, because it is clear that the racial classifications employed by the districts are not narrowly tailored to the goal of achieving the educational and social benefits asserted to flow from racial diversity. In design and operation, the plans are directed only to racial balance, pure and simple, an objective this Court has repeatedly condemned as illegitimate.

The plans are tied to each district's specific racial demographics, rather than to any pedagogic concept of the level of diversity needed to obtain the asserted educational benefits. . . .

Here the racial balance the districts seek is a defined range set solely by reference to the demographics of the respective school districts.

This working backward to achieve a particular type of racial balance, rather than working forward from some demonstration of the level of diversity that provides the purported benefits, is a fatal flaw under our existing precedent. We have many times over reaffirmed that "[r]acial balance is not to be achieved for its own sake." *Grutter* itself reiterated that "outright racial balancing" is "patently unconstitutional." 539 U.S., at 330.

Accepting racial balancing as a compelling state interest would justify the imposition of racial proportionality throughout American society, contrary to our repeated recognition that "[a]t the heart of the Constitution's guarantee of equal protection lies the simple command that the Government must treat citizens as individuals, not as simply components of a racial, religious, sexual or national class." Allowing racial balancing as a compelling end in itself would "effectively assur[e] that race will always be relevant in American life, and that the 'ultimate goal' of 'eliminating entirely from governmental decisionmaking such irrelevant factors as a human being's race' will never be achieved." . . .

The principle that racial balancing is not permitted is one of substance, not semantics. Racial balancing is not transformed from "patently unconstitutional" to a compelling state interest simply by relabeling it "racial diversity." While the school districts use various verbal formulations to describe the interest they seek to promote — racial diversity, avoidance of racial isolation, racial integration — they offer no definition of the interest that suggests it differs from racial balance. . . .

C

The districts assert, as they must, that the way in which they have employed individual racial classifications is necessary to achieve their stated ends. The minimal effect these classifications have on student assignments, however, suggests that other means would be effective. . . .

While we do not suggest that *greater* use of race would be preferable, the minimal impact of the districts' racial classifications on school enrollment casts doubt on the necessity of using racial classifications. . . . Classifying and assigning schoolchildren according to a binary conception of race is an extreme approach in light of our precedents and our Nation's history of using race in public schools, and requires more than such an amorphous end to justify it.

The districts have also failed to show that they considered methods other than explicit racial classifications to achieve their stated goals. Narrow tailoring requires "serious, good faith consideration of workable race-neutral alternatives," *Grutter, supra*, at 339, and yet in Seattle several alternative assignment plans—many of which would not have used express racial classifications—were rejected with little or no consideration. Jefferson County has failed to present any evidence that it considered alternatives, even though the district already claims that its goals are achieved primarily through means other than the racial classifications.

IV

Justice Breyer's dissent takes a different approach to these cases, one that fails to ground the result it would reach in law. Instead, it selectively relies on inapplicable precedent and even dicta while dismissing contrary holdings, alters and misapplies our well-established legal framework for assessing equal protection challenges to express racial classifications, and greatly exaggerates the consequences of today's decision. . . .

*   *   *

If the need for the racial classifications embraced by the school districts is unclear, even on the districts' own terms, the costs are undeniable. [D]istinctions between citizens solely because of their ancestry are by their very nature odious to a free people whose institutions are founded upon the doctrine of equality. Government action dividing us by race is inherently suspect because such classifications promote "notions of racial inferiority and lead to a politics of racial hostility, reinforce the belief, held by too many for too much of our history, that individuals should be judged by the color of their skin," and "endorse race-based reasoning and the conception of a Nation divided into racial blocs, thus contributing to an escalation of racial hostility and conflict." . . .

All this is true enough in the contexts in which these statements were made—government contracting, voting districts, allocation of broadcast licenses, and electing state officers—but when it comes to using race to assign children to schools, history will be heard. In *Brown v. Board of Education*, 347 U.S. 483 (*Brown I*), we held that segregation deprived black children of equal educational opportunities regardless of whether school facilities and other tangible factors were equal, because government classification and separation on grounds of race themselves denoted inferiority. *Id.*, at 493–494. It was not the inequality of the facilities but the fact of legally separating children on the basis of race on which the Court relied to find a constitutional violation in 1954 . . .

Before *Brown*, schoolchildren were told where they could and could not go to school based on the color of their skin. The school districts in these cases have not carried the heavy burden of demonstrating that we should allow this once again—even for very different reasons. For schools that never segregated on the basis of race, such as Seattle, or that have removed the vestiges of past segregation, such as Jefferson County, the way "to achieve a system of determining admission to the public schools on a nonracial basis," Brown II, 349 U.S., at 300–301, is to stop assigning students on a racial basis. The way to stop discrimination on the basis of race is to stop discriminating on the basis of race.

The judgments of the Courts of Appeals for the Sixth and Ninth Circuits are reversed, and the cases are remanded for further proceedings.

It is so ordered.

JUSTICE THOMAS, concurring.

Today, the Court holds that state entities may not experiment with race-based means to achieve ends they deem socially desirable. I wholly concur in The Chief Justice's opinion. I write separately to address several of the contentions in Justice Breyer's dissent (hereinafter the dissent). Contrary to the dissent's arguments, resegregation is not occurring in Seattle or Louisville; these school boards have no present interest in remedying past segregation; and these race-based student-assignment programs do not serve any compelling state interest. Accordingly, the plans are unconstitutional. Disfavoring a color-blind interpretation of the Constitution, the dissent would give school boards a free hand to make decisions on the basis of race—an approach reminiscent of that advocated by the segregationists in *Brown v. Board of Education*. This approach is just as wrong today as it was a half-century ago. The Constitution and our cases require us to be much more demanding before permitting local school boards to make decisions based on race. . . . [Justice Thomas' concurring opinion is a lengthy defense of the "colorblind" interpretation of the Equal Protection Clause, as he and Justice Scalia have repeatedly advanced. Since they have made these arguments in previous opinions, this opinion is heavily edited, leaving primarily "new" materials.]

I

Contrary to the dissent's rhetoric, neither of these school districts is threatened with resegregation, and neither is constitutionally compelled or permitted to undertake race-based remediation. Racial imbalance is not segregation, and the mere incantation of terms like resegregation and remediation cannot make up the difference. . . .

A

Although there is arguably a danger of racial imbalance in schools in Seattle and Louisville, there is no danger of resegregation. No one contends that Seattle has established or that Louisville has reestablished a dual school system that separates students on the basis of race. The statistics cited in Appendix A to the dissent are not to the contrary. At most, those statistics show a national trend toward classroom racial imbalance. However, racial imbalance without intentional state action to separate the races does not amount to segregation. To raise the specter of resegregation to defend these programs is to ignore the meaning of the word and the nature of the cases before us. . . .

1

The Constitution does not permit race-based government decisionmaking simply because a school district claims a remedial purpose and proceeds in good faith with arguably pure motives. Rather, race-based government decisionmaking is categorically prohibited unless narrowly tailored to serve a compelling interest. . . .

II

Lacking a cognizable interest in remediation, neither of these plans can survive strict scrutiny because neither plan serves a genuinely compelling state interest. The dissent avoids reaching that conclusion by unquestioningly accepting the assertions of selected social scientists while completely ignoring the fact that those assertions are the subject of fervent debate. Ultimately, the dissent's entire analysis is corrupted by the considerations that lead it initially to question whether strict scrutiny should apply at all. What emerges is a version of "strict scrutiny" that combines hollow assurances of harmlessness with reflexive acceptance of conventional wisdom. When it comes to government race-based decisionmaking, the Constitution demands more. . . .

A

. . . .

3

Finally, the dissent asserts a "democratic element" to the integration interest. It defines the "democratic element" as "an interest in producing an educational environment that reflects the 'pluralistic society' in which our children will live." Environmental reflection, though, is just another way to say racial balancing. And "[p]referring members of any one group for no reason other than race or ethnic origin is discrimination for its own sake." *Bakke*, 438 U.S., at 307 (opinion of Powell, J.). "This the Constitution forbids."

Navigating around that inconvenient authority, the dissent argues that the racial balancing in these plans is not an end in itself but is instead intended to "teac[h] children to engage in the kind of cooperation among Americans of all races that is necessary to make a land of three hundred million people one Nation." These "generic lessons in socialization and good citizenship" are too sweeping to qualify as compelling interests. . . .

Moreover, the democratic interest has no durational limit, contrary to *Grutter*'s command. In other words, it will always be important for students to learn cooperation among the races. If this interest justifies race-conscious measures today, then logically it will justify race-conscious measures forever. . . .

III

Most of the dissent's criticisms of today's result can be traced to its rejection of the color-blind Constitution. The dissent attempts to marginalize the notion of a color-blind Constitution by consigning it to me and Members of today's plurality. But I am quite comfortable in the company I keep. My view of the Constitution is Justice Harlan's view in *Plessy*: "Our Constitution is color-blind, and neither knows nor tolerates classes among citizens." And my view was the rallying cry for the lawyers who litigated *Brown*. See, *e.g.*, Brief for Appellants in *Brown v. Board of Education*, O.T.1953, Nos. 1, 2, and 4 p. 65 ("That the Constitution is color blind is our dedicated belief"). . . .

What was wrong in 1954 cannot be right today. Whatever else the Court's rejection of the segregationists' arguments in *Brown* might have established, it certainly made clear that state and local governments cannot take from the Constitution a right to make decisions on the basis of race by adverse possession. The fact that state and local governments had been discriminating on the basis of race for a long time was irrelevant to the *Brown* Court. The fact that racial discrimination was preferable to the relevant communities was irrelevant to the *Brown* Court. And the fact that the state and local governments had relied on statements in this Court's opinions was irrelevant to the *Brown* Court. The same principles guide today's decision.

JUSTICE KENNEDY, concurring in part and concurring in the judgment.

The Nation's schools strive to teach that our strength comes from people of different races, creeds, and cultures uniting in commitment to the freedom of all. In these cases two school districts in different parts of the country seek to teach that principle by having classrooms that reflect the racial makeup of the surrounding community. That the school districts consider these plans to be necessary should remind us our highest aspirations are yet unfulfilled. But the solutions mandated by these school districts must themselves be lawful. To make race matter now so that it might not matter later may entrench the very prejudices we seek to overcome. In my view the state-mandated racial classifications at issue, official labels proclaiming the race of all persons in a broad class of citizens—elementary school students in one case, high school students in another—are unconstitutional as the cases now come to us.

I agree with The Chief Justice that we have jurisdiction to decide the cases before us and join Parts I and II of the Court's opinion. I also join Parts III-A and III-C for reasons provided below. My views do not allow me to join the balance of the opinion by The Chief Justice, which seems to me to be inconsistent in both its approach and its implications with the history, meaning, and reach of the Equal Protection Clause. Justice Breyer's dissenting opinion, on the other hand, rests on what in my respectful submission is a misuse and mistaken interpretation of our precedents. This leads it to advance propositions that, in my view, are both erroneous and in fundamental conflict with basic equal protection principles. As a consequence, this separate opinion is necessary to set forth my conclusions in the two cases before the Court. . . .

II

Our Nation from the inception has sought to preserve and expand the promise of liberty and equality on which it was founded. Today we enjoy a society that is remarkable in its openness and opportunity. Yet our tradition is to go beyond present achievements, however significant, and to recognize and confront the flaws and injustices that remain. This is especially true when we seek assurance that opportunity is not denied on account of race. The enduring hope is that race should not matter; the reality is that too often it does.

This is by way of preface to my respectful submission that parts of the opinion by The Chief Justice imply an all-too-unyielding insistence that race cannot be a factor in instances when, in my view, it may be taken into account. The plurality opinion is too dismissive of the legitimate interest government has in ensuring all people have equal opportunity regardless of their race. The plurality's postulate that "[t]he way to stop discrimination on the basis of race is to stop discriminating on the basis of race," is not sufficient to decide these cases. Fifty years of experience since *Brown v. Board of Education*, should teach us that the problem before us defies so easy a solution. . . .

In the cases before us it is noteworthy that the number of students whose assignment depends on express racial classifications is limited. I join Part III-C of the Court's opinion because I agree that in the context of these plans, the small number of assignments affected suggests that the schools could have achieved their stated ends through different means. These include the facially race-neutral means set forth above or, if necessary, a more nuanced, individual evaluation of school needs and student characteristics that might include race as a component. The latter approach would be informed by *Grutter*, though of course the criteria relevant to student placement would differ based on the age of the students, the needs of the parents, and the role of the schools. . . .

JUSTICE STEVENS, dissenting.

While I join Justice Breyer's eloquent and unanswerable dissent in its entirety, it is appropriate to add these words.

There is a cruel irony in The Chief Justice's reliance on our decision in *Brown v. Board of Education*. The first sentence in the concluding paragraph of his opinion states: "Before *Brown*, schoolchildren were told where they could and could not go to school based on the color of their skin." This sentence reminds me of Anatole France's observation: "[T]he majestic equality of the la [w], forbid[s] rich and poor alike to sleep under bridges, to beg in the streets, and to steal their bread." The Chief Justice fails to note that it was only black schoolchildren who were so ordered; indeed, the history books do not tell stories of white children struggling to attend black schools. In this and other ways, The Chief Justice rewrites the history of one of this Court's most important decisions. . . .

The Court has changed significantly since it decided *School Comm. of Boston* in 1968. It was then more faithful to *Brown* and more respectful of our precedent than it is today. It is my firm conviction that no Member of the Court that I joined in 1975 would have agreed with today's decision.

JUSTICE BREYER, with whom JUSTICE STEVENS, JUSTICE SOUTER, and JUSTICE GINSBURG join, dissenting.

These cases consider the longstanding efforts of two local school boards to integrate their public schools. The school board plans before us resemble many others adopted in the last 50 years by primary and secondary schools throughout the Nation. All of those plans represent local efforts to bring about the kind of racially integrated education that *Brown v. Board of Education*, long ago promised—efforts that this Court has repeatedly required, permitted, and encouraged local authorities to undertake. This Court has recognized that the public interests at stake in such cases are "compelling." We have approved of "narrowly tailored" plans that are no less race-conscious than the plans before us. And we have understood that the Constitution *permits* local communities to adopt desegregation plans even where it does not *require* them to do so.

The plurality pays inadequate attention to this law, to past opinions' rationales, their language, and the contexts in which they arise. As a result, it reverses course and reaches the wrong conclusion. In doing so, it distorts precedent, it misapplies the relevant constitutional principles, it announces legal rules that will obstruct efforts by state and local governments to deal effectively with the growing resegregation of public schools, it threatens to substitute for present calm a disruptive round of race-related litigation, and it undermines *Brown*'s promise of integrated primary and secondary education that local communities have sought to make a reality. This cannot be justified in the name of the Equal Protection Clause. . . . [Justice Breyer submitted a long dissenting opinion. It is heavily edited here. It argues against the colorblindness theory and the plurality opinion.]

I

Facts

The historical and factual context in which these cases arise is critical. . . .

Beyond those minimum requirements, the Court left much of the determination of how to achieve integration to the judgment of local communities. . . .

Overall these efforts brought about considerable racial integration. More recently, however, progress has stalled. Between 1968 and 1980, the number of black children attending a school where minority children constituted more than half of the school fell from 77% to 63% in the Nation (from 81% to 57% in the South) but then reversed direction by the year 2000, rising from 63% to 72% in the Nation (from 57% to 69% in the South). . . .

The upshot is that myriad school districts operating in myriad circumstances have devised myriad plans, often with race-conscious elements, all for the sake of eradicating earlier school segregation, bringing about integration, or preventing retrogression. Seattle and Louisville are two such districts, and the histories of their present plans set forth typical school integration stories. . . .

II

The Legal Standard

A longstanding and unbroken line of legal authority tells us that the Equal Protection Clause permits local school boards to use race-conscious criteria to achieve positive race-related goals, even when the Constitution does not compel it. . . .

Nonetheless, in light of *Grutter* and other precedents, see, *e.g., Bakke*, 438 U.S., at 290 (opinion of POWELL, J.), I shall . . . apply the version of strict scrutiny that those cases embody. I shall consequently ask whether the school boards in Seattle and Louisville adopted these plans to serve a "compelling governmental interest" and, if so, whether the plans are "narrowly tailored" to achieve that interest. If the plans survive this strict review, they would survive less exacting review *a fortiori*. Hence, I conclude that the plans before us pass both parts of the strict scrutiny test. Consequently I must conclude that the plans here are permitted under the Constitution.

III

Applying the Legal Standard

A

Compelling Interest

The principal interest advanced in these cases to justify the use of race-based criteria goes by various names. Sometimes a court refers to it as an interest in achieving racial "diversity." Other times a court, like the plurality here, refers to it as an interest in racial "balancing." I have used more general terms to signify that interest, describing it, for example, as an interest in promoting or preserving greater racial "integration" of public schools. By this term, I mean the school districts' interest in eliminating school-by-school racial isolation and increasing the degree to which racial mixture characterizes each of the district's schools and each individual student's public school experience. . . .

The compelling interest at issue here, then, includes an effort to eradicate the remnants, not of general "societal discrimination," (plurality opinion), but of primary and secondary school segregation, see *supra*; it includes an effort to create school environments that provide better educational opportunities for all children; it includes an effort to help create citizens better prepared to know, to understand, and to work with people of all races and backgrounds, thereby furthering the kind of democratic government our Constitution foresees. If an educational interest that combines these three elements is not "compelling," what is? . . .

B

Narrow Tailoring

I next ask whether the plans before us are "narrowly tailored" to achieve these "compelling" objectives. I shall not accept the school board's assurances on faith, cf. *Miller v. Johnson*, 515 U.S. 900 (1995), and I shall subject the "tailoring" of their plans to "rigorous judicial review." *Grutter*, 539 U.S., at 388 (KENNEDY, J., dissenting). Several factors, taken together, nonetheless lead me to conclude that the boards' use of race-conscious criteria in these plans passes even the strictest "tailoring" test. . . .

Finally, I recognize that the Court seeks to distinguish *Grutter* from these cases by claiming that *Grutter* arose in " 'the context of higher education.' " But that is not a meaningful legal distinction. . . . These are not affirmative action plans, and hence "individualized scrutiny" is simply beside the point.

The upshot is that these plans' specific features—(1) their limited and historically-diminishing use of race, (2) their strong reliance upon other non-race-conscious elements, (3) their history and the manner in which the districts developed and modified their approach, (4) the comparison with prior plans, and (5) the lack of reasonably evident alternatives—together show that the districts' plans are "narrowly tailored" to achieve their "compelling" goals. In sum, the districts' race-conscious plans satisfy "strict scrutiny" and are therefore lawful. . . .

VI

Conclusions

To show that the school assignment plans here meet the requirements of the Constitution, I have written at exceptional length. But that length is necessary. . . .

Finally, what of the hope and promise of *Brown*? For much of this Nation's history, the races remained divided. It was not long ago that people of different races drank from separate fountains, rode on separate buses, and studied in separate schools. In this Court's finest hour, *Brown v. Board of Education* challenged this history and helped to change it. For *Brown* held out a promise. It was a promise embodied in three Amendments designed to make citizens of slaves. It was the promise of true racial equality—not as a matter of fine words on paper, but as a matter of everyday life in the Nation's cities and schools. It was about the nature of a democracy that must work for all Americans. It sought one law, one Nation, one people, not simply as a matter of legal principle but in terms of how we actually live. . . .

NOTES AND QUESTIONS

(1) *The Use of Race in Public School Admissions and Transfers: Parents Involved in Community Schools v. Seattle School District No. 1 and Meredith v. Jefferson Bd. of Educ., 127 S. Ct. 2738 (2007).* In these post-*Grutter* decisions, both the Seattle and Louisville school districts used race as the determinant factor under certain circumstances in admissions and student transfers. In both cases, the school districts defended their use of race as a voluntary program seeking to achieve "diversity," under the *Grutter* decision. The *Seattle School District* Court, per Chief Justice Roberts, distinguished *Grutter* and ruled against the districts. The Court (5-4) applied strict scrutiny and held that neither district satisfied the narrow tailoring prong.

By distinguishing *Grutter*, the Court avoided considering whether the *Grutter* concept of "educational diversity" should be reexamined. The Chief Justice concluded that the districts were pursuing "racial balance." He added that "[r]acial balancing is not transformed from 'patently unconstitutional' to a compelling state interest simply be relabeling it 'racial diversity'." The Chief Justice's plurality opinion ultimately adopted a colorblindness interpretation of the Equal Protection Clause. Justice Thomas wrote a concurring opinion further supporting the colorblindness theory (as well as addressing arguments from Justice Breyer's dissent).

(2) *The Kennedy Concurrene: The Future Controlling Opinion?* Justice Kennedy declined to adopt the colorblindness position. He stated that, consistent with *Grutter* (from which he had dissented), public schools can use race as a non-determinant factor in an individualized assessment. He concluded that the Seattle and Louisville school districts had not done that and, instead, had utilized racial quotas. Justice Kennedy's concurrence also argued that "preventing racial isolation" could constitute a compelling governmental interest. With respect to both these governmental interests, Justice Kennedy's position is broader than Roberts plurality opinion.

(3) *The Breyer Dissent.* Justice Breyer dissented for Justices Ginsburg, Stevens, and Souter. Justice Breyer's rejected the colorblindness theory. He focused on the "effects" of residential segregation and argued that the Seattle District should be permitted to voluntarily address this situation. Justice Breyer defended his analysis because he did not characterize the "voluntary" student placement plans as "affirmative action" plans. Justice Breyer also argued that the districts had a compelling interest in preventing "resegregation" of the schools. Note Justice Breyer's assertion that the school admission plans at issue "are not affirmative action plans."

(4) *The Status of Educational Diversity as a Compelling Governmental Interest: Bakke to Grutter to Seattle School District.* While *Grutter* either expanded the concept of "intellectual diversity" or added "educational diversity" to the set of compelling interests, the *Seattle School District* Court limited the use of *Grutter*'s educational diversity to the post-secondary setting. If *Grutter* diversity would not apply even to other educational settings, it would be unlikely to apply to employment or public services. One likely consequence of the *Seattle School District* decision will be litigation in other school districts with "voluntary diversity" programs.

SHAW v. HUNT
517 U.S. 899 (1996)

CHIEF JUSTICE REHNQUIST delivered the opinion of the Court.

[After the 1990 census, the North Carolina Legislature sought to adopt a reapportionment plan for its increased congressional delegation. The Legislature's first plan included one majority-minority district (District 1). The first plan was submitted to the United States Justice Department for preclearance under Section 5 of the Voting Rights Act. The Justice Department rejected the first plan essentially because it did not have a second majority-minority congressional district. "Duly chastened," the Legislature produced a second plan that had two districts (Districts 1 and 12) in which racial minority members were the majority of the voters.

[Five North Carolinians sued the state officials, alleging that the redistricting plan violated their equal protection rights. In *Shaw v. Reno*, 509 U.S. 630 (1993) ("*Shaw I*"), the Court determined that the appellants had stated a claim under the Equal Protection Clause and remanded for trial. The Court recognized the North Carolina redistricting plan as an affirmative action program. In this decision ("*Shaw II*"), the Court concluded, based on the findings of the trial court, that the geographic boundaries of Districts 1 and 12 were "unconventional." The Court called District 12 "snake-like." The Court also concluded, from the totality of the evidence, that the Districts were "deliberately drawn to produce one or more districts of a certain racial composition." The Court then proceeded, as follows, to define the standard for review of voting districts based "predominantly" on race as strict scrutiny, and it then examined whether there was a narrowly tailored compelling interest in this case.]

[W]e explained in *Miller v. Johnson*, 515 U.S. 900 (1995), that a racially gerrymandered districting scheme, like all laws that classify citizens on the basis of race, is constitutionally suspect. *See also Adarand Constructors, Inc. v. Pena.* This is true whether or not the reason for the racial classification is benign or the purpose remedial. . . .

Applying traditional equal protection principles in the voting-rights context is "a most delicate task," however, because a legislature may be conscious of the voters' races without using race as a basis for assigning voters to districts. The constitutional wrong [in a redistricting case] occurs when race becomes the "dominant and controlling" consideration. The plaintiff bears the burden of proving the race-based motive and may do so either through "circumstantial evidence of a district's shape and demographics" or through "more direct evidence going to legislative purpose." *Miller, supra.*

[The majority here reviewed the evidence demonstrating that North Carolina had purposefully created a racial gerrymander.] First, the District Court had evidence of [District 12's] shape and demographics. The [District] Court observed "the obvious fact" that the district's shape is "highly irregular and geographically non-compact by any objective standard that can be conceived." . . .

The District Court also had direct evidence of the legislature's objective. The State's submission for preclearance expressly acknowledged that the [second legislative plan's] "overriding purpose was to comply with the dictates of the [Justice Department] and to create two congressional districts with effective black voting majorities." This admission was confirmed by [the testimony of] Gerry Cohen, the plan's principal draftsman. . . . Indeed, appellees in their first appearance before the District Court "formally concede[d] that the state legislature deliberately created the two districts in a way to assure black-vote majorities," *Shaw v. Barr,* 808 F.Supp. 461, 470 (E.D.N.C.1992), and that concession again was credited by the District Court on remand. . . .

[W]e do not quarrel with the dissent's claims that, in shaping District 12, the State [also] effectuated its [non-racial] interest in creating one rural and one urban district, and that partisan politicking was actively at work in the districting process. That the legislature addressed these interests does not in any way refute the fact that race was the legislature's predominant consideration [in creating these two particular districts]. Race was the criterion that, in the State's view, could not be compromised; respecting communities of interest and protecting Democratic incumbents came into play only after the race-based decision had been made.

[N]orth Carolina, therefore, must show not only that its redistricting plan was in pursuit of a compelling state interest, but also that "its districting legislation is narrowly tailored to achieve [that] compelling interest." *Miller.*

Appellees point to three separate compelling interests to sustain District 12: to eradicate the effects of past and present discrimination; to comply with § 5 of the Voting Rights Act [prohibiting discrimination and requiring preclearance of voting law changes by the Justice Department]; and to comply with § 2 of that Act [which requires that all groups have equal opportunity to elect candidates of their choice]. We address each in turn.

[First: Remedying Past and Present Discrimination Generally.] A State's interest in remedying the effects of past or present racial discrimination may in the proper case justify a government's use of racial distinctions. *Croson.* For that interest to rise to the level of a compelling state interest, it must satisfy two conditions. First, the discrimination must be " 'identified discrimination.' " . . . A generalized assertion of past discrimination in a particular industry or region is not adequate because it "provides no guidance for a legislative body to determine the precise scope of the injury it seeks to remedy." Accordingly, an effort to alleviate the effects of societal discrimination is not a compelling interest. Second, the institution that makes the racial distinction must have had a "strong basis in evidence" to conclude that remedial action

was necessary, "before it embarks on an affirmative-action program."

In this case, the District Court found that an interest in ameliorating past discrimination did not actually precipitate the use of race in the redistricting plan. [The Supreme Court here upholds this finding and rejects the State's argument.] . . .

[*Second: The § 5 Argument.*] With respect to § 5 of the Voting Rights Act, we believe our decision in *Miller* forecloses the argument, adopted by the District Court, that failure to engage in the race-based districting would have violated that section.

[N]orth Carolina's first plan [i.e., the plan rejected by the Justice Department as violative of the Voting Rights Act] indisputably was ameliorative, having created the first majority-black district in recent history. Thus, that plan, "even if [it] fall[s] short of what might be accomplished in terms of increasing minority representation," "cannot violate § 5 unless the new apportionment itself so discriminates on the basis of race or color as to violate the Constitution." *Miller, supra.*

[I]t appears that the Justice Department was pursuing in North Carolina the same policy of maximizing the number of majority-black districts that it pursued in [the *Miller* case] . . . A North Carolina legislator recalled being told by the Assistant Attorney General that "you have twenty-two percent black people in this State, you must have as close to twenty-two percent black Congressmen, or black Congressional Districts in this State." We explained in *Miller* that this maximization policy is not properly grounded in § 5 and the Department's authority thereunder. . . .

[*Third: The § 2 Argument.*] We assume, arguendo, for the purpose of resolving this case, that compliance with § 2 could be a compelling interest, and we likewise assume, arguendo, that the General Assembly believed a second majority-minority district was needed in order not to violate § 2, and that the legislature at the time it acted had a strong basis in evidence to support that conclusion. We hold that even with the benefit of these assumptions, the North Carolina plan does not survive strict scrutiny because the remedy—the creation of District 12—is not narrowly tailored to the asserted end. . . . [*Reversed*]

JUSTICE STEVENS, with whom JUSTICE GINSBURG and JUSTICE BREYER join [in part], dissenting.

As I have explained on prior occasions, I am convinced that the Court's aggressive supervision of state action designed to accommodate the political concerns of historically disadvantaged minority groups is seriously misguided. A majority's attempt to enable the minority to participate more effectively in the process of democratic government should not be viewed with the same hostility that is appropriate for oppressive and exclusionary abuses of political power.

But even if we accept the Court's refusal to recognize any distinction between two vastly different kinds of situations, we should affirm the judgment of the District Court in this case. . . .

[D]istrict 12's noncompact appearance also fails to show that North Carolina engaged in suspect race-based districting. There is no federal statutory or constitutional requirement that state electoral boundaries conform to any particular ideal of geographic compactness. . . .

[T]here is a more fundamental flaw in the majority's conclusion that racial concerns predominantly explain the creation of District 12. The evidence of shape and intent relied on by the majority cannot overcome the basic fact that North Carolina did not have to draw Districts 1 and 12 in order to comply with the Justice Department's finding that federal law required the creation of two majority-minority districts. That goal could have been more straightforwardly accomplished by simply adopting the [Justice Department's] recommendation to draw a geographically compact district in the southeastern portion of the State in addition to the majority-minority district that had already been drawn in the northeastern and Piedmont regions.

That the legislature chose to draw Districts 1 and 12 instead surely suggests that something more than the desire to create a majority-minority district took precedence.

[H]ere, no evidence suggests that race played any role in the legislature's decision to choose the winding contours of District 12 over the more cartographically pleasant boundaries proposed by the [Justice Department]. Rather, the record reveals that two race-neutral, traditional criteria determined District 12's shape: The interest in ensuring that incumbents would remain residents of the districts they have previously represented; and the interest in placing predominantly rural voters in one district and predominantly urban voters in another. . . .

[M]oreover, the record reveals that District 12's lines were drawn in order to unite an African-American community whose political tradition was quite distinct from the one that defines African-American voters in the Coastal Plain, which District 1 surrounds. . . .

[T]he majority's implicit equation of the intentional consideration of race in order to comply with the Voting Rights Act with intentional racial discrimination reveals the inadequacy of the framework it adopts for considering the constitutionality of race-based districting. . . .

NOTES AND QUESTIONS

(1) *Determining the Applicable Standard for Electoral Districting Cases: (Strict Scrutiny): Shaw v. Hunt, 517 U.S. 899 (1996).* The *Shaw II* decision confirms the Court's position that cases involving alleged racial gerrymanders will be governed by the strict scrutiny standard. This standard places the burden on the government to show that the plan serves a "compelling state interest" and that the means chosen were "narrowly tailored" to achieving that compelling interest. Note that this standard is the same test as the Court will use in other "affirmative action" cases.

(2) *Another Redistricting Decision Suggesting the Types of Evidence Relevant to Satisfying the "Predominant Factor" Standard: Bush v. Vera, 517 U.S. 952 (1996).* The *Bush* case was challenge to state electoral redistricting efforts in Texas. The Court treated it as a "mixed motive case" since Texas argued that, in addition to producing majority-minority districts, it had other "race-neutral" goals, such as protecting incumbents. The Court, per Justice O'Connor's plurality opinion, held that race was the "predominant factor" in the Texas redistricting plans and, hence, strict scrutiny was the standard. The Court reviewed evidence of the districts' irregular shapes, the traditional redistricting practices in Texas and the "detailed racial data" in the computer programs used by the Legislature to develop the redistricting plan. Four Justices dissented.

(3) *Further Developments in the Racial Gerrymandering Jurisprudence: Abrams v. Johnson, 521 U.S. 74 (1997).* In *Miller v. Johnson, 521 U.S. 74 (1995),* the Supreme Court invalidated Georgia's congressional redistricting plan, deciding that race was the "predominant factor" in the Legislature's creation of three majority-black districts (out of eleven). On remand, after the Georgia Legislature failed to submit an acceptable plan, the federal district court ordered the use of a plan with only one majority-black district. The district court's plan was challenged, on constitutional and statutory grounds, by minority voters and by the federal government. (The challengers wanted at least a two black-majority plan.) The Supreme Court, per Justice Kennedy, held in *Abrams* that the one majority-black district plan did not violate equal protection doctrine. Justice Breyer, joined by Justices Stevens, Souter, and Ginsburg, dissented.

(4) *Is Strict Scrutiny of Minority-Majority Voting Districts Appropriate, Given That Legislatures Unavoidably Are Cognizant of Racial Residence Patterns and Must Attempt to Comply with the Voting Rights Act?* By a 5-4 majority, the Court in these cases has indicated that it will review "race-based" redistricting activities with strict scrutiny. While this approach is consistent with the Court's approach to other governmental "affirmative action" activities, is this level of judicial review appropriate or

does it unduly restrict legitimate efforts to remedy post discrimination? Notice that the dissenters acknowledge that strict scrutiny may be appropriate for even "benign" or remedial uses of race in some contexts, such as jury selection (*Batson*) or government contracting (*Adarand*), but they distinguish voting rights cases and argue that strict scrutiny should not apply. Consider whether the Legislature's unavoidable awareness of racial population distribution, the need to comply with the Voting Rights Act, and the goal of opening up the political process to persons disadvantaged in the past, combined together, justify avoidance of strict scrutiny—or whether these factors instead demand strict scrutiny, for an issue as important as the political process.

(5)   *A More Cynical View: Majority-Minority Districts, "Bleached-Out" Non-Minority Districts, and Allegations of a Strange Alliance between Majority Conservatives and Minority Leaders.* The political consequence of crowding as many minority voters into one district as possible, of course, is to remove them from other nearby districts. Critics refer to this effect as the "bleaching" of suburban districts. The result in political terms, then, is that not only do majority-minority districts elect minority representatives who otherwise would not be elected, but also, the suburban districts elect representatives more oriented toward protection of wealth and privilege than they might. The political "center" is the loser, under this view. Critics charge that some administrations sought this result by enforcement of the Voting Rights Act. Does this argument strengthen the justification for strict scrutiny?

(6)   *Resolving "Mixed Motive" Issues in the Electoral Districting Cases: Hunt v. Cromartie, 526 U.S. 541 (1999).* The *Cromartie* decision is the subsequent generation of litigation following the main case, *Shaw v. Hunt*, above. After *Shaw*, the North Carolina Legislature established a new Twelfth Congressional District. Believing that it, too, was unconstitutional as a decision motivated by racial factors, plaintiffs sued. The State's defense was that the irregularly shaped District was the product of "political" factors, not "racial" factors. The federal District court resolved the dispute about the Legislature's "predominant motive" without a trial and granted summary judgment for the challengers. The Supreme Court, per Justice Thomas, reversed, holding that "it was error in this case . . . to resolve the disputed fact of motivation at the summary judgment stage." Four Justices concurred only in the judgment.

With respect to the issues raised by Notes (4) and (5) above, the *Cromartie* decision may be important, despite its procedural posture, because: (1) it concluded, by analogy to Title VII law, that the issue of legislative intent (or purpose) is a *factual* question for a jury (and not a legal question for a Judge); and (2) it asserted that, to resolve disputes about whether the Legislature had a "discriminatory purpose," a court should use the *Arlington Heights* framework." [*See* § 10.03[A][3] above.] Regarding the issue of purposefulness (or invidiousness), *see generally* Laurence H. Tribe, *The Mystery of Motive, Private and Public: Some Notes Inspired By The Problems Of Hate Crime and Animal Sacrifice*, 1993 SUP. CT. REV. 1.

(7)   *Evidence in Racial Gerrymandering — "Predominant Motive" Issues: Hunt v. Cromarte, 532 U.S. 234 (2001).* In *Cromarte II*, the federal district court (three judge panel) had found, as a factual conclusion, that race had been the "predominant motive" of the North Carolina Legislature in drawing the congressional district. *See Hunt v. Shaw* and Note (6) above. The Supreme Court, per Justice O'Connor, reversed. The majority held that the burden to establish that race was the predominant motive was on the challengers and that, in *Hunt II*, the challengers had not satisfied the burden. (Therefore, review with the strict scrutiny standard was not triggered.)

The Court held that the district court's factual finding was clearly erroneous even though it had some factual support in the record. The majority faulted the district court for relying on evidence of *voter registration statistics* rather than on the State's evidence of *voting behavior*. The majority also concluded that the district court should have given more weight to the State's expert witness and relied less on the challengers' expert witness.

The four dissenters, in an opinion by Justice Thomas, said the majority "ignores its role as a reviewing court and engages in its own fact-finding enterprise." The dissenters concluded that the "direct evidence" regarding the role of race in the redistricting process (*e.g.*, an email by the primary drafter of the plan) combined with the indirect evidence (*e.g.*, statistical data) was sufficient to uphold the district court.

Resolution of the dispute regarding this North Carolina congressional district took nearly a decade and *four* decisions by the Supreme Court. (Although the district was upheld, the 2000 Census will require a new redistricting plan.) While there are many "grey" areas, we suggest that the racial gerrymandering doctrine presently looks like the following:

> (1) The initial burden is on the challengers to show that race was the "predominant motive" of the legislature. This is analogous to the burden on the challenger in other equal protection cases to show purposefulness. *See* § 10.03[A][3] above. As *Hunt II* indicates, this may be a difficult burden.

> (2) If the challengers would satisfy the "predominant motive" burden, the burden is on the State to satisfy strict scrutiny. The doctrine presently seems "fluid," and the new Census may bring many new cases.

[7] Other Suspect (or Conditionally Suspect) Classifications: Alienage and Nationality

GRAHAM v. RICHARDSON, 403 U.S. 365 (1971). Arizona denied welfare benefits to properly admitted aliens unless they had resided in the United States for a total of fifteen years. Pennsylvania limited assistance to citizens of the United States. Both statutes were attacked by resident aliens who otherwise qualified for public assistance. The Court, per Justice Blackmun, held that lawfully admitted resident aliens were "persons" protected by the Fourteenth Amendment. It then struck down the Arizona and Pennsylvania statutes:

> [C]lassifications based on alienage, like those based on nationality or race, are inherently suspect and subject to close judicial scrutiny. Aliens as a class are a prime example of a "discrete and insular minority . . . for whom such heightened judicial solicitude is appropriate". . . .

> Arizona and Pennsylvania seek to justify their restrictions on the eligibility of aliens for public assistance solely on the basis of a state's "special public interest" in favoring its own citizens over aliens in the distribution of limited resources such as welfare benefits.

> . . . [S]ince an alien as well as a citizen is a "person" for equal protection purposes, a concern for fiscal integrity is [not a] compelling . . . justification for the questioned classification in these cases. . . .

BERNAL v. FAINTER
467 U.S. 216 (1984)

JUSTICE MARSHALL delivered the opinion of the court. . . .

Petitioner, a native of Mexico, is a resident alien who has lived in the United States since 1961. He works as a paralegal for Texas Rural Legal Aid, Inc., helping migrant farm-workers on employment and civil rights matters. In order to administer oaths to these workers and to notarize their statements for use in civil litigation, petitioner applied in 1978 to become a notary public. [T]he Texas Secretary of State denied petitioner's application because he failed to satisfy the statutory requirement that a notary public be a citizen of the United States. . . .

ARL

As a general matter, a state law that discriminates on the basis of alienage can be sustained only if it can withstand strict judicial scrutiny. In order to withstand strict scrutiny, the law must advance a compelling state interest by the least restrictive means available. Applying this principle, we have invalidated an array of state statutes that denied aliens the right to pursue various occupations. In *Sugarman v. Dougall*, 413 U.S. 634 (1973), we struck down a state statute barring aliens from employment in permanent positions in the competitive class of the state civil service. In *In re Griffiths*, 413 U.S. 717 (1973), we nullified a state law excluding aliens from eligibility for membership in the State Bar. And in *Examining Board v. Flores de Otero*, 426 U.S. 572 (1976), we voided a state law that excluded aliens from the practice of civil engineering.

We have, however, developed a narrow exception to the rule that discrimination based on alienage triggers strict scrutiny. This exception has been labeled the "political function" exception and applies to laws that exclude aliens from positions intimately related to the process of democratic self-government. The contours of the "political function" exception are outlined by our prior decisions. . . .

The rationale behind the political-function exception is that within broad boundaries a State may establish its own form of government and limit the right to govern to those who are full-fledged members of the political community. Some public positions are so closely bound up with the formulation and implementation of self-government that the State is permitted to exclude from those positions persons outside the political community, hence persons who have not become part of the process of democratic self-determination. . . .

To determine whether a restriction based on alienage fits within the narrow political-function exception, we devised in *Cabell* a two-part test:

"First, the specificity of the classification will be examined: a classification that is substantially overinclusive or underinclusive tends to undercut the governmental claim that the classification serves legitimate political ends. . . . Second, even if the classification is sufficiently tailored, it may be applied in the particular case only to 'persons holding state elective or important nonelective executive, legislative, and judicial positions,' those officers who 'participate directly in the formulation, execution, or review of broad public policy' and hence 'perform functions that go to the heart of representative government.'"

We now turn to [the Texas law] to determine whether it satisfies the *Cabell* test. Unlike the statute invalidated in *Sugarman*, [the statute] does not indiscriminately sweep within its ambit a wide range of offices and occupations but specifies only one particular post with respect towhich the State asserts a right to exclude aliens. Clearly, then, the statute is not overinclusive. . . . Less clear is whether [it] is fatally underinclusive. Texas does not require court reporters to be United States citizens even though they perform some of the same services as notaries. Nor does Texas require that its Secretary of State be a citizen, even though he holds the highest appointive position in the State and performs many important functions, including supervision of the licensing of all notaries public. We need not decide this issue, however, because of our decision with respect to the second prong of the *Cabell* test. . . .

[A] notary's duties, important as they are, hardly implicate responsibilities that go to the heart of representative government. Rather, these duties are essentially clerical and ministerial. . . .

JUSTICE REHNQUIST, dissenting.

I dissent for the reasons stated in my dissenting opinion in *Sugarman v. Dougall*, 413 U.S. 634, 649 (1973).

NOTES AND QUESTIONS

(1) *Legal Aliens as a Suspect Class and the Political Function Exception: Bernal v. Fainter, 467 U.S. 216 (1984).* Texas required that a person wishing to be a public notary had to be a citizen. A legal alien challenged this state law. Under *Graham*, legal aliens are a suspect class and would receive strict scrutiny. Texas defended by arguing that public notaries were important government officials and fell within the political function exception to strict scrutiny. In *Bernal*, the Court, per Justice Marshall, held that, while there was a political function exception, public notaries were not the sort of officials who engaged directly in the "formulation, execution, or review of broad public policy" that deserved the exception from heightened scrutiny. Justice Rehnquist dissented.

(2) *Strict Scrutiny Applies to the States but Does Not Apply to Most Federal Regulation of Aliens: Mathews v. Diaz, 426 U.S. 67 (1976).* The *Bernal* holding applies to the states, not to the federal government. In *Mathews v. Diaz*, the Court considered the equal protection component of the Fifth Amendment Due Process Clause and determined that it did not require strict scrutiny of Congress' exercise of its authority to regulate immigration and naturalization.

(3) *Is Preemption Analysis, Based Upon Congress' Control of Aliens' Status, a Better Approach? Toll v. Moreno, 458 U.S. 1 (1982).* The broad Congressional power to regulate immigration suggests another conclusion. Rather than use an equal protection analysis to protect aliens whom Congress has admitted, it might be preferable for the Court to view Congress' regulation of immigration as establishing their protected status (or the lack thereof), and thus to apply preemption analysis. For example, in *Toll v. Moreno*, the University of Maryland barred aliens with certain kinds of visas from qualifying for in-state tuition. The Court, per Justice Brennan, said: "[W]e cannot conclude that Congress ever contemplated that a state . . . might impose discriminatory tuition charges and fees solely on account of [a] federal immigration classification." Therefore, the University's policy was preempted.

[B] Fundamental Rights

AUSTIN v. MICHIGAN CHAMBER OF COMMERCE, 494 U.S. 652 (1990). A Michigan statute prohibited corporations from expending general treasury funds to provide independent support to candidates in elections. However, the statute exempted unincorporated associations (including labor unions) from its prohibition. [Note: The Court had previously held that money (political contributions) was "speech," protected by Free Speech doctrine.] The Court, per Justice Marshall, held that strict scrutiny must be applied since the statutes affected the fundamental right of speech, but it nevertheless rejected an equal protection challenge:

> [C]orporations are "by far the most prominent example of entities that enjoy legal advantages enhancing their ability to accumulate wealth." The desire to counterbalance those advantages unique to the corporate form is the state's compelling interest in this case; thus, excluding from the statute's coverage unincorporated entities that also have the capacity to accumulate wealth "does not undermine its justification for regulating corporations."

Justices Kennedy, O'Connor, and Scalia dissented on first amendment grounds. [Question: Does Justice Marshall's opinion reflect correct application of strict scrutiny—or is the result justifiable, if at all, on the ground that strict scrutiny is *too* strict and that a lower level of review should be applied?]

[1] The Right To Vote

[a] Denial Of The Right To Vote

KRAMER v. UNION FREE SCHOOL DISTRICT
395 U.S. 621 (1969)

Mr. Chief Justice Warren delivered the opinion of the Court.

In this case we are called on to determine whether § 2012 of the New York Education Law . . . is constitutional. The legislation provides that in certain New York school districts residents . . . may vote in the school district election only if they (1) own (or lease) taxable real property within the district or (2) are parents (or have custody of) children enrolled in the local public schools. Appellant, a bachelor who neither owns nor leases taxable real property [claimed] that § 2012 denied him equal protection of the laws. . . .

At the outset, it is important to note what is *not* at issue in this case. The requirements of § 2012 that school district voters must (1) be citizens of the United States, (2) be bona fide residents of the school district, and (3) be at least 21 years of age, are not challenged. Appellant agrees that the states have the power to impose reasonable citizenship, age, and residency requirements on the availability of the ballot. . . .

[W]e must give the statute a close and exacting examination. "[S]ince the right to exercise the franchise in a free and unimpaired manner is preservative of other basic civil and political rights, any alleged infringement of the right of citizens to vote must be carefully and meticulously scrutinized." [T]his careful examination is necessary because statutes distributing the franchise constitute the foundation of our representative society. Any unjustified discrimination in determining who may participate in political affairs or in the selection of public officials undermines the legitimacy of representative government. [A]ccordingly, when we are reviewing statutes which deny some residents the right to vote, the general presumption of constitutionality afforded state statutes and the traditional approval given state classifications if the Court can conceive of a "rational basis" for the distinctions made are not applicable. The presumption of constitutionality and the approval given "rational" classifications in other types of enactments are based on an assumption that the institutions of state government are structured so as to represent fairly all the people. However, when the challenge to the statute is in effect a challenge of this basic assumption, the assumption can no longer serve as the basis for presuming constitutionality.

The need for exacting judicial scrutiny of statutes distributing the franchise is undiminished simply because, under a different statutory scheme, the offices subject to election might have been filled through appointment. States do have latitude in determining whether certain public officials shall be selected by election or chosen by appointment and whether various questions shall be submitted to the voters. . . . [A]ll members of the community have an interest in the quality and structure of public education, appellant says, and he urges that "the decisions taken by local boards . . . may have grave consequences to the entire population." Appellant also argues that the level of property taxation affects him, even though he does not own property, as property tax levels affect the price of goods and services in the community.

We turn therefore to question whether the exclusion is necessary to promote a compelling state interest. . . .

Appellees argue that it is necessary to limit the franchise to those "primarily interested" in school affairs because "the ever increasing complexity of the many interacting phases of the school system and structure make it extremely difficult for the electorate fully to understand the whys and wherefores of the detailed operations of the school system." Appellees say that many communications of school boards and school administrations are sent home to the parents through the district pupils and are "not broadcast to the general public"; thus, nonparents will be less informed than parents. Further, appellees argue, those who are assessed for local property taxes (either directly or indirectly through rent) will have enough of an interest "through the burden on their pocketbooks, to acquire such information as they may need."

[A]ssuming, *arguendo*, that New York legitimately might limit the franchise in these school districts to those "primarily interested in school affairs," close scrutiny of the § 2012 classification demonstrates that they do not accomplish this purpose with sufficient precision to justify denying appellant the franchise. . . .

[T]he classifications must be tailored so that the exclusion of appellant and members of his class is necessary to achieve the articulated state goal. Section 2012 does not meet the exacting standard of precision we require of statutes which selectively distribute the franchise. . . .

MR. JUSTICE STEWART, with whom MR. JUSTICE BLACK, and MR. JUSTICE HARLAN join, dissenting.

Although at times variously phrased, the traditional test of a statute's validity under the Equal Protection Clause is a familiar one: a legislative classification is invalid only "if it rests[s] on grounds wholly irrelevant to achievement of the regulation's objectives." A similar premise underlies the proposition, consistently endorsed by this Court, that a State may exclude non-residents from participation in its elections. Such residence requirements, designed to help ensurethat voters have a substantial stake in the outcome of elections and an opportunity to become familiar with the candidates and issues voted upon, are entirely permissible exercises of state authority. Indeed the appellant explicitly concedes, as he must, the validity of voting requirements relating to residence, literacy, and age. Yet, he argues—and the Court accepts the argument—that the voting qualifications involved here somehow have a different constitutional status. I am unable to see the distinction.

Clearly a State may reasonably assume that its residents have a greater stake in the outcome of elections held within its boundaries than do other persons. Likewise, it is entirely rational for a state legislature to suppose that residents, being generally better informed regarding state affairs than are nonresidents, will be more likely than nonresidents to vote responsibly. And the same may be said of legislative assumptions regarding the electoral competence of adults and literate persons on the one hand, and of minors and illiterates on the other. . . . So long as the classification is rationally related to a permissible legislative end, therefore . . . there is no denial of equal protection.

SALYER LAND CO. v. TULARE LAKE BASIN WATER STORAGE DISTRICT, 410 U.S. 719 (1973). This decision should be contrasted to *Kramer*, above. Landowners and registered voters challenged certain provisions of the California Water Code governing the Tulare Lake Basin Water Storage District. The district existed for the purpose of storage and distribution of irrigation waters and had certain flood control responsibilities, but it provided no other general public services. Its costs were assessed against land in proportion to benefits received. The right to vote therefore was limited to landowners (whether they were residents or not), and residents who did not own land were excluded from the franchise. The Court, per Justice Rehnquist, held that this limitation of votes did not violate equal protection:

The appellee district in this case, although vested with some typical government powers, has relatively limited authority. . . .

Not only does the district not exercise what might be thought of as "normal governmental" authority, but its actions disproportionately affect landowners. [I]n short, there is no way that the economic burdens of district operations can fall on residents *qua* residents, and the operations of the districts primarily affect the land within their boundaries.

Under these circumstances, it is quite understandable that the statutory framework for election of directors for the appellee focuses on the land benefited, rather than on people as such. [T]he franchise is extended to landowners, whether they reside in the district or out of it, and indeed whether or not they are natural persons who would be entitled to vote in a more traditional political election.

No doubt residents within the district may be affected by its activities. But this argument proves too much. Since assessments imposed by the district become a cost of doing business for those who farm within it, and that cost must ultimately be passed along to the consumers of the produce, food shoppers in far away metropolitan areas are to some extent likewise"affected" by the activities of the district. [T]he state could rationally conclude that [landowners,] to the exclusion of residents, should be charged with responsibility for the [district's] operation. We conclude, therefore, that nothing in the equal protection clause precluded California from limiting the voting for directors of appellee district by totally excluding those who merely reside within the district.

Justice Douglas, joined by Justice Brennan and Marshall, dissented. They pointed out that, first, farmland lessees were denied the vote; second, residents who faced the "perils of flood which the district is supposed to control are disfranchised;" third, only agricultural landowners were entitled to vote; and fourth, "the corporate voter is put in the saddle."

NOTES AND QUESTIONS

(1) *Limiting the Franchise to Interested Voters: Are Kramer and Salyer Consistent?* Note that, in *Salyer*, the Court approves limiting the franchise to voters interested in (or affected by) the district. Of course, there always are attenuated effects upon some other residents, but *Salyer* upholds the classification. Consider whether *Kramer* is distinguishable. Didn't New York, in *Kramer*, simply attempt to limit the franchise to those interested in and affected by the special-purpose district (school district) at issue, *i.e.*, parents and landowners?

(2) *Strict Scrutiny or Rational Basis?* Notice that *Kramer* recognizes the right to vote in a state election is a fundamental right and applies strict scrutiny, while *Salyer* uses the rational basis test. Are the two decisions consistent in this regard, and if not, which test should be applicable?

(3) *Expansion of Salyer: Ball v. James, 451 U.S. 355 (1981). Ball* concerned a "one acre, one vote" system as opposed to "one person, one vote." In this respect, it resembled *Salyer.* But there was a major difference from *Salyer:* the district in question, in addition to water operations, sold electricity to hundreds of thousands of Arizona residents. Nevertheless, a five-member majority of the Court upheld the Arizona scheme in question, using the rational basis test. The Court emphasized that the district's purposes were of a "narrow, special sort." Interestingly, the Court did not emphasize the issue of who was affected by, or interested in, the district, as it had in *Salyer.* Is this reasoning appropriate? The four dissenters argued that the Arizona system violated equal protection because the district provided general government services.

(4) *State Law Requiring a Photo ID for Voters Did Not Violate the Equal Protection Rights of Poor or Elderly Voters: Crawford v. Marion County Election Board, 128 S. Ct. 1610 (2008).* In the post-*Bush v. Gore* era, Indiana passed a state law requiring that citizens voting in person present state-issued photo identification. A political party and elected government officials challenged this "photo-ID" requirement as an unconstitutional burden ("denial") on the fundamental right to vote, particularly of

certain groups of poor or elderly voters. As they relate to the "burden" imposed by the photo ID law, the facts were that the photo IDs were free, did not apply to absentee voting, and a voter without the photo ID could always cast a "provisional ballot" that would be counted if an affidavit was subsequently filed at the circuit court clerk's office. Under these circumstances, the Court, per Justice Stevens' plurality opinion, ruled: (1) that the burden on the challengers was not a sufficient denial to violate their equal protection rights; and (2) that even if the burden might be considered "substantial," it was outweighed by the state's interests in preventing voter fraud and protecting public confidence in state elections.

The plurality used a precedential analysis, relying on *Burdick v. Takushi*, above. The plurality did not use strict scrutiny. The concurring three Justices, in an opinion by Justice Scalia, relied on a broader doctrinal approach. Justice Scalia considered the Indiana law to be a facially neutral, generally applicable regulation; he concluded that the challengers had not demonstrated a "purposeful" burden, citing to *Washington v. Davis*. The three dissenters, Justices Souter, Ginsburg, and Breyer, evaluated the burden as much more severe. The dissenters also emphasized that Indiana had not presented any evidence of voter fraud.

[b] Voting Apportionment: "One Person, One Vote"

THE EARLY DECISIONS: *BAKER v. CARR* AND ITS PROGENY

Baker v. Carr. The fundamental decision establishing the justiciability of apportionment issues, *Baker v. Carr*, 369 U.S. 186 (1962), is set out in ch. 1, the judicial power chapter. *Baker* did not mandate the one-person-one-vote principle, but its justiciability holding led to substantive cases that established the principle.

Gray v. Sanders, 372 U.S. 368 (1963), was the first post-*Baker* apportionment decision. Georgia's "county unit" system effectively apportioned votes by counties, rather than by population. The Court, per Justice Douglas, held this system unconstitutional:

> Once the geographical unit for which a representative is to be chosen is designated, all who participate in the election are to have an equal vote. . . .

> [T]he conception of political equality, from the Declaration of Independence, to Lincoln's Gettysburg Address, to the fifteenth, seventeenth, and nineteenth amendments, can mean only one thing—one person, one vote.

Justice Harlan dissented: "The Court's holding surely flies in the face of history. For, as impressively shown by the opinion of Frankfurter, J., in *Baker v. Carr*. . . , 'one person, one vote' has never been the universally accepted political philosophy in England, the American colonies, or in the United States." [You should consider whether Justice Douglas' conclusion can be justified. If so, from what doctrine?]

Federal Congressional Elections: Wesberry v. Sanders, 376 U.S. 1 (1964). *Wesberry* concerned a challenge to the apportionment of federal Congressional districts, which presents a different question than apportionment for state offices because Article I, § 2 expressly requires that representatives be chosen "by the people of the several states." The apportionment, therefore, was more precisely controlled by the Constitution than in the case of state elections, which are subject only to the more general standards of the equal protection clause. The Court's conclusion: The Constitution requires that "as nearly as practicable one man's vote in a Congressional election is to be worth as much as another's." This "as nearly as practicable" standard for congressional elections appears to be more exacting in minimization of deviations than the general one-person, one-vote principle.

The Issues: The Extent of the One-Person-One-Vote Principle; Exceptions; and Deviations. Since *Gray* concerned statewide offices, and *Wesberry* concerned the separate issue of Congressional elections, the question remained, to what extent would the one-person-one-vote principle be extended to state legislative apportionment?

REYNOLDS v. SIMS
377 U.S. 533 (1964)

MR. CHIEF JUSTICE WARREN delivered the opinion of the Court.

[Alabama legislative districts were malapportioned because the legislature had not redistricted since 1901, despite a state constitutional requirement that it do so each ten years. Counties with only 25.7 percent of the state's population had the ability to elect a majority of the House of Representatives, and only 25.1 percent of the state's total population resided in districts represented by a majority of the members of the Senate. Jefferson County, with over 600,000 people, was given only one Senator, as was Lowndes County, with only 15,417. Here, the Court holds this apportionment unconstitutional. It similarly invalidated the apportionment schemes of several other states, in companion cases.]

Gray and *Wesberry* are of course not dispositive of or directly controlling on our decision in these cases involving state legislative apportionment controversies. [B]ut neither are they wholly inapposite. *Gray* [involved] the weighting of votes in statewide elections. . . . And our decision in *Wesberry* was of course grounded on that language of the Constitution which prescribes that members of the Federal House of Representatives are to be chosen "by the People," while attacks on state legislative apportionment schemes, such as that involved in the instant cases, are principally based on the Equal Protection Clause of the Fourteenth Amendment. Nevertheless, *Wesberry* clearly established that the fundamental principle of representative government in this country is one of equal representation for equal numbers of people. . . .

[S]uch a case "touches a sensitive and important area of human rights," and "involves one of the basic civil rights of man. . . ." Undoubtedly, the right of suffrage is a fundamental matter in a free and democratic society. Especially since the right to exercise the franchise in a free and unimpaired manner is preservative of other basic civil and political rights, any alleged infringement of the right of citizens to vote must be carefully and meticulously scrutinized. . . .

Legislators represent people, not trees or acres. Legislators are elected by voters, not farms or cities or economic interests. As long as ours is a representative form of government, and our legislatures are those instruments of government elected directly by and directly representative of the people, the right to elect legislators in a free and unimpaired fashion is a bedrock of our political system. It could hardly be gainsaid that a constitutional claim had been asserted by an allegation that certain otherwise qualified voters had been entirely prohibited from voting for members of their state legislature. And, if a State should provide that the votes of citizens in one part of the State should be given two times, or five times, or 10 times the weight of votes of citizens in another part of the State, it could hardly be contended that the right to vote of those residing in the disfavored areas had not been effectively diluted. Their right to vote is simply not the same right to vote as that of those living in a favored part of the State. . . . One must be ever aware that the Constitution forbids "sophisticated as well as simpleminded modes of discrimination. . . ."

Logically, in a society ostensibly grounded on representative government, it would seem reasonable that a majority of the people of a State could elect a majority of that State's legislators. [T]he concept of equal protection has been traditionally viewed as requiring the uniform treatment of persons standing in the same relation to the governmental action questioned or challenged. With respect to the allocation of legislative representation, all voters, as citizens of a State, stand in the same relation regardless of where they live. . . .

We are told that the matter of apportioning representation in a state legislature is a complex and many-faceted one. We are advised that States can rationally consider factors other than population in apportioning legislative representation. We are admonished not to restrict the power of the States to impose differing views as to political philosophy on their citizens. We are cautioned about the dangers of entering into political thickets and mathematical quagmires. Our answer is this: a denial of constitutionally protected rights demands judicial protection; our oath and our office require no less of us. . . .

[W]e hold that, as a basic constitutional standard, the Equal Protection Clause requires that the seats in both houses of a bicameral state legislature must be apportioned on a population basis. Simply stated, an individual's right to vote for state legislators is unconstitutionally impaired when its weight is in a substantial fashion diluted when compared with votes of citizens living in other parts of the State. . . .

Since neither of the houses of the Alabama Legislature, under any of the three plans considered by the District Court, was apportioned on a population basis, we would be justified in proceeding no further. However, one of the proposed plans, that contained in the so-called 67-Senator Amendment, at least superficially resembles the scheme of legislative representation followedin the Federal Congress. Under this plan, each of Alabama's 67 counties is allotted one senator, and no counties are given more than one Senate seat. . . .

[W]e agree with the District Court, and find the federal analogy inapposite and irrelevant to state legislative districting schemes. [T]he Founding Fathers clearly had no intention of establishing a pattern or model for the apportionment of seats in state legislatures when the system of representation in the Federal Congress was adopted. . . .

The system of representation in the two Houses of the Federal Congress is one ingrained in our Constitution, as part of the law of the land. [A]rising from unique historical circumstances, it is based on the consideration that in establishing our type of federalism a group of formerly independent States bound themselves together under one national government.

Political subdivisions of States—counties, cities, or whatever—never were and never have been considered as sovereign entities. . . .

We do not believe that the concept of bicameralism is rendered anachronistic and meaningless when the predominant basis of representation in the two state legislative bodies is required to be the same—population. A prime reason for bicameralism, modernly considered, is to insure mature and deliberate consideration of, and to prevent precipitate action on, proposed legislative measures. Simply because the controlling criterion for apportioning representation is required to be the same in both houses does not mean that there will be no differences in the composition and complexion of the two bodies. . . .

By holding that as a federal constitutional requisite both houses of a state legislature must be apportioned on a population basis, we mean that the Equal Protection Clause requires that a State make an honest and good faith effort to construct districts, in both houses of its legislature, as nearly of equal population as is practicable. We realize that it is a practical impossibility to arrange legislative districts so that each one has an identical number of residents, or citizens, or voters. Mathematical exactness or precision is hardly a workable constitutional requirement. . . .

We do not consider here the difficult question of the proper remedial devices which federal courts should utilize in state legislative apportionment cases. . . .

[The concurring opinions of JUSTICES CLARK and STEWART are omitted.]

MR. JUSTICE HARLAN, dissenting. . . .

Had the Court paused to probe more deeply into the matter, it would have found that the equal protection clause was never intended to inhibit the states in choosing any democratic method they pleased for the apportionment of their legislatures. This is shown by the language of the fourteenth amendment taken as a whole, by the understanding of those who proposed and ratified it, and by the political practices of the states at the time the amendment was adopted. It is confirmed by numerous state and Congressional actions since the adoption of the fourteenth amendment, and by the common understanding of the amendment as evidenced by subsequent Constitutional amendments in decisions of this Court before *Baker v. Carr*, . . . made an abrupt break with the past in 1962.

[Mr. Justice Harlan's opinion contains a substantial discussion of the language and history of the fourteenth amendment, as well as the practices in the states with respect to apportionment before and after the adoption of the amendment. The history documents the states' acceptance of malapportionment.]

Generalities cannot obscure the cold truth that cases of this type are not amenable to the development of judicial standards. No set of standards can guide a Court which has to decide how many legislative districts a state shall have, or what the shape of the district shall be, or where to draw a particular district line. . . .

[I]n one or another of today's opinions, the Court declares it unconstitutional for a state to give effective consideration to any of the following in establishing legislative districts: (1) history; (2) "economic or other sorts of group interests"; (3) area; (4) geographical considerations; (5) a desire to "insure effective representation for sparsely settled areas"; (6) "availability of access of citizens to their representatives"; (7) theories of bicameralism (except those approved by the Court); (8) occupation; (9) "an attempt to balance urban and rural power"; (10) the preference of a majority of voters in the state. . . .

I know of no principle of logic or practical or theoretical politics, still less any constitutional principle, which establishes all or any of these exclusions. . . .

NOTES AND QUESTIONS

(1) *Companion Cases to Reynolds, Including Invalidation of Malapportionment Even if Popularly Approved by Statewide Referendum: Lucas v. Colorado General Assembly, 377 U.S. 713 (1964).* As Justice Harlan's opinion indicates, there actually were six state systems considered in *Reynolds* and its companion cases. The Court applied the one person, one vote principle to all six cases. The most interesting is *Lucas*, above, in which the *entire* Colorado electorate had voted, by statewide referendum, to approve a system of apportionment that did *not* conform to one person, one vote(!) The Court struck down the apportionment nonetheless, on the ground that "a citizen's constitutional rights can hardly be infringed simply because a majority of the people choose that it be." [*See Cooper v. Aaron, supra*, in Chapter 1.] Justices Stewart and Clark dissented from this holding, on the ground that "I could not join in . . . a constitutional mandate which . . . forever freezes one theory of political thought."

Is the majority in *Lucas* correct, or is the dissent? [Note that one reason for the majority's decision in *Baker v. Carr*, holding apportionment justiciable, was that significant deviations were not subject to correction by the political process. Doesn't this reason disappear if the apportionment scheme is approved in an election involving all of the voters of the state, particularly if they have the continuing ability, through initiative and referendum, to supervise the apportionment system?]

(2) *How Much Deviation From Mathematical Equality is Tolerable? From Mahan v. Howell, 410 U.S. 315 (1973), to White v. Regester, 412 U.S. 755 (1973), and Brown v. Thompson, 462 U.S. 835 (1983).* One of the major questions left open in *Reynolds* was, just how much deviation would be acceptable if not justified by the state, and how much could be justified by such factors as existing political boundaries? In *Mahan*, the Virginia apportionment included one district overrepresented by 6.8 percent and one underrepresented by 9.6 percent, for a maximum deviation of 16.4 percent; the Court held that the state had justified these differences by basing the apportionment on the boundaries of its political units. An even greater deviation was permitted in *Brown*. There, the Wyoming apportionment system provided each county at least one representative, which meant that the least populous county received a representative even though it had a population roughly 60 percent below the average population served by Wyoming's representatives. The Court, by a bare five-to-four majority, held that this scheme could be justified by the use of political boundaries.

In other cases, the Court has evolved what might be called a de minimis doctrine. In *White v. Regester*, for example, the Court upheld a system in which the most overrepresented district exceeded the mean by 5.8 percent and the most underrepresented deviated by 4.1 percent, so that the maximum difference was 9.9 percent. The Court required no justification for this minor deviation. It thus appears that apportionments exhibiting maximum variations of less than 10 percent will be upheld. *Cf. Connor v. Finch*, 431 U.S. 407 (1977) (maximum variations of 16.5 percent for Senate and 19.3 percent for House of Representatives held unconstitutional).

(3) *"Supermajority" Requirements Can Be Constitutional: Gordon v. Lance, 403 U.S. 1 (1971).* The *Gordon* case involved a requirement of 60 percent referendum approval for the issuance of bonds or for certain tax increases by political subdivisions. The Court upheld this requirement, distinguishing the malapportionment cases by saying that this "supermajority" requirement did not involve a "denial or dilution of voting power because of group characteristics that bore no valid relation to the interests of those groups" in the election. Here, "no section of the population may be said to be 'fenced out.'" [Question: Is *Gordon* inconsistent with *Reynolds v. Sims*?]

(4) *Requiring Multiple Votes to Protect Different Constituencies May Be Constitutional: Town of Lockport v. Citizens for Community Action, 430 U.S. 259 (1977).* For adoption of a county charter, New York required approval by a majority of all city voters, followed by *separate* approval by a majority of *non-* city voters. The Court upheld this multiple-majority requirement: "[S]eparate voter approval requirements are based on the perception that the real and long-termimpact of a restructuring of local government is felt quite differently" by the different groups. [Question: Is *Town of Lockport* consistent with *Reynolds v. Sims*?]

(5) *Political and Ethnic Gerrymandering; Single-Member or At-Large Representation.* Gerrymandering consists of the drawing of district lines so as to increase the voting advantages of one group or another. Sometimes redistricting is designed as an affirmative action in political representation programs. *See* § 10.03[A][6] above. Since it is impossible to draw district lines without having *some* effect upon any given voters' ability to influence elections, gerrymandering is a matter of degree. Furthermore, it is a matter of judgment: if black voters are concentrated into a single district, they may have greater possibility of electing a representative satisfactory to the majority of black citizens in that district; however, if they are divided into two districts, they may have the ability in some elections to elect two such representatives. There also is the question of gerrymandering along party lines: the majority party in the legislature has the power to redistrict, and it naturally will do so to maximize votes by those sympathetic to it. Should this practice be illegal? Consider again *Shaw v. Hunt* in § 10.03[A][6] regarding ethnic or racial gerrymandering.

DAVIS v. BANDEMER, 478 U.S. 109 (1986). Republican majorities of the Indiana House and Senate redistricted the state. In elections held under the reapportioned plan,

Democrat candidates received 51.9 percent of the popular vote statewide but only 43 out of 100 seats in the House. They received 53.1 percent of the Senate votes statewide, but only 13 out of 25 Democrat candidates were elected. Based upon such facts as these, the district court invalidated the redistricting plan. The Supreme Court, with a plurality opinion by Justice White, reversed. The Court first concluded that issues of political gerrymandering were justiciable. [This portion of the opinion is summarized in Ch. 1 (the judicial review chapter), above.] Then, the Court went on to hold that the record did not support invalidation of the plan:

> [W]here unconstitutional vote dilution is alleged in the form of statewide political gerrymandering, the mere lack of proportional representation will not be sufficient to prove unconstitutional discrimination. . . . Rather, unconstitutional discrimination occurs only when the electoral system is arranged in a manner that will consistently degrade a voter's or a group of voters' influence on the political process as a whole. . . .

> Based on these views, we would reject the district court's apparent holding that *any* interference with an opportunity to elect a representative of one's choice would be sufficient to allege or make out an equal protection violation, unless justified by some acceptable state interest that the state would be required to demonstrate. [S]uch a low threshold for legal action would invite attack on all or almost all reapportionment statutes. . . . [I]nviting attack on minor departures from some supposed norm would too much embroil the judiciary in second-guessing what has consistently been referred to as a political task for the legislature, a task that should not be monitored too closely unless the express or tacit goal is to effect its removal from legislative halls. We decline to take a major step toward that end, which would be so much at odds with our history and experience. . . .

Justice O'Connor, joined by the Chief Justice and Justice Rehnquist, concurred, stating: "I would hold that the partisan gerrymandering claims of major political parties raise a nonjusticiable political question that the judiciary should leave to the legislative branch as the framers of the Constitution unquestionably intended." [Excerpts from this concurring opinion are reproduced in Ch. 1, above.]

Finally, Justice Powell, joined by Justice Stevens, dissented from the reversal.

PROBLEM H

COMPLAINT OF THE EL PASO COUNTY BAR ASSOCIATION REGARDING REPRESENTATION IN THE (MANDATORY) STATE BAR OF TEXAS. The State Bar of Texas is a mandatory or "integrated" bar association, meaning that one must be a member to practice law in Texas. Furthermore, the State Bar of Texas has a number of regulatory and related functions: It charges dues, makes assessments, investigates and presents cases of lawyer discipline or disbarment, regulates designation of specialization, and carries out similar functions. Its governing body is a board of directors, consisting primarily of attorneys elected by other attorneys in geographic districts throughout the state. The El Paso County Bar Association presented a complaint to the Board of Directors, because its representative on the Board was from Odessa, Texas. The district in which El Paso is located also includes Odessa, and the two districts have sharp ethnic, cultural and other differences. The complaint caused an investigation that raised a series of different, but related and fascinating, questions.

(1) *Should Districts Be Cohesive?* Does El Paso have a valid complaint, in that it is districted with an area with which it shares few values, and consequently its representative does not represent it to its satisfaction? Does this complaint rise to constitutional dimensions? [Will it ever be possible to satisfy this condition, and also comply with one-person, one-vote, the Voting Rights Act, and other non-dilution principles?]

(2) *Is the Entire Electoral Scheme Unconstitutional, Because the (Mandatory) Texas State Bar is a Kramer-Type General State Agency Rather than a Salyer-Type "Special Purpose" Agency?* Can't a substantial argument be made that the entire system for electing the State Bar's Board of Directors is unconstitutional? Since only attorneys vote, it certainly does not provide the franchise to all qualified voters, as the *Kramer* case seems to require. Nor does it provide "one person, one vote." Note that attorneys hardly are the only persons interested in or affected byregulation of attorneys, or by disbarment, specialization, or advertising by attorneys. Consider whether the State Bar of Texas is a "special purpose" agency within the holding of *Salyer Land* or *Ball v. James,* or whether it is governed by the general rule of *Kramer v. Union Free School District.*

(3) *Appointed Members.* At the time, five members of the State Bar Board of Directors were non-attorneys, or so-called "public" members, appointed by the state Supreme Court. Does this factor affect the constitutional issues?

(4) *Apportionment and Discrepancies.* The districting inquiry discloses the fact that there are significant discrepancies among districts. For example, Harris County (Houston), Texas has considerably fewer representatives per capita than some rural areas; an adjustment that gave Harris County two or three more directors might bring the system closer to equalization. Do Harris County attorneys have a constitutional argument? [What should be the size of permitted deviations in such a case?]

[This problem is based upon a real situation, raised by a real complaint by the El Paso County Bar Association, although certain facts are changed in the problem for the sake of simplicity.]

[2] The "Right" to be a Candidate for Election: "Flexible Balancing"

NOTES AND QUESTIONS

(1) *Striking Down "Virtually Impossible" Requirements for Getting on the Ballot: Williams v. Rhodes, 393 U.S. 23 (1968).* The election laws of the State of Ohio made it "virtually impossible for a new political party, even though it has hundreds of thousands of members, or an old party, which has a very small number of members, to be placed on the state ballot" to elect the President and Vice-President. A new party, or a minor party that received less than ten percent of the votes in the previous gubernatorial election, was required to obtain petitions signed by fifteen percent of the number of ballots cast in the last preceding gubernatorial election. In addition, it was required to have an elaborate party structure and hold a primary election under "detailed and rigorous standards." The American Independent Party and Socialist Labor Party claimed a violation of equal protection because their nominees were excluded from the 1968 presidential ballot. The Court majority, per Justice Black, held that these statutes infringed two kinds of fundamental interests: (1) the right to associate for political purposes and (2) the right of voters to "cast their votes effectively." The state's interests in preventing ballot proliferation, avoiding voter confusion, minimizing run-offs, and promoting the two-party system, were not sufficiently compelling to salvage the statute:

> [T]he state has here failed to show any "compelling interest" which justifies imposing such heavy burdens on the right to vote and to associate.

> [The state] claims that the state may validly promote a two-party system in order to encourage compromise and political stability. The fact is, however, that the Ohio system does not merely favor a "two-party system"; it favors two particular parties—the Republicans and the Democrats—and in effect tends to give them a complete monopoly. . . .

See also Norman v. Reed, 502 U.S. 279 (1992) (striking down Illinois ballot access laws requiring a new political party to run a complete slate in each county, and thus to obtain

25,000 signaturesin every county, before it could run statewide candidates; using "least restrictive means" approach).

(2)   *Upholding Restrictions on Ballot Access: Jenness v. Fortson, 403 U.S. 431 (1971). Jenness* illustrates the kind of restriction that will be upheld. Georgia required candidates who had not won a primary election to obtain petition signatures totaling at least five percent of the vote in the previous general election. Time deadlines were more liberal than in *Williams v. Rhodes*, which the Court described as involving an "entangling web of election laws." The Court upheld this Georgia law, reasoning that requiring a demonstration of "substantial support" avoided both waste and confusion. The Court did not expressly apply strict scrutiny, as it had in *Williams v. Rhodes. See also* American Party of Texas v. White, 415 U.S. 767 (1974) *(upholding ballot access requirements under strict scrutiny standard).*

(3)   *Filing Fees: Lubin v. Panish, 415 U.S. 709 (1974).* California imposed a filing fee of two percent of the annual salary for the position sought. In plaintiff's case, the fee was just over $700. A unanimous Court struck down this statute, as applied to an indigent, in the absence of alternate means of ballot access (such as by petition).

(4)   *When and How May Filing Fees Be Used?* One question is whether non-indigents may be required to pay filing fees, and if so, of what size. Very high fees may be unconstitutional even in the absence of indigency. *E.g., Bullock v. Carter*, 405 U.S. 134 (1972) (fees that reached as high as $8,900 held "patently exclusionary" and unconstitutional).

(5)   *What Is the "Fundamental" Right at Issue—The Right to Be a Candidate, Or the Right to Vote for One? Lubin v. Panish* comes as close as any case to recognizing a fundamental interest in being a candidate for election. An alternative way to view the issue is that the fundamental right is not the candidates', but the voters'—to have candidates that reasonably conform to their choices. The identification of the right may be important to the outcomes of cases such as *Williams* and *Lubin*. If the fundamental right is solely that of the voter, the issue becomes one of adequate choice, not one of each individual's right of access to the ballot.

(6)   *Should Candidate Restrictions Be Subjected to Strict Scrutiny—Or to the Rational Basis Test?* Some of the cases in this area (*e.g., Williams*, above) apply strict scrutiny to ballot access issues, whereas others use the rational basis test. Which test is more appropriate (and if the answer depends upon the circumstances, in which circumstances should which test be used)? Consider the following case.

(7)   *Rejecting Strict Scrutiny in Favor of a Test That Is a "Matter of Degree": Clements v. Fashing, 457 U.S. 957 (1982).* Texas prohibited judges and certain other officials from running for the legislature during their term of office. It also had what was known as the "resign-to-run" or "automatic resignation" provision, which stated that any official who became a candidate for any other office when there was an unexpired term exceeding one year was deemed to have submitted an "automatic resignation." The Court upheld these provisions; a plurality rejected strict scrutiny:

> Far from recognizing candidacy as a "fundamental right," we have held that the existence of barriers to a candidate's access to the ballot "does not of itself compel close scrutiny." [D]ecision in this area of constitutional adjudication is a matter of degree, and involves a consideration of the facts and circumstances behind the law, the interests the State seeks to protect by placing restrictions on candidacy, and the nature of the interests of those who may be burdened by the restrictions.
>
> [T]his Court has departed from traditional equal protection analysis in recent years in two essentially separate, although similar, lines of ballot access cases. [O]ne line of ballot access cases involves classifications based on wealth. In invalidating candidate filing-fee provisions, for example, we have departed from traditional equal protection analysis because such a "system falls with unequal

weight on voters, as well as candidates, according to their economic status". . . .

The second line of ballot access cases involves classification schemes that impose burdens on new or small political parties or independent candidates. . . .

The provisions of the Texas Constitution challenged in this case do not contain any [wealth classifications or] special burdens on minority political parties or independent candidates. . . .

Justice Stevens concurred separately. Justice Brennan, joined by Justices Marshall, Blackmun and White dissented.

[3]   The Right To Travel In Interstate Commerce

SHAPIRO v. THOMPSON
394 U.S. 618 (1969)

MR. JUSTICE BRENNAN delivered the opinion of the Court.

[Connecticut, the District of Columbia, and Pennsylvania each had one-year durational residency requirements to qualify for public assistance. The lower courts held the statutes unconstitutional, and here, the Supreme Court affirms their invalidation.]

[Each of the State plans was approved by the Secretary of Health, Education and Welfare as mandated by Congress. The Court holds this approval irrelevant, however, on the ground that Congress cannot authorize the States to violate the Equal Protection Clause.]

There is no dispute that the effect of the waiting-period requirement in each case is to create two classes of needy resident families indistinguishable from each other except that one is composed of residents who have resided a year or more, and the second of residents who have resided less than a year, in the jurisdiction. On the basis of this sole difference the first class is granted, and the second class is denied, welfare aid upon which may depend the ability of the families to obtain the very means to subsist—food, shelter, and other necessities of life. . . .

[A]ppellees' central contention is that the statutory prohibition of benefits to residents of less than a year creates a classification which constitutes an invidious discrimination denying them equal protection of the laws. We agree. The interests which appellants assert are promoted by the classification either may not constitutionally be promoted by government or are not compelling governmental interests.

Primarily, appellants justify the waiting-period requirement as a protective device to preserve the fiscal integrity of the state public assistance programs. It is asserted that people who require welfare assistance during their first year of residence in a State are likely to become continuing burdens on state welfare programs. Therefore, the argument runs, if such people can be deterred from entering the jurisdiction by denying them welfare benefits during the first year, state programs to assist long-time residents will not be impaired by a substantial influx of indigent newcomers. . . .

We do not doubt that the one-year waiting period device is well suited to discourage the influx of poor families in need of assistance. . . . But the purpose of inhibiting migration by needy persons into the State is constitutionally impermissible. . . .

Alternatively, appellants argue that even if it is impermissible for a State to attempt to deter the entry of all indigents, the challenged classification may be justified as a permissible state attempt to discourage those indigents who would enter the State solely to obtain larger benefits. We observe first that none of the statutes before us is tailored to serve that objective. Rather, the class of barred newcomers is all-inclusive, lumping the great majority who come to the State for other purposes with those who come for the sole purpose of collecting higher benefits. . . .

More fundamentally, a State may no more try to fence out those indigents who seek higher welfare benefits than it may try to fence out indigents generally. [B]ut we do not perceive why a mother who is seeking to make a new life for herself and her children should be regarded as less deserving because she considers, among other factors, the level of a State's public assistance. Surely such a mother is no less deserving than a mother who moves into a particular State in order to take advantage of its better educational facilities.

Appellants argue further that the challenged classification may be sustained as an attempt to distinguish between new and old residents on the basis of the contribution they have made to the community through the payment of taxes. [A]ppellants' reasoning would logically permit the State to bar new residents from schools, parks, and libraries or deprive them of police and fire protection. . . .

. . . [I]n moving from State to State or to the District of Columbia appellees were exercising a constitutional right, and any classification which serves to penalize the exercise of that right, unless shown to be necessary to promote a *compelling* governmental interest, is unconstitutional. . . .

We conclude [furthermore] that appellants in these cases do not use and have no need to use the one-year requirement for the governmental purposes suggested. Thus, even under traditional equal protection tests a classification of welfare applicants according to whether they have lived in the State for one year would seem irrational and unconstitutional. . . .

Mr. Chief Justice Warren, with whom Mr. Justice Black joins, dissenting.

In my opinion the issue before us can be simply stated: May Congress, acting under one of its enumerated powers, impose minimal nationwide residence requirements or authorize the States to do so? Since I believe that Congress does have this power and has constitutionally exercised it in these cases, I must dissent. . . .

Mr. Justice Harlan, dissenting. . . .

I think that . . . the "compelling interest" doctrine is sound when applied to racial classifications, for historically the Equal Protection Clause was largely a product of the desire to eradicate legal distinctions founded upon race. However, I believe that the more recent extensions have been unwise. . . .

I think this branch of the "compelling interest" doctrine particularly unfortunate and unnecessary. It is unfortunate because it creates an exception which threatens to swallow the standard equal protection rule. Virtually every state statute affects important rights. This Court has repeatedly held, for example, that the traditional equal protection standard is applicable to statutory classifications affecting such fundamental matters as the right to pursue a particular occupation, the right to receive greater or smaller wages or to work more or less hours, and the right to inherit property. . . .

[B]ut when a statute affects only matters not mentioned in the Federal Constitution and is not arbitrary or irrational, I must reiterate that I know of nothing which entitles this Court to pick out particular human activities, characterize them as "fundamental," and give them added protection under an unusually stringent equal protection test. . . .

NOTES AND QUESTIONS

(1) *Residence (As Opposed to Durational Residence) May be a Constitutionally Valid Criterion: Martinez v. Bynum, 461 U.S. 321 (1983).* In *Martinez,* a Texas statute allowed school districts to deny tuition-free education to any child who lived apart from his parent or guardian "for the primary purpose" of attending school in the district. The Court, per Justice Powell, said: "A bona fide residence requirement, appropriately defined and uniformly applied, furthers the substantial state interest in assuring that services provided for its residents are enjoyed only by residents." The Court rejected strict scrutiny, holding that no suspect classification or fundamental right was at issue; the right to travel interstate was not impaired, and the right to education was not fundamental. Justice Marshall was the sole dissenter.

(2) *Durational Residence Requirements that have been Upheld: Starns v. Malkerson, 401 U.S. 985 (1971), and Sosna v. Iowa, below.* In *Starns,* the Court summarily affirmed a district court decision that upheld Minnesota's one-year waiting period for students to be considered residents of the state for purposes of lower tuition. And consider the decision that follows.

SOSNA v. IOWA, 419 U.S. 393 (1975). An Iowa court dismissed Sosna's petition for divorce because she had not complied with a state statute requiring that a divorce petitioner be a resident of the state for at least one year before the filing of the petition. The Supreme Court, per Justice Rehnquist, upheld the Iowa statute:

> State statutes imposing durational residency requirements were, of course, invalidated when imposed by states as a qualification for welfare payments, *Shapiro.* . . ; for voting. . . ; and for medical care, *Maricopa County.* [W]hat those cases had in common was that the durational residency requirements they struck down were justified on the basis of budgetary or recordkeeping considerations which were held insufficient to outweigh the constitutional claims of the individuals. But Iowa's divorce residency requirement is of a different stripe. Appellant was not irretrievably foreclosed from obtaining some part of what she sought. [S]he would eventually qualify for the same sort of adjudication which she demanded virtually upon her arrival in the state. . . .

> Iowa's residency requirement may reasonably be justified on grounds other than purely budgetary considerations or administrative convenience. [A] decree of divorce is not a matter in which the only interested parties are the state as a sort of "grantor," and a divorce petitioner such as appellant in the role of "grantee." Both spouses are obviously interested. . . . Where a married couple has minor children, a decree of divorce would usually include provisions for their custody and support. [I]owa may insist that one seeking to initiate such a proceeding have the modicum of attachment to the state required here.

> Such a requirement additionally furthers the state's parallel interest both in avoiding officious intermeddling in matters in which another state has a paramount interest, and in minimizing the susceptibility of its own divorce decrees to collateral attack. . . .

Justices Marshall and Brennan dissented: "The Court today departs sharply from the course we have followed in analyzing durational residency requirements since *Shapiro.* . . ." The dissenters reasoned that "any classification that penalizes exercise of the constitutional right to travel is invalid unless it is justified by a compelling governmental interest." The dissenters were "of the view that the 'rational basis' test has no place in equal protection analysis when important individual interests [such as those affecting marriage, divorce or interstate travel] . . . are at stake. . . ."

SAENZ v. ROE

526 U.S. 489 (1999)

JUSTICE STEVENS delivered the opinion of the Court.

[C]alifornia is not only one of the largest, most populated, and most beautiful States in the Nation; it is also one of the most generous. Like all other States, California has participated in several welfare programs authorized by the Social Security Act and partially funded by the Federal Government. Its programs, however, provide a higher level of benefits and serve more needy citizens than those of most other States. . . . In California the cash benefit for a family of two—a mother and one child—is $456 a month, but in the neighboring State of Arizona, for example, it is only $275.

In 1992, in order to make a relatively modest reduction in its vast welfare budget, the California Legislature enacted § 11450.03 of the state Welfare and Institutions Code. That section sought to change the California AFDC program by limiting new residents, for the first year they live in California, to the benefits they would have received in the State of their prior residence. [The Court reviewed the procedural history of the case. See § 1.02, Note (7) above.] [§] 11450.03 remained inoperative until after Congress enacted the Personal Responsibility and Work Opportunity Reconciliation Act of 1996 (PRWORA).

PRWORA replaced the AFDC program with TANF. The new statute expressly authorizes any State that receives a block grant under TANF to "apply to a family the rules (including benefit amounts) of the [TANF] program . . . of another State if the family has moved to the State from the other State and has resided in the State for less than 12 months." With this federal statutory provision in effect, California no longer needed specific approval from the Secretary to implement § 11450.03.

II

[In this action,] the State relied squarely on the undisputed fact that the statute would save some $10.9 million in annual welfare costs—an amount that is surely significant even though only a relatively small part of its annual expenditures of approximately $2.9 billion for the entire program. It contended that this cost saving was an appropriate exercise of budgetary authority as long as the residency requirement did not penalize the right to travel. The State reasoned that the payment of the same benefits that would have been received in the State of prior residency eliminated any potentially punitive aspects of the measure. [The trial court] concluded, however, that the relevant comparison was not between new residents of California and the residents of their former States, but rather between the new residents and longer term residents of California. He therefore again enjoined the implementation of the statute.

III

The word "travel" is not found in the text of the Constitution. Yet the "constitutional right to travel from one State to another" is firmly embedded in our jurisprudence. *United States v. Guest*, 383 U.S. 745 (1966). . . .

In *Shapiro*, we reviewed the constitutionality of three statutory provisions that denied welfare assistance to residents of Connecticut, the District of Columbia, and Pennsylvania, who had resided within those respective jurisdictions less than one year immediately preceding their applications for assistance. [W]e squarely held that it was "constitutionally impermissible" for a State to enact durational residency requirements for the purpose of inhibiting the migration by needy persons into the State. We further held that a classification that had the effect of imposing a penalty on the exercise of the right to travel violated the Equal Protection Clause "unless shown to be necessary to promote a compelling governmental interest," and that no such showing had been made.

In this case California argues that § 11450.03 was not enacted for the impermissible purpose of inhibiting migration by needy persons and that, unlike the legislation reviewed in *Shapiro*, it does not penalize the right to travel because new arrivals are not ineligible for benefits during their first year of residence. California submits that, instead of being subjected to the strictest scrutiny, the statute should be upheld if it is supported by a rational basis and that the State's legitimate interest in saving over $10 million a year satisfies that test. . . . The debate about the appropriate standard of review, together with the potential relevance of the federal statute, persuades us that it will be useful to focus on the source of the constitutional right on which respondents rely.

IV

The "right to travel" discussed in our cases embraces at least three different components. It protects the right of a citizen of one State to enter and to leave another State, the right to be treated as a welcome visitor rather than an unfriendly alien when temporarily present in the second State, and, for those travelers who elect to become permanent residents, the right to be treated like other citizens of that State.

It was the right to go from one place to another, including the right to cross state borders while en route, that was vindicated in *Edwards v. California*, 314 U.S. 160 (1941), which invalidated a state law that impeded the free interstate passage of the indigent. . . .

The second component of the right to travel is, however, expressly protected by the text of the Constitution. The first sentence of Article IV, § 2, provides:

> "The Citizens of each State shall be entitled to all Privileges and Immunities of Citizens in the several States."

Thus, by virtue of a person's state citizenship, a citizen of one State who travels in other States, intending to return home at the end of his journey, is entitled to enjoy the "Privileges and Immunities of Citizens in the several States" that he visits. . . . Those protections are not "absolute," but the Clause "does bar discrimination against citizens of other States where there is no substantial reason for the discrimination beyond the mere fact that they are citizens of other States." . . .

What is at issue in this case, then, is this third aspect of the right to travel—the right of the newly arrived citizen to the same privileges and immunities enjoyed by other citizens of the same State. That right is protected not only by the new arrival's status as a state citizen, but also by her status as a citizen of the United States. That additional source of protection is plainly identified in the opening words of the Fourteenth Amendment:

> "All persons born or naturalized in the United States, and subject to the jurisdiction thereof, are citizens of the United States and of the State wherein they reside. No State shall make or enforce any law which shall abridge the privileges or immunities of citizens of the United States; . . .

Despite fundamentally differing views concerning the coverage of the Privileges or Immunities Clause of the Fourteenth Amendment, most notably expressed in the majority and dissenting opinions in the *Slaughter-House Cases* [above, § 6.02], it has always been common ground that this Clause protects the third component of the right to travel. That newly arrived citizens "have two political capacities, one state and one federal," adds special force to their claim that they have the same rights as others who share their citizenship. Neither mere rationality nor some intermediate standard of review should be used to judge the constitutionality of a state rule that discriminates against some of its citizens because they have been domiciled in the State for less than a year. The appropriate standard may be more categorical than that articulated in *Shapiro*, but it is surely no less strict.

V

Because this case involves discrimination against citizens who have completed their interstate travel, the State's argument that its welfare scheme affects the right to travel only "incidentally" is beside the point. Were we concerned solely with actual deterrence to migration, we might be persuaded that a partial withholding of benefits constitutes a lesser incursion on the right to travel than an outright denial of all benefits. *See Dunn v. Blumstein*, 405 U.S. 330, 339 (1972). But since the right to travel embraces the citizen's right to be treated equally in her new State of residence, the discriminatory classification is itself a penalty. . . .

The classifications challenged in this case—and there are many—are defined entirely by (a) the period of residency in California and (b) the location of the prior residences of the disfavored class members. The favored class of beneficiaries includes all eligible California citizens who have resided there for at least one year, plus those new arrivals who last resided in another country or in a State that provides benefits at least as generous as California's. Thus, within the broad category of citizens who resided in California for less than a year, there are many who are treated like lifetime residents. And within the broad sub-category of new arrivals who are treated less favorably, there are many smaller classes whose benefit levels are determined by the law of the States from whence they came. To justify § 11450.03, California must therefore explain not only why it is sound fiscal policy to discriminate against those who have been citizens for less than a year, but also why it is permissible to apply such a variety of rules within that class.

These classifications may not be justified by a purpose to deter welfare applicants from migrating to California for three reasons. First, although it is reasonable to assume that some persons may be motivated to move for the purpose of obtaining higher benefits, the empirical evidence reviewed by the District Judge, which takes into account the high cost of living in California, indicates that the number of such persons is quite small—surely not large enough to justify a burden on those who had no such motive. Second, California has represented to the Court that the legislation was not enacted for any such reason. Third, even if it were, as we squarely held in Shapiro such a purpose would be unequivocally impermissible.

Disavowing any desire to fence out the indigent, California has instead advanced an entirely fiscal justification for its multitiered scheme. The enforcement of § 11450.03 will save the State approximately $10.9 million a year. The question is not whether such saving is a legitimate purpose but whether the State may accomplish that end by the discriminatory means it has chosen. An evenhanded, across-the-board reduction of about 72 cents per month for every beneficiary would produce the same result. But our negative answer to the question does not rest on the weakness of the State's purported fiscal justification. It rests on the fact that the Citizenship Clause of the Fourteenth Amendment expressly equates citizenship with residence . . . It is equally clear that the Clause does not tolerate a hierarchy of 45 subclasses of similarly situated citizens based on the location of their prior residence. Thus § 11450.03 is doubly vulnerable: Neither the duration of respondents' California residence, nor the identity of their prior States of residence, has any relevance to their need for benefits. Nor do those factors bear any relationship to the State's interest in making an equitable allocation of the funds to be distributed among its needy citizens. As in *Shapiro*, we reject any contributory rationale for the denial of benefits to new residents . . . .

VI

The question that remains is whether congressional approval of durational residency requirements in the 1996 amendment to the Social Security Act somehow resuscitates the constitutionality of § 11450.03. That question is readily answered, for we have consistently held that Congress may not authorize the States to violate the Fourteenth

Amendment. Moreover, the protection afforded to the citizen by the Citizenship Clause of that Amendment is a limitation on the powers of the National Government as well as the States.

* * *

Citizens of the United States, whether rich or poor, have the right to choose to be citizens "of the State wherein they reside." U.S. Const., Amdt. 14, § 1. The States, however, do not have any right to select their citizens. . . . [Affirmed]

CHIEF JUSTICE REHNQUIST, with whom JUSTICE THOMAS joins, dissenting.

The Court today breathes new life into the previously dormant Privileges or Immunities Clause of the Fourteenth Amendment—a Clause relied upon by this Court in only one other decision, *Colgate v. Harvey*, 296 U.S. 404 (1935), overruled five years later by *Madden v. Kentucky*, 309 U.S. 83 (1940). It uses this Clause to strike down what I believe is a reasonable measure falling under the head of a "good- faith residency requirement." Because I do not think any provision of the Constitution—and surely not a provision relied upon for only the second time since its enactment 130 years ago—requires this result, I dissent.

I

The Court wisely holds that because Cal. Welf. & Inst.Code Ann. § 11450.03 (West Supp.1999) imposes no obstacle to respondents' entry into California, the statute does not infringe upon the right to travel. Thus, the traditional conception of the right to travel is simply not an issue in this case.

But I cannot see how the right to become a citizen of another State is a necessary "component" of the right to travel, or why the Court tries to marry these separate and distinct rights. A person is no longer "traveling" in any sense of the word when he finishes his journey to a State which he plans to make his home. Indeed, under the Court's logic, the protections of the Privileges or Immunities Clause recognized in this case come into play only when an individual stops traveling with the intent to remain and become a citizen of a new State. The right to travel and the right to become a citizen are distinct, their relationship is not reciprocal, and one is not a "component" of the other. . . .

If States can require individuals to reside in-state for a year before exercising the right to educational benefits, the right to terminate a marriage, or the right to vote in primary elections that all other state citizens enjoy, then States may surely do the same for welfare benefits. . . .

JUSTICE THOMAS, with whom THE CHIEF JUSTICE joins, dissenting.

I join THE CHIEF JUSTICE's dissent. I write separately to address the majority's conclusion that California has violated "the right of the newly arrived citizen to the same privileges and immunities enjoyed by other citizens of the same State." In my view, the majority attributes a meaning to the Privileges or Immunities Clause that likely was unintended when the Fourteenth Amendment was enacted and ratified. . . .

Because I believe that the demise of the Privileges or Immunities Clause has contributed in no small part to the current disarray of our Fourteenth Amendment jurisprudence, I would be open to reevaluating its meaning in an appropriate case. . . .

NOTES AND QUESTIONS

(1) *The Right to Travel: Simply Shapiro Revisited or is Saenz Something Constitutionally New?: Saenz v. Roe, 526 U.S. 489 (1999).* Thirty years after *Shapiro* struck down a one-year residency requirement for the receipt of welfare benefits, even though

Congress had authorized the requirement, the Supreme Court struck down a more modest limitation on welfare benefits (again, even though Congress had given the states authority to impose such limitations). Although not one Justice remained from the 1969 Court, the Supreme Court, per Justice Stevens, held that California's condition on the receipt of welfare benefits—that, for one year, recipients' benefits would be limited to the level paid by the state of their former residence—violated the newly-arrived recipients right to travel under the Equal Protection doctrine. The Court, 7-2, held that the right to travel was "fundamental" and the majority applied strict scrutiny. The Chief Justice, in dissent, echoed many of the themes from Justice Harlan's dissent in *Shapiro*. Justice Thomas also dissented and suggested that he would be willing to revisit the *Slaughter-House Cases* and the Privileges and Immunities Clause of the Fourteenth Amendment. [*See* § 6.02[B] and § 9.04 above.]

(2) *The Sources of a Fundamental Right to Travel: Revisiting Judicial Review When it is Not Based Squarely on a Textually Explicit Provision.* The dispute between the *Saenz* majority and the dissenters (particularly Justice Thomas) centers on the recurring theme of much of American constitutional law: whether a counter-majoritarian form of judicial review should be exercised in the particular case, by federal judges with lifetime tenure and little, if any, political accountability, when there is no textually explicit provision seeming to authorize such "activist" review? You have repeatedly confronted this question. [*See Griswold v. Connecticut,* § 9.02, above.]

Note in *Saenz* that the majority exhibits concern for the lack of a textually explicit provision. Justice Stevens, at some length, identifies three "sources" of a right to travel: (1) a precedentially recognized right of "interstate passage" [*see* § 9.04 above]; and (2) Privileges and Immunities Clause of Article IV, § 2 [*see* § 3.04 above]; and (3) the Privileges or Immunities Clause of the Fourteenth Amendment [*see* § 6.02 above]. Do these provisions, singularly or combined, establish a basis for strict scrutiny or, as the *Saenz* dissenters argued, should rational basis be the appropriate standard? Regarding the two Privileges and Immunities Clauses, *see generally* Timothy S. Bishop, Comment, *The Privileges or Immunities Clause of the Fourteenth Amendment: The Original Intent,* 79 Nw. U. L. Rev. 142 (1984).

[4] Other Fundamental Rights: Marriage, Family, Speech, Association, and Privacy

Other Fundamental Rights. The Court has identified other fundamental rights, including those listed in the title to this section. For the most part, those rights are dealt with in other chapters, and we simply mention them here.

Fundamental Rights of Privacy and Autonomy. As we have seen in chapter 9, certain rights falling under the rubric of privacy autonomy have been deemed fundamental. *E.g.,* contraception, *Griswold v. Connecticut;* abortion, *Roe v. Wade.* In these areas, a type of equal protection analysis similar to that involving rights to vote or to travel would be invoked. Indeed, in *Skinner v. Oklahoma,* in which the Court invalidated a habitual criminal sterilization statute, the Court actually relied directly upon equal protection analysis, while recognizing the fundamental right of reproduction.

Marriage and Family. Similarly, issues in the marriage and family area may implicate fundamental rights. See, *e.g., Loving v. Virginia,* in this Chapter *above; Meyer v. Nebraska,* ch. 4, *above; Zablocki v. Redhall,* ch. 4, *above.*

Speech and Association. The freedoms protected by the first amendment, including both the freedom of speech and the (implied) right of association, are considered fundamental. We shall analyze the freedoms of speech and association in greater depth in a later chapter.

Rights That are Not "Fundamental." As we shall see in other sections of this chapter, below, there is a wide range of rights or interests that the Court has refused to deem fundamental. In some instances, these rights may seem to be of equal or greater importance to some rights that have been deemed fundamental; examples might be the right to basic subsistence or welfare payments, the right to housing, the right to education, and the right to employment. Consider the following.

VACCO v. QUILL, 521 U.S. 793 (1997). [This case is a companion to *Washington v. Glucksberg*, the Washington assisted suicide case, which appears in the preceding chapter of this book, covering substantive due process, privacy and autonomy. *Quill* instead concerned primarily an equal protection challenge, brought by patients and doctors to New York's prohibition on assisted suicide. Although the federal district court upheld the New York law, the court of appeals, applying a form of "heightened scrutiny," overturned it. The court of appeals rejected the distinction between the recognized right to refuse life support and the claimed right to assistance in hastening death, holding that the state could not constitutionally recognize one but not the other. Here, the Supreme Court, per Chief Justice Rehnquist, applies only rational basis scrutiny and upholds New York's ban on assisted suicide.]

[The Equal Protection Clause] creates no substantive rights. Instead, it embodies a general rule that States must treat like cases alike but may treat unlike cases accordingly. If a legislative classification or distinction "neither burdens a fundamental right nor targets a suspect class, we will uphold [it] so long as it bears a rational relation to some legitimate end." . . .

[New York's statutes] neither infringe fundamental rights nor involve suspect classifications. These laws are therefore entitled to a "strong presumption of validity." . . .

On their faces, neither New York's ban on assisting suicide nor its statutes permitting patients to refuse medical treatment treat anyone differently than anyone else or draw any distinctions between persons. Everyone, regardless of physical condition, is entitled, if competent, to refuse unwanted lifesaving medical treatment; no one is permitted to assist a suicide. Generally speaking, laws that apply evenhandedly to all "unquestionably comply" with the Equal Protection Clause. . . .

Unlike the Court of Appeals, we think the distinction between assisting suicide and withdrawing life-sustaining treatment, a distinction widely recognized and endorsed in the medical profession and in our legal traditions, is both important and logical; it is certainly rational.

The distinction comports with fundamental legal principles of causation and intent. First, when a patient refuses life-sustaining medical treatment, he dies from an underlying fatal disease or pathology; but if a patient ingests lethal medication prescribed by a physician, he is killed by that medication. *See, e.g., People v. Kevorkian*, 447 Mich. 436, 470–472, . . .

Furthermore, a physician who withdraws, or honors a patient's refusal to begin, life-sustaining medical treatment purposefully intends, or may so intend, only to respect his patient's wishes and "to cease doing useless and futile or degrading things to the patient when [the patient] no longer stands to benefit from them." . . . A doctor who assists a suicide, however, "must, necessarily and indubitably, intend primarily that the patient be made dead." Similarly, a patient who commits suicide with a doctor's aid necessarily has the specific intent to end his or her own life, while a patient who refuses or discontinues treatment might not. . . .

The law has long used actors' intent or purpose to distinguish between two acts that may have the same result. Put differently, the law distinguishes actions taken "because of" a given end from actions taken "in spite of" their unintended but foreseen consequences.

For all these reasons, we disagree with respondents' claim that the distinction between refusing lifesaving medical treatment and assisted suicide is "arbitrary" and "irrational." Granted, in some cases, the line between the two may not be clear, but certainty is not required, even were it possible. . . .

New York's reasons for recognizing and acting on this distinction—including prohibiting intentional killing and preserving life; preventing suicide; maintaining physicians' role as their patients' healers; protecting vulnerable people from indifference, prejudice, and psychological and financial pressure to end their lives; and avoiding a possible slide towards euthanasia—are discussed in greater detail in our opinion in *Glucksberg*, ante. These valid and important public interests easily satisfy the constitutional requirement that a legislative classification bear a rational relation to some legitimate end. The judgment of the Court of Appeals is reversed.

Justice O'Connor wrote a separate concurrence. Justices Stevens, Souter, Ginsburg and Breyer concurred only in the judgment. *See generally Symposium on Glucksberg and Quill at Ten: Death, Dying and the Constitution*, 106 Mich. L. Rev. 1463 (2008).

§ 10.04   THE "MIDDLE TIER": SHIFTING AREAS OF GREATER-THAN-NORMAL (BUT NOT FUNDAMENTAL) PROTECTION

[A]   How Should Claims for Heightened Scrutiny Be Determined? The Example of Age

MASSACHUSETTS BOARD OF RETIREMENT v. MURGIA, 427 U.S. 307 (1976) (per curiam). Should age classifications be subjected to heightened scrutiny? *issue* More importantly, how should we determine the proper level of review when a litigant claims his status or interests should trigger strict scrutiny, on grounds other than race or other suspect classifications or fundamental rights? The Court addressed this question in *Murgia*. State law required state police officers to retire at age 50. The Court applied the rational basis standard to uphold the law. It rejected both the argument that there was a "fundamental" right to government employment and the contention that age was subject to heightened scrutiny:

> While the treatment of the aged in this nation has not been wholly free of discrimination, such persons, unlike, say, those who have been discriminated *constitutional* against on the basis of race or national origin, have not experienced a "history of purposeful unequal treatment" or been subjected to unique disabilities on the basis of stereotyped characteristics not truly indicative of their abilities. [E]ven old age does not define a "discrete and insular" group [citing *Carolene Products*], in need of "extraordinary protection from the majoritarian political process." Instead, it marks a stage that each of us will reach if we live out our normal span. . . .

Justice Marshall, reiterating the position stated in his dissent in *Dandridge v. Williams* and *San Antonio Independent School District v. Rodriguez*, rejected the "rigid two-tier model" in favor of a more "flexible" standard taking into account the nature of the classification, the importance of the benefit denied, and the strength of the state interest. *dissent!* Because of the importance of employment, the "undoubted" history of discrimination against the elderly, and the lack of a "reasonably substantial interest in the state," Justice Marshall would have held the statute unconstitutional.

[In *City of Cleburne v. Cleburne Living Center*, below, and *Frontiero v. Richardson*, below, the Court considered another factor for defining a quasi-suspect class: whether the characteristic was "immutable." Should this factor also be used? Why or why not?]

[B] Gender

INTRODUCTORY NOTE

The Pre-1971 View of Gender Discrimination: From Bradwell v. Illinois, 83 U.S. (16 Wall.) 130 (1873), *to Goesaert v. Cleary*, 335 U.S. 464 (1948). In *Bradwell*, the Supreme Court upheld a denial of a license to practice law solely because the applicant was a woman, with concurring Justices saying that the "timidity and delicacy which belongs to the female sex evidently unfits it for many of the occupations of civil life." This was "the law of the Creator." Later, in *Muller v. Oregon*, 208 U.S. 412 (1908), the Court upheld a statute limiting women's hours in factories to ten, while no such restriction was placed upon men. More recently, in *Goesaert v. Cleary*, the Court upheld a Michigan law that prohibited females from working as bartenders, except for wives and daughters of licensed establishment owners. The Court applied a rational basis test, determining that the legislation was within "the allowable legislative judgment" because work as bartenders would create moral and social difficulties for women.

Is the Reasoning of Bradwell and Goesaert Backwards? If There is To Be "Protective" Legislation, Should It Instead "Protect" Men From Stressful Occupations? Consider the following excerpt, which suggests that it may be more rational for a legislature to "protect" men rather than women from stressful occupations such as that of lawyer, bartender, or corporate president:

> Washington (UPI)—Women in the United States live longer than men, but a noted physiologist has a way for males to boost their odds against the Grim Reaper: take half an aspirin a day.
>
> Estelle Ramey, a Georgetown University professor of physiology and biophysics, says studies have shown aspirin reduces the effect of stress on the male metabolism and can help ward off heart attacks and other serious coronary events, offering the potential of longer life for many men.
>
> "Male animals are fragile. They need a great deal of protection. They are delicate," Ramey said Thursday at a National Press Club luncheon. . . .
>
> "Why do men die sooner than women? Of course, they deserve it, but that's not a scientific answer."
>
> The reason, she said, is bound up in evolution, which gave men a more powerful physique so they could protect the species and a brain designed to induce a more forceful response to stress.
>
> Men under pressure experience a greater output of stress-related hormones and a stronger heart rate, said Ramey. In general, their blood clots more quickly. . . .
>
> Government statistics show men in the United States have an average life span of 71.2 years while women live an average of 78.2 years.[*] Do (or should) the scientific facts justify gender-based "protective" legislation—but to protect men, instead of women? (At the very least, Ramey's remarks make the protective legislation in *Bradwell* and *Goesaert* seem ironic.)

The Modern View. In 1971, in *Reed v. Reed*, below, the Court employed what appeared to be a modified rational basis analysis to invalidate an "arbitrary" gender-based preference. Later, in *Frontiero v. Richardson*, below, a plurality of the Court used a kind of strict scrutiny, holding that gender classifications are "like classifications based upon race, alienage, or national origin;" as such, they were "inherently suspect" and must be narrowly drafted to serve a compelling interest. More recently, however, a majority of the Court has rejected strict scrutiny and settled into a kind of middle-tier or "intermediate" level of scrutiny for gender classifications.

---

[*] Reprinted with permission of United Press International, Copyright © 1987.

REED v. REED, 404 U.S. 71 (1971). An Idaho statute provided that, as between persons equally qualified to serve as estate administrators, "males must be preferred to females." Sally Reed sought appointment as administrator of her deceased son's estate. Acting under the Idaho statute, however, the court appointed the decedent's father, Cecil Reed. Upon Sally Reed's appeal, the Supreme Court, per Chief Justice Burger, struck down the Idaho statute:

> [T]he equal protection clause . . . [denies] to states the power to legislate that different treatment be accorded to persons placed by a statute into different classes on the basis of criteria wholly unrelated to the objective of that statute. A classification "must be reasonable, not arbitrary, and must rest upon some fair ground of difference having a fair and substantial relation to the object of the legislation, so that all persons in similar circumstances shall be treated alike. . . ."

> In upholding the [statute], the Idaho Supreme Court concluded that its objective was to eliminate one area of controversy when two or more persons . . . seek letters of administration. . . .

> [T]o give a mandatory preference to members of either sex over members of the other, merely to accomplish the elimination of hearings on the merits, is to make the very kind of arbitrary legislative choice forbidden by the equal protection clause. . . ; and whatever may be said as to the positive values of avoiding intrafamily controversy, the choice in this context may not lawfully be mandated solely on the basis of sex. . . .

Another Early Decision Regarding Gender-Based Discrimination: Geduldig v. Aiello, 417 U.S. 484 (1974). What significance should be accorded to actual physical differences between the genders? In *Geduldig,* the Court upheld California's plan of medical insurance even though it excluded disability accompanying "normal pregnancy and childbirth." Justice Stewart, for the Court, concluded that the statute simply did not exclude "because of gender" and applied only the rational basis standard, like *Reed.* Only women can become pregnant, but Justice Stewart reasoned that the legislative classification was not necessarily therefore based on gender. Unless it could be shown that the physiological characteristic was a mere pretext, lawmakers were free to include or exclude pregnancy "on any reasonable basis," just as they would be to exclude any other "physical condition." Justices Brennan, Douglas, and Marshall dissented, concluding that gender discrimination was present in part because men were covered for disabilities affecting predominantly their gender, including prostatectomies and circumcision.

Does the majority's "physical condition" or "unique characteristic" reasoning in *Geduldig* provide a stronger basis for distinctions, at least to the extent that it more narrowly confines gender differences in treatment? Today, after the 1976 decision of *Washington v. Davis* (above § 10.03[A][3]), the *Geduldig* decision is sometimes read as a case where the challengers (the women denied insurance coverage) failed to demonstrate purposeful (or invidious) discrimination on the part of the state. The *Geduldig* Court did not speak in those terms, but the purposefulness standard was not part of the doctrine until two years after *Geduldig.*

FRONTIERO v. RICHARDSON
411 U.S. 677 (1973)

MR. JUSTICE BRENNAN announced the judgment of the Court in an opinion in which MR. JUSTICE DOUGLAS, MR. JUSTICE WHITE, and MR. JUSTICE MARSHALL joined.

[Federal statutes allowed a uniformed serviceman to claim his wife as a "dependent" for the purpose of certain allowances, but required a female member of the uniformed services to prove that her husband was "dependent" in fact in order to obtain the allowance. Here, the Court invalidates this distinction. The major question before the Court was whether women should be considered as a suspect class and afforded strict scrutiny.]

At the outset, appellants contend that classifications based upon sex, like classifications based upon race, alienage, and national origin, are inherently suspect and must therefore be subjected to close judicial scrutiny. We agree and, indeed, find at least implicit support for such an approach in our unanimous decision only last Term in *Reed v. Reed.*

There can be no doubt that our Nation has had a long and unfortunate history of sex discrimination. Traditionally, such discrimination was rationalized by an attitude of "romantic paternalism" which, in practical effect, put women, not on a pedestal, but in a cage.

As a result of notions such as these, our statute books gradually became laden with gross, stereotyped distinctions between the sexes and, indeed, throughout much of the 19th century the position of women in our society was, in many respects, comparable to that of blacks under the pre-Civil War slave codes. Neither slaves nor women could hold office, serve on juries, or bring suit in their own names, and married women traditionally were denied the legal capacity to hold or convey property or to serve as legal guardians of their own children.

Moreover, since sex, like race and national origin, is an immutable characteristic determined solely by the accident of birth, the imposition of special disabilities upon the members of a particular sex because of their sex would seem to violate "the basic concept of our system that legal burdens should bear some relationship to individual responsibility. . . ." [A]nd what differentiates sex from such non-suspect statuses as intelligence or physical disability, and aligns it with the recognized suspect criteria, is that the sex characteristic frequently bears no relation to ability to perform or contribute to society. As a result, statutory distinctions between the sexes often have the effect of invidiously relegating the entire class of females to inferior legal status without regard to the actual capabilities of its individual members.

With these considerations in mind, we can only conclude that classifications based upon sex, like classifications based upon race, alienage, or national origin, are inherently suspect, and must therefore be subjected to strict judicial scrutiny. Applying the analysis mandated by that stricter standard of review, it is clear that the statutory scheme now before us is constitutionally invalid. . . .

Reversed.

MR. JUSTICE STEWART concurs in the judgment, agreeing that the statutes before us work in invidious discrimination in violation of the Constitution. *Reed v. Reed.*

MR. JUSTICE REHNQUIST dissents for the reasons stated by Judge Rives in his opinion for the District Court.

MR. JUSTICE POWELL, with whom THE CHIEF JUSTICE and MR. JUSTICE BLACKMUN join, concurring in the judgment.

I agree that the challenged statutes constitute an unconstitutional discrimination against servicewomen in violation of the Due Process Clause of the Fifth Amendment, but I cannot join the opinion of Mr. Justice Brennan . . . *Reed v. Reed*, which abundantly supports our decision today, did not add sex to the narrowly limited group of classifications which are inherently suspect. In my view, we can and should decide this case on the authority of *Reed* and reserve for the future any expansion of its rationale.

There is another, and I find compelling, reason for deferring a general categorizing of sex classifications as invoking the strictest test of judicial scrutiny. The Equal Rights Amendment, which if adopted will resolve the substance of this precise question, has been approved by the Congress and submitted for ratification by the States. If this Amendment is duly adopted, it will represent the will of the people accomplished in the manner prescribed by the Constitution. By acting prematurely and unnecessarily, as I view it, the Court has assumed a decisional responsibility at the very time when state legislatures, functioning within the traditional democratic process, are debating the proposed Amendment. . . .

NOTES AND QUESTIONS

(1) *Strict Scrutiny, Intermediate Scrutiny, or Rational Basis: Which is Appropriate?* Justice Brennan's plurality opinion points out that gender is an "immutable" characteristic, like race; also, it has been the basis of vicious discrimination, creating economic and social disadvantages that parallel those based on race to some degree. Given these factors, is Justice Brennan correct in urging strict scrutiny of gender classifications?

On the other hand, there are differences between men and women that no society can ignore; for example, women become pregnant and men do not. These and a host of other differences make necessary a wide variety of differences in treatment. Does this consideration justify a level of review that is less than strict scrutiny? Consider, also, whether society has a legitimate interest in preserving customary differences between genders. For example, a court may require male attorneys to wear ties, but accept different-but-equally-formal dress on the part of females. Could such a discrimination ever be upheld if required to be justified by a "compelling" state interest? In this regard, consider the following cases.

(2) *The Court Retreats to an Ostensible "Rational Basis" Test to Uphold Gender Classifications: Kahn v. Shevin, 416 U.S. 351 (1974), and Schlesinger v. Ballard, 419 U.S. 498 (1975).* In these two cases, the Court retreated from the plurality position in *Frontiero. Kahn* concerned a Florida statute that provided a $500 property tax exemption to widows but denied such an exemption to widowers. The Court distinguished *Frontiero*, in part, because the Florida statute was designed to remedy "the effects of past discrimination against women." Having reached that conclusion, the Court, per Justice Douglas, reasoned that the Florida statute was "reasonably designed" to cushion the financial impact upon the gender for which spousal death imposed a "disproportionately heavy burden."

In *Schlesinger*, the Court upheld a federal statute that required discharge of male Navy officers not promoted for *nine* years, but stretched the non-promotion period to *thirteen* years for women before requiring discharge. The Court pointed out that women were excluded from combat and from most kinds of sea duty, and therefore Congress reasonably could have concluded that women had less opportunity for promotion than men.

(3) *Invalidating Gender-Based Distinctions: Weinberger v. Wiesenfeld, 420 U.S. 636 (1975).* But this rational basis rhetoric did not prevent the Court from striking down less justifiable gender-based distinctions. In *Wiesenfeld*, for example, the Court (per Justice Brennan) struck down a statute that provided death benefits to the widow and minor children of a deceased husband, but only to the minor children of a deceased wife. The Court compared the case to the "archaic and overbroad" generalization at issue in *Frontiero* and distinguished *Kahn* on the ground that this distinction was not designed to remedy any special disadvantages to women.

(4) *Discrimination Against Men.* Statistically, it seems probable that invidious discrimination has been practiced much more often against women than against men. But to the extent one accepts the proposition that individuals rather than classes suffer from discrimination, gender-based disadvantages to men also have sometimes been a substantial problem. Consider the following case, *Craig v. Boren.*

CRAIG v. BOREN, 429 U.S. 190 (1976). Oklahoma statutes prohibited the sale of 3.2

percent beer to males under the age of 21 and to females under the age of 18. The Court, per Justice Brennan, struck down this differential statute:

> [T]o withstand constitutional challenge, previous cases establish that classifications by gender must serve important government objectives and must be substantially related to achievement of those objectives [citing, among other cases, *Reed, Frontiero, and Schlesinger*].

> *Reed v. Reed* had also provided the underpinning for decisions that have invalidated statutes employing gender as an inaccurate proxy for other, more germane bases of classification. Hence, "archaic and overbroad" generalizations, *Schlesinger*, concerning the financial position of servicewomen, *Frontiero v. Richardson*, . . . and working women, could not justify use of gender lines in determining eligibility for certain governmental benefits. . . .

> The appellees introduced a variety of statistical surveys. First, an analysis of arrest statistics for 1973 demonstrated that 18-to-20-year-old male arrests for "driving under the influence" and "drunkenness" substantially exceeded female arrests for that same age period. Similarly, youth age 17–21 were found to be overrepresented among those killed or injured in traffic accidents, with males again numerically exceeding females in this regard. . . .

> Even with this statistical evidence accepted as accurate, it nevertheless offers only a weak answer to the equal protection question presented here. [V]iewed in terms of the correlation between sex and the actual activity that Oklahoma seeks to regulate—driving while under the influence of alcohol—the statistics broadly establish that.18 percent of females and 2 percent of males in that age group were arrested for that offense. While such a disparityis not trivial in a statistical sense, it hardly can form the basis for employment of a gender line as a classifying device. . . .

> There is no reason to belabor this line of analysis. [T]he relationship between gender and traffic safety becomes far too tenuous to satisfy *Reed's* requirement that the gender-based difference be substantially related to achievement of the statutory objective. . . .

Justice Powell concurred separately to express reservations as to the appropriate standard for analysis: "*Reed* and subsequent cases involving gender-based classifications make clear that the Court subjects such classification to a more critical examination than is normally applied when 'fundamental' constitutional rights and 'suspect classes' are not present," but in this "relatively easy case" there was no showing that the means employed bore a "fair and substantial relation" to the important objective of highway safety. Similarly, Justice Stevens concurred: Here, the classification was not "totally irrational," but it nevertheless was unacceptable because "it does not seem to me that an insult to all of the young men of the state can be justified by visiting the sins of the two percent on the ninety-eight percent." Justice Stewart also concurred, characterizing the Oklahoma policy as one of "total irrationality." With the adoption of the intermediate scrutiny standard, the Court had developed a three tier model for equal protection.

Finally, Chief Justice Burger and Justice Rehnquist dissented. Justice Rehnquist flatly rejected the intermediate scrutiny standard. See the VMI decision, below. As Justice Rehnquist saw it, "the only redeeming feature of the Court's opinion, to my mind, is that it apparently signals a retreat by those who joined the plurality opinion in *Frontiero v. Richardson* . . . from their view that sex is a 'suspect' classification. [I] think the Oklahoma statute challenged here need pass only the 'rational basis' equal protection analysis. . . , and I believe that it is constitutional under that analysis."

CALIFANO v. WEBSTER
430 U.S. 313 (1977)

PER CURIAM.

[Section 215 of the Social Security Act, for purposes of Old Age Insurance benefits, employed a formula that resulted in a slightly higher "average monthly wage" and a correspondingly higher level of monthly benefits for most retired female wage earners than males. Later, in 1972, Congress amended the statute to equalize treatment of the genders. Here, in a case that arose under the earlier version of the statute, the Court upholds the unequal formula, using middle-tier scrutiny.]

To withstand scrutiny under the equal protection component of the Fifth Amendment's Due Process Clause, "classifications by gender must serve important governmental objectives and must be substantially related to achievement of those objectives." *Craig v. Boren.* Reduction of the disparity in economic condition between men and women caused by the long history of discrimination against women has been recognized as such an important governmental objective. *Schlesinger v. Ballard, Kahn v. Shevin.* But "the mere recitation of a benign, compensatory purpose is not an automatic shield which protects against any inquiry into the actual purposes underlying a statutory scheme." *Weinberger v. Wiesenfeld.* Accordingly, we have rejected attempts to justify gender classifications as compensation for past discrimination against women when the classifications in fact penalized women wage earners, or when the statutory structureand its legislative history revealed that the classification was not enacted as compensation for past discrimination.

The statutory scheme involved here is more analogous to those upheld in *Kahn* and *Ballard* than to those struck down in *Wiesenfeld* and *Goldfarb.* The more favorable treatment of the female wage earner enacted here was not a result of "archaic and overbroad generalizations" about women, *Schlesinger v. Ballard, supra,* or of "the role-typing society has long imposed" upon women, such as casual assumptions that women are "the weaker sex" or are more likely to be child-rearers or dependents. Rather, "the only discernible purpose of [§ 215's more favorable treatment is] the permissible one of redressing our society's longstanding disparate treatment of women." *Califano v. Goldfarb, supra.*

The legislative history of § 215(b) (3) also reveals that Congress directly addressed the justification for differing treatment of men and women in the former version of that section and purposely enacted the more favorable treatment for female wage earners to compensate for past employment discrimination against women. . . .

That Congress changed its mind in 1972 and equalized the treatment of men and women does not, as the District Court concluded, constitute an admission by Congress that its previous policy was invidiously discriminatory. Congress has in recent years legislated directly upon the subject of unequal treatment of women in the job market. Congress may well have decided that "[t]hese congressional reforms . . . have lessened the economic justification for the more favorable benefit computation formula in § 215(b) (3). . . ."

MR. CHIEF JUSTICE BURGER, with whom MR. CHIEF JUSTICE STEWART, MR. JUSTICE BLACKMUN, and MR. JUSTICE REHNQUIST join, concurring in the judgment.

While I am happy to concur in the Court's judgment, I find it somewhat difficult to distinguish the Social Security provision upheld here from that struck down so recently in *Califano v. Goldfarb,* 430 U.S. 199 (1977). Although the distinction drawn by the Court between this case and *Goldfarb* is not totally lacking in substance, I question whether certainty in the law is promoted by hinging the validity of important statutory schemes on whether five Justices view them to be more akin to the "offensive" provisions struck down in *Weinberger v. Wiesenfeld,* or more like the "benign" provision upheld in *Schlesinger v. Ballard* and *Kahn v. Shevin.* I therefore concur in the judgment of the Court for reasons stated by Mr. Justice Rehnquist in his dissenting opinion in *Goldfarb*, in which Mr. Justice Stewart, Mr. Justice Blackmun, and I joined.

NOTES AND QUESTIONS

(1) *The Emergence of Intermediate Scrutiny: Craig v. Boren, 429 U.S. 190 (1976).* With the *Craig* decision, the Court, per Justice Brennan, resolved the competition between strict scrutiny (*Frontiero*) and rational basis (*Reed*) by holding that gender classifications are "quasi-suspect classifications" and that they would be tested against the "intermediate scrutiny" standard. Under the *Craig* intermediate scrutiny standard, the government has the burden of persuasion. The government must demonstrate that the classification serves an "important government interest" *and* that its regulatory means are "substantially related" to the achievement of those important objectives. The Court would use this standard for other quasi-suspect classifications such as classifications based on illegitimacy.

(2) *Affirmative Action on Behalf of Women: The Standard in Intermediate Scrutiny.* One of the major underpinnings of *Kahn, Ballard*, and *Webster* is the idea that general societal discrimination against women in the past justifies gender classifications that favor women and thereby remedy the past discrimination. Consider whether this purpose, which differs from remedying past discrimination by an identified employer and also from gender classifications based upon actual physical characteristics, is or should be constitutional. Might such "remedial" distinctions actually disadvantage women by justifying subtle discriminations against them? The distinctions may disadvantage men that may be innocent of the discriminatory conduct that is being "remedied."

MICHAEL M. v. SUPERIOR COURT, 450 U.S. 464 (1981). California defined the offense of statutory rape as "an act of sexual intercourse . . . where the female is under the age of 18 years." Petitioner, who was a 17-year-old male, sought to set aside the charge against him under this statute on the theory that it violated equal protection by not similarly covering intercourse with under-age males. The Court upheld the statute, with a plurality opinion by Justice Rehnquist:

> [W]e have not held that gender-based classifications are "inherently suspect" and thus we do not apply so-called "strict scrutiny" to those classifications. [O]ur cases have held, however, that the traditional minimum rationality test takes on a somewhat "sharper focus" when gender-based classifications are challenged. [I]n *Reed v. Reed*. . . , for example, the Court stated that a gender-based classification will be upheld if it bears a "fair and substantial relationship" to legitimate state ends, while in *Craig v. Boren*. . . , the Court restated the test to require the classification to bear a "substantial relationship" to "important governmental objectives." . . .

> Because virtually all of the significant harmful and inescapably identifiable consequences of teenage pregnancy fall on the young female, a legislature acts well within its authority when it elects to punish only the participant who, by nature, suffers few of the consequences of his conduct. [M]oreover, the risk of pregnancy itself constitutes a substantial deterrence to young females. No similar natural sanctions deter males. A criminal sanction imposed solely on males thus serves to roughly "equalize" the deterrence on the sexes. Justice Stewart concurred, concluding that a legislative classification "realistically based upon [physical] differences is not unconstitutional." Justice Blackmun also concurred separately.

Justice Brennan, joined by Justices White and Marshall, dissented, emphasizing the issue whether the statute bore a "sufficient relationship to the state's asserted goal of preventing teenage pregnancies to survive the 'mid-level' constitutional scrutiny mandated by *Craig v. Boren*." The dissenters concluded that the statute was not "*substantially* related to the achievement of that goal." At least thirty-seven states had enacted gender-neutral statutory rape laws, which would have served the interests of the state as well. Finally, Justice Stevens dissented, emphasizing the appropriateness of a gender-neutral statutory rape law.

NOTES AND QUESTIONS

(1) *Middle-Tier Review: Is It Really Different From Rational Basis Review?* Notice the meaning of middle-tier review: the statute must "substantially" advance an "important" governmental interest, not merely be "rationally" related to a "legitimate" interest. Justice Rehnquist's opinion has been criticized for "watering down" the intermediate scrutiny standard. As the level of review is applied in *Michael M.*, does it truly differ from rational basis review, or is the Court excessively willing to accept the government's claimed justifications of the statute?

(2) *Upholding Distinctions in Draft Registration: Rostker v. Goldberg, 453 U.S. 57 (1981).* In *Rostker*, men brought suit challenging the Military Selective Service Act because it provided for draft registration by males but not females. Justice Rehnquist, for the Court, upheld the statute, beginning with the statement: "The case arises in the context of Congress' authority over national defense and military affairs, and perhaps in no other area has the Court accorded Congress greater deference." His opinion pointed out that the draft was based upon Congress' decision that men, but not women, should be subject to compulsory military service. Congress held extensive hearings on the matter, and the decision to exempt women from registration was not the "accidental byproduct of a traditional way of thinking about females":

> We do not think that the substantive guarantee of due process or certainty in the law will be advanced by any further "refinement" in the applicable tests. [A]nnounced degrees of "deference" to legislative judgments, just as levels of "scrutiny" which this Court announces that it applies to particular classifications made by a legislative body, may all too readily become facile abstractions used to justify a result. . . .

> Women as a group, . . . unlike men as a group, are not eligible for combat. In the words of the Senate Report: "The principle that women should not intentionally and routinely engage in combat is fundamental, and enjoys wide support among our people. It is universally supported by military leaders who have testified before the Committee. [C]urrent law and policy exclude women from being assigned to combat in our military forces, and the Committee reaffirms this policy." [W]e must examine appellee's constitutional claim concerning registration with these combat restrictions firmly in mind. . . .

Justice White, joined by Justice Brennan, dissented. Justice Marshall, also joined by Justice Brennan, separately dissented.

MISSISSIPPI UNIVERSITY FOR WOMEN v. HOGAN, 458 U.S. 719 (1982). The Mississippi University for Women ("MUW") was "the oldest state-supported all-female college in the United States." It denied admittance to Hogan, a male who wished to study nursing, "[a]lthough he was otherwise qualified, . . . solely because of his sex." MUW allowed men to audit classes, although not to take them for credit, and Mississippi offered a nursing program at another university in a different part of the State that men were allowed to attend. Here, using intermediate-level scrutiny, the Court, per Justice O'Connor, holds that Mississippi's policy is unconstitutional, over dissents that would allow the choice of single-gender education:]

> . . . Our decisions . . . establish that the party seeking to uphold a statute that classifies individuals on the basis of their gender must carry the burden of showing an "exceedingly persuasive justification" for the classification. . . .

> . . . [T]he burden is met only by showing at least that the classification serves "important governmental objectives and that the discriminatory means

employed" are "substantially related to the achievement of those objectives." . . .

The State's primary justification for maintaining the single-sex admissions policy of MUW's School of Nursing is that it compensates for discrimination against women and, therefore, constitutes educational affirmative action. As applied to the School of Nursing, we find the State's argument unpersuasive.

In limited circumstances, a gender-based classification favoring one sex can be justified if it intentionally and directly assists members of the sex that is disproportionately burdened. *See Schlesinger v. Ballard.* However, we consistently have emphasized that "the mere recitation of a benign, compensatory purpose is not an automatic shield which protects against any inquiry into the actual purposes underlying a statutory scheme." *Weinberger v. Wiesenfeld* . . .

. . . Mississippi has made no showing that women lacked opportunities to obtain training in the field of nursing or to attain positions of leadership in that field when the MUW School of Nursing opened its door or that women currently are deprived of such opportunities. In fact, in 1970, the year before the School of Nursing's first class enrolled, women earned 94 percent of the nursing baccalaureate degrees conferred in Mississippi and 98.6 percent of the degrees earned nationwide. . . .

The policy is invalid also because it fails the second part of the equal protection test, for the State has made no showing that the gender-based classification is substantially and directly related to its proposed compensatory objective. To the contrary, MUW's policy of permitting men to attend classes as auditors fatally undermines it claim that women, at least those in the School of Nursing, are adversely affected by the presence of men. . . .

Justice Blackman dissented, pointing out that Hogan could attend an equivalent program elsewhere, but he " 'wants in' at this particular [women's] location in his home city." He added that "rigid rules in this area" easily can "destroy . . . values that mean much to some people by forbidding the State to offer them a choice while not depriving others of an alternative choice." Chief Justice Burger dissented with a separate opinion, observing that the present decision applied only to a professional school; an all-women liberal arts or business school, however, "might well be justified" even after this, he thought. Finally, Justice Powell, joined by Justice Rehnquist, dissented from what they saw as the destruction of the choice of a state-supported women's school.

The Court's opinion bows deeply to conformity. Left without honor—indeed, held unconstitutional—is an element of diversity that has characterized much of American education and enriched much of American life. The Court in effect holds today that no State now may provide even a single institution of higher learning open only to women students. . . .

Nor is respondent significantly disadvantaged by MUW's all-female tradition. His constitutional complaint is based upon a single asserted harm: that he must *travel* to attend the state-supported nursing schools that concededly are available to him. . . .

. . . I would sustain Mississippi's right to continue MUW on a rational-basis analysis. But I need not apply this "lowest tier" of scrutiny. I can accept for present purposes the standard applied by the Court; that there is a gender-based distinction that must serve an important governmental objective by means that are substantially related to its achievement. . . .

The record in this case reflects that MUW has a historic position in the State's education system dating back to 1884. More than 2,000 women presently evidence their preference for MUW by having enrolled there. The choice is one that discriminates invidiously against no one. And the State's purpose in preserving that choice is legitimate and substantial. . . .

NOTES AND QUESTIONS

(1) *Gender-Segregated Education: Can It Be Justified When Racial Segregation Cannot?* In Hogan, the Court, per Justice O'Connor, applied the intermediate scrutiny (from Craig) and struck down the state's gender-segregated education system even though the women-only program was designed to benefit women. Consider whether segregation by gender in education can be justified more easily than segregation by race. Do the preferences of students, as Justice Powell argues, make a difference? Is gender segregation justifiable by reference to privacy-based notions, on the assumption that living arrangements and daily activities will be more easily maintained and the educational mission of the institution more easily achieved in an all-female or all-male environment? On the other hand, consider the possibility that separate-but-equal in the gender context may prove to be de facto unequal, or may be subtly demeaning, in a manner similar to that of separate-but-equal in the racial context.

(2) *Extending Batson to Invalidate Peremptory Challenges Based on Gender: J.E.B. v. Alabama, 511 U.S. 127 (1994).* Alabama filed a paternity and child support action against petitioner J.E.B. During jury selection, Alabama used 9 of its 10 peremptory challenges to remove male jurors while J.E.B. used 9 of his 10 strikes to remove females. Over J.E.B's timely objection based on *Batson v. Kentucky*, 476 U.S. 79 (1986), [§ 10.03, *supra*] the trial court empaneled an all-female jury consisting of six women and no men. This jury found that J.E.B. was the father, and he was ordered to pay child support. Although J.E.B. was denied relief in the Alabama courts, the Supreme Court, per Justice Blackmun, here reverses and holds that intentional discrimination on the basis of gender in the use of peremptory strikes violates the Equal Protection Clause.

. . . [W]e hold that gender, like race, is an unconstitutional proxy for juror competence and impartiality.

[D]iscrimination on the basis of gender in the exercise of peremptory challenges is a relatively recent phenomenon. Gender-based peremptory strikes were hardly practicable formost of our country's existence, since, until the 19th century, women were completely excluded from jury service. . . .

[R]espondents suggest that "gender discrimination in this country . . . has never reached the level of discrimination" against African-Americans, and therefore gender discrimination, unlike racial discrimination, is tolerable in the courtroom . . . .

While the prejudicial attitudes toward women in this country have not been identical to those held toward racial minorities, the similarities between the experiences of racial minorities and women, in some contexts, "overpower those differences." . . . Certainly, with respect to jury service, African-Americans and women share a history of total exclusion, a history which came to an end for women many years after the embarrassing chapter in our history came to an end for African-Americans.

We need not determine, however, whether women or racial minorities have suffered more at the hands of discriminatory state actors during the decades of our Nation's history. It is necessary only to acknowledge that "our Nation has had a long and unfortunate history of sex discrimination," . . . Thus, the only question is whether discrimination on the basis of gender in jury selection substantially furthers the State's legitimate interest in achieving a fair and impartial trial. [In a footnote, the Court adds: "Because we conclude that gender-based peremptories are not substantially related to an important government objective, we once again need not decide whether classifications based on gender are inherently suspect."]

[F]ar from proffering an exceptionally persuasive justification for its gender-based peremptory challenges, [Alabama] maintains that its decision to strike virtually all the males from the jury in this case "may reasonably have been based upon the perception, supported by history, that men otherwise totally qualified to serve upon a jury might be more sympathetic and receptive to the arguments of a man alleged in a paternity action to be the father of an out-of-wedlock child, while women equally qualified to serve upon a jury might be more sympathetic and receptive to the arguments of the complaining witness who bore the child."

We shall not accept as a defense to gender-based peremptory challenges "the very stereotype the law condemns." [Alabama] offers virtually no support for the conclusion that gender alone is an accurate predictor of juror's attitudes; yet it urges this Court to condone the same stereotypes that justified the wholesale exclusion of women from juries and the ballot box. . . .

In recent cases we have emphasized that individual jurors themselves have a right to nondiscriminatory jury selection procedures. *See Powers, Edmonson, and McCollum, supra.* . . . Striking individual jurors on the assumption that they hold particular views simply because of their gender is "practically a brand upon them, affixed by law, an assertion of their inferiority." *Strauder v. West Virginia,* 100 U.S. 303 (1880). . . .

. . . Parties still may remove jurors whom they feel might be less acceptable than others on the panel; gender simply may not serve as a proxy for bias. Parties may also exercise their peremptory challenges to remove from the venire any group or class of individuals normally subject to "rational basis" review . . . Even strikes based on characteristics that are disproportionately associated with one gender could be appropriate, absent a showing of pretext.

Justice O'Connor concurred with a separate opinion to point out, "[T]oday's [decision] is not costless. . . . One need not be a sexist to share the intuition that in certain cases a person'sgender and resulting life experience will be relevant to his or her view of the case." Justice Kennedy wrote a separate opinion concurring in the judgment.

Chief Justice Rehnquist dissented with the observation, among others, that "race and sex discrimination are different . . . our equal protection jurisprudence affords different levels of protection." Finally, Justice Scalia, joined by the Chief Justice and Justice Thomas, dissented: "[F]or every man struck by the government, petitioner's own lawyer struck a woman." The dissenters concluded that "*all* peremptory strikes based on *any* group characteristic [are] at risk, since they all can be denominated 'stereotypes.'" Today's extension of the equal protection clause, the dissenters also concluded, would "damage. . . the entire justice system" by creating "extensive collateral litigation" detracting from the ultimate goal of resolving cases.

UNITED STATES v. VIRGINIA
518 U.S. 515 (1996)

JUSTICE GINSBURG delivered the opinion of the Court. . . .

[Virginia Military Institute (VMI) was the sole single-sex school (male only) among Virginia's state-supported institutions of higher learning. VMI's distinctive educational mission was to prepare men for leadership roles in civilian and military life. To this end, VMI used an "adversative method" of military-life training not otherwise available in Virginia's public school institutions. The United States sued Virginia and VMI, alleging that VMI's exclusively male admissions policy violated the Fourteenth Amendment's Equal Protection Clause.

[After the initial round of litigation in which the federal government prevailed, Virginia established a parallel program for women, the Virginia Women's Institute for Leadership (VWIL), at a private women's college. Virginia then argued that the existence of the VWIL program satisfied equal protection requirements created by

VMI's male-only admissions. Although both the lower federal courts found that VWIL satisfied the equal protection requirement, the Supreme Court here reverses, holding that Virginia has failed to satisfy the applicable standard for gender-based governmental action. The six-Justice majority opinion identifies two basic issues: (1) whether VMI's exclusion of women violated the equal protection guarantee and (2), if so, whether Virginia's providing the alternative VWIL program for women was a sufficient remedy. The Court here answers both issues against Virginia:]

We note, once again, the core instruction of this Court's pathmarking decisions. . . . : Parties who seek to defend gender-based government action must demonstrate an "exceedingly persuasive justification" for that action.

[T]o summarize the Court's current directions for cases of official classification based on gender: Focusing on the differential treatment or denial of opportunity for which relief is sought, the reviewing court must determine whether the proffered justification is "exceedingly persuasive." The burden of justification is demanding and it rests entirely on the State. See *Mississippi Univ. For Women*, 458 U.S., at 724. The State must show "at least that the [challenged] classification serves 'important governmental objectives and that the discriminatory means employed' are 'substantially related to the achievement of those objectives.' " The justification must be genuine, not hypothesized or invented post hoc in response to litigation. And it must not rely on overbroad generalizations about the different talents, capacities, or preferences of males and females . . .

"Inherent differences" between men and women, we have come to appreciate, remain cause for celebration, but not for denigration of the members of either sex or for artificial constraints on an individual's opportunity. Sex classifications may be used to compensate women "for particular economic disabilities [they have] suffered," *Califano v. Webster*, 430 U.S. 313, 320 (1977) (per curiam), to "promote equal employment opportunity," *see California Federal Sav. & Loan Assn. v. Guerra*, 479 U.S. 272, 289 (1987), to advance full development of the talent and capacities of our Nation's people. But such classifications may not be used, as they once were, *see Goesaert v. Cleary*, 335 U.S., at 467 [the 1948 decision upholding a state law excluding women from working as bartenders], to create or perpetuate the legal social, and economic inferiority of women.

[M]easuring the record in this case against the review standard just described, we conclude that Virginia has shown no "exceedingly persuasive justification" for excluding all women from the citizen-soldier training afforded by VMI. We therefore affirm the Fourth Circuit's initial judgment, which held that Virginia had violated the Fourteenth Amendment's Equal Protection Clause. Because the remedy proffered by Virginia—the . . . VWIL program—does not cure the constitutional violation, i.e., it does not provide equal opportunity, we reverse the Fourth Circuit's final judgment in this case.

[I]n sum, we find no persuasive evidence in this record that VMI's male-only admission policy "is in furtherance of a state policy of 'diversity.' " No such policy, the Fourth Circuit observed, can be discerned from the movement of all other public colleges and universities in Virginia away from single-sex education. . . . A purpose genuinely to advance an array of educational options, as the Court of Appeals recognized, is not served by VMI's historic and constant plan—a plan to "afford a unique educational benefit only to males." However "liberally" this plan serves the State's sons, it makes no provision whatever for her daughters. That is not equal protection . . .

Women's successful entry into the federal military academies, and their participation in the Nation's military forces, indicate that Virginia's fears for the future of VMI may not be solidly grounded. The State's justification for excluding all women from "citizen-soldier" training for which some are qualified, in any event, cannot rank as "exceedingly persuasive," as we have explained and applied that standard.

[A]s earlier stated, generalizations about "the way women are," estimates of what is appropriate for most women, no longer justify denying opportunity to women whose talent and capacity place them outside the average description. Notably, Virginia never asserted that VMI's method of education suits most men.

[I]n myriad respects other than military training, VWIL does not qualify as VMI's equal. VWIL's student body, faculty, course offerings, and facilities hardly match VMI's. Nor can the VWIL graduate anticipate the benefits associated with VMI's 157-year history, the school's prestige, and its influential alumni network.

[V]irginia, in sum, while maintaining VMI for men only, has failed to provide any "comparable single-gender women's institution." Instead, the Commonwealth has created a VWIL program fairly appraised as a "pale shadow" of VMI in terms of the range of curricular choices and faculty stature, funding, prestige, alumni support and influence.

CHIEF JUSTICE REHNQUIST, concurring in the judgment. . . .

Two decades ago in *Craig v. Boren*, 429 U.S. 190, 197 (1976), we announced that "to withstand constitutional challenge, ... classifications by gender must serve important governmental objectives an must be substantially related to achievement of those objectives." We have adhered to that standard of scrutiny ever since. While the majority adheres to this test today, it also says that the State must demonstrate an " 'exceedingly persuasive justification' " to support a gender-based classification. It is unfortunate that the Court thereby introduces an element of uncertainty respecting that appropriate test. . . .

While terms like "important governmental objective" and "substantially related" are hardly models of precision, they have more content and specificity than does the phrase "exceedingly persuasive justification." That phrase is best confined, as it was first used, as an observation on the difficulty of meeting the applicable test, not as formulation of the test itself.

[O]ur cases dealing with gender discrimination also require that the proffered purpose for the challenged law be the actual purpose. It is on this ground that the Court rejects the first of two justifications Virginia offers for VMI's single-sex admissions policy, namely, the goal of diversity among its public educational institutions. While I ultimately agree that the State has not carried the day with this justification, I disagree with the Court's method of analyzing the issue.

[B]efore this Court, Virginia has sought to justify VMI's single-sex admissions policy primarily on the basis that diversity in education is desirable, and that while most of the public institutions of higher learning in the State are coeducational, there should also be room for single-sex institutions. I agree with the Court that there is scant evidence in the record that this was the real reason that Virginia decided to maintain VMI as men only. . . .

Even if diversity in educational opportunity were the State's actual objective, the State's position would still be problematic. The difficulty with its position is that the diversity benefited only one sex; there was single-sex public education available for men at VMI, but no corresponding single-sex public education available for women.

[V]irginia offers a second justification for the single-sex admissions policy: maintenance of the adversative method. I agree with the Court that this justification does not serve an important governmental objective. A State does not have substantial interest in the adversative methodology unless it is pedagogically beneficial. While considerable evidence shows that a single-sex education is pedagogically beneficial for some students, and hence a State may have a valid interest in promoting that methodology, there is no similar evidence in the record that an adversative method is pedagogically beneficial or is any more likely to produce character traits than other methodologies.

[T]he Court defines the constitutional violation in this case as "the categorical exclusion of women from an extraordinary educational opportunity afforded to men." . . . As the foregoing discussion suggests, I would not define the violation in this way; it is not the "exclusion of women" that violates the Equal Protection Clause, but the maintenance of an all-men school without providing any—much less a comparable—institution for women.

JUSTICE SCALIA, dissenting. . . .

The virtue of a democratic system with a First Amendment is that it readily enables the people, over time, to be persuaded that what they took for granted is not so, and to change their laws accordingly. That system is destroyed if the smug assurances of each age are removed from the democratic process and written into the Constitution. So to counterbalance the Court's criticism of our ancestors, let me say a word in their praise: they left us free to change. The same cannot be said of this most illiberal Court, which has embarked on a course of inscribing one after another of the current preferences of the society (and in some cases only the counter-majoritarian preferences of the society's law-trained elite) into our Basic Law.

[I] shall devote most of my analysis to evaluating the Court's opinion on the basis of our current equal-protection jurisprudence, which regards this Court as free to evaluate everything under the sun by applying one of three tests: "rational basis" scrutiny, intermediate scrutiny, or strict scrutiny. These tests are no more scientific than their names suggest, and a further element of randomness is added by the fact that it is largely up to us which test will be applied in each case. . . . We have not established criterion for "intermediate scrutiny" either, but essentially apply it when it seems like a good idea to load the dice.

[T]o reject the Court's disposition today, however, it is not necessary to accept my view that the Court's made-up tests cannot displace longstanding national traditions as the primary determinant of what the Constitution means. It is only necessary to apply honestly the test the Court has been applying to sex-based classifications for the past two decades. . . .

[U]nder the constitutional principles announced and applied today, single-sex public education is unconstitutional.

[A]nd the rationale of today's decision is sweeping: for sex-based classifications, a redefinition of intermediate scrutiny that makes it indistinguishable from strict scrutiny. . . .

NOTES AND QUESTIONS

(1) *The VMI Court's Redefinition of the Standard: Does It Stay with the Middle Tier Craig v. Boren Test—or Does It Move to a "Heightened" Intermediate Scrutiny Nearly Equivalent to Strict Scrutiny, Requiring an "Exceedingly Persuasive Justification?"* Relying on the *Mississippi University for Women v. Hogan*, and *J.E.B. v. Alabama*, the VMI Court, per Justice Ginsburg, holds that Virginia's gender segregated military school did not satisfy intermediate scrutiny. The Court also restates the middle tier requirements of an "important governmental objective" to which the state's policy is "substantially" related. But it also says that the state must demonstrate an "exceedingly persuasive justification" for its male-only admissions policy. This "exceedingly persuasive justification" requirement is suggested in earlier decisions, but the Court here emphasizes it in a way that arguably gives it greater weight. Is there any real difference between an "exceedingly persuasive justification" and a "compelling" state interest as these standards apply in the real world? As Justice Scalia's dissent argued, has the middle tier applicable to gender really been replaced by strict scrutiny?

(2) *Whither "Intermediate Scrutiny:" Ratcheting Up The Standard Applicable to Claims of Gender-Based Discrimination?* Even if the result in the case had been generally anticipated, the Court's methodology in *VMI* was somewhat of a surprise.

Although the majority referred to the intermediate scrutiny standard from *Craig v. Boren*, the Court's emphasis on the phrase "exceedingly persuasive justification" appeared to create a new and higher standard (or at least a more rigorous application of the *Craig* test). Certainly the concurring and dissenting Justices both thought that the majority was using a more rigorous standard than intermediate scrutiny. After reviewing the decision, do you find that the non-majority Justices were right or is the majority's terminology more likely explainable as a rhetorical technique? Note that Chief Justice Rehnquist concurs and uses what he characterizes as the true *Craig v. Boren* intermediate scrutiny. There is a certain irony here in that Justice Rehnquist had dissented in *Craig* and rejected intermediate scrutiny altogether.

(3) *"Substantial Equivalency" as Required for an Alternative in the Case of Gender Segregation: The VMI Court's Treatment of the VWIL Remedy.* The Court applies to the women's alternative the test of "substantial equivalency," which Virginia's VWIL alternative for women fails because of course offerings, tradition, etc. Is this standard so high that no state will be able to meet it? If so, is its strictness justified as a test for "separate but equal" education (or should single-sex education be more easily tolerated than separate education in the racial context)?

(4) *The Application of the VMI Standard: Intermediate Scrutiny Satisfied: Nguyen v. INS, 533 U.S. 53 (2001).* In the first application of the gender discrimination standard since *VMI*, the Court addressed a case brought against the federal government (under the Fifth Amendment). Nguyen was born in Vietnam to a Vietnamese mother and an American citizen father, Boulais. Under federal law, for a person like Nguyen to establish American citizenship, the American citizen father must, by the child's eighteenth birthday, take one of three affirmative steps: legitimize the child; make a declaration of paternity; or secure a court order of paternity. These extra steps are not required when the child has an American citizen mother. Although Nguyen lived with his father in the United States for 12 years (before age 18), none of the three alternatives was accomplished.

To defeat a deportation order, Nguyen and his father claimed that the statutory scheme discriminated against men. Applying intermediate scrutiny, the Court, per Justice Kennedy, disagreed. The Court (5-4) held that the government scheme served two substantial governmental interests and that the means were substantially related to the governmental interests in facilitating a parent-child relationship. Justice Scalia (a dissenter in *VMI*) concurred. Justice O'Connor, for Justices Souter, Ginsburg, and Breyer, dissented.

PROBLEM I

IS IT (OR SHOULD IT BE) UNCONSTITUTIONAL FOR A STATE TO PROVIDE SEPARATE LIBERAL ARTS COLLEGES FOR MEN AND WOMEN?: REVISITING MUW v. HOGAN AFTER THE VMI DECISION—A CONSTITUTIONAL CHALLENGE TO "BETSY ROSS COLLEGE." The (fictional) state of West York has several dozen colleges located in it, some state-supported and some private, some coeducational and some single-sex. All but a few offer liberal arts degrees. There are four single-sex colleges that are state supported, two men's and two women's, each offering liberal arts educations, each located roughly in one of the four corners of the State. A man named Bill Jones wants to attend one of these colleges designated for women, which is called "Betsy Ross College." His reasons include (1) it is the closest college to his home and (2) it has a somewhat more extensive curriculum in Renaissance history, which he is interested in studying, than the publicly-supported men's colleges.

West York adamantly insists that Betsy Ross College's policy of confining admissions to women serves "important" goals. The West York Attorney General cites sociological studies indicating, for example, that women have significantly greater opportunities for leadership roles, classroom participation, faculty attention and advanced studies in women's colleges than in coeducational settings. This goal is "substantially related" to the State's policy, she argues, because by definition it depends on single-sex education. The Attorney General (who happens to be a graduate of Wellesley College) also relies on the less scientific rationale that both women and men may arguably perform better in educational endeavors when collateral distractions about dress, grooming, sexually charged dialogue, and dating are reduced in the immediate environment. And she adds, "Mr. Jones has a choice of several dozen other colleges in this state, some of which are nearly as close and offer nearly as extensive curricula in Renaissance history." There is no denying that the state-supported women's colleges offer fewer engineering courses and more humanities courses than the state-supported men's colleges, but the Attorney General explains, "That's in response to different demands from different student bodies. As it happens, fewer of our States' women than men choose to become engineers."

Questions: (1) *Intermediate Scrutiny.* Can Betsy Ross College survive the intermediate scrutiny imposed by *MUW v. Hogan?* (Note Chief Justice Burger's effort to distinguish the relatively unique professional nursing program there at issue from a liberal arts program, which he thought "might well be justified"—although the other dissenters suggested otherwise.) (2) *"Exceedingly Persuasive Justification."* In any event, can Betsy Ross College survive the requirement, after the VMI case, of an "exceedingly persuasive justification?" (3) *"Substantial Equivalency."* Are the state-supported men's liberal arts colleges that Bill Jones can attend the substantial equal of the women's colleges, or close enough to be called equal in this context? (What about a woman who desires a career as an engineer but who believes she would benefit from a single-sexeducation?) (4) *The "Right" Result?* Assuming that the test mandated by the Supreme Court might lead it to hold Betsy Ross College unconstitutional, is this the proper result of Equal Protection analysis?

PROBLEM J

THE MALE STUDENT WHO DESIRES TO JOIN THE STATE UNIVERSITY TENNIS TEAM (AND THE WOMAN WHO WANTS TO WRESTLE). Title IX of the Civil Rights Act of 1968 requires certain kinds of equivalency between men's and women's educational programs, including sports. This law is credited with enormous increases in college sports participation by women, which has pervaded other areas of our national life (*e.g.*, the WNBA). It has, however, produced some anomalous effects. To keep their football teams and other male-dominated sports and yet comply with Title IX, some state universities have resorted to dropping men's teams in certain sports while setting up (and heavily funding) those sports for women's teams.

Assume (a) that Bill Jones has decided, after all, that he does not want to attend Betsy Ross College (see the preceding problem), and he happily is studying Renaissance history at West York State University. But there is one problem. He is a nationally-ranked amateur tennis player, and the University has no men's tennis team, only a women's team. He files suit requesting an injunction to prevent this policy. Meanwhile, (b) his sister, Melissa Jones, sues because in high school, she was a competitive wrestler, and WYSU has only a men's wrestling team. And if that is not enough, even though WYSU has both men's and women's basketball teams, (c) Paul Jones sues for the right to play on the women's team because he likes the women's basketball team's coach better than the men's team's (who treats him in an "adversitative" manner and lets him play only infrequently), and (d) Sally Jones sues to be allowed to play on the men's basketball team because her abilities exceed those of other members of the women's team, which lacks the "tradition" and other attributes of the men's team considered important in the VMI case. Questions: (1) Is there an "exceedingly persuasive justification" for any of these distinctions, sufficient to uphold them under the version of intermediate scrutiny that applies after VMI? (2) Are women's and men's teams sufficiently equivalent after VMI?

NOTE ON THE PROPOSED EQUAL RIGHTS AMENDMENT

The Equal Rights Amendment and the Ratification Process. The proposed Equal Rights Amendment provided, "[e]quality of rights under the law shall not be denied or abridged by the United States or by any state on account of sex." At the Congressionally-set deadline in 1982, the Amendment remained at least three states short of ratification.

The Meaning of the Equal Rights Amendment. Opponents argued that the interpretation of this terse language could not be predicted. For example, the opponents said, it might invalidate rape statutes or even outlaw separate bathrooms for men and women. A possible interpretation is that the Equal Rights Amendment would have an effect similar to that of making gender a suspect classification; *i.e.,* gender classifications, like those based on race, could only be justified by a compelling interest, to which the statute was narrowly targeted. *See* Susan Crump, *An Overview of the Equal Rights Amendment in Texas,* 11 Hous. L. Rev. 136 (1973). Does this interpretation seem appropriate?

Unique Characteristics and the Privacy Qualification. Perhaps male-on-female rape statutes can be upheld by reasoning based upon physiological differences or "unique characteristics" assignable to one gender only, in the manner of the reasoning of *Michael M. v. Superior Court, above. See* Susan Crump, *supra.* As for such matters as separate bathrooms, or such mundane issues as requirements that male attorneys but not female ones wear neckties, perhaps privacy considerations would yield sensible results. The privacy principle, like that of equal rights if the Amendment were adopted, would be a part of the Constitution, of presumably equal dignity. *Id.* Thus, some separate facilities and separate treatment of the different genders for purposes of bodily functions and apparel arguably could be justified.

Sexual Orientation and Sexual Activity. Another open issue raised by the language of the Amendment was whether sexual orientation or sexual activity was a characteristic protected from invidious classification. Since the amendment is written in language that prohibits denial of quality on account of "sex," it is ambiguous in this regard. *Id.*

[C]   Sexual Orientation: The Arguments of Gays, Lesbians, and Others

NOTES AND QUESTIONS

(1) *Sexual Orientation May Be Different from Sexual Activity.* In *Bowers,* the Court held that homosexual conduct was not an activity fundamentally protected by the due process clause. *Bowers* was overruled by *Lawrence v. Texas,* again on substantive due process grounds. *But* by its terms, *Bowers* does not control the question whether sexual orientation can properly be the basis for classification by the state in any other situation. This question could arise in the context of same-sex marriages, domestic partner legislation, military service, and a variety of other situations in which sexual conduct is not determinative of the claims by gays, lesbians, and transgender persons to equal protection.

(2) *Considering the Factors Underlying Heightened Scrutiny in Murgia and Frontiero, supra: Does Sexual Orientation Share Characteristics of Immutability, Stereotyping, History of Repressive Legislation, Discreteness and Insularity, Etc. with Recognized Suspect Classes?* The prior cases suggest consideration of such factors as whether the status is (1) an immutable one, or an accident of birth; (2) often targeted by stereotypical legislation not related to individual responsibility; (3) characterized by a history of repressive legislation; (4) visible; and (5) a status as a "politically powerless" group. Under these criteria, is sexual orientation properly to be treated as a suspect classification? [What is the relevance of scientific inquiries into whether sexual orienta-

tion has a physiological basis? Of past efforts by some opponents to link pedophilia to sexual orientation? Of the fact that the sexual orientation of large percentages of gays is not publicly identified?]

(3) *Different Results, on Different Theories, with Different Levels of Scrutiny.* The cases show mixed results. Among those in which sexual orientation claims have succeeded is *Meinhold v. Department of Defense*, 808 F. Supp. 1455 (D.C. Cal. 1993) (using rational basis standard to strike down Navy's policy, based on status rather than conduct, excluding gays and lesbians frommilitary service). Although Meinhold's own victory was affirmed on appeal, 34 F.3d 1469 (9th Cir. 1994), the court of appeals later upheld certain other regulations. *Holmes v. California Army National Guard*, 124 F.3d 1126 (9th Cir. 1997) (upholding "Don't Ask, Don't Tell" rules (see below). One of the more unusual decisions is *Baehr v. Lewin*, 852 P.2d 44 (Hawaii 1993). Plaintiffs' suit alleged that the denial of marriage licenses to them on the ground that they were of the same sex violated the Hawaii state constitution. The trial court rejected the claims and granted judgment on the pleadings. The Hawaii Supreme Court held (1) that the express right-of-privacy provision in Hawaii Const. art. I, § 6 did not create a fundamental right to same-sex marriage, but (2) that under the state equal-protection provision, art. I, § 5, the state's consideration of gender triggered strict scrutiny. The court remanded for a determination whether the state could demonstrate a narrowly targeted compelling interest.

On the other hand, a federal court of appeals held, in Equality Foundation of Greater Cincinnati, Inc. v. Cincinnati, 54 F.3d 261 (6th Cir. 1995), that "gays, lesbians and bisexuals cannot constitute either a 'suspect class' or a 'quasi-suspect class.' . . ."

(4) *What Governmental Interests Are Relevant?* Consider whether governmental interests in the marriage institution would survive strict scrutiny, intermediate review, or rational basis review, to support a prohibition of same-sex marriages (or a refusal to allow government employees' domestic partners recoveries of pensions or insurance). Also, consider the following problem.

PROBLEM K

SEVEN GAYS IN MILITARY SUE OVER NEW [DON'T ASK, DON'T TELL] RULES: COMPROMISE FACES FIRST COURT CHALLENGE, Houston Chronicle, July 28, 1993, § A, at 2, col. 5. Before 1993, federal law banned gays' service in the military. President Clinton's efforts to reverse this prohibition, based on his campaign promises, drew substantial opposition. Therefore, new regulations resulted in a compromise between the President's position and the desires of military leaders and Congress to keep the ban. This new policy was popularly known as "Don't Ask, Don't Tell." It "permit[ted] homosexuals to serve in the military as long as they remain[ed] silent, except in the most private of settings, about their sexual orientation and [did] not engage in homosexual acts."

Seven plaintiffs, who were gay or lesbians actually serving in the armed forces, claimed that this policy was unconstitutional under both the First Amendment and the Equal Protection Clause. Questions: 1) What level of scrutiny applies to their Equal Protection claim? (2) Can the regulations be justified by the government's interests in discipline, recruitment, esprit de corps, and protection of the privacy of combat soldiers and sailors in close quarters? [The Ninth Circuit has upheld the rules, on the ground that there is a rational basis for concluding that sexual orientation will likely lead persons to engage in sexual acts. *Holmes, supra.*]

ROMER v. EVANS
517 U.S. 620 (1996)

JUSTICE KENNEDY delivered the opinion of the Court.

[In a statewide referendum, the voters of Colorado added an amendment to their state constitution ("Amendment 2"). The impetus for Amendment 2 came largely from the passage of ordinances in certain cities (*e.g.*, Denver) that banned discrimination in many transactions and activities by reason of a person's "sexual orientation." To the extent that these various municipal and state ordinances protected "homosexual, lesbian, or bisexual orientation, conduct or practices or relationships," Amendment 2 repealed them. The challengers also alleged that Amendment 2 prohibited legislative, executive or judicial action at any level of Colorado state or local government which would be designed to protect homosexual persons. The actual impact and effect of Amendment 2 was one of the issues contested in the case.

[Soon after Amendment 2 was adopted, the respondents challenged it in state court. Eventually, the Supreme Court of Colorado determined that Amendment 2 was subject to "strict scrutiny" because it infringed on the fundamental right of gays and lesbians to participate in the political process. The Colorado Supreme Court concluded that the State's interests failed strict scrutiny. In this decision, the United States Supreme Court affirmed but relied upon a different rationale. Instead of applying strict scrutiny, the United States Supreme Court determined that Amendment 2 could not survive even rational basis scrutiny.]

The State's principal argument in defense of Amendment 2 is that it puts gays and lesbians in the same position as all other persons. So, the State says, the measure does no more than deny homosexuals special rights. This reading of the amendment's language is implausible. We rely not upon our own interpretation of the amendment but upon the authoritative construction of Colorado's Supreme Court.

[T]he change that Amendment 2 works in the legal status of gays and lesbians, in the private sphere is far-reaching, both on its own terms and when considered in light of the structure and operation of modern anti-discrimination laws. . . .

Amendment 2 bars homosexuals from securing protection against the injuries that these public-accommodations laws address. That in itself is a severe consequence, but there is more. Amendment 2, in addition, nullifies specific legal protections for this targeted class in all transactions in housing, sale of real estate, insurance, health and welfare services, private education, and employment. . . .

Not confined to the private sphere, Amendment 2 also operates to repeal and forbid all laws or policies providing specific protection for gays or lesbians from discrimination by every level of Colorado government. . . .

Amendment 2's reach may not be limited to specific laws passed for the benefit of gays and lesbians. It is a fair, if not necessary, inference from the broad language of the amendment that it deprives gays and lesbians even of the protection of general laws and policies that prohibit arbitrary discrimination in governmental and private settings. . . .

In any event, even if, as we doubt, homosexuals could find some safe harbor in laws of general application, we cannot accept the view that Amendment 2's prohibition on specific legalprotections does no more that deprive homosexuals of special rights. To the contrary, the amendment imposes a special disability upon those persons alone. Homosexuals are forbidden the safeguards that others enjoy or may seek without constraint. They can obtain specific protection against discrimination only by enlisting the citizenry of Colorado to amend the state constitution or perhaps, on the State's view, by trying to pass helpful laws of general applicability. This is so no matter how local or discrete the harm, no matter how public and widespread the injury. We find nothing special in the protections Amendment 2 withholds. These are protections taken for granted by most people either because they already have them or do not need them; these are protections against exclusion from an almost limitless number of transactions and endeavors that constitute ordinary civic life in a free society.

III

The Fourteenth Amendment's promise that no person shall be denied the equal protection of the laws must coexist with the practical necessity that most legislation classifies for one purpose or another, with resulting disadvantage to various groups or persons. We have attempted to reconcile the principle with the reality by stating that, if a law neither burdens a fundamental right nor targets a suspect class, we will uphold the legislative classification so long as it bears a rational relation to some legitimate end.

Amendment 2 fails, indeed defies, even this conventional inquiry. First, the amendment has the peculiar property of imposing a broad and undifferentiated disability on a single named group, an exceptional and as we shall explain, invalid form of legislation. Second, its sheer breadth is so discontinuous with the reasons offered for it that the amendment seems inexplicable by anything but animus toward the class that it affects; it lacks a rational relationship to legitimate state interests. . . .

. . . By requiring that the classification bear a rational relationship to an independent and legitimate legislative end, we ensure that classifications are not drawn for the purpose of disadvantaging the group burdened by the law.

Amendment 2 confounds this normal process of judicial review. It is at once too narrow and too broad. It identifies persons by a single trait and then denies them protection across the board. The resulting disqualification of a class of persons from the right to seek specific protection from the law is unprecedented in our jurisprudence . . .

It is not within our constitutional tradition to enact laws of this sort. Central both to the idea of the rule of law and to our own Constitution's guarantee of equal protection is the principle that government and each of its parts remain open on impartial terms to all who seek its assistance." 'Equal protection of the laws is not achieved through indiscriminate imposition of inequalities.' " *Sweatt v. Painter*, 339 U.S. 629, 635 (1950) (quoting *Shelley v. Kraemer*, 334 U.S. 1, 22 (1948)). Respect for this principle explains why laws singling out general hardships are rare. A law declaring that in general it shall be more difficult for one group of citizens than for all others to seek aid from the government is itself a denial of equal protection of the laws in the most literal sense. . . .

A second and related point is that laws of the kind now before us raise the inevitable inference that the disadvantage imposed is born of animosity toward the class of persons affected. [E]ven laws enacted for broad and ambitious purposes often can be explained by reference to legitimate public policies which justify the incidental disadvantages they impose on certain persons. Amendment 2, however, in making a general announcement that gays and lesbians shall not have any particular protections from the law, inflicts on them immediate, continuing, and real injuries that outrun and belie any legitimate justifications that may be claimed for it. We conclude that, in addition to the far-reaching deficiencies of Amendment 2 that we have noted, the principles it offends, in another sense, are conventional and venerable; a law must bear a rational relationship to a legitimate government purpose, . . . and Amendment 2 does not.

The primary rationale the State offers for Amendment 2 is respect for other citizens' freedom of association, and in particular the liberties of landlords or employers who have personal or religious objections to homosexuality. Colorado also cites its interest in conserving resources to fight discrimination against other groups. The breadth of the Amendment is so far removed from these particular justifications that we find it impossible to credit them. . . . It is a status-based enactment divorced from any factual context from which we could discern a relationship to legitimate state interests; it is a classification of persons undertaken for its own sake, something the Equal Protection Clause does not permit. . . .

We must conclude that Amendment 2 classifies homosexuals not to further a proper legislative end but to make them unequal to everyone else. This Colorado cannot do. A State cannot so deem a class of persons a stranger to its laws. Amendment 2 violates the Equal Protection Clause, and the judgment of the Supreme Court of Colorado is affirmed.

JUSTICE SCALIA, with whom THE CHIEF JUSTICE and JUSTICE THOMAS join, dissenting. . . .

In holding that homosexuality cannot be singled out for disfavorable treatment, the Court contradicts a decision, unchallenged here, pronounced only 10 years ago, *see Bowers v. Hardwick*, 478 U.S. 186 (1986) [Note: As you saw in Chapter 9, *Bowers* was subsequently overruled by *Lawrence v. Texas, supra*, Chapter 9.] and places the prestige of this institution behind the proposition that opposition to homosexuality is as reprehensible as racial or religious bias. Whether it is or not is *precisely* the cultural debate that gave rise to the Colorado constitutional amendment (and to the preferential laws against which the amendment was directed). Since the Constitution of the United States says nothing about this subject, it is left to be resolved by normal democratic means, including the democratic adoption of provisions in state constitutions. This Court has no business imposing upon all Americans the resolution favored by the elite class from which the Members of this institution are selected, pronouncing that "animosity" toward homosexuality is evil. I vigorously dissent.

[T]he amendment prohibits *special treatment* of homosexuals, and nothing more.

[D]espite all of its hand-wringing about the potential effect of Amendment 2 on general antidiscrimination laws, the Court's opinion ultimately does not dispute all this, but assumes it to be true. The only denial of equal treatment it contends homosexuals have suffered is this: They may not *obtain preferential* treatment without amending the state constitution. That is to say, the principle underlying the Court's opinion is that one who is accorded equal treatment under the laws, but cannot as readily as others obtain *preferential* treatment under the laws, has been denied equal protection of the laws. If merely stating this alleged "equal protection" violation does not suffice to refute it, our constitutional jurisprudence has achieved terminal silliness.

The central thesis of the Court's reasoning is that any group is denied equal protection when, to obtain advantage (or, presumably, to avoid disadvantage), it must have recourse to a more general and hence more difficult level of political decisionmaking than others. The world has never heard of such a principle, which is why the Court's opinion is so long on emotive utterance and so short on relevant legal citation. . . .

III . . .

[B]ut though Coloradans are, as I say, *entitled to* be hostile toward homosexual conduct, the fact is that the degree of hostility reflected by Amendment 2 is the smallest conceivable. The Court's portrayal of Coloradans as a society fallen victim to pointless, hate-filled "gay-bashing" is so false as to be comical. Colorado not only is one of the 25 States that have repealed their antisodomy laws, but was among the first to do so. But the society that eliminates criminal punishment for homosexual acts does not necessarily abandon the view that homosexuality is morally wrong and socially harmful; often, abolition simply reflects the view that enforcement of such criminal laws involves unseemly intrusion into the intimate lives of citizens. . . .

There is a problem, however, which arises when criminal sanction of homosexuality is eliminated but moral and social disapprobation of homosexuality is meant to be retained. TheCourt cannot be unaware of that problem; it is evident in many cities of the country, and occasionally bubbles to the surface of the news, in introduction into local schools of books teaching that homosexuality is an optional and fully acceptable "alternate life style." The problem (a problem, that is, for those who wish to retain social disapprobation of homosexuality) is that, because those who engage in homosexual conduct tend to reside in disproportionate numbers in certain communities, *see* Record, have high disposable income, *see id.;* and of course care about homosexual-rights issues much more ardently than the public at large, they possess political power much greater than their numbers, both locally and statewide. Quite understandably, they devote this political power to achieving not merely a grudging social toleration, but full social acceptance, of homosexuality.

[I] do not mean to be critical of these legislative successes; homosexuals are as entitled to use the legal system for reinforcement of their moral sentiments as are the rest of society. But they are subject to being countered by lawful, democratic countermeasures as well.

That is where Amendment 2 came in. It sought to counter both the geographic concentration and the disproportionate political power of homosexuals by (1) resolving the controversy at the statewide level, and (2) making the election a single-issue contest for both sides. . . . The Court today asserts that this most democratic of procedures is unconstitutional. Lacking any cases to establish that facially absurd proposition, it simply asserts that it must be unconstitutional, because it has never happened before.

[Justice Scalia offered the following "analogy" to Amendment 2:] Polygamists, and those who have a polygamous "orientation," have been "singled out" by [various federal and state laws] for much more severe treatment than merely denial of favored status; and that treatment can only be changed by achieving amendment of the state constitutions. The Court's disposition today suggests that these provisions are unconstitutional, and that polygamy must be permitted in these States on a state-legislated, or perhaps even local-option, basis—unless, of course, polygamists for some reason have fewer constitutional rights than homosexuals. . . .

When the Court takes sides in the culture wars, it tends to be with the knights rather than the villains—and more specifically with the Templars, reflecting the views and values of the lawyer class from which the Court's Members are drawn. How that class feels about homosexuality will be evident to anyone who wishes to interview job applicants at virtually any of the Nation's law schools. The interviewer may refuse to offer a job because the applicant is a Republican; because he is an adulterer; because he went to the wrong prep school or belongs to the wrong country club; because he eats snails; because he is a womanizer; because she wears real-animal fur; or even because he hates the Chicago Cubs. But if the interviewer should wish not to be an associate or partner of an applicant because he disapproves of the applicant's homosexuality, *then* he will have violated the pledge which the Association of American Law Schools requires all its member-schools to exact from job interviewers: "assurance of the employer's willingness" to hire homosexuals. Bylaws of the Association of American Law Schools, Inc. § 6-4(b). . . .

NOTES AND QUESTIONS

(1) *Gay Rights and Equal Protection: Romer v. Evans, 517 U.S. 620 (1996).* The Court, per Justice Kennedy, holds that the standard applicable to Colorado's Amendment 2 is the rational basis standard and that Amendment 2 fails rational basis scrutiny. The Court declined to consider gays and lesbians as a "suspect class" or as a "quasi-suspect class." The Colorado Supreme Court had relied on a fundamental rights approach (*i.e.,* a right of political participation), and it had accordingly applied strict scrutiny. The Court rejects any fundamental rights analysis. Since it did not find a

suspect class or a fundamental right, the Court determined that the appropriate standard was rational basis.

Although it purports to use the rational basis standard, the Court struck down Amendment 2. "We must conclude that Amendment 2 classifies homosexuals not to further a proper legislative end, but to make them unequal to everyone else. This Colorado cannot do. A state cannot so deem a class of person a stranger to its laws." The subsequent Notes explore various issues. Note: You should review *Lawrence v. Texas* from Chapter 9.

(2) *If Rational Basis Is the Court's Approach in Romer, Where Does Amendment 2 Fail?* Is there really no legitimate governmental interest in Amendment 2? Does the Court mean to say that Colorado's means (i.e., a constitutional ban on preferences) are irrational? Or does the Court suggest that Colorado failed both prongs of the rational basis test? Or, does the *Romer* majority confuse the analysis in the two prongs of rational basis?

(3) *Is There Really No Legitimate Interest Here?* Colorado argued that one of its legitimate interests was in protecting scarce state resources from being deployed in the name of what would turn out to be "false claims" regarding discrimination and employment or housing. Assume that we know, from our experience with housing and employment discrimination laws, that there are inevitably a certain number of false claims. This would be true also with claims based upon gender. Can Colorado legitimately protect its scarce public enforcement resources against various kinds of false claims? Aren't there also various privacy interests, especially amongst people who are renting out certain housing units? Again, the Colorado Supreme Court had found that there was a fundamental right of political participation and that Amendment 2 therefore had to be scrutinized under enhanced scrutiny. Would the use of heightened scrutiny be a more satisfactory resolution of this matter?

(4) *Justice Scalia's Dissent: The Majority's "Terminal Silliness."* Justice Scalia's dissent would have found that Colorado had legitimate interests and means which were rationally related to those ends. He called Justice Kennedy's analysis "terminal silliness." He also would have considered Colorado to have a legitimate interest in upholding "traditional moral values." Note that the Court addresses this argument in *Lawrence v. Texas*, overruling *Bowers* (the authority upon which Justice Scalia's dissent relies). Justice Scalia argues that the gay rights issues should be resolved through the political process—and not by judicial review.

(5) *Can the Result Be Defended Because This Case Involved a Classification Drawn Along the Lines of Personal, Intimate Characteristics or because It Involves the Political Process?* The classifications established by Amendment 2 relate to intimate personal relationships. Are personal characteristics less legitimate subjects for so-called democratic regulation? Is the majority institutionally competent to make decisions about personal, intimate sexual activities?

(6) *Is the Court Correct in Concluding that Disqualification of a Class of Persons from the Right to Seek Specific Protection from the Law Is "Unprecedented"?* This statement by the Court is, to put it charitably, overbroad. Constitutional provisions, as well as other laws, often prevent classes of people from seeking "specific protection from the law." A couple of examples: (a) *Public Figures Subject to Frequent Invasions of Privacy in the Tabloid Press Have No Remedy, Owing to the First Amendment.* Imagine that a group of famous people were to approach a state legislature seeking protection from misleading or intrusive tabloid stories. The First Amendment "disqualifies" them from this "specific protection." (b) *Polygamists.* This example comes from Justice Scalia. Isn't the point of a constitutional provision, after all, to "disqualify" some class of people from using the political process to obtain a "specific protection" from the law?

Again, the Colorado Supreme Court employed strict scrutiny once it determined that a "fundamental right" was involved. Would this be a more satisfactory approach? The

Romer decision has generated a large volume of scholarly commentary. To assist your consideration of the issues posed by these Notes, you might examine the articles in the Symposium issue of the University of Colorado Law Review, *Gay Rights and the Court: The Amendment 2 Controversy*, 68 U. COLO. L. REV. 285 (1997). *See also* Daniel Farber & Suzanna Sherry, *The Pariah Principle*, 13 CONST. COMM. 257 (1996).

PROBLEM L

CALIFORNIA'S PROPOSITION 209: IS IT MADE UNCONSTITUTIONAL BY THE REASONING IN ROMER v. EVANS (OR IS ITS EFFECT AFTER ADARAND CONSTITUTIONALLY MANDATED)? In 1995, the Regents of the University of California voted to end preferences in admission based upon race or certain other factors. (This development somewhat paralleled the *Hopwood* decision outlined in an earlier problem, except that it was decided not by a court, but by the State itself.) After the University of California action, Regent Ward Connerly, an African-American, led the effort for adoption of Proposition 209, a California ballot initiative that broadened the ban on racial preferences. It provided, "The State shall not discriminate against, or grant preferential treatment to, any individual or group on the basis of race, sex, color, ethnicity or national origin in the operation of public employment, public education, or public contracting." A federal district court enjoined enforcement, but the Ninth Circuit reversed, *Coalition for Economic Equality v. Wilson*, 110 F.3d 1431 (1997), and the Supreme Court denied certiorari. On August 28, 1997, Proposition 209 went into effect.

Questions: (1) *If You Apply the Reasoning of Romer v. Evans, Is Proposition 209 Unconstitutional?* The proposition, like Colorado's Amendment 2, makes it impossible for members of certain groups, *i.e.*, racial minorities, to obtain preferences by ordinary ballot. To obtain preferences, they would need to get the state constitution amended. (2) *Is Proposition 209 Distinguishable as Outlawing Consideration of All Races as Bases for Preferences?* You may conclude that California's Proposition 209 is broader than Colorado's Amendment 2 in that it bans preferences for people of all races, not just those for members of minority groups. But is this really a difference? Proposition 209's real effect is upon preferences for minority groups, isn't it? (3) *Does Adarand, as Interpreted in Hopwood, Indicate that Proposition 209's Effect Is Constitutionally Mandated?* On the other hand, instead of striking it down, perhaps the effect of the decisions actually is to mandate a result similar to that of Proposition 209 (this is the holding of *Hopwood*, at least for academic preferences). Is this reasoning correct? (4) *If Romer* v. Evans Means that Proposition 209 Is Unconstitutional, Would It Be Constitutional If Rewritten to Protect All Persons from Denial of Any Government Benefit on Grounds of Race? If rewritten this way, wouldn't it mean the same thing?

[D] Illegitimacy

INTRODUCTORY NOTES AND QUESTIONS

(1) *Groping for a Standard to Review Illegitimacy Classifications: Levy v. Louisiana, 391 U.S. 68 (1968).* Levy concerned a Louisiana statute that denied illegitimate children the right to recover for the wrongful death of their mothers, even if the illegitimates were acknowledged. The Court struck down this statute, employing some rhetoric that implied that a mere "rational classification" was required and other rhetoric that implied stricter scrutiny.

(2) *Retrenchment: Matthews v. Lucas, 427 U.S. 495 (1976).* The Social Security Act conditioned eligibility for survivors' insurance benefits to illegitimate children upon a demonstration that the deceased wage earner was the claimant child's parent and, at the time of his death, was living with the child or contributing to his support. The Court, per Justice Blackmun, upheld the Act:

[Appellees argue] that legislation treating legitimate and illegitimate off-spring differently is constitutionally suspect . . . and requires the judicial scrutiny traditionally devoted to cases involving discrimination along lines of race or national origin. [W]e disagree.

It is true, of course, that the legal status of illegitimacy, . . . is, like race or national origin, a characteristic determined by causes not within the control of the illegitimate individual, and it bears no relation to the individual's ability to participate in and contribute to society. [But] irrationality in some classifications does not itself demonstrate that other, possibly rational, distinctions made in part on the basis of legitimacy are inherently untenable. . . .

We therefore adhere to [the view] that . . . discrimination between individuals on the basis of their legitimacy does not "command extraordinary protection from the majoritarian political process," which our most exacting scrutiny would entail. . . .

Congress' purpose in adopting the statutory presumptions of dependency was obviously to serve administrative convenience. [S]uch presumptions in aid of administrative functions, though they may approximate, rather than precisely mirror, the results that case-by-case adjudication would show, are permissible under the fifth amendment, so long as the lack of precise equivalence does not exceed the bounds of substantiality tolerated by the applicable level of scrutiny. . . .

Justice Stevens, joined by Justices Brennan and Marshall dissented: "The Court's reason for approving discrimination against this class—'administrative convenience'—is opaque and insufficient: [i]nsufficient because it unfairly evaluates the competing interests at stake." Since certain other children were eligible for benefits regardless of actual dependency, the classification of illegitimates did not bear any "substantial relationship" to the fact of dependency.

(3) *Establishing the Middle Level of Scrutiny: Trimble v. Gordon*, 430 U.S. 762 (1977). *Trimble* concerned an Illinois statute providing that an illegitimate could recover from his father only if (1) the child had been acknowledged by the father and (2) the parents had married at a later date so as to legitimate the child. The purpose of the statute was to avoid the problems of contested paternity hearings after the death of the putative father and to prevent false claims. Although the Court, per Justice Powell, recognized these aims as valid and important, it held that the Illinois statute was not substantially related to the State's interest. In fact, the decedent in *Trimble* had been found in a paternity proceeding to be the claimant's father. Thus, "difficulties of proving paternity in some situations do not justify the total statutory disinheritance of illegitimate children whose fathers die intestate. The facts of this case graphically illustrate the constitutional defect."

Four members of the Court dissented. Justice Rehnquist's dissent began with the proposition that "when the Court has been required to adjudicate equal protection claims not based on race or national origin, it has faced a much more difficult task." *Trimble*, as Justice Rehnquist saw it, was "a source of confusion, since the unanswered question remains as to the precise sort of scrutiny to which classifications based on illegitimacy will be subject." In this regard, consider the following case.

LALLI v. LALLI
439 U.S. 259 (1978)

MR. JUSTICE POWELL announced the judgment of the Court and delivered an opinion in which THE CHIEF JUSTICE and MR. JUSTICE STEWART join.

[Section 4-1.2 of New York's Estate, Powers and Trust Law provided that an illegitimate could inherit from his intestate father only if a court had, "during the lifetime of the father, made an order of filiation declaring paternity." The proceedings that produced the order of paternity, furthermore, had to have been commenced during the mother's pregnancy or within two years of the illegitimate's birth. Here, the Court begins its analysis by citing *Trimble v. Gordon*, which is dealt with in note (3), *above*. It upholds the New York statute by distinguishing *Trimble.*]

We begin our analysis with *Trimble*. At issue in that case was the constitutionality of an Illinois statute providing that a child born out of wedlock could inherit from his intestate father only if the father had "acknowledged" the child and the child had been legitimated by the intermarriage of the parents.

We concluded that the Illinois statute discriminated against illegitimate children in a manner prohibited by the Equal Protection Clause. Although . . . classifications based on illegitimacy are not subject to "strict scrutiny," they nevertheless are invalid under the Fourteenth Amendment if they are not substantially related to permissible state interests. Upon examination, we found that the Illinois law failed that test.

Two state interests were proposed which the statute was said to foster: the encouragement of legitimate family relationships and the maintenance of an accurate and efficient method of disposing of an intestate decedent's property. Granting that the State was appropriately concerned with the integrity of the family unit, we viewed the statute as bearing "only the most attenuated relationship to the asserted goal."

Illinois' interest in safeguarding the orderly disposition of property at death was more relevant to the statutory classification. . . .

The Illinois statute, however, was constitutionally flawed because, by insisting upon not only an acknowledgment by the father, but also the marriage of the parents, it excluded "at least some significant categories of illegitimate children of intestate men [whose] inheritance rights can be recognized without jeopardizing the orderly settlement of estates or the dependability of titles to property passing under intestacy laws. . . ."

The New York statute, enacted in 1965, was intended to soften the rigors of previous law which permitted illegitimate children to inherit only from their mothers.

At the outset we observe that § 4-1.2 is different in important respects from the statutory provision overturned in *Trimble*. The Illinois statute required, in addition to the father's acknowledgment of paternity, the legitimation of the child through the intermarriage of the parents as an absolute precondition to inheritance. [A]s illustrated by the facts in *Trimble*, even a judicial declaration of paternity was insufficient to permit inheritance.

Under § 4-1.2, by contrast, the marital status of the parents is irrelevant. The single requirement at issue here is an evidentiary one that the paternity of the father be declared in a judicial proceeding sometime before his death. The child need not have been legitimated in order to inherit from his father. Had the appellant in *Trimble* been governed by § 4-1.2, she would have been a distributee of her father's estate. . . .

Although the overarching purpose of the proposed statute was "to alleviate the plight of the illegitimate child," the [New York State] Commission [that proposed the law] considered it necessary to impose the strictures of § 4-1.2 in order to mitigate serious difficulties in the administration of the estates of both testate and intestate decedents. The Commission's perception of some of these difficulties was described by Surrogate Sobel. . . :

> An illegitimate, if made an unconditional distributee in intestacy, must be served with process in the estate of his parent or if he is a distributee in the estate of the kindred of a parent. . . . How does one cite and serve an illegitimate of whose existence neither family nor personal representative may be aware? And of greatest concern, how achieve finality of decree in *any* estate when there always exists the possibility however remote of a secret illegitimate lurking in the buried past of a parent or an ancestor of a class of beneficia-

ries? . . . The point made in the commission discussions was that instead of affecting only a few estates, procedural problems would be created for many—some members suggested a majority—of estates. . . .

As the State's interests are substantial, we now consider the means adopted by New York to further these interests. . . . Accuracy is enhanced by placing paternity disputes in a judicial forum during the lifetime of the father. As the New York Court of Appeals observed in its first opinion in this case, the "availability [of the putative father] should be a substantial factor contributing to the reliability of the fact-finding process." In addition, requiring that the orderbe issued during the father's lifetime permits a man to defend his reputation against "unjust accusations in paternity claims," which was a secondary purpose of § 4-1.2.

We do not question that there will be some illegitimate children who would be able to establish their relationship to their deceased fathers without serious disruption of the administration of estates and that, as applied to such individuals, § 4-1.2 appears to operate unfairly. But few statutory classifications are entirely free from the criticism that they sometimes produce inequitable results. Our inquiry under the Equal Protection Clause does not focus on the abstract "fairness" of a state law, but on whether the statute's relation to the state interests it is intended to promote is so tenuous that it lacks the rationality contemplated by the Fourteenth Amendment. . . .

Even if, as Mr. Justice Brennan believes, § 4-1.2 could have been written somewhat more equitably, it is not the function of a court "to hypothesize independently on the desirability or feasibility of any possible alternative[s]" to the statutory scheme formulated by New York. *Mathews v. Lucas.* "These matters of practical judgment and empirical calculation are for [the State]. . . ."

We conclude that the requirement imposed by § 4-1.2 on illegitimate children who would inherit from their fathers is substantially related to the important state interests the statute is intended to promote. We therefore find no violation of the Equal Protection Clause.

For the reasons stated in his dissent in *Trimble v. Gordon*, 430 U.S. 762, 777 (1977), Mr. Justice Rehnquist concurs in the judgment of affirmance.

[The concurring opinion of Justice Stewart is omitted.]

Mr. Justice Blackmun, concurring in the judgment.

I agree with the result the Court has reached and concur in its judgment. I also agree with much that has been said in the plurality opinion. My point of departure, of course, is at the plurality's valiant struggle to distinguish, rather than overrule, *Trimble v. Gordon*, decided just the Term before last, and involving a small probate estate (an automobile worth approximately $2,500) and a sad and appealing fact situation. . . .

I would overrule *Trimble*, but the Court refrains from doing so on the theory that the result of *Trimble* is justified because of the peculiarities of the Illinois Probate Act there under consideration. This, of course, is an explanation, but, for me, it is an unconvincing one. If *Trimble* is not a derelict, the corresponding statutes of other States will be of questionable validity until this Court passes on them, one by one, as being on the *Trimble* side of the line or the *Labine-Lalli* side.

Mr. Justice Brennan, with whom Mr. Justice White, Mr. Justice Marshall, and Mr. Justice Stevens join, dissenting.

Two interests are said to justify this discrimination against illegitimates. First, it is argued, reliance upon mere formal public acknowledgments of paternity would open the door to fraudulent claims of paternity. I cannot accept this argument. I adhere to the view that when "a father has formally acknowledged his child . . . there is no possible difficulty of proof, and no opportunity for fraud or error. . . ."

But even if my confidence in the accuracy of formal public acknowledgments of paternity were unfounded, New York has available less drastic means of screening out fraudulent claims of paternity. [N]ew York might require illegitimates to prove paternity by an elevated standard of proof, *e.g.*, clear and convincing evidence, or even beyond a reasonable doubt. Certainly here, where there is no factual dispute as to the relationship between Robert and Mario Lalli, there is no justification for denying Robert Lalli his intestate share. . . .

NOTES AND QUESTIONS

(1) *Are Illegitimacy Classifications after Lalli Subject to Intermediate-Level Review—And If So, of What Kind?* The plurality in *Lalli* says that illegitimacy classifications, while not subject to strict scrutiny, must be "substantially related" to "permissible" state interests. What sort of intermediate review is applicable to illegitimacy, if any?

(2) *Illegitimates and Citizenship: The Court's Continued Use of an Intermediate-Level Scrutiny for Classifications Concerning Illegitimates: Miller v. Albright, 523 U.S. 420 (1998).* In a 1998 decision involving both classifications based on illegitimacy and the gender of the parent, the Court, in a plurality opinion by Justice Stevens, applied a version of intermediate scrutiny. Pursuant to its plenary power under the Citizenship Clause, Congress has imposed various requirements on the ability of illegitimate children born outside the United States who have one American citizen parent to secure citizenship. Under 8 U.S.C. § 1409, the requirements are greater when the American citizen is the father rather than the mother; in particular, the American father must take affirmative steps to legitimize the child before the child reaches the age of 18 while the illegitimate child's mother need not satisfy this requirement. The Court, citing to *Trimble*, *supra*, required that the government have "an important governmental objective" for such differential requirements and that the governmental means be "well tailored to serve" those interests. In *Albright*, the Court found that the federal government satisfied this standard.

The two concurring opinions, by Justices O'Connor and Scalia, did not rely on an intermediate scrutiny. Justice Breyer, for Justices Souter and Ginsburg, dissented and treated the case as a "gender discrimination" issue. Under these circumstances, the doctrinal standard for classifications based on illegitimacy is apparently some level of intermediate scrutiny.

[E] Court Access As Influenced By Poverty

INTRODUCTORY NOTE

As we shall see in a later section of this chapter, the Court has declined to apply heightened scrutiny solely because particular legislation has had different impact on the poor than on the rest of the population. It has, however, found equal protection violations in laws that constrict access by the poor to certain kinds of proceedings in the courts. It is this subject that we take up here.

DOUGLAS v. CALIFORNIA, 372 U.S. 353 (1963). The indigent defendants were convicted of thirteen felonies after being represented by a public defender in the trial court. Upon exercising their statutory rights to appeal, they were denied appointed counsel by the appellate court. In accordance with California practice, that court had "gone through" the record itself and, on that basis, had concluded that "no good whatever could be served by appointment of [appellate] counsel." The Supreme Court, per Justice Douglas, reversed:

In *Griffin v. Illinois*, 351 U.S. 12, we held that a state may not grant appellate review in such a way as to discriminate against some convicted defendants on account of their poverty. There . . . the right to a free transcript on appeal was in issue. [I]n either case, [*Griffin* or the present one], the evil is the same: discrimination against the indigent. For there can be no equal justice when the kind of appeal a man enjoys "depends on the amount of money he has. . . ."

Three Justices dissented. Justice Harlan, in his dissenting opinion, pointed out that "The states, of course, are prohibited by the equal protection clause from discriminating between 'rich' and 'poor' *as such.* . . . But it is a far different thing to suggest that the [equal protection clause] prevents the state from adopting a law of general applicability that may affect the poor more harshly than it does the rich, or, on the other hand, from making some effort to redress economic imbalances while not eliminating them entirely."

BODDIE v. CONNECTICUT
401 U.S. 371 (1971)

Mr. Justice Harlan delivered the opinion of the Court.

[Plaintiffs, who were indigents dependent upon welfare, challenged the constitutionality of a $60 filing fee required for obtaining a divorce in the State of Connecticut. The Court here holds the requirement unconstitutional.]

[O]ur conclusion is that, given the basic position of the marriage relationship in this society's hierarchy of values and the concomitant state monopolization of the means for legally dissolving this relationship, [due] process does prohibit a State from denying, solely because of inability to pay, access to its courts to individuals who seek judicial dissolution of their marriages. . . .

[Previous case law] has, however, typically involved rights of defendants—not, as here, persons seeking access to the judicial process in the first instance. This is because our society has been so structured that resort to the courts is not usually the only available, legitimate means of resolving private disputes. . . .

[A]s this Court on more than one occasion has recognized, marriage involves interests of basic importance in our society. *See, e.g., Loving v. Virginia.*

[I]t is not surprising, then, that the States have seen fit to oversee many aspects of that institution. Without a prior judicial imprimatur, individuals may freely enter into and rescind commercial contracts, for example, but we are unaware of any jurisdiction where private citizens may covenant for or dissolve marriages without state approval. . . .

[R]esort to the judicial process by these plaintiffs is no more voluntary in a realistic sense than that of the defendant called upon to defend his interests in court. . . .

[W]e conclude that the State's refusal to admit these appellants to its courts, the sole means in Connecticut for obtaining a divorce, must be regarded as the equivalent of denying them an opportunity to be heard upon their claimed right to a dissolution of their marriages, and, in the absence of a sufficient countervailing justification for the State's action, a denial of due process. . . .

[W]e go no further than necessary to dispose of the case before us, a case where the *bona fides* of both appellants' indigency and desire for divorce are here beyond dispute. We do not decide that access for all individuals to the courts is a right that is, in all circumstances, guaranteed by the Due Process Clause of the Fourteenth Amendment. . . .

[The separate concurrences of Justice Douglas and Justice Brennan are omitted.]

Mr. Justice Black, dissenting. . . .

Civil lawsuits . . . are not like government prosecutions for crime. . . . In such cases the government is not usually involved as a party, and there is no deprivation of life, liberty, or property as punishment for crime. Our federal Constitution, therefore, does not place such private disputes on the same high level as it places criminal trials and punishment. There is consequently no necessity, no reason, why government should in civil trials be hampered or handicapped by the strict and rigid due process rules the Constitution has provided to protect people charged with crime. . . .

NOTES AND QUESTIONS

(1) *Poverty Per Se Does Not Trigger Heightened Scrutiny; It is Poverty Associated With Certain Issues of Court Access That Does.* In both *Douglas* and *Boddie*, the Court finds fundamental interests at stake—the defendant's rights in the criminal process and the spouse's interest in the marriage relationship. Reconsider Justice Harlan's statement, in *Douglas*, that the states are prohibited "from discriminating between 'rich' and 'poor' *as such*." What does Justice Harlan mean? Notice that he goes on to state that laws of general applicability may be sustained even though they have harsher impact upon the poor.

(2) *Distinguishing Boddie in the Case of Bankruptcy: United States v. Kras, 409 U.S. 434 (1973).* In *Kras*, an indigent petitioner in bankruptcy challenged the required filing fee, totaling $50, as a denial of due process. In cases of voluntary bankruptcy all fees "may be paid in installments" upon a proper showing. The Court, per Justice Blackmun, distinguished *Boddie* and upheld the filing fee:

> The appellants in *Boddie*, on the one hand, and Robert Kras, on the other, stand in materially different postures. . . . Kras' alleged interest in the elimination of his debt burden, and in obtaining his desired new start in life, although important and so recognized by the enactment of the Bankruptcy Act, does not rise to the same constitutional level [as *Boddie*'s interest in marriage dissolution.] [W]e see no fundamental interest that is gained or lost depending on the availability of a discharge in bankruptcy.

> Nor is the government's control over the establishment, enforcement, or dissolution of debts nearly so exclusive as Connecticut's control over the marriage relationship in *Boddie*. . . .

> We are also of the opinion that the filing fee requirement does not deny Kras the equal protection of the laws. Bankruptcy is hardly akin to free speech or marriage or to those other rights . . . that the Court has come to regard as fundamental. [T]his being so, the applicable standard . . . is that of rational justification. . . .

Four members of the Court dissented, in an opinion by Justice Stewart: "[T]he debtor, like the married plaintiffs in *Boddie*, originally entered into his contract freely and voluntarily. But it is the government nevertheless that continues to enforce that obligation, and under our legal system that debt is effective only because the judicial machinery is there to collect it. . . ." Thus, for the indigent bankrupt, Justice Stewart concluded, the government provided the only effective means of avoiding a "lifetime burden of debt."

[F] The Court Limits the Use of Heightened Scrutiny: Education, Housing, and Subsistence as Subject to "Mere Rationality" Review

DANDRIDGE v. WILLIAMS
397 U.S. 471 (1970)

MR. JUSTICE STEWART delivered the opinion of the Court.

[Maryland administered Aid to Families with Dependent Children by providing for most families according to the full ascertained standard of need, but it imposed a $250 upper limit on the total amount of money any one family unit could receive. Here, the Court holds that this "maximum grant regulation" does not violate equal protection.]

[M]aryland says that its maximum grant regulation is wholly free of any invidiously discriminatory purpose or effect, and that the regulation is rationally supportable on at least four entirely valid grounds. The regulation can be clearly justified, Maryland argues, in terms of legitimate state interests in encouraging gainful employment, in maintaining an equitable balance in economic status as between welfare families and those supported by a wage-earner, in providing incentives for family planning, and in allocating available public funds in such a way as fully to meet the needs of the largest possible number of families. The District Court, while apparently recognizing the validity of at least some of these state concerns, nonetheless held that the regulation "is invalid on its face for overreaching," that it violates the Equal Protection Clause "[b]ecause it cuts too broad a swath on an indiscriminate basis as applied to the entire group of AFDC eligibles to which it purports to apply. . . ."

If this were a case involving government action claimed to violate the First Amendment guarantee of free speech, a finding of "overreaching" would be significant and might be crucial. . . .

[B]ut the concept of "overreaching" has no place in this case. For here we deal with state regulation in the social and economic field, not affecting freedoms guaranteed by the Bill of Rights, and claimed to violate the Fourteenth Amendment only because the regulation results in some disparity in grants of welfare payments to the larger AFDC families. For this Court to approve the invalidation of state economic or social regulation as "overreaching" would be far too reminiscent of an era when the Court thought the Fourteenth Amendment gave it power to strike down state laws "because they may be unwise, improvident, or out of harmony with a particular school of thought." *Williamson v. Lee Optical of Oklahoma, Inc.* . . .

In the area of economics and social welfare, a State does not violate the Equal Protection Clause merely because the classifications made by its laws are imperfect. If the classification has some "reasonable basis," it does not offend the Constitution simply because the classification "is not made with mathematical nicety or because in practice it results in some inequality." . . .

Under this long-established meaning of the Equal Protection Clause, it is clear that the Maryland maximum grant regulation is constitutionally valid. We need not explore all the reasons that the State advances in justification of the regulation. It is enough that a solid foundation for the regulation can be found in the State's legitimate interest in encouraging employment and in avoiding discrimination between welfare families and the families of the working poor. By combining a limit on the recipient's grant with permission to retain money earned, without reduction in the amount of the grant, Maryland provides an incentive to seek gainful employment. And by keying the maximum family AFDC grants to the minimum wage a steadily employed head of a household receives, the State maintains some semblance of an equitable balance between families on welfare and those supported by an employed breadwinner.

We do not decide today that the Maryland regulation is wise, that it best fulfills the relevant social and economic objectives that Maryland might ideally espouse, or that a more just and humane system could not be devised. Conflicting claims of morality and intelligence are raised by opponents and proponents of almost every measure, certainly including the one before us. But the intractable economic, social, and even philosophical problems presented by public welfare programs are not the business of this Court. . . .

[Reversed.]

Mr. Justice Marshall, whom Mr. Justice Brennan joins, dissenting. . . .

This case simply defies easy characterization in terms of one or the other of [the recognized] "tests." The cases relied on by the Court, in which a "mere rationality" test was actually used, *e.g., Williamson v. Lee Optical of Oklahoma, Inc.,* are most accurately described as involving the application of equal protection reasoning to the regulation of business interests. . . .

[T]his case, involving the literally vital interests of a powerless minority—poor families without breadwinners—is far removed from the area of business regulation, as the Court concedes. Why then is the standard used in those cases imposed here? We are told no more than that this case falls in "the area of economics and social welfare," with the implication that from there the answer is obvious. In my view, equal protection analysis of this case is not appreciably advanced by the *a priori* definition of a "right," fundamental or otherwise. Rather, concentration must be placed upon the character of the classification in question, the relative importance to individuals in the class discriminated against of the governmental benefits that they do not receive, and the asserted state interests in support of the classification. . . .

[The separate opinions of Justices Black, Harlan and Douglas are omitted.]

[Justice Black, joined by the Chief Justice, concurred; so did Justice Harlan, emphasizing that a compelling interest should be required only in the case of racial classifications, "to which unique historical considerations apply." Justice DOUGLAS dissented on the ground that the Maryland regulation was inconsistent with the Social Security Act.]

NOTES AND QUESTIONS

(1) *What Test? Justice Stewart's Rational Basis Approach Versus Justice Marshall's "Sliding Scale" Theory.* The Court holds that public welfare is not a fundamental right. Justice Stewart's majority opinion uses the rational basis approach. Consider whether this test, developed in business regulation cases, is appropriate here. Justice Marshall's alternative approach is sometimes described as a "sliding scale" theory. Instead of two or three specific "tiers" of review, Justice Marshall would create a sliding scale, in which the level of scrutiny is adjusted according to three factors: (1) the nature of the classification, (2) the "relative importance to individuals . . . of the government benefits that they do not receive," and (3) the strengths of the interests asserted by the state. *Compare* to the *Mathews v. Eldridge* standard in procedural due process doctrine, in Chapter 8. Since Justice Marshall sees the individual's interest as great and the state's as relatively small, he regards the Maryland regulation as invalid. Note, however, that he also concludes that the Maryland law cannot be sustained even under the majority's "reasonableness" test.

(2) *The Arguments for Stricter Scrutiny of Government Decisions Affecting Subsistence.* The argument in favor of stricter scrutiny in a case such as *Dandridge* is not difficult to recognize and is eloquently stated by Justice Marshall. The importance of having enough to eat is such that it is "fundamental" at least in the vernacular sense, if not in the legal. The rights to vote, to associate with others, or to travel would have little value if the person exercising them did not have minimum subsistence. Thus, subsistence is necessary for the exercise of other fundamental rights. Finally, it could be argued that the courts should attempt to counteract upper-middle class bias in the definition of fundamental rights, rather than protecting solely those abstract rights that are significant in the philosophy of the "upper middle, professional class from which most lawyers and judges . . . are drawn." *See* J. Ely, *Democracy and Distrust, supra,* at 59. *Cf.* Rich, *Equal Protection for the Poor: Fair Distribution to Meet Brutal Needs,* 24 San Diego L. Rev. 1117 (1987).

(3) *The Case against Stricter Scrutiny.* On the other hand, the imposition of a strict scrutiny or even intermediate level of review for a right to subsistence would create other difficulties:

  a. *Defining the Proper Level of "Subsistence."* How does one decide what is the "minimally acceptable" level of subsistence? Is it that which will maintain life, or that which will maintain robust health? Perhaps the only way to resolve these questions is by societal consensus, which is better expressed through a legislature.

b. *Defining the Appropriate Level of Government Involvement, Particularly in Conjunction With Private Efforts.* Many fundamental rights concern matters in which the government is deeply involved or even has a monopoly (as in the case of access to the courts or voting rights). On the other hand, the question of subsistence is one that generally is answered by private efforts. Even with those whom it assists or subsidizes, the state may reasonably expect and encourage private contributions by others or by the recipients, and court scrutiny of legislative calibrations in this area would make for complex line drawing.

c. *Ineffectiveness of Court Action.* If there is anything that characterizes the problem of welfare assistance, it is the intractability of the problem. Paradox abounds. Many theorize that consistent support creates dependence or other kinds of disadvantage for the recipients. It is unlikely that sporadic court intervention can improve upon legislative and administrative experience in terms of pragmatic workability of a welfare system.

d. *General Absence of Unconstitutional Motivations in Efforts to Conserve Welfare Funds.* When the state affirmatively regulates the self-motivated conduct of private individuals, there always is the concern that it may act with discriminatory motive. When, however, the state sets a level of public assistance that arguably is below some "minimal subsistence" level, its aim generally is to conserve the public fisc, an aim that, in this area, more arguably is legitimate. The United States is dependent upon a market economy, one in which motivations are heavily influenced by such matters as government benefits. The efficiency of such a system depends upon the avoidance of overspending by government. Accordingly, the ostensible rationale is economic; it stands in contradistinction to affirmative regulation, for which discriminatory motives may be clandestine and need to be discovered by strict scrutiny.

(4) *Extending the Dandridge Reasoning to Housing and Shelter: Lindsey v. Normet, 405 U.S. 56 (1972).* Lindsey concerned the constitutionality of the Oregon forcible entry and wrongful detainer statute, which required trial no later than six days after service of an eviction complaint (unless security for rent was provided) and which limited triable issues to the tenant's default, specifically excluding any consideration of the landlord's breach of duty to maintain the premises. The Court, per Justice White, applied the rational basis test and upheld the statute. The Court expressly rejected the argument that the "need for decent shelter" and the "right to retain peaceful possession of one's home" were fundamental interests that should be protected by the requirement of a compelling government interest:

> We do not denigrate the importance of decent, safe, and sanitary housing. But the Constitution does not provide judicial remedies for every social and economic ill. . . . Absent constitutional mandate, the assurance of adequate housing and the definition of landlord-tenant relationships are legislative, not judicial, functions.

Justices Douglas and Brennan filed separate dissents.

(5) *Education: Is the Right to a Public School Education Fundamental or a Proper Subject for Heightened Scrutiny?* Another undeniably important area of human need is education. The argument can be made that the equal protection clause is violated if some categories of persons are denied any such public education at all, or if there is different quality of education in low-income and high-income areas. Consider the following case.

SAN ANTONIO INDEPENDENT SCHOOL DISTRICT v. RODRIGUEZ
411 U.S. 1 (1973)

MR. JUSTICE POWELL delivered the opinion of the Court.

[Parents of school children, who were members of minority groups or who were poor and resided in school districts having low property tax bases, filed suit attacking the Texas system of financing public education. Approximately half of the educational expenditures in Texas were funded on a statewide basis by the Minimum Foundation School Program, to which the state contributed approximately eighty percent; the districts' share, known as the local fund assignment, was apportioned among the school districts under a formula designed to reflect each district's relative tax paying ability.]

[The Edgewood School District, in which appellees resided, was approximately ninety-six percent black and Mexican American, had the lowest assessed property value per pupil in the San Antonio metropolitan area, and contributed only $26 above its local fund assignment to the education of each child for the 1967–68 school year. The total, with local state, and federal funds, was $356 per pupil per year in the Edgewood District. On the other hand, Alamo Heights (the most affluent school district in San Antonio) supplemented other expenditures by $330 per pupil from the local tax base, for a total expenditure of $594 per pupil in the 1967–68 school year.]

[On the basis of facts and statistics such as these, the district court held the Texas school financing system unconstitutional, after concluding that wealth was a "suspect" classification and that education was a "fundamental" interest. Here, the Supreme Court reverses, upholding the Texas system.] *PH + hold.*

The wealth discrimination discovered by the District Court in this case, and by several other courts that have recently struck down school-financing laws in other States is quite unlike any of the forms of wealth discrimination heretofore reviewed by this Court. Rather than focusing on the unique features of the alleged discrimination, the courts in these cases have virtually assumed their findings of a suspect classification through a simplistic process of analysis: since, under the traditional systems of financing public schools, some poorer people receive less expensive educations than other more affluent people, these systems discriminate on the basis of wealth. This approach largely ignores the hard threshold questions, including whether it makes a difference for purposes of consideration under the Constitution that the class of disadvantaged "poor" cannot be identified or defined in customary equal protection terms, and whether the relative—rather than absolute—nature of the asserted deprivation is of significant consequence. . . .

[I]n *Douglas v. California* [in this Chapter, *above*], a decision establishing an indigent defendant's right to court appointed counsel on direct appeal, the Court dealt only with defendants who could not pay for counsel from their own resources and who had no other way of gaining representation. *Douglas* provides no relief for those on whom the burdens of paying for a criminal defense are relatively speaking, great but not insurmountable. Nor does it deal with relative differences in the quality of counsel acquired by the less wealthy.

Only appellees' first possible basis for describing the class disadvantaged by the Texas school-financing system—discrimination against a class of definably "poor" persons—might arguablymeet the criteria established in [our] prior cases. Even a cursory examination, however, demonstrates that neither of the two distinguishing characteristics of wealth classifications can be found here. First, in support of their charge that the system discriminates against the "poor," appellees have made no effort to demonstrate that it operates to the peculiar disadvantage of any class fairly definable as indigent, or as composed of persons whose incomes are beneath any designated poverty level. Indeed, there is reason to believe that the poorest families are not necessarily clustered in the poorest property districts. . . .

Second, neither appellees nor the District Court addressed the fact that, unlike each of the foregoing cases, lack of personal resources has not occasioned an absolute deprivation of the desired benefit. The argument here is not that the children in districts having relatively low assessable property values are receiving no public education; rather, it is that they are receiving a poorer quality education than that available to children in districts having more assessable wealth. Apart from the unsettled and disputed question whether the quality of education may be determined by the amount of money expended for it, a sufficient answer to appellees' argument is that, at least where wealth is involved, the Equal Protection Clause does not require absolute equality or precisely equal advantages. Nor indeed, in view of the infinite variables affecting the educational process, can any system assure equal quality of education except in the most relative sense. . . .

However described, it is clear that appellees' suit asks this Court to extend its most exacting scrutiny to review a system that allegedly discriminates against a large, diverse, and amorphous class, unified only by the common factor of residence in districts that happen to have less taxable wealth than other districts. The system of alleged discrimination and the class it defines have none of the traditional indicia of suspectness: the class is not saddled with such disabilities, or subjected to such a history of purposeful unequal treatment, or relegated to such a position of political powerlessness as to command extraordinary protection from the majoritarian political process.

. . . But in recognition of the fact that this Court has never heretofore held that wealth discrimination alone provides an adequate basis for invoking strict scrutiny, appellees have not relied solely on this contention. They also assert that the State's system impermissibly interferes with the exercise of a "fundamental" right. . . . It is this question—whether education is a fundamental right . . . which has so consumed the attention of courts and commentators in recent years. In *Brown v. Board of Education*, a unanimous Court recognized that "education is perhaps the most important function of state and local governments."

Nothing this court holds today in any way detracts from our historic dedication to public education. But the importance of a service performed by the State does not determine whether it must be regarded as fundamental for purposes of examination under the Equal Protection Clause. Mr. Justice Harlan, dissenting from the Court's application of strict scrutiny to a law impinging upon the right of inter-state travel, admonished that "[v]irtually every state statute affects important rights." *Shapiro v. Thompson*. . . .

Similarly, in *Dandridge v. Williams*, the Court's explicit recognition of the fact that the "administration of public welfare assistance . . . involves the most basic economic needs of impoverished human beings," provided no basis for departing from the settled mode of constitutional analysis of legislative classifications involving questions of economic and social policy. . . .

[I]t is not the province of this Court to create substantive constitutional rights in the name of guaranteeing equal protection of the laws. . . . Rather, the answer lies in assessing whether there is a right to education explicitly or implicitly guaranteed by the Constitution. . . .

Education, of course, is not among the rights afforded explicit protection under our Federal Constitution. Nor do we find any basis for saying it is implicitly so protected. [I]t is appellees' contention . . . that education is distinguishable from other services and benefits provided by the State because it bears a peculiarly close relationship to other rights and liberties accorded protection under the Constitution. Specifically, they insist that education is itself a fundamental personal right because it is essential to the effective exercise of First Amendment freedoms and to intelligent utilization of the right to vote. . . .

We need not dispute any of these propositions. [Y]et we have never presumed to possess either the ability or the authority to guarantee to the citizenry the most *effective* speech or the most *informed* electoral choice. . . .

Even if it were conceded that some identifiable quantum of education is a constitutionally protected prerequisite to the meaningful exercise of either right, we have no indication that the present levels of educational expenditures in Texas provide an education that falls short. Whatever merit appellees' argument might have if a State's financing system occasioned an absolute denial of educational opportunities to any of its children, that argument provides no basis for finding an interference with fundamental rights where only relative differences in spending levels are involved. . . .

Furthermore, the logical limitations on appellees' nexus theory are difficult to perceive. How, for instance, is education to be distinguished from the significant personal interests in the basics of decent food and shelter? Empirical examination might well buttress an assumption that the ill-fed, ill-clothed, and ill-housed are among the most ineffective participants in the political process, and that they derive the least enjoyment from the benefits of the First Amendment. If so, appellees' thesis would cast serious doubt on the authority of *Dandridge v. Williams, supra* and *Lindsey v. Normet.*

We need not rest our decision, however, solely on the inappropriateness of the strict-scrutiny test. A century of Supreme Court adjudication under the Equal Protection Clause affirmatively supports the application of the traditional standard of review, which requires only that the State's system be shown to bear some rational relationship to legitimate state purposes. This case represents far more than a challenge to the manner in which Texas provides for the education of its children. [W]e are asked to condemn the State's judgment in conferring on political subdivisions the power to tax local property to supply revenues for local interests. In so doing, appellees would have the Court intrude in an area in which it has traditionally deferred to state legislatures. . . .

[I]t would be difficult to imagine a case having a greater potential impact on our federal system than the one now before us, in which we are urged to abrogate systems of financing public education presently in existence in virtually every State. . . .

[T]he people of Texas may be justified in believing that other systems of school financing, which place more of the financial responsibility in the hands of the State, will result in a comparable lessening of desired local autonomy. [A]ny scheme of local taxation—indeed the very existence of identifiable local governmental units—requires the establishment of jurisdictional boundaries that are inevitably arbitrary. It is equally inevitable that some localities are going to be blessed with more taxable assets than others. Nor is local wealth a static quantity. . . .

Moreover, if local taxation for local expenditures were an unconstitutional method of providing for education, then it might be an equally impermissible means of providing other necessary services customarily financed largely from local property taxes, including local police and fire protection, public health and hospitals, and public utility facilities of various kinds. . . .

[W]e hardly need add that this Court's action today is not to be viewed as placing its judicial imprimatur on the status quo. The need is apparent for reform in tax systems which may well have relied too long and too heavily on the local property tax. And certainly innovative thinking as to public education, its methods, and its funding is necessary to assure both a higher level of quality and greater uniformity of opportunity. . . . But the ultimate solutions must come from the lawmakers and from the democratic pressures of those who elect them.

Reversed.

Mr. Justice Brennan, dissenting.

Although I agree with my Brother White that the Texas statutory scheme is devoid of any rational basis, and for that reason is violative of the Equal Protection Clause, I also record my disagreement with the Court's rather distressing assertion that a right may be deemed "fundamental" for the purposes of equal protection analysis only if it is "explicitly or implicitly guaranteed by the Constitution." . . .

Mr. Justice White, with whom Mr. Justice Douglas and Mr. Justice Brennan join, dissenting.

The Equal Protection Clause permits discriminations between classes but requires that the classification bear some rational relationship to a permissible object sought to be attained by the statute. It is not enough that the Texas system before us seeks to achieve the valid, rational purpose of maximizing local initiative; the means chosen by the State must also be rationally related to the end sought to be achieved. . . . Neither Texas nor the majority heeds this rule. If the State aims at maximizing local initiative and local choice, by permitting school districts to resort to the real property tax if they choose to do so, it utterly fails in achieving its purpose in districts with property tax bases so low that there is little if any opportunity for interested parents, rich or poor, to augment school district revenues. [I]n my view, the parents and children in Edgewood, and in like districts, suffer from an invidious discrimination violative of the Equal Protection Clause.

Mr. Justice Marshall, with whom Mr. Justice Douglas concurs, dissenting.

[I] must once more voice my disagreement with the Court's rigidified approach to equal protection analysis. [T]he Court apparently seeks to establish today that equal protection cases fall into one of two neat categories which dictate the appropriate standard of review—strict scrutiny or mere rationality. But this Court's decisions in the field of equal protection defy such easy categorization. . . .

I therefore cannot accept the majority's labored efforts to demonstrate that fundamental interests, which call for strict scrutiny of the challenged classification, encompass only established rights which we are somehow bound to recognize from the text of the Constitution itself. . . .

[Justice Marshall also concluded that the Texas system was unconstitutional as a discrimination based on wealth.]

[The concurring opinion of Justice Stewart is omitted.]

NOTES AND QUESTIONS

(1) *Public Education as a Fundamental Right: San Antonio School District v. Rodriguez, 411 U.S. 1 (1973).* The State of Texas relied, as most states, on property taxes to fund public schools. Texas had a "cap" on the amount of self-help a district could do. This system resulted in substantial disparities between local districts. Parent-taxpayers in the "poorest" per-pupil district challenged the scheme as a violation of equal protection. In this landmark fundamental rights decision (decided after *Roe v. Wade*), the Court, per Justice Powell, rejected both of the challengers' theories. The Court rejected the theory that the "poor" were a suspect class. Poverty was not visible or immutable. The Court also rejected the theory that education was a "fundamental right." The Court applied the rational basis standard and upheld the Texas funding scheme. As such, the Court deferred to the political process to cure the disparate funding problem.

(2) *The Plaintiffs Later Achieved Their Goal by Invoking the State Constitution: See ch. 16, Below.* After this decision, many states reached a different result under their state constitutions. In Texas, the state supreme court did so by interpretation of a state

constitutional requirement for "efficient" education. *See* Ch. 16, *below.* Thus, the plaintiffs ultimately achieved their goal by a different route.

(3)   *Denial of All Access to Education: Plyler v. Doe, 457 U.S. 202 (1982).* Note that, in discussing whether education is a fundamental right, Justice Powell expressly reserves the question whether complete denial of access to public education to some individuals would trigger heightened scrutiny. What is meant by this distinction? In *Plyler v. Doe*, Texas had a statute that excluded from the public schools those alien children who were present in the United States illegally, and who thus were subject to deportation. The majority opinion, by Justice Brennan, declined to find either a suspect class or a fundamental right. Instead, it struck down the statute purportedly by applying the lowest level of scrutiny and finding "no sufficient rational basis for the denial to these children of access to education." Justice Powell joined the majority, based on his determination that this regulation constituted the "total denial" he had identified in *Rodriquez.* Four justices dissented, in an opinion by Chief Justice Burger: "Without laboring what will undoubtedly seem obvious to many, it simply is not 'irrational' for a state to conclude that it does not have the same responsibility to provide benefits for persons whose very presence in the state and this country is illegal as it does to provide for persons lawfully present."

[G]   Are There Other "Middle Tier" Classifications?: The Case of Mental Retardation

CITY OF CLEBURNE v. CLEBURNE LIVING CENTER
473 U.S. 432 (1985)

Justice White delivered the opinion of the Court.

[Cleburne Living Center anticipated leasing a building for a home for the mentally retarded. However, the city informed it that the home would be classified as a "hospital for the feeble minded" under the city's zoning ordinances and that a special use permit therefore would be required. The city then denied the permit after a public hearing. CLC sued, alleging a denial of equal protection both by the face of the statute and in its application.

[The district court upheld the ordinance and its application, but the court of appeals reversed, holding that mental retardation was a "quasi-suspect" classification and that under the applicable "heightened scrutiny" test, the ordinance was facially invalid because it did not substantially further an important governmental purpose. The court of appeals also held the ordinance invalid as applied. Here, the Supreme Court holds that the special use permit could not be constitutionally required in this case, although it does not adopt the court of appeals' "quasi-suspect classification" reasoning.]

[T]he general rule is that legislation is presumed to be valid and will be sustained if the classification drawn by the statute is rationally related to a legitimate state interest. [T]he Constitution presumes that even improvident decisions will eventually be rectified by the democratic processes.

The general rule gives way, however, when a statute classifies by race, alienage or national origin. These factors are so seldom relevant to the achievement of any legitimate state interest that laws grounded in such considerations are deemed to reflect prejudice and antipathy. . . . For these reasons and because such discrimination is unlikely to be soon rectified by legislative means, these laws are subjected to strict scrutiny and will be sustained only if they are suitably tailored to serve a compelling state interest.

Legislative classifications based on gender also call for a heightened standard of review. "[W]hat differentiates sex from such nonsuspect statuses as intelligence or physical disability . . . is that the sex characteristic frequently bears no relation to ability to perform or contribute to society". . . .

We have declined, however, to extend heightened review to differential treatment based on age [citing *Murgia*]. . . .

The lesson of *Murgia* is that where individuals in the group affected by a law have distinguishing characteristics relevant to interests the state has the authority to implement, the courts have been very reluctant, as they should be in our federal system and with our respect for the separation of powers, to closely scrutinize legislative choices as to whether, how and to what extent those interests should be pursued. In such cases, the Equal Protection Clause requires only a rational means to serve a legitimate end.

Against this background, we conclude for several reasons that the Court of Appeals erred in holding mental retardation a quasi-suspect classification calling for a more exacting standard of judicial review than is normally accorded economic and social legislation. First, it is undeniable, and it is not argued otherwise here, that those who are mentally retarded have a reduced ability to cope with and function in the everyday world. [A]s the testimony in this record indicates, they range from those whose disability is not immediately evident to those who must be constantly cared for. They are thus different, immutably so, in relevant respects, and the states' interest in dealing with and providing for them is plainly a legitimate one. How this large and diversified group is to be treated under the law is a difficult and often a technical matter. . . . Heightened scrutiny inevitably involves substantive judgments about legislative decisions, and we doubt thatthe predicate for such judicial oversight is present where the classification deals with mental retardation.

Second, the distinctive legislative response, both national and state, to the plight of those who are mentally retarded demonstrates not only that they have unique problems, but also that the lawmakers have been addressing their difficulties in a manner that belies a continuing antipathy or prejudice and a corresponding need for more intrusive oversight by the judiciary. Thus, the federal government has not only outlawed discrimination against the mentally retarded in federally funded programs, see § 504 of the Rehabilitation Act of 1973, 29 U.S.C. § 794, but it has also provided the retarded with the right to receive "appropriate treatment, services, and habilitation" in a setting that is "least restrictive of [their] personal liberty." Developmental Disabilities Assistance and Bill of Rights Act, 42 U.S.C. § § 6010(1), (2). [Here the Court cites additional federal legislation protecting the mentally retarded in education and employment]. . . .

Third, the legislative response, which could hardly have occurred and survived without public support, negates any claim that the mentally retarded are politically powerless in the sense that they have no ability to attract the attention of the lawmakers. Any minority can be said to be powerless to assert direct control over the legislature, but if that were a criterion for higher level scrutiny by the courts, much economic and social legislation would now be suspect.

Fourth, if the large and amorphous class of the mentally retarded were deemed quasi-suspect for the reasons given by the Court of Appeals, it would be difficult to find a principled way to distinguish a variety of other groups who have perhaps immutable disabilities setting them off from others, who cannot themselves mandate the desired legislative responses, and who can claim some degree of prejudice from at least part of the public at large. One need mention in this respect only the aging, the disabled, the mentally ill, and the infirm. We are reluctant to set out on that course, and we decline to do so.

Our refusal to recognize the retarded as a quasi-suspect class does not leave them entirely unprotected from invidious discrimination. To withstand equal protection review, legislation that distinguishes between the mentally retarded and others must be rationally related to a legitimate governmental purpose. . . .

The constitutional issue is clearly posed. The City does not require a special use permit in an R-3 zone for apartment houses, multiple dwellings, boarding and lodging houses, fraternity or sorority houses, dormitories, apartment hotels, hospitals, sanitariums, nursing homes for convalescents or the aged (other than for the insane or feeble-minded or alcoholics or drug addicts), private clubs or fraternal orders, and other specified uses. It does, however, insist on a special permit for the [Cleburne Living Center] home, and it does so, as the District Court found, because it would be a facility for the mentally retarded. [B]ecause in our view the record does not reveal any rational basis for believing that the [Cleburne Living Center] home would pose any special threat to the city's legitimate interests, we affirm the judgment below insofar as it holds the ordinance invalid as applied in this case.

The District Court found that the City Council's insistence on the permit rested on several factors. First, the Council was concerned with the negative attitude of the majority of propertyowners located within 200 feet of the . . . facility, as well as with the fears of elderly residents of the neighborhood. But mere negative attitudes, or fear, unsubstantiated by factors which are properly cognizable in a zoning proceeding, are not permissible bases for treating a home for the mentally retarded differently from apartment houses, multiple dwellings, and the like. . . .

Second, the Council had two objections to the location of the facility. It was concerned that the facility was across the street from a junior high school, and it feared that the students might harass the occupants. . . . But the school itself is attended by about 30 mentally retarded students, and denying a permit based on such vague, undifferentiated fears is again permitting some portion of the community to validate what would otherwise be an equal protection violation. The other objection to the home's location was that it was located on "a five hundred year flood plain." This concern with the possibility of a flood, however, can hardly be based on a distinction between the [Cleburne Living Center] home and, for example, nursing homes, homes for convalescents or the aged, or sanitariums or hospitals, any of which could be located on the Featherston site without obtaining a special use permit.

Fourth, the Council was concerned with the size of the home and the number of people that would occupy it. The District Court found, and the Court of Appeals repeated, that "[i]f the potential residents of the Featherston Street home were not mentally retarded, but the home was the same in all other respects, its use would be permitted under the city's zoning ordinance." [I]n the words of the Court of Appeals, "[t]he City never justifies its apparent view that other people can live under such 'crowded' conditions when mentally retarded persons cannot." . . .

The short of it is that requiring the permit in this case appears to us to rest on an irrational prejudice against the mentally retarded, including those who would occupy the . . . facility and who would live under the closely supervised and highly regulated conditions expressly provided for by state and federal law.

The judgment of the Court of Appeals is affirmed insofar as it invalidates the zoning ordinance as applied to the [Cleburne Living Center] home. The judgment is otherwise vacated.

JUSTICE STEVENS, with whom the CHIEF JUSTICE joins, concurring.

The Court of Appeals disposed of this case as if a critical question to be decided were which of three clearly defined standards of equal protection review should be applied to a legislative classification discriminating against the mentally retarded. In fact, our cases have not delineated three—or even one or two—such well-defined standards.

Rather, our cases reflect a continuum of judgmental responses to differing classifications which have been explained in opinions by terms ranging from "strict scrutiny" at one extreme to "rational basis" at the other. I have never been persuaded that these so called "standards" adequately explain the decisional process. Cases involving classifications based on alienage, illegal residency, illegitimacy, gender, age, or—as in this case—mental retardation, do not fit well into sharply defined classifications. . . .

JUSTICE MARSHALL, with whom JUSTICE BRENNAN and JUSTICE BLACKMUN join, concurring in the judgment in part and dissenting in part. . . .

The Court holds that all retarded individuals cannot be grouped together as the "feebleminded" and deemed presumptively unfit to live in a community. [W]ith this holding and principle I agree. . . .

I cannot agree, however, with the way in which the Court reaches its result or with the narrow, as-applied remedy it provides for the City of Cleburne's equal protection violation. The Court holds the ordinance invalid on rational basis grounds and disclaims that anything special, in the form of heightened scrutiny, is taking place. Yet Cleburne's ordinance surely would be valid under the traditional rational basis test applicable to economic and commercial regulation. In my view, it is important to articulate, as the Court does not, the facts and principles that justify subjecting this zoning ordinance to the searching review—the heightened scrutiny—that actually leads to its invalidation. . . .

I have long believed the level of scrutiny employed in an equal protection case should vary with "the constitutional and societal importance of the interest adversely affected and the recognized invidiousness of the basis upon which the particular classification is drawn." *San Antonio Independent School District v. Rodriguez*, 411 U.S. 1, 99 (1973) (Marshall, J., dissenting). . . .

NOTES AND QUESTIONS

(1) *Are There Other Quasi-Suspect Classes?: City of Cleburne v. Cleburne Living Center, 473 U.S. 432 (1985).* In *Cleburne*, the Court, per Justice White, rejected the challengers' argument for heightened scrutiny. The Court held that the developmentally disabled were not a quasi-suspect class. The Court, therefore, applied the rational basis standard. But, it held that the City's denial of the special use permit was irrational, and the Court ruled for the challengers. The concurring Justices agreed with the result, but they disagreed with the majority's reasoning. Note that the Court rejected the argument that the challengers were politically powerless because they had powerful allies in the political process. Justice Marshall denies that the Court really is applying the kind of traditional rational basis review that is applicable to economic regulations. Is he correct, and if he is, how does it matter that the Court misstates its standard?

(2) *Distinguishing the Mentally Ill from the Mentally Retarded and Treating the Latter with Lesser Procedural Protection: Heller v. Doe, 509 U.S. 312 (1993).* Kentucky required proof beyond a reasonable doubt for commitment of the mentally ill, but it allowed the mentally retarded to be committed on a lesser standard of clear and convincing evidence. The Court, per Justice Kennedy, applied rational basis review, citing *FCC v. Beach Communications, Inc.* for the proposition that any plausible or arguable justification would suffice. The Court then found several rational bases and upheld the classifications because retardation is easier to diagnose, danger to self or others is easier to determine in the case of retardation, and methods of treating the retarded are less invasive than treatment of the mentally ill. Justices Souter, Blackmun, and O'Connor dissented on the ground that the difference in treatment was not supported by any rational basis. Only Justice Blackmun advocated heightened scrutiny, alone among the nine justices. [Doesn't *Cleburne* dictate the lowest standard of review, and doesn't it ordain the outcome since it is difficult to maintain that the state's arguments are not even plausible? And if this reasoning is sufficient, should it be?]

PROBLEM M

LEFT-HANDEDNESS AS A POTENTIAL DISCRIMINANT; WHAT LEVEL OF SCRUTINY?: LIVES OF LEFT-HANDERS FALL SHORT, HOUSTON CHRONICLE, April 4, 1991, at 4A, col. 1. In 1991, a study reported in the New England Journal of Medicine concluded that left-handed people died at an average age of 66. Right handed people, however, lived to an average age of 75—nine years longer. Researchers also concluded that left-handers were nearly six times more likely to die in accidents, and they speculated that left-handed people die sooner because they live in a world designed for right-handers. [Later research cast serious doubt on the validity of these conclusions. But consider whether the study still would provide a rational basis for legislation if lowest-tier review is the correct standard.] Question: If the government were to adopt restrictive policies toward left-handed people (e.g., requiring left-handed drivers to have additional items of safety equipment on their automobiles, or excluding them from Army paratroop units), what level of scrutiny should apply, and would such a law be constitutional?

PROBLEM N

HOMELESS PEOPLE AFFECTED BY UNIFORM RULES FOR HYGIENE AND BEHAVIOR IN PUBLIC PLACES; WHAT LEVEL OF EQUAL PROTECTION REVIEW?: KREIMER v. BUREAU OF POLICE, 958 F.2d 1242 (3d Cir. 1992). Richard R. Kreimer, a homeless man in Morristown, N.J., frequented the Public Library to read or to sit in silent contemplation. The Library, however, contended that he stared at and followed other patrons to such an extent as to disturb them, talked loudly to himself and others, and exuded an odor so strong and offensive that it prevented patrons from using certain areas of the Library. The Library adopted policies against "noisy or boisterous activities, unnecessary staring, [and] following another person," as well as a requirement that "personal hygiene shall conform to the standard of the community for public places." Kreimer sued, asserting claims under the First Amendment, the Equal Protection Clause, and other laws. The District Court held that the Library's policy was facially invalid because it violated the Due Process and Equal Protection Clauses in two ways. First, the policy made "personal attributes such as appearance, smell, and manner of cleanliness determinative." Since this "prohibition on offensive hygiene is in no way restricted to instances of actual, material disruptions which are incompatible with the library's function, . . . the restriction impinges upon individual liberty and sanctions that which may not be sanctioned merely on the basis of 'annoyance.'" Second, the District Court found that the Library adopted the policy "with the explicit intention of limiting [homeless persons'] access to the Library," thus denying homeless persons equal protection.

Question: What level of scrutiny was the District Court thus applying? What level should apply to these classifications: strict scrutiny, rational basis review, or some other standard? [The Court of Appeals reversed the District Court's holding of facial invalidity. It held that the rules were not arbitrary, that there was no evidence of discriminatory intent in their adoption, and that homeless people were not a suspect class anyway so that only the lowest standard of review would have applied. It might appear from this that the Library had won; that conclusion, however, would fail to take into account the nature of constitutional litigation. The Court of Appeals remanded to the District Court for a determination of other issues, including the propriety of application of the Library rules individually to Kreimer. Most of the defendants, having heard the reasoning of the District Court once before and being aware of the huge cost of litigation already incurred, settled; it was reported that $ 150,000 was paid on behalf of police and municipal officials, and that the library's insurer paid $ 80,000, for a total of $ 230,000. *Settlement Ends Portion of Morristown Homeless Case*, N.J.L.J. March 9, 1992, at 5, col.l.]

CHAPTER 11
SPEECH, PRESS, AND ASSOCIATION

§ 11.01 POLICIES, PRINCIPLES, AND HISTORY OF THE FIRST AMENDMENT

[A] History and Purposes of the First Amendment

NOTE ON THE HISTORICAL DEVELOPMENT OF THE FREEDOM OF SPEECH

Press Licensing and Sedition Laws. The pre-constitutional history was not one of protection for the freedom of speech. Most developed nations had rulers who claimed authority from God, and they considered that they had a strong proprietary interest in what was published. Sedition laws were based upon the sincere belief that the national interest precluded allowing citizens to criticize government, and prior restraints on the press, implemented by licensing laws, subjected the publishing industry to censorship. These traditions were imported to the American colonies.

Adoption and Purposes of the First Amendment. The First Amendment was prepared, debated and adopted by the First Congress under the new Constitution. It was part of the Bill of Rights. *See generally* THE COMPLETE BILL OF RIGHTS (Neil Cogan, ed. 1997); DANIEL A. FARBER & SUZANNA SHERRY, A HISTORY OF THE AMERICAN CONSTITUTION 313 (2d ed. 2005). *One* major theme in England had been resistance to press censorship through licensing laws, with such writers as John Milton campaigning for the right to publish without government permission. Therefore, it seems that the Founders conceived of the First Amendment as prohibiting prior restraints. Ironically, this theory contemplated that the author and publisher still could be subjected to subsequent punishment if they printed illegal speech, including libel—of which seditious libel, or criticism of government, was one prohibited species. *See generally* J. NOWAK, R. ROTUNDA & J. YOUNG, CONSTITUTIONAL LAW ch. 18, § II (3d ed. 1986). This was Blackstone's theory of the freedom of speech, and in the colonies, it was typified by the famous trial of publisher John Peter Zenger for seditious libel. Andrew Hamilton defended Zenger and secured his acquittal by a jury, but the threat of sedition prosecutions remained. *Id.*

Sedition Laws After the Adoption of the Bill of Rights. In light of the historical understanding, it is not surprising that the early years of the First Amendment were quite inconsistent with our views of the freedom of speech today. For example, the Sedition Act of 1798 made it a crime to publish "any false, scandalous and malicious writing [against] the government of the United States, or either house of Congress, [or] the President, [with] intent [to] bring them [into] contempt or disrepute." The Federalist administration of President John Adams became unpopular and lost the next election in part because of its use of the Sedition Act to prosecute members of Jefferson's Republican (or Anti-Federalist) Party for criticizing the administration. And Jefferson's administration retaliated by similarly prosecuting Federalists. Congress later repealed the Sedition Act and repaid fines levied under it, and Jefferson, as President, pardoned those who had been convicted. *See New York Times v. Sullivan,* 376 U.S. 254, 273 (1964) (concluding belatedly that the Sedition Act was unconstitutional) (dictum).

The Modern View of the First Amendment as a Recent Development; The Schenck Case. Although the Sedition Act "first crystallized a national awareness of the central meaning of the first amendment," *id.,* it was not until the middle of the Twentieth Century that the view that citizens freely may criticize government assumed its modern form. For example, in *Schenck v. United States* [in the next section, below], Justice

Holmes wrote for the Court in upholding a conviction under the Espionage Act for the speaker's criticism of draft laws during World War I.

NOTE: WHY PROTECT THE FREEDOM OF SPEECH?

Although the purposes of the First Amendment are not clear from its history, the interpretation of the amendment sometimes depends upon inferring those purposes. Thus, courts and commentators often have had occasion to develop the values that the freedom of speech may protect. There are generally considered to be four constitutional goals of the First Amendment (although they vary from Clause to Clause within the First Amendment): protecting the marketplace of ideas; protecting the democratic decision-making process; protecting individual liberty of self-realization; and providing a safety valve against violence or social disruption. *See generally* THOMAS EMERSON, THE SYSTEM OF FREEDOM OF EXPRESSION (1970).

Democratic Self-Government, Informed Voting, and Checking Abuses of Power. First of all, free speech informs and educates voters, and thus it is a foundation of democratic self-government. Free speech serves what has been called a "checking" value, in that speech can effectively limit or check abuses of power by public officials. Because of the importance of this complex of functions, the courts sometimes emphasize that political speech is especially deserving of first amendment protection.

Development of Culture, Science, Art, Technology, and Commerce. But the protection of speech has not been limited to that which is directly political. Publication and discussion of new theories develops scientific knowledge. Speech about how to apply this knowledge advances technology, generally to the benefit of the society. Speech also produces art and makes it available to citizens as a part of the culture, which it also causes to be passed on to new generations. In the business context, speech is necessary to make markets function efficiently to allocate resources and spur innovation, and hence even "commercial" speech arguably deserves a measure of protection. These functions of the freedom of speech are important not only for their direct benefits, but also because speech about science, art, technology, culture, and commerce is necessary to inform the voters in a democracy. J. NOWAK, R. ROTUNDA, & J. YOUNG, CONSTITUTIONAL LAW ch. 18 § II (E) (3d ed. 1986); *but cf.* Bork, *Neutral Principles and Some First Amendment Problems*, 47 IND. L.J. 1 (1971) (arguing that only political speech should be protected—a conclusion that Judge Bork later revised). *See also* EMERSON, THE SYSTEM OF FREEDOM OF EXPRESSION.

Protecting the Pre-existing "Marketplace of Ideas." The Framers certainly understood that, in political life and otherwise, there was a marketplace where different ideas were in competition. After all, they were experimenting with a truly revolutionary idea of government: democracy rather than monarchy or theocracy. They were also familiar with the competition of ideas in the business and social spheres. (Remember the competition between Jefferson and Hamilton about how to structure the new national economy.) A closely related function is to develop political ideas that can be adopted by public servants and to select those ideas that are "best" to be adopted as government policy. Freedom of speech also gives competing groups and individuals the satisfaction of participating in policymaking.

Individual Self-Realization, Association, and Enjoyment. Speech also allows individuals to develop themselves through education, self-expression, and related means. It allows groups of individuals to associate with each other as families, clubs, or other groups to enhance their self-fulfillment (as well as their political expression). Finally, the freedom of speech enables individuals to utter or receive communications for the purpose of pure enjoyment. These "individualized" functions of the freedom of speech have been afforded some protection—and perhaps they are related to political speech in that development of the individual is a requisite of democracy. *See generally* T. EMERSON, *supra*. A related justification for protecting free speech is the "safety valve theory." The concept is that it is preferable for people to express their discontent with words rather than with bullets or bombs. *See* Z. Chafee, Jr., Free Speech in the United States 433–34 (1941). *Cf. Texas v. Johnson*, 491 U.S. 397 (1989) (Kennedy, J., concurring).

[B] An Introduction to the Principles Contained in First Amendment Decisions

NOTE ON MAJOR THEMES IN FIRST AMENDMENT DECISIONS

In this section, we shall introduce the major themes that you will encounter in reading First Amendment cases. The principles are set out here in generalities, and you should remember that they are subject to important limitations. We shall use incomplete citations whenever the cited cases appear in the chapter below.

(1) *First Amendment Freedoms as "Preferred" Rights; Strict Scrutiny.* Because they are preservative of other freedoms [see the preceding section], First Amendment rights are said to be in a "preferred" position. *Murdock v. Pennsylvania*, 319 U.S. 105, 115 (1943). In other words, they are afforded more extensive immunity from government interference than most other human endeavors. *See generally* Wellington, *On Freedom of Expression*, 88 Yale L.J. 1105 (1979). Some cases provide this enhanced protection by subjecting regulations that impinge upon First Amendment freedoms to strict scrutiny, requiring narrow tailoring to a compelling governmental interest. This analysis also may inquire whether the regulation adopts the least restrictive means available. *E.g., Talley v. California*, below.

(2) *Two Approaches to the Limits of the First Amendment: (1) "Balancing" or (2) "Absolute" Protection?* The words of the first amendment ostensibly are absolute: "Congress shall make *no* law . . . abridging the freedom of speech. . . ." This textual feature of the amendment arguably supports the view that the freedom of speech is absolutely protected, a view most closely associated with Justices Black and Douglas. *Cf.* Powe, *Evolution to Absolutism: Justice Douglas and the First Amendment*, 74 Colum. L. Rev. 341 (1974). (This theory led these Justices consistently to dissent from the upholding of convictions in obscenity cases. *E.g., Roth v. United States*, below.) The opposing view is that the amendment is not absolute but must be weighed against other constitutional principles or governmental purposes; this "balancing" view is associated particularly with Justice Harlan. *E.g., Street v. New York*, below; *cf. Cohen v. California*, below. But Justice Harlan's view, like that of most balancing advocates, does not favor ad hoc balancing, but rather seeks to evolve a system of analysis that can be applied consistently.

(3) *The Hierarchy of Protected Speech Categories.* Given its history and purposes, it is not surprising that in some cases, the first amendment has been interpreted in the context of a "hierarchy" of speech values. Political speech of a kind related to the function of democratic self-government, predictably, ranks highest. On the other hand, other categories of speech generally have been given lesser protection. *E.g., Central Hudson Gas & Electric Corp. v. Public Service Commission*, below (expressly giving lesser protection to commercial speech).

(4) *"Speech That is Not Protected" Obscenity, "Fighting Words," and Other "Unprotected Utterances."* One way to approach the limits of the first amendment is by defining "speech" so that it does not cover every kind of "utterance." In other words, this approach divides communications into two categories, consisting of "protected speech" on the one hand and "unprotected utterances" on the other. Balancing advocates tend to arrive at these categorizations by weighing competing values, while absolutists tend to take a definitional approach. Generally recognized categories of unprotected utterances include libel, false advertising, immediate incitement to crime, and obscenity. They also include face-to-face "fighting words," of the type that have little communicative content and high potential for precipitating breaches of the peace. *Chaplinsky v. New*

Hampshire, below. Furthermore, some categories analogous to these unprotected areas are fluid and depend upon a balancing process that varies with the context. *E.g., FCC v. Pacifica Foundation*, below ("indecent" daytime radio broadcasts).

(5) *The "Breathing Space" Doctrine (and the New York Times Rule as an Example).* Because protected speech has a preferred constitutional status, the cases recognize a "breathing space" doctrine: Even some kinds of utterances that are apparently valueless in themselves must be afforded a measure of protection to prevent self-censorship, or to give breathing space to protected speech. For this reason, in *New York Times v. Sullivan*, below, the Court made defamation of public officials non-actionable unless accompanied by "actual malice" (which is a term of artmeaning either intentional falsehood or reckless indifference to truth or falsity). The Court expressly recognized that this standard would result in constitutional protection for some defamatory falsehoods, but this result was necessary if political speech was to remain "robust" and "wide-open."

(6) *The Overbreadth and Vagueness Doctrines.* For similar reasons, vague statutes are particularly disfavored when they impinge upon the freedom of speech. And although the Court has been willing to make some allowances for the inherent imprecision of language used in drafting statutes, "overbroad" laws (those that sweep excessively into protected speech with their prohibitions) also are disfavored. *E.g., Broaderick v. Oklahoma*, below.

(7) *Prior Restraints as Virtually Per Se Invalid.* Both the doctrine of preferred rights and the historical resistance to licensing laws [set forth in the preceding section] support the idea that prior restraints on publication are virtually per se invalid. Thus an injunction against a newspaper, preventing publications in advance, is unconstitutional unless the case is an "exceptional" one—of which the Court has given as an example the publication of military secrets in wartime. *New York Times Co. v. United States* (the "Pentagon Papers" case), below.

(8) *The Two-Track System: "Content-Based" versus "Content-Neutral" Regulation.* A regulation is more likely to be upheld if it is "content-neutral." Conversely, regulation that depends upon the expressive content of the communication faces stricter scrutiny than regulation of the "time, place, and manner." *Compare, e.g., Cox v. New Hampshire*, below (upholding narrowly drawn parade ordinance) *with Lovell v. Griffin* (striking down restrictions on distribution of leaflets affording such broad discretion to public officials as to enable them to censor message content). This theme is generally called as the "Two-Track System."

(9) *The Context of the Expression: Special Forums, Special Technologies, or Special Circumstances.* There are certain kinds of cases in which the context, including the type of forum or the circumstances, significantly affects the state's ability to regulate. For example, traditional "public forums," even if government property, generally are not subject to content-based regulation; other types of forums, including what are called "limited public forums" or "nonpublic forums" may be. *E.g., Perry Education Association v. Perry Local Educators Association*, below. Education, also, is a special context; administrators in the public schools are allowed greater latitude in certain areas of content-based regulation, particularly as concerns the curriculum. *Hazelwood School District v. Kuhlmeier*, below. Other special circumstances include election campaigns, speech by government or its employees, and broadcasting. *E.g., Red Lion Broadcasting Co. v. FCC*, below. *Cf.* Dienes, *When the First Amendment Is Not Preferred: The Military and Other "Special Contexts,"* 56 U. Cin. L. Rev. 779 (1988). More recently, technological changes involving cable television, satellite broadcasting, and the internet have challenged the courts' abilities to apply consistent principles.

(10) *The "Marketplace of Ideas" Metaphor.* Justice Holmes, in *Abrams v. United States*, below, introduced an influential metaphor by likening the objective of the First Amendment to the protection of a "marketplace of ideas." This idea further was developed by Professor Alexander Meikeljohn. *See generally* A. Meikeljohn, Free

SPEECH AND ITS RELATIONSHIP TO SELF-GOVERNMENT (1948). This metaphor is based on the concept that ideas compete for attention and acceptance just as products compete for the acceptance of consumers in the marketplace. Through individual choices in the marketplace, the "best" (or most appealing) ideas emerge as most influential.

(11) *Two Approaches to the "Marketplace" Theory: (1) Insuring "Access to the Press" by Government Regulation and (2) Protecting Editorial Independence by Regarding Government Interference as Unconstitutional.* But the marketplace metaphor may have limited utility in resolving real questions, because it does not say what the role of government should be. What if speech is limited by the number of outlets, as, for example, the number of major television networks is limited? Some theorists argue, then, that the government should intervene in the allocation of speech opportunities by insuring "access to the press" for different viewpoints. But on the other hand, the marketplace metaphor might be interpreted to support private (as opposed to government) editorial decisions in the "marketplace," and in this view, government allocations of speech opportunities countermanding private editorial decisions can be seen as compromising the independence of the press. *Compare, e.g., Red Lion Broadcasting Co. v. FCC*, below (upholding broadcasting content regulation to assure forum for minority viewpoints and protect public's right to receive information) with *Miami Herald Publishing Co. v. Tornillo*, below (rejecting similar content regulation of newspapers, emphasizing freedom of editorial decisions from government control). *Cf.* Francione, *Experimentation and the Marketplace Theory of the First Amendment*, 136 U. PA. L. REV. 417 (1987).

(12) *"Freedom of Association."* Although the First Amendment does not expressly create a right of association, the right has been inferred from it (as well as from other sources). The right of assembly (which the First Amendment expressly protects), as well as the implication that expression may require group activity, both support this right. Thus, the first amendment may be interpreted in some contexts to protect concerted action with expressive content, such as group boycotts. *E.g., NAACP v. Clairborne Hardware Co.*, below. And the right of individuals to associate and exclude others, such as in the context of private clubs that discriminate on racial or gender lines, is a controversial contemporary issue. *E.g., Board of Directors of Rotary International v. Rotary Club of Duarte*, below.

(13) *The Right to Speak as "Including the Right Not to Listen": The Problem of the "Captive Auditor."* One of the many facets of the freedom of speech is a kind of "reverse" right: the right not to listen. Thus, for example, government may take steps to protect a captive audience from being forced to listen to obnoxious expression in some contexts, such as "loud and raucous" sound trucks in residential neighborhoods, *Kovacs v. Cooper*, below, or certain kinds of indecent speech, *Bethel School District v. Fraser*. However, the right not to listen does not always outweigh the interest in expression. *Cf. Cohen v. California*, below (words "Fuck the Draft" held constitutionally protected although exposed to strangers at courthouse).

(14) *Freedom of Speech as Including the Right Not to Speak: Freedom of Belief.* Another of the facets of the First Amendment is that it protects the right *not* to speak, which is a foundation of the freedom of belief (or freedom of conscience). As a general rule, government cannot force citizens to confess their allegiance to any particular idea, *see West Virginia Board of Education v. Barnette*, below (holding that children may not be forced to salute the flag).

Read U.S. Const. Amend. I (freedoms of speech, press, assembly, and petition).

§ 11.02   THE "PREFERRED" POSITION OF THE FREEDOM OF SPEECH: UTTERANCES THAT POSE ALLEGED DANGERS OF VIOLENCE OR INSURRECTION

INTRODUCTORY NOTE

Utterances that create dangers of violence pose a particularly sensitive constitutional problem. If courts interpret the First Amendment to protect all of these utterances indiscriminately, they may legitimize direct and immediate incitements to crime, thereby exposing citizens unnecessarily to harm. On the other hand, if the courts enable governments to criminalize expression merely because it is characterized vaguely as "dangerous," they may censor political speech of the most valuable kind. It is with this dilemma that we begin the cases in this chapter. The first opinion, by Justice Holmes, introduces the famous "clear and present danger" test.

[A]   The "Clear and Present Danger" Doctrine

[1]   The Early History: The Holmes-Brandeis Formulation

SCHENCK v. UNITED STATES
249 U.S. 47 (1919)

MR. JUSTICE HOLMES delivered the opinion of the Court.

[The indictment] charges a conspiracy to violate the Espionage Act . . . by causing and attempting to cause insubordination . . . in the military and naval forces of the United States, and to obstruct the recruiting and enlistment service of the United States, when the United States was at war with the German empire, to wit, that the defendant willfully conspired to have printed and circulated to men who had been called and accepted for military service . . ., a document set forth and alleged to be calculated to cause such insubordination and obstruction. [T]he defendants were found guilty. They set up [as a defense] the first amendment to the Constitution forbidding Congress to make any law abridging the freedom of speech . . ., and [they bring] the case here on that ground. . . .

The document in question upon its first printed side recited the first section of the Thirteenth Amendment, said that the idea embodied in it was violated by the conscription act and that a conscript is little better than a convict. In impassioned language it intimated that conscription was despotism in its worst form and a monstrous wrong against humanity in the interest of Wall Street's chosen few. It said, "Do not submit to intimidation," but in form at least confined itself to peaceful measures such as a petition for the repeal of the act. The other and later printed side of the sheet was headed "Assert Your Rights." It stated reasons for alleging that any one violated the Constitution when he refused to recognize "your right to assert your opposition to the draft," and went on, "If you do not assert and support your rights, you are helping to deny or disparage rights which it is the solemn duty of all citizens and residents of the United Statesto retain." It described the arguments on the other side as coming from cunning politicians and a mercenary capitalist press, and even silent consent to the conscription law as helping to support an infamous conspiracy. It denied the power to send our citizens away to foreign shores to shoot up the people of other lands, and added that words could not express the condemnation such cold-blooded ruthlessness deserves, etc., etc., winding up, "You must do your share to maintain, support and uphold the rights of the people of this country." Of course the document would not have been sent unless it had been intended to have some effect, and we do not see what effect it could be expected to have upon persons subject to the draft except to influence them to obstruct the carrying of it out. The defendants do not deny that the jury might find against them on this point.

But it is said, suppose that that was the tendency of this circular, it is protected by the First Amendment to the Constitution. Two of the strongest expressions are said to be quoted respectively from well-known public men. . . .

[W]e admit that in many places and in ordinary times the defendants in saying all that was said in the circular would have been within their constitutional rights. But the character of every act depends upon the circumstances in which it is done. . . .

[T]he most stringent protection of free speech would not protect a man in falsely shouting fire in a theatre and causing a panic. It does not even protect a man from an injunction against uttering words that may have all the effect of force. . . .

[T]he question in every case is whether the words used are used in such circumstances and are of such a nature as to create a clear and present danger that they will bring about the substantive evils that Congress has a right to prevent. It is a question of proximity and degree. When a nation is at war many things that might be said in time of peace are such a hindrance to its effort that their utterance will not be endured so long as men fight and that no Court could regard them as protected by any constitutional right. It seems to be admitted that if an actual obstruction of the recruiting service were proved, liability for words that produced that effect might be enforced. The statute of 1917 in section 4 (Comp. St. 1918, § 10212d) punishes conspiracies to obstruct as well as actual obstruction. If the act (speaking, or circulating a paper), its tendency and the intent with which it is done are the same, we perceive no ground for saying that success alone warrants making the act a crime. . . .

NOTES AND QUESTIONS

(1) *Does Holmes' "Clear and Present Danger" Test Adequately Protect Speech, Given That Controversial Speech Often Imposes Costs on Society?* The sad but undeniable fact is that controversial speech often imposes costs upon society, and those costs may even be severe. For example, a newspaper story about a crime victim may invade the victim's privacy and subject him or her to humiliation, embarrassment, and psychological damage. A legislature certainly has an interest in minimizing this harm, and thus the newspaper story creates a "clear and present danger" of causing a "substantive evil" which the legislature has a right to prevent. But does it follow that the legislature therefore can prevent publication of the newspaper story in question? Consider whether Justice Holmes' clear-and-present-danger test provides adequate protection for speech.

(2) *Distinguishing the Case of Shouting "Fire" in a Crowded Theater; Distinguishing Explicit Advocacy of Illegal Conduct.* Is Holmes' example of shouting "fire!" in a crowded theater apposite? That sort of utterance would be perceived as an exhortation to immediate action, without thought or debate. Furthermore, it would be perceived as a statement of fact that misrepresents the circumstances, whereas Schenck's utterances were matters of opinion. Do these considerations distinguish Schenck's remarks? Consider, also, the absence of any explicit advocacy by Schenck of illegal conduct. We shall revisit this question in *Brandenburg v. Ohio*, below.

(3) *The Frohwerk and Debs Cases Expand the Application of the Espionage Act by Extending Holmes' Test: Frohwerk v. United States, 249 U.S. 204 (1919), and Debs v.*

United States, 249 U.S. 211 (1919). Frohwerk involved an editorial criticizing the draft. Holmes' opinion for a unanimous Court upheld the writers' Espionage Act convictions by reasoning that it was possible the editorial could have "kindle[d] a flame" of draft evasion. The *Debs* case concerned the Espionage Act conviction of Socialist Party presidential candidate Eugene V. Debs for giving an antiwar speech, in which he praised socialism, expressed support for persons convicted of obstructing the recruiting service, and told the audience they were "fit for something better than slavery and cannon fodder." Justice Holmes' opinion pointed out that the jury had been instructed that they could not find the defendant guilty unless the words used "had as their natural tendency and reasonably probable effect to obstruct the recruiting service" and unless Debs had the "specific intent to do so in his mind." Does this transmutation of the clear and present danger test create an unacceptable risk that speakers may be convicted for general criticisms of government rather than for incitement of unlawful conduct? *Debs* should be compared to *Bond v. Floyd*, 385 U.S. 116 (1966), in which the speakers made expressions of support for draft resisters. The Court, in *Bond*, held the remarks protected because they did not include express advocacy of illegal action.

(4) *Learned Hand's Alternative Formulation of the Test—A Prohibition on "Counsel[ing] Others to Violate the Law": Masses Publishing Co. v. Patten, 244 F. 535 (S.D.N.Y. 1917).* Judge Learned Hand's formulation of the test in *Masses Publishing* provides an alternative approach to *Schenck, Frohwerk,* and *Debs* that arguably avoids some of the difficulties of the clear and present danger test. The plaintiffs in *Masses* were denied use of the mails under the Espionage Act for publishing cartoons and text critical of the war effort. The court upheld an injunction in plaintiffs' favor, although it recognized that the speech in question might arouse "a mutinous and insubordinate temper among the troops." The test, according to Judge Hand, was that "[o]ne may not counsel or advise others to violate the law as it stands." Mere criticism of government, on the other hand, could not be criminalized. The Learned Hand formulation has the advantages of greater clarity and (perhaps) more narrow confinement than Holmes' test. On the other hand, consider whether this test has disadvantages. [For example, might it fail to identify persons who properly ought to be convicted, such as the person who shouts fire in a crowded theater, because it contains no express "incitement"?] You should reconsider Judge Hand's approach in the context of *Brandenburg v. Ohio*, below.

(5) *Justice Holmes' Dissent in Abrams v. United States, below.* Having written opinions upholding application of the Espionage Act in *Schenck, Frohwerk,* and *Debs,* Justice Holmes dissented from an Espionage Act conviction in *Abrams v. United States.* Perhaps Justice Holmes' dissent indicates a change in position.

ABRAMS v. UNITED STATES, 250 U.S. 616 (1919). Socialists who supported the Bolsheviks distributed leaflets that urged workers not to make bullets that could be used againstthe Russian revolution. They were convicted of interfering with the war with Germany, even though they strongly opposed German militarism, because the burden of their argument was that bullets ostensibly made for use against Germany could readily be shifted to use against Bolsheviks. The Court majority upheld the conviction using the Holmesian clear and present danger standard. But, Holmes himself disagreed. The most famous aspect of *Abrams* is the dissent of Justice Holmes:

> But as against dangers peculiar to war . . ., the principle of the right to free speech is always the same. [C]ongress certainly cannot forbid all effort to change the mind of the country. Now nobody can suppose that the surreptitious publishing of a silly leaflet by an unknown man, without more, would present any immediate danger that its opinions would hinder the success of the government arms. . . .

> [T]he best test of truth is the power of the thought to get itself accepted in the competition of the market. . . . That at any rate is the theory of our Constitution. [W]e should be eternally vigilant against attempts to check the expression of opinions that we loathe and believe to be fraught with death,

unless they so imminently threaten immediate interference with the lawful and pressing purposes of the law that an immediate check is required to save the country. . . .

[2]　The Hostile Crowd (and the Hecklers' Veto)

FEINER v. NEW YORK
340 U.S. 315 (1951)

MR. CHIEF JUSTICE VINSON delivered the opinion of the Court.

[Feiner was convicted of disorderly conduct. The proof showed that he had addressed a crowd through a loudspeaker, making derogatory remarks concerning President Truman, the American Legion, the Mayor of Syracuse, and other politicians. He spoke in a "loud, high-pitched voice" and "gave the impression that he was endeavoring to arouse the negro people against the whites, urging that they rise up in arms and fight for equal rights."]

[T]he statements before such a mixed audience "stirred up a little excitement." Some of the onlookers made remarks to the police about their inability to handle the crowd and at least one threatened violence if the police did not act. There were others who appeared to be favoring petitioner's arguments. Because of the feeling that existed in the crowd both for and against the speaker, the officers finally "stepped in to prevent it from resulting in a fight." One of the officers approached the petitioner, not for the purpose of arresting him, but to get him to break up the crowd. [D]uring all this time, the crowd was pressing closer around petitioner and the officer. Finally, the officer told petitioner he was under arrest and ordered him to get down from the box, reaching up to grab him. Petitioner stepped down, announcing over the microphone that "the law has arrived, and I suppose they will take over now." In all, the officer had asked petitioner to get down off the box three times over a space of four or five minutes. Petitioner had been speaking for over a half hour. . . .

Petitioner was thus neither arrested nor convicted for the making or the content of his speech. Rather, it was the reaction which it actually engendered.

When clear and present danger of riot, disorder, interference with traffic upon the public streets, or other immediate threat to public safety, peace, or order, appears, the power of the State to prevent or punish is obvious.

We are well aware that the ordinary murmurings and objections of a hostile audience cannot be allowed to silence a speaker, and are also mindful of the possible danger of giving overzealous police officials complete discretion to break up otherwise lawful public meetings.

But we are not faced here with such a situation. It is one thing to say that the police cannot be used as an instrument for the suppression of unpopular views, and another to say that, when as here the speaker passes the bounds of argument or persuasion and undertakes incitement to riot, they are powerless to prevent a breach of the peace. [T]he findings of the state courts as to the existing situation and the imminence of greater disorder coupled with petitioner's deliberate defiance of the police officers convince us that we should not reverse this conviction in the name of free speech.

Affirmed.

MR. JUSTICE BLACK, dissenting.

The record before us convinces me that petitioner, a young college student, has been sentenced to the penitentiary for the unpopular views he expressed on matters of public interest while lawfully making a street-corner speech in Syracuse, New York. . . . The end result of the affirmance here is to approve a simple and readily available technique by which cities and states can with impunity subject all speeches, political or otherwise, on streets or elsewhere, to the supervision and censorship of the local police. I will have no part or parcel in this holding which I view as a long step toward totalitarian authority.

Moreover, assuming that the "facts" did indicate a critical situation, I reject the implication of the Court's opinion that the police had no obligation to protect petitioner's constitutional right to talk. The police of course have power to prevent breaches of the peace. But if, in the name of preserving order, they ever can interfere with a lawful public speaker, they first must make all reasonable efforts to protect him. Here the policemen did not even pretend to try to protect petitioner. Instead, they shirked that duty and acted only to suppress the right to speak. . . .

[The opinion of JUSTICE FRANKFURTER, who concurred in the result, is omitted. The dissenting opinion of MR. JUSTICE DOUGLAS, joined by MR. JUSTICE MINTON, asserted some positions similar to those of Justice BLACK. In addition, JUSTICE DOUGLAS refuted the majority's reference to "incitement to riot": "[T]his record shows no such extremes."]

TERMINIELLO v. CITY OF CHICAGO, 337 U.S. 1 (1949). This decision should be contrasted to *Feiner, supra,* although it actually was decided more than two years before *Feiner.* Justice Douglas, for a five-to-four Court, described a speech in which Terminiello "condemned the conduct of the crowd outside and vigorously, if not viciously, criticized various political and racial groups whose activities he denounced as inimical to the nation's welfare." The speech was to a meeting of the Christian Veterans of America in an auditorium filled with over 800 persons; a crowd of about one thousand gathered outside to protest against the meeting. A cordon of policemen was unable to prevent disturbances, and the crowd grew "angry and turbulent." On these facts, Terminiello was convicted of breach of the peace. The Court reversed:

> [A] function of free speech under our system of government is to invite dispute. It may indeed best serve its high purpose when it induces a condition of unrest, createsdissatisfaction with conditions as they are, or even stirs people to anger. Speech is often provocative and challenging. It may strike at prejudices and preconceptions and have profound unsettling effects as it presses for acceptance of an idea. That is why freedom of speech, though not absolute . . ., is nevertheless protected against censorship or punishment, unless shown likely to produce a clear and present danger of a serious substantive evil that rises far above public inconvenience, annoyance, or unrest. [T]he alternative would lead to standardization of ideas either by legislatures, courts, or dominant political or community groups.

NOTES AND QUESTIONS

(1) *Is the "Clear and Present Danger" Test an Adequate Means of Addressing the Problem of the "Heckler's Veto?"* The hostile crowd in *Feiner* is often characterized as having exercised a "heckler's veto." Consider whether the clear and present danger test is adequate to avoid this kind of incursion upon the freedom of speech. If speech prompts listeners to assault the speaker, there always will be a "clear and present danger" in the form of a probability that there will be a breach of the peace or actual physical harm, if only to the speaker himself. Presumably, government has a legitimate interest in preventing this "substantive evil." Where is the flaw in this analysis? [Is it in the clear and present danger test itself?] Another reading of *Feiner,* according to subsequent decisions, is that the *Feiner* facts actually satisfied the clear and present danger test. Notice that, in *Terminiello,* Justice Douglas reaches the opposite result by basing his reasoning on the clear and present danger test. Does that test justify the result?

(2) *May Government Ever Regulate Speech By Taking Into Account Its Tendency to Disturb Others?* Presumably, at some point the "disturbance" to others that is created

by obnoxious speech can become severe enough so that government has sufficient interest in preventing it to justify regulation or prohibition. For example, can't government prohibit face-to-face four-letter insults, or "fighting words"? In such a situation the marketplace of ideas is served little by the utterance, and the interest in its prohibition rests both upon the listener's right not to hear it and the likelihood of breach of the peace. *See Chaplinsky v. New Hampshire*, in this chapter below (upholding prohibition of "fighting words"). As another illustration, consider the following problem.

PROBLEM A

THE NAZIS IN SKOKIE-COLLIN v. SMITH, 578 F.2d 1197 (7th Cir.), *cert. denied*, 439 U.S. 916 (1978). A Nazi organization planned a demonstration for approximately a half an hour in front of the village hall of Skokie, Illinois, whose population was heavily Jewish and included a large proportion of Holocaust survivors. Skokie responded to the planned demonstration by passing a "racial slur" ordinance, which prohibited the dissemination of any material, including "markings and clothing of symbolic significance," that incited racial or religious hatred. May the city enforce this ordinance to prevent the Nazis from demonstrating with Swastikas?

(1) *The Danger of Violence From a Hostile Audience.* Can the application of the ordinance be sustained by reference to the "clear and present danger" that police may be inadequate to the task of preventing hostile onlookers from attacking the demonstrators, or vice versa? [Thevillage did not assert this argument. As the court put it, the village "does not rely on a fear of responsive violence . . ., and does not even suggest that there will be any physical violence if the march is held. This concession takes the case out of the scope of . . . *Feiner*." Would the result have been different if Skokie had not taken this position?]

(2) *The Danger of Psychic Harm to Residents.* The village argued that the Nazi march would inflict "psychic trauma on resident holocaust survivors and other Jewish residents." Did this factor create a clear and present danger of a substantive evil that government had a right to prohibit, as the village argued? [The court answered in the negative, concluding that this kind of disturbance was indistinguishable from that in *Terminiello.*]

(3) *Lack of Speech Content.* May the ordinance be applied because the "expression" in question is so lacking in communicative content that it is unprotected by the First Amendment? [The court rejected Skokie's argument that the march was "not speech," but instead was an "invasion."]

PROBLEM B

TINY DEMONSTRATION, LARGER COUNTER-DEMONSTRATION, HUGE LAW ENFORCEMENT COSTS: "FIVE SUPREMACISTS RALLY IN ATLANTA UNDER WATCH OF TWENTY-FIVE HUNDRED LAWMEN," HOUSTON CHRONICLE, Jan. 21, 1990, § A, at 6, col. 3 (Associated Press). On the day following the King National Holiday in 1990, five white supremacists demonstrated by gathering for less than an hour near the tomb of the Rev. Martin Luther King, Jr. About 75 counter demonstrators appeared. The State of Georgia provided 2,500 police and national guard troops to protect the five (5) supremacists and maintain order, at a cost of more than $500,000 to the state and $100,000 to the local jurisdiction. Different groups led by two of the white supremacists had been pelted with rocks in past demonstrations, and of course the state had no way to predict the number of counter demonstrators. Question: Does the provision of security naturally required by a speech—related activity when it deliberately is located in a way that heightens security concerns, amount to a subsidy of that activity, which the state would have reasonable arguments for avoiding or shifting? May the state, for example, require demonstrators to pay the anticipated cost of security, or may it require the demonstration to take place in a secure (but perhaps less newsworthy) location?

The Problem Continues, with Violence. During the year following the above incident, several other demonstrations involving white supremacists resulted in actual violence. For example, on Martin Luther King Jr.'s birthday in 1992 in Denver, about 100 white supremacists gathered for a rally at the state capitol. At one point, there were more than 10,000 people demonstrating for the opposite view. Police attempted to move the white supremacists to safety in a school bus, whereupon a crowd of about 1,000 people throwing bottles, bricks, and snowballs attacked the bus. The crowd damaged five police cars, engaged in looting of nearby businesses, and caused injuries to seven people (including three police officers). HOUSTON CHRONICLE, Jan. 21, 1992, § A, at 3, col. 1. Consider the following decision.

FORSYTH COUNTY v. NATIONALIST MOVEMENT
505 U.S. 123 (1992)

JUSTICE BLACKMUN delivered the opinion of the Court.

[Forsyth County's Ordinance 34 mandated permits for private demonstrations and other uses of public property; declared that the cost of police protection for those activities exceeded the usual cost of law enforcement and should be paid by participants; required every permit applicant to pay a fee of not more than $1,000; and authorized the county administrator to adjust the amount of the fee to meet the expense incident to the administration of the ordinance and the "maintenance of public order." The ordinance had been passed "as a direct result" of two demonstrations, in which white supremacists had confronted demonstrators led by civil rights personality Hosea Williams, one of which had cost over $670,000 in police protection.

[In January 1989, the Nationalist Movement proposed to demonstrate in opposition to the federal holiday commemorating the birthday of Martin Luther King Jr. The county imposed a $100 fee under the ordinance. The fee did not include any expenses incurred for police protection, but was based solely on ten hours of the county administrator's time in issuing the permit. The Movement did not pay the fee and did not hold the rally; instead, it filed suit against the County.

[The District Court upheld the ordinance. The Court of Appeals reversed, holding that an ordinance that charges more than a nominal fee for the use of a public forum for speech on a public issue is facially unconstitutional. Here, the Supreme Court affirms that decision on other grounds and strikes down the ordinance on its face.]

II . . .

A

[The Court held that the ordinance delegated overly broad licensing discretion to county officials. (This part of the opinion is excerpted in section 11.06 of this Chapter, below, in connection with public forum issues.) The Court then went on to analyze the heckler's veto issues.]

B

The Forsyth County ordinance contains more than the possibility of censorship through uncontrolled discretion. As construed by the county, the ordinance often requires that the fee be based on the content of the speech. The county envisions that the administrator, in appropriate instances, will assess a fee to cover "the cost of necessary and reasonable protection of persons participating in or observing said . . . activit[y]." In order to assess accurately the cost of security for parade participants, the administrator "must necessarily examine the content of the message that is conveyed," estimate the response of others to that content, and judge the number of policenecessary to meet that response. The fee assessed will depend on the administrator's measure of the amount of hostility likely to be created by the speech based on its content. Those wishing to express views unpopular with bottle—throwers, for example, may have to pay more for their permit.

Although petitioner agrees that the cost of policing relates to content, it contends that the ordinance is content—neutral because it is aimed only at a secondary effect—the cost of maintaining public order. It is clear, however, that, in this case, it cannot be said that the fee's justification "ha[s] nothing to do with content."

The costs to which petitioner refers are those associated with the public's reaction to the speech. Listeners' reaction to speech is not a content—neutral basis for regulation. Speech cannot be financially burdened, any more than it can be punished or banned, simply because it might offend a hostile mob. *See Gooding v. Wilson*, 405 U.S. 518 (1972); *Terminiello v. Chicago*, 337 U.S. 1 (1949).

[T]he county offers only one justification for this ordinance: raising revenue for police services. While this undoubtedly is an important government responsibility, it does not justify a content—based permit fee.

Petitioner insists that its ordinance cannot be unconstitutionally content—based because it contains much of the same language as did the state statute upheld in *Cox v. New Hampshire*, 312 U.S. 569 (1941). Although the Supreme Court of New Hampshire had interpreted the statute at issue in *Cox* to authorize the municipality to charge a permit fee for the "maintenance of public order," no fee was actually assessed. Nothing in this Court's opinion suggests that the statute, as interpreted by the New Hampshire Supreme Court, called for charging a premium in the case of a controversial political message delivered before a hostile audience. In light of the Court's subsequent First Amendment jurisprudence, we do not read *Cox* to permit such a premium. . . .

C

[N]either the $1,000 cap on the fee charged, nor even some lower nominal cap, could save the ordinance because in this context, the level of the fee is irrelevant. [T]he lower courts derived their requirement that the permit fee be "nominal" from a sentence in the opinion in *Murdock v. Pennsylvania*, 319 U.S. 105 (1943). In *Murdock*, the Court invalidated a flat license fee levied on distributors of religious literature. In distinguishing the case from *Cox*, where the Court upheld a permit fee, the Court stated: "And the fee is not a nominal one, imposed as a regulatory measure and calculated to defray the expense of protecting those on the streets and at home against the abuses of solicitors." This sentence does not mean that an invalid fee can be saved if it is nominal, or that only nominal charges are constitutionally permissible. . . .

The tax at issue in *Murdock* was invalid because it was unrelated to any legitimate state interest, not because it was of a particular size. Similarly, the provision of the Forsyth County ordinance relating to fees is invalid because it unconstitutionally ties the amount of the fee to the content of the speech and lacks adequate procedural safeguards; no limit on such a fee can remedy these constitutional violations.

The judgment of the Court of Appeals is affirmed.

CHIEF JUSTICE REHNQUIST, with whom JUSTICE WHITE, JUSTICE SCALIA, and JUSTICE THOMAS join, dissenting.

We granted certiorari in this case to consider the following question: "Whether the provisions of the First Amendment to the United States Constitution limit the amount of a license fee assessed pursuant to the provisions of a county parade ordinance to a nominal sum or whether the amount of the license fee may take into account the actual expense incident to the administration of the ordinance and the maintenance of public order in the matter licensed, up to the sum of $1,000.00 per day of the activity."

The Court's discussion of this question is limited to an ambiguous and noncommittal paragraph toward the very end of the opinion. The rest of the opinion takes up and decides other perceived unconstitutional defects in the Forsyth County ordinance. None of these claims were passed upon by the Court of Appeals; that court decided only that the First Amendment forbade the charging of more than a nominal fee for a permit to parade on public streets. . . .

I

The answer to this question seems to me quite simple, because it was authoritatively decided by this Court more than half a century ago in *Cox v. New Hampshire*, 312 U.S. 569 (1941). There we confronted a State statute which required payment of a license fee of up to $300 to local governments for the right to parade in the public streets. The Supreme Court of New Hampshire had construed the provision as requiring that the amount of the fee be adjusted based on the size of the parade, as the fee "for a circus parade or a celebration procession of length, each drawing crowds of observers, would take into account the greater public expense of policing the spectacle, compared with the slight expense of a less expansive and attractive parade or procession." Under the state court's construction, the fee provision was "not a revenue tax, but one to meet the expense incident to the administration of the Act and to the maintenance of public order in the matter licensed." This Court, in a unanimous opinion by Chief Justice Hughes, upheld the statute.. . .

Two years later, in *Murdock v. Pennsylvania*, 319 U.S. 105 (1943), this Court confronted a municipal ordinance that required payment of a flat license fee for the privilege of canvassing door-to-door to sell one's wares. [T]he Court held that the flat license tax, as applied against the hand distribution of religious tracts, was unconstitutional, on the ground that it was "a flat tax imposed on the exercise of a privilege granted by the Bill of Rights." [T]he situations in *Cox* and *Murdock* were clearly different; the first involved a sliding fee to account for administrative and security costs incurred as a result of a parade on public property, while the second involved a flat tax on protected religious expression. I believe that the decision in *Cox* squarely controls the disposition of the question presented in this case, and I therefore would explicitly hold that the Constitution does not limit a parade license fee to a nominal amount.

II

[B]ecause there are no [relevant] factual findings, I would not decide at this point whether the ordinance fails for lack of adequate standards to guide discretion or for incorporation of a "heckler's veto," but would instead remand the case to the lower courts to initially consider these issues. [I dissent.]

NOTES AND QUESTIONS

(1) *What Has Happened to Feiner?* Neither the majority nor the dissent in this case cited *Feiner v. New York*. What has happened to *Feiner*? If it isn't good law anymore, why didn't the Court overrule it (can it be that *Feiner* still has some minimal vitality if officials must interrupt a demonstration as the only means of preventing mayhem)?

(2) *What About a Greater-than-"Nominal" Fee (or a Fee Including "Normal" Police Protection)?* The dissent expressly approves a fee exceeding "nominal" amounts if not tied to the "heckler's veto." The majority is unclear, but implies that its decision would not affect a fee merely because it is greater than nominal. If a greater-than-nominal fee is constitutional, will it result in greater ability of wealthy persons to engage in speech (and if so, is such a result unconstitutional, or does it parallel the superior ability of the wealthy to buy printing presses)? A further question: Can the city incorporate a fee to cover police protection based on the size of the demonstration or other ostensibly content—neutral factors? Consider the following.

(3) *Reasonable Regulations of Large-Scale Events Are Upheld Under Time, Place, and Manner Standard: Thomas v. Chicago Park District, 534 U.S. 316 (2002).* Some municipalities have permit schemes that do not involve any fee, and these jurisdictions may not face a problem under *Forsyth County.* Non-fee permit schemes still must satisfy certain standards—basically the content-neutral standards of the time, place, and manner doctrine. [*See* § 11.06[A].] In the *Thomas* case, the challengers primarily argued that a Chicago content-neutral permit scheme was also required to meet the higher procedural standards established for subject matter regulation of movies in *Freedman v. Maryland,* 380 U.S. 51 (1965). The Supreme Court, unanimously per Justice Scalia, rejected this argument. The Court emphasized that the Chicago permit scheme contained sufficient procedural protections to satisfy the time, place, and manner standard.

PROBLEM C

CAN A "NARROWLY DEFINED, SLIDING SCALE" PARADE FEE BE UPHELD?: THE EXAMPLE OF THE HOUSTON PARADE PERMIT ORDINANCE, Houston Chronicle, June 20, 1992, § A, at 3, col. 1. After the decision in *Forsyth County v. Nationalist Movement,* officials for the City of Houston (as well as free—speech advocates) promptly stated that the decision did not threaten Houston's analogous ordinance. Fees under this ordinance, according to Houston's Director of Traffic and Transportation, are guided by a "narrowly defined sliding scale that is capped at $3,000." The amount varies according to the number of participants and the length of the parade, "not the nature of the group." The city attorney added: "The reason for that is that the size of the participants mandates how much police involvement is required." A spokesperson for the American Civil Liberties Union stated that her main concerns about the Houston ordinance did not involve the fee. What would be the effect of such a fee on the Nationalist Movement? (Presumably, the cost would be small, because it would depend upon the number of participants expected.) Is Houston's ordinance constitutional?

[B] Advocacy of Unlawful Conduct (or of Unpopular Ideas)

[1] The Historical Background: "Criminal Anarchy," Sedition, Communism, and the Gravity-of-the-Evil Test

NOTE ON THE COMMUNIST PARTY CASES

The Clear and Present Danger Test and the Fear of Communism: Distant Possibilities of Government Overthrow Provide Justification for Sweeping Laws Against Expression. After the Bolshevik Revolution, America took the possibility of Communist dictatorship seriously, and the clear and present danger test provided only an uncertain bulwark. Violent overthrow of the government was regarded as an extremely clear and serious danger: a danger so clear, in fact, that it often dispensed with the necessity of proving that the threat was present or imminent. Thus, the long-shot possibility that a lone pamphleteer might kindle the flame of proletarian struggle, and might in the distant future succeed in organizing a rebellion, was so frightening that it sufficed to overcome the unlikelihood that the ideas could ever be translated into action. The clear and present danger test arguably lent itself to this kind of reasoning.

The Theory of the Revolutionary Spark: Gitlow v. New York, 268 U.S. 652 (1925). The *Gitlow* case was an example. Gitlow's crime was that he published a manifesto advocating a communist revolution. He was convicted of violating New York's criminal anarchy statute, which prohibited advocating the overthrow of the government by violent means. The Supreme Court affirmed, reasoning that "A single revolutionary spark may kindle a flame, that smoldering for a time, may burst into a sweeping and destructive conflagration." Justice Holmes, joined by Justice Brandeis, dissented: "Every idea is an incitement. [B]ut [Gitlow's] redundant discourse [h]ad no chance of starting a present conflagration."

Communist Party Membership as a Crime: Whitney v. California, 274 U.S. 357 (1927). Two years later, Whitney was convicted under California's Criminal Syndicalism Act because she joined the Communist Party, even though she defended by showing that she was committed to "a legitimate policy of political reform by the use of the ballot." The majority of the Supreme Court affirmed by citing *Gitlow.*

Justice Brandeis' Dissent in Whitney: "The Remedy [Is] More Speech." The most memorable aspect of the *Whitney* case was Justice Brandeis' dissent: "Fear of serious injury alone cannot justify suppression of free speech and assembly. Men feared witches and burnt women. [I]n order to support a finding of clear and present danger, it must be shown either that immediate serious violence was to be expected or was advocated, or that the past conduct furnished reason to believe that such advocacy was contemplated." The most widely quoted sentence: "If there be time to expose through discussion the falsehood and fallacies, to avert the evil through the processes of education, the remedy to be applied is more speech, not enforced silence."

Background to the Dennis Case: The "Gravity of the Evil [D]iscounted by Its Improbability." The latter 1940s and early 1950s saw the execution of Julius and Ethel Rosenberg for espionage, the development of nuclear weapons by the Soviet Union, the perjury conviction of Alger Hiss in connection with alleged espionage, and the accusations of Senator Joseph McCarthy that communists were in important positions in the army and State Department. The temper of thetimes may have defined the mood of the Supreme Court. In *Dennis,* below, the Court modified the clear and present danger test to ask a question more loaded toward suppression of speech: "whether the gravity of the 'evil' [*i.e.,* violent overthrow of the government], discounted by its improbability, justifies such invasion of free speech as is necessary to avoid the danger." The implication was that suppression was justifiable, given such a grave danger, even if the probability of its occurrence was small and distant.

DENNIS v. UNITED STATES, 341 U.S. 494 (1951). Dennis and others were convicted of violating the Smith Act, which was functionally similar to the New York Criminal Anarchy Statute at issue in *Gitlow.* Their crime was organizing the Communist Party and advocating the necessity of overthrowing the government by force. The majority affirmed by using the gravity-of-the-evil test:

> Overthrow of the Government by force and violence is certainly a substantial enough interest for the Government to limit speech. Indeed, this is the ultimate value of any society, for if a society cannot protect its very structure from armed internal attack, it must follow that no subordinate value can be protected. If, then, this interest may be protected, the literal problem which is presented is what has been meant by the use of the phrase "clear and present danger" of the utterances bringing about the evil within the power of Congress to punish.

> Obviously, the words cannot mean that before the Government may act, it must wait until the *putsch* is about to be executed, the plans have been laid and the signal is awaited. [W]e must therefore reject the contention that success or probability of success is the criterion. . . .

> Chief Judge Learned Hand, writing for the majority below, interpreted the phrase as follows: "In each case [courts] must ask whether the gravity of the 'evil,' discounted by its improbability, justifies such invasion of free speech as is necessary to avoid the danger." We adopt this statement of the rule. . . .

> [T]he formation by petitioners of such a highly organized conspiracy, with rigidly disciplined members subject to call when the leaders, these petitioners, felt that the time had come for action, coupled with the inflammable nature of world conditions, similar uprisings in other countries, and the touch-and-go

nature of our relations with countries with whom petitioners were in the very least ideologically attuned, convince us that their convictions were justified on this score. . . .

Justices Black and Douglas dissented. Justice Black flatly said that the clear and present danger test was constitutionally inadequate: "[I] believe that the 'clear and present danger' test does not 'mark the constitutional boundaries of protected expression.' " . . .

NOTES AND QUESTIONS

(1) *Should the Focus of the Inquiry Be upon the Nature of the Utterance Rather than upon Clear and Present Danger?* Is this case an indication that the clear and present danger test should be replaced (or at least supplemented) by a test that focuses upon the nature of the utterance, linking it to the urging of action, rather than weighing the proximity or remoteness of success? Consider whether such a test could better identify harmful utterances that the government legitimately may criminalize and at the same time may better protect the freedom of speech.

(2) *A New Direction Six Years Later— The Court Distinguishes Between "Advocacy of Ideas" and "Advocacy of Action" to Invalidate Convictions of Lesser Communist Leaders: Yates v. United States, 354 U.S. 298 (1957).* Six years after *Dennis*, in 1957, the convictions of "second string" Communist leaders reached the Court in *Yates*. Although sentiment against Communism remained strong, the times had changed. The country had been made aware of the danger of excess by such events as the censure of Senator McCarthy by the Senate. Without overruling *Dennis* or its predecessors, the Court drew a sharper line, in *Yates*, between advocacy of action and advocacy of ideas:

> In failing to distinguish between advocacy of forcible overthrow as an abstract doctrine and advocacy of action to that end, the district court appears to have been led astray by the holding in *Dennis* that advocacy of violent action to be taken at some future time was enough. . . .

> [T]he view of the district court here [was] that mere doctrinal justification of forcible overthrow . . . is punishable per se under the Smith Act. That sort of advocacy . . . is too remote from concrete action to be regarded as the kind of indoctrination preparatory to action which was condemned in *Dennis*. . . .

Justices Black and Douglas dissented in part because they would have "reverse[d] every one of these convictions and direct[ed] that all of the defendants be acquitted." They viewed the Smith Act as facially unconstitutional. Justice Clark dissented because he would have affirmed the convictions.

(3) *The Post-Yates "Communist Party Membership" Case: Noto v. United States, 367 U.S. 290 (1961).* In *Noto*, the Court reversed a conviction because the party's teaching, there, fell under the realm of "abstract doctrine" rather than "advocacy of action." After *Noto*, the government ceased to bring prosecutions under the Smith Act.

[2]　The Modern Test for Criminalizing Speech Urging Illegal Action

BRANDENBURG v. OHIO
395 U.S. 444 (1969)

PER CURIAM.

The appellant, a leader of a Ku Klux Klan group, was convicted under the Ohio Criminal Syndicalism Statute for "advocat[ing] . . . the duty, necessity, or propriety of crime, sabotage, violence, or unlawful methods of terrorism as a means of accomplishing industrial or political reform" and for "voluntarily assembl[ing] with any society, group, or assemblage of persons formed to teach or advocate the doctrines of criminal syndicalism."

The record shows that a man, identified at trial as the appellant, telephoned an announcer-reporter on the staff of a Cincinnati television station and invited him to come to a Ku KluxKlan "rally" to be held at a farm in Hamilton County. With the cooperation of the organizers, the reporter and a cameraman attended the meeting and filmed the events. . . .

The prosecution's case rested on the films and on testimony identifying the appellant as the person who communicated with the reporter and who spoke at the rally. . . .

One film showed 12 hooded figures, some of whom carried firearms. They were gathered around a large wooden cross, which they burned. No one was present other than the participants and the newsmen who made the film. Most of the words uttered during the scene were incomprehensible when the film was projected, but scattered phrases could be understood that were derogatory of Negroes and, in one instance, of Jews.[1] Another scene on the same film showed the appellant, in Klan regalia, making a speech. The speech, in full, was as follows:

> This is an organizers' meeting. We have had quite a few members here today which are—we have hundreds, hundreds of members throughout the State of Ohio. I can quote from a newspaper clipping from the Columbus, Ohio Dispatch, five weeks ago Sunday morning. The Klan has more members in the State of Ohio than does any other organization. We're not a revengent organization, but if our President, our Congress, our Supreme Court, continues to suppress the white, Caucasian race, it's possible that there might have to be some revengeance taken.

> We are marching on Congress July the Fourth, four hundred thousand strong. From there we are dividing into two groups, one group to march on St. Augustine, Florida, the other group to march into Mississippi. Thank you.

The second film showed six hooded figures one of whom, later identified as the appellant, repeated a speech very similar to that recorded on the first film. The reference to the possibility of "revengeance" was omitted, and one sentence was added: "Personally, I believe the nigger should be returned to Africa, the Jew returned to Israel." Though some of the figures in the films carried weapons, the speaker did not.

The Ohio Criminal Syndicalism Statute was enacted in 1919. From 1917 to 1920, identical or quite similar laws were adopted by 20 States and two territories. In 1927, this Court sustained the constitutionality of California's Criminal Syndicalism Act [in] *Whitney v. California*. The Court upheld the statute on the ground that, without more, "advocating" violent means to effect political and economic change involves such danger

---

[1] The significant portions that could be understood were:

How far is the nigger going to—yeah.

This is what we are going to do to the niggers.

A dirty nigger.

Send the Jews back to Israel.

Let's give them back to the dark garden

Save America.

Let's go back to constitutional betterment.

Bury the niggers.

We intend to do our part.

Give us our state rights.

Freedom for the whites.

Nigger will have to fight for every inch he gets from now on.

to the security of the State that the State may outlaw it. . . .

[B]ut *Whitney* has been thoroughly discredited by later decisions. *See Dennis v. United States*. These later decisions have fashioned the principle that the constitutional guarantees of free speech and free press do not permit a State to forbid or proscribe advocacy of the use of force or of law violation except where such advocacy is directed to inciting or producing imminent lawless action and is likely to incite or produce such action. As we said in *Noto v. United States*, "the mere abstract teaching . . . of the moral propriety or even moral necessity for a resort to force and violence, is not the same as preparing a group for violent action and steeling it to such action."

Measured by this test, Ohio's Criminal Syndicalism Act cannot be sustained. The Act punishes persons who "advocate or teach the duty, necessity, or propriety" of violence "as a means of accomplishing industrial or political reform"; or who publish or circulate or display any book or paper containing such advocacy; or who "justify" the commission of violent acts "with intent to exemplify, spread or advocate the propriety of the doctrines of criminal syndicalism"; or who "voluntarily assemble" with a group formed "to teach or advocate the doctrines of criminal syndicalism." Neither the indictment nor the trial judge's instructions to the jury in any way refined the statute's bald definition of the crime in terms of mere advocacy not distinguished from incitement to imminent lawless action.

Accordingly, we are here confronted with a statute which, by its own words and as applied, purports to punish mere advocacy and to forbid, on pain of criminal punishment, assembly with others merely to advocate the described type of action. Such a statute falls within the condemnation of the First and Fourteenth Amendments. The contrary teaching of *Whitney v. California* cannot be supported, and that decision is therefore overruled.

Reversed.

MR. JUSTICE BLACK, concurring.

I agree with the views expressed by MR. JUSTICE DOUGLAS in his concurring opinion in this case that the "clear and present danger" doctrine should have no place in the interpretation of the First Amendment. I join the Court's opinion, which, as I understand it, simply cites *Dennis v. United States*, but does not indicate any agreement on the Court's part with the "clear and present danger" doctrine on which *Dennis* purported to rely.

MR. JUSTICE DOUGLAS, concurring.

While I join the opinion of the Court, I desire to enter a *caveat*.

The "clear and present danger" test was adumbrated by Mr. Justice Holmes in a case arising during World War I. [T]he dissents in *Abrams* show how easily "clear and present danger" is manipulated to crush what Brandeis called "[t]he fundamental right of free men to strive for better conditions through new legislation and new institutions" by argument and discourse even in time of war. Though I doubt if the "clear and present danger" test is congenial to the First Amendment in time of a declared war, I am certain it is not reconcilable with the First Amendment in days of peace. . . .

[I] see no place in the regime of the First Amendment for any "clear and present danger" test, whether strict and tight as some would make it, or free-wheeling as the Court in *Dennis* rephrased it. . . .

The line between what is permissible and not subject to control and what may be made impermissible and subject to regulation is the line between ideas and overt acts.

The example usually given by those who would punish speech is the case of one who falsely shouts fire in a crowded theatre.

This is, however, a classic case where speech is brigaded with action. . . .

[A]part from rare instances of that kind, speech is, I think, immune from prosecution. . . .

NOTES AND QUESTIONS

(1) *The Brandenburg "Directed-To-Inciting-And-Likely-To-Incite" Test. Brandenburg* cites *Dennis* and *Yates*, saying that these decisions have fashioned the principle that the advocacy of law violation may not be proscribed "except where such advocacy [1] is directed to inciting or producing imminent lawless action and [2] is likely to incite or produce such action." Is this statement consistent with the holding in *Dennis* and *Yates*? To what extent is it different from those holdings, and does it protect speech better? On the facts of *Brandenburg*, the state could not satisfy the imminence requirement of the second prong. The way that Justice Fortas presented the content of the speech, it is questionable if the state could satisfy the imminence requirement of the first prong. The *Brandenburg* version of clear and present danger is far more protective than the *Schenck* or *Dennis* versions. *See generally* ERWIN CHEMERINSKY, CONSTITUTION LAW 999 (3d ed. 2006).

(2) *The Relationship of Brandenburg to Learned Hand's Formula in the Masses Press Case.* Hand's opinion stated that utterances could be criminalized if they "counsel or advise others to violate the law as it stands." Does *Brandenburg* vindicate this approach—and does it implicitly demonstrate that the clear and present danger test was a signpost in the wrong direction?

(3) *Applying the Brandenburg Test in the Disorderly Conduct Context: Hess v. Indiana, 414 U.S. 105 (1973).* Hess and others conducted a demonstration in which they blocked the passage of vehicles on a public street. The sheriff and his deputies attempted to clear the street. Hess was convicted of disorderly conduct on evidence that showed that, during this effort by the sheriff, he loudly stated, "We'll take the fucking street later." The court held that this remark could not be punished as incitement of illegal action under the *Brandenburg* test:

> Since the uncontroverted evidence showed that Hess' statement was not directed to any person or group of persons, it cannot be said that he was advocating, in the normal sense, any action. And since there was no evidence or rational inference from the import of the language, that his words were intended to produce, and likely to produce, *imminent* [law violations], those words could not be punished by the state on the ground that they had a "tendency to lead to violence." (emphasis in original)

Justice Rehnquist, joined by Chief Justice Burger and Justice Blackmun, dissented: "Surely the sentence 'we'll take the fucking street later . . .' is susceptible of characterization as an exhortation, particularly when uttered in a loud voice while facing a crowd." Is the majority's approach in *Hess* naively unwilling to accept "indirect" incitement, or are the dissenters too willing to accept inferences about the dangerous effects of speech?

(4) *Commentary on the Brandenburg Standard.* For some of the most recent scholarly commentary on the *Brandenburg* standard, *see* David Crump, *Camouflaged Incitement, Freedom of Speech, Communicative Torts, and the Borderland of the Brandenburg Test*, 29 GA. L. REV. 1 (1994); Andrew B. Sims, *Tort Liability for Physical Injuries Allegedly Resulting From Media Speech: A Comprehensive First Amendment Approach*, 34 ARIZ. L. REV. 231 (1992).

PROBLEM D

THE REFUSAL TO ALLOW TELEVISING OF DEATH PENALTY EXECUTIONS— THE GARY GILMORE CASE: KEARNS TRIBUNE CORP. v. UTAH BOARD OF CORRECTIONS, 2 MEDIA L. RPTR. 1353 (D. Utah, Jan. 13, 1977).

The execution of multiple murderer Gary Gilmore by the State of Utah was the first imposition of the death penalty under modern statutes. Members of the press filed suit, seeking an injunction requiring Utah to allow them to televise this event. The Ninth Circuit denied the injunction, pointing out several arguable state interests supporting the refusal. First, psychological expert testimony in the trial court indicated a probability that the graphic portrayal of violence that would be televised would prompt modeling by impressionable individuals, who might attempt to imitate the execution in their own backyards. Second, television coverage might induce inmates to engage in undesirable forms of behavior, including possibly waiving appeals for the purpose of appearing on camera. Other state interests also were relied upon.

Is the rule of *Brandenburg v. Ohio* applicable in this case? Are the state's interests sufficient to support the refusal to allow television access?

PROBLEM E

DEPICTIONS OF VIOLENCE SUFFICIENTLY GRAPHIC AS TO PRODUCE MODELING. Graphic depictions of violence pose the danger that they may be imitated. In attempting to determine whether the state has valid interests that would support some control of this kind of expression, consider the following two incidents, both of which were reported in a single month in the same metropolitan newspaper:

> Beckville, Texas (Associated Press)—[A] man arrested in the beating death of an eighteen-year-old legally blind woman returned to a graduation party with "blood up to his elbows. . . ."
>
> David E. Metcalf, 19, was released from the Panola County Jail on $75,000 bond Tuesday after being charged with murder in the death of classmate Teresa Ann Downing. . . .
>
> One of the films shown at the party [before the murder] was *The Faces of Death.* [T]he movie, a four-part unrated film, includes real-life footage of executions, violent deaths, autopsies, cannibalism and animal slaughter.

HOUSTON CHRONICLE, June 3, 1987, at 16, Col. 2.*

> Two teen-age cousins who set fire to a prize-winning dog after seeing a similar act in a movie surrendered to police accompanied by their parents, officials said Thursday.
>
> "They said they had seen a movie where an individual was setting dogs and cats on fire," Pasadena Police Spokeswoman, Betty Parks, said. Police were uncertain which movie the boys had watched prior to the June 2 attack. . . .

HOUSTON CHRONICLE, Friday, June 12, 1987, Col. 1 at 21, Col. 1.** After *Brandenburg,* can the state assert interests sufficient to allow it to regulate or prohibit the kinds of depictions of violence that (apparently) led to these two incidents (and if so, what sorts of regulations or prohibitions, and how can they be defined)? Or are we left with the conclusion that such incidents simply are one of the unavoidable costs that our society pays for protecting the freedom of speech? *Cf.* Powe, *Televised Violence: First Amendment Principles and Social Science Theory,* 64 VA. L. REV. 1123 (1978).

PROBLEM F

TORT SUITS AGAINST MERCHANDISERS OF "COP KILLER" RAP MUSIC: DENNIS R. MARTIN, THE MUSIC OF MURDER, 2 WM. & MARY BILL OF RTS. J. 159 (1993). In July 1992, two Las Vegas police officers were ambushed and shot by four juveniles who explained that they were induced to commit the offense by a recording by Rapper Ice-T, published by Time Warner. They continued to chant the lyrics after their

---

arrest. Ice-T's rap speaks through an alleged "cop killer" ("I'm'bout to bust some shots off/I'm'bout to dust some cops off") and contains a chorus and coda as follows:

(Chorus) DIE, DIE, DIE, PIG, DIE! FUCK THE POLICE! (repeat)

FUCK THE POLICE! (repeat). . . .

FUCK THE POLICE, for Rodney King.

FUCK THE POLICE, for my dead homies.

FUCK THE POLICE, for your freedom.

FUCK THE POLICE, don't be a pussy. . . .

FUCK THE POLICE, sing along. . . .

I'm a muthafuckin' COP KILLER! COP KILLER! (repeat)

Time Warner also distributed rap by 2 Pac; and after listening to 2 Pac's lyrics, Ronald Howard shot and killed Texas officer Bill Davidson during a routine traffic stop. According to Martin, *The Music of Murder, supra,* "[t]wo psychiatrists found that the music still affects [Howard's] psycho-social behavior." Davidson's widow, Linda Davidson, sued Time Warner for his wrongful death. The company announced a voluntary suspension of "Cop Killer," right after it "flooded the United States market with an additional half-million copies" shipped in miniature body bags. As for the litigation, Time Warner defended it by pleading the First Amendment.

Questions: (1) Given the *Brandenburg* case and its progeny, will Time Warner's First Amendment defense defeat these tort suits—and if so, should it? [Martin (who is president of the National Association of Chiefs of Police and who displays in his article substantial knowledge of the history of music), offers a restrained assessment of the plaintiffs' prospects: "Given the current state of American law, one can only hope that Time Warner will tire of the expense of defending [lawsuits] prompted by such lyrics and attacks on police." A jury convicted Howard of capital murder and implicitly rejected arguments that rap displaced his responsibility by sentencing him to death.] (2) Would it make a difference in the tort suits if expert witnesses testified to a likelihood that impressionable people would act on the rappers' suggestions? [Martin refers to the "predictability" of this result.] (3) Does it make a difference under Brandenburg that Ice-T ends the recording by urging the listener to "sing along" with the words "I'm a [C]OP KILLER?" (4) Time Warner explained that "Ice-T is attempting to express the rage and frustration of a young black person. . . . Our job as a society is to address the causes of this anger, not to suppress its articulation." Is this view persuasive?

PROBLEM G

THE "HIT MAN" CASE: RICE v. PALADIN ENTERPRISES, INC., 128 F.3d 233 (4th Cir. 1997). Paladin Press publishes a murder-for-hire instruction manual called *Hit Man: A Technical Manual for Independent Contractors.* The manual contains the prefatory statement: "Within the pages of this book you will learn one of the most successful methods of operation used by an independent contractor. . . . Step by step you will be taken from research to equipment selection to job preparation to successful job completion." James Horn plotted with James Perry to have Perry murder his ex-wife, Mildred Horn, and their severely disabled child Trevor. Horn's motive was to inherit a large medical malpractice settlement that had been obtained for Trevor. Perry, the prospective hit man, ordered a copy of the manual *Hit Man* from Paladin by mail and studied it. A little over a year later, he used techniques learned from the *Hit Man* manual to murder Mildred Horn, Trevor Horn, and Janice Saunders (Trevor's private duty nurse).

In committing the three murders, James Perry followed at least twenty-two detailed instructions in the *Hit Man* manual. Among others, these included specific instructions to use an AR-7 rifle, obliterate the serial number just above the clip port in a detailed way, construct a silencer in a specific manner, shoot from three to six feet to cause a close kill but avoid blood splatters on the killer, shoot the victim through the eye sockets, change the rifling in a specified manner, and "[u]sing a rattail file, alter the gun barrel" as well as other specified parts of the gun. Perry also followed detailed instructions in *Hit Man* about soliciting clients, collecting up-front money, traveling, covering up the scene, and other aspects of the crime. Perry had been convicted and sentenced to death at the time of this litigation.

Rice was the guardian and next friend of Tamielle Horn, the daughter of Mildred Horn. Together with the estate representatives of the murder victims, Rice filed suit against Paladin, alleging that it had caused, aided and abetted their wrongful deaths. Paladin filed a motion for summary judgment that invoked the First Amendment. The summary judgment evidence included not only the facts listed above, but also a stipulation agreed to both by the plaintiffs and by Paladin. In the stipulation, Paladin admitted (for purposes of summary judgment only) (1) that it had knowledge and intended that the *Hit Man* manual would be used on receipt by criminals and would-be criminals to plan and execute murders for hire in the manner set forth, (2) that it had engaged in a marketing strategy intended to attract criminals and would-be criminals as customers, and (3) that it had assisted James Perry in his perpetration of the murders. The parties further agreed that Paladin also marketed its manuals to maximize sales to the general public, including authors desiring information about crime, law enforcement officers, criminologists, people who wanted to read about crime, and people who fantasized about committing crimes. [You may have heard of Paladin in connection with the Oklahoma City federal building bombing, because the evidence suggested that similar how-to bombmaking manuals were involved there.]

Questions: (1) *The "Incitement" Prong of Brandenburg.* Can the plaintiffs satisfy the *Brandenburg* "incitement" prong (*i.e.*, do the circumstances show that Paladin's utterances were "directed to inciting or producing . . . and likely to incite or produce" lawless action)? (2) *The "Imminence" Prong of Brandenburg.* Can the plaintiffs satisfy the "imminence" requirement (i.e., is Paladin's incitement, if any, directed to "imminent" lawless action)? [Note that the sale to Perry was by mail, and he did not act until more than a year later.] (3) *Is Brandenburg an Appropriate Standard Here?* Perhaps *Brandenburg* is aimed at utterances that have some claim of relationship to political speech. Should the *Brandenburg* standard apply to a case in whichthe evidence arguably shows that the defendant intentionally has aided and abetted the commission of a crime?

[The District Court, relying on *Brandenburg* and other theories, granted summary judgment for Paladin. Rice et al. appealed. Amici curiae supporting Paladin ranged from television networks and major print media to the Society of Professional Journalists, ACLU, and the Horror Writers Association (which filed a well-written brief). Amici supporting the plaintiffs included the National Victim Center and other Victim's Rights groups and, also, Professor Crump, who filed as "a Professor of Constitutional Law and Recipient of the Friend of the First Amendment Award" (given by the Society of Professional Journalists, although he supported the plaintiffs here). The Fourth Circuit reversed and ordered the suit to proceed, holding that a jury could find Paladin liable on a theory of intentionally aiding and abetting crime. The court relied heavily on the stipulation of intent and the instructional nature of the text. It reasoned that these factors would readily distinguish cases in which news reports or fiction inspired copycat crimes, and it concluded that these same factors also distinguished the *Brandenburg* line of cases. Are these holdings correct, or are the media amici correct in fearing a threat from this decision?

On May 21, 1999, the parties settled. Paladin paid a confidential sum, which the plaintiffs' attorneys described only as a "multi-million dollar settlement," and it also agreed to stop selling the Hit Man book. *See* HOUSTON CHRONICLE, May 22, 1999, at 16.]

§ 11.03   SOME GENERAL PRINCIPLES: THE TWO-TRACK SYSTEM AND THE OVERBREADTH AND VAGUENESS DOCTRINES

[A]   "Track One" and "Track Two" Analysis: Content-Based Regulation Versus Content-Neutral Regulation

INTRODUCTORY NOTE: THE TWO-TRACK SYSTEM

To borrow Professor Laurence Tribe's terminology, the Supreme Court's modern decisions categorize regulations of free speech interests as falling in one of two "Tracks." Content-based regulations are categorized as "Track One" and content-neutral regulations are categorized as "Track Two." Content-based regulations generally are scrutinized more closely (*e.g.*, strict scrutiny). Content-neutral regulations generally receive an "intermediate scrutiny."

Before examining the materials below, note two further considerations. First, before the Court considers the Track of a challenged regulation, the Court must be satisfied that (A) "speech" rather than "conduct" is being regulated and (B) the speech is "protected speech." *See generally* Laurence H. Tribe, American Constitutional Law 789-804 (2d ed. 1988). Second, although the Supreme Court has an extensive body of case law using the "content-based" distinction, the Court has certain alternative doctrinal vehicles for deciding cases. The most important of these are the "vagueness" and "overbreadth" doctrines, which also are examined in this section. But, initially, this section examines the concept of content-based regulation.

POLICE DEPARTMENT OF CHICAGO v. MOSLEY, 408 U.S. 92 (1972). A Chicago city ordinance, in the interest of maintaining an educational atmosphere, prohibited all picketing within 150 feet of a school—except for peaceful picketing of any school involved in a labor dispute. The challenger, Earl Mosley, had frequently picketed on the public sidewalk by Jones Commercial High School with a picket sign claiming that the school "practices black discrimination." When Mosley was informed that the ordinance prohibited his picketing, he sued. TheSupreme Court, per Justice Marshall, concluded that Chicago's ordinance was "unconstitutional because it makes an impermissible distinction:"

> Because Chicago treats some picketing differently from others, we analyze this ordinance in terms of the Equal Protection Clause of the Fourteenth Amendment. Of course, the equal protection claim in this case is closely intertwined with First Amendment interests. . . .

> The central problem with Chicago's ordinance is that it describes permissible picketing in terms of its subject matter. . . . The operative distinction is the message on the picket sign. But, above all else, the First Amendment means that the government has no power to restrict expression because of its message, its ideas, its subject matter or its content. . . . The essence of . . . forbidden censorship is content control.

BOOS v. BARRY, 485 U.S. 312 (1988). A District of Columbia ordinance prohibited anyone from displaying any sign within 500 feet of a foreign embassy that tended to bring the foreign government into "public disrepute" (the "display clause"). The ordinance also made it unlawful for persons to congregate within 500 feet of such an embassy and to refuse to obey a police dispersal order (the "congregation clause").

The court of appeals upheld both clauses. It reasoned that the display clause was a content-based restriction on speech, but it held that the clause was narrowly drawn to serve a compelling governmental interest. The court of appeals narrowed the congregation clause so that it applied only when the police reasonably believed that "a threat to the security or peace of the embassy is present" and concluded that, as narrowed, it was constitutional.

The Supreme Court unanimously reversed as to the display clause, holding it unconstitutional, and affirmed as to the congregation clause, holding it constitutional as narrowed. The Court noted that the Vienna Convention on Diplomatic Relations required signatories to "take all appropriate steps to protect the premises of [an embassy] against any intrusion or damage and to prevent any disturbance of the peace of the embassy or impairment of its dignity." But the Court also noted that Congress had not gone so far as the District of Columbia ordinance in protecting embassies; its enactments prohibited only willful acts or attempts to "intimidate, coerce, threaten, or harass . . . or obstruct a foreign official." Moreover, Congress had repealed an earlier anti-picketing ordinance that was similar to (but more narrowly drawn than) the D.C. ordinance, because of First Amendment concerns. In an opinion by Justice O'Connor (with Justices Brennan and Marshall concurring separately), the Court reasoned:

> [A]s a *content-based* restriction on political speech in a public forum, [the ordinance] must be subjected to the most exacting scrutiny. . . .

> [W]hen considered together with earlier congressional action implementing the Vienna Convention, the claim that the display clause is sufficiently narrowly tailored is gravely weakened; if ever it did so, Congress no longer considers this statute necessary to comply with our international obligations. Relying on congressional judgment in this delicate area, we conclude that the availability of alternatives . . . amply demonstrates that the display clause is not crafted with sufficient precision to withstand first amendment scrutiny. It may serve an interest in protecting the dignity of foreign missions, but it is not narrowly tailored. . . .

> [The congregation clause] does not reach a substantial amount of constitutionally protected conduct; it merely regulates the place and manner of certain demonstrations. [It] issite-specific; it applies only within 500 feet of foreign embassies. *Cf. Cox v. Louisiana* ["*Cox II*"]. Moreover, the congregation clause [as narrowed] does not prohibit peaceful congregations; its reach is limited to groups posing a security threat. [T]hese two limitations . . . make the clause consistent with the first amendment.

NOTES AND QUESTIONS

(1) *Professor Tribe's "Two Track" Analysis: Differentiating Content-Based Regulation from Content-Neutral Regulation.* "Track One" covers government intervention aimed at the content of the ideas or information expressed, either (1) by singling out its message (as in *Boos v. Barry*) or (2) by targeting the reactions produced by listeners' awareness of the message (as in the Forsyth County case). "Track Two" concerns regulation targeted at other legitimate goals rather than at the content of the expression.

(2) *The Evolution of the "Track One" Standard: From Equal Protection to the First Amendment?* The case law indicates that the "content distinction" is firmly entrenched in First Amendment analysis. Some critics charge that the two "Track" approach is really, in *Mosley*, an equal protection analysis and that it should not govern free speech cases. For commentary, *see, e.g.*, Geoffrey Stone, *Restrictions of Speech Because of Its Content: The Peculiar Case of Subject Matter Restrictions*, 46 U. CHI. L. REV. 81 (1978); Susan Williams, *Content Discrimination and the First Amendment*, 139 U. PA. L. REV. 615 (1991).

(3) *What Is a Content-Based Regulation?: The Threshold to Getting on Track One.* Since the decision that a particular governmental regulation is content-based will lead in most situations to the use of strict scrutiny, it is obviously important to examine how the Court decided that the regulation at issue is content-based (instead of content-neutral

and, therefore, on Track Two). Sometimes, as in *Boos v. Barry*, the regulation is *facially* content-based. Sometimes, as in *Mosley*, the Court determines a content-based approach from the "exceptions" to the regulation. Sometimes, as in *Forsyth County*, the impact on the audience determines that the otherwise facially neutral regulation is content-based. Under the Two Track system, the government will always have an incentive (*i.e.*, lower levels of scrutiny) to argue that its regulation is content-neutral. Watch for this argument in the following cases.

SIMON & SCHUSTER, INC. v. MEMBERS OF THE NEW YORK STATE CRIME VICTIMS BOARD
502 U.S. 105 (1991)

JUSTICE O'CONNOR delivered the opinion of the Court.

[New York enacted a statute, as a result of the "Son of Sam" serial killer episode, which required "any entity contracting with an accused or convicted person for a depiction of the crime" to turn over any income generated by the depiction to the State Crime Victims Board for a five-year escrow period. The Board could award the monies to appropriate crime victims. Thisprovision, which was called the "Son of Sam Law," applied both to persons convicted and those who "voluntarily and intelligently admitted" criminal acts, and it was a supplement to other statutory provisions benefitting crime victims.

[In 1986, the Board became aware that Henry Hill had written a best-selling book, Wiseguy: Life in a Mafia Family, that described his participation in various criminal activities. Pursuant to the Son of Sam Law, the Board ordered the publisher, Simon & Schuster, Inc., to turn over the monies owed to Hill. Simon & Schuster sued to enjoin enforcement, but the federal District Court ruled in favor of the Board, and the court of appeals affirmed. The Supreme Court here unanimously reverses.]

II

A

A statute is presumptively inconsistent with the First Amendment if it imposes a financial burden on speakers because of the content of their speech. As we emphasized in invalidating a content—based magazine tax, "official scrutiny of the content of publications as the basis for imposing a tax is entirely incompatible with the First Amendment's guarantee of freedom of the press." *Arkansas Writers' Project, Inc. v. Ragland*, 481 U.S. 221, 230 (1987).

This is a notion so engrained in our First Amendment jurisprudence that last Term we found it so "obvious" as to not require explanation. It is but one manifestation of a far broader principle: "Regulations which permit the Government to discriminate on the basis of the content of the message cannot be tolerated under the First Amendment."

[T]he Son of Sam law is such a content-based statute. It singles out income derived from expressive activity for a burden the State places on no other income, and it is directed only at works with a specified content. . . .

The Board [a]rgues that discriminatory financial treatment is suspect under the First Amendment only when the legislature intends to suppress certain ideas. This assertion is incorrect; our cases have consistently held that "[i]llicit legislative intent is not the *sine qua non* of a violation of the First Amendment." *Minneapolis Star & Tribune Co. v. Minnesota Comm'r of Revenue*, 460 U.S. 575, 592 (1983). Simon & Schuster need adduce "no evidence of an improper censorial motive. . . . "

The Son of Sam law establishes a financial disincentive to create or publish works with a particular content. In order to justify such differential treatment, "the State must show that its regulation is necessary to serve a compelling state interest and is narrowly drawn to achieve that end."

B

The Board disclaims, as it must, any state interest in suppressing descriptions of crime out of solicitude for the sensibilities of readers. As we have often had occasion to repeat, "[T]he fact that society may find speech offensive is not a sufficient reason for suppressing it". . . .

There can be little doubt, on the other hand, that the State has a compelling interest in ensuring that victims of crime are compensated by those who harm them. Every State has a body of tort law serving exactly this interest. . . .

The State likewise has an undisputed compelling interest in ensuring that criminals do not profit from their crimes. Like most if not all States, New York has long recognized the "fundamental equitable principle," that "[n]o one shall be permitted to profit by his own fraud, or to take advantage of his own wrong, or to found any claim upon his own iniquity, or to acquire property by his own crime". . . .

[T]he Board attempts to define the State's interest more narrowly, as "ensuring that criminals do not profit from storytelling about their crimes before their victims have a meaningful opportunity to be compensated for their injuries." Here the Board is on far shakier ground. The Board cannot explain why the State should have any greater interest in compensating victims from the proceeds of such "storytelling" than from any of the criminal's other assets. . . .

In short, the State has a compelling interest in compensating victims from the fruits of the crime, but little if any interest in limiting such compensation to the proceeds of the wrongdoer's speech about the crime. We must therefore determine whether the Son of Sam law is narrowly tailored to advance the former, not the latter, objective.

C

As a means of ensuring that victims are compensated from the proceeds of crime, the Son of Sam law is significantly overinclusive. As counsel for the Board conceded at oral argument, the statute applies to works on any subject, provided that they express the author's thoughts or recollections about his crime, however tangentially or incidentally. In addition, the statute's broad definition of "person convicted of a crime" enables the Board to escrow the income of any author who admits in his work to having committed a crime, whether or not the author was ever actually accused or convicted.

[H]ad the Son of Sam law been in effect . . ., it would have escrowed payment for such works as *The Autobiography of Malcolm X*, which describes crimes committed by the civil rights leader before he became a public figure; *Civil Disobedience*, in which Thoreau acknowledges his refusal to pay taxes and recalls his experience in jail; and even the *Confessions of Saint Augustine*, in which the author laments "my past foulness and the carnal corruptions of my soul," one instance of which involved the theft of pears from a neighboring vineyard. [T]he Son of Sam law clearly reaches a wide range of literature that does not enable a criminal to profit from his crime while a victim remains uncompensated.

Should a prominent figure write his autobiography at the end of his career, and include in an early chapter a brief recollection of having stolen (in New York) a nearly worthless item as a youthful prank, the Board would control his entire income from the book for five years, and would make that income available to all of the author's creditors, despite the fact that the statute of limitations for this minor incident had long since run. That the Son of Sam law can produce such an outcome indicates that the statute is, to say the least, not narrowly tailored to achieve the State's objective of compensating crime victims from the profits of crime.

III

The Federal Government and many of the States have enacted statutes designed to serve purposes similar to that served by the Son of Sam law. Some of these statutes may be quite different from New York's, and we have no occasion to determine the constitutionality of these other laws. We conclude simply that in the Son of Sam law, New York has singled out speech on a particular subject for a financial burden that it places on no other speech and no other income.

[*Reversed.*]

JUSTICE THOMAS took no part in the consideration or decision of this case.

[The concurring opinion of JUSTICE BLACKMUN is omitted.]

JUSTICE KENNEDY, concurring in the judgment.

The New York statute we now consider imposes severe restrictions on authors and publishers, using as its sole criterion the content of what is written. The regulated content has the full protection of the First Amendment and this, I submit, is itself a full and sufficient reason for holding the statute unconstitutional. In my view it is both unnecessary and incorrect to ask whether the State can show that the statute "is necessary to serve a compelling state interest and is narrowly drawn to achieve that end". . . .

Borrowing the compelling interest and narrow tailoring analysis is ill—advised when all that is at issue is a content—based restriction, for resort to the test might be read as a concession that States may censor speech whenever they believe there is a compelling justification for doing so. Our precedents and traditions allow no such inference. . . .

NOTES AND QUESTIONS

(1) *The Applicable Tests: Strict Scrutiny for Track One; Forms of Intermediate Scrutiny for Track Two.* As the *Son of Sam* case demonstrates, a majority of the Court applies strict scrutiny to Track One cases, requiring a regulation that is "narrowly drawn" to serve a "compelling state interest." Track Two cases, on the other hand, invoke a more flexible balancing analysis. The analysis in these cases, which involve content—neutral regulations, is less rigorous than Track One analysis, because it must take account of regulatory interests of varying strengths. The level of scrutiny, however, generally should be lower in Track Two.

(2) *"Time, Place, and Manner" Regulations: Ward v. Rock Against Racism, 491 U.S. 781 (1989).* In the *Ward* case, New York City imposed restrictions on amplified music in its Central Park Bandshell, requiring use of a city—furnished technician and sound equipment. (Other approaches had proved unsatisfactory: general prohibitions of "excessive" noise had been unenforceable, and even decibel limits would not work because listener impact is influenced also by air temperature, foliage and audience size and reaction.) The Court upheld this "time, place, or manner" restriction on the ground that it was "content-neutral" and was "narrowly tailored" to serve a "substantial" government interest. The Court expressly rejected a requirement, imposed by the lower court, that the city use the "least-restrictive or least-intrusive" means, holding instead that narrow tailoring in this context implies only that the governmental interest "would be achieved less effectively without the regulation."

Is this a Track Two analysis? Or is it instead a Middle Track, addressed to ostensibly content-neutral regulations that nevertheless are tied to content because their concern with "time, place, or manner" actually depends on content? Alternatively, is it possible that there are Multiple Tracks, or even an infinite number (like the sliding scale advanced by Justice Marshall in the equal protection jurisprudence)?

(3) *The Threshold Issue of the Two Track System— Determining Whether a Particular Regulation Is Content-Based: Bartnicki v. Vopper, 532 U.S. 514 (2001)*. The significant threshold (and often determinative) issue in the Court's Two Track system is whether the regulation in controversy is content-based or a content-neutral regulation of general applicability. In *Vopper*, the Court, per Justice Stevens, relied on a long line of precedent establishing that "as a general rule, laws that by their terms distinguish favored speech from disfavored speech on the basis of the ideas or views expressed are content-based.. . . In determining whether a regulation is content based or content neutral, we look to the purpose behind the regulation . . .." In *Vopper*, an unknown person intercepted the cell phone conversation of two union officials; this interception was illegal under federal law (the Electronic Communication Privacy Act of 1986). The illegally intercepted conversation was given to the media (Vopper), and Vopper repeatedly broadcast the conversation. The union officials sued Vopper and the other media.

The Court held that the federal prohibition on publication of illegally intercepted communications was a content-neutral regulation because: "the communications at issue are singled out by virtue of the fact that they were illegally intercepted—by virtue of the source, rather than the subject matter." Nevertheless, even though the regulation was content-neutral, the Court subjected it to a rigorous level of scrutiny and held that the federal statute violated the First Amendment protection of the media. For further doctrinal background regarding *Vopper*, *see* § 11.04[D][3] below.

(4) *A Case Upholding Content—Based Regulation because It Survives Strict Scrutiny—Tennessee's Ban on Campaign Expression within 100 Feet of Polls: Burson v. Freeman, 504 U.S. 191 (1992)*. This case demonstrates that although a Track One statute is "presumptively" unconstitutional, the presumption can be overcome. Tennessee enacted a law that prohibited displays of campaign materials or electioneering within 100 feet of the entrance to any polling place on election day. The Court upheld the law. Justice Blackmun's plurality opinion explained the result as follows:

> Tennessee asserts that its campaign—free zone serves two compelling interests. First, the state argues that its regulation serves its compelling interest in protecting the right of its citizens to vote freely for the candidates of their choice. Second, Tennessee argues that its restriction protects the right to vote in an election conducted with integrity and reliability.

> The interests advanced by Tennessee obviously are compelling ones. This Court has recognized that the "right to vote freely for the candidate of one's choice is of the essence of a democratic society." *Reynolds v. Sims*.

> [Justice Blackmun here reviewed history from the colonial period to the present, demonstrating that voter intimidation and election fraud historically was common, in that employers, political parties or others observed and interfered with voters, until the enactment of comprehensive secrecy and "campaign-free zone" statutes.]

> [W]e find that this wide-spread and time-tested consensus demonstrates that some restricted zone is necessary in order to serve the state's compelling interest in preventing voter intimidation and election fraud. . . .

> The real question then is how large a restricted zone is permissible or sufficiently tailored. . . .

> [R]equiring proof that a 100-foot boundary is perfectly tailored to deal with voter intimidation and election fraud "would necessitate that a state's political system sustain some level of damages before the legislature could take corrective action. Legislatures [s]hould be permitted to respond to potential deficiencies in the electoral process with foresight ratherthan reactively, provided that the response is reasonable and does not significantly impinge on constitutionally protected rights." [T]hus, we simply do not view the question

whether the 100-foot boundary line could be somewhat tighter as a question of "constitutional dimension". . . .

Justice Kennedy concurred separately. He would have upheld the Tennessee statute because "the justification for the speech restriction is to protect another constitutional right," the right to vote. Justice Scalia also concurred separately, because he though that the Tennessee statute, "though content-based[,] [i]s a reasonable, viewpoint-neutral regulation of a nonpublic forum."

Justice Stevens, joined by Justices O'Connor and Souter, dissented: "The plurality's reasoning combines two logical errors: first, the plurality assumes that a practice's long life itself establishes its necessity; and second, the plurality assumes that a practice that was once necessary remains necessary until it is ended."

(5) *Justice Kennedy's Rejection of "Balancing" (Even the Strict Scrutiny Type) in Track One Cases, in Favor of a "Categorical" Approach.* Justice Kennedy rejects balancing approaches in Track One cases, including the strict scrutiny approach illustrated in *Son of Sam* and *Freeman v. Burson.* Instead, he prefers to deal with content—based regulations by recognizing categories of unprotected utterances (such as obscenity) as well as categories requiring accommodation of other interests (such as regulations designed to protect other rights, or time, place, or manner restrictions). This "categories" approach differs from a "balancing" approach in that it arguably prevents even strict scrutiny from resulting in censorship by a content—based regulation. Is this approach more likely to protect expression?

PROBLEM H

REWRITING THE SON OF SAM LAW. Perhaps New York's Son of Sam law could be rewritten as a general turnover law. (A "turnover law" typically supplements execution of judgments by authorizing a court of equity to use injunctions or other equitable relief to reach a debtor's present or future rights to property that is not exempt but cannot readily be levied on by ordinary legal process.) Specifically, the New York Crime Victims Board might be authorized to use turnover methods to reach all present or future "fruits [or 'profits'] of crime," defined as those rights or interests that a convicted or confessed criminal would not have obtained without commission of the crime. This definition would cover Hill's royalties from *Wiseguy*—but it would also cover all other fruits of his crimes, without expressly targeting the content of any expression. Would this approach be constitutional?

TURNER BROADCASTING SYSTEM, INC. v. FEDERAL COMMUNICATIONS COMMISSION, 520 U.S. 180 (1997) (*Turner II*). Congress passed a statute providing that cable television operators "must carry" certain local stations' programs, even if the operators would prefer not to because of economics, preference for other channels, or dislike of the local stations' messages. Turner Broadcasting challenged these "must carry" rules in a Supreme Court decision (*Turner I*) that is dealt with in § 11.06[C]. On remand, the lower court upheld the "must-carry" rules. In this decision, *Turner II*, the Supreme Court, per Justice Kennedy (in a 5-4 decision), affirmed.

The threshold issue addressed by the Court was whether the purpose of the regulation was "unrelated to the suppression of free expression." The Court held three Congressional interests underlying the "must carry" requirements satisfied the "unrelatedness" prong: (1) preserving the benefits of free, over-the-air local broadcasts; (2) promoting widespread dissemination of information from a multiplicity of sources; and (3) promoting fair economic competition in the market for television programming ("the fair economic competition interest"). Although Justice Kennedy's opinion relied primarily on the "fair economic competition" rationale, Justice Breyer's concurrence relied on a combination of the other interests—providing public access to a multiplicity of information sources—to agree with the majority. Having decided the "unrelatedness" issue in favor of the Government, the Court went on to apply a complex, intermediate level of scrutiny to the means used by Congress (i.e., the must-carry regulation). The Court gave deference to Congress's predictions about the effects of future competition in cable television markets.

On the "unrelatedness" issue, Justice O'Connor's dissent, for Justices Scalia, Thomas and Ginsburg concluded that the governmental interests were content-based and, accordingly, that strict scrutiny should have been the applicable standard. Regarding the "unrelatedness" issue, *Turner II* suggests that a broad range of governmental interests may allow the government to avoid strict scrutiny.

[B]   The Overbreadth and Vagueness Doctrines

INTRODUCTORY NOTE

The Overbreadth and Vagueness Doctrines. The overbreadth doctrine limits the degree to which a prohibition of utterances can include expression protected under the first amendment. The vagueness doctrine refers to the notion that an unduly vague statute cannot support criminal conviction. This vagueness principle is one of general application, not confined to the first amendment area. Thus, if a statute is so vague that "[persons] of common intelligence must necessarily guess at its meaning" it is unenforceable. *Connally v. General Construction Co.*, 269 U.S. 385, 391 (1926). The doctrine that the freedom of speech is fundamental or preferred, however, has given rise to stricter vagueness standards.

Relationship Between the Two Doctrines. Although these two doctrines generally are treated as distinct, they have a close relationship. A statute that is vague is likely to be overbroad too, and since legislatures have an incentive to avoid deliberate drafting of overbroad statutes, those that exhibit this vice often also are vague.

"As Applied" Challenges and "Limiting Constructions." Sometimes, a statute that otherwise might be attacked facially as vague or overbroad can be invalidated instead in a particular application. This kind of challenge allows a limiting construction, which may have the effect of acceptably limiting or redefining the statutory coverage.

The Limits of the Vagueness and Overbreadth Doctrines; the Imprecision of Language. The vagueness and overbreadth concepts necessarily are flexible, because it is virtually impossible to draft a statute so that all possibility of improper application is foreclosed. Accordingly, inits modern cases, the Supreme Court has retreated from more extreme statements of the doctrine, upholding statutes in spite of some degree of overbreadth or vagueness. One salient statement of the test, which appears in *Broaderick v. Oklahoma*, below, is that "the overbreadth of a statute must not only be real, but substantial as well, judged in relation to the statute's plainly legitimate sweep," before the statute will be invalidated.

UNITED STATES CIVIL SERVICE COMMISSION v. NATIONAL ASSOCIATION OF LETTER CARRIERS, 413 U.S. 548 (1973). The Hatch Act prohibited federal employees from taking an "active part" in political "management" or in political "campaigns." The statute defined this phrase by reference to existing Civil Service rules in effect in 1940. The purpose of the provision was to avoid a "threat [to] good administration" and to avoid the "danger to the service in that political rather than official effort may earn advancement and to the public in that governmental favor may be channeled through political connections." The Court had previously upheld the Hatch Act in *United Public Workers v. Mitchell*, 330 U.S. 75 (1947). Nevertheless, in response to the arguments of the Letter Carriers, the lower court had held the statute to be both vague and overbroad. The Supreme Court, per Justice White, reversed and upheld the Act:

> As we see it, our task is not to destroy the Act if we can, but to construe it, if consistent with the will of Congress, so as to comport with constitutional limitations. . . .

[T]here might be quibbles about taking an "active part in managing" or about "actively participating in . . . fund raising" or about the meaning of becoming a "partisan" candidate for office; but there are limitations in the English language with respect to being both specific and manageably brief, and it seems to us that although the prohibitions may not satisfy those intent on finding fault at any cost, they are set out in terms that the ordinary person exercising ordinary common sense can sufficiently understand and comply with without sacrifice to the public interest. "[T]he general class of offenses to which [the provisions are] directed is plainly within [their] terms, [and they] will not be struck down as vague, even though marginal cases could be put where doubts might arise. . . ."

It is also important in this respect that the Commission has established a procedure by which an employee in doubt about the validity of a proposed course of conduct may seek and obtain advice from the Commission and thereby remove any doubt there may be as to the meaning of the law, at least insofar as the Commission itself is concerned. . . .

Even if the provisions forbidding partisan campaign endorsements and speech making were to be considered in some respects unconstitutionally overbroad, we would not invalidate the entire statute as the District Court did. The remainder of the statute, as we have said, governs a whole range of easily identifiable and constitutionally proscribable partisan conduct on the part of federal employees, and the extent to which pure expression is impermissibly threatened, if at all, . . . does not in our view make the statute substantially overbroad and so invalid on its face. . . .

Justice Douglas, joined by Justices Brennan and Marshall, dissented: "The Act incorporates over 3,000 rulings of the Civil Service Commission between 1886 and 1940 and many hundreds of rulings since 1940. But even with that gloss on the Act, the critical phrases lack precision." Some acts prohibited by the regulations, said the dissenters, were "pregnant with ambiguity" (for example, a provision concerning "participat[ing] fully in public affairs, except as prohibited by law, in a manner which does not materially compromise").

NOTES AND QUESTIONS

(1) *Vagueness Doctrine Used to Strike Down a Municipal "Anti-Gang" Ordinance: City of Chicago v. Morales, 527 U.S. 41 (1999).* In the *Morales* case, the City of Chicago passed an anti-loitering ordinance as part of a program to combat gang crime and violence. The Chicago ordinance required a police officer, on observing any person that the officer reasonably believed to be a criminal gang member loitering in any public place with one or more other persons, to order all such persons to disperse and made failure to disperse promptly a violation of the ordinance. In three years, over 89,000 dispersal orders were issued by police and over 42,000 people were arrested. The ordinance was challenged on overbreadth [below] and vagueness grounds. The Supreme Court, in a plurality opinion by Justice Stevens, held that the ordinance was not overbroad, but that it violated due process by being impermissibly vague. The Court held, first, that loitering is part of the "liberty" interest protected by the Due Process Clause. The Court then concluded that the anti-loitering ordinance was vague for two reasons: (1) that the ordinance was so standardless that it left the public uncertain as to the conduct it prohibited; and (2) that the ordinance, even as augmented by administrative guidelines, failed to establish minimal guidelines to govern law enforcement.

With concurrences by three Justices, the *Morales* Court was somewhat splintered. Justices Scalia and Thomas (joined by Chief Justice Rehnquist) filed dissents. This application of the vagueness doctrine appeared to rely on the "tighter" standards used where First Amendment interests (here, associational interests) are implicated.

(2) *Policy Considerations and The Vagueness Doctrine: Some Limits on Judicial Review.* The *Morales* decision, and an earlier decision, *Kolander v. Lawson*, 461 U.S. 352 (1983), illustrate the two, somewhat overlapping policy considerations underlying the vagueness doctrine. To avoid vagueness, laws must both: (1) give "fair notice" to a reasonable person regarding the prohibited conduct; and (2) provide enforcement officials with sufficient guidance to avoid discriminatory treatment. It is the second, anti-discretionary, consideration that is often controversial, as in *Morales*. *See generally* Anthony Amsterdam, *The Void-For-Vagueness Doctrine in the Supreme Court*, 109 U. Pa. L. Rev. 67 (1960); David S. Day, *Termination of Parental Rights Statutes and the Void For Vagueness Doctrine: A Successful Attack on the Parens Patriae Rationale*, 16 J. of Fam. Law 213 (1977).

BROADERICK v. OKLAHOMA
413 U.S. 601 (1973)

Mr. Justice White delivered the opinion of the court.

§ 818 of Oklahoma's Merit System of Personnel Administration Act contained provisions that paralleled the Hatch Act, which was considered in *Letter Carriers*, above. As the Court stated, "Without question, a broad range of political activities and conduct is proscribed [to state employees] by the section." Oklahoma public employees challenged two parts of the statute. One of the contested provisions provided that "[n]o employee in the classified service . . . shall, directly or indirectly, solicit, receive, or in any manner be concerned in soliciting or receiving any . . . contribution for any political organization, candidacy or other political purposes." The other challenged paragraph provided that no employee "shall be a member of any national, state, or local committee of a political party, or an officer or member of a committee of a partisan political club, or a candidate for nomination or election to any paid public office." The latter paragraph further prohibited employees from "tak[ing] part in the management or affairs of any political party or any political campaign, except to exercise his right as a citizen privately to express his opinion and to cast his vote." State employees, although conceding that Oklahoma constitutionally could restrict partisan political conduct of state employees, challenged these provisions as unconstitutionally vague and overbroad.

[The Court began by citing *Connally v. General Construction Co.*, 269 U.S. 385, 391 (1926), which held that a statute is unconstitutionally vague if ["persons] of common intelligence must necessarily guess at its meaning." It also quoted its holding in *Letter Carriers*, above: "There are limitations in the English language with respect to being both specific and manageably brief. . . ."]

[M]oreover, even if the outermost boundaries of § 818 may be imprecise, any such uncertainty has little relevance here, where appellants' conduct falls squarely within the "hard core" of the statute's proscriptions and appellants concede as much.

[Having rejected the vagueness challenge, the Court addressed the overbreadth claim.] Appellants assert that § 818 has been construed as applying to such allegedly protected political expression as the wearing of political buttons or the displaying of bumper stickers. But appellants did not engage in any such activity. They are charged with actively engaging in partisan political activities—including the solicitation of money—among their co-workers for the benefit of their superior. Appellants concede—and correctly so, *see Letter Carriers, supra*—that § 818 would be constitutional as applied to this type of conduct. They nevertheless maintain that the statute is overbroad and purports to reach protected, as well as unprotected conduct, and must therefore be struck down on its face and held to be incapable of any constitutional application. We do not believe that the overbreadth doctrine may appropriately be invoked in this manner here. . . .

It has long been recognized that the First Amendment needs breathing space and that statutes attempting to restrict or burden the exercise of First Amendment rights must be narrowly drawn and represent a considered legislative judgment that a particular mode of expression has to give way to other compelling needs of society. [A]s a corollary, the Court has altered its traditional rules of standing to permit—in the First Amendment area—"attacks on overly broad statuteswith no requirement that the person making the attack demonstrate that his own conduct could not be regulated by a statute drawn with the requisite narrow specificity." Litigants, therefore, are permitted to challenge a statute not because their own rights of free expression are violated, but because of a judicial prediction or assumption that the statute's very existence may cause others not before the court to refrain from constitutionally protected speech or expression.

Such claims of facial overbreadth have been entertained in cases involving statutes which, by their terms, seek to regulate "only spoken words." . . . Overbreadth attacks have also been allowed where the Court thought rights of association were ensnared in statutes which, by their broad sweep, might result in burdening innocent associations. Facial overbreadth claims have also entertained where statutes, by their terms, purport to regulate the, and manner of expressive or communicative conduct, . . . and where such conduct has required official approval under laws that delegated standardless discretionary power to local functionaries, resulting in virtually unreviewable prior restraints on First Amendment rights. . . .

The consequence of our departure from traditional rules of standing in the First Amendment area is that any enforcement of a statute thus placed at issue is totally forbidden until and unless a limiting construction or partial invalidation so narrows it as to remove the seeming threat or deterrence to constitutionally protected expression. Application of the overbreadth doctrine in this manner is, manifestly, strong medicine. It has been employed by the Court sparingly and only as a last resort. Facial overbreadth has not been invoked when a limiting construction has been or could be placed on the challenged statute. [E]qually important, overbreadth claims, if entertained at all, have been curtailed when invoked against ordinary criminal laws that are sought to be applied to protected conduct. . . .

. . . Although such laws, if too broadly worded, may deter protected speech to some unknown extent, there comes a point where that effect—at best a prediction—cannot, with confidence, justify invalidating a statute on its face and so prohibiting a State from enforcing the statute against conduct that is admittedly within its power to proscribe.

[T]o put the matter another way, particularly where conduct and not merely speech is involved, we believe that the overbreadth of a statute must not only be real, but substantial as well, judged in relation to the statute's plainly legitimate sweep. It is our view that § 818 is not substantially overbroad and that whatever overbreadth may exist should be cured through case-by-case analysis of the fact situations to which its sanctions, assertedly, may not be applied.

Unlike ordinary breach-of-the-peace statutes or other broad regulatory acts, § 818 is directed, by its terms, at political expression which if engaged in by private persons would plainly be protected by the First and Fourteenth Amendments. But at the same time, § 818 is not a censorial statute, directed at particular groups or viewpoints. [T]he statute, rather, seeks to regulate political activity in an even-handed and neutral manner. As indicated, such statutes have in the past been subject to a less exacting overbreadth scrutiny. Moreover, the fact remains that § 818 regulates a substantial spectrum of conduct that is as manifestly subject to state regulation as the public peace or criminal trespass. . . .

[A]ppellants further point to the Board's interpretive rules purporting to restrict such allegedly protected activities as the wearing of political buttons or the use of bumper stickers. It may be that such restrictions are impermissible and that § 818 may be susceptible of some other improper applications. But, as presently construed, we do not believe that § 818 must be discarded *in toto* because some persons' arguably protected conduct may or may not be caught or chilled by thestatute. Section 818 is not substantially overbroad and is not, therefore, unconstitutional on its face.

Affirmed.

MR. JUSTICE DOUGLAS, dissenting.

If this were a regulation of business or commercial matters the Court's citation of *Connally v. General Construction Co.* would be apt. . . .

But the problem here concerns not commerce but the First Amendment. The First Amendment goes further than protecting a person for "privately" expressing his opinion. Public as well as private discourse is included; and the emphasis in § 818, par. 7, that *private* expression of views is tolerated emphasizes that public expression is not tolerated.

MR. JUSTICE BRENNAN, with whom MR. JUSTICE STEWART and MR. JUSTICE MARSHALL join, dissenting.

[F]or the purposes of this decision, the Court assumes—perhaps even concedes—that the statute at issue here sweeps too broadly, barring speech and conduct that are constitutionally protected. [N]evertheless, the Court rejects appellants' contention that the statute is unconstitutional on its face, reasoning that "where conduct and not merely speech is involved, . . . the overbreadth of a statute must not only be real, but substantial as well, judged in relation to the statute's plainly legitimate sweep. . . .

[I]n *Letter Carriers*, the Court concluded that the terms could be defined by reference to a complex network of Civil Service Commission regulations developed over many years and comprehensively restated in 1970. . . .

By contrast, the critical phrase of the Oklahoma Act—no employee shall "take part in the management or affairs of any political party or in any political campaign"—is left almost wholly undefined. . . .

Although the Court does not expressly hold that the statute is vague and overbroad, it does assume not only that the ban on the wearing of badges and buttons may be "impermissible," but also that the Act "may be susceptible of some other improper applications." Under principles that I had thought were established beyond dispute, that assumption requires a finding that the statute is unconstitutional on its face. . . .

NOTES AND QUESTIONS

(1) *Defining Unconstitutional Overbreadth: It Must "Not Only Be Real, but Substantial as Well, Judged in Relation to the Statute's Plainly Legitimate Sweep."* What does the majority's test mean? It appears to say that unconstitutionality is relative. On the one hand, a tiny incursion upon protected speech is tolerable if it is the byproduct of a statute that targets a much larger range of unprotected conduct; but on the other hand, if the prohibition of speech becomes significant enough to be "substantial" in comparison to the unprotected conduct that it also covers, then the statute is unconstitutional. Note that this test has the virtue of discouraging statutes targeted at protected content, because the government can achieve this objective only by proscribing a much larger range of unprotected content. The majority's test appears to be based upon a frank recognition that no statute is perfect. The dissent of Justice Brennan, however, saysthat establishing that the statute is susceptible to some amount of impermissible application "requires a finding that the statute is unconstitutional on its face." Which is the better approach?

(2) *The Preference for Limiting Constructions and "the Normal Rule That Partial Rather than Facial Invalidation Is the Required Course": Brockett v. Spokane Arcades,*

472 U.S. 491 (1985). In *Broaderick,* the majority implies that there is a preference for invalidating particular applications of a statute when they appear, rather than invalidating the entire statute on its face. In *Brockett,* the Court made this preference more definite. The Court of Appeals had struck down an entire state statute on its face because the statute prohibited not only obscene materials, but also those that incited "lust." The Supreme Court reversed; although the statute was indeed overbroad, it should be subjected to a limiting construction that salvaged all but the part that covered protected speech that incited lust:

> Facial invalidation of the statute was . . . improvident. We call to mind two of the cardinal rules governing the federal courts: "[O]ne, never to anticipate a question of constitutional law in advance of the necessity of deciding it; the other, never to formulate a rule of constitutional law broader than is required by the precise facts to which it is to be applied". . . .

> The cases before us are ones governed by the normal rule that partial rather than facial invalidation is the required course. The Washington statute was faulted by the court of appeals only because it reached material that incited normal as well as healthy interest in sex. . . . Unless there are countervailing considerations, the Washington law should have been invalidated only insofar as the word "lust" is to be understood as reaching protected materials. . . .

For a more recent application of the Court's overbreadth doctrine, *see Los Angeles Police Department v. United Reporting Publishing Corp.*, 528 U.S. 32 (1999), rejecting a "facial challenge" to a California statute regulating commercial users' access to arrestee addresses in police records.

§ 11.04 UNPROTECTED SPEECH (OR SPEECH "THAT IS NOT PROTECTED SPEECH")

[A] Unprotected Speech Categories: An Overview

INTRODUCTORY NOTE

Although the text of the free speech clause does not contain any exceptions, certain types of speech (or, to use the *Chaplinsky* language, "certain well-defined and narrowly limited classes of speech") were considered exceptions to the norm of heightened protection. Instead of receiving heightened judicial protection, these types of speech only received rational basis scrutiny. It is in this regard that these types of speech are doctrinally labeled as "unprotected speech."

CHAPLINSKY v. NEW HAMPSHIRE, 315 U.S. 568 (1942). The defendant was accused of having addressed a city official, face to face, as a "racketeer" and a "damned fascist." He was convicted under a city ordinance that made it a crime to "address any offensive, derisive or annoying word to any other person who is lawfully in a street or other public place. . . ." The New Hampshire courts upheld the conviction. The Supreme Court, per Justice Murphy, rejected defendant's constitutional challenge to the statute and affirmed:

> [I]t is well understood that the right of free speech is not absolute at all times and under all circumstances. There are certain well-defined and narrowly limited classes of speech, the prevention and punishment of which has never been thought to raise any constitutional problem. These include the lewd and obscene, the profane, the libelous, and the insulting or "fighting words"—those which by their very utterance inflict injury or tend to incite an immediate breach of the peace. [S]uch utterances are no essential part of any exposition of ideas, and are of such slight social value as a step to truth that any benefit that may be derived from them is clearly outweighed by the social interest in order and morality. "Resort to epithets or personal abuse is not in any proper sense

communication of information or opinion safeguarded by the Constitution, and its punishment as a criminal act would raise no question under that instrument." . . .

On the authority of its earlier decisions, the state court declared that the statute's purpose was to preserve the public peace, no words being "forbidden except such as have a direct tendency to cause acts of violence by the person to whom, individually, the remark is addressed." It was further said: "The word 'offensive' is not to be defined in terms of what a particular addressee thinks. . . . The test is what men of common intelligence would understand would be words likely to cause an average addressee to fight. [T]he statute, as construed, does no more than prohibit the face-to-face words plainly likely to cause a breach of the peace by the addressee, words whose speaking constitute a breach of the peace by the speaker-including 'classical fighting words' . . . and other disorderly words, including profanity, obscenity and threats."

NOTES AND QUESTIONS

(1) *Unprotected Speech: The Chaplinsky List.* The *Chaplinsky* Court held that there were "certain well-defined and narrowly limited classes of speech" that were not protected by heightened judicial scrutiny (from either of the two Tracks). The Court provided a listing ("the *Chaplinsky* List") of the categories of unprotected speech: "the lewd and obscene, the profane, the libelous, and the insulting or 'fighting words' . . . ." The *Chaplinsky* List has been changed over the years: some categories have gained protected status while new categories of unprotected speech (*e.g.,* child porn and "true threats") have been added to the *Chaplinsky* List.

(2) *Unprotected Speech: The Chaplinsky Standard.* In addition to providing a list, the *Chaplinsky* Court identified the standard for determining a category of unprotected speech: "[S]uch utterances are of no essential part of any exposition of ideas, and are of such slight social value as a step to truth that any benefit that may be derived from them is clearly outweighed by the social interest in order and morality." This standard was used by the Court in the *Ferber* decision to hold that child pornography is an unprotected category; it used by the Court in *Texas v. Johnson* to hold that flag-burning was, under the circumstances, not unprotected speech.

It is important to remember that there is a significant doctrinal distinction between "unprotected speech" and "speech that is ultimately not protected." For example, in the *Burson* decision, political campaign speech within 100 of a polling place was *ultimately not protected* because the government could satisfy strict scrutiny. This is very different than saying, in the case of "unprotected speech," the government need only satisfy rational basis. *See generally* U.S. DEPT. OF JUSTICE, *Final Report of the Attorney General's Commission on Pornography* 39 (Rutledge Hill ed., 1986) (Fredrick Schauer).

[B] Obscenity

[1] Development of the Basic Doctrine

ROTH v. UNITED STATES, 354 U.S. 476 (1957). Roth was convicted under the federal obscenity statute, which then covered every "obscene, lewd, lascivious, or filthy" communication. Alberts was convicted under a parallel California statute. The court, per Justice Brennan, upheld the convictions:

The dispositive question is whether obscenity is utterance within the area of protected speech and press. Although this is the first time the question has been squarely presented to this court, . . . expressions found in numerous opinions indicate that this court has always assumed that obscenity is not protected [citing *Chaplinsky v. New Hampshire* and other cases]. . . .

All ideas having even the slightest redeeming social importance-unorthodox ideas, controversial ideas, even ideas hateful to the prevailing climate of opinion-have the full protection of the guarantees [of freedom of speech and press]. [B]ut implicit in the history of the first amendment is the rejection of obscenity as utterly without redeeming social importance. . . .

However, sex and obscenity are not synonymous. Obscene material is material which deals with sex in a manner appealing to prurient interests. The portrayal of sex, *e.g.*, in art, literature, and scientific works, is not itself sufficient reason to deny material the constitutional protection of freedom of speech and press. . . .

The early leading standard of obscenity allowed material to be judged merely by the effect of an isolated excerpt upon particularly susceptible persons. *Regina v. Hicklin*, [1868] L.R. 3 Q.B. 360. Some American courts adopted this standard, but later decisions have rejected it and substituted this test: Whether to the average person, applying contemporary community standards, the dominant theme of the material taken as a whole appeals to prurient interests. The *Hicklin* test . . . might well encompass material legitimately treating with sex, and so it must be rejected. . . .

Chief Justice Warren concurred in the result only, emphasizing that "the conduct of the defendant is the central issue, not the obscenity of a book or picture," and stating that he concurred only because proof of scienter was required under both statutes (each required that the conduct be "knowingly" or "willfully" engaged in). Justice Harlan dissented from Roth's conviction, although not that of Alberts, emphasizing that the "disarming generalizations" made by the majority concealed a "number of problems," including the issue whether the court had an independent constitutional duty to review the material.

Finally, Justice Douglas, joined by Justice Black, dissented:

I would give the broad sweep of the first amendment full support. I have the same confidence in the ability of our people to reject noxious literature as I have in their capacity to sort out the true from the false in theology, economics, politics, or any other field.

NOTES AND QUESTIONS

(1) *The Three-Part Test of Roth-and Its Survival, in Altered Form In Later Cases.* *Roth* tests obscenity by whether the material (1) is "utterly without redeeming social importance," (2) "deals with sex in a manner appealing to prurient interest," and (3) taken as a whole, "offend[s] the common conscience of the community by present-day standards." The elements of this three-part test have survived, in altered form, in the Supreme Court's later obscenity decisions. For a comparative view, *see* Davidow, *Obscenity Laws in England and the United States: A Comparative Analysis*, 56 NEB. L. REV. 249 (1977).

(2) *The "Prurient" Interest Standard.* The concept of "prurient" interest is central to the definition of obscenity, and the Court, recognizing that it might otherwise contain an element of ambiguity, quoted a dictionary definition: "Itching; longing; uneasy with desire or longing; of persons, having itching, morbid, or lascivious longings; of desire, curiosity or propensity, lewd. . . ." It also quoted the Model Penal Code definition: "A shameful or morbid interest in nudity, sex, or excretion [that] goes substantially beyond customary limits of candor in description or representation of such matters. . . ." How significant is the problem of ambiguity in the word "prurient," and do these definitions provide helpful guidance?

(3) *Scienter, or Knowledge of Obscene Contents, as a Requirement for Conviction: Smith v. California, 361 U.S. 147 (1959).* Chief Justice Warren, in *Roth*, emphasized the requirement of defendant's conduct, and the requirement that that conduct be commit-

ted knowingly. The state might be tempted to regard this requirement as posing an impossible barrier to conviction, since it might be difficult to prove that a bookseller knew the contents of the hundreds of books he sold. In *Smith*, California enacted a statute that made it clear that knowledge was not a requirement. The Court held the statute unconstitutional.

(4) *The "I Know It When I See It" Test— And the Court's Self-Imposed Duty of "Independent" Review of the Questioned Materials: Jacobellis v. Ohio, 378 U.S. 184 (1964).* In *Jacobellis*, the Court observed that "in obscenity cases, as in all others involving rights derived from the first amendment guarantee of free expression, this Court cannot avoid making an independent constitutional judgment . . . as to whether the material involved in constitutionally protected." Therefore, the allegedly obscene material must be made a part of the record of conviction-and the Court must view it itself. After this kind of review, the *Jacobellis* Court pronounced the material in question not obscene.

> In a famous concurring opinion, Justice Stewart proposed his own test:

> I have reached the conclusion, which I think is confirmed at least by negative implication, in the Court's decisions since *Roth* . . ., that under the first and fourteenth amendments criminal laws in this area are constitutionally limited to hard-core pornography. I shall not today attempt further to define the kinds of material I understand to be embraced within that shorthand description; and perhaps I could never succeed in intelligibly doing so. But I know it when I see it, and the motion picture involved in this case is not that.

Perhaps the truest criterion for a constitutional "test" is whether the words make judges categorize each case accurately. In that regard, is Justice Stewart's pornography test— *i.e.*, only "hard core" pornography qualifies, and you know it when you see it-a useful one?

(5) *The "Utterly Without Redeeming Social Importance" Element of the Test and the "Fanny Hill" Case: A Book Named John Cleland's Memoirs of a Woman of Pleasure v. Attorney General, 383 U.S. 413 (1966).* In the *Memoirs* case, which concerned a book popularly known as "Fanny Hill," the Court (per Justice Brennan) applied the three different elements of the Roth test independently. Therefore, even if it appealed to the prurient interest, the book was not obscene, because it had at least some artistic value. However, the *Memoirs* case also caused another issue to arise. If the material must be proved to be "utterly" without redeeming social importance, and if even the most infinitesimal glimmer of artistic or literary value salvages it, how can the jury ever find obscenity beyond a reasonable doubt?

NOTE ON *REDRUP v. NEW YORK* AND ITS AFTERMATH

The Court Throws up Its Hands: Redrup v. New York, 386 U.S. 767 (1967). A year after *Fanny Hill*, the Court found itself seized with a paralysis produced by fragmentation and disagreement in the application of the *Roth-Memoirs* test. The short per curiam opinion in *Redrup v. New York* contained the following:

> Two members of the Court have consistently adhered to the view that a state is utterly without power to suppress, control, or punish the distribution of any writings or pictures on the grounds of their "obscenity." A third has held to the opinion that a state's power in this area is narrowly limited to a distinct and clearly identifiable class of material. Others have subscribed to a not dissimilar standard [consisting of the three-part *Roth* test, as refined in *Memoirs*]. Another Justice has not viewed the "social value" element as an independent factor in the judgment of obscenity. Whichever of these constitutional views is brought to bear upon the cases before us, it is clear that the judgment cannot stand.

The Aftermath of Redrup. At least thirty-one subsequent cases followed *Redrup*, reversing obscenity determinations without reasoning or consensus. *See Paris Adult Theatre I v. Slaton*, 413 U.S. 49, 82 (1973).

The Court Redefines the Elements of the Three-Part Test: Miller v. California, below. Finally, the Supreme Court restructured the *Roth-Memoirs* test is such a way as to make it practical to identify obscenity. There are several redefinitions, but one of the most important is the transformation of the "utterly without redeeming social importance" element, which probably was the most difficult hurdle for proof of obscenity, into the question "whether the work, taken as a whole, lacks serious literary, artistic, political, or scientific value," a test that was intended to draw a sharper line.

MILLER v. CALIFORNIA
413 U.S. 15 (1973)

Mr. Chief Justice Burger delivered the opinion of the Court. . . .

Appellant conducted [an unsolicited] mass mailing campaign to advertise the sale of illustrated books, euphemistically called "adult" material. After a jury trial, he was convicted of violating [a section of the] California Penal Code by knowingly distributing obscene matter. . . .

The brochures advertised four books entitled "Intercourse," "Man-Woman," "Sex Orgies Illustrated," and "An Illustrated History of Pornography," and a film entitled "Marital Intercourse." [P]rimarily they consist of pictures and drawings very explicitly depicting men and women in groups of two or more engaging in a variety of sexual activities, with genitals often prominently displayed. . . .

While *Roth* presumed "obscenity" to be "utterly without redeeming social importance," *Memoirs* required that to prove obscenity it must be affirmatively established that the material is "*utterly* without redeeming social value." Thus, even as they repeated the words of *Roth*, the *Memoirs* plurality produced a drastically altered test that called on the prosecution to prove a negative, *i.e.*, that the material was "*utterly* without redeeming social value"—a burden virtually impossible to discharge under our criminal standards of proof. . . .

Apart from the initial formulation in the *Roth* case, no majority of the Court has at any given time been able to agree on a standard to determine what constitutes obscene, pornographic material subject to regulation under the States' police power. *See, e.g., Redrup v. New York.* . . .

This much has been categorically settled by the Court, that obscene material is unprotected by the First Amendment. [W]e acknowledge, however, the inherent dangers of undertaking to regulate any form of expression. [A]s a result, we now confine the permissible scope of such regulation to works which depict or describe sexual conduct. That conduct must be specifically defined by the applicable state law, as written or authoritatively construed. A state offense must also be limited to works which, taken as a whole, appeal to the prurient interest in sex, which portray sexual conduct in a patently offensive way, and which, taken as a whole, do not have serious literary, artistic, political, or scientific value.

The basic guidelines for the trier of fact must be: (a) whether "the average person, applying contemporary community standards" would find that the work, taken as a whole, appeals to the prurient interest, (b) whether the work depicts or describes, in a patently offensive way, sexual conduct specifically defined by the applicable state law; and (c) whether the work, taken as a whole, lacks serious literary, artistic, political, or scientific value. We do not adopt as a constitutional standard the "*utterly* without redeeming social value" test of *Memoirs;* that concept has never commanded the adherence of more than three Justices at one time. . . .

We emphasize that it is not our function to propose regulatory schemes for the States. That must await their concrete legislative efforts. It is possible, however, to give a few plain examples of what a state statute could define for regulation under part (b) of the standard announced in this opinion, *supra*:

(a) Patently offensive representations or descriptions of ultimate sexual acts, normal or perverted, actual or simulated.

(b) Patently offensive representation or descriptions of masturbation, excretory functions, and lewd exhibition of the genitals.

Sex and nudity may not be exploited without limit by films or pictures exhibited or sold in places of public accommodation any more than live sex and nudity can be exhibited or sold without limit in such public places. At a minimum, prurient, patently offensive depiction or description of sexual conduct must have serious literary, artistic, political, or scientific value to merit First Amendment protection. [F]or example, medical books for the education of physicians and related personnel necessarily use graphic illustrations and descriptions of human anatomy. In resolving the inevitably sensitive questions of fact and law, we must continue to rely on the jury system, accompanied by the safeguards that judges, rules of evidence, presumption of innocence, and other protective features provide, as we do with rape, murder, and a host of other offenses against society and its individual members. [P]aradoxically, Mr. Justice Brennan indicates that suppression of unprotected obscene material is permissible to avoid exposure to unconsenting adults, as in this case, and to juveniles, although he gives no indication of how the division between protected and nonprotected materials may be drawn with greater precision for these purposes than for regulation of commercial exposure to consenting adults only. Nor does he indicate where in the Constitution he finds the authority to distinguish between a willing "adult" one month past the state law age of majority and a willing "juvenile" one month younger.

Under the holdings announced today, no one will be subject to prosecution for the sale or exposure of obscene materials unless these materials depict or describe patently offensive "hard core" sexual conduct specifically defined by the regulating state law, as written or construed. We are satisfied that these specific prerequisites will provide fair notice. [I]f the inability to define regulated materials with ultimate, god-like precision altogether removes the power of the States or the Congress to regulate, then "hard core" pornography may be exposed without limit to the juvenile, the passerby, and the consenting adult alike, as, indeed, Mr. Justice Douglas contends. . . .

Mr. Justice Brennan also emphasizes "institutional stress" in justification of his change of view. [B]ut no amount of "fatigue" should lead us to adopt a convenient "institutional" rationale-an absolutist, "anything goes" view of the First Amendment-because it will lighten our burdens. . . .

Under a National Constitution, fundamental First Amendment limitations on the powers of the States do not vary from community to community, but this does not mean that there are, or should or can be, fixed, uniform national standards of precisely what appeals to the "prurient interest" or is "patently offensive." [W]hen triers of fact are asked to decide whether "the average person, applying contemporary community standards" would consider certain materials "prurient," it would be unrealistic to require that the answer be based on some abstract formulation. The adversary system, with lay jurors as the usual ultimate factfinders in criminal prosecutions, has historically permitted triers of fact to draw on the standards of their community, guided always by limiting instructions on the law. . . .

We conclude that neither the State's alleged failure to offer evidence of "national standards," nor the trial court's charge that the jury consider state community standards, were constitutional errors. . . .

It is neither realistic nor constitutionally sound to read the First Amendment as requiring that the people of Maine or Mississippi accept public depiction of conduct found tolerable in Las Vegas, or New York City. . . .

There is no evidence, empirical or historical, that the stern 19th century American censorship of public distribution and display of material relating to sex, *see Roth v. United States*, in any way limited or affected expression of serious literary, artistic, political, or scientific ideas. We do not see the harsh hand of censorship of ideas—good or bad, sound or unsound—and "repression" of political liberty lurking in every state regulation of commercial exploitation of human interest in sex. . . .

MR. JUSTICE DOUGLAS, dissenting. . . .

[O]bscenity—which even we cannot define with precision-is a hodge-podge. To send men to jail for violating standards they cannot understand, construe, and apply is a monstrous thing to do in a Nation dedicated to fair trials and due process. . . .

MR. JUSTICE BRENNAN, with whom MR. JUSTICE STEWART and MR. JUSTICE MARSHALL join, dissenting.

In my dissent in *Paris Adult Theatre I v. Slaton* [immediately following, below], I noted that I had no occasion to consider the extent of state power to regulate the distribution of sexually oriented material to juveniles or the offensive exposure of such material to unconsenting adults.

[S]ince my view in *Paris Adult Theatre* I represents a substantial departure from the course of our prior decisions, and since the state courts have as yet had no opportunity to consider whether a "readily apparent construction suggests itself as a vehicle for rehabilitating the [statute] in a single prosecution," [I] would reverse the judgment of the Appellate Department of the Superior Court [in this case] and remand the case for proceedings not inconsistent with this opinion.

PARIS ADULT THEATRE I v. SLATON, 413 U.S. 49 (1973). In this companion case to *Miller v. California* [above], defendants commercially displayed two films, "Magic Mirror" and "It All Comes Out in the End," characterized by the state supreme court as "hard-core pornography" leaving "little to the imagination." The exhibition was in a conventional, inoffensive theater, with signs warning, "Adult theater You must be 21 and able to prove it. If viewing the nude body offends you, please do not enter." The Court, per Chief Justice Burger, held that "nothing precludes the State of Georgia from the regulation of the allegedly obscene material exhibited [here], provided that the applicable Georgia law . . . meets the first amendment standards set forth in *Miller*." In reaching that holding, the Court rejected the argument that exhibition of obscenity to consenting adults in a closed environment was constitutionally protected:

> We categorically disapprove the theory . . . that obscene, pornographic films acquire a constitutional immunity from state regulation simply because they are exhibited for consenting adults only. . . .

> In particular, we hold that there are legitimate state interests at stake in stemming the tide of commercialized obscenity, even assuming it is feasible to enforce effective safeguards against exposure to juveniles and to passersby. [T]hese include the interest of the public in the quality of life and the total community environment, the tone of commerce in the great city centers and, possibly the public safety itself. The Hill-Link Minority Report of the Commission on Obscenity and Pornography indicates that there is at least an arguable correlation between obscene material and crime. Quite apart from sex crimes, however, there remains one problem of large proportions aptly described by Professor Bickel:

>> It concerns the tone of the society, the mode, or to use terms that have perhaps greater currency, the style and quality of life, now and in the future. A man may be entitled to read an obscene book in his room, or expose himself indecently there. . . . [W]e should protect his privacy. But if he demands a right to obtain the books and pictures he wants in the market, and to foregather in public places-discreet, if you will, but accessible to all—with

others who share his taste, then to grant him his right is to affect the world about the rest of us, and to impinge on other privacies. Even supposing that each of us can, if he wishes, effectively avert the eye and stop the ear (which in truth, we cannot), what is commonly read and seen and heard and done intrudes upon us all, wanted or not.

Justice Brennan, joined by Justices Stewart and Marshall, dissented. The dissent extended also to the holding in *Miller v. California*, above:

Our experience with the *Roth* approach has certainly taught us that the outright suppression of obscenity cannot be reconciled with the fundamental principles of the first and fourteenth amendments. . . .

The severe problems arising from the lack of fair notice, from the chill on protected expression, and from the stress imposed on the state and federal judicial machinery persuade me that a significant change in direction is urgently required. I turn, therefore, to the alternatives that are now open.

[T]he approach requiring the smallest deviation from our present course would be to draw a new line between protected and unprotected speech, still permitting the states to suppress all material on the unprotected side of the line. In my view, clarity cannot be obtained pursuant to this approach, except by drawing a line that resolves all doubt in favor of state power and against the guarantees of the first amendment. We could hold, for example, that any depiction or description of human sexual organs . . . is outside the protection of the first amendment. . . . [B]ut such a standard would be appallingly overbroad, permitting the suppression of a vast range of literary, scientific, and artistic masterpieces. . . .

The alternative adopted by the court today recognizes that a prohibition against any depiction or description of human sexual organs could not be reconciled with the guarantees of the first amendment. But the court does retain the view that certain sexually oriented material can be considered obscene and therefore unprotected. . . . *Miller v. California*. . . .

The differences between this formulation and the three-pronged *Memoirs* test are, for the most part, academic. . . .

Ultimately, the reformulation must fail because it still leaves in this court the responsibility of determining in each case whether the materials are protected by the first amendment. . . .

I have also considered the possibility of reducing our own role, and the role of appellate courts generally, in determining whether particular matter is obscene. Thus, we might conclude that juries are best suited to determine obscenity *vel non* and that jury verdicts in this area should not be set aside except in cases of extreme departure from prevailing standards. . . . Plainly, the institutional gain would be more than offset by the unprecedented infringement of first amendment rights.

Finally, I have considered the view, urged so forcefully since 1957 by our brothers Black and Douglas, that the first amendment bars the suppression of any sexually oriented expression. . . . I am convinced that it would achieve [the] desirable goal [of removing uncertainty] only by stripping the states of power to an extent that cannot be justified by the commands of the Constitution. . . .

[At this point, Justice Brennan set out a proposal that would allow regulation of obscenity to prevent exposure to juveniles and unconsenting adults.]

In short, while I cannot say that the interests of the state-apart from the question of juveniles and unconsenting adults-are trivial or non-existent, I am compelled to conclude that these interests cannot justify the substantial damage to constitutional rights and to this nation's judicial machinery that inevitably results from state efforts to bar the distribution even of unprotected material to consenting adults. . . .

Mr. Justice Douglas also dissented, restating his position in *Roth* that rejected "the basic decision that held that 'obscenity' was not protected by the first amendment."

NOTES AND QUESTIONS

(1) *What Has Happened to the Three-Part Test?* You should carefully compare the elements of the three-part test after *Miller* with the elements of the *Roth-Memoirs* test. Has the test become more focused, refined, and specific? Has it become more practicably workable—and, if so, will obscenity prosecutors or obscenity defense lawyers be the ones to applaud it?

(2) *Vagueness.* Both Justice Douglas and the Brennan group of dissenters are concerned about ambiguities in the *Miller* refinement of the test. Consider whether these concerns are well taken. Consider whether it is possible that the test is, indeed, more sharply focused, with a brighter dividing line, but nevertheless poses difficulties because the universe of prohibited materials is larger under *Miller*. If so, is *Miller* a better decision or a worse one than *Roth* and *Memoirs*?

(3) *"Serious" Literary, Artistic, Political, or Scientific Value: Is This a Meaningful Standard?* Imagine that a publisher intersperses commentary on the history of pornography with hard-core photographs otherwise qualifying as obscene. Does the commentary qualify the work, taken as a whole, as having "serious" literary, political, or scientific value?

(4) *An Example of the "Serious . . . Value" Problem—"The Illustrated Presidential Report of the Commission on Obscenity and Pornography": Hamling v. United States, 418 U.S. 87 (1974).* Defendants in *Hamling* mailed a brochure advertising an "Illustrated Version" of the report of a Presidential Commission on Obscenity and Pornography. The brochure had been mailed, unsolicited, to approximately 55,000 persons in various parts of the United States. The Court adopted the following description of the contents of the brochure:

> The folder opens to a full page splash of pictures portraying heterosexual and homosexual intercourse, sodomy, and a variety of deviate sexual acts. Specifically, [there is] a group picture of nine persons, one male engaged in masturbation, a female masturbating two males, [and] two couples engaged in intercourse in reverse fashion while one female participant engages in fellatio of a male; a second group picture of six persons, two males masturbating, two fellatrices practicing the act, each bearing a clear depiction of ejaculated seminal fluid on their faces; two persons with the female engaged in the act of fellatio and the male in female masturbation by hand; two separate pictures of males engaged in cunnilinction; a film strip of six frames depicting lesbian love scenes including a cunnilinguist in action and female masturbation with another's hand and a vibrator, and two frames, one depicting a woman mouthing the penis of a horse and second poising the same for entrance into her vagina.

> [The brochure also contained the following]:

> THANKS A LOT, MR. PRESIDENT. A monumental work of research and investigation has now become a giant of a book. All the facts, all the statistics, presented in the best possible format . . . and . . . completely illustrated in black and white and full color. Every facet of the most controversial public report ever issued is covered in detail.

The Court majority applied *Miller* to affirm these defendants' convictions. Justices Douglas, Brennan, Stewart, and Marshall dissented. Question: Did the brochure, taken as a whole, lack "serious literary, scientific, artistic, or political value?"

(5) *A Case Arguably Demonstrating the Vagueness of Obscenity Tests: Jenkins v. Georgia, 418 U.S. 153 (1974).* A Georgia jury convicted Jenkins, and the Georgia

Supreme Court affirmed, because he exhibited the film "Carnal Knowledge." The film was a major Hollywood production starring Jack Nicholson, Candice Bergen, and Art Garfunkel, and it "appeared on many 'Ten Best' lists for 1971, the year in which it was released. Many but not all of the reviews were favorable." The Supreme Court, per Justice Rehnquist, unanimously reversed: "Appellant's showing of the film 'Carnal Knowledge' is simply not the 'public portrayal of hard-core sexual conduct for its own sake, and for the ensuing commercial gain' which we said was punishable in *Miller*." Does *Jenkins* confirm the validity of the Brennan or Douglas positions that the display of obscenity, at least to consenting adults, should be protected (or does the clarity, brevity and unanimity of the Supreme Court's vindication of Jenkins support the opposite conclusion)?

(6) *The "Tone of Commerce" Argument.* Is there any validity to the argument, set out by the majority in *Paris Art Theatre I* and supported by Bickel's reasoning, that the "tone" of commerce (and of the society) is adversely affected by commercial obscenity? [Imagine that you conduct a general civil litigation practice and may choose, as the building to be located next to your office, either a flower shop or a plain brown adult motion picture theater with appropriate warnings.] A second—and less explicitly developed—theme of the Bickel-*Paris* argument is that "unconsenting adults," in truth, really cannot effectively avoid obscene material by averting their gaze. If prohibitions upon commercial display to consenting adults were removed, would this argument be valid? As a third undercurrent of the argument, consider whether it truly would be possible to avoid exposure to juveniles whose parents do not consent if commercial obscenity were not restricted. Finally, consider the extent to which these interests, if valid, can support the suppression of obscenity in conformity with the first amendment.

PROBLEM I

A FEMINIST ANTI-PORNOGRAPHY ORDINANCE— AMERICAN BOOKSELLERS ASSOCIATION, INC. v. HUDNUT, 771 F.2d 323 (7th Cir. 1985), aff'd, 475 U.S. 1001 (1986). Indianapolis enacted an ordinance defining "pornography" in terms of its discrimination against women. "Pornography" was "the graphic sexually explicit subordination of women, whether in pictures or in words, that also include[d] one or more" of the following:

(1) Women are presented as sexual objects who enjoy pain or humiliation; or (2) Women are presented as sexual objects who experience sexual pleasure in being raped; or (3) Women are presented as sexual objects, tied up or cut up or mutilated or bruised or physically hurt, or as dismembered or truncated or fragmented or severed into body parts; or (4) Women are presented as being penetrated by objects or animals; or (5) Women are presented in scenarios of degradation, injury, abasement, torture, shown as filthy or inferior, bleeding, bruised, or hurt in a context that makes these conditions sexual; or (6) Women are presented as sexual objects for domination, conquest, violation, exploitation, possession, or use, or through postures or positions of servility or submission or display.

The statute also provided that the use of "men, children, or transsexuals in the place of women" would also constitute pornography. "Sexually explicit" was defined to mean actual or simulated intercourse or the uncovered exhibition of the genitals, buttocks or anus. Finally, the ordinance contained prohibitions against "trafficking" in pornography, "coercing" others into performing in pornographic works, "forcing" pornography on anyone, or committing an "assault, physical attack, or injury" in a way "directly caused by specific pornography." The terms of these offenses, in turn, were further defined.

However, the Indianapolis ordinance did not refer to the prurient interest, to offensiveness, or to the standards of the community as the *Roth-Memoirs-Miller* test did. Nor did it depend upon whether any particular work had literary, artistic, political, or scientific value. Its supporters defended these omissions as virtues, arguing that the ordinance was designed to prevent discrimination against women, rather than to vindicate community standards of offensiveness. As one of the principal drafters of the ordinance asked, "[i]f a woman is subjected, why should it matter that the work has other value?" MacKinnon, *Pornography, Civil Rights, and Speech*, 20 HARV. CIV. RTS.-CIV. LIB. L. REV. 1, 21 (1985).

Consider the following questions: (1) Is the ordinance constitutional? (2) If not, why not? (3) Can the premises, or central thrust, of the ordinance be reformulated into another ordinance, differently drawn but retaining the same core values, that would be constitutional?

[The Seventh Circuit held the ordinance unconstitutional, and the Supreme Court affirmed without opinion. The Seventh Circuit began by accepting the premises of the legislation: "Depictions of subordination tend to perpetuate subordination. The subordinate status of women in turn leads to affront and lower pay at work, insult and injury at home, battery and rape on the streets. [T]he bigotry and contempt [pornography] produces, with the acts of aggression it fosters, harm women's opportunities for equality and rights [of all kinds]." The court then squarely rejected this premise as a basis for the prohibition: "Yet this simply demonstrates the power of pornography as speech. All of these unhappy effects depend on mental intermediation. [H]itler's orations affected how some Germans saw Jews. Communism is a world view, not simply a manifesto by Marx and Engels or a set of speeches. [T]he Alien and Sedition Acts passed during the administration of John Adams rested on a sincerely held belief that disrespect for the government leads to social collapse and revolution. . . . Most governments of the world act on this empirical regularity, suppressing critical speech. In the United States, however, the strength of the support for this belief is irrelevant."]

NOTE: CANADA ACCEPTS THE FEMINIST ANTI-PORNOGRAPHY APPROACH

Although the *Hudnut* court rejected the pornography as discrimination against women theory, the highest Court in Canada recently accepted a similar justification for a criminal obscenity law. *Regina v. Butler*, 1 S.C.R. 452 (Can. 1992). Professor MacKinnon declared that Butler was "a stunning victory for women." *See* Daniel O. Conkle, *Harm, Morality, and Feminist Religion: Canada's New—But Not So New— Approach to Obscenity*, 10 CONST. COMM. 105 (1993). Is Canada's approach better?

[2] "Variable" Obscenity and Related Issues

STANLEY v. GEORGIA
394 U.S. 557 (1969)

MR. JUSTICE MARSHALL delivered the opinion of the court.

[By accident, officers executing a warrant to search for suspected bookmaking activities found three reels of sexually explicit film. Defendant was convicted of knowingly possessing obscene matter on this basis. Here, the Court reverses the conviction.]

[W]e do not believe that this case can be decided simply by citing *Roth*. [T]hat holding cannot foreclose an examination of the constitutional implications of a statute forbidding mere private possession of such material.

It is now well established that the Constitution protects the right to receive information and ideas. [M]oreover, in the context of this case—a prosecution for mere possession of printed or filmed matter in the privacy of a person's own home—that right takes on an added dimension. For also fundamental is the right to be free, except in very limited circumstances, from unwanted governmental intrusions into one's privacy. . . .

[I]f the First Amendment means anything, it means that a State has no business telling a man, sitting alone in his own house, what books he may read or what films he may watch. Our whole constitutional heritage rebels at the thought of giving government the power to control men's minds.

[A]nd yet, in the face of these traditional notions of individual liberty, Georgia asserts the right to protect the individual's mind from the effects of obscenity. We are not certain that this argument amounts to anything more than the assertion that the State has the right to control the moral content of a person's thoughts. [N]or is it relevant that obscene materials in general, or the particular films before the Court, are arguably devoid of any ideological content. The line between the transmission of ideas and mere entertainment is much too elusive for this Court to draw, if indeed such a line can be drawn at all. Whatever the power of the state to control public dissemination of ideas inimical to the public morality, it cannot constitutionally premise legislation on the desirability of controlling a person's private thoughts.

Perhaps recognizing this, Georgia asserts that exposure to obscene materials may lead to deviant sexual behavior or crimes of sexual violence. There appears to be little empirical basis for that assertion. But more important, if the State is only concerned about printed or filmed materials inducing antisocial conduct, we believe that in the context of private consumption of ideas and information we should adhere to the view that "[a]mong free men, the deterrents ordinarily to be applied to prevent crime are education and punishment for violations of the law. . . ."

Finally, we are faced with the argument that prohibition of possession of obscene materials is a necessary incident to statutory schemes prohibiting distribution. That argument is based on alleged difficulties of proving an intent to distribute or in producing evidence of actual distribution. We are not convinced that such difficulties exist, but even if they did we do not think that they would justify infringement of the individual's right to read or observe what he pleases. Because that right is so fundamental to our scheme of individual liberty, its restriction may not be justified by the need to ease the administration of otherwise valid criminal laws. . . .

We hold that the First and Fourteenth Amendments prohibit making mere private possession of obscene material a crime. *Roth* and the cases following that decision are not impaired by today's holding. . . .

[The concurring opinions of MR. JUSTICE BLACK and of MR. JUSTICE STEWART, joined by JUSTICES BRENNAN and WHITE, are omitted.]

NOTES AND QUESTIONS

(1) *Did the Court Adequately Assess All of the State's Interests?* If a person privately possessed large amounts of child pornography, would there be an additional State interest at issue? A legislature presumably could conclude that indeterminate numbers of children are forcibly abducted for the purpose of manufacturing such material. In any event, child pornography is produced without the minors' mature consent or parental concurrence. The possessor of the material creates the market for this chain of distribution, and a state well may conclude that it must attack all links in the chain to combat this problem. Is the *Stanley* Court's treatment of the distribution issue convincing?

(2) *Distinguishing Commercial Exploitation: Paris Art Theatre I, above.* After *Stanley*, in the *Paris Art Theatre* case, the Court held that commercial exhibition of an obscene film to consenting adults, even in a closed environment, could constitutionally be prohibited. Can *Paris Art Theatre* be distinguished from *Stanley*?

[C] Certain Types of "Offensive" Speech: Profanity, "Fighting Words" and "Indecent" Speech

[1] Profane Speech

COHEN v. CALIFORNIA
403 U.S. 15 (1971)

Mr. Justice Harlan delivered the opinion of the court.

[Note that the *Chaplinsky* List included profanity as unprotected speech. Cohen wore a jacket bearing the words "Fuck the Draft" inside the Los Angeles County Courthouse and was convicted under California Penal Code § 415 which made it an offense to "maliciously and willfully disturb the peace or quiet of any neighborhood or person . . . [by] . . . offensive conduct. . . ." In affirming the conviction, the California appellate court said: "There were women and children present in the corridor. . . . The defendant testified that he wore the jacket, knowing that the words were on the jacket as a means of informing the public of the depth of his feelings against the Vietnam War and the draft." . . . The California court reasoned that "offensive conduct," including "behavior which has a tendency to provoke *others* to acts of violence or to in turn disturb the peace," could be prohibited. Here, the Supreme Court reverses the conviction.]

The conviction quite clearly rests upon the asserted offensiveness of the *words* Cohen used to convey his message to the public. The only "conduct" which the State sought to punish is the fact of communication. Thus, we deal here with a conviction resting solely upon "speech," not upon any separately identifiable conduct which allegedly was intended by Cohen to be perceived by others as expressive of particular views but which, on its face, does not necessarily convey any message and hence arguably could be regulated without effectively repressing Cohen's ability to express himself. . . .

[F]urther, the State certainly lacks power to punish Cohen for the underlying content of the message the inscription conveyed. At least so long as there is no showing of an intent to incite disobedience to or disruption of the draft, Cohen could not, consistently with the First and Fourteenth Amendments, be punished for asserting the evident position on the inutility or immorality of the draft his jacket reflected.

Appellant's conviction, then, rests squarely upon his exercise of the "freedom of speech" protected from arbitrary governmental interference by the Constitution and can be justified, if at all, only as a valid regulation of the manner in which he exercised that freedom, not as a permissible prohibition on the substantive message it conveys. This does not end the inquiry, of course, for the First and Fourteenth Amendments have never been thought to give absoluteprotection to every individual to speak whenever or wherever he pleases or to use any form of address in any circumstances that he chooses. In this vein, too, however, we think it important to note that several issues typically associated with such problems are not presented here.

In the first place, Cohen was tried under a statute applicable throughout the entire State. Any attempt to support this conviction on the ground that the statute seeks to preserve an appropriately decorous atmosphere in the courthouse where Cohen was arrested must fail in the absence of any language in the statute that would have put appellant on notice that certain kinds of otherwise permissible speech or conduct would nevertheless, under California law, not be tolerated in certain places. . . .

In the second place, as it comes to us, this case cannot be said to fall within those relatively few categories of instances where prior decisions have established the power of government to deal more comprehensively with certain forms of individual expression simply upon a showing that such a form was employed. This is not, for example, an obscenity case. . . .

This Court has also held that the States are free to ban the simple use, without a demonstration of additional justifying circumstances, of so-called "fighting words," those personally abusive epithets which, when addressed to the ordinary citizen, are, as a matter of common knowledge, inherently likely to provoke violent reaction. *Chaplinsky v. New Hampshire.* While the four-letter word displayed by Cohen in relation to the draft is not uncommonly employed in a personally provocative fashion, in this instance it was clearly not "directed to the person of the hearer." . . . Nor do we have here an instance of the exercise of the State's police power to prevent a speaker from intentionally provoking a given group to hostile reaction. *Cf. Feiner v. New York; Terminiello v. Chicago.* . . .

Finally, in arguments before this Court much has been made of the claim that Cohen's distasteful mode of expression was thrust upon unwilling or unsuspecting viewers, and that the State might therefore legitimately act as it did in order to protect the sensitive from otherwise unavoidable exposure to appellant's crude form of protest. Of course, the mere presumed presence of unwitting listeners or viewers does not serve automatically to justify curtailing all speech capable of giving offense. [T]he ability of government, consonant with the Constitution, to shut off discourse solely to protect others from hearing it is, in other words, dependent upon a showing that substantial privacy interests are being invaded in an essentially intolerable manner. Any broader view of this authority would effectively empower a majority to silence dissidents simply as a matter of personal predilections.

In this regard, persons confronted with Cohen's jacket were in a quite different posture than, say, those subjected to the raucous emissions of sound trucks blaring outside their residences. Those in the Los Angeles courthouse could effectively avoid further bombardment of their sensibilities simply by averting their eyes. And, while it may be that one has a more substantial claim to a recognizable privacy interest when walking through a courthouse corridor than, for example, strolling through Central Park, surely it is nothing like the interest in being free from unwanted expression in the confines of one's own home. . . .

Against this background, the issue flushed by this case stands out in bold relief. It is whether California can excise, as "offensive conduct," one particular scurrilous epithet from the public discourse, either upon the theory of the court below that its use is inherently likely to cause violent reaction or upon a more general assertion that the States, acting as guardians of public morality, may properly remove this offensive word from the public vocabulary. . . .

To many, the immediate consequence of [the freedom of speech] may often appear to be only verbal tumult, discord, and even offensive utterance. These are, however, within established limits, in truth necessary side effects of the broader enduring values which the process of open debate permits us to achieve. [W]e cannot lose sight of the fact that, in what otherwise might seem a trifling and annoying instance of individual distasteful abuse of a privilege, these fundamental societal values are truly implicated. That is why "[w]holly neutral futilities . . . come under the protection of free speech as fully as do Keats' poems or Donne's sermons. . . ."

Against this perception of the constitutional policies involved, we discern certain more particularized considerations that peculiarly call for reversal of this conviction. First, the principle contended for by the State seems inherently boundless. How is one to distinguish this from any other offensive word? Surely the State has no right to cleanse public debate to the point where it is grammatically palatable to the most squeamish among us. For, while the particular four-letter word being litigated here is perhaps more distasteful than most of its genre, it is nevertheless true that one man's vulgarity is another's lyric. . . .

Additionally, we cannot overlook the fact, because it is well illustrated by the episode involved here, that much linguistic expression serves a dual communicative function: it conveys not only ideas capable of relatively precise, detached explication, but otherwise inexpressible emotions as well. In fact, words are often chosen as much for their emotive as their cognitive force.

Finally, and in the same vein, we cannot indulge the facile assumption that one can forbid particular words without also running a substantial risk of suppressing ideas in the process. . . .

It is, in sum, our judgment that, absent a more particularized and compelling reason for its actions, the State may not, consistently with the First and Fourteenth Amendments, make the simple public display here involved of this single four-letter expletive a criminal offense. Because that is the only arguably sustainable rationale for the conviction here at issue, the judgment below must be reversed.

MR. JUSTICE BLACKMUN, with whom THE CHIEF JUSTICE and MR. JUSTICE BLACK join, [dissenting]. . . .

Cohen's absurd and immature antic, in my view, was mainly conduct and little speech. [F]urther, the case appears to me to be well within the sphere of *Chaplinsky v. New Hampshire*, 315 U.S. 568 (1942), where Mr. Justice Murphy, a known champion of First Amendment freedoms, wrote for a unanimous bench. As a consequence, this Court's agonizing over First Amendment values seems misplaced and unnecessary.

NOTES AND QUESTIONS

(1) *The Chaplinsky List of "Unprotected" Speech Categories and "Profanity" as Protected Speech: Cohen v. California, 403 U.S. 15 (1971).* The *Cohen* decision tested the continued validity of the *Chaplinsky* assertion that "profane" speech would be considered a category of "unprotected" speech (*i.e.*, could be regulated based on the rational basis standard). Cohen wore a jacket with the words "Fuck the Draft" inside the Los Angeles County Courthouse (but not actually inside the courtroom). He was convicted for "offensive conduct" under a California statute. On appeal, Cohen was represented by Professor Melville Nimmer from UCLA. Cohen testified that he wore the phrase to communicate his "feelings against the Vietnam War and the draft." Cohen's use of the phrase therefore satisfied the *Spence* standard for "speech." The remaining issue was whether the profane/offensive phrase "Fuck the Draft" should be considered as unprotected speech. The Supreme Court, per Justice Harlan, held that "the State may not . . . make the simple public display here involved of this single four-letter expletive a criminal offense." Just because the word was profane or offensive, it could not constitutionally be considered as "unprotected speech."

Justice Blackmun dissented, relying on the speech/conduct distinction that had, in 1971, some followers. Today, after the development of the *Spence* standard and the symbolic speech cases, that theory would not gather many votes—except perhaps Justice Thomas. *See generally* William Cohen, *A Look Back at Cohen v. California*, 34 U.C. L. REV. 1595 (1987).

(2) *The Rationale in Cohen.* The *Cohen* Court was primarily concerned with protecting the free speech of "dissidents" from majoritarian abridgment. The Court concluded that "the State has no right to cleanse public debate to the point where it is grammatically palatable to the most squeamish among us." The Court's rationale was that the government (*i.e.*, the majority) could not be trusted to "cleanse public debate" because "one man's vulgarity is another's lyric." Since free speech was a fundamental right, the majority was not institutionally competent to regulate the individual's decisions about protected speech, including "profane" speech.

(3) *The Cohen Decision and the Goals of the Modern Free Speech Doctrine.* You will recall, from the Chapter's Introductory Notes, that modern free speech doctrine is premised on four goals: (1) the search for truth; (2) the preservation of democratic

self-government; (3) protection of individual self-realization; and (4) providing a "safety valve" for discontent. *See generally* THOMAS EMERSON, THE SYSTEM OF FREEDOM OF EXPRESSION (1970).

It is hard to see how the phrase "Fuck the Draft" serves the search for truth. Moreover, it does not seem that democratic self-government would be greatly impaired by suppression of the phrase at the Courthouse. (Note, however, that suppression in the aggregate does present a risk of undermining collective dissent.) So, *Cohen* is best understood as a self-realization decision.

The controversy regarding the *Cohen* decision focuses primarily on the Court's reliance on the self-realization rationale. Critics of the *Cohen* decision, such as Judge Robert Bork, consider reliance on this goal to be nothing more than an exercise of "moral relativism." *See* ROBERT BORK, THE TEMPTING OF AMERICA (1990). If self-realization would not be a permissible goal for free speech judicial review, then *Cohen* might seem suspect or improperly decided.

These themes will reoccur frequently in this chapter. As you review the many free speech decisions, consider whether those based on the self-realization goal should be abandoned or otherwise marginalized.

(4) *The "Captive Audience" Issue.* The protection of the captive auditor from obnoxious expression is a well established principle of first amendment jurisprudence. It is considered in a later section of this chapter. *See, e.g., Frisby v. Schultz*, in this chapter, below. Can it be argued that people at a courthouse are more properly viewed as even more "captive" than people in their homes, because most people go to the courthouse involuntarily? Did the Court afford inadequate attention to this interest?

[2] Fighting Words and Hate Speech

R.A.V. v. CITY OF ST. PAUL, MINNESOTA
505 U.S. 377 (1992)

JUSTICE SCALIA delivered the opinion of the Court.

[Note that the *Chaplinsky* Court listed "fighting words" as unprotected speech. In the pre-dawn hours of June 21, 1990, petitioner R.A.V. and other teenagers allegedly assembled a crudely-made cross by taping together broken chair legs. They then allegedly burned the cross inside the fenced yard of a black family that lived across the street from the house where R.A.V. was staying. Respondent City of St. Paul charged R.A.V. (then a juvenile) under its Bias-Motivated Crime Ordinance, which provided:

> Whoever places on public or private property a symbol, object, appellation, characterization or graffiti, including, but not limited to, a burning cross or Nazi swastika, which one knows or has reasonable grounds to know arouses anger, alarm or resentment in others on the basis of race, color, creed, religion or gender commits disorderly conduct and shall be guilty of a misdemeanor.

Although the trial court dismissed this charge on the ground that the ordinance was facially invalid under the First Amendment, the Minnesota Supreme Court reversed, holding on the basis of its prior decisions that the modifying phrase "arouses anger, alarm or resentment in others" limited the reach of the ordinance to conduct that amounts to "fighting words," *i.e.*, "conduct that itself inflicts injury or tends to incite immediate violence." The Supreme Court reversed and held the ordinance facially invalid.

[The Court began by recognizing that there are certain "categories of expression" that are "not within the area of constitutionally protected speech," such as obscenity and "fighting words." This "limited categorical approach" had remained an important part of the Court's First Amendment jurisprudence. The Court cited *Chaplinsky* for the proposition that certain kinds of expression are "of such slight social value as a step to truth that any benefit that may be derived from them is clearly outweighed by the social interest in order and morality."

[The Court further explained that "[w]hat [these statements] mean is that these areas of speech can, consistently with the First Amendment, be regulated because of their constitutionally proscribable content (obscenity, defamation, etc.)—not that they are categories of speech entirely invisible to the Constitution, so that they may be made the vehicles for content discrimination unrelated to their distinctively proscribable content." Thus, "the government may proscribe libel; but it may not make the further content discrimination of proscribing only libel critical of the government."

[The Court thus analogized bans on these categories of "unprotected" utterances to content—neutral regulation. Thus, "[f]ighting words are [a]nalogous to a noisy sound truck: [b]oth can be used to convey an idea; but neither has, in and of itself, a claim upon the First Amendment. As with the sound truck, however, so also with fighting words: The government may not regulate use based on hostility—or favoritism—towards the underlying message expressed." The Court then concluded:]

[A]lthough the [o]rdinance [h]as been limited by the Minnesota Supreme Court's construction to reach only those symbols or displays that amount to "fighting words," [it] applies only to "fighting words" that insult, or provoke violence, "on the basis of race, color, creed, religion or gender." Displays containing abusive invective [a]re permissible unless they are addressed to one of the specified disfavored topics. Those who wish to use "fighting words" in connection with other ideas—to express hostility, for example, on the basis of political affiliation, union membership, or homosexuality—are not covered. The First Amendment does not permit St. Paul to impose special prohibitions on those speakers who express views on disfavored subjects. See Simon & Schuster [the Son of Sam case].

In its practical operation, moreover, the ordinance goes even beyond mere content discrimination, to actual viewpoint discrimination. "[F]ighting words" that do not themselves invoke race, color, creed, religion, or gender—aspersions upon a person's mother, for example—would seemingly be usable ad libitum in the placards of those arguing in favor of racial, color, etc. tolerance and equality, but could not be used by that speaker's opponents. One could hold up a sign saying, for example, that all "anti-Catholic bigots" are misbegotten; but not that all "papists" are, for that would insult and provoke violence "on the basis of religion." St. Paul has no such authority to license one side of a debate to fight freestyle, while requiring the other to follow Marquis of Queensbury Rules. What we have here, it must be emphasized, is not a prohibition of fighting words that are directed at certain persons or groups (which would be facially valid if it met the requirements of the Equal Protection Clause); but rather, a prohibition of fighting words that contain (as the Minnesota Supreme Court repeatedly emphasized) messages of "bias-motivated" hatred and in particular, as applied to this case, messages "based on virulent notions of racial supremacy." One must wholeheartedly agree with the Minnesota Supreme Court that "[i]t is the responsibility, even the obligation, of diverse communities to confront such notions in whatever form they appear," but the manner of that confrontation cannot consist of selective limitations upon speech. St. Paul's brief asserts that a general "fighting words" law would not meet the city's needs because only a content—specific measure can communicate to minority groups that the "group hatred" aspect of such speech "is not condoned by the majority." The point of the First Amendment is that majority preferences must be expressed in some fashion other than silencing speech on the basis of its content. . . .

Finally, St. Paul and its amici defend the conclusion of the Minnesota Supreme Court that, [t]his discrimination is nonetheless justified because it is narrowly tailored to serve compelling state interests. Specifically, they assert that the ordinance helps to ensure the basic human rights of members of groups that have historically been subjected to discrimination, including the right of such group members to live in peace where they wish. We do not doubt that these interests are compelling, and that the ordinance can be said to promote them. But the "danger of censorship" presented by a facially content—based statute requires that that weapon be employed only where it is "necessary to serve the asserted [compelling] interest," *Burson v. Freeman*. The existence of adequate content—neutral alternatives thus "undercut[s] significantly" any defenseof such a statute. . . . An ordinance not limited to the favored topics, for example, would have precisely the same beneficial effect. In fact the only interest distinctively served by the content limitation is that of displaying the city council's special hostility towards the particular biases thus singled out. That is precisely what the First Amendment forbids. . . .

JUSTICE WHITE concurred only in the judgment, and was joined by JUSTICES Blackmun, O'CONNOR and (in part) STEVENS:

This Court's decisions have plainly stated that expression falling within certain limited categories so lacks the values the First Amendment was designed to protect that the Constitution affords no protection to that expression. *Chaplinsky v. New Hampshire.* . . .

All of these categories are content based. But the Court has held that the First Amendment does not apply to them because their expressive content is worthless or of de minimis value to society. [T]his categorical approach has provided a principled and narrowly focused means for distinguishing between expression that the government may regulate freely and that which it may regulate on the basis of content only upon a showing of compelling need. Today, however, the Court announces that earlier Courts did not mean their repeated statements that certain categories of expression are "not within the area of constitutionally protected speech." The present Court submits that such clear statements "must be taken in context" and are not "literally true."

To the contrary, those statements meant precisely what they said: The categorical approach is a firmly entrenched part of our First Amendment jurisprudence. . . .

Therefore, the Court's insistence on inventing its brand of First Amendment underinclusiveness puzzles me. The overbreadth doctrine has the redeeming virtue of attempting to avoid the chilling of protected expression, *Broadrick v. Oklahoma;* but the Court's new "underbreadth" creation serves no desirable function. Instead, it permits, indeed invites, the continuation of expressive conduct that in this case is evil and worthless in First Amendment terms, until the city of St. Paul cures the underbreadth by adding to its ordinance a catch—all phrase such as "and all other fighting words that may constitutionally be subject to this ordinance. . . ."

Although I disagree with the Court's analysis, I do agree with its conclusion: The St. Paul ordinance is unconstitutional. However, I would decide the case on overbreadth grounds. . . .

JUSTICE BLACKMUN, although he joined JUSTICE WHITE'S opinion, wrote separately to observe: "I fear that the Court has been distracted from its proper mission by the temptation to decide the issue over 'politically correct speech' and 'cultural diversity,' neither of which is presented here."

JUSTICE STEVENS (joined in part by JUSTICES WHITE and BLACKMUN) concurred only in the judgment:

[I] disagree with both the Court's and part of Justice White's analysis. . . . Unlike the Court, I do not believe that all content—based regulations are equally infirm and presumptively invalid; unlike Justice White, I do not believe that fighting words are wholly unprotected by the First Amendment. To the contrary, I believe our decisions establish a more complex and subtle analysis, one that considers the content and context of the regulated speech, and the nature and scope of the restriction on speech. Applying this analysis and assuming arguendo (as the Court does) that the St. Paul ordinance is not overbroad, I conclude that such a selective, subject—matter regulation on proscribable speech is constitutional. . . .

NOTES AND QUESTIONS

(1) *Is Unprotected Speech Really "Unprotected"?* Justice White argues that the Court's past decisions about traditionally unprotected utterances mean what they say, categorically. But Justice Scalia and those who join him, as well as Justice Stevens, disagree: "unprotected" utterances can be communications, and therefore they sometimes are protected; in any event, they areprotected (according to Justice Scalia) against content or "viewpoint" discrimination. Who is correct?

(2) *Is a "Categorical" Approach Better than a "Balancing" Approach?* Justice White supports his categorical approach by arguing that it is more "principled" than balancing and ultimately protects speech more consistently. Is this an accurate description of the cases you have read? If the balancing analysis requires a fuzzy "consideration of a host of variables," isn't Justice White correct?

(3) *"Underinclusion," "Overinclusion," and the "Substantial Overbreadth" Doctrine.* The *Broadrick* decision (excerpted in a previous section) established the doctrine of substantial overbreadth. Justice White contends that, rather than use this doctrine appropriately, Justice Scalia has invented a new theory of "underinclusion," whereby a regulation that bans unprotected utterances is not valid unless it bans "all" of the category in question; *i.e.*, it is invalid unless it prohibits more speech than the government thought it needed to. Justice Scalia, on the other hand, defends his holding as an application of the familiar presumption against content-based regulation or viewpoint discrimination. Who is correct?

(4) *Motive Can Properly Be a Factor When the Gist of the Offense Is Proscribable Conduct Rather than Expression—"Hate Crimes" Distinguished from "Hate Speech": Wisconsin v. Mitchell, 508 U.S. 476 (1993).* In this case, the Court held that Wisconsin's "hate crimes penalty enhancement" statute did not violate the free speech guarantee. Wisconsin's statute permitted enhancement of the length of a criminal sentence if the convicted defendant had "intentionally selected" the crime victim or the particular property "because of the race, religion, color, disability, sexual orientation, national origin or ancestry of that person or occupant of the property." Wis. Stat. §939. 645 (1) (b). The trial court, in conformity with this statute, had doubled the sentence of black man's assault conviction when the jury found that the assault on a Caucasian victim was motivated by racial animus. The Supreme Court held that Wisconsin could enhance criminal penalties based on the defendant's motive without violating the First Amendment. It distinguished *R.A.V.* on the ground that the Wisconsin statute was "aimed at conduct unprotected by the First Amendment." Is this distinction of *R.A.V.* persuasive? *See generally* Edward J. Eberle, *Hate Speech, Offensive Speech, and Public Discourse in America*, 29 WAKE FOREST L. REV. 1135 (1994) (reviewing *R.A.V.* and suggesting the Court's concern for viewpoint discrimination underlies the use of more rigorous scrutiny in such cases).

(5) *After Mitchell, The Court Strikes Down A Hate Crime Sentence Enhancement Scheme: Apprendi v. New Jersey, 530 U.S. 466 (2000).* In its first decision regarding a hate crime scheme since the 1993 *Mitchell* decision, the Court faced a case where the defendant, a Caucasian male, was charged with a firearms offense after he fired several bullets into a neighboring black family's home. At the request of the prosecution, and over the defense objections, the New Jersey state court determined that the crime had been motivated by racial bias and increased the sentence by two years. The Supreme Court, per Justice Stevens, overturned the sentence enhancement for two reasons. First, the Court decided that the essential finding of bias must be by the jury—not the Judge. Second, the Court held that, in a "hate crime," the crucial determination of bias must be made under the beyond reasonable doubt standard. There were two concurrences and four dissenters with a decision over 70 pages long. The *Apprendi* decision

places constraints on a state's ability to punish "hate crimes," but *Apprendi* does not seem to address the distinction between "hate speech" and "hate crime."

(6) *Racial or Gender Discrimination Laws after R.A.V. and Mitchell: What Effect?* There are numerous laws at all levels of government that prohibit racial and gender discrimination. Virtually all depend upon motives, and some can be triggered at least in part by expression, expressive conduct, or utterances that may or may not be protected in all contexts (a sexual harassment suit alleging an offensive workplace owing to sexually charged utterances is an example). How will the enforcement of such laws be affected, if at all, by *R.A.V.* and *Mitchell?*

PROBLEM J

CAN A SEXUALLY SUGGESTIVE BEER ADVERTISEMENT BE HELD ILLEGAL AS SEXUAL HARASSMENT OF FEMALE BREWERY WORKERS?: "STROH'S ADS TARGETED; BIKINIS AND BEER LEAD TO HARASSMENT AT WORK," ABA JOURNAL, Feb. 1992, at 20. Several female employees of Stroh Brewery Company filed a sexual harassment suit. For the most part, the allegations concerned conduct recognized as illegal, such as offensive touching and sexist comments that pervaded the work environment. What was unusual about the suit was that it also alleged that the company's public advertising was a part of the illegal environment. The suit particularly targeted an ad campaign for Old Milwaukee Beer featuring the "Swedish Bikini Team," a fictional group of scantily dressed women who appear at a men's camping trip in television commercials. The complaints of harassment included the display at the jobsite of posters from the company's own advertising, depicting attractive women.

Question: Can either the posters displayed at the worksite, or the national advertising campaign, be considered as illegally contributing to sexual harassment, consistently with the First Amendment? [The ACLU, through a spokesperson, sided with Stroh, but the lawyer for the plaintiff, noting that she was "into free speech" herself, dismissed the ACLU because it "coddles the Klan, Nazis and pornographers." She added that commercial speech was entitled to a lesser degree of protection than other kinds of expression; that subject is covered in another section, below. The lawsuit ultimately was settled.]

[3] "Indecent" Speech

FCC v. PACIFICA FOUNDATION
438 U.S. 726 (1978)

MR. JUSTICE STEVENS delivered the opinion of the Court (Parts I, II, III, and IV-C) and an opinion in which the CHIEF JUSTICE and MR. JUSTICE REHNQUIST joined (Parts IV-A and IV-B).

[Pacifica's radio station broadcast a twelve-minute monologue entitled "Filthy Words" by humorist George Carlin at about two o'clock in the afternoon on Tuesday, October 30, 1973. The monologue referred to the "the words you couldn't say on the public, ah, airways, um, the ones you definitely wouldn't say, ever." Carlin listed seven words: "Shit, piss, fuck, cunt, cocksucker, mother—fucker, and tits. Those are the ones that will curve your spine, grow hair on your hands and (laughter) maybe even bring us . . . peace without honor (laughter). . . ." He then proceeded to repeat the words in various contexts.

[A few weeks later a listener who had heard the broadcast while driving with his young son wrote a letter of complaint to the Federal Communications Commission. The FCC issued an order holding that Pacifica "could have been the subject of administrative sanctions." It did not impose formal sanctions, but did state that the order would be "associated with the station's license file" and could be a basis for sanctions in the event of subsequent complaints. The Commission reasoned that the language was not obscene, but that it was "indecent" and therefore prohibited by a section of the Communications Act, 18 U.S.C. § 1464, which prohibited the use of any "obscene, indecent or profane language" by radio stations. In a later opinion, the Commission stated that it never intended to place an absolute prohibition on the broadcast of this type of language, but rather sought to channel it to "times of day when children most likely would not be exposed to it."

[The Court began by determining that the Commission's action was not "forbidden 'censorship'" within the meaning of the Communications Act and that the broadcast in question was properly characterized as "indecent" within the meaning of that Act. "The words 'obscene, indecent, or profane' are written in the disjunctive, implying that each has a separate meaning. Prurient appeal is an element of the obscene, but the normal definition of 'indecent' merely refers to non-conformance with accepted standards of morality." Having thus defined "indecent," the Court here proceeds to uphold the Commission's orders.]

When the issue is narrowed to the facts of this case, the question is whether the First Amendment denies government any power to restrict the public broadcast of indecent language in any circumstances. For if the government has any such power, this was an appropriate occasion for its exercise.

The words of the Carlin monologue are unquestionably "speech" within the meaning of the First Amendment. It is equally clear that the Commission's objections to the broadcast were based in part on its content. The order must therefore fall if, as Pacifica argues, the First Amendment prohibits all governmental regulation that depends on the content of speech. Our past cases demonstrate, however, that no such absolute rule is mandated by the Constitution.

The question in this case is whether a broadcast of patently offensive words dealing with sex and excretion may be regulated because of its content. . . . [I]t is a central tenet of the First Amendment that the government must remain neutral in the marketplace of ideas. If there were any reason to believe that the Commission's characterization of the Carlin monologue as offensive could be traced to its political content or even to the fact that it satirized contemporary attitudes about four letter words— First Amendment protection might be required. But that is simply not this case. These words offend for the same reasons that obscenity offends. Their place in the hierarchy of First Amendment values was aptly sketched by Mr. Justice Murphy when he said: "Such utterances are no essential part of any exposition of ideas, and are of such slight social value as a step to truth that any benefit that may be derived from them is clearly outweighed by the social interest in order and morality." *Chaplinsky v. New Hampshire.*

Although these words ordinarily lack literary, political, or scientific value, they are not entirely outside the protection of the First Amendment. Some uses of even the most offensive words are unquestionably protected. Indeed, we may assume, *arguendo*, that this monologue would be protected in other contexts. Nonetheless, the constitutional protection accorded to a communication containing such patently offensive sexual and excretory language need not be the same in every context. It is a characteristic of speech such as this that both its capacity to offend and its "social value," to use Mr. Justice Murphy's term, vary with the circumstances. Words that are commonplace in one setting are shocking in another. To paraphrase Mr. Justice Harlan, one occasion's lyric is another's vulgarity. *Cf. Cohen v. California.*

In this case it is undisputed that the content of Pacifica's broadcast was "vulgar," "offensive," and "shocking." Because content of that character is not entitled to absolute constitutional protection under all circumstances, we must consider its context in order to determine whether the Commission's action was constitutionally permissible.

We have long recognized that each medium of expression presents special First Amendment problems. [A]nd of all forms of communication, it is broadcasting that has received the most limited First Amendment protection. . . .

The reasons for these distinctions are complex, but two have relevance to the present case. First, the broadcast media have established a uniquely pervasive presence in the lives of all Americans. Patently offensive, indecent material presented over the airwaves confronts the citizen, not only in public, but also in the privacy of the home, where the individual's right to be left alone plainly outweighs the First Amendment rights of an intruder. [B]ecause the broadcast audience is constantly tuning in and out, prior warnings cannot completely protect the listener or viewer from unexpected program content. To say that one may avoid further offense by turning off the radio when he hears indecent language is like saying that the remedy for an assault is to run away after the first blow. . . .

Second, broadcasting is uniquely accessible to children, even those too young to read. Although Cohen's written message might have been incomprehensible to a first grader, Pacifica's broadcast could have enlarged a child's vocabulary in an instant. . . .

It is appropriate, in conclusion, to emphasize the narrowness of our holding. This case does not involve a two-way radio conversation between a cab driver and a dispatcher, or a telecast of an Elizabethan comedy. We have not decided that an occasional expletive in either setting would justify any sanction or, indeed, that this broadcast would justify a criminal prosecution. The Commission's decision rested entirely on a nuisance rationale under which context is all—important. The concept requires consideration of a host of variables. The time of day was emphasized by the Commission. The content of the program in which the language is used will also affect the composition of the audience, and differences between radio, television, and perhaps closed—circuit transmissions, may also be relevant. As Mr. Justice Sutherland wrote, a "nuisance may be merely a right thing in the wrong place—like a pig in the parlor instead of the barnyard." Euclid v. Ambler Realty Co., 272 U.S. 365, 388. We simply hold that when the Commission finds that a pig has entered the parlor, the exercise of its regulatory power does not depend on proof that the pig is obscene.

The judgment of the Court of Appeals is *reversed.*

Mr. Justice Powell, with whom Mr. Justice Blackmun joins, concurring in part and concurring in the judgment.

The issue . . . is whether the Commission may impose civil sanctions on a licensee radio station for broadcasting the monologue at two o'clock in the afternoon. The Commission's primary concern was to prevent the broadcast from reaching the ears of unsupervised children who were likely to be in the audience at that hour. In essence, the Commission sought to "channel" the monologue to hours when the fewest unsupervised children would be exposed to it. In my view, this consideration provides strong support for the Commission's holding. . . .

In most instances, the dissemination of [indecent] speech to children may be limited without also limiting willing adults' access to it. The difficulty is that such a physical separation of the audience cannot be accomplished in the broadcast media. [I]n my view, the Commission was entitled to give substantial weight to this difference in reaching its decision in this case. . . .

[H]owever, . . . I do not subscribe to the theory that the Justices of this Court are free generally to decide on the basis of its content which speech protected by the First Amendment is most "valuable" and hence deserving of the most protection, and which is less "valuable" and hence deserving of less protection. . . .

The result turns instead on the unique characteristics of the broadcast media, combined with society's right to protect its children from speech generally agreed to be inappropriate for their years, and with the interest of unwilling adults in not being assaulted by such offensive speech in their homes. Moreover, I doubt whether today's decision will prevent any adult who wishes to receive Carlin's message in Carlin's own words from doing so, and from making for himself a value judgment as to the merit of the message and words. . . .

MR. JUSTICE BRENNAN, with whom MR. JUSTICE MARSHALL joins, dissenting.

I agree with Mr. Justice Stewart that, under Hamling v. United States, the word "indecent" in 18 U.S.C. § 1464 (1976 ed.) must be construed to prohibit only obscene speech. I would, therefore, normally refrain from expressing my views on any constitutional issues implicated in this case. However, I find the Court's misapplication of fundamental First Amendment principles so patent, and its attempt to impose *its* notions of propriety on the whole of the American people so misguided, that I am unable to remain silent. . . .

Whatever the minimal discomfort suffered by a listener who inadvertently tunes into a program he finds offensive during the brief interval before he can simply extend his arm and switch stations or flick the "off" button, it is surely worth the candle to preserve the broadcaster's right to send, and the right of those interested to receive, a message entitled to full First Amendment protection. To reach a contrary balance, as does the Court, is clearly, to follow Mr. Justice Stevens' reliance on animal metaphors, "to burn the house to roast the pig. . . ."

[I]n this context, the Court's decision may be seen for what, in the broader perspective, it really is: another of the dominant culture's inevitable efforts to force those groups who do not share its mores to conform to its way of thinking, acting, and speaking. *See Moore v. East Cleveland* [in ch. 9, *above*].

MR. JUSTICE STEWART, with whom MR. JUSTICE BRENNAN, MR. JUSTICE WHITE, and MR. JUSTICE MARSHALL join, dissenting. . . .

I would hold . . . that Congress intended, by using the word "indecent" in § 1464, to prohibit nothing more than obscene speech. Under that reading of the statute, the Commission's order in this case was not authorized, and on that basis I would affirm the judgment of the Court of Appeals.

NOTES AND QUESTIONS

(1) *The Pacifica Foundation Plurality.* All justices in *Pacifica* agreed that the "indecent" words were protected speech in some contexts, but they could be prohibited in the particular context, precisely because of their content. The characteristic of that content that subjects them to prohibition is closely associated with their capacity to offend. Given these conclusions, how does *Pacifica* compare to the problems of *Feiner* and *Terminiello* (the "heckler's veto" cases) and the demonstration by the Nazis in Skokie? Consider whether the *Pacifica* reasoning would justify prohibition in those cases on the basis of the offense given the audience. *Cf.* Hogue, *On Keeping Pigs Out of the Parlor: Speech as Public Nuisance after FCC v. Pacifica Foundation*, 31 SUP. CT. REV. 377 (1980).

(2) *Some Limits on the Scope of Pacifica Foundation's Rationale: Sable Communications of California, Inc. v. FCC, 492 U.S. 115 (1989).* Following the Court's decision in *Pacifica Foundation*, Congress amended the Communications Act to impose a 24-hour, complete ban on "indecent" and "obscene" interstate commercial telephone messages (or "dial-a-porn"). Note that this was an extension of the type of ban at issue in Pacifica Foundation. The Supreme Court, per Justice White, upheld the complete ban on "obscene" commercial telephone messages; three Justices dissented. In contrast, the Court unanimously struck down the complete ban on "indecent" commercial telephone messages. The Court distinguished *Pacifica Foundation* because it had not involved a "total ban."

Further limits on the persuasiveness of *Pacifica Foundation* are indicated by the Court's decision in *United States v. Playboy Entertainment Group, Inc.*, 529 U.S. 803 (2000). [*See* Note (3) below after the *Reno* decision.]

RENO v. AMERICAN CIVIL LIBERTIES UNION
521 U.S. 844 (1997)

JUSTICE STEVENS delivered the opinion of the Court.

[Congress overwhelmingly passed, and the President signed, the Communications Decency Act of 1996 ("CDA" or "the Act"). The CDA was an effort to regulate communication on the Internet (or "Cyberspace"). At issue in this case are two provisions of the CDA relating to communications involving minors: one makes it a felony to knowingly communicate "indecent" messages with minors and a second provision makes it a crime to knowingly display to minors messages which are "patently offensive." The CDA provided certain "good faith" defenses, but these were affirmative defenses which must be raised by the speaker, and their effect was such that a communication indiscriminately aimed at adults but received by children could be proscribed in some circumstances, as is analyzed below.

[The provisions of the CDA were challenged by a consortium of plaintiffs. After extensive fact—finding, a three-judge District Court held that the CDA provisions violated the free speech interests of the adult plaintiffs. The federal government appealed. Here, the Supreme Court affirms, holding that the "indecent transmission" and "patently offensive display" provisions violate the cyberspace speakers' free speech rights.]

In arguing for reversal [of the District Court], the Government contends that the CDA is plainly constitutional under three of our prior decisions: (1) *Ginsberg v. New York*, (2) *FCC v. Pacifica Foundation*, and (3) *Renton v. Playtime Theatres, Inc.* A close look at these cases, however, raises—rather than relieves-doubts concerning the constitutionality of the CDA.

In *Ginsberg*, we upheld the constitutionality of a New York statute that prohibited selling to minors under 17 years of age material that was considered obscene as to them even if not obscene as to adults. . . .

In four important respects, the statute upheld in *Ginsberg* was narrower than the CDA. . . .

[The Court here distinguishes *Ginsberg* on the grounds (1) that the New York law did not bar parents from purchasing any materials for their children, (2) that it applied only to commercial transactions, (3) that its definition was clearer, not merely covering "indecency" but setting up a 3-part obscenity standard adapted to minors, and (4) that it applied to persons under 17, whereas the CDA included 17-year olds.]

In *Pacifica*, we upheld a declaratory order of the Federal Communications Commission, holding that the broadcast of a recording of a 12-minute monologue entitled "Filthy Words" that had previously been delivered to a live audience "could have been the subject of administrative sanctions." . . .

As with the New York statute at issue in *Ginsberg*, there are significant differences between the order upheld in *Pacifica* and the CDA. First, the order in *Pacifica*, issued by an agency that had been regulating radio stations for decades, targeted a specific broadcast that represented a rather dramatic departure from traditional program content in order to designate when—rather than whether—it would be permissible to air such a program in that particular medium. The CDA's broad categorical prohibitions are not limited to particular times and are not dependent on any evaluation by an agency familiar with the unique characteristics of the Internet. Second, unlike the CDA, the Commission's declaratory order was not punitive; we expressly refused to decide whether the indecent broadcast "would justify a criminal prosecution." Finally, the Commission's order applied to a medium (i.e., broadcasting) which as a matter of history had "received the most limited First Amendment protection," in large part because warnings could not adequately protect the listener from unexpected program content. The Internet, however, has no comparable history. . . .

In *Renton*, we upheld a zoning ordinance that kept adult movie theatres out of residential neighborhoods. The ordinance was aimed, not at the content of the films shown in the theaters, but rather at the "secondary effects"—such as crime and deteriorating property values—that these theaters fostered. . . . According to the Government, the CDA is constitutional because it constitutes a sort of "cyberzoning" on the Internet. But the CDA applies broadly to the entire universe of cyberspace. And the purpose of the CDA is to protect children from the primary effects of "indecent" and "patently offensive" speech, rather than any "secondary" effect of such speech. Thus, the CDA is a content-based blanket restriction on speech, and, as such, cannot be "properly analyzed as a form of, and manner regulation." . . .

These precedents, then, surely do not require us to uphold the CDA and are fully consistent with the application of the most stringent review of its provisions.

Some of our cases have recognized special justifications for regulation of the broadcast media that are not applicable to other speakers, *see Red Lion Broadcasting Co. v. FCC*, 395 U.S. 367 (1969). In these cases, the Court relied on the history of extensive government regulation of the broadcast medium, *see, e.g., Red Lion*, 395 U.S., at 399–400; the scarcity of available frequencies at its inception, *see, e.g., Turner Broadcasting System, Inc. v. FCC*, 512 U.S. 622 (1994); and its "invasive" nature, *see Sable Communications of Cal., Inc. v. FCC*, 492 U.S. 115 (1989).

Those factors are not present in cyberspace. Neither before nor after the enactment of the CDA have the vast democratic fora of the Internet been subject to the type of government supervision and regulation that has attended the broadcast industry. Moreover, the Internet is not as "invasive" as radio or television. The District Court specifically found that "[c]ommunications over the Internet do not 'invade' an individual's home or appear on one's computer screen unbidden. Users seldom encounter content 'by accident.'" . . .

Finally, unlike the conditions that prevailed when Congress first authorized regulation of the broadcast spectrum, the Internet can hardly be considered a "scarce" expressive commodity. It provides relatively unlimited, low-cost capacity for communication of all kinds. . . . Our cases provide no basis for [reducing] the level of First Amendment scrutiny that should be applied to this medium.

Regardless of whether the CDA is so vague that it violates the Fifth Amendment, the many ambiguities concerning the scope of its coverage render it problematic for purposes of the First Amendment. . . .

The vagueness of the CDA is a matter of special concern for two reasons. First, the CDA is a content based regulation of speech. The vagueness of such a regulation raises special First Amendment concerns because of its obvious chilling effect on free speech. Second, the CDA is a criminal statute. In addition to the opprobrium and stigma of a criminal conviction, the CDA threatens violators with penalties including up to two years in prison for each act of violation. The severity of criminal sanctions may well cause speakers to remain silent rather than communicate even arguably unlawful words, ideas, and images. . . .

VII

We are persuaded that the CDA lacks the precision that the First Amendment requires when a statute regulates the content of speech. In order to deny minors access to potentially harmful speech, the CDA effectively suppresses a large amount of speech that adults have a constitutional right to receive and to address to one another. That burden on adult speech is unacceptable if less restrictive alternatives would be at least as effective in achieving the legitimate purpose that the statute was enacted to serve. . . .

The District Court found that at the time of trial existing technology did not include any effective method for a sender to prevent minors from obtaining access to its communications on the Internet without also denying access to adults. . . . These limitations must inevitably curtail a significant amount of adult communication on the Internet. . . .

The breadth of the CDA's coverage is wholly unprecedented. Unlike the regulations upheld in *Ginsberg* and *Pacifica*, the scope of the CDA is not limited to commercial speech or commercial entities. Its open-ended prohibitions embrace all nonprofit entities and individuals posting indecent messages or displaying them on their own computers in the presence of minors. The general, undefined terms "indecent" and "patently offensive" cover large amounts of nonpornographic material with serious educational or other value.

The breadth of this content-based restriction of speech imposes an especially heavy burden on the Government to explain why a less restrictive provision would not be as effective as the CDA. It has not done so. . . . Particularly in the light of the absence of any detailed findings by the Congress, or even hearings addressing the special problems of the CDA, we are persuaded that the CDA is not narrowly tailored if that requirement has any meaning at all. . . .

IX

The Government's . . . remaining arguments focus on the defenses provided in § 223(e)(5). First, relying on the "good faith, reasonable, effective, and appropriate actions" provision, the Government suggests that "tagging" provides a defense that saves the constitutionality of the Act. The suggestion assumes that transmitters may encode their indecent communications in a way that would indicate their contents, thus permitting recipients to block their reception with appropriate software. It is the requirement that the good faith action must be "effective" that makes this defense illusory. The Government recognizes that its proposed screening software does not currently exist. Even if it did, there is no way to know whether a potential recipient will actually block the encoded material. Without the impossible knowledge that every guardian in America is screening for the "tag," the transmitter could not reasonably rely on its action to be "effective." . . .

We agree with the District Court's conclusion that the CDA places an unacceptably heavy burden on protected speech, and that the defenses do not constitute the sort of "narrow tailoring" that will save an otherwise patently invalid unconstitutional provision. . . .

XI

In this Court, though not in the District Court, the Government asserts that-in addition to its interest in protecting children—its "[e]qually significant" interest in fostering the growth of the Internet provides an independent basis for upholding the constitutionality of the CDA. The Government apparently assumes that the unregulated availability of "indecent" and "patently offensive" material on the Internet is driving countless citizens away from the medium because of the risk of exposing themselves or their children to harmful material.

We find this argument singularly unpersuasive. The dramatic expansion of this new marketplace of ideas contradicts the factual basis of this contention. The record demonstrates that the growth of the Internet has been and continues to be phenomenal. As a matter of constitutional tradition, in the absence of evidence to the contrary, we presume that governmental regulation of the content of speech is more likely to interfere with the free exchange of ideas than to encourage it. . . .

For the foregoing reasons, the judgment of the district court is affirmed.

JUSTICE O'CONNOR, with whom THE CHIEF JUSTICE joins, concurring in the judgment in part and dissenting in part.

I write separately to explain why I view the Communications Decency Act of 1996 (CDA) as little more than an attempt by Congress to create "adult zones" on the Internet. Our precedent indicates that the creation of such zones can be constitutionally sound. Despite the soundness of its purpose, however, portions of the CDA are unconstitutional because they stray from the blueprint our prior cases have developed for constructing a "zoning law" that passes constitutional muster. . . .

Our cases make clear that a "zoning" law is valid only if adults are still able to obtain the regulated speech. If they cannot, the law does more than simply keep children away from speech they have no right to obtain-it interferes with the rights of adults to obtain constitutionally protected speech and effectively "reduce[s] the adult population . . . to reading only what is fit for children." Butler v. Michigan, 352 U.S. 380, 383 (1957). The First Amendment does not tolerate such interference. . . .

NOTES AND QUESTIONS

(1) *"Indecent" Speech In Cyberspace.* The Court held, in *Reno*, that the "indecent speech" and "patently offensive speech" provisions, as these were defined relating to minors, were unconstitutional abridgments of the free speech rights of adults. In a doctrinally eclectic opinion, the Court found that, although the concern for minors was a constitutionally significant end, Congress had used impermissibly vague and over-broad means. Note that the Justice Department had argued that indecent cyberspeech should be considered unprotected, following the broadcasting model.

(2) *What Level of Scrutiny Applies (or Is the Court Here Forsaking Calculation of the "Level" for a Multi-Factor Approach)?* The *Reno* Court first held that indecent "cyberspeech" is protected speech. The *Reno* Court then addressed the issue of what level of protection should be afforded, and the Court's analysis here is far less clear. While the Court referred to the CDA as a "content-based regulation of speech," the Court did not directly apply the strict scrutiny test from the Two Track model, § 11.03[A] above, as had the District Court. Although Justice Stevens distinguished the *Pacifica Foundation* plurality opinion, the *Reno* opinion is presented in a multi-factored manner, like *Pacifica Foundation*. (Of course, the *Reno* result is largely inconsistent with *Pacifica Foundation*.) Apart from the similarity of authorship (Justice Stevens), why might the Court eschew the Two Track model in favor of the multi-factored approach?

(3) *Congressional Restriction of Indecent Speech on Cable Television Struck Down as a Content-Based Regulation: United States v. Playboy Entertainment Group, Inc., 529 U.S. 803 (2000).* In the Telecommunications Act, Congress attempted to regulate sexually explicit programing, and the accompanying "signal bleed" problem, by requiring that programers either fully "scramble" such programming or "channel" such adult entertainment only to certain nighttime hours (as in *Pacifica Foundation*). Playboy Entertainment challenged the signal bleed provisions as a content-based regulation. The record at trial showed that, although the cable programers had a theoretical choice of means to comply, the problems with technology forced the programers to use the "channel" approach resulting in a "national daytime speech ban." The government argued that the signal bleed regulations should be considered as a Track Two regulation.

The Supreme Court, per Justice Kennedy, disagreed with the government. The Court held that, as applied, the signal bleed provision was a content-based regulation. Then, applying strict scrutiny, the Court held that the government had failed the means prong. The Court noted that a less restrictive alternative of allowing individual households to request blockage of undesired channels existed and was even used as a regulatory alternative in other provisions of the Telecommunications Act. Doctrinally, the decision is significant for confirming that, in strict scrutiny, the burden to prove that the government regulator is using the least restrictive alternative rests on the government. Four Justices dissented.

(4) *Reno Revisited: Ashcroft v. American Civil Liberties Union, 535 U.S. 564 (2002)*. After the Court struck down the CPA in *Reno*, Congress made another effort, in the interest of protecting children, to regulate indecent speech in cyberspace. The new Child Online Protection Act (COPA) prohibits the commercial display of "materials harmful to minors." The term "harmful to minors" was defined by reference to the "contemporary community standards" language in the *Miller* obscenity test. The Supreme Court, in a plurality opinion by Justice Thomas, concluded that Congressional reliance on the community standards concept to define what is "harmful to minors" did not, by itself, render COPA substantially overbroad.

The Court was doctrinally splintered with five Justices concurring only in the judgment. Justice's Kennedy's concurrence emphasized the sequence of events, suggesting that Congress may have been attempting to override the *Reno* decision.

(5) *COPA II— More Litigation Regarding Adult Pornography and COPA: Ashcroft v. American Civil Liberties Union, 542 U.S. 656 (2004)*. Although the Court upheld the Child Online Protection Act (COPA) against an overbreadth challenge predicated on its reliance on community standards [above at Note (4)], the lower court enjoined the enforcement of COPA because, as a content-based regulation, it failed to satisfy the strict scrutiny standard, particularly the "least restrictive means" prong. The federal government appealed, but the Supreme Court, per Justice Kennedy, affirmed the preliminary injunction. The case was remanded for a trial on the application of the least restrictive alternative means.

Justice Kennedy applied strict scrutiny, relying on his *Playboy Entertainment Group* decision [above at Note (3)]. The majority held that parental utilization of filters at the "user end" may constitute a less restrictive alternative to COPA's criminalization of "commercial" material "harmful to minors" at the "provider end." Justice Stevens concurred. Justice Scalia, only for himself, dissented on the grounds that "commercial pornography" is simply not protected speech. Justice Breyer, for Chief Justice Rehnquist and Justice O'Connor, submitted a lengthy dissent. While there are many doctrinal nuances, it appears that Justice Breyer would apply a lesser standard than traditional strict scrutiny, especially regarding the "modest nature" of any burden on the speaker.

PROBLEM K

THE FCC'S EFFORTS TO REGULATE THE "SHOCK JOCKS." Since the Communications Act forbids broadcasting of "obscene, indecent or profane" language, the FCC arguably has a nondiscretionary duty to enforce the "indecency" prohibition. After *Pacifica*, citing its duty to enforce the law, the Commission determined that it would not limit its regulatory action to the Carlin glossary of Seven Dirty Words, but would enforce more broadly the provision against indecent broadcasts. Public complaints triggered at least three FCC investigations of programs. In one, the FCC issued a warning to a Los Angeles station that had broadcast explicit descriptions of one speaker's feelings during anal intercourse. In another case, the Commission warned a station licensed to the Regents of the University of California for broadcasting a song with lyrics containing repeated references to anal and oral sex. A third case is described as follows:

> The Philadelphia station, WYSP-FM, . . . broadcast comments by so-called "shock jock" Howard Stern in which he described the arrangement of his testicles and made other comments that the Commission found indecent.

Indicating that it was not intending to prohibit the broadcast of sexual innuendo, double entendre, or even explicit sexual discussions, the Commission noted a long list of topics addressed by Stern, including "[m]asturbation, ejaculation, breast size, penis size, sexual intercourse, nudity, urination, oral genital contact, erections, sodomy, bestiality, menstruation and testicles." The agency said, "[N]one of these subjects is *per se* beyond the realm of acceptable broadcast discussion," but, in the context of Stern's discussions, "There is not merely an occasional off-color reference or expletive but a dwelling on matters sexual and excretory, in a pandering and titillating fashion."

[The FCC defined its standard as prohibiting "material regarding sexual activity, reproductive organs or excretory functions in a manner that is patently offensive, measured against contemporary community standards for broadcasters." It also indicated that a different standard, allowing more latitude, would apply after ten p.m.]

In all three cases, the Commission limited its sanctions to warnings, citing the need to "clarify" its stance on what constitutes indecency, and in what context and at what hours such programming might be broadcast.

Are these three warnings, based upon the standard enunciated by the FCC, consistent with the statutory prohibition of indecency and with the First Amendment?

PROBLEM L

COLLEGE CONDUCT CODES PROHIBITING RACIST AND ANTI-MINORITY SPEECH: reported in France, *Hate Goes to College,* 76 A.B.A.J. 44 (1990). In response to perceptions that anti-minority slurs were increasing, several universities considered or implemented prohibitory rules. Consider the following disciplinary provision adopted at the University of Wisconsin: Discriminatory comments or expressive behavior "directed at an individual that intentionally demean the race, sex, religion, color, creed, disability, sexual orientation, national origin, ancestry or age of the individual, and create a demeaning environment for education" are prohibited. [Does the "directed at an individual" proviso bring this rule within the coverage of the "fighting words" coverage of *Chaplinsky*? Isn't it broader than "fighting words"? Can the holding in *R.A.V. v. St. Paul* be distinguished? Do the cases following *Pacifica* and dealing with indecency provide any guidance?] Also, analyze the proposed prohibition at Stanford University, considered but not adopted, upon forms of expression that "degrade, victimize, stigmatize, or pejoratively characterize [individuals or groups] on the basis of personal, cultural or intellectual diversity." This provision would not have been limited to individually-directed remarks. [How would such a regulation apply in the case of a University of Connecticut student who posted a sign on the door of her dormitory room stating that various groups, including "bimbos" and "preppies," were unwelcome? *Id.* at 47.]

[D] Child Pornography

GINSBERG v. NEW YORK
390 U.S. 629 (1968)

[Ginsberg was convicted of selling what the court described as "two 'girlie' magazines" to a sixteen-year-old boy. A New York statute prohibited the distribution to minors of materials containing female buttocks or breasts "with less than a fully opaque covering of any portion thereof below the top of the nipple," if the materials were "harmful to minors." The latter term was defined to include nudity that predominantly appealed to the prurient, shameful or morbid interests of minors, was patently offensive to prevailing standards in the adult community as a whole with respect to what was suitable for minors, and was utterly without redeeming social importance for minors.

The court, per Justice Brennan, upheld the conviction:]

> The "girlie" picture magazines involved in the sales here are not obscene for adults. *Redrup v. New York.* . . .

> The New York Court of Appeals "upheld the legislature's power to employ variable concepts of obscenity" in a [similar] case. . . . In sustaining state power to enact the law, the Court of Appeals said:

> [M]aterial which is protected for distribution to adults is not necessarily constitutionally protected from restriction upon its dissemination to children. In other words, the concept of obscenity or of unprotected matter may vary according to the group to whom the questionable material is directed or from whom it is quarantined. . . .

> The well being of its children is of course a subject within the state's constitutional power to regulate, and, in our view, two interests justify the limitations in the [the New York statute] upon the availability of such materials to minors under age seventeen. [F]irst of all, constitutional interpretation has consistently recognized that parents' claim to authority in their own household to direct the rearing of their children is basic in the structure of our society. . . .

> The state also has an independent interest in the well being of its youth. [It] has an interest "to protect the welfare of children" and to see that they are "safeguarded from abuses" which might prevent their "growth into free and independent well-developed [citizens.]" . . .

Justice Douglas, joined by Justice Black, dissented.

NEW YORK v. FERBER
458 U.S. 747 (1982)

Justice White delivered the opinion of the Court.

At issue in this case is the constitutionality of a New York criminal statute which prohibits persons from knowingly promoting sexual performances by children under the age of 16 by distributing material which depicts such performances. [Note that "child pornography" was *not* listed in *Chaplinsky* as a category of unprotected speech. Here New York attempts to expand the set of unprotected categories.]

In recent years, the exploitive use of children in the production of pornography has become a serious national problem. The Federal Government and 47 States have sought to combat the problem with statutes specifically directed at the production of child pornography. At least half of such statutes do not require that the materials produced be legally obscene. Thirty-five States and the United States Congress have also passed legislation prohibiting the distribution of such materials; 20 States prohibit the distribution of material depicting children engaged in sexual conduct without requiring that the material be legally obscene.

New York is one of the 20. In 1977, the New York Legislature enacted Article 263 of its Penal Law [the statute at issue].

This case arose when Paul Ferber, the proprietor of a Manhattan bookstore specializing in sexually oriented products, sold two films to an undercover police officer. The films are devoted almost exclusively to depicting young boys masturbating.

The Court of Appeals proceeded on the assumption that the standard of obscenity incorporated in § 263.10, which follows the guidelines enunciated in *Miller v. California*, constitutes the appropriate line dividing protected from unprotected expression by which to measure a regulation directed at child pornography. It was on the premise that "nonobscene adolescent sex" could not be singled out for special treatment that the court found [the New York Statute] "strikingly underinclusive."

[W]e believe our inquiry should begin with the question of whether a State has somewhat more freedom in proscribing works which portray sexual acts or lewd exhibitions of genitalia by children.

[L]ike obscenity statutes, laws directed at the dissemination of child pornography run the risk of suppressing protected expression by allowing the hand of the censor to become unduly heavy. For the following reasons, however, we are persuaded that the States are entitled to greater leeway in the regulation of pornographic depictions of children.

First. It is evident beyond the need for elaboration that a State's interest in "safeguarding the physical and psychological well-being of a minor" is "compelling." [I]n *Ginsberg v. New York, supra,* we sustained a New York law protecting children from exposure to nonobscene literature.

The prevention of sexual exploitation and abuse of children constitutes a government objective of surpassing importance. The legislative findings accompanying passage of the New York laws reflect this concern: "[T]here has been a proliferation of exploitation of children as subjects in sexual performances. The care of children is a sacred trust and should not be abused by those who seek to profit through a commercial network based upon the exploitation of children. The public policy of the state demands the protection of children from exploitation through sexual performances."

Second. The distribution of photographs and films depicting sexual activity by juveniles is intrinsically related to the sexual abuse of children in at least two ways. First, the materials produced are a permanent record of the children's participation and the harm to the child is exacerbated by their circulation.[10] Second, the distribution network for child pornography mustbe closed if the production of material which requires the sexual exploitation of children is to be effectively controlled. [T]he most expeditious if not the only practical method of law enforcement may be to dry up the market for this material by imposing severe criminal penalties on persons selling, advertising, or otherwise promoting the product.

Respondent does not contend that the State is unjustified in pursuing those who distribute child pornography. Rather, he argues that it is enough for the State to prohibit the distribution of materials that are legally obscene under the *Miller* test. While some States may find that this approach properly accommodates [their] interests, it does not follow that the First Amendment prohibits a State from going further. The *Miller* standard, like all general definitions of what may be banned as obscene, does not reflect the State's particular and more compelling interest in prosecuting those who promote the sexual exploitation of children. Thus, the question under the *Miller* test of whether a work, taken as a whole, appeals to the prurient interest of the average person bears no connection to the issue of whether a child has been physically or psychologically harmed in the production of the work. . . .

Third. The advertising and selling of child pornography provide an economic motive for and are thus an integral part of the production of such materials, an activity illegal throughout the Nation.

Fourth. The value of permitting live performances and photographic reproductions

---

[10] As one authority has explained:

Pornography poses an even greater threat to the child victim than does sexual abuse or prostitution. Because the child's actions are reduced to a recording, the pornography may haunt him in future years, long after the originalmisdeed took place. A child who has posed for a camera must go through life knowing that the recording is circulating within the mass distribution system for child pornography. Shouvlin, *Preventing the Sexual Exploitation of Children: A Model Act,* 17 WAKE FOREST L. REV. 535, 545 (1981).

of children engaged in lewd sexual conduct is exceedingly modest, if not *de minimis*. We consider it unlikely that visual depictions of children performing sexual acts or lewdly exhibiting their genitals would often constitute an important and necessary part of a literary performance or scientific or educational work.

Fifth. Recognizing and classifying child pornography as a category of material outside the protection of the First Amendment is not incompatible with our earlier decisions. "The question whether speech is, or is not protected by the First Amendment often depends on the content of the speech."

[W]e think the balance of competing interests is clearly struck and that it is permissible to consider these materials as without the protection of the First Amendment.

We hold that [the statute] sufficiently describes a category of material the production and distribution of which is not entitled to First Amendment protection. It is therefore clear that there is nothing unconstitutionally "underinclusive" about a statute that singles out this category of material for proscription.

[W]e hold that [the statute] is not substantially overbroad. We consider this the paradigmatic case of a state statute whose legitimate reach dwarfs its arguably impermissible applications. [W]hile the reach of the statute is directed at the hard core of child pornography, the Court of Appeals was understandably concerned that some protected expression, ranging from medical textbooks to pictorials in the National Geographic, would fall prey to the statute. How often, if ever, it may be necessary to employ children to engage in conduct clearly within the reach of [the statute] in order to produce educational, medical, or artistic works cannot be known with certainty. Yet we seriously doubt, and it has not been suggested, that these arguably impermissible applications of the statute amount to more than a tiny fraction of the materials within the statute'sreach. [U]nder these circumstances, [the statute] is "not substantially overbroad and . . . whatever overbreadth may exist should be cured through case-by-case analysis of the fact situations to which its sanctions, assertedly, may not be applied." *Broadrick v. Oklahoma.* . . .

. . . The judgment of the New York Court of Appeals is reversed, and the case is remanded to that court for further proceedings not inconsistent with this opinion.

JUSTICE BLACKMUN concurs in the result.

JUSTICE O'CONNOR, concurring.

Although I join the Court's opinion, I write separately to stress that the Court does not hold that New York must except "material with serious literary, scientific, or educational value" from its statute. The Court merely holds that, even if the First Amendment shelters such material, New York's current statute is not sufficiently overbroad to support respondent's facial attack.

JUSTICE BRENNAN, with whom JUSTICE MARSHALL joins, concurring in the judgment.

I agree with much of what is said in the Court's opinion. As I made clear in the opinion I delivered for the Court in *Ginsberg v. New York*, the State has a special interest in protecting the well-being of its youth.

But in my view application of [this] or any similar statute to depictions of children that in themselves do have serious literary, artistic, scientific, or medical value, would violate the First Amendment. [I]n short, it is inconceivable how a depiction of a child that is itself a serious contribution to the world of art or literature or science can be deemed "material outside the protection of the First Amendment."

[The opinion of JUSTICE STEVENS, concurring in the judgment, is omitted.]

NOTES AND QUESTIONS

(1) *Child Pornography As An Unprotected Speech Category: New York v. Ferber, 458 U.S. 747 (1982).* New York, and many other states, had a law criminalizing the sale of possession of material which, although not obscene, constituted "child pornography." The New York statute prohibited materials showing sexual activity by children under age 16. To defend the law against Ferber's challenge, New York argued that the Court should recognize "child porn" as a new category of unprotected speech. [Note that, if the speech would not be considered unprotected, then New York would have to satisfy strict scrutiny because the law was a content-based, Track One regulation.]

Using the *Chaplinsky* standard, the Court, per Justice White, held that child pornography was unprotected speech. The Court held that the social value of child porn was very low and the harm caused by child porn was very great,

The Court saw the harm arising in the *production* process in two ways: (1) the children who make the movies are in all cases being sexually abused in the production process; and (2) these child actors are repeatedly harmed again when the movies are played in the future.

All Justices concurred. Justices Brennan and Marshall expressed reservations about the breadth of the majority's statement. Justice Brennan reminded the Court that, under New York's law, the play/movie *Romeo and Juliet* might qualify. After all Shakespeare's play (universally read by American 14—16 year olds' in public high schools) involved sexual activities by children under 16.

What happens if states "experiment" with the scope of child pornography? South Dakota, for example, has set the age at 18. Same result as *Ferber?*

(2) *A Problem: Combining Stanley and Ferber to Consider Private Possession of Child Pornography.* Consider what the result would have been if, in *Stanley*, the officers had found motion pictures of child pornography, rather than merely material that could be characterized as obscene. Would the result be different? [*Stanley* appears to give absolute protection to private possession within the home, but it does not recognize the interest that is determinative in *Ferber*, which is the interest in breaking the chain of distribution.] Are *Stanley* and *Ferber* inconsistent? Cf. Potuto, *Stanley Plus Ferber Equals The Constitutional Crime of At—Home Child Pornography*, 76 Ky. L.J. 15 (1987).

(3) *Practical Difficulties and Doctrinal Limitations of Ferber.* Among the practical difficulties raised by the *Ginsberg* approach is the difficulty of compartmentalization of materials "harmful" to minors, as well as the difficulty of compartmentalization of individuals as minors. Might there be a difference if the standard is that for all minors, including those under ten, or whether it focuses upon the particular minor to whom the item is sold or displayed, who may be seventeen years old? If so, does the concept of "harmfulness" to minors conceal considerably more ambiguity even than is present in the definition of obscenity for adults? Note that the *Ferber* reasoning has not been applied to "adult pornography" which is protected speech—subject to the Two Track system.

(4) *The "National Geographic Hypothetical" Contained in Ferber: Would the Speech at Issue be Protected?* To follow a hypothetical situation raised in the *Ferber* opinion, consider the possibility that a respected national magazine publishes a photograph otherwise falling within the definition of child pornography, but constituting part of an inquiry into the culture of a particular geographical region. Is its distribution in New York a crime? If not, why not?

ASHCROFT v. THE FREE SPEECH COALITION, 535 U.S. 564 (2002). Under the *Ferber* decision, above, the category of speech considered to be "child pornography" is unprotected speech (*i.e.*, it can be regulated with only rational basis judicial review). While the precise definition of "child pornography" was ambiguous, the *Ferber* decision did not apply to so-called "adult" pornography. *Ferber* had involved the sale of child pornography; in *Osborne v. Ohio*, 495 U.S. 103 (1990), the Court upheld a ban on the *possession* of child of pornography.

Based on *Ferber* and *Osborne*, Congress passed the Child Pornography Prevention Act of 1996 (CPPA). The CPPA extended the federal prohibitions on child pornography to include two types of sexually explicit images: (1) "virtual child pornography" which were images produced by use of youthful-looking adults or computer imaging technology; and (2) the advertisement of any sexually explicit image "in such a manner that conveys the impression" it depicts a minor. Adult entertainment businesses challenged both of CPPA's attempted extensions on overbreadth and vagueness grounds. The Supreme Court, per Justice Kennedy, held that both prohibitions were overbroad and unconstitutional. As a matter of free speech doctrine, the decision is significant for its clarification (and narrowing) of the *Ferber* decision.

Justice Thomas concurred. Justice O'Connor concurred in part. While she agreed with the majority on the "conveys the impression" advertising issue, she partially dissented on the "virtual child pornography" issue. Doctrinally, her opinion went beyond the "unprotected speech" issue and addressed the application of strict scrutiny. Finally, Chief Justice Rehnquist dissented, primarily on the grounds that any "chill felt by the Court . . . has apparently never been felt by those who actually make [adult] movies." The dissent argued that the CPPA did not actually burden any speech interests.

In general, *Free Speech Coalition* represents a limitation on regulatory efforts based on child pornography since it concluded that "*Ferber*'s judgment about child pornography was based on how it was made, not what it communicated." The *Free Speech Coalition* decision therefore limited the definition of child pornography to speech produced by sexual abuse of actual children.

NOTES AND QUESTIONS

The Congressional Response to Free Speech Coalition: United States v. Williams, 128 S. Ct. 1830 (2008). Shortly after *Free Speech Coalition*, Congress enacted the PROTECT Act, adding a new pandering and solicitation provision criminalizing offers to provide or requests to obtain visual depictions of actual minors engaging in sexually explicit conduct. Because the offer or request for the child pornography constitutes the crime, the Act does not require the government to establish that actual children were sexually abused. Nevertheless, the Supreme Court, per Justice Scalia, upheld the Act against overbreadth and vagueness challenges. The Court reasoned that, because offers to engage in illegal transactions are categorically excluded from free speech protection, the First Amendment likewise did not prevent Congress from criminalizing offers to provide and requests to obtain child pornography involving real children, regardless of whether the underlying pornography actually exists. And, unlike the pandering provision in *Free Speech Coalition* that also prohibited the possession of virtual child pornography, the Court held the Act targeted only the proscribable "collateral speech" introducing materials in the child pornography network. Justice Souter, joined by Justice Ginsburg, dissented, contending that the Act undermined the actual child sexual abuse rationale of the Court's prior decisions.

PROBLEM M

A LAW RESTRICTING SALES OF VIOLENT VIDEOS TO CHILDREN, BASED UPON THE OBSCENITY-FOR-MINORS STANDARD: VIDEO SOFTWARE DEALERS ASS'N v. WEBSTER, 60 U.S.L.W. 2051 (W.D. Mo. 1991). Missouri passed a statute designed to prevent sales or rentals of excessively violent video cassettes to minors. The statute defined the prohibited material by adapting the obscenity definition to include such phrases as cassettes that appeal to a "morbid interest in violence," for minors, are "patently offensive" when considered by contemporary community standards, for minors, etc. Reconsider Problem E, above (reproducing two instances in which graphic violence apparently caused children to exhibit violent behavior by modeling); consider, also, American Psychological Ass'n, Big World, Small Screen (1992) (concluding that children learn violent behavior from television programs: "TV violence can cause aggression and can cultivate values favoring the use of aggression to resolve conflicts"), reported in *Kids Learn Violence from TV, Report Says*, HOUSTON CHRONICLE, Feb. 26, 1992, at 4D, col.5.

Can the Missouri law, patterned on the law upheld in *Ginsberg v. New York*, withstand a First Amendment attack? [The district court struck it down. Violent speech, it reasoned, was not an unprotected category like obscenity or child pornography; strict scrutiny therefore applied; and although the state has a compelling interest in protecting minors, the statute was not narrowly drawn because of the overbreadth and vagueness inherent in the morbid interest and contemporary standards phrases.] You should also reconsider this Missouri law in light of the upholding of a prohibition upon indecent speech in *Pacifica Foundation*, below.

[E]   Adult Pornography: Zoning and Other Regulation

YOUNG v. AMERICAN MINI-THEATERS, INC.
427 U.S. 50 (1976)

MR. JUSTICE STEVENS delivered the opinion of the Court [Part III of which is joined only by the CHIEF JUSTICE, MR. JUSTICE WHITE, and MR. JUSTICE REHNQUIST].

[Detroit zoning ordinances prohibited "adult motion picture theaters" and "adult bookstores" from operating within 1,000 feet of any two other "regulated uses" or within 500 feet of a residential area. "Regulated uses" included ten different kinds of establishments, ranging from bars to hotels. The court of appeals struck down the ordinances. Here, the Supreme Court reverses and upholds the ordinances.]

[R]espondents contend (1) that the ordinances are so vague that they violate the due process clause of the fourteenth amendment; (2) that they are invalid under the first amendment as prior restraints on protected communication; and (3) that the classification of theaters on the basis of the content of their exhibitions violates the equal protection clause of the fourteenth amendment. . . .

[Respondents] claim that the ordinances are too vague. . . . They argue that they cannot determine how much of the described activity may be permissible before the exhibition is "characterized by an emphasis" on such matter [and this phrase is used in defining the covered businesses]. [Citing to *Broadrick v. Oklahoma*, the plurality concluded that the zoning ordinance was not impermissibly vague.] . . .

[R]espondents [next] argue that the ordinances are . . . invalid as prior restraints on free speech.

The ordinances are not challenged on the ground that they impose a limit on the total number of adult theaters which may operate in the City of Detroit. There is no claim that distributors or exhibitors of adult film are denied access to the market, or, conversely, that the viewing public is unable to satisfy its appetite for sexually explicit fare. Viewed as an entity, the market for this commodity is essentially unrestrained.

It is true, however, that adult films may only be exhibited commercially in licensed theaters, but that is also true of all motion pictures. The city's general zoning laws require all motion picture theaters to satisfy certain locational as well as other requirements. [T]he mere fact that the commercial exploitation of material protected by the first amendment is subject to zoning and other licensing requirements is not a sufficient reason for invalidating these ordinances.

Putting to one side for the moment the fact that adult motion picture theaters must satisfy a locational restriction not applicable to other theaters, we are also persuaded that the 1,000 foot restriction does not, in itself, create an impermissible restraint on protected communication. The city's interest in planning and regulating the use of property for commercial purposes is clearly adequate to support that kind of restriction applicable to all theaters within the city limits. In short, apart from the fact that the ordinances treat adult theaters differently from other theaters and the fact that the classification is predicated on the content of material shown in the respective theaters, the regulation of the place where such films may be exhibited does not offend the first amendment. We turn, therefore, to the question whether the classification is consistent with the equal protection clause.

[Voltaire] said: "I disapprove of what you say, but I will defend to the death your right to say it. . . ."

[Above] all else, the first amendment means that government has no power to restrict expression because of its message, its ideas, its subject matter, or its content. . . .

[But] [t]he question whether speech is, or is not, protected by the first amendment often depends on the content of the speech. . . .

Such a line may be drawn on the basis of content without violating the government's paramount obligation of neutrality in its regulation of protected communication. For the regulation of the places where sexually explicit films may be exhibited is unaffected by whatever social, political, or philosophical message a film may be intended to communicate; whether a motion picture ridicules or characterizes one point of view or another, the effect of the ordinances is exactly the same. Moreover, even though we recognize that the first amendment will not tolerate the total suppression of erotic materials that have some arguable artistic value, it is manifest that society's interest in protecting this type of expression is of a wholly different, and lesser, magnitude than the interest in untrammeled political debate that inspired Voltaire's immortal comment. Whether political oratory or philosophical discussion moves us to applaud or despise what is said, every schoolchild can understand why our duty to defend the right to speak remains the same. But few of us would march our sons or daughters off to war to preserve the citizens' rights to see "specified sexual activities" exhibited in the theaters of our choice.

The remaining question is whether the line drawn by these ordinances is justified by the city's interest in preserving the character of its neighborhoods. [T]he record discloses a factual basis for the [Detroit] council's conclusion that this kind of restriction will have the desired affect. It is not our function to appraise the wisdom of its decision to require adult theaters to be separated rather than concentrated in the same areas. [M]oreover, the city must be allowed a reasonable opportunity to experiment with solutions to admittedly serious problems. . . .

Reversed.

Mr. Justice Powell, concurring in the judgment and portions of the opinion.

Although I agree with much of what is said in the court's opinion, and concur in Part I and II, my approach to the resolution of this case is sufficiently different to prompt me to write separately. I view the case as presenting an example of innovative land-use regulation, implicating first amendment concerns only incidentally and to a limited extent. [Because he saw the zoning regulation as having only an "incidental" effect on free speech, Justice Powell applied the standard from *United States v. O'Brien*, § 11.06 below.] . . .

The inquiry for first amendment purposes is not concerned with economic impact; rather, it looks only to the effect of this ordinance upon freedom of expression. This prompts essentially two inquiries: (i) does the ordinance impose any content limitation on the creators of adult movies or their ability to make them available to whom they desire, and (ii) does it restrict in any significant way the viewing of these movies by those who desire to see them. On the record in this case, these inquiries must be answered in the negative. . . .

Mr. Justice Stewart with whom Mr. Justice Brennan, Mr. Justice Marshall, and Mr. Justice Blackmun join, dissenting. . . .

This case does not involve a simple zoning ordinance, or a content-neutral, and manner restriction, or a regulation of obscene expression or other speech that is entitled to less than the full protection of the first amendment. . . .

What this case does involve is the constitutional permissibility of selective interference with protected speech whose content is thought to produce distasteful effects. It is elementary that a prime function of the first amendment is to guard against just such interference. By refusing to invalidate Detroit's ordinance the court rides roughshod over cardinal principles of first amendment law, which require that, and manner regulations that affect protected expression be content neutral except in the limited context of a captive or juvenile audience. . . .

The fact that the "offensive" speech here may not address "important" topics—"ideas of social and political significance," in the court's terminology . . .—does not mean that it is less worthy of constitutional protection. [M]oreover, in the absence of judicial determination of obscenity, it is by no means clear that the speech is not "important" even on the court's terms. . . .

The court must never forget that the consequences of rigorously enforcing the guarantees of the first amendment are frequently unpleasant. Much speech that seems to be of little or no value will enter the marketplace of ideas, threatening the quality of our social discourse and, more generally, the serenity of our lives. But that is the price to be paid for constitutional freedom.

[The separate dissent of Mr. Justice Blackmun, joined by Justices Brennan, Stewart, and Marshall, is omitted.]

NOTES AND QUESTIONS

(1) *The Court Reaffirms and Extends Young to a Case in Which Available Zoned Space is Limited and Concentrated: City of Renton v. Playtime Theatres, Inc., 475 U.S. 41 (1986).* The City of Renton, Washington, enacted an ordinance prohibiting adult motion picture theaters from locating within 1,000 feet of any residential zone, single- or multiple-family dwelling, church, park, or school. The Court, per Justice Rehnquist, upheld the ordinance, even though noting that it concentrated the land zoned for availability of adult theaters, rather than dispersing it, as had the Detroit ordinance in *Young.* The Court applied the time, place, and manner standard and found the available land adequate:

> Respondents argue, however, that some of the land in question is already occupied by existing business, that "practically none" of the undeveloped land is currently for sale or lease, and that in general there are no "commercially viable" adult theaters sites within the 520 acres left open by the Renton ordinance. . . .

> [T]hat respondents must fend for themselves in the real estate market on an equal footing with other prospective purchasers and lessees, does not give rise to a first amendment violation. . . .

Justices Brennan and Marshall dissented.

(2) *May Government Prohibit Drive-In Theaters From Showing Nudity Visible to Those Outside?: Erznoznik v. City of Jacksonville, 422 U.S. 205 (1975).* Erznoznik concerned a Jacksonville ordinance making it a public nuisance for a drive-in movie theater to exhibit non-obscene films containing nudity when the screen was visible from

a public street or place. The Court, per Justice Powell, struck down the ordinance as a violation of the first amendment:

> [A] state or municipality may protect individual privacy by enacting reasonable time, place, and manner regulations applicable to all speech irrespective of content. [B]ut when the government, acting as censor, undertakes selectively to shield the public from some kinds of speech on the ground that they are more offensive than others, the first amendment strictly limits its power. . . . Such selective restrictions have been upheld only when the speaker intrudes on the privacy of the home, . . . or the degree of captivity makes it impractical for the unwilling viewer or auditor to avoid exposure. . . .

Chief Justice Burger and Justices Rehnquist and White dissented. Justice White was particularly critical of the Court's limitations of privacy concerns to the home or to situations involving high degrees of captivity of an unwilling listener. *Erznoznik* was decided just one year before *Young v. American Mini-Theaters, Inc.* Are the two decisions consistent?

(3) *Renton Revisited and Reinterpreted: City of Los Angeles v. Alameda Books, Inc., 535 U.S. 425 (2002).* Based on a 1977 study, Los Angeles adopted a zoning dispersion ordinance for adult entertainment businesses (like the ordinance in *Young*, above). When the city learned that a loophole allowed "adult-oriented department store" arrangements, the city amended to prohibit "multiuse adult establishments." Alameda Books, which had a video business and a book business, sued. The district court granted Alameda summary judgment, which was affirmed by the court of appeals. The Supreme Court, per Justice O'Connor's plurality opinion, reversed, holding that the 1977 study and the city's experience were sufficient evidence of the "secondary effects" of adult entertainment to demonstrate the city's "substantial governmental interest" under the time, place, and manner standard.

Doctrinally, the plurality opinion relied on the *Renton* decision. Justice Kennedy's (the swing vote) opinion, concurring only in the judgment, offered a reinterpretation of *Renton*, explicitly limiting it to zoning cases. The dissent, by Justice Souter, sought to reconfigure the entire subdoctrine of "secondary effects" and even offered a new label—"content correlated zoning restrictions"—for this line of decisions.

[F]   "True Threats" as Unprotected Speech

VIRGINIA v. BLACK
538 U.S. 343 (2003)

JUSTICE O'CONNOR delivered the opinion of the Court.

[This decision involved a Virginia anti-cross burning statute (§ 18.2-423) which was first enacted in 1950, before *Brown v. Board of Education.* The statute provided:

> It shall be unlawful for any person or persons, with the intent of intimidating any person or group of persons, to burn or cause to be burned, a cross on the property of another, a highway or other public place.

Violation of the statute was a felony. Since a 1968 amendment, the statute contained a "prima facie provision" which provided that any cross burning "shall be prima facie evidence of an intent to intimidate a person or group of persons."

The Virginia statute, therefore, was distinguishable in at least three doctrinally significant ways from the ordinance in *R.A.V.* First, the Virginia statute was broader in some respects than the ordinance at issue in *R.A.V.*; it was not "underinclusive" as in *R.A.V.* Second, the Virginia statute had the prima facie provision. Third, the Virginia statute had been enacted many years ago; unlike the *R.A.V.* ordinance, the Virginia statute was not a recent enactment perhaps motivated by political correctness.

There were three defendants in this case (consolidated on appeal by the Virginia Supreme Court). Defendant Black was charged with cross burning when he led a Ku Klux Klan rally for 30 people in an open field on private property and a cross was burned some 300 yards away from any road. The other two defendants, Elliot and O'Mara, were charged with burning a cross on the yard of an African-American neighbor of Elliot's. Apparently, the African-American neighbors had complained about Elliot's "hobby" of shooting firearms in his backyard, and the defendants retaliated with the cross burning.

All three defendants were convicted. The prima facie provision was an issue only in Black's case; his lawyers timely objected, on Free Speech grounds, to the jury instruction. The Virginia Supreme Court, relying on *R.A.V.*, overturned all three convictions. The United States Supreme Court here affirmed in the case of Black and vacated and remanded regarding the other defendants.]

II

Cross burning originated in the 14th century as a means for Scottish tribes to signal each other. . . . Cross burning in this country, however, long ago became unmoored from its Scottish ancestry. Burning a cross in the United States is inextricably intertwined with the history of the Ku Klux Klan. . . .

From the inception of the second Klan, cross burnings have been used to communicate both threats of violence and messages of shared ideolog. . . .

The new Klan's ideology did not differ much from that of the first Klan. . . . Violence was also an elemental part of this new Klan. By September 1921, the New York World newspaper documented 152 acts of Klan violence, including 4 murders, 41 floggings, and 27 tar-and-featherings. Wade 160.

Often, the Klan used cross burnings as a tool of intimidation and a threat of impending violence. . . .

These incidents of cross burning, among others, helped prompt Virginia to enact its first version of the cross-burning statute in 1950.

The decision of this Court in *Brown v. Board of Education*, 347 U.S. 483 (1954), along with the civil rights movement of the 1950s and 1960s, sparked another outbreak of Klan violence. These acts of violence included bombings, beatings, shootings, stabbings, and mutilations. Members of the Klan burned crosses on the lawns of those associated with the civil rights movement, assaulted the Freedom Riders, bombed churches, and murdered blacks as well as whites whom the Klan viewed as sympathetic toward the civil rights movement. . . .

At Klan gatherings across the country, cross burning became the climax of the rally or the initiation. . . .

For its own members, the cross was a sign of celebration and ceremony. . . . In short, a burning cross has remained a symbol of Klan ideology and of Klan unity.

To this day, regardless of whether the message is a political one or whether the message is also meant to intimidate, the burning of a cross is a "symbol of hate." *Capitol Square Review and Advisory Bd. v. Pinette*, 515 U.S., at 771 (THOMAS, J., concurring). And while cross burning sometimes carries no intimidating message, at other times the intimidating message is the *only* message conveyed. . . . Indeed, as the cases of respondents Elliott and O' Mara indicate, individuals without Klan affiliation who wish to threaten or menace another person sometimes use cross burning because of this association between a burning cross and violence.

In sum, while a burning cross does not inevitably convey a message of intimidation, often the cross burner intends that the recipients of the message fear for their lives. And when a cross burning is used to intimidate, few if any messages are more powerful. . . .

III

A

The protections afforded by the First Amendment, however, are not absolute, and we have long recognized that the government may regulate certain categories of expression consistent with the Constitution. . . .

Thus, for example, a State may punish those words "which by their very utterance inflict injury or tend to incite an immediate breach of the peace." *Chaplinsky v. New Hampshire, supra*, at 572; see also *R.A.V. v. City of St. Paul, supra*, at 383 (listing limited areas where the First Amendment permits restrictions on the content of speech). We have consequently held that fighting words—"those personally abusive epithets which, when addressed to the ordinary citizen, are, as a matter of common knowledge, inherently likely to provoke violent reaction"—are generally proscribable under the First Amendment. *Cohen v. California*, 403 U.S. 15 (1971); see also *Chaplinsky v. New Hampshire, supra*, at 572. . . . And the First Amendment also permits a State to ban a "true threat." *Watts v. United States*, 394 U.S. 705 (1969) (*per curiam*).

"True threats" encompass those statements where the speaker means to communicate a serious expression of an intent to commit an act of unlawful violence to a particular individual or group of individuals. See *Watts v. United States, supra*, at 708 ("political hyberbole" is not a true threat); *R.A.V. v. City of St. Paul*, 505 U.S., at 388. The speaker need not actually intend to carry out the threat. Rather, a prohibition on true threats "protect[s] individuals from the fear of violence" and "from the disruption that fear engenders," in addition to protecting people "from the possibility that the threatened violence will occur." *Ibid.* Intimidation in the constitutionally proscribable sense of the word is a type of true threat, where a speaker directs a threat to a person or group of persons with the intent of placing the victim in fear of bodily harm or death. Respondents do not contest that some cross burnings fit within this meaning of intimidating speech, and rightly so. As noted in Part II, *supra*, the history of cross burning in this country shows that cross burning is often intimidating, intended to create a pervasive fear in victims that they are a target of violence. . . .

B

In *R.A.V.*, we held that a local ordinance that banned certain symbolic conduct, including cross burning, when done with the knowledge that such conduct would " 'arouse anger, alarm or resentment in others on the basis of race, color, creed, religion or gender' " was unconstitutional. *Id.*, at 380 (quoting the St. Paul Bias-Motivated Crime Ordinance, St. Paul, Minn., Legis. Code § 292.02 (1990)). We held that the ordinance did not pass constitutional muster because it discriminated on the basis of content by targeting only those individuals who "provoke violence" on a basis specified in the law. 505 U.S., at 391. The ordinance did not cover "[t]hose who wish to use 'fighting words' in connection with other ideas—to express hostility, for example, on the basis of political affiliation, union membership, or homosexuality." *Ibid.* This content-based discrimination was unconstitutional because it allowed the city "to impose special prohibitions on those speakers who express views on disfavored subjects." *Ibid.*

We did not hold in *R.A.V.* that the First Amendment prohibits *all* forms of content-based discrimination within a proscribable area of speech. . . .

Consequently, while the holding of *R.A.V.* does not permit a State to ban only obscenity based on "offensive *political* messages," *ibid.*, or "only those threats against the President that mention his policy on aid to inner cities," *ibid.*, the First Amendment permits content discrimination "based on the very reasons why the particular class of speech at issue . . . is proscribable," *id.*, at 393.

Similarly, Virginia's statute does not run afoul of the First Amendment insofar as it bans cross burning with intent to intimidate. Unlike the statute at issue in *R.A.V.*, the Virginia statute does not single out for opprobrium only that speech directed toward "one of the specified disfavored topics." . . .

The First Amendment permits Virginia to outlaw cross burnings done with the intent to intimidate because burning a cross is a particularly virulent form of intimidation. Instead of prohibiting all intimidating messages, Virginia may choose to regulate this subset of intimidating messages in light of cross burning's long and pernicious history as a signal of impending violence. Thus, just as a State may regulate only that obscenity which is the most obscene due to its prurient content, so too may a State choose to prohibit only those forms of intimidation that are most likely to inspire fear of bodily harm. . . .

IV

The Supreme Court of Virginia ruled in the alternative that Virginia's cross-burning statute was unconstitutionally overbroad due to its provision stating that "[a]ny such burning of a cross shall be prima facie evidence of an intent to intimidate a person or group of persons." . . .

The prima facie evidence provision, as interpreted by the jury instruction, renders the statute unconstitutional. . . . As construed by the jury instruction, the prima facie provision strips away the very reason why a State may ban cross burning with the intent to intimidate. The prima facie evidence provision permits a jury to convict in every cross-burning case in which defendants exercise their constitutional right not to put on a defense. And even where a defendant like Black presents a defense, the prima facie evidence provision makes it more likely that the jury will find an intent to intimidate regardless of the particular facts of the case. The provision permits the Commonwealth to arrest, prosecute, and convict a person based solely on the fact of cross burning itself. . . .

For these reasons, the prima facie evidence provision, as interpreted through the jury instruction and as applied in Barry Black's case, is unconstitutional on its face. . . .

JUSTICE STEVENS, concurring.

Cross burning with "an intent to intimidate," Va. Code Ann. § 18.2-423 (1996), unquestionably qualifies as the kind of threat that is unprotected by the First Amendment. For the reasons stated in the separate opinions that Justice White and I wrote in *R.A.V. v. St. Paul*, that simple proposition provides a sufficient basis for upholding the basic prohibition in the Virginia statute even though it does not cover other types of threatening expressive conduct. With this observation, I join Justice O'Connor's opinion.

JUSTICE SCALIA, with whom JUSTICE THOMAS joins as to Parts I and II, concurring in part, concurring in the judgment in part, and dissenting in part.

I agree with the Court that, under our decision in *R.A.V. v. St. Paul*, a State may, without infringing the First Amendment, prohibit cross burning carried out with the intent to intimidate. Accordingly, I join Parts I–III of the Court's opinion. I also agree that we should vacate and remand the judgment of the Virginia Supreme Court so that that Court can have an opportunity authoritatively to construe the prima-facie-evidence provision of Va. Code Ann. § 18.2-423 (1996). I write separately, however, to describe what I believe to be the correct interpretation of § 18.2-423, and to explain why I believe there is no justification for the plurality's apparent decision to invalidate that provision on its face. . . .

JUSTICE SOUTER, with whom JUSTICE KENNEDY and JUSTICE GINSBURG join, concurring in the judgment in part and dissenting in part.

I agree with the majority that the Virginia statute makes a content-based distinction within the category of punishable intimidating or threatening expression, the very type of distinction we considered in *R.A.V. v. St. Paul.* I disagree that any exception should save Virginia's law from unconstitutionality under the holding in *R.A.V.* or any acceptable variation of it. . . .

JUSTICE THOMAS, dissenting.

In every culture, certain things acquire meaning well beyond what outsiders can comprehend. That goes for both the sacred, see *Texas v. Johnson,* (Rehnquist, C. J., dissenting) (describing the unique position of the American flag in our Nation's 200 years of history), and the profane. I believe that cross burning is the paradigmatic example of the latter.

Although I agree with the majority's conclusion that it is constitutionally permissible to "ban. . . cross burning carried out with intent to intimidate," I believe that the majority errs in imputing an expressive component to the activity in question,. . . In my view, whatever expressive value cross burning has, the legislature simply wrote it out by banning only intimidating conduct undertaken by a particular means. A conclusion that the statute prohibiting cross burning with intent to intimidate sweeps beyond a prohibition on certain conduct into the zone of expression overlooks not only the words of the statute but also reality.

A

"In holding [the ban on cross burning with intent to intimidate] unconstitutional, the Court ignores Justice Holmes' familiar aphorism that 'a page of history is worth a volume of logic.' " *Texas v. Johnson, supra,* at 421 (REHNQUIST, C. J., dissenting). . . .

It strains credulity to suggest that a state legislature that adopted a litany of segregationist laws self-contradictorily intended to squelch the segregationist message. Even for segregationists, violent and terroristic conduct, the Siamese twin of cross burning, was intolerable. The ban on cross burning with intent to intimidate demonstrates that even segregationists understood the difference between intimidating and terroristic conduct and racist expression. It is simply beyond belief that, in passing the statute now under review, the Virginia legislature was concerned with anything but penalizing conduct it must have viewed as particularly vicious.

Accordingly, this statute prohibits only conduct, not expression. And, just as one cannot burn down someone's house to make a political point and then seek refuge in the First Amendment, those who hate cannot terrorize and intimidate to make their point. In light of my conclusion that the statute here addresses only conduct, there is no need to analyze it under any of our First Amendment tests. . . .

NOTES AND QUESTIONS

(1) *The Second Cross-Burning Decision: Virginia v. Black, 538 U.S. 343 (2003).* In *Black,* three defendants had been convicted of felony cross-burning under Virginia's criminal statute. The Virginia statute did not have the underinclusive features of the ordinance in *R.A.V.,* but the Virginia statute did include a "prima facie provision" that allowed the fact-finder to infer an "intent to intimidate" from the act of cross-burning itself. Despite these differences, the Virginia Supreme Court considered *R.A.V.* controlling and struck down the statute. The Supreme Court, per Justice O'Connor, affirmed, but used different reasoning.

(2) *A Category of Unprotected Speech: Cross Burning As A "True Threat."* Like the *R.A.V.* Court, the Black Court resisted the state's argument that cross burning should

be considered "unprotected speech" as "fighting words." Instead, the *Black Court* appeared to analogize cross burning done only for intimidation and not for a communicative purpose to what it considered to be another category of "unprotected speech": what it called "true threats."

Justice Souter's concurrence declined to join this analogy, and the Souter opinion explicitly identified the doctrinal shift away from the *R.A.V.* reasoning. Also, note that, even if cross-burning would be analogous to a "true threat," there is still a question, under the *Chaplinsky* standard, whether a particular "threat" is unprotected speech.

(3) *Justice Thomas and the Second Cross-Burning Decision.* Justice Thomas dissented. In his view, because of its history, cross-burning is not "speech" at all. Justice Thomas' opinion has the virtue of simplicity: if cross-burning would not qualify as speech, all of the other (sometimes complex) issues are moot. For authority, Justice Thomas cites to the Chief Justice's opinion in the first flag burning decision where the Chief Justice argued that flag burning was not speech because it was only an "inarticulate grunt." Of course, the Chief Justice's *Johnson* opinion was only a dissent; it was not the position of the Court.

Although he did not reference it, Justice Thomas apparently disagrees with the settled doctrine on the standard for determining when symbolic conduct will be considered "speech." You have reviewed the decisions, and the standard is the *Spence* test (as confirmed by the flag-burning decisions). In either case, no other Justice joined Justice Thomas.

[G] Defamation and Invasion of Privacy

[1] Defamation in the Public Arena

NEW YORK TIMES CO. v. SULLIVAN
376 U.S. 254 (1964)

MR. JUSTICE BRENNAN delivered the opinion of the court.

[The New York Times published a paid editorial advertisement signed by the "Committee to Defend Martin Luther King and the Struggle for Freedom in the South." The advertisement described indignities suffered by Martin Luther King and other blacks in the south, including expulsion from school, an incident in which "truckloads of police armed with shotguns and tear-gas ringed the Alabama State College Campus," padlocking of a dining hall, bombing of King's home, assaults, and arrests. Sullivan, who was Commissioner of Public Affairs in Montgomery, Alabama, sued for defamation and recovered damages of $500,000. The state supreme court affirmed, noting that it was uncontroverted that some of the statements contained in the advertisement were not accurate descriptions of the relevant events. The jury had been instructed that the statements in the advertisement were "libelous per se" and were not privileged, so that the Times would be held liable if it merely had published the advertisement and if the statements were made "of and concerning" Sullivan. Note that this jury instruction relied (at least implicitly) on the *Chaplinsky* assertion that libel was unprotected speech. Here, the United States Supreme Court reverses.]

We hold that the rule of law applied by the Alabama courts is constitutionally deficient for failure to provide the safeguards for freedom of speech and of the press that are required by the First and Fourteenth Amendments in a libel action brought by a public official against critics of his official conduct. We further hold that under the proper safeguards the evidence presented in this case is constitutionally insufficient to support the judgment for respondent.

Respondent relies heavily, as did the Alabama courts, on statements of this Court to the effect that the Constitution does not protect libelous publications. Those statements do not foreclose our inquiry here. None of the cases sustained the use of libel laws to impose sanctions upon expression critical of the official conduct of public officials.

[I]n deciding the question now, we are compelled by neither precedent nor policy to give any more weight to the epithet "libel" than we have to other "mere labels" of state law. Like insurrection, contempt, advocacy of unlawful acts, breach of the peace, obscenity, solicitation of legal business, and the various other formulae for the repression of expression that have been challenged in this Court, libel can claim no talismanic immunity from constitutional limitations. It must be measured by standards that satisfy the First Amendment. . . .

Thus we consider this case against the background of a profound national commitment to the principle that debate on public issues should be uninhibited, robust, and wide-open, and that it may well include vehement, caustic, and sometimes unpleasantly sharp attacks on government and public officials. *See Terminiello v. Chicago.* The present advertisement, as an expression of grievance and protest on one of the major public issues of our time, would seem clearly to qualify for the constitutional protection. The question is whether it forfeits that protection by the falsity of some of its factual statements and by its alleged defamation of respondent.

Authoritative interpretations of the First Amendment guarantees have consistently refused to recognize an exception for any test of truth-whether administered by judges, juries, or administrative officials-and especially one that puts the burden of proving truth on the speaker. [A]s Madison said, "Some degree of abuse is inseparable from the proper use of every thing; and in no instance is this more true than in that of the press." 4 Elliot's Debates on the Federal Constitution (1876), p. 571.

[E]rroneous statement is inevitable in free debate, and . . . it must be protected if the freedoms of expression are to have the "breathing space" that they "need . . . to survive". . . .

[I]njury to official reputation error affords no more warrant for repressing speech that would otherwise be free than does factual error. Where judicial officers are involved, this Court has held that concern for the dignity and reputation of the courts does not justify the punishment as criminal contempt of criticism of the judge or his decision. *Bridges v. California*, 314 U.S. 252. This is true even though the utterance contains "half-truths" and "misinformation". . . .

If neither factual error nor defamatory content suffices to remove the constitutional shield from criticism of official conduct, the combination of the two elements is no less inadequate. This is the lesson to be drawn from the great controversy over the Sedition Act of 1798, 1 Stat. 596, which first crystallized a national awareness of the central meaning of the First Amendment. That statute made it a crime, punishable by a $5,000 fine and five years in prison, "if any person shall write, print, utter or publish . . . any false, scandalous and malicious writing or writings against the government of the United States, or either house of the Congres s. . . or the President . . ., with intent to defame . . . or to bring them, or either of them, into contempt or disrepute; or to excite against them, or either or any of them, the hatred of the good people of the United States." The Act allowed the defendant the defense of truth, and provided that the jury were to be judges both of the law and the facts. Despite these qualifications, the Act was vigorously condemned as unconstitutional in an attack joined in by Jefferson and Madison. . . .

Although the Sedition Act was never tested in this Court, the attack upon its validity has carried the day in the court of history. Fines levied in its prosecution were repaid by Act of Congress on the ground that it was unconstitutional.

What a State may not constitutionally bring about by means of a criminal statute is likewise beyond the reach of its civil law of libel. The fear of damage awards under a rule such as that invoked by the Alabama courts here may be markedly more inhibiting than the fear of prosecution under a criminal statute. [P]resumably a person charged with violation of [a criminal libel] statute enjoys ordinary criminal-law safeguards such as the requirements of an indictment and of proof beyond a reasonable doubt. These safeguards are not available to the defendant in a civil action. The judgment awarded in this case-without the need for any proof of actual pecuniary loss-was one thousand times greater than the maximum fine provided by the Alabama criminal [libel] statute, and one hundred times greater than that provided by the Sedition Act.

And since there is no double-jeopardy limitation applicable to civil lawsuits, this is not the only judgment that may be awarded against petitioners for the same publication. Whether or not a newspaper can survive a succession of such judgments, the pall of fear and timidity imposed upon those who would give voice to public criticism is an atmosphere in which the First Amendment freedoms cannot survive. . . .

The state rule of law is not saved by its allowance of the defense of truth. A defense for erroneous statements honestly made is no less essential here. . . . A rule compelling the critic of official conduct to guarantee the truth of all his factual assertions-and to do so on pain of libel judgments virtually unlimited in amount-leads to a comparable "self-censorship." Allowance of the defense of truth, with the burden of proving it on the defendant, does not mean that only false speech will be deterred. Even courts accepting this defense as an adequate safeguard have recognized the difficulties of adducing legal proofs that the alleged libel was true in all its factual particulars. . . .

. . . The rule thus dampens the vigor and limits the variety of public debate. It is inconsistent with the First and Fourteenth Amendments.

The constitutional guarantees require, we think, a federal rule that prohibits a public official from recovering damages for a defamatory falsehood relating to his official conduct unless he proves that the statement was made with "actual malice"—that is, with knowledge that it was false or with reckless disregard of whether it was false or not. . . .

Since respondent may seek a new trial, we deem that considerations of effective judicial administration require us to review the evidence in the present record to determine whether it could constitutionally support a judgment for respondent.

[We] consider that the proof presented to show actual malice lacks the convincing clarity which the constitutional standard demands, and hence that it would not constitutionally sustain the judgment for respondent under the proper rule of law. . . .

[T]he statement by the Times' Secretary that, apart from the padlocking allegation, he thought the advertisement was "substantially correct," affords no constitutional warrant for the Alabama Supreme Court's conclusion that it was a "cavalier ignoring of the falsity of the advertisement [from which], the jury could not have but been impressed with the bad faith of The Times, and its maliciousness inferable therefrom." The Times' failure to retract upon respondent's demand, although it later retracted upon the demand of Governor Patterson, is likewise not adequate evidence of malice for constitutional purposes. Whether or not a failure to retract may ever constitute such evidence, there are two reasons why it does not here. *First*, the letter written by the Times reflected a reasonable doubt on its part as to whether the advertisement could reasonably be taken to refer to respondent at all. *Second*, it was not a final refusal, since it asked for an explanation on this point—a request that respondent chose to ignore.

Finally, there is evidence that the Times published the advertisement without checking its accuracy against the news stories in the Times' own files. The mere presence of the stories in the files does not, of course, establish that the Times "knew" the advertisement was false, since the state of mind required for actual malice would have to be brought home to the persons in the Times' organization having responsibility for the publication of the advertisement. With respect to the failure of those persons to make the check, the record shows that they relied upon their knowledge of the good reputation of many of those whose names were listed as sponsors of the advertisement, and upon the letter from A. Philip Randolph, known to them as a responsible individual, certifying that the use of the names was authorized. . . .

[*Reversed.*]

Mr. Justice Black, with whom Mr. Justice Douglas joins [concurring].

[T]he Court [holds] that a state can subject . . . critics [of public officials] to damages if "actual malice" can be proved against them. "Malice," even as defined by the Court, is an elusive, abstract concept, hard to prove and hard to disprove. The requirement that malice be proved requires at best an evanescent protection for the right critically to discuss public affairs and certainly measure up to the sturdy safeguard embodied in the first amendment. Unlike the court, therefore, I vote to reverse exclusively on the ground that the . . . defendants had an absolute, unconditional right to publish . . . their criticisms of the Montgomery agencies and officials. . . .

The half-million-dollar verdict [here] [gives] dramatic proof . . . that state libel laws threaten the very existence of an American press . . . bold enough to criticize the conduct of public officials. [I]n fact, briefs before us show that in Alabama there are now pending eleven libel suits by local and state officials against the Times seeking $5,600,000, and five such suits against the Columbia Broadcasting System seeking $1,700,000. Moreover, this technique for harassing and punishing a free press-now that it has been shown to be possible-is by no means limited to cases with racial overtones. . . .

In my opinion, the federal Constitution has dealt with this deadly danger to the press in the only way possible . . . by granting the press an absolute immunity for criticism of the way public officials do their public duty.

[The concurring opinion of Justice Goldberg, joined by Justice Douglas, is omitted.]

NOTES AND QUESTIONS

(1) *The Famous New York Times v. Sullivan Decision.* The initial holding in *Sullivan* is that "libel can claim no talismanic immunity from constitutional limitations. It must be measured by standards that satisfy the First Amendment." In other words, Justice Brennan's famous opinion held that libel would not be considered unprotected speech. The Court then proceeded to announce the standard it would use ("actual malice") and applied that standard. With the adoption of the actual malice standard, Justice Brennan is credited with having "constitutionalized the law of libel."

(2) *The Argument that the New York Times "Actual Malice" Standard Tips the Balance Excessively in Favor of the Press.* Can it be argued that the *New York Times* standard excessively favors the press? By placing the burden of proof on the defamed individual, and requiring that he prove not only falsity and defamation but also the recklessness of the defendant's operative, it erects a barrier that few will be able to surmount, even if they have been defamed and seriously injured by the fault of the defendant. In most areas of human endeavor, businesses are required to compensate for the external effects of their activity, even if no particular injury is intentional or even reckless. A derivative disadvantage is that, as a reaction to this favored status for the press, our society, including juries and courts, may deal punitively with those members of the press whom they do have the power to sanction. Finally, a standard for professional malpractice that requires "actual malice" may lower the level of accuracy throughout the press.

(3) *The Contrary Argument—That the New York Times Rule Fails Adequately to Protect the Press.* But can't the opposite argument also be made? There always is some step that the publisher could have taken that would have alerted it to possible falsity but that it chose not to undertake, usually because of economic or similar reasons. When that choice results in defamation and injury, and when it is viewed in hindsight, it often will

appear reckless. The plaintiff's burden of proof may not protect the defendant, particularly since it will be subjected to extensive discovery, which itself is undesirable to the press because it has subtle effects in compromising investigations. Furthermore, reliance on a constitutional defense, in which a newspaper "wraps itself in the First Amendment," makes press defendants appear arrogant and may produce undeserved negative verdicts. The lack of any coherent measure of actual damages, and the potential size of punitive damages, produce a chilling effect. Do these arguments support the conclusion of Justice Black, that criticism of public officials should be "absolutely" protected under the first amendment even if they are false and defamatory?

(4) *What Does "Actual Malice" or "Reckless Disregard" Mean? The "Serious Doubt" Standard of St. Amant v. Thompson, 390 U.S. 727 (1968).* It is clear that the *New York Times* standard requires more than negligence. It is not enough to show that the defendant failed to exercise reasonable care or that a person of ordinary prudence would not have published the defamatory statement. Instead, the evidence must support a finding that "the defendant in fact entertained serious doubts as to the truth of his publication." *St. Amant v. Thompson.* Consider whether this standard disadvantages the thorough reporter who amasses contrary information and weighs it carefully, and gives license to the reporter who instead remains inadvertently ignorant. Paradoxically, mightn't a reporter who remains too ignorant even to "entertain serious doubts" be better off? For a thorough analysis of proof issues in these cases, *see Bloom, Proof of Fault in Media Defamation Litigation*, 38 VAND. L. REV. 247 (1985).

(5) *Applying the New York Times Actual Malice Standard to "Hot" News Stories—and to "Think Pieces": Associated Press v. Walker, 388 U.S. 130 (1967), and Curtiss Publishing Co. v. Butts, 388 U.S. 130 (1967).* The *Walker* case arose out of the distribution of a news dispatch giving an eyewitness account alleging that Walker had taken command of a violent crowd opposing the enrollment of a black student, James Meredith, at the University of Mississippi. Walker denied inciting the crowd, claimed that he had counseled restraint, and showed that there was a discrepancy between oral and written accounts furnished to the defendant. The Court set aside a libel award. The plurality opinion, authored by Justice Harlan, emphasized the need for "immediate dissemination" of this breaking news story, the "trustworthiness and competence" of this reporter, his actual "presence" at the scene of the events, the internal consistency of the dispatches with one minor discrepancy, the lack of a motive to distort, and the consistency of the reported conduct with Walker's previous history. On this basis, the plurality concluded that the *New York Times* standard could not be satisfied because of the absence of evidence showing intent or recklessness. In *Butts*, on the other hand, the Saturday Evening Post accused the Athletic Director of the University of Georgia of participating in a "football fix" and stated "[C]areers will be ruined, that is sure." Plaintiff's expert witnesses analyzed the reporter's notes, concluded they were inadequate to support the charges reported, and "severely contradicted" the Post version of the events. The plurality reasoned: "The evidence showed that the Butts story was in no sense 'hot news,' and the editors of the magazine recognized the need for thorough investigation of the serious charges. Elementary precautions were, nevertheless, ignored." On this basis, the Court upheld a jury verdict under the actual malice standard. Taken together, *Butts and Walker* show the kind of factors that will influence the actual malice decision. In particular, they show that recklessness is less likely to be found in the context of a "hot news" story that in the context of a "muckraking" feature article or "think piece."

(6) *Butts and Walker as Establishing a Trichotomy of "Public Officials," "Public Figures," and "Private Figures" for Purposes of the New York Times Standard.* The *New Times* case concerned a public official as plaintiff. *Walker* and *Butts*, on the other hand, were not public officials. Nevertheless, extending the *New York* Times rule, the plurality denominated *Butts* and *Walker* as "public figures," and concluded: "We . . . hold that a 'public figure' who is not a public official may also recover damages for a defamatory falsehood whose substance makes substantial danger to reputation appar-

ent, on a showing of highly unreasonable conduct constituting an extreme departure from the standards of investigation and reporting ordinarily adhered to by responsible publishers." How does this standard differ, if meaningfully it does, from the standard enunciated in *New York Times*? By implication, those who are not public officials or public figures are subject to a different constitutional standard. We consider the treatment of these so-called "private figures" in the next section of this chapter, below.

(7) *The New York Times Standard in Actual Practice: Press Defendants Usually Win on the Law, But Usually Lose With Juries if Plaintiffs Can Reach Them.* Empirical study shows that roughly three out of four contested libel cases do not reach trial, being disposed of by summary judgments or similar means. But in those cases that do reach trial, juries hold against media defendants in the overwhelming majority of cases. (Survey results vary between 80 and 90 percent. Bench trials, interestingly, result in a much lower percentage of plaintiff's judgments, approximately 50 percent; it appears that judges do not share the predispositions of jurors.) On appeal, however, the majority of plaintiff's verdicts are reversed (approximately 64 percent, or nearly two-thirds). In summary, the clear majority of libel cases cannot be supported on the law, and thus result in pretrial disposition; and the clear majority of those that are tried result in defendant's judgments by application of the law on appeal—despite jury antagonism to the press. *See generally* Franklin, *Suing Media for Libel: A Litigation Study*, 1981 ABA Foundation Research J. 795; Libel Defense Research Center, Bulls. No. 4, 6 (Aug. 15, 1982; Mar. 15, 1983). Franklin points out that, even in cases resulting in defendant's judgments, costs of litigation are significant, and they probably far exceed the amounts paid in satisfaction of judgments. Question: What do these empirical findings show about whether the *Times* standard is too tight-or too loose?

MILKOVICH v. LORAIN JOURNAL, 497 U.S. 1 (1990). The Lorain Journal published an article implying that Michael Milkovich, a local high school wrestling coach, had lied under oath in a judicial proceeding about an incident involving petitioner and his team which occurred at a wrestling match. The article gave factual reasons for its conclusion, which was: "Anyone who attended the meet, whether he be from Maple Heights, Mentor, or impartial observer, knows in his heart that Milkovich and [former Superintendent] Scott lied at the hearing after each having giving his solemn oath to tell the truth." Milkovich sued for defamation.

The trial court granted summary judgment for the newspaper on the ground that the article was "opinion" protected by "constitutional law" from a libel action. The Ohio Supreme Court reversed; it concluded that Milkovich was neither a public figure nor a public official, and it found that "the statements in issue are factual assertions as a matter of law, and are not constitutionally protected as opinions of the writer. . . . The plain import of the author's assertions is that Milkovich [c]ommitted the crime of perjury in a court of law." The United States Supreme Court, per Chief Justice Rehnquist, affirmed and agreed that the statements could be treated as actionable. The Court proceeded to consider whether "opinion" was protected:

> Respondents would have us recognize, in addition to the established safe-guards . . ., still another first amendment-based protection for defamatory statements which are categorized as "opinion" as opposed to "fact". . . .

> If a speaker says, "in my opinion John Jones is a liar," he implies a knowledge of facts which lead to the conclusion that Jones told an untruth. Even if the speaker states the facts upon which he bases his opinion, if those facts are either incorrect or incomplete, or if his assessment of them is erroneous, the statement may still imply a false assertion of fact. Simply couching such statements in terms of opinion does not dispel these implications; and the statement, "in my opinion Jones is a liar," can cause as much damage to reputation as the statement, "Jones is a liar." As Judge Friendly aptly stated:

> "[It] would be destructive of the law of libel if a writer could escape liability for accusations of [defamatory conduct] simply by using, explicitly or implicitly,

the words 'I think.' "

Foremost, we think [prior case law] stands for the proposition that a statement on matters of public concern must be provable as false before there can be liability under state defamation law, at least in situations, like the present, where a media defendant is involved. Thus, unlike the statement, "In my opinion Mayor Jones is a liar," the statement "In my opinion Mayor Jones shows his abysmal ignorance by accepting the teachings of Marx and Lenin," would not be actionable. [This rule] insures that a statement of opinion relating to matters of public concern which does not contain a provably false factual connotation will receive full constitutional protection. . . .

We are not persuaded that, in addition to these protections, an additional separate constitutional privilege for "opinion" is required to ensure the freedom of expression guaranteed by the first amendment. . . .

Justice Brennan, joined by Justice Marshall, dissented. He agreed with most of the propositions of law stated by the Court. In particular, he agreed that there was no "so-called opinion privilege" wholly in addition to other first amendment protections. However, he disagreed with the Court in its application of those principles to the case before it:

[A]lthough statements of opinion *may* imply an assertion of a false and defamatory fact, they do not *invariably* do so. . . .

[In this case, the newspaper's writer] not only reveals the facts upon which he is relying, but he makes it clear at which point he runs out of facts and is simply guessing. Read in context, the statements cannot reasonably be interpreted as implying such an assertion as fact. . . .

The format of the piece is a signed editorial column with a photograph of the columnist and the logo "TD says. . . ."

[C]onjecture is intrinsic to "the free flow of ideas and opinions on matters of public interest and concern" that is at "the heart of the first amendment". . . .

[The newspaper's writer] is guilty of jumping to conclusions, of benightedly assuming that court decisions are always based on the merits, and of looking foolish to lawyers. He is not, however, liable for defamation. . . .

PROBLEM N

GO OR NO GO ON A HOT NEWS STORY OR A FEATURE STORY?—DOUBLEDAY, INC. v. ROGERS, 674 S.W.2d 751 (Tex. 1984). Imagine that a news reporter or book author has submitted a manuscript stating in one short passage, that a named person "was appointed to the state Optometry Board by [the governor], despite [the appointee's] three indictments for practicing without a license." If you were the attorney for the publisher, what substantiation of this statement would you insist upon? In *Doubleday*, the author responded to the attorney's inquiry by citing a legislative journal. But he did not re-inspect that original source, which was located in another city some distance away. After publication, the named person sued for libel—since the author, apparently from confusion, had substituted his name for his brother's(!) The jury awarded $2.5 million in punitive damages. Question 1: Should the award stand, either in the context of a "hot" news story or of a feature story? Question 2: What substantiation should we as a society desire that a publisher insist upon in these circumstances? Question 3: How closely does the *New York Times* standard, as refined in *Butts* and *Walker*, correspond to the proper balance? [In *Doubleday*, the Texas Supreme Court ultimately reversed, holding that the requisite proof of actual malice was lacking in these circumstances.]

[2]   Libel Law in the Context of Private Figures or Events

GERTZ v. ROBERT WELCH, INC.
418 U.S. 323 (1974)

Mr. Justice Powell delivered the opinion of the Court.

[Defendant published a periodical called American Opinion, which the Court described as "a monthly outlet for the views of the John Birch Society." It published an article charging that Gertz was the "architect of [a] 'frame-up.'" It also falsely stated that he was a "Leninist," a "Communist-fronter," a member of the "Marxist League for Industrial Democracy," and a member of the "Intercollegiate Socialists Society," among other statements. Because some of the statements in the article constituted libel per se under applicable state law, the trial court submitted the case to the jury under instructions that withdrew from its consideration all issues except the measure of damages. The jury awarded $50,000 to Gertz.

[The district judge, however, concluded that the *New York Times* standard should govern, even though Gertz was not a public official or public figure. He reasoned that the standard protected discussion of any public issue, without regard to the status of a person allegedly defamed. Therefore, the district court granted the defendant's motion for judgment notwithstanding the verdict. The court of appeals affirmed. Here, the Supreme Court reverses and opts for a lesser standard in the context of libel of private figures.]

We begin with the common ground. Under the First Amendment there is no such thing as a false idea. [B]ut there is no constitutional value in false statements of fact. Neither the intentional lie nor the careless error materially advances society's interest in "uninhibited, robust, and wide-open" debate on public issues. *New York Times Co. v. Sullivan.* They belong to that category of utterances which "are no essential part of any exposition of ideas, and are of such slight social value as a step to truth that any benefit that may be derived from them is clearly outweighed by the social interest in order and morality." *Chaplinsky v. New Hampshire.*

Although the erroneous statement of fact is not worthy of constitutional protection, it is nevertheless inevitable in free debate. [T]he First Amendment requires that we protect some falsehood in order to protect speech that matters.

The need to avoid self-censorship by the news media is, however, not the only societal value at issue. If it were, this Court would have embraced long ago the view that publishers and broadcasters enjoy an unconditional and indefeasible immunity from liability for defamation. *See New York Times Co. v. Sullivan* (Black, J., concurring). . . . [A]bsolute protection for the communications media requires a total sacrifice of the competing value served by the law of defamation.

The legitimate state interest underlying the law of libel is the compensation of individuals for the harm inflicted on them by defamatory falsehood. "[T]he protection of private personality, like the protection of life itself, is left primarily to the individual States under the Ninth and Tenth Amendments. But this does not mean that the right is entitled to any less recognition by this Court as a basic of our constitutional system."

[F]or the reasons stated below, we conclude that the state interest in compensating injury to the reputation of private individuals requires that a different rule should obtain with respect to them.

[B]ecause an *ad hoc* resolution of the competing interests at stake in each particular case is not feasible, we must lay down broad rules of general application. . . .

With that caveat we have no difficulty in distinguishing among defamation plaintiffs. The first remedy of any victim of defamation is self-help-using available opportunities to contradict the lie or correct the error and thereby to minimize its adverse impact on reputation. Public officials and public figures usually enjoy significantly greater access to the channels of effective communication and hence have a more realistic opportunity to counteract false statements then private individuals normally enjoy. Private individuals are therefore more vulnerable to injury, and the state interest in protecting them is correspondingly greater.

More important than the likelihood that private individuals will lack effective opportunities for rebuttal, there is a compelling normative consideration underlying the distinction between public and private defamation plaintiffs. An individual who decides to seek governmental office must accept certain necessary consequences of that involvement in public affairs. . . .

Those classed as public figures stand in a similar position. Hypothetically, it may be possible for someone to become a public figure through no purposeful action of his own, but the instances of truly involuntary public figures must be exceedingly rare. More commonly, those classed as public figures have thrust themselves to the forefront of particular public controversies in order to influence the resolution of the issues involved. In either event, they invite attention and comment.

[N]o such assumption is justified with respect to a private individual. He has not accepted public office or assumed an "influential role in ordering society". . . .

We hold that, so long as they do not impose liability without fault, the States may define for themselves the appropriate standard of liability for a publisher or broadcaster of defamatory falsehood injurious to a private individual. [W]e endorse this approach in recognition of the strong and legitimate state interest in compensating private individuals for injury to reputation. But this countervailing state interest extends no further than compensation for actual injury. For the reasons stated below, we hold that the States may not permit recovery of presumed or punitive damages, at least when liability is not based on a showing of knowledge of falsity or reckless disregard for the truth. . . .

[I]n most jurisdictions jury discretion over the amounts [of punitive damages] awarded is limited only by the gentle rule that they not be excessive. Consequently, juries assess punitive damages in wholly unpredictable amounts bearing no necessary relation to the actual harm caused. And they remain free to use their discretion selectively to punish expressions of unpopular views. . . . [I]n short, the private defamation plaintiff who establishes liability under a less demanding standard than that stated by *New York Times* may recover only such damages as are sufficient to compensate him for actual injury.

Notwithstanding our refusal to extend the *New York Times* privilege to defamation of private individuals, respondent contends that we should affirm the judgment below on the ground that petitioner is . . . a public figure. . . .

Respondent's characterization of petitioner as a public figure raises a different question. That designation may rest on either of two alternative bases. In some instances an individual may achieve such pervasive fame or notoriety that he becomes a public figure for all purposes and in all contexts. More commonly, an individual voluntarily injects himself or is drawn into a particular public controversy and thereby becomes a public figure for a limited range of issues.

[W]e would not lightly assume that a citizen's participation in community and professional affairs rendered him a public figure for all purposes. Absent clear evidence of general fame or notoriety in the community, and pervasive involvement in the affairs of society, an individual should not be deemed a public personality for all aspects of his life. It is preferable to reduce the public-figure question to a more meaningful context by looking to the nature and extent of an individual's participation in the particular controversy giving rise to the defamation.

In this context it is plain that petitioner was not a public figure. He played a minimal role at the coroner's inquest [on which the defamatory report was based], and his participation related solely to his representation of a private client. He took no part in the criminal prosecution [at issue]. Moreover, he never discussed either the criminal or civil litigation with the press and was never quoted as having done so. He plainly did not thrust himself into the vortex of this public issue, nor did he engage the public's attention in an attempt to influence its outcome. . . .

We therefore conclude that the *New York Times* standard is inapplicable to this case and that the trial court erred in entering judgment for respondent. Because the jury was allowed to impose liability without fault and was permitted to presume damages without proof of injury, a new trial is necessary. We reverse and remand for further proceedings in accord with this opinion. . . .

Reversed and remanded.

[The concurring opinion of MR. JUSTICE BLACKMUN is omitted. The dissenting opinion of MR. CHIEF JUSTICE BURGER also is omitted.]

MR. JUSTICE DOUGLAS, dissenting. . . .

It is only the hardy publisher who will engage in discussion in the face of [the] risk [created by this decision], and the court's preoccupation with proliferating standards in the area of libel increases the risk. It matters little whether the standard be articulated as "malice" or "reckless disregard of the truth" or "negligence," for jury determinations by any of these criteria are virtually unreviewable. . . .

Since in my view the first and fourteenth amendments prohibit the imposition of damages upon respondent for this discussion of public affairs, I would affirm the judgment below.

MR. JUSTICE BRENNAN, dissenting . . .

[I] adhere to my view . . . that we strike the proper accommodation between avoidance of media self-censorship and protection of individual reputations only when we require states to apply the *New York Times Co. v. Sullivan* . . . knowing-or-reckless-falsity standard in civil libel actions concerning media reports of the involvement of private individuals in events of public or general interest. . . .

MR. JUSTICE WHITE, dissenting.

For some 200 years . . . the law of defamation and right to the ordinary citizen to recover for false publication injuries to his reputation have been almost exclusively the business of state courts and legislatures. . . .

. . . Under the new rule, the plaintiff can lose, not because the statement is true, but because it was not negligently made. . . .

The Court evinces a deep-seated antipathy to "liability without fault." But this catch—phrase has no talismanic significance and is almost meaningless in this context where the Court appears to be addressing those libels and slanders that are defamatory on their face and where the publisher is no doubt aware from the nature of the material that it would be inherently damaging to reputation. He publishes notwithstanding, knowing that he will inflict injury. . . .

In these circumstances, the law has heretofore put the risk of falsehood on the publisher where the victim is a private citizen and no grounds of special privilege are involved. . . .

The communications industry has increasingly become concentrated in a few powerful hands operating very lucrative businesses reaching . . . into almost every home. Neither the industry as a whole nor its individual components are easily intimidated, and we are fortunate that they are not. Requiring them to pay for the occasional damage they do to private reputation will play no substantial part in their future performance or their existence.

NOTES AND QUESTIONS

(1) *The Four Approaches Advocated By Different Justices in Gertz: Actual Malice (or Reckless Disregard), Fault (or Negligence), Strict Liability, Or Absolute Immunity?* Notice the fragmentation of the Justices in *Gertz*. The majority allows liability to be imposed upon proof of "fault" (*i.e.*, negligence), since the defamed individual is a private figure. In this regard, the *Gertz* Court limited (or narrowed) the *Sullivan* decision. On the other hand, Justice Brennan would apply the actual malice standard (requiring reckless disregard of truth or falsity), because even though the case involves a private individual, the report concerned "events of public or general interest." A third position is staked out by Justice White, who would permit imposition of strict liability in these circumstances. Finally, Justice Douglas would afford the defendant absolute immunity for "discussion of public affairs." Which of these four approaches is most appropriate?

(2) *Just Who Is a "Public Figure" and Who Is a "Private Figure" after Gertz?: Time, Inc. v. Firestone, 424 U.S. 448 (1976).* If *New York Times* was good news for the media, *Firestone* was very bad news for them. Firestone sued for separate maintenance and her husband counterclaimed for divorce on grounds of extreme cruelty and adultery. Time Magazine published an item attributing the grounds to "extreme cruelty and adultery." Firestone then sued *Time* and recovered judgment for $100,000, having proved that the divorce decree, although it recited the grounds stated in the counterclaim and "granted" the counterclaim, actually was based upon lesser grounds. The Supreme Court, per Justice Rehnquist, remanded the case for a determination whether there was "fault" on *Time*'s part, implicitly indicating that if there was, the judgment could be upheld.

In the course of reaching that holding, Justice Rehnquist quoted *Gertz* to the effect that most public figures "have assumed roles of special prominence" and most "have thrust themselves into the forefront of particular public controversies in order to influence the resolution of the issues involved." Applying this concept, the Court held that Firestone was a private figure:

> Respondent did not assume any role of special prominence in the affairs of society, other than perhaps Palm Beach society, and she did not thrust herself to the forefront of any particular public controversy in order to influence the resolution of the issues involved in it. . . .

> Dissolution of a marriage through judicial proceedings is not the sort of "public controversy" referred to in *Gertz*, even though the marital difficulties of extremely wealthy individuals may be of interest to some portions of the reading public.

Justice Brennan dissented, stressing that "a trial is a public event." He would have applied the *New York Times* standard. Justice White, on the other hand, dissented because he would have affirmed the judgment outright.

Finally, Justice Marshall dissented: "I consider the respondent . . . to be a public figure within the meaning of our prior decisions. . . ." [S]he was "prominent among the 'four hundred' of Palm Beach society." [S]he was "hardly in a position to suggest that she lacked access to the media," particularly since she had held several press conferences in the course of the divorce proceedings.

(3) *A Lesser Proof Standard for Matter That Is Not "of Public Concern": The Defamatory Credit Report Case (Greenmoss).* What if defamation is said to have occurred in the context of a commercial relationship or in an employment reference? Should the case be governed by the same considerations of "breathing space" and avoiding "chilling effects" as apply to media defendants? *Cf.* Note, *American Defama-*

tion Law: From Sullivan through Greenmoss and Beyond, 48 Ohio St. L.J. 513 (1987). In *Dun & Bradstreet, Inc. v. Greenmoss Builders, Inc.*, 472 U.S. 749 (1985), the plaintiff claimed that defendant had defamed it by a false credit report, which erroneously stated that plaintiff had filed a bankruptcy petition. The Supreme Court upheld the resulting damage award, with the plurality reasoning that a lesser proof standard applied when the speech was not on a "matter of public concern." Proof of actual malice was therefore not required.

[3] Invasion of Privacy and Intentional Infliction of Emotional Distress

FLORIDA STAR v. B.J.F.
491 U.S. 524 (1989)

JUSTICE MARSHALL delivered the opinion of the Court.

Florida Stat. section 794.03 (1987) makes it unlawful to "print, publish, or broadcast . . . in any instrument of mass communication" the name of the victim of a sexual offense. Pursuant to this statute, appellant The Florida Star was found civilly liable for publishing the name of a rape victim which it had obtained from a publicly released police report. The issue presented here is whether this result comports with the First Amendment. We hold that it does not.

I

[O]n October 20, 1983, appellee B.J.F. reported to the Duval County, Florida, Sheriff's Department (the Department) that she had been robbed and sexually assaulted by an unknown assailant. The Department prepared a report on the incident which identified B.J.F., by her full name. The Department then placed the report in its press room. The Department does not restrict access either to the press room or to the reports made available therein.

A Florida Star reporter-trainee sent to the press room copied the police report verbatim, including B.J.F.'s full name, on a blank duplicate of the Department's forms. A Florida Star reporter then prepared a one-paragraph article about the crime, derived entirely from the trainee's copy of the police report. The article included B.J.F.'s full name. It appeared in the "Robberies" subsection of the "Police Reports" section on October 29, 1983, one of fifty-four police blotter stories in that day's edition. The article read:

> [B.J.F.] reported on Thursday, October 20, she was crossing Brentwood Park, which is in the 500 block of Golfair Boulevard, enroute to her bus stop, when an unknown black man ran up behind the lady and placed a knife to her neck and told her not to yell. The suspect then undressed the lady and had sexual intercourse with her before fleeing the scene with her 60 cents, Timex watch and gold necklace. Patrol efforts have been suspended concerning this incident because of a lack of evidence.

In printing B.J.F.'s full name, The Florida Star violated its internal policy of not publishing the names of sexual offense victims.

On September 26, 1984, B.J.F. filed suit in the Circuit Court of Duval County against the Department and The Florida Star, alleging that these parties negligently violated section 794.03. Before trial, the Department settled with B.J.F. for $2,500. . . .

At the ensuing day-long trial, B.J.F. testified that she had suffered emotional distress from the publication of her name. She stated that she had heard about the article from fellow workers and acquaintances; that her mother had received several threatening phone calls from a man who stated that he would rape B.J.F. again; and that these events had forced B.J.F. to change her phone number and residence, to seek police protection, and to obtain mental health counseling. In defense, The Florida Star put forth evidence indicating that the newspaper had learned B.J.F.'s name from the incident report released by the Department, and that the newspaper's violation of its internal rule against publishing the names of sexual offense victims was inadvertent.

[The trial court granted judgment on the jury's verdict of $75,000 and $25,000 punitive damages, less the $2,500 settlement. The court of appeals affirmed. The Supreme Court here reverses.]

[T]he parties to this case frame their contentions in light of a trilogy of cases [*Cox Broadcasting Corp. v. Cohn*, 420 U.S. 469 (1975), *Oklahoma Publishing Co. v. District Court*, 430 U.S. 308 (1977) and *Smith v. Daily Mail Publishing Co.*, 443 U.S. 97 (1979)] which have presented, in different contexts, the conflict between truthful reporting and state—protected privacy interests.

[I]n our view, this case is appropriately analyzed with reference to [a] limited First Amendment principle . . . which we articulated in *Daily Mail* in our synthesis of prior cases involving attempts to punish truthful publication: "[I]f a newspaper lawfully obtains truthful information about a matter of public significance then state officials may not constitutionally punish publication of the information, absent a need to further a state interest of the highest order." According the press the ample protection provided by that principle is supported by at least three separate considerations, in addition to, of course, the overarching "public interest, secured by the Constitution, in the dissemination of truth". . . .

First, because the *Daily Mail* formulation only protects the publication of information which a newspaper has "lawfully obtain[ed]," the government retains ample means of safeguarding significant interests upon which publication may impinge, including protecting a rape victim's anonymity. . . .

A second consideration undergirding the *Daily Mail* principle is the fact that punishing the press for its dissemination of information which is already publicly available is relatively unlikely to advance the interests in the service of which the State seeks to act. . . .

A third and final consideration is the "timidity and self-censorship" which may result from allowing the media to be punished for publishing certain truthful information. *Cox Broadcasting* noted this concern with overdeterrence in the context of information made public through official court records, but the fear of excessive media self-suppression is applicable as well to other information released, without qualification, by the government. . . .

Applied to the instant case, the *Daily Mail* principle clearly commands reversal. It is undisputed that the news article describing the assault on B.J.F. was accurate. In addition, appellant lawfully obtained B.J.F.'s name. . . . Even assuming the Constitution permitted a State to proscribe receipt of information, Florida has not taken this step. It is clear, furthermore, that the news article concerned "a matter of public significance," in the sense in which the *Daily Mail* synthesis of prior cases used that term. That is, the article generally, as opposed to the specific identity contained within it, involved a matter of paramount public import: the commission, and investigation, of a violent crime which had been reported to authorities.

The second inquiry is whether imposing liability on appellant pursuant to section 794.03 serves "a need to further a state interest of the highest order." Appellee argues that a rule punishing publication furthers three closely related interests: the privacy of victims of sexual offenses; the physical safety of such victims, who may be targeted for retaliation if their names become known to their assailants; and the goal of encouraging victims of such crimes to report these offenses without fear of exposure.

At a time in which we are daily reminded of the tragic reality of rape, it is undeniable that these are highly significant interests, a fact underscored by the Florida Legislature's explicit attempt to protect these interests by enacting a criminal statute prohibiting much dissemination of victim identities. We accordingly do not rule out the possibility that, in a proper case, imposing civil sanctions for publication of the name of a rape victim might be so overwhelmingly necessary to advance these interests as to satisfy the *Daily Mail* standard. For three independent reasons, however, imposing liability for publication under the circumstances of this case is too precipitous a means of advancing these interests to convince us that there is a "need" within the meaning of the *Daily Mail* formulation for Florida to take this extreme step.

First is the manner in which appellant obtained the identifying information in question. As we have noted, where the government itself provides information to the media, it is most appropriate to assume that the government had, but failed to utilize, far more limited means of guarding against dissemination than the extreme step of punishing truthful speech. . . .

A second problem with Florida's imposition of liability for publication is the broad sweep of the negligence per se standard applied under the civil cause of action implied from section 794.03. Unlike claims based on the common law tort of invasion of privacy, *see* Restatement (Second) of Torts section 652D (1977), civil actions based on section 794.03 require no case-by-case findings that the disclosure of a fact about a person's private life was one that a reasonable person would find highly offensive. On the contrary, under the per se theory of negligence adopted by the courts below, liability follows automatically from publication. . . .

Third, and finally, the facial underinclusiveness of section 794.03 raises serious doubts about whether Florida is, in fact, serving, with this statute, the significant interests which appellee invokes. . . . Section 794.03 prohibits the publication of identifying information only if this information appears in an "instrument of mass communication," a term the statute does not define. An individual who maliciously spreads word of the identity of a rape victim is thus not covered. . . . [W]ithout more careful and inclusive precautions against alternative forms of dissemination, we cannot conclude that Florida's selective ban on publication by the mass media satisfactorily accomplishes its stated purpose.

[W]e hold only that where a newspaper publishes truthful information which it has lawfully obtained, punishment may lawfully be imposed, if at all, only when narrowly tailored to a state interest of the highest order, and that no such interest is satisfactorily served by imposing liability under section 794.03 to appellant under the facts of this case.

[Reversed.]

[The opinion of Justice SCALIA, concurring in the judgment, is omitted.]

Justice WHITE, with whom the CHIEF JUSTICE and JUSTICE O'CONNOR join, dissenting.

Short of homicide, [rape] is the "ultimate violation of self." For B.J.F., however, the violation she suffered at a rapist's knifepoint marked only the beginning of her ordeal. . . .

Finding *Cox Broadcasting* inadequate to support its result, the Court relies on *Smith v. Daily Mail Publishing Co.* as its principal authority. But the flat rule from *Daily Mail* on which the Court places so much reliance—"[I]f a newspaper lawfully obtains truthful information . . . then state officials may not constitutionally punish publication of the information, absent a need to further a state interest of the highest order"—was introduced in *Daily Mail* with the cautious qualifier that such a rule was "suggest[ed]" by our prior cases, "[n]one of [which] . . . directly control[led]" in *Daily Mail*. The rule the Court takes as a given was thus offered only as a hypothesis in *Daily Mail*: it should not be so uncritically accepted as constitutional dogma.

More importantly, at issue in *Daily Mail* was the disclosure of the name of the perpetrator of an infamous murder of a 15-year-old student. Surely the rights of those accused of crimes and those who are their victims must differ with respect to privacy concerns. [T]he rights of crime victims to stay shielded from public view must be infinitely more substantial. *Daily Mail* was careful to state that the "holding in this case is narrow . . . *there is no issue here of privacy*." But in this case, there is an issue of privacy-indeed, that is the principal issue-and therefore, this case falls outside of *Daily Mail's* "rule" (which, as I suggest above, was perhaps not even meant as a rule in the first place). . . .

We are left, then, to wonder whether the three "independent reasons" the Court cites for reversing the judgment for B.J.F. support its result.

The first of these reasons relied on by the Court is the fact "appellant gained access to (B.J.F.'s name) through a government news release." [But] the "release" of information provided by the government was not, as the Court says, "without qualification." As the *Star's* own reporter conceded at trial, the crime incident report that inadvertently included B.J.F.'s name was posted in a room that contained signs making it clear that the names of rape victims were not matters of public record, and were not to be published. [U]nfortunately, as this case illustrates, mistakes happen; even when States take measures to "avoid" disclosure, sometimes rape victim's names are found out. As I see it, it is not too much to ask the press, in instances such as this, to respect simple standards of decency and refrain from publishing a victim's name, address, and/or phone number.

Second, the Court complains that appellant was judged here under too strict a liability standard. The Court contends that a newspaper might be found liable under the Florida courts' negligence per se theory without regard to a newspaper's scienter or degree of fault. The short answer to this complaint is that whatever merit the Court's argument might have, it is wholly inapposite here, where the jury [in order to award punitive damages] found that appellant acted with "reckless indifference towards the rights of others," a standard far higher than the *Gertz* standard the Court urges as a constitutional minimum today. . . .

Third, the Court faults the Florida criminal statute for being underinclusive. . . . [The Florida statute] excludes neighborhood gossips because presumably the Florida Legislature has determined that neighborhood gossips do not pose the danger and intrusion to rape victims that "instrument[s] of mass communication" do. Simply put: Florida wanted to prevent the widespread distribution of rape victim's names, and therefore enacted a statute tailored almost as precisely as possible to achieving that end. . . .

Of course, the right to privacy is not absolute. [T]his right inevitably conflicts with the public's right to know about matters of general concern. . . . Resolving this conflict is a difficult matter, and I do not fault the court for attempting to strike an appropriate balance between the two, but rather, for according too little weight to B.J.F.'s side of the equation, and too much on the other. . . .

NOTES AND QUESTIONS

(1) *Constitutional Protections for Claims Against Invasions of Privacy that Cast the Plaintiff in a "False Light:" Time, Inc. v. Hill, 385 U.S. 374 (1967).* Life Magazine reported that a play called *The Desperate Hours* was a "re-enactment" of the story of the James Hill family, who had been held hostage by three escaped convicts in their home. In several respects, however, the play did not accurately reflect the Hills' ordeal—for example, it depicted them as subjected to violence which had not occurred—and Hill therefore sued *Life's* publisher, Time, Inc., on the theory that it had invaded his privacy by placing him in a "false light." Time defended on the theory that the article was a subject of legitimate news interest and that it had published in good faith and without malice.

The New York Court of Appeals upheld an award for Hill; the Supreme Court, per Justice Brennan, however, reversed and remanded for a new trial with different jury instructions incorporating the *New York Times* standard:

> The [New York] Court of Appeals held that *New York Times* had no application. The court [reasoned:] "The free speech which is encouraged and essential to the operation of a healthy government is something quite different from an individual's attempt to enjoin the publication of a fictitious biography of him. No public interest is served by protecting the dissemination of the latter". . . .

> If this is meant to imply that proof of knowing or reckless falsity is not essential to a constitutional [invasion of privacy judgment], we disagree with the Court of Appeals. We hold that the constitutional protections for speech and press preclude [recovery for] false reports of matters of public interest in the absence of proof that the defendant published the report with knowledge of its falsity or in reckless disregard of the truth. . . .

Justices Black and Douglas concurred separately, to emphasize their rejection of a balancing test in favor of absolute protection for speech. Justice Harlan wrote separately to argue that negligent fictionalization, rather than the actual malice standard of *New York Times*, was all that should constitutionally be required. Finally, Justice Fortas, joined by the Chief Justice and Justice Clark, dissented.

(2) *Evaluating Hill and Florida Star: Do These Cases Strike the Right Balance Between Individual Privacy and Freedom of Speech?* Justice Fortas expressed the concern that the holding in *Time, Inc. v. Hill* will allow a sloppy press to "ride roughshod" over the interests of individuals. When private figures assert "false light" invasion of privacy, would a standard of negligence be more appropriate, as the Court has adopted in the defamation context (*Gertz*)? Consider, also, whether *Florida Star* strikes the right balance: Are Justice White's criticisms persuasive?

HUSTLER MAGAZINE v. FALWELL, 485 U.S. 46 (1988). This case involved a $150,000 judgment recovered by nationally known minister and political commentator Jerry Falwell against Hustler Magazine for the tort known as "intentional infliction of emotional distress." The Court, per Justice Rehnquist, described the offending publication as follows:

> The inside front cover of the November 1983 issue of Hustler Magazine featured a "parody" of an advertisement for Campari liqueur that contained the name and picture of respondent and was entitled "Jerry Falwell Talks about His First Time." The parody was modelled after actual Campari ads that included interviews with various celebrities about their "first times." Although it was apparent by the end of each interview that this meant the first time they sampled Campari, the ads clearly played on the sexual double entendres of the general subject of "first times." Copying the form and layout of these Campari ads, Hustler's editors chose [Falwell] as the featured celebrity and drafted an alleged "interview" with him in which he states that his "first time" was during a drunken incestuous rendezvous with his mother in an outhouse. The Hustler parody portrays respondent and his mother as drunk and immoral. . . . In small print at the bottom of the page, the ad contains the disclaimer, "ad parody not to be taken seriously." The magazine's table of contents also lists the ad as "Fiction; Ad and Personality Parody."

The Court unanimously reversed the judgment, holding that the first amendment precluded recovery. It pointed out that the parody could not be actionable as libel because it did not purport to be true. The Court also held that Falwell was a public figure. The Court's reasoning included the following:

> Generally speaking the law does not regard the intent to inflict emotional distress as one which should receive much solicitude, and it is quite understand-

able that most if not all jurisdictions have chosen to make it civilly culpable where the conduct in question is sufficiently "outrageous." But in the world of debate about public affairs, many things done with motives that are less than admirable are protected by the first amendment. . . .

Were we to hold otherwise, there can be little doubt that political cartoonists and satirists would be subjected to damages awards without any showing their work falsely defamed its subject. [T]he art of the cartoonist is often not reasoned or evenhanded, but slashing and one-sided. . . .

Respondent contends, however, that the caricature in question here was so "outrageous" as to distinguish it from more traditional political cartoons. There is no doubt that the caricature of respondent and his mother published in Hustler is at best a distant cousin of the political cartoons described above, and a rather poor relation at that. If it were possible by laying down a principled standard to separate the one from the other, public discourse would probably suffer little or no harm. But we doubt there is any such standard, and we are quite sure that the pejorative description "outrageous" does not supply one. "Outrageousness" . . . has an inherent subjectiveness about it which would allow a jury to impose liability on the basis of the jurors' taste or views, or perhaps on the basis of their dislike of a particular expression. . . .

We conclude that public figures and public officials may not recover for the tort of intentional infliction of emotional distress by reason of publications such as the one here at issue without showing in addition that the publication contains a false statement of fact which was made with "actual malice," *i.e.*, with knowledge that the statement was false or with reckless disregard as to whether or not it was true. *New York Times [v. Sullivan].* . . .

NOTES AND QUESTIONS

(1) *The Expansion of the Use of the "Actual Malice" Standard: Hustler Magazine v. Falwell, 485 U.S. 46 (1988).* In *Falwell*, the Court, per Chief Justice Rehnquist, unanimously decided that the Free Press Clause required that a state law regarding intentional infliction of emotional distress could impose liability on the media only if the plaintiff could satisfy the "actual malice" standard from *Sullivan*, above. The actual malice standard (generally recognized as a functional equivalent to strict scrutiny) provides a significant immunity for the media. More generally, the decisions in this section raise the issue whether the media could ever be punished for the publication of truthful information, even though the publication might be harmful to privacy or other personal interests.

(2) *Media Liability for Publication of Illegally Intercepted Cell Phone Conversations: Bartnicki v. Vopper, 532 U.S. 1753 (2001).* From *Sullivan* and the *Pentagon Papers* decisions, through *Florida Star* (above), the Court had demonstrated "its repeated refusal to answer categorically whether the publication of truthful information may ever be punished consistent with the First Amendment." In *Vopper* (also noted above in § 11.03), the Court again faced this issue. In *Vopper*, a cell phone conversation of two union officials was illegally intercepted and recorded by a person who gave the tape to Vopper, a radio commentator. Vopper repeatedly played the tape as part of a "talk news" program. The union officials sued under the federal statute, and the media raised the First Amendment as a defense. The Court, per Justice Stevens, ruled in favor of the media even though the union officials advanced important "privacy" interests. The Court concluded, relying on *Sullivan* and *Florida Star*, that "a stranger's illegal conduct does not suffice to remove the First Amendment shield from speech about a matter of public concern."

Justices Breyer and O'Connor concurred on narrower grounds. Chief Justice Rehnquist (author of *Falwell*, above), for Justices Scalia and Thomas dissented. The dissent argued that the majority was applying a "strict scrutiny" standard when a lesser level of scrutiny was appropriate because of the significant privacy interests involved. While the Court declined to announce a "categorical" immunity for the publication of truthful information, the level of protection for the media appears, after *Florida Star*, *Falwell*, and *Vopper*, to be very high and, correspondingly, the protection of "privacy" interests is reduced. Did the Court strike the appropriate balance? Did the Framers?

[H] Copyright Infringement

HARPER & ROW, PUBLISHERS, INC. v. NATION ENTERPRISES, 471 U.S. 539 (1985). *The Nation* magazine used "generous verbatim excerpts of [President] Ford's unpublished manuscript to lend authenticity to its account of [his] forthcoming memoirs," which were protected by copyright. In doing so, *The Nation* "effectively arrogated to itself the right of first publication, an important marketable subsidiary right" protected by legislation enacted under Congress' copyright power. *The Nation* defended on the theory, among others, that its lifting of verbatim quotes was a "fair use" within the meaning of the Copyright Act. After considering the meaning of fair use, which is a "a privilege . . . to use the copyrighted material in a reasonable manner without [the owner's] consent," the Court, per Justice O'Connor, rejected the argument. In the course of its reasoning, the court recognized the underlying constitutional issues and dealt with them as follows:

> Respondents . . . contend that first amendment values require a different rule [of fair use] under the circumstances of this case. The thrust of the decision below is that "[T]he scope of [fair use] is undoubtedly wider when the information conveyed relates to matters of high public concern." [R]espondents argue that the public's interest in learning this news as fast as possible outweighs the right of the author to control its first publication. . . .

> Respondent's theory, however, would expand fair use to effectively destroy any expectation of copyright protection in the work of a public figure. Absent such protection, there would be little incentive to create or profit in financing such memoirs and the public would be denied an important source of significant historical information.

> In view of the first amendment protection already embodied in the Copyright Act's distinction between copyrightable expression and uncopyrightable facts and ideas, and the latitude for scholarship and comment traditionally afforded by fair use, we see no warrant for expanding the doctrine of fair use to create what amounts to a public figure exception to copyright.

Justice Brennan, joined by Justices White and Marshall, dissented: "[T]his zealous defense of the copyright owner's prerogative will, I fear, stifle the broad dissemination of ideas and information copyright is intended to nurture."

§ 11.05 THE FREE PRESS CLAUSE: PRIOR RESTRAINT, SUBSEQUENT REGULATION, AND PRESS ACCESS

[A] The "Prior Restraint" Doctrine

NEAR v. MINNESOTA, 283 U.S. 697 (1931). A Minnesota statute provided that any "malicious, scandalous and defamatory newspaper" was "a nuisance, and all persons guilty of such nuisance may be enjoined" from publication. On the basis of this statute, a Minnesota County Attorney obtained an injunction against Near, the owner of The Saturday Press, which had published a series of articles charging law enforcement officers with graft and neglect of duty in dealing with gangsters. The injunction, which prevented publication of any "malicious, scandalous or defamatory newspaper" or of a "nuisance under the name and title of said Saturday Press or any other name or title," was affirmed by the state supreme court. The United States Supreme Court, per Chief Justice Hughes, reversed:

[T]he reason for the enactment, as the state court has said, is that prosecutions to enforce penal statutes for libel do not result in "efficient repression or suppression of the evils of scandal". . . .

In determining the extent of the constitutional protection, it has been generally, if not universally, considered that it is the chief purpose of the guarantee [of freedom of speech and press] to prevent previous restraints upon publication. [T]he liberty deemed to be established was thus described by Blackstone: "The liberty of the press . . . consists in laying no *previous* restraints upon publications. [E]very free man has an undoubted right to lay what sentiments he pleases before the public. . . . But if he publishes what is improper, mischievous, or illegal, he must take the consequences of his own temerity." [T]he preliminary freedom extends as well to the false as to the true. . . .

[T]he protection even as to previous restraint is not absolutely unlimited. But the limitation has been recognized only in exceptional cases. [N]o one would question but that a government [at war] might prevent actual obstruction to its recruiting service or the publication of the sailing dates of transports or the number and location of troops. [T]hese limitations are not applicable here.

Justice Butler, joined by Justice Van Devanter, McReynolds, and Sutherland, dissented: "The doctrine that measures such as the one before us are invalid because they operate as previous restraints . . . exposes the peace and good order of every community and the business and private affairs of every individual to the constant and protracted false and malicious assaults of any insolvent publisher who may have purpose and sufficient capacity to contrive and put into effect a scheme or program for oppression, blackmail, or extortion."

NEW YORK TIMES CO. v. UNITED STATES
(THE "PENTAGON PAPERS" CASE)
403 U.S. 713 (1971)

Per Curiam.

[T]he United States seeks to enjoin the New York Times and the Washington Post from publishing the contents of a classified study entitled "History of U.S. Decision-Making Process on Viet Nam Policy."

"Any system of prior restraints of expression comes to this Court bearing a heavy presumption against its constitutional validity" [citing *Near v. Minnesota*, inter alia]. The Government "thus carries a heavy burden of showing justification for the imposition of such a restraint." [T]he District Courts . . . held that the Government had not met that burden. We agree.

[T]he stays entered June 25, 1971, by the Court are vacated. The judgments shall issue forthwith. . . .

Mr. Justice Black, with whom Mr. Justice Douglas joins, concurring.

I adhere to the view that the Government's case against the Washington Post should have been dismissed and that the injunction against the New York Times should have been vacated without oral argument when the cases were first presented to this Court. I believe that every moment's continuance of the injunctions against these newspapers amounts to a flagrant, indefensible, and continuing violation of the First Amendment. . . .

The Government's case here is based on premises entirely different from those that guided the Framers of the First Amendment. The Solicitor General has carefully and emphatically stated:

Now, Mr. Justice [Black], your construction of . . . [the First Amendment] is well known, and I certainly respect it. You say that no law means no law, and that should be obvious. I can only say, Mr. Justice, that to me it is equally obvious that "no law" does not mean "no law", and I would seek to persuade the Court that is true. . . . [T]here are other parts of the Constitution that grant powers and responsibilities to the Executive, and . . . the First Amendment was not intended to make it impossible for the Executive to function or to protect the security of the United States.

And the Government argues in its brief that in spite of the First Amendment, "[t]he authority of the Executive Department to protect the nation against publication of information whose disclosure would endanger the national security stems from two interrelated sources: the constitutional power of the President over the conduct of foreign affairs and his authority as Commander-in-Chief."

[T]he Government does not even attempt to rely on any act of Congress. [T]o find that the President has "inherent power" to halt the publication of news by resort to the courts would wipe out the First Amendment and destroy the fundamental liberty and security of the very people the Government hopes to make "secure." No one can read the history of the adoption of the First Amendment without being convinced beyond any doubt that it was injunctions like those sought here that Madison and his collaborators intended to outlaw in this Nation for all time.

MR. JUSTICE DOUGLAS, with whom MR. JUSTICE BLACK joins, concurring.

While I join the opinion of the Court I believe it necessary to express my views more fully. . . .

There is . . . no statute barring the publication by the press of the material which the Times and the Post seek to use. . . .

So any power that the Government possesses must come from its "inherent power."

The power to wage war is "the power to wage war successfully." But the war power stems from a declaration of war. The Constitution by art. 1, § 8, gives Congress, not the President, power "[t]o declare War." Nowhere are presidential wars authorized. We need not decide therefore what leveling effect the war power of Congress might have.

These disclosures may have a serious impact. But that is no basis for sanctioning a previous restraint on the press. . . .

MR. JUSTICE BRENNAN, concurring. . . .

I write separately in these cases only to emphasize what should be apparent: that our judgments in the present cases may not be taken to indicate the propriety, in the future, of issuing temporary stays and restraining orders to block the publication of material sought to be suppressed by the Government. So far as I can determine, never before has the United States sought to enjoin a newspaper from publishing information in its possession.

The error that has pervaded these cases from the outset was the granting of any injunctive relief whatsoever, interim or otherwise. The entire thrust of the Government's claim throughout these cases has been that publication of the material sought to be enjoined "could," or "might," or "may" prejudice the national interest in various ways. But the First Amendment tolerates absolutely no prior judicial restraints of the press predicated upon surmise or conjecture that untoward consequences may result. Our cases, it is true, have indicated that there is a single, extremely narrow class of cases in which the First Amendment's ban on prior judicial restraint may be overridden. Our cases have thus far indicated that such cases may arise only when the Nation "is at war," *Schenck v. United States*, during which times "[n]o one would question but that a government might prevent actual obstruction to its recruiting service or the publication of the sailing dates of transports or the number and location of troops." *Near v. Minnesota.*

Thus, only governmental allegation and proof that publication must inevitably, directly, and immediately cause the occurrence of an event kindred to imperiling the safety of a transport already at sea can support even the issuance of an interim restraining order. In no event may mere conclusions be sufficient. . . .

Mr. Justice Stewart, with whom Mr. Justice White joins, concurring. . . .

[W]e are asked, quite simply, to prevent the publication by two newspapers of material that the Executive Branch insists should not, in the national interest, be published. I am convinced that the Executive is correct with respect to some of the documents involved. But I cannot say that disclosure of any of them will surely result in direct, immediate, and irreparable damage to our Nation or its people. That being so, there can under the First Amendment be but one judicial resolution of the issues before us. I join the judgments of the Court.

Mr. Justice White, with whom Mr. Justice Stewart joins, concurring.

I concur in today's judgments, but only because of the concededly extraordinary protection against prior restraints enjoyed by the press under our constitutional system. I do not say that in no circumstances would the First Amendment permit an injunction against publishing information about government plans or operations. Nor, after examining the materials the Government characterizes as the most sensitive and destructive, can I deny that revelation of these documents will do substantial damage to public interests. Indeed, I am confident that their disclosure will have that result. But I nevertheless agree that the United States has not satisfied the very heavy burden that it must meet to warrant an injunction against publication in these cases, at least in the absence of express and appropriately limited congressional authorization for prior restraints in circumstances such as these. . . .

Mr. Justice Marshall, concurring.

[W]ith all due respect, I believe the ultimate issue in this case is even more basic than the one posed by the Solicitor General. The issue is whether this Court or the Congress has the power to make law. . . .

It would [b]e utterly inconsistent with the concept of separation of powers for this Court to use its power of contempt to prevent behavior that Congress has specifically declined to prohibit.

Mr. Chief Justice Burger, dissenting. . . . [The Chief Justice emphasized that the Court was considering the case only a few days after the trial court's decision, owning to its emergency nature.]

[W]e literally do not know what we are acting on. As I see it, we have been forced to deal with litigation concerning rights of great magnitude without an adequate record, and surely without time for adequate treatment either in the prior proceedings or in this Court. It is interesting to note that counsel, on both sides, in oral argument before this Court, were frequently unable to respond to questions on factual points. Not surprisingly they pointed out that they had been working literally "around the clock" and simply were unable to review the documents that give rise to these cases and were not familiar with them. This Court is in no better posture. I agree generally with Mr. Justice Harlan and Mr. Justice Blackmun, but I am not prepared to reach the merits. . . .

MR. JUSTICE HARLAN, with whom The CHIEF JUSTICE and MR. JUSTICE BLACKMUN join, dissenting. . . .

It is a sufficient basis for affirming the Court of Appeals for the Second Circuit in the *Times* litigation to observe that its order must rest on the conclusion that because of the time elements the Government had not been given an adequate opportunity to present its case to the District Court. At the least this conclusion was not an abuse of discretion.

. . . But I think there is another and more fundamental reason why this judgment cannot stand. [I]t is plain to me that the scope of the judicial function in passing upon the activities of the Executive Branch of the Government in the field of foreign affairs is very narrowly restricted. This view is, I think, dictated by the concept of separation of powers upon which our constitutional system rests.

In a speech on the floor of the House of Representatives, Chief Justice John Marshall, then a member of that body, stated:

> The President is the sole organ of the nation in its external relations, and its sole representative with foreign nations. . . .

The power to evaluate the "pernicious influence" of premature disclosure is not, however, lodged in the Executive alone. I agree that, in performance of its duty to protect the values of the First Amendment against political pressures, the judiciary must review the initial Executive determination to the point of satisfying itself that the subject matter of the dispute does lie within the proper compass of the President's foreign relations power. [M]oreover the judiciary may properly insist that the determination that disclosure of the subject matter would irreparably impair the national security be made by the head of the Executive Department concerned—here the Secretary of State or the Secretary of Defense—after actual personal consideration by that officer.

But in my judgment the judiciary may not properly go beyond these two inquiries and redetermine for itself the probable impact of disclosure on the national security. . . .

Pending further hearings in each case conducted under the appropriate ground rules, I would continue the restraints on publication. . . .

MR. JUSTICE BLACKMUN, dissenting. . . .

The First Amendment, after all, is only one part of an entire Constitution. Article II of the great document vests in the Executive Branch primary power over the conduct of foreign affairs and places in that branch the responsibility for the Nation's safety. Each provision of the Constitution is important, and I cannot subscribe to a doctrine of unlimited absolutism for the First Amendment at the cost of downgrading other provisions. *See, for example, Near v. Minnesota.* . . .

NOTES AND QUESTIONS

(1) *The Government Is Not Allowed To Regulate With A "Prior Restraint" Unless Exceptional Circumstances Are Proven: New York Times Co. v. United States, 403 U.S. 713 (1971) ("The Pentagon Papers Case").* In a *per curiam* (6-3) opinion, the Court denied the injunction sought by the Nixon Administration (during the Vietnam War) against the publication, by the *New York Times* and *The Washington Post*, of the Pentagon Papers. The time pressure contributed to the Court's highly splintered opinions (9 separate opinions). It is generally understood that the standard articulated in Justice Stewart's concurring opinion has emerged, over time, as the governing standard for justifying a prior restraint. To satisfy the standard, the government must show that publication will "surely result in direct, immediate, and irreparable damage to our Nation or its people." The "directness," "immediacy" and "irreparable" elements seem similar to the clear and present danger standard.

(2) *What do the Justices' Nine Separate Opinions Mean?* Each Justice wrote an individual opinion in the *Pentagon Papers* Case. First, the position of Justices Black and Douglas is absolute: There can be no prior restraint. [Do you believe that they would have disapproved an injunction during World War II against publication of highly classified information about the Normandy Invasion immediately before D-Day?]

Secondly, Justices Brennan, White, Stewart, and Marshall all would recognize extraordinary circumstances in which a prior restraint could be upheld, but each believes that either the proof,or congressional authorization, or both, are missing here. Finally, Justices Harlan, Burger, and Blackmun would continue the restraints, at least until the issues could be studied more carefully.

Notice Justice Harlan's formula: courts may review executive foreign policy determinations of this kind, but only to the extent of determining (1) whether the effort to restrict disclosure is within the President's constitutional competence, and (2) whether the President (or department head) personally has considered and decided the matter. Does Justice Harlan's approach adequately protect the freedom of speech? For commentary on the Court's apparent confusion, *see* Arenson, *Prior Restraint: A Rational Doctrine or an Elusive Compendium of Hackneyed Phrases?*, 36 DRAKE L. REV. 265 (1987). For further commentary, relying on sources recently disclosed under the Freedom of Information Act, *see* John Cary Sims, *Triangulating The Boundaries of Pentagon Papers*, 2 WM. & MARY BILL OF RIGHTS J. 341 (1993).

(3) *Should Misappropriation of Secrets, or "Receipt of Stolen Goods," Trigger Prior Restraint?: The Ellsberg Connection.* That Daniel Ellsberg leaked the Pentagon Papers to the press, after having confidentially been given access to them by the Government, is well known. Should this fact make a difference? Consider whether, if it does, it will obliterate the prior restraint doctrine. In the alternative, should it make a difference if the newspapers knew of, encouraged, or participated in the unlawful misappropriation?

(4) *Subsequent Liability for Disclosure, as Versus Prior Restraint by Injunction: Snepp v. United States, 444 U.S. 507 (1980).* In *Snepp*, a CIA agent had signed a contractual agreement that he would not publish confidential information "without specific prior approval by the Agency." The contract explicitly recognized that the agent was entering into a trust relationship and had fiduciary obligations. In willful breach of the agreement, Snepp published without pre-clearance a book about certain CIA activities in South Vietnam. Undisputed evidence showed that a CIA agent's violation of the review obligation would dry up confidential sources, destroy arrangements with other governments, and "even endanger the personal safety of foreign agents." The Supreme Court upheld a district court order impressing a constructive trust on all profits that Snepp might earn from this book in violation of the contract.

(5) *Prior Restraint Doctrine And Judicial Injunctions: Tory v. Cochran, 544 U.S. 734 (2005).* Attorney Johnnie L. Cochran, Jr. (part of OJ's "Dream Team") brought a defamation action against a former client and others because the defendants had picketed, displayed signs and made defamatory statements about Cochran's law firm. The state trial court had entered a permanent injunction against the defendants' conduct outside the law firm. The client-defendant appealed, arguing that the injunction was an impermissible prior restraint. Although the California courts sided with Cochran, the Supreme Court, per Justice Breyer, ruled for the defendants.

After ruling that the claim was not moot, the Court, in a very short opinion, held that the injunction "amounts to an overly broad prior restraint upon speech, lacking plausible justification." Only Justices Thomas and Scalia dissented. As a matter of prior restraint doctrine, the opinion interestingly relied on the *Nebraska Press Ass'n v. Stuart*, 427 U.S. 539 (1976) decision (below) rather than the *Pentagon Papers* case (above) for the applicable prior restraint standard.

NEBRASKA PRESS ASS'N v. STUART, 427 U.S. 539 (1976). One Simants was charged with a sensational mass-murder of six members of a family, committed during the course of sexual assault. The state trial judge, expecting prejudicial publicity, entered an order prohibiting those in attendance from publishing or broadcasting accounts of confessions made by the accused or facts "strongly implicative of the accused." The order applied during pretrial proceedings, and it was to expire upon the empaneling of a jury. The Supreme Court, per Chief Justice Burger, struck down this "press gag" order:

> The first amendment provides that "Congress shall make no law . . . abridging the freedom . . . of the press". . . . The Court has interpreted these guarantees to afford special protection against orders that prohibit the publication or broadcast of particular information or commentary-orders that impose a "previous" or "prior" restraint on speech [citing *Near v. Minnesota, New York Times Co. v. United States* (Pentagon Papers), and other cases]. . . .

> Our review of the pretrial record persuades us that the trial judge was justified in concluding that there would be intense and pervasive pretrial publicity concerning this case. He could also reasonably conclude, based on common human experience, that publicity might impair the defendant's right to a fair trial. . . .

> [But] [w]e find little in the record that goes to another aspect of our task, determining whether measures short of an order restraining all publication would have insured the defendant a fair trial. [The court here discussed the measures approved in *Sheppard v. Maxwell*, including change of venue, postponement, searching questioning during voir dire, instructions against publicity to jurors, sequestration, "gag" orders binding counsel and state employees, and, finally, courtroom closure.]

> [T]here is no finding that alternative measures would not have protected Simants' rights, and the Nebraska Supreme Court did no more than imply that such measures might not be adequate. Moreover, the record is lacking in evidence to support such a finding. . . .

> To the extent that this order prohibited the reporting of evidence adduced at the open preliminary hearing, it plainly violated several [first amendment] principles. "[T]here is nothing that proscribes the press from reporting events that transpire in the courtroom." [O]nce a public hearing had been held, what transpired there could not be subject to prior restraint.

Justice Brennan, joined by Justices Stewart and Marshall concurred in the judgment only: "I would hold . . . that resort to prior restraints on the freedom of the press is a constitutionally impermissible method for enforcing [the right to a fair trial]; judges have at their disposal a broad spectrum of devices for insuring that fundamental fairness is accorded the accused without necessitating so drastic an incursion on the equally fundamental . . . constitutional mandate that discussion of public affairs in a free society cannot depend on the preliminary grace of judicial censors."

NOTES AND QUESTIONS

(1) *A "Gag Order" Treated as a Prior Restraint: Nebraska Press Association v. Stuart, 427 U.S. 539 (1976).* In this post-*Pentagon Papers* decision, a state trial court entered a "gag order" in a highly sensationalized mass murder case. The gag order prohibited the press from printing stories about the case; it was based on a concern about prejudicial pretrial publicity. The Court, per Justice Burger (a dissenter in *Pentagon Papers*), treated the gag order as a prior restraint and applied a four-part standard based on *Pentagon Papers*. A gag order could be valid only if (1) the publication was directed at creating imminent pretrial prejudice; (2) was likely to create imminent pretrial prejudice; (3) served a compelling government interest; and (4) was narrowly tailored to that compelling interest.

Chief Justice Burger found that the gag order was designed to protect the compelling interest in providing a fair trial, but that the trial court had not considered less restrictive alternatives such as change of venue, postponement, jury instructions, jury sequestration, courtroom closure, or carefully tailored combinations of such alternatives. Hence, the gag order failed the standard and was ruled unconstitutional, by relying on the narrow tailoring prong avoided addressing the "immediacy" requirement of the first two prongs.

(2) *"Gag" Orders Versus Courtroom Closing or Other Remedies.* If a court closes a courtroom, it conducts proceedings in secret, and this practice may appear more violative of First Amendment concerns than the "gag" order at issue in *Nebraska Press*. On the other hand, as a direct, prior restraint, the order in *Nebraska Press* placed government in the position of controlling press content—and this practice may induce self-censorship by the press or abuses by government officials. (Note that "gag" orders against attorneys arguably are narrower and less restrictive than restraints on the press itself; indeed, such orders were approved in *Sheppard*.) Which "remedy" is more harmful—courtroom closure or restraining the press?

PROBLEM O

THE "HYDROGEN BOMB RECIPE" CASE: UNITED STATES v. PROGRESSIVE, INC., 467 F. Supp. 990 (W.D. Wis. 1979). *The Progressive* magazine intended to publish an article that was headlined: "The H-Bomb Secret—How We Got It, Why We're Telling It." *The Progressive*'s stated purpose was to debunk the regime of government secrecy and to make the public better informed about nuclear weapons. The government sued for, and obtained, an injunction against publication. Both the Secretary of State and the Secretary of Defense testified that publication would increase nuclear proliferation and impair national security, although the government admitted that some if not most of *The Progressive*'s information had come from declassified sources or sources in the public domain.

The district court observed that, in the nation's history, this injunction was "the first instance of a prior restraint against a publication in this fashion," but also noted that the injunction extended only to "restricted data" as defined by the Atomic Energy Act of 1954. The balance of equities, which pitted First Amendment rights against thermonuclear war in which "our right to life [would be] extinguished and the right to publish [would become] moot," weighed in favor of theinjunction. The court distinguished *New York Times (Pentagon Papers)* by pointing out that in that case, "no cogent reasons were advanced by the government as to why the article affected national security," whereas this case involved specific and concrete proof. Furthermore, a specific statute was involved, in the form of the Atomic Energy Act. Therefore, the district court held that the case fell "within the extremely narrow exception to the rule against prior restraint" for "exceptional" cases, citing *Near.*

Questions: (1) After *Pentagon Papers, Near,* and *Snepp,* what should be the result have been if *The Progressive* had appealed? [The Supreme Court denied mandamus sub nom. *Morland v. Sprecher,* 443 U.S. 709 (1979).] (2) In July, 1993, Newsweek magazine published a diagram for an "implosion"—type bomb, complete with the required amounts of uranium and other ingredients. What result if the federal government sought to enjoin this publication?

[B] Regulation of The Press Other than by Prior Restraint: Judicial Review of "Subsequent Regulation."

MINNEAPOLIS STAR AND TRIBUNE COMPANY v. MINNESOTA COMMISSIONER OF REVENUE.
460 U.S. 575 (1983)

JUSTICE O'CONNOR delivered the opinion of the Court.

This case presents the question of a State's power to impose a special tax on the press and, by enacting exemptions, to limit its effect to only a few newspapers.

I

[Minnesota imposed a sales tax on most retail sales of goods. Certain publications, including newspapers, were exempted from the sales tax, largely because of the difficulties associated with collecting the sales tax. Minnesota imposed a "use tax" on the cost of paper and ink products used in the production of the publications. Minnesota then established an exemption for the first $100,000 worth of ink and paper. As a consequence of the use tax exemption, only the eleven largest publishers actually paid the use tax. The plaintiff *Minneapolis Star and Tribune*, was one of the eleven and it paid $608,634 in use taxes (nearly two-thirds of all the use taxes paid in 1974). The newspaper commenced this action, under 42 U.S.C. § 1983, challenging the use tax scheme as an abridgment of freedom of the press and under equal protection doctrine. The Minnesota Supreme Court upheld the use tax scheme, and the Supreme Court here reversed.]

II

[The Court first addressed arguments based on precedent.] Star Tribune argues that we must strike this tax on the authority of *Grosjean v. American Press Co., Inc.*, 297 U.S. 233 (1936). Although there are similarities between the two cases, we agree with the State that *Grosjean* is not controlling.. . .

We think that the result in *Grosjean* may have been attributable in part to the perception on the part of the Court that the state imposed the tax with an intent to penalize a selected group of newspapers. In the case currently before us, however, there is no legislative history and no indication, apart from the structure of the tax itself, of any impermissible or censorial motive on the part of the legislature. We cannot resolve the case by simple citation to *Grosjean*. Instead, we must analyze the problem anew under the general principles of the First Amendment.

III

Clearly, the First Amendment does not prohibit all regulation of the press. It is beyond dispute that the States and the Federal Government can subject newspapers to generally applicable economic regulations without creating constitutional problems. Minnesota, however, has not chosen to apply its general sales and use tax to newspapers. Instead, it has created a special tax that applies only to certain publications protected by the First Amendment. Although the State argues now that the tax on paper and ink is part of the general scheme of taxation, the use tax provision is facially discriminatory, singling out publications for treatment that is, to our knowledge, unique in Minnesota tax law. . . .

By creating this special use tax . . . Minnesota has singled out the press for special treatment. We then must determine whether the First Amendment permits such special taxation. A tax that burdens rights protected by the First Amendment cannot stand unless the burden is necessary to achieve an overriding governmental interest.

See, e.g., *United States v. Lee*, 455 U.S. 252 (1982). Any tax that the press must pay, of course, imposes some "burden." But, as we have observed, this Court has long upheld economic regulation of the press. The cases approving such economic regulation, however, emphasized the general applicability of the challenged regulation to all businesses, e.g., *Oklahoma Press Publishing Co. v. Walling, supra,* 327 U.S., at 194, . . . suggesting that a regulation that singled out the press might place a heavier burden of justification on the State, and we now conclude that the special problems created by differential treatment do indeed impose such a burden.

There is substantial evidence that differential taxation of the press would have troubled the Framers of the First Amendment.[1] [The Court engaged in an extended historical analysis.] The role of the press in mobilizing sentiment in favor of independence was critical to the Revolution. When the Constitution was proposed without an explicit guarantee of freedom of the press, the Antifederalists objected. Proponents of the Constitution, relying on the principle of enumerated powers, responded that such a guarantee was unnecessary because the Constitution granted Congress no power to control the press. . . .

The concerns voiced by the Antifederalists led to the adoption of the Bill of Rights. . . .

The fears of the Antifederalists were well-founded. A power to tax differentially, as opposed to a power to tax generally, gives a government a powerful weapon against the taxpayer selected. When the State imposes a generally applicable tax, there is little cause for concern. We need not fear that a government will destroy a selected group of taxpayers by burdensome taxation if it must impose the same burden on the rest of its constituency. See *Railway Express Agency v. New York*, 336 U.S. 106 (1949) (Jackson, J., concurring). When the State singles out the press, though, the political constraints that prevent a legislature from passing crippling taxes of general applicability are weakened, and the threat of burdensome taxes becomes acute. That threat can operate as effectively as a censor to check critical comment by the press, undercutting the basic assumption of our political system that the press will often serve as an important restraint on government. . . .

Further, differential treatment, unless justified by some special characteristic of the press, suggests that the goal of the regulation is not unrelated to suppression of expression, and such a goal is presumptively unconstitutional. See, e.g., *Police Department of the City of Chicago v. Mosley*, 408 U.S. 92, 95–96 (1972). Differential taxation of the press, then, places such a burden on the interests protected by the First Amendment that we cannot countenance such treatment unless the State asserts a counterbalancing interest of compelling importance that it cannot achieve without differential taxation.

IV

The main interest asserted by Minnesota in this case is the raising of revenue. Of course that interest is critical to any government. Standing alone, however, it cannot

---

[1] It is true that our opinions rarely speculate on precisely how the Framers would have analyzed a given regulation of expression. In general, though, we have only limited evidence of exactly how the Framers intended the First Amendment to apply. There are no recorded debates in the Senate or in the States, and the discussion in the House of Representatives was couched in general terms, perhaps in response to Madison's suggestion that the representatives not stray from simple acknowledged principles. . . . see also Z. Chafee, Freedom of Speech in the United States 16 (1941). Consequently, we ordinarily simply apply those general principles, requiring the government to justify any burdens on First Amendment rights by showing that they are necessary to achieve a legitimate overriding governmental interest, see note 7, *infra*. But when we do have evidence that a particular law would have offended the Framers, we have not hesitated to invalidate it on that ground alone. Prior restraints, for instance, clearly strike to the core of the Framers' concerns, leading this Court to treat them as particularly suspect.

justify the special treatment of the press, for an alternative means of achieving the same interest without raising concerns under the First Amendment is clearly available: the State could raise the revenue by taxing businesses generally, avoiding the censorial threat implicit in a tax that singles out the press.

[F]urther, even assuming that the legislature did have valid reasons for substituting another tax for the sales tax, we are not persuaded that this tax does serve as a substitute. The State asserts that this scheme actually favors the press over other businesses, because the same rate of tax is applied, but, for the press, the rate applies to the cost of components rather than to the sales price. We would be hesitant to fashion a rule that automatically allowed the State to single out the press for a different method of taxation as long as the effective burden was no different from that on other taxpayers or the burden on the press was lighter than that on other businesses. One reason for this reluctance is that the very selection of the press for special treatment threatens the press not only with the current differential treatment, but with the possibility of subsequent differentially more burdensome treatment. Thus, even without actually imposing an extra burden on the press, the government might be able to achieve censorial effects, for "[t]he threat of sanctions may deter [the] exercise of [First Amendment] rights almost as potently as the actual application of sanctions." *NAACP v. Button*, 371 U.S. 415 (1963).

A second reason to avoid the proposed rule is that courts as institutions are poorly equipped to evaluate with precision the relative burdens of various methods of taxation. The complexities of factual economic proof always present a certain potential for error, and courts have little familiarity with the process of evaluating the relative economic burden of taxes. In sum, the possibility of error inherent in the proposed rule poses too great a threat to concerns at the heart of the First Amendment, and we cannot tolerate that possibility. Minnesota, therefore, has offered no adequate justification for the special treatment of newspapers.

V

Minnesota's ink and paper tax violates the First Amendment not only because it singles out the press, but also because it targets a small group of newspapers. . . . Again, there is no legislative history supporting the State's view of the purpose of the amendment. Whatever the motive of the legislature in this case, we think that recognizing a power in the State not only to single out the press but also to tailor the tax so that it singles out a few members of the press presents such a potential for abuse that no interest suggested by Minnesota can justify the scheme. . . .

VI

We need not and do not impugn the motives of the Minnesota legislature in passing the ink and paper tax. Illicit legislative intent is not the *sine qua non* of a violation of the First Amendment. We have long recognized that even regulations aimed at proper governmental concerns can restrict unduly the exercise of rights protected by the First Amendment. E.g., *Schneider v. State*, 308 U.S. 147 (1939). A tax that singles out the press, or that targets individual publications within the press, places a heavy burden on the State to justify its action. Since Minnesota has offered no satisfactory justification for its tax on the use of ink and paper, the tax violates the First Amendment, and the judgment below is

Reversed.

JUSTICE WHITE, concurring in part and dissenting in part.

This case is not difficult. The exemption for the first $100,000 of paper and ink limits the burden of the Minnesota tax to only a few papers. This feature alone is sufficient reason to invalidate the Minnesota tax and reverse the judgment of the Minnesota Supreme Court. The Court recognizes that Minnesota's tax violates the First Amendment for this reason, and I subscribe to Part V of the Court's opinion and concur in the judgment. . . .

JUSTICE REHNQUIST, dissenting.

Today we learn from the Court that a State runs afoul of the First Amendment proscription of laws "abridging the freedom of speech, or of the press" where the State structures its taxing system to the advantage of newspapers. This seems very much akin to protecting something so overzealously that in the end it is smothered. While the Court purports to rely on the intent of the "Framers of the First Amendment," I believe it safe to assume that in 1791 "abridge" meant the same thing it means today: to diminish or curtail. Not until the Court's decision in this case, nearly two centuries after adoption of the First Amendment has it been read to prohibit activities which in no way diminish or curtail the freedoms it protects. . . .

[T]he record further indicates that the Minneapolis Star & Tribune paid $608,634 in use taxes in 1974 and $636,113 in 1975—a total liability of $1,244,747. We need no expert testimony from modern day Euclids or Einsteins to determine that the $1,224,747 paid in use taxes is significantly less burdensome than the $3,685,092 that could have been levied by a sales tax. *A fortiori*, the Minnesota taxing scheme which singles out newspapers for "differential treatment" has benefitted, not burdened, the "freedom of speech, [and] of the press."

Ignoring these calculations, the Court concludes that "differential treatment" alone in Minnesota's sales and use tax scheme requires that the statutes be found "presumptively unconstitutional" and declared invalid "unless the State asserts a counterbalancing interest of compelling importance that it cannot achieve without differential taxation." The "differential treatment" standard that the Court has conjured up is unprecedented and unwarranted. . . .

The State is required to show that its taxing scheme is rational. But in this case that showing can be made easily. . . . [N]ewspapers are commonly sold in a different way than other goods. The legislature could have concluded that paper boys, corner newsstands, and vending machines provide an unreliable and unsuitable means for collection of a sales tax. . . .

NOTES AND QUESTIONS

(1) *Governmental Regulation of the Press Other than by Prior Restraint: Minneapolis Star and Tribune Co. v. Minnesota Commissioner of Revenue, 406 U.S. 575 (1983).* In *Minneapolis Star* the Court addressed the standard for judicial review of governmental regulation of the press through sanctions subsequent to publication. The Court, per Justice O'Connor, held that "subsequent regulation" of the press must be justified by strict scrutiny. The Court applied strict scrutiny to Minnesota's sales and use tax scheme. The Court determined that, although the Legislature had not had a censorial motive, the tax scheme "singled out the press for special treatment." The Court rejected Minnesota's asserted interest in the "raising of revenue" as not compelling and also determined that Minnesota failed the means test of strict scrutiny. Justice White concurred only on equal protection grounds. Justice Rehnquist dissented. *See generally* RANDALL P. BEZANSON, TAXES ON KNOWLEDGE IN AMERICA 252–286 (1994).

(2) *The Use of Strict Scrutiny to Protect Press Interests: Justice Rehnquist's Minneapolis Star Dissent.* The *Minneapolis Star* Court had relied heavily on history to support a "Framers Intent" analysis. Justice Rehnquist disagreed, suggesting that the history of the press clause was more ambiguous. As a matter of policy, Justice Rehnquist also argued that the newspaper was not "burdened" by the State's tax scheme: it was better off financially under the use tax than if it had been subject to the sales tax. Thus,

the dissent argued that the press had not suffered any "abridgment," and the dissent contended that the rational basis standard should be applied. Justice Rehnquist's dissent forced the majority to argue that the mere "potential for abuse" was enough to trigger strict scrutiny. This expansive notion of judicial review would be revisited by the Rehnquist Court in the *Cohen* decision, below.

COHEN v. COWLES MEDIA COMPANY
501 U.S. 663 (1991)

JUSTICE WHITE delivered the opinion of the Court.

The question before us is whether the First Amendment prohibits a plaintiff from recovering damages, under state promissory estoppel law, for a newspaper's breach of a promise of confidentiality given to the plaintiff in exchange for information. We hold that it does not.

During the closing days of the 1982 Minnesota gubernatorial race, Dan Cohen, an active Republican associated with Wheelock Whitney's Independent-Republican gubernatorial campaign, approached reporters from the St. Paul Pioneer Press Dispatch (Pioneer Press) and the Minneapolis Star and Tribune (Star Tribune) and offered to provide documents relating to a candidate in the upcoming election. Cohen made clear to the reporters that he would provide the information only if he was given a promise of confidentiality. Reporters from both papers promised to keep Cohen's identity anonymous and Cohen turned over copies of two public court records concerning Marlene Johnson, the Democratic—Farmer-Labor candidate for Lieutenant Governor. The first record indicated that Johnson had been charged in 1969 with three counts of unlawful assembly, and the second that she had been convicted in 1970 of petit theft. Both newspapers interviewed Johnson for her explanation and one reporter tracked down the person who had found the records for Cohen. As it turned out, the unlawful assembly charges arose out of Johnson's participation in a protest of an alleged failure to hire minority workers on municipal construction projects, and the charges were eventually dismissed. The petit theft conviction was for leaving a store without paying for $6 worth of sewing materials. The incident apparently occurred at a time during which Johnson was emotionally distraught, and the conviction was later vacated.

After consultation and debate, the editorial staffs of the two newspapers independently decided to publish Cohen's name as part of their stories concerning Johnson. In their stories, both papers identified Cohen as the source of the court records, indicated his connection to the Whitney campaign, and included denials by Whitney campaign officials of any role in the matter. The same day the stories appeared, Cohen was fired by his employer.

Cohen sued respondents, the publishers of the Pioneer Press and Star Tribune, in Minnesota state court, alleging fraudulent misrepresentation and breach of contract. The trial court rejected respondents' argument that the First Amendment barred Cohen's lawsuit. A jury returned a verdict in Cohen's favor, awarding him $200,000 in compensatory damages and $500,000 in punitive damages. . . .

A divided Minnesota Supreme Court reversed the compensatory damages award. After affirming the Court of Appeals' determination that Cohen had not established a claim for fraudulent misrepresentation, the court considered his breach-of-contract claim and concluded that "a contract cause of action is inappropriate for these particular circumstances." The court then went on to address the question whether Cohen could establish a cause of action under Minnesota law on a promissory estoppel theory. Apparently, a promissory estoppel theory was never tried to the jury, nor briefed nor argued by the parties; it first arose during oral argument in the Minnesota Supreme Court when one of the justices asked a question about equitable estoppel. . . .

Respondents rely on the proposition that "if a newspaper lawfully obtains truthful information about a matter of public significance then state officials may not constitutionally punish publication of the information, absent a need to further a state interest of the highest order." *Smith v. Daily Mail Publishing Co.*, 443 U.S. 97 (1979). That proposition is unexceptionable, and it has been applied in various cases that have found insufficient the asserted state interests in preventing publication of truthful, lawfully obtained information.

This case, however, is not controlled by this line of cases but, rather, by the equally well-established line of decisions holding that generally applicable laws do not offend the First Amendment simply because their enforcement against the press has incidental effects on its ability to gather and report the news. As the cases relied on by respondents recognize, the truthful information sought to be published must have been lawfully acquired. The press may not with impunity break and enter an office or dwelling to gather news. Neither does the First Amendment relieve a newspaper reporter of the obligation shared by all citizens to respond to a grand jury subpoena and answer questions relevant to a criminal investigation, even though the reporter might be required to reveal a confidential source. *Branzburg v. Hayes*, 408 U.S. 665 (1972). The press, like others interested in publishing, may not publish copyrighted material without obeying the copyright laws. See *Zacchini v. Scripps-Howard Broadcasting Co.*, 433 U.S. 562 (1977). Similarly, the media must obey the National Labor Relations Act, *Associated Press v. NLRB*, 301 U.S. 103 (1937), and the Fair Labor Standards Act, *Oklahoma Press Publishing Co. v. Walling*, 327 U.S. 186 (1946); may not restrain trade in violation of the antitrust laws, *Associated Press v. United States*, 326 U.S. 1 (1945); and must pay non-discriminatory taxes, *Minneapolis Star & Tribune Co. v. Minnesota Comm'r of Revenue*, 460 U.S. 575 (1983). It is, therefore, beyond dispute that "[t]he publisher of a newspaper has no special immunity from the application of general laws. He has no special privilege to invade the rights and liberties of others." *Associated Press v. NLRB*, *supra*. Accordingly, enforcement of such general laws against the press is not subject to stricter scrutiny than would be applied to enforcement against other persons or organizations.

There can be little doubt that the Minnesota doctrine of promissory estoppel is a law of general applicability. It does not target or single out the press. Rather, insofar as we are advised, the doctrine is generally applicable to the daily transactions of all the citizens of Minnesota. The First Amendment does not forbid its application to the press.

Justice Blackmun suggests that applying Minnesota promissory estoppel doctrine in this case will "punish" respondents for publishing truthful information that was lawfully obtained. This is not strictly accurate because compensatory damages are not a form of punishment, as were the criminal sanctions at issue in *Smith v. Daily Mail, supra*. . . . In any event, as indicated above, the characterization of the payment makes no difference for First Amendment purposes when the law being applied is a general law and does not single out the press. Moreover, Justice Blackmun's reliance on cases like *Florida Star v. B.J.F.*, *supra*, and *Smith v. Daily Mail* is misplaced. In those cases, the State itself defined the content of publications that would trigger liability. Here, by contrast, Minnesota law simply requires those making promises to keep them. The parties themselves, as in this case, determine the scope of their legal obligations, and any restrictions that may be placed on the publication of truthful information are self-imposed. . . .

Respondents and amici argue that permitting Cohen to maintain a cause of action for promissory estoppel will inhibit truthful reporting because news organizations will have legal incentives not to disclose a confidential source's identity even when that person's identity is itself newsworthy. Justice Souter makes a similar argument. But if this is the case, it is no more than the incidental, and constitutionally insignificant, consequence of applying to the press a generally applicable law that requires those who make certain kinds of promises to keep them. . . .

JUSTICE BLACKMUN, with whom JUSTICE MARSHALL and JUSTICE SOUTER join, dissenting.

[T]he majority concludes that this case is not controlled by the decision in *Smith v. Daily Mail Publishing Co.*, 443 U.S. 97 (1979), to the effect that a State may not punish the publication of lawfully obtained, truthful information "absent a need to further a state interest of the highest order." Instead, we are told, the controlling precedent is "the equally well-established line of decisions holding that generally applicable laws do not offend the First Amendment simply because their enforcement against the press has incidental effects on its ability to gather and report the news." I disagree. . . .

Contrary to the majority, I regard our decision in *Hustler Magazine, Inc. v. Falwell*, 485 U.S. 46 (1988), to be precisely on point. There, we found that the use of a claim of intentional infliction of emotional distress to impose liability for the publication of a satirical critique violated the First Amendment. There was no doubt that Virginia's tort of intentional infliction of emotional distress was "a law of general applicability" unrelated to the suppression of speech. Nonetheless, a unanimous Court found that, when used to penalize the expression of opinion, the law was subject to the strictures of the First Amendment. . . .

As in *Hustler*, the operation of Minnesota's doctrine of promissory estoppel in this case cannot be said to have a merely "incidental" burden on speech; the publication of important political speech is the claimed violation. Thus, as in *Hustler*, the law may not be enforced to punish the expression of truthful information or opinion. In the instant case, it is undisputed that the publication at issue was true. . . .

JUSTICE SOUTER, with whom JUSTICE MARSHALL, JUSTICE BLACKMUN, and JUSTICE O'CONNOR join, dissenting.

I agree with Justice Blackmun that this case does not fall within the line of authority holding the press to laws of general applicability where commercial activities and relationships, not the content of publication, are at issue. Even such general laws as do entail effects on the content of speech, like the one in question, may of course be found constitutional, but only, as Justice Harlan observed,

> "when [such effects] have been found justified by subordinating valid governmental interests, a prerequisite to constitutionality which has necessarily involved a weighing of the governmental interest involved.. . . Whenever, in such a context, these constitutional protections are asserted against the exercise of valid governmental powers a reconciliation must be effected, and that perforce requires an appropriate weighing of the respective interests involved."
> *Konigsberg v. State Bar of California*, 366 U.S. 36.

Thus, "[t]here is nothing talismanic about neutral laws of general applicability," *Employment Div., Dept. of Human Resources of Ore. v. Smith*, 494 U.S. 872, (1990) (O'CONNOR, J., concurring in judgment), for such laws may restrict First Amendment rights just as effectively as those directed specifically at speech itself. Because I do not believe the fact of general applicability to be dispositive, I find it necessary to articulate, measure, and compare the competing interests involved in any given case to determine the legitimacy of burdening constitutional interests, and such has been the Court's recent practice in publication cases. . . .

NOTES AND QUESTIONS

(1) *The Fundamental Right of Press Freedom is Subject to Purposefulness: Cohen v. Cowles Media Company, 501 U.S. 663 (1991).* The *Minneapolis Star* decision, *supra*, had determined that, without requiring proof of an impermissible motive, a state tax scheme would be tested against strict scrutiny. Relying on this standard for state regulation of the press defendant Cowles Media sought to defend itself against a claim for damages, under Minnesota's promissory estoppel law, based on its breach of a promise of confidentiality. The Court, per Justice White (who had not joined the Court's

Press Clause analysis in *Minneapolis Star*), held that "generally applicable laws do not offend [the Press Clause] simply because their enforcement against the press has incidental effects. . . ." After determining that Minnesota's promissary estoppel law was a "law of general applicability," the majority applied only rational basis scrutiny and upheld the trial court's damage award. There were four dissenters, including Justice O'Connor, the author of *Minneapolis Star.*

(2) *The Free Press Clause Doctrine and The Purposefulness Requirement.* The *Cowles Media* Court's analysis indicates that it was imposing a purposefulness requirement on the claim under the Press Clause. Note that *Cowles Media* was decided only one year after the Court had imposed the purposefulness requirement on the Free Exercise Clause, in the *Smith v. Employment Division* decision [§ 12.03[C] below]; the same five Justices in the *Cowles Media* decision had been the five-Justice majority in *Smith.*

As you have seen in equal protection doctrine [§ 10.03[A][3] above] and in the Free Exercise doctrine, the Court's use of a purposefulness threshold (in the case of facially neutral, generally applicable laws) limits the judicial use of strict scrutiny as a judicial review standard. By avoiding strict scrutiny, judicial review will be more deferential (to the majoritarian decision-maker). In the case of a fundamental right (*e.g.*, freedom of the press), is such deference appropriate or should judicial review be more counter-majoritarian?

[C]   Newsgathering

BRANZBURG v. HAYES
408 U.S. 665 (1972)

MR. JUSTICE WHITE delivered the opinion of the Court.

[Newspaper reporter Branzburg wrote articles in which he described actual drug use and manufacture that he personally had observed. Kentucky courts applied a state statute immunizing Branzburg from testimony about confidential sources, but held that he could not invoke a privilege against testifying about events that he had observed personally, including the identities of persons he had observed.

[Television photographer Pappas agreed with Black Panthers to remain inside their headquarters and avoid disclosure of anything he saw or heard, except an anticipated police raid. When called before a grand jury, he refused to testify to his observations inside Panther headquarters, claiming a First Amendment privilege to protect confidential informants and their information. The Massachusetts courts rejected the claimed privilege.

[New York Times reporter Caldwell, who also covered Black Panthers, was subpoenaed to bring his notes and tape recordings of interviews with Panthers. The Ninth Circuit held that the First Amendment provided a qualified testimonial privilege to news reporters, who could withhold testimony absent "compelling reasons for requiring" it. The Ninth Circuit also held that, absent some special showing of necessity by the government, Caldwell had a privilege to refuse to attend a secret meeting of the grand jury because of the potential impact of such an appearance on the flow of news to the public.

[Here, the Supreme Court affirms in Branzburg's and Pappas' cases, but reverses in Caldwell's, holding that the claimed First Amendment privilege does not exist.]

Petitioners Branzburg and Pappas and respondent Caldwell press First Amendment claims that may be simply put: that to gather news it is often necessary to agree either not to identify thesource of information published or to publish only part of the facts revealed, or both; that if the reporter is nevertheless forced to reveal these confidences to a grand jury, the source so identified and other confidential sources of other reporters will be measurably deterred from furnishing publishable information, all to the detriment of the free flow of information protected by the First Amendment. Although the newsmen in these cases do not claim an absolute privilege against official interrogation in all circumstances, they assert that the reporter should not be forced either to appear or to testify before a grand jury or at trial until and unless sufficient grounds are shown for believing that the reporter possesses information relevant to a crime the grand jury is investigating, that the information the reporter has is unavailable from other sources, and that the need for the information is sufficiently compelling to override the claimed invasion of First Amendment interests occasioned by the disclosure. . . .

We do not question the significance of free speech, press, or assembly to the country's welfare. Nor is it suggested that news gathering does not qualify for First Amendment protection. . . .

It is clear that the First Amendment does not invalidate every incidental burdening of the press that may result from the enforcement of civil or criminal statutes of general applicability. [T]he Court has emphasized that "[t]he publisher of a newspaper has no special immunity from the application of general laws. He has no special privilege to invade the rights and liberties of others". . . .

Despite the fact that news gathering may be hampered, the press is regularly excluded from grand jury proceedings, our own conferences, the meetings of other official bodies gathered in executive session, and the meetings of private organizations. Newsmen have no constitutional right of access to the scenes of crime or disaster when the general public is excluded, and they may be prohibited from attending or publishing information about trials if such restrictions are necessary to assure a defendant a fair trial before an impartial tribunal. . . .

It is thus not surprising that the great weight of authority is that newsmen are not exempt from the normal duty of appearing before a grand jury and answering questions relevant to a criminal investigation. . . .

A number of States have provided newsmen a statutory privilege of varying breadth, but the majority have not done so, and none has been provided by federal statute. Until now the only testimonial privilege for unofficial witnesses that is rooted in the Federal Constitution is the Fifth Amendment privilege against compelled self-incrimination. We are asked to create another by interpreting the First Amendment to grant newsmen a testimonial privilege that other citizens do not enjoy. This we decline to do. . . .

This conclusion itself involves no restraint on what newspapers may publish or on the type or quality of information reporters may seek to acquire, nor does it threaten the vast bulk of confidential relationships between reporters and their sources. [O]nly where news sources themselves are implicated in crime or possess information relevant to the grand jury's task need they or the reporter be concerned about grand jury subpoenas. Nothing before us indicates that a large number or percentage of *all* confidential news sources falls into either category and would in any way be deterred by our holding that the Constitution does not, as it never has, exempt the newsman from performing the citizen's normal duty of appearing and furnishing information relevant to the grand jury's task.

The preference for anonymity of those confidential informants involved in actual criminal conduct is presumably a product of their desire to escape criminal prosecution, and this preference,while understandable, is hardly deserving of constitutional protection. It would be frivolous to assert—and no one does in these cases—that the First Amendment, in the interest of securing news or otherwise, confers a license on either the reporter or his news sources to violate valid criminal laws. . . .

There remain those situations where a source is not engaged in criminal conduct but has information suggesting illegal conduct by others. [S]uch informants presumably desire anonymity in order to avoid being entangled as a witness in a criminal trial or grand jury investigation. They may fear that disclosure will threaten their job security or personal safety or that it will simply result in dishonor or embarrassment.

The argument that the flow of news will be diminished by compelling reporters to aid the grand jury in a criminal investigation is not irrational, nor are the records before us silent on the matter. But we remain unclear how often and to what extent informers are actually deterred from furnishing information when newsmen are forced to testify before a grand jury. The available data indicate that some newsmen rely a great deal on confidential sources and that some informants are particularly sensitive to the threat of exposure and may be silenced if it is held by this Court that, ordinarily, newsmen must testify pursuant to subpoenas, but the evidence fails to demonstrate that there would be a significant constriction of the flow of news to the public if this Court reaffirms the prior common-law and constitutional rule regarding the testimonial obligations of newsmen. Estimates of the inhibiting effect of such subpoenas on the willingness of informants to make disclosures to newsmen are widely divergent and to a great extent speculative. It would be difficult to canvass the views of the informants themselves: surveys of reporters on this topic are chiefly opinions of predicted informant behavior and must be viewed in the light of the professional self-interest of the interviewees.[33] Reliance by the press on confidential informants does not mean that all such sources will in fact dry up because of the later possible appearance of the newsman before a grand jury.

Accepting the fact, however, that an undetermined number of informants not themselves implicated in crime will nevertheless, for whatever reason, refuse to talk to newsmen if they fear identification by a reporter in an official investigation, we cannot accept the argument that the public interest in possible future news about crime from undisclosed, unverified sources must take precedence over the public interest in pursuing and prosecuting those crimes reported to the press by informants and in thus deterring the commission of such crimes in the future. . . .

The argument for [a] constitutional privilege rests heavily on those cases holding that the infringement of protected First Amendment rights must be no broader than necessary to achieve a permissible governmental purpose. . . . We do not deal, however, with a governmental institution that has abused its proper function, as a legislative committee does when it "expose[s] for the sake of exposure." [N]othing in the record indicates that these grand juries were "prob[ing] at will and without relation to existing need." [N]or did the grand juries attempt to invade protected First Amendment rights by forcing wholesale disclosure of names and organizational affiliations for a purpose that was not germane to the determination of whether crime has beencommitted. [A]nd the characteristic secrecy of grand jury proceedings is a further protection against the undue invasion of such rights. . . .

The privilege claimed here is conditional, not absolute; given the suggested preliminary showings and compelling need, the reporter would be required to testify. [I]f newsmen's confidential sources are as sensitive as they are claimed to be, the prospect of being unmasked whenever a judge determines the situation justifies it is hardly a satisfactory solution to the problem. For them, it would appear that only an absolute privilege would suffice.

[T]he administration of a constitutional newsman's privilege would present practical and conceptual difficulties of a high order. Sooner or later, it would be necessary to define those categories of newsmen who qualified for the privilege, a questionable

---

[33] In his Press Subpoenas: An Empirical and Legal Analysis, Study Report of the Reporters' Committee on Freedom of the Press 6-12, Prof. Vince Blasi discusses these methodological problems. Prof. Blasi's survey found that slightly more than half of the 975 reporters questioned said that they relied on regular confidential sources for at least 10% of their stories. *Id.*, at 21. Of this group of reporters, only 8% were able to say with some certainty that their professional functioning had been adversely affected by the threat of subpoena; another 11% were not certain whether or not they had been adversely affected. *Id.*, at 53.

procedure in light of the traditional doctrine that liberty of the press is the right of the lonely pamphleteer who uses carbon paper or a mimeograph just as much as of the large metropolitan publisher who utilizes the latest photocomposition methods. . . .

Finally, as we have earlier indicated, news gathering is not without its First Amendment protections, and grand jury investigations if instituted or conducted other than in good faith, would pose wholly different issues for resolution under the First Amendment. Official harassment of the press undertaken not for purposes of law enforcement but to disrupt a reporter's relationship with his news sources would have no justification. . . .

MR. JUSTICE POWELL, concurring.

I add this brief statement to emphasize what seems to me to be the limited nature of the Court's holding. The Court does not hold that newsmen, subpoenaed to testify before a grand jury, are without constitutional rights with respect to the gathering of news or in safeguarding their sources. Certainly, we do not hold, as suggested in Mr. Justice Stewart's dissenting opinion, that stateand federal authorities are free to "annex" the news media as "an investigative arm of government". . . .

MR. JUSTICE STEWART, with whom MR. JUSTICE BRENNAN and MR. JUSTICE MARSHALL join, dissenting.

The Court . . . invites state and federal authorities to undermine the historic independence of the press by attempting to annex the journalistic profession as an investigative arm of government. Not only will this decision impair performance of the press' constitutionally protected functions, but it will, I am convinced, in the long run, harm rather than help the administration of justice. . . .

No less important to the news dissemination process is the gathering of information. [A]ccordingly, a right to gather news, of some dimensions, must exist. . . .

The right to gather news implies, in turn, a right to a confidential relationship between a reporter and his source. This proposition follows as a matter of simple logic once three factual predicates are recognized: (1) newsmen require informants to gather news; (2) confidentiality . . . is essential to the creation and maintenance of a news-gathering relationship with informants; and (3) an unbridled subpoena power . . . will either deter sources from divulging information or deter reporters from gathering and publishing information. . . .

After today's decision, the potential informant can never be sure that his identity or off-the-record communications will not subsequently be revealed through the compelled testimony of a newsman. . . .

The reporter must speculate about whether contact with a controversial source or publication of controversial material will lead to a subpoena. In the event of a subpoena, under today's decision, the newsman will know that he must choose between being punished for contempt if he refuses to testify, or violating his profession's ethics and impairing his resourcefulness as a reporter if he discloses confidential information. . . .

Accordingly, when a reporter is asked to appear before a grand jury and reveal confidences, I would hold that the government must (1) show that there is probable cause to believe that the newsman has information that is clearly relevant to a specific probable violation of law; (2) demonstrate that the information sought cannot be obtained by alternative means less destructive of First Amendment rights; and (3) demonstrate a compelling and overriding interest in the information. . . .

[The dissenting opinion of JUSTICE DOUGLAS is omitted.]

NOTES AND QUESTIONS

(1) *Applying the Branzburg Holding in the Context of Civil Libel Suits Between Private Persons: Herbert v. Lando, 441 U.S. 153 (1979).* May a private litigant, suing a media defendant for libel, obtain broad discovery from that defendant under applicable rules of civil procedure? In *Herbert*, the Supreme Court rejected arguments for a general privilege against this kind of discovery. Consider whether this result is consistent with that in *Branzburg v. Hayes*, which relies heavily upon the public purposes served by the grand jury. Are the interests of the private litigant less compelling and less narrowly tailored?

(2) *Press Shield Laws Passed by the States: In re Farber, 78 N.J. 259, 394 A.2d 330 (1978).* A majority of the states have passed laws, called "press shield laws," that extend a privilege to newsgathering, usually by exempting from disclosure certain kinds of confidential information received from news sources. In *Farber*, above, the court rejected a claim of privilege even though it was supported by a state statute, on the ground that the reporter's testimony was essential to preservation of a murder defendant's sixth amendment right to compulsory process. Is this conclusion correct? [Note that most other privileges, ranging from the attorney-client privilege to the patient-physician privilege, are not abrogated merely because the context happens to be that of a criminal prosecution.]

(3) *Prohibiting Grand Jury Witnesses From Disclosing Their Own Testimony as a First Amendment Violation: Butterworth v. Smith, 494 U.S. 624 (1990).* What happens when the state subpoenas a reporter before the grand jury, orders him to testify concerning his investigations—and then prohibits him from revealing subjects underlying his testimony in any manner? Smith was a reporter for a newspaper in Florida and wished to publish a news story—and perhaps a book—on the subject matter of such an investigation, a publication that would include his own testimony and experiences in dealing with the grand jury. The Supreme Court, per Chief Justice Rehnquist, acknowledged that it was proper to maintain the traditional secrecy of grand jury testimony, which had been acknowledged by the Court's decisions. But it held that, when an investigation ends, suppressing the reporter's revelation of his own testimony was a violation of the First Amendment. The state advanced a number of interests—prevention of escape by investigation targets, concern for deterrence of witnesses due to fears of retribution, preventing subornation of grand jury witnesses who later testify at trial, and protecting exonerated persons—but the Court concluded that they were "not sufficient to overcome respondent's First Amendment right to make a truthful statement of information he acquired on his own."

[D]   Press Access to Government Institutions

INTRODUCTORY NOTES AND QUESTIONS

(1) *In the Prison Context, the Court Rejects Press Access: Pell v. Procunier, 417 U.S. 817 (1974), Saxbe v. Washington Post Co., 417 U.S. 843 (1974), and Houchins v. KQED, Inc., 438 U.S. 1 (1978).* In the *Pell* and *Saxbe* cases, the Court, per Justice Stewart, upheld state and federal prison regulations that prohibited press interviews with specific individual inmates. The majority reasoned that members of the public have no right to demand access to individual inmates, and consequently the press did not either. Given the non-existence of the claimed right of access, the regulations were supportable if they had a rational basis, which the court found in such rationales as the federal government's "wheel" theory: press attention could make a particular, notorious inmate into a "big wheel," with undesirable consequences for prison discipline and security. Four Justices dissented.

Later, in *Houchins*, Chief Justice Burger reaffirmed the *Pell-Saxbe* holdings for the Court majority, writing that the media had "no special right of access . . . different or greater than that accorded the public generally." Since "the Constitution affords no guidelines, . . . hundreds of judges would be at large to fashion ad hoc standards in individual cases, according to their own ideas of what seems 'desirable' or 'expedient.' "

(2) *Strict Scrutiny of Courtroom Closure, Even in Sexual Assault Cases: Globe Newspaper Co. v. Superior Court, 457 U.S. 596 (1982).* In *Globe Newspaper*, the Court considered a Massachusetts statute that required the trial judge to exclude the public, including the press, from the courtroom during the victim's testimony in any sexual assault case. The Court struck down the statute, after applying strict scrutiny. Saving the victim from further invasion of privacy was a compelling interest, but since a case-by-case review of the need for closure would be less restrictive, the mandatory statute was not sufficiently narrow to survive. The *Globe Newspaper* decision is the background against which Chief Justice Burger writes the *Press Enterprises II* decision.

PRESS ENTERPRISE CO. v. SUPERIOR COURT OF CALIFORNIA
478 U.S. 1 (1986)

CHIEF JUSTICE BURGER delivered the opinion of the Court.

[California charged Robert Diaz, a nurse, with murdering 12 patients with massive overdoses of a drug, and the State sought the death penalty. At the preliminary hearing, upon Diaz's motion, the Judge excluded the public and the press. The preliminary hearing continued for 41 days. Only the State submitted evidence, but Diaz's counsel cross-examined most witnesses. Diaz was held to answer all charges. At the conclusion of the hearing, petitioner Press-Enterprise Co. moved to have the transcript of the preliminary hearing released. The Judge, with concern for fair trial rights, refused. After six months, the State joined petitioner's motion, but Diaz continued to oppose release of the transcript. Petitioner filed a peremptory writ, but it was denied when the California Supreme Court decided that all that was needed to close the hearing was a "reasonable likelihood" of prejudice to the defendant's fair trial rights. The United States Supreme Court previously had reviewed this case in what was labeled *Press Enterprise I*. Here, in *Press Enterprise II*, the Supreme Court, after holding that the case was not moot, reversed the State courts on the First Amendment press access issue.]

. . . .

III

It is important to identify precisely what the California Supreme Court decided:

"[W]e conclude that the magistrate shall close the preliminary hearing upon finding a reasonable likelihood of substantial prejudice which would impinge upon the right to a fair trial. Penal code section 868 makes clear that the primary right is the right to a fair trial and that the public's right of access must give way when there is conflict." 37 Cal.3d, at 781.

It is difficult to disagree in the abstract with that court's analysis balancing the defendant's right to a fair trial against the public right of access. It is also important to remember that these interests are not necessarily inconsistent. Plainly, the defendant has a right to a fair trial but, as we have repeatedly recognized, one of the important means of assuring a fair trial is that the process be open to neutral observers.

The right to an open public trial is a shared right of the accused and the public, the common concern being the assurance of fairness.

[T]he right asserted here is that of the public under the First Amendment. The California Supreme Court concluded that the First Amendment was not implicated because the proceeding was not a criminal trial, but a preliminary hearing. However, the First Amendment question cannot be resolved solely on the label we give the event, *i.e.*, "trial" or otherwise, particularly where the preliminary hearing functions much like a full-scale trial.

In cases dealing with the claim of a First Amendment right of access to criminal proceedings, our decisions have emphasized two complementary considerations. First, because, a ' "tradition of accessibility implies the favorable judgment of experience' " *Globe Newspaper Co. v. Superior Court*, 457 U.S. 596, 605 (1982) (quoting *Richmond Newspapers, Inc. v. Virginia*, 448 U.S., at 555 (1980) (BRENNAN, J., concurring in judgment)), we have considered whether the place and process have historically been open to the press and general public. . . .

Second, in this setting the Court has traditionally considered whether public access plays a significant positive role in the functioning of the particular process in question. *Globe Newspaper, supra.* Although many governmental processes operate best under public scrutiny, it takes little imagination to recognize that there are some kinds of government operations that would be totally frustrated if conducted openly. A classic example is [the grand jury]. . . .

These considerations of experience and logic are, of course, related, for history and experience shape the functioning of governmental processes. If the particular proceeding in question passes these test of experience and logic, a qualified First Amendment right of public access attaches. But even when a right of access attaches, it is not absolute. *Globe Newspaper Co. v. Superior Court, supra.* While open criminal proceedings give assurances of fairness to both the public and the accused, there are some limited circumstances in which the right of the accused to a fair trial might be undermined by publicity. In such cases, the trial court must determine whether the situation is such that the rights of the accused override the qualified First Amendment right of access. In *Press-Enterprise I* we stated:

> "[T]he presumption may be overcome only by an overriding interest based on findings that closure is essential to preserve higher values and is narrowly tailored to serve that interest. . . .

IV

A

The considerations that led the Court to apply the First Amendment right of access to criminal trials in *Richmond Newspapers* and *Globe* and the selection of jurors in *Press-Enterprise I* lead us to conclude that the right of access applies to preliminary hearings as conducted in California.

First, there has been a tradition of accessibility to preliminary hearings of the type conducted in California. Although grand jury proceedings have traditionally been closed to the public and the accused, preliminary hearings conducted before neutral and detached magistrates have been open to the public. . . .

The second question is whether public access to preliminary hearings as they are conducted in California plays a particularly significant positive role in the actual functioning of the process. We have already determined in *Richmond Newspapers*, *Globe*, and *Press-Enterprise I* that public access to criminal trials and the selection of jurors is essential to the proper functioning of the criminal justice system. California preliminary hearings are sufficiently like a trial to justify the same conclusion. . . .

It is true that unlike a criminal trial, the California preliminary hearing cannot result in the conviction of the accused and the adjudication is before a magistrate or other judicial officer without a jury. But these features, standing alone, do not make public access any less essential to the proper functioning of the proceedings in the overall criminal justice process. Because of its extensive scope, the preliminary hearing is often the final and most important step in the criminal proceeding. . . .

We therefore conclude that the qualified First Amendment right of access to criminal proceedings applies to preliminary hearings as they are conducted in California.

B

Since a qualified First Amendment right of access attaches to preliminary hearings in California . . . the proceedings cannot be closed unless specific, on the record findings are made demonstrating that "closure is essential to preserve higher values and is narrowly tailored to serve that interest." *Press-Enterprise I, supra.* If the interest asserted is the right of the accused to a fair trial, the preliminary hearing shall be closed only if specific findings are made demonstrating that, first, there is a substantial probability that the defendant's right to a fair trial will be prejudiced by publicity that closure would prevent and, second, reasonable alternatives to closure cannot adequately protect the defendant's fair trial rights. . . .

The First Amendment right of access cannot be overcome by the conclusory assertion that publicity might deprive the defendant of that right. And any limitation must be "narrowly tailored to serve that interest." *Press-Enterprise I, supra.*

. . . Accordingly, the judgment of the California Supreme Court is reversed.

Justice Stevens, with whom Justice Rehnquist joins as to Part II, dissenting.

The constitutional question presented by this case is whether members of the public have a First Amendment right to insist upon access to the transcript of a preliminary hearing during the period before the public trial, even though the accused, the prosecutor, and the trial judge have all agreed to the sealing of the transcript in order to assure a fair trial. . . .

In view of the [one-sided presentation of evidence at the hearing], the trial judge had an obvious and legitimate reason for refusing to make the transcript public any sooner than he did. His decision plainly did not violate the defendant's right to a public trial under the Sixth Amendment, for it was the defendant who objected to release of the transcript. In my opinion, the judge's decision did not violate the First Amendment either.

Although perhaps obvious, it bears emphasis that the First Amendment right asserted by petitioner is not a right to publish or otherwise communicate information lawfully or unlawfully acquired. That right, which lies at the core of the First Amendment and which erased the legacy of restraints on publication against which the drafters of that Amendment rebelled, . . . may be overcome only by a governmental objective of the highest order attainable in a no less intrusive way. . . .

The First Amendment right asserted by petitioner in this case, in contrast, is not the right to publicize information in its possession, but the right to acquire access thereto.

I have long believed that a proper construction of the First Amendment embraces a right of access to information about the conduct of public affairs. . . .

But it has always been apparent that the freedom to obtain information that the government has a legitimate interest in not disclosing is far narrower than the freedom to disseminate information, which is "virtually absolute" in most contexts. In this case, the risk of prejudice to the defendant's right to a fair trial is perfectly obvious. For me, that risk is far more significant than the countervailing interest in publishing the transcript of the preliminary hearing sooner rather than later.

. . . The obvious defect in the Court's approach is that its reasoning applies to the traditionally secret grand jury with as much force as it applies to California preliminary hearings. . . .

NOTES AND QUESTIONS

(1) *The Court's Test For Press Access to Courtroom Activities.* Prior to the *Press-Enterprise II* decision above, the Court's decisions were mixed (some would say "confused") as to when the trial court should use strict scrutiny to evaluate a request to close part of a criminal proceeding to the press and public. In particular, it was unclear whether the use of strict scrutiny was required any time the press sought access to part of a criminal proceeding. Although some decisions could be read to support that position, *Press-Enterprise II* seemed to limit the use of strict scrutiny with its holding that strict scrutiny was invoked only after the threshold issue of "historic openness" was resolved in favor of the press.

(2) *Distinguishing the Prison Cases (Pell, Saxbe and Houchins) From the Open Courts Cases (Press Enterprise etc.).* Can *Press Enterprise* persuasively be distinguished from the *Pell-Saxbe-Houchins* line of prison non-access cases? Consider the following: (1) the cases may reflect differences in traditions of access, in that court proceedings historically have been open whereas prisons typically have not; (2) there are differences in rationales for closure, in that prisons create security and discipline issues that judicial proceedings do not; (3) there are differences in availability of substitute information, such as communications with prisoners by mail and inspection of facilities in the case of prisons, whereas no similar substitute is available for a closed judicial proceeding. Are any of these distinctions meritorious?

(3) *Reliance on Voir Dire Examination and On the Jury's Hearing of the Evidence as Predominant Protectors of a Fair Trial: Press-Enterprise, Above.* In *Press-Enterprise*, the Court applied a similar test to that used for other judicial closures to pretrial hearings (specifically, a preliminary hearing). The Court expressed the view that closure of an entire pretrial proceeding will "rarely" be justified, because problems of pretrial publicity can be avoided through voir dire examination of prospective jurors. "Through *voir dire*, . . . a court can identify those jurors whose prior knowledge of the case would disable them from rendering an impartial verdict." Won't testimony under oath have so much more impact as to minimize the effect of prior press accounts? But what about pretrial hearings that widely publicize evidence such as a confession that is excluded at trial?

(4) *The Fair Trial, Free Press Cases.* In the next section, we concentrate in greater detail on the fair trial, free press issue.

NOTE ON THE FAIR TRIAL, FREE PRESS ISSUE:
THE *ESTES* AND *SHEPPARD* CASES

Television as "a Powerful Weapon": Estes v. Texas, 381 U.S. 532 (1965). In *Estes*, the Court (per Justice Clark) held that the defendant had been deprived of due process by the televising of his sensational criminal trial. Texas law would have permitted the sequestering of jurors, so that their contamination was not the Court's only, or even its principal concern; instead, the Court identified four kinds of interests that might be harmed by the presence of the battery of cameras covering *Estes'* trial:

> The potential impact of television on the jurors is perhaps of the greatest significance. . . . It is true that in states like Texas where they are required to be sequestered in trials of this nature, the jurors will probably will not see any of the proceedings as televised from the courtroom. But the inquiry cannot end there. From the moment the trial judge announces that a case will be televised it becomes a *cause celebre.* [T]he conscious or unconscious effect that this may have on the juror's judgment cannot be evaluated, but experience indicates that it is not only possible, but highly probable, that it will have a direct bearing on his vote as to guilt or innocence. . . .

Justice Clark concluded that the television camera "is a powerful weapon." Chief Justice Warren, in a concurring opinion, included photographs of bulky camera equipment massed together in the courtroom.

The Concern for Contamination of Jurors by Pretrial Publicity: Sheppard v. Maxwell, 384 U.S. 333 (1966). In *Sheppard,* newspaper publicity about the defendant's alleged murder of his wife contained considerable amounts of evidence not introduced at trial, including polygraph results, a confession under the influence of truth serum, information about alleged marital infidelity by Sheppard, and blood test results. Although jurors were subject to continuing press coverage, the trial judge merely "admonished" them not to read or watch news reports of the case. The Supreme Court reversed Sheppards' conviction, holding that the trial judge should have (1) avoided the "carnival atmosphere" in the courtroom; (2) insulated the witnesses; (3) "made some effort to control the release of leads, information, and gossip to the press by police officers, witnesses and the counsel for both sides"; and (4) insured "an impartial jury free from outside influences" by continuing the proceedings, transferring the case, sequestering the jury, or otherwise protecting the jury from publicity during trial.

Harmonizing the Right of a Free Press With the Right of a Fair Trial. As you read the following materials, consider whether in retrospect, the rhetoric of *Estes*— particularly the reference to television as "a powerful weapon"—may have been a signpost in the wrong direction. The *Sheppard* holding must be understood in light of options available to the trial judge, short of censorship, that could have protected the defendant's rights. *Cf.* Frank, *Cameras in the Courtroom: A First Amendment Right of Access,* 9 COMM./ENT. L.J. 749 (1987).

Access for Television Cameras: Should Less Obtrusive Technology Lead to a Reversal of the Estes Approach?— Chandler v. Florida, 449 U.S. 560 (1981). The *Chandler* case concerned a Florida statute that allowed the trial judge, under certain conditions and with various protections, to permit access by a television camera for the broadcast media in criminal trials, even over the defendant's objection. Despite the implications of *Estes v. Texas,* above, the Court upheld the statute. Does the existence of more compact technology and press pooling arrangements (which allow a single camera to serve multiple broadcasters) mitigate the concerns of the *Estes* case, or would television still adversely affect the performance of jurors, witnesses, judges and defendants?

PROBLEM P

A RIGHT OF ACCESS TO GOVERNMENT AGENCY DATA?— CAPITAL CITIES MEDIA, INC. v. CHESTER, 797 F.2d 1164 (3d Cir. 1986). If no law covers a particular item of information, is there a generalized First Amendment right of access? In *Chester,* a newspaper sought information from the Pennsylvania Department of Environmental Resources concerning an outbreak of intestinal illness caused by contaminated drinking water. The agency provided some of the materials sought, but it refused to supply copies of citizens' complaints and memoranda generated by technical personnel, among other documents. The newspaper then sued, claiming the First Amendment as a basis for requiring disclosure of the information. It argued that, after *Richmond Newspapers* and its progeny, a governmental agency must either furnish requested information or justify its refusal to do so. Question: Should the court order the requested disclosure?

[A majority of the Third Circuit, sitting en banc, held that the answer is no. "Our national experience has shown that reliance upon the political process to provide information has not been misplaced, and the peoples' representatives have not been unresponsive to political pressure when increased public access is needed [citing state and federal freedom of information acts]." As for the *Richmond Newspapers* line of cases, they "hold no more than that the government may not close government proceedings that historically have been open."]

[E] Regulation Of Broadcasters: Rationales And Results

INTRODUCTORY NOTE ON THE DIFFERENT CONSTITUTIONAL TREATMENT OF THE BROADCAST MEDIA

For an excellent treatment of the general subject, *see* L. Powe, American Broadcasting and the First Amendment (1987). The broadcast media traditionally have been subject to different constitutional treatment. For example, television broadcasters have been subjected to regulations of program content that would be unacceptable if applied to the print media, including requirements of program "balance" (mandating that each broadcaster carry a mix of differentkinds of programs), requirements of equal time for political candidates, the "fairness" doctrine (which is discussed in a later section of this Chapter, below), and other program content regulations. The constitutionality of the different treatment of broadcasters has been established for many years, although it lately has undergone re-examination in a world that includes a proliferation of cable television, satellite broadcasting, VHF, UHF, and numerous AM and FM radio stations. What is the rationale for this different treatment? Consider the following.

CRUMP, REGULATION OF PROGRAMMING AND PROGRAM CONTENT, IN TELEVISION BROADCASTING AND THE FCC
46 Texas L. Rev. 1100, 1190–92 (1968)*

First, it is often argued that broadcasters are regulated because they use public property [*i.e.*, the broadcast spectrum]. [R]easonable regulation of broadcasting, however, could be confined to the allocation of broadcast frequencies.

Secondly, it is said that broadcasters are public trustees having some degree of governmental character in their licenses. The government selects broadcasters and gives them valuable economic and political powers. . . .

Thirdly, there is the [scarcity] rationale that inherent limitations on the broadcast media make them constitutionally distinguishable from other media. This argument has been criticized on the ground that all communications media are limited. Thus, it has been pointed out that each of our fifty largest cities, on the average, has four television stations but only two newspaper publishers. Comparing broadcast outlets with major newspapers, however, is misleading. Austin, Texas, for example, has two television stations and one major newspaper publisher; it also has at least five newspapers serving its ethnic minorities, several college newspapers, and a myriad of smaller media serving communities or special groups. [A]t the simplest level, any person may pass out leaflets. No one, however, on pain of federal penalties, may broadcast without a license. . . .

Fourthly, it has been argued that regulation is needed to protect the first amendment rights of individuals and of the public. [This rationale] seems to be a basis for the equal time and fairness doctrines when considered in light of the limitations on broadcasting. . . .

Finally, some types of program regulation are arguably constitutional because they do not infringe upon the broadcaster's freedom of speech. Objectionable material, for example, may be constitutionally prohibited if it is not protected expression. More importantly, economic regulation is permissible even if it affects speech. Thus broadcast programming is regulated, primarily because of spectrum limitations, for economic and first amendment reasons. . . .

[F]   "Access" To The Press

[1]   Access Theory versus the "Checking Value"

BARRON, ACCESS TO THE PRESS—A NEW FIRST AMENDMENT RIGHT
80 HARV. L. REV. 1641 (1967)[*]

There is an anomaly in our constitutional law. While we protect expression after it has come to the fore, our law is indifferent to creating opportunities for expression. Our constitutional theory is in the grip of a romantic conception of free expression, a belief that the "marketplace of ideas" is freely accessible. But if ever there were a self-operating marketplace of ideas, it has long ceased to exist. The mass media's development of antipathy to ideas requires legal intervention if novel and unpopular ideas are to be assured a forum—unorthodox points of view which have no claim on broadcast time and newspaper space as a matter of right are in a poor position to compete with those aired as a matter of grace.

[T]o those who can obtain access to the media of mass communications first amendment case law furnishes considerable help. But what of those whose ideas are too unacceptable to secure access to the media? To them the mass communications industry replies: The first amendment guarantees our freedom to do as we choose with our media. Thus the constitutional imperative of free expression becomes a rationale for repressing competing ideas. First amendment theory must be re-examined, for only by responding to the present reality of the mass media's repression of ideas can the constitutional guarantee of free speech best serve its original purposes. . . .

[I]t is the writer's position that it is open to the courts to fashion a remedy for a right of access, at least in the most arbitrary cases, independently of legislation. If such an innovation is judicially resisted, I suggest that our constitutional law authorizes a carefully framed right of access statute which would forbid an arbitrary denial of space, hence securing an effective forum for the expression of divergent opinions. . . .

BLASI, THE CHECKING VALUE IN FIRST AMENDMENT THEORY
1977 AM. BAR FOUND. RES. J. 521.[**]

In this article, I examine . . . the idea that free expression is valuable in part because of the function it performs in checking the abuse of official power, an idea I shall hereafter refer to as "the checking value. . . ."

The tendency of officials to abuse their public trust is a theme that has permeated political thought from classical times to the present. John Locke devoted much of his second *Treatise on Civil Government*, first published in 1690, to this specific problem. [Blasi traces the sources of this idea through various pre-constitutional writers, including Madison and Jefferson.]

The central premise of the checking value is that the abuse of official power is an especially serious evil—more serious than the abuse of private power, even by institutions such as large corporations which can affect the lives of millions of people. . . .

The government's monopoly of legitimized violence means also that there is no concentrated force available to check the government in the way government is available to check even the most powerful private parties. The check upon government must come from the power of public opinion, which in turn rests on the power of the populace to retire officials at the polls, to withdraw the minimal cooperation required for effective governance, and ultimately to make a revolution. . . .

In this age of radio, television, and wire services, the basic reading and listening fare of most people emanates from a fairly limited number of sources—those persons who control or have access to the channels of mass communication. [S]ome commentators have even argued that the first amendment by its own force grants individuals and private groups a right of access to the channels of mass communication. . . .

[Blasi discusses the broadcast regulation cases and concludes that, since they discern first amendment limits on such regulations, "[T]he subtle pull of the checking value is evident in several of the opinions. . . ." He then turns to a decision striking down a state statute that gave a mandatory right of access to newspapers, *Miami Herald Publishing Co. v. Tornillo*, discussed in this section below. He examines the reasons for this holding.]

[O]ne possible explanation consistent with the checking value is that such a narrow right of reply could have the effect of shifting newspaper coverage away from topics that are central to the checking function—discussions of the fitness of candidates, particularly those with records in office—and toward less valued subjects for which the reply right would be inapplicable. A more likely reason is that the Justices perceived the print media as having historically enjoyed an adversary relationship with government which could only be compromised, symbolically as well as materially, if officials could dictate, for what ever reason, what the content of a particular publication must be. It is significant in this respect that the only justice who elaborated on the concept of journalistic discretion as it relates to newspapers, Mr. Justice White, stressed the role of the press as a watchdog over government. . . .

[I]f one considers journalistic autonomy as a means of serving the checking value rather than as derivative from the diversity and self-government values, a strong case can be made that news organizations should be constitutionally protected against government intervention in their internal operations. For the process of checking official misconduct sometimes requires the press to behave as a vigorous, unabashed partisan, campaigning with all available resources against a corrupt official or improper government practice. In most instances, a press campaign to discredit will have more credibility if the object of attack is given an opportunity to present a defense. But whether granting access to outsiders will serve the partisan campaign, and if so precisely what format of access will best do so, are tactical questions that are better left to be decided by the news organization itself . . . than by means of a legislative or judicial generalization. . . .

[2] Different Treatment of Access in Broadcast and in Print Media

RED LION BROADCASTING CO. v. FCC
395 U.S. 367 (1969)

MR. JUSTICE WHITE delivered the opinion of the Court.

[The Federal Communications Commission, which licenses radio and television broadcasters, promulgated what was called the "fairness doctrine," which required broadcasters to provide coverage of each side whenever they covered a controversial issue. Two regulations implementing this doctrine were at issue in *Red Lion*: (1) The "personal attack rule," which required the broadcaster to furnish a tape or transcript and free response time whenever an attack upon the "honesty, character, integrity or like personal qualities of an identified person or group" was aired; and (2) the "political editorial rule," which required a broadcaster that endorsed or opposed a candidate for office to furnish a tape or transcript and a reasonable opportunity for response. Here, the Supreme Court upholds both rules.]

Before 1927, the allocation of frequencies was left entirely to the private sector, and the result was chaos. It quickly became apparent that broadcast frequencies constituted a scarce resource whose use could be regulated and rationalized only by the Government. Without government control, the medium would be of little use because of the cacophony of competing voices, none of which could be clearly and predictably heard. Consequently, the Federal Radio Commission was established to allocate frequencies among competing applicants in a manner responsive to the public "convenience, interest, or necessity. . . ."

The broadcasters challenge the fairness doctrine and its specific manifestations in the personal attack and political editorial rules on conventional First Amendment grounds, alleging that the rules abridge their freedom of speech and press. Their contention is that the First Amendment protects their desire to use their allotted frequencies continuously to broadcast whatever they choose, and to exclude whomever they choose from ever using that frequency. [T]his right, they say, applies equally to broadcasters.

Although broadcasting is clearly a medium affected by a First Amendment interest, differences in the characteristics of new media justify differences in the First Amendment standards applied to them. . . .

Just as the Government may limit the use of sound-amplifying equipment potentially so noisy that it drowns out civilized private speech, so may the Government limit the use of broadcast equipment. . . .

Where there are substantially more individuals who want to broadcast than there are frequencies to allocate, it is idle to posit an unabridgeable First Amendment right to broadcast comparable to the right of every individual to speak, write, or publish. If 100 persons want broadcast licenses but there are only 10 frequencies to allocate, all of them may have the same "right" to a license; but if there is to be any effective communication by radio, only a few can be licensed and the rest must be barred from the airwaves. It would be strange if the First Amendment [p]revented the Government from making radio communication possible by requiring licenses to broadcast and by limiting the number of licenses so as not to overcrowd the spectrum. . . .

By the same token, as far as the First Amendment is concerned those who are licensed stand no better than those to whom licenses are refused. A license permits broadcasting, but the licensee has no constitutional right [to] monopolize a radio frequency to the exclusion of his fellow citizens. There is nothing in the First Amendment which prevents the Government from requiring a licensee to share his frequency with others and to conduct himself as a proxy or fiduciary with obligations to present those views and voices which are representative of his community and which would otherwise, by necessity, be barred from the airwaves.

This is not to say that the First Amendment is irrelevant to public broadcasting. [B]ecause of the scarcity of radio frequencies, the Government is permitted to put restraints on licensees in favor of others whose views should be expressed on this unique medium. But the people as a whole retain their interest in free speech by radio and their collective right to have the medium function consistently with the ends and purposes of the First Amendment. It is the right of the viewers and listeners, not the right of the broadcasters, which is paramount. [I]t is the purpose of the First Amendment to preserve an uninhibited marketplace of ideas in which truth will ultimately prevail, rather than to countenance monopolization of that market, whether it be by the Government itself or a private licensee. . . .

In terms of constitutional principle, and as enforced sharing of a scarce resource, the personal attack and political editorial rules are indistinguishable from the equal-time provision of § 315, a specific enactment of Congress requiring stations to set aside reply time under specified circumstances and to which the fairness doctrine and these constituent regulations are important complements. . . .

It is strenuously argued, however, that if political editorials or personal attacks will trigger an obligation in broadcasters to afford the opportunity for expression to speakers who need not pay for time and whose views are unpalatable to the licensees, then broadcasters will be irresistibly forced to self-censorship and their coverage of controversial public issues will be eliminated or at least rendered wholly ineffective. Such a result would indeed be a serious matter, for should licensees actually eliminate their coverage of controversial issues, the purposes of the doctrine would be stifled.

At this point, however, as the Federal Communications Commission has indicated, that possibility is at best speculative. [A]nd if experience with the administration of those doctrines indicates that they have the net effect of reducing rather than enhancing the volume and quality of coverage, there will be time enough to reconsider the constitutional implications. The fairness doctrine in the past has had no such overall effect. . . .

MIAMI HERALD PUBLISHING CO. v. TORNILLO
418 U.S. 241 (1974)

CHIEF JUSTICE BURGER delivered the opinion of the Court.

The issue in this case is whether a state statute granting a political candidate a right to equal space to reply to criticism and attacks on his record by a newspaper violates the guarantee of a free press.

[A Florida statute, § 104.38, provided a "right of reply" for a candidate for nomination or election whose personal character or official record was criticized by a newspaper, allowing the candidate to demand that the newspaper print the candidate's reply. The Miami Herald printed an editorial criticizing Tornillo, a candidate for the legislature. It refused his reply and argued that the Florida statute was unconstitutional. Here, the Supreme Court agrees and strikes it down.]

Access advocates submit that although newspapers of the present are superficially similar to those of 1791 the press of today is in reality very different from that known in the early years of our national existence. . . .

The elimination of competing newspapers in most of our large cities, and the concentration of control of media that results from the only newspaper's being owned by the same interests which own a television station and a radio station, are important components of this trend toward concentration of control of outlets to inform the public. . . .

However much validity may be found in these arguments, at each point the implementation of a remedy such as an enforceable right of access necessarily calls for some mechanism, either governmental or consensual. If it is governmental coercion, this at once brings about a confrontation with the express provisions of the First Amendment and the judicial gloss on that Amendment developed over the years. . . .

The clear implication [of prior cases] has been that any [c]ompulsion to publish that which " 'reason' tells [newspapers] should not be published" is unconstitutional. A responsible press is an undoubtedly desirable goal, but press responsibility is not mandated by the Constitution and like many other virtues it cannot be legislated.

Appellee's argument that the Florida statute does not amount to a restriction of appellant's right to speak because "the statute in question here has not prevented the *Miami Herald* from saying anything it wished" begs the core question. Compelling editors or publishers to publish that which " 'reason' tells them should not be published" is what is at issue in this case. The Florida statute operates as a command in the same sense as a statue or regulation forbidding appellant to publish specified matter. [T]he Florida statute exacts a penalty on the basis of the content of a newspaper. The first phase of the penalty resulting from the compelled printing of a reply is exacted in terms of the cost in printing and composing time and materials and in taking up space that could be devoted to other material the newspaper may have preferred to print. It is correct, as appellee contends, that a newspaper is not subject to the finite technological limitations of time that confront a broadcaster but it is not correct to say that, as an economic reality, a newspaper can proceed to infinite expansion of its column space to accommodate the replies that a government agency determines or a statute commands the readers should have available.

Faced with the penalties that would accrue to any newspaper that published news or commentary arguably within the reach of the right-of-access statute, editors might well conclude that the safe course is to avoid controversy. Therefore, under the operation of the Florida statute, political and electoral coverage would be blunted or reduced. . . .

Even if a newspaper would face no additional costs to comply with a compulsory access law and would not be forced to forgo publication of news or opinion by the inclusion of a reply, the Florida statute fails to clear the barriers of the First Amendment because of its intrusion into the function of editors. A newspaper is more than a passive receptacle or conduit for news, comment, and advertising. The choice of material to go into a newspaper, and the decisions made as to limitations on the size and content of the paper, and treatment of public issues and public officials—whether fair or unfair—constitute the exercise of editorial control and judgment. It has yet to be demonstrated how governmental regulation of this crucial process can be exercised consistent with First Amendment guarantees of a free press as they have evolved to this time. Accordingly, the judgment of the Supreme Court of Florida is reversed.

[The concurring opinions of JUSTICE BRENNAN, joined by JUSTICE REHNQUIST, and of JUSTICE WHITE, are omitted.]

NOTES AND QUESTIONS

(1) *State Mandated Right of Reply to Print Media Criticism Is Unconstitutional: Miami Herald Publishing Co. v. Tornillo, 418 U.S. 241 (1974).* Florida had a statute requiring the print media to give equal space for purposes of a right-of-reply to any political candidate who had been criticized by the newspaper. Florida argued that it was just responding to the increased concentration of newspaper ownership. The Court, per Chief Justice Burger, rejected this argument. The Court held that the statute was an unconstitutional abridgment of the free press interests of the newspaper: (1) It added costs to production; and (2) Independent of additional costs, the statute was an impermissible "intrusion" into the protected editorial function. There were three concurring Justices.

(2) *The Different Treatment of Print Media in Miami Herald and Broadcast Media in Red Lion: Is the Distinction Justifiable?* Consider whether the different treatment of the broadcast and print media in these two cases is justified. Doesn't the Court's "scarcity" rationale, in *Red Lion*, apply equally or with greater force to the print media, since most metropolitan areas have only one or two major newspapers but have a wide variety of broadcast outlets? Conversely, aren't the Court's "compulsion" and "penalty" rationales in *Miami Herald* equally applicable to the broadcast media—that is, when the government requires a broadcaster to give free air time to an individual, isn't the broadcaster "compelled," and isn't it subject to the same kind of "penalty" that was imposed by the newspaper-right-of-reply statute in *Miami Herald*?

(3) *The Checking Value: Blasi's View of the Fairness Doctrine.* Reconsider *Blasi, The Checking Value.* Is the personal attack rule consistent with the checking value? The political editorial rule? The general fairness doctrine (which simply applies to "controversial issues")? Blasi's own conclusion is that "the general fairness doctrine . . . should be considered a violation of the first amendment. [It] undercuts the conception of journalistic autonomy that grows out of the checking value. . . . [But] [m]ore narrowly defined access regulations designed to give persons who are criticized on the air a right to reply stand on a different footing. The FCC's personal attack and political editorial rules . . . are examples. . . ."

(4) *Did the Red Lion Court Underestimate the Discouragement that the Fairness Doctrine Could Have Upon the Broadcasting of Controversial Issues?* First, consider the generality of the fairness doctrine. What does it mean, for example, to give "fair" coverage to a complex subject (*e.g.,* the Vietnam War)? Is it possible that the uncertainty of the broadcaster's obligations in such a situation might cause a talk show producer to decide to cover a subject that is not such a "can of worms?" Secondly, consider the possibility that the broadcaster might avoid a given subject because of the absence of available responsible spokespersons, or because the broadcaster simply concludes that the opposing spokesperson is one that his audience strongly would prefer not to hear. For example, what if a broadcaster does not air a program criticizing the American Nazi Party, because of a concern that he might be legally required to sponsor utterances by a Nazi spokesperson? Will the fairness doctrine, in this way, be a bonanza for speakers with more extreme views? Finally, to what extent will the broadcaster be deterred by the need to give free time to fairness doctrine subjects?

COLUMBIA BROADCASTING SYSTEM, INC. v. DEMOCRATIC NATIONAL COMMITTEE, 412 U.S. 94 (1973). CBS had a policy of refusing paid public issue announcements (or political commercials). The court of appeals held that the FCC's refusal to countermand this policy by regulation violated the First Amendment, at least when other sorts of paid announcements (or non-political commercials) were accepted. The Supreme Court, per Chief Justice Burger, reversed and held in favor of CBS:

> [T]he licensee's policy against accepting editorial advertising cannot be examined as an abstract proposition, but must be viewed in the context of its journalistic role. It does not help to press on us the idea that editorial ads are "like" commercial ads, for the licensee's policy against editorial spot ads is expressly based on a journalistic judgment that ten-to-sixty-second spot announcements are ill-suited to intelligible and intelligent treatment of public issues; the broadcaster has chosen to provide a balanced treatment of controversial questions in a more comprehensive form. Obviously the licensee's evaluation is based on its own journalistic judgment of priorities and newsworthiness. . . .
>
> Were we to read the first amendment to spell out governmental action in the circumstances presented here, few licensee decisions on the content of broadcasts or the processes of editorial evaluation would escape constitutional scrutiny. . . .
>
> More profoundly, it would be anomalous for us to hold, in the name of promoting the constitutional guarantees of free expression, that the day-to-day editorial decisions of broadcast licensees are subject to the kind of restraints urged by respondents. [J]ournalisticdiscretion would in many ways be lost to the rigid limitations that the first amendment imposes on government. . . .

Justices Stewart, Blackmun, Powell, and Douglas wrote or joined in concurring opinions. Mr. Justice Douglas, in particular, declined to concur in the Court's opinion, and concurred only in the judgment, because he did not accept the Court's reasoning with respect to the legitimacy of broadcast regulation under the fairness doctrine:

> My conclusion is that T.V. and radio stand in the same protected position under the first amendment as do newspapers and magazines. The philosophy of the first amendment requires that result, for the fear that Madison and Jefferson had of government intrusion is perhaps even more relevant to T.V. and radio than it is to newspapers and other like publications. That fear was founded not only on the specter of a lawless government but of government under the control of a faction that desired to foist its views of the common good on the people. . . .

Justice Brennan, joined by Justice Marshall, dissented: "[I]ndividual licensees have often attained their present position," not as a result of free market pressures, but, rather, "because of their initial government selection." Therefore, the absolute ban on the sale of air time for editorials was "government action" and implicated the First Amendment. And "in light of the strong interests of broadcasters in maximizing their audience, and therefore their profits, it seems almost naive to expect a majority of broadcasters to produce the variety and controversiality of material necessary to reflect a full spectrum of viewpoints."

NOTES AND QUESTIONS

(1) *If it is the Public's Right to Receive Information that Is Paramount, Shouldn't It Be the Public's Choices, Exercised in the Marketplace, that Control?: FCC v. WNCN Listener's Guild, 449 U.S. 946 (1980).* In *WNCN*, the FCC had promulgated a policy relying upon market forces rather than regulation to govern radio entertainment formats. The Supreme Court upheld this policy: "The Commission [relies] on market forces to promote diversity . . . and to satisfy the entertainment preferences of radio listeners. This policy does not conflict with the first amendment." Notice that Justice Brennan, in *CBS v. DNC*, criticizes the editorial judgment of broadcasters because they will follow viewers' preferences. Are the two views—that of the Court in *WNCN Listener's Guild* and that of Justice Brennan in *CBS v. DNC*—inconsistent? If so, which is more nearly correct?

(2) *Criticizing "Fairness"—Krattenmaker and Powe, The Fairness Doctrine Today: A Constitutional Curiosity and an Impossible Dream,* 1985 DUKE L.J. 151.[*] Krattenmaker and Powe's article is one of the most outspoken and readable denunciations of the fairness doctrine:

> [O]ur conclusion is that the fairness doctrine does not—and cannot—work. Accordingly, it should be repealed either by legislative or administrative action. . . .

> [A]t best, the fairness doctrine is, like the 1962 New York Mets, a glorious but futile symbol, full of wondrous pretension and promise, yet utterly devoid of performance.

> As a practical matter, the fairness doctrine is a failure for two distinct reasons. First, viewed as an exercise of regulatory power, there is no reason to believe that the doctrine achieves its purposes or does so in an efficient manner. Second, as a legal principle, it is utterly meaningless. In our view, these practical considerations are sufficiently compelling that, even were the constitutional issues more nearly balanced on both sides, the case for abolishing the fairness doctrine would be clear. . . .

> [W]hen one considers critically the probable affects of the doctrine, its public and private costs, and the results that can be achieved by relying on alternative and cost-free techniques, the doctrine's principal net effects appear to be: (1) To foist upon broadcast licensees the FCC's view of what are important positions on public issues and (2) to reduce incentives among broadcasters to compete for listeners' and viewers' attention by offering programs that address controversial issues. To the extent that these effects are not realized, this is due to the fact that (1) systematic monitoring of compliance with the fairness doctrine is impossible, given the relative size of the industry and resources of the [FCC]; and (2) competition with other media for the public's attention and trust are likely to force broadcasters to cover many sides of significant public issues. At best, then, it is difficult to grasp how anyone who shares the goals purportedly sought by the fairness doctrine can argue that we are better off with it than without it. . . .

PROBLEM Q

THE FCC VOTES TO SCRAP THE FAIRNESS DOCTRINE—IS ITS ACTION (1) UNCONSTITUTIONAL, (2) CONSTITUTIONALLY MANDATED, (3) NEITHER, OR (4) BOTH? On August 4, 1987, the Federal Communications Commission voted to repeal the general fairness doctrine. *See FCC Scraps Fairness Doctrine*, HOUSTON CHRONICLE, August 4, 1987, § 1, at 3, col. 4. FCC Chairman Dennis Patrick asserted that the vote "should be cause for celebration" because "the fairness doctrine chills speech and contravenes the first amendment and the public interest." But Andrew J. Schwartzman, Executive Director of Media Access Project, said, "Today is a bad day for the first amendment, but listeners will win in the end. The fairness doctrine has always had the support of Congress and the courts, and it will prevail."

Questions: Was the FCC's vote (1) an unconstitutional violation of the first amendment, in that it sanctions government-licensed monopolies arguably unresponsive to some radio and television users? Or, was the FCC's vote (2) constitutionally required, in that the fairness doctrine is an unconstitutional penalty on broadcasting controversial views and an unlawful intrusion into the function of editors? Or, was this action (3) neither unconstitutional nor constitutionally mandated, but simply a matter of policy to be decided by the Commission?

[3]   Revisiting the Red Lion Doctrine

TURNER BROADCASTING SYSTEM, INC. v. FEDERAL COMMUNICATIONS COMMISSION, 509 U.S. 952 (1994) (*"Turner I"*). In the 1992 Cable Television Consumer Protection and Competition Act, Congress imposed "must-carry" requirements on cable television operators and programmers as part of the Act's effort to maintain balance between cable andtraditional television broadcasters. The challengers claimed that these must-carry provisions, which require cable operators to dedicate a percentage of their channels to carrying local broadcast stations, were content-based restrictions and, accordingly, that strict scrutiny must be applied [§ 11.03 *supra*]. The FCC defended, *inter alia*, on the ground that the free speech rights of cable broadcasters should be controlled by *Red Lion*, below. The Court, per Justice Kennedy, rejected the FCC's argument and held, on this issue, that cable television would not be subject to the lower level of scrutiny used for the broadcast television media:

> It is true that our cases have permitted more intrusive regulation of broadcast speakers than of speakers in other media [citing *Red Lion* and *Miami Herald*]. But the rationale for applying a less rigorous standard of First Amendment scrutiny to broadcast regulation, whatever its validity in the cases elaborating it, does not apply in the context of cable regulation.

> The scarcity of broadcast frequencies . . . required the establishment of some regulatory mechanism to divide the electromagnetic spectrum and assign specific frequencies to particular broadcasters. . . .

> Although courts and commentators have criticized the scarcity rationale since its inception, we have declined to question its continuing validity as support for our broadcast jurisprudence and see no reason to do so here. . . . In light of [the] fundamental technological differences between broadcast and cable transmission, application of the more relaxed standard of scrutiny adopted in *Red Lion* and the other broadcast cases is inapt when determining the First Amendment validity of cable regulation. . . .

Despite this holding, the lower court, on remand, upheld the "must carry" law. The Supreme Court, on its second review of the case, also upheld it. Among other conclusions, the Court decided that the rationale for "must carry" was "unrelated to the suppression of free expression." Cable television operators were more like a conduit or channel of communication than an editor, as in *Miami Herald*. Note the arguable inconsistency of this result, in *Turner II* with *Turner I* and its distinction of *Red Lion*. (*Turner II* is excerpted above in § 11.03[A], dealing with "Tracks" One and Two).

§ 11.06   TRACK TWO REGULATION

[A]   Time, Place, or Manner Regulations

[1]   Licensing: Historical Development

LOVELL v. GRIFFIN
303 U.S. 444 (1938)

MR. CHIEF JUSTICE HUGHES delivered the opinion of the Court.

[Lovell was convicted under an ordinance of the City of Griffin, Georgia, which provided that "the practice of distributing, either by hand or otherwise, circulars, handbooks, advertising, or literature of any kind, . . . without first obtaining written permission from the City Manager . . ., shall be deemed a nuisance, punishable as an offense. . . ." The Supreme Court here strikes down the ordinance.]

The ordinance in its broad sweep . . . manifestly applies to pamphlets, magazines, and periodicals. The evidence against appellant was that she distributed a certain pamphlet and a magazine called the "Golden Age." [T]he ordinance is not limited to "literature" that is obscene or offensive to public morals or that advocates unlawful conduct. . . .

The ordinance is comprehensive with respect to the method of distribution. It covers every sort of circulation "either by hand or otherwise." There is thus no restriction in its application with respect to time or place. It is not limited to ways which might be regarded as inconsistent with the maintenance of public order, or as involving disorderly conduct, the molestation of the inhabitants, or the misuse or littering of the streets. The ordinance prohibits the distribution of literature of any kind at any time, at any place, and in any manner without a permit from the city manager.

We think that the ordinance is invalid on its face. [T]he struggle for the freedom of the press was primarily directed against the power of the licensor. It was against that power that JohnMilton directed his assault by his "Appeal for the Liberty of Unlicensed Printing." And the liberty of the press became initially a right to publish "*without* a license what formerly could be published only *with* one. . . ."

Reversed and remanded.

COX v. NEW HAMPSHIRE, 312 U.S. 569 (1941). Cox and others, who were Jehovah's Witnesses, conducted a "parade or procession" on a public street in Manchester, New Hampshire, without a parade license. The state supreme court construed the governing statute to require that "no measures for controlling or suppressing the publication on the highways of facts and opinions" could be used by the Licensing Board. The Board was required to exercise its discretion with "uniformity of method of treatment upon the facts of each application, free from improper or inappropriate considerations and from unfair discrimination," using a "systematic, consistent and just order of treatment." The purpose of the license requirement was "to prevent confusion by overlapping parades or processions, to secure convenient use of the streets by other travelers, and to minimize the risk of disorder." Any applicant would have a right to a permit "if after a required investigation it was found that the convenience of the public in the use of the streets would not thereby be unduly disturbed, upon such conditions or changes in time, place, and manner as would avoid disturbance."

The Court, per Chief Justice Hughes, upheld both the statute and the conviction:

> If a municipality has authority to control the use of its public streets for parades or processions, as it undoubtedly has, it cannot be denied authority to give consideration, without unfair discrimination, to time, place, and manner in relation to the other proper uses of the streets. . . .

> There remains the question of license fees, which, as the court said, had a permissible range from $300 to a nominal amount. The court construed the Act as requiring "a reasonable fixing of the amount of the fee." [T]he fee was held to be "not a revenue tax, but one to meet the expense incident to the administration of the Act and to the maintenance of public order in the matter licensed." There is nothing contrary to the Constitution in the charge of a fee limited to the purpose stated. . . .

> The decisions upon which appellants rely are not applicable. In *Lovell v. Griffin*, the ordinance prohibited the distribution of literature of any kind at any time, at any place, and in any manner without a permit from the City Manager, thus striking at the very foundation of the freedom of the press by subjecting it to license and censorship. . . .

NATIONALIST MOVEMENT v. FORSYTH COUNTY, 505 U.S. 123 (1992). This case appears in an earlier section of this chapter and should be reconsidered here. It holds the Forsyth County parade permit fee unconstitutional because of (1) "unbridled" official discretion to set the amount of the fee and (2) consideration of hostile reaction as a factor in setting the fee. The majority purports to distinguish *Cox v. New Hampshire;* the dissent regards *Cox* as upholding a fee ordinance, but would remand for findings on the discretion and heckler's veto issues. The majority's reasoning on the issue of excessive discretion included the following:

> [A]lthough there is a "heavy presumption" against the validity of a prior restraint, the Court has recognized that government, in order to regulate competing uses of public forums, may impose a permit requirement on those wishing to hold a march, parade, or rally. *See Cox v. New Hampshire*, 312 U.S. 569, 574—576 (1941). Such a scheme, however, must meet certain constitutional requirements. It may not delegate overly broad licensing discretion to a government official. . . .

> Respondent contends that the county ordinance is facially invalid because it does not prescribe adequate standards for the administrator to apply when he sets a permit fee. "[A] law subjecting the exercise of First Amendment freedoms to the prior restraint of a license" must contain "narrow, objective, and definite standards to guide the licensing authority." The reasoning is simple: If the permit scheme "involves appraisal of facts, the exercise of judgment, and the formation of an opinion," *Cantwell v. Connecticut*, 310 U.S. 296, 305 (1940), by the licensing authority, "the danger of censorship and of abridgment of our precious First Amendment freedoms is too great" to be permitted. . . .

> In this case, according to testimony at the District Court hearing, the administrator based the fee on his own judgment of what would be reasonable. [T]he administrator also attested that he had deliberately kept the fee low by undervaluing the cost of the time he spent processing the application. [H]e further testified that, in this instance, he chose not to include any charge for expected security expense. . . .

> [A]t oral argument in this Court, counsel for Forsyth County stated that the administrator had levied a $5 fee on the Girl Scouts for an activity on county property. Finally, the administrator testified that in other cases the county required neither a permit nor a fee for activities in other county facilities or on county land.

Based on the county's implementation and construction of the ordinance, it simply cannot be said that there are any "narrowly drawn, reasonable and definite standards". . . . The First Amendment prohibits the vesting of such unbridled discretion in a government official.

NOTES AND QUESTIONS

(1) *How Much of Cox v. New Hampshire Is Left After the Nationalist Movement Decision?* On the face of it, the discretion given by the ordinance in *Nationalist Movement* does not appear to exceed that given by the ordinance in *Cox*. Of course, the discretion to consider hostile reaction is a new factor not (expressly) present in *Cox*—but if this were the only distinction, presumably the majority's treatment of "unbridled" discretion would be unnecessary. Does *Nationalist Movement* overrule *Cox* (or if not, how much is left of *Cox*)?

(2) *Distinguishing Cox from Lovell: Limiting the Licensor's Discretion to Time, Place, and Manner Considerations; Content-Neutral Regulation.* Consider the distinction between *Cox* and *Lovell.* Both involved discretion on the part of licensors, but in *Cox*, the construction placed upon the statute by the state supreme court restricted that discretion much more than in *Lovell.* Consider whether this difference explains the difference in result. Consider also whether the regulation, in *Cox*, truly will be content-neutral. Does the ability of the licensor to set the fee, or to set "such conditions . . . as would avoid disturbance," provide excessive authority to discriminate on the basis of content? *See generally* David S. Day, *The Hybridization of the Content-Neutral Standards for the Free Speech Clause,* 19 Ariz. St. L.J. 195 (1987).

(3) *Further Distinguishing Cox from Lovell—The Purposes of the Regulation: Leaflets as Versus Parades.* Or, is the distinction between *Cox* and *Lovell* really that, in *Lovell*, the regulation was not sufficiently tied to legitimate purposes? Consider whether the state has a lesser interest in licensing distribution of literature than in regulating parades through the streets.

(4) *The Open Forum and the Clash With Breach-of-the-Peace and Public-Passage Laws: Cox v. Louisiana, 379 U.S. 536 (1965) ("Cox I").* Cox led a group of approximately 2,000 demonstrators protesting racial discrimination and opposing the arrests of certain individuals. The demonstration involved noisy cheering, clapping, and singing, but was peaceful. Police officers ordered dispersal when Cox encouraged sit-in demonstrations; the demonstrators did not disperse, and ultimately were separated by tear gas. Cox was convicted of breach of the peace and obstructing public passages. The Supreme Court, per Justice Goldberg, reversed the convictions:

> We have no occasion in this case to consider the constitutionality of the uniform, consistent, and non-discriminatory application of a statute forbidding all access to streets and other public facilities for parades and meetings. [I]t appears that the authorities . . . permit or prohibit parades or street meetings in their completely uncontrolled discretion. . . .

> [T]he lodging of such broad discretion in a public official allows him to determine which expressions of view will be permitted and which will not. This [ordinance] sanctions a device for the suppression of the communication of ideas and permits the official to act as a censor. . . .

Question: If Cox had been convicted under an ordinance such as that in *Cox v. New Hampshire*, rather than the ordinance at issue in *Cox v. Louisiana*, would the conviction have been upheld?

(5) *Closing the Public Forum— By Making the Courthouse Off Limits: Cox v. Louisiana, 379 U.S. 559 (1965) ("Cox II").* In this companion case to *Cox I*, above, the court reviewed a conviction of the same defendant for picketing "in or near a building housing a court of the state." The Court, per Justice Goldberg, upheld this conviction even though Cox's other convictions had been invalidated. The Court concluded that the

prohibition upon picketing "near" a courthouse was not unconstitutionally vague, and "there can be no question that a state has a legitimate interest in protecting its judicial system from the pressures which picketing near a courthouse might create":

> [A]dministrative discretion to construe the term "near" concerns a limited control of the streets and other areas in the immediate vicinity of the courthouse and is the type of narrow discretion which this Court has recognized as the proper role of responsible officials in making determinations concerning the time, place, duration, and manner of demonstrations.

Question: Is *Cox II* consistent with *Cox I*, with *Lovell v. Griffin*, or with the decisions on overbreadth and vagueness?

(6)   *The Constitutionality of Permit Requirements For Door-To-Door Advocacy and Solicitation: Watchtower Bible and Tract Society of New York, Inc. v. Village of Stratton, 536 U.S. 150 (2002).* The *Forsyth County* decision, above, addressed the standards for the imposition of permit fees. Many municipalities, however, attempted to regulate door-to-door solicitation and advocacy without resorting to any monetary fees. In *Watchtower Bible*, the Court focused on such non-fee permit schemes.

Watchtower Bible challengers were Jehovah's Witnesses, whose religious beliefs mandate door-to-door activities. The Village's ordinance made it a misdemeanor to engage in door-to-door advocacy without first registering with the mayor and receiving a permit. The Court, per Justice Stevens, held that, as applied to religious proselytizing, anonymous political speech and the distribution of handbills, the ordinance violated the First Amendment.

Justice Breyer (for Souter and Ginsburg) concurred. Justice Scalia (for Thomas) concurred only in the judgment. Justice Scalia criticized the Court's analysis as it relied on a hypothetical political activist: "If our free speech jurisprudence is to be determined by the predicted behavior of such crackpots, we are in a sorry state indeed." Chief Justice Rehnquist dissented on several grounds and argued that the decision implicitly overruled 60 years of precedent. The decision seems more expansive than the *Lovell* analysis above.

[2]   The Modern Time, Place, or Manner Doctrine

The Seminal Decision of the Modern Time, Place, or Manner Regulation: Grayned v. City of Rockford, 408 U.S. 104 (1972). Grayned and others participated in a demonstration to present their grievances concerning the administration of West Senior High School in the city of Rockford, Illinois. They were convicted under an anti-noise ordinance that prohibited any person "adjacent to any building in which a school . . . is in session [from] willfully mak[ing] . . . any noise or diversion which . . . tends to disturb the peace or good order of such school session or class thereof." The Court, per Justice Marshall, upheld the ordinance and the conviction: "[R]ockford's anti-noise ordinance does not permit punishment for the expression of an unpopular point of view, and it contains no broad invitation to subjective or discriminatory enforcement. [T]here must be demonstrated interference with school activities. As always, enforcement requires the exercise of some degree of police judgment, but, as confined, that degree of judgment here is permissible." *Compare Mosley, supra*, as the companion decision (a content-based regulation).

HEFFRON v. INTERNATIONAL SOCIETY FOR KRISHNA CONSCIOUSNESS
452 U.S. 640 (1981)

MR. JUSTICE WHITE delivered the opinion of the Court.

[The State of Minnesota promulgated a rule called Rule 6.05, applicable to its State Fair, requiring persons desiring to sell, exhibit, or distribute materials or to solicit contributions to do so only from assigned booths. The International Society for Krishna

Consciousness ("ISKCON") sought an injunction against the enforcement of this rule. ISKCON's members engaged in a religious practice called "Sankirtan" that required them to solicit donations and sell items in public places, and they wished to do so at the State Fair. The Minnesota Supreme Court applied the strict scrutiny standard (requiring a compelling government interest and the use of least restrictive means) and held in favor of ISKCON. The United States Supreme Court here reverses and upholds the Minnesota rule.]

[T]he First Amendment does not guarantee the right to communicate one's views at all times and places or in any manner that may be desired . . .; see *Cox v. Louisiana*, 379 U.S. 536, 554 (1965). As the Minnesota Supreme Court recognized, the activities of ISKCON, like those of others protected by the First Amendment, are subject to reasonable time, place, and manner restrictions. *Grayned v. City of Rockford.* . . .

A major criterion for a valid time, place, and manner restriction is that the restriction "may not be based upon either the content or subject matter of speech." [R]ule 6.05 qualifies in this respect, since as the Supreme Court of Minnesota observed, the Rule applies evenhandedly to all who wish to distribute and sell written materials or to solicit funds. No person or organization, whether commercial or charitable, is permitted to engage in such activities except from a booth rented for those purposes.

Nor does Rule 6.05 suffer from the more covert forms of discrimination that may result when arbitrary discretion is vested in some governmental authority. The method of allocating space is a straightforward first-come, first-served system. The Rule is not open to the kind of arbitrary application that this Court has condemned as inherently inconsistent with a valid time, place, and manner regulation because such discretion has the potential for becoming a means of suppressing a particular point of view. . . .

A valid time, place, and manner regulation must also "serve a significant governmental interest." [S]ee *Grayned v. City of Rockford.* Here, the principal justification asserted by the State in support of Rule 6.05 is the need to maintain the orderly movement of the crowd given the large number of exhibitors and persons attending the Fair.

The fairgrounds comprise a relatively small area of 125 acres, the bulk of which is covered by permanent buildings, temporary structures, parking lots, and connecting thoroughfares. There were some 1,400 exhibitors and concessionaires renting space for the 1977 and 1978 Fairs, chiefly in permanent and temporary buildings. The Fair is designed to exhibit to the public an enormous variety of goods, services, entertainment, and other matters of interest. This is accomplished by confining individual exhibitors to fixed locations, with the public moving to and among the booths or other attractions, using streets and open spaces provided for that purpose. Because the Fair attracts large crowds, it is apparent that the State's interest in the orderly movement and control of such an assembly of persons is a substantial consideration.

. . . [C]onsideration of a forum's special attributes is relevant to the constitutionality of a regulation since the significance of the governmental interest must be assessed in light of the characteristic nature and function of the particular forum involved. [T]his observation bears particular import in the present case since respondents make a number of analogies between the fairgrounds and city streets which have "immemorially been held in trust for the use of the public and . . . have been used for purposes of assembly, communicating thoughts between citizens, and discussing public questions. . . ."

[B]ut it is clear that there are significant differences between a street and the fairgrounds. [T]he flow of the crowd and demands of safety are more pressing in the context of the Fair. As such, any comparisons to public streets are necessarily inexact.

The Minnesota Supreme Court recognized that the State's interest in the orderly movement of a large crowd and in avoiding congestion was substantial and that Rule 6.05 furthered that interest significantly. Nevertheless, the Minnesota Supreme Court declared that the case did not turn on the "importance of the state's undeniable interest in preventing the widespread disorder that would surely exist if no regulation such as Rule 6.05 were in effect" but upon the significance of the State's interest in avoiding whatever disorder would likely result from granting members of ISKCON an exemption from the Rule. . . .

As we see it, the Minnesota Supreme Court took too narrow a view of the State's interest in avoiding congestion and maintaining the orderly movement of fair patrons on the fairgrounds. [ISKCON] and its ritual of Sankirtan have no special claim to First Amendment protection as compared to that of other religions who also distribute literature and solicit funds. . . .

If Rule 6.05 is an invalid restriction on the activities of ISKCON, it is no more valid with respect to the other social, political, or charitable organizations that have rented booths at the Fair and confined their distribution, sale, and fund solicitation to those locations. Nor would it be valid with respect to other organizations that did not rent booths [b]ut that would in all probability appear in the fairgrounds to distribute, sell, and solicit if they could freely do so. . . .

Given these considerations, we hold that the State's interest in confining distribution, selling, and fund solicitation activities to fixed locations is sufficient to satisfy the requirement that a place or manner restriction must serve a substantial state interest. . . .

For Rule 6.05 to be valid as a place and manner restriction, it must also be sufficiently clear that alternative forums for the expression of respondents' protected speech exist despite the effects of the Rule. Rule 6.05 is not vulnerable on this ground. First, the Rule does not prevent ISKCON from practicing Sankirtan anywhere outside the fairgrounds. [More importantly,] the Rule does not exclude ISKCON from the fairgrounds, nor does it deny that organization the right to conduct any desired activity at some point within the forum. Its members may mingle with the crowdand orally propagate their views. The organization may also arrange for a booth and distribute and sell literature and solicit funds from that location on the fairgrounds itself. The Minnesota State Fair is a limited public forum in that it exists to provide a means for a great number of exhibitors temporarily to present their products or views, be they commercial, religious, or political, to a large number of people in an efficient fashion. . . .

The judgment of the Supreme Court of Minnesota is reversed, and the case is remanded for further proceedings not inconsistent with this opinion.

JUSTICE BRENNAN, with whom JUSTICE MARSHALL and *Justice Stevens* join, concurring in part and dissenting in part. . . .

The Court errs . . . failing to apply its analysis separately to each of the protected First Amendment activities restricted by Rule 6.05. Thus, the Court fails to recognize that some of the State's restrictions may be reasonable while other may not. . . .

I quite agree with the Court that the State has a significant interest in maintaining crowd control on its fairgrounds. *See Grayned v. City of Rockford, Cox v. New Hampshire.* I also have no doubt that the State has a significant interest in protecting its fairgoers from fraudulent or deceptive solicitation practices. [I]ndeed, because I believe on this record that this latter interest is substantially furthered by a Rule that restricts sales and solicitation activities to fixed booth locations, where the State will have the greatest opportunity to police and prevent possible deceptive practices, I would hold that Rule 6.05's restriction on those particular forms of First Amendment expression is justified as an antifraud measure. Accordingly, I join the judgment of the Court insofar as it upholds Rule 6.05's restriction on sales and solicitations. However, because I believe that the booth Rule is an overly intrusive means of achieving the State's interest in crowd control, and because I cannot accept the validity of the State's third asserted justification, I dissent from the Court's approval of Rule 6.05's restriction on the distribution of literature. . . .

NOTES AND QUESTIONS

(1) *The Three-Part Test in Heffron.* The *Heffron* decision applied a three-part test. A valid time, place, and manner regulation must be (1) "content-neutral"; (2) further a "substantial government interest"; and (3) leave the speaker with "alternative forums for expression." Is this the right approach?

(2) *Is the Minnesota Rule at Issue in Heffron a Content-Neutral "Time, Place, or Manner" Regulation?* The Minnesota rule treated all sales or solicitations alike. However, it distinguished those kinds of communications from other activity protected by the first amendment. Furthermore, the Court's recognition of a valid state interest in avoiding ISKCON's "intercepting fair patrons as they move about" may conceal a purpose of protecting patrons from obnoxious or disturbing speech. Can the state validly concern itself with this annoyance to fair patrons, if that motive is a part of the reason for the ordinance?

(3) *The Continuing Evolution of the Time, Place, and Manner Standard Into a Four-Part Test: Ward v. Rock Against Racism, 491 U.S. 781 (1989).* The *Heffron* test, discussed in Note (1) above, applied a three-part standard. In a series of post-*Heffron* decisions, the Court has added a fourth part to the standard: in addition to (1) content-neutrality, (2) a substantial (or significant) governmental interest and (3) ample alternative channels, a valid time, place, and manner regulation must be (4) "narrowly tailored." *See, e.g., Clark v. Community For Creative Non-Violence,* 468 U.S. 288 (1984); *Ward v. Rock Against Racism, supra.* In *Rock Against Racism,* the City of New York sought to regulate excessive noise from musical performances at the bandshell in Central Park. New York's regulations required that all performers use city-owned sound equipment controlled by a city technician. Rock Against Racism was a rock band that claimed that this regulation was not "narrowly tailored." The Supreme Court disagreed; it emphasized that a regulation did not have to be the "least restrictive alternative" (as in strict scrutiny [§ 11.03]) in order to satisfy the "narrow tailoring" requirement. *See generally* Gregory L. Lippetz, Note, *The Day the Music Died: Ward v. Rock Against Racism,* 25 U.S.F. L. REV. 627 (1991).

(4) *The "Ample Alternative Channels" Prong of the Time, Place, and Manner Standard: City of Ladue v. Gilleo, 512 U.S. 43 (1994).* Gilleo was a resident who placed signs on her home arguing against United States participation in the Persian Gulf war. The city threatened to enforce against her an ordinance which constituted a total ban on non-commercial signs located on private residential property. She argued that the ordinance was content-based. The city argued that the ordinance was merely a content-neutral time, place, and manner regulation. The Court, per Justice Stevens, held that, even if the ordinance were content-neutral [and the Court emphasized that the regulation was content-based in its effect], it failed the ample alternative channels prong of the *Rock Against Racism* standard. The Court suggested that a regulation will not be "content-neutral" simply because it is a "total ban"; rather, in determining the appropriate level of scrutiny, the Court will independently determine the *effect* of a total ban.

MADSEN v. WOMEN'S HEALTH CENTER, INC., 512 U.S. 753 (1994). In the post-*Roe v. Wade* era, antiabortion demonstrations around abortion clinics has become a nation-wide experience. These demonstrations (including verbal communication, picketing, and "counseling") have often generated counter-demonstrations (with similar "protest" tactics).

When this interplay of protest and counterprotest occurred around a Florida clinic (and the residences of clinic employees), the clinic sought to enjoin the antiabortion protesters. After an initial injunction proved to be ineffective in preserving access to the clinic and patient security, the state court entered a second, broader injunction. The second injunction contained the following provisions, which were the main object of this decision: (1) a 36-foot buffer zone regarding clinic premises (2) a 36-foot buffer zone regarding private properties adjacent to the clinic; (3) a ban on picketing with "images observable" to patients within the clinic; (4) a 300-foot "no approach" zone around the clinic; (5) a 300-foot buffer zone around the residences of clinic employees; (6) a limit on "excessive noise" within patient hearing range. Applying a version of the modern time, place, and manner standard, the Court, per Chief Justice Rehnquist, held all the provisions except the 36-foot buffer zone around the clinic and the noise level provision unconstitutional.

We begin by addressing petitioners' contention that the state court's order, because it is an injunction that restricts only the speech of antiabortion protesters, is necessarily content or viewpoint based. . . . To accept petitioners' claim would be to classify virtually every injunction as content or viewpoint based.

[T]he fact that the injunction in the present case did not prohibit activities of those demonstrating in favor of abortion is justly attributable to the lack of any similar demonstrations by those in favor of abortion, and of any consequent request that their demonstrations be regulated by injunction. There is no suggestion in this record that Florida law would not equally restrain similar conduct directed at a target having nothing to dowith abortion; none of the restrictions imposed by the court were directed at the contents of petitioner's message. . . .

[I]f this were a content-neutral, generally applicable statute, instead of an injunctive order, its constitutionality would be assessed under the standard set forth in *Ward v. Rock Against Racism*. . . . Given that the forum around the clinic is a traditional public forum, *see Frisby v. Schultz*, 487 U.S., at 480, we would determine whether the time, place, and manner regulations were "narrowly tailored to serve a significant governmental interest." *Ward, supra,* at 791.

[T]here are obvious differences, however, between an injunction and a generally applicable ordinance. Ordinances represent a legislative choice regarding the promotion of particular societal interests. Injunctions, by contrast, are remedies imposed for violations (or threatened violations) of a legislative or judicial decree. *See United States v. W. T. Grant Co.*, 345 U.S. 629, 632–633 (1953). Injunctions also carry greater risks of censorship and discriminatory application than do general ordinances.

[W]e believe that these differences require a somewhat more stringent application of general First Amendment principles in this context. [A]ccordingly, when evaluating a content-neutral injunction, we think that our standard time, place, and manner analysis is not sufficiently rigorous. We must ask instead whether the challenged provisions of the injunction burden no more speech than necessary to serve a significant government interest.

[Applying the "heightened" *Ward* standard, the Court held that the regulation served significant governmental interests. It then turned to the "means" prong to determine whether each part of the injunction was narrowly tailored.]

We begin with the 36-foot buffer zone. The state court prohibited petitioners from "congregating, picketing, patrolling, demonstrating or entering" any portion of the public right-of-way or private property within 36 feet of the property line of the clinic as a way of ensuring access to the clinic.

[T]he need for a complete buffer zone near the clinic entrances and driveway may be debatable, but some deference must be given to the state court's familiarity with the facts and the background of the dispute between the parties even under our heightened review. . . . We also bear in mind the fact that the state court originally issued a much narrower injunction, providing no buffer zone, and that this order did not succeed in protecting access to the clinic. The failure of the first order to accomplish its purpose may be taken into consideration in evaluating the constitutionality of the broader order. *National Society of Professional Engineers v. United States*, 435 U.S. 679, 697–698 (1978). On balance, we hold that the 36-foot buffer zone around the clinic entrances and driveway burdens no more speech than necessary to accomplish the governmental interest at stake.

Justice Souter concurred. Justice Stevens concurred in part and dissented in part. Justice Scalia, for Justices Kennedy and Thomas, dissented; he concluded that the injunction's 36-foot buffer around the clinic premises was content-based and that strict scrutiny should be the test.

Later, in an application of the standard announced in *Madsen*, the Supreme Court, in *Schenk v. Pro-Choice Network of Western New York*, 519 U.S. 357 (1997), struck down an injunction which had established so-called "floating buffer zones" around abortion clinic patrons and vehicles. The Court, per Chief Justice Rehnquist, upheld "fixed buffer zones" of fifteen (15) feet around the abortion clinic under the *Madsen* standards for time, place, or manner regulations. Justice Scalia, for Justices Thomas and Kennedy, dissented largely on the grounds of his dissent in *Madsen*.

In *Hill v. Colorado*, 530 U.S. 703 (2000), the Court, per Justice Stevens, upheld a Colorado statute which prohibited speakers from approaching within eight (8) feet of an unwilling listener, as this statute was applied to sidewalk "counselors" outside an abortion clinic. Justices Scalia, Thomas, and Kennedy dissented.

[B]　The "Public Forum" Doctrine

[1]　What Is a "Public Forum?": Defining The Boundaries

BROWN v. LOUISIANA, 383 U.S. 131 (1966). Defendants were five black individuals who refused to leave the reading room of a public library maintained on a segregated basis after being asked to do so by the Sheriff. They were convicted of breach of the peace. The Supreme Court reversed the convictions. The plurality opinion of Justice Fortas expressly recognized that the defendants' conduct was intended as an expression of protest against segregation, but held that this "peaceful and orderly protest demonstration was constitutionally protected in the library":

> [T]he issue, asserts the state, is simply that petitioners were using the library room "as a place in which to loaf or make a nuisance of themselves." The state argues that the "test"—the permissible civil rights demonstration—was concluded when petitioners entered the library, asked for service and were served. Having satisfied themselves, the argument runs, that they could get service, they should have departed. Instead, they simply sat there "staring vacantly," and this was "enough to unnerve a woman in the situation Mrs. Reeves [a library employee] was in."

> [W]e are here dealing with an aspect of a basic constitutional right—the right under the first and fourteenth amendments guaranteeing freedom of speech and of assembly, and freedom to petition the government for a redress of grievances. [T]hese rights are not confined to verbal expression. They embrace appropriate types of action which certainly include the right in a peaceable and orderly manner to protest by silent and reproachful presence, in a place where the protestant has every right to be, the unconstitutional segregation of public facilities. . . .

> A state or its instrumentality may, of course, regulate the use of its libraries or other public facilities. But it must do so in a reasonable and non-discriminatory manner. . . .

ADDERLEY v. FLORIDA
385 U.S. 39 (1966)

Mr. Justice Black delivered the opinion of the Court.

[Adderley and thirty-one other persons were convicted of trespassing after demonstrating on the driveway at the entrance to a county jail in Florida. The Supreme Court here affirms.]

Petitioners have insisted from the beginning of this case that it is controlled by and must be reversed because of our prior cases of *Edwards v. South Carolina*, 372 U.S. 229, and *Cox v. Louisiana*. [W]e cannot agree.

[I]t was on [the] ground of vagueness that in *Cox v. State of Louisiana*, . . . the Louisiana breach-of-the-peace law used to prosecute Cox was invalidated.

The Florida trespass statute under which these petitioners were charged cannot be challenged on this ground. It is aimed at conduct of one limited kind, that is, for one person or persons to trespass upon the property of another with a malicious and mischievous intent. . . .

[T]he question [is] whether conviction . . . unconstitutionally deprives petitioners of their rights to freedom of speech, press, assembly or petition. We hold [that] it does not. The Sheriff, as jail custodian, had power, as the state's courts have here held, to direct that this large crowd of people get off the grounds. There is not a shred of evidence in this record that this power was exercised . . . because the Sheriff objected to what was being sung or said by the demonstrators or because he disagreed with the objectives of the protest. The record reveals that he objected only to their presence on that part of the jail grounds reserved for jail uses. [N]othing in the Constitution of the United States prevents Florida from even-handed enforcement of its general trespass statute. . . .

The state, no less than a private owner of property, has power to preserve the property under its control for the use to which it is lawfully dedicated. For this reason, there is no merit to the petitioners' argument that they had a constitutional right to stay on the property, over the jail custodian's objections, because this "area chosen for the peaceful civil rights demonstration was not only 'reasonable' but also particularly appropriate. . . ." Such an argument has as its major unarticulated premise the assumption that people who want to propagandize protests or views have a constitutional right to do so whenever and however and wherever they please. That concept of constitutional law was vigorously and forthrightly rejected in [*Cox v. Louisiana II, above*]. We reject it again. . . .

Mr. Justice Douglas, with whom the Chief Justice, Mr. Justice Brennan and Mr. Justice Fortas concur, dissenting. . . .

The jailhouse, like an executive mansion, a legislative chamber, a courthouse, or the state house itself . . . is one of the seats of government, whether it be the Tower of London, the Bastille, or a small county jail. And when it houses political prisoners or those who many think are unjustly held, it is an obvious center for protest. . . .

There may be some public places which are so clearly committed to other purposes that their use for the airing of grievances is anomalous. [A] noisy meeting may be out of keeping with the serenity of the state house or the quiet of the courthouse. [B]ut this is quite different from saying that all public places are off limits to people with grievances. [A]nd it is farther yet from saying that the custodian of the public property in his discretion can decide when public places shall be used for the communication of ideas, especially the constitutional right to assemble and petition for redress of grievances. . . .

NOTES AND QUESTIONS

(1) *Can Brown and Adderley Persuasively Be Distinguished? Brown* (the library case) and *Adderley* (the jail grounds case) both involved public facilities used for dedicated purposes. Consider whether the two cases can be distinguished on the basis of Justice Fortas' observation that the demonstrators in *Brown* had a lawful right to be where they were. Is this distinction persuasive? Notice that the opinion in *Adderley* placed heavy emphasis on the idea that the government as property owner had the same rights as a private property owner.

(2) *Is a Military Reservation a Public Forum?: Greer v. Spock, 424 U.S. 828 (1976).* Federal regulations prohibited speeches and demonstrations of a partisan political nature on a military reservation and prohibited distribution of literature without prior approval of post headquarters. Spock and others sought an injunction against enforcement of these regulations at Fort Dix. The Court, per Justice Stewart, upheld the regulations and their application:

> [We reject the argument] that whenever members of the public are permitted freely to visit a place owned or operated by the government, then that place becomes a "public forum." [S]uch a principle of constitutional law has never existed and does not exist now [citing *Adderley v. Florida*]. . . .
>
> A necessary concomitant of the basic function of a military installation has been "the historically unquestioned power of [its] commanding officer summarily to exclude civilians from the area of his command." [T]he notion that federal military reservations, like municipal streets and parks, have traditionally served as a place for free public assembly and communication of thoughts by private citizens is thus historically and constitutionally false.

Justice Brennan, joined by Justice Marshall, dissented.

(3) *The Standard for Identifying the Three Types of Fora in the Modern Doctrine: Perry Education Ass'n v. Perry Local Educator's Ass'n, 460 U.S. 37 (1983).* In *Perry*, which is cited in *Lee* and is generally regarded as the "seminal" case, the school district gave the teachers' recognized union exclusive access to the interschool mail system, including teacher mailboxes, to the exclusion of a rival union which was seeking recognition. The Court, per Justice White, held that public property that is not by tradition or designation a public forum may be reserved by the state for its intended purposes, as long as regulations on speech are reasonable and are not merely an effort to suppress expression because of opposition to the speaker's views. The court rejected the rival union claim that the school had created a "limited public forum":

> [I]f by policy or by practice the Perry School District had opened its mail system for indiscriminate use by the general public, then [the rival union] could justifiably argue a public forum had been created. This, however, is not the case. . . . [T]he schools do allow some outside organizations such as the YMCA, Cub Scouts, and other civic and church organizations to use the facilities. This type of selective access does not transform government property into a public forum. . . .
>
> Moreover, even if we assume that by granting access to the Cub Scouts, YMCA, and parochial schools, the school district has created a "limited" public forum, the constitutional right of access would in any event extend only to other entities of similar character. While the school mail facilities thus might be a forum generally open for use by the Girl Scouts, the local Boy's Club, and other organizations that engage in activities of interest and educational relevance to students, they would not as a consequence be open to an organization such as [the rival union], which is concerned with the terms and conditions of teacher employment.

The majority also concluded that the recognized union was different from its rival because it was the teachers' exclusive bargaining representative and therefore had a special need to communicate with teachers. Is the Court's reasoning, which distinguishes the rival union both from the recognized union and from organizations such as the Girl Scouts, persuasive? Justices Brennan, Marshall, Powell, and Stevens concluded that it was not persuasive—and they dissented, believing that access by the rival union was constitutionally mandated.

(4) *The Forum Status of Residential Streets: Frisby v. Schultz, 487 U.S. 474 (1988).* In the *Frisby* case, a municipal ordinance prohibited all picketing "before or about the residence of any individual in the Town of Brookfield," Wisconsin. Anti-abortion activists filed suit because they wished to picket in the street in front of the home of a physician who apparently performed abortions. The district court struck down the ordinance as not "narrowly tailored" enough for a public forum.

The Supreme Court, per Justice O'Connor, reversed and upheld the ordinance. The Court reasoned, first, that the streets, even residential streets, were a "traditional public forum." Therefore, regulations of speech must meet "stringent" standards. But this ordinance was "content neutral." Furthermore, it allowed for "ample alternative channels" of expression. For example, picketing even in residential areas was not prohibited if not focused on a particular residence, and protesters could go door to door or use the mail. Finally, the ordinance served the "significant" government interest of protecting residential privacy, and it was narrowly tailored to remove only the evil of picketing targeted at a "captive" home audience.

Justices Brennan, Marshall, and Stevens dissented.

(5) *Rejecting Heightened Scrutiny, in Favor of Reasonableness, for Government-Controlled Access to Government Employees: Cornelius v. NAACP Legal Defense and Educational Fund, Inc., 473 U.S. 788 (1985).* In *Cornelius*, the federal government excluded legal defense and political advocacy organizations from participation in the Combined Federal Campaign (CFC), a charity drive aimed at federal employees. It alleged that the charity drive was a non-public forum, and that its interests in minimizing disruption of the federal workplace, insuring the success of the fundraising effort, and avoiding the appearance of political favoritism, justified its action. The Supreme Court, per Justice O'Connor, held that the government would not violate the first amendment under these conditions (but that a remand was necessary for a determination whether the government had impermissibly excluded the organizations in question because it disagreed with their viewpoints). In so holding, the Court required only that the regulations be "reasonable." Justices Blackmun, Brennan, and Stevens dissented.

(6) *Is the Curtilage of a Post Office a Public Forum (or a Forum for Limited Purposes)?: United States v. Kokinda, 497 U.S. 720 (1990).* Postal regulations made the curtilage of a United States Post Office unavailable for any kind of solicitation (including the walkway to the entrance). Is this regulation constitutional? The Court, per Justice O'Connor, held that it was: "The postal sidewalk was constructed solely to assist postal patrons to negotiate the space between the parking lot and the front door of the post office, not to facilitate the daily commerce and life of the neighborhood or city." Three Justices dissented. For more on the history, *see* David S. Day, *The End of the Public Forum Doctrine*, 78 IA. L. REV. 143 (1992).

[2]　Different Kinds of Forums (with Different Levels of Protection): Traditional, Designated, and Nonpublic Forums

INTERNATIONAL SOCIETY FOR KRISHNA CONSCIOUSNESS, INC. v. LEE
505 U.S. 672 (1992)

CHIEF JUSTICE REHNQUIST delivered the opinion of the Court.

[The Society ("ISKCON") wished to have its members perform a religious ritual known as "sankirtan," consisting of distributing literature and soliciting money, in airport terminals operated by the New York Port Authority. These are among the world's busiest airports. The Authority adopted a regulation that effectively prevented ISKCON from distributing or soliciting, as follows:

> The following conduct is prohibited within the interior areas of buildings or structures at an air terminal if conducted by a person to or with passers-by in a continuous or repetitive manner:
>
> (a) The sale or distribution of any merchandise, including but not limited to jewelry, food stuffs, candles, flowers, badges and clothing.
>
> (b) The sale or distribution of flyers, brochures, pamphlets, books or any other printed or written material.
>
> (c) Solicitation and receipt of funds.

Solicitation and distribution still were allowed on adjacent outside sidewalks, however, because the regulation covered only the terminal buildings themselves.

[ISKCON sued to void this regulation. The District Court struck down the regulation because it decided that the terminals were "traditional public forums," akin to public streets. The Court of Appeals, based upon the then-recent decision in *United States v. Kokinda* held that the airport terminals were not public forums, that the regulation need only satisfy a "reasonableness" standard, and that the ban on solicitation was constitutional under this standard but the ban on distribution was not.

[Here, the Supreme Court affirms and upholds the ban on solicitation. In the companion case, which follows this decision, the Court affirms the decision striking down the distribution ban.]

It is uncontested that the solicitation at issue in this case is a form of speech protected under the First Amendment. *Heffron*, 452 U.S. 640 (1981); *Kokinda, supra.* But it is also well settled that the government need not permit all forms of speech on property that it owns and controls. Where the government is acting as a proprietor, managing its internal operations, rather than acting as lawmaker with the power to regulate or license, its action will not be subjected to the heightened review to which its actions as a lawmaker may be subject. *Kokinda.* . . .

These cases reflect, either implicitly or explicitly, a "forum-based" approach for assessing restrictions that the government seeks to place on the use of its property. Under this approach, regulation of speech on government property that has traditionally been available for public expression is subject to the highest scrutiny. Such regulations survive only if they are narrowly drawn to achieve a compelling state interest. The second category of public property is the designated public forum, whether of a limited or unlimited character—property that the state has opened for expressive activity by part or all of the public. Regulation of such property is subject to the same limitations as that governing a traditional public forum. Finally, there is all remaining public property. Limitations on expressive activity conducted on this last category of property must survive only a much more limited review. The challenged regulation need only be reasonable, as long as the regulation is not an effort to suppress the speaker's activity due to disagreement with the speaker's view.

The parties do not disagree that this is the proper framework. Rather, they disagree whether the airport terminals are public fora or nonpublic fora. They also disagree whether the regulation survives the "reasonableness" review governing nonpublic fora, should that prove the appropriate category. Like the Court of Appeals, we conclude that the terminals are nonpublic fora and that the regulation reasonably limits solicitation. . . .

Our recent cases provide additional guidance on the characteristics of a public forum. [We have] noted that a traditional public forum is property that has as "a principal purpose . . . thefree exchange of ideas." Moreover, [t]he government does not create a public forum by inaction. Nor is a public forum created "whenever members of the public are permitted freely to visit a place owned or operated by the Government." The decision to create a public forum must instead be made "by intentionally opening a nontraditional forum for public discourse." Finally, we have recognized that the location of property also has bearing because separation from acknowledged public areas may serve to indicate that the separated property is a special enclave, subject to greater restriction.

These precedents foreclose the conclusion that airport terminals are public fora. [G]iven the lateness with which the modern air terminal has made its appearance, it hardly qualifies for the description of having "immemorially . . . time out of mind" been held in the public trust and used for purposes of expressive activity. . . . [N]or can we say that these particular terminals, or airport terminals generally, have been intentionally opened by their operators to such activity; the frequent and continuing litigation evidencing the operators' objections belies any such claim. . . .

[I]t cannot fairly be said that an airport terminal has as a principal purpose "promoting the free exchange of ideas". . . .

[T]hus, we think that neither by tradition nor purpose can the terminals be described as satisfying the standards we have previously set out for identifying a public forum.

The restrictions here challenged, therefore, need only satisfy a requirement of reasonableness. [W]e have no doubt that under this standard the prohibition on solicitation passes muster. . . .

The inconveniences to passengers and the burdens on Port Authority officials flowing from solicitation activity may seem small, but viewed against the fact that "pedestrian congestion is one of the greatest problems facing the three terminals," the Port Authority could reasonably worry that even such incremental effects would prove quite disruptive. Moreover, "the justification for the Rule should not be measured by the disorder that would result from granting an exemption solely to ISKCON." For if petitioner is given access, so too must other groups. [A]s a result, we conclude that the solicitation ban is reasonable. [Affirmed.]

[The concurring opinion of JUSTICE KENNEDY is omitted. Part I of Justice Kennedy's opinion, which is joined by the dissenting Justices (see below), concludes that the airport terminals are traditional public forums. However, in Part II, Justice Kennedy concludes that the ban on solicitation is constitutional, because it is content-neutral: It is "either a reasonable time, place, and manner restriction or [a] regulation directed to the nonspeech element of expressive conduct."]

[The concurring opinion of JUSTICE O'CONNOR also is omitted.]

JUSTICE SOUTER, with whom JUSTICE BLACKMUN and JUSTICE STEVENS join, concurring in the judgment in [the companion case, *Lee v. International Society for Krishna Consciousness*, below, involving the ban on distribution of literature], and dissenting in [this case]:

I

I join in Part I of Justice Kennedy's opinion and the judgment of affirmance in [the companion case, striking down the distribution ban]. I agree with Justice Kennedy's view of the rule that should determine what is a public forum and with his conclusion that the public areas of the airports at issue here qualify as such.. . . .

[P]ublic forum analysis is stultified not only by treating its archetypes as closed categories, but by treating its candidates so categorically as to defeat their identification with the archetypes. [T]o find one example of a certain property type (*e.g.*, airports, post offices, etc.) that is not a public forum is not to rule out all properties of that sort. [O]ne can imagine a public airport of a size or design or need for extraordinary security that would render expressive activity incompatible with its normal use. But that would be no reason to conclude that one of the more usual variety of metropolitan airports is not a public forum.

I also agree with Justice Kennedy's statement of the public forum principle: we should classify as a public forum any piece of public property that is "suitable for discourse" in its physical character, where expressive activity is "compatible" with the use to which it has actually been put. [A]pplying this test, I have no difficulty concluding that the unleased public areas at airports like the metropolitan New York airports at issue in this case are public forums.

II . . .

[E]ven if I assume *arguendo* that the ban on the petitioners' activity at issue here is both content neutral and merely a restriction on the manner of communication, the regulation must be struck down for its failure to satisfy the requirements of narrow tailoring to further a significant state interest, and availability of "ample alternative channels for communication." . . .

LEE v. INTERNATIONAL SOCIETY FOR KRISHNA CONSCIOUSNESS, INC.
505 U.S. 830 (1992)

PER CURIAM.

For the reasons expressed in the opinions of JUSTICE O'CONNOR, JUSTICE KENNEDY, and JUSTICE SOUTER in [*International Society for Krishna Consciousness, Inc. v. Lee*], the judgment of the Court of Appeals holding that the ban on distribution of literature in the Port Authority airport terminals is invalid under the First Amendment is Affirmed.

CHIEF JUSTICE REHNQUIST, with whom JUSTICE WHITE, JUSTICE SCALIA and JUSTICE THOMAS join, dissenting.

Leafletting presents risks of congestion similar to those posed by solicitation. It presents, in addition, some risks unique to leafletting. And of course, as with solicitation, these risks must be evaluated against a backdrop of the substantial congestion problem facing the Port Authority and with an eye to the cumulative impact that will result if all groups are permitted terminal access. Viewed in this light, I conclude that the distribution ban, no less than the solicitation ban, is reasonable. I therefore dissent from the Court's holding striking the distribution ban.

[T]he weary, harried, or hurried traveler may have no less desire and need to avoid the delays generated by having literature foisted upon him than he does to avoid delays from a financial solicitation. . . . Moreover, those who accept material may often simply drop it on the floor once out of the leafletter's range, creating an eyesore, a safety hazard, and additional clean-up work for airport staff. . . .

NOTES AND QUESTIONS

(1) *The "Airport" Decisions and the Standards for Forum Status Determination: Lee v. International Society for Krishna Consciousness, Inc., 505 U.S. 672 (1992).* Following its decisions since *Heffron* (and despite the academic criticism), the Court, per Chief Justice Rehnquist, used the New York airport cases as the vehicle to confirm the standards for the various types of fora in the public forum doctrine. First, the traditional forum was established only by history and was limited to those types of locations that the Framers might have envisioned for public debate: parks and streets (and some types of sidewalks). Second, the designated forum was created by the government's intent. A forum was a designated forum only if the government intended it to be open. Third, all other government property (or programs) were nonforums. Here the government regulation needed to satisfy only rational basis, unless the regulation was viewpoint based. *See* the Note below.

(2) *If It's a Public Forum, the Government Must Be Content-Neutral, and This Includes the Klan—The Ku Klux Klan Cross case: Capitol Square Review and Advisory Board v. Pinette, 515 U.S. 753 (1995).* In *Pinette*, the city had allowed various displays on the Capitol Square outside the Ohio Statehouse, but the government contested the attempt by a Ku Klux Klan group to place a cross on the Square. While the Klan claimed the cross was intended as a religious symbol, the city's position was that the cross was an offensive symbol of the Klan's oppression of minorities. Recent decisions, especially *United States v. Kokinda*, above § 11.06[A][3] at Note (3) (post office access sidewalk was not a traditional public forum), had suggested that the set of places which might qualify as traditional public forums was narrowing. In *Pinette*, the plurality, per Justice Scalia, determined that the Capitol Square was a traditional public forum. In a decision also involving Establishment Clause issues, § 12.02 below, the Court held that the government's content-based regulation of private religious speech did not satisfy strict scrutiny.

(3) *Viewpoint Discrimination Is Unconstitutional Irrespective of Forum Category: Lamb's Chapel v. Center Moriches Union Free School District, 508 U.S. 384 (1993).* In this case, the Court, per Justice White, held that a public school district cannot maintain a policy of excluding religious speakers from using its buildings during non-school hours when it has otherwise opened the buildings for use by civic, social and recreational groups. It reasoned that content discrimination is impermissible irrespective of the category of forum involved. Does this holding mean the government must avoid viewpoint discrimination even in a nonforum? *See also Rosenberger v. Rector, University of Virginia*, 515 U.S. 819 (1995) (viewpoint discrimination in funding decisions from the public University's student activities fund, which was created by mandatory student fees, violated Free Speech rights of religious speakers).

(4) *Commentary.* The modern public forum doctrine has generated a large volume of academic commentary. *See, e.g.*, G. Sidney Buchanan, *The Case of the Vanishing Public Forum*, 1991 U. ILL. L. REV. 949; David S. Day, *The End of the Public Forum Doctrine*, 78 IA. L. REV. 143 (1992); Robert C. Post, *Between Governance and Management: The History and Theory of the Public Forum*, 34 UCLA L. REV. 1713 (1987); Richard B. Saphire, *Reconsidering the Public Forum Doctrine*, 59 U. CIN. L. REV. 739 (1991).

(5) *The Forum Status of Candidate Debates on Public Television: Arkansas Educational Television Commission v. Forbes, 523 U.S. 666 (1998).* The *Forbes* case arose from the decision by a state owned television station to exclude a minority party candidate from a televised candidate debate. Although the court of appeals had determined that the debate was a "public forum," the Supreme Court per Justice Kennedy, reversed. In *Forbes*, the Supreme Court held: (1) that the claim by the ballot-qualified candidate to participate in the televised debate on public television would be subjected to the modern public forum doctrine; (2) that the public television debate was a nonpublic forum; and (3) that the decision to exclude Forbes survived the

applicable standard of review because it was not based on his viewpoint and was otherwise journalistically reasonable. The *Forbes* facts involve the application of the public forum doctrine to a "metaphysical" forum—a forum not defined by location or places. Should this doctrine be so extended? *See* David S. Day, *The Public Forum Doctrine's 'Government Intent Standard': What Happened To Justice Kennedy?* 2000 M.S.U.— D.C.L. L. Rev. 173.

(6) *The Standard for the "Designated" Forum.* The *Forbes* Court clarified the standard for a "designated" forum. A designated forum must be "created by purposeful government action," and this action must constitute "general access for a class of speakers" or the public generally. The Court has held that the government's intent will determine the nonpublic forum status and that such status will not be lost simply because the government allows "selective access" (in *Forbes*, allowing only the major party candidates into the debate). The Court, in *Lee* and *Forbes*, has established that the test for the "designated" forum and the "nonpublic" forum will be the intent of the government entity. Is this a prudent means to allocate the government's managerial resources or a judicial standard that mistakenly defers to the intentions of the very government officials who are supposedly restrained by the Free Speech clause? *Compare* Lillian R. Bevier, *Rehabilitating Public Forum Doctrine: In Defense of Categories*, 1992 Sup. Ct. Rev. 79 *with* David S. Day, *The End of the Public Forum Doctrine*, 78 Ia. L. Rev. 143 (1992) *supra*. The category of a "limited forum" has been introduced into the doctrine. In *Heffron*, this was a synonym for a "designated forum." Recent usage suggests that the "limited forum" may be a subset of the designated forum.

PROBLEM R

THE PUBLIC FORUM DOCTRINE AND AMERICA'S NATIONAL MONUMENTS AND MEMORIALS. The Vietnam Veterans Memorial is one of the most heavily visited national memorials. Since 1982, the National Park Service has allowed private vendors to sell various items on the walk near the Memorial; the items range, in expense, from five-dollar T-shirts to 23-carat gold enhanced stones reproducing some of the 58,000 names engraved on the Memorial. While many of the private vendors (including highly-decorated Vietnam veterans) assert that their sales are fully protected speech, critics of the National Park Service (including highly-decorated Vietnam veterans) have claimed that the Park Service has allowed "K-Mart on the Mall" and have called for the revocation of the vendors' permits. Associated Press, *Vendors at Vietnam Memorial Say They Have a Right to Be There*, Sioux City Journal, at 10, col. 1.

Assume that you are an attorney with the Department of the Interior, and the Park Service seeks your advice concerning whether it constitutionally may ban the vendors. Consider whether the Mall is a traditional public forum, a designated one, a limited one, or a nonpublic one; and consider, also, whether this status can be changed by designation. For example, can the Park Service designate the Memorial to be a nonforum (or a limited forum) and revoke (or non-renew)the vendors' permits? Alternatively, can it selectively revoke only the permits of the more obnoxious vendors? [You might reach a different result if you pursued a commercial speech theory; see the Section on that subject, below.]

[C] The Incidental Regulation Standard: The Standard for Regulation of "Symbolic Speech"

TINKER v. DES MOINES SCHOOL DISTRICT, 393 U.S. 503 (1969). Tinker, a high school student, wore a black armband in the classroom to publicize his opposition to the War in Vietnam. Pursuant to a school policy prohibiting the wearing of armbands, he was suspended. The Supreme Court, per Justice Fortas, reversed the suspension:

The district court recognized that the wearing of an armband for the purpose of expressing certain views is the type of symbolic act that is within the free speech clause of the first amendment. [T]he wearing of armbands in the circumstances of this case was entirely divorced from actually or potentially disruptive conduct by those participating in it. It was closely akin to "pure speech" which, we have repeatedly held, is entitled to comprehensive protection under the first amendment [citing *Cox v. Louisiana* and *Adderley v. Florida*].

The Court held that the wearing of the black armband on a day of nation-wide protest against the Vietnam War was "speech."

Justice Black dissented: "Even a casual reading of the record shows that this armband did divert students' minds from their regular lessons and that talk, comments, etc., made John Tinker 'self-conscious' in attending school with his armband. While the absence of obscene remarks or boisterous and loud disorder perhaps justifies the Court's statement that the few armband students did not actually 'disrupt' the classwork, I think the record overwhelmingly shows that the armbands did exactly what the elected school officials and principals foresaw they would, that is, put the student's minds off their class work and diverted them to thoughts about the highly emotional subject of the Vietnam War."

UNITED STATES v. O'BRIEN
391 U.S. 367 (1968)

MR. CHIEF JUSTICE WARREN delivered the opinion of the Court.

[O'Brien and three companions burned their Selective Service registration certificates publicly on the steps of the South Boston Courthouse to dramatize their opposition to the draft and the War in Vietnam. O'Brien was convicted of violating 50 U.S.C. § 462(b), as amended in 1965, which provides that any person who "knowingly destroys, knowingly mutilates, or in any manner changes any [registration] certificate" commits a crime. Here, the Supreme Court upholds the conviction.]

O'Brien first argues that the 1965 Amendment is unconstitutional as applied to him because his act of burning his registration certificate was protected "symbolic speech" within the First Amendment. His argument is that the freedom of expression which the First Amendment guarantees includes all modes of "communication of ideas by conduct," and that his conduct is within this definition because he did it in "demonstration against the war and against the draft."

We cannot accept the view that an apparently limitless variety of conduct can be labeled "speech" whenever the person engaging in the conduct intends thereby to express an idea. However, even on the assumption that the alleged communicative element in O'Brien's conduct is sufficient to bring into play the First Amendment, it does not necessarily follow that the destruction of a registration certificate is constitutionally protected activity. This Court has held that when "speech" and "nonspeech" elements are combined in the same course of conduct, a sufficiently important governmental interest in regulating the nonspeech element can justify incidental limitations on First Amendment freedoms. To characterize the quality of the governmental interest which must appear, the Court has employed a variety of descriptive terms: compelling; substantial; subordinating; paramount; cogent; strong. Whatever imprecision inheres in these terms, we think it clear that a government regulation is sufficiently justified if [1] it is within the constitutional power of the Government; [2] if it furthers an important or substantial governmental interest; [3] if the governmental interest is unrelated to the suppression of free expression; and [4] if the incidental restriction on alleged First Amendment freedoms is no greater than is essential to the furtherance of that interest. We find that the 1965 Amendment to § 12 (b) (3) of the Universal Military Training and Service Act meets all of these requirements, and consequently that O'Brien can be constitutionally convicted for violating it.

The constitutional power of Congress to raise and support armies and to make all laws necessary and proper to that end is broad and sweeping. [P]ursuant to this power, Congress may establish a system of registration for individuals liable for training and service, and may require such individuals within reason to cooperate in the registration system. The issuance of certificates indicating the registration and eligibility classification of individuals is a legitimate and substantial administrative aid in the functioning of this system. And legislation to insure the continuing availability of issued certificates serves a legitimate and substantial purpose in the system's administration.

O'Brien's argument to the contrary is necessarily premised upon his unrealistic characterization of Selective Service certificates. He essentially adopts the position that such certificates are so many pieces of paper designed to notify registrants of their registration or classification, to be retained or tossed in the wastebasket according to the convenience or taste of the registrant. Once the registrant has received notification, according to this view, there is no reason for him to retain the certificates. [T]his circumstance, however, does not lead to the conclusion that the certificate serves no purpose, but that, like the classification certificate it serves purposes in addition to initial notification. Many of these purposes would be defeated by the certificates' destruction or mutilation. Among these are:

1. The registration certificate serves as proof that the individual described thereon has registered for the draft. . . .

2. The information supplied on the certificates facilitates communication between registrants and local boards, simplifying the system and benefiting all concerned. To begin with, each certificate bears the address of the registrant's local board, an item unlikely to be committed to memory. Further, each card bears the registrant's Selective Service number. [F]inally, a registrant's inquiry, particularly through a local board other than his own, concerning his eligibility status is frequently answerable simply on the basis of his classification certificate. . . .

3. Both certificates carry continual reminders that the registrant must notify his local board of any change of address, and other specified changes in his status. . . .

4. The regulatory scheme involving Selective Service certificates includes clearly valid prohibitions against the alteration, forgery, or similar deceptive misuse of certificates. [T]he destruction or mutilation of certificates obviously increases the difficulty of detecting and tracing abuses such as these. Further, a mutilated certificate might itself be used for deceptive purposes.

The many functions performed by Selective Service certificates establish beyond doubt that Congress has a legitimate and substantial interest in preventing their wanton and unrestrained destruction and assuring their continuing availability by punishing people who knowingly and wilfully destroy or mutilate them.

It is equally clear that the [statute] specifically protects this substantial governmental interest. We perceive no alternative means that would more precisely and narrowly assure the continuing availability of issued Selective Service certificates than a law which prohibits their wilful mutilation or destruction. [T]he [statute] prohibits such conduct and does nothing more. In other words, both the governmental interest and the operation of the [statute] are limited to the noncommunicative aspect of O'Brien's conduct. The governmental interest and the scope of the [statute] are limited to preventing harm to the smooth and efficient functioning of the Selective Service System. . . .

The case at bar is therefore unlike one where the alleged governmental interest in regulating conduct arises in some measure because the communication allegedly integral to the conduct is itself thought to be harmful. In *Stromberg v. California*, 283 U.S. 359 (1931), for example, this Court struck down a statutory phrase which punished people who expressed their "opposition to organized government" by displaying "any flag, badge, banner, or device." Since the statute there was aimed at suppressing communication it could not be sustained as a regulation of noncommunicative conduct. . . .

[The concurring opinion of Justice Harlan, and the dissenting opinion of Justice Douglas (which raised the question whether conscription is permissible in the absence of a declaration of war), are omitted.]

NOTES AND QUESTIONS

(1) *The O'Brien Four-Part Test: United States v. O'Brien, 391 U.S. 367 (1968).* The *O'Brien* Court first held (*i.e.,* "assumed") that draft-card burning was "speech." The Court, per Chief Justice Warren, then held that the test of a government regulation of conduct that impinges on first amendment interests is that (1) it must be within the constitutional power of the government; (2) it must further an important or substantial government interest; (3) the governmental interest must be unrelated to the suppression of free expression; and (4) the incidental restriction on alleged first amendment freedoms must be no greater than is essential to the furtherance of that interest. Consider whether the analysis of the Court, in *O'Brien*, adequately applies this four-part test.

(2) *Flag "Misuse" as Symbolic Speech: Spence v. Washington, 418 U.S. 405 (1974).* In *Spence*, the defendant affixed a large peace symbol, fashioned of removable tape, to a United States flag and displayed it out of the window of his apartment. He was convicted under a Washington state statute forbidding the exhibition of a United States flag with superimposed figures, symbols or other extraneous material. In a per curiam opinion, the Supreme Court reversed the conviction on the ground "that as applied to appellant's activity the Washington statute impermissibly infringed protected expression." The Court emphasized that the flag was privately owned, displayed on private property, and devoid of any demonstrated breach of peace. It then turned to the symbolic speech issue:

On this record there can be little doubt that appellant communicated through the use of symbols. The symbolism included not only the flag but also the superimposed peace symbol. . . .

It may be noted, further, that this was not an act of mindless nihilism. Rather, it was a pointed expression of anguish by appellant about the then-current domestic and foreign affairs of his government. An intent to convey a particularized message was present, and in the surrounding circumstances the likelihood was great that the message would be understood by those who viewed it. . . .

We are brought, then, to the state court's thesis that Washington has an interest in preserving the national flag as an unalloyed symbol of our country. [P]resumably, this interest might be seen as an effort to prevent the appropriation of a revered national symbol by an individual, interest group, or enterprise where there was a risk that association of the symbol with a particular product or viewpoint might be taken erroneously as evidence of governmental endorsement. Alternatively, it might be argued that the interest is based on the uniquely universal character of the national flag as a symbol. [If] it may be destroyed or permanently disfigured, it could be argued that it will lose its capability of mirroring the sentiments of all who view it.

[We] assume, *arguendo*, that [this interest is valid]. The statute is nonetheless unconstitutional as applied to appellant's activity. There was no risk that appellant's acts would mislead viewers into assuming that the [government] endorsed his viewpoint. [G]iven the protected character of his expression and in light of the fact that no interest the state may have in preserving the physical integrity of a privately owned flag was significantly impaired on these facts, the conviction must be invalidated.

Justice Rehnquist, joined by the Chief Justice and Justice White, dissented:

> The statute under which appellant was convicted is no stranger to this Court, a virtually identical statute having been before the Court in *Halter v. Nebraska*, 205 U.S. 34 (1907). In that case the Court held that the state of Nebraska could enforce its statute to prevent use of a flag representation on beer bottles . . .
>
> The true nature of the state's interest in this case is not only one of preserving "the physical integrity of the flag," but also one of preserving the flag as "an important symbol of nationhood and unity."
>
> [Mr.] Justice Fortas, for example, noted in *Street v. New York*, . . . that "the flag is a special kind of personalty," a form of property "burdened with peculiar obligations and restrictions." [M]r. Justice White has observed that "[t]he flag is a national property, and the nation may regulate those who would make, imitate, sell, possess, or use it". . . .

Which, if any, of these asserted interests are valid? Is the majority or the dissent more nearly correct in its analysis of the state interests as balanced against the symbolic-speech component of Spence's activity? And, finally: Can this case be distinguished from the draft card burning in *O'Brien*?

(3) *"Parades" as Symbolic Speech: Hurley v. Irish-American Gay, Lesbian and Bisexual Group, 515 U.S. 557 (1995).* In *Hurley*, the private organizers of an annual parade refused to allow a homosexual group to march peacefully. The parade organizers contended that, under the *Spence* test above, their parade was "speech" and that a state court order, under state laws protecting against discrimination based on sexual orientation, was a content-based regulation. *See* § 11.03[A] above. The Supreme Court, per Justice Souter, unanimously agreed. Relying on *Spence*, the Court held that parades are "speech." Asserting "the fundamental rule of protection under the First Amendment, that a speaker has the autonomy to choose the content of his own message," the Court applied free speech doctrine to defeat a claim, based largely on equal protection principles, for "inclusion" in the parade. Is a claim for "inclusion" less of a burden (*i.e.*, "abridgment") than the kind of censorship normally faced in free speech cases? *See also* § 11.09 below. Or is it like an "intrusion" into the "function of editors," as in the case of a newspaper forced to carry a viewpoint it would rather reject? *See* § 11.05, above.

(4) *The "Spence" Standard and Access by Military Recruiters to Law Schools: Rumsfeld v. FAIR, 547 U.S. 47 (2006).* A consortium of law schools (FAIR) challenged the requirement of the Solomon Amendment that law schools provide "equal" access for military recruiters even though the law schools disagreed with the military's policies on gay rights. [*See* § 2.03 above for further discussion of the Spending Clause analysis.] FAIR argued, under *Spence* and *Hurley*, that the Solomon Amendment violated FAIR's free speech rights because it abridged FAIR's symbolic speech. The Court, per Chief Justice Roberts, disagreed. The unanimous Court distinguished *Hurley, Texas v. Johnson*, and *O'Brien*. The Court never cited to *Spence*, but *Spence* is a basis for the holdings in *Johnson* and *Hurley*. The FAIR Court stated: "we have extended First Amendment protection only to conduct that is inherently expressive." The *FAIR* Court's "inherently expressive" standard seems narrower than Spence's two prong analysis. Wouldn't one person's "inherent expression" be another person's "lyric"? *See Cohen v. California, supra.*

TEXAS v. JOHNSON
491 U.S. 397 (1989)

JUSTICE BRENNAN delivered the opinion of the Court.

[Johnson doused an American flag with kerosene and burned it while demonstrators chanted, "America, the red, white and blue, we spit on you." The incident took place outside the Dallas, Texas City Hall, during the Republican National Convention of 1984. Another demonstrator had taken the flag from a pole outside one of the targeted buildings and handed it to Johnson. Several witnesses testified that they were offended (and one retrieved and buried the ashes), but no physical violence resulted or was threatened. Johnson was convicted of "desecration of a venerated object," in violation of § 42.09(a) (3) of the Texas Penal Code.[1]

[The Texas Court of Criminal Appeals reversed the conviction, holding that Johnson's conduct was protected under the first amendment. The Supreme Court here affirms the invalidation of the conviction.]

II

Johnson was convicted of flag desecration for burning the flag rather than for uttering insulting words. This fact somewhat complicates our consideration of his conviction under the FirstAmendment. We must first determine whether Johnson's burning of the flag constituted expressive conduct, permitting him to invoke the First Amendment in challenging his conviction. *See, e.g., Spence v. Washington*, 418 U.S. 405, 409–411 (1974). If his conduct was expressive, we next decide whether the State's regulation is related to the suppression of free expression. *See, e.g., United States v. O'Brien*, 391 U.S. 367, 377 (1968). . . . If the State's regulation is not related to expression, then the less stringent standard we announced in *United States v. O'Brien* for regulations of noncommunicative conduct controls. If it is, then we are outside of *O'Brien's* test, and we must ask whether this interest justifies Johnson's conviction under a more demanding standard.[3] A third possibility is that the State's asserted interest is simply not implicated on these facts, and in that event the interest drops out of the picture. . . .

In deciding whether particular conduct possesses sufficient communicative elements to bring the First Amendment into play, we have asked whether "[a]n intent to convey a particularized message was present, and [whether] the likelihood was great that the message would be understood by those who viewed it". . . .

---

[1] Tex. Penal Code Ann. section 42.09 (1989) provides in full: Section 42.09. Desecration of Venerated Object

(a) A person commits an offense if he intentionally or knowingly desecrates:

(1) a public monument;

(2) a place of worship or burial; or

(3) a state or national flag.

(b) For purposes of this section, "desecrate" means deface, damage, or otherwise physically mistreat in a way that the actor knows will seriously offend one or more persons likely to observe or discover his action.

(c) An offense under this section is a Class A misdemeanor.

[3] Although Johnson has raised a facial challenge to Texas' flag-desecration statute, we choose to resolve this case on the basis of his claim that the statute as applied to him violates the First Amendment. [B]ecause the prosecution of a person who had not engaged in expressive conduct would pose a different case, and because we are capable of disposing of this case on narrower grounds, we address only Johnson's claim that section 42.09 as applied to political expression like his violates the First Amendment.

Especially pertinent to this case are our decisions recognizing the communicative nature of conduct relating to flags. Attaching a peace sign to the flag, *Spence, supra,* at 409–410; saluting the flag; and displaying a red flag, *Stromberg v. California,* 283 U.S. 359, 368–369 (1931), we have held, all may find shelter under the First Amendment. . . .

We have not automatically concluded, however, that any action taken with respect to our flag is expressive. Instead, [w]e have considered the context in which it occurred. . . .

The State of Texas conceded for purposes of its oral argument in this case that Johnson's conduct was expressive conduct. . . . Johnson burned an American flag as part—indeed, as the culmination—of a political demonstration that coincided with the convening of the Republican party and its renomination of Ronald Reagan for President. [I]n these circumstances, Johnson's burning of the flag was conduct "sufficiently imbued with elements of communication," *Spence,* to implicate the First Amendment.

III

The Government generally has a freer hand in restricting expressive conduct than it has in restricting the written or spoken word. *See O'Brien.* . . . It may not, however, proscribe particular conduct *because* it has expressive elements. . . . A law *directed* at the communicative nature of conduct must, like a law directed at speech itself, be justified by the substantial showing of need that the First Amendment requires. It is, in short, not simply the verbal or nonverbal nature of the expression, but the governmental interest at stake, that helps to determine whether a restriction on that expression is valid.

In order to decide whether *O'Brien's* test applies here, therefore, we must decide whether Texas has asserted an interest in support of Johnson's conviction that is unrelated to the suppression of expression. If we find that an interest asserted by the State is simply not implicated on the facts before us, we need not ask whether *O'Brien's* test applies. The State offers two separate interests to justify this conviction: [A] preventing breaches of the peace, and [B] preserving the flag as a symbol of nationhood and national unity. We hold that the first interest is not implicated on this record and that the second is related to the suppression of expression.

A

Texas claims that its interest in preventing breaches of the peace justifies Johnson's conviction for flag desecration. [N]o disturbance of the peace actually occurred or threatened to occur because of Johnson's burning of the flag. [T]he only evidence offered by the State at trial to show the reaction to Johnson's actions was the testimony of several persons who had been seriously offended by the flag-burning.

The State's position, therefore, amounts to a claim that an audience that takes serious offense at particular expression is necessarily likely to disturb the peace and that the expression may be prohibited on this basis. Our precedents do not countenance such a presumption. . . .

[T]o accept Texas' arguments that it need only demonstrate "the potential for a breach of the peace," and that every flag-burning necessarily possesses that potential, would be to eviscerate our holding in *Brandenburg.* This we decline to do.

Nor does Johnson's expressive conduct fall within that small class of "fighting words" that are "likely to provoke the average person to retaliation, and thereby cause a breach of the peace." *Chaplinsky v. New Hampshire.* No reasonable onlooker would have regarded Johnson's generalized expression of dissatisfaction with the policies of the Federal Government as a direct personal insult or an invitation to exchange fisticuffs.

We thus conclude that the State's interest in maintaining order is not implicated on these facts. . . .

B

The State also asserts an interest in preserving the flag as a symbol of nationhood and national unity. In *Spence*, we acknowledged that the Government's interest in preserving the flag's special symbolic value "is directly related to expression in the context of activity" such as affixing a peace symbol to a flag. We are equally persuaded that this interest is related to expression in the case of Johnson's burning of the flag. The State, apparently, is concerned that such conduct will lead people to believe either that the flag does not stand for nationhood and national unity, but instead reflects other, less positive concepts, or that the concepts reflected in the flag do not in fact exist, that is, we do not enjoy unity as a Nation. These concerns blossom only when a person's treatment of the flag communicates some message, and thus are related "to the suppression of free expression" within the meaning of *O'Brien*. We are thus outside of *O'Brien's* test altogether.

IV

It remains to consider whether the State's interest in preserving the flag as a symbol of nationhood and national unity justifies Johnson's conviction. [J]ohnson was not, we add, prosecuted for the expression of just any idea; he was prosecuted for his expression of dissatisfaction with the policies of this country, expression situated at the core of our First Amendment values.

Moreover, Johnson was prosecuted because he knew that his politically charged expression would cause "serious offense". . . .

Whether Johnson's treatment of the flag violated Texas law thus depended on the likely communicative impact of his expressive conduct. Our decision in *Boos v. Barry* tells us that this restriction on Johnson's expression is content-based. . . .

According to the principles announced in *Boos*, Johnson's political expression was restricted because of the content of the message he conveyed. We must therefore subject the State's asserted interest in preserving the special symbolic character of the flag to "the most exacting scrutiny."

Texas argues that its interest in preserving the flag as a symbol of nationhood and national unity survives this close analysis. [A]ccording to Texas, if one physically treats the flag in a way that would tend to cast doubt on either the idea that nationhood and national unity are the flag's referents or that national unity actually exists, the message conveyed thereby is a harmful one and therefore may be prohibited.

If there is a bedrock principle underlying the First Amendment, it is that the Government may not prohibit the expression of an idea simply because society finds the idea itself offensive or disagreeable. . . .

[For example,] [i]n [*Board of Education v.*] *Barnette* [319 U.S. 24 (1943),] [J]ustice Jackson described one of our society's defining principles in words deserving of their frequent repetition: "If there is any fixed star in our constitutional constellation, it is that no official, high or petty, can prescribe what shall be orthodox in politics, nationalism, religion, or other matters of opinion or force citizens to confess by word or act their faith therein". . . .

In short, nothing in our precedents suggests that a State may foster its own view of the flag by prohibiting expressive conduct relating to it.[10] To bring its argument outside

---

[10] Our decision in *Halter v. Nebraska*, 205 U.S. 34 (1907), addressing the validity of a state law prohibiting certain commercial uses of the flag, is not to the contrary. [T]hat case involved purely commercial rather than political speech. . . .

our precedents, Texas attempts to convince us that even if its interest in preserving the flag's symbolic role does not allow it to prohibit words or some expressive conduct critical of the flag, it does permit it to forbid the outright destruction of the flag. The State's argument cannot depend here on the distinction between written or spoken words and nonverbal conduct. That distinction, we have shown, is of no moment where the nonverbal conduct is expressive, as it is here, and where the regulation of that conduct is related to expression, as it is here. . . .

We never before have held that the Government may ensure that a symbol be used to express only one view of that symbol or its referents. . . .

[T]o conclude that the Government may permit designated symbols to be used to communicate only a limited set of messages would be to enter territory having no discernible or defensibleboundaries. Could the Government, on this theory, prohibit the burning of state flags? Of copies of the Presidential seal? Of the Constitution? In evaluating these choices under the First Amendment, how would we decide which symbols were sufficiently special to warrant this unique status? To do so, we would be forced to consult our own political preferences, and impose them on the citizenry, in the very way that the First Amendment forbids us to do.

There is, moreover, no indication—either in the text of the Constitution or in our cases interpreting it—that a separate juridical category exists for the American flag alone. [T]he First Amendment does not guarantee that other concepts virtually sacred to our Nation as a whole—such as the principle that discrimination on the basis of race is odious and destructive—will go unquestioned in the marketplace of ideas. . . .

Johnson was convicted for engaging in expressive conduct. The State's interest in preventing breaches of the peace does not support his conviction because Johnson's conduct did not threaten to disturb the peace. Nor does the State's interest in preserving the flag as a symbol of nationhood and national unity justify his criminal conviction for engaging in political expression. The judgment of the Texas Court of Criminal appeals is therefore

Affirmed.

JUSTICE KENNEDY, concurring. . . .

The hard fact is that sometime we must make decisions we do not like. We make them because they are right, right in the sense that the law and the Constitution, as we see them, compel the result. And so great is our commitment to the process that, except in the rare case, we do not pause to express distaste for the result, perhaps for fear of undermining a valued principle that dictates the decision. This is one of those rare cases. . . .

[W]hether or not [Johnson] could appreciate the enormity of the offense he gave, the fact remains that his acts were speech, in both the technical and the fundamental meaning of the Constitution. So I agree with the Court that he must go free.

CHIEF JUSTICE REHNQUIST, with whom JUSTICE WHITE and JUSTICE O'CONNOR join, dissenting.

In holding this Texas statute unconstitutional, the Court ignores Justice Holmes' familiar aphorism that "a page of history is worth a volume of logic." For more than 200 years, the American flag has occupied a unique position as the symbol of our Nation, a uniqueness that justifies a governmental prohibition against flag burning in the way respondent Johnson did here. . . .

The American flag, then, throughout more than 200 years of history, has come to be the visible symbol embodying our Nation. It does not represent the views of any particular political party, and it does not represent any particular political philosophy.

The flag is not simply another "idea" or "point of view" competing for recognition in the marketplace of ideas. . . .

More than 80 years ago in *Halter v. Nebraska*, 205 U.S. 34 (1907), this Court upheld the constitutionality of a Nebraska statute that forbade the use of representations of the American flag for advertising purposes upon articles of merchandise. The Court there said: "For that flag every true American has not simply an appreciation but a deep affection. . . . Hence, it has often occurred that insults to a flag have been the cause of war, and indignities put upon it, in the presence of those who revere it, have often been resented and sometimes punished on the spot." . . .

[I]n *Chaplinsky v. New Hampshire*, a unanimous Court said: "[T]here are certain well-defined and narrowly limited classes of speech, the prevention and punishment of which have never been thought to raise any Constitutional problem. [I]t has been well observed that such utterances are no essential part of any exposition of ideas, and are of such slight social value as a step to truth that any benefit that may be derived from them is clearly outweighed by the social interest in order and morality". . . .

. . . [Johnson's] act, like Chaplinsky's provocative words, conveyed nothing that could not have been conveyed and was not conveyed just as forcefully in a dozen different ways. As with "fighting words," so with flag burning, for purposes of the First Amendment: It is "no essential part of any exposition of ideas, and [is] of such slight social value as a step to truth that any benefit that may be derived from [it] is clearly outweighed" by the public interest in avoiding a probable breach of the peace. . . .

[F]lag burning is the equivalent of an inarticulate grunt or roar that, it seems fair to say, is most likely to be indulged in not to express any particular idea, but to antagonize others. [T]he Texas statute deprived Johnson of only one rather inarticulate symbolic form of protest [a]nd left him with a full panoply of other symbols and every conceivable form of verbal expression to express his deep disapproval of national policy. Thus, in no way can it be said that Texas is punishing him because his hearers [w]ere profoundly opposed to the message that he sought to convey. [I]t was Johnson's use of this particular symbol, and not the idea that he sought to convey by it or by his many other expressions, for which he was punished.

Our prior cases dealing with flag desecration statutes have left open the question that the Court resolves today. [The Chief Justice reviewed the Court's prior decisions involving various forms of flag desecration.] . . .

[T]he government may conscript men into the Armed Forces where they must fight and perhaps die for the flag, but [as a result of this decision,] the government may not prohibit the public burning of the banner under which they fight. I would uphold the Texas statute as applied in this case.

JUSTICE STEVENS, dissenting.

The question [here presented] is unique. In my judgment rules that apply to a host of other symbols [a]re not necessarily controlling. . . .

The value of the flag as a symbol cannot be measured. [T]he interest in preserving that value for the future is both significant and legitimate. Conceivably that value will be enhanced by the Court's conclusion that our national commitment to free expression is so strong that even the United States as ultimate guarantor of that freedom is without power to prohibit the desecration of its unique symbol. But I am unpersuaded. The creation of a federal right to post bulletin boards and graffiti on the Washington Monument might enlarge the market for free expression, but at a cost I would not pay. Similarly, in my considered judgment, sanctioning the public desecration of the flag will tarnish its value—both for those who cherish the ideas for which it waves and for those who desire to don the robes of martyrdom by burning it. That tarnish is not justified by the trivial burden on free expression occasioned by requiring that an available, alternative mode of expression—including uttering words critical of the flag, *see Street v. New York*—be employed. . . .

The Court is therefore quite wrong in blandly asserting that respondent was prosecuted for his expression of dissatisfaction with the policies of this country, expression situated at the core of our First Amendment values. Respondent was prosecuted because of the method he chose to express his dissatisfaction with those policies. Had he chosen to spray paint—or perhaps convey with a motion picture projector—his message of dissatisfaction on the facade of the Lincoln Memorial, there would be no question about the power of the Government to prohibit his means of expression. The prohibition would be supported by the legitimate interest in preserving the quality of an important national asset. Though the asset at stake in this case is intangible, given its unique value, the same interest supports a prohibition on the desecration of the American flag.

NOTES AND QUESTIONS

(1) *The First Flag-Burning Decision: Texas v. Johnson, 491 U.S. 397 (1989).* An anti-Reagan Administration demonstrator burned a United States flag outside the 1984 Republican National Convention and was convicted of a misdemeanor under Texas law. In a highly visible 5-4 decision, the Supreme Court, per Justice Brennan, overturned the conviction.

There were multiple issues on these facts. (It was almost "hypothetical" quality.) The Court first held that, under the *Spence* standard, flag-burning constituted "speech." Second, the Court held that flag-burning was protected speech. Third, the Court held that, under *O'Brien*, the State's asserted interests were not "unrelated to the suppression of free expression" and, hence, the lower *O'Brien* test would not apply. Considering the Texas statute as a content-based regulation, the Court applied strict scrutiny; since the State did not have a compelling governmental interest, the conviction was overturned.

The *Johnson* decision features a remarkable concurrence by Justice Kennedy. Justice Stevens dissented, largely on the theory that flag-burning should be considered as "unprotected speech." (Is flag-burning like child pornography? *See Ferber* above.) There is also a famous dissent by Chief Justice Rehnquist. The Chief Justice, a WWII veteran, discussed American history and American literature (including famous poems which were once required reading for public school students). The Chief Justice argued that flag-burning was not "speech" at all—just "the equivalent of an inarticulate grunt or roar." There was no separate opinion by Justice Scalia, who joined the Brennan majority.

(2) *Desecration Implicating High Likelihood of Breach of the Peace: Would It Call for a Different Result?* Imagine that an anti-war protestor enters an ongoing American Legion meeting and burns a flag beside the podium while face to face with veterans sitting in the front row; later, he is convicted under a statute such as Texas' § 42.09. Would such a case call for a different result? [Consider such holdings as *Chaplinsky, Brandenburg, Terminiello, Pacifica*, and *Feiner* (to the extent *Feiner* is not discredited today); note that the *Johnson* majority, in a footnote, appears to reserve decision in such a case.]

(3) *Low Speech Value?* The *Chaplinsky* conception of unprotected utterances rests on two factors: (1) high likelihood of social harm and (2) low speech value, found in utterances that are "no essential part of any exposition of ideas." Is the dissent correct when it asserts that flag-burning "is the equivalent of an inarticulate grunt or roar [i]ndulged in not to express any particular idea but to antagonize others?"

(4) *The "National Property" Issue.* The government presumably may retain the intellectual property rights in symbols or works of art that it establishes, pursuant to the copyright power (or the national property clause). If so, isn't the dissent correct when

it says (quoting Justice White) that the design of the flag "is a national property, and the Nation may regulate those who would make, imitate, sell, possess, or use it?" Analogous rights would inhere even in a private copyright holder who had created an artistic design.

(5) *Commercial Versus Political Misuse of the Flag: Distinguishing Halter v. Nebraska.* But perhaps an answer to the dissent's national property arguments can be found in the majority's treatment of *Halter*, in which the Court upheld a prohibition on the exploitation of a state flag by its inclusion on a beer label. The majority points out that *Halter* is a case of commercial speech, which is subject to lesser protection. Can the interest in intellectual property (such as it is) be given whatever protection it deserves by allowing persons to appropriate the design at issue in political speech but not commercial speech?

(6) *Desecration of Other Venerated Objects: Doesn't Johnson Imply that the Freedom of Speech Broadly Protects the Act of Desecration Itself, because Desecration Must by Definition Contain an Element of Expression to Qualify as "Desecration"—and Consideration of This Element Is Essential to Meaningful Prohibition?* Justice Stevens gives the example of a hypothetical protestor who extinguishes the eternal flame at the grave of President Kennedy; can such a case be distinguished from *Johnson*, if the actor is expressing distaste for the policiesof the Kennedy Administration? Consider, also, other instances of expressive desecration of venerated objects: demonstrators urinate on the Alamo to express outrage at mistreatment of ethnic groups to which they belong; vandals use water-soluble paint to spray Swastikas on a synagogue. *Cf. Shaare Tefila Congregation v. Cobb,* ch. 10, above (upholding verdict under civil rights legislation against persons who defaced synagogue). Are these cases distinguishable from *Johnson* or is the expression that is inherent in any act of "desecration" itself protected by the first amendment precisely *because* it is desecration?

THE RESPONSE TO THE FLAG—BURNING DECISION: FLAG PROTECTION LEGISLATION AND A PROPOSED CONSTITUTIONAL AMENDMENT

A Proposed Constitutional Amendment to Authorize Prohibitions of Flag Desecration. President Bush promptly called for a constitutional amendment to reverse the effect of *Johnson:* "Congress and the States shall have the power to prohibit the physical desecration of the flag of the United States."

The Gambit of the Opposition: The Flag Protection Act of 1989. Sentiment in favor of the proposed constitutional amendment was strong, both in Congress and with a clear majority of the American people. *See generally* HOUSTON CHRONICLE, June 26, 1989, § A, at 1, col. 5. Opponents adopted two distinct strategies. First, they argued that it was a bad idea, for the "first time," to "revise the Bill of Rights we adopted two centuries ago." Testimony of Professor Walter Dellinger before the Senate Committee on the Judiciary, Sept. 14, 1989. Second, they suggested that a "Flag Protection Act" that would focus "not on the likely reaction of the audience to perceiving an act of flag desecration, or on the expressive motive of the actor," could be "sharply distinguish[ed]" from the Texas law at issue in *Texas v. Johnson.* Testimony of Laurence H. Tribe before the House Judiciary Committee, July 18, 1989.

Would the Flag Amendment Really Be the "First" Revision of the Bill of Rights? Shortly after passing the first ten amendments, the United States adopted the eleventh—which prohibits enforcement of the Bill of Rights by damage remedies against the states in federal courts. Several amendments and legislation promulgated under them have amended (and arguably, for some, diluted) the right to vote—which is a "fundamental" right with underpinnings in several of the first ten amendments.

Opponents Forestall the Constitutional Amendment By Arguing That the Flag Protection Act "Might" Be Constitutional. Professors Tribe and Dellinger rallied law professors to write that they saw a "reasonable basis" for believing that the current

Supreme Court "might" uphold the Flag Protection Act. Letters from Professor Walter Dellinger and Laurence Tribe, September 29, 1989. [What do you suppose the legislative strategy was?] Based upon this and other arguments, the Flag Protection Act passed instead of the constitutional amendment. It promptly was struck down, as applied, by the Supreme Court in the decision that follows. By that time, proponents of a constitutional amendment were unable to muster the requisite two-thirds in both houses that was necessary to amend the Constitution, and the amendment was defeated. *See House Kills Flag-Burning Amendment*, HOUSTON CHRONICLE, June 22, 1990, § A, at 1, col. 1.

UNITED STATES v. EICHMAN, 496 U.S. 310 (1990). The Flag Protection Act of 1989, passed in response to the Johnson decision, provided that whoever "knowingly mutilates, defaces,physically defiles, burns, maintains on the floor or ground, or tramples upon any flag of the United States" could be fined and imprisoned for not more than one year. It contained an exception for "disposal of a flag when it has become worn or soiled." The appellants had burned United States flags, some while protesting various aspects of the government's domestic and foreign policy, and others while protesting the Flag Protection Act itself. Two different district courts dismissed the charges on First Amendment grounds. On direct appeal, the Supreme Court, per Justice Brennan, affirmed the dismissal and held that the Flag Protection Act could not be applied to the appellants:

> The government [i]nvites us to reconsider our rejection in *Johnson* of the claim that flag-burning as a mode of expression, like obscenity or "fighting words," does not enjoy the full protection of the first amendment. *Cf. Chaplinsky.* This we decline to do. The only remaining question is whether the Flag Protection Act is sufficiently distinct from the Texas statute [construed in *Johnson*] that it may constitutionally be applied to proscribe appellees' expressive conduct.

> The government contends that the Flag Protection Act is constitutional because, unlike the statute addressed in *Johnson*, the Act does not target expressive conduct on the basis of the content of its message. [B]y contrast, the Texas statute expressly prohibited only those acts of physical flag desecration "that the actor knows will seriously offend" onlookers, and the former federal statute prohibited only those acts of desecration that "cas[t] contempt upon" the flag.

> Although the Flag Protection Act contains no explicit content-based limitation on the scope of prohibited conduct, it is nevertheless clear that the government's asserted *interest* is "related 'to the suppression of free expression' " [citing *Johnson*], and concerned with the content of such expression. . . .

Justice Stevens, joined by the Chief Justice, Justice White and Justice O'Connor, dissented.

PROBLEM S

CAN SOME FLAG DESECRATION STILL BE PROHIBITED, AND DOES THE FLAG PROTECTION ACT STILL HAVE ANY VITALITY?: UNITED STATES v. CARY, 897 F.2d 917 (8th Cir. 1990). On March 18, 1988, a large crowd gathered at the Armed Services Recruitment Center in Minneapolis to protest the sending of U.S. troops to Honduras. Defendant Cary entered, dressed in a flag slit like a poncho; the crowd broke windows, a man shot a roman candle into the Recruitment Center, someone handed Cary a flag and told him to light it, and he did—and then threw it into the building. The Eighth Circuit, per Judge Magill, held that *Johnson*—which, like *Eichman*, was an "as applied" decision—did not protect flag-burning when it threatens to "breach the peace." "The government's interest in punishing Cary's violation [w]as to prevent further breaches of the peace which would likely result from the reaction of vandals to Cary's means of communicating his message in the context of violence, not to the message itself. [C]ary's punishment is akin to a time, place, and manner restriction, and not to a content restriction." Is this decision correct?

NOTES AND QUESTIONS

(1) *Commentary Supporting the Johnson Holding: Gressman, Bicentennializing Freedom of Expression, 20 Seton Hall L. Rev. 378 (1990).* Gressman examines the historical promulgation of the First Amendment and concludes that it reflects a "natural rights theory": "In sum, the First Amendment protection of freedom of expression is historically and thoroughly permeated with the concept of natural, human, or funda-mental rights, rights that stem from the unique human capacity to think, to reason and to communicate rationally with others." He finds in this theory the justification for the Court's protection of flag-burning:[*]

[U]nder the natural or fundamental rights theory that we have examined, Johnson as a human being has a natural right, an individually autonomous right of choice, to express himself in a peaceable manner in opposition to majoritarian or governmental policies. [I]f we are faithful to the natural rights underpinning of the First Amendment, we can only conclude, as did the Court, that the government cannot force Johnson to change his opinion as to what the flag symbolized to him.

Consider for a moment the inadequacy of any other First Amendment justification for Johnson's expressive conduct:

1. Johnson's conduct contributes little if anything to the search for truth with respect to our government's nuclear war policies. Nor can we confidently say, in the words of Justice Holmes, that the best test of truth as to those policies "is the power of the [flag-burning] thought to get itself accepted in the competition of the market."

2. It is equally difficult to find very much "democracy-promotion" in Johnson's expressive act of burning the flag. [I]t is unlikely that government or the public will be very responsive to Johnson's form of discussing our nuclear issues. . . .

3. Finally, it is difficult to premise Johnson's expressive burning of the flag on his innate desire for self-fulfillment, or realization of his character, or advance-ment of potentialities as a human being. We can doubt whether the First Amendment was designed primarily to create a public therapeutic forum wherein Johnson can satisfy his self-fulfillment needs of expression by way of a flag-burning. There must be more value to the First Amendment than that.

And so perforce we return to the original purposes and values that inspired the framers to draft the First Amendment. [Johnson] gave expression to his natural and fundamental right to speak freely, to criticize governmental policies, to utilize a mode of expression that is unorthodox and to the extreme—but not to the point of creating an imminent threat of violent reaction or being in violation of some other reasonable time, place, or manner restriction. . . .

In short, *Johnson* properly treats the First Amendment as preservative of the individual's natural right to speak out in unorthodox ways, to speak in the form of expressive conduct distasteful to the majority. The First Amendment is directed toward protection of that natural right, not toward preservation of venerable or patriotic symbols, not toward prescribing or forcing orthodox forms of expressive conduct. . . .

See also, e.g., Loewy, *The Flag-Burning Case: Freedom of Speech When We Need It Most,* 68 N.C.L. REV. 165 (1989) ("perhaps the ultimate irony is that *Johnson* has done more to preserve the flag as a symbol of liberty than any prior decision, while the decision's detractors would allow real desecration of the flag by making it a symbol of political oppression").

(2) *Commentary Objecting to the Flag-Burning Decision.* There has been little law review commentary that opposes the result in the flag-burning case. [Since a clear majority of the American people opposed the decision, is this absence of literature a reflection of law professors' greater understanding of the problem—or does it reflect attitudes determined by occupational selection?] To provide an opposing view to that of co-author Professor Gressman, Professor Crump respectfully has written the following:

Unprotected speech categories generally reflect two characteristics: (1) low speech value and (2) significant potential for harmful effects. These characteristics are to be found in such unprotected areas as incitement to crime, obscenity, contextually prohibited indecent speech, defamation, copyright infringement, and child pornography. *See, e.g., Chaplinsky; Osborne. But cf. Cohen.*

The speech content of flag-burning is nil. It is analogous to inarticulate noise. Professor Gressman's careful analysis all but says so. And if it is correct that the First Amendment is permeated with the concept of natural rights that "stem from the unique human capacity to think, to reason and to communicate rationally with others," as Professor Gressman says, then flag-burning does not qualify.

But one might be suspicious of this natural rights orientation, because (as Justice Iredell said, *see* ch. 1) it is regulated "by no fixed standard." For example, if one accepted the natural rights theory, one might just as well find a "natural right" to venerate an object one holds sacred without its being desecrated. Thus, in *Shaare Tefila* (ch. 10), the Supreme Court said that desecration of a synagogue with swastikas may be prohibited. Professor Gressman's argument logically protects the desecrator, at least if he acts while temple members who might punch him in the nose are at a distance. If one uses a historical, fundamental, or cross-cultural means of defining "natural" rights, one might conclude even that the temple members' right is "more natural" than the desecrator's—but again, I am suspicious of this reason for reaching the result.

Johnson's act also was harmful, whether or not it was calculated to provoke immediate violence. It was the use of a national property, created by the United States. The United States—not Gregory Johnson—created the combination of colors and figures comprising the flag, and it was entitled, just as a copyright holder is for his works, to protect it. If a great painter sold a portrait on condition that the buyer not deface it by painting a moustache on it, Congress presumably could protect his interest under the copyright power—and so should the United States be able to protect the flag, under various of the powers of Congress, including the national property clause.

The United States may again need the inspirational value of the flag. Perhaps the world has become peaceable enough so that we never will be involved in conflicts such as World War I, World War II, the Korean conflict or the Vietnam War; if we do, however, the flag desecration decision will have significantly decreased the value of the United States' interest in this singular piece of intellectual property. The value of the undiluted flag as an inspirational device is reflected well in Crane's *The Red Badge of Courage,* and for that matter, in Justice Rehnquist's *Johnson* opinion; the effect of its dilution is illustrated bythe demoralization of some our military in the Vietnam War. As for the violence-provoking potential of flag-burning, it is present whenever the act is done publicly in the presence of strangers. It may not invariably provoke physical violence, but then neither do fighting words.

Flag desecration prohibitions can be drafted consistently with other first amendment principles. For example, they can be done in a narrow, specific way, they need not be overbroad, and they probably can be written with no more vagueness than other permitted legislation.

Is there anything to these observations? Is there *any* middle ground between Professor Gressman's and Professor Crump's positions? [Professor Gressman graciously waived the right to file a reply brief.] *See also* Douglas W. Kmiec, *In the Aftermath of Johnson and Eichmann: The Constitution Need Not Be Mutilated To Preserve The Government's Speech and Property Interests in the Flag*, 1990 B.Y.U.. REV. 577.

BARNES v. GLEN THEATRE, INC.
501 U.S. 560 (1991)

The CHIEF JUSTICE [REHNQUIST] delivered the opinion of the Court.

[An Indiana state public indecency law prohibited public nudity. It had the effect of requiring exotic dancers to wear pasties and a G-string. Two Indiana establishments (Glen Theatre and the Kitty Kat Lounge), joined by individual dancers, claimed that non-obscene nude dancing performed for entertainment was protected expression and that the statute was unconstitutional. The court of appeals agreed and struck down the statute, holding that it was an improper infringement of erotic activity because its purpose was to prevent the message of eroticism and sexuality conveyed by the dancers.

[The Supreme Court, in a plurality opinion by Chief Justice Rehnquist, employed a four-part analysis based upon the *O'Brien* test:]

Applying the four-part *O'Brien* test . . ., we find that Indiana's public indecency statute is justified despite its incidental limitations on some expressive activity. [P]ublic indecency statutes of this sort are of ancient origin, and presently exist in at least forty-seven states. [P]ublic indecency statutes such as the one before us reflect moral disapproval of people appearing in the nude among strangers in public places. . . .

Thus, the public indecency statute furthers a substantial government interest in protecting order and morality.

This interest is unrelated to the suppression of free expression. Some may view restricting nudity on moral grounds as necessarily related to expression. We disagree. . . .

Respondents contend that even though prohibiting nudity in public generally may not be related to suppressing expression, prohibiting the performance of nude dancing is related to expression because the state seeks to prevent its erotic message. Therefore, they reason that the application of the Indiana statute to the nude dancing in this case violates the First Amendment, becauseit fails the third part of the *O'Brien* test, *viz*: The governmental interest must be unrelated to the suppression of free expression.

But we do not think that when Indiana applies its statute to the nude dancing in these night clubs it is prescribing nudity because of the erotic message conveyed by the dancers. [T]he perceived evil that Indiana seeks to address is not erotic dancing, but public nudity. The appearance of people of all shapes, sizes and ages in the nude at a beach, for example, would convey little if any erotic message, yet the state still seeks to prevent it. . . .

The fourth part of the *O'Brien* test requires that the incidental restriction on First Amendment freedom be no greater than is essential to the furtherance of the government interests. [T]he governmental interests served by the text of the prohibition is societal disapproval of nudity in public places and among strangers. The statutory prohibition is not a means to some greater end, but an end in itself. It is without cavil that the public indecency statute is "narrowly tailored;" Indiana's requirement that the dancers wear at least pasties and a G-string is modest, and a bare minimum necessary to achieve the state's purpose. . . .

[JUSTICE SCALIA concurred only in the judgment. He concluded that the statute was subject only to rational basis review, as a "general" law regulating conduct and not directed at expression:]

[I]n my view [t]he challenged regulation must be upheld, not because it survives some lower level of First-Amendment scrutiny, but because, as a general law regulating conduct and not specifically directed at expression, it is not subject to First-Amendment scrutiny at all. . . .

On its face, this law is not directed at expression in particular. As Judge Easterbrook put it in his dissent below: "Indiana does not regulate dancing. It regulates public nudity. . . . Almost the entire domain of Indiana's statute is unrelated to expression, unless we view nude beaches and topless hotdog vendors as speech". . . .

[I]ndiana's first public nudity statute predated by many years the appearance of nude barroom dancing. It was general in scope, directed at all public nudity, and not just at public nude expression; and all succeeding statutes, down to the present one, have been the same. . . .

The dissent confidently asserts that the purpose of restricting nudity in public places in general is to protect nonconsenting parties from offense; and argues that since only consenting, admission-paying patrons see respondents dance, that purpose cannot apply and the only remaining purpose must relate to the communicative elements of the performance. Perhaps the dissenters believe that "offense to others" ought to be the only reason for restricting nudity in public places generally, but there is no basis for thinking that our society has ever shared that Thoreauvian "you-may-do-what-you-like-so-long-as-it-does-not-injure-someone-else" Beau ideal—much less for thinking that it was written into the Constitution. The purpose of Indiana's nudity law would be violated, I think, if 60,000 fully consenting adults crowded into the Hoosierdome to display their genitals to one another, even if there were not an offended innocent in the crowd. Our society prohibits, and all human societies have prohibited, certain activities not because they harm others but because they are considered, in the traditional phrase, "*contra bonos mores*," i.e., immoral. In American society, such prohibitions have included, for example, sadomasochism, cock fighting, bestiality, suicide, drug use, prostitution, and sodomy. [S] ee Bowers v. Hardwick. [T]he dissent has no basis for positing that, where only thoroughly edified adults are present, the purpose must be repression of expression.[3]

[W]hen any law restricts speech, even for a purpose that has nothing to do with the suppression of communication (for instance, to reduce noise, . . . to regulate election campaigns, . . . or to prevent littering . . .), we insist that it meet the high, First Amendment standard of justification. But virtually every law restricts conduct, and virtually any prohibited conduct can be performed for an expressive purpose—if only expressive of the fact that the actor disagrees with the prohibition. *See, e.g., Florida Free Beaches, Inc. v. Miami*, 734 F.2d 608, 609 (1984) (nude sunbathers challenging public indecency law claimed their "message" was that nudity is not indecent). It cannot

---

[3] The dissent [m]isunderstands what is meant by the term "general law." I do not mean that the law restricts the targeted conduct in all places at all times. A law is "general" for the present purposes if it regulates conduct withoutregard to whether that conduct is expressive. Concededly, Indiana bans nudity in public places, but not within the privacy of the home. [B]ut that confirms, rather than refutes the general nature of the law: One may not go nude in public, whether or not one intends thereby to convey a message, and similarly one may go nude in private, again, whether or not that nudity is expressive.

reasonably be demanded, therefore, that every restriction of expression incidentally produced by a general law regulating conduct pass normal First-Amendment scrutiny or even—as some of our cases have suggested, *see, e.g., United States v. O'Brien*—that it be justified by an "important or substantial" government interest. . . .

This is not to say that the First Amendment affords no protection to expressive conduct. Where the government prohibits conduct precisely because of its communicative attributes, we hold the regulation unconstitutional. *See, e.g., United States v. Eichman* (burning flag). . . .

[JUSTICE SOUTER concurred in the judgment. He agreed with the plurality that the appropriate analysis was the four-part test of *United States v. O'Brien*. He wrote separately to rest his concurrence not on the possible sufficiency of society's moral views to justify the statute, but "on the state's substantial interest in combatting the secondary effects of adult entertainment establishments of the sort typified by respondents' establishments." Accordingly, he would have considered Indiana's "assertion that the statute is applied to nude dancing because such dancing 'encourages prostitution, increases sexual assaults, and attracts other criminal activity.' " He rejected the dissent's reasoning in this regard.]

[JUSTICE WHITE, joined by JUSTICES MARSHALL, BLACKMUN, and STEVENS, dissented, concluding that strict scrutiny was required, and that in any event the statute did not pass even the *O'Brien* test:]

[T]he purpose of forbidding people from appearing nude in parks, beaches, hotdog stands, and like public places is to protect others from offense. But that could not possibly be the purpose of preventing nude dancing in theaters and barrooms since the viewers are exclusively consenting adults who pay money to see these dances. The purpose of the proscription in these contexts is to protect the viewers from what the state believes is the harmful message that nude dancingcommunicates. [A]s the state now tells us, and as Justice Souter agrees, the state's goal in applying what it describes as its "content neutral" statute to the nude dancing in this case is "deterrence of prostitution, sexual assaults, criminal activity, degradation of women, and other activities which break down family structure." The attainment of these goals, however, depends on preventing an expressive activity.

The Court nevertheless holds that the third requirement of the *O'Brien* test, that the governmental interest be unrelated to the suppression of free expression, is satisfied because in applying the statute to nude dancing, the state is not "proscribing nudity because of the erotic message conveyed by the dancers." [T]his analysis is transparently erroneous. . . .

The Court and Justice Souter do not go beyond saying that the state interests asserted here are important and substantial. But even if they were compelling interests, the Indiana statute is not narrowly drawn. If the state is genuinely concerned with prostitution and associated evils, [i]t can adopt restrictions that do not interfere with the expressiveness of non-obscene nude dancing performances. . . .

[T]he premise for [Justice Scalia's] position—that the statute is a general law of the type our cases contemplate—is nonexistent in this case. [W]e agree with Justice Scalia that the Indiana statute would not permit 60,000 consenting Hoosiers to expose themselves to each other in the Hoosierdome. No one can doubt, however, that those same 60,000 Hoosiers would be perfectly free to drive to their respective homes all across Indiana and, once there, to parade around, cavort, and revel in the nude for hours in front of relatives and friends. It is difficult to see why the state's interest in morality is any less in that situation. . . .

NOTES AND QUESTIONS

(1) *The First Exotic Nude Dancing Decision: Barnes v. Glenn Theater, Inc., 501 U.S. 560 (1991).* The Indiana Public Indecency Law prohibited public nudity. To apply this law to exotic nude dancing in adult entertainment establishments, the State developed regulations requiring all dancers to wear at least pasties and a g-string. Various dancers (who sought to perform totally nude) and exotic entertainment businesses challenged these regulations as violating their free speech rights. The Court, per Chief Justice Rehnquist's plurality opinion, rejected the challenge and upheld the regulations as the "bare minimum" necessary to achieve the state's substantial interest in traditional public morality. The Court first held that exotic nude dancing was, under *Spence* and *O'Brien*, speech. Since the state interest was "unrelated to the suppression of free speech," the plurality utilized the *O'Brien* test and found it satisfied (unlike *Johnson*). Justice Souter provided the fifth vote on a secondary effects theory. The four dissenters thought this was a Track One, content regulation case.

(2) *What Test: The O'Brien Four Part Substantial Interest Test, Strict Scrutiny, or the Rational Basis Test?* The Justices use three different approaches in the nude dancing case. Justice Rehnquist uses the four part test that focuses upon whether the state's interest is substantial and unrelated to expression; Justice Scalia uses rational basis review (but would use strict scrutiny if the regulation were enacted because of the expressive element); and the dissenters prefer strict scrutiny. Which approach is most appropriate? Regarding these different standards, *see generally*, David S. Day, *The Incidental Regulation of Free Speech*, 42 U. OF MIAMI L. REV. 491 (1988).

(3) *The Barnes Plurality's Reasoning Confirmed— But by Another Plurality: City of Erie v. Pap's A.M., 529 U.S. 277 (2000).* After the *Barnes* decision, the City of Erie passed an ordinance essentially mirroring the Indiana regulation upheld in *Barnes*: erotic dancers had to wear "pasties" and a "g-string." *Pap's A.M.*, the operator of the "Kandyland," sued and prevailed in the Pennsylvania state courts.

The Supreme Court, per Justice O'Connor's plurality opinion, reversed. The *Pap's* plurality concluded that the *O'Brien* incidental regulation standard would be applied [*see* Note 2 above] and that the City satisfied all four prongs. Justice Scalia concurred in the judgment, tracking his reasoning from *Barnes* (*e.g.*, a purposefulness standard). Justice Stevens dissented on the ground that the ordinance was a content-based regulation.

Justice Souter—who had provided the crucial fifth vote in *Barnes*—also dissented from the plurality's reasoning. Justice Souter in essence offered an apology for his vote in *Barnes*. [It was Justice Souter's first Term.] Justice Souter commented: "I may not be less ignorant of nude dancing than I was nine years ago, but after many subsequent occasions to think further about the needs of the First Amendment, I have come to believe that a government must tow the mark more carefully than I first insisted." Do Justices change their views over time? Should they?

§ 11.07 COMMERCIAL SPEECH

NOTES AND QUESTIONS

(1) *The Earlier Position That Commercial Speech Did Not Qualify for First Amendment Protection: Valentine v. Chrestensen, 316 U.S. 52 (1942).* The Court's conclusion in *Bates* that commercial speech was entitled at least to some First Amendment protection may seem obvious, but was not always clearly accepted. In *Valentine v. Chrestensen*, the Court stated the earlier position, which was that purely commercial advertising did not qualify at all for First Amendment protection, and it was subject to the same kind of business regulation as other economic activity. Consider whether this position can be defended, particularly if one accepts the premise that the most important purposes of the freedom of speech are political in nature.

(2) *"Commercial Speech" Gains the Status of "Protected Speech": Virginia Board of Pharmacy v. Virginia Citizens Consumer Council, Inc., 425 U.S. 748 (1976).* The Court's earlier position in *Valentine* and *Chaplinsky v. New Hampshire* that commercial speech was not protected by the First Amendment (*i.e.*, it could be regulated as long as the government could satisfy only the rational basis standard), was overruled by the *Virginia Citizens Consumer Council* decision. The Court, per Justice Blackmun, concluded that individual interests in the commercial speech at issue (price advertising for prescription medications), were as significant as individual interests might be in "political speech" and that the categorical exclusion of commercial speech was not constitutionally justified. The dissenters argued that the majority had misapplied the protected speech standard from *Chaplinsky*. The Court did not announce what the standard for commercial speech would be. For that, you should read the *Central Hudson* decision below.

BATES v. STATE BAR, 433 U.S. 350 (1977). In this post-*Virginia Citizens Consumer Council* case, *Bates* and his partner violated an Arizona Supreme Court rule by placing an advertisement for their legal clinic in the newspaper. The advertisement stated that the lawyers were offering "legal services at very reasonable fees," and it listed their fees for certain services. The Supreme Court, per Justice Blackmun, held that the advertisement constituted protected speech and that the Arizona rule was unconstitutional as applied to it:

> [C]ommercial speech [is] entitled to the protection of the first amendment.

> [T]he [l]istener's interest is substantial; the consumer's concern for the free flow of commercial speech often may be far keener than his concern for urgent political dialogue. Moreover, significant societal interests are served by such speech. [A]nd commercial speech serves to inform the public of the availability, nature, and prices of products and services, and does perform an indispensable role in the allocation of resources in a free enterprise system. . . .

> [The Court then proceeded to examine and reject arguments that attorney advertising would (1) have adverse effects on professionalism; (2) be inherently misleading; (3) have an adverse effect on the administration of justice; (4) have undesirable economic effects; (5) have adverse effects on the quality of service; and (6) create difficulties in enforcement.]

Justice Powell, joined by Justice Stewart, dissented from this holding: "The supervisory power of the courts over members of the bar . . . and the authority of the respective states to oversee the regulation of the profession have been weakened."

NOTES AND QUESTIONS

(1) *A Mere "Potential" For Misleading Cannot Be the Basis For a Broad Prohibition: In re RMJ, 455 U.S. 191 (1982).* In the *RMJ*, case, a lawyer listed the jurisdictions in which he was admitted to practice, including the United States Supreme Court (in large type). While notingthat the reference to it was in "bad taste" and disclosed only a "relatively uninformative fact," the Supreme Court held that the state could not prohibit the advertising. "Actually" or "inherently" misleading advertising could be flatly prohibited, but in the prevention of "potentially" misleading advertising, the state must tailor its regulation narrowly: The prohibition must be "No broader than [is] reasonably necessary to prevent the deception." *See also Peel v. Illinois Attorney Registration and Disciplinary Commission*, 496 U.S. 91 (1990) (states cannot categorically prohibit lawyers from advertising their certifications as "specialists" by bona fide private organizations).

(2) *Prohibition of In-Person Solicitation: The State Can Stop Lawyers, but Not Accountants; Ohralik v. Ohio State Bar Ass'n, 436 U.S. 447 (1978).* The *Bates* Court also expressly reserved decision on "the problems associated with in-person solicitation of clients—at the hospital room or the accident site, or in any other situation that breeds

undue influence—by attorneys or their agents or 'runners.' Activity of that kind might well pose dangers of overreaching and misrepresentation". . . .

The Court later answered the question in *Ohralik*. There, the petitioner had been indefinitely suspended for his face-to-face solicitation of two accident victims, one in a hospital room and one on the day of her return from the hospital, and his inducement of them to employ him to represent them. The Court, per Justice Powell, labeled in-person solicitation by a lawyer as "a business transaction in which speech is an essential but subordinate component." The Court distinguished the advertisement at issue in *Bates:* "The aim and effect of in-person solicitation may be to provide a one-sided presentation and to encourage speedy and perhaps uninformed decision making; there is no opportunity for intervention or counter-education. [I]t actually may disserve the individual and societal interest, identified in *Bates*, in facilitating 'informed and reliable decision making.'" *But cf. Edenfield v. Fane*, 507 U.S. 761 (1993) (states cannot categorically prohibit in-person solicitation of clients by certified public accountants). The Court distinguished *Ohralik* on the ground that the relationship between accountants and potential clients whom they might personally solicit is not as conducive to overreaching as that between lawyers and potential clients. Is this distinction persuasive?

(3) *Direct Mail Advertising.* What about direct mail advertising? The Court struck down a blanket prohibition on targeted direct mail solicitation by lawyers in *Shapiro v. Kentucky Bar Ass'n*, 486 U.S. 466 (1988), but upheld a ban on direct mail solicitation of accident victims within 30 days of an accident in *Florida Bar v. Went For It, Inc.*, 515 U.S. 618 (1995).

CENTRAL HUDSON GAS & ELECTRIC CORP. v. PUBLIC SERVICE COMMISSION
447 U.S. 557 (1980)

Mr. Justice Powell delivered the opinion of the Court.

This case presents the question whether a regulation of the Public Service Commission of the State of New York ["PSC"] violates the first and fourteenth amendments because it completely bans promotional advertising by an electrical utility. [The PSC's regulation originated in response to a situation in which the utility system in New York State did not have sufficient fuel stocksto service all consumer demand. The order prohibited even advertising that would result in a net energy savings if it encouraged consumption of additional electricity. Here, the Supreme Court strikes down this total ban on promotional advertising.]

II

The Commission's order restricts only commercial speech, that is, expression related solely to the economic interests of the speaker and its audience. [C]ommercial expression not only serves the economic interest of the speaker, but also assists consumers and furthers the societal interest in the fullest possible dissemination of information. In applying the First Amendment to this area, we have rejected the "highly paternalistic" view that government has complete power to suppress or regulate commercial speech. Even when advertising communicates only an incomplete version of the relevant facts, the First Amendment presumes that some accurate information is better than no information at all.

Nevertheless, our decisions have recognized "the 'commonsense' distinction between speech proposing a commercial transaction, which occurs in an area traditionally subject to government regulation, and other varieties of speech." *Ohralik v. Ohio State Bar Ass'n.* [T]he Constitution therefore accords a lesser protection to commercial speech than to other constitutionally guaranteed expression. The protection available for particular commercial expression turns on the nature both of the expression and of the governmental interests served by its regulation. . . .

In commercial speech cases, then, a four-part analysis has developed. At the outset, we must determine whether the expression is protected by the First Amendment. For commercial speech to come within that provision, it at least must concern lawful activity and not be misleading. Next, we ask whether the asserted governmental interest is substantial. If both inquiries yield positive answers, we must determine whether the regulation directly advances the governmental interest asserted, and whether it is not more extensive than is necessary to serve that interest.

III

We now apply this four-step analysis for commercial speech to the Commission's arguments in support of its ban on promotional advertising.

A

The Commission does not claim that the expression at issue either is inaccurate or relates to unlawful activity. Yet the New York Court of Appeals questioned whether Central Hudson's advertising is protected commercial speech. Because appellant holds a monopoly over the sale of electricity in its service area, the state court suggested that the Commission's order restricts no commercial speech of any worth. The court stated that advertising in a "noncompetitive market" could not improve the decisionmaking of consumers. . . .

Even in monopoly markets, the suppression of advertising reduces the information available for consumer decisions and thereby defeats the purpose of the First Amendment. . . .

B

The Commission offers two state interests as justifications for the ban on promotional advertising. The first concerns energy conservation. Any increase in demand for electricity—during peak or off-peak periods—means greater consumption of energy. [I]n view of our country's dependence on energy resources beyond our control, no one can doubt the importance of energy conservation. Plainly, therefore, the state interest asserted is substantial.

The Commission also argues that promotional advertising will aggravate inequities caused by the failure to base the utilities' rates on marginal cost. The utilities argued to the Commission that if they could promote the use of electricity in periods of low demand, they would improve their utilization of generating capacity. The Commission responded that promotion of off-peak consumption also would increase consumption during peak periods. [T]he choice among rate structures involves difficult and important questions of economic supply and distributional fairness. The State's concern that rates be fair and efficient represents a clear and substantial governmental interest.

C

Next, we focus on the relationship between the State's interests and the advertising ban. Under this criterion, the Commission's laudable concern over the equity and efficiency of appellant's rates does not provide a constitutionally adequate reason for restricting protected speech. [A]dvertising to increase off-peak usage would have to increase peak usage, while other factors that directly affect the fairness and efficiency of appellant's rates remained constant. Such conditional and remote eventualities simply cannot justify silencing appellant's promotional advertising.

In contrast, the State's interest in energy conservation is directly advanced by the Commission order at issue here. There is an immediate connection between advertising and demand for electricity. Central Hudson would not contest the advertising ban unless it believed that promotion would increase its sales. Thus, we find a direct link between the state interest in conservation and the Commission's order.

D

We come finally to the critical inquiry in this case: whether the Commission's complete suppression of speech ordinarily protected by the First Amendment is no more extensive than necessary to further the State's interest in energy conservation. The Commission's order reaches all promotional advertising, regardless of the impact of the touted service on overall energy use. But the energy conservation rationale, as important as it is, cannot justify suppressing information about electric devices or services that would cause no net increase in total energy use. In addition, no showing has been made that a more limited restriction on the content of promotional advertising would not serve adequately the State's interests. . . .

The Commission's order prevents appellant from promoting electric services that would reduce energy use by diverting demand from less efficient sources, or that would consume roughly thesame amount of energy as do alternative sources. In neither situation would the utility's advertising endanger conservation or mislead the public. To the extent that the Commission's order suppresses speech that in no way impairs the State's interest in energy conservation, the Commission's order violates the First and Fourteenth Amendments and must be invalidated.

[T]o further its policy of conservation, the Commission could attempt to restrict the format and content of Central Hudson's advertising. It might, for example, require that the advertisements include information about the relative efficiency and expense of the offered service, both under current conditions and for the foreseeable future. . . .

[Reversed.]

[The concurring opinion of JUSTICE BRENNAN is omitted.]

MR. JUSTICE BLACKMUN, with whom MR. JUSTICE BRENNAN joins, concurring in the judgment.

[Justice Blackmun described the Court's approach as an "intermediate" level of scrutiny. He agreed with the Court that it was a generally appropriate approach.]

I do not agree, however, that the Court's four-part test is the proper one to be applied when a state seeks to suppress information about a product in order to manipulate a private economic decision that the state cannot or has not regulated or outlawed directly. . . .

MR. JUSTICE STEVENS, with whom MR. JUSTICE BRENNAN joins, concurring in the judgment.

Because "commercial speech" is afforded less constitutional protection than other forms of speech, it is important that the commercial speech concept not be defined too broadly lest speech deserving of greater constitutional protection be inadvertently suppressed. The issue in this case is whether New York's prohibition on the promotion of the use of electricity through advertising is a ban on nothing but commercial speech.

[W]hatever the precise contours of the concept [of commercial speech], I am persuaded that it should not include the entire range of communication that is embraced within the term "promotional advertising." . . .

Mr. Justice Rehnquist, dissenting. . . .

The Court's analysis in my view is wrong in several respects. Initially, I disagree with the Court's conclusion that the speech of a state-created monopoly, which is the subject of a comprehensive regulatory scheme, is entitled to protection under the first amendment. I also think that the Court errs here in failing to recognize that the state law is most accurately viewed asan economic regulation and that the speech involved (if it falls within the scope of the first amendment at all) occupies a significantly more subordinate position in the hierarchy of first amendment values that the Court gives it today. Finally, the Court in reaching its decision improperly substitutes its own judgment for that of the state in deciding how a proper ban on promotional advertising should be drafted. With regard to this latter point, the Court adopts as its final part of a four-part test a "no more extensive than necessary" analysis that will unduly impair a state legislature's ability to adopt legislation reasonably designed to promote interests that have always been rightfully thought to be of great importance to the state. . . .

NOTES AND QUESTIONS

(1) *Defining Commercial Speech: Does Central Hudson Do It Appropriately?* At one point, the *Central Hudson* majority defines commercial speech as "speech proposing a commercial transaction," quoting *Ohralik*. This definition seems relatively narrow. However, the majority elsewhere defines commercial speech as "expression related solely to the economic interests of the speaker and its audience." This latter definition seems much broader, and it could encompass many issues that are important to political government in a democracy. In another portion of his opinion, omitted above, Justice Stevens says, "Neither a labor leader's exhortation to strike, nor an economist's dissertation on the money supply, should receive any lesser protection because the subject matter concerns only the economic interests of the audience. [A]n electric company's advocacy of the use of electric heat for environmental reasons, as opposed to woodburning stoves, would seem to fall squarely within New York's promotional advertising ban and also within the bounds of maximum first amendment protection." Does the *Central Hudson* formula relegate some speech that is politically valuable to the lesser-protected "commercial" status?

(2) *The Four-Part Test: Too Much Protection for Commercial Speech—Or Too Little?* The four-part test appears to lump together, as commercial speech, utterances that range from philosophical advocacy about the importance of a product in a free society, to crass hucksterism. As such, it may, as Justice Blackmun seems to argue, provide inadequate protection for the former type of speech—and, arguably, excessive protection for the latter. Consider whether this criticism of the four-part test is meritorious. [Might it be that these difficulties would be taken into account in the "balancing" phase of the application of the test—that is, in weighing the significance of the state interest and determining whether the regulation is sufficiently narrow?] *See generally* Edward J. Eberle, *Practical Reason: The Commercial Speech Paradigm*, 42 Case W. L. Rev. 411 (1992).

(3) *Refinement of the Central Hudson "Means" Test: Board of Trustees v. Fox, 492 U.S. 469 (1989).* [This is the famous "Tupperware Speech" decision.] A public university in New York had regulations which banned "commercial sales" in dormitories including "Tupperware parties." The challenger argued that the ban was overly broad under *Central Hudson*. The Court, per Justice Scalia, disagreed. The Court specifically held that the "no more extensive than necessary" prong was not the "least restrictive alternative" test (from Track One analysis or the strict scrutiny standard you have studied). The *Fox* decision provided an early confirmation that the standard for regulation of commercial speech was less than the Track One standard otherwise applicable to content-based regulations.

(4) *A Law Reflecting Content Discrimination Fails the Close Fit Requirement: City of Cincinnati v. Discovery Network, Inc., 507 U.S. 410 (1993).* This case is notable because it is one of the "commercial speech" cases that the government has lost. The Court, per Justice Stevens, used the four-pronged test from *Central Hudson* and *Fox* to invalidate a Cincinnati ordinance barring the challengers, Discovery Network and Harmon Publishing Co., from distributing theirfree magazines from newsracks. While banning the challengers' 62 newsracks, Cincinnati did not ban the remaining 1500-2000 newsracks (mainly for newspapers) existing in the city. The Court held that this content discrimination did not provide the requisite close fit:

> The city argues that there is close fit between its ban on newsracks dispensing "commercial handbills" and its interest in safety and esthetics because every decrease in the number of such dispensing devices necessarily effects an increase in safety and an improvement in the attractiveness of the cityscape. In the city's view, the prohibition is thus entirely related to its legitimate interests in safety and esthetics.

> We accept the validity of the city's proposition, but consider it an insufficient justification for the discrimination against respondents' use of newsracks that are no more harmful than the permitted newsracks, and have only a minimal impact on the overall number of newsracks on the city's sidewalks. The major premise supporting the city's argument is the proposition that commercial speech has only a low value. Based on that premise, the city contends that the fact that assertedly more valuable publications are allowed to use newsracks does not undermine its judgment that its esthetic and safety interests are stronger than the interest in allowing commercial speakers to have similar access to the reading public.

> We cannot agree. In our view, the city's argument attaches more importance to the distinction between commercial and noncommercial speech than our cases warrant and seriously underestimates the value of commercial speech.

Chief Justice Rehnquist, joined by Justices White and Thomas, dissented. The Chief Justice agreed with the use of the *Central Hudson* standard, but he concluded that Cincinnati's regulation achieved a "reasonable fit." Justice Scalia, the author of the *Fox* opinion, joined the majority.

(5) *An Application of the "Directly Advances" and "Not More Extensive Than Is Necessary" Parts of the Central Hudson Test: Prohibition of Labeling Beer by Alcohol Content Is Struck Down in Rubin v. Coors Brewing Co., 514 U.S. 476 (1995).* The federal government prohibited beer labels from displaying alcohol content. The Court, per Justice Thomas, determined that, although the federal government had a substantial interest in preventing "strength wars" between brewers, the regulation failed two parts of the *Central Hudson* test. The federal government did not satisfy the "directly advances" part because the government's "failure to prohibit the disclosure of alcohol content in advertising, which would seem to constitute a more influential weapon in any strength war than labels, makes no rational sense if the government's true aim is to suppress strength wars." The Court also determined that, since the government had "several alternatives" *e.g.* "prohibiting marketing efforts emphasizing high alcohol strength (which is apparently the policy in some other Western nations)," the government failed to satisfy the "no more extensive than necessary" part of the *Central Hudson* test.

(6) *Ratcheting Up the Central Hudson Standard?: Prohibition of Liquor Price Advertising Is Struck Down in 44 Liquormart, Inc. v. Rhode Island, 517 U.S. 484 (1996).* Rhode Island, in the interest of promoting temperance, prohibited the inclusion of prices in advertisements for alcoholic beverages except at the point of sale. The Court unanimously held the prohibitions to be an unconstitutional restriction on commercial speech. The Court, however, failed to reach a majority on the method of analysis to be given restrictions on commercial speech. Justice Stevens authored the plurality opinion,

in which he concluded that not all commercial speech restrictions should be given the more relaxed scrutiny of the *Central Hudson* test, but "[w]hen a State entirely prohibits the dissemination of truthful, nonmisleading commercial messages for reasons unrelated to the preservation of a fair bargaining process, there is far less reason to departfrom the rigorous review that the First Amendment generally demands." Justice Stevens found that a restriction of commercial speech must not only directly advance a substantial state interest but must do so in a significant manner, thus creating an additional burden for the State to meet. Since the studies introduced as evidence in this case were contradictory as to the effect of the prohibitions on alcohol sales and consumption, the State did not meet its burden of proving that the prohibitions *significantly* advanced Rhode Island's interest in temperance. Additionally, a majority of justices found that the restrictions failed the fourth prong of the *Central Hudson* test because other regulations (*i.e.*, direct regulation and taxation) would have been less extensive.

Justice O'Connor, joined by Chief Justice Rehnquist and Justices Souter and Breyer, concurred in the judgment but rejected the plurality opinion's modifications to the *Central Hudson* standard. Using the existing standard, Justice O'Connor decided that the price prohibitions failed the "not more extensive than necessary" prong as there were less restrictive means of advancing Rhode Island's interest in temperance. Justice Scalia concurred separately by relying on *Central Hudson*. Justice Thomas, noting that the government had paternalistically restricted speech to prevent legal use of a legal product, would not have applied *Central Hudson* but would have found the regulation per se invalid.

(7) *Continued Litigation of the Central Hudson Standard: Greater New Orleans Broadcast Association, Inc. v. United States, 527 U.S. 173 (1999).* In a decision indicating continued allegiance to the *Central Hudson* standard, *Greater New Orleans Broadcast Association, Inc. v. United States*, 527 U.S. 173 (1999), the Supreme Court unanimously struck down a federal regulation of advertising in the gambling industry. In *Greater New Orleans*, the Court, per Justice Stevens, held that an FCC regulation that prohibited advertising about privately operated commercial casino gambling failed the last two prongs of the *Central Hudson* standard. The Court found that the federal government had created numerous exceptions to the ban and reasoned that, because of these "exemptions and inconsistencies," the advertising ban failed the "directly advances" and "not more extensive than necessary" tests. Chief Justice Rehnquist, a dissenter from *Central Hudson* in 1980, applied *Central Hudson* and concurred. Justice Thomas concurred in the judgment and argued, again, that *Central Hudson* is not sufficiently protective of speech interests. Doctrinally, the *Greater New Orleans* will be significant because it reflected a majority of the Court, thus confirming the plurality opinion in *44 Liquormart* above.

(8) *Application of the Four-Pronged Central Hudson Test and State Regulation of Tobacco Advertising: Lorillard Tobacco Co. v. Reilly, 533 U.S. 525 (2001).* The Federal Cigarette Labeling and Advertising Act ("FCLAA") prescribes mandatory health warnings for packaging and preempts similar state legislation. Massachusetts, in the interest of reducing tobacco use by children, promulgated extensive additional regulations regarding advertising and sale of tobacco products. At issue here were two state regulations which were more restrictive than the FCLAA: (1) an outdoor regulation of advertising banning tobacco products advertising within 1,000 feet of a school or playground (the "school zone regulations"); and (2) a point-of-sale regulation for indoor advertising of smokeless tobacco and cigars which required sellers to place advertising (and products) at least five feet above the floor (the "5-foot rule"). Although the lower courts essentially upheld the state regulations, the Supreme Court, per Justice O'Connor, held that both regulations were pre-empted by FCLAA [*see* § 3.01 above] and, alternatively, that both regulations failed the *Central Hudson* standard for commercial speech. There were several concurrences. Four Justices—Stevens, Souter, Ginsburg, and Breyer—dissented, at least in part.

This Note focuses on the Court's application of the *Central Hudson* standard. The Court concluded that the school zone regulation would constitute nearly a complete ban in major metropolitan areas. The Court therefore held that school zone regulations failed the means test: "no more extensive than necessary." As for the 5-foot rule, the Court concluded that it failed both the "no more extensive than necessary" prong and the "directly advances" prong. While recognizing the important goal of preventing minors from using tobacco, the Court observed that: "Not all children are less than 5 feet tall, and those who are certainly have the ability to look up and take in their surroundings." Given that factual predicate, the Court concluded that the 5-foot rule did not "directly advance" the State's asserted goal.

Finally, the Court rejected the State's argument that *Central Hudson* should not apply when the burden on commercial speech is "de minimis." Use this decision to assist your analysis of Problem T above.

(9) *Certain FDA Regulations Fail the Central Hudson Test: Thompson v. Western States Medical Center, 535 U.S. 357 (2002).* The Food and Drug Administration has certain standard drug approval requirements which mandate an expensive scientific testing process. Certain "compounded drugs" are exempt from the approval requirements as long as the providers meet requirements including a ban on the providers advertising or promoting particular compounded drugs. ("Compounded drugs" are created by a pharmacist or physician to meet the needs of an individual patient.) Not all licensed pharmacists perform drug compounding. Licensed pharmacists who perform compounding sued the FDA, claiming their rights to commercial speech were violated by the FDA prohibition.

The Supreme Court, per Justice O'Connor, applied the *Central Hudson* standard and held that the FDA prohibition failed both the "not more extensive than necessary" prong and the "directly advances" prong. Justice Thomas concurred, repeating his call for using the basic Two Track analysis for such commercial speech. The four dissenters, per Justice Breyer, expressed concern that permitting the pharmacist-to-patient advertising would initiate compound drug decisions by patients rather than doctors. The dissenters argued for "a more flexible test," which would be more deferential to the federal government's assessment of the public health consequences of permitting such advertising.

PROBLEM T

IS PROHIBITION OF CIGARETTE ADVERTISING CONSTITUTIONAL? The FCC, by regulation, has prohibited cigarette advertising in the broadcast media. Is this regulation sustainable on the ground that (1) it concerns "pure" commercial speech advertising a "harmful" product, or (2) broadcasting is a licensed profession, or (3) both rationales combined? In addition, there have been various proposals, supported by such prestigious organizations as the American Medical Association, to ban cigarette advertising in the print media, on billboards, etc. Would such a prohibition be constitutional after *Central Hudson, Fox,* and *Posadas*?

§ 11.08   WHEN GOVERNMENT FUNCTIONS ARE INTERTWINED WITH SPEECH: PUBLIC SCHOOLS, ELECTIONS, GOVERNMENT EMPLOYEES, AND GOVERNMENT SUBSIDY

[A]   Education: The Public Schools

INTRODUCTORY NOTE

It is generally accepted that the Court's decision in *Tinker v. Des Moines Independent Community School Dist.*, 393 U.S. 503 (1969), is the seminal decision in the area of First Amendment law in the public school setting. The *Tinker* decision is addressed in § 11.06[B] above. *Tinker* first held that wearing the black armbands was "speech." The Court then held that the speech of schoolchildren was "protected speech." Given that the school regulation was content-based, the *Tinker* Court applied a version of strict scrutiny, examining whether the speech materially and substantially interfered with schoolwork or discipline. For present purposes, the Court's statement in *Tinker* that students in public schools do not "shed their constitutional rights to freedom of speech or expression at the schoolhouse gate" is the starting point for reviewing the subsequent caselaw. Watch how the scope of this statement changes (*i.e.*, narrows) over the next thirty years.

BETHEL SCHOOL DISTRICT v. FRASER, 478 U.S. 675 (1986). After consulting teachers who counseled him against doing so, high school student Fraser delivered a speech containing "an elaborate, graphic, and explicit sexual metaphor" to nominate a fellow student for a class office, before approximately 600 high school students, many of whom were fourteen-year-olds. Specifically, Fraser described his candidate as "firm—he's firm in his pants . . . but most . . . of all, his belief in you, the students of Bethel, is firm. Jeff . . . is a man who takes his point and pounds it in. If necessary, he'll take an issue and nail it to the wall. He doesn't attack things in spurts—he drives hard. . . . Jeff is a man who will go to the very end—even the climax, for each and every one of you". . . .

Fraser was suspended pursuant to a high school rule prohibiting "[c]onduct which materially and substantially interferes with the educational process . . ., including the use of obscene,profane language or gestures." The Court, per Chief Justice Burger, held that the suspension was constitutional:

> The pervasive sexual innuendo in Fraser's speech was plainly offensive to both teachers and students—indeed to any mature person. By glorifying male sexuality, and in its verbal content, the speech was acutely insulting to teenage girl students. [T]he speech could well be seriously damaging to its less mature audience, many of whom were only fourteen years old and on the threshold of awareness of human sexuality. Some students were reported as bewildered by the speech and the reaction of mimicry it provoked.

> This court's first amendment jurisprudence has acknowledged limitations on the otherwise absolute interest of the speaker in reaching an unlimited audience where the speech is sexually explicit and the audience may include children [citing *Ginsberg v. New York, FCC v. Pacifica Foundation*, and other cases]. These cases recognize the obvious concern on the part of parents, and school authorities acting in loco parentis to protect children—especially in a captive audience—from exposure to sexually explicit, indecent, or lewd speech.

Justice Blackmun and Brennan concurred in the result. Justice Marshall dissented, as he stated, "because in my view the school district failed to demonstrate that the respondent's remarks were indeed disruptive. [W]here speech is involved we may not unquestioningly accept a teacher's or administrator's assertion that certain pure speech interfered with education." Finally, Justice Stevens dissented, because although he believed that "a school faculty must regulate the content as well as the style of student speech in carrying out its educational mission," he concluded that the school policy was too vague to give Fraser "fair notice."

NOTES AND QUESTIONS

(1) *The Public Schools' Duty to "Inculcate Fundamental Values": Board of Education v. Pico, 457 U.S. 853 (1982).* The decisions clearly recognize the public schools' function to inculcate fundamental values of the society. This is one of the factors that makes public education a special setting. Consider whether the duty to inculcate values and the demands of the First Amendment might conflict.

(2) *Required School Activities and the First Amendment: Searching for a Standard in Bethel School District v. Fraser and Comparing It to Tinker (the Black Armbands Case).* Consider thedifferences between the holding in the case above and the black armbands decision in *Tinker v. Des Moines School District*, above. Perhaps there is a difference between (1) a case in which a student individually engages in expression and (2) a case in which a student uses a platform provided by the school, either to prevent the school's activity or to speak as though the school had conferred its authority on the speech. Is this distinction useful, and does it explain the differing results?

(3) *May the Principal Censor the High School Newspaper, and if So, When?: Distinguishing Individual Student Expression from Speech That Carries the Authority of the School.* Consider whether the following decision appropriately uses the distinction between individual student expression and speech that partakes of the authority of the school itself. *See also* Levin, *Educating Youth for Citizenship: The Conflict between Authority and Individual Rights in the Public School*, 95 YALE L.J. 1647 (1986).

(4) *Narrowing Tinker (Again) and the War on Drugs in Public Schools: Morse v. Frederick, 127 S. Ct. 2618 (2007).* At a school-sanctioned and school-supervised event to watch the Olympic Torch Relay, the school principal, Morse, saw some students unfurl a banner stating "BONG HiTS 4 JESUS." The principal interpreted the banner as promoting illegal drug use. Even though the students were located on the public sidewalk (facing the high school), the principal confiscated the banner and eventually suspended one of the students, Frederick. Frederick sued under 42 U.S.C. § 1983. The Supreme Court, per Chief Justice Roberts, held that the principal could take reasonable steps to protect other students from speech that could be reasonably regarded as encouraging illegal drug use.

The decision was basically a 5-4 split, but some Justices in the majority filed separate concurrences that were highly splintered in their rationales. Justice Thomas concurred, calling for *Tinker* to be overruled. Justice Alito, joined by Justice Kennedy, filed a concurring opinion stating their view that the majority opinion only applied to advocating illegal drug use rather than commenting on political or social issues. Justice Breyer's opinion concurred on the qualified immunity issue, but he otherwise dissented on the free speech merits. Justice Stevens dissented for Justices Souter and Ginsburg. Justice Stevens did not think the student was advocating illegal drug use; rather, the student was just trying to exploit "a rare chance to appear on national television." Justice Stevens extensively discussed the "marketplace of ideas" theory of free speech doctrine. He relied, in part, on "two personal recollections" including his experience "when I was a student" under Prohibition. He thought the majority's reasoning interfered with the national marketplace of ideas about the wisdom of the War on Drugs. *See Gonzales v. Raich*, 545 U.S. 1 (2005) above in Chapter 2 (Justice Stevens' further discussion of the political processes and the War on Drugs).

(5) *High School Prohibitions on "Recruiting" and Free Speech Doctrine: Tennessee Secondary School Athletic Association v. Brentwood Academy, 127 S. Ct. 2489*

(2007). The first time Brentwood Academy's challenge to the anti-recruiting rule of the TSSAA (the governing entity of secondary school athletics in Tennessee) reached the Supreme Court, the Court held, 5-4, that TSSAA was a state actor. *See* § 13.03 below. After remand, the lower courts ruled for Brentwood Academy, reasoning that, as applied to a letter sent by the football coach to eighth grade boys inviting them to participate in spring practice, the anti-recruiting rule was a content-based regulation that failed strict scrutiny. The Supreme Court, per Justice Stevens, reversed and held that a rule prohibiting high school coaches from recruiting middle school athletes did not violate the First Amendment. [The Court also ruled against Brentwood Academy's procedural due process claim; *see* § 8.03 above.]

It is hard to characterize the approach by Justice Stevens, except to suggest that he used common law, precedential reasoning. In a section joined only by a plurality, he relied on certain commercial speech decisions, *see* § 11.06 above, particularly *Ohralik v. Ohio State Bar Assn.*, 436 U.S. 447 (1978). He also relied, for the Court, on the public employee speech decisions, *see* § 11.07[C] above, because Brentwood Academy was a "voluntary" participant in TSSAA. Justice Stevens also emphasized the facts, reasoning that, "[a]fter all it is a heady thing for an eighth grade student to be contacted directly by a coach—here 'Your Coach'—and invited to join a high school sports team." Calling the coach's letter "a potent entreaty," Justice Stevens concluded that the potential for "undue pressure" outweighed Brentwood Academy's free speech interests. [Professor Day's children—girls and boys—have received such letters, and other invitations to participate, even as early as sixth grade. His children did not seem to be unduly influenced and certainly didn't view the form letters as a "heady experience." Justice Stevens' characterization of the facts seems similar to his opinion in *Fraser*, above.]

The precedential importance of *Brentwood Academy II* will be limited by the fact that five Justices concurred but disagreed with core features of the reasoning employed by Justice Stevens. Justice Kennedy (for Roberts, Scalia, and Alito) concurred in part because he disagreed with the use of the *Ohralik* and other commercial speech decisions. Justice Thomas concurred only in the judgment. Justice Thomas said reliance on *Ohralik* "is outright wrong." As for the Court's reliance on the public employee speech cases, Justice Thomas called this "the bizarre exercise of extending obviously inapplicable First Amendment doctrine to these circumstances."

The Court's reliance on two factors—(1) the non-core nature of the speech involved; and (2) the so-called voluntariness of Brentwood Academy's participation—does seem to stray far from the Two Track Model. *See* § 11.03 above. But, the decision may portend some modification of the Two Track Model by the Roberts Court.

HAZELWOOD SCHOOL DISTRICT v. KUHLMEIER, 484 U.S. 260 (1988). The principal of Hazelwood East High School censored two articles from Spectrum, the school newspaper. One of the articles described three students' experiences with pregnancy, and the other discussed the impact of divorce on students at the school. The principal "was concerned that, although the pregnancy story used false names 'to keep the identity of these girls a secret,' the pregnant students still might be identifiable from the text. He also believed that the article's references to sexual activity and birth control were inappropriate for some of the younger students at the school. In addition, [he] was concerned that a student identified by name in the divorce story had complained [about her father's behavior]. [The principal] believed that the student's parents should have been given an opportunity to respond to these remarks or to consent to their publication."

Spectrum was written and edited by the Journalism II class at the high school. Most of the costs were paid by the school board. The district court held that Spectrum was "a part of the school adopted curriculum," but it also held that the paper was a "public forum," "intended to be and operated as a conduit for student viewpoint," and that it could not be censored except when "necessary to avoid material and substantial interference with school work or discipline . . . or the rights of others." The court of appeals, affirming, held that the school board had violated the student editors' first amendment rights by deleting the articles.

The Supreme Court, per Justice White, reversed and held in favor of the school board:

> Students in the public schools do not "shed their constitutional rights to freedom of speech or expression at the school house gate." *Tinker* [*v. Des Moines Independent School District*]. They cannot be punished merely for expressing their personal views on the school premises . . . unless school authorities have reason to believe that such expression will "substantially interfere with the work of the school or impinge upon the rights of other students."
>
> We have nonetheless recognized that the first amendment rights of students in the public schools "are not automatically coextensive with the rights of adults in the settings," *Bethel School District v. Fraser*, and must be "applied in light of the special characteristics of the school environment." . . .
>
> We deal first with the question whether Spectrum may appropriately be characterized as a forum for public expression. The public schools do not possess all of the attributes of streets, parks, and other traditional public forums that "time out of mind, have been usedfor purposes of assembly, communicating thoughts between citizens, and discussing public questions". . . .
>
> [S]chool officials did not evince either "by policy or by practice," any intent to open the pages of Spectrum to "indiscriminate use" by its student reporters and editors, or by the student body generally. Instead, they "reserve[d] the forum for its intended purpos[e]," as a supervised learning experience for journalism students. Accordingly, school officials were entitled to regulate the contents of Spectrum in any reasonable manner. It is this standard, rather than our decision in *Tinker*, that governs this case.
>
> The question whether the first amendment requires a school to tolerate particular student speec—the question that we addressed in *Tinker*—is different from the question whether the first amendment requires a school affirmatively to promote particular speech. The former question addresses educators' ability to silence a student's personal expression that happens to occur on the school premises. The latter questions concerns educators' authority over school-sponsored publications, theatrical productions, and other expressive activities that students, parents, and members of the public might reasonably perceive to bear the imprimatur of the school. . . .

Justice Brennan, joined by Justices Marshall and Blackmun, dissented. Relying on such cases as *Tinker*, the dissenters argued that "[o]nly speech that 'materially and substantially interferes with the requirements of appropriate discipline' can be found unacceptable and therefore prohibited."

[B] Election Campaigns

BUCKLEY v. VALEO, 424 U.S. 1 (1976) (per curiam). The Federal Election Campaign Act, a post-Watergate measure, imposed various limits upon contributions and spending. Individual contributions to any candidate were limited to $1000, and no contributor could give more than $25,000 in total. Independent expenditures "relative to a clearly identified candidate" were limited to $1000 per year. Candidates were subjected to limitations upon their spending; the limits depended upon the particular office. Finally, committees and candidates were required to keep detailed records of contributions and expenditures. Here, the court upholds the contribution limits and reporting requirements, but it invalidates the limits on "independent" expenditures and the spending limits placed on candidates.

a. *General Principles.* The Act's contribution and expenditure limitations operate in an area of the most fundamental first amendment activities. Discussion of public issues and debate on the qualifications of candidates are integral to the operation of the system of government established by our Constitution. . . .

The expenditure limitations contained in the Act represent substantial rather than merely theoretical restraints on the quantity and diversity of political speech. . . .

In sum, although the Act's contribution and expenditure limitations both implicate fundamental first amendment interests, its expenditure ceilings impose significantly more severe restrictions on protected freedoms of political and association than do its limitations on financial contributions.

b. *Contribution Limitations.* [I]n view of the fundamental nature of the right to associate, governmental action which may have the effect of curtailing the freedom to associate is subject to the closest scrutiny. . . .

Appellees argue that the Act's restrictions on large campaign contributions are justified by [various compelling] governmental interests. [T]he primary interest served by the limitations, and, indeed, by the Act as a whole, is the prevention of corruption and the appearance of corruption spawned by the real or imagined coercive influence of large financial contributions on candidate's positions and on their actions if elected to office. . . .

We find that, under the rigorous standard of review established by our prior decisions, the weighty interests served by restricting the size of financial contributions to political candidates are sufficient to justify the limited effect upon first amendment freedoms caused by the $1,000 contribution ceiling. . . .

c. *Expenditure Limitations [Including the Candidate's Own Funds].* [W]e find that the governmental interest in preventing corruption and the appearance of corruption is inadequate to justify [the] ceiling on independent expenditures. First, assuming, *arguendo*, that large independent expenditures pose the same dangers of actual or apparent *quid pro quo* arrangements as do large contributions, [the Act] does not provide an answer that sufficiently relates to the elimination of those dangers. [S]o long as persons and groups eschew expenditures that in express terms advocate the election or defeat of a clearly identified candidate, they are free to spend as much as they want to promote the candidate and his views. . . .

Second, [t]he independent advocacy restricted by the provision does not presently appear to pose dangers of real or apparent corruption comparable to those identified with large campaign contributions. . . .

The Act also sets limits on expenditures by a candidate "from his personal funds, or the personal funds of his immediate family, in connection with his campaigns during any calendar year". . . .

The primary government interest served by the Act [d]oes not support the limitation of the candidate's expenditure of his own personal funds. Indeed, the use of personal funds reduces the candidate's dependence on outside contributions and thereby counteracts the coercive pressures and attendant risks of abuse to which the Act's contribution limitations are directed.

The ancillary interests in equalizing the relative financial resources of candidates competing for elective office, therefore, provides the sole relevant rationale for [the ceiling on the candidate's own expenditures]. That interest is clearly not sufficient to justify the provision's infringement of fundamental first amendment rights. [W]e therefore hold that [the] restriction on a candidate's personal expenditures is unconstitutional. . . .

The Court went on to uphold the recording and disclosure requirements of the Act. The Court also upheld a complex scheme for public financing of presidential campaigns. The opinions of Chief Justice Burger and Justice White, concurring in part and dissenting in part, are omitted.

AUSTIN v. MICHIGAN CHAMBER OF COMMERCE, 494 U.S. 652 (1990). A Michigan statute prohibited even "independent" expenditures by corporations favoring political candidates.The Michigan State Chamber of Commerce challenged the constitutionality of this statutory scheme. The Supreme Court, per Justice Marshall, applied the strict scrutiny standard and upheld the statute:

> The State contends that the unique legal and economic characteristics of corporations necessitate some regulation of their expenditures to avoid corruption or the appearance of corruption. [S]tate law grants corporations special advantages—such as limited liability, perpetual life, and favorable treatment of the accumulation and distribution of assets. . . . These state-created advantages not only allow corporations to play a dominant role in the Nation's economy, but also permit them to use resources amassed in the economic marketplace to obtain "an unfair advantage in the political marketplace". . . . "[T]he resources in the treasury of a business corporation . . . are not an indication of popular support for the corporation's political ideas". . . .

> [W]e therefore hold that the state has articulated a sufficiently compelling rationale to support its restriction on independent expenditures by corporations. . . .

Justices Brennan and Stevens concurred with separate opinions.

Justice Scalia dissented:

> "Attention all citizens. To assure the fairness of elections by preventing disproportionate expression of the views of any single powerful group, your government has decided that the following associations of persons shall be prohibited from speaking or writing in support of any candidate: _____." In permitting Michigan to make private corporations the first object of this Orwellian announcement, the Court today endorses the principle that too much speech is an evil that the democratic majority can prescribe. I dissent because that principle is contrary to our case law and incompatible with the absolutely central truth of the first amendment: That government cannot be trusted to assure, through censorship, the "fairness" of political debate. . . .

Justice Kennedy, joined by Justices O'Connor and Justice Scalia, also dissented.

NOTES AND QUESTIONS

(1) *Should Expenditure Limits Be Valid if the Candidate Accepts Public Funds?: FEC v. National Conservative Political Action Committee, 518 U.S. 604 (1985).* What if the candidate accepts public funds? Consider whether there is a *quid pro quo* for which the government may insist upon limiting spending by the candidate—or by his supporters. In the *National Conservative Political Action Committee* case, the Court (per Justice Rehnquist) struck down a statute prohibiting independent groups from spending more than $1,000 to support a candidate who accepted public financing, saying: "[T]he effort to link either corruption or the appearance of corruption to independent expenditures by [political action committees], whether large or small, simply does not pass [the strict scrutiny] standard of review." Justice White, joined by Justices Brennan and Marshall, dissented.

(2) *The Refinement—or Potential Reconsideration—;of Buckley?:* Colorado Republican Federal Campaign Committee v. Federal Election Commission, 518 U.S. 604 (1996). The Federal Election Commission (FEC) charged the Colorado Republican Party with violating the "PartyExpenditure Provision" (PEP) of the Federal Campaign Act upheld in *Buckley, supra.* The Colorado Party defended on several grounds including a claim that they satisfied the PEP requirement that party expenditures be "independent" and also on the grounds that PEP was unconstitutional, as applied and facially. In a plurality opinion, the Court, per Justice Breyer, rejected the FEC's argument that the Colorado Party's expenditures were not independent and declined to decide the constitutional claims.

This case, like others in the Term, spawned several concurring opinions. Justice Kennedy, joined by two other Justices, would have overturned the Party Expenditure Provision, as applied in this case. The concurrence by Justice Thomas, joined by Justice Scalia, went further and would have overturned the contribution limitations upheld in *Buckley.* Justice Stevens, joined by Justice Ginsburg, dissented. Reconsider *Buckley*'s distinction between limits on contributions (constitutional) and expenditures (unconstitutional). In light of *Colorado Republican Federal Campaign Committee,* do you think the Court might decide *Buckley* differently today?

(3) *Contributions or Speech by Corporations During Elections: Does the Complete Ban in the Austin Case Set the Proper Standard?* The Court's holding, that a complete ban on a corporation's independent speech supporting a candidate is justified by compelling interests in preventing corporate wealth advantages from influencing elections, draws sharp dissents. Is this holding proper, or does it deny freedom of speech to corporations?

The Court has reaffirmed, per Justice Souter, the constitutionality of the federal ban on campaign contributions by corporations—even nonprofit corporations. *Federal Election Commission v. Beaumont,* 539 U.S. 146 (2003). The majority's rationale was based on: (1) the fact that federal law does permit corporate contributions to Political Action Committees (thus providing some reasonable alternatives); and (2) the Court's continued concern for the disruptive impact of the ability of corporations to raise money.

(4) *Censorship of Endorsements as Unconstitutional: Eu v. San Francisco County Democratic Central Committee, 489 U.S. 214 (1989).* The California Elections Code prohibited the official governing bodies of political parties from endorsing candidates in party primaries. The Supreme Court, per Justice Marshall, invalidated these provisions: "[F]reedom of association means not only that an individual voter has the right to associate with the political party of her choice, but also that a political party has a right to 'identify the people who constitute the association,' and to select a 'standard bearer who best represents the party's ideologies and preferences.'" The state had attempted to defend the ban on endorsements, as well as the other measures, by advancing its interest in "party stability" (an interest that it claimed was contained within the compelling interest in stable government) and reducing "intra-party friction which may endanger the party's general election prospects"—an interest the Court rejected by referring to the party's self-interest. Is this reasoning persuasive?

(5) *A Confirmation of Buckley: Nixon v. Shrink Missouri Government, 528 U.S. 377 (2000).* After the *Buckley* decision, Missouri adopted a campaign finance law limiting contributions to candidates for state office. An unsuccessful candidate in the state primary and a political action committee challenged Missouri's restrictions. Although the Court of Appeals had agreed with the challengers, the Supreme Court, per Justice Souter, ruled for the State and upheld Missouri's contribution limits.

The Court's opinion (6-3) followed *Buckley* and determined that the Missouri law was sufficiently tailored to withstand a First Amendment scrutiny. Justices Kennedy, Thomas and Scalia dissented. One of the main issues of contention was whether the Court's opinion was actually applying strict scrutiny; the dissenters argued that the

Court was not using an appropriately high standard. See the dissenting opinion in *Austin* above.

(6) *The Further Progeny of Buckley: Federal Election Commission v. Colorado Republican Federal Campaign Committee, 533 U.S. 431 (2001).* Buckley v. Valeo, the main case, established a distinction between *campaign contributions* and *campaign expenditures*: restrictions (in the interests of electoral system integrity) on contributions can be constitutional while restrictions on expenditures will generally be unconstitutional. Understandably, given the *Buckley* dichotomy, political candidates and campaign groups would prefer to have political funds considered as "expenditures" rather than "contributions." One of the "grey" areas in the *Buckley* dichotomy has been the spending of so-called "independent" committees. While the political campaign spending of independent committees has been protected as "expenditures," the Court, per Justice Souter, held, in *Colorado Republican Federal Campaign Committee,* that some spending is more appropriately characterized as "contributions" (and, thereby, constitutionally subject to regulation). For the majority, the evidence in the record demonstrated that certain coordinated campaign spending was not truly "independent" and actually was a campaign contribution subject to regulation. Four Justices, in an opinion by Justice Thomas, dissented.

(7) *The "Blanket Primary" Violated the Freedom of Association Rights of Political Parties: California Democratic Party v. Jones, 530 U.S. 567 (2000).* Many states use so-called "open primaries" to select the candidates for political parties. In California, an extreme version known as a "blanket primary" was used: all voters, regardless of party affiliation, vote on a single ballot and can vote for primary candidates of any party. The Supreme Court, per Justice Scalia, held that California's primary, although defended as an effort to make the political process more "centrist," violated the First Amendment association rights of the political party members. Justices Stevens and Ginsburg dissented, arguing that the majority's approach threatened the constitutionality of all open primaries.

Although the *Jones* decision concerned an "open" primary system (where the State required a political party to allow any registered voter to vote in the party's primary), it was the controlling authority in a case involving Oklahoma's "semi-closed" primary system. *Clingman v. Beaver,* 544 U.S. 581 (2005). In Oklahoma's system, a political party may invite only its own members and registered Independents to vote, and this was challenged as a violation of the free association rights of nonparty members. The Supreme Court, per Justice Thomas' plurality opinion, rejected the challenge. The Court held that not every burden on association rights is subject to strict scrutiny and that the burden imposed by Oklahoma was not sufficiently severe to trigger strict scrutiny.

[C] Government Speech: The Government as Speaker or the Government's Message

YUDOF, WHEN GOVERNMENT SPEAKS
3–4, 172–73 (1983)*

This book arose from my concern that legal scholars and courts have failed to grapple with the realities of communications in the twentieth century. With few exceptions, they are taken with the dying metaphor of the marketplace of ideas; they concern themselves with government attempts to regulate private speech and ignore the massive role of governments in communications networks. . . .

[But] [i]f government dominates the flow of ideas and information, the ideal of the

---

self-controlled citizen, making informed choices about his government, is destroyed. [T]he First Amendment then should be perceived as protecting the processes of consent. . . . Conversely, even democratic governments must lead, inform, teach, and seek to expand the knowledge of people. . . .

The idea that government expression can be inconsistent with democratic consent and majoritarian processes can be framed in constitutional terms. [S]ources of limitation of government communications may be sought in the First Amendment. . . . The interpretation is based [not literally on the constitutional text but] on the relationship between the text and the structure of democratic government embodied in the Constitution and American institutions and in the pervasive assumptions and general purposes underlying the First Amendment. . . .

The identification of unconstitutional government expression is a complex matter, and, as in the larger communications system, this complexity requires that we look at many interdependent factors. First, does the government body label the communication as a government message? A public official may fear to take responsibility for a statement and attempt to hide behind the anonymity of a government agency publication or news release. [S]econd, to what extent have the resources of the agency in question been mobilized? [T]hird, is the content of the speech inappropriate to the agency's mission and yet frequently repeated? For example, required Bible readings in public schools, not tied to the immediate educational objectives of the school and repeated daily, may aptly be characterized as a form of government speech. Fourth, to whom are the communications addressed? Is the audience captive? Does it have alternate sources of information and opinion? Are the audience characteristics (maturity, intelligence, etc.) such that judgment distortion appears likely?

In any given case, these factors may be difficult to weigh, and where the character of the speech is unclear, courts should err on the side of expansively protecting the individual First Amendment rights of government officials and employees.

[1] Government Subsidy

FCC v. LEAGUE OF WOMEN VOTERS, 468 U.S. 364 (1984). The Public Broadcasting Act prohibited any public, non-commercial, or educational broadcasting station that received federal grants from "editorializing." The Court, per Justice Brennan, determined that even though this regulation concerned broadcasting, it was subject to heightened scrutiny and could be upheld only if it was "narrowly tailored to further a substantial government interest," since it resulted in a flat ban upon speech by the stations in question. The Court then proceeded to strike down the prohibition:

> [T]o the extent that federal financial support creates a risk that stations will lose their independence through the bewitching power of governmental largesse, the elaborate structure established by the Public Broadcasting Act already operates to insulate local stations from governmental interference. . . .

> [T]here are literally hundreds of public radio and television stations in communities scattered throughout the United States and its territories. . . . [T]he risk that localeditorializing will place all of public broadcasting in jeopardy is not sufficiently pressing to warrant [the] broad suppression of speech. . . .

Justice Rehnquist, joined by the Chief Justice and Justice White, dissented: "Congress has rationally determined that the bulk of taxpayers [w]ould prefer not to see the management of local education stations promulgate its own private views on the air at taxpayer expense. Accordingly, Congress simply has decided not to subsidize stations which engage in that activity."

RUST v. SULLIVAN, 500 U.S. 173 (1991). Regulations promulgated by the Secretary of Health and Human Services, pursuant to congressional legislation, prohibited the use of federal funds to family planning projects for counseling or referral for abortion. Petitioners, who were grantees and doctors, alleged that the challenged regulations violated the First Amendment, among other arguments. The Court, per Chief Justice Rehnquist, rejected this argument:

> The challenged regulations implement the statutory prohibition by prohibiting counseling, referral, and the provision of information regarding abortion as a method of family planning. They are designed to insure that the limits of the federal program are observed. The Title X program is designed not for prenatal care, but to encourage family planning. A doctor who wished to offer prenatal care to a project patient who became pregnant could properly be prohibited from doing so because such service is outside the scope of the federally funded program. [T]his is not a case of the government "suppressing a dangerous idea," but of a prohibition on a project grantee or its employees from engaging in activities outside of its scope.

> To hold that the government unconstitutionally discriminates on the basis of viewpoint when it chooses to fund a program dedicated to advance certain permissible goals, because the program in advancing those goals necessarily discourages alternate goals, would render numerous government programs constitutionally suspect. When Congress established a National Endowment for Democracy to encourage other countries to adopt democratic principles, it was not constitutionally required to fund a program to encourage competing lines of political philosophy such as communism and fascism. Petitioners' assertions ultimately boil down to the position that if the government chooses to subsidize one protected right, it must subsidize analogous counterpart rights. But the Court has soundly rejected that proposition. . . .

> Petitioners also contend that the restrictions on the subsidization of abortion-related speech contained in the regulations are impermissible because they condition the receipt of a benefit, in this case Title X funding, on the relinquishment of a constitutional right, the right to engage in abortion advocacy and counseling. . . .

> [T]he Secretary's regulations do not force the Title X grantee to give up abortion-related speech; they merely require that the grantee keep such activity separate and distinct from Title X activities. [T]he Title X *grantee* can continue to perform abortions, provide abortion-related services, and engage in abortion advocacy; it simply is required to conduct those activities through programs that are separate and independent from the project that receives Title X funds. . . . [I]n *FCC v. League of Women Voters*, 468 U.S. 364 (1984), we invalidated a federal law providing that noncommercial television and radio stations that receive federal grants may not "engage in editorializing." [T]he effect of the law was that "a noncommercial educational station that receives only one percent of its overall income from [federal] grants is barred absolutely from all editorializing" and "barred from using even wholly private funds to finance its editorial activity."

Justices Blackmun, Marshall, Stevens, and O'Connor dissented from the Court's holding. As Justice Blackmun concluded, "Until today, the Court never has upheld viewpoint-based suppression of speech simply because that suppression was a condition upon the acceptance of public funds. Further, as Justice Blackmun saw it, "By manipulating the content of the doctor/patient dialogue, the regulations upheld today force each of the petitioners 'to be an instrument for fostering public adherence to an ideological point of view [he or she] finds unacceptable.' "

NATIONAL ENDOWMENT FOR THE ARTS v. FINLEY
524 U.S. 569 (1998)

JUSTICE O'CONNOR delivered the opinion of the Court.

The National Foundation on the Arts and Humanities Act, as amended in 1990, requires the Chairperson of the National Endowment for the Arts (NEA) to ensure that "artistic excellence and artistic merit are the criteria by which [grant] applications are judged, taking into consideration general standards of decency and respect for the diverse beliefs and values of the American public." 20 U.S.C. § 954(d)(1) [the decency and respect provision]. . . . We conclude that § 954(d)(1) is facially valid, as it neither inherently interferes with First Amendment rights nor violates constitutional vagueness principles.

[The application process for the NEA award at issue here starts with application review by "advisory panels" composed of experts and "knowledgeable" lay persons. These panels report to a National Council (Council) which then advises the NEA Chairperson. A negative recommendation by the Council kills an application. The Chairperson makes the final awards. The Chairperson's decisions are subject to the "decency and respect" provision.

Although only a few of the NEA's awards had generated formal complaints, two works funded by the NEA generated public controversy in 1989. One involved "homoerotic photographs" and the other was a photograph of a "crucifix immersed in urine." Congress reacted to these two controversial works by cutting the NEA budget and by imposing a condition on the awards process whereby all grantees had to certify that they would not use the award to create "obscene" works. This certification condition was eventually declared unconstitutional by lower courts, and the NEA did not appeal. Congress, meanwhile, created a Commission to study the awards process. Against this background, the Congress passed, as a compromise measure, the decency and respect provision.

The four individual plaintiffs (here, respondents) were "performance artists" whose applications, although initially approved before the passage of the decency and respect provision, were disapproved by the Council and denied by the Chairperson. The respondents sued on free speech grounds. When respondents' action survived the NEA's summary judgment motion, the NEA settled the respondents "as-applied" free speech claims. The respondents also prevailed on the remaining "facial" challenge to the decency and respect provision, but the Supreme Court eventually reversed and upheld the constitutionality of the decency and respect provision.]

II

Respondents raise a facial constitutional challenge to §954(d)(1), and consequently they confront "a heavy burden" in advancing their claim. *Rust, supra,* at 183. [T]o prevail, respondents must demonstrate a substantial risk that application of the provision will lead to the suppression of speech.

Respondents argue that the provision is a paradigmatic example of viewpoint discrimination because it rejects any artistic speech that either fails to respect mainstream values or offends standards of decency. The premise of respondents' claim is that § 954(d)(1) constrains the agency's ability to fund certain categories of artistic expression. The NEA, however, reads the provision as merely hortatory, and contends that it stops well short of an absolute restriction. Section 954(d)(1) adds "considerations" to the grant-making process; it does not preclude awards to projects that might be deemed "indecent" or "disrespectful," nor place conditions on grants, or even specify that those factors must be given any particular weight in reviewing an application. . . . It is clear, however, that the text of § 954(d)(1) imposes no categorical requirement. . . .

Furthermore, like the plain language of §954(d), the political context surrounding the adoption of the "decency and respect" clause is inconsistent with respondents' assertion that the provision compels the NEA to deny funding on the basis of viewpoint discriminatory criteria. The legislation was a bipartisan proposal introduced as a counterweight to amendments aimed at eliminating the NEA's funding or substantially constraining its grant-making authority. . . .

That § 954(d)(1) admonishes the NEA merely to take "decency and respect" into consideration, and that the legislation was aimed at reforming procedures rather than precluding speech, undercut respondents' argument that the provision inevitably will be utilized as a tool for invidious viewpoint discrimination. In cases where we have struck down legislation as facially unconstitutional, the dangers were both more evident and more substantial. . . .

In contrast, the "decency and respect" criteria do not silence speakers by expressly "threaten[ing] censorship of ideas." *See* ibid. Thus, we do not perceive a realistic danger that § 954(d)(1) will compromise First Amendment values. As respondents' own arguments demonstrate, the considerations that the provision introduces, by their nature, do not engender the kind of directed viewpoint discrimination that would prompt this Court to invalidate a statute on its face. . . .

Respondents' claim that the provision is facially unconstitutional may be reduced to the argument that the criteria in § 954(d)(1) are sufficiently subjective that the agency could utilize them to engage in viewpoint discrimination. Given the varied interpretations of the criteria and the vague exhortation to "take them into consideration," it seems unlikely that this provision will introduce any greater element of selectivity than the determination of "artistic excellence" itself. . . .

We recognize, of course, that reference to these permissible applications would not alone be sufficient to sustain the statute against respondents' First Amendment challenge. But neither are we persuaded that, in other applications, the language of § 954(d)(1) itself will give rise to the suppression of protected expression. Any content-based considerations that may be taken into account in the grant-making process are a consequence of the nature of arts funding. The NEA has limited resources and it must deny the majority of the grant applications that it receives, including many that propose "artistically excellent" projects. . . .

Respondents do not allege discrimination in any particular funding decision. (In fact, after filing suit to challenge §954(d)(1), two of the individual respondents received NEA grants.) Thus, we have no occasion here to address an as-applied challenge in a situation where the denial of a grant may be shown to be the product of invidious viewpoint discrimination. If the NEA were to leverage its power to award subsidies on the basis of subjective criteria into a penalty on disfavored viewpoints, then we would confront a different case. We have stated that, even in the provision of subsidies, the Government may not "ai[m] at the suppression of dangerous ideas," and if a subsidy were "manipulated" to have a "coercive effect," then relief could be appropriate. . . . Unless and until § 954(d)(1) is applied in a manner that raises concern about the suppression of disfavored viewpoints, however, we uphold the constitutionality of the provision. . . .

JUSTICE SCALIA, with whom JUSTICE THOMAS joins, concurring in the judgment.

"The operation was a success, but the patient died." What such a procedure is to medicine, the Court's opinion in this case is to law. It sustains the constitutionality of 20 U.S.C. § 954(d)(1) by gutting it. The most avid congressional opponents of the provision could not have asked for more. I write separately because, unlike the Court, I think that § 954(d)(1) must be evaluated as written, rather than as distorted by the agency it was meant to control. By its terms, it establishes content- and viewpoint-based criteria upon which grant applications are to be evaluated. And that is perfectly constitutional.

I

More fundamentally, of course, all this legislative history has no valid claim upon our attention at all. . . . It matters not whether this enactment was the product of the most partisan alignment in history or whether, upon its passage, the Members all linked arms and sang, "The more we get together, the happier we'll be." . . . The law at issue in this case is to be found in the text of §954(d)(1), which passed both Houses and was signed by the President, U.S. Const., Art. I, §7. And that law unquestionably disfavors—discriminates against—indecency and disrespect for the diverse beliefs and values of the American people. I turn, then, to whether such viewpoint discrimination violates the Constitution.

II

The Court devotes so much of its opinion to explaining why this statute means something other than what it says that it neglects to cite the constitutional text governing our analysis. The First Amendment reads: "Congress shall make no law . . . abridging the freedom of speech." U.S. Const., Amdt. 1 (emphasis added). To abridge is "to contract, to diminish; to deprive of." T. Sheridan, A Complete Dictionary of the English Language (6th ed. 1796). With the enactment of § 954(d)(1), Congress did not abridge the speech of those who disdain the beliefs and values of the American public, nor did it abridge indecent speech. Those who wish to create indecent and disrespectful art are as unconstrained now as they were before the enactment of this statute. Avant-garde artists such as respondents remain entirely free to epater les bourgeois; they are merely deprived of the additional satisfaction of having the bourgeoisie taxed to pay for it. . . .

JUSTICE SOUTER, dissenting. . . .

The decency and respect proviso mandates viewpoint-based decisions in the disbursement of government subsidies, and the Government has wholly failed to explain why the statute should be afforded an exemption from the fundamental rule of the First Amendment that viewpoint discrimination in the exercise of public authority over expressive activity is unconstitutional. The Court's conclusions that the proviso is not viewpoint based, that it is not a regulation, and that the NEA may permissibly engage in viewpoint-based discrimination, are all patently mistaken. . . .

I

"If there is a bedrock principle underlying the First Amendment, it is that the government may not prohibit the expression of an idea simply because society finds the idea itself offensive or disagreeable." *Texas v. Johnson*, 491 U.S. 397, 414 (1989). . . .

It goes without saying that artistic expression lies within this First Amendment protection. The constitutional protection of artistic works turns not on the political significance that may be attributable to such productions, though they may indeed comment on the political, but simply on their expressive character, which falls within a spectrum of protected "speech" extending outward from the core of overtly political declarations. . . .

Just as self-evidently, a statute disfavoring speech that fails to respect America's "diverse beliefs and values" is the very model of viewpoint discrimination; it penalizes any view disrespectful to any belief or value espoused by someone in the American populace. Boiled down to its practical essence, the limitation obviously means that art that disrespects the ideology, opinions, or convictions of a significant segment of the American public is to be disfavored, whereas art that reinforces those values is not. . . .

NOTES AND QUESTIONS

(1) *The Constitutionality of "Subsidies" and Other Speech-Related Conditions: National Endowment For The Arts v. Finley, 524 U.S. 569 (1998).* The individual artist plaintiffs in *NEA* challenged the imposition of "decency and respect" criteria in the NEA's award process. Trying to avoid any "public forum" analysis, *see* § 11.06[A] above, the challengers claimed that the decency and respect criteria inevitably discriminated on the basis of viewpoint. The Supreme Court rejected this claim, determining that Congress intended: (1) that these criteria were only additional "considerations" for the already subjective award process and (2) that the additional considerations were a bipartisan compromise aimed at reforming NEA "procedures," and not a purposeful restriction on speech. Thus, the Court did not see a "realistic danger" to free speech values. The *NEA* decision, by Justice O'Connor, seems to suggest that, since Congress did not intend the NEA "subsidies" as an "abridgment" of free speech values, the Court will not interfere with the political branch's decisionmaking. This appears to be consistent with the *Rust* holding that the condition on grant recipients did not "significantly impinge" on free speech. *See Rust* above.

(2) *Justice Scalia's Concurrence in Finley: A Simpler Standard or a Categorical Narrowing of Free Speech Protection?* Because the decency and respect provision did not impose a "categorical" restraint, the Court concludes there was no viewpoint regulation. Justice Scalia disagreed with the majority and concluded that the NEA subsidies were viewpoint discrimination. (Thus, his opinion agreed in this regard with Justice Souter's dissent.) Justice Scalia would exempt the category of subsidies from free speech analysis. In contrast, the majority requires that governmental subsidies be viewpoint neutral. Which approach—the Court's or Justice Scalia's—provides greater protection for free speech values? Is this the right question? *See generally* Randall P. Bezanson, *The Quality of First Amendment Speech*, 20 Hastings Comm/Ent. L.J. 275 (1998).

(3) *Speech by Participants in Government-Funded Programs—A Case Distinguished from Rust: Legal Services Corp. v. Velazquez, 531 U.S. 533 (2001).* Congress funds the Legal Service Corp. (LSC) to provide legal assistance to certain low income persons. As a condition of the subsidy, Congress in 1996 banned LSC attorneys from participating in any lawsuit (or lobbying effort) challenging the constitutionality of a federal or state welfare system. When this ban on litigation was challenged, Congress defended based on its reading of *Rust*, above: subsidies do not directly restrict speech and are unconstitutional only if the funding scheme is "coercive." Despite the seeming similarity to *Rust*, the Supreme Court, per Justice Kennedy, distinguished *Rust*, and struck down the LSC litigation ban.

The *Velazquez* Court said that *Rust* depended "on the rationale that the counseling activities of the doctors under Title X amounted to government speech; . . . ." In contrast, the Court found that "the LSC program was designed to facilitate private speech, not to promote a government message." The dissenting opinion, by Justice Scalia (for the Chief Justice and Justices O'Connor and Thomas), did not find this distinction persuasive and argued that *Rust* and *Finley* were being eroded.

Two aspects of the majority's opinion might be noted for your consideration (*e.g.*, how these factors might apply in a future "subsidy" case). First, the Court explicitly drew an analogy between its public forum doctrine [§ 11.06[A] above] and its subsidized speech doctrine. This suggests that the public forum doctrine decisions may have more significant precedential weight. Second, the Court concluded that the LSC ban "threatens severe impairment of the judicial function" because it "prohibits speech and expression upon which the courts must depend for the proper exercise of judicial power." This purported impact on the judiciary might distinguish *Velazquez* from *Rust* and *Finley*. Note that Justice Kennedy had joined the majorities in *Rust* and *Finley*.

(4) *Rereading The Rust Decision After the Narrowing Interpretation of Legal Services Corp.: United States v. American Library Ass'n, 539 U.S. 194 (2003).* As part

of its effort to protect children using the Internet from adult pornography (as well as unprotected speech such as child pornography and obscenity), Congress passed the Children's Internet Protection Act (CIPA). [*See* § 11.04 for the *Reno* (CPA) and *The Free Speech Coalition* (CPPA) decisions above.] The CIPA required, pursuant to the spending power (§ 2.03 above), that public libraries must install software to block obscenity, child pornography images or certain adult pornography harmful to minors as a condition of receiving federal funding for Internet access (under the E-rate program or the Library Services and Technology Act). The CIPA was challenged by libraries, patrons, and Web site publishers as violating their free speech rights. Although the lower court had ruled for the challengers, the Supreme Court, per Chief Justice Rehnquist's plurality opinion, upheld CIPA (at least against this facial challenge).

The challengers' theory was that the CIPA filtering software was a content-based restriction on access to a public forum and was, therefore, subject to strict scrutiny. The plurality rejected the public forum argument, relying on *Finley* and *Forbes*. The plurality rejected any heightened scrutiny, relying on the *Rust* decision (another plurality opinion by the Chief Justice) and pointedly not adopting the narrowing interpretation of *Rust* offered by the *Velazquez* decision (written by Justice Kennedy). Ultimately, the plurality treated the case as though it were a spending power issue [*see* § 2.03 above] rather than a First Amendment case. The case hinged factually on whether a library could unblock the CIPA filtering mechanism for adult patrons. The district court had held that, even so, free speech rights were violated (*i.e.*, "chilled") because some adults would be too embarrassed to request unblocking. In an epigram rivaling Justice Holmes, Chief Justice Rehnquist responded to the lower court's "embarrassment analysis": "But the Constitution does not guarantee the right to acquire information at a public library without any risk of embarrassment."

The Court's majority was formed by two Justices, Kennedy and Breyer, who filed concurrences only in the judgment. Both concurrences relied upon the government's assertion that the CIPA filters would be removed for any adult patron upon request. Justice Breyer also relied on the line of commercial speech decisions, although his reasoning was not explained. [See § 11.06 above.] Justices Stevens and Souter dissented.

(5) *Generic Advertising Funded by "Beef Check-Off" Tax is "Government Speech": Johanns v. Livestock Marketing Association, 544 U.S. 550 (2005).* The Beef Promotion and Research Act (Beef Act) established a federal policy promoting and marketing beef and beef products. The goals of the Beef Act were implemented through the Secretary of Agriculture by creating a Cattleman's Beef Promotion and Research Board (Beef Board) and an Operating Committee and by imposing an assessment, or check off, on all sales and importation of cattle. The assessment funds (a tax) were used to pay for beef promotional campaigns approved by the Operating Committee and, more generally, the Secretary. Certain producers objected to the advertising run by the Beef Board, mainly on the grounds the advertising was "generic." The dissenting producers wanted the advertising to focus on an "American Beef" theme. The dissenting producers brought their claim based upon the *United Foods* decision. The lower courts held that the generic advertising was compelled speech of the dissenting producers and that the compelled funding did not constitute government speech.

Although the dissenting producers had prevailed at the lower courts, the Supreme Court, per Justice Scalia, reversed. The Court held that the generic advertising was "government speech" and was not susceptible to a First Amendment compelled subsidy challenge. The dissenting producers had argued against the government speech theory mainly on the grounds that the generic advertising was actually developed and paid for by non-governmental entities, the Beef Board and the Operating Committee. The Court majority found that the message of the generic advertising was "effectively controlled" by the federal government. Congress and the Secretary established the overarching message and a number of the campaign elements. The Court found that the Secretary had final approval authority over every word of the promotional campaigns. The Court also found that, although details of the advertising were left to the Operating Committee, half the members of the Operating Committee were appointed by the Secretary and all members of the committee were subject to removal by the Secretary. In addition, the Court found that the Secretary's subordinates attended and participated in the meetings at which the generic advertising proposals were developed. The Court said that the evidence in the record was sufficient to establish that the generic advertising was "government speech" and thereby not subject to a compelled speech analysis. The Court did leave open questions regarding the possible attribution of the generic advertising to the dissenting producers, saying that the record was not sufficiently developed on this point.

There were two concurrences. Justice Ginsburg concurred only in the judgment. Justice Kennedy filed a dissenting opinion and Justices Souter and Stevens also dissented. The dissenters disagreed with the majority's conclusion on government speech and would have applied the analysis from *United Foods*. Note that Justice Kennedy was the author of *United Foods*, and he was not persuaded to adopt the government speech theory. The implications for the many other product promotion schemes (*e.g.*, pork) are significant.

Professor Day was part of the trial team in the Beef Checkoff case (held before the Honorable Charles Kornmann, U.S. District Court for the District of South Dakota), representing the Nebraska Cattleman's Association which was Intervenor-Defendant, siding with the federal government in the case. Former students of Professor Day's were on the other side of the case. The lawyers for the Nebraska Cattleman's Association, in conjunction with the Department of Justice lawyers, built the record on the "government speech" issue. Although neither lower court was persuaded, the depth of that record proved to be significant to Justice Scalia's analysis of the government speech issue. This case is an excellent example of how you sometimes litigate a case not just for the immediate decision-maker, but with an eye towards the eventual appeal.

Since Professor Yudof's seminal work in the area, the leading authority on the topic of "government speech" is Randall P. Bezanson and William G. Buss, *The Many Faces of Government Speech*, 86 IA. L. REV. 1377 (2001).

[2] Speech By Government Employees

INTRODUCTORY NOTES

(1) *Public Employee Speech — The Traditional Lack of Protection: McAuliff v. Mayor of New Bedford, 29 N.E. 517 (1892)*. Traditionally, public employees did not have job protection. Public employees could be discharged at will—including for their exercise of free speech. As Justice Holmes (then on the Massachusetts Supreme Court) stated in *McAuliff*: "a [policeman] may have a constitutional right to talk politics, but he has no constitutional right to be a policeman." If a government employer could condition public employment on a waiver of free speech rights, then the government employee would be forced to choose between the job and the exercise of fundamental rights.

It is important for a student to recognize that the Holmesian position is not the modern constitutional law doctrine. As you will see in the cases below, today a governmental employer may not, as a general matter, treat employees adversely when they exercise their free speech rights as a citizen. Note that the public employee speech doctrine is part of the "unconstitutional conditions" doctrine.

(2) *The Development of the Modern Two-Step Doctrine: Connick v. Myers, 461 U.S. 138 (1983)*. In *Connick*, Myers was an assistant district attorney. After winning the election, Connick sought to reorganize the office and to reward his political supporters. Myers circulated a questionnaire to other employees asking, inter alia, whether they believed that Connick's decisions were based on politics rather than "efficiency." When

Connick learned of the questionnaire, he treated it as "insubordination" and fired Myers. She sued under a theory that her discharge was in retaliation for exercising her free speech rights.

The *Connick* Court, per Justice White, rejected Myers' argument. The Court identified the two-part standard which would control public employee speech doctrine for the next decade. The *Connick* standard required: (1) that the employee demonstrate that the speech was regarding a "matter of public concern;" and (2) if that were established, then the government employer must establish that the speech was "disruptive" of the employer's business or operation. In *Connick*, the Court decided that the questionnaire was not a matter of public concern, and it accordingly ruled against Myers.

Justice Brennan (for Marshall, Blackmun, and Stevens) dissented. He argued that the Court's conclusion that the questionnaire was not speech on a matter of public concern was too narrow and not sufficiently protective of free speech values. Note that the public employee speech doctrine, like commercial speech doctrine, is not fully integrated into the Two Track system.

RANKIN v. McPHERSON
483 U.S. 378 (1987)

JUSTICE MARSHALL delivered the opinion of the Court.

[McPherson was a clerical employee in a county constable's office and was terminated after she remarked to a co-worker, after hearing of an attempt to assassinate the President, "If they go for him again, I hope they get him." She was not a commissioned peace officer, did not wear a uniform, was not authorized to make arrests or carry a weapon, and was not in contact with the public in her job. The statement was made during a private conversation in a room not accessible to the public. Upon ascertaining that McPherson actually had made the remark and hearing her verify that she "meant" it, the constable terminated her, explaining that she should not be able to "ride with the cops while she cheers for the robbers." The court of appeals held that McPherson's remark had addressed a matter of public concern and that the government's interest in maintaining efficiency in the workplace did not outweigh the first amendment interest in protecting McPherson's speech. Here, the Supreme Court affirms.]

The determination whether a public employer has properly discharged an employee for engaging in speech requires "a balance between the interests of the [employee], as a citizen, in commenting upon matters of public concern and the interest of the State, as an employer, in promoting the efficiency of the public services it performs through its employees." *Pickering v. Board of Education*, 391 U.S. 563, 568 (1968); *Connick v. Myers*, 461 U.S. 138 (1983). This balancing is necessary in order to accommodate the dual role of the public employer as a provider of public services and as a government entity operating under the constraints of the First Amendment. . . .

A

The threshold question in applying this balancing test is whether McPherson's speech may be "fairly characterized as constituting speech on a matter of public concern." Considering the statement in context, as *Connick* requires, discloses that it plainly dealt with a matter of public concern. The statement was made in the course of a conversation addressing the policies of the President's administration. It came on the heels of a news bulletin regarding what is certainly a matter of heightened public attention: an attempt on the life of the President. While a statement that amounted to a threat to kill the President would not be protected by the First Amendment, the District Court concluded, and we agree, that McPherson's statement did not amount to a threat punishable under 18 U.S.C. § 871(a) or 18 U.S.C. § 2385, or, indeed, that could properly be criminalized at all. . . .

B

Because McPherson's statement addressed a matter of public concern, *Pickering* next requires that we balance McPherson's interest in making her statement against "the interest of the State, as an employer, in promoting the efficiency of the public services it performs through its employees." The State bears a burden of justifying the discharge on legitimate grounds. *Connick.*

In performing the balancing, the statement will not be considered in a vacuum; the manner, time, and place of the employee's expression are relevant, as is the context in which the dispute arose. . . .

These considerations, and indeed the very nature of the balancing test, make apparent that the state interest element of the test focuses on the effective functioning of the public employer's enterprise. Interference with work, personnel relationships, or the speaker's job performance can detract from the public employer's function; avoiding such interference can be a strong state interest. From this perspective, however, petitioner fails to demonstrate a state interest that outweighs McPherson's First Amendment rights. While McPherson's statement was made at the workplace, there is no evidence that it interfered with the efficient functioning of the office. The Constable was evidently not afraid that McPherson had disturbed or interrupted other employees—he did not inquire to whom respondent had made the remark. . . .

Nor was there any danger that McPherson had discredited the office by making her statement in public. . . .

[N]or is there any evidence that employees other than [the co-worker] who worked in the room even heard the remark. Not only was McPherson's discharge unrelated to the functioning of the office, it was not based on any assessment by the constable that the remark demonstrated a character trait that made respondent unfit to perform her work.

[I]n weighing the State's interest in discharging an employee based on any claim that the content of a statement made by the employee somehow undermines the mission of the public employer, some attention must be paid to the responsibilities of the employee within the agency. The burden of caution employees bear with respect to the words they speak will vary with the extent of authority and public accountability the employee's role entails. Where, as here, an employee serves no confidential, policymaking, or public contact role, the danger to the agency's successful function from that employee's private speech is minimal. . . .

Affirmed.

Justice Powell concurring. . . .

There is no dispute that McPherson's comment was made during a private conversation with a co-worker who happened also to be her boyfriend. She had no intention or expectation that it would be overheard or acted on by others. Given this, I think it is unnecessary to engage in the extensive analysis normally required by *Connick v. Myers.* . . . If a statement is on a matter of public concern, as it was here, it will be an unusual case where the employer's legitimate interests will be so great as to justify punishing an employee for this type of private speech that routinely takes place at all levels in the workplace. The risk that a single, offhand comment directed to only one other worker will lower morale, disrupt the work force, or otherwise undermine the mission of the office borders on the fanciful. To the extent that the full constitutional analysis of the competing interests is required, I generally agree with the Court's opinion. . . .

Justice Scalia, with whom The Chief Justice, Justice White, and Justice O'Connor join, dissenting.

I agree with the proposition, felicitously put by Constable Rankin's counsel, that no law enforcement agency is required by the First Amendment to permit one of its employees to "ride with the cops and cheer for the robbers". . . .

[W]e have held that the First Amendment's protection against adverse personnel decisions extends only to speech on matters of "public concern," *Connick, supra.* . . .

McPherson fails this threshold requirement. The statement for which she was fired—and the only statement the Constable heard—was, "If they go for him again, I hope they get him." It is important to bear in mind the District Judge's finding that this was *not* hyperbole. . . .

Given the meaning of the remark, there is no basis for the Court's suggestion that McPherson's criticisms of the president's policies that immediately preceded the remark can illuminate it insuch fashion as to render it constitutionally protected. [T]he majority's magical transformation of the *motive* for McPherson's statement into its *content* is as misguided as viewing a political assassination preceded by a harangue as nothing more than a strong denunciation of the victim's political views. . . .

McPherson's statement is indeed so different from [statements protected in prior decisions] that it is only one step removed from statements that we have previously held entitled to no First Amendment protection, even in the nonemployment context—including assassination threats against the President (which are illegal under 18 U.S.C. § 871), *see Frohwerk v. United States,* 249 U.S. 204, 206 (1919); "fighting words," *Chaplinsky v. New Hampshire,* 315 U.S. 568, 572 (1942); epithets or personal abuse; and advocacy of force or violence. . . .

Even if I agreed that McPherson's statement was speech on a matter of "public concern," I would still find it unprotected. . . . [W]e are asked to determine whether, given the interests of this law enforcement office McPherson had a *right* to say what she did—;so that she could not only not be fired for it, but could not be formally reprimanded for it, or even prevented from repeating it endlessly into the future. It boggles the mind to think that she has such a right.

[In *Connick,*] [a]lthough we held that one [part of the employee's expression]—dealing with pressure in the office to participate in political campaigns—satisfied the "public concern" requirement, we held that the discharge nonetheless did not violate the First Amendment because the [expression] itself "carrie[d] the clear potential for undermining office relations." Statements like McPherson's obviously carry a similar potential in an office devoted to law enforcement. . . .

The Court's sweeping assertion (and apparent holding) that where an employee "serves no confidential, policymaking, or public contact role, the danger to the agency's successful function from that employee's private speech is minimal," is simply contrary to reason and experience. Nonpolicymaking employees (the assistant district attorney in *Connick,* for example) can hurt working relationships and undermine public confidence in an organization every bit as much as policymaking employees. . . .

In sum, since Constable Rankin's interest in maintaining both an esprit de corps and a public image consistent with his office's law enforcement duties outweighs any interest his employees may have in expressing on the job a desire that the President be killed, even assuming that such an expression addresses a matter of public concern it is not protected by the First Amendment from suppression. . . .

NOTES AND QUESTIONS

(1) *Holmes' "No Constitutional Right to be a Policeman" Statement.* Reconsider Holmes' famous epigram that "a policeman may have a constitutional right to talk politics, but he has no constitutional right to be a policeman." How much is left of this "traditional" principle?

(2) *"Private" Speech: The Proper Definition and Balance.* The *Connick-Rankin* approach affords constitutional protection to "private" speech, but the protection is less than that given to speech "on a matter of public concern." Is "private" speech, then, in a category similar to that of "commercial" speech, in the sense that it is entitled to a lesser degree of protection? *Cf. Dun & Bradstreet, Inc. v. Greenmoss Builders, Inc.*, above (lesser protection for credit reportthan upon "other types of utterances" in the libel context, apparently because it has less value as "private" than "public" speech.)

(3) *"Public Concern."* *Rankin* obviously makes the outcome depend heavily upon whether the speech is characterized as dealing with a "matter of public concern." Does the majority correctly characterize McPherson's statement as concerning a "matter of public concern," or does Justice Scalia come closer to the mark by asserting that this characterization "boggles the mind," since McPherson would have a right to "repeat it endlessly?"

(4) *What Constitutes "Disruptive" Speech by a Public Employee?: Waters v. Churchill, 511 U.S. 661 (1994).* Churchill was an obstetrics nurse at a public hospital. According to her supervisors ("defendants"), she was fired after she allegedly made disparaging remarks about her supervisors during a work break to another nurse and discouraged that nurse from joining the obstetrics staff. Churchill's version of the conversation was that she made only nondisruptive comments about the hospital's policies. After Churchill sued, the district court granted summary judgment to the defendants on the ground that neither version of Churchill's comments was a "matter of public concern." The Court disagreed and reversed the summary judgment and remanded for a trial on the merits.

The Court's plurality, per Justice O'Connor, concluded that, while the *Connick* test should be applied to what the government employer actually believed the facts were, the government employer's belief about the employee's speech must be *reasonable* and that the employer must conduct an investigation to satisfy this reasonableness requirement. *See also* United States v. National Treasury Employees Union, 513 U.S. 454 (1995) (confirming the burden of proof on this issue rests on the government). The *Churchill* plurality also determined that, if the government employer actually believed the supervisors' version of the facts, Churchill's speech was sufficiently "disruptive" to justify the firing.

(5) *The Expansion of Public Employee Free Speech Protection to "Independent Contractors": Board of County Commissioners v. Umbehr, 518 U.S. 668 (1996).* Umbehr had an at-will contract to haul trash for the County, but Umbehr was an "outspoken critic" of the County Board of Commissioners: he wrote letters to the editor, accused the commissioners of financial mismanagement, and even ran (unsuccessfully) for the Board. The Commissioners eventually voted to terminate (non-renew) Umbehr's trash-hauling contract. Relying on the "similarities between government employees and government contractors," the Supreme Court, per Justice O'Connor, held that independent contractors could not be terminated in retaliation for exercising First Amendment rights. Justice Scalia, joined by Justice Thomas, dissented.

(6) *The Public Employee Speech Doctrine in the Roberts Court: Garcetti v. Ceballos, 547 U.S. 410 (2006).* Ceballos was a calendar (supervising) deputy district attorney in Los Angeles County. Part of his job responsibilities required that he review criminal prosecutions by his office. In one instance, he reviewed the Sheriff's affidavit regarding a search, and he informed his supervisors in a written "disposition memo" that the affidavit was flawed. He also alleged wrongdoing by the Sheriff's Office. His supervisors ignored his advice and continued the prosecution. Ceballos was also called

as a witness by the defendant at the suppression hearing, but the court ruled in favor of the prosecution. Ceballos alleged that, as a result of his memo (and testimony), he was subjected to a demotion and other adverse employment actions. Ceballos sued under 42 U.S.C. § 1983 for "retaliation" against his free speech rights.

Although the court of appeals had decided that Ceballos' memo alleging wrongdoing was protected as employee speech on a matter of "public concern," the Supreme Court, per Justice Kennedy in a 5-4 decision, ruled for the County. The Court concluded that Ceballos' expressions were made "pursuant to his duties as a calendar deputy." The Court held that "when employees make statements pursuant to their official duties, the employees are not speaking as citizens for First Amendment purposes. . . ." Thus, the majority did not apply the two-part *Connick/Rankin* standard. *See also City of San Diego v. Roe*, 543 U.S. 77 (2004). There were four dissenters. Justice Breyer's dissent, only for himself, seemed to reject the entire *Connick/Rankin* standard. When reviewing the majority opinion, students should consider the "government speech" materials in § 11.07[8][1] above. Note that, as the concept of government speech would expand, the scope of protected employee speech about matters of public concern will shrink. For discussion of the difficulties in determining when speech is pursuant to an employee's job duties, *see* Charles W. "Rocky" Rhodes, *Public Employee Speech Rights Fall Prey to An Emerging Doctrinal Formalism*, 15 WM. & MARY BILL OF RIGHTS J. 1173 (2007).

PROBLEM U

HOW MUCH FREEDOM OF EXPRESSION FOR AN AIR FORCE GENERAL?: TRASHING CLINTON DRAWS REPRIMAND, HOUSTON CHRONICLE, June 19, 1993, § A, at 2, col. 5. At an awards dinner, Air Force General Harold Campbell publicly called President Clinton a "pot-smoking," "womanizing," "draft-dodging" Commander-in-Chief. Despite the general's honorable 32-year career, the response was swift: the Air Force Chief of Staff announced a few days later that General Campbell had agreed to punishment that included a fine "in the neighborhood of $7,000," a letter of reprimand, and retirement from the service. President Clinton called this response "appropriate," and the Chief of Staff said it would "sustain integrity [of] and respectfor the chain of command." (Reportedly, however, the Chief of Staff privately disclosed that he considered the penalty insufficient and actually wanted to court-martial General Campbell). Questions: (1) Does this speech deal with a matter of public concern? (2) Does it make a difference if Campbell can demonstrate that his statements were true? (3) Is the General's punishment consistent with *Rankin v. McPherson?* (4) If so, does an Air Force general have any First Amendment protection at all?

[3]   Government Employees' or Licensees' Freedom of Belief or Association

ELROD v. BURNS, 427 U.S. 347 (1976). In 1970, the Sheriff of Cook County, a Republican, was replaced by Elrod, a Democrat. Burns and others were employees of the Sheriff's office, and all Republicans; they had no civil service protection. It had been the practice of the Sheriff of Cook County, upon assuming office from a Sheriff of a different political party, to replace non-civil service employees with members of his own party, and consequently Elrod discharged Burns and others. The Supreme Court, with a plurality opinion by Justice Brennan, held that these political patronage dismissals violated rights of political belief and association protected by the first amendment:

> Patronage practice is not new to American politics. It has existed at the federal level at least since the presidency of Thomas Jefferson, although its popularization and legitimation primarily occurred later, in the presidency of Andrew Jackson [who followed the principle that, to the victor belong the spoils]. More recent times have witnessed a strong decline in its use. . . .

It is not only belief and association which are restricted where political patronage is the practice. The free functioning of the electoral process also suffers. Conditioning public employment on partisan support prevents support of competing political interests. [P]atronage thus tips the electoral process in favor of the incumbent party. . . .

Although the practice of patronage dismissals clearly infringes first amendment interests, our inquiry is not at an end, for the prohibition on encroachment of first amendment protections is not any absolute. Restraints are permitted for appropriate reasons. . . .

One interest which has been offered as a justification of patronage is the need to insure effective government and the efficiency of public employees. It is argued that employees of political persuasions not the same as that of the party in control of public office will not have the incentive to work effectively and may even be motivated to subvert the incumbent administration's efforts to govern effectively. We are not persuaded. The inefficiency resulting from the wholesale replacement of large numbers of public employees every time political office changes hands belies this justification. [F]urther, it is not clear that dismissal in order to make room for a patronage appointment will result in replacement by a person more qualified to do the job since appointment often occurs in exchange for the delivery of votes, or other party service, not job capability. More fundamentally, however, the argument does not succeed because it is doubtful that the mere difference of political persuasion motivates poor performance; nor do we think it legitimately may be used as basis for imputing such behavior.

A second interest advanced in support of patronage is the need for politically loyal employees, not to the end that effectiveness and efficiency be insured, but to the end thatrepresentative government not be undercut by tactics obstructing the implementation of policies of the new administration, policies presumably sanctioned by the electorate. [L]imiting patronage dismissals to policymaking positions is sufficient to achieve this governmental end. Nonpolicymaking individuals usually have only limited responsibility and are therefore not in a position to thwart the goals of the in-party. . . .

It is argued that a third interest supporting patronage dismissals is the preservation of the democratic process. According to petitioners, "We have contrived no system for the support of party that does not place considerable reliance on patronage. The party organization makes a democratic government work and charges a price for its services". . . .

Patronage dismissals . . . are not the least-restrictive alternative to achieving the contribution they may make to the democratic process. The process functions as well without the practice, perhaps even better, for patronage dismissals clearly also retard that process. . . .

Justice Stewart, joined by Justice Blackmun, concurred only in the judgment. Chief Justice Burger, Justice Powell, and Justice Rehnquist dissented, with Justice Powell maintaining that the majority's decision "may well disserve—rather than promote—core values of the first amendment:"

[W]e deal here with a highly practical and rather fundamental element of our political system, not the theoretical abstractions of a political science seminar. In concluding that patronage hiring practices are unconstitutional, the plurality seriously underestimates the strength of the government interest—especially at the local level—in allowing some patronage hiring practices, and it exaggerates the perceived burden on first amendment rights.

[P]atronage hiring practices have contributed to American democracy by stimulating political activity and by strengthening parties, thereby helping to make government accountable. [W]e also have recognized the strong government interest in encouraging stable political parties and avoiding excessive political fragmentation.

Without analysis, however, the plurality opinion disparages the contribution of patronage hiring practices in advancing the state interest.

I . . . conclude that patronage hiring practices sufficiently serve important state interests, including some interests sought to be advanced by the first amendment, to justify a tolerable intrusion on the first amendment interests of employees or potential employees. . . .

NOTES AND QUESTIONS

(1) *Comparing the Plurality, Concurrence, and Dissent in Elrod: Is the Dissent Correct in Comparing the Plurality Approach to "The Theoretical Abstractions of a Political Science Seminar?"* Justice Brennan's plurality opinion in *Elrod* is subject to the criticism that it makes a political judgment that is better left to other branches. For example, Justice Brennan concludes that "[T]he [democratic] process functions as well without the [patronage] practice, perhaps even better, for patronage dismissals clearly also retard that process." Consider whether Justice Stewart's approach, that a non-policy making employee cannot be discharged "upon the sole ground of his political beliefs," is better. Does this holding mean that the incumbent sheriff can require employees to conform their behavior to his political preferences, including joining theparty or at least not working against it, as long as he does not invade their "beliefs?" Finally, consider whether the dissent is correct in rejecting "the theoretical abstractions of a political science seminar" in preference for "a highly practical and rather fundamental element of our political system." *See also Rutan v. Republican Party*, 497 U.S. 62 (1990) (just as termination of employees based upon spoils system violates their right of association, so may hiring, promotion, transfer, and recall after layoff).

(2) *The First Amendment's Protection of Political Belief and Affiliation Extended to "Independent Contractors":O'Hare Truck Service, Inc. v. City of Northlake, 518 U.S. 712 (1996).* O'Hare Truck Service had been a participating contractor on the City of Northlake's "rotation" list for towing services for nearly thirty years, but O'Hare's owner refused to contribute to the mayor's reelection campaign and openly supported the mayor's opponent. "[S]oon, after, O'Hare was removed from the rotation list" in response. Although the lower courts refused to extend protection to O'Hare Truck Service, the Supreme Court, per Justice Kennedy, held that a government's interest in political patronage "does not justify the coercion of a person's political beliefs and associations," and the Court further held that this principle applied to independent contractors as well as public employees. Because of the procedural posture of the case, the Court remanded for discovery and trial. Justice Scalia, joined by Justice Thomas, dissented.

(3) *Union Shops and Exclusive Collective Bargaining on Behalf of Public Employees: Abood v. Detroit Board of Education, 431 U.S. 209 (1977).* Abood concerned a Michigan statute that permitted an "agency shop" arrangement, whereby every employee exclusively was represented by a union as collective bargaining agent, and, even though not a union member, was required to pay to the union a service charge equal in amount to union dues. The Supreme Court, per Justice Stewart, held that forced payments to finance collective-bargaining, contract administration, and grievance adjustment were valid. However, the first amendment protected Abood's freedom of belief and association, so that he constitutionally could not be forced to contribute to the support of ideological causes advanced by the union:

Our decisions establish with unmistakable clarity that the freedom of an individual to associate for the purpose of advancing beliefs and ideas is protected by the first and fourteenth amendments. *E.g., Elrod v. Burns.* . . .

We do not hold that a union cannot constitutionally spend funds for the expression of political views, on behalf of political candidates, or toward the advancement of other ideological causes not germane to its duties as collective-bargaining representative. Rather, the constitution requires only that such expenditures be financed from charges, dues, or assessments paid by employees who do not object to advancing those ideas and who are not coerced into doing so against their will by the threat of loss of government employment.

Consider whether the logical extensions of this decision make sense. For example, does this decision mean that a mandatory bar association cannot lobby the legislature or engage in other kinds of political advocacy?

(4) *Political Activities and Law-Reform Lobbying By Bar Associations With Compulsory Dues: Keller v. California State Bar, 496 U.S. 1 (1990)*. This case concerned the California State Bar, which used compulsory dues of members to lobby for law reform concerning general criminal, tax, and other legislation, as well as filing amicus curiae briefs. Since the California State Bar is a "mandatory" bar—meaning that an attorney must be a member to practice law—members were compelled to pay dues which were used to support these activities, whether individual members agreed with them or not. The Court, per Chief Justice Rehnquist, citing *Abood*, heldthis use of compulsory dues to be unconstitutional, unless the expenditures were incurred for the purpose of regulating the legal profession or improving the quality of legal services.

(5) *Mandatory Assessments on Agricultural Growers To Finance Collective "Generic Advertising" Do Not Violate Free Speech Rights: Glickman v. Wileman Brothers & Elliot, Inc., 521 U.S. 457 (1997)*. Under the Agricultural Marketing Agreement Act of 1937 and regulations of the Secretary of Agriculture, a "tree fruit" commodity committee imposed mandatory assessments on Wileman Brothers to cover various costs of operating the committee, including paying for generic advertising promotion of "tree fruit" product consumption. Certain growers objected to the mandatory assessments for the generic advertising on free speech grounds. The Supreme Court, per Justice Stevens, upheld the mandatory assessments. The majority determined that the mandatory assessments "cannot be said to engender any crisis of conscience," and thereby distinguished *Abood* and *Keller*, above. The Court, therefore, refused to apply any form of heightened scrutiny (Track One, Track Two or even the commercial speech standard) to the claim. Justice Souter, joined by Chief Justice Rehnquist and Justices Scalia and Thomas, dissented: "forced payment for commercial speech should be subject to the same level of judicial scrutiny as any restriction on communications in that category."

§ 11.09 FREEDOM OF ASSOCIATION AND RELATED CONCEPTS

[A] Associational Privacy

NAACP v. ALABAMA, 377 U.S. 288 (1964). Alabama sought to require the NAACP to disclose the names and addresses of its Alabama members. The NAACP demonstrated that members whose identities had been disclosed had been subjected to threats, job losses, and other hostility. The Court held the required disclosure unconstitutional: "Privacy in group association may in many circumstances be indispensable in preservation of freedom of association, particularly where a group espouses dissident beliefs." To overcome the association rights at issue, only a compelling or "subordinating" state interest, which could not be achieved by less restrictive means, would suffice.

TALLEY v. CALIFORNIA
362 U.S. 60 (1960)

Mr. Justice Black delivered the opinion of the Court.

[A Los Angeles ordinance provided, "No person shall distribute any handbill in any place under any circumstances, which does not have printed on the cover, or the face thereof, the name and address of the [printer and distributor of the handbill]. Talley was convicted for passing out handbills for the National Consumers Mobilization. Here, the Supreme Court reverses the conviction. The Court describes the Los Angeles ordinance as "broad," and emphasizes that it bars "distribution of 'any handbill in any place under any circumstances.' "]

Anonymous pamphlets, leaflets, brochures and even books have played an important role in the progress of mankind. Persecuted groups and sects from time to time throughout history havebeen able to criticize oppressive practices and laws either anonymously or not at all. The obnoxious press licensing law of England, which was also enforced in the Colonies, was due in part to the knowledge that exposure of the names of printers, writers and distributors would lessen the circulation of literature critical of the government. The old seditious libel cases in England show the lengths to which government had to go to find out who was responsible for books that were obnoxious to the rulers. John Lilburne was whipped, pilloried and fined for refusing to answer questions designed to get evidence to convict him or someone else for the secret distribution of books in England. Two Puritan Ministers, John Penry and John Udal, were sentenced to death on charges that they were responsible for writing, printing or publishing books. Before the Revolutionary War colonial patriots frequently had to conceal their authorship or distribution of literature that easily could have brought down on them prosecutions by English-controlled courts. [E]ven the Federalist Papers, written in favor of the adoption of our Constitution, were published under fictitious names. It is plain that anonymity has sometimes been assumed for the most constructive purposes.

We have recently had occasion to hold . . . that there are times and circumstances when States may not compel members of groups engaged in the dissemination of ideas to be publicly identified. [T]he reason for those holdings was that identification and fear of reprisal might deter perfectly peaceful discussions of public matters of importance. This broad Los Angeles ordinance is subject to the same infirmity. . . .

Mr. Justice Harlan, concurring. . . .

Here the state says that this ordinance is aimed at the prevention of "fraud, deceit, false advertising, negligent use of words, obscenity, and libel. [I] think it will not do for the state simply to say that the circulation of all anonymous handbills must be suppressed in order to identify the distributors of those that may be of an obnoxious character. . . .

Mr. Justice Clark, whom Mr. Justice Frankfurter and Mr. Justice Whittaker joined, dissenting. . . .

[T]alley makes no showing whatsoever to support his contention that a restraint upon his freedom of speech will result from the enforcement of the ordinance. The existence of such a restraint is necessary before we can strike the ordinance down.

[T]his Court has approved laws requiring no less than Los Angeles' ordinance. I submit that they control this case and require its approval under the attack made here. First, Lewis Publishing Co. v. Morgan, 229 U.S. 288 (1913), upheld an act of Congress requiring any newspaper using the second-class mails to publish the names of its editor, publisher, owner, and stockholders. [S]econd, in the Federal Regulation of Lobbying Act, . . . Congress requires those engaged in lobbying to divulge their identity and to give "a modicum of information" to Congress. *United States v. Harriss*, 347 U.S. 612 (1954). Third, the several states have corrupt practices acts outlawing, *inter alia*, the distribution of anonymous publications with respect to political candidates. While these statutes are levelled at political campaign and election practices, the underlying ground sustaining their validity applies with equal force here. . . .

PROBLEM V

DRAFTING THE WEST YORK CAMPAIGN REPORTING AND DISCLOSURE ACT— PRINTING INDUSTRIES OF THE GULF COAST, INC. v. HILL, 382 F. Supp. 801 (S.D. Tex. 1974), *judgment vacated*, 422 U.S. 937 (1975). The West York Secretary of State has promulgated a report indicating that legislation is needed to combat "dirty tricks" in election campaigns. One of the most serious of these is the "falsely attributed smear:" A candidate issues a false smear of a rival candidate, then attributes the smear to *another* rival candidate, and thus misleadingly embarrasses both rivals. In order to combat this deceptive practice within the time frame of an election campaign, the Secretary of State believes that every piece of campaign literature must disclose both the name and address of the printer and the name and address of the person distributing the advertisement. A falsely attributed smear thus can be traced, or, if the literature does not conform to the law, that fact may be pointed out.

Question: Would such a law be constitutional? Notice that it contains many of the characteristics of the ordinance condemned in *Talley*, above—but it also is far more narrowly circumscribed and is directed to a specific evil, as the dissenters in *Talley* point out. [The Court in *Printing Industries*, above, held such a statute unconstitutional on its face, as a violation of the freedoms of speech and association.] Consider the following case.

BROWN v. SOCIALIST WORKERS' '74 CAMPAIGN COMMITTEE, 459 U.S. 87 (1982). The disclosure provisions of the Ohio Campaign Expense Reporting Law required every candidate for political office to report the names and addresses of campaign contributors and recipients of campaign disbursements. The Court, per Justice Marshall, held that these requirements could not constitutionally be applied to the Socialist Workers' Party (SWP), which was a minor political party that historically had been the object of harassment by government officials and private parties:

> [A]ppellants seriously understate the threat to first amendment rights that would result from requiring minor parties to disclose the recipients of campaign disbursements. Expenditures by a political party often consist of reimbursements, advances, or wages paid to party members, campaign workers, and supporters, whose activities lie at the very core of the first amendment. Disbursements may also go to persons who choose to express their support for an unpopular cause by providing services rendered scarce by public hostility and suspicion. Should their involvement be publicized, these persons would be as vulnerable to threats, harassment, and reprisals as are contributors whose connection with the party is solely financial. Even individuals who receive disbursements for "merely" commercial transactions may be deterred. . . .

Justice O'Connor, joined by Justices Rehnquist and Stevens, dissented in part.

NOTES AND QUESTIONS

(1) *Anonymous Literature about Referenda Issued by Ad Hoc Groups: McIntyre v. Ohio Elections Comm'n, 514 U.S. 334 (1995).* Ohio's election law prohibited the distribution of campaign literature that did not contain the name and address of the person or campaign issuing the literature. The Ohio Elections Commission fined Margaret McIntyre when, in opposing a proposed school tax levy, she distributed

leaflets whose authorship was identified only as CONCERNED PARENTS AND TAX PAYERS. Although the Ohio Supreme Court upheld the ban on anonymous campaign literature, the Supreme Court, per Justice Stevens, reversed. TheCourt held that anonymous speech is protected and that the Ohio statute was a content-based regulation. Applying strict scrutiny, the Court held that, although Ohio may have a compelling interest in preventing election fraud, the prohibition on all anonymous campaign literature failed the means prong of strict scrutiny because it was not "narrowly tailored." The holding was based on the "blunderbuss approach" of Ohio's law, prohibiting all uses of anonymous campaign literature, and thus the opinion leaves open the possibility of disclosure requirements directed to candidates, ballot-registered parties, or other circumstances.

(2) *"Anti-Fusion" Statutes that Prevent a Minor Party from "Double-Nominating" a Major-Party Candidate Already on the Ballot: Timmons v. Twin Cities Area New Party, 520 U.S. 351 (1997).* In *Timmons*, the Court examined the constitutionality of "anti-fusion" statutes. A minority political party in Minnesota (the New Party) wanted to nominate a candidate for political office who already held a nomination from another party. This process, called "fusion," was prohibited by statute in Minnesota. The New Party challenged the prohibition as a restriction on its associational rights under the First and Fourteenth Amendments. The Court, per Chief Justice Rehnquist, upheld the restriction using a form of the rational basis standard. The Court determined that the burdens placed upon the rights of the New Party were slight since it could nominate another candidate or could endorse the candidate of another party without that candidate being formally associated with the party on the ballot. Due to the insignificance of the burden on the associational rights of the New Party, the Court subjected the ban to "less exacting review."

[B] Concerted Action As "Speech"

NAACP v. CLAIBORNE HARDWARE CO.
458 U.S. 886 (1982)

JUSTICE STEVENS delivered the opinion of the Court.

[The local NAACP organized a boycott of white merchants in Claiborne County, Mississippi. Claiborne Hardware Co. and other merchants sued the NAACP and certain participants in the boycott and recovered judgment holding them jointly and severally liable for all of the merchants' lost earnings during a seven-year period on three separate conspiracy theories, including the tort of malicious interference with the merchants' businesses. The Mississippi Supreme Court upheld the imposition of liability on this basis. Here, the Supreme Court reverses and holds that the non-violent elements of the boycott were entitled to the protection of the first amendment.]

The boycott of white merchants at issue in this case took many forms. The boycott was launched at a meeting of a local branch of the NAACP attended by several hundred persons. Its acknowledged purpose was to secure compliance by both civic and business leaders with a lengthy list of demands for equality and racial justice. The boycott was supported by speeches and nonviolent picketing. Participants repeatedly encouraged others to join in its cause.

Each of these elements of the boycott is a form of speech or conduct that is ordinarily entitled to protection under the First and Fourteenth Amendments. "[T]he practice of persons sharing common views banding together to achieve a common end is deeply embedded in the American political process". . . .

. . . Petitioners admittedly sought to persuade others to join the boycott through social pressure and the "threat" of social ostracism. Speech does not lose its protected character, however, simply because it may embarrass others or coerce them into action. . . .

The presence of protected activity, however, does not end the relevant constitutional inquiry. Governmental regulation that has an incidental effect on First Amendment freedoms may be justified in certain narrowly defined instances. *See United States v. O'Brien*, 391 U.S. 367. A nonviolent and totally voluntary boycott may have a disruptive effect on local economic conditions. This Court has recognized the strong governmental interest in certain forms of economic regulation, even though such regulation may have an incidental effect on rights of speech and association. *See Giboney v. Empire Storage & Ice Co.*, 336 U.S. 490. The right of business entities to "associate" to suppress competition may be curtailed. *National Society of Professional Engineers v. United States*, 435 U.S. 679. Unfair trade practices may be restricted. Secondary boycotts and picketing by labor unions may be prohibited, as part of "Congress' striking of the delicate balance between union freedom of expression and the ability of neutral employers, employees, and consumers to remain free from coerced participation in industrial strife. . . ."

While States have broad power to regulate economic activity, we do not find a comparable right to prohibit peaceful political activity such as that found in the boycott in this case. This Court has recognized that expression on public issues "has always rested on the highest rung of the hierarchy of First Amendment values". . . .

[T]he "right of petition is one of the freedoms protected by the Bill of Rights, and we cannot, of course, lightly impute to Congress an intent to invade these freedoms". . . .

It is not disputed that a major purpose of the boycott in this case was to influence governmental action. . . . [T]he petitioners certainly foresaw—and directly intended—that the merchants would sustain economic injury as a result of their campaign. . . . [H]owever, the purpose of petitioners' campaign was not to destroy legitimate competition. Petitioners sought to vindicate rights of equality and of freedom that lie at the heart of the Fourteenth Amendment itself. The right of the States to regulate economic activity could not justify a complete prohibition against a nonviolent, politically motivated boycott designed to force governmental and economic change and to effectuate rights guaranteed by the Constitution itself.

[The Court went on to analyze acts of violence that had occurred during the boycott. The Mississippi Supreme Court had held that these acts of violence, which it imputed attributed to the NAACP and other petitioners, were a partial basis for liability. The Supreme Court held that the record did not support this imposition of liability.]

NOTES AND QUESTIONS

(1) *Distinguishing Association for "Political" Purposes, as in Claiborne Hardware, From Association for "Economic" Purposes.* As the cases cited in *Claiborne Hardware* indicate, concerted action for economic ends, even if it involves the same sort of speech components at issue in *Claiborne Hardware*, may be regulated. Consider whether the distinction drawn in *Claiborne Hardware* is persuasive. Wasn't the issue, with which the NAACP and other petitioners in *Claiborne Hardware* were concerned, at least partially "economic" in nature?

(2) *The Right of Petition.* Notice that the Court refers not only to the right of association, but also to the right to petition the government for a redress of grievances, an express First Amendment right. Consider whether the result in *Claiborne Hardware* can be defended better on the ground that the speech and conduct at issue were protected by the right of petition, rather than by freedom-of-association reasoning.

[C]   The Right to Exclude (or Meet Privately With) Others: Private (and Not-So-Private) Clubs

BOARD OF DIRECTORS OF ROTARY INTERNATIONAL v. ROTARY CLUB OF DUARTE
481 U.S. 537 (1987)

Justice Powell delivered the opinion of the Court.

[California's Unruh Civil Rights Act provides, in part: "All persons within the jurisdiction of this state are free and equal, and no matter what their sex, race, color, religion, ancestry, or national origin are entitled to the full and equal accommodations, advantages, facilities, privileges, or services in all business establishments of every kind whatsoever."

[The Rotary Club of Duarte admitted three women to active membership. Rotary Club International then revoked its charter, because the International Club was limited to male members. In response, the Duarte Club and two of its women members sued Rotary International, alleging that enforcement of its male-only policy violated the Unruh Act. International argued that this application of the Unruh Act would violate its, and its members', constitutionally protected rights of private association and expression.

[There were more than 19,000 Rotary Clubs, with a total membership of more than 900,000. The membership system was designed to insure a representative of "every worthy and recognized business, professional, or institutional activity." Evidence showed that members enjoyed certain business advantages from the Association, performed public services, and appreciated the "fellowship enjoyed by the present male membership." Based upon these facts, the California Court of Appeal held that Rotary Clubs were business establishments covered by the Unruh Act and rejected Rotary International's First Amendment arguments. Here, the Supreme Court affirms.]

The Court has recognized that the freedom to enter into and carry on certain intimate or private relationships is a fundamental element of liberty protected by the Bill of Rights. . . . *See Moore v. East Cleveland*. We have not attempted to mark the precise boundaries of this type of constitutional protection. The intimate relationships to which we have accorded constitutional protection include marriage, *Zablocki v. Redhail*, . . .; the begetting and bearing of children, *Carey v. Population Services International*, . . .; child rearing and education, *Pierce v. Society of Sisters*, . . .; and cohabitation with relatives, *Moore v. East Cleveland* [each of these cases is reproduced or discussed in Chapter 9, above]. [W]e have emphasized that the first amendment protects those relationships . . . that presuppose "deep attachments and commitments to thenecessarily few other individuals with whom one shares not only a special community of thoughts, experiences, and beliefs but also distinctively personal aspects of one's life."

The evidence in this case indicates that the relationship among Rotary Club members is not the kind of intimate or private relationship that warrants constitutional protection. The size of local Rotary Clubs ranges from fewer than 20 to more than 900. There is no upper limit. . . . About ten percent of the membership of a typical club moves away or drops out during a typical year. [T]he clubs therefore are instructed to "keep a flow of prospects coming." [T]he purpose of Rotary "is to produce an inclusive, not exclusive, membership, making possible the recognition of all useful local occupations, and enabling the club to be a true cross section of the business and professional life of the community". . . .

Many of the Rotary Clubs' central activities are carried on in the presence of strangers. [I]n sum, Rotary Clubs, rather than carrying on their activities in an atmosphere of privacy, seek to keep their "windows and doors open to the whole world". . . . We therefore conclude that application of the Unruh Act to local Rotary Clubs does not interfere unduly with the members' freedom of private association.

[The Court went on to hold that application of the Unruh Act did not infringe either Rotary's or its members right to free expression. "As a matter of policy, Rotary Clubs do not take positions on 'public questions' including political or international issues." Furthermore, "[e]ven if the Unruh Act does work some slight infringement on Rotary members' right of expressive association, that infringement is justified because it serves the state's compelling interest in eliminating discrimination against women."] . . .

The judgment of the Court of Appeal of California is affirmed.

NOTES AND QUESTIONS

(1) *The Nature of the Right of Association.* The Court in *Rotary Club* appears to test the existence of the right of association, at least in the sense of the right to exclude others, by such concerns as privacy, permanence, and intimacy. Is this test appropriate? Might there be instances in which relatively brief, non-private, non-intimate associations should be protected, particularly if they impinge upon other fundamental liberties (such as expression)? *Cf.* Note, *Private Club Membership: Where Does Privacy End and Discrimination Begin?*, 61 St. John's L. Rev. 474 (1987).

(2) *The Unruh Act—Could It, by Its Breadth and Vagueness, Result in the Infringement Rather than Protection of Civil Liberties?* The Unruh Act applies only to "business establishments," but as this case indicates, it can be applied to entities that are not very similar to traditional business establishments. Is the breadth of the enactment such that it could threaten the rights of association, or privacy, or expression?

(3) *Is There a "Right to Dance" With a Person of a Different Age—Under the Rubric of the Freedom of Association?: City of Dallas v. Stanglin, 490 U.S. 19 (1989).* The City of Dallas adopted an ordinance restricting admission to certain dance halls to persons between the ages of fourteen and eighteen, plus certain designated adults (such as parents and dance hall personnel). A Texas court of appeals held that the ordinance violated the first amendment right of personsbetween the ages of fourteen and eighteen to associate with persons outside that age group. The Supreme Court, per Chief Justice Rehnquist, unanimously reversed and upheld the ordinance:

> It is clear beyond cavil that dance-hall patrons, who may number one thousand on any given night, are not engaged in the sort of "intimate human relationships" referred to in [previous cases dealing with the freedom of association]. . . .

(4) *Upholding a Right to Associate By Membership in a Prison Gang: Dawson v. Delaware, 503 U.S. 159 (1992).* Dawson escaped from a Delaware prison and committed a series of crimes, including a brutal murder. Based upon his lengthy criminal record and other aggravating evidence, the jury recommended that Dawson be sentenced to death. The evidence in the sentencing hearing, however, included proof that Dawson was a member of a prison gang (the Aryan Brotherhood), together with a brief stipulation showing only that "an Aryan Brotherhood prison gang originated in California in the 1960s, that it entertains white racist beliefs, and that a separate gang in the Delaware prison system calls itself the Aryan Brotherhood." The Court reversed on the ground that "the First Amendment protects an individual's right to join groups and associate with others holding similar beliefs." If the prosecution had shown (as it offered at trial to do) that the Aryan Brotherhood advocated crimes such as drugs, violent escape, and murder, "we would have a much different case"; but the mere fact of membership in a group entertaining racist beliefs having no relevance to the crime or sentence, said the Court, was protected association.

(5) *Private Organization's Right to Exclude Based on Free Speech Principles: Boy Scouts of America v. Dale, 520 U.S. 640 (2000).* [Regarding this decision, you should also

review the *Hurley* decision below in § 11.09 and the materials on Sexual Orientation in § 10.04[C].] Plaintiff Dale was a former Eagle Scout who, upon reaching 18, became an adult Boy Scout troop leader in Monmouth, New Jersey. Later, at college, Dale became openly homosexual and a gay rights activist. The troop then dismissed him on the grounds that his sexual orientation was inconsistent with the values which the Boy Scouts sought to instill in scouts. Dale sued under New Jersey's public accommodations law which protected against discrimination based on sexual orientation. Distinguishing the *Hurley* decision [below], the New Jersey courts upheld Dale's claim to be reinstated as an adult troop member.

The Supreme Court, per Chief Justice Rehnquist, reversed and remanded. The Court first determined that the Boy Scouts were a "private" entity (and not state action). Then, applying the analysis in *Hurley*, the Court held that the Boy Scouts' first amendment rights of expression and association would be impermissibly violated by the application of the New Jersey public accommodations law: "Forcing a group to accept certain members may impair the ability of the group to express those views, and only those views, that it intends to express." The Court distinguished *Rotary International* and other decisions in this section. Justices Stevens, Souter, Ginsburg and Breyer dissented. Doesn't this decision interfere with a state's ability to protect its citizens against "discrimination"?

§ 11.10   THE RIGHT NOT TO SPEAK—AND NOT TO LISTEN

[A]   Freedom Not to Speak and Loyalty Oaths

WOOLEY v. MAYNARD, 430 U.S. 705 (1977). Maynard, a Jehovah's Witness, obscured a part of his automobile license plate containing the state motto of New Hampshire, "Live Free or Die," because he found it objectionable on religious grounds. He was convicted under a state statute that made it a misdemeanor knowingly to obliterate "the figures or letters on any number plate." The Supreme Court, per Chief Justice Burger, reversed the conviction:

> We begin with the proposition that the right of freedom of thought protected by the first amendment against state action includes both the right to speak freely and the right to refrain from speaking at all. [A] system which secures the right to proselytize religious, political, and ideological causes must also guarantee the concomitant right to decline to foster such concepts. . . .
>
> New Hampshire's statute in effect requires that appellees use their private property as a "mobile billboard" for the state's ideological message—or suffer a penalty, as Maynard already has. As a condition to driving an automobile—a virtual necessity for most Americans—the Maynards must display "Live Free or Die" to hundreds of people each day. . . .
>
> Identifying the Maynards' interests as implicating first amendment protections does not end our inquiry, however. We must also determine whether the state's countervailing interest is sufficiently compelling to justify requiring appellees to display the state motto on their license plates. *See, e.g., United States v. O'Brien.* . . .
>
> The state first points out that passenger vehicles, but not commercial, trailer, or other vehicles are required to display the state motto. Thus, the argument proceeds, officers of the law are more easily able to determine whether passenger vehicles are carrying the proper plates. . . . Even were we to credit the state's reasons, "[t]hat purpose cannot be pursued by means that broadly stifle fundamental personal liberties when the end can be more narrowly achieved. . . ."
>
> The state's second claimed interest [that the motto on the license "promotes appreciation of history, individualism, and state pride"] is not ideologically

neutral. [O]f course, the state may legitimately pursue such interests in a number of ways. However, . . . no matter how acceptable to some, such interests cannot outweigh an individual's first amendment right to avoid becoming the courier for such [a] message. . . .

Justice Rehnquist, joined by Justice Blackmun, dissented: "I . . . agree with the [district] court's implicit recognition that there is no protected 'symbolic speech' in this case . . . The state has not forced appellees to 'say' anything. . . The state has simply required that *all* non-commercial automobiles bear license tags with the state motto. . . Appellees have not been forced to affirm or reject that motto. . . ." Justice Rehnquist compared Maynard's argument to the claim of a hypothetical atheist who might wish to deface United States currency containing the words "In God We Trust" or "E Pluribus Unum" to avoid an affirmation of belief, a result that the dissenters viewed as "startling [and] totally unacceptable."

COLE v. RICHARDSON
405 U.S. 676 (1972)

MR. CHIEF JUSTICE BURGER delivered the opinion of the Court.

[Richardson's employment at the Boston State Hospital was terminated because she refused to take the following statutorily required oath: "I do solemnly swear (or affirm) that I will uphold and defend the Constitution of the United States of America and the Constitution of the Commonwealth of Massachusetts and that I will oppose the overthrow of the government of the United States of America or of this Commonwealth by force, violence, or by any illegal or unconstitutional method." The district court held this loyalty oath statute unconstitutional. Here, the Supreme Court reverses and upholds it.]

A review of the oath cases in this Court will put the instant oath into context. We have made clear that neither federal nor state government may condition employment on taking oaths that impinge on rights guaranteed by the First and Fourteenth Amendments respectively, as for example those relating to political beliefs. Nor may employment be conditioned on an oath that one has not engaged, or will not engage, in protected speech activities such as the following: criticizing institutions of government; discussing political doctrine that approves the overthrow of certain forms of government; and supporting candidates for political office. Employment may not be conditioned on an oath denying past, or abjuring future, associational activities within constitutional protection; such protected activities include membership in organizations having illegal purposes unless one knows of the purpose and shares a specific intent to promote the illegal purpose. [A]nd, finally, an oath may not be so vague that "men of common intelligence must necessarily guess at its meaning and differ as to its application. . . ." . . .

Several cases recently decided by the Court stand out among our oath cases because they have upheld the constitutionality of oaths, addressed to the future, promising constitutional support in broad terms. These cases have begun with a recognition that the Constitution itself prescribes comparable oaths in two articles. Article II, § 1, cl. 8, provides that the President shall swear that he will "faithfully execute the Office . . . and will to the best of [his] Ability preserve, protect and defend the Constitution of the United States." Article VI, cl. 3, provides that all state and federal officers shall be bound by an oath "to support this Constitution." The oath taken by attorneys as a condition of admission to the Bar of this Court identically provides in part "that I will support the Constitution of the United States"; it also requires the attorney to state that he will "conduct [himself] uprightly, and according to law."

[T]he second clause of the oath contains a promise to "oppose the overthrow of the government of the United States of America or of this Commonwealth by force, violence or by any illegal or unconstitutional method." The District Court sought to give a dictionary meaning to this language and found "oppose" to raise the specter of vague, undefinable responsibilities actively to combat a potential overthrow of the government. That reading of the oath understandably troubled the court because of what it saw as vagueness in terms of what threats would constitute sufficient danger of overthrow to require the oath giver to actively oppose overthrow, and exactly what actions he would have to take in that respect. . . .

But such a literal approach to the second clause is inconsistent with the Court's approach to the "support" oaths. One could make a literal argument that "support" involves nebulous, undefined responsibilities for action in some hypothetical situations. [W]e have rejected such rigidly literal notions and recognized that the purpose leading legislatures to enact such oaths, just as the purpose leading the Framers of our Constitution to include the two explicit constitutional oaths, was not to create specific responsibilities but to assure that those in positions of public trust were willing to commit themselves to live by the constitutional processes of our system. . . . The second clause does not expand the obligation of the first: it simply makes clear the application of the first clause to a particular issue. Such repetition, whether for emphasis or cadence, seems to be the wont of authors of oaths. That the second clause may be redundant is no ground to strike it down; we are not charged with correcting grammar but with enforcing a constitution. . . .

Since there is no constitutionally protected right to overthrow a government by force, violence, or illegal or unconstitutional means, no constitutional right is infringed by an oath to abide by the constitutional system in the future. . . .

[The concurring opinion of JUSTICE STEWART, joined by JUSTICE WHITE WHITE is omitted.]

MR. JUSTICE DOUGLAS, dissenting. . . .

Advocacy of basic fundamental changes in government, which might popularly be described as "overthrow" is within the protection of the first amendment even when it is restrictively construed. . . .

[T]his oath, however, requires that appellee "oppose" that which she has an indisputable right to advocate. [I would affirm the judgment below.]

MR. JUSTICE MARSHALL, with whom MR. JUSTICE BRENNAN joins, [dissented on the grounds of vagueness and overbreadth].

NOTES AND QUESTIONS

(1) *The Barnette Dictum: Board of Education v. Barnette, 319 U.S. 624 (1943).* In *Barnette*, a state statute required public school students to honor the flag both with words and with traditional salute gestures. The Supreme Court regarded this act as "a ceremony so touching on matters of opinion and political attitude [that it] may [not] be imposed upon the individual by official authority." Further, as Justice Jackson said for the Court:

> If there is any fixed star in our constitutional constellation, it is that no official, high or petty, can proscribe what shall be orthodox in politics, nationalism, religion, or other matter of opinion or force citizens to confess by word or act their faith therein.

Chief Justice Burger relied heavily upon *Barnette* in his opinion in *Wooley*; he did not cite it, however, in his opinion in *Cole v. Richardson.* Consider whether the *Barnette* dictum, though useful as a hortatory expression, actually is less useful as a principle for line-drawing in more difficult cases such as *Cole.* Doesn't that case indicate that there are at least some minimal contexts in which "officials, high or petty" indeed can prescribe demonstrations of loyalty?

(2) *Is the Speech-Conduct Distinction Useful for Differentiating Permissible from Impermissible Loyalty Oaths?* Consider whether the result in *Cole v. Richardson* can be defended on the ground that the promise concerns not abstract "loyalty" but future conduct relevant to the performance of the job of a state employee. Couldn't Massachusetts, for example, require state employees to promise, "I will carry out the legitimate and lawful directives of my supervisors?" Wouldn't the job-related promise in such an oath differentiate it from a hypothetical (unconstitutional) one, "I will never publicly criticize the government and will maintain political beliefs conforming to those of the governor?"

(3) *Free Speech Protection Against "Compelled Speech" (Even for Commercial Speech): United States v. United Foods, Inc., 533 U.S. 405 (2001).* Under the Mushroom Promotion, Research and Consumer Information Act, producers are subject to assessments used to fund generic advertisements promoting mushroom sales. A mushroom producer (who disagreed with the advertising campaign) challenged the assessment as "compelled speech." Although the federal government relied on the *Glickman* decision, § 11.07 above, the Supreme Court, per Justice Kennedy, held that the assessment requirement constituted compelled speech from the dissenting producer and that, absent satisfying a form of strict scrutiny, the mushroom assessment program violated the free speech rights of the dissenting producer.

The Court distinguished *Glickman* on the grounds that the assessment program there (regarding "tree fruit" producers) was merely "incidental" to a comprehensive regulatory program while the mushroom assessment was used only for advertising. Justice Stevens concurred because the mushroom assessment was "government compulsion to finance objectionable speech." Justice Thomas concurred, arguing for broader protection for commercial speech. Justices Breyer, Ginsburg, and O'Connor dissented, arguing mainly that *Glickman* should be the controlling precedent.

HURLEY v. IRISH-AMERICAN GAY, LESBIAN AND BISEXUAL GROUP OF BOSTON, 515 U.S. 557 (1995). Since 1947, the South Boston Allied War Veterans Council (Council), a private organization, has conducted an annual St. Patrick's Day parade under a permit from the city. The Irish-American Gay, Lesbian and Bisexual Group (GLIB) applied to march in the parade, but the Council refused to admit GLIB. GLIB eventually won a state court order requiring its inclusion, and the highest Massachusetts court affirmed on the ground that GLIB's rejection was based on the sexual orientation of its members (a "protected category" under Massachusetts law). The Massachusetts courts rejected the Council's defense based upon the theory that the parade was protected speech and the state court order was a content-based regulation. The Supreme Court, per Justice Souter, unanimously reversed on free speech grounds.

> If there were no reason for a group of people to march from here to there except to reach a destination, they could make the trip without expressing any message beyond the fact of the march itself. . . . Hence, we use the word "parade" to indicate marchers who are making some sort of collective point, not just to each other but to bystanders along the way. . . . Parades are thus a form of expression, not just motion, and the inherent expressiveness of marching to make a point explains our cases involving protest marchers.

> The protected expression that inheres in a parade is not limited to its banners and songs, however, for the Constitution looks beyond written or spoken words as mediums of expression. Noting that "[s]ymbolism is a primitive but effective way of communicating ideas," *West Virginia Bd. of Ed. v. Barnette*, 319 U.S. 624, 632 (1943), our cases have recognized that the First Amendment shields such acts as saluting a flag (and refusing to do so). . . . [A] narrow, succinctly articulable message is not a condition of constitutional protection, which if confined to expressions conveying a "particularized message," would never reach the unquestionably shielded painting of Jackson Pollock, music of Arnold Schonberg, or Jabberwocky verse of Lewis Carroll.

Provisions like [Massachusetts public accommodations law] are well within the State's usual power to enact when a legislature has reason to believe that a given group is the target of discrimination, and they do not, as a general matter, violate the First or Fourteenth Amendments. . . .

In the case before us, however, the Massachusetts law has been applied in a peculiar way. . . . [O]nce the expressive character of both the parade and the marching GLIB contingent is understood, it becomes apparent that the state courts' application of the statute had the effect of declaring the sponsors' speech itself to be the public accommodation. . . . [T]his use of the State's power violates the fundamental rule of protection under the First Amendment, that a speaker has the autonomy to choose the content of his own message.

"Since all speech inherently involves choices of what to say and what to leave unsaid," one important manifestation of the principle of free speech is that one who chooses to speak may also decide "what not to say." . . .

[The Council's] claim to the benefit of this principle of autonomy to control one's own speech is as sound as the South Boston parade is expressive. Rather like a composer, the Council selects the expressive units of the parade from potential participants, and though the score may not produce a particularized message, each contingent's expression in the Council's eyes comports with what merits celebration on that day. Even if this view gives the Council credit for a more considered judgment than it actively made, the Council clearly decided to exclude a message it did not like from the communication it chose to make, and that is enough to invoke its right as a private speaker to shape its expression by speaking on one subject while remaining silent on another. . . .

It might, of course, have been argued that [the state has] a broader objective . . . that the ultimate point of forbidding acts of discrimination toward certain classes is to produce a society free of the corresponding biases. [B]ut if this indeed is the point of applying the state law to expressive conduct, it is a decidedly fatal objective. . . . [T]he very idea that a noncommercial speech restriction be used to produce thoughts and statements acceptable to some groups or, indeed, all people, grates on the First Amendment, for it amounts to nothing less than a proposal to limit speech in the service of orthodox expression. . . .

NOTES AND QUESTIONS

(1) *Parades As "Speech" And State Antidiscrimination Laws As Regulations of Compelled Speech.* The *Hurley* Court unanimously held: (1) that the Council's parade was, under the circumstances, "speech" for purposes of Free Speech doctrine, and (2) that the imposition of the state antidiscrimination law would impermissibly compel speech from the Council.

(2) *Some Implications of Hurley For "Hate Speech" Codes.* Earlier, at Problem M in § 11.04, you examined the issues whether university officials might constitutionally prohibit or inhibit certain speech on campus which, in the view of the government, constituted anti-minority slurs or was otherwise degrading or offensive to some (if not almost all) members of the campus community. You also considered the *R.A.V. v. St. Paul* decision (the "hate speech" decision) in § 11.04. Reconsider the constitutionality of a campus hate speech code in light of *Hurley.* Or, can *Hurley*, like *R.A.V.*, be distinguished because a campus hate speech code applies in an educational setting?

(3) *Compelled Speech and Required Equal Access for Military Recruiters: Rumsfeld v. FAIR, 547 U.S. 47 (2006).* A consortium of law schools (FAIR) challenged the Solomon Amendment's requirement that law schools provide "equal" access for military recruiters even though the law schools disagreed with the military's policies on gays in the military-(*i.e.*, Don't Ask; Don't Tell). One of FAIR's theories, based on *Barnette,*

Wooley, and *Hurley*, was that the Solomon Amendment compelled the schools to speak the government's message. The unanimous Court, in an opinion by Chief Justice Roberts, disagreed, distinguishing FAIR's case authorities. The Court held that the Solomon Amendment "does not dictate the content of the speech at all.. . .." The Court then rejected FAIR's compelled speech argument by stating "it trivializes the freedom protected in *Barnette* and *Wooley* to suggest that [hosting military recruiters under equal access is compelled speech]." *See* § 11.06 for other aspects of the *FAIR* decision.

[B] Protection of the "Captive Auditor"

KOVACS v. COOPER, 336 U.S. 77 (1949). Kovacs emitted music and speech from a sound truck and was convicted under a city ordinance prohibiting "loud and raucous noises" from any vehicle on a public street. The Supreme Court, with a plurality opinion by Justice Reed, affirmed:

> [A] satisfactory judgment of the conflicting interests is difficult. . . . [U]nrestrained use throughout a municipality of all sound amplifying devices would be intolerable. Absolute prohibition within municipal limits of all sound amplification, even though reasonably regulated in place, time and volume, is undesirable and probably unconstitutional as an unreasonable interference with normal activities. . . .

> This ordinance is not of that character. [I]t is an exercise of the authority granted to the city . . . "to prevent disturbing noises," . . . nuisances well within the municipality's power to control. . . .

> [T]he preferred position of freedom of speech . . . does not require legislatures to be insensible to claims by citizens to comfort and convenience. . . .

Justice Black, joined by Justice Douglas and Justice Rutledge, dissented. He concluded that the ordinance properly was interpreted to ban sound trucks generally. "There are many people who have ideas that they wish to disseminate but do not have enough money to own or control publishing plants, newspapers, radios, moving picture studios, or chains of show places. . . ."

NOTES AND QUESTIONS

(1) *The Unconstitutionality of Discretionary Bans on Loud Noises: Saia v. New York, 334 U.S. 558 (1948).* In *Saia*, the Court struck down an ordinance similarly concerned with loudspeakers, but that allowed exceptions from the prohibition to be made "under permission obtained from Chief of Police." The Court focused upon the vagueness of the standards contained in the ordinance: "The right to be heard is placed in the uncontrolled discretion of the Chief of Police. [A] more effective previous restraint is difficult to imagine." The *Kovacs* Court distinguished *Saia* on this ground. But consider whether the ordinance in *Kovacs* avoids the vagueness problem, in that it does not define, either for the speaker or for the law enforcement officer, just how loud a "loud and raucous" sound must be to violate it.

(2) *Solicitations in Private Homes by Mail or by Personal Visits: From Rowan v. Post Office Dept., 397 U.S. 728 (1970), toBreard v. City of Alexandria, 341 U.S. 622 (1951).* What about the right of a homeowner to cut off all communication at the door of his or her home—or, as a proxy, the authority of a municipality to enact an ordinance having this effect? In *Rowan v. Post Office*, the Court upheld a federal statute allowing a homeowner to determine in his own opinion that certain material was erotic or "sexually provocative" and to refuse to receive it, by obtaining an order of the Post Office requiring that the sender remove him from its mailing list. "The right of every person 'to be let alone' must be placed in the scales with the right of others to communicate," said the Court.

As for personal home solicitation, the Court in *Breard* upheld a municipal ordinance that prohibited door-to-door visits by persons seeking orders for consumer goods. But

Breard should be compared with *Martin v. Struthers*, 319 U.S. 141 (1943), which concerned a law that flatly prohibited home visits to residents for delivery of hand-bills. The Court reversed the conviction of the defendant, who was a Jehovah's Witness distributing religious materials door-to-door. The city's broad prohibition of canvassing was "a naked restriction on the dissemination of ideas" and was unconstitutional under less-restrictive-means analysis.

(3) *Modern Home-Solicitation Cases— Heightened Scrutiny: Schaumburg v. Citizens for a Better Environment, 444 U.S. 620 (1980).* Schaumburg concerned a municipal ordinance that prohibited home solicitation by charities that failed to expend at least 75% of their receipts for "charitable purposes" as opposed to administration and solicitation expenses. The Court applied heightened scrutiny, holding that any "direct and substantial" impairment of protected expression could be upheld only if it was "substantially" related to a "strong, subordinating interest" of the state. The Court concluded that the city's purposes—which included prevention of fraud or annoyance and protection of residential safety—were not sufficiently "substantially related" to the ordinance.

FRISBY v. SCHULTZ, 487 U.S. 474 (1988). Brookfield, Wisconsin, a Milwaukee suburb, adopted an ordinance because of perceived intrusions on residential privacy interests and a concern for public safety: "It is unlawful for any person to engage in picketing before or about the residence or dwelling of any individual in the Town of Brookfield." The appellees, Schultz and Braun, along with others, had been picketing outside a doctor's home in Brookfield to protest the doctor's performance of abortions. Although the picketing had been "generally orderly and peaceful," it had generated "substantial controversy and numerous complaints." Brookfield's ordinance was passed in response to this anti-abortion protest, and the picketers sought injunctive relief in federal court. Although the District Court granted an injunction and the Court of Appeals affirmed, the Supreme Court, per Justice O'Connor, reversed and upheld the ordinance.

The Supreme Court initially concluded that "public issue picketing" was protected speech and that Brookfield's ban on residential picketing should be considered as a content-neutral "place" regulation. The Supreme Court also concluded that "in order to fall within the scope of the ordinance the picketing must be directed at a single residence." With the ordinance accordingly narrowed, the Court examined whether Brookfield could satisfy the time, place, and manner standard.

> We readily agree that the ordinance preserves ample alternative channels of communication and thus move on to inquire whether the ordinance serves a significant government interest. . . .

> The State's interest in protecting the well-being, tranquility, and privacy of the home is certainly of the highest order in a free and civilized society. . . .

> One important aspect of residential privacy is protection of the unwilling listener. Although in many locations, we expect individuals simply to avoid speech they do not want to hear, *cf. Cohen v. California*, 403 U.S. 15, 21–22 (1971), the home is different. . . .

> It remains to be considered, however, whether the Brookfield ordinance is narrowly tailored to protect only unwilling recipients of the communications. A statute is narrowly tailored if it targets and eliminates no more than the exact source of the "evil" it seeks to remedy. . . .

> In this case, for example, appellees subjected the doctor and his family to the presence of a relatively large group of protesters on their doorstep in an attempt to force the doctor to cease performing abortions. But the actual size of the group is irrelevant; even a solitary picket can invade residential privacy. . . .

The First Amendment permits the government to prohibit offensive speech as intrusive when the "captive" audience cannot avoid the objectionable speech. . . . The target of the focused picketing banned by the Brookfield ordinance is just such a "captive." . . . Accordingly, the Brookfield ordinance's complete ban of that particular medium of expression is narrowly tailored.

Justice White concurred. Justice Brennan, joined by Justice Marshall, dissented on the grounds that the ordinance was not narrowly tailored. Justice Stevens dissented because of overbreadth concerns: "My hunch is that the town will probably not enforce its ban against friendly, innocuous or even brief unfriendly picketing. . . . The scope of the ordinance gives the town official far too much discretion. . . ."

NOTES AND QUESTIONS

(1)   *What About a Billboard Ordinance Permitting Commercial, But Not Political, Advertising?: Metromedia, Inc. v. City of San Diego, 453 U.S. 490 (1981).* Metromedia concerned the validity of a city ordinance that permitted commercial signs if they were on site, but prohibited all other kinds of billboards, including political ones. The plurality concluded that this preference of commercial over non-commercial speech was unconstitutional. In addition, Justices Brennan and Blackmun, who concurred separately, appeared to view as unconstitutional any approach that would allow city officials the power to distinguish between commercial and non-commercial messages. Did the plurality appropriately consider the interests of the audience that may be forced to view these billboards?

(2)   *Loud Rock Music is Protected Speech but the Government May Regulate with Time, Place, or Manner Restrictions: Ward v. Rock Against Racism, 491 U.S. 781 (1989)* Is there a right to listen to rock music, protected under the first amendment? The Supreme Court answered this question in the affirmative. And if government creates a public or limited public forum, it may be required to provide rock groups access in appropriate circumstances. Reasonable noise restrictions, however, constitutionally may be enforced.

THE STORY OF A FIRST AMENDMENT CASE—SELECTED MATERIALS FROM *RANKIN v. McPHERSON*

INTRODUCTORY NOTE

The Supreme Court's opinions in *Rankin v. McPherson* appear in Chapter 11, above, in the section entitled "Speech by Government Employees." McPherson was discharged from her employment by Constable Rankin because of a statement she made in an unofficial conversation in the office of the Constable shortly after the attempted assassination of President Reagan: "I hope if they go for him again, they get him." The Supreme Court held that under the circumstances, this remark was protected speech.

In this appendix, we reproduce excerpts from *McPherson's* complaint, the evidentiary record, the parties' briefs, and other materials. Our objective is to show the context in which first amendment cases are litigated.

PLAINTIFF'S COMPLAINT

IN THE UNITED STATES DISTRICT COURT
FOR THE SOUTHERN DISTRICT OF TEXAS
HOUSTON DIVISION

ARDITH McPHERSON, **Plaintiff,** **v.** **WALTER RANKIN, Individually** **and in his Official Capacity as Constable,** **Precinct One (1), of Harris County, Texas;** **and HARRIS COUNTY, TEXAS,** **Defendants**	**CIVIL ACTION NO. H-81-1442**

ORIGINAL COMPLAINT

I. INTRODUCTORY STATEMENT

1. Plaintiff seeks to enjoin Defendants from conditioning continuing public employment on espousal of only those personal or political opinions and ideas found acceptable to the Constable. Plaintiff also seeks declaratory judgment and damages. . . .

II. JURISDICTION

2. Plaintiff alleges that Defendants' actions have deprived her of rights secured her under the First and Fourteenth Amendments to the Constitution of the United States, and further assured to her by 42 U.S.C. §§ 1983 and 1988, and corresponding provisions under Texas laws.

3. Pursuant to 28 U.S.C. § 1343(3) and (4), this Court has jurisdiction. . . .

III. PARTIES

5. Plaintiff ARDITH McPHERSON is an adult citizen of the United States, and resident of Harris County, Texas.

6. Defendant WALTER RANKIN is Constable of Precinct One (1) of Harris County,

Texas. He is an elected official, and is sued both individually and in his official capacity as constable. Defendant may be served with process at his office address at the Harris County Criminal Courts Building, 301 San Jacinto, Houston, Texas.

7. Defendant HARRIS COUNTY, TEXAS, is a county of the State of Texas, and process may be had by serving its statutorily designated agent for service. . . .

IV. COLOR OF LAW

8. At all times mentioned herein, all Defendants acted under color of the laws, statutes, customs, usages, and regulations of the State of Texas, of Harris County, Texas, and of the office of Constable, Precinct One, of said County.

V. FACTUAL ALLEGATIONS

. . . 11. Plaintiff ARDITH McPHERSON was hired by Defendant RANKIN on January 14, 1981, as a Deputy Clerk of Harris County, Texas. Her job duties concerned entry of information about civil process into the computer records of said County. . . .

13. On Monday, March 30, 1981, an assassination attempt was made on the President of the United States.

14. Plaintiff first learned of the attempt as a result of a radio broadcast on said date, during a time that the Constable's office in which Plaintiff was sitting was emptied for lunch.

15. Upon hearing the news of the assassination attempt, Plaintiff and another employee of said Constable's office began a private discussion concerning the current administration of President Reagan, and its proposed budget reductions, and the employees discussed how proposed money cuts would generate anger in this Country.

16. During the course of said private discussion, Plaintiff stated to the other employee, "I hope if they go for him [President Reagan] again, they get him," and the conversation turned to other personal topics.

17. Said verbal statement made by Plaintiff was overheard by a Captain Levrier, and Plaintiff alleges on knowledge and belief that said Captain reported Plaintiff's statement to Defendant RANKIN. . . .

20. In Defendant RANKIN's office, the Defendant RANKIN informed Plaintiff that his office is "for Reagan," and further, that he would not tolerate expression of any opinions against President Reagan.

21. Plaintiff attempted to explain her comment, but Defendant RANKIN would not allow Plaintiff to respond.

22. Defendant RANKIN immediately thereafter terminated Plaintiff's employment with Harris County, and instructed an employee to remove Plaintiff's name from the payroll. . . .

VI. CLAIMS FOR RELIEF

26. Defendants' actions described above were arbitrary, capricious, and in willful violation of Plaintiff's freedom of speech, in that Plaintiff was terminated based upon expression of personal and political opinion, said expression being in the context of a private conversation; thus Defendants violated Plaintiff's rights under the First and Fourteenth Amendments to the United States Constitution, and deprived Plaintiff of rights secured by 42 U.S.C. § 1983. . . .

RELIEF REQUESTED

Plaintiff requests that each Defendant be cited to appear and answer herein, that this cause be expedited for trial and that, upon trial of this action, the Court grant

Plaintiff the following relief against Defendants, jointly and severally:

A. Adjudge and declare that Defendants' actions are in violation of the First and Fourteenth Amendments to the United States Constitution, and 42 U.S.C. § 1983; and

B. Incident to such declaration, and in exercise of its equitable powers, this Court order that Defendants reinstate Plaintiff to her job position; and

C. Order that Defendants publicize Plaintiff's reinstatement and advise the news media of such action; and

D. Award Plaintiff back pay for the time during which she was not employed by Defendants; [and]

E. Permanently enjoin Defendants from conditioning employment with said Harris County, Texas, Constable's office on the expression of only those ideas found personally acceptable by said Defendant RANKIN; [and]

F. Permanently enjoin Defendants from again summarily terminating employees with said Harris County, Texas Constable's office based on expression of ideas found personally unacceptable by said Defendant RANKIN, without notice and hearing; and

G. Award Plaintiff her costs of court and reasonable attorneys' fees; and

H. Grant such other relief as may be just and proper in the opinion of this Court.

Respectfully submitted,
STEFAN PRESSER, . . .
Attorney-in-Charge for Plaintiff. . . .
Greater Houston Civil Liberties Union . . .

NOTES AND QUESTIONS

(1) *Contested Facts: The Trial Judge's Findings Differed Somewhat from the Allegations of the Complaint.* At this point, no "facts" are established; only the plaintiff has made allegations. The defendants contested some of the allegations, asserting that the constable had asked the plaintiff about her remark and that she told the constable that she *did* "mean it," and denying that the constable stated anything about not tolerating expression of opinions against President Reagan. The trial judge's findings implicitly accepted the latter version. Question: Is this a case that depended upon the resolution of contested facts? [Whether or not *this* case so depended, what does the factual controversy tell you about how a plaintiff's lawyer should *evaluate* a constitutional case that he is asked to take on?]

(2) *The Defendants' Answers.* The constable and the county each filed separate answers, both through the county attorney. Fed. R. Civ. P. 8 requires a federal defendant to answer by admitting or denying each allegation of the complaint. The defendants' answers did not contain complete admissions or denials, but consisted of narratives of the defendants' versions of facts and positions. Question: To what dangers might an attorney answering in this manner expose his or her case?

(3) *Discovery.* It normally would be expected that discovery in a case of this nature would consist of depositions of plaintiff and defendant and other fact and expert witnesses (in addition to the possible use of interrogatories or requests to produce). In an unusual proceeding, the trial judge held a hearing on the defendant's motion for summary judgment at which live witnesses testified.

(4) *Initial Grant of Summary Judgment for Defendant—and Findings of Fact.* The trial judge's hearing of evidence resulted in findings of fact and conclusions of law, upon which the trial court in April 1983 granted summary judgment for the defendant. (Summary judgment usually is based upon pleadings, affidavits and discovery products, in accordance with Rule 56.) The findings included the following:

4. Defendants at all times mentioned herein acted under color of state law. . . .

7. Defendant Walter Rankin employed Plaintiff for a ninety-day probationary period. At the time Plaintiff was terminated, she had two weeks of her probationary period remaining. . . .

10. Plaintiff's notarized oath of office . . . read: "I, Ardith S. McPherson, do solemnly swear (or affirm), that I will [to] the best of my ability preserve, protect and defend the Constitution and laws of the United States and of this State. . . ."

11. Pursuant to Texas law, all employees of the Constable's office, regardless of job function, are deputy constables and must give the prescribed oath of office. *See* Vernon's Rev. Civ. Stat. Ann. art. 6879a and 6879b. . . .

12. On March 30, 1981, during the lunch hour, Plaintiff and some other employees heard on an office radio, an announcement of the assassination attempt on President Reagan. Plaintiff concluded a discussion with a coworker about that event and about Reagan administration economic policies with the statement, "I hope if they go for him (President Reagan) again, they get him."

14. Plaintiff testified that she told Constable Rankin, "Yes, but I didn't mean anything by it." Plaintiff claims her statement did not signify an actual intent on her part to harm or to participate in harming the President.

15. Constable Rankin, Captain Levrier, and Captain Abercia each testified that Plaintiff repeated the statement in the Constable's office. The Constable testified that when he asked her whether she meant it, Plaintiff replied, "I sure do". . . .

18. Constable Rankin testified that he lost all confidence in the Plaintiff's ability to be a Deputy Constable and as an employee of a law enforcement agency when she repeated (or acknowledged) her statement. . . .

19. The Court finds that, regardless of the seriousness of Plaintiff's intent, the fact that she did make such a statement while on the job indicated to her superiors that she did not appreciate or possess the sensitivity and discretion required of a public employee. The Constable sincerely and earnestly believes that an individual possessing an attitude such as Plaintiff's is not a suitable employee of a law enforcement agency. . . .

(5) *Reversal of the Summary Judgment by the Court of Appeals.* The plaintiff's attorneys filed appropriate appellate documents and briefed and argued the case. In July 1984, a panel of the Fifth Circuit reversed the summary judgment. Its opinion, after recitation of the facts, included the following:

In reviewing a district court's grant of summary judgment, we are required to consider the evidence presented in the light most favorable to the party opposing the motion. [T]he standard is simply that the evidence shows "that there is no genuine issue as to any material fact and that the moving party is entitled to judgment as a matter of law." Fed. R. Civ. P. 56(c). . . .

In this instance, the statement was made by McPherson during the lunch hour in a conversation between McPherson and her boyfriend, a coworker. . . .

At the evidentiary hearing, Ardith McPherson testified that her statement—[was] intended only as a verbal expression of her anger with the Reagan administration's social and economic policies. The plaintiff maintained that "it is just like if I ask my sister to pick me up somewhere and she's late and I say, 'Where is she,' and I said 'Wait till she get[s] here, I'm going to kill her.' . . ." Hence, the essence of McPherson's contention is that her statement was merely a form of political hyperbole and was not intended to advocate harm to the President.

[C]onstable Rankin testified that when he asked Ms. McPherson whether she meant what she said, her reply was "I sure do."

The issue of McPherson's intent is relevant to the present inquiry because it is imperative that a court's characterization of speech as political expression, for purposes of First Amendment protection, be predicated upon consideration of its "content, form, and context." *See Connick v. Myers*, 103 S. Ct. 1684, 1690 (1983). . . .

The Court's task is to fully consider each of these factors in "[arriving] at a balance between the interests of the [employee], as a citizen, in commenting upon matters of public concern and the interest of the State, as an employer in promoting the efficiency of the public services it performs through its employees." *Pickering v. Board of Education*, 391 U.S. 563, 568 (1968). . . .

[*Reversed.*]

(6) *Significance of Fact Findings.* How important is the submission of evidence and advocacy to obtain favorable fact findings in a case such as this?

(7) *Trial of the Case.* In January 1985, almost four years after plaintiff's discharge, trial was held before the district court. [Consider what impact a delay of this magnitude has upon the parties in a first amendment case.] Excerpts from the trial record follow.

EXCERPTS FROM THE TRIAL RECORD

[At trial, plaintiff McPherson was represented by Bruce V. Griffiths, ACLU staff counsel. Defendants Rankin and Harris County were represented by Assistant County Attorney Billy E. Lee.]

[Mr. Griffiths began by calling Constable Rankin, an adverse witness, as his first witness. He immediately added, "Your Honor, at this time the Plaintiff would invoke the rule." This was a request to the judge to sequester all witnesses except the parties, McPherson and Rankin. The judge accordingly instructed other witnesses to remain outside and talk to no one but the attorneys about the case. Mr. Griffiths then examined Constable Rankin:]

DIRECT EXAMINATION

By Mr. Griffiths: Q. Constable Rankin, would you state your name for the record, please?

A. Walter H. Rankin.

Q. And you are, sir, the elected Constable of Precinct 1 of Harris County, Texas? Is that correct?

A. Yes, sir. . . .

[The examination detailed Constable Rankin's duties and authority; the function and organization of his office; his relationship to other county offices; his deputies' primary tasks of serving papers, carrying out evictions, and protecting visiting dignitaries; plaintiff McPherson's employment and duties as a "deputy assigned to [a] clerical position;" Rankin's learning of McPherson's remark; his reaction; and the aftermath, among other subjects. The examination included the following:]

Q. Mr. Rankin, [y]ou are elected on a party ticket; is that correct?

A. Yes, sir.

Q. So you have, for the 20 years that you have been constable of Precinct 1, been selected as a Democrat; is that correct?

A. That's correct, sir.

Q. Would you consider that your office essentially is a partisan political office?

A. Counselor, in the work I do, I don't care whether a man is Democrat, Republican or an Independent. It's just that we don't look at that. We carry out the enforcement of the laws, and I don't think law enforcement has a party. . . .

Q. So someone with—who was either for or against the Reagan Administration could still work in your office, notwithstanding their opinion on that subject?

A. I don't ask them how they vote or who they vote for, Counselor.

Q. The people who work for you are all deputy constables, but the jobs that they do are different jobs. [F]irst of all, what do you call, in terms of job description, the job of taking data off the court papers and putting them into the computer system?

A. I call them deputies assigned to clerical positions.

Q. And when you hire somebody for a job, clerical position, it's true, is it not, that you do not require them to be a commissioned law enforcement officer?

A. No, sir. But if they so request later on, want to go to school, then I'll assist them in training, which I have done in the past, which I am doing now. . . .

Q. And, in fact, when Ardith McPherson applied for a job in your office, she was not required to undergo the psychological testing, for example, that a peace officer is required to undergo before he gets commissioned as a peace officer?

A. No, sir. . . .

Q. And I presume that you did not require her to do those things because you didn't think that that was necessary for her to perform her job. . . .

A. Not unless she proved her desire, or wanted to go further up into law enforcement. Then she would have. . . .

Q. And what conversation took place at the time that Ms. McPherson, Chief Abercia and Captain Levrier were in your office?

A. [I asked] if she made the remark about hoping that the President, the next time he was shot, that they would get him. And I said, do you mean that. And no doubt in my mind, she said, yes. And that is when I took my action. . . .

Q. Your action—did you ever ask Ms. McPherson to whom she had made that remark?

A. I did not.

Q. Did you ever ask Captain Abercia—or Chief Abercia to whom she had made the remark?

A. I was not concerned who she had made it to, because she had made it to me, and when she made the remark to me, then I lost all confidence at all that I could ever be comfortable in a law enforcement office and agency that I could permit her to be. . . .

Q. Did you ever ask Ms. McPherson whether she was working or on her lunch hour during this conversation?

A. No, I did not ask her.

Q. As far as you know, except for Captain Levrier's decision to report this matter to Mr. Riley, that conversation or that comment did not disrupt the work that was going on in that data processing area, did it?

A. I did not base my action on whether the work was interrupted or not. I based my action on a statement that was made to me direct. . . .

Q. Okay. Constable Rankin, if you and I were having lunch together last Wednesday, let's say, and I said to you, I sure hope those 49'ers kill the Dolphins on Sunday, you would in fact understand that as not being a serious threat on the lives of the Miami Dolphin football team, would you not?

A. It's a lot different in playing football than it is the life of the President of the United States. . . .

Q. Suppose Mr. Lee [the Assistant County Attorney; opposing counsel] was at lunch with you, talking about the case, and he said to you, I hope the 49'ers kill the Miami Dolphins on Sunday. You wouldn't take that as being a threat that Mr. Lee would go out and kill the Miami football team, would you?

A. I have never heard Mr. Lee have a desire to kill anyone, or make any kind—so I couldn't say that would be in Mr. Lee's mind. If he did and he meant it, I would be very greatly disappointed in him, and I have a lot of respect for Mr. Lee. . . .

Q. Constable Rankin, you are a member of the White race, are you not?

A. Yes, sir.

Q. And Ms. McPherson is a member of the black race; is that true?

A. Yes, sir. . . .

Mr. Griffiths: Pass the witness, Your Honor.

The Court: Mr. Lee.

Mr. Lee: [Reserved examination until presentation of defendant's case.]

[Plaintiff next called CAPTAIN JOHN M. LEVRIER as an adverse witness. Captain Levrier corroborated the testimony of Constable Rankin, to the effect that McPherson had said that she "meant" the remark about President Reagan, which Levrier also had overheard. DEPUTY JOHN ABERCIA, plaintiff's next witness and also an adverse witness, did not recall whether McPherson had said she "meant it." Plaintiff's counsel made such points as the non-law-enforcement nature of plaintiff's duties and the lack of actual observed disruption from plaintiff's remark.

[Plaintiff's counsel then called ARDITH McPHERSON, the plaintiff, who (among other matters) testified that she had *not* told the Constable that she "meant" the remark. On the contrary, she testified that she had told the Constable that she did not mean it, creating a square conflict in the testimony.

[Plaintiff next called PROFESSOR THOMAS KOCHMAN, a sociologist, who provided some of the more innovative evidence in the trial. His testimony was that the fact that the remark in question was made between two black individuals made some difference in the speaker's intention. Black culture, he maintained, tolerates a greater degree of verbal flamboyance than white culture, and hence it could more readily be inferred that McPherson did not truly desire the assassination of the President.

[Plaintiff then briefly called LAWRENCE JACKSON (identified as plaintiff's boyfriend and a commissioned peace officer) and rested.

[Defendant then recalled Constable Rankin, as follows:]

DIRECT EXAMINATION

By Mr. Lee: Q. Constable Rankin, [is] your office . . . engaged in security work?

A. When we are requested to assist, or called upon, yes.

Q. All right. Since February of 1983, has your office been in any security work involving President Reagan in Houston?

A. Since '83, I don't recall. We have furnished personnel for so many, and it's almost on a regular—if he was in here, I'm sure that we had personnel assigned.

Q. All right. Tell the court some of the people whom you have represented in just the past year, and furnishing personal security for them.

A. Well, within the last year, one of the main functions for a week was Billy Graham, when he was here, and we handled all security there. The last most important assignment that we have had recently was for Jesse Jackson, on two occasions. . . .

Q. When you are handling a personal security assignment, would you tell the court what kind of information is made available to you, that is not available to the general public?

A. We know arrival, which airport, which plane he is coming in, we know how many people will be with them, what route they will be taking, where they will be staying, and where they will be going and different places, because we furnish automobiles, and we furnish drivers and security to get them there and bring them back. . . .

Q. All right. Is there any danger in your office that any of your deputies will, with malice or just with negligence, make this confidential information available to other than your office staff?

A. I must have complete trust in the people I'm working there, because I—whoever might be typing, or the information there, or for my officers, is that I have to be comfortable with the people that I work with. . . .

Q. Is there any doubt in your mind—and especially since Ms. McPherson, from the stand there, has told you that she didn't mean anything by her verbal comments on wanting the President to be killed—[that] you would reconsider in taking her back as your deputy?

A. I could not. . . .

CROSS-EXAMINATION

By Mr. Griffiths: Q. Constable Rankin, [are] you seriously telling this Court that you expect every member of your staff to be entrusted with secret information about the travels of the President of the United States and similar dignitaries, and that the only investigation you made before you hired Ardith McPherson was to give her a typing test?

A. I'm not going to get on a mountain top and shout it out. It is there, and if I call upon Ms. McPherson to type up a work schedule for me, I want to be comfortable with her. . . .

ARGUMENT OF COUNSEL TO TRIAL COURT

Mr. Griffiths: We have nothing on rebuttal, Your Honor. We do have an argument.

The Court: All right, sir.

Mr. Griffiths: Your Honor, I think that this issue, this question, is very clear. I think the evidence is essentially all on one side. The *Connick v. Myers* decision emphasizes that when we are talking about the First Amendment rights of a public employee, we are balancing the interest of the public office in operating and doing its job, versus the interest of the employee in question, in having a right to free speech. . . .

The dichotomy between public concern and internal affairs weighs down completely on the side of public concern. [T]he only way that this statement could be understood as interfering with the operation of this office, of the constable's office—would be essentially if it were to be understood as saying that I, Ardith McPherson, intend to actively work for the assassination of President Reagan. . . .

I think it was clearly a statement made under exciting circumstances. It was something that essentially amounted to, I don't like Ronald Reagan and Ronald Reagan has been thrust to my attention by this radio report.

The fact that it could not interfere with the operation of this office is shown quite clearly by Constable Rankin's testimony. It's absolutely clear Ardith McPherson, without some 400 hours of training could not—and considerable screening—could not have been assigned to guard any visiting dignitary. . . .

So the question is intent. And if we listen to Professor Kochman, he tells us [that] Black culture tolerates a greater degree of sort of verbal flamboyance. . . .

Finally, Your Honor, I would like to talk briefly about the First Amendment, in general, because after all, that is what we are litigating in this case. One of the reasons for having the First Amendment is that we have a democracy, and we need a free marketplace of ideas to assure that democracy makes a wise choice, and that is why politically—

The Court: How would you respond to a comment, let's kill all the ACLU lawyers, as free speech, counsel?

Mr. Griffiths: Your Honor, [i]n fact, I have received such comments in the mail regularly, and I respond to it as being free speech, Your Honor.

The Court: Okay. A man of principle.

Mr. Griffiths: The First Amendment is involved with great ideas, political discourse, and I would submit that this is political discourse on a very down-to-earth level. . . .

The Court: Go ahead, Mr. Lee.

Mr. Lee: Thank you, Your Honor.

The Court: I hope you are not going to stress too much her position as a quasi-secret service agent.

Mr. Lee: I will do my best to eliminate that from my prepared speech, Your Honor.

The Court: All right.

Mr. Lee: [C]onstable Rankin was looking at her when he [asked her if she had said that she would like to see the President killed], and her statement to him [was] that she would.

Now, this is his alter ego. . . .

He is sworn to a constitutional oath. His deputies are sworn to the same constitutional oath. And in the eyes of the public, his deputy is him. . . .

It was disruptive to the Constable's office to have someone who is not marching in step to our drummer, here in our midst as one of us. If we were talking about the Dolphins and the 49'ers, this would be just like a guard on the Dolphins coming back to the huddle there and telling the quarterback, "Marino, that I hope that linebacker for the 49'ers smears you on the next play". . . .

THE DISTRICT COURT'S OPINION (FROM THE BENCH)

[Immediately after the arguments, the district court ruled from the bench. Excerpts follow:]

The Court: [I] suppose while listening to the testimony this second time and re-reading the Fifth Circuit's opinion and re-reading *Connick v. Myers*, I think I understand what the courts are trying to tell us.

[T]here is no question that Ms. McPherson was a probationary public employee; no question but that she was discharged. I really don't believe there is any question about what she said. . . .

I think that the constable was entitled to listen to the words that were said by Ms. McPherson, when she repeated them to him, were confirmed that she had said them to him, and judge those words by their ordinary English context. . . .

Then I suppose we get down to the serious question, what did she "mean." I don't believe she meant nothing, as she said here today, and I don't believe that those words were mere political hyperbole. They were something more than political hyperbole. They expressed such dislike of a high public government official as to be violent words, in context. This is not the situation where one makes an idle threat to kill someone for not picking them up on time, or not picking up their clothes. It was more than that.

It's not like the *Myers* case where Ms. Myers was trying to comment upon the internal affairs of the office, or matters upon public concern. I don't think it is a matter of public concern to approve . . . the second attempt at assassination.

Certainly, [Constable Rankin] had some concern about the security questions that Ms. McPherson would have access to delicate information about the whereabouts of the President. I think that is far less significant in his motivation than the question of the statement by Ms. McPherson, indicating to him she was the kind of person who would be a bad employee, would be a negative influence in the office.

I think what we have at this point is the *Pickering v. Board of Education* balance test. . . .

In looking at the balancing test, I have got to go with Constable Rankin, as I did on the initial hearing. [I]s the communication protected, no, I do not believe it is. I do not believe that that is protected speech. But applying the second part of the test, it certainly was a substantial part in the decision to fire her, and I doubt that he would have fired her had she not made that comment. I know I'm not required to reach the second [point], having found against the plaintiff on the first. . . .

Mr. Griffiths: Your Honor, is the court—is that opinion from the bench the court's opinion?

The Court: Those will be my Findings of Fact and Conclusions of Law. . . .

NOTES AND QUESTIONS

(1) *Strategy.* Consider the following matters of strategy, and evaluate the wisdom of each:

(a) Plaintiff's decision to call Constable Rankin as plaintiff's first witness.

(b) Plaintiff's invocation of "the rule" (sequestering witnesses).

(c) Plaintiff's emphasis of the private context of the remark, the public nature of the underlying political issue, McPherson's duties, her lack of training, and the absence of actual disruption.

(d) Plaintiff's use of Professor Kochman (who testified to the alleged "verbal flamboyance" of black culture).

(e) Defendants' emphasis of security concerns of visiting dignitaries.

(f) Defendant's emphasis of the "team" aspect of the constable's office.

(2) *The Security Issue.* The trial judge downplayed the issue of security of visiting dignitaries during argument—but then mentioned it in his bench opinion. The Supreme Court did not emphasize the issue. Is the desire (if it exists) of a clerical employee for the assassination of the President, in an office that handles confidential information regarding security of visiting dignitaries, a more serious issue than the Supreme Court made it? Was this de-emphasis the result of an oversight of the Supreme Court—or of counsel?

NOTE ON COURT OF APPEALS OPINION

[In March, 1986, five years after McPherson's discharge, the court of appeals reversed the district court and held for McPherson. *McPherson v. Rankin,* 786 F.2d 1233 (5th Cir. 1986). The opinion was by Judge Higginbotham, who happened to have been appointed by President Reagan(!) After setting out the facts and citing *Connick* and *Pickering,* the opinion included the following:]

[F]or the purpose of applying the *Pickering/Connick* balancing test, we accept the district court's conclusion that McPherson actually hoped that the President would be assassinated. . . .

Regardless of her intent, however, McPherson's comment clearly addressed a matter of public concern. [T]hus, the value of protecting her right to express her opinion, however loathsome, must be weighed against the competing interests of the constable's office in the effective and efficient fulfillment of its law enforcement responsibilities.

We are persuaded that the government's interest in maintaining an efficient office does not outweigh the first amendment interest in protecting McPherson's freedom of expression. Her comment was made to a co-worker who, with the benefit of the remark's full context, was not offended. Constable Rankin specifically denied having fired her because of any disruption caused by her comment, and the evidence did not show that the remark threatened the future efficiency or morale of the office.

The government's strongest argument lies in Constable Rankin's contention that he should not have to employ *anyone* who "rides with the cops and cheers for the robbers." [J]ust as a hospital has a legitimate interest in ensuring that its employees are not committed to euthanasia, so a law enforcement agency cannot be expected to carry out its mission through officers who favor political assassination. We therefore agree that Constable Rankin's action [w]as based on an important and legitimate government interest.

The difficulty with the government's position in this case, however, is that McPherson's duties were so utterly ministerial and her potential for undermining the office's mission so trivial. [H]owever ill-considered Ardith McPherson's opinion was, it did not make her unfit for her lowly job in Constable Rankin's office.

REVERSED and REMANDED for determination of an appropriate remedy.

NOTE ON SUPREME COURT'S GRANT OF CERTIORARI

The defendants timely filed a petition for certiorari in June of 1986, after the Court of Appeals' judgment had become final. [You should recall that a petition seeking review in the Supreme Court differs from an ordinary brief in that its function is not to persuade on the merits but to establish the need for decision of the issue. An example of such a document in a different context appears in Chapter 7.]

The Supreme Court granted certiorari on October 20, 1986, roughly five and one-half years after McPherson's discharge. The Petitioners (*i.e.*, Defendants Rankin and Harris County) then were required to file a brief on the merits.

PETITIONERS' BRIEF ON THE MERITS

NO. 85-2068

IN THE
SUPREME COURT OF THE UNITED STATES
OCTOBER TERM, 1985

CONSTABLE WALTER H. RANKIN and HARRIS COUNTY, TEXAS,
Petitioners
v.
ARDITH McPHERSON, Respondent

On Writ of Certiorari to the United States Court of Appeals for the Fifth Circuit

PETITIONERS' BRIEF ON THE MERITS . . .

QUESTIONS PRESENTED FOR REVIEW

(1) Does a Deputy Constable serving at the pleasure of the Constable have a constitutional right to speak out favoring the assassination of the President of the United States?

(2) Does a law enforcement officer have a constitutional right to speak out in favor of violations of the law the officer has undertaken to enforce? . . .

[Certain formal parts of the brief, including the listing of interested parties, index, table of contents, citations to judgments below, jurisdictional grounds, constitutional and statutory provisions, and statement of the case, are omitted.]

SUMMARY OF ARGUMENT

Under Texas law, a Constable appoints a Deputy to assist him in the performance of his duties. The Deputy serves at the pleasure of the Constable. The Deputy is the alter ego of the Constable. [T]he public rightly holds the Constable responsible for whatever the Deputy does.

The Constable is a law enforcement officer of the State of Texas. By force of law, his Deputies are also law enforcement officers. He, and his Deputies, are sworn to preserve, protect, and defend the Constitution and laws of the United States and of this State. [M]urder of the President is prohibited by Congressional statute. It is inconsistent for a Deputy sworn to preserve, protect and defend the Constitution and laws of the United States and Texas to voice a desire for some of those same laws to be violated. [A] Constable, with a responsibility to the people who elected him to enforce the laws, cannot have confidence in a Deputy, who is his alter ego to the public, who wants a very heinous crime perpetrated.

ARGUMENT

[The argument, which is here omitted, did not cite either the *Pickering* or the *Connick* case. It cited more Texas cases than Supreme Court cases, and it basically expanded upon the Summary of Argument, above.]

Respectfully submitted,

County Attorney, Harris County,
Texas . . .

NOTES AND QUESTIONS ON QUALITY OF ADVOCACY
AND AMICUS BRIEFS

(1) *The Quality of Advocacy.* What is the quality of the advocacy reflected in the preceding brief? How does the quality of advocacy affect the quality of decision?

(2) *Amicus Curiae Brief by Law Enforcement Groups that Included the International Association of Chiefs of Police and National District Attorneys Association; Amicus Curiae Brief of the United States.* The United States, through the Solicitor General, filed an amicus curiae brief carefully discussing the *Connick* and *Pickering* cases, among others, and since the Supreme Court's decision clearly would affect them, other groups interested in law enforcement issues also filed an amicus curiae brief addressing the *Connick-Pickering* balance, as well as other issues. Excerpts from that brief follow.

AMICUS CURIAE BRIEF SUPPORTING PETITIONERS

. . . ARGUMENT AND AUTHORITIES

THE EMPLOYEE'S [S]TATEMENT IN THIS CASE, ADVOCATING THE CRIME OF MURDER, WAS NOT THE KIND OF EXPRESSION ON A MATTER OF "PUBLIC CONCERN" THAT WOULD OVERCOME THE LEGITIMATE CONCERNS OF HER EMPLOYER IN A LAW ENFORCEMENT OFFICE.

The court of appeals correctly recognized that *Connick v. Myers,* 461 U.S. 138 (1983) provides the framework for analysis of this case. Furthermore, that court correctly held; "We . . . agree that Constable Rankin's action in dismissing McPherson was based on an important and legitimate government interest." 786 F.2d at 1238. However, the court incorrectly held that her advocacy of the crime of murder, even though in the form of "an actual wish for . . . assassination," was "addressed to serious matters of public concern." *Id.*

A. *Statements That Merely Have Private Shock Value, and That Have No Possibility of Advancing Discussion of Any Public Issue Whatsoever, Cannot Be Characterized as Expression on "Matters of Public Concern."*

McPherson's statement contributed nothing to any public debate on any issue. Indeed, it was deliberately phrased to have nothing to do with any public debate. [T]o frame the question in the terminology of *Connick v. Myers*, amici submit that "Publication of [McPherson's] remark would provide no basis for determining [any person's] qualifications for continuing in public office." *Connick v. Myers*, 461 U.S. at 1690; *Pickering v. Board of Education*, 391 U.S. 571–72 (1968).

The only possible motivation for this statement was to give vent to anger. That is a private purpose, not a "serious matter of public concern." Furthermore, a law enforcement office is the last place on earth where actions or utterances produced solely by uncontrolled temper should be encouraged. . . .

The decisions of this Court clearly indicate that remarks having merely private shock value cannot appropriately be labeled as "serious matters of public concern." For example, in *Bethel School District v. Fraser*, 54 U.S.L.W. 5054 (U.S. S. Ct. Mar. 3, 1986), the court held that an offensive speech, inconsistent with the mission of the institution, was not protected when given by a high school student at a school assembly. That was so, even though the student mentioned a candidate for office, and even though his speech might have been protected as dealing with "public concern" if he had not chosen to abandon that purpose, and, instead, merely shock and offend. . . .

In *FCC v. Pacifica Foundation*, 438 U.S. 726 (1978), the Court dealt with the power of the Federal Communications Commission to regulate a radio broadcast in which a comedian described his own performance as being in "the words you couldn't say on the public, ah, airwaves, um, the ones you definitely wouldn't say ever." [I]ts opinion said: "Such utterances are no essential part of any exposition of ideas, and are of such slight social value as a step to truth that any benefit that may be derived from them is clearly outweighed by the social interest in order and morality." These words (which fit the present case perfectly) were quoted from *Chaplinsky v. New Hampshire*, 355 U.S. 568, 572 (1942), which held that "insulting or 'fighting' words" are not expressions on serious matters of public concern. *Cf. New York v. Ferber*, 458 U.S. 747 (1982); *Cantwell v. Connecticut*, 310 U.S. 296 (1940) (carving out "personal abuse" as unprotected) (by implication). . . .

B. *A Statement Made By a Law Enforcement Employee [t]o a Captive Audience [is of] Concern to the Law Enforcement Employer.* . . .

Police officers have rights of association, too. [F]urthermore, the right to speak includes the right not to listen. Constable Rankin was entitled to consider the fact that employees in his office are a captive audience for other employees, with whom they work side by side. [What] the court of appeals failed to recognize was that all personnel in the office, from Constable Rankin on down, had a *first amendment* interest to that effect. *See also Bethel School District v. Fraser, supra* (teenage girl students had a valid interest in avoiding treatment as captive audience during speech that, "[b]y glorifying male sexuality, . . . was acutely insulting"); *Erzoznik v. Jacksonville*, 422 U.S. 205 (1975) (rights of listener become particularly important when "the degree of captivity makes it impractical for the unwilling viewer or auditor to avoid exposure"); Lehman v. Shaker Heights, 418 U.S. 298 (1974) (bus riders can be protected from involuntary exposure to political advertising); *Kovacks v. Cooper*, 336 U.S. 77 (1949) (freedom of speech protects efforts to reach the minds of "willing listeners" . . .).

Perhaps the most uncareful statement by the court of appeals is its conclusion that "the evidence did not show that the remark threatened the future efficiency or morale of the office". . . .

It is fortunate that this Court has avoided the court of appeals' analysis of this "work environment" issue. In *Bethel School District v. Fraser, supra*, for example, the Court said:

> The first amendment does not prevent the school officials from determining that to permit a vulgar and lewd speech such as respondent's would undermine

the school's basic educational mission. . . . Accordingly, it was perfectly appropriate for the school to disassociate itself to make the point to the people that vulgar speech and lewd conduct is wholly inconsistent with the "fundamental values" of public school education.

Similarly, Constable Rankin's office had proper authority to disassociate itself from the utterances that would contradict its "basic . . . mission" in this case.

But there is something even more fundamentally wrong with the court of appeals' finding that there was no "disruption caused by [McPherson's comment" and that the remark did not "[threaten] the future efficiency or morale of the office." A more perceptive analysis is given by Diamond, *The First Amendment and Public Schools: The Case Against Judicial Intervention*, 59 Texas L. Rev. 477, 479–98 (1981):

> The judiciary cannot know the extent to which any kind of distraction during the course of the day interferes with learning. A court can observe that fist fights did not break out and that no one complained about being prevented from doing his work. But the court cannot begin to know even the amount of distraction that actually occurred, either in the students' minds or beyond their awareness. . . .

It is not necessary for an "employer to allow events to unfold to the extent that the disruption of the office and the destruction of working relationships is manifest before taking action." *Perry Education Ass'n v. Perry Local Educators' Ass'n*, 460 U.S. 37, 52 (1983).

In this regard, amici are proud that the modern law enforcement ideal—and in the overwhelming majority of cases, the actual practice—is courtesy toward those who provoke personal frustration, including the most repugnant arrested citizen. This Court can take judicial notice, based upon widespread news reports, of the professionalism that New York City detectives displayed when they arrested David Berkowitz (who designated himself as the "Son of Sam") . . . [A]mici emphatically submit that these examples of professionalism do not happen by accident. They happen because officers such as Constable Rankin promptly, habitually, and systematically reject behavior such as McPherson's. By taking away their ability to do so, the court of appeals' opinion would decrease that professionalism. . . .

C. *While Law Enforcement Employees Clearly Have the Protection of the First Amendment, They Do Not Have the Kind of "Super First Amendment Status" That Respondent in Effect Claims For Them.*

Amici agree with this Court's view, expressed in *Pickering v. Board of Education*, 391 U.S. 563 (1968), that a public employee is free to voice criticism against his employer. Law enforcement personnel are also privileged to raise criticism. In Illinois, for example, one appellate court upheld a firefighter's right publicly to accuse the mayor of stealing an election. *Shewmake v. Board of Fire & Police Commrs*, 390 N.E.2d 536 (Ill. App. Ct. 1979). In another case, an Illinois appellate court upheld another firefighter who called an alderman a "dummy" in connection with a public issue. Hasenstab v. Board of Fire & Police Commrs, 389 N.E.2d 588 (Ill. App. Ct. 1979). [Amici agree with these decisions.] . . .

[But] an employee in a purely private business (one without the difficult public mission of a law enforcement office) obviously could be fired for behavior such as McPherson's. [I]ronically, what ACLU actually argues for is lower performance standards for law enforcement employees. [T]he Court should reject this "super first amendment status" advocated by McPherson and ACLU.

D. *The Fact That the Employee in This Case Was Not, Herself, a Law Enforcement Officer Should Not Exempt Her From Reasonable Policies Generally Applicable in the Law Enforcement Office in which She Worked.*

[I]t is impossible to compartmentalize a given functionary so that he or she has no influence on law enforcement activities. If McPherson may perform her civil process job in the manner disclosed here, why not protect advocacy of murder by a radio dispatcher? Must Constable Rankin retain a radio dispatcher who "dispatches for the cops, but cheers for the criminals?" In the second place, a civilian employee like McPherson has great influence in the way that the rights and interests of citizens are protected. McPherson's responsibilities could determine records concerning whether citizens have warrants out for their arrests, or whether they are subject to eviction, or whether their civil papers have been served. [F]inally, the court of appeals' opinion fails to recognize that police chiefs are like any other kind of employer in that they wish for, and deserve, the kind of employees they will want to retain and promote. . . .

Of course, these responsible, positive employees are initially hired as probationary employees, in positions where their responsibility for public contact is minimal. The court of appeals failed to recognize that McPherson was likely to have limited responsibilities, which should be expected to expand. . . .

CONCLUSION

The decision of the court of appeals should be reversed.

Respectfully submitted,

David Crump. . . .
Attorney for Amici Curiae

RESPONDENT MCPHERSON'S BRIEF ON THE MERITS

[The style and certain other parts of the brief are omitted,
as are many citations.]

RESPONDENT MCPHERSON'S BRIEF ON THE MERITS

[The style and certain other parts of the brief are omitted, as are many citations.]

QUESTION PRESENTED FOR REVIEW

Can a nonpolicymaking, nonconfidential county employee be constitutionally discharged for a private expression of her views on the policies of the President, where those views were wholly unrelated to office matters and were found to have had no disruptive effect upon the office, merely because her deplorable choice of words caused her superior to "los[e] confidence" in her? . . .

ARGUMENT . . .

I. MS. McPHERSON'S PRIVATE CONVERSATION CRITICIZING GOVERN-MENT POLICIES WAS AN EXPRESSION OF POLITICAL BELIEFS THAT WAS CLEARLY DIRECTED TO MATTERS OF PUBLIC CONCERN AND IS ENTITLED TO FIRST AMENDMENT PROTECTION. . . .

B. An Independent Examination of the Content, Form, and Context of Ms. McPherson's Statement Compels the Conclusion That It Was a Protected Form of Political Hyperbole.

Ms. McPherson's challenged statement is milder than that involved in *Watts v. United States*, 394 U.S. 705 (1967) (per curiam). Watts took part in a rally on the Washington Monument grounds protesting American involvement in the Vietnam War. He referred to his upcoming physical examination for the draft and then stated, "If they ever make me carry a rifle the first man I want to get in my sights is L.B.J." This Court reversed Watts' conviction under 18 U.S.C. § 871 for threatening the life of the President. . . .

[M]s. McPherson's statement, like that in *Watts*, was not meant literally. As she testified, "It doesn't mean that I want the man dead." The "content, form, and context, . . . as revealed by the whole record," demonstrate that she intended her statement only to illustrate how strongly she "disagreed with [the President's] policy". . . .

Constable Rankin and Captain LeVrier testified that Ms. McPherson told them that she "meant" her final remark. Deputy Chief Abercia, however, could recall no such statement by her. Ms. McPherson and Mr. Jackson (the only person to who she was speaking and the only person who heard the entire conversation in full context) testified that she did not mean it. It is clear from the district court's two opinions in this case that it was unwilling to accord any probative value to the testimony of Constable Rankin and Captain LeVrier on the point. The court never found that she said that she meant the remark, and never found what she did mean by it, except that it was "something more" than hyperbole. . . .

C. Whatever She Meant by Her Remark, Ms. McPherson's Conversation Was Protected Political Speech on a Matter of Public Concern.

Even if Ms. McPherson could be found to have meant her statement literally, such a hope for the President's death, in the context in which it was made, was clearly protected speech on a matter of public concern. It was certainly not "advocacy" of assassination, much less incitement to imminent lawless action. As this Court noted about the remark in *Watts*, her remark was conditional; she began by saying, "*If* they go for him again . . ." (emphasis added). Its intended recipient, Mr. Jackson, was certainly unmoved to engage in unlawful action; indeed, he thought nothing of the remark and was shocked at her discharge because of it. The abstract expression of a hope that "they" might be successful in the future is deplorable, but it cannot be characterized as advocacy or incitement of "them" to assassination.

Of course, as the United States points out, certain other narrowly limited types of speech have been held not entitled to First Amendment protection. These include "fighting words" which "by their very utterance . . . tend to incite an immediate breach of the peace," certain forms of libelous speech, and obscenity. But Ms. McPherson's expression of political views—including her final remark—was far removed from any of these categories of speech. . . .

Nor was Ms. McPherson's expression of her opposition to the President's policies one that "occupies at best a 'subordinate position in the scale of First Amendment values'" (citing *Ohralik v. Ohio State Bar Ass'n*, 436 U.S. 447, 456 (1978)). [A]nd it was not misinformation about anyone's financial assets and liabilities (citing *Dun & Bradstreet, Inc. v. Greenmoss Builders, Inc.*, 472 U.S. 749 (1985)). It was a conversation about the political, social, and economic policies of a national Administration.

[The brief also addressed the "balancing" issue and the countervailing interests of the government office. It concluded that the Fifth Circuit's decision "should be affirmed."]

	Respectfully submitted,
Bruce V. Griffiths	Lloyd N. Cutler . . .
[Counsel of Record] . . .	Wilmer, Cutler & Pickering

NOTE ON SUPREME COURT DECISION

The Supreme Court's opinions appear in Chapter 11, above, in the section on "Speech by Government Employees." They should be reconsidered in light of these materials.

Chapter 12
FREEDOM OF RELIGION

§ 12.01 THE RELIGION CLAUSES: AN OVERVIEW

Purpose of the Religion Clauses. The Supreme Court has written that the Establishment Clause was a reaction to laws that compelled citizens to attend or to support, by taxes, churches established by government. *Everson v. Board of Education,* below. In *Abington School Dist. v. Schempp,* below, Justice Goldberg summarized the purposes of both clauses as a requirement "that government neither engage in nor compel religious practices, that it affect no favoritism among sects or between religion and nonreligion, and that it work deterrence of no religious belief."

Difficulty of Interpreting the Religion Clauses. Chief Justice Burger interpreted the Establishment Clause as "a blurred, indistinct, and variable barrier depending on all the circumstances of a particular relationship." *Lemon v. Kurtzman,* below. In the same decision, the Chief Justice said: "We can only dimly perceive the lines of demarcation in this extraordinary area of constitutional law."

The Clash Between the Establishment Clause and the Free Exercise Clause. There are two clauses addressed to two separate concerns. The two religion clauses "are cast in absolute terms, and either, if expanded to a logical extreme, would tend to clash with the other." *Walz v. Tax Comm'n,* below. For example, consider the issue of military chaplains (which is discussed in a concurring opinion in *Abington School Dist. v. Schempp*). If the government posts a conscripted soldier overseas where he does not have access to a member of the clergy, it may deny him the free exercise of his religion. On the other hand, if it provides clergy, it risks creating an establishment of religion. This conflict between the clauses is a recurring theme in some of the cases.

"Neutrality" and "Accommodation." Many of the cases indicate that government must be "neutral" among religions, and as between religion and irreligion; also, it must avoid providing any "aid" to any particular religion. This idea of neutrality, however, is more easily stated than explained, since government arguably "aids" religion by such apparently "neutral" acts as providing fire protection to churches or furnishing police officers to direct traffic in streets in front of them. Another theme that is seen in some of the cases is that of official "accommodation" of religion, when government adapts its activities so as to recognize or allow, but not to "aid," the exercise of religion. Just how far "accommodation" may go without running afoul of the Establishment Clause is an issue that recurs in the cases—as is the question whether a failure to accommodate may violate the Free Exercise Clause.

The "Wall of Separation" Metaphor—and Criticisms of the Metaphor. Thomas Jefferson is credited with the famous statement that the First Amendment created a "wall of separation" between church and state. Several of the Court's decisions quote this statement, and it has been quite influential. However, it must be remembered that this figure of speech was not the universal view among the founders, and that it may not be helpful in resolving all religion clause issues. Neither clause uses the word "separation" at all. In *Lynch v. Donnelly,* Chief Justice Burger stated that the wall metaphor was not "a wholly accurate description of the practical relationship that in fact exists between church and state."

The Three-Part Test of Lemon v. Kurtzman and the Retreat from It. In *Lemon v. Kurtzman,* below, the Supreme Court set out a three-part test for Establishment Clause issues: "First, the statute must have a secular legislative purpose; second, its principal or primary effect must be one that neither advances nor inhibits religion. . . . finally, the statute must not foster 'an excessive government entanglement with religion.'" The Court has applied this method of analysis in many of its cases. However, there have been cases in which the Court has avoided relying on the test. *E.g., Marsh v. Chambers,* below; *Lynch v. Donnelly*, below. As you read these cases, use *Everson* and *Lemon* as benchmarks to consider the various levels of judicial scrutiny applied to Establishment Clause claims.

Read U.S. Const. Amend. I (the Establishment Clause; the Free Exercise Clause).

---

§ 12.02   THE ESTABLISHMENT CLAUSE

INTRODUCTORY NOTE

In Considering the Establishment Clause and Its Interpretation by the Modern Court, It Is Important to Keep the Text In Mind. The text states "Congress shall make no law respecting an establishment of religion. . . ." For purposes of interpreting this Clause, whether under an originalist approach or otherwise, it is important to understand what was meant by "an establishment of religion." You will see in the following cases a great deal of debate among Justices about what that term meant in 1791 and what that term should mean today. In all cases, it is important to remember that the term "establishment" is referring to a constitutionally appropriate arrangement between church and state.

Different countries around the world have taken various approaches to the relationship between church and state. For example, in countries such as Iran and Pakistan there is the merging of religion and the state. Some nations have established state churches (one supported by the government), including Greece and the United Kingdom. There are a number of countries with *de facto* established churches, such as in Spain or Portugal. In countries such as Germany there is a high level of church-state cooperation. In other countries such as Mexico there is a strict sense of separation between church and state. It is important to recognize that there is a range of possibilities for arranging affairs of church and state.

Against this backdrop, the one question that American courts must resolve, whether considering original intent or modern policy analysis under judicial review, is the constitutionally appropriate arrangement of affairs between religion and the state in the American constitutional democracy. *See generally* Edward J. Eberle, *Religion in the Classroom in Germany and the United States*, 81 TUL. L. REV. 67 (2006).

The Role of History in Establishment Clause Interpretation. Starting with the *Everson* decision below, history has played a significant role in the judicial review of the Establishment Clause and the Free Exercise Clause. The *Everson* decision, in fact, is one of the most easily recognizable examples of *original intentionism* in the modern case law. Watch for the use of history by the various Justices, either in formulating the majority opinions or in the concurring and dissenting opinions. *See generally* Erwin Chemerinsky, *Why Separate Church and State?*, 85 ORE. L. REV. 351 (2006).

It might be helpful to review the various historical periods relevant to the Establishment Clause, at least for purposes of any type of originalism analysis: the "early" colonial period; the later colonial period including colonial charters; the state constitutions in the post-Revolutionary era; the state constitutions during the Articles of Confederation; the constitutional convention itself (*e.g.*, religious oath provision of Article VI); the ratification period including the anti-federalist sentiments so prominent in the development of the Bill of Rights; the legislative history of the development of the Bill of Rights including the First Amendment; and the ratification of the Bill of Rights. Watch for various types of history that are utilized and the arguments that are developed.

There obviously are two centuries of history since the ratification of the First Amendment. As you discussed in Chapter 5, such post-adoption and ratification history might be considered, as Justice Frankfurter said in the *Steel Seizure* case, as a "gloss" regarding the interpretation of these Clauses. Even under the skillful theorizing of Justice Frankfurter, however, the post-ratification history or interpretation of these clauses is not germane to the original intent of the Framers. *See, e.g., District of Columbia v. Heller*, 128 S. Ct. 2783 (2008) (Scalia, J.): *Boumediene v. Bush*, 128 S. Ct. 2229 (2008) (Kennedy, J.). That is, some history is more important to any kind of originalism analysis than any kind of post-adoption history.

One example of a post-adoption history that has had a significant doctrinal life is Jefferson's famous statement that the First Amendment was designed to create a "wall" between Church and State. This is a statement made by Jefferson many years after the First Amendment (and the Establishment Clause) had been ratified. At best, the wall concept might be considered part of a historical gloss. Note that the *Everson* Court may not have appreciated that distinction; on the other hand, the *Everson* Court's use of the "wall" metaphor may have been used as a straw man by the critics of the result in the *Everson* decision.

[A] Aid to Religion or Religious Institutions

[1] Financial Aid

EVERSON v. BOARD OF EDUCATION
330 U.S. 1 (1947)

MR. JUSTICE BLACK delivered the opinion of the Court.

[A New Jersey statute authorized school districts to provide bus transportation or reimbursement to individuals for transportation to either public or private schools, including Catholic parochial schools. Everson, a taxpayer, challenged the statute as a "law respecting an establishment of religion." Here, the Court upholds the statute.]

A large proportion of the early settlers of this country came here from Europe to escape the bondage of laws which compelled them to support and attend government favored churches. [W]ith the power of government supporting them, at various times and places, Catholics had persecuted Protestants, Protestants had persecuted Catholics, Protestant sects had persecuted other Protestant sects, Catholics of one shade of belief had persecuted Catholics of another shade of belief, and all of these had from time to time persecuted Jews. . . .

These practices became so commonplace as to shock the freedom-loving colonials into a feeling of abhorrence. The imposition of taxes to pay ministers' salaries and to build and maintain churches and church property aroused their indignation. It was these feelings which found expression in the First Amendment. . . .

The movement toward this end reached its dramatic climax in Virginia in 1785–'86 when the Virginia legislative body was about to renew Virginia's tax levy for the support of the established church. Thomas Jefferson and James Madison led the fight against this tax. [W]hen the proposal came up for consideration at that session, it not only died in committee, but the assembly enacted the famous "Virginia Bill for Religious Liberty" originally written by Thomas Jefferson. . . .

This Court has previously recognized that the provisions of the First Amendment . . . had the same objective and were intended to provide the same protection against government intrusion on religious liberty as the Virginia statute. . . .

The "establishment of religion" clause of the First Amendment means at least this:

Neither a state nor the federal government can set up a church. Neither can pass laws which aid one religion, aid all religions, or prefer one religion over another. Neither can force nor influence a person to go to or remain away from church against his will or force him to profess a belief or disbelief in any religion. No person can be punished for entertaining or professing religious beliefs or disbeliefs, for church attendance or non-attendance. No tax in any amount, large or small, can be levied to support any religious activities or institutions, whatever they may be called, or whatever form they may adopt to teach or practice religion. Neither a state nor the federal government can, openly or secretly, participate in the affairs of any religious organizations or groups and vice versa. In the words of Jefferson, the clause against establishment of religion by law was intended to erect "a wall of separation between church and state". . . .

. . . On the other hand, other language of the amendment commands that New Jersey cannot hamper its citizens in the free exercise of their own religion. Consequently, it cannot exclude individual Catholics, Lutherans, . . . non-believers, Presbyterians, or other members of any other faith, *because of their faith, or lack of it,* from receiving the benefits of public welfare legislation. While we do not mean to intimate that a state could not provide transportation only to children attending public schools, we must be careful, in protecting the citizens of New Jersey against state-established churches, to be sure that we do not inadvertently prohibit New Jersey from extending its general State law benefits to all its citizens without regard to their religious belief.

Measured by these standards, we cannot say that the First Amendment prohibits New Jersey from spending tax-raised funds to pay the bus fares of parochial school pupils as part of a general program under which it pays the fares of people attending public and other schools. There is even a possibility that some of the children might not be sent to the church schools if the parents were compelled to pay their children's bus fares out of their own pockets when transportation to a public school would have been paid for by the state. [M]oreover, state-paid policemen, detailed to protect children going to and from church schools from the very real hazards of traffic, would serve much the same purpose. [S]imilarly, parents might be reluctant to permit their children to attend schools which the state had cut off from such general government services as ordinary police and fire protection, connections for sewage disposal, public highways and sidewalks. Of course, cutting off church schools from these services, so separate and so indisputably marked off from the religious function, would make it far more difficult for the schools to operate. But such is obviously not the purpose of the First Amendment. That amendment requires the state to be a neutral in its relations with groups of religious believers and nonbelievers; it does not require the state to be their adversary. State power is no more to be used so as to handicap religions, than it is to favor them.

[T]he state contributes no money to the schools. It does not support them. . . .

The First Amendment has erected a wall between church and state. [W]e could not approve the slightest breach. New Jersey has not breached it here. . . .

JUSTICE JACKSON, dissenting:

The Court's opinion marshals every argument in favor of state aid and puts the case in its most favorable light, but much of its reasoning confirms my conclusions that there are no good grounds upon which to support the present legislation. In fact, the undertones of the opinion, advocating complete and uncompromising separation of Church from State, seem utterly discordant with its conclusion yielding support to their commingling in educational matters. . . .

MR. JUSTICE RUTLEDGE, with whom MR. JUSTICE FRANKFURTER, MR. JUSTICE JACKSON, and MR. JUSTICE BURTON agree, dissenting. . . .

Not simply an established church, but any law respecting an establishment of religion is forbidden. . . .

The amendment's purpose was not to strike merely at the official establishment of a single sect, creed or religion, outlawing only a formal relation such as had prevailed in England and some of the colonies. [I]t was to create a complete and permanent separation of the spheres of religious activity and civil authority by comprehensively forbidding every form of public aid or support for religion. . . .

No provision of the Constitution is more closely tied to or given content by its generating history than the religious clause of the First Amendment. [T]he history includes not only Madison's authorship and the proceedings before the First Congress, but also the long and intensive struggle for religious freedom in America, more especially in Virginia, . . .

The reasons underlying the Amendment's policy have not vanished with time or diminished in force. [T]he great condition of religious liberty is that it be maintained free from sustenance, as also from other interferences, by the state. For when it comes to rest upon that secular foundation it vanishes with the resting. Public money devoted to payment of religious costs, educational or other, brings the quest for more. It brings too the struggle of sect against sect for the larger share or for any. [I]t is the very thing Jefferson and Madison experienced and sought to guard against, whether in its blunt or in its more screened forms. The end of such strife cannot be other than to destroy the cherished liberty. The dominating group will achieve the dominant benefit; or all will embroil the state in their dissensions. . . .

NOTES AND QUESTIONS

(1) *The Seminal Establishment Clause Decision: Everson v. Board of Education, 330 U.S. 1 (1947).* In the post-WWII population boom, the state of New Jersey passed a statutory program authorizing public school districts to provide bus transportation—or reimbursement to individuals for transportation—to public or private schools, including parochial schools. The New Jersey statute was challenged under the Establishment Clause. The Supreme Court, per Justice Black, held that the New Jersey transportation reimbursement statute did not constitute an impermissible establishment of religion. Four Justices dissented, with Justices Jackson and Rutledge writing famous dissents.

The nine Justices all seemed to agree on the Framers' intent and the goals of the Establishment Clause. The Justices disagreed, however, on how the Establishment Clause doctrine applied to the facts of the New Jersey transportation reimbursement program. The case involved only an Establishment Clause challenge. There was no claim under the Free Exercise Clause; note that Court stated that there would be no problem if a public school district only provided transportation to public school students. (At this time and well into the 1970s, it was a common practice to publicly fund transportation only for public school students.) The *Everson* decision will be frequently cited in the subsequent caselaw.

(2) *The "Wall of Separation" Theory, the "Neutrality" Theory, and the "Prohibition of Official Religion" Theory.* Notice that Justice Black advances the wall-of-separation theory, but the dissents chide him for failing to use it. Justice Black also relies upon the separate notion that the statute is "neutral" as to religion, because it is "general" in application and merely removes an impediment that otherwise would encourage the parents of school children to send them to public, not private, schools. (Notice that this "neutrality" theory would allow more government involvement with religion than the wall-of-separation metaphor would.) Finally, notice the implication that the basic purpose of the First Amendment was to prohibit the historical practice of

officially established religions, or compulsory attendance or support of them. This theory presumably would allow even broader government action than the neutrality theory in that it would permit government action short of an official church.

(3) *The Difficulty of Ascertaining the Original Understanding.* As often happens, the original understanding of the Founders in drafting the amendment is difficult exactly to determine. The history of official establishment may be used to argue certain theories, the statements of Jefferson and Madison can be used to argue others, and the understandings of other members of Congress may be different still.

(4) *The Post-Everson Doctrinal Developments: The Apparent Search for a Less Rigorous Standard.* The *Everson* decision eventually came to stand for the judicial review standard of the Establishment Clause known as "strict neutrality." While the majority and the dissenters all agreed on the intent of the Framers, the 5-Justice majority held that New Jersey's transportation reimbursement program was sufficiently neutral and did not violate the Establishment Clause. In addition to textual and historical analysis, the *Everson* decision reveals the role of policy analysis. Justice Rutledge's dissent is noted for identifying policy concerns confronting the Framers: (1) maintaining religious liberty "free from [public] sustenance"; and (2) avoiding "the struggle of sect against sect for the larger share or for any." Are these still "dangers" against which the Establishment Clause must protect or are these policy concerns just historic relics?

(5) *Avoiding "Excessive Entanglement with Religion"—The Constitutionality of Tax Exemptions for Churches; Walz v. Tax Comm'n, 397 U.S. 664 (1970).* In *Walz*, the Court upheld an exemption from taxes for "property used exclusively for religious, educational or charitable purposes." Speaking through Chief Justice Burger, the Court said:

> Each value judgment under the religion clauses must [t]urn on whether particular acts in question are intended to establish or interfere with religious beliefs and practices or have the effect of doing so. . . . The legislative purpose of a property tax exemption is neither the advancement nor the inhibition of religion; it is neither sponsorship nor hostility. . . .

> Determining that the legislative purpose of tax exemption is not aimed at establishing, sponsoring, or supporting religion does not end the inquiry, however. We must also be sure that the end result—the effect—is not an excessive government entanglement with religion. . . . Either course, taxation of churches or exemption, occasions some degree of involvement with religion. Elimination of exemptions would tend to expand the involvement of government by giving rise to tax valuation of church property, tax liens, tax foreclosures, and the direct confrontations and conflicts that would follow in the train of those legal processes.

> Granting tax exemptions to churches necessarily operates to afford an indirect economic benefit and also gives rise to some, but yet a lesser, involvement than taxing them.

Justice Douglas dissented: "[N]on-believers who own realty are taxed at the usual rate." The exemption was not neutral, as he saw it, because it amounted to a subsidy.

LEMON v. KURTZMAN
403 U.S. 602 (1971)

MR. CHIEF JUSTICE BURGER delivered the opinion of the Court.

[The Rhode Island Salary Supplement Act] rests on the legislative finding that the quality of education available in nonpublic elementary schools has been jeopardized by the rapidly rising salaries needed to attract competent and dedicated teachers. The Act authorizes state officials to supplement the salaries of teachers of secular subjects in nonpublic elementary schools by paying directly to a teacher an amount not in excess of 15% of his current annual salary. [The Act also required teachers to teach only subjects offered in the State's public schools, to use only teaching materials used in the public schools, and to agree in writing not to teach any courses in religion.]

Pennsylvania has adopted a program that has some but not all of the features of the Rhode Island Program. [Pennsylvania authorized the State to "purchase" specified "secular educational services" from nonpublic schools by contracts that reimbursed the schools for their actual expenditures for teachers' salaries, textbooks, and educational materials. Schools were required to maintain prescribed accounting procedures to identify the "separate" cost of "secular" education. Reimbursement was limited to mathematics, language, physical science, and physical education classes, using approved textbooks, without "expressing religious teaching."]

Every analysis in this area must begin with consideration of the cumulative criteria developed by the Court over many years. Three such tests may be gleaned from our cases. First, the statute must have a secular legislative purpose; second, its principal or primary effect must be one that neither advances nor inhibits religion . . .; [and] finally, the statute must not foster "an excessive government entanglement with religion" [citing *Walz v. Tax Comm'n*]. . . .

Inquiry into the legislative purposes of the Pennsylvania and Rhode Island statutes affords no basis for a conclusion that the legislative intent was to advance religion. On the contrary, the statutes themselves clearly state that they are intended to enhance the quality of the secular education in all schools covered by the compulsory attendance laws. . . .

[W]e need not decide whether these legislative precautions restrict the principal or primary effect of the programs to the point where they do not offend the religion clauses, for we conclude that the cumulative impact of the entire relationship arising under the statutes in each state involves excessive entanglement between government and religion. . . .

Our prior holdings do not call for total separation between church and state; total separation is not possible in an absolute sense. Some relationship between government and religious organizations is inevitable. . . .

[In Rhode Island], the district court made extensive findings on the grave potential for excessive entanglement that inheres in the religious character and purpose of the Roman Catholic elementary schools of Rhode Island, to date the sole beneficiaries of the Rhode Island Salary Supplement Act.

[T]he district court concluded that the parochial schools constituted "an integral part of the religious mission of the Catholic church." The various characteristics of the schools make them "a powerful vehicle for transmitting the Catholic faith to the next generation." [I]n short, parochial schools involve substantial religious activity and purpose. . . .

[I]n terms of potential for involving some aspect of faith or morals in secular subjects, a textbook's content is ascertainable, but a teacher's handling of a subject is not. We cannot ignore the danger that a teacher under religious control and discipline poses to the separation of the religious from the purely secular aspects of pre-college education. . . .

A comprehensive, discriminating, and continuing state surveillance will inevitably be required to insure that these restrictions are obeyed and the first amendment otherwise respected. Unlike a book, a teacher cannot be inspected once so as to determine the extent and intent of his or her personal beliefs and subjective acceptance of the limitations imposed by the first amendment. These prophylactic contacts will involve excessive and enduring entanglement between state and church.

There is another area of entanglement in the Rhode Island program that gives concerns. The statute excludes teachers employed by non-public schools whose average per-pupil expenditures on secular education equal or exceed the comparable figures for public schools. In the event that the total expenditures of an otherwise eligible school exceed this norm, the program requires the government to examine the school's records in order to determine how much of the total expenditures is attributable to secular education and how much to religious activity. This kind of state inspection and evaluation of the religious organization is fraught with the sort of entanglement that the Constitution forbids. . . .

The Pennsylvania statute also provides state aid to church-related schools for teachers' salaries. . . .

The Pennsylvania statute, moreover, has the further defect of providing state financial aid directly to the church-related schools. This factor distinguishes [*Everson*], for [there] the Court was careful to point out that state aid was provided to the student and his parents—not to the church-related school. . . .

A broader base of entanglement of yet a different character is presented by the divisive political potential of these state programs. In a community where such a large number of pupils are served by church-related schools, it can be assumed that state assistance will entail considerable political activity. Partisans of parochial schools . . . will inevitably champion this cause and promote political action to achieve their goals. [C]andidates will be forced to declare and voters to choose. It would be unrealistic to ignore the fact that many people confronted with issues of this kind will find their votes aligned with their faith.

[I]n *Waltz*, we dealt with a status under state tax laws for the benefit of all religious groups. Here we are confronted with successive and very likely permanent annual appropriations that will benefit relatively few religious groups. Political fragmentation and divisiveness on religious lines are thus likely to be intensified. . . .

[W]e have no long history of state aid to church-related educational institutions comparable to 200 years of tax-exemption for churches [as in *Waltz*]. . . .

[The concurring opinion of JUSTICE DOUGLAS, joined by JUSTICE BLACK, is omitted. JUSTICE WHITE dissented, in an opinion appended to *Tilton v. Richardson*, below.]

TILTON v. RICHARDSON, 403 U.S. 672 (1971). This was the companion case to *Lemon v. Kurtzman*, and its application of the *Lemon* test provides perspective on the degree of scrutiny afforded there. Chief Justice Burger wrote the plurality opinion for the Court. The Higher Education Facilities Act of 1963 provided for federal construction grants to colleges for buildings, excluding sectarian and religious buildings. The United States retained a twenty-year interest in any facility constructed with funds under the Act, and if the recipient violated the statutory conditions during this period, the government was entitled to recovery of certain funds. Appellants attempted to show that grants to church-related colleges were unconstitutional by showing pervasive religious influence through curricula. Here, the Court upholds the Act as constitutional, except for the portion providing for a twenty-year limitation on the religious use of the facilities:

> [W]e consider four questions: First, does the Act reflect a secular legislative purpose? Second, is the primary effect of the Act to advance or inhibit religion? Third, does the administration of the Act foster an excessive government entanglement with religion? Fourth, does the implementation of the Act inhibit the free exercise of religion?

> The stated legislative purpose [is to encourage and to assist colleges and universities to accommodate growing numbers of youth who aspire to a higher education]. This expresses a legitimate secular objective entirely appropriate for governmental action. . . .

> [T]he crucial question is not whether some benefit accrues to a religious institution as a consequence of the legislative program, but whether its principal or primary effect advances religion.

[A]ppellants' position depends on the validity of the proposition that religion so permeates the secular education provided by church-related colleges and universities that their religious and secular educational functions are in fact inseparable. . . .

This record . . . provides no basis for any such assumption here. Two of the five federally financed buildings involved in this case are libraries. The district court found that no classes had been conducted in either of these facilities and that no restrictions were imposed by the institutions on the books that they acquired. [T]he third building was a language laboratory at Albertus Magnus College. [F]ederal grants were also used to build a science building at Fairfield University and a music, drama, and arts building at Annhurst College.

There is no evidence that religion seeps into the use of any of these facilities. . . .

Although we reject Appellants' broad constitutional arguments we do perceive an aspect in which the statute's enforcement provisions are inadequate to insure that the impact of the federal aid will not advance religion. If a recipient institution [within twenty years] violates any of the statutory restrictions on the use of a federally financed facility, § 754(B)(2) permits the government to recover an amount equal to the proportion of the facilities' present value that the federal grant bore to its original cost.

[Because of this provision] the Act therefore trespasses on the religion clauses. [The Court therefore excised the twenty-year limit from this statute.]

We next turn to the question of whether excessive entanglements characterize the relationship between government and church under the Act. . . .

There are generally significant differences between the religious aspects of church-related institutions of higher learning and parochial elementary and secondary schools. . . . Many church-related colleges and universities are characterized by a high degree of academic freedom and seek to evoke free and critical responses from their students. . . .

The entanglement between church and state is also lessened here by the nonideological character of the aid that the government provides. [I]n *Lemon*, . . . the state programs subsidized teachers. [S]ince teachers are not necessarily religiously neutral, greater governmental surveillance would be required to guarantee that state salary aid would not in fact subsidize religious instruction. [H]ere, on the other hand, the government provides facilities that are themselves religiously neutral. . . .

Finally, government entanglements with religion are reduced by the circumstance that, unlike the direct and continuing payments under the Pennsylvania program, and all the incidents of regulation and surveillance, the government aid here is a one-time, single-purpose construction grant. There are no continuing financial relationships or dependencies, no annual audits, and no government analysis of an institutions expenditures on secular as distinguished from religious activities. . . .

We think that cumulatively, these three factors also substantially lessen the potential for divisive religious fragmentation in the political arena. . . .

[The concurring opinion of JUSTICE DOUGLAS, joined by JUSTICE BLACK, is omitted, as is the separate opinion of JUSTICE BRENNAN.]

MR. JUSTICE WHITE, concurring in part and dissenting in part [in an opinion also applicable to *Lemon v. Kurtzman*].

It is enough for me that the states and the federal government are financing a separable secular function of overriding importance in order to sustain the legislation here challenged. That religion and private interests other than education may substantially benefit does not convert these laws into impermissible establishments of religion. . . .

NOTES AND QUESTIONS

(1) *The Three-Part Test of Lemon v. Kurtzman.* Notice the three-part test laid down by *Lemon.* It requires (1) a "secular legislative purpose;" (2) a primary effect that "neither advances nor inhibits religion;" and (3) the avoidance of excessive "entanglement" with religion. Is this test workable? Note that the level of scrutiny seems less than that of the wall-of-separation theory from *Everson.*

(2) *The Application of the Lemon Test to Related Issues.* In practice, the *Lemon* test proved to be difficult to apply, and the results were not easy to predict. Consider the following cases. A relatively early post-*Lemon* decision involved an Ohio law authorizing various forms of aid (*e.g.*, standardized testing) to nonpublic schools, most of whom were sectarian. The Supreme Court, per Justice Blackmun, held that most of the forms of aid survived the *Lemon* test—although funding certain instructional materials and field trips did not. *Wohlman v. Walter,* 433 U.S. 229 (1977).

Justice Powell concurred in part and dissented in part. Consider Justice Powell's observations below concerning the use of the Framers' Intent in Establishment Clause analysis:

> It is important to keep these issues in perspective. At this point in the 20th century we are quite far removed from the dangers that prompted the Framers to include the Establishment Clause in the Bill of Rights. *See Walz v. Tax Comm'n,* 397 U.S. 664, 668 (1970). The risk of significant religious or denominational control over our democratic processes—or even of deep political division along religious lines—is remote, and when viewed against the positive contributions of sectarian schools, any such risk seems entirely tolerable in light of the continuing oversight of this Court. Our decisions have sought to establish principles that preserve the cherished safeguard of the Establishment Clause without resort to blind absolutism. If this endeavor means a loss of some analytical tidiness, then that too is entirely tolerable. . . .

Although the Framers may have been prompted by historical circumstances to draft a "wall" for an Establishment Clause, should the Court today limit its interpretation to the Framers' intentions when, arguably, the historic foundation for the Framers' views no longer exist. Or, was Justice Powell too optimistic about the demise of "deep political division along religious lines"?

(3) *State Tax Credits for "Tuition, Textbooks, and Transportation:" Upheld in Mueller v. Allen, 463 U.S. 388 (1983).* The State of Minnesota allowed state taxpayers, in computing their state income tax, to deduct expenses incurred in providing "tuition, textbooks, and transportation" for their children attending elementary or secondary school. As far as "primary effect," the effect of the deduction "overwhelmingly" benefitted the children attending religious private schools. Nevertheless, the Court, per Justice Rehnquist, upheld these tax credits:

> A state's decision to defray the cost of educational expenses incurred by parents—regardless of the type of school their children attend—evidences a purpose that is both secular and understandable. . . .

> We turn, therefore, to the more difficult but related question whether the Minnesota statute has "the primary effect of advancing the sectarian aims of the non-public schools". . . .

> [T]he deduction is available for educational expenses incurred by *all* parents, including those whose children attend public schools and those whose children attend non-sectarian private schools or sectarian private schools. . . .

[U]nder Minnesota's arrangement public funds become available only as a result of numerous private choices of individual parents of school-age children.

Turning to the third part of the *Lemon* inquiry, we have no difficulty in concluding that the Minnesota statute does not "excessively entangle" the state in religion. The only plausible source of [difficulty] would lie in the fact that state officials must determine whether particular textbooks qualify for a deduction.

[S]tate officials must disallow deductions taken for "instructional books and materials used in the teaching of religious tenets, doctrines, or worship. . . ." Making decisions such as this does not differ substantially from making the types of decisions approved in earlier opinions of this Court.

Justice Marshall, joined by Justices Brennan, Blackmun, and Stevens dissented. "By insuring that parents will be reimbursed for tuition payments they make, the Minnesota statute requires that taxpayers in general pay for the cost of parochial education and extends [to parents] a financial 'incentive to send their children to sectarian schools,' " wrote the dissenters. Thus, the Minnesota program failed the second prong of the *Lemon* test because, according to the dissenters, its "primary effect" was "to aid and advance . . . religious institutions."

(4) *Upholding Congress's Mandate for Inclusion of Religiously Affiliated Organizations in a Government Program to Prevent Teen Premarital Sex and Pregnancy: Bowen v. Kendrick, 487 U.S. 589 (1988).* Congress passed the Adolescent Family Life Act (AFLA) in 1981 to provide grants to public or nonprofit private organizations "for services and research in the area of premarital sexual relations and pregnancy." AFLA was administered by the Secretary of Health and Human Services, and 141 applicants (out of 1,088) were awarded grants. Religiously affiliated organizations or organizations with institutional ties to various religious denominations were some of the grant recipients. In fact, the Act required grantees to consider how to include these religiously affiliated organizations. Some of the religious grantees had programs relying on theological and doctrinal concepts. Various taxpayers, clergymen and religious organizations challenged AFLA, on its face and as applied. Although the District Court ruled for the plaintiffs, the Supreme Court, per Justice Rehnquist, applying the *Lemon* standard, upheld AFLA against the facial challenge and remanded the as-applied challenge.

[W]e assess the constitutionality of [this] enactment by reference to the three factors first articulated in *Lemon v. Kurtzman*, 403 U.S. 602 (1971). Under the *Lemon* standard, [a] court may invalidate a statute only if it is motivated wholly by an impermissible purpose, if its primary effect is the advancement of religion, or if it requires excessive entanglement between church and state. . . .

As we see it, it is clear from the face of the statute that the AFLA was motivated primarily, if not entirely, by a legitimate secular purpose—the elimination or reduction of social and economic problems caused by teenage sexuality, pregnancy, and parenthood. . . .

As usual in establishment clause cases, the more difficult question is whether the primary effect of the challenged statute is impermissible. . . .

[T]here are two ways in which the statute, considered "on its face," might be said to have the impermissible primary effect of advancing religion. First, it can be argued that the AFLA advances religion by expressly recognizing that "religious organizations have a role to play" in addressing the problems associated with teenage sexuality. *Senate Report* at 16. [S]econdly, it can be argued that the AFLA is invalid on its face because it allows religiously affiliated organizations to participate as grantees or subgrantees in AFLA programs. . . .

We consider the former objection first. . . .

[T]he statute reflect[s] at most Congress' considered judgment that religious organizations can help solve the problems to which the AFLA is addressed. Nothing in our previous cases prevents Congress from making such a judgment or from recognizing the important part that religion or religious organizations may play in resolving certain secular problems. Particularly when, as Congress found, "prevention of adolescent sexual activity and adolescent pregnancy depends primarily upon developing strong family values and close family ties," it seems quite sensible for Congress to recognize that religious organizations can influence values and can have some influence on family life, including parents' relations with their adolescent children to the extent that this Congressional recognition has any effect of advancing religion, the effect is at most "incidental and remote." *See Lynch* [*v. Donnelly*]. . . .

This brings us to the second grounds for objecting the AFLA: the fact that it allows religious institutions to participate as recipients of federal funds. . . . [A] fairly wide spectrum of organizations is eligible to apply for and receive funding under the Act, and nothing on the face of the Act suggests that the AFLA is anything but neutral with respect to the grantee's status as a sectarian or purely secular institution. . . .

This, of course, brings us to the third prong of the *Lemon* establishment clause "test"—the question whether the AFLA leads to "an excessive government entanglement with religion." There is no doubt that the monitoring of AFLA grants is necessary if the Secretary is to insure that public money is to be spent in the way that Congress intended and in a way that comports with the establishment clause. Accordingly, this case presents us with yet another "catch-22" argument: The very supervision of the aid to assure that it does not further religion renders the statute invalid. [M]ost of the cases in which the Court has divided over the "entanglement" part of the Lemon test have involved aid to parochial schools. . . .

Here, by contrast, there is no reason to assume that the religious organizations which may receive grants are "pervasively sectarian." . . .

Justices O'Connor, Kennedy, and Scalia concurred separately.

Four Justices, Blackmun, Brennan, Marshall and Stevens, dissented in an opinion by Justice Blackmun:

[I]t is unclear whether Congress ever envisioned that public funds would pay for a program during a session of which parents and teenagers would be instructed:

You want to know the church teachings on sexuality. . . . You are the church. You people sitting here are the body of Christ. The teachings of you and the things you value are, in fact, the values of the Catholic Church.

Or of curricula that taught:

The church has always taught that the marriage act, or intercourse, seals the union of husband and wife. . . . Christ commits himself to us when we come to ask for the sacrament of marriage. . . .

Or the teaching of a method of family planning described on the grant application as "not only a method of birth regulation but also a philosophy of procreation," [a]nd as "facilitat[ing] the evangelization of homes." [The dissenters cite to the Record to support these quotations.]

It is true, of course, that the Court has recognized that the Constitution does not prohibit the government from supporting secular social-welfare services solely because they are provided by a religiously affiliated organization. But such recognition has been closely tied to the nature of the subsidized social service: "The state may send a cleric, indeed even a clerical order, to perform *a wholly secular task*." There is a very real and important difference between running a soup kitchen or a hospital, and counseling pregnant teenagers on how to make the difficult decisions facing them. . . . [F]or some religious organizations, the answer to a teenager's question "Why shouldn't I have an abortion?" or "Why shouldn't I use a barrier contraceptive?" will undoubtedly be different from an answer based solely on secular considerations. Public funds may not be used to endorse the religious message.

NOTES ON THE *LEMON* TEST

(1) *The Many Proposed Replacements for the Lemon Test.* One of the major doctrinal developments observable in later cases is the proposal of new tests to replace the *Lemon* standard: (1) the "endorsement" standard, *Lynch v. Donnelly* (O'Connor, Jr., concurring), below and *County of Allegheny*, below; (2) the "nonpreferentialist" standard, *Wallace v. Jaffree* (Rehnquist, J., dissenting), below; and (3) the "coercion" standard, *County of Allegheny* (Kennedy, J., dissenting), below and *Lee v. Weismann*, below. Note these various "tests" as you read the cases. Despite their many differences, they all share a common feature: they would impose a lesser degree of judicial scrutiny than either the *Lemon* test or the wall-of-separation theory (from *Everson*). *See generally* Steven G. Gey, *Reconciling The Supreme Court's Four Establishment Clauses*, 8 U. Pa. J. Const. L. 725 (2006).

(2) *Continued Reliance on the Lemon Test.* While these various substitutes have been suggested to replace the *Lemon* standard, the Supreme Court has continued, with a number of exceptions, to use the three pronged test. A concurrent pattern suggested by the cases has been the Court's application of the *Lemon* test with varying degrees of rigor. In other words, the Supreme Court does not always apply the *Lemon* test as strictly as the original decisions (*Lemon* and *Tilton*) did.

KIRYAS JOEL VILLAGE SCHOOL DISTRICT v. GRUMET, 512 U.S. 687 (1994). The Village of Kiryas Joel was populated exclusively by members of the Satmar Hasidic sect, a Jewish religious faith which sought to avoid assimilation into the modern secular world. Although most Village children attend private, religious schools, children requiring special education services received these from the public school district encompassing the Village. When the Satmar special education children experienced problems (because of their dress and insularity) at the public schools, the state legislature (aware that the Village was exclusively Satmar) created a new school district just for the Village. This provided state funding for the Village's special education students. This was challenged under the Establishment Clause, and the state courts ruled for the challengers. The Supreme Court, per Justice Souter, affirmed:

> [The Act creating the District] departs from [the Establishment Clause] by delegating the State's discretionary authority over public schools to a group defined by its character as a religious community, in a legal and historical context that gives no assurance that governmental power has been or will be exercised neutrally.

> [T]he Establishment Clause problem presented by [the Act] is more subtle, but it resembles the issue raised in Larkin [*supra*] to the extent that the earlier case teaches that a State may not delegate its civic authority to a group chosen according to a religious criterion.

> [W]here "fusion" is an issue, the difference lies in the distinction between a government's purposeful delegation on the basis of religion and a delegation on principles neutral to religion, to individuals whose religious identities are incidental to their receipt of civic authority.

> [T]he fact that this school district was created by a special and unusual Act of the legislature also gives reason for concern whether the benefit received by the Satmar community is one that the legislature will provide equally to other religious (and nonreligious) groups. . . .

[B]ut accommodation is not a principle without limits, and what petitioners seek is an adjustment to the Satmars' religiously grounded preferences that our cases do not countenance. [W]e have never hinted that an otherwise unconstitutional delegation of political power to a religious group could be saved as a religious accommodation.

Justice Stevens concurred, noting that "the State could have taken steps to alleviate the [special education] children's fear by teaching their schoolmates to be tolerant and respectful of Satmar customs." Justice O'Connor concurred in the judgment. Justice Kennedy concurred in the judgment, reasoning that: "[T]he Establishment Clause forbids the government to draw political boundaries on the basis of religious faith."

Justice Scalia dissented, arguing that the creation of the school district was a permissible "accommodation" to the Satmar religious community. He critiqued the plurality and the concurring opinions:

> The Court today finds that the Powers That Be, up in Albany, have conspired to effect an establishment of the Satmar Hasidim. I do not know who would be more surprised at this discovery: the Founders of our Nation or Grand Rebbe Joel Teitelbaum, founder of the Satmar. . . . I, however, am not surprised. Once this Court has abandoned text and history as guides, nothing prevents it from calling religious toleration the establishment of religion.

> [J]ustice Souter believes that the present case "resembles" [*Larkin*]. . . . [Justice Souter] misdescribes both what that case taught (which is that a state may not delegate its civil authority to a church), and what this case involves (which is a group chosen according to cultural characteristics). The statute at issue there gave churches veto power over the State's authority to grant a liquor license to establishments in the vicinity of the church. . . .

> I have little doubt that Justice Souter would laud this humanitarian legislation if all of the distinctiveness of the students of Kiryas Joel were attributable to the fact that their parents were nonreligious commune-dwellers, or American Indians, or gypsies. The creation of a special, one-culture school district for the benefit of those children would pose no problem. The neutrality demanded by the Religion Clauses requires the same indulgence towards cultural characteristics that are accompanied by religious belief. . . .

For commentary, *see* Ira C. Lupu, *Uncovering The Village of Kiryas Joel*, 96 COLUM. L. REV. 104 (1996).

NOTES AND QUESTIONS

The Substantial Erosion of the Lemon Standard: Agostini v. Felton, 521 U.S. 203 (1997). In *Agostini*, the Court, per Justice O'Connor, held that a federally funded "shared time" program which provided remedial instruction on a religion-neutral basis did not violate the Establishment Clause simply because the instruction occurred on the premises of a parochial school. (In essence, the remedial services could move from trailers adjacent to the parochial school buildings). The Court overruled two 1985 "shared time" decisions.

Regarding the *Lemon* test, the Court reasoned that the same "factors" were used to assess both the effect prong and the entanglement prong. The Court concluded, therefore, that the entanglement inquiry should be considered as part of the effect inquiry. The Court also concluded that the challengers should not enjoy three substantive "presumptions." In combination, this analysis seemed to reduce the *Lemon* test from three prongs to only two: a secular purpose inquiry and an effect inquiry. Four Justices, led by Justice Souter, dissented. *Agostini* was a stepping stone on the road to the *Zelman* decision below.

ZELMAN v. SIMMONS-HARRIS
536 U.S. 639 (2002)

CHIEF JUSTICE REHNQUIST delivered the opinion of the Court.

The State of Ohio has established a pilot program designed to provide educational choices to families with children who reside in the Cleveland City School District. The question presented is whether this program offends the Establishment Clause of the United States Constitution. We hold that it does not.

There are more than 75,000 children enrolled in the Cleveland City School District. The majority of these children are from low-income and minority families. Few of these families enjoy the means to send their children to any school other than an inner-city public school. For more than a generation, however, Cleveland's public schools have been among the worst performing public schools in the Nation. . . .

The program provides two basic kinds of assistance to parents of children in a covered district. First, the program provides tuition aid for students in kindergarten through third grade, expanding each year through eighth grade, to attend a participating public or private school of their parent's choosing. Second, the program provides tutorial aid for students who choose to remain enrolled in public school.

The tuition aid portion of the program is designed to provide educational choices to parents who reside in a covered district. Any private school, whether religious or nonreligious, may participate in the program and accept program students so long as the school is located within the boundaries of a covered district and meets statewide educational standards. . . .

Tuition aid is distributed to parents according to financial need. Families with incomes below 200% of the poverty line are given priority and are eligible to receive 90% of private school tuition up to $2,250. Where tuition aid is spent depends solely upon where parents who receive tuition aid choose to enroll their child. If parents choose a private school, checks are made payable to the parents who then endorse the checks over to the chosen school.

The tutorial aid portion of the program provides tutorial assistance through grants to any student in a covered district who chooses to remain in public school. . . .

The program has been in operation within the Cleveland City School District since the 1996–1997 school year. In the 1999–2000 school year, 56 private schools participated in the program, 46 (or 82%) of which had a religious affiliation. None of the public schools in districts adjacent to Cleveland have elected to participate. More than 3,700 students participated in the scholarship program, most of whom (96%) enrolled in religiously affiliated schools. Sixty percent of these students were from families at or below the poverty line. . . .

The Establishment Clause of the First Amendment, applied to the States through the Fourteenth Amendment, prevents a State from enacting laws that have the "purpose" or "effect" of advancing or inhibiting religion. *Agostini v. Felton.* There is no dispute that the program challenged here was enacted for the valid secular purpose of providing educational assistance to poor children in a demonstrably failing public school system. Thus, the question presented is whether the Ohio program nonetheless has the forbidden "effect" of advancing or inhibiting religion.

To answer that question, our decisions have drawn a consistent distinction between government programs that provide aid directly to religious schools, and programs of true private choice, in which government aid reaches religious schools only as a result of the genuine and independent choices of private individuals. While our jurisprudence with respect to the constitutionality of direct aid programs has "changed significantly" over the past two decades, *Agostini, supra,* at 236, our jurisprudence with respect to true private choice programs has remained consistent and unbroken. Three times we have confronted Establishment Clause challenges to neutral government programs that provide aid directly to a broad class of individuals, who, in turn, direct the aid to religious schools or institutions of their own choosing. Three times we have rejected such challenges. . . .

Mueller, Witters, and *Zobrest* thus make clear that where a government aid program is neutral with respect to religion, and provides assistance directly to a broad class of citizens who, in turn, direct government aid to religious schools wholly as a result of their own genuine and independent private choice, the program is not readily subject to challenge under the Establishment Clause. A program that shares these features permits government aid to reach religious institutions only by way of the deliberate choices of numerous individual recipients. The incidental advancement of a religious mission, or the perceived endorsement of a religious message, is reasonably attributable to the individual recipient, not to the government, whose role ends with the disbursement of benefits.

We believe that the program challenged here is a program of true private choice, consistent with *Mueller, Witters,* and *Zobrest,* and thus constitutional. As was true in those cases, the Ohio program is neutral in all respects toward religion. It is part of a general and multifaceted undertaking by the State of Ohio to provide educational opportunities to the children of a failed school district. It confers educational assistance directly to a broad class of individuals defined without reference to religion, *i.e.,* any parent of a school-age child who resides in the Cleveland City School District. The program permits the participation of *all* schools within the district, religious or nonreligious. Adjacent public schools also may participate and have a financial incentive to do so. Program benefits are available to participating families on neutral terms, with no reference to religion. The only preference stated anywhere in the program is a preference for low-income families, who receive greater assistance and are given priority for admission at participating schools.

There are no "financial incentive[s]" that "ske[w]" the program toward religious schools. . . . The program here in fact creates financial disincentives for religious schools, with private schools receiving only half the government assistance given to community schools and one-third the assistance given to magnet schools. . . .

Respondents suggest that even without a financial incentive for parents to choose a religious school, the program creates a "public perception that the State is endorsing religious practices and beliefs." But we have repeatedly recognized that no reasonable observer would think a neutral program of private choice, where state aid reaches religious schools solely as a result of the numerous independent decisions of private individuals, carries with it the *imprimatur* of government endorsement. . . .

There also is no evidence that the program fails to provide genuine opportunities for Cleveland parents to select secular educational options for their school-age children. . . . That 46 of the 56 private schools now participating in the program are religious schools does not condemn it as a violation of the Establishment Clause. . . . The Establishment Clause question is whether Ohio is coercing parents into sending their children to religious schools, and that question must be answered by evaluating *all* options Ohio provides Cleveland school children, only one of which is to obtain a program scholarship and then choose a religious school.

In sum, the Ohio program is entirely neutral with respect to religion. It provides benefits directly to a wide spectrum of individuals, defined only by financial need and residence in a particular school district. It permits such individuals to exercise genuine choice among options public and private, secular and religious. The program is therefore a program of true private choice. In keeping with an unbroken line of decisions rejecting challenges to similar programs, we hold that the program does not offend the Establishment Clause.

The judgment of the Court of Appeals is reversed.

JUSTICE O'CONNOR, concurring.

The Court holds that Ohio's Pilot Project Scholarship Program, (voucher program), survives respondents' Establishment Clause challenge. While I join the Court's opinion, I write separately for two reasons. First, although the Court takes an important step, I do not believe that today's decision, when considered in light of other longstanding government programs that impact religious organizations and our prior Establishment Clause jurisprudence, marks a dramatic break from the past. Second, given the emphasis the Court places on verifying that parents of voucher students in religious schools have exercised "true private choice," I think it is worth elaborating on the Court's conclusion that this inquiry should consider all reasonable educational alternatives to religious schools that are available to parents. To do otherwise is to ignore how the educational system in Cleveland actually functions. . . .

Nor does today's decision signal a major departure from this Court's prior Establishment Clause jurisprudence. A central tool in our analysis of cases in this area has been the *Lemon* test. As originally formulated, a statute passed this test only if it had "a secular legislative purpose," if its "principal or primary effect" was one that "neither advance[d] nor inhibit[ed] religion," and if it did "not foster an excessive government entanglement with religion." *Lemon v. Kurtzman*, 403 U.S. 602, 612–613 (1971) (internal quotation marks omitted). In *Agostini v. Felton*, we folded the entanglement inquiry into the primary effect inquiry. This made sense because both inquiries rely on the same evidence, *see ibid.*, and the degree of entanglement has implications for whether a statute advances or inhibits religion. The test today is basically the same as that set forth in *School Dist. of Abington Township v. Schempp*, 374 U.S. 203; *McGowan v. Maryland*, 366 U.S. 420, 442 (1961)), over 40 years ago.

The Court's opinion in these cases focuses on a narrow question related to the *Lemon* test: how to apply the primary effects prong in indirect aid cases? Specifically, it clarifies the basic inquiry when trying to determine whether a program that distributes aid to beneficiaries, rather than directly to service providers, has the primary effect of advancing or inhibiting religion, *Lemon v. Kurtzman, supra*, at 613–614, or, as I have put it, of "endors[ing] or disapprov[ing] . . . religion," *Lynch v. Donnelly, supra*, at 691–692 (concurring opinion); *see also Wallace v. Jaffree*, 472 U.S. 38, 69–70 (1985) (O'Connor, J., concurring in judgment). Courts are instructed to consider two factors: first, whether the program administers aid in a neutral fashion, without differentiation based on the religious status of beneficiaries or providers of services; second, and more importantly, whether beneficiaries of indirect aid have a genuine choice among religious and nonreligious organizations when determining the organization to which they will direct that aid. If the answer to either query is "no," the program should be struck down under the Establishment Clause. . . .

JUSTICE THOMAS, concurring.

The dissents and respondents wish to invoke the Establishment Clause of the First Amendment, as incorporated through the Fourteenth, to constrain a State's neutral efforts to provide greater educational opportunity for underprivileged minority students. Today's decision properly upholds the program as constitutional, and I join it in full. . . .

I

To determine whether a federal program survives scrutiny under the Establishment Clause, we have considered whether it has a secular purpose and whether it has the primary effect of advancing or inhibiting religion. I agree with the Court that Ohio's program easily passes muster under our stringent test, but, as a matter of first principles, I question whether this test should be applied to the States. . . .

Consequently, in the context of the Establishment Clause, it may well be that state action should be evaluated on different terms than similar action by the Federal Government. . . . Thus, while the Federal Government may "make no law respecting an establishment of religion," the States may pass laws that include or touch on religious matters so long as these laws do not impede free exercise rights or any other individual religious liberty interest. By considering the particular religious liberty right alleged to be invaded by a State, federal courts can strike a proper balance between the demands of the Fourteenth Amendment on the one hand and the federalism prerogatives of States on the other. . . .

II

The wisdom of allowing States greater latitude in dealing with matters of religion and education can be easily appreciated in this context. Respondents advocate using the Fourteenth Amendment to handcuff the State's ability to experiment with education. . . .

While the romanticized ideal of universal public education resonates with the cognoscenti who oppose vouchers, poor urban families just want the best education for their children, who will certainly need it. . . . The failure to provide education to poor urban children perpetuates a vicious cycle of poverty, dependence, criminality, and alienation that continues for the remainder of their lives. If society cannot end racial discrimination, at least it can arm minorities with the education to defend themselves from some of discrimination's effects. . . .

JUSTICE STEVENS, dissenting.

Is a law that authorizes the use of public funds to pay for the indoctrination of thousands of grammar school children in particular religious faiths a "law respecting an establishment of religion" within the meaning of the First Amendment? In answering that question, I think we should ignore three factual matters that are discussed at length by my colleagues.

First, the severe educational crisis that confronted the Cleveland City School District when Ohio enacted its voucher program is not a matter that should affect our appraisal of its constitutionality. . . .

Second, the wide range of choices that have been made available to students *within the public school system* has no bearing on the question whether the State may pay the tuition for students who wish to reject public education entirely and attend private schools that will provide them with a sectarian education. The fact that the vast majority of the voucher recipients who have entirely rejected public education receive religious indoctrination at state expense does, however, support the claim that the law is one "respecting an establishment of religion." The State may choose to divide up its public schools into a dozen different options and label them magnet schools, community schools, or whatever else it decides to call them, but the State is still required to provide a public education and it is the State's decision to fund private school education over and above its traditional obligation that is at issue in these cases.

Third, the voluntary character of the private choice to prefer a parochial education over an education in the public school system seems to me quite irrelevant to the question whether the government's choice to pay for religious indoctrination is constitutionally permissible. . . .

For the reasons stated by JUSTICE SOUTER and JUSTICE BREYER, I am convinced that the Court's decision is profoundly misguided. Admittedly, in reaching that conclusion I have been influenced by my understanding of the impact of religious strife on the decisions of our forbears to migrate to this continent, and on the decisions of neighbors in the Balkans, Northern Ireland, and the Middle East to mistrust one another. Whenever we remove a brick from the wall that was designed to separate religion and government, we increase the risk of religious strife and weaken the foundation of our democracy.

JUSTICE SOUTER, with whom JUSTICE STEVENS, JUSTICE GINSBURG, and JUSTICE BREYER join, dissenting.

The Court's majority holds that the Establishment Clause is no bar to Ohio's payment of tuition at private religious elementary and middle schools under a scheme that systematically provides tax money to support the schools' religious missions. The occasion for the legislation thus upheld is the condition of public education in the city of Cleveland. The record indicates that the schools are failing to serve their objective, and the vouchers in issue here are said to be needed to provide adequate alternatives to them. If there were an excuse for giving short shrift to the Establishment Clause, it would probably apply here. But there is no excuse. Constitutional limitations are placed on government to preserve constitutional values in hard cases, like these. . . .

III

I do not dissent merely because the majority has misapplied its own law, for even if I assumed *arguendo* that the majority's formal criteria were satisfied on the facts, today's conclusion would be profoundly at odds with the Constitution. . . .

Justice Breyer has addressed this issue in his own dissenting opinion, which I join, and here it is enough to say that the intensity of the expectable friction can be gauged by realizing that the scramble for money will energize not only contending sectarians, but taxpayers who take their liberty of conscience seriously. Religious teaching at taxpayer expense simply cannot be cordoned from taxpayer politics, and every major religion currently espouses social positions that provoke intense opposition. . . . Views like these, and innumerable others, have been safe in the sectarian pulpits and classrooms of this Nation not only because the Free Exercise Clause protects them directly, but because the ban on supporting religious establishment has protected free exercise, by keeping it relatively private. With the arrival of vouchers in religious schools, that privacy will go, and along with it will go confidence that religious disagreement will stay moderate. . . .

JUSTICE BREYER, with whom JUSTICE STEVENS and JUSTICE SOUTER join, dissenting.

I join Justice Souter's opinion, and I agree substantially with Justice Stevens. I write separately, however, to emphasize the risk that publicly financed voucher programs pose in terms of religiously based social conflict. I do so because I believe that the Establishment Clause concern for protecting the Nation's social fabric from religious conflict poses an overriding obstacle to the implementation of this well-intentioned school voucher program. . . .

I

The First Amendment begins with a prohibition, that "Congress shall make no law respecting an establishment of religion," and a guarantee, that the government shall not prohibit "the free exercise thereof." These Clauses embody an understanding, reached in the 17th century after decades of religious war, that liberty and social stability demand a religious tolerance that respects the religious views of all citizens, permits those citizens to "worship God in their own way," and allows all families to "teach their children and to form their characters" as they wish. C. Radcliffe, The Law & Its Compass 71 (1960). The Clauses reflect the Framers' vision of an American Nation free of the religious strife that had long plagued the nations of Europe. . . . Whatever the Framers might have thought about particular 18th century school funding practices, they undeniably intended an interpretation of the Religion Clauses that would implement this basic First Amendment objective. . . .

The 20th century Court was fully aware, however, that immigration and growth had changed American society dramatically since its early years. By 1850, 1.6 million Catholics lived in America, and by 1900 that number rose to 12 million. Jeffries & Ryan, *A Political History of the Establishment Clause*, 100 MICH. L. REV. 279, 299–300 (2001). There were similar percentage increases in the Jewish population. Not surprisingly, with this increase in numbers, members of non-Protestant religions, particularly Catholics, began to resist the Protestant domination of the public schools. . . .

These historical circumstances suggest that the Court, applying the Establishment Clause through the Fourteenth Amendment to 20th century American society, faced an interpretive dilemma that was in part practical. The Court appreciated the religious diversity of contemporary American society. *See Schempp*, 374 U.S., at 240 (Brennan, J., concurring). It realized that the status quo favored some religions at the expense of others. And it understood the Establishment Clause to prohibit (among other things) any such favoritism. Yet *how* did the Clause achieve that objective? Did it simply require the government to give each religion an equal chance to introduce religion into the primary schools—a kind of "equal opportunity" approach to the interpretation of the Establishment Clause? Or, did that Clause avoid government favoritism of some religions by insisting upon "separation"—that the government achieve equal treatment by removing itself from the business of providing religious education for children? This interpretive choice arose in respect both to religious activities in public schools and government aid to private education.

In both areas the Court concluded that the Establishment Clause required "separation," in part because an "equal opportunity" approach was not workable. . . .

With respect to government aid to private education, did not history show that efforts to obtain equivalent funding for the private education of children whose parents did not hold popular religious beliefs only exacerbated religious strife? As Justice Rutledge recognized:

> "Public money devoted to payment of religious costs, educational or other, brings the quest for more. It brings too the struggle of sect against sect for the larger share or for any. Here one [religious sect] by numbers [of adherents] alone will benefit most, there another. This is precisely the history of societies which have had an established religion and dissident groups." *Everson v. Board of Ed. of Ewing*, 330 U.S. 1, 53–54, (dissenting opinion).

The upshot is the development of constitutional doctrine that reads the Establishment Clause as avoiding religious strife, *not* by providing every religion with an *equal opportunity* (say, to secure state funding or to pray in the public schools), but by drawing fairly clear lines of *separation* between church and state—at least where the heartland of religious belief, such as primary religious education, is at issue.

II

The principle underlying these cases—avoiding religiously based social conflict—remains of great concern. As religiously diverse as America had become when the Court decided its major 20th century Establishment Clause cases, we are exponentially more diverse today. America boasts more than 55 different religious groups and subgroups with a significant number of members. . . .

V

The Court, in effect, turns the clock back. It adopts, under the name of "neutrality," an interpretation of the Establishment Clause that this Court rejected more than half a century ago. In its view, the parental choice that offers each religious group a kind of equal opportunity to secure government funding overcomes the Establishment Clause concern for social concord. . . . In a society composed of many different religious creeds, I fear that this present departure from the Court's earlier understanding risks creating a form of religiously based conflict potentially harmful to the Nation's social fabric. . . .

NOTES AND QUESTIONS

(1) *"True Private Choice"— An Educational Voucher System Ruled Constitutional: Zelman v. Simmons-Harris, 536 U.S. 639 (2002).* The Ohio school voucher program included sectarian schools, as well as public and "charter" schools as potential recipients of the public treasury dollars. Although the lower courts struck down the program, the Supreme Court, per Chief Justice Rehnquist, held that the program did not violate the Establishment Clause.

According to the majority, the facts established that Ohio's program relied upon the true private choice of private decisionmakers—and not the government. Ohio's program was targeted at the severely failing Cleveland Schools. All types of private and parochial schools were eligible, as well as adjacent suburban schools. The program included special funding for tutorial assistance in the public schools. Most significantly, the vouchers were given to the parents, and then the parents made "private choices" on where to place their children. Under these circumstances, the majority concluded that the program was "neutral" and, therefore, constitutional. Although the voucher scheme may have had the effect of supporting religious groups, the Chief Justice concluded that this effect was merely "incidental" and not constitutionally determinate. *See generally* Charles Fried, *Five To Four: Reflections On The School Voucher Case,* 116 Harv. L. Rev. 163 (2002); Daniel O. Conkle, Indirect Funding and the Establishment Clause: Rehnquist's Triumphant Vision of Neutrality and Private Choice, The Rehnquist Legacy (2006).

(2) *The Voucher Concurrences.* Justice O'Connor concurred, and most of her opinion was aimed at refuting Justice Souter's dissenting arguments based on "statistics" (which she calls "alarmist claims"). She also argues that the *Lemon* test is now just two prongs. The "excessive entanglement" prong has been dropped.

Justice Thomas also concurred. Part of Justice Thomas' sweeping opinion seemed to call for a reconsideration of the "incorporation doctrine" in Establishment Clause cases. [*See* Chapter 8.] This may remind students of Justice Thomas's concurrences in *Lopez* and *Morrison* decisions from Chapter 2. Justice Thomas expressed concern about the fate of "poor urban children" and argued that certain Fourteenth Amendment values override any Establishment Clause concerns. In this vein, Justice Thomas argued the opponents of vouchers were "cognoscenti" who were indifferent to the plight of "urban minority students." *See generally* Mark Tushnet, *Clarence Thomas' Black Nationalism,* 47 Howard L. Rev. 323 (2004).

(3) *The Voucher Dissents: Justices Stevens, Souter, and Breyer (for Justice Ginsburg).* In the shortest dissent, Justice Stevens, once a law clerk to Justice Rutledge, argued that the decision permitted "religious indoctrination at state expense," and his dissent rejected consideration of the "severe educational crisis" in Cleveland.

Justice Souter argued that scale of state aid to religious schools is "unprecedented." His dissent focused on the effects of the voucher aid program. Justice Souter also pursued a "structural" argument that "the ban on supporting religious establishment has protected free exercise, by keeping it relatively private." Based on your study of these materials, has the separationism interpretation of the Establishment Clause helped, or hurt, free exercise?

Finally, Justice Breyer dissented because of "the risk that publicly financed vouchers programs pose in terms of religiously based social conflict." Is there, in this new century of American society, a "risk" of political conflict along sectarian lines or is Justice Breyer's concern overstated? *See* also Justice Breyer's concurrences on the *Ten Commandments* Cases below. Compare Justice Breyer's concern about political conflict along sectarian lines *with* Justice Powell's assessment in *Wolhman v. Walter,* above.

[2] Non-Financial Aid: "Accommodation" or Official Recognition

WIDMAR v. VINCENT, 454 U.S. 263 (1981). The University of Missouri at Kansas City made its facilities generally available for activities by registered student groups. A registered student religious group known as "Cornerstone," which previously had received permission to conduct its meetings in university facilities, was informed that it would no longer be able to do so because of a university regulation prohibiting the use of facilities "for purposes of religious worship or religious teaching." Eleven members of Cornerstone sued the university, claiming that its action violated their rights to free exercise of religion, equal protection, and freedom of speech. The court of appeals held for the students, reasoning that the "primary effect" of allowing Cornerstone to use university facilities would not be to advance religion but rather to further the "neutral purpose" of developing students' "social and cultural awareness as well as [their] intellectual curiosity." The Supreme Court, per Justice Powell, also agreed with the students and affirmed, primarily on freedom-of-speech grounds:

> Through its policy of accommodating their meetings, the university has created a forum generally open for use by student groups. Having done so, the university has assumed the obligation to justify its discriminations and exclusions under applicable constitutional norms. . . .

> Here the UMKC has discriminated against student groups and speakers based on their desire to use a generally open forum to engage in religious worship and discussion. These are forms of speech and association protected by the first amendment. [To prevail, the university] must show that its regulation is necessary to serve a compelling state interest and that it is narrowly drawn to achieve that end. . . .

> In this case two prongs of the [*Lemon*] test are clearly met. Both the district court and the court of appeals held that an open-forum policy, including non-discrimination against religious speech, would have a secular purpose and would avoid entanglement with religion. But . . . the university argues [that] allowing religious groups to share the limited public forum would have the primary effect of advancing religion. . . .

> We are satisfied that any religious benefits of an open forum at UMKC would be "incidental" within the meaning of our cases. Two factors are especially relevant.

> First, an open forum in a public university does not confer any imprimatur of state approval on religious sects or practices. . . .

> Second, the forum is available to a broad class of nonreligious as well as religious speakers; there are over 100 recognized student groups at UMKC. The provision of benefits to so broad a spectrum of groups is an important index of secular effect. . . .

> [R]espondents' first amendment rights [to engage in religious worship and discussion] are entitled to special constitutional solicitude. [T]he state interest asserted here—in achieving greater separation of church and state than is already insured under the establishment clause of the federal constitution—is limited by the free exercise clause and in this case by the free speech clause as well. In this constitutional context, we are unable to recognize the state's interests as sufficiently "compelling" to justify content-based discrimination against respondents' religious speech.

Justice White dissented: "There may be instances in which a state's attempt to disentangle itself from religious worship would intrude upon secular speech about religion. [T]his is not such a case. This case involves religious worship only; the fact that worship is accomplished through speech does not add anything to respondents' argument. That argument must rely upon the claim that the state's action impermissibly interferes with the free exercise of respondents' religious practices. Although this is a close question, I conclude that it does not." As Justice White saw it, if religious worship were protected by the freedom of speech, "the religion clauses would be emptied of any independent meaning."

NOTES AND QUESTIONS

(1) *"Accommodation" of Religion Versus "Establishment" of Religion: What is the Difference?* Although government is prohibited from "establishing" religion, the Free Exercise Clause, or the freedom of speech, or other principles may permit or even require government to "accommodate" religion. It can be quite difficult, however, to identify just where accommodation shades into establishment.

(2) *Neutral Financial Aid Used to Pay for Religious Study—"Accommodation" or "Establishment?": Witters v. Washington Department of Services for the Blind, 474 U.S. 481 (1986).* The Washington State Commission for the Blind, which provided financial vocational assistance for blind persons in their studies, refused assistance to Witters because he was studying at a Christian college and seeking to become a clergyman. Question: Was the state in this manner avoiding an "establishment" of religion; or was it refusing to "accommodate" religion; or was it in actual violation of the free exercise or free speech clauses?

In *Witters* the Supreme Court unanimously reversed a decision of the state supreme court excluding Witters from receiving aid. Justice Marshall's opinion for the Court held that the use of "neutrally available state aid to help pay for . . . religious education" did not violate the establishment clause. However, the Court declined to hold that the Free Exercise Clause *required* the extension of aid, and it left open the possibility that Washington's stricter state constitution might prohibit the assistance in question. Is this holding correct?

(3) *Financial Aid Used to Pay for Sign Language Assistance in Parochial Schools: Is this an "Establishment?" Zobrest v. Catalina Foothills Schools, 509 U.S. 1 (1993).* The parents of a profoundly deaf high school student requested, under the federal Individuals with Disabilities Education Act, 20 U.S.C. § 1400(a), that the public school district pay for the services of a certified sign language interpreter for their son while he attended classes at a parochial high school. The Court held that the board's payment for sign language services to a parochial school student did not have any impermissible effect or create any unconstitutional entanglement. Following its loss in the Supreme Court, the School District was liable for Zobrest's legal fees (over $100,000.00). The District residents faced a one-time tax increase. ARGUS LEADER (Sioux Falls), July 21, 1993, § A, at 7, col. 6.

(4) *Commentary on the "Accommodation" Debate. See, e.g.,* Stephen G. Gey, *Why is Religion Special?: Reconsidering the Accommodation of Religion Under the Religion Clauses of the First Amendment,* 52 U. PITT. L. REV. 75 (1990); Ira C. Lupu, *Reconstructing the Establishment Clause: The Case Against Discretionary Accommodation of Religion,* 140 U. PA. L. REV. 555 (1991); Michael W. McConnell, *Accommodation of Religion,* 1985 SUP. CT. REV. 1.

(5) *The Application of Widmar in Public Secondary Schools: Good News Club v. Milford Central School, 533 U.S. 98 (2001).* Following *Widmar,* there remained open the issue whether the reasoning in *Widmar* would also apply to "building utilization" decisions by secondary and elementary schools. In *Good News Club,* a Christian Club for children sought to use school facilities for after-school activities which were fundamentally religious in nature; the Club was willing to satisfy all generally applicable conditions for usage under the School's policies. The School denied the Club solely because of the religious content of the Club's activities, and the Club sued for the violation of their free speech rights. The Court, per Justice Thomas, agreed with the Club. The Court held that the denial of the Club's usage was impermissible viewpoint

discrimination and that the School would not violate the Establishment Clause by allowing the Club's usage of the building. Justices Scalia and Breyer concurred. Justices Stevens, Souter, and Ginsburg dissented.

(6) *The Legislative Chaplain Case: Marsh v. Chambers, 463 U.S. 783 (1983).* In *Marsh*, the Court upheld the practice of the Nebraska legislature in beginning each of its sessions with a prayer by a chaplain paid by the state. The Court did not rely upon the three-part *Lemon* test; instead, it emphasized the "unbroken practice for two centuries in the national Congress and for more than a century in Nebraska" of legislative prayers. Was this reasoning correct, and if so, does it demonstrate a deficiency in the three-part test?

(7) *Congressional Protection of Religious Freedom Rights of Institutionalized Persons: Cutter v. Wilkinson, 544 U.S. 709 (2005).* Section 3 of the Religious Land Use and Institutionalized Persons Act of 2000 (RLUIPA) requires that no level of government, including States, impose a "substantial burden" on the religious exercise rights of persons residing in or confined to any institution unless the government can justify the burden under strict scrutiny. Prisoners in the Ohio system sued the State under Section 3 of RLUIPA because the State allegedly failed to accommodate their "nonmainstream" religions (*e.g.*, Satanism, Wicca, and Asatru). For present purposes, the State defended by arguing that Section 3 impermissibly violated the Establishment Clause. Although the lower court agreed with the State, the Supreme Court, per Justice Ginsburg, ruled in favor of the prisoners.

The unanimous Court held that RLUIPA "does not, on its face, exceed the limits of permissible government accommodation of religious practices." Justice Thomas submitted a concurring opinion, expressing his narrow view of the Establishment Clause.

LYNCH v. DONNELLY
465 U.S. 668 (1984)

CHIEF JUSTICE BURGER delivered the opinion of the Court.

[The City of Pawtucket, R.I., included a creche (or nativity scene) in its annual Christmas display, including traditional figures of the infant Jesus, Mary, and Joseph with angels, shepherds, kings and animals. The creche, which had been included in the display for forty or more years, was part of an overall display that included a Santa Claus house, reindeer pulling Santa's sleigh, candy-striped poles, a Christmas tree, carolers, cut-out figures representing such characters as a clown, various Disney characters, an elephant, and a teddy bear, hundreds of colored lights, a large banner that read, "Seasons Greetings," and the creche. Although the display was located on privately owned property, all components of the display were owned by the city and cost about $20 per year for erection and dismantling. In a suit by Pawtucket residents and the American Civil Liberties Union and its members, the district court enjoined the city against displaying the creche, and the court of appeals affirmed. Here, the Supreme Court reverses.]

This Court has explained that the purpose of the establishment and free exercise clauses of the first amendment is "to prevent, as far as possible, the intrusion of either [the church or the state] into the precincts of the other." *Lemon v. Kurtzman.* At the same time, however, the Court has recognized that "total separation is not possible in an absolute sense. Some relationship between government and religious organizations is inevitable." *Ibid.* . . .

The Court has sometimes described the religion clauses as erecting a "wall" between church and state, *see, e.g., Everson v. Board of Education.* The concept of a "wall" of separation is a useful figure of speech probably deriving from views of Thomas Jefferson. The metaphor has served as a reminder that the establishment clause forbids an established church or anything approaching it. But the metaphor itself is not a wholly accurate description of the practical aspects of the relationship that in fact exists between church and state.

No significant segment of our society and no institution within it can exist in a vacuum or in total or absolute isolation from all the other parts, much less from government. [N]or does the Constitution require complete separation of church and state; it affirmatively mandates accommodation, not merely tolerance, of all religions, and forbids hostility toward any. *See, e.g., Zorach v. Clauson* [below]. . . . Indeed, we have observed, such hostility would bring us into "war with our national tradition as embodied in the first amendment's guarantee of the free exercise of religion". . . .

The Court's interpretation of the establishment clause has comported with what history reveals was the contemporaneous understanding of its guarantees. [I]n the very week that Congress approved the establishment clause as part of the Bill of Rights for submission to the states, it enacted legislation providing for paid chaplains for the House and Senate. In *Marsh v. Chambers*, 463 U.S. 783 (1983), . . . [w]e saw no conflict with the establishment clause when Nebraska employed members of the clergy as official legislative chaplains to give opening prayers at sessions of the state legislature. . . .

There is an unbroken history of official acknowledgment by all three branches of government of the role of religion in American life from at least 1789. Seldom in our opinions was this more affirmatively expressed than in Justice Douglas' opinion for the Court validating a program allowing release of public school students from classes to attend off-campus religious exercises. [T]he Court asserted pointedly: "We are a religious people whose institutions presuppose a Supreme Being." *Zorach v. Clauson, supra.*

[P]resident Washington and his successors proclaimed Thanksgiving, with all its religious overtones, a day of national celebration and Congress made it a national holiday more than a century ago. That holiday has not lost its theme of expressing thanks for divine aid any more than has Christmas lost its religious significance. . . .

[T]he [Establishment] Clause erects a "blurred, indistinct, and variable barrier depending on all the circumstances of a particular relationship." *Lemon* [*v. Kurtzman*].

In the line-drawing process we have often found it useful to inquire whether the challenged law or conduct has a secular purpose, whether its principal or primary effect is to advance or inhibit religion, and whether it creates an excessive entanglement of government with religion. *Lemon, supra.* But, we have repeatedly emphasized our unwillingness to be confined to any single test or criterion in this sensitive area.

[I]n this case, the focus of our inquiry must be on the creche in the context of the Christmas season. *See, e.g., Stone v. Graham*, 449 U.S. 39 (1980). [F]ocus[ing] exclusively on the religious component of any activity would inevitably lead to its invalidation under the establishment clause. . . .

[W]hen viewed in the proper context of the Christmas holiday season, it is apparent that, on this record, there is insufficient evidence to establish that the inclusion of the creche is a purposeful or surreptitious effort to express some kind of subtle governmental advocacy of a particular religious message. In a pluralistic society a variety of motives and purposes are implicated. The city, like the Congresses and Presidents, however, has principally taken note of a significant historical religious event long celebrated in the western world. The creche in the display depicts the historical origins of this traditional event long recognized as a national holiday. . . .

[T]he district court's inference, drawn from the religious nature of the creche, that the city has no secular purpose was on this record, clearly erroneous.

The district court found that the primary effect of including the creche is to confer a substantial and impermissible benefit on religion in general and on the Christian faith in particular. [B]ut to conclude that the primary effect of including the creche is to advance religion . . . would require that we view it as more beneficial to and more an endorsement of religion, for example, than expenditure of large sums of public money for textbooks supplied throughout the country to students attending church-sponsored schools, *Board of Education v. Allen, supra;* expenditure of public funds for transportation of students to church-sponsored schools, *Everson v. Board of Education, supra;* federal grants for college buildings of church-sponsored institutions of higher education combining secular and religious education, *Tilton v. Richardson,* [above]; [and other holdings in other cases].

[W]hat was said about the legislative prayers in *Marsh, supra,* . . . is true of the city's inclusion of creche: Its "reason or effect merely happens to coincide or harmonize with the tenets of some . . . religions". . . .

[The district court held] that some political divisiveness was engendered by this litigation. [T]his persuaded the Court that there was "excessive entanglement". . . .

[A] litigant cannot, by the very act of commencing a lawsuit, . . . create the appearance of divisiveness and then exploit it as evidence of entanglement.

Of course the creche is identified with one religious faith but no more so than the examples we have set out from prior cases in which we found no conflict with the establishment clause. To forbid the use of this one passive symbol—the creche—at the very time people are taking note of the season with Christmas hymns and carols in public schools and other public places, and while the Congress and legislatures open sessions with prayers by paid chaplains, would be a stilted overreaction contrary to our history and to our holdings. . . .

The Court has acknowledged that the "fears and political problems" that gave rise to the religion clauses in the eighteenth century are of far less concern today. *Everson.* We are unable to perceive the Archbishop of Canterbury, the Bishop of Rome, or other powerful religious leaders behind every public acknowledgement of the religious heritage long officially recognized by the three constitutional branches of government. Any notion that these symbols pose a real danger of establishment of a state church is far-fetched indeed.

[Reversed.]

JUSTICE O'CONNOR, concurring.

[I] write separately to suggest a clarification of our establishment clause doctrine. . . .

The establishment clause prohibits government from making adherence to a religion relevant in any way to a person's standing in the political community. Government can run afoul of that prohibition in two principal ways. One is excessive entanglement with religious institutions. . . . [T]he second and more direct infringement is government endorsement or approval of religion. . . .

In this case, as even the district court found, there is no institutional entanglement. Nevertheless, the respondents contend that the political divisiveness caused by Pawtucket's display of its creche violates the excessive-entanglement prong of the *Lemon* test. In my view, political divisiveness along religious lines should not be an independent test of constitutionality. . . .

The central issue in this case is whether Pawtucket has endorsed Christianity by its display of the creche. To answer that question, we must examine both what Pawtucket intended to communicate in displaying the creche and what message the city's display actually conveyed. The purpose and effect prongs of the *Lemon* test represent these two aspects of the meaning of the city's action. . . .

The purpose prong of the *Lemon* test asks whether government's actual purpose is to endorse or disapprove of religion. The effect prong asks whether, irrespective of government's actual purpose, the practice under review in fact conveys a message of endorsement or disapproval. An affirmative answer to either question should render the challenged practice invalid.

The purpose prong of the *Lemon* test requires that a government activity have a secular purpose. [T]he proper inquiry under the purpose prong of *Lemon*, I submit, is whether the government intends to convey a message of endorsement or disapproval of religion.

Applying that formulation to this case, I would find that Pawtucket did not intend to convey any message of endorsement of Christianity or disapproval of non-Christian religions. [C]elebration of public holidays, which have cultural significance even if they also have religious aspects, is a legitimate secular purpose. . . .

Focussing on the evil of government endorsement or disapproval of religion makes clear that the effect prong of the *Lemon* test is properly interpreted not to require invalidation of a government practice merely because it in fact causes, even as a primary effect, advancement or inhibition of religion. The laws upheld in *Walz v. Tax Comm'n* (tax exemption for religious, educational, and charitable organizations), in *McGowan v. Maryland*, 366 U.S. 420 (1961) (mandatory Sunday closing law), and in *Zorach v. Clauson* (release time from school for off-campus religious instruction), had such effects, but they did not violate the establishment clause. What is crucial is that a government practice does not have the effect of communicating a message of government endorsement or disapproval of religion. . . .

Pawtucket's display of its creche, I believe, does not communicate a message that the government intends to endorse the Christian beliefs represented by the creche. [T]he creche is a traditional symbol of the holiday that is very commonly displayed along with purely secular symbols, as it was in Pawtucket. . . .

JUSTICE BRENNAN, with whom JUSTICE MARSHALL, JUSTICE BLACKMUN, and JUSTICE STEVENS join, dissenting.

Applying the three-part test [of *Lemon v. Kurtzman*] to Pawtucket's creche, I am persuaded that the city's inclusion of the creche and its Christmas display simply does not reflect a "clearly secular . . . purpose." . . .

The "primary effect" of including a nativity scene in the city's display is, as the district court found, to place the government's imprimatur of approval on the particular religious beliefs exemplified by the creche. [T]he effect on minority religious groups, as well as on those who may reject all religion, is to convey the message that their views are not similarly worthy of public recognition nor entitled to public support. It was precisely this sort of religious chauvinism that the establishment clause was intended forever to prohibit. . . .

Finally, it is evident that Pawtucket's inclusion of a creche as part of its annual Christmas display does pose a significant threat of fostering "excessive entanglement". . . . Jews and other non-Christian groups, prompted perhaps by the mayor's remark that he will include a Menorah in future displays, can be expected to press government for inclusion of their symbols, and faced with such requests, government will have to become involved in accommodating the various demands. [M]ore importantly, although no political divisiveness was apparent in Pawtucket prior to the filing of respondents' lawsuit, that act, as the district court found, unleashed powerful emotional reactions which divided the city along religious lines. . . .

The Court advances two principal arguments to support its conclusion that the Pawtucket creche satisfies the *Lemon* test. Neither is persuasive.

First. The Court, by focussing on the holiday "context" in which the nativity scene appeared, seeks to explain away the clear religious import of the creche. . . . But it blinks reality to claim, as the Court does, that by including such a distinctively religious object as the creche in its Christmas display, Pawtucket has done no more than make use of a traditional symbol of the holiday, and thereby has purged the creche of its religious content and conferred only an "incidental and indirect" benefit on religion. . . .

Second. [T]he Court [notes] that government may recognize Christmas day as a public holiday; the Court then asserts that the creche is nothing more than a traditional element of Christmas celebration. The vice of this dangerously superficial argument is that it overlooks the fact that the Christmas holiday in our national culture contains both secular and sectarian elements. . . .

[The dissenting opinion of JUSTICE BLACKMUN, joined by JUSTICE STEVENS, is omitted.]

NOTES AND QUESTIONS

(1) *"Accommodation," "Official Recognition," or "Establishment" of Religion?* *Lynch v. Donnelly* demonstrates, once again, the difficulty of drawing the line between accommodation and establishment of religion.

(2) *What Has Happened to the Three-Part Lemon Test? Comparing the Views of the Majority, Justice O'Connor's Concurrence and the Dissent.* Chief Justice Burger's opinion for the Court describes the *Lemon* test as "often . . . useful"—but it pointedly emphasizes the Court's "unwillingness to be confined to any single test or criterion in this sensitive area." It also emphasizes cases in which the Court has approved accommodations of religion without relying upon the *Lemon* approach. Is the majority advancing a "watered-down" version of the *Lemon* test? *Cf.* Smith, *Symbols, Perceptions, and Doctrinal Illusions: Establishment Neutrality and the "No Endorsement" Test,* 86 MICH. L. REV. 266 (1987).

Justice O'Connor's concurrence, on the other hand, reinterprets the three-part test in accordance with the purposes that she concludes underlie the establishment clause. The purpose and effect prongs are to be interpreted so as to avoid government endorsement of religion. Is this "endorsement standard" a useful recasting of the *Lemon* test?

Finally, the dissent applies the three-part test more rigorously. But would this rigorous approach have the effect of preventing accommodations of religion that neither are harmless or actually are required by the Free Exercise Clause?

(3) *What is the Role of "Political Divisiveness" in Establishment Clause Analysis?* Note that, in *Lemon,* Chief Justice Burger's opinion expressly considered the prospect that financial aid to the religious schools might engender political controversy within the community as a factor in at least the entanglement prong of the *Lemon* test. In *Lynch,* however, Chief Justice Burger appears to reject any consideration of political divisiveness because it might be generated by a litigant who would then, in the *Lemon* test, benefit from the existence of such political controversy. Should the potential for political divisiveness be considered in applying the *Lemon* test?

(4) *Denial of Funding To a Student Publication Because of Its "Religious" Viewpoint Violates the Neutrality Required by the Establishment Clause: Rosenberger v. Rector, University of Virginia, 515 U.S. 819 (1995).* The University of Virginia, a public institution, provided cost reimbursement for the publication costs incurred by authorized student organizations. But the university refused to fund one organization's publication, "Wide Awake: A Christian Perspective," solely because of the publication's pervasive religious content. The Court, per Justice Kennedy, followed *Widmar, supra,* and held that the University's action violated the principle of governmental neutrality required by the Establishment Clause. Four Justices dissented from this holding.

The *Rosenberger* decision also involved a public forum issue, which is discussed at § 11.06[A], above. Finally, the most interesting aspect of *Rosenberger* may be Justice Thomas's concurrence. In an opinion similar to Justice Rehnquist's dissent in *Wallace v. Jaffree,* below, Justice Thomas presents an historical analysis of the Establishment Clause, which suggests that the traditional understanding of the Framers' Intent, as stated, for example, in *Everson* above, is flawed, because the Framers considered establishment of religion far more narrowly.

(5) *The "Reindeer Rule?"* Perhaps *Lynch v. Donnelly* stands for the proposition that if religious symbols are joined with secular ones (*e.g.,* reindeer), they become sanitized from establishment clause claims. In connection with this concept, which sometimes is called the "reindeer rule," consider the following.

COUNTY OF ALLEGHENY v. AMERICAN CIVIL LIBERTIES UNION GREATER PITTSBURGH CHAPTER, 492 U.S. 573 (1989). This case presents a variation upon *Lynch v. Donnelly, supra.* At issue were two holiday displays. The County displayed a creche at the base of the county courthouse's "Grand Staircase." Unlike the creche in *Lynch*, this creche was essentially a solitary item. In the other display, the City located two items at the entrance of a city office building: a large, decorated evergreen with the title "Salute to Liberty" and next to it an "18-foot Chanukah menorah," which has religious and civic significance to Jewish religious groups. The local ACLU chapter sued the City and the County. In a highly fragmented decision, the Supreme Court held that, while the creche display violated the Establishment Clause, the City's menorah and Christmas tree did not. Justice Blackmun's plurality opinion applied a version of the "endorsement" standard:

> [I]n recent years, we have paid particularly close attention to whether the challenged governmental practice either has the purpose or effect of "endorsing" religion. . . .

> Under [*Lynch*], the effect of a creche display turns on its setting. Here, unlike *Lynch*, nothing in the context of the display detracts from the creche's religious message [and, hence, the creche display violated the Establishment Clause].

> [T]he display of the Chanukah menorah in front of the City-County Building may well present a closer constitutional question. [Although the menorah is a religious symbol,] [t]he menorah's message is not exclusively religious. [M]oreover, the menorah here stands next to a Christmas tree and a sign saluting liberty.

> [G]iven [the placement of the tree and the Liberty sign], it is not "sufficiently likely" that residents of Pittsburgh will perceive the combined display . . . as an "endorsement" or "disapproval . . . of their individual religious choices."

Justice O'Connor concurred separately. She concluded that the menorah-tree-sign display was not an endorsement because it conveyed only a "message of pluralism." Justice Brennan (with Justices Marshall and Stevens) dissented in part; he would have held that both displays violated the Establishment Clause. Justice Stevens also dissented in part, rejecting the use of the endorsement standard.

Justice Kennedy (with Chief Justice Rehnquist and Justices White and Scalia) dissented in part for the opposite reason: he would have upheld both displays. He saw the constitutional standard in this context as depending on government "coercion." He concluded that, because no governmental "coercion" was present, the solitary creche was not violative of the Establishment Clause, and he charged that the majority of the Justices were engaged in "an Orwellian rewriting of history as many understand it." The creche cases demonstrate how the law can change. Two new standards are introduced: (1) the endorsement standard, and (2) Justice Kennedy's proposed coercion.

THE TEN COMMANDMENTS CASES. Although the Court had found that the mandatory posting of the Ten Commandments in public schools was, in *Stone v. Graham*, a violation of the Establishment Clause, the issue remained a politically-charged question and numerous cases arose—in a variety of settings. In the two cases below, the Supreme Court revisited the question of what limitations on the majority's will were created by the Establishment Clause. The companion decisions are remarkably parallel to the first and second "creche" cases above.

As in the creche cases, the determining factor appeared to be the context, including the *historical* context, in which the particular display of the Ten Commandments was set. The two decisions are highly fractured with multiple opinions, and this indicates that the Court is struggling to identify the proper framework for evaluating the constitutionality of governmental displays of religious symbols. Only Justice Breyer voted on the winning side of both cases; in that regard, he was the "swing vote" position, often previously held by Justice O'Connor.

VAN ORDEN v. PERRY, 545 U.S. 677 (2005). The "Texas" case involved a 10 foot high granite monument inscribed with the Ten Commandments. The monument was located, along with 17 other monuments and 21 historical markers, on the 22 acres of the Texas State Capitol grounds. The monument had been donated by the Fraternal Order of Eagles in 1961. The Texas monument was only one of many donated by the Eagles and Cecil B. DeMille following DeMille's Biblical screen epic—The Ten Commandments. The constitutionality of the Texas monument was not questioned until Van Orden filed his Establishment Clause challenge.

As you can see, the Texas monument case has both a physical context (much like the first creche case) and a historical context. These factors would be determinative (especially in Justice Breyer's concurrence).

The Supreme Court, in a plurality opinion by Chief Justice Rehnquist, upheld the Texas monument display. The Chief Justice relied on an historical analysis similar to *Marsh v. Chambers* above. As such, the plurality stepped outside of the *Lemon* standard—or any other competing doctrinal standard. The plurality reasoned that:

> Of course, the Ten Commandments are religious—they were so viewed at their inception and so remain. . . . But, Moses was a lawgiver as well as a religious leader. And the Ten Commandments have an undeniable historical meaning. . . .

The plurality concluded: "The placement of the Ten Commandments monument on the Texas State Capitol grounds is a far more passive use of those texts than was the case in *Stone*. . . ."

Justice Breyer's concurrence in the judgment provided the fifth vote. He rejected the plurality's reasoning. He also rejected the *Lynch* Court's reasoning. For Justice Breyer, the critical issue is whether the display of a religious symbol will create the type of political divisiveness the Establishment Clause was designed to prevent. Calling this a "close case," Justice Breyer concluded that "as a practical matter of *degree* this display is unlikely to prove divisive."

There were four dissenters in *Van Orden*, with Justice Stevens, O'Connor, and Souter submitting opinions. As a general matter, the dissenters rejected the plurality's "historical" approach and argued for the heightened scrutiny of the *Lemon* or endorsement standards. The dissenters would, with Justice Breyer, become the majority in the companion case.

McCREARY COUNTY, KY v. AMERICAN CIVIL LIBERTIES UNION, 545 U.S. 844 (2005). In *McCreary County*, two Kentucky courthouses had displayed framed copies of the Ten Commandments. Initially, these framed copies were displayed in a solitary manner, and they became part of a broader display of historical documents only after the County was threatened with litigation (and even changed defense counsel). The Supreme Court, per Justice Souter, struck down the courthouse displays as a violation of the Establishment Clause. The majority concluded that the Counties lacked a "secular purpose." The "evolution" of the displays was the main evidence that the Counties had a "religious" purpose. The majority rejected the Counties' argument that the Court should eliminate the purpose prong from the *Lemon* test.

Justice O'Connor provided a concurrence. Since she has been a long-time critic of the

Lemon test, her position may be influential in future cases. She argued that religion should be "a matter for the individual conscience, not for the prosecutor or bureaucrat." As for the critics of *Lemon* or other "separationist" standards, Justice O'Connor asserted that: "Those who would renegotiate the boundaries between church and state must therefore answer a difficult question: why would we trade a system that has served us so well for one that has served others so poorly?"

This defense of a separationist position provoked a lengthy dissent by Justice Scalia (joined partly by Justice Kennedy). Justice Scalia invoked several themes from his dissents in prior cases (*e.g.*, *Weisman*). Justice Scalia would not find even the sole display of the Ten Commandments to be a violation of the Establishment Clause because he concluded that the Ten Commandments always has sufficient historical significance to provide a secular purpose. Of course, Justice Scalia has previously rejected the *Lemon* test.

PROBLEM A

IS A COURTROOM PRAYER UNCONSTITUTIONAL?: NORTH CAROLINA CIVIL LIBERTIES UNION LEGAL FOUNDATION v. CONSTANGY, 947 F.2d 1145 (4th Cir. 1991). A North Carolina state judge opened each court session by saying, "Let us pause for a moment of prayer" and by reciting a short, nondenominational prayer directed to "our God, our Father in Heaven" and asking for guidance and protection. What test, *Lemon* or *Marsh*, applies to this activity, and if the *Lemon* test applies, is the ingredient of "endorsement" under Justice O'Connor's approach (or "coercion" under Justice Kennedy's approach) sufficient to invalidate it?

[The Fourth Circuit, here, held the prayer to be a religious ceremony rather than solemnization of the atmosphere (this holding was based upon district court findings particular to the exact facts). The Court further rejected *Marsh*-type reasoning because it found no history of prayers in courtrooms analogous to those in legislatures. And it held that the prayer failed the *Lemon* test, since its primary effect was "endorsement" of religion and since it constituted an excessive "entanglement." Is this reasoning persuasive?]

[B] Religion in the Public Schools

NOTES AND QUESTIONS

(1) *Religion in the Public Schools.* Controversies regarding the Establishment Clause (and the Free Exercise Clause) have occurred in a number of settings, but one of the most problematic has been the public schools. We have placed the following materials in this subsection because the controversies have arisen in the context of public school properties and programs. The controversies generally involve the proponents of the majoritarian religious views seeking, sometimes in the name of their Free Exercise rights, to hold prayers or other religious observance during public school events or activities. Generally, members of non-majoritarian religious groups object, usually on Establishment Clause grounds.

(2) *The Right to Choose Religious Education: Meyer v. Nebraska, 262 U.S. 390 (1923), and Pierce v. Society of Sisters, 268 U.S. 510 (1925).* In *Meyer*, the Supreme Court invalidated a law prohibiting the teaching of foreign languages. Later, in *Pierce*, the Court invalidated a statute that limited children to attending the public schools, preventing them from obtaining a parochial education. *Pierce* emphasized the "liberty of parents . . . to direct the upbringing and education of children."

ZORACH v. CLAUSON, 343 U.S. 306 (1952). New York City had a program that permitted public schools to release students during the school day so that they could leave the school grounds and go to religious centers for religious instruction or devotional exercises. Those not released by written request of their parents were required to stay in classrooms. The Supreme Court, per Justice Douglas, upheld this "release time" program:

> There is a suggestion that the system involves the use of coercion to get public school students into religious classrooms. There is no evidence in the record before us that supports that conclusion. The present record indeed tells us that the school authorities are neutral in this regard. . . . If in fact coercion were used, . . . a wholly different case would be presented.

> Moreover, apart from that claim of coercion, we do not see how New York by this type of "release time" program has made a law respecting an establishment of religion within the meaning of the first amendment. [T]he first amendment within the scope of its coverage permits no exception; the prohibition is absolute. The first amendment, however, does not say that in every and all respects there shall be a separation of church and state. Rather, it studiously defines the manner, the specific ways, in which there shall be no concert or union or dependency one on the other. That is the common sense of the matter. Otherwise the state and religion would be aliens to each other—hostile, suspicious, and even unfriendly. Churches could not be required to pay even property taxes. Municipalities would not be permitted to render police or fire protection to religious groups. Policemen who helped parishioners into their places of worship would violate the Constitution. Prayers in our legislative halls; the appeals to the Almighty in the message of the Chief Executive; the proclamations making Thanksgiving Day a holiday; "so help me God" in our courtroom oaths—these and all other references to the Almighty that run through our laws, our public rituals, our ceremonies would be flouting the first amendment. A fastidious atheist or agnostic could even object to the supplication with which the Court opens each session: "God save the United States and this honorable Court." . . .

> We are a religious people whose institutions presuppose a Supreme Being. [Government] may not coerce anyone to attend church, to observe a religious holiday, or to take religious instruction. But it can close its doors or suspend its operations as to those who want to repair to their religious sanctuary for worship or instruction. No more than that is undertaken here.

Justice Black dissented: "The Court's validation of the New York system rests in part on its statement that Americans are a 'religious people whose institutions presuppose a Supreme Being.' [I]t was precisely because eighteenth century Americans were a religious people divided into many fighting sects [that] we were given the constitutional mandate to keep church and state completely separate."

In addition, Justice Frankfurter dissented, observing, " '[c]oercion' in the abstract is acknowledged to be fatal. But the Court disregards the fact that as the case comes to us, there could be no proof of coercion, for the appellants were not allowed to make proof of it." Justice Frankfurter thought that the plaintiffs should be allowed to introduce evidence in support of their allegation that the release time program had resulted in the exercise of pressure upon parents and children to secure attendance at religious instruction. Finally, Justice Jackson dissented on the ground that, during the released time, the school room "serves as a temporary jail for a pupil who will not go to church" and therefore operates "in support of religion."

ENGEL v. VITALE, 370 U.S. 421 (1962). The Board of Education of Union Free School District No. 9, in New Hyde Park, New York, promulgated the following prayer to be said aloud by each class in the presence of a teacher at the beginning of each school day: "Almighty God, we acknowledge our dependence upon thee, and we beg thy blessings upon us, our parents, our teachers and our country." The Court, per Justice Black, held this practice unconstitutional:

> There can, of course, be no doubt that New York's program of daily classroom invocation of God's blessings as prescribed in the Regents' prayer is

a religious activity. . . .

[W]e think that the constitutional prohibition against laws respecting an establishment of religion must at least mean that in this country it is not part of the business of government to compose official prayers for any group of the American people to recite as part of a religious program carried on by government.

Justice Stewart dissented: "I cannot see how an 'official religion' is established by letting those who want to say a prayer say it. On the contrary, I think that to deny the wish of these school children to join in reciting this prayer is to deny them the opportunity of sharing in the spiritual heritage of our nation."

SCHOOL DISTRICT OF ABINGTON TOWNSHIP v. SCHEMPP
374 U.S. 203 (1963)

Mr. Justice Clark delivered the opinion of the Court.

[A Pennsylvania statute required that "at least ten verses from the Holy Bible shall be read, without comment, at the opening of each public school on each school day." The statute also provided that any child would be excused on the written request of his parent or guardian. The Schempps sought an injunction to prevent this practice as a violation of the First Amendment. The district court granted the injunction, and the Supreme Court here affirms.

[The evidence showed that individual schools carried out the statute by a recitation of the ten Bible verses over an intercom system, followed by a recitation of the Lord's Prayer, during which students were asked to stand and join in repeating the prayer in unison. In schools without an intercom, the home-room teacher conducted the exercise. The Schempps testified that these religious doctrines "were contrary to [their] religious beliefs." Expert testimony also indicated that these exercises were "offensive to Jewish tradition" and, in some parts, were "practically blasphemous."]

The wholesome "neutrality" of which this Court's cases speak . . . stems from a recognition of the teachings of history that powerful sects or groups might bring about a fusion of governmental and religious functions or a concert or dependency of one upon the other to the end that official support of the state or federal government would be placed behind the tenets of one or of all orthodoxies. This the establishment clause prohibits. And a further reason for neutrality is found in the free exercise clause, which recognizes the value of religious training, teaching and observance, and, more particularly, the right of every person to freely choose his own course with reference thereto, free of any compulsion from the state.

[T]he two clauses may overlap. [The Court] has consistently held that the [establishment] clause withdrew all legislative power respecting religious belief or the expression thereof. The test may be stated as follows: what are the purpose and the primary effect of the enactment? If either is the advancement or inhibition of religion then the enactment exceeds the scope of legislative power as circumscribed by the Constitution. . . .

. . . These exercises are prescribed as part of the curricular activities of students who are required by law to attend school. They are held in the school buildings under the supervision and with the participation of teachers employed in those schools. None of these factors, other than compulsory school attendance, was present in the program upheld in *Zorach v. Clauson*. . . .

The conclusion follows that in both cases the laws require religious exercises and such exercises are being conducted in direct violation of the rights of the appellees and petitioners. Nor are these required exercises mitigated by the fact that individual students may absent themselves upon parental request, for that fact furnishes no defense to a claim of unconstitutionality under the establishment clause. *See Engel v.*

Vitale, supra. Further, it is no defense to urge that the religious practices here may be relatively minor encroachments on the first amendment. The breach of neutrality that is today a trickling stream may all too soon become a raging torrent and, in the words of Madison, "it is proper to take alarm at the first experiment on our liberties." [Madison,] *Memorial and Remonstrance against Religious Assessments.* . . .

It is insisted that unless these religious exercises are permitted a "religion of secularism" is established in the schools. We agree of course that the state may not establish a "religion of secularism" in the sense of affirmatively opposing or showing hostility to religion, thus "preferring those who believe in no religion over those who do believe." *Zorach.* [W]e do not agree, however, that this decision in any sense has that effect. . . . They are religious exercises, required by the states in violation of the command of the first amendment. . . .

[The concurring opinion of JUSTICE DOUGLAS is omitted.]

MR. JUSTICE BRENNAN, concurring. . . .

It is true that the Framers' immediate concern was to prevent the setting up of an official federal church of the kind which England and some of the colonies had long supported. But nothing in the text of the establishment clause supports the view that the prevention of the setting up an official church was meant to be the full extent of the prohibitions against official involvements in religion. . . .

A too literal quest for the advice of the Founding Fathers upon the issues of these cases seems to me futile and misdirected for several reasons: First, on our precise problem the historical record is at best ambiguous, and statements can readily be found to support either side of the proposition. . . .

Second, the structure of American education has greatly changed since the first amendment was adopted. . . .

Third, our religious composition makes us a vastly more diverse people than were our forefathers. They knew differences chiefly among Protestant sects. . . .

Fourth, the American experiment in free public education available to all children has been guided in large measure by the dramatic evolution of the religious diversity among the population which our public schools serve. . . .

The use of prayers and Bible readings at the opening of the school day long antedates the founding of our Republic.

[U]nlike the Sunday closing laws, these exercises appear neither to have been divorced from their religious origins nor deprived of their centrally religious character by the passage of time. . . .

[W]hat the Framers meant to foreclose, and what our decisions under the establishment clause have forbidden, are those involvements of religious with secular institutions which (a) serve the essentially religious activities of religious institutions; (b) employ the organs of government for essentially religious purposes; or (c) use essentially religious means to serve governmental ends, where secular means would suffice. [O]n the other hand, there may be myriad forms of involvements of government with religion which do not import such dangers and therefore, should not, in my judgment, be deemed to violate the establishment clause. . . .

[I] think a brief survey of certain of these forms of accommodation will reveal that the first amendment commands not official hostility toward religion, but only a strict neutrality in matters of religion. . . .

A. *The Conflict Between Establishment and Free Exercise.*—There are certain practices conceivably violative of the establishment clause, the striking down of which might seriously interfere with certain religious liberties also protected by the first amendment. Provisions for churches and chaplains at military establishments for those in the armed service may afford one such example. The like provision by state and federal governments for chaplains in penal institutions may afford another example. It is argued that such provisions may [be] sustained on constitutional grounds as necessary to secure to the members of the armed forces and prisons those rights of worship guaranteed under the free exercise clause. . . .

C. *Non-Devotional Use of the Bible in the Public Schools.*—The holding of the Court today plainly does not foreclose teaching *about* the Holy Scriptures or about the differences between religious sects in classes in literature or history. . . .

D. *Uniform Tax Exemptions Incidentally Available to Religious Institutions.*—Nothing we hold today questions the propriety of certain tax deductions or exemptions which incidentally benefit churches and religious institutions, along with many secular charities and non-profit organizations. If religious institutions benefit, it is in spite of rather than because of their religious character. . . .

E. *Religious Considerations in Public Welfare Programs.*—Since government may not support or directly aid religious *activities* without violating the establishment clause, there might be some doubt whether non-discriminatory programs of government aid may constitutionally include *individuals* who become eligible wholly or partially for religious reasons. [T]herefore, the argument runs, the state may avoid an establishment only by singling out and excluding such persons on the ground that religious beliefs or practices have made them potential beneficiaries. Such a construction would, it seems to me, require government to impose religious discriminations and disabilities, thereby jeopardizing the free exercise of religion. . . .

F. *Activities Which, Though Religious in Origin, Have Ceased to Have Religious Meaning.*—As we noted in our Sunday Law decisions, nearly every criminal law in the books can be traced to some religious principle or inspiration, [but] "the establishment clause does not ban federal or state regulation of conduct whose reason or effect merely happens to coincide or harmonize with the tenets of some or all religions." This rationale suggests that the use of the motto "In God We Trust" on currency, on documents and public buildings and the like may not offend the clause. [We] have simply interwoven the motto so deeply into the fabric of our civil polity that its present use may well not present that type of involvement which the first amendment prohibits. . . .

MR. JUSTICE GOLDBERG, with whom MR. JUSTICE HARLAN joins, concurring. . . .

It is said, and I agree, that the attitude of government toward religion must be one of neutrality. But untutored devotion to the concept of neutrality can lead to invocation or approval of results which partake not simply of that non-interference and non-involvement with the religious which the Constitution commands, but of a brooding and pervasive devotion to the secular and a passive, or even active, hostility to the religious. Such results are not only not compelled by the Constitution, but, it seems to me, are prohibited by it. . . .

The practices here involved do not fall within any sensible or acceptable concept of compelled or permitted accommodation and involve the state so significantly and directly in the realm of the sectarian as to give rise to those very divisive influences and inhibitions of freedom which both religion clauses of the first amendment preclude. . . .

MR. JUSTICE STEWART, dissenting. . . .

[T]here is involved in these cases a substantial free exercise claim on the part of those who affirmatively desire to have their children's school day open with the reading of passages from the Bible. . . .

It might also be argued that parents who want their children exposed to religious influences can adequately fulfill that wish off school property and outside school time. [T]his argument seriously misconceives the basic constitutional justification for permitting the exercises at issue in these cases. For a compulsory state educational system so structures a child's life that if religious exercises are to be an impermissible activity in schools, religion is placed at an artificial and state-created disadvantage . . . and a refusal to permit religious exercises thus is seen, not as the realization of state neutrality, but rather as the establishment of a religion of secularism, or at the least, as government support of the beliefs of those who think that religious exercises should be conducted only in private. . . .

PROBLEM B

THE "SECULAR HUMANISM SCHOOL BOOKS" CASES— MOZERT v. HAWKINS COUNTY BOARD OF EDUCATION, 827 F.2d 1058 (6th Cir. 1987) *AND SMITH v. BOARD OF SCHOOL COMMISSIONERS*, 827 F.2d 684 (11th Cir. 1987). In the *Mozert* case, "born again Christian" families in a Tennessee county sued on the theory that textbooks that exposed students to conclusions that they found contrary to their religious beliefs violated the Free Exercise Clause. For example, some of the books espoused the theory that individuals were able to determine their own destiny, a belief that clashed with the plaintiff's faith in control of their destiny by the Deity. (Similar issues arose in the *Smith* case.) If faced with evidence that school books contain significant amounts of such secular notions, and that students whose religious beliefs contradict them are required to use them, should a district court grant relief?

[In both *Mozert* and *Smith*, the district courts granted the requested injunctions. In both cases, the court of appeals reversed. The Sixth Circuit in *Mozert* reasoned that there was no government compulsion and hence no violation of the Free Exercise Clause or establishment of religion since the schools merely required students to read and discuss the books, rather than to affirm or deny beliefs contrary to their religious faith. The Eleventh Circuit in *Smith* applied the three-part test of *Lemon v. Kurtzman*, concluding that the books served the secular purpose of educating students, had a primary effect that neither advanced nor inhibited religion, and avoided excessive entanglement. Are these conclusions correct?] *Cf.* Davidow, *"Secular Humanism" as an "Established Religion:" A Response to Whitehead and Conian*, 11 TEXAS TECH L. REV. 51 (1979), and authorities therein cited; Mitchell, *Secularism in Public Education: The Constitutional Issues*, 67 B.U. L. REV. 603 (1987); Note, *"Secular Humanism:" A Blight on the Establishment Clause*, 18 LOY. U. CHI. L.J. 1245 (1987).

NOTES AND QUESTIONS

(1) *Is the Issue in These Cases One of "Coercion" (A Free Exercise Concern) or of a State Religious Ceremony (An Establishment Concern)?* To what extent is the decision in *Schempp* based upon the Free Exercise Clause, in that students arguably may be coerced into participation by indirect means despite the option not to participate, and to what extent is it based upon the Establishment Clause, in that state facilities and funds are used to conduct a religious exercise?

(2) *Comparing Schempp to Marsh v. Chambers: Does Uniform Acceptance of the Practice at the Time of the Adoption of the Constitution Make a Difference?* In *Marsh v. Chambers*, the Court upheld the use of legislative chaplains, largely on the ground that it was sanctioned by an unbroken history of acceptance since preconstitutional times. A similar history underlies the practice of school prayer. Is *Marsh* inconsistent with *Schempp*—and if so, which decision is incorrect?

(3) *Striking Down Prayers at Graduation on Coercion Grounds: Lee v. Weisman, 505 U.S. 577 (1992).* The plaintiffs in this case sought an injunction preventing principals of public schools from selecting clergy to deliver invocations and benedictions at public middle school and high school graduations. The school officials exercised a degree of control of the content of these prayers by issuing "guidelines" to the clergy. Citing *Schempp* and *Allegheny*, the Court (per Justice Kennedy) rejected an analogy to *Marsh v. Chambers* because of "inherent differences between the public school system and a session of a state legislature." Instead, Justice Kennedy (consistently with his position

in *Allegheny*) emphasized "heightened concerns with protecting freedom of conscience from subtle coercive pressure in the elementary and secondary public schools" and observed that "prayer exercises in public schools carry a particular risk of indirect coercion":

> [T]he undeniable fact is that the school district's supervision and control of a high school graduation ceremony places public pressure, as well as peer pressure, on attending students to stand as a group or, at least, maintain respectful silence during the invocation and benediction. This pressure, though subtle and indirect, can be as real as any overt compulsion. . . .

> [A]nd to say a teenage student has a real choice not to attend her high school graduation is formalistic in the extreme. [E]veryone knows that in our society and in our culture high school graduation is one of life's most significant occasions. . . .

Justice Blackmun, joined by Justices Stevens and O'Connor, concurred separately, as did Justice Souter, joined by Justices Stevens and O'Connor. Justice Scalia, joined by Chief Justice Rehnquist, Justice White and Justice Thomas, dissented. The dissenters saw "no warrant for expanding the concept of coercion beyond acts backed by [p]enalty," and they saw the case as one involving official accommodation of longstanding tradition.

(4) *Expansion of "Graduation Prayer" Decision's Reasoning to Certain Student-Initiated, Student-Conducted Prayers: Sante Fe Independent School District v. Doe, 530 U.S. 290 (2000).* Following the *Weisman* decision, various school boards around the country (*e.g.*, northwest Iowa, etc.) sought strategies for continuing various group prayers. In the Santa Fe, Texas district, the Board and Administrators adopted a policy based on the theory that a student-initiated, student-directed and student-conducted prayer (by the elected "student council chaplain") before each home varsity football game would be distinguishable from *Weisman* as essentially "private speech." In a closely-watched case, the Supreme Court, per Justice Stevens, disagreed and struck down the pre-game prayers.

The Court rejected the District's "private speech" argument by pointing to certain facts: the pre-game prayer was held on school property; at school-sponsored events; over the school's public address system; by a speaker elected by a majoritarian process; under supervision of school faculty; and (more controversially) pursuant to the explicit and implicit "encouragement" of the school. As to the District's argument that the pre-game prayer did not involve any governmental "coercion," the Court held that "the school may not force this difficult choice" on students for whom the majoritarian religious prayer is a "personally offensive religious ritual."

The second holding appears to use a broader notion of "coercion" than *Weisman*, probably because the facts of *Sante Fe* seem to involve "voluntary" attendance. Chief Justice Rehnquist, for Justices Scalia and Thomas, dissented, arguing much along the themes of the *Weisman* dissent [above]. Is this decision "hostile" to free exercise values generally or limited to constraining majoritarian attempts to subject students with minority religious views to constitutionally improper messages? *See generally* Ira C. Lupa, *Government Messages and Government Money: Santa Fe, Mitchell v. Helms and The Arc of the Establishment Clause*, 42 Wm & Mary L. Rev. 771 (2001).

(5) *The "Ten Commandments" Case: Use of the Bible for Religious Purposes as Versus Study of the Bible in History, Literature, Ethics, or Comparative Religion Classes: Stone v. Graham, 449 U.S. 39 (1980). Stone* concerned a Kentucky statute that required a copy of the Ten Commandments, purchased with private contributions, to be posted on the wall of each public classroom in the state, with a legend saying that the "secular application of the Ten Commandments is clearly seen in its adoption as the fundamental legal code of Western civilization and the common law of the United States."

The Court held that this requirement had "no secular legislative purpose, and is therefore unconstitutional." Justice Rehnquist dissented, reasoning that Kentucky had simply decided to make students aware that "religion has been closely identified with our history and government" and that "the history of man is inseparable from the history of religion."

(6) *Religious Speech in Public School Buildings During Non-School Hours: Lamb's Chapel v. Center Moriches Union Free School, 508 U.S. 384 (1993).* The school board had a regulation allowing community groups to use the school buildings during non-school hours except when the group intended to use the facility for religious worship or speech. The Court struck down this categorical ban as a viewpoint regulation of free speech, holding that a group wishing to show a Christian family values film must be allowed to do so on a basis comparable to that given other groups during non-school use.

The Court treated the *Lamb's Chapel* case as a Free Speech issue (specifically, a viewpoint-based regulation in a nonpublic forum). Does the fact that the Court used a Free Speech rationale (rather than the Establishment Clause) affect its precedential weight, or your view of the result?

(7) *The Pledge of Allegiance to the Flag—Whether Congressional Addition of the Phrase "Under God" Violates the Establishment Clause: Elk Grove Unified School District v. Newdow, 542 U.S. 1 (2004).*

In *Newdow*, the plaintiff was an atheist. His daughter attended a public school near Sacramento. Her elementary school class, pursuant to state law, recited the pledge of allegiance each day, led by the teacher. While she was not required to salute the flag or say the pledge because of the *Barnette* decision, Newdow claimed that the daughter was harmed merely by being in the room while the rest of the class recited the pledge. Plaintiff Newdow appeared on a *pro se* basis, even before the Supreme Court. Although the district court had dismissed his claim, the Ninth Circuit panel ruled that the inclusion of the phrase "under God" in the Pledge violated Newdow's Establishment Clause rights.

The Supreme Court, per Justice Stevens, held that Newdow lacked prudential standing [*see* Chapter 1] to bring the challenge and reversed. Chief Justice Rehnquist (for Justices O'Connor and Thomas) concurred in the dismissal, but he would have reached the substantive merits (and rejected the claim). Justice Thomas concurred only in the judgment. In an opinion that will certainly attract academic attention, Justice Thomas argued that the Establishment Clause does not create any "individual" rights and that the Fourteenth Amendment did not incorporate the Establishment Clause against the States. Both of these propositions, if adopted, would cause a radical transformation of the current Establishment Clause doctrine. It appears likely that the "under God" controversy will reemerge in the near future.

WALLACE v. JAFFREE, 472 U.S. 38 (1985). An Alabama statute authorized a period of silence in public schools each day "for meditation or voluntary prayer." (Other, pre-existing Alabama statutes, not at issue in the case, authorized a one-minute period of silence "for meditation" and also authorized teachers to lead "willing students" in a prescribed prayer to "Almighty God . . . the Creator and Supreme Judge of the world.") Jaffree, a parent of Alabama school children, sought an injunction preventing the application of the minute-of-silence statute. The Supreme Court, per Justice Stevens, struck down the statute.

The Court first examined the district court's decision, based upon the historical understanding of the First and Fourteenth Amendments, to the effect that the federal Constitution imposed no obstacle to Alabama's establishment of a state religion. Labeling this conclusion "remarkable," the Court observed that the First Amendment was adopted to curtail only the power of Congress, but "when the Constitution was amended to prohibit any state from depriving any person of liberty without due process of law, that amendment imposed the same substantive limitations on the states' power to legislate that the first amendment had always imposed on the Congress' power."

The Court then analyzed the Alabama statute pursuant to the three-part test of *Lemon v. Kurtzman* and relied only on the "secular purpose" part of the test:

> [N]o consideration of the second or third criteria [of *Lemon*] is necessary if a statute does not have a clearly secular purpose. . . .

> In applying the purpose test, it is appropriate to ask "whether government's actual purpose is to endorse or disapprove of religion." In this case, the answer to that question is dispositive. For the record not only provides us with an unambiguous affirmative answer, but also reveals that the enactment of [the Alabama statute] was not motivated by any clearly secular purpose—indeed, the statute had *no* secular purpose.

> The sponsor of the bill that became [the statute], Senator Donald Holmes, inserted into the legislative record—apparently without dissent—a statement indicating that the legislation was an "effort to return voluntary prayer" to the public schools. [In testimony before the district court,] he stated, "No, I did not have no other purpose in mind." The state did not present evidence of *any* secular purpose.

> The unrebutted evidence of legislative intent contained in the legislative record and in the testimony of the sponsor . . . is confirmed by a consideration of the relationship between this statute and the two other measures that were considered in this case. . . .

> [T]he earlier statute refers only to "meditation" whereas [this statute] refers to "meditation or voluntary prayer". . . .

> The addition of "or voluntary prayer" indicates that the state intended to characterize prayer as a favored practice. Such an endorsement is not consistent with the established principle that the government must pursue a course of complete neutrality toward religion. . . .

Justice Powell concurred on "factual" grounds (as compared to the doctrinal analysis of the majority and O'Connor opinions):

> I concur in the Court's opinion and judgment that Ala. Code § 16-1-2011 (Supp. 1984) violates the Establishment Clause of the First Amendment. My concurrence is prompted by Alabama's persistence in attempting to institute state-sponsored prayer in the public schools by enacting three successive statutes. I agree fully with Justice O'Connor's assertion that some moment-of-silence statutes may be constitutional, a suggestion set forth in the Court's opinion as well.

From these facts, Justice Powell inferred a "sectarian purpose" which, under the *Lemon* standard, violated the Establishment Clause.

Chief Justice Burger dissented from "today's curious holding," observing that "it makes no sense to say that Alabama has 'endorsed prayer' by merely enacting a new statute 'to specify expressly that voluntary prayer is *one* of the authorized activities during a moment of silence.'" Justice White also dissented: "As I read the filed opinions, a majority of the Court would approve statutes that provided for a moment of silence but did not mention prayer. [I]f that is the case, I would not invalidate a statute that at the outset provided the legislative answer to the question, 'May I pray?'"

Finally, Justice Rehnquist dissented, urging a significant re-examination of the Framers' intent:

> It seems indisputable from . . . glimpses of Madison's thinking . . . that he saw the [first] amendment as designed to prohibit the establishment of a national religion, and perhaps to prevent discrimination among sects. He did not see it as requiring neutrality on the part of government between religion and irreligion. . . .

[There] is simply no historical foundation for the proposition that the Framers intended to build the "wall of separation" that was constitutionalized in *Everson*. . . .

The Framers intended the Establishment Clause to prohibit the designation of any church as a "national" one. The Clause was also designed to stop the Federal Government from asserting a preference for one religious denomination or sect over others. . . .

The Court strikes down the Alabama statute . . . because the state wished to "endorse prayer as a favored practice". . . . It would come as much of a shock to those who drafted the Bill of Rights as it will to a large number of thoughtful Americans today to learn that the Constitution, as construed by the majority, prohibits the Alabama legislature from "endorsing" prayer.

NOTES AND QUESTIONS

(1)   *A "Moment of Silence" Statute and the Introduction of the Nonpreferentialism Theory: Wallace v. Jaffree, 472 U.S. 38 (1985).* Alabama had passed a statute authorizing the public schools to begin the school day with a "moment of silence." An earlier version of the statute had stated that the moment of silence was "for meditation," but the Legislature amended the statute to permit "for meditation or prayer." A contemporaneous statute had authorized teacher-led prayers for "willing students." The State did not introduce evidence of any secular purpose for the moment of silence statute. The challenger produced testimony from the statute's legislative sponsor that his only purpose was to "return voluntary prayer" to the public schools.

The Supreme Court used the *Lemon* standard. The majority, per Justice Stevens, held that the state failed to demonstrate a secular purpose and, thus, failed the first prong of *Lemon*. Justices Powell and O'Connor concurred. Justices White and Rehnquist and Chief Justice Burger dissented.

(2)   *The Nonpreferentialism Theory of the Establishment Clause: Justice Rehnquist's Dissent in Jaffree.* The main (and certainly most interesting) dissent was by then-Justice Rehnquist. Justice Rehnquist called for a rejection of the *Lemon* standard (and Justice O'Connor's "endorsement" standard). Justice Rehnquist necessarily had to call for rejection of the "strict neutrality" standard of *Everson*. He argued that *Everson* was wrong about the history of the Establishment Clause. Applying what he called an original intentionist approach (remember: the *Everson* Court claimed to be an original intentionist decision), Justice Rehnquist stated that the Framers had intended only two results with the Establishment Clause:

(1) to prohibit a national church; and

(2) to prevent Congress from preferring one sect over another.

Put another way, as long as government is nonpreferentialist (between sects), it does not violate the Establishment Clause. One critical difference, therefore, between the *Jaffree* majority and Justice Rehnquist is that Rehnquist would allow government to "prefer" religion over non-religion. As such, the nonpreferential first theory would be narrower (*i.e.*, prohibit fewer majoritarian actions) than *Lemon* or endorsement (or any other theory you have studied).

Justice Rehnquist's nonpreferentialism theory was met with much academic criticism. Justice Rehnquist was questioned by the Senate Judiciary Committee during his 1986 confirmation hearings about his nonpreferentialist theory. Perhaps the leading article is Douglas Laycock, *Nonpreferential Aid to Religion: A False Claim About Original Intent*, 27 WILLIAM & MARY L. REV. 875 (1986). The leading response to Professor Laycock is found in Rodney K. Smith, *Nonpreferentialism in Establishment Clause Analysis: A Response to Professor Laycock*, 65 ST. JOHN'S L. REV. 245 (1991).

PROBLEM C

THE NEW JERSEY MINUTE-OF-SILENCE CASE: MAY v. COOPERMAN, 780 F.2d 240 (3d Cir. 1985). As did a large percentage of the states, New Jersey had a statute that authorized a minute of silence at the beginning of the day in public schools. Unlike the Alabama statute at issue in *Wallace v. Jaffree*, above, the New Jersey statute did *not* mention prayer or religious activity explicitly as permitted purposes. Plaintiffs attacking the statute, however, introduced considerable evidence purporting to show that the subjective purpose of legislators who voted for the New Jersey enactment was to return voluntary prayer to the public schools, including statements by those legislators. If this case were presented to the Supreme Court, would it uphold the New Jersey statute—or strike it down?

[The Third Circuit struck down the statute as unconstitutional. The Supreme Court granted certiorari, but it did not reach the merits because it determined that the appellants who brought the case before it on behalf of the state lacked standing to do so.] For a different perspective, *see* Baker, *The Religion Clauses Reconsidered: The Jaffree Case*, 18 CUMBERLAND L. REV. 125 (1985) (article by attorney for Alabama officials).

[C] Discrimination or Preferences Among Religions

UNITED STATES v. BALLARD, 322 U.S. 78 (1944). Ballard was convicted in the district court of mail fraud and related charges. The indictment charged that Ballard and others, "alias St. Germain, Jesus, George Washington, and Godfrey Ray King," had claimed that they had been "selected as divine messengers" and had, "by reason of supernatural attainments, the power to heal persons of ailments and diseases [including] diseases which are ordinarily classified . . . as being incurable diseases. . . ." The indictment further charged that the defendants knew that these representations were false and untrue and intended to use them to defraud. The Supreme Court, per Justice Douglas, reversed the convictions:

> Men may believe what they cannot prove. They may not be put to the proof of their religious doctrines or beliefs. Religious experiences which are as real as life to some may be incomprehensible to others. Yet the fact that they may be beyond the ken of mortals does not mean that they can be made suspect before the law.

> [I]f one could be sent to jail because a jury in a hostile environment found those teachings false, little indeed would be left of religious freedom. The Fathers of the Constitution were not unaware of the varied and extreme views of religious sects, of the violence of disagreement among them, and of the lack of any one religious creed on which all men would agree. They fashioned a charter of government which envisaged the widest possible toleration of conflicting views. . . .

LARSON v. VALENTE
456 U.S. 228 (1982)

JUSTICE BRENNAN delivered the opinion of the Court.

[A Minnesota statute imposed certain onerous registration and reporting requirements upon only those religious organizations that solicited more than fifty percent of their funds from nonmembers. The Unification Church and certain of its members sought an injunction against enforcement of this law on the ground that it violated the Establishment Clause. The Supreme Court here holds (1) that the statute must be subjected to strict scrutiny since it grants denominational preferences, (2) that the state's interest in preventing fraud, even if compelling, is not sufficiently "closely fitted" to the statute, and (3) that the statute creates an unacceptable "risk of politicizing religion." Therefore, the Court holds the statute unconstitutional.]

The clearest command of the establishment clause is that one religious denomination cannot be officially preferred over another. . . .

This constitutional prohibition of denominational preferences is inextricably connected with the continuing vitality of the free exercise clause. . . .

The fifty percent rule of [the Minnesota statute] clearly grants denominational preferences of the sort consistently and firmly deprecated in our precedents. Consequently, that rule must be invalidated unless it is justified by a compelling governmental interest, *cf. Widmar v. Vincent*, and unless it is closely fitted to further that interest, *Murdock v. Pennsylvania*, 319 U.S. 105 (1943). . . .

Appellants assert, and we acknowledge, that the State of Minnesota has a significant interest in protecting its citizens from abusive practices in the solicitation of funds for charity, and that this interest retains importance when the solicitation is conducted by a religious organization. [W]e will therefore assume, *arguendo*, that the Act generally is addressed to a sufficiently "compelling" governmental interest. But . . . appellants must demonstrate that the challenged fifty percent rule is closely fitted to further the interest that it assertedly serves.

[Appellants'] argument is based on three distinct premises: that members of a religious organization can and will exercise supervision and control over the organization's solicitation activities when membership contributions exceed fifty percent; that membership control, assuming its existence, is an adequate safeguard against abusive solicitations of the public by the organization; and that the need for public disclosure rises in proportion with the *percentage* of nonmember contributions. Acceptance of all three of these premises is necessary to appellants' conclusion, but we find no substantial support for any of them in the record.

We accordingly conclude that appellants have failed to demonstrate that the fifty percent rule . . . is "closely fitted" to further a "compelling governmental interest."

[The Court also applied the *Lemon* test and concluded that Minnesota's fifty percent rule violated the "entanglement" prong.]

[Thus,] we hold that appellees cannot be compelled to register and report under the Act. . . .

[The concurring opinion of JUSTICE STEVENS is omitted. The dissenting opinion of JUSTICE REHNQUIST, joined by CHIEF JUSTICE BURGER, JUSTICE WHITE and JUSTICE O'CONNOR, concluding that the appellees lack standing, also is omitted.]

JUSTICE WHITE, with whom JUSTICE REHNQUIST joins, dissenting. . . .

[The majority states that the fifty percent rule is not simply a facially neutral statute but one that makes explicit and deliberate distinctions between different religious organizations.] The rule itself, however, names no churches or denominations that are entitled to or denied the exemption. It neither qualifies nor disqualifies a church based on the kind or variety of its religious beliefs. Some religions will qualify and some will not, but this depends on the source of their contributions, not on their brand of religion.

To say that the rule on its face represents an explicit and deliberate preference for some religious beliefs over others is not credible. The Court offers no support for this assertion other than to agree with the court of appeals that the limitation might burden the less well organized denominations. . . .

NOTES AND QUESTIONS

(1) *Must Discrimination be "Intentional," or Will "Disparate Impact" Do?* Both the majority and the dissent in *Larson* seem to agree that disparate impact upon religions is not sufficient to make out a case for strict scrutiny; intentional or deliberate discrimination or preference seems (at least by implication, in the majority opinion) to

be required. Is this approach correct? Of course, disparate impact, particularly if severe and unjustified, may be evidence of discriminatory intent, as in the equal protection area. Notice the analogy to equal protection cases.

(2) The *Larson* majority, after finding that the Minnesota statute created a denominational preference, applied the strict scrutiny standard. How does the level of scrutiny in this standard compare to the scrutiny required by *Lemon*? Note that, while the government must have a "compelling" interest or purpose to satisfy strict scrutiny, only a "secular purpose" is demanded by *Lemon*.

(3) *Involving Churches "In the Exercise of Substantial Government Powers:" Larkin v. Grendel's Den, Inc., 459 U.S. 116 (1982).* A related problem concerns government grants of quasi-governmental powers to religious denominations. For example, in *Larkin v. Grendel's Den*, a Massachusetts statute vested power in governing bodies of churches effectively to veto applications for liquor licenses within a 500-foot radius of any church. The Court, per Chief Justice Burger, held the statute unconstitutional under the Establishment Clause.

The Court recognized that the state had a valid interest in enforcing neutral zoning laws, including those that would protect the character of schools, churches, and other activities. But it concluded that the Massachusetts statute was not a mere zoning ordinance but instead "delegates to private, nongovernmental entities power to veto certain liquor license applications, . . . a power ordinarily vested in agencies of government." Therefore, the deference normally due a zoning enactment was not merited.

Justice Rehnquist dissented. He concluded that the Massachusetts statute did not "sponsor or subsidize any religious group or activity. It does not encourage, much less compel, anyone to participate in religious activities or to support religious institutions. To say it 'advances' religion is to strain at the meaning of that word." Furthermore, as Justice Rehnquist saw it, the statute was more flexible, and less an establishment of religion, than the sort of absolute ban that the majority had indicated would be constitutional.

(4) *Sunday Closing Laws: McGowan v. Maryland, 366 U.S. 420 (1961).* In the *McGowan* case, which is also set out in Chapter 7, above, the Court considered the constitutionality of so-called Sunday Closing Laws or "Blue Laws," which prohibit the sale of given items or the conduct of certain types of activities on Sundays. The Court, per Chief Justice Warren, upheld such a law against an Establishment Clause claim that included arguments that the statute preferred certain religions:

> [The] establishment clause does not ban federal or state regulation of conduct whose reason or effect merely happens to coincide or harmonize with the tenets of some or all religions. In many instances, the Congress or state legislatures conclude that the general welfare of society, wholly apart from any religious considerations, demands such regulation. Thus, for temporal purposes, murder is illegal. And the fact that this agrees with the dictates of the Judeo-Christian religions while it may disagree with others does not invalidate the regulation. So too with the questions of adultery and polygamy. [T]he same could be said of theft, fraud, etc., because those offenses were also proscribed in the Decalogue.

> [We] accept the state supreme court's determination that the statute's present purpose and effect is not to aid religion but to set aside a day of rest and recreation.

See also Braunfeld v. Brown, 366 U.S. 599 (1961) (prohibition of Sunday retail sale of certain enumerated commodities did not violate establishment clause and did not interfere with the free exercise of plaintiffs' Orthodox Jewish religion). In both *McGowan* and *Braunfeld*, the Court recognized that Sunday closing laws had originally had religious purposes, but it concluded that the secular purpose of providing a uniform day of rest underlay the modern enactments.

Are these decisions correct, or do Sunday Closing Laws enact an unconstitutional preference for religions that observe Sunday as their Sabbath [and an unconstitutional discrimination against religions that do not]?

§ 12.03   THE FREE EXERCISE CLAUSE

[A]   What is a "Religion?"

NOTE ON THE DIFFICULTY OF DETERMINING THE "RELIGIOUS" BASIS OF A BELIEF OR PRACTICE

Defining "Religion." A threshold question for purposes of the Free Exercise Clause is whether the belief or practice in which the claimant is engaged is, indeed, a "religious" one. Hard core beliefs or practices of traditional religions generally are readily identified, but other cases are more difficult. Particular difficulty arises when the religious belief in question is not connected to a God or Supreme Being, or when it rests upon grounds resembling secular philosophical, ethical, or even scientific or economic grounds, or when its recognition would give rise to suspicion that its assertion may have been motivated by temporal advantages.

Should a Belief in a God or Supreme Being be a Requisite of a Religion?: Torcaso v. Watkins, 367 U.S. 488 (1961), and United States v. Seeger, 380 U.S. 163 (1965). In *Torcaso*, the Court struck down a state statute that required affirmation of belief in the existence of God as a condition for public office. The Court reasoned that a state could not "aid . . . religions based on a belief in the existence of God against those religions founded on different beliefs." The Court's opinion emphasized the existence of "religions in this country which do not teach what would generally be considered a belief in the existence of God[, including] Buddhism, Taoism, Ethical Culture, Secular Humanism and others." Later, in *Seeger*, the Court construed military draft laws that exempted conscientious objectors if their objections were based upon belief "in a relation to a Supreme Being involving duties superior to those arising from any human relation, but [not including] essentially political, sociological, or philosophical views or a merely personal moral code." Seeger stated that his conscientious objection was based upon his "belief in and devotion to goodness and virtue for their own sakes, and a religious faith in a purely ethical creed," although he "preferred to leave the question as to his belief in a Supreme Being open." The Court reasoned that "the test of belief 'in a relation to a Supreme Being' is whether a given belief that is sincere and meaningful occupies a place in the life of its possessor parallel to that filled by the orthodox belief in God of one who clearly qualifies for the exemption." Is the reasoning in these cases correct? Couldn't members of the American Communist Party claim protection for their beliefs as "religious" under the tests of *Torcaso* and *Seeger*?

Testing the Validity of an Individual's Claim of Religious Belief: The Focus Upon "Sincerity" Rather than Upon "Truth." The Supreme Court's decisions indicate that the probable "truth" of a given belief is irrelevant to the question of whether it is protected. For an eloquent example of such a holding, consider *United States v. Ballard* in the preceding section of this chapter ("Men may believe what they cannot prove. They may not be put to the proof of their religious doctrines or beliefs."). On the other hand, the Court frequently has indicated that the sincerity of a belief is a valid consideration. *E.g., Ballard, supra* (by implication); *Frazee v. Illinois Dept. of Employment Security*, 489 U.S. 829 (1989). (Although the claimant did not belong to a particular Christian sect, the Court found that his refusal to work on Sundays "was based on a sincerely held religious belief. Under our cases, he was entitled to invoke first amendment protection.") But when does a "sincerely" held belief, which incidentally provides the holder of the belief with important secular or temporal advantages over others in the population, become so driven by those nonreligious concerns, or simply so bizarre, that it no longer qualifies for First Amendment protection? Consider whether the following is an appropriate statement: "One can, of course, imagine an asserted claim so bizarre, so clearly nonreligious in motivation, as not to be entitled to protection under the free exercise clause. . . ." *Thomas v. Review Board*, 450 U.S. 707 (1981). Mightn't an observer from another culture regard beliefs in such events as the immaculate conception or the resurrection as so "bizarre" that Orthodox Christianity could not qualify (and if so, is this an indication that whether the belief appears "bizarre" should be irrelevant)?

[B]　Should Free Exercise be Protected by Strict Scrutiny?: The Search for a Standard

SHERBERT v. VERNER
374 U.S. 398 (1963)

Mr. Justice Brennan delivered the opinion of the Court.

Appellant, a member of the Seventh-Day Adventist Church, was discharged by her South Carolina employer because she would not work on Saturday, the Sabbath Day of her faith. When she was unable to obtain other employment because she would not take Saturday work, she filed a claim for unemployment compensation benefits. [T]he appellee Employment Security Commission [found] that appellant's restriction upon her availability for Saturday work brought her within [a statutory] provision disqualifying for benefits insured workers who fail, without good cause, to accept "suitable work when offered. . . ." The Commission's finding was sustained by [the South Carolina Supreme Court]. [South Carolina's law also contained an exemption for Sunday worshipers that the Court says "saves the Sunday worshiper from having to make the kind of choice that [the] Sabbatarian" does.] [W]e reverse the judgment of the South Carolina Supreme Court and remand for further proceedings not inconsistent with this opinion.

[I]f [t]he decision of the South Carolina Supreme Court is to withstand appellant's constitutional challenge, it must be either because her disqualification as a beneficiary represents no infringement by the state of her constitutional rights of free exercise, or because any incidental burden on the free exercise of appellant's religion may be justified by a "compelling state interest in the regulation of a subject within the state's constitutional power to regulate. . . ."

We turn first to the question whether the disqualification for benefits imposes any burden on the free exercise of appellant's religion. We think it is clear that it does. . . . [H]ere not only is it apparent that appellant's declared ineligibility for benefits derives solely from the practice of her religion, but the pressure upon her to forego that practice is unmistakable. . . . Governmental imposition of such a choice puts the same kind of burden upon the free exercise of religion as would a fine imposed against appellant for her Sunday worship. . . .

We must next consider whether some compelling state interest enforced in the eligibility provisions of the South Carolina statute justifies the substantial infringement of appellant's first amendment right. . . . No such [interest] has been advanced in the present case. The appellees suggest no more than a possibility that the filing of fraudulent claims by unscrupulous claimants feigning religious objections to Saturday work might not only dilute the unemployment compensation fund but also hinder the scheduling by employers of necessary Saturday work. [Even] if the possibility of spurious claims did threaten to dilute the fund and disrupt the scheduling of work, it would plainly be incumbent upon the appellees to demonstrate that no alternative forms of regulation would combat such abuses without infringing first amendment rights. . . .

In these respects, then, the state interest asserted in the present case is wholly dissimilar to the interests which were found to justify the less direct burden upon religious practices in *Braunfeld v. Brown, supra*. The Court recognized that the Sunday closing law which that decision sustained undoubtedly served "to make the practice of [the Orthodox Jewish merchants'] religious beliefs more expensive." [B]ut the statute was nevertheless saved by a countervailing factor which finds no equivalent in the instant case—a strong state interest in providing one uniform day of rest for all workers. [R]equiring exemptions for Sabbatarians, while theoretically possible, appeared to present an administrative problem of such magnitude, or to afford the exempted class so great a competitive advantage, that such a requirement would have rendered the entire statutory scheme unworkable. . . .

In holding as we do, plainly we are not fostering the "establishment" of the Seventh-Day Adventist religion in South Carolina, for the extension of unemployment benefits to Sabbatarians in common with Sunday worshipers reflects nothing more than the government obligation of neutrality in the face of religious differences, and does not represent that involvement of religious with secular institutions which it is the object of the establishment clause to forestall. *See School District of Abington Township v. Schempp.* [N]or do we, by our decision today, declare the existence of a constitutional right to unemployment benefits on the part of all persons whose religious convictions are the cause of their unemployment. This is not a case in which an employee's religious convictions serve to make him a nonproductive member of society. . . .

Reversed and remanded.

Mr. Justice Douglas, concurring. . . .

Religious scruples of Moslems require them to attend a mosque on Friday and to pray five times daily. Religious scruples of a Sikh require him to carry a regular or a symbolic sword. . . . Religious scruples of a Jehovah's Witness teach him to be a colporteur, going from door to door, from town to town, distributing his religious pamphlets. . . .

The examples could be multiplied, including those of the Seventh-Day Adventist whose Sabbath is Saturday and who is advised not to eat some meats.

These suffice, however, to show that many people hold beliefs alien to the majority of our society—beliefs that are protected by the first amendment but which could easily be trod upon under the guise of "police" or "health" regulations reflecting the majority's views.

Some have thought that a majority of a community can, through state action, compel a minority to observe their particular religious scruples so long as the majority's rule can be said to perform some valid secular function. That was the essence of this Court's decision in the Sunday blue law cases [citing *Braunfeld v. Brown, McGowan v. Maryland*, and other cases], a ruling from which I then dissented. . . .

[The] harm is the interference with the individual's scruples or conscience. [T]he interference here is as plain as it is in Soviet Russia, where a churchgoer is given a second-class citizenship. . . .

Mr. Justice Stewart, concurring in the result.

Although fully agreeing with the result which the Court reaches in this case, I cannot join the Court's opinion. . . .

[What] this Court has said about the establishment clause must inevitably lead to a diametrically opposite result. If the appellant's refusal to work on Saturdays were based on indolence, or on a compulsive desire to watch the Saturday television programs, no one would say that South Carolina could not hold that she was not "available for work" within the meaning of the statute. That being so, the establishment clause as construed by this Court not only *permits* but affirmatively *requires* South Carolina equally to deny the appellant's claim for unemployment compensation when her refusal to work on Saturdays is based upon her religious creed [citing *Everson v. Board of Education, Schempp,* and *Engel v. Vitale, supra*]. . . .

To require South Carolina to so administer its laws as to pay public money to the appellant under the circumstances of this case is thus clearly to require the state to violate the establishment clause as construed by this Court. This poses no problem for me, because I think the Court's mechanistic concepts of the establishment clause is historically unsound and constitutionally wrong. [I] think that the guarantee of religious liberty embodied in the free exercise clause affirmatively requires government to create an atmosphere of hospitality and accommodation to individual belief or disbelief. In short, I think our Constitution demands the positive protection by government of religious freedom—not only for a minority, however small—not only for the majority, however large—but for each of us. . . .

MR. JUSTICE HARLAN, with whom MR. JUSTICE WHITE joins, dissenting. . . .

[The] purpose of the [South Carolina Unemployment Compensation Law] was to tide people over, and to avoid social and economic chaos, during periods when *work was unavailable.* . . .

The South Carolina Supreme Court has uniformly applied this law in conformity with its clearly expressed purpose. It has consistently held that one is not "available for work" if his unemployment has resulted not from the inability of industry to provide a job but rather from personal circumstances, no matter how compelling. . . .

In the present case all that the state court has done is to apply these accepted principles. . . . The fact that [appellant's] personal consideration sprang from her religious convictions was wholly without relevance to the state court's application of the law. Thus in no proper sense can it be said that the state discriminated against the appellant on the basis of her religious beliefs or that she was denied benefits *because* she was a Seventh-Day Adventist. She was denied benefits just as any other claimant would be denied benefits who was not "available for work" for personal reasons.

[W]hat the Court is holding is that if the state chooses to condition unemployment compensation on the applicant's availability for work, it is constitutionally compelled to *carve out an exception*—and to provide benefits—for those whose unavailability is due to their religious convictions. . . .

NOTES AND QUESTIONS

(1) *Comparing Sherbert v. Verner with the Sunday Closing Law Cases.* In *Sherbert,* the majority distinguishes *Braunfeld v. Brown* and *McGowan v. Maryland,* the Sunday Closing Law cases. But Justice Stewart and the dissenters claim that the Sunday closing law cases compel the opposite result. Who is correct?

The majority opinion in *Sherbert* says, first, that the Sunday Closing Law cases involved a "less direct burden upon religious practices." Is that argument persuasive? (The Sunday Closing Law cases did not require any person to commit an act in violation of his religious beliefs, and this factor may support the majority's reasoning—but on the other hand, the Sunday Closing Laws actually required the population to observe a custom prescribed by majoritarian religions.) The majority opinion in *Sherbert* also distinguishes Sunday Closing Laws on the ground that they are supported by a "strong" state interest in a uniform day of rest. (The creation of exceptions, according to the majority opinion, would have made the "entire statutory scheme unworkable" because it would have presented a huge administrative problem and afforded the exempted class a great competitive advantage.) Are these distinctions persuasive?

(2) *Reaffirming Sherbert: Thomas v. Review Board, 450 U.S. 707 (1981), and Hobbie v. Unemployment Appeals Commission, 480 U.S. 136 (1987).* In the *Thomas* case, a Jehovah's Witness was transferred within his company to a department that produced turrets for military tanks. He refused for religious reasons to participate in the production of armaments, was denied transfer or layoff, and resigned. The state then denied him unemployment compensation benefits under a statutory scheme similar to that in *Sherbert v. Verner.* The Court, per Chief Justice Burger, held that the denial of benefits was unconstitutional. Justice Rehnquist dissented. He argued that the majority had misread both the Free Exercise Clause and the Establishment Clause. *See Hobbie v. Unemployment Appeals Commission*, 480 U.S. 136 (1987) (following *Sherbert* and *Thomas* even when the claimant's religiously-based objection arose after her initial hiring). *See also* Katz, *Caesar, God and Mammon: Business and the Religion Clauses,* 21 VAL. U. L. REV. 387 (1987); Note, *A New Category of Free Exercise Clause Claims: Protection for Individuals Objecting to Governmental Actions that Impede Their Religions*, 135 U. PA. L. REV. 1557 (1987); *cf.* Ivankovich, *The "Religious" Employee and Reasonable Accommodation Requirements*, 13 CAN. BUS. L.J. 313 (1987).

(3) *Later Refusal to Extend Strict Scrutiny: The Smith Case, Below.* In the next section, we shall encounter a case in which the Court rejected strict scrutiny. You will need to decide for yourself whether the cases can be reconciled.

WISCONSIN v. YODER
406 U.S. 205 (1972)

MR. CHIEF JUSTICE BURGER delivered the opinion of the Court.

[Wisconsin's compulsory school-attendance law required, through criminal sanctions, members of the Amish religion to cause their children to attend public or private school until reaching age 16. The respondents, Yoder and others, refused to do so beyond the eighth grade, on the ground that it was "contrary to the Amish religion and way of life." The dispute centered, therefore, essentially on the two years of compulsory school beyond eighth grade. The Amish respondents believed that by compliance with the statute, they would "endanger their own salvation and that of their children." The state stipulated that respondents' religious beliefs were sincere. Here, the Court upholds respondents' claim under the Free Exercise Clause.]

There is no doubt as to the power of a state, having a high responsibility for education of its citizens, to impose reasonable regulations for the control and duration of basic education. *See, e.g., Pierce v. Society of Sisters.* [Y]et even this paramount responsibility was, in *Pierce,* made to yield to the right of parents to provide an equivalent education in a privately operated system. . . .

[In] order for Wisconsin to compel school attendance . . . against a claim that such attendance interferes with the practice of a legitimate religious belief, it must appear either that the state does not deny the free exercise of religious belief by its requirement, or that there is a state interest of sufficient magnitude to override the interest claiming protection under the free exercise clause. . . .

[In] evaluating [respondents'] claims we must be careful to determine whether the Amish religious faith and their mode of life are, as they claim, inseparable and independent. . . .

[The Court reviewed the evidence regarding the Amish way of life, which involved emphasis of family and home, a church-oriented community, separation from the outside world, rejection of telephones, automobiles, radios and television, particular modes of dress and speech, habits of manual work, and other symbolic and practical customs.] Giving no weight to . . . secular considerations, . . . we see that the record in this case abundantly supports the claim that the traditional way of the life of the Amish is not merely a matter of personal preference, but one of deep religious conviction, shared by an organized group, and intimately related to daily living. . . .

The impact of the compulsory-attendance law on respondents' practice of the Amish religion is not only severe, but inescapable, for the Wisconsin law affirmatively compels them, under threat of criminal sanction, to perform acts undeniably at odds with fundamental tenets of their religious beliefs. [A]s the record shows, compulsory school attendance to age 16 for Amish children carries with it a very real threat of undermining the Amish community and religious practice as they exist today; they must either abandon belief and be assimilated into society at large, or be forced to migrate to some other and more tolerant region.

Wisconsin concedes that under the religion clauses religious beliefs are absolutely free from the state's control, but it argues that "actions," even though religiously grounded, are outside the protection of the first amendment. [S] ee, e.g., *Gillette v. United States* [below]. But to agree that religiously grounded conduct must often be subject to the broad police power of the state is not to deny that there are areas of conduct protected by the free exercise clause of the first amendment and thus beyond the power of the state to control, even under regulations of general applicability. *E.g., Sherbert v. Verner* [below]. [I]n this context belief and action cannot be neatly confined in logic-tight compartments. *Cf. Lemon v. Kurtzman.* . . .

[A] regulation neutral on its face may, in its application, nonetheless offend the constitutional requirement for governmental neutrality if it unduly burdens the free exercise of religion. . . .

We turn, then, to the State's broader contention that its interest in its system of compulsory education is so compelling that even the established religious practices of the Amish must give way. . . .

The State advances two primary arguments in support of its system of compulsory education. It notes, as Thomas Jefferson pointed out early in our history, that some degree of education is necessary to prepare citizens to participate effectively and intelligently in our open political system if we are to preserve freedom and independence. Further, education prepares individuals to be self-reliant and self-sufficient participants in society. We accept these propositions. . . .

The State, however, supports its interest in providing an additional one or two years of compulsory high school education to Amish children because of the possibility that some such children will choose to leave the Amish community, and that if this occurs they will be ill-equipped for life. [This] argument of the State appears to rest primarily on the State's mistaken assumption, [t]hat the Amish do not provide any education for their children beyond the eighth grade, but allow them to grow in "ignorance". . . .

Insofar as the State's claim rests on the view that a brief additional period of formal education is imperative to enable the Amish to participate effectively and intelligently in our democratic process, it must fall. The Amish alternative for formal secondary school education has enabled them to function effectively in their day-to-day life under self-imposed limitations on relations with the world. . . .

Finally, the State . . . argues that a decision exempting Amish children from the State's requirement fails to recognize the substantive right of the Amish child to a secondary education, and fails to give due regard to the power of the State as *parens patriae* to extend the benefit of secondary education to children regardless of the wishes of their parents. . . .

[I]t seems clear that if the State is empowered, as *parens patriae*, to "save" a child from himself or his Amish parents by requiring an additional two years of compulsory formal high school education, the state will in large measure influence, if not determine, the religious future of the child. [Therefore], this case involves the fundamental interests of parents, as contrasted with that of the State, to guide the religious future and education of their children. The history and culture of Western civilization reflect a strong tradition of parental concern for the nurture and upbringing of their children [citing *Pierce v. Society of Sisters* and *Meyer v. Nebraska*].

For the reasons stated we hold . . . that the first and fourteenth amendments prevent the State from compelling respondents to cause their children to attend formal high school to age 16. . . .

[The concurring opinions of Justice Stewart, joined by Justice Brennan, and of Justice White, joined by Justices Brennan and Stewart, are omitted.]

Mr. Justice Douglas, dissenting in part. . . .

[The] Court's analysis assumes that the only interests at stake in the case are those of the Amish parents on the one hand, and those of the State on the other. The difficulty with this approach is that, despite the Court's claim, the parents are seeking to vindicate not only their own free exercise claims, but also those of their high-school-aged children. . . .

[If] the parents in this case are allowed a religious exemption, the inevitable effect is to impose the parents' notions of religious duty upon their children. Where the child is mature enough to express potentially conflicting desires, it would be an invasion of the child's rights to permit such an imposition without canvassing his views. . . . And, if an Amish child desires to attend high school, and is mature enough to have that desire respected, the state may well be able to override the parents' religiously motivated objections.

NOTES AND QUESTIONS

(1) *The Further Development of the Free Exercise Standard in the Smith Case, below.* In *Employment Division v. Smith*, below, we shall encounter a holding that uses rational basis review for neutral regulations that impair religious practices, but you will need to decide for yourself the impact that decision would have upon *Yoder*.

(2) *Under Yoder, What is the Test for a Religious Practice Protected Against Neutral General Regulation?* At no point in *Yoder* does the Court set forth a readily applicable test for determining what religious practices are protected, and what are not, against a given kind of neutral general police power regulation. Consider whether the Court may actually have been employing a multi-factor balancing approach that may have included some or all of the following elements, possibly together with others: (a) the pervasiveness of the religious practice in the claimant's belief system; (b) the severity of impairment of the practice by the regulation; (c) the comprehensiveness or generality of the regulation in questions; and (d) the nature and quality of the state's reasons for the regulation. [Notice that, if the regulation severely impairs free exercise rights, the Court does hold that a "compelling" state interest is required. However, it does not set out a test for determining when a neutral law infringes free exercise rights in the first place.]

(3) *From Yoder to Smith.* Between the *Yoder* decision and the *Smith* decision, the Court decided a number of free exercise cases. In most instances, these decisions claimed to follow the standard from *Sherbert* and *Yoder*, but the outcome in each case was in favor of the government. Thus, these *results* seemed inconsistent with the use of strict scrutiny, and a great deal of academic and other commentary was directed at attempting to explain these decisions. These decisions included: *United States v. Lee*, 455 U.S. 252 (1982); *Goldman v. Weinberger*, 475 U.S. 503 (1986); *Bowen v. Roy*, 476 U.S. 693 (1986); *O'Lone v. Estate of Shabazz*, 482 U.S. 342 (1987); and *Lyng v. Northwest Indian Cemetery Protective Association*, 485 U.S. 439 (1988).

For present purposes, the rationale of the *O'Lone* decision was probably the most readily understandable because the Court, by a 5-4 majority, declared that a free exercise claim brought by a *prisoner* against a prison facility would receive only rational basis scrutiny. In that instance, the Court explicitly created an exception to the *Sherbert* and *Yoder* precedent. The other decisions were anything but clear, and they engendered a great deal of academic commentary. In any case, these decisions were superceded by the reasoning in *Smith*. We note them here for familiarity with the general free exercise doctrine and with the doctrinal awkwardness that accompanies a transition as significant as that from *Sherbert* to *Smith*.

PROBLEM D

GENDER DISCRIMINATION BY RELIGIONS. Assume that a state, as part of its effort to eradicate gender discrimination, enacts a law that prohibits any employer (including a religious institution or school acting as an employer) from engaging in any form of gender discrimination in employment. Also assume that the (hypothetical) New Zion Christian Church firmly maintains a religious tenet, based upon its hierarchy's interpretation of the scriptures, that only men can properly administer its sacraments, and it therefore excludes women from employment as clergy. If a woman denied employment as a member of the clergy of this hypothetical church complains or sues under the state anti-discrimination law, can the church successfully defend on the ground that the application of the law to it would violate the Free Exercise Clause?

You may find it interesting to compare this hypothesis with Title VII of the Civil Rights Act of 1968, 42 U.S.C. § 2000e-2 (1981), which provides that it is *not* an unlawful employment practice for an employer to distinguish on the basis of religion, sex, or national origin "in those certain instances where religion, sex, or national origin is a bona fide occupational qualification reasonably necessary to the normal operation of that particular business or enterprise." Is this limited exemption required by the Free Exercise Clause with respect to religious institutions?

[C] Conflict with Nondiscriminatory Secular Regulation: The Modern Court Limits the Use of Strict Scrutiny

EMPLOYMENT DIVISION v. SMITH
494 U.S. 872 (1990)

JUSTICE SCALIA delivered the opinion of the Court.

[Respondents Smith and Black were fired by a private drug rehabilitation organization because they ingested peyote as part of a ceremony at their Native American Church. The employment division of the State of Oregon denied their applications for unemployment compensation under a state law disqualifying employees discharged for work-related "misconduct." The state supreme court held that the denial violated Smith and Black's first amendment free exercise rights. The United States Supreme Court vacated the judgment and remanded for a determination whether sacramental peyote use was prohibited by the state's criminal laws. On remand, the state supreme court held that the sacramental use of peyote violated the state's criminal Controlled Substances Act and was not exempted from that Act, but also held that this prohibition was unconstitutional under the free exercise clause. The United States Supreme Court here reverses and holds that the sacramental use of peyote is not constitutionally protected under the circumstances.]

II

Respondents' claim for relief rests on our decisions in *Sherbert v. Verner* [below], *Thomas v. Review Board, Indiana Employment Security Div.* [below], and *Hobbie v. Unemployment Appeals Comm'n of Florida*, 480 U.S. 136 (1987), in which we held that a State could not condition the availability of unemployment insurance on an individual's willingness to forgo conduct required by his religion. As we observed in *Smith I*, however, the conduct at issue in those cases was not prohibited by law. [N]ow that the Oregon Supreme Court has confirmed that Oregon does prohibit the religious use of peyote, we proceed to consider whether that prohibition is permissible under the Free Exercise Clause.

A

The Free Exercise Clause of the First Amendment, which has been made applicable to the States by incorporation into the Fourteenth Amendment, provides that "Congress shall make no law respecting an establishment of religion, or *prohibiting the free exercise thereof. . . .*" U.S. Const. Am. I (emphasis added). The free exercise of religion means, first and foremost, the right to believe and profess whatever religious doctrine one desires. Thus, the First Amendment obviously excludes all "governmental regulation of religious *beliefs* as such. . . ."

But the "exercise of religion" often involves not only belief and profession but the performance of (or abstention from) physical acts. . . .

Respondents in the present case, however, seek to carry the meaning of "prohibiting the free exercise [of religion]" one large step further. They contend that their religious motivation for using peyote places them beyond the reach of a criminal law that is not specifically directed at their religious practice, and that is concededly constitutional as applied to those who use the drug for other reasons. They assert, in other words, that "prohibiting the free exercise [of religion]" includes requiring any individual to observe a generally applicable law that requires (or forbids) the performance of an act that his religious belief forbids (or requires). As a textual matter, we do not think the words must be given that meaning. . . .

[W]e have never held that an individual's religious beliefs excuse him from compliance with an otherwise valid law prohibiting conduct that the State is free to regulate. On the contrary, the record of more than a century of our free exercise jurisprudence contradicts that proposition. As described succinctly by Justice Frankfurter in *Minersville School Dist. Bd. of Educ. v. Gobitis*, 310 U.S. 586, 594–595 (1940): "Conscientious scruples have not, in the course of the long struggle for religious toleration, relieved the individual from obedience to a general law not aimed at the promotion or restriction of religious beliefs. The mere possession of religious convictions which contradict the relevant concerns of a political society does not relieve the citizen from the discharge of political responsibilities (footnote omitted). . . ."

[The Court turned from a textual analysis to a discussion of its free exercise precedents.] [T]he only decisions in which we have held that the First Amendment bars application of a neutral, generally applicable law to religiously motivated action have involved not the Free Exercise Clause alone, but the Free Exercise Clause in conjunction with other constitutional protections such as freedom of speech and of the press, or the right of parents, acknowledged in *Pierce v. Society of Sisters*, 268 U.S. 510 (1925), to direct the education of their children, *see Wisconsin v. Yoder*, 406 U.S. 205 (1972) (invalidating compulsory school-attendance laws as applied to Amish parents who refused on religious grounds to send their children to school). [A]nd it is easy to envision a case in which a challenge on freedom of association grounds would likewise be reinforced by Free Exercise Clause concerns.

The present case does not present such a hybrid situation but a free exercise claim unconnected with any communicative activity or parental right. Respondents urge us to hold, quite simply, that when otherwise prohibitable conduct is accompanied by religious convictions, not only the convictions but the conduct itself must be free from governmental regulation. We have never held that, and decline to do so now. . . .

B

Respondents argue that even though exemption from generally applicable criminal laws need not automatically be extended to religiously motivated actors, at least the claim for a religious exemption must be evaluated under the balancing test set forth in

Sherbert v. Verner, 374 U.S. 398 (1963). Under the *Sherbert* test, governmental actions that substantially burden a religious practice must be justified by a compelling governmental interest. [I]n recent years we have abstained from applying the *Sherbert* test (outside the unemployment compensation field) at all. In *Bowen v. Roy*, [discussed *supra*], [for example,] we declined to apply *Sherbert* analysis to a federal statutory scheme that required benefit applicants and recipients to provide their Social Security numbers. The plaintiffs in that case asserted that it would violate their religious beliefs to obtain and provide a Social Security number for their daughter. We held the statute's application to the plaintiffs valid regardless of whether it was necessary to effectuate a compelling interest. [The Court briefly discussed several other decisions.]

[E]ven if we were inclined to breathe into *Sherbert* some life beyond the unemployment compensation field, we would not apply it to require exemptions from a generally applicable criminal law. The *Sherbert* test, it must be recalled, was developed in a context that lent itself to individualized governmental assessment of the reasons for the relevant conduct. As a plurality of the Court noted in *Roy*, a distinctive feature of unemployment compensation programs is that their eligibility criteria invite consideration of the particular circumstances behind an applicant's unemployment. . . .

The "compelling government interest" requirement seems benign, because it is familiar from other fields. But using it as the standard that must be met before the government may accord different treatment on the basis of race, or before the government may regulate the content of speech, is not remotely comparable to using it for the purpose asserted here. What it produces in those other fields—equality of treatment, and an unrestricted flow of contending speech—are constitutional norms; what it would produce here—a private right to ignore generally applicable laws—is a constitutional anomaly.[1]

Nor is it possible to limit the impact of respondents' proposal by requiring a "compelling state interest" only when the conduct prohibited is "central" to the individual's religion. It is no more appropriate for judges to determine the "centrality" of religious beliefs before applying a "compelling interest" test in the free exercise field, than it would be for them to determine the "importance" of ideas before applying the "compelling interest" test in the free speech field. . . .

If the "compelling interest" test is to be applied at all, then, it must be applied across the board, to all actions thought to be religiously commanded. Moreover, if "compelling interest" really means what it says (and watering it down here would subvert its rigor in the other fields where it is applied), many laws will not meet the test. Any society adopting such a system would be courting anarchy, but that danger increases in direct proportion to the society's diversity of religious beliefs, and its determination to coerce or suppress none of them. Precisely because "we are a cosmopolitan nation made up of people of almost every conceivable religious preference," and precisely because we value and protect that religious divergence, we cannot afford the luxury of deeming *presumptively invalid*, as applied to the religious objector, every regulation of conduct that does not protect an interest of the highest order. The rule respondents favor would

---

[1] Justice O'Connor suggests that . . . all laws burdening religious practices should be subject to compelling-interest scrutiny because "the First Amendment unequivocally makes freedom of religion, like freedom from race discrimination and freedom of speech, a 'constitutional norm,' not an 'anomaly.' " . . . But this comparison with other fields supports, rather than undermines, the conclusion we draw today. Just as we subject to the most exacting scrutiny laws that make classifications based on race, or on the content of speech, so too we strictly scrutinize governmental classifications based on religion, . . . But we have held that race-neutral laws that have the effect of disproportionately disadvantaging a particular racial group do not thereby become subject to compelling-interest analysis under the Equal Protection Clause, see *Washington v. Davis*, 426 U.S. 229 (1976) (police employment examination); . . . Our conclusion that generally applicable, religion-neutral laws that have the effect of burdening a particular religious practice need not be justified by a compelling government interest is the only approach compatible with these precedents.

open the prospect of constitutionally required religious exemptions from civic obligations of almost every conceivable kind—ranging from compulsory military service, to the payment of taxes, to health and safety regulation such as manslaughter and child neglect laws, compulsory vaccination laws, drug laws, and traffic laws; to social welfare legislation such as minimum wage laws, child labor laws, animal cruelty laws, environmental protection laws, and laws providing for equality of opportunity for the races [the Court, in each of these instances, cites a case presenting a claim for exemption from the laws]. The First Amendment's protection of religious liberty does not require this.

Values that are protected against government interference through enshrinement in the Bill of Rights are not thereby banished from the political process. Just as a society that believes in the negative protection accorded to the press by the First Amendment is likely to enact laws that affirmatively foster the dissemination of the printed word, so also a society that believes in the negative protection accorded to religious belief can be expected to be solicitous of that value in its legislation as well. It is therefore not surprising that a number of States have made an exception to their drug laws for sacramental peyote use. . . . But to say that a nondiscriminatory religious-practice exemption is permitted, or even that it is desirable, is not to say that it is constitutionally required, and that the appropriate occasions for its creation can be discerned by the courts. It may fairly be said that leaving accommodation to the political process will place at a relative disadvantage those religious practices that are not widely engaged in; but that unavoidable consequence of democratic government must be preferred to a system in which each conscience is a law unto itself or in which judges weigh the social importance of all laws against the centrality of all religious beliefs. . . .

[The concurring opinion of JUSTICE O'CONNOR concludes:]

I would [a]dhere to our established free exercise jurisprudence and hold that the State in this case has a compelling interest in regulating peyote use by its citizens and that accommodating respondents' religiously motivated conduct "will unduly interfere with fulfillment of the governmental interest." Accordingly, I concur in the judgment of the Court.

JUSTICE BLACKMUN, with whom JUSTICE BRENNAN and JUSTICE MARSHALL join, dissenting. . . .

This Court over the years painstakingly has developed a consistent and exacting standard to test the constitutionality of a state statute that burdens the free exercise of religion. Such a statute may stand only if the law in general, and the State's refusal to allow a religious exemption in particular, are justified by a compelling interest that cannot be served by less restrictive means. [The dissent applied the strict scrutiny standard.] . . .

I

[T]he State's interest in enforcing its prohibition, in order to be sufficiently compelling to outweigh a free exercise claim, cannot be merely abstract or symbolic. The State cannot plausibly assert that unbending application of a criminal prohibition is essential to fulfill any compelling interest, if it does not, in fact, attempt to enforce that prohibition. In this case, the State actually has not evinced any concrete interest in enforcing its drug laws against religious users of peyote. Oregon has never sought to prosecute respondents, and does not claim that it has made significant enforcement efforts against other religious users of peyote. . . .

The State proclaims an interest in protecting the health and safety of its citizens from the dangers of unlawful drugs. It offers, however, no evidence that the religious use of peyote has ever harmed anyone. . . .

[Moreover,] the Native American Church's internal restrictions on, and supervision of, its members' use of peyote substantially obviate the State's health and safety concerns. . . .

The State also seeks to support its refusal to make an exception for religious use of peyote by invoking its interest in abolishing drug trafficking. There is, however, practically no illegal traffic in peyote. . . .

Finally, the State argues that granting an exception for religious peyote use would erode its interest in the uniform, fair, and certain enforcement of its drug laws. The State fears that, if it grants an exemption for religious peyote use, a flood of other claims to religious exemptions will follow. It would then be placed in a dilemma, it says, between allowing a patchwork of exemptions that would hinder its law enforcement efforts, and risking a violation of the Establishment Clause by arbitrarily limiting its religious exemptions. This argument, however, could be made in almost any free exercise case.

[F]inally, although I agree [t]hat courts should refrain from delving into questions of whether, as a matter of religious doctrine, a particular practice is "central" to the religion, [I] do not think this means that the courts must turn a blind eye to the severe impact of a State's restrictions on the adherents of a minority religion. . . .

NOTES AND QUESTIONS

(1) *Is Smith Consistent With Precedent, Including Yoder and Sherbert?* The majority distinguishes *Yoder* on the ground that *Yoder* was a "hybrid" case and relied on the *Pierce* doctrine that parents have a right to direct the education of their children. It distinguishes *Sherbert* and other unemployment compensation cases on the ground that the context lends itself to individualized government treatment of the reasons for the relevant conduct, since the "misconduct" must be inquired into in any event—and in *Sherbert* and its progeny, the asserted "misconduct" did not include violations of state criminal laws. Although *Sherbert* was distinguished in *Smith* as not involving a state criminal statute, note that *Yoder* did involve a criminal statute. *Yoder* followed *Sherbert* and applied strict scrutiny. Are the distinctions in *Smith* consistent with the reasoning of the prior cases?

(2) *A Criminal Prohibition of Christian Communion?* Could a state that prohibited possession or consumption of alcoholic beverages, as some have done, refuse to exempt the use of wine in Christian communion? Consider whether the state should be required to advance a "compelling" interest, or merely a legitimate one, to support such a regulation. A version of this question was posed in Justice Blackmun's dissent in *Smith*, but Justice Scalia's majority opinion made no response. The *Smith* decision generated a large volume of academic commentary, almost all of which was highly critical of the majority's reasoning. *See, e.g.*, Douglas Laycock, *The Remnants of Free Exercise*, 1990 SUP. CT. REV. 1; Michael W. McConnell, *Free Exercise Revisionism and the Smith Decision*, 57 U. CHI. L. REV. 1109 (1990). For one of the defenses of the result in *Smith*, see William P. Marshall, *In Defense of Smith and Free Exercise Revisionism*, 58 U. CHI. L. REV. 308 (1991). *See also* McConnell, *A Response to Professor Marshall*, *id.* at 329. Professor Marci Hamilton has provided a defense of the result in SMITH IN GOD vs. THE GAVEL (2005).

(3) *The Congressional Response: The Religious Freedom Restoration Act.* Religious groups persuaded Congress to pass an unusual, broadly applicable law called the Religious Freedom Restoration Act to reverse the *Smith* decision. The Supreme Court later held the Act unconstitutional. We shall consider both the Act and its demise later.

(4) *Further Congressional Response to the Smith Decision.* Besides passing RFRA, the Congress responded to the *Smith* decision in two other ways. Remember that the *Smith* decision refused to create a constitutionally based exemption for the religious use

of peyote by the Native American religion. In 1994, Congress passed a statute creating an exemption from Schedule I of the Controlled Substances Act ("CSA") for peyote use by all members of every recognized Indian Tribe. *See* 42 U.S.C. § 1996 a (b)(1) (1994). What does that indicate, if anything, about the Congressional (*i.e.*, majoritarian) reaction to the *Smith* reasoning?

A second Congressional response, after RFRA was struck down by the Court in the *Flores* decision, was the passage of the Religious Land Use and Institutionalized Persons Act of 2000. The RLUIPA was a narrower and less burdensome version of RFRA. It was upheld, at least against an Establishment Clause challenge, in *Cutter v. Wilkinson*, 544 U.S.709 (2005). *See* § 12.02 above.

(5) *Potential Judicial Reinterpretation of Smith: Gonzales v. O Centro Espirita Beneficente Uniao Do Vegetal, 546 U.S. 418 (2006).* In the *O Centro* case, a religious sect (UDV) with origins in the Amazon Rainforest received communion by drinking a sacramental tea, brewed from Amazon-region plants, that contained a hallucinogen (DMT) banned by Schedule I of the CSA. When the Customs Service intercepted the shipments of the tea and the federal government threatened criminal action, UDC sued under RFRA. The Court emphasized that the American chapter of UDV had only 130 members. In light of the Congressional exemption for "hundreds of thousands of Native Americans practicing their faith," *see* Note (4) above, the Court concluded that RFRA's imposition of the strict scrutiny standard justified an "exception for the 130 or so American members of the UDV who want to practice theirs." The Court, in an opinion by Chief Justice Roberts, upheld the application of RFRA against a federal law. In *O Centro*, the unanimous Court stated *Smith* "held that the Constitution does not require judges to engage in a case-by-case assessment of the religious burdens imposed by facially constitutional laws." This rereading of *Smith* seems to focus only on the means test of the strict scrutiny standard and ignores the compelling interest prong of the test. *See Smith supra.*

Was the Court retreating from a broad reading of *Smith* or merely reacting to an arguably overzealous enforcement policy of the Attorney General? How should the "small size" of the religious group factor into the Free Exercise doctrine?

CHURCH OF THE LUKUMI BABALU AYE, INC. v. CITY OF HIALEAH, 508 U.S. 520 (1993). The congregants of the Church of Lukumi Babaluaye practice the Santerian religion. One of its principal forms of devotion is animal sacrifice using "chickens, pigeons . . . [and] turtles." To avoid persecution, Santerians practiced the rituals in secret until a new policy of "openness" was announced. Then, the city council of Hialeah held public hearings and, for the stated purposes of protecting public health and preventing animal cruelty, passed several ordinances. While the ordinances contained various exemptions, including an exemption for the "Kosher" slaughter of animals, they effectively banned the Santerian religious ritual. Although the lower courts ruled in favor of the City, the Supreme Court, per Justice Kennedy, unanimously reversed:

> [O]ur cases establish the general proposition that a law that is neutral and of general applicability need not be justified by a compelling governmental interest even if the law has the incidental effect of burdening a particular religious practice. [*Smith.*] [N]eutrality and general applicability are interrelated. [A] law failing to satisfy these requirements must be justified by a compelling governmental interest and must be narrowly tailored to advance that interest.

> [I]t becomes evident that these ordinances target Santeria sacrifice when the ordinances' operation is considered. Apart from the text, the effect of a law in its real operation is strong evidence of its object.

> [T]he design of these laws accomplishes [a] "religious gerrymander," an impermissible attempt to target petitioners and their religious practices.

[W]e also find significant evidence of the ordinances' improper targeting of Santeria sacrifice in the fact that they proscribe more religious conduct than is necessary to achieve their stated ends.

[A]s in equal protection cases, we may determine the city council's object from both direct and circumstantial evidence [citing *Arlington Heights v. Metropolitan Housing Development Corp.*, 429 U.S. 252, 266 (1977).] Relevant evidence includes, among other things, the historical background of the decision under challenge, the specific series of events leading to the enactment or official policy in question, as well as the legislative or administrative history, including contemporaneous statements made by members of the decisionmaking body. . . .

[Hialeah] claims that the ordinances advance two interests: protecting the public health and preventing cruelty to animals. The ordinances are underinclusive for those ends. . . . Despite the city's proffered interest in preventing cruelty to animals, the ordinances are drafted with care to forbid few killings but those occasioned by religious sacrifice. Many types of animal deaths or kills for nonreligious reasons are either not prohibited or approved by express provision. . . .

[Having thus determined that Hialeah's ordinances failed the "neutrality" and "general applicability" requirements of *Smith*, the Court applied strict scrutiny.] [T]o satisfy the commands of the First Amendment, a law restrictive of religious practice must advance "interests of the highest order" and must be narrowly tailored in pursuit of those interests. . . . It follows from what we have already said that these ordinances cannot withstand this scrutiny. First, even were the governmental interests compelling, the ordinances are not drawn in narrow terms to accomplish those interests. [Reversed.]

Justice Scalia (joined by Chief Justice Rehnquist) concurred in part and in the judgment. Regarding the appropriate evidence of government intent, Justice Scalia disagreed with the majority's consideration of the "subjective motivation of the lawmakers." Justice Souter concurred in part and in the judgment, expressing his "doubts whether the *Smith* rule merits adherence." Justice Blackmun (joined by Justice O'Connor) concurred only in the judgment. Justice Blackmun viewed the case as "an easy one to decide . . .," and he called for the use of strict scrutiny "beyond those rare occasions on which the government explicitly targets religion (or a particular religion) for disfavored treatment, as is done in [Hialeah]."

NOTES AND QUESTIONS

(1) *"Neutrality" and "General Applicability."* The *Hialeah* majority concluded that the case fit within the "general proposition" established in *Smith*. Remember that the *Hialeah* decision thwarts the will of the political majority who had legitimate interests in community health, aesthetics and preventing cruelty to animals. Consider the following report published shortly after the Court's decision, entitled *Animal Sacrifices Celebrate Court Victory*, HOUSTON CHRONICLE, June 27, 1993, § A, at 4, col. 3 (from Aminda Marques Gonzales, Miami Herald News Service):

The first offering, a goat, bleated twice as it was hoisted out of a crate. [A Santerian initiate] held the animal above basins that catch the sacrificial blood.

With a 7-inch knife in his right hand, [the Santerian priest] pierced the goat's jugular. The knife was apparently dull; he traded it for a larger one.

The blood was poured over the rocks and shells. Finally, [the priest] twisted off the goat's head and placed the offering in a bowl. . . .

After two hours, 15 animals had been sacrificed to four deities. All had their throats slit. The guinea hens were stunned first, slammed against the terrago floor. . . .

Is this really a case of improper targeting of religious practices *because* they are religious, or is it instead a case of distinguishing a particularly cruel kind of killing, in a neutral way, from less cruel killings? Doesn't the City of Hialeah have a sufficient interest to prevent these cruel acts, even if it still permits humane killing of stray animals, extermination of mice and rats, medical experiments, and preparation of Kosher food?

(2) *An "Easy Case"?* Was *Hialeah* such an "easy case"? Even if Justice Blackmun's assessment would be accurate, consider whether the Santerian free exercise argument would prevail against a uniform governmental ban on all cruelty to animals. Justice Blackmun suggests that even then, strict scrutiny should apply. This result is inconsistent with the result in *Smith*. Is *Smith*, then, incorrectly decided?

(3) *The Congressional Reaction to the Smith Decision: The Religious Freedom Restoration Act of 1993 (RFRA).* In 1993, Congress passed the "Religious Freedom Restoration Act," 42 U.S.C. § 2000bb, intended to overrule the central holding in *Smith*. Selected provisions are provided below to assist you in examining the Problems below. As a general matter, did Congress appropriately understand the *Smith* decision? The *Hialeah* decision? *See also* Eugene Gressman & Angela Carmella, *The RFRA Revision of the Free Exercise Clause*, 57 OHIO ST. L.J. 65 (1996). [The Supreme Court, in *City of Boerne, Texas v. Flores*, 521 U.S. 507 (1997), held that RFRA was unconstitutional. *See* § 14.02, below.]

(4) *A Narrow Reading of Hialeah: Locke v. Davey, 540 U.S. 712 (2004).* It was over a decade before the Court again addressed a Free Exercise case. In *Locke*, the state of Washington had a scholarship program for a set of high-achieving high school graduates. The scholarship program could be used at any eligible institution; the eligible institutions included private and parochial colleges. There was one exception to the scholarship program: because of the Washington state constitution and certain Washington statutes, the scholarship could not be used to subsidize a degree in theology or training for ministerial professions. The challenger, who desired to pursue a major in theology, sued the state of Washington under, *inter alia*, a Free Exercise theory. The challenger claimed that the Washington scholarship program singled out religion and, under *Hialeah*, could not survive strict scrutiny. Although the court of appeals had agreed, the United States Supreme Court, in an opinion by Chief Justice Rehnquist, disagreed.

There are several dimensions to the Chief Justice's opinion. There is, for example, a concern about federalism in the majority's opinion. For present purposes, it is notable that the Chief Justice read *Hialeah* narrowly: "In *Lukumi*, the City of Hialeah made it a crime to engage in certain kinds of animal slaughter. We found that the law sought to suppress ritualistic animal sacrifices of the Santeria Religion." Having read *Hialeah* narrowly (as a regulation that *sought to suppress*), the Chief Justice was able to distinguish the *Locke* case from *Hialeah* and reach a different result because the Washington constitutional provision did not target religious belief and left open many alternatives for a scholarship recipient to study religious topics and courses. The *Locke* decision confirmed that *Smith* and *Hialeah* imposed a purposefulness requirement on a Free Exercise claim. Justice Scalia dissented (for Justice Thomas), disagreeing with the *Locke* opinion's narrow reading of *Hialeah*. For further examination of the status of Free Exercise doctrine, including a comparative analysis, consider Edward J. Eberle, *Free Exercise of Religion in Germany and the United States*, 78 TULANE L. REV. 1023 (2004).

THE RELIGIOUS FREEDOM RESTORATION ACT
42 U.S.C. § 2000bb (1993)

SECTION 2. CONGRESSIONAL FINDINGS AND DECLARATION OF PURPOSES

(a) FINDINGS.—The Congress finds that—. . .

(2) laws "neutral" toward religion may burden RELIGIOUS exercise as surely as laws intended to interfere with RELIGIOUS exercise; . . .

(4) in *Employment Division v. Smith*, 494 U.S. 872 (1990), the Supreme Court virtually eliminated the requirement that the government justify burdens on RELIGIOUS exercise imposed by laws neutral toward religion; and

(5) the compelling interest test as set forth in prior Federal court rulings is a workable test for striking sensible balances between RELIGIOUS liberty and competing prior governmental interests.

(b) PURPOSES.—The purposes of this Act are—

(1) to RESTORE the compelling interest test as set forth in *Sherbert v. Werner*, 374 U.S. 398 (1963) and *Wisconsin v. Yoder*, 406 U.S. 205 (1972) and to guarantee its application in all cases where free exercise of religion is substantially burdened; and

(2) to provide a claim or defense to persons whose religious exercise is substantially burdened by government.

SEC. 3. FREE EXERCISE OF RELIGION PROTECTED.

(a) IN GENERAL.—Government shall not substantially burden a person's exercise of religion even if the burden results from a rule of general applicability, except as provided in subsection (b).

(b) EXCEPTION.—Government may substantially burden a person's exercise of religion only if it demonstrates that application of the burden to the person—

(1) is in furtherance of a compelling governmental interest; and

(2) is the least restrictive means of furthering that compelling governmental interest.

(c) JUDICIAL RELIEF.—A person whose religious exercise has been burdened in violation of this section may assert that violation as a claim or defense in a judicial proceeding and obtain appropriate relief against a government. Standing to assert a claim or defense under this section shall be governed by the general rules of standing under article III of the Constitution. . . .

SEC. 6. APPLICABILITY.

(a) IN GENERAL.—This Act applies to all Federal and State law, and the implementation of that law, whether statutory or otherwise, and whether adopted before or after the enactment of this Act.

PROBLEM E

HOW DOES A COURT DECIDE WHETHER A LAW IMPACTING RELIGION IS DISCRIMINATORY? THE EXAMPLE OF CIRCUMCISION: SORAYA MIRE, "CHILDHOOD MUTILATION HAUNTS SOMALI NATIVE," HOUSTON CHRONICLE, Aug. 18, 1993, at 3D, col.5. In this editorial, Soraya Mire, who now is a filmmaker in Pasadena, California, describes female circumcision, which she underwent as a child in Somalia. There, the practice is usually performed on girls aged 5 to 10 and includes removing the clitoris, labia minora and majora without anesthetic and sewing the remaining tissues to leave only a small opening for urine and menstrual blood. Mire calls for a global movement against female genital mutilation, which she reports has been banned in England, France, Sweden, Switzerland, and the Netherlands. Questions: (1) If the United States similarly prohibited female circumcision, would the approach of the *Hialeah* case categorize the ban as discriminatory? (Presumably, such a law would not prohibit the widespread practice of male circumcision by some established religions in America, and you should remember that a similar exception of Kosher animal killings was a reason for labeling Hialeah's law "discriminatory.") (2) If a female genital mutilation law unaccompanied by a prohibition of religious male circumcision were characterized as "discriminatory" on this ground, could it be upheld under the strict scrutiny mandated by the *Hialeah* decision (which upholds cruel killings of animals)? (3) Does the assertion in the *Hialeah* concurrence that the case was an easy one mask inadequate treatment of a more difficult question, namely, how to determine whether an ostensibly general law with some exceptions is "discriminatory"?

NOTE ON THE INVALIDATION OF RFRA

The Supreme Court Invalidates RFRA in Flores v. City of Boerne. Ultimately, the Supreme Court struck down the Religious Freedom Restoration Act on the grounds that it exceeded the power of Congress, violated the separation of powers, and infringed the judicial role. RFRA had been passed under the purported authority of section 5 of the Fourteenth Amendment, which gives Congress power to enforce the amendment. We therefore defer consideration of the case to Chapter 14, below.

Chapter 13
STATE ACTION vs. PRIVATE ACTION

INTRODUCTORY NOTE

See § 8.01, in Chapter 8, for an Introduction to State Action. The beginning of Chapter 8 contains a short description of three different theories of state action. You should read that text at this time.

Weighing All the Facts. As the cases in this chapter will show, the doctrine of state action does not boil down to one standard. Instead, the issue often turns on the individual facts of the case. "Only by sifting facts and weighing circumstances can the non-obvious involvement of the state in private conduct be attributed its true significance." *Burton v. Wilmington Parking Authority*, 365 U.S. 715, 722 (1961).

The Court has reaffirmed the fact-intensive nature of the "state action" issue. In *Brentwood Academy v. Tennessee Secondary School Athletic Association*, 531 U.S. 288 (2001), the Court observed that: "From the range of circumstances that could point toward the State behind an individual face, no one fact can function as a necessary condition across the board for finding state action; nor is there any set of circumstances absolutely sufficient for there may be some counter-vailing reason against attributing activity to the government." As you will see, there are several—sometimes overlapping—standards for "state action."

§ 13.01 THE "GOVERNMENT FUNCTION" DOCTRINE

INTRODUCTORY NOTE

A private person engaged in a governmental function may be treated as a state actor. A broad test for a government function would encompass private acts which have any parallel function conducted by the state. A more restrictive view would limit the application of the doctrine to functions "traditionally" and "exclusively" performed by the state. When reading the cases, consider how far the doctrine should extend.

Note that, today, a claim against a restaurant for discriminatory conduct would be brought under the 1964 Civil Rights Act and, probably, under a parallel state statute. As such, there would be no need for a claim directly under the Fourteenth Amendment and no need to establish that the restaurant was a "state action." In the modern era, the incidence of state action issues has diminished.

[A] Expansion

NOTE ON THE "WHITE PRIMARY" CASES

State-Sponsored Primaries for Whites Only: Smith v. Allwright, 321 U.S. 649 (1944). The White Primary cases involved the exclusion of African-Americans from the electoral process within the Democratic Party. In *Smith v. Allwright*, the Court held that the exclusion of African-Americans from the regular Democratic primary violated the Fifteenth Amendment. The Court found that "state delegation to a party of the power to fix the qualifications of primary elections is delegation of a state function that may make the party's action the action of the state."

What about Discriminatory Primaries Conducted by "Private" Groups? Terry v. Adams, 345 U.S. 461 (1953). The Court in *Smith* dealt with a primary election conducted under power delegated by the state. *Terry v. Adams*, in contrast, involved a "private and voluntary" political organization called the Jaybird Association, which excluded blacks from the organization's "pre-primary" elections. The Jaybird organization was a clear effort to accomplish the same discriminatory result as in *Smith v. Allwright*, but (its sponsors hoped) without triggering the Fifteenth Amendment. Although there was not a majority opinion, eight justices agreed that state action was involved. Justice Black's plurality opinion concluded:

[T]he Jaybird Party thus brings into being and holds precisely the kind of election that the Fifteenth Amendment seeks to prevent. When it produces the equivalent of the prohibited election, the damage has been done.

For a state to permit such a duplication of its election processes is to permit a flagrant abuse of those processes to defeat the purposes of the Fifteenth Amendment. The use of the county-operated primary to ratify the result of the prohibited election merely compounds the offense. . . .

MARSH v. ALABAMA
326 U.S. 501 (1946)

MR. JUSTICE BLACK delivered the opinion of the Court.

In this case we are asked to decide whether a State, consistently with the First and Fourteenth Amendments, can impose criminal punishment on a person who undertakes to distribute religious literature on the premises of a company-owned town contrary to the wishes of the town's management. The town, a suburb of Mobile, Alabama, known as Chickasaw, is owned by the Gulf Shipbuilding Corporation. Except for that it has all the characteristics of any other American town. The property consists of residential buildings, streets, a system of sewers, a sewage disposal plant and a "business block" on which business places are situated. A deputy of the Mobile County Sheriff, paid by the company, serves as the town's policeman. [A]ccording to all indications the residents use the business block as their regular shopping center. [I]ntersecting company-owned roads at each end of the business block lead into a four-lane public highway which runs parallel to the business block at a distance of thirty feet. [I]n short the town and its shopping district are accessible to and freely used by the public in general and there is nothing to distinguish them from any other town and shopping center except the fact that the title to the property belongs to a private corporation.

Appellant, a Jehovah's Witness, came onto the sidewalk we have just described, stood near the post-office and undertook to distribute religious literature. In the stores the corporation had posted a notice which read as follows: "This Is Private Property, and Without Written Permission, No Street, or House Vendor, Agent or Solicitation of Any Kind Will Be Permitted." Appellant was warned that she could not distribute the literature without a permit and told that no permit would be issued to her. The deputy sheriff arrested her and she was charged in the state court with violating Title 14, Section 426 of the 1940 Alabama Code which makes it a crime to enter or remain on the premises of another after having been warned not to do so. Appellant contended that to construe the state statute as applicable to her activities would abridge her right to freedom of press and religion contrary to the First and Fourteenth Amendments to the Constitution. This contention was rejected and she was convicted. . . .

. . . Our question then narrows down to this: Can those people who live in or come to Chickasaw be denied freedom of press and religion simply because a single company has legal title to all the town? . . .

[T]he State urges in effect that the corporation's right to control the inhabitants of Chickasaw is coextensive with the right of a homeowner to regulate the conduct of his guests. We can not accept that contention. [T]he more an owner, for his advantage, opens up his property for use by the public in general, the more do his rights become circumscribed by the statutory and constitutional rights of those who use it. . . .

[H]ad the corporation here owned the segment of the four-lane highway which runs parallel to the "business block" and operated the same under a State franchise, doubtless no one would have seriously contended that the corporation's property interest in the highway gave it power to obstruct through traffic or to discriminate against interstate commerce. . . .

We do not think it makes any significant constitutional difference as to the relationship between the rights of the owner and those of the public that here the State, instead of permitting the corporation to operate a highway, permitted it to use its property as a town. . . .

Many people in the United States live in company-owned towns. [T]here is no more reason for depriving these people of the liberties guaranteed by the First and Fourteenth Amendments than there is for curtailing these freedoms with respect to any other citizen. . . .

NOTES AND QUESTIONS

(1) *Function or Power?* What were the particular governmental functions that caused the Court to find state action in *Marsh*? Was the Court really more concerned with the degree of power that the company possessed over the town's affairs?

(2) *The Existence of Reasonable Alternatives.* Justice Reed, in dissent, noted that the appellants could have used the public highway located nearby, instead of the privately owned business area of the company town, in order to convey their message. Should the presence of an alternative forum make a difference? Compare the result with *Hudgens v. NLRB, infra.*

(3) *State Action as Part of the Substantive Constitutional Calculus.* In *Marsh*, the Court balanced the property rights of the company town owners against the freedom of religion and the press. Should state action serve as a balancing factor in weighing these interests? Consider Glennon & Nowak, *A Functional Analysis of the Fourteenth Amendment "State Action" Requirement*, 1976 Sup. Ct. Rev. 221, 231–32:[*]

> Confronted with a conflict between individual rights, the Court must determine whether the Fourteenth Amendment dictates a preference for one over the other. The Court must balance the relative merits of permitting the challenged practice to continue against the limitation which is imposed on the asserted right. If the value of the right clearly outweighs the value of the challenged practice, the Amendment proscribes the practice. If the importance of the right is not clearly greater than that of the challenged practice, the effect of the practice of the right does not violate the Amendment. The impact of the practice on the asserted right is in accordance with the Amendment not because state action is missing, but because it is permissible for the state to prefer the challenged practice rather than the asserted right.

PROBLEM A

STATE UNIVERSITY "INVOLVEMENT" IN AWARDING GENDER-RESTRICTED SCHOLARSHIPS— SHAPIRO v. COLUMBIA UNION NATIONAL BANK & TRUST CO., 576 S.W.2d 310 (Mo. 1978). Victor Wilson's will created a trust to help "deserving boys" attend either "Yale University or the University of Kansas City, Missouri." The "deserving boys" were to be selected by judges "appointed by the Yale Alumni of Kansas City, Missouri, and the University of Kansas City, Missouri," after which they would be "approved by the [private] Trustee" appointed under Wilson's will. The University of Kansas City later became a state university (the University of Missouri at Kansas City). A female law student, Marilyn Shapiro, sued on the claim that her exclusion from the fund, since it was restricted to deserving "boys," violated the Fourteenth Amendment. Question: Does the university's involvement, in

---

[*] Copyright © 1976 by the University of Chicago Press. Reprinted by permission.

the form of appointment of judges, amount to sufficient state action to trigger the Fourteenth Amendment? Does the same result apply to a private university, such as Yale, on a government function theory?

[The Missouri Supreme Court held that the state university's involvement did *not* convert the selection into state action, since the university only appointed judges who made a "tentative award" and forwarded names to a trustee, who made the final selection. A situation "where the *trustee* is a state body" would be different, said the court, as would one in which "the 'selection committee' is composed of public officials." Three judges dissented.]

[B] Contraction

NOTE ON THE SHOPPING CENTER CASES

Expansion of the Government Function Doctrine Followed by Contraction: The Shopping Center Cases. The decisions of the Burger Court contracted the reach of the government function doctrine—a development illustrated by the "shopping center" cases. In *Amalgamated Food Employees Union v. Logan Valley Plaza,* 391 U.S. 308 (1968), the Warren Court extended the government function doctrine to cover a shopping center. Members of a union had picketed a supermarket in the shopping center. The center obtained an injunction preventing picketing inside the center. The Court, per Marshall, J., found the shopping center sidewalks to be like the "business block" in *Marsh*: "[T]he shopping center premises are open to the public to the same extent as the commercial center of a normal town."

In *Lloyd Corp. v. Tanner,* 407 U.S. 51 (1972), however, the Court limited the application of *Logan Valley.* The Court, per Powell, J., held that a shopping center's refusal to permit the distribution of antiwar handbills on its premises was not state action. Justice Marshall, the author of *Logan Valley,* joined by Justices Brennan, Douglas, and Stewart, dissented.

The apparent conflict between *Logan Valley* and *Lloyd* was resolved in *Hudgens v. NLRB,* 424 U.S. 507 (1976). The Court, in the following opinion by Justice Stewart, held that *Logan Valley* was overruled by *Lloyd.*

HUDGENS v. NLRB
424 U.S. 507 (1976)

MR. JUSTICE STEWART delivered the opinion of the Court.

The petitioner, Scott Hudgens, is the owner of the North DeKalb Shopping Center, located in suburban Atlanta, Ga. [O]ne of the lessees is the Butler Shoe Co. Most of the stores, including Butler's, can be entered only from the interior mall.

In January 1971, warehouse employees of the Butler Shoe Co. went on strike to protest the company's failure to agree to demands made by their union in contract negotiations. [T]he general manager of the shopping center informed the employees that they could not picket within the mall or on the parking lot and threatened them with arrest if they did not leave. . . . [The lower court held this exclusion unconstitutional; the Supreme Court here reverses.]

The Court in its *Lloyd* opinion did not say that it was overruling the *Logan Valley* decision. Indeed a substantial portion of the Court's opinion in *Lloyd* was devoted to pointing out the differences between the two cases, noting particularly that, in contrast to the hand-billing in *Lloyd,* the picketing in *Logan Valley* had been specifically directed to a store in the shopping center and the pickets had had no other reasonable opportunity to reach their intended audience. But the fact is that the reasoning of the Court's opinion in *Lloyd* cannot be squared with the reasoning of the Court's opinion in *Logan Valley.*

[N]ot only did the *Lloyd* opinion incorporate lengthy excerpts from two of the dissenting opinions in *Logan Valley*, the ultimate holding in *Lloyd* amounted to a total rejection of the holding in *Logan Valley*:

[R]espondents contend . . . that the property of a large shopping center is "open to the public," serves the same purposes as a "business district" of a municipality, and therefore has been dedicated to certain types of public use. . . .

The argument reaches too far. [T]he closest decision in theory, *Marsh v. Alabama*, involved the assumption by a private enterprise of all of the attributes of a state-created municipality and the exercise by that enterprise of semi-official municipal functions as a delegate of the State. [I]n the instant case there is no comparable assumption or exercise of municipal functions or power. . . .

It [follows,] therefore, that if the respondents in the *Lloyd* case did not have a First Amendment right to enter that shopping center to distribute handbills concerning Vietnam, then the pickets in the present case did not have a First Amendment right to enter this shopping center for the purpose of advertising their strike against the Butler Shoe Co. . . .

MR. JUSTICE MARSHALL, with whom MR. JUSTICE BRENNAN joins, dissenting. . . .

[T]he roadways, parking lots, and walkways of the modern shopping center may be as essential for effective speech as the streets and sidewalks in the municipal or company-owned town. I simply cannot reconcile the Court's denial of any role for the First Amendment in the shopping center with *Marsh's* recognition of a full role for the First Amendment [in] the company-owned town. . . .

JACKSON v. METROPOLITAN EDISON CO.
419 U.S. 345 (1974)

MR. JUSTICE REHNQUIST delivered the opinion of the Court. . . .

[The Metropolitan Edison Co., a privately owned utility operating under a certificate of public convenience issued by the Pennsylvania Public Utility Commission, cut off the petitioner's power because of her non-payment of electric bills. The petitioner filed suit under 42 U.S.C. § 1983 seeking damages for the termination and an injunction requiring the utility to continue providing power to her home until she had been afforded notice, a hearing and an opportunity to pay any amounts found due. The district court granted the utility's motion to dismiss and the Third Circuit affirmed, finding that the termination did not constitute state action. Here, the Supreme Court affirms.]

[T]he action complained of was taken by a utility company which is privately owned and operated, but which in many particulars of its business is subject to extensive state regulation. [I]t may well be that acts of a heavily regulated utility with at least something of a governmentally protected monopoly will more readily be found to be "state" acts than will the acts of an entity lacking these characteristics. But the inquiry must be whether there is a sufficiently close nexus between the State and the challenged action of the regulated entity so that the action of the latter may be fairly treated as that of the State itself. . . .

Petitioner first argues that "state action" is present because of the monopoly status allegedly conferred upon Metropolitan by the State of Pennsylvania. As a factual matter, it may well be doubted that the State ever granted or guaranteed Metropolitan a monopoly. But assuming that it had this fact is not determinative in considering whether Metropolitan's termination of service to petitioner was "state action" for purposes of the Fourteenth Amendment. . . .

Petitioner next urges that state action is present because respondent provides an essential public service required to be supplied on a reasonably continuous basis by Pa.Stat.Ann., Tit. 66, § 1171 (1959), and hence performs a "public function." We have, of course, found state action present in the exercise by a private entity of powers traditionally exclusively reserved to the State.

If we were dealing with the exercise by Metropolitan of some power delegated to it by the State which is traditionally associated with sovereignty, such as eminent domain, our case would be quite a different one. But while the Pennsylvania statute imposes an obligation to furnish service on regulated utilities, it imposes no such obligation on the State. . . .

The nature of governmental regulation of private utilities is such that a utility may frequently be required by the state regulatory scheme to obtain approval for practices a business regulated in less detail would be free to institute without any approval from a regulatory body. [A]t most, the Commission's failure to overturn this practice amounted to no more than a determination that a Pennsylvania utility was authorized to employ such a practice if it so desired. Respondent's exercise of the choice allowed by state law where the initiative comes from it and not from the State, does not make its action in doing so "state action" for purposes of the Fourteenth Amendment.

MR. JUSTICE DOUGLAS, dissenting. . . .

It is not enough to examine seriatim each of the factors upon which a claimant relies and to dismiss each individually as being insufficient to support a finding of state action. It is the aggregate that is controlling. . . .

In the aggregate, these factors depict a monopolist providing essential public services as a licensee of the State and within a framework of extensive state supervision and control. [I]n that perspective, what the Court does today is to make a significant departure from our previous treatment of state-action issues.

JUSTICE MARSHALL, dissenting. . . .

The Metropolitan Edison Co. provides an essential public service to the people of York, Pa. It is the only entity public or private, that is authorized to supply electric service to most of the community. As a part of its charter to the company, the State imposes extensive regulations, and it cooperates with the company in myriad ways. Additionally, the State has granted its approval to the company's mode of service termination—the very conduct that is challenged here. Taking these factors together, I have no difficulty finding state action in this case. . . .

NOTES AND QUESTIONS

(1) *Monopoly Power.* Should it matter that the state conferred a monopoly on the electric company? Metropolitan was "the only public utility furnishing electricity to the city." Why shouldn't the decision of the government to permit the monopoly the right to deny service at its discretion suffice to show state action?

(2) *Institutional Power.* In his dissent in the *Civil Rights Cases*, 109 U.S. 3 (1883), Justice Harlan noted that actions of corporations should be considered state action. Does this notion have currency today, given the nature of some modern day corporations? One commentator has argued: "[A]s rights that were once vulnerable only to the power of government become subject to private determination, the courts should be generous in their protection of civil liberties." Note, *State Action: Theories for Applying Constitutional Restrictions to Private Activity*, 74 COLUM. L. REV. 656, 698 (1974). Is this view persuasive?

(3) *The Viability of the "Traditionally Exclusive Government Function" Test; Private Schools.* The Court has continued to use the standard whether an activity is "traditionally exclusively reserved to the State" in making state action determinations. For example, in *Rendell-Baker v. Kohn*, 457 U.S. 830 (1982), the Court, per Burger, C.J.,

held that a private school for troubled high school students was not a state actor subject to constitutional restraints. The Court found that operating such a school was a public function, but it was not one that was "traditionally" the "exclusive" prerogative of the state.

Nevertheless, serious questions remain whether a government function test of activities "traditionally exclusively reserved to the State" is workable. In *Garcia v. San Antonio Metropolitan Transit Authority*, 469 U.S. 528 (1985) [reproduced in Chapter 3, *above*], the Court found the traditional government function test to be unworkable as the standard for limiting the reach of federal legislation directly against the states. Moreover, does the standard really have any content? If the function were exclusively the state's, why would a private entity be performing it?

(4) *Are There Different State Action Standards for Different Constitutional Rights?* Would the result in *Jackson* have been the same if the claim were that the utility discriminated against racial minorities rather than that the utility terminated service without following adequate procedures? In his dissent in *Jackson*, Justice Marshall concluded that it would:

> The Court has not adopted the notion, accepted elsewhere, that different standards should apply to state action analysis when different constitutional claims are presented. [T]hus, the majority's analysis would seemingly apply as well to a [utility] company that refused to extend service to Negroes, welfare recipients, or any other group that the company preferred, for its own reasons, not to serve.

PROBLEM B

A CITY-OWNED UTILITY; A RACIALLY DISCRIMINATORY PRIVATE UTILITY. Suppose that a city owns and operates a utility. Would this be an easier case for finding state action? [Should it be? The utility is providing the same service that a private monopoly would provide. Should a finding of state action turn on mere government ownership?]

Furthermore, consider Justice Marshall's suggestion of the possibility of a private utility monopoly that deliberately refuses to serve racial minorities. If truly insulated from state action findings, the corporation may claim it is not violating the Fourteenth Amendment. Is this the result under the Supreme Court's jurisprudence?

§ 13.02   STATE INVOLVEMENT OR MUTUAL BENEFITS

NOTE ON STATE LICENSING, LEASING, OR REGULATION

When the government is entangled with private activity, the Court often has found state action. The Court's focus is the nature and extent of contacts between the state and the private actor. Clearly, state support of a private activity may show state action. But what about less concrete forms of involvement or assistance, such as granting a license to a private actor that discriminates?

BURTON v. WILMINGTON PARKING AUTHORITY
365 U.S. 715 (1961)

MR. JUSTICE CLARK delivered the opinion of the Court.

In this action for declaratory and injunctive relief it is admitted that the Eagle Coffee Shoppe, Inc., a restaurant located within an off-street automobile parking building in Wilmington, Delaware, has refused to serve appellant food or drink solely because he is a Negro. The parking building is owned and operated by the Wilmington Parking Authority, an agency of the State of Delaware, and the restaurant is the

Authority's lessee. [T]he Supreme Court of Delaware has held that Eagle was acting in "a purely private capacity" under its lease; that its action was not that of the Authority and was not, therefore, state action within the contemplation of the prohibitions contained in [the Fourteenth] Amendment. . . .

The Authority was created by the City of Wilmington pursuant to 22 Del. Code, §§ 501–515. [I]ts statutory purpose is to provide adequate parking facilities for the convenience of the public and thereby relieve the "parking crisis, which threatens the welfare of the community. . . ."

Before it began actual construction of the facility, the Authority was advised by its retained experts that the anticipated revenue from the parking of cars and proceeds from sale of its bonds would not be sufficient to finance the construction costs of the facility. [T]o secure additional capital needed for its "debt-service" requirements, and thereby to make bond financing practicable, the Authority decided it was necessary to enter long-term leases with responsible tenants for commercial use of some of the space available in the projected "garage building". . . .

In April 1957 such a private lease [was] made with Eagle Coffee Shoppe, Inc. . . .

[T]he Delaware Supreme Court seems to have placed controlling emphasis on its conclusion, as to the accuracy of which there is doubt, that only some 15% of the total cost of the facility was "advanced" from public funds; that the cost of the entire facility was allocated three-fifths to the space for commercial leasing and two-fifths to parking space; that anticipated revenue from parking was only some 30.5% of the total income, the balance of which was expected to be earned by the leasing; that the Authority had no original intent to place a restaurant in the building, it being only a happenstance resulting from the bidding; that Eagle expended considerable moneys on furnishings; that the restaurant's main and marked public entrance is on Ninth Street without any public entrance direct from the parking area; and that "the only connection Eagle has with the public facility . . . is the furnishing of the sum of $28,700 annually in the form of rent which is used by the Authority to defray a portion of the operating expense of an otherwise unprofitable enterprise." While these factual considerations are indeed validly accountable aspects of the enterprise upon which the State has embarked, we cannot say that they lead inescapably to the conclusion that state action is not present. Their persuasiveness is diminished when evaluated in the context of other factors which must be acknowledged.

The land and building were publicly owned. As an entity, the building was dedicated to "public uses" in performance of the Authority's "essential governmental functions." 22 Del. Code, §§ 501, 514. The costs of land acquisition, construction, and maintenance are defrayed entirely from donations by the City of Wilmington, from loans and revenue bonds and from the proceeds of rentals and parking services out of which the loans and bonds were payable.

[U]pkeep and maintenance of the building, including necessary repairs, were responsibilities of the Authority and were payable out of public funds. It cannot be doubted that the peculiar relationship of the restaurant to the parking facility in which it is located confers on each an incidental variety of mutual benefits. Guests of the restaurant are afforded a convenient place to park their automobiles even if they cannot enter the restaurant directly from the parking area. Similarly, its convenience for diners may well provide additional demand for the Authority's parking facilities. Should any improvements effected in the leasehold by Eagle become part of the realty, there is no possibility of increased taxes being passed on to it since the fee is held by a tax-exempt government agency. [P]rofits earned by discrimination not only contribute to, but also are indispensable elements in, the financial success of a governmental agency.

Addition of all these activities, obligations and responsibilities of the Authority, the benefits mutually conferred, together with the obvious fact that the restaurant is operated as an integral part of a public building devoted to a public parking service, indicates that degree of state participation and involvement in discriminatory action which it was the design of the Fourteenth Amendment to condemn. [T]he State has so far insinuated itself into a position of interdependence with Eagle that it must be recognized as a joint participant in the challenged activity, which, on that account, cannot be considered to have been so "purely private" as to fall without the scope of the Fourteenth Amendment.

Because readily applicable formulae may not be fashioned, the conclusions drawn from the facts and circumstances of this record are by no means declared as universal truths on the basis of which every state leasing agreement is to be tested. Owing to the very "largeness" of government, a multitude of relationships might appear to some to fall within the Amendment's embrace, but that, it must be remembered, can be determined only in the framework of the peculiar facts or circumstances present.

NOTES AND QUESTIONS

(1) *What Is the Basis of Decision: Is Mere Neutral Involvement of the State Enough, or Is Some Degree of Symbiosis (Mutual Benefits) Required?* What factor, if any, was essential in *Burton* for the Court's finding of state action? Was it significant that the land and building were publicly owned? Was it significant that the restaurant conferred "mutual benefits?" Was it significant that Eagle Coffee Shop was a financially integral part of the state's plan to undertake the project?

(2) *State Subsidization of Private Activity.* Does *Burton* mean that state subsidization of discriminatory conduct is unconstitutional? If so, what constitutes subsidization? A government grant? Tax exempt status? Providing ordinary municipal services to a private entity?

In *Norwood v. Harrison,* 413 U.S. 455 (1973), the Court enjoined Mississippi's lending of textbooks to racially segregated private schools. The Court noted that a state does not violate its constitutional duty merely by providing *any* state services that benefit a discriminatory private school. Instead, the Court found:

> Textbooks are a basic educational tool and . . . are provided only in connection with schools. They are distinguished from general services, like electricity and water, which the government provides to schools and others.

Is this a valid distinction?

(3) *Is Regulation or Other Adversary Action by the State Different from Symbiosis or Subsidy?* Neutral regulation may seem different. If the state neutrally sets health or safety requirements by regulation, perhaps it is not involved in private discrimination. But what if it grants a license or permit to a person who invidiously discriminates?

MOOSE LODGE NO. 107 v. IRVIS
407 U.S. 163 (1972)

Mr. Justice Rehnquist delivered the opinion of the Court.

Appellee Irvis, a Negro (hereafter appellee), was refused service by appellant Moose Lodge, a local branch of the national fraternal organization located in Harrisburg, Pennsylvania. . . .

Moose Lodge is a private club in the ordinary meaning of that term. It is a local chapter of a national fraternal organization having well-defined requirements for membership. It conducts all of its activities in a building that is owned by it. It is not publicly funded. Only members and guests are permitted in any lodge of the order; one may become a guest only by invitation of a member or upon invitation of the house committee.

Appellee, while conceding the right of private clubs to choose members upon a discriminatory basis, asserts that the licensing of Moose Lodge to serve liquor, by the Pennsylvania Liquor Control Board, amounts to such state involvement with the club's activities as to make its discriminatory practices forbidden by the Equal Protection Clause of the Fourteenth Amendment. . . .

The Court has never held, of course, that discrimination by an otherwise private entity would be violative of the Equal Protection Clause if the private entity receives any sort of benefit or service at all from the State, or if it is subject to state regulation in any degree whatever. Since state-furnished services include such necessities of life as electricity, water, and police and fire protection, such a holding would utterly emasculate the distinction between private as distinguished from state conduct. . . .

[U]nlike *Burton*, the Moose Lodge building is located on land owned by it, not by any public authority. Far from apparently holding itself out as a place of public accommodation, Moose Lodge quite ostentatiously proclaims the fact that it is not open to the public at large. Nor is it located and operated in such surroundings that although private in name, it discharges a function or performs a service that would otherwise in all likelihood be performed by the State. In short, while Eagle was a public restaurant in a public building, Moose Lodge is a private social club in a private building.

With the exception hereafter noted, the Pennsylvania Liquor Control Board plays absolutely no part in establishing or enforcing the membership or guest policies of the club that it licenses to serve liquor. . . .

However detailed [liquor] regulation may be in some particulars, it cannot be said to in any way foster or encourage racial discrimination. Nor can it be said to make the State in any realistic sense a partner or even a joint venturer in the club's enterprise. . . .

The District Court found that the regulations of the Liquor Control Board adopted pursuant to statute affirmatively require that "[e]very club licensee shall adhere to all of the provisions of the Constitution and By-Laws". . . .

The effect of this particular regulation on Moose Lodge [w]ould be to place state sanctions behind its discriminatory membership rules, but not behind its guest practices, which were not embodied in the constitution of the lodge. . . .

Even though the Liquor Control Board regulation in question is neutral in its terms, the result of its application in a case where the constitution and by-laws of a club required racial discrimination would be to invoke the sanctions of the State to enforce a concededly discriminatory private rule. . . .

Appellee was entitled to a decree enjoining the enforcement of § 113.09 of the regulations promulgated by the Pennsylvania Liquor Control Board insofar as that regulation requires compliance by Moose Lodge with provisions of its constitution and bylaws containing racially discriminatory provisions. He was entitled to no more.

PROBLEM C

A PRIVATE LAW SCHOOL. Suppose a private law school is being charged with a constitutional violation. On what basis could it be characterized as a state actor? Consider whether any or all of the following kinds of government involvement would warrant a finding of state action: (1) the receipt of government grants; (2) the availability of federal financial assistance; (3) the provision of a license approved by a state body; (4) accreditation by the state; (5) automatic admission of the school's graduate's to the state bar; or (6) the provision of normal city services like electricity and water to the school.

Would it be easier to find state action under another test? For example, would a government function approach be appropriate since states provide for higher education? Does it matter that access to the legal profession is limited by admission to law school in most states?

NATIONAL COLLEGIATE ATHLETIC ASSOCIATION v. TARKANIAN, 488 U.S. 179 (1988). Jerry Tarkanian, once called "the 'winningest' active basketball coach," allegedly participated in ten violations of rules of the National Collegiate Athletic Association. The NCAA placed his employer, the University of Nevada at Las Vegas (UNLV), on probation for two years and threatened further sanctions unless UNLV severed its ties to Tarkanian during the period of probation. After offering opposition, UNLV complied. The NCAA is an unincorporated association of approximately nine hundred and sixty members, including virtually all public and private universities conducting major athletic programs in the United States. Member universities agree to cooperate with enforcement programs of NCAA.

Tarkanian filed suit, and he ultimately obtained a judgment against the NCAA for damages and other relief, on the ground that the NCAA had denied him procedural due process—a holding that was sustainable only if the NCAA had engaged in state action. The Supreme Court, per Justice Stevens, held that the NCAA was not liable because it was not a state actor:

> [I]n the typical case raising a state action issue, a private party has taken the decisive step that caused the harm to the plaintiff, and the question is whether the state was sufficiently involved to treat that decisive conduct as state action. . . .

> The mirror image presented in this case requires us to step through an analytical looking glass to resolve it. [I]t was UNLV, the state entity, that actually suspended Tarkanian. Thus, the question is not whether UNLV participated to a critical extent in the NCAA's activities, but whether UNLV's actions in compliance with the NCAA rules and recommendations turn the NCAA's conduct into state action.

> [U]NLV is among the NCAA's members and participated in promulgating the association's rules; it must be assumed, therefore, that Nevada had some impact on the NCAA's policy determinations. Yet the NCAA's several hundred other public and private member institutions each similarly affected those policies. Those institutions, the vast majority of which were located in states other than Nevada, did not act under color of Nevada law. It necessarily follows that the source of the legislation adopted by the NCAA is not Nevada but the collective membership, speaking through an organization that is independent of any particular state. . . .

> Tarkanian further asserts that the NCAA's investigation, enforcement proceedings, and consequent recommendations constituted state action because they resulted from a delegation of power by UNLV. But UNLV delegated no power to the NCAA to take specific action against any university employee. . . .

> [D]uring the several years that the NCAA investigated the alleged violations, the NCAA and UNLV acted much more like adversaries than like partners engaged in a dispassionate search for the truth. [J]ust as a state-compensated public defender acts in a private capacity when she represents a private client in a conflict against the state, *Polk County v. Dodson*, 454 U.S. 312, 320 (1981), the NCAA is properly viewed as a private actor at odds with the state when it represents the interests of its entire membership in an investigation of one public university. . . .

> Finally, Tarkanian argues that the power of the NCAA is so great that the UNLV had no practical alternative to compliance with its demands. We are not at all sure this is true, but even if we assume that a private monopolist can impose its will on a state agency by a threatened refusal to deal with it, it does not follow that such a private party is therefore acting under color of state law. *Cf. Jackson* [*v. Metropolitan Edison Co.*]. . .

JUSTICE WHITE, joined by JUSTICES BRENNAN, MARSHALL, and O'CONNOR, dissented:

[I]n both *Adickes v. S.H. Kress & Co.*, 398 U.S. 144 (1970), and *Dennis v. Sparks*, 449 U.S. 24 (1980), we faced the question of whether private parties could be held to be state actors in cases in which the final or decisive act was carried out by a state official. In both cases we held that the private parties could be found to be state actors, if they were "jointly engaged with state officials in the challenged action. . . ."

On the facts of the present case, the NCAA acted jointly with UNLV in suspending Tarkanian. [T]arkanian was suspended for violations of NCAA rules, which UNLV embraced in its agreement with the NCAA. . . .

The majority states in conclusion that [i]t would be ironic indeed to conclude that the NCAA's imposition of sanctions against UNLV—sanctions that UNLV and its council, including the Attorney General of Nevada, steadfastly opposed during protracted adversary proceedings—is fairly attributable to the State of Nevada. I agree. Had UNLV refused to suspend Tarkanian, and the NCAA responded by imposing sanctions against UNLV, it would be hard indeed to find any state action that harmed Tarkanian. But that is not this case. Here, UNLV did suspend Tarkanian. . . . Under these facts, I would find that the NCAA acted jointly with UNLV and therefore is a state actor.

NOTES AND QUESTIONS

(1) *"Joint" Action or "Adversary" Postures?* The majority correctly points out that the NCAA sanctions were not themselves state action and indeed were vigorously opposed by the state; the dissenters agree. But aren't the dissenters also correct in arguing that the larger scheme of things involved joint activity? Nevada participated in NCAA activities, and ultimately it acted in concert with NCAA to separate from Tarkanian. Do these circumstances show the kind of joint conduct that should qualify as state action?

(2) *"Multi-State Action"—Is There Such a Thing?* The majority concludes that diffuse, multi-state participation in NCAA prevents its action from being that of Nevada—and therefore prevents it from being the action of any state. But can't a multi-state entity—such as an interstate compact commission, for example—exercise governmental authority of a kind that should qualify as state action?

(3) *Symbiosis—What Has Become of Burton v. Wilmington Parking Authority?* The suspension of Tarkanian seems to be more the result of "joint" and symbiotic action than the discriminatory policies of the Eagle Coffee Shoppe in *Burton*, because NCAA needs to affiliate with state entities more than Eagle did. Is *Tarkanian* consistent with *Burton*?

LEBRON v. NATIONAL RAILROAD PASSENGER CORP., 513 U.S. 374 (1995). Lebron, an artist, wanted to lease a huge illuminated billboard at the National Railroad Passenger Corporation's ("Amtrak") New York train station. With a take off of the "Silver Bullet" beer ads, Lebron wanted to display text and photographs that would criticize the Coors family for its support of certain "right-wing causes." When Amtrak officials disapproved the ads because they would constitute "political advertising," Lebron sued, claiming that Amtrak, although a private corporation, constituted government action and that the denial of the leased advertisements violated his Free Speech rights. (In this decision, the Court addressed only the "state action" issue.) The court of appeals had held that Amtrak was not a government entity, but the Supreme Court, per Justice Scalia, reversed.

Amtrak claims that whatever its relationship with the Federal Government, its charter's disclaimer of agency status [provided by Congress in 1970] prevents it from being considered a Government entity in the present case. . . . But it is not for Congress to [decide] Amtrak's status as a government entity for purposes of determining the constitutional rights of citizens affected by its actions. If Amtrak is, by its very nature, what the Constitution regards as Government, congressional pronouncement that it is not such can no more relieve it of its First Amendment restrictions than a similar pronouncement could exempt the [FBI] from the Fourth Amendment. . . .

Amtrak was created by a special statute, explicitly for the furtherance of federal government goals. [Additionally,] six of [Amtrak's] eight externally named directors [from a total of nine] are appointed directly by the President—four of [the directors] with the advice and consent of the Senate. . . . Moreover, Amtrak is not merely in the temporary control of the Government . . . it is established and organized under federal law for the very purpose of pursuing federal governmental objectives, under the direction and control of federal governmental appointees. . . .

We hold that where, as here, the Government creates a corporation by special law, for the furtherance of governmental objectives, and retains for itself permanent authority to appoint a majority of the directors of that corporation, the corporation is part of the Government for purposes of the First Amendment. . . .

JUSTICE O'CONNOR dissented.

NOTES AND QUESTIONS

(1) *The Degree of Government Involvement in Lebron?* The majority relies on several factors to hold that Amtrak's refusal to lease the billboard was "governmental action," including the President's authority to name six of the nine Amtrak directors. What if the Government controlled the appointment of fewer than a majority of the directors? Would this remove Government "control"? Doesn't the *Lebron* approach to the state action issue hinder governmental efforts to "privatize" various governmental activities while maintaining some protection for the investment by taxpayers?

(2) *Should There Be Different Standards for Different Constitutional Rights?* *Lebron* suggests that the issue posed in § 13.01 above has not been definitely addressed: should the nature of "state action" vary from one Amendment's guarantees to another? While the Court's holding is phrased in terms of the "First Amendment," above, Justice Scalia's majority opinion analogized to the Fourth Amendment. The "state action" issues, it seems, may require Amendment-by-Amendment litigation.

(3) *Further Implications of the "State Action "Doctrine for the "Privatization" of Government Functions: Richardson v. McKnight, 521 U.S. 399 (1997).* McKnight, a prisoner at a Tennessee prison whose management had been privatized, sued certain guards under 42 U.S.C. § 1983 for physical injuries allegedly inflicted by the guards. Even though the guards were employed by a private entity, the Supreme Court, per Justice Breyer, held that they were potentially liable for action "under color of state law" and, further, that they would not be able to assert the qualified immunity defense available to state officials in 1983 suits.

One reason a State might "privatize" its facilities or operations would be to avoid liability under 42 U.S.C. § 1983. The *McKnight* decision, taken together with *Lebron, supra,* suggests that the State cannot easily avoid § 1983 liability by privatization, at least not of traditional government functions or by less-than-complete divestment of control, and that the employees in a "privatized" operation may have less protection against liability than their counterparts who are employed by the State.

§ 13.03   STATE ENCOURAGEMENT, ENFORCEMENT, OR APPROBATION

NOTE ON STATE ACTION BY "ENCOURAGEMENT"

Just as government involvement may provide state action, state encouragement or enforcement of a private activity may also amount to state action. This is the broadest theory and most controversial aspect of the state action doctrine. It provides the potential for finding state action where the state is a passive party. It raises the question, to what extent should state inaction be considered state action?

SHELLEY v. KRAEMER, 334 U.S. 1 (1948). The Petitioners were African-Americans who purchased land that was subject to racially restrictive covenants—provisions in the documents affecting title that barred the sale of the land to blacks. The respondents, their neighbors, sued to enforce the racially restrictive covenants and prevent the sale of the property to the petitioners. Both petitioners and respondents were private parties. The state courts upheld and enforced the covenants. The Supreme Court, in an opinion by Chief Justice Vinson, reversed:

> [T]he restrictive agreements standing alone cannot be regarded as a violation of any rights guaranteed to petitioners by the Fourteenth Amendment. So long as the purposes of those agreements are effectuated by voluntary adherence to their terms, it would appear clear that there has been no action by the State and the provisions of the Amendment have not been violated. . . .

> [But] the action of the States to which the Fourteenth Amendment has reference includes action of state courts and state judicial officials. . . .

> These are not cases, as has been suggested, in which the States have merely abstained from action, leaving private individuals free to impose such discriminations as they see fit. Rather, these are cases in which the States have made available to such individuals the full coercive power of the government to deny to petitioners, on the grounds of race or color, the enjoyment of property rights in premises which petitioners are willing and financially able to acquire and which the grantors are willing to sell. The difference between judicial enforcement and nonenforcement of the restrictive covenants is the difference to petitioners between being denied rights of property available to other members of the community and being accorded full enjoyment of those rights on an equal footing.

NOTES AND QUESTIONS

(1) *What Was the Precise State Action in Shelley?* Wasn't the Court merely enforcing a private agreement that expressed the intent and choices of the parties to it? The discrimination originated with private parties, not with the judge. Is the state action, then, really the state's failure to prohibit racial discrimination?

Alternatively, it might be possible to view *Shelley* as a case in which the state courts were being used to compel discrimination by the seller, who did not want to be bound by the restrictive covenant and did not want to discriminate. *See* Henkin, *Shelley v. Kraemer: Notes for a Revised Opinion*, 110 U. PA. L. REV. 473 (1962).

(2) *The "Black Hole" Potential of Shelley.* How far does the reasoning of *Shelley* extend? "If obtaining court aid to carry out 'private' activity converts such private action into state action, then there could never be any private action in any practical sense. So entwined are our lives with the law that the logical result would be that almost *all* action, to be effective, must result in state action." Comment, 44 CALIF. L. REV. 718, 733 (1956). However, despite its expansive potential, *Shelley* has not been given such a broad

reading. Note, when reading *Brentwood Academy*, this student Comment's use of the term "entwined."

REITMAN v. MULKEY
387 U.S. 369 (1967)

MR. JUSTICE WHITE delivered the opinion of the Court.

[S]ection 26 of [California Constitution] Art. I, an initiated measure submitted to the people as Proposition 14 in a statewide ballot in 1964, provides in part as follows:

> Neither the State nor any subdivision or agency thereof shall deny, limit or abridge, directly or indirectly, the right of any person, who is willing or desires to sell, lease or rent any part or all of his [residential] real property, to decline to sell, lease or rent such property to such person or persons as he, in his absolute discretion, chooses. . . .

[The] Mulkeys who are husband and wife and respondents here, sued under § 51 and § 52 of the California Civil Code [which prohibited discrimination in certain transactions before Proposition 14 was adopted,] alleging that petitioners had refused to rent them an apartment solely on account of their race. An injunction and damages were demanded. Petitioners moved for summary judgment on the ground that §§ 51 and 52, insofar as they were the basis for the Mulkeys' action, had been rendered null and void by the adoption of Proposition 14 after the filing of the complaint. [The California Supreme Court held that Proposition 14, as adopted in § 26, was invalid as violative of the Equal Protection Clause.]

We affirm the judgment of the California Supreme Court. We first turn to the opinion of that court in *Reitman*, which quite properly undertook to examine the constitutionality of § 26 in terms of its "immediate objective," its "ultimate effect" and its "historical context and the conditions existing prior to its enactment". . . .

First, the [California] court considered whether § 26 was concerned at all with private discriminations in residential housing. This involved a review of past efforts by the California Legislature to regulate such discriminations. The Unruh Act, Civ. Code §§ 51–52, on which respondents based their cases, was passed in 1959. The Hawkins Act [f]ollowed and prohibited discriminations in publicly assisted housing. In 1961, the legislature enacted proscriptions against restrictive covenants. Finally, in 1963, came the Rumford Fair Housing Act, [s]uperseding the Hawkins Act and prohibiting racial discriminations in the sale or rental of any private dwelling containing more than four units. . . .

It was against this background that Proposition 14 was enacted. Its immediate design and intent, the California court said, were "to overturn state laws that bore on the right of private sellers and lessors to discriminate," the Unruh and Rumford Acts, and "to forestall future state action that might circumscribe this right." This aim was successfully achieved: the adoption of Proposition 14 [e]stablishes "a purported constitutional right to *privately* discriminate on grounds which admittedly would be unavailable under the Fourteenth Amendment *should state action* be involved."

Second, the court conceded that the State was permitted a neutral position with respect to private racial discriminations and that the State was not bound by the Federal Constitution to forbid them. But, because a significant state involvement in private discriminations could amount to unconstitutional state action, *Burton v. Wilmington Parking Authority*, the court deemed it necessary to determine whether Proposition 14 invalidly involved the State in racial discriminations in the housing market. Its conclusion was that it did. . . .

It concluded that a prohibited state involvement could be found "even where the state can be charged with only encouraging," rather than commanding discrimination. . . .

There is no sound reason for rejecting this judgment. Petitioners contend that the

California court has misconstrued the Fourteenth Amendment since the repeal of any statute prohibiting racial discrimination, which is constitutionally permissible, may be said to "authorize" and "encourage" discrimination because it makes legally permissible that which was formerly proscribed. But, as we understand the California court, it did not posit a constitutional violation on the mere repeal of the Unruh and Rumford Acts. [T]he court dealt with § 26 as though it expressly authorized and constitutionalized the private right to discriminate. Third, the court assessed the ultimate impact of § 26 in the California environment and concluded that the section would encourage and significantly involve the State in private racial discrimination contrary to the Fourteenth Amendment.

[P]rivate discriminations in housing were now not only free from Rumford and Unruh but they also enjoyed a far different status than was true before the passage of those statutes. The right to discriminate, including the right to discriminate on racial grounds, was now embodied in the State's basic charter, immune from legislative, executive, or judicial regulation at any level of the state government. . . .

[W]e accept this holding of the California court. . . .

[H]ere we are dealing with a provision which does not just repeal an existing law forbidding private racial discriminations. Section 26 was intended to authorize, and does authorize, racial discrimination in the housing market. The right to discriminate is now one of the basic policies of the State. The California Supreme Court believes that the section will significantly encourage and involve the State in private discriminations. We have been presented with no persuasive considerations indicating that these judgments should be overturned.

Affirmed.

Mr. Justice Harlan, whom Mr. Justice Black, Mr. Justice Clark, and Mr. Justice Stewart join, dissenting.

I consider that this decision, which cuts deeply into state political processes, is supported neither by anything "found" by the Supreme Court of California nor by any of our past cases decided under the Fourteenth Amendment. [I] must respectfully dissent.

The facts of this case are simple and undisputed. The legislature of the State of California has in the last decade enacted a number of statutes restricting the right of private landowners to discriminate on the basis of such factors as race in the sale or rental of property. These laws aroused considerable opposition, causing certain groups to organize themselves and to take advantage of procedures embodied in the California Constitution permitting a "proposition" to be presented to the voters for a constitutional amendment. "Proposition 14" was thus put before the electorate in the 1964 election and was adopted by a vote of 4,526,460 to 2,395,747. . . .

[T]he provision is neutral on its face, and it is only by in effect asserting that this requirement of passive official neutrality is camouflage that the Court is able to reach its conclusion. In depicting the provision as tantamount to active state encouragement of discrimination the Court essentially relies on the fact that the California Supreme Court so concluded. . . .

The only "factual" matter relied on by the majority of the California Supreme Court was the context in which Proposition 14 was adopted, namely, that several strong antidiscrimination acts had been passed by the legislature and opposed by many of those who successfully led the movement of adoption of Proposition 14 by popular referendum. [T]his, of course, is nothing but a legal conclusion as to federal constitutional law, the California Supreme Court not having relied in any way upon the State Constitution. . . .

[T]he core of the Court's opinion is that § 26 is offensive to the Fourteenth

Amendment because it effectively *encourages* private discrimination. By focusing on "encouragement" the Court, I fear, is forging a slippery and unfortunate criterion by which to measure the constitutionality of a statute simply permissive in purpose and effect, and inoffensive on its face. . . .

NOTES AND QUESTIONS

(1) *The Ratchet Effect of Reitman.* Does *Reitman* effectively mean that a law passed to protect civil rights or prevent discrimination may never be repealed? What prevents the case from being so read? The California Supreme Court's "finding" concerning the "intent" with which the amendment was enacted? Remember, the Court was dealing not with the intent of a legislative body, which is difficult enough to ascertain, but with the intent of some 7 million California voters. *See also Cooper v. Aaron, supra,* Chapter 1.

(2) *The "Black Hole" Potential of Reitman.* At the most fundamental level, there are only two possible relationships between state law and private action. Either the action is permitted under state law or it is prohibited. Should it matter that the state has no provision governing private discrimination in the sale of property instead of a law which declares explicitly that private parties are free to sell their property to whomever they choose? Doesn't the absence of such a law have precisely the same effect? Taken to its extreme, does *Reitman* mean that state action exists when the state fails to prohibit private discrimination?

FLAGG BROS. v. BROOKS
436 U.S. 149 (1978)

MR. JUSTICE REHNQUIST delivered the opinion of the Court.

The question presented by this litigation is whether a warehouseman's proposed sale of goods entrusted to him for storage, as permitted by New York Uniform Commercial Code § 7-210 (McKinney 1964), is an action properly attributable to the State of New York. . . .

Respondents' primary contention is that New York has delegated to Flagg Brothers a power "traditionally exclusively reserved to the State." *Jackson* [*v. Metropolitan Edison Co.*] They argue that the resolution of private disputes is a traditional function of civil government, and that the State in § 7-210 has delegated this function to Flagg Brothers. Respondents, however, have read too much into the language of our previous cases. While many functions have been traditionally performed by governments, very few have been "exclusively reserved to the State."

Although the elections held by the Democratic Party and its affiliates [in *Terry v. Adams*] were the only meaningful elections in Texas, and the streets owned by the Gulf Shipbuilding Corp. [in *Marsh v. Alabama*] were the only streets in Chickasaw, the proposed sale by Flagg Brothers under § 7-210 is not the only means of resolving this purely private dispute. Respondent Brooks has never alleged that state law barred her from seeking a waiver of Flagg Brothers' right to sell her goods at the time she authorized their storage. Presumably, respondent Jones, who alleges that she never authorized the storage of her goods, could have sought to replevy her goods at any time under state law. *See* N.Y.Civ.Prac.Law § 7101 *et seq.* (McKinney 1963). The challenged statute itself provides a damages remedy against the warehouseman for violations of its provisions. N.Y. U.C.C. § 7-210(9) (McKinney 1964). This system of rights and remedies, recognizing the traditional place of private arrangements in ordering relationships in the commercial world, can hardly be said to have delegated to Flagg Brothers an exclusive prerogative of the sovereign. . . .

[E]ven if we were inclined to extend the sovereign-function doctrine outside of its present carefully confined bounds, the field of private commercial transactions would be a particularly inappropriate area into which to expand it. We conclude that our sovereign-function cases do not support a finding of state action here.

Respondents further urge that Flagg Brothers' proposed action is properly attributable to the State because the State has authorized and encouraged it in enacting § 7-210. Our cases state "that a State is responsible for the act . . . of a private party when the State, by its law, has compelled the act." This Court, however, has never held that a State's mere acquiescence in a private action converts that action into that of the State. The Court rejected a similar argument in *Jackson.*

It is quite immaterial that the State has embodied its decision not to act in statutory form. If New York had no commercial statutes at all, its courts would still be faced with the decision whether to prohibit or to permit the sort of sale threatened here the first time an aggrieved bailor came before them for relief. A judicial decision to deny relief would be no less an "authorization" or "encouragement" of that sale than the legislature's decision embodied in this statute. [I]f the mere denial of judicial relief is considered sufficient encouragement to make the State responsible for those private acts, all private deprivations of property would be converted into public acts whenever the State, for whatever reason, denies relief sought by the putative property owner.

Here, the State of New York has not compelled the sale of a bailor's goods, but has merely announced the circumstances under which its courts will not interfere with a private sale. Indeed, the crux of respondents' complaint is not that the State *has* acted, but that it has *refused* to act. This statutory refusal to act is no different in principle from an ordinary statute of limitations whereby the State declines to provide a remedy for private deprivations of property after the passage of a given period of time.

Mr. Justice Stevens, with whom Mr. Justice White and Mr. Justice Marshall join, dissenting.

There is no question in this case but that respondents have a property interest in the possessions that the warehouseman proposes to sell. It is also clear that, whatever power of sale the warehouseman has, it does not derive from the consent of the respondents. The claimed power derives solely from the State, and specifically from § 7-210 of the New York Uniform Commercial Code. The question is whether a state statute which authorizes a private party to deprive a person of his property without his consent must meet the requirements of the Due Process Clause of the Fourteenth Amendment. This question must be answered in the affirmative unless the State has virtually unlimited power to transfer interests in private property without any procedural protections.

In determining that New York's statute cannot be scrutinized under the Due Process Clause, the Court reasons that the warehouseman's proposed sale is solely private action because the state statute "*permits* but does not compel" the sale (emphasis added), and because the warehouseman has not been delegated a power "*exclusively* reserved to the State" (emphasis added). Under this approach a State could enact laws authorizing private citizens to use self-help in countless situations without any possibility of federal challenge. A state statute could authorize the warehouseman to retain all proceeds of the lien sale, even if they far exceeded the amount of the alleged debt; it could authorize finance companies to enter private homes to repossess merchandise; or indeed, it could authorize "any person with sufficient physical power" to acquire and sell the property of his weaker neighbor. . . . The Court's rationale would characterize action pursuant to such a statute as purely private action, which the State permits but does not compel, in an area not exclusively reserved to the State.

As these examples suggest, the distinctions between "permission" and "compulsion" on the one hand, and "exclusive" and "nonexclusive," on the other, cannot be determinative factors in state-action analysis. . . .

NOTES AND QUESTIONS

(1) *Can Flagg Bros. be Reconciled With Reitman?* Does the finding in *Reitman* of an intent to authorize discrimination make a difference that allows *Flagg Bros.* to be distinguished from *Reitman?* Was it significant that *Flagg Bros.* involved a state statute, while *Reitman* involved a state constitutional amendment? *Cf.* Rowe, *The Emerging Threshold Approach to State Action Determinations: Trying to Make Sense of Flagg Brothers, Inc. v. Brooks,* 69 GEO. L.J. 745 (1981); *see also* Buchanan, *State Authorization, Class Discrimination, and the Fourteenth Amendment,* 21 HOUS. L. REV. 1 (1984).

(2) *Action vs. Inaction: A Matter of Characterization.* Is the state's posture in *Flagg Bros.* really one of inaction and passivity? Didn't the legislature make an affirmative decision to vest warehousemen with the power to sell goods? Consider Brest, *State Action and Liberal Theory: A Casenote on Flagg Bros. v. Brooks,* 130 U. PA. L. REV. 1296, 1313 (1982):

> Although the state did not assist the creditor in gaining possession, it treats his possession as the occasion for transferring to him, and protecting against the debtor, property interests (the right to possess and dispose of the goods) that were formerly the debtor's. Even if the creditor's gaining of possession cannot be characterized as action of the state, the state surely acts when it protects the possessor's interest once gained.

But if one accepts this view, the recurring problem of limiting the scope of state actions arises. Would there be any private activity?

(3) *Beyond Flagg Bros: Skinner v. Railway Labor Executives Association, 489 U.S. 602 (1989).* In *Flagg Bros.,* the state had limited itself to allowance of the questioned private conduct. In *Skinner,* the federal government's Federal Railroad Administration ("FRA") had issued drug testing regulations. These were implemented by private companies. The Court, per Justice Kennedy, held that the private companies were "state action." The Court emphasized that the private companies could not contract away (such as by collective bargaining) the obligation to conduct the drug testing. The FRA regulations also gave the government the right to receive certain drug test results procured by the private companies. Under these circumstances, the Court found that the government had gone beyond mere "allowance" or acquiescence in private conduct.

(4) *The Development of a Two-Part Standard for "State Action": Edmonson v. Leesville Concrete Co., 500 U.S. 614 (1991).* In *Batson v. Kentucky,* 476 U.S. 79 (1986) [§ 10.03], the Court prohibited the prosecutors in a criminal case from exercising peremptory challenges on the basis of race. In *Edmonson,* the Court addressed the issue whether the exercise of peremptory challenges by private litigants in a civil case constituted state action (thereby subject to equal protection analysis). The Court, per Justice Kennedy, concluded that such conduct by private litigants was state action.

The Court articulated a two part standard: "We asked first whether the claimed constitutional deprivation resulted from the exercise of a right or privilege having its source in state authority, and second, whether the private party charged with the deprivation could be described in all fairness as a state actor." The first issue apparently addresses the actual cause of the alleged constitutional violation while the second issue determines, on a totality of circumstances basis, whether the imposition of liability would be "reasonable." This two part standard from *Edmonson* and *Lugar* has been applied in subsequent decisions. The results, as you can see below, vary.

§ 13.04   THE ENTWINEMENT THEORY

BRENTWOOD ACADEMY v. TENNESSEE SECONDARY SCHOOL ATHLETIC ASSOCIATION
531 U.S. 288 (2001)

JUSTICE SOUTER delivered the opinion of the Court.

[In *Brentwood Academy*, the Court reaffirmed the fact-intensive nature of the state action issue. The Court purported to apply the two-part standard from *Edmonson*, although the author of *Edmonson*, Justice Kennedy, dissented. When reading this decision, watch for the Court's treatment of the facts.

Brentwood Academy, a private parochial high school, belonged to the Tennessee Secondary School Athletic Association ("TSSAA"). The Association controlled all interscholastic athletic activity in Tennessee by a membership rule prohibiting members from competing with nonmember schools unless the Association granted a special permission. This case arose when the Association found that Brentwood Academy had violated "recruiting" rules and handed out a harsh penalty: four years of probation; two years of play-off ineligibility for boys football and basketball; and a $3,000 fine. Although the District Court found the Association to be a state action, the Court of Appeals had reversed. The Supreme Court, by a 5-4 margin, held that a private corporation established to run interscholastic athletics in Tennessee, is a state action and, therefore, the Fourteenth Amendment's guarantees apply.]

The issue is whether a statewide association incorporated to regulate interscholastic athletic competition among public and private secondary schools may be regarded as engaging in state action when it enforces a rule against a member school. The association in question here includes most public schools located within the State, acts through their representatives, draws its officers from them, is largely funded by their dues and income received in their stead, and has historically been seen to regulate in lieu of the State Board of Education's exercise of its own authority. We hold that the association's regulatory activity may and should be treated as state action owing to the pervasive entwinement of state school officials in the structure of the association, there being no offsetting reason to see the association's acts in any other way.

I

Respondent Tennessee Secondary School Athletic Association (Association) is a not-for-profit membership corporation organized to regulate interscholastic sport among the public and private high schools in Tennessee that belong to it. . . .

Ever since the Association was incorporated in 1925, Tennessee's State Board of Education (State Board) has (to use its own words) acknowledged the corporation's functions "in providing standards, rules and regulations for interscholastic competition in the public schools of Tennessee." More recently, the State Board cited its statutory authority, Tenn.Code Ann. § 49-1-302, when it adopted language expressing the relationship between the Association and the Board. Specifically, in 1972, it went so far as to adopt a rule expressly "designat[ing]" the Association as "the organization to supervise and regulate the athletic activities in which the public junior and senior high schools in Tennessee participate on an interscholastic basis." . . . Thus, on several occasions over the next 20 years, the State Board reviewed, approved, or reaffirmed its approval of the recruiting Rule at issue in this case. In 1996, however, the State Board dropped the original Rule 0520-1-2-.08 expressly designating the Association as regulator; it substituted a statement "recogniz[ing] the value of participation in interscholastic athletics and the role of [the Association] in coordinating interscholastic athletic competition," while "authoriz[ing] the public schools of the state to voluntarily maintain membership in [the Association]."

The action before us responds to a 1997 regulatory enforcement proceeding brought against petitioner, Brentwood Academy, a private parochial high school member of the Association. . . . When these penalties were imposed, all the voting members of the board of control and legislative council were public school administrators. . . .

II

A

Our cases try to plot a line between state action subject to Fourteenth Amendment scrutiny and private conduct (however exceptionable) that is not. *Jackson v. Metropolitan Edison Co.*, 419 U.S. 345, 349 (1974). The judicial obligation is not only to " 'preserv[e] an area of individual freedom by limiting the reach of federal law' and avoi[d] the imposition of responsibility on a State for conduct it could not control," but also to assure that constitutional standards are invoked "when it can be said that the State is *responsible* for the specific conduct of which the plaintiff complains." If the Fourteenth Amendment is not to be displaced, therefore, its ambit cannot be a simple line between States and people operating outside formally governmental organizations, and the deed of an ostensibly private organization or individual is to be treated sometimes as if a State had caused it to be performed. Thus, we say that state action may be found if, though only if, there is such a "close nexus between the State and the challenged action" that seemingly private behavior "may be fairly treated as that of the State itself." *Jackson*, supra.

What is fairly attributable is a matter of normative judgment, and the criteria lack rigid simplicity. From the range of circumstances that could point toward the State behind an individual face, no one fact can function as a necessary condition across the board for finding state action; nor is any set of circumstances absolutely sufficient, for there may be some countervailing reason against attributing activity to the government.

Our cases have identified a host of facts that can bear on the fairness of such an attribution . . . .

Amidst such variety, examples may be the best teachers, and examples from our cases are unequivocal in showing that the character of a legal entity is determined neither by its expressly private characterization in statutory law, nor by the failure of the law to acknowledge the entity's inseparability from recognized government officials or agencies. *Lebron v. National Railroad Passenger Corporation*, 513 U.S. 374 (1995), held that Amtrak was the Government for constitutional purposes, regardless of its congressional designation as private; it was organized under federal law to attain governmental objectives and was directed and controlled by federal appointees. . . . Ostensibly the converse situation occurred in *Evans v. Newton, supra*, which held that private trustees to whom a city had transferred a park were nonetheless state actors barred from enforcing racial segregation, since the park served the public purpose of providing community recreation, and "the municipality remain[ed] entwined in [its] management [and] control."

These examples of public entwinement in the management and control of ostensibly separate trusts or corporations foreshadow this case, as this Court itself anticipated in *Tarkanian, supra*. . . .

To be sure, it is not the strict holding in *Tarkanian* that points to our view of this case, for we found no state action on the part of the NCAA. We could see, on the one hand, that the university had some part in setting the NCAA's rules, and the Supreme Court of Nevada had gone so far as to hold that the NCAA had been delegated the university's traditionally exclusive public authority over personnel. But on the other side, the NCAA's policies were shaped not by the University of Nevada alone, but by several hundred member institutions, most of them having no connection with Nevada, and exhibiting no color of Nevada law. Since it was difficult to see the NCAA, not as a collective membership, but as surrogate for the one State, we held the organization's connection with Nevada too insubstantial to ground a state action claim. . . .

B

Just as we foresaw in *Tarkanian*, the "necessarily fact-bound inquiry," leads to the conclusion of state action here. The nominally private character of the Association is overborne by the pervasive entwinement of public institutions and public officials in its composition and workings, and there is no substantial reason to claim unfairness in applying constitutional standards to it. . . .

In sum, to the extent of 84% of its membership, the Association is an organization of public schools represented by their officials acting in their official capacity to provide an integral element of secondary public schooling. . . .

To complement the entwinement of public school officials with the Association from the bottom up, the State of Tennessee has provided for entwinement from top down. State Board members are assigned ex officio to serve as members of the board of control and legislative council, and the Association's ministerial employees are treated as state employees to the extent of being eligible for membership in the state retirement system.

It is, of course, true that the time is long past when the close relationship between the surrogate association and its public members and public officials acting as such was attested frankly. As mentioned, the terms of the State Board's Rule expressly designating the Association as regulator of interscholastic athletics in public schools was deleted in 1996, the year after a Federal District Court held that the Association was a state actor because its rules were "caused, directed and controlled by the Tennessee Board of Education."

But the removal of the designation language from Rule 0520-1-2-.08 affected nothing but words. Today the State Board's member-designees continue to sit on the Association's committees as nonvoting members, and the State continues to welcome Association employees in its retirement scheme. The close relationship is confirmed by the Association's enforcement of the same preamendment rules and regulations reviewed and approved by the State Board (including the recruiting Rule challenged by Brentwood), and by the State Board's continued willingness to allow students to satisfy its physical education requirement by taking part in interscholastic athletics sponsored by the Association. The most one can say on the evidence is that the State Board once freely acknowledged the Association's official character but now does it by winks and nods.[1] The amendment to the Rule in 1996 affected candor but not the "momentum" of the Association's prior involvement with the State Board. . . .

The entwinement down from the State Board is therefore unmistakable, just as the entwinement up from the member public schools is overwhelming. Entwinement will support a conclusion that an ostensibly private organization ought to be charged with a

---

[1] The significance of winks and nods in state-action doctrine seems to be one of the points of the dissenters' departure from the rest of the Court. In drawing the public-private action line, the dissenters would emphasize the formal clarity of the legislative action providing for the appointment of Gerard College's trustees, see *supra*, at—, *post*, at—, in preference to our reliance on the practical certainty in this case that public officials will control operation of the Association under its bylaws. Similarly, the dissenters stress the express formality of the special statute defining Amtrak's ties to the Government, see *supra*, at—, *post*, at—, in contrast to the reality in this case that the Association's organizers structured the Association's relationships to the officialdom of public education. But if formalism were the sine qua non of state action, the doctrine would vanish owing to the ease and inevitability of its evasion, and for just that reason formalism has never been controlling.

public character and judged by constitutional standards; entwinement to the degree shown here requires it.

C

Entwinement is also the answer to the Association's several arguments offered to persuade us that the facts would not support a finding of state action under various criteria applied in other cases. These arguments are beside the point, simply because the facts justify a conclusion of state action under the criterion of entwinement, a conclusion in no sense unsettled merely because other criteria of state action may not be satisfied by the same facts. . . .

D

This is not to say that all of the Association's arguments are rendered beside the point by the public officials' involvement in the Association, for after application of the entwinement criterion, or any other, there is a further potential issue, and the Association raises it. Even facts that suffice to show public action (or, standing alone, would require such a finding) may be outweighed in the name of some value at odds with finding public accountability in the circumstances. . . .

The assertion of such a countervailing value is the nub of each of the Association's two remaining arguments, neither of which, however, persuades us. The Association suggests, first, that reversing the judgment here will somehow trigger an epidemic of unprecedented federal litigation. . . .

Nor do we think there is anything to be said for the Association's contention that there is no need to treat it as a state actor since any public school applying the Association's rules is itself subject to suit under § 1983 or Title IX of the Education Amendments. If Brentwood's claim were pushing at the edge of the class of possible defendant state actors, an argument about the social utility of expanding that class would at least be on point, but because we are nowhere near the margin in this case, the Association is really asking for nothing less than a dispensation for itself. . . .

[Reversed.]

JUSTICE THOMAS, with whom THE CHIEF JUSTICE, JUSTICE SCALIA, and JUSTICE KENNEDY join, dissenting.

We have never found state action based upon mere "entwinement." Until today, we have found a private organization's acts to constitute state action only when the organization performed a public function; was created, coerced, or encouraged by the government; or acted in a symbiotic relationship with the government. The majority's holding—that the Tennessee Secondary School Athletic Association's (TSSAA) enforcement of its recruiting rule is state action—not only extends state-action doctrine beyond its permissible limits but also encroaches upon the realm of individual freedom that the doctrine was meant to protect. I respectfully dissent. . . .

I

A

The State of Tennessee did not create the TSSAA. The State does not fund the TSSAA and does not pay its employees. In fact, only 4% of the TSSAA's revenue comes from the dues paid by member schools; the bulk of its operating budget is derived from gate receipts at tournaments it sponsors. The State does not permit the TSSAA to use state-owned facilities for a discounted fee, and it does not exempt the TSSAA from state taxation. No Tennessee law authorizes the State to coordinate interscholastic athletics or empowers another entity to organize interscholastic athletics on behalf of the State. The only state pronouncement acknowledging the TSSAA's existence is a rule providing that the State Board of Education permits public schools to maintain membership in the TSSAA if they so choose. . . .

B

Even approaching the issue in terms of any of the Court's specific state-action tests, the conclusion is the same: The TSSAA's enforcement of its recruiting rule against Brentwood Academy is not state action. . . . The TSSAA has not performed a function that has been "traditionally exclusively reserved to the State." *Jackson v. Metropolitan Edison Co.*, 419 U.S. 345, 352 (1974). The organization of interscholastic sports is neither a traditional nor an exclusive public function of the States. . . . The TSSAA no doubt serves the public, particularly the public schools, but the mere provision of a service to the public does not render such provision a traditional and exclusive public function.

It is also obvious that the TSSAA is not an entity created and controlled by the government for the purpose of fulfilling a government objective, as was Amtrak in *Lebron v. National Railroad Passenger Corporation*, 513 U.S. 374, 394 (1995). Indeed, no one claims that the State of Tennessee played any role in the creation of the TSSAA as a private corporation in 1925. The TSSAA was designed to fulfill an objective—the organization of interscholastic athletic tournaments—that the government had not contemplated, much less pursued. . . .

Although the TSSAA's enforcement activities cannot be considered state action as a matter of common sense or under any of this Court's existing theories of state action, the majority presents a new theory. Under this theory, the majority holds that the combination of factors it identifies evidences "entwinement" of the State with the TSSAA, and that such entwinement converts private action into state action. . . .

NOTES AND QUESTIONS

(1) *A Private Corporation Running High School Athletics Constitutes State Action: Brentwood Academy v. Tennessee Secondary School Athletic Association, 531 U.S. 288 (2001).* In the main case, the Court, per Justice Souter, held that a private corporation which ran essentially all interscholastic athletic activity in Tennessee was a state actor, subject to the Fourteenth Amendment's limitations. The Court's analysis relied on the two-part standard from *Edmonson/Lugar*, and the decision was fact-intensive. The Court found a degree of "pervasive entwinement" sufficient to establish state action. Notice how Justice Souter read *Tarkanian* narrowly—and thereby distinguished it.

Justice Thomas wrote for the four dissenters—disagreeing with any notion of entwinement and with the majority's characterization of many facts. The dissent reviews each of the theories of state action and concludes that the actions of TSSAA do not satisfy any of them. The dissent asserted that the majority "entwinement" analysis was a more expansive theory. As a matter of policy, an expansive theory of state action is more restrictive of the state's discretion. Should the Court interpret the state action requirement expansively or narrowly?

(2) *Brentwood Academy and "Privatization."* You reviewed the *Lebron* decision above in § 13.02; it raised issues regarding the government's ability to privatize state businesses or activities. In *Brentwood Academy*, the athletic association had always been nominally private. Starting in the 1970s, however, the State agency governing secondary education had, for approximately 20 years, expressly established a regulatory scheme allowing TSSAA, the private corporation, to govern athletic activities. In the 1990s, the State agency formally privatized (or, "reprivatized") the interscholastic athletic activities. This decision, like *Lebron*, indicates that the Court's analysis on the

first prong of the *Edmonson* standard will look behind the formalities. *See generally* David Lust, Note, *What To Do When Faced With a Novel State Action Question? Punt: The Eighth Circuit's Decision in Reinhart v. City of Brookings*, 42 S.D. L. Rev. 508 (1997).

PROBLEM D

WOULD DEREGULATING MARDI GRAS BE UNCONSTITUTIONAL?: "VOTERS [SAY] REPEAL MARDI GRAS LAW [AGAINST RACE AND GENDER DISCRIMINATION]", New Orleans Times-Picayune, Feb. 2, 1992, at 1A, col. 1. A New Orleans ordinance requires krewes to open their membership without regard to race and gender. (Krewes are private membership societies, privately organized and privately funded, through which Mardi Gras parades and balls are held.) A majority of 86 percent of white voters wanted this ordinance repealed; interestingly, a majority of 51 percent of black voters also wanted it repealed (and only 36 percent of blacks supported the law.) Unfortunately, several of the krewes decided to discontinue parades, either to protest the ordinance or because "the fun and the excitement are gone." Houston Chronicle, Aug. 19, 1992, at 5A, col. 1. Yet these parades are the "backbone of a multimillion dollar tourist boost for New Orleans in the late winter." Question: If New Orleans were to repeal the ordinance, would the krewes' subsequent discrimination amount to unconstitutional state action? Consider (1) a government function theory (given the identification of Mardi Gras with New Orleans), (2) a state involvement theory (given the mutual benefits, the economics of Mardi Gras, and the state's accommodation of street parades), or (3) a state encouragement theory (given the implications of repeal); and also consider (4) the private organization and funding of the krewes.

Chapter 14

CONGRESSIONAL ENFORCEMENT OF THE CIVIL RIGHTS AMENDMENTS

§ 14.01 AN OVERVIEW OF THE STATUTES

(1) *The Civil Rights Act of 1866: Equal Contract, Property, and Other Rights; Criminal Penalties.* Congress passed the Civil Rights Act of 1866 pursuant to the Thirteenth Amendment. It was the first Reconstruction Act designed "to protect all persons in the United States in their civil rights." Several provisions of the 1866 Act remain in force today with only minor revisions. They include:

> *42 U.S.C. § 1981. Equal rights under the law.* All persons within the jurisdiction of the United States shall have the same right in every State and Territory to make and enforce contracts, to sue, be parties, give evidence, and to the full and equal benefit of all laws and proceedings for the security of persons and property as is enjoyed by white citizens, and shall be subject to like punishment, pains, penalties, taxes, licenses, and exactions of every kind, and to no other.

> *42 U.S.C. § 1982. Property rights of citizens.* All citizens of the United States shall have the same right, in every State and Territory, as is enjoyed by white citizens thereof to inherit, purchase, lease, sell, hold, and convey real and personal property.

Also, the 1866 Act imposed criminal penalties on those who denied these rights under color of law. The current version of that provision provides:

> *18 U.S.C. § 242. Deprivation of rights under color of law.* Whoever, under color of any law, statute, ordinance, regulation, or custom, willfully subjects any inhabitant of any State, Territory, or District to the deprivation of any rights, privileges, or immunities secured or protected by the Constitution or laws of the United States, or to different punishments, pains, or penalties, on account of such inhabitant being an alien or by reason of his color, or race, than are prescribed for the punishment of citizens, shall be fined not more than $1,000 or imprisoned not more than one year, or both; and if death results shall be subject to imprisonment for any term of years or for life.

(2) *Was the 1866 Act Constitutional?* The 1866 Act was passed over the veto of President Johnson, who believed it to be unconstitutional. Fear that the Supreme Court would agree with President Johnson, and fear that the southern Black Codes would emasculate the Thirteenth Amendment, led the Congress to pass the Fourteenth Amendment in 1868. Two years later, Congress passed the Fifteenth Amendment, which did what the Fourteenth Amendment had only implicitly done—guarantee the right to vote. Using these two amendments as their constitutional foundation, Congress passed several acts to further enforce all civil rights guaranteed by these three amendments.

(3) *The Act of May 31, 1870: Protecting the Right to Vote.* This Act was designed principally to protect the right to vote. Although few of the provisions protecting the right to vote survived, one important provision barring private conspiracies has survived:

> *18 U.S.C. § 241. Conspiracy against rights of citizens.* If two or more persons conspire to injure, oppress, threaten, or intimidate any citizen in the free exercise or enjoyment of any right or privilege secured to him by the Constitution or laws of the United States, or because of his having exercised the same; or

> If two or more persons go on the highway, or on the premises of another, with intent to prevent or hinder his free exercise or enjoyment of any right or

privilege so secured—

They shall be fined not more than $10,000 or imprisoned not more than ten years, or both; and if death results, they shall be subject to imprisonment for any term of years or for life.

(4) *The Ku Klux Klan Act of 1871: The Most Pervasive of the Early Enactments Providing for Civil Suits to Redress Deprivations of Civil Rights.* This Act established, among other things, civil liabilities for the deprivation of rights. This provision has evolved into the principal tool in the enforcement of civil liberties. It is codified as:

42 U.S.C. § 1983. Civil action for deprivation of rights. Every person who, under color of any statute, ordinance, regulation, custom, or usage, of any State or Territory, subjects, or causes to be subjected, any citizen of the United States or other persons within the jurisdiction thereof to the deprivation of any rights, privileges or immunities secured by the Constitution and laws, shall be liable to the person injured in an action of law, suit in equity, or other proper proceedings for redress.

This legislation today is involved in a very large percentage of the litigation that occurs in federal courts.

(5) *Modern Legislation: The Civil Rights Acts of 1964 and 1968; the Voting Rights Act.* We encountered the Civil Rights Act of 1964 in Chapter 2, above, in the cases of *Heart of Atlanta Motel, Inc. v. United States* and *Katzenback v. McClung.* Those decisions upheld the public accommodations sections of the 1964 Act, which prohibited private discrimination in such places of public accommodation as motels and restaurants. (You should recall the Court's decision to uphold the enactment on the basis of the Commerce Clause instead of the Fourteenth Amendment, upon which Congress also had relied.) The 1964 Act also contains Title VII, which prohibits employment discrimination by private persons. As for the Civil Rights Act of 1968, its best-known provision probably is its open housing protections. Finally, the Voting Rights Act is described in greater depth in the materials that follow. Because it displaces democratically determined state and local government power, the Voting Rights Act is the vehicle for several landmark decisions dealing with the limits of Congress' power to enforce the civil rights amendments.

> Read U.S. Const. Amend. XIII, § 2; Amend. XIV, § 5; and Amend. XV, § 2 (Congress' power to enforce the Thirteenth, Fourteenth, and Fifteenth Amendments).

§ 14.02   ENFORCING THE FOURTEENTH AND FIFTEENTH AMENDMENTS AGAINST STATE ACTION

HISTORICAL BACKGROUND OF THE VOTING RIGHTS ACT

Despite the apparently clear and direct language of the Fifteenth Amendment, it was many years before blacks were able to exercise effectively their right to vote. Congress passed the Enforcement Act of 1870 under the Fifteenth Amendment to provide for detailed federal supervision of the electoral process at all levels. However, the enforcement of these laws become spotty and ineffective, and most of their provisions were repealed in 1894. Through the use of poll taxes, literacy tests, residency requirements and other devices, certain states were able to disenfranchise most potential black voters.

It was not until the Civil Rights Act of 1957 that Congress again attempted to cure this problem by facilitating case-by-case litigation against the discriminatory uses of these barriers to voting. Congress revised the 1957 Act with the Civil Rights Acts of 1960 and 1964 in an effort to further ease the heavy procedural burdens incurred in bringing such a suit and to strengthen the remedies that could be ordered once a suit was won. Despite these efforts, reform was still severely hampered by the difficulties of litigation and the outright defiance of some localities, which would merely replace an enjoined restrictive practice with another that was equally restrictive.

This history prompted Congress to abandon the strategy of encouraging piecemeal litigation as a means of achieving voting reform, and to adopt the sweeping provisions of the Voting Rights Act of 1965. The first constitutional challenge to this Act came almost immediately in *South Carolina v. Katzenbach.*

SOUTH CAROLINA v. KATZENBACH, 383 U.S. 301 (1966). South Carolina challenged the constitutionality of the Voting Rights Act of 1965. The Act provided, *inter alia*, that an electoral subdivision was "covered" by the Act if (a) the Attorney General found the use of a "test or device" to qualify for voting rights, and (b) the Director of the Census determined that less than fifty percent of the voting age residents were registered. Once it was determined that a political subdivision was "covered" by the Act, the Act suspended the use of literacy tests and similar voting qualifications for a period of five years from the last occurrence of substantial voting discrimination.

The subdivision could avoid the coverage of the Act in two ways. The first was to obtain the Attorney General's approval of its voting rules. The second was to obtain a declaratory judgment from a three-judge District Court for the District of Columbia that its "tests or devices" had not been used to abridge the vote on racial grounds within the last five years.

The constitutionality of these provisions was upheld by the Court in an opinion by Chief Justice Warren:

> [A]s against the reserved powers of the States, Congress may use any rational means to effectuate the constitutional prohibition of racial discrimination in voting. . . .
>
> The basic test to be applied in a case involving sec. 2 of the Fifteenth Amendment is the same as in all cases concerning the express powers of Congress with relation to the reserved powers of the states. Chief Justice Marshall laid down the classic formulation 50 years before the Fifteenth Amendment was ratified [citing *McCulloch v. Maryland*, in Chapter 2, above]. . . .
>
> We therefore reject South Carolina's argument that Congress may appropriately do no more than to forbid violations of the Fifteenth Amendment in general terms—that the task of fashioning specific remedies or of applying them to particular localities must necessarily be left entirely to the courts. Congress is not circumscribed by any such artificial rules under sec. 2 of the Fifteenth Amendment. . . .

KATZENBACH v. MORGAN
384 U.S. 641 (1966)

Mr. Justice Brennan delivered the opinion of the Court. . . .

[Section 4(e) of the Voting Rights Act of 1965 provides that a person who has completed the sixth grade in a Puerto Rican school in which the predominant language was not English may not be denied the right to vote in any election because of his or her inability to read or write English. This provision prohibited the enforcement of the election laws of New York, which required that a voter be able to read and write English. The appellees, registered voters in New York, challenged the constitutionality of that provision as applied, claiming that it exceeded the powers granted to Congress and usurped powers reserved to the States by the Tenth Amendment. A three-judge District Court for the District of Columbia, one judge dissenting, agreed with the appellees.

[The Supreme Court had earlier held that English literacy requirements did not violate the Fourteenth and Fifteenth Amendments. *Lassiter v. Northampton County Board of Election*, 360 U.S. 45 (1959). Nevertheless, in an opinion by Justice Brennan, the Court here upholds the congressional enactment of section 4(e).]

The Attorney General of the State of New York argues that an exercise of congressional power under § 5 of the Fourteenth Amendment that prohibits the enforcement of a state law can only be sustained if the judicial branch determines that the state law is prohibited by the provisions of the Amendment that Congress sought to enforce. More specifically, he urges that § 4(e) cannot be sustained as appropriate legislation to enforce the Equal Protection Clause unless the judiciary decides—even with the guidance of a congressional judgment—that the application of the English literacy requirement prohibited by § 4(e) is forbidden by the Equal Protection Clause itself. We disagree. Neither the language nor history of § 5 supports such a construction. As was said with regard to § 5 in *Ex parte Virginia*, 100 U.S. 339, 345, "It is the power of Congress which has been enlarged. Congress is authorized to *enforce* the prohibitions by appropriate legislation. Some legislation is contemplated to make the amendments fully effective." A construction of § 5 that would require a judicial determination that the enforcement of the state law precluded by Congress violated the Amendment [w]ould depreciate both congressional resourcefulness and congressional responsibility for implementing the Amendment. It would confine the legislative power in this context to the insignificant role of abrogating only those state laws that the judicial branch was prepared to adjudge unconstitutional, or of merely informing the judgment of the judiciary by particularizing the "majestic generalities" of § 1 of the Amendment.

Thus our task in this case is not to determine whether the New York English literacy requirement as applied to deny the right to vote to a person who successfully completed the sixth grade in a Puerto Rican school violates the Equal Protection Clause. Accordingly, our decision in *Lassiter v. Northampton County Bd. of Election*, sustaining the North Carolina English literacy requirement as not in all circumstances prohibited by the first sections of the Fourteenth and Fifteenth Amendments, is inopposite.

[L] *assiter* did not present the question before us here: Without regard to whether the judiciary would find that the Equal Protection Clause itself nullifies New York's English literacy requirement as so applied, could Congress prohibit the enforcement of the state law by legislating under § 5 of the Fourteenth Amendment? In answering this question, our task is limited to determining whether such legislation is, as required by § 5, appropriate legislation to enforce the Equal Protection Clause.

By including § 5 the draftsmen sought to grant to Congress, by a specific provision applicable to the Fourteenth Amendment, the same broad powers expressed in the Necessary and Proper Clause, Art. I, § 8, cl. 18. The classic formulation of the reach of those powers was established by Chief Justice Marshall in *McCulloch v. Maryland*. . . .

We therefore proceed to the consideration whether § 4(e) is "appropriate legislation" to enforce the Equal Protection Clause, that is, under the *McCulloch v. Maryland* standard, whether § 4(e) may be regarded as an enactment to enforce the Equal Protection Clause, whether it is "plainly adapted to that end" and whether it is not prohibited by but is consistent with "the letter and spirit of the constitution."

There can be no doubt that § 4(e) may be regarded as an enactment to enforce the Equal Protection Clause. [I]t was well within congressional authority to say that this need of the Puerto Rican minority for the vote warranted federal intrusion upon any state interests served by the English literacy requirement. [I]t is not for us to review the congressional resolution of these factors. It is enough that we be able to perceive a basis upon which the Congress might resolve the conflict as it did. There plainly was such a basis to support § 4(e) in the application in question in this case. . . .

NOTES AND QUESTIONS

(1) *Congressional Power to Remedy Judicially Defined Rights.* In *South Carolina v. Katzenbach,* the Court upheld the constitutionality of the Voting Rights Act of 1965 even though Congress went beyond simply providing for judicially enforceable remedies once a violation of civil rights was proven in the courts through litigation. Did the Court expand the traditional powers of Congress as against those reserved to the States under the Tenth Amendment? *Cf.* Buchanan, *Katzenbach v. Morgan and Congressional Enforcement Power under the Fourteenth Amendment: A Study in Conceptual Confusion,* 17 Hous. L. Rev. 69 (1979).

(2) *The Scope of Congressional Power to Formulate a Remedy.* In *Katzenbach v. Morgan,* the Court adopted a very low standard of review of Congress' determination. The Court stated that if it could "perceive a basis" for Congress' determination, that was sufficient to satisfy the constitutionality of the provision. In dissent, Justice Harlan argued that there was an insufficient legislative record upon which Congress could devise such a remedy. How much factual data had Congress actually collected? Professor Bickel contends that:

> The only relevant evidence cited (but not quoted, or even paraphrased) by the Court is the following letter received in 1962 by the Subcommittee on Constitutional Rights of the Senate Committee on the Judiciary, and incorporated in the record of hearings the subcommittee held in the course of that year on literacy tests and other voter qualifications.

The author of the letter wrote:

> I could write volumes on the cruelty, brutality, murder, mayhem and general abuse delivered upon the disfranchised Spanish-speaking citizens in New York by the various agencies of our Government, all of which is directly due to their disenfranchisement. Having no vote, they have no representation and no means of redress.

Bickel, *The Voting Rights Cases,* 1966 Sup. Ct. Rev. 79, 99 n.80.[*]

(3) *Should the Extent of Congress' Data Collection Matter?* There is much to suggest that Justice Harlan is incorrect in suggesting that "factual data" or "voluminous testimony" has been a precondition for upholding civil rights legislation. As Professor Cox has written:

> [Harlan's view] is at odds with the presumption of constitutionality and with a long line of precedents holding that a statute must be judged constitutional if any set of facts which can reasonably be conceived would sustain it. No case has ever held that a record is constitutionally required.

Cox, *Forward: Constitutional Adjudication and the Promotion of Human Rights,* 80 Harv. L. Rev. 91, 105 (1966). For example, the Court reaffirmed Congress' broad remedial power to enforce judicially determined rights in *Fullilove v. Klutznick* [in Chapter 10, above], in which the Court stated that Congress did not have to recite any preamblary "findings" when it had an "abundant historical basis."

(4) *Congressional Power to Define the Scope of Civil Rights.* Another rationale of the Court in *Morgan* was that Congress may have constitutionally determined that literacy tests were a violation of the Fourteenth Amendment, even though the Court had refused to so hold in *Lassiter v. Northampton Bd. of Election.* Reaction to this rationale

---

is fairly summarized in Gordon, *The Nature and Uses of Congressional Power Under Section Five of the Fourteenth Amendment to Overcome Decisions of the Supreme Court*, 72 Nw. U. L. Rev. 656, 657 (1977):

> The *Morgan* principle, as we shall refer to this holding, touched off a heated debate. Justices Harlan and Stewart, as well as constitutional scholars off the Court, were troubled by the suggestion that Congress might change a constitutional decision of the Court and the implications such a result would have on the judicial function as defined in *Marbury v. Madison*. Sympathetic commentators, on the other hand, envisioned *Morgan* as a charter for Congress to make a significant contribution to the cause of civil rights, and as a doctrinal tour de force whereby the tremendous resources of Congress could be creatively marshaled by the Court to deal with the bewildering problems of equal protection and due process.

Would the broad reading of *Morgan* suggested by the "sympathetic commentators" noted above be consistent with the limits on congressional powers enunciated in *McCulloch v. Maryland*?

(5) *The Arguable "One-Way Ratchet" Limitation of Congressional Power to Define Civil Rights*. In his dissenting opinion, Justice Harlan attacked the rationale of *Morgan* as also giving Congress the power to restrict the scope of substantive rights as defined by the Court. If Congress had power to redefine rights secured by the Constitution so as to expand them, perhaps it also had the power to restrict those rights. Justice Brennan's response to this criticism appeared in footnote 10 of his opinion for the Court:

> Contrary to the suggestion of the dissent, § 5 does not grant Congress power to exercise discretion in the other direction and to enact "statutes so as in effect to dilute equal protection and due process decisions of this Court." We emphasize that Congress' power under § 5 is limited to adopting measures to enforce the guarantees of the Amendment; § 5 grants Congress no power to restrict, abrogate, or dilute these guarantees. Thus, for example, an enactment authorizing the States to establish racially segregated systems of education would not be—as required by § 5—a measure "to enforce" the Equal Protection Clause since that clause of its own force prohibits such state laws.

For obvious reasons, this theory has been referred to as the "ratchet" or "one-way ratchet" doctrine. Is Justice Brennan correct in claiming that his holding limits Congress' power to expanding civil rights?

(6) *Problems in the Application of the One-Way Ratchet Limitation*. Even assuming the existence of a ratchet limitation, it may not be clear whether a particular congressional interpretation of the scope of substantive rights under the Fourteenth Amendment enlarges or restricts those rights. For example, Congress might enact a law that places constitutionally questionable restrictions on a woman's right to an abortion because it finds that the law is necessary to ensure the rights of the unborn. What guidelines should be used in determining whether Congress' interpretation is expansive or restrictive? Who should make this determination?

(7) *The Scope of Section One of the Fifteenth Amendment and State "Affirmative Action" Voting Programs: Rice v. Cayetano, 528 U.S. 495 (2000)*. The Hawaiian Constitution limited the eligible electorate for a state agency known as the Office of Hawaiian Affairs (OHA) to a subclass of all citizens of the state; only "Hawaiians" (*i.e.*, citizens not less than one half part of the races inhabiting the Islands before 1778) may vote in the OHA elections. Rice, a Hawaiian citizen without the requisite ancestry, sued under 42 U.S.C. § 1983. Although the lower courts sided with the State, the Supreme Court, per Justice Kennedy, reversed, agreeing with plaintiff Rice that the OHA voting eligibility scheme violated the Fifteenth Amendment.

The Court reasoned that the Hawaiian scheme explicitly limited the right to vote in a state election to a certain ancestry and that this "native" ancestry was a proxy for "race." Thus, the Fifteenth Amendment applied. The Court rejected the State's argument based on *Morton v. Mancari*, 417 U.S. 535 (1974), and limited the scope of that decision. (For certain Indian Law issues, this may have the consequence of undercutting the defense of various affirmative action programs.) Justices Breyer and Souter concurred in the result. Justices Stevens and Ginsburg dissented.

(8) *The Continuing Controversy Regarding Congressional Power to Define the Substantive Scope of Fourteenth Amendment Rights: Oregon v. Mitchell, 400 U.S. 112 (1970).* Between the *Morgan* and *Flores* (below) decisions, the Court decided a number of cases. In *Oregon v. Mitchell*, Congress had passed amendments to the Voting Rights Act that changed the voting age—in both federal and state elections—from 21 to 18. This was challenged by Oregon as outside the scope of the Section 5 power. In *Oregon v. Mitchell*, the Court held that Congress did not have the power to direct the States to lower their voting age for state elections.

The *Oregon* decision was highly splintered, and its analysis was complex. Its precedential value was, accordingly, questionable. In addition, *Oregon* has been superceded by the adoption of the "searching scrutiny" standard for Section 5 in *Flores* and subsequent decisions. The *Oregon* decision, however, was relied upon by Justice Kennedy's majority opinion in *Flores*, below. For that reason, it is noted here.

(9) *The Ongoing Question of Congress' Power to Define Substantive Constitutional Rights.* After *Oregon v. Mitchell* and *Morgan*, what is the status of Congress' power to determine the scope of the rights guaranteed by the Fourteenth and Fifteenth Amendments?

PROBLEM A

THE "HUMAN LIFE STATUTE." The following "Human Life Statute" was proposed in Congress in 1981 and again in 1983 in the form of the Helms-Hyde Bill, S. 158, H.R. 900. It has not been passed for lack of support and for doubts about its constitutionality. If Congress did pass the statute, what would be its effect in the wake of *Morgan, Mitchell*, and other cases?

SECTION I. The Congress finds that present-day scientific evidence indicates a significant likelihood that actual human life exists from conception.

The Congress further finds that the Fourteenth Amendment to the Constitution of the United States was intended to protect all human beings.

Upon the basis of these findings, and in the exercise of the powers of the Congress, including its powers under section 5 of the Fourteenth Amendment to the Constitution of the United States, the Congress hereby declares that for the purpose of enforcing the obligation of the States under the Fourteenth Amendment not to deprive persons of life without due process of law, human life shall be deemed to exist from conception, without regard to race, sex, age, health, defect, or condition of dependency; and for this purpose "person" shall include all human life as defined herein.

Among the issues you should consider in assessing the effect of the law are the following:

(1) *The "One-Way Ratchet" Theory: "Dilution" or "Expansion?"* Does the Bill dilute the constitutional rights of women, or enlarge the rights of unborn fetuses? If it does both, who should reconcile these competing constitutional considerations?

(2) *What Significance for Congress' "Superior Fact-Finding Ability?"* Is Congress' "finding" that human life begins at conception based upon its superior fact finding ability, or is it primarily a value judgment? Should this matter?

CITY OF BOERNE, TEXAS v. FLORES
521 U.S. 507 (1997)

JUSTICE KENNEDY delivered the opinion of the Court.

A decision by local zoning authorities to deny a church a building permit was challenged under the Religious Freedom Restoration Act of 1993 (RFRA). The case calls into question the authority of Congress to enact RFRA. We conclude the statute exceeds Congress' power.

[A Roman Catholic parish in the city of Boerne (which rhymes with "journey") had outgrown its 1923 building and sought to construct an addition. The city denied a building permit because of an historic preservation ordinance. The parish challenged the ordinance under several theories, including RFRA. Although the District Court had concluded that RFRA was unconstitutional, the court of appeals had upheld RFRA. Here, the Supreme Court reverses the Court of Appeals and holds RFRA unconstitutional.]

II

Congress enacted RFRA in direct response to the Court's decision in *Employment Div. v. Smith*, 494 U.S. 872 (1990) [*see* Chapter 12, above]. There we considered a Free Exercise Clause claim brought by members of the Native American Church who were denied unemployment benefits when they lost their jobs because they had used peyote. In evaluating the claim, we declined to apply the [strict scrutiny] test set forth in *Sherbert v. Verner*, 374 U.S. 398 (1963) [also in Chapter 12], under which we would have asked whether Oregon's prohibition substantially burdened a religious practice and, if it did, whether the burden was justified by a compelling government interest. . . .

Smith held that neutral, generally applicable laws may be applied to religious practices even when not supported by a compelling governmental interest.

Four Members of the Court disagreed. They argued the law placed a substantial burden on the Native American Church members so that it could be upheld only if the law served a compelling state interest and was narrowly tailored to achieve that end. . . . These points of constitutional interpretation were debated by Members of Congress in hearings and floor debates. Many criticized the Court's reasoning, and this disagreement resulted in the passage of RFRA. . . .

RFRA [is excerpted in the last section of Chapter 12; it] prohibits "[g]overnment" from "substantially burden[ing]" a person's exercise of religion even if the burden results from a rule of general applicability unless the government can demonstrate the burden "(1) is in furtherance of a compelling governmental interest; and (2) is the least restrictive means of furthering that compelling governmental interest." The Act's mandate applies to any "branch, department, agency, instrumentality, and official (or other person acting under color of law) of the United States," as well as to any "State, or . . . subdivision of a State." . . .

III

A

Under our Constitution, the Federal Government is one of enumerated powers. *McCulloch v. Maryland*, 4 Wheat. 316 (1819); see also The Federalist No. 45, p. 292 (C. Rossiter ed. 1961) (J. Madison). The judicial authority to determine the constitutionality of laws, in cases and controversies, is based on the premise that the "powers of the legislature are defined and limited; and that those limits may not be mistaken, or forgotten, the constitution is written." *Marbury v. Madison*, 1 Cranch 137 (1803).

Congress relied on its Fourteenth Amendment enforcement power in enacting the

Congress relied on 14th Am. enforcement power

most far-reaching and substantial of RFRA's provisions, those which impose its requirements on the States. The Fourteenth Amendment provides, in relevant part: . . . "Section 5. The Congress shall have power to enforce, by appropriate legislation, the provisions of this article."

In defense of the Act respondent contends, with support from the United States as amicus, that RFRA is permissible enforcement legislation. Congress, it is said, is only protecting by legislation one of the liberties guaranteed by the Fourteenth Amendment's Due Process Clause, the free exercise of religion, beyond what is necessary under *Smith*. It is said the congressional decision to dispense with proof of deliberate or overt discrimination and instead concentrate on a law's effects accords with the settled understanding that § 5 includes the power to enact legislation designed to prevent as well as remedy constitutional violations. It is further contended that Congress' § 5 power is not limited to remedial or preventive legislation.

All must acknowledge that § 5 is "a positive grant of legislative power" to Congress. *Katzenbach v. Morgan*, 384 U.S. 641 (1966). . . .

Legislation which deters or remedies constitutional violations can fall within the sweep of Congress' enforcement power even if in the process it prohibits conduct which is not itself unconstitutional and intrudes into "legislative spheres of autonomy previously reserved to the States." *Fitzpatrick v. Bitzer*, 427 U.S. 445 (1976).

It is also true, however, that "[a]s broad as the congressional enforcement power is, it is not unlimited." *Oregon v. Mitchell* (opinion of Black, J.). In assessing the breadth of § 5's enforcement power, we begin with its text. Congress has been given the power "to enforce" the "provisions of this article." . . .

textual argument

Congress' power under § 5 . . . extends only to "enforc[ing]" the provisions of the Fourteenth Amendment. The Court has described this power as "remedial," *South Carolina v. Katzenbach*. The design of the Amendment and the text of § 5 are inconsistent with the suggestion that Congress has the power to decree the substance of the Fourteenth Amendment's restrictions on the States. Legislation which alters the meaning of the Free Exercise Clause cannot be said to be enforcing the Clause. ✳ Congress does not enforce a constitutional right by changing what the right is. It has been given the power "to enforce," not the power to determine what constitutes a constitutional violation. Were it not so, what Congress would be enforcing would no longer be, in any meaningful sense, the "provisions of [the Fourteenth Amendment]."

While the line between measures that remedy or prevent unconstitutional actions and measures that make a substantive change in the governing law is not easy to discern, and Congress must have wide latitude in determining where it lies, the distinction exists and must be observed. There must be a congruence and proportionality between the injury to be prevented or remedied and the means adopted to that end. . . .

1

The Fourteenth Amendment's history confirms the remedial, rather than substantive, nature of the Enforcement Clause. The Joint Committee on Reconstruction of the 39th Congress began drafting what would become the Fourteenth Amendment in January 1866. The objections to the Committee's first draft of the Amendment [the Bingham draft, which granted broad power to Congress to legislate protections of citizens], and the rejection of the draft, have a direct bearing on the central issue of defining Congress' enforcement power. . . .

As a result of these objections having been expressed from so many different quarters, the House voted to table the [Bingham draft] until April. The congressional action was seen as marking the defeat of the proposal. The Amendment in its early form was not again considered. Instead, the Joint Committee began drafting a new article of Amendment, which it reported to Congress on April 30, 1866.

remedial not plenary

Section 1 of the new draft Amendment imposed self-executing limits on the States. Section 5 prescribed that "[t]he Congress shall have power to enforce, by appropriate legislation, the provisions of this article." Under the revised Amendment, Congress' power was no longer plenary but remedial. Congress was granted the power to make the substantive constitutional prohibitions against the States effective. . . . After revisions not relevant here, the new measure passed both Houses and was ratified in July 1868 as the Fourteenth Amendment.

The significance of the defeat of the Bingham draft was apparent even then. . . .

The design of the Fourteenth Amendment has proved significant also in maintaining the traditional separation of powers between Congress and the Judiciary. The first eight Amendments to the Constitution set forth self-executing prohibitions on governmental action, and this Court has had primary authority to interpret those prohibitions. The Bingham draft, some thought, departed from that tradition by vesting in Congress primary power to interpret and elaborate on the meaning of the new Amendment through legislation. . . . As enacted, the Fourteenth Amendment confers substantive rights against the States which, like the provisions of the Bill of Rights, are self-executing. The power to interpret the Constitution in a case or controversy remains in the Judiciary.

2

S.C. v. Katzenbach

The remedial and preventive nature of Congress' enforcement power, and the limitation inherent in the power, were confirmed in our earliest cases on the Fourteenth Amendment. . . .

Recent cases have continued to revolve around the question of whether § 5 legislation can be considered remedial. In *South Carolina v. Katzenbach, supra*, we emphasized that "[t]he constitutional propriety of [legislation adopted under the Enforcement Clause] must be judged with reference to the historical experience . . . it reflects." . . .

After *South Carolina v. Katzenbach*, the Court continued to acknowledge the necessity of using strong remedial and preventive measures to respond to the widespread and persisting deprivation of constitutional rights resulting from this country's history of racial discrimination. . . .

3

Any suggestion that Congress has a substantive, non-remedial power under the Fourteenth Amendment is not supported by our case law. In *Oregon v. Mitchell*, a majority of the Court concluded Congress had exceeded its enforcement powers by enacting legislation lowering the minimum age of voters from 21 to 18 in state and local elections. The five Members of the Court who reached this conclusion explained that the legislation intruded into an area reserved by the Constitution to the States. . . .

There is language in our opinion in *Katzenbach v. Morgan*, 384 U.S. 641 (1966), which could be interpreted as acknowledging a power in Congress to enact legislation that expands the rights contained in § 1 of the Fourteenth Amendment. This is not a necessary interpretation, however, or even the best one. . . . Both rationales for upholding [the Congressional action in *Morgan*] rested on unconstitutional discrimination by New York and Congress' reasonable attempt to combat it. . . .

If Congress could define its own powers by altering the Fourteenth Amendment's meaning, no longer would the Constitution be "superior paramount law, unchangeable by ordinary means." It would be "on a level with ordinary legislative acts, and, like other acts, . . . alterable when the legislature shall please to alter it." *Marbury v. Madison*. Under this approach, it is difficult to conceive of a principle that would limit congressional power. Shifting legislative majorities could change the Constitution and effectively circumvent the difficult and detailed amendment process contained in Article V.

We now turn to consider whether RFRA can be considered enforcement legislation under § 5 of the Fourteenth Amendment.

B

Respondent contends that RFRA is a proper exercise of Congress' remedial or preventive power. The Act, it is said, is a reasonable means of protecting the free exercise of religion as defined by *Smith*. . . .

[margin note: resp. arg.]

While preventive rules are sometimes appropriate remedial measures, there must be a congruence between the means used and the ends to be achieved. The appropriateness of remedial measures must be considered in light of the evil presented. Strong measures appropriate to address one harm may be an unwarranted response to another, lesser one.

A comparison between RFRA and the Voting Rights Act is instructive. In contrast to the record which confronted Congress and the judiciary in the voting rights cases, RFRA's legislative record lacks examples of modern instances of generally applicable laws passed because of religious bigotry. The history of persecution in this country detailed in the hearings mentions no episodes occurring in the past 40 years. . . .

[margin note: no evid. unlike the Voting Rights Act]

It is difficult to maintain that [the laws that prompted RFRA] are examples of legislation enacted or enforced due to animus or hostility to the burdened religious practices or that they indicate some widespread pattern of religious discrimination in this country. Congress' concern was with the incidental burdens imposed, not the object or purpose of the legislation. This lack of support in the legislative record, however, is not RFRA's most serious shortcoming. . . .

Regardless of the state of the legislative record, RFRA cannot be considered remedial, preventive legislation, if those terms are to have any meaning. RFRA is so out of proportion to a supposed remedial or preventive object that it cannot be understood as responsive to, or designed to prevent, unconstitutional behavior. It appears, instead, to attempt a substantive change in constitutional protections. Preventive measures prohibiting certain types of laws may be appropriate when there is reason to believe that many of the laws affected by the congressional enactment have a significant likelihood of being unconstitutional. . . .

The stringent test RFRA demands of state laws reflects a lack of proportionality or congruence between the means adopted and the legitimate end to be achieved. If an objector can show a substantial burden on his free exercise, the State must demonstrate a compelling governmental interest and show that the law is the least restrictive means of furthering its interest. Claims that a law substantially burdens someone's exercise of religion will often be difficult to contest. . . . We make these observations not to reargue the position of the majority in *Smith* but to illustrate the substantive alteration of its holding attempted by RFRA. . . . This is a considerable congressional intrusion into the States' traditional prerogatives and general authority to regulate for the health and welfare of their citizens.

[margin note: test RFRA applies to state laws is wrong]

The substantial costs RFRA exacts, both in practical terms of imposing a heavy litigation burden on the States and in terms of curtailing their traditional general regulatory power, far exceed any pattern or practice of unconstitutional conduct under the Free Exercise Clause as interpreted in *Smith*. Simply put, RFRA is not designed to identify and counteract state laws likely to be unconstitutional because of their treatment of religion. In most cases, the state laws to which RFRA applies are not ones which will have been motivated by religious bigotry. . . . When the exercise of religion has been burdened in an incidental way by a law of general application, it does not follow that the persons affected have been burdened any more than other citizens, let alone burdened because of their religious beliefs. In addition, the Act imposes in every case a least restrictive means requirement—a requirement that was not used in the pre-*Smith* jurisprudence RFRA purported to codify—which also indicates that the legislation is broader than is appropriate if the goal is to prevent and remedy constitutional violations. . . .

. . . When the Court has interpreted the Constitution, it has acted within the province of the Judicial Branch, which embraces the duty to say what the law is. *Marbury v. Madison*, 1 Cranch, at 177. When the political branches of the Government act against the background of a judicial interpretation of the Constitution already issued, it must be understood that in later cases and controversies the Court will treat its precedents with the respect due them under settled principles, including stare decisis, and contrary expectations must be disappointed. RFRA was designed to control cases and controversies, such as the one before us; but as the provisions of the federal statute here invoked are beyond congressional authority, it is this Court's precedent, not RFRA, which must control.

. . . Broad as the power of Congress is under the Enforcement Clause of the Fourteenth Amendment, RFRA contradicts vital principles necessary to maintain separation of powers and the federal balance. The judgment of the Court of Appeals sustaining the Act's constitutionality is reversed.

JUSTICE STEVENS, concurring.

In my opinion, the Religious Freedom Restoration Act of 1993 (RFRA) is a "law respecting an establishment of religion" that violates the First Amendment to the Constitution. . . .

JUSTICE SCALIA, with whom JUSTICE STEVENS joins, concurring in part.

I write to respond briefly to the claim of Justice O'Connor's dissent (hereinafter "the dissent") that historical materials support a result contrary to the one reached in *Employment Div. v. Smith*. . . . The material that the dissent claims is at odds with *Smith* either has little to say about the issue or is in fact more consistent with *Smith* than with the dissent's interpretation of the Free Exercise Clause. . . .

JUSTICE O'CONNOR, with whom JUSTICE BREYER joins except as to a portion of Part I, dissenting.

[A]s a yardstick for measuring the constitutionality of RFRA, the Court uses its holding in *Employment Div. v. Smith*, the decision that prompted Congress to enact RFRA as a means of more rigorously enforcing the Free Exercise Clause. I remain of the view that *Smith* was wrongly decided, and I would use this case to reexamine the Court's holding there. . . .

I agree with much of the reasoning set forth in Part III-A of the Court's opinion. Indeed, if I agreed with the Court's standard in Smith, I would join the opinion. . . . In short, Congress lacks the ability independently to define or expand the scope of constitutional rights by statute. Accordingly, whether Congress has exceeded its § 5 powers turns on whether there is a "congruence and proportionality between the injury to be prevented or remedied and the means adopted to that end." . . .

[JUSTICES SOUTER and BREYER also dissented.]

NOTES AND QUESTIONS

(1) *Congressional Power Under § 5 of the Fourteenth Amendment and RFRA: City of Boerne v. Flores, 521 U.S. 507 (1997).* The Court here identifies two major flaws in RFRA. First, for an enforcement measure to be valid under § 5, it must have "congruence between the means used and the ends to be achieved." Under this

congruence or proportionality test, "RFRA is so out of proportion to a supposed remedial or preventive object that it cannot be understood as responsive to, or designed to prevent, unconstitutional behavior." The second flaw appears to be that, with the passage of RFRA, Congress invaded the "province of the Judicial Branch" and violated the separation of powers doctrine. The majority determined that "RFRA was designed to control cases and controversies . . .; but as the provisions of the federal statute here invoked are beyond congressional authority, it is this Court's precedent, not RFRA, which must control." The Court determined that Congress could not overturn one of the Court's constitutional rulings by a mere statute. Is either (or are both) of these arguments persuasive? *See* Eugene Gressman, *The Necessary and Proper Downfall of RFRA*, 2 NEXUS 73 (1997).

(2) *Flores as a Limitation on Morgan.* The *Morgan* decision, as you saw above, treated the § 5 power as a plenary power of Congress and, accordingly, reviewed its exercise by Congress with the deferential rational basis standard. *Flores* rejected the interpretation in *Morgan*: "This is not a necessary interpretation, however, or even the best one. . . ." The *Flores* Court, thirty years after *Morgan*, decided that the § 5 power was not a plenary power. The *Flores* Court then applied the congruence and proportionality standard which, while somewhat ambiguous, was clearly a higher level of scrutiny than rational basis.

The Court's determination that the § 5 power was not a "plenary power" was controversial. The Court's analysis seemed inconsistent not only with the *Morgan* Court but also with the text. The Framers of the Fourteenth Amendment used the term "by appropriate legislation," and the term "appropriate" derived from the *McCulloch* decision [Ch. 2]—the seminal plenary powers decision. For a review of the Framers' reliance on the *McCulloch* decision in designing the Enforcement powers, *see* AKHIL REED AMAR, AMERICA'S CONSTITUTION 351–401 (2005).

(3) *Some Implications of Flores: What About Congressional "Affirmative Action" Efforts Under Section 5?* As is noted below with the *Adarand Constructors* decision, an important issue in the Court's "affirmative action" jurisprudence concerns the scope of Congressional authority under § 5, particularly the issue whether Congress may require State and local governments to use racial or gender diversity as a decision-making factor in employment or awarding government contracts. After *Flores*, can racial or gender "diversity" requirements be considered constitutionally appropriate "enforcement" measures? After *Flores*, what record of a need for a "remedy" will be sufficient to satisfy the "congruence and proportionality" test for § 5?

ADARAND CONSTRUCTORS INC. v. PENA, 515 U.S. 200 (1995). This affirmative action decision is set forth in § 10.03[6] above, but it should also be considered here. The Congressional program in *Adarand* provided a financial incentive to prime contractors for federal highway projects who hired subcontractors which qualified, under federal regulations, as Disadvantaged Business Enterprises ("DBE's"). Also, the federal regulations imposed a (rebuttable) presumption that subcontractors who were racial minorities or women would qualify as DBE's.

The primary issue in *Adarand* was what level of judicial scrutiny would be applied: the *J.A. Croson*, 488 U.S. 469 (1989), decision's use of *strict scrutiny* (for state affirmative action programs) or the *Metro Broadcasting*, 497 U.S. 547 (1990), decision's use of *intermediate scrutiny* (for Congressional programs). The *Adarand* majority, per Justice O'Connor, explicitly overruled *Metro Broadcasting* and held that Congressional affirmative action programs must meet the demanding burdens of the strict scrutiny standard.

For present purposes, the *Adarand* decision apparently leaves open the issue whether, under § 5 of the Fourteenth Amendment, Congress may employ the "One-Way Ratchet" theory. (The program in *Adarand* was established by Congress as an exercise of the Commerce and Spending Powers. *See* § 2.02 above.) Justice Souter's dissent in *Adarand* observed that "it is worth noting that nothing in today's opinion implies any view of Congress' § 5 power and the deference due its exercise . . ." Should Congress receive more deference when it exercises its § 5 power than when it exercises one of its Art. I, § 8 plenary powers? Does *Adarand*, by requiring strict scrutiny, narrow the scope of Congressional power, even under § 5 of the Fourteenth Amendment?

NOTES AND QUESTIONS

(1) *Developments Regarding Congressional Enforcement Powers: Florida Prepaid Postsecondary Education Expense Board v. College Savings Bank, 527 U.S. 627 (1999).* After the *Flores* decision, above, the Supreme Court applied and developed its standards for determining the constitutionality of Congressional action under the Reconstruction Amendments. In *College Savings Bank*, Congress had passed the Patent Remedy Act and expressly abrogated the State's Eleventh Amendment immunity for patent infringement. [*See* § 3.06 above.] While the Court, per Chief Justice Rehnquist, recognized that Congress had sufficiently expressed its intent to abrogate, the Court held that Congress did not validly exercise its § 5 power under the Due Process Clause.

The Court applied the "congruence and proportionality" test from *Flores*. More importantly, the Court restated the § 5 standard: "to invoke § 5, [Congress] must identify the conduct transgressing the Fourteenth Amendment's substantive provisions, and must tailor its legislative scheme to remedying or preventing such conduct . . .." The Court determined that Congress had failed both the "identification" prong and the "tailoring" prong of this standard. The *College Savings Bank* standard appears to be a higher standard than the *Flores* "congruence and proportionality" standard. Justices Stevens, Souter, Ginsburg and Breyer dissented.

(2) *Further Refinement of the § 5 Standard: United States v. Morrison, 529 U.S. 598 (2000).* [You have examined *Morrison* in § 2.02 above; this Note focuses on *Morrison's* holding regarding Congressional power under § 5.] In *Morrison*, Congress had created, pursuant to § 5, a private federal civil cause of action against persons who commit crimes of violence "motivated by gender." Proponents saw the Violence Against Women Act (VAWA) as the equivalent of the Civil Rights Act of 1964. The Supreme Court, per Chief Justice Rehnquist, held that the § 5 power of Congress was not sufficient to sustain this provision of the VAWA.

In reviewing the exercise of § 5 power, the Court applied the standard from *College Savings Bank* above: (1) sufficient identification of state action transgressing the Fourteenth Amendment; and (2) appropriate tailoring of the remedy to fit the "evil" identified. The majority found that Congress had sufficiently identified a problem of gender motivated violence, but that Congress failed the tailoring requirement by using overbroad means. The same four Justices from *College Savings Bank* dissented, although the dissenters focused primarily on the Commerce Clause issue.

BOARD OF TRUSTEES OF THE UNIVERSITY OF ALABAMA v. GARRETT
531 U.S. 356 (2001)

CHIEF JUSTICE REHNQUIST delivered the opinion of the Court.

[Two state employees brought separate actions under the Americans with Disabilities Act ("ADA") against state entities which were their respective employers. For present purposes, you should understand that the ADA prohibits certain employers (including a State) from discriminating against qualified individuals because of a disability. To this end, the ADA requires employers to make "reasonable accommodations" unless the employer demonstrates that such an accommodation would impose an "undue hardship" on the employer.

Garrett, a registered nurse, was diagnosed with breast cancer and underwent various therapies; upon her return, the University Hospital required her to give up her position for a lower paying job. Plaintiff Ash suffered from chronic asthma and requested that his state employer adjust his duties to minimize exposure to cigarette smoke. His state employer refused to make any accommodations.

The state of Alabama moved for summary judgment based on the Eleventh Amendment. Although the court of appeals had held that Congress had validly abrogated the Eleventh Amendment with the ADA, the Supreme Court here reversed. The Eleventh Amendment aspects of this opinion are noted in § 3.06 above. The focus here is on the Court's discussion of the scope of Congressional power under § 5 of the Fourteenth Amendment.]

We decide here whether employees of the State of Alabama may recover money damages by reason of the State's failure to comply with the provisions of Title I of the Americans with Disabilities Act of 1990 (ADA or Act). We hold that such suits are barred by the Eleventh Amendment. . . .

I

Although by its terms the [Eleventh] Amendment applies only to suits against a State by citizens of another State, our cases have extended the Amendment's applicability to suits by citizens against their own States. The ultimate guarantee of the Eleventh Amendment is that nonconsenting States may not be sued by private individuals in federal court.

We have recognized, however, that Congress may abrogate the States' Eleventh Amendment immunity when it both unequivocally intends to do so and "act[s] pursuant to a valid grant of constitutional authority." The first of these requirements is not in dispute here. The question, then, is whether Congress acted within its constitutional authority by subjecting the States to suits in federal court for money damages under the ADA.

Congress may not, of course, base its abrogation of the States' Eleventh Amendment immunity upon the powers enumerated in Article I. . . . As a result, we concluded, Congress may subject nonconsenting States to suit in federal court when it does so pursuant to a valid exercise of its § 5 power. Our cases have adhered to this proposition. Accordingly, the ADA can apply to the States only to the extent that the statute is appropriate § 5 legislation.

Section 1 of the Fourteenth Amendment provides, in relevant part:

> "No State shall make or enforce any law which shall abridge the privileges or immunities of citizens of the United States; nor shall any State deprive any person of life, liberty, or property, without due process of law; nor deny to any person within its jurisdiction the equal protection of the laws."

Section 5 of the Fourteenth Amendment grants Congress the power to enforce the substantive guarantees contained in § 1 by enacting "appropriate legislation." See *City of Boerne v. Flores*, 521 U.S. 507 (1997). Congress is not limited to mere legislative repetition of this Court's constitutional jurisprudence. "Rather, Congress' power 'to enforce' the Amendment includes the authority both to remedy and to deter violation of rights guaranteed thereunder by prohibiting a somewhat broader swath of conduct, including that which is not itself forbidden by the Amendment's text."

City of Boerne also confirmed, however, the long-settled principle that it is the responsibility of this Court, not Congress, to define the substance of constitutional guarantees. Accordingly, § 5 legislation reaching beyond the scope of § 1's actual guarantees must exhibit "congruence and proportionality between the injury to be prevented or remedied and the means adopted to that end."

II

The first step in applying these now familiar principles is to identify with some precision the scope of the constitutional right at issue. Here, that inquiry requires us to examine the limitations § 1 of the Fourteenth Amendment places upon States' treatment of the disabled. As we did last Term in *Kimel*, we look to our prior decisions under the Equal Protection Clause dealing with this issue.

In *Cleburne v. Cleburne Living Center, Inc.*, 473 U.S. 432 (1985), [we concluded] that such legislation incurs only the minimum "rational-basis" review applicable to general social and economic legislation.. . . .

Under rational-basis review, where a group possesses "distinguishing characteristics relevant to interests the State has the authority to implement," a State's decision to act on the basis of those differences does not give rise to a constitutional violation. . . .

Thus, the result of *Cleburne* is that States are not required by the Fourteenth Amendment to make special accommodations for the disabled, so long as their actions towards such individuals are rational. They could quite hard headedly—and perhaps hardheartedly—hold to job-qualification requirements which do not make allowance for the disabled. If special accommodations for the disabled are to be required, they have to come from positive law and not through the Equal Protection Clause.[1]

III

Once we have determined the metes and bounds of the constitutional right in question, we examine whether Congress identified a history and pattern of unconstitutional employment discrimination by the States against the disabled. Just as § 1 of the Fourteenth Amendment applies only to actions committed "under color of state law," Congress' § 5 authority is appropriately exercised only in response to state transgressions. The legislative record of the ADA, however, simply fails to show that Congress did in fact identify a pattern of irrational state discrimination in employment against the disabled.. . . .

Several of these incidents undoubtedly evidence an unwillingness on the part of state officials to make the sort of accommodations for the disabled required by the ADA. Whether they were irrational under our decision in *Cleburne* is more debatable, particularly when the incident is described out of context. But even if it were to be determined that each incident upon fuller examination showed unconstitutional action on the part of the State, these incidents taken together fall far short of even suggesting the pattern of unconstitutional discrimination on which § 5 legislation must be based.. . .

Even were it possible to squeeze out of these examples a pattern of unconstitutional discrimination by the States, the rights and remedies created by the ADA against the States would raise the same sort of concerns as to congruence and proportionality as were found in *City of Boerne, supra*. For example, whereas it would be entirely rational (and therefore constitutional) for a state employer to conserve scarce financial resources by hiring employees who are able to use existing facilities, the ADA requires employers to "mak[e] existing facilities used by employees readily accessible to and usable by individuals with disabilities." The ADA does except employers from the "reasonable accommodatio[n]" requirement where the employer "can demonstrate that the accommodation would impose an undue hardship on the operation of the business of such covered entity." However, even with this exception, the accommodation duty far exceeds what is constitutionally required in that it makes unlawful a range of alternate responses that would be reasonable but would fall short of imposing an "undue burden" upon the employer. The Act also makes it the employer's duty to prove that it would suffer such a burden, instead of requiring (as the Constitution does) that the complaining party negate reasonable bases for the employer's decision.

The ADA also forbids "utilizing standards, criteria, or methods of administration"

---

[1] It is worth noting that by the time that Congress enacted the ADA in 1990, every State in the Union had enacted such measures. At least one Member of Congress remarked that "this is probably one of the few times where the States are so far out in front of the Federal Government, it's not funny."

that disparately impact the disabled, without regard to whether such conduct has a rational basis. § 12112(b)(3)(A). Although disparate impact may be relevant evidence of racial discrimination, see *Washington v. Davis*, 426 U.S. 229 (1976), such evidence alone is insufficient even where the Fourteenth Amendment subjects state action to strict scrutiny.

The ADA's constitutional shortcomings are apparent when the Act is compared to Congress' efforts in the Voting Rights Act of 1965 to respond to a serious pattern of constitutional violations. . . . [See *South Carolina v. Katzenbach*, 383 U.S. 301 (1966)].

In [the Voting Rights Act], Congress documented a marked pattern of unconstitutional action by the States. State officials, Congress found, routinely applied voting tests in order to exclude African-American citizens from registering to vote. Congress also determined that litigation had proved ineffective and that there persisted an otherwise inexplicable 50-percentage-point gap in the registration of white and African-American voters in some States. Congress' response was to promulgate in the Voting Rights Act a detailed but limited remedial scheme designed to guarantee meaningful enforcement of the Fifteenth Amendment in those areas of the Nation where abundant evidence of States' systematic denial of those rights was identified.

The contrast between this kind of evidence, and the evidence that Congress considered in the present case, is stark. Congressional enactment of the ADA represents its judgment that there should be a "comprehensive national mandate for the elimination of discrimination against individuals with disabilities." Congress is the final authority as to desirable public policy, but in order to authorize private individuals to recover money damages against the States, there must be a pattern of discrimination by the States which violates the Fourteenth Amendment, and the remedy imposed by Congress must be congruent and proportional to the targeted violation. Those requirements are not met here, and to uphold the Act's application to the States would allow Congress to rewrite the Fourteenth Amendment law laid down by this Court in *Cleburne*.[2] Section 5 does not so broadly enlarge congressional authority.

no pattern?
→no authority!

Reversed.

JUSTICE KENNEDY, with whom JUSTICE O'CONNOR joins, concurring. . . .

One of the undoubted achievements of statutes designed to assist those with impairments is that citizens have an incentive, flowing from a legal duty, to develop a better understanding, a more decent perspective, for accepting persons with impairments or disabilities into the larger society. The law works this way because the law can be a teacher. So I do not doubt that the Americans with Disabilities Act of 1990 will be a milestone on the path to a more decent, tolerant, progressive society.

It is a question of quite a different order, however, to say that the States in their official capacities, the States as governmental entities, must be held in violation of the Constitution on the assumption that they embody the misconceived or malicious perceptions of some of their citizens. . . .

---

[2] Our holding here that Congress did not validly abrogate the States' sovereign immunity from suit by private individuals for money damages under Title I does not mean that persons with disabilities have no federal recourse against discrimination. Title I of the ADA still prescribes standards applicable to the States. Those standards can be enforced by the United States in actions for money damages, as well as by private individuals in actions for injunctive relief under *Ex parte Young*, 209 U.S. 123 (1908). In addition, state laws protecting the rights of persons with disabilities in employment and other aspects of life provide independent avenues of redress.

JUSTICE BREYER, with whom JUSTICE STEVENS, JUSTICE SOUTER and JUSTICE GINSBURG join, dissenting.

Reviewing the congressional record as if it were an administrative agency record, the Court holds the statutory provision before us, 42 U.S.C. § 1220 2, unconstitutional. The Court concludes that Congress assembled insufficient evidence of unconstitutional discrimination, that Congress improperly attempted to "re-write" the law we established in *Cleburne v. Cleburne Living Center, Inc.*, and that the law is not sufficiently tailored to address unconstitutional discrimination.

Section 5, however, grants Congress the "power to enforce, by appropriate legislation" the Fourteenth Amendment's equal protection guarantee. U.S. Const., Amdt. 14, § 5. As the Court recognizes, state discrimination in employment against persons with disabilities might "'run afoul of the Equal Protection Clause'" where there is no "'rational relationship between the disparity of treatment and some legitimate governmental purpose.'" In my view, Congress reasonably could have concluded that the remedy before us constitutes an "appropriate" way to enforce this basic equal protection requirement. And that is all the Constitution requires. . ..

The evidence in the legislative record bears out Congress' finding that the adverse treatment of persons with disabilities was often arbitrary or invidious in this sense, and thus unjustified. . . . A complete listing of the hundreds of examples of discrimination by state and local governments that were submitted to the task force is set forth in Appendix C. Congress could have reasonably believed that these examples represented signs of a widespread problem of unconstitutional discrimination.

II

The Court's failure to find sufficient evidentiary support may well rest upon its decision to hold Congress to a strict, judicially created evidentiary standard, particularly in respect to lack of justification. . . .

The problem with the Court's approach is that neither the "burden of proof" that favors States nor any other rule of restraint applicable to *judges* applies to *Congress* when it exercises its § 5 power. . . . Rational-basis review—with its presumptions favoring constitutionality—is "a paradigm of *judicial* restraint." *FCC v. Beach Communications, Inc.*, 508 U.S. 307, 314 (1993) (emphasis added). And the Congress of the United States is not a lower court.

There is simply no reason to require Congress, seeking to determine facts relevant to the exercise of its § 5 authority, to adopt rules or presumptions that reflect a court's institutional limitations. Unlike courts, Congress can readily gather facts from across the Nation, assess the magnitude of a problem, and more easily find an appropriate remedy. Unlike courts, Congress directly reflects public attitudes and beliefs, enabling Congress better to understand where, and to what extent, refusals to accommodate a disability amount to behavior that is callous or unreasonable to the point of lacking constitutional justification. Unlike judges, Members of Congress can directly obtain information from constituents who have first-hand experience with discrimination and related issues.

Moreover, unlike judges, Members of Congress are elected. When the Court has applied the majority's burden of proof rule, it has explained that we, *i.e.*, the courts, do not "'sit as a superlegislature to judge the wisdom or desirability of legislative policy determinations.'" To apply a rule designed to restrict courts as if it restricted Congress' legislative power is to stand the underlying principle—a principle of judicial restraint—on its head. But without the use of this burden of proof rule or some other unusually stringent standard of review, it is difficult to see how the Court can find the legislative record here inadequate. Read with a reasonably favorable eye, the record indicates that state governments subjected those with disabilities to seriously adverse, disparate treatment. And Congress could have found, in a significant number of instances, that this treatment violated the substantive principles of justification—shorn of their judicial-restraint-related presumptions—that this Court recognized in *Cleburne*. . ..

IV

The Court's harsh review of Congress' use of its § 5 power is reminiscent of the similar (now-discredited) limitation that it once imposed upon Congress' Commerce Clause power. . . .

The Court, through its evidentiary demands, its non-deferential review, and its failure to distinguish between judicial and legislative constitutional competencies, improperly invades a power that the Constitution assigns to Congress. Its decision saps § 5 of independent force, effectively "confin[ing] the legislative power . . . to the insignificant role of abrogating only those state laws that the judicial branch [is] prepared to adjudge unconstitutional." Whether the Commerce Clause does or does not enable Congress to enact this provision, in my view, § 5 gives Congress the necessary authority.

NOTES AND QUESTIONS

(1) *Judicial Review of Congress's Section 5 Enforcement Power—A "Non-Deferential Review": Board of Trustees of the University of Alabama v. Garrett, 531 U.S. 356 (2001).* In *Garrett*, the Court held that Congress had not validly abrogated the States' Eleventh Amendment immunity. Although Congress had acted pursuant to its § 5 enforcement power, Congress had not satisfied the post-*Flores* standard. Congress failed to sufficiently identify a pattern of state action of discrimination and also to tailor its remedy to the "evil" identified. As a result, although private employers are still subject to liability under ADA, the States can be held liable only if the federal government would bring an appropriate action. *See* note 2 in the decision.

(2) *Developments Regarding the Section 5 Standard: A Further Trend Away from Deferential, Rational Basis Review.* In applying the § 5 standard (from *College Savings Bank*), the *Garrett* Court appeared to "ratchet up" the level of judicial review. For example, the identification prong now required Congress to demonstrate "a history and pattern of unconstitutional [conduct]." Regarding the tailoring prong, the *Garrett* majority found that the ADA's nationwide application was not "congruent or proportional." Note that the Court contrasted the ADA to the 1965 Voting Rights Act, upheld in *South Carolina v. Katzenbach* above. The Voting Rights Act was upheld because its applicability was limited to "those areas of the Nation where abundant evidence of States' systematic denial" of rights was identified. In sum, *Garrett* indicates that both prongs of the § 5 standard have been tightened and that the standard has become less deferential than in *South Carolina* or *Morgan* above.

(3) *Further Research on the Section 5 Enforcement Power.* The Court's decisions from *Flores* to *Garrett* have engendered a great volume of scholarly and other commentary. In addition to the sources cited earlier in this chapter such as Professor Buchanan's article, you might consider the following articles. *See* Judith Olans Brown & Peter D. Enrich, *Nostalgic Federalism*, 28 HAST. CON. L. Q. 1 (2000); Evan H. Caminker, *"Appropriate" Means-Ends Constraints On Section 5 Powers*, 53 STAN. L. REV. 1127 (2001); Ruth Colker, *City of Boerne Revisited*, 70 U. CINCINNATI L. REV. 455 (2002); David S. Day, *New Dimensions of the Section 5 Enforcement Power*, 47 S.D. L. REV. 366 (2002); Robert C. Post & Reva B. Siegel, *Equal Protection by Law: Federal Antidiscrimination Legislation After Morrison and Kimel*, 110 YALE L.J. 441 (2001); Tracy Thomas, *Congress' Section 5 Power and Remedial Right*, 34 U.C. DAVIS L. REV. 673 (2001).

NEVADA DEPARTMENT OF HUMAN RESOURCES v. HIBBS
538 U.S. 721 (2003)

CHIEF JUSTICE REHNQUIST delivered the opinion of the Court.

[The Family and Medical Leave Act (FMLA) entitles eligible employees to take up to 12 weeks of unpaid leave for a variety of reasons, including serious illness of a spouse, parent or child. The FMLA created a private right of action, for damages and equitable relief, against employers, including public employers, for denial or interference with FMLA rights. The Court decided that the Congressional purpose underlying the FMLA was the eradication of certain sexual stereotypes regarding women and employment. The Court also concluded that two previous Congressional efforts to control such employment discrimination and stereotypes, Title VII of the 1964 Civil Rights Act and the 1978 Pregnancy Discrimination Act, had not been successful.

Hibbs was an employee of the State of Nevada. He sought FMLA leave to care for an injured spouse. He eventually had a dispute with his employer about his FMLA leave, and he was terminated. He sued for damages and the district court ruled that the Eleventh Amendment barred his claim. The Ninth Circuit held that Congress had validly abrogated the State's Eleventh Amendment immunity, either under Art. I, § 8 or under § 5 of the Fourteenth Amendment. Here, the Supreme Court affirmed, holding that Congress had validly exercised its Section 5 power.]

[T]wo provisions of the Fourteenth Amendment are relevant here: Section 5 grants Congress the power 'to enforce' the substantive guarantees of § 1—among them, equal protection of the laws—by enacting 'appropriate legislation.' Congress may, in the exercise of its § 5 power, do more than simply proscribe conduct that we have held unconstitutional. 'Congress' power 'to enforce' the Amendment includes the authority both to remedy and to deter violation of rights guaranteed thereunder by prohibiting a somewhat broader swath of conduct, including that which is not itself forbidden by the Amendment's text.' *Garrett, supra,* at 365 (quoting *Kimel, supra,* at 81); *City of Boerne v. Flores,* 521 U. S. 507, 536 (1997); *Katzenbach v. Morgan,* 384 U. S. 641, 658 (1966). In other words, Congress may enact so-called prophylactic legislation that proscribes facially constitutional conduct, in order to prevent and deter unconstitutional conduct.

City of Boerne also confirmed, however, that it falls to this Court, not Congress, to define the substance of constitutional guarantees . . . Section 5 legislation reaching beyond the scope of § 1's actual guarantees must be an appropriate remedy for identified constitutional violations, not "an attempt to substantively redefine the States' legal obligations." *Id.,* at 88. We distinguish appropriate prophylactic legislation from 'substantive redefinition of the Fourteenth Amendment right at issue,' *id.,* at 81, by applying the test set forth in *City of Boerne:* Valid § 5 legislation must exhibit "congruence and proportionality between the injury to be prevented or remedied and the means adopted to that end."

The FMLA aims to protect the right to be free from gender-based discrimination in the workplace. We have held that statutory classifications that distinguish between males and females are subject to heightened scrutiny. See, *e.g., Craig v. Boren,* 429 U. S. 190, 197–199 (1976). For a gender-based classification to withstand such scrutiny, it must 'serv[e] important governmental objectives,' and 'the discriminatory means employed [must be] substantially related to the achievement of those objectives.' *United States v. Virginia,* 518 U. S. 515, 533 (1996) (citations and internal quotation marks omitted). The State's justification for such a classification 'must not rely on overbroad generalizations about the different talents, capacities, or preferences of males and females.' *Ibid.* We now inquire whether Congress had evidence of a pattern of constitutional violations on the part of the States in this area.

The history of the many state laws limiting women's employment opportunities is chronicled in—and, until relatively recently, was sanctioned by—this Court's own opinions. . . .

Congress responded to this history of discrimination by abrogating States' sovereign immunity in Title VII of the Civil Rights Act of 1964, and we sustained this abrogation in *Fitzpatrick, supra*. But state gender discrimination did not cease.. . . According to evidence that was before Congress when it enacted the FMLA, States continue to rely on invalid gender stereotypes in the employment context, specifically in the administration of leave benefits. Reliance on such stereotypes cannot justify the States' gender discrimination in this area. *Virginia, supra*, at 533. The long and extensive history of sex discrimination prompted us to hold that measures that differentiate on the basis of gender warrant heightened scrutiny; here, as in *Fitzpatrick*, the persistence of such unconstitutional discrimination by the States justifies Congress' passage of prophylactic § 5 legislation. . . .

Finally, Congress had evidence that, even where state laws and policies were not facially discriminatory, they were applied in discriminatory ways. . . . Testimony supported that conclusion. . . .

Furthermore, the dissent's statement that some States 'had adopted some form of family-care leave' before the FMLA's enactment, *post*, at 7, glosses over important shortcomings of some state policies. . . . Against the above backdrop of limited state leave policies, no matter how generous petitioner's own may have been, Congress was justified in enacting the FMLA as remedial legislation. In sum, the States' record of unconstitutional participation in, and fostering of, gender-based discrimination in the administration of leave benefits is weighty enough to justify the enactment of prophylactic § 5 legislation.

We reached the opposite conclusion in *Garrett* and *Kimel*. In those cases, the § 5 legislation under review responded to a purported tendency of state officials to make age- or disability-based distinctions. Under our equal protection case law, discrimination on the basis of such characteristics is not judged under a heightened review standard, and passes muster if there is 'a rational basis for doing so at a class-based level, even if it 'is probably not true' that those reasons are valid in the majority of cases.' Thus, in order to impugn the constitutionality of state discrimination against the disabled or the elderly, Congress must identify, not just the existence of age- or disability-based state decisions, but a 'widespread pattern' of irrational reliance on such criteria. *Kimel, supra*, at 90. We found no such showing with respect to the ADEA and Title I of the Americans with Disabilities Act of 1990 (ADA).

Here, however, Congress directed its attention to state gender discrimination, which triggers a heightened level of scrutiny. See, *e.g., Craig*, 429 U.S. at 197–199. Because the standard for demonstrating the constitutionality of a gender-based classification is more difficult to meet than our rational-basis test—it must 'serv[e] important governmental objectives' and be 'substantially related to the achievement of those objectives,' *Virginia*, 518 U. S., at 533—it was easier for Congress to show a pattern of state constitutional violations. Congress was similarly successful in South *Carolina v. Katzenbach*, 383 U. S. 301, 308–313 (1966), where we upheld the Voting Rights Act of 1965: Because racial classifications are presumptively invalid, most of the States' acts of race discrimination violated the Fourteenth Amendment. . . .

We believe that Congress' chosen remedy, the family-care leave provision of the FMLA, is 'congruent and proportional to the targeted violation,' *Garrett, supra*, at 374. Congress had already tried unsuccessfully to address this problem through Title VII and the amendment of Title VII by the Pregnancy Discrimination Act, 42 U. S. C. § 2000e(k). Here, as in *Katzenbach, supra*, Congress again confronted a 'difficult and intractable proble[m],' *Kimel, supra*, at 88, where previous legislative attempts had failed. Such problems may justify added prophylactic measures in response. . . .

tried to address the problem before but failed

The dissent characterizes the FMLA as a 'substantive entitlement program' rather than a remedial statute because it establishes a floor of 12 weeks' leave. In the dissent's view, in the face of evidence of gender-based discrimination by the States in the provision of leave benefits, Congress could do no more in exercising its § 5 power than simply proscribe such discrimination. But this position cannot be squared with our recognition that Congress 'is not confined to the enactment of legislation that merely parrots the precise wording of the Fourteenth Amendment,' but may prohibit 'a somewhat broader swath of conduct, including that which is not itself forbidden by the Amendment's text.' *Kimel, supra,* at 81. . . .

Unlike the statutes at issue in *City of Boerne, Kimel,* and *Garrett,* which applied broadly to every aspect of state employers' operations, the FMLA is narrowly targeted at the fault line between work and family—precisely where sex-based overgeneralization has been and remains strongest—and affects only one aspect of the employment relationship.

We also find significant the many other limitations that Congress placed on the scope of this measure. The FMLA requires only unpaid leave, 29 U. S. C. § 2612(a)(1), and applies only to employees who have worked for the employer for at least one year and provided 1,250 hours of service within the last 12 months, § 2611(2)(A). Employees in high-ranking or sensitive positions are simply ineligible for FMLA leave; of particular importance to the States, the FMLA expressly excludes from coverage state elected officials, their staffs, and appointed policymakers. §§ 2611(2)(B)(i) and (3), 203(e)(2)(C). Employees must give advance notice of foreseeable leave, § 2612(e), and employers may require certification by a health care provider of the need for leave, § 2613. In choosing 12 weeks as the appropriate leave floor, Congress chose 'a middle ground, a period long enough to serve 'the needs of families' but not so long that it would upset 'the legitimate interests of employers.' Moreover, the cause of action under the FMLA is a restricted one: The damages recoverable are strictly defined and measured by actual monetary losses, and the accrual period for backpay is limited by the Act's 2-year statute of limitations (extended to three years only for willful violations).

For the above reasons, we conclude that [the private cause of action] is congruent and proportional to its remedial object, and can 'be understood as responsive to, or designed to prevent, unconstitutional behavior.'

JUSTICE SOUTER, with whom JUSTICE GINSBURG and JUSTICE BREYER join, concurring.

Even on this Court's view of the scope of congressional power under § 5 of the Fourteenth Amendment, the Family and Medical Leave Act is undoubtedly valid legislation, and application of the Act to the States is constitutional; the same conclusions follow *a fortiori* from my own understanding of § 5. . . [*i.e.,* only the rational basis standard should be used]. . . .

JUSTICE SCALIA, dissenting.

I join JUSTICE KENNEDY's dissent, and add one further observation: The constitutional violation that is a prerequisite to 'prophylactic' congressional action to 'enforce' the Fourteenth Amendment is a violation *by the State against which the enforcement action is taken.* . . .

Today's opinion for the Court does not even attempt to demonstrate that each one of the 50 States covered by 29 U. S. C. § 2612(a)(1)(C) was in violation of the Fourteenth Amendment. It treats 'the States' as some sort of collective entity which is guilty or innocent as a body. '[T]he States' record of unconstitutional participation in, and fostering of, gender-based discrimination,' it concludes, 'is weighty enough to justify the enactment of prophylactic § 5 legislation.' *Ante,* at 12. This will not do. Prophylaxis in the sense of extending the remedy beyond the violation is one thing; prophylaxis in the sense of extending the remedy beyond the violator is something else. . . .

JUSTICE KENNEDY, with whom JUSTICE SCALIA and JUSTICE THOMAS join, dissenting.

The Family and Medical Leave Act of 1993 makes explicit the congressional intent to invoke § 5 of the Fourteenth Amendment to abrogate state sovereign immunity and allow suits for money damages in federal courts. The specific question is whether Congress may impose on the States this entitlement program of its own design, with mandated minimums for leave time, and then enforce it by permitting private suits for money damages against the States. . . .

Congress does not have authority to define the substantive content of the Equal Protection Clause; it may only shape the remedies warranted by the violations of that guarantee. *City of Boerne, supra*, at 519–520. This requirement has special force in the context of the Eleventh Amendment, which protects a State's fiscal integrity from federal intrusion by vesting the States with immunity from private actions for damages pursuant to federal laws. The Commerce Clause likely would permit the National Government to enact an entitlement program such as this one; but when Congress couples the entitlement with the authorization to sue the States for monetary damages, it blurs the line of accountability the State has to its own citizens. . . .

In examining whether Congress was addressing a demonstrated 'pattern of unconstitutional employment discrimination by the States,' the Court gives superficial treatment to the requirement that we 'identify with some precision the scope of the constitutional right at issue.' *Garrett*, 531 U. S., at 365, 368. . . .

Respondents [Hibbs] fail to make the requisite showing. The Act's findings of purpose are devoid of any discussion of the relevant evidence. . . .

The federal-state equivalence upon which the Court places such emphasis is a deficient rationale at an even more fundamental level, however; for the States appear to have been ahead of Congress in providing gender-neutral family leave benefits. Thirty States, the District of Columbia, and Puerto Rico had adopted some form of family-care leave in the years preceding the Act's adoption. . . .

Considered in its entirety, the evidence fails to document a pattern of unconstitutional conduct sufficient to justify the abrogation of States' sovereign immunity. The few incidents identified by the Court 'fall far short of even suggesting the pattern of unconstitutional discrimination on which § 5 legislation must be based.'. . .

NOTES AND QUESTIONS

(1) *The FMLA is a Valid Exercise of the Section 5 Power: Nevada Dept. of Human Resources v. Hibbs, 538 U.S. 721 (2003)*. Congress passed the Family and Medical Leave Act (FMLA) in 1993. It basically provides employees with a statutory entitlement to 12 weeks of unpaid leave for certain family illnesses and emergencies. The FMLA also created a private right of action for employees—against both private and public employers. In *Hibbs*, the State of Nevada argued that its Eleventh Amendment immunity barred any liability for damages. Hibbs contended that Congress had abrogated the Eleventh Amendment pursuant to its Section 5 power. Although the Court had, since 1997, struck down a series of federal statutes attempting to abrogate a state's sovereign immunity, the Court, per Chief Justice Rehnquist, upheld the FMLA.

(2) *The Standard for the Exercise of Congress' Section 5 Power*. The result in the *Hibbs* decision surprised many who were following developments in the Section 5 power cases. In *Hibbs*, the four dissenting Justices from *Garrett* were joined by Justice O'Connor and Chief Justice Rehnquist. It seemed especially curious that the Chief Justice, who wrote most of the decisions narrowing the Section 5 power, would write the opinion upholding the FMLA. The Chief Justice's opinion appeared to confirm that judicial review of the Section 5 power would be a "searching scrutiny"—higher than the rational basis standard from *Morgan*. Nevertheless, the Chief Justice distinguished the other Section 5 decisions. The Court reasoned that, because the FMLA was a

Congressional effort to remedy gender discrimination and because gender discrimination is judicially reviewed with the intermediate scrutiny standard, it was easier for the Congress to satisfy the Section 5 standard. The Court also distinguished the race discrimination remedy decisions.

While the difference in the judicial review standards (between gender and age) would seem to distinguish certain of the prior decisions from *Hibbs*, the majority did not directly address how the FMLA was distinguishable from the Violence Against Women Act (VAWA) (Note (2) above). The VAWA was also a Congressional effort to remedy gender discrimination. In *Morrison*, the Court, per Chief Justice Rehnquist, found that Congress had not satisfied the Section 5 standard. The *Hibbs* opinion, as dissenting Justices Kennedy, Scalia, and Thomas noted, did not explain how the *Morrison* decision was distinguishable. More generally, the Court has not explained why a lower burden of proof for Congress under § 5 is derived from a heightened level of scrutiny in judicial review.

(3)   *The Role of the States in Remedying "Problems": Should Congress Be Able To Act Under Its Section 5 Power If the States Have Adequately and Reasonably Addressed "The Problem"?* In *Lopez*, the Court struck down the Gun Free School Zone Act in part because it concluded that almost all States had enacted legislation addressing guns and violence in schools. The States, in other words, were adequately handling the "problem." In *Morrison*, the Court struck down the Violence Against Women Act in part because the Congress had not assembled sufficient evidence that the States were not adequately addressing the issue of violence based on gender (*e.g.*, domestic abuse; rape; sexual assault). Again, the Court suggested that, if the States had adequately addressed a problem, then Congress would not have the power under Section 5 to pass legislation. In this context, review the debate between the majority and Justice Kennedy's dissent as to the adequacy of state laws on family leave and whether the States actually were the "leaders" in solving this "problem."

(4)   *Title II of the ADA Upheld Under the Section 5 "Searching Scrutiny" Standard: Tennessee v. Lane, 541 U.S. 509 (2004).* In the *Garrett* decision, above, the Court had held that Congress lacked authority, under its Section 5 power, to abrogate the State's Eleventh Amendment immunity regarding Title I (employment) of the Americans With Disability Act ("ADA"). *In Tennessee v. Lane*, the challengers sued the State for money damages under Title II of the ADA (access to public facilities and accommodations) when they were denied access to a county courthouse. Tennessee defended on Eleventh Amendment grounds and relied on the *Garrett* decision (which, after all, concerned another Title of the ADA). The lower courts distinguished *Garrett* as relying on equal protection principles while the *Lane* case arguably relied on due process principles. [Reconsider the *Garrett* reasoning; note that the *Hibbs* decision did not suggest that such a distinction was important.]

The Supreme Court, per Justice Stevens, relied on other reasoning, but it upheld Congressional power to pass Title II of the ADA and to abrogate the State's Eleventh Amendment immunities. Justice Stevens applied the searching scrutiny standard of *Garrett* and *Hibbs* and found it satisfied. The *Garrett* dissenters were joined by Justice O'Connor, as a swing vote.

The Chief Justice, author of *Garrett* and *Hibbs*, dissented. He provided a lengthy explanation why the Congressional record for Title II did not satisfy the Section 5 standard. Justice Scalia also dissented—mainly to emphasize that he had predicted in *Hibbs* that the *Hibbs* application of the Section 5 standard was too lenient and would lead to results such as *Lane*. After *Hibbs*, and especially *Lane*, the Section 5 standard does not appear to be as restrictive as much of the academic literature feared. *See generally* William D. Araiza, *The Section 5 Power After Tennessee v. Lane*, 32 Pepp. L. Rev. 39 (2004). *See also United States v. Georgia*, 546 U.S. 151 (2006) where, in an opinion by *Lane*—dissenter Justice Scalia, the Court reaffirmed that Title II of the ADA validly abrogated the states' sovereign immunity.

§ 14.03 ENFORCING THE THIRTEENTH AND FOURTEENTH AMENDMENTS AGAINST PRIVATE CONDUCT

[A] Legislating Against Private Action Under the Fourteenth Amendment

INTRODUCTORY NOTE

The Narrow Early View: No Congressional Power to Regulate Private Conduct under § 5. The substantive provisions of the Fourteenth Amendment guarantee rights against state action. Section 5 of the amendment grants Congress the power to protect those rights by "appropriate legislation." The question arises whether Congress constitutionally can determine that it is "appropriate" to legislate against private action as a means of protecting those rights. This issue was first addressed in the *Civil Rights Cases*, 109 U.S. 3 (1883), in which the Court narrowly construed Congress' power under Section 5 to limit it from reaching private action.

> [T]he last section of the [fourteenth] amendment invests Congress with power to enforce it by appropriate legislation. To enforce what? . . . It does not authorize Congress to create a code of municipal law for the regulation of private rights; but to provide modes of redress against the operation of state laws, and the action of state officers.

Expanded Views of Congressional Power. In the twentieth century, the holding of the *Civil Rights Cases* has been undermined in several ways. First, through the Civil Rights Act of 1964, most civil rights legislation was upheld under the expanded scope of the Commerce Clause, and not under the Fourteenth Amendment. Second, the Court expanded the definitions of "state action" and the related "under color of law" concept found in several civil rights statutes.

The Price Decision: Expanded Construction of "Under Color of [State Law.]" For example, in *United States v. Price*, 383 U.S. 787 (1966), Mississippi law enforcement officers were accused of removing three civil rights workers from their cells and taking them to a place where fifteen private persons were waiting, and where the victims were beaten to death. All eighteen defendants were charged under 18 U.S.C. § 242 for "punishing" the victims "under color of law" without "due process." The Supreme Court upheld the district court's determination that the officers, although acting contrary to state law, were still acting "under color of law." The Court relied on *Screws v. United States*, 325 U.S. 91 (1945), in which it was held that, "Misuse of power, possessed by virtue of state law and made possible only because the wrongdoer is clothed with the authority of state law, is action taken 'under color of state law.'" The Supreme Court went farther than the district court, and found that the fifteen private defendants were also acting "under color of law" because they were participating in "joint activity with the State or its agents."

UNITED STATES v. GUEST, 383 U.S. 745 (1966). The defendants were charged with violating of 18 U.S.C. § 241. In contrast to § 242—the provision involved in *Price*—§ 241 contains no "color of law" requirement. Instead, § 241 makes it a crime for private citizens to conspire "to injure, oppress, threaten, or intimidate any citizen in the free exercise or enjoyment of any right or privilege secured to him by the Constitution or laws of the United States."

The second paragraph of the indictment alleged that the defendants had conspired to injure, oppress, threaten and intimidate black citizens in the free exercise and enjoyment of "The right to the equal utilization, without discrimination upon the basis of race, of public facilities in the vicinity of Athens, Georgia. . . ." The fourth paragraph of the indictment charged that the defendants conspired to injure, oppress, threaten and intimidate black citizens in the free exercise and enjoyment of "the right to travel freely to and from the State of Georgia and to use highway facilities and other instrumentalities of interstate commerce within the State of Georgia." The defendants succeeded in having the district court quash the indictment on the ground that it did not charge an offense. On direct appeal, the Supreme Court reversed.

Writing for the Court, Justice Stewart held both the second and fourth paragraphs of the indictment sufficient to state an offense. With respect to the second paragraph, Justice Stewart reasoned:

> It is a commonplace that rights under the Equal Protection Clause itself arise only where there has been involvement of the State or of one acting under the color of its authority. . . .
>
> This is not to say, however, that the involvement of the State need be either exclusive or direct. In a variety of situations the Court has found state action of a nature sufficient to create rights under the Equal Protection Clause even though the participation of the State was peripheral, or its action was only one of several cooperative [forces].
>
> This case, however, requires no determination of the threshold level that state action must attain in order to create rights under the Equal Protection Clause [because] the indictment in fact contains an express allegation of state involvement sufficient at least to require the denial of a motion to dismiss. One of the means of accomplishing the object of the conspiracy, according to the indictment, was "By causing the arrest of Negroes by means of false reports that such Negroes had committed criminal acts." Although it is possible that a bill of particulars, or the proof at trial, would disclose no cooperative action of that kind by officials of the State, the allegation is enough to prevent dismissal of this branch of the indictment.

With respect to the fourth paragraph, Justice Stewart wrote:

> The constitutional right to travel from one State to another, and necessarily to use the highways and other instrumentalities of interstate commerce in doing so, occupies a position fundamental to the concept of our Federal Union. . . .
>
> This does not mean, of course, that every criminal conspiracy affecting an individual's right of free interstate passage is within the sanction of [§ 241]. A specific intent to interfere with the federal right must be proved, and at a trial the defendants are entitled to a jury instruction phrased in those terms. . . . Thus, for example, a conspiracy to rob an interstate traveler would not, of itself, violate § 241. But if the predominant purpose of the conspiracy is to impede or prevent the exercise of the right of interstate travel, or to oppress a person because of his exercise of that right, then, whether or not motivated by racial discrimination, the conspiracy becomes a proper object of the federal law under [§ 241].

Justice Brennan, joined by Chief Justice Warren and Justice Douglas, concurred in part and dissented in part:

> I do not agree with [that part of the Court's opinion] which holds, as I read the opinion, that a conspiracy to interfere with the exercise of the right to equal utilization of state facilities is not within the meaning of § 241 . . . unless discriminatory conduct by state officers is involved in the alleged conspiracy. . . .
>
> I believe that § 241 reaches such a private conspiracy, not because the Fourteenth Amendment of its own force prohibits such a conspiracy, but because § 241, as an exercise of congressional power under § 5 of that Amendment, prohibits *all* conspiracies to interfere with the exercise of a "right . . . secured . . . by the Constitution" and because the right to equal utilization of state facilities is a "right . . . secured . . . by the Constitution"

within the meaning of that phrase as used in § 241. . . .

In reversing the District Court's dismissal of the second numbered paragraph, I would therefore hold that proof at the trial of the conspiracy charged to the defendants in that paragraph will establish a violation of § 241 without regard to whether there is also proof that state law enforcement officers actively connived in causing the arrests of Negroes by means of false reports. . . .

I acknowledge that some of the decisions of this Court, most notably an aspect of the *Civil Rights Cases* . . ., have declared that Congress' power under § 5 is confined to the adoption of "appropriate legislation for correcting the effects of . . . prohibited state law and state acts, and thus to render them effectually null, void, and innocuous." I do not accept—and a majority of the Court today rejects—this interpretation of § 5. It reduces the legislative power to enforce the provisions of the Amendment to that of the judiciary; and it attributes a far too limited objective to the Amendment's sponsors.

Justice Harlan wrote an opinion concurring in the Court's decision with respect to the second paragraph of the indictment, but dissenting from the Court's decision that § 241 reaches private conspiracies to interfere with the right to travel.

NOTES AND QUESTIONS

(1) *Are There Different State Action Requirements for Legislation Affecting Different Constitutional Rights?* Although Justice Stewart was careful to require *some* activity by state actors in order to support a conviction under § 241 with respect to the equal protection aspect of the indictment, he did not indicate that state action was necessary to convict the defendants of interfering with the victims' right to travel. Is this because the right to travel stems from constitutional sources other than the Fourteenth Amendment?

(2) *Limiting the Reach of § 241.* There are many actions private individuals can take that interfere with another's "right to travel." If one person kills or seriously injures another in a garden-variety murder or assault case, he clearly interferes with his victim's right to travel. But neither Congress nor the Court seem to have contemplated making every murder into a federal case. Therefore, Justice Stewart required that a "specific intent to interfere with the federal right [to travel] must be proved." Was this requirement included to limit the sweep of the statute, and thus to prevent Congress' ability to regulate purely private action that was traditionally the concern of state criminal law?

[B] Enforcement Of The Thirteenth Amendment Against Private Action

INTRODUCTORY NOTE

The Absence of a State Action Requirement in the Thirteenth Amendment; Its Reach into Private Conduct. The Thirteenth Amendment was passed in 1865 to abolish slavery in the United States. It has no requirement of state action, and thus it prohibits all activity that violates an individual's right to be free from "involuntary servitude." Under the Thirteenth Amendment, Congress passed the Civil Rights Act of 1875. One of the sections of the Act provided that all persons were entitled to equal access to inns, public transportation, and theaters. The constitutionality of this Act was first challenged in the *Civil Rights Cases*, 109 U.S. 3 (1883).

The "Badge of Slavery" Theory: Confinement in the Civil Rights Cases. The Court found that the Thirteenth Amendment "clothes Congress with power to pass all laws necessary and proper for abolishing all badges and incidents of slavery." Nevertheless, the Court held that Congress had gone beyond its powers in attempting to adjust "social rights" and found the provisions of the Act invalid. Justice Harlan, the sole dissenter, wrote that discrimination on the basis of race could constitute a "badge of slavery." After the *Civil Rights Cases* were decided, the Thirteenth Amendment lay dormant for nearly a century.

Revival of the Thirteenth Amendment in Modern Times. In the wake of *Katzenbach v. Morgan*, Congress attempted to tackle the problem of discrimination in housing by passing the Open Housing Act of 1968. But one of the sharpest blows to discriminatory housing practices came from the Supreme Court, relying not on the 1968 Act, but on one of the surviving provisions of the Civil Rights Act of 1866— 42 U.S.C. § 1982.

JONES v. ALFRED H. MAYER CO.
392 U.S. 409 (1968)

MR. JUSTICE STEWART delivered the opinion of the Court.

[Joseph Lee Jones sued the housing developer, Alfred H. Mayer Co., when he was denied the opportunity to buy housing because he was black. No state action was involved because all services in the development were provided by the defendants, and there was no federal aid given to the project.]

In this case we are called upon to determine the scope and constitutionality of an Act of Congress, 42 U.S.C. § 1982, which provides that:

> All citizens of the United States shall have the same right, in every State and Territory, as is enjoyed by white citizens thereof to inherit, purchase, lease, sell, hold, and convey real and personal property.

[T]he District Court sustained the respondents' motion to dismiss the complaint, and the Court of Appeals for the Eighth Circuit affirmed, concluding that § 1982 applies only to state action and does not reach private refusals to sell. [F]or the reasons that follow, we reverse the judgment of the Court of Appeals. We hold that § 1982 bars *all* racial discrimination, private as well as public, in the sale or rental of property, and that the statute, thus construed, is a valid exercise of the power of Congress to enforce the Thirteenth Amendment. . . .

[A]s its text reveals, the Thirteenth Amendment "is not a mere prohibition of state laws establishing or upholding slavery, but an absolute declaration that slavery or involuntary servitude shall not exist in any part of the United States." *Civil Rights Cases*. It has never been doubted, therefore, "that the power vested in Congress to enforce the article by appropriate legislation," includes the power to enact laws "direct and primary, operating upon the acts of individuals, whether sanctioned by state legislation or not."

[T]he constitutional question in this case, therefore, comes to this: Does the authority of Congress to enforce the Thirteenth Amendment "by appropriate legislation" include the power to eliminate all racial barriers to the acquisition of real and personal property? We think the answer to that question is plainly yes.

"By its own unaided force and effect," the Thirteenth Amendment "abolished slavery, and established universal freedom." *Civil Rights Cases*. Whether or not the Amendment *itself* did any more than that—a question not involved in this case—it is at least clear that the Enabling Clause of that Amendment empowered Congress to do much more. For that clause clothed "Congress with power to pass *all laws necessary and proper for abolishing all badges and incidents of slavery in the United States.*" (Emphasis added.) . . .

Surely Congress has the power under the Thirteenth Amendment rationally to determine what are the badges and the incidents of slavery, and the authority to translate that determination into effective legislation. Nor can we say that the determination Congress has made is an irrational one. For this Court recognized long ago that [t]he badges and incidents of slavery [i]ncluded restraints upon "those fundamental rights which are the essence of civil freedom, namely, the same right . . .

to inherit, purchase, lease, sell and convey property, as is enjoyed by white citizens." *Civil Rights Cases.* Just as the Black Codes, enacted after the Civil War to restrict the free exercise of those rights, were substitutes for the slave system, so the exclusion of Negroes from white communities became a substitute for the Black Codes. And when racial discrimination herds men into ghettos and makes their ability to buy property turn on the color of their skin, then it too is a relic of slavery. . . .

MR. JUSTICE HARLAN, whom MR. JUSTICE WHITE joins, dissenting. . . .

I have concluded that this is one of those rare instances in which an event which occurs after the hearing of argument so diminishes a case's public significance, when viewed in light of the difficulty of the questions presented, as to justify this Court in dismissing the writ as improvidently granted.

The occurrence to which I refer is the recent enactment of the Civil Rights Act of 1968, Pub.L. 90-284, 82 Stat.73. Title VIII of that Act contains comprehensive "fair housing" provisions, which by the terms of § 803 will become applicable on January 1, 1969, to persons who, like the petitioners, attempt to buy houses from developers. [T]hus, the type of relief which the petitioners seek will be available within seven months' time under the terms of a presumptively constitutional Act of Congress. . . .

NOTES AND QUESTIONS

(1) *Extensions of Jones: The Sullivan and Runyon Cases.* In *Sullivan v. Little Hunting Park, Inc.,* 396 U.S. 229 (1969), the Court construed § 1982 to cover private discrimination with respect to personal property as well as real property, and to support an action for damages as well as injunctive relief. In *Runyon v. McCrary,* 427 U.S. 160 (1976), the Court relied on *Jones* and *Sullivan* to hold that 42 U.S.C. § 1981, which guarantees to "all persons . . . the same right . . . to make and enforce contracts . . . as is enjoyed by white citizens," provides a damages remedy against purely private conduct. *Runyon* involved a suit by a black parent against two private schools that refused to enroll the plaintiff's children because they were not white.

(2) *The Court Reaffirms but Limits Runyon: Patterson v. McLean Credit Union, 491 U.S. 164 (1989).* In *Patterson,* the Court announced that it would reexamine *Runyon.* The announcement occasioned great press attention and some denunciations of the Court (including those by Court members dissenting from the reexamination). *Patterson* involved claims for racial harassment as well as racially motivated refusal of promotion and discharge, all brought under 42 U.S.C. § 1981. Rather than repudiating *Runyon,* the Court reaffirmed it—but held the racial harassment claim not actionable under § 1981. This restriction of liability resulted from the Court's narrow construction of statutory language: § 1981 protected the right to "make and enforce contracts," and thus it did not extend to harassment that was not part of the contract formation issue.

(3) *Extensions of the Civil Rights Act to Groups Other than African-Americans: The St. Francis and Shaare Tefila Cases.* The Court has construed §§ 1981 and 1982 to reach private discrimination and private acts against members of ethnic groups generally. In *Saint Francis College v. Al-Khazraji,* 481 U.S. 604 (1987), the plaintiff, a U.S. citizen born in Iraq, sued under § 1981 claiming that he was denied tenure because of his Arab ancestry. The Court reviewed the legislative history of § 1981 and the understanding of the concept of "race" at the time it was enacted, and held:

> Based on the history of sec. 1981, we have little trouble in concluding that Congress intended to protect from discrimination identifiable classes of persons who are subject to intentional discrimination solely because of their ancestry or ethnic characteristics. Such discrimination is racial discrimination that Congress intended sec. 1981 to forbid, whether or not it would be classified as racial in terms of modern scientific theory.

In *Shaare Tefila Congregation v. Cobb*, 481 U.S 615 (1987), the Court relied on this historical analysis to hold that § 1982 also reaches discrimination against groups defined by religious affiliation. *Shaare Tefila* involved a suit by a Jewish synagogue against private individuals who had spray-painted the synagogue with anti-Semitic symbols and slogans.

Chapter 15

THE RIGHT TO KEEP AND BEAR ARMS AND THE MILITIA CLAUSES

§ 15.01 THE CONSTITUTIONAL TEXT: CONGRESS'S MILITIA POWERS AND THE PHRASEOLOGY OF THE SECOND AMENDMENT

> Read U.S. Const. Art. I, § 8, cl. 15–16 (militia powers of Congress); also, read Amend. II (militia clause and right to keep and bear arms).

INTRODUCTORY NOTE

Remember How Your High School English Teacher Warned You Against "Dangling Modifiers"? Perhaps your English class should have used the Second Amendment as an example. The trouble with dangling participles is that it is difficult to tell what, if anything, they modify. So it is with the Second Amendment. Those who seek to restrict the Second Amendment argue that the (dangling) militia clause modifies—and therefore confines—the right to keep and bear arms. This interpretation is used to support the "collective-rights" theory, which is that the purpose of the Amendment is to protect the power of States to maintain state militias. On the other hand, those who seek to read the Amendment broadly argue that the militia clause amplifies the (individual) right to keep and bear arms, adding to it without confining it. This reasoning supports an "individual rights" theory.

What is Meant By the Right of "the People" to Keep and Bear Arms? Advocates of gun control argue the collective-rights theory: that "the people" means the people in a body politic, or in other words, the States. But gun-rights advocates point out that historically a "militia" consisted of the entire population (or at least, the entire able-bodied free male population), and they interpret "the people" as though it referred to every person, consistently with the individual-rights theory. The words "the people" appear also in the First and Fourth Amendments, in contexts that seem to protect individual rights. The Tenth Amendment reserves rights "to the States respectively, or to the people." And although people may "bear" arms collectively, the right to "keep" them seems to imply individual retention or ownership. *See* Michael Kinsley, *Second Thoughts: Gun Control Unconstitutional?* THE NEW REPUBLIC, Feb. 26, 1990, at 4.

Few Supreme Court Decisions, Blurring of Ideological Lines Among Commentators, and Scholarship Calling the Second Amendment "Embarrassing" and "Terrifying." The Supreme Court has decided only a very few cases seriously addressing the Second Amendment, until the *Heller* decision, below. The Amendment makes strange bedfellows: "Conservative columnist George Will and liberal New York Congressman Major Owens have urged repeal of the provision guaranteeing a right to keep and bear arms." ROBERT J. COTTROL, GUN CONTROL AND THE CONSTITUTION: SOURCES AND EXPLORATIONS ON THE SECOND AMENDMENT, at ix (1994). The individual-rights theory has been embraced not only by the National Rifle Association, but also by commentators sometimes thought of as "liberal," and the collective-rights view is not only the preserve of gun-control groups, but also is supported by commentators sometimes thought of as "conservative." Scholars have described the Second Amendment as "embarrassing" and even "terrifying" (*see* below).

Collective Rights or Individual Rights (or Some of Both)?: Text and History. In addition to the text, history sometimes is used to interpret the Amendment. Perhaps the originalist view may vary from obvious interpretations of the text. Above all, the gap between collective-rights and individual-rights theorists is one of the principal difficulties of Second Amendment interpretation.

§ 15.02 THE HISTORICAL CONTEXT: SAFEGUARDING STATE MILITIA POWER, OR INDIVIDUAL SELF-DEFENSE AGAINST CRIMES—OR, PERHAPS, PRESERVING AN ARMED CITIZENRY AS A BULWARK AGAINST TYRANNY?

UNITED STATES v. MILLER
307 U.S. 174 (1939)

MR. JUSTICE MCREYNOLDS delivered the opinion of the Court.

[The] indictment [c]harged that Jack Miller and Frank Layton [had transported in interstate commerce a sawed-off shotgun, defined by the National Firearms Act as "a shotgun or rifle having a barrel of less than eighteen inches." The trial court held the Act unconstitutional under the Second Amendment and quashed the indictment. The Supreme Court here reverses, reinstating the indictment.]

In the absence of any evidence tending to show that possession or use of a "shotgun having a barrel of less than eighteen inches in length" at this time has some reasonable relationship to the preservation or efficiency of a well regulated militia, we cannot say that the Second Amendment guarantees the right to keep and bear such an instrument. Certainly it is not within judicial notice that this weapon is any part of the ordinary military equipment or that its use could contribute to the common defense.

The Constitution as originally adopted granted to the Congress power—"To provide for calling forth the Militia to execute the Laws of the Union, suppress Insurrections and repel Invasions; To provide for organizing, arming, and disciplining, the Militia, and for governing such Part of them as may be employed in the Service of the United States, reserving to the States respectively, the Appointment of the Officers, and the Authority of training the Militia according to the discipline prescribed by Congress." With obvious purpose to assure the continuation and render possible the effectiveness of such forces the declaration and guarantee of the Second Amendment were made. It must be interpreted and applied with that end in view.

The Militia which the States were expected to maintain and train is set in contrast with Troops which they were forbidden to keep without the consent of Congress. The sentiment of the time strongly disfavored standing armies; the common view was that adequate defense of country and laws could be secured through the Militia—civilians primarily, soldiers on occasion.

The signification attributed to the term Militia appears from the debates in the Convention, the history and legislation of Colonies and States, and the writings of approved commentators. These show plainly enough that the Militia comprised all males physically capable of acting in concert for the common defense. [A]nd further, that ordinarily when called for service these men were expected to appear bearing arms supplied by themselves and of the kind in common use at the time. . . .

"The American Colonies In The 17th Century," Osgood, Vol. 1, ch. XIII, affirms in reference to the early system of defense in New England—"In all the colonies, as in England, the militia system was based on the principle of the assize of arms. This implied the general obligation of all adult male inhabitants to possess arms, and, with certain exceptions, to cooperate in the work of defence." . . . "A year later [1632] it was ordered that any single man who had not furnished himself with arms might be put out to service, and this became a permanent part of the legislation of the colony [Massachusetts]." . . . [The Court also traces analogous militia laws in England and in Colonial New York and Virginia.]

Most if not all of the States have adopted provisions touching the right to keep and bear arms. [B]ut none of them seem to afford any material support for the challenged ruling of the court below . . . [*Reversed.*]

NOTES AND QUESTIONS

(1) *Miller as "Steer[ing] an Almost Perfect Middle Course": Don B. Kates, Jr., Handgun Prohibition and the Original Meaning of the Second Amendment, 82 Mich. L. Rev. 204, 249–50 (1983).* Kates says that *Miller* has been attacked both by individual-rights theorists and by collective-rights advocates "because it steers an almost perfect middle course between today's contending extremes—those who claim that the Amendment guarantees nothing to individuals versus those who claim that its guarantee is unlimited." Thus, on the one hand, the Court treated the Amendment as protecting the defendants as individuals, without requiring that they show that they were in fact part of a well-regulated militia. On the other hand, the Court's focus on common military use ties the scope of the individual right to militia equipment and thereby limits the individual right (although not as strictly as collective-rights theorists would prefer). Earlier, in *Presser v. Illinois*, 116 U.S. 252 (1886), the Court upheld state laws prohibiting the unlicensed organization, training and marching of paramilitary groups, holding that group arms-bearing is governed by the congressional militia clauses in Art. I § 8. In addition, the *Presser* Court held that the Bill of Rights was not applicable to the States (this was standard doctrine prior to the incorporation of the Bill of Rights).

(2) *The Constitutionality of Handgun Bans: Quilici v. Morton Grove, 532 F. Supp. 1169 (N.D. Ill. 1981) aff'd, 695 F.2d 261 (7th Cir. 1982).* One of the best known cases involving a handgun ban involved a city ordinance of Morton Grove, Illinois, which prohibited civilian possession of handguns. The district court concluded that it was bound by *Presser* and other holdings to the effect that the Amendment did not apply to States or cities. (Is this holding countermanded by the cases since *Presser*, selectively incorporating the Bill of Rights?) *See also* Thomas J. Walsh, *The Limits and Possibilities of Gun Control*, 23 Capital U. L. Rev. 639 (1994).

(3) *Differing Arguments Based Upon Text, History, Structure, Doctrine, and Prudentialism: The Second Amendment as a Bulwark Against Tyranny—Sanford Levinson, The Embarrassing Second Amendment, 99 Yale L.J. 637 (1989).* In addition to the argument from the text, which can be used to support either individual-right or collective-right theories, one can argue about the second amendment from history. As Professor Levinson shows, such an originalist argument furnishes support for an individual right to engage in armed self-defense against criminal conduct. Furthermore, historically, the militia included the entire full citizenry, as an alternative to a standing army. Perhaps most interestingly, history supports a view of the Second Amendment that links it to political order in a republic. In this view, an armed citizenry is not merely a response to external enemies or to crime, but is a bulwark against tyranny. Thus, the National Rifle Association has argued that if all Chinese citizens kept arms, their rulers would hardly have dared to massacre the demonstrators in Tiananmin Square. Levinson uses others of Professor Bobbit's approaches to constitutional interpretation, including structural, doctrinal, prudential and ethical arguments. *See* Ch. 1 appendix, above. The Amendment is "embarrassing," Levinson concludes, because advocates of broad readings of the First, Fourth, Fifth and other Amendments should read the Second Amendment consistently and take it as seriously.

(4) *The Response of the Center to Prevent Handgun Violence to the Argument That an Armed Citizenry Protects Political Order: Dennis A. Henigan, Arms, Anarchy and*

the Second Amendment, 26 Valparaiso U. L. Rev. 107 (1991). Levinson's article prompted one critic to accuse him of "manipulating his supporting material." Thus, Henigan, the Director of the Legal Action Project at the Center to Prevent Handgun Violence, argued that the "insurrectionist theory" was inconsistent with the constitutional language (including the Second Amendment's reference to "the security of a free State," the concept of a "well-regulated" militia, and the militia powers of Congress). Historically, Henigan also argues that the purpose of the militia was as an instrument of state government. Further, Henigan argues that what he calls the "insurrectionist theory" logically extends itself to the position that courts are powerless to punish armed insurrection as long as revolutionaries believe in good faith that the government has become a tyranny. Ultimately, he maintains, this position would destroy the Bill of Rights. (But is it necessary to adopt a theory justifying armed rebellion against the constitutional government, or an "insurrectionist theory," to argue that the existence of an armed citizenry might restrain an overbearing government at a point short of armed conflict, so that actual "insurrection" is not necessary to the political theory?)

(5)   *Further Debate on the Allegedly "Embarrassing" Second Amendment.* Wendy Brown responds to Levinson by arguing that the republican right of revolution depended upon the existence of a virtuous citizenry, of a kind that does not exist in these heterogeneous United States. Thus, even if we believe in the political theory today, the premise for an armed citizenry may be lacking. Brown also points out that sexism and violence underlie the Second Amendment. Wendy Brown, *Guns, Cowboys, Philadelphia Mayors and Civic Republicanism: On Sanford Levinson's The Embarrassing Second Amendment,* 99 YALE L.J. 61 (1989). On the other hand, David C. Williams concludes that the Second Amendment's republicanism is not just embarrassing—"it is terrifying." Self-government is internally contradictory because "Republics can never successfully survive unless their citizens act in a virtuous manner . . . , but citizens will not act virtuously except in a republic that fosters such virtuous conduct." Among the "structures to aid in this task . . . [is] the universal militia." David C. Williams, *Civic Republicanism and the Citizen Militia: The Terrifying Second Amendment,* 101 YALE L.J. 551, 553 (1991). Finally, from an African-American perspective, it can be argued that "a society with a dismal record of protecting a people [*e.g.,* African-American citizens] has a dubious claim on the right to disarm them . . . [T]he framers of the Second Amendment understood . . . that it is unwise to place the means of protection totally in the hands of the state, and that self-defense is also a civil right." Robert J. Cottrol & Raymond T. Diamond, *The Second Amendment: Toward an Afro-Americanist Reconsideration,* 80 GEO. L.J. 309, 361 (1991).

DISTRICT OF COLUMBIA v. HELLER
128 S. Ct. 2783 (2008)

JUSTICE SCALIA delivered the opinion of the Court.

[The District of Columbia ("DC") generally prohibits, through criminal penalties, the possession of handguns. No one may carry a handgun without a license, issued by the chief of police. In addition, DC required lawfully owned handgun and non-handgun weapons to be "unloaded and dissembled or bound by a trigger lock or similar device." Heller was a "special police officer" at the "Federal Judicial Center." After his application for a DC handgun license was denied, Heller sued claiming that the broad regulatory scheme violated his rights under the Second Amendment. Heller argued that the total ban on handguns and the requirement that firearms in the home be nonfunctional, taken together, burdened his Second Amendment right to self-defense. In a 5-4 decision, the Supreme Court ruled for Heller.

The threshold issue was, as noted above, whether the Second Amendment protected an individual right. Justice Scalia, as an originalist, analyzed the text and history of the

Second Amendment; he also addressed the *Miller* precedent, especially since it was the basis of the dissents.]

II

We turn first to the meaning of the Second Amendment.

A

The Second Amendment provides: "A well regulated Militia, being necessary to the security of a free State, the right of the people to keep and bear Arms, shall not be infringed." In interpreting this text, we are guided by the principle that "[t]he Constitution was written to be understood by the voters; its words and phrases were used in their normal and ordinary as distinguished from technical meaning." Normal meaning may of course include an idiomatic meaning, but it excludes secret or technical meanings that would not have been known to ordinary citizens in the founding generation.

The two sides in this case have set out very different interpretations of the Amendment. Petitioners and today's dissenting Justices believe that it protects only the right to possess and carry a firearm in connection with militia service. Respondent argues that it protects an individual right to possess a firearm unconnected with service in a militia, and to use that arm for traditionally lawful purposes, such as self-defense within the home.

The Second Amendment is naturally divided into two parts: its prefatory clause and its operative clause. The former does not limit the latter grammatically, but rather announces a purpose. The Amendment could be rephrased, "Because a well regulated Militia is necessary to the security of a free State, the right of the people to keep and bear Arms shall not be infringed." See J. Tiffany, A Treatise on Government and Constitutional Law § 585, p. 394 (1867); Brief for Professors of Linguistics and English as *Amici Curiae* 3 (hereinafter Linguists' Brief). Although this structure of the Second Amendment is unique in our Constitution, other legal documents of the founding era, particularly individual-rights provisions of state constitutions, commonly included a prefatory statement of purpose. See generally Volokh, The Commonplace Second Amendment, 73 N.Y.U. L. Rev. 793, 814–821 (1998).

Logic demands that there be a link between the stated purpose and the command. . . . Therefore, while we will begin our textual analysis with the operative clause, we will return to the prefatory clause to ensure that our reading of the operative clause is consistent with the announced purpose.

1. Operative Clause.

a. "Right of the People." The first salient feature of the operative clause is that it codifies a "right of the people." The unamended Constitution and the Bill of Rights use the phrase "right of the people" two other times, in the First Amendment's Assembly-and-Petition Clause and in the Fourth Amendment's Search-and-Seizure Clause. The Ninth Amendment uses very similar terminology ("The enumeration in the Constitution, of certain rights, shall not be construed to deny or disparage others retained by the people"). All three of these instances unambiguously refer to individual rights, not "collective" rights, or rights that may be exercised only through participation in some corporate body.. . .

Reading the Second Amendment as protecting only the right to "keep and bear Arms" in an organized militia therefore fits poorly with the operative clause's description of the holder of that right as "the people."

We start therefore with a strong presumption that the Second Amendment right is exercised individually and belongs to all Americans.

b. "Keep and bear Arms." We move now from the holder of the right—"the people"—to the substance of the right: "to keep and bear Arms."

Before addressing the verbs "keep" and "bear," we interpret their object: "Arms." The 18th-century meaning is no different from the meaning today. . . .

The term was applied, then as now, to weapons that were not specifically designed for military use and were not employed in a military capacity. . . .

We turn to the phrases "keep arms" and "bear arms.". . . No party has apprised us of an idiomatic meaning of "keep Arms." Thus, the most natural reading of "keep Arms" in the Second Amendment is to "have weapons.". . .

At the time of the founding, as now, to "bear" meant to "carry." When used with "arms," however, the term has a meaning that refers to carrying for a particular purpose—confrontation. . . .

2. Prefatory Clause.

The prefatory clause reads: "A well regulated Militia, being necessary to the security of a free State. . . ."

a. "Well-Regulated Militia." In *United States v. Miller*, 307 U.S. 174, 179 (1939), we explained that "the Militia comprised all males physically capable of acting in concert for the common defense." That definition comports with founding-era sources. . . .

Petitioners take a seemingly narrower view of the militia, stating that "[m]ilitias are the state- and congressionally-regulated military forces described in the Militia Clauses (art. I, § 8, cls. 15–16)." Although we agree with petitioners' interpretive assumption that "militia" means the same thing in Article I and the Second Amendment, we believe that petitioners identify the wrong thing, namely, the organized militia. Unlike armies and navies, which Congress is given the power to create ("to raise . . . Armies"; "to provide . . . a Navy," Art. I, § 8, cls. 12–13), the militia is assumed by Article I already to be *in existence*. Congress is given the power to "provide for calling forth the militia," § 8, cl. 15; and the power not to create, but to "organiz[e]" it—and not to organize "a" militia, which is what one would expect if the militia were to be a federal creation, but to organize "the" militia, connoting a body already in existence, *ibid.*, cl. 16. This is fully consistent with the ordinary definition of the militia as all able-bodied men. From that pool, Congress has plenary power to organize the units that will make up an effective fighting force. That is what Congress did in the first militia Act. . . .

Finally, the adjective "well-regulated" implies nothing more than the imposition of proper discipline and training. . . .

b. "Security of a Free State." The phrase "security of a free state" meant "security of a free polity," not security of each of the several States as the dissent below argued. Joseph Story wrote in his treatise on the Constitution that "the word 'state' is used in various senses [and in] its most enlarged sense, it means the people composing a particular nation or community." 1 Story § 208; see also 3 *id.*, § 1890 (in reference to the Second Amendment's prefatory clause: "The militia is the natural defence of a free country"). It is true that the term "State" elsewhere in the Constitution refers to individual States, but the phrase "security of a free state" and close variations seem to have been terms of art in 18th-century political discourse, meaning a " 'free country' " or free polity. See Volokh, Necessary to the Security of a Free State, 83 Notre Dame L. Rev. 1, 5 (2007); see, *e.g.*, 4 Blackstone 151 (1769); Brutus Essay III (Nov. 15, 1787), in The Essential Antifederalist 251, 253 (W. Allen & G. Lloyd eds., 2d ed.2002). Moreover, the other instances of "state" in the Constitution are typically accompanied by modifiers making clear that the reference is to the several States—"each state," "several states," "any state," "that state," "particular states," "one state," "no state." And the presence of the term "foreign state" in Article I and Article III shows that the word "state" did not have a single meaning in the Constitution.

There are many reasons why the militia was thought to be "necessary to the security of a free state." See 3 Story § 1890. First, of course, it is useful in repelling invasions and suppressing insurrections. Second, it renders large standing armies unnecessary—an argument that Alexander Hamilton made in favor of federal control over the militia. The Federalist No. 29, pp. 226, 227 (B. Wright ed.1961) (A. Hamilton). Third, when the able-bodied men of a nation are trained in arms and organized, they are better able to resist tyranny.

3. Relationship between Prefatory Clause and Operative Clause

We reach the question, then: Does the preface fit with an operative clause that creates an individual right to keep and bear arms? It fits perfectly, once one knows the history that the founding generation knew and that we have described above. That history showed that the way tyrants had eliminated a militia consisting of all the able-bodied men was not by banning the militia but simply by taking away the people's arms, enabling a select militia or standing army to suppress political opponents. This is what had occurred in England that prompted codification of the right to have arms in the English Bill of Rights.

The debate with respect to the right to keep and bear arms, as with other guarantees in the Bill of Rights, was not over whether it was desirable (all agreed that it was) but over whether it needed to be codified in the Constitution. During the 1788 ratification debates, the fear that the federal government would disarm the people in order to impose rule through a standing army or select militia was pervasive in Antifederalist rhetoric. . . . It was understood across the political spectrum that the right helped to secure the ideal of a citizen militia, which might be necessary to oppose an oppressive military force if the constitutional order broke down.

It is therefore entirely sensible that the Second Amendment's prefatory clause announces the purpose for which the right was codified: to prevent elimination of the militia. The prefatory clause does not suggest that preserving the militia was the only reason Americans valued the ancient right; most undoubtedly thought it even more important for self-defense and hunting. But the threat that the new Federal Government would destroy the citizens' militia by taking away their arms was the reason that right—unlike some other English rights—was codified in a written Constitution. . . .

B

Our interpretation is confirmed by analogous arms-bearing rights in state constitutions that preceded and immediately followed adoption of the Second Amendment. Four States adopted analogues to the Federal Second Amendment in the period between independence and the ratification of the Bill of Rights. . . .

We therefore believe that the most likely reading of all four of these pre-Second Amendment state constitutional provisions is that they secured an individual right to bear arms for defensive purposes. . . .

C

JUSTICE STEVENS relies on the drafting history of the Second Amendment-the various proposals in the state conventions and the debates in Congress. It is dubious to rely on such history to interpret a text that was widely understood to codify a pre-existing right, rather than to fashion a new one. But even assuming that this legislative history is relevant, JUSTICE STEVENS flatly misreads the historical record. . . .

D

We now address how the Second Amendment was interpreted from immediately after its ratification through the end of the 19th century. Before proceeding, however, we take issue with JUSTICE STEVENS' equating of these sources with postenactment legislative history, a comparison that betrays a fundamental misunderstanding of a court's interpretive task. "Legislative history," of course, refers to the pre-enactment statements of those who drafted or voted for a law; it is considered persuasive by some, not because they reflect the general understanding of the disputed terms, but because the legislators who heard or read those statements presumably voted with that understanding. *Ibid.* "Postenactment legislative history," *ibid.*, a deprecatory contradiction in terms, refers to statements of those who drafted or voted for the law that are made after its enactment and hence could have had no effect on the congressional vote. It most certainly does not refer to the examination of a variety of legal and other sources to determine *the public understanding* of a legal text in the period after its enactment or ratification. That sort of inquiry is a critical tool of constitutional interpretation. As we will show, virtually all interpreters of the Second Amendment in the century after its enactment interpreted the amendment as we do.

1. Post-ratification Commentary

Three important founding-era legal scholars interpreted the Second Amendment in published writings. All three understood it to protect an individual right unconnected with militia service. . . .

We have found only one early 19th-century commentator who clearly conditioned the right to keep and bear arms upon service in the militia—and he recognized that the prevailing view was to the contrary. . . .

2. Pre-Civil War Case Law

The 19th-century cases that interpreted the Second Amendment universally support an individual right unconnected to militia service. . . .

Many early 19th-century state cases indicated that the Second Amendment right to bear arms was an individual right unconnected to militia service, though subject to certain restrictions. . . .

3. Post-Civil War Legislation.

In the aftermath of the Civil War, there was an outpouring of discussion of the Second Amendment in Congress and in public discourse, as people debated whether and how to secure constitutional rights for newly free slaves. See generally S. Halbrook, Freedmen, the Fourteenth Amendment, and the Right to Bear Arms, 1866–1876 (1998) (hereinafter Halbrook); Brief for Institute for Justice as *Amicus Curiae.* Since those discussions took place 75 years after the ratification of the Second Amendment, they do not provide as much insight into its original meaning as earlier sources. Yet those born and educated in the early 19th century faced a widespread effort to limit arms ownership by a large number of citizens; their understanding of the origins and continuing significance of the Amendment is instructive.

Blacks were routinely disarmed by Southern States after the Civil War. Those who opposed these injustices frequently stated that they infringed blacks' constitutional right to keep and bear arms. Needless to say, the claim was not that blacks were being prohibited from carrying arms in an organized state militia. . . .

It was plainly the understanding in the post-Civil War Congress that the Second Amendment protected an individual right to use arms for self-defense.

4. Post-Civil War Commentators.

Every late-19th-century legal scholar that we have read interpreted the Second Amendment to secure an individual right unconnected with militia service. The most famous was the judge and professor Thomas Cooley, who wrote a massively popular 1868 Treatise on Constitutional Limitations. . . .

All other post-Civil War 19th-century sources we have found concurred with Cooley. . . .

E

We now ask whether any of our precedents forecloses the conclusions we have reached about the meaning of the Second Amendment. . . .

Justice Stevens places overwhelming reliance upon this Court's decision in *United States v. Miller*, 307 U.S. 174 (1939).. . . . And what is, according to Justice Stevens, the holding of *Miller* that demands such obeisance? That the Second Amendment "protects the right to keep and bear arms for certain military purposes, but that it does not curtail the legislature's power to regulate the nonmilitary use and ownership of weapons."

Nothing so clearly demonstrates the weakness of Justice Stevens' case. *Miller* did not hold that and cannot possibly be read to have held that. The judgment in the case upheld against a Second Amendment challenge two men's federal convictions for transporting an unregistered short-barreled shotgun in interstate commerce, in violation of the National Firearms Act, 48 Stat. 1236. It is entirely clear that the Court's basis for saying that the Second Amendment did not apply was *not* that the defendants were "bear[ing] arms" not "for . . . military purposes" but for "nonmilitary use." Rather, it was that the *type of weapon at issue* was not eligible for Second Amendment protection: "In the absence of any evidence tending to show that the possession or use of a [short-barreled shotgun] at this time has some reasonable relationship to the preservation or efficiency of a well regulated militia, we cannot say that the Second Amendment guarantees the right to keep and bear *such an instrument*." . . .

It is particularly wrongheaded to read *Miller* for more than what it said, because the case did not even purport to be a thorough examination of the Second Amendment. Justice Stevens claims that the opinion reached its conclusion "[a]fter reviewing many of the same sources that are discussed at greater length by the Court today." Not many, which was not entirely the Court's fault. The respondent made no appearance in the case, neither filing a brief nor appearing at oral argument; the Court heard from no one but the Government (reason enough, one would think, not to make that case the beginning and the end of this Court's consideration of the Second Amendment). See Frye, The Peculiar Story of *United States v. Miller*, 3 N.Y.U. J. L. & Liberty 48, 65–68 (2008). The Government's brief spent two pages discussing English legal sources, concluding "that at least the carrying of weapons without lawful occasion or excuse was always a crime" and that (because of the class-based restrictions and the prohibition on terrorizing people with dangerous or unusual weapons) "the early English law did not guarantee an unrestricted right to bear arms.". . . The Government's *Miller* brief thus provided scant discussion of the history of the Second Amendment—and the Court was presented with no counterdiscussion. As for the text of the Court's opinion itself, that discusses *none* of the history of the Second Amendment. It assumes from the prologue that the Amendment was designed to preserve the militia (which we do not dispute), and then reviews some historical materials dealing with the nature of the militia, and in particular with the nature of the arms their members were expected to possess. Not a word *(not a word)* about the history of the Second Amendment. This is the mighty rock upon which the dissent rests its case. . . .

We conclude that nothing in our precedents forecloses our adoption of the original understanding of the Second Amendment. It should be unsurprising that such a significant matter has been for so long judicially unresolved. For most of our history, the Bill of Rights was not thought applicable to the States, and the Federal Government did not significantly regulate the possession of firearms by law-abiding citizens. . . .

III

Like most rights, the right secured by the Second Amendment is not unlimited. From Blackstone through the 19th-century cases, commentators and courts routinely explained that the right was not a right to keep and carry any weapon whatsoever in any manner whatsoever and for whatever purpose. . . . Although we do not undertake an exhaustive historical analysis today of the full scope of the Second Amendment, nothing in our opinion should be taken to cast doubt on longstanding prohibitions on the possession of firearms by felons and the mentally ill, or laws forbidding the carrying of firearms in sensitive places such as schools and government buildings, or laws imposing conditions and qualifications on the commercial sale of arms.

We also recognize another important limitation on the right to keep and carry arms. *Miller* said, as we have explained, that the sorts of weapons protected were those "in common use at the time." We think that limitation is fairly supported by the historical tradition of prohibiting the carrying of "dangerous and unusual weapons.". . .

It may be objected that if weapons that are most useful in military service—M-16 rifles and the like—may be banned, then the Second Amendment right is completely detached from the prefatory clause. But as we have said, the conception of the militia at the time of the Second Amendment's ratification was the body of all citizens capable of military service, who would bring the sorts of lawful weapons that they possessed at home to militia duty. It may well be true today that a militia, to be as effective as militias in the 18th century, would require sophisticated arms that are highly unusual in society at large. Indeed, it may be true that no amount of small arms could be useful against modern-day bombers and tanks. But the fact that modern developments have limited the degree of fit between the prefatory clause and the protected right cannot change our interpretation of the right. [*Note Justice Scalia's succinct summation of originalism.*]

IV

We turn finally to the law at issue here. As we have said, the law totally bans handgun possession in the home. It also requires that any lawful firearm in the home be disassembled or bound by a trigger lock at all times, rendering it inoperable.

As the quotations earlier in this opinion demonstrate, the inherent right of self-defense has been central to the Second Amendment right. The handgun ban amounts to a prohibition of an entire class of "arms" that is overwhelmingly chosen by American society for that lawful purpose. The prohibition extends, moreover, to the home, where the need for defense of self, family, and property is most acute. Under any of the standards of scrutiny that we have applied to enumerated constitutional rights, banning from the home "the most preferred firearm in the nation to 'keep' and use for protection of one's home and family," would fail constitutional muster.

Few laws in the history of our Nation have come close to the severe restriction of the District's handgun ban. And some of those few have been struck down. . . . That was so even though the statute did not restrict the carrying of long guns.

It is no answer to say, as petitioners do, that it is permissible to ban the possession of handguns so long as the possession of other firearms (*i.e.*, long guns) is allowed. It is enough to note, as we have observed, that the American people have considered the handgun to be the quintessential self-defense weapon. There are many reasons that a citizen may prefer a handgun for home defense: It is easier to store in a location that is readily accessible in an emergency; it cannot easily be redirected or wrestled away by an attacker; it is easier to use for those without the upper-body strength to lift and aim a long gun; it can be pointed at a burglar with one hand while the other hand dials the police. Whatever the reason, handguns are the most popular weapon chosen by Americans for self-defense in the home, and a complete prohibition of their use is invalid.

We must also address the District's requirement (as applied to respondent's handgun) that firearms in the home be rendered and kept inoperable at all times. This makes it impossible for citizens to use them for the core lawful purpose of self-defense and is hence unconstitutional. . . .

Apart from his challenge to the handgun ban and the trigger-lock requirement respondent asked the District Court to enjoin petitioners from enforcing the separate licensing requirement "in such a manner as to forbid the carrying of a firearm within one's home or possessed land without a license." App. 59a. The Court of Appeals did not invalidate the licensing requirement, but held only that the District "may not prevent [a handgun] from being moved throughout one's house.". . . We therefore assume that petitioners' issuance of a license will satisfy respondent's prayer for relief and do not address the licensing requirement.

Justice Breyer has devoted most of his separate dissent to the handgun ban. He says that, even assuming the Second Amendment is a personal guarantee of the right to bear arms, the District's prohibition is valid. He first tries to establish this by founding-era historical precedent, pointing to various restrictive laws in the colonial period. These demonstrate, in his view, that the District's law "imposes a burden upon gun owners that seems proportionately no greater than restrictions in existence at the time the Second Amendment was adopted." Of the laws he cites, only one offers even marginal support for his assertion. . . . In any case, we would not stake our interpretation of the Second Amendment upon a single law, in effect in a single city, that contradicts the overwhelming weight of other evidence regarding the right to keep and bear arms for defense of the home. The other laws Justice Breyer cites are gunpowder-storage laws that he concedes did not clearly prohibit loaded weapons, but required only that excess gunpowder be kept in a special container or on the top floor of the home. Nothing about those fire-safety laws undermines our analysis; they do not remotely burden the right of self-defense as much as an absolute ban on handguns. Nor, correspondingly, does our analysis suggest the invalidity of laws regulating the storage of firearms to prevent accidents. . . .

Justice Breyer moves on to make a broad jurisprudential point: He criticizes us for declining to establish a level of scrutiny for evaluating Second Amendment restrictions. He proposes, explicitly at least, none of the traditionally expressed levels (strict scrutiny, intermediate scrutiny, rational basis), but rather a judge-empowering "interest-balancing inquiry" that "asks whether the statute burdens a protected interest in a way or to an extent that is out of proportion to the statute's salutary effects upon other important governmental interests." After an exhaustive discussion of the arguments for and against gun control, Justice Breyer arrives at his interest-balanced answer: because handgun violence is a problem, because the law is limited to an urban area, and because there were somewhat similar restrictions in the founding period (a false proposition that we have already discussed), the interest-balancing inquiry results in the constitutionality of the handgun ban. . . .

We know of no other enumerated constitutional right whose core protection has been subjected to a freestanding "interest-balancing" approach. The very enumeration of the right takes out of the hands of government—even the Third Branch of Government—the power to decide on a case-by-case basis whether the right is *really worth* insisting upon. A constitutional guarantee subject to future judges' assessments of its usefulness is no constitutional guarantee at all. Constitutional rights are enshrined with the scope they were understood to have when the people adopted them, whether or not future legislatures or (yes) even future judges think that scope too broad. We would not apply an "interest-balancing" approach to the prohibition of a peaceful neo-Nazi march through Skokie. See *Nationalist Socialist Party of America v. Skokie*, 432 U.S. 43 (1977) *(per curiam)*. The First Amendment contains the freedom-of-speech guarantee that the people ratified, which included exceptions for obscenity, libel, and disclosure of state secrets, but not for the expression of extremely unpopular and wrong-headed views. The Second Amendment is no different. Like the First, it is the very *product* of an interest-balancing by the people—which Justice Breyer would now conduct for them anew. And whatever else it leaves to future evaluation, it surely elevates above all other interests the right of law-abiding, responsible citizens to use arms in defense of hearth and home.

Justice Breyer chides us for leaving so many applications of the right to keep and bear arms in doubt, and for not providing extensive historical justification for those regulations of the right that we describe as permissible. But since this case represents this Court's first in-depth examination of the Second Amendment, one should not expect it to clarify the entire field, any more than *Reynolds v. United States*, 98 U.S. 145 (1879), our first in-depth Free Exercise Clause case, left that area in a state of utter certainty. And there will be time enough to expound upon the historical justifications for the exceptions we have mentioned if and when those exceptions come before us.

In sum, we hold that the District's ban on handgun possession in the home violates the Second Amendment, as does its prohibition against rendering any lawful firearm in the home operable for the purpose of immediate self-defense. Assuming that Heller is not disqualified from the exercise of Second Amendment rights, the District must permit him to register his handgun and must issue him a license to carry it in the home.

*   *   *

We are aware of the problem of handgun violence in this country, and we take seriously the concerns raised by the many *amici* who believe that prohibition of handgun ownership is a solution. The Constitution leaves the District of Columbia a variety of tools for combating that problem, including some measures regulating handguns. But the enshrinement of constitutional rights necessarily takes certain policy choices off the table. These include the absolute prohibition of handguns held and used for self-defense in the home. Undoubtedly some think that the Second Amendment is outmoded in a society where our standing army is the pride of our Nation, where well-trained police forces provide personal security, and where gun violence is a serious problem. That is perhaps debatable, but what is not debatable is that it is not the role of this Court to pronounce the Second Amendment extinct.

We affirm the judgment of the Court of Appeals.

Justice Stevens, with whom Justice Souter, Justice Ginsburg, and Justice Breyer join, dissenting.

The question presented by this case is not whether the Second Amendment protects a "collective right" or an "individual right." Surely it protects a right that can be enforced by individuals. But a conclusion that the Second Amendment protects an individual right does not tell us anything about the scope of that right.

Guns are used to hunt, for self-defense, to commit crimes, for sporting activities, and to perform military duties. The Second Amendment plainly does not protect the right to use a gun to rob a bank; it is equally clear that it *does* encompass the right to use weapons for certain military purposes. Whether it also protects the right to possess and use guns for nonmilitary purposes like hunting and personal self-defense is the question presented by this case. The text of the Amendment, its history, and our decision in *United States v. Miller*, 307 U.S. 174 (1939), provide a clear answer to that question.

The Second Amendment was adopted to protect the right of the people of each of the several States to maintain a well-regulated militia. It was a response to concerns raised during the ratification of the Constitution that the power of Congress to disarm the state militias and create a national standing army posed an intolerable threat to the sovereignty of the several States. Neither the text of the Amendment nor the arguments advanced by its proponents evidenced the slightest interest in limiting any legislature's authority to regulate private civilian uses of firearms. Specifically, there is no indication that the Framers of the Amendment intended to enshrine the common-law right of self-defense in the Constitution. . . .

I

. . . .

"A well regulated Militia, being necessary to the security of a free State"

The preamble to the Second Amendment makes three important points. It identifies the preservation of the militia as the Amendment's purpose; it explains that the militia is necessary to the security of a free State; and it recognizes that the militia must be "well regulated." In all three respects it is comparable to provisions in several State Declarations of Rights that were adopted roughly contemporaneously with the Declaration of Independence. Those state provisions highlight the importance members of the founding generation attached to the maintenance of state militias; they also underscore the profound fear shared by many in that era of the dangers posed by standing armies. While the need for state militias has not been a matter of significant public interest for almost two centuries, that fact should not obscure the contemporary concerns that animated the Framers. . . .

The preamble thus both sets forth the object of the Amendment and informs the meaning of the remainder of its text. Such text should not be treated as mere surplusage, for "[i]t cannot be presumed that any clause in the constitution is intended to be without effect." *Marbury v. Madison*, 1 Cranch 137, 174 (1803).

The Court today tries to denigrate the importance of this clause of the Amendment by beginning its analysis with the Amendment's operative provision and returning to the preamble merely "to ensure that our reading of the operative clause is consistent with the announced purpose." That is not how this Court ordinarily reads such texts, and it is not how the preamble would have been viewed at the time the Amendment was adopted. While the Court makes the novel suggestion that it need only find some "logical connection" between the preamble and the operative provision, it does acknowledge that a prefatory clause may resolve an ambiguity in the text. Without identifying any language in the text that even mentions civilian uses of firearms, the Court proceeds to "find" its preferred reading in what is at best an ambiguous text, and then concludes that its reading is not foreclosed by the preamble. Perhaps the Court's approach to the text is acceptable advocacy, but it is surely an unusual approach for judges to follow. . . .

* * *

When each word in the text is given full effect, the Amendment is most naturally read to secure to the people a right to use and possess arms in conjunction with service in a well-regulated militia. So far as appears, no more than that was contemplated by its drafters or is encompassed within its terms. Even if the meaning of the text were genuinely susceptible to more than one interpretation, the burden would remain on those advocating a departure from the purpose identified in the preamble and from settled law to come forward with persuasive new arguments or evidence. The textual analysis offered by respondent and embraced by the Court falls far short of sustaining that heavy burden. And the Court's emphatic reliance on the claim "that the Second Amendment . . . codified a *pre-existing* right," is of course beside the point because the right to keep and bear arms for service in a state militia was also a pre-existing right.

Indeed, not a word in the constitutional text even arguably supports the Court's overwrought and novel description of the Second Amendment as "elevat[ing] above all other interests" "the right of law-abiding, responsible citizens to use arms in defense of hearth and home."

II

The proper allocation of military power in the new Nation was an issue of central concern for the Framers. The compromises they ultimately reached, reflected in Article I's Militia Clauses and the Second Amendment, represent quintessential examples of the

Framers' "splitting the atom of sovereignty." [*Note that the "splitting the atom" phrase belongs to Justice Kennedy—the fifth vote in the majority.*] . . .

[The] original Constitution's retention of the militia and its creation of divided authority over that body did not prove sufficient to allay fears about the dangers posed by a standing army. For it was perceived by some that Article I contained a significant gap: While it empowered Congress to organize, arm, and discipline the militia, it did not prevent Congress from providing for the militia's *dis*armament. . . .

This sentiment was echoed at a number of state ratification conventions; indeed, it was one of the primary objections to the original Constitution voiced by its opponents. The Anti-Federalists were ultimately unsuccessful in persuading state ratification conventions to condition their approval of the Constitution upon the eventual inclusion of any particular amendment. But a number of States did propose to the first Federal Congress amendments reflecting a desire to ensure that the institution of the militia would remain protected under the new Government. . . .

Madison, charged with the task of assembling the proposals for amendments sent by the ratifying States, was the principal draftsman of the Second Amendment. He had before him, or at the very least would have been aware of, all of these proposed formulations. . . .

With all of these sources upon which to draw, it is strikingly significant that Madison's first draft omitted any mention of nonmilitary use or possession of weapons. Rather, his original draft repeated the essence of the two proposed amendments sent by Virginia, combining the substance of the two provisions succinctly into one, which read: "The right of the people to keep and bear arms shall not be infringed; a well armed, and well regulated militia being the best security of a free country; but no person religiously scrupulous of bearing arms, shall be compelled to render military service in person."

Madison's decision to model the Second Amendment on the distinctly military Virginia proposal is therefore revealing, since it is clear that he considered and rejected formulations that would have unambiguously protected civilian uses of firearms. When Madison prepared his first draft, and when that draft was debated and modified, it is reasonable to assume that all participants in the drafting process were fully aware of the other formulations that would have protected civilian use and possession of weapons and that their choice to craft the Amendment as they did represented a rejection of those alternative formulations.

Madison's initial inclusion of an exemption for conscientious objectors sheds revelatory light on the purpose of the Amendment. It confirms an intent to describe a duty as well as a right, and it unequivocally identifies the military character of both. . . .

The history of the adoption of the Amendment thus describes an overriding concern about the potential threat to state sovereignty that a federal standing army would pose, and a desire to protect the States' militias as the means by which to guard against that danger. But state militias could not effectively check the prospect of a federal standing army so long as Congress retained the power to disarm them, and so a guarantee against such disarmament was needed.

III

Although it gives short shrift to the drafting history of the Second Amendment, the Court dwells at length on four other sources: the 17th-century English Bill of Rights; Blackstone's Commentaries on the Laws of England; postenactment commentary on the Second Amendment; and post-Civil War legislative history. All of these sources shed only indirect light on the question before us, and in any event offer little support for the Court's conclusion. . . .

V

The Court concludes its opinion by declaring that it is not the proper role of this Court to change the meaning of rights "enshrine[d]" in the Constitution. But the right the Court announces was not "enshrined" in the Second Amendment by the Framers; it is the product of today's law-changing decision. The majority's exegesis has utterly failed to establish that as a matter of text or history, "the right of law-abiding, responsible citizens to use arms in defense of hearth and home" is "elevate[d] above all other interests" by the Second Amendment. . . .

For these reasons, I respectfully dissent.

JUSTICE BREYER, with whom JUSTICE STEVENS, JUSTICE SOUTER, and JUSTICE GINSBURG join, dissenting.

. . . .

I

The majority's conclusion is wrong for two independent reasons. The first reason is that set forth by Justice Stevens—namely, that the Second Amendment protects militia-related, not self-defense-related, interests. . . . [Self]-defense alone, detached from any militia-related objective, is not the Amendment's concern.

The second independent reason is that the protection the Amendment provides is not absolute. The Amendment permits government to regulate the interests that it serves. Thus, irrespective of what those interests are—whether they do or do not include an independent interest in self-defense—the majority's view cannot be correct unless it can show that the District's regulation is unreasonable or inappropriate in Second Amendment terms. This the majority cannot do. . . .

III

I therefore begin by asking a process-based question: How is a court to determine whether a particular firearm regulation (here, the District's restriction on handguns) is consistent with the Second Amendment? What kind of constitutional standard should the court use? How high a protective hurdle does the Amendment erect?

The question matters. The majority is wrong when it says that the District's law is unconstitutional "[u]nder any of the standards of scrutiny that we have applied to enumerated constitutional rights." How could that be? It certainly would not be unconstitutional under, for example, a "rational basis" standard, which requires a court to uphold regulation so long as it bears a "rational relationship" to a "legitimate governmental purpose." The law at issue here, which in part seeks to prevent gun-related accidents, at least bears a "rational relationship" to that "legitimate" life-saving objective. And nothing in the three 19th-century state cases to which the majority turns for support mandates the conclusion that the present District law must fall. . . .

Respondent proposes that the Court adopt a "strict scrutiny" test, which would require reviewing with care each gun law to determine whether it is "narrowly tailored to achieve a compelling governmental interest." But the majority implicitly, and appropriately, rejects that suggestion by broadly approving a set of laws—prohibitions on concealed weapons, forfeiture by criminals of the Second Amendment right, prohibitions on firearms in certain locales, and governmental regulation of commercial firearm sales—whose constitutionality under a strict scrutiny standard would be far from clear. . . .

I would simply adopt . . . an interest-balancing inquiry explicitly. The fact that important interests lie on both sides of the constitutional equation suggests that review of gun-control regulation is not a context in which a court should effectively presume either constitutionality (as in rational-basis review) or unconstitutionality (as in strict scrutiny). Rather, "where a law significantly implicates competing constitutionally protected interests in complex ways," the Court generally asks whether the statute burdens a protected interest in a way or to an extent that is out of proportion to the statute's salutary effects upon other important governmental interests. See *Nixon v. Shrink Missouri Government PAC*, 528 U.S. 377, 402 (2000) (Breyer, J., concurring). Any answer would take account both of the statute's effects upon the competing interests and the existence of any clearly superior less restrictive alternative. Contrary to the majority's unsupported suggestion that this sort of "proportionality" approach is unprecedented, the Court has applied it in various constitutional contexts, including election-law cases, speech cases, and due process cases. See 528 U.S., at 403 (citing examples where the Court has taken such an approach); see also, *e.g., Thompson v. Western States Medical Center*, 535 U.S. 357, 388 (2002) (Breyer, J., dissenting) (commercial speech); *Burdick v. Takushi*, 504 U.S. 428, 433 (1992) (election regulation); *Mathews v. Eldridge*, 424 U.S. 319, 339–349 (1976) (procedural due process); *Pickering v. Board of Ed. of Township High School Dist. 205, Will Cty.*, 391 U.S. 563, 568 (1968) (government employee speech).

In applying this kind of standard the Court normally defers to a legislature's empirical judgment in matters where a legislature is likely to have greater expertise and greater institutional factfinding capacity. See *Turner Broadcasting System, Inc. v. FCC*, 520 U.S. 180 (1997); see also *Nixon, supra*, at 403 (BREYER, J., concurring). Nonetheless, a court, not a legislature, must make the ultimate constitutional conclusion, exercising its "independent judicial judgment" in light of the whole record to determine whether a law exceeds constitutional boundaries. *Randall v. Sorrell*, 548 U.S. 230 (2006) (opinion of Breyer, J.).

The above-described approach seems preferable to a more rigid approach here for a further reason. Experience as much as logic has led the Court to decide that in one area of constitutional law or another the interests are likely to prove stronger on one side of a typical constitutional case than on the other. See, *e.g., United States v. Virginia*, 518 U.S. 515 (1996) (applying heightened scrutiny to gender-based classifications, based upon experience with prior cases); *Williamson v. Lee Optical of Okla., Inc.*, 348 U.S. 483 (1955) (applying rational-basis scrutiny to economic legislation, based upon experience with prior cases). Here, we have little prior experience. Courts that *do* have experience in these matters have uniformly taken an approach that treats empirically-based legislative judgment with a degree of deference. See Winkler, Scrutinizing the Second Amendment, 105 Mich. L. Rev. 683, 687, 716–718 (2007) (describing hundreds of gun-law decisions issued in the last half-century by Supreme Courts in 42 States, which courts with "surprisingly little variation," have adopted a standard more deferential than strict scrutiny). While these state cases obviously are not controlling, they are instructive. And they thus provide some comfort regarding the practical wisdom of following the approach that I believe our constitutional precedent would in any event suggest. . ..

V

The majority derides my approach as "judge-empowering." I take this criticism seriously, but I do not think it accurate. As I have previously explained, this is an approach that the Court has taken in other areas of constitutional law. Application of such an approach, of course, requires judgment, but the very nature of the approach—requiring careful identification of the relevant interests and evaluating the law's effect upon them—limits the judge's choices; and the method's necessary transparency lays bare the judge's reasoning for all to see and to criticize.

The majority's methodology is, in my view, substantially less transparent than mine. At a minimum, I find it difficult to understand the reasoning that seems to underlie certain conclusions that it reaches.

The majority spends the first 54 pages of its opinion attempting to rebut Justice Stevens' evidence that the Amendment was enacted with a purely militia-related purpose. In the majority's view, the Amendment also protects an interest in armed personal self-defense, at least to some degree. But the majority does not tell us precisely what that interest is. . . .

The majority does, however, point to one type of confrontation that counts, for it describes the Amendment as "elevat[ing] above all other interests the right of law-abiding, responsible citizens to use arms in defense of hearth and home." What is its basis for finding that to be the core of the Second Amendment right? The only historical sources identified by the majority that even appear to touch upon that specific matter consist of an 1866 newspaper editorial discussing the Freedmen's Bureau Act, two quotations from that 1866 Act's legislative history, and a 1980 state court opinion saying that in colonial times the same [weapons] were used to defend the home as to maintain the militia. How can citations such as these support the far-reaching proposition that the Second Amendment's primary concern is not its stated concern about the militia, but rather a right to keep loaded weapons at one's bedside to shoot intruders?

Nor is it at all clear to me how the majority decides *which* loaded "arms" a homeowner may keep. The majority says that that Amendment protects those weapons "typically possessed by law-abiding citizens for lawful purposes." This definition conveniently excludes machineguns, but permits handguns, which the majority describes as "the most popular weapon chosen by Americans for self-defense in the home." . . .

At the same time the majority ignores a more important question: Given the purposes for which the Framers enacted the Second Amendment, how should it be applied to modern-day circumstances that they could not have anticipated? Assume, for argument's sake, that the Framers did intend the Amendment to offer a degree of self-defense protection. Does that mean that the Framers also intended to guarantee a right to possess a loaded gun near swimming pools, parks, and playgrounds? That they would not have cared about the children who might pick up a loaded gun on their parents' bedside table? . . . One cannot answer those questions by combining inconclusive historical research with judicial *ipse dixit*.

The argument about method, however, is by far the less important argument surrounding today's decision. Far more important are the unfortunate consequences that today's decision is likely to spawn. Not least of these, as I have said, is the fact that the decision threatens to throw into doubt the constitutionality of gun laws throughout the United States. I can find no sound legal basis for launching the courts on so formidable and potentially dangerous a mission. In my view, there simply is no untouchable constitutional right guaranteed by the Second Amendment to keep loaded handguns in the house in crime-ridden urban areas.

NOTES AND QUESTIONS

(1) *The Second Amendment Protects an Individual Right: District of Columbia v. Heller, 128 S. Ct. 2783 (2008).* The District of Columbia had a total ban on possession of handguns and other regulations on non-handguns that rendered firearms nonfunctional for self-defense in the home. The regulatory scheme was challenged by a federally employed police officer. The Supreme Court, per Justice Scalia, held that the Second Amendment protected an individual right to bear arms to keep a loaded handgun at home for self-defense. The Court rejected the position that the Second Amendment created only a state (or collective) right to have arms as part of a state militia. The Court determined that the Framers intended the Second Amendment to protect a *pre-existing right* to self-defense, especially in the home. The Court relied on an originalist (text and history) approach. [For more background on originalism, review Chapter 1 Appendix.] The Court distinguished (or narrowed) the *Miller* decision. Without specifying a standard (in traditional terms), the Court further held that D.C.'s total ban on handguns was unconstitutional.

(2) *The Unanswered Second Amendment Issues.* Both majority and dissenting opinions recognized that future litigation is likely, as the courts proceed on a case-by-case basis. One issue unanswered in *Heller* was, assuming the Second Amendment creates an individual right, whether the individual right is a *fundamental right* (and, thereby, tested under strict scrutiny). Another unanswered issue is what will be the Second Amendment standard: strict scrutiny; intermediate scrutiny; the undue burden standard; etc. Another unanswered issue is whether the individual right recognized in *Heller* will be applied outside the home setting (which more clearly implicates self-defense). There also will be issues regarding the use of guns for non-self-defense (*e.g.*, recreational) purposes.

In some ways, these questions will be as challenging as the individual v. state/collective right issues in *Heller*. For example, the Court's decision (*Virginia Citizens Consumer Council*) that commercial speech was protected speech was not nearly as difficult (or prolonged) as the subsequent disputes about whether particular regulations would satisfy the commercial speech standard as announced in *Central Hudson. See* Chapter 11.

(3) *The Dissents.* The lead dissent was by Justice Stevens. Justice Stevens contested the Court on both textual and historical grounds. Justice Stevens argued that the Framers did not intend to codify any individual right of self-defense—whether pre-existing or newly created in the Bill of Rights. The second dissent, by Justice Breyer, focused on a policy argument about the empirical evidence linking handguns to urban violence. As an originalist, Justice Scalia would not directly respond in policy terms. But, note that Justice Scalia did rely on the fact that "handguns are the most popular weapon chosen by Americans for self-defense in the home. . .." The choice of the majority of the public thus apparently trumped any other policy considerations. *See generally* Linda Greenhouse, *D.C. Ban Rejected*, N.Y. TIMES June 27, 2008, at 1.

(4) *Justice Breyer's Dissent: His Precedential "Interest-Balancing" Test.* Justice Breyer, the former law professor, critiqued Justice Scalia's majority opinion in a classic format: arguing that the majority is both overbroad and underinclusive in its use of historical evidence. Justice Breyer rejected the originalist approach in favor of a policy-based, "evolving constitution" position.

Justice Breyer argued that the Court should adopt an "interest-balancing inquiry" or "proportionality" test for Second Amendment cases. The majority, of course, declined to take such a step. Justice Breyer derived his proposed standard from precedent. So, what precedent did he cite? The main case authority is the *Shrink Missouri Government* decision, above in Chapter 11, but he cites only to his concurring opinion. His subsequent authorities include citing to one of his dissenting opinions.

Nevertheless, could Justice Breyer be correct that "interest balancing" is commonplace (although perhaps not explicitly recognized) in constitutional law? Would this standard be a way to reconcile some of the Court's precedents that do not comfortably fit within the traditional tiers of strict scrutiny, intermediate scrutiny, and rational basis review? For an argument that a number of due process strands (including the personal jurisdiction doctrine that you studied in Civil Procedure) can only be understood as engaging in a similar concept, which Professor Rhodes called "rationality balancing," *see* Charles W. "Rocky" Rhodes, *Liberty, Substantive Due Process, and Personal Jurisdiction*, 82 TULANE L. REV. 567 (2007).

Chapter 16
STATE CONSTITUTIONAL LAW

§ 16.01 THE CASE FOR AND AGAINST EXPANSION OF STATE CONSTITUTIONAL LAW

INTRODUCTORY NOTE

The Significance of State Constitutional Law; the Case for Its Expansion. Both liberals and conservatives have rediscovered state constitutional law. They have used it for the protection of rights that are not protected by the federal Constitution and that allegedly are infringed by state legislatures. According to Justice William J. Brennan Jr., "rediscovery by state supreme courts of the broader protections afforded their own citizens by their state constitutions . . . is probably the most important development in constitutional jurisprudence of our times." Nat. L.J., Sept. 29, 1986, at S-1, col. 1. Commentators have argued that state constitutional law provides something for everyone: "For the liberal," writes California Supreme Court Justice Stanley Mosk, "there is the prospect of continued expansion of individual rights and liberties. . . . For the conservative, state constitutionalism represents the triumph of federalism; crucial decisions about apportionment of rights and benefits are decided by state courts responsive to local needs, rather than by a distant United States Supreme Court, perceived as insensitive." Mosk, *State Constitutionalism: Both Liberal and Conservative,* 63 Tex. L. Rev. 1081 (1985). *See also, e.g.,* Alloway, *Florida Constitutional Law,* 14 Miami L. Rev. 501 (1960); Symposium, *The Georgia Constitution and the New Ascendancy of State Constitutional Law,* 3 Ga. St. U. L. Rev. 1 (1986); Project, *Developments in the Law: The Interpretation of State Constitutional Rights,* 95 Harv. L. Rev. 1324 (1982). *Cf.* Collins, *Reliance on State Constitutions: The Montana Disaster,* 63 Tex. L. Rev. 1095 (1985).

The Subjects of State Constitutional Law. State constitutionalism runs very nearly the gamut of federal constitutional issues. The main difference is that state constitutions are more extensive than the federal one, and the issues are broader. Thus, in addition to speech, privacy, criminal justice, and other issues analogous to federal ones, state constitutions often include "open courts" or "due course of law" provisions, which trace back to Magna Carta and which have been made the basis of a surprising array of individual rights; sometimes, firmer guarantees of separation of powers (embodied in explicit provisions); protection for specific governmental functions (*e.g.,* education, an area in which state decisions departing from federal constitutional norms have been frequent); and many others. Sometimes, state provisions contain different language that explicitly protects interests not covered by the federal Constitution; in other instances, state judges have interpreted parallel language to provide broader protection.

The Case Against Expansive State Constitutional Law. But the state constitutionalism movement is not without its critics, who eloquently argue against expansive reading of state constitutions. For example, Professor Earl M. Maltz argues that state constitutionalism "will merely duplicate already existing federal review, while decreasing the ability of local legislatures to respond to changing conditions and increasing uncertainty about the state of constitutional rights." Maltz, *The Dark Side of State Court Activism,* 63 Tex. L. Rev. 995, 1023 (1985); *see also* Liberato, *Keeping Up With Constitutional Law,* 11 Houston Law. 52 (1987). The concerns about government by judiciary, constitutionalization of judges' idiosyncratic preferences, and inconsistency with democracy, which are major criticisms of federal judicial activism, would be multiplied if state constitutional activism increased. *See also* Hudnut, *State*

Constitutions and Individual Rights: The Case for Judicial Restraint, 63 DENVER L. REV. 85 (1985); Deukmejian & Thompson, *All Sail and No Anchor*, 6 HAST. CONST. L.Q. 975 (1979).

§ 16.02 STATE CONSTITUTIONAL PROVISIONS PARALLEL TO FEDERAL PROVISIONS

[A] The Most Frequent Construction: Similar Meaning

NOTE ON SIMILAR CONSTRUCTION OF PARALLEL PROVISIONS

Despite the touted importance of state constitutionalism, many state provisions are parallel to analogous federal ones—and the most frequent resolution of questions under these provisions is that they have meanings similar to the federal ones. The litigation in *South Dakota v. Neville* provides a striking example.

South Dakota v. Neville. Neville was arrested for drunk driving. As authorized by a state statute, the prosecution intended to introduce evidence that Neville had refused to take a breath test. Neville challenged this evidence as a violation of the Fifth Amendment guarantee against self-incrimination. The trial court agreed and suppressed the evidence. The decisions of the South Dakota Supreme Court, the United States Supreme Court, and the South Dakota Supreme Court on remand illustrate the point:

> *Neville I: Neville v. State*, 312 N.W.2d 723 (S.D. 1981). The South Dakota Supreme Court, in its first decision, agreed with Neville, affirming the suppression under the Fifth Amendment to the United State Constitution.

> *Neville II: South Dakota v. Neville*, 459 U.S. 553 (1983). The United States Supreme Court reversed. It reasoned that Neville had not been "compelled" to be a "witness against himself," and there was no Fifth Amendment violation.

> *Neville III: Neville v. State*, 346 N.W.2d 425 (S.D. 1984) (on remand). On remand, the South Dakota Supreme Court considered whether the evidence of the refusal should be suppressed under the South Dakota Constitution, which (like most state constitutions) has a provision against self-incrimination parallel to that of the Fifth Amendment. This time, the court held for the state. Despite its initial holding, that the introduction of the evidence violated the (federal) Fifth Amendment, it construed the parallel state provision to conform to the holding of the United States Supreme Court construing the federal provision.

It should be remembered that state constitutions, like the federal Constitution, are not involved in a very large percentage of litigation, and the differences should not be exaggerated.

[B] Greater Extension Of Protection Under State Constitutions

NOTE ON BROADER STATE PROTECTION BY DIFFERENT CONSTRUCTION OF SIMILAR PROVISIONS

On the other hand, there are numerous decisions in which similar (and sometimes identical) language has been construed by state courts to provide greater protection under state than under federal constitutions. *Cf.* Hogue, *Regulating Business Activity by Means of the Substantive Due Process and Equal Protection Doctrines under the Georgia Constitution: An Analysis and a Proposal*, in *Symposium*, 3 GA. ST. L. REV. 1 (1986); Williams, *In the Supreme Court's Shadow: Legitimacy of State Court Rejection of Supreme Court Reasoning and Result*, 35 S.C. L. REV. 353 (1984). The *Serrano, Baehr,* and *Pruneyard* cases provide interesting examples.

Serrano v. Priest, 18 Cal. 3d 728, 135 Cal. Rptr. 345, 557 P.2d 929 (1977), involved a challenge to financing of public education dependent upon local tax bases. The United States Supreme Court had rejected such a challenge that was based on the federal Equal Protection Clause. *San Antonio Independent School District v. Rodriquez* [Chapter 10, above]. But Serrano's challenge was based on the *state* equal protection clause, and the California Supreme Court upheld it:

> [O]ur state equal protection provisions, while "substantially the equivalent of" the guarantees contained in the Fourteenth Amendment to the United States Constitution, are possessed of an independent vitality which, in a given case, may demand an analysis different from that which would obtain if only the federal standard were applicable. "[In this area,] we sit as a court of last resort, subject only to the qualification that our interpretations may not restrict the guarantees accorded the national citizenry under the federal charter". . . .

The California court then proceeded to hold, contrary to the reasoning of *Rodriguez*, that the wealth-based distinctions created by California's funding system created a suspect classification and that education was a fundamental right—and for these reasons, it struck down California's system.

In *Robins v. Pruneyard Shopping Center*, 23 Cal.3d 899, 153 Cal. Rptr. 854, 592 P.2d 341 (1979), Robins and others were high school students who set up a card table in a corner of Pruneyard's shopping center courtyard and sought to solicit signatures for a petition to be sent to the White House in Washington. Employees of Pruneyard required them to leave. Robins brought suit, alleging that this action denied him the freedom of speech guaranteed by the California State Constitution.

The California Supreme Court recognized that the federal Constitution would not extend protection to Robins' speech because it was not infringed by state action. *Lloyd Corp. v. Tanner*, 407 U.S. 551 (1972) [this issue is discussed in Chapter 14, above]. Nevertheless, it held for the plaintiffs, extending protection beyond that of the federal Constitution under Cal. Const. Art. I, 2, which reads: "Every person may freely speak, write and publish his or her sentiments on all subjects, being responsible for the abuse of this right. A law may not restrain or abridge liberty of speech or press." [Later, the United States Supreme Court held that this decision did not violate the federal Constitution.]

In *Baehr v. Lewin*, 852 P.2d 44 (Hawaii 1993), plaintiffs claimed a right to same-sex marriage licenses under two provisions of the Hawaii state constitution. A plurality of the Hawaii Supreme Court first rejected their argument under Hawaii's express provision protecting the right of privacy (see below), concluding that there was no fundamental right to same-sex marriages. But then the plurality proceeded to reason that because it was based on gender, the refusal to issue licenses triggered strict scrutiny under the equal protection clause of the state constitution, and the court remanded to the trial court for consideration of this and other issues.

[C] Parallel Provisions With Significantly Different Language

NOTES AND QUESTIONS

(1) *"Taking 'or Destruction' of Property" Provisions.* The Fifth Amendment to the federal Constitution prohibits the "taking" of private property for public use. Some state constitutions provide that private property may not be taken *"or destroyed"* for a public purpose. *E.g.*, Tex. Const. Art. I, § 17. Imagine a situation in which police efforts to arrest dangerous suspects results in a gun battle, which in turn causes a fire that consumes a building owned by an innocent, uninvolved citizen. Has this private property, under the circumstances, been "taken" by the government? Or, to apply state constitutional language, has it been "destroyed?" Which of the two variations, federal or state, would provide better arguments for compensation?

(2) *Frontier Thinking on Obscenity— Oregon Interprets the Freedom of Speech to Protect Obscene Material: State v. Henry, 302 Or. 510, 732 P.2d 9 (1987).* Article I, § 8 of the Oregon Constitution provides, "No law shall be passed restraining the free expression of opinion, or restricting the right to speak or print freely on any subject whatever; but every person shall be responsible for the abuse of this right." The Oregon Supreme Court pointed out that at the time of adoption of the Oregon Constitution, "[t]he only relevant Oregon territorial legislation . . . included prohibitions against [o]bscene writing or pictures which manifestly tended to corrupt the morals of youth." The court then proceeded to hold that obscenity was broadly protected under the (different) language of the state constitution:

> [T]he prime reason that "obscene" expression cannot be restricted is that it is speech that does not fall within any historical exception to the plain wording of the Oregon Constitution that "no law shall be passed [restricting the right to speak] freely on any subject whatsoever."

If this decision protects child pornography, so-called "snuff" films (those depicting actual rape and murder in the course of obscene acts), or materials depicting bestiality, is it correctly decided? [Does it protect them? Consider the following.]

(3) *More Frontier Thinking on Obscenity— Hawaii Construes Its Constitutional Privacy Doctrines to Protect Obscenity: State v. Kam, 748 P.2d 372 (Haw. 1988).* Article I, § 6 of the Hawaii Constitution provides, "the right of the people to privacy is recognized and shall not be infringed without the showing of a compelling state interest. The legislature shall take affirmative steps to implement this right." The Hawaii Supreme Court, in *Kam,* observed that the state Constitution "affords much greater privacy rights than the federal right to privacy, so we are not bound by the United States Supreme Court precedents." The court then proceeded to strike down the state's prohibition not only upon the possession, but also upon the sale of obscene materials:

> [S]ince a person has the right to view pornographic items at home, there necessarily follows a correlative right to purchase such materials for this personal use, or the underlying privacy right becomes meaningless.

The defense lawyer in *Kam* expressed the opinion that the ruling would "allow pornography to be shown in theaters and private booths," and both the prosecutor and the defense lawyer "agreed it also allows the selling of films depicting bestiality and 'snuff' films of killings." Is the decision correct?

§ 16.03 AMENDMENT OF STATE CONSTITUTIONS TO ADD (OR DELETE) RIGHTS

NOTE ON STATE CONSTITUTIONAL AMENDMENTS

The Amendment Process. State constitutions are easier to amend than the federal Constitution. It is not necessary to persuade multiple jurisdictions to vote in favor of the amendment, as the federal Constitution requires; instead, a legislative vote followed by a single popular vote within the same state typically suffices. For this reason, state constitutions often are longer and more detailed than the federal Constitution.

Examples: California's Death Penalty Authorization and "Victim's Bill of Rights." In 1972, the people of California adopted Cal. Const. Art. I, § 27, which provides: "the death penalty . . . shall not be deemed to be, or to constitute, the infliction of cruel or unusual punishments within the meaning of Article I, § 6, nor shall such punishment for such offenses be deemed to contravene any other provision of this Constitution." This provision was a reaction to, and a popular overruling of, decisions of the California Supreme Court restricting capital punishment.

Ten years later, in 1982, the people added Cal. Const. Art. I, § 28, popularly known as the California "Victim's Bill of Rights." Section 28 begins with a declaration that a Bill of Rights for victims of crime, "including safeguards in the criminal justice system to fully protect those rights, is a matter of grave statewide concern." Other provisions required victim restitution ("all persons who suffer losses as a result of criminal activity shall have the right to restitution from the persons convicted"); safe schools ("all students . . . have the inalienable right to attend campuses which are safe, secure and peaceful"); "truth in evidence" ("relevant evidence shall not be excluded in any criminal proceeding," with limited exceptions); public safety bail (no release on own recognizance for a "serious felony," procedural safeguards required before release, and "protection of the public" to be considered); and use of prior convictions ("any prior felony conviction . . . shall subsequently be used without limitation for purposes of impeachment or enhancement of sentence in any criminal proceeding").

Another Example: Texas' Prohibition on Garnishment of Wages, and Its Amendment for Enforcement of Child Support. As a "debtors' haven" (largely owing to the history of its settlement), Texas long had an absolute provision that no current wages "shall ever be subject to garnishment." In 1983, by popular vote, Tex. Const. Art I, § 28 was amended to add the following: "except for the enforcement of court-ordered child support payments." Was the pre-1983 absolute prohibition wise? Is the current provision wise? (Together with homestead exemptions, it precludes the recovery of most judgments against most individuals!)

§ 16.04   STATE PROVISIONS NOT SHARED BY THE FEDERAL CONSTITUTION

[A]   "Open Courts" And "Due Course Of Law" Provisions: Language Found In The Majority Of State, But Not The Federal, Constitutions

LeCROY v. HANLON, 713 S.W.2d 335 (Tex. 1986). Tex. Const. Art. I, § 13 provides, "[a]ll courts shall be open, and every person for an injury done him, in his lands, goods, person or reputation, shall have remedy by due course of law." Similar "open courts" or "remedy by due course of law" provisions appear in the majority of state constitutions—but not in the federal Constitution. In *LeCroy*, the state legislature had enacted a special filing fee for state court actions, payable to state general revenues. The state supreme court held this tax unconstitutional as a violation of the state "open courts . . . due course of law" provision:

> [The open courts provision] originates from Chapter 40 of Magna Carta, the great charter of English liberties obtained from King John in 1215: "To none will we sell, to none deny or delay, right or justice." Colonists brought to America and then to Texas their belief in the historic rights guaranteed by Magna Carta. . . .

> [T]he open courts provision must have been intended to provide rights in addition to those in the due process provision or the former would be surplusage. . . .

> We hold that filing fees that go to state general revenues—in other words taxes on the right to litigate that pay for other programs besides the judiciary—are unreasonable impositions on the state constitutional right of access to the courts. Regardless of its size, such a filing fee is unconstitutional, for filing fees cannot go for non-court related purposes.

NOTES AND QUESTIONS

(1) *Similar Decisions, Based Upon Other States' Open Courts Provisions.* Other states, including Florida, Illinois, and Missouri have construed similar open courts provisions to reach the same result as that in *LeCroy. Farabee v. Board of Trustees*, 254

So. 2d 1 (Fla. 1971); *Crocker v. Finley*, 99 Ill. 2d 444, 459 N.E.2d 1346 (1984); *Hayes v. C.C. & H. Mining & Mill Co.*, 126 S.W. 1051 (Mo. 1910).

(2) *The Broad Array of Uses of "Open Courts" and "Due Course of Law" Provisions—the Texas Example: Striking Down Statutes of Limitations, Guest Statutes, and "Tort Reform."* The Texas Supreme Court has applied the open courts and due course of law provisions, as construed in *LeCroy*, above, to strike down the state's guest statute, certain statutes of limitations, and tort reform legislation, including "caps" on medical malpractice awards. *See Lucas v. United States*, 31 Tex. Sup. Ct. J. 423, 757 S.W.3d 687 (Tex. 1988); *Sax v. Votteler*, 648 S.W.2d 661, 666 (Tex. 1983); *Nelson v. Krusen*, 678 S.W.2d 918 (Tex. 1984). There have been numerous other state decisions addressing the constitutionality, under state constitutions, of "tort reform." *E.g., Johnson v. St. Vincent Hospital*, 404 N.E.2d 585 (1980) (cap upheld as against open courts challenge); *Sibley v. Board of Supervisors*, 462 So. 2d 149 (La. 1985) (cap upheld as against open courts challenge); *Smith v. Department of Insurance*, 507 So. 2d 1080 (Fla. 1987) (cap struck down under open courts provision similar to Texas'). *See generally* Morrison & Morrison, *Constitutional Challenges to Tort Reform: Equal Protection and State Constitutions*, 64 Denver L. Rev. 719 (1988).

(3) *Magnitude of Impact of Open Courts Provisions.* Given the large number of open courts provisions in state constitutions, and the variety and numbers of "bread-and-butter" cases that are affected by rulings such as those in Note (2), is it possible to argue that recent decisions under state open courts provisions have had more impact of a direct nature upon more litigation than most of the recent decisions construing federal constitutional provisions emphasized in this book?

[B]   Education

NOTE ON STATE CONSTITUTIONAL "OVERRULINGS" OF *SAN ANTONIO INDEPENDENT SCHOOL DISTRICT v. RODRIGUEZ*

Numerous state constitutions describe educational systems extensively. Some require that the state establish an "effective" or an "efficient" system of public education. In *San Antonio Independent School District v. Rodriguez* [in Chapter 10, above], the United States Supreme Court held that equality of education was not a fundamental right, and it refused to strike down a system of public education based upon local financing, dependent upon local tax bases.

Several states have construed state constitutional provisions either governing school systems, or guaranteeing equal protection, or providing for uniform taxation, to reach results contrary to that of *Rodriguez*. *E.g., Serrano v. Priest*, 18 Cal. 3d 728, 135 Cal. Rptr. 345, 557 P.2d 929 (1977) (state equal protection provision is "substantially the equivalent of" the federal provision but possesses "an independent vitality which, in a given case, may demand an analysis different from that which would obtain if only the federal standard were applicable;" discrimination in educational opportunity on the basis of district wealth involves suspect classification and education is a fundamental interest); *Dupree v. Alma School District*, 651 S.W.2d 90 (Ark. 1983); *Buse v. Smith*, 247 N.W.2d 141 (Wisc. 1976) (relying upon uniform taxation provision).

In Texas, a state district court initially held the same state financing system that was upheld in *Rodriguez* to be a violation of the state constitutional provisions governing the public education system. The state constitution requires an "efficient" system, which the trial court held the Texas system was not. *Edgewood Independent School District v. Kirby*, reported in *Texas Lawyer*, May 16, 1988, at 20, col. 1. A state court of appeals reversed and upheld the state financing system. *Kirby v. Edgewood Independent School Dist.*, 761 S.W.2d 859, (Tex. App.—Aus. 1988). Finally, however, the Texas Supreme Court unanimously reversed the intermediate court and reinstated the trial court's judgment of unconstitutionality. *Edgewood Independent School Dist. v.*

Kirby, 777 S.W.2d 391 (Tex. 1989). Thus an issue that, over the years, will affect billions of public dollars was decided as a matter of state constitutional law.

Similar challenges were brought in other states. *See School Finance System Overturned in N.J. to Aid Poor Districts*, Houston Chronicle, June 6, 1990, § A, at 5, col. 1 (reporting on pending challenges in "Kansas, Wisconsin, California, Connecticut, Washington, West Virginia, Wyoming, and Arkansas," as well as successful challenges in "Montana, Kentucky, Texas, and New Jersey.")

TABLE OF SECONDARY AUTHORITIES

[References are to pages]

[References are to pages]

[References are to pages]

[References are to pages]

[References are to pages]

[References are to pages]

[References are to pages]

[References are to pages]

[References are to pages]

[References are to pages]

T

[References are to pages]

[References are to pages]

TABLE OF CASES

[References are to pages]

[References are to pages]

[References are to pages]

[References are to pages]

[References are to pages]

[References are to pages]

[References are to pages]

T

[References are to pages]

[References are to pages]

INDEX

[References are to pages.]

[References are to pages.]

[References are to pages.]

[References are to pages.]

[References are to pages.]

[References are to pages.]

T

[References are to pages.]